Oxford Wordpower

قاموس اكسفورد
الحديث

لدارسي اللغة الانكليزية

انكليزي - انكليزي - عربي

طبعة موسعة

OXFORD
UNIVERSITY PRESS

OXFORD
UNIVERSITY PRESS

Great Clarendon Street, Oxford OX2 6DP

Oxford University Press is a department of the University of Oxford.
It furthers the University's objective of excellence in research, scholarship, and education by publishing worldwide in

Oxford New York

Auckland Cape Town Dar es Salaam Hong Kong Karachi
Kuala Lumpur Madrid Melbourne Mexico City Nairobi
New Delhi Shanghai Taipei Toronto

With offices in

Argentina Austria Brazil Chile Czech Republic France Greece
Guatemala Hungary Italy Japan Poland Portugal Singapore
South Korea Switzerland Thailand Turkey Ukraine Vietnam

First published 1999
Second edition 2006
Third edition 2011

2015 2014 2013
10 9 8 7 6 5 4 3

OXFORD UNIVERSITY PRESS
ISBN: 978 019 431611 8 (PACK FOR DICTIONARY AND CD-ROM)
ISBN: 978 0 19 431631 6 (DICTIONARY IN PACK)
ISBN: 978 0 19 431632 3 (CD-ROM IN PACK)

Data capture by Oxford University Press
Typesetting by Data Standards Limited

Printed in China

Contents

تمهيد

نقدم للقاريء الكريم الطبعة الجديدة من معجم اكسفورد الحديث، وهو كسابقه قد أعدّ خصيصاً ليفيَ بحاجات دارسي اللغة الانكليزية ممّن بلغوا مرحلة متوسطة أو متقدمة.

مزايا هذا المعجم

هذا معجم انكليزي ـ انكليزي ـ عربي أي أن كل مادة فيه قد شرحت أولاً بالانكليزية شرحاً بسيطاً واضحاً، ثم أعطي ما يقابلها باللغة العربية زيادة في ايضاحها. فهو، إذن، يجمع مزايا المعجم وحيد اللغة ومزايا المعجم ثنائي اللغة. وقد أضفنا إلى هذه الطبعة مئات الكلمات الجديدة التي تعكس التقدم اللغوي السريع المواكب للتغيّرات الحضارية والتكنولوجية في عصرنا.

وممّا يفخر به هذا المعجم، الذي اشرفت على اعداده الدكتورة نجاح الشمعة، هو الأمثلة الكثيرة المأخوذة من اللغة اليومية الحيّة، والتي تساعد الطالب في استخدام العبارات استخداماً صحيحاً، وتوضح له المواقف والظروف المرافقة لاستخدامها. ويضم النص ٣١،٠٠٠ مثال وما ينوف عن ١،٥٠٠ تعليق وملاحظة. وقد حرصنا كل الحرص أن نعطي ترجمة عربية خاصّة بكل من الكلمة الرئيسية ومعانيها المجازية والاصطلاحات المتعلقة بها.

وفي المعجم أيضاً العديد من الشروح التي تتناول قواعد اللغة وتصريف الأفعال، والكلمات المتلازمة، والشواذ في اللغة، والأفعال الاصطلاحية، وأصول التنقيط، وكتابة الرسائل، ولفظ الكلمات وصفحات تتعلق بجغرافية العالم العربي. وقد أضفنا قائمة ببعض الكلمات الانكليزية المأخوذة عن العربية. أما الصفحات الملونة، فتحوي كل منها مجموعة من الصور تمثل موضوعاً واحداً؛ وهي تهدف إلى أن تضع في متناول الطالب وبشكل منهجي بسيط، معظم المفردات التي يحتاجها لمعالجة بعض نواحي حياتنا اليومية.

أكسفورد ٢٠٠٦

The information in the dictionary

Spellings

alternative spelling shown in brackets

realize (*also* **realise**) /ˈriːəlaɪz/ *verb* [T] **1** to know and understand That sth is true or that sth has happened: *I'm sorry I mentioned the subject, I*

The small numbers show that two or more main words have the **same spelling.**

moor[1] /mʊə(r); *Brit also* mɔː(r)/ (*also* **moorland** /-lənd/) *noun* [C,U] a wild open area of high land that is covered with grass and other low plants أرض بَراح، أرض مغطاة بالأعشاب والخَلَنْج

moor[2] /mʊə(r); *Brit also* mɔː(r)/ *verb* [I,T] to fasten a boat to the land or to an object in the water, with a rope or chain يرسي أو يربط القارب بالشاطئ
▸ **mooring** *noun* [C] a place where a boat is moored مرسى

American spelling

harbour (*US* **harbor**) /ˈhɑːbə(r)/ *noun* [C] a place

Words and phrases related to the main word

Idioms are listed together in a section marked IDM.

The arrow → shows that the idiom is explained at the word following the arrow.

IDM **ahead of your time** so modern that people do not understand you طليعي، سابق لأوانه
go ahead (used to give sb permission to do sth): *'Can I take this chair?' 'Sure, go ahead.'* لا مانع، افعل ذلك!
streets ahead → STREET

Phrasal verbs are listed together in a section marked PHR V. Look at Appendix 3 for more information about phrasal verbs.

PHR V **bring sth about** to cause sth to happen: *to bring about changes in people's lives* يحْدث
bring sb/sth back to return sb/sth: *You can borrow the DVD if you bring it back tomorrow morning.* يعيد
bring sth back 1 to cause sth that existed before to be introduced again: *Nobody wants to bring back the days of child labour.* يعيد

derivatives of the main word (words with the same spelling but a different part of speech; or the main word plus an ending such as *-ly*, *-ness*, etc)

characteristic /ˌkærəktəˈrɪstɪk/ *noun* [C] a quality that is typical of sb/sth and that makes him/her/it different from other people or things: *The chief characteristic of reptiles is that they are cold-blooded.* صفة ، سمة
▸ **characteristic** *adj*: *Thatched cottages are characteristic of this part of England.* ❶ The opposite is **uncharacteristic**. مميَّز
characteristically /-kli/ *adv*: *'No' he said, in his characteristically direct manner.* على الوجه المعهود

Meaning

The **meaning** of words and phrases is given in simple English followed by an **Arabic translation or translations**. If there are several meanings, each one has a number.

scoop /sku:p/ *noun* [C] **1** a tool like a spoon used for picking up ice cream, flour, grain, etc. مِغرفة
2 the amount that one scoop contains: *apple pie served with a scoop of ice cream* غَرْفة
3 an exciting piece of news that is reported by one newspaper, TV or radio station before it is reported anywhere else سَبْق صحفي

The **example sentences** help you understand the meaning of the word and show how it is used.

arrive /ə'raɪv/ *verb* [I] **1** to reach the place to which you were travelling: *We arrived home at about midnight.* ○ *What time does the train arrive in Newcastle?* ○ *They arrived at the station ten minutes late.* ○ *Has my letter arrived yet?* يصل

a word which has the **same meaning**

comedian /kə'mi:diən/ (*also* **comic**) *noun* [C] a person whose job is to entertain people and make them laugh, e.g. by telling jokes كوميدي ، ممثل هَزْلي

a word with the **same meaning** used in **American English**

maize /meɪz/ (*US* **corn**) *noun* [U] a tall plant that produces yellow grains in a large mass (a cob) ➲ Look at **sweet corn**. الذُّرة

a **figurative** use of the word (the word is not used in its basic meaning, but in an imaginative way)

gnaw /nɔ:/ *verb* [I,T] **gnaw (at) sth** to bite a bone, etc. many times: *The dog lay on the carpet gnawing its bone.* ○ *(figurative) Fear of the future gnawed away at her all the time.* يَقْضم، يقرض

Grammar

the **part of speech** (whether the word is a noun, verb, adjective, etc)

coin /kɔɪn/ *noun* [C] a piece of money made of metal: *a pound coin* قطعة نقود
▸ **coin** *verb* [T] to invent a new word or phrase: *Who was it who coined the phrase 'a week is a long time in politics'?* يبتكر ، يأتي بِ

countable and uncountable nouns
[U] marks an uncountable noun.
[C] marks a countable noun.
Look at *countable* and *uncountable* in the dictionary.

coffee /'kɒfi; *US* 'kɔ:fi/ *noun* **1** [U] the roasted seeds of a tropical tree, made into powder and used for making a drink: *Coffee is the country's biggest export.* بُن
2 [U] a drink made by adding hot water to this: *Would you prefer tea or coffee?* ○ *a cup of coffee* قهوة
3 [C] a cup of this drink: *Two coffees please.* فنجان قهوة

a singular noun

forefront /'fɔ:frʌnt/ *noun* [sing.] the leading position; the position at the front: *Our department is right at the forefront of scientific research.* طليعة

a plural noun

roadworks /'rəʊdwɜ:ks/ *noun* [plural] work that involves repairing or building roads: *The sign said 'Slow down. Roadworks ahead.'* (ورشة عمل) إصلاح الطرق

a noun that can be used with either **a singular or a plural verb**

crew /kru:/ *noun* [C, with sing. or pl. verb] **1** all the people who work on a ship, plane, etc: *The captain and his crew hope you had a pleasant flight* طاقم الطائرة مثلاً

irregular plural

tooth /tu:θ/ *noun* [C] (*pl.* **teeth** /ti:θ/) **1** one of the hard white parts in your mouth that you use for biting: *to have a tooth out* ○ *The old man took out his false teeth.* ○ *wisdom teeth* سِن

transitive and intransitive verbs

[I] shows that a verb is intransitive (is never followed by an object).

[T] shows that a verb is transitive (is followed by an object).

exercise² /'eksəsaɪz/ *verb* **1** [I] to do some form of physical movement in order to stay fit and healthy: *It is important to exercise regularly.* يمارس الرياضة البدنيّة، يتمرّن
2 [T] to make use of sth (e.g. a power, right, etc.): *You should exercise your right to vote.* يمارس، يستخدم

irregular forms of verbs

draw² /drɔ:/ *verb* (*pt* **drew** /dru:/; *pp* **drawn** /drɔ:n/) **1** [I,T] to make a picture or diagram of sth with a pencil, pen, etc: *Shall I draw you a map of how to get there?* يرسم

When the **last letter** of a verb **is doubled** before you add *-ed* or *-ing*, this is shown.

cram /kræm/ *verb* (cramming; crammed) **1** [T] to push people or things into a small space:

The **comparative** and **superlative** forms of adjectives are shown if they are not regular.

funny /'fʌni/ *adj* (**funnier**; **funniest**) **1** that makes you smile or laugh: *a funny story* ○ *He's an extremely funny person* (= he can make people laugh). ○ *I didn't think it was very funny when somebody tipped a cup of coffee over me.* مُضْحِك

a note giving **grammatical information**

advice /əd'vaɪs/ *noun* [U] an opinion that you give sb about what he/she should do or how he/she should behave: *She took her doctor's advice and gave up smoking.* ○ *You should get some legal advice* (= ask a lawyer to tell you what to do). ○ *Let me give you some advice ...* نصيحة ، إرشاد

Advice is an uncountable noun, so we cannot say 'an advice' or 'some advices'. We can say: *a piece of advice* and : *a lot of advice*.

Using words

how a word is used in a sentence (sb = somebody; sth = something)

agree /ə'gri:/ *verb* **1** [I,T] **agree (with sb/sth); agree (that...)** to have the same opinion as sb/sth: *'I think we should talk to the manager about this.' 'Yes, I agree.'* ○ *I agree with Paul.* ○ *Do you agree that we should travel by train?* ○ *I'm afraid*

the particular **preposition** that is used after a word

increase² /'ɪŋkri:s/ *noun* [C,U] **increase (in sth)** a rise in the number, amount or level of sth: *a steady increase in the number of people taking*

The adjective is used only after a verb like *be*, *seem*, etc, not before a noun.

asleep /ə'sli:p/ *adj* (not before a noun) not awake; sleeping: *The baby is asleep.* ○ *to be sound/fast asleep* ○ *to fall asleep* ➲ Look at the note at **sleep**². نائم

The adjective is used only before a noun, not after a verb like **be**, **seem**, etc.

lifelong /'laɪflɒŋ; *US* -lɔːŋ/ *adj* (only *before* a noun) for all of your life: *a lifelong friend* طول العمر ، (دائم) مدى الحياة

Style labels show when words are used only in particular situations:

formal (= used in formal written English)

informal (= used in informal conversation, not written in an essay, for example)

slang (= very informal)

couch² /kaʊtʃ/ *verb* [T] (usually passive) (*formal*) to express a thought, idea, etc. (in the way mentioned): *His reply was couched in very polite terms.* يصوغ بطريقة معيّنة

'couch potato *noun* [C] (*informal*) a person who spends a lot of time sitting and watching television جليس التلفزيون

Choosing the right word and building vocabulary

a key shows that a word belongs to the Oxford 3000 – the most important words for students to know

explain /ɪk'spleɪn/ *verb* [I,T] **1** to make sth clear or easy to understand: *A dictionary explains the meaning of words.* ○ *She explained how I should fill in the form.* ○ *I don't understand this. Can you explain?* يشرح

a note explaining the **difference between words** that might be confused

You can **see** something without paying attention to it: *I saw a girl riding past on a horse.* If you **look** at something you pay attention to it with your eyes: *Look carefully. Can you see anything strange?*

notes giving **related vocabulary**

flower /'flaʊə(r)/ *noun* [C] **1** the beautiful coloured part of a plant or tree from which seeds or fruit grow ❶ A flower consists of several **petals**. It grows from a **bud** on the end of a **stem**. زهرة
2 a plant that is grown for its flowers; a flower and its stem: *She grows a lot of flowers but no vegetables.* ○ *a lovely bunch of flowers* نبات مزهر؛ زهرة

We **pick** flowers and **arrange** them in a vase. Flowers that are given or carried on a special occasion are called a **bouquet**.

members of a **word family**

wide /waɪd/ *adj* **1** measuring a large amount from one side or edge to the other: *The road was not wide enough for two cars to pass.* ○ *a wide river* ❶ The noun is **width**. The opposite is **narrow**. ➲ Look at the note at **broad**. واسع

Pronunciation

the **pronunciation** of each word

emoticon /ɪ'məʊtɪkɒn/ *noun* [C] (*computing*) a short set of keyboard symbols that represents the expression on sb's face, used in email, etc. to show the feelings of the person sending the message. For example :-) represents a smiling face (when you look at it sideways). رموز (كمبيوتر)

where the **stress** falls in a word or phrase

ˌend-'user *noun* [C] a person who actually uses a product rather than one who makes or sells it, especially a person who uses a product connected with computers: *Programs are tailored to meet the*

Dictionary Quiz

Use the dictionary to find the answers to this quiz and you will see how much information is given in the dictionary and how it can help you.

1a Which of these can you eat?
- **a** a baguette
- **b** a couch potato

b Where could you find an **inbox**?

c What does **SUV** stand for?

Meaning

The dictionary explains what words mean in simple English, as well as giving an Arabic translation. Example sentences show you how to use the word correctly. Abbreviations are listed in alphabetical order in the main part of the dictionary.

2a What is the link between **hang up** and **put sb/sth through**?

b Where do you **book in** – at a library or a hotel?

Phrasal verbs

Verbs that have a different meaning when they combine with a preposition or adverb like *out*, *on*, or *down* are given in a separate section marked PHR V after the main meanings of the verb. Look also at Appendix 3.

3a If you **lose your temper**, should you go to the lost property office?

b If you **give somebody a ring**, do you have to go to the jeweller's?

Idioms

Expressions with special meanings are given in a separate section marked IDM IDM after the main meanings of the word.

4a What is another word for **inconsiderate**?

b What is the opposite of **accurate**?

c Name four ways that **eggs** can be cooked.

d Choose the right word for this sentence:
I am very interested/interesting in art.

Vocabulary

There are notes (shown by the ❶ symbol or in a grey box) that give useful extra vocabulary associated with a word and explain the difference between words that people often confuse. A note that begins ➲ shows you where there is more information on related words.

5a Is the word **hub** a noun or a verb?

b Is the word **information** countable or uncountable?

c What is the past tense of **teach**?

d Correct the mistake in this sentence:
Most the boxes are empty.

Grammar

The dictionary tells you whether a word is a noun, verb, adjective, etc., and whether nouns are countable or uncountable. It also gives irregular forms, e.g. irregular past tenses of verbs, and notes on difficult points of grammar and usage.

6a How do you spell the plural of **allergy**?

b How do you spell the *–ing* form of the verb **cancel**?

c How do you spell the superlative form of **happy**?

Spelling

You can use the dictionary to check how a word is spelt. It also tells you about small spelling changes in the other forms of a word, (e.g. irregular plurals).

7a Which letter is silent in the word **lamb**?
b Where is the stress in the word **thermometer**?

Pronunciation

The dictionary gives the pronunciation of words, and at the bottom of each page there is a key that shows you how to read the phonetic spelling. Look also at the marks (ˌ ˈ) that show you where the main stress of the word is.

8a Which word in this sentence would you NOT use in a formal essay?
He was gobsmacked at the news.
b Which word in this sentence is too formal for a normal conversation?
I rose early this morning.

Style

The dictionary tells you if a word is formal or informal, and often suggests another word that you can use in most situations.

9a What noun is related to adjective **obstinate**?
b Which two adjectives can be formed from the verb **detach**?

Words formed from other words

Derivatives (**happily** and **happiness** are derivatives of **happy**) are given in a group after the main meanings of the word. This section begins with the symbol ▶.

10a What is the American English word for **drawing pin**?
b How do Americans spell the word **favourable**?

American English

The dictionary tells you about words that are different in British and American English, and also gives American spelling.

11a Write down the names of three types of ship.
b Name three parts of a plant.

Topic pages

The colour pages in the middle of the dictionary show you words related to 15 different topics. The **More to explore** boxes tell you where to find more vocabulary on these topics in the dictionary.

12a What is the past participle of **tear**?
b Is a **pint** more or less than half a litre?
c What is the meaning of the prefix **quad-**?

Appendices

The appendices include
— a list of irregular verbs
— a list of expressions using numbers, including weights and measures
— a list of prefixes and suffixes used to make other words.

Now turn the page upside down and check your answers.

Answers
1a a
1b on a computer
1c sports utility vehicle
2a the telephone
2b at a hotel
3a No, it means you're angry.
3b No, it means you're going to make a phone call.
4a thoughtless
4b inaccurate
4c Eggs can be boiled, fried, poached or scrambled.
4d interested
5a noun
5b uncountable
5c taught
5d Most of the boxes …
6a allergies
6b cancelling
6c happiest
7a b
7b thermometer
8a gobsmacked
8b rose
9a obstinacy
9b detached, detachable
10a thumbtack
10b favorable
11a oil tanker, ferry, hydrofoil
11b bud/bulb/leaf/seed/stalk
12a torn
12b more
12c four

A a

A, a /eɪ/ *noun* [C] (*pl.* **As**; **A's**; **a's** /eɪz/) **1** the first letter of the English alphabet: *'Andy' begins with (an) 'A'.* الحرف الأول من الأبجدية الإنكليزية

2 the highest grade given for an exam or piece of work: *I got an 'A' for my essay.* أعلى درجة (في امتحان مثلاً)

⚷ **a** /ə; *strong form* eɪ/ (*also* **an** /ən; *strong form* æn/) *indefinite article* ❶ The form **an** is used before a vowel sound.

1 one: *A cup of coffee, please.* ○ *an apple and a pear* (أداة تنكير تسبق حروف العلة)

2 (used when you are talking about sth in general, not one particular example of it): *A lion is a dangerous animal.* (أداة تنكير تستعمل للتعميم)

3 (used with sb's name to show that the speaker does not know the person): *There's a Ms Mills to see you.* (أداة تنكير تدلّ على عدم معرفة شخص ما)

4 (used for showing that sb/sth is a member of a group, class or profession): *She's a Muslim.* ○ *Their car's a Mini.* ○ *He's a doctor.* ○ *She's an MP.* (للدلالة على الانتماء إلى فئة ما)

5 (used with some expressions of quantity): *a lot of money* ○ *a few cars* (تستعمل مع بعض التعابير الدالة على الكمية)

6 (used with prices, rates, measurements) each: *They cost 50p a pound.* ○ *twice a week* ○ *He was travelling at about 80 miles an hour.* في ؛ كلّ

A2 (level) /ˌeɪ 'tu: levl/ *noun* [C,U] a British exam usually taken in Year 13 of school or college (= the final year) when students are aged 18. Students must first have studied a subject at AS level before they can take an A2 exam. Together AS and A2 level exams form the A-level qualification, which is needed for entrance to universities: *He's doing an A2 in history.* ○ *Students will normally take three A2 subjects.* جزء من الشهادة الثانوية

AA /ˌeɪ 'eɪ/ *abbrev* (*Brit*) Automobile Association; an organization for motorists. If you are a member of the AA and your car breaks down, you can phone them and they will send someone to help you. رابطة السيارات

aback /ə'bæk/ *adv*

IDM **take sb aback** to surprise or shock sb يدهش، يذهل

⚷ **abandon** /ə'bændən/ *verb* [T] **1** to leave sb/sth that you are responsible for, usually permanently: *an abandoned car* يترك ، يتخلّى عن

2 to stop doing sth without finishing it or without achieving what you wanted to do: *The search for the missing sailors was abandoned after two days.* يترك ، يوقف

▸ **abandonment** *noun* [U] هجر

abashed /ə'bæʃt/ *adj* ashamed and embarrassed because of having done sth bad خجل

abattoir /'æbətwɑ:(r); *US* ˌæbə'twɑ:r/ *noun* [C] (*Brit*) = SLAUGHTERHOUSE

abbess /'æbes/ *noun* [C] a woman who is the head of a religious community for women (nuns) رئيسة دَيْر الراهبات

abbey /'æbi/ *noun* [C] a building where monks or nuns live or used to live دَيْر

abbot /'æbət/ *noun* [C] a man who is the head of a religious community for men (monks) رئيس دَيْر الرهبان

abbreviate /ə'bri:vieɪt/ *verb* [T] **1** to make a word or phrase shorter by leaving out some letters يختصر

2 to make a story or a piece of writing or speech shorter: *the abbreviated version of the story* يختصر

▸ **abbreviation** /əˌbri:vi'eɪʃn/ *noun* [C] (*abbr* **abbr**; **abbrev**) a short form of a word or phrase: *In this dictionary 'sth' is the abbreviation for 'something'.* اختصار

ABC /ˌeɪ bi: 'si:/ *noun* [sing.] **1** the alphabet; the letters of English from A to Z الأبجدية ؛ الأبجدية الإنكليزية

2 the simple facts about sth: *the ABC of Gardening* المبادئ الأساسيّة (لشيء ما)

abdicate /'æbdɪkeɪt/ *verb* **1** [I] to give up being King or Queen: *The Queen abdicated and her son became King.* يتنازل عن العرش

2 [T] to give sth up, especially power or a position: *to abdicate responsibility* (= to refuse to be responsible for sth) يتخلّى عن ، يرفض (تحمّل مسؤولية ما)

▸ **abdication** /ˌæbdɪ'keɪʃn/ *noun* [C,U] تنازل؛ تنصّل

abdomen /'æbdəmən/ *noun* [C] a part of the body below the chest, in which the stomach is contained بَطْن

▸ **abdominal** /æb'dɒmɪnl/ *adj* بطْني

abduct /æb'dʌkt/ *verb* [T] to take hold of sb and take him/her away illegally: *He has been abducted by a terrorist group.* يخطف

▸ **abduction** /æb'dʌkʃn/ *noun* [C,U] خَطْف

abet /ə'bet/ *verb* [T] (**abetting**; **abetted**)

IDM **aid and abet** → AID

abhor /əb'hɔ:(r)/ *verb* [T] (**abhorring**; **abhorred**) to hate sth very much: *All civilized people abhor the use of torture.* يمقت

▸ **abhorrence** /əb'hɒrəns; *US* -'hɔ:r-/ *noun* [U] كراهية

abhorrent /əb'hɒrənt; *US* -'hɔ:r-/ *adj* كريه ، فظيع

abide /ə'baɪd/ *verb*
IDM **can't/couldn't abide sb/sth/doing sth** to dislike sth very much يكره
PHRV **abide by sth** to obey a law, etc; to do what you have agreed or decided: *You must abide by the rules of the game.* يتقيّد (بقانون) يلتزم

ability /ə'bɪləti/ *noun* [C,U] (*pl.* **abilities**) the mental or physical power or skill that makes it possible to do sth: *A person of his ability will have no difficulty getting a job.* ○ *an ability to make decisions* قدرة

ablaze /ə'bleɪz/ *adj* (not before a noun) burning strongly; completely on fire: *Within ten minutes, the whole house was ablaze.* مشتعل

able[1] /'eɪbl/ *adj* **be able to do sth** (used as a modal verb) to have the ability, power, opportunity, time, etc. to do sth: *Will you be able to come to a meeting next week?* ○ *I'll be able to give you the money back in a few days.* ○ *I was able to solve the problem quickly.* ❶ In the passive **can/could** are used, not **be able**: *The arrangement can't be changed.* يقدر على

able[2] /'eɪbl/ *adj* clever; doing your job well: *one of the ablest students in the class* ○ *an able politician* متمكّن، بارع، قدير
▸ **ably** *adv* باقتدار

ˌable-'bodied *adj* physically healthy and strong; having full use of your body قويّ البنية

abnormal /æb'nɔːml/ *adj* different from what is normal or usual, in a way that worries you or that is unpleasant: *abnormal levels of sugar in the blood* ○ *abnormal weather conditions* شاذّ ؛ غير طبيعي، غير سوي
▸ **abnormality** /ˌæbnɔː'mæləti/ *noun* [C,U] (*pl.* **abnormalities**) شذوذ ؛ خلاف المعتاد
abnormally /æb'nɔːməli/ *adv* على نحو غير طبيعي

aboard /ə'bɔːd/ *adv, prep* on or into a train, ship, aircraft or bus: *We went aboard the boat and found our cabins.* ○ *Welcome aboard this flight to Caracas.* على متن (قطار أو سفينة أو طائرة أو باص)

abode /ə'bəʊd/ *noun* [usually sing.] (*formal*) the place where you live: *They have the right of abode in this country* (= they are officially allowed to live there). مسكن ، إقامة
IDM **(of) no fixed abode/address** → FIX[1]

abolish /ə'bɒlɪʃ/ *verb* [T] to put an end to or stop a law or system officially: *When was capital punishment abolished here?* يلْغي
▸ **abolition** /ˌæbə'lɪʃn/ *noun* [U]: *the abolition of slavery in the US* إلغاء

abominable /ə'bɒmɪnəbl; *US* -mən-/ *adj* very unpleasant; very bad كريه؛ شنيع؛ رديء
▸ **abominably** /ə'bɒmɪnəbli; *US* -mən-/ *adv* على نحو رديء أو شنيع

Aboriginal /ˌæbə'rɪdʒənl/ (*also* **Aborigine** /ˌæbə'rɪdʒəni/) *noun* [C] a member of the race of people who were the original inhabitants of Australia من سكان أستراليا الأصليين
▸ **Aboriginal** (*also* **Aborigine**) *adj*: *Aboriginal traditions* متعلق بسكان أستراليا الأصليين

abort /ə'bɔːt/ *verb* [I,T] **1** to end a pregnancy intentionally and cause the baby inside to die يجهض
2 to end sth before it is complete يجهِض (امراً ما)

abortion /ə'bɔːʃn/ *noun* [C,U] an operation to end a pregnancy intentionally, causing the baby inside to die: *to have an abortion* ○ *Abortion is illegal in that country.* إجهاض

abortive /ə'bɔːtɪv/ *adj* not completed successfully: *an abortive attempt* مخْفِق

abound /ə'baʊnd/ *verb* [I] **1** to exist in large numbers: *Animals abound in the forest.* يكْثر
2 **abound with sth** to contain large numbers of sth يزخَر بـ

about[1] /ə'baʊt/ *adv* **1** (*especially US* **around**) a little more or less than; approximately: *It's about three miles from here to the city centre.* ○ *I got home at about half past seven.* نحو
2 (*informal*) almost; nearly: *Dinner's just about ready.* تقريباً
3 (*also* **around**) in many directions or places: *I could hear people moving about upstairs.* في كلّ الاتجاهات
4 (*also* **around**) here and there, in different positions: *clothes lying about all over the floor* هنا و هناك
5 (*also* **around**) (used after certain verbs) without doing anything in particular: *People were standing about in the street.* (يقف) متبطّلاً
6 (*also* **around**) present in a place; existing: *It was very late and there were few people about.* في أنحاء المكان؛ موجود
IDM **be about to do sth** to be going to do sth very soon: *The film's about to start.* ○ *I was just about to explain when she interrupted me.* على وشك

about[2] /ə'baʊt/ *prep* **1** on the subject of: *a book about Spain* ○ *Let's talk about something else.* ○ *I don't like it, but there's nothing I can do about it.* عن ، بشأن
2 (*also* **around**) in many directions or places; in different parts of sth: *We wandered about the town for an hour or two.* في أنحاء (المكان)
3 in the character of sb: *There's something about him that I don't quite trust.* متعلّق به ، في شخصيته
IDM **how/what about...? 1** (used when asking for information about sb/sth or for sb's opinion or wish): *How about Ruth? Have you heard from her lately?* ○ *I'm going to have chicken. What about you?* عن ، بشأن
2 (used when making a suggestion): *What about going to a film tonight?* عن ، بشأن ، ما رأيك في...؟

aˌbout-'turn (*US* **aˌbout-'face**) *noun* [C] a turn in the opposite direction; a change of opinion تحوّل للاتجاه المعاكس ، تغيير في الرأي

above /ə'bʌv/ *adv, prep* **1** in a higher place: *The people in the flat above make a lot of noise.* ○ *I live in a small house above the village.* ○ *He looked up at the sky above.* فوق
2 in an earlier part (of sth written): *When replying, quote the reference number above.* أعلاه

3 more than a number, amount, price, etc: *children aged 11 and above ○ A score of 70 and above will get you a grade B. ○ You must get above 50% to pass. ○ above-average temperatures* أكبر، أعلى، أكثر

4 too good, etc. to do sth: *She's not above telling a few lies, if it makes life easier.* أرفع ، أسمى

5 with a higher rank: *The person above me is the department manager.* أعلى

IDM **above all** most importantly: *Above all, stay calm!* أهمّ من كلّ شيء

(be) above board (used especially about a business deal, etc.) honest and open فوق الشبهات ، شريف

abrasive /ə'breɪsɪv/ *adj* **1** rough and likely to scratch: *Do not use abrasive cleaners on the bath.* كاشط ، مخرِّش

2 (used about a person) rude and rather aggressive (شخص) غير مهذب

abreast /ə'brest/ *adv* **abreast (of sb/sth)** next to or level with and going in the same direction: *The soldiers marched two abreast.* جنباً إلى جنب

IDM **be/keep abreast of sth** to have all the most recent information about sth يتابع آخر الأخبار و المعلومات

abridge /ə'brɪdʒ/ *verb* [T] to make sth (usually a book) shorter by removing parts of it: *an abridged version of a novel* يختصر

▸ **abridgement** (*also* **abridgment**) *noun* [C,U] (نص روائي) مختصر

abroad /ə'brɔːd/ *adv* in or to another country or countries: *My mother has never been abroad. ○ They found it difficult to get used to living abroad.* خارج البلاد

abrupt /ə'brʌpt/ *adj* **1** sudden and unexpected: *an abrupt change of plan* مفاجئ ، غير متوقع

2 (used about a person's behaviour) rather rude and unfriendly فظّ ، جافّ

▸ **abruptly** *adv* فجأةً

abruptness *noun* [U] مباغتة ؛ فظاظة

abscess /'æbses/ *noun* [C] a swelling on or in the body, containing a poisonous liquid (pus) خُرَاج

abscond /əb'skɒnd/ *verb* [I] (*formal*) to run away from a place where you should stay, sometimes with sth that you should not take: *She absconded with all the company's money.* يفِرّ

abseil /'æbseɪl/ (*US* **rappel**) *verb* [I] to go down a steep cliff or rock while attached to a rope, pushing against the slope or rock with your feet هبوط المنحدرات الصخرية بالحبال

absence /'æbsəns/ *noun* **1** [C,U] a time when sb is away from somewhere; the fact of being away from somewhere: *Frequent absences due to illness meant he was behind with his work. ○ I have to make all the decisions in my boss's absence.* غَيْبة ، غياب

2 [U] the fact of sth not being there; lack: *The first thing I noticed about the place was the absence of noise.* غياب ، انعدام

absent /'æbsənt/ *adj* **1** not present somewhere: *He was absent from work because of illness. ○ absent friends* غائب

2 thinking about sth else, and so not paying attention: *an absent stare* شارد الذهن

▸ **absently** *adv* بذهن شارد

absentee /ˌæbsən'tiː/ *noun* [C] a person who is absent and should be present غائب

ˌabsent-'minded *adj* often forgetting or not noticing things, because you are thinking about sth else شارد الذهن

▸ **ˌabsent-'mindedly** *adv* بذهن شارد

ˌabsent-'mindedness *noun* [U] شرود الذهن ، غَفْلة

absolute /'æbsəluːt/ *adj* **1** complete; total: *The whole trip was an absolute disaster. ○ None of the parties had an absolute majority* (= more votes, etc. than all the other parties together). كامل ، مطلق

2 not measured in comparison with sth else: *Spending on the Health Service has increased in absolute terms.* مطلق

absolutely *adv* **1** /'æbsəluːtli/ completely; totally: *What you're saying is absolutely wrong. ○ I absolutely refuse to believe that. ○ He made absolutely no effort* (= no effort at all) *to help me.* كلياً، قطعاً

2 /ˌæbsə'luːtli/ (used when you are agreeing with sb) yes; certainly: *'It is a good idea, isn't it?' 'Oh, absolutely!'* تماماً ؛ حتماً

absolve /əb'zɒlv/ *verb* [T] **absolve sb (from/of sth)** to state formally that sb is free from guilt or blame: *The driver was absolved from any responsibility for the train crash.* يبرِّئ

absorb /əb'sɔːb; -zɔːb/ *verb* [T] **1** to take in and hold sth (a liquid, heat, etc.): *a drug that is quickly absorbed into the bloodstream* يمتصّ

2 to take sth into the mind and understand it: *I found it impossible to absorb so much information so quickly.* يستوعب ، يفهم

3 to take sth into sth larger, so that it becomes part of it: *Over the years many villages have been absorbed into the city.* يستوعب ، يبتلع

4 to hold sb's attention completely or interest sb greatly: *History is a subject that absorbs her.* يستحوذ على انتباهه أو اهتمامه

5 to reduce the effect of a sudden violent knock, hit, etc: *The front of the car is designed to absorb most of the impact of a crash.* يمتص

▸ **absorbed** *adj* with sb's attention completely held: *He was absorbed in his work and didn't hear me come in.* مستغرِق ، منهمك

absorbent /-ənt/ *adj* able to take in and hold liquid: *an absorbent cloth* ماصّ ، نشّاف

absorbing *adj* holding the attention completely: *an absorbing story* يستحوذ على الذهن

absorption /əb'sɔːpʃn; -zɔːp-/ *noun* [U] امتصاص

abstain /əb'steɪn/ *verb* [I] **abstain (from sth)**

1 to stop yourself from doing sth that you enjoy: *to abstain from eating during daylight hours* يمنع نفسه من، يمسك عن

ℹ The noun is **abstinence**.

2 (in a vote) to say that you are not voting either

for or against sth: *Two people voted in favour, two voted against and one abstained.* ❶ The noun is **abstention**. يمتنع عن التصويت

abstention /əb'stenʃn/ *noun* [C,U] the act of not voting either for or against sth امتناع

abstinence /'æbstɪnəns/ *noun* [U] stopping yourself from having or doing sth that you enjoy امتناع ؛ تقشّف

abstract¹ /'æbstrækt/ *adj* **1** existing only as an idea, not as a physical or real thing: *I find it hard to think about abstract ideas like the meaning of life.* مجرد

2 (used about art) not showing things as they really look: *an abstract painting* تجريدي

abstract² /'æbstrækt/ *noun* [C] an example of abstract art عمل (فني) تجريدي

IDM in the abstract without mentioning particular people, objects, etc: *I find it hard to think about the problem in the abstract.* على نحو تجريدي ، نظرياً

absurd /əb'sɜːd/ *adj* that should be laughed at; ridiculous; not seeming sensible: *You look absurd in that hat.* ○ *Don't be absurd! I can't possibly do all this work in one day.* مضحك ؛ سخيف ؛ غير معقول

▸ **absurdity** *noun* [C,U] (*pl.* **absurdities**) سَخافة
absurdly *adv*: *The rules of the game are absurdly complicated.* بشكل غير معقول

abundance /ə'bʌndəns/ *noun* [U, sing.] a very large quantity of sth غزارة ، وَفْرة

abundant /ə'bʌndənt/ *adj* existing in very large quantities; more than enough: *abundant supplies of food* غزير ، وفير
▸ **abundantly** *adv* بكثرة ، بوفرة ، بغزارة

⚷**abuse¹** /ə'bjuːz/ *verb* [T] **1** to use sth in the wrong way, e.g. dishonestly: *He was accused of abusing his position for personal gain.* يُسيء استعمال (شيء)

2 to say rude things to sb يسب

3 to treat sb badly, often violently: *Social workers discovered that the girl had been sexually abused by her father.* ينتهك

⚷**abuse²** /ə'bjuːs/ *noun* **1** [C,U] using sth in the wrong way: *an abuse of power* ○ *the dangers of drug abuse* إساءة الاستعمال

2 [U] rude words, used to insult another person: *The other driver leaned out of the car and hurled abuse at me.* شتائم ، سِباب

3 [U] bad, usually violent treatment of sb: *child abuse* انتهاك

abusive /ə'bjuːsɪv/ *adj* using rude language to insult sb: *an abusive remark* مسيء ، بَذيء

abysmal /ə'bɪzməl/ *adj* very bad; of very poor quality رديء للغاية
▸ **abysmally** *adv* بشكل سيئ للغاية

⚷**academic** /ˌækə'demɪk/ *adj* **1** connected with the educational activities of schools, colleges and universities: *The academic year begins in September.* أكاديمي ، دراسي

2 connected with subjects of interest to the mind rather than technical or practical subjects: *academic subjects such as history* أكاديمي ، فكري

3 not connected with reality; not affecting the facts of a situation: *It's academic which one I prefer because I can't have either of them.* نظري
▸ **academic** *noun* [C] a person who teaches and/or does research at a university or college (شخص) أكاديمي ، جامعي
academically /-kli/ *adv* أكاديمياً

academy /ə'kædəmi/ *noun* [C] (*pl.* **academies**)
1 a school for special training: *a military academy* أكاديمية ، كلية

2 (*also* **Academy**) a society of people who are important in art, science or literature: *the Royal Academy of Arts* أكاديمية ، مجمع

accelerate /ək'seləreɪt/ *verb* [I,T] to go faster; to make sth go faster or happen more quickly: *I accelerated and left the other cars behind.* يُسْرِع ؛ يُسرّع
▸ **acceleration** /əkˌselə'reɪʃn/ *noun* [U] تسارع

accelerator /ək'seləreɪtə(r)/ *noun* [C] the pedal in a car, etc. that you press in order to increase speed دوّاسة البنزين ، مسرّع

⚷**accent** /'æksent; -sənt/ *noun* **1** [C,U] a particular way of pronouncing words that is connected with the country, area or social class that you come from: *a strong Scottish accent* لهجة

2 [C] the act of emphasizing a word or part of a word by pronouncing it with greater force: *In the word 'because' the accent is on the second syllable.* نَبْرة

3 [C] (in writing) a mark, usually above a letter, that shows that it has to be pronounced in a certain way علامة كتابية

4 [C, usually sing.] the particular importance that is given to sth: *In all our products the accent is on quality.* توكيد ، تركيز الاهتمام

accentuate /ək'sentʃueɪt/ *verb* [T] to make sth easier to notice يبرِز ، يوضح

⚷**accept** /ək'sept/ *verb* **1** [I,T] to take sth willingly that sb offers you: *Please accept this small gift.* ○ *Do I have to pay in cash or will you accept a cheque?* ○ *Why won't you accept my advice?* يقبَل

2 [I,T] to say yes to sth or to agree to sth: *Thank you for your invitation. I am happy to accept.* ○ *He asked her to marry him and she accepted him.* ○ *I'd be pleased to accept your offer.* يقبَل ، يوافق

3 [T] to admit or recognize that sth unpleasant is true: *They refused to accept responsibility for the accident.* يسلّم بـ

4 [T] to recognize that sth cannot be changed: *It is hard to accept the death of a child.* يتقبّل ، يسلّم بـ

5 [T] to believe sth: *I'm afraid I don't accept that. It simply isn't true.* ○ *She didn't accept that I was telling the truth.* يصدّق

6 [T] to allow sb to join a group, etc: *I had a letter from the university saying that I had been accepted on the course.* يقبل، يوافق على

acceptable /ək'septəbl/ *adj* **1** allowed, often by people in general: *One or two mistakes are acceptable but no more than that.* مقبول

2 satisfactory; good enough: *We hope that you will consider our offer acceptable.* مرضٍ

ℹ The opposite is **unacceptable**.

▸ **acceptability** /əkˌseptə'bɪləti/ *noun* [U] قبول ، درجة التقبُّل

acceptably /-bli/ *adv* بشكل معقول

acceptance /ək'septəns/ *noun* [C,U] the act of accepting or being accepted: *a letter of acceptance from the university* ○ *the acceptance of a difficult situation* (= seeing that it cannot be changed) ○ *He quickly gained acceptance in the group* (= the other people thought of him as equal to them). قبول ، موافقة

access /'ækses/ *noun* [U] **1 access (to sth)** a way of entering or reaching a place: *Access to the garden is through the kitchen.* مدخل ، وسيلة الوصول

2 access (to sth) the chance or right to use or have sth: *Do you have access to a personal computer?* فرصة استعمال ، حقّ استعمال

3 access (to sb) permission, especially legal or official, to see sb: *They are divorced, but he has regular access to the children.* إذن رسمي (بمقابلة شخص مثلاً)

▸ **access** *verb* [T] to find information on a computer: *Click on the icon to access a file.* يصل إلى، يحصل على

accessible /ək'sesəbl/ *adj* **1** possible to be reached or entered: *Because of the snow, the village was not accessible by car.* يَسهُل الوصول إليه

2 easy to get, use or understand سهل المنال

ℹ The opposite is **inaccessible**.

▸ **accessibility** /əkˌsesə'bɪləti/ *noun* [U] سهولة الوصول إلى ، انفتاح

accession /æk'seʃn/ *noun* [U] the act of taking a very high position or rank, especially as ruler of a country or head of sth: *the accession of Queen Elizabeth to the throne in 1952* اعتلاء (العرش)

accessory /ək'sesəri/ *noun* [C] (*pl.* **accessories**) **1** an extra item that is added to sth and is useful or attractive but not essential: *The car has accessories such as an electronic alarm.* مُلْحَق

2 [usually pl.] a small item that is worn or carried with the main items of clothing (e.g. shoes, a bag, etc.) مكمِّل للزينة

3 an accessory (to sth) (in law) a person who helps sb to do sth illegal مساعد (في ارتكاب جريمة)

accident /'æksɪdənt/ *noun* [C] an unpleasant event that happens unexpectedly and causes damage, injury or death: *I hope they haven't had an accident.* ○ *a car accident* ○ *a fatal accident* (= when sb is killed) ○ *I didn't mean to kick you, it was an accident.* حادثة ، حادث

IDM **by accident** by chance; without being planned: *We met each other again completely by accident.* مصادفةً

accidental /ˌæksɪ'dentl/ *adj* happening by chance; not having been planned بالمصادفة ؛ عَرَضي

▸ **accidentally** /-təli/ *adv* بالمصادفة ؛ عَرَضاً ؛ دونَ قصد

ˌaccident and e'mergency *noun* (*abbr* **A & E**) (*Brit*) (*Brit also* **casualty**; *US* **emergency room**) the part of a hospital where people who have been injured in accidents are taken for immediate treatment قسم الحوادث (في مستشفى)

'accident-prone *adj* more likely to have accidents than other people معرَّض للحوادث، عرضة لـ

acclaim /ə'kleɪm/ *verb* [T] to praise sb/sth greatly: *The novel has been acclaimed as a modern classic.* يهلِّل لـ ؛ يمدح

▸ **acclaim** *noun* [U]: *The film received widespread critical acclaim.* ترحيب، مديح

acclimatize (*also* **acclimatise**) /ə'klaɪmətaɪz/ *verb* [I,T] **acclimatize (yourself) (to sth)** to get used to a new climate, a new situation, etc. so that it is not a problem any more: *It took me a long time to get acclimatized to the heat when I went to live in Africa.* يتأقلم

▸ **acclimatization** (*also* **acclimatisation**) /əˌklaɪmətaɪ'zeɪʃn; *US* -tɪ'z-/ *noun* [U] تأقلم

accommodate /ə'kɒmədeɪt/ *verb* [T] **1** to have enough space for sb/sth (especially a certain number of people): *Each apartment can accommodate up to six people.* يتّسع لـ

2 to provide sb with a place to stay, live or work: *During the conference, you will be accommodated in a nearby hotel.* ينْزِل

3 to do or provide what sb wants or needs: *Should you have any special requirements, our staff will do their best to accommodate you.* يزوِّد

▸ **accommodating** *adj* (used about a person) willing to do or provide what sb wants خدوم ؛ متسامح ، ليِّن العريكة

accommodation /əˌkɒmə'deɪʃn/ *noun* [U] a place for sb to live or stay: *We lived in rented accommodation before buying this house.* ○ *The price of the holiday includes flights and accommodation.* سَكَن

> **Accommodation** is uncountable. We cannot say, 'I will help you to find an accommodation.' In this case we could say, 'I will help you to find somewhere to live.'

accompaniment /ə'kʌmpənimənt/ *noun* **1** [C] something that naturally or pleasantly goes with sth else (especially food or drink): *Chocolates were provided as an accompaniment to the coffee.* متمِّم

2 [C,U] music that is played with singing or the main instrument: *a violin piece with a piano accompaniment* مُصاحَبة (موسيقية)

accompany /ə'kʌmpəni/ *verb* [T] (*pres part* **accompanying**; *3rd pers sing pres* **accompanies**; *pt, pp* **accompanied**) **1** to go with sb to a place: *Children must be accompanied by an adult.* يرافق

2 to happen or exist at the same time as, or because of, sth: *Massive publicity accompanied the film's release.* يرافق

3 to give or send sth together with sth else, in

addition to it: *The letter was accompanied by a cheque for £50.* يرفق

4 to play music for a singer or another instrument: *She accompanied him on the guitar.* يصاحب

accomplice /əˈkʌmplɪs; *US* əˈkɒm-/ *noun* [C] a person who helps sb to do sth bad, especially a crime شريك في جريمة

accomplish /əˈkʌmplɪʃ; *US* əˈkɒm-/ *verb* [T] to succeed in doing sth requiring effort and/or skill; to achieve: *Very little was accomplished in the meeting.* ينجز

▸ **accomplished** *adj* skilled: *an accomplished pianist* بارع

accomplishment /əˈkʌmplɪʃmənt; *US* əˈkɒm-/ *noun* **1** [U] the act of completing sth successfully إنجاز

2 [C] something impressive that sb has achieved; a skill that sb has إنجاز ؛ براعة : موهبة

accord¹ /əˈkɔːd/ *noun* [C] *(formal)* an agreement, e.g. between countries: *the Helsinki accords on human rights* اتّفاق

IDM **in accord** in agreement about sth على وفاق

of your own accord without being forced or asked: *He wasn't sacked from his job, he left of his own accord.* طَوْعاً

accord² /əˈkɔːd/ *verb* **1** [T] to give sth to sb: *The diplomats were accorded every respect during their visit.* يمنَح

2 [I] *(formal)* to match; to agree with: *The information did not accord with what I had been told previously.* ينسجم : يتّفق

accordance /əˈkɔːdns/ *noun*

IDM **in accordance with sth** in a way that follows or obeys sth: *to act in accordance with instructions* وفقاً ل

accordingly /əˈkɔːdɪŋli/ *adv* **1** in a way that is suitable after what has happened: *I realized that I was in danger and acted accordingly.* طِبْقاً لذلك

2 *(formal)* therefore; for that reason: *We accept that the mistake was ours and, accordingly, have pleasure in refunding your money.* لذلك

according to /əˈkɔːdɪŋ tə/ *prep* **1** as stated by sb; as shown by sth: *According to Mick, it's a brilliant film.* ○ *More people now have a high standard of living, according to the statistics.* حَسْبَ

2 in a way that matches, follows or depends on sth: *Everything went off according to plan* (= as we had planned it). ○ *The salary will be fixed according to age and experience.* طِبْقاً ل

accordion /əˈkɔːdiən/ *noun* [C] a musical instrument that you hold in both hands and play by pulling the two sides apart and then pushing them together, while pressing the keys with your fingers أكورديون: آلة موسيقية

accost /əˈkɒst; *US* əˈkɔːst/ *verb* [T] to approach and talk to a stranger in a way that is considered unpleasant or frightening يدنو منه و يتعرّض له بالكلام

account¹ /əˈkaʊnt/ *noun* [C] **1** a report or description of sth that has happened: *She gave the police a full account of the robbery.* تقرير ، وصف

2 the arrangement by which a bank looks after your money for you: *to open/close an account* ○ *an account with Barclays* ○ *My salary is paid into my bank account.* ○ *How much money have I got left in my account?* ○ *Can I withdraw £500 from my account?* حساب

> We use a **current** account to pay for things with a **cheque**. We can save money in a **deposit** or **savings** account.

3 [usually pl.] a record of all the money that a person or business has received or paid out: *He takes care of the business and his wife keeps the accounts.* الحسابات

4 an arrangement with a shop, etc. that allows you to pay for goods or services at a later date: *Could you charge that to my account?* حساب

IDM **by all accounts** according to what everyone says: *By all accounts, she's a very good doctor.* حسب كل الراويات ، بإجماع الآراء

on account of because of: *Our flight was delayed on account of bad weather.* بسبب

on no account; not on any account not for any reason: *On no account should you walk home by yourself.* مهما يكن السبب ، مطلقاً

take account of sth; take sth into account to consider sth, especially when deciding or judging sth: *We'll take account of your comments.* يدخله في اعتباره

account² /əˈkaʊnt/ *verb*

PHRV **account for sth 1** to explain or give a reason for sth: *How can we account for these changes?* ○ *I was asked by my boss to account for all the money I had spent* (= to say what I had spent it on). يفسِّر ، يعلّل : يبيّن

2 to supply the amount that is mentioned: *Sales to Europe accounted for 80% of our total sales last year.* يبلغ

accountable /əˈkaʊntəbl/ *adj* expected to give an explanation of your actions, etc; responsible: *She is too young to be held accountable for what she did.* مسؤول

▸ **accountability** /-əbɪləti/ *noun* [U]: *The new law requires greater accountability from the police.* محاسبة ، مسؤولية

accountant /əˈkaʊntənt/ *noun* [C] a person whose job is to keep or examine the financial accounts of a business, etc. محاسب

▸ **accountancy** /əˈkaʊntənsi/ *noun* [U] the profession of an accountant: *a career in accountancy* (علم) المحاسبة

accumulate /əˈkjuːmjəleɪt/ *verb* **1** [T] to collect a number or quantity of sth over a period of time: *Over the years, I've accumulated hundreds of records.* يجمع ، يراكم

2 [I] to increase over a period of time: *Dust soon accumulates if you don't clean the house for a week or so.* يتراكم

▸ **accumulation** /əˌkjuːmjəˈleɪʃn/ *noun* [C,U] تراكم

accuracy /ˈækjərəsi/ *noun* [U] the quality of

being exact and correct ℹ The opposite is **inaccuracy**. دقّة

⚷ **accurate** /ˈækjərət/ *adj* careful and exact; without mistakes: *an accurate description of the house* ○ *That clock isn't very accurate.* ℹ The opposite is **inaccurate**. دقيق ؛ مضبوط
▸ **accurately** *adv* بدِقّة

accusation /ˌækjuˈzeɪʃn/ *noun* [C,U] a statement that says that sb has done sth wrong: *He said that a false accusation had been made against him.* ○ *There was a note of accusation in her voice* (= she sounded critical). اتّهام

⚷ **accuse** /əˈkjuːz/ *verb* [T] **accuse sb (of sth)** to say that sb has done wrong or broken the law: *I accused her of cheating.* ○ *He was accused of murder and sent for trial.* يتّهم
▸ **the accused** *noun* [C] (*pl.* **the accused**) (used in a court of law) the person who is said to have broken a law: *Will the accused please stand.* المتّهم
accusing /əˈkjuːzɪŋ/ *adj* that shows that you think sb has done sth wrong: *He gave me an accusing look.* معبّر عن اللوم ، اتّهامي
accusingly /əˈkjuːzɪŋli/ *adv* على نحو يوحي بالاتّهام

accustomed /əˈkʌstəmd/ *adj* **1 accustomed to sth** if you are accustomed to sth, you are used to it and it is not strange for you: *She's accustomed to travelling a lot in her job.* ○ *It took a while for my eyes to get accustomed to the dark room.* متعوّد على
2 (*formal*) usual; regular: *He took his accustomed walk after lunch.* معتاد

ace /eɪs/ *noun* [C] **1** a playing card which has a single shape on it. An ace has either the lowest or the highest value in a game of cards: *the ace of spades* الآس في ورق اللعب
2 (in tennis) a serve (the first stroke of a game) that is so good that the person playing against you cannot hit it back (في التنس): ضربة أولى لا تُردّ

ache /eɪk/ *noun* [C,U] a pain that lasts for a long time: *to have toothache, earache, stomach ache, etc.* ألم متواصل

> **Ache** is often used in compounds. In British English it is usually used without 'a' or 'an': *I've got toothache.* But we always use 'a' with 'headache': *I've got a headache.* In American English, ache is usually used with 'a' or 'an', especially when talking about a particular attack of pain: *I have an awful toothache.*

▸ **ache** *verb* [I] to feel a continuous pain: *His legs ached after playing football for two hours.* ○ *She was aching all over.* يتألم طويلاً

⚷ **achieve** /əˈtʃiːv/ *verb* [T] **1** to gain sth, usually by effort or skill: *You have achieved the success you deserve.* يحقّق ، يحرز
2 to get sth done; to complete: *They have achieved a lot in a short time.* يحقّق ؛ ينجز
▸ **achievement** *noun* **1** [C] something that is done successfully, especially through hard work or skill: *She felt that the book was her greatest achievement.* إنجاز
2 [U] the act of finishing sth successfully; the feeling that you get when you have finished sth successfully: *Climbing the mountain gave him a sense of achievement.* إنجاز

⚷ **acid** /ˈæsɪd/ *noun* [C,U] (in chemistry) a liquid substance that can dissolve metal and may burn your skin or clothes: *sulphuric acid* ➲ Look at **alkali**. حمض أو حامض
▸ **acid** *adj* **1** (used about a fruit, etc.) with a sharp, sour taste لاذع ، حامض
2 (*also* **acidic**) containing an acid: *an acid solution* ➲ Look at **alkaline**. حمضي
acidity /əˈsɪdəti/ *noun* [U] the quality of being acid حموضة

ˌacid ˈrain *noun* [U] rain that is polluted by acid substances from the chimneys of factories and that causes damage to trees, buildings and rivers أمطار حمضية ، أمطار ملوّثة

⚷ **acknowledge** /əkˈnɒlɪdʒ/ *verb* [T] **1** to accept or admit that sth is true or exists: *He acknowledged the fact that he had been wrong.* ○ *They wouldn't acknowledge defeat.* ○ *It is acknowledged that he is the country's greatest writer.* ○ *He is acknowledged to be the country's greatest writer.* يقرّ ب ، يعترف
2 to show that you have seen sb by raising your hand, smiling, etc: *She refused to acknowledge him and walked straight past.* يُبدي تعرفه (على شخص)
3 to say that you have received a letter, etc: *I would be grateful if you could acknowledge my letter.* يشعر بالاستلام
4 to show or say that you are grateful for sth: *I should like to acknowledge all the help I have received from my family.* يعبر عن شكره
▸ **acknowledgement** (*also* **acknowledgment**) *noun* **1** [U] the act of acknowledging: *I have received no acknowledgement for all the work I did.* اعتراف (بتقدير)
2 [C] a letter, etc. stating that sth has been received خطاب (يشعِر) بالاستلام
3 [C] a few words of thanks that an author writes at the beginning or end of a book to the people who have helped him/her كلمة شكر

acne /ˈækni/ *noun* [U] a type of skin disease, usually affecting young people, that causes a lot of spots on the face and neck حَبّ الشباب

acorn /ˈeɪkɔːn/ *noun* [C] a small nut that is the fruit of the oak tree جوزة البلّوط

acoustic /əˈkuːstɪk/ *adj* **1** connected with sound or the sense of hearing صوتي
2 (of a musical instrument) not electric: *an acoustic guitar* (آلة موسيقية) غير كهربائية
▸ **acoustics** *noun* [plural] **1** the qualities of a room, etc. that make it good or bad for you to hear music, etc: *The theatre has excellent acoustics.* الخصائص السمعية (لحجرة أو قاعة مثلاً)
2 [with sing. verb] the scientific study of sound علم الصوت ، علم السمعيات

acquaintance /əˈkweɪntəns/ *noun* **1** [C] a person that you know but who is not a close friend أحد المعارف

2 [U] **acquaintance with sb/sth** a slight knowledge of sb/sth معرفة قليلة بـ

IDM make sb's acquaintance; make the acquaintance of sb to meet sb for the first time: *I made his acquaintance at a party in London.* يتعرَّف على

acquainted /ə'kweɪntɪd/ *adj* (*formal*) **1 acquainted with sth** knowing sth: *Are you acquainted with the facts?* مطّلع على

2 acquainted (with sb) knowing sb, but usually not very closely: *The two women had been acquainted since they were children.* على معرفة بشخص

acquiesce /ˌækwi'es/ *verb* [I] (*formal*) to accept sth without argument, although you may not agree with it يذْعِن ، يقبل

▸ **acquiescence** /ˌækwi'esns/ *noun* [U] إذعان ، قبول

🔑**acquire** /ə'kwaɪə(r)/ *verb* [T] to get or obtain sth: *The company has acquired shares in a rival business.* ○ *Children do not automatically acquire British citizenship if they are born in this country.* ○ *She acquired an American accent while living in New York.* ○ *He's acquired a reputation for being difficult to work with.* ينال ، يكتسب

acquisition /ˌækwɪ'zɪʃn/ *noun* **1** [C] something that you have obtained or bought, especially sth you are pleased with: *This painting is my latest acquisition.* مقتنى

2 [U] the act of obtaining sth: *the acquisition of wealth* اكتساب : اقتناء : تملُّك

acquit /ə'kwɪt/ *verb* [T] (acqui**tt**ing; acqui**tt**ed)

1 acquit sb (of sth) to declare formally that a person is not guilty of a crime: *The jury acquitted her of murder.* ❶ The opposite is **convict**. يبرِّئ

2 acquit yourself ... (*formal*) to behave in the way that is mentioned: *He acquitted himself quite well in his first match as a professional.* يتصرَّف (وفق ما هو مذكور) ، يقوم بالعمل

▸ **acquittal** /ə'kwɪtl/ *noun* [C,U] تبرئة

acre /'eɪkə(r)/ *noun* [C] a measure of land; 0.405 of a hectare: *a farm of 20 acres/a 20-acre farm* فدّان إنكليزي

acrobat /'ækrəbæt/ *noun* [C] a person who performs difficult movements of the body or difficult balancing acts (e.g. walking on a wire), especially in a circus بَهْلوان

▸ **acrobatic** /ˌækrə'bætɪk/ *adj* بهلواني

acrobatics *noun* [U] (the art of performing) acrobatic acts بهلوانيات

acronym /'ækrənɪm/ *noun* [C] a short word that is made from the first letters of a group of words: *TEFL is an acronym for Teaching English as a Foreign Language.* كلمة مؤلفة من أوائل حروف مجموعة من الكلمات

🔑**across** /ə'krɒs; *US* ə'krɔːs/ *adv, prep* **1** from one side of sth to the other: *The stream was too wide to jump across.* ○ *He walked across the field.* ○ *I drew a line across the page.* ○ *A smile spread across his face.* عَبْر

2 on the other side of sth: *There's a bank just across the road.* في الجانب الآخر

> We can use **across** or **over** to mean 'on or to the other side': *I ran across/over the road.* But when we talk about crossing something high, we usually use **over**: *I can't climb over that wall.* With 'room' we usually use **across**: *I walked across the room to the door.*

3 measuring from side to side: *The river was about 20 metres across.* عَرضاً

IDM across the board involving or affecting all groups, members, cases, etc: *a 10% pay increase across the board* يمس كل القطاعات : للجميع

acrylic /ə'krɪlɪk/ *adj* of a material that is made artificially by a chemical process and used in making sweaters and other clothes أكريليك: نسيج صناعي

🔑**act¹** /ækt/ *verb* **1** [I] to do sth; to take action: *There's no time to lose – you must act now.* ○ *The government were slow to act over the problem of dangerous dogs.* ○ *The man we met on the plane to Tokyo was kind enough to act as our guide* (= to perform the function of guide). يقوم بعمل ، يفعل

2 [I] to behave in the manner stated: *Don't act like a fool.* يتصرَّف

3 [I,T] to perform or have a part in a play or film: *I've never acted before.* ○ *He's always wanted to act the part of Hamlet.* يُمثِّل

▸ **acting** *noun* [U] the art or profession of performing in plays or films تمثيل

🔑**act²** /ækt/ *noun* **1** [C] a thing that you do: *In a typical act of generosity they refused to accept any money.* فعل ، عمل ، صنيع

> **Act** and **action** can have the same meaning: *It was a brave act/action.* **Act**, not **action** can be followed by **of**: *It was an act of bravery.* **Activity** is used for something that is done regularly: *I like outdoor activities such as walking and gardening.* **Deed** is a formal and rather old-fashioned word and often refers to very important acts: *Robin Hood was famous for his brave deeds.* It is the word usually used with **good**: *I wanted to pay back the good deed he had done.*

2 often **Act** [C] one of the main divisions of a play or opera: *How many scenes are there in Act 4?* فصْل في مسرحية

3 [C] a short piece of entertainment that is usually part of a show or circus: *Ladies and gentlemen, please welcome our next act, the Roncalli brothers.* فصْل، فقرة

4 often **Act** [C] a law made by a government: *the Prevention of Terrorism Act* قانون

5 [C] (*informal*) a piece of behaviour that hides your true feelings: *She seems very happy but she's just putting on an act.* تظاهر

IDM get your act together to get organized so that you can do sth properly ينظِّم نفسه

in the act (of doing sth) while doing sth, especially sth wrong: *He was looking through the* *papers on her desk and she caught him in the act.* متلبساً (بفعل شيء)

acting *adj* (only *before* a noun) doing the job mentioned for a short time: *Helen will be the acting director of studies while Susan White is away.* نائب (عن)

⚷**action** /ˈækʃn/ *noun* **1** [U] doing things, often for a particular purpose: *Now is the time for action.* ➲ Look also at **course** (7). عمل، نشاط أو فعالية

2 [C] something that you do: *The doctor's quick action saved the child's life.* ○ *They should be judged by their actions, not by what they say.* ➲ Look at the note at **act**². تصرّف

3 [sing.] the most important events in a story or play: *The action is set in London during the Second World War.* أحداث (قصة أو مسرحية)

4 [U] exciting things that happen: *I didn't like the film, there wasn't much action in it.* أحداث مثيرة، حركة

5 [sing.] the effect that one substance has on another: *The building has been damaged by the action of acid rain.* تأثير

6 [U] the fighting that takes place in battle: *Their son was killed in action.* معركة ، قتال

7 [C,U] the process of settling an argument in court: *He is going to take legal action against the hospital.* اجراء قانوني، مقاضاة

IDM **in action** in operation; while working or doing sth: *We shall have a chance to see their new team in action next week.* أثناء العمل

into action into operation: *We'll put the plan into action immediately.* موضع التنفيذ

out of action not working; unable to function as normal: *The coffee machine's out of action again.* مُعطّل ، متَعطّل

take action to do sth, in order to solve a problem, etc: *The government must take action over unemployment.* يتّخذ إجراء

activate /ˈæktɪveɪt/ *verb* [T] to make sth start working: *A slight movement can activate the car alarm.* يشغّل ، يحرّك

⚷**active** /ˈæktɪv/ *adj* **1** able and willing to do things; energetic: *My grandfather is very active for his age.* ○ *Students should take an active part in college life.* ○ *He was on active service for five years during the war* (= he served in the armed forces). نشيط : فعّال : فعلي

2 that produces an effect; that is in operation: *What is the active ingredient in this medicine?* ○ *an active volcano* (= one that can still erupt) فعّال : نشط

3 (used about the form of a verb or a sentence when the subject of the sentence performs the action of the verb): *In the sentence 'The dog bit him', the verb is active.* ❶ You can also say: 'The verb is in the active'. Look at **passive**. صيغة المعلوم

⚷**activity** /ækˈtɪvəti/ *noun* (*pl.* **activities**) **1** [U] a situation in which there is a lot of action or movement: *The house was full of activity on the morning of the wedding.* ❶ The opposite is **inactivity**. نشاط ، حركة

2 [C] something that you do, usually regularly and for enjoyment: *The hotel offers a range of leisure activities.* ➲ Look at the note at **act**². نشاط

⚷**actor** /ˈæktə(r)/ *noun* [C] a person whose job is to act in a play, film or television programme ممثّل

⚷**actress** /ˈæktrəs/ *noun* [C] a woman whose job is to act in a play, film or television programme ممثّلة

⚷**actual** /ˈæktʃuəl/ *adj* (only *before* a noun) real; that happened, etc. in fact: *The actual damage to the car was not as great as we had feared.* ○ *They seemed to be good friends but in actual fact they hated each other.* فعلي ، حقيقيّ

▸ **actually** /ˈæktʃuəli/ *adv* **1** really; in fact: *You don't actually believe her, do you?* ○ *I can't believe that I'm actually going to America!* في الواقع ، في الحقيقة

2 although it may seem strange: *He actually expected me to cook his meal for him!* في الواقع (رغم غرابته)

> **Actually** is often used in conversation to get somebody's attention or to correct somebody politely: *Actually, I wanted to show you something. Have you got a minute?* ○ *We aren't married, actually.* ○ *I don't agree about the book. I think it's rather good, actually.*

acupuncture /ˈækjupʌŋktʃə(r)/ *noun* [U] a way of treating an illness or stopping pain by putting thin needles into parts of the body بالوخز بالإبر

acute /əˈkjuːt/ *adj* **1** severe; very great: *an acute shortage of food* ○ *acute pain* حادّ ، شديد

2 (used about an illness) reaching a dangerous stage quickly: *acute appendicitis* ❶ The opposite is **chronic**. حاد

3 (used about feelings or the senses) very strong: *Dogs have an acute sense of smell.* شديد ، حادّ

4 showing that you are able to understand things easily: *The report contains some acute observations on the situation.* ذكي ، ثاقب

▸ **acutely** *adv*: *They are acutely aware of the problem.* بشدّة ، إلى حدّ كبير

aˌcute ˈangle *noun* [C] an angle of less than 90° زاوية حادّة

AD (*US* **A.D.**) /ˌeɪ ˈdiː/ *abbrev* anno domini; used in dates for showing the number of years after the time it was traditionally believed that Jesus Christ was born: *44 AD.* ➲ Look at **CE**. بعد الميلاد

⚷**ad** /æd/ *noun* (*informal*) = ADVERTISEMENT: *I saw your ad in the local paper.*

adamant /ˈædəmənt/ *adj* (*formal*) (used about a person) very sure; not willing to change your mind: *He was adamant that he had not made a mistake.* صُلب الرأي ، عنيد

▸ **adamantly** *adv* بإصرار ، بعناد

⚷**adapt** /əˈdæpt/ *verb* **1** [I] **adapt (to sth)** to change your behaviour because the situation you are in has changed: *He was quick to adapt to the new system.* يتكيَّف مع

2 [T] **adapt sth (for sth)** to change sth so that you can use it in a different situation: *The car was adapted for use as a taxi.* يكيِّف ، يعدِّل

3 [T] to change a book, etc. so that it can be shown as a film, etc: *Tonight's play has been adapted for radio from the novel by Charles Dickens.* يحوِّر، يعدّ (للإذاعة)

▸ **adaptable** /-əbl/ *adj* able and willing to change to suit new conditions: *You have to be adaptable if you want to live in a foreign country.* مرِن، قابل للتكيُّف

adaptation /ˌædæpˈteɪʃn/ *noun* [C] **1** a play or film that is based on a novel, etc: *a television adaptation of 'Wuthering Heights'* مسرحية أو فيلم مقتبس من رواية

2 the state or process of adapting: *a period of adaptation* تكيُّف ؛ تعديل

adaptor (*also* **adapter**) *noun* [C] **1** a device that allows more than one plug to be connected to an electricity supply point (socket) قابس متعدد المآخذ

2 a device that fits on an electrical plug and allows you to use a piece of electrical equipment with a different type of socket: *You'll need an adaptor to use your hairdryer in Spain.* وَصْلة مهايئة

add /æd/ *verb* **1** [I,T] **add (sth) (to sth)** to put sth together with sth else, so that you increase the size, number, value, etc: *Next, add some milk to the mixture.* ○ *He wanted to add his name to the letter.* ○ *They had invited an entertainer to the party, just to add to the fun.* يضيف

2 [T] to put numbers or amounts together so that you get a total: *If you add 3 and 3 together, you get 6.* ○ *Add £8 to the total, to cover postage and packing.* ❶ The opposite is **subtract**. ❶ We often use the word **plus** when we add two numbers: *2 plus 2 is 4.* يجمَع ، يضيف

3 [T] to say sth more: *'Don't forget to write to us,' she added.* يضيف ، يردِف (قائلاً)

PHRV **add sth on (to sth)** to include: *10% will be added on to your bill as a service charge.* يضيف

add up to seem as if it could be true: *I'm sorry, but your story just doesn't add up.* يقبل التصديق

add (sth) up to find the total of several numbers: *The waiter hadn't added up the bill correctly.* يجمع

add up to sth to have as a total: *The bill should add up to about £40.* يبلغ

adder /ˈædə(r)/ *noun* [C] a small poisonous snake أفعى

addict /ˈædɪkt/ *noun* [C] a person who cannot stop taking or doing sth harmful: *a drug addict* مدْمِن

▸ **addicted** /əˈdɪktɪd/ *adj* **addicted (to sth)** unable to stop taking or doing sth harmful: *He is addicted to heroin.* ○ *He's addicted to football.* مدْمِن على

addiction /əˈdɪkʃn/ *noun* [C,U]: *the problem of teenage drug addiction* إدمان

addictive /əˈdɪktɪv/ *adj*: *addictive drugs* يؤدّي إلى الإدمان

addition /əˈdɪʃn/ *noun* **1** [U] the process of adding sth, especially of adding up two or more numbers ➲ Look at **subtraction**. جَمْع

2 [C] **addition (to sth)** a person or thing that is added to sth: *They've got a new addition to the family* (= another child). شخص أو شيء إضافيّ

IDM **in addition (to sth)** as well as: *She speaks five foreign languages in addition to English.* علاوة على ، إضافةً إلى

▸ **additional** /-ʃənl/ *adj* added; extra: *a small additional charge for the use of the swimming pool* إضافي

additionally /-ʃənəli/ *adv* بالإضافة إلى ذلك

additive /ˈædətɪv/ *noun* [C] a substance that is added in small amounts for a special purpose: *food additives* (= to add colour or flavour) مادة مضافة

address[1] /əˈdres; *US* ˈædres/ *noun* [C] **1** the number of the house and the name of the street and town where you live or work: *Let me give you my home/business address.* ○ *She no longer lives at this address.* ○ *Please inform the office of any change of address.* ○ *an address book* (= a small book that you keep the addresses of people you know in) ○ *an email address* عُنوان

2 a formal speech that is given to an audience خطبة

address[2] /əˈdres/ *verb* [T] **1** **address sth (to sb/sth)** to write (on a letter, etc.) the name and address of the person you are sending it to: *The parcel was returned because it had been wrongly addressed.* يعَنْوِن

2 to make an important or formal speech to a crowd or audience يخاطب ؛ يلقي خطبة

3 **address sth to sb** (*formal*) make a remark, etc. to sb: *Would you kindly address any complaints you have to the manager.* يوجِّه

4 to talk or write to sb using a particular name or title: *She prefers to be addressed as 'Ms'.* يخاطب (بلقب)

5 **address yourself to sth** (*formal*) to try to deal with a problem, etc: *He had to address himself to the task of finding a new job.* ينصرف إلى ، يجدّ في

adept /əˈdept/ *adj* **adept (at sth)** very good or skilful at sth بارع ، حاذق

adequate /ˈædɪkwət/ *adj* **1** enough for what you need: *The food they eat is barely adequate to keep them alive.* ○ *Make sure you take an adequate supply of water with you.* كافٍ

2 good enough; acceptable: *Your work is adequate but I'm sure you could do better.* وافٍ (بالحاجة) ؛ لا بأس به

❶ The opposite is **inadequate**.

▸ **adequacy** /ˈædɪkwəsi/ *noun* [U] كفاية ، وفاء (بالحاجة)

adequately *adv*: *The work has been done adequately, but not well.* ○ *The mystery has never been adequately explained.* على نحو كافٍ

adhere /əd'hɪə(r)/ *verb* [I] (*formal*) **1 adhere (to sth)** to stick firmly: *Make sure that the paper adheres firmly to the wall.* يلتصق

2 adhere to sth to continue to support an idea, etc.; to follow a rule: *This rule has never been strictly adhered to by members of staff.* يلتزم بِ

▸ **adherent** *noun* [C] somebody who supports a particular idea مشايع، نصير

adherence /-əns/ *noun* [U]: *His adherence to his principles cost him his job.* التزام، تمسك

adhesive /əd'hi:sɪv/ *noun* [C] a substance that makes things stick together: *a fast-drying adhesive* مادة لاصقة، لزاق

▸ **adhesive** *adj* that can stick, or can cause two things to stick together: *He sealed the parcel with adhesive tape.* (شريط) لزّاق أو لاصق

ad hoc /ˌæd 'hɒk/ *adj* made or formed for a particular purpose: *They set up an ad hoc committee to discuss the matter.* لغرض محدّد

adjacent /ə'dʒeɪsnt/ *adj* situated next to or close to sth: *There was a fire in the adjacent building.* ○ *She works in the office adjacent to mine.* مجاور

adjective /'ædʒɪktɪv/ *noun* [C] (*grammar*) a word used with a noun that tells you more about it: *The adjective 'asleep' cannot come before a noun.* صفة، نَعْت

▸ **adjectival** /ˌædʒek'taɪvl/ *adj* that contains or is used like an adjective: *an adjectival phrase* وصفي، نَعْتي

adjoining /ə'dʒɔɪnɪŋ/ *adj* joining sth or situated next or nearest to sth: *A scream came from the adjoining room.* ملاصق

adjourn /ə'dʒɜ:n/ *verb* [I,T] to stop sth (a meeting, a trial, etc.) for a short period of time and start it again later: *This court will adjourn until tomorrow.* ○ *The meeting was adjourned until the following week.* يؤجّل، يرجئ

▸ **adjournment** *noun* [C]: *The lawyers asked for an adjournment.* تأجيل

adjudicate /ə'dʒu:dɪkeɪt/ *verb* [I,T] (*formal*) to act as an official judge in a competition or to decide who is right when two sides disagree about sth يحكم، يفصل

▸ **adjudicator** *noun* [C] a person who acts as a judge, especially in a competition حَكَم، فيصل

🔑 **adjust** /ə'dʒʌst/ *verb* **1** [T] to change sth slightly, especially because it is not in the right position: *There's something wrong with the brakes on the car – they need adjusting.* ○ *The figures have been adjusted to take account of inflation.* يعدّل، يضبط

2 [I] **adjust (to sth)** to get used to new conditions or a new situation: *She found it hard to adjust to working at night.* يتأقلم مع، يتعوّد على

▸ **adjustable** /-əbl/ *adj* that can be adjusted: *an adjustable mirror* قابل للتعديل أو الضبط

adjustment *noun* [C,U] تعديل؛ تأقلم

ad lib /ˌæd 'lɪb/ *adj, adv* done or spoken without preparation: *She had to speak ad lib because she couldn't find her notes.* ارتجالاً

▸ **ad lib** *verb* [I] (ad lib**b**ing; ad lib**b**ed) يرتجل

administer /əd'mɪnɪstə(r)/ *verb* [T] **1** to control or manage sth: *The system is very complicated and difficult to administer.* يدير

2 (*formal*) to make sb take sth (especially medicine): *The doctor administered a pain-killing drug.* يناول، يعطي دواء

administration /ədˌmɪnɪ'streɪʃn/ *noun* **1** [U] the control or management of sth (e.g. a system, an organization or a business): *The administration of a large project like this is very complicated.* إدارة

2 [sing.] the group of people who organize or control sth: *the hospital administration* هيئة الإدارة

3 often **the Administration** [C] the government of a country, especially the USA: *the Bush Administration* الإدارة، الحكومة

▸ **administrative** /əd'mɪnɪstrətɪv; *US* -streɪtɪv/ *adj* connected with the organization and management of a country or business, etc: *London is still the most important administrative centre.* ○ *an administrative assistant* إداري

administrator /əd'mɪnɪstreɪtə(r)/ *noun* [C] a person whose job is to organize or manage a system, a business, etc. مدير؛ وكيل أو وصيّ

admirable /'ædmərəbl/ *adj* deserving admiration or praise: *an admirable example of good planning* جدير بالإعجاب، رائع

▸ **admirably** /-əbli/ *adv*: *She dealt with the problem admirably.* بشكل يستحق الإعجاب

admiral /'ædmərəl/ *noun* [C] an officer of very high rank in the navy who commands a group (fleet) of ships أميرال، أمير البحر

🔑 **admiration** /ˌædmə'reɪʃn/ *noun* [U] a feeling that you have when you like and respect sb/sth very much: *I have great admiration for his work.* إعجاب

🔑 **admire** /əd'maɪə(r)/ *verb* [T] to respect or like sb/sth very much; to look at sb/sth with pleasure: *Everyone admired the way he dealt with the problem.* ○ *I've always admired her for being such a wonderful mother.* ○ *We walked round the house, admiring the furniture and decorations.* يُعجَب بِ؛ يتأمّل معجباً

▸ **admirer** *noun* [C] a person who admires sb/sth مُعْجَب

admiring *adj* feeling or expressing admiration: *an admiring look* معبِّر عن الإعجاب

admiringly *adv* بإعجاب

admission /əd'mɪʃn/ *noun* **1** [C,U] permission to enter a school, club, public place, etc: *Admissions to British universities have increased by 15% this year.* ○ *All those who were not wearing a tie were refused admission to the club.* دخول، قبول

2 [U] the amount of money that you pay to enter a place: *The museum charges £3 admission.* رسْم الدخول

3 [C] a statement that something, usually unpleasant, is true: *I viewed her silence as an admission of guilt.* إقرار، اعتراف

🔑 **admit** /əd'mɪt/ *verb* (admit**t**ing; admit**t**ed) **1** [I,T] **admit to sth/doing sth**; **admit (that...)** to agree, often without wanting to, that sth is true:

a b c d e f g h i j k l m n o p q r s t u v w x y z

He refused to admit to the theft. ○ *You should admit your mistake.* ○ *I have to admit that I was wrong.* ○ *'I was wrong,' he admitted.* ○ *She admitted having broken the vase.* يقرّ ، يعترف

2 [T] **admit sb/sth (into/to sth)** to allow sb/sth to enter; to take sb into a place: *I have a ticket that admits a member plus one guest to the gardens.* ○ *He was admitted to hospital with suspected appendicitis.* يسمح بالدخول ؛ يدخل

▸ **admittedly** *adv* it must be admitted (that): *The work is very interesting. Admittedly, I do get rather tired.* لا نكران

admittance /əd'mɪtns/ *noun* [U] being allowed to enter a place (especially a private one); the right to enter: *The journalist tried to gain admittance to the minister's office.* ○ *No admittance* (= as a warning on a door that people should keep out). دخول ؛ حقّ الدخول

adolescence /ˌædə'lesns/ *noun* [U] the period of a person's life between being a child and becoming an adult, i.e. between the ages of about 13 and 17 (سن) المراهقة

▸ **adolescent** /ˌædə'lesnt/ *noun* [C] a young person who is no longer a child and not yet an adult: *the problems of adolescents* ○ *an adolescent daughter* ➲ Look at **teenager**. مراهق

⚷**adopt** /ə'dɒpt/ *verb* **1** [I,T] to take a child into your family and treat him/her as your own child by law يتبنّى

2 [T] to take and use sth: *She decided not to adopt her husband's name when she got married.* ○ *All his suggestions have been adopted.* يتّخذ ؛ يتبنّى ، يُقرّ

▸ **adopted** *adj*: *an adopted child* متبنّى ، (طفل) بالتبنّي

adoption /ə'dɒpʃn/ *noun* [C,U]: *The party is considering the adoption of a new transport policy.* ○ *We can't have children so we're interested in adoption.* ○ *The number of adoptions has risen in the past year* (= the number of children being adopted). التبنّي

adoptive /ə'dɒptɪv/ *adj* متبنّي

adorable /ə'dɔːrəbl/ *adj* (used for expressing affection for a child or animal) very attractive محبوب ؛ جذّاب

adore /ə'dɔː(r)/ *verb* [T] **1** to love and admire sb/sth very much: *Kim adores her older sister.* يحب بشغف ؛ يعشق

2 (*informal*) to like sth very much: *I adore strawberries.* يهوى، يولع بِ

▸ **adoration** /ˌædə'reɪʃn/ *noun* [U] عشق، عبادة

adorn /ə'dɔːn/ *verb* [T] to add sth in order to make a thing or person more attractive or beautiful: *a building adorned with flags* يزيّن

adrenalin /ə'drenəlɪn/ *noun* [U] a substance that your body produces when you are very angry, frightened or excited and that makes your heart beat faster أدرينالين

adrift /ə'drɪft/ *adj* (not before a noun) not tied to anything or controlled by anybody (used about a boat) (قارب) سائب

⚷**adult** /'ædʌlt; ə'dʌlt/ *noun* [C] a person or animal that is fully grown: *This film is suitable for both adults and children.* بالغ ، راشد

▸ **adult** *adj*: *She was born here but has spent her adult life in Chile.* ناضج ، راشد

adultery /ə'dʌltəri/ *noun* [U] sexual relations between a person who is married and sb who is not that person's wife/husband زنى

⚷**advance**[1] /əd'vɑːns; *US* -'væns/ *verb* **1** [I] to move forward: *The army advanced towards the city.* ➲ Look at **retreat**. يتقدم نحو

2 [I,T] to make progress or help sth make progress: *Our research has not advanced much recently.* يتقدّم ؛ يساعد على تقدّمه

▸ **advanced** *adj* **1** of a high level: *an advanced English class* متقدّم ؛ على مستوى عال

2 highly developed: *a country that is not very advanced industrially* متقدّم ، متطوّر

⚷**advance**[2] /əd'vɑːns; *US* -'væns/ *noun* **1** [C, usually sing.] forward movement: *the army's advance towards the border* تقدّم ، زحف

2 [C,U] progress in sth: *advances in computer technology* تقدّم

3 [C] an amount of money that is paid to sb before the time when it is usually paid سلفة

IDM in advance (of sth) before a particular time or event: *You should book tickets for the concert well in advance.* سلفاً ، مقدماً

advance[3] /əd'vɑːns; *US* -'væns/ *adj* (only before a noun) that happens before sth: *There was no advance warning of the earthquake* مسبق

Ad'vanced level = A LEVEL

⚷**advantage** /əd'vɑːntɪdʒ; *US* -'væn-/ *noun* **1** [C] **an advantage (over sb)** something that may help you to do better than other people: *Her secretarial experience gave her an advantage over the other people applying for the job.* ○ *Our team had the advantage of playing at our home ground.* ميزة، أفضليّة

2 [C,U] something that helps you or that will bring you a good result: *the advantages and disadvantages of a plan* ○ *The traffic is so bad here that there is no advantage in having a car.* فائدة

🛈 The opposite is **disadvantage**.

IDM take advantage of sth 1 to make good or full use of sth: *Take advantage of the cheap prices while they last.* يستفيد من ، ينتهز الفرصة

2 to make unfair use of sb or of sb's kindness, etc. in order to get what you want: *You shouldn't let him take advantage of you like this.* يستغلّ

▸ **advantageous** /ˌædvən'teɪdʒəs/ *adj* that will help you or bring you a good result مفيد ؛ موات ؛ مربح

advent /'ædvent/ *noun* [sing.] **1** (*formal*) the arrival or coming of sb/sth: *This area was very isolated before the advent of the railway.* قدوم ، وصول

2 Advent (in the Christian year) the period which includes the four Sundays before Christmas الأسابيع الأربعة قبل عيد الميلاد

⚷**adventure** /əd'ventʃə(r)/ *noun* [C,U] an experience or event that is very unusual, exciting or dangerous: *She left home to travel, hoping for excitement and adventure.* ○ *an adventure story* مغامرة ؛ مخاطرة

▸ **adventurous** *adj* **1** (used about a person) liking to try new things or have adventures مغامر ؛ محبّ لتجريب الأشياء الجديدة

2 involving adventure: *For a more adventurous holiday try mountain climbing.* مثير ، مليء بالمغامرات

adverb /ˈædvɜːb/ *noun* [C] a word that adds information to a verb, adjective, phrase or another adverb: *In the sentence 'Please speak slowly', 'slowly' is an adverb.* ○ *'Happily', 'well', 'always', 'very' and 'too' are all adverbs.* ظرف ، حال

▸ **adverbial** /ædˈvɜːbiəl/ *adj* used like an adverb: *'In the afternoon' is an adverbial phrase.* عبارة ظَرفيّة

adversary /ˈædvəsəri; *US* -seri/ *noun* [C] (*pl.* **adversaries**) (*formal*) an enemy, or an opponent in a competition عدوّ ، خصم

adverse /ˈædvɜːs/ *adj* (*formal*) making sth difficult for sb; not favourable: *Our flight was cancelled because of adverse weather conditions.* معاد ؛ معاكس

▸ **adversely** *adv* على نحو سيّئ

adversity /ədˈvɜːsəti/ *noun* [C,U] (*pl.* **adversities**) (*formal*) difficulties or problems: *to show strength in the face of adversity* محنة ، شدّة

advert /ˈædvɜːt/ *noun* [C] (*Brit informal*) = ADVERTISEMENT

advertise /ˈædvətaɪz/ *verb* **1** [I,T] to put information in a newspaper, on television, on a poster, etc. in order to persuade people to buy sth, apply for a job, etc: *a poster advertising a new type of biscuit* ○ *The job was advertised in the local newspapers.* ○ *It's very expensive to advertise on television.* يعلن ؛ يروّج

2 [I] **advertise for sb/sth** to say publicly in a newspaper, on a noticeboard, etc. that you need sb to do a particular job, want to buy sth, etc: *The shop is advertising for a part-time sales assistant.* يعلن عن

▸ **advertisement** /ədˈvɜːtɪsmənt; *US* ˌædvərˈtaɪzmənt/ *noun* [C] (*also* **advert**; **ad**) a piece of information in a newspaper, on television, on a poster, etc. that tries to persuade people to buy sth, apply for a job, etc: *a television advert for a new brand of washing powder* ○ *If you want to sell your car, why don't you put an advertisement in the local newspaper?* إعلان

advertising *noun* [U]: *The magazine gets a lot of money from advertising.* ○ *an advertising campaign* إعلان، حملة دعائيّة

advice /ədˈvaɪs/ *noun* [U] an opinion that you give sb about what he/she should do or how he/she should behave: *She took her doctor's advice and gave up smoking.* ○ *You should get some legal advice* (= ask a lawyer to tell you what to do). ○ *Let me give you some advice ...* نصيحة ، إرشاد

> **Advice** is an uncountable noun, so we cannot say 'an advice' or 'some advices'. We can say: *a piece of advice* and : *a lot of advice.*

advisable /ədˈvaɪzəbl/ *adj* (*formal*) that sb would recommend you to do; sensible: *It is advisable to reserve a seat.* مستحسن ، صائب

advise /ədˈvaɪz/ *verb* **1** [I,T] **advise (sb) (to do sth); advise (sb) (against sth/against doing sth)** to tell sb what you think he/she should do: *I would strongly advise you to take the job.* ○ *They advised us not to travel on a Friday.* ○ *The newspaper article advised against buying a house in that area.* ○ *He did what the doctor advised.* ○ *She advises the Government on economic affairs.* ينصح ؛ يشير على

2 [T] (*formal*) to inform sb: *We would like to advise you that the goods are now ready for collection.* يحيط علماً ، يبلّغ

▸ **adviser** (*US* **advisor**) *noun* [C] a person who gives advice to a company, government, etc: *an adviser on economic affairs* مستشار

advisory /ədˈvaɪzəri/ *adj* giving advice only; not having the power to make decisions: *an advisory committee* استشاري

advocate /ˈædvəkeɪt/ *verb* [T] (*formal*) to recommend or say that you support a particular plan or action: *The Minister advocated a reform of the tax system.* يوصي بِ

▸ **advocate** /ˈædvəkət/ *noun* [C] **1 advocate (of sth)** a person who supports a particular plan or action, especially in public: *an advocate of nuclear disarmament* نصير

2 a lawyer who defends sb in a court of law محامي دفاع

A & E /ˌeɪ ənd ˈiː/ *abbrev* = ACCIDENT AND EMERGENCY

aerial[1] /ˈeəriəl/ (*especially US* **antenna**) *noun* [C] a long metal stick on a building, car, etc. that receives radio or television signals هوائي

aerial[2] /ˈeəriəl/ *adj* **1** from or in the air: *an aerial attack on the city* ○ *aerial warfare* جوّي

2 taken from an aircraft: *an aerial photograph of the village* مأخوذ من الجوّ

aerobics /eəˈrəʊbɪks/ *noun* [U] energetic physical exercises that increase the amount of oxygen in your blood. Aerobics is often done to music: *I do aerobics twice a week to keep fit.* تمرينات رياضيّة

aerodynamics /ˌeərəʊdaɪˈnæmɪks/ *noun* [U] the scientific study of the way that things move through the air علم الديناميك الهوائي

▸ **aerodynamic** *adj* ديناميكي هوائي

aeroplane /ˈeərəpleɪn/ *noun* [C] = PLANE

aerosol /ˈeərəsɒl; *US* -sɔːl/ *noun* [C] a container in which a liquid substance is kept under pressure. When you press a button the liquid comes out in a fine spray. بخّاخة ، مرذاذ

aesthetic /iːsˈθetɪk/ (*US also* **esthetic** /esˈθetɪk/) *adj* involving people's sense of beauty: *The columns are there for purely aesthetic reasons* (= only to look beautiful). جمالي

▸ **aesthetically** (*US also* **esthetically**) /-kli/ *adv*: *to be aesthetically pleasing* جماليّاً

afar /əˈfɑː(r)/ *adv* (*formal*)

a b c d e f g h i j k l m n o p q r s t u v w x y z

IDM from afar from a long distance away: *The lights of the city were visible from afar.* من بعيد

affair /ə'feə(r)/ *noun* **1** [C] an event or situation: *The wedding was a very grand affair.* ○ *The whole affair has been extremely unpleasant.* حَدَث ؛ وضع

2 affairs [plural] important personal, business, national, etc. matters: *The organization should have control of its own financial affairs.* ○ *the Irish minister for foreign affairs* ○ *current affairs* (= the political and social events that are happening at the present time) أمور ، شؤون

3 [sing.] something private that you do not want other people to know about: *What happened between us is my affair. I don't want to discuss it.* أمر خاص

4 [C] a sexual relationship between two people who are not married to each other: *They are having an affair.* علاقة غراميّة

IDM state of affairs → STATE[1]

affect /ə'fekt/ *verb* [T] **1** to influence or cause sb/sth to change in a particular way: *Her personal problems seem to be affecting her work.* ○ *Loud music can affect your hearing.* ➲ Look at the note at **influence**. يؤثّر على

2 to cause sb to feel very sad, angry, etc: *The whole community was affected by the terrible tragedy.* يؤثّر في ، يحزن ؛ يضر بـ

> Notice that **affect** is a verb and **effect** is a noun: *Smoking can affect your health.* ○ *Smoking can have a bad effect on your health.*

affected /ə'fektɪd/ *adj* (used about a person or a person's behaviour) not natural or sincere متكلّف ، متصنّع

▸ **affectation** /ˌæfek'teɪʃn/ *noun* [C,U] تصنّع ، تظاهر

affection /ə'fekʃn/ *noun* [U] **affection (for/towards sb/sth)** a feeling of loving or liking sb/sth: *Mark felt great affection for his sister.* حبّ ، حنان ، مودّة

▸ **affectionate** /ə'fekʃənət/ *adj* showing that you love or like sb very much: *a very affectionate child* محبّ ، حنون

affectionately *adv*: *He looked at her affectionately.* بحبّ ، بحنان

affiliate /ə'fɪlieɪt/ *verb* [T] (usually passive) **affiliate sth (to sth)** to connect an organization to a larger organization: *Our local club is affiliated to the national association.* يلحق بـ ، يضمّ إلى

▸ **affiliated** *adj*: *the NUJ and other affiliated unions* ملحق ، منتسب

affiliation /əˌfɪli'eɪʃn/ *noun* [C,U] a connection made by affiliating: *The group has affiliations with the Conservative Party.* ارتباط ؛ انتساب

affinity /ə'fɪnəti/ *noun* [C,U] (*pl.* **affinities**) **1 affinity (for/with sb/sth)** a strong feeling that you like and understand sb/sth, usually because you feel similar to him/her/it in some way: *He had always had an affinity for wild and lonely places.* ميل إلى ؛ تقارب

2 affinity (with sb/sth); affinity (between A and B) a similar quality in two or more people or things: *His music has certain affinities with Brahms.* تشابه

affirm /ə'fɜːm/ *verb* [T] (*formal*) **1** to say clearly that you hold a particular belief: *The people affirmed their country's right to independence.* يؤكّد ؛ يصرّح

2 to say that sth is a fact: *She affirmed that he would resign.* يؤكّد

▸ **affirmation** /ˌæfə'meɪʃn/ *noun* [C,U] إثبات ، تأكيد

affirmative /ə'fɜːmətɪv/ *adj* (*formal*) meaning 'yes': *an affirmative answer* ❶ We can also say 'an answer in the affirmative'. ❶ The opposite is **negative**. إيجابي

afflict /ə'flɪkt/ *verb* [T] (usually passive) (*formal*) to cause sb/sth to suffer pain, sadness, etc: *He had been afflicted with a serious illness since childhood.* يصيب ، يبتلي

▸ **affliction** /ə'flɪkʃn/ *noun* [C,U] a thing that causes suffering: *Poor sight and hearing are common afflictions of old age.* بلوى ؛ ألم

affluent /'æfluənt/ *adj* having a lot of money موسر ، غني

▸ **affluence** /-əns/ *noun* [U] غنى ، نعمة

afford /ə'fɔːd/ *verb* [I,T] **1** (usually after *can, could* or *be able to*) to have enough money or time to be able to do sth: *We couldn't afford a television in those days.* ○ *There's a lot to do. We can't afford to waste any time.* يقدر مالياً ؛ يملك الوقت الكافي ...

2 can't/couldn't afford to not be able to do sth or let sth happen because it would have a bad result for you: *The other team was very good so we couldn't afford to make mistakes.* ليس في وسعه أن...

affront /ə'frʌnt/ *noun* [C] something that you say or do that is insulting to another person or thing إهانة ، إساءة

afield /ə'fiːld/ *adv*

IDM far afield → FAR[2]

afloat /ə'fləʊt/ *adj* (not before a noun) **1** on the surface of the water; not sinking عائم ، طافٍ

2 (used about a business, an economy, etc.) having enough money to survive: *We will need to borrow ten million pounds to keep the company afloat.* شغّال ، مستمرّ في العمل

afoot /ə'fʊt/ *adj* (not before a noun) being planned or prepared: *There was a plan afoot to build a new theatre.* قيد الإعداد

afraid /ə'freɪd/ *adj* (not before a noun) **1 afraid (of sb/sth); afraid (of doing sth/to do sth)** having or showing fear; frightened: *Why are some people afraid of spiders?* ○ *Sue is afraid of going out after dark.* ○ *I was too afraid to answer the door.* خائف

2 afraid (that...); afraid (of doing sth) worried about sth: *We were afraid that you would be angry.* ○ *to be afraid of offending sb* قلِق

> Compare **afraid** and **frightened**. You can only use **afraid** after a noun, but you can use

frightened before or after a noun: *a frightened animal* ○ *The animal was afraid/frightened.*

IDM **I'm afraid (that...)** (used for saying politely that you are sorry about sth): *I'm afraid I can't come on Sunday.* آسف (أنّ...)

afresh /ə'freʃ/ *adv* (*formal*) again, in a new way: *to start afresh* ثانيةً ، مجدداً

African-American /ˌæfrɪkən ə'merɪkən/ *noun* [C] an American citizen whose family was originally from Africa مواطن أمريكي من أصل افريقي
▸ **African-American** *adj* أمريكي من أصل افريقي

Afrobeat /'æfrəʊbiːt/ *noun* [U] a type of music that combines traditional Nigerian rhythms and singing styles with jazz and funk موسيقى الأفروبيت: خليط من الموسيقى النيجيرية و موسيقى الجاز

Afro-Caribbean /ˌæfrəʊ kærɪ'biːən; *US* -kə'rɪbiən/ *noun* [C] **1** a person from the Caribbean whose family was originally from Africa كاريبيّ من أصل إفريقي
2 a person from a different country whose family was originally Afro-Caribbean (1) شخص من أصل كاريبيّ-أفريقيّ
▸ **Afro-Caribbean** *adj*: *the Afro-Caribbean community in West London* كاريبيّ-افريقي

after¹ /'ɑːftə(r); *US* 'æf-/ *prep* **1** later than sth: *Ian phoned just after six o'clock.* ○ *the week, month, year, etc. after next* ○ *I hope to arrive some time after lunch.* ○ *We spent three days in Edinburgh and after that we went to Glasgow.* ○ *After doing my homework, I went out for a walk.* بَعْدَ
2 ...after... repeated many times or continuing for a long time: *day after day of hot weather* ○ *I've told the children time after time not to do that.* بَعْدَ ، (مرّة) بَعْدَ (مرّة)
3 following or behind sb/sth: *Shut the door after you.* ○ *The dog ran after its master.* ○ *After you* (= used for politely allowing sb to use sth, go through a door, etc. first) خلفَ ، وراء
4 following in order: *C comes after B in the alphabet.* بَعْدَ
5 because of sth: *After the way he behaved I won't invite him here again.* بِسَبَب
6 looking for or trying to catch or get sb/sth: *The police were after him.* ○ *Nicky is after a job in advertising.* يفتّش عن
7 (used when sb/sth is given the name of another person or thing): *The street is called Wellington Street, after the famous general.* نسبةً إلى

IDM **after all 1** (used when sth happens that you did not expect to happen, or when you discover that sth that you thought was not true is, in fact, true): *So you decided to come after all!* (= I thought you weren't going to come) ○ *Maybe he's not so stupid after all.* إذَنْ! ; كما ظننت
2 (used for reminding sb of a certain fact): *She can't understand. After all, she's only two.* لا تنسَ أنّ...

after² /'ɑːftə(r); *US* 'æf-/ *conj* at a time later than sth: *They arrived at the station after the train had left.* ○ *After we had finished our dinner, we went into the garden.* بَعْدَ ، عَقِب

after³ /'ɑːftə(r); *US* 'æf-/ *adv* at a later time: *That was in 1986. Soon after, I heard that he was ill.* ○ *They lived happily ever after* (= for ever). بعد ذلك

It is more common to use **afterwards** at the end of a sentence: *We played tennis and then went to Angela's house afterwards.*

'after-effect *noun* [C] an unpleasant result of sth that comes some time after it has happened: *the after-effects of a serious illness* عاقبة ، نتيجة وخيمة

aftermath /'ɑːftəmæθ; *Brit also* 'ɑːftəmɑːθ/ *noun* [sing.] a situation that is the result of an important or unpleasant event: *the aftermath of a war* عاقبة ، آثار (الكارثة)

afternoon /ˌɑːftə'nuːn; *US* ˌæf-/ *noun* [C,U] the part of a day between midday and about six o'clock: *I'll see you tomorrow afternoon.* ○ *We sat in the garden all afternoon.* ○ *He goes swimming every afternoon.* ○ *She arrived at four o'clock in the afternoon.* ○ *Tom works two afternoons a week.* ○ *Are you busy on Friday afternoon?* ○ *afternoon tea* ○ *Where were you on the afternoon of February 26th?* بعد الظهر

IDM **good afternoon** (used as a formal greeting when you see sb for the first time in the afternoon) ❶ Often we just say *Afternoon*: *'Good afternoon, Mrs Davies.' 'Afternoon, Jack.'* ➲ Look at the note at **morning**. تحية (تقال بعد الظهر)

aftershave /'ɑːftəʃeɪv/ *noun* [C,U] a liquid with a pleasant smell that men put on their faces after shaving كولونيا بعد الحلاقة

afterthought /'ɑːftəθɔːt/ *noun* [C, usually sing.] something that you think of or add to sth else at a later time: *He did the shopping, and then bought some flowers on the way home as an afterthought.* فكرة لاحقة ، استدراك

afterwards /'ɑːftəwədz; *US* 'æf-/ (*US also* **afterward**) *adv* at a later time: *I met her at a party and saw her again soon afterwards.* ○ *Afterwards, Nick said he hadn't enjoyed the film.* بعد ذلك ، فيما بعد

again /ə'gen; ə'geɪn/ *adv* **1** once more; another time: *Could you say that again, please?* ○ *She was out. I'll phone again later.* ○ *Don't ever do that again!* ثانيةً ، مرّة ثانية
2 in the place or condition that sb/sth was in before: *It's great to be home again.* ○ *I hope you'll soon be well again.* من جديد
3 (used for expressing that sth you have just said may not happen or be true): *She might pass her test, but then again she might not.* أعودُ وأستدرك
4 in addition: *'Is that enough?' 'No, I'd like half as much again, please'* (= one-and-a-half times the original amount). إضافة إلى ذلك

IDM **again and again** many times: *He said he was sorry again and again.* مراراً و تكراراً
(but) then again = THEN

a b c d e f g h i j k l m n o p q r s t u v w x y z

yet again → YET

🔑**against** /ə'genst; ə'geɪnst/ *prep* **1** touching or leaning on sb/sth for support: *Put the cupboard over there against the wall.* مُستند إلى

2 in the opposite direction to sth: *We had to cycle against the wind.* بِعكس ، في الاتّجاه المعاكس لـ

3 opposing sb/sth in a game, competition, war, etc: *Leeds are playing against Everton on Saturday.* ضِدّ

4 not agreeing with or supporting sb/sth: *Are you for or against the plan?* ○ *She felt that everybody was against her.* ضِدّ

5 what a law, rule, etc. says you must not do: *It's against the law to buy cigarettes before you are sixteen.* مخالف لـ

6 in order to protect yourself from sb/sth: *Take these pills as a precaution against malaria.* ضِدّ

🔑**age**[1] /eɪdʒ/ *noun* **1** [C,U] the length of time that sb has lived or that sth has existed: *Nigel is seventeen years of age.* ○ *She left school at the age of sixteen.* ○ *When I was your age I never did anything like that!* ○ *Children of all ages will enjoy this film.* ○ *He needs some friends of his own age.* عُمْر ، سِنّ

When you want to ask about somebody's age, you usually say: *How old is she?* and the answer can be: *She's eighteen* or: *She's eighteen years old* but NOT: *She's eighteen years.* Here are some examples of other ways of talking about age: *I'm nearly nineteen.* ○ *a girl of eighteen* ○ *an eighteen-year-old girl* ○ *The girl, aged 18, said she came from Perth.* ○ *I first went abroad when I was fifteen.*

2 [U] one of the periods of sb's life: *a problem that often develops in middle age* عُمْر

3 [U] the state of being old: *a face lined with age* ➲ Look at **youth**. شيخوخة ، كِبَر السِّنّ

4 [C] a particular period of history: *We are now living in the computer age.* ○ *the history of art through the ages* عصر

5 ages [plural] (*informal*) a very long time: *We had to wait ages at the hospital.* لمدّة طويلة جداً

IDM under age not old enough by law to do sth قاصر

age[2] /eɪdʒ/ *verb* [I,T] (*pres part* **ageing** or **aging**; *pt, pp* **aged** /eɪdʒd/) to become or look old; to cause sb to look old: *My father seems to have aged a lot recently.* يَشيخ ؛ تظهر عليه علائم الشيخوخة

▸ **aged** /eɪdʒd/ *adj* (not before a noun) of a particular age (1): *The woman, aged 26, was last seen at Victoria Station.* بالغ من العمر

the aged /'eɪdʒɪd/ *noun* [plural] old people كِبار السِّنّ

'age group *noun* [C] people of a particular age (1): *This club is very popular with the 20-30 age group.* مجموعة أفراد من سِنّ معيّنة

🔑**agency** /'eɪdʒənsi/ *noun* [C] (*pl.* **agencies**) **1** a business that provides a particular service: *an advertising agency* وكالة

2 (*US*) a government department: *the Central Intelligence Agency* دائرة حكوميّة ؛ وكالة

agenda /ə'dʒendə/ *noun* [C] a list of all the subjects that are to be discussed at a meeting جدول أعمال

🔑**agent** /'eɪdʒənt/ *noun* [C] **1** a person whose job is to do business for a company or for another person: *Our company's agent in Rio will meet you at the airport.* ○ *Most actors and musicians have their own agents.* ○ *a travel agent* ○ *an estate agent* وكيل

2 = SECRET AGENT

aggravate /'ægrəveɪt/ *verb* [T] **1** to make sth worse or more serious: *The country's food problems were aggravated by the hot dry summer.* يَزيد (الوضع) سوءاً

2 (*informal*) to make sb angry or annoyed يغيظ ، يزعج

▸ **aggravation** /,ægrə'veɪʃn/ *noun* [C,U] تفاقم ، اشتداد

aggregate /'ægrɪgət/ *noun*

IDM on aggregate in total: *Our team won 3-1 on aggregate.* إجمالاً

aggression /ə'greʃn/ *noun* [U] **1** the act of starting a fight or war without reasonable cause: *This is an intolerable act of aggression against my country.* اعتداء ، عدوان

2 angry feelings or behaviour that make you want to attack other people: *People often react to this kind of situation with fear or aggression.* روح عدائيّة

▸ **aggressor** /ə'gresə(r)/ *noun* [C] a person or country that attacks sb/sth or starts fighting first المعتدي

🔑**aggressive** /ə'gresɪv/ *adj* **1** ready or likely to fight or argue: *an aggressive dog* ○ *Some people get aggressive after drinking alcohol.* مستعد أو محبّ للشجار ، عدواني

2 using or showing force or pressure in order to succeed: *an aggressive salesman* مِلحاح ، جسور

▸ **aggressively** *adv* بعنف

aggrieved /ə'griːvd/ *adj* (*formal*) upset or angry مستاء ، ممتعض؛ غاضب

agile /'ædʒaɪl; *US* ædʒl/ *adj* able to move quickly and easily خفيف الحركة، رشيق

▸ **agility** /ə'dʒɪləti/ *noun* [U] خِفّة الحركة ، نشاط

agitate /'ædʒɪteɪt/ *verb* [I] **agitate (for/against sth)** to make other people feel very strongly about sth so that they want to do sth to help you achieve it: *to agitate for reform* يحرِّض على ، يهيِّج المشاعر

▸ **agitated** *adj* worried or excited: *She became more and more agitated when her son did not appear.* مضطرب ، قلق

agitation /,ædʒɪ'teɪʃn/ *noun* [U] اضطراب ، اهتياج

AGM /,eɪ dʒiː 'em/ *abbrev* (*Brit*) Annual General Meeting الاجتماع السنوي العام

agnostic /æg'nɒstɪk/ *noun* [C] a person who believes that you cannot know whether or not God exists اللاأدري

🔑**ago** /ə'gəʊ/ *adv* in the past; back in time from now: *Patrick left ten minutes ago* (= if it is twelve o'clock now, he left at ten to twelve). ○ *That was a long time ago.* ○ *How long ago did this happen?* منذ ، من : في الماضي

Ago is used with the simple past tense and not the present perfect tense: *I arrived in Britain three months ago.* Compare **ago** and **before**. **Ago** means 'before now' and **before** means 'before then' (i.e. before a particular time in the past): *Anne married Simon two years ago.* ○ *She had left her first husband six years before* (= six years before she married Simon).

agonize (*also* **agonise**) /ˈæɡənaɪz/ *verb* [I] to worry or think about sth for a long time: *to agonize over a difficult decision* يتعذّب ، يتألّم

▸ **agonized** (*also* **agonised**) *adj* showing extreme pain or worry: *an agonized cry* معذّب ، متألّم

agonizing (*also* **agonising**) *adj* causing extreme worry or pain: *an agonizing choice* ○ *an agonizing headache* مؤلم ، مبرح

agony /ˈæɡəni/ *noun* [C,U] (*pl.* **agonies**) great pain or suffering: *to scream in agony* ألم مبرح ، عذاب

agree /əˈɡriː/ *verb* **1** [I,T] **agree (with sb/sth)**; **agree (that...)** to have the same opinion as sb/sth: *'I think we should talk to the manager about this.' 'Yes, I agree.'* ○ *I agree with Paul.* ○ *Do you agree that we should travel by train?* ○ *I'm afraid I don't agree.* ➲ Look at **disagree**. يوافق ، يتّفق في الرأي

2 [I] **agree (to sth)** to say yes to sth: *I asked if I could go home early and she agreed.* ○ *Andrew has agreed to lend me his car for the weekend.* ➲ Look at **refuse**[1]. يوافق ، يقبل

3 [I,T] **agree (to do sth)**; **agree (on) (sth)** to make an arrangement or agreement with sb: *They agreed to meet again the following day.* ○ *Can we agree on a price?* ○ *We agreed a price of £500.* يتّفق على

4 [I] **agree with sth** to think that sth is right: *I don't agree with experiments on animals.* يرضى بـ ، يوافق على

5 [I] to be the same as sth: *The two accounts of the accident do not agree.* يتطابق

agreeable /əˈɡriːəbl/ *adj* (*formal*) **1** pleasant; nice ❶ The opposite is **disagreeable**. لطيف ، حلو المعشر : سائغ

2 ready to agree: *If you are agreeable, we would like to visit your offices on 21 May.* موافق

▸ **agreeably** /-əbli/ *adv* بصورة ممتعة

agreement /əˈɡriːmənt/ *noun* **1** [C] a contract or decision that two or more people have made together: *Please sign the agreement and return it to us.* ○ *The leaders reached an agreement after five days of talks.* اتّفاقية: اتفاق

2 [U] the state of agreeing with sb/sth: *She nodded her head in agreement.* ❶ The opposite is **disagreement**. موافقة

agriculture /ˈæɡrɪkʌltʃə(r)/ *noun* [U] keeping animals and growing crops for food; farming: *the Minister of Agriculture* زراعة

▸ **agricultural** /ˌæɡrɪˈkʌltʃərəl/ *adj*: *agricultural land* زراعي

ah /ɑː/ *interj* (used for expressing surprise, pleasure, sympathy, etc.): *Ah, there you are.* ○ *Ah well, never mind.* صيحة تدلّ على الدهشة أو الغبطة..الخ

aha /ɑːˈhɑː/ *interj* (used when you suddenly find or understand sth): *Aha! Now I understand.* ها هو (وجدته!) : أيوه (فهمت!)

ahead /əˈhed/ *adv, adj* **ahead (of sb/sth) 1** in front of sb/sth: *I could see the other car about half a mile ahead of us.* ○ *The path ahead looked narrow and steep.* ○ *Look straight ahead and don't turn round!* أماماً...

2 before or in advance of sb/sth: *Jane and Nicky arrived a few minutes ahead of us.* ○ *London is about five hours ahead of New York.* قبل...

3 into the future: *He's got a difficult time ahead of him.* ○ *We must think ahead and make a plan.* في المستقبل

4 doing better than another person or team in a game, competition, etc: *The third goal put Italy ahead.* في المقدمة ، متفوّق

5 more advanced than sb/sth else: *The Japanese are way ahead of us in their research.* سبّاق، متقدّم عن

IDM **ahead of your time** so modern that people do not understand you طليعي، سابق لأوانه

go ahead (used to give sb permission to do sth): *'Can I take this chair?' 'Sure, go ahead.'* لا مانع، افعل ذلك!

streets ahead → STREET

aid /eɪd/ *noun* **1** [U] help: *to walk with the aid of a stick* ○ *to go to sb's aid* (= to go and help sb) ➲ Look at **first aid**. مساعدة ، عوْن

2 [C] a person or thing that helps you: *a hearing aid* مساعد ، معين : إداة معينة

3 [U] money, food, etc. that is sent to a country or people in order to help them: *We sent aid to the earthquake victims.* ○ *Oxfam and other aid agencies* معونة

IDM **in aid of sb/sth** in order to raise money for sb/sth: *a concert in aid of Children in Need* إعانة لـ

▸ **aid** *verb* [T] (*formal*) to help sb يساعد

IDM **aid and abet** to help sb to do sth that is against the law يساعد شخصاً في مخالفة القانون

aide /eɪd/ *noun* [C] a person who is an assistant to sb important in the government, etc. مساعد (لشخصيّة هامّة)

AIDS (*Brit usually* **Aids**) /eɪdz/ *noun* [U] an illness which destroys the body's ability to fight infection: *an AIDS victim* ○ *Thousands of people have died of Aids.* ❶ 'AIDS' is short for **Acquired Immune Deficiency Syndrome**. مرض الإيدز

ailing /ˈeɪlɪŋ/ *adj* not in good health; weak: (*figurative*) *an ailing economy* معتلّ الصحّة ، مريض : متدهور

ailment /ˈeɪlmənt/ *noun* [C] (*formal*) an illness (that is not very serious) اعتلال ، مرض خفيف

aim[1] /eɪm/ *noun* **1** [C] something that you intend to do or achieve: *Our aim is to open offices in Paris* *and Rome before the end of the year.* ○ *His only aim in life is to make money.* هدف ، غاية

2 [U] the act of pointing sth at sb/sth before trying to hit him/her/it with it: *Get ready to shoot. Take aim – fire!* ○ *Her aim was good and she hit the target.* هدف

▸ **aimless** *adj* having no purpose: *an ˌaimless discussion* بلا هدف ، متخبِّط

aimlessly *adv* على غير هدى

aim² /eɪm/ *verb* **1** [I] **aim to do sth; aim at/for sth** to intend to do or achieve sth: *We aim to leave after breakfast.* ○ *The company is aiming at a 25% increase in profit.* ○ *You should always aim for perfection in your work.* يهدف أو يرمي إلى ، ينوي

2 [T] **aim sth at sb/sth** to direct sth at a particular person or group: *The advertising campaign is aimed at young people.* يوجِّه إلى

3 [I,T] **aim (sth) (at sb/sth)** to point sth at sb/sth before trying to hit him/her/it with it: *She picked up the gun, aimed, and fired.* يسدِّد ، يصوِّب

IDM be aimed at sth to be intended to achieve sth: *The new laws are aimed at reducing heavy traffic in cities.* يهدف إلى

ain't /eɪnt/ (*informal*) *short for* AM NOT, IS NOT, ARE NOT, HAS NOT, HAVE NOT ❶ **Ain't** is considered to be incorrect English.

air¹ /eə(r)/ *noun* **1** [U] the mixture of gases that surrounds the earth and that people, animals and plants breathe: *the pure mountain air* ○ *The air was polluted by smoke from the factory.* هواء

2 [U] the space around and above things: *to throw a ball high into the air* ○ *in the open air* (= outside) الهواء ، (في) الهواء الطلْق

3 [U] travel or transport in an aircraft: *to travel by air* ○ *an air ticket* جوّاً : (بطاقة) طائرة

4 [C] **an air (of sth)** the impression that sb gives or the impression you get of a place, event, etc: *a confident air* ○ *There was a general air of confusion outside the President's palace.* جوّ ، إحساس

IDM a breath of fresh air → BREATH

in the air probably going to happen soon: *A feeling of change was in the air.* متوقَّع الحدوث

in the open air → OPEN¹

on (the) air broadcasting on the radio or television: *This radio station is on the air 24 hours a day.* يبثّ ، يذيع

vanish, etc. into thin air → THIN

air² /eə(r)/ *verb* **1** [I,T] to put clothes, etc. in a warm place or outside in the fresh air to make sure they are completely dry; to be put in this place: *Put the sleeping bag on the washing line to air.* يهوّي الغسيل: يتهوّى

2 [I,T] to make a room, etc. fresh by letting air into it; to become fresh in this way: *Open the window to air the room.* يهوّي : يتهوّى

3 [T] to tell people what you think about sth: *The discussion gave people a chance to air their views.* يبدي رأيه

airbag /ˈeəbæg/ *noun* [C] a device in a car that fills with air if there is an accident, to protect the people in the car كيس هواء، "بالون"

airbase /ˈeəbeɪs/ *noun* [C] an airport for military aeroplanes قاعدة جويّة

airborne /ˈeəbɔːn/ *adj* flying in the air: *airborne missiles* جوّي، محمول جوّاً

ˈ**air-conditioned** *adj* having air conditioning: *air-conditioned offices* مكيَّف

ˈ**air conditioning** *noun* [U] the system that keeps the air in a room, building, etc. cool and dry تكييف الهواء

aircraft /ˈeəkrɑːft; *US* -kræft/ *noun* [C] (*pl.* **aircraft**) any vehicle that can fly in the air, e.g. an aeroplane, a helicopter, etc. طائرة

ˈ**aircraft carrier** *noun* [C] a ship that carries military aircraft and that has a long flat area where they can take off and land حاملة طائرات

airfield /ˈeəfiːld/ *noun* [C] an area of land where aeroplanes can land or take off. An airfield is smaller than an airport. مطار صغير ، مهبِط طائرات

ˈ**air force** *noun* [C, with sing. or pl. verb] the part of a country's military organization that fights in the air ➲ Look at **army** and **navy**. سلاح الطيران ، السلاح الجوّي

ˈ**air hostess** (*also* **hostess**) *noun* [C] (*old-fashioned*) a woman who looks after the passengers on an aeroplane مضيفة طائرة

ˈ**airing cupboard** *noun* [C] a warm cupboard that you use for airing² (1) clothes in خزانة (دولاب) تهوية الثياب

airless /ˈeələs/ *adj* not having enough fresh air: *The room was hot and airless.* غير مهوّى

airline /ˈeəlaɪn/ *noun* [C] a company that provides regular flights for people or goods in aeroplanes: *an airline pilot* شركة طيران

airliner /ˈeəlaɪnə(r)/ *noun* [C] a large aeroplane that carries passengers طائرة ركّاب كبيرة

airmail /ˈeəmeɪl/ *noun* [U] the system for sending letters, parcels, etc. by aeroplane البريد الجوّي

airplane /ˈeəpleɪn/ *noun* [C] (*US*) = PLANE

airport /ˈeəpɔːt/ *noun* [C] a place where aircraft can land and take off and that has buildings for passengers to wait in مطار

ˈ**air raid** *noun* [C] an attack by military aeroplanes غارة جويّة

airsick /ˈeəsɪk/ *adj* feeling sick or vomiting as a result of travelling on a plane ➲ Look at **carsick**, **seasick** and **travel-sick**. دائخ من السفر جوّاً

airspace /ˈeəspeɪs/ *noun* [U] the part of the sky that is above a country and that belongs to that country by law المجال الجوّي ، الأجواء

airstrip /ˈeəstrɪp/ (*also* **landing strip**) *noun* [C] a narrow piece of land where aircraft can take off and land مهبط طائرات

airtight /ˈeətaɪt/ *adj* that air cannot get into or out of محكَم السدّ

ˌ**air traffic conˈtroller** *noun* [C] a person whose job is to organize routes for aircraft, and to tell pilots by radio when they can land and take off مراقب الحركة الجويّة

airy /'eəri/ *adj* (**airier**; **airiest**) having a lot of fresh air: *a light and airy room* مهوًى

aisle /aɪl/ *noun* [C] a passage between the rows of seats in a church, theatre, etc. ممَرّ (بين المقاعد)

ajar /ə'dʒɑː(r)/ *adj* (not before a noun) slightly open (used about a door) (الباب) موارَب ، مفتوح جزئياً

akin /ə'kɪn/ *adj* **akin to sth** similar to or like sth قريب من ، شبيه

à la carte /ˌɑː lɑː 'kɑːt/ *adj, adv* (used about a meal in a restaurant) where each dish on the menu has a separate price and there is not a fixed price for a complete meal بالصحن، بالطلب

alarm /ə'lɑːm/ *noun* **1** [U] a sudden feeling of fear or worry: *She jumped up in alarm.* ذُعْر

2 [sing.] a warning of danger: *A small boy saw the smoke and raised the alarm.* إنذار بالخطر

3 [C] a machine that warns you of danger, e.g. by ringing a loud bell: *a burglar alarm* ○ *a fire alarm* جرس الإنذار

4 [C] = ALARM CLOCK

IDM **a false alarm** → FALSE

▸ **alarm** *verb* [T] to make sb/sth feel suddenly frightened or worried: *The news of the escaped prisoner alarmed the local people.* يرعب : يقلق

alarmed *adj* **alarmed (at/by sth)** frightened or worried: *Government ministers are alarmed at the recent rise in unemployment.* خائف : قلق

alarming *adj* that makes you frightened or worried: *The population of the world is increasing at an alarming rate.* مفزع : مقلق

alarmingly *adv* بصورة مقلقة

a'larm clock (*also* **alarm**) *noun* [C] a clock that you can set to make a noise at a particular time to wake you up: *She set the alarm clock for half past six.* ○ *My alarm clock goes off at seven o'clock.* ساعة منبِّهة

alas /ə'læs/ *interj* (*formal*) (used for expressing sadness about sth) وا أسفاه

albino /æl'biːnəʊ; *US* -'baɪ-/ *noun* [C] (*pl.* **albinos**) a person or animal with very white skin, white hair and pink eyes أمْهَق

album /'ælbəm/ *noun* [C] a book in which you can keep stamps, photographs, etc. that you have collected, or a collection of pieces of music that have been recorded on one record, CD or cassette ألبوم

alcohol /'ælkəhɒl; *US* -hɔːl/ *noun* [U] **1** the colourless liquid in drinks such as beer, whisky and wine that can make you drunk كحول ، غَوْل

2 the drinks (e.g. beer, whisky, wine) that contain alcohol (مشروب) مسْكِر

▸ **alcoholic** /ˌælkə'hɒlɪk; *US* -'hɔːl-/ *adj*: *alcoholic drinks* ❶ The opposite is **non-alcoholic**. Drinks without alcohol are also called **soft drinks**. (مشروب) كحولي

alcoholic *noun* [C] a person who is dependent on alcohol and drinks a large amount of it every day ❶ A person who does not drink alcohol at all is a **teetotaller**. المدمن على المسكرات

alcoholism /-ɪzəm/ *noun* [U] the medical condition that is caused by regularly drinking too much alcohol إدمان المسكرات ، الكحولية

alcove /'ælkəʊv/ *noun* [C] a small area in a room where one part of the wall is further back than the rest of the wall تجويف في غرفة

ale /eɪl/ *noun* [U] beer ❶ In modern English we use the word **beer**, not **ale**, except when we are talking about certain types of beer. نوع من البيرة

alert /ə'lɜːt/ *adj* **alert (to sth)** watching, listening, etc. for sth with full attention: *Security guards must be alert at all times.* ○ *to be alert to possible changes* منتبه ، يقظ

▸ **alert** *noun* [C] a warning of possible danger: *a bomb alert* إنذار

IDM **on the alert (for sth)** ready or prepared for danger or an attack: *The public were warned to be on the alert for possible terrorist attacks.* على استعداد (لمواجهة خطر)

alert *verb* [T] **alert sb (to sth)** to warn sb of danger or a problem ينبّه ، ينذر

A level /'eɪ levl/ (*also* **Advanced level**) *noun* a British exam taken in a particular subject, usually in the final year of school at the age of 18: *How many A levels have you got?* ○ *I'm doing my A levels this summer.* ➲ Look at **AS** level **A2** and **GCSE**. امتحان الثانوية العامة (لدخول الجامعات البريطانية)

algae /'ældʒiː; 'ælgiː/ *noun* [plural, with sing. or pl. verb] very simple plants that grow mainly in water: *During the hot summer algae spread to levels which made it impossible to swim at some beaches.* طُحْلُب

algebra /'ældʒɪbrə/ *noun* [U] a type of mathematics in which letters and symbols are used to represent numbers (علم) الجبر

alias /'eɪliəs/ *noun* [C] a false name, e.g. one that is used by a criminal اسم مستعار

▸ **alias** *adv* (used for giving sb's false name): *Mrs Phillips, alias Maria Jones* المعروف باسم

alibi /'æləbaɪ/ *noun* [C] a statement by sb that says you were in a different place at the time of a crime and so cannot be guilty of the crime: *He had a good alibi for the night of the robbery.* دَفع بالغيبة ، وجود المتهم في غير مكان الجريمة

alien /'eɪliən/ *noun* [C] **1** (*formal*) a person who comes from another country أجنبي

2 a creature that comes from another planet مخلوق من كوكب آخر

▸ **alien** *adj* **1** of another country; foreign: *an alien land* أجنبي

2 very strange and completely different from your normal experience: *Cruelty was alien to him.* خارج عن المألوف، غريب

alienate /'eɪliəneɪt/ *verb* [T] **1** to make people feel that they cannot share your opinions any more: *The Prime Minister's new policies on defence have alienated many of his supporters.* ينفِّر ، يُبعِد

2 alienate sb (from sb/sth) to make sb feel

that he/she does not belong somewhere or is not part of sth: *Many young unemployed people feel completely alienated from the rest of society.* يعزل ، يبعد

▸ **alienation** /ˌeɪliəˈneɪʃn/ *noun* [U] اغتراب ، نفور : عزلة

alight[1] /əˈlaɪt/ *adj* on fire; burning: *The petrol had been set alight* (= made to start burning) *by a cigarette.* مشتعل

> **Alight** can only be used after a noun, but you can use **burning** before a noun: *The whole building was alight.* ○ *a burning building.*

alight[2] /əˈlaɪt/ *verb* [I] (*formal*) **alight (from sth)** to get off a bus, train, etc. ينزل (من حافلة أو قطار الخ)

align /əˈlaɪn/ *verb* [T] **1 align sth (with sth)** to arrange things in a straight line or so that they are parallel to sth else: *to align the wheels of a car* يَصُفّ

2 align yourself with sb to say that you support the opinions of a particular group, country, etc: *The Green Party has aligned itself with the Socialists over this issue.* ➲ Look at **non-aligned.** يقف في صفّه ، ينحاز إلى

▸ **alignment** *noun* **1** [U] arrangement in a straight line or parallel to sth else اصطفاف

2 [C,U] an agreement between political parties, countries, etc. to support the same thing: *the alignment of Japan with the West* انحياز

alike /əˈlaɪk/ *adj* like one another; the same: *The two children are very alike.* متشابه

> **Alike** can only be used after a noun, but you can use **similar-looking** before a noun: *The houses in this street are all alike.* ○ *a street of similar-looking houses.*

▸ **alike** *adv* in the same way: *We try to treat women and men alike in this company.* ○ *The musical has been a success with adults and children alike.* على السواء

alimony /ˈælɪməni; *US* -moʊni/ *noun* [U] money that you have to pay by law to your former wife or husband after a divorce نَفَقة شرعية

alive /əˈlaɪv/ *adj* **1** not dead; living: *The young woman was still alive when the ambulance reached the hospital.* ○ *He kept the little cat alive by feeding it warm milk.* حيّ

> **Alive** can only be used after a noun, but you can use **living** before a noun: *Are her parents still alive?* ○ *Does she have any living relatives?*

2 full of life: *In the evening the town really comes alive.* ممتلئ بالحياة

3 continuing to exist: *Many old traditions are very much alive in this area of Britain.* حيّ

alkali /ˈælkəlaɪ/ *noun* [C,U] any of the chemical substances with a pH value of more than 7 ➲ Look at **acid.** مادة قلوية ، قلي

▸ **alkaline** *adj* قلوي

all[1] /ɔːl/ *det, pron* **1** the whole of a thing: *All (of) the food has gone.* ○ *They've eaten all of it.* ○ *They've eaten it all.* ○ *This money is all yours.* ○ *All of it is yours.* كلّ ، جميع

2 the whole of the period of time: *It rained all day.* ○ *all week/month/year* ○ *He worked hard all his life.* كلّ ، طوال

3 every one of a group: *All cats are animals but not all animals are cats.* ○ *All (of) my children can swim.* ○ *My children can all swim.* ○ *She's read all (of) these books.* ○ *She's read them all.* ○ *The people at the meeting all voted against the plan.* ○ *All of them voted against the plan.* كلّ (فرد)

4 everything that; the only thing that: *I wrote down all I could remember.* ○ *All I've eaten is a slice of toast.* كلّ شيء

IDM above all → ABOVE

after all → AFTER[1]

in all in total: *There were ten of us in all.* جملةً ، في المجموع

not all that... not very: *The film wasn't all that good.* ليس في المستوى المتوقع

(not) at all in any way: *I didn't enjoy it at all.* ❶ We can say **not at all** as a reply when somebody thanks us for something. مطلقا

all[2] /ɔːl/ *adv* **1** completely; very: *He has lived all alone since his wife died.* ○ *I didn't watch that programme – I forgot all about it.* ○ *They got all excited about it.* تماماً ؛ جداً

2 (in sport) for each side: *The score was two all.* للطرفين

IDM all along from the beginning: *I knew you were joking all along.* منذ البداية

all right; (*informal*) **alright 1** good or good enough: *Is everything all right?* على ما يرام

2 safe; not hurt; well: *The children are all right. Don't worry.* ○ *Do you feel all right?* سليم ؛ بخير

3 (showing you agree): *'You go on ahead.' 'Oh, all right.'* حسناً، طيّب! (للتعبير عن الموافقة)

> You say 'That's all right,' when sb thanks you for sth or when sb says sorry for sth he/she has done: *'Thanks for the lift home.' 'That's (quite) all right.'* ○ *'I'm so sorry I'm late.' 'That's all right. We haven't started yet anyway.'*

all the better, harder, etc. better, harder, etc. than before: *It will be all the more difficult with two people missing.* أفضل، أصعب الخ من السابق

Allah /ˈælə/ the Arabic name for God الله

allay /əˈleɪ/ *verb* [T] (*formal*) to make sth less strong: *to allay sb's fears* يخفّف

the ˌall-ˈclear *noun* [sing.] a signal telling you that danger is over إشارة الأمان

allege /əˈledʒ/ *verb* [T] (*formal*) to say that sb has done sth wrong, but without proving that this is true: *The woman alleged that Williams had attacked her with a knife.* يزعم

▸ **allegation** /ˌæləˈɡeɪʃn/ *noun* [C]: *to make allegations of police corruption* زعم ، ادعاء

alleged /əˈledʒd/ *adj*: *the alleged criminal* (= people say this person is a criminal but nobody has proved that this is true) مزعوم

allegedly /əˈledʒɪdli/ *adv*: *The man was allegedly shot while trying to escape.* كما يزعم

allegiance /ə'li:dʒəns/ *noun* [U,C] (*formal*) support for or loyalty towards a leader, government, belief, etc: *to swear your allegiance to the Queen* ولاء

allergy /'ælədʒi/ *noun* [C] (*pl.* **allergies**) **an allergy (to sth)** a medical condition that makes you ill when you eat, touch or breathe sth that does not normally make other people ill: *an allergy to cats, shellfish, pollen, etc.* تحسّس أو حساسية، أرجيّة

▸ **allergic** /ə'lɜ:dʒɪk/ *adj* **1 allergic (to sth)** having an allergy: *I can't drink cow's milk. I'm allergic to it.* عنده حساسية، أرجي

2 caused by an allergy: *an allergic reaction to house dust* تحسّسي ، تسبّبه حساسية

alleviate /ə'li:vieɪt/ *verb* [T] to make sth less strong or bad: *The doctor gave me an injection to alleviate the pain.* يخفّف

▸ **alleviation** /ə,li:vi'eɪʃn/ *noun* [U] تخفيف

alley /'æli/ (*also* **'alleyway** /'æliweɪ/) *noun* [C] a narrow passage between buildings ممرّ ضيق ، زقاق

alliance /ə'laɪəns/ *noun* [C] an agreement between people, groups, countries, etc. to work together and support each other: *the country's military alliance with France* ○ *The two parties formed an alliance.* ➲ Look at **ally**. تحالف

🔑**allied** /ə'laɪd; 'ælaɪd/ *adj* **1** (used about organizations, countries, etc.) having an agreement to work together and support each other: *allied forces* ○ *Allied Irish Banks* متحالف

2 allied (to sth) connected with; similar: *coal mining and allied industries* ذو صلة بـ ؛ شبيه

alligator /'ælɪgeɪtə(r)/ *noun* [C] a large animal with a long body and sharp teeth that lives in the lakes and rivers of the southern United States and China. An alligator is similar to a crocodile. تمساح أمريكي

,all-'in *adj* including everything: *an all-in price* شامل

allocate /'æləkeɪt/ *verb* [T] **allocate sth (to sb/sth)** to give sth to sb as his/her share or to decide to use sth for a particular purpose: *6 000 seats for next Saturday's football match have been allocated to Liverpool supporters.* ○ *The BBC has allocated £160 000 for each new programme.* يخصّص : يوزّع

▸ **allocation** /,ælə'keɪʃn/ *noun* [C,U] giving sth for a particular purpose; the amount that is given: *the allocation of resources for health care* تخصيص : حصّة

allot /ə'lɒt/ *verb* [T] (allotting; allotted) **allot sth (to sb/sth)** to give sb money, a piece of work, etc. as his/her share or to decide to allow a certain amount of time for sth: *Different tasks were allotted to each member of the class.* ○ *We all finished the exam in the allotted time.* يخصّص : يوزّع

allotment /ə'lɒtmənt/ *noun* [C] (*Brit*) a small area of land in a town that you can rent for growing vegetables on قطعة أرض تستأجر لزراعة الخضراوات

,all 'out *adj, adv* using all your strength, etc: *We're going all out for the Cup.* ○ *an all-out effort* (يبذل) قصارى جهده

🔑**allow** /ə'laʊ/ *verb* [T] **1 allow sb/sth to do sth; allow sth** to give permission for sb/sth to do sth or for sth to happen: *Children under sixteen are not allowed to buy cigarettes.* ○ *I'm afraid we don't allow people to bring dogs into this restaurant.* ○ *Photography is not allowed inside the cathedral.* يسمح

> Compare **allow, permit** and **let. Allow** can be used in both formal and informal English. The passive form **be allowed to** is especially common. **Permit** is a formal word and is usually used only in written English. **Let** is an informal word, and very common in spoken English. You **allow sb to do sth** but **let sb do sth** (no 'to'). **Let** cannot be used in the passive: *Visitors are not allowed/permitted to smoke in this area.* ○ *Smoking is not allowed/permitted.* ○ *I'm not allowed to smoke in my bedroom.* ○ *My Dad won't let me smoke in my bedroom.*

2 to give permission for sb/sth to be or go somewhere: *No dogs allowed.* ○ *I'm only allowed out on Friday and Saturday nights.* يسمح

3 allow sb sth to let sb have sth: *My contract allows me four weeks' holiday a year.* يمنح ، يجيز

4 allow sb/sth to do sth to make it possible for sb/sth to do sth: *Working part-time would allow me to spend more time with my family.* يتيح

5 allow sth (for sb/sth) to provide money, time, etc. for sb/sth: *You should allow about 30 minutes for each examination question.* يخصّص

PHR V allow for sb/sth to think about possible problems when you are planning sth and include extra time, money, etc. for them: *The journey should take about two hours, allowing for heavy traffic.* يأخذ بعين الاعتبار

allowance /ə'laʊəns/ *noun* [C] **1** an amount of sth that you are allowed: *Most flights have a 20 kg baggage allowance.* حصّة

2 an amount of money that you receive regularly to help you pay for sth that you need (مبلغ) مخصّص

IDM make allowances for sb/sth to judge a person or a person's actions more kindly because he/she has a particular problem or disadvantage: *You really should make allowances for her. She's very inexperienced.* يراعي ، يأخذ بعين الاعتبار

alloy /'ælɔɪ/ *noun* [C] a metal that is formed by mixing two types of metal together, or by mixing metal with another substance: *Brass is an alloy of copper and zinc.* سبيكة خليطة

,all-'rounder *noun* [C] a person who can do many different things well شخص متعدد البراعات

'all-time *adj* (used when you are comparing things or saying how good or bad sth is) of any time: *one of the all-time great players* ○ *my all-time favourite song* ○ *Unemployment reached an all-time record of 3 million.* ○ *Profits are at an all-time high/low.* على مر العصور، في أي وقت كان

allude /ə'lu:d/ *verb* [I] **allude to sb/sth** (*formal*) to speak about sb/sth in an indirect way: *He mentioned no names but we all knew who he was alluding to.* يلمّح

▸ **allusion** /əˈluːʒn/ *noun* [C,U] an act of speaking about sth indirectly: *The play is full of allusions to classical mythology.* تلميح ، إشارة خفيفة

ally /ˈælaɪ/ *noun* [C] (*pl.* **allies**) **1** a country that has an agreement to support another country, especially in a war: *France and its European allies* ➲ Look at **alliance** and **allied**. دولة حليفة

2 a person who helps and supports you, especially when other people are against you: *the Prime Minister's political allies* حليف ، نصير

almighty /ɔːlˈmaɪti/ *adj* **1** having the power to do anything: *Almighty God* ذو قدرة كليّة

2 (only *before* a noun) (*informal*) very great: *Suddenly we heard the most almighty crash.* ضخم ، هائل

almond /ˈɑːmənd/ *noun* [C] an oval nut that is often used in cooking: *trout with almonds* لوز

almost /ˈɔːlməʊst/ *adv* not quite; very nearly: *By nine o'clock almost everybody had arrived.* ○ *Careful! I almost fell into the water then!* ○ *The film has almost finished.* ○ *She almost always cycles to school.* ○ *There's almost nothing left.* تقريباً

alone /əˈləʊn/ *adj, adv* **1** without any other person: *The old man lives alone.* ○ *Are you alone? Can I speak to you for a moment?* ○ *I don't like walking home alone after dark.* وحيد ؛ بمفرده

> **Alone** and **lonely** both mean that you are not with other people. **Lonely** (*US* **lonesome**) means that you are unhappy about this, but **alone** does not usually suggest either happiness or unhappiness. **Alone** cannot be used before a noun. You can also use **on your own** and **by yourself** to mean 'alone'. These expressions are more informal and very common in spoken English.

2 (after a noun or pronoun) only: *You alone can help us.* ○ *The food alone cost £40. The wine was extra.* وحْده

IDM **go it alone** to do sth on your own without help from anyone دون الاعتماد على أحد

leave sb/sth alone → LEAVE[1]

let alone → LET[1]

along /əˈlɒŋ; *US* əˈlɔːŋ/ *prep* **1** from one end to or towards the other end of sth: *I walked slowly along the road.* ○ *David looked along the corridor to see if anyone was coming.* ○ *Carry on along this street until you get to the traffic lights.* على طول

2 in a line that follows the side of sth long: *Wild flowers grew along both sides of the river.* بمحاذاة

3 at a particular point on or beside sth long: *Our house is about halfway along Hope Street.* في

▸ **along** *adv* **1** forward: *We moved along slowly with the crowd.* إلى الأمام

2 (*informal*) with sb: *We're going to the pub. Why don't you come along too?* مع (شخص ما)

IDM **all along** → ALL[2]

along with sb/sth together with sb/sth: *Along with hundreds of others, she lost her job when the factory closed.* مع ، بصحبة

alongside /əˌlɒŋˈsaɪd; *US* -ˌlɔːŋ-/ *adv, prep* **1** next to or along the side of sth: *a garden with a small river running alongside* ○ *The boat moored alongside the quay.* بمحاذاة

2 together with sb/sth: *the opportunity to work alongside experienced musicians* مع ، في صحبة

aloof /əˈluːf/ *adj* **1** not friendly or open to other people; distant متحفّظ ؛ متباعد

2 not involved in sth; apart: *The President can no longer remain aloof from the problem.* مبتعد، منعزل

aloud /əˈlaʊd/ (*also* **out loud**) *adv* in a normal speaking voice that other people can hear; not silently: *to read aloud from a book* بصوت عالٍ ، جهاراً

alphabet /ˈælfəbet/ *noun* [C] the set of letters that you use when you are writing a particular language, especially when they are arranged in a fixed order: *There are 26 letters in the English alphabet.* الأبجدية

▸ **alphabetical** /ˌælfəˈbetɪkl/ *adj* arranged in the same order as the letters of the alphabet: *The poems are listed in alphabetical order.* أبجدي

alphabetically /-kli/ *adv* أبجدياً

alpine /ˈælpaɪn/ *adj* of or found in high mountains: *alpine flowers* موجود على الجبال الشاهقة

already /ɔːlˈredi/ *adv* **1** (used for talking about sth that has happened before now or before a particular time in the past, especially if it happened earlier than you expected): *'Would you like some lunch?' 'No, I've already eaten, thanks.'* ○ *We got there at 6.30 but Martin had already left.* ○ *Sarah was already awake when I went into her room.* من قبل ، مسبقاً

2 (used in negative sentences and questions for expressing surprise) so early; as soon as this: *Have you finished already?* ○ *Surely you're not going already!* مبكّراً هكذا!!

alright /ɔːlˈraɪt/ *adv* (*informal*) = ALL RIGHT

Alsatian /ælˈseɪʃn/ *noun* [C] (*US* **German shepherd**) a large dog with smooth hair, that is often trained to help the police or as a guard dog كلب حراسة كبير، كلب بوليسي

also /ˈɔːlsəʊ/ *adv* (not with negative verbs) in addition; too: *Mark Wilson paints and writes novels in his spare time. He also speaks Chinese.* ○ *Please bring some paper, a pen and also a calculator.* ○ *The food is wonderful, and also very cheap.* أيضاً ؛ علاوة على ذلك

> **Too** and **as well** are less formal than **also** and are very common in spoken English. **Also** usually goes before a main verb or after 'is', 'are', 'were', etc: *He also enjoys reading.* ○ *He has also been to Australia.* ○ *He is also intelligent.* **Too** and **as well** usually go at the end of a phrase or sentence: *I really love this song, and I liked the first one too/as well.* Do not confuse **also** with **even**: *Even (NOT also) in the middle of summer, the nights can be cold.*

IDM **not only ... but also** → ONLY[2]

altar /ˈɔːltə(r)/ *noun* [C] the holy table in a church or temple هيكل : مذبح

alter /ˈɔːltə(r)/ *verb* [I,T] to make sth different in some way, but without changing it completely; to become different: *They've altered the plan for the new building. The main entrance will now be in Queen Street.* ○ *This does not alter the fact that the company is in serious financial difficulty.* ○ *This skirt is too big for me now. I'll have to alter it* (= make it smaller by sewing it). ○ *The village seems to have altered very little in the last twenty years.* يغيِّر؛ يتغيَّر
▶ **alteration** /ˌɔːltəˈreɪʃn/ *noun* [C,U] a small change in sb/sth: *We want to make a few alterations to the house before we move in.* ○ *The travel company will inform you of any alteration in the time of departure.* تغيير ، تعديل

alternate[1] /ɔːlˈtɜːnət; *US* ˈɔːltərnət/ *adj* **1** (used about two types of events, things, etc.) happening or following regularly one after the other: *Helen and Nick take the children to school on alternate days* (= Helen takes them on Monday, Nick on Tuesday, Helen on Wednesday, etc.). متعاقب ، متناوب

2 one of every two: *He works alternate weeks* (= he works the first week, he doesn't work the second week, he works again the third week, etc.). (أسابيع مثلاً) متخالفة
▶ **alternately** *adv* بالتعاقب ، بالتناوب

alternate[2] /ˈɔːltəneɪt/ *verb* **1** [I] **alternate with sth; alternate between A and B** (used about two types of events, things, etc.) to happen or follow regularly one after the other: *It's exciting music. Quiet violin passages alternate with sudden bursts of trumpet sound.* ○ *She seemed to alternate between hating him and loving him.* يتعاقب ، يتناوب

2 [T] **alternate A with B** to cause two types of events or things to happen or follow regularly one after the other: *He alternated periods of work with periods of rest.* يناوب
▶ **alternation** /ˌɔːltəˈneɪʃn/ *noun* [C,U] تعاقب ، تناوب

alternative /ɔːlˈtɜːnətɪv/ *adj* (only *before* a noun) that you can use, do, etc. instead of sth else: *There is heavy traffic on the A34. Drivers are advised to find an alternative route.* بديل ، آخر
▶ **alternative** *noun* [C] one of two things that you can choose between: *The Minister suggested community service as an alternative to imprisonment.* خِيار آخر

> **Alternative** is now often used for talking about more than two things: *There are several alternatives open to us at the moment.*

alternatively *adv*: *Trains leave London Paddington every half hour. Alternatively, there is a regular coach service from Victoria Coach Station.* بدلاً من ذلك

although /ɔːlˈðəʊ/ *conj* **1** (used for introducing a statement that makes the main statement in a sentence seem surprising): *Although she was tired, she stayed up to watch the late-night film on television.* رغم أنّ

2 (used for introducing a statement that modifies the main statement) and yet; but: *There will be heavy rain in many parts of Britain tonight, although it is unlikely to reach the South West until morning.* إلاّ أنّ

> You can also use **though** but it is less formal than **although**. **Even** can be used with **though** for emphasis, but not with **although**: *She didn't want to go to the party, although/though/even though she knew all her friends would be there.* **Though**, but not **although** can be used at the end of a sentence: *She knew all her friends would be there. She didn't want to go, though.*

altitude /ˈæltɪtjuːd; *US* -tuːd/ *noun* **1** [sing.] the height of sth above sea: *The plane climbed to an altitude of 10 000 metres.* ارتفاع (فوق مستوى البحر)

2 [C, usually pl] a place that is high above sea level: *You need to carry oxygen when you are climbing at high altitudes.* الأماكن المرتفعة

Alt key (*also* **ALT key**) /ˈɔːlt kiː/ *noun* a key on a computer keyboard which you press while pressing other keys, in order to change their function مفتاح التبديل

alto /ˈæltəʊ/ *noun* [C] (*pl.* **altos**) the lowest normal singing voice for a woman, the highest for a man; a woman or man with this voice إحدى الطبقات الصوتية : مغنٍ بهذا الصوت

altogether /ˌɔːltəˈgeðə(r)/ *adv* **1** completely: *I don't altogether agree with you.* ○ *At the age of 55 he stopped working altogether.* تماماً

2 including everything: *We've got about £65 altogether.* جملةً

3 when you consider everything; generally: *Altogether, Oxford is a pleasant place to live.* عموماً

> **Altogether** is not the same as **all together**. **All together** means 'everything or everybody together': *Put your books all together on the table.* ○ *Let's sing. All together now!*

aluminium /ˌæljəˈmɪniəm; ˌæla-/ (*US* **aluminum** /əˈluːmɪnəm/) (*symbol* **Al**) *noun* [U] a light silver-coloured metal that is used for making cooking equipment, etc: *aluminium foil* (معدن) الألومنيوم

always /ˈɔːlweɪz/ *adv* **1** at all times; regularly: *We almost always go to Scotland for our holidays.* ○ *Why is the train always late when I'm in a hurry?* دائماً

2 all through the past until now: *Tom has always been shy.* ○ *I've always liked music.* دوماً

3 for ever: *I shall always remember this moment.* أبداً

4 (with continuous tenses) again and again, usually in an annoying way: *She's always complaining about something.* لا ينفكّ (يفعل شيئاً)

> **Always** does not usually go at the beginning of a sentence. It usually goes before the main verb or after 'is', 'are', 'were', etc: *He always wears*

those shoes. ○ *I have always wanted to visit Egypt.* ○ *Fiona is always late.* However, **always** can go at the beginning of a sentence when you are telling somebody to do something: *Always stop and look before you cross the road.*

5 (used with 'can' or 'could' for suggesting sth that sb could do, especially if nothing else is possible): *If you haven't got enough money, I could always lend you some.* إذا لزم الأمر

Alzheimer's disease /ˈæltshaɪməz dɪziːz/ *noun* [U] a disease that affects the brain and makes you become more and more confused as you get older مرض ألزايمر

AM /ˌeɪ ˈem/ *abbrev* amplitude modulation; one of the systems of broadcasting radio signals تضمين الذروة (راديو)

a.m. (*US also* **A.M.**) /ˌeɪ ˈem/ *abbrev* before midday: *10 am* (= 10 o'clock in the morning) قبل الظهر

am → BE

amalgamate /əˈmælgəmeɪt/ *verb* [I,T] (used especially about organizations, groups, etc.) to join together to form a single organization, group, etc: *If the two unions amalgamated, they would be much more powerful.* يندمج؛ يدمج
▸ **amalgamation** /əˌmælgəˈmeɪʃn/ *noun* [C,U] اندماج

amass /əˈmæs/ *verb* [T] to gather together a large quantity of sth: *We've amassed a lot of information on the subject.* يكدِّس

amateur /ˈæmətə(r)/ *noun* [C] **1** a person who takes part in a sport or an activity for pleasure, not for money as a job: *Only amateurs can take part in the tournament; no professionals will be allowed.* الهاوي (ضد المحترف)

2 (usually used when being critical) a person who does not have skill or experience when doing sth: *The repair work on this house was clearly done by a bunch of amateurs.* غير خبير
▸ **amateur** *adj* **1** done, or doing sth, for pleasure (not for money as a job): *an amateur photographer* هاوٍ

2 (*also* **amateurish**) done without skill or experience بلا خبرة، بلا براعة

amaze /əˈmeɪz/ *verb* [T] to surprise sb very much; to seem incredible to sb: *Sometimes your behaviour amazes me!* ○ *It amazes me that anyone could be so stupid!* يُدهش
▸ **amazed** *adj* extremely surprised; feeling that you cannot believe sth: *She was amazed to discover the truth about her husband.* ○ *I was amazed by the change in his attitude.* منذهل، مندهش

amazement *noun* [U]: *He looked at me in amazement.* ○ *To my amazement, I passed the test easily.* اندهاش، استغراب
amazing *adj* causing you to be very surprised: *She has shown amazing courage.* ○ *I've got an amazing story to tell you.* عجيب، مدهش
amazingly *adv* لدرجة مذهلة

ambassador /æmˈbæsədə(r)/ *noun* [C] a diplomat of high rank who represents his/her country in a foreign country: *the Spanish Ambassador to Britain* ➲ Look at **embassy**. سفير

amber /ˈæmbə(r)/ *noun* [U] **1** a hard clear yellow-brown substance used for making jewellery or ornaments كهرمان

2 a yellow-brown colour: *The three colours in traffic lights are red, amber and green.* لون أصفر ضارب للحمرة
▸ **amber** *adj* كهرماني

ambiguity /ˌæmbɪˈgjuːəti/ *noun* [C,U] (*pl.* **ambiguities**) the possibility of being understood in more than one way; sth that can be understood in more than one way غموض؛ شيء غامض

ambiguous /æmˈbɪgjuəs/ *adj* having more than one possible meaning: *That's a rather ambiguous remark – what exactly do you mean?* غامض
▸ **ambiguously** *adv* على نحوٍ غامض

ambition /æmˈbɪʃn/ *noun* **1** **ambition (to be/do sth)** [U] strong desire to be successful, to have power, etc: *One problem of young people today is their lack of ambition.* طموح

2 [C] something that you very much want to have or do: *It has always been her ambition to travel the world.* تَوق، مطمح

ambitious /æmˈbɪʃəs/ *adj* **1** **ambitious (to be/do sth)** having a strong desire to be successful, to have power, etc: *I'm not particularly ambitious – I'm content with my life the way it is.* طَموح

2 difficult to achieve or do because it takes a lot of work or effort: *The company have announced ambitious plans for expansion.* طموح، صعب التحقيق

ambivalent /æmˈbɪvələnt/ *adj* having or showing a mixture of feelings or opinions about sth or sb: *I have always felt rather ambivalent about having children.* متناقض المشاعر
▸ **ambivalence** /-əns/ *noun* [U] تناقض المشاعر

ambulance /ˈæmbjələns/ *noun* [C] a special motor vehicle for taking ill or injured people to and from hospital سيّارة الإسعاف

ambush /ˈæmbʊʃ/ *noun* [C] a surprise attack from a hidden position كمين
▸ **ambush** *verb* [T] يهاجم من مكمن

amen /ɑːˈmen; *US* eɪˈmen/ *interj* (used at the end of a prayer by Christians) let this be so: *In the name of the Father, the Son and the Holy Ghost. Amen.* آمين

amenable /əˈmiːnəbl/ *adj* willing to accept sth; willing to be guided: *I'm amenable to any suggestions you may have.* على استعداد للقبول، قابل للتوجيه

amend /əˈmend/ *verb* [T] to change sth slightly, often in order to make it better: *The law needs to be amended.* يعدِّل
▸ **amendment** *noun* **1** [C] a part that is added or a small change that is made to a piece of writing, especially to a law تعديل

2 [U] an act of amending: *The bill was passed without amendment.* تعديل

amends /əˈmendz/ *noun* [plural]
IDM **make amends** to do sth for sb, that shows that you are sorry for sth bad that you have done

before: *I bought her a present to make amends for the horrible things I had said to her.* يكفِّر عن

amenity /ə'mi:nəti; *US* ə'menəti/ *noun* [C] (*pl.* **amenities**) something in a place that helps to make living there pleasant or easy: *Among the town's amenities are two cinemas and a sports centre.* مِرفَق من مرافق الراحة أو المتعة

American /ə'merɪkən/ *adj* from or connected with the USA: *Have you met Bob? He's American.* ○ *an American accent* ○ *In American English 'theatre' is spelt 'theater'.* أمريكيّ

▸ **American** *noun* [C] a person who comes from the USA: *His wife is an American.* (شخص) أمريكي

A,merican 'football (*US* **football**) *noun* [U] a form of football played in the USA with an oval-shaped ball. The players wear helmets and other protective clothing and are allowed to pick up and carry, as well as kick, the ball. كرة القدم الأمريكيّة

A,merican 'Indian = NATIVE AMERICAN

amiable /'eɪmiəbl/ *adj* friendly and pleasant لطيف

▸ **amiably** /-əbli/ *adv* بودّ

amicable /'æmɪkəbl/ *adj* made or done in a friendly way, without argument: *I'm sure we can find an amicable way of settling the dispute.* وِدّيّ، سلمي

▸ **amicably** /-əbli/ *adv* على نحوٍ وِدّي

amid /ə'mɪd/ (*also* **amidst** /ə'mɪdst/) *prep* (*formal*) in the middle of; among: *Amid all the confusion, the thieves got away.* وسط

amiss /ə'mɪs/ *adj, adv* wrong; not as it should be: *When I walked into the room I could sense that something was amiss.* غلط، مختَلّ

IDM **not come/go amiss** to be welcome: *Things are fine, although a bit more money wouldn't come amiss.* ○ *An apology wouldn't go amiss.* مستحبّ

take sth amiss to be upset by sth, perhaps because you have understood it in the wrong way: *Please don't take my remarks amiss.* ينزعج، يسيء فهم الشيء

ammunition /,æmju'nɪʃn/ *noun* [U] **1** the supply of bullets, etc. that you need to fire from a weapon: *The troops surrendered because they had run out of ammunition.* ذخيرة

2 (*figurative*) facts or information that can be used against sb/sth ذخيرة

amnesia /æm'ni:ziə/ *noun* [U] loss of memory فقدان الذاكرة

amnesty /'æmnəsti/ *noun* [C] (*pl.* **amnesties**) **1** a time when a government forgives political crimes عفو

2 a time when people can give in illegal weapons عفو عام

⚷**among** /ə'mʌŋ/ (*also* **amongst** /ə'mʌŋst/) *prep* **1** surrounded by; in the middle of: *I often feel nervous when I'm among strangers.* ○ *The modern block looks wrong among all the old buildings.* ○ *I found the missing letter amongst a heap of old newspapers.* بين، وسطَ

2 in the group or number of: *She is among the nicest people I have ever met.* ○ *Among the city's attractions are its museums and art galleries.* بين

3 to each one (of a group): *On his death, his money will be divided among his children.* بين

4 inside (a group): *Discuss it amongst yourselves and let me know your decision.* ➲ Look at the note at **between**. بين

⚷**amount** /ə'maʊnt/ *noun* [C] **1** the amount of sth is how much of it there is; quantity: *I spent an enormous amount of time preparing for the exam.* ○ *I have a certain amount of sympathy with her.* كميّة، قدْر

2 total or sum of money: *You are requested to pay the full amount within seven days.* مجموع؛ مبلغ

▸ **amount** *verb* [I] **amount to sth 1** to add up to; to total: *The cost of the repairs amounted to £5 000.* يبلغ

2 to be the same as: *Whether I tell her today or tomorrow, it amounts to the same thing.* يتساوى مع

amp /æmp/ (*also formal* **ampere** /'æmpeə(r); *US* 'æmpɪər/) *noun* [C] a unit for measuring electric current أمْبير

amphibian /æm'fɪbiən/ *noun* [C] an animal that can live both on land and in water. Amphibians have cold blood and skin without scales. برمائي

ample /'æmpl/ *adj* **1** enough or more than enough: *We've got ample time to make a decision.* ○ *I'm not sure how much the trip will cost, but I should think £500 will be ample.* كافٍ، وافٍ

2 large; having a great deal of space: *There is space for an ample car park.* متّسع

▸ **amply** /'æmpli/ *adv*: *The report makes it amply clear whose mistake it was.* على نحوٍ وافٍ

amplify /'æmplɪfaɪ/ *verb* [T] (*pres part* **amplifying**; *3rd pers sing pres* **amplifies**; *pt, pp* **amplified**) **1** to increase the strength of a sound, using electrical equipment يكبِّر

2 (*formal*) to add details to sth in order to explain it more fully: *Would you like to amplify your recent comments, Minister?* يفصِّل

▸ **amplification** /,æmplɪfɪ'keɪʃn/ *noun* [U]: *These comments need further amplification.* تفصيل

amplifier *noun* [C] a piece of electrical equipment for making sounds louder or signals stronger مكبِّر

amputate /'æmpjuteɪt/ *verb* [I,T] to cut off a person's arm or leg (or part of it) for medical reasons: *His leg was so badly injured that it had to be amputated.* يبتر

▸ **amputation** /,æmpju'teɪʃn/ *noun* [C,U] بتْر

⚷**amuse** /ə'mju:z/ *verb* [T] **1** to make sb laugh or smile; to seem funny to sb: *Everybody laughed but I couldn't understand what had amused them.* يضحك، يسلّي

2 to make time pass pleasantly for sb; to stop sb

from getting bored: *I did some crosswords to amuse myself on the journey.* ○ *I've brought a few toys to amuse the children.* يتسلّى، يسلّي

▸ **amused** *adj* **1** if you are amused, you think that sth is funny and it makes you want to laugh or smile: *You may think it's funny, but I'm not amused.* ○ *I was amused to hear his account of what happened.* مبتهج

2 if sth keeps you amused, it makes you pass the time pleasantly, without getting bored متسلٍّ، غير شاعر بالملل

amusement *noun* **1** [U] the feeling caused by sth that makes you laugh or smile, or by sth that entertains you and that stops you from being bored: *There was a look of amusement on his face.* ○ *Much to the pupils' amusement, the teacher fell off his chair.* انبساط، تسلية

2 [C] something that makes time pass pleasantly; an entertainment: *The holiday centre offers a wide range of amusements, including golf and tennis.* تسلية، لهو

amusing *adj* causing you to laugh or smile: *He's a very amusing person and he makes me laugh a lot.* ○ *an amusing story* مسلٍّ

an → A[2]

anaemia (*US* **anemia**) /ə'ni:miə/ *noun* [U] a medical condition in which there are not enough red cells in the blood الأنيميا: فقر الدّم

▸ **anaemic** (*US* **anemic**) /ə'ni:mɪk/ *adj* suffering from anaemia مصاب بفقر الدّم

anaesthetic (*US* **anesthetic**) /,ænəs'θetɪk/ *noun* [C,U] a substance that stops you feeling pain, e.g. when a doctor is performing an operation on you: *You'll need to be under anaesthetic for the operation.* ○ *a local anaesthetic* (= one that only affects part of the body and does not make you unconscious) ○ *a general anaesthetic* (= one that makes you unconscious) مخدِّر

▸ **anaesthetist** (*US* **anesthetist**) /ə'ni:sθətɪst/ *noun* [C] a person who is qualified to give anaesthetics to patients طبيب التخدير

anaesthetize (*also* **anaesthetise**; *US* **anesthetize**) /ə'ni:sθətaɪz/ *verb* [T] to give an anaesthetic to sb يخدِّر

anagram /'ænəgræm/ *noun* [C] a word or phrase that is made by arranging the letters of another word or phrase in a different order: *'Worth' is an anagram of 'throw'.* الجناس التصحيفي

analogous /ə'næləgəs/ *adj* (*formal*) **analogous (to/with sth)** similar in some way; that you can compare شبيه بـ، نظير لـ

analogy /ə'nælədʒi/ *noun* [C] (*pl.* **analogies**) **an analogy (between sth and sth)** a comparison between two things that shows a way in which they are similar: *You could make an analogy between the human body and a car engine.* تشبيه، قياس

IDM **by analogy** If you explain sth by analogy to sth else you compare it to the other thing and show how it is similar. بالقياس

⚷ **analyse** (*US* **analyze**) /'ænəlaɪz/ *verb* [T] to look at or think about the different parts or details of sth carefully in order to understand or explain it: *The water samples are now being analysed in a laboratory.* ○ *to analyse statistics* ○ *She analysed the situation and then decided what to do.* يحلّل

⚷ **analysis** /ə'næləsɪs/ *noun* (*pl.* **analyses** /-si:z/) **1** [C,U] the careful examination of the different parts or details of sth: *Some samples of the water were sent to a laboratory for analysis.* ○ *They carried out an analysis of the causes of the problem.* تحليل

2 [C] the result of such an examination: *Your analysis of the situation is different from mine.* نتيجة التحليل

▸ **analytical** /,ænə'lɪtɪkl/ (*also* **analytic**) *adj* looking carefully at the different parts of sth in order to understand or explain it: *analytic techniques* تحليلي

analyst /'ænəlɪst/ *noun* [C] a person whose job is to analyse things as an expert: *a food analyst* محلّل

anarchy /'ænəki/ *noun* [U] a situation in which people do not obey rules and laws; a situation in which there is no government in a country: *While the civil war went on, the country was in a state of anarchy.* فوضى

▸ **anarchic** /ə'nɑ:kɪk/ *adj* without rules or laws فوضوي

anarchism /'ænəkɪzəm/ *noun* [U] the political theory that there should be no government or laws in a country نظريّة الفوضوية

anarchist *noun* [C] a person who believes in this theory, especially one who takes action to achieve it الفوضوي

anatomy /ə'nætəmi/ *noun* (*pl.* **anatomies**) **1** [U] the scientific study of the structure of human or animal bodies علم التشريح

2 [C] the structure of a living thing: *the anatomy of the frog* التركيب البنيَوي

▸ **anatomical** /,ænə'tɒmɪkl/ *adj* تشريحي، جسمي

ancestor /'ænsestə(r)/ *noun* [C] a person in your family who lived a long time before you, from whom you are descended: *My ancestors settled in this country a hundred years ago.* جَدّ، سَلَف

▸ **ancestry** /'ænsestri/ *noun* [C,U] (*pl.* **ancestries**) all of a person's ancestors, when you think of them as a group: *He was of Irish ancestry.* نَسَب

anchor /'æŋkə(r)/ *noun* [C] a heavy metal object at the end of a chain that you drop into the water from a boat in order to keep the boat in one place: *They dropped anchor 400 yards offshore.* مِرساة

▸ **anchor** *verb* **1** [I,T] to drop an anchor; to stop a boat moving by using an anchor: *We anchored in the harbour and went ashore.* يرسو؛ يرسي

2 [T] to fix sth firmly so that it is held in a place and cannot move: *They anchored the tent with strong ropes.* يثبِّت

anchovy /'æntʃəvi; *US* -əʊvi/ *noun* [C,U] (*pl.* **anchovies**) a small fish with a strong salty flavour بلَم مملّح

⚷ **ancient** /'eɪnʃənt/ *adj* **1** belonging to or connected with the distant past: *ancient civilizations* قديم، عتيق

2 having existed for a long time: *The annual festival is one of the ancient traditions of the region.* قديم

3 (*informal*) very old: *I can't believe he's only 30, he looks ancient!* متقدِّم في السن

and /ənd; ən; *strong form* ænd/ *conj* **1** (used to connect words or parts of sentences) also; in addition to: *bread and butter* ○ *one woman, two men and three children* ○ *a boy and a girl* ○ *an apple and a pear* ○ *Do it slowly and carefully.* ○ *We were singing and dancing all evening.* وَ (حرف عطف)

> When the two things are closely linked, you do not need to repeat the 'a', etc: *a knife and fork* ○ *my mother and father*

2 (used when you are saying numbers) plus: *Twelve and six is eighteen.* ○ *It cost me a hundred and sixty pounds.* وَ

> When you are saying large numbers *and* is used after the word 'hundred': *We say 2 264 as two thousand, two hundred and sixty-four.*

3 then; following this or that: *Come in and sit down.* ثُمَّ

4 as a result of this or that; because of this or that: *It was a terrible shock and he was very upset.* ○ *Say that again and I'll lose my temper.* بِسَبَب ذلك

5 (used between repeated words to show that sth is increasing or continuing): *The situation is getting worse and worse.* ○ *I shouted and shouted but nobody answered.* (للتدليل على استفحال أمر أو استمراره)

6 (used between repeated words for saying that there are important differences between things of the same kind): *City life can be very exciting but there are cities and cities.* (لتأكيد الفرق)

7 (used instead of 'to' after certain verbs e.g. 'go', 'come', 'try'): *Go and answer the door for me, will you?* ○ *I'll try and find out what's going on.* ○ *Why don't you come and stay with us one weekend?* (بعد بعض الأفعال)

anecdote /ˈænɪkdəʊt/ *noun* [C] a short interesting story about a real person or event حكاية، نادرة

anemia, anemic (*US*) = ANAEMIA, ANAEMIC

anesthetic (*US*) = ANAESTHETIC

anew /əˈnjuː; *US* əˈnuː/ *adv* (*formal*) again; in a new or different way: *They started life anew in Canada.* مجدداً، مرّة أخرى

angel /ˈeɪndʒl/ *noun* [C] **1** a servant of God: *In pictures angels are usually dressed in white, with wings.* مَلاك، مَلَك

2 a person who is very kind: *Be an angel and wash these clothes for me, will you?* شخص لطيف

▸ **angelic** /ænˈdʒelɪk/ *adj* looking or acting like an angel ملائكي

angelically /-kli/ *adv* بملائكيّة

anger /ˈæŋɡə(r)/ *noun* [U] the strong feeling that you have when sth has happened or sb has done sth that you do not like: *He could not hide his anger at the news.* ○ *She was shaking with anger.* غَضَب

▸ **anger** *verb* [T] to cause sb to become angry: *It angers me that such things can be allowed to happen.* يُغضِب

angles

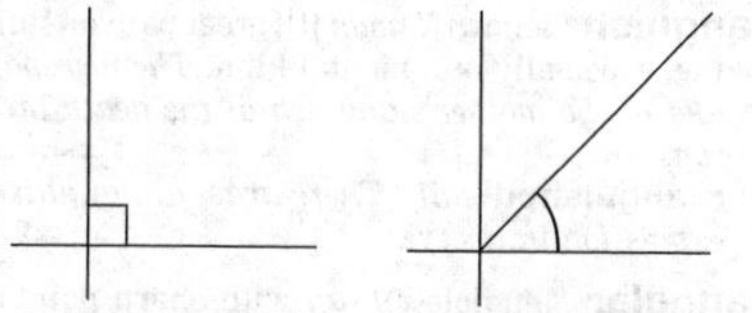

a right angle an angle of 45°

angle¹ /ˈæŋɡl/ *noun* [C] **1** the space between two lines or surfaces that meet, measured in degrees: *a right angle* (= a angle of 90°) ○ *at an angle of 40°* ○ *The three angles of a triangle add up to 180°.* زاوية

2 the direction from which you look at sth: *Viewed from this angle, the building looks bigger than it really is.* ○ *If we look at the problem from another angle, it might be easier to solve it.* زاوية، جهة

IDM **at an angle** not straight: *This hat is meant to be worn at an angle.* بانحراف

▸ **angle** *verb* [T] **1** to put sth in a position that is not straight; to be in this position: *Angle the lamp towards the desk.* يميل

2 angle sth (at/to/towards sb) to present sth from a particular point of view; to aim sth at a particular person: *The new magazine is angled at young professional people.* يعرض من زاوية معيّنة، يستهدف

angle² /ˈæŋɡl/

PHR V **angle for sth** to try to make sb give you sth, without asking for it directly: *She was angling for a free ticket to the match.* يحتال لِنَيل شيء

angler /ˈæŋɡlə(r)/ *noun* [C] a person who catches fish as a hobby هاوي صيد سمك

▸ **angling** *noun* [U] fishing as a sport or hobby: *He goes angling at weekends.* صَيْد السمك (هواية)

Anglican /ˈæŋɡlɪkən/ *noun* [C] a member of the Church of England, or of a related church in another English-speaking country أنكليكاني: تابع للكنيسة الأنكليكانيّة

Anglo- /ˈæŋɡləʊ/ (in compounds) English or British; connected with England or Britain (and another country or countries): *Anglo-American relations* إنكليزي، متعلّق بانكلترا أو بريطانيا

Anglo-Saxon /ˌæŋɡləʊ ˈsæksn/ *noun* **1** [C] a person whose ancestors were English شخص من أصل انكليزي

2 [C] an English person who lived in the period before the Norman Conquest انكلوسكسوني

3 (*also* **Old English**) [U] the English language before about 1150 اللغة الانكلوسكسونية

▸ **Anglo-Saxon** *adj* الانكلوسكسوني

angry /ˈæŋɡri/ *adj* (**angrier**; **angriest**) **angry (with sb) (at/about sth)** feeling or showing anger: *Calm down, there's no need to get angry.*

a b c d e f g h i j k l m n o p q r s t u v w x y z

○ *My parents will be angry with me if I get home late.* ○ *I'm very angry with them for letting me down at the last moment.* ○ *He's always getting angry about something.* غاضب
▸ **angrily** /-əli/ *adv* بغضب

anguish /ˈæŋɡwɪʃ/ *noun* [U] great pain or suffering, especially of a mental kind: *The newspaper told of the mother's anguish at the death of her son.* ألم مبرِّح، حسرة
▸ **anguished** *adj*: *There was an anguished expression in his eyes.* متألِّم، كَمِد

angular /ˈæŋɡjələ(r)/ *adj* with sharp points or corners: *an angular face* (= one where you can see the bones clearly) حادّ الزّوايا؛ بارز العظام

animal /ˈænɪml/ *noun* [C] **1** a living creature that is not a plant: *the animal kingdom* ○ *Humans are a social animals.* حيوان

2 a living creature of this kind, but not including humans: *She thinks that zoos are cruel to animals.* ○ *They keep cows, chickens and other animals on their farm.* حيوان

3 a living creature that is not a human, bird, fish, insect or reptile: *He studied the animals and birds of Southern Africa.* ○ *Domestic animals such as cats and dogs are not very popular in my country.* حيوان

animated /ˈænɪmeɪtɪd/ *adj* **1** lively and interesting: *an animated discussion* مفعَم بالحيويّة

2 (used about films) using a technique by which drawings or models appear to move: *an animated cartoon* (أفلام) الرسوم المتحركة
▸ **animation** /ˌænɪˈmeɪʃn/ *noun* [U] **1** the state of being lively: *She spoke with great animation on the subject.* حيويّة، حماس

2 the technique of making films, videos and computer games with drawings that appear to move رسوم متحرِّكة

ankle /ˈæŋkl/ *noun* [C] the part of the body where the foot joins the leg: *The water only came up to my ankles.* ○ *I tripped and sprained my ankle.* الكاحل: رسغ القدم

annex /əˈneks/ *verb* [T] to take possession and control of another country or region يضُمّ
▸ **annexation** /ˌænekˈseɪʃn/ *noun* [C,U]: *the annexation of Austria* ضمّ

annexe (*especially US* **annex**) /ˈæneks/ *noun* [C] a building that is joined to or near a larger one ملحَق

annihilate /əˈnaɪəleɪt/ *verb* [T] to destroy or defeat sb/sth completely: *The army was annihilated in the battle.* ○ *They weren't just beaten in the match, they were annihilated.* يبيد
▸ **annihilation** /əˌnaɪəˈleɪʃn/ *noun* [U]: *Modern weapons have placed mankind in danger of annihilation.* إبادة

anniversary /ˌænɪˈvɜːsəri/ *noun* [C] (*pl.* **anniversaries**) a day that is exactly a year or a number of years after a special or important event: *the hundredth anniversary of the country's independence* ○ *a twenty-fifth wedding anniversary* ذكرى سنويّة
➲ Look at **birthday**.

annotated /ˈænəteɪtɪd/ *adj* (used about a book, etc.) with notes added to it that explain and give extra information about the contents مذيَّل بحواش

announce /əˈnaʊns/ *verb* [T] **1** to make sth known publicly, in an official way: *We are pleased to announce the opening of our new department store.* ○ *The winners will be announced in next week's paper.* ○ *The champion was defeated and announced his retirement from the sport.* يعلِن

2 to say sth in a loud voice or in an aggressive way: *She stormed into my office and announced that she was leaving.* يعلِن
▸ **announcement** *noun* **1** [C] a statement that tells people about sth: *Ladies and gentlemen, may I have your attention. I have an important announcement to make.* إعلان

2 [U] the act of telling people about sth: *The announcement of the election results takes place at the Town Hall.* إعلان
announcer *noun* [C] a person who introduces or gives information about programmes on radio or television مذيع

annoy /əˈnɔɪ/ *verb* [T] to make sb quite angry: *It really annoys me when you act so selfishly.* ○ *Close the door if the noise is annoying you.* يزعج
▸ **annoyance** /-əns/ *noun* **1** [U] the feeling of being annoyed: *Much to my annoyance, the train had just left when I got to the station.* انزعاج

2 [C] something that annoys: *Low-flying planes are an annoyance in this area.* إزعاج
annoyed *adj* angry or fairly angry: *I shall be extremely annoyed if he turns up late again.* ○ *She's annoyed with herself for making such a stupid mistake.* ○ *He's annoyed that nobody believes him.* ○ *I was annoyed to see that they had left the door open.* منزعج
annoying *adj* making you feel rather angry: *Oh, how annoying! I've left my money at home.* مزعج

annual /ˈænjuəl/ *adj* **1** happening or done once a year or every year: *the company's annual report* ○ *an annual festival* سنوي

2 for the period of one year: *Her annual income is £20 000.* ○ *the annual sales figures* سنوي
▸ **annual** *noun* [C] a book or magazine that is published once a year, with the same title but different contents: *the 2006 Football Annual* كتاب سنويّ، مجلّة سنويّة
annually /ˈænjuəli/ *adv*: *Payment will be made annually.* ○ *China produces about 60 tonnes of gold annually.* سنويّاً، كلّ سنة

anon. /əˈnɒn/ *abbrev* (used to show that we do not know who the author of a piece of writing is) anonymous مجهول

anonymity /ˌænəˈnɪməti/ *noun* [U] the situation where a person's name is not known مجهوليّة: عدم معرفة الاسم

anonymize /əˈnɒnɪmaɪz/ *verb* [T] **1** if you anonymize a test result, especially a medical test result, you remove any information that shows who it belongs to يخفي (هوية الشخص)
2 if you anonymize data that is sent or received

over the Internet, you remove any information that identifies which particular computer that data originally came from يخفي (هوية المَصدر)

anonymous /əˈnɒnɪməs/ *adj* **1** (used about a person) with a name that is not known or made public: *An anonymous caller told the police that the robbery was going to take place.* مجهول الاسم

2 done, written, given, etc. by sb whose name is not known or made public: *He received an anonymous letter.* مجهول المصدر، (فاعله) غير مسمّى

▸ **anonymously** *adv* دون ذكر الاسم

anorak /ˈænəræk/ *noun* [C] **1** a short coat with a hood that protects you from rain, wind and cold سترة مع غطاء للرأس

2 (*Brit informal*) a person who enjoys learning boring facts or collecting things that most people think are boring: *He's a real anorak – he can name every player in the World Cup.* من يشغل نفسه بأمور مملّة

anorexia /ˌænəˈreksiə/ (*also* **anorexia nervosa** /ˌænəreksiə nɜːˈvəʊsə/) *noun* [U] an illness, especially affecting young women. It makes them afraid of being fat and so they do not eat. قَهَم

▸ **anorexic** /ˌænəˈreksɪk/ *adj* قَهِم

⚷**another** /əˈnʌðə(r)/ *det, pron* **1** one more; an additional thing or person: *Would you like another drink?* ○ *'Have you finished yet?' 'No, I've still got another three questions to do.'* ○ *They've got three children already and they're having another.* ○ *Is this another of your silly jokes?* آخَر

2 a different thing or person: *I'm afraid I can't see you tomorrow, could we arrange another day?* ○ *She discovered that he was having an affair with another woman.* ○ *If you've already seen that film, we can go and see another.* ➲ Look also at **one another**. آخَر

IDM **one after another/the other** → ONE[1]

⚷**answer**[1] /ˈɑːnsə(r); *US* ˈænsər/ *verb* [I,T] **1** to say or write sth back to sb who has asked you sth: *I asked her what the matter was but she didn't answer.* ○ *I've asked you a question, now please answer me.* ○ *Answer all the questions on the form.* ○ *When I asked him how much he earned, he answered that it was none of my business.* يجيب، يردّ

> **Answer** and **reply** are the most common verbs used for speaking or writing in reaction to questions, letters, etc: *I asked him a question but he didn't answer.* ○ *I sent my application but they haven't replied yet.* Note that you **answer** a person, a question or a letter (no 'to') but you **reply to** a letter. **Respond** is less common and more formal with this meaning: *Applicants must respond within seven days.* It is more commonly used with the meaning of 'reacting in a way that is desired': *Despite all the doctor's efforts the patient did not respond to treatment.*

2 to do sth as a reply: *Can you answer the phone for me, please?* ○ *I rang their doorbell but nobody answered.* ○ *He hasn't answered my letter yet* (= written a letter back to me). يجيب، يردّ

PHR V **answer back** to defend yourself against sth bad that has been written or said about you: *It's wrong to write things like that about people who can't answer back.* يردّ (دفاعاً عن النفس)

answer (sb) back to reply rudely to sb يردّ بخشونة، يتواقح

answer for sb/sth 1 to accept responsibility or blame for: *Somebody will have to answer for all the damage that has been caused.* يتحمّل المسؤوليّة

2 to speak in support of sb/sth: *I can certainly answer for her honesty.* يؤكّد

▸ **answerable** /-əbl/ **answerable to sb (for sth)** having to explain and give good reasons for your actions to sb; responsible to sb محاسَب لدى، مسؤول

⚷**answer**[2] /ˈɑːnsə(r); *US* ˈænsər/ *noun* [C] **answer (to sb/sth) 1** something that you say, write or do as a reply: *The answer to your question is that I don't know.* ○ *They've made me an offer and I have to give them an answer by Friday.* ○ *I wrote to them two weeks ago and I'm still waiting for an answer.* ○ *I knocked on the door and waited but there was no answer.* إجابة، ردّ

2 a solution to a problem: *I didn't have any money so the only answer was to borrow some.* حلّ

3 something that is written or said, trying to give the correct information asked for in a test or exam: *What was the answer to question 4?* إجابة

IDM **in answer (to sth)** as a reply (to sth): *They sent me some leaflets in answer to my request for information.* استجابةً لِ

ˈ**answering machine** (*Brit* **answerphone** /ˈɑːnsəfəʊn; *US* ˈæns-/) *noun* [C] a machine that answers the telephone and records messages from callers: *I rang him and left a message on his answerphone.* آلة تسجيل الرسائل التليفونيّة

ant /ænt/ *noun* [C] a very small insect that lives in large groups and works very hard: *an army of ants* نملة

antagonism /ænˈtæɡənɪzəm/ *noun* [U] **antagonism (towards sb/sth)**; **antagonism (between A and B)** a feeling of hate and of being opposed to sb/sth عداوة

antagonize (*also* **antagonise**) /ænˈtæɡənaɪz/ *verb* [T] to make sb angry or to annoy sb: *She tends to antagonize people with her outspoken remarks.* يستعدي (على نفسه)

Antarctic /ænˈtɑːktɪk/ *adj* connected with the coldest, most southern parts of the world: *an Antarctic expedition* ➲ Look at **Arctic**. متعلّق بالقطب الجنوبي

▸ **the Antarctic** *noun* [sing.] the most southern part of the world القطب الجنوبي

antelope /ˈæntɪləʊp/ *noun* [C] (*pl.* **antelope** or **antelopes**) an animal with horns that has long, thin legs, looks like a deer and can run very fast. It is found especially in Africa. ظبي

antenatal /ˌæntiˈneɪtl/ *adj* happening or existing before birth: *an antenatal clinic* (= for pregnant women) قبل الولادة

a b c d e f g h i j k l m n o p q r s t u v w x y z

antenna /æn'tenə/ *noun* [C] **1** (*pl.* **antennae** /-niː/) one of the two long thin parts on the heads of insects and some animals that live in shells. It is used for feeling things with. قرن الاستشعار (لدى الحشرة)

2 (*pl.* **antennas**) (*US*) = AERIAL[1]

anthem /'ænθəm/ *noun* [C] a song, especially one that is sung in church or on special occasions: *the national anthem* (= the special song of a country) ترتيلة (دينيّة)، نشيد

anthology /æn'θɒlədʒi/ *noun* [C] (*pl.* **anthologies**) a book that contains pieces of written work or poems, often on the same subject, by different authors: *an anthology of love poetry* مجموعة نثرية أو شعريّة

anthropology /ˌænθrə'pɒlədʒi/ *noun* [U] the study of human beings, especially of their origin, development, customs and beliefs الأنثروبولوجيا: عِلم الإنسان

antibiotic /ˌæntibaɪ'ɒtɪk/ *noun* [C] a medicine which is used for destroying bacteria and curing infections: *The doctor gave me some antibiotics for a chest infection.* مضادّ حيَوي

antibody /'æntibɒdi/ *noun* [C] (*pl.* **antibodies**) a substance that the body produces to fight disease الضدّ (طبّ)

anticipate /æn'tɪsɪpeɪt/ *verb* [T] to expect sth to happen (and to prepare for it): *to anticipate a problem* ○ *Traffic jams are anticipated on all coastal roads this weekend.* ○ *I anticipate that the situation will get worse.* ○ *We anticipate an increase in sales over the next few months.* يتوقّع

anticipation /ænˌtɪsɪ'peɪʃn/ *noun* [U] **1** the state of expecting sth to happen (and preparing for it): *The government has reduced tax in anticipation of an early general election.* تحسُّب

2 the state of feeling excited about sth that is going to happen: *They queued outside the cinema in excited anticipation.* توقُّع، انتظار

anticlimax /ˌænti'klaɪmæks/ *noun* [C,U] an event, etc. that is less exciting than you had expected or than what has already happened: *a mood/feeling of anticlimax* ○ *The ending of the film was a dreadful anticlimax.* هبوط (لنهاية مخيّبة للآمال مثلاً)

anticlockwise /ˌænti'klɒkwaɪz/ (*US* **counterclockwise**) *adv, adj* in the opposite direction to the movement of the hands of a clock: *Turn the lid anticlockwise/in an anticlockwise direction.* عكس حركة عقارب الساعة

antics /'æntɪks/ *noun* [plural] funny, strange or silly ways of behaving: *The children roared with laughter at the clown's antics.* تهريج

antidote /'æntidəʊt/ *noun* [C] **1** a medical substance that is used to prevent a poison or a disease from having an effect: *an antidote to snakebites* ترياق

2 anything that helps you to deal with sth unpleasant: *Many people find music a marvellous antidote to stress.* مُضاد

antipathy /æn'tɪpəθi/ *noun* [U] **antipathy (to/towards sb/sth)** (a strong feeling of) dislike نفُور

antiperspirant /ˌænti'pɜːspərənt/ *noun* [C,U] a liquid, cream, etc. that you use to reduce sweating, especially under the arms قاطع التعرُّق، مزيل رائحة العرق

antiquated /'æntɪkweɪtɪd/ *adj* old-fashioned and not suitable for the modern world: *antiquated ideas/methods* مهجور، قديم، فات زمانه

antique /æn'tiːk/ *adj* very old and therefore unusual and valuable: *an antique vase, table, etc.* ○ *antique furniture, jewellery, etc.* عتيق، أثري

▶ **antique** *noun* [C] an old and valuable object, e.g. a piece of furniture: *He collects antiques.* ○ *an antique shop* (= one that sells antiques) ○ *That vase is an antique.* شيء عتيق، أثري

antiquity /æn'tɪkwəti/ *noun* (*pl.* **antiquities**) **1** [U] ancient times, especially those of the Egyptians, Greeks and Romans: *myths and legends from antiquity* عهد قديم

2 [C, usually pl.] a building, work of art or other object that remains from ancient times: *Greek, Roman, etc. antiquities* أثر (من عهد قديم)

3 [U] great age: *priceless objects of great antiquity* عمر طويل

anti-Semitism /ˌænti 'semətɪzəm/ *noun* [U] prejudice against Jewish people اللاساميّة: معاداة اليهود

antiseptic /ˌænti'septɪk/ *noun* [C,U] a liquid or cream that prevents a cut, etc. from becoming infected: *Put an antiseptic/some antiseptic on that scratch.* مطهِّر

▶ **antiseptic** *adj*: *antiseptic cream* كَريم مطهِّر

antisocial /ˌænti'səʊʃl/ *adj* **1** not considered acceptable by other people or the rest of society: *antisocial behaviour/activities* ○ *Some people regard smoking as antisocial.* ضارّ بالآخرين

2 not willing to be with other people; unfriendly غير اجتماعي، مجافٍ

antivirus /'æntivaɪrəs/ *adj* designed to find and destroy computer viruses: *antivirus software* مضاد فيروسات

antler /'æntlə(r)/ *noun* [C, usually pl.] a horn on the head of a male deer: *a pair of antlers* قرن الوَعل

anus /'eɪnəs/ *noun* [C] (*pl.* **anuses**) the hole through which solid waste substances leave the body إسْت، شَرَج

anxiety /æŋ'zaɪəti/ *noun* [C,U] (*pl.* **anxieties**) a feeling of worry or fear, especially about the future: *a feeling/a state of anxiety* ○ *There are anxieties over the effects of unemployment.* قلق، هَمّ

anxious /'æŋkʃəs/ *adj* **1** **anxious (about/for sb/sth)** worried and afraid: *I began to get anxious when they still hadn't arrived at 9 o'clock.* ○ *an anxious look, expression, etc.* قَلِق، مُضْطرِب الخاطر

2 causing worry and fear: *For a few anxious*

moments we thought we'd missed the train. مثير للقلق

3 anxious to do sth wanting sth very much; eager for sth: *Police are anxious to find the owner of the white car.* حريص، متلهِّف (على فعل شيء)

▸ **anxiously** *adv* بِقَلَق، بانزعاج

any /'eni/ *det, pron* **1** (used in negative sentences and in questions, also after *if/whether*) some: *We didn't have any lunch.* ○ *I speak hardly any Spanish.* ○ *I don't know any Canadians.* ○ *He asked if we had any questions.* ○ *I wanted chips but there aren't any.* ○ *I don't like any of his books.* ➲ Look at the note at **some**. أيّ

2 (used for saying that it does not matter which thing or person you choose): *Take any book you want.* ○ *Any teacher would say the same.* ○ *Come round any time – I'm usually in.* ○ *I'll take any that you don't want.* أيّ

▸ **any** *adv* (used in negative sentences and questions) at all; to any degree: *I can't run any faster.* ○ *Is your father any better?* مطلقاً، إلى أيّ حدّ

anybody /'enibɒdi/ (*also* **anyone**) *pron* **1** (usually in questions or negative statements) any person: *I didn't know anybody at the party.* ○ *Is there anybody here who can speak Japanese?* ○ *Would anybody else* (= any other person) *like to come with me?* أيّ أحد

The difference between **somebody** and **anybody** is the same as the difference between **some** and **any**. Look at the notes at **some** and **somebody**.

2 any person, it does not matter who: *Anybody* (= all people) *can learn to swim.* ○ *Can anybody come? Or are there special invitations?* أيّ شخص

anyhow /'enihaʊ/ *adv* **1** (*also* **anyway**) (used to add an extra point or reason) in any case: *Spain will be terribly hot in August and anyhow we can't afford a holiday abroad.* على أيّة حال

2 (*also* **anyway**) (used when saying or writing sth which contrasts in some way with what has gone before) however: *It's a very difficult exam but anyway you can try.* ○ *I'm afraid I can't come to your party, but thanks anyway.* على كلّ حال

3 (*also* **anyway**) (used for correcting sth you have just said and making it more accurate) at least: *Everybody wants to be rich – well, most people anyhow.* على الأقلّ

4 (*also* **anyway**) (used after a pause in order to change the subject or go back to a subject being discussed before): *Anyway, that's enough about my problems. How are you?* على أيّة حال

5 in a careless way; with no order: *She threw her clothes on anyhow and dashed out of the door.* كيفما اتّفق

anyone /'eniwʌn/ *pron* = ANYBODY

anyplace (*US*) = ANYWHERE

anything /'eniθɪŋ/ *pron* **1** (usually in questions or negative statements) one thing (of any kind): *The fog was so thick that I couldn't see anything at all.* ○ *There isn't anything interesting in the newspaper today.* ○ *Did you buy anything?* ○ *'I'd like a pound of apples please.' 'Anything else?'* (= any other thing?) أيّ شيء

The difference between **something** and **anything** is the same as the difference between **some** and **any**. Look at the note at **some**.

2 any thing or things: it does not matter what: *I'm starving. I'll eat anything.* ○ *I'll do anything you say.* أيّ شيء

IDM **anything like sb/sth** at all similar to sb/sth; nearly: *She isn't anything like her sister, is she?* ○ *This car isn't anything like as fast as mine.* لا يشبه، لا يقارب

like anything → LIKE[2]

not come to anything → COME

anyway /'eniweɪ/ *adv* = ANYHOW

anywhere /'eniweə(r)/ (*US also* **anyplace**) *adv* **1** (usually in questions or negative statements) in, at or to any place: *I can't find my keys anywhere.* ○ *Is there a post office anywhere near here?* ○ *You can't buy the book anywhere else* (= in another place). ○ *If we want to go anywhere in August we'd better book it now.* في أيّ مكان

The difference between **somewhere** and **anywhere** is the same as the difference between **some** and **any**. Look at the note at **some**.

2 any place; it does not matter where: *'Where shall we go to eat?' 'Oh, anywhere will do.'* في أيّ مكان

apart /ə'pɑːt/ *adv* **1** away from sb/sth or each other; not together: *The doors slowly slid apart.* ○ *They always quarrel so it's best to keep them apart.* منفرداً، بِمَعْزِل

2 away from each other by the distance mentioned: *Plant the potatoes two feet apart.* ○ *I'm afraid our ideas are too far apart.* بعيداً

3 into pieces: *to fall apart* ○ *The material was so old that it just fell/came apart in my hands.* ○ *Their relationship was clearly falling apart* (= about to end). يتكسّر، يتهشّم

IDM **take sth apart** to separate sth into pieces: *He took the whole bicycle apart.* يفكّ

tell A and B apart to see the difference between A and B: *It's very difficult to tell the twins apart.* يميّز

a'part from (*especially US* **aside from**) *prep* **1** except for: *I've finished my homework apart from some reading we have to do.* ○ *There's nobody here apart from me.* ما عدا

2 as well as; in addition to: *Apart from their house in the country they've got a flat in London.* فضلاً عن

apartheid /ə'pɑːthaɪt; *US* -heɪt/ *noun* [U] the former official government policy in South Africa of separating people of different races and making them live apart (سياسة) التّفرقة العنصريّة

apartment /ə'pɑːtmənt/ *noun* [C] **1** (*especially US*) = FLAT[1]

2 [usually pl.] one of a number of rooms in a large house, used by an important person: *the Duke's private apartments* حجْرة أو شقّة، مقصورة

a b c d e f g h i j k l m n o p q r s t u v w x y z

a'partment block *noun* [C] a large building containing several apartments عمارة متعددة الشقق

apathy /ˈæpəθi/ *noun* [U] a lack of interest in things or of a desire to do anything لا مبالاة
▸ **apathetic** /ˌæpəˈθetɪk/ *adj* lacking interest or a desire to act: *Don't be so apathetic!* لا مبالٍ

ape /eɪp/ *noun* [C] a type of animal like a large monkey with no tail or only a very short tail: *Chimpanzees and gorillas are apes.* قِرد
▸ **ape** *verb* [T] to copy sb/sth يقلّد، يحاكي

aperitif /əˌperəˈtiːf; US əˌperəˈtiːf/ *noun* [C] a drink of alcohol that you have before a meal مشروب كحولي فاتح للشهية

apiece /əˈpiːs/ *adv* each: *He gave the children £1 apiece.* لكلٍّ

apologetic /əˌpɒləˈdʒetɪk/ *adj* feeling or showing that you are sorry for sth you have done: *He was most apologetic about his son's bad behaviour.* ○ *I wrote him an apologetic letter.* اعتذاري
▸ **apologetically** /-kli/ *adv* باعتذار

apologize (*also* **apologise**) /əˈpɒlədʒaɪz/ *verb* [I] **apologize (to sb) (for sth)** to say that you are sorry for sth you have done: *I do apologize for taking so long to reply to your letter.* ○ *You'll have to apologize to your teacher for forgetting to do your homework.* ❶ When you apologize, the actual words you use are usually **'I'm sorry'**. يعتذر

apology /əˈpɒlədʒi/ *noun* [C,U] (*pl.* **apologies**) **apology (to sb) (for sth)** a spoken or written statement that you are sorry for sth you have done, etc: *Please accept our apologies for the problems you experienced during your stay in the hotel.* ○ *He was full of apology for having missed my birthday.* اعتذار

apostle /əˈpɒsl/ *noun* [C] one of the twelve men chosen by Christ to spread his teaching حَوارِيّ

apostrophe /əˈpɒstrəfi/ *noun* [C] **1** the sign (') used for showing that you have left a letter or number out of a word (as in 'I'm', 'can't', 'we'll', etc.) الفاصلة العليا (للدلالة على حذف حرف أو عدد)
2 the sign (') used for showing who or what sth belongs or relates to as in 'John's chair', 'the boy's room' or 'the book's title'. الفاصلة العليا (للدلالة على الإضافة)

appal (*US* **appall**) /əˈpɔːl/ *verb* [T] (appalling; appalled) (usually passive) to shock sb deeply: *We were appalled by the poverty and starvation we saw everywhere.* يرتاع؛ يُفزع
▸ **appalling** *adj* shocking or terrible: *appalling cruelty* ○ *The food is appalling.* فظيع، شنيع
appallingly *adv* بشكل فظيع

apparatus /ˌæpəˈreɪtəs; US -ˈrætəs/ *noun* [U] a set of tools, instruments or equipment used for doing a job or an activity: *the scientific apparatus necessary for carrying out experiments* جهاز

apparent /əˈpærənt/ *adj* **1** (only *before* a noun) perhaps not true or real although seeming to be so: *His apparent interest in the proposal didn't last very long.* ظاهري، بادٍ
2 apparent to sb clear; easy to see: *It was apparent to everyone that the man could not be trusted.* ○ *For no apparent reason she suddenly burst into tears.* واضح
▸ **apparently** *adv* **1** according to what people say (but perhaps not true): *Apparently, he's already been married twice.* حَسْبَما يقال
2 according to how sth seems or appears (but perhaps not true): *He was apparently undisturbed by the news.* على مايبدو

appeal /əˈpiːl/ *verb* [I] **1 appeal to sb (for sth)**; **appeal for sth** to make a serious request for sth you need or want very much: *Relief workers in the disaster area are appealing for more help and supplies.* ○ *She appeared on television to appeal to the men for her child's safe return.* يُناشد، يلتمس
2 appeal (to sb) to be attractive or interesting (to sb): *The idea of living in the country doesn't appeal to me at all.* يجذب؛ يروق لِ
3 appeal to sth to influence sb's feelings or thoughts so that he/she will do sth you want: *to appeal to sb's honour, sense of justice, etc.* ○ *We aim to appeal to people's generosity.* يحتكم إلى، يخاطب
4 appeal (to sb) (for/against sth) to ask sb in authority to change a decision: *He decided to appeal against his conviction.* ○ *The team appealed against the referee's decision.* يستأنف
▸ **appeal** *noun* **1** [C] a serious request for sth you need or want very much: *The police have made an urgent appeal for witnesses to come forward.* ○ *a television, radio, etc. appeal* (= a television or radio programme asking for help or money for a particular cause) مناشدة، التماس
2 [C] **appeal to sth** a written or spoken statement that tries to influence sb's feelings or thoughts so that he/she will do what you want: *a powerful appeal to our sense of loyalty* نداء، مناشدة
3 [C] a formal request to sb in authority to change a decision: *The judge turned down the defendant's appeal.* استئناف
4 [U] attraction or interest: *I can't understand the appeal of stamp collecting.* جاذبيّة، فتنة
appealing *adj* **1** attractive or interesting: *The idea of a Greek holiday sounds very appealing!* جذّاب
2 showing that you need help, etc: *an appealing glance in my direction* مستنجِد
appealingly *adv* على نحو جذّاب؛ مستنجداً

appear /əˈpɪə(r)/ *verb* [I] **1** to be seen; to come into sight: *The bus appeared round the corner.* يَظهر، يبدو
2 to begin to exist: *The disease is thought to have appeared in Africa.* يَظهر، يبدأ
3 to be published or printed: *The article appeared in the 'Daily Mail' on Friday.* يَظهر، يُنشر
4 to present yourself in public to speak, perform, act, etc: *to appear on television* ○ *A man will appear in court today charged with murder.* ○ *She is currently appearing in 'Macbeth'.* يَظهر، يَمْثُل (أمام محكمة)
5 to seem: *She appears to be very happy in her*

job. ○ *It appears that you were given the wrong information.* ○ *'Do you think there will be an election?' 'It appears so/not.'* ❶ The adjective is **apparent**. يبدو

appearance /ə'pɪərəns/ *noun* **1** [sing.] the arrival of sb/sth: *I was surprised by her unexpected appearance at the party.* ظهور، وصول

2 [sing.] the beginning (of sth never seen or used before): *the appearance of television in the home in the 1950s* ظهور

3 [C] an act of appearing in public, especially on stage, television, etc: *His last appearance before his death was in 'Julius Caesar'.* ظهور، مثول (أمام محكمة)

4 [C,U] the way that sb/sth looks: *A different hairstyle can completely change your appearance.* ○ *He gives the appearance of being extremely confident.* مظهر

appendicitis /əˌpendə'saɪtɪs/ *noun* [U] an illness in which your appendix becomes extremely painful and usually has to be removed التهاب الزائدة الدوديّة

appendix /ə'pendɪks/ *noun* [C] **1** (*pl.* **appendixes**) a small tube inside your body which is attached to the intestine الزائدة الدوديّة

2 (*pl.* **appendices** /-dɪsiːz/) a section at the end of a book, etc. that gives extra information ملحق

appetite /'æpɪtaɪt/ *noun* **1** [C,U] the desire for food: *a good/healthy appetite* ○ *My two teenage sons have enormous appetites!* ○ *Some fresh air and exercise should give you an appetite* (= make you hungry). شهيّة (للطعام)

2 [C,U] a natural desire: *sexual appetites* شهوة

IDM whet sb's appetite → WHET

appetizer (*also* **appetiser**) /'æpɪtaɪzə(r)/ *noun* [C] a small amount of food or a drink that you have before a meal فاتح الشهية

appetizing (*also* **appetising**) /'æpɪtaɪzɪŋ/ *adj* (used about food, etc.) attractive and tempting: *an appetizing smell* مشهٍّ

applaud /ə'plɔːd/ *verb* **1** [I,T] to clap your hands in order to show that you like sb/sth: *The audience applauded loudly.* ○ *The team was applauded as it left the field.* يصفّق

2 [T] (usually passive) to praise sb/sth: *The decision was applauded by everybody.* يمتدح

applause /ə'plɔːz/ *noun* [U] the noise made by a group of people, clapping their hands to show their approval and enjoyment: *The performance got terrific applause from the audience.* ○ *The actor was greeted by a round of applause.* تصفيق

apple /'æpl/ *noun* [C] a hard, round fruit with a smooth green, red or yellow skin: *cooking/eating apples* ○ *an apple pie* تفّاحة

appliance /ə'plaɪəns/ *noun* [C] a piece of equipment for a particular purpose in the house: *electrical appliances* أداة

applicable /ə'plɪkəbl; 'æplɪkəbl/ *adj* (not before a noun) **applicable (to sb/sth)** that concerns or relates to: *This part of the form is only applicable to married women.* ينطبق على

applicant /'æplɪkənt/ *noun* [C] a person who applies for sth, especially a job طالب (عمل)

application /ˌæplɪ'keɪʃn/ *noun* **1** [C,U] **application (to sb) (for sth)** a formal written request, especially for a job or a place in a school, club, etc: *Applications for the job should be made to the Personnel Manager.* ○ *an application form* (= a special form on which you apply for a job, etc.) طلب (وظيفة مثلاً)

2 [C,U] a/the practical use (of sth): *The lecture was about the application of educational theory to the classroom.* تطبيق

3 [C] a computer program designed to do a particular job; a piece of software: *a database application* برنامج محدد الغرض

4 [U] hard work; effort مثابرة، جهد

apply /ə'plaɪ/ *verb* (*pres part* **applying**; *3rd pers sing pres* **applies**; *pt, pp* **applied**) **1** [I] **apply (to sb) (for sth)** to ask for sth in writing: *I'm going to apply for that job they advertised.* ○ *My daughter's applying for a place at university.* يتقدّم (لوظيفة)

2 [T] **apply yourself/sth (to sth/to doing sth)** to make yourself concentrate on sth: *to apply your mind to sth* ○ *He applied himself to his studies.* يركّز، ينكبّ

3 [I] **apply (to sb/sth)** to concern or relate (to sb/sth): *This information applies to all children born after 2003.* ينطبق على

4 [T] **apply sth (to sth)** to make practical use of sth: *new technology which can be applied to solving problems in industry* يطبّق

5 [T] (usually passive) to use a word, a name, etc. to refer to sb/sth: *I don't think the word 'antique' can be applied to this old table, do you?* ينطبق

6 [T] **apply sth (to sth)** to put or spread sth (onto sth): *Apply the cream to the infected area twice a day.* يضع

▶ **applied** *adj* (used about a subject) having a practical use: *applied mathematics* (e.g. as used in engineering) تطبيقي

appoint /ə'pɔɪnt/ *verb* [T] **1 appoint sb (to sth)** to choose sb for a job, etc: *The committee have appointed a new chairperson.* ○ *He's been appointed (as) Assistant Secretary to the Minister of Education.* يعيّن

2 appoint sth (for sth) (*formal*) to arrange or decide on sth: *the date appointed for the next meeting* يحدّد

appointment /ə'pɔɪntmənt/ *noun* **1** [C,U] **appointment (with sb)** an arrangement to see sb at a particular time: *a doctor's, dentist's, hairdresser's, etc. appointment* ○ *I'd like to make an appointment to see the manager.* ○ *I'm afraid I won't be able to keep our appointment on Monday.* ○ *to cancel an appointment* ○ *Visits are by appointment only* (= at a time that has been arranged in advance). موعد

2 [C] a job or position of responsibility: *a temporary/permanent appointment* وظيفة

3 [U] **appointment (to sth)** the act of choosing sb for a job: *Many people criticized the appointment of such a young man to the post.* تعيين

appraise /ə'preɪz/ *verb* [T] (*formal*) to form an opinion about the value or quality of sb/sth يقوّم، يقيّم

▸ **appraisal** /ə'preɪzl/ *noun* [C,U] an opinion about the value or quality of sb/sth; a judgement تقويم، تقييم

appreciable /ə'priːʃəbl/ *adj* noticeable or important: *There has been an appreciable drop in the rate of inflation.* مقدر، ملحوظ

appreciate /ə'priːʃieɪt/ *verb* **1** [T] to enjoy sth or to understand the value of sth: *The art of Van Gogh was not appreciated during his own lifetime.* يقدّر

2 [T] to understand sth (a problem, situation, etc.): *I don't think you appreciate how serious this situation is.* يدرك

3 [T] to be grateful for sth: *Thanks for your help. We did appreciate it.* يقدّر

4 [I] to increase in value: *Houses in this area have appreciated faster than elsewhere.* ترتفع (قيمته)

▸ **appreciative** /ə'priːʃətɪv/ *adj* **1** feeling or showing pleasure or admiration: *'You look lovely,' he said, with an appreciative smile.* ينم عن التقدير أو الاعجاب

2 appreciative (of sth) grateful for sth: *He was very appreciative of our efforts to help.* ممتَن

appreciation /əˌpriːʃi'eɪʃn/ *noun* **1** [U] understanding and enjoyment (of the value of sth): *I'm afraid I have little appreciation of modern architecture.* فهم، استمتاع

2 [U] the feeling of being grateful for sth: *We bought him a present to show our appreciation for all the work he had done.* ○ *Please accept these flowers as a token* (= a sign) *of my appreciation.* عِرفان

3 [U, sing.] understanding of what sth involves: *None of us had the slightest appreciation of the seriousness of the situation.* إدراك

4 [U] increase in value: *the appreciation of antiques and works of art* زيادة (في القيمة)

apprehension /ˌæprɪ'henʃn/ *noun* [C,U] (*formal*) worry or fear about sth in the future: *feelings of apprehension* تخوُّف

apprehensive /ˌæprɪ'hensɪv/ *adj* worried or afraid: *to be/feel apprehensive* ○ *The students were apprehensive about their forthcoming exams.* متخوّف

apprentice /ə'prentɪs/ *noun* [C] a person who works for sb for low wages, in order to learn an occupation or skill: *an apprentice electrician* تلميذ الصنعة

▸ **apprenticeship** /-tɪʃɪp/ *noun* [C,U] the state or time of being an apprentice فترة التتلمذ على صنعة

approach /ə'prəʊtʃ/ *verb* **1** [I,T] to come near or nearer to sb/sth: *The day of her wedding approached.* ○ *When you approach the village you will see a garage on your left.* يقترب

2 [T] to speak to sb usually in order to ask for sth: *I'm going to approach my bank manager about a loan.* يكلّم، يفاتح

3 [T] to begin to deal with sth (a problem, a situation, etc.): *What is the best way to approach this problem?* يعالج

4 [T] to almost reach sth (a certain standard, level, etc.): *at a depth approaching 50 feet under water* يناهز

▸ **approach** *noun* **1** [sing.] the act of coming nearer (to sb/sth): *The children stopped talking at the teacher's approach.* دنوّ، اقتراب

2 [C] a discussion about getting sth; a request for sth: *The company has made an approach to us for financial assistance.* مفاتحة، طلب

3 [C] a road or path, etc. leading to sth: *the approach to the village* طريق

4 [C] a way of dealing with sb/sth: *Parents don't always know what approach to take with teenage children.* وسيلة (للتعامل)

approachable /-əbl/ *adj* **1** friendly and easy to talk to: *She's nice but her husband's not very approachable.* ❶ The opposite is **unapproachable.** سهل الجانب، يسهل التعامل معه

2 (not before a noun) able to be reached: *The area was easily approachable by bus.* سهل الوصول

appropriate /ə'prəʊpriət/ *adj* **appropriate (for/to sth)** suitable or right: *The matter will be dealt with by the appropriate authorities.* ○ *This card is rather appropriate for the occasion, isn't it?* ○ *Please take whatever action you think is appropriate.* ❶ The opposite is **inappropriate.** ملائم، مناسب

▸ **appropriately** *adv* على نحو ملائم

approval /ə'pruːvl/ *noun* [U] feeling, showing or saying that you think sth is good; agreement: *Everybody gave their approval to the proposal.* ○ *I'm afraid I can't sign these papers without my partner's approval.* ○ *She was always anxious to win her mother's approval.* استحسان، موافقة

approve /ə'pruːv/ *verb* **1** [I] **approve (of sb/sth)** to be pleased about sth; to like sb/sth: *His father didn't approve of his leaving school at 16.* ○ *Her parents don't approve of her friends.* ❶ The opposite is **disapprove.** يستحسن، يوافق

2 [T] to agree to sth or to accept sth as correct: *We need to get an accountant to approve these figures.* يصدّق على

▸ **approving** *adj* showing support or admiration for sth: *'I agree entirely,' he said with an approving smile.* موافق، معجب بـ

approvingly *adv* باستحسان، بموافقة

approximate /ə'prɒksɪmət/ *adj* (*abbr* **approx**) almost correct but not completely accurate: *The approximate time of arrival is 3 o'clock.* ○ *I can only give you an approximate idea of the cost.* تقريبي

▸ **approximately** *adv* (*abbr* **approx**) about: *It's approximately fifty miles from here.* تقريباً

approximation /əˌprɒksɪ'meɪʃn/ *noun* [C] a

number, answer, etc. which is nearly, but not exactly, right تقريب

apricot /ˈeɪprɪkɒt/ *noun* [C] a small, round, yellow or orange fruit with soft flesh and a stone inside مِشْمِش

April /ˈeɪprəl/ *noun* [C,U] (*abbr* **Apr.**) the fourth month of the year, coming before May ℹ For examples of the use of the months in sentences, look at **January**. أبريل/نيسان

ˌApril ˈFool *noun* [C] a person who has a joke or trick played on him/her on 1 April ضحيّة كذبة أبريل

ˌApril ˈFool's Day *noun* [sing.] 1 April يوم كذبة أبريل

On this day it is traditional for people to play tricks on each other, especially by inventing silly stories and trying to persuade other people that they are true. If somebody believes such a story he/she is called an April Fool.

apron /ˈeɪprən/ *noun* [C] a piece of clothing that you wear over the front of your usual clothes in order to keep them clean, especially when cooking مِئْزَر، مَرْيَلة

apt /æpt/ *adj* **1** suitable: *a very apt reply* مناسب

2 apt to do sth having a tendency to do sth; likely: *You'd better remind me. I'm rather apt to forget.* ميّال لـ، عرْضة لـ

▸ **aptly** *adv* suitably: *The house was aptly named 'Sea View'* (= because it had a view of the sea). على نحوٍ ملائم

aptitude /ˈæptɪtjuːd; *US* -tuːd/ *noun* [C,U] **aptitude (for sth/for doing sth)** (a) natural ability: *She has an aptitude for learning languages.* ○ *He's shown no aptitude for music.* استعداد طبيعي

aquarium /əˈkweəriəm/ *noun* [C] (*pl.* **aquariums** or **aquaria** /-riə/) **1** a glass container filled with water, in which fish and water animals are kept حوض الأسماك

2 a building, often in a zoo, where fish and water animals are kept معرض الأسماك والأحياء المائيّة

Aquarius /əˈkweəriəs/ *noun* [C,U] the eleventh sign of the zodiac, the Water-carrier; a person who was born under this sign برج الدلو ؛ شخص من مواليد هذا البرج

aquatic /əˈkwætɪk/ *adj* **1** (used about an animal or a plant) living in water (حيوان أو نبات) مائي

2 (used about a sport) performed on or in water (رياضة) مائيّة

Arab /ˈærəb/ *noun* [C] a member of a people who lived originally in Arabia and who now live in many parts of the Middle East and North Africa العربي

▸ **Arab** *adj*: *Arab countries* عربي

Arabic /ˈærəbɪk/ *noun* [sing.] **1** the language that is spoken by Arab people اللغة العربية

2 the religious language of Islam اللغة العربية

arable /ˈærəbl/ *adj* (in farming) connected with growing crops for sale, not keeping animals زراعي

arbitrary /ˈɑːbɪtrəri; *US* ˈɑːrbɪtreri/ *adj* not based on any principle or reason; not thinking about the wishes of the other people involved: *The choice he made seemed completely arbitrary. I couldn't see any reason for it, anyway.* عشوائي ، اعتباطي ؛ تعسّفي

▸ **arbitrarily** *adv* اعتباطاً

arbitrate /ˈɑːbɪtreɪt/ *verb* [I,T] to settle an argument between two people or groups by finding a solution that both can accept يفصِل (في نزاع)

arbitration /ˌɑːbɪˈtreɪʃn/ *noun* [U] the process of settling an argument between two people or groups by a third person (who has been chosen by them): *The union and the management decided to go to arbitration.* تحكيم

arc /ɑːk/ *noun* [C] a curved line, part of a circle قوس

arcade /ɑːˈkeɪd/ *noun* [C] a large covered passage or area with shops along one or both sides; a passage with arches: *a shopping arcade* رواق مغطى فيه حوانيت ؛ ممرّ بقناطر

arch /ɑːtʃ/ *noun* [C] **1** a structure made with two columns joined over the top in a curve. An arch may support a bridge or the roof of a large building or it may be above a door or a window. ➲ Look at **archway**. قنطرة ؛ قوس

2 a monument in the shape of an arch: *Marble Arch in London* نصب مقوّس ، قوس

3 the middle part of the inside of your foot قوس القدم

▸ **arch** *verb* [I,T] to make a curve: [T]: *The cat arched its back and hissed.* يقوّس

archaeology (*especially US* **archeology**) /ˌɑːkiˈɒlədʒi/ *noun* [U] the study of ancient civilizations, based on objects or parts of buildings that are found in the ground علم الآثار

▸ **archaeological** (*especially US* **archeological**) *adj* connected with archaeology متعلق بالآثار القديمة

archaeologist (*especially US* **archeologist**) *noun* [C] an expert in archaeology عالم آثار

archaic /ɑːˈkeɪɪk/ *adj* old-fashioned; no longer in common use قديم ؛ مهجور الاستعمال

archbishop /ˌɑːtʃˈbɪʃəp/ *noun* [C] a priest in some branches of the Christian church who is in charge of all the bishops, priests and churches in a large area of a country: *the Archbishop of Canterbury* مَطْران: رئيس الأساقفة

archer /ˈɑːtʃə(r)/ *noun* [C] a person who shoots with a bow and arrow رامي السّهام أو النبال

▸ **archery** *noun* [U] the sport of shooting with a bow and arrow رياضة رمي السّهام

architect /ˈɑːkɪtekt/ *noun* [C] a person whose job is to design buildings مهندس معماري

architecture /ˈɑːkɪtektʃə(r)/ *noun* [U] **1** the study of how buildings are planned and constructed الهندسة المعمارية

2 the style or design of a building or buildings:

the architecture of the fifteenth century ○ *modern architecture* فن العمارة

▶ **architectural** /ˌɑːkɪˈtektʃərəl/ *adj* connected with the design of buildings معماري

archives /ˈɑːkaɪvz/ *noun* [plural] (*also* **archive** /ˈɑːkaɪv/ *noun* [C]) a collection of historical documents, etc. which record the history of a place or an organization; the place where they are kept: *In the city archives they found letters dating from the Middle Ages.* ○ *archive material on the First World War* أرشيف ، مكان حفظ السجلات

archway /ˈɑːtʃweɪ/ *noun* [C] a passage or entrance with an arch over it ممر مقنطر

Arctic /ˈɑːktɪk/ *adj* **1** connected with the region round the North Pole (the most northern point of the world) ➲ Look at **Antarctic**. متعلّق بالقطب الشمالي

2 arctic very cold: *The mountaineers faced arctic conditions near the top of the mountain.* قارس البرد

▶ **the Arctic** *noun* [sing.] the area round the North Pole منطقة القطب الشمالي

the ˌArctic ˈCircle *noun* [sing.] the line of latitude 66° 30´N الدائرة القطبية الشمالية

ardent /ˈɑːdnt/ *adj* showing strong feelings, especially a strong liking for sb/sth: *He was an ardent supporter of the Government.* متحمّس

▶ **ardently** *adv* بحماس

arduous /ˈɑːdjuəs; *US* -dʒu-/ *adj* full of difficulties; needing a lot of effort: *an arduous journey* عسير ؛ شاقّ

are, aren't → BE

area /ˈeəriə/ *noun* **1** [C] a part of a town, a country or the world: *Housing is very expensive in the London area.* ○ *The wettest areas are in the West of the country.* ○ *a built-up area* (= where there are buildings) ○ *The high winds scattered litter over a wide area.* ➲ Look at the note at **district**. منطقة ، حيّ

2 [C,U] the size of a surface, that you can calculate by multiplying the length by the width: *The area of the office is 35 square metres.* ○ *The office is 35 square metres in area.* مساحة

3 [C] a space used for a particular activity: *The restaurant has a non-smoking area.* ○ *the penalty area* (= the space in front of the goal, in football) منطقة ؛ قسم

4 [C] a particular part of a subject or activity: *Training is one area of the business that we could improve.* مجال

arena /əˈriːnə/ *noun* [C] **1** an area with seats around it where public entertainments (sporting events, concerts, etc.) are held ميدان ، ساحة ، حلبة

2 where a particular activity happens: *The Foreign Secretary was well-respected in the international political arena.* ساحة ؛ صعيد

arguable /ˈɑːgjuəbl/ *adj* **1** that can be argued; probably true: *It is arguable that no one should have to pay for hospital treatment.* قابل للتأييد ؛ محتمل الصحّة

2 not certain; that you do not accept without question: *It is arguable whether the case should have ever gone to trial* (= perhaps it should not have). قابل للأخذ و الردّ

▶ **arguably** *adv* probably; you can argue that: *'King Lear' is arguably Shakespeare's best play.* من المحتمل ؛ على الأرجح

argue /ˈɑːgjuː/ *verb* **1** [I] **argue (with sb) (about/over sth)** to say things (often angrily) that show that you do not agree with sb about sth: *The couple next door are always arguing.* ○ *I never argue with my husband about money.* يجادل ، يختلف مع

2 [I,T] **argue that; argue (for/against sth)** to give reasons that support your opinion about sth: *John argued that buying a new computer was a waste of money.* ○ *He argued against buying a new computer.* يقدّم حجّة

argument /ˈɑːgjumənt/ *noun* **1** [C,U] **argument (with sb) (about/over sth)** an angry discussion between two or more people who disagree with each other: *Sue had an argument with her father about politics.* ○ *He accepted the decision without argument.* ❶ A **quarrel** is usually about something less serious. جدال ، نزاع

2 [C] the reason(s) that you give to support your opinion about sth: *His argument was that if they bought a smaller car, they would save money.* حُجّة

argumentative /ˌɑːgjuˈmentətɪv/ *adj* often involved in or enjoying arguments محبّ للجدال ، شديد الخصام

arid /ˈærɪd/ *adj* (used about land or climate) very dry; with little or no rain جاف ، مجدب

Aries /ˈeəriːz/ *noun* [C,U] the first sign of the zodiac, the Ram; a person who was born under this sign برج الحَمَل ؛ شخص من مواليد هذا البرج

arise /əˈraɪz/ *verb* [I] (*pt* **arose**; *pp* **arisen**) to begin to exist; to appear: *If any problems arise, let me know.* ينشأ ، يبرز ؛ يحصل

aristocracy /ˌærɪˈstɒkrəsi/ *noun* [C, with sing. or pl. verb] (*pl.* **aristocracies**) the people of the highest social class who often have special titles الأرستقراطية: طبقة النبلاء

aristocrat /ˈærɪstəkræt; *US* əˈrɪst-/ *noun* [C] a member of the highest social class, often with a special title أرستقراطي

▶ **aristocratic** *adj* أرستقراطي

arithmetic /əˈrɪθmətɪk/ *noun* [U] the branch of mathematics which involves counting with numbers (adding, subtracting, multiplying and dividing) علم الحساب

arm[1] /ɑːm/ *noun* [C] **1** the limb at each side of the human body from the shoulder to the hand: *He was carrying a newspaper under his arm.* ○ *They waved their arms in the air and shouted at us.* ○ *I put my arm round her and tried to comfort her.* ذراع

2 the part of a piece of clothing that covers your arm; a sleeve: *He had a hole in the arm of his jumper.* كُمّ

3 something shaped like an arm: *the arm of a chair* (= where you rest your arm) يد (الكرسي مثلاً)

IDM **arm in arm** with your arm linked together with sb else's arm: *The two friends walked arm in arm.* متشابك الذراعين

cross/fold your arms to cross your arms in front of your chest: *She folded her arms and waited.* ○ *James was sitting with his arms crossed.* يشبك الذراعين أمام صدره

twist sb's arm → TWIST[1]

with open arms → OPEN[1]

arm² /ɑːm/ *verb* [I,T] to prepare sb/yourself to fight by supplying weapons: *The country is beginning to arm itself for war.* ➲ Look at **armed** and **arms**. يُسلّح : يتسلّح

armaments /ˈɑːməmənts/ *noun* [plural] weapons and military equipment عدّة حربية

armband /ˈɑːmbænd/ *noun* [C] **1** a piece of material that you wear around your sleeve شريط يلفّ حول الذراع

2 a plastic ring filled with air which you can wear on your arms when you are learning to swim طوق سباحة يلبس حول الذراع

armchair /ˈɑːmtʃeə(r)/ *noun* [C] a soft comfortable chair with sides which support your arms كرسي مريح ذو مرفقين

armed /ɑːmd/ *adj* carrying a gun or other weapon; involving weapons: *All the terrorists were armed.* ○ *armed robbery* ○ *the armed forces* (= the army, navy and air force) ○ *(figurative) They came to the meeting armed with all the latest information.* مسلّح

armful /ˈɑːmfʊl/ *noun* [C] the amount that you can carry in your arms ملء الذراعين

armhole /ˈɑːmhəʊl/ [C] the opening in a piece of clothing where your arm goes through فتحة الذراع في الثوب

armistice /ˈɑːmɪstɪs/ *noun* [C] an agreement between two countries who are at war that they will stop fighting هُدْنة

armour (*US* **armor**) /ˈɑːmə(r)/ *noun* [U] clothing, often made of metal, that soldiers wore in earlier times to protect themselves: *a suit of armour* دِرْع

▸ **armoured** (*US* **armored**) *adj* (used about a vehicle) covered with metal to protect it in an attack (سيارة) مصفحة

armpit /ˈɑːmpɪt/ [C] the part of the body under the arm at the point where it joins the shoulder ابط

arms /ɑːmz/ *noun* [plural] **1** weapons, especially those that are used in war: *a reduction in nuclear arms* أسلحة

2 = COAT OF ARMS

IDM **be up in arms** very angry; protesting about sth: *The workers were up in arms over the news that the factory was going to close.* غاضب جداً : محتج

army /ˈɑːmi/ *noun* [C, with sing. or pl. verb] (*pl.* **armies**) the military forces of a country which are trained to fight on land; a large group of soldiers: *the British Army* ○ *She joined the army at the age of eighteen.* ○ *He's a sergeant in the army.* ○ *an army officer* ➲ Look at **air force** and **navy**. جيش

ˈA-road *noun* [C] (*Brit*) a major road, usually not as wide as a motorway طريق رئيسي

aroma /əˈrəʊmə/ *noun* [C] a smell (usually one that is pleasant) رائحة ذكيّة : شذا ، عبير

aromatherapy /əˌrəʊməˈθerəpi/ *noun* [U] the use of natural oils that smell pleasant for controlling pain or for massage (=rubbing into the body) العلاج بالزيوت العطرية

arose *pt* of ARISE

around¹ /əˈraʊnd/ *adv* **1** (*also* **about**) in or to various places or directions: *We walked around for hours looking for a cafe.* ○ *I don't want to buy anything – I'm just looking around.* ○ *This is our office – David will show you around* (= show you the different parts of it). هنا وهناك

2 moving so as to face in the opposite direction: *Turn around and go back the way you came.* إلى الوراء

3 on all sides; forming a circle: *The garden is very nice with a wall all around.* ○ *Gather around so that you can all see.* حول : على شكل دائرة

ℹ In senses **1**, **2** and **3** **round** can be used instead of **around**.

4 (*also* **about**) present or available: *I went to the house but there was nobody around.* ○ *That isn't a new book. It's been around for ages.* موجود : متوفّر

5 (*also* **about**) (used for activities with no real purpose): *'What are you doing?' 'Nothing, just lazing around.'* ○ *John likes messing around with cars.* ○ *I found this pen lying around on the floor.* (للدلالة على نشاط بلا هدف)

around² /əˈraʊnd/ *prep* **1** in various directions inside an area; in different places in a particular area: *They wandered around the town, looking at the shops.* حول : هنا وهناك

2 in a circle or following a curving path: *We sat down around the table.* ○ *The athlete ran around the track ten times.* ○ *Go around the corner and it's the first house on the left.* ○ *She had a bandage around her leg.* ○ *(figurative) There doesn't seem to be any way around the problem.* حول

3 near a place: *Is there a bank around here?* قريب (من)

ℹ In senses **1**, **2** and **3** **round** can also be used.

4 (*also* **about**) (at) approximately: *It's around three hours' drive from here.* ○ *I'll see you around seven* (= at about 7 o'clock). حوالي ، تقريباً

arouse /əˈraʊz/ *verb* [T] to cause a particular reaction in people: *His actions have aroused a lot of criticism.* يثير

▸ **arousal** *noun* [U] إثارة

arr. *abbrev* arrives: *arr New York 07.15* وقت الوصول

arrange /ə'reɪndʒ/ *verb* **1** [T] to put sth in order or in a particular pattern: *The books were arranged in alphabetical order.* ○ *Arrange the chairs in a circle.* ○ *She arranged the flowers in a vase.* ينظّم، يرتّب

2 [I,T] to make plans and preparations so that sth can happen in the future: *Isobel's parents arranged a big party for her eighteenth birthday.* ○ *He arranged for Peter to stay with friends in France.* ○ *She arranged to meet Stuart after work.* يدبّر؛ ينظّم

arrangement /ə'reɪndʒmənt/ *noun* **1** [C, usually pl.] plans or preparations for sth that will happen in the future: *We're just making the final arrangements for the concert.* ترتيبات؛ تدابير

2 [C,U] something that you have agreed or settled with sb else; the act of doing this: *They made an arrangement to share the cost of the food.* ○ *Under the new arrangement it will be possible to pay monthly instead of weekly.* ○ *Use of the swimming pool will be by special arrangement only.* اتفاق

3 [C] a group of things that have been placed in a particular pattern: *a flower arrangement* ترتيب، تشكيل فنيّ

array /ə'reɪ/ *noun* [C] a large collection of things, especially one that is impressive and is seen by other people: *There was a colourful array of vegetables on the market stall.* مجموعة بديعة، عرض جميل

arrears /ə'rɪəz/ *noun* [plural] money that should have been paid by an earlier date or that is owed for work which has been done: *I'm in arrears with the rent* (= I owe some money). ○ *You will be paid monthly in arrears* (= at the end of month for the work done during the month). متأخّرات، ديون لم تسدّد بعد

arrest /ə'rest/ *verb* [T] when the police arrest sb they take him/her prisoner in order to question him/her about a crime يوقف، يعتقل

▸ **arrest** *noun* [C] the act of arresting sb: *The police made ten arrests after the riot.* اعتقال

IDM **be under arrest**: *He was under arrest for murder.* معتقل

arrival /ə'raɪvl/ *noun* **1** [U] the act of reaching the place to which you were travelling: *On our arrival we were told that our rooms had not been reserved.* ○ *We apologize for the late arrival of this train.* وصول

2 [C] people or things that have arrived: *We brought in extra chairs for the late arrivals.* ○ *I'll look on the arrivals board to see when the train gets in.* (شخص) وافد، قادم

arrive /ə'raɪv/ *verb* [I] **1** to reach the place to which you were travelling: *We arrived home at about midnight.* ○ *What time does the train arrive in Newcastle?* ○ *They arrived at the station ten minutes late.* ○ *Has my letter arrived yet?* يصل

We use **arrive in** with the name of a town, country, etc. and **arrive at** with a place, building, etc.

2 to come or happen: *The day of the wedding had finally arrived.* ○ *Paula's baby arrived* (= was born) *two weeks late.* يجيء

PHR V **arrive at** to reach sth: *After months of discussions they finally arrived at a decision.* يتوصّل إلى

arrogant /'ærəgənt/ *adj* thinking that you are better and more important than other people and not caring about their feelings; proud متعجرف، متكبّر

▸ **arrogance** /'ærəgəns/ *noun* [U] عجرفة، غطرسة

arrogantly *adv* بعجرفة

arrow /'ærəʊ/ *noun* [C] **1** a thin piece of wood or metal, with one pointed end and feathers at the other end, that is shot from a bow سهم

2 the sign (→) which is used to show direction: *The arrow is pointing left.* إشارة السهم

arsenic /'ɑ:snɪk/ *noun* [U] a type of very strong poison زرنيخ

arson /'ɑ:sn/ *noun* [U] the crime of setting fire to a building on purpose جريمة إحراق الممتلكات عمداً

▸ **arsonist** a person who deliberately sets fire to a building محرق المباني إجراماً

art /ɑ:t/ *noun* **1** [U] the producing of beautiful things such as paintings, drawings, etc.; the objects that are produced: *an art class* ○ *She studied History of Art at university.* ○ *the art of the Italian Renaissance* ○ *modern art* ○ *an art gallery* ➲ Look at **work of art**. فن؛ أعمال فنيّة

2 [C, usually sing.] a skill or sth that requires skill: *There's an art to writing a good letter.* فن، براعة

3 the arts [plural] activities such as painting, writing literature or writing and performing music: *The government has agreed to spend £2 million extra on the arts next year.* الفنون والآداب

4 arts [plural] subjects such as history or languages that you study at school or university ❶ We usually contrast **arts** (or **arts subjects**) with **sciences** (or **science subjects**). الآداب

artery /'ɑ:təri/ *noun* [C] (*pl.* **arteries**) one of the tubes which take blood from the heart to other parts of the body ➲ Look at **vein**. شريان

artful /'ɑ:tfl/ *adj* clever at getting what you want, perhaps by deceiving people داهية، ماكر

arthritis /ɑ:'θraɪtɪs/ *noun* [U] a disease which causes swelling and pain in the joints of your body (where you bend your arms, fingers, etc.) التهاب المفاصل

artichoke /'ɑ:tɪtʃəʊk/ (*also* **globe 'artichoke**) *noun* [C] a plant whose flower looks like pointed leaves. The bottoms of the leaves and the centre of the flower can be eaten as a vegetable. أرضي شوكي/ خرشوف/ حَرشَف

article /'ɑ:tɪkl/ *noun* [C] **1** a thing or object, especially one of a set: *Articles of clothing were lying all over the room.* شيء؛ قطعة

2 a piece of writing in a newspaper or magazine: *There's an article about cycling holidays in today's paper.* مقال

3 (*grammar*) the words 'a/an' (the indefinite

article) or 'the' (the definite article) أداة (التنكير أو التعريف)

articulate[1] /ɑːˈtɪkjələt/ *adj* good at expressing your ideas clearly فصيح ، مبين

articulate[2] /ɑːˈtɪkjuleɪt/ *verb* [I,T] to say sth clearly or to express your ideas or feelings ينطق بوضوح : يفصح

articulated /ɑːˈtɪkjuleɪtɪd/ *adj* (*Brit*) (used about a vehicle such as a lorry) made of two sections which are connected in a special way so that the lorry can turn corners easily (شاحنة) مفصلة

artificial /ˌɑːtɪˈfɪʃl/ *adj* not genuine or natural but made by people to seem like something natural: *artificial flowers* ○ *an artificial lake* اصطناعي

▸ **artificially** /-ʃəli/ *adv*: *This drug cannot be produced artificially.* صناعياً

ˌartificial inseміˈnation *noun* [U] a scientific technique to introduce male seed into a female, so that babies or young can be produced without sex تلقيح صناعي

ˌartificial inˈtelligence *noun* [U] (the study of) the way in which computers can be made to imitate human thought ذكاء اصطناعي

artillery /ɑːˈtɪləri/ *noun* [U] a number of large guns on wheels; the part of the army which uses them مدفعية: سلاح المدفعية

artist /ˈɑːtɪst/ *noun* [C] somebody who produces art, especially paintings or drawings: *I like that picture – who is the artist?* ○ *an exhibition of paintings by the English artist, Constable* فنان

artistic /ɑːˈtɪstɪk/ *adj* **1** connected with art: *the artistic director of the theatre* فني

2 showing a skill in art: *Helen is very artistic – her drawings are excellent.* ذو نزعة فنية

▸ **artistically** /ɑːˈtɪstɪkli/ *adv*: *The garden was laid out very artistically.* بذوق فني

artistry /ˈɑːtɪstri/ *noun* [U] the skill of an artist براعة فنية

as /əz; *strong form* æz/ *conj, prep, adv* **1** while sth else is happening: *The phone rang just as I was leaving the house.* ○ *As she walked along the road, she thought about her father.* بينما

2 as... as (used for comparing people or things): *Tom's almost as tall as me.* ○ *Tom's almost as tall as I am.* ○ *It's not as cold as it was yesterday.* ○ *I'd like an appointment as soon as possible.* مثل ، بقدر

3 as... as (used with 'much' or 'many' for comparing people or things): *She earns twice as much as her husband.* ○ *I haven't got as many books as you have.* مثل

4 (used for talking about sb's job): *He works as a train driver.* كـ

5 (used for describing sb/sth's role): *Think of me as your friend, not as your boss.* كـ

6 (used for describing sb/sth in an unusual role or function): *I went to the party dressed as a policeman.* ○ *You could use this white sheet as a tablecloth.* كـ

7 in a particular way, state, etc: *Please do as I tell you.* ○ *Leave the room as it is. Don't move anything.* مثلما

8 (used at the beginning of a comment about what you are saying): *As you know, I've decided to leave at the end of the month.* كما

9 because: *I didn't buy the dress, as I decided it was too expensive.* لأنّ

IDM as for; as to (used when you are starting to talk about a different person or thing): *Jane's in Paris at the moment. As for Andrew, I've no idea where he is.* أمّا (فيما يتعلّق بـ)

as if; as though (used for saying how sb/sth appears): *She looks as if she's just got out of bed.* ○ *He behaved as though nothing had happened.* كأنّ

as it were (used for saying that sth is only true in a certain way): *She felt, as it were, a stranger in her own house.* إن صحّ التعبير

as of; as from starting from a particular time: *As from next week, Tim Shaw will be managing this department.* ابتداءً من

as to about a particular thing: *I was given no instructions as to how to begin.* فيما يتعلّق بـ

asap /ˌeɪ es eɪ ˈpiː/ *abbrev* as soon as possible باسرع ما يكون

asbestos /æsˈbestəs/ *noun* [U] a soft grey material which does not burn and which is used to protect against heat الأسبستوس أو الحرير الصخري

ascend /əˈsend/ *verb* [I,T] (*formal*) to go or come up يطلع ، يصعد

▸ **ascending** *adj*: *The questions are arranged in ascending order of difficulty* (= the most difficult ones are at the end). ➲ Look at **descend**. صاعد : متصاعد ، متزايد

Ascension Day /əˈsenʃn deɪ/ the day forty days after Easter when Christians remember Christ leaving the earth and going to heaven عيد الصعود

ascent /əˈsent/ *noun* [C] **1** the act of climbing or going up: *Their aim was the ascent of the highest mountains in the Himalayas.* صعود ، تسلّق

2 a path or slope leading upwards: *There was a steep ascent before the path became flat again.* مرتقى

ascertain /ˌæsəˈteɪn/ *verb* [T] (*formal*) to find out: *It was difficult to ascertain who was telling the truth.* يتحقّق أو يتثبّت من

ascribe /əˈskraɪb/ *verb* [T] **ascribe sth to sb/sth** to say that sth was written by or belonged to sb, or that sth was caused by sth: *This piece of music was ascribed to Bach, although we now believe it was written by another composer.* ○ *He ascribed his forgetfulness to old age.* ينسب أو يعزو إلى

ash[1] /æʃ/ *noun* [C] a type of tree that is found in British forests شجرة الدردار أو المرّان

ash[2] /æʃ/ *noun* **1** [U] (*also* **ashes** [plural]) the grey or black powder which is left after sth has burned: *cigarette ash* ○ *They found the ring in the ashes of the fire.* رماد

2 ashes [plural] what remains after a human body has been burned رماد، رفات

ashamed /ə'ʃeɪmd/ *adj* **ashamed (of sth/sb/yourself)**; **ashamed (that...)**; **ashamed (to...)** (not before a noun) feeling sorry or embarrassed about sb/sth or about yourself or sth you have done: *She was ashamed of her old clothes.* ○ *He was ashamed of himself for having made such an unkind remark.* ○ *How could you be so rude? I'm ashamed of you!* ○ *She felt ashamed that she hadn't visited her aunt more often.* ○ *He knew that it was his fault but he was ashamed to admit his mistake.* خجلان، مستحٍ

ashore /ə'ʃɔ:(r)/ *adv* onto the land: *The passengers went ashore for an hour while the ship was in port.* على أو إلى البرّ

ashtray /'æʃtreɪ/ *noun* [C] a small dish for cigarette ash منفضة (سجاير)

Asian /'eɪʃn; *US* 'eɪʒn/ *noun* [C] a person from Asia or whose family was originally from Asia: *British Asians* آسيوي

▸ **Asian** *adj*: *the Asian community in Birmingham* آسيوي

aside /ə'saɪd/ *adv* **1** on or to one side; out of the way: *She took Richard aside to tell him her secret.* جانباً، على انفراد

2 to be kept separately, for a special purpose: *They are setting aside £50 a month for their summer holiday.* يضع جانباً

▸ **aside** *noun* [C] something which a character in a play says to the audience, but which the other characters on stage do not hear مخاطبة جانبيّة للجمهور في المسرح

a'side from *prep* (*especially US*) = APART FROM

ask /ɑ:sk/ *verb* **1** [I,T] **ask (sb) (about sb/sth)** to put a question to sb in order to find out some information: *We need to ask about the price.* ○ *I'll ask the salesman how much the jacket is.* ○ *Did you ask Sarah about the bike?* ○ *She asked whether I wanted tea or coffee.* ○ *'What's the time?' he asked.* ○ *He asked what the time was.* ○ *He asked me the time.* ○ *She asked the little boy his name.* ○ *I got lost coming here and I had to ask somebody the way.* يسأل

2 [I,T] **ask (sb) for sth**; **ask sth (of sb)**; **ask sb to do sth** to request that sb gives you sth or does sth for you: *She sat down at the table and asked for a cup of coffee.* ○ *Don't ask John for money – he hasn't got any.* ○ *You are asking too much of him – he can't possibly do all that!* ○ *Ring this number and ask for Mrs Smith* (= ask to speak to Mrs Smith). ○ *I asked him if he would drive me home.* ○ *I asked him to drive me home.* يطلب

3 [T] to say the price that you want for sth: *They're asking £2 000 for their car.* يطلب (ثمن شيء)

4 [I,T] to request permission to do sth: *I'm sure she'll let you go if you ask.* ○ *He asked to use our phone.* ○ *We asked permission to go early.* ○ *We asked if we could go home early.* يستأذن، يلتمس

5 [T] **ask sb (to sth)** to invite sb: *They asked six friends to dinner.* ○ *He's asked Eileen out on Saturday* (= asked her to go out with him). يدعو

IDM **ask for trouble/it** to behave in a way that will almost certainly cause trouble: *Not wearing a seat belt is just asking for trouble.* يبحث عن المتاعب

if you ask me if you want my opinion: *If you ask me, she's too young to travel alone.* إن كنت تريد سماع رأيي

PHR V **ask after sb** to inquire about sb's health or to ask for news of sb: *I saw Miss Black today. She asked after you.* يستفسر عن

askew /ə'skju:/ *adv, adj* (not before a noun) not in a straight or level position بانحراف ؛ منحرف

AS (level) /eɪ 'es levl/ *noun* [C,U] Advanced subsidiary (level); a British exam usually taken in Year 12 of school or college (= the year before the final year) when students are aged 17. Together with A2 exams, AS levels form the A-level qualification, which is needed for entrance to universities. (في الشهادة الثانوية) السنة قبل النهائية

asleep /ə'sli:p/ *adj* (not before a noun) not awake; sleeping: *The baby is asleep.* ○ *to be sound/fast asleep* ○ *to fall asleep* ➲ Look at the note at **sleep**². نائم

> Notice that you can only use **asleep** after the noun. **Sleeping** can be used before or after the noun: *a sleeping child*

asparagus /ə'spærəgəs/ *noun* [U] a plant with long green stems that you can cook and eat as a vegetable (نبات) الهِلْيَون

aspect /'æspekt/ *noun* [C] one of the qualities or parts of a situation, idea, problem, etc: *information about many aspects of British life* وجه ، مظهر

asphalt /'æsfælt; *US* -fɔ:lt/ *noun* [U] a thick black substance that is used for making the surface of roads, etc. أسفلت ، زِفْت

asphyxiate /əs'fɪksieɪt/ *verb* [T] (usually passive) (used about gas, smoke, etc.) to cause sb to be unable to breathe: *He was asphyxiated by the smoke while he was asleep.* يخنق ؛ يختنق

▸ **asphyxiation** /əsˌfɪksi'eɪʃn/ *noun* [U] اختناق

aspic /'æspɪk/ *noun* [U] a clear jelly made from meat juices and served with or around meat, fish, eggs, etc: *chicken in aspic* هلام المرق

aspiration /ˌæspə'reɪʃn/ *noun* [C,U] (often plural) a strong desire to have or do sth: *She has aspirations to become an opera singer.* طموح ، أمنية

aspire /ə'spaɪə(r)/ *verb* [I] **aspire to sth/to do sth** (*formal*) to have a strong desire to have or do sth: *She aspired to become managing director.* ○ *an aspiring ballet dancer* يطمح

aspirin /'æsprɪn; 'æspərɪn/ *noun* [C,U] a type of medicine that reduces pain and fever: *I've taken two aspirins* (= two tablets). أسبيرين

ass /æs/ *noun* [C] **1** = DONKEY

2 (*informal*) a stupid person حمار ؛ شخص غبيّ

assailant /əˈseɪlənt/ *noun* [C] a person who attacks sb مهاجم ، معتدٍ

assassin /əˈsæsɪn; *US* -sn/ *noun* [C] a person who kills a famous or important person for money or for political reasons مُغتال : قاتل مأجور

assassinate /əˈsæsɪneɪt; *US* -sən-/ *verb* [T] to kill a famous or important person for money or for political reasons ➲ Look at the note at **kill**. يغتال

▸ **assassination** /əˌsæsɪˈneɪʃn; *US* əˌsæsəˈneɪʃn/ *noun* [C,U]: *an assassination attempt* اغتيال

assault /əˈsɔːlt/ *noun* [C,U] **assault (on sb/sth)** a sudden attack on sb/sth: *Assaults on the police are becoming more common.* هجوم ، اعتداء

▸ **assault** *verb* [T]: *a prison sentence for assaulting a police officer* يهاجم ، يعتدي على

assemble /əˈsembl/ *verb* **1** [I,T] to come together in a group; to gather or collect: *The leaders assembled in Strasbourg for the summit meeting.* ○ *I've assembled all the information I need for my essay.* يجتمع : يجمع

2 [T] to fit the parts of sth together: *We spent all day trying to assemble our new bookshelves.* يركّب

assembly /əˈsembli/ *noun* (*pl.* **assemblies**) **1** [C,U] a large group of people who come together for a particular purpose: *school assembly* (= a regular meeting for all the students and teachers of a school) ○ *The regional assembly has the power to raise local taxes.* اجتماع ، مجلس

2 [U] the act of fitting the parts of sth together: *the assembly of cars by robots* تركيب

asˈsembly line *noun* [C] a line of people and machines in a factory that fit the parts of sth together in a fixed order: *the assembly-line workers at the Toyota car plant* صفّ التجميع في مصنع

assent /əˈsent/ *noun* [U] (*formal*) agreement: *The committee gave their assent to the proposed changes.* موافقة

▸ **assent** *verb* [I] **assent (to sth)** to say that you agree to sth يوافق

assert /əˈsɜːt/ *verb* [T] **1** to say sth clearly and firmly: *He asserted that the allegations were untrue.* يؤكّد

2 to behave in a way that makes other people listen to you and take notice of you: *You ought to assert yourself more.* ○ *to assert your authority* يفرض أو يثبت (شخصيته)

assertion /əˈsɜːʃn/ *noun* **1** [U] the act of asserting sth/yourself: *the assertion of power* توكيد : فرض

2 [C] something that you say firmly and clearly: *his confident assertion that he would win* توكيد ، جزم

assertive /əˈsɜːtɪv/ *adj* expressing your opinion clearly and firmly so that people listen to you and take notice of you: *to speak in an assertive manner* جازم : توكيدي

▸ **assertively** *adv* بحزم

assertiveness *noun* [U] فرض أو إثبات الشخصية

assess /əˈses/ *verb* [T] **1** to estimate or decide the amount or value of sth: *The value of the house was assessed at £75 000.* ○ *to assess the cost of repairs* يقدّر ، يخمّن

2 to judge or form an opinion about sth: *It's too early to assess the effects of the price rises.* يقدّر ، يقيّم، يحكم على

▸ **assessment** *noun* [C,U] the act of judging or forming an opinion about sb/sth: *Students' marks are based on continuous assessment of their work.* ○ *to make a careful assessment of a situation* تقدير ، تقييم

asset /ˈæset/ *noun* [C] **1 an asset (to sb/sth)** a person or thing that is useful to sb/sth: *She's a great asset to the organization.* ○ *It's an asset to be able to drive.* شخص أو شيء مفيد

2 [usually pl.] something of value that a person, company, etc. owns: *The company is having to sell its assets.* موجودات ، ممتلكات

assign /əˈsaɪn/ *verb* [T] **1 assign sth to sb** to give sth to sb for him/her to use or do يخصص

2 assign sb to sth to give sb a particular job or type of work to do: *She was assigned to the publicity department.* ○ *A detective was assigned to the case.* يعيّن

▸ **assignment** *noun* [C] a job or type of work that you are given to do: *Kate is on an assignment for the BBC.* ○ *to give pupils an assignment to do during the holidays* مهمّة : وظيفة معيّنة

assimilate /əˈsɪməleɪt/ *verb* **1** [I,T] (to allow sb/sth) to become part of a country or social group: *Many immigrants have difficulty in assimilating.* ○ *to assimilate people from other cultures* يندمج : يدمج

2 [T] to learn and understand sth: *to assimilate new facts/information/ideas* يستوعب

▸ **assimilation** /əˌsɪməˈleɪʃn/ *noun* [U] تمثّل ، استيعاب : اندماج

⚷ **assist** /əˈsɪst/ *verb* [I,T] **assist (sb) in/with sth**; **assist (sb) in doing sth** (*formal*) to help: *A man is assisting the police with their inquiries.* يساعد ، يعاون

▸ **assistance** /-əns/ *noun* [U] (*formal*) help: *Can I be of any assistance?* ○ *financial assistance for poorer families* مساعدة ، عون

assistant *noun* [C] **1** a person who helps sb of higher rank: *The director is away today. Would you like to speak to her assistant?* ○ *the assistant manager* مساعد ، معاون

2 (*US* **clerk**) a person who sells things to people in a shop: *a shop/sales assistant* بائع في مخزن

Assoc (*also* **assoc**) *abbrev* = ASSOCIATION

⚷ **associate**[1] /əˈsəʊʃiət; -siət/ *adj* (only *before* a noun) of a slightly lower rank or status: *associate members of the organization* منتسب

▸ **associate** *noun* [C] a person that you meet and get to know through your work: *a business associate* رفيق أو زميل في العمل

⚷ **associate**[2] /əˈsəʊʃieɪt; -sieɪt/ *verb* **1** [T] **associate sb/sth (with sb/sth)** to connect sb/sth with sb/sth else (in your mind): *lung cancer and* *other illnesses associated with smoking* ○ *Somehow, I don't associate Sweden with skiing.* يربط

2 [I] **associate with sb** to spend time with sb يخالط ، يختلط بِ

3 [T] **associate yourself with sth** to say that you support sth or agree with sth: *I do not wish to associate myself with any organization that promotes violence.* يؤيّد ، يرتبط بِ

association /əˌsəʊʃiˈeɪʃn; -siˈeɪʃn/ *noun* **1** [U] the act of joining or working with another person or group: *We work in association with our New York office.* مشاركة

2 [C] a group of people or organizations who join or work together for a particular purpose: *a housing association* ○ *the British Medical Association* ○ *the Football Association* رابطة ، جمعية

3 [C,U] the act of connecting sb/sth to sb/sth else in your mind ربط ذهني

assorted /əˈsɔːtɪd/ *adj* of different types; mixed: *a packet of assorted sweets* متنوع : مشكّل

▶ **assortment** /əˈsɔːtmənt/ *noun* [C] a group of different things or of different types of the same thing; a mixture: *You'll find a wide assortment of different gifts in our shop.* تنويعة : تشكيلة

Asst (*especially US* **Asst.**) *abbrev* = ASSISTANT

assume /əˈsjuːm; *US* əˈsuːm/ *verb* [T] **1** to accept or believe that sth is true even though you have no proof; to expect sth to be true: *I assume that you have the necessary documents.* ○ *You'll be going to the meeting, I assume?* ○ *We can assume profits of around 5%.* ○ *Everyone assumed Ralph was guilty.* ○ *Everyone assumed Ralph to be guilty.* يفترض ؛ يفرِض

2 to falsely pretend to have or be sb/sth: *to assume a false name* ينتحل

3 to begin to use power or to have a powerful position: *to assume control of sth* ○ *to assume political power* ○ *to assume a position of responsibility* يتقلّد (منصباً)

assumption /əˈsʌmpʃn/ *noun* **1** [C] something that you accept is true even though you have no proof: *Our figures are based on the assumption that the rate of inflation will be 5% by the end of the year.* ○ *a reasonable, false, etc. assumption* افتراض

2 [U] **assumption of sth** the act of taking power or of starting an important job: *the assumption of power by the army* تقلّد منصب : تولّي الحكم

assurance /əˈʃʊərəns; *Brit also* əˈʃɔːrəns/ *noun* **1** (*also* **self-assurance**) [U] the belief that you can do or succeed at sth; confidence: *He spoke with assurance* (= confidently). تأكد : ثقة

2 [C] a promise that sth will certainly happen or be true: *They gave me an assurance that the work would be finished by Friday.* وعد : تأكيد

assure /əˈʃʊə(r); *Brit also* əˈʃɔː(r)/ *verb* [T] **1** to promise sb that sth will certainly happen or be true, especially if he/she is worried: *I assure you that it is perfectly safe.* ○ *Let me assure you of my full support.* يؤكّد ، يطمْئن

2 to make sth sure or certain: *The survival of the species is assured.* يضمن

▶ **assured** (*also* **self-assured**) *adj* believing that you can do sth or succeed at sth; confident: *a calm and self-assured young woman* واثق من نفسه

asterisk /ˈæstərɪsk/ *noun* [C] the sign (*) that you use to call attention to sth in a piece of writing علامة النجمة

asteroid /ˈæstərɔɪd/ *noun* [C] any of the many small planets that go round the sun كوكب صغير سيّار

asthma /ˈæsmə; *US* ˈæzmə/ *noun* [U] a medical condition that causes difficulty in breathing الرّبو

▶ **asthmatic** /æsˈmætɪk; *US* æzˈm-/ *noun* [C] a person who suffers from asthma مصاب بالرّبو

astonish /əˈstɒnɪʃ/ *verb* [T] to cause sb to be very surprised: *She astonished everybody by announcing her engagement.* يدْهش

▶ **astonished** *adj*: *I was astonished by the decision.* مندهش

astonishing *adj*: *astonishing news* مدهش

astonishingly *adv*: *astonishingly successful* لدرجة مذهلة

astonishment *noun* [U] very great surprise: *To my absolute astonishment the scheme was a huge success.* ○ *A look of astonishment crossed her face.* ○ *He dropped his book in astonishment.* دهشة ، استغراب

astound /əˈstaʊnd/ *verb* [T] (usually passive) to cause sb to be very surprised: *We were astounded at how well he performed.* يذْهل

▶ **astounding** *adj* very surprising: *an astounding success* مذهِل

astray /əˈstreɪ/ *adv* away from the right way: *The young are easily led astray* (= persuaded to do bad things by other people). في ضلال

IDM **go astray** to become lost: *My new pen seems to have gone astray.* يضيع

astride /əˈstraɪd/ *adv, prep* with one leg on each side of sth: *to sit astride a horse* منفرج الساقين

astrology /əˈstrɒlədʒi/ *noun* [U] the study of the positions and movements of the stars and planets and the way that they are supposed to affect people and events ➲ Look at **astronomy** and also at **horoscope** and **zodiac**. علم التنجيم

▶ **astrologer** /-ədʒə(r)/ *noun* [C] a person who is an expert in astrology منجّم

astronaut /ˈæstrənɔːt/ *noun* [C] a person who travels in a spaceship رائد الفضاء

astronomy /əˈstrɒnəmi/ *noun* [U] the scientific study of the sun, moon, stars, etc. ➲ Look at **astrology**. علم الفلَك

▶ **astronomer** /-nəmə(r)/ *noun* [C] a person who studies or is an expert in astronomy فلكي

astronomical /ˌæstrəˈnɒmɪkl/ *adj* **1** connected with astronomy فلكي

2 very large, often too large (describing a price, number, amount, etc.): *astronomical house prices* (سعر) باهظ أو خيالي

astute /ə'stjuːt; *US* ə'stuːt/ *adj* very clever; good at judging people or situations داهية، ثاقب البصيرة

asylum /ə'saɪləm/ *noun* **1** [U] protection that a government gives to people who have left their own country for political reasons: *The leaders of the coup were given political asylum by the US* (= invited to stay in the US where they would be safe). لجوء (سياسي)

2 [C] an old-fashioned word for a hospital for people who are mentally ill مستشفى أمراض عقلية

at /ət; *strong form* æt/ *prep* **1** (showing the position of sth or where sth happens): *at the bottom of the page* ○ *at the top of the hill* ○ *He was standing at the door.* ○ *Change trains at Didcot.* ○ *We were at home all weekend.* ○ *Are the children at school?* ○ *at the theatre* ○ *'Where's Peter?' 'He's at Sue's.'* (= at Sue's house) في ، عند

The sign used in email addresses @ is pronounced 'at'.

2 (showing when sth happens): *I start work at 9 o'clock.* ○ *at the weekend* ○ *at night* ○ *at Christmas* ○ *She got married at 18* (= when she was 18). في

3 in the direction of sb/sth: *What are you looking at?* ○ *He pointed a gun at the policeman.* ○ *Somebody threw a tomato at the Prime Minister.* ○ *Don't shout at me!* إلى : نحو : على

4 because of: *I was surprised at her behaviour.* ○ *We laughed at his jokes.* بسبب : على

5 (showing what sb is doing or what is happening): *They were hard at work.* ○ *The two countries were at war.* (منشغل) في

6 (showing the price, rate, speed, etc. of sth): *What price are you selling at?* ○ *We were travelling at about 50 miles per hour.* بِ (سعر أو سرعة كذا)

7 (used with adjectives that show how well sb/sth does sth): *She's not very good at French.* ○ *I'm hopeless at hockey.* في

ate *pt* of EAT

atheism /'eɪθiɪzəm/ *noun* [U] the belief that there is no God إلحاد

▸ **atheist** /'eɪθiɪst/ *noun* [C] a person who believes that there is no God ملحد

athlete /'æθliːt/ *noun* [C] a person who can run, jump, etc. very well, especially one who takes part in sports competitions, etc. رياضي

athletic /æθ'letɪk/ *adj* **1** connected with athletes or athletics رياضي ، متعلّق بالرياضة

2 (used about a person) having a fit, strong, and healthy body ذو لياقة بدنية

athletics /æθ'letɪks/ *noun* [U] sports such as running, jumping, throwing, etc: *an athletics meeting/track* ألعاب القوى

atishoo /ə'tɪʃuː/ *interj* (used for expressing the sound that you make when you sneeze) (للتعبير عن صوت العطس)

atlas /'ætləs/ *noun* [C] (*pl.* **atlases**) a book of maps أطلس

ATM /ˌeɪ tiː 'em/ *noun* automated teller machine = CASH MACHINE

atmosphere /'ætməsfɪə(r)/ *noun* **1** [C, usually sing.] **the atmosphere** the mixture of gases that surrounds the earth or any other star, planet, etc: *the earth's atmosphere* الجوّ ، الغلاف الجوّي

2 [sing.] the air in a place: *a smoky atmosphere* هواء ، جو

3 the mood or feeling of a place or situation: *There was a tense atmosphere during the final minutes of the game.* جو

atmospheric /ˌætməs'ferɪk/ *adj* connected with the atmosphere (1) جَوّي

atom /'ætəm/ *noun* [C] the smallest part into which an element can be divided: (*figurative*) *She hasn't got an atom of common sense* (= she hasn't got any). ➲ Look at **molecule**. ذَرّة

atomic /ə'tɒmɪk/ *adj* of or concerning an atom or atoms: *atomic physics* ذرّي

aˌtomic 'bomb (*also* **'atom bomb**) *noun* [C] a bomb that explodes using the energy that is produced when an atom or atoms are split قنبلة ذَرّيّة

aˌtomic 'energy *noun* [U] the energy that is produced when an atom or atoms are split. Atomic energy can be used to produce electricity. طاقة ذَرّيّة

atrocious /ə'trəʊʃəs/ *adj* very bad or cruel: *What atrocious weather!* فظيع

▸ **atrociously** *adv*: *The children behaved atrociously.* على نحو سيّئ جداً

atrocity /ə'trɒsəti/ *noun* [C,U] (*pl.* **atrocities**) (an act of) great cruelty: *Both sides were guilty of dreadful atrocities during the war.* عمل وحشي : فظاعة

attach /ə'tætʃ/ *verb* [T] **1 attach sth (to sth)** to fasten or join sth to sth: *A note was attached to the document with a paper clip.* يرفق ، يربط بِ

2 attach yourself to sb/sth; attach sb to sb/sth to join another person or group; to make sb do this: *Tom will be attached to the finance department for the next six months.* يلتحق ، يلحق

3 attach sth to sb/sth to think that sth has a particular quality: *Don't attach too much importance to what they say.* ○ *No blame was attached to him.* يعلّق : يلحق (به)

IDM (with) no strings attached; without strings → STRING[1]

▸ **attached** *adj* **attached to sb/sth** liking sb/sth very much: *He's become very attached to you.* مولع أو متعلّق بِ

attachment *noun* **1** [C] something that can be fitted on sth else: *a bath with a shower attachment* (شيء) ملحق : وصلة

2 [C,U] **attachment (to/for sb/sth)** the feeling of liking sb/sth very much: *an emotional attachment* ○ *I feel a strong attachment to this house.* تعلّق ، ولوع

3 a document that you send to sb using email ملحقات

attack /ə'tæk/ *noun* **1** [C,U] **an attack (on sb/**

sth) an act of trying to hurt or defeat sb/sth by using force: *The rebel forces launched an attack on the capital.* ○ *to be under attack* (= to be attacked by sb/sth) هجوم

2 [C,U] **attack (on sb/sth)** an act of saying strongly that you do not like or agree with sb/sth: *an outspoken attack on government policy* هجوم

3 [C] a short period when you suffer badly from a disease, medical condition, etc: *an attack of asthma, flu, etc.* إصابة : نوبة

4 [C] an act of trying to score a point in a game of sport: *England made several strong attacks but failed to score a goal.* ○ *The home team went on the attack again.* هجمة ، هجوم

▸ **attack** *verb* **1** [I,T] to try to hurt or defeat sb/sth by using force: *The enemy attacked at night.* ○ *to be attacked by a wild animal* يهاجم

2 [T] to say strongly that you do not like or agree with sb/sth: *The minister attacked the press for misleading the public.* يهاجم ، يحمل على

3 [T] to damage or harm sb/sth: *a virus that attacks the nervous system* يهاجم

4 [I,T] to try to score a point in a game of sport يهاجم

attacker *noun* [C] a person who attacks sb/sth مهاجم

attain /əˈteɪn/ *verb* [T] to succeed in getting or achieving sth, especially after great effort: *to attain a goal* ينال ، يحصل على

▸ **attainable** /-əbl/ *adj* that can be attained ممكن تحقيقه

attainment *noun* **1** [U] the act of achieving sth: *the attainment of the government's objectives* تحقيق ، إحراز

2 [C] a skill or achievement: *students with few academic attainments* إنجاز : مهارة ، موهبة

attempt /əˈtempt/ *verb* [T] to try to do sth that is difficult: *The prisoner was shot while attempting to escape.* ○ *She was accused of attempted murder* (= she didn't succeed). ○ *Don't attempt to argue with him.* يحاول

▸ **attempt** *noun* [C] **1 attempt (to do sth/at doing sth)** an act of trying to do sth: *He managed to hit the target at the first attempt.* ○ *They failed in their attempt to reach the North Pole.* محاولة

2 attempt (on sb/sth) an act of trying to attack or beat sb/sth: *She hopes to make an attempt on the world record in tomorrow's race.* ○ *an attempt on sb's life* (= to kill sb) محاولة (قتل مثلاً)

attend /əˈtend/ *verb* **1** [T] to go to or be present at a place: *Do you attend church regularly?* ○ *I'm afraid I will be unable to attend tonight's meeting.* ○ *The children attend the local school.* يحضر ، يذهب إلى

2 [I] **attend to sb/sth** (*formal*) to give your care, thought or attention to sb/sth or look after sb/sth: *Please attend to this matter immediately.* يرعى ، يهتمّ بِ

attendance /əˈtendəns/ *noun* **1** [U] being present somewhere: *Attendance at lectures is not compulsory.* حضور

2 [C,U] the number of people who go to or are present at a place: *There was a large attendance at the meeting.* ○ *Attendance has decreased in recent months.* عدد الحاضرين (في مكان)

attendant /əˈtendənt/ *noun* [C] **1** a person who looks after a public place: *a swimming-pool attendant* مشرف : مساعد : خادم

2 a person who looks after an important person: *the Queen's attendants* مرافق

▸ **attendant** *adj* (only *before* a noun) (*formal*) that goes with or results from sth: *unemployment and all its attendant social problems* مصاحب ، ملازم

attention /əˈtenʃn/ *noun* [U] **1** the act of watching, listening to or thinking about sb/sth carefully: *to call/draw sb's attention to sth* ○ *The bride is always the centre of attention* (= the person that everybody is watching). ○ *I shouted in order to attract her attention.* ○ *to hold sb's attention* (= to keep them interested in sth) انتباه : اهتمام

2 special care or action: *The hole in the roof needs urgent attention.* ○ *to require medical attention* عناية ، اهتمام : عمل

3 a position in which a soldier stands up straight and still: *to come/stand to attention* وقفة الاستعداد (عسكرية)

IDM **catch sb's attention/eye** → CATCH[1]
draw sb's attention to sth → DRAW[2]
pay attention → PAY[2]

▸ **attention** *interj* (used for asking people to listen to sth carefully): *Attention, please! The boat will be leaving in five minutes.* انتبه! ، انتباه!

attentive /əˈtentɪv/ *adj* watching, listening to or thinking about sb/sth carefully: *The staff at the hotel were very attentive.* ○ *an attentive audience* مصغ ، منتَبِه : كثير العناية بِ

▸ **attentively** *adv*: *to listen attentively to sth* بانتباه ، باهتمام

attic /ˈætɪk/ *noun* [C] the space or room under the roof of a house ➲ Look at **loft**. علِّية ، سقيفة

attitude /ˈætɪtjuːd; *US* -tuːd/ *noun* [C] **attitude (to/towards sb/sth)** the way that you think, feel or behave: *social attitudes and beliefs* ○ *She shows a very positive attitude to her work.* موقف

attorney /əˈtɜːni/ *noun* [C] (*pl.* **attorneys**) (*US*) a lawyer محام

attract /əˈtrækt/ *verb* [T] **1** to cause sb/sth to go to or give attention to sth: *to attract sb's attention* ○ *Moths are attracted to light.* ○ *The new film has attracted a lot of publicity.* يجذب ، يجتذب

2 to cause sb to like sb/sth: *She's attracted to older men.* يجتذب : يفتن

attraction /əˈtrækʃn/ *noun* **1** [U] attracting or being attracted: *I can't understand the attraction of fishing.* ○ *sexual attraction* جاذبية ، فتنة

2 [C] something that attracts sb/sth: *The city offers all kinds of tourist attractions.* ○ *One of the attractions of the job is having a company car.* شيء مغرٍ ، مغريات

attractive /əˈtræktɪv/ *adj* **1** that pleases or interests you; that you like: *an attractive idea* جذّاب ؛ شيّق

2 pretty, beautiful or handsome: *an attractive room* ○ *an attractive man/woman* جذّاب ، جميل
▸ **attractively** *adv* بشكل جذّاب
attractiveness *noun* [U] جاذبية ؛ جَمال

attribute¹ /əˈtrɪbjuːt/ *verb* [T] **attribute sth to sb/sth** to believe that sth was caused or done by sb/sth: *Terry attributes his success to hard work.* ○ *a poem attributed to Shakespeare* يعزو أو ينسِب إلى

attribute² /ˈætrɪbjuːt/ *noun* [C] a quality or feature of sb/sth: *physical attributes* خاصيّة، صفة

atypical /ˌeɪˈtɪpɪkl/ *adj* (*formal*) not typical of a particular type, group, etc: *atypical behaviour* غير نموذجي

aubergine /ˈəʊbəʒiːn/ (*especially US* **eggplant**) *noun* [C,U] a long vegetable with dark purple skin باذنجان

auburn /ˈɔːbən/ *adj* (usually used about hair) reddish-brown (شَعْر) بنّي محمرّ

auction /ˈɔːkʃn/ *noun* [C,U] a public sale at which items are sold to the person who offers to pay the most money: *The house will be sold by auction.* مزاد علني
▸ **auction** *verb* [T] to sell sth at an auction يبيع بالمزاد العلني

auctioneer /ˌɔːkʃəˈnɪə(r)/ *noun* [C] a person who organizes the selling at an auction دلاّل (للبيع بالمزاد)

audible /ˈɔːdəbl/ *adj* that can be heard: *Her speech was only just audible.* ➲ Look at **inaudible.** مسموع
▸ **audibly** /-əbli/ *adv*: *to sigh audibly* على نحو مسموع

audience /ˈɔːdiəns/ *noun* [C] **1** [with sing. or pl. verb] the group of people who are watching or listening to a play, concert, speech, the television, etc: *The audience was/were wild with excitement.* ○ *There were only about 200 people in the audience.* ○ *Television can reach an audience of millions.* الحضور : جمهور المستمعين

2 a formal meeting with a very important person: *an audience with the Pope* مقابلة (رسمية)

audio /ˈɔːdiəʊ/ *adj* connected with the recording of sound: *audio equipment* ○ *audio tape* سمعي

ˌaudio-ˈvisual *adj* using both sound and pictures: *A video recorder is an excellent audio-visual aid in the classroom.* سمعي بصري

audit /ˈɔːdɪt/ *noun* [C] an official examination of the present state of sth, especially of a company's financial records: *to carry out an audit* تدقيق الحسابات

▸ **auditor** /ˈɔːdɪtə(r)/ *noun* [C] a person whose job is to examine a company's financial records مدقق الحسابات

audition /ɔːˈdɪʃn/ *noun* [C] a short performance by a singer, actor, musician, etc. to find out if he/she is good enough to be in a play, show, concert, etc. اختبار صلاحيّة الشخص للغناء أو التمثيل و غير ذلك

auditorium /ˌɔːdɪˈtɔːriəm/ *noun* [C] (*pl.* **auditoriums** or **auditoria**) the part of a theatre, etc. where the audience sits قاعة الحضور ؛ قاعة المحاضرات

augur /ˈɔːgə(r)/ *verb*
IDM **augur well/ill for sb/sth** (*formal*) to be a good/bad sign of what will happen in the future: *The opinion polls augur well for the government.* يتكهّن ؛ يبشّر/ينذر

August /ˈɔːgəst/ *noun* [C,U] (*abbr* **Aug.**) the eighth month of the year, coming before September ❶ For examples of the use of the months in sentences, look at **January**. أغسطس/آب

aunt /ɑːnt; *US* ænt/ (*also informal* **auntie**; **aunty** /ˈɑːnti; *US* ˈænti/) *noun* [C] the sister of your father or mother; the wife of your uncle: *Aunt Ann* ➲ Look at the note at **uncle**. خالة ، عمّة

au pair /ˌəʊ ˈpeə(r)/ *noun* [C] a person, usually a young woman, from another country who comes to live with a family in order to learn the language. An au pair helps with the housework and looking after the children.
فتاة أجنبية تساعد في شؤون المنزل

aura /ˈɔːrə/ *noun* [C] (*formal*) the quality that sb/sth seems to have: *The village had an aura of peace and tranquility.* هالة

aural /ˈɔːrəl/ *adj* of or concerning the ear or hearing: *an aural comprehension test* ➲ Look at **oral.** سمعي ، أذني

auspices /ˈɔːspɪsɪz/ *noun* [plural]
IDM **under the auspices of sb/sth** with the help and support of sb/sth: *a conference under the auspices of the UN* تحت رعاية (شخص أو شيء)

auspicious /ɔːˈspɪʃəs/ *adj* (*formal*) that seems likely to succeed or be pleasant in the future ميمون الطالع ، مبَشّر بالنجاح

austere /ɒˈstɪə(r)/ *adj* **1** not having pleasures or luxuries متقشّف

2 very plain and simple; without decoration بسيط ؛ بلا زينة
▸ **austerity** /ɒˈsterəti/ *noun* [U] the quality of being austere تقشّف ، بساطة

authentic /ɔːˈθentɪk/ *adj* that you know is true or genuine: *an authentic Van Gogh painting* أصيل ، حقيقي

▸ **authenticity** /ˌɔːθenˈtɪsəti/ *noun* [U]: *to check the authenticity of a document* صحّة ، موثوقيّة

author /ˈɔːθə(r)/ *noun* [C] a person who writes a book, play, etc: *a well-known author of detective novels* مؤلّف
▸ **authorship** *noun* [U]: *The authorship of the play is unknown.* تأليف

authoritarian /ɔːˌθɒrɪˈteəriən/ *adj* not allowing people the freedom to decide things for themselves: *The authoritarian government crushed all signs of opposition.* ○ *authoritarian parents* مستبدّ

authoritative /ɔːˈθɒrətətɪv; *US* -teɪtɪv/ *adj*

a b c d e f g h i j k l m n o p q r s t u v w x y z

1 having authority; demanding or expecting that people obey you: *an authoritative tone of voice* مسيّطر ، آمر
2 that you can trust because it/he/she has a lot of knowledge and information: *They will be able to give you authoritative advice on the problem.* موثوق به

authority /ɔːˈθɒrəti/ *noun* (*pl.* **authorities**) **1** [C] (often plural) a person, group or government department that has the power to give orders, make official decisions, etc: *Cases of the illness must be reported to the health authority.* ○ *The French authorities refused permission for the hijacked plane to land.* سُلْطة
2 [U] the power and right to give orders and make others obey: *Children often begin to question their parents' authority at a very early age.* ○ *You must get this signed by a person in authority* (= who has a position of power). سُلْطة ، نفوذ
3 [U] **authority (to do sth)** the right to act in a particular way: *The police have the authority to question anyone they wish.* تفويض ، سُلْطة
4 [U] a quality that sb has which makes it possible to influence and control other people: *He spoke with authority and everybody listened.* سُلْطان ، نفوذ ، قوة الشخصيّة
5 [C] a person with special knowledge: *He's an authority on ancient Egypt.* حجّة، مرجع

authorize (*also* **authorise**) /ˈɔːθəraɪz/ *verb* [T] to give official permission for sth or for sb to do sth: *Any new buildings have to be authorized by the planning department.* ○ *He authorized his secretary to sign letters in his absence.* يخوّل : يرخّص لـ
▶ **authorization** (*also* **authorisation**) /ˌɔːθəraɪˈzeɪʃn; *US* -rɪˈz-/ *noun* [U] official permission for sth: *I can't give you the information without authorization from the manager.* ترخيص؛ تفويض

autistic /ɔːˈtɪstɪk/ *adj* having a serious mental illness which makes it very difficult to form relationships with other people: *an autistic child* منطوٍ ذاتيًا، متوحّد

autobiography /ˌɔːtəbaɪˈɒɡrəfi/ *noun* [C,U] (*pl.* **autobiographies**) the story of a person's life written by that person ➲ Look at **biography**. سيرة ذاتية
▶ **autobiographic** /ˌɔːtəbaɪəˈɡræfɪk/**autobiographical** /ˌɔːtəˌbaɪəˈɡræfɪkl/ *adj* متعلّق بالسيرة الذاتية

autograph /ˈɔːtəɡrɑːf; *US* -ɡræf/ *noun* [C] the signature of a famous person: *People were waiting at the stage door to get the dancer's autograph.* توقيع (شخص مشهور)
▶ **autograph** *verb* [T] to put your signature on or in sth: *a painting autographed by the artist* يوقّع

automate /ˈɔːtəmeɪt/ *verb* [T] (usually passive) to make sth operate by machine, without needing people: *The system in the factory has been fully automated.* يُشغّل أو يضبط آليًا

automatic /ˌɔːtəˈmætɪk/ *adj* **1** (used about a machine) that can work by itself without direct human control: *an automatic washing machine* أوتوماتيكي، آليّ
2 (used about actions) done without thinking or like a machine; unconscious: *Practise this exercise until it becomes automatic.* تلقائيّ ، (يعمل) دون تفكير
3 certain to happen because it is part of a normal process: *Not everyone with a British passport has the automatic right to live in Britain.* تلقائي
▶ **automatic** *noun* [C] an automatic machine, gun or car: *This car is an automatic* (= has automatic gears). آلة أو سلاح أوتوماتيكي
automatically /-kli/ *adv*: *The lights will come on automatically when it gets dark.* ○ *You will automatically receive a reminder when your next payment is due.* تلقائيا؛ بصورة آليّة

automation /ˌɔːtəˈmeɪʃn/ *noun* [U] the use of machines, instead of people, to do work: *Unemployment is rising because of increased automation.* استعمال الآلة بدلاً من الإنسان

automobile /ˈɔːtəməbiːl/ *noun* [C] (*especially US*) = CAR (1)

autonomous /ɔːˈtɒnəməs/ *adj* having the right to govern or control its own affairs: *The people in this region want to be completely autonomous.* مستقلّ ذاتياً
▶ **autonomy** /ɔːˈtɒnəmi/ *noun* [U] the right of an organization, region, etc. to govern or control its own affairs استقلال ذاتي

autopsy /ˈɔːtɒpsi/ *noun* [C] (*pl.* **autopsies**) an examination of a dead body to find out the cause of death تشريح الجثة

autumn /ˈɔːtəm/ (*US usually* **fall**) *noun* [C,U] the season of the year that comes between summer and winter: *It was a very cold autumn that year.* ○ *In autumn the leaves on the trees begin to fall.* ○ *autumn weather* فصل الخريف
▶ **autumnal** /ɔːˈtʌmnəl/ *adj* خريفي

auxiliary /ɔːɡˈzɪliəri/ *adj* (only *before* a noun) giving extra help: *auxiliary nurses, troops, etc.* ○ *auxiliary equipment* مساعد

auˌxiliary ˈverb *noun* [C] (*grammar*) a verb (e.g. *be*, *do* or *have*) that is used with a main verb to show tense, etc. or to form questions فعل مساعد

avail /əˈveɪl/ *noun* [U] (*formal*)
IDM **of little/no avail** not helpful or effective: *All our efforts to persuade her were of little avail.* بلا جدوى
to little/no avail; **without avail** without success: *They had searched everywhere, but to no avail.* بلا طائل

available /əˈveɪləbl/ *adj* **1** (used about things) that you can get, buy, use, etc: *Do you know if there are any flats available in this area?* ○ *I'm afraid that material is no longer available, Madam.* ○ *This information is easily available to everyone at the local library.* ○ *Refreshments are available at the snack bar.* موجود ، متوفّر
2 (used about people) free to be seen, talked to,

etc: *The minister was not available for comment.* موجود

▸ **availability** /əˌveɪləˈbɪləti/ *noun* [U] the state of being available: *You will receive the colour you order, subject to availability* (= if it is available). تواجد ، تيسّر ، توفر

avalanche /ˈævəlɑːnʃ; *US* -læntʃ/ *noun* [C] a very large amount of snow that slides quickly down the side of a mountain: *Two skiers are still missing after yesterday's avalanche.* ○ *(figurative) The company received an avalanche of complaints.* انهيار ثلجي

avant-garde /ˌævɒŋ ˈɡɑːd/ *adj* (used especially about art and literature) extremely new and modern طليعي

avatar /ˈævətɑː(r)/ *noun* [C] a picture of a person or an animal that represents a particular computer user, on a computer screen, especially in a computer game or chat room "أفاتار": صورة رمزية افتراضية

avenge /əˈvendʒ/ *verb* [T] **avenge sth**; **avenge yourself on sb** to punish sb for hurting you, your family, etc. in some way: *He wanted to avenge his father's murder.* ○ *He wanted to avenge himself on his father's murderer.* ➲ Look at **revenge.** يثأر ، ينتقم

avenue /ˈævənjuː; *US* -nuː/ *noun* [C] **1** (*abbr* **Ave.**; **Av.**) a wide street, especially one with trees or tall buildings on each side: *The house is on Beech Avenue.* ○ *I live at 12 Tennyson Avenue.* ○ *Fifth Avenue, New York* ➲ Look at the note at **road.** شارع مشجّر

2 a way of doing or getting sth: *We must explore every avenue open to us* (= try every possibility). سبيل

🔑**average** /ˈævərɪdʒ/ *noun* **1** [C] the number you get when you add two or more figures together and then divide the total by the number of figures you added: *The average of 14, 3 and 1 is 6* (= 18 divided by 3 is 6). المعدّل ، الوسطي

2 [sing., U] the normal standard, amount or quality: *Only 60% of the students passed the exam. That's well below the national average.* ○ *On average, I buy a newspaper about twice a week.* المعدّل ، المتوسط

▸ **average** *adj* **1** (only *before* a noun) (used about a number) found by calculating the average(1): *What's the average age of your students?* متوسط ، وسطي

2 normal or typical: *People on average incomes are finding it hard to manage at the moment.* ○ *children of above/below average intelligence* عادي

average *verb* [T] to do, get, etc. a certain amount as an average: *If we average 50 miles an hour we should arrive at about 4 o'clock.* يبلغ معدّله

PHR V **average out (at sth)** to result in an average (of sth): *The meal averaged out at about £20 each.* يبلغ معدّله

averse /əˈvɜːs/ *adj* **averse to sth** (*formal*) (often with a negative) against or opposed to sth: *He is not averse to trying out new ideas.* ممانع : كاره لـ ، نافر من

aversion /əˈvɜːʃn; *US* əˈvɜːrʒn/ *noun* [C] **1** [usually sing.] **an aversion (to sb/sth)** a feeling of great dislike: *Some people have an aversion to spiders.* نفور ، كره

2 a thing that you greatly dislike: *Mathematics was always one of my particular aversions.* شيء بغيض

avert /əˈvɜːt/ *verb* [T] to prevent sth unpleasant; to avoid: *The accident could have been averted.* يتفادى؛ يتجنّب

aviary /ˈeɪviəri; *US* -vieri/ *noun* [C] (*pl.* **aviaries**) a large cage or area in which birds are kept بيت أو قفص كبير للطيور

aviation /ˌeɪviˈeɪʃn/ *noun* [U] the flying or building of aircraft طيران

avid /ˈævɪd/ *adj* keen and eager; greedy: *an avid collector of antiques* ○ *The people crowded round the radio, avid for news.* نهم، متعطّش

▸ **avidly** *adv*: *He read avidly as a child.* بنهم

avocado /ˌævəˈkɑːdəʊ/ *noun* [C] (*pl.* **avocados**) a fruit shaped like a pear with a tough dark green skin and a large stone inside أفوكادو: نوع من الفواكه

🔑**avoid** /əˈvɔɪd/ *verb* [T] **1 avoid (doing sth)** to prevent sth happening or try not to do sth: *He always tried to avoid an argument if possible.* ○ *It was so dark that we managed to avoid being seen.* ○ *She has to avoid eating fatty food* (= she must make an effort not to eat it). يتفادى : يمتنع عن

2 to keep away from (sb/sth): *I leave home at 7 o'clock in order to avoid the rush hour.* ○ *Jane is trying to avoid him at the moment.* يتجنّب

▸ **avoidable** /-əbl/ *adj* that can be prevented; unnecessary: *We have been asked to cut down on any avoidable expense.* ❶ The opposite is **unavoidable.** يمكن تجنّبه : غير ضروري

avoidance /-əns/ *noun* [U] تجنّب

await /əˈweɪt/ *verb* [T] (*formal*) **1** (used about people) to wait for sb/sth: *Please await further instructions.* ينتظر

2 (used about things or events) to be ready or waiting for sb/sth: *We were unaware of the danger that awaited us.* ينتظر؛ يتربّص لـ

awake[1] /əˈweɪk/ *verb* (*pt* **awoke** /əˈwəʊk/; *pp* **awoken** /əˈwəʊkən/) **1** [I,T] to wake up; to make sb/sth wake up: *I awoke to find that it was already 9 o'clock.* ○ *A sudden loud noise awoke us all.* ❶ **Wake up** is more common than **awake.** يستيقظ : يوقظ

2 [T] to make sb have a particular feeling, attitude, etc: *His words awoke fear and hatred in the boy.* يثير

🔑**awake**[2] /əˈweɪk/ *adj* (not before a noun) not sleeping: *I was awake most of the night, worrying.* ○ *The children are always wide* (= completely) *awake at 6 o'clock in the morning.* ○ *They were so tired that they found it difficult to keep awake.* ❶ The opposite is **asleep.** مستيقظ

awaken /əˈweɪkən/ *verb* **1** [I,T] (*formal*) to wake

a b c d e f g h i j k l m n o p q r s t u v w x y z

up; to make sb/sth wake up: *I awakened to find the others already up.* ○ *We were awakened by a loud knock at the door.* ❶ **Wake up** is much more common than **awaken**. يستيقظ ؛ يوقظ

2 [T] (*formal*) to produce a particular feeling, attitude, etc. in sb: *The film awakened memories of her childhood.* يثير

PHR V **awaken sb to sth** to make sb become aware of sth: *The letter awakened me to the seriousness of the situation.* ينبّه

▸ **awakening** /əˈweɪkənɪŋ/ *noun* [C, usually sing.] **1** the start (of a feeling, etc.): *the awakening of an interest in the opposite sex* استفاقة ، بداية

2 an act of realizing: *It was a rude* (= unpleasant) *awakening when I suddenly found that I was unemployed.* صحوة ، تنبّه

award /əˈwɔːd/ *verb* [T] **award sth (to sb/sth)** to give sth to sb as a prize, payment, etc: *She was awarded first prize in the gymnastics competition.* ○ *The novel was awarded the Booker Prize.* ○ *The court awarded £10 000 each to the workers injured in the factory accident.* يمنح

▸ **award** *noun* [C] **1** a prize, etc. that sb gets for doing sth well: *This year the awards for best actor and actress went to two Americans.* جائزة ، مكافأة

2 an amount of money given to sb as the result of a court decision: *She received an award of £5 000 for damages.* تعويض : حكم بِـ

aware /əˈweə(r)/ *adj* **1 aware (of sb/sth)**; **aware (that)** knowing about or realizing sth; conscious of sb/sth: *I am aware of the difficulties you face.* ○ *I am aware that you will face difficulties.* ○ *I suddenly felt aware of somebody watching me.* ○ *There is no other entrance, as far as I am aware.* ❶ The opposite is **unaware**. مدرك ؛ واعٍ لـ

2 interested and informed: *to be politically aware* مطّلع

▸ **awareness** *noun* [U] knowledge, consciousness or interest: *People's awareness of healthy eating has increased in recent years.* معرفة ؛ وعي

awash /əˈwɒʃ/ *adj* (not before a noun) covered with water; flooded: *The bathroom was awash because the bath had overflowed.* ○ (*figurative*) *The city was awash with rumours.* مغمور بالماء ، غارق

away /əˈweɪ/ *adj, adv* ➲ Look also at phrasal verbs, e.g. **give away**, **take away**.

1 away (from sb/sth) to a different place or in a different direction: *Go away! I'm busy!* ○ *I asked him a question, but he just looked away.* بعيداً ، إلى مكان آخر

2 at a distance from a place: *My parents live five miles away.* ○ *The village is two miles away from the sea.* على بُعد

3 away (from sth) (used about people) not present; absent: *My neighbours are away on holiday at the moment.* ○ *Tom was away from school for two weeks with measles.* غائب

4 away (from sth) in the future: *Our summer holiday is only three weeks away.* بَعْد: (للتعبير عن المستقبل)

5 into a safe place: *Put your books away now.* ○ *He tidied his clothes away.* ○ *They cleared the dishes away* (= off the table). ❶ Contrast **throw that away** (= put it in the rubbish bin). (في مكان آمِن)

6 (used about a football, etc. team) on the other team's ground: *Our team's playing away on Saturday.* ○ *an away match/game* على ملعب الفريق الآخر

7 until it disappears completely: *The crash of thunder slowly died away.* ○ *The writing has almost faded away.* (حتى يتلاشى تماماً)

8 continuously, without stopping: *They chatted away for hours.* باستمرار ، دون توقّف

IDM **right/straight away** immediately; without any delay: *I'll phone the doctor right away.* ○ *I understood straight away what she wanted me to do.* في الحال

awe /ɔː/ *noun* [U] a feeling of respect and either fear or admiration: *We watched in awe as the rocket took off into space.* ○ *As a young boy he was very much in awe of his uncle.* رَهْبة

▸ **awesome** /-səm/ *adj* impressive and rather frightening: *an awesome task* مهول ، مرهِب

ˈawe-inspiring *adj* causing a feeling of respect and fear or admiration مهيب، يبعث على الرهبة

awful /ˈɔːfl/ *adj* **1** very bad or unpleasant: *We had an awful holiday. It rained every day.* ○ *What an awful thing to say!* فظيع ، سيّئ للغاية

2 terrible; very serious: *I'm afraid there's been some awful news.* شنيع : بغيض : مقلق للغاية

3 (only *before* a noun) (*informal*) very great: *I'm in an awful hurry. See you later.* ○ *We've got an awful lot of work to do.* شديد ، كبير ، هائل

▸ **awfully** /ˈɔːfli/ *adv* (*informal*) very; very much: *I'm awfully sorry.* جداً ؛ كثيراً

awkward /ˈɔːkwəd/ *adj* **1** not convenient, difficult: *My mother always phones at an awkward time.* ○ *You've put me in an awkward position.* ○ *That's an awkward question.* ○ *It's awkward for her to get home by bus.* ○ *This tin-opener is very awkward to clean.* غير مناسِب : صعب

2 (used about people) causing difficulties; unreasonable: *He keeps asking for different things – he's just being awkward.* عسير : مشتطّ : شكِس

3 embarrassed; not relaxed: *There was an awkward silence when no one could think of anything to say.* محْرِج : متوتّر

4 without grace or skill: *an awkward gesture* أخرق

▸ **awkwardly** *adv* على نحو أخرق : بصورة محرجة أو غير ملائمة

awkwardness *noun* [U] صعوبة: حرج: عدم مهارة

awoke *pt* of AWAKE

awoken *pp* of AWAKE

awry /əˈraɪ/ *adv* wrong, not in the way that was planned: *Our plans went awry.* منحرفاً عن هدفه : فاشلاً : سدىً

▸ **awry** *adj* (not before a noun) untidy; in the wrong position: *Her hair was all awry.* مشوّش : منحرِف: مشعّث

axe (*especially US* **ax**) /æks/ *noun* [C] a tool with a

wooden handle and a metal blade used for cutting wood, etc: *He chopped the tree down with an axe.* فأس
▸ **axe** (*especially US* **ax**) *verb* [T] **1** to remove or end sth: *Hundreds of jobs have been axed.* يُنهي ، يلغي ؛ يقضي على

2 to reduce sth greatly: *School budgets are to be axed.* يُخفِّض تخفيضاً كبيراً

axis /'æksɪs/ *noun* [C] (*pl.* **axes** /'æksi:z/) **1** an imaginary line through the middle of an object that turns: *The earth rotates on its axis.* مِحْوَر

2 a fixed line used for marking measurements on a graph: *the horizontal/vertical axis* مِحْوَر

axle /'æksl/ *noun* [C] a bar that connects a pair of wheels on a vehicle مِحور أو جزْء (الدولاب)

ayatollah /ˌaɪə'tɒlə; *US* -təʊl/ *noun* [C] a religious leader of Shiite Muslims in Iran آية الله

aye (*also* **ay**) /aɪ/ *interj* yes ❶ **Aye** is common in Scotland and the North of England. نعم ، بَلَى

B b

B, b /bi:/ *noun* [C] (*pl.* **Bs**; **B's**; **b's**) the second letter of the English alphabet: *'Billy' begins with (a) 'B'.* الحرف الثاني في الأبجدية الإنكليزية

BA (*US* **B.A.**) /ˌbi: 'eɪ:/ *abbrev* Bachelor of Arts; the degree that you receive when you complete a university or college course in an arts subject بكالوريوس في الآداب

b. *abbrev* born: *J S Bach, b. 1685* وُلِد في...

baa /bɑ:/ *noun* [C] the sound that a sheep or lamb makes ثُغاء الخراف

babble /'bæbl/ *verb* [I] **1** to talk quickly or in a way that is difficult to understand يتكلّم على نحو يصعب فهمه ، يغمغم

2 to make the sound of water running over stones يخِرّ كالماء
▸ **babble** *noun* [U] **1** the sound of many voices talking at the same time: *I could hear a babble of voices coming from downstairs.* أصوات مختلطة

2 the sound of water running over stones خرير (الماء)

babe /beɪb/ *noun* [C] **1** (*old-fashioned*) a baby طفل رضيع

2 (*US slang*) (used when talking to sb, especially a girl or young woman): *It's OK, babe.* عبارة تدليع: "يا حلوة"

🔑**baby** /'beɪbi/ *noun* [C] (*pl.* **babies**) **1** a very young child: *I've got wonderful news. I'm going to have a baby.* ○ *She's expecting a baby early next year* (= she's pregnant and the baby will be born early next year). ○ *When's the baby due?* (= when will it be born?) ○ *Babies can usually sit up when they are about six months old.* ○ *a baby boy/girl* طفل (رضيع)

2 a very young animal or bird: *a baby rabbit* صغير الحيوان أو الطير

3 (*US slang*) a person, especially a girl or young woman that you are fond of حبيبة ، صغيرة
▸ **babyish** *adj* like or suitable for a baby: *Don't be so babyish – stop crying.* ○ *This book is a bit too babyish for Tom now.* طفولي

'**baby boom** *noun* [C] a time when more babies are born than usual, for example after a war فترة ازدهار الولادات
▸ '**baby boomer** *noun* [C] a person born during a baby boom مولود في فترة ازدهار الولادات

'**baby carriage** *noun* [C] (*US*) = PRAM

'**babysit** /'beɪbisɪt/ *verb* [I] (babysi**tt**ing; *pt, pp* babysat) to look after a child for a short time while the parents are out: *We have friends who babysit for us if we go out in the evening.* يرعى الأطفال
▸ '**babysitter** *noun* [C]: *We can't come this evening. We couldn't find a babysitter.* راعي الأطفال

bachelor /'bætʃələ(r)/ *noun* [C] **1** a man who has not yet married ❶ Nowadays **single** is the most usual word that is used to describe a man or a woman who is not married: *a single man/woman* أعزب

2 a person who has a first university degree: *a Bachelor of Arts* ○ *a Bachelor of Science* مُجاز جامعيّ ؛ حامل بكالوريوس

back

back to front   inside out

🔑**back¹** /bæk/ *noun* [C] **1** the part of a person's or animal's body between the neck and the bottom: *Do you sleep on your back or on your side?* ○ *She was standing with her back to me so I couldn't see her face.* ○ *He swung himself up onto the horse's back.* ظهر

2 the part or side of sth that is furthest from the front: *David couldn't see the blackboard because he was sitting at the back of the class.* ○ *Jane sat*

next to the driver and Anne and I sat in the back of the car. ○ *The back of the house is much prettier than the front.* ○ *There's some information about the author at the back of the book.* مؤخَرة ، خَلف

3 the part of a chair that you lean against when you sit down: *Don't climb on the back of the sofa, children!* ظهر

IDM **back to front** with the back where the front should be: *Wait a minute – you've got your jumper on back to front.* معكوس ، "بالمقلوب"

behind sb's back without sb's knowledge or agreement: *They criticized her behind her back.* من وراء ظهره ، غيْبةً

get off sb's back (*informal*) to stop bothering or annoying sb: *I wish she'd get off my back!* يتركه في سلام

know sth inside out/like the back of your hand → KNOW

a pat on the back → PAT[1]

back² /bæk/ *adj* **1** (only *before* a noun) furthest from the front: *Have you locked the back door?* ○ *the back row of the theatre* ○ *back teeth* خَلْفي

2 owed for a time in the past: *back pay* مؤخَّر

back³ /bæk/ *adv* **1** in or to a place or state that sb/sth was in before: *Bye! I'll be back about 6 o'clock* (= back home again). ○ *When is your brother coming back from Australia?* ○ *Go back to sleep.* ○ *Could I have my pen back, please?* (يعود) لبيته أو حالته السابقة

2 away from the direction you are facing or moving in: *She walked away without looking back.* ○ *Could everyone move back a bit, please?* بعيداً ، إلى الخلف

3 away from sth; under control: *The police were unable to keep the crowds back.* ○ *She tried to keep back her tears.* (بعيداً عن شيء) ؛ (تحت سيطرته)

4 in return or in reply: *He said he'd phone me back in half an hour.* كردٍّ أو جواب لـ

5 in or into the past; ago: *I met him a few years back, in Madrid.* ○ *Think back to your first day at school.* منذ ، في الماضي

IDM **back and forth** from one place to another and back again, all the time: *Travelling back and forth to work takes up quite a bit of time.* جيئة و ذهاباً

back⁴ /bæk/ *verb* **1** [I,T] to move backwards or to make sth move backwards: *I'll have to back into that parking space.* ○ *He backed the car into the parking space.* يرجع للخلف ؛ يُرجع للخلف

2 [I] to face sth at the back: *Many of the colleges back onto the river.* يطلّ من الخلف (على النهر مثلاً)

3 [T] to give help or support to sb/sth: *We can go ahead with the scheme if the bank will agree to back us.* يساند ، يدعم

4 [T] to bet money that a particular horse, team, etc. will win in a race or game: *Which horse are you backing in the 2 o'clock race?* يراهن على

PHR V **back away (from sb/sth)** to move backwards because you are afraid, shocked, etc: *He began to back slowly away from the snake.* يتراجع ، يرتدّ ، يبتعد

back down to stop insisting that you are right: *I think you are right to demand an apology. Don't back down now.* يتنازل ؛ يتراجع

back out (of sth) to decide not to do sth that you had promised to do: *You promised you would come with me. You can't back out of it now!* يتراجع عن ، يتنصّل من

back sb/sth up to support sb; to say or show that sth is true: *I'm going to say exactly what I think at the meeting. Will you back me up?* ○ *All the evidence backed up what the woman had said.* يدعَم

back sth up (*computing*) to make a copy of a computer program, etc. in case the original one is lost or damaged: *If you don't back up your files you risk losing data.* يدعم بنسخة أخرى

▸ **backer** *noun* [C] a person who gives support or money to another person, a scheme, etc. مموِّل ، داعم (المشروع)

backing *noun* [U] help or support to do sth, often in the form of money: *financial backing* تمويل ، دعْم

ˌback ˈbench *noun* [C, usually pl.] (*Brit*) a seat in the House of Commons for an ordinary member of Parliament: *to sit on the back benches* المقعد الخلفي (في البرلمان الإنكليزي)

▸ **ˌback-ˈbencher** *noun* [C] (*Brit*) a member of Parliament who does not have an important position in a political party عضو برلمان يشغل مقعداً خلفياً

backbone /ˈbækbəʊn/ *noun* **1** [C] the line of bones down the back of your body ➲ Look at **spine**. العمود الفقري

2 [sing.] the main strength or support: *Volunteer workers are the backbone of the organization.* عماد

backdate /ˌbækˈdeɪt/ *verb* [T] to make sth valid from an earlier date: *The pay rise will be backdated to 1 April.* يجعله ساري المفعول من تاريخ سابق

backfire /ˌbækˈfaɪə(r)/ *verb* [I] to have an unexpected and unwanted result, often the opposite of what was intended يتمخّض عن نتيجة عكسية

background /ˈbækgraʊnd/ *noun* **1** [C] the type of family and social class you come from and the education and experience you have: *We get on very well together in spite of our different backgrounds.* ○ *a working-class background* خلفيّة اجتماعية، بيئة

2 [sing., U] the facts or events that are connected with a situation: *The talks are taking place against a background of increasing tension.* ○ *I need some background information.* خلفيّة

3 [sing.] the part of a view, scene, picture, etc. which is furthest away from the person looking at it: *You can see the mountains in the background of the photo.* ➲ Look at **foreground**. خلفيّة

4 [sing.] a position where sb/sth can be seen/heard, etc. but is not the centre of attention: *The film star's husband prefers to stay in the background.* ○ *All the time I was speaking to her, I could hear a child crying in the background.* ○ *The restaurant kept playing the same back-*

ground music again and again. خلفيّة : بُعْد عن الأنظار

backhand /ˈbækhænd/ *noun* [sing.] a stroke in tennis, etc. that is made with the back of your hand facing forward ➲ Look at **forehand**. ضربة في التنس بظهر اليد

backlash /ˈbæklæʃ/ *noun* [sing.] a strong reaction against a political or social event or development ردّ فعل عنيف

backlog /ˈbæklɒg/ *noun* [C, usually sing.] an amount of work, etc. that has not yet been done and needs doing: *I've got an enormous backlog of letters to write.* متأخّرات ، عمل متراكم

backpack /ˈbækpæk/ *noun* [C] (*especially US*) = RUCKSACK

▶ **backpack** *verb* [I] to go walking or travelling with your clothes, etc. in a backpack ℹ **Go backpacking** is used when you are talking about spending time backpacking: *We went backpacking round Europe last summer.* يسافر حاملا حقيبته على ظهره

backpacker *noun* [C] مسافر يحمل امتعته على ظهره

backside /ˈbæksaɪd/ *noun* [C] (*informal*) the part of the body that you sit on; your bottom عجيزة : مؤخّرة

backslash /ˈbækslæʃ/ *noun* [C] a mark (\ ) used in computer commands شَرطة مائلة (كمبيوتر)

backstage /ˌbækˈsteɪdʒ/ *adv* behind the stage in a theatre, where the actors get dressed, etc. وراء الكواليس

backstroke /ˈbækstrəʊk/ *noun* [U] a style of swimming that you do on your back: *Can you do backstroke?* السباحة على الظهر

backup /ˈbækʌp/ *noun* **1** [U] extra help or support: *Her success is partly due to the backup she gets from her team.* مساندة ، دعم

2 [C] a copy of a computer disk that you can use if the original one is lost or damaged: *Always make a backup of your files.* نسخة دَعْم

🔑**backward** /ˈbækwəd/ *adj* **1** (only *before* a noun) directed towards the back: *a backward step, glance, etc.* خلفي : متجه الى الوراء

2 slow to learn or develop: *Considerable modernization is needed in the more backward areas of the country.* متخلّف

▶ **backwards** (*especially US* **backward**) *adv* **1** away from the front; towards the back: *Could everybody take a step backwards?* ○ *He fell backwards and hit the back of his head.* ○ *We seem to be going backwards, not forwards.* إلى الوراء

2 the opposite way to usual; with the end first: *It was a very easy code. All the words were written backwards.* بالمعكوس، بالمقلوب

3 towards an earlier time: *The film was about some people who travelled backwards in time.* إلى الماضي

IDM **backward(s) and forward(s)** first in one direction and then in the other, all the time: *The dog ran backwards and forwards, barking loudly.* إلى الأمام و إلى الوراء

backwater /ˈbækwɔːtə(r)/ *noun* [C] a place that is not affected by new ideas or outside events مكان معزول عن المدنيّة

backyard /ˌbækˈjɑːd/ *noun* [C] an area behind a house, usually of concrete or stone, with a wall or fence around it فناء مسوّر خلف البيت

bacon /ˈbeɪkən/ *noun* [U] thin pieces of salted or smoked meat from the back or sides of a pig شرائح لحم خنزير

🔑**bacteria** /bækˈtɪəriə/ *noun* [plural] very small living things that can only be seen with a microscope. Bacteria exist in large numbers in air, water, soil, plants and the bodies of people and animals. Some bacteria cause disease. ➲ Look at **virus**. بكتيريا ، جراثيم

🔑**bad** /bæd/ *adj* (**worse** /wɜːs/, **worst** /wɜːst/)

1 not good or pleasant: *Our family's had rather a bad time recently.* ○ *The weather forecast for the weekend is very bad.* رديء : مكدِّر

2 severe or serious: *The traffic was extremely bad on the way to work.* ○ *She went home with a bad headache.* ○ *That was a bad mistake!* سيّئ : شديد : (خطأ) فاحش

3 of poor quality; of a low standard: *Many accidents are caused by bad driving.* ○ *Some of the company's problems are the result of bad management.* رديء

4 bad (at sth/at doing sth) not able to do sth well or easily; not skilful or reliable: *a bad teacher, driver, cook, etc.* ○ *I've always been bad at sport, but Liz is even worse than me.* ○ *He's very bad at keeping us informed* (= we can't rely on him to give us information). غير ماهر : غير موثوق

5 (used about food) not fresh or fit to eat; rotten: *Smell this meat – I think it's gone bad.* فاسد : متعفّن

6 (used about parts of the body) not healthy; painful: *He's always had a bad heart.* معتلّ : مؤلم

7 (used about a person or behaviour) not good; morally wrong: *He was not a bad man, just rather weak.* شرّير

8 (not before a noun) **bad for sb/sth** likely to damage or hurt sb/sth: *Too many sweets are bad for you.* ضارّ

9 bad (for sth/to do sth) difficult or unsuitable: *This is a bad time to phone – everyone's out to lunch.* صعب : غير ملائم

IDM **not bad** (*informal*) quite good: *'What was the lecture like?' 'Not bad.'* ○ *He earned £100 – not bad for four hours' work!* حسَن : لا بأس به

too bad (*informal*) (used to show that nothing can be done to change a situation): *'I'd much rather stay at home.' 'Well that's just too bad. We've said we'll go.'* (أمر) سيّئ للغاية

▶ **baddy** *noun* [C] (*pl.* **baddies**) (*informal*) a bad person in a film, book, etc. ℹ The opposite is a **goody**. الشخص الشرّير في فيلم و نحوه

badge /bædʒ/ *noun* [C] a small piece of metal or cloth with a design or words on it which you pin or sew onto your clothing. A badge can show position, rank, membership of a club, etc., or express a message: *The players all have jackets with the club badge on them.* شارة : شعار : وسام

badger /ˈbædʒə(r)/ *noun* [C] an animal with black and white stripes on its head that lives in holes in the ground and comes out at night غُرَيْر

ˌ**bad ˈlanguage** *noun* [U] words that are used for swearing: *You'll get into trouble if you use bad language.* لغة بذيئة

⚿ **badly** /ˈbædli/ *adv* (**worse**; **worst**) **1** in a way that is not satisfactory; not well: *'Can you speak French?' 'Well, only very badly.'* ○ *Some modern houses are very badly built.* ○ *She did badly in the exams.* على نحو غير مُرْضٍ : بشكل رديء

2 greatly or severely: *He was badly hurt in the accident.* بشدّة : (يجرح جرحاً) بليغاً

3 very much: *He badly needed a holiday.* كثيراً جداً

IDM badly off poor; not having enough of sth: *They don't seem too badly off – they have smart clothes and a nice house.* ❶ The opposite is **well off**. فقير ، معْوِز

badminton /ˈbædmɪntən/ *noun* [U] a game for two or four people in which players hit a type of light ball with feathers (shuttlecock) over a high net, using rackets: *to play badminton* لعبة الرِّيشة الطائرة

⚿ ˌ**bad-ˈtempered** *adj* often angry or impatient: *a bad-tempered old man* سريع الغضب ، سيِّئ الطبع

baffle /ˈbæfl/ *verb* [T] to be impossible for sb to understand; to confuse greatly: *His illness baffled the doctors.* يستغلق على : يحيِّر

▸ **baffled** *adj* very confused; unable to understand: *The instructions were so complicated that I was absolutely baffled.* مشوَّش : عاجز عن الفهم

baffling *adj*: *I find English a baffling language.* محيِّر ، صعب الفهم

⚿ **bag¹** /bæg/ *noun* [C] **1** a container made of paper, plastic, cloth or leather that is open at the top, often with handles, in which you can carry things: *The assistant took my money and put the book in a paper bag.* ○ *She brought some sandwiches in a plastic bag.* ○ *Are carrier bags free in this supermarket?* ○ *a shopping bag* ○ *a shoulder bag* ○ *a sports bag* ○ *a handbag* ○ *She took her purse out of her bag* (= handbag). كيس : حقيبة

2 a container made of paper or plastic that is closed at the top; a packet: *a bag of sweets, crisps, sugar, etc.* كيس

3 a thing that looks like a bag: *bags under the eyes* (= folds of skin under the eyes, often caused by lack of sleep) انتفاخ

4 (*slang*) an unpleasant woman امرأة ممقوتة

5 bags (of sth) [plural] a lot (of sth); plenty (of sth): *There's no hurry, we've got bags of time.* كثيرٌ من

bag² /bæg/ *verb* [T] (**bagg**ing; **bagg**ed) (*informal*) to try to reserve sth for yourself so that other people cannot have it: *Somebody's bagged the seats by the pool!* يستولي على ، يحتلّ

⚿ **baggage** /ˈbægɪdʒ/ *noun* [U] = LUGGAGE: *We loaded our baggage into the car.* ○ *Baggage should be checked in* (= given to an airline employee at a counter) *at least an hour before the flight.* ○ *excess baggage* (= baggage weighing more than the airline's permitted limit)

baggy /ˈbægi/ *adj* (**baggier**; **baggiest**) (used about a piece of clothing) hanging loosely on the body: *a baggy pullover* فضفاض

bagpipes /ˈbægpaɪps/ (*also* **pipes**) *noun* [plural] a musical instrument, popular in Scotland, that is played by blowing air through a pipe into a bag and then pressing the bag so that the air comes out of other pipes مِزمار القِربة

baguette /bæˈget/ *noun* [C] a loaf of white bread

bags

in the shape of a long thick stick that is crisp on the outside and soft inside خبز فرنسي

bail /beɪl/ *noun* [U] **1** money that sb agrees to pay if a person accused of a crime does not appear in front of the court on the day he/she is called. When bail has been arranged, the accused person can go free until that day: *She was released on bail of £2 000.* ○ *The judge set bail at £10 000.* كفالة ماليّة

2 permission for sb who is accused of a crime to be free until the trial if a sum of money is handed over to the court: *The judge felt that he was a dangerous man and refused him bail.* ○ *She was granted bail.* كَفالة

▶ **bail** *verb*

PHRV **bail sb out 1** to obtain sb's freedom by paying his/her bail(1): *After she had been charged, her parents bailed her out.* يدفع كفالة لإطلاق سراح متّهم

2 to rescue sb or sth from a difficult situation (especially by providing money) يستنقذ (بعون مالي)

bailiff /ˈbeɪlɪf/ *noun* [C] an officer whose job is to make sure that a court order is carried out, especially by taking possession of people's goods when they owe money مأمور قضائي

bait /beɪt/ *noun* [U] **1** food or sth that looks like food that is put onto a hook to catch fish, or placed in a trap to catch animals or birds طُعْم

2 something that is used for tempting or attracting sb: *Free offers are often used as bait to attract customers.* إغراء

bake /beɪk/ *verb* [I,T] **1** to cook in an oven in dry heat: *I could smell bread baking in the oven.* ○ *On his birthday she baked him a cake.* ○ *Would you like boiled or baked potatoes?* ➲ Look at the note at **cook**. يخبِز

2 to become or to make sth hard by heating it: *The hot sun baked the earth.* يتحمّص : يحمّص ، يشوي

▶ **baking** *adj* (*informal*) very hot: *The workers complained of the baking heat in the office in the summer.* محْرق

baker /ˈbeɪkə(r)/ *noun* [C] a person who bakes and sells bread, cakes, etc: *Get a loaf at the baker's.* ℹ Note that **the baker** is the person who runs the shop and **the baker's** is the shop. خبّاز

▶ **bakery** /ˈbeɪkəri/ *noun* [C] (*pl.* **bakeries**) (*US* ˈ**bake shop**) a place where bread, cakes, etc. are baked to be sold مَخْبَز ، فرْن

balance¹ /ˈbæləns/ *verb* **1** [I,T] to be or to put sb/sth in a steady position in which weight is evenly spread: *I had to balance on the top step of the ladder to paint the ceiling.* ○ *Carefully, she balanced a glass on top of the pile of plates.* يتوازن : يوازن

2 [I,T] to have equal totals of money spent and money received: *I must have made a mistake – the accounts don't balance.* ○ *She is always very careful to balance her weekly budget.* يرصّد الحساب : يوازن بين الدخل و النفقات

3 [T] **balance sth (out) (with sth)** to have or give sth equal value, importance, etc. in relation to other parts: *It's difficult to balance the demands of a career with caring for an elderly relative.* ○ *The loss in the first half of the year was balanced out by the profit in the second half.* يساوي (بين) ؛ يعدل

4 [T] **balance sth against sth** to consider and compare one matter in relation to another: *In planning the new road, we have to balance the benefit to motorists against the damage to the environment.* يوازن ، يقارن

▶ **balanced** *adj* **1** including all different sides, opinions, etc. equally; fair: *I like this newspaper because it gives a balanced view.* متوازن ، شامل لآراء مختلفة

2 consisting of parts that are in the correct or pleasing proportions: *A balanced diet plays an important part in good health.* متكامل

balance² /ˈbæləns/ *noun* **1** [U] the state of being in a steady position in which weight is evenly spread: *You need a good sense of balance to ride a motor bike.* توازن

2 [sing.] **(a) balance (between A and B)** a situation in which different or opposite things are of equal importance, size, etc. or are in the correct proportions: *The course provides a good balance between academic and practical work.* ○ *Man has upset the environmental balance of the world.* توازن

3 [C] (*technical*) an instrument used for weighing things ➲ Look at **scales**. ميزان

4 [C] the amount of money in sb's bank account: *While I was in the bank I asked the cashier for my balance.* رصيد

5 the balance [sing.] the amount that still has to be paid; the amount that remains after some has been used, taken, etc: *You can pay a 10% deposit now, with the balance due in one month.* ○ *I took most of my annual holiday in the summer and I'm taking the balance over Christmas.* باقي الحساب

IDM **in the balance** uncertain: *Following poor results, the company's future is in the balance.* غير مؤكّد

keep/lose your balance to remain/not to remain steady and upright: *It's difficult to keep your balance on this icy path.* ○ *She tripped, lost her balance and fell over.* يحفظ/يفقد توازنه

(catch/throw sb) off balance (to find or put sb) in an unsteady position from which it is easy to fall: *A strong gust of wind caught me off balance and I nearly fell over.* يفقده توازنه

on balance having taken all sides, facts, etc. into consideration: *On balance, I've had a pretty good year.* بعد أخذ كل شيء بعين الاعتبار

strike a balance → STRIKE²

ˌ**balance of** ˈ**payments** *noun* [sing.] the difference between the amount of money one country receives from other countries from exports, etc. and the amount it pays to them for imports, etc. ميزان المدفوعات

ˌ**balance of** ˈ**power** *noun* [sing.] **1** a situation in which power is evenly divided among the various sides, parties, groups, etc. involved توازن القوى

2 the power that a smaller political party has when the larger parties need its support because they do not have enough votes on their own (يحمل) ميزان القوى

ˈbalance sheet *noun* [C] a written record of money received and money paid out, showing the difference between the totals of each بيان الميزانية

balcony /ˈbælkəni/ *noun* [C] (*pl.* **balconies**) **1** a platform built on an upstairs outside wall of a building, with a wall or rail around it: *Our hotel room had a balcony where we could sit and look at the lake.* شُرفة، بلكون

2 the rows of seats high up and near the back of a theatre البلكون في المسرح

bald /bɔːld/ *adj* **1** (used about people) having little or no hair on the head: *He went bald when he was only 30.* ○ *He has a bald patch on the top of his head.* أصلع

2 (used about sth that is said) simple; without extra words: *the bald truth* بسيط ، مجرّد

▶ **balding** *adj* becoming bald: *a balding man in his fifties* آخذ بالصلَع

bale /beɪl/ *noun* [C] a large quantity of sth (paper, hay, cloth, etc.) tied together in a bundle so that it can be transported بالة ، رِزْمة

balk = BAULK

🔑 **ball¹** /bɔːl/ *noun* [C] **1** a round object that you hit, kick, throw, etc. in games and sports: *a tennis ball* ○ *a golf ball* ○ *a football* ○ *The children were playing with a ball in the garden.* ○ *The ball bounced over the fence.* كُرة

2 any object that has this shape or has been formed into this shape: *a ball of wool* ○ *The cat curled up into a ball and went to sleep.* ○ *The children threw snowballs at each other.* ○ *We had meatballs and pasta for dinner.* كرة ، كُبّة

IDM **(be) on the ball** (*informal*) (to be) aware of what is happening and able to react to or deal with it quickly: *With so many new developments, you really have to be on the ball.* يَقِظ ، متنبّه ؛ مطّلع

set/start the ball rolling to start sth (an activity, conversation, etc.) that involves or is done by a group: *I made the first contribution to the collection to set the ball rolling.* يستهلّ أمراً أو حديثاً

ball² /bɔːl/ *noun* [C] a large formal party at which people dance حفلة راقصة

ballad /ˈbæləd/ *noun* [C] a long song or poem in simple language, telling a story قصيدة قصصيّة

ˌball ˈbearing *noun* [C] one of a number of metal balls put between parts of a machine to make them move smoothly محمل كريّات (في آلة)

ballerina /ˌbæləˈriːnə/ *noun* [C] a woman who dances in ballets راقصة باليه

ballet /ˈbæleɪ; *US* bæˈleɪ/ *noun* **1** [U] a style of dancing that tells a story with music but without words: *I like opera but I'm not keen on ballet.* رقص باليه

2 [C] a performance or work that consists of this type of dancing: *They went to see a performance of Tchaikovsky's ballet 'The Nutcracker'.* (حفلة أداء) باليه

ˈballet dancer *noun* [C] a person who dances in ballets راقص أو راقصة باليه

ˈball game *noun* **1** [C] any game played with a ball: *Tennis, football, golf – he's good at all ball games.* لعبة كرة

2 [C] (*US*) a baseball match مباراة بيسبول

3 [sing.] (*informal*) a situation; a set of circumstances: *After living in a village for so long, living in the big city is a whole new ball game for me.* وضع ، ظرف

balloon /bəˈluːn/ *noun* [C] **1** a small coloured rubber bag that you blow air into and use as a toy or for decoration: *We hung balloons around the room for the party.* ○ *The child cried when his balloon burst.* بالون

2 (*also* **hot-ˈair balloon**) a large bag that is filled with gas or hot air so that it can rise into and fly through the air, carrying people in a basket attached below it: *They crossed the Atlantic in a balloon.* منْطاد

ballot /ˈbælət/ *noun* [C,U] a secret written vote: *A ballot will be held to elect a new chairman.* ○ *The members of the union voted in a ballot to accept the pay rise.* ○ *The committee are elected by ballot every year.* تصويت سري

▶ **ballot** *verb* [T] **ballot sb (about/on sth)** to ask sb to vote in a ballot; to arrange and hold a ballot: *The union is balloting its members on strike action.* يجعله يقترع؛ يجري اقتراعاً

ballpark /ˈbɔːlpɑːk/ *noun* [C] a place where baseball is played ملعب بيسبول

IDM **in the ballpark** (*informal*) (used about figures or amounts) that are within the same limits: *All the bids for the contract were in the same ballpark.* متقارب، ضمن الحدود

a ballpark figure/estimate a number, amount, etc. that is approximately correct: *We asked the builders for a ballpark figure, to give us an idea of how much it would cost.* (سعر) تقريبي

ballpoint /ˈbɔːlpɔɪnt/ (*also* **ˌballpoint ˈpen**) *noun* [C] a pen with a very small metal ball at the end that rolls ink onto paper ➲ Look at **Biro**. قلم حبر جاف

ballroom /ˈbɔːlruːm; -rʊm/ *noun* [C] a large room used for dancing قاعة رقص

ˌballroom ˈdancing *noun* [U] a formal type of dance in which couples dance together using particular steps and movements رقص ثنائي يخضع لخطوات معيّنة

bamboo /ˌbæmˈbuː/ *noun* [C,U] a tall tropical plant of the grass family. Young bamboo shoots can be eaten; the hard, hollow stems are used for making furniture, etc: *a bamboo chair* خَيْزران

🔑 **ban** /bæn/ *verb* (banning; banned) [T] **1** to forbid officially, often by law: *The government has banned the import of products from that country.* يمنَع، يحظر

2 ban sb (from sth/from doing sth) to officially forbid sb to do sth, often by law: *He was fined £400 and banned from driving for a year.* يمنعه من

▸ **ban** *noun* [C] **a ban (on sth/sb)**: *There is a ban on smoking in this office.* منع ، حظر

banal /bəˈnɑːl; *US* ˈbeɪnl/ *adj* not original or interesting: *a banal comment* مُبتَذَل ، سخيف

banana /bəˈnɑːnə; *US* bəˈnænə/ *noun* [C] a long curved fruit that has a yellow skin and that can be eaten: *a bunch of bananas* ○ *a banana milk-shake* مَوْزة

band /ˈbænd; bænd/ *noun* [C] **1** a thin, flat, narrow piece of material used for fastening sth, or put round sth, often to hold it together: *She rolled up the papers and put an elastic band round them.* ○ *The cards were held together by a rubber band.* ○ *He was wearing a white hat with a black band round it.* شريط ، شريطة

2 a line of a colour or design that is different from the one on either side of it: *She wore a red pullover with a green band across the middle.* خط أو "قلم" ملوّن (على ثوب مثلاً)

3 [with sing. or pl. verb] a group of people who have joined together with a common purpose: *The attack was made by a small band of rebels.* عصبة ، جماعة

4 a group of musicians: *a brass band* ○ *a jazz band* ○ *a rock band* فرقة (موسيقية)

5 = WAVEBAND

bandage /ˈbændɪdʒ/ *noun* [C] a long piece of soft white material that is wrapped round a wound or injury ضمادة

▸ **bandage** *verb* [T] **bandage sth/sb (up)**: *She played the game with a bandaged knee.* يضمِّد

Band-Aid™ /ˈbænd eɪd/ *noun* [C] (*especially US*) = PLASTER (2)

B and B (*also* **b and b**) /ˌbiː ən ˈbiː/ *abbrev* = BED AND BREAKFAST

bandit /ˈbændɪt/ *noun* [C] an armed robber, usually in a wild place قاطع طريق

bandwagon /ˈbændwægən/ *noun*

IDM **climb/jump on the bandwagon** to copy what other people are doing because it is fashionable or successful
يقلّد الآخرين ؛ يلتحق بالجانب المتوقع فوزه

bang[1] /bæŋ/ *verb* [I,T] **1** to make a loud noise by hitting sth hard, closing sth, or putting sth down: *The people downstairs banged on their ceiling to complain about the noise.* ○ *Somewhere in the house, I heard a door bang.* ○ *She stormed out of the room, banging the door behind her.* ○ *He banged his fist on the table and started shouting.* يخبِط ؛ ينخبط

2 to knock against sth by accident: *As I was crossing the room in the dark I banged into a table.* ○ *Be careful not to bang your head on the ceiling. It's quite low.* يصطدم ؛ يصدم بعنف

PHR V **bang about/around** to move around a place making loud noises: *I could hear him banging about in the kitchen.* يحدث ضجة عالية

bang[2] /bæŋ/ *noun* [C] **1** a sudden, short, very loud noise: *There was an enormous bang when the bomb exploded.* ○ *The balloon burst with a bang.* صوت انفجار ، دويّ

2 a short, strong knock or blow, especially one that causes pain and injury: *He received a nasty bang on the head and was unconscious for several minutes.* ضربة عنيفة

▸ **bang** *interj* (used to sound like the noise of a gun, etc.): *The children were running around with toy guns, shouting, 'Bang! Bang!'* طاخ!

bang[3] /bæŋ/ *adv* (*informal*) exactly; directly; right: *She phoned bang in the middle of dinner.* ○ *The shot was bang on target.* بالضبط ؛ تماماً

IDM **bang goes sth** (*informal*) (used for expressing the idea that sth is now impossible): *'It's raining!' 'Ah well, bang goes our picnic!'* لا أمل الآن في...

banger /ˈbæŋə(r)/ *noun* [C] (*Brit informal*) **1** a sausage سجق

2 an old car that is in very bad condition سيارة قديمة و بحالة رديئة

3 a small firework that explodes with a short loud noise مفرقعة أو لعبة نارية صغيرة

bangle /ˈbæŋgl/ *noun* [C] a large bracelet or metal band that is worn round the arm for decoration سِوار

bangs /bæŋz/ *noun* [plural] (*US*) = FRINGE (1)

banish /ˈbænɪʃ/ *verb* [T] **1** to send sb away (especially out of the country), usually as a punishment: *They were banished from the country for demonstrating against the government.* ○ *The children were banished to the garden for making too much noise in the house.* ينفي ، يطرد من البلاد

2 to remove sth completely; to force out: *She banished all hope of winning from her mind.* يطرد، يستبعد

banister /ˈbænɪstə(r)/ *noun* [C] (often plural) a rail supported by upright bars at the side of a staircase, that you hold on to when you are going up- or downstairs درابزين

banjo /ˈbændʒəʊ/ *noun* [C] (*pl.* **banjos**) a musical instrument with a long thin neck, a round body and four or more strings, played with the fingers البانجو: آلة موسيقية

bank[1] /bæŋk/ *noun* [C] **1** an organization which keeps money safely for its customers; the office or building of such an organization. You can take money out, save, borrow or exchange money at a bank: *My salary is paid directly into my bank.* ○ *He went to the bank and got some money out of his account.* ○ *She got a loan from the bank to buy a new car.* بنك، مصرف

2 a store of things, which you keep to use later: *a data bank* ○ *a blood bank in a hospital* بنك ، مصرف

▸ **banker** *noun* [C] a person who owns or has an important job in a bank مدير أو موظف كبير في بنك

banking *noun* [U] the type of business done by banks: *She decided on a career in banking.* العمل المصرفي

bank² /bæŋk/ *noun* [C] **1** the ground along the side of a river or canal: *People were fishing along the banks of the river.* ○ *We rowed to the bank and got out of the boat.* ضفة

2 any area of sloping ground: *There were grassy banks on either side of the road.* جرف ، منحدر

3 (used about certain features of weather) a mass of sth: *a bank of cloud* ركام ، كومة

bank³ /bæŋk/ *verb*

PHR V **bank on sb/sth** to expect and trust sb to do sth, or sth to happen: *I suppose you might be lucky but I wouldn't bank on it.* ○ *We haven't booked a hotel – we're banking on finding somewhere to stay when we get there.* يعتمد على

ˌbank ˈholiday *noun* [C] a public holiday (not a Saturday or Sunday) when banks are officially closed عطلة رسمية

banknote /ˈbæŋknəʊt/ *noun* [C] = NOTE¹ (4)

bankrupt /ˈbæŋkrʌpt/ *adj* not having enough money to pay your debts: *The company went bankrupt owing thousands of pounds.* مفلس

▸ **bankrupt** *verb* [T] to cause sb/sth to become bankrupt يفلّس

bankruptcy /ˈbæŋkrʌpsi/ *noun* [C,U] the state when a person or an organization is bankrupt: *During this period of economic difficulty, bankruptcies are becoming more common.* ○ *Competition from larger companies drove them to bankruptcy.* إفلاس

ˈbank statement (*also* **statement**) *noun* [C] a printed list of all the money going into or out of a bank account during a certain period كشف حساب

banner /ˈbænə(r)/ *noun* [C] a long piece of cloth with words or signs on it, which can be hung up or carried through the streets on two poles: *The demonstrators carried banners saying 'Stop the War'.* راية

banquet /ˈbæŋkwɪt/ *noun* [C] a formal dinner for a large number of people, usually as a special event at which speeches are made مأدبة

baptism /ˈbæptɪzəm/ *noun* [C,U] a ceremony in which a person becomes a member of the Christian Church by being placed briefly under water or having drops of water put onto his/her head. Often he/she is also formally given a name. ➲ Look at **christening**. تعميد (ديني)

▸ **baptize** (*also* **baptise**) /bæpˈtaɪz/ *verb* [T] to perform the ceremony of baptism: *Were you baptized as a child?* ○ *He was baptized 'George David'.* يعمد

Baptist /ˈbæptɪst/ *noun* [C], *adj* (a member) of a Protestant Church that believes that baptism should only be for people who are old enough to understand the meaning of the ceremony and should be done by placing the person fully under water معمداني

bar¹ /bɑː(r)/ *noun* [C] **1** a place where you can buy and drink (especially alcoholic) drinks and sometimes have sth to eat: *They had a drink in*

a bar of chocolate/soap

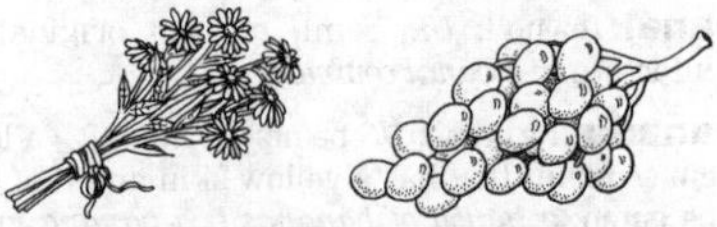

a bunch of flowers/grapes

a slice of lemon/cake

a lump of coal

a drop of water

the bar before the meal. ○ *a wine bar* ○ *a coffee bar* ○ *a snack bar* بار ، مشرب

2 a long, narrow, high table or counter where drinks are served: *We sat on stools at the bar.* ○ *He works behind the bar in the local pub.* بار ، طاولة المشروبات

3 a long, thin, straight piece of metal, often placed across a window or door, etc. to make it strong or to prevent people from passing through it: *They escaped by sawing through the bars of their prison cell.* ○ *To open the emergency exit door, push the bar.* قضيب معدني

4 a small block of solid material, longer than it is wide: *a bar of soap* ○ *a bar of chocolate* لوح ، قطعة

5 a thing that prevents you from doing sth: *Lack of education is not always a bar to success in business.* حائل ، عائق

6 one of the short, equal units of time into which music is divided: *If you sing a few bars of the song I might recognize it.* فاصلة موسيقية

IDM **behind bars** (*informal*) in prison مسجون ، وراء القضبان

bar² /bɑː(r)/ *verb* [T] (barring; barred) **1** to fasten with a bar¹ (3) or bars: *The heavy door was barred and bolted.* يقفل بمزلاج

2 to stop sb going through or into a place: *A line of police barred the entrance to the embassy.* يسد

3 **bar sb from sth/from doing sth** to forbid sb officially to do, use or enter sth: *She was barred from the club for bad behaviour.* يحظر ، يمنع

bar³ /bɑː(r)/ *prep* except: *All the seats were taken, bar one.* ما عدا

barbarian /bɑːˈbeəriən/ *noun* [C] a wild, uncivilized person همجي ، غير متمدن

barbaric /bɑːˈbærɪk/ *adj* very cruel and violent: *barbaric punishments* ○ *barbaric treatment of prisoners* همجي ، وحشي
▸ **barbarism** /ˈbɑːbərɪzəm/ *noun* [U]: *acts of barbarism committed in war* همجية ، وحشية

barbecue /ˈbɑːbɪkjuː/ *noun* [C] (*abbr* **BBQ**) **1** a metal frame on which food is cooked over an open fire outdoors شوّاية توضع في الهواء الطلق
2 an outdoor party at which food is cooked in this way: *Let's have a barbecue.* شِواء في الهواء الطلق
▸ **barbecue** *verb* [T]: *barbecued steak* يشوي في الهواء الطلق

barbed wire /ˌbɑːbd ˈwaɪə(r)/ *noun* [U] strong wire with sharp points on it: *a barbed wire fence* أسلاك شائكة

barber /ˈbɑːbə(r)/ *noun* [C] a man who cuts men's hair: *Your hair's getting rather long. It's time you went to the barber's.* ℹ Note that **the barber** is the person who runs the shop and **the barber's** is the shop. حلاّق

ˈ**bar chart** *noun* [C] a diagram that uses narrow bands of different heights to show different amounts so that they can be compared أعمدة الرسم البياني

ˈ**bar code** *noun* [C] a pattern of thick and thin lines that is printed on things you buy. It contains information that a computer can read. خطوط الترميز

bare /beə(r)/ *adj* **1** (used about part of the body) not covered by clothing: *bare arms* ○ *a bare chest* ○ *She killed him with her bare hands* (= without a weapon). ➲ Look at **naked** and **nude**. عارٍ ، مكشوف
2 without anything covering it: *They had taken the paintings down, so the walls were all bare.* عارٍ ، اجرد
3 minimum, basic and no more: *We were so poor that we didn't even have the bare necessities of life.* ○ *Just give me the bare facts as quickly as you can.* أساسي ؛ مجرد
4 empty; without its usual contents: *I looked for some food but the cupboards were bare.* خالٍ ، خاوٍ
▸ **barely** *adv* only just; hardly; almost not: *You've barely eaten anything – are you feeling all right?* ○ *She's barely older than you.* بالكاد

bareback /ˈbeəbæk/ *adj, adv* on a horse without a saddle: *bareback riders in the circus* ○ *She likes riding bareback.* دون سَرْج

barefoot /ˈbeəfʊt/ (*also* **barefooted** /ˌbeəˈfʊtɪd/) *adj, adv* with nothing (e.g. shoes, socks, etc.) on the feet: *I was barefoot because my shoes and socks had got wet.* ○ *We walked barefoot along the beach.* عاري القدمين ، حافٍ

🔑**bargain** /ˈbɑːgən/ *noun* [C] **1** an agreement between people or groups about what each of them will do for the other or others: *Let's make a bargain. I'll lend you the money if you'll help me with my work.* ○ *I hope he keeps his side of the bargain.* صَفْقة ، اتفاق
2 something that is cheaper or at a lower price than usual: *At that price, it's an absolute bargain!* ○ *I found a lot of bargains in the sale.* شروة رخيصة ، "لقطة"
IDM **into the bargain** (used for emphasizing sth) as well; in addition; also: *They gave me free tickets and a free meal into the bargain.* علاوة على (البيعة) ، أيضاً
strike a bargain → STRIKE²
▸ **bargain** *verb* [I] **bargain (with sb) (about/over/for sth)** to discuss the form of an agreement, a price, etc: *I'm sure that if you bargain with him, he'll drop the price.* ○ *They bargained over the price.* يساوم
PHRV **bargain for/on sth** to expect sth or to be prepared for sth: *When I agreed to help him I didn't bargain for how much it would cost me.* يتوقع ، يتهيأ

bargaining *noun* [U] discussion about the form of an agreement, the price for a sale, etc., in which people are trying to get a result that is to their own advantage: *Hours of bargaining failed to produce an agreement.* مساومة ، تفاوض

barge /bɑːdʒ/ *noun* [C] a long narrow boat with a flat bottom that is used for transporting goods or people on a canal or river مركب نهري لنقل البضائع خاصة

baritone /ˈbærɪtəʊn/ *noun* [C] a singing voice that is fairly low, between tenor and bass الجهير الأول (صوت غنائي)

bark¹ /bɑːk/ *noun* [U] the hard outer covering of a tree لحاء (الشجر)

bark² /bɑːk/ *verb* **1** [I] **bark (at sb/sth)** (used about dogs) to make a loud, short noise or noises: *Their dog always barks at anyone who rings the doorbell.* ينبح
2 [I,T] **bark (sth) (out) (at sb)** to speak to sb in a loud voice with an angry or aggressive tone: *The boss came in, barked some orders and left again.* يزعق ، يصيح غاضباً
▸ **bark** *noun* [C]: *The dog next door has a very loud bark.* نباح

barley /ˈbɑːli/ *noun* [U] **1** a plant similar to grass that produces grain that is used for food or for making beer and other drinks شعير
2 the grain produced by this plant حب الشعير

barmaid /ˈbɑːmeɪd/ *noun* [C] a woman who serves drinks from behind a bar in a pub, etc. بائعة المشروب (في حانة) ، نادلة

barman /ˈbɑːmən/ *noun* [C] (*pl.* **barmen** /-mən/) a man who serves drinks from behind a bar in a pub, etc. نادل أو ساقٍ (في حانة)

barn /bɑːn/ *noun* [C] a large building on a farm in which crops or animals are kept مخزن الحبوب ؛ حظيرة الماشية

barometer /bəˈrɒmɪtə(r)/ *noun* [C] **1** an instrument that measures air pressure and indicates changes in weather بارومتر: ميزان الضغط الجوي
2 something that indicates the state of sth (a situation, a feeling, etc.): *Results of local elections are often a barometer of the government's popularity.* مقياس

baron /ˈbærən/ *noun* [C] **1** a man who belongs to the lowest rank of the aristocracy بارون

2 a person who controls a large part of a particular industry or type of business: *an oil baron* قطب (في صناعة أو تجارة)

baroness /ˈbærənəs/ *noun* [C] a woman who is of the same rank as a baron or is the wife of a baron بارونة

baroque /bəˈrɒk; *US* bəˈrəʊk/ *adj* having the highly decorated and elaborate style that was fashionable in the arts, especially architecture, in Europe in the 17th and 18th centuries (طراز) باروك

barracks /ˈbærəks/ *noun* [C, with sing. or pl. verb] (*pl.* **barracks**) a building or group of buildings in which soldiers live: *Guards were on duty at the gate of the barracks.* ثُكْنة

barrage /ˈbærɑːʒ; *US* bəˈrɑːʒ/ *noun* [C] **1** a continuous attack with a large number of guns in a particular direction قصف مدفعي متواصل

2 a large number of questions, remarks, etc., aimed at a person very quickly: *The minister faced a barrage of questions from reporters.* وابل، سيل من الاسئلة

barrel /ˈbærəl/ *noun* [C] **1** a large, round, often wooden container for liquids, that has a flat top and bottom and is wider in the middle; the amount contained in a barrel: *The price of oil is usually given per barrel.* بَرْميل

2 the long metal tube of a gun, through which the bullet passes when it is fired أنبوبة البندقية ، سبطانة

barren /ˈbærən/ *adj* **1** (used about land) not good enough to grow crops on قاحل ، (أرض) جدباء

2 (used about trees or plants) not producing fruit or seeds (شجر) غير مثمر

barricade /ˌbærɪˈkeɪd/ *noun* [C] an object or line of objects that is placed (usually quickly) across a road, entrance, etc. to stop people getting through: *The demonstrators put up barricades to keep the police away.* مِتْراس

▸ **barricade** *verb* [T] to block sth with a barricade: *Rioters barricaded the road with cars.* يقيم الحواجز ، يسدّ بمتاريس

PHR V **barricade yourself in** to defend yourself by putting up a barricade: *Demonstrators took over the university building and barricaded themselves in.* يتمترس ، يتحصّن

⚷**barrier** /ˈbæriə(r)/ *noun* [C] **1** an object that keeps people or things apart or prevents them moving from one place to another: *The police put up barriers along the pavement to stop the crowd getting on to the road.* ○ *You must show your ticket at the barrier before going onto the platform.* حاجز

2 something that causes problems or makes it impossible for sth to happen: *Old-fashioned attitudes are a barrier to progress.* ○ *When you live in a foreign country, the language barrier is often the most difficult problem to overcome.* ○ *trade barriers* عائق

barring /ˈbɑːrɪŋ/ *prep* **1** except for: *Barring one or two small problems, everything's fine at the moment.* فيما عدا ، باستثناء

2 if there is/are not: *Barring any unforeseen problems, we'll be moving house in a month.* في حالة عدم حدوث ، ما لَمْ (يحدث)

barrister /ˈbærɪstə(r)/ *noun* [C] (in English law) a lawyer who is trained to speak in the higher courts ➲ Look at the note at **lawyer**. محام (أمام المحاكم العليا)

barrow /ˈbærəʊ/ *noun* [C] **1** = WHEELBARROW

2 a small cart on which fruit, vegetables, etc. are moved or sold in the street, especially in markets عربة يد

barter /ˈbɑːtə(r)/ *verb* [I,T] **barter sth (for sth)** to exchange goods for other goods, not for money: *I bartered my watch for a guitar with a man in the street.* يقايض

▸ **barter** *noun* [U] the exchange of goods for other goods, not for money: *Spices were used for barter many years ago.* مقايضة

⚷**base¹** /beɪs/ *noun* [C] **1** the lowest part of sth, especially the part on which it stands or at which it is attached to sth: *The sculptor's name can be found at the base of the statue.* ○ *I felt a terrible pain at the base of my spine.* قاعدة

2 a starting point from which sth develops or is made: *With these ingredients as a base, you can create all sorts of interesting dishes.* أساس

3 a strong foundation on which sth is built or maintained: *The country needs a strong economic base.* أساس

4 a place used as a centre from which activities are done or controlled: *This hotel is an ideal base for touring the region.* ○ *Taxi drivers are in contact with their base so that they know where to go to next.* مركز ؛ نقطة انطلاق

5 a military centre from which forces operate: *an army base* ○ *a naval base* قاعدة

⚷**base²** /beɪs/ *verb* [T] **1** **base sth on sth** to form or develop sth from a particular starting point or source: *This film is based on a true story.* يبني أو يقيم على، يسند

2 (usually passive) **base sb/sth in...** to make one place the centre from which sb/sth can work or move around: *I'm based in New York, although my job involves a great deal of travel.* يستقر ، يقيم

baseball /ˈbeɪsbɔːl/ *noun* [U] a team game that is popular in the USA in which players hit the ball with a bat and run round four points (bases). They have to touch all four bases in order to score a point (run). البيسبول: لعبة كرة أمريكية

basement /ˈbeɪsmənt/ *noun* [C] the lowest room or rooms of a building which are partly or completely below ground level: *The toy department is in the basement of the store.* ○ *a basement flat* قبو ، دور تحتاني

bases 1 *pl.* of BASIS

2 *pl.* of BASE

bash /bæʃ/ *verb* (*informal*) **1** [T] to hit sb/sth very hard يضرب بعنف

2 [I] **bash against/into sb/sth** to crash into sb/sth يصطدم

3 [T] to criticize sb/sth strongly يصنف يؤنب

▸ **bash** *noun* [C] **1** a hard blow ضربة عنيفة

2 a large party or celebration حفلة

IDM **have a bash (at sth)** (*informal*) to try: *I don't know whether I can do it, but I'll have a bash.* يحاول

bashful /ˈbæʃfl/ *adj* shy and embarrassed خجول

basic /ˈbeɪsɪk/ *adj* **1** forming a starting point or basis on which other ideas rest: *The basic question is, can we afford it?* أساسي

2 simplest or most elementary; including only what is most necessary: *This course teaches basic skills in First Aid.* ○ *The basic pay is £100 a week – with extra for overtime.* ○ *The rooms in the cheapest hotels are very basic – they have no bathrooms or televisions.* أساسي ، أوّلي : بسيط

▸ **basically** /-kli/ *adv* looking at what is most important or basic in a person or an object or in a particular situation: *She seemed to me to be basically a very nice person.* ○ *The design of the new car is basically the same as the old one.* ○ *Basically, all I want is to be left alone.* أساسياً ، في جوهر الأمر

basics *noun* [plural] the things that you need most or that are the most important: *You can get all the basics at the local shop.* ضروريات

basil /ˈbæzl/ *noun* [U] a sweet-smelling herb that is used in cooking ريحان، حبق

basin /ˈbeɪsn/ *noun* [C] **1** = WASHBASIN

2 a round open bowl often used for mixing or cooking food: *a pudding basin* طاسة ، سلطانيّة ، "زبديّة"

3 an area of land from which water flows into a river: *the Congo Basin* حوض النهر

basis /ˈbeɪsɪs/ *noun* [C] (*pl.* **bases** /ˈbeɪsiːz/) **1** the way sth is done or organized: *They meet on a regular basis.* ○ *The changes have been introduced on a voluntary basis this year but will become compulsory next year.* أساس

2 the principle or reason which lies behind sth: *We made our decision on the basis of the reports which you sent us.* أساس

3 a starting point, from which sth can develop: *Her diaries formed the basis of the book she later wrote.* مُنْطَلَق ، أساس

bask /bɑːsk; *US* bæsk/ *verb* [I] to sit or lie in a place where you can enjoy the warmth: *The snake basked in the sunshine on the rock.* ○ (*figurative*) *He basked in the admiration of his fans.* يتشمّس ، ينْعَم بـ

basket /ˈbɑːskɪt; *US* ˈbæskɪt/ *noun* [C] a container for carrying or holding things, made of strips of light material such as cane or wire that are woven together: *a waste-paper basket* ○ *a shopping basket* ○ *a basket of shopping* (= one that is full of shopping) سلّة

IDM **put all your eggs in one basket** → EGG

basketball /ˈbɑːskɪtbɔːl; *US* ˈbæs-/ *noun* [C] a game for two teams of five players. There is a net (basket) fixed to a metal ring high up at each end of the court and the players try to throw a ball through the other team's net in order to score points (baskets). كرة السلّة

bass /beɪs/ *noun* **1** [C] the lowest male singing voice; a singer with this kind of voice الجهير: صوت غنائي

2 [U] the lowest part in music القراري ، الخفيض

3 [C] = DOUBLE BASS

4 [C] (*also* **bass guitar**) an electric guitar which plays very low notes جيتار خفيض النغمات

▸ **bass** *adj* producing a deep sound; connected with the lowest part in music: *a bass drum* ○ *Can you sing the bass part in this song?* ذو صوت خفيض ؛ قراري

bassoon /bəˈsuːn/ *noun* [C] a musical instrument of the woodwind family which makes a very deep sound زَمْخر: مزْمار بأنبوبين

bastard /ˈbɑːstəd; *US* ˈbæs-/ *noun* [C] (*slang*) (used as an insult) an unpleasant or cruel person ابن حرام ، نذل

bat[1] /bæt/ *noun* [C] a small animal, like a mouse with wings, which comes out and flies around at night وطواط ، خفّاش

bat[2] /bæt/ *noun* [C] a piece of wood for hitting the ball in sports such as table tennis, cricket or baseball: *a cricket bat* ➲ Look at **club**[2](2), **racket**[1] and **stick**[1](3). مِضرب

IDM **off your own bat** without anyone asking you or helping you من تلقاء نفسه ؛ بمفرده

▸ **bat** *verb* [I] (batting; batted) (used about one player or a whole team) to have a turn hitting the ball in sports such as cricket or baseball يأخذ دوره في ضرب كرة الكريكيت مثلاً

bat[3] /bæt/ *verb* (batting; batted)

IDM **not bat an eyelid** to show no reaction لا يطرف له جفن

batch /bætʃ/ *noun* [C] a number of things or people that belong together as a group: *The bus returned to the airport for the next batch of tourists.* دُفْعة

bated /ˈbeɪtɪd/ *adj*

IDM **with bated breath** excited or afraid, because you are waiting for sth to happen كاتم أنفاسه (خوفاً أو ترقّباً)

bath /bɑːθ; *US* bæθ/ *noun* (*pl.* **baths** /bɑːðz; *US* bæðz/) **1** [C] (*especially US* **bathtub**) a large container for water in which you sit to wash your body: *All the rooms have a private bath or shower.* ○ *Can you answer the phone? I'm in the bath!* حمّام ؛ حوض استحمام (بانيو)

2 [sing.] an act of washing the whole of your body when you sit or lie in a bath filled with water: *to have a bath* ○ *Would you prefer to take a bath or a shower?* ○ *bath oil* استحمام

3 baths [plural] (*Brit old-fashioned*) an indoor

public swimming pool or a building where you can take a bath مسبح وحمّامات
▶ **bath** *verb* **1** [T] to give sb a bath: *bath the baby* يحمّم
2 [I] (*old-fashioned*) to have a bath: *I prefer to bath in the mornings.* يستحمّ

bathe /beɪð/ *verb* **1** [I] to swim in the sea or in a lake or river يسبح
2 [T] to wash or put part of the body in water, often for medical reasons: *She bathed the wound with antiseptic.* يغسل
▶ **bathed** *adj* (not before a noun) covered with or surrounded by sth: *The room was bathed in light.* مغمور بِ
bathing *noun* [U] the act of swimming in the sea, etc. (not in a swimming pool): *Bathing is possible at a number of beaches along the coast.* سباحة (في البحر)

bathrobe /ˈbɑːθrəʊb; *US* bæθ-/ *noun* [C] = DRESSING GOWN

bathroom /ˈbɑːθruːm; -rʊm; *US* bæθ-/ *noun* [C] **1** a room where there is a bath and usually a washbasin (and sometimes a toilet) حمّام
2 (*US*) a room with a toilet ➲ Look at the note at **toilet**. مِرحاض

bathtub /ˈbɑːθtʌb; *US* bæθ-/ *noun* [C] = BATH (1)

baton /ˈbætɒn; *US* bəˈtɒn/ *noun* [C] **1** a short thin stick used by the conductor of an orchestra مِخصرة: عصا قائد الفرقة الموسيقية
2 = TRUNCHEON
3 a stick which a runner in a relay race passes to the next person in the team عصا يتبادلها المتنافسون في سباق

battalion /bəˈtæliən/ *noun* [C] a large unit of soldiers forming part of another larger unit in the army كتيبة

batter[1] /ˈbætə(r)/ *verb* [I,T] to hit sb/sth hard, many times: *The wind battered against the window.* ○ *He battered the door down.* ○ *High winds battered Britain again yesterday.* ○ *The parents were accused of battering the child* (= of hitting him/her often and violently). يضرب تكراراً و بقوة
▶ **battered** *adj* no longer looking new; damaged or out of shape: *a battered old hat* بالٍ : مهشّم

batter[2] /ˈbætə(r)/ *noun* [U] a mixture of flour, eggs and milk used to make pancakes, etc. or to cover food such as fish before frying عجينة سائلة

battery /ˈbætri/ *noun* [C] (*pl.* **batteries**) **1** a device which provides electricity for a torch, radio, car, etc: *He couldn't start the car because the battery was flat.* ❶ When a car battery is flat, you need to **recharge** it. بطارية
2 a large number of very small cages in which hens are kept: *a battery chicken* ➲ Look at **free-range**. مركز تفريخ الدجاج

battle /ˈbætl/ *noun* **1** [C,U] a fight, especially between armies in a war: *the battle of Trafalgar* ○ *They won the first battle but still they lost the war.* ○ *to die/be killed in battle* معركة
2 [C] a struggle of any kind: *After three years she lost her battle against cancer.* ○ *the battle against inflation* صراع ، كفاح
IDM **a losing battle** → LOSE
▶ **battle** *verb* [I] **battle (with/against sb/sth) (for sth)**; **battle (on)** to fight hard; to struggle: *Mark is battling with his maths homework.* ○ *The little boat battled against the wind.* ○ *The two brothers were battling for control of the family business.* ○ *Life is hard at the moment but we're battling on.* يصارع ، يتعارك مع

battlefield /ˈbætlfiːld/ (*also* **battleground** /ˈbætlgraʊnd/) *noun* [C] the place where a battle is fought ميدان القتال ، معترك

battleship /ˈbætlʃɪp/ *noun* [C] the largest type of ship used in war سفينة حربية

baulk (*also* **balk**) /bɔːk/ *verb* [I] **baulk (at sth)** to be unwilling to do or agree to sth because it seems difficult, dangerous or unpleasant: *She liked the flat but she baulked at paying so much for it.* يحجِم عن

bawl /bɔːl/ *verb* [I,T] to shout or cry loudly يزعَق

bay[1] /beɪ/ *noun* [C] a part of the coast where the land forms a curve inwards: *the Bay of Bengal* ○ *The harbour was in a sheltered bay.* خليج

bay[2] /beɪ/ *noun* [C] a part of a building, aircraft or area which has a particular purpose: *the loading bay of the factory* قسم (في مبنى) لغرض خاص

bay[3] /beɪ/ *noun*
IDM **hold/keep sb at bay** to stop sb who is chasing you from coming near; to stop sb/sth reaching you يمنع من الاقتراب ؛ يصدّ

bayonet /ˈbeɪənət/ *noun* [C] a knife which can be fixed to the end of a gun حربة البندقية

ˌbay ˈwindow *noun* [C] a window in a part of a room that sticks out from the wall of a house نافذة بارزة

bazaar /bəˈzɑː(r)/ *noun* [C] **1** (in Eastern countries) a market بازار ، سوق
2 a sale where the money that is made goes to charity: *a church bazaar* سوق خيريّة

BBC /ˌbiː biː ˈsiː/ *abbrev* British Broadcasting Corporation; one of the national radio and television companies in Britain: *a BBC documentary* ○ *watch a programme on BBC 1* هيئة الاذاعة البريطانية

BBQ *abbrev* = BARBECUE

BC (*especially US* **B.C.**) /ˌbiː ˈsiː/ *abbrev* before Christ; used in dates to show the number of years before the time it was traditionally believed that Jesus Christ was born: *300 BC.* ➲ Look at **BCE**. قبل الميلاد

BCE (*especially US* **B.C.E.**) /ˌbiː siː ˈiː/ *abbrev* before the Common Era (may be used instead of BC) قبل الميلاد

be[1] /bi; *strong form* biː/ *auxiliary verb* **1** (used to form the continuous tense of verbs): *You're sitting on my book.* ○ *We were listening to the radio.* ○ *Is he coming?* ○ *How long have we been waiting?* يوجد، هناك... (للدلالة على الاستمرار)

2 (used to form the passive): *This cheese is made in France.* ○ *We were taken to the police station.* ○ *The car has been repaired.* (لتكوين صيغة المجهول)

3 (used to show that sth must happen or that sth has been arranged): *You are to leave here at 10 o'clock at the latest.* ○ *They are to be married in June.* (للدلالة على وجوب شيء أو ترتيبه حدوثه)

4 (used to show that sth is possible but not very likely): *If they were to offer me the job, I'd probably take it.* (شيء ممكن و لكنه غير محتمل)

be² /bi; *strong form* biː/ *verb* **1** (used with *there* to say that sb/sth exists or is in in a particular place): *Is there a God?* ○ *I tried phoning them but there was no answer.* ○ *There are some people outside.* ○ *There are a lot of trees in our garden.* يوجد، هناك...

2 (used when you are naming people or things, describing them or giving more information about them): *That's Jane over there.* ○ *I'm Alan.* ○ *He's Italian. He's from Milan.* ○ *Sue is 18. She's at university.* ○ *He's a doctor.* ○ *What's that?* ○ *A lion is a mammal.* ○ *Where are the scissors?* ○ *'What colour is your car?' 'It's green.'* ○ *It's 6 o'clock.* ○ *It was Tuesday yesterday.* ○ *How much was your ticket?* ○ *The film was excellent.* ○ *She's very friendly.* (لتسمية الناس و الأشياء أو لوصفهم)

3 (only used in the perfect tenses) to go to a place (and return): *Have you ever been to Japan?* يزور (مع الفعل الماضي فقط)

Compare **has/have gone**: *Julia's gone to the doctor's* (= she hasn't returned yet). ○ *Julia's been to the doctor's today* (= she has returned).

IDM **be yourself** to act naturally: *Don't be nervous; just be yourself and the interview will be fine.* يتصرّف بشكل طبيعي

-to-be (in compounds) future: *his wife-to-be* المستقبلي ، في المستقبل

beach /biːtʃ/ *noun* [C] the piece of sandy or rocky land next to the sea: *a nice sandy beach* شاطئ

beacon /ˈbiːkən/ *noun* [C] a fire or light on a hill, a tower or near the coast, which is used as a signal منارة

bead /biːd/ *noun* [C] **1** a small ball of wood, glass or plastic with a hole in the middle for threading a string through خرَزة

2 beads [plural] a necklace made of beads عِقد من الخرَز

3 a drop of liquid: *There were beads of sweat on his forehead.* قَطْرة

beak /biːk/ *noun* [C] the hard pointed part of a bird's mouth منْقار

beaker /ˈbiːkə(r)/ *noun* [C] **1** a tall cup for drinks, sometimes without a handle كأس كبيرة

2 a glass container used in laboratories for pouring liquids قدح أو كوب كيميائي

beam /biːm/ *noun* [C] **1** a long piece of wood, metal, concrete, etc. that is used to support weight, e.g. in the floor or ceiling of a building دعامة

2 a line of light: *the beam of a car's headlights* ○ *a laser beam* شعاع

3 a happy smile ابتسامة مشرقة

▶ **beam** *verb* **1** [I] to send out light and warmth: *The sun beamed down on them.* يشعّ

2 [I] to smile happily: *Beaming with pleasure she stepped forward to receive her prize.* يبتسم بإشراق

3 [T] to broadcast a signal: *The programme was beamed live by satellite to many different countries.* يبثّ

bean /biːn/ *noun* [C] **1** the seeds or seed containers (pods) from a climbing plant which are eaten as vegetables: *broad beans* ○ *runner beans* ○ *soya beans* ○ *a tin of baked beans* (= beans in a tomato sauce) باقلاء: مثل الفول و الفاصولياء

2 similar seeds from other plants: *coffee beans* حَبّ

bear¹ /beə(r)/ *noun* [C] a large, heavy wild animal with thick fur: *a brown bear* ○ *a polar bear* دُبّ
➲ Look at **teddy bear**.

bear² /beə(r)/ *verb* [T] (*pt* **bore** /bɔː(r)/; *pp* **borne** /bɔːn/) **1** to support sth: *Twelve pillars bear the weight of the roof.* يحمل ، يسند

2 (*formal*) to carry sth: *The waiters came in bearing trays of food.* ○ (*figurative*) *In her position as Minister she bears a great responsibility.* ○ (*figurative*) *Customers will bear the full cost of the improvements.* يحمل ؛ يتحمّل

3 to suffer sth without complaining or giving in: *She bore her illness bravely.* ○ *The heat is too much to bear.* ○ *These figures won't bear close examination* (= when you look closely you will find mistakes). يتحمّل

4 (with *can/could* in negative sentences or in questions) to dislike strongly; to hate: *I can't bear spiders.* ○ *Joanne can't bear people who are late.* ○ *She can't bear waiting for people.* ○ *She can't bear to wait for people.* ○ *How can you bear to listen to that music?* يكره ، لا يطيق

5 (*formal*) to give birth to children: *She bore four children, all sons.* تنجب أو تلِد

A more common expression is 'She has had four children.' When you talk about a person's own birth you use 'to be born': *Robert was born in 1986.* ○ *The baby will be born in spring.*

6 to produce flowers or fruit: *The tree in our garden bears more apples than we can eat.* ○ (*figurative*) *Our plan is beginning to bear fruit – these are the first signs of success.* يحمل ؛ يثمر

7 to show the mark of sth: *The coins bear the date and the Queen's head on them.* ○ *He still bears the scars of his accident.* ○ *She bears a strong resemblance to her mother* (= she is very like her). يحمل علامة ؛ يشبه

8 (*formal*) to have a feeling: *I offended him once and he bore me a grudge for years.* يكِنّ شعوراً، يضمر

9 to turn or go in the direction that is mentioned: *At the crossroads, bear left.* ينعطف

IDM **bear the brunt of sth** to suffer the main

force of sth: *The west bore the brunt of the storm.* يتحمّل وطأة الشيء

bear in mind (that) to remember that: *You can have something to eat now but bear in mind that there'll be a big meal later.* يتذكّر، يضع في الاعتبار

bear/keep sb/sth in mind → MIND[1]

bear witness (to sth) to show evidence of sth: *The burning buildings and empty streets bore witness to a recent attack.* يشهد على

PHRV **bear sb/sth out** to show that sb is right or that sth is true: *The figures bear him out.* ○ *The figures bear out what he says.* يثبت صحته

bear with sb/sth to be patient with: *Bear with me – I won't be much longer.* يصبر على

bearable /ˈbeərəbl/ *adj* that you can bear (3): *It was extremely hot but the breeze made it more bearable.* ❶ The opposite is **unbearable**. محتمل

beard /bɪəd/ *noun* [C,U] the hair which grows on a man's cheeks and chin: *He's got a beard.* ○ *He's growing a beard.* ○ *He's had his beard shaved off.* لحية

▸ **bearded** *adj* with a beard ذو لحية

bearer /ˈbeərə(r)/ *noun* [C] a person who carries or brings sth: *I'm sorry to be the bearer of bad news.* الحامل؛ رسول

bearing /ˈbeərɪŋ/ *noun* **1** [U] **bearing on sth** relation or connection to the subject being discussed: *Her comments had no bearing on our decision.* علاقة

2 [C] a direction measured by a compass اتجاه

IDM **lose your bearings** to become confused about where you are يضلّ طريقه

beast /biːst/ *noun* [C] **1** (*formal*) an animal, especially a large one: *a wild beast* حيوان، بهيمة

2 (*informal*) an unpleasant or cruel person شخص جلف، متوحّش

▸ **beastly** *adj* (*informal*) very unpleasant فظيع، سيئ جداً؛ فظ

beat[1] /biːt/ *verb* (*pt* **beat**; *pp* **beaten**) **1** [I,T] to hit many times, usually very hard: *The man was beating the donkey with a stick.* ○ *The rain was beating on the roof of the car.* يضرب بشدة

2 [T] to mix quickly with a fork, etc: *Beat the eggs and sugar together.* يخفق (البيض مثلاً)

3 [I,T] to make a regular sound or movement: *Her heart beat faster as she ran to pick up her child.* ○ *We could hear the drums beating as the band marched towards us.* ○ *The bird beat its wings and tried to fly away.* ينبض؛ يضرب

4 [T] to defeat sb; to be better than sth: *He always beats me at tennis.* ○ *We're hoping to beat the world record.* ○ *You can't beat a nice cup of tea.* ○ (*informal*) *This question beats me* (= it is too difficult for me). يهزم؛ يفوق

IDM **beat about the bush** to talk about sth without mentioning the main point يدور حول الموضوع

beat time (to sth) to move sth (a stick, your foot or your hand) following the rhythm of a piece of music يحرك بتوافق مع الإيقاع الموسيقي

off the beaten track in a place where people do not often go بعيداً عن الأماكن المطروقة

PHRV **beat sb/sth off** to fight until sb/sth goes away: *The thieves tried to take his wallet but he beat them off.* يصدّ، يردّ

beat sb to sth to get somewhere or do sth before sb else: *She beat me back to the house.* ○ *I wanted to ring him first but Sheila beat me to it.* يسبق

beat sb up to attack sb by hitting or kicking يضرب، يركل

▸ **beating** *noun* [C] **1** a punishment that you give to sb by hitting him/her: *The boys got a beating when they were caught stealing.* ضرب، "علقة"، "قتلة"

2 a defeat هزيمة

IDM **take a lot of/some beating** to be so good that it would be difficult to find sth better: *Mary's cooking takes some beating.* تصعُب منافسته

beat[2] /biːt/ *noun* **1** [C] a single stroke or blow that comes at regular intervals in a series; the sound it makes: *a heartbeat* ○ *the beat of the drums* خفقة، دقة

2 [sing.] the strong rhythm that a piece of (especially pop) music has إيقاع موسيقي قوي

3 [sing.] the route along which a policeman or woman regularly walks: *Having more police officers on the beat helps reduce crime.* منطقة تجوال رجل البوليس، دورية

beautician /bjuːˈtɪʃn/ *noun* [C] a person whose job is to improve the way people look, e.g. with beauty treatments and make-up خبير تجميل

beautiful /ˈbjuːtɪfl/ *adj* lovely; attractive; giving pleasure to the senses: *The view from the top of the hill was really beautiful.* ○ *What a beautiful day – the weather's perfect!* ○ *He has a beautiful voice.* ○ *A beautiful perfume filled the air.* ○ *a beautiful woman* جميل؛ جذاب؛ ممتع

> **Beautiful** is usually used for women and girls. It is stronger than **pretty**, which is also used of women and girls only. Men are described as **handsome** or **good-looking**.

▸ **beautifully** /-fli/ *adv*: *He plays the piano beautifully.* ○ *She was beautifully dressed.* على نحو جميل؛ بمهارة

beauty /ˈbjuːti/ *noun* (*pl.* **beauties**) **1** [U] the quality which gives pleasure to the senses; the state of being beautiful: *Thousands of tourists are attracted to Cornwall by the beauty of its coast.* ○ *Brahms wrote music of great beauty.* جمال

2 [C] a beautiful woman: *She grew up to be a beauty.* حسناء

3 [C] a particularly good example of sth: *Look at this tomato – it's a beauty!* نموذج رائع

ˈbeauty spot *noun* [C] a place which is famous for its attractive scenery بقعة اشتهرت بجمالها الطبيعي

beaver /ˈbiːvə(r)/ *noun* [C] an animal with brown fur, a long, broad tail and sharp teeth, with which it cuts branches to make dams across rivers قندس

became *pt* of BECOME

because /bɪˈkɒz; *US* -kɔːz/ *conj* for the reason

that: *They didn't go for a walk because it was raining.* لأن
▸ **because of** *prep* by reason of, as a result of: *They didn't go for a walk because of the rain.* بسبب

beck /bek/ *noun*
IDM **at sb's beck and call** always ready to obey sb's orders طوع إشارته

beckon /ˈbekən/ *verb* [I,T] to show sb (often with a movement of your finger or hand) that you want him/her to come closer: *She beckoned me over to speak to her.* يومئ له بالاقتراب

become /bɪˈkʌm/ *verb* [I] (*pt* **became** /bɪˈkeɪm/; *pp* **become**) to begin to be sth: *Mr Saito became Chairman in 2002.* ○ *She wants to become a pilot.* ○ *They became friends.* ○ *She became nervous as the exam date came closer.* ○ *He is becoming more like you every day.* ○ *It became clear that she wanted to stay.* يصبح

> **Get** is also used with adjectives in this sense: *She got nervous as the exam date came closer.* ○ *He's getting more like you every day.* It is very common in conversation and is less formal than **become**.

PHR V **become of sb/sth** to happen to sb/sth: *What became of Eileen? – I haven't seen her for years!* يحدث له

bed[1] /bed/ *noun* **1** [C,U] a piece of furniture that you lie on when you sleep: *a single/double bed* ○ *twin beds* (= two single beds in one room) ○ *The children sleep in bunk beds.* ○ *to make a bed* (= to arrange the sheets, etc. so that the bed is tidy and ready for sb to sleep in) ○ *What time do you usually go to bed?* ○ *When he rang I was already in bed.* ○ *It's late. It's time for bed.* ○ *to get into/out of bed* سرير ، فراش
2 [C] the ground at the bottom of a river or the sea قاع
3 = FLOWER BED

IDM **bed and breakfast** (*abbr* **B and B**; **b and b**) accommodation in a house or small hotel that consists of a room for the night and breakfast; a place that provides this: *Bed and breakfast costs £23 per night.* ○ *We stayed in a nice bed and breakfast near Cork.* منامة وفطور في نزل، استراحة
go to bed with sb (*informal*) to have sex with sb يضاجع ، يمارس الجنس

bed[2] /bed/ *verb* [T] (be**dd**ing; be**dd**ed) to place sth firmly in or on sth يغرس ، يدفن ، يثبّت
PHR V **bed down** to make yourself comfortable and sleep somewhere: *We couldn't find a hotel so we bedded down for the night in the back of the van.* يفترش
▸ **-bedded** (in compounds) having the stated type or number of beds: *a twin-bedded room* ○ *a three-bedded room* (للتعبير عن عدد الاسرة)
bedding *noun* [U] the sheets, etc. that are used on a bed, sometimes including the mattress أغطية و شراشف السرير

bedclothes /ˈbedkləʊðz/ *noun* [plural] the sheets, etc. that you use on a bed أغطية وشراشف السرير

bedroom /ˈbedruːm; -rʊm/ *noun* [C] a room which is used for sleeping in: *You can sleep in the spare bedroom.* حجرة النوم

bedside /ˈbedsaɪd/ *noun* [sing.] the area that is next to a bed: *She sat at his bedside all night long.* ○ *a bedside table* جانب السرير

bedsit /ˈbedsɪt/ (*also* **bedsitter** /ˈbedsɪtə(r)/) *noun* [C] (*Brit*) a room which is used for both living and sleeping in غرفة مشتركة للجلوس والنوم

bedspread /ˈbedspred/ *noun* [C] an attractive cover for a bed that you put on top of the sheets and blankets غطاء السرير

bedtime /ˈbedtaɪm/ *noun* [C,U] the time that you normally go to bed وقت النوم

bee /biː/ *noun* [C] a black and yellow striped in-

beds

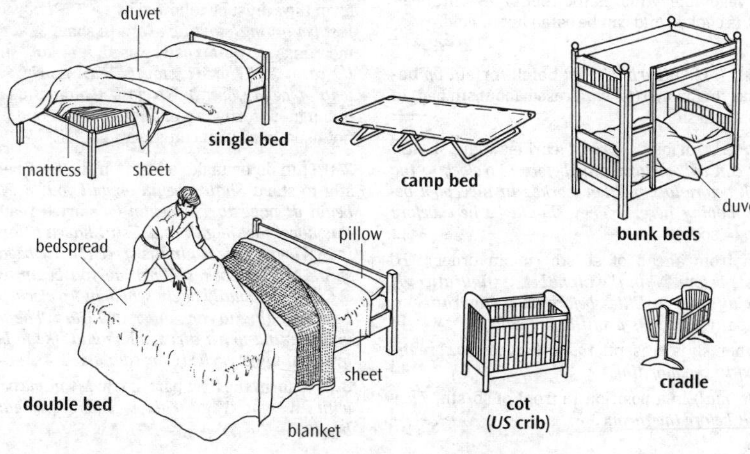

sect that lives in large groups and that makes honey نحلة

A large number of bees together is a **swarm**. Bees **buzz** or **hum** when they make a noise. They may **sting** if they are angry.

beech /biːtʃ/ (*also* **'beech tree**) *noun* [C,U] a large tree with a smooth trunk that has small three-sided nuts شجر الزّان

⚷ **beef** /biːf/ *noun* [U] the meat of a cow: *a slice of roast beef* ➲ Look at the note at **meat**. لحم بقر

beefburger /'biːfbɜːgə(r)/ *noun* [C] minced beef in a flat round shape, often served in a bread roll ➲ Look at **hamburger**. قرص من اللحم البقري المفروم

beehive /'biːhaɪv/ (*also* **hive**) *noun* [C] a type of box that people use for keeping bees in خلية النحل

been /biːn/ *pp* of BE, GO

Been is used as the past participle of both **be** and **go**: *I've never been seriously ill.* ○ *I've never been to Lisbon.* **Gone** is also a past participle of **go**. Note the difference in meaning: *They've been to the cinema* (= They went and have come back). ○ *They've gone to the cinema* (= They went and have not yet come back).

beep /biːp/ *noun* [C] a short high noise, e.g. made by the horn of a car تزمير ، صوت عالٍ و قصير
▶ **beep** *verb* [I] to make a beep يزمّر ، يصفّر

⚷ **beer** /bɪə(r)/ *noun* **1** [U] a type of alcoholic drink that is made from grain بيرة ، جعَة
2 [C] a type or glass of beer بيرة ، كأس من البيرة

beet /biːt/ *noun* [U,C] a type of plant with a root which is used for feeding animals or for making sugar: *sugar beet* شمندر سكري، بَنْجر

beetle /'biːtl/ *noun* [C] an insect that has hard coverings for its wings and often a black shiny body. There are many different types of beetle. خُنْفُساء

beetroot /'biːtruːt/ (*US* **beet**) *noun* [C,U] a dark red vegetable which is the root of a plant. Beetroot is cooked and can be eaten hot or cold. شمندر ، بَنْجر

befall /bɪ'fɔːl/ *verb* [I,T] (*pt* **befell** /bɪ'fel/; *pp* **befallen** /bɪ'fɔːlən/) (*formal*) (used about sth bad) to happen to sb يصيب

⚷ **before**[1] /bɪ'fɔː(r)/ *prep* **1** earlier than sb/sth: *You can call me any time before 10 o'clock.* ○ *the week before last* ○ *Ellen worked in Liverpool before moving here.* ○ *They should be here before long* (= soon). قبل
2 in front/ahead of sb/sth (in an order): *'H' comes before 'N' in the alphabet.* ○ (*figurative*) *A very difficult task lies before us.* ○ (*figurative*) *a company that puts profit before safety* قبل : أمام
3 when sb is present: *You will appear before the court in the morning.* أمام
4 (*formal*) in a position in front of sb/sth: *They knelt before the throne.* أمام : في حضرة

⚷ **before**[2] /bɪ'fɔː(r)/ *conj* **1** earlier than the time that: *Turn the lights off before you leave.* قبل
2 (*formal*) rather than: *I'd die before I apologized to him!* أفضل من

⚷ **before**[3] /bɪ'fɔː(r)/ *adv* at an earlier time: *I think we've met somewhere before.* ○ *It was fine yesterday but it rained the day before.* قبلاً ، قبل ذلك

beforehand /bɪ'fɔːhænd/ *adv* at an earlier time than sth: *We prepared most of the food for the party beforehand.* سلفاً ، مُقدّماً

befriend /bɪ'frend/ *verb* [T] (*formal*) to act as a friend to sb; to be kind to sb يصادق

beg /beg/ *verb* [I,T] (begging; begged) **1 beg (for) sth (from/of sb)** to ask sb for food, money, etc., e.g. because you are very poor: *There are people begging for food in the streets of London.* ○ *She begged some money for her children's clothes.* يشحَذ ، يتسوّل
2 beg sth (of sb); **beg (sb) for sth** to ask sb for sth strongly, or with great emotion: *He begged for forgiveness.* ○ *Can I beg a favour of you?* ○ *We begged him to let the children go free.* يتوسّل ، يرجو

IDM **I beg your pardon 1** I'm sorry: *I beg your pardon. I picked up your bag by mistake.* أعْتَذِر ، آسف
2 (used for asking sb to repeat sth because you did not hear it properly) آسف، لم أسمعك جيداً

began *pt* of BEGIN

beggar /'begə(r)/ *noun* [C] a person who lives by asking people for money, food, etc. on the streets شحّاذ ، متسوّل

⚷ **begin** /bɪ'gɪn/ *verb* (*pres part* **beginning**; *pt* **began** /bɪ'gæn/; *pp* **begun** /bɪ'gʌn/) **1** [I] to take place from a particular time; to start: *What time does the concert begin?* يبدأ

Begin and **start** are very similar in meaning but **start** is more often used in informal speech. They can be followed by *to* or by the *-ing* form of a verb: *The baby began/started to cry/crying.* When **begin** or **start** are themselves in the *-ing* form they must be followed by *to*: *The baby was just beginning/starting to cry.* In some meanings only **start** can be used: *I couldn't start the car.* ○ *We'll have to start* (= leave) *early if we want to be in Dover by 8 o'clock.* **Commence** is much more formal than **begin** or **start** and is not usually used in conversation.

2 [I,T] to do or make a start on the first part of sth; to start: *Shall I begin or will you?* ○ *Please begin at page 10.* ○ *I began* (= started reading) *this novel last month and I still haven't finished it.* ○ *When did he begin his speech?* ○ *He began to speak at 11 o'clock.* ○ *When do you begin work?* ○ *Children usually begin school at 9 o'clock.* ○ *We began writing to each other in 1970.* ○ *The paint is beginning to get dirty.* ○ *I should like to begin by thanking everybody for coming.* يشرع : يبدأ
3 [I] to form the first part of sth: *My name begins with 'W' not 'V'.* ○ *This is where our garden begins.* يبدأ

IDM **to begin with 1** (used for giving your first reason for sth): *We can't possibly go. To begin with it's too far and we can't afford it either.* السبب الأول، باديء ذي بدء

2 at first: *To begin with they were very happy.* في البداية

▸ **beginner** *noun* [C] a person who has just begun learning sth مبتدئ

beginning *noun* [C,U] the first part of sth; the time when or place where sth starts: *The beginning of the book is quite interesting but it gets boring towards the end.* ○ *I've read the article from beginning to end.* ○ *We're going away at the beginning of the school holidays.* بداية

begonia /bɪˈɡəʊniə/ *noun* [C] a garden plant with brightly coloured leaves and flowers بغونية

begrudge /bɪˈɡrʌdʒ/ *verb* [T] **begrudge (sb) sth 1** to feel angry or upset because sb has sth that you think that he/she does not deserve: *He's worked hard. I don't begrudge him his success.* يحسده ، يستكثر عليه

2 to be unwilling to give sb sth يضِنّ عليه بِـ

behalf /bɪˈhɑːf; *US* -ˈhæf/ *noun*

IDM **on behalf of sb; on sb's behalf** for sb; as the representative of sb: *Mary couldn't be present so her husband accepted the prize on her behalf.* ○ *I should like to thank you all on behalf of my colleagues and myself.* نيابةً عن

behave /bɪˈheɪv/ *verb* **1** [I] **behave well, badly, etc. (towards sb)** to act in a particular way: *Don't you think that Ellen has been behaving very strangely recently?* ○ *I think you behaved very badly towards your father.* ○ *He behaves as if he was the boss.* يتصرّف ، يسلك

2 [I,T] **behave (yourself)** to act in the correct or proper way: *The children behaved themselves while we were out.* يتصرّف بأدب

▸ **-behaved** (in compounds) behaving in a particular way: *a well-behaved child* (يتصرّف بطريقة معينة)

behaviour (*US* **behavior**) /bɪˈheɪvjə(r)/ *noun* [U] the way that you act or behave: *Her behaviour has been very strange recently.* ○ *'I will not tolerate this sort of behaviour', said the teacher.* تصرّف ، سلوك

behind[1] /bɪˈhaɪnd/ *prep* **1** in, at or to the back of sb/sth: *I was sitting behind a very tall woman and I couldn't see anything at all.* ○ *There's a small garden behind the house.* ○ *The sun went behind a cloud.* ○ *Look behind you before you drive off.* ○ (*figurative*) *It's time you put your problems behind you* (= forgot about them). خلف

2 later or less good than sb/sth: *The train is twenty minutes behind schedule.* ○ *Jane is behind the rest of the class in maths.* متأخّر: متخلف

3 supporting or agreeing with sb/sth: *Most people are behind the President's policies.* وراء

4 causing or starting sth: *What is the reason behind his sudden change of opinion?* يسبّب ؛ وراء

behind[2] /bɪˈhaɪnd/ *adv* **1** in, at or to the back of sb/sth: *You go on ahead. I'll follow on behind.* ○ *Try not to look behind.* ○ *He ran off but the police were close behind.* وراءه ؛ إلى الوراء

2 in the place where sb/sth is or was: *Oh no! I've left the tickets behind* (= at home). حيث كان الشخص

3 behind (in/with sth) later or less good than sb/sth: *We are a month behind with the rent.* ○ *Arsenal were behind at half-time.* ➲ Look at **ahead**. متخلّف

behind[3] /bɪˈhaɪnd/ *noun* [C] (*informal*) the part of your body that you sit on ➲ Look at **bottom** and **buttocks**. مؤخّرة

beige /beɪʒ/ *adj, noun* [U] (of) a light-brown colour بيج: لون رملي

being /ˈbiːɪŋ/ *noun* **1** [U] the state of existing: *When did the organization come into being?* (= when did it start) وجود

2 [C] a living person or thing: *a human being* ○ *a strange being from another planet* ➲ Look also at **be**. كائن حي

belated /bɪˈleɪtɪd/ *adj* coming late: *a belated apology* متأخّر

▸ **belatedly** *adv*: *They have realized, rather belatedly, that they have made a big mistake.* متأخّراً

belch /beltʃ/ *verb* **1** [I] to let gas out from your stomach through your mouth with a sudden noise, e.g. because you have eaten a lot يتجشأ

2 [T] to send out smoke, etc: *The volcano belched smoke and ashes.* يقذف بِـ، يطلق دخاناً ونحوه

▸ **belch** *noun* [C]: *Julia gave a loud belch.* جشأة

belie /bɪˈlaɪ/ *verb* [T] (*pres part* **belying**; *3rd pers sing pres* **belies**; *pt, pp* **belied**) to give a false or untrue idea of sth: *His smiling face belied his true feelings.* يكذّب ، يخالف

belief /bɪˈliːf/ *noun* (*pl.* **beliefs**) **1** [sing., U] **belief in sb/sth** a feeling that sb/sth is true, good or right, or that sb/sth really exists: *She has lost her belief in God.* ○ *The amount of money we spend has increased beyond belief* (= very much). ➲ Look at **disbelief**. اعتقاد ؛ تصوّر

2 [sing., U] **belief that...** (*formal*) something you accept as true; what you believe: *It's my belief that people are basically good.* ○ *There is a general belief that things will soon get better.* ○ *The man was killed in the mistaken belief that he was a member of a terrorist organization.* ○ *Contrary to popular belief* (= in spite of what many people think) *the North of the country is not poorer than the South.* اعتقاد ؛ إيمان

3 [C] an idea about religion, politics, etc: *Divorce is contrary to their religious beliefs.* معتقد

believe /bɪˈliːv/ *verb* (not used in the continuous forms) **1** [T] to feel sure that sth is true or that sb is telling the truth: *He said he hadn't taken any money but I didn't believe him.* ○ *Nobody believes a word she says.* ○ *When they said they were getting married, I just couldn't believe it.* يصدّق

2 [T] **believe (that)...** to think or suppose: *I believe they have moved to Peterborough.* ○ *Ian*

has joined the army, I believe. ○ *The escaped prisoner is believed to be in this area.* يعتقد ، يظنّ

3 [I] to have religious faith يعتقد ، يؤمن

IDM **believe it or not** it may be surprising but it is true: *Believe it or not, English food can sometimes be quite good.* قد لا تصدّق و لكنه صحيح

give sb to believe/understand (that) → GIVE[1]

PHRV **believe in sb/sth** to be sure that sb/sth exists: *Do you believe in God?* ○ *Most young children believe in Father Christmas.* يؤمن

believe in sb/sth; believe in doing sth to think that sb/sth is good or right: *I believe in the value of a good education.* ○ *He doesn't believe in going by car if he can walk.* يؤمن ؛ يحبِّذ

▶ **believable** /-əbl/ *adj* that can be believed ➲ Look at **unbelievable**. قابل للتصديق

believer *noun* [C] a person who has religious faith مؤمن

IDM **be a (great/firm) believer in sth** to think that sth is good or right: *He is a great believer in getting things done on time.* يؤمن بِ، (يكون) من الأنصار

belittle /bɪ'lɪtl/ *verb* [T] to make sb/sth seem unimportant or not very good يقلِّل من شانه

⚷ **bell** /bel/ *noun* [C] **1** a hollow metal object, usually shaped like a cup, that makes a ringing sound when it is hit: *the sound of church bells* جَرَس ، ناقوس

2 an object that makes a ringing sound; the sound that it makes, often used as a signal: *a bicycle bell* ○ *a doorbell* ○ *Ring the bell and see if they're in.* ○ *There's the bell for the end of the lesson.* جرس ؛ صوت الجرس

IDM **ring a bell** → RING[2]

bellow /'beləʊ/ *verb* **1** [I] to make a deep low sound, like a bull يخور ، يجأر

2 [I,T] to shout in a loud deep voice يجأر ؛ يصرخ

▶ **bellow** *noun* [C] خوار ؛ صرخة

belly /'beli/ *noun* [C] (*pl.* **bellies**) the stomach or the part of the body between the chest and the legs: *a full/empty belly* بَطن

⚷ **belong** /bɪ'lɒŋ; *US* -lɔːŋ/ *verb* [I] **1 belong to sb** to be owned by sb: *Who does this pen belong to?* ○ *Don't take anything that doesn't belong to you.* يخص

2 belong to sth to be a member of a group or organization: *Do you belong to any political party?* ينتمي

3 to have a proper or usual place: *The plates belong in the cupboard over there.* ○ *I don't think this paragraph really belongs here.* ○ *It took quite a long time before we felt we belonged in the village* (= until we felt at home). يوضع عادة في ؛ يلائم

▶ **belongings** *noun* [plural] the things that you own that can be moved, i.e. not land and buildings: *The tourists lost all their belongings in the hotel fire.* أمتعة ، ممتلكات

beloved /bɪ'lʌvɪd; bɪ'lʌvd/ *adj* (*formal*) much loved: *They had always intended to return to their beloved Ireland.* ❶ When 'beloved' comes before a noun, the pronunciation is /bɪ'lʌvɪd/. محبوب ، معشوق

⚷ **below** /bɪ'ləʊ/ *prep* at or to a lower position or level than sb/sth: *Do not write below this line.* ○ *It hurts here – just below my knee.* ○ *The temperature fell below freezing during the night.* ○ *Her marks in the exam were below average.* ○ *A sergeant in the police force is below an inspector.* ➲ Look at the note at **under**. تحت

▶ **below** *adv* at or to a lower position or level: *I don't live on the top floor. I live on the floor below.* ○ *For further explanation of this point, please see below* (= a later part of the book, etc.). ○ *temperatures of 30° and below* تحت ؛ أدناه ؛ أدنى

⚷ **belt** /belt/ *noun* [C] **1** a thin piece of cloth, leather, etc. that you wear around your waist: *I've lost the belt for this dress.* ○ *I need a belt to keep these trousers up.* ○ *to do up/undo a belt* ➲ Look at **seat belt**. حِزام ، زنّار

2 a long strip of rubber, etc. in a circle, that is used for carrying things or for making parts of a machine move: *The suitcases were carried round on a conveyor belt.* ○ *the fan belt of a car* سَيْر متحرك

3 an area of land that has a particular quality: *the Green Belt around London* (= an area of countryside where you are not allowed to build houses, factories, etc.) حِزام (زراعي مثلاً) ؛ منطقة خاصة

IDM **below the belt** (*informal*) unkind or not fair: *That remark was rather below the belt.* قاسٍ ؛ جائر

under your belt (*informal*) that you have already done or achieved: *She's already got four tournament wins under her belt.* شيء تم إنجازه

▶ **belt** *verb* [T] (*informal*) **1** to hit sb hard يضرب بشدّة

2 to run or move very fast يسرع

PHRV **belt up 1** to fasten your seat belt in a car يربط حزام السيارة

2 (*informal*) to be quiet: *Belt up! I can't think with all this noise.* يسكت

bemused /bɪ'mjuːzd/ *adj* not knowing what to think or do; confused or puzzled حائر ، مشوّش ؛ مذهول

bench /bentʃ/ *noun* [C] **1** a long wooden or metal seat for two or more people, often outdoors: *a park bench* مقعد طويل

2 (*Brit*) (in the British parliament) the seats where a particular group of Members of Parliament sit: *the Government front bench* ○ *the Labour benches* مقعد (برلماني)

3 a long narrow table that people work at, e.g. in a factory or laboratory: *a carpenter's bench* طاولة الورشة ؛ دكّة (النجار)

benchmark /'bentʃmɑːk/ *noun* [C] a standard that other things can be compared to: *These new safety features set a benchmark for other manufacturers to follow.* مقياس، (مثال يحتذى به)

⚷ **bend**[1] /bend/ *verb* (*pt, pp* **bent** /bent/) **1** [T] to make sth that was straight into a curved shape; to make sth that was upright lean forward: *Bend your legs when you pick up something heavy.* ○ *to* *bend a piece of wire into an S shape* ○ *She sat with her head bent forward, thinking about what he had said.* يثني ، يحني ، يلوي

2 [I] to be or become curved: *The road bends to the left here.* ينثني ، يلتوي

3 [I] to move your body forwards and downwards: *He bent down to tie up his shoelaces.* ○ *She had to bend forward to hear what the child was saying.* ينحني

IDM bend the rules to change the rules a little in order to allow sth for a particular reason يكيِّف الأنظمة قليلاً

bend² /bend/ *noun* [C] a curve or turn, e.g. in a road: *a sharp bend in the road* مُنعطف

IDM round the bend (*informal*) mad; crazy: *His behaviour is driving me round the bend* (= annoying me very much). مجنون ، مخبَّل

beneath /bɪˈniːθ/ *prep* **1** in, at or to a lower position than sb/sth; under: *The ship disappeared beneath the waves.* ○ *I love to feel the grass beneath my feet again.* ○ *He seemed a nice person but there was a lot of anger beneath the surface.* ➲ Look at the note at **under**. تحت

2 not good enough for sb: *She felt that washing up for other people was beneath her.* دون مرتبته

▸ **beneath** *adv* (*formal*) in, at or to a lower position: *From the top of the tower we gazed down on the city beneath.* تحت

benefactor /ˈbenɪfæktə(r)/ *noun* [C] a person who helps or gives money to a person or an organization محْسن

beneficial /ˌbenɪˈfɪʃl/ *adj* **beneficial (to sb/sth)** having a good or useful effect: *a beneficial effect/influence on sb/sth* مفيد

benefit /ˈbenɪfɪt/ *noun* **1** [U] the advantage or good or useful effect of sth: *Most parents want to give their children the benefit of a good education.* ○ *a change in the law would be to everyone's benefit* ○ *I can't see the benefit of doing things this way.* فائدة ، منفعة

2 [C] a thing that has a good or useful effect: *the benefits of modern technology* منفعة

3 [U] money that the government gives to people who are ill, poor, unemployed, etc: *I'm not entitled to unemployment benefit.* إعانة

IDM for sb's benefit especially to help, please, etc. sb: *For the benefit of the newcomers, I will explain again what we are planning to do.* لمصلحة ، لفائدة

give sb the benefit of the doubt to believe that what sb says is true because there is no clear proof that it is not يبرِّئه أو يصدِّقه لعدم توفّر البراهين ضدّه

▸ **benefit** *verb* (*pt, pp* **benefited**; *US also* **benefitted**) **1** [T] to have a good or useful effect: *The new tax laws will benefit small businesses.* ينفع ، يفيد

2 benefit (from sth) [I] to receive an advantage from sth: *We've certainly benefited from the changes in the law.* يستفيد

benevolent /bəˈnevələnt/ *adj* (*formal*) kind, friendly and helpful to others محْسِن

▸ **benevolence** /bəˈnevələns/ *noun* [U] إحسان

benign /bɪˈnaɪn/ *adj* **1** (used about people) kind or gentle لطيف، طيِّب

2 (used about a disease, etc.) not causing death: *a benign tumour* ➲ Look at **malignant**. (ورم) غير خبيث

bent¹ *pt, pp* of BEND¹

bent² /bent/ *adj* **1** not straight: *Do this exercise with your knees bent.* ○ *This knife is bent.* ○ *It was so funny we were bent double with laughter.* منحني أو مقوّس الظهر

2 (*slang*) not honest: *a bent policeman* غير نزيه

3 bent on sth/on doing sth wanting to do sth very much, so that you cannot accept not doing it: *They seem bent on moving house, whatever the difficulties.* مصمِّم على

bent³ /bent/ *noun* [C, usually sing.] **a bent for sth/doing sth** a natural skill at sth or interest in sth: *She has a bent for music.* ميل ؛ موهبة

bequeath /bɪˈkwiːð/ *verb* [T] (*formal*) **bequeath sth (to sb)** to arrange for sth to be given to sb after you have died: *He bequeathed £1 000 to his favourite charity.* ℹ **Leave** is a more common word. يورِّث ، يوصي بِ

bequest /bɪˈkwest/ *noun* [C] (*formal*) something that you arrange to be given to sb after you have died: *He left a bequest to each of his grandchildren.* تَرِكة ، إرث

bereaved /bɪˈriːvd/ *adj* having had a relative or close friend die فاقد (شخصاً عزيزاً) ، مفجوع

▸ **the bereaved** *noun* [C] a person whose relative or close friend has died recently ℹ The plural is also **the bereaved**. المصاب ، المفجوع

bereavement *noun* (*formal*) **1** [U] the state of being bereaved فجيعة (بفقد شخص عزيز)

2 [C] the death of a relative or close friend: *There has been a bereavement in the family.* فقدان شخص عزيز

beret /ˈbereɪ; *US* bəˈreɪ/ *noun* [C] a soft flat round hat "بيْريه"، طاقية صوف

berry /ˈberi/ *noun* [C] (*pl.* **berries**) a small soft fruit with seeds: *Those berries are poisonous.* ○ *a raspberry* توت

berth /bɜːθ/ *noun* [C] **1** a place for sleeping on a ship or train: *a cabin with four berths* سرير في باخرة أو قطار

2 a place where a ship can be tied up in a harbour مَرْسى

beside /bɪˈsaɪd/ *prep* at the side of, or next to sb/sth: *Come and sit beside me.* ○ *He kept his bag close beside him at all times.* قرب ، جانب

IDM beside the point not connected with the subject you are discussing لا علاقة له بالموضوع

beside yourself (with sth) not able to control yourself because of a very strong emotion: *Emily was almost beside herself with grief.* يفقد السيطرة على نفسه

besides /bɪˈsaɪdz/ *prep* in addition to or as well

as sb/sth: *There will be six people coming, besides you and David.* علاوة على
▸ **besides** *adv* in addition; also: *I thought the hotel was too expensive. Besides, it was very close to the main road.* علاوة على ذلك ، أيضاً

besiege /bɪˈsiːdʒ/ *verb* [T] to surround a place with an army: *(figurative) The actor was besieged by fans and reporters.* يحاصر

best[1] /best/ *adj* (the superlative of *good*) of the highest quality or level; most suitable: *Who's your best friend?* ○ *His latest book is by far his best.* ○ *It's best to arrive early if you want a good seat.* ○ *Who in the class is best at maths?* ○ *What's the best way to get to York from here?* ○ *The best thing to do is to forget all about it.* أفضل
IDM **your best bet** (*informal*) the best thing for you to do in a particular situation: *There's nowhere to park in the city centre. Your best bet is to go in by bus.* أفضل ما يمكن أن تفعله
the best/better part of sth → PART[1]

best[2] /best/ *adv* (the superlative of *well*) **1** in the most excellent way: *He works best in the morning.* أفضل ما يكون
2 to the greatest degree; most: *Which of these dresses do you like best?* ○ *one of Britain's best-loved TV stars* ○ *Next week would suit me best.* ○ *Ask Peter. He'll know best what to do.* أعظم
IDM **as best you can** as well as you can even if it is not perfectly على قدر المستطاع

best[3] /best/ *noun* [sing.] **1** something that is of the highest quality or level: *When you pay that much for a meal you expect the best.* ○ *I'm not in the best of health.* ○ *They are the best of friends.* ○ *The best we can hope for is that the situation doesn't get any worse.* ➲ Look at **second-best**. الأفضل
2 the best [with sing. or pl. verb] a person that is best: *Even the best of us make mistakes sometimes.* الأفضل ، أفضل شخص
IDM **all the best** (*informal*) (used when you are saying goodbye to sb and wishing him/her success): *All the best! Keep in touch, won't you?* مع السلامة و أتمنى لك التوفيق
at best if everything is as favourable as possible; taking the most hopeful view: *We won't be able to deliver the goods before March, or, at best, the last week in February.* في أحسن الأحوال
at its/your best in its/your best state or condition: *This is an example of Beckett's work at its best.* ○ *No one is at their best first thing in the morning.* في أحسن حالاته
be (all) for the best to be good in the end even if it does not seem good at first: *He didn't go to London after all, but as it turned out it was all for the best* (= because he was able to do something that was better). يكون خيراً له في النهاية
bring out the best/worst in sb to show sb's best/worst qualities: *The crisis really brought out the best in Tony.* يظهر أفضل/أسوأ ما في الشخص
do/try your best to do all or the most that you can: *It doesn't matter whether you win or not. The important thing is doing your best.* يبذل قصارى جهده
look your best to look as beautiful or attractive as possible يبدو بأجمل صورة
make the best of sth/a bad job to accept a difficult situation and try to be as happy as possible يحاول الانتفاع من وضع سيِّئ

ˌ**best ˈman** *noun* [C] a man who helps and supports the bridegroom at his wedding ➲ Look at the note at **wedding**. وكيل العريس

ˌ**best-ˈseller** *noun* [C] a book or other product that has been bought by large numbers of people أروج (كتاب مثلاً)

ˌ**best-ˈselling** *adj* (not *before* a noun) very popular: *Frederick Forsyth has written many best-selling novels.* رائج جداً

bet /bet/ *verb* [I,T] (*pres part* **betting**; *pt, pp* **bet** or **betted**) **bet (sth) (on sth)** to risk some money on the result of sth (e.g. a horse race). If you are wrong about the result, you have to pay some money: *I bet him £10 he couldn't stop smoking for a week.* يراهن
IDM **I bet (that)...** (*informal*) I'm sure that...: *I bet he arrives late – he always does.* أراهن أنّ ، أنا متأكد أنّ
you bet (*informal*) a way of saying, 'Yes, of course!': *'Are you coming too?' 'You bet.'* بالطبع
▸ **bet** *noun* [C] **1** an act of betting: *to win/lose a bet* رِهان
2 an opinion: *My bet is that he's missed the train.* رأي
IDM **your best bet** → BEST[1]
hedge your bets → HEDGE

betray /bɪˈtreɪ/ *verb* [T] **1** to be disloyal to a person or thing; to harm a person or organization that trusts you: *By taking the money he had betrayed the trust that she had put in him.* ○ *When parents get divorced the children often feel betrayed.* ○ *to betray your country* يغدر بـ؛ يخون
2 to make facts about sb/sth known to an enemy; to make a secret known: *She betrayed all the members of the group to the secret police.* ○ *He refused to betray the information.* يكشف؛ يفشي سراً
3 to show a feeling or quality that you would like to keep hidden: *Her steady voice did not betray the emotion she was feeling.* يفضح
▸ **betrayal** /bɪˈtreɪəl/ *noun* [C,U] the act of betraying sb/sth خيانة، غدر

better[1] /ˈbetə(r)/ *adj* **1** (the comparative of *good*) **better (than sth)** of a higher quality or level or more suitable: *I think her second novel was much better than her first.* ○ *He's better at chemistry than physics.* ○ *It's a long way to drive. It would be better to take the train.* ○ *You'd be better getting the train than driving* (= it would be more suitable or sensible). أفضل
2 less ill or fully recovered from an illness: *I feel a bit better today.* ○ *You can't go swimming until you're better.* أحسن (صحيّاً) : معافى

better[2] /ˈbetə(r)/ *adv* (the comparative of *well*) in a better way; to a greater or higher degree: *I think you could have done this better.* ○ *Sylvie speaks*

English better than I do. ○ *She is much better known than her sister.* على وجه أفضل : أكثر

IDM **the best/better part of sth** → PART[1]

(be) better off 1 to be in a more pleasant or suitable situation: *You look terrible. You'd be better off at home in bed.* من الأفضل له أن

2 with more money: *We're much better off now I go out to work.* في وضع مالي أفضل

you, etc. had better you should; you would be wise to: *I think we'd better go before it gets dark.* ○ *You'd better take a pen and paper. You might want to take notes.* من الأفضل أن، يجدر أن...

know better → KNOW

think better of (doing) sth → THINK[1]

better[3] /ˈbetə(r)/ *noun* [sing.] something that is of higher quality: *The hotel wasn't very good. I must say we'd expected better.* شيء أفضل : شيء أرقى

IDM **get the better of sb/sth** to defeat or be stronger than sb/sth: *When we have an argument she always gets the better of me.* يتغلّب أو يتفوق على

between/among

a small house between two large ones   a house among some trees

between /bɪˈtwiːn/ *prep* **1** in the space that separates two things, people, etc.; somewhere in the middle: *I was sitting between Anne and Derek.* ○ *a village between Cambridge and Ely* بين

2 from one place to another and back again: *There aren't any direct trains between here and Milton Keynes.* ○ *the journey between home and the office* بين

3 involving or linking two people, groups or things: *There's some sort of disagreement between them.* ○ *There may be a connection between the two crimes.* بين

4 (used about two amounts, distances, ages, times, etc.) at a point that is greater or later than the first and smaller or earlier than the second; somewhere in the middle: *She must be between about thirty and thirty-five.* ○ *They said they would arrive between 4 and 5 o'clock.* ○ *a cost of between £200 and £300* ما بين

5 choosing one and not the other (of two things): *to choose between two jobs* ○ *What's the difference between 'some' and 'any'?* بين

6 by putting together the actions, efforts, etc. of two or more people: *We've got over a thousand pounds saved up between us.* فيما بين

7 giving each person a share: *The money was divided equally between the two children.* ○ *We ate all the chocolates between us.* فيما بين

Between is usually used of two people or things: *sitting between her mother and father* ○ *between the ages of 12 and 14.* However, **between** can sometimes be used of more than two when the people or things are being considered as individuals, especially when the meaning is that of number 7 (above): *We drank a bottle between the three of us.* **Among** is always used of more than two people or things considered as a group rather than as individuals: *You're among friends here.*

▸ **between** (*also* **in between**) *adv* in the space or period of time that separates two things, points, people, times, etc: *We can't get to the beach this way. There's a railway line in between.* ○ *I've got a meeting at 10 and one at 11 but I should manage to see you in between.* في الوسط

beverage /ˈbevərɪdʒ/ *noun* [C] (*formal*) (used especially on menus) a drink مشروب

beware /bɪˈweə(r)/ *verb* [I] (only in the imperative or infinitive) **beware (of sb/sth)** (used for giving a warning) to be careful: *Beware of the dog!* (= written on a sign) ○ *We were told to beware of strong currents in the sea.* احترس! ، احذر! ؛ يحترس

bewilder /bɪˈwɪldə(r)/ *verb* [T] to confuse: *I was completely bewildered by his sudden change of mood.* يحتار

▸ **bewildered** *adj*: *He seemed bewildered by all the fuss.* متحيِّر

bewildering *adj*: *a bewildering experience* مُحيِّر : مذْهِل

bewilderment *noun* [U]: *to stare at sb in bewilderment* حَيْرة ، اندهاش

bewitch /bɪˈwɪtʃ/ *verb* [T] to fascinate sb and be very attractive to them يفتِن ، يسحَر اللبّ

beyond /bɪˈjɒnd/ *prep* **1** on the other side of: *beyond the distant mountains* خلف ، وراء

2 further than; later than: *Does the motorway continue beyond Birmingham?* ○ *Most people don't go on working beyond the age of 65.* وراء ، إلى ما بعد

3 out of the range or reach of sth (so that sth is not possible): *The house was beyond what I could afford.* ○ *The car was completely beyond repair.* ○ *His success was beyond all our expectations* (= more than we expected). ○ *The fact that she is guilty is beyond doubt* (= there is no doubt about it). أكثر من المستطاع : فوق

4 except for or apart from: *I haven't heard anything beyond a few rumours.* عدا

IDM **be beyond sb** (*informal*) to be impossible for sb to understand or imagine: *Why she wants to go and live there is quite beyond me.* لا يفهَمه ، لا يتصوّره

▸ **beyond** *adv* on the other side or further on: *We could see the mountains and the sea beyond.* (فيما) وراء ذلك

bias /ˈbaɪəs/ *noun* [C,U, usually sing.] (*pl.* biases)

1 an opinion, feeling or attitude that is not fair and not based on facts: *a bias against women drivers* تحامل

2 giving one side in an argument an advantage over the other; not being neutral: *The BBC has been accused of political bias.* تحيُّز : انحياز

▸ **bias** *verb* [T] (biasing; biased or biassing;

a b c d e f g h i j k l m n o p q r s t u v w x y z

biassed) to influence sb/sth, especially unfairly; to give an advantage to one group, etc: *Good newspapers should not be biased towards a particular point of view.* ○ *Our schools are biased in favour of middle-class children.* ○ *a biased* (= unfair) *report* ينحاز : يحابي

bib /bɪb/ *noun* [C] a piece of cloth or plastic that a baby or small child wears under the chin to protect its clothes while it is eating مريلة ، صدريّة الطفل

bible /ˈbaɪbl/ (*also* **the Bible**) *noun* [C] the holy book of the Christian and Jewish people الكتاب المقدّس

▸ **biblical** /ˈbɪblɪkl/ *adj* توراتي ، متعلّق بالكتاب المقدس

bibliography /ˌbɪbliˈɒɡrəfi/ *noun* [C] (*pl.* **bibliographies**) **1** a list of the books and articles that a writer used when he/she was writing a particular book بيبلوغرافيا ، مسرد المراجع

2 a list of books on a particular subject (قائمة) مَراجع

bicentenary /ˌbaɪsenˈtiːnəri; *US* -ˈsentəneri/ *noun* [C] (*pl.* **bicentenaries**) (*US* **bicentennial** /ˌbaɪsenˈteniəl/) the day or year two hundred years after sth happened or began: *the bicentenary of the French Revolution* ذكرى مرور مئتي سنة

biceps /ˈbaɪseps/ *noun* [C] (*pl.* **biceps**) the large muscle at the front of the top part of your arms العضلة ذات الرأسين

bicker /ˈbɪkə(r)/ *verb* [I] to quarrel about unimportant things: *The boys were bickering about whose turn it was to play with the train.* يتشاحن، يناكف

🔑 **bicycle** /ˈbaɪsɪkl/ (*also informal* **bike**) *noun* [C] a vehicle with two wheels, which you sit on and ride by moving your legs: *to ride a bicycle* ○ *to go somewhere by bicycle* ➲ Look at **cycle**. This is usually used as the verb. **Cyclist** is the usual noun. درّاجة

🔑 **bid**[1] /bɪd/ *verb* (**bidding**; *pt, pp* **bid** or, in sense 2 *pt* **bade** /bæd/; *pp* **bidden** /ˈbɪdn/) **1** [I,T] **bid (sth) (for sth)** to offer a sum of money in order to buy sth: *to bid for sth at an auction* ○ *Somebody bid £5 000 for the painting.* يزايد أو يناقص، يعرض مبلغاً من المال

2 [T] (*old-fashioned, formal*) to say as a greeting: *He bade us good day and got up to leave.* يُحَيِّي أو يودِّع

▸ **bidder** *noun* [C] a person who offers a sum of money in order to buy sth: *The house was sold to the highest bidder* (= the person who offered the most money). مزايد : من يعرض مبلغاً من المال

🔑 **bid**[2] /bɪd/ *noun* [C] **1** an attempt to do, obtain, etc. sth: *a bid to slow down traffic and prevent accidents* ○ *her bid to win the championship* ○ *His bid for power had failed.* محاولة ، مسعى

2 an offer of a sum of money in order to buy sth: *We made a bid of £100 for the chair.* عَرْض

3 (*especially US*) = TENDER[2]

bide /baɪd/ *verb*

IDM **bide your time** to wait for a good opportunity: *I'll bide my time until the situation improves.* ينتظر (فرصة سانحة)

bidet /ˈbiːdeɪ; *US* biːˈdeɪ/ *noun* [C] a small bath that you can sit on in order to wash your bottom "بِيْديه": مغسلة منخفضة

🔑 **big** /bɪɡ/ *adj* (**bigger**; **biggest**) **1** large; not small: *a big house, town, salary, etc.* ○ *This dress is too big for me.* ضخم : كبير

2 great or important: *They had a big argument yesterday.* ○ *That was the biggest decision I've ever had to make.* ○ *some of the big names in Hollywood* كبير ، هام

3 (only *before* a noun) (*informal*) older: *a big brother/sister* أكبر (سِنّاً)

Big and **large** can both be used when talking about size or number. **Large** is more formal and is not usually used for describing people: *a big/large house* ○ *a big boy.* **Great** is mostly used when talking about the importance, quality, etc. of a person or thing. It can also be used with uncountable nouns to mean 'a lot of': *a great*

bicycle

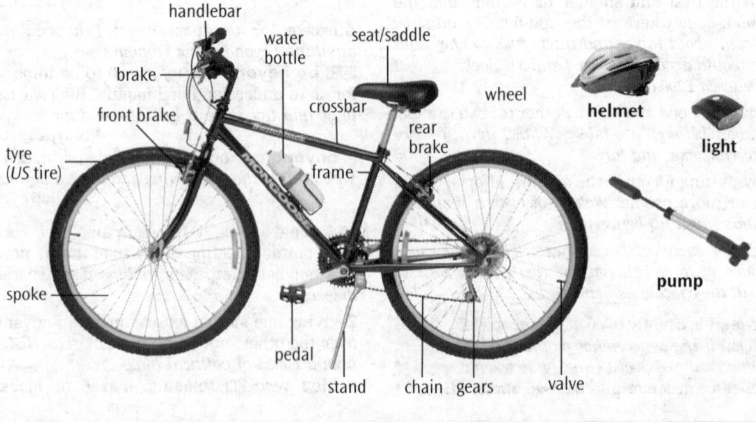

occasion ○ *a great musician* ○ *great happiness, care, etc.*

IDM **big deal!** (*informal*) used to say that you think sth is not important or interesting: *'Look at my new bike!' 'Big deal! It's not as nice as mine.'* (يعني أيه!). ما هذا الأمر العظيم!

a big deal (*informal*) something that is very important or exciting: *Birthday celebrations are a big deal in our family.* شيء مهم

no big deal (*informal*) something that is not very important or exciting: *A 2% pay increase is no big deal.* أمرٌ ليس بذي بال

give sb/get a big hand to clap sb/to be clapped loudly: *The audience gave the little girl a big hand when she finished her song.* يصفق أو يتلقى التصفيق

▶ **big** *adv* (*slang*) in a grand or ambitious way: *You have to think big if you want to be successful.* بطموح ، على مقياس كبير

bigamy /ˈbɪɡəmi/ *noun* [U] the crime of being married to two people at the same time الزواجٍ من امرأتين أو رجلين في نفس الوقت

▶ **bigamist** *noun* [C] متزوج من اثنين

ˌ**big ˈbox** *noun* (*US informal*) a very large shop, built on one level and located outside a town, which sells goods at low prices مخزن ضخم خارج المدن يبيع بأسعار رخيصة

ˈ**big-head** *noun* (*informal*) a person who thinks he/she is very important or clever because of sth he/she has done الشخص المغرور

▶ ˌ**big-ˈheaded** *adj* مغرور

bigot /ˈbɪɡət/ *noun* [C] a person who has very strong and unreasonable opinions and refuses to change them or listen to other people: *religious/racial bigot* متعصب

▶ **bigoted** /ˈbɪɡətɪd/ *adj* متعصّب

bigotry /ˈbɪɡətri/ *noun* [U] التعصّب

ˈ**big time** *noun* [sing.] success; fame: *This is the role that could help her make it to the big time in Hollywood.* النجاح، عالم الشهرة

▶ **big time** *adv* (*slang*) much: *You screwed up big time, Wayne!* كثيراً، جداً

big-time *adj* (only *before* a noun) important or famous: *a big-time drug dealer/politician* ذائع الصيت، مشهور

⚷ **bike** /baɪk/ *noun* [C] (*informal*) a bicycle or a motorcycle: *Mary's just learned to ride a bike.* درّاجة هوائية ؛ درّاجة بخارية

bikini /bɪˈkiːni/ *noun* [C] a piece of clothing, in two pieces, that women wear for swimming مايوه نسائي من قطعتين

bilingual /ˌbaɪˈlɪŋɡwəl/ *adj* **1** having or using two languages: *a bilingual dictionary* ثنائي اللغة

2 able to speak two languages equally well: *Our children are bilingual in English and Spanish.* ذو لغتين

⚷ **bill**[1] /bɪl/ *noun* **1** [C] (*US* **check**) a piece of paper that shows how much money you owe for goods or services: *an electricity bill* ○ *Can I have the bill, please* (e.g. in a restaurant)? ○ *to pay a bill* فاتورة ، بيان الحساب

2 [C] (*US*) = NOTE[1] (4): *a ten-dollar bill*

3 [C] a plan for a possible new law: *The bill was discussed in Parliament.* ○ *The bill was passed/defeated.* مشروع قانون

4 [sing.] the programme of entertainment offered in a show, concert, etc: *Which bands are on the bill at the festival?* ○ *a double bill of 'Swan Lake' and 'The Nutcracker'* برنامج ترفيهي

IDM **foot the bill** → FOOT[2]

▶ **bill** *verb* [T] **1 bill sb (for sth)** to send sb a bill for sth: *Please bill me for the books.* يقدم فاتورة

2 to announce to the public with an advertisement, etc: *The show is billed as a musical comedy.* يعلن للجمهور

bill[2] /bɪl/ *noun* [C] a bird's beak مِنْقار

billboard /ˈbɪlbɔːd/ *noun* [C] (*US*) = HOARDING

billfold /ˈbɪlfəʊld/ *noun* [C] (*US*) = WALLET

billiards /ˈbɪliədz/ *noun* [U] a game played on a big table covered with cloth. You use a long stick (a cue) to hit balls into pockets at the corners and sides of the table: *to play billiards* ○ *to have a game of billiards* (لعبة) البلياردو

▶ **billiard** /ˈbɪliəd-/ (in compounds) used for billiards: *a billiard table* (متعلّق بالبلياردو)

⚷ **billion** /ˈbɪljən/ *number* 1 000 000 000; one thousand million: *billions of dollars* بليون ، ألف مليون

> Notice that when you are counting you use billion without 's': *nine billion pounds.* Formerly, 'billion' was used with the meaning 'one million million'. We now say **trillion** for this.

billow /ˈbɪləʊ/ *verb* [I] to rise or move slowly in the wind, like waves: *curtains billowing in the breeze* يتماوج

⚷ **bin** /bɪn/ *noun* [C] **1** a container that you put rubbish in: *to throw sth in the bin* ○ *a litter bin* ○ *The dustmen come to empty the bins on Wednesdays.* صفيحة الزبالة، صندوق القمامة

2 a container, usually with a lid, for storing bread, flour, etc: *a bread bin* علبة لحفظ الخبز أو الدقيق الخ

binary system /ˈbaɪnəri sɪstəm/ *noun* [sing.] (*technical*) a system of numbers using only the numbers 0 and 1. It is used especially with computers. النظام الثنائي

bind /baɪnd/ *verb* [T] (*pt, pp* **bound** /baʊnd/)
1 bind A (to B); **bind A and B (together)** to tie or fasten with string or rope: *They bound the prisoner's hands behind his back.* ○ (*figurative*) *The two men were bound together* (= united or held together) *by the strength of their beliefs.* يقيّد ، يربِط

2 bind sb/yourself (to sth) to cause or force sb to do sth: *to be bound by a law, an agreement, etc.* ○ *The contract binds you to completion of the work within two years.* يقيّد

3 (usually passive) to fasten sheets of paper into a cover to form a book: *The book was bound in leather.* يجلّد

a b c d e f g h i j k l m n o p q r s t u v w x y z

▸ **bind** *noun* [sing.] (*informal*) something that you find boring or annoying; a nuisance: *I find housework a real bind.* شيء ممل ، شيء مزعج
binder *noun* [C] a hard cover for holding loose sheets of paper together غلاف مقوّى (لحفظ الأوراق)
binding *noun* **1** [C] a cover that holds the pages of a book together جِلد الكتاب
2 [U] material that you use for making the edge of sth stronger or more attractive حافة أو حاشية (للتقوية أو التزيين)
binding *adj* making it necessary for sb to do sth they have promised or to obey a law, etc: *This contract is legally binding.* ملْزِم

binge /bɪndʒ/ *noun* [C] (*informal*) a period of eating or drinking too much فترة إفراط في المأكل و المشرب

bingo /ˈbɪŋɡəʊ/ *noun* [U] a game in which each player has a different card with numbers on it. The person in charge of the game calls numbers out and the winner is the first player to have all the numbers on their card called out. البِنغو: لعبة قمار

binoculars /bɪˈnɒkjələz/ *noun* [plural] an instrument with two lenses which you look through in order to make distant objects seem nearer: *a pair of binoculars* ➲ Look at **telescope**. منظار مزدوج

biochemistry /ˌbaɪəʊˈkemɪstri/ *noun* [U] the study of the chemistry of living things الكيمياء الحيوية

biodegradable /ˌbaɪəʊdɪˈɡreɪdəbl/ *adj* that can decay naturally: *Most plastic packaging is not biodegradable.* قابل للانحلال الطبيعي

biodiversity /ˌbaɪəʊdaɪˈvɜːsəti/ *noun* [U] the existence of a large number of different kinds of animals and plants which make a balanced environment التعدّد الحيوي

biofuel /ˈbaɪəʊfjuːəl/ *noun* [C,U] fuel made from plant or animal sources and used in engines: *biofuels made from sugar cane and sugar beet* وقود حيوي

biography /baɪˈɒɡrəfi/ *noun* [C,U] (*pl.* **biographies**) the story of a person's life written by sb else: *a biography of Napoleon* ○ *I enjoy reading history and biography.* ➲ Look at **autobiography**. سِيرة
▸ **biographer** /baɪˈɒɡrəfə(r)/ *noun* [C] a person who writes a story of sb else's life كاتب السيرة
biographical /ˌbaɪəˈɡræfɪkl/ *adj* containing information about sb's life: *interesting biographical details* متعلّق بسيرة شخص

biological /ˌbaɪəˈlɒdʒɪkl/ *adj* **1** connected with the scientific study of animals, plants and other living things: *biological research* بيولوجي ، متعلّق بعلم الأحياء
2 involving the use of living things to destroy or damage other living things: *biological weapons* ○ *a biological detergent* (= one that uses enzymes to destroy dirt) بيولوجي ، جرثومي

⚷ **biology** /baɪˈɒlədʒi/ *noun* [U] the scientific study of living things علم الأحياء

▸ **biologist** /-dʒɪst/ *noun* [C] a person who studies or is an expert in biology عالم أحياء

biotechnology /ˌbaɪəʊtekˈnɒlədʒi/ *noun* [U] the use of living cells and bacteria in industrial and scientific processes: *biotechnological research* التكنولوجيا الحيوية

birch /bɜːtʃ/ *noun* [C,U] a type of tree with a smooth trunk and thin branches شجرة البتولا

⚷ **bird** /bɜːd/ *noun* [C] a creature with feathers and wings which can (usually) fly ❶ Birds **fly** and **sing**. They build **nests** and **lay eggs**. طائر
IDM **kill two birds with one stone** → KILL

ˌ**bird of ˈprey** *noun* [C] a bird that kills and eats other animals and birds طائر جارح

birdwatcher /ˈbɜːdwɒtʃə(r)/ *noun* [C] a person who studies birds in their natural surroundings ❶ The formal word is **ornithologist**. راصِد الطير

Biro™ /ˈbaɪrəʊ/ *noun* [C] (*pl.* **Biros**) a type of pen in which ink comes out of a small metal ball at the end ➲ Look at **ballpoint**. قلم حبر جاف

⚷ **birth** /bɜːθ/ *noun* **1** [C,U] being born; coming out of a mother's body: *It was a difficult birth.* ○ *The baby weighed six pounds at birth* (= when it was born). ○ *She's been slightly deaf since birth.* ○ *What's your date of birth?* (= the date on which you were born) مَوْلِد ؛ ولادة
2 [U] your nationality or your place of birth: *She's always lived in England but she's German by birth.* مولد ، أصل
3 [sing.] the beginning of sth: *the birth of an idea* نشوء
IDM **give birth (to sb/sth)** to produce a baby: *She gave birth to her second child at home.* تَلِد

ˈ**birth certificate** *noun* [C] an official piece of paper that states the date and place of a person's birth شهادة ميلاد

ˈ**birth control** *noun* [U] ways of controlling or limiting the number of children you have ➲ Look at **contraception**. تحديد النسل

⚷ **birthday** /ˈbɜːθdeɪ/ *noun* [C] the day in each year which is the same date as the one when you were born: *My birthday's (on) November 15th.* ○ *my eighteenth birthday* ○ *a birthday present* ○ *a birthday card* عيد ميلاد

An **anniversary** is not the same as a **birthday**. It is the day in each year which is the same date as an important past event: *our wedding anniversary* ○ *the fiftieth anniversary of the sinking of the Titanic* (= exactly fifty years after it happened). When it is a person's birthday we say **Happy Birthday**! or **Many happy returns**! If we know the person well we send a special card to them or a present. Your eighteenth birthday is an important occasion when you legally become an adult.

birthmark /ˈbɜːθmɑːk/ *noun* [C] a permanent mark on your body, that you are born with وحمة: علامة خَلْقيّة دائمة

birthplace /ˈbɜːθpleɪs/ *noun* **1** [C] the house or area where a person was born مكان الميلاد

2 [sing.] the place where sth began: *in Greece, the birthplace of the Olympic Games* منشأ

ˈbirth rate *noun* [C] the number of babies born in a particular group of people during a particular period of time: *The birth rate is falling/rising.* نسبة المواليد

⚷**biscuit** /ˈbɪskɪt/ *noun* [C] (*US* **cookie**) a type of small cake that is thin, hard and usually sweet: *a chocolate biscuit* ○ *a packet of biscuits* بسكويت

bisexual /ˌbaɪˈsekʃuəl/ *adj* sexually attracted to both men and women ثنائي الانجذاب الجنسي: من ينجذب للجنسين

bishop /ˈbɪʃəp/ *noun* [C] a senior person in the Christian Church, who is in charge of the churches in a city or a district: *the Bishop of Durham* ➲ Look at **archbishop**. أسقف

⚷**bit¹** /bɪt/ *noun* **1** [C] a small piece or amount of sth: *There were bits of broken glass all over the floor.* ○ *I think these strawberries need a bit more sugar.* ○ *Could you give me a bit of advice?* قطعة صغيرة ، قليل من : بعض

2 [sing.] (especially with *quite*) (*informal*) a lot: *It must have rained quite a bit during the night.* كثيراً

IDM **a bit 1** slightly; rather: *I'm afraid I'll be a bit late tonight.* ○ *I was a bit annoyed with him.* بعض الشيء

2 a short time or distance: *Could you move forward a bit?* قليلاً

bit by bit slowly or a little at a time: *Bit by bit we managed to get the information we needed.* تدريجياً : شيئاً فشيئاً

a bit much (*informal*) annoying or unpleasant: *It's a bit much expecting me to work on Sundays.* (أمر) مزعج

a bit of a (*informal*) rather a: *I've got a bit of a problem...* ○ *He's a bit of a tyrant, isn't he?* شيء من : بعض الشيء

bits and pieces (*informal*) small things of different kinds: *I've finished packing except for a few bits and pieces.* متفرّقات

do your bit (*informal*) to do your share of sth; to help with sth: *It won't take long to finish if we all do our bit.* يساهم : يعاون

not a bit not at all: *The holiday was not a bit what we had expected.* بتاتاً

to bits into small pieces: *She angrily tore the letter to bits.* مِزعاً ، (مزّقه) إرْباً

bit² /bɪt/ *noun* [C] a metal bar that you put in a horse's mouth when you ride it شكيمة (اللّجام)

⚷**bit³** /bɪt/ *noun* [C] (*computing*) the smallest unit of information that is stored in a computer's memory, represented by the numbers 0 or 1 أصغر وحدة معلومات في ذاكرة الكمبيوتر

bit⁴ *pt* of BITE¹

bitch /bɪtʃ/ *noun* [C] **1** a female dog كلبة

2 (*slang*) a very unpleasant woman: *She's a real bitch.* ○ *You bitch!* (= used to insult a woman) امرأة سليطة أو بغيضة

▸ **bitchy** (**bitchier**; **bitchiest**) *adj* (usually used about women or their behaviour) tending to talk about other people in an unkind way: *a bitchy remark* لئيم، مليء بالضغينة والنميمة

⚷**bite¹** /baɪt/ *verb* (*pt* **bit** /bɪt/; *pp* **bitten** /ˈbɪtn/) **1** [I,T] **bite (into sth)** to cut or attack with the teeth: *Don't worry about the dog. She never bites.* ○ *The dog bit me.* ○ *He picked up the bread and bit into it hungrily.* يعض ، يَقضم

2 [T] (used about insects or snakes) to prick your skin and cause pain: *He was bitten by a snake.* ❶ Wasps and bees do not **bite** you. They **sting** you. يلسَع ، يلدغ

3 [I] to begin to have an effect, usually in an unpleasant way: *In the South the job losses are starting to bite.* يَظهر تأثيره السَّيّئ

⚷**bite²** /baɪt/ *noun* **1** [C] a piece of food that you can put into your mouth: *She took a big bite of the apple.* لقمة ، قضمة

2 [C] a painful place on the skin made by an insect, snake, dog, etc: *a mosquito bite* لسعة ، لدغة

3 [sing.] (*informal*) some food: *Would you like a bite to eat before you go?* لقمة ، قليل من الطعام

bitten *pt* of BITE¹

⚷**bitter** /ˈbɪtə(r)/ *adj* **1** (used about a person) very unhappy or angry about sth that has happened; disappointed: *She was very bitter about the break-up of her marriage.* شاعر بالمرارة : خائب الأمل

2 causing unhappiness or anger for a long time; difficult to accept: *His son has been a bitter disappointment to him.* مرير : عسير القبول

3 caused by anger or hatred: *a bitter quarrel* مرير

4 (used about the weather) very cold: *a bitter wind* قارس البرد

5 having a sharp, unpleasant taste; not sweet: *bitter coffee* مرّ

▸ **bitter** *noun* [U] (*Brit*) a type of dark beer with a bitter taste نوع من البيرة

bitterly *adv* **1** (used for describing strong negative feelings or cold weather) extremely: *bitterly disappointed* ○ *a bitterly cold winter* جداً ، إلى أبعد حدّ

2 in a bitter(1) way: *'I've lost everything,' he said bitterly.* بمرارة

bitterness *noun* [U] anger and unhappiness as a result of sth bad happening مرارة

bitty /ˈbɪti/ (**bittier**; **bittiest**) *adj* made up of lots of parts which do not seem to be connected: *a bitty letter* غير مترابط الأجزاء

bizarre /bɪˈzɑː(r)/ *adj* very strange: *The story had a most bizarre ending.* غريب

bk (*pl.* **bks**) *abbrev* = BOOK

⚷**black¹** /blæk/ *adj* **1** of the darkest colour possible, the colour of the night sky أسود

2 belonging to a race of people with dark skins: *the black population of Britain* ○ *black culture* أسود

a b c d e f g h i j k l m n o p q r s t u v w x y z

3 (used about coffee or tea) without milk or cream: *black coffee with sugar* (قهوة مثلاً) دون حليب

4 (used about a situation) without hope; depressing: *The economic outlook for the coming year is rather black.* قاتم ، غير مبشّر

5 funny in a cruel or unpleasant way: *The film was a black comedy.* مضحِك على نحو مؤلم أو مخيف

6 very angry: *a black mood* ○ *to give sb a black look* ساخط

IDM black and blue covered with bruises مغطًى بالكدْمات

► **blacken** /ˈblækən/ *verb* [T] **1** to make sth black: *The soldiers had to blacken their faces at night.* يسوِّد

2 to make sth seem bad, by saying unpleasant things about it: *to blacken sb's name* يلطّخ (سمعته)

blackness *noun* [U] سواد ؛ ظلام

black² /blæk/ *noun* **1** [U] the darkest colour, like the night sky: *People usually wear black* (= black clothes) *at funerals.* سواد

2 usually **Black** [C] a person who belongs to a race of people with dark skins ➲ Look at **African-American.** أسود

IDM be in the black to have some money in the bank ➲ Look at **in the red.** له رصيد

black and white (used about television, photographs, etc.) showing no colours except black, white and grey: *a black and white television* أسود وأبيض

in black and white in writing or in print: *I won't believe we've got the contract till I see it in black and white.* كتابةً

black³ /blæk/ *verb*

PHRV black out to lose consciousness for a short time: *I remember losing control of the car and then I blacked out.* يفقد وعيه

blackberry /ˈblækbərɪ; *US* -berɪ/ *noun* [C] (*pl.* **blackberries**) a small black fruit that grows wild on bushes توت بري

BlackBerry™ /ˈblækbəri/ *noun* [C] (**pl. BlackBerries**) a very small computer that you can hold in your hand and that you can use for storing information, sending and receiving emails and text messages, making and receiving phone calls and looking at the Internet: *Check your emails via your BlackBerry.* ○ *He was talking on his BlackBerry.*
"بلاك بيري": جهاز محمول يزاوج ما بين تطبيقات الحاسب وخدمات الهاتف النقال

blackbird /ˈblækbɜːd/ *noun* [C] a common European bird. The male is black with a yellow beak and the female is brown. شَحْرور

blackboard /ˈblækbɔːd/ (*US* **chalkboard**) *noun* [C] a piece of dark board used for writing on, especially with chalk and in a classroom سَبورة

blackcurrant /ˌblækˈkʌrənt/ *noun* [C] a small round black fruit that grows in bunches on bushes الكشمش الأسود

ˌblack ˈeye *noun* [C] an eye with dark-coloured skin around it as the result of a blow: *He got a black eye in the fight.* كَدمة حول العين

blackhead /ˈblækhed/ *noun* [C] a small spot on the skin with a black centre بثرة صغيرة برأس أسود، "زيوانة"

blacklist /ˈblæklɪst/ *noun* [C] a list of people who are considered bad or dangerous: *to be on sb's blacklist* القائمة السوداء

► **blacklist** *verb* [T] يضعه في القائمة السوداء

ˌblack ˈmagic *noun* [U] a type of magic that is used for evil purposes السحر الأسود ، سحر شرّير

blackmail /ˈblækmeɪl/ *noun* [U] the crime of forcing a person to give you money or do sth for you, usually by threatening to make known sth which they want to keep secret ابتزاز

► **blackmail** *verb* [T]: *He was blackmailed into paying an enormous amount of money.* يبتز

blackmailer *noun* [C] مبتز

ˌblack ˈmarket *noun* [C] the buying and selling of goods or foreign money in a way that is not legal: *to buy/sell sth on the black market* السوق السوداء

blackout /ˈblækaʊt/ *noun* [C] **1** a period of time during a war, when all lights must be turned off or covered so that the enemy cannot see them تعتيم

2 a period when you lose consciousness for a short time: *to have a blackout* فقدان الوعي

blacksmith /ˈblæksmɪθ/ *noun* [C] a person whose job is to make and repair things made of metal, especially horses' shoes حدّاد

bladder /ˈblædə(r)/ *noun* [C] the part of the body where waste liquid (urine) collects before leaving the body مَثانة

blade /bleɪd/ *noun* [C] **1** the flat, sharp part of a knife, sword, etc. شَفْرة

2 one of the flat, wide parts that spin round on a plane, helicopter, etc. ريشة المروحة

3 a long, thin leaf of grass, wheat, etc: *a blade of grass* ورقة (عشب)

blame /bleɪm/ *verb* [T] **1 blame sb (for sth); blame sth on sb** to think or say that a certain person or thing is responsible for sth bad that has happened: *The teacher blamed me for the accident.* ○ *Some people blame the changes in the climate on pollution.* يلوم

2 not blame sb (for sth) to think that sb is not wrong to do sth: *'I'd like to leave school and get a job.' 'I don't blame you.'* (= I can understand why). ○ *I don't blame you for feeling fed up.* يفهم السبب

IDM be to blame (for sth) to be responsible for sth bad: *The police say that careless driving was to blame for the accident.* يكون مسؤولاً

► **blame** *noun* [U] **blame (for sth)** responsibility for sth bad: *to take the blame for sth* ○ *The report puts the blame on rising prices.* مسؤولية، لائمة

blameless *adj* deserving no blame; not guilty: *He insisted that his wife was blameless and hadn't known about his activities.* لا لوم عليه ، بريء

bland /blænd/ *adj* **1** showing no strong feelings; calm ساكن ، هادئ

2 (used about food) mild or lacking in taste قليل الطعم ، قليل التوابل

3 ordinary or uninteresting: *a rather bland style of writing* عادي، غير مثير

▸ **blandly** *adv* بهدوء ؛ بدماثة

blank /blæŋk/ *adj* **1** without writing or anything else on it: *a blank cassette* ○ *a blank piece of paper* ○ *a blank wall* فارغ ، خالٍ

2 without feelings, understanding or interest: *a blank expression on his face* ○ *My mind went blank when I saw the exam questions* (= I couldn't think properly or remember anything). أجوف

▸ **blank** *noun* [C] an empty space: *Fill in the blanks in the following exercise.* ○ *(figurative) I couldn't remember his name – my mind was a complete blank.* فراغ

IDM **draw a blank** → DRAW[2]

blankly *adv* with a blank expression (ينظر) نظرة جوفاء أو خالية من التعبير

ˌ**blank ˈcheque** *noun* [C] a cheque that has been signed but that has an empty space so that the amount to be paid can be filled in later شيك على بياض

blanket /ˈblæŋkɪt/ *noun* [C] a cover made of wool, etc. that is put on beds to keep people warm بطّانية

IDM **a wet blanket** → WET

▸ **blanket** *verb* [T] to cover sth completely: *The countryside was blanketed in snow.* يغطّي تغطية تامّة

blanket *adj* (only *before* a noun) affecting everybody or everything: *a blanket ban on journalists reporting the case* شامل

blare /bleə(r)/ *verb* [I,T] **blare (sth) (out)** to make a loud, unpleasant noise: *The radio was blaring in the room next to ours.* ○ *The loudspeaker blared out a warning.* يدوّي

▸ **blare** *noun* [U]: *the blare of a siren* زعيق ، دويّ

blasphemy /ˈblæsfəmi/ *noun* [U] writing or speaking about God in a way that shows a lack of respect تجديف ، كفر

▸ **blasphemous** /ˈblæsfəməs/ *adj* مُجَدِّف، تجديفيّ

blast[1] /blɑːst; *US* blæst/ *noun* [C] **1** an explosion, especially one caused by a bomb: *The windows of the nearby shops were shattered in the blast.* انفجار

2 a sudden strong rush of air: *a blast of cold air* هبّة

3 a loud sound made by a musical instrument such as a horn: *a few blasts on his trumpet* نَفْخَة ، صَفْرة

blast[2] /blɑːst; *US* blæst/ *verb* [I,T] to make a hole, a tunnel, etc. in sth with an explosion: *They had to blast their way through the mountainside.* يفجّر مُحدثاً ثقباً الخ

PHR V **blast off** (used about a spacecraft) to leave the ground; to take off يقلع ؛ ينطلق

▸ **blast** *interj* a mild swear word, used to show that you are angry: *Blast! I've cut my finger.* (كلمة للشتم تعبر عن الغضب)

blasted *adj* (*informal*) very annoying: *Can you turn that blasted music down?* مزعج جداً

ˈ**blast-off** *noun* [U] the time when a spacecraft leaves the ground انطلاق (الصاروخ مثلاً)

blatant /ˈbleɪtnt/ *adj* very clear or obvious: *their blatant dislike for each other* ○ *a blatant lie*
ⓘ This word is used in a critical way. صريح ؛ واضح

▸ **blatantly** *adv* بوضوح

blaze[1] /bleɪz/ *noun* **1** [C] a large and often dangerous fire: *It took firemen four hours to put out the blaze.* حريق ، لَهب

2 [sing.] **a blaze of sth** a very bright display of light or colour: *In the summer the garden was a blaze of colour.* ○ *(figurative) The new theatre was opened in a blaze of publicity* (= the newspapers, television, etc. gave it a lot of attention). شُعْلة ، تأجّج

blaze[2] /bleɪz/ *verb* [I] **1** to burn with bright strong flames: *a blazing log fire* يتقد ، يتوهج

2 **blaze (with sth)** to be extremely bright; to shine brightly: *I woke up to find that the room was blazing with sunshine.* ○ *(figurative) 'Get out!' she shouted, her eyes blazing with anger.* يتوهّج ؛ يتألّق

blazer /ˈbleɪzə(r)/ *noun* [C] a jacket, especially one that has the colours or sign (badge) of a school, club, team, etc. on it; usually worn by men, or by schoolchildren as part of their uniform: *a school blazer* سُتْرة ذات شارة

bleach /bliːtʃ/ *verb* [T] to make sth white or lighter in colour (by using a chemical or by leaving it in the sun) يبيّض ؛ يفتّح اللون

▸ **bleach** *noun* [C,U] a strong chemical substance used for making clothes, etc. whiter or for cleaning things مادة (كيماوية) مبيِّضة

bleak /bliːk/ *adj* **1** (used about a situation) bad; not encouraging or hopeful: *a bleak future for the next generation* غير مبشّر بالخير ، قاتم

2 (used about a place) cold, bare and grey: *the bleak Yorkshire Moors* (مكان) كئيب ، يثير الانقباض

3 (used about the weather) cold and grey: *a bleak winter's day* كئيب

▸ **bleakly** *adv* بكآبة

bleakness *noun* [U] قتامة ؛ رداءة الوضع

bleary /ˈblɪəri/ *adj* (**blearier**; **bleariest**) (used about the eyes) red, tired and unable to see clearly: *We were all rather bleary-eyed after the journey.* (عيون) محمرة ومتعبة

▸ **blearily** *adv*: *'What's the time?' he said blearily, switching on the light.* بعيون متعبة وغبشة

bleat /bliːt/ *verb* **1** [I] to make the sound of a sheep or goat يثغو

2 [I,T] to speak in a weak, uncertain way يتكلّم بصوت ضعيف

▸ **bleat** *noun* [C] ثغاء

bleed /bliːd/ *verb* [I] (*pt*, *pp* **bled** /bled/) to lose blood: *He was bleeding badly from a cut on his head.* ○ *Is your finger bleeding?* ينزف

▸ **bleeding** *noun* [U] blood flowing from a cut, etc: *He wrapped a scarf around his arm to try to stop the bleeding.* نزيف

ˌbleeding ˈedge *noun* [sing.] technology that is so advanced that there may be problems when you use it: *They were working at the bleeding edge of chip design.*
تكنولوجيا متقدمة جدا (لدرجة قد تسبب عوائق عند الاستخدام)

bleep /bliːp/ *noun* [C] a short, high sound made by an electronic machine صفير أو تزمير متقطّع

▸ **bleep** *verb* **1** [I] (used about machines) to make a short high sound: *Why is the computer bleeping?* يصفر أو يزمّر بصورة متقطّعة

2 [T] to attract a person's attention using a bleeper يناديه بمنبّه الكتروني

bleeper *noun* [C] a small piece of equipment that makes bleeps to let a person (e.g. a doctor) know when sb is trying to contact them
منبّه أو صفّارة الكترونية

blemish /ˈblemɪʃ/ *noun* [C] a mark that spoils the way sb/sth looks: *make-up to hide spots and other blemishes* عيب ، شائبة

▸ **blemish** *verb* [T] to spoil sth يعيب (شيئاً) ؛ يلوّث

blend /blend/ *verb* **1** [T] **blend A with B**; **blend A and B (together)** to mix: *First blend the flour and the melted butter together.* يمزج

2 [I] **blend with sth** to look or sound good with sth else: *new buildings that don't blend with their surroundings* ينسجم مع

3 [I] **blend (into sth)** to be difficult to tell apart from sth else: *These animals' ability to blend into their surroundings provides a natural form of defence.* يندمج

PHR V **blend in (with sth)** to look or sound good with sth else because the two things are similar: *The new room is decorated to blend in with the rest of the house.* ينسجم ، يتوافق مع

▸ **blend** *noun* [C] a mixture: *a blend of China and Indian tea* ○ *He had the right blend of enthusiasm and experience.* مزيج

ˌblended ˈlearning *noun* [U] a way of studying a subject that combines being taught in class with the use of different technologies, including learning over the Internet
التعليم المدمج: الربط بين التعليم في الفصل والتعلم الالكتروني

blender /ˈblendə(r)/ *noun* [C] (*Brit also* **liquidizer**; **liquidiser**) *noun* [C] an electric machine that is used for liquidizing food
آلة كهربائية صغيرة لتمييع الاطعمة

bless /bles/ *verb* [T] (*pt, pp* **blessed** /blest/) to ask for God's help and protection for sb/sth: *At the end of the marriage service, the vicar will bless the young couple.* يبارك

IDM **be blessed with sth/sb** to be lucky enough to have sth/sb: *The West of Ireland is an area blessed with many fine sandy beaches.* ينعم

bless you! what you say to a person who has just sneezed صحة! ، يرحمك الله!

blessed /ˈblesɪd/ *adj* **1** (in religious language) holy: *the Blessed Virgin Mary* مقدّس

2 (in religious language) lucky; fortunate: *Blessed are the pure in heart.* مبارك

3 giving great pleasure: *The cool breeze brought blessed relief from the heat.* ممتع ، لذيذ

4 (used for expressing anger or surprise): *Where's the blessed train?*
اللعين! (للتعبير عن الغضب أو الاستغراب)

blessing /ˈblesɪŋ/ *noun* [C] **1** a thing that you are grateful for or that brings happiness: *It's a great blessing that we have two healthy children.* ○ *a blessing in disguise* (= something which seems unlucky but turns out to be a good thing) ○ *to count your blessings* نعمة

2 [usually sing.] approval or support: *They got married without their parents' blessing.* موافقة

3 [usually sing.] (a prayer asking for) God's help and protection: *to ask for God's blessing* ○ *The priest said a blessing.* بركة ، رضا

blew *pt of* BLOW[1]

🔑 **blind**[1] /blaɪnd/ *adj* **1** unable to see: *a blind person* ○ *to be completely/partially blind* ℹ We can also describe a person as **visually impaired**.
أعمى ، ضرير

2 blind (to sth) not willing to notice or understand sth: *He was completely blind to her faults.* أعمى ، متغاضٍ عن

3 without reason or thought: *her blind acceptance of fate* ○ *He drove down the motorway in a blind panic.* جامح ، متهور

4 impossible to see round: *You should never overtake on a blind corner.*
مستور ، (منعطف) حاجب للرؤية

IDM **turn a blind eye (to sth)** to pretend not to notice sth يتعامى عن ، يتجاهل

▸ **the blind** *noun* [plural] people who are blind: *ways of making homes safer for the blind*
المكفوفون

blindly *adv* بصورة عمياء

blindness *noun* [U] عمى

blind[2] /blaɪnd/ *verb* [T] **1** to make sb unable to see: *Her grandfather had been blinded in an accident* (= permanently). ○ *For a minute I was blinded by the lights of the oncoming car* (= for a short time). يعمي ، يبهر

2 blind sb (to sth) to prevent sb from being aware of sth يعمي ، يضلّ

blind[3] /blaɪnd/ *noun* [C] a piece of cloth or other material that you pull down to cover a window
حاجب (للنور) ، ستارة

ˌblind ˈdate *noun* [C] an arranged meeting between a man and a woman who have never met before to see if they like each other enough to begin a romantic relationship
ترتيب تعارف بين رجل و امرأة

blinders /ˈblaɪndəz/ *noun* [plural] (*US*) = BLINKERS

blindfold /ˈblaɪndfəʊld/ *verb* [T] to cover a per-

son's eyes with a piece of cloth, etc. so that he/she cannot see يعصب العينين
▸ **blindfold** *noun* [C] a piece of cloth, etc. that is used for covering sb's eyes عِصابة للعينين

ˈ**blind spot** *noun* [C] **1** if you have a blind spot about sth, you cannot understand or accept it موضوع لا يفهمه الشخص ولا يتقبّله
2 the part of the road that you cannot see when driving a car, i.e. the part which is just behind you بقْعة عمياء (لا يراها السائق)

blink /blɪŋk/ *verb* **1** [I,T] to shut your eyes and open them again very quickly: *Oh dear! You blinked just as I took the photograph!* ➲ Look at **wink**. تطرِف العين
2 [I] (used about a light) to come on and go off again quickly (النور) يَمِض
▸ **blink** *noun* [C] غمضة أو طَرفة عين

blinkers /ˈblɪŋkəz/ (*US* **blinders**) *noun* [plural] pieces of leather fixed beside a horse's eyes so that it can only look straight in front غمامة (الفرس)

blip /blɪp/ *noun* [C] **1** a short sound made by an electronic machine صوت قصير يصدر عن آلة الكترونية
2 a small point of light on a screen نقطة منيرة على شاشة
3 a small problem that does not last for long مشكلة صغيرة و عارضة

bliss /blɪs/ *noun* [U] perfect happiness: *fifteen years of domestic bliss with his wife Mary* نعيم، سعادة
▸ **blissful** /-fl/ *adj* هنيء ؛ سعيد
blissfully /-fəli/ *adv* بسعادة ، في نعيم

blister /ˈblɪstə(r)/ *noun* [C] a small painful area of skin that looks like a bubble and contains clear liquid. Blisters are usually caused by rubbing or burning: *These shoes give me blisters.* نَفْطة ، بقبوقة، "فقفولة"
▸ **blister** *verb* [I,T] to get or cause blisters يتنفّط أو "يبقبق": يسبّب نَفْطة
blistering /ˈblɪstərɪŋ/ *adj* **1** very great or severe: *the blistering midday heat* قاسٍ ، شديد
2 showing great anger: *a blistering attack on his political enemies* مهتاج ؛ غاضب ؛ لاذع

blitz /blɪts/ *noun* [C] **1** a sudden heavy military attack, especially from the air هجوم (جوي) صاعق
2 a blitz (on sth) (*informal*) a sudden great effort: *I had a blitz on the garden and it's looking quite nice now.* حملة مركّزة

blizzard /ˈblɪzəd/ *noun* [C] a very bad snowstorm with strong winds ➲ Look at the note at **storm**. عاصفة ثلجية

bloated /ˈbləʊtɪd/ *adj* unusually or uncomfortably large and full because of liquid, food or gas inside: *I felt a bit bloated after all that food.* منتفخ

blob /blɒb/ *noun* [C] a small piece of a thick liquid: *a blob of paint, cream, etc.* كتلة صغيرة

bloc /blɒk/ *noun* [C, with sing. or pl. verb] a group of countries, political parties, etc. who have similar political ideas and who act together كُتْلَة

🔑**block**[1] /blɒk/ *noun* [C] **1** a large, heavy piece of sth, usually with flat sides: *a block of wood* ○ *huge concrete blocks* كُتلة مُضلّعة
2 a large building that is divided into separate flats or offices: *a block of flats* ○ *an office block* مجمّع ، بناية كبيرة
3 a group of buildings in a town which has streets on four sides: *I went for a walk around the block.* مجموعة أبنية تشكّل كتلة واحدة
4 [usually sing.] a thing that makes movement or progress difficult or impossible: *a block to further progress in the talks* عائق
IDM **to have a block (about sth)** to be unable to think or understand sth properly: *I had a complete mental block. I just couldn't remember his name.* ينشلّ تفكيره

🔑**block**[2] /blɒk/ *verb* [T] **1 block sth (up)** to make it difficult or impossible for anything or anybody to pass: *Many roads are completely blocked by snow.* ○ *I'm afraid the sink's blocked up.* يسُدّ
2 to prevent sth from being done: *The management tried to block the deal.* يمنع
3 to prevent sth from being seen by sb: *Get out of the way, you're blocking the view!* يحجب
PHR V **block sth off** to separate one area from another with sth solid: *This section of the motorway has been blocked off by the police.* يقفل، يعزل
block sth out to try not to think about sth unpleasant: *She tried to block out the memory of the crash.* يطرد
▸ **blockage** /ˈblɒkɪdʒ/ *noun* [C] a thing that is blocking sth; the state of being blocked: *a blockage in the drainpipe* ○ *blockages on some major roads* انسداد ؛ عائق

blockade /blɒˈkeɪd/ *noun* [C] a situation in which a place is surrounded by soldiers or ships in order to prevent goods or people from reaching it حصار
▸ **blockade** *verb* [T] يحاصر

blockbuster /ˈblɒkbʌstə(r)/ *noun* [C] a book or film with an exciting story which is very successful and popular كتاب أو فيلم ذو نجاح كاسح

ˌ**block ˈletter** (*also* ˌ**block ˈcapital**) *noun* [C, usually pl.] a capital letter: *Please write your name in block letters.* حرف كبير

blog /blɒg/ *noun* [C] = WEBLOG

blogosphere /ˈblɒgəsfɪə(r)/ *noun* [sing.] (*informal*) usually **the blogosphere** all the personal websites that exist on the Internet, viewed as a network of people communicating with each other: *It's one of the top stories in the blogosphere.* فضاء المدوّنات

blogroll /ˈblɒgrəʊl/ *noun* [C] a list on a website of other linked websites that the website owner thinks are useful or interesting قائمة المواقع المفيدة أو الطريفة

bloke /bləʊk/ *noun* [C] (*Brit informal*) a man: *He's a really nice bloke.* ○ *What does her bloke (= boyfriend) do?* رَجل ، شخص

🔑**blond** (*also* **blonde**) /blɒnd/ *noun* [C], *adj* (a person) with fair or yellow hair: *Most of our family have blond hair.* أشقر، شقراء

When describing women the spelling **blonde** is used: *She's tall, slim and blonde.* The noun is usually only used of women and is spelt **blonde**: *She's a blonde.*

blood /blʌd/ *noun* [U] the red liquid that flows through the body: *Blood was pouring from a cut on his knee.* ○ *The heart pumps blood around the body.* دم
IDM **in your blood** a strong part of your character: *A love of the countryside was in his blood.* (يجري) في دمه، طبيعة
in cold blood → COLD[1]

bloodbath /ˈblʌdbɑːθ; *US* -bæθ/ *noun* [C] an act of violently killing many people حمّام دم، سفك دماء

ˈ**blood-curdling** *adj* horrible and frightening: *a blood-curdling scream* تقشعرّ له الأبدان

ˈ**blood donor** *noun* [C] a person who gives his/her blood for use in medical operations المتبرع بدمه

ˈ**blood group** (*also* ˈ**blood type**) *noun* [C] any of several different types of human blood: *'What blood group are you?' 'O.'* فصيلة الدم

bloodless /ˈblʌdləs/ *adj* **1** (used about a part of the body) very pale شاحب
2 without killing or violence: *a bloodless coup* غير دموي، (ثورة) بيضاء

ˈ**blood pressure** *noun* [U] the force with which the blood travels round the body: *to have high/low blood pressure* ضغط الدّم

bloodshed /ˈblʌdʃed/ *noun* [U] the killing or wounding of people: *Both sides in the war want to avoid further bloodshed.* سفك الدّماء

bloodshot /ˈblʌdʃɒt/ *adj* (used about the white part of the eyes) full of red lines, e.g. when sb is tired محتقن بالدّم

ˈ**blood sport** *noun* [C] a sport such as fox-hunting, in which animals are killed رياضة دموية (يُقتل فيها الحيوان)

bloodstained /ˈblʌdsteɪnd/ *adj* having marks of blood on it ملطّخ بالدّماء

bloodstream /ˈblʌdstriːm/ *noun* [sing.] the blood as it flows through the body: *drugs injected straight into the bloodstream* مجرى الدّم

bloodthirsty /ˈblʌdθɜːsti/ *adj* eager to use violence or to watch scenes of violence متعطّش للدّماء

ˈ**blood transfusion** *noun* [C] an injection of blood into a person's body: *to have a blood transfusion* نقل الدّم

ˈ**blood vessel** *noun* [C] any of the tubes in the body which blood flows through وعاء دموي

bloody[1] /ˈblʌdi/ *adj* (**bloodier**; **bloodiest**) **1** involving a lot of violence and killing: *a bloody war* دموي، مليء بالعنف
2 covered with blood: *a bloody knife* مغطّى بالدّم

bloody[2] /ˈblʌdi/ *adj, adv* (*Brit informal*) (used for emphasizing anger, annoyance or just an opinion): *The bloody train was late again this morning.* ○ *What a bloody stupid idea!* ○ *We had a bloody good time.* ❶ Some people think that it is rude to use this word. (لتأكيد الغضب أو الانزعاج أو فكرة ما)

ˌ**bloody-**ˈ**minded** *adj* (*Brit informal*) difficult and unhelpful, often on purpose صعب المراس (عن قصد)

bloom /bluːm/ *noun* [C] a flower زَهْرة
IDM **in bloom** with its flowers open: *All the wild plants are in bloom.* مزْهِر، متَفتّح
▸ **bloom** *verb* [I] to produce flowers: *This shrub blooms in May.* ○ (*figurative*) *You look blooming* (= very healthy)*!* يزْهِر، يتفتّح

blossom /ˈblɒsəm/ *noun* [C,U] a flower or a mass of flowers, especially on a fruit tree: *The apple tree is covered in blossom.* زهر (على شجرة مثمرة)
▸ **blossom** *verb* [I] **1** (used especially about trees) to produce flowers يزهر
2 blossom (out) (into sth) to develop well: *This young runner has blossomed into a top-class athlete.* يترعرع، يتفتّح

blot[1] /blɒt/ *noun* [C] **1** a spot or stain, especially one made by ink on paper لطخة، بقعة
2 a blot on sth a thing that spoils sb's reputation, character, future, etc. وصمة

blot[2] /blɒt/ *verb* [T] (**blotting**; **blotted**) **1** to make a spot or stain on sth, especially one of ink on paper يلطّخ، يلوّث
2 to dry spots of liquid on sth by pressing it with soft paper or cloth ينشّف (الحبر مثلاً)
PHR V **blot sth out** to cover or hide: *Heavy fog blotted out the view completely.* ○ *She kept herself busy, hoping to blot out her unhappy memories* (= trying not to think of them). يمحو؛ يطمس

blotch /blɒtʃ/ *noun* [C] a mark or an area of different colour, especially on sb's skin: *The blotches on her face showed that she had been crying.* لطخة، بقعة
▸ **blotched** (*also* **blotchy**) *adj* covered in blotches ملطّخ، مبقّع

ˈ**blotting paper** *noun* [U] soft paper that you use for drying wet ink on writing paper, etc. ورق نشّاف

blouse /blaʊz; *US* blaʊs/ *noun* [C] a piece of clothing like a shirt, that women wear بلوزة

blow[1] /bləʊ/ *verb* (*pt* **blew** /bluː/; *pp* **blown** /bləʊn/) **1** [I] (used about wind, air, etc.) to move: *Out at sea, a gentle breeze was blowing.* يهبّ
2 [I] to send air out of the mouth: *Take a deep breath and then blow.* ينفخ، ينفث
3 [T] to make or shape sth by blowing air out of your mouth: *to blow bubbles* ينفخ
4 [I,T] to produce sound from a musical instrument, whistle, etc. by means of air: *The referee's whistle blew for the end of the match.* ○ *He blew a few notes on the trumpet.* ○ *All the drivers behind me were blowing their horns.* يصفّر، ينفخ
5 [T] (*informal*) to waste an opportunity of

succeeding in sth: *I think I've blown my chances of promotion.* يضيّع الفرصة

6 [T] **blow sth (on sth)** (*informal*) to spend or waste a lot of money on sth: *She blew all her savings on a trip to China.* ينفق أو يبعثر نقوده

7 [I,T] (used about an electric fuse) to stop working suddenly because the electric current is too strong; to make sth do this: *A fuse has blown.* ○ *I think the kettle's blown a fuse.* (المِصْهَر) يحترق

8 [I,T] (*informal*) (used for expressing anger, annoyance or the fact that you do not care about sth): *Oh, blow! It's raining.* ○ *'What will the neighbours think?' 'Oh blow the neighbours* (= I don't care about them)*!'* (للتعبير عن السخط أو الضيق أو اللامبالاة)

IDM **blow your nose** to clear your nose by blowing strongly through it into a handkerchief, etc. يتمخّط

PHR V **blow (sb/sth) down, off, over, etc.** to move or make sth move through the air in the direction mentioned, because of the wind, etc: *My papers blew all over the garden.* ○ *The balloons blew away into the sky.* ○ *The wind suddenly blew my hat off.* يطير؛ يُطيِّر

blow sth out to make sth stop burning by blowing air at it: *to blow out the candles on a birthday cake* يطفئ

blow over to pass away; to end: *I expect those black clouds will soon blow over.* ○ *We often have arguments but they usually blow over fairly quickly.* يزول ، ينتهي ، يمرّ (بسلام)

blow up 1 to explode or to be destroyed in an explosion: *A bomb blew up near Oxford Street this morning.* ○ *The car blew up when the door was opened.* ينفجر

2 to start suddenly and strongly: *A storm blew up in the night.* ○ *An argument blew up about money.* يعصف ، يهبّ فجأة

blow sth up 1 to make sth explode or to destroy sth in an explosion: *The terrorists tried to blow up the plane.* ينسف ، يفجِّر

2 to fill sth with air or gas: *to blow up a balloon* ينفخ (بالهواء أو الغاز)

▸ **blow** *noun* [C] an act of blowing: *Give your nose a blow!* نَفْخة : نفّ الأنف

blow² /bləʊ/ *noun* [C] **1** a hard knock from your hand, a weapon, etc. that hits or is intended to hit sb/sth: *He felt a blow on the back of his head and fell down unconscious.* ○ *She aimed a blow at me.* ضربة

2 a blow (to sb/sth) a sudden shock or disappointment: *It was rather a blow when I heard that I hadn't got the job.* صدمة

IDM **a blow-by-blow account, description, etc. (of sth)** an account, etc. of an event that gives all the exact details of it وصف تفصيلي

come to blows (over sth) to start fighting or arguing (about sth) يتشاجر ، يتضارب

deal sb/sth a blow; deal a blow to sb/sth → DEAL²

ˈblow-dry *verb* [T] (*pt, pp* **blow-dried**) to dry and shape sb's hair using a hairdryer that you hold and a brush يجفّف الشعر بآلة التجفيف الكهربائية

▸ **ˈblow-dry** *noun* [sing.]: *an appointment at the hairdresser's for a cut and blow-dry* تجفيف الشعر

blown *pp* of BLOW¹

blue¹ /bluː/ *adj* **1** having the colour of a clear sky on a sunny day: *His eyes were bright blue.* ○ *light/dark blue* أزرق

2 (*informal*) (often used in popular songs) sad حزين

3 (used about jokes, films, etc.) connected with sex جنسي

IDM **black and blue** → BLACK¹

blue² /bluː/ *noun* **1** [C,U] the colour of a clear sky on a sunny day: *I'd like some curtains with some blue in them.* ○ *dressed in blue* (= blue clothes) زُرْقة

2 the blues [plural, with sing. or pl. verb] a type of slow sad music similar to jazz: *a blues singer* موسيقى جاز حزينة

3 the blues [plural] (*informal*) the state of feeling sad or depressed: *to have the blues* حالة اكتئاب

IDM **once in a blue moon** → ONCE

out of the blue suddenly; without being expected: *I didn't hear from him for years and then this letter came out of the blue.* فجأة

bluebell /ˈbluːbel/ *noun* [C] a plant with blue or white flowers shaped like bells ياقوتية الكرم

blueberry /ˈbluːbəri; *US* -beri/ *noun* a small dark blue berry that grows on low bushes in North America عنب الأحراج، عنب الدب

ˌblue-ˈcollar *adj* doing or involving physical work with the hands rather than office work (عامل) يدوي (أي ليس في مكتب)

blueprint /ˈbluːprɪnt/ *noun* [C] a plan or description of how to make, build or achieve sth مُخطَّط

bluff /blʌf/ *verb* [I,T] to try to convince people of sth that is not really true, usually by appearing very confident: *Don't take any notice of him, he's just bluffing.* ○ *They tried to bluff their parents into believing there was no school that day.* يخدَع ، يبلِف

PHR V **bluff your way in, out, through, etc. sth** to trick sb in order to get into, out of a place, etc: *We managed to bluff our way into the stadium by saying we were journalists.* يخادع

▸ **bluff** *noun* [C,U]: *John keeps threatening to leave home but I'm sure it's only bluff!* خِداع ، تهديد دون تنفيذ

bluish (*also* **blueish**) /ˈbluːɪʃ/ *adj* (*informal*) slightly blue: *bluish green* مائل للزرقة

blunder /ˈblʌndə(r)/ *noun* [C] a silly mistake: *I'm afraid I've made a terrible blunder.* خطأ فاحش

▸ **blunder** *verb* [I] to make a blunder يرتكب خطأ فاحشاً

PHR V **blunder about, around, etc.** to move in an uncertain or careless way, as if blind: *We blundered about in the dark, trying to find the light switch.* يتخبَّط

blunt /blʌnt/ *adj* **1** (used about a person, remark, etc.) saying exactly what you think in a not very polite way: *I'm sorry to be so blunt, but I'm afraid you're just not good enough.* صريح بشكل جارح

2 (used about a knife, pencil, tool, etc.) not sharp: *blunt scissors* غير حادّ ، متثلّم

▸ **blunt** *verb* [T] to make sth less sharp or less strong يثلّم (الحد)

bluntly *adv* بصراحة فظة

bluntness *noun* [U] صراحة جارحة

blur /blɜː(r)/ *noun* [C, usually sing.] something that you cannot see or remember clearly: *Through the window of the train the countryside was just a blur.* شيء غير واضح المعالم

▸ **blur** *verb* [I,T] (blu**rr**ing; blu**rr**ed) to become unclear; to make sth less clear: *The words on the page blurred as tears filled her eyes.* ○ *His thoughts were blurred and confused.* يصبح غير واضح : يطمس

blurt /blɜːt/ *verb*

PHRV **blurt sth out** to say sth suddenly or without thinking: *We didn't want to tell Mum but Ann blurted the whole thing out.* تفلت منه الكلمات دون تفكير

blush /blʌʃ/ *verb* [I] to become red in the face, especially because of shame or embarrassment: *She blushed with embarrassment.* يحمّر وجهه (خجلاً أو ارتباكاً)

▸ **blush** *noun* [C, usually sing.]: *She admitted, with a blush, that she had been lying.* تورّد أو إحمرار الوجه

boa /ˈbəʊə/ (*also* ˈ**boa constrictor**) *noun* [C] a large snake that kills animals by squeezing them بواء أو أصلة عاصرة

boar /bɔː(r)/ *noun* [C] (*pl.* **boar** or **boars**) **1** a male pig خنزير "ذكر"

2 a wild pig خنزير بري

⚷ **board**[1] /bɔːd/ *noun* **1** [C] a long, thin, flat piece of wood used for making floors, walls, etc: *The old house needed new floorboards.* لوح خشبي

2 [C] a thin flat piece of wood, etc. used for a particular purpose: *an ironing board* ○ *a diving board* ○ *a blackboard* ○ *a surfboard* لوح (لأغراض معيّنة) : منضدة

3 [C] a flat and usually square piece of wood, cardboard, etc. that you play certain games on: *a chessboard* ○ *board games* (= games you play on a board) رقعة ألعاب (الشطرنج مثلاً)

4 [C, with sing. or pl. verb] a group of people who control an organization, company, etc: *The board of directors is/are meeting to discuss the firm's future.* ○ *the Irish Tourist Board* مجلس ، هيئة

5 [U] the meals that are provided when you stay in a hotel, etc: *The prices are for a double room and full board* (= all the meals). طعام (في فندق الخ)

IDM **above board** → ABOVE

across the board → ACROSS

on board on a ship or aeroplane: *All the passengers were safely on board.* على ظهر (السفينة أو الطائرة)

⚷ **board**[2] /bɔːd/ *verb* [I,T] to get on a plane, ship, bus, etc: *We said goodbye and boarded the train.* ○ *Lufthansa flight LH120 to Hamburg is now boarding* (= ready to take passengers) *at Gate 27.* يركب (الطائرة مثلاً)

PHRV **board sth up** to cover with boards[1](1): *Nobody lives there now – it's all boarded up.* يغطي بالواح خشبية

▸ **boarder** *noun* [C] **1** a person who pays to live at sb's house مستأجر ، نزيل

2 a pupil who lives at a school during term-time تلميذ داخلي

ˈ**boarding card** *noun* [C] a card that you must show in order to board a plane or ship بطاقة الركوب (في طائرة أو سفينة)

ˈ**boarding house** *noun* [C] a private house where you can pay to stay and have meals for a period of time نزل

ˈ**boarding school** *noun* [C] a school that pupils live at during term-time مدرسة داخلية

boardroom /ˈbɔːdruːm; -rʊm/ *noun* [C] the room where a company's board of directors meets قاعة مجلس الإدارة

boast /bəʊst/ *verb* **1** [I,T] to talk with too much pride about sth that you have or can do: *I wish she wouldn't boast about her family so much.* ○ *He's always boasting that he's the fastest runner in the school.* يتبجّح، يتفاخر ، يتباهى

2 [T] (used about a place) to have sth that it can be proud of: *The town boasts over a dozen restaurants.* يفتخر بِ

▸ **boast** *noun* [C] **1** something you say that is too proud: *I didn't believe his boasts about how well he played.* تفاخر ، تباه

2 a thing that you are proud of: *It is our proud boast that our city is the most exciting in Europe.* فخر

boastful /-fl/ *adj* (used about a person or the things that he/she says) showing too much pride متفاخِر ، متبجّح

⚷ **boat** /bəʊt/ *noun* [C] a small vehicle that is used for travelling across water: *The cave can only be reached by boat/in a boat.* ○ *a rowing boat* ○ *a fishing boat* ○ *a motor boat* قارب ، مَرْكَب

> Usually **boat** means a small vessel but it can also be used for a large ship, especially one that carries passengers: *When does the next boat to France sail?*

bob /bɒb/ *verb* (bo**bb**ing; bo**bb**ed) [I,T] to move quickly up and down; to make sth do this: *The boats in the harbour were bobbing up and down in the water.* يتنطّط : ينطط

PHRV **bob up** to appear suddenly: *He disappeared and then bobbed up again on the other side of the pool.* يظهر فجاة ، ينبق

bobby /ˈbɒbi/ *noun* [C] (*pl.* **bobbies**) (*Brit informal*) a policeman شرطي

bode /bəʊd/ *verb* (*formal*)

IDM **bode well/ill (for sb/sth)** to be a good/bad sign for sb/sth يبشّر بخير أو ينذر بشرّ

bodily /ˈbɒdɪli/ *adj* of the human body; physical: *First we must attend to their bodily needs* (= make

boats

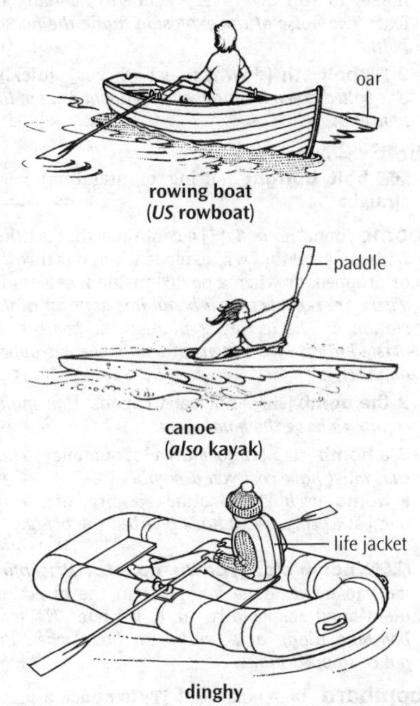

sure that they have a home, enough to eat, etc.). جسدي ، بدني

▶ **bodily** *adv* by taking hold of the body: *She picked up the child and carried him bodily from the room.* جسدياً

body /ˈbɒdi/ *noun* (*pl.* **bodies**) **1** [C] the whole physical form of a person or animal: *the human body* جسد ، بدن

2 [C] the body apart from the legs, arms and head: *She had injuries to her head and body.* جذع

3 [C] a dead human body: *The police have found a body in the canal.* جثّة

4 [sing.] the main part of sth: *The main body of the guests will arrive at about 7 o'clock.* الجزء الأساسي (من شيء)

5 [C, with sing. or pl. verb] a group of people who work or act together, especially in an official way: *The governing body of the college meets/meet once a month.* هيئة

6 [C] an object: *The doctor removed a foreign body* (= something that should not be there) *from the child's ear.* شيء ، جسم

IDM **in a body** all together: *The students went in a body to complain to their teacher.* جميعاً

bodybuilding /ˈbɒdibɪldɪŋ/ *noun* [U] making the muscles of the body stronger and larger by exercise (رياضة) كمال الأجسام

bodyguard /ˈbɒdigɑːd/ *noun* [C] a person or group of people whose job is to protect sb حارس شخصي، حرس

When **bodyguard** means a group of people, it can be used with either a singular or plural verb: *His bodyguard is/are armed.*

ˈ**body language** *noun* [U] showing how you feel by the way you move, stand, sit, etc., rather than by what you say لغة الجسد

ˈ**body odour** *noun* [U] (*abbr* **BO**) the unpleasant smell of a person's body when it is sweating رائحة العرق

ˈ**body piercing** (*also* **piercing**) *noun* [U] the making of holes in parts of the body as a decoration: *tattooing and body piercing* ثقب الجسم بأدوات الزينة

bog /bɒg/ *noun* [C,U] an area of ground that is very soft and wet: *the peat bogs of central Ireland* مستنقع

▶ ˌ**bogged ˈdown** *adj* **1** if a vehicle is bogged down, it has sunk into mud, etc. and cannot move غائص أو مغرز في الوحل (مثلاً)

2 if a person is bogged down in sth, he/she cannot make any progress: *We got bogged down in a long discussion and didn't have time to make any decisions.* عاجز عن التقدم

boggy /ˈbɒgi/ *adj* (**boggier**; **boggiest**) (used about land) soft and wet, so that your feet sink into it مستنقعي ، سبخ

boggle /ˈbɒgl/ *verb* [I] to be very surprised at sth, or to find it difficult to imagine: *Bob Brown as headteacher? The mind boggles!* يحتار ؛ يعجز عن التصوّر

BOGOF /ˈbɒgɒf/ *abbrev* (*informal*) buy one, get one free (a type of special offer used in shops): *BOGOF offers and bargains* الإثنان بسعر الواحد:(عرض للبيع)

bogus /ˈbəʊgəs/ *adj* pretending to be sth that it is not; not genuine: *He made a bogus claim to the insurance company.* زائف

boil[1] /bɔɪl/ *verb* **1** [I] (used about a liquid) to reach a high temperature where bubbles rise to the surface and the liquid changes to a gas: *Water boils at 100°C.* ○ *The kettle's boiling* (= the water inside the kettle). يَغْلي

2 [T] to heat a liquid until it boils and let it keep boiling: *Boil all drinking water for five minutes.* يُغْلي

3 [I,T] to cook in boiling water: *Put the potatoes on to boil, please.* ○ *He doesn't even know how to boil an egg.* يسلق

4 [I] (used about a person) to feel very angry: *She was boiling with rage.* يَغْلي غضباً

PHR V **boil down to sth** to have sth as the most important point: *What it all boils down to is that you don't want to spend too much money.* يخلص الأمر إلى

boil over 1 (used about a liquid) to boil and flow over the sides of a pan: *You let the soup boil over.* يغلي حتى يفيض ، يفور

2 (used about an argument or sb's feelings) to become more serious or angry يحتد ، يفور غضبه

▶ **boil** *noun* [sing.] an act or period of boiling غليان

IDM **bring sth to the boil** to heat sth until it boils: *Bring the soup to the boil, then allow to simmer for five minutes* يسخّن لدرجة الغليان ، يفوّر
come to the boil to begin to boil يغْلي
boiling (*also* ˌ**boiling** ˈ**hot**) *adj* (*informal*) very hot: *Open a window – it's boiling hot in here.* ○ *Can I have a drink? I'm boiling.* حارّ جداً ؛ "محموم"

boil[2] /bɔɪl/ *noun* [C] a painful swelling under your skin, like a large spot: *The boil on my neck has burst.* بَثْرة

boiler /ˈbɔɪlə(r)/ *noun* [C] **1** a metal container used for providing hot water in a house غلّاية

2 a large metal container used for producing steam in an engine مِرجَل

ˈ**boiler suit** *noun* [C] a piece of clothing that covers your body, arms and legs, worn especially for dirty work رداء من قطعة واحدة للوقاية من الاتساخ

ˈ**boiling point** *noun* [C] the temperature at which a liquid starts to boil نقطة الغليان

boisterous /ˈbɔɪstərəs/ *adj* (used about a person or his/her behaviour) noisy and full of energy: *Their children are very nice but they can get a bit too boisterous.* صخّاب
▸ **boisterously** *adv* بصخب

bold /bəʊld/ *adj* **1** (used about a person or his/her behaviour) brave and confident; not afraid: *Not many people are bold enough to say exactly what they think.* ○ *We need somebody with bold new ideas.* جريء ؛ شجاع

2 that you can see clearly: *The new fashion is for bold, bright colours.* واضح

3 (used about printed letters) in thick, dark type: *The title was written in bold type.* (حرف طباعة) ثخين وأسود
▸ **boldly** *adv* بجراءة ، بشجاعة
boldness *noun* [U] جراءة ، شجاعة

bollard /ˈbɒlɑːd/ *noun* [C] a short thick concrete post in the middle or at the side of a road. Bollards divide the two sides of the road, or they are used to stop cars passing or parking. عمود قصير غليظ (لتقسيم شارع أو منع المرور)

bolster /ˈbəʊlstə(r)/ *verb* [T] **bolster sb/sth (up)** to support or encourage sb/sth; to make sth stronger: *His remarks did nothing to bolster my confidence.* يسند ، يعزّز

bolt[1] /bəʊlt/ *noun* [C] **1** a small piece of metal (shaped like a screw without a point) that is used with another piece of metal (a nut) for fastening things together. The nut screws onto the bolt. مسمار ملوْلب

2 a bar of metal that you can slide across the inside of the door in order to fasten it مِزلاج ، رِتاج
▸ **bolt** *verb* [T] **1** to fasten one thing to another using a bolt: *All the tables have been bolted to the floor so that nobody can steal them.* يثبّت بمسامير ملولبة

2 to fasten a door, etc. with a bolt: *Make sure that the door is locked and bolted.* يحكم الإغلاق بمزلاج ، يتَربّس

bolt[2] /bəʊlt/ *verb* **1** [I] (used especially about a horse) to run away very suddenly, usually in fear: *The noise of the explosion made the horses bolt.* ينفر

2 [T] **bolt sth (down)** to eat sth very quickly: *She bolted down a sandwich and dashed out of the house.* يزدرد ، يلتهم

bolt[3] /bəʊlt/ *adv*
IDM **bolt upright** (sitting or standing) very straight باستقامة ، منتصباً

bomb /bɒm/ *noun* **1** [C] a container that is filled with material that will explode when it is thrown or dropped, or when a device inside it sets it off: *There are reports that a bomb has gone off at the station.* ○ *The terrorists planted the bomb in a waste bin.* ○ *Several tons of bombs were dropped on the city.* قنبلة

2 the bomb [sing.] nuclear weapons: *How many countries have the bomb now?* قنبلة ذرية

3 a bomb [sing.] (*informal*) a lot of money: *That coat must have cost you a bomb!* مال كثير
▸ **bomb** *verb* [T] to attack a city, etc. with bombs: *Enemy forces have bombed the bridge.* يقذف بالقنابل

PHR V **bomb along, down, up, etc.** (*Brit informal*) to move along very fast in the direction mentioned, especially in a vehicle: *He was bombing along at 90 miles an hour when the police stopped him.* يندفع

bombard /bɒmˈbɑːd/ *verb* [T] to attack a place with bombs or guns: *They bombarded the city until the enemy surrendered.* ○ (*figurative*) *The reporters bombarded the minister with questions.* يقذف بالقنابل ؛ يمطر بالأسئلة
▸ **bombardment** /bɒmˈbɑːdmənt/ *noun* [C,U] an attack with bombs or guns: *The main radio station has come under enemy bombardment.* قذف بالقنابل

ˈ**bomb disposal** *noun* [U] the removing or exploding of bombs in order to make an area safe: *a bomb-disposal expert* إبطال مفعول القنابل

bomber /ˈbɒmə(r)/ *noun* [C] **1** a type of plane that drops bombs قاذفة القنابل

2 a person who throws bombs or leaves them to explode in a public place مفجّر قنابل في مكان عام

bombshell /ˈbɒmʃel/ *noun* [C, usually sing.] an unexpected piece of news, usually about sth unpleasant خبر صاعق

bona fide /ˌbəʊnə ˈfaɪdi/ *adj* real or genuine: *This car park is for the use of bona fide customers only.* حقيقي ، غير زائف

bon appetit /ˌbɒn æpəˈtiː/ *interj* (used to wish sb an enjoyable meal) "بالهنا والشفا!"

bond /bɒnd/ *noun* **1** [C] (often plural) something that links two or more people or groups of people together, such as a feeling of friendship: *Our two countries are united by bonds of friendship.* رابطة ، علاقة

2 [C] a certificate that you can buy from a government or company that promises to pay you interest on the money you have lent: *National Savings Bonds* سَنَد

bone /bəʊn/ *noun* **1** [C] one of the hard parts inside the body of a person or animal that are covered with flesh and skin: *He's broken a bone in his hand.* ○ *This fish has got a lot of bones in it.* عَظْمة
2 [U] the substance that bones are made of عَظْم
IDM **have a bone to pick with sb** to have sth that you want to complain to sb about يودّ أنْ يشتكي أو يعاتب شخصاً
make no bones about (doing) sth to do sth without hesitating or feeling worried about it: *She made no bones about telling him exactly what she thought about him.* لا يتحرّج
▶ **bone** *verb* [T] to take the bones out of sth: *to bone a fish, chicken, etc.* ينزع العظم

ˌbone ˈdry *adj* completely dry: *Give that plant some water. It's bone dry.* جاف تماماً

ˈbone marrow (*also* **marrow**) *noun* [U] the soft substance that is inside the bones of a person or animal مخ العظم ، نخاع

bonfire /ˈbɒnfaɪə(r)/ *noun* [C] a large fire that you build outside to burn rubbish, etc. نار كبيرة في العراء

ˈBonfire Night *noun* [C] the night of 5 November. On this day people in Britain light bonfires and fireworks to celebrate the failure of Guy Fawkes to blow up the Houses of Parliament in the seventeenth century. ليلة إشعال النيران (في بريطانيا)

bonkers /ˈbɒŋkəz/ *adj* (*Brit slang*) mad; crazy مجنون ؛ مخبول

bonnet /ˈbɒnɪt/ *noun* [C] **1** (*US* **hood**) the front part of a car that covers the engine غطاء محرّك السيارة
2 a type of hat which covers the sides of the face and is fastened with strings under the chin قُبّعة (تربط بشريط)

bonus /ˈbəʊnəs/ *noun* (*pl.* **bonuses**) **1** a payment that is added to what is usual: *All our employees will receive a Christmas bonus.* علاوة إكرامية
2 something good that you get in addition to what you expect: *As a special bonus, all our holidays will include use of a car for a week.* مكافأة ، إضافة

bony /ˈbəʊni/ *adj* (**bonier**; **boniest**) so thin that you can see the shape of the bones: *long bony fingers* نحيل، ناتيء العظام

boo /buː/ *interj, noun* [C] (*pl.* **boos**) **1** a sound you make to show that you do not like sb/sth: *The minister's speech was met with boos from the audience.* (صوت للتعبير عن الاستخفاف أو الاستهجان)
2 a sound you make to frighten or surprise sb: *He jumped out from behind the door and said 'boo'.* (صوت للتخويف أو للمباغتة)
▶ **boo** *verb* [I,T]: *The crowd booed when they were told that the show had been cancelled.* يصيح استهجاناً

boob¹ /buːb/ *noun* [C] (*informal*) a silly mistake: *to make a boob* خطأ سخيف
▶ **boob** *verb* [I]: *I'm afraid I've boobed again.* يرتكب خطأ سخيفاً

boob² /buːb/ *noun* [C, usually pl.] (*slang*) a woman's breast ثدي

booby prize /ˈbuːbi praɪz/ (*also* **wooden spoon**) *noun* [C] a prize that is given as a joke to the person who is last in a competition جائزة تافهة تُعطى للخاسر دعابةً

booby trap /ˈbuːbi træp/ *noun* [C] something dangerous, like a bomb, which is hidden inside sth that seems harmless فخ متفجر ؛ شَرَك خداعي
▶ **booby-trap** *verb* [T]: *The car had been booby-trapped.* يخبئ شركاً ، يُفخّخ

book¹ /bʊk/ *noun* **1** [C] a number of sheets of paper, fastened together inside a cover, with words printed on them for people to read: *I'm reading a book on astrology.* ○ *She's writing a book about her life abroad.* ○ *Do you have any books by William Golding?* ○ *Open your books, please.* ○ *to publish a book* ○ *a library book* ○ *a cookery book* كتاب
2 [C] a number of pieces of paper, fastened together inside a cover, for people to write on: *Please write down all the new vocabulary in your exercise books.* كرّاسة ، دفتر
3 [C] a small number of things fastened together in the form of a book: *a book of stamps* دفتر
4 books [plural] the records that a company, etc., keeps of the amount of money it spends or receives: *We employ an accountant to keep the books.* دفتر تجاري
IDM **be in sb's good/bad books** (*informal*) to have someone pleased/angry with you: *He's been in his girlfriend's bad books since he forgot her birthday.* مَرْضي عنه/مغضوب عليه
by the book exactly according to the rules: *A policeman must always do things by the book.* حسب القوانين

book² /bʊk/ *verb* **1** [I,T] to arrange to have or do sth at a particular time: *You must book weeks in advance if you want to travel on Christmas Eve.* ○ *Have you booked a table, sir?* ○ *to book a seat on a plane/train/bus* ○ *I've booked a hotel room for you/I've booked you a hotel room.* ○ *I'm sorry, but this evening's performance is fully booked* (= there are no seats left). يحجز
2 [T] to write the name of a person who has done sth wrong in a book: *The police booked her for dangerous driving* (= charged her with dangerous driving). ○ *The player was booked twice during the match and then sent off.* يسجّل
PHR V **book in** to say that you have arrived at a hotel, etc. (and sign your name on a list) يقوم بالحجز (في فندق مثلاً)
book sb in to arrange a room for sb at a hotel, etc. in advance: *I've booked you in at the George Hotel.* يحجز لشخص (في فندق مثلاً)
▶ **booking** *noun* [C,U] the arrangement you make in advance to have a hotel room, a seat on a plane, etc: *Did you manage to make a*

booking? ○ *Booking for the new musical does not start until October.* حَجْز

bookcase /ˈbʊkkeɪs/ *noun* [C] a piece of furniture with shelves to keep books on خزانة كتب

bookie /ˈbʊki/ *noun* [C] (*informal*) = BOOKMAKER

ˈbooking office *noun* [C] an office where you buy tickets مكتب بيع التذاكر

bookkeeping /ˈbʊkkiːpɪŋ/ *noun* [U] keeping the accounts of the money that a company, etc., spends or receives مسك الدفاتر

booklet /ˈbʊklət/ *noun* [C] a small thin book, usually with a soft cover, that gives information about sth كُتَيِّب

bookmaker /ˈbʊkmeɪkə(r)/ (*also informal* **bookie**) *noun* [C] a person whose job is to take bets on horse races, etc. شخص يبيع تذاكر الرِّهان

bookmark /ˈbʊkmɑːk/ *noun* [C] a narrow piece of card, etc. that you put between the pages of a book so that you can find the same place again easily علامة كتاب

bookseller /ˈbʊkselə(r)/ *noun* [C] a person whose job is selling books بائع كتب

bookshop /ˈbʊkʃɒp/ (*US* **ˈbookstore** /ˈbʊkstɔː(r)/) *noun* [C] a shop that sells books ➲ Look at **library**. مكتبة (تجارية)

bookstall /ˈbʊkstɔːl/ (*US* **ˈnews-stand**) *noun* [C] a type of small shop, which is open at the front, selling newspapers, magazines and books, e.g. on a station كشك الكتب

bookworm /ˈbʊkwɜːm/ *noun* [C] a person who likes reading books very much قارئ نهم

boom[1] /buːm/ *noun* [C] a period in which sth increases or develops very quickly: *There was a boom in car sales in the 1980s.* ○ *a boom year for exports* ازدهار ، فترة رواج

▸ **boom** *verb* [I] to grow very quickly in size or value: *Business was booming in the Japanese car industry.* ينمو بازدهار

boom[2] /buːm/ *verb* [I,T] **boom (sth) (out)** to make a loud, deep, hollow sound: *guns booming in the distance* ○ *The loudspeaker boomed out instructions to the crowd.* يدوّي بِ

boomerang /ˈbuːməræŋ/ *noun* [C] a curved piece of wood that returns to you when you throw it in the right way, used for hunting by the first people who lived in Australia البُومِرانغ: قطعة خشبية يرميها الصائد و تعود اليه

boon /buːn/ *noun* [C] a thing that is very helpful and that you are grateful for هِبة ، نعمة

boost /buːst/ *verb* [T] to increase sth in number, value or strength: *If we lower the price, that should boost sales.* ○ *The good exam result boosted her confidence.* يرفع ، يزيد

▸ **boost** *noun* [C] an increase; sth that encourages people: *The fall in the value of the pound has led to a boost in exports.* ○ *The president's visit gave a boost to the soldiers' morale.* زيادة : تشجيع ، تعزيز

⚷ **boot** /buːt/ *noun* [C] **1** a type of shoe that covers your foot and ankle and sometimes part of your leg: *a pair of ladies' boots* ○ *ski boots* ○ *walking/climbing boots* ○ *football boots* حذاء عالي الرقبة ، جزمة

2 (*US* **trunk**) the part of a car where you put luggage, usually at the back صندوق السيارة

▸ **boot** *verb* [T] to kick sth/sb hard: *He booted the ball over the fence.* يركل

PHR V **boot sb/sth out** to force sb/sth to leave a place: *The boys were booted out of the cub for fighting.* يلقي أو يرمي خارجاً

booth /buːð; *US* buːθ/ *noun* [C] a small enclosed place with thin walls that divide it from the rest of the room or area: *He called from a public phone booth at the station.* ○ *a ticket booth* كُشك

booty /ˈbuːti/ *noun* [U] things that are taken by thieves or captured by soldiers in war غنيمة

⚷ **border** /ˈbɔːdə(r)/ *noun* [C] **1** a line that divides two countries, etc.; the land close to this line: *The refugees escaped across/over the border.* ○ *We crossed the border into Switzerland.* ○ *the Swiss border* ○ *the border between France and Italy* ○ *Italy's border with France* حدّ ، تخم

> We use **border** and **frontier** to talk about the line that divides two countries or states. We usually use **border** to talk about natural divisions: *The river forms the border between the two countries.* **Boundary** is usually used for the line that divides smaller areas: *the county boundary.*

2 a band or strip around the edge of sth, often for decoration: *a white tablecloth with a blue border* حافّة ، زِيق

▸ **border** *verb* [T] to be a border to; to be on the border of: *The road was bordered with trees.* ○ *Which English counties border Scotland?* يحدّ ؛ يتاخم ؛ يحفّ بِ

PHR V **border on sth 1** to be next to sth: *Our garden borders on the railway line.* يحاذي ، يجاور

2 to be almost the same as sth: *The dictator's ideas bordered on madness.* يشابه، يقارب

borderline /ˈbɔːdəlaɪn/ *noun* [sing.] the line that marks a division between two different cases, conditions, etc: *The novel is on the borderline between fiction and non-fiction.* ○ *He's a borderline case – he may pass the exam or he may fail.* حافّة ، خط فاصل

⚷ **bore**[1] /bɔː(r)/ *verb* [T] to make sb tired and uninterested: *I hope I'm not boring you.* ○ *Those old jokes bore me.* يضجر

▸ **bore** *noun* **1** [C] a person who talks or behaves in an uninteresting way: *Her husband is such a bore.* شخص ثقيل الدم، مملّ

2 [sing.] (*informal*) something that you have to do that you find uninteresting: *It's such a bore having to learn these lists of irregular verbs.* شيء مضجِر

bored *adj* feeling uninterested and tired because sth is not exciting or because you do not have anything to do: *I'm bored. There's nothing to do at home.* ○ *The children get bored in the long* *holidays.* ○ *He gave a bored yawn.* ○ *The play was awful. We were bored stiff* (= extremely bored). شاعر بالضجر

boredom /-dəm/ *noun* [U] the state of being bored: *People say that many young people turn to crime out of boredom.* ضجر ، سأم

boring /ˈbɔːrɪŋ/ *adj* uninteresting; dull: *a boring film* ○ *boring work* مضْجِر ، يبعث على السأم

bore² /bɔː(r)/ *verb* [I,T] to make a round hole or passage through sth: *The drill can bore through solid rock.* ○ *They are boring a tunnel through the mountain.* يثقب

bore³ /bɔː(r)/ *pt* of BEAR²

born /bɔːn/ *verb* **be born** to come into the world by birth; to start existing: *Where were you born?* ○ *My parents were born in Wales, but they grew up in England.* ○ *Peter Jones, born 1932, died 1992.* ○ *He was born in Frankfurt, of Italian parents.* ○ *I'm going to give up work after the baby is born.* ○ *Their baby was born deaf.* ○ *The idea of free education for all was born in the nineteenth century.* ○ *His unhappiness was born out of a feeling of frustration.* يولد ؛ ينشأ

▸ **born** *adj* having a natural ability to do the task mentioned: *She's a born leader.* مطبوع أو مفطور (على) ،

-born (in compounds) born in the place or state mentioned: *Samuel Beckett, the Irish-born writer, lived in Paris most of his life.* مولود

ˌ**born-aˈgain** *adj* having found new, strong faith in a religion: *a born-again Christian* متجدِّد الإيمان (بدين ما)

borne /bɔːn/ *pp* of BEAR²

borough /ˈbʌrə; *US* -rəʊ/ *noun* [C] a town, or an area within a large town, that has some form of local government مدينة أو ج زء من مدينة يتمتع بحكم ذاتي، منطقة

borrow /ˈbɒrəʊ/ *verb* [I,T] **borrow (sth) (from/off sb/sth) 1** to take or receive sth from sb/sth that you intend to give back, usually after a short time: *I had to borrow from the bank to pay for my car.* ○ *They borrowed £10 000 to buy a new car.* ○ *Could I borrow your pen for a minute?* ○ *Can I borrow £10? I'll pay you back next week.* ○ *He's always borrowing off his mother.* ○ *I borrowed a book from the library.* ❶ Be careful not to confuse **borrow** with its opposite **lend**. يستعير ، يقترض

2 to take sth and use it as your own; to copy: *That idea is borrowed from another book.* يستمدّ ، يقلِّد

▸ **borrower** *noun* [C] a person who borrows مستدين ، مُقْتَرِض ؛ مستعير

bosom /ˈbʊzəm/ *noun (formal)* [C, usually sing.] a person's chest, especially a woman's breasts: *She clutched the child to her bosom.* صدر ، ثديا المرأة

IDM **in the bosom of sth** close to; with the protection of: *He was glad to be back in the bosom of his family.* في كَنَف ، في أحضان

ˌ**bosom ˈfriend** *noun* [C] a very close friend صديق حميم

boss /bɒs/ *noun* [C] *(informal)* a person whose job is to give orders to others at work; an employer; a manager: *I'm going to ask the boss for a day off work.* ○ *Who's in charge when the boss is away?* ○ *OK. You're the boss* (= you make the decisions). رئيس ؛ موظِّف ؛ مدير

▸ **boss** *verb* [T] **boss sb (about/around)** to give orders to sb, especially in an annoying way: *I wish you'd stop bossing me around.* يتأمّر على

bossy *adj* (**bossier**; **bossiest**) liking to give orders to other people, often in an annoying way: *His mother was a strong, bossy woman.* متأمِّر ، محبّ للترؤس، متَسلّط

bossily *adv* بتأمّر

bossiness *noun* [U] تأمّر

botany /ˈbɒtəni/ *noun* [U] the scientific study of plants علم النبات

▸ **botanical** /bəˈtænɪkl/ *adj*: *botanical gardens* (= a type of park where plants are grown for scientific study) نباتي

botanist /ˈbɒtənɪst/ *noun* [C] a person who studies plants عالم النبات

botch /bɒtʃ/ *verb* [T] **botch sth (up)** to do or repair sth badly because you are not very skilful: *I've made rather a botched job of this typing, I'm afraid.* يفسد العمل لعدم مهارته

both¹ /bəʊθ/ *det, pron* the two; the one as well as the other: *Both women were French.* ○ *Both the women were French.* ○ *Both of the women were French.* ○ *I talked to the women. Both of them were French/They were both French.* ○ *I liked them both.* ○ *We were both very tired.* ○ *Both of us were tired.* ○ *They have both seen the film.* ○ *I've got two sisters. They both live in London/Both of them live in London.* ○ *Both of my sisters live in London.* ❶ Note that we CANNOT say: *the both women* or: *my both sisters.* كلا ، كلتا

both² /bəʊθ/ *adv* **both... and...** not only... but also...: *I like both him and his wife.* ○ *They were both hungry and thirsty.* معاً ؛ على السواء

bother /ˈbɒðə(r)/ *verb* **1** [T] to disturb or annoy sb: *I'm sorry to bother you, but could I speak to you for a moment?* ○ *Don't bother Sue with that now – she's busy.* يزعج ، يضايق

2 [T] to worry sb: *You don't look very happy. Is something bothering you?* يقلق

3 [I,T] **bother (to do sth)**; **bother about sth** (usually negative) to make the effort to do sth: *'Shall I make you something to eat?' 'No, don't bother – I'm not hungry.'* ○ *He didn't even bother to say thank you.* ○ *Don't bother about the washing-up. I'll do it later.* ○ *Don't bother waiting for me – I'll catch you up later.* يكلّف أو يُتعب نفسه

▸ **bother** *noun* [U] trouble or difficulty: *Thanks for all your help. It's saved me a lot of bother.* تعب ، عُسر

bother *interj* (used when you are annoyed): *Oh bother! I've left my keys in the car!* (للتعبير عن الضيق)

bothered *adj* worried: *I'm a bit bothered about my sister – she doesn't look very well.* قلق

IDM **can't be bothered (to do sth)** If sb can't be bothered to do sth, he/she does not want to make the effort and is not going to do it: *I can't be*

a b c d e f g h i j k l m n o p q r s t u v w x y z

bothered to do my homework now. I'll do it tomorrow. لا يرغب في القيام بعمل ما

I'm not bothered I don't mind: *'What would you like to do this evening?' 'I'm not bothered really.'* لا فرقَ عندي

bottle /ˈbɒtl/ *noun* [C] **1** a glass or plastic container with a narrow neck for keeping liquids in: *a milk bottle ○ an empty bottle* زجاجة ، قنّينة

2 the amount of liquid in a bottle: *a bottle of milk* (ما تحويه الزجاجة من سائل)

▸ **bottle** *verb* [T] to put sth into bottles: *After three or four months the wine is bottled.* يعبّئ في زجاجات

bottled *adj* that you can buy in bottles: *bottled water* معبّأ في زجاجات

ˈ**bottle bank** *noun* [C] a large container in a public place where people can leave their empty bottles so that the glass can be used again (recycled) صندوق كبير لجمع الزجاجات

bottleneck /ˈbɒtlnek/ *noun* [C] **1** a narrow piece of road that causes traffic to slow down or stop زنقة ، مختَنَق (في طريق)

2 something that slows down progress, especially in business of industry عنق الزجاجة

bottom /ˈbɒtəm/ *noun* **1** [C, usually sing.] the lowest part of sth: *The house is at the bottom of a hill. ○ Look at the picture at the bottom of page 23. ○ I think I've got a pen in the bottom of my bag.* أسفل : قعر

2 [C] the flat surface on the outside of an object, on which it stands: *There's a label on the bottom of the box.* قاعدة

3 [sing.] the far end of sth: *The bus stop is at the bottom of the road.* آخر

4 [sing.] the least important position in relation to other people: *She started at the bottom and now she's the Managing Director.* دَرَك ، حضيض

5 [sing.] the ground under the sea, a river, a swimming pool, etc: *The water was so clear that we could see the bottom.* قاع

6 [C] the part of your body that you sit on: *He fell over and landed on his bottom.* عجيزة ، كَفَل

7 bottoms [plural] the lower part of a piece of clothing that is in two parts: *pyjama bottoms ○ track suit bottoms* بنطلون (البيجاما مثلاً)

IDM **be at the bottom of sth** to be the real cause of sth: *I'm sure Kate Mills is at the bottom of all this.* (يكون) المسبّب الحقيقي لشيء

get to the bottom of sth to find out the real cause of sth يكتشف حقيقة الأمر

▸ **bottom** *adj* in the lowest position: *the bottom shelf ○ I live on the bottom floor of a block of flats.* أسفل

bottomless *adj* very deep; without limit عميق ، لا حدّ له

ˌ**bottom** ˈ**line** *noun* [sing.] **1** the most important thing to consider when you are discussing or deciding sth, etc: *A musical instrument should look and feel good, but the bottom line is how it sounds.* خلاصة الأمر

2 the final profit or loss that a company has made in a particular period of time صافي الارباح والخساره للشركة في فترة ما

3 the lowest price that sb will accept for sth أدنى سعر مقبول

bough /baʊ/ *noun* [C] one of the main branches of a tree غصن ، فرع

bought /bɔːt/ *pt, pp* of BUY

boulder /ˈbəʊldə(r)/ *noun* [C] a very large rock صخرة ضخمة ، جلْمُود

boulevard /ˈbuːləvɑːd; *US* ˈbʊl-/ *noun* [C] a wide street in a city with trees on each side شارع عريض على جانبيه أشجار

bounce /baʊns/ *verb* **1** [I,T] (used about a ball, etc.) to move away quickly after it has hit a hard surface; to make a ball do this: *In tennis, the ball can only bounce once before you hit it back. ○ The stone bounced off the wall and hit her on the head. ○ A small boy came down the street, bouncing a ball.* يرتدّ ؛ ينطّط

2 [I] to jump up and down continuously: *The children were bouncing on their beds.* ينط ، يتنطّط

3 [I] (used about a cheque) to be returned by a bank without payment because there is not enough money in the account يرتدّ (الشيك)

PHR V **bounce back** to recover from a failure, disappointment, etc. and return quickly to your normal life with the same energy as before يرتدّ إلى حاله (بعد نكسة)

▸ **bounce** *noun* [C]: *I couldn't reach the ball before the second bounce.* ارتداد (الكرة) ، وثبة

bouncy (**bouncier**; **bounciest**) *adj* (كرة) نطّاطة: كثير الحيوية

bound[1] /baʊnd/ *adj* **bound to do sth 1** certain to do sth: *You've done so much work that you're bound to pass the exam. ○ There are bound to be problems in a situation like this.* لا بدّ أن

2 (not before a noun) having a legal or moral duty to do sth: *The company is bound by UK employment law. ○ She felt bound to refuse the offer.* ملْزم

IDM **bound up with sth** very closely connected with sth متّصل بالشيء (اتصالاً وثيقاً)

bound[2] /baʊnd/ *adj* **bound (for...)** travelling to a particular place: *a ship bound for Australia* متّجه إلى

bound[3] /baʊnd/ *verb* [I] to run quickly with jumping movements: *She bounded up the stairs in a state of great excitement.* يقفز ، يثب

▸ **bound** *noun* [C]: *With a couple of bounds he had crossed the room.* قفزة ، وثبة

bound[4] *pt, pp* of BIND

boundary /ˈbaʊndri/ *noun* [C] (*pl.* **boundaries**) **1** a line that marks the limits of a place and divides it from other places: *The main road is the boundary between the two districts.* حدّ ، تخم

2 the farthest limit of sth: *Scientists continue to push back the boundaries of human knowledge.* حد ، تخم
➲ Look at the note at **border**.

boundless /ˈbaʊndləs/ *adj* having no limit: *boundless energy* لا حدّ له

bounds /baʊndz/ *noun* [plural] limits that cannot or should not be passed: *Price rises must be kept within reasonable bounds.* حدود (لا يمكن تجاوزها)

IDM **out of bounds** forbidden; not to be entered by sb: *This area is out of bounds to all staff.* محظور ، يمنع دخوله

bouquet /buˈkeɪ/ *noun* [C] a bunch of flowers that is arranged in an attractive way: *The actress received a huge bouquet of roses.* باقة زهور

bourgeois /ˈbʊəʒwɑː; ˌbʊərˈʒwɑː/ *adj* typical of fairly rich middle-class people: *bourgeois attitudes, ideas, values, etc.* برجوازي ، متعلق بالطبقة الوسطى

▶ **bourgeoisie** /ˌbʊəʒwɑːˈziː/ *noun* [sing., with sing. or pl. verb] the middle class البرجوازية ، الطبقة الوسطى

bout /baʊt/ *noun* [C] **1** a short period of great activity: *a bout of hard work* فترة نشاط قصيرة

2 a period of illness: *I'm just recovering from a bout of flu.* نَوبَة مرض

boutique /buːˈtiːk/ *noun* [C] a small shop that sells fashionable clothes or expensive presents دكان صغير لبيع الملابس الأنيقة

bovine /ˈbəʊvaɪn/ *adj* (*formal*) connected with cows بقري

bow¹ /baʊ/ *verb* **1** [I,T] to bend your head or the upper part of your body forward and down, as a sign of respect: *At the end of the play all the actors came onto the stage and bowed.* ○ *He bowed his head respectfully.* ينحني

2 bow to sth [I] to accept sth: *I do not think the unions should bow to pressure from the Government.* يخضع ، يذعن

PHRV **bow out (of sth)** to retire from an important position or stop taking part in sth: *After 12 years on the committee, she decided to bow out.* ينسحب، يتقاعد

▶ **bow** *noun* [C] an act of bowing (1): *The audience were still clapping so the actors came back for another bow.* انحناءة

bow² /bəʊ/ *noun* [C] **1** a knot with two loops and two loose ends that you use when you are tying shoes, ribbons, etc: *He tied the ribbon into a bow.* ○ *She had a black bow in her hair.* أنشوطة

2 a weapon for shooting arrows. A bow is a curved piece of wood that is held in shape by a tight string. قوس

3 a long thin piece of wood with horsehair stretched along it that you use for playing a violin, etc. قوس الكمنجة

bow³ /baʊ/ *noun* [C] the front part of a ship ➲ Look at **stern**. قيدوم السفينة

bowel /ˈbaʊəl/ *noun* [C, usually pl.] one of the tubes that takes waste food from the stomach so that it can pass out of the body أمعاء

⚷ **bowl¹** /bəʊl/ *noun* [C] **1** a deep round dish without a lid that is used for holding food or liquid: *a sugar bowl* ○ *a mixing bowl* سلطانية، زبدية

2 the amount of sth that is in a bowl: *I usually have a bowl of cereal for breakfast.* سلطانيّة من

3 a large plastic container that is used for washing up, washing clothes, etc. طست بلاستيكي

⚷ **bowl²** /bəʊl/ *verb* [I,T] (in cricket) to throw the ball in the direction of the batsman (في الكريكيت) يرمي الكرة

PHRV **bowl sb over 1** to knock sb down when you are moving quickly يطرحه أرضاً

2 to astonish sb in a pleasant way: *I was absolutely bowled over by the beautiful scenery.* يذهل ، يسحر

bowler /ˈbəʊlə(r)/ (*also* ˌ**bowler ˈhat**) (*US* **derby**) *noun* [C] a round hard black hat, usually worn by men قبعة مستديرة سوداء

bowling /ˈbəʊlɪŋ/ *noun* [U] a game in which you roll a ball towards a group of wooden objects and try to knock down as many of them as you can: *tenpin bowling* لعبة البولنغ

bowls /bəʊlz/ *noun* [U] a game in which you try to roll large wooden balls as near as possible to a smaller ball لعبة البولز (دحرجة الكرات للاقتراب من كرة صغيرة)

ˌ**bow ˈtie** *noun* [C] a tie in the shape of a bow (1), that is worn by men, especially on formal occasions "بابيون": ربطة عنق على شكل الفراشة

⚷ **box¹** /bɒks/ *noun* **1** [C] a square or rectangular container for solid objects. A box often has a lid: *We opened the lid and looked inside the box.* ○ *I keep the letters in an old shoebox.* صندوق

2 [C] a box and the things inside it: *a box of chocolates, matches, tissues, etc.* علبة أو صندوق (شوكولاتة مثلاً)

3 [C] an empty square or rectangle on a form in which you have to write sth: *Write your full name in the box below.* مربع صغير في استمارة

4 [C] an enclosed area that is used for a particular purpose: *a telephone box* ○ *a witness box* (= in a court of law) كشك (تليفون) ؛ قفص (الشاهد)

5 [C] an enclosed area in a theatre in which a small group of people can sit and watch the play مقصورة

6 the box [sing.] (*Brit informal*) television: *What's on the box tonight?* التلفزيون

▶ **box** *verb* [T] to put sth into a box: *a boxed set of CDs* يضع في صندوق

box² /bɒks/ *verb* [T] to fight in the sport of boxing: *He used to box when he was in the Army.* يلاكم

▶ **boxer** *noun* [C] a person who boxes as a sport, often professionally ملاكم

boxing *noun* [U] a sport in which two people fight by hitting each other with their hands inside large gloves: *the world middleweight boxing champion* ○ *boxing gloves* ملاكمة

ˈ**boxer shorts** *noun* [plural] men's underpants that are similar to shorts سروال تحتاني قصير للرجال

Boxing Day /ˈbɒksɪŋ deɪ/ *noun* [U] the day after Christmas Day; 26 December ❶ In England and Wales Boxing Day is a public holiday. اليوم التالي لعيد الميلاد

a b c d e f g h i j k l m n o p q r s t u v w x y z

'box number *noun* [C] a number that is given in a newspaper advertisement as part of the address to which replies should be sent رقم بريدي

'box office *noun* [C] the place in a cinema, theatre, etc. where the tickets are sold شبّاك التذاكر

boy¹ /bɔɪ/ *noun* **1** [C] a male child: *They've got three children – two boys and a girl.* صبي ، ولد

2 the boys [plural] (*informal*) a group of male friends مجموعة أصدقاء من الرجال

▶ **boyhood** /-hʊd/ *noun* [U] the time of being a boy: *My father told me some of his boyhood memories.* (فترة) الصبا

boyish *adj* like a boy: *a boyish smile* صبياني

boy² /bɔɪ/ *interj* (*informal*) (*especially US*) (used for expressing a strong feeling): *Boy, it's hot today!* (للتعبير عن شعور حادّ)

boycott /'bɔɪkɒt/ *verb* [T] to refuse to buy things from a particular company, take part in an event, etc. because you strongly disapprove of it: *Several countries boycotted the Olympic Games in protest.* يقاطع

▶ **boycott** *noun* [C]: *a boycott of the local elections* مقاطعة

boyfriend /'bɔɪfrend/ *noun* [C] a man or boy with whom a person has a romantic and/or sexual relationship صديق ، صاحب

,Boy 'Scout = SCOUT (2)

bra /brɑː/ *noun* [C] a piece of clothing that women wear under their other clothes to support their breasts حمّالة الثديين ، سوتيان

brace¹ /breɪs/ *noun* **1** [C] a metal frame that is attached to a child's teeth in order to make them straight دعامة لتقويم الأسنان

2 braces (*US* **suspenders**) [plural] a pair of straps for holding your trousers up. You put the braces over your shoulders and attach them to the top of your trousers at the front and back. حمّالة البنطلون

brace² /breɪs/ *verb* [T] **1 brace (yourself)** to make your body stiff or press it against sth in order to prepare yourself, e.g. if sth is going to hit you, or to stop yourself from falling: *He braced himself as the big man came towards him.* يستجمع قواه ، يتوتّر

2 brace yourself (for sth) to prepare yourself for sth difficult or unpleasant: *You'd better brace yourself for some bad news.* يتجلّد ، يستجمع قواه

▶ **bracing** *adj* (used about a type of air, etc.) making you feel healthy and lively: *bracing sea air* منْعِش

bracelet /'breɪslət/ *noun* [C] a piece of jewellery (e.g. a metal chain or band) that you wear around your wrist or arm سوار

bracken /'brækən/ *noun* [U] a plant with long leaves like feathers that grows thickly on hills and in woods. In autumn it turns brown. سرخس، خنشار

bracket /'brækɪt/ *noun* [C] **1** [usually pl.] (*especially US* **parenthesis**; **parentheses**) one of two marks, () or [ ], that you put round extra information in a piece of writing قوس ، هلال

2 a piece of metal or wood that is attached to a wall and used as a support for a shelf, lamp, etc. كتيفة أو ذراع (تحت رف مثلاً)

3 a group of people whose ages, incomes, etc. are between two limits: *to be in a high income bracket* ○ *The magazine is aimed at people in the 30-40 age bracket.* فئة

▶ **bracket** *verb* [T] **1** to put brackets (1) round a word, number, etc. يضع بين قوسين

2 bracket A and B (together); **bracket A with B** to think of two or more people or things as similar in some way يقرن ، يجمل مع

brag /bræg/ *verb* [I,T] (bra**gg**ing; bra**gg**ed) to talk too proudly about sth: *She's always bragging about how clever she is.* يتبجّح ، يتفاخر

braid /breɪd/ *noun* **1** [U] a narrow piece of material that is used to decorate clothes, curtains, etc: *a uniform with gold braid on it* شريط ، ضفيرة

2 [C] (*US*) = PLAIT: *You look nice with your hair in braids.*

Braille /breɪl/ *noun* [U] a way of printing for blind people, using raised dots that they read by touching them with their fingers طريقة بْرايل (القراءة للمكفوفين)

brain /breɪn/ *noun* **1** [C] the part of the body inside the head that controls your thoughts, feelings and movements: *He suffered serious brain damage in a road accident.* ○ *a brain surgeon* مخ ، دماغ

2 [C,U] the ability to think clearly; intelligence: *She has a very quick brain and learns fast.* ○ *He hasn't got the brains to be a doctor.* فهم ؛ ذكاء، نجابة

3 [C] (*informal*) a very clever person: *He's one of the best brains in the country.* شخص ذكي

4 the brains [sing.] the person who plans or organizes sth: *She's the real brains in the organization.* العقل المدبّر

IDM **have sth on the brain** (*informal*) to think about sth all the time: *I've had that song on the brain all day.* ينشغل فكره (بالشيء)

rack your brains → RACK²

▶ **brainless** *adj* very silly سخيف ، مغفّل

brainy *adj* (**brainier**; **brainiest**) (*informal*) clever ذكي

brainchild /'breɪntʃaɪld/ *noun* [sing.] the idea or invention of a particular person: *The music festival was the brainchild of a young teacher.* (من) بنات الأفكار ؛ اختراع

'brain-dead *adj* **1** having serious brain damage and needing a machine to stay alive ميت الدماغ

2 unable to think clearly; stupid: *He's brain-dead from watching too much TV.* غبي

brainstorm /'breɪnstɔːm/ *verb* [I,T] to solve problems or make decisions by asking all the members of a group to think of as many ideas as possible يستشير عدداً من الأدمغة

brainwash /'breɪnwɒʃ/ *verb* [T] to force sb to believe sth by using strong mental pressure: *Televi-*

sion advertisements try to brainwash people into believing they need these things. يغسل دماغه
▶ **brainwashing** *noun* [U] غسل الدماغ

brainwave /ˈbreɪnweɪv/ (*US* **brainstorm**) *noun* [C] (*informal*) a sudden clever idea فكرة عبقرية، إلهام مفاجئ

braise /breɪz/ *verb* [T] to cook meat or vegetables slowly in a little liquid in a covered dish يطهو ببطء

brake /breɪk/ *noun* [C] **1** the part of a vehicle that makes it go slower or stop: *She put her foot on the brake and just managed to stop in time.* ○ *I'm taking my car to the garage today – there's something wrong with the brakes.* مكبح، "فرملة"
2 something that makes sth else slow down or stop: *The Government must try to put a brake on inflation.* مكبح
▶ **brake** *verb* [I] to make a vehicle go slower or stop by using the brakes: *If the driver hadn't braked in time, the car would have hit me.* يكبح (السرعة)

bramble /ˈbræmbl/ *noun* [C] (*especially Brit*) a wild bush with sharp thorns and red or black berries; a blackberry bush عليق

bran /bræn/ *noun* [U] the brown outer parts of wheat grains that have been separated from the flour نخالة

branch /brɑːntʃ; *US* bræntʃ/ *noun* [C] **1** one of the main parts of a tree that grows from its trunk and often has leaves, flowers or fruit on it: *The little boy climbed the tree and sat on a branch.* غصن
2 an office, shop, etc. that is part of a larger organization: *The company I work for has branches in Paris, Milan and New York.* ○ *the High Street branch of Barclays Bank* فرع
3 a part of an academic subject: *Psychology is a branch of medicine.* فرع
▶ **branch** *verb*
PHR V **branch off** (used about a road) to leave a larger road and go off in another direction: *A bit further on, the road branches off to the left.* يتفرع
branch out (into sth) to start doing sth new and different from the things you usually do: *The company sells radios and stereo equipment and has recently branched out into computers.* يتوسع

brand /brænd/ *noun* [C] **1** the name of a product that is made by a particular company: *a well-known brand* علامة تجارية، ماركة
2 a particular type of sth: *a strange brand of humour* نوع، ضرب
▶ **brand** *verb* [T] **1** to mark an animal with a hot iron to show who owns it يسم (حيواناً بالنار)
2 brand sb (as sth) to say that sb has a bad character so that people have a bad opinion of him/her: *She was branded as a troublemaker after she complained about her long working hours.* يصم، يدمغ

brandish /ˈbrændɪʃ/ *verb* [T] to wave sth in the air in an aggressive or excited way: *The attacker stood in front of me, brandishing a knife.* يلوّح (مهدداً أو مهتاجاً)

brand ˈnew *adj* completely new جديد تماماً

brandy /ˈbrændi/ *noun* [C,U] a strong alcoholic drink that is made from wine براندي أو كونياك

brash /bræʃ/ *adj* too confident and direct: *Her brash manner makes her unpopular with strangers.* عديم الخجل، مفرط في الثقة بنفسه عارم
▶ **brashness** *noun* [U] اندفاع

brass /brɑːs; *US* bræs/ *noun* **1** [U] a yellow metal that is a mixture of copper and zinc: *brass buttons on a uniform* نحاس أصفر
2 [sing., with sing. or pl. verb] the group of musical instruments that are made of brass, e.g. the trumpet, the trombone: *the brass section in an orchestra* ○ *a brass band* آلات موسيقية نحاسية

brat /bræt/ *noun* [C] (*informal*) a child who behaves badly and annoys you طفل مشاكس

bravado /brəˈvɑːdəʊ/ *noun* [U] behaviour that makes you appear to be brave and confident when you are not, in order to impress people تظاهر بالشجاعة

brave /breɪv/ *adj* ready to do things that are dangerous or difficult without showing fear: *the brave soldiers who fought in the war* ○ *'This may hurt a little, so try and be brave,' said the dentist.* شجاع
▶ **brave** *verb* [T] to face sth dangerous or difficult without showing fear: *She braved the rain and went out into the street.* يواجه بشجاعة
bravely *adv*: *The men bravely defended the town for three days.* ○ *She smiled bravely and continued walking.* بشجاعة
bravery /ˈbreɪvəri/ *noun* [U]: *After the war he received a medal for bravery.* شجاعة

bravo /ˌbrɑːˈvəʊ/ *interj* a word that you shout to show that you like sth that sb has done, e.g. an actor's performance in a play مرحى! ، برافو!

brawl /brɔːl/ *noun* [C] a noisy fight among a group of people, usually in a public place شجار صاخب
▶ **brawl** *verb* [I] يتشاجر بصخب

brazil nut /brəˈzɪl nʌt/ *noun* [C] a nut that we eat with a very hard shell الجوز البرازيلي

breach /briːtʃ/ *noun* **1** [C,U] an act that breaks an agreement, a law, etc: *Giving private information about clients is a breach of confidence.* ○ *The company was found to be in breach of contract.* خرق
2 [C] a break in friendly relations between people, groups, etc: *a breach between two countries* قطع (العلاقة)
3 [C] an opening in a wall, etc. that defends or protects sb/sth: *The waves made a breach in the sea wall.* ثغرة
▶ **breach** *verb* [T] **1** to an agreement, a law, etc: *He accused the Government of breaching international law.* يخرق

a b c d e f g h i j k l m n o p q r s t u v w x y z

2 to make an opening in a wall, etc. that defends or protects sb/sth يحدث ثغرة

bread

bread /bred/ *noun* [U] a type of food. To make bread you mix together flour and water (and yeast if you want the bread to rise) and bake the mixture in an oven: *a piece/slice of bread* ○ *We had bread and cheese for lunch.* ○ *Would you like some bread and butter?* خبز

A **loaf** of bread is bread that has been shaped and cooked in one piece. **Wholemeal** bread is made from flour that contains all the grain.

breadcrumbs /ˈbredkrʌmz/ *noun* [plural] very small bits of bread that are used in cooking فتات الخبز

breadth /bredθ/ *noun* **1** [C,U] the distance between the two sides of sth: *We measured the length and breadth of the garden.* عرض

2 [U] the wide range of sth: *I was amazed by the breadth of her knowledge.* سعة

ℹ The adjective is **broad**.

IDM **the length and breadth of sth** → LENGTH

breadwinner /ˈbredwɪnə(r)/ *noun* [C, usually sing.] the person who earns the money that his/her family needs المعيل ، كاسب الرزق

break¹ /breɪk/ *verb* (*pt* **broke** /brəʊk/; *pp* **broken** /ˈbrəʊkən/) **1** [I,T] to separate, or make sth separate, into two or more pieces: *She dropped the vase onto the floor and it broke.* ○ *I've broken one of your dinner plates.* ○ *He broke his leg in a car accident.* يكسر ؛ ينكسر

2 [I,T] (used about a machine, etc.) to stop working; to stop a machine, etc. working: *The photocopier has broken.* ○ *Be careful with my camera – I don't want you to break it.* يتعطّل ؛ يُعطِب

3 [T] to do sth that is against the law, or to not keep a promise, etc: *A policeman told me that I was breaking the law.* ○ *Slow down! You're breaking the speed limit.* ○ *to break a contract* ○ *Don't worry – I never break my promises.* يخرق ؛ يحنث (بوعده)

4 [T] **break a record** to do sth better or faster than anyone has ever done before: *She broke the world record for the 100 metres.* يحطّم الرقم القياسي

5 [I,T] to stop doing sth for a short time: *Let's break for coffee now.* ○ *We decided to break the journey by stopping for lunch in Chester.* يأخذ راحة قصيرة ، يتوقّف ؛ يقطع

6 [T] to interrupt sth so that it ends suddenly: *Suddenly, the silence was broken by the sound of a bird singing.* يقطع

7 [T] to make sth end by force or strong action: *It's very difficult to break the habit of smoking.* ○ *Two days of talks failed to break the deadlock between the two countries.* ينهي، يضع حداً ل

8 [I] (used about a day or the dawn) to begin: *Dawn was breaking as I walked home after the party.* يبزغ ، ينبلج

9 [I] (used about a storm) to begin suddenly: *We ran indoors when the storm broke.* يهبّ

10 [I] (used about a wave) to curl over and fall: *I watched the waves breaking on the rocks.* يتكسّر

11 [I,T] (used about a piece of news) to become, or to make sth, known: *When the story broke in the newspapers, nobody could believe it.* ○ *He broke the news to her last night.* يذيع ، ينتشر (الخبر)

12 [I] (used about a boy's voice) to become permanently deeper, usually at about the age of 13 or 14 يتغيّر صوته (عند البلوغ)

For idioms containing **break**, look at the entries for nouns, adjectives, etc. For example, **break even** is at **even**.

PHR V **break away (from sb/sth) 1** to escape suddenly from sb who is holding you ينفلت ، يفْلت

2 to leave a political party, state, etc. in order to form a new one: *Several politicians broke away from the Labour Party and formed the SDP.* ينشقّ ، ينفصل

break down 1 (used about a vehicle or machine) to stop working: *Jill's car broke down on the way to work this morning.* يتعطّل

2 (used about a system, discussion, etc.) to fail: *Talks between the two countries have completely broken down.* يفشَل

3 to lose control of your feelings and start crying: *He broke down in tears when he heard the news.* ينهار

break sth down to make a substance separate into parts or change into a different form in a chemical process: *Food is broken down in our bodies by the digestive system.* يحلّل إلى

break in 1 to enter a building by force, usually in order to steal sth يسطو على ؛ يقتحم

2 to interrupt when sb else is speaking: *'But that's not true!' she broke in angrily.* يقاطع

break into sth 1 to enter a building by force, usually in order to steal sth يسطو على ؛ يقتحم

2 to start doing sth suddenly: *He broke into a smile when he heard the good news.* ○ *She broke into a run and disappeared into the distance.* يبدأ ، يأخذ في (الغناء) فجأة

break off to suddenly stop doing or saying sth: *He started speaking and then broke off in the middle of a sentence.* يتوقّف

break (sth) off to remove a part of sth by force; to come off in this way: *Could you break off another bit of chocolate for me?* ○ *Oh no, part of my tooth has broken off!* يكسر؛ ينكسر

break sth off to end a relationship suddenly: *They broke off their engagement after a argument.* ○ *to break off diplomatic relations with another country* يفسَخ (خطوبة) ، يقطع (علاقة)

break out (used about fighting, wars, fires, etc.) to start suddenly يندلع ، ينشب

break out (of sth) to escape from a prison, etc. يهرب (من السجن مثلاً)

break up 1 (used about events that involve a group of people) to come to an end: *The meeting broke up just before lunch.* ينتهي ؛ يتفرق الحضور

2 (*Brit*) to start school holidays at the end of a term: *When do you break up for the summer holidays?* يبدأ الإجازة المدرسية

3 when a person who is talking on a mobile phone breaks up, you can no longer hear them clearly because the signal has been interrupted: *You're breaking up.* يفقِد الإتصال

break up (with sb) to end a relationship with a wife, husband, girlfriend or boyfriend: *My marriage broke up when I was 25.* ○ *She's broken up with her boyfriend.* ينقصم، ينهي علاقته بشخص

break (sth) up to separate into parts: *The ship broke up on the rocks.* يتحطّم

break sth up to end an event by separating the people who are involved in it: *The police arrived and broke up the fight.* يفرّق

break with sth to end a relationship or connection with sb/sth: *to break with tradition, the past, etc.* يقطع صلته بـ

break[2] /breɪk/ *noun* [C] **1** a place where sth has been broken: *a break in a pipe* كَسر

2 an opening or space in sth: *Wait for a break in the traffic before you cross the road.* ○ *a break in the clouds* انفراج ، تغيّر

3 a short period of rest: *We worked all day without a break.* ○ *to take a break* ○ *a tea/coffee break* ➲ Look at the note at **interval**. استراحة

4 break (in sth); **break (with sb/sth)** a change from what usually happens or an end to sth: *a break with tradition* ○ *She wanted to make a complete break with the past.* ○ *The incident led to a break in diplomatic relations.* انقطاع ؛ قطع

5 (*informal*) a piece of good luck: *to give sb a break* (= to help sb by giving him/her a chance to be successful) فرصة

IDM **break of day** the time when light first appears in the morning; dawn فجر

breakage /ˈbreɪkɪdʒ/ *noun* [C, usually pl.] something that has been broken: *Customers must pay for any breakages* (e.g. in a shop selling glass). شيء مكسور

breakaway /ˈbreɪkəweɪ/ *adj* (only *before* a noun) used about a political group, an organization, or a part of a country) that has separated from a larger group or country منشق

breakdown /ˈbreɪkdaʊn/ *noun* [C] **1** a time when a vehicle, machine, etc. stops working: *We had a breakdown on the motorway.* تعطّل

2 the failure or end of sth: *The breakdown of the talks means that a strike is likely.* فشل ، انهيار

3 = NERVOUS BREAKDOWN

4 a list of all the details of sth: *I would like a full breakdown of how the money was spent.* قائمة تفصيلية

breakfast /ˈbrekfəst/ *noun* [C,U] the meal which you have when you get up in the morning: *to have breakfast* ○ *to eat a big breakfast* فطور

> In a hotel, etc. an **English** breakfast means cereal, fried eggs, bacon, sausages, tomatoes, toast, etc. A **Continental** breakfast means bread and jam with coffee.

IDM **bed and breakfast** → BED

ˈbreak-in *noun* [C] entering a building by force, especially in order to steal sth: *The police say there have been several break-ins in this area.* اقتحام ، سَطو

breakneck /ˈbreɪknek/ *adj* (only *before* a noun) very fast and dangerous: *at breakneck speed* (سرعة) خطرة، متهورة

breakthrough /ˈbreɪkθruː/ *noun* [C] an important discovery or development: *Scientists have made a major breakthrough in cancer research.* ○ *The agreement represents a breakthrough in relations between the two countries.* اكتشاف حاسم ، فتح (علمي) : تطوّر هام

breakup /ˈbreɪkʌp/ *noun* [C] **1** the end of a relationship between two people: *the breakup of a marriage* انهيار ، انحلال

2 the separation of a group or organization into smaller parts: *the breakup of the Soviet Union* تجزئة

breast /brest/ *noun* [C] **1** one of the two soft round parts of a woman's body that can produce milk ثدي

2 a word used especially in literature for the upper part of the front of your body: *to clasp sb to your breast* صدر

3 the front part of the body of a bird صدر الطائر

breastfeed /ˈbrestfiːd/ *verb* [I,T] (*pt, pp* **ˈbreastfed** /ˈbrestfed/) to feed a baby with milk from the breast ترضع من الثدي (وليس من الزجاجة)

breaststroke /ˈbreststrəʊk/ *noun* [U] a style of swimming on your front in which you start with your hands together, push both arms forward and then pull them outwards and back through the water السباحة على الصدر

breath /breθ/ *noun* **1** [U] the air that you take into and blow out of your lungs: *to have bad breath* (= breath which smells unpleasant) نَفَس

2 [C] an act of taking air into or blowing air out of your lungs: *Take a deep breath.* تنفّس

IDM **a breath of fresh air** the clean air which you breathe outside, especially when compared to the air inside a room or building: *Let's go for a* *walk. I need a breath of fresh air.* ○ *(figurative) Her happy face is like a breath of fresh air in that miserable place.* نسمة هواء منعشة

get your breath (again/back) to rest after physical exercise so that your breathing returns to normal يسترجع أنفاسه

hold your breath to stop breathing for a period of time, e.g. when swimming underwater or because of fear or excitement: *We all held our breath as we waited for her reply.* يكتم نفَسه

(be) out of/short of breath to be breathing very quickly, e.g. after physical exercise (يكون) منقطع النفَس، يلهث

say sth, speak, etc. under your breath to say sth very quietly, usually because you do not want people to hear what you are saying يهمس

take your breath away to surprise sb very much: *The spectacular view took our breath away.* ℹ The adjective is **breathtaking**. يبهر

with bated breath → BATED

breathalyse /ˈbreθəlaɪz/ *verb* [T] (used about a police officer) to test the breath of a driver with a special machine (a breathalyser) to measure how much alcohol he/she has drunk يختبر النفَس

breathe /briːð/ *verb* [I,T] to take air, etc. into your lungs and blow it out again: *She was unconscious but still breathing.* ○ *to breathe in/out* (= to take air in/to blow air out) ○ *I hate sitting in restaurants breathing in other people's cigarette smoke.* يتنفّس؛ يستنشق؛ يزفر

IDM **not breathe a word (of/about sth) (to sb)** to not tell sb about sth that is secret: *If you breathe a word of this to my mother, I'll never speak to you again!* (لا) يفشي سراً، لا يتفوه بكلمة

▸ **breathing** *noun* [U]: *heavy, irregular, etc. breathing* تنفّس

breather /ˈbriːðə(r)/ *noun* [C] (*informal*) a short rest: *to have/take a breather* راحة قصيرة

breathless /ˈbreθləs/ *adj* **1** breathing quickly or with difficulty, e.g. after physical exercise لاهث

2 not able to breathe because you are so excited, frightened, etc: *to be breathless with excitement* منقطع النفَس

▸ **breathlessly** *adv* لاهثاً

breathtaking /ˈbreθteɪkɪŋ/ *adj* very exciting, beautiful, etc: *breathtaking mountain scenery* باهر، خلاّب

ˈ**breath test** *noun* [C] a test by the police on the breath of a driver to measure how much alcohol he/she has drunk اختبار النفَس (لقياس كمية الكحول فيه)

breed /briːd/ *verb* (*pt, pp* **bred** /bred/) **1** [I] (used about animals or plants) to produce young animals or plants: *Many animals won't breed in zoos.* يتوالد؛ يتكاثر

2 [T] to keep animals or plants in order to produce young from them: *cattle which are bred to produce high yields of milk* يربّي

3 [T] to cause sth: *This kind of thinking breeds intolerance and violence.* يولِّد، يسبِّب

▸ **breed** *noun* [C] a type of animal: *a breed of cattle* سلالة، نوع

breeder *noun* [C] a person who breeds animals or plants: *a dog breeder* مربّي (حيوانات مثلاً)

breeding *noun* [U] **1** the act of producing young plants or animals: *The breeding of fighting dogs has been banned.* تربية، استيلاد

2 good manners and behaviour as a result of coming from an upper-class family: *a man and woman of breeding* تهذيب

ˈ**breeding ground** *noun* [C] **1** a place where wild animals go to breed مكان توالد (الحيوانات)

2 a place where sth can develop: *a breeding ground for crime* مرتع (الجريمة)

breeze /briːz/ *noun* [C] a light wind: *A warm breeze was blowing.* نسيم

▸ **breeze** *verb*

PHR V **breeze along, in, out, etc.** (*informal*) to move in a cheerful relaxed way, even when this is not suitable behaviour: *He just breezed in twenty minutes late without a word of apology.* ينساب كالنسيم (إلى أو خارج المكان)

breezy *adj* (**breezier**; **breeziest**) **1** a little windy (يوم) فيه ريح خفيفة

2 cheerful and relaxed: *You're bright and breezy this morning!* مرح

brevity /ˈbrevəti/ *noun* [U] the state of being short or quick ℹ The adjective is **brief**. إيجاز

brew /bruː/ *verb* **1** [T] to make beer يخمّر (الجعة)

2 [T] to make a drink of tea or coffee by adding hot water: *to brew a pot of tea* يغلي، يعدّ (الشاي مثلاً)

3 [I] (used about tea) to stand in hot water before it is ready to drink: *Leave it to brew for a few minutes.* يتخمّر

IDM **be brewing** (used about sth bad) to develop or grow: *There's trouble brewing.* يتجمّع؛ يتدبّر

▸ **brewery** /ˈbruːəri/ *noun* [C] (*pl.* **breweries**) a place where beer is made مصنع الجعة

bribe /braɪb/ *noun* [C] money, etc. that is given to sb such as an official to persuade him/her to do sth to help you, especially when you want him/her to do sth dishonest: *to offer a bribe to sb* ○ *to accept/take bribes* رشوة

▸ **bribe** *verb* [T] **bribe sb (with sth)**: *They got a visa by bribing an official.* يرشو

bribery /ˈbraɪbəri/ *noun* [U] ارتشاء

bric-a-brac /ˈbrɪk ə bræk/ *noun* [U] ornaments, small items of furniture and other objects of little value: *market stalls selling an array of cheap bric-a-brac* خردة، طرف منوّعة

brick /brɪk/ *noun* [C,U] a hard block of baked clay that is used for building houses, etc: *a lorry carrying bricks* ○ *a house built of red brick* طوب، آجُرّ

bricklayer /ˈbrɪkleɪə(r)/ *noun* [C] a person whose job is to build walls with bricks بنّاء يبني بالطوب

brickwork /ˈbrɪkwɜːk/ *noun* [U] the part of a building that is made of bricks مشيّد بالطوب

bridal /ˈbraɪdl/ *adj* (only *before* a noun) connected with a bride or a wedding: *the bridal suite in a hotel* عرائسي، متعلق بالعروس أو الزفاف

bride /braɪd/ *noun* [C] a woman on or just before

her wedding day: *the bride and groom* ➲ Look at the note at **wedding**. عروس

bridegroom /ˈbraɪdɡruːm/ (*also* **groom**) *noun* [C] a man on or just before his wedding day ➲ Look at the note at **wedding**. عريس

bridesmaid /ˈbraɪdzmeɪd/ *noun* [C] a woman or girl who helps the bride at her wedding ➲ Look at the note at **wedding**. إشبينة العروس

⚷**bridge**[1] /brɪdʒ/ *noun* [C] **1** a structure that carries a road or railway, across a river, valley, road or railway: *a bridge over the River Thames* ○ *a motorway bridge* جِسْر ، قنطرة

2 the high part of a ship where the captain and the people who control the ship stand برج القيادة في السفينة

▸ **bridge** *verb* [T] to build a bridge over sth يبني جِسْراً

IDM **bridge a/the gap** to fill a space between two people, groups or things or to bring them closer together يقرّب الشقّة

bridge[2] /brɪdʒ/ *noun* [U] a card game for four people لعبة البريدج

bridle /ˈbraɪdl/ *noun* [C] the leather straps that you put over a horse's head so that you can control it when you are riding it لجام

⚷**brief**[1] /briːf/ *adj* short or quick: *a brief description* ○ *a brief phone call* ○ *Please be brief. We don't have much time.* ❶ The noun is **brevity**.

موجز ، قصير

IDM **in brief** using only a few words: *News in Brief* (= in a newspaper) بإيجاز؛ بالاختصار

▸ **briefly** *adv* **1** for a short time; quickly: *She glanced briefly at her mother.* ○ *We met briefly in London yesterday* لمدة وجيزة ؛ سريعا

2 using only a few words: *I'd like to comment very briefly on that last statement.* بإيجاز

brief[2] /briːf/ *noun* [C] instructions or information about a job or task: *When he was appointed he was given the brief of improving the image of the organization.* تعليمات

▸ **brief** *verb* [T] to give sb information or instructions about sth: *The minister has been fully briefed on what questions to expect.*

يحيطه علماً ؛ يزوّده بالتعليمات

briefing *noun* [C,U] instructions or information that you are given before sth happens: *a press/news briefing* (= where information is given to journalists) بيان موجز

briefcase /ˈbriːfkeɪs/ *noun* [C] a flat case that you use for carrying papers, etc., especially when you go to work حقيبة أوراق و غيرها

briefs /briːfs/ *noun* [plural] pants for men or women سروال تحتاني قصير

brigade /brɪˈɡeɪd/ *noun* [C] **1** a unit of soldiers in the army لواء

2 a group of people who work together for a particular purpose: *the fire brigade* فرقة

▸ **brigadier** /ˌbrɪɡəˈdɪə(r)/ *noun* [C] an officer of high rank in the army عميد

⚷**bright** /braɪt/ *adj* **1** having a lot of light: *a bright, sunny day* ○ *eyes bright with happiness* مشرق ، نيِّر

2 (used about a colour) strong: *a bright yellow jumper* زاه ، ساطع

3 clever, or able to learn things quickly: *a bright child* ○ *a bright idea* ذكي

4 likely to be pleasant or successful: *The future looks bright.* باسم ، مشرق

5 cheerful, happy: *You seem very bright and cheerful today.* مَرِح ، بشوش

▸ **brighten** /ˈbraɪtn/ *verb* [I,T] **brighten (sth) (up)** to become brighter or happier; to make sth brighter: *His face brightened when he saw her.* ○ *to brighten up sb's day* (= make it happier) يشرق ؛ يُبهِج

brightly *adv*: *brightly-coloured clothes* بألوان زاهية ؛ بابتهاج ؛ بإشراق

brightness *noun* [U] تألّق ، زهاء

⚷**brilliant** /ˈbrɪliənt/ *adj* **1** having a lot of light; very bright: *brilliant sunshine* ساطع ؛ متألّق

2 very clever or intelligent: *a brilliant young scientist* ذكي جداً ، ألمعي

3 very good: *a brilliant performance by Pavarotti* رائع

▸ **brilliance** /ˈbrɪliəns/ *noun* [U]

تألّق ، ضياء ؛ ألمعيّة

brilliantly *adv* بتألّق؛ ببراعة

brim /brɪm/ *noun* [C] **1** the top edge of a cup, glass, etc: *The cup was full to the brim.* حافّة ، شفة (الفنجان)

2 the bottom part of a hat, that is wider than the rest حافّة (القُبَّعة)

▸ **brim** *verb* [I] (brimming; brimmed) **brim (with sth)** to be full of sth: *His eyes were brimming with tears.* يمتلئ؛ يغرورق بِ

PHR V **brim over (with sth)** (used about a cup, glass, etc.) to have more liquid than it can hold: *The bowl was brimming over with water.* ○ *(figurative) to be brimming over with health/happiness* يطفح

⚷**bring** /brɪŋ/ *verb* [T] (*pt, pp* **brought** /brɔːt/) **1** to come to a place with sb/sth: *We will be out all day so bring some sandwiches with you.* ○ *Is it all right if I bring a friend to the party?* ○ *Bring me two coffees, please.* ○ *The prisoner was brought into the court by two policewomen.* ○ *(figurative) He will bring valuable skills and experience to the team.* يُحضِر ، يجلب

2 to cause or result in sth: *The sight of her brought a smile to his face.* ○ *Money doesn't always bring happiness.* يجلب ، يسبِّب

3 to cause sb/sth to be in a certain place or condition: *Their screams brought people running from all directions.* ○ *Add water to the mixture and bring it to the boil.* ○ *What brings you here? Business or pleasure?* ○ *to bring sth to an end* يجعل؛ يجيء بِ

4 to force yourself to do sth: *The film was so horrible that I couldn't bring myself to watch it.* يجْبِر ، يكْرِه

PHR V **bring sth about** to cause sth to happen: *to bring about changes in people's lives* يُحْدِث

bring sb/sth back to return sb/sth: *You can*

a b c d e f g h i j k l m n o p q r s t u v w x y z

borrow the DVD if you bring it back tomorrow morning. يعيد
bring sth back 1 to cause sth that existed before to be introduced again: *Nobody wants to bring back the days of child labour.* يعيد
2 to cause sb to remember sth: *The photographs brought back memories of his childhood.* يعيد
bring sb sth back to return with sth for sb: *My sister went to Spain on holiday and brought me back a T-shirt.* يجلب ، يحمل له
bring sb/sth down to cause sb/sth to be defeated or to lose a position of power: *to bring down a government* يسقط ، يطيح بـ
bring sth down to make sth lower in level: *to bring down the price of sth* يخفّض
bring sth forward 1 to move sth to an earlier time: *The date of the wedding has been brought forward by two weeks.* يقدّم
2 to suggest sth for discussion يطرح (للنقاش)
bring sb in to ask or appoint sb to do a particular job: *A specialist was brought in to set up the new computer system.* يستجلب ، يعيّن
bring sth in to introduce sth: *The government have brought in a law on dangerous dogs.* يُقدّم (مشروع قانون مثلاً)
bring sth off (*informal*) to manage to do sth difficult: *The team brought off an amazing victory.* يحقّق
bring sth on to cause sth: *Her headaches are brought on by stress.* يسبّب
bring sth out to produce or cause sth to appear: *When is the company bringing out its next new model?* ○ *A crisis can sometimes bring out the best in people.* ينتج ، يصدِر ؛ يظهر
bring sb round to cause sb to become conscious again يعيد شخصاً إلى وعيه ، ينعش
bring sb round (to sth) to persuade sb to agree with your opinion: *After a lot of discussion we finally brought them round to our point of view.* يقنع
bring sth round to sth to direct a conversation to a particular subject: *I finally brought the conversation round to the subject of money.* يحول أو يوجّه (النقاش) إلى
bring sb up to look after a child until he/she is adult and to teach him/her how to behave: *After her parents were killed the child was brought up by her uncle.* ○ *a well-brought up child* يربّي
bring sth up 1 to be sick so that food that you have swallowed comes back out of your mouth; to vomit يتقيأ
2 to introduce sth into a discussion or conversation: *I intend to bring the matter up at the next meeting.* يعرض ، يطرح

brink /brɪŋk/ *noun* [sing.] the edge at the top of a high place: (*figurative*) *The firm was close to disaster but the new director brought it back from the brink.* حافّة ؛ شفا الهاوية
IDM **be on the brink (of sth/of doing sth)** to be about to do or experience sth exciting or dangerous على شفا (شيء)

brisk /brɪsk/ *adj* **1** quick or using a lot of energy; busy: *They set off at a brisk pace.* ○ *Trading has been brisk this morning.* سريع ؛ نشيط
2 confident and efficient; wanting to do things quickly: *a brisk manner* واثق ؛ حثيث
▸ **briskly** *adv* بهمّة ونشاط
briskness *noun* [U] نشاط ، سرعة

bristle /ˈbrɪsl/ *noun* [C] **1** a short thick hair on a person or animal شعرة قصيرة وغليظة
2 one of the short thick hairs of a brush شعرة من شعرات الفرشاة
▸ **bristle** *verb* [I] **1** (used about hair or an animal's fur) to stand up straight because of fear, anger, cold, etc. يقف شعره (خوفاً مثلاً)
2 bristle (with sth) to show that you are angry يحتدم غضباً
PHR V **bristle with sth** to be full of sth يمتلئ بالشيء

Brit /brɪt/ *noun* [C] (*informal*) a British person (شخص) بريطاني

Britain /ˈbrɪtn/ = GREAT BRITAIN ➲ Look at the note at **United Kingdom**.

British /ˈbrɪtɪʃ/ *adj* of the United Kingdom (= Great Britain and Northern Ireland): *British industry* ○ *to hold a British passport* بريطاني
▸ **the British** *noun* [plural] the people of the United Kingdom البريطانيون

the ˌBritish ˈIsles *noun* [plural] Great Britain and Ireland with all the islands that are near their coasts. The British Isles are a geographical but not a political unit. الجزر البريطانية

Briton /ˈbrɪtn/ *noun* [C] a person who comes from Great Britain (شخص) بريطاني

> This is normally only used in newspapers, or when talking about the inhabitants of Britain in earlier times: *Three Britons killed in air crash!* ○ *the Ancient Britons*. Otherwise we say 'a British man', 'a British woman'.

brittle /ˈbrɪtl/ *adj* hard but easily broken: *brittle fingernails* هشّ ، سريع الانكسار

broach /brəʊtʃ/ *verb* [T] to start talking about a particular subject, especially one which is difficult or embarrassing: *Have you broached the subject of the money he owes us?* يطرق (موضوعاً)

ˈB-road *noun* [C] (in Britain) a road that is not as wide or important as a motorway or an A-road: *Turn right onto the B427.* (في بريطانيا) طريق ثانويّ

⚷ **broad** /brɔːd/ *adj* **1** large in size from one side to the other; wide: *a broad river valley* ○ *the broad boulevards of the capital* عريض

> **Wide** is more often used than **broad** when you are talking about the distance between one side of something and the other: *The gate is four metres wide.* ○ *The table is too wide to go through the door.* **Broad** is often used about geographical features: *a broad expanse of desert* and in particular phrases such as: *broad shoulders*. The noun from **broad** is **breadth**. The opposite is **narrow**.

2 easily noticeable; very clear: *She spoke with a broad Somerset accent.* لافت للنظر ؛ واضح

3 without a lot of detail; general: *Just give me a broad outline of your plan.* عريض ؛ عامّ

4 including many different people or things: *We sell a broad range of products.* متنوّع

5 felt or believed by a lot of people: *There seems to be broad support for stronger anti-pollution laws.* واسع النطاق

IDM (in) broad daylight during the day, i.e. not at night: *He was attacked in broad daylight.* وضَح النهار

▶ **broaden** /ˈbrɔːdn/ *verb* [I,T] **broaden (out)** to become broader; to make sth broader: *The river broadens out beyond the bridge.* ○ *(figurative) Travel broadens the mind* (= it makes you understand other people better). يتّسع ؛ يوسّع

broadly *adv* **1** (used to describe a way of smiling): *to smile broadly* (= to have a very big, wide smile) (يبتسم) ابتسامة عريضة

2 generally: *Broadly speaking, the scheme will work as follows...* عموماً

broadband /ˈbrɔːdbænd/ *noun* [U] a way of connecting a computer to the Internet, which allows you to receive information, including pictures, etc., very quickly المجال الواسع

ˌ**broad ˈbean** *noun* [C] a type of large flat green bean that can be cooked and eaten as a vegetable فول

🔑**broadcast** /ˈbrɔːdkɑːst; *US* ˈbrɔːdkæst/ *verb* (*pt, pp* **broadcast**) **1** [I,T] to send out radio or television programmes: *The BBC World Service broadcasts to most countries in the world.* ○ *The Olympics are broadcast live by satellite.* يذيع، يبثّ

2 [I] to speak or appear on radio or on television: *The President broadcasts to the nation at times of crisis.* يذيع ، يتحدّث

▶ **broadcast** *noun* [C] something that is sent out by radio or television: *a news broadcast* (شيء) مذاع

broadcaster *noun* [C] a person who speaks on serious subjects on the radio or on television مذيع

ˌ**broad-ˈminded** *adj* willing to listen to and accept beliefs and ways of life that are different from your own; tolerant ❶ The opposite is **narrow-minded.** منفتح العقل ؛ متسامح

broccoli /ˈbrɒkəli/ *noun* [U] a plant with green or purple flower-heads that can be cooked and eaten as a vegetable ضرب من القرنبيط

brochure /ˈbrəʊʃə(r); *US* brəʊˈʃʊər/ *noun* [C] a small book with pictures in it that gives you information about sth: *a holiday brochure* كرّاسة (للدعاية مثلاً)

broil /brɔɪl/ *verb* [T] *(especially US)* = GRILL

broke[1] *pt* of BREAK[1]

broke[2] /brəʊk/ *adj* (not before a noun) *(informal)* having no money: *I can't come out tonight. I'm absolutely broke.* مفلس

broken[1] *pp* of BREAK[1]

🔑**broken**[2] /ˈbrəʊkən/ *adj* **1** damaged or in pieces; not working: *The washing machine's broken.* ○ *Watch out! There's broken glass on the floor.* ○ *a broken leg* مهشّم ، مكسور ؛ معطّل

2 not continuous; interrupted: *a broken line* ○ *a broken night's sleep* منقطع؛ متقطّع

3 not kept: *a broken promise* (وعد) مخْلَف

4 (used about a foreign language) spoken slowly with a lot of mistakes: *to speak in broken English* متكسّر

ˌ**broken-ˈdown** *adj* **1** in a very bad condition: *a broken-down old shed* مهلهل

2 (used about a vehicle) not working: *A broken-down bus was blocking the road.* متعطّل،خرب

ˌ**broken-ˈhearted** *adj* = HEARTBROKEN

ˌ**broken ˈhome** *noun* [C] a family in which the parents do not live together, e.g. because they are separated or divorced: *Many of the children came from broken homes.* أسرة متصدّعة أو مفككة

ˌ**broken ˈmarriage** *noun* [C] a marriage that has ended because the partners have got divorced زواج منحلّ (أي انتهى بالطلاق)

broker /ˈbrəʊkə(r)/ *noun* [C] **1** a person who buys and sells things (e.g. shares in a business) for other people: *an insurance broker* سِمسار ، وسيط

2 = STOCKBROKER

bronchitis /brɒŋˈkaɪtɪs/ *noun* [U] an illness of part of the lungs (bronchial tubes) that causes a very bad cough التهاب رئوي

bronze /brɒnz/ *noun* **1** [U] a brown-coloured metal that is made from copper and tin برونز

2 [U] the colour of bronze اللون البرونزي

3 [C] (*also* **bronze medal**) a round piece of bronze that you get as a prize for coming third in a race or a competition ➲ Look at **gold** and **silver medal.** مدَالية برونزية

▶ **bronze** *adj* of the colour of bronze برونزي

brooch /brəʊtʃ/ *noun* [C] a piece of jewellery with a pin at the back that women wear on a dress, blouse or jacket البروش: مِشبك للزينة

brood /bruːd/ *noun* [C] all the young birds that belong to one mother حضْنة: كلّ فراخ الأم الواحدة

▶ **brood** *verb* [I] **1** (used about a female bird) to sit on her eggs يحضن (الطائر بيضه)

2 brood (on/over sth) to worry, or to think a lot about sth that makes you sad: *to brood on a failure* يطيل التفكير في همومه

broody *adj* **1** (used about a female bird) ready to have or sit on eggs: *a broody hen* (دجاجة) حضون

2 (used about a woman) wanting to have a baby (امرأة) تشتهي الإنجاب

brook /brʊk/ *noun* [C] a small stream جدول

broom /bruːm/ *noun* [C] a brush with a long handle that you use for sweeping the floor مِكْنسة

broomstick /ˈbruːmstɪk/ *noun* [C] the handle of a broom. In stories witches are sometimes said to fly on broomsticks. عصا المِكْنسة

a b c d e f g h i j k l m n o p q r s t u v w x y z

Bros *abbrev* (used in the name of companies) Brothers: *Wentworth Bros Ltd* إخوان...

broth /brɒθ; *US* brɔːθ/ *noun* [U] thin soup: *chicken broth* حَساء رقيق

brothel /ˈbrɒθl/ *noun* [C] a place where men can go and pay to have sex with a woman (a prostitute) ماخور ، بيت دعارة

brother /ˈbrʌðə(r)/ *noun* [C] **1** a man or boy who has the same parents as another person: *Michael and Jim are brothers.* ○ *Michael is Jim's brother.* ○ *a younger/older brother* ○ *a twin brother* أخ

> Look at **half-brother** and **stepbrother**. Notice that there is not a common English word that means 'both brothers and sisters': *Have you got any brothers and sisters?* The word **sibling** is very formal.

2 a man who is a member of a Christian religious community: *Brother John* أخ ، راهب

▸ **brotherhood** /-hʊd/ *noun* **1** [U] a feeling of great friendship and loyalty between people: *the brotherhood of Man* (= a feeling of friendship between all the people in the world) أخوّة

2 [C, with sing. or pl. verb] an organization which is formed for a particular, often religious, purpose جمعية (دينية)

brotherly *adv* of or like a brother: *brotherly love* أخوي

ˈbrother-in-law *noun* [C] (*pl.* **brothers-in-law**) **1** the brother of your husband or wife أخو الزوج أو الزوجة

2 the husband of your sister زوج الأخت

brought *pt, pp* of BRING

brow /braʊ/ *noun* [C] **1** [usually pl.] = EYEBROW

2 = FOREHEAD: *Sweat was pouring from his brow.*

3 the top part of a hill or slope: *Suddenly a car came over the brow of the hill.* أعلى المنحدر : قمّة الهضبة

brown /braʊn/ *adj* **1** having the colour of soil or wood: *brown eyes* ○ *brown shoes* ○ *dark brown hair* بنّي

2 having skin of this colour: *They were very brown when they got back from their holiday.* أسمر

▸ **brown** *noun* [C,U] the colour brown: *the yellows and browns of the trees in autumn* ○ *You don't look nice in brown* (= in brown clothes). اللون البنّي أو الأسمر

brown *verb* [I,T] to become or cause sth to become brown يَسمر؛ يسمِّر

brownish *adj* slightly or fairly brown: *She has brownish eyes.* ضارب إلى اللون البنّي

brownie /ˈbraʊni/ *noun* [C] **1** **ˈBrownie** a young girl who is a member of the junior branch of the Girl Guides organization فتاة صغيرة في فرقة كشفية

2 a type of heavy chocolate cake that often contains nuts نوع من حلويات الشوكولاته

ˌbrown ˈpaper *noun* [U] strong, thick paper used for wrapping parcels, etc. ورق لفّ أسمر

browse /braʊz/ *verb* [I] **1** to spend time pleasantly, looking round a shop, without a clear idea of what you are looking for: *I spent hours browsing in the local bookshop.* يتفرج على المعروضات في دكان

2 **browse through sth** to look through a book or magazine without reading every part or studying it carefully: *I enjoyed browsing through the catalogue but I didn't order anything.* يتصفح (كتاباً أو مجلة)

3 (*computing*) to look for and read information on a computer: *I've just been browsing the Internet for information on Iceland.* يتصفح

▸ **browse** *noun* [sing.]: *I had a browse through the newspapers on the plane.* تصفّح

browser *noun* [C] a computer program that lets you look at words and pictures from other computer systems by receiving information through telephone wires: *an Internet browser* متصفح

bruise /bruːz/ *noun* [C] a dark mark on the skin caused by a blow that injures but does not break the skin: *He didn't break any bones but he suffered cuts and bruises to his face.* ❶ A bruise on your eye is a **black eye**. كَدْمة ، رضة

▸ **bruise** *verb* **1** [T] to cause a bruise or bruises: *I fell over and bruised my arm.* ○ *She had a badly bruised face.* ○ *Handle the fruit carefully or you'll bruise it.* يرضّ، يسبّب كدمات

2 [I] to get a bruise or bruises: *I've got the sort of skin that bruises easily.* يرتض : تظهر عليه الكدمات

brunette /bruːˈnet/ *noun* [C] a white woman with dark brown hair ➲ Look at **blond**. امرأة بيضاء ذات شعر بني داكن

brunt /brʌnt/ *noun*

IDM **bear the brunt of sth** → BEAR[2]

brush[1] /brʌʃ/ *noun* **1** [C] an object that is used for cleaning things, painting, tidying your hair, etc: *I took a brush and swept the snow from the path.* ○ *a clothes brush* ○ *a toothbrush* ○ *a paintbrush* ○ *a hairbrush* فُرشاة

2 [sing.] an act of sweeping, cleaning, tidying the hair, etc. with a brush: *Your coat needs a brush.* تنظيف بالفرشاة

3 [C] **a brush with sb** a short argument or fight with sb خناقة، مناوشة قصيرة

brush[2] /brʌʃ/ *verb* **1** [T] to clean, tidy, sweep, etc. with a brush: *Make sure you brush your teeth twice a day.* ○ *She was brushing her hair in front of a mirror.* ➲ Look at the note at **clean[2]**. ينظّف بالفرشاة

2 [I,T] to touch sb/sth lightly when passing: *Her hand brushed his cheek.* ○ *Leaves brushed against the car as we drove along the narrow road.* يمس مسّاً رفيقاً

PHR V **brush sb/sth aside** **1** to refuse to pay attention to sb/sth: *She brushed aside the protests and continued with the meeting.* يتجاهل

2 to get past sb/sth: *He hurried through the crowd, brushing aside the reporters who tried to stop him.* يزيح جانباً

brush sth away/off to remove sth with a brush

or with the hand, as if using a brush: *I brushed the dust off my jacket.* ينفض

brush sth up/brush up on sth to study or practise sth in order to get back knowledge or skill that you had before and have lost: *She took a course to brush up her Spanish.* يستعيد أو يصقل

ˈbrush-off *noun* [sing.] (*informal*) an act of refusing to be friendly to sb: *He asked her to go out with him but she gave him the brush-off.* رفض

brusque /bruːsk; *US* brʌsk/ *adj* not taking time to be polite when you are dealing with people: *He gave a brusque 'No comment!' and walked off.* مقتضب و جافّ

▸ **brusquely** *adv* بفظاظة : بجفاء

Brussels sprout /ˌbrʌslz ˈspraʊt/ (*also* **sprout**) *noun* [C, usually pl.] a green vegetable that looks like a very small cabbage كُرُنب بروكسل

brutal /ˈbruːtl/ *adj* very cruel and violent; without pity: *a brutal murder* ○ *brutal treatment of prisoners* ○ *a brutal dictatorship* وحشي : قاسٍ

▸ **brutality** /bruːˈtæləti/ *noun* [C,U] (*pl.* **brutalities**) very cruel and violent behaviour; acts that show no pity: *There have been many complaints of police brutality.* وحشية : قسوة

brutally *adv*: *The girl had been brutally attacked.* ○ *He was brutally honest and told her that he didn't love her any more.* بوحشية ، بقسوة

brute /bruːt/ *noun* [C] **1** a large animal حيوان هائل

2 a cruel, violent man: *Don't you dare hit him again, you brute!* وحش

▸ **brute** *adj* (only *before* a noun) without the use of thought; using a violent method: *I think you'll have to use brute force to get this window open.* أعمى : عنيف

BSc /ˌbiː es ˈsiː/ *abbrev* Bachelor of Science; the degree that you receive when you complete a university or college course in a science subject بكالوريوس علوم

BSE /ˌbiː es ˈiː/ *noun* (*also informal* **mad ˈcow disease**) bovine spongiform encephalopathy, a disease of cows which affects their brains and usually kills them. ➲ Look also at **CJD**. مرض جنون البقر

BST /ˌbiː es ˈtiː/ *abbrev* British Summer Time; the system used in Britain between March and October, when clocks are put one hour ahead of Greenwich Mean Time توقيت بريطانيا الصيفي

🔑 **bubble** /ˈbʌbl/ *noun* [C] a hollow ball containing air or gas, in liquid or floating in the air: *The children were blowing bubbles with washing-up liquid.* ○ *the bubbles in a glass of champagne* فقّاعة

▸ **bubble** *verb* [I] **1** to produce bubbles or to rise with bubbles: *Cook the pizza until the cheese starts to bubble.* ○ *The clear water bubbled up out of the ground.* يبقبق (عند الغليان) ، يفور

2 bubble (over) (with sth) to be full of happy feelings يجيش (بشعور سعيد)

bubbly /ˈbʌbli/ *adj* (**bubblier**; **bubbliest**) **1** full of bubbles: *a bubbly drink* مليء بالفقاعات ، فوّار

2 (used about a person) lively and happy: *She has a naturally bubbly personality.* مَرِح ، مليء بالحيوية

bubblegum /ˈbʌblɡʌm/ *noun* [U] chewing gum that can be blown into bubbles out of the mouth علكة أو لبان ينفخ إلى فقاعات

buck[1] /bʌk/ *noun* [C] (*US informal*) a US dollar: *Could you lend me a few bucks?* دولار أمريكي

buck[2] /bʌk/ *noun* [C] (*pl.* **buck** or **bucks**) a male deer or rabbit ➲ Look at the note at **deer**. ذكر الظبي أو الأرنب

buck[3] /bʌk/ *noun*

IDM pass the buck → PASS[2]

buck[4] /bʌk/ *verb* [I] (used about a horse) to jump into the air with all four feet off the ground: *His horse suddenly bucked and he fell off.* يثب (الفرس)

PHR V buck up (*informal*) to hurry up: *Come on, buck up! We have to leave in a minute.* يسرع

buck (sb) up (*informal*) to become or to make sb more cheerful or less unhappy: *Buck up! It's not the end of the world.* يبتهج : يبهج

bucket /ˈbʌkɪt/ *noun* [C] **1** a round, open container, usually made of metal or plastic, with a handle, that is used for carrying or holding liquids or sand جَرْدَل ، سَطْل

2 (*also* ˈ**bucketful** /-fʊl/) the amount that a bucket contains: *How many buckets of cement do you think we'll need?* مِلء جَرْدَل

buckle /ˈbʌkl/ *noun* [C] a piece of metal or plastic at the end of a belt or strap that is used for fastening it إبزيم

▸ **buckle** *verb* [I,T] **1** to fasten or be fastened with a buckle يثبّت بإبزيم

2 to bend because of heat, force, weakness, etc: *Some railway lines buckled in the heat.* يلتوي ، يتقوّس

bud /bʌd/ *noun* [C] a small lump on a tree or plant that opens and develops into a flower or leaf: *rosebuds* ○ *At this time of year all the trees are in bud* (= have buds on them). برْعم

▸ **budding** *adj* wanting or starting to develop and be successful: *Have you got any tips for budding young photographers?* ناشئ ، صاعد

Buddhism /ˈbʊdɪzəm/ *noun* [U] an Asian religion that was founded in India by Buddha (الديانة) البوذية

▸ **Buddhist** /ˈbʊdɪst/ *noun* [C] a person whose religion is Buddhism (شخص) بوذي

Buddhist *adj*: *a Buddhist temple* بوذي

buddy /ˈbʌdi/ *noun* [C] (*pl.* **buddies**) (*informal*) a friend, especially a male friend of a man صديق ، صاحب

budge /bʌdʒ/ *verb* [I,T] **1** to move or cause sth to move a little: *I tried as hard as I could to loosen the screw but it simply wouldn't budge.* ○ *We just couldn't budge the car when it got stuck in the mud.* يتزحزح : يزحزح

2 to change or cause sb to change a firm opinion: *Neither side in the dispute is prepared to budge.* ○ *Once he's made up his mind, nothing*

will budge him. يتزحزح (عن رأيه) : يزحزح (شخصاً عن رأيه)

budgerigar /ˈbʌdʒərigɑː(r)/ (*also informal* **budgie**) *noun* [C] a small, brightly-coloured bird that people often keep as a pet in a cage طائر صغير من نوع الببغاء

🔑**budget** /ˈbʌdʒɪt/ *noun* [C] **1** a plan of how to spend an amount of money over a particular period of time; the amount of money that is mentioned: *What's your monthly budget for food?* ○ *The government has announced reductions in the country's defence budget.* ○ *The new product was launched with an advertising budget of £2 million.* ميزانية

2 (*also* **Budget**) a statement by a government saying how much money it plans to spend on particular things in the next year and how it plans to collect money: *Do you think taxes will go up in this year's budget?* ميزانية (الحكومة)

▸ **budget** *verb* [I,T] **budget (sth) (for sth)** to plan carefully how much money to spend on sth: *Don't forget to budget for possible increased costs.* ○ *Costs for the new building are already far greater than the £10 million originally budgeted.* يضع في الميزانية : ينظم الإنفاق

budget *adj* (*informal*) (used in advertisements) very cheap رخيص جداً

budgie /ˈbʌdʒi/ *noun* [C] (*informal*) = BUDGERIGAR

buff /bʌf/ *noun* [C] (*informal*) a person who knows a lot about a particular subject and is very interested in it: *a film/computer buff* خبير

buffalo /ˈbʌfələʊ/ *noun* [C] (*pl.* **buffalo** or **buffaloes**) a large wild animal that looks like a cow with long curved horns: *a herd of buffalo* جاموس

buffer /ˈbʌfə(r)/ *noun* [C] **1** a flat round piece of metal with a spring behind it that is put on the front or back of a train or at the end of a railway track. Buffers reduce the shock when sth hits them. مخفف الصدمات

2 a thing or person that reduces the unpleasant effects of sth مخفّف للأذى أو للتصادم

buffet[1] /ˈbʊfeɪ; *US* bəˈfeɪ/ *noun* [C] **1** a meal (usually at a party or a special occasion) at which food is placed on a long table and people serve themselves: *Lunch was a cold buffet.* ○ *a buffet lunch* بوفيه: مأدبة ذات خدمة ذاتية

2 a counter where passengers can buy food and drinks on a train; a cafe at a station: *The buffet car is situated at the rear of the train.* مَقْصَف صغير في قطار : مطعم في محطة

buffet[2] /ˈbʌfɪt/ *verb* [T] to knock or push sth in a rough way from side to side: *The boat was buffeted by the rough sea.* تتقاذفه (الأمواج) : يلطم ، يدفع

bug /bʌg/ *noun* **1** [C] a small insect, especially one that causes damage or is found in dirty places بقّة : حشرة صغيرة

2 [C] an illness that is not very serious and that people get from each other: *I don't feel very well – I think I've got the bug that's going round.* جرثومة ، عدوى

3 [C] something wrong in a system or machine, especially a computer: *There's a bug in the software.* خلل

4 usually **the bug** [sing.] (*informal*) a sudden interest in sth: *They've been bitten by the golf bug.* اهتمام مفاجئ (بشيء) ، حماس

5 [C] a tiny hidden microphone that secretly records people's conversations ميكرفون بالغ الصغر للتنصّت

▸ **bug** *verb* [T] (bugging; bugged) **1** to hide a tiny microphone somewhere so that people's conversations can be recorded secretly: *Be careful what you say. This room is bugged.* يتنصّت (بإخفاء ميكرفون بالغ الصغر)

2 (*informal*) to annoy or worry sb: *It bugs him that he's not as successful as his brother.* يضايق : يُقلق

buggy /ˈbʌgi/ *noun* [C] (*pl.* **buggies**) (*Brit*) **1** (*US* **cart**) a small car, often without a roof or doors, used for a particular purpose: *a golf buggy* كارة

2 = PUSHCHAIR

🔑**build** /bɪld/ *verb* (*pt, pp* **built** /bɪlt/) **1** [T] to make sth by putting pieces, materials, etc. together: *How long ago was your house built?* ○ *They've built a new bridge across the river.* ○ *The house is built of stone and brick.* يبني ، يشيِّد

2 [I] to build buildings in a place: *There's plenty of land to build on around here.* يبني ، يشيِّد

3 [T] to develop or increase sth: *The government is trying to build a more modern society.* ○ *This book claims to help people to build their self-confidence.* ينمّي

PHR V **build sth in; build sth into sth 1** (used about furniture) fixed into a wall so that it cannot be moved: *We're going to have new cupboards built in in the kitchen.* يُثبّت في الحائط

2 to make sth a part of sth else: *They've made sure that a large number of checks are built into the system.* يدخل في، يضمن

build on sth to use sth as a base from which you can make further progress: *Now that we're beginning to make a profit, we must build on this success.* يتّخذه أساساً

build sth on sth to base sth on sth: *a society built on the principle of freedom and democracy* يقيم

build up to become greater in amount or number; to increase: *The traffic starts to build up at this time of day.* يستفحل : يتزايد

build sth up 1 to make sth seem more important or greater than it really is: *I don't think it's a very serious matter, it's just been built up in the newspapers.* يضخّم

2 to increase or develop sth over a period: *You'll need to build up your strength again slowly after the operation.* ينمّي ، يعزّز تدريجياً

▸ **build** *noun* [C,U] the shape and size of sb's body: *She has a very athletic build.* ○ *Police are looking for a young man of slim build.* بنية

Compare **build** and **figure**. **Build** usually describes size in connection with strength and muscle and is used for both men and women. **Figure** usually describes shape, especially w whether it is attractive or not, and is usually used only for women.

builder *noun* [C] a person whose job is to build houses and other buildings بنّاء

-built (in compounds) having a body with a particular shape and size: *a tall well-built man* ذو بنية (معيّنة)

building /ˈbɪldɪŋ/ *noun* **1** [C] a structure, such as a house, church or school, that has a roof and walls: *There are a lot of very old buildings in this town.* مبنى

2 [U] the process or business of making buildings: *building materials* ○ *the building industry* بناء، تشييد

ˈbuilding site *noun* [C] an area of land on which a building is being built موقع بناء

ˈbuilding society *noun* [C] (*Brit*) (*pl.* **building societies**) an organization rather like a bank with which people can save money and get interest on it and which lends money to people who want to buy houses or flats بنك عقاري

ˈbuild-up *noun* [C, usually sing.] **1 a build-up (of sth)** an increase of sth over a period: *The build-up of tension in the area has made war seem more likely.* تراكم؛ استفحال ، زيادة

2 a build-up (to sth) a period of preparation or excitement before an event: *The players started to get nervous in the build-up to the big game.* (فترة) تهيّؤ

ˌbuilt-ˈin *adj* **1** (used about furniture) built so it is fixed into a wall and cannot be moved: *built-in cupboards* مثبّت

2 made a part of sth else: *There is built-in unfairness in the system.* داخلي

ˌbuilt-ˈup *adj* covered with buildings: *a built-up area* مكتظّ بالمباني

bulb /bʌlb/ *noun* [C] **1** (*also* **ˈlight bulb**) the glass part of an electric lamp that gives out light: *The bulb's gone* (= it no longer works) – *I'll have to put a new one in.* ○ *a 60-watt light bulb* مصباح كهربائي

2 the round root of certain plants: *a tulip bulb* بَصَلة النبات

bulge /bʌldʒ/ *noun* [C] an outward curve or lump on sth that is usually flat نتوء ، انتفاخ

▶ **bulge** *verb* [I] **1** to stick out from sth that is usually flat; to swell outwards: *My stomach is starting to bulge. I must get more exercise.* يبرز ، ينتفخ

2 bulge with sth to be full of sth: *His bags were bulging with presents for the children.* مليء بـ

bulging *adj* **1** sticking out: *He had a thin face and rather bulging eyes.* بارز ، جاحظ

2 very full: *She came home with bulging carrier bags.* منتفخ ، مليء

bulimia /buˈlɪmiə; -liːmiə/ (*also* **bulimia nervosa** /buˈlɪmiə nɜːˈvəʊsə/) *noun* [U] an emotional disorder in which a person repeatedly eats too much and then forces him- or herself to vomit النهام

bulk /bʌlk/ *noun* **1** [U] the large size or amount of sth: *The cupboard isn't especially heavy, it's its bulk that makes it hard to move.* حجم كبير

2 [C] a very large body: *He slowly lifted his vast bulk out of the chair.* جسم ضخم

3 the bulk (of sth) [sing.] the main part of sth; most of sth: *The bulk of the work has been done, there's only a bit left.* معْظم

IDM in bulk in large quantities: *If you buy in bulk, it is 10% cheaper.* بمقادير كبيرة ، بالجملة

▶ **bulky** *adj* (**bulkier**; **bulkiest**) large and heavy and therefore difficult to move or carry: *a bulky parcel* ضخم ؛ جسيم

bull /bʊl/ *noun* [C] **1** an adult male of the cow family ➲ Look at the note at **cow**. ثور

2 the male of certain other animals, e.g. the elephant and the whale ذكر بعض الحيوانات

bulldog /ˈbʊldɒg/ *noun* [C] a strong dog with short legs, a large head and a short, thick neck البلدوغ: نوع من الكلاب

bulldoze /ˈbʊldəʊz/ *verb* [T] to make ground flat or knock down a building with a bulldozer: *The old buildings were bulldozed and new ones were built.* يهدم أو يمهّد بجرّافة

▶ **bulldozer** /ˈbʊldəʊzə(r)/ *noun* [C] a large, powerful tractor with a broad piece of metal at the front, used for clearing ground or knocking down buildings جرّافة

bullet /ˈbʊlɪt/ *noun* [C] a small rounded piece of metal with a pointed end that is fired from a gun: *The bullet hit her in the arm.* ○ *a bullet wound* ○ *There were bullet holes in the window.* رصاصة

bulletin /ˈbʊlətɪn/ *noun* [C] **1** a short news report on TV or radio; an official statement about a situation: *The next news bulletin on this channel is at nine o'clock.* نشرة أخبار ؛ بلاغ

2 a short newspaper that a club or organization produces نشرة

ˈbulletin board *noun* [C] (*US*) = NOTICEBOARD

bulletproof /ˈbʊlɪtpruːf/ *adj* made of a strong material that stops bullets from passing through it مضادّ أو مانع للرصاص

bullfight /ˈbʊlfaɪt/ *noun* [C] a traditional public entertainment, especially in Spain, Portugal and Latin America, in which a man makes a bull angry, fights it and often kills it مصارعة الثيران

▶ **bullfighter** *noun* [C] a man who takes part in a bullfight مصارع الثيران

bullfighting *noun* [U] the public entertainment in which men fight bulls in a special stadium (bullring) مصارعة الثيران

bullion /ˈbʊliən/ *noun* [U] bars of gold or silver: *The dollar price of gold bullion has risen by more than 10%.* سبيكة

bull's eye /ˈbʊlzaɪ/ *noun* [C] **1** the centre of a target that you aim at when you are shooting or throwing sth مركز أو قلب الهدف

2 a shot that hits this target الرّمية الصائبة

bully /ˈbʊli/ *noun* [C] (*pl.* **bullies**) a person who uses his/her greater strength or power to hurt

a b c d e f g h i j k l m n o p q r s t u v w x y z

or frighten people who are weaker
بلطجي ؛ المعتدي على الضعيف

▶ **bully** *verb* (*pres part* **bullying**; *3rd pers sing pres* **bullies**; *pt, pp* **bullied**) to use your strength or power to hurt or frighten sb who is weaker: *The older children bullied him at school.*
إرعاب أو اعتداء على الضعيف

PHR V **bully sb into doing sth** to force sb to do sth by frightening him/her
يجبره (على فعل شيء بالتهديد)

bulrush /ˈbʊlrʌʃ/ *noun* [C] a type of tall plant like a reed that grows in or near water تيفا، عشبة البِرَك

bum[1] /bʌm/ *noun* [C] (*especially Brit informal*) the part of the body on which you sit; bottom
عجيزة ، كَفَل

bum[2] /bʌm/ *noun* [C] (*especially US informal*)
1 a person who moves from place to place and lives by begging متشرّد يعيش على التسول
2 a lazy or useless person شخص كسول أو عديم القيمة

bumbag /ˈbʌmbæg/ *noun* [C] a small bag worn around the waist to keep money, etc. in
محفظة تحمل على الخصر

bump /bʌmp/ *verb* **1** [I] **bump against/into sb/sth** to hit sth solid by accident when you are moving: *She bumped into a lamp post because she wasn't looking where she was going.* يصطدم

2 [T] **bump sth (against/on sth)** to hit sth against or on sth by accident when moving it: *I bumped my knee on the edge of the table.*
يصدم ، يخبط

3 [I] to move in an uneven way as if going over bumps: *We bumped along the track to the cottage.* يتخبّط

PHR V **bump into sb** to meet sb by chance: *I bumped into a old friend on the bus today.*
يلتقي (بشخص) مصادفةً

bump sb off (*slang*) to kill or murder sb يقتل

▶ **bump** *noun* [C] **1** a sudden strong blow caused by sth hard hitting sth else; the sound of such a blow: *She fell and hit the ground with a bump.* ○ *We heard a loud bump from upstairs. One of the children had fallen out of bed.*
خبطة ، صدمة قوية

2 a lump on the body, often caused by a blow
ورم

3 a part of a flat surface that is raised above the rest of it: *There are a lot of bumps in the road, so drive carefully.* نتوء

bumpy *adj* (**bumpier**; **bumpiest**) **1** (used about a surface) having a lot of bumps (3): *We drove along a bumpy road until we reached the farm.*
ذو نتوءات ، وعِر

2 (used about a journey) rough and uncomfortable; not smooth: *Because of the stormy weather, it was a very bumpy flight.*
وَعِر ، مليء بالمطبّات ؛ غير مريح

bumper[1] /ˈbʌmpə(r)/ *noun* [C] the bar fixed to the front and back of a motor vehicle to reduce the effect if it hits sth مِصَدّ: مُخفِّف الصدمات

bumper[2] /ˈbʌmpə(r)/ *adj* larger than usual: *The unusually fine weather has produced a bumper harvest this year.* وافر جداً

bun /bʌn/ *noun* [C] **1** a small round, often sweet cake: *a currant bun* كعكة صغيرة مستديرة

2 hair fastened tightly into a round shape at the back of the head: *She wears her hair in a bun.*
عِقْصة أو كعكة (شعر)

bunch /bʌntʃ/ *noun* **1** [C] a number of things, usually of the same type, fastened or growing together: *He bought her a bunch of flowers for her birthday.* ○ *a bunch of bananas/grapes* ○ *a bunch of keys*
باقة ؛ عنقود ؛ حُزْمة

2 bunches [plural] long hair that is tied on each side of the head شعر طويل محزوم على جانبي الرأس

3 [C, with sing. or pl. verb] (*informal*) a group of people: *My colleagues are the best bunch of people I've ever worked with.* مجموعة

▶ **bunch** *verb* [I,T] **bunch (sth/sb) (up/together)** to stay together in a group; to form sth into a group or bunch: *The athletes bunched up as they came round the final bend.* ○ *He kept his papers bunched together in his hand.*
يتجمّع ؛ يُجمِّع

bundle /ˈbʌndl/ *noun* [C] a number of things tied or wrapped together: *a bundle of letters with an elastic band round them* رزمة

▶ **bundle** *verb* [T] **1 bundle sth (up)** to make or tie sth into a bundle or bundles: *I bundled up the old newspapers.* يحزم

2 to put or push sb or sth quickly and in a rough way in a particular direction: *He was arrested and bundled into a police car.*
يدفع بعنف ، يقذف به إلى

bung /bʌŋ/ *noun* [C] a round piece of wood or rubber that is used for closing the hole in certain containers e.g. a barrel, a jar, etc.
سدّادة برميل أو جرّة

▶ **bung** *verb* [T] (*Brit informal*) to put or throw sth somewhere in a rough or careless way: *We bunged the suitcases into the car and drove away.* يلقي بإهمال

bunged up *adj* blocked, so that nothing can get through: *I feel terrible. I've got a cold and my nose is all bunged up.* مسدود

bungalow /ˈbʌŋgələʊ/ *noun* [C] a house that is all on one level, without an upstairs
بيت من طابق واحد

bungee jumping /ˈbʌndʒi dʒʌmpɪŋ/ *noun* [U] a sport in which a person jumps from a high place, such as a bridge or a cliff قفز "بنجي"

bungle /ˈbʌŋgl/ *verb* [I,T] to do sth badly: *The men fled after bungling a raid on a bank in Oxford Road.* يفسد العمل

bunk[1] /bʌŋk/ *noun* [C] **1** a bed that is fixed to a wall (e.g. on a ship or train)
سرير مثبّت بجدار (في سفينة أو قطار مثلاً)

2 (*also* ˈ**bunk bed**) one of a pair of single beds built as a unit with one above the other
سريران يعلو أحدهما الآخر

bunk[2] /bʌŋk/ *noun*
IDM **do a bunk** (*Brit informal*) to run away or escape; to leave without telling anyone يهرب

bunker /ˈbʌŋkə(r)/ *noun* [C] **1** a strongly built

underground shelter that gives protection in a war مأوى محصّن تحت الأرض

2 an area of sand on a golf course, where it is difficult to hit the ball مجال رملي في لُعْبة الغولف يصعب ضرب الكرة منه

bunny /ˈbʌni/ *noun* [C] (used by and to small children) a rabbit أرنب

buoy /bɔɪ/ *noun* [C] a floating object, fastened to the bottom of the sea or a river, that shows ships and boats where dangerous places are الطافية

▸ **buoy** *verb* [T] **buoy sb/sth (up) 1** to keep sb cheerful: *His encouragement buoyed her up during that difficult period.* يفرح، يرفع روحه المعنوية

2 to keep sth high by supporting it: *Share prices were buoyed by news of a takeover.* يرفع

buoyant /ˈbɔɪənt/ *adj* **1** (used about a material) floating or able to float قابل للطفو

2 happy and cheerful: *The team were in buoyant mood after their win.* مبتهج

3 (used about economic and business life) successful, with a lot of activity: *Despite the recession, the property market remained buoyant.* منتعش ، مزدهر

4 (used about prices) rising or keeping at a high level مرتفع

▸ **buoyancy** /-ənsi/ *noun* [U]: *a buoyancy aid* (= something that helps you float) ○ *the buoyancy of the economy* طفو : انتعاش

burden /ˈbɜːdn/ *noun* [C] **1** a heavy load that is difficult to carry حِمْل

2 a responsibility or difficult task that causes a lot of work or worry: *Having to make all the decisions is a terrible burden for me.* ○ *I don't want to be a burden to my children when I'm old.* عبء

▸ **burden** *verb* [T] **burden sb/yourself (with sth)** to give sb/yourself a responsibility or task that causes a lot of work or worry: *If I were you, I wouldn't burden myself with other people's problems.* يثقل كاهله ، يحمّل (نفسه)

bureau /ˈbjʊərəʊ; *US* bjʊˈrəʊ/ *noun* [C] (*pl.* **bureaux** or **bureaus** /-rəʊz/) **1** (*Brit*) a writing desk with drawers and a lid طاولة للكتابة

2 (*US*) = CHEST OF DRAWERS

3 (*especially US*) one of certain government departments: *the Federal Bureau of Investigation* مكتب : دائرة حكومية

4 an organization that provides information: *a tourist information bureau* مكتب

bureaucracy /bjʊəˈrɒkrəsi/ *noun* (*pl.* **bureaucracies**) **1** [C,U] a system of government by a large number of officials in various departments بيروقراطية

2 [U] (often used in a critical way) the system of official rules that an organization has for doing sth, that people often think are too complicated: *With all the bureaucracy involved, it takes ages to get a visa.* بيروقراطية

▸ **bureaucrat** /ˈbjʊərəkræt/ *noun* [C] (often used in a critical way) an official in an organization or government department (شخص) بيروقراطي ، ديواني

bureaucratic /ˌbjʊərəˈkrætɪk/ *adj* connected with a bureaucracy, especially when it follows official rules too closely: *You have to go through a complex bureaucratic procedure if you want to get your money back.* بيروقراطي ، ديواني

bureau de change /ˌbjʊərəʊ də ˈʃɑːnʒ/ *noun* [C] (*pl.* **bureaux de change**) an office at an airport, in a hotel, etc. where you can change the money of one country to the money of another country صرّاف، مكتب صرافة

burger /ˈbɜːɡə(r)/ *noun* [C] = HAMBURGER

▸ **-burger** (in compounds) **1** a hamburger with sth else on top: *a cheeseburger* برجر: قرص من اللحم

2 something that is cooked like and looks like a hamburger, but is made of sth else: *a fishburger* طعام معدّ على شكل برجر

burglar /ˈbɜːɡlə(r)/ *noun* [C] a person who enters a building illegally in order to steal: *The burglars broke in by smashing a window.* ➲ Look at the note at **thief**. لص (يسطو على البيوت والمباني)

▸ **burglary** /ˈbɜːɡləri/ *noun* [C,U] (*pl.* **burglaries**) the crime of entering a building illegally in order to steal: *There was a burglary at the house next door last week.* ○ *He is in prison for burglary.* سطو على المباني

ˈ**burglar alarm** *noun* [C] a piece of equipment, usually fixed on a wall, that makes a loud noise if a thief enters a building إنذار أو منبّه ضد السطو

burgle /ˈbɜːɡl/ *verb* [T] to enter a building illegally in order to steal from it: *Our flat was burgled while we were out.* ○ *Lock all doors and windows or you might get burgled.* يسطو على مبنى

burial /ˈberiəl/ *noun* [C,U] the ceremony when a dead body is put in the ground (buried): *The burial took place on Friday.* ○ *The victims of the disaster were flown home for burial.* ➲ Look at the note at **funeral**. دَفْن

burka (*also* **burkha**) /ˈbɜːkə; *Brit also* ˈbʊəkə/ *noun* [C] a long loose piece of clothing that covers the whole body, including the head and face, worn in public by Muslim women in some countries برقع

burly /ˈbɜːli/ *adj* (**burlier**; **burliest**) (used about a person or sb's body) strong and heavy ضخم الجثّة

🔑 **burn** /bɜːn/ *verb* (*pt, pp* **burnt** /bɜːnt/ or **burned** /bɜːnd/) **1** [T] to destroy, damage or injure sb/sth with fire or heat: *We took all the rubbish outside and burned it.* ○ *It was a terrible fire and the whole building was burnt to the ground* (= completely destroyed). ○ *The water was so hot that I burned my hands.* ○ *If you get too close to the fire you'll burn yourself.* ○ *The people inside the building couldn't get out and they were all burnt to death.* يحرق ؛ يحترق

2 [I] to be destroyed, damaged or injured by fire or heat: *If you leave the cake in the oven for much longer, it will burn.* ○ *I can't spend too much time in the sun because I burn easily.* ○ *They were trapped by the flames and they burned to death.* يحترق

a b c d e f g h i j k l m n o p q r s t u v w x y z

3 [T] to produce a hole or mark in or on sth by burning: *He dropped his cigarette and it burned a hole in the carpet.* يحرق أو يسم بالحرق

4 [I] to be on fire: *Firemen raced to the burning building.* يشتعل ، يلتهب

5 [I] to produce light: *I don't think he went to bed at all – I could see his light burning all night.* يشتعل ، يضيء

6 [I] to feel unpleasantly hot: *You must have a temperature, your forehead's burning.* ترتفع درجة حرارته ، يتّقد

7 [I] **burn (with sth)** to be filled with a very strong feeling: *She was burning with indignation.* يشتعل أو يتّقد بِ

PHR V **burn (sth) down** (used about a building) to destroy or be destroyed completely by fire: *The fire could not be brought under control and the school burned down.* ○ *The house was burnt down in a fire some years ago.* يدمّر بالحرق ، يحترق عن آخره

burn sth off 1 to remove sth by burning: *Burn off the old paint before repainting the door.* يزيل بالحرق

2 to use energy by doing exercise: *This workout helps you to burn off fat and tone up muscles.* يحرق (الحريرات)

burn sth out (usually passive) to completely destroy sth by burning: *the burnt-out wreck of a car* يحرق (شيئاً) حرقاً تاماً

burn up to be destroyed by fire or strong heat: *The space capsule burnt up on its re-entry into the earth's atmosphere.* يحترق

burn sth up to destroy sth by fire: *When all the rubbish had been burnt up I put out the fire.* يتلف بالاحراق

▶ **burn** *noun* [C] an injury or piece of damage caused by fire or heat: *He has been treated for burns to his face and hands.* ○ *the burns unit of a hospital* حرْق

burner (*US*) = RING[1] (5)

burp /bɜːp/ *verb* [I] to make a noise with the mouth when air rises from the stomach and is forced out: *He sat back when he had finished his meal and burped loudly.* يتجشأ

▶ **burp** *noun* [C]: *a loud burp* تجشّؤ

burrow /ˈbʌrəʊ/ *noun* [C] a hole in the ground made by certain animals (e.g. rabbits) in which they live جحر

▶ **burrow** *verb* **1** [I,T] to dig a hole in the ground يحفر جحراً

2 [I] to search for sth, using your hands as if you were digging: *She burrowed in her handbag for her keys.* ينقّب

bursar /ˈbɜːsə(r)/ *noun* [C] the person who manages the financial matters of a school, college or university أمين صندوق في مؤسسة دراسيّة

▶ **bursary** /ˈbɜːsəri/ *noun* [C] (*pl.* **bursaries**) a sum of money given to a specially chosen student to pay for his/her studies at a college or university منحة دراسيّة

⚷ **burst[1]** /bɜːst/ *verb* (*pt, pp* **burst**) **1** [I,T] to break open suddenly and violently, usually because there is too much pressure inside; to cause this to happen: *The balloon burst with a loud bang.* ○ *You'll burst that balloon if you blow it up any more.* [I] (*figurative*) *'Would you like some more to eat?' 'No, thanks. If I have any more, I'll burst!'* ○ *If it rains much more, the river will burst its banks.* ينفجر ، يتفتق : يجعله ينفجر الخ

2 [I] **be bursting (with sth)** to be so full that it is in danger of breaking open: *I packed so many clothes that my suitcases were bursting.* ○ (*figurative*) *He was bursting with happiness on his wedding day.* يطفح : يكاد يتفتّق؛ ينضح بِ

IDM **be bursting to do sth** to want to do sth very much: *I'm bursting to tell someone the news but it's a secret.* يتشوّق

PHR V **burst in on sb/sth** to interrupt sb/sth by arriving suddenly: *I'm sorry to burst in on you like this but there's an urgent phone call.* يقتحم أو يقاطع فجاة

burst into sth to start doing sth suddenly: *On hearing the news she burst into tears* (= started crying). ○ *The lorry hit a wall and burst into flames* (= started burning). ينفجر (باكياً) : ينفجر (مشتعلاً)

burst into, out of, through, etc. to move suddenly in a particular direction, often using force: *She burst into the manager's office and demanded to speak to him.* يقتحم ، يندفع

burst out 1 to start doing sth suddenly: *He looked so ridiculous that I burst out laughing.* ينفجر (ضاحكاً مثلاً)

2 to say sth suddenly and with strong feeling: *Finally she burst out, 'I can't stand it any more!'* ينفجر (قائلاً مثلاً)

⚷ **burst[2]** /bɜːst/ *noun* [C] **1** an occasion when sth bursts or explodes; a crack caused by an explosion: *a burst in a water pipe* انفجار : شقّ أو صدع

2 a short period of a particular activity, that often starts suddenly: *With a burst of speed, she left the other runners behind.* ○ *He prefers to work in short bursts.* ○ *There were several bursts of applause during her speech.* فَوْرة

⚷ **bury** /ˈberi/ *verb* [T] (*pres part* **burying**; *3rd pers sing pres* **buries**; *pt, pp* **buried**) **1** to put a dead body in a grave: *She wants to be buried in the village graveyard.* ○ *Anne Brontë is buried in Scarborough.* يدفن

2 to put sth in a hole in the ground to cover it up: *Our dog always buries its bones in the garden.* ○ *They say there's buried treasure somewhere on the island!* يدفن ، يطمر

3 (usually passive) to cover or hide: *At last I found the photograph, buried at the bottom of a drawer.* ○ *After the earthquake, hundreds of people were buried under the rubble.* ○ (*figurative*) *Sally didn't hear us come in. She was buried in a book.* مدفون : غارق (في كتاب)

⚷ **bus** /bʌs/ *noun* [C] (*pl.* **buses**; *US also* **busses**) a big public vehicle which takes passengers from one stopping-place to another along a fixed route: *Where do you usually get on/off the bus?* ○ *We'll have to hurry up if we want to catch the 9 o'clock bus.* ○ *It's so difficult to park your car in town. It's better to go by bus.* حافلة، أوتوبيس

The **bus driver** may also take the money (your **fare**) and give you your **ticket**, or there may be a **conductor** who collects the fares. You can get on or off at a **bus stop** and the central point where most buses start is the **bus station**. Note that we travel **by bus**. We can also say **on the bus**: *'How do you get to work?' 'On the bus.'*

bush /bʊʃ/ *noun* **1** [C] a plant like a small, thick tree with many low branches: *a rose bush* ○ *The house was surrounded by thick bushes.* شُجَيرة

2 often **the bush** [U, sing.] wild land that is not cultivated, especially in Africa and Australia دَغَل

IDM **beat about the bush** → BEAT[1]

▶ **bushy (bushier; bushiest)** *adj* growing thickly: *bushy hair* ○ *bushy eyebrows* كثيف

busier, busiest, busily → BUSY

business /ˈbɪznəs/ *noun* **1** [U] buying and selling as a way of earning money; commerce: *She has set up in business as a hairdresser.* ○ *They are very easy to do business with.* ○ *He teaches English for Business.* عمل تجاريّ

2 [U] the work that you do as your job: *The manager will be away on business next week.* ○ *a business trip* عمل ، مهمّة

3 [U] the amount of trade done: *Business has been good for the time of year.* الحركة التجاريّة

4 [C] a firm, a shop, a factory, etc. which produces or sells goods or provides a service: *She started an antique business of her own.* ○ *Small businesses are finding it hard to survive at the moment.* مشروع تجاري

5 [U] something that concerns a particular person: *The friends I choose are my business, not yours.* ○ *Our business is to collect the information, not to comment on it.* ○ *'How much did it cost?' 'It's none of your business!'* (= I don't want to tell you. It's private.) شأن ، عمل ، مهمّة

6 [sing.] a situation or an event: *The divorce was an awful business.* ○ *I found the whole business very depressing.* أمر ، قضيّة

IDM **get down to business** to start the work that must be done: *Let's just have a cup of coffee before we get down to business.* يشرع في إداء العمل

go out of business to have to close because there is no more money available: *The shop went out of business because it couldn't compete with the new supermarket.* ينهي عمله التجاري ، يفلس

have no business to do sth/doing sth to have no right to do sth: *You have no business to read/reading my letters without asking me.* ليس له حق

mind your own business → MIND[2]

businesslike /ˈbɪznəslaɪk/ *adj* efficient and practical: *She has a very businesslike manner.* عملي ، منظّم ، جدّي

businessman /ˈbɪznəsmæn; -mən/, **businesswoman** /ˈbɪznəswʊmən/ *noun* [C] (*pl.* **businessmen** /-mən/, **businesswomen** /-wɪmɪn/) **1** a person who works in business (1) especially in a top position رجل أعمال ، سيدة أعمال

2 a person who is skilful at dealing with money: *My brother can advise you on your investments – he's a better businessman than I am.* خبير بشؤون المال

ˈ**business studies** *noun* [U, with sing. or pl. verb] the study of how to control and manage a business (4): *a course in business studies* دراسات أعمال ، دراسات تجارية

busk /bʌsk/ *verb* [I] to sing or play music in the street so that people will stop and give you money يعزف أو يغني في الشوارع (بقصد الارتزاق)

▶ **busker** *noun* [C] a street musician عازف أو مغنّي شوارع

bust[1] /bʌst/ *noun* [C] **1** a model in stone, etc. of a person's head, shoulders and chest تمثال نصفي

2 a woman's breasts; the measurement round a woman's chest: *This blouse is a bit tight around the bust.* صدر (المرأة) : محيط صدر المرأة

3 an unexpected visit by the police in order to arrest people for doing sth illegal: *a drugs bust* مداهمة

bust[2] /bʌst/ *verb* [T] (*pt, pp* **bust** or **busted**) (*informal*) to break or damage sth so that it cannot be used يكسر ، يعطب

▶ **bust** *adj* (not before a noun) (*informal*) broken or not working: *The zip on these trousers is bust.* مكسور : معطّل

IDM **go bust** (*informal*) (used about a business) to have to close because it has lost so much money: *During the recession thousands of businesses went bust.* يفلس

bustle /ˈbʌsl/ *verb* [I,T] **1** to move in a busy, noisy or excited way; to make sb move somewhere quickly: *He bustled about the kitchen making tea.* ○ *They bustled her out of the room before she could see the body.* يروح و يجيء بنشاط ؛ يستحث ، يخرجه بسرعة

2 bustle (with sth) to be full of sth (people, noise, activity, etc.): *It was the week before Christmas and the streets were bustling with shoppers.* يعج بِ

▶ **bustle** *noun* [U] excited and noisy activity: *She loved the bustle of city life.* صخب

ˈ**bust-up** *noun* [C] (*informal*) a serious quarrel شِجار حاد

busy /ˈbɪzi/ *adj* (**busier; busiest**) **1 busy (at/with sth); busy (doing sth)** having a lot of work or tasks to do; not free; working on sth: *Mr Smith is busy until 4 o'clock but he could see you after that.* ○ *Don't disturb him. He's busy.* ○ *She's busy with her preparations for the party.* ○ *We're busy decorating the spare room before our visitors arrive.* مشغول

2 (used about a period of time) full of activity and things to do: *I've had rather a busy week.* مليئ بالمشاغل

3 (used about a place) full of people, movement and activity: *Oxford Street was so busy that I could hardly move.* كثير الحركة ، يعجّ بِ مزدحم

4 (*US*) = ENGAGED (2): *The line's busy at the moment. I'll try again later.*

IDM **get busy** start working: *We'll have to get busy if we're going to be ready in time.* يبدأ العمل

▶ **busy** *verb* [T] (*pres part* **busying**; *3rd pers sing*

a b c d e f g h i j k l m n o p q r s t u v w x y z

pres **busies**; *pt, pp* **busied**) **busy yourself with sth; busy yourself doing sth** to keep yourself busy; to find sth to do ينشغل ، يشغل نفسه بـ
busily *adv*: *When I came in she was busily writing something at her desk.* بانهماك

busybody /ˈbɪzibɒdi/ *noun* [C] (*pl.* **busybodies**) a person who is too interested in other people's affairs فضولي

but¹ /bət; *strong form* bʌt/ *conj* **1** (used for introducing an idea which contrasts with or is different from what has just been said): *The weather will be sunny but cold.* ○ *Theirs is not the first but the second house on the left.* ○ *James hasn't got a car but his sister has.* لكن
2 however; and yet: *She's been learning Italian for five years but she doesn't speak it very well.* ○ *I'd love to come but I can't make it till 8 o'clock.* إلاّ أنّ
3 (used with an apology): *Excuse me, but is your name Peter Watkins?* ○ *I'm sorry, but I can't stay any longer.* (تصاحب الاعتذار)
4 (used for introducing a statement that shows that you are surprised or annoyed or that you disagree): *'Here's the money I owe you.' 'But that's not right – it was only £6.'* (للتعبير عن الاندهاش أو الانزعاج أو الاختلاف)
IDM but then however; on the other hand: *We could go swimming. But then perhaps it's too cold.* ○ *He's brilliant at the piano. But then so was his father* (= however, this is not surprising because...). إلاّ أنّ : ليس مستغرباً

but² /bət; *strong form* bʌt/ *prep* except: *I've told no one but you about this.* ○ *We've had nothing but trouble with this washing machine!* إلاّ ، ما عدا
IDM but for sb/sth except for or without sb/sth: *We wouldn't have managed but for your help.* لولا

butcher /ˈbʊtʃə(r)/ *noun* [C] **1** a person who sells meat: *The butcher cut me four lamb chops.* ○ *She went to the butcher's for some sausages.*
ℹ Note that **the butcher** is the person who runs the shop and **the butcher's** is the shop. جزار ، قصّاب ، لحّام
2 a person who kills many people in a cruel way سفّاح ، جزار
▸ **butcher** *verb* [T] to kill a lot of people in a cruel way يسفك الدماء ، يقوم بمذبحة
butchery *noun* [U] unnecessary or cruel killing سفْك (الدماء)

butler /ˈbʌtlə(r)/ *noun* [C] the most important male servant in a big house كبير الخدم

butt¹ /bʌt/ *noun* [C] **1** the thicker, heavier end of a weapon or tool: *the butt of a rifle* كعب أو عقِب (البندقية)
2 a short piece of a cigarette or cigar which is left when it has been smoked عقِب (السيجارة)
3 (*especially US informal*) your bottom: *Get up off your butt and do some work!* عجيزة ، مؤخّر
4 the act of hitting sb with your head نَطحة

butt² /bʌt/ *noun* [C] a person who is often laughed at or talked about unpleasantly: *Fat children are often the butt of other children's jokes.* أضحوكة

butt³ /bʌt/ *verb* [T] to hit or push sb/sth with the head ينطح
PHR V butt in (on sb/sth) to interrupt sb/sth or to join in sth without being asked: *I'm sorry to butt in but could I speak to you urgently for a minute?* يقاطع (حديثه مثلاً)

butter /ˈbʌtə(r)/ *noun* [U] a soft yellow fat that is made from cream and used for spreading on bread, etc. or in cooking زُبْدَة
▸ **butter** *verb* [T] to spread butter on bread, etc: *I'll cut the bread and you butter it.* ○ *hot buttered toast* يدهن بالزّبدة

ˈ**butter bean** *noun* [C] a large pale yellow bean. Butter beans are often sold dried فاصوليا ليميّة

buttercup /ˈbʌtəkʌp/ *noun* [C] a wild plant with bright yellow flowers shaped like small cups حَوْذان

butterfly /ˈbʌtəflaɪ/ *noun* [C] (*pl.* **butterflies**) an insect with a long, thin body and four brightly coloured wings: *Caterpillars develop into butterflies.* فراشة
IDM have butterflies (in your stomach) (*informal*) to feel very nervous before doing sth يشعر بالاضطراب والهلع

buttermilk /ˈbʌtəmɪlk/ *noun* [U] the liquid that is left when butter has been separated from milk مخيض (اللبن)

buttock /ˈbʌtək/ *noun* [C, usually pl.] the part of the body which you sit on عجيزة ، ردف

button /ˈbʌtn/ *noun* [C] **1** a small, often round, piece of plastic, wood or metal that you use for fastening your clothes: *One of the buttons on my jacket has come off.* ○ *a coat, shirt, trouser, etc. button* ○ *This blouse is too tight. I can't fasten the buttons.* زرّ
2 a type of small switch on a machine, etc. that you press in order to operate sth: *Press this button to ring the bell.* ○ *Which button turns the volume down?* ○ *the buttons on a telephone* ○ *Double-click the right mouse button.* زرّ

buttonhole /ˈbʌtənhəʊl/ *noun* [C] **1** a hole in a piece of clothing that you push a button through in order to fasten it عُروة
2 (*Brit*) a flower that you pin to your coat or jacket or push through your buttonhole زهرة توضع في عروة السُتْرة
▸ **buttonhole** *verb* [T] to make sb stop and listen to what you want to say: *I'll try to buttonhole the headmaster before he goes home.* يجبره على الاستماع إليه

buy /baɪ/ *verb* [T] (*pt, pp* **bought** /bɔːt/) to get sth by paying money for it: *I'm going to buy a new dress for the party.* ○ *We bought this book for you in London.* ○ *Can I buy you a coffee?* ○ *He bought the car from a friend.* ○ *Did you buy this sofa new?* ○ *He bought the necklace as a present for his wife.* يشتري
▸ **buy** *noun* [C] an act of buying sth or a thing that you can buy: *I think your house was a very*

good buy (= worth the money you paid). شروة، صفقة

buyer *noun* [C] **1** a person who is buying sth or may buy sth: *I think we've found a buyer for our house!* مشترٍ

2 a person whose job is to choose and buy goods to be sold in a large shop مسؤول مشتريات

buyout /ˈbaɪaʊt/ *noun* [C] the act of buying enough or all of the shares in a company in order to get control of it شراء معظم أسهم الشركة

buzz /bʌz/ *verb* **1** [I] to make the sound that bees, etc. make when flying: *A large fly was buzzing against the window pane.* يطِنّ، يزن

2 [I] **buzz (with sth)** to be full of (talk, thoughts, etc.): *Her head was buzzing with questions that she wanted to ask.* ○ *The office was buzzing with rumours about the proposed changes.* يضج

3 [I,T] to call sb by using an electric bell, etc: *The doctor will buzz for you when he's ready.* يستدعي بضغط جرس كهربائي الخ

▸ **buzz** *noun* **1** [C] the sound that a bee, etc. makes when flying: *the buzz of insects* طنين : أزيز، زن

2 [sing.] the low sound made by many people talking at the same time: *I could hear the buzz of conversation in the next room.* غمغمة

3 [sing.] (*informal*) a strong feeling of excitement or pleasure: *a buzz of expectation* ○ *She gets a buzz out of shopping for expensive clothes.* ابتهاج

IDM **give sb a buzz** (*informal*) to telephone sb يتصل تلفونياً

buzzer *noun* [C] a piece of equipment that makes a buzzing sound: *You'll hear the buzzer on the cooker when the meal's ready.* طنّان أو زنّان كهربائي

buzzword /ˈbʌzwɜːd/ *noun* [C] a word or phrase, especially one connected with a particular subject, that has become fashionable and popular العبارة الرائجة أو (آخر موضة)

by[1] /baɪ/ *adv* **1** past: *We stopped to let the ambulance get by.* ○ *If we sit here we can watch the boats sail by.* ○ *Time seemed to be going by very slowly.* ماراً (من أمامنا)

2 near: *The shops are close by.* على مقربة من

IDM **by and large** mostly; in general: *By and large the school is very efficient.* بشكل عام : غالباً

by the way → WAY[1]

by[2] /baɪ/ *prep* **1** beside; very near: *Come and sit by me.* ○ *We stayed in a cottage by the sea.* قرب

2 past: *He walked straight by me without speaking.* ماراً بِ

3 not later than; before: *I'll be home by 7 o'clock.* ○ *He should have telephoned by now/by this time.* ○ *By this time tomorrow you'll be married!* في وقت لا يتجاوز (كذا)، قبلَ

4 (usually without *the*) during a period of time; in particular circumstances: *By day we covered about thirty miles and by night we rested.* ○ *The electricity went off so we had to work by candlelight.* في، خلال : بِ

5 (after a passive verb) (used for showing who or what did or caused sth): *She was knocked down by a car.* ○ *The event was organized by local people.* ○ *I was deeply shocked by the news.* ○ *The building was designed by Stirling.* ○ *Who was the book written by?/Who is the book by?* بِ : من قِبَل

6 through doing sth: *You can get hold of me by phoning this number.* بِ

7 using sth: *Will you be paying by cheque?* ○ *The house is heated by electricity.* ○ *'How do you go to work?' 'By train, usually.'* ○ *by bus, car, plane, bicycle, etc.* بِ، بواسطة

8 as a result of; due to: *I got on the wrong bus by mistake/accident.* ○ *I met an old friend by chance.* نتيجةً لِ، بِ (الصدفة)

9 according to: *It's 8 o'clock by my watch.* ○ *By law you have to attend school from the age of five.* حسب، وفقاً لـ

10 (used for multiplying or dividing): *4 multiplied by 5 is 20.* ○ *6 divided by 2 is 3.* (مضروباً) في : (مقسوماً) على

11 (used for showing the measurements of an area): *The table is six feet by three feet* (= six feet long and three feet wide). بِ

12 (with *the*) in quantities or periods of: *We buy material by the metre.* ○ *You can rent a car by the day, the week or the month.* ○ *Copies of the book have sold by the million.* بِ

13 in groups or units of: *They came in one by one.* ○ *Bit by bit I began to understand.* ○ *Day by day she was getting better.* فَ

14 to the amount of: *Prices have gone up by 10 per cent.* ○ *I missed the bus by a few minutes.* بمقدار، بِ

15 (used with a part of the body or an article of clothing) holding: *He grabbed me by the arm.* من

16 with regard to: *She's French by birth.* ○ *He's a doctor by profession.* ○ *By nature she's a very gentle person.* بِ، (فيما يتعلّق) بِ

bye /baɪ/ (*also* **ˈbye-bye**) *interj* (*informal*) goodbye: *Bye! See you tomorrow.* وداعاً : مع السلامة

ˈby-election *noun* [C] an election to choose a new Member of Parliament for a particular town or area (a constituency). It is held when the previous member has resigned or died. ➲ Look at **general election**. انتخاب فرعي

bypass /ˈbaɪpɑːs; *US* -pæs/ *noun* [C] a road which traffic can use to go round a town, instead of through it طريق حول المدينة يتجنّب دخولها

▸ **bypass** *verb* [T] to go around or to avoid sth using a bypass: *Let's try to bypass the city centre.* ○ (*figurative*) *It's no good trying to bypass the problem.* يتحاشى، يتجنّب

ˈby-product *noun* [C] **1** something that is formed during the making of sth else محصول ثانوي

2 something that happens as the result of sth else حصيلة أو نتيجة ثانوية

bystander /ˈbaɪstændə(r)/ *noun* [C] a person who is standing near and sees sth that happens, without being involved in it: *Several innocent by-*

a b c d e f g h i j k l m n o p q r s t u v w x y z

standers were hurt when the two gangs attacked each other. متفرِّج، مشاهِد، أحد الموجودين

byte /baɪt/ *noun* [C] (*computing*) a unit of information that can represent one item, such as a letter or a number. A byte is usually made up of a series of eight smaller units (bits). في الكمبيوتر: وحدة معلومات

C c

C, c /siː/ *noun* [C] (*pl.* **Cs; C's; c's**) the third letter of the English alphabet: *'Come' begins with (a) 'C'.* الحرف الثالث من الأبجدية الإنكليزية

C *abbrev* = CELSIUS

c (*also* **ca**) *abbrev* (before dates) about, approximately: *c 1770* حوالي

cab /kæb/ *noun* [C] **1** (*especially US*) = TAXI: *Let's take a cab/go by cab.*
2 the part of a lorry, train, bus, etc. where the driver sits مكان جلوس السائق في شاحنة أو قطار وغيره

cabaret /ˈkæbəreɪ; *US* ˌkæbəˈreɪ/ *noun* [C,U] an entertainment with singing, dancing, etc. in a restaurant or nightclub ملهى ليلي

cabbage /ˈkæbɪdʒ/ *noun* [C,U] a large round vegetable with thick green, or sometimes dark red leaves, often eaten cooked: *We've planted cabbages in the garden.* ○ *Shall we have cabbage with the sausages?* كُرُنْب ، مَلْفوف

cabin /ˈkæbɪn/ *noun* [C] **1** a small room in a ship or boat, where a passenger sleeps: *We've booked a cabin on the ferry as we'll be travelling overnight.* قَمَرة ، حجرة في سفينة
2 one of the parts of a plane, at the front or where the passengers sit: *I prefer to have a seat at the front of the cabin.* ○ *the pilot's cabin* المقصورة: مكان الجلوس في الطائرة
3 a small wooden house or hut: *We stayed in a log cabin in Sweden.* كوخ

ˈcabin cruiser *noun* [C] = CRUISER (2)

⚷**cabinet** /ˈkæbɪnət/ *noun* [C] **1** a cupboard with shelves or drawers, used for storing things: *a medicine cabinet* ○ *a filing cabinet* خزانة
2 (*also* **the Cabinet**) [with sing. or pl. verb] the most important ministers in a government, who have regular meetings with the Prime Minister: *The Cabinet is/are meeting today to discuss the crisis.* ○ *a cabinet meeting, minister, etc.* مجلس الوزراء

⚷**cable** /ˈkeɪbl/ *noun* **1** [C] a very strong, thick rope or chain, etc. حبل غليظ : سلسلة معدنية
2 [C,U] a set of wires covered with plastic, etc., for carrying electricity or signals: *an underground electrical cable* ○ *a telephone cable* ○ *fibre-optic cable* كابل: سلك كهربائي غليظ
3 [C] (*old-fashioned*) = TELEGRAM
4 [U] = CABLE TELEVISION

ˈcable car *noun* [C] a carriage that hangs on a moving cable (1) and carries passengers up and down a mountain مركبة معلقة على سلك

ˌcable ˈtelevision (*also* **cable**) *noun* [U] a system of broadcasting television programmes by cable (2) instead of by radio signals البثّ التلفزيوني بواسطة الكابلات

ˈcab stand (*US*) = TAXI RANK

cackle /ˈkækl/ *noun* [C] **1** the loud sound that a hen makes after laying an egg قوقأة الدجاج
2 a loud, unpleasant laugh ضحكة عالية مزعجة
▸ **cackle** *verb* [I] تقوقئ (الدجاجة) ؛ يضحك ضحكة عالية مزعجة

cactus /ˈkæktəs/ *noun* [C] (*pl.* **cactuses** or **cacti** /ˈkæktaɪ/) a type of plant that grows in hot, dry areas, especially deserts. A cactus has a thick stem and sharp points (prickles) but no leaves. صبّار

cadet /kəˈdet/ *noun* [C] a young person who is training to be in the army, navy, air force or police طالب في كلية عسكرية

cadge /kædʒ/ *verb* [I,T] **cadge (sth) (from/off sb)** (*informal*) to try to persuade sb to give or lend you sth: *He's always cadging meals from people without repaying them!* يستجدي (من أصدقائه) ، يتطفل

Caesarean (*also* **Caesarian**; *US also* **Cesarian, Cesarean**) /sɪˈzeəriən/ *noun* [C] an operation to remove a baby from its mother's body when a normal birth would be impossible or dangerous عملية (ولادة) قيصرية

cafe /ˈkæfeɪ; *US* kæˈfeɪ/ *noun* [C] a small restaurant that serves drinks and light meals مقهى ، مطعم صغير

cafeteria /ˌkæfəˈtɪəriə/ *noun* [C] a restaurant, especially one for staff or workers, where people collect their meals on trays and carry them to their tables ➲ Look at **canteen**. مطعم يقوم على الخدمة الذاتية

caffeine /ˈkæfiːn/ *noun* [U] the substance found in coffee and tea which makes you feel more awake and lively ➲ Look at **decaffeinated**. كافين: المادة المنشّطة في القهوة أو الشاي

cage /keɪdʒ/ *noun* [C] a box made of bars or wire, or a space surrounded by wire or metal bars, in which a bird or animal is kept so that it cannot escape: *The tiger paced up and down its cage.* ○ *The parrot has escaped from its cage.* قفص
▸ **caged** /keɪdʒd/ *adj*: *He felt like a caged animal in the tiny office.* محبوس في قفص

cagey /ˈkeɪdʒi/ *adj* **cagey (about sth)** (*informal*) not wanting to give information or to talk about sth ❶ A more formal word is **secretive**. حَذِر ، محترس (في كلامه)

cagoule /kəˈɡuːl/ *noun* [C] a long waterproof jacket with a hood سترة بغطاء للرأس واقية من المطر

cakes

🔑**cake** /keɪk/ *noun* **1** [C,U] a sweet food made by mixing flour, eggs, butter, sugar, etc. together and baking the mixture in the oven: *a birthday cake* ○ *a wedding cake* ○ *a chocolate cake* ○ *a fruit cake* ○ *a sponge cake* ○ *The bride and bridegroom cut the cake.* ○ *Would you like some more cake?* ○ *a piece of birthday cake* كعكة ، "كاتو"

> After **making** or **baking** a cake we often **ice** or (*US*) **frost** the top and sides of it.

2 [C] a mixture of other food, cooked in a round, flat shape: *fish cakes* ○ *potato cakes* قرص من (السمك المهروس مثلاً)

IDM **have your cake and eat it** to enjoy the advantages of sth without its disadvantages; to have both things that are available: *You can't go out every night and save for your holiday. You can't have your cake and eat it.* يربح على الوجهين ، يجمع بين النقيضين

a piece of cake → PIECE[1]

▸ **cake** *verb* [T] (usually passive) to cover sth thickly with a substance that becomes hard when it dries: *boots caked in/with mud* يكسو بطبقة يابسة

calamity /kəˈlæməti/ *noun* [C,U] (*pl.* **calamities**) a terrible event that causes a lot of damage or harm كارثة ، فاجعة

calcium /ˈkælsiəm/ *noun* [U] (*symbol* **Ca**) a chemical element. Calcium is found in bones, teeth and chalk. كَلسيوم

🔑**calculate** /ˈkælkjuleɪt/ *verb* [T] **1** to find sth out by using mathematics: *I've been calculating the costs involved and it's too expensive.* ○ *It's difficult to calculate how long the project will take.* يحسُب ، يقدّر

2 to consider or expect sth: *We calculated that the advantages would be greater than the disadvantages.* يتوقّع

IDM **be calculated to do sth** to be intended or designed to do sth: *His remark was clearly calculated to annoy me.* متعمّد ؛ يقصد به

▸ **calculating** *adj* planning things in a very careful and selfish way in order to achieve exactly what you want: *Her cold, calculating approach made her many enemies.* ذو كيد ، ماكر

calculation /ˌkælkjuˈleɪʃn/ *noun* **1** [C,U] finding an answer by using mathematics: *Several of his calculations are wrong.* ○ *Calculation of the exact cost is impossible.* حساب ، عملية حسابية

2 [U] (*formal*) careful thought and planning in order to achieve your own, selfish aims: *His actions were clearly the result of deliberate calculation.* مكر، تخطيط مدروس

calculator /ˈkælkjuleɪtə(r)/ *noun* [C] a small electronic machine used for calculating figures: *a pocket calculator* آلة حاسبة

caldron (*especially US*) = CAULDRON

calendar /ˈkælɪndə(r)/ *noun* [C] **1** a list that shows the days, weeks and months of a particular year: *She had ringed the important dates on her calendar in red.* ○ *There was a calendar hanging on the back of the door.* تقويم

> A **calendar** is often hung on a wall and may have a separate page for each month, sometimes with a picture or photograph. A **diary** is a little book which you can carry around with you and which has spaces next to the dates so that you can write in appointments, etc.

2 a system for dividing time into fixed periods and for marking the beginning and end of a year: *the Muslim calendar* تقويم

3 a list of dates and events in a year that are important in a particular area of activity: *Wimbledon is a major event in the sporting calendar.* تقويم ، برنامج سنوي

ˌcalendar ˈmonth *noun* [C] = MONTH (1,2)

ˌcalendar ˈyear *noun* [C] = YEAR (2)

calf[1] /kɑːf; *US* kæf/ *noun* [C] (*pl.* **calves** /kɑːvz; *US* kævz/) **1** a young cow ❶ The meat from a calf is called **veal**. Look at the note at **meat**. ➲ Look at the note at **cow**. عِجْل

2 the young of some other animals, e.g. elephants صغير بعض الحيوانات (مثل الفيل)

calf[2] /kɑːf; *US* kæf/ *noun* [C] (*pl.* **calves** /kɑːvz; *US* kævz/) the back of your leg, below your knee بطّة أو ربلة الساق

calibre (*US* **caliber**) /ˈkælɪbə(r)/ *noun* [sing., U] the quality or ability of a person or thing: *The company's employees are of the highest calibre.* مقدرة ، مستوى

🔑**call[1]** /kɔːl/ *noun* **1** [C] a loud sound that is made to attract attention; a shout: *a call for help* ○ *That bird's call is easy to recognize.* نداء ؛ صيحة

2 (*also* **ˈphone call**) [C] an act of telephoning or a conversation on the telephone: *Were there any calls for me while I was out?* ○ *I'll give you a call at the weekend.* ○ *The manager is on the line. Will you take the call?* ○ *a local call* ○ *a long-distance call* مخابرة تليفونية

3 [C] a short visit, especially to sb's house: *We could pay a call on Dave on our way home.* ○ *The*

doctor has several calls to make this morning. زيارة قصيرة

4 [C] a request, demand for sth: *There have been calls for the President to resign.* دعوة ، مطالبة

5 [C,U] **call for sth** a need for sth: *The doctor said there was no call for concern.* ضرورة ، لزوم

IDM at sb's beck and call → BECK

(be) on call to be ready to work if necessary: *Dr Young will be on call this weekend.* (يكون) تحت الاستدعاء

call² /kɔːl/ *verb* **1** [I,T] **call (out) to sb; call (sth) (out)** to say sth loudly or to shout in order to attract attention: *'Hello, is anybody there?' she called.* ○ *I could hear a voice calling for help.* ○ *He called out the names and the winners stepped forward.* ○ *Call the children. Breakfast is ready.* ينادي ؛ يصرخ ؛ يتلو بصوت عالٍ

2 [I,T] to telephone sb: *Who's calling, please?* ○ *Thank you for calling.* ○ *I'll call you tomorrow.* ○ *We're just in the middle of dinner. Can I call you back later?*

3 be called to have as your name: *What's your wife called?* ○ *What was that village called?* يُسمَّى

4 [T] to name or describe a person or thing in a certain way: *They called the baby Martin.* ○ *My name is Elizabeth but I'm often called Liz.* ○ *Can you really call this picture 'art'?* ○ *It was very rude to call her fat.* ○ *Are you calling me a liar?* يسمّي ، يدعو

5 [T] to order or ask sb to come to a certain place: *Can you call everybody in for lunch?* ○ *The President called his advisers to the White House.* ○ *I think we had better call the doctor.* يدعو ، يستدعي

6 [T] to arrange for sth to take place at a certain time: *to call a meeting, an election, a strike, etc.* يعلن ؛ ينظِّم

7 [I] **call (in/round) (on sb/at...)** to make a short visit to a person or place: *Can I call in/round after supper?* ○ *We called at his house but there was nobody in.* يزور زيارة قصيرة

8 [I] **call at...** (used about a train, etc.) to stop at: *This train is for Poole, calling at Reading and Southampton.* يتوقّف في

IDM call it a day (*informal*) to decide to stop doing sth: *Let's call it a day. I'm exhausted.* يتوقّف عن العمل

PHR V call by (*informal*) to make a short visit to a place or person as you pass: *I'll call by to pick up the book on my way to work.* يمرّ على

call for sb/sth (*Brit*) to collect: *I'll call for you when it's time to go.* يأخذ

call for sth to demand or need: *The opposition is calling for an early general election.* ○ *The crisis calls for immediate action.* ○ *This calls for a celebration!* ○ *Their rudeness was not called for* (= there was no need for it). يطالب بـ ؛ يستدعي ، يتطلّب

call sth off to cancel sth: *The football match was called off because of the bad weather.* يلغي

call sb out to ask or tell sb to go somewhere: *We had to call out the doctor in the middle of the night.* ○ *The police were called out to control the riot.* يستدعي

call sb/sth up 1 (*especially US*) to telephone sb: *He called me up to tell me the good news.* يتلفن ، يخابر تليفونياً

2 to order sb to join the army, navy or air force: *All the men between the ages of 18 and 25 were called up.* يستدعي (للخدمة العسكرية)

call sth up to look at sth that is stored in a computer: *The bank clerk called up my account details on screen.* ينادي

▸ **caller** *noun* [C] a person who telephones or visits sb: *I don't know who the caller was. He rang off without giving his name.* من يتصل تليفونياً ؛ زائر

'call box *noun* [C] = PHONE BOX

'call centre (*US* **'call center**) *noun* [C] an office in which a large number of people work using telephones, for example arranging insurance for people, or taking customers' orders and answering questions مركز لخدمات العملاء هاتفياً

'call-in (*US*) = PHONE-IN

callous /ˈkæləs/ *adj* not caring about the suffering of other people قاسي القلب

calm /kɑːm/ *adj* **1** not worried or angry; quiet: *Try to keep calm – there's no need to panic.* ○ *She spoke in a calm voice.* ○ *The city is calm again after last night's riots.* رابط الجاش ؛ هادئ

2 without big waves: *a calm sea* ساكن ، هادئ

3 without much wind: *calm weather* ساكن

▸ **calm** *noun* [C,U] a period of time or a state when everything is peaceful: *After living in the city, I enjoyed the calm of country life.* هدوء ، سكون

calm *verb* [I,T] **calm (sb/sth) (down)** to become or to make sb quiet or calm: *Calm down! Shouting at everybody won't help.* ○ *She calmed the horses by talking quietly to them.* ○ *He read the children a story to calm them down.* يهدأ؛ يهدّئ، يسكّن

calmly *adv*: *Len told the police very calmly exactly what he had seen.* بهدوء

calmness *noun* [U] هدوء ، سكون

Calor gas™ /ˈkælə gæs/ *noun* [U] gas that is kept in special bottles and used for cooking, heating, etc. غاز البوتان أو بوتوغاز (للاستعمالات المنزلية)

calorie /ˈkæləri/ *noun* [C] **1** a unit for measuring the energy that a certain amount of food will produce حريرة ، سعْر (حراري)

2 a unit for measuring heat سعر حراري ، حريرة

calves *pl.* of CALF

camcorder /ˈkæmkɔːdə(r)/ *noun* [C] a camera that you can carry with you and use for recording pictures and sound on a video cassette آلة تصوير فيديو

came *pt* of COME

camel /ˈkæml/ *noun* **1** [C] an animal that lives in the desert and has a long neck and either one or two humps on its back. It is used for carrying people and goods. جمل

2 [U] a light brown colour (لون) بنّي فاتح

camellia /kəˈmiːliə/ *noun* [C] a bush, originally from China and Japan, with shiny leaves and white, red or pink flowers كاميليا

camera /ˈkæmərə/ *noun* [C] a piece of equipment that you use for taking photographs or moving pictures: *I need a new film for my camera.* ○ *a digital camera* ○ *a television camera* ○ *a video camera* كاميرا ، آلة تصوير

cameraman /ˈkæmərəmən/ *noun* [C] (*pl.* **cameramen** /-men/) a person whose job is to operate a camera for a film or a television company مُصوّر

camomile = CHAMOMILE

camouflage /ˈkæməflɑːʒ/ *noun* [U] materials or colours that soldiers use to make themselves and their equipment less easy to see (وسيلة) تمويه

▶ **camouflage** *verb* [T] to make sb/sth difficult to see in a particular place يموّه

camp /kæmp/ *noun* [C,U] a place where people live in tents or huts for a short time: *a scout camp* ○ *a holiday camp* ○ *a training camp* (= for soldiers) ○ *We returned to camp tired after our long hike.* ○ *The climbers set up camp at the foot of the mountain.* معسكر ، مخيّم

▶ **camp** *verb* [I] **camp (out)** to put up a tent and sleep in it: *Where shall we camp tonight?* ○ *The children like to camp out in summer.* ❶ **Go camping** is a common way of talking about camping for pleasure: *They went camping in France last year.* يعسكر ، يخيّم

camper *noun* [C] **1** a person who camps مُعَسْكِر ، مُخيِّم

2 (*Brit*) (*also* ˈ**motor home**; *Brit also* ˈ**camper van**; *US also* **recreational vehicle**) a large vehicle designed for people to live and sleep in when they are travelling سيارة تستخدم للسكن والترحال

camping *noun* [U] sleeping or spending a holiday in a tent: *Camping is cheaper than staying in hotels.* ○ *a camping holiday* تخييم

campaign /kæmˈpeɪn/ *noun* [C] **1** a plan to do a number of things in order to achieve a special aim: *an advertising campaign* حملة

2 a planned series of attacks in a war حملة عسكرية

▶ **campaign** *verb* [I] **campaign (for/against sb/sth)** to take part in a campaign (1) in order to make sth happen or to prevent sth يقوم بحملة

campaigner *noun* [C]: *a campaigner for equal rights for women* داعٍ (لقضية)

campsite /ˈkæmpsaɪt/ (*also* ˈ**camping site**) *noun* [C] a place where you can camp معسكر ، مخيّم

campus /ˈkæmpəs/ *noun* [C,U] (*pl.* **campuses**) the area of land where the main buildings of a college or university are: *the college campus* ○ *About half the students live on campus – the other half rent rooms in the town.* الحرم الجامعي، المدينة الجامعية

can[1] /kən; *strong form* kæn/ *modal verb* (*negative* **cannot** /ˈkænɒt/ short form **can't** /kɑːnt; *US* kænt/; *pt* **could** /kəd/ strong form /kʊd/; *negative* **could not** short form **couldn't** /ˈkʊdnt/) **1** (used for showing that it is possible for sb/sth to do sth or that sb/sth has the ability to do sth): *I can catch a bus from here.* ○ *Can you ride a bike?* ○ *He can't speak French.* ○ *She couldn't answer the question.* يستطيع ، يقدر ، يتمكّن من

> **Can** has no infinitive or participle forms. To make the future and perfect tenses, we use **be able to**: *One day people will be able to travel to Mars.* ○ *He's been able to swim for almost a year.* **Could have** is used when we say that somebody had the ability to do something but did not do it: *She could have passed the exam but she didn't really try.*

2 (asking or giving permission): *Can I have a drink, please?* ○ *He asked if he could have a drink.* ○ *You can't go swimming today.* يسمح لـ ، يمكن

> When we are talking about general permission in the past **could** is used: *I could do anything I wanted when I stayed with my grandma.* When we are talking about one particular occasion we do not use **could**: *They were allowed to visit him in hospital yesterday.*

3 (asking sb to do sth): *Can you help me carry these books?* هل من الممكن

4 (offering to do sth): *Can I help at all?* أتريد المساعدة

5 (talking about sb's typical behaviour or of a typical effect): *You can be very annoying.* ○ *Wasp stings can be very painful.* قد يكون

6 (used in the negative for saying that you are sure sth is not true): *That can't be Mary – she's in London.* ○ *Surely you can't be hungry. You've only just had lunch.* لا يمكن أن يكون

7 (used with the verbs 'feel', 'hear', 'see', 'smell', 'taste') ❶ These verbs are not used in the continuous tenses. If we want to talk about seeing, hearing, etc. at a particular moment, we use **can**: *I can smell something burning.* NOT *I'm smelling...* (مع بعض الأفعال)

can[2] /kæn/ *noun* [C] **1** a metal or plastic container that is used for holding or carrying liquid: *an oil can* ○ *a can of oil* ○ *a watering can* صفيحة ، تنكة

2 a metal container for food that is sealed so that the food stays fresh: *a can of sardines* ○ *a can of lemonade* ❶ In British English the more usual word is **tin**. (**Can** is used for drinks.) عُلْبة

▶ **can** *verb* [T] (canning; canned) to put food, drink, etc. into a can in order to keep it fresh for a long time: *canned fruit* يعلّب

canal /kəˈnæl/ *noun* [C] a channel that is cut through land so that boats or ships can travel along it or so that water can flow to an area where it is needed: *the Suez Canal* قناة

canary /kəˈneəri/ *noun* [C] (*pl.* **canaries**) a small yellow bird that sings and is often kept in a cage as a pet طائر الكَنار

cancel /ˈkænsl/ *verb* [T] (cancelling; cancelled;

US canceling; canceled) **1** to decide that sth that had been planned or arranged will not happen: *Because of the bad weather the picnic was cancelled.* ➲ Look at **postpone**. يُلْغِي

2 to stop sth that you asked for or agreed to: *We shall have to cancel the reservation.* ○ *I wish to cancel my order for these books.* يُلْغِي

PHR V cancel (sth) out to be equal or have an equal effect: *What I owe you is the same as what you owe me, so our debts cancel each other out.* يتعادل مع ؛ يبطل

▸ **cancellation** /ˌkænsəˈleɪʃn/ *noun* [C,U] the act of cancelling sth: *We've had several cancellations for this evening's concert.* ○ *The cancellation of the match was a great disappointment.* إلغاء ؛ حجز ملغى

cancer /ˈkænsə(r)/ *noun* [C,U] **1** a very serious disease in which lumps grow in the body in an uncontrolled way: *She has lung cancer.* ○ *He died of cancer.* سرطان

2 Cancer the fourth sign of the zodiac, the Crab; a person who was born under this sign برج السرطان ؛ شخص من مواليد هذا البرج

candid /ˈkændɪd/ *adj* honest and frank; saying exactly what you think ❶ The noun is **candour**. صريح

▸ **candidly** *adv* بصراحة

candidate /ˈkændɪdət; *US* -deɪt/ *noun* [C] **1** a person who applies for a job or wants to be elected to a particular position: *We have some very good candidates for the post.* مُرَشَّح

2 a person who is taking an examination الطالب المُمتحَن

▸ **candidacy** /ˈkændɪdəsi/ *noun* [U] being a candidate ترشيح

candle /ˈkændl/ *noun* [C] a round stick of wax with a piece of string (a wick) through the middle that you can burn to give light: *to light/blow out a candle* شمعة

candlelight /ˈkændllaɪt/ *noun* [U] the light that a candle produces: *They had dinner by candlelight.* ضوء الشمعة

ˈcandlestick /ˈkændlstɪk/ *noun* [C] a holder for a candle or candles شَمْعَدان

candour (*US* **candor**) /ˈkændə(r)/ *noun* [U] the quality of being honest; saying exactly what you think ❶ The adjective is **candid**. صراحة

candy /ˈkændi/ *noun* [C,U] (*pl.* **candies**) (*US*) = SWEET² (1): *You eat too much candy.*

cane /keɪn/ *noun* **1** [C,U] the long, hollow stem of certain plants, such as the sugar plant قصب ، خيزران

2 [C] a stick, for example a walking stick or a stick used to hit sb with عصا ، عكاز

▸ **cane** *verb* [T] to punish sb by hitting him/her with a cane (2) يضرب (بعصا أو خيزرانة)

canine /ˈkeɪnaɪn/ *adj* connected with dogs or like a dog كلبيّ: متعلّق بالكلاب

canister /ˈkænɪstə(r)/ *noun* [C] a small metal container عُلبة صغيرة

cannabis /ˈkænəbɪs/ *noun* [U] a drug made from a plant (hemp) that some people smoke for pleasure, but which is illegal in many countries حشيش

cannibal /ˈkænɪbl/ *noun* [C] a person who eats other people أكل لحم البشر

▸ **cannibalism** /ˈkænɪbəlɪzəm/ *noun* [U] أكل لحم البشر

cannon /ˈkænən/ *noun* [C] (*pl.* **cannon** or **cannons**) **1** a large old-fashioned gun that was used for firing stone or metal balls (cannon balls) مدفع

2 a large modern gun on a ship, tank, plane, etc. مدفع

cannot /ˈkænɒt/ = CAN NOT

canoe /kəˈnuː/ *noun* [C] a light, narrow boat for one or two people that you can move through the water using a flat piece of wood (a paddle) ➲ Look at **kayak**. الكنو: قارب خفيف طويل يدفع بمجداف

▸ **canoe** *verb* [I] (*pres part* **canoeing**; *3rd pers sing pres* **canoes**; *pt, pp* **canoed**) to travel in a canoe يتحرك بالكنو

We can say 'He is learning to canoe' or 'They canoed down the river', but when we are talking about spending time in a canoe it is more usual to say **go canoeing**: *We're going canoeing on the Thames tomorrow.*

canon /ˈkænən/ *noun* [C] a Christian priest who works in a cathedral قسيس في كاتدرائية

canopy /ˈkænəpi/ *noun* [C] (*pl.* **canopies**) a cover, often a piece of cloth, that hangs above sth: *a throne with a purple silk canopy over it* ظُلّة ، سدَّة

can't *short for* CAN NOT

canteen /kænˈtiːn/ *noun* [C] the place in a school, factory, office, etc. where the people who work there can get meals: *the staff canteen* ➲ Look at **cafeteria**. مطعم في مدرسة أو مصنع الخ

canter /ˈkæntə(r)/ *verb* (used about a horse and its rider) to run fairly but not very fast يخبّ، يهرول

canvas /ˈkænvəs/ *noun* **1** [U] a type of strong cloth that is used for making tents, sails, bags, etc. خَيْش ، جنفاص

2 [C] a piece of canvas for painting a picture on; the painting itself قماش الرسم الزيتي ؛ لوحة زيتية

canvass /ˈkænvəs/ *verb* **1** [I,T] to go around an area trying to persuade people to vote for a particular person or political party in an election: *He's canvassing for the Conservative Party.* يجول ملتمساً أصوات الناخبين

2 [T] to find out what people's opinions are about sth يستطلع الآراء

canyon /ˈkænjən/ *noun* [C] a deep valley with very steep sides: *the Grand Canyon, Arizona* وادٍ عميق

canyoning /ˈkænjənɪŋ/ *noun* [U] a sport in which you jump into a mountain stream and allow yourself to be carried down at high speed رياضة الانجراف في نهر جبلي سريع

cap /kæp/ *noun* [C] **1** a soft flat hat that is usually worn by men or boys قُبعة ، طاقيّة

2 a hat that is worn for a particular purpose: *a shower cap* قُبعة ، طاقيّة

3 a covering for the end or top of sth: *Please put the cap back on the bottle.* ○ *Take the lens cap off before you take the photo!* ➲ Look at the note at **top**[1]. غطاء

▸ **cap** *verb* [T] (capping; capped) **1** to cover the top of sth: *mountains capped with snow* يغَطّي (قمة شيء)، يكلّل

2 to follow sth with sth bigger or better يبزّ ، يفوق

IDM **to cap it all** as a final piece of bad luck: *What a holiday! The plane was delayed for 24 hours, they lost their luggage and to cap it all he broke his leg skiing.* والأنكى من ذلك

capability /ˌkeɪpəˈbɪləti/ *noun* [C,U] (*pl.* **capabilities**) the quality of being able to do sth: *Animals in the zoo have lost the capability to catch/of catching food for themselves.* ○ *I tried to fix the computer, but it was beyond my capabilities.* قُدرة

capable /ˈkeɪpəbl/ *adj* **1** **capable of (doing) sth** able to do sth; having the power to do sth: *He's capable of passing the exam if he tries harder.* ○ *That car is capable of 180 miles per hour.* ○ *I do not believe that she's capable of stealing* (= she is not the sort of person who would steal). ❶ The opposite is **incapable**. قادر على (فعل شيء)

2 having a lot of skill; good at doing sth: *She's a very capable teacher.* ○ *We need a capable person to organize the concert.* قدير ، بارع

▸ **capably** *adv* بكفاءة ، بمقدرة

capacity /kəˈpæsəti/ *noun* (*pl.* **capacities**) **1** [sing., U] the greatest amount that a container or space can hold: *The tank has a capacity of 1 000 litres.* ○ *The stadium was filled to capacity.* سعة

2 [sing., U] the amount that a factory or machine can produce: *The power station is working at full capacity.* طاقة ، قدرة

3 [sing.] **capacity (for sth)** the ability to understand or do sth: *That book is beyond the capacity of children who are still learning to read.* استيعاب ، مقدرة عقلية : مقدور

4 [C] the official position that a person has: *In his capacity as chairman of the council...* اعتبار ، صفة

cape[1] /keɪp/ *noun* [C] a piece of clothing with no sleeves that hangs from your shoulders ❶ A **cape** is shorter than a **cloak**. رداء بلا كمّين يتدلّى من الكتفين

cape[2] /keɪp/ *noun* [C] a piece of land that sticks out into the sea: *the Cape of Good Hope* رأس (في الجغرافيا)

capital[1] /ˈkæpɪtl/ *noun* [C] **1** (*also* **capital city**) the town or city where the government of a country is: *Madrid is the capital of Spain.* عاصمة

2 (*also* ˌ**capital ˈletter**) the large form of a letter that is used at the beginning of a name or sentence: *Write your name in capitals.* حرف كبير (في الأحرف اللاتينية)

▸ **capital** *adj* (only *before* a noun) written in the large form that we use at the beginning of a name, a sentence, etc: *'David' begins with a capital 'D'.* حرف كبير ، حرف استهلالي

capital[2] /ˈkæpɪtl/ *adj* connected with punishment by death: *a capital offence* (= a crime for which sb can be sentenced to death) ○ *capital punishment* (= punishment by death) متعلّق بعقوبة الإعدام

capital[3] /ˈkæpɪtl/ *noun* [U] an amount of money that you use to start a business or to invest so that you earn more money (interest) on it: *When she had enough capital, she bought a shop.* ○ *The firm has been trying to raise extra capital.* رأس المال

IDM **make capital (out) of sth** to use a situation to your own advantage يستغل ، ينتفع بـ

capitalism /ˈkæpɪtəlɪzəm/ *noun* [U] the economic system in which businesses are owned and run for profit by individuals and not by the state ➲ Look at **communism** and **socialism**. الرأسمالية ، النظام الرأسمالي

▸ **capitalist** *noun* [C], *adj* رأسمالي

capitalize (*also* **capitalise**) /ˈkæpɪtəlaɪz/ *verb*

PHR V **capitalize on sth** to use sth to your advantage: *We can capitalize on the mistakes that our rivals have made.* يستغل ، ينتفع بـ

capitulate /kəˈpɪtʃuleɪt/ *verb* [I] (*formal*) to stop fighting and say that you have lost; to give in to sb and do what he/she wants يستسلم ؛ يذْعِن

▸ **capitulation** /kəˌpɪtʃuˈleɪʃn/ *noun* [C,U] استسلام

Capricorn /ˈkæprɪkɔːn/ *noun* [C,U] the tenth sign of the zodiac, the Goat; a person who was born under this sign بُرج الجدي : شخص من مواليد هذا البرج

capsize /kæpˈsaɪz; *US* ˈkæpsaɪz/ *verb* [I,T] (used about boats) to turn over in the water: *The yacht capsized.* ○ *She capsized the yacht.* يقلِب أو ينقلب (القارب)

capsule /ˈkæpsjuːl; *US* kæpsl/ *noun* [C] **1** a very small tube containing medicine that you swallow whole كبسولة (دواء)

2 the part of a spaceship in which the crew live and work غرفة القيادة والمعيشة في سفينة فضائية

captain /ˈkæptɪn/ *noun* [C] (*abbr* **Capt.**) **1** the person who is in command of a ship or a plane رُبّان؛ قبطان

2 an officer of middle rank in the Army or Navy نقيب

3 a person who is the leader of a group or team: *Who's (the) captain of the French team?* قائد ، رئيس

▸ **captain** *verb* [T] to be the captain of a group or team يقود

caption /ˈkæpʃn/ *noun* [C] the words that are written above or below a picture, cartoon, etc. to explain what it is about تعليق على صورة في مجلة وغيرها

captivate /ˈkæptɪveɪt/ *verb* [T] to attract and hold sb's attention يفتن ، يأسر ، يخلب الألباب
▸ **captivating** *adj* ساحر ، جذاب

captive /ˈkæptɪv/ *noun* [C] a prisoner أسير
▸ **captive** *adj* kept as a prisoner; (of animals) kept in a cage, zoo, etc. أسير : حبيس

IDM **hold sb captive** to keep sb as a prisoner and not allow him/her to escape يأسِر ؛ يحبّس
take sb captive to catch sb and hold him/her as your prisoner يأسِر ، يحتجز

ℹ It is also possible to say **hold sb prisoner** and **take sb prisoner**.

captivity /kæpˈtɪvəti/ *noun* [U] the state of being kept as a captive: *Wild animals are often unhappy in captivity.* أسر ، حَبْس

captor /ˈkæptə(r)/ *noun* [C] a person who takes or keeps a person as a prisoner آسر ، معتقل

⚷ **capture** /ˈkæptʃə(r)/ *verb* [T] **1** to take a person or animal prisoner: *The lion was captured and taken back to the zoo.* يقبض على
2 to take or win sth from your enemy by force: *The town has been captured by the rebels.* يستولي على
3 to succeed in representing sth in words, pictures, etc: *This poem captures the atmosphere of the carnival.* يعكس ، ينجح في تصوير..
▸ **capture** *noun* [U] a time when a person, animal or thing is captured أَسْر

⚷ **car** /kɑː(r)/ *noun* [C] **1** (*also* **motor car**) (*especially US* **automobile**) a vehicle with an engine and four wheels that up to four or five people can ride in: *a new/second-hand car* ○ *Where can I park the car?* ○ *He's having the car serviced tomorrow.* ○ *They had a car crash.* ○ *She gave me a lift in her car.* ○ *to get into/out of a car* ○ *an estate car*

ℹ Note that we go **by car**. We can also say **in the car**: *Do you prefer going on holiday by coach or by car?* ○ *I come to work in the car.* سيّارة ، عربيّة

2 a railway carriage that is used for a particular purpose: *a dining car* ○ *a sleeping car* عربة (في قطار)

caramel /ˈkærəmel/ *noun* **1** [U] sugar that has been burned so that it is dark brown. It is used in food because of its colour and taste الكرميلة: سكر محروق
2 [C,U] a type of sticky sweet that is made from boiled sugar حلوى الكرميلة أو الكراميل

carat (*US* **karat**) /ˈkærət/ *noun* [C] a unit of measurement used to describe how pure gold is or how heavy jewels are: *a 20-carat gold ring* قيراط

caravan /ˈkærəvæn/ *noun* [C] **1** (*US* **trailer**) a large vehicle that can be pulled by a car or horse. You can sleep, cook, etc. in a caravan when you are travelling or on holiday: *They're touring in Wales with a caravan.* ○ *a caravan holiday* مسكن متنقل (يُقطر بسيارة أو حصان)

When we are talking about using a caravan for holidays we say **go caravanning**: *We're going caravanning in Scotland this summer.*

2 a group of people and animals that travel together, e.g. across a desert قافلة

caraway /ˈkærəweɪ/ *noun* [C,U] a plant with seeds that have a strong taste and are used for giving flavour to bread, cakes, etc: *Add a teaspoon of caraway seed(s).* كراوية

carbohydrate /ˌkɑːbəʊˈhaɪdreɪt/ *noun* [C,U] one of the substances in food, e.g. sugar, that gives your body energy: *Athletes need a diet that is high in carbohydrate and low in fat.* ○ *Bread,*

car

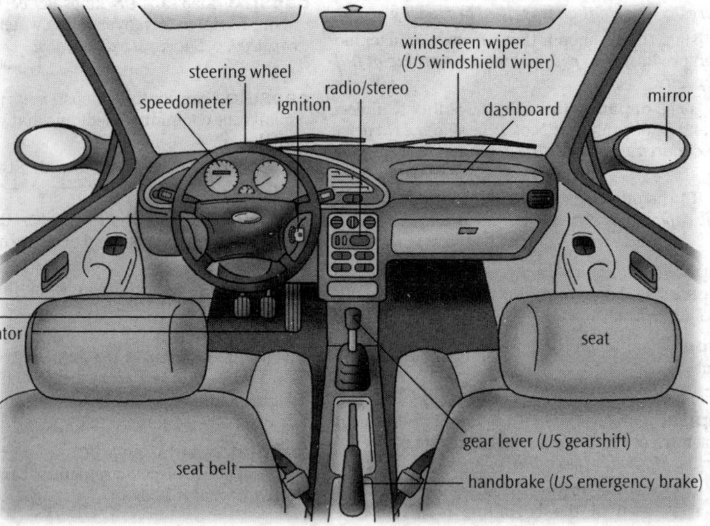

potatoes and rice all contain carbohydrates. النشويّات و السكَّريات ، الكربوهيدرات

carbon /ˈkɑːbən/ *noun* [U] (*symbol* **C**) a chemical substance that is found in all living things, for example in a pure form in diamonds and in an impure form in coal فحم/كربون

ˌcarbon ˈcopy *noun* [C] (*pl.* **carbon copies**)
1 a copy of a letter, etc. that was made by using carbon paper نسخة كربونيّة
2 an exact copy of sth نسخة مطابقة (للأصل)

ˌcarbon diˈoxide *noun* [U] (*symbol* CO_2) a gas that has no colour or smell that people and animals breathe out of their lungs ثاني أكسيد الكربون

ˌcarbon ˈfootprint *noun* [C] a measure of the amount of carbon dioxide that is produced by the daily activities of a person or company: *Recycling waste is a good way of reducing our carbon footprint.* البصمة الكربونية

ˌcarbon monˈoxide *noun* [U] (*symbol* **CO**) the poisonous gas that is produced when carbon is burned in a small amount of air. Motor vehicles produce a lot of carbon monoxide. أول أكسيد الكربون

ˌcarbon ˈneutral *adj* in which the amount of carbon dioxide produced has been reduced to nothing or is balanced by actions that protect the environment: *The company aims to become carbon neutral within ten years.* ذو أثر محايد بالنسبة لطرح الكربون

ˌcarbon ˈoffset *noun* [C,U] a way for a company or person to reduce the level of carbon dioxide for which they are responsible by paying money to a company that works to reduce the total amount produced in the world, for example by planting trees كفارة تدفع تعويضا عن إصدار الكربون و تُنفق في تخفيض انبعاثه

ˈcarbon paper *noun* [U] thin paper with carbon on one side that you put between two pieces of paper. When you write or type on the top piece of paper a copy is produced on the second piece. ورق كربون

ˌcar ˈboot sale *noun* [C] a sale in an outdoor place where people sell things they do not want from the back of their cars ➲ Look at **jumble sale**. بيع الزوائد المنزلية من السيارات

carburettor /ˌkɑːbəˈretə(r)/ (*US* **carburetor** /ˈkɑːrbəreɪtər/) *noun* [C] the piece of equipment in a car's engine that mixes petrol and air المكَرْبِن في السيارة

carcass /ˈkɑːkəs/ *noun* [C] the dead body of an animal ➲ Look at **corpse**. جثّة (الحيوان)

🔑card /kɑːd/ *noun* **1** [U] thick paper that does not bend easily ورق سميك
2 [C] a piece of card or plastic that has information on it: *Here is my business card with my address and telephone number on it.* ○ *a membership card* ○ *an identity card* ○ *a credit card* بِطاقة
3 [C] a piece of card with a picture on it that you use for sending greetings or a message to sb: *a Christmas card* ○ *a birthday card* ○ *a get-well card* (= one that you send to sb who is ill) ○ *We've had a card* (= a postcard) *from Diana in Portugal.* بِطاقة

4 (*also* **playing card**) [C] one of a set of 52 small pieces of card with shapes or pictures on them that are used for playing games: *a pack of cards* ورقة لعب
5 cards [plural] games that are played with cards: *Let's play cards.* ○ *Let's have a game of cards.* ○ *I never win at cards!* لَعِب الورق
IDM on the cards (*informal*) likely to happen على قدر كبير من الاحتمال

🔑cardboard /ˈkɑːdbɔːd/ *noun* [U] very thick paper that is used for making boxes, etc: *The groceries were delivered in large cardboard boxes.* ورق مقوى

cardiac /ˈkɑːdiæk/ *adj* connected with the heart قلبيّ

cardigan /ˈkɑːdɪgən/ *noun* [C] a piece of clothing for the top part of the body, often made from wool, that has long sleeves and buttons at the front ➲ Look at the note at **sweater**. جاكيت أو سُترة من الصوف

cardinal¹ /ˈkɑːdɪnl/ *noun* [C] a priest of high rank in the Roman Catholic church كاردينال (في الكنيسة الكاثوليكية)

cardinal² /ˈkɑːdɪnl/ (*also* **ˌcardinal ˈnumber**) *noun* [C] a whole number, e.g. 1, 2, 3 that shows quantity ➲ Look at **ordinal**. عدد أصلي

ˈcard index *noun* [C] → INDEX (2)

🔑care¹ /keə(r)/ *verb* **1** [I,T] **care (about sth)** to be worried about or interested in sth; to mind: *I shall be late and my mother will be cross, but I don't care.* ○ *Money is the thing that she cares about most.* ○ *I don't care what you do.* يهتم بِ ، يحرص على ؛ يكترث
2 [I] **care for sth; care to do sth** (*formal*) to like or want: *Would you care for a drink?* ○ *Would you care to leave a message, sir?* ❶ **Care for** in this sense is used in questions and always with 'would'. يرغَب ، يريد

3 [I] **care for sb/sth** to like: *I don't care for that colour very much.* ○ *Do you think she still cares for him although he married someone else?* يحبّ

IDM **I, etc. couldn't care less** (*informal*) it does not matter to me, etc. at all: *'You don't look very smart.' 'Well, quite honestly, I couldn't care less.'* لا يهمني الأمر

who cares? (*informal*) nobody is interested; it is not important to anyone: *'I wonder who'll win the match.' 'Who cares?'* غير مهم!

PHR V **care for sb** to look after sb: *Who cared for her while she was ill?* يَرعى ، يعتني بِ

▸ **caring** /ˈkeərɪŋ/ *adj* showing that you care about other people: *We must work towards a more caring society.* مهتمّ بالآخرين ، عطوف

care² /keə(r)/ *noun* **1** [U] **care (over sth/in doing sth)** thinking about what you are doing so that you do it well or do not have an accident: *You should take more care over your homework.* ○ *This box contains glasses – please handle it with care.* اهتمام ، عناية

2 [U] **care (for sb)** looking after people so that they have things they need; responsibility for sb/sth: *All the children in their care were healthy and happy.* ○ *health care* ○ *medical care* ○ *She's in intensive care* (= the part of the hospital for people who are very seriously ill). عناية : رعاية

Children **in care** live in a home which is organized by the government or the local council.

3 [C,U] worry, anxiety: *She went on holiday to try to forget all her cares.* ○ *It was a happy life, free from care.* قَلَق ، هَمّ

IDM **care of sb** (*abbr* **c/o**) words used on an envelope when you are writing to sb at another person's address: *Mary Jenkins, c/o Mrs Brown, 10 Riverside Way, Oxford.* ○ *You can write to the author, care of his publisher.* لعناية (فلان)، بواسطة

take care (that.../to do sth) to be careful: *Goodbye and take care!* ○ *Take care that you don't spill your tea.* ○ *He took care not to arrive too early.* ينتبه ، يحترس

take care of sb/sth to deal with sb/sth; to organize or arrange sth: *I'll take care of the food for the party.* يتولّى أمر شخص أو شيء

take care of yourself/sb/sth to keep yourself/sb/sth safe from injury, illness, damage, etc: *You should take more care of yourself. You look tired.* ○ *Could you take care of the cat while we are away on holiday?* ○ *She always takes great care of her books.* يعتني بِ

ˈcare assistant = CARE WORKER

career¹ /kəˈrɪə(r)/ *noun* [C] **1** a job or profession for which you are trained and which you do for a long time, often with the chance to move to a higher position: *Sarah is considering a career in engineering.* ○ *His career was always more important to him than his family.* ○ *a successful career in politics* مهنة

2 your working life: *She spent most of her career working in India.* الحياة المهنيّة

career² /kəˈrɪə(r)/ *verb* [I] to move quickly and dangerously: *The car careered off the road and crashed into a wall.* يندفع بسرعة ، يفلت دون ضابط

carefree /ˈkeəfriː/ *adj* happy because you have no problems or worries لا همّ له ، ناعم البال

careful /ˈkeəfl/ *adj* **1 careful (of/with sth)** thinking about what you are doing so that you do not have an accident or make mistakes, etc: *Be careful! There's a car coming.* ○ *Be careful of that knife – it's very sharp.* ○ *Please be very careful with those glasses.* ○ *That ladder doesn't look very safe. Be careful you don't fall.* ○ *I was careful not to say anything about the money.* ○ *Don't worry – she's a careful driver.* منتبه ، محترس

2 showing care and attention to details: *I'll need to give this matter some careful thought.* دقيق

▸ **carefully** /ˈkeəfəli/ *adv*: *Please listen carefully. It's important that you remember all this.* بانتباه : بدقّة

carefulness *noun* [U] عناية ، دقّة

careless /ˈkeələs/ *adj* **careless (about/with sth)** not thinking enough about what you are doing so that you make mistakes, lose or damage things, etc: *It was careless of you to go out without locking the door.* ○ *Here's another careless mistake – you've forgotten the full stop at the end of the sentence.* ○ *The accident was caused by careless driving.* مُهمِل : طائش

▸ **carelessly** *adv*: *She threw her coat carelessly on the chair.* بلا مبالاة

carelessness *noun* [U] إهمال : استهتار

carer /ˈkeərə(r)/ (*US* **caregiver** /ˈkeəgɪvə(r)/) *noun* [C] a person who takes care of a sick or old person at home من يرعى مريضاً أو عاجزاً

caress /kəˈres/ *verb* [T] to stroke sb in a gentle and loving way: *He caressed her hand and looked deep into her eyes.* يداعب ، يلامس بحبّ

▸ **caress** *noun* [C] ملاطفة ، ملامسة بحبّ

caretaker /ˈkeəteɪkə(r)/ (*US* **janitor**) *noun* [C] a person whose job is to look after a large building (e.g. a school or a block of flats) and to do small repairs and other services قيّم ، فرّاش مؤسّسة

ˈcare worker (*also* **care assistant**) *noun* a person whose job is to help and take care of people who are mentally ill, sick or disabled, especially those who live in special homes or hospitals من يرعى المرضى أو العجزة في مؤسسة

cargo /ˈkɑːgəʊ/ *noun* [C,U] (*pl.* **cargoes**; *US also* **cargos**) the goods that are carried in a ship or aircraft: *The ship was carrying a cargo of wheat.* حمولة

Caribbean /ˌkærəˈbiːən; kəˈrɪbiən/ *noun* [sing.] **the Caribbean** the area in the Caribbean Sea where the group of islands called the West Indies are situated منطقة البحر الكاريبي

▸ **Caribbean** *adj*: *the Caribbean islands* كاريبي

caricature /ˈkærɪkətʃʊə(r)/ *noun* [C] a picture or description of sb that makes his/her appearance or behaviour funnier and more extreme than it really is: *She drew a very funny caricature of the Prime Minister.* ○ *Many of the people in the* *book are caricatures of the author's friends.* رسم كاريكاتوري

carnation /kɑːˈneɪʃn/ *noun* [C] a white, pink or red flower with a pleasant smell قرنفل

carnival /ˈkɑːnɪvl/ *noun* [C] a public festival that takes place outdoors, during which there is a procession in the streets with music and dancing: *the carnival in Rio* كارنفال ، احتفال

carob /ˈkærəb/ *noun* [C] a southern European tree with dark brown fruit that can be made into a powder that tastes like chocolate شجرة الخروب

carol /ˈkærəl/ *noun* [C] a Christian religious song that people sing at Christmas: *carol singers* (= groups of people who sing carols outside people's houses in order to collect money for charity) أنشودة (في عيد الميلاد)

carousel /ˌkærəˈsel/ *noun* [C] **1** (*US*) = ROUNDABOUT[2] (2)

2 (at an airport) a moving belt that carries luggage for passengers to collect سَيْر متحرك للحقائب (في مطار)

carp /kɑːp/ *noun* [C,U] (*pl.* **carp**) a large fish that you can eat that lives in rivers, lakes, etc. سمك الشبوط

ˈcar park (*US* **parking lot**) *noun* [C] an area or building where you can leave your car: *a multi-storey car park* موقف (سيارات)

carpenter /ˈkɑːpəntə(r)/ *noun* [C] a person whose job is to make and repair wooden objects نجّار

▸ **carpentry** /-tri/ *noun* [U] the skill or work of a carpenter نجارة

carpet /ˈkɑːpɪt/ *noun* **1** [C,U] (a piece of) thick, flat material that is used for covering floors and stairs: *We need a new carpet in the bedroom.* ○ *a fitted carpet* (= one that has been cut to the exact shape of a room) ➲ Look at **rug**. سجّادة ، بساط

2 [C] a thick layer of sth that covers the ground: *The fields were under a carpet of snow.* طبقة سميكة ، بساط

▸ **carpeted** *adj*: *All the rooms are carpeted.* مغطّى بسجّاد

carriage /ˈkærɪdʒ/ *noun* **1** [C] (*also* **coach**) a vehicle with wheels that is pulled by horses عربة تجرّها الخيول

2 [C] (*also* **coach**) (*US* **car**) one of the separate parts of a train where people sit: *a first-class carriage* عربة أو حافلة (في قطار)

3 [U] the cost of transporting goods from one place to another: *Carriage must be paid by the receiver.* أجرة النقل

carriageway /ˈkærɪdʒweɪ/ *noun* [C] one of the two sides of a motorway or major road on which vehicles travel in one direction only: *the southbound carriageway of the motorway* ➲ Look at **dual carriageway**. أحد جزئي طريق رئيسي

carrier /ˈkæriə(r)/ *noun* [C] **1** (in business) a company that transports people or goods: *the Dutch carrier, KLM* (شركة) نقل

2 a military vehicle or ship that is used for transporting soldiers, planes, weapons, etc: *an armoured personnel carrier* ○ *an aircraft carrier* ناقلة (جنود أو عتاد حربي)

3 a person or animal that can give an infectious disease to others but does not show the signs of the disease: *Some insects are carriers of tropical diseases.* حامل (المرض)

4 (*Brit also* **ˈcarrier bag**) a plastic or paper bag for carrying shopping كيس الحاجيات

carrot /ˈkærət/ *noun* **1** [C,U] a long thin orange vegetable that grows under the ground: *A pound of carrots, please.* ○ *grated carrot* جزر

2 [C] something attractive that is offered to sb in order to persuade him/her to do sth: *The management have offered them the carrot of a £500 bonus if they agree to work extra hours.* شيء مغرٍ ، حافز : مكافأة

carry /ˈkæri/ *verb* (*pres part* **carrying**; *3rd pers sing pres* **carries**; *pt, pp* **carried**) **1** [T] to hold sb/sth in your hand, arms or on your back while you are moving from one place to another: *Could you carry this bag for me? It's terribly heavy.* ○ *She was carrying a rucksack on her back.* يحمل

> You use **wear**, not **carry**, to talk about having clothes, jewellery, etc. on your body: *He was wearing a black jacket.*

2 [T] to have with you as you go from place to place: *I never carry much money with me when I go to London.* ○ *Do the police carry guns in your country?* يحمل

3 [T] to transport sb/sth from one place to another: *A train carrying hundreds of passengers crashed yesterday.* ○ *The waves carried the boat to the shore.* ينقل

4 [T] to have an infectious disease that can be given to others, usually without showing any signs of the disease yourself: *Rats carry all sorts of diseases.* يحمل

5 [T] (usually passive) to accept a proposal in a meeting because a majority of people vote for it: *The motion was carried by 12 votes to 9.* يوافق على

6 [I] (used about a sound) to reach a long distance: *You'll have to speak louder if you want your voice to carry to the back of the room.* يصل

IDM **be/get carried away** to be so excited that you forget what you are doing: *I got so carried away watching the race that I forgot how late it was.* يستخفّه (الحماس مثلاً)

carry weight to have great influence on the opinion of sb else: *Nick's views carry a lot of weight with our manager.* له وزن أو قيمة

PHR V **carry it/sth off** to succeed in doing sth difficult: *He felt nervous before he started his speech but he carried it off very well.* ينجز (شيئاً صعباً) بنجاح

carry on (with sth/doing sth); carry sth on to continue: *How long did the party carry on after I left?* ○ *Carry on* (= continue speaking). *What happened next?* ○ *They ignored me and carried on* *with their conversation.* ○ *She intends to carry on studying after the course has finished.* يستمر

carry sth on to take part in sth: *I can't carry on a normal conversation while you're making that noise.* يشارك ، يقوم بـ

carry sth out 1 to do sth that you have been ordered to do: *The soldiers carried out their orders without question.* ينفِّذ

2 to do or perform sth, e.g. a test, repair, etc: *I think we should wait until more tests have been carried out.* ○ *The owner is responsible for carrying out repairs to the building.* يقوم بـ ، يجري

'carry-all *noun* [C] (*US*) = HOLDALL

carrycot /'kærikɒt/ *noun* [C] a small bed, like a box with handles, that you can carry a baby in سرير صغير نقّال للأطفال

carsick /'kɑːsɪk/ *adj* feeling sick or vomiting as a result of travelling in a car: *to get/feel/be carsick* دائخ من ركوب السيارة

cart /kɑːt/ *noun* [C] a wooden vehicle with wheels that is used for transporting things: *a horse and cart* عربة (نقل)

▶ **cart** *verb* [T] (*informal*) to take or carry sth somewhere, often with difficulty: *We left our luggage at the station because we didn't want to cart it around all day.* ○ *Six of the women were carted off to the police station.* ينقل

cartilage /'kɑːtɪlɪdʒ/ *noun* [C,U] a strong substance that surrounds the places where your bones join غَضْروف

carton /'kɑːtn/ *noun* [C] a small container made of cardboard or plastic: *a carton of milk, orange juice, etc.* علبة

cartoon /kɑː'tuːn/ *noun* [C] **1** a funny drawing, especially one in a newspaper or magazine that makes a joke about a current event رسم هزلي

2 a film that tells a story by using moving drawings instead of real people and places: *a Donald Duck cartoon* فيلم كرتون

▶ **cartoonist** *noun* [C] a person who draws cartoons رسّام الكاريكاتير ، رسّام هزلي

cartridge /'kɑːtrɪdʒ/ *noun* [C] **1** a small tube that contains explosive powder and a bullet. You put a cartridge into a gun when you want to fire it. خَرْطوشة

2 a closed container that holds camera film, typewriter ribbon, ink for a pen, etc. It is easy to change a cartridge when you want to put in a new one. خرطوشة: علبة خاصة مغلقة

carve /kɑːv/ *verb* **1** [I,T] **carve sth (out of sth)** to cut wood or stone in order to make an object or to put a pattern or writing on it: *The statue had been carved out of marble.* ○ *He carved his name on the desk.* ينحت

2 [I,T] to cut a piece of cooked meat into slices: *Can you carve while I serve the vegetables?* ○ *to carve a chicken* يشرِّح اللحم المطبوخ

▶ **carving** *noun* [C,U] an object or design that has been carved: *There are ancient carvings on the walls of the cave.* (شيء) منحوت

cascade /kæ'skeɪd/ *noun* [C] **1** a waterfall شلاّل

2 something that hangs or falls in a way that seems similar to a waterfall: *The wall of the villa was covered in a cascade of flowers.* شيء كالشلاّل

▶ **cascade** *verb* [I] ينهمر كشلاّل

⚷ **case**[1] /keɪs/ *noun* **1** [C] a particular situation or a situation of a particular type: *In some cases, people have had to wait two weeks for a doctor's appointment.* ○ *Most of us travel to work by tube – or, in Susie's case, by train and tube.* ○ *There's no secret to success in this business. It's just a case of hard work.* حالة

2 the case [sing.] the true situation: *The man said he worked in Cardiff, but we discovered later that this was not the case.* الأمر الحقيقي

3 [C] an example of an illness; a person who is suffering from an illness: *Cases of the disease are very unusual in this country.* ○ *The most serious cases were taken to hospital immediately.* إصابة : حالة مرضيّة

4 [C] a crime that is being investigated by the police: *a murder case* جريمة (تحت التحقيق)

5 [C] something that is decided in a court of law; a trial: *The case will come to court in a few months.* دعوى : قضية

6 [C, usually sing.] the facts and reasons that support one side in a discussion or legal matter: *She made a case for shorter working hours, but the others disagreed.* (يقدّم) الحجج والبراهين

IDM **as the case may be** (used when you are not sure which of two or more possibilities will be true in a particular situation): *The money will be received by the husband or wife, as the case may be.* كما يقتضي الأمر

in any case 1 whatever happens or has happened: *We've decided to go in any case.* على أية حال

2 anyway: *He didn't say anything about it at the meeting and in any case it's too late now.* على أية حال

in case because sth might happen: *I think I'll take an umbrella in case it rains.* ○ *Take my number in case you need to phone me.* ○ *I wasn't intending to buy anything but I took my credit card just in case.* تحسباً لـ : في حالة

in case of sth if sth happens: *In case of fire, break this glass.* في حالة (حدوث شيء)

in that case if that is the situation: *'I'm busy on Tuesday.' 'Oh well, in that case we'll have to meet another day.'* في هذه الحالة

prove your/the case/point → PROVE

⚷ **case**[2] /keɪs/ *noun* [C] **1** (especially in compounds) a container or cover for sth: *a pencil case* ○ *a pillowcase* ○ *a bookcase* ○ *She put her glasses back in the case.* علبة : غطاء : غلاف : حقيبة

2 = SUITCASE: *Would you like me to carry your case?*

'case study *noun* [C] (*pl.* **case studies**) a study of the development of a person or group of people, especially in social research دراسة حالة

⚷ **cash** /kæʃ/ *noun* [U] **1** money in the form of coins or notes and not cheques, credit cards, etc:

Would you prefer me to pay in cash or by cheque? ○ *How much cash have you got with you?* نَقد

We use **cash** when we are talking about coins and notes, but **change** when we are talking about coins only.

2 (*informal*) money in any form: *I'm a bit short of cash this month so I can't afford to go out much.* نقود

▶ **cash** *verb* [T] to exchange a cheque, traveller's cheque, etc. for coins and notes: *I'm just going to the bank to cash a cheque.* يصرِف (شيكاً)

PHR V cash in (on sth) to take advantage of a situation يستغل

cashback /ˈkæʃbæk/ *noun* [U] **1** an offer of money as a present that is made by some banks, companies selling cars, etc. in order to persuade customers to do business with them مبلغ يدفع للترويج

2 a system in some large shops which allows the customer to take money out of his/her bank account at the same time as paying for the goods with a cash card نقود يمكن سحبها عند شراء الحاجيات

ˈcash card *noun* [C] (*US* **ATM card**) a plastic card given by a bank to its customers so that they can get money from a cash dispenser بطاقة سحب نقود

ˈcash desk *noun* [C] the place in a large shop where you pay for things مكان الدفع (في متجر)

cashew /ˈkæʃuː; kæˈʃuː/ (*also* **ˈcashew nut**) *noun* [C] a small nut with a curved shape that you can eat ثمرة الأكاجو

ˈcash flow *noun* [sing.] the movement of money into and out of a business as goods are bought and sold حركة النقود

cashier /kæˈʃɪə(r)/ *noun* [C] the person in a bank, shop, etc. that customers pay money to or get money from أمين الصندوق ، صرّاف

ˈcash machine (*also* **ˈcash dispenser**; **Cashpoint™** /ˈkæʃpɔɪnt/; *US also* **ATM**) *noun* [C] a machine inside or outside a bank from which you can get money at any time of day by putting in a special card آلة صرف النقود (في داخل مصرف أو خارجه)

cashmere /ˌkæʃˈmɪə(r)/ *noun* [U] a type of wool that is very fine and soft الكشمير: صوف ناعم

casino /kəˈsiːnəʊ/ *noun* [C] (*pl.* **casinos**) a place where people play roulette and other games in which you can win or lose money كازينو ، ملهى قمار

cask /kɑːsk; *US* kæsk/ *noun* [C] a large wooden container in which alcoholic drinks, etc. are stored; barrel برميل خشبي

casserole /ˈkæsərəʊl/ *noun* **1** [C,U] a type of food that you make by cooking meat and vegetables in liquid for a long time in the oven: *chicken casserole* الكسرولة: نمط من الطبيخ

2 [C] a large dish with a lid for cooking casseroles in الكسرولة: طبق كبير بغطاء

cassette /kəˈset/ *noun* [C] a flat case with magnetic tape inside that you use for recording and playing music and other sounds ❶ Another word for **cassette** is **tape**. When you want to go back to the beginning of a cassette you **rewind** it. When you want to go forward you **fast forward** it. ➲ Look at **video**. كاسيت

casˈsette recorder *noun* [C] a machine that you use for recording and playing cassettes مسجِّلة كاسيت

🔑 **cast¹** /kɑːst; *US* kæst/ *noun* [C, with sing. or pl. verb] all the actors in a play, film, etc: *The film has an excellent cast.* الممثلون (في مسرحية أو فيلم الخ)

🔑 **cast²** /kɑːst; *US* kæst/ *verb* (*pt, pp* **cast**) **1** [T] (often passive) to choose an actor for a particular role in a play, film, etc: *She always seems to be cast in the same sort of role.* يختار (ممثلاً) لدور

2 [T] to make an object by pouring hot liquid metal into a shaped container (a mould): *a statue cast in gold* يصبّ ، يسبك

3 [I,T] to throw a fishing line or net into the water يلقِي

IDM cast doubt on sth to make people unsure about sth: *The newspaper report casts doubts on the truth of the Prime Minister's statement.* يُشكِّك (في شيء)

cast an eye/your eye(s) over sb/sth to look at sth quickly يلقي نظرة خاطفة

cast light on sth to help to explain sth: *I'd be grateful if you could cast any light on the problem.* يلْقي ضوءاً على

cast a shadow (across/over sth) to cause a shadow to appear somewhere: *The tree cast a long shadow across the garden.* ○ (*figurative*) *The accident cast a shadow over the rest of the holiday* (= stopped people enjoying it fully). يلْقي ظلاً على

cast a/your vote to vote: *The MPs will cast their votes in the leadership election tomorrow.* يصوّت

PHR V cast sb/sth off to remove or make yourself free of sb/sth: *He cast off the stress of city life and went to live in the country.* يزيل ، يتحرّر من

castaway /ˈkɑːstəweɪ; *US* kæst-/ *noun* [C] a person who is left in a place far from civilization after a shipwreck ناجٍ من سفينة غارقة في مكان منعزل

caste /kɑːst; *US* kæst/ *noun* **1** [C] one of the social classes into which Hindus are divided طبقة اجتماعية

2 [U] the system of dividing people in this way نظام الطبقات (عند الهندوس)

ˌcast ˈiron *noun* [U] a hard type of iron حديد مسبوك ، حديد الصّب

▶ **ˌcast-ˈiron** *adj* made of cast iron: (*figurative*) *a cast-iron alibi* (= one that people cannot doubt) مصنوع من حديد الصّب : محكَم

🔑 **castle** /ˈkɑːsl; *US* ˈkæsl/ *noun* [C] a large building with high walls and towers that was built in the past to defend people against attack: *a medieval castle* ○ *Edinburgh Castle* قلعة

ˈcast-off *noun* [C, usually pl.] a piece of clothing that you no longer want and that you give to sb else or throw away: *When I was little I had to wear my sister's cast-offs.* ثوب مستغنى عنه

castrate /kæˈstreɪt; *US* ˈkæstreɪt/ *verb* [T] to remove part of the sexual organs of a male animal or person يخصي
▸ **castration** /kæˈstreɪʃn/ *noun* [U] خِصاء

casual /ˈkæʒuəl/ *adj* **1** relaxed and not worried; not showing great effort or interest: *She tried to appear casual as he walked towards her.* ○ *The manager is not happy about your casual attitude to your work.* ○ *It was only a casual remark so I don't know why he got so angry.*
غير مبالٍ ؛ غير مقصود

2 (used about clothes) not formal: *I always change into casual clothes as soon as I get home from work.* (لباس) غير رسمي

3 (used about work) done only for a short period; not regular or permanent: *Most of the building work was done by casual labour.* ○ *She had a number of casual jobs during the university holidays.* قصير ؛ متقطِّع ؛ مؤقَّت
▸ **casually** /ˈkæʒuəli/ *adv*: *She walked in casually and said, 'I'm not late, am I?'* ○ *Dress casually, it won't be a formal party.*
بلا مبالاة ؛ على نحو غير رسمي

casualty /ˈkæʒuəlti/ *noun* (*pl.* **casualties**) **1** [C] a person who is killed or injured in a war or an accident: *After the accident the casualties were taken to hospital.* ○ *The army retreated after suffering heavy casualties.* خسائر ، إصابات

2 [C] a person or thing that suffers as a result of sth else: *Many small companies have been casualties of the country's economic problems.* ضحيّة

3 [U] (*Brit*) = ACCIDENT AND EMERGENCY

ʔ **cat** /kæt/ *noun* [C] **1** a small furry animal with four legs and a tail. People often keep cats as pets. قِطّ ، هِرّ

> A young cat is called a **kitten**. A male cat is called a **tom**. When a cat makes a soft sound of pleasure, it **purrs**. When it makes a louder sound, it **miaows**.

2 any larger wild animal that is related to a cat, e.g. a lion or tiger: *We went to the zoo to see the big cats.* أي حيوان من السنّوريات

catalogue (*US* **catalog** /ˈkætəlɒg; *US* -lɔːg/) *noun* [C] **1** a list of all the things that you can buy from a company, all the books in a library, all the paintings in an art exhibition, etc.
كتالوج ، كشف ، مدرك

2 a series, especially of bad things: *a catalogue of disasters* سلسلة (مصائب مثلاً)
▸ **catalogue** *verb* [T] to list things in a catalogue: *She started to catalogue all the new library books.* يدرج في قائمة

catalytic converter /ˌkætəˌlɪtɪk kənˈvɜːtə(r)/ *noun* [C] (*technical*) a device used in motor vehicles to reduce the damage caused to the environment by poisonous gases مخفّف التلوّث

catapult /ˈkætəpʌlt/ *noun* [C] a Y-shaped stick with a piece of elastic attached to each side that is used by children for shooting stones
مِرْجام ، "نِبلة" ، "نقّيفة"
▸ **catapult** *verb* [T] **1** to shoot sth from a catapult يقذف بالمِرْجام

2 to throw sb/sth suddenly and with great force: *When the train crashed, several people were catapulted through the windows.* ○ (*figurative*) *The success of his first film catapulted him to stardom.* يقذف به بقوة

cataract /ˈkætərækt/ *noun* [C] a diseased area that can grow on a person's eye and cause difficulty in seeing الماء الأزرق في العين

catarrh /kəˈtɑː(r)/ *noun* [U] a thick liquid that forms in the nose and throat when you have a cold افراز زكامي

catastrophe /kəˈtæstrəfi/ *noun* [C] a sudden event that causes great suffering or damage; disaster: *Major catastrophes like floods and earthquakes happen regularly in that part of the world.* ○ *a financial catastrophe* كارثة ؛ نكبة
▸ **catastrophic** /ˌkætəˈstrɒfɪk/ *adj*: *The war had a catastrophic effect on the whole country.*
فاجع

ʔ **catch¹** /kætʃ/ *verb* (*pt, pp* **caught** /kɔːt/) **1** [T] to take hold of sth that is moving, usually with your hand or hands: *She threw the ball and he caught it in one hand.* ○ *The dog caught the ball in its mouth.* يمسك بـ

2 [T] to capture sb/sth that you have been chasing or looking for: *Two policemen ran after the thief and caught him at the end of the street.* ○ *The murderer still hasn't been caught.* ○ *to catch a fish* يقبض على

3 [T] to discover sb who is doing sth bad: *I caught her taking money from my purse.*
يجده متلبِّساً

4 [T] to get on a form of public transport: *I caught the bus into town.* ○ *to catch a train, plane, etc.* يركب أو يأخذ (وسيلة مواصلات)

5 [T] to be in time for sth; not to miss sb/sth: *If I take the letter now, I should catch the post.* ○ *We arrived just in time to catch the beginning of the film.* ○ *I'll phone her now. I might just catch her before she leaves the office.* يدْرِك ، يلحق بـ

6 [T] to hear or understand sth that sb says: *I'm sorry, I didn't quite catch what you said. Could you repeat it?* يسمع ، يفهم

7 [I,T] to become or cause sth to become accidentally attached to or trapped in sth: *His jacket caught on a nail.* ○ *I caught my finger in the drawer as I shut it.* ○ *I'm sorry I'm late. I got caught in the traffic.* يعلق ؛ ينحبس

8 [T] to get an illness: *I've got a terrible cold. I must have caught it from someone at work.*
يصيب

IDM **catch sb's attention/eye** to make sb notice sth: *I tried to catch the waiter's eye so that I could get the bill.* يجذب انتباهه
catch fire to start burning, often accidentally: *Nobody knows how the building caught fire.*
يشتعل
catch sb red-handed to find sb just as he/she is doing sth wrong: *A policeman noticed the ladder at the window and caught the burglars red-handed.* يقبض عليه متلبِّساً
catch sight/a glimpse of sb/sth to see sb/sth for a moment: *I caught sight of the man at the end*

of the street. ○ *We waited outside the theatre, hoping to catch a glimpse of the actress.* يلمح

catch the sun to become burned or tanned by the sun: *Your face looks red. You've really caught the sun, haven't you?* تلوّحه الشمس

catch/take sb unawares → UNAWARE

PHR V **catch on** (*informal*) **1** to understand or realize sth: *She's sometimes a bit slow to catch on.* يفهم ، يستوعب

2 to become popular or fashionable: *The idea has never really caught on in this country.* ينتشر ، يروج

catch sb out to cause sb to make a mistake by asking a clever question: *Ask me anything you like – you won't catch me out.* يوقع

catch up (with sb); **catch sb up 1** to reach sb/sth who is ahead of you: *Jackie was walking very fast and I had to run to catch up with her.* ○ *I'll just finish this letter. You go on and I'll catch you up in a minute.* يدرك ، يلحق بـ

2 to reach the same level as sb/sth else: *Our economy is developing fast and we should soon catch up with other countries in the western world.* يدرك، يلحق بـ

catch up on sth to spend time doing sth that you have not been able to do until now: *I'll have to go into the office at the weekend to catch up on my work.* يعوض ما فاته

be/get caught up in sth to be or get involved in sth, usually without intending to: *I seem to have got caught up in a rather complicated situation.* يتورط

catch² /kætʃ/ *noun* [C] **1** an act of taking hold of sth that is moving, usually with your hand or hands إمساك (بشيء)

2 the amount of fish that sb has caught: *The fishermen brought their catch to the harbour.* كمية السمك المصطاد

3 a device for fastening sth and keeping it closed: *I can't close my suitcase – the catch is broken.* ○ *a window catch* ماسكة ، مزلاج

4 a hidden disadvantage to sth that seems attractive: *It looks like a good offer but I'm sure there must be a catch in it.* عيب خفي

catchment area /ˈkætʃmənt eəriə/ *noun* [C] the area from which a school gets its pupils, a hospital gets its patients, etc. منطقة استمداد

catchphrase /ˈkætʃfreɪz/ *noun* [C] a phrase that becomes famous for a while because it is used by a famous person قول دارج

catchy /ˈkætʃi/ *adj* (**catchier**; **catchiest**) (used about a tune or song) easy to remember يعلق بسرعة ، سهل التذكر

categorical /ˌkætəˈɡɒrɪkl; *US* -ˈɡɔːr-/ *adj* completely definite: *The answer was a categorical 'no'.* قطعي

▸ **categorically** /-kli/ *adv*: *The Minister categorically denied the rumour.* بشكل قطعي

category /ˈkætəɡəri; *US* -ɡɔːri/ *noun* [C] (*pl.* **categories**) a group of people or things that are similar to each other: *There were two categories in the competition: children under 5 and 6-8 year-olds.* ○ *These books are divided into categories according to subject.* فئة ، صنف

▸ **categorize** (*also* **categorise**) /ˈkætəɡəraɪz/ *verb* [T] to divide people or things into groups, or to say that sb/sth belongs to a particular group يصنّف

cater /ˈkeɪtə(r)/ *verb* [I] **1 cater for sb/sth**; **cater to sth** to provide what sb/sth needs or wants: *We need a hotel that caters for small children.* ○ *a newspaper that caters to people's love of gossip* يخدم ، يؤمّن ما يحتاجه

2 cater (for sb/sth) to provide and serve food and drink for a social event: *the firm that catered at our wedding* يقوم بخدمات الطعام والشراب

▸ **caterer** *noun* [C] a person or business that provides food and drink for social events متعهّد (بخدمات الطعام والشراب)

catering *noun* [U] the activity or business of providing food and drink for social events: *the hotel and catering industry* خدمة الحفلات العامة (بالطعام والشراب)

caterpillar /ˈkætəpɪlə(r)/ *noun* [C] an animal like a small hairy worm with legs, which changes into a butterfly or moth يسروع أو سرفة

cathedral /kəˈθiːdrəl/ *noun* [C] a large church that is the most important one in a district كاتدرائية

Catholic /ˈkæθlɪk/ *noun* [C], *adj* = ROMAN CATHOLIC

▸ **Catholicism** /kəˈθɒləsɪzəm/ *noun* [U] = ROMAN CATHOLICISM

cattle /ˈkætl/ *noun* [plural] male and female cows, e.g. on a farm: *a herd of cattle* (= a group of them) ➲ Look at the note at **cow**. ماشية

Caucasian /kɔːˈkeɪziən; kɔːˈkeɪʒn/ *noun, adj* (of) a member of the race of people who have white or light-coloured skin قوقازي: ينتمي للعرق الأبيض

caught *pt, pp* of CATCH¹

cauldron (*also* **caldron**) /ˈkɔːldrən/ *noun* [C] a large, deep, metal pot that is used for cooking things over a fire مرجل

cauliflower /ˈkɒliflaʊə(r); *US* ˈkɔːli-/ *noun* [C,U] a large vegetable with green leaves and a round white centre that you eat when it is cooked قرنبيط

cause /kɔːz/ *noun* **1** [C] a thing or person that makes sth happen: *The police do not know the cause of the accident.* ○ *Smoking is one of the causes of heart disease.* سبب

2 [U] **cause (for sth)** reason: *I don't think you have any real cause for complaint.* موجب ، داع

3 [C] an aim or principle that a group of people believe in and support: *We are all committed to the cause of racial equality.* ○ *I don't mind giving money to a good cause.* قضية

IDM **a lost cause** → LOST

▸ **cause** *verb* [T] to make sth happen: *The fire was caused by an electrical fault.* ○ *High winds caused many trees to fall during the night.* ○ *Is your leg causing you any pain?* يسبّب ، يحدث

a b c d e f g h i j k l m n o p q r s t u v w x y z

caustic /ˈkɔːstɪk/ *adj* **1** (used about a substance) able to burn or destroy things by chemical action كاوٍ

2 (used about a comment or type of humour) cruel and unpleasant لاذع

caution /ˈkɔːʃn/ *noun* **1** [U] great care, because of possible danger: *Caution! Falling rocks!* (= on a road sign) حَذَر

2 [C] a spoken warning that a judge or policeman gives to sb who has committed a small crime تحذير ، تنبيه

▸ **caution** *verb* [I,T] to warn sb about sth: *He cautioned me not to believe everything I heard.* ○ *The President's advisers have cautioned against calling an election too early.* يحذّر

cautionary /ˈkɔːʃənəri; US ˈkɔːʃəneri/ *adj* giving a warning: *a cautionary tale* تحذيري ، للعظة والعبرة

cautious /ˈkɔːʃəs/ *adj* taking great care to avoid possible danger: *I'm very cautious about expressing my opinions in public.* حَذِر

▸ **cautiously** *adv* بحذر

cavalry /ˈkævlri/ *noun* [sing., with sing. or pl. verb] **1** the part of the army which fights in fast, heavily protected vehicles (سلاح) المدرّعات

2 the group of soldiers who fought on horses in the past (سلاح) الفرسان

cave /keɪv/ *noun* [C] a large hole in the side of a cliff or hill, or under the ground: *When it started to rain, we ran to shelter in a cave.* كهف ، مغارة

▸ **cave** *verb*

PHR V **cave in 1** to fall in: *The roof of the tunnel had caved in and we could go no further.* يتقوّض، ينهار

2 to suddenly stop arguing or opposing sth: *He finally caved in and agreed to the plan.* يستسلم ، يذعن

cavern /ˈkævən/ *noun* [C] a large, deep cave كهف ، مغارة كبيرة

caviare (*also* **caviar**) /ˈkæviɑː(r)/ *noun* [U] the eggs of a large fish (a sturgeon) that are eaten as food. Caviare is usually very expensive. الكافيار: نوع من البطرخ

cavity /ˈkævəti/ *noun* [C] (*pl.* **cavities**) **1** an empty space inside sth solid: *a wall cavity* فجوة ، تجويف

2 a hole in a tooth فجوة ، نخر

cc /ˌsiː ˈsiː/ *abbrev* **1** cubic centimetre(s): *a 1200 cc engine* سنتمتر مكعب

2 carbon copy: *cc Harriet Symes* صورة طبق الأصل: نسخة إلى

CCTV /ˌsiː siː tiː ˈviː/ *abbrev* = CLOSED-CIRCUIT TELEVISION

🔑 **CD** /ˌsiː ˈdiː/ *abbrev* compact disc; a small, round piece of hard plastic, like a record, on which sound is recorded or information stored قرص مضغوط (أو مركز أو مدمّج)

CD-ROM (*US* **CD/ROM**) /ˌsiː diː ˈrɒm/ *abbrev* compact disc read-only memory; a compact disc which can be used in a computer and which has a lot of information recorded on it. The information cannot be changed or removed. قرص مدمّج للقراءة فقط

CE /ˌsiː ˈiː/ *abbrev* Common Era (may be used instead of AD) بعد الميلاد

🔑 **cease** /siːs/ *verb* [I,T] (*formal*) to stop or end: *Fighting in the area has now ceased.* ○ *That organization has ceased to exist.* ○ *500 people lost their jobs when the company ceased trading.* يتوقّف ؛ يوقف ؛ ينهي

▸ **ceaseless** *adj* continuing for a long time without stopping مستمر، متواصل

ceaselessly *adv* باستمرار ، بلا انقطاع

ceasefire /ˈsiːsfaɪə(r)/ *noun* [C] an agreement between two groups to stop fighting each other وقف إطلاق النار

cede /siːd/ *verb* [T] (*formal*) to give land or control of sth to another country or person يتنازل عن

🔑 **ceiling** /ˈsiːlɪŋ/ *noun* [C] **1** the top surface of the inside of a room: *We painted the walls pink and the ceiling white.* ○ *a room with a high/low ceiling* سقف الغرفة

2 a top limit on wages, prices, etc: *The Government has put a 10% ceiling on wage increases.* حدّ أعلى

🔑 **celebrate** /ˈselɪbreɪt/ *verb* **1** [I,T] to do sth special and enjoyable on an important day or because of an important event: *When I got the job we celebrated by going out for a meal.* ○ *Mrs Halford celebrated her 80th birthday yesterday.* يحتفل بـ

2 [T] (used about a priest) to lead a religious ceremony: *to celebrate Mass* يقوم بالشعائر

▸ **celebration** /ˌselɪˈbreɪʃn/ *noun* [C,U] the act or occasion of doing sth enjoyable because sth good has happened or because it is a special day: *Christmas celebrations* ○ *I think this is an occasion for celebration!* احتفال

celebrated /ˈselɪbreɪtɪd/ *adj* (*formal*) famous: *a celebrated poet* مشهور

celebrity /səˈlebrəti/ *noun* [C] (*pl.* **celebrities**) a famous person (شخص) مشهور

celery /ˈseləri/ *noun* [U] a vegetable with long green stems that is eaten raw in salads and sometimes used in cooking: *a stick of celery* ○ *celery soup* الكَرَفْس

celibate /ˈselɪbət/ *adj* (*formal*) remaining unmarried or never having sexual relations, often because of religious beliefs متبتّل ؛ عَزَب

▸ **celibacy** /ˈselɪbəsi/ *noun* [U] تبتّل ؛ عزوبة

🔑 **cell** /sel/ *noun* [C] **1** the smallest living part of an animal or a plant body: *The human body consists of millions of cells.* ○ *red blood cells* خليّة

2 a small room in a prison or police station in which a prisoner is locked زنزانة

cellar /ˈselə(r)/ *noun* [C] an underground room that is used for storing things ➲ Look at **basement**. قَبْو

cello /'tʃeləʊ/ *noun* [C] (*pl.* **cellos**) a musical instrument like a large violin. You sit down to play it and hold it between your knees. فيولونسيل: كمنجة كبيرة

▸ **cellist** /'tʃelɪst/ *noun* [C] a person who plays the cello عازف فيولونسيل

Cellophane™ /'seləfeɪn/ *noun* [U] thin transparent material that is used for wrapping things ورق سلوفان

cellphone /'selfəʊn/ (*also* ˌ**cellular** '**phone**) *noun* = MOBILE PHONE

cellular /'seljələ(r)/ *adj* consisting of cells (1): *cellular tissue* خلوي

Celsius /'selsiəs/ (*also* **Centigrade**) *adj* (*abbr* **C**) the name of a scale for measuring temperatures, in which water freezes at 0° and boils at 100°: *The temperature tonight will fall to 7°C.* ❶ We say 'seven degrees Celsius'. Look also at **Fahrenheit**. (مقياس حرارة) مئوي

Celtic /'keltɪk; *US* 'seltɪk/ *adj* connected with the people (the Celts) who lived in Wales, Scotland Ireland and Brittany in ancient times, or with their culture كلتي

cement /sɪ'ment/ *noun* [U] **1** a grey powder, that becomes hard after it is mixed with water and left to dry. It is used in building for sticking bricks or stones together or for making very hard surfaces. إسمنت

2 a type of glue لصاق

▸ **cement** *verb* [T] **1** to cover sth with cement يغطي بالاسمنت

2 to stick things together يلصق

3 to make a relationship very strong: *This agreement has cemented the relationship between our two companies.* يعزّز

cemetery /'semətri; *US* 'seməteri/ *noun* [C] (*pl.* **cemeteries**) a place where dead people are buried (that does not belong to a church) ➲ Look at **graveyard**. مقْبرة

censor /'sensə(r)/ *noun* [C] an official who examines books, films, plays, etc. and removes any parts that might offend people, or who examines letters, newspaper reports, etc. and removes any parts which contain secret information رقيب

▸ **censor** *verb* [T]: *The journalist said that all the information they sent back to Britain was being censored.* يراقب

censorship *noun* [U]: *state censorship of radio and television programmes* مراقبة

censure /'senʃə(r)/ *verb* [T] (*formal*) to tell sb, in a strong and formal way, that he/she has done sth wrong: *The minister was censured for not revealing the information earlier.* يقرّع ، يوبّخ

▸ **censure** *noun* [U]: *a vote of censure in parliament* تقريع ، توبيخ

census /'sensəs/ *noun* [C] (*pl.* **censuses**) an official count of the people who live in a country, including information about their ages, jobs, etc. إحصاء أو تعداد (السكّان)

cent /sent/ *noun* [C] (*abbr* **c, ct**) a unit of money that is worth 100th part of the main unit of money in many countries e.g. the euro or the US dollar ➲ Look also at **per cent**. السِّنْت

centenary /sen'tiːnəri; *US* 'sentəneri/ *noun* [C] (*pl.* **centenaries**) (*US also* **centennial** /sen'teniəl/) the year that comes exactly one hundred years after an important event or the beginning of sth: *2005 is the centenary of Norway's independence.* ○ *centenary celebrations* مئوي

center /'sentə(r)/ *noun* [C] (*US*) = CENTRE

centigrade /'sentɪgreɪd/ *adj* = CELSIUS

centilitre (*US* **centiliter**) /'sentɪliːtə(r)/ *noun* [C] (*abbr* **cl**) a unit for measuring liquids. There are 100 centilitres in a litre. سنتيلتر

centimetre (*US also* **centimeter**) /'sentɪmiːtə(r)/ *noun* [C] (*abbr* **cm**) a measure of length. There are 100 centimetres in a metre: *The insect was about two centimetres long.* سنتيمتر

central /'sentrəl/ *adj* **1** in the centre of sth: *a map of central Europe* ○ *The flat is in Edgware Road, which is very central* (= near the centre of the city and therefore very convenient). أوسط ، مركزي

2 (only *before* a noun) (used about an office, group, etc.) having control of all other parts of an organization: *central government* (= the government of a whole country, not local government) ○ *the Conservative Central Office* مركزي

3 most important; main: *The film's central character is a fifteen-year-old girl.* رئيسي

▸ **centralize** (*also* **centralise**) /'sentrəlaɪz/ *verb* [T] (usually passive) to make sth come under central control: *Our educational system is becoming increasingly centralized.* يُمَركِز: يضع تحت السلطة المركزية

centralization (*also* **centralisation**) /ˌsentrəlaɪ'zeɪʃn; *US* -lɪ'z-/ *noun* [U] مركزية : مركزة

centrally /'sentrəli/ *adv* in or from the centre: *a centrally located hotel* (= near the centre of the town) ○ *a centrally heated house* في أو من المركز

ˌ**central** '**heating** *noun* [U] a system for heating a building from one main point. Air or water is heated and carried by pipes to all parts of the building: *The house has gas central heating.* تدفئة مركزية

centre (*US* **center**) /'sentə(r)/ *noun* **1** [C, usually sing.] the middle point or part of sth: *There was a vase of flowers in the centre of the table.* ○ *I work in the centre of London.* ○ *Which way is the town centre, please?* ➲ Look at the note at **middle**. مركز، وَسَط ، قلْب

2 [C] a building or place where a particular activity or service is based: *a sports, leisure, arts, shopping, etc. centre* ○ *a job, information, health, etc. centre* مركز

3 [C] a person or thing that receives a lot of attention: *She always likes to be the centre of attention.* محور ، محَطّ

4 the centre [sing., with sing. or pl. verb] a political position that is not extreme: *the centre parties* الوَسَط

▶ **centre** *verb*

PHRV **centre on/around sb/sth** to have sb/sth as its centre: *The life of the village centres on the church, the school and the pub.* يتركز في : يتمحور حول

century /ˈsentʃəri/ *noun* [C] (*pl.* **centuries**) **1** a particular period of 100 years that is used for giving dates: *the 20th century* (= the period between the years 1901 and 2000) قرْن

2 any period of 100 years: *His family have owned this farm for centuries.* قرْن

ceramic /səˈræmɪk/ *adj* made of clay that has been baked: *ceramic tiles* خزفيّ، من السيراميك

▶ **ceramic** *noun* [C] a pot or other object made of clay: *an exhibition of ceramics by Picasso* إناء خزفي

ceramics *noun* [U] the art of making and decorating clay pots, etc. فن أو صناعة الخزف

cereal /ˈsɪəriəl/ *noun* [C,U] **1** a plant such as wheat, rice, etc. that is grown to produce grain: *These fields are usually planted with cereals.* ○ *cereal crops* حبوب ، غلال

2 food that is made from the grain of cereals: *10 different varieties of breakfast cereal* طعام من الحبوب

cerebral /ˈserəbrəl; *US* səˈriːbrəl/ *adj* connected with the brain: *He died of a cerebral haemorrhage.* دماغي أو مخي

ceremonial /ˌserɪˈməʊniəl/ *adj* relating to a ceremony: *a ceremonial occasion* احتفالي

▶ **ceremonially** /-niəli/ *adv* على نحو احتفالي : بصورة رسميّة

ceremony /ˈserəməni; *US* -məʊni/ *noun* (*pl.* **ceremonies**) **1** [C] a formal public or religious event: *the opening ceremony of the Olympic Games* ○ *a wedding ceremony* احتفال رسميّ

2 [U] formal behaviour, speech, actions, etc. that are expected on special occasions: *The Queen was welcomed with great ceremony.* مراسم

certain¹ /ˈsɜːtn/ *adj* **1** (not before a noun) **certain (that...); certain (of sth)** completely sure; without any doubts: *She's absolutely certain that there was somebody outside her window.* ○ *I think this is the man, but I can't be certain.* ○ *We're not quite certain what time the train leaves.* ○ *I'm certain of one thing – he didn't take the money.* متأكّد : واثق

2 certain (that...); certain (to do sth) sure to happen or to do sth; definite: *It is almost certain that unemployment will increase this year.* ○ *The Director is certain to agree.* ○ *Nothing is certain at the moment. Wait and see.* ○ *We must rescue them today, or they will face certain death.* ➲ Look at the note at **sure**. مؤكّد : محتوم

IDM **for certain** without doubt: *I don't know for certain what time we'll arrive.* على وجه التأكيد

make certain (that...) to do sth in order to be sure that sth else happens: *They're doing everything they can to make certain that they win.* يتأكّد ، يستوثق

▶ **certainly** *adv* **1** without doubt; definitely: *The number of students will certainly increase after 2010.* ○ *It certainly was a very good party.* ○ *I certainly don't think you should tell him now.* بلا شك : حتماً

2 (used in answer to questions) of course: *'Do you think I could borrow your notes?' 'Certainly.'* ○ *'Can I take your car to France?' 'Certainly not!'* طبعاً

certainty /ˈsɜːtnti/ *noun* (*pl.* **certainties**) **1** [U] the state of being completely sure about sth: *We can't say with certainty that there is life on other planets.* ❶ The opposite is **uncertainty**. يقين

2 [C] something that is sure to happen: *It's now almost a certainty that Italy will play in the World Cup Final.* أمر مؤكّد

certain² /ˈsɜːtn/ *adj* (only *before* a noun) **1** (used for talking about a particular thing or person without naming them): *You can only contact me at certain times of the day.* ○ *There are certain reasons why I'd prefer not to meet him again.* مُعيّن

2 noticeable but difficult to describe: *There was a certain feeling of autumn in the air.* (شعور) مبهم

3 (used before a person's name to show that you do not know him/her): *I received a letter from a certain Mrs Berry.* شخص ما اسمه...

▶ **certain** *pron* **certain of...** (*formal*) (used for talking about some members of a group of people or things without giving their names): *Certain of our hotels are only open in the summer months.* بعض

certificate /səˈtɪfɪkət/ *noun* [C] an official piece of paper that says that sth is true or correct: *a birth certificate* شهادة

certify /ˈsɜːtɪfaɪ/ *verb* [T] (*pres part* **certifying**; *3rd pers sing pres* **certifies**; *pt, pp* **certified**) **1** to say formally that sth is true or correct: *We need someone to certify that this is her signature.* يشهد

2 to give sb a certificate to show that he/she has successfully completed a course of training for a particular profession يمنح شهادة

Cesarian, **Cesarean** (*US*) = CAESAREAN

cf /ˌsiː ˈef/ *abbrev* compare: *cf note on p 20* أنظر

CFC /ˌsiː ef ˈsiː/ *noun* [C] a type of gas used especially in aerosols. CFCs are harmful to the layer of ozone in the earth's atmosphere. CFC stands for 'chlorofluorocarbon'. فحم الكلور والفلور

ch (*also* **chap**) *abbrev* = CHAPTER

chador /tʃɑːdɔː(r)/ *noun* [C] a large piece of cloth that covers a woman's head and upper body so that only the face can be seen, worn by some Muslim women شادور

chain /tʃeɪn/ *noun* **1** [C,U] a line of metal rings that are joined together: *They used heavy chains to pull the boat out of the water.* ○ *a bicycle chain* ○ *She was wearing a silver chain round her neck.* ○ *a length of chain* سلسلة

2 [C] a number of things in a line: *a chain of mountains/a mountain chain* سلسلة

3 [C] a group of shops, hotels, etc. that are owned by the same person or company: *a chain*

of supermarkets/a supermarket chain سلسلة مؤسسات تجارية

4 [C] a number of connected events that happen one after another: *The book examines the complex chain of events that led to the Russian Revolution.* سلسلة أحداث

▸ **chain** *verb* [T] **chain sb/sth (to sth)**; **chain sb/sth (up)** to fasten sb/sth to sth else with a chain: *The prisoners had been chained to the walls.* يقيِّد بالسلاسل

'chain-smoker *noun* [C] a person who smokes continuously, lighting one cigarette after another مدخِّن لا يتوقف عن التدخين

'chain store *noun* [C] one of a number of similar shops that are owned by the same company متجر في سلسلة (متاجر متماثلة)

chairs

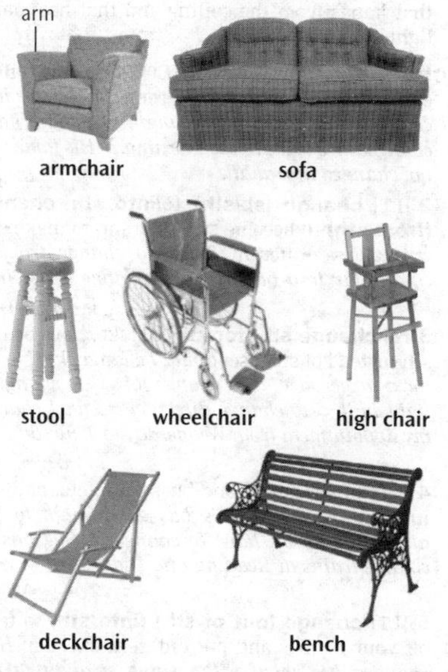

chair /tʃeə(r)/ *noun* **1** [C] a piece of furniture for one person to sit on. It has a seat, a back and usually four legs. It sometimes has two arms: *a kitchen chair ○ an armchair ○ a wheelchair* كُرسي

2 [sing.] the person who is controlling a meeting: *Please address your questions to the chair.* رئيس (رئيسة) الاجتماع

3 [C] the position of a university professor: *the chair of economics at London University* كرسي (الأستاذية)

▸ **chair** *verb* [T] to be the chairman or chairwoman of a meeting: *Who's chairing the meeting this evening?* يرأس

chairman /ˈtʃeəmən/ *noun* [C] (*pl.* **chairmen**) **1** the head of a committee, company or other organization: *the Chairman of IBM* رئيس (لجنة الخ)

2 a person who controls a meeting رئيس الاجتماع

▸ **chairmanship** /ˈtʃeəmənʃɪp/ *noun* [sing.] being the chairman of sth; the time during which sb is chairman of sth رئاسة؛ مدة الرئاسة

chairperson /ˈtʃeəpɜːsn/ *noun* [C] (*pl.* **chairpersons**) a person who controls a meeting رئيس (رئيسة) الاجتماع

chairwoman /ˈtʃeəwʊmən/ (*pl.* **chairwomen**) *noun* [C] a woman who controls a meeting رئيسة الاجتماع

chalet /ˈʃæleɪ; *US* ʃæˈleɪ/ *noun* [C] a house or hut that is made of wood, especially in a mountain area or holiday camp الشاليه: منزل أو كوخ خشبي

chalk /tʃɔːk/ *noun* **1** [U] a soft, white rock: *chalk cliffs* طباشير، حوار

2 [C,U] a small stick of this that is used for writing or drawing on a blackboard: *a piece of chalk* حوّارة أو طباشيرة

▸ **chalk** *verb* [I,T] to write or draw sth with a piece of chalk: *Somebody had chalked a message on the wall.* يكتب أو يرسم بالطباشير

PHR V **chalk sth up** to succeed in getting sth: *The team has chalked up five wins this summer.* يحرز

chalkboard /ˈtʃɔːkbɔːd/ *noun* [C] (*US*) = BLACKBOARD

challenge¹ /ˈtʃælɪndʒ/ *noun* **1** [C,U] something new and difficult that forces you to make a lot of effort: *I'm finding my new job an exciting challenge. ○ Reducing unemployment will be the main challenge for the new government.* تحدٍّ

2 [C] **a challenge (to sb) (to do sth)** an invitation from sb to fight, play, argue, etc. against him/her: *The Prime Minister should accept our challenge and call a new election now.* دعوة للمواجهة

challenge² /ˈtʃælɪndʒ/ *verb* [T] **1 challenge sb (to sth)** to invite sb to fight, play, argue, etc. against you: *They've challenged us to a football match this Saturday.* يدعو للمنازلة ، يتحدّى

2 to question whether sth is true or right: *She hates anyone challenging her authority.* يعترض على ، يتحدّى

▸ **challenger** *noun* [C] a person who invites you to take part in a competition, because he/she wants to win a title or position that you already have متحدٍّ، مناجز

challenging *adj* forcing you to make a lot of effort: *a challenging job* شاقّ ، مجهِد

chamber /ˈtʃeɪmbə(r)/ *noun* [C] **1** a large room that is used for formal meetings: *a council chamber* غرفة اجتماعات

2 a room that is used for a particular purpose: *a torture chamber* حجرة (لغرض معين)

chambermaid /ˈtʃeɪmbəmeɪd/ *noun* [C] a woman whose job is to clean and tidy hotel bedrooms خادمة في فندق

'chamber music *noun* [U] music that is written for a small group of instruments موسيقى لعدد محدود من الآلات

chameleon /kəˈmiːliən/ *noun* [C] a small lizard

that can change colour according to its surroundings حرباء

chamomile (*also* **camomile**) /ˈkæməmaɪl/ *noun* [U] a sweet-smelling plant with small white and yellow flowers whose leaves and flowers are used in medicine, etc: *camomile tea* ○ *camomile shampoo* بابونج

champagne /ʃæmˈpeɪn/ *noun* [U] a French white wine which has a lot of bubbles in it and is often very expensive شمبانيا

champion /ˈtʃæmpiən/ *noun* [C] **1** a person, team, etc. that has won a competition: *a world champion* ○ *a champion swimmer* بطل

2 a person who speaks and fights for a particular group, idea, etc: *a champion of free speech* مدافع عن ، نصير

▸ **champion** *verb* [T] to support or fight for a particular group or idea: *to champion the cause of human rights* يدافع عن ، يناصر

championship *noun* [C] **1** (often plural) a competition or series of competitions to find the best player or team in a sport or game: *to win the world championship* ○ *the World Hockey Championships* بطولة

2 the position or title of a champion (1) بطولة

chance¹ /tʃɑːns; US tʃæns/ *noun* **1** [C,U] **chance of (doing) sth**; **chance (that...)** (a) possibility: *The plan didn't really have a chance of succeeding.* ○ *I think there's a good chance that she'll be the next Prime Minister.* ○ *I'm afraid he has very little chance of winning.* ○ *Is there any chance of getting tickets for tonight's concert?* إمكانية ، احتمال

2 [C] **chance (of doing sth/to do sth)** an opportunity: *If you get the chance of going to America, you should take it!* ○ *Be quiet and give her a chance to explain.* ○ *I think you should tell him now. You may not get another chance.* ➲ Look at the note at **occasion**. فرصة

3 [C] a risk: *We may lose some money but that's a chance we'll have to take.* مخاطرة ، مجازفة

4 [U] luck or fortune (= sth that you cannot control): *I don't know what will happen – we'll have to leave it to chance.* ○ *We met by chance* (= we had not planned to meet) *as I was walking down the street.* حظ ، صُدفة

IDM **by any chance** (used for asking sth politely) perhaps or possibly: *Are you, by any chance, going into town this afternoon?* ربّما ، لعلّك...

the chances are (that)... (*informal*) it is probable that...: *The chances are that it will rain tomorrow.* من المحتمل

no chance (*informal*) there is no possibility of that happening: *'Perhaps your mother will give you the money.' 'No chance!'* هذا غير ممكن!

on the off chance in the hope that sth might happen, although it is not very likely: *I didn't think you'd be at home, but I just called in on the off chance.* على أمل (حدوث شيء غير محتمل)

stand a chance (of sth/of doing sth) to have a possibility of achieving sth: *I think she stands a good chance of winning the competition.* يمكنه أن يحقّق شيئاً

chance² /tʃɑːns; US tʃæns/ *verb* **1** [T] (*informal*) to risk sth: *Shall we take umbrellas or shall we chance it* (= risk getting wet)? يخاطر ، يجازف

2 [I] (*formal*) to do sth without planning or trying to do it: *I chanced to see the letter on his desk.* يصادف ، يحدُث اتفاقاً

chance³ /tʃɑːns; US tʃæns/ *adj* (only *before* a noun) not planned: *a chance meeting* (لقاء) مصادفة

chancellor /ˈtʃɑːnsələ(r); US ˈtʃæns-/ *noun* [C] **1** the head of government in some countries: *the German chancellor* مستشار ؛ رئيس وزراء

2 (*also* **ˌChancellor of the Exˈchequer**) (*Brit*) the government minister who makes decisions about taxes and government spending وزير المالية (في بريطانيا)

chandelier /ˌʃændəˈlɪə(r)/ *noun* [C] a large light that hangs from the ceiling and that has many light bulbs or candles ثُريّة/ثُريّا ، نجفة

change¹ /tʃeɪndʒ/ *verb* **1** [I,T] to become different or to make sb/sth different: *This town has changed a lot since I was young.* ○ *Our plans have changed. We leave in the morning.* ○ *His fame has not changed him at all.* يتغيّر ؛ يُغيّر

2 [I,T] **change (sb/sth) to/into sth**; **change (from sth)** to become sth different; to make sb/sth take a different form: *to change from a caterpillar to a butterfly* ○ *to change water into ice* يتحوّل ؛ يُغيّر ، يحوّل

3 [T] **change sth (for sth)** to take, have or use sth instead of sth else: *Could I change this blouse for a larger size?* ○ *to change jobs* ○ *to change a light bulb* ○ *to change direction* ○ *Can I change my appointment from Wednesday to Thursday?* يغيّر ، يستبدل

4 [I,T] to get out of one bus, train, etc. and get into another: *Does this bus go through to the airport or do we have to change?* ○ *She has to change trains at Reading and Didcot.* يغيّر واسطة النقل

5 [I,T] **change (out of sth) (into sth)** to take off your clothes and put different ones on: *He's changed his shirt.* ○ *I'm going straight to the party from work, so I'll change when I get there.* ○ *She changed out of her gardening clothes and into a clean dress.* ℹ **Get changed** is a common expression meaning 'to change your clothes': *You can get changed in the bedroom.* يغيّر ملابسه

6 [T] to put clean things onto sb/sth: *to change the bed* (= to put clean sheets on) ○ *The baby's nappy needs changing.* يغيّر

7 [T] **change sth (for/into sth)** to give sb money and receive the same amount back in money of a different type: *Can you change a ten-pound note for two fives?* ○ *I'd like to change fifty pounds into Swiss francs.* يحوّل ، يصرف

IDM **change hands** to pass from one owner to another تنتقل ملكيته

change your mind to change your decision or opinion: *I'll have the green one. No, I've changed my mind. I want the red one.* يعدل عن رأيه

change/swap places (with sb) → PLACE[1]
change the subject to start talking about sth different يغيِّر الموضوع
change your tune (*informal*) to change your opinion or feelings about sth يغيِّر موقفه
chop and change → CHOP[3]
PHR V **change over (from sth) (to sth)** to stop doing or using one thing and start doing or using sth else: *The theatre has changed over to a computerized booking system.* يتغيَّر؛ ينقلب إلى
▸ **changeable** /ˈtʃeɪndʒəbl/ *adj* likely to change; often changing: *English weather is very changeable.* متقلِّب

change² /tʃeɪndʒ/ *noun* **1** [C,U] **change (in/to sth)** the process of becoming or making sth different: *There was little change in the patient's condition overnight.* ○ *After two hot summers, people were talking about a change in the climate.* تغيُّر، تغيير
2 [C] **change (of sth)** something that you take, have or use instead of sth else: *We must notify the bank of our change of address.* تغيير
3 [U] coins or notes of lower value that together make up the same value as a larger coin or note: *Have you got change for a pound?* فكّة، فراطة
4 [U] coins of low value: *He needs some change for the phone.* فكّة، فراطة
5 [U] the money that you get back if you pay more than the amount sth costs: *If a paper costs 60p and you pay with a pound coin, you will get 40p change.* كمالة النقود (التي يعيدها البائع)
IDM **a change of heart** a change in your opinion or the way that you feel تغيُّر في الموقف : تغيير الرأي
for a change in order to do sth different from usual: *We always spend our holidays by the sea. Let's go to the mountains for a change this year.* على سبيل التغيير
make a change to be enjoyable or pleasant because it is different from what you usually do يخلق تغييراً ممتعاً

changeover /ˈtʃeɪndʒəʊvə(r)/ *noun* [C] a change from one system to another تغيير؛ تبدُّل

ˈchanging room *noun* [C] a room for changing clothes in, e.g. before or after playing sport غرفة تبديل الملابس

channel /ˈtʃænl/ *noun* [C] **1** [C] a television or radio station. Each channel broadcasts on its own frequency or wavelength: *There's an interesting programme on Channel 4 tonight.* ○ *Can I switch over to the other channel?* قناة (تلفزيونية أو إذاعية)
2 [C] a narrow area of water between two seas قناة ، قنال
3 the Channel [sing.] the sea between England and France القنال الإنكليزي ، بحر المانش
4 [C] an open passage along which liquids can flow: *a drainage channel* مجرى
5 [C] the part of a river, etc. which is deep enough for boats to pass along مجرى النهر
6 [C] a way or route along which news, information, etc. is sent: *a channel of communication* قناة
▸ **channel** *verb* [T] (channelling; channelled; *US also* channeling; channeled) to make sth move along a particular path or route: *Water is channelled from the river to the fields.* ○ (*figurative*) *You should channel your energies into something constructive.* يوصِّل ؛ يوجِّه

the ˌChannel ˈTunnel *noun* [sing.] the tunnel under the sea that connects England and France نفق القنال الإنكليزي

chant /tʃɑːnt/ *noun* [C] a word or phrase that is sung or shouted many times: *A chant of 'we are the champions' went round the stadium.* هتاف مكرَّر؛ ترنيمة
▸ **chant** *verb* [I,T] to sing or shout a word or phrase many times: *The protestors marched by, chanting slogans.* يغني؛ يرنِّم؛ يهتِف

chaos /ˈkeɪɒs/ *noun* [U] a state of great disorder; confusion: *The meeting ended in chaos when demonstrators threw tomatoes at the speakers.* ○ *The accident has caused chaos on the M25 motorway.* فوضى
▸ **chaotic** /keɪˈɒtɪk/ *adj* in a state of chaos: *With no one in charge the situation became chaotic.* فوضوي ، في حالة فوضى

chap /tʃæp/ *noun* [C] (*especially Brit informal*) a man or boy رجل ، فتى

chapel /ˈtʃæpl/ *noun* **1** [C] a small part of a large church that can be used for private prayer جناح في كنيسة
2 [C] a small building or room in a prison, hospital, school, etc. that is used as a church مصلّى خاص
3 [C,U] (*Brit*) a church for some Protestant groups: *a Methodist chapel* كنيسة (بروتستانتية)

chaperone (*Brit also* **chaperon**) /ˈʃæpərəʊn/ *noun* [C] an older person, usually a woman, who goes to public places with a young unmarried woman to look after her and to make sure that she behaves correctly مرافقة لفتاة شابّة لحمايتها
▸ **chaperone** (*Brit also* **chaperon**) *verb* [T] يرافق فتاة لحمايتها

chaplain /ˈtʃæplɪn/ *noun* [C] a priest who works in a hospital, school, prison, army, etc. قسيس خاص

chapter /ˈtʃæptə(r)/ *noun* [C] (*abbr* **ch**; **chap**) one of the parts into which a book is divided: *Please read Chapter 2 for homework.* ○ *In the opening chapter, the author sets the scene of the novel.* ○ (*figurative*) *The last few years have been a difficult chapter in the country's history.* فصل؛ سورة

character /ˈkærəktə(r)/ *noun* **1** [C,U, sing.] the quality that makes sb/sth different from other people or things; the nature of sb/sth: *Although they are twins, their characters are quite different.* ○ *The introduction of more practical work has completely changed the character of the science course.* ○ *Modern houses often seem to lack character* (= they all seem the same). شخصية ؛ طبيعة

2 [U] a person's inner strength: *The match developed into a test of character rather than just physical strength.* ○ *Military service is said to be character-building.* قوة الشخصية

3 [C] (*informal*) a person: *There was a suspicious-looking character hanging around outside so I phoned the police.* شخص

4 [U] the good opinion that people have of you: *The article was a vicious attack on the President's character.* سمعة، شخصية

5 [C] a person who is very interesting or amusing: *Neil's quite a character.* شخصية طريفة

6 [C] a person in a book, story, etc: *The main character in the book is a boy who meets an alien.* شخصية (في قصة الخ)

7 [C] a letter or sign that you use when you are writing or printing: *Chinese characters* حرف ، علامة (كتابية)

IDM **in/out of character** typical/not typical of sb/sth ينسجم مع شخصيته/لا ينسجم مع شخصيته، ليس من طبعه

characteristic /ˌkærəktəˈrɪstɪk/ *noun* [C] a quality that is typical of sb/sth and that makes him/her/it different from other people or things: *The chief characteristic of reptiles is that they are cold-blooded.* صفة ، سمة

▶ **characteristic** *adj*: *Thatched cottages are characteristic of this part of England.* ❶ The opposite is **uncharacteristic**. مميز

characteristically /-kli/ *adv*: *'No' he said, in his characteristically direct manner.* على الوجه المعهود

characterize (*also* **characterise**) /ˈkærəktəraɪz/ *verb* [T] **1** (often passive) to be typical of sb/sth: *The 1980s were characterized by the pursuit of money.* يتميز بِ

2 characterize sb/sth as sth to describe the nature of sb/sth or to show a person's character in a particular way: *The President characterized the meeting as friendly and positive.* يصف

charade /ʃəˈrɑːd; *US* ʃəˈreɪd/ *noun* **1 charades** [U] a game that is played at a party, etc. in which one person or team acts out a word for others to guess ازاي عروستي: لعبة جماعية تمثّل فيها معاني الكلمات

2 [C] a situation or event that is clearly false but in which people pretend to do or be sth: *They pretend to be friends but it's all a charade. Everyone knows they hate each other.* زَيْف

charcoal /ˈtʃɑːkəʊl/ *noun* [U] a black substance that is produced when you burn wood in an oven with very little air. Charcoal can be used for drawing with or as a fuel. فحم حطب

charge¹ /tʃɑːdʒ/ *noun* **1** [C,U] the price that you must pay for sth: *The hotel makes a small charge for changing currency.* ○ *We deliver free of charge.* ○ *A small charge is made for admission.* ➲ Look at the note at **price**. رَسْم: مبلغ يدفع

2 [C] an official statement that says that sb has done sth which is against the law: *He was arrested on a charge of theft.* تهمة

3 [C] a sudden attack where sb/sth runs directly at sb/sth else: *a cavalry charge* حَملة ، هجوم (مفاجئ)

4 [C] the amount of electricity that is put into a battery or carried by a substance: *a positive/negative charge* شحنة

IDM **in charge (of sb/sth)** in control or command (of sb/sth): *Who is in charge of the office while Alan's away?* ○ *I'd like to speak to the person in charge.* مشرف على ، مسؤول

reverse the charges → REVERSE³

take charge (of sth) to take control of or responsibility for sth يكون مسؤولاً عن

charge² /tʃɑːdʒ/ *verb* **1** [I,T] **charge (sb/sth) for sth** to ask sb to pay a particular amount of money: *Do you charge for postage and packing?* ○ *We charge £35 per night for a single room.* ○ *He charged me 30 pence for the onions.* يطلب ثمناً ؛ يتقاضى أجراً

2 [T] **charge sb (with sth)** to accuse sb officially of doing sth which is against the law: *Six men are to be charged with attempted robbery.* يتّهم

3 [I,T] to attack sb/sth by running directly at him/her/it: *The bull put its head down and charged.* ○ (*figurative*) *The children charged down the stairs and into the garden.* يهجم ، يندفع

4 [T] to put electricity into sth: *to charge a battery* يشحَن

chariot /ˈtʃæriət/ *noun* [C] an open vehicle with two wheels, that was pulled by a horse or horses in ancient times عربة بعجلتين يجرها حصان

charisma /kəˈrɪzmə/ *noun* [U] the power that some people have to attract and influence people كارزما: جاذبيّة شخصية

▶ **charismatic** /ˌkærɪzˈmætɪk/ *adj*: *a charismatic politician* كارزمي ، ذو جاذبية قوية

charitable /ˈtʃærətəbl/ *adj* **1** kind; generous: *Some people accused him of lying, but a more charitable explanation was that he had made a mistake.* ❶ The opposite is **uncharitable**. طيب النفس ؛ كريم

2 connected with a charity (1) خيري

charity /ˈtʃærəti/ *noun* (*pl.* **charities**) **1** [C,U] an organization that collects money to help people who are poor, sick, etc. or to do work that will be of benefit to society: *We went on a sponsored walk to raise money for charity.* ○ *He supports a charity that helps disabled people.* منظمة خيرية ؛ عمل خيري

2 [U] kindness towards other people: *to act out of charity* إحسان

ˈcharity shop *noun* [C] a shop that sells clothes, books, etc. given by people to make money for charity دكان خيريّ

charm¹ /tʃɑːm/ *noun* **1** [C,U] the quality of being pleasant or attractive: *The charm of the island lies in its unspoilt beauty.* ○ *One of his charms was his ability to talk amusingly on any topic.* سِحْر، فتنة

2 [C] something that you wear because you believe it will bring you good luck: *a necklace with a lucky charm on it* رقية ، تعويذة

charm² /tʃɑːm/ *verb* [T] to please sb; to influence people by your power to attract them: *Her draw-*

ings have charmed children all over the world. يُبْهِج ؛ يسحَر

▸ **charming** *adj* very pleasing or attractive: *Everyone enjoyed talking to them because they're such a charming couple.* ○ *What a charming little cottage!* مبهِج ؛ جذّاب

charmingly *adv*: *She smiled charmingly.* بجاذبية؛ بلباقة

charred /tʃɑːd/ *adj* black and partly burnt by fire محترق ، متفحّم

⚷ **chart** /tʃɑːt/ *noun* **1** [C] a drawing which shows information in the form of a diagram, etc: *a temperature chart* ○ *a bar chart* رسم بياني

2 [C] a map of the sea or the sky: *navigation charts* خريطة

3 the charts [plural] an official list of the songs or CDs, etc., that have sold the most in a particular week قائمة الأغاني الرائجة

▸ **chart** *verb* [T] **1** to make a map of one area of the sea or sky: *an uncharted coastline* يرسم خريطة

2 to follow or record sth carefully and in detail: *This television series charts the history of the country since independence.* يسجِّل (تسجيلاً تفصيلياً)

charter /ˈtʃɑːtə(r)/ *noun* [C,U] **1** an official written statement of the rights, beliefs and purposes of an organization or a particular group of people: *The club's charter does not permit women to become members.* دستور ، ميثاق

2 the hiring of a ship, plane, etc. for a particular purpose or for a particular group of people: *a charter airline* استئجار سفينة أو طائرة الخ لغرض محدّد

▸ **charter** *verb* [T] **1** to hire a ship, plane, etc. for a particular purpose or for a particular group of people يستأجر سفينة أو طائرة الخ لغرض محدد

2 to give a charter (1) to an organization or a particular group of people يزوِّد بدستور أو ميثاق

chartered /ˈtʃɑːtəd/ *adj* (only *before* a noun) (used about people in certain professions) fully qualified: *He's training to be a chartered accountant.* (محاسب) قانوني

ˈ**charter flight** *noun* [C] a flight in which all seats are paid for by a travel company and then sold to their customers, usually at a lower price than a scheduled flight رحلة بطائرة مستأجرة لغرض محدد

⚷ **chase¹** /tʃeɪs/ *verb* [I,T] to run after sb/sth in order to catch him/her/it: *The dog chased the cat up a tree.* ○ *The police car chased the stolen van along the motorway.* يطارد

⚷ **chase²** /tʃeɪs/ *noun* [C] the act of following sb/sth in order to catch him/her/it; chasing or being chased: *an exciting car chase* مطاردة

IDM give chase to begin to run after sb/sth in order to try to catch him/her/it: *The robber ran off and the policeman gave chase.* يطارد

chasm /ˈkæzəm/ *noun* [C] **1** a long deep hole in the ground فلق أو شق عميق

2 (*figurative*) a wide difference of feelings, interests, etc. هوّة

chassis /ˈʃæsi/ *noun* [C] (*pl.* **chassis** /ˈʃæsiz/) the metal frame of a vehicle onto which the other parts fit هيكل (السيارة)

chaste /tʃeɪst/ *adj* **1** never having had a sexual relationship, or only with your husband/wife عفيف ، محصن

2 not involving thoughts and feelings about sex طاهر

▸ **chastity** /ˈtʃæstəti/ *noun* [U]: *The nuns took a vow of chastity.* عفّة ، طهارة

⚷ **chat** /tʃæt/ *noun* [C,U] a friendly informal conversation: *Why don't you come in for a cup of coffee and a chat?* محادثة

▸ **chat** *verb* [I] (cha**tt**ing; cha**tt**ed) **1** to talk to sb in a friendly, informal way: *The two grandmothers sat chatting about the old days.* يتآنس بالحديث

2 to exchange messages with other people on the Internet, especially in a chat room مسامرة

PHR V chat sb up (*Brit informal*) to talk to sb in a friendly way because you are sexually attracted to him/her يغازل ، يتودّد إلى

chatty *adj* (chattier; chattiest) **1** fond of talking: *My neighbour's very chatty – she tells me all the news.* محبّ للحديث

2 in an informal style: *a chatty letter* ذو أسلوب غير رسمي

ˈ**chat room** *noun* [C] (*computing*) an area on the Internet where people can communicate with each other, usually about one particular topic غرفة المحادثة

ˈ**chat show** *noun* [C] a television or radio programme on which well-known people are interviewed برنامج مقابلة

chatter /ˈtʃætə(r)/ *verb* [I] **1** to talk quickly or for a long time about sth unimportant: *The children chattered away continuously.* يثرثر

2 (used about your teeth) to knock together because you are cold or frightened تصطك (الأسنان)

▸ **chatter** *noun* [U]: *Stop that chatter and get on with your work.* ثرثرة

chauffeur /ˈʃəʊfə(r); *US* ʃəʊˈfɜːr/ *noun* [C] a person whose job is to drive a car for sb else: *a chauffeur-driven limousine* سائق

▸ **chauffeur** *verb* [T] يسوق

chauvinism /ˈʃəʊvɪnɪzəm/ *noun* [U] **1** a strong belief that your country is better and more important than all others شوفينية ، تعصّب مفرط للوطن

2 = MALE CHAUVINISM

▸ **chauvinist** /ˈʃəʊvɪnɪst/ *noun* [C] a person who believes in or shows chauvinism المتعصّب لوطنه

chauvinist, **chauvinistic** /ˌʃəʊvɪˈnɪstɪk/ *adj* believing in or showing chauvinism متعصب لوطنه

⚷ **cheap** /tʃiːp/ *adj* **1** low in price, costing little money: *Oranges are cheap at the moment.* ○ *It's cheaper to buy a return ticket than two singles.* ❶ The opposite is **expensive**. رخيص

2 charging low prices: *We are looking for a cheap hotel for the night.* رخيص

3 low in price and quality and therefore not attractive مبتذل

▶ **cheap** *adv* (*informal*) for a low price: *I got this coat cheap in the sales.* بسعر رخيص

IDM **be going cheap** (*informal*) to be selling at a low price: *They've got strawberries going cheap at the market.* يباع بسعر رخيص

cheaply *adv* for a low price: *You can travel quickly and cheaply all over the town by bus.* بسعر رخيص

cheat /tʃiːt/ *verb* [I] to act in a dishonest or unfair way in order to get an advantage for yourself: *Len was caught cheating in the exam.* ○ *to cheat at cards* يغش

PHRV **cheat sb (out) of sth** to take sth from sb in a dishonest or unfair way: *They tried to cheat the old lady out of her savings.* يحتال على

▶ **cheat** *noun* [C] a person who cheats غشاش، محتال

check[1] /tʃek/ *verb* **1** [I,T] **check (up)** to examine sth in order to make sure that it is safe, correct, in good condition, etc: *He wasn't sure whether he had locked the door, so he went to check.* ○ *I expect they're coming by car but I'll ring them and check up.* ○ *Check your work through for mistakes before you hand it in.* ○ *Can you check that we've got everything that's on the list?* ○ *She looked in her diary to check what time her appointment was.* يتحقّق (من)

2 [T] to stop or go more slowly; to make sb/sth stop or go more slowly: *A tight bandage should check the flow of blood from a wound.* يتوقّف؛ يوقف؛ يبطئ

3 [T] (*US*) to write a cross on a form, etc., to show your choice: *Check the box next to the right answer.* ➲ Look at **tick**. يضع علامة

PHRV **check in (at...)**; **check into...** to go to a hotel/airline desk and say that you have arrived: *Passengers should check in two hours before their departure time.* يسجّل وصوله في فندق أو في مطار

check sth off to mark names or items on a list: *The boxes were all checked off as they were unloaded.* يضع علامة أمام بنود القائمة

check (up) on sb/sth to find out more information about sb/sth: *The boss is checking up on how much work we've done.* يستعلم سراً

check out (of...) to pay your bill and leave a hotel يدفع الحساب ويغادر الفندق

check sb/sth out 1 to find out if sth is correct, or if sb is acceptable: *The police are checking out his alibi.* يدقّق، يتأكد من

2 (*especially US*) to look at or examine a person or thing that seems interesting or attractive: *Check out the prices at our new store!* ينظر إلى؛ يتفحص

check[2] /tʃek/ *noun* **1** [C] **a check (on sth)** a close look at sth to make sure that it is safe, correct, in good condition, etc: *We do regular checks on our products to make sure that they are of high quality.* ○ *a security check* مراقبة : تدقيق

2 [C] an act of going more slowly or stopping or of making sb/sth go more slowly or stop توقّف : ايقاف ، كبح

3 [sing.] (in the game of chess) the situation in which a player must move to protect his/her king ➲ Look at **checkmate**. (في الشطرنج) كش ملك!

4 [C] (*US*) = CHEQUE

5 [C] (*US*) = BILL[1] (1)

6 [C] (*US*) = TICK[1] (3)

IDM **hold/keep sth in check** to stop sth from advancing or increasing too quickly: *government measures to keep inflation in check* يضبط ، يتحكّم في، يكبح

check[3] /tʃek/ *noun* [C,U] a pattern of squares, often of different colours: *a check jacket* ○ *a pattern of blue and red checks* رسم ذو مربعات ملوّنة

▶ **checked** /tʃekt/ *adj* with a pattern of squares: *a red-and-white checked tablecloth* ذو مربعات

checkbook *noun* [C] (*US*) = CHEQUEBOOK

checkers /ˈtʃekəz/ *noun* [U] (*US*) = DRAUGHTS

ˈcheck-in *noun* [C] **1** the act of checking in at an airport: *Our check-in time is 10.30 am.* تسجيل المسافر عند وصوله إلى المطار

2 the place where you check in at an airport: *the check-in desk* نقطة القيام بإجراءات السفر في المطار

ˈchecking account *noun* [C] (*US*) = CURRENT ACCOUNT

checklist /ˈtʃeklɪst/ *noun* [C] a list of things that you must do or have جدول التحقّق

checkmate /ˈtʃekmeɪt/ (*also* **mate**) *noun* [sing.] (in the game of chess) the situation in which you cannot protect your king and so have lost the game ➲ Look at **check**[2](3). (في الشطرنج) شاه مات!

checkout /ˈtʃekaʊt/ *noun* [C] the place in a supermarket where you pay for the things you have bought نقطة الدفع (في سوبرماركت)

checkpoint /ˈtʃekpɔɪnt/ *noun* [C] a place where all people and vehicles must stop and be checked: *an army checkpoint* نقطة تفتيش

ˈcheck-up *noun* [C] a general medical examination to find out whether you are healthy: *You should visit your dentist for a check-up twice a year.* فحص طبّي (عام)

cheddar /ˈtʃedə(r)/ *noun* [U] a type of hard yellow cheese that can be eaten cooked or raw نوع من الجبن

cheek /tʃiːk/ *noun* **1** [C] one of the two parts of your face that are on each side of your nose and mouth and below your eyes: *Their cheeks were red when they came in out of the cold.* ○ *Tears rolled down her cheeks.* خدّ

2 [U, sing.] (*informal*) rude or impolite behaviour; lack of respect: *What cheek! Asking for my help after saying such horrible things about me.* ○ *He's got a cheek!* سلوك وَقِح ، صفاقة

IDM **(with) tongue in cheek** → TONGUE

▶ **cheeky** *adj* (**cheekier**; **cheekiest**) impolite; not showing respect: *Don't be so cheeky! Of course I'm not fat!* غير مؤدب ، متجرّئ

cheekily *adv* بتجرؤ

cheekbone /ˈtʃiːkbəʊn/ *noun* [C] the bone that is below your eye عظم الوَجْنَة

cheer[1] /tʃɪə(r)/ *verb* **1** [I,T] to shout to show that you like sth or to encourage sb who is taking part in competition, sport, etc: *The crowd clapped and cheered.* ○ *Everyone cheered the winner as he crossed the finishing line.* يهتف ، يشجّع

2 [T] to make sb happy or more hopeful: *They were all cheered by the good news.* يبهج

PHR V **cheer sb on** to cheer (1) sb in order to encourage him/her to do better: *As the runners started the last lap the crowd cheered them on.* يُشجّع ، يهتف له مشجّعاً

cheer (sb/sth) up to become or to make sb happier; to make sth look more attractive: *Cheer up! Things aren't that bad.* ○ *A few pictures would cheer this room up a bit.* يبتهج ؛ يبهج ؛ يزيّن

cheer[2] /tʃɪə(r)/ *noun* [C] a loud shout to show that you like sth or to encourage sb who is taking part in a competition, sport, etc: *Three cheers for the winning team!* (= 'Hip, hip, hurrah' three times) هتاف

cheerful /ˈtʃɪəfl/ *adj* happy: *Tom remained cheerful throughout his illness.* ○ *a cheerful smile* بشوش ، مرح

▶ **cheerfully** /-fəli/ *adv* بابتهاج ، بمرح

cheerfulness *noun* [U] ابتهاج ، بشاشة ، مرح

cheerio /ˌtʃɪəriˈəʊ/ *interj* (*Brit informal*) goodbye إلى اللقاء

cheers /tʃɪəz/ *interj* (*especially Brit informal*) **1** (used to express good wishes before you have a drink): *'Cheers,' she said, raising her glass.* في صحتك!

2 goodbye إلى اللقاء

3 thank you شكراً

cheese /tʃiːz/ *noun* **1** [U] a type of solid food that is made from milk. Cheese is white or yellow in colour: *a simple lunch of bread and cheese* ○ *a cheese sandwich* ○ *Sprinkle the top of the pizza with grated cheese.* جُبن

2 [C] a type of cheese: *a wide selection of cheeses* نوع من الجُبن

cheesecake /ˈtʃiːzkeɪk/ *noun* [C,U] a type of cake that is made from soft cheese and sugar on a pastry or biscuit base كعكة الجبن

cheetah /ˈtʃiːtə/ *noun* [C] a large wild animal of the cat family that comes from Africa and can run very fast فَهْد

chef /ʃef/ *noun* [C] a person who works as the chief cook in a hotel, restaurant, etc. كبير الطهاة

chemical /ˈkemɪkl/ *adj* connected with chemistry; produced by processes that involve changing the structure of a substance: *a chemical reaction* ○ *the chemical industry* ○ *Farmers are using too many chemical fertilizers.* كيميائي أو كيماوي

▶ **chemical** *noun* [C] a substance that is used or produced in a chemical process: *Sulphuric acid is a dangerous chemical.* مادة كيماوية

chemically /-kli/ *adv* كيماوياً

chemist /ˈkemɪst/ *noun* [C] **1** (*also* **pharmacist**) (*US* **druggist**) a person who prepares and sells medicines: *I got my tablets from the chemist's.* ○ *The doctor gave me a prescription to take to the chemist's.* ℹ A chemist's shop usually sells soap, perfume, etc., as well as medicines. صيدليّ

2 a person who is a specialist in chemistry (خبير) كيميائي

chemistry /ˈkemɪstri/ *noun* [U] **1** the scientific study of the structure of substances and what happens to them in different conditions or when mixed with each other: *We did an experiment in the chemistry lesson today.* ○ *a chemistry laboratory* الكيمياء

2 the structure of a particular substance and the way that it may change under different conditions التركيب الكيميائي (للمادة)

chemotherapy /ˌkiːməʊˈθerəpi/ *noun* [U] the treatment of disease, especially cancer, with the use of chemical substances علاج كيميائي

cheque (*US* **check**) /tʃek/ *noun* [C,U] a piece of paper printed by a bank that you can fill in, sign and use to pay for things: *She wrote out a cheque for £20.* ○ *I went to the bank to cash a cheque.* ○ *Can I pay by cheque?* صك أو شيك

chequebook (*US* **ˈcheckbook**) /ˈtʃekbʊk/ *noun* [C] a book of cheques دفتر شيكات

ˈcheque card *noun* [C] (*Brit*) a small plastic card that you get from your bank. A cheque card guarantees that any cheques you write will be paid, up to a certain amount. بطاقة شيكات

cherish /ˈtʃerɪʃ/ *verb* [T] **1** to love sb/sth: *The ring was her most cherished possession.* يعزّ

2 to look after sb/sth carefully يرعى بحنان

3 to keep a thought, feeling, etc. in your mind and think about it often: *a cherished ambition* يكِنّ

cherry /ˈtʃeri/ *noun* [C] (*pl.* **cherries**) **1** a small round black or red fruit that has a stone inside it كَرَز

2 (*also* **ˈcherry tree**) the tree that produces cherries: *a flowering cherry* شجرة الكرَز

cherub /ˈtʃerəb/ *noun* [C] (*pl.* **cherubim** /ˈtʃerəbɪm/, **cherubs**) a beautiful child often shown in religious paintings as having wings and a round face; a small angel ملاك بصورة طفل

chess /tʃes/ *noun* [U] a game for two people that is played on a board with 64 black and white squares (a chessboard). Each player has sixteen pieces which can be moved according to fixed rules. شطرنج

chest /tʃest/ *noun* [C] **1** a container, often a large strong one, that is used for storing or transporting things صندوق كبير

2 the upper part of the front of your body: *What is your chest measurement?* ○ *This jacket is a 40-inch chest.* ○ *to have a hairy chest* ○ *Linda went to the doctor complaining of chest pains.* صدر

IDM **get sth off your chest** (*informal*) to talk about sth that you have been thinking about or that has been worrying you يبوح بما في نفسه

chestnut /ˈtʃesnʌt/ *noun* [C] **1** (*also* **ˈchestnut tree**) a tree with large leaves that produces smooth reddish-brown nuts in prickly shells شجرة الكَستناء

2 one of the nuts from the chestnut tree. You can eat some chestnuts: *roast chestnuts* ➲ Look at **conker**. كَستناء

ˌchest of ˈdrawers (*US* **bureau**) *noun* [C] a piece of furniture with drawers in it that is used for storing clothes, etc. خِزانة ذات أدراج

⚿ **chew** /tʃuː/ *verb* [I,T] to break up food in your mouth with your teeth before you swallow it: *You should chew your food thoroughly.* يمضَغ

ˈchewing gum (*also* **gum**) *noun* [U] a sweet sticky substance that you chew in your mouth but do not swallow لبان ، علكة ، مضغة

chic /ʃiːk/ *adj* fashionable; elegant أنيق

chick /tʃɪk/ *noun* [C] a young bird, especially a young chicken كتكوت ، صوص

⚿ **chicken** /ˈtʃɪkɪn/ *noun* **1** [C] a bird that people often keep for its eggs and its meat فرخة ، دجاجة

2 [U] the meat of this bird: *roast chicken* ○ *cold chicken and salad*

> Notice that chicken is the general word for the bird and its meat. A male chicken is called a **cock** (*US* **rooster**), a female is called a **hen** and a young bird is called a **chick**.

لحم الدجاج

▸ **chicken** *verb*

PHR V **chicken out (of sth)** (*informal*) to decide not to do sth because you are afraid: *He wanted to swim across the river but he chickened out when he saw how far it was.* يجبن ، ينسحب خوفاً

chickenpox /ˈtʃɪkɪnpɒks/ *noun* [U] a disease, especially of children. When you have chickenpox you have a temperature and get red spots on your skin that itch a lot. جدري الماء ، حماق

chickpea /ˈtʃɪkpiː/ *noun* [C] a hard round seed, like a light brown pea, that is cooked and eaten as a vegetable حمص

chicory /ˈtʃɪkəri/ (*US* **endive**) *noun* [U] a plant with slightly bitter-tasting leaves that can be eaten in salads الهندباء البرية

⚿ **chief** /tʃiːf/ *noun* [C] **1** the leader or ruler of a group of people: *African tribal chiefs* ○ *Indian chiefs* زعيم

2 the person who has command or control over an organization: *the chief of police* رئيس

▸ **chief** *adj* (only *before* a noun) **1** most important; main: *One of the chief reasons for his decision was money.* هام ؛ رئيسي

2 of the highest rank: *the chief executive of a company* الأعلى

chiefly *adv* mainly; mostly: *His success was due chiefly to hard work.* بشكل رئيسي ؛ غالباً

chieftain /ˈtʃiːftən/ *noun* [C] the leader of a tribe زعيم قبيلة

chilblain /ˈtʃɪlbleɪn/ *noun* [C] a painful red area on your foot, hand, etc. that can be caused by cold weather تثليج: ورم مؤلم يسببه البرد

⚿ **child** /tʃaɪld/ *noun* [C] (*pl.* **children** /ˈtʃɪldrən/) **1** a boy or girl; a human who is not yet fully grown: *A group of children were playing in the park.* ○ *a six-year-old child* طفل

2 a son or daughter of any age: *She has two children but both are married and have moved away.* ○ *He is married with three children.* ابن ، ابنة

> An **only child** is a child who has no brothers or sisters. People may **adopt** a child who is not their own son or daughter (for example if the child's parents are dead). A **foster child** is looked after for a certain period of time by a family that is not his/her own.

▸ **childhood** /ˈtʃaɪldhʊd/ *noun* [C,U] the time when you are a child: *Harriet had a very unhappy childhood.* ○ *childhood memories* طفولة

childless *adj* having no children: *a childless marriage* بلا ولد ، بلا عَقِب

ˌchild ˈbenefit *noun* [U] (*Brit*) a sum of money that is paid every week by the government to parents for each child that they have علاوة طفل

childbirth /ˈtʃaɪldbɜːθ/ *noun* [U] the act of giving birth to a baby: *His wife died in childbirth.* ولادة

childcare /ˈtʃaɪlkeə(r)/ *noun* [U] the job of looking after children, especially while the parents are at work: *Some employers provide childcare facilities.* خدمة ورعاية الأطفال

childish /ˈtʃaɪldɪʃ/ *adj* like a child طفولي ؛ صبياني

> If you say that people or their behaviour are **childlike**, you mean that they are like children in some way: *childlike innocence* ○ *His childlike enthusiasm delighted us all.* If you say that an adult's behaviour is **childish**, you are criticizing it because you think it is silly and that he/she should be more sensible: *Don't be so childish! You can't always have everything you want.*

▸ **childishly** *adv*: *to giggle childishly* بصبيانية ؛ بصورة سخيفة

childlike /ˈtʃaɪldlaɪk/ *adj* like a child ➲ Look at **childish**. طِفْلي ، بريء كالطفل

childminder /ˈtʃaɪldmaɪndə(r)/ *noun* [C] (*Brit*) a person whose job is to look after a child while his/her parents go out to work راعي أطفال

ˈchildren's home *noun* [C] an institution where children live whose parents cannot look after them مأوى الأطفال

chili (*US*) = CHILLI

chill /tʃɪl/ *noun* **1** [sing.] an unpleasant coldness: *There's a chill in the air.* ○ (*figurative*) *A chill of fear went down my spine.* برد شديد

2 [C] an illness like a cold that is caused by being cold or damp: *to catch a chill* برد ، زكام

▸ **chill** *verb* [I,T] to become or to make sb/sth

colder: *Chill the melon before you serve it.* يبرد ؛ يبرّد

chilling /'tʃɪlɪŋ/ *adj* frightening: *a chilling ghost story* مخيف ، مرعب

chilly /'tʃɪli/ *adj* (**chillier**; **chilliest**) unpleasantly cold: *It's a chilly morning. You need a coat on.* ○ (*figurative*) *a chilly reception* بارد ، فيه قرصة برد

chilli (*US* **chili**) /'tʃɪli/ *noun* [C,U] (*pl.* **chillies**; *US* **chilies**) a small green or red vegetable that has a very strong hot taste: *chilli powder* فليفلة أو فلفل حارّ

chime /tʃaɪm/ *verb* **1** [I] (used about a bell) to ring (الجرس) يدقّ أو يرن

2 [T] (used about a bell or a clock) to show the time by ringing: *The town-hall clock chimed midnight.* يدقّ (معلناً الوقت)

PHRV **chime in (with sth)** (*informal*) to interrupt a conversation and add your own comments يقاطع لإبداء ملاحظة

▸ **chime** *noun* [C] the sound of a bell or a clock chiming رنين الجرس ؛ دقّات الساعة

chimney /'tʃɪmni/ *noun* [C] (*pl.* **chimneys**) the passage through which smoke, etc. can get out of a building. A chimney in a house usually goes up from the fireplace, behind the walls and to a hole in the roof: *The chimney is sooty and needs sweeping.* ○ *Smoke poured out of the factory chimneys.* مَدْخَنة

'**chimney sweep** (*also* **sweep**) *noun* [C] a person whose job is to clean chimneys by sweeping them with long brushes منظّف المداخن

chimpanzee /ˌtʃɪmpæn'ziː/ (*also informal* **chimp**) *noun* [C] a type of small ape that lives in Africa الشمبانزي

chin /tʃɪn/ *noun* [C] the part of your face that is below your mouth: *He sat listening, his chin resting on his hand.* ذَقَن

china /'tʃaɪnə/ *noun* [U] **1** the substance of which cups, plates, etc. can be made. China is made from fine white baked clay: *a china vase* (خزف) الصيني

2 cups, saucers, plates, etc. that are made from china: *We only use the best china when we have visitors.* (آنية) الصيني

chink¹ /tʃɪŋk/ *noun* [C] a small narrow opening صَدْع ، شقّ

chink² /tʃɪŋk/ *verb* [I,T] to make a light ringing sound; to cause this sound, e.g. by knocking two pieces of china or glass together gently يَرِنّ ؛ يجعله يرن

▸ **chink** *noun* [C] رنّة

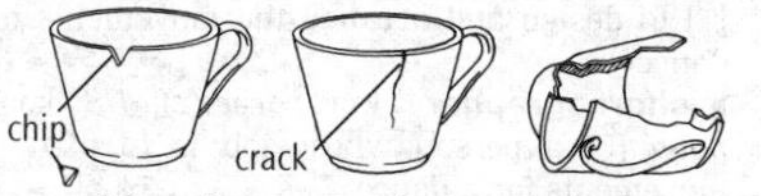

chip¹ /tʃɪp/ *noun* [C] **1** a small piece of wood, stone, glass, etc. that has broken off sth شظيّة ، كسرة

2 a place where a piece has broken off sth: *This dish has a chip in it.* كسْر صغير ، ثَلْم

3 (*US* **French fry**) [usually pl.] a thin piece of potato that is fried in hot fat or oil: *Would you like boiled potatoes or chips?* ○ *fish and chips* أصابع بطاطس مقليّة

4 (*also* **potato chip**) (*US*) = CRISP²

5 a flat round piece of plastic that you use instead of money when you are playing some games فِيشة (في اللعب)

6 = MICROCHIP

IDM **have a chip on your shoulder** (*informal*) to be angry about sth for a long time, especially because you think you have been treated unfairly دائم الشعور بالسخط والظلامة

chip² /tʃɪp/ *verb* [I,T] (**chipping**; **chipped**) to lose or to knock a small piece off the edge or surface of sth: *They chipped the paint trying to get the table through the door.* يقشط ، ينقر ، يثلم

PHRV **chip in (with sth)** (*informal*) **1** to interrupt when sb else is talking يقاطع (حديث شخص آخر)

2 to give some money as part of the cost of sth: *We all chipped in and bought him a present when he left.* يتشارك (في دفع مبلغ)

chiropodist /kɪ'rɒpədɪst/ (*US* **podiatrist**) *noun* [C] a person whose job is to care for people's feet مختص بمعالجة الأقدام

chirp /tʃɜːp/ *noun* [C] the short high sound that a small bird makes زقزقة أو شقشقة (الطائر)

▸ **chirp** *verb* [I] يزقزق أو يشقشق

chisel /'tʃɪzl/ *noun* [C] a tool with a sharp end that is used for cutting or shaping wood, stone, etc. إزميل

chivalry /'ʃɪvəlri/ *noun* [U] behaviour which shows particular respect, usually of men towards women شهامة، تهذيب

▸ **chivalrous** /'ʃɪvlrəs/ *adj* شَهْم ، رفيع الأخلاق

chives /tʃaɪvz/ *noun* [plural] a plant with purple flowers and long thin leaves that are used in cooking. Chives taste similar to onions. ثوم معمّر

chloride /'klɔːraɪd/ *noun* [U] a chemical compound of chlorine and another chemical الكلوريد

chlorine /'klɔːriːn/ *noun* [U] (*symbol* **Cl**) a greenish-yellow gas with a strong smell, that is used for making water safe to drink or to swim in (غاز) الكلور

chock-a-block /ˌtʃɒk ə 'blɒk/ *adj* (not before a noun) completely full: *The High Street was chock-a-block with shoppers.* غاصّ ، مكتظ

chocolate /'tʃɒklət/ *noun* **1** [U] a sweet brown substance that you usually buy in the form of a hard block (bar). Chocolate is made from cocoa beans: *milk chocolate* (= sweet and light in colour) ○ *plain chocolate* (= more bitter and darker in colour) شوكولاتة

2 [C] a small sweet that is made from chocolate with a nut or another sweet substance inside: *a box of chocolates* قطعة شوكولاتة

3 [C,U] a drink made from powdered chocolate

with hot milk or water: *a mug of hot chocolate* مشروب شوكولاتة أو كاكاو

▶ **chocolate** *adj* **1** made from or covered with chocolate: *chocolate cake* ○ *a chocolate biscuit* (مصنوع من أو مغطى بـ) الشوكولاتة

2 dark brown بنّي: لون الشوكولاتة

🔑choice /tʃɔɪs/ *noun* **1** [C] **a choice (between A and B)** an act of choosing between two or more people or things: *to make the right/wrong choice* ○ *David faced a difficult choice between moving house and losing his job.* ○ *You can have first choice of all the cakes* (= you can choose first). اختيار

2 [U] the right or chance to choose: *There was a rail strike so we had no choice but to stay on in Paris.* ○ *to have freedom of choice* خيار

3 [C,U] two or more things from which you can or must choose: *This cinema offers a choice of six different films every night.* ○ *You get more choice of vegetables at the market.* مجموعة يمكن الاختيار منها

4 [C] a person or thing that has been chosen: *What is your choice of colour?* المنتقى ، المختار

IDM **out of/from choice** because you want to; of your own free will: *I wouldn't have gone to America out of choice. I was sent there on business.* عن رغبة ؛ بملء اختياره

▶ **choice** *adj* of very good quality: *choice beef* فاخر ، من أحسن صنف

choir /ˈkwaɪə(r)/ *noun* [C, with sing. or pl. verb] a group of people who sing together: *Dennis sings in the church choir.* ○ *The choir meets/meet on Thursday to rehearse.* جوقة مغنّين

choke /tʃəʊk/ *verb* **1** [I,T] to be or to make sb unable to breathe because sth is stopping air getting into the lungs: *The child swallowed a pen top and choked to death.* ○ *The smoke choked us.* ○ *She was choking on a fish bone.* يختنق ؛ يخنق

2 [T] (usually passive) **choke sth (up) (with sth)** to fill a passage, space, etc., so that nothing can pass through: *The roads to the coast were choked with traffic.* مسدود ؛ يسدّ

PHR V **choke sth back** to hide or control a strong emotion: *to choke back tears* يكبح ، يتماسك عن (البكاء)

▶ **choke** *noun* [C] **1** an act or a sound of choking (1) خنق

2 the piece of equipment in a car, etc. that controls the amount of air going into the engine. If you pull out the choke it makes it easier to start the car. شرّاقة السيارة

cholera /ˈkɒlərə/ *noun* [U] a serious disease that causes diarrhoea and vomiting. Cholera is most common in hot countries and can be carried by water. كوليرا

cholesterol /kəˈlestərɒl/ *noun* [U] a substance that is found in the bodies of people and animals, and that helps to carry fats. Too much cholesterol is thought to be a cause of heart disease: *a high/low level of cholesterol* كوليسترول

🔑choose /tʃuːz/ *verb* [I,T] (*pt* **chose** /tʃəʊz/; *pp* **chosen** /ˈtʃəʊzn/) **1 choose (between A and/or B); choose (A) (from B); choose sb/sth as sth** to pick or select the person or thing that you prefer: *Choose carefully before you make a final decision.* ○ *Amy had to choose between getting a job or going to college.* ○ *You can choose three questions from the five on the exam paper.* ○ *The viewers chose this programme as their favourite.* يختار

2 to decide or prefer to do sth: *You are free to leave whenever you choose.* ○ *They chose to resign rather than work for the new manager.* يقرّر ؛ يفضّل

choosy (*also* **choosey**) /ˈtʃuːzi/ *adj* (**choosier**; **choosiest**) (*informal*) careful in choosing; difficult to please مدقّق في اختياره ؛ صعب الإرضاء

🔑chop¹ /tʃɒp/ *verb* [T] (chopp**ing**; chopp**ed**) **chop sth (up) (into sth)** to cut sth into pieces with an axe or knife: *They chopped the logs up.* ○ *finely chopped herbs* ○ *Chop the onions up into small pieces.* يُقطّع ، يفرم

PHR V **chop sth down** to cut a tree, etc. at the bottom so that it falls down يقطع (بفأس مثلاً)

chop sth off (sth) to remove sth from sth by cutting it with an axe or knife: *to chop a branch off a tree* يقطع

chop² /tʃɒp/ *noun* [C] **1** an act of chopping sth فرم ، تقطيع

2 a thick slice of meat with a piece of bone in it شريحة لحم بعظمها

➲ Look at **steak**.

chop³ /tʃɒp/ *verb* (chopp**ing**; chopp**ed**)

IDM **chop and change** to change your plans or opinions several times يغيّر ويبدّل في آرائه

chopper /ˈtʃɒpə(r)/ *noun* [C] **1** (*informal*) = HELICOPTER

2 a heavy tool that is used for cutting wood, meat, etc. ساطور

choppy /ˈtʃɒpi/ *adj* (**choppier**; **choppiest**) (used about the sea) having a lot of small waves, slightly rough (بحر) مائج نوعاً ما

chopsticks /ˈtʃɒpstɪks/ *noun* [plural] two thin sticks that people in China, Japan, etc. use for picking up food عودا الأكل (عند الصينيين الخ)

choral /ˈkɔːrəl/ *adj* written for or involving a group of singers (a choir) كورالي ، متعلّق بجوقة غنائية

chord /kɔːd/ *noun* [C] two or more musical notes that are played at the same time نغمات متآلفة

IDM **strike a chord** → STRIKE²

chore /tʃɔː(r)/ *noun* [C] a job that is not interesting but that you must do: *household chores* عمل مُسئِم ، شغل روتيني

choreograph /ˈkɒriəɡrɑːf; *US* ˈkɔːriəɡræf/ *verb* [T] to design and arrange the movements of a dance يصمّم حركات الرقص

▶ **choreographer** /ˌkɒriˈɒɡrəfə(r); *US* ˌkɔːri-/ *noun* [C] a person whose job is to plan the movements for a dance مصمّم حركات الرقص

choreography /ˌkɒriˈɒɡrəfi; *US* ˌkɔːri-/ *noun* [U] the arrangement of movements for a dance, especially ballet تصميم حركات الرقص وخاصة الباليه

chorus /ˈkɔːrəs/ *noun* [C] **1** [with sing. or pl. verb] a large group of people who sing together كورس: جوقة غنائية

2 the part of a song that is repeated at the end of each verse: *The audience joined in with the choruses.* لازمة الأغنية

3 a piece of music for a large group to sing قطعة موسيقية تغنيها جوقة كبيرة

4 something that a lot of people say together: *a chorus of cheers, boos, criticism, etc.* هتاف (مثلاً) بصوت واحد

5 [with sing. or pl. verb] a group of singers and dancers in a show: *She was always in the chorus, never a star.* كورس: جماعة المغنين والراقصين

▸ **chorus** *verb* [T] (used about a group of people) to sing or say sth together: *'That's not fair!' the children chorused.* يغنون أو يقولون جماعياً

chose *pt* of CHOOSE

chosen *pp* of CHOOSE

Christ /kraɪst/ (*also* **Jesus**; **Jesus Christ** /ˌdʒiːzəs 'kraɪst/) the man who Christians believe is the son of God and who established the Christian religion المسيح

christen /'krɪsn/ *verb* [T] **1** to give a person, often a child, a name during a Christian ceremony in which he/she is made a member of the Church: *The baby was christened Simon Mark.* ➲ Look at **baptize**. يسمّي (عند التعميد)

2 to give sb/sth a name: *People drive so dangerously on this stretch of road that they've christened it 'The Mad Mile'.* يسمّي

▸ **christening** /'krɪsnɪŋ/ *noun* [C] the church ceremony in which a baby is given a name حفل التعميد

Christian /'krɪstʃən/ *noun* [C] a person whose religion is Christianity: *Christians all over the world will join in prayers for peace today.* (شخص) مسيحي

▸ **Christian** *adj*: *the Christian Church, faith, religion, etc.* مسيحي

Christianity /ˌkrɪsti'ænəti/ *noun* [U] the religion that is based on the teachings of Jesus Christ: *to be converted to Christianity* المسيحيّة

'**Christian name** (*especially US* '**given name**) *noun* [C] the name given to a child when he/she is born; first name ➲ Look at the note at **name**[1]. الاسم (الأول)

Christmas /'krɪsməs/ (*also informal* **Xmas**) *noun* [C,U] the period of time before and after Christmas Day: *We wish you a merry Christmas.* ○ *Where are you spending Christmas this year?* ○ *the Christmas holidays* عيد الميلاد

'**Christmas card** *noun* [C] a card with a picture on the front and a greeting inside that people send to their friends and relatives at Christmas بطاقة عيد الميلاد

ˌ**Christmas 'cracker** *noun* [C] = CRACKER (2)

ˌ**Christmas 'Day** *noun* [C] the day on which Christians celebrate the birth of Christ each year. For most Christians Christmas Day is 25 December. يوم عيد الميلاد

ˌ**Christmas 'dinner** *noun* [C] the traditional meal eaten on Christmas Day, often with roast turkey as the main dish, followed by Christmas pudding عشاء عيد الميلاد

ˌ**Christmas 'Eve** *noun* [C] the day before Christmas Day, 24 December عشية عيد الميلاد

ˌ**Christmas 'pudding** *noun* [C] a sweet made from dried fruit and eaten hot with sauce at Christmas dinner بودنغ عيد الميلاد

'**Christmas tree** *noun* [C] a tree such as a fir, or an artificial tree, which people bring into their homes and decorate with bright lights and coloured balls شجرة عيد الميلاد

chrome /krəʊm/ (*also* **chromium** /'krəʊmiəm/) *noun* [U] a hard shiny metal that is used for covering other metals: *chrome-plated taps* (معدن) الكروم

chromosome /'krəʊməsəʊm/ *noun* [C] the part of the cells of living things that contains the genes الكروموزوم ، الصِّبْغي

chronic /'krɒnɪk/ *adj* (used about a disease or a problem) that continues for a long time: *chronic bronchitis* ○ *There is a chronic shortage of housing in the city.* ➲ Look at **acute**. مزمن

▸ **chronically** /'krɒnɪkli/ *adv* على نحو مزْمن

chronicle /'krɒnɪkl/ *noun* [C] (often plural) a record of events that happened in the past سِجلّ (لأحداث ماضية)

chronological /ˌkrɒnə'lɒdʒɪkl/ *adj* arranged in the order in which the events happened: *This book describes the main events in his life in chronological order.* مرتّب حسب التسلسل الزمني

▸ **chronologically** /-kli/ *adv* طبقاً للتسلسل الزمني

chrysanthemum /krɪ'sænθəməm; krɪ'zæ-/ *noun* [C] a garden plant with brightly coloured flowers أقحوان

chubby /'tʃʌbi/ *adj* (**chubbier**; **chubbiest**) rather fat; round: *chubby cheeks* سمين نوعاً ما، ممتلئ (الخدين)

chuck /tʃʌk/ *verb* [T] (*informal*) **1** to throw sth in a careless way: *Chuck that magazine over here.* ○ *You can chuck those old shoes in the bin.* يلقي بإهمال

2 chuck sth (in) to give sth up: *He's chucked his job in because he was fed up.* يترك ، يستقيل

PHR V **chuck sb out (of sth)** to force sb to leave a place: *They were chucked out of the cinema for making too much noise.* يُخرِج ، يطرد

chuckle /'tʃʌkl/ *verb* [I] to laugh quietly: *Bruce chuckled to himself as he read the letter.* يضحك بصوت خافت

▸ **chuckle** *noun* [C]: *He put down the phone with a chuckle.* ضحكة خافتة

chug /tʃʌg/ *verb* [I] (chu**gg**ing; chu**gg**ed) (used about a machine or engine) to make short repeated knocking sounds while it is working or moving slowly يقرقع

PHR V **chug along, down, up, etc.** to move in a particular direction making this sound: *The train chugged out of the station.* يقرقع في سيره

chum /tʃʌm/ *noun* [C] (*informal, old-fashioned*) a friend صديق

chunk /tʃʌŋk/ *noun* [C] a large or thick piece of sth: *chunks of bread and cheese* قطعة كبيرة

chunky /ˈtʃʌŋki/ *adj* (**chunkier**; **chunkiest**)
1 short and rather fat قصير مائل للسمنة
2 made of thick material or thick pieces: *chunky jewellery* ○ *a chunky sweater* مصنوع من قطع كبيرة ؛ سميك

church /tʃɜːtʃ/ *noun* **1** [C,U] a building where Christians go to pray: *Services are held in this church every Sunday morning at 10.* ○ *They are getting married in the village church.* ○ *the church tower* ○ *Do you go to church regularly?* كنيسة

Notice that when you are talking about going to a ceremony (a service) in a church you say 'in church', 'to church' or 'at church' without '**a**' or '**the**': *Was Mrs Stevens at church today?*

2 Church [C] a particular group of Christians: *the Anglican, Catholic, Methodist, etc. Church* كنيسة ، طائفة مسيحيّة

churchgoer /ˈtʃɜːtʃɡəʊə(r)/ *noun* [C] a person who goes to church regularly المواظب على الكنيسة

the ˌChurch of ˈEngland *noun* [sing.] the Protestant Church which is the official church in England ➲ Look at **Anglican**. الكنيسة الأنكليكانية

churchyard /ˈtʃɜːtʃjɑːd/ *noun* [C] the area of land that is around a church ➲ Look at **cemetery** and **graveyard**. مقبرة حول الكنيسة

churn /tʃɜːn/ *verb* **1** [T] to beat milk or cream so that it turns into butter يمخض اللبن (الحليب)
2 [I,T] **churn (sth) (up)** to move, or to make sth move with great force: *The motor boat churned up the water of the lake.* ينخض أو يخضّ بعنف
PHRV **churn sth out** (*informal*) to produce large numbers of sth very quickly: *Modern factories can churn out cars at an amazing speed.* ينتج بغزارة

chute /ʃuːt/ *noun* [C] a passage down which you can drop or slide things, so that you do not have to carry them: *a laundry chute* مِزلقة (للنفايات مثلاً)

chutney /ˈtʃʌtni/ *noun* [U] a thick sweet sauce that is made from fruit or vegetables with sugar, vinegar and spices. You eat chutney cold with cheese or meat. نوع من الصلصة والمخلّلات الحارة

CIA /ˌsiː aɪ ˈeɪ/ *abbrev* (*US*) Central Intelligence Agency; the US government organization that tries to discover political and military information about other countries وكالة المخابرات المركزية الامريكية

cider /ˈsaɪdə(r)/ *noun* [U] an alcoholic drink that is made from apples مشروب كحولي من التفاح

cigar /sɪˈɡɑː(r)/ *noun* [C] a roll of dried tobacco leaves that people smoke. Cigars are larger and more expensive than cigarettes: *cigar smoke* سيجار

cigarette /ˌsɪɡəˈret; US ˈsɪɡərət/ *noun* [C] a roll of tobacco in a tube of thin white paper that people smoke: *a packet of cigarettes* ○ *to smoke a cigarette* ○ *She lit another cigarette.* ○ *John put out his cigarette.* سيجارة

cigaˈrette lighter (*also* **lighter**) *noun* [C] an object which produces a small flame for lighting cigarettes and cigars ولاّعة أو قدّاحة

cinder /ˈsɪndə(r)/ *noun* [C] a very small piece of coal, wood, etc. that has been burning and may still be hot جمْرة غير تامة الإنطفاء

cinema /ˈsɪnəmə; US ˈsɪnəmə/ *noun* (*US also* **the movies**) **1** [C] a place where you go to see a film: *Let's go to the cinema this evening* (= go and see a film). ○ *What's on at the cinema this week?* سينما

In American English, you use **movie theater** to talk about the building where films are shown: *There are five movie theaters in this town* but **the movies** when you are talking about going to see a film there: *Let's go to the movies this evening.*

2 [U] films in general: *Are you interested in cinema?* السينما

cinnamon /ˈsɪnəmən/ *noun* [U] a brown powder that is used for giving flavour to sweet food قرْفة

circa /ˈsɜːkə/ *prep* (*abbr* **c**) (*formal*) (used with dates) about: *The vase was made circa 600 AD.* حوالى (تاريخ معين)

circle /ˈsɜːkl/ *noun* **1** [C] a line which curves round to form the shape of a ring. Every point on the line is the same distance from the centre: *The children were drawing circles and squares on a piece of paper.* ○ *We all stood in a circle and held hands.* دائرة ، حَلقة
2 [C] a flat, round area: *She cut out a circle of paper.* دائرة
3 [C] a group of people who are friends, or who have the same interest or profession: *He has a large circle of friends.* ○ *Her name was well known in artistic circles.* دائرة ، وَسط
4 [sing.] an area of seats that is upstairs in a cinema, theatre, etc: *We've booked seats in the front row of the circle.* الشرْفة (في السينما أو المسرح الخ)
IDM **a vicious circle** → VICIOUS
▸ **circle** *verb* **1** [I,T] to move, or to move round sth, in a circle, especially in the air: *The plane circled the town several times before it landed.* يحلّق حول ، يحوّم
2 [T] to draw a circle round sth, e.g. on an examination paper: *There are three possible answers to each question. Please circle the correct one.* يرسم دائرة (حول شيء)

circuit /ˈsɜːkɪt/ *noun* [C] **1** a complete circular path that an electric current can flow around دارة أو دائرة كهربائيّة
2 a number of competitions or other events that take place every year in a particular sport. People often take part in all the events, moving round from place to place: *She's one of the best players on the tennis circuit.* نشاط (رياضي) دوري

3 a circular journey round sth: *The cars have to complete ten circuits of the track.* جولة حول

circular /ˈsɜːkjələ(r)/ *adj* **1** round and flat; shaped like a circle: *a circular table* دائري ، مستدير

2 (used about a journey, etc.) going round in a circle: *The bus will take you on a circular tour of Oxford.* دائري ، (جولة) حول

3 (used about a theory, etc.) using the point it is trying to prove as evidence for its conclusion (نظرية) دائرية

▶ **circular** *noun* [C] a printed letter, notice or advertisement that is sent to a large number of people تعميم ، منشور

circulate /ˈsɜːkjəleɪt/ *verb* [I,T] **1** to go from one person to another; to pass information from one person to another: *Stories were circulating about the Minister's private life.* ○ *We've circulated a copy of the report to each department.* ينتشر ، تتناقله الألسن ؛ يوزِّع

2 (used about a substance) to move or make sth move round continuously: *Blood circulates round the body.* يدور ؛ يدوِّر

circulation /ˌsɜːkjəˈleɪʃn/ *noun* **1** [U] the passing of sth from one person or place to another: *the circulation of news, information, rumours, etc.* ○ *Old five pence coins are no longer in circulation* (= being used by people). دوران ؛ تداول

2 [C] the number of copies of a newspaper, magazine, etc. that are sold each time it is produced: *This newspaper has a circulation of over a million.* عدد النسخ التي تبيعها صحيفة مثلاً

3 [sing.] the movement of blood around the body: *If you have bad circulation, your hands and feet get cold easily.* الدورة الدموية

circumcise /ˈsɜːkəmsaɪz/ *verb* [T] to cut off the skin at the end of a man's penis, for religious or medical reasons يختِن

▶ **circumcision** /ˌsɜːkəmˈsɪʒn/ *noun* [C,U] ختان

circumference /səˈkʌmfərəns/ *noun* [C,U] the distance round a circle or sth circular: *The circumference of the Earth is about 40 000 kilometres.* ○ *The Earth is about 40 000 kilometres in circumference.* محيط الدائرة

⚷**circumstance** /ˈsɜːkəmstəns/ *noun* **1** [C, usually pl.] the facts and events that affect what happens in a particular situation: *We need to know the exact circumstances surrounding the accident.* ○ *In normal circumstances I would not have accepted the job, but at that time I had very little money.* حالة ، ظرف

2 circumstances [plural] (*formal*) the amount of money that you have: *The company has promised to repay the money when its financial circumstances improve.* الوضع المالي

IDM **in/under no circumstances** never, for any reason: *You must in no circumstances mention this subject again.* مهما تكن الظروف

in/under the circumstances as the result of a particular situation: *My father was very ill at that time, so under the circumstances I decided not to apply for the job.* ○ *Well, it's not an ideal solution, but it's the best we can do in the circumstances.* في تلك الظروف

circumstantial /ˌsɜːkəmˈstænʃl/ *adj* (used in connection with the law) containing details and information that strongly suggest sth is true but are not actual proof of it: *circumstantial evidence* ظرفيّ، عرَضي

circus /ˈsɜːkəs/ *noun* [C] a show performed in a large tent by a company of people and animals: *We saw clowns, acrobats, lions and elephants at the circus.* سيرك

cistern /ˈsɪstən/ *noun* [C] a tank for water, especially one that is connected to a toilet صِهْريج

cite /saɪt/ *verb* [T] (*formal*) to mention sth as an example to support what you are saying: *She cited the high unemployment figures as an example of the Government's bad management.* يستشهد بـ ، يذكر

⚷**citizen** /ˈsɪtɪzn/ *noun* [C] **1** a person who is legally accepted as a member of a particular country: *a British citizen* ○ *She was born in Japan, but became an American citizen in 1981.* مواطن

2 a person who lives in a town or city: *Many of the citizens of Paris leave the town for the seaside during the summer.* ➲ Look at **senior citizen**. ساكن (مدينة)

▶ **citizenship** *noun* [U] the state of being a citizen of a particular country: *After living in Spain for twenty years, he decided to apply for Spanish citizenship.* جِنْسية

citrus fruit /ˈsɪtrəs fruːt/ *noun* [C,U] a fruit such as an orange or lemon فاكهة حَمضيّة

⚷**city** /ˈsɪti/ *noun* (*pl.* **cities**) **1** [C] a large and important town: *Venice is one of the most beautiful cities in the world.* ○ *Tokyo is the capital city of Japan.* ○ *Many people are worried about housing conditions in Britain's inner cities* (= the central parts where there are often social problems). ○ *the city centre* مدينة

2 the City [sing.] the oldest part of London, which is now Britain's financial centre: *She works in a bank in the City.* مركز لندن المالي

civic /ˈsɪvɪk/ *adj* of a city or town: *civic pride* (= feeling proud because you belong to a particular town or city) ○ *Guildford Civic Centre* مَدينيّ، مدنيّ

civil[1] /ˈsɪvl/ *adj* polite, but not very friendly: *I know you don't like the director, but do try and be civil to him.* مهذّب

▶ **civilly** /ˈsɪvəli/ *adv* بأدب

⚷**civil**[2] /ˈsɪvl/ *adj* **1** (only *before* a noun) connected with the state, not with the army or the Church: *civil aviation* ○ *civil engineering* (= the designing and building of roads, railways, bridges, etc.) ○ *a civil wedding* (= not a religious one) مَدَني

2 (in law) relating to the rights of ordinary people, and not criminal offences: *civil courts* مَدَني

civilian /səˈvɪliən/ *noun* [C] a person who is not

in the army, navy, air force or police force: *Two soldiers and one civilian were killed when the bomb exploded.* ○ *He left the army and returned to civilian life.* مدني

civilization (*also* **civilisation**) /ˌsɪvəlaɪˈzeɪʃn; *US* -ələˈz-/ *noun* **1** [C,U] a society which has its own highly developed culture and way of life: *the civilizations of ancient Greece and Rome* ○ *Western civilization* حضارة

2 [U] an advanced state of social and cultural development, or the process of reaching this state: *China had reached a higher level of civilization than Europe at that time.* ○ *The civilization of the human race has taken thousands of years.* حضارة ، مدنيّة

civilize (*also* **civilise**) /ˈsɪvəlaɪz/ *verb* [T] to make people or a society develop from a low social and cultural level to a more advanced one يحضِّر ، يمدِّن

▸ **civilized** (*also* **civilised**) /ˈsɪvəlaɪzd/ *adj* **1** (used about a society) having a high level of social and cultural development: *In a civilized society there should not be people sleeping on the streets.* متحضِّر ، متمدِّن

2 polite and reasonable: *a civilized conversation* مهذَّب ؛ معقول

civilly *adv* → CIVIL[1]

ˌ**civil ˈrights** (*also* ˌ**civil ˈliberties**) *noun* [plural] a citizen's legal right to freedom and equality whatever his/her sex, race or religion حقوق مدنيّة

ˌ**civil ˈservant** *noun* [C] a person who works in the Civil Service موظف مدني

the ˌ**Civil ˈService** *noun* [sing.] all the government departments (except for the armed forces) and all the people who work in them دوائر الحكومة وموظفوها

ˌ**civil ˈwar** *noun* [C,U] a war between different groups of people who live in the same country حرب أهلية

CJD /ˌsiː dʒeɪ ˈdiː/ *abbrev* Creutzfeldt-Jakob disease; a disease of the brain caused by eating infected meat مرض كرويتسفلت جاكوب

cl *abbrev* (*pl.* **cl** or **cls**) = CENTILITRE(S)

clad /klæd/ *adj* (not before a noun) (*old-fashioned, formal*) dressed: *The children were warmly clad in coats, hats and scarves.* لابس ، مرتدٍ

⚷ **claim[1]** /kleɪm/ *verb* **1** [T] to say that sth is true, without having any proof: *The bus driver claimed that she had not seen the cyclist.* ○ *Colin claims the book belongs to him.* ○ *The woman claims to be the oldest person in Britain.* ○ *No one has claimed responsibility for the bomb attack.* يدّعي

2 [I,T] **claim (for sth)** to ask for sth because you think you should have it or that it belongs to you: *The police are keeping the animal until somebody claims it.* ○ *If you are disabled you can claim a special allowance from the Government.* ○ *Don't forget to claim for your travel expenses when you get back.* يطالب بـ

3 [T] (*formal*) to cause death: *The earthquake claimed thousands of lives.* يتسبب في قتل

⚷ **claim[2]** /kleɪm/ *noun* [C] **1** a statement that sth is true, that does not have any proof: *I do not believe the Government's claim that they can reduce unemployment by the end of the year.* ادِّعاء

2 claim (for sth) a demand for sth that you think you have a right to: *to make an insurance claim* ○ *After the accident he decided to put in a claim for compensation.* ○ *a pay claim* طلب (تعويض مثلاً)

3 claim (to sth) the right to have sth: *You will have to prove your claim to the property in a court of law.* حقّ (المطالبة بشيء) ، حقّ الملكية

IDM stake a/your claim → STAKE[1]

claimant /ˈkleɪmənt/ *noun* [C] a person who believes he/she has the right to have sth: *The insurance company refused to pay the claimant any money.* المطالب، المدّعي

clairvoyant /kleəˈvɔɪənt/ *noun* [C] a person who some people believe has special mental powers and can see what will happen in the future منجِّم، كاشف الغيب، بصّار

clam[1] /klæm/ *noun* [C] a type of shellfish سمك صَدَفي

clam[2] /klæm/ *verb* (clamming; clammed)

PHRV clam up (*informal*) to stop talking and refuse to speak: *She always clams up when I ask her about her past.* يمتنع عن الكلام ، يصمت؛ يحرس

clamber /ˈklæmbə(r)/ *verb* [I] to climb with difficulty, usually using both your hands and feet: *She managed to clamber up the hillside.* يتسلّق بصعوبة

clammy /ˈklæmi/ *adj* (**clammier**; **clammiest**) damp and sticky: *clammy hands* رطب ودَبِق

clamour (*US* **clamor**) /ˈklæmə(r)/ *verb* [I] **clamour for sth** to demand sth in a loud or angry way: *The public are clamouring for an answer to all these questions.* يضجّ بالطلب ، يطالب بغضب

▸ **clamour** (*US* **clamor** /ˈklæmə(r)/) *noun* [sing.]: *We could hear the clamour of angry voices.* ضجيج ، صخب

clamp /klæmp/ *noun* [C] **1** a tool that you use for holding two things together very tightly ملزمة ، مضبَّة

2 (*also* **wheel clamp**) (*Brit*) a metal object that is fixed to the wheel of a car that has been parked illegally, so that it cannot drive away مضبَّة الاطارات

▸ **clamp** *verb* [T] **1** to fasten two things together with a clamp: *The metal rods were clamped together.* ○ *Clamp the wood to the table so that it doesn't move.* يشدّ بملزمة ، يضبّ

2 to put or hold sth very firmly in a particular place: *He kept his pipe clamped between his teeth.* يثبّت ، يضغط (على)

3 (*also* **wheelclamp**) to attach a metal object to the wheel of a vehicle that has been parked in an illegal place, so that it cannot move: *Oh no! My car's been clamped.* يثبّت (سيارة بملزمة)

PHRV clamp down on sb/sth (*informal*) to

take strong action against sb/sth in order to stop or control sth: *The police are clamping down on people who drink and drive.* يضيّق الخناق على ، يشدِّد على

clampdown /ˈklæmpdaʊn/ *noun*: *a clampdown on tax evasion* قمع ، إجراء صارم

clan /klæn/ *noun* [C, with sing. or pl. verb] a group of families who are related to each other, especially in Scotland عشيرة

clandestine /klænˈdestɪn/ *adj* (*formal*) secret and often not legal سرّي

clang /klæŋ/ *noun* [C] a loud ringing sound that is made when a metal object hits sth: *The huge metal door closed with a clang.* رنين ، ضجيج

▸ **clang** *verb* [I,T] to make or cause sth to make this sound يرن ، يضج

clank /klæŋk/ *noun* [C] a loud sound that is made when a metal object (e.g. a heavy chain) hits sth قعقعة ، صلصلة

▸ **clank** *verb* [I,T] to make or cause sth to make this sound يقعقع ، يصلصل

⚷**clap** /klæp/ *verb* (clap**p**ing; clap**p**ed) **1** [I,T] to put your hands together quickly in order to make a loud sound, usually to show that you like sth: *The audience clapped as soon as the singer walked onto the stage.* ○ *Everybody was clapping their hands in time to the music.* يصفّق

2 [T] to put sth onto sth quickly and firmly: *'Oh no, I shouldn't have said that,' she said, clapping a hand over her mouth.* يصفق

▸ **clap** *noun* [C] **1** an act of clapping: *Let's have a big clap for our next performer!* تصفيق

2 a sudden loud noise of thunder: *a clap of thunder* قصفة رعد

clarify /ˈklærəfaɪ/ *verb* [T] (*pres part* **clarifying**; *3rd pers sing pres* **clarifies**; *pt, pp* **clarified**) to make sth become clear and easier to understand: *I hope that what I say will clarify the situation.* يوضّح

▸ **clarification** /ˌklærɪfɪˈkeɪʃn/ *noun* [U]: *We'd like some clarification of exactly what your company intends to do.* توضيح

clarinet /ˌklærəˈnet/ *noun* [C] a musical instrument that is made of wood. You play a clarinet by blowing through it. كلارينت ، مِزمار

clarity /ˈklærəti/ *noun* [U] the quality of being clear and easy to understand: *clarity of expression* وضوح

clash /klæʃ/ *verb* **1** [I] **clash (with sb) (over sth)** to fight or disagree seriously about sth: *A group of demonstrators clashed with police outside the Town Hall.* ○ *Conservative and Labour politicians have clashed again over defence cuts.* يصطدم (مع) ، يشتبك

2 [I] **clash (with sth)** (used about two events) to happen at the same time: *It's a pity the two concerts clash. I wanted to go to both of them.* يتضارب (مع)

3 [I] **clash (with sth)** (used about colours, etc.) not to match or look nice together: *I don't think you should wear that tie – it clashes with your shirt.* يتنافر

4 [I,T] (used about two metal objects) to hit together with a loud noise; to cause two metal objects to do this: *Their swords clashed.* يصطدم محدثاً صليلاً : يجعله يصل

▸ **clash** *noun* [C] **1** a fight or serious disagreement: *a clash between police and demonstrators* اصطدام ، اشتباك

2 a big difference: *a clash of opinions* ○ *There was a personality clash between the two men.* تضارب

3 a loud noise, made by two metal objects hitting each other: *the clash of cymbals* قعقعة ، صليل

clasp[1] /klɑːsp; *US* klæsp/ *noun* [C] an object, usually of metal, which fastens or holds sth together: *the clasp on a necklace, brooch, handbag, etc.* مِشبك

clasp[2] /klɑːsp; *US* klæsp/ *verb* [T] to hold sb/sth tightly: *She was clasping a knife.* ○ *Kevin clasped the child in his arms.* يقبض (على) : يضم

⚷**class** /klɑːs; *US* klæs/ *noun* **1** [C] a group of pupils or students who are taught together: *Jane and I are in the same class at school.* ❶ In the singular **class** can be used with either a singular or a plural verb: *The whole class is/are going to the theatre tonight.* فصل أو صف (في مدرسة)

2 [C,U] a lesson: *Classes begin at 9 o'clock in the morning.* ○ *I go to evening classes in local history on Wednesdays.* ○ *We watched an interesting video in class* (= during the lesson) *yesterday.* درس

3 [U] the way people are divided into social groups: *The idea of class still divides British society.* ○ *class differences* الطبقية ، النظام الطبقي

4 [C,U] a group of people who are at the same social and economic level: *the working/middle/upper class* ❶ In the singular **class** can be used with either a singular or a plural verb. طبقة (اجتماعية)

5 [C] a group of things of a similar type: *There are several different classes of insects.* صنف

6 [U] (*informal*) high quality or style: *Pele was a football player of great class.* رتبة ، مقام

7 [C] (especially in compounds) of a certain level of quality or comfort: *a first-class compartment on a train* درجة

8 [C] (*Brit*) (especially in compounds) a grade that you get when you pass your final university examination: *a first-/second-/third-class degree* مرتبة ، درجة

▸ **class** *verb* [T] **class sb/sth (as sth)** to put sb/sth in a particular group or type: *The house has recently been classed as a 'historic building'.* يصنِّف

classy /ˈklɑːsi; *US* ˈklæsi/ *adj* (**classier**; **classiest**) (*informal*) of high quality or style; expensive: *She took me to a classy restaurant in Soho.* راقٍ ؛ غالٍ

⚷**classic** /ˈklæsɪk/ *adj* **1** typical: *This painting is a classic example of the French Impressionist style.*

○ *It was a classic case of bad management.* نموذجي

2 (used about a book, play, etc.) important and having a value that will last: *the classic film 'Gone With The Wind'* كلاسيكي، (أثر) خالد

▸ **classic** *noun* **1** [C] a famous book, play, etc. which has a value that will last: *All of Charles Dickens' novels are classics.* أثر أدبي خالد

2 Classics [U] the study of ancient Greek and Roman language and literature دراسة اليونانية واللاتينية وآدابهما

classical /'klæsɪkl/ *adj* **1** (used about music) serious and having a value that lasts: *I prefer classical music to pop or jazz.* (موسيقى) كلاسيكية

2 traditional, not modern: *classical ballet* ○ *classical scientific methods* تقليدي

3 relating to ancient Greece or Rome: *classical architecture* متعلّق باليونان أو روما القديمتين

▸ **classically** /'klæsɪkəli/ *adv* (مؤهّل) كلاسيكياً

ˌclassified adˈvertisements (*also* (*Brit informal*) **classified ads**; **small ads**) *noun* [plural] small advertisements that you put in a newspaper if you want to buy or sell sth, employ sb, find a flat, etc. إعلان صغير مبوب

classify /'klæsɪfaɪ/ *verb* [T] (*pres part* **classifying**; *3rd pers sing pres* **classifies**; *pt, pp* **classified**) **classify sb/sth (as sth)** to put sb/sth into a group with other people or things of a similar type: *The books in a library are usually classified according to subject.* يصنّف ، يرتّب

▸ **classification** /ˌklæsɪfɪ'keɪʃn/ *noun* [C,U]: *His job involves the classification of the different species of butterfly.* تصنيف

classified *adj* officially secret: *classified information* سري

classmate /'klɑːsmeɪt; *US* 'klæs-/ *noun* [C] a person who is in the same class as you at school or college زميل في الصفّ أو الفصل

classroom /'klɑːsruːm; -rʊm; *US* 'klæs-/ *noun* [C] a room in a school, college, etc. where classes are taught غرفة التدريس ، صفّ أو فصْل

clatter /'klætə(r)/ *noun* [sing.] a series of short loud repeated sounds that is made when hard objects hit against each other: *the clatter of knives and forks* قرقعة ، طقطقة

▸ **clatter** *verb* [I,T] to make or cause sth to make this noise: *The horses clattered down the street.* يقرقع ، يطقطق

clause /klɔːz/ *noun* [C] **1** a paragraph in a legal document فقرة (في قانون)

2 (*grammar*) a group of words that includes a subject and a verb. A clause is usually only part of a sentence: *The sentence, 'After we had finished eating, we watched a video' contains two clauses.* شبه جملة

claustrophobia /ˌklɔːstrə'fəʊbiə/ *noun* [U] great fear of being in a small or closed space الخوف من الأماكن المغلقة

▸ **claustrophobic** /ˌklɔːstrə'fəʊbɪk/ *adj* **1** afraid in this way: *I always feel claustrophobic in lifts.* خائف من الأماكن المغلقة

2 (used about sth that makes you feel afraid in this way): *a claustrophobic little room* مسبّب للضيق والخوف

claw /klɔː/ *noun* [C] **1** one of the pointed nails on the feet of some animals and birds: *Cats have sharp claws.* مِخلب

2 the part of a leg on some types of insects and sea animals which they use for holding things كلّابة

clay /kleɪ/ *noun* [U] heavy earth that is soft when it is wet and becomes hard when it is baked or dried: *The students were modelling heads out of clay.* ○ *clay pots* طين الفخّار ، صلصال

clean[1] /kliːn/ *adj* **1** not dirty: *The whole house was beautifully clean.* ○ *Are your hands clean?* ○ *I think I'll change into some clean clothes.* نظيف

2 (used about animals and people) having clean habits: *Cats are very clean animals.* محبّ للنظافة

3 (used about humour) not about sex, etc.; not dirty: *a clean joke* غير بذيء

4 having no record of offences: *a clean driving licence* خالٍ من المخالفات

5 not owning or carrying anything illegal such as drugs or weapons: *The police searched her but she was clean.* لايحمل الممنوعات

IDM **a clean sweep** a complete victory in a sports competition, election, etc. that you get by winning all the different parts of it: *The Russians made a clean sweep of all the gymnastics events.* انتصار كامل

▸ **clean** *adv* (*informal*) completely: *The lorry went clean through the wall.* ○ *I clean forgot it was your birthday.* تماماً

IDM **come clean (with sb) (about sth)** (*informal*) to tell the truth about sth that you have been keeping secret: *She decided to come clean with them about the mistake she had made.* يكشِف (الحقيقة) ، يعترف

clean[2] /kliːn/ *verb* **1** [T] to remove dirt and marks from sth: *to clean the house, the windows, the kitchen floor, etc.* ○ *Don't forget to clean your teeth!* ○ *Oh dear, my shoes need cleaning.* ينظّف

> **Clean** is a general word for removing dirt from something. If you **wash** something you clean it with water and often soap. You can **wipe** a surface by rubbing it with a wet cloth; you **dust** a surface by rubbing it with a dry cloth. If you **brush** something you clean it with a brush that has a short handle; if you **sweep** the floor you use a brush with a long handle.

2 [I] to make the inside of a house, office, etc. free from dust and dirt: *Mr Burrows comes in to clean after office hours.* ينظّف البيت

PHR V **clean sth out** to clean the inside of sth thoroughly: *I'm going to clean out all the kitchen cupboards next week.* ينظّف (داخل الشيء) نظافة تامة

clean (sth) up 1 to remove all the dirt from a place that is particularly dirty: *I'm going to clean up the kitchen before Mum and Dad get back.* ينظّف (مكاناً قذراً)

2 to remove sth that has just been spilled: *Oh no,*

you've spilt coffee on the new carpet! Can you clean it up? يزيل أو ينظّف (بسرعة)

cleaner /'kli:nə(r)/ *noun* **1** [C] a person whose job is to clean the rooms and furniture inside a house or other building: *an office cleaner* المنظّف

2 [C] a substance or an instrument that you use for cleaning sth: *liquid floor cleaners* ○ *a carpet cleaner* ➲ Look at **vacuum cleaner**. (مادة أو أداة) منظّفة

3 cleaner's = DRY-CLEANER'S: *Could you take my coat to the cleaner's?*

cleanliness /'klenlinəs/ *noun* [U] being clean: *High standards of cleanliness are extremely important in a hotel kitchen.* نظافة

cleanly /'kli:nli/ *adv* easily or smoothly: *The knife cut cleanly through the rope.* بسهولة ، بيسر

cleanse /klenz/ *verb* [T] to make sth thoroughly clean: *to cleanse a cut* ينظّف (نظافة تامة) ؛ يطهّر

▸ **cleanser** *noun* [C] a substance that you use for cleaning sth, especially your skin مادة منظّفة (للبشرة)

ˌclean-'shaven *adj* (used about men) not having a beard or a moustache حليق: بلا لحية أو شارب

clear[1] /klɪə(r)/ *adj* **1** easy to see through: *clear glass* ○ *The water was so clear that we could see the bottom of the lake.* شفّاف

2 easy to see, hear or understand: *We get a very clear picture on our new television.* ○ *His voice wasn't very clear on the telephone.* ○ *She gave me clear directions on how to get there.* واضح

3 free from marks: *a clear sky* (= without clouds) ○ *a clear skin* (= without spots) خالٍ (من الغيوم أو الشوائب الخ) ، صافٍ

4 free from things that are blocking the way: *The police say that most roads are now clear of snow.* خالٍ من العوائق ، سالك

5 clear (to sb) easy to see; obvious: *There are clear advantages to the second plan.* ○ *It was clear to me that he was not telling the truth.* ○ *The answer to the problem is quite clear.* واضح

6 clear (about/on sth) sure or definite; without any doubts: *I'm not quite clear about the arrangements for tomorrow.* متأكّد

7 not confused: *Clear thinking is very important in this job.* ○ *We need to get a clear understanding of the situation.* واضح ، غير متشوّش

8 free from guilt: *It wasn't your fault. You can have a completely clear conscience.* صافٍ ، مرتاح

IDM make yourself clear; make sth clear/plain (to sb) to speak so that there can be no doubt about what you mean: *'I do not want you to go to that concert,' said my mother. 'Do I make myself clear?'* ○ *He made it quite clear that he was not happy with the decision.* يوضّح توضيحاً تاماً

▸ **clearly** *adv* **1** in a way that is easy to see, hear or understand: *It was so foggy that we couldn't see the road clearly.* بوضوح

2 in a way that is not confused: *I'm so tired that I can't think clearly.* بوضوح ، بصفاء

3 obviously; without doubt: *She clearly doesn't want to speak to you any more.* من الواضح ؛ بلا شك

clear[2] /klɪə(r)/ *adv* **1** = CLEARLY (1): *We can hear the telephone loud and clear from here.*

2 clear (of sth) away from sth; not touching sth: *Stand clear of the doors* (= on a train). بعيداً عن (شيء)

IDM keep/stay/steer clear (of sb/sth) to avoid sb/sth: *It's best to keep clear of the town centre during the rush hour.* يتجنّب

clear[3] /klɪə(r)/ *verb* **1** [T] to remove sth that is not wanted or needed: *to clear the roads of snow/to clear snow from the roads.* ○ *It's your turn to clear the table* (= to take away the dirty plates, etc. after a meal). ○ *Shall I help you clear away the plates?* يزيل ؛ ينظّف ، يرفع الصحون عن المائدة

2 [I] (used about fog, smoke, etc.) disappear: *The fog slowly cleared and the sun came out.* ينقشع

3 [I] (used about the sky, the weather or water) to become free of clouds, rain, or mud: *After a cloudy start, the weather will clear during the afternoon.* يصفو

4 [T] to jump over or get past sth without touching it: *The horse cleared the first jump but knocked down the second.* يثب (فوق شيء) دون مسّه

5 [T] to give permission for sth to happen: *At last the plane was cleared for take-off.* يأذن ، يسمح

6 [I] (used about a cheque) to go through the system that transfers money from one account to another: *The cheque will take three days to clear.* يتمّ تسديده

7 [T] **clear sb (of sth)** to prove that sb is not guilty of a crime or mistake: *The man has finally been cleared of murder.* يبرئ

IDM clear the air to remove tension by talking openly about worries, doubts, etc: *I'm sure if you discuss your feelings with her it will help to clear the air between you.* ينقّي الجو

clear your throat to cough slightly in order to make it easier to speak: *He cleared his throat and then began his speech.* يتنحنح

PHR V clear off (*informal*) (used especially as an order) to go away: *'Clear off,' shouted the farmer, 'you're on my land!'* ينصرف

clear sth out to tidy sth and throw away things that you do not want: *I really must clear out the kitchen cupboards.* يرتّب و يرمي ما لا يحتاج إليه

clear up (used about the weather or an illness) to get better: *We can go out for a walk if it clears up later on.* ○ *The doctor told him to stay at home until his cold cleared up.* يصحو؛ يزول

clear (sth) up to make sth tidy: *Make sure you clear up properly before you leave.* يرتّب (المكان)

clear sth up to find the solution to a problem, mystery, etc: *There's been a slight misunderstanding but we've cleared it up now.* يحلّ (مشكلة أو لغزاً الخ)

clearance /'klɪərəns/ *noun* [U] **1** the removing of sth that is old or not wanted: *slum clearance* ○ *The shop is having a clearance sale* (= selling things cheaply in order to get rid of them). إزالة ، تخلّص ؛ تصفية

2 the distance between an object and something that is passing under or beside it, e.g. a ship or vehicle: *There was not enough clearance for the bus to pass under the bridge safely.* فسحة مرور

a b c d e f g h i j k l m n o p q r s t u v w x y z

3 official permission for sb/sth to do sth: *clearance to work at the nuclear research establishment* تصريح رسمي

ˌclear-ˈcut *adj* definite and easy to see or understand: *It was a clear-cut case of police corruption.* قاطع ، واضح المعالم

ˌclear-ˈheaded *adj* able to think clearly, especially if there is a problem صافي الذهن

clearing /ˈklɪərɪŋ/ *noun* [C] a small area without trees in the middle of a wood or forest رقْعَة صغيرة بلا شجر

clearly *adv* → CLEAR¹

ˌclear-ˈsighted *adj* able to understand situations well and to see what might happen in the future بصير ، بعيد النظر

cleavage /ˈkliːvɪdʒ/ *noun* [C,U] the space between a woman's breasts الفلق بين الثديين

clef /klef/ *noun* [C] (in music) a sign (𝄞, 𝄢) at the beginning of a line of written music that shows the range of the notes المفتاح: علامة موسيقية

clematis /ˈklemətɪs; kləˈmeɪtɪs/ *noun* [U,C] a climbing plant with white, purple or pink flowers ظيّان، ياسمين البرّ

clementine /ˈkleməntiːn/ *noun* [C] a type of small orange نوع من اليوسفي

clench /klentʃ/ *verb* [T] to close or hold tightly: *He clenched his teeth in pain.* ○ *She clenched her fists and looked as if she was about to hit him.* يشدّ على، يصك (أسنانه)

clergy /ˈklɜːdʒi/ *noun* [plural] the people who perform religious ceremonies in the Christian church: *a member of the clergy* رجال الدين المسيحي

clergyman /ˈklɜːdʒimən/ *noun* [C] (*pl.* **clergymen** /-mən/) a member of the clergy قِسيس

clerical /ˈklerɪkl/ *adj* **1** connected with the work of a clerk in an office: *clerical work* كتابي

2 of or concerning the clergy كَهنوتي، إكليروسي

🔑**clerk** /klɑːk; *US* klɜːrk/ *noun* [C] **1** a person whose job is to do written work or look after records or accounts in an office, bank, court of law, etc. كاتب: موظف في مكتب

2 (*also* **sales clerk**) (*US*) = SHOP ASSISTANT

🔑**clever** /ˈklevə(r)/ *adj* **1** able to learn, understand or do sth quickly and easily; intelligent: *a clever student* ○ *How clever of you to mend my watch!* ○ *She's so clever with her hands – she makes all her own clothes.* بارع : ذكي

2 (used about things, ideas, etc.) showing skill or intelligence: *a clever device* ○ *a clever plan* ذكيّ ، بارع

▸ **cleverly** *adv* ببراعة ، بذكاء

cleverness *noun* [U] ذكاء ، نباهة : براعة

cliché (*also* **cliche**) /ˈkliːʃeɪ; *US* kliːˈʃeɪ/ *noun* [C] a phrase or idea that has been used so many times that it no longer has any real meaning or interest: *The story was full of clichés.* كليشيه، فكرة مبتذلة

🔑**click¹** /klɪk/ *noun* [C] **1** a short sharp sound: *I heard the click of a key in the lock.* ○ *the click of a switch* طقة

2 (*computing*) the act of pressing the button on a computer mouse نقرة

🔑**click²** /klɪk/ *verb* **1** [I,T] to make a short sharp sound; to cause sth to do this: *The door clicked shut.* ○ *He clicked the switch.* يطقّ؛ يضغط على (محدثاً صوتاً)

2 [I, T] **click (on sth)** (*computing*) to press one of the buttons on a mouse: *To open a file, click on the menu.* ينقر على

3 [I] (*Brit informal*) (used about two people) to become friendly immediately: *We met at a party and just clicked.* ينسجم (مع شخص) من أول وهلة

4 [I] (*informal*) (used about a problem, etc.) to become suddenly clear or understood: *Once I'd found the missing letter, everything clicked into place.* يتوضّح الأمر فجأة

clickable /ˈklɪkəbl/ *adj* if text or an image is clickable, you can click on it with the mouse or touch pad in order to make sth happen: *a clickable map* قابل للنّقر

🔑**client** /ˈklaɪənt/ *noun* [C] someone who receives a service from a professional person زبون ، عميل

clientele /ˌkliːənˈtel; *US* ˌklaɪənˈtel/ *noun* [U] the group of people who regularly go to a particular shop, hotel, etc. ❶ This word is more formal than alternatives such as **customers** or **guests**. عملاء أو زبائن دائمون

cliff /klɪf/ *noun* [C] a high, very steep area of rock, especially one next to the sea: *the white cliffs of Dover* منحدر صخري ، جرْف

🔑**climate** /ˈklaɪmət/ *noun* [C] **1** the normal weather conditions of a particular region: *a dry, humid, tropical, etc. climate* ○ *What are the effects of global warming on our climate?* مناخ

2 the general opinions, etc. that people have at a particular time: *What is the current climate of opinion regarding the death penalty?* ○ *the political climate* مناخ ، جو

▸ **climatic** /klaɪˈmætɪk/ *adj* connected with climate: *a conference to discuss climatic change* مناخي

ˈclimate change *noun* [U] changes in the earth's weather, including changes in temperature, wind patterns and rainfall, especially the increase in the temperature of the earth's atmosphere that is caused by the increase of particular gases, especially carbon dioxide التغير المناخي

climax /ˈklaɪmæks/ *noun* [C] the most important and exciting part of a book, play, piece of music, event, etc: *the novel's climax in the final chapter* ○ *The election victory marked the climax of his political career.* ذروة ، أوج

▸ **climax** *verb* [I] to reach a climax يصل إلى الذروة

🔑**climb** /klaɪm/ *verb* **1** [I,T] to move up to the top of sth: *The cat managed to climb to the top of the tree.* ○ *to climb a tree, mountain, rope, etc.* ○ *She* *climbed the stairs to bed.* ○ *to climb up a ladder* يتسلّق ، يصعَد

2 [I] to move, with difficulty, in the direction mentioned: *I managed to climb out of the window.* يتسلّق بصعوبة

3 [I] to go up mountains, etc. as a sport ❶ **Go climbing** is a common way of talking about climbing for pleasure: *I go climbing in the Alps most summers.* يمارس رياضة التسلّق

4 [I] to rise to a higher position: *The plane climbed steadily.* ○ *The road climbed steeply up the side of the mountain.* ○ *(figurative) The value of the dollar against the pound has climbed to a record level.* يصعد، يرتفع

IDM climb/jump on the bandwagon → BANDWAGON

PHR V climb down (over sth) (*informal*) to admit that you have made a mistake; to change your opinion about sth يعترف بخطئه ؛ يغيّر رأيه

▸ **climb** *noun* [C] an act of climbing or a journey made by climbing: *The monastery could only be reached by a three-hour climb.* صعود ، ارتقاء

climber *noun* [C] a person who climbs mountains or rocks as a sport متسلّق

climbdown /ˈklaɪmdaʊn/ *noun* [C] an act of admitting you have been wrong: *a government climbdown* إقرار بالخطأ

clinch /klɪntʃ/ *verb* [T] (*informal*) to settle or decide sth finally, e.g. an argument or business agreement: *to clinch a deal* يحسم (أمراً) : يعقد (صفقة)

cling /klɪŋ/ *verb* [I] (*pt, pp* **clung** /klʌŋ/) **1 cling (on) to sb/sth; cling together** to hold on tightly to sb/sth: *to cling to a rope* ○ *They clung together for warmth.* يتمسك أو يتعلّق (بشيء) : يلتصق بِ

2 to continue to believe that sth is true, often when it is not reasonable to do so: *They were still clinging to the hope that the girl would be found alive.* يتشبّث

3 to stick firmly to sth: *Her wet clothes clung to her.* يلتصق

ˈcling film *noun* [U] a thin transparent material used for covering food to keep it fresh غشاء بلاستيكي لاصق

clinic /ˈklɪnɪk/ *noun* [C] **1** a small hospital or a part of a hospital where you go to receive special medical treatment: *He's being treated at a private clinic.* ○ *The ante-natal clinic is part of the maternity department.* مستوصف : عيادة

2 a time when a doctor in a hospital sees patients and gives special treatment or advice: *Dr Greenall's clinic is from 2 to 4 on Mondays.* مواعيد العيادة في مستشفى

clinical /ˈklɪnɪkl/ *adj* **1** of or relating to the examination and treatment of patients at a clinic or hospital: *Clinical trials of the new drug have proved successful.* سريري

2 (used about a person) cold and not emotional بارد (المشاعر)

▸ **clinically** /-kli/ *adv* **1** according to medical examination: *to be clinically dead* طبّياً ، سريرياً

2 in a clinical (2) way بشكل مجرّد من العواطف

clink /klɪŋk/ *noun* [sing.] the short sharp sound that objects made of glass, metal, etc. make when they touch each other: *the clink of glasses* رنين : صليل : صوت قرع (الكؤوس)

▸ **clink** *verb* [I,T] يرن، يصِل ؛ يقرع (الكؤوس)

clip¹ /klɪp/ *noun* [C] a small object, usually made of metal or plastic, used for holding things together: *a paper clip* مِشْبك ، "شكّالة" : دبوس شعر

▸ **clip** *verb* [I,T] (clip**p**ing; clip**p**ed) to be fastened with a clip; to fasten sth to sth else with a clip: *Do your earrings clip on?* ○ *Clip the photo to the letter, please.* ينشبك : يشبك : يربط بدبوس

clip² /klɪp/ *verb* [T] (clip**p**ing; clip**p**ed) to cut sth, especially by cutting small parts off: *The hedge needs clipping.* يقصّ ، يقلّم

▸ **clip** *noun* [C] **1** an act of cutting sth قص

2 (*informal*) a short sharp blow: *She gave the boy a clip round the ear.* صفعة ، لطمة

3 a small section of a film that is shown separately so that people can see what the rest of the film is like مقطع قصير من فيلم

clipping (*US*) *noun* [C] = CUTTING¹ (1)

clipboard /ˈklɪpbɔːd/ *noun* [C] a small board with a clip at the top for holding papers, so that you can write while you are standing or moving around لوحة كتابة في أعلاها ملقط للأوراق

clippers /ˈklɪpəz/ *noun* [plural] a small metal tool used for cutting things (e.g. hair or fingernails): *a pair of nail clippers* مقلّمة الأظافر

clique /kliːk/ *noun* [C] a small group of people with the same interests who do not want others to join their group عصبة

cloak /kləʊk/ *noun* **1** [C] a type of loose coat without sleeves, more common in former times معطَف فضفاض دون أكمام ، عباءة

2 [sing.] a thing that hides sth else ستار : ذريعة

cloakroom /ˈkləʊkruːm; -rʊm/ *noun* [C] **1** a room near the entrance to a theatre, school, club, etc. where you can leave your coat, bags, etc. حجرة إيداع المعاطف والحقائب الخ

2 (*Brit*) a lavatory in a public building: *Excuse me. Where are the ladies' cloakrooms, please?* مِرحاض في مبنى عام

clobber /ˈklɒbə(r)/ *verb* [T] (*Brit informal*) to hit sb hard يضرب بشدة

🔑**clock¹** /klɒk/ *noun* [C] **1** an instrument that shows you what time it is, often found on the wall of a house or building (not worn like a watch): *an alarm clock* ○ *That clock is five minutes slow* (= it says 10.55 when it is really 11 o'clock). ○ *The clock is five minutes fast* (= it says 6.05 when it is really 6 o'clock). ○ *The clock struck midnight.* ساعة حائط

2 an instrument in a car that measures how far it has travelled: *My car has only 10 000 miles on the clock.* عدّاد المسافة المقطوعة (في السّيارة)

IDM around/round the clock all day and all night: *They are working round the clock to repair the bridge.* ليلاً نهاراً

put the clock/clocks forward/back to change

a b **c** d e f g h i j k l m n o p q r s t u v w x y z

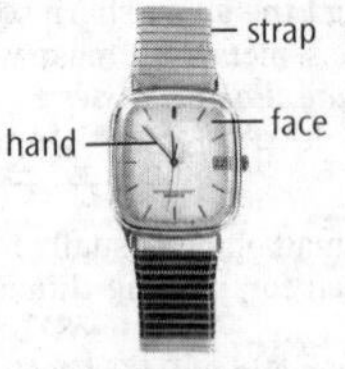

watch

digital watch

clock

alarm clock

the time, usually by one hour, at the beginning/end of summer يقدم/يؤخر الساعة (في بداية/نهاية الصيف)

▸ **clockwise** *adv, adj* in the same direction as the hands of a clock: *Turn the handle clockwise.* ○ *to move in a clockwise direction* ❶ The opposite is **anticlockwise**. في اتجاه عقارب الساعة

clock² /klɒk/ *verb*

PHRV **clock in/on**; **clock off** to record the time that you arrive at or leave work, especially by putting a card into a type of clock يسجّل زمن الوصول للعمل أو الخروج منه

clock sth up to achieve a certain number or total: *Our car clocked up over 2 000 miles while we were on holiday.* يسجّل أو يصل رقماً معيناً

clockwork /ˈklɒkwɜːk/ *noun* [U] a type of machinery found in certain toys, etc. that you operate by winding a key: *a clockwork toy* ○ *The plan went like clockwork* (= smoothly and without any problems). آلية تعمل بزنبرك ، انتظام (آلي)

clog¹ /klɒg/ *noun* [C] a type of shoe made completely of wood or with a thick wooden bottom: *a pair of clogs* قَبْقاب

clog² /klɒg/ *verb* (clogging; clogged) [I,T] **clog (sth) (up) (with sth)** to block or become blocked: *The drain is clogged up with leaves.* ○ *You've clogged up the machine.* ○ *The roads were clogged with traffic.* يسدّ : ينسدّ

clone /kləʊn/ *noun* [C] an identical copy of a plant or animal that is produced by artificial methods نبات أو حيوان مستنسخ

▸ **clone** *verb* [T] to cause sth to grow as a clone يستنسخ

close¹ /kləʊs/ *adj* **1** (not before a noun) **close (to sb/sth)**; **close (together)** near: *Is our hotel close to the beach?* ○ *It's close to midnight.* ○ *The edges are quite close together.* قريب

2 (used about a friend, etc.) known very well and liked: *They invited only close friends to the wedding.* (صديق) مقرّب

3 near in a family relationship: *a close relative* قريب ، لصيق

4 (used about a competition, etc.) only won by a small amount: *a close match* (فوز) بفارق ضئيل

5 careful; thorough: *On close examination, you could see that the banknote was a forgery.* دقيق : شامل

6 (used about the weather, etc.) warm in an uncomfortable way and with little movement of air: *It's so close today that there might be a storm.* (جو) ثقيل

IDM **a close shave/thing** a bad thing that almost happened: *I wasn't injured, but it was a close shave.* نجاة بأعجوبة

at close quarters at or from a position that is very near من مكان قريب ، عن كَثَب

keep a close watch on sb/sth to watch sb/sth very carefully: *The police kept a close watch on the gang.* يراقب مراقبة دقيقة

▸ **closely** *adv* in a close way: *to watch sb closely* ○ *The insect closely resembles a stick.* عن كَثَب ؛ بإمعان ؛ إلى حدّ كبير

closeness *noun* [U] the state of being close قُرب

close² /kləʊs/ *adv* near: *The child stood close to his mother.* ○ *to follow close behind someone* ○ *I held her close* (= tightly). قريباً من

IDM **close by (sb/sth)** at a short distance from sb/sth: *She lives close by.* على مَقْرُبة من....

close on nearly; almost: *He was born close on a hundred years ago.* تقريباً

close up (to sb/sth) at or from a very short distance to sb/sth: *You can't tell it's a forgery until you look at it close up.* عن قُرْب

close³ /kləʊs/ *noun* [C] part of the name of a street, especially one that is closed off at one end: *5 Devon Close* حي مسدود في آخره

close⁴ /kləʊz/ *verb* [I,T] **1** to shut: *The door closed quietly.* ○ *to close a door, window, cupboard, etc.* ○ *Close your eyes – I've got a surprise.* ينغلق ؛ يُغلِق

2 to be, or to make sth, not open to the public: *What time do the shops close?* ○ *The police have closed the road to traffic.* يقفل ، يُغلِق

3 to come or bring sth to an end: *The meeting closed at 10p.m.* ○ *Detectives have closed the case on the missing girl.* ينتهي ، يختتم

PHRV **close (sth) down** to stop all business or work permanently, at a shop or factory: *The factory has had to close down because of the recession.* ○ *Health inspectors have closed the restaurant down.* يقفل نهائياً

close in (on sb/sth) to come nearer and gradually surround sb/sth, especially in order to attack: *The army is closing in on the enemy troops.* يطبق على

close⁵ /kləʊz/ *noun* [sing.] the end, especially of a period of time or an activity: *the close of trading on the stock market* انتهاء ، اختتام

IDM **bring sth/come/draw to a close** to end: *The chairman brought the meeting to a close.* ○ *The guests began to leave as the evening drew to a close.* يختتم : ينتهي

closed /kləʊzd/ *adj* not open; shut: *Keep your mouth closed.* ○ *with closed eyes* مُقْفَل ، مُغْلَق

ˌclosed-ˌcircuit ˈtelevision *noun* [C,U] (*abbr* **CCTV**) a type of television system that works

within a limited area, for example a public building, to protect it from crime
كاميرا (الدائرة المغلقة) للمراقبة

closet /ˈklɒzɪt/ *noun* [C] (*US*) a large cupboard that is built into a room خزانة (مشيّدة داخل حجرة)

ˈ**close-up** *noun* [C] a photograph or film of sb/sth that you take from a very short distance away: *Here's a close-up of our wedding cake.* صورة مقرّبة

ˈ**closing time** *noun* [C] the time when a shop, etc. closes وقت انتهاء (العمل)

closure /ˈkləʊʒə(r)/ *noun* [C,U] the permanent closing, e.g. of a business: *Miners are protesting against pit closures.* ○ *The firm is threatened with closure.* إقفال ، إغلاق

clot /klɒt/ *noun* [C] **1** a lump formed by blood as it dries جلطة

2 (*Brit informal*) a stupid person شخص غبي

▸ **clot** *verb* (clotting; clotted) [I,T] to form or cause sth to form clots يتجلّط ، يتخثّر

cloth /klɒθ; *US* klɔːθ/ *noun* (*pl.* **cloths** /klɒθs; *US* klɔːðz/) **1** [U] a material made of cotton, wool, etc. that you use for making clothes, curtains, etc: *a metre of cloth* قماش

2 [C] a piece of cloth that you use for a particular purpose: *a tablecloth* ○ *Where can I find a cloth to wipe this up?* قطعة قماش

clothe /kləʊð/ *verb* [T] to provide clothes for sb; *to feed and clothe a child* يلبِس ، يكسو

▸ **clothed** *adj* **clothed (in sth)** dressed: *He was clothed in leather from head to foot.* ○ *Luckily I was fully clothed when they arrived.* مرتدٍ ، لابس

clothes /kləʊðz; *US* kləʊz/ *noun* [plural] the things that you wear, e.g. trousers, shirts, dresses, coats, etc. (when thought of all together): *Take off those wet clothes.* ○ *She was wearing new clothes.* ملابس

> Remember that clothes is always plural. We can use an **item/piece/article of clothing** to describe a single thing that you wear: *A kilt is an item of clothing worn in Scotland.* Look also at **garment**.

ˈ**clothes hanger** *noun* [C] = HANGER

ˈ**clothes line** *noun* [C] a thin rope that you hang clothes on so that they can dry حبل الغسيل

ˈ**clothes peg** (*US* ˈ**clothespin**) *noun* [C] = PEG[1] (3)

clothing /ˈkləʊðɪŋ/ *noun* [U] the clothes that you wear: *You will need waterproof clothing.* ❶ **Clothing** is more formal than **clothes**. ملابس ، ثياب

ˌ**clotted** ˈ**cream** *noun* [U] (*Brit*) a type of thick rich cream قشدة متخثّرة

cloud[1] /klaʊd/ *noun* **1** [C,U] a mass of very small drops of water that floats in the sky and is usually grey or white: *The sun disappeared behind a cloud.* ○ *A band of thick cloud is spreading from the west.* سحابة ، سحاب

2 [C] a mass of smoke, dust, sand, etc: *Clouds of smoke were pouring from the burning building.*
سحابة

IDM **under a cloud** with the disapproval of the people around you: *She left her job under a cloud because she'd been accused of stealing.*
محاط باستهجان الآخرين ، موضع نقمة

▸ **cloudless** *adj* (used about the sky, etc.) clear; without any clouds صافٍ ؛ صاحٍ

cloudy *adj* (**cloudier**; **cloudiest**) **1** (used about the sky, etc.) full of clouds غائم

2 (used about liquids, etc.) not clear: *cloudy water* غير صافٍ ، عكر

cloud[2] /klaʊd/ *verb* **1** [I,T] to become or make sth difficult to see through: *His eyes clouded with tears.* يعتم ؛ يغشّي

2 [T] to make sth less clear or easy to understand يعتّم ؛ يبهم

3 [T] to make sth less enjoyable; to spoil: *Illness has clouded the last few years of his life.* يفسد

PHRV **cloud over 1** (used about the sky) to become full of clouds يتلبّد بالسحب

2 (used about a person's face) to start to look sad يتكدّر (الوجه بالحزن)

cloudburst /ˈklaʊdbɜːst/ *noun* [C] a sudden heavy fall of rain وابل (من المطر)

ˈ**cloud computing** *noun* [U] a way of using computers in which data and software are stored mainly on a central computer, to which users have access over the Internet الحَوسبة السَحابية

clout /klaʊt/ *noun* (*informal*) **1** [C] a heavy blow, usually with the hand: *to give someone a clout* لطمة قوية

2 [U] influence and power: *He's an important man – he has a lot of clout in the company.* نفوذ ، سلطة

clove[1] /kləʊv/ *noun* [C] the small dried flower of a tropical plant, used to give a special flavour in cooking بهار أو كَبْش القَرَنْفل

clove[2] /kləʊv/ *noun* [C] a section of a garlic bulb فصّ الثوم

clover /ˈkləʊvə(r)/ *noun* [C] a small plant with pink or white flowers and leaves with three parts to them ❶ Sometimes clover leaves have four parts and it is thought to be very lucky if you find one of these. بِرْسِيم

clown /klaʊn/ *noun* [C] a person who wears funny clothes and makes people laugh, especially in a circus مهرج

▸ **clown** *verb* [I] **clown (about/around)** to act in a funny or foolish way, like a clown: *Stop clowning around and get some work done!* يتصرّف كالمهرّج

club[1] /klʌb/ *noun* [C] **1** a group of people who meet to share an interest; the place where they meet: *to join a club* ○ *to be a member of a club* ○ *a social club* ○ *a tennis, football, golf, etc. club* نادٍ

2 = NIGHTCLUB

Going dancing and drinking in a club is known as **clubbing** or **going clubbing**. A person who often goes to nightclubs is called a **clubber**.

PHR V **club together (to do sth)** to share the cost of sth, e.g. a present: *We clubbed together to buy him a leaving present.* يتشارك

club² /klʌb/ *noun* [C] **1** a heavy stick, usually with one end that is thicker than the other, used as a weapon هراوة

2 a long stick that is specially shaped at one end and used for hitting a ball when playing golf ➲ Look at **bat²**, **racket¹** and **stick¹**(3). مضرب الغولف

▸ **club** *verb* (clubbing; clubbed) [T] to hit sb/sth hard with a heavy object, especially a club² (1): *to club somebody to death* يضرب بهراوة

club³ /klʌb/ *noun* **1 clubs** [plural] the set (suit) of playing cards with black three-leafed shapes on them السباتي (في ورق اللعب)

2 [C] a playing card from this suit ورقة لعب سباتي

clubber /ˈklʌbə(r)/ *noun* [C] a person who goes to nightclubs regularly مرتاد النوادي الليلية

cluck /klʌk/ *noun* [C] the noise made by a hen نقيق أو قَرْق الدجاج

▸ **cluck** *verb* [I] تنِق أو تقْرق (الدجاجة)

clue /kluː/ *noun* [C] a piece of information that helps you solve a problem, answer a question, etc: *The police were looking for clues to his disappearance.* ○ *the clues for solving a crossword puzzle* مفتاح لحلّ لغْز

IDM **not have a clue** (*informal*) to know nothing; to be unable to help or understand: *I haven't a clue where you left your watch.* ليس لديه أدنى فكرة

▸ **clued up** /ˌkluːd ˈʌp/ *adj* knowing a lot about sth: *I'm not really clued up on the technical details.* عالم أو خبير بـ

clueless *adj* not able to understand; stupid: *I'm absolutely clueless about computers.* غبي؛ جاهل

clump /klʌmp/ *noun* [C] a small group of plants or trees, growing together أجَمَة ، شجراء

clumsy /ˈklʌmzi/ *adj* (**clumsier**; **clumsiest**) **1** (used about a person) careless or awkward and likely to drop things or do things badly: *I'm afraid I've broken the glass – it was very clumsy of me.* ○ *She undid the parcel with clumsy fingers.* أخرق

2 (used about a remark, etc.) not showing enough understanding of the feelings of other people; likely to upset or offend people: *He made a clumsy apology.* ○ *her clumsy attempts at humour* غير لبق ؛ ثقيل

3 large, awkward to use, and not attractive in design: *a clumsy piece of furniture* ضخم يعوزه التناسب

▸ **clumsily** *adv* على نحو غير مصقول ؛ بشكل أخرق
clumsiness *noun* [U] خرق ؛ عدم رشاقة

clung *pt, pp of* CLING

cluster /ˈklʌstə(r)/ *noun* [C] a group of people, plants or things that stand or grow close together: *a cluster of schoolchildren* ○ *a cluster of berries* مجموعة ؛ عنقود

▸ **cluster** *verb*

PHR V **cluster/be clustered round sb/sth** to form a group around sb/sth: *The tourists clustered around their guide.* يتجمع حول

clutch /klʌtʃ/ *verb* [T] to hold sth tightly, especially because you are afraid or excited: *He clutched his mother's hand in fear.* ○ *The girl ran off, clutching her prize.* يقبض بقوة ، يمْسك بـ

PHR V **clutch at sth** to try to take hold of sth: *She clutched at the money but the wind blew it away.* يمسك بـ

▸ **clutch** *noun* **1** [C] the part of a car that you press with your foot before you change gear; the apparatus that it is connected to: *to press/release the clutch* قابض ؛ جهاز تعشيق التروس في السيارة

2 clutches [plural] the power or control of a person or group: *He fell into the enemy's clutches.* براثن ، سيطرة

3 [C] an act of seizing or clutching: *to make a clutch at sth* قبْضة شديدة

clutter /ˈklʌtə(r)/ *noun* [U] things that are where they are not wanted or needed and make a place untidy: *Who left all this clutter on the table?* أشياء مبعثرة ، فوضى ، "كركبة"

▸ **clutter** *verb* [T] **clutter sth (up)** to cover or fill sth with lots of objects in an untidy way: *Don't leave those books there – they're cluttering up the table.* يبعثر ، "يكركب"

cluttered *adj*: *a cluttered desk* مليء بالفوضى، يعوزه النظام

⚷ **cm** *abbrev* (**cm** or **cms**) = CENTIMETRE(S)

Co. **1** /kəʊ/ = COMPANY: *W Smith and Co.*

2 = COUNTY: *Co. Down*

c/o /ˌsiː ˈəʊ/ *abbrev* (used for addressing a letter to somebody who is staying at another person's house) care of: *Mr Peter Boyes, c/o Mr and Mrs B. Jay* بواسطة، عناية، طرف

⚷ **coach¹** /kəʊtʃ/ *noun* [C] **1** a comfortable bus used for long journeys: *It's cheaper by coach than by train.* ○ *a coach trip* حافلة

2 = CARRIAGE

3 a large carriage with four wheels pulled by horses and used especially in former times: *the royal coach* عربة تجرها الجياد

⚷ **coach²** /kəʊtʃ/ *noun* [C] a person who trains people to compete in certain sports: *a tennis coach* مدرّب رياضي

▸ **coach** *verb* [I,T] to train or teach sb, especially to compete in a sport or pass an examination: *She is coached by a former Olympic champion.* يدرّب ، يعلّم

⚷ **coal** /kəʊl/ *noun* **1** [U] a type of black mineral that is dug (mined) from the ground and is burned to give heat and energy: *a lump of coal* ○ *a coal fire* فحم حجري

2 coals [plural] burning pieces of coal فحم مشتعل أو جَمر

coalition /ˌkəʊəˈlɪʃn/ *noun* [C, with sing. or pl. verb] the joining of two or more political parties, often for a temporary period, usually in order to form a government: *a coalition between the socialists and the Green Party* ○ *a coalition government* تحالف ، ائتلاف

ˈ**coal mine** (*also* **pit**) *noun* [C] a place, usually underground, where coal is dug from the ground ➲ Look at **colliery**. مَنجم فحم حجري

ˈ**coal miner** (*also* **miner**) *noun* [C] a person whose job is to dig coal in a coal mine عامل مَنجم

coarse /kɔːs/ *adj* **1** consisting of large, not fine pieces; rough, not smooth: *coarse salt* ○ *coarse cloth* خشن

2 (used about a person or sb's behaviour) rude, likely to offend people; having bad manners: *His coarse remarks about women offended her.* فظّ ، جِلف

▸ **coarsely** *adv*: *Coarsely chop the onion* (= into pieces which are not too small). ○ *He laughed coarsely.* بخشونة ؛ بفظاظة

coarsen /ˈkɔːsn/ *verb* [I,T] to become or to make sth coarse يخشُن ؛ يخشّن

coast[1] /kəʊst/ *noun* [C] the area of land that is next to or close to the sea: *After sailing for an hour we could finally see the coast.* ○ *Holidaymakers reported seeing sharks just off the coast.* ○ *It was a sunny weekend and the roads were full of people going to the coast.* ○ *Scarborough is on the east coast.* ساحل

▸ **coastal** *adj* at or near a coast: *coastal areas* ○ *fishing in coastal waters* ساحلي

coast[2] /kəʊst/ *verb* [I] **1** to move (especially down a hill) without using power يسير أو يهبط تلقائياً

2 to achieve sth without much effort: *They coasted to victory.* يحقّق بسهولة

coastguard /ˈkəʊstgɑːd/ *noun* [C] a person or group of people whose job is to watch the sea near the coast in order to warn or help ships that are in danger or to stop illegal activities خَفَر السواحل

coastline /ˈkəʊstlaɪn/ *noun* [C] the edge or shape of a coast: *a rocky coastline* خطّ الساحل

coat /kəʊt/ *noun* [C] **1** a piece of clothing, usually with long sleeves, that you wear on top of other clothes to keep warm: *Put your coat on – it's cold outside.* ○ *Take off your coat and sit down.* ➲ Look at **overcoat** and **raincoat**. معطف

2 the fur or hair covering an animal's body: *a dog with a smooth coat* شعر أو فراء الحيوان

3 a layer of sth covering a surface: *The walls will probably need two coats of paint.* طبقة

▸ **coat** *verb* [T] **coat sth (with/in sth)** to cover sth with a layer of sth: *biscuits coated with milk chocolate* يغطّي بطبقة من ، يلبّس بِ

coating *noun* [C] a thin layer of sth that covers sth else: *a coating of dust* طبقة رقيقة

ˈ**coat hanger** *noun* [C] = HANGER

ˌ**coat of ˈarms** (*also* **arms**) *noun* [C] a design that is used as the symbol of a family, a town, a university, etc. شعار النَّسَب

coax /kəʊks/ *verb* [T] to persuade sb gently: *The child wasn't hungry, but his mother coaxed him into eating a little.* ○ *They coaxed the cat out of the basket.* يقْنِع بالملاطفة

PHR V **coax sth out of/from sb** to get sth from sb by gently persuading: *At last he coaxed a smile out of her.* ينال بالملاطفة

cobble[1] /ˈkɒbl/ (*also* ˈ**cobblestone**) *noun* [C] a rounded stone used (in the past) for covering the surface of streets حجر خاصّ لرصف الشوارع

▸ **cobbled** *adj*: *cobbled streets* مرصوف بالحجارة

cobble[2] /ˈkɒbl/ *verb*

PHR V **cobble sth together** to make sth or put sth together quickly and without much care يصنعه بسرعة ودون إتقان

cobbler /ˈkɒblə(r)/ *noun* [C] (*old-fashioned*) a person who repairs shoes إسكاف

cobra /ˈkəʊbrə/ *noun* [C] a poisonous snake found in Africa and Asia صِل: ثعبان سامّ

cobweb /ˈkɒbweb/ *noun* [C] a net of threads made by a spider in order to catch insects بيت أو نسج العنكبوت

Coca-Cola™ /ˌkəʊkə ˈkəʊlə/ (*also* **Coke™**) *noun* [C,U] a brown, sweet, non-alcoholic drink الكوكا كولا

cocaine /kəʊˈkeɪn/ *noun* [U] a drug that some people take for pleasure but to which they can become addicted (= they cannot stop using it) (مخدّر) الكوكائين

cock[1] /kɒk/ *noun* [C] **1** (*US* **rooster**) an adult male chicken: *cocks crowing at dawn* ➲ Look at the note at **chicken**. ديك

2 an adult male bird of any type: *a cock sparrow* ذكر الطائر

cock[2] /kɒk/ *verb* [T] to raise or move part of the body: *The horse cocked its ears on hearing the noise.* ينصب أو يرهف (أذنيه)

PHR V **cock sth up** (*Brit slang*) to do something very badly and inefficiently; to spoil sth "يطصلق" أو يفسد العمل

cock-a-doodle-doo /ˌkɒk ə ˌduːdl ˈduː/ *interj* the noise made by a cock صياح الديك

cockerel /ˈkɒkərəl/ *noun* [C] a young male chicken ديك صغير

cockney /ˈkɒkni/ *noun* **1** [C] person who was born and grew up in London, especially the East End شخص من الحيّ الشعبي في لندن

2 [U] the way of speaking English that is typical of cockneys لهجة لندن الشعبيّة

▸ **cockney** *adj*: *a cockney accent* متعلّق بهذه اللهجة

cockpit /ˈkɒkpɪt/ *noun* [C] **1** the part of an aircraft where the pilot sits غرفة الطيّار

2 the part of a racing car in which the driver sits مقعد السائق في سيارات السباق

cockroach /ˈkɒkrəʊtʃ/ (*US* **roach**) *noun* [C] a large dark brown insect, often found in dirty rooms or damp places صرصور، صرصار

cocktail /ˈkɒkteɪl/ *noun* [C] **1** an alcoholic

drink made from a mixture of drinks: *a cocktail party* مزيج من مشروبات كحوليّة

2 a mixture of small pieces of food, usually served as the first part of a meal: *a prawn cocktail* طعام من قطع صغيرة

'cock-up *noun* [C] (*slang*) something that was badly done; a mistake that spoils sth: *What a cock-up! You'll have to start again.* إفساد العمل ، لخبطة

cocoa /'kəʊkəʊ/ *noun* **1** [U] a dark brown powder made from the seeds of a tropical tree and used in making chocolate الكاكاو

2 [C,U] a hot drink made from this powder mixed with milk or water مشروب الكاكاو

coconut /'kəʊkənʌt/ *noun* [C,U] the large brown fruit of a tropical tree. Coconuts have very hard, hairy shells and are filled with a white liquid that you can drink. The white substance inside the shell is often eaten in sweets and cakes. جوزة الهند

cocoon /kə'ku:n/ *noun* [C] a fine covering like silk threads made by an insect to protect itself during one stage of its development شرنقة، فَيْلجة

cod /kɒd/ *noun* [C,U] (*pl.* **cod**) a large sea fish that you can eat سمك القدّ

code /kəʊd/ *noun* **1** [C,U] a system of words, letters, numbers, etc. used instead of other words, letters, etc. so that messages, information, etc. can be kept secret: *They succeeded in breaking/cracking the enemy code* (= in finding out what it was). ○ *They wrote letters to each other in code.* شِفْرة

2 [C] a group of numbers, letters, etc. that is used for identifying sth: *What's the code* (= the telephone number) *for Stockholm?* ○ *a bar code* (= a pattern of lines printed on goods, that a computer can read) مِفْتاح ، رمز

3 [C] a set of rules for behaviour: *a code of practice* (= a set of standards agreed and accepted by a particular profession) ○ *the Highway Code* (= the rules for driving on the roads) قواعد ، مجموعة قوانين

▸ **code** *verb* [T] **1** to put or write sth in code (1): *coded messages* يشفّر

2 to use a particular system for identifying things: *The files are colour-coded: blue for Europe, green for Africa.* ينظّم حسب قواعد معينة

co-educational /ˌkəʊedʒu'keɪʃənl/ *adj* (used about a school) with both boys and girls together in the same classes (تعليم) مختلَط

coerce /kəʊ'ɜ:s/ *verb* [T] (*formal*) to force sb to do sth, e.g. by threatening him/her يجْبر ، يكْره

▸ **coercion** /kəʊ'ɜ:ʃn; *US* -ʒn/ *noun* [U] إجبار ، إكراه

coexist /ˌkəʊɪg'zɪst/ *verb* [I] to exist together at the same time or in the same place: *Is it possible for these different ethnic groups to coexist peacefully?* يتعايش

▸ **coexistence** /-əns/ *noun* [U] تعايش

C of E /ˌsi: əv 'i:/ *abbrev* = CHURCH OF ENGLAND

coffee /'kɒfi; *US* 'kɔ:fi/ *noun* **1** [U] the roasted seeds of a tropical tree, made into powder and used for making a drink: *Coffee is the country's biggest export.* بُن

2 [U] a drink made by adding hot water to this: *Would you prefer tea or coffee?* ○ *a cup of coffee* قهوة

3 [C] a cup of this drink: *Two coffees please.* فنجان قهوة

> **Black coffee** is made without milk; **white coffee** is with milk. **Decaffeinated coffee** has had the caffeine taken out. Coffee can be **weak** or **strong**. **Instant coffee** is made by pouring hot water or milk onto coffee powder. **Fresh coffee** is made in a coffee pot from coffee beans that have just been ground.

'coffee table *noun* [C] a small low table, usually in a living room طاولة القهوة

coffin /'kɒfɪn/ *noun* [C] a box in which a dead body is buried ➲ Look at the note at **funeral**. تابوت

cog /kɒg/ *noun* [C] one of the tooth-shaped parts on the edge of a wheel in a piece of machinery. The cogs fit into those on another wheel so that, as it moves, the other wheel moves too. سِنّ الدولاب

cohabit /kəʊ'hæbɪt/ *verb* [I] (*formal*) (used about an unmarried couple) to live together as if they were married يعاشر (من غير زواج)

coherent /kəʊ'hɪərənt/ *adj* connected in a way that makes sense; clear and easy to understand: *a coherent plan* متماسك ؛ مترابط منطقياً

▸ **coherence** /-əns/ *noun* [U] تماسك ، ترابط

coherently *adv* بشكل يسهل فهمه ؛ بصورة منطقية مترابطة

cohesion /kəʊ'hi:ʒn/ *noun* [U] the ability to stay or fit together well: *What the team lacks is cohesion – all the players play as individuals.* تماسك ، ترابط

coil /kɔɪl/ *verb* [I,T] to wind sth into a round shape: *The snake coiled itself round a tree.* ○ *He coiled up the cable and put it into his tool bag.* يلتفّ ؛ يلفّ

▸ **coil** *noun* [C] **1** a length of rope, wire, etc. that has been wound into a round shape: *a coil of rope* لفّة

2 a small piece of plastic or metal that a woman can wear inside her body to prevent her becoming pregnant لولب

coin /kɔɪn/ *noun* [C] a piece of money made of metal: *a pound coin* قطعة نقود

▸ **coin** *verb* [T] to invent a new word or phrase: *Who was it who coined the phrase 'a week is a long time in politics'?* يبتكر ، يأتي بـ

coinage *noun* [U] the system of coins used in a country: *decimal coinage* عملة

coincide /ˌkəʊɪn'saɪd/ *verb* [I] **coincide (with sth) 1** (used about events) to happen at the same time as sth else: *The Queen's visit is timed to coin-*

cide with the country's centenary celebrations. يتزامن ، يتوافق

2 to be exactly the same or very similar: *Our views coincide completely.* يتطابق

coincidence /kəʊˈɪnsɪdəns/ *noun* [C,U] the surprising fact of two or more similar things happening at the same time by chance; an occasion when this happens: *By an incredible coincidence I found myself sitting next to someone I hadn't seen for years.* ○ *We hadn't planned to meet, it was just coincidence.* مصادفة ، اتفاق

coincidental /kəʊˌɪnsɪˈdentl/ *adj* resulting from two similar or related events happening at the same time by chance اتفاقي ، عَرَضي
▸ **coincidentally** /-təli/ *adv* اتفاقاً ، بالمصادفة

Coke™ /kəʊk/ *noun* [C,U] = COCA-COLA

coke /kəʊk/ *noun* [U] a solid black substance produced from coal and used as a fuel (فحم) الكوك

Col. *abbrev* = COLONEL

cola /ˈkəʊlə/ *noun* [C,U] a brown, sweet non-alcoholic drink; a glass, can, etc. of this كوكا (كولا)

colander /ˈkʌləndə(r)/ *noun* [C] a metal or plastic bowl with a lot of small holes in it, used for draining water from food مِصْفاة

🔑cold¹ /kəʊld/ *adj* **1** having a low temperature; not hot or warm: *If I were you, I'd put a coat on. It's cold outside.* ○ *I'm not going into the sea, the water's too cold.* ○ *Shall I put the heating on? I'm cold.* بارد

> Compare **cold**, **hot**, **cool**, and **warm**. **Cold** indicates a lower temperature than **cool** and may describe a temperature that is unpleasantly low: *a terribly cold winter.* **Cool** means 'fairly cold' and may describe a pleasantly low temperature: *It's terribly hot outside but it's nice and cool in here.* **Hot** indicates a higher temperature than warm and may describe a temperature that is unpleasantly high: *I can't drink this yet, it's too hot.* **Warm** means 'fairly hot' and may describe a pleasantly high temperature: *Come and sit by the fire, you'll soon get warm again.*

2 (used about food or drink) not heated or cooked; having become cold after being heated or cooked: *I don't feel like coffee, I'd rather have a cold drink.* ○ *Have your soup before it gets cold.* بارد

3 (used about a person or sb's behaviour) very unfriendly; not showing kindness, sympathy, etc: *She gave him a cold, hard look.* بارد : غير وِدّي

IDM **get/have cold feet** (*informal*) to become/be afraid to do sth: *She started to get cold feet as her wedding day approached.* يخاف ، يرتعب

in cold blood cruelly and without pity: *to kill sb in cold blood* بوحشية ، بلا رحمة

▸ **coldly** *adv* in an unfriendly way; in a way that shows no kindness or sympathy: *He looked at her coldly and did not reply.* ببرود : بفتور ، بجفاء

coldness *noun* [U] unfriendliness; a lack of kindness or sympathy برود : فتور ، جفاء

🔑cold² /kəʊld/ *noun* **1** [sing., U] lack of heat; low temperature; cold weather: *We walked home in the snow, shivering with cold.* ○ *He seldom wears a coat because he doesn't feel the cold.* ○ *Come on, let's get out of the cold and go indoors.* بَرْد : جوّ بارد

2 [C,U] a common illness of the nose and throat. When you have a cold you sneeze a lot, you have a sore throat and often cannot breathe through your nose: *I think I'm getting a cold.* ○ *Wear some warm clothes when you go out or you'll catch cold.* زكام

ˌcold-ˈblooded *adj* **1** having a blood temperature that varies with the temperature of the surroundings: *Reptiles are cold-blooded.* بارد الدّم

2 cruel; having or showing no pity: *cold-blooded killers* وحشي ، قاس

ˌcold-ˈhearted /-ˈhɑːtɪd/ *adj* unkind; showing no kindness, sympathy, etc. قاسٍ : فظ

coleslaw /ˈkəʊlslɔː/ *noun* [U] raw cabbage and carrots, etc., chopped and mixed with mayonnaise and eaten as a salad سلطة الملفوف (الكرنب) المفروم

colic /ˈkɒlɪk/ *noun* [U] pain in the stomach area, which especially babies get مَغْص

collaborate /kəˈlæbəreɪt/ *verb* [I] **1 collaborate (with sb)(on sth)** to work together (with sb), especially to create or produce sth: *She collaborated with another author on the book.* يتعاون

2 collaborate (with sb) to help the enemy forces who have taken control of your country ❶ This word shows disapproval. يتعاون مع العدو

▸ **collaboration** /kəˌlæbəˈreɪʃn/ *noun* [U] **1** working together to create or produce sth تعاون

2 help given to enemy forces who have taken control of your country تعاون مع العدو

collaborator /kəˈlæbəreɪtə(r)/ *noun* [C] **1** a person who works together with sb else, especially in order to create or produce sth متعاون

2 a person who helps the enemy forces who have taken control of his/her country متعاون مع العدو

collage /ˈkɒlɑːʒ; *US* kəˈlɑːʒ/ *noun* **1** [C] a picture made by fixing pieces of paper, cloth, photographs, etc. onto a surface كولاج

2 [U] the art of making these pictures فنّ الكولاج

🔑collapse /kəˈlæps/ *verb* [I] **1** to fall down or inwards suddenly: *A lot of buildings collapsed in the earthquake.* ينهار

2 (used about a person) to fall down and perhaps become unconscious: *The winner collapsed at the end of the race.* ينهار : يُغمى عليه

3 to fail or break down suddenly or completely: *The company collapsed, leaving hundreds of people out of work.* ينهار

▸ **collapse** *noun* **1** [sing., U] a sudden fall: *the collapse of the motorway bridge* انهيار

2 [sing., U] (used about a person) falling down and perhaps becoming unconscious: *a state of collapse* انهيار

3 [C,U] sudden or complete failure: *economic collapse* إخفاق تامّ: انهيار

collapsible *adj* able to be folded into a shape that makes it easy to store: *a collapsible chair* قابل للطي

collar /ˈkɒlə(r)/ *noun* [C] **1** the part of a shirt, coat, dress, etc. that fits round the neck and is often folded over ياقة

2 a band of leather that is put round an animal's neck (especially a dog or cat) طوق

▸ **collar** *verb* [T] (*informal*) to catch and keep or hold sb: *She collared me during the party and asked me for advice on her problems.* يُمْسِك بِـ ، يحصر

collarbone /ˈkɒləbəʊn/ *noun* [C] one of the two bones that connect the chest bones to the shoulder عظم التّرقوة

collateral /kəˈlætərəl/ *noun* [U] property or sth valuable that you agree to give if you cannot pay back money that you have borrowed ضمانة موازية

colleague /ˈkɒliːɡ/ *noun* [C] a person that you work with in a job, especially in a profession زميل

collect /kəˈlekt/ *verb* **1** [T] **collect sth (up)** to bring a number of things together: *All the exam papers will be collected at the end.* يجمع

2 [I] to come together; to gather: *A crowd collected to see what was going on.* يحتشد : يجتمع

3 [I,T] to ask for money from a number of people: *Hello, I'm collecting for a local charity. Would you like to make a contribution?* ○ *The landlord collects the rent at the end of each month.* يجمع، يحصِّل

4 [T] to gather a number of objects of a particular type over a period of time as a hobby: *He used to collect stamps.* يجمع

5 [T] to go and fetch sb/sth from a particular place: *My daughter's at a party and I have to collect her in half an hour.* يجلب

6 [T] **collect yourself/sth** to get control of yourself, your feelings, thoughts, etc: *She collected herself and went back into the room as if nothing had happened.* ○ *I tried to collect my thoughts before the exam.* يستجمع (رباطة جأشه، أفكاره الخ)

▸ **collect** *adj*, *adv* (*US*) (used about a telephone call) to be paid for by the person who receives the call: *a collect call* ○ *She called me collect because she hadn't any money.* مكالمة تليفونية محولة الأجرة (على مستلمها)

collected *adj* in control of yourself, your feelings, thoughts, etc.; calm رابط الجأش : هادئ

collection /kəˈlekʃn/ *noun* **1** [C,U] the act of getting sth from a place or from people: *The repairs won't take long and your car will be ready for collection tomorrow.* استلام

2 [C] a group of objects of a particular type that sb has collected as a hobby: *a stamp collection* مجموعة

3 [C] a number of poems, stories, letters, articles, etc. published in one book: *a collection of modern poetry* مجموعة

4 [C] the act of asking for money from a number of people (for charity, in church, etc.): *a collection for the poor* ○ *The staff had a collection to buy him a present when he retired.* تَبرُّع ، جمع تبرُّعات

5 [C] a group of people or things; a pile: *a large collection of papers on the desk* مجموعة ، حشد : كومة

collective /kəˈlektɪv/ *adj* shared by a group of people together; not individual: *collective responsibility* جماعي : مشترك

▸ **collective** *noun* [C, with sing. or pl. verb] an organization or business that is owned and controlled by the people who work in it (منظمة) تعاونية

collectively *adv*: *We took the decision collectively at a meeting.* جماعياً

collector /kəˈlektə(r)/ *noun* [C] (often in compounds) a person who collects things: *a stamp collector* ○ *a ticket collector* جامع (طوابع مثلاً)

college /ˈkɒlɪdʒ/ *noun* **1** [C,U] an institution where you can study after you leave school: *an art college* ○ *a college of education* ○ *He first got interested in politics when he was at college.*

> We talk about **college**, without **the**, when we mean that somebody is attending it as a student: *He's at college in York.* ○ *She's going to college in October*, but not if somebody goes there for any other reason: *I went to an art exhibition at the college last night.*

كليّة

2 [C] (in Britain) one of the separate institutions into which certain universities are divided: *Kings College, London* كليّة

3 [C] (in the US) a university, or part of one, where students can study for a degree جامعة

collide /kəˈlaɪd/ *verb* [I] **collide (with sb/sth)** to crash; to hit sb/sth very hard while moving: *He ran along the corridor and collided with his teacher.* ○ *The lorry collided with a coach but fortunately nobody was injured.* يصطدم

collie /ˈkɒli/ *noun* [C] a dog with long hair and a long pointed nose. Some types of collie are used for guarding and looking after sheep. كولي: كلب للحراسة ورعي الغنم

colliery /ˈkɒliəri/ *noun* [C] (*pl.* **collieries**) (*especially Brit*) a coal mine and its buildings مَنْجَم الفحم (ومبانيه)

collision /kəˈlɪʒn/ *noun* [C,U] a crash; an occasion when things or people collide: *It was a head-on collision and the driver was killed instantly.* ○ *The two planes were in collision with each other and exploded.* اصطدام

colloquial /kəˈləʊkwiəl/ *adj* (used about words, phrases, etc.) used in conversation, not in formal situations or formal writing عاميّ ، دارج

▸ **colloquially** /-kwiəli/ *adv* باللغة الدارجة أو العاميّة

cologne /kəˈləʊn/ *noun* [U] = EAU DE COLOGNE

colon /ˈkəʊlən/ *noun* [C] a punctuation mark (:)

used before a list, an explanation, an example, etc. نقطتان متراكبتان أو علامة تفصيل

colonel /ˈkɜːnl/ *noun* [C] (*abbr* **Col.**) an officer with a high rank in the army عقيد

colonial /kəˈləʊniəl/ *adj* connected with or owning a colony (1): *Spain used to be a major colonial power.* استعماري

▸ **colonialism** *noun* [U] the practice of keeping countries as colonies استعمار

colonist /ˈkɒlənɪst/ *noun* [C] a person who goes to live in a colony (1) when it is first established as one مستوطن ، مستعمر

colonize (*also* **colonise**) /ˈkɒlənaɪz/ *verb* [T] to take control of a place as a colony; to establish a colony in a place يستعمر : يقيم مستعمرة

▸ **colonization** (*also* **colonisation**) /ˌkɒlənaɪˈzeɪʃn; *US* -nɪˈz-/ *noun* [U]: *the colonization of South America by the Spanish* استعمار

colony /ˈkɒləni/ *noun* (*pl.* **colonies**) **1** [C] a country or area that is ruled by another, more powerful country: *Kenya used to be a British colony.* مستعمرة

2 [C, with sing. or pl. verb] a group of people from the same country living in a foreign country or city: *the English colony on the Spanish coast* جالية

3 [C, with sing. or pl. verb] a group of people with the same interests, profession, etc. living together in the same place: *an artist's colony* مستعمرة (فنّانين مثلاً)

4 [C] a group of the same type of animals, insects or plants living or growing in the same place: *a colony of ants* قرية : جماعة : مستوطنة ، مستعمرة

⚷ **color** (*US*) = COLOUR

colossal /kəˈlɒsl/ *adj* extremely large; huge: *a colossal building* ○ *a colossal amount* هائل : ضخم

⚷ **colour¹** (*US* **color**) /ˈkʌlə(r)/ *noun* **1** [C,U] the quality that makes sth red, green, yellow, etc: *'What colour is your car?' 'Red.'* ○ *Brown isn't my favourite colour.* ○ *What colours do the Swedish team play in?* ○ *a dark/light colour* ○ *a bright colour* ○ *a deep/pale colour* ○ *Those flowers certainly give the room a bit of colour.* ❶ We say that a thing **is** a certain colour, not that it **has** a colour. لون

2 [U] the use of all the colours, not just black and white: *All the pictures in the book are in colour.* ○ *a colour television* (بِ) الألوان

3 [U, sing.] redness in your face, particularly showing how healthy you are: *You look much better now, you've got a bit more colour.* تورّد الوجه

4 [C,U] the colour of a person's skin, showing the person's race: *people of all colours and religions* ○ *Discrimination on the grounds of colour is illegal.* لون

5 [U] interesting or exciting details: *It's a busy area, full of activity and colour.* حيوية : تنوّع

IDM **off colour** ill: *I didn't go out because I was feeling a bit off colour.* متوعّك

with flying colours → FLYING

▸ **colourful** (*US* **colorful**) /-fl/ *adj* **1** with bright colours; full of colour: *a colourful shirt* زاهي الألوان

2 full of interest or excitement: *a colourful story* ○ *He has a rather colourful past.* نابض بالحياة : مثير

colourless (*US* **colorless**) *adj* **1** without colour: *a colourless liquid, like water* عديم اللون

2 dull and uninteresting: *a colourless description* باهت

⚷ **colour²** (*US* **color**) /ˈkʌlə(r)/ *verb* [T] **1** to put colour on sth, e.g. by painting it: *Colour the picture with your crayons.* ○ *The area coloured yellow on the map is desert.* يلوّن

2 to influence thoughts, opinions, etc: *You shouldn't let one bad experience colour your attitude to everything.* يؤثّر على : يصبغ

PHR V **colour sth in** to fill a shape, a picture, etc. with colour using pencils, chalk, etc: *The children were colouring in pictures of animals.* يلوّن (صورة مثلاً)

▸ **coloured** (*US* **colored**) *adj* **1** having colour; a particular colour: *She always writes letters on coloured paper.* ○ *a coffee-coloured dress* ○ *brightly-coloured lights* ملوّن

2 (used about a person) belonging to a race that does not have white skin ❶ This word is old-fashioned and may offend some people. To refer to a person belonging to a particular racial group, you should use black, Asian, etc. as appropriate. (شخص) ملوّن

colouring (*US* **coloring**) *noun* **1** [U] the colour of a person's hair, skin, etc: *People with such fair colouring get sunburnt easily.* لون (الشعر، البشَرة الخ)

2 [C,U] a substance that is used for giving a particular colour to sth, especially food مادة ملوّنة ، صِبغَة

ˈ**colour-blind** (*US* **color-blind**) *adj* unable to distinguish between certain colours, especially red and green مصاب بعمى الألوان

ˈ**colour scheme** (*US* **color scheme**) *noun* [C] the way in which colours are arranged, especially in a room تنسيق الألوان

colt /kəʊlt/ *noun* [C] a young male horse مُهْر

⚷ **column** /ˈkɒləm/ *noun* [C] **1** a tall solid vertical post made of stone, supporting or decorating a building or standing alone عمود

2 something that has the shape of a column: *a column of smoke* عمود

3 one of the vertical sections into which a printed page, especially in a newspaper, is divided عمود

4 a series of numbers written one under the other: *to add up a column of figures* عمود

5 a piece of writing in a newspaper or magazine that is part of a regular series or written by the same writer: *the travel column* عمود: زاوية

6 a long line of people, vehicles, etc., one following behind another: *a column of troops* صف طويل ، طابور

▸ **columnist** /ˈkɒləmnɪst/ *noun* [C] a journalist who writes regular articles in a newspaper or magazine: *a gossip columnist* ○ *a political columnist* صحفيّ (يكتب عموداً خاصاً)

coma /ˈkəʊmə/ *noun* [C] a state of deep unconsciousness, often lasting for a long time and caused by serious illness or injury: *She went into a coma and a few days later she died.* غيبوبة

comb /kəʊm/ *noun* **1** [C] a piece of metal or plastic with a row of teeth that you use for making your hair tidy مُشْط

2 [C, usually sing.] an act of combing the hair: *Give your hair a comb before you go out.* تمشيطة

▸ **comb** *verb* [T] **1** to make the hair tidy using a comb يمشط ، يسرح

2 comb sth (for sb/sth) to search thoroughly: *Police are combing the area for the escaped prisoners.* يمَشِّط ، يفتّش تفتيشاً دقيقاً

combat /ˈkɒmbæt/ *noun* [C,U] a fight, especially in war: *unarmed combat* (= without weapons) ○ *He got a medal for bravery in combat.* قتال

▸ **combat** *verb* [T] to fight against sth; to try to stop, reduce or defeat sth: *This government will do everything in its power to combat terrorism.* يقاتل : يكافح

combatant /ˈkɒmbətənt/ *noun* [C] a person who takes part in fighting, especially in war مقاتل

combination /ˌkɒmbɪˈneɪʃn/ *noun* [C,U] a number of people or things mixed or joined together; a mixture: *He left the job for a combination of reasons.* ○ *The team manager still hasn't found the right combination of players.* ○ *On this course, you may study French in combination with Spanish or Italian.* مجموعة : تضافر : مزيج من

combine¹ /kəmˈbaɪn/ *verb* **1** [I,T] **combine (with sb/sth); combine A and B/A with B** to join or mix two or more things together: *The two organizations combined to form one company.* ○ *Bad planning, combined with bad luck, led to the company's collapse.* يتّحد؛ يضم

2 [T] **combine A and B/A with B** to do two or more things at the same time or have two or more qualities at the same time: *to combine business with pleasure.* ○ *This car combines speed and reliability.* يجمع

▸ **combined** *adj* done by a number of people joining together, resulting from the joining of two or more things: *The combined efforts of the emergency services prevented a major disaster.* ○ *I use that room as a spare bedroom and office combined* (= it can be used as either). متّحد، مُجتَمِع؛ معاً

combine² /ˈkɒmbaɪn/ (*also* **ˌcombine ˈharvester**) *noun* [C] an agricultural machine that both cuts corn and separates the seed from the stem حصّادة دراسة

combustion /kəmˈbʌstʃən/ *noun* [U] the process of burning احتراق

come /kʌm/ *verb* [I] (*pt* **came** /keɪm/; *pp* **come**)

1 to move to or towards the person who is speaking or the place that sb is talking about: *Come here, please.* ○ *Come and see what I've found.* ○ *I hope you can come to my party.* ○ *They're coming to stay for a week.* ○ *The children came running into the room.* يجيء ، يأتي

2 to arrive or reach: *What time are you coming home?* ○ *Has the newspaper come yet?* ○ *The news came as a complete surprise.* ○ *The time has come to say goodbye.* يأتي ، يصل

3 to have a particular position: *March comes after February.* ○ *Charlie came second in the exam.* يقع ، يجيء

4 to be available: *This blouse comes in a choice of four colours.* يوجَد

5 to be produced by or from sth: *Wool comes from sheep.* يؤخذ (من)

6 to become: *Your blouse has come undone.* يصبح

7 come to do sth (used for talking about how, why or when sth happened): *How did you come to lose your passport?* يحدث ، يحصل : يصادف

8 (used with *to/into* and a noun) to reach a particular state: *We were all sorry when the holiday came to an end.* ○ *The military government came to power in a coup d'état.* يصل ، يبلغ

IDM **come and go** to be present for a short time and then go away: *The pain in my ear comes and goes.* يأتي ويذهب

come easily, etc. to sb to be easy, etc. for sb to do: *Apologizing does not come easily to her.* يسهل عليه

come to nothing; not come to anything to be unsuccessful: *Unfortunately, all his efforts came to nothing.* يخفق

how come...? (*informal*) why or how: *How come you're back so early?* ○ *How come I didn't get one too?* لماذا أو كيف...؟

to come (used after a noun) in the future: *You'll regret it in years to come.* في المستقبل

when it comes to sth/to doing sth when it is a question of sth: *When it comes to value for money, these prices are hard to beat.* فيما يتعلّق بِ

PHR V **come about** to happen: *How did this situation come about?* يحدث ، يقع

come across/over to make an impression of a particular type: *Elizabeth comes across as being rather shy.* يعطي انطباعاً

come across sb/sth to meet or find sb/sth by chance: *I came across this book in a second-hand shop.* يصادف ؛ يجد بالمصادفة

come along 1 to arrive or appear: *An old man was coming along the road.* يأتي ، يَقْدم ؛ يظهر

2 = COME ON (2)

3 = COME ON (3)

come apart to break into pieces: *This old coat is coming apart at the seams.* يتفكك ، يتحطّم ؛ يتفتّق

come away (from sth) to become loose or unfastened: *The cover of the book is coming away* (= from the pages). ينفصل (عن) ، ينفك

come away with sth to leave a place with a particular opinion or feeling: *We came away with a very favourable impression of Cambridge.* يرجع حاملاً انطباعاً معيناً

come back 1 to return: *I don't know what time I'll be coming back.* يعود ، يرجع

2 to become popular or fashionable again: *Flared trousers are coming back again.* يستعيد رواجه

come back (to sb) to be remembered: *When I*

went to Italy again, my Italian started to come back. يعود إلى الذاكرة
come before sb/sth to be more important than sb/sth else: *Mark feels his family comes before his career.* يتقدم على ، يفوق في أهميته
come between sb and sb to damage the relationship between two people: *Arguments over money came between the two brothers.* يفسد العلاقة (بين شخصين)
come by sth to get sth: *Fresh vegetables are hard to come by in the winter.* يجد ، يحصل على
come down 1 to fall down: *The power lines came down in the storm.* ينهار ، يسقط

2 (used about an aircraft, etc.) to land: *The helicopter came down in a field.* يهبط ، يحطّ

3 to become lower: *The price of land has come down in the past year.* ينزل ، ينخفض
come down to sth/to doing sth (*informal*) to have as the main feature or most important fact: *It all comes down to having the right qualifications.* جوهر الأمر
come down to sth to reach down to a particular point: *Her hair comes down to her waist.* يتدلّى
come down with sth to become ill with sth: *I think I'm coming down with flu.* يصاب (بمرض)
come forward to offer help: *The police are asking witnesses to come forward.* يساعد ، يتقدّم للمساعدة
come from... to live in or have been born in a place: *Where do you come from originally?* يسكن في مكان أو يكون مولوداً فيه
come from (doing) sth to be the result of sth: *'I'm tired.' 'That comes from all the late nights you've had.'* ينتج أو ينشأ عن
come in 1 (used about the tide) to move towards the land يرتفع (المدّ)

2 to become popular or fashionable: *Punk fashions came in in the seventies.* يصبح شائعاً ، يروج

3 (used about news or information) to be received: *Reports are coming in of fighting in Beirut.* يصل
come in for sth to receive blame, etc: *The government came in for a lot of criticism.* يتعرّض (للنقد مثلاً)
come of sth/of doing sth to be the result of sth: *We've written to several companies asking for help but nothing has come of it yet.* يثْمر ، ينتج
come off 1 to be able to be removed: *Does the collar come off?* ينفكّ ، ينفصل

2 (*informal*) to be successful: *The deal seems unlikely to come off.* ينجح

3 (*informal*) (followed by an adverb) to be in a good, bad, etc. situation as a result of sth: *Unfortunately, Dennis came off worst in the fight.* يطلع منه بنتيجة حسنة (أو سيئة)
come off (sth) 1 to fall off sth: *Kim came off her bicycle and broke her leg.* يسقط عن

2 to become removed from sth: *One of the legs has come off this table.* ينفكّ ، ينفصل
come off it (*informal*) (used for showing that you do not believe sb/sth or that you strongly disagree with sb): *'I thought it was quite a good performance.' 'Oh, come off it – it was awful!'* لا أصدّق ذلك : لا أوافق

come on 1 to start to act, play in a game of sport, etc: *The audience jeered every time the villain came on.* ○ *The substitute came on in the second half.* يبدأ في التمثيل أو اللعب الخ ، يخرج

2 (*also* **come along**) to make progress or to improve: *Your English is coming on nicely.* يتحسّن ، يتقدّم

3 (*also* **Come on!**; **Come along!**) (used for telling sb to hurry up, try harder, etc.): *Come on or we'll be late!* ○ *Come on! You can do better work than that.* هيّا ، أسْرِع!

4 to begin: *I think I've got a cold coming on.* يبدأ

come out 1 to appear: *The rain stopped and the sun came out.* ○ *The report came out in 1988.* يطلع ، يصدر

2 to become known: *It was only after his death that the truth came out.* يظهر ، ينكشف

3 (used about a photograph, etc.) to be produced successfully: *Only one of our photos came out.* (الصورة) تطلع أو تنجح
come out (of sth) to be removed from sth: *Red wine stains don't come out easily.* يزول
come out against sth to say in public that you do not like or agree with sth: *The Prime Minister came out against capital punishment.* يعارض علانية
come out in sth to become covered in spots, etc: *Heat makes him come out in a rash.* يصاب بطفْح جلدي وغيره
come out with sth to say sth: *The children came out with all kinds of stories.* يطلع (بفكرة) ، يحكي
come over = COME ACROSS
come over (to...) (from...) to move from one place to another: *They've invited us to come over to Australia for a holiday.* يأتي ؛ يسافر
come over sb (used about a feeling) to affect sb; *A feeling of despair came over me.* يصيب ، ينتاب
come round 1 (used about an event that happens regularly) to happen: *The end of the holidays always comes round very quickly.* يحدث ؛ يأتي

2 (*also* **come to**) to become conscious again يستردّ وعيه ، يفيق من إغماء
come round (to...) to visit a person or place: *Why don't you come round to see us on Saturday?* يزور
come round (to sth) to change your opinion so that you agree with sb/sth: *They finally came round to our way of thinking.* يغيّر رأيه ، يتنازل عن موقفه
come through (used about news, information, etc.) to arrive: *The football results are just coming through.* يصل
come through (sth) to escape injury or death in a dangerous situation, illness, etc: *to come through a heart attack* ينجو من
come to = COME ROUND
come to sth 1 to equal or total a particular amount: *The bill for the meal came to £35.* يبلغ

2 to reach a bad situation: *We will sell the house to pay our debts if we have to but we hope it won't come to that.* يتدنّى الوضع (إلى ذلك)
come under to be included in a particular

section, department, etc: *Garages that sell cars come under 'car dealers' in the telephone book.* يصنّف ، يقع تحت اسم

come up 1 (used about a plant) to appear above the soil ينمو

2 (used about the sun and moon) to rise يشرق ، يبزغ

3 to be about to happen in the future: *I have an important meeting coming up next week.* يحدث أو يأتي قريباً

4 to be discussed: *The subject of religion came up.* يَعرض للمناقشة

come up against sb/sth to find a problem or difficulty that you have to deal with: *The developers came up against a lot of opposition from the local residents.* يواجه

come up to sth 1 to reach up as far as a particular point: *The water in the pool came up to our knees.* يبلغ ، يصل

2 to be as good as usual or as necessary: *This piece of work does not come up to your usual standard.* يرقى

come up with sth to find an answer or solution to sth: *Engineers have come up with new ways of saving energy.* يجد حلاً ، يبتكر

comeback /ˈkʌmbæk/ *noun* [C] a return to a position of strength or importance that you had before: *The former world champion is hoping to make a comeback.* استعادة مجد سابق

comedian /kəˈmiːdiən/ (*also* **comic**) *noun* [C] a person whose job is to entertain people and make them laugh, e.g. by telling jokes كوميدي ، ممثل هَزْلي

comedown /ˈkʌmdaʊn/ *noun* [C, usually sing.] (*informal*) a loss of importance or social position: *It's a bit of a comedown for her having to move to a smaller house.* انخفاض في المنزلة

comedy /ˈkɒmədi/ *noun* (*pl.* **comedies**) **1** [C] an amusing play, film, etc. that has a happy ending ➲ Look at **tragedy**. كوميديا ، مسرحية أو فيلم هَزْلي

2 [U] the quality of being amusing or making people laugh: *There is a hint of comedy in all her novels.* كوميديا ، هَزْل

comet /ˈkɒmɪt/ *noun* [C] an object that looks like a bright star with a tail and that moves around the sun (نجم) مذنّب

comfort /ˈkʌmfət/ *noun* **1** [U] the state of having everything your body needs, or of having a pleasant life: *Most people expect to live in comfort in their old age.* ○ *to travel in comfort* راحة ، رفاهية

2 [U] the state of being relaxed: *This furniture is not designed for comfort.* راحة

3 [U] help or kindness to sb who is suffering: *I tried to offer a few words of comfort.* عزاء ، مواساة

4 [sing.] a person or thing that helps you when you are very sad or worried: *You've been a real comfort to me.* سلوى

5 [C] something that makes your life easier or more pleasant: *After a week's camping we really appreciated the comforts of home.* ➲ Look at **discomfort**. وسيلة راحة

▸ **comfort** *verb* [T] to try to make sb feel less worried or unhappy: *to comfort a crying child* يعزّي ، يسكّن ، يطيّب خاطره

comfortable /ˈkʌmftəbl; *US* -fərt-/ (*also informal* **comfy**) *adj* **1** allowing you to feel relaxed and providing you with everything your body needs: *Our hotel room was large and comfortable.* ○ *a comfortable temperature* (= not too hot or too cold) ○ *Sit down and make yourselves comfortable.* ❶ The opposite is **uncomfortable**. مريح

2 not having or causing worry, pain, difficulty, etc: *He did not feel comfortable in the presence of so many women.* مرتاح

3 having or providing enough money for all your needs: *They are not wealthy but they're quite comfortable.* ميسور ، مكْتَفٍ مالياً

▸ **comfortably** /-təbli/ *adv* in a comfortable way: *You can't live comfortably on such low wages.* على نحو مريح أو كافٍ

comfy /ˈkʌmfi/ *adj* (**comfier**; **comfiest**) (*informal*) comfortable (1): *a comfy chair* مريح ، وثير

comic /ˈkɒmɪk/ *adj* that makes you laugh; funny: *a comic scene in a play* هَزلي ؛ مضحك

▸ **comic** *noun* [C] **1** = COMEDIAN

2 a magazine for children that tells stories through pictures مجلة أطفال مصوّرة

comical /ˈkɒmɪkl/ *adj* that makes you laugh مُضْحك ، مثير للضحك

comically /-kli/ *adv* على نحو مضحك أو هزْلي

ˈ**comic strip** (*also* ˈ**strip cartoon**) *noun* [C] a series of pictures that tell a story, e.g. in a newspaper, etc. قصّة مصوّرة

coming /ˈkʌmɪŋ/ *noun* [C] the arrival of sth: *The coming of the computer meant the loss of many jobs.* قدوم

comma /ˈkɒmə/ *noun* [C] the punctuation mark (,) used for dividing parts of a sentence or items in a list فاصلة ، فارزة

command¹ /kəˈmɑːnd; *US* -ˈmænd/ *verb* **1** [I,T] to tell or order sb to do sth: *The men did as their officer had commanded.* يأمر

2 [T] to control or be in charge of sb/sth: *to command a ship, regiment, army, etc.* يقود ؛ يرأس

3 [T] to deserve and get sth: *The old man commanded great respect.* يحظى بِ ، يستحق

▸ **commanding** *adj* **1** (used about a person who commands (2) sb/sth): *Who is your commanding officer?* قائد

2 having or showing power or authority: *to speak in a commanding tone of voice* آمر (وناه)

3 strong: *The castle occupied a commanding position at the head of the valley.* قوي ، مسيطر على ما حوله

command² /kəˈmɑːnd/ *noun* **1** [C] an order: *The captain's commands must be obeyed without question.* أمر

2 [U] control over sb/sth: *Who is in command of the expedition?* ○ *to take command of a situation* قيادة ؛ إشراف ؛ سلطة

3 [sing.] the state of being able to do or use sth: *She has a good command of French.* تمكّن

IDM **at/by sb's command** (*formal*) because you were ordered by sb: *At the command of their officer the troops opened fire.* بأمر من

be at sb's command to be ready to obey sb: *I'm completely at your command.* تحت أمر (شخص)

commandeer /ˌkɒmənˈdɪə(r)/ *verb* [T] to take control or possession of sth for military use يصادر لغرض عسكري

commander /kəˈmɑːndə(r); *US* -ˈmæn-/ *noun* [C] **1** a person who controls or is in charge of sb/sth قائد ، آمر

2 (*Brit*) an officer in the Navy ضابط بحرية

commandment (*also* **Commandment**) /kəˈmɑːndmənt; *US* -ˈmænd-/ *noun* [C] (*formal*) one of the ten important laws that Christian people should obey وصية (من الوصايا العشر)

commando /kəˈmɑːndəʊ; *US* -ˈmæn-/ *noun* [C] (*pl.* **commandos**) one of a group of soldiers who are trained to make quick attacks in enemy areas أحد المغاوير، فدائي

commemorate /kəˈmeməreɪt/ *verb* [T] to keep a special event in people's memories; to exist in order to make people remember a special event: *a statue commemorating all the soldiers who died in the last war* يحيي ذكرى

▶ **commemoration** /kəˌmeməˈreɪʃn/ *noun* [C,U]: *The concerts were held in commemoration of the 200th anniversary of the composer's death.* إحياء ذكرى

commence /kəˈmens/ *verb* [I,T] (*formal*) **commence sth/doing sth** to start or begin ➲ Look at the note at **begin**. يبدأ، يشرع

▶ **commencement** *noun* [C,U] بدء

commend /kəˈmend/ *verb* [T] to say that sb/sth is very good: *Dean was commended for his excellent work.* يشيد بـ، يثني على

▶ **commendable** /-əbl/ *adj* that you must praise: *She acted with commendable honesty and fairness.* جدير بالثناء

comment /ˈkɒment/ *noun* [C,U] **comment (on sth)** something that you say or write that gives your opinion or feeling about sth: *The chancellor was not available for comment.* ○ *I have heard both favourable and unfavourable comments about the film.* تعليق

IDM **no comment** (used in reply to a question when you do not want to say anything at all): *'Mr President, how do you feel about these latest developments?' 'No comment.'* لا أريد أن أعلّق

▶ **comment** *verb* [I,T] **comment (on sth)** to give your opinion or feeling about sth: *Several people commented on how lovely the garden looked.* ○ *Somebody commented that it didn't seem very fair.* يعلّق (على)

commentary /ˈkɒməntri; *US* -teri/ *noun* (*pl.* **commentaries**) **1** [C,U] a spoken description on the radio or television of sth as it is happening: *the commentary on a football match* تعليق

2 [C] a written explanation of sth: *a translation of Shakespeare's plays with a commentary* شرح

commentate /ˈkɒmənteɪt/ *verb* [I] to give a spoken description on the radio or television of sth as it is happening يعلّق تعليقاً حيّاً

▶ **commentator** /ˈkɒmənteɪtə(r)/ *noun* [C] **1** a person who commentates on sth: *a sports commentator* معلّق

2 a person who gives his/her opinion about sth on the radio, on television or in a newspaper: *a political commentator* معلّق

commerce /ˈkɒmɜːs/ *noun* [U] the activities that are involved in buying and selling things: *the Minister for Industry and Commerce* تجارة

commercial /kəˈmɜːʃl/ *adj* **1** connected with buying and selling goods: *a specialist in commercial law* تجاري

2 making a profit: *Although it won a lot of awards, the film was not a commercial success.* مربِح (تجارياً)

▶ **commercial** *noun* [C] an advertisement on the radio or on television دعاية أو إعلان تجاري

commercialism /kəˈmɜːʃəlɪzəm/ *noun* [U] the attitude that making a profit is more important than anything else النزعة التجارية ، التركيز على الكسب

commercialize (*also* **commercialise**) /kəˈmɜːʃəlaɪz/ *verb* [T] to try to make a profit out of sth, even if it means spoiling it: *Christmas has become very commercialized over recent years.* يجعله تجارياً؛ يستغل للربح

commercially /-ʃəli/: *The factory was closed down because it was no longer commercially viable.* تجارياً

commiserate /kəˈmɪzəreɪt/ *verb* [I] **commiserate (with sb) (on/over sth)** (*formal*) to feel or show sympathy for sb who is very unhappy or in difficulty يواسي ، يتعاطف مع

commission /kəˈmɪʃn/ *noun* **1** [C] an act of asking sb to do a piece of work for you: *He received a commission to write a play for the festival.* تكليف

2 often **Commission** [C, with sing. or pl. verb] an official group of people who are asked to find out about sth: *A Commission was appointed to investigate the causes of the accident.* لجنة تحقيق

3 [C,U] money that you get for selling sth: *Agents get 10% commission on everything they sell* (= 10% of the value of the things they sell). عمولة

▶ **commission** *verb* [T] to ask sb to do a piece of work: *to commission an architect to design a building* يكلّف

commissioner /kəˈmɪʃənə(r)/ *noun* [C] an official of high rank in an organization مفوّض، مندوب

commit /kəˈmɪt/ *verb* [T] (committing; committed) **1** to do sth bad or illegal: *to commit a crime* ○ *to commit suicide* يرتكب (جريمة)

2 (*formal*) to send sb to a prison, mental hospital, etc: *He was committed to Broadmoor for the rest of his life.* يودِع (في سجن أو مصحّة الخ)

3 commit sb/yourself (to sth/to doing sth) to promise to do sth: *I can't commit myself to helping you tomorrow. I'm still not sure if I will be free.* يتعهّد أو يلتزم بـ

a b c d e f g h i j k l m n o p q r s t u v w x y z

4 to decide to use sth for a particular purpose يوجّه (لغرض معين) : يودع

5 commit yourself (on sth) to say openly what you think or believe: *When asked for her opinion she refused to commit herself.* ➲ Look at **non-committal**. يعلن رأيه بصراحة

▶ **commitment** *noun* **1** [U] **commitment (to sth)** the state of giving a lot of your time and attention to sth because you believe it is right or important: *We are looking for a teacher with enthusiasm and commitment.* ○ *commitment to an ideal* التزام

2 [C] something that you have promised to do; a responsibility: *Marriage is a great commitment.* ○ *We usually have family commitments on Sunday.* ○ *Japan has made a commitment to respect the new agreement.* تعهّد : مسؤولية ، التزام

committed *adj* giving a lot of your time and attention to sth because you believe it is right or important: *a committed Christian* ○ *The company is committed to providing quality products.* ملتزم

committee /kəˈmɪti/ *noun* [C, with sing. or pl. verb] a group of people who have been chosen to discuss sth or decide on sth: *They have set up a committee to look into ways of reducing traffic in the city centre.* ○ *to be/sit on a committee* ○ *The planning committee meets/meet twice a week.* لجنة

commodity /kəˈmɒdəti/ *noun* [C] (*pl.* **commodities**) something that you buy or sell: *Salt was once a very valuable commodity.* سلعة ، بِضاعة

commodore /ˈkɒmədɔː(r)/ *noun* [C] an officer of middle rank in the Navy قائد أو عميد بحري

common¹ /ˈkɒmən/ *adj* **1** happening or found often or in many places; usual: *Nowadays it is quite common for people to go abroad for their holidays.* ○ *The word is no longer in common use.* ○ *The daisy is a common wild flower.* شائع : عادي

2 common (to sb/sth) shared by or belonging to two or more people or groups, or by most or all people: *The Americans and the British share a common language.* ○ *This type of behaviour is common to most children of that age.* ○ *We have a common interest in gardening.* مشترك

3 (only *before* a noun) not special; ordinary: *The officers had much better living conditions than the common soldiers.* عادي

4 (*informal*) having or showing a lack of education: *Don't speak like that. It's common!* مبتذل ، سوقيّ

IDM **be common/public knowledge** → KNOWLEDGE

▶ **commonly** *adv* often; usually: *These insects are commonly known as midges.* عموماً : عادة

common² /ˈkɒmən/ *noun* [C] an area of open land where the public is free to walk: *cricket on the village common* أرض مشاع

IDM **have sth in common (with sb/sth)** to share sth with sb/sth else: *They seem to be good friends although they have few interests in common.* ○ *to have a lot in common with sb* يشترك

in common with sb/sth like sb/sth: *This company, in common with many others, is losing a lot of money.* على غِرار

commoner /ˈkɒmənə(r)/ *noun* [C] an ordinary person, i.e. not a member of a noble or royal family من عامة الشعب

ˌcommon ˈground *noun* [U] beliefs, interests, etc. that two or more people or groups share: *They have very little common ground.* آراء أو هوايات الخ...مشتركة

ˌcommon ˈlaw *noun* [U] laws in England that are based on decisions that judges have made, not laws that were made by Parliament قانون العرف والعادة

commonplace /ˈkɒmənpleɪs/ *adj* not very exciting or unusual; ordinary: *Foreign travel has become commonplace in recent years.* عادي : مألوف

ˈcommon room *noun* [C] a room in a school, university, etc. where students or teachers can go to relax when they are not in class غرفة الاستراحة (في مدرسة أو جامعة الخ)

Commons /ˈkɒmənz/ *noun* [plural] **the Commons** (*Brit*) = THE HOUSE OF COMMONS ➲ Look at the note at **Parliament**.

ˌcommon ˈsense *noun* [U] the ability to make good sensible decisions because of your experience of life, not because of what you have learned at school or from books: *Safety precautions are basically just common sense.* التفكير أو الحسّ السليم

Commonwealth /ˈkɒmənwelθ/ *noun* [sing.] **the Commonwealth** the group of countries that once formed the British Empire and that try to work and to trade together in a friendly way (دول) الكومونولث

commotion /kəˈməʊʃn/ *noun* [sing., U] great noise or excitement: *People looked out of their windows to see what all the commotion was about.* جَلَبة ، هَرْج ومَرْج

communal /ˈkɒmjənl; kəˈmjuːnl/ *adj* shared by a group of people: *a communal kitchen* جماعي ، مشترك

commune /ˈkɒmjuːn/ *noun* [C, with sing. or pl. verb] a group of people, not from the same family, who live together and share their property and responsibilities مجموعة تعيش حياة اشتراكية

communicate /kəˈmjuːnɪkeɪt/ *verb* **1** [I,T] to make information or your opinions, feelings, etc. known to sb: *Parents often have difficulty communicating with their teenage children* (= understanding them and being understood). ○ *They communicate by sign language.* ○ *Our boss is good at communicating her ideas to the team.* ينقل (المعلومات الخ) : يتواصل

2 [I] **communicate (with sth)** to be joined or connected with sth: *two rooms with a communicating door* يربط أو يتّصل بـ

communication /kəˌmjuːnɪˈkeɪʃn/ *noun* **1** [U] the act of communicating: *There is little real communication between father and daughter.* ○ *verbal/non-verbal communication* ○ *Radio is the* *only means of communication in remote areas.* اتصال

2 communications [plural] the methods that are used for travelling to and from a place or for sending messages between places: *The telephone lines are down so communications are very difficult.* وسائل الاتصال

3 [C] (*formal*) a message: *a communication from our chairman* رسالة

IDM **be in communication with sb/sth** (*formal*) to be in regular contact with: *The astronauts are in direct communication with the control centre in Houston.* (يكون) على اتصال

communicative /kə'mju:nɪkətɪv; *US* -keɪtɪv/ *adj* willing to talk or give information: *Daphne seems shy and not very communicative.* ❶ The opposite is **uncommunicative**. على استعداد للكلام ، غير متحفّظ

communion /kə'mju:niən/ *noun* **1 Communion** (*also* **Holy Communion**) [U] the ceremony in the Christian Church in which people share bread and wine as symbols of Christ's body and blood: *to take/go to Communion* العشاء الرباني ، القربان المقدّس

2 (*formal*) [U] the sharing of thoughts or feelings: *Modern man is no longer in communion with nature.* تبادل المشاعر ؛ مناجاة

communiqué /kə'mju:nɪkeɪ; *US* kə,mju:nə'keɪ/ *noun* [C] an official statement, especially from a government, a political group, etc. بيان (رسمي)

communism /'kɒmjunɪzəm/ *noun* [U] the political and economic system or theory in which the state owns and controls the means of production and in which everybody is supposed to be equal الشيوعية

▸ **communist** /'kɒmjənɪst/ *noun* [C] a person who believes in or supports communism (شخص) شيوعي

communist *adj*: *communist sympathies* شيوعي

> When we are talking about a particular society or political party which is organized according to the principles of communism we often use a capital letter for **communism** and **communist**: *Russian Communism* ○ *He was a member of the Communist Party.*

🔑 **community** /kə'mju:nəti/ *noun* (*pl.* **communities**) **1 the community** [sing.] the group of people who live in a particular place, area or country: *She was given an award for her work with young people in the community.* ○ *Recent increases in crime have disturbed the whole community.* جماعة ، مجتمع

2 [C, with sing. or pl. verb] a group of people who have sth (e.g. nationality, interests, type of work, etc.) in common: *the Asian community in Britain* ○ *the business community* مجتمع ، جالية

3 [U] the feeling of belonging to a group in the place where you live: *There is a strong sense of community in the neighbourhood.* روح الجماعة

com'munity centre (*US* **community center**) *noun* [C] a building where local people can take part in classes, sports, etc. مركز ثقافي ورياضي لخدمة الأهالي

com,munity 'service *noun* [U] work helping people in the local community that sb does without being paid, sometimes because he/she has been ordered to do it by a court of law as a punishment خدمة اجتماعية

commute /kə'mju:t/ *verb* [I] to travel a long distance from home to work every day: *A lot of people commute to London from nearby towns.* يسافر يومياً إلى مكان عمله

▸ **commuter** *noun* [C]: *The trains are always full of commuters at this time of day.* مسافر يومياً

compact /kəm'pækt; *US* 'kɒmpækt/ *adj* small, neat and taking up little space: *a compact camera* ○ *The compact design of the iron makes it ideal for travel.* مدمَج؛ صغير مركز

,compact 'disc *noun* [C] = CD

companion /kəm'pæniən/ *noun* [C] a person or animal with whom you spend a lot of time or go somewhere: *They were constant companions at school.* ○ *a travelling companion* رفيق

▸ **companionship** *noun* [U] friendship or company: *A lot of people get married for companionship.* رِفقة

🔑 **company** /'kʌmpəni/ *noun* (*pl.* **companies**) **1** [C, with sing. or pl. verb] a business organization selling goods or services: *an engineering company* ○ *Is the telephone company here private or state-owned?* ○ *She applied to several companies for a job.* ○ *The company is/are planning to build a new factory in Derby.* ❶ In names company is written with a capital letter. The abbreviation is **Co.**: *the Walt Disney Company* ○ *Milton & Co.* شركة

2 [U] being with a person: *I always enjoy her company because she always has amusing stories to tell.* ○ *She was very good company* (= pleasant to be with) *and I thoroughly enjoyed our evening together.* رِفقة

3 [U] a visitor or visitors: *We were surprised when the doorbell rang because we weren't expecting company.* زائر ، زوّار

4 [C, with sing. or pl. verb] a group of actors, singers, dancers, etc: *a ballet company* ○ *the Royal Shakespeare Company* فرقة (مسرحية مثلاً)

IDM **keep sb company** to go or be with sb so that he/she is not alone: *She was nervous so I went with her to keep her company.* يرافق ، يبقى مع

part company → PART²

comparable /'kɒmpərəbl/ *adj* **comparable (to/with sb/sth)** of a similar standard or size; that can be compared with sth: *A comparable flat in my country would be a lot cheaper.* مُشابِه ؛ قابل للمقارنة

comparative /kəm'pærətɪv/ *adj* **1** compared with sth else or with what is usual or normal: *He had problems with the written exam but passed the practical exam with comparative ease.* نسبي

2 involving comparing things of the same kind:

a b **c** d e f g h i j k l m n o p q r s t u v w x y z

a comparative study of systems of government مقارَن

3 (*grammar*) (used about the form of an adjective or adverb) expressing a greater amount, quality, size, etc: *'Hotter' is the comparative form of 'hot'.* في صيغة التفضيل

▸ **comparative** *noun* [C] (*grammar*) the form of an adjective or adverb that expresses a greater amount, quality, size, etc: *'Worse' is the comparative of 'bad'.* صيغة التفضيل

comparatively *adv* as compared with sth else or with what is usual: *The disease is comparatively rare nowadays.* ○ *Most of the houses are old but this one was built comparatively recently.* نسبياً

compare /kəm'peə(r)/ *verb* **1** [T] **compare A and B; compare A with/to B** to consider people or things in order to find ways in which they are similar or different: *If you compare the old and the new models, you'll see the changes we've made.* ○ *When the police compared the two letters, they realized that they had been written by the same person.* ○ *Write an essay comparing Britain in the eighteenth century with Britain today.* يقارن

2 [T] **compare A to B** to say that things or people are similar in a way or ways: *When it was built, people compared the cathedral to a huge tent.* يشبِّه

3 [I] **compare with sb/sth** to be of the same quality as sb/sth: *Her last film was brilliant but this one simply doesn't compare.* ○ *There is nothing to compare with the taste of bread fresh from the oven.* يشبِه ، يعادل في النوعيّة

IDM **compare notes (with sb)** to discuss your opinions, ideas, experiences, etc. with sb else: *At the beginning of term we met and compared notes about the holidays.* يتبادل الآراء

▸ **compared** *adj* **compared to/with** in comparison with; considered in relation to: *I'm quite a patient person, compared with him.* ○ *Compared to the place where I grew up, this town is exciting.* مقارنةً بِ ، بالنسبة لِ

comparison /kəm'pærɪsn/ *noun* [C,U] an act of comparing; a statement in which people or things are compared: *Put the new one and the old one side by side, for comparison.* ○ *A comparison of this year's figures with last year's shows that the economy is improving.* ○ *It's hard to make comparisons between Ian's painting and Sheila's because he's been learning so much longer.* مقارنة

IDM **by/in comparison (with sb/sth)** when compared: *He's quite tall, by comparison with some of the older boys.* ○ *In comparison with many other people, they're quite well off.* ○ *When she told me about her problems I realized that mine were small by comparison.* بالنسبة لِ ، بالمقارنة مع

draw a comparison/a parallel → DRAW[2]

compartment /kəm'pɑːtmənt/ *noun* [C] **1** one of the separate sections into which some railway carriages are divided: *a first-class compartment* مقصورة (في قطار)

2 one of the separate sections into which certain containers are divided: *The drugs were discovered in a secret compartment in his suitcase.* ○ *the glove compartment* (= the space where you can keep maps, etc. in a car) قسم

compasses

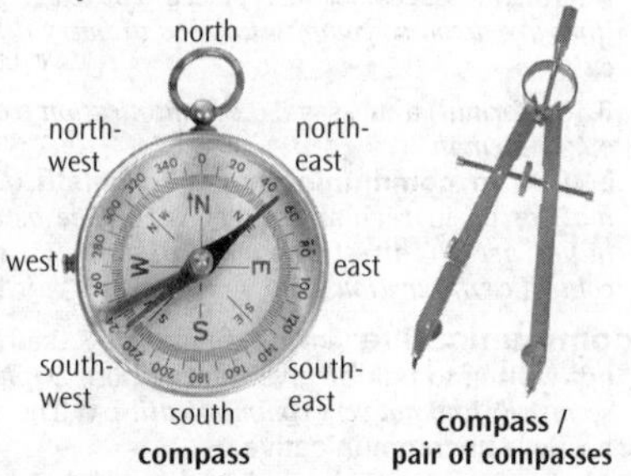

compass /'kʌmpəs/ *noun* [C] **1** an instrument for finding direction, with a needle that always points north: *a ship's compass* ○ *They had to find their way back to the camp using a map and a compass.* بوصلة

2 (*also* **compasses**) [plural] a V-shaped instrument that is used for drawing circles, etc: *a pair of compasses* فرجار

compassion /kəm'pæʃn/ *noun* [U] **compassion (for sb)** sympathy or pity for sb who is suffering شفقة ، رحمة

▸ **compassionate** /kəm'pæʃənət/ *adj* having or showing sympathy or pity for sb who is suffering شفوق ، رحيم

compatible /kəm'pætəbl/ *adj* **compatible (with sb/sth)** suitable to live together or to be used together: *As a couple, they are simply not compatible.* ○ *compatible software* ❶ The opposite is **incompatible.** متوافق ، متناسب

▸ **compatibility** /kəm,pætə'bɪləti/ *noun* [U] تلاؤم، توافق

compatriot /kəm'pætriət; *US* -'peɪt-/ *noun* [C] a person who comes from the same country as another مواطن: من وطن واحد

compel /kəm'pel/ *verb* [T] (compelling; compelled) (*formal*) to force sb to do sth: *I felt compelled to tell her what I really thought of her.* يُجبِر

▸ **compelling** *adj* **1** very exciting; holding your attention: *a compelling story* شيِّق ، مثير

2 forcing sb to do sth; convincing: *I felt that there was no compelling reason to stay, so I left.* ❶ The noun is **compulsion**. قاهر ؛ مُقنِع

compensate /'kɒmpenseɪt/ *verb* **compensate (sb) for sth 1** [I,T] to pay sb money because you have injured him/her or lost or damaged his/her property: *To compensate for the loss of my luggage, the airline sent me a cheque.* يعوِّض (على)

2 [I] to remove or reduce the bad effect of sth; to make up for sth: *His willingness to work hard compensates for his lack of skill.* يعوِّض (عن)

▸ **compensation** /,kɒmpen'seɪʃn/ *noun* **compensation (for sth) 1** [U] money that you pay to sb because you have injured him/her or lost or damaged his/her property: *She claimed compensation from the company for the injury she suffered while working there.* تعويض

2 [C,U] a fact or action that removes or reduces the bad effect of sth: *City life can be very tiring but there are compensations* (= good things about it). ○ *He took the children to the zoo as compensation for not taking them on holiday.* شيء مُعوِّض ؛ حسنة

compère /ˈkɒmpeə(r)/ *noun* [C] (*Brit*) a person who introduces the different performers in a show at the theatre or on television مُقدِّم برنامج فني

▸ **compère** *verb* [T] (*Brit*) to act as a compère يقدِّم برنامجاً فنياً

compete /kəmˈpiːt/ *verb* [I] **compete (against/with sb) (for sth)** to try to win or achieve sth, or to try to be better than sb else: *The world's best athletes compete in the Olympic Games.* ○ *The teams are competing for a silver trophy.* ○ *As children, they always used to compete with each other.* ○ *They had to compete against several larger companies to get the contract.* ○ *We can't compete with overseas firms unless we improve the quality of our goods.* يتنافس

competent /ˈkɒmpɪtənt/ *adj* **1** having the ability or skill needed for sth: *a highly competent player* ○ *She is competent at her job.* ○ *He is not competent to be a manager.* ❶ The opposite is **incompetent**. كفء ، مقتدر

2 satisfactory but not excellent: *a competent, but not particularly exciting, performance* لا بأس به

▸ **competence** /ˈkɒmpɪtəns/ *noun* [U] having the ability or skill that is needed: *She quickly proved her competence in her new position.* ❶ The opposite is **incompetence**. كفاءة ، مقدرة

competently *adv* باقتدار ، بكفاءة

competition /ˌkɒmpəˈtɪʃn/ *noun* **1** [C] an organized event in which people try to win sth: *She entered a competition in the newspaper and won a car.* ○ *They're holding a competition to find the best name for the new magazine.* ○ *He came second in an international piano competition.* مسابقة

2 [U] a situation where two or more people are trying to achieve the same thing or gain an advantage: *There was fierce competition among the players for places in the team.* ○ *He is in competition with three other people for promotion.* ○ *Competition from the supermarkets means that many small shops have had to close.* منافسة

3 the competition [sing., with sing. or pl. verb] the other people, companies, etc. who are trying to achieve the same as you: *If we are going to succeed, we must offer a better product than the competition.* المنافسون

competitive /kəmˈpetətɪv/ *adj* **1** involving people competing against each other: *The travel industry is a highly competitive business.* ○ *competitive sports* مزاحم؛ تنافسي

2 able to be as successful as or more successful than those competing: *They are trying to make the company competitive in the international market.* ○ *Our prices are highly competitive* (= as low as or lower than those of the others). قادر على المزاحمة التجارية

3 (used about people) eager to win or to be more successful than others: *She's a very competitive player.* مزاحم، مغرم بالفوز

▸ **competitively** *adv* بتنافس

competitor /kəmˈpetɪtə(r)/ *noun* a person, company, product, etc. that is competing with another or others: *All competitors must wear a number in the race.* ○ *Two local companies are our main competitors.* متسابق ؛ متنافس

compile /kəmˈpaɪl/ *verb* [T] to collect information and arrange it in a list, book, etc: *to compile a list of addresses* يجمع ، يصنِّف

▸ **compilation** /ˌkɒmpɪˈleɪʃn/ *noun* **1** [U] the act of compiling: *The compilation of the encyclopedia took many years.* جمع

2 [C] something that has been compiled: *This CD is a compilation of the band's previous hits.* مجموعة

complacent /kəmˈpleɪsnt/ *adj* feeling so satisfied with yourself or with the situation that you think (perhaps wrongly) that there is no need to worry: *He had won his matches so easily that he was in danger of becoming complacent.* راضٍ عن نفسه ؛ متواكل

▸ **complacency** /kəmˈpleɪsnsi/ *noun* [U]: *We have achieved a high standard but there is no cause for complacency. We can still improve.* الرضا عن النفس ؛ التواكل

complacently *adv*: *We had complacently assumed that it was not our problem.* دون مبالاة

complain /kəmˈpleɪn/ *verb* **1** [I,T] **complain (about sth)**; **complain (that...)** to say that you are not satisfied with or happy about sth: *I wish you wouldn't keep complaining.* ○ *People are always complaining about the weather.* ○ *We complained to the hotel manager that the room was too noisy.* ➲ Look at the notes at **grumble** and **protest**. يشكو ، يتذمّر

2 [I] **complain of sth** to say that you have a pain or illness: *He went to the doctor, complaining of chest pains.* يشكو (من مرض)

complaint /kəmˈpleɪnt/ *noun* **complaint (about sth)**; **complaint (that...)** **1** [U] an act or acts of complaining: *I wrote a letter of complaint to the manager about the service I had received.* ○ *a cause for complaint* شكوى

2 [C] a statement that you are not satisfied with sth: *You should make a complaint to the company that made the machine.* شكوى

3 [C] an illness or disease: *a heart complaint* ○ *minor complaints* مرض ، عِلّة

complement /ˈkɒmplɪmənt/ *noun* [C] **1** a thing that goes together well with sth else: *A cream sauce is the perfect complement to this dessert.* مُكمِّل لـ

2 the total number that makes a group complete: *Without a full complement of players, the*

team will not be able to take part in the match. تكملة

3 (*grammar*) a word or words, especially a noun or adjective, used after a verb such as 'be' or 'become' and describing the subject of that verb: *In 'He's friendly' and 'He's a fool', 'friendly' and 'fool' are complements.* عبارة متممة للخبر

▸ **complement** *verb* [T] to go together well with: *The colours of the furniture and the carpet complement each other.* يلائم ، يناسب

complementary /ˌkɒmplɪ'mentri/ *adj* going together well with sth; adding sth which the other thing does not have: *They work well together because their skills are complementary: he's practical and she's creative.* مكمِّل (لبعضه البعض)

complete[1] /kəm'pliːt/ *adj* **1** having or including all parts; with nothing missing: *I gave a complete list of the stolen items to the police.* ○ *a complete set of Dickens' novels* ○ *The book explains the complete history of the place.* كامل

2 (not before a noun) finished or ended: *The repair work should be complete by Friday.* مكتمل ، منتهٍ

3 (only *before* a noun) as great as is possible; total; in every way: *the complete reorganization of the department* ○ *It was a complete waste of time.* تامّ ، كلّي

▸ **completely** *adv* as much as is possible; totally; in every way: *The building was completely destroyed by fire.* ○ *We're trying a completely new method.* تماماً ، كلّياً

completeness *noun* [U] تمام : اكتمال

complete[2] /kəm'pliːt/ *verb* [T] **1** to make sth whole: *We need two more players to complete the team.* ○ *I finally managed to complete my collection.* يُكمِّل

2 to finish sth; to bring sth to an end: *When the building has been completed, it will look impressive.* ○ *He completed his teacher training course in June 2001.* يكمِل ، ينهي

3 to fill in sth (e.g. a form): *Please complete the following in capital letters.* يملأ

completion /kəm'pliːʃn/ *noun* [U] the act of completing or the state of being complete: *The new motorway is due for completion within two years.* إكمال

complex[1] /'kɒmpleks; *US* kəm'pleks/ *adj* made up of several connected parts and often difficult to understand; complicated: *a complex system of taxation* ○ *You can't expect to find a simple solution when the problem is so complex.* مُعقَّد : مركَّب

▸ **complexity** /kəm'pleksəti/ *noun* (*pl.* **complexities**) **1** [U] the state of being complex: *an issue of great complexity* تعقيد

2 [C] one of the many details that make sth complicated: *I haven't time to explain the complexities of the chemical process now.* تعقيد : تركيب

complex[2] /'kɒmpleks/ *noun* [C] **1** a group or set of things, especially buildings, designed for a particular purpose: *a shopping complex* ○ *a sports complex* مجمّع (مبانٍ)

2 a complex (about sth) a mental problem that causes sb to worry or be upset about sth: *He's got a complex about his height.* ○ *an inferiority complex* عُقدة

complexion /kəm'plekʃn/ *noun* [C] **1** the natural colour and quality of the skin or the face: *a fair complexion* ○ *a healthy complexion* بَشرة

2 [usually sing.] the general nature or character of sth: *This news puts a completely different complexion on our situation.* طبيعة : مظهر عام

compliant /kəm'plaɪənt/ *adj* (*formal*) **compliant (with sth)** working or done in agreement with particular rules, orders, etc: *All new products must be compliant with EU specifications.* مطابق، موافق لـ

▸ **compliance** /-əns/ *noun* [U]: *A hard hat must be worn at all times in compliance with safety regulations.* مراعاة (النظام)

complicate /'kɒmplɪkeɪt/ *verb* [T] to make sth difficult to understand: *Let's not complicate things by adding too many details.* يعقّد

▸ **complicated** *adj* difficult to understand; made up of many parts: *a novel with a very complicated plot* ○ *a complicated mathematical calculation* ○ *I can't tell you all the details now, it's too complicated.* معقّد : صعب

complication /ˌkɒmplɪ'keɪʃn/ *noun* [C] **1** something that complicates sth: *Unless there are any unexpected complications, I'll be arriving next month.* ○ *The fact that she changed her mind was yet another complication.* تعقيد : صعوبة

2 a new illness that you get when you are already ill مضاعفة (في المرض)

complicity /kəm'plɪsəti/ *noun* [U] being involved, with sb else, in a crime تواطؤ

compliment /'kɒmplɪmənt/ *noun* **1** [C] **a compliment (on sth)** a statement or action that praises or expresses admiration for sb: *People have often paid her compliments on her piano playing.* إطراء : مجاملة

2 compliments [plural] (*formal*) greetings or good wishes given in a message: *Tea and coffee are provided with the compliments of the hotel management* (= without charge). مع تحيات

▸ **compliment** /'kɒmplɪment/ *verb* [T] **compliment sb (on sth)** to praise or express admiration for sb: *She complimented them on their smart appearance.* يطري ، يثني على

complimentary /ˌkɒmplɪ'mentri/ *adj* **1** praising or expressing admiration for sb: *He made several complimentary remarks about her work.* إطرائي

2 given free of charge: *a complimentary theatre ticket* مجّاني

comply /kəm'plaɪ/ *verb* [I] (*pres part* **complying**; *3rd pers sing pres* **complies**; *pt, pp* **complied**) **comply (with sth)** (*formal*) to obey an order or request: *All office buildings must comply with the fire and safety regulations.* يمتثل ، يطيع

component /kəm'pəʊnənt/ *noun* [C] one of the parts that together form sth, especially a machine: *car components* ○ *the components of a video recorder* جزء : عنصر مركّب

▸ **component** *adj* being one of the parts that together form sth: *the component parts of an engine* مكوِّن

compose /kəm'pəʊz/ *verb* **1** [I,T] to write music: *Mozart composed forty-one symphonies.* يؤلِّف (قطعة موسيقية)

2 [T] to produce a piece of writing, using careful thought: *I sat down and composed a letter of reply.* يكتب (بعناية) ، يؤلِّف

3 [T] to be the parts that form sth: *the parties that compose the coalition government* يؤلِّف، يشكِّل

4 [T] **compose yourself/sth** to make yourself, your feelings, etc. become calm and under control: *The news came as such a shock that it took me a while to compose myself.* ○ *She tried to compose her thoughts and answer calmly.* يهدّئ نفسه ، يضبط (أعصابه)

▸ **composed** *adj* **1 composed of sth** made up of sth; having as its parts: *The committee is composed of politicians from all parties.* مؤلَّف من

2 calm, in control of your feelings: *Although he felt very nervous, he managed to appear composed.* هادئ ، رابط الجأش

composer /kəm'pəʊzə(r)/ *noun* [C] a person who writes music professionally مؤلِّف موسيقي

composite /'kɒmpəzɪt/ *adj* consisting of different parts, substances or materials مركَّب

composition /ˌkɒmpə'zɪʃn/ *noun* **1** [C] a piece of music that has been written by sb: *'Finlandia' is probably Sibelius' best-known composition.* قطعة موسيقية

2 [U] the act of composing a piece of music or writing تأليف (قطعة موسيقية أو كتاب)

3 [U] the skill or technique of writing music: *She studied both musical theory and composition.* تأليف موسيقي

4 [C] a short piece of writing done as part of an educational course or exam: *Write a composition of about 500 words on one of the following subjects.* (قطعة) إنشاء

5 [U] the parts that form sth: *the chemical composition of a substance* ○ *the composition of the population* تركيب ، تكوين

compost /'kɒmpɒst/ *noun* [U] a mixture of decaying substances, such as plants and waste material, that is added to soil to help plants to grow سماد طبيعي

composure /kəm'pəʊʒə(r)/ *noun* [U] the state of being calm and having your feelings under control ضبط الأعصاب

compote /'kɒmpɒt; *US* 'kɒmpəʊt/ *noun* [C,U] fruit cooked with sugar فاكهة مطبوخة مع السكّر

compound[1] /'kɒmpaʊnd/ *noun* **1** something that consists of two or more things or substances combined: *a chemical compound* مركَّب

2 (*grammar*) a word or phrase consisting of two or more parts that combine to make a single meaning: *'General election' and 'bad-tempered' are compounds.* كلمة أو تعبير مركَّب

compound[2] /kəm'paʊnd/ *verb* [T] **1** to make sth (a problem, etc.) worse يزيد الأمر سوأ

2 (usually passive) to form by combining two or more things يركِّب

compound[3] /'kɒmpaʊnd/ *noun* [C] an area of land with a group of buildings on it, surrounded by a wall or fence قطعة أرض مسيَّجة عليها مبانٍ

comprehend /ˌkɒmprɪ'hend/ *verb* [T] (*formal*) to understand sth completely: *She's too young to comprehend what has happened.* يفهم

comprehensible /ˌkɒmprɪ'hensəbl/ *adj* easy to understand: *The book is written in clear, comprehensible language.* ❶ The opposite is **incomprehensible**. سهل الفهم

comprehension /ˌkɒmprɪ'henʃn/ *noun* **1** [U] the ability to understand or the act of understanding: *How such a peculiar thing could happen is beyond my comprehension.* ❶ The opposite is **incomprehension**. فهم

2 [C,U] an exercise that tests how well you understand spoken or written language: *a listening comprehension* ○ *The first part of the exam is reading comprehension.* اختبار الاستيعاب أو الفهم

comprehensive /ˌkɒmprɪ'hensɪv/ *adj* **1** including everything or nearly everything that is connected with a particular subject: *a guide book giving comprehensive information on the area* ○ *The store offers a comprehensive range of kitchen equipment.* شامِل

2 (*Brit*) (used about education) educating pupils of all levels of ability in the same school: *a comprehensive education system* (نظام تعليمي) عام أو شامل

▸ **comprehensively** *adv* thoroughly; completely على نحو شامل

compre'hensive school (*also* **comprehensive**) *noun* [C] (*Brit*) a secondary school in which pupils of all levels of ability are educated: *I went to the local comprehensive.* (في بريطانيا) مدرسة إعدادية شاملة لقدرات مختلفة

compress /kəm'pres/ *verb* [T] **compress sth (into sth) 1** to press sth together so that it takes up less space يضغط

2 to express sth briefly or in a shorter form يركِّز ، يختصر

▸ **compression** /kəm'preʃn/ *noun* [U] ضغط

comprise /kəm'praɪz/ *verb* [T] **1** to consist of; to have as parts or members: *The set comprises a pen, pencil, ruler and rubber.* ○ *a house comprising three bedrooms, kitchen, bathroom and a living room* يتألّف من

2 to be the parts or members that make up sth; to form: *Women comprise 62% of the staff.* يؤلِّف ، يشكِّل

compromise /'kɒmprəmaɪz/ *noun* [C,U] **a compromise (between/on sth)** an agreement that is reached when each side allows the other side part of what it wanted: *Unless the union and* *the management can reach a compromise on pay, there will be a strike.* ○ *It's difficult to find a compromise between the protection of the countryside and the need for more housing.* ○ *'There can be no compromise on the subject of terrorism,' a government minister said.* تسوية بالتراضي ، حل وسط

▸ **compromise** *verb* **1** [I] **compromise (with sb) (on sth)** to reach an agreement by which each side gets sth it wants and allows the other side to have sth it wants يتوصلان إلى حل وسط

2 [T] **compromise yourself** to put yourself in a position in which other people can criticize you for not being honest: *He compromised himself by accepting money from them.* يعرّض نفسه للشبهة

3 [T] to do sth that is harmful to sth: *She refused to compromise her principles by signing the letter.* يسيء إلى، يخالف

compulsion /kəm'pʌlʃn/ *noun* **1** [U] forcing sb to do sth or being forced to do sth: *There is no compulsion to take part. You can decide yourself.* ❶ The verb is **compel.** إكراه

2 [C] a strong desire that you cannot control, often to do sth that you should not do رغبة جامحة

▸ **compulsive** /kəm'pʌlsɪv/ *adj* **1** (used about a bad or harmful habit) caused by a strong desire that you cannot control: *compulsive eating* قاهِر، لا يقاوم

2 (used about a person) having a bad habit that he/she cannot control: *a compulsive liar* عبد لرغباته ، مدمن

3 so interesting or exciting that you cannot take your attention away from it: *This book makes compulsive reading.* اجباري ، آسر

compulsively *adv* على نحو لا يقاوَم

compulsory /kəm'pʌlsəri/ *adj* that must be done, by law, rules, etc: *Maths and English are compulsory subjects on this course; Art and Music are optional.* ○ *It is compulsory to wear a hard hat on the building site.* ❶ Something that you do not have to do is **non-compulsory**, **voluntary** or **optional.** إلزامي ، إجباري

compute /kəm'pju:t/ *verb* [T] (*formal*) to calculate sth يحسب

🔑**computer** /kəm'pju:tə(r)/ *noun* [C] an electronic machine that can store and arrange information, make calculations and control other machinery: *The bills are all done by computer.* ○ *a computer program* ○ *a computer programmer* ○ *a home computer* ○ *a personal computer* ○ *computer software* ○ *computer games* ○ *These days the whole process is done by computer.* ○ *First of all, the details are fed into a computer.* الكمبيوتر، الحاسوب

▸ **computerize** (*also* **computerise**) /-təraɪz/ *verb* [T] **1** to put computers in a place of work: *The whole factory has been computerized.* يجهز بكمبيوترات

2 to deal with sth by computer; to store information in a computer: *We have now computerized the library catalogue.* يعالج أو يحفظ بالكمبيوتر

computerization (*also* **computerisation**) /kəm,pju:təraɪ'zeɪʃn; *US* -rɪ'z-/ *noun* [U] استعمال الكمبيوتر في مجالات مختلفة

computing *noun* [U] the skill of using computers: *She did a course in computing.* استعمال الكمبيوتر

comrade /'kɒmreɪd; *US* -ræd/ *noun* [C] **1** (used by members of a union or of a socialist party when they talk about or to each other) رفيق

2 (*formal*) a friend or companion, especially one with whom you share a difficult experience رفيق (السلاح مثلاً)

▸ **comradeship** /'kɒmreɪdʃɪp/ *noun* [U] رفقة، روح الزمالة

Con (*also* **Cons**) *abbrev* = CONSERVATIVE

con¹ /kɒn/ *verb* [T] (conning; conned) **con sb (into doing sth/out of sth)** (*informal*) to cheat sb, especially in order to get money: *He conned her into investing in a company that didn't really exist.* ○ *The old lady was conned out of her life savings.* يحتال على، ينصب

▸ **con** *noun* [C] (*informal*) a trick, especially in order to cheat sb out of some money: *I didn't sign anything because I suspected that the whole scheme was a con.* احتيال : ابتزاز

con² /kɒn/ *noun*

IDM **the pros and cons** → PRO

concave /kɒn'keɪv/ *adj* (used about a surface) curving inwards ➲ Look at **convex.** مقعَّر

conceal /kən'si:l/ *verb* [T] **conceal sth/sb (from sb/sth)** to hide sb/sth; to prevent sb/sth from being seen or discovered: *She tried to conceal her anger from her friend.* ○ *The film was taken with a concealed camera.* يخفي : يحجب

▸ **concealment** *noun* [U]: *the concealment of the facts of the case* إخفاء ، حجب

concede /kən'si:d/ *verb* [T] **1** to admit that sth is true, often unwillingly: *When it was clear that he would lose the election, he conceded defeat.* ○ *She conceded that the problem was mostly her fault.* يسلِّم ب

2 concede sth (to sb) to allow sb to take sth, often unwillingly: *They lost the war and had to concede territory to their enemy.* ○ *Despite conceding two late goals, they still won.* ❶ The noun is **concession.** يتنازل عن

conceit /kən'si:t/ *noun* [U] too much pride in yourself, too high an opinion of your abilities and importance غرور

▸ **conceited** *adj* too proud of yourself, your abilities, your importance, etc: *He's so conceited – he thinks he's the best at everything!* مغرور

conceive /kən'si:v/ *verb* **1** [I,T] to become pregnant: *Tests showed that she was unable to conceive.* ○ *Their first child was conceived soon after they got married.* تحمل (المرأة)

2 [T] to form or think of sth (an idea, plan, etc.); to imagine: *He conceived the idea for the novel during his journey through India.* ○ *I cannot conceive that she would lie to me.* يخطر في باله : يتخيّل

3 [I] **conceive (of) sb/sth (as sth)** to think of

sb/sth in a particular way: *He started to conceive of the world as a dangerous place.* يتصوّر، يرى

🛈 The noun is **conception**.

▸ **conceivable** /-əbl/ *adj* possible to imagine or believe: *I made every conceivable effort to succeed.* 🛈 The opposite is **inconceivable**. ممكن تصوره ؛ معقول

conceivably /-əbli/ *adv*: *She might just conceivably be telling the truth.* من الممكن ؛ من المعقول

⚷**concentrate** /ˈkɒnsntreɪt/ *verb* [I,T] **1 concentrate (sth) (on sth/doing sth)** to give all your attention or effort to sth: *How can you concentrate on your work with so much noise going on?* ○ *It is important to concentrate on the road when you are driving.* ○ *I tried to concentrate my thoughts on the problem.* يركّز على

2 to come together or to bring people or things together in one place: *The general concentrated most of his tanks on the border.* يركّز، يحشد

▸ **concentrated** *adj* **1** aimed at one particular point: *With another concentrated attack we should break through the enemy's defences.* مركّز

2 made stronger by the removal of some liquid: *This is concentrated orange juice. You have to add water before you drink it.* مركّز

⚷**concentration** /ˌkɒnsnˈtreɪʃn/ *noun* **1** [U] **concentration (on sth)** the act of giving all your attention or effort to sth: *This type of work requires total concentration.* ○ *She lost her concentration when she heard a door bang.* تركيز

2 [C] **concentration (of sth)** a large amount of people or things in one place: *There are high concentrations of nitrates in the drinking water here.* تركيز ؛ كثافة

concenˈtration camp *noun* [C] a prison (usually a number of buildings inside a high fence) where political prisoners are kept in very bad conditions: *Millions of Jews died in Nazi concentration camps.* معسكر اعتقال

concentric /kənˈsentrɪk/ *adj* (used about circles) having the same centre متّحد المركز

⚷**concept** /ˈkɒnsept/ *noun* [C] **concept (of sth/that...)** an idea; a basic principle: *The basic concepts of physics can be quite difficult to understand.* ○ *The concept that 'big is beautiful' is no longer as popular as it was.* مفهوم ؛ مبدأ

conception /kənˈsepʃn/ *noun* [C,U] **1** the beginning of a new life inside a female person or animal: *an embryo 14 days after conception* حمْل (الجنين)

2 an idea or a plan: *We have no real conception of what people suffered during the war.* فكرة ؛ تخيّل

🛈 The verb is **conceive**.

⚷**concern¹** /kənˈsɜːn/ *verb* [T] **1** to affect or be of importance to sb: *The destruction of the world's forests concerns everybody in some way.* ○ *This does not concern you. Please go away.* ○ *The closure of the factory came as a shock to all those concerned.* ○ *It is important that no risks are taken where safety is concerned.* يهمّ، يخصّ

2 concern yourself with sth to give your attention to sth: *You needn't concern yourself with the hotel booking. The travel agent will take care of it.* يهتمّ

3 to worry sb: *What concerns the experts most is the increasing level of pollution in our cities.* يُقلِق

IDM **as/so far as sb/sth is concerned** → FAR²

to be concerned in sth to have a connection with or be involved in sth: *Everyone who was directly concerned in the incident has now resigned.* متورّط (في شيء)

to be concerned with sth to be about sth: *Tonight's programme is concerned with the effects of the law on ordinary people.* متعلّق بِ

▸ **concerned** *adj* **concerned (about/for sth); concerned (that...)** worried or anxious: *If you are concerned about your baby's health you should consult a doctor immediately.* 🛈 The opposite is **unconcerned**. قلِق على

concerning *prep* about; on the subject of: *She refused to answer questions concerning her private life.* عن ، بشأن

⚷**concern²** /kənˈsɜːn/ *noun* **1** [U] **concern (for/about/over sb/sth); concern (that...)** worry: *Following the accident there is growing concern over the safety of rail travel.* ○ *Don't worry. There is no cause for concern.* قلَق

2 [C,U] something that affects you or is of importance to you: *Edward's family problems are not my concern.* ○ *He showed great concern for the poor.* شأن، اهتمام

3 [C] a company or business: *a large industrial concern* شركة ، مؤسسة تجاريّة

IDM **a going concern** → GOING²

⚷**concert** /ˈkɒnsət/ *noun* [C] a performance of music: *a rock concert* ○ *The concert was held in the Albert Hall.* ○ *The orchestra is giving concerts in Liverpool, Glasgow and London.* حفلة موسيقية

concerted /kənˈsɜːtɪd/ *adj* done by a group of people working together: *We must all make a concerted effort.* متناسق ، جماعي ، موحّد

concertina /ˌkɒnsəˈtiːnə/ *noun* [C] a musical instrument that you hold in your hands and play by pressing the ends together and pulling them apart, so that the material in the middle folds and unfolds 🛈 A concertina is like a small **accordion**. الكونسرتينا: آلة موسيقية

concerto /kənˈtʃɜːtəʊ/ *noun* [C] (*pl.* **concertos**) a piece of music for an orchestra with one instrument playing an important part (solo): *Tchaikovsky's piano concerto* الكونشيرتو: قطعة موسيقية

concession /kənˈseʃn/ *noun* **1** [C,U] **concession (to sb/sth)** something that you agree to do or give up in order to end an argument: *Employers have been forced to make concessions to the union.* 🛈 The verb is **concede**. تنازل

2 [C] a lower price for certain groups of people: *Concessions are available for students and pensioners.* سعر مخفّض

3 [C] a special right to do sth that is given or sold to sb/sth: *mining concessions* امتياز

a b c d e f g h i j k l m n o p q r s t u v w x y z

▸ **concessionary** /kən'seʃənəri; *US* -neri/ *adj* having a lower price for certain groups of people: *a concessionary fare* مُخَفَّض

conciliate /kən'sɪlieɪt/ *verb* [I,T] (*formal*) to try to end a disagreement between two groups يصالح ، يوفق (بين)

▸ **conciliation** /kən,sɪli'eɪʃn/ *noun* [U] the process of ending a disagreement: *All attempts at conciliation have failed and civil war seems inevitable.* مصالحة ، توفيق

conciliatory /kən'sɪliətəri; *US* -tɔ:ri/ *adj*: *a conciliatory speech* مهادن ، استرضائي

concise /kən'saɪs/ *adj* giving a lot of information in a few words; short: *He gave a clear and concise summary of what had happened.* موجَز

▸ **concisely** *adv* بإيجاز

conciseness (*also* **concision** /kən'sɪʒn/) *noun* [U] إيجاز

⚷**conclude** /kən'klu:d/ *verb* **1** [I,T] (*formal*) to end or to bring sth to an end: *May I conclude by thanking our guest speaker.* ○ *The Prince concluded his tour with a visit to a charity concert.* يختتم

2 [T] **conclude sth from sth** to reach a belief or opinion as a result of thought or study: *From their studies the archaeologists concluded that the area was the site of an ancient temple.* يستنتج

3 [T] **conclude sth (with sb)** to arrange or agree to sth formally: *to conclude a treaty, business deal, etc.* يعقد ؛ يبرم

⚷**conclusion** /kən'klu:ʒn/ *noun* **1** [C, usually sing.] the end: *The conclusion of the novel was quite unexpected.* ○ *to bring sth to a conclusion* ○ *The conclusion is just as important a part of your essay as the introduction.* خاتمة

2 [C] **the conclusion (that...)** a belief or opinion that you reach after considering sth carefully: *We came to the conclusion that he was right.* ○ *What conclusions can you draw from her remarks?* ○ *Have you reached any conclusions from your studies?* استنتاج

3 [U] an act of arranging or agreeing to sth formally: *The summit ended with the conclusion of an arms-reduction treaty.* عقد ، إبرام

IDM **a foregone conclusion** → FOREGONE

in conclusion finally; lastly: *In conclusion, I would like to wish you continued success in the future.* ختاماً ، أخيراً

jump to conclusions → JUMP¹

conclusive /kən'klu:sɪv/ *adj* that shows sth is definitely true or real: *conclusive proof of sb's guilt* ❶ The opposite is **inconclusive**. قاطع ، حاسم

▸ **conclusively** *adv*: *Tests can now prove conclusively who is the father of a child.* بشكل قاطع

concoct /kən'kɒkt/ *verb* [T] **1** to make sth by mixing different things together يعِدّ (بالخلط)

2 to make up or invent sth (an excuse, a story, etc.) يلفِّق ، يختلق

▸ **concoction** /kən'kɒkʃn/ *noun* [C,U] خليط ؛ إعداد

concourse /'kɒŋkɔ:s/ *noun* [C] a large hall or space inside a building such as a station or an airport قاعة كبيرة أو باحة داخل محطّة أو مطار

⚷**concrete¹** /'kɒŋkri:t/ *adj* **1** that can be touched, felt, etc.; real: *a concrete object* ➲ Look at **abstract**. (شيء) ملموس ؛ حقيقي

2 definite; particular: *Can you give me a concrete example of the behaviour you're complaining about?* محدَّد ، معيَّن

▸ **concretely** *adv* على نحو ملموس أو محدّد

⚷**concrete²** /'kɒŋkri:t/ *noun* [U] a hard substance made from cement mixed with sand, water, small stones (gravel), etc., that is used in building: *a modern office building of glass and concrete* اسمنت، خَرَسانة

▸ **concrete** *verb* [T] **concrete sth (over)** to cover sth with concrete يغَطّي بالاسمنت

concur /kən'kɜ:(r)/ *verb* [I] (concurring; concurred) (*formal*) **concur (with sb/sth) (in sth)** to agree يوافق ؛ يتّفق مع

concurrent /kən'kʌrənt/ *adj* existing or happening at the same time as sth else متزامن

▸ **concurrently** *adv*: *The semi-finals are played concurrently, so it is impossible to watch both.* في نفس الوقت

concuss /kən'kʌs/ *verb* [T] (often passive) to injure sb's brain by hitting his/her head: *to be badly concussed* يرجّ المخ

▸ **concussion** /kən'kʌʃn/ *noun* [U] an injury to the brain that was caused by a blow to the head: *He was rushed to hospital suffering from concussion.* ارتجاج في المخ

condemn /kən'dem/ *verb* [T] **1 condemn sb/sth (for/as sth)** to say strongly that you think sb/sth is very bad or wrong: *A government spokesman condemned the bombing as a cowardly act of terrorism.* يدين ، يستنكر

2 condemn sth (as sth) to say officially that sth is not good enough to use: *The building was condemned and had to be demolished.* يحكم رسمياً بعدم صلاحيته للاستعمال

3 condemn sb (to sth/to do sth) to say what sb's punishment will be: *The murderer was condemned to death.* ○ (*figurative*) *Their poor education condemns them to a series of low-paid jobs.* يحكم على

▸ **condemnation** /,kɒndem'neɪʃn/ *noun* [C,U] the act of condemning sth; a statement that condemns: *The bombing of the airport brought condemnation from all around the world.* إدانة ، استنكار

condensation /,kɒnden'seɪʃn/ *noun* [U] small drops of liquid that are formed when warm air touches a cold surface: *On cold mornings the windows are covered in condensation.* قطرات مكثَّفة

condense /kən'dens/ *verb* **1** [I,T] to change from gas to liquid; to make a gas change to liquid: *Steam condenses into water when it touches a cold surface.* ➲ Look at **evaporate**. يتكثّف أو يكثِّف (الغاز)

2 [I,T] to become or to make sth thicker: *condensed soup* يتكثّف ؛ يكثِّف ، يركِّز

3 [T] **condense sth (into sth)** to make a piece of writing shorter: *We'll have to condense these three chapters into one.* يلخّص

condescend /ˌkɒndɪˈsend/ *verb* [I] **1** to do sth that you believe is below your level of importance: *Celia only condescends to speak to me when she wants me to do something for her.* يتنازل ، يتكرّم

2 condescend (to sb) to behave towards sb in a way that shows that you think you are better or more important than him/her: *The teacher must be able to explain things at the right level for the children without condescending to them.* يعامله بشيء من التعالي

▶ **condescending** *adj*: *a condescending smile* مُتنازل ، متكرّم

condescendingly *adv* بتنازل ، بلهجة متعطّفة

condescension /ˌkɒndɪˈsenʃn/ *noun* [U] تنازل ، تكرم

⚷ **condition**[1] /kənˈdɪʃn/ *noun* **1** [sing., U] the state that sb/sth is in: *The car is three years old but it is still in very good condition.* ○ *He looks really ill. He is certainly not in a condition to drive home.* حالة

2 [C] something that must happen so that sth else can happen or be possible: *One of the conditions of the job is that you agree to work on Sundays.* ○ *We agreed to the conditions that the landlord laid down.* شَرْط

3 conditions [plural] a situation or circumstances: *The prisoners were kept in terrible conditions.* ○ *poor housing conditions* ○ *The weather conditions were very favourable for the expedition.* أحوال ، ظروف

4 [C] an illness: *to have a heart condition* مرض

IDM **on condition (that...)** only if: *I agreed to help on condition that I got half the profit.* شرط ، شريطة

on no condition (*formal*) not at all; for no reason: *On no condition must the press find out about this.* بتاتاً : لاي سبب من الاسباب

out of condition not very healthy; unfit: *I need to get more exercise. I'm really out of condition.* سيِّئ الصحة : سيِّئ اللياقة البدنية

condition[2] /kənˈdɪʃn/ *verb* [T] **1** to affect or control the way that sb/sth behaves: *Boys are conditioned to feel that they are stronger than girls.* ○ *to be conditioned by your environment* يكيِّف (السلوك)

2 to keep sth in a good condition: *a cream that moisturizes and conditions your skin* يحسّن

▶ **conditioner** /kənˈdɪʃənə(r)/ *noun* [C,U] a substance that keeps sth in a good condition: *hair conditioner* (مادة) محسِّنة

conditional /kənˈdɪʃənl/ *adj* **1 conditional (on/upon sth)** if sth is conditional on sth else, it can only happen if this other thing happens first; the one thing depends on the other: *My university place is conditional on my getting good marks in the exams.* مشروط بِـ

2 (*grammar*) (used about a phrase or sentence) expressing a condition: *A conditional clause usually begins with 'if' or 'unless'.* شَرْطي

▶ **conditionally** /-ʃənəli/ *adv* شرطياً

condolence /kənˈdəʊləns/ [C, usually pl., U] an expression of sympathy to sb whose relative or close friend has just died: *Please accept my condolences on your sister's death.* تعزية

condom /ˈkɒndɒm/ (*also informal* **rubber**) *noun* [C] a rubber covering that a man wears over his penis during sexual intercourse to prevent the woman from becoming pregnant or as protection against disease (الوقاء) العازل

condominium /ˌkɒndəˈmɪniəm/ *noun* [C] (*US*) a flat or block of flats owned by the people who live in them شقة (أو مجمع شقق) يملكها ساكنوها

condone /kənˈdəʊn/ *verb* [T] to accept sth; not to consider sth to be wrong: *I can never condone violence – no matter what the circumstances are.* يقبل ، يؤيِّد

conducive /kənˈdjuːsɪv; *US* -ˈduːs-/ *adj* **conducive (to sth)** helping or making sth likely to happen: *This hot weather is not conducive to hard work.* باعث أو معين على

⚷ **conduct**[1] /ˈkɒndʌkt/ *noun* [U] **1** a person's behaviour: *His conduct has always been of the highest possible standard.* ○ *a code of conduct* (= a set of rules for behaviour) تصرّف ، سلوك

2 conduct of sth the act of controlling or organizing sth: *She was criticized for her conduct of the bank's affairs.* إدارة ، تنظيم

⚷ **conduct**[2] /kənˈdʌkt/ *verb* [T] **1** to carry out or organize sth: *Tests are being conducted to find the cause of the accident.* يقوم بِ : ينظِّم

2 to stand in front of an orchestra and direct the musicians: *The orchestra was conducted by Karajan.* يقود

3 conduct yourself well, badly, etc. (*formal*) to behave in a particular way يتصرّف

4 to allow heat or electricity to pass along or through sth: *Rubber does not conduct electricity.* يوصّل

5 to lead or guide sb/sth: *a conducted tour of the cathedral* يرشِد

conductor /kənˈdʌktə(r)/ *noun* [C] **1** a person who stands in front of an orchestra and directs the musicians قائد أوركسترا

2 (*Brit*) a person who collects the fares on a bus قاطع التذاكر في حافلة

3 (*US*) = GUARD[2] (4)

4 a substance that allows heat or electricity to pass through or along it: *Water is a good conductor.* موصّل (كهربائي)

cone /kəʊn/ *noun* [C] **1** a solid shape that has a round base and gets narrower, making a point at the top ❶ The adjective is **conical**. المخروط

2 an object of this shape: *Orange cones marked off the area where the roadworks were.* ○ *an ice-cream cone* شيء مخروطي

3 the hard fruit of a pine or a fir tree ➲ Look at **conifer**. كوز (صنوبر أو تنّوب)

confectionery /kənˈfekʃənəri; *US* -ʃənerɪ/ *noun* [U] sweets, cakes, chocolates, etc. حلويات

a b c d e f g h i j k l m n o p q r s t u v w x y z

confederation /kən,fedə'reɪʃn/ *noun* [C,U] an organization of smaller groups which have joined together: *a confederation of independent republics* ○ *The Confederation of British Industry represents employers.* كونفدرالية، اتحاد

confer /kən'fɜː(r)/ *verb* (conferring; conferred) **1** [I] **confer (with sb) (on/about sth)** to discuss sth with sb before making a decision: *The President is conferring with his advisers.* يتباحث ، يتشاور

2 [T] **confer sth (on sb)** to give sb a special right or advantage: *Oxford University first conferred degrees on women in 1920.* يمنح

conference /'kɒnfərəns/ *noun* [C] a meeting for discussion, often one held every year where representatives of a particular profession, political party, etc. meet for several days to hear speeches and vote on the matters discussed: *The Conservative Party conference is held in the autumn.* ○ *an international conference on global warming* ○ *a press conference* (= when a politician, etc. talks to reporters) مؤتمر

confess /kən'fes/ *verb* [I,T] **1 confess (to sth/ to doing sth); confess (sth) (to sb)** to say that you have done sth bad or wrong: *The young woman confessed to the murder of her boyfriend/ to murdering her boyfriend.* ○ *Frank confessed that he had stolen the car.* ○ *They confessed to their mother that they had spent all the money.* ○ *I must confess I didn't understand a word of that talk!* يعترف ، يقرّ بِ

2 confess (sth) (to sb) to tell a priest or God what you have done that is bad or wrong: *to confess a sin* يعترف

confession /kən'feʃn/ *noun* [C,U] an act of confessing sth: *The young man made a full confession to the police.* ○ *She goes to confession* (= with a priest) *twice a year.* اعتراف

confetti /kən'feti/ *noun* [U] small pieces of coloured paper that people throw at the bride and bridegroom after a wedding نثار (أوراق ملوّنة)

confide /kən'faɪd/ *verb* [T] **confide sth to sb** to tell sb sth that is secret: *She did not confide her love to anyone – not even to her best friend.* يبوح (بسرّه)

PHR V confide in sb to talk to sb whom you trust about sth that is secret or private. يأتمنه (على سرّه)

confidence /'kɒnfɪdəns/ *noun* [U] **1 confidence (in sb/sth)** trust or strong belief in sb/ sth: *I have every confidence in Emily's ability to do the job.* ○ *They don't have much confidence in him.* ○ *The public is losing confidence in the government's ability to improve the economy.* ثقة

2 the feeling that you are sure about your own abilities, opinion, etc: *I didn't have the confidence to tell her I thought she was wrong.* ○ *to be full of confidence* ○ *'Of course we will win,' the team captain said with confidence.* ➲ Look at **self-confidence**. ثقة بالنفس

IDM in (strict) confidence as a secret: *The information was given to me in the strictest confidence.* بوصفه سرّاً

take sb into your confidence to tell sb a secret (يثق به) ويفضي له بسرّ

'confidence trick *noun* [C] a way of getting money by cheating sb احتيال (لنيل المال)

confident /'kɒnfɪdənt/ *adj* **confident (of sth/ that...)** feeling or showing that you are sure about your own abilities, opinions, etc: *Kate feels confident of passing/that she can pass the exam.* ○ *to be confident of success* ○ *Donald has a very confident manner.* ➲ Look at **self-confident**. واثق

▸ **confidently** *adv*: *She stepped confidently onto the stage and began to sing.* ○ *We confidently expect an improvement in sales next year.* بثقة ، باعتداد

confidential /,kɒnfɪ'denʃl/ *adj* secret; not to be shown or told to other people: *The letter was marked 'private and confidential'.* سرّي

▸ **confidentiality** /,kɒnfɪ,denʃi'æləti/ *noun* [U] سرّية

confidentially /-ʃəli/ *adv*: *She told me confidentially that she is going to retire early.* سرّاً، بشكل سرّي

confine /kən'faɪn/ *verb* [T] **1 confine sb/sth (in/to sth)** to keep a person or animal in a particular place, usually a small place: *The prisoners are confined to their cells for long periods at a time.* يحتجز

2 confine sb/sth/yourself to sth to stay within the limits of sth: *Please confine your questions and comments to the topic we are discussing.* يقتصر على ، يتقيّد بِ

▸ **confined** *adj* (used about a space) very small: *Sailors on submarines must get used to living in confined spaces.* ضيّق، محصور

confinement *noun* [U] being kept in a small space: *to be kept in solitary confinement* حَبْس ، عَزْل (في مكان ضيّق)

confines /'kɒnfaɪnz/ *noun* [plural] (*formal*) the limits or outer edges of sth: *Patients are not allowed beyond the confines of the hospital grounds.* حدود

confirm /kən'fɜːm/ *verb* [T] **1** to say or show that sth is true; to make sth definite: *Please confirm your telephone booking in writing.* ○ *Seeing the two of them together confirmed our suspicions.* ○ *Can you confirm that you will be able to attend?* يُثبِت ، يؤكّد

2 to accept sb as a full member of a Christian Church: *He was baptized as a baby and confirmed at the age of thirteen.* يمنحه التثبيت الديني

▸ **confirmation** /,kɒnfə'meɪʃn/ *noun* **1** [C,U] a statement that confirms sth: *We are waiting for confirmation of the report.* ○ *You will receive a written confirmation of your reservation.* تأكيد ، تثبيت

2 [C] a religious service at which a person is confirmed (2) تثبيت ديني ، تثبيت التعميد

confirmed *adj* (only *before* a noun) fixed in a particular habit or way of life: *a confirmed bachelor* ثابت ، مترسّخ

confiscate /'kɒnfɪskeɪt/ *verb* [T] to take sth away from sb as a punishment: *Any cigarettes found in school will be confiscated.* يصادر
▶ **confiscation** /ˌkɒnfɪ'skeɪʃn/ *noun* [C,U] مصادرة

conflict /'kɒnflɪkt/ *noun* [C,U] **1** a fight or an argument: *an armed conflict* ○ *The new laws have brought the Government into conflict with the unions.* صِراع ، صدام
2 a difference between two or more ideas, wishes, etc: *When both my wife and father were taken ill, I had a serious conflict of loyalties.* ○ *a conflict of interests* تضارب ، تعارض
▶ **conflict** /kən'flɪkt/ *verb* [I] **A and B conflict; A conflicts with B** to disagree with or be different from sb/sth: *The statements of the two witnesses conflict.* ○ *John's statement conflicts with yours.* ○ *The two studies came up with conflicting results.* يتعارض ، يتضارب

conform /kən'fɔːm/ *verb* [I] **conform (to sth)**
1 to obey a rule or law; to come up to a particular standard: *This building does not conform to fire regulations.* يتوافق (مع قانون) ، يطابق
2 to behave in the way that other people and society expect you to behave: *Children are under a lot of pressure to conform when they first start school.* يراعي ، يجاري
▶ **conformist** /kən'fɔːmɪst/ *noun* [C] a person who behaves in the way that people are expected to behave by society من يراعي متطلّبات المجتمع
conformity /kən'fɔːməti/ *noun* [U] (*formal*) behaviour which conforms to rules and customs مراعاة القواعد والأعراف

confront /kən'frʌnt/ *verb* [T] **1 confront sth; confront sb with sb/sth** to think about, or to make sb think about, sth that is difficult or unpleasant: *to confront a problem, difficulty, etc.* ○ *When the police confronted him with the evidence, he confessed.* يواجه ، يجابه
2 to stand in front of sb, e.g. because you want to fight him/her: *The unarmed demonstrators were confronted by a row of soldiers.* يتصدّى لِ ، يجابه
▶ **confrontation** /ˌkɒnfrʌn'teɪʃn/ *noun* [C,U] a fight or an argument مجابهة ، صدام

confuse /kən'fjuːz/ *verb* [T] **1** (usually passive) to make sb unable to think clearly or to know what to do: *I'm a bit confused. Could you explain that again?* ○ *He confused everybody with his pages of facts and figures.* يربِك ، يشوّش
2 confuse A and/with B to mistake sb/sth for sb/sth else: *I often confuse Lee with his brother. They look very much alike.* ○ *Don't confuse 'complement' with 'compliment'.* يخلط (بين شيئين)
3 to make sth unclear: *The situation is confused by the fact that so many organizations are involved.* يشوّش
▶ **confused** *adj* **1** not able to think clearly: *When he regained consciousness he was dazed and confused.* مشوّش ، مضطرب
2 difficult to understand: *The article is very confused – I don't know what the main point is.* عسير الفهم (لتشوّشه)
confusedly /-ədli/ *adv* بارتباك

confusing *adj* difficult to understand: *Her instructions were contradictory and confusing.* صعب الفهم ؛ محيِّر
confusingly *adv* ممّا يصعب فهمه

confusion /kən'fjuːʒn/ *noun* [U] **1** the state of not being able to think clearly or to know what to do: *He stared in confusion at the crowd of people in front of his house.* ارتباك ، اضطراب
2 a state of disorder: *In the panic and confusion two people were trampled to death.* ○ *Their unexpected visit threw all our plans into confusion.* فوضى ، اضطراب ، لخبطة
3 the act of mistaking sb/sth for sb/sth else: *To avoid confusion, all luggage should be labelled with your name and destination.* خَلْط بين الأشياء ، لخبطة
4 the state of being uncertain or unclear: *There is still a great deal of confusion as to the true facts.* إشكال ، عدم وضوح

congeal /kən'dʒiːl/ *verb* [I,T] to become solid; to make a liquid solid: *congealed blood* يتخثّر ؛ يخثّر

congenial /kən'dʒiːniəl/ *adj* (*formal*) pleasant: *We spent an evening in congenial company.* لطيف ، أنيس

congenital /kən'dʒenɪtl/ *adj* (used about a disease) beginning at and continuing since birth: *congenital brain damage* خِلْقي ، ولادي

congested /kən'dʒestɪd/ *adj* so full of sth that nothing can move: *The streets of London are congested with traffic.* مكتظّ ؛ مسدود

congestion /kən'dʒestʃən/ *noun* [U] the state of being very full of sth: *severe traffic congestion* اكتظاظ ، ازدحام

conglomerate /kən'glɒmərət/ *noun* [C] a large firm made up of several different companies شركة ضخمة تتألف من عدة شركات
▶ **conglomeration** /kənˌglɒmə'reɪʃn/ *noun* [C] a group of many different things that have been gathered together خليط ؛ مجموعة

congratulate /kən'grætʃuleɪt/ *verb* [T] **congratulate sb (on sth)** to praise sb or tell sb that you are pleased about sth he/she has done: *I congratulated Sue on passing her driving test.* ○ *They sent a card to congratulate the couple on their engagement.* يهنّئ

congratulations /kənˌgrætʃu'leɪʃnz/ *noun* [plural] (used for praising sb or telling sb that you are pleased about sth he/she has done): *Congratulations on the birth of your baby boy!* ○ *Congratulations! Your painting has won first prize.* مبروك! ، تهانينا!

congregate /'kɒŋgrɪgeɪt/ *verb* [I] to come together in a crowd يحتشد ، يجتمع

congregation /ˌkɒŋgrɪ'geɪʃn/ *noun* [C, with sing. or pl. verb] a group of people who attend church جماعة (المصلين في كنيسة)

congress /'kɒŋgres; *US* -grəs/ *noun* [C, with sing. or pl. verb] **1** a large formal meeting or series of meetings: *a medical congress* ○ *When is the Trades Union Congress held?* مؤتمر ، اجتماع

a b c d e f g h i j k l m n o p q r s t u v w x y z

2 Congress the name in some countries (e.g. the USA) for the group of people who are elected to make the laws ℹ The US Congress is made up of the **Senate** and the **House of Representatives**. الكونغرس: الهيئة التشريعية

▶ **congressional** /kənˈɡreʃənl/ *adj* connected with a congress or Congress: *a congressional committee* متعلق بالكونغرس

conical /ˈkɒnɪkl/ *adj* having a round base and getting narrower towards a point at the top ℹ The noun is **cone**. مخروطي

conifer /ˈkɒnɪfə(r); ˈkəʊn-/ *noun* [C] a tree with long, very thin leaves (needles) that stay green all through the year and that has hard brown fruit (cones) شجرة الصنوبر

▶ **coniferous** /kəʊˈnɪfərəs; *US* kəʊˈn-/ *adj* صنوبري

conjecture /kənˈdʒektʃə(r)/ *verb* [I,T] to guess about sth without real proof or evidence يحدس ، يخمّن

▶ **conjecture** *noun* [C,U] حدْس ، تخمين

conjugate /ˈkɒndʒəɡeɪt/ *verb* [T] to give the different forms of a verb يصرّف (الفعل)

▶ **conjugation** /ˌkɒndʒuˈɡeɪʃn/ *noun* [C,U] تصريف (الأفعال)

conjunction /kənˈdʒʌŋkʃn/ *noun* [C] a word that is used for joining other words, phrases or sentences: *'And', 'but' and 'or' are conjunctions.* حرف عطف

IDM **in conjunction with sb/sth** together with sb/sth: *Various charities are working in conjunction with the United Nations to help the disaster victims.* بالاشتراك مع

conjure /ˈkʌndʒə(r)/ *verb* [I] to do tricks by clever, quick hand movements, that appear to be magic يشعوذ ، يقوم بألعاب سحرية

PHR V **conjure sth up** to cause a picture to appear in your mind: *Hawaiian music conjures up images of sunshine, flowers and sandy beaches.* يبعث ، يستثير

conjure sth up; **conjure sth (up) from/out of sth** to make sth appear quickly or suddenly يستحضر (شيئاً بسرعة أو فجأة)

▶ **conjurer** (*also* **conjuror**) /ˈkʌndʒərə(r)/ *noun* [C] a person who does clever tricks that appear to be magic ➲ Look at **magician**. حاوٍ ، مشعوذ

conjuring /ˈkʌndʒərɪŋ/ *noun* [U]: *to perform conjuring tricks* ألعاب سحرّية

conker /ˈkɒŋkə(r)/ (*informal*) (*Brit*) (*also* **horse chestnut**) *noun* [C] the seed of the horse chestnut tree, used in a popular children's game ثمرة شجرة الكستناء المرّة

🔑 **connect** /kəˈnekt/ *verb* **1** [I,T] **connect (sth) (up) (to/with sth)** to be joined or linked to sth; to join or link sth to sth else: *The tunnels connect (up) ten metres further on.* ○ *This pipe connects with the main drain outside the house.* ○ *The printer is connected to the computer.* ○ *This motorway connects Oxford with Birmingham.* ○ *The plumber hasn't connected the shower up yet.* ➲ Look at **disconnect**. يتّصل : يربِط ، يوصِل

2 [T] (usually passive) **connect sb/sth (with sb/sth)** to associate sb/sth with sb/sth; to consider sb/sth to be related to sb/sth else: *There was no evidence that she was connected with the crime.* ○ *Doctors believe that the increase in asthma is connected with pollution levels.* يرتبط : يربِط

3 [I] **connect (with sth)** (used about a bus, train, plane, etc.) to arrive at a particular time so that passengers can change to another bus, train, plane, etc: *This train connects with the ferry to Le Havre.* يربط بـ ، يوصل إلى

4 [T] **connect sb (with sb)** to link sb by telephone: *Hold the line, please. I'm just trying to connect you.* يوصل (بالتليفون)

🔑 **connection** (*Brit also* **connexion**) /kəˈnekʃn/ *noun* **1** [C,U] **connection between A and B**; **connection with/to sth** connecting or being connected: *There is a clear connection between crime and poverty.* ○ *Is there any connection between the two organizations?* ○ *What is your connection with the school? Do you work here?* علاقة ، ارتباط

2 [C] a place where two wires, pipes, etc. join together: *The radio doesn't work. There must be a loose connection somewhere.* وصْلة

3 [C] a bus, train, plane, etc. that leaves soon after another arrives: *Our bus was late so we missed our connection.* وسيلة مواصلات لمتابعة الرحلة

4 [C, usually pl.] a person that you know who is important or of high rank: *Chris got a good job because of his mother's connections.* صلة ، واسطة

IDM **in connection with sb/sth** (*formal*) about or concerning: *I am writing to you in connection with your application.* بشأن ، بصدد

in this/that connection (*formal*) about or concerning this/that بهذا الصدد ، فيما يتعلّق بهذا

connive /kəˈnaɪv/ *verb* [I] **1 connive at sth** to do nothing to stop sth that is illegal or wrong يتغاضى عن

2 connive (with sb) (to do sth) to work together with sb to do sth that is wrong يتواطأ

connoisseur /ˌkɒnəˈsɜː(r)/ *noun* [C] a person who knows a lot about art, good food, music, etc: *a connoisseur of modern art* خبير ، ذوّاقة

connotation /ˌkɒnəˈteɪʃn/ *noun* [C] an impression that a word gives in addition to its meaning: *'Spinster' means a single woman but it has negative connotations.* المضمون ، إيحاء المعنى

conquer /ˈkɒŋkə(r)/ *verb* [T] **1** to take control of an area by winning a war: *Napoleon's ambition was to conquer Europe.* ○ (*figurative*) *The young singer conquered the hearts of audiences all over the world.* يستولي على

2 to defeat an enemy, an army, etc.; to overcome sth: *The Spanish conquered the Incas.* ○ *She's trying to conquer her fear of flying.* يهزم ، يقهر

▶ **conqueror** /ˈkɒŋkərə(r)/ *noun* [C] a person who has conquered (1) sth منتصر ، فاتح

conquest /ˈkɒŋkwest/ *noun* **1** [C, U] an act of conquering sth: *the Norman conquest* (= of England in 1066) ○ (*figurative*) *the conquest of Mount Everest* انتصار على ، فَتْح

2 [C] an area of land that has been taken by war أرض مفتوحة حرباً

conscience /ˈkɒnʃəns/ *noun* [C,U] your own feeling about whether what you are doing is right or wrong: *a clear/a guilty conscience* ضمير ، وجدان

IDM **have sth on your conscience** to feel guilty because of sth that you have done that was wrong يؤنّبه ضميره

conscientious /ˌkɒnʃiˈenʃəs/ *adj* **1** (used about people) careful to do sth correctly and well: *He's a very conscientious worker.* متقن (لعمله)، صاحب وجدان

2 (used about actions) done with great care and attention: *conscientious work* (عمل) مُتْقَن
▸ **conscientiously** *adv* بإتقان

ˌ**conscientious obˈjector** *noun* [C] a person who refuses to join the army, etc. because he/she believes it is morally wrong to kill other people المعارض الاخلاقي

conscious /ˈkɒnʃəs/ *adj* **1** able to see, hear, feel, etc. things; awake: *She was badly injured but conscious and able to tell the doctor what had happened.* ℹ The opposite is **unconscious**. واعٍ ، مُدْرِك

2 conscious of sth/that... noticing or aware of sth: *He suddenly became conscious that someone was following him.* ○ *She didn't seem conscious of the danger.* مُدْرِك لِـ ، شاعر بِـ

3 that you do on purpose or for a particular reason: *We made a conscious effort to treat both children equally.* ➲ Look at **deliberate**. It has a similar meaning. ℹ The opposite is **unconscious**. مقصود

4 being particularly interested in or aware of sth: *Young people today are very fashion-conscious.* مهتمّ بِـ
▸ **consciously** *adv*: *I have never consciously harmed another human being.* عمداً

consciousness /ˈkɒnʃəsnəs/ *noun* **1** [U] the state of being conscious (1); being able to see, hear, feel, etc. things: *As he fell, he hit his head and lost consciousness.* ○ *She regained consciousness after two weeks in a coma.* وعي ، شعور

2 [U, sing.] the state of being aware of sth: *There is growing consciousness of the need to save energy.* إدراك ، اهتمام ، وعي

conscript /kənˈskrɪpt/ *verb* [T] to make sb join the army, navy or air force: *When war broke out all the young men were conscripted.* يجنّد (إلزامياً)
▸ **conscript** /ˈkɒnskrɪpt/ *noun* [C] a person who has been conscripted مجنّد
conscription /kənˈskrɪpʃn/ *noun* [U] the system of making sb join the army, etc. تجنيد

consecrate /ˈkɒnsɪkreɪt/ *verb* [T] to make a place or an object holy in a special ceremony يقدّس ، يبارك
▸ **consecration** /ˌkɒnsɪˈkreɪʃn/ *noun* [C,U] ترسيم (بغرض إسباغ القداسة عليه)

consecutive /kənˈsekjətɪv/ *adj* coming or happening one after the other: *We have had three consecutive hot summers.* متوالٍ ، متعاقب
▸ **consecutively** *adv* على التوالي ، بالتعاقب

consensus /kənˈsensəs/ *noun* [sing., U] agreement among a group of people: *to reach a consensus after a long discussion* ○ *There is no consensus among experts about the causes of global warming.* اتفاق أو اجماع الآراء

consent /kənˈsent/ *verb* [I] **consent (to sth)** to agree to sth; to allow sth to happen يوافق ؛ يسمح
▸ **consent** *noun* [U] agreement; permission: *The child's parents had to give their consent to the operation.* موافقة ؛ إذن

consequence /ˈkɒnsɪkwəns; *US* -kwens/ *noun* **1** [C] something that follows as a result or effect of sth else: *The power station was shown to be dangerous and, as a consequence, was closed down.* ○ *The error had tragic consequences.* نتيجة ، عاقبة

2 [U] (*formal*) importance: *It is of no consequence.* أهمية

consequent /ˈkɒnsɪkwənt/ *adj* (*formal*) following as the result of sth else: *The lack of rain and consequent poor harvests have led to food shortages.* تالٍ ، ناتج
▸ **consequently** *adv*: *She didn't work hard enough, and consequently failed the exam.* وبالتالي، ونتيجة لذلك

conservation /ˌkɒnsəˈveɪʃn/ *noun* [U] **1** not allowing sth to be wasted, damaged or destroyed: *the conservation of energy* حفظ

2 the protection of the natural world: *Conservation groups are protesting against the plan to build a road through the forest.* ℹ The verb is **conserve**. حماية ، حِفظ
▸ **conservationist** /-ʃənɪst/ *noun* [C] a person who believes in conservation (2) المحافظ على البيئة

conservatism /kənˈsɜːvətɪzəm/ *noun* [U] **1** the dislike of new ideas and change محافظة على القديم

2 usually **Conservatism** the beliefs of the Conservative Party معتقدات حزب المحافظين

conservative /kənˈsɜːvətɪv/ *adj* **1** not liking change; traditional: *They have very conservative tastes. This design is too modern for them.* محافظ ؛ تقليدي

2 Conservative connected with the British Conservative Party: *Conservative voters* محافظ

3 (used about a guess, estimate, etc.) cautious, not extreme; rather low: *At a conservative estimate I would say the damage will cost about £4 000 to repair.* حَذِر ؛ معتدل
▸ **conservative** *noun* [C] **1** a conservative (1) person (شخص) محافظ

2 usually **Conservative** a member of the British Conservative Party عضو حزب المحافظين البريطاني
conservatively *adv*: *We have estimated the costs conservatively.* على نحو معتدل

Conˈservative Party *noun* [C] one of the main political parties in Britain. The Conservative Party supports a free market and is opposed to

the state controlling industry ➲ Look at **Labour Party** and **Liberal Democrats**.
حزب المحافظين البريطاني

conservatory /kən'sɜːvətri; *US* -tɔːri/ *noun* [C] (*pl.* **conservatories**) a room with a glass roof and walls often built against the outside wall of a house غرفة من زجاج ملحقة بالبيت

conserve /'kɒnsɜːv/ *verb* [T] to avoid wasting sth: *Higher charges will encourage people to conserve water.* ❶ The noun is **conservation**.
يحافظ على، يصون

consider /kən'sɪdə(r)/ *verb* [T] **1 consider sb/sth (for/as sth); consider doing sth** to think about sb/sth, often before making a decision: *We must consider the matter carefully before we make our choice.* ○ *They are considering him for the part of Romeo.* ○ *She had never considered nursing as a career.* ○ *He is still considering what material to include in the book.* ○ *We're considering going to Spain for our holidays.* يفكّر في ، يقلّب الرأي

2 to have sth as your opinion; to think about sb/sth in a particular way: *He considered that the risk was too great.* ○ *He considered the risk (to be) too great.* يعتبر ، يرى

3 to remember or pay attention to sth: *I can't just move abroad. I have to consider my family.* ○ *Be tactful. Consider how other people feel.*
يراعي ، يضع في اعتباره

considerable /kən'sɪdərəbl/ *adj* great in amount or size: *We had considerable difficulty in getting tickets for the flights we wanted.* ○ *A considerable number of people preferred the old building to the new one.* كثير ؛ ضخم

▸ **considerably** /-əbli/ *adv*: *This flat is considerably larger than our last one.* بكثير، إلى حدّ كبير

considerate /kən'sɪdərət/ *adj* careful not to upset people; thinking of others: *It was very considerate of you to offer to drive me home.* ❶ The opposite is **inconsiderate**. مراعٍ لمشاعر الآخرين

consideration /kən,sɪdə'reɪʃn/ *noun* **1** [U] (*formal*) an act of thinking about sth carefully or for a long time: *I have given some consideration to the idea but I don't think it would work.* ○ *After careful consideration, we regret that we cannot offer you the position.* تفكير مليّ ، إمعان النظر

2 [U] **consideration (for sb/sth)** the quality of thinking about other people's wishes and feelings: *You should keep your music turned down low out of consideration for your neighbours.*
مراعاة (لمشاعر الآخرين)

3 [C] something that you think about when you are making a decision: *If he changes his job, the salary will be an important consideration.*
اعتبار

IDM **take sth into consideration** to think about sth when you are forming an opinion or making a decision يأخذ بعين الاعتبار

considering /kən'sɪdərɪŋ/ *prep, conj* (used for introducing a surprising fact) when you think about or remember sth: *He coped with the long journey well, considering his age.* ○ *Considering you've only been studying for a year, you speak English very well.* إذا أخذنا بعين الاعتبار

consign /kən'saɪn/ *verb* [T] (*formal*) **1** to put sb/sth in, or to send sb/sth to, a particular place يودع ؛ يرسِل

2 to send goods to sb يشحَن (بضاعة)

▸ **consignment** *noun* **1** [U] sending sb/sth to a particular place إرسال ، شحن

2 [C] goods that are being sent to sb/sth: *We are expecting a new consignment of bicycles very soon.* شحنة (بضائع)

consist /kən'sɪst/ *verb*

PHR V **consist in sth** to have sth as its main point or feature: *Her job consisted in welcoming the guests as they arrived.* يقوم على

consist of sth to be made up of sth: *Pastry consists of flour, fat and water.* ○ *The band consists of a singer, two guitarists and a drummer.* يتألف من

consistency /kən'sɪstənsi/ *noun* (*pl.* **consistencies**) **1** [U] the quality of being consistent (1); always having the same standard, opinions, etc: *Your work lacks consistency. Sometimes it's excellent but at other times it's full of mistakes.* ❶ The opposite is **inconsistency**.
ثبات على مبدأ واحد ؛ إتّباع طريقة واحدة

2 [C, U] the degree of thickness or firmness that a liquid substance has: *The mixture should have a thick, sticky consistency.* قوام

consistent /kən'sɪstənt/ *adj* **1** always having the same opinions, standard, behaviour, etc.; not changing: *You must be consistent. If you punish Jason, you must punish Paul for doing the same thing.* ❶ The opposite is **inconsistent**.
ثابت في مبدئه ؛ مطّرد

2 consistent (with sth) agreeing with or similar to sth: *I'm afraid your statement is not consistent with what the other witnesses said.*
متوافق مع ، مطابِق لِ

▸ **consistently** *adv*: *We must try to maintain a consistently high standard.* باطّراد ؛ بصورة ثابتة

consolation /,kɒnsə'leɪʃn/ *noun* **1** [U] making sb feel better when they are sad: *It was some consolation to me to know that I wasn't the only one who had failed the exam.* عزاء

2 [C] a person or thing that consoles you: *Having his children near him was a great consolation when his wife died.* عزاء ، سلوى

console[1] /kən'səʊl/ *verb* [T] to make sb happier when he/she is very sad or disappointed; to comfort sb يعزي

console[2] /'kɒnsəʊl/ *noun* [C] a flat surface which contains all the controls and switches for a machine, a piece of electronic equipment, etc. لوحة التحكم

consolidate /kən'sɒlɪdeɪt/ *verb* [I,T] to become or to make sth firmer or stronger: *We're going to consolidate what we've learned so far by doing some revision exercises today.*
يتعزّز؛ يثبّت، يقوّي ، يوحّد

▸ **consolidation** /kənˌsɒlɪˈdeɪʃn/ *noun* [U] تعزيز ، تقوية

consonant /ˈkɒnsənənt/ *noun* [C] **1** a sound that you make by partly stopping the air as it comes out through your mouth صوت ساكن

2 a letter that represents this sound: *The letters 't', 'm', 's' and 'b' are all consonants.* ➲ Look at **vowel**. حرف ساكن

consortium /kənˈsɔːtiəm; *US* -ʃiəm/ *noun* [C] (*pl.* **consortiums** or **consortia** /-tiə; *US* -ʃiə/) a group of companies that work closely together for a particular purpose اتحاد شركات

conspicuous /kənˈspɪkjuəs/ *adj* easily seen or noticed: *As a tall, blond American he was very conspicuous in China.* ❶ The opposite is **inconspicuous**. بارز (للعيان) ، ملفِت للنظر

▸ **conspicuously** *adv*: *She was conspicuously dressed in bright colours.* بشكل ملفِت للأنظار

conspiracy /kənˈspɪrəsi/ *noun* (*pl.* **conspiracies**) **1** [U] planning sth, especially a crime, together with other people: *They were accused of conspiracy to murder.* مؤامرة

2 [C] a secret plan to do sth bad or illegal: *Investigators have uncovered a conspiracy to defraud the bank of thousands of pounds.* مؤامرة

conspire /kənˈspaɪə(r)/ *verb* [I] **1** to plan sth, especially a crime, together with other people: *A group of terrorists were conspiring to blow up the plane.* يتآمر

2 conspire (against sb/sth) to work together to produce a particular, usually bad, result for sb/sth: *When we both lost our jobs in the same week, we felt that everything was conspiring against us.* يتواطأ

▸ **conspirator** /kənˈspɪrətə(r)/ *noun* [C] a person who conspires (1) متآمر

constable /ˈkʌnstəbl; *US* ˈkɒn-/ *noun* [C] = POLICE CONSTABLE

▸ **constabulary** /kənˈstæbjələri; *US* -leri/ *noun* [C] (*pl.* **constabularies**) the police force of a particular area: *the West Yorkshire Constabulary* قوى الشرطة (في منطقة معينة)

⚷ **constant** /ˈkɒnstənt/ *adj* **1** happening or existing all the time or again and again: *The constant noise gave me a headache.* ○ *Don't lock this door. It's in constant use.* ○ *There were constant interruptions so we didn't get the work finished.* دائم ، مستمرّ

2 that does not change: *You use less petrol if you drive at a constant speed.* ثابت

▸ **constantly** *adv* always; again and again: *The situation is constantly changing.* باستمرار

constellation /ˌkɒnstəˈleɪʃn/ *noun* [C] a number of stars that are considered as a group مجموعة نجوم ، كوكبة

consternation /ˌkɒnstəˈneɪʃn/ *noun* [U] surprise and worry or fear: *We stared at each other in consternation.* دهشة : ذُعْر

constipated /ˈkɒnstɪpeɪtɪd/ *adj* not able to pass waste material easily from the bowels: *If you are constipated you should eat more fibre and fresh fruit.* مصاب بالإمساك

▸ **constipation** /ˌkɒnstɪˈpeɪʃn/ *noun* [U] إمساك

constituency /kənˈstɪtjuənsi/ *noun* [C] (*pl.* **constituencies**) a district which has its own Member of Parliament دائرة (انتخابية)

constituent /kənˈstɪtjuənt/ *noun* [C] **1** a person who lives in the district for which a particular Member of Parliament is responsible أحد أفراد دائرة انتخابية معيّنة

2 one of the parts of sth (عنصر) مكوّن

constitute /ˈkɒnstɪtjuːt/ *verb* [T] (*formal*) (not used in the continuous tenses) to make up or form sth: *Women constitute a high proportion of part-time workers.* ○ *The presence of the troops constitutes a threat to peace.* يشكّل

constitution /ˌkɒnstɪˈtjuːʃn; *US* -ˈtuːʃn/ *noun* **1** [C] the laws or rules of a country or organization: *the United States constitution* دستور

2 [U] the way sth is put together تكوين

3 [C] (*old-fashioned*) the condition of your body; your health بنية الجسم

constitutional /ˌkɒnstɪˈtjuːʃənl; *US* -ˈtuː-/ *adj* connected with a constitution (1) دستوري

constrain /kənˈstreɪn/ *verb* [T] (*formal*) to set limits on sth, especially sb's freedom; to force sb to do sth يقيِّد : يجبِر

constraint /kənˈstreɪnt/ *noun* [C,U] a limit on sth, or on your freedom to do sth: *There are always some financial constraints on a project like this.* ○ *He signed the document under constraint* (= he was forced to do it). قيد : إكراه

constrict /kənˈstrɪkt/ *verb* [T] **1** to make sth tighter or narrower; to reduce sth يضيّق : يقلّص

2 to limit a person's freedom to do sth يحدّ (من حرية شخص)

▸ **constriction** /kənˈstrɪkʃn/ *noun* [C,U] **1** a reduction in the space or the range of possibilities available تضييق : تقلّص

2 making sth tighter or narrower: *a feeling of constriction in the chest* ضيق

⚷ **construct** /kənˈstrʌkt/ *verb* [T] to build or make sth: *Early houses were constructed out of mud and sticks.* ❶ **Construct** is more formal than **build**. يبني ، يشيّد

⚷ **construction** /kənˈstrʌkʃn/ *noun* **1** [U] the act or method of building or making sth: *A new bridge is now under construction.* ○ *He works in the construction industry.* بناء ، تشييد

2 [C] something that has been built or made: *The new pyramid was a construction of glass and steel.* بناء ، مبنى

3 [C] the way that words are used together in a phrase or sentence: *a complex sentence construction* ○ *Which construction is more common – 'to dress' or 'to get dressed'?* تركيب لغويّ

constructive /kənˈstrʌktɪv/ *adj* useful or helpful: *She made a number of constructive criticisms to help us to improve our work.* بنّاء ، مفيد

▶ **constructively** *adv* على نحو بنّاء

construe /kən'stru:/ *verb* [T] (*formal*) **construe sth (as sth)** to understand the meaning of sth in a particular way: *Her confident manner is often construed as arrogance.* يؤوِّل، يفسِّر بشكل معيَّن

consul /'kɒnsl/ *noun* [C] an official who works in a foreign city helping people from his/her country who are living or visiting there ➲ Look at **ambassador**. قنصل

▶ **consular** /'kɒnsjələ(r); *US* -səl-/ *adj* connected with a consul قنصلي

consulate /'kɒnsjələt; *US* -səl-/ *noun* [C] the office of a consul قنصليّة

consult /kən'sʌlt/ *verb* **1** [T] **consult sb/sth (about sth)** to ask sb or to look sth up in a book, etc. to get information or advice: *You should consult a doctor if the symptoms get worse.* ○ *He consulted the map to find the shortest route.* يستشير (طبيباً الخ) : يستعين بِ

2 [I] **consult with sb** to discuss sth with sb يتباحث أو يتشاور مع

consultancy /kən'sʌltənsi/ *noun* [C] **1** a company that gives expert advice on a particular subject مكتب استشاري

2 [U] expert advice that sb is paid to provide on a particular subject مشورة، إستشارة

consultant /kən'sʌltənt/ *noun* [C] **1** a person who gives advice to people on business, law, etc: *a firm of management consultants* مستشار

2 (*Brit*) a hospital doctor of high rank who is a specialist in a particular area of medicine (طبيب) أخصائي أو استشاري

consultation /ˌkɒnsl'teɪʃn/ *noun* **1** [U] discussing sth or looking sth up in a book to get information or advice استشارة : مراجعة

2 [C,U] a meeting at which sth is discussed: *Diplomats met for consultations on the hostage crisis.* ○ *The measures were introduced without consultation.* اجتماع تشاوري ، تشاور

consume /kən'sju:m; *US* -'su:m/ *verb* [T] (*formal*) **1** to use sth: *The United States imports 45% of the oil it consumes.* يستهلك

2 to eat or drink sth يأتي على، يأكل أو يشرب

3 (used about fire) to destroy sth تلتهم (النار)

4 (used about an emotion) to affect sb very strongly: *She was consumed by grief when her son was killed.* يضني : يأكله (الحزن)

▶ **consuming** *adj* (only *before* a noun) that takes up a lot of your time and attention: *Sport is her consuming passion.* مستحوذ على عقله ووقته

consumer /kən'sju:mə(r); *US* -su:-/ *noun* [C] a person who buys things or uses services: *Consumers should complain if they are not satisfied with the service they receive.* ○ *the rights of the consumer* ○ *Consumer spending has risen in the past few months.* مُستَهلِك

consummate /'kɒnsəmeɪt/ *verb* [T] (*formal*) **1** to make sth complete يكمل، ينجز

2 to make a marriage legal or complete by having sexual intercourse يبني (بزوجته)

▶ **consummation** /ˌkɒnsə'meɪʃn/ *noun* [C,U] إكمال، إتمام

consumption /kən'sʌmpʃn/ *noun* [U] **1** the act of using, eating, etc. sth: *This fish is unfit for human consumption* (= for people to eat). استهلاك

2 the amount of fuel, etc. that sth uses: *a car with low fuel consumption* استهلاك

cont. (*also* **contd**) *abbrev* continued: *cont. on p 91* يتبع

contact /'kɒntækt/ *noun* **1** [U] the state of touching sb/sth: *Don't let the wires come into contact with each other.* احتكاك

2 [U] meeting, talking to or writing to sb else: *We are in close contact with our office in New York.* ○ *I've lost contact with most of my old school friends.* ○ *They are trying to make contact with the kidnappers.* ○ *Tom has not been in contact since he moved to Edinburgh.* ○ *Tom broke off contact with his family after a quarrel.* اتّصال

3 [C] a person that you know who may be able to help you: *I have some useful business contacts in Berlin.* واسطة ، أحد المعارف

▶ **contact** /'kɒntækt/ *verb* [T] to telephone, write to, etc. sb: *Is there a phone number where I can contact you?* يتّصل بِ

'**contact lens** *noun* [C] a small piece of plastic that fits onto your eye to help you to see better عدسة لاصقة

contagious /kən'teɪdʒəs/ *adj* (used about a disease) that you can catch by touching sb/sth: *Smallpox is a contagious disease.* ○ (*figurative*) *contagious laughter* ➲ Look at **infectious**. معْدٍ

contain /kən'teɪn/ *verb* [T] **1** to have sth inside (or as part of) itself: *Each box contains 24 tins.* ○ *petrol containing lead* يحوي ، يحتوي على

2 to keep sth within limits: *efforts to contain inflation* ○ *The children couldn't contain themselves – they burst out laughing.* ○ *She found it hard to contain her anger.* يحصر ، يحدّ من

> **Contain** or **include**? **Contain** is used when we are talking about objects which have other things inside them: *a jar containing olives* ○ *The parcel contained six books.* **Include** is used to show that several things are part of a whole or thought to belong to something: *The price of the holiday includes accommodation and evening meals but not lunch.* ○ *a team of seven people including a cameraman and a doctor*

container /kən'teɪnə(r)/ *noun* [C] **1** a box, bottle, packet, etc. in which sth is kept: *a plastic container* ○ *a watertight container* وعاء ، إناء

2 a large metal box that is used for transporting goods by sea, road or rail: *a container lorry, ship, etc.* خزان نقل ، صهريج

contaminate /kən'tæmɪneɪt/ *verb* [T] to add a substance which will make sth dirty, harmful or dangerous: *The town's drinking water was contaminated with poisonous chemicals.* يلوِّث

▶ **contamination** /kənˌtæmɪ'neɪʃn/ *noun* [U]:

containers

There was widespread radioactive contamination of farmland after the accident at the nuclear power station. تلوّث

contemplate /ˈkɒntəmpleɪt/ *verb* [T] **1** to think about sth or the possibility of doing sth: *The idea was too awful to contemplate.* ○ *Before her illness she had never contemplated retiring.* يفكّر (في فعل شيء) ، يعتزم

2 to look at sb/sth, often quietly or for a long time يتأمّل

▸ **contemplation** /ˌkɒntəmˈpleɪʃn/ *noun* [U]

1 looking at sth quietly تأمّل

2 thinking deeply about sth تفكّر (عميق)

🔑**contemporary** /kənˈtemprəri; *US* -pəreri/ *adj* **1** belonging to the same time as sb/sth else: *Samuel Pepys' diary gives us a contemporary account of the Great Fire of London in 1666.* معاصر

2 of the present time; modern: *contemporary music, art, etc.* معاصر : حديث

▸ **contemporary** *noun* [C] (*pl.* **contemporaries**) a person who lived or did sth at the same time as sb else: *Telemann, a contemporary of Bach* (شخص) معاصر ا

contempt /kənˈtempt/ *noun* [U] **contempt (for sb/sth)** the feeling that sb/sth does not deserve to be respected or is unimportant: *That country has shown contempt for human rights.* احتقار

▸ **contemptuous** /kənˈtemptʃuəs/ *adj* feeling or showing contempt for sb/sth محتقِر

contend /kənˈtend/ *verb* **1** [I] **contend with/against sb/sth; contend for sth** to struggle to overcome sth or to win sth: *She's had a lot of problems to contend with.* ○ *Two athletes are contending for first place.* يصارع : يتنافس

2 [T] (*formal*) to declare or argue that sth is true: *The young man contended that he had never met the murdered girl.* يؤكّد : يجادل

▸ **contender** *noun* [C] a person who takes part in a competition: *There were three contenders for the leadership.* متنافس ، متبارٍ

content¹ /kənˈtent/ *adj* (not before a noun) **content (with sth); content to do sth** satisfied with what you have: *She is quite content to stay at home looking after her children.* راضٍ ، قانع

▸ **content** *noun* [U] the state of being happy or satisfied: *His face was a picture of content.* رضا ، قناعة

content *verb* [T] **content yourself with sth** to accept sth even though it was not exactly what you wanted: *The castle was closed, so we contented ourselves with a walk round the park.* يقنع بِ

contented *adj* happy or satisfied: *The baby gave a contented chuckle.* قانع ، سعيد

contentedly *adv*: *The cat purred contentedly.* برضا

contentment *noun* [U]: *a sigh of contentment* رضا

🔑**content²** /ˈkɒntent/ *noun* **1 contents** [plural] the thing or things that are inside sth: *Add the contents of this packet to a pint of cold milk and mix well.* ○ *The contents page tells you what is inside a book.* محتويات أو محتوى

2 [sing.] the main subject, ideas, etc. of a book, article, television programme, etc: *The content of the essay is good, but there are too many grammatical mistakes.* محتوى ، مضمون

3 [sing.] the level or amount of a particular substance that sth contains: *Many processed foods have a high sugar content.* محتوى

contention /kənˈtenʃn/ *noun* **1** [U] the situation of competing for sth: *Four players are still in contention for the cup.* منافسة

2 [U] arguing; disagreement نزاع ؛ خلاف

3 [C] your opinion; sth that you declare to be true: *The government's contention is that unemployment will start to fall next year.* رأي ؛ زَعْم

contentious /kən'tenʃəs/ *adj* likely to cause argument: *a contentious issue* موضع جدال ؛ مثير للنزاع

contest /kən'test/ *verb* [T] **1** to say that sth is wrong or that it was not done properly: *They contested the decision, saying that the judges had not been fair.* يعارض ، يطعن في

2 to take part in a competition or try to win sth: *a hotly contested world-championship fight* ينافس ، يباري

▸ **contest** /'kɒntest/ *noun* [C] a competition to find out who is the best, strongest, most beautiful, etc: *a boxing contest* ○ *The by-election will be a contest between the two main parties.* مباراة ؛ مسابقة

contestant /kən'testənt/ *noun* [C] a person who takes part in a contest: *Four contestants appear on the quiz show each week.* متسابق ، متبارٍ

context /'kɒntekst/ *noun* [C,U] **1** the words that come before or after a word, phrase, sentence, etc. and that help you to understand its meaning: *You can often guess the meaning of a word from its context.* ○ *Taken out of context, his comment made no sense.* سِياق ، قرينة الكلام

2 the situation in which sth happens or that caused sth to happen: *The rise in nationalism must be seen in the context of changing attitudes in Europe.* سِياق ، إطار

continent /'kɒntɪnənt/ *noun* **1** [C] one of the seven main areas of land on the Earth: *Asia, Africa and Antarctica are continents.* قارّة

2 the Continent [sing.] (*Brit*) the main part of Europe, i.e. not the British Isles: *Hotels on the Continent are much cheaper than in Britain.* أوروبا (عدا بريطانيا)، القارّة الأوروبية

▸ **continental** /ˌkɒntɪ'nentl/ *adj* **1** connected with or typical of a continent: *Moscow has a continental climate: hot summers and cold winters.* قارّي

2 (*also* **Continental**) (*Brit*) connected with the main part of Europe: *continental holidays* أوروبي

ˌcontinental 'breakfast *noun* [C] a breakfast of bread and jam with coffee ➲ Look at **English breakfast**. فطور أوروبي

contingency /kən'tɪndʒənsi/ *noun* [C] (*pl.* **contingencies**) a possible future situation or event: *contingency plans* حدث محتمل الوقوع ، طارئ

contingent /kən'tɪndʒənt/ *noun* [C, with sing. or pl. verb] **1** a group of people from the same country, organization, etc. who are attending an event: *the Irish contingent at the conference* فريق ، مجموعة ؛ جالية

2 a group of armed forces forming part of a larger force فرقة (عسكرية)

continual /kən'tɪnjuəl/ *adj* happening again and again: *His continual phone calls started to annoy her.* مستمر

▸ **continually** /kən'tɪnjuəli/ *adv*: *She continually criticizes his behaviour.* بشكل متلاحق ، باستمرار

Continual or **continuous?** We use **continuous** to describe an action or state that goes on without stopping: *There has been a continuous improvement in his work.* ○ *After climbing continuously for three hours, we were exhausted.* **Continual** is used to describe something that happens repeatedly, especially something that annoys us: *They have had continual problems with the heating.*

continuation /kənˌtɪnju'eɪʃn/ *noun* **1** [sing., U] continuing to do sth without stopping; starting to do sth again after you have stopped متابعة ؛ استئناف

2 [sing.] something that continues sth else or makes it longer: *a continuation of recent trends* ○ *The track was a continuation of the road.* امتداد ، تتمّة

continue /kən'tɪnju:/ *verb* **1** [I,T] **continue (doing/to do sth)**; **continue (with sth)** to go on happening or existing, or to make sth go on happening or existing: *If the pain continues, see your doctor.* ○ *They ignored me and continued their conversation.* ○ *He continued working/to work late into the night.* ○ *I shall continue with the lessons after the exam.* يستمرّ ، يتابع

2 [I,T] to begin to do or say sth again after you had stopped: *The meeting will continue after lunch.* ○ *I'm sorry I interrupted. Please continue.* ○ *The next day we continued our journey.* يستمرّ ، يستأنف

3 [I,T] to go further or to make sth go further: *We continued along the path until we came to the river.* يستمرّ ، يواصل

4 [I] to remain in a particular situation or condition: *He will continue as headmaster until the end of term.* يبقى

▸ **continued** *adj* going on without stopping: *There are reports of continued fighting near the border.* مستمرّ ، متواصل

continuity /ˌkɒntɪ'nju:əti; *US* -'nu:-/ *noun* [U] the state of continuing without interruption; linking one thing smoothly with the next: *The pupils will have the same teacher for two years to ensure continuity.* استمرارية

continuous /kən'tɪnjuəs/ *adj* happening or existing without stopping: *a period of continuous economic growth* ○ *a continuous process* ○ *There was a continuous line of cars stretching for miles.* مستمرّ، متواصل

▸ **continuously** *adv*: *It has rained continuously here for three days.* ➲ Look at the note at **continual**. باستمرار ، بلا انقطاع

con'tinuous tense (*also* **progressive tense**) *noun* [C] (*grammar*) the form of a verb such as 'I am waiting' or 'It was raining' which is made from a part of 'be' and a verb ending in '-ing' and is used to describe an action that continues for a period of time صيغة الفعل الدالّة على الاستمرار

contort /kən'tɔːt/ *verb* [I,T] to move or to make sth move into an unnatural shape: *His face contorted/was contorted with pain.* يتلوّى ؛ يلتوي
▸ **contortion** /kən'tɔːʃn/ *noun* [C] تلوية الجسم بحركات بهلوانية

contour /'kɒntʊə(r)/ *noun* [C] **1** the outline or shape of the outer surface of sth: *I could just make out the contours of the house in the dark.* الخطّ الخارجي ، الكفاف
2 (*also* '**contour line**) a line on a map joining places of equal height: *From the contour lines I could tell that there was a steep hill to climb.* الخط الكنتوري أو التسامقي

contraception /ˌkɒntrə'sepʃn/ *noun* [U] the means of preventing a woman from becoming pregnant: *Your doctor will be happy to advise you about contraception.* ○ *a reliable form of contraception* منع الحَمْل
▸ **contraceptive** /ˌkɒntrə'septɪv/ *noun* [C] a pill or object that prevents a woman from becoming pregnant: *an oral contraceptive* ○ *a packet of contraceptives* وسيلة لمنع الحَمْل
contraceptive *adj*: *a contraceptive pill* مانع للحَمْل

contract¹ /'kɒntrækt/ *noun* [C] a written legal agreement: *They signed a three-year contract with a major record company.* ○ *The company has just won a contract to supply machinery to the government.* ○ *a temporary contract* عَقْد ، اتفاقية
▸ **contractual** /kən'træktʃuəl/ *adj* connected with or included in a contract تعاقدي

contract² /kən'trækt/ *verb* **1** [I,T] to make a written legal agreement with sb to do sth or to have sb work for you: *His firm has been contracted to supply all the furniture for the new building.* يتعاقد ؛ يعقد
2 [T] to get an illness or disease: *She contracted pneumonia.* يُصاب (بمرض)
▸ **contractor** *noun* [C] a person or company that does work, especially building work, by contract: *a building contractor* مقاول ، متعهّد

contract³ /kən'trækt/ *verb* [I,T] to become or to make sth smaller or shorter: *Metals contract as they cool.* ○ *'I'm' is the contracted form of 'I am.'*
➲ Look at **expand**. It is the opposite for the first example. يتقلّص ؛ يختزل ، يقصّر
▸ **contraction** /kən'trækʃn/ *noun* **1** [U] the process of getting smaller or of making sth smaller تقلّص ، انكماش
2 [C] a contracted form of a word or words: *'Mustn't' is a contraction of 'must not.'* صيغة مختصرة
3 [C] a strong tightening of muscles that happens to a woman as her baby is born تقلّص (العضلات)

contradict /ˌkɒntrə'dɪkt/ *verb* **1** [I,T] to say that sth is wrong or untrue; to say the opposite of sth: *'We haven't got any tea.' 'Yes, we have,' she contradicted.* ○ *I didn't dare contradict him, but I think he was wrong.* يكذّب (شخصاً آخر) ؛ يناقض
2 [T] (used about a statement, fact, etc.) to be different from or opposite to sth: *These instructions seem to contradict previous ones.* يناقض ، يخالف
▸ **contradiction** /ˌkɒntrə'dɪkʃn/ *noun* **1** [C] a statement or fact that is opposite to or different from another;: *There were a number of contradictions in what he told the police.* تناقض، اختلاف
2 [C,U] **(a) contradiction (between sth and sth)** the fact of two things being opposite to or not matching each other: *There is a contradiction between the two sets of figures.* ○ *This letter is in complete contradiction to their previous one.* تعارض
contradictory /ˌkɒntrə'dɪktəri/ *adj* being opposite to or not matching sth else: *Contradictory reports appeared in the newspapers.* متناقض ، متعارض

contraflow /'kɒntrəfləʊ/ *noun* [C] an arrangement where part of a wide road is closed, usually for repairs, and traffic going in both directions has to use one side of the road استخدام جزء من الطريق لحركة المرور في الاتجاهين

contraption /kən'træpʃn/ *noun* [C] a strange or complicated piece of equipment أداة غريبة الشكل أو معقّدة

contrary¹ /'kɒntrəri; *US* -treri/ *adj* completely different; opposite: *I thought it was possible but she took the contrary view.* مخالف ؛ معاكس
▸ **contrary to** *prep* completely different from; opposite to; against: *He's actually very nice, contrary to what people say about him.* عكسَ ، على عكس

contrary² /'kɒntrəri; *US* -treri/ *noun*
IDM **on the contrary** the opposite is true; certainly not: *'You look as if you're not enjoying yourself.' 'On the contrary, I'm having a great time'.* على العكس
to the contrary saying the opposite: *Unless I hear anything to the contrary, I shall assume that the arrangements haven't changed.* بما يؤكّد العكس

contrast¹ /kən'trɑːst; *US* -'træst/ *verb* **1** [T] **contrast (A and/with B)** to compare people or things in order to show the differences between them: *It's interesting to contrast the various styles of architecture here.* ○ *The film contrasts his poor childhood with his later life as a millionaire.* يقارن ، يبرز الفروق بين
2 [I] **contrast with sb/sth** to be clearly different when compared: *The red cushions contrast dramatically with the black sofa.* ○ *This comment contrasts sharply with his previous remarks.* يتغاير ، يتباين

contrast² /'kɒntrɑːst; *US* -træst/ *noun* **contrast (to/with sb/sth); contrast (between A and B)** **1** [U] comparison between two people or things that shows the differences between them: *In contrast to previous years, we've had a very successful summer.* ○ *He was friendly and talkative; she, by contrast, said nothing.* مقارنة ؛ بالمقارنة مع
2 [C,U] a clear difference between two things or people that is seen when they are compared: *There is a tremendous contrast between the climate in the valley and the climate in the hills.* فارق ، تباين

3 [C] something that is clearly different from sth else when the two things are compared: *This house is quite a contrast to your old one!* شيء مختلف جداً

contravene /ˌkɒntrəˈviːn/ *verb* [T] (*formal*) to break a law or a rule ينتهك (قانوناً) ، يخالف، يخرق
▶ **contravention** /ˌkɒntrəˈvenʃn/ *noun* [C,U] انتهاك ، تعارض ، خرق، مخالفة

contribute /kənˈtrɪbjuːt/ *verb* **1** [I,T] to give a part of the total, together with others: *Would you like to contribute towards our collection for famine relief?* ○ *He didn't contribute anything to the conversation.* ○ *We contributed £5 each towards a retirement present for her.* يساهم ، يتبرع بـ
2 [I] to help to produce sth; to play a part in sth: *Every member of the team contributed to the victory.* يسهم
3 [I,T] to write articles for a magazine or newspaper يساهم بالكتابة في الصحف أو المجلات
▶ **contributor** *noun* [C] a person who contributes to sth مساهم ، متبرع

contribution /ˌkɒntrɪˈbjuːʃn/ *noun* [C,U] something that you give or do together with others; the act of giving your share: *All contributions to the appeal will be gratefully received.* ○ *He made a significant contribution to the country's struggle for independence.* مساهمة ، تبرع

contributory /kənˈtrɪbjətəri; *US* -tɔːri/ *adj* helping to cause or produce sth: *a contributory factor* (عامل) مساعد

contrive /kənˈtraɪv/ *verb* [T] **1** to plan or invent sth clever and/or dishonest يحتال للأمر
2 to manage to do or make sth, although there are difficulties يتدبر الأمر
▶ **contrived** *adj* clearly artificial or invented, not natural: *The ending of the film seemed rather contrived.* مصطنع

control¹ /kənˈtrəʊl/ *noun* **1** [U] **control (of/over sb/sth)** power over sth; the ability to organize, direct or guide sb/sth: *Rebels took control of the radio station.* ○ *He lost control of the car and crashed.* ○ *There's nothing I can do about the problem, it's outside my control.* ○ *I was late because of circumstances beyond my control.* سيطرة : تحكم
2 [C,U] **(a) control (on/over sth)** a limit on sth; a way of keeping sb/sth within certain limits: *price controls* ○ *crowd control* ضبط : تنظيم
3 [C] one of the parts of a machine that is used for operating it: *the controls of an aeroplane* جهاز تحكم
4 [sing.] the place from which sth is operated or where sth is checked: *We went through passport control and then got onto the plane.* نقطة تفتيش أو مراقبة
5 (*also* **con'trol key**) (on a computer keyboard) a key that you press when you want to perform a particular operation مفتاح التحكم
IDM **be in control (of sth)** to be in command of sth; to have the power or ability to deal with sth: *The police are again in control of the area following last night's violence.* يدير، يشرف على، يسيطر على
be/get out of control to be/become impossible to deal with or guide: *The demonstration got out of control and fighting broke out.* يفقد التحكم في ؛ يفلت الزمام
under control being dealt with, directed or run successfully: *It took several hours to bring the fire under control.* ○ *She finds it difficult to keep her feelings under control.* تحكم (في الأمر)، "تحت السيطرة"

control² /kənˈtrəʊl/ *verb* [T] (controlling; controlled) **1** to have power over sth or the ability to organize, direct or guide sth: *One family controls the company.* ○ *Police struggled to control the crowd.* ○ *I couldn't control myself any longer and burst out laughing.* يسيطر على : يضبط
2 to keep sth within certain limits: *measures to control price rises* يضبط ، ينظم
▶ **controller** *noun* [C] a person who directs sth: *air traffic controllers* مراقب : مدير

controversial /ˌkɒntrəˈvɜːʃl/ *adj* causing public discussion and disagreement: *a controversial TV programme* ○ *a controversial new law* مثير للجدل ، موضع خلاف

controversy /ˈkɒntrəvɜːsi; *Brit also* kənˈtrɒvəsi/ *noun* [C,U] (*pl.* **controversies**) public discussion and disagreement about sth: *The plans for changing the city centre caused a great deal of controversy.* جدال ، خلاف

conurbation /ˌkɒnɜːˈbeɪʃn/ *noun* [C] a group of towns that have grown and joined together مدن صغيرة متلاصقة

convalesce /ˌkɒnvəˈles/ *verb* [I] to rest and recover from an illness over a period of time يتماثل للشفاء
▶ **convalescence** /ˌkɒnvəˈlesns/ *noun* [sing., U] نقاهة
convalescent /ˌkɒnvəˈlesnt/ *adj* نقاهي : متماثل للشفاء

convene /kənˈviːn/ *verb* [I,T] to come together or to bring people together for a meeting, etc. يجتمع ؛ يعقد اجتماعاً

convenience /kənˈviːniəns/ *noun* **1** [U] the quality of being suitable or practical for a particular purpose: *a building designed for the convenience of disabled people* ○ *For convenience, you can pay for everything at once.* ملاءمة ، راحة
2 [C] something that is useful or suitable: *houses with all modern conveniences* وسيلة راحة، (مجهز بوسائل الراحة)
3 [C] (*Brit*) a public toilet: *public conveniences* ➲ Look at the note at **toilet**. دورة مياه أو مرحاض عام

con'venience food *noun* [C,U] food that you buy frozen or in a box or can, that you can prepare very quickly and easily طعام جاهز

con'venience store *noun* [C] a shop/store that sells food, newspapers, etc. and often stays open 24 hours a day دكان للحاجيات يفتح طويلاً

convenient /kənˈviːniənt/ *adj* **1** suitable or practical for a particular purpose; not causing difficulty: *I'm willing to meet you on any day* *that's convenient for you.* ○ *It isn't convenient to talk at the moment, I'm in the middle of a meeting.* ملائم ، مناسب

2 close to sth; in a useful position: *The hotel is convenient for the beach.* ❶ The opposite is **inconvenient**. قريب : مفيد

▸ **conveniently** *adv*: *Conveniently, a bus was waiting when I got there.* ○ *She had conveniently forgotten that she owed me some money.* على نحو ملائم

convent /ˈkɒnvənt; *US* -vent/ *noun* [C] a place where women (nuns) live in a religious community ➲ Look at **monastery**. دَيْر راهبات

⚷ **convention** /kənˈvenʃn/ *noun* **1** [C] a large meeting or conference: *the Democratic Party Convention* مؤتمر ، اجتماع كبير

2 [C,U] a traditional way of behaving or of doing sth: *A speech by the bride's father is one of the conventions of a wedding.* ○ *The film shows no respect for convention.* تقليد ، عرف

3 [C] a formal agreement, especially between nations: *the Geneva Convention* اتفاقية

⚷ **conventional** /kənˈvenʃənl/ *adj* following what is traditional or considered to be normal, sometimes too closely: *conventional attitudes* ○ *The house was built with conventional materials but in a totally new style.* ○ *I quite like him but he's so conventional* (= boring, because of this). ❶ The opposite is **unconventional**. تقليدي : متمسّك بالتقاليد

▸ **conventionally** /-ʃənəli/ *adv*: *He always dresses conventionally.* على نحو تقليدي : وفق الطراز المألوف

converge /kənˈvɜːdʒ/ *verb* [I] **converge (on sb/sth)** to move towards or meet at the same point from different directions: *People from the surrounding areas converge on the village during the annual festival.* ○ *The paths converge at the bottom of the hill.* يتجمّع ، يلتقي في نقطة واحدة

⚷ **conversation** /ˌkɒnvəˈseɪʃn/ *noun* [C,U] informal talk: *I had a long conversation with her about her plans for the future.* ○ *His job is his only topic of conversation.* ○ *They sat in the corner, deep in conversation.* ○ *She finds it difficult to make conversation* (= to think of things to say). محادثة

converse /kənˈvɜːs/ *verb* [I] (*formal*) to talk informally; to have a conversation يتحدث مع : يحادث

conversely /ˈkɒnvɜːsli/ *adv* (*formal*) in a way that is opposite to sth: *People who earn a lot of money have little time to spend it. Conversely, many people with limitless time do not have enough money to do what they want.* وعلى العكس

conversion /kənˈvɜːʃn; *US* kənˈvɜːrʒn/ *noun* **(a) conversion (from sth) (into/to sth) 1** [C,U] change from one form, system or use to another: *a conversion table for miles and kilometres* تحويل

2 [C,U] becoming a member of a different religion: *conversion to Catholicism* اعتناق دين آخر

⚷ **convert**[1] /kənˈvɜːt/ *verb* [I,T] **1 convert (sth) (from sth) (into/to sth)** to change from one form, system or use to another: *a sofa that converts into a double bed* ○ *How do you convert pounds into kilos?* ○ *They're converting the house into four flats.* يتحوّل إلى : يحوِّل

2 convert (sb) (from sth) (to sth) to change to, or persuade sb to change to a new religion: *As a young man he converted to Islam.* ○ *to convert people to Christianity* يعتنق ديناً آخر : يحوّل (لدين آخر)

convert[2] /ˈkɒnvɜːt/ *noun* [C] **a convert (to sth)** a person who has been persuaded to become a member of a particular religion معتنق أو متحوّل لدين آخر

convertible /kənˈvɜːtəbl/ *adj* able to be changed into another form: *a convertible sofa* (= one that unfolds to make a bed) ○ *convertible currencies* (= those that can be exchanged for other currencies) قابل للتحويل

▸ **convertible** *noun* [C] a car with a roof that can be folded down or taken off سيّارة مكشوفة

convex /ˈkɒnveks/ *adj* having a surface that curves outwards: *a convex lens* ➲ Look at **concave**. محدّب

convey /kənˈveɪ/ *verb* [T] **1 convey sth (to sb)** to make ideas, thoughts, feelings, etc. known to sb; to communicate sth: *The film conveys a lot of information but in an entertaining manner.* ○ *Please convey my sympathy to her at this sad time.* يوصِّل ، يحمل ، يبلِّغ

2 (*formal*) to transport sb/sth from one place to another ينقل

conˈveyor belt *noun* [C] a continuous moving belt that carries objects from one place to another, e.g. in a factory حزام أو سَيْر متحرك

convict /kənˈvɪkt/ *verb* [T] **convict sb (of sth)** to declare in a court of law that sb is guilty of a crime: *He was convicted of armed robbery and sent to prison.* ○ *a convicted criminal* ❶ The opposite is **acquit**. يدين

▸ **convict** /ˈkɒnvɪkt/ (*formal*) *noun* [C] a person who has been found guilty of a crime and put in prison مدان ، محكوم عليه

conviction /kənˈvɪkʃn/ *noun* **1** [C,U] an occasion when sb is found guilty of a crime in a court of law; the act of finding sb guilty in this way: *He has several previous convictions for burglary.* إدانة

2 [C] very strong opinion or belief: *religious convictions* إيمان ، عقيدة

3 [U] being certain and able to convince others about what you are doing: *He played without conviction and lost easily.* اقتناع

⚷ **convince** /kənˈvɪns/ *verb* [T] **1 convince sb (of sth/that...)** to succeed in making sb believe sth: *She convinced him of the need to go back.* ○ *I couldn't convince her that I was right.* يُقنِع

2 convince sb (to do sth) to persuade sb to do sth: *The salesman convinced them to buy it.* ❶ Some people feel that this second use of 'convince' is incorrect. يقنع

▸ **convinced** *adj* completely sure about sth: *He's convinced of his ability to win.* ○ *I'm con-*

vinced that she said it but she denies it. واثق ، متأكّد

convincing *adj* **1** able to make sb believe sth: *Her explanation for her absence wasn't very convincing.* مقْنِع

2 (used about a victory) complete; clear: *a convincing win* تامّ، قاطع، مبين

convincingly *adv*: *She argued convincingly that the law should be changed.* ○ *He won the race convincingly.* بشكل مقنع ، بصورة قاطعة

convoy /ˈkɒnvɔɪ/ *noun* [C,U] a group of vehicles or ships travelling together: *a convoy of lorries* ○ *warships travelling in convoy* قافلة (سيارات أو سفن)

convulse /kənˈvʌls/ *verb* [I,T] to make sudden violent movements that you cannot control; to make sb move in this way يتشنّج ؛ يشنّج

convulsion /kənˈvʌlʃn/ *noun* [C, usually pl.] a sudden violent movement of the body that you cannot control: *Children sometimes have convulsions when their temperature goes up.* تشنّج

coo /kuː/ *verb* [I] **1** to make the sound that a dove or pigeon makes يهدِل (الحمام)

2 to speak in a soft, gentle voice: *He went to the cot and cooed over the baby.* يتحدّث بصوت ناعم

⚷ **cook** /kʊk/ *verb* **1** [I,T] to prepare food for eating by heating it: *My mother taught me how to cook.* ○ *The sauce should be cooked on low heat for twenty minutes.* ○ *He cooked us a meal.* يطبخ

2 [I] (used about food) to be prepared for eating by being heated: *I could smell something cooking in the kitchen.* يطبخ، يطهو

> Food can be cooked in various ways: by **boiling** in a saucepan of hot water; by **frying** in a frying pan with hot oil or fat; or by **grilling** under a grill, which heats the food from above. We can **toast** bread under a grill or in a toaster to make it crisp and brown. Cakes and bread are **baked** in the oven, but we use the word **roast** for cooking meat or potatoes in the oven.

PHRV **cook sth up** (*informal*) to invent sth that is not true: *She cooked up an excuse for not arriving on time.* يلفّق ، يختلق

▸ **cook** *noun* [C] a person who cooks: *My sister is an excellent cook.* ○ *He works as a cook in a hotel restaurant.* طبّاخ ، طاهٍ

cooking *noun* [U] **1** the preparation of food for eating: *Cooking is one of her hobbies.* ❶ A common way of talking about the activity of preparing food is **do the cooking**: *In our house, I do the cleaning and my husband does the cooking.* طبْخ

2 food produced by cooking: *He missed his mother's cooking when he left home.* طعام

cookbook /ˈkʊkbʊk/ *noun* [C] = COOKERY BOOK

⚷ **cooker** /ˈkʊkə(r)/ *noun* [C] a piece of kitchen equipment for cooking using gas or electricity, consisting of an oven, a flat top on which pans can be placed and often a grill جهاز أو موقد طبخ

cookery /ˈkʊkəri/ *noun* [U] the skill or methods of cooking: *My new recipe book is called 'Chinese Cookery for Beginners'.* فنّ الطبْخ

ˈ**cookery book** (*also* **cookbook**) *noun* [C] a book of recipes and instructions for cooking كتاب فنّ الطبخ

⚷ **cookie** /ˈkʊki/ *noun* [C] (*pl.* **cookies**) **1** (*US*) = BISCUIT

2 a computer file with information in it that is sent to the central server each time a particular person uses a network or the Internet كوكي (كمبيوتر)

⚷ **cool**[1] /kuːl/ *adj* **1** fairly cold; not hot or warm: *It was a cool evening so I put on a pullover.* ○ *This product should be stored in a cool place.* ○ *What I'd like is a nice cool drink.* ➲ Look at the note at **cold**. معتدل البرودة

2 calm; not excited or affected by strong emotions: *She always manages to remain cool under pressure.* هادئ الأعصاب ، غير انفعاليّ

3 very good or fashionable: *Those are cool shoes you are wearing.* ممتاز، رائع

4 unfriendly; not showing interest: *When we first met, she was rather cool towards me, but later she became friendlier.* بارد ، فاتِر

▸ **cool** *noun* [sing.] **the cool** a cool temperature or place; the quality of being cool: *We sat in the cool of a cafe, out of the sun.* برودة معتدلة (محبّبة)

IDM **keep/lose your cool** to remain calm/to stop being calm and become angry, nervous, etc. يحافظ على/يفقد هدوء أعصابه

coolly /ˈkuːlli/ *adv* in a calm way; without showing much interest or excitement: *At first she was very angry; then she explained the problem coolly.* ○ *My offer was received rather coolly.* بهدوء ؛ بفتور

coolness *noun* [U] the quality or state of being cool: *the coolness of the water* ○ *his coolness under stress* ○ *their coolness towards strangers* برودة محبّبة ؛ هدوء ؛ فتور

⚷ **cool**[2] /kuːl/ *verb* **1** [I,T] **cool (sth/sb) (down/off)** to lower the temperature of sth; to become cool (1): *Let the soup cool (down).* ○ *After the game we needed to cool off.* ○ *A nice cold drink will soon cool you down.* يبرد ؛ يبرّد

2 [I] (used about feelings) to become less strong يفتر

PHRV **cool (sb) down/off** to become or make sb calmer يهدّئ؛ يهدأ

ˌ**cooling-ˈoff period** *noun* [C] a delay when sb is given time to think about sth فترة تريّث ؛ فترة لتهدئة الخواطر

coop /kuːp/ *verb*

PHRV **coop sb/sth up (in sth)** to keep sb/sth inside a small space: *The children were cooped up indoors all day because the weather was so bad.* يحصر، يحبس (في مكان ضيّق)

cooperate (*also* **co-operate**) /kəʊˈɒpəreɪt/ *verb* [I] **1** to work with sb else to achieve sth: *Our company is cooperating with a Danish firm on this project.* يتعاون

2 to be helpful by doing what sb asks you to do: *If everyone cooperates by following the instructions, there will be no problem.* ○ *to cooperate*

with the police (e.g. by giving them information) يتعاون

cooperation (*also* **co-operation**) /kəʊˌɒpəˈreɪʃn/ *noun* [U] **1 cooperation (with sb)** working together with sb else to achieve sth: *international cooperation to protect the ozone layer* ○ *Schools are working in close cooperation with parents to improve standards.* تعاون

2 willingness to be helpful by doing what sb asks you to do: *The police asked the public for their cooperation in the investigation.* تعاون ، مساعدة

cooperative (*also* **co-operative**) /kəʊˈɒpərətɪv/ *adj* **1** done by people working together: *a cooperative business venture* تعاوني

2 helpful; doing what sb asks you to do: *My firm were very cooperative and allowed me to have time off.* ❶ The opposite is **uncooperative**. متعاون ، محبّ للمساعدة

▸ **cooperative** *noun* [C] a business or organization that is owned and run by all of the people who work for it: *a workers' cooperative* (شركة) تعاونية

coordinate¹ (*also* **co-ordinate**) /kəʊˈɔːdɪnət/ *noun* [C] one of the two sets of numbers and/or letters that are used for finding the position of a point on a map إحداثي

coordinate² (*also* **co-ordinate**) /kəʊˈɔːdɪneɪt/ *verb* [T] to organize different things or people so that they work together efficiently: *It is her job to coordinate the various departments.* ينسّق (ما بين)

▸ **coordination** /kəʊˌɔːdɪˈneɪʃn/ *noun* [U] **1** the organization of different things or people so that they work together efficiently تنسيق

2 the ability to control the movements of your body properly: *You need good coordination between eye and hand to play badminton well.* تناسق الحركة

coordinator *noun* [C] a person who is responsible for organizing different things or people so that they work together efficiently: *a project coordinator* منسّق

cop¹ /kɒp/ *noun* [C] (*informal*) a police officer شُرْطي أو شُرْطية

cop² /kɒp/ *verb* (copping; copped) (*informal*)

PHR V cop out (of sth) to avoid sth that you should do, because you are afraid or lazy: *She was going to help me with the cooking but she copped out at the last minute.* ينسحب ؛ يتقاعس أو يتوانى عن

cope /kəʊp/ *verb* [I] **cope (with sb/sth)** to deal successfully with a difficult matter or situation: *She sometimes finds it difficult to cope with all the pressure at work.* ينجح في مواجهة مشكلة

copious /ˈkəʊpiəs/ *adj* in large amounts; plentiful: *She made copious notes at the lecture.* وافر ، غزير

▸ **copiously** *adv* بغزارة

ˈcop-out *noun* [C] (*informal*) a way of avoiding sth that you should do: *I'm paying somebody to do the cooking for the party. It's a bit of a cop-out, I know.* تقاعس ، هروب

copper¹ /ˈkɒpə(r)/ *noun* **1** [U] a common reddish-brown metal: *water pipes made of copper* ○ *copper wire* نحاس

2 [C] a coin of low value made of brown metal: *I only had a few coppers left.* قطعة نقدية صغيرة القيمة

copper² /ˈkɒpə(r)/ *noun* [C] (*informal*) a police officer شُرْطي أو شُرْطية

copse /kɒps/ *noun* [C] a small group of trees or bushes that are close together غَيْضة صغيرة

copulate /ˈkɒpjuleɪt/ *verb* [I] (*formal*) (used especially about animals) to have sexual intercourse يجامع

▸ **copulation** /ˌkɒpjuˈleɪʃn/ *noun* [U] جِماع

copy¹ /ˈkɒpi/ *noun* [C] (*pl.* **copies**) **1** something that is made to look exactly like sth else: *I kept a copy of the letter I wrote.* ○ *The painting isn't an original, of course, it's only a copy.* ○ *the master copy* (= the original piece of paper from which copies are made) ○ *to make a copy of a computer file* ➲ Look at **photocopy**. نُسخة ، صورة

2 a book, newspaper, record, etc. of which many have been printed or produced: *I managed to buy the last copy of the book left in the shop.* نُسخة

copy² /ˈkɒpi/ *verb* (*pres part* **copying**; *3rd pers sing pres* **copies**; *pt, pp* **copied**) **1** [T] **copy sth (down/out)** to write down sth exactly as it is written somewhere else: *The students copied what was written on the board.* ○ *I copied down the address on the brochure.* ○ *I copied out the letter more neatly.* ينسَخ

2 [T] to make a copy of a video, computer information, etc: *It is illegal to copy videos.* ينسَخ

3 [T] = PHOTOCOPY

4 [T] to do or try to do the same as sb else; to imitate: *She copies everything her friends do.* يقلّد

5 [I] **copy (from sb)** to cheat by writing what sb else has written: *He was caught copying from his neighbour in the exam.* ينقل

copyright /ˈkɒpiraɪt/ *noun* [C,U] the legal right to be the only person who may print, copy, perform, etc. a piece of original work, such as a book, a song or a computer program. Other people who want to use work must ask permission of the person who holds the copyright. حقوق الطبع والنشر

coral /ˈkɒrəl; *US* ˈkɔːrəl/ *noun* [U] a hard red, pink or white substance formed from the bones of very small sea animals, often used for making jewellery: *a coral reef* (= a line of rock in the sea formed by coral) ○ *a coral necklace* مرجان

cord /kɔːd/ *noun* **1** [C,U] (a piece of) strong, thick string حَبْل ؛ شريط كهربائي

2 [C,U] (*especially US*) = FLEX¹

3 cords [plural] corduroy trousers بنطلون من قماش الكوردروي

▸ **cordless** /ˈkɔːdləs/ *adj* without a cord (2): *a cordless phone* بلا شريط كهربائي

a b c d e f g h i j k l m n o p q r s t u v w x y z

cordial /ˈkɔːdiəl; *US* ˈkɔːrdʒəl/ *adj* friendly: *a cordial greeting* ○ *a cordial meeting* وُدّي
▸ **cordiality** /ˌkɔːdiˈæləti; *US* ˌkɔːrdʒi-/ *noun* [U] مودّة
cordially /-diəli; *US* -dʒəli/ *adv* بمودّة ، بحرارة

cordon /ˈkɔːdn/ *noun* [C] a line or ring of police or soldiers that prevents people from entering or leaving an area نطاق من الشرطة أو الجنود
▸ **cordon** *verb*
PHR V **cordon sth off** to close an area by surrounding it with a ring of police or soldiers: *The street where the bomb was discovered was quickly cordoned off.* يطوّق ويمنع الدخول إلى

corduroy /ˈkɔːdərɔɪ/ *noun* [U] a thick soft cotton cloth with raised lines on it, used for making clothes: *a corduroy jacket* الكوردروي: قماش قطني محزّز

core /kɔː(r)/ *noun* **1** [C] the hard centre of certain fruits, containing seeds: *an apple core* قَلب الثمرة
2 [sing.] the central or most important part of sth: *the core curriculum* (= the subjects that all pupils have to study) ○ *the core vocabulary of a language* (= the most common and important words) نواة ، لُبّ ، صميم
3 [C] the central part of a planet: *the earth's core* مركز
IDM **to the core** completely; in every way: *The system is rotten to the core* (= bad in every part). ○ *The news shook him to the core* (= shocked him very much). كلياً ، إلى الصميم

coriander /ˌkɒriˈændə(r); *US* ˌkɔːr-/ *noun* [U] a plant whose fresh leaves and dried seeds are used in cooking كزبرة أو كسبرة

cork /kɔːk/ *noun* **1** [U] a light but tough substance which comes from the outside of a type of tree. It floats on water: *cork floor tiles* الفلّين
2 [C] a round piece of cork that you push into the end of a bottle to close it فلّينة: سِدادة الزجاجة

corkscrew /ˈkɔːkskruː/ *noun* [C] a tool that you use for pulling corks out of bottles بريمة لنزع فلّينة الزجاجة

corn¹ /kɔːn/ *noun* [U] **1** (*especially Brit*) a general word for grain crops such as wheat, or the seeds from these crops: *a field of corn* ○ *a cornfield* ○ *sacks of corn* حنطة، حبوب
2 (*US*) = MAIZE

corn² /kɔːn/ *noun* [C] a small, painful area of hard skin on the toe مسمار القدم

corner¹ /ˈkɔːnə(r)/ *noun* [C] **1** a place where two lines, edges, surfaces or roads meet: *in a corner of the room* ○ *Write your address in the top right-hand corner.* ○ *The pub is on the corner of Wall Street and Long Road.* ○ *He went round the corner at top speed.* زاوية
2 a quiet or secret place or area: *a remote corner of Scotland* ناحية ، ركن
3 a difficult situation which you cannot escape from: *to get yourself into a corner* مأزق

The lamp is in the corner

The bank is on the corner

4 (*also* **ˈcorner kick**) (in football) a kick from the corner of a field ضربة ركنية
IDM **cut corners** to do sth quickly and not as well as you should يفعل الشيء على عجل وبلا إتقان
(just) round the corner very near: *There's a phone box just round the corner.* قريب جداً

corner² /ˈkɔːnə(r)/ *verb* [T] **1** to get a person or an animal into a position from which it is difficult or impossible to escape: *He cornered me at the party and started telling me all his problems.* يحصر ، يسدّ عليه السبل
2 to get control in some area of business so that there is no room for anybody else to have any success: *That company's really cornered the market in health foods.* يسيطر على

cornflakes /ˈkɔːnfleɪks/ *noun* [plural] food made of small pieces of dried corn and eaten with milk for breakfast: *a bowl of cornflakes* رقائق من الذرة المحمّصة

cornflour /ˈkɔːnflaʊə(r)/ *noun* [U] very fine flour often used for making puddings, sauces, etc. نشاء

cornflower /ˈkɔːnflaʊə(r)/ *noun* [C] a small plant with blue flowers, that often grows wild زهرة الحقول

ˌcorn on the ˈcob *noun* [U] the long round part of the maize plant with yellow grains on it that is cooked and eaten as a vegetable كوز الذرة

corny /ˈkɔːni/ *adj* (**cornier**; **corniest**) (*informal*) too ordinary or familiar to be interesting or amusing: *a corny joke* سخيف ، مبتذل

coronary /ˈkɒrənri; *US* ˈkɔːrəneri/ *adj* connected with the heart قلبي ، تاجي
▸ **coronary** *noun* [C] (*pl.* **coronaries**) a type of heart attack in which the blood cannot flow to the heart because a tube (artery) is blocked. Coronaries can cause damage to the heart and death. نوبة قلبية

coronation /ˌkɒrəˈneɪʃn; *US* ˌkɔːr-/ *noun* [C] a ceremony at which a king or queen is crowned (حفل) تتويج

coroner /ˈkɒrənə(r); *US* ˈkɔːr-/ *noun* [C] an official whose job is to find out the causes of death of people who have died in violent or unusual ways المحقّق في أسباب الوفاة

Corp. (*US*) *abbrev* = CORPORATION

corporal /ˈkɔːpərəl/ *noun* [C] a person of low rank in the army or air force عريف (في الجيش أو الطيران)

ˌ**corporal ˈpunishment** *noun* [U] the punishment of people by hitting them, especially the punishment of children by parents or teachers عقوبة بدنية

corporate /ˈkɔːpərət/ *adj* of or shared by all the members of a group or organization: *corporate responsibility* مشترك ، متضامن (في المسؤولية)

corporation /ˌkɔːpəˈreɪʃn/ *noun* [C, with sing. or pl. verb] **1** (*abbr* **Corp.**) a large business company: *the Nikon Corporation* ○ *multinational corporations* ○ *the British Broadcasting Corporation* شركة ، هيئة

2 a group of people elected to govern a particular town or city مجلس بلدي

corps /kɔː(r)/ *noun* [C, with sing. or pl. verb] (*pl.* **corps** /kɔː(r)/) **1** a part of an army with special duties: *the medical corps* فيلق، سلاح

2 a group of people involved in a special activity: *the diplomatic corps* سلك دبلوماسي ؛ هيئة

corpse /kɔːps/ *noun* [C] a dead body, especially of a person جثة

correct[1] /kəˈrekt/ *adj* **1** with no mistakes; right or true: *Well done! All your answers were correct.* ○ *Have you got the correct time, please?* صحيح ، مضبوط

2 (used about behaviour, manners, dress, etc.) suitable according to normal customs and ideas: *What's the correct form of address for a vicar?* سليم ، لائق

ℹ The opposite for **1** and **2** is **incorrect**.

▸ **correctly** *adv* على نحو صحيح
correctness *noun* [U] صِحّة

correct[2] /kəˈrekt/ *verb* [T] **1** to make a mistake, fault, etc. right or better: *to correct a spelling mistake* ○ *to correct a test* (= mark the mistakes in it) يصحّح

2 to point out the mistakes or faults of sb: *He's always correcting me when I'm talking to people.* يصحّح

correction /kəˈrekʃn/ *noun* [C,U] (an act of) making sth right or changing sth: *Can you do your corrections to the essay, please?* ○ *Some parts of the report needed correction.* تصحيح ؛ تعديل

corrective /kəˈrektɪv/ *adj* intended to put right sth that is wrong: *to take corrective action* تصحيحي

correlate /ˈkɒrəleɪt; US ˈkɔːr-/ *verb* [I,T] to have or to show a relationship or connection يربط بين شيئين ؛ يرتبط بِ

▸ **correlation** /ˌkɒrəˈleɪʃn; US ˌkɔːr-/ *noun* [C,U]: *a correlation between diet and height* ارتباط ، علاقة

correspond /ˌkɒrəˈspɒnd; US ˌkɔːr-/ *verb* [I] **1 correspond (to sth)** to be similar or equal (to sth): *American High Schools correspond to British comprehensives.* يماثل ، يقابل

2 correspond (with sth) to be the same as; to match: *Does the name on the envelope correspond with the name inside the letter?* يطابق

3 correspond (with sb) to write letters to and receive them from sb: *They corresponded for a year before they got married.* يتراسل

▸ **corresponding** *adj* (only *before* a noun) related or similar: *Sales are up 10% compared with the corresponding period last year.* مماثل
correspondingly *adv* بالمقابل

correspondence /ˌkɒrəˈspɒndəns; US ˌkɔːr-/ *noun* **1** [U] the act of writing letters; the letters themselves: *There hasn't been any correspondence between them for years.* ○ *Please address all correspondence to the Arts Editor.* مراسلة ؛ رسائل

2 [C,U] a close connection or relationship: *There is no correspondence between the two sets of figures.* مطابقة

correspondent /ˌkɒrəˈspɒndənt; US ˌkɔːr-/ *noun* [C] **1** a person who provides news or writes articles for a newspaper, etc., especially from abroad: *our Middle East correspondent, Andy Jenkins* مراسِل

2 a person who writes letters مكاتِب ، مراسل

corridor /ˈkɒrɪdɔː(r); US ˈkɔːr-/ *noun* [C] a long narrow passage in a building or train, with doors that open into rooms, etc: *to walk along a corridor* رواق ، دهليز

corroborate /kəˈrɒbəreɪt/ *verb* [T] (*formal*) to support a statement, idea, etc. by providing new evidence: *The witness corroborated Mr Patton's statement about the night of the murder.* يعزِّز، يؤيِّد

▸ **corroboration** /kəˌrɒbəˈreɪʃn/ *noun* [U] إثبات ، تعزيز

corrode /kəˈrəʊd/ *verb* [I,T] (used about metals) to become weak or to be destroyed by chemical action; to cause a metal to do this: *Parts of the car were corroded by rust.* يتآكل ؛ يأكله (الصدأ)

▸ **corrosion** /kəˈrəʊʒn/ *noun* [U] the process of being destroyed by chemical action; the damage caused when sth is corroded تآكل
corrosive /kəˈrəʊsɪv/ *adj* (عامل) أكّال

corrugated /ˈkɒrəgeɪtɪd/ *adj* (used about metal or cardboard) shaped into folds; not smooth and flat: *corrugated iron* (حديد) متموّج

corrupt /kəˈrʌpt/ *adj* not honest, moral or legal: *corrupt business practices* ○ *corrupt officials who accept bribes* فاسد

▸ **corrupt** *verb* [I,T] to cause sb/sth to become dishonest or to have lower moral standards: *Too many people are corrupted by power.* يُفسِد
corruption /kəˈrʌpʃn/ *noun* [U] **1** behaviour that is not honest or legal, especially by people in official positions: *There were accusations of corruption among senior police officers.* فساد ؛ رشوة

2 the process of making sb/sth corrupt: *the corruption of an innocent young boy* إفساد ؛ تحريف

corset /ˈkɔːsɪt/ *noun* [C] a tight piece of clothing worn by some women close to their skin in order to make themselves look thinner مِشدّ

cosmetic /kɒz'metɪk/ *noun* [C] a substance that you put on your face or hair to make yourself look more attractive: *I only use cosmetics that are not tested on animals.* مستحضر تجميلي

▸ **cosmetic** *adj* **1** used or done in order to improve your appearance: *cosmetic products* ○ *cosmetic surgery* تجميلي

2 done in order to improve only the appearance of sth, without changing it in any other way: *changes in government policy which are purely cosmetic* تجميلي ، ظاهري

cosmic /'kɒzmɪk/ *adj* of the whole universe كَوْنيّ

cosmopolitan /,kɒzmə'pɒlɪtən/ *adj* **1** containing people from all over the world: *a cosmopolitan city* عالمي: فيه أناس من مختلف القوميّات

2 having, or influenced by, wide experience of other countries and cultures: *the cosmopolitan atmosphere of the bars and cafes* ○ *a cosmopolitan and sophisticated young woman* عالمي

cosmos /'kɒzmɒs/ *noun* [sing.] **the cosmos** the universe الكون

cost[1] /kɒst; *US* kɔːst/ *noun* **1** [C,U] the money that you have to pay for sth: *The cost of petrol has gone up again.* ○ *the cost of living* (= the general level of prices for things that you need to live a normal life) ○ *The damage will have to be put right regardless of cost.* ➲ Look at the note at **price**. ثمن ، تكلفة

2 [sing., U] what you have to give or lose in order to obtain sth else: *He achieved great success but only at the cost of a happy family life.* (على) حساب؛ ثمن

3 costs [plural] the cost of settling sth in a court of law; the amount of money that the losing side has to pay to the winning side: *a £250 fine and £100 costs* نفقات (الدعوى)

IDM **at all costs** using whatever means are necessary to achieve sth: *We must win at all costs.* بأي ثمن ، بكلّ الوسائل

to your, etc. cost as you, etc. experienced it yourself: *Life can be lonely at university, as I found out to my cost.* على حساب تجربة الشخص

cost[2] /kɒst; *US* kɔːst/ *verb* [T] (*pt, pp* **cost**) **1** to have the price of: *These apples cost 60p a pound.* ○ *How much does it cost?* ○ *It cost me £10 to go by train.* يكلّف

2 to make you lose sth: *That one mistake cost him his job.* يفقد

3 to estimate the price to be asked for some goods, a service, etc: *Engineers costed the repairs at £2 million.* ❶ The past tense and past participle for this sense is **costed**. يقدر التكاليف مثلاً

co-star /'kəʊ stɑː(r)/ *verb* (co-starring; co-starred) **1** [T] (used of a film, play, etc.) to have two or more famous actors as its stars: *a film co-starring Kate Winslet and Leonardo di Caprio* (فيلم) يشارك في تمثيله

2 [I] (used of actors) to be one of two or more stars in a film, play, etc: *Michael Caine co-stars with Sean Connery in the film.* يمثّل بالاشتراك مع

▸ **co-star** /'kəʊ stɑː(r)/ *noun* [C] a famous actor or actress who has one of the most important parts in a film, play, etc. in which another famous actor or actress also appears: *His co-star was Marilyn Monroe.* شريك (في التمثيل)

costly /'kɒstli; *US* 'kɔːst-/ *adj* (**costlier**; **costliest**) **1** costing a lot of money; expensive: *a costly repair bill* غالٍ ، مكلف

2 involving great loss of time, effort, etc: *a costly mistake* فادح

costume /'kɒstjuːm; *US* -tuːm/ *noun* [C,U] a set or style of clothes worn by people in a particular country or at a particular time: *She designs costumes for the theatre.* ○ *17th century costume* ○ *the Welsh national costume* ➲ Look at **swimming costume**. زي ، لباس

cosy /'kəʊzi/ *adj* (**cosier**; **cosiest**) (*US* **cozy**) warm and comfortable: *The room looked cosy and inviting in the firelight.* دافئ ومريح

cot /kɒt/ (*US* **crib**) *noun* [C] a bed for a baby or young child, with high sides to stop it from falling out مهد ، سرير أطفال

cottage /'kɒtɪdʒ/ *noun* [C] a small and usually old house, especially in the country: *a pretty village with little thatched cottages* كوخ

,cottage 'cheese *noun* [U] a type of soft white cheese in small lumps نوع من الجبن الأبيض

,cottage 'pie *noun* [C] = SHEPHERD'S PIE

cotton[1] /'kɒtn/ *noun* [U] **1** a natural cloth or thread; the tall tropical plant that produces it: *This shirt is 60% cotton and 40% polyester.* ○ *cotton fields in Mississippi* ○ *a reel of cotton* (= for sewing with) قطن ، شجر القطن

2 (*US*) = COTTON WOOL

cotton[2] /'kɒtn/ *verb*

PHR V **cotton on** (*informal*) to understand sth: *It took me ages to cotton on.* يفهم

,cotton 'wool (*US* **cotton**) *noun* [U] soft, loose cotton in a mass, used for cleaning the skin قطن طبّي

couch[1] /kaʊtʃ/ *noun* [C] a long seat, often with a back and arms, for sitting or lying on: *They were sitting on the couch in the living room.* ○ *a doctor's couch* أريكة

couch[2] /kaʊtʃ/ *verb* [T] (usually passive) (*formal*) to express a thought, idea, etc. (in the way mentioned): *His reply was couched in very polite terms.* يصوغ بطريقة معيّنة

'couch potato *noun* [C] (*informal*) a person who spends a lot of time sitting and watching television جليس التلفزيون

cough /kɒf; *US* kɔːf/ *verb* **1** [I] to send air out of your throat and mouth with a sudden loud noise, especially when you have a cold, have sth in your throat, etc: *I could hear him coughing all night.* يسعل ، يكحّ

2 [T] **cough (sth) (up)** to send sth out of your throat and mouth with a sudden loud noise: *He was coughing blood.* يسعل ، يخرج بالسعال

PHR V **cough (sth) up** (*Brit informal*) to give

N	ن	G	غ	[illegible]	ش	O	خ	A	ا
?	ه ة	F	ف	X	ص	D	د d	B	ب
W	و	Q	ق	V	ض	Z	ذ	T	ت
F	ي ى	K	ك	U	ط	R	ر	C	ث
E	ء	L	ل	Y	ظ	i	ز	J	ج
		M	م	x	ع	S	س	H	ح

money or information unwillingly: *Come on, cough up what you owe me!* يعطي مكرَهاً

▶ **cough** *noun* [C] **1** an act or the sound of coughing: *He gave a nervous cough before he started to speak.* سعال

2 an illness or infection that makes you cough a lot: *She's had a cough for weeks.* ○ *cough medicine* ○ *coughs and colds* سعال

could /kəd; *strong form* kʊd/ *modal verb* (*negative* **could not**; *short form* **couldn't** /ˈkʊdnt/) **1** (used as the past form of 'can' when you report what sb says): *She said that she couldn't come.* (صيغة الماضي لـ can في الإفادة عما يقوله شخص)

2 (used for saying that sth is, will be, or was possible): *I could do it now if you like.* ○ *She could be famous one day.* ○ *Couldn't you come earlier?* (= I wish you could) ○ *He could have gone to university but he didn't want to.* ○ *I can't find my purse. I could have left it in the bank.* ○ *You could have said you were going to be late!* (= I wish that you had) يستطيع ، يمكن

If something was possible on one occasion in the past use **was/ were able to**: *The firemen were able to rescue the children.* But in negative sentences **could not** can be used, too: *The firemen couldn't rescue the children.*

3 (used for saying that sb had the ability in the past to do sth): *I could run two miles without stopping when I was younger.* ○ *My mother could cook beautifully.* كان في استطاعته

4 (used for asking permission politely): *Could I possibly borrow your car?* هل يمكنني أن...

5 (used for asking sb politely to do sth for you): *Could you open the door? My hands are full.* هل يمكنك أن...

6 I could/could have I would like/have liked to: *I could scream, I'm so angry.* ○ *I was so angry I could have screamed.* أودّ أن...؛ كان بودّي لو...

7 (used with the verbs 'feel', 'hear', 'see', 'smell', 'taste') (مع أفعال معيّنة)

These verbs are not used in the continuous tenses. If we want to talk about seeing, hearing, etc. at a particular moment in the past, we use **could**: *We could hear the birds singing.* (NOT *We were hearing...*)

council (*also* **Council**) /ˈkaʊnsl/ *noun* [C, with sing. or pl. verb] **1** a group of people who are elected to manage affairs for a town, city, country, etc: *The county council has/have decided to build a new road.* ○ *a council decision* ○ *Oxford City Council* ○ *a council house* (= one built and owned by a city or county council and rented out) مجلس (بلدي)

2 a group of people elected to give advice, manage affairs, etc. for a particular organization or area of activity: *a student council* ○ *the Arts Council* مَجلس

▶ **councillor** /ˈkaʊnsələ(r)/ *noun* [C] a member of a council: *to elect new councillors* عضو مجلس بلدي

counsel[1] /ˈkaʊnsl/ *verb* [T] (counselling; counselled; *US* counseling; counseled) **1** (*formal*) to advise or recommend: *Mr Dean's lawyers counselled him against making public statements.* ينصح ، يشير عليه بـ

2 to give professional advice to sb with a problem ينصح ، يرشد

▶ **counselling** (*US* **counseling**) /-səlɪŋ/ *noun* [U] professional advice given to people with problems: *Many students come to us for counselling.* ○ *psychiatric counselling* استشارة؛ تقديم النصح والإرشاد

counsellor (*US* **counselor**) /ˈkaʊnsələ(r)/ *noun* [C] a person whose job is to give advice: *a student counsellor* مستشار

counsel[2] /ˈkaʊnsl/ *noun* **1** [U] (*formal*) advice نصيحة ، مشورة

2 [C] (*pl.* **counsel**) a lawyer who speaks in a court of law: *the counsel for the defence/prosecution* محام ، مستشار قانوني

count[1] /kaʊnt/ *verb* **1** [I] to say numbers one after another in order: *Close your eyes and count (up) to 20.* ○ *to count from 0 to 100* يعُدّ

2 [T] **count sth (up)** to calculate the total number or amount of sth: *The teacher counted the children as they got on the bus.* يعدّ ، يحصي

3 [I] **count (for sth)** to be important or valuable: *Your opinion really counts.* يُقدَّر، له قيمته

4 [I] **count (as sth)** to be accepted: *'I won,' shouted Tom. 'But you cheated so it doesn't count,' replied Sarah.* ○ *Will my driving licence count as identification?* يُقبَل

5 [T] to consider to be: *You should count yourself lucky to have a good job.* يعتبر

6 [T] to include sb/sth when you are calculating an amount or number: *The holiday costs about £1 000, not counting the flights.* يشمل، يُدخل في الاعتبار

PHR V **count against sb** to be considered as a disadvantage: *Do you think my age will count against me?* يُعتَبر عائقاً

count on sb/sth to expect sth with confidence; to rely on sb/sth: *In England you can't count on good weather in May.* ○ *Can I count on you to help me?* يتوقع بثقة ، يعتمد على

count sb/sth out 1 to count things slowly, one by one: *She carefully counted out £100 in five pound notes.* يَعُدّ بعناية

2 (*informal*) not include sb/sth: *If you're going swimming, you can count me out!* يستثنيه ، لا يدخله في الحساب

▶ **countable** /-əbl/ *adj* that can be counted ❶ The opposite is **uncountable**. قابل للعدّ

count[2] /kaʊnt/ *noun* [C] **1** [usually sing.] an act of counting or a number that you get after counting: *At the latest count, there were nearly 2 million unemployed.* إحصاء

2 [usually pl.] a point that is made in a discussion, argument, etc: *I proved her wrong on all counts.* وجه (في حجة) ، نقطة

IDM **keep/lose count (of sth)** to know/not know how many there are of sth: *I've lost count of the number of times he's told that joke!* يذكر/لا يذكر عدد المرات

count[3] (*also* **Count**) /kaʊnt/ *noun* [C] a title for a man of noble birth in some European countries الكونت: نبيل أوروبي

ˌ**countable 'noun** (*also* '**count noun**) *noun* [C] (*grammar*) a noun that can be used in the plural, and with words like 'a', 'many' and 'few': *Countable nouns are marked [C] in this dictionary.* الأسماء القابلة للعدّ

countdown /'kaʊntdaʊn/ *noun* [C] the act of saying numbers backwards to zero just before sth important happens: *the countdown to take-off* عدّ تنازلي

counter[1] /'kaʊntə(r)/ *noun* [C] **1** a long, flat surface or table in a shop, bank, etc., where customers are served منضدة البائع

2 a small object (usually round and made of plastic) that is used in some games to show where a player is on the board فيشة: بديل العملة

counter[2] /'kaʊntə(r)/ *adv* **counter to sth** in the opposite direction to sth: *The results of these experiments run counter to previous findings.* عكس

counter[3] /'kaʊntə(r)/ *verb* [I,T] to answer or react to sb/sth with a different opinion or a return attack: *He countered our criticism with a powerful defence of his actions.* يعارض ، يردّ على

counteract /ˌkaʊntər'ækt/ *verb* [T] to reduce the effect of sth by acting against it: *measures to counteract traffic congestion* يقاوم ، يعاكس ، يبطِل

'**counter-attack** *noun* [C] an attack made in reaction to an enemy's attack هجوم مضادّ
▶ **counter-attack** *verb* [I,T] يقوم بهجوم مضادّ

counterclockwise /ˌkaʊntə'klɒkwaɪz/ (*US*) = ANTICLOCKWISE

counterfeit /'kaʊntəfɪt/ *adj* not genuine, but copied so that it looks like the real thing: *counterfeit money* مزيّف

counterfoil /'kaʊntəfɔɪl/ *noun* [C] the part of a cheque or receipt that you keep as a record أرومة أو كَعْب الشيك أو الإيصال

counterpart /'kaʊntəpɑːt/ *noun* [C] a person or thing that has a similar position or function to sb/sth else: *She's my counterpart in our New York office* (= she does the same job there that I do here). نظير

ˌ**counter-pro'ductive** *adj* having the opposite effect to the one you want ذو أثر معاكس

countess /'kaʊntəs/ *noun* [C] a woman who is married to a count or earl, or who has the same rank as one الكونتيسة: نبيلة أوروبية

countless /'kaʊntləs/ *adj* (only *before* a noun) very many: *I've tried to telephone him countless times.* لا يُعَدّ

country /'kʌntri/ *noun* (*pl.* **countries**) **1** [C] an area of land with its own people, government, etc: *France, Spain and other European countries* ○ *There was snow over much of the country during the night.* بلد ، قطر

> **State** is used for talking about a country as an organized political community controlled by one government. It can also mean the government itself: *a politically independent state* ○ *the member states of the EU* ○ *You get a pension from the state when you retire.* ○ *state education.* **Land** is more formal or literary: *explorers who set out to discover new lands.*

2 the country [sing.] the people who live in a country: *a survey to find out what the country really thinks* السكّان، الشعب

3 the country [sing.] land which is away from towns and cities: *Do you live in the town or the country?* ○ *country life* ريف

> The word **country** is used for emphasizing that an area of land is away from towns, etc: *city workers who like to get out into the country at weekends.* The word **countryside** also refers to areas of land that are away from towns but it emphasizes the natural features such as hills, rivers, trees, etc. that you find there: *beautiful countryside* ○ *the destruction of the countryside by new roads.* **Landscape** refers to everything you see when you look across an area of land either in the town or the country: *a dreary landscape of factories and chimneys* ○ *a landscape of forests and lakes*

4 [U] an area of land (especially considering its physical features): *We looked down over miles of open country.* ○ *hilly country* أرض ، منطقة

ˌ**country-and-'western** *noun* [U] a type of popular music that comes from the southern and western USA الموسيقى الشعبية لجنوب وغرب الولايات المتحدة الأمريكية

ˌ**country 'house** *noun* [C] a large house in the country, usually owned by an important family and often with a lot of land منزل كبير في الريف

countryman /'kʌntrimən/ *noun* [C] (*pl.* **countrymen**; *feminine* **countrywoman** /'kʌntriwʊmən/; *pl.* **countrywomen**) **1** a person from your own country مواطن أو مواطنة من بلدك

2 a person who lives in the country (3) قرويّ ، ريفي

countryside /'kʌntrisaɪd/ *noun* [U, sing.] **the countryside** land which is away from towns and cities, consisting of farms, woods, etc: *the French countryside* ○ *The countryside near York is very beautiful.* ➲ Look at the note at **country**. الريف

county /'kaʊnti/ *noun* [C] (*pl.* **counties**) an area in Britain, Ireland or the USA which has its own local government: *the county of Kent* مقاطعة ، إقليم ذو حكومة محلية

coup /kuː/ *noun* [C] (*pl.* **coups** /kuːz/) **1** (*also* **coup d'état** /ˌkuː deɪ'tɑː/ (*pl.* **coups d'état** /ˌkuː deɪ'tɑː/)) a sudden and often violent change of government organized by a small group of people: *a coup to overthrow the President* ○ *an attempted coup* (= one which did not succeed) انقلاب (عسكري)

2 a clever and successful thing to do: *Getting that promotion was a real coup.* ضربة موفقة

couple¹ /ˈkʌpl/ *noun* [C] two people who are married, living together, etc: *A very nice couple have moved in next door.* ○ *a married couple* زوجان

IDM a couple of people/things 1 two people/things: *I need a couple of glasses.* زوج

2 a few (not saying an exact number): *I last saw her a couple of months ago.* عِدّة ، بِضع

couple² /ˈkʌpl/ *verb* [T] (usually passive) to join or link sb/sth to sb/sth else: *The fog, coupled with the amount of traffic on the roads, made driving very difficult.* يقرن بـ ؛ يربط

coupon /ˈkuːpɒn/ *noun* [C] **1** a small piece of paper which you can use to buy goods at a lower price, or which you can collect and then exchange for goods: *a coupon worth £1 off your next purchase* كوبون ، قسيمة

2 a small form in a newspaper or magazine which you fill in with your name and address and send off, in order to get information or to enter a competition: *To place your order, simply fill in the coupon at the bottom of this page.* قسيمة

courage /ˈkʌrɪdʒ/ *noun* [U] the ability to control fear in a situation that may be dangerous or unpleasant: *It took real courage to go back into the burning building.* ○ *She showed great courage all through her long illness.* شجاعة

IDM pluck up courage → PLUCK

▸ **courageous** /kəˈreɪdʒəs/ *adj* having or showing courage; brave شجاع

courageously *adv* بشجاعة

courgette /kʊəˈʒet/ (*especially US* **zucchini**) *noun* [C] a long vegetable with a dark green skin that is eaten cooked. A courgette is a small marrow. قَرْع صيفي ، كوسى

courier /ˈkʊriə(r)/ *noun* [C] **1** a person whose job is to carry letters, important papers, etc., especially when they are urgent الساعي ، رسول خاص

2 (*Brit*) a person whose job is to look after a group of tourists مشرف على السّياح

▸ **courier** *verb* [T] to send sth by courier(1) يرسل مع ساعٍ خاص

course /kɔːs/ *noun* **1** [C] one of the parts of a meal: *a three-course lunch* ○ *I had chicken for the main course.* لون (من ألوان الطعام)

2 [C] **a course (in/on sth)** a complete series of lessons or studies: *I've enrolled on an English course.* ○ *I'm taking a course in self-defence.* ○ *At some universities the course lasts for four years.* دورة دراسية

3 [C] an area where golf is played or where certain types of race take place: *a golf course* ○ *a racecourse* (= where horse races take place) ○ *Several of the horses didn't complete the course.* ميدان الغولف ، مِضْمار

4 [C] **a course (of sth)** a series of medical treatments: *The doctor put her on a course of tablets.* سلسلة من العلاجات الطبية

5 [C,U] the route or direction that sth, especially a plane, ship or river, takes: *We changed course and sailed towards land.* ○ *to be on/off course* (= going in the right/wrong direction) ○ *the course of the Rhine* ○ (*figurative*) *I'm on course* (= making the right amount of progress) *to finish this work by the end of the week.* اتجاه ، خط (السير)، مجرى

6 [sing.] the development of sth over a period of time: *events that changed the course of history* ○ *In the normal course of events* (= the way things normally happen) *such problems do not arise.* مسار ، مجرى

7 (*also* **course of action**) [C] a way of acting in or dealing with a particular situation: *In that situation resignation was the only course open to him.* تصرف ، إجراء

IDM in the course of sth during sth: *He mentioned it in the course of conversation.* أثناء ، في غضون

in (the) course of time eventually; when enough time has passed: *I'm sure that all these problems will be sorted out in the course of time.* في آخر الأمر ؛ مع الزمن

in due course → DUE¹

a matter of course → MATTER¹

of course naturally; certainly: *Of course, having children has changed their lives a lot.* ○ *Of course it can be repaired but I think it will be too expensive to do it.* ○ *'Can I use your phone?' 'Of course you can.'* ○ *'You're not annoyed with me, are you?' 'Of course not.'* بالطبع ، طبعاً

coursebook /ˈkɔːsbʊk/ *noun* [C] a book for studying from that is used regularly in class كتاب دراسي مقرّر

court¹ /kɔːt/ *noun* **1** [C,U] a place where trials take place in front of a judge or a jury, to decide whether a person has broken the law: *a magistrate's court* ○ *A man has been charged and will appear in court tomorrow.* محكمة

2 **the court** [sing.] the people in a court, especially those taking part in the trial: *Please tell the court exactly what you saw.* أعضاء المحكمة

3 often **Court** [C,U] the official home of a king or queen بَلاط ، قَصْر

4 [C,U] an area where certain ball games are played: *a tennis, squash, etc. court* ○ *The players have been on court for nearly three hours.* ملعب

IDM take sb to court to take legal action against sb in a court of law: *She took the company to court for breaking the contract.* يقاضي ، يقيم دعوى

court² /kɔːt/ *verb* **1** [T] to try to gain sb's support by paying special attention to them: *Politicians from all parties will be courting voters this week.* يحاول استمالته

2 [T] to do sth that might lead to sth unpleasant: *Britain is courting ecological disaster if it continues to dump waste in the North Sea.* يلعب بالنار ، يجلب على نفسه المتاعب

3 [I] (*old-fashioned*) (used about two people) to spend time together in a relationship that may

lead to marriage: *There were a lot of courting couples in the park.* يتودّد إلى ، يغازل
▸ **courtship** /ˈkɔːtʃɪp/ *noun* [C,U] (*old-fashioned*) the period or situation of having a relationship that leads or may lead to marriage: [C]: *They got married after a brief courtship.* فترة خطوبة أو تودّد

courteous /ˈkɜːtiəs/ *adj* polite and pleasant, showing respect for other people ❶ The opposite is **discourteous**. مهذب ، مجامل
▸ **courteously** *adv* بلطف ، بكياسة

courtesy /ˈkɜːtəsi/ *noun* (*pl.* **courtesies**) **1** [U] polite and pleasant behaviour that shows respect for other people: *She didn't even have the courtesy to say that she was sorry.* لطف ، كياسة
2 [C] (*formal*) a polite action or remark: *The two presidents exchanged courtesies before their meeting.* مجاملة
IDM **(by) courtesy of sb** with the permission or because of the kindness of sb: *These pictures are being shown by courtesy of BBC TV.* بإذن من : تكرّماً من

courtier /ˈkɔːtiə(r)/ *noun* [C] (especially in the past) a companion of a king or queen at his/her court أحد أفراد البلاط

court martial /ˌkɔːt ˈmɑːʃl/ *noun* [C] (*pl.* courts martial or court martials) a military court that deals with matters of military law; a trial that takes place in such a court: *His case will be heard by a court martial.* محكمة أو محاكمة عسكرية
▸ **court-martial** *verb* [T] (court-martialling; court-martialled; *US* court-martialing; court-martialed) to try sb in a military court يحاكم أمام محكمة عسكرية

ˌcourt of ˈlaw *noun* [C] (*pl.* **courts of law**) = LAW COURT

courtship *noun* → COURT[2]

courtyard /ˈkɔːtjɑːd/ *noun* [C] an area of ground, without a roof, that has walls or buildings around it, e.g. in a castle, or between houses or flats ساحة ، فناء

couscous /ˈkʊskʊs; ˈkuːskuːs/ *noun* [U] a type of N African food made from crushed wheat; a dish of meat and/or vegetables with couscous كسكس، مغربية

cousin /ˈkʌzn/ (*also* **ˌfirst ˈcousin**) *noun* [C] the child of your aunt or uncle: *Have you met Lizzie? We're cousins.* ❶ The same word is used for both male and female cousins. A **second cousin** is the child of your cousin. ابن أو بنت العم أو العمة أو الخال أو الخالة

cove /kəʊv/ *noun* [C] a small bay on the coast: *a sandy cove* خليج صغير

cover[1] /ˈkʌvə(r)/ *verb* [T] **1 cover sb/sth (up/over) (with sth)** to put sth on or in front of sth in order to hide or protect it: *Could you cover the food and put it in the fridge?* ○ *She couldn't look any more and covered her eyes.* ○ *She was asleep on the sofa so he covered her over with a blanket.* ○ *I covered the floor with newspaper before I started painting.* يغطّي
2 to be across or over the surface of sth: *Snow covered the ground.* يكسو ، يغطّي
3 cover sb/sth in/with sth to form a layer on sb/sth: *A car went through the puddle and covered me with mud.* يغطّي
4 to fill or be spread over a certain area: *The smoke from the fire now covers about 15 000 square kilometres.* يغطّي ؛ يملأ
5 to include or to deal with sth: *Part-time workers are not covered by the law.* ○ *The course covered both British and European history.* ○ *I think we've covered everything. Now, does anyone have a question?* يشمَل ؛ يعالج
6 to travel a certain distance: *We covered about 500 kilometres that day.* يقطع
7 to be enough money for sth: *Will £20 cover your expenses?* يكفي ، يغطّي (النفقات)
8 (used about the media) to report on or show sth: *All the papers covered the election in depth.* يغطّي
9 cover sb/sth against/for sth to protect sb/sth by insurance: *The insurance policy covers us for any damage to our property.* ○ *The policy even covers your garden furniture* (= it is insured). يؤمّن على
PHRV **cover (sth) up** to prevent people hearing about a mistake or sth bad: *The police have been accused of trying to cover up the facts of the case.* يخفي
cover up for sb to hide a person's mistakes or crimes in order to protect him/her: *His wife covered up for him to the police.* يُخفي بقصد الحماية ، يتستّر على
▸ **covered** *adj* **1 covered in/with sth** having a layer or a large amount of sth on sb/sth: *The victim was lying on the floor, covered in blood.* ○ *The whole room was covered in dust.* مغطّى ، مكسوّ
2 having a cover, especially a roof: *a covered shopping centre* مسقوف
covering /ˈkʌvərɪŋ/ *noun* [C] something that covers the surface of sth: *A thick covering of snow lay on the ground.* غطاء، لحاف

cover[2] /ˈkʌvə(r)/ *noun* **1** [C] something that is put on or over sth, especially in order to protect it: *a plastic cover for a computer* ○ *a duvet cover* غطاء
2 [C] the outside part of a book or magazine: *I can't remember the title of the book but I know it has a green cover.* ○ *I read the magazine from cover to cover* (= from beginning to end). غلاف
3 the covers [plural] the blankets, sheets, etc. that cover sb in bed: *She pulled the covers off him and said: 'Get up!'* غطاء، لحاف
4 [U] **cover (against sth)** insurance against sth, so that if sth bad happens you get money or help in return: *The policy provides cover against theft.* تأمين ، ضمان
5 [U] shelter or protection from the weather, damage, etc: *When the storm started we took cover in a shop doorway.* ○ *The soldiers had no cover and were easy targets.* حماية ؛ ملاذ
6 [C, usually sing.] **a cover (for sth)** something

that hides the real nature of sth, especially sth illegal: *The whole company was just a cover for all kinds of criminal activities.* ستار

7 [U] doing sb's job for him/her while he/she is away from work: *Joanne's off next week, so we'll have to arrange cover.* موظف بديل

IDM **under cover of sth** hidden by sth; not noticed because of sth: *They attacked under cover of darkness.* تحت ستار (شيء) ، تحت جنْح (الظلام)

coverage /ˈkʌvərɪdʒ/ *noun* [U] the act or amount of reporting on or showing an event in the media: *TV coverage of the Olympic Games was excellent.* تغطية إعلاميّة

coveralls /ˈkʌvərɔːlz/ *noun* [plural] (*US*) = OVERALLS

ˌcovering ˈletter *noun* [C] a letter that you send with a parcel, job application, etc. explaining it or giving more information about it رسالة توضيحية

covert /ˈkʌvət; *US* ˈkəʊvɜːrt/ *adj* done secretly, not openly: *a covert police operation* سرّي
▸ **covertly** *adv* سرّاً

ˈcover-up *noun* [C] an act of preventing sth bad or dishonest from becoming known: *Several newspapers have claimed that there has been a government cover-up.* تَستُّر ، إخفاء الحقائق

covet /ˈkʌvət/ *verb* [T] (*formal*) to want very much to have sth (especially sth that belongs to sb else) يشتهي (ما عند الغير)

cow /kaʊ/ *noun* [C] **1** a large female animal that is kept on farms to produce milk: *to milk a cow* ○ *a herd of cows* بقرة

> **Cow** is often used for both male and female members of the **cattle** family. The special word for a male is **bull**. A young cow is a **calf**. A number of cows together can be called **cattle**. Look at the note at **meat**.

2 the adult female of certain large animals, e.g the elephant أنثى بعض الحيوانات الكبيرة مثل الفيل

3 (*slang*) an insulting word for a woman: *She's a real cow!* امرأة (كلمة مسيئة)

coward /ˈkaʊəd/ *noun* [C] (used when disapproving) a person who has no courage and is afraid in dangerous or unpleasant situations: *I hate going to the dentist's because I'm a terrible coward.* ○ *He was too much of a coward to argue.* جبان
▸ **cowardice** /ˈkaʊədɪs/ *noun* [U] a lack of courage: *I was ashamed at the cowardice I showed in running away.* جُبْن
cowardly *adj* جبان

cowboy /ˈkaʊbɔɪ/ *noun* [C] **1** a man whose job is to look after cows (usually on a horse) in certain parts of the USA: *a cowboy film* راعي بقر

2 (*Brit informal*) a person in business who is not honest or who does work badly: *a cowboy builder* عامل غشّاش أو غير متقن لعمله

cower /ˈkaʊə(r)/ *verb* [I] to move back or into a low position because of fear: *The dog cowered under the table.* ينكمش خائفاً

cowslip /ˈkaʊslɪp/ *noun* [C] a small wild plant with sweet-smelling yellow flowers زهرة الربيع المَرجيّة

coy /kɔɪ/ *adj* **1** pretending to be shy or modest: *She lifted her head a little and gave him a coy smile.* متظاهر بالحياء

2 unwilling to say sth directly or to give information: *Don't be coy, tell me how much you earn.* يتمنّع (في إعطاء معلومات)
▸ **coyly** *adv* باستحياء

cozy (*US*) = COSY

crab /kræb/ *noun* [C] a sea animal with a flat body covered by a shell and five pairs of curved legs. The front two legs have long claws (pincers) on them. Crabs move sideways. سرَطان (البحر)

crack[1] /kræk/ *noun* [C] **1** a line on the surface of sth where it has broken, but not into separate pieces: *a pane of glass with a crack in it* كَسْر ، صَدْع ، شَعْر

2 a narrow opening: *The wind blew through the cracks in the roof.* شَقّ

3 a sudden loud, sharp sound: *There was a crack and he realized that he had broken his leg.* طقّة ، فرقعة

4 an amusing, often critical, remark; a joke: *She made a crack about his clothes.* تعليق فكاهي ساخر ؛ نكتة

IDM **the crack of dawn** very early in the morning في مطلع الفجر

have a crack (at sth/at doing sth) (*informal*) to try to do sth: *I'm not sure how to play but I'll have a crack at it.* يحاول (فعل شيء)

▸ **crack** *adj* (used especially about soldiers) very well-trained and skilful: *crack troops* (جندي) فائق التدريب والمهارة

crack[2] /kræk/ *verb* **1** [I,T] to break so that a line appears, but without breaking into pieces; to make sth do this: *Don't put boiling water into that glass, it'll crack.* ○ *You can crack this sort of glass but you can't break it.* ○ *Oh no, this glass is cracked.* يصدّع ؛ يتصدّع

2 [T] to break sth open: *Crack two eggs into a bowl.* يكسِر ؛ يفلق

3 [I,T] to make a sudden loud, sharp sound; to cause sth to make this sound: *He cracked his whip.* يفرقع ، يطقطق

4 [T] to hit a part of your body against sth: *She stood up and cracked her head on the cupboard door.* يصدم (رأسه بالخزانة مثلاً)

5 [I] to stop being able to deal with pressure and so lose control: *She cracked under the strain of all her problems.* ينهار

6 [T] (*informal*) to solve a problem: *I think I've cracked it!* ○ *The police have cracked an international drug-smuggling ring.* يحلّ (مشكلة) يدرك كنه شيء

7 [T] to tell or make a joke ينكّت

IDM **get cracking** (*informal*) to start doing sth immediately: *I have to finish this job today so I'd better get cracking.* يشرع في فعل شيء حالاً

PHR V **crack down (on sb/sth)** (used about people in authority) to start dealing severely with bad or illegal behaviour: *The police have started to crack down on drug dealers.* يقمع ، يضرِب بيد من حديد

crack up (*informal*) to be unable to deal with pressure and so lose control and become mentally ill: *He cracked up when his wife left him.* ينهار

crackdown /ˈkrækdaʊn/ *noun* [C] action to stop bad or illegal behaviour: *a police crackdown on street crime* قمع ، مكافحة

cracker /ˈkrækə(r)/ *noun* [C] **1** a thin flat dry biscuit that is often eaten with cheese بسكوتة رقيقة (توكل مع الجبن)

2 (*also* **Christmas cracker**) a cardboard tube wrapped in coloured paper and containing a small present. Crackers are pulled apart by two people, each holding one end, at Christmas parties. They make a loud sharp noise as they break. فرقاعة صغيرة تحوي هدية

crackle /ˈkrækl/ *verb* [I] to make a series of short, sharp sounds: *The radio started to crackle and then it stopped working.* يطقطق ، يخشخش

▸ **crackle** *noun* [sing.]: *the crackle of dry wood burning* طقطقة ، خشخشة

cradle /ˈkreɪdl/ *noun* [C] a small bed for a baby. Cradles can often be moved from side to side. مَهْد

▸ **cradle** *verb* [T] to hold sb/sth carefully and gently in your arms: *He cradled her head in his arms until the ambulance came.* يحتضن برفق

craft[1] /krɑːft; *US* kræft/ *noun* [C] **1** a job or activity for which you need skill with your hands: *an arts and crafts exhibition* ○ *the craft of basket making* ➲ Look at **handicraft**. حِرفة

2 any job or activity for which you need skill: *He regards acting as a craft.* مهنة تتطلب مهارة

▸ **craftsman** /ˈkrɑːftsmən; *US* ˈkræfts-/ *noun* [C] (*pl.* **craftsmen** /-mən/) a person who makes things skilfully, especially with the hands: *All the furniture we sell is individually made by craftsmen.* حرفي ، عامل يدوي ماهر

craftsmanship *noun* [U] the skill used by sb to make sth of high quality with the hands مهارة يدوية : جودة الصنعة

craft[2] /krɑːft; *US* kræft/ *noun* [C] (*pl.* **craft**) a boat, aircraft or spaceship: *There were a few sailing craft on the lake.* قارب أو طائرة أو سفينة فضائية

crafty /ˈkrɑːfti; *US* ˈkræfti/ *adj* (**craftier**; **craftiest**) clever at getting or achieving things by deceiving people or using indirect methods مكّار ، خبيث

▸ **craftily** *adv* بمكر

crag /kræg/ *noun* [C] a steep, rough rock on a hill or mountain صخرة وعرة شديدة الانحدار

cram /kræm/ *verb* (cramming; crammed) **1** [T] to push people or things into a small space: *I managed to cram all my clothes into the bag but I couldn't zip it up.* ○ *How many more people can they cram onto this train?* ○ (*figurative*) *We only spent two days in Rome but we managed to cram a lot of sightseeing in.* يحشو يحشر ، يحشك

2 [I] to move, with a lot of other people, into a small space: *He only had a small car but they all managed to cram in.* ينحشر ، ينحشك

3 [I] to study very hard and learn a lot in a short time before an examination: *She's cramming for her exams.* ينكبّ على الدراسة قبل الامتحان

▸ **crammed** *adj* very or too full: *That book is crammed with useful information.* ○ *Athens is crammed with tourists at that time of year.* ممتلئ ، مكتظ

cramp /kræmp/ *noun* [U] a sudden pain that you get in a muscle, that makes it difficult to move: *One of the swimmers got cramp and we had to pull him out of the water.* تشنّج

cramped /kræmpt/ *adj* not having enough space: *The flat was terribly cramped with so many of us living there.* مكتظّ ، محشور : ضيق

cranberry /ˈkrænbəri; *US* -beri/ *noun* [C] (*pl.* **cranberries**) a small red berry with a slightly sour taste نوع من التوت البري

crane[1] /kreɪn/ *noun* [C] a large machine with a long metal arm that is used for moving or lifting heavy objects رافعة ، ونْش

crane[2] /kreɪn/ *verb* [I,T] to stretch your neck forward in order to see or hear sth: *We all craned forward to get a better view.* يمدّ عنقه

crank /kræŋk/ *noun* [C] a person with strange ideas or who behaves in a strange way: *Lots of cranks phoned the police confessing to the murder.* شخص غريب الأطوار

cranny /ˈkræni/ *noun* [C] (*pl.* **crannies**) a small opening in a wall, a rock, etc. صَدْع ، شقّ

IDM **every nook and cranny** → NOOK

crash[1] /kræʃ/ *noun* [C] **1** a sudden loud noise made by sth breaking, hitting sth, etc: *I heard a crash and ran outside.* صوت تهشّم أو ارتطام

2 an accident when a car or other vehicle hits sth and is damaged: *She was injured in a serious car crash.* ○ *a plane crash with no survivors* اصطدام ، حادث

3 an occasion when there is a failure in the business world: *the Stock Market crash of 1987* انهيار

▸ **crash** *adj* done with a lot of effort in a short period of time: *She did a crash course in Spanish before going to work in Madrid.* مكثّف وقصير

crash[2] /kræʃ/ *verb* **1** [I] to fall or move suddenly, making a loud noise: *The tree crashed through the window.* ○ *The elephant went crashing through the jungle.* ينهار فجأة محدثاً ضجيجاً : يتخبّط

2 [I,T] to have an accident in a vehicle; to cause a vehicle to have an accident: *He braked too late and crashed into the car in front.* ○ *He crashed his father's car.* يصطدم ، يصدِم

3 [I] to make a loud noise: *I could hear thunder crashing outside.* يدوّي ، يفرقع

4 [I] (used about a business or a financial organization) to fail suddenly ينهار

5 [I] (used about a computer) to stop working

suddenly: *We lost the data when the computer crashed.* يعطب فجأة

'crash barrier *noun* [C] a fence that keeps people or vehicles apart, e.g. when there are large crowds, or between the two sides of the road حاجز الوقاية من التصادم

'crash helmet *noun* [C] a hard hat worn by motorcyclists, racing drivers, etc. to protect their heads in an accident خوذة واقية

crass /kræs/ *adj* **1** stupid, showing that you do not understand sth: *It was a crass comment to make when he knew how upset she was.* أحمق

2 extreme: *crass carelessness* مفرط

crate /kreɪt/ *noun* [C] a large box in which goods are transported or stored. Sometimes crates are divided into sections, for carrying bottles: *We had to pack everything into crates when we moved house.* ○ *a crate of beer* صندوق كبير (للشحن)

crater /'kreɪtə(r)/ *noun* [C] **1** a large hole in the ground: *The bomb left a large crater.* ○ *craters on the moon* حفرة ، فجوة

2 the hole in the top of a volcano فوهة

cravat /krə'væt/ *noun* [C] a wide piece of cloth that men tie around their neck and wear inside the collar of their shirt لفاع للعنق

crave /kreɪv/ *verb* [I,T] **crave (for) sth** to want and need to have sth very much: *He craves attention from other people.* يتوق إلى : يشتهي

▶ **craving** *noun* [C] a strong desire for sth: *When she was pregnant she had cravings for all sorts of peculiar food.* شهوة : وَحَم

crawl /krɔːl/ *verb* [I] **1** to move slowly with the body on or close to the ground, or on the hands and knees: *An insect crawled across the floor.* ○ *Their baby has just started to crawl.* يزحَف ، يحبو

2 (used about vehicles) to move very slowly: *The traffic crawls through the centre of town in the rush hour.* يزحَف ، يسير ببطء

3 crawl (to sb) (*informal*) to be too polite or pleasant to sb in order to be liked or to gain sth: *He only got promoted because he crawled to the manager.* يداهن، يتملّق

IDM **crawling with sth** to be completely full of or covered with sb/sth that is moving and that is considered unpleasant: *The kitchen was crawling with insects.* ○ *The village is always crawling with tourists at this time of year.* يعجّ أو يغصّ بِ

▶ **crawl** *noun* [sing.] **1** a very slow speed: *The traffic slowed to a crawl.* حركة بطيئة

2 often **the crawl** a style of swimming which you do on your front. When you do the crawl, you move first one arm and then the other over your head, turn your face to one side so that you can breathe and kick up and down with your legs. نوع من السباحة

crayon /'kreɪən/ *noun* [C,U] a soft, thick, coloured pencil sometimes made of wax, used for drawing or writing, especially by children قلم طباشير ملوّن

▶ **crayon** *verb* [I,T] يرسم بقلم طباشير ملوّن

craze /kreɪz/ *noun* [C] **a craze (for sth) 1** a strong interest in sth, that usually only lasts for a short time: *There was a craze for that kind of music years ago.* هوس

2 something that a lot of people are very interested in: *Pocket TVs are the latest craze among teenagers.* جنون ، "صرعة"

crazy /'kreɪzi/ *adj* (**crazier**; **craziest**) (*informal*) **1** very silly or foolish: *I think that that's a crazy idea.* ○ *You must be crazy to turn down such a wonderful offer.* سخيف ، أحمق

2 very angry: *She goes crazy when people criticize her.* غاضب ، محتدّ

3 crazy about sth very interested in sth; liking sth very much: *He's always been crazy about horses.* مغرم أو مهووس بِ

4 crazy about sb very much in love with sb مُغرَم بِ ، شديد الولع بِ

5 showing great excitement: *The fans went crazy when their team scored the first goal.* شديد الاهتياج والحماس

▶ **crazily** *adv* على نحو أحمق

craziness *noun* [U] جنون ؛ حماقة

creak /kriːk/ *verb* [I] to make the noise of wood bending or of sth not moving smoothly: *The floorboards creaked when I walked across the room.* ○ *The lift creaked to a halt.* يَصِرّ، يحدث صوتاً

▶ **creak** *noun* [C] صرير

creaky *adj*: *creaky stairs* يحدث صوتاً كالصرير

cream[1] /kriːm/ *noun* **1** [U] the thick yellowish-white liquid that is the fatty part of milk and that rises to the top of it: *coffee with cream* ○ *strawberries and cream* ○ *whipped cream* (= cream that has been beaten) قِشْدة (اللبن)

2 [C,U] a substance that you rub into your skin to keep it soft or as a medical treatment كْريم: مستحضر تجميل

3 the cream [sing.] the best part of sth or the best people in a group زبدة (الشيء) ، صَفْوة (الناس)

▶ **cream** *adj* having a yellowish-white colour ذو لون أبيض مائل للصفرة

creamy *adj* (**creamier**; **creamiest**) **1** containing cream: *a creamy sauce* يحوي قشدة

2 thick, smooth and soft; looking or feeling like cream: *Beat the mixture until it is creamy and light.* ذو قوام كالقشدة

cream[2] /kriːm/ *verb*

PHR V **cream sb/sth off** to take away the best people or part from sth for a particular purpose: *The big clubs cream off the country's best young players.* يأخذ الصفوة

,cream 'tea *noun* [C] (*Brit*) a meal taken in the afternoon consisting of tea with a special type of cake (scone) that is eaten with jam and cream وجبة من الشاي ونوع معين من الكعك مع القشدة

crease /kriːs/ *noun* [C] **1** an untidy line on paper, material, a piece of clothing, etc. that is caused by not treating it carefully: *Your shirt needs ironing, it's full of creases.* ○ *When I unrolled the poster, there was a crease in it.* غضَن ، تجعيدة، "كرمشة"

2 a neat line that is put on paper, material, a piece of clothing, etc. intentionally: *He had a sharp crease in his trousers.* ثنية رفيعة ، "كسرة"

▶ **crease** *verb* [I,T] to get creases (1); to make sth get creases: *Hang up your jacket or it will crease.* ○ *I creased my skirt by sitting on the floor.* يتغضّن ، "يتكرمش" : "يكرمش"

create /kriˈeɪt/ *verb* [T] to cause sth new to happen or exist: *God created the world.* ○ *a plan to create new jobs in the area* ○ *All these changes will simply create confusion.* ○ *He created a bad impression at the interview.* يخلق

creation /kriˈeɪʃn/ *noun* **1** [U] the act of causing sth new to happen or exist: *the creation of new independent states* خَلق

2 usually **the Creation** [sing.] the act of making the whole universe, as described in the Bible الخلق ، خَلق السموات والأرض

3 [C] something that sb has made or produced, especially using skill or imagination: *This dish is a new creation, I didn't use a recipe.* ابتكار

creative /kriˈeɪtɪv/ *adj* **1** using skill or imagination to make or do new things: *She's a fantastic designer – she's so creative.* ○ *We need some creative thinking to solve this problem.* خلاّق ، مبدع

2 connected with producing new things, especially works of art: *His creative life went on until he was well over 80.* خلاّق ، مُبْدِع

▶ **creatively** *adv*: *They haven't got a very big house but they use the space creatively.* على نحو خلاّق : بخيال إبداعي

creativity /ˌkriːeɪˈtɪvəti/ *noun* [U] the ability to make or produce new things, especially using skill or imagination: *We want teaching that encourages children's creativity.* روح الإبداع

creator /kriˈeɪtə(r)/ *noun* **1** [C] a person who makes or produces sth new, especially using skill or imagination: *He was the creator of some of the best-known characters in literature.* خالق ، مبدع

2 the Creator [sing.] God الخالق ، الله

creature /ˈkriːtʃə(r)/ *noun* [C] a living thing such as an animal, a bird, a fish or an insect, but not a plant: *a living creature* ○ *a small black furry creature* ○ *creatures from other planets* مخلوق

crèche (*also* **creche**) /kreʃ/ *noun* [C] (*Brit*) a place where small children are looked after while their parents are working دار حضانة

credentials /krəˈdenʃlz/ *noun* [plural] **1** something that shows that a person is qualified or suitable for sth: *He has perfect credentials for the top job.* مؤهّلات

2 a document that proves that sb is who he/she claims to be, or that he/she is qualified to do sth وثيقة اعتماد

credible /ˈkredəbl/ *adj* **1** that you can believe: *It's hardly credible that such a thing could happen without him knowing it.* ❶ The opposite is **incredible**. قابل للتصديق

2 that you can trust or take seriously: *We need to think of a credible alternative to nuclear energy.* جدير بالثقة

▶ **credibility** /ˌkredəˈbɪləti/ *noun* [U] the quality of being able to be believed or trusted and taken seriously: *The Prime Minister had lost all credibility and had to resign.* مصداقية ، صدقية

credibly /-əbli/ *adv* على نحو معقول أو قابل للتصديق

credit¹ /ˈkredɪt/ *noun* **1** [U] the system of buying goods or services and not paying for them until later: *I bought the television on credit.* ○ *interest-free credit* (= payment over a period without any extra charges) ○ *Read the credit terms carefully before signing.* نظام الشراء بالدين

2 [U] having money in an account at a bank: *No bank charges are made if your account remains in credit.* رصيد دائن ، حساب اعتماد

3 [C] a payment made into an account at a bank ➲ Look at **debit**. نقدة أو دفعة

4 [C,U] a sum of money that a bank, etc. lends: *The company was not able to get any further credit and went bankrupt.* تسليفة

5 [U] praise for sth good that a person has done: *He got all the credit for the success of the project.* ○ *I can't take any credit; the others did all the work.* ○ *She didn't do very well but at least give her credit for trying.* فضل ، شرَف : مديح

6 credits [plural] the list of the names of the people who made a film or TV programme, shown at the beginning or end of the film أسماء المشاركين في إنتاج فيلم أو برنامج تلفزيوني

7 [sing.] **a credit to sb/sth** a person or thing that gives honour: *She is a lovely girl and a credit to her school.* مفخرة

8 [C] (*US*) a part of a course at a college or university, that a student has completed and that appears on his/her record قسم من برنامج دراسي مقبول رسمياً

IDM **do sb credit** to make sb deserve to be praised or respected: *His courage and optimism do him credit.* يشرِّف ، يجعله جديراً بالثناء

have sth to your credit to have finished sth that is successful: *He has three best-selling novels to his credit.* يكمل بنجاح

(be) to sb's credit (used for showing that you approve of sth that sb has done, although you have criticized sth else): *The company, to its credit, apologized and refunded my money.* والحق يقال

credit² /ˈkredɪt/ *verb* [T] **1 credit sb/sth with sth; credit sth to sb/sth** to accept or believe that sb/sth has a particular quality or is responsible for sth good or successful: *Of course I wouldn't do such a stupid thing – credit me with a bit more sense than that!* ○ *He credited his success to a lot of hard work.* يعزو أو ينسب إلى

2 to record that money has been added to an account: *Has the cheque been credited to my account yet?* يضيف للحساب

3 (especially in negative sentences and questions) to believe: *I simply cannot credit that he has made the same mistake again!* يصدّق

creditable /ˈkredɪtəbl/ *adj* deserving to be praised or respected (even if it is not excellent): *It was a creditable result considering that three players were injured.* جدير بالثناء ، جدير بالاحترام

🔑 **'credit card** *noun* [C] a small plastic card that allows sb to get goods or services without using money. You usually receive a bill once a month for what you have bought: *Can I pay by credit card?* بطاقة ائتمان/اعتماد

'credit crunch *noun* [usually sing.] an economic condition in which it suddenly becomes difficult and expensive to borrow money أزمة الائتمان

creditor /'kredɪtə(r)/ *noun* [C] a person or company to whom money is owed دائن

creed /kri:d/ *noun* [C] a set of beliefs or principles (especially religious ones) that strongly influence sb's life عقيدة

creek /kri:k/ *noun* [C] **1** (*Brit*) a narrow piece of water where the sea flows into the land خليج ضيِّق ، شَرْم ، خَوْر

2 (*US*) a small river or stream نُهَيْر ، جدول

creep[1] /kri:p/ *verb* [I] (*pt, pp* **crept** /krept/) **1** to move very quietly and carefully, often with the body in a low position, so that nobody will notice you: *The cat crept silently towards the bird.* ○ *She crept into the room so as not to wake him up.* يزحف ، يتسلّل

2 to move forward slowly: *His latest record has crept up to number 10 in the charts.* يتقدّم ببطء

PHRV **creep in** to begin to appear: *All sorts of changes are beginning to creep into the education system.* يظهر ، ينسل إلى

creep[2] /kri:p/ *noun* [C] (*informal*) a person that you dislike because they try too hard to be liked by people in authority (شخص) متملّق أو مداهن

IDM **give sb the creeps** (*informal*) to give sb an unpleasant feeling; to make sb feel frightened: *There's something about the way he laughs that gives me the creeps.* يضايق ؛ يرعب

creeper /'kri:pə(r)/ *noun* [C] a plant that grows up trees or walls or along the ground نبات مدّاد أو متسلّق

creepy /'kri:pi/ *adj* (**creepier**; **creepiest**) (*informal*) that makes you feel rather nervous and frightened مخيف ، موحش

cremate /krə'meɪt/ *verb* [T] to burn the body of a dead person as part of a funeral service يحرق جثة الميّت (بدل دفنها)

▶ **cremation** /krə'meɪʃn/ *noun* [C,U] an act of cremating a dead person ➲ Look at the note at **funeral.** إحراق جثة الميّت

crematorium /ˌkremə'tɔ:riəm/ *noun* [C] (*pl.* **crematoriums** or **crematoria** /-ɔ:riə/) (*US* **crematory** /'kremətəri/ or /-tɔ:ri/) a place where dead people are cremated مكان إحراق جثث الموتى

crêpe paper /'kreɪp peɪpə(r)/ *noun* [U] a type of thin brightly coloured paper that stretches and has a surface covered in lines and folds, used especially for making decorations ورق رقيق مكرمش (مجعّد)

crept *pt, pp* of CREEP

crescendo /krə'ʃendəʊ/ *noun* [C] (*pl.* **crescendos**) a noise or piece of music that is very loud or that gets louder and louder تصعيد الصوت أو النغمة ؛ مقطع تصعيديّ

crescent /'kresnt/ *noun* [C] **1** the shape of the moon in its first and last stages; a curved shape that is pointed at both ends هلال

2 a street or row of houses that is curved حيّ سكنيّ على هيئة هلال

cress /kres/ *noun* [U] a small plant with small green leaves that is eaten raw in salads رشاد ، حُرف ، قُرّة

crest /krest/ *noun* [C] **1** a group of attractive feathers on the top of a bird's head عرف الطائر ، قنبرة

2 the top of a hill قمة ، ذروة

3 the white part at the top of a wave قمة الموجة المزبدة

crestfallen /'krestfɔ:lən/ *adj* sad or disappointed حزين ، خائب الأمل ، كسير الخاطر

cretin /'kretɪn; *US* kri:tn/ *noun* [C] (*slang*) a stupid person غبيّ ، ضعيف العقل

crevasse /krə'væs/ *noun* [C] a deep crack in thick ice صدع عميق في الجليد

crevice /'krevɪs/ *noun* [C] a narrow crack in a rock, wall, etc. شقّ ، صدع

crew /kru:/ *noun* [C, with sing. or pl. verb] **1** all the people who work on a ship, plane, etc: *The captain and his crew hope you had a pleasant flight* طاقم الطائرة مثلاً

2 a group of people who work together: *a camera crew* (= people who film things for television, etc.) طاقم ، هيئة

'crew cut *noun* [C] a very short hairstyle for men قصّة شعر قصيرة للرجال

crewman /'kru:mən/ *noun* [C] (*pl.* **-men** /-mən/) a member of a crew(1): *Four crewmen were drowned.* أحد أفراد الطاقم

crib[1] /krɪb/ *noun* [C] (*especially US*) = COT

crib[2] /krɪb/ *verb* [I,T] (cri**bb**ing; cri**bb**ed) **crib (sth) (from/off sb)** to copy sb else's work and pretend it is your own: *She cribbed some of the answers off her friend.* يغشّ في الامتحان ؛ ينقل من غيره

crick /krɪk/ *noun* [sing.] a pain in your neck, back, etc. that makes it difficult for you to move easily: *I've got a crick in my neck.* تصلّب أو تشنّج مؤلم

▶ **crick** *verb* [T]: *I've cricked my neck.* يصاب بتشنّج مؤلم

cricket[1] /'krɪkɪt/ *noun* [U] a game that is played with a bat and ball on a large area of grass by two teams of eleven players لعبة الكريكيت

> In cricket the **bowler** bowls the ball to the **batsman** who tries to hit it with a **bat** and then score a **run** by running from one end of the pitch to the other.

▶ **cricketer** *noun* [C] a person who plays cricket, especially as their job لاعب الكريكيت

cricket[2] /'krɪkɪt/ *noun* [C] an insect that makes a

loud noise by rubbing its wings together جُدجُد، صرّار الليل

crime /kraɪm/ *noun* **1** [C] something which is against the law and which people are punished for, e.g. by being sent to prison: *to commit a crime* ○ *serious crimes such as murder and armed robbery* جريمة ، جناية

2 [U] illegal behaviour in general: *There has been an increase in car crime recently.* ○ *to lead a life of crime* ○ *to fight crime* ○ *crime prevention measures* إجرام ، مخالفة القوانين

3 usually **a crime** [sing.] something that is morally wrong: *It is a crime to waste food when people are starving.* عمل لا أخلاقي

▸ **criminal** /ˈkrɪmɪnl/ *adj* **1** (only *before* a noun) connected with crime: *Deliberate damage to public property is a criminal offence.* ○ *criminal law* اجراميّ ؛ جنائيّ

2 morally wrong: *a criminal waste of taxpayers' money* غير أخلاقي

criminal *noun* [C] a person who has committed a crime مجرم

crimson /ˈkrɪmzn/ *adj, noun* [U] (of) a dark red colour ➲ Look at **maroon** and **scarlet**. قرمزيّ ؛ اللون القرمزيّ

cringe /krɪndʒ/ *verb* [I] **1** to move away from sb/sth because you are frightened: *The dog cringed in terror when the man raised his arm.* ينكمش خوفاً ، ينفر

2 to feel embarrassed: *awful family photographs that make you cringe in embarrassment* يخجل ، يشعر بالحرج

crinkle /ˈkrɪŋkl/ *verb* [I,T] **crinkle (sth) (up)** (to cause sth) to have thin folds or lines in it: *He crinkled the silver paper up into a ball.* يتجعّد أو يجعّد

▸ **crinkly** /ˈkrɪŋkli/ *adj*: *a type of soft crinkly material* مجعّد

cripple /ˈkrɪpl/ *verb* [T] **1** (usually passive) to cause sb to be a cripple: *He was crippled in a road accident.* يشلّ ، يقعد

2 to damage sth badly: *The recession has crippled the motor industry.* يشلّ ، يعطّل

▸ **crippling** *adj* that causes very great damage; that has a very harmful effect: *They had crippling debts and had to sell their house.* مُشلّ للحركة ؛ فظيع

crisis /ˈkraɪsɪs/ *noun* [C,U] (*pl.* **crises** /ˈkraɪsiːz/) a time of great danger or difficulty; the moment when things change and either improve or get worse: *the international crisis caused by the invasion* ○ *Events reached a crisis during the summer of 1939.* ○ *a friend you can rely on in times of crisis* أزمة

crisp¹ /krɪsp/ *adj* **1** hard and dry: *Store the biscuits in a tin to keep them crisp.* جافّ وهشّ

2 firm and fresh or new: *a crisp salad* ○ *a crisp apple* ○ *a crisp new £10 note* ○ *a crisp cotton dress* طازج ، ناضر ؛ جديد

3 (used about the air or weather) cold and dry: *a crisp winter morning* منعش

4 (used about the way sb speaks) quick, clear but not very friendly: *a crisp reply* (كلام) واضح جازم

▸ **crisply** *adv* in a crisp¹ (4) way: *'I disagree,' she said crisply.* بِجَزم ، بشيء من الحدّة

crispy *adj* (**crispier**; **crispiest**) (*informal*) = CRISP¹ (1,2): *fish in crispy batter* هش ؛ طازج

crisp² /krɪsp/ (*also* **poˌtato ˈcrisp**) (*US* **potato chip**; **chip**) *noun* [C] a very thin piece of potato that is fried in oil, dried and then sold in packets. Crisps usually have salt or another flavouring on them: *a packet of crisps* رقاقة بطاطا مقليّة

crispbread /ˈkrɪspbred/ *noun* [C,U] a thin crisp biscuit that is usually made from rye and often eaten with cheese بسكوت خاص من الشعير

criss-cross /ˈkrɪs krɒs; *US* -krɔːs/ *adj* (only *before* a noun) with many lines that cross over each other: *a criss-cross pattern* ذو خطوط متقاطعة

▸ **criss-cross** *verb* [I,T]: *the footpaths which criss-cross the countryside* يتقاطع أو يتصالب ؛ يقطع بخطوط متصالبة

criterion /kraɪˈtɪəriən/ *noun* [C] (*pl.* **criteria** /-riə/) the standard that you use when you make a decision or form an opinion about sb/sth: *What is the criterion for deciding who gets a place on the course?* معيار ، مقياس

critic /ˈkrɪtɪk/ *noun* [C] **1** a person who says what he/she thinks is bad or wrong with sb/sth: *He is a long-standing critic of the council's transport policy.* منتقد

2 a person whose job is to give his/her opinion about a play, film, book, work of art, etc: *a film critic* (= in a newspaper, etc.). ناقد

critical /ˈkrɪtɪkl/ *adj* **1** **critical (of sb/sth)** saying what is wrong with sb/sth; disapproving: *The report was very critical of safety standards on the railways.* ○ *critical remarks* ℹ The opposite is **uncritical**. انتقادي ، مظهر للعيوب

2 (only *before* a noun) describing the good and bad points of a play, film, book, work of art, etc: *a critical guide to this month's new films* نقديّ

3 dangerous or serious: *The patient is in a critical condition.* خطِر ؛ عصيب

4 very important; at a time when things can suddenly become better or worse: *The talks between the two leaders have reached a critical stage.* حرج ، حاسم

▸ **critically** /-ɪkli/ *adv*: *a critically ill patient* ○ *a critically important decision* بصورة خطيرة ؛ ذو نتائج هامّة

criticism /ˈkrɪtɪsɪzəm/ *noun* **1** [C,U] (an expression of) what you think is bad about sb/sth: *My main criticism is that it is too expensive.* ○ *The council has come in for severe criticism over the plans.* انتقاد

2 [U] the act of describing the good and bad points of a play, film, book, work of art, etc: *literary criticism* نقد ، عرض نقدي

criticize (*also* **criticise**) /ˈkrɪtɪsaɪz/ *verb* **criticize sb/sth (for sth)** to say what is bad or wrong with sb/sth: *The doctor was criticized for not* *sending the patient to hospital.* ○ *Stop criticizing!* ينتقد

critique /krɪ'ti:k/ *noun* [C] a piece of writing that describes the good and bad points of sb/sth نقد، عرض نقدي

croak /krəʊk/ *noun* [C] a deep low sound, like the noise that a frog makes نقيق (الضفدع) : صوت أجش
▸ **croak** *verb* [I,T] to make a noise like a croak, e.g. because you have a cold and are losing your voice يتكلم بصوت خافت أجش

crochet /'krəʊʃeɪ; US krəʊ'ʃeɪ/ *noun* [U] a way of making clothes, cloth, etc. by using wool or cotton and one needle with a hook at one end "كروشيه"، شغل الصنّارة
▸ **crochet** *verb* [T] (*pt, pp* **crocheted** /-ʃeɪd/): *to crochet a shawl* ➲ Look at **knit**. يحيك بالصنّارة، يشتغل الكروشيه

crockery /'krɒkəri/ *noun* [U] cups, plates and dishes ➲ Look at **cutlery**. أواني الطعام الخزفية

crocodile /'krɒkədaɪl/ *noun* [C] **1** a large, long animal with hard skin that lives in rivers in hot countries. A crocodile is a dangerous animal because it has a large mouth with a lot of sharp teeth in it. It is a reptile. ➲ Look at **alligator**. تمساح
2 (*Brit*) a line of children standing or walking in pairs صفّ طويل مزدوج من التلاميذ

crocus /'krəʊkəs/ *noun* a small plant that produces yellow, purple or white flowers early in spring (زهر) الكركم: زعفران

croissant /'krwæsɒ̃; US krwæ'sɒ̃/ *noun* [C] a type of light bread roll, shaped in a curve, that is eaten with butter at breakfast "كِرواسان"، كعكة خفيفة هلاليّة

crony /'krəʊni/ *noun* [C] (*pl.* **cronies**) (*informal*) (often used in a critical way) a friend صديق، خليل

crook /krʊk/ *noun* [C] **1** (*informal*) a dishonest person; a criminal محتال، نصّاب
2 a bend or curve in sth: *the crook of your arm* (= the inside of your elbow) عقفة، حنية

crooked /'krʊkɪd/ *adj* **1** not straight or even: *That picture is crooked.* ○ *crooked teeth* معقوف، ملتوٍ، غير مستقيم
2 (*informal*) not honest: *a crooked accountant* غير أمين، غشّاش

crop /krɒp/ *noun* **1** [C] all the grain, fruit, vegetables, etc. that grow or are collected at one time or place: *a crop of apples* ○ *Another year of crop failure would mean starvation for many people.* غلّة، محصول
2 [C, usually pl.] plants that are grown on farms for food: *Rice and soya beans are the main crops here.* محصولات غذائيّة
3 [sing.] a number of people or things which have appeared at the same time: *the recent crop of movies about aliens* مجموعة أو طائفة من
▸ **crop** *verb* (cropping; cropped) **1** [T] to cut sth very short: *cropped hair* يقصّ (الشّعر) قصيراً
2 [I] to produce a crop (1) يغلّ، ينتج

PHRV **crop up** to appear suddenly, when you are not expecting it: *Some problems have cropped up that we weren't expecting.* يحدث أو يبرز فجأة

cropper /'krɒpə(r)/ *noun*
IDM **come a cropper** (*informal*) **1** to fall over يسقط على الأرض، يكبو
2 to fail; to have an accident يخفق؛ يُصاب بحادث

croquet /'krəʊkeɪ; US krəʊ'keɪ/ *noun* [U] a game that you play on grass. When you play croquet you use wooden sticks (mallets) to hit balls through metal arches (hoops). لعبة الكروكي

cross[1] /krɒs; US krɔ:s/ *noun* **1** [C] a mark that you make by drawing one line across another (e.g. x). The sign is used for showing the position of sth, for showing that sth is not correct, etc: *The cross on the map shows where our house is.* ○ *Incorrect answers were marked with a cross.* صليب، إشارة الضرب أو الجمع
2 (*also* **the Cross**) [sing.] the two pieces of wood in the shape of a cross on which people were killed as a punishment in former times: *Christ's death on the cross* الصليب
3 [C] something in the shape of the cross (2) that is used as a symbol of the Christian religion: *She wore a gold cross round her neck.* ○ *The priest made the sign of the cross* (= by moving his right hand in front of his face and chest in the shape of a cross). ➲ Look at **crucifix**. صليب
4 [C, usually sing.] **a cross (between A and B)** something (especially a plant or an animal) that is a mixture of two different types of thing: *a fruit which is a cross between a peach and an apple* خليط، هجين
5 [C] (*formal*) something that makes you unhappy or worried or that makes your life more difficult: *We all have our own cross to bear.* محنة، بلوى

cross[2] /krɒs; US krɔ:s/ *verb* **1** [I,T] **cross (over) (from sth/to sth)** to go from one side of sth to the other: *to cross the road* ○ *You can't cross here, there's too much traffic.* ○ *Where did you cross the border?* يعبر، يجتاز
2 [I] (used about lines, roads, etc.) to pass across each other: *The two roads cross just north of the village.* ○ (*figurative*) *Our letters crossed in the post.* يتقاطع
3 [T] to put sth across or over sth else: *to cross your arms* يضع بشكل متقاطع، يشبك
4 [T] **cross yourself** to make the sign of a cross in front of your face and chest as a symbol of the Christian religion يصلّب، يرسم علامة الصليب
5 [T] to refuse to do what sb wants you to do; to oppose sb: *He's an important man. It could be dangerous to cross him.* يخالف، يعارض
6 [T] **cross sth with sth** to produce a new type of plant or animal by mixing two different types: *If you cross a horse with a donkey you get a mule.* يهجّن
IDM **cross your fingers** to hope that things will happen in the way that you want; to wish for good luck: *There's nothing more we can do now –*

just cross our fingers and hope for the best. يتمنى له النجاح ، يدعو له بالخير

If a person says they are 'crossing their fingers' or 'keeping their fingers crossed' it doesn't mean that they are really doing this with their hands. It means that they are wishing somebody luck or hoping very much that something good will happen.

cross my heart (and hope to die) (*informal*) (used for emphasizing that what you are saying is true) أحلف بحياتي! (تعبير لتأكيد صحة ما تقول)

cross your mind (used about a thought, idea, etc.) to come into your mind: *It never once crossed my mind that she was lying.* يخطر في باله

PHR V **cross sth off (sth)** to remove sth from a list, etc. by drawing a line through it: *Cross Dave's name off the guest list – he can't come.* يحذف ، يشطب

cross sth out to draw a line through sth that you have written because you have made a mistake, etc: *to cross out a spelling mistake* يشطب على

cross[3] /krɒs; US krɔːs/ *adj* **cross (with sb) (about sth)** (*informal*) angry or annoyed: *I was really cross with her for leaving me with all the work.* ○ *What are you so cross about?* ℹ **Cross** is less formal than **angry**. غاضب : منزعج

▸ **crossly** *adv*: *'Be quiet,' Dad said crossly.* بغضب ، بانزعاج

crossbar /ˈkrɒsbɑː(r); US krɔːs-/ *noun* [C] **1** the piece of wood over the top of a goal in football, etc. عارضة المرمى

2 the metal bar that joins the front and back of a bicycle قضيب مستعرض

ˌcross-ˈcountry *adj, adv* across fields, etc.; not using main roads: *a cross-country run* عبر الريف

ˌcross-eˈxamine *verb* [T] to ask sb a lot of questions (e.g. in a court) in order to find out the truth about sth: *to cross-examine a witness in a court of law* يستجوب ، يستنطق

▸ **ˌcross-examiˈnation** *noun* [C,U] استجواب ، استنطاق

cross-eyed /ˈkrɒs aɪd; US ˈkrɔːs-/ *adj* having one or both your eyes looking towards your nose أحول

crossfire /ˈkrɒsfaɪə(r); US ˈkrɔːs-/ *noun* [U] situation in which guns are being fired from two or more different directions: *The journalist was killed in crossfire.* ○ (*figurative*) *When my parents argued, I sometimes got caught in the crossfire.* (تبادل) اطلاق النار

crossing /ˈkrɒsɪŋ; US ˈkrɔːs-/ *noun* [C] **1** a journey across water: *a rough sea crossing* رحلة بحريّة

2 a place where roads or railway lines cross each other: *a level crossing* (= where a road crosses a railway line) تقاطع طرق

3 a place where you can cross over sth: *to cross the road at a pedestrian crossing* ○ *a border crossing* نقطة عبور

cross-legged /ˌkrɒs ˈleɡd; -ˈleɡɪd; US ˌkrɔːs-/ *adj, adv* sitting on the floor with your legs pulled up in front of you and with one leg or foot over the other: *to sit cross-legged* واضعاً رجلاً على رجل : متصالب الساقين

ˌcross ˈpurposes *noun*

IDM **at cross purposes** in a state of confusion and misunderstanding between people who are talking about different things but think they are talking about the same thing: *I think we've been talking at cross purposes. You mean next Saturday but I'm talking about this one.* سوء تفاهم

ˌcross-ˈreference *noun* [C] a note in a book, etc. that tells you to look in another place in the book for more information إحالة ، إشارة إلى جزء آخر من الكتاب

crossroads /ˈkrɒsrəʊdz; US ˈkrɔːs-/ *noun* [C] (*pl.* **crossroads**) a place where two or more roads cross each other: *When you come to the next crossroads turn right.* تقاطع طرق

ˌcross ˈsection *noun* [C] **1** a picture of what the inside of sth would look like if you cut through it: *a diagram of a cross-section of the human brain* مقطع عرضي

2 a group of people that are typical of a larger group: *a representative cross-section of society* شريحة ، قطاع

crosswalk /ˈkrɒswɔːk; US ˈkrɔːs-/ *noun* [C] (*US*) = PEDESTRIAN CROSSING

crossword /ˈkrɒswɜːd; US ˈkrɔːs-/ (*also* **ˈcrossword puzzle**) *noun* [C] a word game with black and white squares where you write the words in the white squares, either across or down. The correct words are the answers to special questions (clues): *to do a crossword* (أحجية) الكلمات المتقاطعة

crotch /krɒtʃ/ (*also* **crutch**) *noun* [C] the place where a person's legs, or trouser legs, join at the top نقطة التقاء الساقين في الأعلى: "السرج"

crouch /kraʊtʃ/ *verb* [I] to bend down so that your body is close to the ground and leaning forward slightly: *The cat crouched in front of the hole waiting for the mouse to appear.* ○ *He crouched down behind the sofa.* يجثم ، ينحني قريباً من الأرض

crow[1] /krəʊ/ *noun* [C] a large black bird that makes a loud noise غراب

IDM **as the crow flies** (used for describing distances) in a straight line: *It's a kilometre as the crow flies but three kilometres by road.* على خط مستقيم

crow[2] /krəʊ/ *verb* [I] **1** to make a loud noise, such as a male chicken (a cock) makes, e.g. early in the morning يصيح (الديك)

2 (*informal*) to speak very proudly about sth; to boast يتبجح

crowbar /ˈkrəʊbɑː(r)/ *noun* [C] a long iron bar that is used for forcing sth open عتلة

🔑 **crowd**[1] /kraʊd/ *noun* **1** [C, with sing. or pl. verb] a large number of people in one place: *The crowd was/were extremely noisy.* ○ *A large crowd gathered to hear the President speak.* ○ *He pushed his* *way through the crowd.* ○ *There were crowds of people waiting outside the cinema.* حشد ، جمهور

2 the crowd [sing.] most people: *to follow the crowd* (= to do what everybody else does) الناس ، الأغلبيّة

3 [C, with sing. or pl. verb] (*informal*) a group of people who know each other: *John, Linda and Barry will be there – all the usual crowd.* "شلّة"

crowd² /kraʊd/ *verb* **1** [I] **crowd around/round (sb)** (used about a lot of people) to come together in one place: *Fans crowded round the singer hoping to get his autograph.* يحتشد ، يتجمهر

2 [T] (used about a lot of people) to fill an area: *Groups of tourists crowded the main streets.* يحشد ، يملأ المكان

PHR V **crowd into sth; crowd in** to go into a small place and make it very full: *Somehow we all crowded into their small living room.* ينحشر
crowd sb/sth into sth; crowd sb/sth in to put a lot of people into a small place: *Ten prisoners were crowded into one small cell.* يحشر
▸ **crowded** *adj* full of people: *The town was crowded with Christmas shoppers.* ○ *a crowded bus* مكتظ ، مزدحم

crown¹ /kraʊn/ *noun* **1** [C] a round ornament made of gold and jewels, that a king or queen wears on the head on official occasions تاج

2 the Crown [sing.] the state as represented by a king or queen: *an area of land belonging to the Crown* السلطة الملكيّة

3 [sing.] the top of your head or of a hat قمة الرأس

4 [sing.] the top of a hill قمة ، ذروة

crown² /kraʊn/ *verb* [T] **1** to put a crown on the head of a new king or queen in an official ceremony: *Elizabeth was crowned in 1952.* ○ (*figurative*) *the newly crowned British champion* يتوّج

2 crown sth (with sth) (*formal*) to cover the top of sth: *The mountain was crowned with snow.* يغطّي القمة ، يكلّل

3 to be a good or successful end to sth: *years of hard work that were finally crowned with success* يكلّل (بالنجاح)

IDM **to crown it all** to be the last in a number of lucky or unlucky events: *She failed her exam, her boyfriend left her and to crown it all her handbag was stolen.* يختتم ختاماً حسناً ؛ يزيد الطين بلّة
▸ **crowning** *adj* (only *before* a noun) the best or most important: *Winning the World Championship was the crowning moment of her career.* أهمّ (لحظة) ، أسمى (نقطة)

ˌcrown ˈprince (*feminine* **ˌcrown prinˈcess**) *noun* [C] the person who has the right to become the next king or queen وليّ العهد

crucial /ˈkruːʃl/ *adj* **crucial (to/for sth)** very important: *Early diagnosis of the illness is crucial for successful treatment.* هامّ جداً : حاسم
▸ **crucially** /-ʃəli/ *adv*: *a crucially important decision, meeting, etc.* بصورة تترتب عليها نتائج هامة

crucifix /ˈkruːsəfɪks/ *noun* [C] a small model of a cross with a figure of Jesus on it تمثال المسيح المصلوب

crucifixion /ˌkruːsəˈfɪkʃn/ *noun* [C,U] the act of crucifying sb: *the Crucifixion of Christ* صلب : صلب السيّد المسيح

crucify /ˈkruːsɪfaɪ/ *verb* [T] (*pres part* **crucifying**; *3rd pers sing pres* **crucifies**; *pt, pp* **crucified**) to kill sb by nailing or tying him/her to a cross يصلب

crude /kruːd/ *adj* **1** in its natural state: *crude oil* خام

2 done or made in a simple way; not skilful: *The method was crude but very effective.* غير متقن ، بدائيّ ، بسيط

3 rude, talking or acting in a way that would offend many people: *He's always telling crude jokes.* وقح ، فظّ ، بذيء
▸ **crudely** *adv* بصورة غير متقنة : بفظاظة

cruel /ˈkruːəl/ *adj* (**crueller**; **cruellest**) causing physical or mental pain or suffering to sb/sth; unkind: *I think it's cruel to keep animals in cages.* ○ *cruel words* ○ *Life can be cruel.* ○ *a cruel punishment* قاسٍ : قاسي القلب
▸ **cruelly** /ˈkruːəli/ *adv* بقسوة

cruelty /ˈkruːəlti/ *noun* (*pl.* **cruelties**) **1** [U] **cruelty (to sb/sth)** cruel behaviour: *cruelty to children* معاملة قاسية ، إيذاء

2 [C, usually pl.] a cruel act: *the cruelties of war* عمل وحشي

cruise /kruːz/ *verb* [I] **1** to travel by boat, visiting a number of places, as a holiday: *to cruise around the Caribbean* يقوم بجولة بحرية

2 to travel by car, plane, etc. staying at the same speed: *cruising at 70 miles an hour* (السيّارة مثلاً) تسير بسرعة ثابتة
▸ **cruise** *noun* [C] a holiday in which you travel on a ship and visit a number of different places: *After they retired they went on a world cruise.* تطواف أو جولة بحريّة
cruiser /ˈkruːzə(r)/ *noun* [C] **1** a large warship طرّاد بحري

2 (*also* **ˈcabin cruiser**) a motor boat which has room for people to sleep on it قارب للرحلات صالح للسكنى

crumb /krʌm/ *noun* [C] a very small piece of bread, cake or biscuit فتاتة (خبز مثلاً)

crumble /ˈkrʌmbl/ *verb* [I,T] **crumble (sth) (into/to sth); crumble (sth) (up)** (to cause sth) to break into very small pieces: *The walls of the church are beginning to crumble.* ○ *We crumbled up the bread and threw it to the birds.* ○ (*figurative*) *Support for the government is beginning to crumble.* يتفتّت : ينهار

crummy /ˈkrʌmi/ *adj* (**crummier**; **crummiest**) (*informal*) bad or unpleasant: *a crummy little backstreet hotel* حقير ، زري

crumpet /ˈkrʌmpɪt/ *noun* [C] (*Brit*) a flat round type of small cake with holes in the top that you eat hot with butter on it كعكة طريّة تشبه القطايف

crumple /ˈkrʌmpl/ *verb* [I,T] **crumple (sth) (into sth); crumple (sth) (up)** (to cause sth) to be folded or pressed in an untidy or irregular

a b c d e f g h i j k l m n o p q r s t u v w x y z

way: *The front of the car crumpled when it hit the wall.* ○ *to crumple a piece of paper into a ball* يجعّد ، "يكرمش" : "يتكرمش"

crunch /krʌntʃ/ *verb* **1** [I,T] **crunch sth (up)** to make a loud noise when you are eating sth hard: *to crunch an apple/a carrot* "يقرقش" ، يجرش الطعام في فمه

2 [I] to make a loud noise like the sound of sth being walked on and crushed: *We crunched through the snow.* ○ *The snow made a crunching noise under our feet.* يتهشّم بصوت مسموع

▸ **crunch** *noun* [sing.] an act or noise of crunching: *There was a loud crunch as he sat on the box of eggs.* تهشيم أو جرش : صوت التهشيم أو الجرش

IDM **if/when it comes to the crunch** if/when you are in a difficult situation and must make a difficult decision: *If it comes to the crunch, I'll stay and fight.* عندما يجدّ الجدّ ، في اللحظة الحاسمة

crunchy *adj* (**crunchier**; **crunchiest**) hard and crisp, so that it makes a noise when you eat it or step on it: *a crunchy apple* (تفّاح مثلاً) مكتنز يقرقش تحت الأسنان

crusade /kruːˈseɪd/ *noun* [C] **1** a fight for sth that you believe to be good or against sth that you believe to be bad: *a crusade against drugs* حملة ، مكافحة

2 Crusade one of the wars that European Christians fought with Muslims in the Middle Ages حملة صليبيّة

▸ **crusader** *noun* [C] a person who takes part in a crusade مشترك في حملة

crush¹ /krʌʃ/ *verb* [T] **1** to press sb/sth hard so that he/she/it is broken, damaged or injured: *Don't pack the cakes at the bottom of the box or they'll get crushed.* ○ *to be crushed to death* يمعس ، يهرس

2 crush sth (up) to break sth hard into very small pieces or a powder: *First crush the garlic and fry in olive oil.* يهرس ، يسحن

3 to defeat sb/sth completely: *The army was sent in to crush the rebellion.* يسحق ، يقمع

▸ **crushing** *adj* (only *before* a noun) that defeats sb/sth completely or upsets sb/sth a lot: *a crushing defeat* ○ *a crushing blow to the country's economy* ساحق ، (ضربة) قاضية

crush² /krʌʃ/ *noun* **1** [sing.] a large group of people in a small space: *There was such a crush that I couldn't get near the bar.* ازدحام ، حشد مكتظّ

2 [C] **a crush (on sb)** (*informal*) a strong feeling of love and admiration for sb that does not usually last for a long time: *to have a crush on your teacher* غرام عابر ، افتتان

crust /krʌst/ *noun* [C,U] **1** the hard part on the outside of a loaf of bread, pie, etc: *I cut the crusts off the bread.* قشرة الرغيف (مثلاً) المحمّصة

2 [C] a hard layer on the outside of sth: *the Earth's crust* قشرة

crusty /ˈkrʌsti/ *adj* (**crustier**; **crustiest**) **1** having a hard crust (1): *crusty bread* ذو قشرة محمّصة

2 (*informal*) bad-tempered and impatient: *a crusty old professor* سيئ الخلق ، سريع الغضب

crutch /krʌtʃ/ *noun* [C] **1** a type of stick that you put under your arm to help you walk when you have hurt your leg or foot: *to be on crutches* (= to walk using crutches) عكّاز

2 = CROTCH

crux /krʌks/ *noun* [sing.] the most important or difficult part of a problem: *Now we come to the crux of the problem.* صلب الموضوع ، النقطة الأساسيّة

cry¹ /kraɪ/ *verb* (*pres part* **crying**; *3rd pers sing pres* **cries**; *pt, pp* **cried**) **1** [I] to make a noise and produce tears in your eyes, e.g. because you are unhappy or have hurt yourself: *The baby never stops crying.* ○ *The child was crying for* (= because she wanted) *her mother.* ○ *to cry yourself to sleep* ○ *They were crying with cold and hunger.* يبكي

2 [I,T] **cry (out)** to shout or make a loud noise: *'Look,' he cried, 'There they are.'* ○ *to cry out in pain* يصيح ، يصرخ

PHR V **cry out for sth** to need sth very much: *London is crying out for a new transport system.* يكون بأمسّ الحاجة إلى

cry² /kraɪ/ *noun* (*pl.* **cries**) **1** [C] a shout or loud noise: *the cries of the children in the playground* ○ *the cry of a seagull* ○ *a cry of pain, fear, joy, etc.* صيحة ، صرخة

2 [sing.] an act of crying¹ (1): *After a good cry I felt much better.* (نوبة) بكاء

IDM **a far cry from sth/from doing sth** → FAR¹

crying /ˈkraɪɪŋ/ *adj* (only *before* a noun) very great (usually used when talking about a bad situation, etc.): *There's a crying need for more doctors.* ○ *It's a crying shame that so many young people can't find jobs.* ملحّ : هائل ، فظيع

crypt /krɪpt/ *noun* [C] a room that is under a church, where dead people are sometimes buried سرداب تحت كنيسة

cryptic /ˈkrɪptɪk/ *adj* having a hidden meaning that is not easy to understand; mysterious: *a cryptic message, remark, etc.* غامض ، سرّي

crystal /ˈkrɪstl/ *noun* **1** [U] a transparent rock or mineral بِلّور

2 [U] very high-quality glass: *a crystal vase* زجاج كريستال

3 [C] a regular shape that some mineral substances form when they are solid: *salt crystals* بِلّورة

ˌcrystal ˈball *noun* [C] a glass ball in which some people believe you can see what is going to happen in the future كرة بلّورية لرؤية الطالع

ˌcrystal ˈclear *adj* very easy to understand: *The meaning is crystal clear.* غاية في الوضوح

cub /kʌb/ *noun* [C] **1** a young fox, bear, lion, tiger or wolf شبل ، جَرْو

2 the Cubs (*US* **the Cub Scouts**) [plural] the part of the Boy Scout organization that is for younger boys الجراميز، الكشافة الصغار السنّ

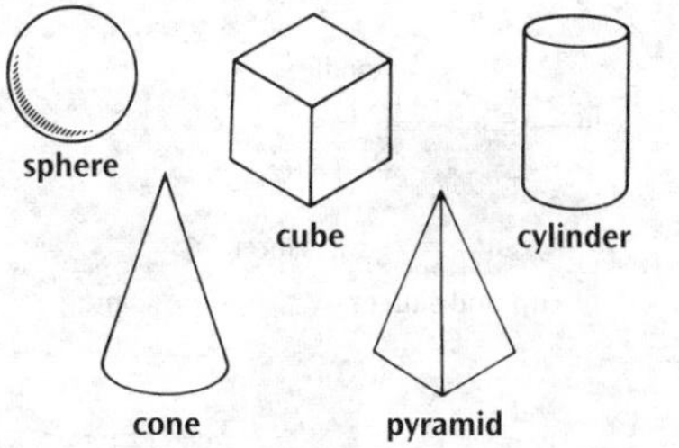

cube /kjuːb/ *noun* [C] **1** a solid shape that has six equal square sides مكعَّب

2 the number that you get if you multiply a number by itself twice: *The cube of 5 (5^3) is 125* (= 5x5x5). مكعَّب

▸ **cube** *verb* [T] (usually passive) to multiply a number by itself twice: *Four cubed (4^3) is 64* (= 4 x 4 x 4). يكعِّب

cubic /ˈkjuːbɪk/ *adj* (*abbr* **cu.**) if a box is 2m long, 2m wide and 2m high, its volume is 8 cubic metres مكعَّب ، تكعيبيّ

cubicle /ˈkjuːbɪkl/ *noun* [C] a small separate section of a larger room, e.g. for changing in at a swimming pool or trying on clothes in a shop مقصورة أو حجيرة مفصولة عن بقية الغرفة

cuckoo /ˈkʊkuː/ *noun* [C] a bird which makes a sound like its name and which lays its eggs in another bird's nest وقواق

cucumber /ˈkjuːkʌmbə(r)/ *noun* [C,U] a long, thin vegetable with a dark green skin and a soft white inside that is often used in salads خيار ، قثّاء

cuddle /ˈkʌdl/ *verb* [I,T] to hold (sb/sth/each other) closely in your arms as a sign of love: *She cuddled her baby until he fell asleep.* يحتضن ، يضمّ إلى صدره

PHR V **cuddle up (to/against sb/sth)**; **cuddle up (together)** to move close to sb and sit or lie comfortably: *She cuddled up to her mother on the sofa.* ○ *They cuddled up together for warmth.* يستكنّ إلى جانبه

▸ **cuddle** *noun* [C]: *He gave the child a cuddle and kissed her goodnight.* ضمّة ، عناق

cuddly /ˈkʌdli/ (**cuddlier**; **cuddliest**) *adj* soft and pleasant to hold close to you: *a cuddly toy* طريّ مستحب ويغري بالمعانقة

cue[1] /kjuː/ *noun* [C] **1** a word or gesture that is the signal for sb else to say or do sth, especially in a play: *When Julia puts the tray on the table, that's your cue to come on stage.* إشارة خاصة ليبدأ (الممثل) دوره

2 an example of how to behave: *I wasn't sure how to behave at a Japanese wedding, so I took my cue from my hosts.* مثال ، نموذج

IDM **(right) on cue** at exactly the moment expected في اللحظة المناسبة

cue[2] /kjuː/ *noun* [C] a long, thin wooden stick, used to hit the ball in games like snooker and billiards عصا البلياردو

cuff[1] /kʌf/ *noun* [C] the end part of a sleeve, which often fastens at the wrist اسوارة أو طرف الكمّ

IDM **off the cuff** (used about a remark, etc.) without previous thought or preparation: *I haven't got the figures here, but, off the cuff, I'd say the rise is about 10%.* ارتجالاً

cuff[2] /kʌf/ *verb* [T] to hit sth (especially sb's head) lightly with your open hand يصفع صفعة خفيفة

cuisine /kwɪˈziːn/ *noun* [U] a style of cooking: *Italian cuisine* ⓘ A less formal word is **cooking**. فنّ الطبخ

cul-de-sac /ˈkʌl də sæk/ *noun* [C] (*pl.* **cul-de-sacs**) a street that is closed at one end طريق غير نافذ

culinary /ˈkʌlɪnəri; *US* -neri/ *adj* connected with cooking متعلّق بالطبخ ، مطبخيّ

cull /kʌl/ *verb* [T] **1** to reduce the size of a group of animals such as deer, by killing its weakest members يقلّل من عدد القطيع بقتل الضعيف منه

2 to gather or select information, ideas, etc., from different sources يجمع ، ينتقي

culminate /ˈkʌlmɪneɪt/ *verb* [I] (*formal*) **culminate in sth** to reach a final result or high point: *The team's efforts culminated in victory in the championships.* ينتهي بِ ، يتوج بِ ؛ يبلغ الذروة

▸ **culmination** /ˌkʌlmɪˈneɪʃn/ *noun* [sing.]: *The joint space mission was the culmination of years of research.* أوج ، ذروة ؛ خاتمة

culottes /kjuːˈlɒts/ *noun* [plural] women's wide shorts that look like a skirt: *a pair of culottes* "الكولوت": مزيج من بنطلون قصير وتنّورة

culpable /ˈkʌlpəbl/ *adj* (*formal*) guilty; deserving blame مذنب ، جدير باللوم

culprit /ˈkʌlprɪt/ *noun* [C] a person who has done sth wrong الجاني ، المذنب

cult /kʌlt/ *noun* [C] **1** a type of religion or religious group, especially one that is considered unusual دين ؛ طائفة دينيّة

2 a person or thing that has become popular with a particular group of people: *His books have become a cult among young people.* موضع إعجاب جمهور معين

cultivate /ˈkʌltɪveɪt/ *verb* [T] **1** to prepare and use land for growing crops: *to cultivate the soil* يفلح ، يحرث

2 to grow crops: *Olives have been cultivated for centuries in Mediterranean countries.* يزرع

3 to try hard to develop sth: *He cultivated links with colleagues abroad.* ينمّي، يطوّر

4 to try to form a friendship with sb who could be useful to you يسعى لمصادقة شخص للاستفادة منه

▸ **cultivated** *adj* **1** well educated, with good manners مثقّف ، مهذّب

2 (used about land) used for growing plants for food or to sell (أرض) مهيّأة للزراعة

3 (used about plants) grown on a farm not wild (نباتات) مزروعة (أي عكس البرّيّة)

cultivation /ˌkʌltɪˈveɪʃn/ *noun* [U] زراعة ؛ تنمية

⚷cultural /ˈkʌltʃərəl/ *adj* **1** connected with the

customs, ideas, art, etc. of a society: *cultural identities* ○ *The country's cultural diversity is a result of taking in immigrants from all over the world.* ثقافيّ، حضاريّ

2 connected with art, music, literature, etc: *The city has a rich cultural life, with many theatres, concert halls and art galleries.* ثقافي

▸ **culturally** /-rəli/ *adv* من الوجهة الحضاريّة؛ ثقافياً

⚷**culture** /ˈkʌltʃə(r)/ *noun* **1** [C,U] the customs, ideas, civilization, etc. of a particular society or group of people: *the language and culture of the Aztecs* ○ *The international conference aims to bring together people from many different cultures.* حضارة

2 [U] achievement in or understanding of art, literature, ideas, etc: *London has always been a centre of culture.* ○ *a man/woman of culture* ثقافة

3 [U] the growing of plants or the keeping of certain types of animals إستنبات

▸ **cultured** *adj* well-educated, showing a good knowledge of the arts, etc: *a cultured manner, mind, person, etc.* مثقف؛ مهذّب؛ مطّلع على الفنون والآداب

ˈ**culture shock** *noun* [U] a feeling of confusion, etc. that you may experience when you go to a country that is very different from your own صدمة حضاريّة

cum /kʌm/ *prep* (used for linking two nouns) also used as; as well as: *a bedroom-cum-study* مع، إضافة إلى كونه

cumbersome /ˈkʌmbəsəm/ *adj* **1** heavy and difficult to carry, use, wear, etc. ثقيل ومربك

2 (used about a system, etc.) slow; too complicated to be efficient: *Collection of the new tax proved cumbersome.* معقّد وبطيء

cumin /ˈkʌmɪn/ *noun* [U] a plant whose seeds are used as a spice in cooking كمّون

cumulative /ˈkjuːmjələtɪv; *US* -leɪtɪv/ *adj* increasing steadily in amount, degree, etc: *a cumulative effect* تراكميّ، متزايد

cunning /ˈkʌnɪŋ/ *adj* clever, especially at deceiving people: *a cunning liar* ○ *a cunning trick* ماكر، شاطر

▸ **cunning** *noun* [U] cunning behaviour مكر، دهاء

cunningly *adv* بمكر وذكاء، بدهاء

⚷**cup**[1] /kʌp/ *noun* [C] **1** a small deep container with a round base and usually a handle, used for drinking liquids: *a cup and saucer* ○ *a teacup* ○ *a cup of coffee* فنجان، كوب

2 (in sport) a large metal cup given as a prize; the competition for such a cup: *Our team won the cup in the basketball tournament.* ○ *Is Scotland in the World Cup?* كأس (البطولة مثلاً)

3 an object shaped like a cup: *an egg cup* وعاء يشبه الفنجان

IDM **(not) sb's cup of tea** not what sb likes or is interested in: *Horror films aren't my cup of tea.* ما يوافق مزاج المرء، هوى

cup[2] /kʌp/ *verb* (cupping; cupped) [T] to form sth, especially your hands, into the shape of a cup; to hold sth with your hands shaped like a cup: *I cupped my hands to take a drink from the stream.* ○ *to cup your chin in your hands* يجعله على شكل كوب؛ يضم بين كفّيه

cup and saucer

mug

plastic cup/beaker

⚷**cupboard** /ˈkʌbəd/ *noun* [C] a piece of furniture, usually with shelves inside and a door or doors at the front, used for storing food, clothes, etc: *a kitchen cupboard* ○ *built-in cupboards* خزانة، دولاب

curable /ˈkjʊərəbl/ *adj* that can be cured: *a curable disease* ❶ The opposite is **incurable**. قابل للشفاء

curate /ˈkjʊərət/ *noun* [C] a priest of the lowest rank in the Church of England, who helps the vicar of a church district (parish) قسّ، مساعد الخوري

curator /kjʊəˈreɪtə(r)/ *noun* [C] a person whose job is to look after the things that are kept in a museum, art gallery, etc. أمين (المكتبة)، قيّم

⚷**curb** /kɜːb/ *noun* [C] **1 a curb (on sth)** something that controls or puts a limit on sth else: *a curb on local government spending* كابح؛ شكيمة

2 (*especially US*) = KERB

▸ **curb** *verb* [T] to control or set a limit on sth: *The law aims to curb pollution of rivers.* يكبح، يحدّ من

curd /kɜːd/ *noun* [U] (*also* **curds** [plural]) a thick soft substance formed when milk turns sour, used in making cheese: *curds and whey* مختّر اللبن؛ روبة

curdle /ˈkɜːdl/ *verb* [I,T] to turn sour or to separate into different parts; to make something do this: (*figurative*) *The scream made her blood curdle* (= made her very frightened). ➲ Look at **blood-curdling**. يتخثّر؛ يخثّر

⚷**cure**[1] /kjʊə(r)/ *verb* [T] **1 cure sb (of sth)** to make sb healthy again: *The treatment cured him of cancer.* ○ *The doctors couldn't cure her.* يشفي

2 to make an illness, injury, etc. end or disappear: *It is still not possible to cure the common cold.* ○ (*figurative*) *The plumber cured the problem with the central heating.* يعالج، يداوي

3 to make certain types of food last longer by drying, smoking or salting them: *cured meat* يحفظ الطعام بالتقديد أو التمليح وغيره

⚷**cure**[2] /kjʊə(r)/ *noun* [C] **1** a medicine or treatment that can cure an illness, etc: *There is no known cure for AIDS.* علاج ، دواء

2 a return to good health; the process of being cured: *The new drug brought about a miraculous cure.* شفاء

curfew /'kɜːfjuː/ *noun* [C] a time after which people are not allowed to go outside their homes, e.g. during a war: *The government imposed a curfew.* منع أو حظر التجول

curiosity /ˌkjʊəri'ɒsəti/ *noun* [C,U] (*pl.* **curiosities**) **1** [U] a desire to know or learn: *I was full of curiosity about their plans.* ○ *Out of curiosity, he opened her letter.* حبّ الاستطلاع ، فضول

2 [C] an unusual and interesting person or thing: *The museum was full of historical curiosities.* طُرفة

⚿ **curious** /'kjʊəriəs/ *adj* **1** eager to know or learn as much as you can: *He was curious to know how the machine worked.* محبّ الاستطلاع

2 too interested in other people's affairs: *Don't be so curious – it's got nothing to do with you.* فضوليّ

3 unusual or strange: *As I was walking home, a curious thing happened.* غريب ، عجيب

▸ **curiously** *adv*: *Curiously enough, we discovered that we had exactly the same name.* من العجيب : بفضول

⚿ **curl¹** /kɜːl/ *noun* [C] **1** a piece of hair that curves round: *Her hair fell in curls round her face.* خصلة شعر ملتفة

2 a thing that has a curved round shape: *a curl of blue smoke* شيء ملتوٍ ، عكفة

▸ **curly** *adj* (**curlier**; **curliest**) full of curls; shaped like a curl: *curly hair* ❶ The opposite is **straight**. مجعّد : ملتوٍ أو ملتفّ

⚿ **curl²** /kɜːl/ *verb* **1** [I,T] to form or to make sth form into a curl or curls: *Does your hair curl naturally?* ○ *The pages had curled with age.* ○ *He curled his lip and laughed scornfully.* يتجعّد ، يلتوي : يلفّ

2 [I] to move round in a curve: *The snake curled around his arm.* يلتفّ

PHR V **curl up** to pull your arms, legs and head close to your body: *I like to curl up on the couch and watch TV.* ○ *The animal curled up into a ball to protect itself.* يتكوّر

▸ **curler** *noun* [C] a small plastic or metal tube that you wrap hair around in order to make it curly لفّافة شعر

currant /'kʌrənt/ *noun* [C] **1** a very small dried grape used to make cakes, etc. زبيب صغير ، كِشْمش

2 (often in compounds) one of several types of small soft fruit: *blackcurrants* كِشْمش

currency /'kʌrənsi/ *noun* (*pl.* **currencies**) **1** [C,U] the system or type of money that a particular country uses: *The currency of Argentina is the austral.* ○ *foreign currency* ○ *a weak, strong, stable, etc. currency* عملة ، نقد

2 [U] the state of being believed, accepted or used by many people: *The new ideas soon gained currency.* شيوع ، قبول

⚿ **current¹** /'kʌrənt/ *adj* **1** of the present time; happening now: *current fashions* ○ *current events* حاليّ ، جارٍ

2 generally accepted; in common use: *Is this word still current?* متداول ، شائع

▸ **currently** *adv* at present: *He is currently working in Spain.* حالياً

⚿ **current²** /'kʌrənt/ *noun* **1** [C] a continuous flowing movement of water, air, etc: *to swim against/with the current* ○ *You shouldn't swim in the river. There are dangerous currents.* ○ (*figurative*) *a current of anti-government feeling* تيّار

2 [U] the flow of electricity through a wire, etc: *Turn on the current.* تيّار

'current account (*US* **checking account**) *noun* [C] a bank account from which you can take out money with a cheque book or cash card حساب جارٍ

ˌcurrent af'fairs *noun* [plural] important political or social events that are happening at the present time قضايا الساعة ، الأحداث الجارية

curriculum /kə'rɪkjələm/ *noun* [C] (*pl.* **curriculums** or **curricula** /-lə/) all the subjects that are taught in a school, college or university; the contents of a particular course of study: *Latin is not on the curriculum at our school.* ○ *The curriculum for foreign languages emphasizes communication skills.* منهج دراسيّ

curriculum vitae /kəˌrɪkjələm 'viːtaɪ/ (*abbr* **CV**) (*US also* **résumé**) *noun* [sing.] a short account of your education and work experience, often used when you are applying for a new job بيان السيرة

curry /'kʌri/ *noun* [C,U] (*pl.* **curries**) a hot-tasting dish of meat, vegetables, etc. usually served with rice: *some Indian vegetable curry* ○ *a hot/mild curry* الكَري: طبق مبهّر حارّ

▸ **curried** *adj* made into a curry: *curried chicken* مضاف إليه بهارات "الكري"

'curry powder *noun* [U] a fine mixture of strongly flavoured substances (spices) that is used to make curry بهارات "الكري"

curse¹ /kɜːs/ *noun* [C] **1** a word used for expressing anger; a swear word شتيمة

2 a word or words expressing the wish that sth terrible will happen to sb: *The witch put a curse on him.* ○ *The family seemed to be under a curse* (= lots of bad things happened to them). لعنة

3 something that causes great harm: *the curse of drug addiction* بلاء

curse² /kɜːs/ *verb* **1** [I,T] to swear at sb/sth; to use rude language to express your anger: *He dropped the box, cursed, and began to pick up the contents.* ○ *They cursed the traffic, realizing they would be late.* يلعن ، يسبّ

2 [T] to use a curse¹(2) against sb/sth: *She cursed his family.* يستنزل اللعنة على

cursor /'kɜːsə(r)/ *noun* [C] a small sign on a computer screen that you can move to indicate a particular position المؤشّر على شاشة الكمبيوتر

a b c d e f g h i j k l m n o p q r s t u v w x y z

cursory /ˈkɜːsəri/ *adj* quick and brief; done in a hurry: *a cursory glance* سريع خاطف ، عابر : متعجّل

curt /kɜːt/ *adj* short and not polite: *She gave him a curt reply and slammed the phone down.* مقتضب ، جافّ

▸ **curtly** *adv* بجفاء، بشيء من الحدّة
curtness *noun* [U] اقتضاب ، جفاء الردّ

curtail /kɜːˈteɪl/ *verb* [T] to make sth shorter or smaller; to reduce يقصّر : يقلّص
▸ **curtailment** *noun* [C,U] تقصير ، تقليص : قطع

⚷ **curtain** /ˈkɜːtn/ *noun* [C] **1** (*US also* **drape**) a piece of material that you can move sideways to cover a window, etc: *Could you draw the curtains, please?* ○ *lace curtains* ○ *The curtain goes up at 7pm* (= in a theatre, the play begins). ستارة

2 a thing that covers or hides sth: *a curtain of mist* ستار، حجاب : غطاء

PHR V **curtain sth off** to divide a room, etc. with a curtain: *The bed was curtained off from the rest of the room.* يفصل شيئاً بستار ، يجزئ (الغرفة) بالستر

curtsy (*also* **curtsey**) /ˈkɜːtsi/ *noun* [C] (*pl.* **curtsies** or **curtseys**) a movement made by a woman as a sign of respect, done by bending the knees, with one foot behind the other انحناءة احترام (تقوم بها النساء)

▸ **curtsy** (*also* **curtsey**) *verb* (*pres part* **curtsying** or **curtseying**; *3rd pers sing pres* **curtsies** or **curtseys**; *pt, pp* **curtsied** or **curtseyed**) [I] to make a curtsy تنحني احتراماً

⚷ **curve** /kɜːv/ *noun* [C] a line that bends round: *a curve on a graph* خطّ منحنٍ : منعطف
▸ **curve** *verb* [I,T] to bend or to make sth bend in a curve: *The bay curved round to the south.* ○ *a curved line* ينحني ، يتقوّس : يحني أو يقوّس

cushion /ˈkʊʃn/ *noun* [C] **1** a bag filled with soft material, e.g. feathers, which you put on a chair, etc. to make it more comfortable: *She sat back in the armchair with a cushion behind her head.* ⓘ A cushion on a bed is a **pillow**. وسادة ، مخدة

2 something that acts or is shaped like a cushion: *a cushion of air* ميثرة: مخدة واقية
▸ **cushion** *verb* [T] **1** to make a blow, etc. less painful: *The snow cushioned his fall.* يخفّف شدّة الصدمة

2 to reduce the unpleasant effect of sth: *She spent her childhood on a farm, cushioned from the effects of the war.* يقي ، يلطّف ، يخفّف الوطأة

cushy /ˈkʊʃi/ *adj* (**cushier**; **cushiest**) (*informal*) too easy, requiring little effort (to a degree that seems unfair to others): *a cushy job* هيّن ليّن

custard /ˈkʌstəd/ *noun* [U] a sweet yellow sauce made from milk and cornflour and eaten hot or cold: *apple pie and custard* "كستردة"

custodian /kʌˈstəʊdiən/ *noun* [C] (*formal*) a person who looks after sth, especially a museum, library, etc. قيّم ، أمين ، سادن

custody /ˈkʌstədi/ *noun* [U] **1** the legal right or duty to take care of sb/sth: *After the divorce, the mother was given custody of the children.* رعاية ، وصاية

2 the state of being guarded, or kept in prison temporarily, especially by the police: *The man was arrested and kept in custody until his trial.* اعتقال ، حجز

⚷ **custom** /ˈkʌstəm/ *noun* **1** [C,U] a way of behaving which a particular group or society has had for a long time: *It's the custom in Britain for a bride to throw her bouquet to the wedding guests.* ○ *according to local custom* ➲ Look at the note at **habit**. عادة ، عرف ، تقليد

2 [C] something that a person regularly does: *They were walking through the park, as was their custom, when a large dog attacked them.* عادة

3 [U] trade; the practice of people buying things regularly from a particular shop, etc: *The local shop lost a lot of custom when the new supermarket opened.* زبانة ، تعامل مع متجر معيّن

customary /ˈkʌstəməri; *US* -meri/ *adj* according to custom; usual: *Is it customary to tip hairdressers in your country?* معتاد ، متعارف عليه
▸ **customarily** /ˈkʌstəmərəli; *US* ˌkʌstəˈmerəli/ *adv* عادة

⚷ **customer** /ˈkʌstəmə(r)/ *noun* [C] **1** a person who buys goods or services: *a regular customer* ○ *The shop assistant was serving a customer.* زبون

2 (*informal*) (after certain adjectives) a person: *a tough, awkward, odd, etc. customer* شخص (غريب، شاذ الخ)

⚷ **customs** (*also* **the Customs**) /ˈkʌstəmz/ *noun* [plural] the place at an airport, etc. where government officials check your luggage to see whether you are bringing goods into the country illegally: *We went straight through customs with nothing to declare.* ○ *a customs officer* الجمرك

⚷ **cut**[1] /kʌt/ *verb* (*pres part* **cutting**; *pt, pp* **cut**) **1** [I,T] to make an opening, wound or mark in sth using a sharp tool, e.g. a pair of scissors or a knife: *I cut my finger with a vegetable knife.* ○ *Be careful not to cut yourself on that broken glass!* ○ *This knife doesn't cut very well.* يجرح : يقطع

2 [T] to remove sth or a part of sth, using a knife, etc: *She cut two slices of bread (from the loaf).* يقطع

3 [T] **cut sth (in/into sth)** to divide sth into pieces with a knife, etc: *She cut the cake into eight (pieces).* ○ *He cut the rope in two.* يقطّع ، يقسم

4 [T] to make sth shorter by using scissors, etc: *I cut my own hair.* ○ *to have your hair cut* (= at the hairdressers). ○ *to cut the grass* يقصّ

5 [T] to make or form sth by removing material with a sharp tool: *She cut a hole in the card and pushed the string through.* ○ *They cut a path through the jungle.* يثقب ، يحفر : يفتح (طريقاً)

6 [T] to reduce sth or make it shorter; to remove sth: *to cut taxes* ○ *Train services have been cut because of the strike.* ○ *Several violent scenes in the film were cut.* يقلّل ، يخفّض : يحذف

7 [T] (*computing*) to remove a piece of text from the screen: *Use the cut and paste buttons to change the order of the paragraphs.* يحذف

IDM **cut sth/sb short** → SHORT[2]

PHR V **cut across sth** to go beyond the limits

of: *The question of aid for the earthquake victims cuts across national boundaries.* يتجاوز ، يتخطّى حدود...

cut across, along, through, etc. (sth) to go across, etc. sth, in order to shorten your journey: *It's much quicker if we cut across the field.* يسلك طريقاً مختصراً

cut sth back; cut back (on sth) to reduce sth: *to cut back on public spending* يقلّل ، ينقّص

cut sth down 1 to make sth fall down by cutting it: *to cut down a tree* يقطع (شجرة)

2 to shorten sth: *I have to cut my essay down to 2 000 words.* يختصر ، يقصّر

cut sth down; cut down (on sth) to reduce the quantity or amount of sth; to do sth less often: *You should cut down on fatty foods.* يخفّف من ، يقلّل

cut in (on sb/sth); cut into sth to interrupt sb/sth: *to cut into a conversation* يقاطع (الحديث)

cut sb off (often passive) to stop or interrupt sb's telephone conversation: *We were cut off before I could give her my message.* يقطع الاتصال التليفوني

cut sb/sth off (often passive) to stop the supply of sth to sb: *If you don't pay your gas bill they'll cut you off.* ○ *The electricity has been cut off.* يقطع

cut sth off to block a road, etc. so that nothing can pass: *We must cut off all possible escape routes.* يسدّ ، يقطع

cut sb/sth off (from sb/sth) (often passive) to prevent sb/sth from moving from a place or contacting people outside: *The farm was cut off from the village by heavy snow.* يقطع ، يعزل

cut sth open to open sth by cutting: *She fell and cut her head open.* يشقّ

cut sth out 1 to remove sth or to form sth into a particular shape by cutting: *to cut out a dress from a piece of cloth* يفصل : يفصّل (ثوباً مثلاً)

2 to leave sth out: *Cut out the boring details!* يحذف

3 (*informal*) (often in orders) to stop saying or doing sth, usually sth annoying: *Cut that out and leave me alone!* يتوقّف عن

4 (*informal*) to stop doing or using sth: *You'll only lose weight if you cut out sweet things from your diet.* يلغي ، يترك

cut sth out (of sth) to remove sth from sth larger by cutting: *He cut the job advertisement out of the newspaper.* يقص ، يقتطع

be cut out for sth; be cut out to be sth to have the qualities to be able to do sth; to be suitable for sth/sb: *You're not cut out to be a soldier.* ○ *David and Janet are cut out for each other.* يصلح لـ ؛ يناسب

cut sth up to cut sth into small pieces with a knife, etc. يقطّع

cut² /kʌt/ *noun* [C] **1** a wound or opening made with a knife, etc: *He had a deep cut on his forehead.* جرح

2 an act of cutting: *to have a cut and blow-dry* (= at a hairdresser's) قصّة شَعْر

3 a cut (in sth) a reduction in size, amount, etc: *a cut in government spending* ○ *a power cut* (= when the electric current is cut off temporarily) تخفيض ، تقليل ؛ قطع

4 a piece of meat from a particular part of an animal قطعة لحم

5 (*informal*) a share, especially in profits حصّة (من الأرباح)

cutback /ˈkʌtbæk/ *noun* [C] a reduction in amount or number: *The management were forced to make cutbacks in staff.* تخفيض ، تقليص ، تقليل

cute /kjuːt/ *adj* (*especially US*) attractive; pretty: *Your little girl is so cute!* ○ *a cute smile* محبّب ، جذّاب

cuticle /ˈkjuːtɪkl/ *noun* [C] the piece of hard skin at the base of a nail on a person's finger or toe جُلَيْدة تغطّي منبت الظفر

cutlery

cutlery /ˈkʌtləri/ *noun* [U] the knives, forks and spoons that you use for eating food: *Where do you keep your cutlery?* ➲ Look at **crockery**. السكاكين والملاعق والشوكات

cutlet /ˈkʌtlət/ *noun* [C] a small, thick piece of meat, e.g. lamb, often with bone in it, that is fried or grilled شريحة من لحم الضلوع

ˈcut-off *noun* [C] the level at which sth stops: *The cut-off date is 12 May. After that we'll end the offer.* آخر موعد (للطلبات) : الحد الأقصى

ˌcut-ˈprice (*US* **ˌcut-ˈrate**) *adj* sold at a reduced price; selling goods at low prices: *cut-price offers* ○ *a cut-price store* (سعر) مخفّض

cutter /ˈkʌtə(r)/ *noun* [C] (*also* **cutters** [plural]) a tool that you use for cutting through sth, e.g. metal: *a pair of wire-cutters* آلة قاطعة

cut-throat /ˈkʌtθrəʊt/ *adj* caring only about success and not worried about hurting anybody: *cut-throat business practices* قاسٍ لا يرحم ، عنيف

cutting¹ /ˈkʌtɪŋ/ *noun* [C] **1** (*US* **clipping**) a piece cut out from a newspaper, etc: *press cuttings* قُصاصة من جريدة

2 a piece cut off from a plant that you use for growing a new plant فسيلة أو "فسخ" من نبات

cutting² /ˈkʌtɪŋ/ *adj* **1** (used about sth you say) unkind; meant to hurt sb's feelings: *a cutting remark* جارح ، قاسٍ

2 (of the wind, etc.) cold, strong and unpleasant قارص ، لاذع

CV /ˌsiː ˈviː/ *abbrev* = CURRICULUM VITAE

cwt. *abbrev* = HUNDREDWEIGHT

cyanide /ˈsaɪənaɪd/ *noun* [U] a poisonous chemical السيانيد: مادّة سامّة

cybercrime /ˈsaɪbəkraɪm/ *noun* [U,C] crime that is committed using the Internet, for example by stealing sb's personal or bank details or infecting their computer with a virus الجريمة الإلكترونية

cyberspace /ˈsaɪbəspeɪs/ *noun* [U] a place that is not real, where electronic messages exist while they are being sent from one computer to another الفضاء الالكتروني

cycle /ˈsaɪkl/ *noun* [C] **1** a series of events, etc. that happen repeatedly in the same order: *the life cycle of a frog* دورة

2 a bicycle or motorcycle: *a cycle shop* درّاجة

▶ **cycle** *verb* [I] to ride a bicycle: *He usually cycles to school.* ⓘ **Go cycling** is a common way of talking about cycling for pleasure: *We like to go cycling at weekends.* يركب درّاجة

cyclist /ˈsaɪklɪst/ *noun* [C] a person who rides a bicycle راكب درّاجة

cyclic /ˈsaɪklɪk; ˈsɪk-/ (*also* **cyclical** /ˈsaɪklɪkl; ˈsɪk-/) *adj* following a repeated pattern دَوْري

cyclone /ˈsaɪkləʊn/ *noun* [C] a violent wind that moves in a circle causing a storm ➲ Look at the note at **storm**. إعصار ، زوبعة دوّارة أو حلزونيّة

cygnet /ˈsɪɡnət/ *noun* [C] a young swan فرخ التّم (البجع)

cylinder /ˈsɪlɪndə(r)/ *noun* [C] **1** a shape or an object with circular ends and straight sides اسطوانة

2 a cylinder-shaped part of an engine, e.g. in a car: *a five-cylinder engine* اسطوانة ، "سلندر"

▶ **cylindrical** /səˈlɪndrɪkl/ *adj* having the shape of a cylinder اسطواني

cymbal /ˈsɪmbl/ *noun* [C, usually pl.] one of a pair of round metal plates used as a musical instrument. Cymbals make a loud ringing sound when you strike them together or hit them with a stick. صَنْج

cynic /ˈsɪnɪk/ *noun* [C] a person who believes that people only do things for selfish reasons: *Don't be such a cynic. He did it to help us, not for the money.* المستخِفّ بنوايا الآخرين ، المتهكِّم

▶ **cynical** /ˈsɪnɪkl/ *adj*: *She takes a cynical view of politics.* ○ *a cynical remark* مستخفّ بنوايا الآخرين ، تهكّمي

cynically /-kli/ *adv* بصورة تهكميّة الاستخفاف بالدنيا ؛

cynicism /ˈsɪnɪsɪzəm/ *noun* [U] الشكّ بوجود الخير

cypress /ˈsaɪprəs/ *noun* [C] a tall straight tree of the kind that does not lose its leaves in winter (an evergreen) السرو

Cyrillic /sɪˈrɪlɪk/ *adj* the Cyrillic alphabet is used in languages such as Russian (الأبجدية) السيريليّة

cyst /sɪst/ *noun* [C] a swelling filled with liquid in the body or under the skin كيس (طبّ)

Dd

D, d /diː/ *noun* [C] (*pl.* **Ds**; **D's**; **d's**) the fourth letter of the English alphabet: *'David' begins with (a) 'D'.* الحرف الرابع من الأبجدية الإنكليزية

d. *abbrev* = DIED

dab /dæb/ *verb* (dab**b**ing; dab**b**ed) [I,T] to touch sth lightly, usually several times: *He dabbed the cut with some cotton wool.* يلمس أو يمسح مسحاً خفيفاً

PHR V **dab sth on/off (sth)** to put sth on or to remove sth with a light stroke or strokes: *to dab some antiseptic on a wound* يدهن ؛ يمسح

▶ **dab** *noun* [C] **1** a light touch: *She gave her eyes a dab with a handkerchief.* مسحة خفيفة

2 a small quantity of sth that is put on a surface: *a dab of paint, perfume, etc.* قليل من ، "نقطة"

dabble /ˈdæbl/ *verb* **1** [T] to put your hands, feet, etc. in water and move them around: *We sat on the bank and dabbled our toes in the river.* يُطبِّش أو "يبلبط" في الماء

2 [I] to become involved in sth in a manner that is not very serious: *to dabble in politics* يقوم بعمل كهواية

dachshund /ˈdækshnd; *US* ˈdɑːkshʊnd/ *noun* [C] a small dog with a long body and short legs كلب صغير قصير القوائم

dad /dæd/ *noun* [C] (*informal*) father: *Is that your dad?* ○ *Come on, Dad!* أب ؛ بابا

daddy /ˈdædi/ *noun* (*pl.* **daddies**) (*informal*) (used by children) father: *I want my daddy!* ○ *Give daddy a kiss.* أب ؛ بابا

daffodil /ˈdæfədɪl/ *noun* [C] a tall yellow flower that grows from a bulb in the spring نرجس بري أو كاذب

daft /dɑːft; *US* dæft/ *adj* (*informal*) silly; foolish: *Don't be daft.* ○ *a daft idea* سخيف ؛ أحمق

dagger /ˈdæɡə(r)/ *noun* [C] a type of knife with a point and two sharp edges used as a weapon, especially in former times: *He plunged a dagger into her heart.* خنجر

daily /ˈdeɪli/ *adj, adv* done, made or happening every day: *Our airline flies to Japan daily.* ○ *a daily routine, delivery, newspaper, etc.* يوميّ ؛ يوميًّا

▶ **daily** *noun* [C] (*pl.* **dailies**) a newspaper that is published every day except Sunday جريدة يوميّة

dainty /ˈdeɪnti/ *adj* (**daintier**; **daintiest**) small or delicate and pretty: *a dainty lace handkerchief* رقيق ، لطيف ، أنيق

▸ **daintily** *adv*: *She walked daintily, with graceful little steps.* بخفّة ، برشاقة

dairy /ˈdeəri/ *noun* [C] (*pl.* **dairies**) **1** a place on a farm where milk is kept and butter, cheese, etc. are made معمل ألبان

2 a shop which sells milk, butter, eggs, etc., or a company that supplies shops with these products مخزن بيع الألبان

ˈ**dairy cattle** *noun* [U] cows which are kept for their milk, not their meat ماشية اللبن

ˈ**dairy farm** *noun* [C] a farm that produces mainly milk and milk products مزرعة ألبان

ˈ**dairy products** *noun* [plural] food made from milk, such as butter, cheese, etc. منتوجات الألبان

daisy /ˈdeɪzi/ *noun* [C] (*pl.* **daisies**) a small white flower with a yellow centre, which usually grows wild on grass أقحوان المروج ، زهرة الربيع

dale /deɪl/ *noun* [C] a valley, especially in Northern England وادٍ (في شمال انكلترة خاصّة)

dalmatian /dælˈmeɪʃn/ *noun* [C] a large dog with short white hair marked with dark spots كلب دَلْماسي

dam /dæm/ *noun* [C] a wall built across a river to hold back the water and form a lake (reservoir) behind it سدّ

▸ **dam** *verb* [T] يبني سداً

⚷**damage** /ˈdæmɪdʒ/ *noun* **1** [U] **damage (to sth)** harm or injury caused when sth is broken or spoiled: *The earthquake caused widespread damage* ○ *It will take weeks to repair the damage done by the vandals.* ○ *The arms scandal did considerable damage to relations between the two countries.* ضرر ، تلف

2 damages [plural] money that you can claim from sb if he/she damages sth of yours or hurts you تعويض ماليّ ، عطَل وضرَر

▸ **damage** *verb* [T] to spoil or harm sth, e.g. by breaking it: *The roof was damaged by the storm.* يحدث ضرراً ؛ يؤذي

damaging *adj* having a bad or harmful effect ضارّ ، مؤذٍ

dame /deɪm/ *noun* [C] **1 Dame** (*Brit*) a title given to a woman as an honour because of sth special that she has done: *Dame Ellen MacArthur* (في بريطانيا) لقب شرف للنساء

2 (*US old-fashioned informal*) a woman سيّدة ، امرأة

damn[1] /dæm/ *verb* [T] **1** (*informal*) (used for expressing anger or annoyance): *Damn that stupid driver!* ○ *Damn! I've left my money behind.* يلعن

2 to describe sth as very bad: *The film was damned by all the critics.* يذمّ ذمّاً شديداً

3 (used about God) to send sb to hell يخلّده في الجحيم

▸ **the damned** *noun* [plural] the people who suffer in hell: *The film was called 'The Journey of the Damned'.* أهل النار ، المعذّبون في الجحيم

damning *adj* very unfavourable; extremely critical: *There was a damning article about the book in the newspaper.* عنيف بانتقاده ، مليء بالذمّ

damn[2] /dæm/ *noun*

IDM not care/give a damn (about sb/sth) (*informal*) not care at all: *I don't give a damn what he thinks about me.* لا يهتم أبداً

▸ **damn** *adj* (only *before* a noun) (*informal*) (used for expressing anger or annoyance): *Some damn fool has parked too close to me.* (تستعمل للتعبير عن الغضب أو الانزعاج): لعين

damn *adv* (*informal*) (used for emphasizing that sth is good or bad) very: *Don't be so damn silly!* ○ *Read it! It's a damn good book.* جداً

⚷**damp**[1] /dæmp/ *adj* a little wet: *The grass is a bit damp. Sit on the rug.* ○ *The house had been empty and felt rather damp.* رطب

▸ **damp** *noun* [U] the state of being a little wet, especially in the air or in a house: *She hated the damp and the cold of the English climate.* ○ *We inspected the walls for signs of damp.* ➲ Look at the note at **wet**. رطوبة

damp[2] /dæmp/ *verb* [T] **damp sth (down)** to make sth less strong or urgent: *He tried to damp down their expectations in case they failed.* يخفّف ، يخمد ؛ يثبّط الهمّة

dampen /ˈdæmpən/ *verb* [T] **1 dampen sth (down)** to make sth less strong or urgent: *Even the awful weather did not dampen their enthusiasm for the trip.* يخفّف، يخمد ؛ يثبّط العزيمة

2 to make sth a little wet: *He dampened his hair to try to stop it sticking up.* يبلّل ، يندّي

damson /ˈdæmzn/ *noun* [C] a small dark purple fruit; a type of plum نوع من البرقوق/الخوخ/الاجاص

⚷**dance**[1] /dɑːns; *US* dæns/ *noun* **1** [C] a series of steps and movements which you do to music: *What sort of dance is this? A waltz?* ○ *Would you like a dance?* رقصة

2 [C] a social meeting at which people dance with each other: *There's usually a dance at the end of term.* رقص ، حفلة راقصة

3 [U] dancing as a form of art or entertainment: *She's very interested in modern dance.* رقص

⚷**dance**[2] /dɑːns; *US* dæns/ *verb* **1** [I,T] to move around to the rhythm of music by making a series of steps: *I can't dance very well.* ○ *to dance the waltz* يرقص

2 [I] to move in a lively way, usually up and down: *She was dancing up and down with excitement.* يقفز (فرحاً) ، "يتنطّط"

▸ **dancer** *noun* [C] a person who dances, often as a job: *a ballet dancer* ○ *She's a good dancer.* راقص أو راقصة

dancing *noun* [U] moving to music: *Will there be dancing at the party?* ➲ Look at **ballet**. رقص

dandelion /ˈdændɪlaɪən/ *noun* [C] a small wild plant with a bright yellow flower هندباء بريّة ، طرخشقون

dandruff /ˈdændrʌf/ *noun* [U] small pieces of dead skin in the hair, that look like white dust قشرة الرأس ، هبريّة

⚷**danger** /ˈdeɪndʒə(r)/ *noun* **1** [U] the chance that

sb/sth may be hurt, killed or damaged or that sth unpleasant may happen: *Danger! Steep hill!* ○ *As a fighter pilot, he had to face danger daily.* ○ *The men kept on running until they thought they were out of danger.* خطر

2 [C] **a danger (to sb/sth)** a person or thing that can cause injury, pain or damage: *Careless drivers are a danger to everyone on the road.* خطر

dangerous /ˈdeɪndʒərəs/ *adj* likely to cause injury or damage: *a dangerous animal, road, illness, etc.* ○ *The strong currents in the sea here are extremely dangerous for swimmers.* خطِر
▸ **dangerously** *adv*: *He was standing dangerously close to the cliff edge.* بصورة تنذر بالخطر

dangle /ˈdæŋgl/ *verb* [I,T] to hang or swing freely; to hold sth so that it hangs in this way: *She sat on the fence with her legs dangling.* ○ *The police dangled a rope from the bridge and the man grabbed it.* يتدلّى ؛ يدلّي

dank /dæŋk/ *adj* damp, cold and unpleasant: *a dank cave* بارد ورطب

dare¹ /deə(r)/ *verb* (usually in negative sentences) to be brave enough to do sth: *I daren't ask her to lend me any more money.* ○ *We were so frightened that we didn't dare go into the room.* ○ *The government dared not increase taxes again that year.* ○ *If you dare say that again, I'll hit you!* يجرؤ ، يتجاسر

> The negative is **dare not** (usually **daren't** /deənt/) or **do not/does not** (= **don't/doesn't**) **dare**. In the past tense it is **did not (didn't) dare**, or (formal) **dared not**. **Dare** is usually followed by an infinitive without 'to': *Nobody dared (to) speak.*

IDM **don't you dare** (used for telling sb very strongly not to do sth): *Don't you dare tell my parents about this.* لا تفعل هذا!
how dare you (used when you are angry about sth that sb has done): *How dare you speak to me like that!* كيف تجرؤ! (تقال بغضب)
I dare say I suppose: *'I think you should accept the offer.' 'I dare say you're right.'* أظنّ ، ربما

dare² /deə(r)/ *verb* [T] to try to persuade sb to do sth in order to prove how brave he/she is: *Can you jump off that wall? Go on, I dare you!* ○ *He dared his friend to put a worm on the teacher's desk.* يتحدّى

dare³ /deə(r)/ *noun* [C, usually sing.] something you do because sb asks you to, to prove how brave you are: *'Why did you try to swim across the river?' 'For a dare.'* تحدٍّ، برهان على الجسارة

daredevil /ˈdeədevl/ *noun* [C] a person who is willing to take risks, often foolishly شخص متهوِّر

daring /ˈdeərɪŋ/ *adj* willing to take risks or to do or say things which other people might not; brave; bold: *a daring attack* جسور ، مخاطِر

dark¹ /dɑːk/ *noun* [sing.] **the dark** the state of having no light: *He's afraid of the dark.* ○ *Why are you sitting alone in the dark?* الظلام ، الظلمة

IDM **before/after dark** before/after the sun goes down قبل أو بعد غياب الشمس
(be/keep sb) in the dark (about sth) (be/keep sb) in a position of not knowing (about sth): *Don't keep me in the dark. Tell me!* يبقي الأمر سراً ، يخفي عنه

dark² /dɑːk/ *adj* **1** with no light or very little light: *It was a dark night, with no moon.* مظلم ، معتم

2 (used about a colour) nearer black than white; not light: *dark blue* قاتم ، داكن

3 (used about a person) having brown or black skin or hair; not fair: *She was small and dark with brown eyes.* أسمر

4 (only *before* a noun) sad; without hope: *the dark days leading up to the start of the war* كئيب ، يائس

5 (only *before* a noun) mysterious or slightly threatening: *He seemed friendly, but there was a dark side to his character.* غامض ، غريب وربما شرّير

IDM **keep it/sth dark (from sb)** to keep sth secret يبقي الأمر سرّاً
▸ **darkness** *noun* [U] the state of being dark: *We sat in complete darkness, waiting for the lights to come back on.* ظلمة ، عتمة

darken /ˈdɑːkən/ *verb* [I,T] to become or to make sth darker: *The sky suddenly darkened and it looked like rain.* يظلم ، يكفهرّ ؛ يعتّم

ˌdark ˈglasses *noun* [plural] = SUNGLASSES

darkroom /ˈdɑːkruːm; -rʊm/ *noun* [C] a room that can be made completely dark so that film can be taken out of a camera and photographs can be produced there غرفة مظلمة (تصوير)

darling /ˈdɑːlɪŋ/ *noun* [C] a person or thing that you like or love: *Hello darling! How lovely to see you.* ○ *He's so kind. He's an absolute darling!* حبيب

darn /dɑːn/ *verb* [I,T] to mend a hole (in clothes) by sewing across it in one direction and then in the other يرفو ، يرتق

dart¹ /dɑːt/ *noun* **1** [C] an object like a small arrow. It is thrown or shot as a weapon or in a game: *They first tranquillize the tiger with a special dart.* نَبْلة ، سهم صغير

2 darts [U] a game in which you throw darts at a round board with numbers on it (a dartboard): *Darts is a popular game in English pubs.* لعبة رمي سهام صغيرة على هدف

dart² /dɑːt/ *verb* [I,T] to move suddenly and quickly in a certain direction; to make sth move in this way: *A rabbit darted across the field.* ○ *She darted an angry glance at me* (= suddenly glanced angrily). ينطلق كالسهم ؛ يرمي أو يقذف فجأة

dash¹ /dæʃ/ *noun* **1** [sing.] a sudden, quick forward movement: *We made a dash for the bus and just got on.* اندفاع مفاجئ

2 [C, usually sing.] a small amount of sth that you add to sth else: *a dash of lemon juice* قليل من ، "رشّة"

3 [C] a small horizontal line (–) used in writing,

especially for adding extra information ➲ Look at **hyphen**. شَرْطة أو قاطعة

dash[2] /dæʃ/ *verb* **1** [I] to go or run suddenly and quickly: *We all dashed for shelter when it started to rain* يندفع فجأة

2 [I,T] to hit sth with great force; to throw sth so that it hits sth else very hard: *The waves dashed against the harbour wall.* ○ *She dashed her racket to the ground.* ○ *(figurative) The accident dashed his hopes of becoming a pianist.*
يرتطم بِ ؛ يحطِّم

PHRV **dash sth off** to write or draw sth very quickly يكتب أو يرسم على عجل

dashboard /ˈdæʃbɔːd/ *noun* [C] the part in a car in front of the driver where most of the switches, etc. are لوحة العدّادات (في السيارة)

data /ˈdeɪtə; ˈdɑːtə (*US also*) ˈdætə/ *noun* [U, plural] facts or information: *to gather data* ○ *The data is/are still being analysed.* ○ *How much data can we store on one disk?* (= on a computer).
معطيات ؛ معلومات؛ بيانات

Data was originally the plural form of a Latin noun, but it is now often used as an uncountable noun: *The data we have is not very interesting.*

database /ˈdeɪtəbeɪs (*US also*) ˈdætə-/ *noun* [C] a large amount of data that is stored in a computer and can easily be used, added to, etc.
قاعدة المعلومات أو البيانات

date[1] /deɪt/ *noun* **1** [C] a particular day of the month or of the year: *What's the date today?* ○ *What date is it today?* ○ *What's your date of birth?* تاريخ

2 [sing.] a particular time: *We can discuss this at a later date.* موعد ، وقت

3 [C] an appointment to meet sb, especially a boyfriend or girlfriend: *Shall we make a date to have lunch together?* ○ *I've got a date with Tom on Friday night.* ميعاد ، موعد لقاء

4 [C] (*especially US*) a boyfriend or girlfriend: *Who's your date – is it Sarah?*
صاحب أو صاحبة (بالمعنى الغرامي)

IDM **out of date 1** unfashionable; no longer useful: *out-of-date methods, machinery, etc.*
قديم العهد ، "موضة" قديمة

2 no longer able to be used: *I must renew my passport. It's out of date.* باطل المفعول

to date (*formal*) until now: *We've had very few complaints to date.* حتى الآن

up to date 1 modern: *The new kitchen will be right up to date, with all the latest gadgets.*
عصريّ، حديث

2 with all the latest information; having done everything that you should have done: *In this report we'll bring you up to date with the latest news from the area.* ○ *Are you up to date with your homework?*
مطّلع على آخر المعلومات؛ مكملاً لواجباته في حينها

date[2] /deɪt/ *verb* **1** [T] to discover or guess how old sth is: *The skeleton has been dated at about 3000 BC.* يحدّد تاريخ أو عمر شيء ما

2 [T] to write the day's date on sth: *The letter is not dated so we can't tell when it was written.*
يؤرِّخ (رسالة)

3 [I,T] to seem, or to make sb/sth seem, unfashionable: *We chose a simple style so that it wouldn't date as quickly.* يقدم عهده، يصبح "موضة" قديمة

4 [I,T] (*especially US informal*) to meet a girlfriend or boyfriend regularly
يواعد فتى أو فتاة بصورة منتظمة

5 [I] **date from.../back to...** to have existed since...: *The house dates back to the seventeenth century.* يرجع عهده إلى

▸ **dated** *adj* unfashionable: *This sort of jacket looks rather dated now.* "موضة" قديمة ، قديم الطراز

date[3] /deɪt/ *noun* [C] a small, sweet, dark brown fruit that comes from a tree which grows in hot countries تمرة ، بلحة

daughter /ˈdɔːtə(r)/ *noun* [C] a female child: *I have two sons and one daughter.* ○ *Janet's daughter is a doctor.* إبنة ، بنت

ˈ**daughter-in-law** *noun* [C] (*pl.* **daughters-in-law**) the wife of your son كَنّة ، زوجة الأبن

daunt /dɔːnt/ *verb* [T] (usually passive) to frighten or to worry sb by being too big or difficult: *I was rather daunted by the sudden responsibility.* يخيف ، يجعله يتهيّب

▸ **daunting** *adj*: *A daunting journey lay ahead.* مرهب

dawdle /ˈdɔːdl/ *verb* [I] to be slow or to move slowly; to waste time: *Stop dawdling! We're waiting for you!* يتباطأ ، يتلكّأ؛ يضيع الوقت

dawn[1] /dɔːn/ *noun* **1** [C,U] the early morning, when light first appears in the sky: *a beautiful winter's dawn, still and cold* ○ *before/at dawn*
فجر ، سَحَر

2 [sing.] the beginning: *the dawn of civilization* مطلع ، بزوغ

IDM **the crack of dawn** → CRACK[1]

dawn[2] /dɔːn/ *verb* [I] **1** to begin to grow light, after the night: *The day dawned bright and cold.* ○ *(figurative) A new era of peace is dawning.*
ينبثق (الفجر) ؛ يبزغ ، يبدأ

2 dawn (on sb) to become clear (to sb): *Suddenly it dawned on her. 'Of course!' she said. 'You're Mike's brother!'* يتّضح الأمر

day /deɪ/ *noun* **1** [C] a period of 24 hours, of which seven make up a week: *'What day is it today?' 'Tuesday.'* ○ *We went to Italy for ten days.* ○ *I saw that film a few days ago.* ○ *There's a meeting in two days' time.* ○ *The next day was Saturday.* ○ *the day before* ○ *the following day* ○ *New Year's Day* يوم

2 [C,U] the time between sunrise and sunset: *The days were warm but the nights were freezing.* ○ *Have a good day! See you tonight.* ○ *It's been raining all day.* ➲ Look at **daily**. نهار

3 [C] the hours of the day when you work: *She's expected to work a seven-hour day.* عدد ساعات العمل

4 [C] (*also* **days**) a particular period of time: *in Shakespeare's day* ○ *in the days of Shakespeare*

○ *In the old days, most houses had an outside toilet.* أيّام ، عهد

IDM **break of day** → BREAK[2]

by day/night during the day/night: *These animals sleep by day and hunt by night.* أثناء النهار

call it a day → CALL[2]

the day after tomorrow not tomorrow, but the next day بعد غد

the day before yesterday not yesterday, but the day before أول أمس

day by day every day; as time passes: *Day by day, she was getting a little bit stronger.* يوماً بعد يوم ؛ كل يوم

day in, day out every day, without any change: *He sits at his desk working, day in, day out.* كلّ يوم دون انقطاع

from day to day; **from one day to the next** within a short period of time: *Things change so quickly that we never know what will happen from one day to the next.* بين عشيّة وضحاها

make sb's day (*informal*) to make sb very happy يسرّ ، يسعد

one day; **some day** at some time in the future: *Some day we'll go back and see all our old friends.* يوماً ما

the other day a few days ago; recently: *I bumped into him in town the other day.* منذ أيّام ، من مدّة قصيرة

the present day → PRESENT[1]

these days in the present age; nowadays: *More and more couples are getting divorced these days.* في هذه الأيّام

daybreak /'deɪbreɪk/ *noun* [U] the time in the early morning when light first appears: *at daybreak* فجر ، انبلاج الصبح

daydream /'deɪdriːm/ *noun* [C] thoughts that are not connected with what you are doing; often pleasant scenes in your imagination: *The child stared out of the window, lost in a daydream.* أحلام اليقظة

▸ **'daydream** *verb* [I] يشرد فكره ، يستغرق في أحلام اليقظة

daylight /'deɪlaɪt/ *noun* [U] the light that there is during the day: *The colours look quite different in daylight.* ○ *daylight hours* ضوء النهار

IDM **broad daylight** → BROAD

ˌday 'off *noun* [C] a day on which you do not go to work: *Wednesday's my day off next week.* يوم عطلة من العمل

ˌday re'turn *noun* [C] (*Brit*) a train or bus ticket which is cheaper than normal. You have to go somewhere and come back on the same day. تذكرة ذهاب وإياب يوميّة

daytime /'deɪtaim/ *noun* [U] the time between sunrise and sunset: *These flowers open in the daytime and close up again at night.* النهار

daze /deɪz/ *verb* [T] (usually passive) to make sb unable to think clearly يذهل ؛ يدوّخ

▸ **daze** *noun*

IDM **in a daze** in a confused state في حالة ذهول

dazed /deɪzd/ *adj* confused; not showing normal reactions: *He had a dazed expression on his face.* مذهول ، مبهوت

dazzle /'dæzl/ *verb* [T] (usually passive) **1** (used about a bright light) to make sb unable to see clearly: *She was dazzled by the other car's headlights.* يخطف أو يبهر (الأبصار)

2 to impress sb very much: *He had been dazzled by her beauty.* يبهر ، يفتن

▸ **dazzling** *adj* very bright or impressive: *a dazzling light* ○ *a dazzling performance* مبهِر للبصر ؛ (نجاح) باهر

deacon /'diːkən/ (*feminine* **deaconess**) *noun* [C] an official who has a rank below a priest, in some Christian churches شمّاس (في الكنيسة)

🔑 **dead** /ded/ *adj* **1** no longer alive: *They rushed him to hospital, but he was dead on arrival.* ○ *There's a dead spider in the bath.* ميّت

2 (not before a noun) no longer able to feel anything (used about a part of the body): *My fingers had gone dead with the cold.* خَدِر ، فاقد الإحساس

3 (not before a noun) no longer working properly (used about a piece of equipment): *I picked up the telephone but the line was dead.* معطّل

4 (only *before* a noun) complete: *There was dead silence when she finished speaking.* شامل ، مطبِق

5 without movement, activity or interest: *This town is completely dead after 11 o'clock at night.* ميّت ، راكد

6 no longer used; over and finished: *Latin is a dead language.* ○ *We've made our decision so the subject is now dead.* بائد ، ميّت ؛ منته

IDM **a dead end 1** a street that is only open at one end طريق مسدود

2 a point, situation, etc. from which you can make no further progress: *a dead-end job* (= one that offers no chance of promotion) (وظيفة) لا مجال فيها للترفيع

drop dead → DROP[1]

▸ **dead** *adv* completely, exactly or very: *The sign said 'Dead slow!'* ○ *He's dead keen to start work.* تماماً ، كليّاً ؛ بالضبط

the dead *noun* [plural] people who have died: *A church service was held in memory of the dead.* الموتى

IDM **in the/at dead of night** in the middle of the night, when it is very dark and quiet في هدأة الليل

deaden /'dedn/ *verb* [T] to make sth less strong, painful, etc: *They gave her drugs to try and deaden the pain.* يخفّف ، يسكّن

ˌdead 'heat *noun* [C] the result in a race when two people finish at exactly the same time: *The race was a dead heat.* تعادل في السباق

deadline /'dedlaɪn/ *noun* [C] a time or date before which sth must be done: *A journalist is used to having to meet deadlines.* آخر موعد (لتقديم الطلبات مثلاً)

deadlock /'dedlɒk/ *noun* [U] a situation in which an agreement between two sides cannot be reached فشل التوصّل إلى إتّفاق

deadly /'dedli/ *adj* (**deadlier**; **deadliest**) **1** causing or likely to cause death: *a deadly poison* مميت ، قاتل ، زعاف

2 very great: *They're deadly enemies.* (عدو) لدود ؛ شديد

3 (*informal*) very boring ممل جداً ، لا حياة فيه

▸ **deadly** *adv* extremely; very: *I'm not joking – I'm deadly serious!* للغاية ، جداً

deadpan /ˈdedpæn/ *adj* without any expression on your face or in your voice: *He told the joke with a completely deadpan face.* (وجه) خالٍ من أي تعبير

deaf /def/ *adj* **1** unable to hear anything or unable to hear very well: *You'll have to speak louder. My father's a bit deaf.* أصمّ ، أطرش

2 deaf to sth not wanting to listen to sth: *I've told her what I think but she's deaf to my advice.* غير راغب في الإصغاء

▸ **the deaf** *noun* [plural] deaf people: *sign language for the deaf* الطُرْش ، الصم

deafness *noun* [U] the state of being deaf طَرَش ، صَمَم

deafen /ˈdefn/ *verb* [T] (usually passive) to make sb unable to hear by making a very loud noise: *We were deafened by the loud music and conversation was impossible.* يصمّ الآذان

▸ **deafening** *adj* very loud عالٍ جداً ، يصمّ الآذان

deal[1] /diːl/ *noun*

IDM **a good/great deal (of sth)** a lot (of sth): *I've spent a great deal of time on this report.* مقدار كبير ، كمّية كبيرة

deal[2] /diːl/ *verb* [I,T] (*pt, pp* **dealt** /delt/) **1 deal sth (out); deal sth (to sb)** to give cards to players in a game of cards: *Start by dealing seven cards to each player.* يوزّع أوراق اللعب على اللاعبين

2 [I, T] (*informal*) to buy and sell illegal drugs يبيع أو يتاجر بالمخدرات

IDM **deal sb/sth a blow; deal a blow to sb/sth 1** to hit sb/sth يضرب ، يسدّد له ضربة

2 to give sb a shock, etc: *This news dealt a terrible blow to my father.* يصيبه بصدمة

PHR V **deal in sth** to buy and sell sth; to trade in sth: *He deals in second-hand cars.* يتاجر بِ

deal sth out to give sth to a number of people: *The profits will be dealt out among us.* يقسّم ، يوزّع

deal with sb to behave towards sb; to handle sb: *He's a difficult man. Nobody quite knows how to deal with him.* يعامل ، يتعامل مع

deal with sth 1 to act in a suitable way in order to solve a problem, complete a task, etc.; to handle sth: *I'm not sure how to deal with the situation at work.* ○ *My secretary will deal with my correspondence while I'm away.* يعالج (المشكلة) ؛ يدبّر

2 to have sth as its subject: *This chapter deals with letter-writing.* يتناول ، يبحث في

deal[3] /diːl/ *noun* [C] an agreement or arrangement, especially in business: *It was part of the deal that they would deliver by May.* ○ *We've done/made a deal with an Italian company.* ○ *a fair deal* ○ *a bad deal* صفقة

IDM **a big deal/no big deal** → BIG

ˈ**deal-breaker** *noun* [C] (*especially US*) something that causes sb to reject a deal in politics or business عامل مسبب لإخفاق صفقة

dealer /ˈdiːlə(r)/ *noun* [C] **1** a person whose business is buying and selling things: *a dealer in gold and silver* ○ *a drug dealer* تاجر

2 the person who gives the cards to the players in a game of cards من يوزّع أوراق اللعب

dealing /ˈdiːlɪŋ/ *noun* **1** [U] buying and selling: *drug dealing* تجارة ، بيع وشراء

2 dealings [plural] relations, especially in business: *We had some dealings with that firm several years ago.* تعامل ، علاقات تجاريّة

dealt *pt, pp of* DEAL[2]

dean /diːn/ *noun* [C] **1** an important official at some universities or colleges عميد

2 a priest who is head of a large church or responsible for a number of small churches رئيس كَنَسيّ ذو مرتبة عالية

dear /dɪə(r)/ *adj* **1** (used at the beginning of a letter before the name or title of the person you are writing to): *Dear Sarah, ...* ○ *Dear Sir or Madam, ...* عزيزي/عزيزتي

2 (only *before* a noun) a word that is used with 'little' or 'old' to express your liking for sb/sth: *Dear old Jane! She always remembers to write at Christmas.* العزيز أو العزيزة (تقال تحبباً)

3 dear (to sb) loved by or important to sb: *She's one of my dearest friends.* ○ *It was a subject that was very dear to him.* عزيز ؛ مهم

4 (*Brit*) expensive: *How can people afford to smoke when cigarettes are so dear?* غالٍ

▸ **dear** *adv* at a high price: *Always buy cheap and sell dear, if possible!* بسعرٍ عالٍ

dear *noun* [C] **1** a kind, gentle person: *She's a kind old lady – an absolute dear.* شخص لطيف محبوب

2 (used for speaking to sb you know well or love): *Would you like a cup of tea, dear?* يا عزيزي

dear *interj* (used for expressing disappointment, sadness, surprise, etc.): *Oh dear! I've spilt the tea.* ○ *Dear me! Aren't you ready?* (صيحة تعبّر عن خيبة الأمل أو الدهشة الخ)

dearly *adv* **1** very much: *He loves her dearly.* ○ *I'd dearly like to go there again.* (حباً) جمّاً ؛ كثيراً

2 (*formal*) at great cost: *I've already paid dearly (= suffered a lot) for that mistake.* (يدفع الثمن) غالياً ، (يعاني) كثيراً

dearth /dɜːθ/ *noun* [sing.] a lack of sth; not enough of sth: *There's a dearth of young people in the village.* قلّة ، ندرة ؛ جدب

death /deθ/ *noun* **1** [C,U] the end of sb/sth's life; dying: *He continued to write until his death.* ○ *There were two deaths and many other people were injured.* ○ *Most people are afraid of death.* ○ *The police do not know the cause of death.* ○ *There was no food and people were starving to death.* موت

2 [U] the end (of sth): *the death of communism* نهاية

IDM **put sb to death** (usually passive) to kill

a b c **d** e f g h i j k l m n o p q r s t u v w x y z

sb, usually as a punishment: *The general had ordered the prisoners to be put to death.* يعدِم
sick to death of sb/sth → SICK
sudden death → SUDDEN

deathly /ˈdeθli/ *adj, adv* like death: *There was a deathly silence.* شبيه بالموت : (صمت) مطبق

ˈ**death penalty** *noun* [sing.] the punishment of being killed عقوبة الإعدام

ˈ**death toll** *noun* [C] the number of people killed in a disaster, war, etc. عدد القتلى

debase /dɪˈbeɪs/ *verb* [T] (usually passive) (*formal*) to reduce the quality or value of sth يخفِّض قيمة (العملة): يحطّ من قدره

debatable /dɪˈbeɪtəbl/ *adj* not certain; something that you could argue about غير مؤكّد : قابل للأخذ والردّ

⚷ **debate** /dɪˈbeɪt/ *noun* **1** [C] a formal argument or discussion of a question at a public meeting or in Parliament. At the end there may be a vote: *a debate in Parliament on educational reform* مناظرة ، مناقشة

2 [C,U] a discussion; talk expressing different opinions: *There's been a lot of debate about the cause of acid rain.* مناقشة، جدال

▸ **debate** *verb* **1** [I,T] to discuss sth in a formal way or at a public debate يناظر ، يشترك في مناقشة

2 [T] to think about or discuss sth before deciding what to do: *They debated whether to go or not.* يفكّر في الأمر

debit /ˈdebɪt/ *noun* [C] a sum of money paid out of a bank account; a written note of this مبلغ مدين أو مسحوب : الإشعار بهذا المبلغ

▸ **debit** *verb* [T] to take a sum of money out of a bank account, etc. usually as a payment; to record this: *The bank hasn't debited my account with the money I paid for the car yet.* ➲ Look at **credit** and **direct debit**. يأخذ مبلغاً من رصيده : يقيد عليه الدين

ˈ**debit card** *noun* [C] a plastic card that can be used to take money directly from your bank account when you pay for sth بطاقة دَيْن

debris /ˈdebriː; *US* dəˈbriː/ *noun* [U] pieces from sth that has crashed to the ground or been destroyed: *debris from the crashed plane* حطام : أنقاض

⚷ **debt** /det/ *noun* **1** [C] a sum of money that you owe sb: *She borrowed a lot of money and she's still paying off the debt.* دَيْن

2 [U] the state of owing money: *After he lost his job, he got into debt.* دَيْن

3 [C, usually sing.] (*formal*) something that you owe sb, e.g. because they have helped or been kind to you: *In his speech he acknowledged his debt to his family and friends for their support.* المديونيّة: كون الإنسان مَديناً ا

IDM **be in/out of debt** to owe/not owe money مديون : غير مديون
be in sb's debt (*formal*) to feel grateful to sb for sth that he/she has done for you مَدين ل

▸ **debtor** /ˈdetə(r)/ *noun* [C] a person who owes money المدين

debut (*also* **début**) /ˈdeɪbjuː; *US* dɪˈbjuː/ *noun* [C] a first appearance in public of an actor, etc: *She made her debut in London in 1959.* أوّل ظهور على المسرح أو في المجتمع

Dec. *abbrev* = DECEMBER

⚷ **decade** /ˈdekeɪd; dɪˈkeɪd/ *noun* [C] a period of ten years عقد ، فترة عشر سنوات

decadence /ˈdekədəns/ *noun* [U] behaviour, attitudes, etc. that show a fall in standards, especially moral ones انحطاط ، انحلال

▸ **decadent** /ˈdekədənt/ *adj*: *a decadent society* منحلّ خُلقيّاً، منحطّ ثقافياً

decaffeinated /ˌdiːˈkæfɪneɪtɪd/ *adj* (used about coffee or tea) with most or all of the caffeine removed مزال منه مادّة الكافيين

decapitate /dɪˈkæpɪteɪt/ *verb* [T] (*formal*) to cut off a person's head يقطع الرأس

⚷ **decay** /dɪˈkeɪ/ *verb* [I] **1** to become bad or fall apart: *The old farm buildings had been left to decay.* ○ *the decaying body of a dead sheep* ○ *Children's teeth will decay if they eat too many sweets.* يبلى: يتفسّخ: يسوّس

2 to become weaker or less efficient: *The Roman Empire had by then begun to decay.* ينحطّ ، ينهار

▸ **decay** *noun* [U] the process of decaying, or the state reached after decaying: *It is better to prevent tooth decay than to treat it.* ○ *Many of the old houses had fallen into decay.* تسوّس ، بِلى، تفسُّخ : انهيار

decayed *adj*: *a decayed tooth* مسوس ، نخِر: متفسخ

decease /dɪˈsiːs/ *noun* [U] (*formal*) the death of a person وفاة

▸ **deceased** *adj* (*formal*) dead: *He inherited the house from his deceased parents.* متوفّى

the deceased *noun* [sing.] (*formal*) a person who has died, especially one who has died recently: *Many friends of the deceased were present at the funeral.* الفقيد ، الراحل ، المرحوم

deceit /dɪˈsiːt/ *noun* [U] dishonest behaviour; trying to make sb believe sth that is not true خداع ، تضليل ، غشّ

▸ **deceitful** /dɪˈsiːtfl/ *adj* dishonest, and intending to make sb believe sth that is not true خدّاع ، مضلّل، غشّاش

deceitfully /-fəli/ *adv* على نحو مضلّل ، بصورة كاذبة
deceitfulness *noun* [U] خداع ، غشّ

deceive /dɪˈsiːv/ *verb* [T] **deceive sb/yourself (into doing sth)** to try to make sb believe sth that is not true: *He deceived his mother into believing that he had earned the money, not stolen it.* ○ *Her story didn't deceive me – I knew it was a lie.* ○ *You're deceiving yourself if you think there's an easy solution to the problem.* ❶ The noun is **deception** or **deceit**. يخدع ، يضلّل

⚷ **December** /dɪˈsembə(r)/ *noun* [C,U] (*abbr* **Dec.**) the twelfth month of the year, coming before January ❶ For examples of the use of the months in sentences, look at **January**. ديسمبر/كانون الأوّل

decency /ˈdiːsnsi/ *noun* [U] moral or correct behaviour: *She had the decency to admit that it was her fault.* احتشام : حسن السلوك

decent /ˈdiːsnt/ *adj* **1** satisfactory; of an acceptable standard: *All she wants is a decent job with decent wages.* معقول ، مناسب

2 (used about people or behaviour) honest and respectable: *All decent people are appalled by such terrible crimes.* شريف ، محترم

3 not likely to embarrass or offend sb: *I can't come to the door, I'm not decent* (= I'm not dressed). ℹ The opposite is **indecent**. لائق ، محتشم : مرتدٍ ملابسه

▸ **decently** *adv* بصورة حسنة

deception /dɪˈsepʃn/ *noun* [C,U] deceiving or being deceived; a trick: *He had obtained the secret papers by deception.* خداع ، تضليل : خدعة أو حيلة

deceptive /dɪˈseptɪv/ *adj* likely to give a false impression or to make sb believe sth that is not true: *The water is deceptive. It's much deeper than it looks.* مضلِّل ، خدّاع

▸ **deceptively** *adv*: *She made the task sound deceptively easy.* بصورة مضلّلة

decibel /ˈdesɪbel/ *noun* [C] a measurement of how loud a sound is وحدة قياس شدّة الصوت

⚷**decide** /dɪˈsaɪd/ *verb* **1** [I,T] to think about two or more possibilities and choose one of them: *There are so many to choose from – I can't decide!* ○ *She decided against borrowing the money.* ○ *They decided on a name for the baby.* ○ *He decided that it was too late to go.* ○ *You'll have to decide what to do.* ○ *We've decided not to invite Isabel.* ○ *The date hasn't been decided yet.* يبتّ ، يقرِّر ؛ يختار

2 [T] to influence sth so that it produces a particular result: *Your votes will decide the winner.* يفصل ، يحسم ، يقرِّر

3 [T] to cause sb to make a decision: *What finally decided you to leave?* ℹ The noun is **decision**. ℹ The adjective is **decisive**. يجعله يقرر ، يحمله على

▸ **decided** *adj* clear; definite: *There has been a decided improvement in his work.* واضح ؛ مؤكّد ، جازم

decidedly *adv*: *The new office is decidedly better than the old one.* حتماً ، قطعاً ، دون ريب

deciduous /dɪˈsɪdʒuəs/ *adj* (used about a tree) of a type that loses its leaves every autumn ➲ Look at **evergreen**. (شجر) متساقط الأوراق

decimal /ˈdesɪml/ *adj* based on or counted in units of ten: *decimal currency* عشري

▸ **decimal** *noun* [C] part of a number, written after a dot (decimal point) and expressed in tenths, hundredths, etc: *Three quarters expressed as a decimal is 0.75.* كسر عشري

decipher /dɪˈsaɪfə(r)/ *verb* [T] to succeed in reading or understanding sth that is not clear: *It's impossible to decipher his handwriting.* يفكّ رموز (الشفرة) ، يتمكن من قراءة شيء غامض

⚷**decision** /dɪˈsɪʒn/ *noun* **1** [C,U] **a decision (on/about sth); a decision (to do sth); a decision (that...)** a choice or judgement that you make after thinking about various possibilities: *'Have you made a decision yet?' 'No, I'm still thinking about it!'* ○ *I took the decision that I believed to be right.* ○ *I realize now that I made the wrong decision.* ○ *There were good reasons for his decision to leave.* ○ *Who made the decision that the school should be closed?* ○ *How you vote is a matter of personal decision.* قرار

2 [U] being able to decide clearly and quickly عزم ، تصميم

decisive /dɪˈsaɪsɪv/ *adj* **1** making sth certain or final: *the decisive battle of the war* حاسم ، فاصل

2 having the ability to make clear decisions quickly: *It's no good hesitating. Be decisive.* جازم

▸ **decisively** *adv* بصورة جازمة

decisiveness *noun* [U] مقدرة على اتّخاذ قرارات حاسمة

deck /dek/ *noun* [C] **1** one of the floors of a ship or bus: *The restaurant is on the upper deck.* طابق في سفينة أو باص

2 (*US*) = PACK[1] (4)

3 a piece of equipment on which you can play records or tapes جهاز للأسطوانات والأشرطة

IDM on deck on the floor of a ship which is in the open air: *I'm going out on deck for some fresh air.* على ظهر السفينة

deckchair /ˈdektʃeə(r)/ *noun* [C] a chair that you use outside, especially on the beach. You can fold it up and carry it. كرسي قابل للطيّ للجلوس على الشاطئ مثلاً

declaration /ˌdekləˈreɪʃn/ *noun* **1** [C,U] a statement: *In his speech he made a strong declaration of support for the rebels.* ○ *Fighting has started without declaration of war.* إعلان ، بيان

2 [C] a written statement giving information on goods or income on which you have to pay tax: *If you're sending a parcel abroad, you have to fill in a customs declaration.* تصريح

⚷**declare** /dɪˈkleə(r)/ *verb* [T] **1** to announce or to make sth known, especially in an official or forceful way: *to declare war on another country* ○ *The republic has declared its independence.* ○ *I declare that the winner of the award is Joan Taylor.* ○ *'I've had enough of this,' she declared and walked out of the room.* يعلن

2 to give information about goods or income on which you have to pay tax: *You must declare all your income on this form.* يصرِّح بِ

⚷**decline**[1] /dɪˈklaɪn/ *verb* **1** [I,T] (*formal*) to refuse, usually politely: *Thank you for the invitation but I'm afraid I have to decline.* ○ *The minister declined to make a statement.* يعتذر عن القبول ، يرفض بأدب

2 [I] to become weaker, smaller or less good: *declining profits* ○ *The standard of education has declined in this country.* ينحطّ ، ينحدر ؛ ينخفض

⚷**decline**[2] /dɪˈklaɪn/ *noun* [C,U] **(a) decline (in sth)** a process or period of becoming weaker, smaller or less satisfactory: *a decline in sales* ○ *As an industrial power, the country is in decline.* انحطاط ، انهيار ، هبوط

declutter /diːˈklʌtə(r)/ *verb* [T] to remove things that you do not use so that you have more space

and can easily find things when you need them
ينسق الأشياء ويرمي ما لا يحتاج إليه

decode /ˌdiːˈkəʊd/ *verb* [T] to find the meaning of sth that is in code ❶ The opposite is **encode**.
يفكّ رموز الشّفرة

▸ **decoder** *noun* [C] a piece of equipment that allows you to receive satellite television channels for which you have to pay extra
(جهاز) فاكّ الرموز

decompose /ˌdiːkəmˈpəʊz/ *verb* [I,T] to decay or to make sth decay: *The body was so badly decomposed that it couldn't be identified.*
يتفسّخ ، يتحلّل ؛ يعفّن

decor /ˈdeɪkɔː(r); *US* deɪˈkɔːr/ *noun* [U, sing.] the furniture and decoration in a place
"ديكور": تزيين داخلي

decorate /ˈdekəreɪt/ *verb* **1** [T] **decorate sth (with sth)** to add sth in order to make a thing more attractive to look at: *Decorate the cake with cherries and nuts.*
يزيّن ، يزخرف

2 [I,T] to put paint and/or wallpaper onto walls, ceilings and doors in a room or building: *I think it's about time we decorated the living room.*
يدهّن أو يطلي (البيت مثلاً)

decoration /ˌdekəˈreɪʃn/ *noun* **1** [C,U] the decorating of a room or building with paint, wallpaper, etc.; the wallpaper, curtains, etc. that have been used in a room or building: *The theatre has been renovated in the style of the original decoration.* ○ *The house is in need of decoration.*
طلاء وغيره ؛ التزيينات الداخليّة

2 [C,U] something that is added to sth in order to make it look more attractive: *Christmas decorations*
تزيين ، زينة

decorative /ˈdekərətɪv; *US* ˈdekəreɪtɪv/ *adj* attractive to look at; added to sth to make it prettier: *The cloth had a decorative lace edge.*
تزييني

decoy /ˈdiːkɔɪ/ *noun* [C] a person or object that is used to lead sb/sth in the wrong direction
شَرَك ؛ تمويه

decrease /dɪˈkriːs/ *verb* [I,T] to become or to make sth smaller or less: *As the temperature decreases, the metal contracts.* ○ *Profits have decreased by 15%.* ○ *Decrease speed when you are approaching a road junction.* ❶ The opposite is **increase**.
ينخفض ، يتناقص ؛ يخفّض

▸ **decrease** /ˈdiːkriːs/ *noun* [C,U] **(a) decrease (in sth)** a process of becoming or making sth smaller or less; a reduction: *a decrease in the number of students* ○ *a 10% decrease in sales*
انخفاض ؛ تضاؤل ؛ تخفيض

decree /dɪˈkriː/ *noun* [C] an official order given by a government, a ruler, etc.
مرسوم ، قرار

▸ **decree** *verb* [T] (*pt, pp* **decreed**) (used about a government, a ruler, etc.) to give an official order
يصدر مرسوماً أو قراراً

decrepit /dɪˈkrepɪt/ *adj* old and in very bad condition
هَرِم متهدّم الصحّة ، عاجز لكبر سنّه

dedicate /ˈdedɪkeɪt/ *verb* [T] **1** to give all your energy, time, efforts, etc. to sth: *He dedicated his life to helping the poor.*
يكرّس ، ينذر

2 dedicate sth to sb to say that sth is in honour of sb: *He dedicated the book he had written to his brother.*
(المؤلّف) يهدي كتابه إلى

▸ **dedicated** *adj* giving a lot of your energy, time, efforts, etc. to sth that you believe to be important: *dedicated nurses and doctors*
مخلص لعمله

dedication /ˌdedɪˈkeɪʃn/ *noun* **1** [U] being willing to give your time and energy to sth: *I admire her dedication to her career.*
تكريس (الوقت) ، إخلاص (للعمل)

2 [C] a message at the beginning of a book or before a piece of music is played, saying that it is for a particular person
إهداء

deduce /dɪˈdjuːs/ *verb* [T] to form an opinion using the facts that you already know: *From his name I deduced that he was Polish.* ❶ The noun is **deduction**.
يستنتج ، يستخلص

deduct /dɪˈdʌkt/ *verb* [T] **deduct sth (from sth)** to take sth such as money or points away from a total amount: *Income tax is deducted from your salary.* ○ *Marks will be deducted for untidy work.*
يحسم ، يخصم ، يطرح

deduction /dɪˈdʌkʃn/ *noun* [C,U] **1** something that you work out from facts that you already know; the skill of reasoning in this way: *It was a brilliant piece of deduction by the detective.*
استنتاج ، استدلال

2 deduction (from sth) taking away an amount or number from a total; the amount or number taken away from the total: *What is your total income after deductions?* (= when tax, insurance, etc. are taken away).
حسم ، خصم ؛ طرح

deed /diːd/ *noun* [C] (*formal*) something that you do; an action: *Deeds are more important than words.*
عمل ، فعل ، صنيع

deem /diːm/ *verb* [T] (*formal*) to consider sth: *He did not even deem it necessary to apologize.*
يعتبر ، يرى

deep[1] /diːp/ *adj* **1** going a long way down from top to bottom: *the deep end of a swimming pool* ○ *to dig a deep hole* ○ *That's a deep cut – I think you'd better see a doctor.* ○ *a coat with deep pockets* ❶ The noun is **depth**.
عميق

2 going a long way from front to back: *deep shelves*
عميق ، عريض

3 measuring a particular amount from top to bottom or from front to back: *The water is only a metre deep at this end of the pool.* ○ *shelves 40 centimetres deep*
بالغ عمقه

4 (used about sounds) low: *a deep voice*
(صوت) خفيض

5 (used about colours) dark; strong: *a deep red*
غامق ، داكن

6 strongly felt; serious: *Please accept my deepest sympathy on this sad occasion.* ○ *The country is in a deep recession and there is massive unemployment.*
قلبيّ ؛ عميق ، شديد

7 (used about a breath) taking in or letting out a lot of air: *Take a few deep breaths.*
عميق

8 concentrating on or involved in sth: *She was*

deep in thought. ○ *deep sleep* ○ *deep in conversation* مستغرق ، غارق

9 thorough, able to deal with the difficult parts of sth: *His books show a deep understanding of human nature.* متعمّق ، دقيق

▸ **deepen** /ˈdiːpən/ *verb* [I,T] to become or to make sth deep or deeper: *The river deepens here.* ○ *This bad news deepened the atmosphere of depression.* يَعمق ؛ يعمّق

deeply *adv*: *a deeply unhappy person* ○ *to breathe deeply* بشدّة ؛ عميقاً ؛ بتعمّق

deep² /diːp/ *adv* a long way down or inside sth: *The ship sank deep into the sea.* ○ *They talked deep into the night.* عميقاً : إلى عمق أو جزء كبير من

IDM **deep down** in what you really think or feel: *I tried to appear optimistic but deep down I knew there was no hope.* في دخيلة النفس ، في حقيقة الأمر

ˌdeep-ˈfreeze *noun* [C] = FREEZER

ˌdeep-ˈfry *verb* [T] (usually passive) to cook food in oil that covers it completely: *deep-fried chicken pieces* يقلي بالغمس في الزيت

deeply *adj* → DEEP¹

ˌdeep-ˈrooted (*also* **ˌdeep-ˈseated**) *adj* strongly felt or believed and therefore difficult to change: *deep-seated prejudices* راسخ ، متأصّل الجذور

deer /dɪə(r)/ *noun* [C] (*pl.* **deer**) a large wild grass-eating animal. The male has horns shaped like branches (antlers). أيّل

A male deer is called a **buck** or, especially if it has fully grown antlers, a **stag**. The female is a **doe** and a young deer a **fawn**. **Venison** is the meat from deer.

deface /dɪˈfeɪs/ *verb* [T] to spoil the way sth looks by writing on or marking the surface of it: *Vandals defaced the statue with graffiti.* يشوّه

default /dɪˈfɔːlt/ *noun* [sing.] (*computing*) a course of action taken by a computer when it is not given any other instruction اختيار افتراضي

IDM **by default** because nothing happened, not because of successful effort: *They won by default, because the other team didn't turn up.* لعدم حدوث شيء معيّن، بسبب غياب...

▸ **default** *verb* [I] **1** not to do sth that you should do by law: *If you default on the credit payments* (= you don't pay them), *the car will be taken back.* يتخلّف عن ؛ يهمل

2 (*computing*) to take a particular course of action when no other command is given يفترض اختياراً معيّناً

defeat /dɪˈfiːt/ *verb* [T] **1** to win a game, a fight, a vote, etc. against sb: *The army defeated the rebels after three days of fighting.* ○ *In the last match France defeated Wales by ten points to six.* يهزم ، يتغلّب على

2 to prevent sth from succeeding: *The local residents are determined to defeat the council's building plans.* يحبط مساعيه

3 to be too difficult for sb to do or understand: *I've tried to work out what's wrong with the car but it defeats me.* يتعذّر فهمه أو عمله

▸ **defeat** *noun* **1** [C] an occasion when sb is defeated: *This season they have had two victories and three defeats.* هزيمة

2 [U] defeating or being defeated: *She refused to admit defeat and kept on trying.* هزيمة ، انهزام

defeatism /-ɪzəm/ *noun* [U] the attitude that you have when you expect sth to end unsuccessfully الانهزاميّة

defeatist /-ɪst/ *noun* [C]: *Don't be such a defeatist, we haven't lost yet!* انهزامي

defecate /ˈdefəkeɪt/ *verb* [I] (*formal*) to pass waste materials from the bowels يتغوّط

defect¹ /ˈdiːfekt/ *noun* [C] something that is wrong with or missing from sb/sth: *a speech defect* ○ *defects in the education system* عيب ، خلل ، علّة

▸ **defective** /dɪˈfektɪv/ *adj*: *If you find any of our goods to be defective, please return them to the shop.* معيوب ، فيه عيب أو خلل

defect² /dɪˈfekt/ *verb* [I] to leave your country, a political party, etc. and go to or join an opposing one: *a spy who defected from the East* ينضمّ إلى جانب العدوّ

▸ **defection** /dɪˈfekʃn/ *noun* [C,U] انضمام إلى جانب العدوّ

defence (*US* **defense**) /dɪˈfens/ *noun* **1** [U] **defence (against sth)** action to protect sb/sth from attack: *Would you fight in defence of your country?* دفاع

2 [C] **a defence (against sth)** something that protects sb/sth from sth or that is used for fighting against attack: *to build up a country's defences* ○ *the body's defences against disease* وسيلة دفاع ، وقاء

3 [U] the military equipment, forces, etc. for protecting a country: *the Defence Minister* ○ *Spending on defence can be cut if fewer weapons are needed.* الدفاع

4 [C,U] something that you say or write to support sb/sth that is being attacked or accused: *In his speech, he made a strong defence of the party's policy.* ○ *I must say in her defence that I have always found her very reliable.* دفاع ، مدافعة

5 [C] (in law) an argument in support of the accused person in a court of law: *His defence was that he was only carrying out orders.* حجّة ، دفاع

6 the defence [sing., with sing. or pl. verb] (in law) the accused person in a court of law and the lawyer or lawyers who are acting for him/her: *The defence claims/claim that many of the witnesses were lying.* ○ *a witness giving evidence for the defence* جهة الدفاع

7 usually **the defence** [sing., with sing. or pl. verb, U] (in sport) action to prevent the other team scoring; the players who try to do this: *The defence was/were unable to stop Brown and he scored.* ○ *They put up no defence and were beaten by five points.* (في الرياضة) الدفاع

▸ **defenceless** *adj* unable to defend yourself against attack عاجز عن حماية نفسه

a b c d e f g h i j k l m n o p q r s t u v w x y z

defend /dɪˈfend/ *verb* **1** [T] **defend sb/sth (against sb/sth)** to act, especially to fight, to protect sb/sth: *Would you be able to defend yourself if someone attacked you in the street?* يدافع عن

2 [T] **defend sb/sth (against sb/sth)** to say or write sth to support sb/sth: *The minister went on television to defend the government's policy.* يدافع عن

3 [T] (in law) to speak for sb who is accused of sth in a court of law يتولّى الدفاع عن متّهم

4 [I,T] to try to stop the other team or player scoring: *They defended well and managed to hold onto their lead.* يدافع

5 [T] to try to win a match so that you remain champion: *She successfully defended her title.* يدافع عن ، يحاول الاحتفاظ بـ

▸ **defender** *noun* [C] a person who defends sb/sth, especially in sport مدافع ، الدفاع

defendant /dɪˈfendənt/ *noun* [C] a person who is accused of sth in a court of law المدّعى عليه

defense (*US*) = DEFENCE

defensive /dɪˈfensɪv/ *adj* **1** used or intended for protecting sb/sth from attack: *The troops took up a defensive position.* دفاعي

2 showing that you feel that sb is accusing or criticizing you: *When I asked him about his new job, he became very defensive and tried to change the subject.* متحفّز للدفاع ، مستعدّ لردّ الاتّهام

▸ **defensive** *noun*

IDM **on the defensive** ready to defend yourself against attack or criticism في موقف دفاعيّ

defer /dɪˈfɜː(r)/ *verb* [T] (deferring; deferred) (*formal*) to leave sth until a later time; to postpone يرجئ ، يؤجّل

deference /ˈdefərəns/ *noun* [U] polite behaviour that you show towards sb/sth, usually because you respect him/her مراعاة ، احترام

IDM **in deference to sb/sth** because you respect and do not wish to upset sb: *In deference to her father's wishes, she didn't mention the subject again.* احتراماً لشعوره

defiance /dɪˈfaɪəns/ *noun* [U] open refusal to obey: *As an act of defiance they continued to play their music loud.* ❶ The verb is **defy**. تحدٍّ ، عصيان

IDM **in defiance of sb/sth** openly refusing to obey sb/sth تحدّياً لـ

defiant /dɪˈfaɪənt/ *adj* showing open refusal to obey متحدٍّ بجسارة ، متمرّد

▸ **defiantly** *adv* بتحدٍّ وجسارة

deficiency /dɪˈfɪʃnsi/ *noun* (*pl.* **deficiencies**)

1 [C,U] a condition of not having enough of sth; a lack: *a deficiency of vitamin C* نقص

2 [C] something that is not good enough or that is wrong with sb/sth: *The problems were caused by deficiencies in the design.* خلل ، نقطة ضعف

deficient /dɪˈfɪʃnt/ *adj* **1 deficient (in sth)** not having enough of sth: *food that is deficient in minerals* ناقص

2 not good enough or not complete فيه خلل ، ضعيف ؛ ناقص

deficit /ˈdefɪsɪt/ *noun* [C] the amount by which the money you receive is less than the money you have spent: *a trade deficit* عجز مالي

define /dɪˈfaɪn/ *verb* [T] **1** to say exactly what a word or idea means: *How would you define 'happiness'?* يعرِّف

2 to explain the exact nature of sth clearly: *We need to define the problem before we can attempt to solve it.* يحدِّد ، يتبيَّن بوضوح

definite /ˈdefɪnət/ *adj* **1** fixed and unlikely to change; certain: *I'll give you a definite decision in a couple of days.* جازم ، أكيد

2 clear; easy to see or notice: *There has been a definite change in her attitude recently.* واضح ، جلي

▸ **definitely** *adv* certainly; without doubt: *I'll definitely consider your advice.* ○ *We definitely can't afford such a high price.* بكل تأكيد ؛ بلا ريب

ˌdefinite ˈarticle *noun* [C] (*grammar*) the name used for the word 'the' ➲ Look at **indefinite article**. أداة التعريف (في النحو)

definition /ˌdefɪˈnɪʃn/ *noun* [C,U] a statement of the exact meaning of a word or idea تعريف ؛ تحديد ؛ وضوح

definitive /dɪˈfɪnətɪv/ *adj* in a form that cannot be changed or that cannot be improved: *This is the definitive version.* ○ *the definitive performance of Hamlet* نهائي ، قاطع ، لا مجال فيه للتحسين

▸ **definitively** *adv* بشكل قاطع

deflate /diːˈfleɪt/ *verb* **1** [I,T] to become or to make sth smaller by letting the air or gas out: *The balloon slowly deflated and began to come down.* ❶ The opposite is **inflate**. ينفِّس : يفرِّغ الهواء من شيء منفوخ

2 [T] to make sb feel less confident, proud or excited يقلّل من غطرسته ؛ يضعف حماسه

deflect /dɪˈflekt/ *verb* **1** [I,T] to change direction after hitting sb/sth; to make sth change direction in this way: *The ball was deflected off a defender and into the net.* ينحرف (بعد ارتطام) ؛ يحرِف

2 [T] to turn sb or sb's attention away from sth: *Nothing could deflect her from her aim.* يثني (عن عزمه)

▸ **deflection** /dɪˈflekʃn/ *noun* [C,U] a change of direction after hitting sb/sth انحراف (بعد ارتطام)

deforestation /diːˌfɒrɪˈsteɪʃn/ *noun* [U] cutting down trees over a large area: *Deforestation is a major cause of global warming.* إتلاف الحراج

deform /dɪˈfɔːm/ *verb* [T] to change the shape of sth so that it is unnatural يمسخ ، يشوّه

▸ **deformed** *adj* having an unnatural or ugly shape ممسوخ ، مشوّه

deformity /dɪˈfɔːməti/ *noun* (*pl.* **deformities**) [C,U] the state of being deformed; a part of the body that is deformed: *The drug caused women to give birth to babies with severe deformities.* تشوّه ؛ عاهة

defraud /dɪˈfrɔːd/ *verb* [T] to get sth from sb by cheating يحتال على، يغبن

defrost /ˌdiːˈfrɒst; *US* ˌdiːˈfrɔːst/ *verb* **1** [T] to re-

move the ice from sth: *to defrost a fridge* (= by switching it off so that the ice melts)
يذيب الجليد (المتراكم في ثلاّجة مثلاً)

2 [I,T] (used about frozen food) to return to a normal temperature; to make food do this: *Defrost the chicken thoroughly before cooking.*
يذيب الأطعمة المتجمّدة

deft /deft/ *adj* (used especially about movements) skilful and quick رشيق ، سريع الحركة
▸ **deftly** *adv* برشاقة ، بخفّة

defunct /dɪˈfʌŋkt/ *adj* no longer existing or in use منقرض ، زائل من الوجود

defuse /ˌdiːˈfjuːz/ *verb* [T] **1** to remove the part of a bomb that would make it explode: *Army experts defused the bomb safely.* يبطل مفعول القنبلة

2 to make a situation calmer or less dangerous: *She defused the tension by changing the subject.* يخفّف من تأزّم الوضع

defy /dɪˈfaɪ/ *verb* [T] (*pp* **defying**; *3rd pers sing pres* **defies**; *pt, pp* **defied**) **1** to openly refuse to obey sb/sth: *She defied her parents and continued seeing him.* ⓘ The adjective is **defiant** and the noun **defiance**. يتحدّى ، يعصي

2 defy sb to do sth to tell sb to do sth that you believe to be impossible: *I defy you to prove me wrong.* يتحدّى

3 to make sth impossible or very difficult: *It's such a beautiful place that it defies description.*
يستعصي على

degenerate /dɪˈdʒenəreɪt/ *verb* [I] to fall to a less satisfactory standard; to become worse: *The calm discussion degenerated into a nasty argument.* يتدهور ، ينحطّ : يسوء
▸ **degeneration** /dɪˌdʒenəˈreɪʃn/ *noun* [U]
تدهور ، انحطاط

degrade /dɪˈɡreɪd/ *verb* [T] to make people respect sb less: *It's the sort of film that really degrades women.* يحطّ من الشأن، يحقّر
▸ **degrading** *adj*: *Having to ask other people for money is degrading.* مهين ، مذلّ
degradation /ˌdeɡrəˈdeɪʃn/ *noun* [U] **1** degrading sb or being degraded: *the degradation of women* حطّ من الشأن ، تحقير : انحطاط

2 causing the condition of sth to become worse: *environmental degradation* تدهور

degree /dɪˈɡriː/ *noun* **1** [C] a measurement of temperature: *Water boils at 212 degrees Fahrenheit (212°F) or 100 degrees Celsius (100° C).* ○ *three degrees below zero/minus three degrees (-3°)*
درجة

2 [C] a measurement of angles: *a forty-five degree (45°) angle* ○ *An angle of 90 degrees is called a right angle.* درجة

3 [C,U] (used about feelings or qualities) a certain amount or level: *There is always some degree of risk involved in mountaineering.* ○ *Our lives have changed to a considerable degree.* ○ *I sympathize with her to some degree.*
حدّ : مقدار

4 [C] a qualification gained by successfully completing a course at university or college: *She's got a degree in Philosophy.* ○ *He's at university, doing an Economics degree.*
شهادة ، درجة علميّة

In Britain **degree** is the usual word for the qualification you get when you complete and pass a university course. You can study for a **diploma** at other types of college. The courses may be shorter and more practical than degree courses.

dehydrate /diːˈhaɪdreɪt; ˌdiːhaɪˈdreɪt/ *verb* **1** [T] (usually passive) to remove all the water from food so that it can be kept longer: *dehydrated vegetables* يجفّف ، يزيل منه الماء

2 [I,T] to lose or to take water from the body: *If you run for a long time in the heat, you start to dehydrate.* يزيل أو يفقد الماء من الجسم
▸ **dehydration** /ˌdiːhaɪˈdreɪʃn/ *noun* [U] جفاف

deign /deɪn/ *verb* [T] to do sth in a way that shows people that you are really too important for it: *He didn't even deign to look up when I entered the room.* يتنازل ، يتكرم

deity /ˈdeɪəti/ *noun* [C] (*pl.* **deities**) (*formal*) a god or goddess إله أو إلهة

dejected /dɪˈdʒektɪd/ *adj* very unhappy, especially because you are disappointed
كسير الخاطر ، مكتئب ، مغموم
▸ **dejectedly** *adv* بيأس ، بكدر
dejection /dɪˈdʒekʃn/ *noun* [U] اكتئاب ، غمّ ، يأس

delay /dɪˈleɪ/ *verb* **1** [T] to make sb/sth slow or late: *The plane was delayed for several hours because of bad weather.* يؤخّر

2 [I,T] **delay (doing sth)** to decide not to do sth until a later time: *I was forced to delay the trip until the following week.* يؤجّل
▸ **delay** *noun* [C,U] a situation or period of time where you have to wait: *Delays are likely on the roads because of heavy traffic.* ○ *Because of an accident, all trains are subject to delay.*
تأخير : تأخُّر

delegate[1] /ˈdelɪɡət/ *noun* [C] a person who has been chosen to speak or take decisions for a group of people, especially at a meeting
مندوب ، ممثّل

delegate[2] /ˈdelɪɡeɪt/ *verb* [I,T] to give sb with a lower job or rank a particular task to carry out: *You can't do everything yourself. You must learn how to delegate.* يفوّض ، يخوّل : ينتدب

delegation /ˌdelɪˈɡeɪʃn/ *noun* **1** [U] giving sb with a lower job or rank a particular task to perform تفويض ، توكيل

2 [C, with sing. or pl. verb] a group of people who have been chosen to speak or take decisions for a larger group of people, especially at a meeting: *The British delegation walked out of the meeting in protest.* وفد

delete /dɪˈliːt/ *verb* [T] to remove sth that is written: *'I will/will not be able to attend the meeting. Delete as appropriate.'* (= on a form, cross out the words which do not apply to you).
يشطب ، يزيل ، يحذف، يمحو

▸ **deletion** /dɪˈliːʃn/ *noun* **1** [U] the act of deleting شطب ، إزالة ، حذف، محو

2 [C] part of sth written or printed (e.g. a word, a sentence, a paragraph, etc.) that is deleted عبارة محذوفة أو مشطوبة

deliberate¹ /dɪˈlɪbərət/ *adj* **1** done on purpose; planned: *Was it an accident or was it deliberate?* متعمّد

2 done slowly and carefully, without hurrying: *She spoke in a calm, deliberate voice.* متأنٍّ ، متمهّل

▸ **deliberately** *adv* **1** on purpose; intentionally: *I didn't break it deliberately, it was an accident.* عمداً ، عن قصد

2 slowly and carefully, without hurrying بتأنٍّ ، متمهّلاً

deliberate² /dɪˈlɪbəreɪt/ *verb* [I,T] (*formal*) to think about or discuss sth thoroughly before making a decision: *The judges deliberated for an hour before announcing the winner.* يفكّر في الأمر مليّاً ؛ يتشاور ، يتداول

deliberation /dɪˌlɪbəˈreɪʃn/ *noun* **1** [C,U] discussion or thinking about sth: *After much deliberation I decided to reject the offer.* تفكير في الأمر ؛ تشاور ، تداول

2 [U] slowness and carefulness; lack of hurry: *He spoke with great deliberation.* تأنٍّ ، تمهّل

delicacy /ˈdelɪkəsi/ *noun* (*pl.* **delicacies**) **1** [U] lightness and gentleness; having a fine or detailed quality: *The pianist played the quiet song with great delicacy.* رقّة ، خفّة

2 [U] using or needing particular care or skill so as not to offend sb: *Be tactful! It's a matter of some delicacy.* حساسية ، رهافة

3 [C] a type of food that is considered particularly good: *Try this dish, it's a local delicacy.* طعام خاص مترف

delicate /ˈdelɪkət/ *adj* **1** fine or thin; easy to damage or break: *delicate skin* ○ *delicate china teacups* ○ *the delicate mechanisms of a watch* رقيق ، ناعم ؛ سريع العطب

2 frequently ill or easily made ill: *He was a delicate child and often in hospital.* رقيق الصحة

3 (used about colours, flavours, etc.) light and pleasant; not strong: *a delicate shade of pale blue* خفيف ، لطيف

4 requiring skilful treatment and care: *Repairing this is going to be a very delicate operation.* دقيق ، متطلب عناية خاصّة

▸ **delicately** *adv* **1** lightly, gently or finely: *delicately painted vases* بشكل لطيف ناعم

2 with skilful and careful movement: *She stepped delicately over the broken glass.* بخفّة ، بحذر

3 carefully so as not to offend sb: *I phrased my comments delicately so as not to upset her.* بلباقة

delicatessen /ˌdelɪkəˈtesn/ *noun* [C] a shop that sells special, unusual or foreign foods, especially cold cooked meat, cheeses, etc. مخزن لبيع أطعمة خاصّة منها اللحوم والأجبان

delicious /dɪˈlɪʃəs/ *adj* having a very pleasant taste or smell: *What are you cooking? It smells delicious.* لذيذ ، شهيّ

delight¹ /dɪˈlaɪt/ *noun* **1** [U] great pleasure; joy: *She laughed with delight as she opened the present.* سرور شديد ، ابتهاج

2 [C] something that gives sb great pleasure: *The story is a delight to read.* مصدر سرور ، مدعاة للبهجة

▸ **delightful** /-fl/ *adj*: *a delightful view* ○ *The people were delightful and I made a lot of friends.* ممتع ، مبهج ؛ لطيف

delightfully /-fəli/ *adv* بشكل جميل ، بصورة تبعث على البهجة

delight² /dɪˈlaɪt/ *verb* [T] to give sb great pleasure: *She delighted the audience by singing all her old songs.* يبهج ، يسر

PHR V **delight in sth/in doing sth** to get great pleasure from sth: *He delights in playing tricks on people.* يجد متعة وسروراً

▸ **delighted** *adj* **delighted (at/with sth)**; **delighted (to do sth/that...)** extremely pleased: *'How do you feel about winning today?' 'Delighted.'* ○ *She was delighted at getting the job/that she got the job.* ○ *They're absolutely delighted with their baby.* ○ *'Would you like to come for dinner?' 'Thanks, I'd be delighted to.'* مسرور جداً ، مبتهج

delinquency /dɪˈlɪŋkwənsi/ *noun* [U] bad or criminal behaviour, usually among young people جنوح (الأحداث)

delinquent /dɪˈlɪŋkwənt/ *adj* (usually used about a young person) behaving badly and often breaking the law: *delinquent children* جانح

▸ **delinquent** *noun* [C]: *a juvenile delinquent* حَدَث جانح

delirious /dɪˈlɪriəs/ *adj* **1** speaking or thinking in a crazy way, often because of a fever مهلوس ، هاذٍ

2 extremely happy في غاية السعادة

▸ **deliriously** *adv* باهتياج

deliver /dɪˈlɪvə(r)/ *verb* **1** [I,T] to take sth (goods, letters, etc.) to the place requested or to the address on it: *Your order will be delivered within five days.* يوصل ، يسلّم

2 [T] to help a mother to give birth to her baby: *The doctor who delivered the baby said she was lucky to be alive.* يولّد

3 [T] to give sth (a speech, a warning, etc.): *He delivered a long lecture to the staff about efficiency.* يلقي (خطاباً مثلاً)

4 [I] **deliver (on sth)** (*informal*) to do or give sth that you have promised: *He's made a lot of promises, but can he deliver?* يفي بالوعد ، ينفّذ

IDM **come up with/deliver the goods** → GOODS

delivery /dɪˈlɪvəri/ *noun* (*pl.* **deliveries**) **1** [U] the act of taking sth (goods, letters, parcels, etc.) to the place or person who has ordered it or whose address is on it: *Please allow 28 days for delivery.* ○ *a delivery van* تسليم ، توصيل

2 [C] an occasion when sth is delivered: *Are there any postal deliveries here on Sundays?* دور توزيع ، توزيعة

3 [C] something (goods, letters, parcels, etc.) that is delivered رسالة أو طرد مثلاً يسلّم بالبريد

4 [C] the process of giving birth to a baby: *an easy delivery* ولادة ، وضع

delta /ˈdeltə/ *noun* [C] an area of flat land shaped like a triangle where a river divides into smaller rivers flowing towards the sea دلتا النهر

delude /dɪˈluːd/ *verb* [T] to make sb believe sth that is not true: *If he thinks he's going to get rich quickly, he's deluding himself.* ❶ The noun is **delusion**. يخدع ، يوهم

deluge /ˈdeljuːdʒ/ *noun* [C] **1** a sudden very heavy fall of rain; a flood أمطار غزيرة مفاجئة : طوفان

2 a very large number of things that happen or arrive at the same time: *The programme was followed by a deluge of complaints from the public.* فيض ، سيل

▶ **deluge** *verb* [T] (usually passive) to send or give sb/sth a very large quantity of sth, all at the same time: *They were deluged with applications for the job.* يغرقه بـ

delusion /dɪˈluːʒn/ *noun* [C,U] a false belief: *He seems to be under the delusion that he's popular.* ❶ The verb is **delude**. وهم

de luxe /dəˈlʌks; -ˈlʊks/ *adj* of extremely high quality and more expensive than usual: *a de luxe hotel* ممتاز ، فاخر ، راقٍ

delve /delv/ *verb* [I] **delve into sth** to search inside sth: *She delved into the bag and brought out a tiny box.* ○ *(figurative) We must delve further into the past to find the origins of the custom.* ينقّب ؛ يتعمّق

Dem. *abbrev* = DEMOCRAT; DEMOCRATIC (PARTY)

🔑**demand**[1] /dɪˈmɑːnd; *US* dɪˈmænd/ *noun* **1** [C] **a demand (for sth/that...)** a strong request or order that must be obeyed: *The demand for the kidnappers to release the hostage has not been met.* ○ *a demand for changes in the law* ○ *I was amazed by their demand that I should leave immediately.* مطالبة

2 [U, sing.] **demand (for sth/sb)** the desire or need for sth/sb among a group of people: *We no longer stock that product because there is no demand for it.* طلب

IDM **in demand** wanted by a lot of people: *I'm in demand this weekend – I've had three invitations!* رائج ، عليه طلب كبير

make demands on sb to require a large amount of effort from sb: *Playing so many matches makes enormous demands on the players.* يتطلّب مجهوداً كبيراً

on demand whenever you ask for it: *This treatment is available from your doctor on demand.* عند الطلب

🔑**demand**[2] /dɪˈmɑːnd; *US* dɪˈmænd/ *verb* [T] **1** to ask for sth in a way that shows you expect to get it: *I walked into the office and demanded to see the manager.* ○ *She demanded that I pay her immediately.* ○ *Your behaviour was disgraceful and I demand an apology.* يطالب ، يطلب بحزم

2 to ask a question in an aggressive way: *'Have you seen her?' he demanded.* يسأل بحدّة

3 to require or need: *a sport that demands skill as well as strength* يتطلّب ، يحتاج إلى

demanding /dɪˈmɑːndɪŋ; *US* dɪˈmændɪŋ/ *adj* **1** (used about a job, task, etc.) requiring a great deal of effort, care, skill, etc: *It will be a demanding schedule – I have to go to six cities in six days.* متطلّب جهداً أو مهارة وغير ذلك

2 (used about a person) constantly wanting attention or expecting very high standards of people: *a demanding child* ○ *a demanding boss* متطلّب عناية كبيرة ؛ ملحف

demise /dɪˈmaɪz/ *noun* [sing.] **1** *(formal)* the death of a person: *the King's demise* وفاة

2 the unsuccessful end of sth: *Poor business decisions led to the company's demise.* زوال ، انتهاء

democracy /dɪˈmɒkrəsi/ *noun* (*pl.* **democracies**) **1** [U] a system in which the government of a country is elected by all of the people الديموقراطيّة

2 [C] a country that has this system: *How long has that country been a democracy?* (دولة) ديموقراطيّة

3 [U] the right of everyone in an organization, etc. to vote on matters that affect them and to be treated equally: *There is a need for more democracy in the company.* ديموقراطيّة

democrat /ˈdeməkræt/ *noun* [C] **1** a person who believes in and supports democracy ديموقراطيّ

2 **Democrat** (*abbr* **Dem.**) a member or supporter of the Democratic Party of the USA ➲ Look at **Republican**. عضو أو مؤيّد للحزب الديموقراطي الأمريكي

democratic /ˌdeməˈkrætɪk/ *adj* **1** based on the system of democracy: *democratic elections* ○ *a democratic government* ديموقراطيّ

2 having or supporting equality for all members: *the democratic traditions of the party* ○ *a fully democratic society* ديموقراطيّ

▶ **democratically** /-kli/ *adv*: *a democratically elected government* بشكل ديموقراطيّ

Demo'cratic Party *noun* [sing.] (*abbr* **Dem.**) one of the two main political parties of the USA الحزب الديموقراطيّ

demolish /dɪˈmɒlɪʃ/ *verb* [T] **1** to knock sth down (e.g. a building): *The old shops were demolished and a supermarket was built in their place.* يهدم

2 to destroy sth (an idea, a belief, etc.): *She demolished his argument in one sentence.* يقوّض ، يدحَض

▶ **demolition** /ˌdeməˈlɪʃn/ *noun* [C,U] the act of knocking down or destroying sth هدم ؛ تقويض

demon /ˈdiːmən/ *noun* [C] an evil spirit: *He thinks he is possessed by demons.* شيطان

🔑**demonstrate** /ˈdemənstreɪt/ *verb* **1** [T] to show clearly that sth exists or is true; to prove: *Scientists demonstrated the presence of radioactiv-*

a b c **d** e f g h i j k l m n o p q r s t u v w x y z

ity in the soil. ○ *The prison escape demonstrates the need for greater security.* يُثبت ، يبرهن على

2 [T] to show and explain to sb how to do sth or how sth works: *The crew demonstrated the use of life jackets just after take-off.* يوضّح عملياً

3 [I] **demonstrate (against/for sb/sth)** to take part in a public protest or march in which a crowd of people express their opposition or support of sb/sth: *Enormous crowds have been demonstrating for human rights.* يشترك في مظاهرة ، يتظاهر

demonstration /ˌdemənˈstreɪʃn/ *noun* **1** [C,U] something that shows clearly that sth exists or is true: *This accident is a clear demonstration of the system's faults.* دليل ، برهان

2 [C,U] an act of showing or explaining to sb how to do sth or how sth works: *The salesman gave me a demonstration of what the computer could do.* ايضاح عمليّ

3 [C] **a demonstration (against/for sb/sth)** a public protest or march in which a crowd of people show how they oppose or support sb/sth: *Many thousands took part in demonstrations for greater political freedom.* مظاهرة

demonstrative /dɪˈmɒnstrətɪv/ *adj* (used about a person) showing feelings, especially affection, openly (شخص) لا يخفي مشاعره

demonstrator /ˈdemənstreɪtə(r)/ *noun* [C] a person who takes part in a public protest or march متظاهر

demoralize (*also* **demoralise**) /dɪˈmɒrəlaɪz; *US* -ˈmɔːr-/ *verb* [T] to make sb lose confidence or the courage to continue doing sth: *Repeated defeats demoralized the team.* يثبّط العزيمة ، يحطِّم المعنويّات

▸ **demoralization** (*also* **demoralisation**) /dɪˌmɒrəlaɪˈzeɪʃn; *US* -ˌmɔːrəlɪˈz-/ *noun* [U] ضعف المعنويّات

demure /dɪˈmjʊə(r)/ *adj* (used especially about a girl or young woman) shy, quiet and well behaved حييّة ، محتشمة

den /den/ *noun* [C] **1** the hidden home of certain wild animals, e.g. lions عرين

2 a secret place, especially for illegal activities: *a gambling den* مخبأ ، وكر

denial /dɪˈnaɪəl/ *noun* **1** [C] a statement that sth is not true: *The minister issued a denial that he was involved in the scandal.* إنكار ، تكذيب

2 [C,U] **(a) denial (of sth)** refusing to allow sb to have or do sth: *a denial of personal freedom* منع ، رفض

ℹ The verb is **deny**.

denim /ˈdenɪm/ *noun* **1** [U] a thick cotton material (often blue) that is used for making clothes, e.g. jeans قماش قطنيّ متين

2 denims [plural] trousers made of denim بَنْطلون مصنوع من هذا القماش

denomination /dɪˌnɒmɪˈneɪʃn/ *noun* [C] a religious group that is part of a larger religious organization: *Anglicans, Methodists and members of other denominations attended the meeting.* طائفة دينية

denote /dɪˈnəʊt/ *verb* [T] to indicate or be a sign of sth; to mean: *What does* [U] *denote in this dictionary?* يدلّ على ، يعني

denounce /dɪˈnaʊns/ *verb* [T] to say publicly that sth is wrong; to be very critical of a person in public: *Opposition MPs have denounced the government's decision.* ○ *The actor has been denounced as a bad influence on young people.* ℹ The noun is **denunciation**. يشجب ، يدين ، يتّهم

dense /dens/ *adj* **1** containing a lot of things or people close together: *dense forests* ○ *areas of dense population* كثيف ، مكتظّ ؛ مكتنز

2 difficult to see through: *dense fog* كثيف

3 (*informal*) not intelligent; stupid بليد ، غبيّ

▸ **densely** *adv*: *densely populated* بكثافة ، بشكل مكتظّ

density /ˈdensəti/ *noun* (*pl.* **densities**) **1** [U] the number of things or people in a place in relation to its area: *the density of population* كثافة ، ازدحام

2 [C,U] (*technical*) the relation of the weight of a substance to the space it occupies الكثافة

dent /dent/ *noun* [C] a hollow place in the surface of sth hard, especially metal, that is the result of sth hitting or pressing against it: *This tin's got a dent in it.* بعجة ، "طعجة" : "فعصة"

▸ **dent** *verb* [T] to damage sth by hitting it and making a hollow place in it: *I hit a wall and dented the front of the car.* يبعج ، "يطعج" ، "يفعص"

dental /ˈdentl/ *adj* connected with teeth: *dental care* ذو علاقة بالأسنان

🔑 **dentist** /ˈdentɪst/ (*also* **ˈdental surgeon**) *noun* [C] a person whose job is to look after people's teeth: *The dentist examined my teeth.* ℹ We refer to the dentist's surgery as 'the dentist's': *I went to the dentist's to have a tooth out.* طبيب أسنان

dentures /ˈdentʃəz/ *noun* [plural] = FALSE TEETH

denunciation /dɪˌnʌnsiˈeɪʃn/ *noun* [C,U] an expression of strong disapproval of sb/sth in public: *a strong denunciation of the invasion* ℹ The verb is **denounce**. شجب ، إدانة ، استنكار

🔑 **deny** /dɪˈnaɪ/ *verb* [T] (*pres part* **denying**; *3rd pers sing pres* **denies**; *pt, pp* **denied**) **1 deny sth/doing sth/that...** to state that sth is not true: *In court he denied all the charges.* ○ *When I challenged her, she denied telling lies/that she had told lies.* يُنكر

2 deny sb sth; deny sth (to sb) to refuse to allow sb to have sth: *She was denied permission to remain in the country.* يمنع من ، يحرم من

ℹ The noun is **denial**.

deodorant /diˈəʊdərənt/ *noun* [C,U] a chemical substance that you put onto your body to destroy or prevent bad smells مزيل للروائح (الكريهة)

dep. *abbrev* = DEPARTS

depart /dɪˈpɑːt/ *verb* [I] (*formal*) to leave a place, usually at the beginning of a journey: *Ferries depart for Spain twice a day.* ○ *The next train to the*

airport departs from platform 2. ❶ The noun is **departure**. ➲ Look at the note at **leave**.
يغادر ؛ يرحل

department /dɪˈpɑːtmənt/ *noun* [C] (*abbr* **Dept**) **1** one of the sections into which an organization (e.g. a school or a business) is divided: *the Modern Languages department* ○ *The book department is on the second floor.* ○ *She works in the accounts department.* إدارة ؛ قسم ؛ شعبة

2 = MINISTRY (1): *the Department of Health*

▶ **departmental** /ˌdiːpɑːtˈmentl/ *adj* concerning a department: *There is a departmental meeting once a month.* متعلّق بالقسم أو الدائرة أو نحو ذلك

deˈpartment store *noun* [C] a large shop that is divided into departments selling many different types of goods متجر ضخم يبيع سلعاً منوّعة

departure /dɪˈpɑːtʃə(r)/ *noun* [C,U] **1** leaving or going away from a place: *Arrivals and departures are shown on the board in the main hall of the station.* ○ *Passengers should check in at least one hour before departure.* مغادرة ، انطلاق

2 an action which is different from what is usual or expected: *a departure from normal practice* انحراف ، تحوّل

depend /dɪˈpend/ *verb*

IDM that depends; it (all) depends (used alone or at the beginning of a sentence) it is not certain; it is influenced or decided by sth: *'Can you lend me some money?' 'That depends. How much do you want?'* ○ *I don't know whether I'll see him. It all depends what time he gets here.* هذا يتوقّف على...

PHR V depend on sb/sth to be sure that sb/sth will help you; to trust sb/sth to do sth: *If you ever need any help, you know you can depend on me.* ○ *You can't depend on the trains. They're always late.* ○ *I was depending on things going according to plan.* ○ *You can always depend on him to say what he thinks* (= you can be sure that he will say what he thinks). يعتمد على ؛ يثق بِ

depend on sb/sth (for sth) to need sb/sth to provide sth: *I depend on my parents for advice.* ○ *Our organization depends on donations from the public.* يعتمد أو يتكّل على

depend on sth to be decided or influenced by sth: *His whole future depends on these exams.* ○ *The starting salary will be between £17 000 and £19 000, depending on age and experience.* يتوقّف على

▶ **dependable** /-əbl/ *adj* that can be trusted: *The bus service is usually very dependable.* يعتمد عليه، موثوق به

dependant (*especially US* **dependent**) /dɪˈpendənt/ *noun* [C] a person who depends on sb else for money, a home, food, etc: *The insurance provides cover for you and all your dependants.* شخص يعتمد على غيره لإعالته

dependence /dɪˈpendəns/ *noun* [U] **dependence on sb/sth** the state of needing sb/sth: *The country wants to reduce its dependence on imported oil.* اعتماد (على) ، تعويل

dependency /dɪˈpendənsi/ *noun* [U] the state of being dependent on sb/sth; the state of being unable to live without sth, especially a drug: *a drug dependency clinic* اعتماد ، تبعيّة ، إدمان

dependent /dɪˈpendənt/ *adj* **1 dependent (on sb/sth)** needing sb/sth to support you: *The industry is heavily dependent on government funding.* ○ *dependent children* معتمد على؛ تابع

2 dependent on sb/sth influenced or decided by sb/sth: *The price you pay is dependent on the number in your group.* متوقّف على

depict /dɪˈpɪkt/ *verb* [T] **1** to show sb/sth in a painting or drawing: *a painting depicting a country scene* يصوّر ، يرسم

2 to describe sb/sth in words: *The novel depicts rural life a century ago.* يَصِف

deplete /dɪˈpliːt/ *verb* [T] to reduce the amount of sth: *We are depleting the world's natural resources.* يستهلك ، يستنزف

▶ **depletion** /dɪˈpliːʃn/ *noun* [U]: *the depletion of the ozone layer* استهلاك ، استنفاد

deplore /dɪˈplɔː(r)/ *verb* [T] (*formal*) to feel or state that sth is morally bad: *I deplore such dishonest behaviour.* يستنكر ، يستهجن ، يندّد بِ

▶ **deplorable** /dɪˈplɔːrəbl/ *adj* morally bad and deserving disapproval مستهجن أو مستنكر ؛ مؤسف

deplorably /-əbli/ *adv* بصورة مؤسفة أو مخزية

deploy /dɪˈplɔɪ/ *verb* [T] **1** to put soldiers or weapons in a position where they can be used ينشر القوات

2 to arrange people or things so that they can be used efficiently يوزّع (الأشخاص أو الأشياء) لتسهيل العمل

▶ **deployment** *noun* [U]: *the deployment of troops* نشر القوّات

deport /dɪˈpɔːt/ *verb* [T] to send a foreigner out of a country officially: *A number of illegal immigrants have been deported.* يرحّل ، يخرج من البلاد

▶ **deportation** /ˌdiːpɔːˈteɪʃn/ *noun* [C,U]: *The illegal immigrants face deportation.* ترحيل ، إخراج

depose /dɪˈpəʊz/ *verb* [T] to remove a ruler or leader from power: *There was a revolution and the dictator was deposed.* يخلع ، يعزل

deposit¹ /dɪˈpɒzɪt/ *verb* [T] **1** to put money into an account at a bank: *He deposited £20 a week into his savings account.* يودع مالاً في حسابه

2 to put sth valuable in a official place where it is safe until needed again: *Valuables can be deposited in the hotel safe.* يودع

3 to pay a sum of money as the first payment for sth, with the rest of the money to be paid later: *You will have to deposit 10% of the cost when you book.* يدفع القسط الأول ؛ يدفع عربوناً

4 to put sth down somewhere: *He deposited his bags on the floor and sat down.* يضع

5 to leave sth lying on a surface, as the result of a natural or chemical process: *mud deposited by a flood* يرسّب ؛ يترك وراءه

deposit² /dɪˈpɒzɪt/ *noun* [C] **1** a sum of money paid into a bank account; the paying of a sum of money into a bank account وديعة ؛ ايداع

2 a deposit (on sth) a sum of money which is

the first payment for sth, with the rest of the money to be paid later: *Once you have paid a deposit, the booking will be confirmed.* قسط أول : عربون

3 a deposit (on sth) a sum of money that you pay when you rent sth and get back when you return it without damage: *Boats can be hired for £5 an hour, plus £20 deposit.* وديعة ، تأمين

4 a substance that has been left on a surface or has developed in the ground as the result of a natural or chemical process: *mineral deposits* راسب : طبقة معدنيّة

de'posit account *noun* [C] a type of bank account where your money earns interest. You cannot take money out of a deposit account without arranging it first with the bank. حساب وديعة ، حساب مع فائدة

depot /'depəʊ; *US* 'di:pəʊ/ *noun* [C] **1** a place where large numbers of vehicles (buses, lorries, etc.) are kept when not in use مستودع سيّارات

2 a place where military supplies are stored مستودع عسكري

3 (*US*) a bus or railway station محطة قطارات أو باصات

depreciate /dɪ'pri:ʃieɪt/ *verb* [I] to lose value, especially as a result of use or age تنخفض قيمته
▸ **depreciation** /dɪˌpri:ʃi'eɪʃn/ *noun* [C,U] انخفاض قيمة (الأسهم مثلاً)

depress /dɪ'pres/ *verb* [T] **1** to make sb unhappy: *The thought of going to work tomorrow really depresses me.* يكدّر ، يغمّ

2 (used especially in connection with business) to cause sth to become less successful or profitable: *The reduction in the number of tourists has depressed local trade.* يكسد (التجارة)

3 (*formal*) to press sth down when operating sth: *To switch off the machine, depress the lever.* يضغط على (إلى الأسفل) ، ينزل

▸ **depressed** *adj* very unhappy, often for a long period. If you are depressed you may be suffering from the medical condition of depression: *He's been very depressed since he lost his job.* مكتئب
depressing *adj* making sb feel sad or without hope: *The outlook for the future of the company is very depressing.* مكدّر ، محزن ، لا يدعو إلى التفاؤل
depressingly *adv* بصورة تبعث على الكآبة

depression /dɪ'preʃn/ *noun* **1** [U] a feeling of unhappiness and hopelessness that lasts for a long time. Depression can be a medical condition and may have physical symptoms. اكتئاب

2 [C] a period when the economic situation is bad, with little business activity and many people without a job كساد : ركود اقتصادي

3 [C] a hollow part in the surface of sth: *a depression in the ground* منخفَض

deprive /dɪ'praɪv/ *verb* [T] **deprive sb/sth of sth** to prevent sb/sth from having sth; to take away sth from sb/sth: *to deprive people of their rights as citizens* ○ *The prisoners were deprived of food.* يحرم
▸ **deprived** *adj* not having enough of the basic things in life, such as food, money, etc: *He came from a deprived background.* فقير ، محروم من أساسيّات الحياة
deprivation /ˌdeprɪ'veɪʃn/ *noun* [C,U] حرمان

Dept (*especially US* **Dept.**) *abbrev* = DEPARTMENT

depth /depθ/ *noun* **1** [C,U] the distance down from the top surface of sth; the measurement of how deep sth is: *What's the depth of the swimming pool?* ○ *The hole should be 3 cm in depth.* عمْق

2 [C,U] the distance from the front to the back: *the depth of a shelf* عرض ، عمق

3 [U] (used about emotions, knowledge, etc.) the amount that a person has: *He tried to convince her of the depth of his feelings for her.* عمق ، مقدار

IDM **in depth** looking at all the details: *to discuss a problem in depth* بالتفصيل ، بتعمّق
out of your depth 1 in water that is too deep for you to stand up in ماء أعمق من أن يقف فيه

2 in a situation that is too difficult for you: *When they start discussing politics I soon get out of my depth.* (موضوع) أصعب من أن يفهمه

deputation /ˌdepju'teɪʃn/ *noun* [C, with sing. or pl. verb] a group of people sent to sb to speak for others وفد ، مندوبون

deputize (*also* **deputise**) /'depjətaɪz/ *verb* [I] **deputize (for sb)** to act for sb who is absent or unable to do sth ينوب عن

deputy /'depjəti/ *noun* [C] (*pl.* **deputies**) the second most important person in a particular organization. A deputy does the work of his/her boss if the boss is absent: *the Deputy Manager* ○ *While I am away my deputy will take over.* نائب الرئيس ، وكيل

derail /dɪ'reɪl/ *verb* [T] to cause a train to come off a railway track يخرج القطار عن الخط الحديدي
▸ **derailment** *noun* [C,U] an occasion when this happens: *Due to a derailment, all trains have been cancelled this morning.* خروج القطار عن الخط الحديدي

deranged /dɪ'reɪndʒd/ *adj* thinking and behaving in a way that is not normal, especially because of mental illness فاقد صوابه ، مشوّش ؛ مجنون

derby /'dɜ:rbi; 'dɑ:bi/ *noun* [C] (*pl.* **derbies**) (*US*) = BOWLER

derelict /'derəlɪkt/ *adj* no longer used and in bad condition: *a derelict house* مخرّب ومهجور

deride /dɪ'raɪd/ *verb* [T] to say that sb/sth is ridiculous; to laugh at sb/sth in a cruel way يسخر أو يهزأ من
▸ **derision** /dɪ'rɪʒn/ *noun* [U]: *Her comments were met with howls of derision.* سخرية أو استهزاء
derisive /dɪ'raɪsɪv/ *adj*: *'What rubbish!' he said with a derisive laugh.* ساخر أو مستهزئ

derisory /dɪ'raɪsəri/ *adj* so small that it is ridiculous or does not deserve to be considered seriously: *He made a derisory offer, which I turned down immediately.* تافه ، ضئيل لا يستحق الذكر

derivation /ˌderɪ'veɪʃn/ *noun* [C,U] the origin from which a word or phrase has developed: *a word of Latin derivation* أصل : اشتقاق

derivative /dɪˈrɪvətɪv/ *adj* copied from sth or influenced by sth and therefore not new or original غير أصليّ ، منقول عن غيره

▸ **derivative** *noun* [C] a form of sth (especially a word) that has developed from the original form: *'Sadness' is a derivative of 'sad.'* المشتقّ : كلمة مشتقّة

derive /dɪˈraɪv/ *verb* **1** [T] (*formal*) to get sth (especially a feeling or an advantage) from sth: *I derive great satisfaction from my work.* يستمدّ، يحصل على

2 [I,T] to come from sth; to have sth as its origin: *'Mutton' derives from the French word 'mouton'.* ○ *The town derives its name from the river on which it was built.* يأتي من ، يشتقّ

derogatory /dɪˈrɒɡətri; *US* -tɔːri/ *adj* expressing a lack of respect for, or a low opinion of sth: *derogatory comments about the standard of my work* معبّر عن الاستخفاف ، حاطّ من القيمة

descend /dɪˈsend/ *verb* [I,T] (*formal*) to go down to a lower place; to go down sth: *The plane started to descend and a few minutes later we landed.* ○ *She descended the stairs slowly.* ❶ The opposite is **ascend**. يهبط ، ينزل

IDM **be descended from sb** to have as a relative or relatives in the distant past: *He says he's descended from a Russian prince.* ينحدر من

▸ **descendant** /-ənt/ *noun* [C] a person who is related to sb who lived a long time ago: *Her family are descendants of one of the first convicts who were sent to Australia.* ➲ Look at **ancestor**. سليل ، شخص منحدر من

descent /dɪˈsent/ *noun* **1** [C] a movement down to a lower place: *The pilot informed us that we were about to begin our descent.* هبوط ، نزول

2 [U] family origins, especially in connection with nationality: *He is of Italian descent.* أصل ، سلالة

describe /dɪˈskraɪb/ *verb* [T] **describe sb/sth (as sth)** to say what sb/sth is like, or what happened: *Can you describe the bag you lost?* ○ *It's impossible to describe how I felt.* ○ *She described what had happened to the reporter.* ○ *The thief was described as tall, thin, and aged about twenty.* ○ *Would you describe yourself as confident?* يصِف

description /dɪˈskrɪpʃn/ *noun* **1** [C,U] a picture in words of sb/sth or an account of sth that happened; the ability to describe sb/sth: *The man gave the police a detailed description of the burglar.* ○ *Her description of the events that evening was most amusing.* وَصْف

2 [C] a type or kind of sth: *It must be a tool of some description, but I don't know what it's for.* نوع أو ضرب من

descriptive /dɪˈskrɪptɪv/ *adj* **1** that describes sb/sth: *a piece of descriptive writing* وصفيّ ، تصويريّ

2 that describes sb/sth in a skilful and interesting way: *She gave a highly descriptive account of the journey.* (وصف) ممتع شيّق

desert¹ /dɪˈzɜːt/ *verb* **1** [T] to leave sb/sth, usually for ever: *Many people have deserted the countryside and moved to the towns.* يهجر، يترك

2 [I,T] (used especially about sb in the armed forces) to leave without permission: *He deserted because he didn't want to fight.* يفرّ (من الجنديّة)

▸ **deserted** *adj* empty, because all the people have left: *a deserted house* مهجور

deserter *noun* [C] a person who leaves military duty without permission الفارّ من الجيش

desertion /dɪˈzɜːʃn/ *noun* [C,U] leaving sb/sth, especially your husband or wife, or leaving military duty without permission هَجْر ، تخلٍّ عن : فرار من الجيش

desert² /ˈdezət/ *noun* [C,U] a large area of land, usually covered with sand, that has very little water and very few plants: *the Gobi Desert* صحراء

ˌdesert ˈisland *noun* [C] an island, especially a tropical one, where nobody lives جزيرة مهجورة

deserve /dɪˈzɜːv/ *verb* [T] (not used in the continuous tenses) to earn sth, especially a suitable reward or punishment, for sth that you have done: *We've done a lot of work and we deserve a break.* ○ *He deserves to be punished severely for such a crime.* يستحقّ

▸ **deservedly** /dɪˈzɜːvɪdli/ *adv* as is deserved; rightly: *He deservedly won the Best Actor award.* عن جدارة ، باستحقاق

deserving /dɪˈzɜːvɪŋ/ *adj* that deserves help: *This charity is a most deserving cause.* مستأهِل أو مستحقّ لـ

design /dɪˈzaɪn/ *noun* **1** [C] a drawing that shows how sth should be made: *The architect showed us her design for the new theatre.* تصميم ، مخطّط ، رسم

2 [U] the way in which sth is planned and made or in which the parts of sth are arranged: *Design faults have been discovered in the car.* تصميم

3 [U] the process and skill of making drawings that show how sth should be made: *to study industrial design* ○ *graphic design* تصميم

4 [C] a pattern of lines, shapes, etc. that decorate sth: *a T-shirt with a geometric design on it* رسم تزييني

▸ **design** *verb* **1** [I,T] to plan and make a drawing of how sth will be made: *She designs the interiors of shops.* يصمّم

2 [T] to invent, plan and develop sth for a particular purpose: *I designed a scheme for increasing profits.* ○ *The bridge wasn't designed for such heavy traffic.* يرسم خطّة : يهدف

designate /ˈdezɪɡneɪt/ *verb* [T] (*formal*) **1** to give sth a name to show that it has a particular purpose: *This has been designated a conservation area.* يسمّي

2 to choose sb for a particular job or task يعيّن

3 to show or mark sth: *These arrows designate the emergency exits.* يدلّ على ، يحدّد

designer /dɪˈzaɪnə(r)/ *noun* [C] a person whose job is to make drawings showing how sth will be made: *a fashion designer* ○ *designer jeans* (= made by a famous designer) مصمَّم (أزياء مثلاً)

desirable /dɪˈzaɪərəbl/ *adj* **1** wanted, often by many people; worth having: *a desirable area* (= one that many people would like to live in) ○ *Experience is desirable but not essential for this job.* مرغوب فيه

2 sexually attractive جذاب (جنسيًا)

desire¹ /dɪˈzaɪə(r)/ *noun* [C,U] **1 (a) desire (for sth/to do sth)** the feeling of wanting sth very much; a strong wish: *the desire for a peaceful solution to the crisis* ○ *I have no desire to visit that place again.* رغبة

2 the wish for sexual relations with sb شهوة

desire² /dɪˈzaɪə(r)/ *verb* [T] **1** (*formal*) to want: *They have everything they could possibly desire.* يرغب ، يشتهي

2 to find sb/sth sexually attractive يشتهي (امرأة مثلاً)

desk /desk/ *noun* [C] **1** a type of table, often with drawers, that you sit at to write or work: *The pupils took their books out of their desks.* ○ *a computer that fits easily onto any desk* مقعد (مدرسيّ) : مكتب : منضدة

2 a table or place in a building where a particular service is provided: *Brochures are available at the information desk.* منصّة ، مكتب ، قسم

desktop /ˈdesktɒp/ *noun* [C] **1** the top of a desk سطح المكتب

2 a computer screen on which you can see symbols showing the programs, information, etc. that are available to be used الشاشة

ˌdesktop ˈpublishing (*abbr* **DTP**) *noun* [U] the use of a small computer and a machine for printing, to produce books, magazines and other printed material الطباعة والنشر بواسطة الكمبيوتر

desolate /ˈdesələt/ *adj* **1** (used about a place) sad, empty and depressing: *desolate wasteland* موحش ، مقفر

2 (used about a person) lonely, very unhappy and without hope تعيس شاعر بالوحدة، قانط

▸ **desolation** /ˌdesəˈleɪʃn/ *noun* [U] **1** the state of being empty because all the people have left: *All the factories closed, leaving the town a scene of desolation.* وحشة ، كآبة ، إقفار

2 the feeling of being lonely and without hope: *He felt utter desolation when his wife died.* تعاسة ، وحدة : قنوط

despair /dɪˈspeə(r)/ *noun* [U] the state of having lost all hope: *I felt like giving up in despair.* ○ *Despair drove him to attempt suicide.* يأس ، قنوط

▸ **despair** *verb* [I] **despair (of sb/sth)** to lose all hope and to feel that there will be no improvement: *Don't despair. Keep trying and I'm sure you'll get it right.* ○ *We began to despair of ever finding somewhere to live.* ييأس ، يقنط

despairing *adj*: *a despairing cry* (صرخة) يائسة

despatch = DISPATCH

desperate /ˈdespərət/ *adj* **1** out of control and willing to do anything to change the situation you are in because it is so terrible: *She became desperate when her money ran out.* ○ *I only took this job because I was desperate.*

مستميت ، متهوّر لشدّة يأسه

2 done with little hope of success, as a last thing to try when everything else has failed: *I made a desperate attempt to persuade her to change her mind.* (محاولة) أخيرة يائسة

3 desperate (for sth/to do sth) wanting or needing sth very much: *Let's go into a cafe. I'm desperate for a drink.* في أشدّ الحاجة إلى

4 terrible, very serious: *There is a desperate shortage of skilled workers.* فظيع ، هائل ، شديد

▸ **desperately** *adv*: *She was desperately* (= extremely) *unlucky not to win.* للغاية ، إلى أقصى حدّ

desperation /ˌdespəˈreɪʃn/ *noun* [U] the feeling or state of being desperate: *She felt she wanted to scream in desperation.* يأس شديد

despicable /dɪˈspɪkəbl/ *adj* deserving to be hated: *a despicable liar* ○ *a despicable act of terrorism* حقير ، دنيء، بغيض

despise /dɪˈspaɪz/ *verb* [T] to hate sb/sth; to consider sb/sth worthless: *I despise him for lying about me to other people.* يحتقر ؛ يكره

despite /dɪˈspaɪt/ *prep* (used to show that sth happened although you would not expect it): *Despite having very little money, they enjoy life.* ○ *The scheme went ahead despite public opposition.*

رغم ، بالرغم من

despondent /dɪˈspɒndənt/ *adj* without hope; expecting no improvement قانط ، يائس

▸ **despondency** /dɪˈspɒndənsi/ *noun* [U]

قنوط ، اكتئاب

dessert /dɪˈzɜːt/ *noun* [C,U] something sweet that is eaten after the main part of a meal: *What would you like for dessert – ice cream or fresh fruit?* ➲ Look at **pudding** and **sweet**.

الحلوى في نهاية الوجبة

dessertspoon /dɪˈzɜːtspuːn/ *noun* [C] a spoon of medium size, used for eating dessert ملعقة متوسطة الحجم

destabilize /ˌdiːˈsteɪbəlaɪz/ *verb* [T] to make a system, government, country, etc. become less safe and successful: *Terrorist attacks were threatening to destabilize the government.*

يزيل الاستقرار، يقلق الوضع

destination /ˌdestɪˈneɪʃn/ *noun* [C] the place where sb/sth is going or being sent: *I finally reached my destination two hours late.*

وجهة السفر : نهاية السَّفْرة : المكان المقصود

destined /ˈdestɪnd/ *adj* **1 destined for sth/to do sth** sure to or intended to be, have or do sth: *I think she is destined for success.* ○ *He was destined to become one of the country's leading politicians.* مكتوب له (النجاح)

2 destined for... on a journey or moving towards a particular place: *I boarded a bus destined for New York.* ○ *They were destined for a new life in a new country.* متّجه نحو، قاصد

destiny /ˈdestəni/ *noun* (*pl.* **destinies**) **1** [U] a power that people believe influences their lives; fate القضاء والقَدَر

2 [C] the things that happen to you in your life, especially things that you do not control: *She felt that it was her destiny to be a great singer.* ○ *The destiny of the country lies in the hands of the people.* قدَر ، قسمة

destitute /ˈdestɪtjuːt; *US* -tuːt/ *adj* not having the things that are necessary in life, such as money, food, a home, etc. فقير معدم

▸ **destitution** /ˌdestɪˈtjuːʃn; *US* -ˈtuːʃn/ *noun* [U] فاقة ، فقر مدقع

destroy /dɪˈstrɔɪ/ *verb* [T] **1** to damage sth so badly that it can no longer be used or no longer exists: *The building was destroyed by fire.* ○ *The defeat destroyed his confidence.* يخرِّب ، يدمِّر ؛ يقضي على

2 to kill an animal, especially because it is injured or dangerous: *The horse broke its leg and had to be destroyed.* يقتل حيواناً (جريحاً مثلاً) تخفيفاً عنه

▸ **destroyer** *noun* [C] **1** a person or thing that destroys sth المدمِّر

2 a small warship المدمِّرة (سفينة حربيّة)

destruction /dɪˈstrʌkʃn/ *noun* [U] destroying or being destroyed: *The war brought death and destruction to the city.* ○ *the destruction of the rainforests* دمار ، خراب ؛ تدمير

destructive /dɪˈstrʌktɪv/ *adj* causing a lot of damage: *destructive weapons* ○ *the destructive effects of drink and drugs* مدمِّر ، مخرِّب ، هدّام

detach /dɪˈtætʃ/ *verb* [T] **detach sth (from sth)** to separate sth from sth it is attached to: *Detach the form at the bottom of the page and send it to this address...* يفصل

▸ **detached** *adj* **1** not being or not feeling personally involved متجرِّد : غير مرتبط عاطفيّاً

2 (used about a house) not joined to any other house (بيت) منفصل

detachable /-əbl/ *adj* that can be separated from sth it is attached to قابل للفصل (عن شيء مربوط به)

detachment /dɪˈtætʃmənt/ *noun* **1** [U] the fact or feeling of not being personally involved تجرّد عاطفي ، عدم تحيز

2 [C] a group of soldiers who have been given a particular task away from the main group مفرزة ، تجريدة عسكريّة

detail[1] /ˈdiːteɪl; *US* dɪˈteɪl/ *noun* [C,U] a small individual fact, point or piece of information: *Just give me the basic facts. Don't worry about the details.* ○ *On the application form you should give details of your education and experience.* ○ *For full details of the offer, contact your local travel agent.* ○ *The work involves close attention to detail.* جزء تفصيليّ : تفصيل

IDM **go into detail(s)** to talk or write about the details of sth: *I can't go into detail now because it would take too long.* يذكر بالتفصيل ، يدخل بالتفاصيل

in detail including the details; thoroughly: *We haven't discussed the matter in detail yet.* بالتفصيل ، بإسهاب

detail[2] /ˈdiːteɪl; *US* dɪˈteɪl/ *verb* [T] to give a full list of sth; to describe sth fully: *He detailed all the equipment he needed for the job.* يعدِّد ، يفصِّل ، يصِف بالتفصيل

▸ **detailed** *adj* having many details or giving a lot of attention to details: *a detailed description of the accident* مفصَّل

detain /dɪˈteɪn/ *verb* [T] to stop sb from leaving a place; to delay sb: *A man has been detained by the police for questioning* (= kept at the police station). ○ *Don't let me detain you if you're busy.*
ⓘ The noun is **detention**. يحتجز : يؤخّر

detect /dɪˈtekt/ *verb* [T] to notice or discover sth that is difficult to see, feel, etc: *I detected a slight change in his attitude.* ○ *Traces of blood were detected on his clothes.* يلاحظ : يكتشف

▸ **detection** /dɪˈtekʃn/ *noun* [U]: *The crime escaped detection for many years.* كشف ، اهتداء إلى

detector *noun* [C] an instrument that is used for detecting sth: *a smoke detector* مكشاف: جهاز كشف

detective /dɪˈtektɪv/ *noun* [C] a person, especially a police officer, who tries to solve crimes and find the person who is guilty "التحرّي" ، بوليس سرّي

de'tective story *noun* [C] (*pl.* **detective stories**) a story about a crime in which sb tries to find out who the guilty person is قصّة بوليسيّة

détente (*also* **detente**) /ˌdeɪˈtɑːnt/ *noun* [U] (*formal*) a more friendly relationship between countries that had previously been very unfriendly towards each other وفاق (دولي)

detention /dɪˈtenʃn/ *noun* [U] **1** the act of stopping a person leaving a place, especially by keeping him/her in prison, often for political reasons
ⓘ The verb is **detain**. حجز : اعتقال

2 the punishment of being kept at school after the other children have gone home حبس

deter /dɪˈtɜː(r)/ *verb* [T] (deterring; deterred) **deter sb (from doing sth)** to make sb decide not to do sth: *The council is trying to deter visitors from bringing their cars into the city centre.* يردع ، يثني عن

detergent /dɪˈtɜːdʒənt/ *noun* [C,U] a chemical liquid or powder that is used for cleaning things مادّة منظِّفة

deteriorate /dɪˈtɪəriəreɪt/ *verb* [I] to become worse: *The political tension is deteriorating into civil war.* يتردّى ، يسوء ، يتدهور

▸ **deterioration** /dɪˌtɪəriəˈreɪʃn/ *noun* [C,U] تدهور ، تردٍّ

determination /dɪˌtɜːmɪˈneɪʃn/ *noun* [U] **1** the quality of having firmly decided to succeed in doing sth, even if it is very difficult or people are against you: *her determination to win* ○ *You need great determination to succeed in business.* عزيمة ، تصميم

2 the act of fixing or deciding sth: *the determination of future council policy* تحديد ، تقرير

determine /dɪˈtɜːmɪn/ *verb* [T] **1** to fix or decide sth: *The results of the tests will determine what treatment you need.* يحدِّد ، يقرِّر

2 to find sth out: *an attempt to determine the exact position of the enemy submarine* يعيِّن ، يحدِّد

3 (*formal*) to decide sth firmly: *He determined to give up smoking in the New Year.* يصمِّم على

determined /dɪˈtɜːmɪnd/ *adj* having firmly decided to succeed in doing sth, even if it is difficult or people are against you: *He is determined to leave school, even though his parents want him to stay.* ○ *She's a very determined athlete.* مصمِّم ، ذو عزيمة، عاقد العزم

determiner /dɪˈtɜːmɪnə(r)/ *noun* [C] (*grammar*) a word that comes before a noun to show how the noun is being used: *'Her', 'most' and 'those' are all determiners.* كلمة تسبق الاسم توضح استعماله

deterrent /dɪˈterənt; *US* -ˈtɜː-/ *noun* [C] something that is intended to stop you doing sth: *Their punishment will be a deterrent to others.* ○ *the belief that nuclear weapons act as a deterrent* رادع
▸ **deterrent** *adj* رادع، مانع

detest /dɪˈtest/ *verb* [T] to hate or dislike sb/sth: *They absolutely detest each other.* يكره ، يبغض

detonate /ˈdetəneɪt/ *verb* [I,T] to explode or to make sth explode ينفجر : يفجِّر

detour /ˈdiːtʊə(r); *US* dɪˈtʊər/ *noun* [C] **1** a longer route that you take from one place to another in order to avoid sth or in order to see or do sth: *Because of the accident we had to make a five-kilometre detour.* طريق غير مباشر

2 (*US*) = DIVERSION

detract /dɪˈtrækt/ *verb* [I] **detract from sth** to make sth seem less good or important: *These criticisms in no way detract from the team's achievements.* ينتقص من قيمته

detriment /ˈdetrɪmənt/ *noun*
IDM **to the detriment of sb/sth** harming or damaging sb/sth: *Doctors claim that the changes will be to the detriment of patients.* فيه ضرر أو أذى لِ
▸ **detrimental** /ˌdetrɪˈmentl/ *adj*: *Eating too much sweet food is detrimental to your health.* ضارّ ، مؤذٍ

deuce /djuːs; *US* duːs/ *noun* [U] a score of 40 points to each player in a game of tennis تعادل أربعين نقطة في التنس

devalue /ˌdiːˈvæljuː/ *verb* [T] to reduce the value of the money of one country in relation to the value of the money of other countries: *The pound has been devalued against the dollar.* يخفِّض قيمة العملة
▸ **devaluation** /ˌdiːˌvæljuˈeɪʃn/ *noun* [U] تخفيض قيمة العملة

devastate /ˈdevəsteɪt/ *verb* [T] to destroy sth or damage it badly: *a land devastated by war* يدمِّر تدميراً شديداً
▸ **devastated** *adj* **1** completely destroyed مدمَّر

2 shocked or very upset: *The community was devastated by the killings.* شديد الاضطراب ، مصاب بهزّة عنيفة

devastating *adj* **1** that destroys sth completely: *a devastating explosion* مدمِّر

2 that shocks or upsets sb very much: *The closure of the factory was a devastating blow to the workers.* مذهل ، مكدِّر للغاية ، محطِّم (للروح)
devastatingly *adv* بشكل هائل
devastation /ˌdevəˈsteɪʃn/ *noun* [U]: *a scene of total devastation* دمار ، خراب

develop /dɪˈveləp/ *verb* **1** [I,T] to grow slowly, increase, or change into sth else; to make sb/sth do this: *to develop from a child into an adult* ○ *Gradually their friendship developed into love.* ○ *a scheme to help pupils develop their natural talents* ينمو ، يتطوّر : ينمّي ، يطور

2 [T] to begin to have sth: *to develop cancer* يصاب بِ : تبدأ عليه أعراض المرض

3 [I] to begin to happen or be noticeable: *A fault developed when we'd only had the car a month.* ○ *Trouble is developing at the border.* يبدأ في الحدوث أو الظهور

4 [T] to make pictures or negatives from a piece of film by using special chemicals: *to develop a film* يحمِّض (فيلماً فوتوغرافياً)

5 [T] to build houses, shops, factories, etc. on a piece of land: *This site is being developed for offices.* يعمِّر الأراضي
▸ **developed** *adj* of a good level or standard: *a highly developed economy* متطوِّر ، نامٍ
developer (*also* **property developer**) *noun* [C] a person or company that develops land شخص أو شركة تتولّى تعمير الأراضي

de'veloping country *noun* [C] (*pl.* **developing countries**) a poor country that is trying to develop or improve its economy دولة نامية

development /dɪˈveləpmənt/ *noun* **1** [U] developing or being developed: *the development of tourism in many Mediterranean resorts* ○ *the history of Japan's development from a feudal to an industrial society* ○ *a child's intellectual development* نموّ ، تطوّر : تنمية

2 [C] a new event: *This week has seen a number of new developments in the crisis.* تطوّر ، حَدَث جديد

3 [C,U] a new product or the act of making a new product: *a technological development* ○ *research and development* مكتَشف جديد : تطوير الانتاج

4 [C] a piece of land on which houses, shops, factories, etc. have been built: *a new housing development* أرض أُقيمت عليها البيوت أو المخازن أو غير ذلك

deviate /ˈdiːvieɪt/ *verb* [I] to change the way you think or behave, or to start to behave in a way that is not acceptable to other people: *He never once deviated from his Christian principles.* يحيد أو ينحرف عن
▸ **deviation** /ˌdiːviˈeɪʃn/ *noun* [C,U] a difference from what is usual or expected, or from what is approved of by society: *sexual deviation* ○ *a deviation from our usual way of doing things* انحراف : شذوذ

device /dɪˈvaɪs/ *noun* [C] **1** a tool or piece of equipment made for a particular purpose: *a security device which detects any movement or change in temperature* ○ *labour-saving devices* *such as washing machines and vacuum cleaners* ➲ Look at the note at **tool**. جهاز ، أداة

2 a trick or plan: *Critics dismissed the speech as a political device for winning support.* حيلة ، وسيلة

devil /'devl/ *noun* [C] **1 the Devil** the most powerful evil being, according to religion ➲ Look at **Satan**. الشيطان ، إبليس

2 an evil being or spirit شيطان

3 (*informal*) a word used when you are describing a person: *The poor devil died in hospital two days later.* ○ *You're a lucky devil!* (تستعمل وصفاً لشخص): المسكين؛ المحظوظ...

IDM speak/talk of the devil used when the person who is being talked about appears unexpectedly تحدّث عن الشيطان يظهر لك، اذكر الديب وهيّئ القضيب!

why, etc. the devil (used for expressing great surprise or annoyance about sth): *It's two o'clock in the morning. Where the devil have you been?* بحق السماء! (تستعمل تعبيراً عن الاستغراب أو الاستياء)

devious /'di:viəs/ *adj* **1** clever but not honest or direct: *I wouldn't trust him – he can be very devious.* مراوغ ، ماكر

2 (used about a route, path, etc.) having many bends and curves; not straight ملتوٍ ، متعرج

devise /dɪ'vaɪz/ *verb* [T] to invent a plan, system, etc: *They've devised a plan for keeping traffic out of the city centre.* يبتكر ، يبتدع : يدبّر

devoid /dɪ'vɔɪd/ *adj* (*formal*) **devoid of sth** not having a particular quality; without sth: *to be devoid of hope* خالٍ أو مجرّد من

devolution /ˌdi:və'lu:ʃn; *US* ˌdev-/ *noun* [U] the transfer of power, especially from central to local government نقل السلطة المركزيّة (إلى المقاطعات مثلاً)

⚷**devote** /dɪ'vəʊt/ *verb* [T] **devote yourself/sth to sb/sth** to give a lot of time, energy, etc. to sb/sth: *She gave up work to devote herself full-time to her music.* ○ *Schools should devote more time to science subjects.* يكرّس ؛ يتفرّغ لـ

▸ **devoted** *adj* loving sb/sth very much: *Neil's absolutely devoted to his wife.* محبّ : مولع بـ ، مخلص

devotee /ˌdevə'ti:/ *noun* [C] a person who likes sb/sth very much: *Devotees of science fiction will enjoy this new film.* عاشق لـ : نصير متحمّس لـ

devotion /dɪ'vəʊʃn/ *noun* [U] **devotion (to sb/sth) 1** great love: *a mother's devotion to her children* تفانٍ ، حبّ شديد

2 the act of giving a lot of your time, energy, etc. to sb/sth: *devotion to duty* تكريس ؛ إخلاص

3 great religious feeling تقوى ، عبادة

devour /dɪ'vaʊə(r)/ *verb* [T] to eat sth quickly and with enjoyment يلتهم ، يزدرد

devout /dɪ'vaʊt/ *adj* very religious: *a devout Muslim family* تقيّ ، ورع

▸ **devoutly** *adv* بشدّة ، بحماس

dew /dju:; *US* du:/ *noun* [U] small drops of water that form on plants, leaves, etc. during the night ندى

dexterity /dek'sterəti/ *noun* [U] skill at doing things, especially with your hands مهارة ، خفّة اليد

diabetes /ˌdaɪə'bi:ti:z/ *noun* [U] a serious disease in which a person's body cannot control the level of sugar in the blood مرض السكّري

▸ **diabetic** /ˌdaɪə'betɪk/ *adj* of or for diabetes or diabetics: *diabetic chocolate* (= safe for diabetics) متعلّق بمرض السكّري : خاصّ بمرضى السكّري

diabetic *noun* [C] a person who suffers from diabetes المصاب بمرض السكّري

diagnose /'daɪəgnəʊz; *US* ˌdaɪəg'nəʊs/ *verb* [T] to find out what is wrong or what illness a person has: *His illness was diagnosed as bronchitis.* يشخّص (المرض)

▸ **diagnosis** /ˌdaɪəg'nəʊsɪs/ *noun* [C,U] (*pl.* **diagnoses** /-'nəʊsi:z/) an act of diagnosing sth: *The doctor's diagnosis was proved right.* ○ *What's your diagnosis of the situation?* تشخيص

diagonal /daɪ'ægənl/ *adj* **1** (used about a straight line) not vertical or horizontal; sloping مائل ، موروب

2 going from one corner to the opposite corner of a square, rectangle, etc. قطريّ

▸ **diagonally** /-nəli/ *adv*: *I was sitting diagonally opposite Diane at the table.* بشكل مائل ، بالورب

⚷**diagram** /'daɪəgræm/ *noun* [C] a simple picture that is used to explain how sth works or what sth looks like: *a diagram of the body's digestive system* مخطّط ، رسم تخطيطيّ

dial[1] /'daɪəl/ *verb* [I,T] (dialling; dialled; *US* dialing; dialed) to move the dial[2] (3) or push the buttons on a telephone in order to call a particular telephone number: *You can now dial direct to Singapore.* ○ *to dial the wrong number* يدير قرص التليفون؛ يتّلفن

dial[2] /'daɪəl/ *noun* [C] **1** the round part of a clock, watch or other piece of equipment that gives you information about the time or about a measurement. A dial has numbers and a hand or pointer on it: *a dial for showing air pressure* وجه الساعة ، لوحة العدّاد

2 the round part on a piece of equipment that you turn to change sth قرص مدرّج

3 the round part with holes in it on some telephones. You put your finger in one of the holes and turn the dial to call a number. قرص التليفون

dialect /'daɪəlekt/ *noun* [C,U] a form of a language that is spoken in one part of a country: *a local dialect* لهجة

'**dialling code** *noun* [C] (*Brit*) the numbers that you must dial for a particular area or country: *The dialling code for York is 01904.* الرمز التليفونيّ (لبلد ما)

'**dialling tone** *noun* [C,U] (*Brit*) the sound that you hear when you pick up a telephone before you begin to dial ونين الخطّ التليفوني

dialogue (*US* **dialog**) /'daɪəlɒg; *US* -lɔ:g/ *noun* [C,U] **1** (a) conversation between people in a book, play, etc. حوار ، محاورة

2 (a) discussion between people who have different opinions: *a dialogue between the major political parties* حوار ، تبادل آراء

dialysis /ˌdaɪˈæləsɪs/ *noun* [U] a process for separating substances from a liquid, especially for taking waste substances out of the blood of people with damaged kidneys دِيال

diameter /daɪˈæmɪtə(r)/ *noun* [C] a straight line that goes from one side to the other of a circle, passing through the centre ➲ Look at **radius**. قطر الدائرة

⚷ **diamond** /ˈdaɪəmənd/ *noun* **1** [C,U] a hard, bright precious stone which is very expensive and is used for making jewellery and in industry. A diamond usually has no colour. ألماسة : ألماس

2 [C] a flat shape that has four sides of equal length and points at two ends المعين

3 diamonds [plural] the group (suit) of playing cards with red shapes like diamonds (2) on them الديناري (في ورق اللّعب)

4 [C] one of the cards from this suit ورقة لعب ديناريّ

ˌ**diamond ˈwedding** *noun* [C] the 60th anniversary of a wedding ➲ Look at **golden wedding** and **silver wedding**. الاحتفال بمرور ستّين عاماً على الزواج

diaper /ˈdaɪəpə(r); *US* ˈdaɪpər/ *noun* [C] (*US*) = NAPPY

diaphragm /ˈdaɪəfræm/ *noun* [C] the muscle between your lungs and your stomach that helps you to breathe الحجاب الحاجز

diarrhoea (*US* **diarrhea**) /ˌdaɪəˈrɪə/ *noun* [U] an illness that causes you to pass waste material (faeces) from your bowels very often and in a more liquid form than usual: *diarrhoea and vomiting* إسهال

⚷ **diary** /ˈdaɪəri/ *noun* [C] (*pl.* **diaries**) **1** a book in which you write down your appointments, etc: *I'll just check in my diary to see if I'm free that weekend.* ➲ Look at the note at **calendar**. مفكّرة

2 a book in which you write down what happens to you each day: *Do you keep a diary?* يوميّات

dice /daɪs/ *noun* [C] (*pl.* **dice**) a small cube with a different number of spots (from one to six) on each side, used in certain games: *Throw the dice to see who goes first.* نَرْد ، أحجار النَرْد

dictate /dɪkˈteɪt; *US* ˈdɪkteɪt/ *verb* **1** [I,T] to say sth aloud so that sb else can write or type it: *to dictate a letter to a secretary* يملي على

2 [I,T] to tell or order sb to do sth: *Parents can't dictate to their children how they should run their lives.* يأمر ، يفرض على

3 [T] to decide or influence sth: *The kind of house people live in is usually dictated by how much they earn.* يتحكّم في ، يوجّه

dictation /dɪkˈteɪʃn/ *noun* [C,U] spoken words that sb else must write or type: *We had a dictation in English today* (= a test in which we had to write down what the teacher said). إملاء

dictator /dɪkˈteɪtə(r); *US* ˈdɪkteɪtər/ *noun* [C] a ruler who has total power in a country, especially one who used force to gain power and who rules the country unfairly دكتاتور ، حاكم مطلق

▸ **dictatorship** *noun* [C,U] government by a dictator; a country that is ruled by a dictator: *a military dictatorship* دكتاتورية ، حكم مطلق

⚷ **dictionary** /ˈdɪkʃənri; *US* -neri/ *noun* [C] (*pl.* **dictionaries**) a book that lists the words of a language in alphabetical order and that tells you what they mean, in the same or another language: *to look up a word in a dictionary* ○ *a bilingual/monolingual dictionary* ○ *a French-English dictionary* مُعجَم ، قاموس

did *pt* of DO

didn't *short for* DID NOT

⚷ **die** /daɪ/ *verb* (*pres part* **dying**; *3rd pers sing pres* **dies**; *pt, pp* **died**) **1** [I] to stop living: *Thousands of people have died from this disease.* ○ *to die of hunger* ○ *to die of a heart attack* ○ *to die for what you believe in* ○ *(figurative) Our love will never die.* يموت ، يقضي نحبه

2 [T] to have a particular kind of death: *to die a natural death* يموت (موتاً طبيعياً مثلاً)

IDM be dying for sth/to do sth to want sth/to do sth very much: *I'm dying for a cup of coffee.* في غاية التلهف أو في أشدّ الحاجة إلى

die hard to change or disappear only slowly or with difficulty: *Old attitudes towards women die hard.* يتغيّر أو يزول بصعوبة

to die for if you think that sth is to die for, you really want it and would do anything to get it: *They have a house in town that's to die for.* يموت في سبيل غرض ما

PHR V die away to slowly become weaker before stopping or disappearing: *The sound of the engine died away as the car drove into the distance.* يضمحلّ، يتلاشى

die down to slowly become less strong: *Let's wait until the storm dies down before we go out.* يخفّ ، يسكن ؛ يخمد

die out to disappear: *The use of horses on farms has almost died out in this country.* يزول ، يختفي ؛ ينقرض

diesel /ˈdiːzl/ *noun* **1** (*also* **ˈdiesel engine**) [C] an engine in buses, trains, and some cars that uses heavy oil محرك ديزل

2 [U] the heavy oil that is used in these engines: *a taxi that runs on diesel* ➲ Look at **petrol**. ديزل

⚷ **diet** /ˈdaɪət/ *noun* **1** [C,U] the food that a person or animal usually eats: *The peasants live on a diet of rice and vegetables.* ○ *Poor diet is a cause of ill health.* الطعام المعتاد

2 [C] certain foods that a person who is ill, or who wants to lose weight is allowed to eat: *a low-fat diet* نظام غذائي ؛ حمية

IDM be/go on a diet to eat only certain foods or a small amount of food because you want to lose weight: *I won't have a cake, thank you. I'm on a diet.* يتّبع نظاماً غذائياً لتخفيف الوزن

▸ **diet** *verb* [I] to be trying to lose weight by eating less food or only certain kinds of food:

You've lost some weight. Have you been dieting? يحاول تخفيف وزنه بالتقليل من الطعام

differ /ˈdɪfə(r)/ *verb* [I] **1 differ (from sb/sth)** to be different: *How does this car differ from the more expensive model?* يختلف عن

2 differ (with sb) (about/on sth) to have a different opinion: *I'm afraid I differ with you on that question.* يختلف مع ، يخالفه في الرأي

difference /ˈdɪfrəns/ *noun* **1** [C] **difference (between A and B)** the way that people or things are not the same or the way that sb/sth has changed: *What's the difference between this computer and that cheaper one?* ○ *From a distance, it's hard to tell the difference between the twins.* اختلاف

2 [C,U] **difference (in sth) (between A and B)** the amount by which people or things are not the same or by which sb/sth has changed: *There's an age difference of three years between the two children.* ○ *There's very little difference in price since last year.* ○ *We paid a 30% deposit and we'll pay the difference when the work is finished* (= the rest of the money). فَرْق

3 [C] a disagreement that is not very serious: *All couples have their differences from time to time.* خلاف

IDM make a, some, etc. difference (to sb/sth) to have an effect (on sb/sth): *A week's holiday made a lot of difference to her health.* يحدث فرقاً أو تغييراً

make no difference (to sb/sth); not make any difference to not be important (to sb/sth): *It makes no difference to us if the baby is a girl or a boy.* لا يهمّ ، لا فرق

different /ˈdɪfrənt/ *adj* **1 different (from/to sb/sth)** not the same: *Cricket is quite different from baseball.* ○ *The play was different to anything I had seen before.* ○ *The two houses are very different in style.* ℹ In US English **different than** is also used. مختلف ، متباين

2 separate; individual: *This coat is available in three different colours.* مختلف

▸ **differently** *adv*: *I think you'll feel differently about it tomorrow.* بصورة مختلفة

differentiate /ˌdɪfəˈrenʃieɪt/ *verb* **1** [I,T] **differentiate between A and B; differentiate A (from B)** to see how things are different: *It is hard to differentiate between these two species of fungus.* يميِّز (بين) ، يفرِّق

2 [T] **differentiate sth (from sth)** to make one thing different from another: *The coloured feathers differentiate the male bird from the plain brown female.* يميِّز (عن)

3 [T] to treat one person or group differently from another: *We don't differentiate between the two groups – we treat everybody alike.* يميِّز واحداً على الآخر

difficult /ˈdɪfɪkəlt/ *adj* **1** not easy to do or understand: *a difficult test* ○ *a difficult problem* ○ *a difficult language to learn* ○ *Dean found it difficult to pass the driving test.* ○ *It was difficult for Dean to pass the driving test.* ○ *I'm in a difficult situation. Whatever I do, somebody will be upset.* صعب ، عسير

2 (used about a person) not friendly, reasonable or helpful: *a difficult customer* صعب الإرضاء ، عسِر

difficulty /ˈdɪfɪkəlti/ *noun* (*pl.* **difficulties**) **1** [U] **difficulty (in sth/in doing sth)** the state of being difficult or of not being able to do sth easily: *Gail had great difficulty in getting a visa to go to America.* ○ *We had no difficulty selling our car.* صعوبة

2 [C, usually pl.] something that is difficult to do or understand; a problem: *There will be some difficulties to start with but things should get easier later.* ○ *If you borrow too much money you may get into financial difficulties.* صعوبة ، مشكلة

diffident /ˈdɪfɪdənt/ *adj* not feeling or showing belief or confidence in your own strengths or abilities: *He has a very diffident manner.* حييّ ، قليل الثقة بنفسه

▸ **diffidence** /-dəns/ *noun* [U] استحياء ، عدم ثقة بالنفس

dig /dɪɡ/ *verb* (*pres part* **digging**; *pt, pp* **dug** /dʌɡ/) [I,T] to move earth and make a hole using your hands, a spade, a machine, etc: *The children are busy digging in the sand.* ○ *to dig a hole* ○ *to dig for gold* يحفر

PHR V dig sth in; dig sth into sth to push sth into sb/sth: *She dug her fingernails into my arm.* يغرز ، ينشب

dig sb/sth out (of sth) 1 to get sb/sth out of sth by digging: *Rescue workers dug the survivors out of the rubble.* ينبش ، يخرج (من تحت الردم)

2 to get or find sb/sth by searching: *Bill went into the attic and dug out some old photos.* يجد أو يستخرج (بعد تفتيش) ، ينتبش

dig sth up 1 to remove sth from the earth by digging: *to dig up potatoes* يستخرج بالحفر

2 to make a hole or take away soil by digging: *Workmen are digging up the road in front of our house.* يحفر

3 to find information by searching or studying: *Newspapers have dug up some embarrassing facts about his private life.* ينبش معلومات

▸ **dig** *noun* **1** [C] a hard push: *to give sb a dig in the ribs* (= with your elbow, etc.) وكزة ، نخسة

2 [C] something that you say to upset sb: *The others kept making digs at him because of the way he spoke.* ملاحظة جارحة

3 digs [plural] (*Brit old-fashioned*) a room in a person's house that you rent and live in: *Some university students have flats, others live in digs.* غرفة مستأجرة

digest /daɪˈdʒest; dɪ-/ *verb* [T] **1** to change food in your stomach so that it can be used by the body يهضم

2 to think about new information so that you understand it fully يهضم أو يتمثل (عقلياً)

▸ **digestion** /daɪˈdʒestʃən; dɪ-/ *noun* [C,U] the process of digesting food هضم

digestive /daɪˈdʒestɪv; dɪ-/ *adj*: *the digestive system* هضميّ ؛ مساعد على الهضم

digit /ˈdɪdʒɪt/ *noun* [C] any of the numbers from 0

to 9: *a six-digit telephone number* رقم (من الصفر إلى التسعة) ، خانة

digital /ˈdɪdʒɪtl/ *adj* **1** using an electronic system that uses the numbers 1 and 0 to record sound or store information, and that gives results of a high quality: *a digital recording* رقمي

2 a digital watch or clock shows the time by numbers alone and does not have hands or a dial ذو أرقام ، رقمي

dignified /ˈdɪgnɪfaɪd/ *adj* behaving in a calm, serious way that makes other people respect you: *dignified behaviour* ❶ The opposite is **undignified.** وقور ، مَهيب

dignity /ˈdɪgnəti/ *noun* [U] **1** calm, serious behaviour that makes other people respect you: *to behave with dignity* ○ *He managed to keep his dignity, even in prison.* وقار ، هيبة

2 the quality of being serious or formal: *the quiet dignity of the funeral service* هيبة

digress /daɪˈgres/ *verb* [I] (*formal*) to stop talking or writing about the main subject under discussion and start talking or writing about another, possibly less important, one يستطرد

▸ **digression** /daɪˈgreʃn/ *noun* [C,U] استطراد

dike → DYKE

dilapidated /dɪˈlæpɪdeɪtɪd/ *adj* (used about a building, furniture, etc.) old and broken متداعٍ ، مخرَّب

▸ **dilapidation** /dɪˌlæpɪˈdeɪʃn/ *noun* [U] تداعٍ ، خراب ، تهدُّم

dilemma /dɪˈlemə/ *noun* [C] a situation in which you have to make a difficult choice between two or more things: *Doctors face the moral dilemma of when to keep patients alive artificially and when to let them die.* ورطة ، خيار بين أمور صعبة

dill /dɪl/ *noun* [U] a herb used in cooking whose seeds have a strong taste: *dill pickles* شِبْت، سَنوت، رز الدجاج

dilute /daɪˈluːt/ *verb* [T] **dilute sth (with sth)** to make a liquid weaker by adding water or another liquid ➲ Look at **concentrate**. يخفِّف أو يمدِّد بالماء مثلاً

▸ **dilute** *adj* مخفَّف ، ممدَّد

dim /dɪm/ *adj* (dimmer; dimmest) **1** not bright or easily seen; not clear: *The light was too dim to read by.* ○ *a dim shape in the distance* ○ *My memories of my grandmother are a bit dim.* خافت ، مُعتِم ؛ ضعيف

2 (*informal*) not very clever; stupid: *He's a bit dim.* بليد ، بطيء الفهم

▸ **dim** *verb* [I,T] (dimming; dimmed) to become or make sth dim (1): *to dim the lights* يخفت (الأضواء) ، يعتِّم ؛ يصبح معتماً أو ضعيفاً

dimly *adv*: *I dimly remember meeting him somewhere before.* بصورة غير واضحة ، بغموض

dime /daɪm/ *noun* [C] a coin used in the USA and Canada that is worth ten cents قطعة نقود أمريكية تعادل 10 سنتات

dimension /daɪˈmenʃn/ *noun* **1** [C,U] a measurement of the length, width or height of sth بُعْد ، مقياس

2 dimensions [plural] the size of sth including its length, width and height: *to measure the dimensions of a room* ○ (*figurative*) *The full dimensions of this problem are only now being recognized.* أبعاد

3 [C] something that affects the way you think about a problem or situation: *Global warming has added a new dimension to the problem of hunger in the world.* بُعْد : عنصر ، معطى

▸ **-dimensional** /-ʃənəl/ (in compounds) with the number of dimensions mentioned: *a three-dimensional object* ذو (ثلاثة) أبعاد

diminish /dɪˈmɪnɪʃ/ *verb* [I,T] (*formal*) to become or to make sth smaller or less important: *The bad news did nothing to diminish her enthusiasm for the plan.* يقلِّل ، يضْعِف : يقل ، يضعف

diminutive /dɪˈmɪnjətɪv/ *adj* (*formal*) very small صغير جداً

dimple /ˈdɪmpl/ *noun* [C] a small round hollow area on your chin, cheek, etc. which can often only be seen when you smile غمّازة

din /dɪn/ *noun* [sing.] a loud unpleasant noise that continues for some time: *Will you stop making such a din!* ضجيج مزعج ، جلبة

dine /daɪn/ *verb* [I] (*formal*) to eat dinner: *We dined at an exclusive French restaurant.* ○ *We dined on fresh salmon.* يتناول العشاء

PHR V **dine out** to eat in a restaurant يتناول العشاء في مطعم

▸ **diner** /ˈdaɪnə(r)/ *noun* [C] **1** a person who is eating at a restaurant متناول الطعام في مطعم

2 (*US*) a small restaurant beside a main road مطعم صغير بجانب طريق عام

ding-dong /ˈdɪŋ dɒŋ/ *noun* [U] the sound that a bell makes صوت الجرس

dinghy /ˈdɪŋi/ *noun* [C] (*pl.* **dinghies**) **1** a small sailing boat ➲ Look at **yacht**. زورق شراعي صغير

2 a small open boat, often used to take people to or from a larger boat زورق صغير

dingy /ˈdɪndʒi/ *adj* (**dingier**; **dingiest**) dirty and not bright or cheerful: *a dark and dingy room* قَذِر معتم

dining → DINE

ˈ**dining room** *noun* [C] a room where you eat meals غرفة الطعام

⚷ **dinner** /ˈdɪnə(r)/ *noun* **1** [C,U] the main meal of the day, eaten either at midday or in the evening: *What time is dinner served?* ○ *That was a lovely dinner you cooked.* ○ *It's dinner time/time for dinner.* الوجبة الرئيسيّة

People from different parts of the country, different backgrounds, etc. have different ways of talking about their meals. As a general rule, if dinner is eaten at midday the lighter meal eaten in the evening is then called **tea** or **supper**. **Supper** is eaten later in the evening than **tea**. **Tea** may also mean a drink with cake or biscuits in the late afternoon. If **dinner** is eaten in the evening, the lighter meal eaten at midday is then called **lunch**.

2 [C] a formal occasion in the evening during which a meal is served: *A dinner was given for the president.* مأدبة عشاء

'dinner jacket (*US* **tuxedo**) *noun* [C] a black or white jacket that a man wears on formal occasions. A dinner jacket is usually worn with a bow tie. بدلة السهرة للرجال

dinosaur /'daɪnəsɔː(r)/ *noun* [C] a very large animal that disappeared from the earth (became extinct) before the appearance of Man دیناصور

diocese /'daɪəsɪs/ *noun* [C] an area containing a number of churches, for which a bishop is responsible أبرشيّة

dip /dɪp/ *verb* (dipping; dipped) **1** [T] **dip sth (into sth)**; **dip sth (in)** to put sth into liquid for a short time: *Julie dipped her toe into the pool to see how cold it was.* يغمس ، يغطّس

2 [I,T] to go down; to lower sth: *The road suddenly dipped down to the river.* ○ *The driver dipped his headlights when a car came in the opposite direction.* ينحدر : يخفض ، يخفّف

PHR V dip into sth 1 to take money out of sth: *Tim had to dip into his savings to pay for his new suit.* ينفق ، يسحب نقوداً

2 to read parts, but not all, of sth: *I've only dipped into the book. I haven't read it all the way through.* يتصفّح

▸ **dip** *noun* **1** [C] a drop; a downwards movement: *a dip in sales* انخفاض ؛ انحدار

2 [C] (*informal*) a quick swim: *We went for a dip before breakfast.* غطسة ، سبحة سريعة

3 [C,U] a thick sauce that you eat by dipping pieces of vegetable, bread, etc. into it صلصة يغمس فيها الطعام

4 [C] an area of lower ground: *The cottage lay in a dip in the hills.* وهدة

diphtheria /dɪf'θɪəriə/ *noun* [U] a serious disease of the throat that makes it difficult to breathe الخناق أو الدفتريا

diphthong /'dɪfθɒŋ; *US* -θɔːŋ/ *noun* [C] two vowel sounds pronounced together, making one sound: *The /aɪ/ sound in 'fine' is a diphthong.* تتابع حرفيْ علّة في مقطع واحد

diploma /dɪ'pləʊmə/ *noun* [C] **1** a qualification that you receive when you complete a course of study, often at a college: *a diploma in hotel management* شهادة دراسيّة

2 the official piece of paper which shows that you have completed a course of study ➲ Look at the note at **degree**. وثيقة (دراسية)

diplomacy /dɪ'pləʊməsi/ *noun* [U] **1** the management of the relations between countries الدبلوماسيّة

2 skill in dealing with people: *He handled the awkward situation with tact and diplomacy.* دبلوماسيّة ، كياسة

diplomat /'dɪpləmæt/ *noun* [C] one of the officials who represent their country abroad: *a diplomat at the embassy in Rome* الدبلوماسيّ

▸ **diplomatic** /ˌdɪplə'mætɪk/ *adj* **1** connected with diplomacy (1): *The two countries will restore diplomatic relations and the embassies will be reopened.* دبلوماسيّ

2 clever at dealing with people: *He searched for a diplomatic reply so as not to offend her.* لبق ، كيّس ، دبلوماسيّ

diplomatically /-kli/ *adv* بالطرق الدبلوماسية ؛ دبلوماسيّاً

dire /'daɪə(r)/ *adj* (*formal*) very bad or serious; terrible: *dire consequences* ○ *dire poverty* فظيع ، وخيم ؛ (فقر) مدقع

⚷ **direct¹** /də'rekt; dɪ-; daɪ-/ *adj* **1** going from one place to another without turning or stopping; straight: *The most direct route is through the city centre.* ○ *a direct flight to Hong Kong* مباشر ؛ دون توقّف

2 with nobody/nothing in between; not involving anybody/anything else: *The Prime Minister is in direct contact with the President.* ○ *a direct attack on the capital* ○ *As a direct result of the new road, traffic jams in the centre have been reduced.* مباشر

3 saying what you mean; clear: *Politicians never give a direct answer to a direct question.* صريح ؛ واضح

ℹ The opposite for senses 1, 2 and 3 is **indirect**.

4 (only *before* a noun) complete; exact: *What she did was in direct opposition to my orders.* تامّ ، جليّ

▸ **direct** *adv* **1** not turning or stopping; straight: *This bus goes direct to London.* رأساً ، دون توقّف

2 not involving anybody/anything else: *I always deal direct with the manager.* مباشرةً

directly *adv* **1** exactly; in a direct way: *The bank is directly opposite the supermarket.* ○ *He refused to answer my question directly.* ℹ The opposite is **indirectly**. تماماً ؛ بصورة صريحة

2 immediately; very soon: *Wait where you are. I'll be back directly.* حالاً ؛ بعد قليل

directly *conj* as soon as: *I phoned him directly I heard the news.* حالما

⚷ **direct²** /də'rekt; dɪ-; daɪ-/ *verb* [T] **1 direct sb (to...)** to tell or show sb how to get somewhere: *I was directed to an office at the end of the corridor.* ➲ Look at the note at **lead³**(1). يدلّ ، يرشد

2 to manage or control sb/sth: *a policeman in the middle of the road, directing the traffic* ○ *to direct a play, film, etc.* يدير

3 direct sth to/towards sb/sth; **direct sth at sb/sth** to turn or aim your attention or actions towards sb/sth: *In recent weeks the media's attention has been directed towards events abroad.* ○ *The advert is directed at young people.* يوجّه

4 (*formal*) to tell or order sb to do sth: *Take the tablets as directed by your doctor.* يوصي ، يُعطي تعليمات

diˌrect 'debit *noun* [C,U] an order to your bank

a b c d e f g h i j k l m n o p q r s t u v w x y z

that allows sb else to take a particular amount of money out of your account on certain dates دفع مباشر: تخويل البنك لتحويل مبلغ معين في موعد معين

direction /də'rekʃn; dɪ-; daɪ-/ *noun* **1** [C] the path or line along which a person or thing is moving, looking or pointing: *When the path divided, they didn't know which direction to take.* ○ *A woman was seen running in the direction of the station.* ○ *The wind has changed direction.* ○ *People began arriving from all directions.* ○ *We met him coming in the opposite direction.* اتّجاه ، جهة

2 [C, usually pl.] information or instructions about how to do sth or how to get to a place إرشادات ، تعليمات

3 [U] management or control: *This department is under the direction of Mrs Walters.* ○ *the direction of a play, film, etc.* إدارة

4 [C,U] a purpose; an aim: *Once again her life seemed lacking in direction.* هدف

directive /də'rektɪv; dɪ-; daɪ-/ *noun* [C] an official order to do sth: *an EU directive on safety at work* تعليمات، توجيه أو أمر رسمي

directly *adv* → DIRECT[1]

di,rect 'object *noun* [C] a noun or phrase that is directly affected by the action of a verb: *In the sentence 'Anna bought a CD', 'a CD' is the direct object.* ➲ Look at **indirect object**. المفعول به (نحو)

director /də'rektə(r); dɪ-; daɪ-/ *noun* [C] **1** a person who manages or controls a company or organization: *the managing director of Rolls Royce* ○ *the director of studies of a language school* مدير

2 a person who tells the actors, camera crew, etc., what to do in a film, play, etc. مخرج

directory /də'rektəri; dɪ-; daɪ-/ *noun* [C] (*pl.* **directories**) **1** an alphabetical list of names, addresses and telephone numbers دليل الهاتف

2 a file containing a group of other files or programs in a computer مرشد، دليل

direct 'speech *noun* [U] the actual words that a person said ➲ Look at **indirect speech**. كلمات المتحدّث كما قالها تماماً

dirt /dɜːt/ *noun* [U] **1** a substance that is not clean, such as dust or mud: *Wipe the dirt off your shoes before you come in.* وَسَخ

2 earth or soil: *a dirt track* تراب

dirty[1] /'dɜːti/ *adj* (**dirtier**; **dirtiest**) **1** not clean: *Your hands are dirty. Go and wash them!* ○ *Lighting the fire can be a dirty job* (= it makes you dirty). وَسخ ، قذر

2 referring to sex in a way that may upset or offend people: *to tell a dirty joke* بذيء ، فاحش

3 unpleasant or dishonest: *He's a dirty player.* ○ *He doesn't sell the drugs himself – he gets kids to do his dirty work for him.* نذل، منحط، لا وازع له

IDM **a dirty word** an idea or thing that you do not like or agree with فكرة بغيضة

dirty[2] /'dɜːti/ *verb* [I,T] (*pres part* **dirtying**; *3rd pers sing pres* **dirties**; *pt, pp* **dirtied**) to become or to make sth dirty يتّسخ ؛ يوسِّخ

disability /,dɪsə'bɪləti/ *noun* (*pl.* **disabilities**) **1** [U] the state of being unable to use a part of your body properly: *physical/mental disability* عجز

2 [C] something that makes you unable to use a part of your body properly: *Because of his disability, he needs constant care.* عاهة

disable /dɪs'eɪbl/ *verb* [T] (often passive) to make sb unable to use a part of his/her body properly: *Many soldiers were disabled in the war.* يُعجِز ، يُكسِح

disabled /dɪs'eɪbld/ *adj* unable to use a part of your body properly: *The car has been adapted for disabled drivers.* عاجز ، مقعَد

▸ **the disabled** *noun* [plural] people who are disabled: *The hotel has improved facilities for the disabled. There are new lifts and wheelchair ramps.* العَجزة

disadvantage /,dɪsəd'vɑːntɪdʒ; *US* -'væn-/ *noun* [C] **1** something that may make you less successful than other people: *Your qualifications are good. Your main disadvantage is your lack of experience.* شيء غير موات ، مَضرّة ، نقص

2 something that is not good or that causes problems: *The main disadvantage of the job is the long hours.* ○ *What are the advantages and disadvantages of nuclear power?* عيب ، سيّئة

IDM **put sb/be at a disadvantage** to put sb/be in a situation where he/she/you may be less successful than other people: *The fact that you don't speak the language will put you at a disadvantage in France.* يقلّل من فرص نجاحه ، يضعه في موقف أضعف

to sb's disadvantage (*formal*) not good or helpful for sb: *The agreement will be to your disadvantage – don't accept it.* ليس من صالحه

▸ **disadvantaged** *adj* in a bad social or economic situation; poor: *extra help for the most disadvantaged members of society* محتاج ، فقير

disadvantageous /,dɪsædvæn'teɪdʒəs/ *adj* causing sb to be in a worse situation compared to other people مضر بالمصلحة، غير مواتٍ

disagree /,dɪsə'griː/ *verb* [I] **1 disagree (with sb/sth) (about/on sth)** to have a different opinion from sb/sth; not agree: *Nigel often disagrees with his father about politics.* ○ *They strongly disagreed with the idea.* يخالفه الرأي ؛ يعارض

2 to be different: *These two sets of statistics disagree.* يختلف ، يتعارض

▸ **disagreement** *noun* **1** [U] **disagreement (about/on sth)** having a different opinion from sb or not agreeing with sb/sth: *There's great disagreement about what causes people to turn to crime.* اختلاف في الرأي

2 [C] an argument: *Mandy resigned after a disagreement with her boss.* خلاف ، نزاع

disagreeable /,dɪsə'griːəbl/ *adj* (*formal*) unpleasant غير مستحبّ ، بغيض ، مزعج

▸ **disagreeably** /-əbli/ *adv* بصورة مزعجة

disallow /,dɪsə'laʊ/ *verb* [T] to not allow or accept sth: *The goal was disallowed because the player was offside.* يرفض ، يردّ : لا يسمح

disappear /ˌdɪsəˈpɪə(r)/ *verb* [I] **1** to become impossible to see; to go away: *He walked away and disappeared into a crowd of people.* ○ *My purse was here a moment ago and now it's disappeared.* يختفي ، يتلاشى

2 to go to a place where you cannot be found: *She disappeared five years ago and has never been heard of since.* يختفي (من الوجود)

3 to stop existing: *Plant and animal species are disappearing at an alarming rate.* ينقرض ، يزول

▸ **disappearance** /-ˈpɪərəns/ *noun* [C,U]: *The mystery of her disappearance was never solved.* اختفاء ؛ زوال

disappoint /ˌdɪsəˈpɔɪnt/ *verb* [T] to make sb sad because what he/she had hoped for has not happened or because sb/sth is less good, interesting, etc. then he/she had hoped: *I'm sorry to disappoint you but I'm afraid you haven't won the prize.* يخيّب الأمل

▸ **disappointed** *adj* **disappointed (about/at sth)**; **disappointed (in/with sb/sth)** sad because you/sb/sth did not succeed or because sth was not as good, interesting, etc. as you had hoped: *They are very disappointed that they can't stay longer.* ○ *We were disappointed with our accommodation – we were expecting a luxury apartment.* ○ *Lucy was deeply disappointed at not being chosen for the team.* ○ *I'm disappointed in you. I thought you could do better.* خائب الأمل ، مخذول

disappointing *adj* making you feel sad because sth was not as good, interesting, etc. as you had hoped: *It has been a disappointing year for the company.* مخيّب للأمل

disappointingly *adv*: *The amount of money they collected was disappointingly small.* بصورة غير متوقّعة ، بشكل مخيّب

disappointment *noun* **1** [U] the state of being disappointed: *To his great disappointment he failed to get the job.* خيبة أمل

2 [C] **a disappointment (to sb)** a person or thing that disappoints you: *Our holiday was a bit of a disappointment.* شخص أو شيء مخيّب للأمل

disapprove /ˌdɪsəˈpruːv/ *verb* [I] **disapprove (of sb/sth)** to think that sb/sth is bad, foolish, etc: *His parents strongly disapproved of him leaving college before he had finished his course.* يستنكر ، يستهجن : لا يستحسن

▸ **disapproval** /-ˈpruːvl/ *noun* [U] a feeling that sth is bad or that sb is behaving badly: *to shake your head in disapproval* استنكار ، استهجان : عدم استحسان

disapproving *adj*: *After he had told the joke there was a disapproving silence.* دالّ على الاستهجان أو الاستنكار

disapprovingly *adv*: *David frowned disapprovingly when I lit a cigarette.* باستنكار، باستهجان ، بعدم استحسان

disarm /dɪsˈɑːm/ *verb* **1** [T] to take weapons away from sb: *The police caught and disarmed the terrorists.* يجرِّد من السلاح

2 [I] (used about a country) to reduce the number of weapons it has ينزع أو يحدّ من التسلّح

3 [T] to make sb feel less angry يلطّف من حدّة غضبه

▸ **disarmament** /dɪsˈɑːməmənt/ *noun* [U] reducing the number of weapons that a country has: *nuclear disarmament* نزع السلاح

disassociate = DISSOCIATE

disaster /dɪˈzɑːstə(r); *US* -ˈzæs-/ *noun* **1** [C] an event that causes a lot of harm or damage: *earthquakes, floods and other natural disasters* كارثة ، نكبة

2 [C] a person or thing that is very bad, harmful or unsuccessful: *The school play was an absolute disaster. Everything went wrong.* حدَث فاشل ، طامّة: شخص أخرق

3 [U] failure; a terrible situation: *The drought brought disaster to the area.* فشل ؛ أوضاع صعبة ، رزء

▸ **disastrous** /dɪˈzɑːstrəs; *US* -ˈzæs-/ *adj* very bad, harmful or unsuccessful: *Our mistake had disastrous results.* فاجع ، وخيم ؛ فاشل

disastrously *adv*: *The plan went disastrously wrong.* بشكل مروّع

disband /dɪsˈbænd/ *verb* [I,T] to stop existing as a group; to break up ينحل: يَحلّ أو يسرّح

disbelieve /ˌdɪsbɪˈliːv/ *verb* [T] to think that sth is not true or that sb is not telling the truth: *I have no reason to disbelieve her.* لا يصدّق ، يكذّبه

▸ **disbelief** /ˌdɪsbɪˈliːf/ *noun* [U] not believing sb/sth: *'It can't be true!' he shouted in disbelief.* عدم تصديق ؛ إنكار

disc (*especially US* **disk**) /dɪsk/ *noun* [C] **1** a round flat object قرص

2 = CD

3 (*Brit*) a disk for a computer قرصْ

4 one of the pieces of thin strong material (cartilage) between the bones in your back غضروف بين الفقرات

5 (*old-fashioned*) = RECORD

discard /dɪsˈkɑːd/ *verb* [T] (*formal*) to throw sth away because it is not useful يطرح ، ينبذ ، يرمي جانباً

discern /dɪˈsɜːn/ *verb* [T] (*formal*) to see or notice sth with difficulty: *I discerned a note of anger in his voice.* يتبيّن ، يشتم

▸ **discernible** *adj* that can only be seen or noticed with difficulty: *The shape of a house was just discernible through the mist.* مشاهَد أو مميّز بصعوبة

discerning /dɪˈsɜːnɪŋ/ *adj* able to recognize the quality of sb/sth: *The discerning music lover will appreciate the excellence of this recording.* بصير ، حصيف، ذو خبرة

discharge /dɪsˈtʃɑːdʒ/ *verb* [T] **1** to send sth out (a liquid, gas, etc.): *Smoke and fumes are discharged from the factory and cause air pollution.* يطلِق ، ينفث

2 to allow sb officially to leave; to send sb away: *to discharge sb from hospital, the army, etc.* يُخرِج ؛ يخلي سبيله ، يسرّح

3 to do or carry sth out (a duty, task, etc.) يقوم (بعمله) ، يؤدّي (واجبه)

a b c d e f g h i j k l m n o p q r s t u v w x y z

▸ **discharge** /ˈdɪstʃɑːdʒ/ *noun* [C,U] **1** the action of sending sb/sth out or away: *The discharge of oil from the leaking tanker could not be prevented.* ○ *The wounded soldier was given a medical discharge.* انطلاق ، خروج ؛ تسريح ؛ تفريغ

2 a substance that has come out of somewhere: *yellowish discharge from a wound* إفراز ، مادة مفرزة ، صديد

disciple /dɪˈsaɪpl/ *noun* [C] a person who follows a teacher, especially a religious one: *the twelve disciples of Jesus* مريد ، تابع ، حواري

discipline /ˈdɪsəplɪn/ *noun* **1** [U] a way of training your mind and body so that you control your actions and obey rules: *military discipline* ○ *It takes a lot of self-discipline to train for three hours a day.* ضبط ، انضباط

2 [U] the result of such training: *A good teacher must be able to maintain discipline in the classroom.* نظام

3 [C] a subject of study; a type of sporting event: *academic disciplines* ○ *Olympic disciplines* موضوع دراسيّ ؛ حدث رياضي

▸ **discipline** *verb* [T] **1** to train sb to obey and to behave in a controlled way: *You should discipline yourself to practise the piano every morning.* يدرّب (على ضبط النفس)

2 to punish sb يعاقب ، يؤدّب

disciplinary /ˈdɪsəplɪnəri; *US* -neri/ *adj* connected with punishment for breaking rules تأديبيّ

ˈ**disc jockey** *noun* [C] (*abbr* **DJ**) a person whose job is to play and introduce pop music on the radio or in a disco مقدّم التسجيلات الموسيقيّة الحديثة

disclaim /dɪsˈkleɪm/ *verb* [T] to say that you do not have sth, especially responsibility or knowledge يتنصّل من ؛ ينكر

disclose /dɪsˈkləʊz/ *verb* [T] (*formal*) to tell sth to sb or to make sth known publicly: *The newspapers did not disclose the victim's name.* يكشف عن ، يعلن ، يفشي

▸ **disclosure** /dɪsˈkləʊʒə(r)/ *noun* [C,U] making sth known; the facts that are made known: *the disclosure of secret information* ○ *He resigned following disclosures about his private life.* كشف عن ؛ فضح ، حقائق تظهر للوجود

disco /ˈdɪskəʊ/ (*also formal* **discotheque**) *noun* [C] (*pl.* **discos**) a place, party, etc. where people dance to popular music مرقص ، "ديسكو"

discolour (*US* **discolor**) /dɪsˈkʌlə(r)/ *verb* **1** [I] to change colour (often by the effect of light, age or dirt) يتغيّر لونه ، يبهت

2 [T] to change or spoil the colour of sth يغيّر اللون أو يفسده

discomfort /dɪsˈkʌmfət/ *noun* **1** [U] a slight feeling of pain: *There may be some discomfort from the wound after the operation.* ألم خفيف ، انزعاج

2 [C] something that makes you feel uncomfortable or that causes a slight feeling of pain: *The beauty of the scenery made up for the discomforts of the journey.* شيء متعب ، مشقّة

3 [U] a feeling of embarrassment حَرَج ، عدم ارتياح

disconcert /ˌdɪskənˈsɜːt/ *verb* [T] (usually passive) to make sb feel confused or worried: *She was disconcerted when everyone stopped talking and listened to her.* يربك ، يقلق

▸ **disconcerting** *adj* مربِك ، مثير للقلق

disconcertingly *adv* بصورة تبعث على القلق ؛ بشكل محرج

disconnect /ˌdɪskəˈnekt/ *verb* [T] to undo two things that are joined or connected together: *If you don't pay your gas bill your supply will be disconnected.* يفكّ ، يفصل ، يقطع

discontent /ˌdɪskənˈtent/ (*also* **discontentment** /ˌdɪskənˈtentmənt/) *noun* [U] the state of being unhappy or not satisfied with sth استياء ، سخط ، تذمّر

▸ **discontented** *adj* unhappy or not satisfied مستاء ، ساخط ، متذمّر

discontinue /ˌdɪskənˈtɪnjuː/ *verb* [T] (*formal*) to stop sth or stop producing sth يوقف ، يتوقّف عن إنتاج شيء

discord /ˈdɪskɔːd/ *noun* (*formal*) **1** [U] disagreement or argument خلاف ، نزاع

2 [C] two or more musical notes that do not sound pleasant when they are played together نشاز

▸ **discordant** /dɪsˈkɔːdənt/ *adj* not producing harmony; causing an unpleasant impression: *Her criticism was the only discordant note in the discussion.* متنافر ، متضارب ، ناشز

discotheque /ˈdɪskətek/ *noun* [C] (*formal*) = DISCO

discount[1] /ˈdɪskaʊnt/ *noun* [C,U] a reduction in the price or cost of sth: *Staff get 20% discount on all goods.* ○ *Do you give a discount for cash?* خَصْم ، حَسْم ، تخفيض

discount[2] /dɪsˈkaʊnt; *US* ˈdɪskaʊnt/ *verb* [T] to consider sth not true or not important: *I think we can discount that idea. It's just not practical.* يهمل ، يصرف النظر عن

discourage /dɪsˈkʌrɪdʒ/ *verb* [T] **1 discourage sb (from doing sth)** to make sb lose hope or feel less confident about sth: *Don't let these little problems discourage you.* يثبّط العزيمة

2 discourage sb from doing sth to try to stop sb doing sth: *Consumers should be discouraged from throwing away glass and tins.* ❶ The opposite is **encourage**. يشجّعه على ألا....

▸ **discouraged** *adj* having lost hope; not feeling confident about sth: *After failing the exam again Paul felt very discouraged.* فاقد الأمل ، ضعيف الثقة بـ ...

discouragement *noun* [C,U] discouraging or being discouraged; something that discourages you: *High parking charges would be a discouragement to people taking their cars into the city centre.* تثبيط العزيمة ؛ شيء غير مشجّع

discover /dɪˈskʌvə(r)/ *verb* [T] **1** to find or learn sth that nobody knew or had found before: *Who discovered Australia?* ○ *Scientists are hoping to discover the cause of the epidemic.* يكتشف

2 to find or learn sth new or unexpected or sth that you did not know before: *I think I've discovered why the computer won't print out.* ○ *We recently discovered that a famous writer used to live in this house.* يكتشف ، يعلم

▶ **discoverer** *noun* [C] a person who discovers sth مكتشف

discovery /dɪ'skʌvəri/ *noun* (*pl.* **discoveries**) **1** [U] finding sth: *The discovery of X-rays changed the history of medicine.* ○ *The discovery of fingerprints in the car helped the police to find the thief.* اكتشاف

2 [C] something that has been discovered: *scientific discoveries* مكتشَف

discredit /dɪs'kredɪt/ *verb* [T] to cause sb/sth to lose people's trust; to damage the reputation of sb/sth يزعزع ثقة الناس به ؛ يشوه سمعته

▶ **discredit** *noun* [U] loss of trust; damage to the reputation of sb/sth فقدان الثقة بِ ؛ تشويه السمعة

discreet /dɪ'skriːt/ *adj* careful not to attract attention and so cause embarrassment or difficulty for sb: *She was too discreet to mention the argument in front of Neil.* ❶ The noun is **discretion**. The opposite is **indiscreet**. كيّس ، حذِر ، متحفّظ

▶ **discreetly** *adv* بحذر ، بتحفظ

discrepancy /dɪs'krepənsi/ *noun* [C,U] (*pl.* **discrepancies**) a difference between two things that should be the same: *Something is wrong here. There is a discrepancy between these two sets of figures.* تضارب أو تفاوت ، اختلاف

discretion /dɪ'skreʃn/ *noun* [U] **1** care not to attract attention and so cause embarrassment or difficulty for sb: *This is confidential but I know I can rely on your discretion.* ❶ The adjective is **discreet**. تحفّظ ، حذر ، لباقة

2 the freedom and ability to make decisions by yourself: *You must decide what is best. Use your discretion.* اجتهاد ؛ حرية الاختيار

IDM at sb's discretion depending on what sb thinks or decides: *Pay increases are awarded at the discretion of the director.* وفق قراره ، (يتوقّف) على اجتهاده

discriminate /dɪ'skrɪmɪneɪt/ *verb* **1** [I] **discriminate (against sb)** to treat one person or group worse than others: *It is illegal to discriminate against any ethnic or religious group.* يتحامل على ، يتحيّز ضد

2 [I,T] **discriminate (between A and B)** to see or make a difference between two people or things: *The immigration law discriminates between political and economic refugees.* يفرّق ، يميّز

▶ **discrimination** /dɪˌskrɪmɪ'neɪʃn/ *noun* [U] **1 discrimination (against sb)** treating one person or group worse than others: *sexual, racial, religious, etc. discrimination* تفرقة ، تمييز ، تحيّز

2 the state of being able to judge what is good, true, etc. حصافة ، حسن التمييز

discus /'dɪskəs/ *noun* [C] a heavy round flat object that is thrown as a sport قرص (رمي القرص)

discuss /dɪ'skʌs/ *verb* [T] **discuss sth (with sb)** to talk or write about sth seriously or formally: *I must discuss the matter with my parents before I make a decision.* ○ *The article discusses the need for a change in the law.* يناقش ، يبحث في

▶ **discussion** /dɪ'skʌʃn/ *noun* [C,U] a time when you talk about sth: *After much discussion we all agreed to share the cost.* ○ *a long discussion on the meaning of life* مناقشة

IDM under discussion being talked about: *Plans to reform the Health Service are under discussion in Parliament.* قيد البحث

disdain /dɪs'deɪn/ *noun* [U] the feeling that sb/sth is not good enough and does not deserve to be respected ترفع ، أنفة ، ازدراء

▶ **disdainful** /-fl/ *adj* مترفع ، ممتهن ، مزدرٍ

disdainfully /-fəli/ *adv* بترفع، بأنفة ، بازدراء

disease /dɪ'ziːz/ *noun* [C,U] an illness of the body in humans, animals or plants: *an infectious disease* ○ *Many diseases can be prevented by vaccination.* ○ *Rats and flies spread disease.* مرض ، داء

▶ **diseased** *adj*: *His diseased kidney had to be removed.* مريض أو ممروض ، معلول

> **Illness** and **disease** can be used in a similar way. However, we use **disease** to describe a type of illness which has a name and is recognized by certain symptoms. Diseases may be caused by bacteria, viruses, etc., and you can often catch and pass them on to others. **Illness** is used to describe the general state of being ill and the time during which you are not well.

disembark /ˌdɪsɪm'bɑːk/ *verb* [I] to get off a ship or a plane: *All foot passengers should disembark from Deck B.* ينزل من سفينة أو طائرة

▶ **disembarkation** /ˌdɪsˌembɑː'keɪʃn/ *noun* [U] نزول من سفينة أو طائرة

disenchanted /ˌdɪsɪn'tʃɑːntɪd; *US* -tʃænt-/ *adj* having lost your good opinion of sb/sth خائب الأمل بِ ، لم يَعد مسحوراً بِ

▶ **disenchantment** *noun* [U]: *There is increasing disenchantment among voters with the government's policies.* خيبة أمل ؛ فقد الثقة

disentangle /ˌdɪsɪn'tæŋgl/ *verb* [T] **1** to remove the knots from sth and make it straight: *to disentangle wool, rope, string, etc.* يحلّ أو يفكّ التعقّد أو التشابك

2 to free sb/sth that was stuck in or attached to sb/sth else: *I helped to disentangle the sheep from the bush.* يفكّ ، يحرر

disfigure /dɪs'fɪgə(r); *US* dɪs'fɪgjər/ *verb* [T] to spoil the appearance of sb/sth يشوّه

disgrace /dɪs'greɪs/ *noun* **1** [U] the state of not being respected by other people, usually because you have behaved badly: *There is no disgrace in not having much money.* عار ، خزي

2 [sing.] **a disgrace (to sb/sth)** a person or thing that gives such a bad impression that other people feel ashamed: *The streets are covered in litter. It's a disgrace!* شيء مخزٍ

IDM (be) in disgrace (with sb) (to be) in a position where other people do not respect you, usually because you have behaved badly في خزي ، في موقف محتقَر

▸ **disgrace** *verb* [T] **1** to cause disgrace to sb/yourself يخزي ، يجلب العار

2 to cause sb to lose his/her position of power: *the disgraced leader* (رئيس) مخلوع

disgraceful /-fl/ *adj* very bad, making other people feel ashamed: *The football supporters' behaviour was absolutely disgraceful.* مخزٍ ، مشين ، مسيء للغاية

disgracefully /-fəli/ *adv* بصورة مخزية

disgruntled /dɪs'grʌntld/ *adj* rather angry; disappointed and annoyed ساخط ، مستاء ، متبرِّم

disguise /dɪs'gaɪz/ *verb* [T] **disguise sb/sth (as sb/sth)** to change the appearance, sound, etc. of sb/sth so that people cannot recognize him/her/it: *They disguised themselves as fishermen and escaped in a boat.* ○ *to disguise your voice* ○ *(figurative) His smile disguised his anger.* يتنكّر ؛ يخفي

▸ **disguise** *noun* [C,U] clothes or items such as false hair, glasses, etc., that you wear to change your appearance so that nobody recognizes you ملابس تنكّرية

IDM **in disguise** wearing or using a disguise متنكِّر ، متخفٍ

disgust /dɪs'gʌst/ *noun* [U] a strong feeling of dislike or disapproval: *She looked round the filthy room with disgust.* ○ *The film was so bad that we walked out in disgust.* اشمئزاز ؛ امتعاض

▸ **disgust** *verb* [T] to cause disgust: *Cruelty towards animals absolutely disgusts me.* يُثير الاشمئزاز أو الامتعاض

disgusted *adj* feeling disgust: *We were disgusted at the standard of service we received.* مشمئزّ ، ممتعض

disgusting *adj* causing disgust: *What a disgusting smell!* مقرِف، مثير للاشمئزاز

disgustingly *adv* على نحو يثير الاشمئزاز

dish[1] /dɪʃ/ *noun* **1** [C] a shallow container for food. You can use a dish to cook sth in the oven, to serve food on the table or to eat from: *Is this dish ovenproof?* صحن ، طبق

2 [C] a type of food prepared in a particular way: *The main dish was curry. It was served with a selection of side dishes.* طبق ، أكلة

3 the dishes [plural] all the plates, cups, etc. that you use during a meal: *I'll cook and you can wash the dishes.* الصحون ، الأطباق

4 = SATELLITE DISH

dish[2] /dɪʃ/ *verb*

PHR V **dish sth out** (*informal*) to give away a lot of sth يوزِّع (بسخاء) ، يغرف أو يسكب الطعام

dish sth up (*informal*) to serve food يسكب الطعام في الصحون

disheartened /dɪs'hɑːtnd/ *adj* sad or disappointed مثبَّط العزيمة

▸ **disheartening** /-hɑːtnɪŋ/ *adj* مثبِّط للعزيمة

dishevelled (*US* **disheveled**) /dɪ'ʃevld/ *adj* (used about a person's appearance) untidy مهمَل الهندام ؛ مشعَّث

dishonest /dɪs'ɒnɪst/ *adj* not honest or truthful كاذب ، غشّاش ، غير أمين

▸ **dishonestly** *adv* بصورة مضلِّلة ، بعدم أمانة

dishonesty *noun* [U] عدم الأمانة ، غش

dishonour (*US* **dishonor**) /dɪs'ɒnə(r)/ *noun* [U, sing.] (*formal*) the state of no longer being respected; shame خِزي ، عار

▸ **dishonour** *verb* [T] (*formal*) to bring shame on sb/sth يجلب العار على

dishonourable /-nərəbl/ *adj* عديم الشرف ، غشّاش

dishwasher /'dɪʃwɒʃə(r); *US* -wɔːʃ-/ *noun* [C] an electric machine that washes plates, cups, knives, forks, etc. جلاّية ، غسّالة صحون

disillusion /ˌdɪsɪ'luːʒn/ *verb* [T] to destroy sb's belief in or good opinion of sb/sth يُخيِّب فأله ؛ يزول وَهْمه

▸ **disillusioned** *adj* disappointed because sb/sth is not as good as you first thought: *She's disillusioned with nursing.* خائب الفأل

disillusionment (*also* **disillusion**) *noun* [U] disappointment because sb/sth is not as good as you first thought خيبة الفأل

disinfect /ˌdɪsɪn'fekt/ *verb* [T] to clean sth with a liquid that destroys bacteria: *to disinfect a toilet* ○ *to disinfect a wound* يطهِّر ، يعقِّم

▸ **disinfectant** /ˌdɪsɪn'fektənt/ *noun* [C,U] a substance that destroys bacteria and is used for cleaning: *wash the floor with disinfectant* مطهِّر

disinfection /ˌdɪsɪn'fekʃn/ *noun* [U] تطهير ، تعقيم

disintegrate /dɪs'ɪntɪgreɪt/ *verb* [I] to break into many small pieces: *The spacecraft exploded and disintegrated.* يتفكّك ، يتفتّت

▸ **disintegration** /dɪsˌɪntɪ'greɪʃn/ *noun* [U]: *the disintegration of the empire* تفكّك ، تفتّت ؛ تداعٍ

disinterested /dɪs'ɪntrəstɪd/ *adj* fair, not influenced by personal feelings: *disinterested advice* ➲ Look at **uninterested**. It has a different meaning. غير مغرِض ، نزيه

disjointed /dɪs'dʒɔɪntɪd/ *adj* (used especially about ideas, writing or speech) not clearly linked and therefore difficult to follow غير مترابط

▸ **disjointedly** *adv* بصورة متقطّعة

disk /dɪsk/ *noun* [C] **1** (*US*) = DISC

2 (*computing*) a flat piece of plastic that stores information for use by a computer ➲ Look at **floppy disk** and **hard disk**. قرص

'**disk drive** *noun* [C] a piece of electrical equipment that passes information to or from a computer disk وحدة دفع الأقراص

diskette /dɪs'ket/ *noun* [C] = FLOPPY DISK

dislike /dɪs'laɪk/ *verb* [T] to think that sb/sth is unpleasant: *I really dislike flying.* ○ *What is it that you dislike about living here?* يكره

▸ **dislike** *noun* [U, sing.] **dislike (of/for sb/sth)** the feeling of not liking sb/sth: *She couldn't hide her dislike for him.* ○ *He seems to have a strong dislike of hard work.* كره؛ نفور

IDM **likes and dislikes** → LIKES

take a dislike to sb/sth to start disliking sb/sth صار يكره

dislocate /'dɪsləkeɪt; *US* 'dɪsləʊkeɪt/ *verb* [T] to put sth (often a bone) out of its proper position: *He dislocated his shoulder during the game.* يخلع

▸ **dislocation** /ˌdɪslə'keɪʃn; *US* ˌdɪsləʊ'keɪʃn/ *noun* [C,U] خَلْع

dislodge /dɪs'lɒdʒ/ *verb* [T] to make sb/sth move from a fixed position يزيح ، يزحزح

disloyal /dɪs'lɔɪəl/ *adj* doing or saying sth that is against sb/sth that you should support; not loyal: *It was disloyal of him to turn against his friends.* غير مخلص ، خائن

▸ **disloyalty** /-'lɔɪəlti/ *noun* [C,U] (*pl.* **disloyalties**) عدم ولاء ، عدم إخلاص

dismal /'dɪzməl/ *adj* **1** depressing; causing sadness: *dismal surroundings* ○ *a dismal failure* قابض للصدر ، موحِش ؛ رهيب

2 (*informal*) of low quality; poor: *a dismal standard of work* رديء ، غير متقَن

dismantle /dɪs'mæntl/ *verb* [T] to take sth to pieces; to separate sth into the parts it is made from: *The photographer dismantled his equipment and packed it away.* يفكِّك

dismay /dɪs'meɪ/ *noun* [U] a strong feeling of worry and shock: *I realized to my dismay that I was going to miss the plane.* قلق ؛ فزع

▸ **dismay** *verb* [T] (usually passive) يقلِق ، يفزع

dismember /dɪs'membə(r)/ *verb* [T] to tear or cut a body apart يقطِّع الأوصال

dismiss /dɪs'mɪs/ *verb* [T] **1** to order an employee to leave his/her job: *He was dismissed for refusing to obey orders.* ℹ **Fire** and **sack** are less formal words for **dismiss**. يطرد ، يفصل عن العمل

2 to allow sb to leave: *The lesson ended and the teacher dismissed the class.* يصرف (التلاميذ)

3 to remove sb/sth from your mind; to stop thinking about sb/sth completely: *She decided to dismiss her worries from her mind.* يطرد، يبعِد من تفكيره

4 dismiss sb/sth (as sth) to say or think that sb/sth is not important or is not worth considering seriously: *He dismissed the idea as nonsense.* ينبذ الفكرة ، يصرف النظر عن

▸ **dismissal** /dɪs'mɪsl/ *noun* **1** [C,U] ordering sb or being ordered to leave a job: *a case of unfair dismissal* طرد ، فصل من العمل

2 [U] refusing to consider sb/sth seriously: *She was hurt at their dismissal of her offer of help.* نَبْذ ، عدم اهتمام بِ

dismissive /dɪs'mɪsɪv/ *adj* saying or showing that you think that sb/sth is not important or is not worth considering seriously: *The boss was dismissive of all the efforts I had made.* نابذ (للفكرة) دون اكتراث

dismount /dɪs'maʊnt/ *verb* [I] to get off sth that you ride (a horse, a bicycle, etc.) يترجّل ، ينزل عن ركْبه

disobedient /ˌdɪsə'biːdiənt/ *adj* not willing to obey; refusing to do what you are told to do; not obedient عاصٍ ، غير مطيع

▸ **disobedience** /-iəns/ *noun* [U] عصيان ، تمرد

disobey /ˌdɪsə'beɪ/ *verb* [I,T] to refuse to do what you are told to do; not to obey: *He was punished for disobeying orders.* يَعصي ، لا يطيع

disorder /dɪs'ɔːdə(r)/ *noun* **1** [U] an untidy, confused or disorganized state: *His financial affairs are in complete disorder.* فوضى

2 [U] violent behaviour by a large number of people: *Disorder broke out on the streets of the capital.* شَغَب ، اضطراب

3 [C,U] an illness in which the mind or part of the body is not working properly: *a stomach disorder* اضطراب ؛ علّة

▸ **disordered** *adj* untidy, confused or disorganized غير منظَّم ، مشوّش

disorderly *adj* **1** very untidy مشوّش ، "ملَخْبَط"

2 (used about people or behaviour) out of control and violent; causing trouble in public: *They were arrested for being drunk and disorderly.* مُشاغِب ؛ مثير للفوضى ، مخِلّ بالنظام

disorganization (*also* **disorganisation**) /dɪsˌɔːɡənaɪ'zeɪʃn; *US* -nɪ'z-/ *noun* [U] a lack of organization عدم تنظيم ، فوضى

▸ **disorganized** /dɪs'ɔːɡənaɪzd/ (*also* **disorganised**) *adj* not organized; badly planned غير منظَّم ، مشوّش

disorientate /dɪs'ɔːriənteɪt/ (*especially US* **disorient** /dɪs'ɔːriənt/) *verb* [T] (usually passive) to make sb lose all sense of direction or become confused about where he/she is: *The road signs were very confusing and I soon became disorientated.* يُفقده وجهته ، يضلّله

▸ **disorientation** /dɪsˌɔːriən'teɪʃn/ *noun* [U] فقدان التعرّف على المكان ، تشوّش

disown /dɪs'əʊn/ *verb* [T] to decide or say that you are no longer associated with sb/sth: *When he was arrested, his family disowned him.* يتبرأ من ، ينكِر

disparage /dɪ'spærɪdʒ/ *verb* [T] (*formal*) to talk about sb/sth in a critical way or to say that sb/sth is of little value or importance ينتقد ، يذمّ ، يحطّ من قيمته

▸ **disparaging** *adj*: *disparaging remarks* مستخِف ، انتقاديّ

dispatch (*also* **despatch**) /dɪ'spætʃ/ *verb* [T] (*formal*) to send: *Your order will be dispatched from our warehouse within 7 days.* يرسل ؛ يبعث ، يوفد

dispel /dɪ'spel/ *verb* [T] (dispelling; dispelled) to make sth disappear; to remove sth from sb's mind: *His reassuring words dispelled all her fears.* يطرد ، يبدِّد ، يزيل

dispensable /dɪ'spensəbl/ *adj* not necessary: *I suppose I'm dispensable. Anybody could do my job.* ℹ The opposite is **indispensable**. غير أساسيّ ، يمكن الاستغناء عنه

dispense /dɪ'spens/ *verb* [T] **1** (*formal*) to give out: *a machine that dispenses hot and cold drinks* يعطي ، يوزع

2 to prepare and give out medicines in a chemist's shop: *a dispensing chemist* يحضِّر ويبيع الأدوية

PHR V **dispense with sb/sth** to get rid of sb/sth that is not necessary: *They decided to dispense with luxuries and live a simple life.* يستغني عن

▸ **dispenser** *noun* [C] a machine or container

from which you can get sth: *a cash dispenser at a bank* آلة أوتوماتيكيّة تعطي نقوداً أو قطع حلوى وغير ذلك

disperse /dɪ'spɜːs/ *verb* [I,T] to separate and go in different directions; to break sth up: *When the meeting was over, the group dispersed.* ○ *Police arrived and quickly dispersed the crowd.* يتفرّق ، يتشتّت : يفرّق أو يشتّت

dispirited /dɪ'spɪrɪtɪd/ *adj* having lost confidence or hope; depressed مثبّط العزيمة ، قانط

displace /dɪs'pleɪs/ *verb* [T] **1** to force sb/sth to move from the usual or correct place يزيح

2 to remove and take the place of sb/sth: *She hoped to displace Williams as the top player in the world.* يزيحه ويحلّ محلّه

display¹ /dɪ'spleɪ/ *verb* [T] **1** to put sth in a place where people will see it or where it will attract attention: *Posters for the concert were displayed throughout the city.* يعرض

2 to show sth (e.g. a feeling or personal quality): *She displayed no interest in the discussion.* يظهِر ، يبدي

display² /dɪ'spleɪ/ *noun* [C] **1** a public event in which sth is shown in action: *a firework display* عرض

2 an arrangement of things for people to see: *The shops take a lot of trouble over their window displays.* معروضات

3 behaviour that shows a particular feeling or quality: *a sudden display of aggression* إظهار ، إبداء

4 (*computing*) words, pictures, etc. that can be seen on a computer screen المعروض على الشاشة ، عرض

IDM on display in a place where people will see it and where it will attract attention: *Treasures from the sunken ship were put on display at the museum.* معروض (في متحف مثلاً)

displease /dɪs'pliːz/ *verb* [T] (*formal*) to annoy sb or to make sb angry or upset يغضب ، يثير استياءه

displeasure /dɪs'pleʒə(r)/ *noun* [U] (*formal*) the feeling of being annoyed or not satisfied: *I wrote to express my displeasure at not having been informed sooner.* استياء

disposable /dɪ'spəʊzəbl/ *adj* intended to be thrown away after being used once or for a short time: *a disposable razor* معدّ للطرح بعد الاستعمال

disposal /dɪ'spəʊzl/ *noun* [U] the act of getting rid of sth: *the disposal of dangerous chemical waste* التخلّص من ، طرح

IDM at sb's disposal available for sb's use at any time: *They put their house at my disposal.* تحت التصرّف

dispose /dɪ'spəʊz/ *verb*

PHRV dispose of sb/sth to throw away or sell sth; to get rid of sb/sth that you do not want يتخلّص من : يبيع

disproportionate /ˌdɪsprə'pɔːʃənət/ *adj* larger or smaller than is acceptable or expected غير متناسب ، غير متكافئ مع

▸ **disproportionately** *adv* بشكل غير متناسب (مع)

disprove /ˌdɪs'pruːv/ *verb* [T] to show or prove that sth is not true يَدحض ، يفنّد ، ينقض

dispute¹ /dɪ'spjuːt; 'dɪspjuːt/ *noun* [C,U] disagreement or argument between people: *There was some dispute about whose fault it was.* ○ *a pay dispute* نزاع ، خلاف

IDM in dispute in a situation of arguing or being argued about: *He is in dispute with the tax office about how much he should pay.* موضع نزاع : في حالة نزاع

dispute² /dɪ'spjuːt/ *verb* [T] to argue about sth or to suggest that sth is not true: *The player disputed the referee's decision.* يخالف ، يشكّ في ، يجادل بشدّة

disqualify /dɪs'kwɒlɪfaɪ/ *verb* [T] (*pres part* **disqualifying**; *3rd pers sing pres* **disqualifies**; *pt, pp* **disqualified**) **disqualify sb (from sth/from doing sth)** to officially forbid sb to do sth or to take part in sth, usually because he/she has broken a rule or law: *The team were disqualified for cheating.* يسقط حقّه، يجرّده من أهليّته (للّعب)

▸ **disqualification** /dɪsˌkwɒlɪfɪ'keɪʃn/ *noun* [C,U] تجريد من الأهليّة، حِرمان (من اللعب)

disregard /ˌdɪsrɪ'ɡɑːd/ *verb* [T] to take no notice of sb/sth; to pay no attention to sb/sth: *These are the latest instructions. Please disregard any you received before.* يهمل ، يتجاهل

▸ **disregard** *noun* [U, sing.] **(a) disregard (for/of sb/sth)** lack of attention to, interest in or care for sb/sth: *He rushed into the burning building with complete disregard for his own safety.* عدم اكتراث ، تجاهل ، صرف النظر

disrepair /ˌdɪsrɪ'peə(r)/ *noun* [U] a bad condition, existing because repairs have not been made: *Over the years the building fell into a state of disrepair.* تداعٍ ، تهدّم ، حاجة إلى الترميم

disreputable /dɪs'repjətəbl/ *adj* not deserving to be trusted; having a bad reputation: *a disreputable area, full of criminal activity* ○ *disreputable business methods* سيّئ السمعة ، مشبوه

disrepute /ˌdɪsrɪ'pjuːt/ *noun* [U] the situation when people no longer respect sb/sth: *Such unfair decisions bring the legal system into disrepute.* سوء سمعة

disrespect /ˌdɪsrɪ'spekt/ *noun* [U] behaviour or words that show that you do not respect sb/sth عدم احترام ، ازدراء

▸ **disrespectful** /-fl/ *adj* عديم الاحترام ، قليل الأدب
disrespectfully /-fəli/ *adv* باستخفاف ، بعدم احترام

disrupt /dɪs'rʌpt/ *verb* [T] to disturb a process or system: *The strike severely disrupted flights to Spain.* يعطّل ، يشوّش

▸ **disruption** /dɪs'rʌpʃn/ *noun* [C,U] تعطيل ، تشويش

disruptive /dɪs'rʌptɪv/ *adj*: *A badly behaved child can have a disruptive influence on the rest of the class.* مشوّش ، مخرّب

dissatisfaction /ˌdɪsˌsætɪs'fækʃn/ *noun* [U] the feeling of not being satisfied or pleased: *There is some dissatisfaction among teachers with the plans for the new exam.* عدم رضى : استياء

dissatisfied /dɪs'sætɪsfaɪd/ *adj* **dissatisfied**

(with sb/sth) not satisfied or pleased: *complaints from dissatisfied customers* غير راضٍ ، مستاء، متبرّم

dissect /dɪˈsekt/ *verb* [T] to cut up a dead body, a plant, etc. in order to examine its structure يُشرِّح
▸ **dissection** /dɪˈsekʃn/ *noun* [C,U] تشريح

dissent¹ /dɪˈsent/ *noun* [U] (*formal*) disagreement with official or generally agreed ideas or opinions: *There is some dissent within the Labour Party on these policies.* انشقاق ، خلاف في الرأي

dissent² /dɪˈsent/ *verb* [I] **dissent (from sth)** (*formal*) to have opinions that are different to those that are officially held ينشقّ على ، يخالف في الرأي
▸ **dissenting** *adj* showing or feeling dissent منشقّ ، مخالف

dissertation /ˌdɪsəˈteɪʃn/ *noun* [C] a long piece of writing on sth that you have studied, especially as part of a university degree ➲ Look at **thesis.** رسالة جامعيّة ، أطروحة

disservice /dɪsˈsɜːvɪs/ *noun* [U, sing.] **(a) disservice to sb/sth** an action that is unhelpful or has a negative effect إساءة ، ضرر

dissident /ˈdɪsɪdənt/ *noun* [C] a person who expresses disagreement with the actions or ideas of a government or organization المنشقّ ، الخارج على
▸ **dissidence** /ˈdɪsɪdəns/ *noun* [U] انشقاق ، تمرّد

dissimilar /dɪˈsɪmɪlə(r)/ *adj* **dissimilar (from/ to sb/sth)** unlike; not similar; different غير مشابه لِ ، مختلف

dissociate /dɪˈsəʊʃieɪt/ (*also* **disassociate** /ˌdɪsəˈsəʊʃieɪt/) *verb* [T] **dissociate sb/sth/ yourself from sth** to say or believe that a thing or a person is not connected with another, or that you do not agree with sth: *She dissociated herself from the views of the extremists in her party.* يتبرأ من ؛ يفرّق أو يفصل بين

🔑**dissolve** /dɪˈzɒlv/ *verb* [I,T] to become liquid or to make sth become liquid: *Sugar dissolves in water.* ○ *Dissolve two tablets in cold water.* ينحلّ ، يذوب ؛ يحلّ أو يذيب

dissuade /dɪˈsweɪd/ *verb* [T] **dissuade sb (from doing sth)** to persuade sb not to do sth: *I tried to dissuade her from spending the money, but she insisted.* يثني (عن) ، يقنعه بالعدول عن

🔑**distance¹** /ˈdɪstəns/ *noun* **1** [C,U] the amount of space between two places or points: *It's only a short distance from my home to work.* ○ *The map tells you the distances between the major cities.* ○ *We can walk home from here, it's no distance* (= it isn't far). ○ *The house is within walking distance of the shops.* مسافة ، بُعْد
2 [sing.] a point that is a long way from sb/sth: *At this distance I can't read the number on the bus.* ○ *From a distance the village looks quite attractive.* بُعْد ، مسافة
IDM **in the distance** far away: *I could hear voices in the distance.* من بعيد ، عن بُعْد
keep your distance to stay away from sb/sth: *Rosie's got a bad cold so I'm keeping my distance until she gets better.* ينأى بنفسه

distance² /ˈdɪstəns/ *verb* [T] **1** to make sb feel less friendly towards sb/sth: *Her wealth and success have distanced her from her old friends.* يقصي ، يخلق جفوة
2 distance yourself from sb/sth to show that you are not involved or connected with sb/sth: *She was keen to distance herself from the views of her colleagues.* يبْعد نفسه عن ، يتبرأ من

distant /ˈdɪstənt/ *adj* **1** a long way away in space or time: *travel to distant parts of the world* ○ *in the not-too-distant future* (= quite soon) بعيد ، ناء
2 (used about a relative) not closely related: *a distant cousin* (قرابة) بعيدة
3 not very friendly: *He has a rather distant manner and it's hard to get to know him well.* متجافٍ ، متحفّظ ، بارد
4 seeming to be thinking about sth else: *She had a distant look in her eyes and clearly wasn't listening to me.* شارد الذهن

distaste /dɪsˈteɪst/ *noun* [U, sing.] **(a) distaste (for sb/sth)** dislike; the feeling that sb/sth is unpleasant or unacceptable: *She viewed business with distaste.* ○ *He seems to have a distaste for hard work.* كُره ، مقْت ؛ نُفور
▸ **distasteful** /dɪsˈteɪstfl/ *adj* causing the feeling of dislike; unpleasant or unacceptable مكروه ، ممقوت ، منفّر

distil (*US* **distill**) /dɪˈstɪl/ *verb* [T] (distilling; distilled) to heat a liquid until it becomes steam and then collect the liquid that forms when the steam cools: *distilled water* يقطّر

distinct /dɪˈstɪŋkt/ *adj* **1** clear; easily seen, heard or understood: *There has been a distinct improvement in your work recently.* ○ *I had the distinct impression that she was lying.* واضح ، جليّ
2 distinct (from sth) clearly different: *Her books fall into two distinct groups: the novels and the travel stories.* ○ *This region, as distinct from other parts of the country, relies heavily on tourism.* متميّز ، منفصل
▸ **distinctly** *adv* **1** clearly: *I distinctly heard her say that she would be here on time.* بوضوح
2 very; particularly: *His behaviour has been distinctly odd recently.* جداً ، بصورة خاصّة

distinction /dɪˈstɪŋkʃn/ *noun* [C,U] **1 (a) distinction (between A and B)** a clear or important difference between things or people: *We must make a distinction between classical and popular music here.* تمييز ، تفريق
2 the quality of being excellent; fame for what you have achieved: *a violinist of some distinction* ○ *She has the distinction of being the only player to win the championship five times.* امتياز ، تفوّق ؛ شهرة
3 the highest mark that is given to students in some exams for excellent work: *James got a distinction in maths.* درجة امتياز
IDM **draw a distinction between sth and sth** → DRAW²

distinctive /dɪˈstɪŋktɪv/ *adj* clearly different from others and therefore easy to recognize: *the soldiers wearing their distinctive red berets* مميز ، متميّز

▸ **distinctively** *adv* بصورة مميزة أو خاصة

distinguish /dɪˈstɪŋɡwɪʃ/ *verb* **1** [I,T] **distinguish between A and B; distinguish A from B** to recognize the difference between things or people: *He doesn't seem able to distinguish between what's important and what isn't.* ○ *People who are colour-blind often can't distinguish red from green.* يميز ، يفرق

2 [T] **distinguish A (from B)** to make sb/sth different from others; to show the difference between people or things: *distinguishing features* (= things by which sb/sth can be recognized) يميّز

3 [T] to see, hear or recognize with effort: *I listened carefully but they were too far away for me to distinguish what they were saying.* يتبيّن

4 [T] **distinguish yourself** to do sth which causes you to be noticed and admired: *She distinguished herself in the exams.* يكتسب شهرة ؛ يبرز

▸ **distinguishable** /-əbl/ *adj* **1** possible to distinguish as different from sb/sth else: *The male bird is distinguishable from the female by the colour of its beak.* مميز عن ، يمكن تمييزه

2 possible to see, hear or recognize with effort: *The letter is so old that the signature is barely distinguishable.* يمكن تبيّنه بصعوبة

distinguished *adj* important and respected: *I am pleased to welcome our distinguished guests to the conference.* بارز ، شهير ، محترم

distort /dɪˈstɔːt/ *verb* [T] **1** to change the shape or sound of sth so that it seems unnatural: *Her face was distorted with grief.* يغيّر المعالم ، يشوّه

2 to change sth and show it falsely: *Foreigners are often given a distorted view of this country.* يحرّف ؛ يعطي صورة زائفة

▸ **distortion** /dɪˈstɔːʃn/ *noun* [C,U] تشوّه ؛ تشويه، تحريف

distract /dɪˈstrækt/ *verb* [T] to take sb's attention away from sth: *Could you stop talking please? You're distracting me from my work.* يلهي ، يَصرِف الانتباه

▸ **distracted** *adj* unable to concentrate because of being worried or thinking about sth else مشوّش أو شارد الذهن

distraction /dɪˈstrækʃn/ *noun* [C,U] something that takes your attention away from what you were doing or thinking about: *I find it hard to work at home because there are so many distractions.* إلهاء ، تلهية : ملهية

distraught /dɪˈstrɔːt/ *adj* extremely sad and upset في غاية الحزن والاضطراب ، مذهول

distress[1] /dɪˈstres/ *noun* [U] **1** the state of being very upset or unhappy or of suffering great pain: *Their distress on hearing the bad news was obvious.* ○ *She was in such distress that I didn't want to leave her on her own.* أسى ، ألم ، لوعة

2 the state of being in great danger and needing immediate help: *The ship's captain radioed that it was in distress.* خطر ؛ محنة

distress[2] /dɪˈstres/ *verb* [T] (often passive) to make sb very upset or unhappy: *She was too distressed to talk.* يحزن ، يؤلم ؛ يقلِق

▸ **distressing** *adj* causing sb to be very upset or unhappy محزن ، مؤلم ، مقلِق

distribute /dɪˈstrɪbjuːt/ *verb* [T] **1 distribute sth (to/among sb/sth)** to give things to a number of people; to divide sth up and give the parts to people or place them in various positions: *Protesters were distributing leaflets in the street.* ○ *Tickets will be distributed to all club members.* ○ *Make sure that the weight is evenly distributed.* يوزّع

2 distribute sth (to sb/sth) to transport and supply sth to various people or places: *They distributed emergency food supplies to the areas that were most in need.* يوزّع

▸ **distribution** /ˌdɪstrɪˈbjuːʃn/ *noun* **1** [sing., U] the act of giving sth: *the distribution of food parcels to the refugees* توزيع

2 [sing., U] the way sth is shared out; the pattern in which sth is found: *The uneven distribution of wealth causes many problems.* ○ *a map to show the distribution of rainfall in India* توزيع ؛ توزّع

3 [U] the transport and supply of goods, etc. to various people or places: *The country produces enough food but distribution is a problem.* التوزيع

distributor /dɪˈstrɪbjətə(r)/ *noun* [C] a person or company that transports and supplies goods to a number of shops and companies الموزّع ، وكيل التوزيع

district /ˈdɪstrɪkt/ *noun* [C] **1** a part of a town or country that has a particular feature or is of a particular type: *railway services in rural districts* حيّ ؛ منطقة

2 an official division of a town or country: *the district council* ○ *postal districts* دائرة ؛ مقاطعة

> A **district** may be part of a town or country, and it may have fixed boundaries: *the district controlled by a council.* A **region** is larger, usually part of a country only and may not have fixed boundaries: *the industrial regions of the country.* An **area** is the most general term and is used with the same meaning as both **district** and **region**: *the poorer areas of a town* ○ *an agricultural area of the country.* We use **part** more often when we are talking about a section of a town: *Which part of Paris do you live in?*

distrust /dɪsˈtrʌst/ *noun* [U, sing.] **(a) distrust (of sb/sth)** the feeling that you cannot believe sb/sth; lack of trust عدم ثقة ، ارتياب

▸ **distrust** *verb* [T]: *She distrusts him because he lied to her once before.* يرتاب في ، لا يثق بِ

disturb /dɪˈstɜːb/ *verb* [T] **1** to interrupt and possibly annoy sb while he/she is doing sth or sleeping; to spoil a peaceful situation: *I'm sorry to disturb you but there's a phone call for you.* ○ *Keep the noise down! You'll disturb the neighbours.*

○ *Their sleep was disturbed by a loud crash.* يزعج : يُقاطع

2 to cause sb to worry: *It disturbed her to think that he might be unhappy.* يقلق

3 to change sth from its normal position or condition: *I noticed a number of things had been disturbed and realized that there had been a burglary.* يقلق ترتيب الأشياء المعهود ، يلخبط

▸ **disturbed** *adj* having mental or emotional problems: *a school for disturbed young people* مصاب باضطراب نفسي

disturbing *adj* causing sb to worry: *These disturbing developments suggest that war is a possibility.* مقلق

disturbance /dɪ'stɜːbəns/ *noun* **1** [C,U] an interruption; something that stops you concentrating, sleeping, etc. مقاطعة ، إزعاج : تشويش

2 [C] an occasion when people behave violently or make a lot of noise in public: *Further disturbances have been reported in the capital city.* شغب ، إخلال بالأمن

disuse /dɪs'juːs/ *noun* [U] the state of not being used any more: *The farm buildings had fallen into disuse.* حالة إهمال ، عدم استعمال

▸ **disused** /ˌdɪs'juːzd/ *adj* not used any more: *a disused railway line* مهمل ، مهجور

ditch /dɪtʃ/ *noun* [C] a long narrow hole that has been dug into the ground, especially along the side of a road or field for water to flow through: *The car left the road and ended up in a ditch.* خندق

▸ **ditch** *verb* [T] (*informal*) to get rid of or leave sb/sth: *She ditched her old friends when she became famous.* يتخلّص من ، يهجر

dither /'dɪðə(r)/ *verb* [I] to hesitate and be unable to decide sth: *Stop dithering and make up your mind!* يتردّد

ditto /'dɪtəʊ/ *noun* [C] (represented by the mark (˝) and used instead of repeating the thing written above it) the same كذلك ، مثله : إشارة التكرار

divan /dɪ'væn; *US* 'daɪvæn/ *noun* [C] a type of bed with only a base and a mattress, not with a frame (سرير) ديوان

dive[1] /daɪv/ *verb* [I] (*pt* **dived**; *US also* **dove** /dəʊv/; *pp* **dived**) **1** to jump into water with your head first: *In Acapulco, men dive off the cliffs into the sea.* ○ *A passer-by dived in and saved the drowning man.* يقفز إلى الماء

2 dive (down) (for sth) to go under water: *people diving for pearls* يغوص (تحت الماء)

3 to move downwards steeply and quickly through the air: *The engines failed and the plane dived.* يهوي بسرعة هائلة

4 to move quickly in a particular direction, especially downwards: *He dived under the table and hid there.* يندفع نحو الأرض : ينقضّ

PHR V **dive into sth/in** to put your hand quickly into sth in order to find or get sth: *She dived into her bag and brought out an old photograph.* يدسّ يده داخل شيء منقّباً

▸ **diver** *noun* [C] a person whose job is going underwater using special equipment: *Police divers searching the lake found the body.* غوّاص ، غطّاس

diving *noun* [U] the activity or sport of diving into water or swimming under water: *The resort has facilities for sailing, waterskiing and diving.* الغوص ، القفز إلى الماء

dive[2] /daɪv/ *noun* [C] **1** the act of diving into the water غوصة ، قفزة إلى الماء

2 (in football, hockey, etc.) a deliberate fall that a player makes when sb tackles them so that the referee awards a foul وقوع أو سقوط مفاجيء

diverge /daɪ'vɜːdʒ/ *verb* [I] **diverge (from sth)** **1** (used about roads, lines, etc.) to separate and go in different directions: *The paths suddenly diverged and I didn't know which one to take.* يتفرّع ، يتشعّب

2 to be or become different (from each other): *Attitudes among teachers diverge on this question.* يختلف

diverse /daɪ'vɜːs/ *adj* very different from each other: *people with diverse social backgrounds* مختلف ، متباين

diversify /daɪ'vɜːsɪfaɪ/ *verb* [I] (*pres part* **diversifying**; *3rd pers sing pres* **diversifies**; *pt, pp* **diversified**) **diversify (into sth)** (used about a business) to increase the range of activities, products, etc: *To remain successful in the future, the company will have to diversify.* يتنوّع ، ينوّع العمل

▸ **diversification** /daɪˌvɜːsɪfɪ'keɪʃn/ *noun* [C, U] تنويع الإنتاج

diversion /daɪ'vɜːʃn/ *noun* **1** [C,U] the act of changing the direction or purpose of sth especially in order to solve or avoid a problem: *the diversion of a river to prevent flooding* ○ *the diversion of government funds to areas of greatest need* تحويل (مجرى النهر مثلاً)

2 [C] (*US* **detour**) a different route which traffic can take when a road is closed: *There are temporary traffic lights and diversions due to roadworks on the A161.* تحويل اتّجاه السير

3 [C] something that takes your attention away from sth: *Some prisoners created a diversion while others escaped.* تسلية ، وسيلة لهو : صرف للانتباه

diversity /daɪ'vɜːsəti/ *noun* [U] the wide range or variety of sth: *a country of tremendous diversity, with landscape ranging from semi-desert to tropical* تنوّع

divert /daɪ'vɜːt/ *verb* [T] **divert sb/sth (from sth) (to sth)** to change the direction or purpose of sb/sth, especially to avoid a problem: *During the road repairs, all traffic is being diverted.* ○ *Government money was diverted from defence to education and training.* يحوّل (المجرى أو الاتجاه)

⚷ **divide** /dɪ'vaɪd/ *verb* **1** [I,T] **divide (sth) (up) (into sth)** to separate into different parts: *The egg divides into two cells.* ○ *a book divided into ten sections* ○ *The house was divided into flats.* ينقسم : يُقسّم

2 [T] **divide sth (out/up) (between/among sb)** to separate sth into parts and give a share to each of a number of people: *The robbers divided the money among themselves.* ○ *When he died, his property was divided up among his children.* يُقسّم ، يوزّع

3 [T] **divide sth (between A and B)** to use different parts or amounts of sth for different purposes: *They divide their time between their two homes.* يقسم

4 [T] to separate two places by being a boundary or area between them: *The river divides the old part of the city from the new.* يفصل

5 [T] to cause people to disagree: *The question of immigration has divided the country.* يسبّب الشقاق

6 [T] **divide sth by sth** to calculate how many times a number will go into another number: *10 divided by 5 is 2.* يقسّم

di͵vided 'highway (*US*) = DUAL CARRIAGEWAY

dividend /'dɪvɪdend/ *noun* [C] a part of a company's profits that is paid to the people who own shares in it حصّة من أرباح الأسهم

divine /dɪ'vaɪn/ *adj* connected with God or a god سماوي ، إلهي
▸ **divinely** *adv* من قبل الآلهة ، سماويّاً

diving /'daɪvɪŋ/ *noun* [U] → DIVE¹

'diving board *noun* [C] a board at the side of a swimming pool from which people can dive into the water منصّة القفز او الغوص

divisible /dɪ'vɪzəbl/ *adj* that can be divided: *9 is divisible by 3.* قابل للقسمة

division /dɪ'vɪʒn/ *noun* **1** [U] the dividing of sth into separate parts: *the division of Germany after the Second World War* تقسيم ، تجزئة

2 [U, sing.] the sharing of sth: *a fair/unfair division of the profits* تقسيم ، توزيع

3 [U] dividing one number by another: *the teaching of multiplication and division* التقسيم ، القسمة

4 [C] a disagreement or difference in thought, way of life, etc: *deep divisions within the Labour Party* انشقاق

5 [C] something that divides or separates: *The division between arts and science subjects is a problem in our education system.* فرق : تفريق، فصل بين

6 [C] a part or section of an organization: *the company's sales division* ○ *the First Division* (= of the football league) قسم : فئة

divisive /dɪ'vaɪsɪv/ *adj* (*formal*) likely to cause disagreements or arguments between people: *a divisive policy* مسبّب للشقاق

divorce¹ /dɪ'vɔːs/ *noun* [C,U] the legal end of a marriage: *to get a divorce* ○ *One in three marriages ends in divorce.* طلاق

divorce² /dɪ'vɔːs/ *verb* [T] **1** to legally end your marriage to sb: *She divorced him a year after their marriage.* يُطلّق

It is more common to say **to get divorced** than **to divorce**: *My parents got divorced when I was three.* However when only one partner wants a divorce or when the reason for the divorce is given, we say **to divorce**: *She divorced her first husband for mental cruelty.*

2 divorce sb/sth from sth to separate sb/sth from sth: *Sometimes these modern novels seem completely divorced from everyday life.* يفصل ، يعزل

▸ **divorced** *adj*: *No, I'm not married – I'm divorced.* مطلّق

divorcee /dɪ͵vɔː'siː/ *noun* [C] a person who is divorced المطلّق أو المطلّقة

divulge /daɪ'vʌldʒ/ *verb* [T] (*formal*) to tell sth secret: *The phone companies refused to divulge details of their costs.* يفشي ، يبوح

DIY /͵diː aɪ 'waɪ/ *abbrev* do it yourself; the activity of making and repairing things yourself around your home: *a DIY expert* اعمل بنفسك!

dizzy /'dɪzi/ *adj* (**dizzier**; **dizziest**) feeling as if everything is spinning round and that you might fall: *to feel/get dizzy* يشعر بدوار ، يدوخ
▸ **dizziness** *noun* [U]: *He had been to the doctor complaining of headaches and dizziness.* دُوار ، دَوْخة

DJ /'diː dʒeɪ/ *abbrev* = DISC JOCKEY

DNA /͵diː en 'eɪ/ *noun* [U] (deoxyribonucleic acid) the chemical in the cells of animals and plants that carries genetic information إختبار الحامض النووي

do¹ /də/ *auxiliary verb* (*negative* **do not**; *short form* **don't** /dəʊnt/; *3rd pers sing pres* **does** /dəz; *strong form* dʌz/; *negative* **does not**; *short form* **doesn't** /'dʌznt/; *pt* **did** /dɪd/; *negative* **did not**; *short form* **didn't** /'dɪdnt/) **1** (used with other verbs to form questions and negative sentences, also in short answers and question tags): *Do you know John?* ○ *He doesn't live in Oxford.* ○ *'Do you agree?' 'No, I don't/yes I do.'* ○ *She works in Paris, doesn't she?* ○ *He didn't say that, did he?* هل.. : لا (يفعل)

2 (used for emphasizing the main verb): *'Why didn't you buy any milk?' 'I did buy some, It's in the fridge.'* (تستعمل للتوكيد)

3 (used to avoid repeating the main verb): *He earns a lot more than I do.* ○ *She's feeling much better than she did last week.* (تستعمل بدلاً من تكرار الفعل)

do² /də; duː/ *verb* (*pres part* **doing**; *3rd pers sing pres* **does** /dʌz/; *pt* **did** /dɪd/; *pp* **done** /dʌn/) **1** [T] to perform an action: *What are you doing?* ○ *We didn't do much yesterday.* ○ *Please do as you're told.* ○ *It's not fair but what can we do about it* (= how can we change it)*?* ○ *What is the government doing about pollution?* ○ *What do you do* (= what is your job)*?* ○ *I don't know what I did with the keys* (= where I put them). يعمل ، يفعل

2 [T] to carry out a particular activity: *Do* (= tidy) *your hair before you go out.* ○ *Has he done his homework?* ○ *Who does the cooking in your house?* ○ *Did you get your essay done* (= finished)*?* يقوم بـ

3 [I] to make progress or develop: *'How's your*

daughter doing at school?' 'She's doing well (= she is successful).*'* يتقدّم ؛ ينجح

4 [T] to travel at a certain speed: *This car does 120 miles per hour.* يَسير (بسرعة كذا)

5 [T] to produce sth: *The photocopier does 60 copies a minute.* يعمل ، ينتج

6 [T] to study a subject: *I'm doing a course on hotel management.* يدرس

7 [T] to have a particular effect: *A holiday will do you good.* ○ *The storm did a lot of damage.* يؤثّر ، يسبّب

8 [I,T] to be good enough: *I don't need much money – £10 will do.* يكفي ؛ يسدّ الحاجة

IDM **be/have to do with sb/sth** to be connected with sb/sth: *Don't ask me about the accident. I had nothing to do with it.* ○ *I'm not sure what Paul's job is, but I think it's something to do with animals.* يتعلّق بـ

could do with sth to want or need sth: *I could do with a holiday.* يودّ ، يحتاج إلى

how do you do? → HOW

make do with sth → MAKE[1]

PHR V **do away with sth** to get rid of sth: *Most European countries have done away with their royal families.* يتخلّص من ، يستغني عن

do sb out of sth to prevent sb having sth in an unfair way: *They've cheated me! They've done me out of £50!* يسلب ، يحرم

do sth up 1 to fasten a piece of clothing: *He can't do his shoelaces up yet.* يربط ؛ يزرّر

2 to repair a building and make it more modern: *They're doing up the old cottage.* يجدّد ، يرمّم

do without (sth) to manage without having sth: *If there isn't any coffee left, we'll just have to do without.* يدبّر أمره ، "يمشّي الحال"

🔑 **do³** /duː/ *noun* [C] (*pl.* **dos** or **do's** /duːz/) (*Brit informal*) a party or other social event: *We're having a bit of a do to celebrate Tim's birthday on Saturday.* حفلة ؛ "جَمْعة"

docile /ˈdəʊsaɪl; *US* ˈdɒsl/ *adj* (used about a person or animal) quiet and easy to control وديع ؛ سهل القياد

dock¹ /dɒk/ **1** [C,U] an area of a port where ships stop to be loaded, unloaded, repaired, etc. رصيف الميناء

2 docks [plural] a group of docks with all the sheds, offices, etc. that are around them: *He works down at the docks.* حوض السفن

▶ **dock** *verb* [I,T] (used about a ship) to sail into a dock: *The ship had docked/was docked at Lisbon.* (السفينة) تلقي مراسيها

dock² /dɒk/ *noun* [C, usually sing.] the place in a court of law where the person accused sits or stands قفص الاتّهام

dock³ /dɒk/ *verb* [T] to take away part of sb's wages, especially as a punishment: *They've docked £20 off my wages because I was late.* يحسم ، يقتطع

🔑 **doctor** /ˈdɒktə(r)/ *noun* [C] (*abbr* **Dr**; **Dr.**) **1** a person who has been trained in medical science and who treats people who are ill: *Our family doctor is Dr Young.* ○ *I've got a doctor's appointment at 10 o'clock.* ○ *What time is the doctor's surgery today?* طبيب ، دكتور صحّة

> We can say **go to the doctor** or **to the doctor's** (= the doctor's surgery). A doctor **sees** or **treats** his/her **patients**. He/she may **prescribe** treatment or **medicine**. This is written on a **prescription**.

2 a person who has got the highest degree from a university: *Doctor of Philosophy* دكتور ، حامل دكتوراه

▶ **doctor** *verb* [T] **1** to change sth that should not be changed in order to gain some advantage: *The results of the survey had been doctored.* يزوّر

2 to add sth harmful to food or drink يدسّ شيئاً ضاراً (في الطعام مثلاً)

doctorate /ˈdɒktərət/ *noun* [C] the highest university degree درجة الدكتوراه

doctrine /ˈdɒktrɪn/ *noun* [C,U] a belief or a set of beliefs that is taught by a church, political party, etc. مذهب ، عقيدة ، تعاليم

🔑 **document** /ˈdɒkjumənt/ *noun* [C] **1** an official piece of writing which gives information, proof or evidence: *Her solicitor asked her to read and sign a number of documents.* وثيقة

2 a computer file that contains writing etc: *Save the document before closing.* ملف معطيات

documentary /ˌdɒkjuˈmentri/ *noun* [C] (*pl.* **documentaries**) a film or television or radio programme that gives facts or information about a particular subject: *a documentary on/about life in Northern Ireland* فيلم وثائقي

doddle /ˈdɒdl/ *noun* [sing.] (*Brit informal*) something that is very easy to do: *The work is an absolute doddle!* شيء سهل جداً

dodge /dɒdʒ/ *verb* **1** [I,T] to move quickly in order to avoid sb/sth: *I managed to dodge the headmaster and slipped into the classroom.* يتجنّب ، يروغ

2 [T] to avoid doing or thinking about sth such as a duty, etc: *Don't try to dodge your responsibilities!* يتملّص من ؛ يتفادى

▶ **dodge** *noun* [C] **1** [usually sing.] a quick movement to avoid sb/sth: *He made a sudden dodge to the right.* روغة ، حركة سريعة للتفادي

2 (*informal*) a clever way of avoiding sth: *The man had been involved in a massive tax dodge.* تهرّب، خدعة

dodgy /ˈdɒdʒi/ *adj* (**dodgier**; **dodgiest**) (*especially Brit informal*) risky; not reliable or honest: *a dodgy business deal* غير مأمون ؛ مشبوه

doe /dəʊ/ *noun* [C] a female deer or rabbit أنثى الغزال أو الأرنب

does → DO[1,2]

🔑 **dog¹** /dɒg; *US* dɔːg/ *noun* [C] **1** an animal that many people keep as a pet, or for working on farms, hunting, etc. ℹ A dog can **bark**, **growl**, **whine** and **wag** its tail. كلب

2 a male dog or fox: *If you're getting a puppy, bitches are gentler than dogs.* ذكر الكلب أو الثعلب

dog² /dɒg; *US* dɔːg/ *verb* [T] (dogging; dogged) to follow closely: *A shadowy figure was dogging their every move.* ○ (*figurative*) *Bad luck and illness has dogged her career from the start.* يلازم ، يقتفي الأثر

'dog collar *noun* [C] (*informal*) a white collar that is worn by priests in the Christian church ياقة القسّيس

'dog-eared *adj* (used about a book or piece of paper) in bad condition and having the corners of the pages turned down because it has been used a lot (زوايا الصفحات) مبرومة أو متفتلة

dogged /'dɒgɪd; *US* 'dɔːgɪd/ *adj* refusing to give up even when sth is difficult: *I was impressed by his dogged determination to succeed.* عنيد ، مصرّ
▸ **doggedly** *adv*: *She doggedly refused all offers of help.* بعناد ، بإصرار

dogma /'dɒgmə; *US* 'dɔːgmə/ *noun* [C,U] a belief or set of beliefs that people are expected to accept as true without questioning عقيدة (لا تناقش)

dogmatic /dɒg'mætɪk; *US* dɔːg'mætɪk/ *adj* insisting that sth is true or right; not prepared to consider other opinions متعنّت ، مصّر على صحة آرائه
▸ **dogmatically** /-kli/ *adv* بتعنُّت ؛ بإصرار على صحة آرائه

dogsbody /'dɒgzbɒdi; *US* 'dɔːg-/ *noun* [C] (*pl.* **dogsbodies**) (*Brit informal*) a person who is made to do the boring or unpleasant jobs that no one else wants to do and who is treated as being less important than other people شخص يوكَل بأحقر الأعمال

doldrums /'dɒldrəmz/ *noun* [plural]
IDM **in the doldrums** (*informal*) **1** not active or busy: *Business has been in the doldrums but should improve later in the year.* في ركود أو كساد
2 sad or depressed مكتئب ، حزين

dole¹ /dəʊl/ *verb* (*informal*)
PHR V **dole sth out** to give sth, especially food, money, etc. to a number of people, in small amounts يوزّع بتقتير

dole² /dəʊl/ *noun* [sing.] **the dole** (*Brit informal*) money that the State gives every week to people who are unemployed: *He's been on the dole* (= receiving this money) *for six months.* إعانة حكوميّة للعاطلين تُدفع أسبوعياً

doleful /'dəʊlfl/ *adj* sad or depressed: *She looked at him with doleful eyes.* حزين ، مكتئب
▸ **dolefully** /-fəli/ *adv* بحزن ، بأسى

doll /dɒl; *US* dɔːl/ *noun* [C] a child's toy that looks like a small person or a baby دمية

⚿dollar /'dɒlə(r)/ *noun* **1** [C] (*symbol* $) a unit of money in the US, Canada, Australia, etc. ❶ There are 100 **cents** in a dollar. دولار
2 [C] a note or coin that is worth one dollar ورقة أو قطعة نقديّة بقيمة دولار
3 **the dollar** [sing.] the value of the US dollar on international money markets سعر الدولار

dollop /'dɒləp/ *noun* [C] (*informal*) a lump of sth soft, especially food غَرفة كبيرة

dolphin /'dɒlfɪn/ *noun* [C] an intelligent animal that lives in the sea and looks like a large fish. Dolphins usually swim in large groups. دلفين

domain /də'meɪn/ *noun* [C] **1** an area of knowledge or activity: *I'm afraid I don't know – that's really outside my domain.* ○ *This issue is now in the public domain* (= the public knows about it). ميدان ، مجال (التخصّص)
2 (*computing*) a set of websites on the Internet which end with the same group of letters, for example.com or.org نِطاق

dome /dəʊm/ *noun* [C] a round roof on a building: *the dome of St Paul's in London* قبّة

⚿domestic /də'mestɪk/ *adj* **1** connected with the home or family: *domestic responsibilities* ○ *domestic water, gas, etc. supplies* عائليّ ؛ منزليّ
2 (used about a person) enjoying doing things in the home, such as cooking and housework محبّ للشؤون المنزليّة
3 not international; of or inside a particular country: *domestic flights* (= within one country) داخليّ
4 (used about animals) kept as pets or on farms; not wild: *domestic animals such as cats, dogs and horses* أهليّ ، أليف

domesticated /də'mestɪkeɪtɪd/ *adj* **1** (used about animals) used to living near people and being controlled by them أليف، داجن
2 (used about people) able to do or good at housework, cooking, etc: *Men are expected to be much more domesticated nowadays.* ماهر في الشؤون المنزليّة

dominant /'dɒmɪnənt/ *adj* **1** the strongest or most important: *His mother was the dominant influence in his life.* مسيطر ؛ سائد
2 that you notice very easily: *The castle stands in a dominant position above the town.* بارز ؛ مشرف على
▸ **dominance** /'dɒmɪnəns/ *noun* [U] control or power: *Japan's dominance of the car industry* سيطرة ، هَيْمَنة

⚿dominate /'dɒmɪneɪt/ *verb* **1** [I,T] to have strong control or influence; to be the most important person or thing in sth: *The Italian team dominated throughout the second half of the game.* ○ *She always tends to dominate the conversation at dinner parties.* يسيطر (على) ، يسود
2 [T] (used about a building or place) to look down on or over: *The cathedral dominates the area for miles around.* يشرف على
▸ **domination** /ˌdɒmɪ'neɪʃn/ *noun* [U] strong control, power or influence سيطرة ، تحكّم في

domineering /ˌdɒmɪ'nɪərɪŋ/ *adj* having a very strong character and wanting to control other people محبّ للسيطرة ؛ مستبدّ

dominion /də'mɪniən/ *noun* **1** [U] (*formal*) the power to rule and control: *to have dominion over an area* سلطة ، سيادة ، حكم
2 [C] (*formal*) an area controlled by one government or ruler: *the dominions of the Roman empire* منطقة سيادة

domino /ˈdɒmɪnəʊ/ *noun* [C] (*pl.* **dominoes**) one of a set of small flat pieces of wood or plastic that are used for playing a game (dominoes). Each domino has a different number of spots on one side of it. قطعة دومينو

donate /dəʊˈneɪt; *US* ˈdəʊneɪt/ *verb* [T] to give money or goods to an organization, especially one for people or animals who need help: *She donated a large sum of money to Cancer Research.* يتبرّع؛ يَهب

▸ **donation** /dəʊˈneɪʃn/ *noun* [C] a gift of money or goods to an organization, especially one for people or animals who need help: *Would you like to make a small donation to the Red Cross?* تبرّع؛ هِبة

done[1] *pp* of DO[2]

done[2] /dʌn/ *adj* (not before a noun) **1** finished: *I've got to go out as soon as this job is done.* منتهٍ، منجَز

2 (used about food) cooked enough: *The meat's ready but the vegetables still aren't done.* (طعام) ناضج، مطبوخ جيداً

IDM **over and done with** completely finished; in the past منتهٍ، (يصبح) في عداد الماضي

▸ **done** *interj* (used for saying that you accept an offer): *'I'll give you twenty pounds for it.' 'Done!'* موافق!

dongle /ˈdɒŋgl/ *noun* [C] **1** a cable that is used to attach a computer to a telephone system or to another computer تَوصيلة شبكة

2 a device or code that is needed in order to use protected software "دونغل"، قفل رقمي

donkey /ˈdɒŋki/ *noun* [C] (*pl.* **donkeys**) (*also* **ass**) an animal like a small horse, with long ears حمار

IDM **donkey's years** (*Brit informal*) a very long time: *They've been going out together for donkey's years.* مدّة طويلة

donor /ˈdəʊnə(r)/ *noun* [C] **1** a person who gives blood or a part of his/her own body for medical use: *a blood donor* ○ *a kidney donor* المتبرّع للطبّ بأجزاء من جسمه

2 a person who gives money or goods to an organization that needs it, especially an organization for helping other people المتبرع

don't → DO[1,2]

donut = DOUGHNUT

doodle /ˈduːdl/ *verb* [I] to draw lines, patterns, etc. without concentrating, especially when you are bored or thinking about sth else يُشَخْبِط أو يرسم وهو شارد الذهن

▸ **doodle** *noun* [C] شخبطة أو رسم عابث

doom /duːm/ *noun* [U] death or a terrible event in the future which you cannot avoid: *In the last scene of the film the villain plunges to his doom in the river.* ○ *a sense of doom* (= that something bad is going to happen) هلاك، حتف؛ قدَر مشؤوم

▸ **doomed** *adj* certain to fail or to suffer sth unpleasant: *The plan was doomed from the start.* ○ *a doomed love affair* مآله الفشل؛ مشؤوم

door /dɔː(r)/ *noun* [C] **1** a piece of wood, glass, etc. that you open and close to get in or out of a room, building, car, etc: *to open/shut/close the door* ○ *Don't forget to lock the door when you leave the house.* ○ *Have you bolted the door?* ○ *Please don't slam the door.* ○ *I could hear someone knocking on the door.* ○ *the front/back door* ○ *the kitchen door* ○ *the fridge door* باب

2 the entrance to a building, room, car, etc: *I peeped through the door and saw her sitting there.* باب، مدخل

IDM **(from) door to door** (from) house to house: *The journey takes about five hours, door to door.* ○ *a door-to-door salesman* (= a person who visits people in their homes to try and sell them things) من الباب إلى الباب؛ (بائع) يزور البيوت

next door (to sb/sth) in the next house, room, etc: *Do you know the people who live next door?* ○ *You'll find the bathroom next door to your bedroom.* في البيت أو في الغرفة المجاورة

out of doors outside: *Shall we eat out of doors today?* ⓘ The opposite is **indoors**. في الهواء الطَّلق

doorbell /ˈdɔːbel/ *noun* [C] a bell on the outside of a house which you ring when you want to go in جرس الباب

doormat /ˈdɔːmæt/ *noun* [C] a mat beside a door which you can wipe your shoes on to clean them before going inside ممسحة الأرجل (عند المدخل)

doorstep /ˈdɔːstep/ *noun* [C] a step in front of a door, usually outside a building عتبة باب البيت

IDM **on your doorstep** very near to you: *The sea was right on our doorstep.* قريب جداً، على بُعْد خطوتَين

doorway /ˈdɔːweɪ/ *noun* [C] an entrance into a building, room, etc: *She was standing in the doorway.* مدخل

dope /dəʊp/ *noun* (*informal*) **1** [U] a drug that is not legal, especially cannabis مخدِّر، حشيش

2 [C] a stupid person: *What a dope!* غبيّ، مغفَّل

▸ **dope** *verb* [T] to give a drug secretly to a person or animal, especially to make them sleep يعطي مخدِّراً

dopey (*also* **dopy**) /ˈdəʊpi/ *adj* (**dopier**; **dopiest**) **1** sleepy and not able to think clearly, especially because of drugs, alcohol or lack of sleep نعسان (وكأنه مخدّر)، مخبول

2 (*informal*) stupid; not very intelligent غبيّ، بليد

dormant /ˈdɔːmənt/ *adj* not active for some time: *a dormant volcano* نائم؛ كامن، ساكن

dormitory /ˈdɔːmətri; *US* -tɔːri/ *noun* [C] (*pl.* **dormitories**) **1** a large bedroom with a number of beds in it, especially in a school, etc. مهجع

2 (*US*) a building at a college or university where students live مسكن الطَّلَبة

dosage /ˈdəʊsɪdʒ/ *noun* [C, usually sing.] the amount of a medicine you should take over a period of time: *The recommended dosage is one tablet every four hours.* مقدار الجرعات

dose /dəʊs/ *noun* [C] **1** an amount of medicine that you take at one time: *You should take a large* *dose of this cough medicine before going to bed.* جرعة

2 an amount of sth, especially sth unpleasant: *a dose of the flu* ○ *I can only stand my mother-in-law in small doses.* مقدار (من شيء غير مستحب)

▸ **dose** *verb* [T] to give sb/yourself a medicine or drug يعطي أو يجرّع دواء

doss /dɒs/ *verb*

PHRV **doss down** (*Brit slang*) to lie down to sleep, without a proper bed: *Do you mind if I doss down on your floor tonight?* ينام (أينما كان)

dot /dɒt/ *noun* [C] **1** a small, round mark: *a white dress with black dots* ○ *The letters i and j have dots above them.* نقطة

2 something that looks like a dot: *He watched until the plane was just a dot in the sky.* نقطة

IDM **on the dot** (*informal*) at exactly the right time or at exactly the time mentioned: *Lessons start at 9 o'clock on the dot.* بالضبط ، تماماً

▸ **dot** *verb* [T] (dotting; dotted) (usually passive) to mark with a dot ينقّط ، يضع نقاطاً على

IDM **be dotted about** to be scattered over an area: *There are little bars and restaurants dotted about all over the centre of town.* يتبعثر أو ينتشر في كلّ مكان

be dotted with to have many things or people in or on it: *a hillside dotted with sheep and cows* منتشِر عليه

dot-com (*also* **dotcom**) /ˌdɒt ˈkɒm/ *adj, noun* [C] a company that sells goods and services on the Internet, especially one whose address ends '.com' شركة على الانترنت

dote /dəʊt/ *verb* [I] **dote on sb/sth** to have or show too much love for sb/sth and think they are perfect: *He's always doted on his eldest son.* يشغَف أو يتولّع بِ ، يدلّل

▸ **doting** *adj* very or too loving: *doting parents* مولَع ، مفرط في الحبّ

dotted 'line *noun* [C] a line of dots which show where sth is to be written on a form, etc. خطّ منقّط (يكتب أو يوقّع عليه)

double¹ /ˈdʌbl/ *adj* **1** twice as much or as many (as usual): *a double helping of ice cream* مضاعَف

2 having two equal or similar parts: *Don't park on double yellow lines.* ○ *double doors* ○ *Does 'necessary' have a double 's'?* ○ *My phone number is two four double 0 four* (= 24004). مزدوج : ثنائي

3 made for or used by two people or things: *a double garage* مزدوج

double² /ˈdʌbl/ *det* twice as much or as many (as usual, as sb/sth, etc.): *His income is double hers.* ○ *We'll need double the amount of food.* ضعْف

double³ /ˈdʌbl/ *adv* in twos or two parts: *When I saw her with her twin sister I thought I was seeing double.* بشكل مزدوج أو ثنائيّ

double⁴ /ˈdʌbl/ *noun* **1** [U] twice the (usual) number or amount: *When you work overtime, you get paid double.* مقدار مضاعف

2 [C] a person who looks very much like another: *I thought it was you I saw in the supermarket You must have a double.* شبيه

3 doubles [plural] (in some sports, e.g. tennis) with two pairs playing: *the Men's Doubles final* ➲ Look at **singles** (4). مباراة ثنائيّة أو زوجيّة

double⁵ /ˈdʌbl/ *verb* [I,T] **1** to become or to make sth twice as much or as many: *The price of houses has almost doubled.* ○ *Think of a number and double it.* يتضاعف : يضاعف

2 double (up) as sth to have a second use or function: *The small room doubles as a study.* يُستعمل لغرض آخر

IDM **double (sb) up** (to cause sb) to bend the body: *to be doubled up in pain, with laughter, etc.* يثني : ينطوي ، يتلوّى

ˌdouble 'bass (*also* **bass**) *noun* [C] the largest instrument of the violin family, that you play standing up أكبر أنواع آلة الكمان

ˌdouble 'bed *noun* [C] a bed made for two people ➲ Look at **single** and **twin**. سرير مزدوج

ˌdouble-'breasted *adj* (used about a coat or jacket) having two rows of buttons down the front (معطف) بصفين من الأزرار

ˌdouble-'check *verb* [I,T] to check sth again, or with great care يدقّق بعناية أو مرة ثانية

ˌdouble-'click *verb* [T] **double-click (on sth)** (*computing*) to choose a particular function or item on a computer screen, etc. by pressing one of the buttons on a mouse twice quickly: *To run an application, just double-click on the icon.* النقر مرتين

ˌdouble-'cross *verb* [T] to cheat sb who believes that he/she can trust you يخون

ˌdouble-'decker *noun* [C] a bus with two floors باص ذو طابقين

ˌdouble 'Dutch *noun* [U] talk or writing that you cannot understand at all كلام غير مفهوم

ˌdouble 'figures *noun* [U] a number that is more than 10: *Inflation is now in double figures.* رقم ذو خانتين (10-99)

ˌdouble-'glaze *verb* [T] to put two layers of glass in a window, so that the building is kept warm or quiet يركّب زجاجاً مزدوجاً للنوافذ

ˌdouble 'glazing *noun* [U] تركيب زجاج مزدوج للنوافذ

doubly /ˈdʌbli/ *adv* **1** in two ways: *He was doubly blessed with both good looks and talent.* بصورة مضاعفة

2 more than usually: *I made doubly sure that the door was locked.* اكثر من المعتاد

doubt¹ /daʊt/ *noun* [C,U] (a feeling of) uncertainty: *If you have any doubts, feel free to ring me and discuss them.* ○ *You'll definitely pass. There's no doubt about it.* ○ *There was some doubt as to whether she was the right person for the job.* شكّ

IDM **cast doubt on sth** → CAST²

give sb the benefit of the doubt → BENEFIT

in doubt not sure or definite غير متأكّد : غير مؤكّد

no doubt (used when you expect sth to happen but you are not sure that it will) probably: *No doubt she'll write when she has time.* ربّما ، قدْ...

without (a) doubt definitely: *It was, without doubt, the coldest winter for many years.* دون شكّ

doubt² /daʊt/ *verb* [T] to think sth unlikely or to feel uncertain (about sth): *She never doubted* (= she was always sure) *that he was telling the truth.* ○ *I doubt whether/if I'll have time to go to the shops today* (= I don't think I'll be able to go). ○ *He had never doubted her support.* يشكّ في

doubtful /'daʊtfl/ *adj* **1** unlikely or uncertain: *It's doubtful whether/if we'll finish in time for Christmas.* ○ *It was doubtful that he was still alive.* مشكوك فيه

2 doubtful (about sth/about doing sth) (used about a person) not sure: *He still felt doubtful about his decision.* شاكّ في : غير متأكد ، متردّد

▶ **doubtfully** /-fəli/ *adv*: *'I suppose it'll be all right,' she said doubtfully.* بشكّ ، بعدم ثقة

doubtless /'daʊtləs/ *adv* almost certainly: *Doubtless she'll have a good excuse for being late!* لا شكّ

dough /dəʊ/ *noun* [U] **1** a mixture of flour, water and sometimes fat and sugar. It is used for baking into bread, etc. عجين

2 (*informal*) money نقود ، فلوس

doughnut (*especially US* **donut**) /'dəʊnʌt/ *noun* [C] a small cake in the shape of a ball or a ring, made from sweet dough cooked in fat كعكة مستديرة مقليّة

dour /daʊə(r); *Brit also* dʊə(r)/ *adj* (used about a person's manner or expression) cold and unfriendly عبوس ، صارم

douse (*also* **dowse**) /daʊs/ *verb* [T] **1 douse sth (with sth)** to stop a fire, etc. burning: *The firemen managed to douse the blaze.* يخمد

2 douse sb/sth (in/with sth) to cover sb/sth with liquid: *to douse yourself in perfume* (= wear too much of it) يرشّ ، يغرّقه بِ

dove¹ /dʌv/ *noun* [C] a type of bird, similar to a pigeon, often used as a sign of peace حمامة ، يمامة

dove² /dəʊv/ (*US*) *pt of* DIVE¹

dowdy /'daʊdi/ *adj* (**dowdier**; **dowdiest**) (used about a person or the clothes he/she wears) dull and unfashionable زريّ الهيئة

down¹ /daʊn/ *adv* **1** to or at a lower level or place; not up: *We sat and watched the sun go down.* ○ *Can you get that book down from the top shelf?* ○ *'Where's Mary?' 'She's down in the basement.'* (إلى) تحت ، نحو الأسفل

2 from a standing or vertical position to a sitting or horizontal one: *I think I'll sit/lie down.* (إلى وضع الجلوس أو الاستلقاء)

3 to or in the south: *We went down to Devon for our holiday.* جنوباً ، في الجنوب

4 (used for showing that the level, amount, strength, etc. of sth is less or lower): *Do you mind if I turn the heating down a bit?* بقدر أقلّ ، إلى حدّ أدنى

5 (written) on paper: *Put these dates down in your diary.* بشكل مكتوب

6 down to sb/sth even including: *Everybody was invited from the Director down to the tea ladies.* بما فيه ، حتّى

IDM **be down to sb** to be sb's responsibility: *When my father died it was down to me to look after the family's affairs.* تقع عليه المسؤوليّة

be down to sth to have only the amount mentioned left: *I can't lend you any money – I'm down to my last £5.* يصل أو ينزل إلى

be/go down with sth to be or become ill with sth: *Simon's gone down with flu.* يمرض ، يصاب بِ

down and out having no money, job or home متشرّد

down under (*informal*) (in) Australia: *He comes from down under.* (من) استراليا

down² /daʊn/ *prep* **1** along: *'Where's the nearest garage?' 'Go down this road and take the first turning on the right.'* على طول

2 from the top towards the bottom of sth: *Her hair hung down her back.* ○ *The snow began to slide down the mountain.* إلى أسفل

3 at or to a lower or further part of sth: *We sailed down the river towards the sea.* (ينزل) إلى ؛ مع مجرى (النهر)

down³ /daʊn/ *verb* [T] (*informal*) to finish a drink quickly: *She downed her drink in one* (= she drank the whole glass without stopping). يزدرد ؛ يشرب بسرعة

down⁴ /daʊn/ *noun*

IDM **ups and downs** → UP

down⁵ /daʊn/ *adj* **1** sad: *You're looking a bit down today.* كئيب

2 lower than before: *Unemployment figures are down for the third month in succession.* منخفض ، أقلّ من السابق

3 (used about computers) not working (الكمبيوتر) معطّل

down⁶ /daʊn/ *noun* [U] very soft feathers: *a duvet filled with down* زَغَب ، وَبَر

'**down-and-out** *noun* [C] a person who has not got money, a job or a home إنسان فقير متشرّد

downcast /'daʊnkɑːst; *US* 'daʊnkæst/ *adj* **1** (used about a person) sad and without hope قانط ، كسير الخاطر

2 (used about eyes) looking down (نظَر) مخفوض

downfall /'daʊnfɔːl/ *noun* [sing.] **1** a loss of power or success: *The government's downfall seemed inevitable.* سقوط ، انهيار

2 a thing that causes a loss of power or success سبب الانهيار أو الخراب

downgrade /'daʊngreɪd/ *verb* [T] to reduce sb/sth to a lower level or position of importance يُخفّض مرتبته أو قيمته

downhearted /ˌdaʊn'hɑːtɪd/ *adj* sad or depressed مكتئب ، قانط

downhill /ˌdaʊn'hɪl/ *adj, adv* (going) down a slope; towards the bottom of a hill: *It's an easy*

a b c d e f g h i j k l m n o p q r s t u v w x y z

walk. The road runs downhill most of the way. ○ *Do you go downhill or cross-country skiing?*
نحو الأسفل ، بانحدار ؛ إلى اسفل التلّ

IDM **go downhill** to get worse: *Their relationship has been going downhill for some time now.* يتدهور

download /ˌdaʊnˈləʊd/ *verb* [T] to copy a computer file, etc. from a large computer system to a smaller one يُنزِل

downmarket /ˌdaʊnˈmɑːkɪt/ *adj* cheap and of not very high quality رخيص ومبتذل ، غير متقن

downpour /ˈdaʊnpɔː(r)/ *noun* [C, usually sing.] a heavy, sudden fall of rain وابل مفاجئ من المطر

downright /ˈdaʊnraɪt/ *adj* (only *before* a noun) (used about sth bad or unpleasant) complete: *The holiday was a downright disaster.* تامّ ؛ صِرف

▸ **downright** *adv* completely or thoroughly: *That road is downright dangerous!* تماماً ؛ كليّاً

downs /daʊnz/ *noun* [plural] an area of low, round hills, especially in the south of England: *the Sussex Downs* منطقة تلال (وخاصّة في جنوب انكلترا)

downside /ˈdaʊnsaɪd/ *noun* [usually sing.] a negative aspect; a disadvantage or set of disadvantages: *All good ideas have a downside.*
جانب سلبي، نقص، عيب

Down's syndrome /ˈdaʊnz sɪndrəʊm/ *noun* [U] a condition that a person is born with. People with this condition have a flat, wide face and lower than average intelligence.
المغوليّة: عيب خِلْقي

⚷ **downstairs** /ˌdaʊnˈsteəz/ *adv, adj* **1** down the stairs: *He fell downstairs and broke his arm.*
إلى اسفل الدَرَج

2 on or to the ground floor or a lower floor: *Dad's downstairs, in the kitchen.* ○ *a downstairs toilet* ❶ The opposite is **upstairs**.
في أو إلى الطابق السفلي ، تحت

downstream /ˌdaʊnˈstriːm/ *adv* in the direction in which a river flows: *We were rowing downstream, towards the sea.* ❶ The opposite is **upstream**. باتّجاه مجرى النهر

ˌ**down-to-ˈearth** *adj* sensible and practical; not complicated or too clever
واقعيّ ، عمليّ ، خالٍ من التعقيد

downtown /ˈdaʊntaʊn/ *adv, adj* (*especially US*) in or towards the centre of a city, especially its main business area: *to go/work downtown* ○ *a downtown store* بالقسم التجاري بالمدينة

▸ **downtown** *noun*: *a hotel in the heart of downtown* القِسم التجاري بالمدينة

downturn /ˈdaʊntɜːn/ *noun* [C] **downturn (in sth)** a reduction in economic or business activity: *hit by a downturn in consumer spending*
هبوط تجاري، ركود

⚷ **downward** /ˈdaʊnwəd/ *adj* (only *before* a noun) towards the ground or a lower level: *a downward movement* ○ *There is still a downward trend in house prices.* نازل ، متّجه نحو الأسفل

▸ **downwards** (*also* **downward**) *adv* towards the ground or a lower level: *She laid the picture face downwards on the table.* ❶ The opposite is **upward(s)**. نحو الأسفل ، مقلوباً

dowry /ˈdaʊri/ *noun* [C] (*pl.* **dowries**) an amount of money or property which a woman's family gives to the man she is marrying or a man's family give to the woman he is marrying
مَهْر ، صَداق ؛ "دوطة"

dowse = DOUSE

doze /dəʊz/ *verb* [I] to sleep lightly and/or for a short time: *He was dozing in front of the television.* ينام نومة قصيرة

PHR V **doze off** to go to sleep, especially during the day: *I'm sorry – I must have dozed off for a minute.* يغفو ، يغلبه النعاس

▸ **doze** *noun* [C, usually sing.] a light, short sleep غفوة ، نومة قصيرة

⚷ **dozen** /ˈdʌzn/ *noun* [C] (*pl.* **dozens** or **dozen**) (*abbr* **doz.**) twelve or a group of twelve: *A dozen eggs, please.* ○ *half a dozen* (= six) ○ *two dozen sheep* دَزّينة ، اثنا عشر

IDM **dozens** (*informal*) very many: *I've tried phoning her dozens of times.* عشرات ، مرّات كثيرة

dozy /ˈdəʊzi/ *adj* (**dozier**; **doziest**) **1** sleepy: *The heat had made her rather dozy.* نعسان ، وسنان

2 (*Brit informal*) stupid: *You dozy thing – look what you've done!* غبيّ ، مغفّل

Dr (*also* **Dr.**) *abbrev* = DOCTOR

drab /dræb/ *adj* (**drabber**; **drabbest**) dull and not interesting or attractive: *a drab grey office building* أغبر اللون ، باهت ؛ كئيب

⚷ **draft¹** /drɑːft; *US* dræft/ *noun* **1** [C] a piece of writing, etc. which will probably be changed and improved; not the final copy: *the first draft of a speech* مُسوّدة

2 a written order to a bank to pay money to sb: *Payment must be made by bank draft.*
حوالة مصرفية

3 (*US*) = DRAUGHT

⚷ **draft²** /drɑːft; *US* dræft/ *verb* [T] **1** to make a first or early copy of a piece of writing: *I'll draft a letter and show it to you before I type it.* يعِدّ مسوّدة

2 (usually passive) (*US*) to order sb to join the armed forces: *He was drafted into the army.*
يستدعي للخدمة العسكريّة

drafty (*US*) = DRAUGHTY

⚷ **drag¹** /dræg/ *noun* **1** [sing.] (*informal*) a person or thing that is boring or annoying: *'The car's broken down.' 'Oh no! What a drag!'*
شخص أو شيء مُملّ أو مزعج

2 [U] (*informal*) the wearing of women's clothes by a man, especially as part of a show, etc.
(رجل) في ملابس امرأة

3 [C] (*informal*) an act of breathing in cigarette smoke: *He took a long drag on his cigarette.*
سحبة (من سيجارة)

⚷ **drag²** /dræg/ *verb* (dra**gg**ing; dra**gg**ed) **1** [T] to pull sb/sth along with difficulty: *The box was so heavy we had to drag it along the floor.*
يجرّ، يسحب بجهد

2 [T] to force or to make sb come or go somewhere: *She dragged the child up the steps by her arm.* ○ *Can I drag you away from the television for a moment?* يجرّ ، يرغِم ؛ يبعِد

3 [I] **drag (on)** to be boring or to seem to last a long time: *The speeches dragged on for hours.* (خطاب) يطول على نحو مملّ

PHR V **drag sth out** to make sth last longer than necessary: *Let's not drag this decision out – shall we go or not?* يمطّ أو يطيل اكثر من اللازم

drag sth out (of sb) to force or persuade sb to give you information that you want يسحب أو يستخرج منه المعلومات

dragon /'drægən/ *noun* [C] (in stories, etc.) an imaginary animal with wings, which can breathe out fire تِنّين

dragonfly /'drægənflaɪ/ *noun* [C] (*pl.* **dragonflies**) an insect with a long thin body and two pairs of transparent wings يعسوب أو سرمان

drain[1] /dreɪn/ *noun* [C] a pipe or hole that dirty water, etc. goes down to be carried away: *The drain outside the kitchen is blocked.* أنبوب التصريف ؛ بالوعة

IDM **a drain on sb/sth** something that uses up time, money, strength, etc: *The cost of travelling is a great drain on our budget.* استنزاف ، تبديد

(go) down the drain (*informal*) (to be) wasted: *All that hard work has gone down the drain.* يذهب هباءً

drain[2] /dreɪn/ *verb* **1** [I,T] to become dry as liquid flows away; to make sth dry in this way: *The whole area will have to be drained before it can be used for farming.* يصرف الماء ، يجفّف

2 [I,T] to flow away; to make a liquid flow: *The sink's blocked – the water won't drain away at all.* ○ *The plumber had to drain the water from the heating system.* يجري ؛ يصرف ، يفرِغ (الماء)

3 [T] to drink all the liquid (in a glass, etc.): *He drained his glass in one gulp.* يشرب (حتى الثمالة)

4 [I] (used about a feeling) to become weaker and weaker until it disappears: *He felt all his anger begin to drain away.* يتلاشى

5 [T] **drain sb/sth (of sth)** to make sb/sth weaker, poorer, etc. by slowly using all the strength, money, etc. available يستنزف (قوته أو ماله)

drainage /'dreɪnɪdʒ/ *noun* [U] a system used for draining water, etc. away from a place تصريف ؛ نظام التصريف

'draining board (*US* **'drainboard**) *noun* [C] the place beside a kitchen sink where you put plates, cups, knives, etc. to dry (في حوض المطبخ) سطح مائل لتجفيف الصحون

drainpipe /'dreɪnpaɪp/ *noun* [C] a pipe which goes down the side of a building, especially one that carries water from the roof into a drain ميزاب ؛ مَصْرِف

drama /'drɑːmə/ *noun* **1** [C] a play for the theatre, radio or television: *a contemporary drama* مسرحيّة

2 [U] plays as a form of writing; the performance of plays: *He wrote some drama, as well as poetry.* ○ *a drama student* مسرحيّات ، الفنّ المسرحي

3 [C] an exciting event حَدَث مثير

4 [U] excitement: *Why is there so little drama in my life?* ○ *...and to add to all the drama, the lights went out!* إثارة

dramatic /drə'mætɪk/ *adj* **1** noticeable or sudden: *a dramatic change* مفاجئ ، مذهل

2 exciting or impressive: *The opening scene of the film was extremely dramatic.* مثير ، رائع

3 (used about a person, a person's behaviour, etc.) showing feelings, etc. in a very obvious way because you want other people to notice you or pay attention to you: *Calm down. There's no need to be so dramatic about everything!* دراميّ ، متصنّع (لجذب الانتباه)

4 connected with plays or the theatre: *Shakespeare's dramatic works* مسرحي

▸ **dramatically** /-kli/ *adv* in a dramatic way: *'I can't go on,' she said dramatically.* بشكل مسرحيّ ، على نحو درامي

dramatist /'dræmətɪst/ *noun* [C] a person who writes plays كاتب مسرحيّ

dramatize (*also* **dramatise**) /'dræmətaɪz/ *verb* **1** [T] to make a book, an event, etc. into a play: *The novel has been dramatized for television.* يضعه في قالب مسرحي

2 [I,T] to make sth seem more exciting or important than it really is: *The newspaper was accused of dramatizing the situation.* يصوّر بشكل دراميّ

▸ **dramatization** (*also* **dramatisation**) /ˌdræmətaɪ'zeɪʃn/ *noun* [C,U] نقْل إلى شكل مسرحيّ

drank *pt of* DRINK

drape /dreɪp/ *verb* [T] **1** **drape sth round/over sth** to put a piece of cloth, clothing, etc. loosely on sth: *He quickly draped a towel round his waist.* يلتحف ، يلتفّ بِ

2 **drape sb/sth (in/with sth)** (usually passive) to cover sb/sth (with cloth, etc.): *The furniture was draped in dust sheets.* يجلّل ، يغطّي بالقماش

▸ **drape** *noun* [C] (*US*) = CURTAIN

drastic /'dræstɪk/ *adj* **1** strong, effective and usually quick: *The situation requires drastic action.* صارم ، فعّال

2 very noticeable or serious: *There has been a drastic rise in crime in the area.* بالغ ، ملحوظ

▸ **drastically** /-kli/ *adv*: *House prices have fallen drastically over the last two years.* بصورة هائلة

draught /drɑːft/ (*US* **draft** /dræft/) *noun* **1** [C] a current of air that comes into a room: *Can you shut the door? There's a draught in here.* جريان، مجرى أو تيّار هوائيّ

2 **draughts** (*Brit*) (*US* **checkers**) [U] a game for two players that you play on a black and white board using round black and white pieces لعبة الداما

▸ **draught** *adj* (used about beer, etc.) served from barrels, not bottles: *draught beer* (شراب) مسحوب من برميل

draughtsman /ˈdrɑːftsmən/ (*US* **draftsman** /ˈdræfts-/) *noun* [C] (*pl.* **draughtsmen**; *US* **draftsmen** /-mən/) a person whose job is to make technical drawings رسّام هندسي

draughty /ˈdrɑːfti/ (*US* **drafty** /ˈdræfti/) *adj* (**draughtier**; **draughtiest**) having currents of air blowing through: *a large, draughty old house* (بيت قديم) تدخله تيارات الهواء

draw¹ /drɔː/ *noun* [C] **1** a result of a game or competition in which both players or teams get the same score so that neither of them wins: *The match ended in a draw.* تعادل

2 an act of deciding sth by chance by pulling out names or numbers from a bag, etc. سحب ورق القرعة أو اليانصيب

draw² /drɔː/ *verb* (*pt* **drew** /druː/; *pp* **drawn** /drɔːn/) **1** [I,T] to make a picture or diagram of sth with a pencil, pen, etc: *Shall I draw you a map of how to get there?* يرسم

2 [I] to move in the direction mentioned: *At last the train drew into/out of the station.* يسير باتّجاه... يدخل أو يخرج

3 [T] **draw sth out of/from sth** to pull sth smoothly out of its present position: *She drew the letter out of her pocket and handed it to me.* يُخرِج

4 [T] to pull sb/sth gently into a new position: *He drew me by the hand into the room.* ○ *Why don't you draw your chairs up to the fire?* يسحب أو يجرّ برفق

5 [T] (used about horses, etc.) to pull sth along: *The Queen's carriage was drawn by six horses.* يجر

6 [T] to open or close curtains, etc: *It was getting dark so I switched on the lights and drew the curtains.* يفتح أو يغلق الستائر وغيرها

7 [T] to pull a gun, sword or knife out of its holder, quickly and in order to attack sb: *The cowboy drew his gun.* يشهَر ، يسحب ، يستلّ

8 [T] **draw sth from sb/sth** to gain sth from sb/sth: *This information has been drawn from a number of sources.* يحصل على ، يستخلص : يكسب

9 [T] **draw sth (from sth)** to learn sth from study, experience, etc: *Can we draw any conclusions from this survey?* يستنتج

10 [T] **draw sth (from sb)** to produce a reaction or response to the thing mentioned: *The advertisement has drawn interest from people all over the country.* يثير الاهتمام

11 [T] **draw sb (to sb/sth)** to attract or interest sb: *She had always been drawn to older men.* ○ *The musicians drew quite a large crowd.* يجذب

12 [I,T] to finish a game, competition, etc. with equal scores so that neither person or team wins: *The two teams drew.* ○ *The match was drawn.* يتعادل ، ينتهي بالتعادل

IDM **bring sth/come/draw to an end** → END¹

draw sb's attention to sth to make sb aware of sth: *Can I draw your attention to point seven on the agenda?* يسترعي انتباهه ، ينبه إلى

draw a blank to get no result or response: *Detectives investigating the case have drawn a blank so far.* تذهب مساعيه سُدى

draw a comparison/a parallel to show how two things compare or are similar: *The programme drew an interesting comparison between education in Japan and Britain.* يقارن

draw a distinction between sth and sth to show how two things are different: *It's important to draw a distinction between the methods used now and those used previously.* يفرّق ، يبيّن أوجه الخلاف

draw the line at sth to say 'no' to sth even though you are prepared to be helpful in other ways: *I do most of the cooking but I draw the line at washing up as well!* يرفض، يتوقف عند حدّ معيّن

draw lots to decide sth by chance: *They drew lots to see who should stay behind.* يجري قرعة

PHR V **draw in 1** (used about the hours of daylight) to get shorter before the winter (ساعات النهار) تأخذ بالقِصر

2 (used about cars, buses, etc.) to go to the side of the road and stop يتوقف عند جانب الطريق

draw out 1 (used about the hours of daylight) to get longer in the spring (ساعات النهار) تأخذ بالطول

2 (used about cars, buses, etc.) to move out from the side of the road where they have stopped (السيّارة) تتحرّك من موقفها

draw sth out to take money out of a bank account: *How much money do I need to draw out?* يسحب

draw up (used about a car, etc.) to drive up and stop in front of or near sth: *A police car drew up outside the building.* (سيّارة) تتوقف عند...

draw sth up to prepare a document, list, etc. and write it out: *Our solicitor is going to draw up the contract.* يصوغ أو يعدّ وثيقة

drawback /ˈdrɔːbæk/ *noun* [C] a disadvantage or problem: *His lack of experience is a major drawback.* علّة ، نَقْص : عائق

drawer /drɔː(r)/ *noun* [C] a container which forms part of a piece of furniture such as a desk, that you can pull out to put things in or take things out: *There's some paper in the top drawer of my desk.* درج ، جارور

drawing /ˈdrɔːɪŋ/ *noun* **1** [C] a picture made with a pencil, pen, etc. صورة مرسومة بالقلم

2 [U] the art of drawing pictures: *She's good at drawing and painting.* فنّ الرسم

ˈdrawing pin (*US* **thumbtack**) *noun* [C] a short pin with a flat top, used for fastening paper, etc. to a board or wall مسمار أو دبّوس كبس

ˈdrawing room *noun* [C] a living room, especially one used mainly for formal occasions غرفة الضيوف

drawl /drɔːl/ *verb* [I,T] to speak slowly, making the vowel sounds very long يمطّ كلامه ، يتشدّق

▶ **drawl** *noun* [sing.]: *a slow Kentucky drawl* مطّ الكلام

drawn¹ /drɔːn/ *adj* (used about a person or his/her face) looking tired, worried or ill: *He looked* *pale and drawn after the long journey.* (وجه) مُتعَب

drawn² *pp of* DRAW²: *The match was drawn.* ○ *The curtains were drawn.*

dread /dred/ *noun* [U, sing.] great fear: *He lived in dread of the same thing happening to him one day.* ○ *a secret dread of what might happen* فزع ، هلع ، رهبة

▶ **dread** *verb* [T] to be very afraid of or worried about sth: *I'm dreading the exams.* ○ *She dreaded having to tell him what had happened.* ○ *I dread to think what my father will say.* يرهب ، يخشى

dreaded *adj* terrible; causing you to feel afraid or worried: *the most dreaded punishment of all* مُريع ، مرعب ، رهيب

dreadful /ˈdredfl/ *adj* very bad, unpleasant or poor in quality: *We had a dreadful journey – traffic jams all the way!* ○ *What a dreadful man!* ○ *I'm afraid there's been a dreadful* (= very serious) *mistake.* رديء للغاية : بغيض : فظيع ، مريع

▶ **dreadfully** /-fəli/ *adv* بصورة مريعة : للغاية

dreadlocks /ˈdredlɒks/ *noun* [plural] hair worn in long curled pieces, especially by some black people ضفائر رفيعة عديدة

dream¹ /driːm/ *noun* **1** [C] a series of events or pictures which happen in your mind while you are asleep: *I had a strange dream last night.* ○ *In my dream I was flying a helicopter...* ➲ Look at **nightmare**. حُلم ، رؤيا

2 [C] an event or situation that you want very much to happen, although it is not very likely that it will: *His dream was to give up his job and live in the country.* ○ *a dream house* (= one that you would like very much to own) حُلم

3 [sing.] a state of mind in which you are not concentrating on what is happening around you: *You've been in a dream all morning!* عالم الخيال ، (سابح في) حلم

dream² /driːm/ *verb* [I,T] (*pt, pp* **dreamt** /dremt/ or **dreamed** /driːmd/) **1** to see or experience pictures and events in your mind while you are asleep: *I dreamed about the house that I lived in as a child.* ○ *I woke up to find that I wasn't really rich. I had only dreamt it.* ○ *I dreamed that I was running but I couldn't get away.* يحلم ، يرى في منامه

2 to imagine sth that you would like to happen: *I've always dreamt about winning lots of money.* ○ *I never dreamt that I would be so lucky!* ➲ Look at **daydream**. يحلم

IDM **I, etc. would not dream of sth** I, etc. would definitely not do sth, under any circumstances: *'Don't tell anybody.' 'Of course not. I wouldn't dream of it.'* لن افعل ذلك بأي حالٍ من الأحوال

PHR V **dream sth up** (*informal*) to think of sth such as a plan, etc. especially sth unusual or slightly foolish: *Which of you dreamt up that idea?* يجيء بفكرة (عجيبة)

▶ **dreamer** *noun* [C] a person who thinks a lot about ideas, plans, etc. which may never happen instead of concentrating on what is really happening من يعيش في دنيا الخيال

dreamy /ˈdriːmi/ *adj* (**dreamier**; **dreamiest**) (used about a person or his/her expression) having or showing thoughts that are far away from the real world: *a dreamy look, expression, etc.* حالم ، سارح

▶ **dreamily** /-ɪli/ *adv* بصورة حالمة

dreary /ˈdrɪəri/ *adj* (**drearier**; **dreariest**) dull, boring or depressing: *What dreary weather! It's so grey.* كئيب؛ مملّ

dredge /dredʒ/ *verb* [T] to clear the mud, etc. from the bottom of a river or harbour using a special machine يجرف الوحل من القاع

PHR V **dredge sth up** to mention again sth unpleasant from the past that it would be better to forget: *The newspaper had dredged up all sorts of embarrassing details about her private life.* ينبش

dregs /dregz/ *noun* [plural] **1** the unwanted liquid left at the bottom of sth, including any solid bits that have sunk down: *'Is there anything left in that bottle?' 'Only the dregs.'* حثالة ، ثُفْل

2 the worst and most useless part of sth: *These people were regarded as the dregs of society.* حثالة (الناس) ، غثاء

drench /drentʃ/ *verb* [T] (usually passive) to make sb/sth completely wet: *We got absolutely drenched in the storm.* يبلّل بللاً شديداً

dress¹ /dres/ *noun* **1** [C] a piece of clothing worn by a girl or a woman. It covers the body from the shoulders to the knees or below and often covers the arms. ثوب ، "فُسْتان"

2 [U] clothes for either men or women: *formal/informal dress* ○ *evening dress* ملابس ، ثياب

dress² /dres/ *verb* **1** [I,T] to put clothes on sb or yourself: *He dressed quickly and left the house with a minute to spare.* ○ *If you don't get dressed soon, we'll be late.* ○ *My husband dressed the children while I got breakfast ready.* ○ *Hurry up, Simon! Aren't you dressed yet?* ℹ It is more common to say **get dressed** than **dress**. يلبس ، يرتدي ؛ يُلبِس

2 [I] to put or have clothes on, in the way or style mentioned: *to dress well, badly, etc.* ○ *to be well dressed, badly dressed, etc.* يلبس

3 [I] to put on formal clothes for the evening: *In the past wealthy families always dressed for dinner.* يرتدي ملابس رسميّة (للعشاء)

4 [T] to clean and put a bandage, etc. on a wound: *to dress a wound* يضمِّد

IDM **(be) dressed in sth** wearing sth: *The people at the funeral were all dressed in black.* مرْتدٍ، لابس

PHR V **dress up 1** to put on special or unusual clothes for fun or for a play: *The children decided to dress up as pirates.* يرتدي ملابس تزيينيّة أو تنكّرية

2 to put on smart clothes, usually for a special occasion: *You don't need to dress up for the party.* يرتدي ملابس أنيقة

dresser /ˈdresə(r)/ *noun* [C] **1** (*especially Brit*) a piece of furniture with cupboards at the bottom and shelves above. It is used for holding dishes, cups, etc. خزانة لحفظ الأطباق والفناجين وما إليها

a b c d e f g h i j k l m n o p q r s t u v w x y z

2 (*US*) a chest of drawers, usually with a mirror on top منضدة الزينة ، "تواليت"

dressing /ˈdresɪŋ/ *noun* **1** [C] a covering that you put on a wound to protect it and keep it clean ضماد

2 [C,U] a sauce for food, especially for salads صلصة وتوابِل السَلَطة

3 [U] the act or action of putting on clothes ارتداء

ˈdressing gown (*also* **bathrobe**; *US* **robe**) *noun* [C] a piece of clothing like a loose coat which you wear before or after a bath or over pyjamas, etc. رداء بيتي

ˈdressing table *noun* [C] a piece of furniture in a bedroom. It has drawers and a mirror. منضدة الزينة

dressmaker /ˈdresmeɪkə(r)/ *noun* [C] a person, especially a woman, who makes women's clothes خيّاطة (أو خيّاط)

▸ **dressmaking** /ˈdresmeɪkɪŋ/ *noun* [U] خياطة الملابس النسائية

drew *pt* of DRAW²

dribble /ˈdrɪbl/ *verb* **1** [I,T] (used about a liquid) to move downwards in a thin stream; to make a liquid move in this way: *The paint dribbled down the side of the pot.* "يشُرّ" ، يسيل أو يجعله يسيل قطرة قطرة

2 [I] to allow liquid (saliva) to run out of the mouth: *Small children often dribble.* يُروِّل ، يسيل لعابه

3 [I,T] (used in ball games) to make a ball move forward by using many short kicks or hits يدفع أو يدحرج الكرة

dried *pt, pp* of DRY²

drier¹ *adj* → DRY¹

drier² *noun* [C] → DRYER

drift /drɪft/ *verb* [I] **1** to be carried or moved along by wind or water: *The boat drifted out to sea.* ينجرف ، ينساق

2 (used about snow or sand) to be moved into piles by wind or water: *The snow drifted up to two metres deep in some places.* (الرمل) ينجرف ويتراكم

3 to move slowly or without any particular purpose: *He drifted from room to room.* ○ *She drifted into acting almost by accident.* ○ *At one time they were close friends, but over the years they've drifted apart.* يسير على غير هدى ، ينساق

▸ **drift** *noun* **1** [C] a slow movement towards sth: *the country's drift into economic decline* انجراف ، انسياق ، جنوح

2 [sing.] the general meaning of sth: *I couldn't understand every word but I got the drift of what he was saying.* معنى عام ، مغزى

3 [C] a pile of snow or sand that was made by wind or water ركام أو كومة (ثلج مثلاً)

drill¹ /drɪl/ *noun* [C] a tool or machine that is used for making holes in things: *a dentist's drill* مثقاب

▸ **drill** *verb* [I,T] to make a hole in sth with a drill: *to drill a hole in sth* ○ *to drill for oil* يحفر بمثقاب ؛ يحفر بئر نفط

drill² /drɪl/ *noun* **1** [U] exercise in marching, etc. that soldiers do تدريب عسكري

2 [C] something that you repeat many times in order to learn sth تمرين أو تدريب

3 [C,U] practice for what you should do in an emergency: *a fire drill* تدريب ؛ تجربة

▸ **drill** *verb* [I,T] to teach sb by making him/her repeat sth many times يعلِّم ، يدرِّب

drily /ˈdraɪli/ *adv* → DRY¹

⚷ **drink** /drɪŋk/ *verb* (*pt* **drank** /dræŋk/; *pp* **drunk** /drʌŋk/) **1** [I,T] to take liquid into your body through your mouth: *You've lost a lot of fluid. You must keep drinking.* ○ *We sat drinking coffee and chatting for hours.* يشرب

2 [I] to drink alcohol: *Don't drink and drive.* يشرب الكحول

PHRV **drink to sb/sth** to wish sb/sth good luck by raising your glass before you drink: *We all drank to the future of the bride and groom.* ➲ Look at **toast**². يشرب نخبه

drink (sth) up to finish drinking sth: *Drink up your tea – it's getting cold.* يشربه كلّه

▸ **drink** *noun* [C,U] **1** liquid for drinking: *Can I have a drink please?* ○ *a drink of milk* ○ *food and drink* شراب ، مشروب

2 alcoholic drink: *the link between drink and crime* ○ *a strong drink* مشروب كحولي

drinker *noun* [C] a person who drinks alcohol: *a heavy drinker* شارب الخمر ، سكّير

drinking *noun* [U] drinking alcohol: *Her drinking became a problem.* شرب أو تعاطي المسكرات

ˌdrink-ˈdriving *noun* [U] driving a vehicle after drinking too much alcohol: *He was convicted of drink-driving and was banned for two years.* قيادة السيارة في حالة سكْر

ˈdrinking water *noun* [U] water that is safe to drink ماء صالح للشرب

drip /drɪp/ *verb* (dri**pp**ing; dri**pp**ed) **1** [I] (used about a liquid) to fall in small drops: *Water was dripping down through the roof.* يقطر ، ينقط

2 [I,T] to have drops of liquid falling: *The tap is dripping.* ○ *Her finger was dripping blood.* يقطر ، ينقط

▸ **drip** *noun* **1** [sing.] the act or sound of water dripping: *the drip of a leaky tap* قَطْر (الماء مثلاً)

2 [C] a drop of water that falls down from sb/sth قطرة ماء متساقطة

3 [C] a piece of medical equipment, like a tube, that is used for putting liquid food or medicine directly into a sick person's blood: *She's on a drip.* محقنة "سيروم"

⚷ **drive¹** /draɪv/ *verb* (*pt* **drove** /drəʊv/; *pp* **driven** /ˈdrɪvn/) **1** [I,T] to control or operate a car, train, bus, etc: *Can you drive?* ○ *to drive a car, train, bus, lorry, etc.* يسوق ، يقود

2 [I,T] to go or take sb somewhere in a car, etc: *I usually drive to work.* ○ *We drove Nancy to the airport.* يذهب أو يوصل بالسيّارة

3 [T] to force people or animals to move in a

particular direction: *The dogs drove the sheep into the field.* يسوق ، يطرد

4 [T] to force sth into a particular position by hitting it: *to drive a post into the ground* يدقّ (المسمار)

5 [T] to cause sb to be in a particular state or to do a particular thing: *That noise is driving me mad.* ○ *to drive sb to despair* ○ *His loneliness drove him to commit suicide.* يقود ، يدفع

6 [T] to make sb/sth work very hard: *You shouldn't drive yourself so hard.* يجهده بالعمل

7 [T] to make a machine work, by giving it power: *What drives the wheels in this engine?* يسيّر ، يحرك

IDM **be driving at** (*informal*) to want to say sth; to mean: *I'm afraid I don't understand what you are driving at.* يعني ، يقصد

drive sth home (to sb) to make sth clear so that people understand it يفهّم ، يوضّح

PHRV **drive off** (used about a car, driver, etc.) to leave ينصرف ، يمضي ؛ يبتعد

drive sb/sth off to force sb/sth to go back or away: *They kept a large dog outside to drive off burglars.* يصدّ ، يدفع

🔑**drive²** /draɪv/ *noun* **1** [C] a journey in a car: *The supermarket is only a five-minute drive away.* ○ *Let's go out for a drive.* نزهة في السيّارة

2 [C] a private road that leads to a house طريق خاص يوصل إلى البيت

3 [U] the energy and determination you need to succeed in doing sth طاقة ، دافع ، عزيمة

4 [C,U] a strong natural need or desire: *a strong sex drive* رغبة ، شهوة

5 [C] a strong effort by a group of people in order to achieve sth: *a sales drive* حملة ؛ مجهود عظيم

'drive-by *adj* (*US*) (only *before* a noun) (used about a shooting) done from a moving car: *drive-by killings* (قتل) من سيارة عابرة مسرعة

'drive-in *noun* [C] a place where you can go to eat, watch a film, etc. in your car سينما في الهواء الطلق تدخلها السيّارات

driven *pp* of DRIVE¹

🔑**driver** /'draɪvə(r)/ *noun* [C] a person who drives a vehicle: *One passenger died in the accident but the driver was unhurt.* سائق

'drive-through *noun* [C] (*especially US*) a restaurant, bank, etc. where you can be served without getting out of your car (مطعم مثلاً) ممكن الشراء منه من السيارة

🔑**driving¹** /'draɪvɪŋ/ *noun* [U] the act of controlling a car, etc: *Driving in the fog is very frightening.* ○ *She was arrested for dangerous driving.* سَوْق ، قيادة

driving² /'draɪvɪŋ/ *adj* very strong: *driving rain* ○ *Who's the driving force behind this plan?* شديد ؛ عاتٍ

'driving licence (*US* **'driver's licence**) *noun* [C] an official piece of paper that says you are allowed to drive a car, etc. You get this piece of paper after you have passed a test. شهادة سَوْق أو قيادة

'driving school *noun* [C] an organization for teaching people to drive a car مدرسة لتعليم قيادة السيّارات

drizzle /'drɪzl/ *noun* [U] light rain that has many small drops: *A cloudy day with rain or drizzle is expected.* رذاذ ، مطر خفيف

▶ **drizzle** *verb* [I] ➲ Look at the note at **weather**. تمطر مطراً خفيفاً

drone /drəʊn/ *verb* [I] to make a continuous low sound: *the sound of the tractors droning away in the fields* يدوي ، يطنّ

PHRV **drone on** to talk in a flat or boring voice يتكلم على وتيرة واحدة

▶ **drone** *noun* [C, usually sing.] a continuous low sound دويّ ، طنين

drool /druːl/ *verb* [I] **1** to let liquid (saliva) come out from your mouth, usually at the sight or smell of sth good to eat يسيل لعابه

2 drool (over sb/sth) to show in a foolish way how much you like or admire sb/sth: *teenagers drooling over photographs of their favourite pop stars* يبدي إعجابه بصورة مزرية

droop /druːp/ *verb* [I] to bend or hang downwards, e.g. because of weakness or tiredness: *The flowers were drooping without water.* يتهدّل ، يتراخى، يذوي

▶ **drooping** *adj*: *drooping shoulders* ○ *a drooping moustache* متهدّل

🔑**drop¹** /drɒp/ *verb* (dro**pp**ing; dro**pp**ed) **1** [T] to allow sth to fall: *The helicopters dropped food and medicine.* ○ *That vase was very expensive. Whatever you do don't drop it!* يسقط ، يلقي ، يرمي

2 [I] to fall: *The parachutist dropped safely to the ground.* يهبط

3 [I,T] to become weaker or lower; to make sth weaker or lower: *The temperature will drop to minus 3 overnight.* ○ *They ought to drop their prices.* ○ *to drop your voice* (= speak more quietly) يهبط ، ينخفض ؛ يخفض أو يخفّض

4 [T] **drop sb/sth (off)** to stop your car, etc. so that sb can get out, or in order to take sth out: *Drop me off at the traffic lights, please.* ○ *I'll drop the parcel at your house.* ينزل (من السيّارة)

5 [T] to no longer include sb/sth in sth: *Joe has been dropped from the team.* يحذف ، يسقط

6 [T] to stop doing sth: *I'm going to drop geography next term* (= stop studying it). ○ *Drop everything – I need your help right now!* يترك ، يلغي

IDM **drop dead** (*informal*) to die suddenly يموت فجأة

drop sb a line to write a letter to sb: *Do drop me a line when you've time.* يكتب رسالة ا

PHRV **drop back**; **drop behind (sb)** to move into a position behind sb else, because you are moving more slowly: *Towards the end of the race she dropped behind the other runners.* يتخلّف عن الآخرين

drop by/in; **drop in on sb** to visit sb informally or without having told them you were coming:

We were in the area so we thought we'd drop in and see you. يزور (دون موعد)

drop off (*informal*) to fall into a light sleep: *I must have dropped off in front of the television.* يغفو

drop out (of sth) to leave or stop doing sth before you have finished: *His injury forced him to drop out of the competition.* ○ *to drop out of college* يترك ، ينقطع عن

drop[2] /drɒp/ *noun* **1** [C] a small round mass of liquid: *I thought I felt a drop of rain.* قطرة ، نقطة

2 drops [plural] liquid medicine that you put into your eyes, ears or nose قطرة (للعيون)

3 [C, usually sing.] a small amount of liquid: *I'll just have a drop more tea.* كميّة صغيرة ، "نقطة"

4 [sing.] a vertical distance down from a place: *a sheer drop of 40 metres to the sea* مسافة الهبوط

5 [sing.] a smaller amount or level of sth: *The job is much more interesting but it will mean a drop in salary.* انخفاض : تنزيل

ˌdrop-down ˈmenu *noun* (*computing*) a menu that appears on a computer screen when you choose it, and that stays there until you choose one of the functions on it
لائحة هابطة، قائمة بالبرامج الموجودة على الكمبيوتر

ˈdrop-out *noun* [C] **1** a person who leaves school, university, etc. before finishing his/her studies منقطع عن الدراسة

2 a person who does not accept the rules of society and who wants to live in a way that is different from one that most people consider is acceptable شاذّ عن المجتمع

droppings /ˈdrɒpɪŋz/ *noun* [plural] waste material from the bodies of small animals or birds: *rabbit droppings* بَعْر الغنم وغيره ، ذَرْق الطيور

drought /draʊt/ *noun* [C,U] a long period of weather which is too dry: *Drought has affected many countries in Africa.* جفاف ، قحط

drove *pt of* DRIVE[1]

drown /draʊn/ *verb* **1** [I,T] to die in water because it is not possible to breathe; to make sb die in this way: *The girl fell into the river and drowned.* ○ *Twenty people were drowned in the floods.* يغرق؛ يغرق

2 [T] (used about a sound) to be so loud that you cannot hear sb/sth else: *His answer was drowned by the music.* يغطّي أو يطغى على

drowsy /ˈdraʊzi/ *adj* (**drowsier**; **drowsiest**) very sleepy: *The heat made me feel drowsy.* نعسان
▸ **drowsily** /-əli/ *adv* شبه نائم ، بنعاس
drowsiness *noun* [U] نعاس : خمول

drudgery /ˈdrʌdʒəri/ *noun* [U] hard and uninteresting work عمل شاقّ ، كدّ وكدح

drug /drʌg/ *noun* [C] **1** a chemical which is used as a medicine: *Some drugs can only be obtained with a prescription from a doctor.* دواء

2 a chemical which people use to give them pleasant or exciting feelings. It is against the law in many countries to use drugs: *hard drugs such as heroin and cocaine* مخدِّر

▸ **drug** *verb* [T] (drug**g**ing; drug**g**ed) **1** to give a person or animal a chemical to make them sleepy or unconscious: *The lion was drugged before the start of the journey.* يخدر ، ينوم

2 to put a drug into food or drink: *drugged food* يدسّ مخدّراً

ˈdrug addict *noun* [C] a person who cannot stop taking drugs مدمن على المخدّرات

ˈdrug addiction *noun* [U] the state of being a drug addict الإدمان على المخدّرات

druggist /ˈdrʌgɪst/ *noun* [C] (*US*) = CHEMIST (1)

drugstore /ˈdrʌgstɔː(r)/ *noun* [C] (*US*) a shop that sells medicine, soap, shampoo, film, etc. as well as drinks and light meals صيدليّة

drum /drʌm/ *noun* [C] **1** a round hollow musical instrument, with plastic or skin stretched across the ends. You play a drum by hitting it with your hands or with sticks: *She plays the drums in a band.* طبل

2 a round hollow container: *an oil drum* برميل

▸ **drum** *verb* (drum**m**ing; drum**m**ed) **1** [I] to play a drum or drums يطبِّل ، يدقّ الطبل

2 [I,T] to make a noise like a drum by hitting sth many times: *to drum your fingers on the table* (= because you are annoyed, impatient, etc.) يدقّ ، ينقر

PHRV **drum sth into sb** to make sb remember sth by repeating it many times: *Road safety should be drummed into children from an early age.* يلقّن بالتكرار

drum sth up to try to get more of sth: *to drum up more custom* يشجّع ، يروّج

drummer *noun* [C] a person who plays a drum or drums طبّال

drunk[1] *pp of* DRINK

drunk[2] /drʌŋk/ *adj* (not before a noun) having drunk too much alcohol: *You're drunk!* سكران ، مخمور

▸ **drunk** *noun* [C] a person who is drunk السكران

drunkard /ˈdrʌŋkəd/ *noun* [C] a person who often gets drunk السكّير

drunken /ˈdrʌŋkən/ *adj* (only *before* a noun) **1** having drunk too much alcohol: *drunken drivers* سكران ، مخمور

2 showing the effects of too much alcohol: *drunken singing* ثمل ، مخمور
▸ **drunkenly** *adv* بثَمَل ، (تكلّم) وهو مخمور
drunkenness *noun* [U] حالة سُكر ، ثَمَل

dry[1] /draɪ/ *adj* (**drier**; **driest**) **1** without liquid in it or on it; not wet: *The washing isn't dry yet.* ○ *The paint is dry now.* ○ *Rub your hair dry with a towel.* ○ *In the hot weather the stream ran dry.* جافّ ، ناشف

2 having little or no rain: *a hot, dry summer* جافّ

3 (used about wine) not sweet (خمر) مزّاي غير حلو

4 (used of a remark, etc.) amusing, although it sounds serious: *a dry sense of humour* (تعليق) مضحك وذكيّ ولو أنه يبدو جاداً

5 dull or boring: *dry legal documents* جافّ وممل

▶ **drily** (*also* **dryly**) /ˈdraɪli/ *adv* in a dry(4) way: *'I can hardly contain my excitement,' Peter said dryly* (= he was not excited at all). بجفاء، دون اكتراث

dryness *noun* [U] جفاف : انعدام الروح أو التشويق

dry² /draɪ/ *verb* [I,T] (*pres part* **drying**; *3rd pers sing pres* **dries**; *pt, pp* **dried**) to become dry; to make sth dry: *Leave your swimsuit in the sun to dry.* ○ *to dry your hands on a towel* يجفّ، ينشف

PHRV **dry (sth) out** (to cause sth wet) to become very dry or too dry: *Don't allow the soil to dry out.* يجفّ أو ينشف : يجفّف أو ينشّف

dry up 1 (used about a river, etc.) to have no more water in it ينضب، يجفّ

2 to stop being available: *Because of the recession a lot of building work has dried up.* ينفد، ينقطع

3 to forget what you intended to say, e.g. because you are very nervous ينسى ما يودّ قوله

dry (sth) up to dry plates, knives, forks, etc. with a towel after they have been washed يجفّف، ينشّف

▶ **dried** *adj* (used about food) with all the liquid removed from it: *dried milk* ○ *dried fruit* مجفّف

dryer (*also* **drier**) /ˈdraɪə(r)/ *noun* [C] a machine that you use for drying sth: *a hairdryer* ○ *a tumble dryer* آلة تجفيف

ˌdry-ˈclean *verb* [T] to clean clothes using special chemicals, without using water التنظيف على الناشف

▶ **ˌdry-ˈcleaner's** (*also* **cleaner's**) *noun* [C] the shop where you take your clothes to be cleaned محل التنظيف على الناشف

ˌdry ˈland *noun* [U] land, not the sea: *I was glad to be back on dry land again.* البرّ، اليابسة

dual /ˈdjuːəl; *US* ˈduːəl/ *adj* (only *before* a noun) having two parts; double: *the dual role of mother and working woman* ○ *to have dual nationality* ثنائيّ أو مزدوج، مضاعف

ˌdual ˈcarriageway (*US* **divided highway**) *noun* [C] a road that has an area of grass or a fence down the middle to separate the lines of traffic going in one direction from the traffic going in the other direction طريق مزدوج ذو اتجاهين

dub /dʌb/ *verb* [T] (du**bb**ing; du**bb**ed) **1** to give sb/sth a new or amusing name (a nickname): *The Belgian actor Jean Claude Van Damme has been dubbed 'Muscles from Brussels'.* يلقّب

2 to change the sound in a film so that what the actors said originally is spoken by actors using a different language: *I don't like foreign films when they're dubbed into English. I prefer subtitles.* يُدَبلَج الفيلم: يجعل الممثّلين يتكلّمون لغة أخرى

dubious /ˈdjuːbiəs; *US* ˈduː-/ *adj* **1 dubious (about sth/about doing sth)** not sure or certain: *I'm very dubious about whether we're doing the right thing.* غير متيقّن، شاكّ

2 that may not be honest or safe: *dubious financial dealings* مشبوه، مشكوك فيه

▶ **dubiously** *adv* بارتياب : بصورة تثير الشبهة

duchess (*also* **Duchess**) /ˈdʌtʃəs/ *noun* [C] **1** the wife of a duke دوقة

2 a woman who is of the same rank as a duke دوقة

duck¹ /dʌk/ *noun* (*pl.* **duck** or **ducks**) **1** [C] a common bird that lives on or near water. Ducks have short legs, special (webbed) feet for swimming and a wide beak. They are kept on farms for their meat and eggs. بطّة

2 [C] a female duck بطّة

A male duck is called a **drake** and a young duck is a **duckling**. A duck **waddles** and **quacks**.

3 [U] the meat of a duck: *roast duck with orange sauce* لحم البطّ

duck² /dʌk/ *verb* **1** [I,T] to move your head down quickly so that you are not seen or hit by sb/sth: *I saw the ball coming towards me and ducked.* يخفض رأسه (تفادياً لشيء)

2 [I,T] (*informal*) **duck (out of) sth** to try to avoid sth difficult or unpleasant: *She tried to duck out of apologizing.* يتهرّب من

3 [T] to push sb's head under water for a short time, especially when playing يغطّس رأسه تحت الماء للمداعبة

duct /dʌkt/ *noun* [C] a tube that carries liquid, gas, etc: *They got into the building through the air duct.* أنبوب، قناة

dud /dʌd/ *noun* [C] (*informal*) a thing that is useless or that does not work properly شيء معطّل أو عديم القيمة

dude /duːd/ *noun* [C] (*slang*) a man رجل، شخص، واحد من الناس

due¹ /djuː; *US* duː/ *adj* **1** (not before a noun) expected or planned to happen or arrive: *The conference is due to start in four weeks' time.* ○ *What time is the plane due?* متوقّع

2 (not before a noun) having to be paid: *The rent is due on the fifteenth of each month.* مستحقّ (الدفع)

3 that is owed to you because it is your right to have it: *Make sure you claim all the benefits that are due to you.* مستحقّ

4 due to sb/sth caused by or because of sb/sth: *His illness is probably due to stress.* ناتج عن؛ بسبب

Some careful speakers only use **due to** after the verb **to be**: *The strike was due to poor working conditions.* However, **due to** is often used in the same way as **owing to** and **because of**: *Due to/owing to/because of the bad weather many trains have been cancelled.*

5 due for sth deserving or expecting to have sth: *I think that I'm due for a pay rise.* مستحقّ لـ، متوقّع

6 (only *before* a noun) (*formal*) suitable or right: *After due consideration I have decided to accept your offer.* ملائم : صحيح

IDM **in due course** at some time in the future, quite soon: *All applicants will be informed of our decision in due course.* قريباً، في الوقت المناسب

due² /djuː; *US* duː/ *noun*

IDM **give sb his/her due** to be fair to a person:

She doesn't work very quickly, but to give her her due, she is very accurate. يُنصف

due³ /djuː; *US* duː/ *adv* (used before 'north', 'south', 'east' and 'west') exactly: *The plane was flying due east.* بالضبط ، مباشرة

duel /ˈdjuːəl; *US* ˈduːəl/ *noun* [C] a formal type of fight with guns or swords which was used in the past to settle an argument between two men: *to challenge sb to a duel* مبارزة

duet /djuˈet; *US* duːˈet/ (*also* **duo**) *noun* [C] a piece of music for two people to sing or play لحن ثنائي

duffel coat (*also* **duffle coat**) /ˈdʌfl kəʊt/ *noun* [C] a coat made of heavy woollen cloth with a hood. A duffel coat has special long buttons (toggles). معطف سميك ذو قلنسوة

dug *pt, pp of* DIG

duke /djuːk; *US* duːk/ (*also* **Duke**) *noun* [C] a nobleman of very high rank: *the Duke of York* ➲ Look at **duchess**. دوق

dull /dʌl/ *adj* **1** not bright: *a dull and cloudy day* معتم ، قاتم

2 not loud, sharp or strong: *Her head hit the floor with a dull thud.* ○ *a dull pain* خافت ، مكتوم

3 not interesting or exciting: *Life is never dull in the city.* ممل

▸ **dullness** *noun* [U] رتابة ؛ ملل ؛ بهوت الألوان

dully /ˈdʌlli/ *adv* **1** in a dull way بصورة مملّة

2 showing no interest: *Sheila didn't answer. She just stared dully at me.* بفتور ، بضجر

duly /ˈdjuːli; *US* ˈduːli/ *adv* (*formal*) in the correct or expected way: *We all duly assembled at 7.30 as agreed.* كما يجب ، على النحو المطلوب

dumb /dʌm/ *adj* **1** not able to speak: *to be deaf and dumb* ○ (*figurative*) *They were struck dumb with amazement.* أخرس ، أبكم

2 (*informal*) stupid: *What a dumb thing to do!* أحمق ، غبي

▸ **dumbly** *adv* without speaking: *Ken dumbly nodded agreement.* بِصمت

dumbfounded /dʌmˈfaʊndɪd/ *adj* very surprised معقود اللسان ، مبهوت

dummy /ˈdʌmi/ *noun* [C] (*pl.* **dummies**) **1** a model of the human body used for putting clothes on in a shop window or while you are making clothes: *a tailor's dummy* تمثال لعرض الأزياء

2 (*US* **pacifier**) a rubber object that you put in a baby's mouth to keep him/her quiet and happy لهّاية ، مصّاصة

3 something that is made to look like sth else but that is not the real thing نسخة مزيّفة عن ، دمية "تقليد"

▸ **dummy** *adj* made to look like sth else but not the real thing: *dummy bullets* كاذب ، زائف

dump /dʌmp/ *verb* [T] **1** to take sth that you do not want to a place, especially a place which is not suitable, and leave it there: *Nuclear waste should not be dumped in the sea.* ○ *piles of rubbish dumped by the side of the road* يرمي ، يتخلص من

2 to put something down quickly or in a careless way: *The children dumped their coats and bags in the hall and ran off to play.* يلقي به على عجل

▸ **dump** *noun* [C] **1** a place where rubbish or waste material from factories, etc. is left: *the municipal rubbish dump* مزبلة

2 (*informal*) a place that is very dirty, untidy or unpleasant: *The flat is cheap but it's a real dump.* مكان قذر حقير

dumpling /ˈdʌmplɪŋ/ *noun* [C] a small ball of fat and flour (dough) that is cooked and usually eaten with meat كرة عجين مطبوخة

dumps /dʌmps/ *noun* [plural] (*informal*)

IDM **down in the dumps** unhappy or depressed مكتئب ، تعيس

dune /djuːn; *US* duːn/ (*also* **sand dune**) *noun* [C] a low hill of sand by the sea or in the desert كثيب رملي

dung /dʌŋ/ *noun* [U] waste material from the bodies of large animals روث

dungarees /ˌdʌŋɡəˈriːz/ *noun* [plural] a piece of clothing, similar to trousers, but covering your chest as well as your legs and with straps that go over the shoulders: *a pair of dungarees* سروال عمل ذو صدر

dungeon /ˈdʌndʒən/ *noun* [C] an underground prison, e.g. in a castle سجن تحت الأرض ، ديماس

duo /ˈdjuːəʊ; *US* ˈduːəʊ/ *noun* [C] **1** two people playing music or singing together ثنائي موسيقي

2 = DUET

dupe /djuːp; *US* duːp/ *verb* [T] (*informal*) to trick sb: *The woman was duped into carrying the drugs.* يحتال على ، يغرّر بـ

duplicate¹ /ˈdjuːplɪkət; *US* ˈduːpləkət/ *adj* (only *before* a noun) exactly the same as sth else: *a duplicate key* (= a copy of another key) مطابق تماماً ، منسوخ عنه

▸ **duplicate** *noun* [C] something that is exactly the same as sth else صورة طبق الأصل

IDM **in duplicate** with two copies (e.g. of an official piece of paper) that are exactly the same: *The contract must be in duplicate.* من نسختين

duplicate² /ˈdjuːplɪkeɪt; *US* ˈduːpləkeɪt/ *verb* [T] **1** to make an exact copy of sth يستنسخ عن

2 to do sth that has already been done: *We don't want to duplicate the work of other departments.* يكرّر ، يعيد

▸ **duplication** /ˌdjuːplɪˈkeɪʃn; *US* ˌduːpləˈkeɪʃn/ *noun* [U] استنساخ ؛ تكرار

durable /ˈdjʊərəbl; *US* ˈdʊə-/ *adj* that is able to last a long time: *a durable fabric* متين ، شديد التحمّل

▸ **durability** /ˌdjʊərəˈbɪləti; *US* ˌdʊə-/ *noun* [U] متانة ، شدّة التحمّل

duration /djuˈreɪʃn; *US* du-/ *noun* [U] the time that sth lasts: *Please remain seated for the duration of the flight.* مدّة ، فترة

duress /djuˈres; *US* du-/ *noun* [U]

IDM **under duress** because of the threat of force

being used; not willingly: *He signed the confession under duress.* إكراه ، إرغام

during /ˈdjʊərɪŋ; *US* ˈdʊər-/ *prep* **1** for all of a period of time: *The audience must remain seated during the performance.* طوال ، خلال

2 on more than one occasion in a period of time: *During the summer holidays we went swimming every day.* أثناء ، خلال

3 at some point in a period of time: *Grandpa was taken very ill during the night.* خلال ، أثناء

Notice that you use **during** to say when something happens and **for** to say how long something lasts: *I went shopping during my lunch break. I was out for about 25 minutes.*

dusk /dʌsk/ *noun* [U] the time in the evening when the sun has already gone down and it is nearly dark ➲ Look at **dawn**. الغسق

dust¹ /dʌst/ *noun* [U] a fine dry powder that is made of very small pieces of earth, dirt, etc: *There is dust everywhere in our house.* ○ *a thick layer of dust* ○ *chalk dust* ○ *The tractor came up the track in a cloud of dust.* ○ *a speck* (= small piece) *of dust* غبار

dust² /dʌst/ *verb* [I,T] to remove dust from furniture, etc. with a cloth: *Let me dust those shelves before you put the books on them.* ➲ Look at the note at **clean**². يمسح الغبار عن

▸ **duster** *noun* [C] a soft cloth that you use for dusting furniture ممسحة غبار

dustbin /ˈdʌstbɪn/ (*US* **garbage can**; **trash can**) *noun* [C] a large container for rubbish that you keep outside your house صفيحة الزبالة

dustman /ˈdʌstmən/ (*pl.* **dustmen** /-mən/) *noun* [C] a person whose job is to take away the rubbish that people put in their dustbins زبّال

dustpan /ˈdʌstpæn/ *noun* [C] a flat container with a handle into which you brush dust or dirt from the floor جاروف الكناسة ، "مجرور" ، "كريك"

dusty /ˈdʌsti/ *adj* (**dustier**; **dustiest**) having a lot of dust: *This shelf has got very dusty.* مغبّر

Dutch *adj* from the Netherlands هولنديّ

dutiful /ˈdjuːtɪfl; *US* ˈduː-/ *adj* (*formal*) willing to respect and obey: *a dutiful daughter* مطيع ، بارّ

duty /ˈdjuːti; *US* ˈduːti/ *noun* (*pl.* **duties**) **1** [C,U] something that you have to do because people expect you to do it or because you think it is right: *A soldier must do his duty.* ○ *a sense of moral duty* ○ *It's your duty to look after your parents when they get older.* واجب

2 [C,U] the tasks that you do when you are at work: *the duties of a policeman* ○ *to be on night duty* (= e.g. as a nurse) عمل ، مهمّة

3 [C] a tax that you pay, especially on goods that you bring into a country ضريبة جمركيّة

IDM on/off duty (used about doctors, nurses, policemen, etc.) to be working/not working: *The porter's on duty from 8 till 4.* ○ *What time does she go off duty?* في/خارج عمله

ˌduty-ˈfree *adj, adv* (used about goods) that you can bring into a country without paying tax: *an airport duty-free shop* ○ *How many cigarettes can you bring into Britain duty-free?* معفى من الضريبة الجمركيّة

duvet /ˈduːveɪ/ *noun* [C] a thick cover filled with feathers or another soft material that is placed on top of a bed instead of a sheet and blankets ➲ Look at **eiderdown** and **quilt**. لحاف

ˈduvet day *noun* [C] (*informal*) a day when you stay at home instead of going to work because you feel tired and want to rest but are not ill يوم غياب عن العمل (بداعي الاسترخاء)

DVD /ˌdiː viː ˈdiː/ *noun* [C] digital videodisc or digital versatile disc; a disk on which large amounts of information, especially photographs and video, can be stored, for use on a computer or DVD-player: *a DVD-ROM drive* اسطوانة فيديو رقمية

DVR /ˌdiː viː ˈɑː(r)/ *noun* [C] a device that records video onto a hard disk or other memory device, using digital technology (the abbreviation for digital video recorder) مسجل فيديو رقمي

dwarf /dwɔːf/ *noun* [C] (*pl.* **dwarfs** or **dwarves** /dwɔːvz/) **1** a person, animal or plant that is much smaller than the usual size قزم

2 (in children's stories) a very small person, often with special powers: *Snow White and the Seven Dwarfs* قزم

▸ **dwarf** *verb* [T] (used about a large object) to make sth seem very small in comparison: *The skyscraper dwarfs all the other buildings around.* يجعله يبدو أصغر

dwell /dwel/ *verb* [I] (*pt, pp* **dwelt** /dwelt/ or **dwelled**) (*old-fashioned, formal*) to live or stay in a place يقيم ، يقطن

PHR V dwell on/upon sth to think, speak or write about sth for a long time: *I don't want to dwell on the past. Let's think about the future.* يطيل التفكير في ؛ يسهب

▸ **dweller** *noun* [C] (often in compounds) a person or animal that lives in the place mentioned: *city-dwellers* ساكن ، قاطن

dwelling *noun* [C] (*formal*) the place where a person lives; a house مسكن ، منزل

dwindle /ˈdwɪndl/ *verb* [I] to become smaller or weaker: *Their savings dwindled away to nothing.* يتضاءل ، يشحّ

dye¹ /daɪ/ *verb* [T] (*pres part* **dyeing**; *3rd pers sing pres* **dyes**; *pt, pp* **dyed**) to colour sth, especially by putting it into a liquid: *Does she dye her hair?* ○ *I'm going to dye this blouse black.* يصبغ

dye² /daɪ/ *noun* [C,U] a substance, usually added to a liquid, that changes the colour of sth, e.g. cloth, hair صبغة

dying *present participle of* DIE

dyke (*also* **dike**) /daɪk/ *noun* [C] **1** a wall made of earth, etc. used for preventing a river or the sea from flooding سور بحري، حاجز لصدّ المياه

2 a channel used for taking water away from land ترعة ، قناة

dynamic /daɪˈnæmɪk/ *adj* **1** (used about a person) full of energy and ideas; active
مفعم بالنشاط : فعّال

2 (used about a force or power) that causes movement حركيّ ، ديناميّ أو ديناميكيّ
▸ **dynamism** /ˈdaɪnəmɪzəm/ *noun* [U]
نشاط فعّال ، ديناميّة

dynamite /ˈdaɪnəmaɪt/ *noun* [U] **1** a type of explosive, used especially in mining ديناميت

2 a thing or person that causes great excitement, shock, etc: *His news was dynamite.*
شخص ديناميّ مثير : (خبر) مذهل

dynamo /ˈdaɪnəməʊ/ *noun* [C] (*pl.* **dynamos**) a device that changes a type of power such as steam or water into electricity مولّد كهربائيّ ، دينامو

dynasty /ˈdɪnəsti; *US* ˈdaɪ-/ *noun* [C] (*pl.* **dynasties**) a series of rulers who are from the same family: *the Ming dynasty* سلالة حاكمة

dysentery /ˈdɪsəntri; *US* -teri/ *noun* [U] a serious disease which causes a severe form of diarrhoea الزُّحار

dyslexia /dɪsˈleksiə; *US* dɪsˈlekʃə/ *noun* [U] a problem in sb's brain that causes difficulties in reading and spelling خلل القراءة
▸ **dyslexic** /dɪsˈleksɪk/ *noun* [C], *adj*
من يعاني من خلل القراءة

E e

E, e /iː/ *noun* [C] (*pl.* **Es**; **E's**; **e's**) the fifth letter of the English alphabet: *'Egg' begins with (an) 'E'.* الحرف الخامس من الأبجدية الإنكليزيّة

E *abbrev* = EAST(ERN)

🔑 **each** /iːtʃ/ *det, pron* every one of two or more things or people in a group, when you think about them individually: *Each lesson lasts an hour.* ○ *Each of the lessons lasts an hour.* ○ *The lessons each last an hour.* ○ *He gave each child a present.* ○ *He gave each of the children a present.* ○ *He gave the children a present each.*
كلّ ، كلّ واحد

🔑 **each 'other** (used for saying that sb feels, does or has the same thing as another person/other people in the group): *They loved each other very much.* ○ *We looked at each other.*
بعضهما أو بعضهم بعضاً

eager /ˈiːɡə(r)/ *adj* full of desire or interest: *He is eager to meet you.* ○ *eager for success*
متلهّف ، توّاق إلى
▸ **eagerly** *adv* بتلهُّف
eagerness *noun* [U] تلهّف

eagle /ˈiːɡl/ *noun* [C] a very large bird that can see very well. It eats small birds and animals.
نَسْر ، عُقاب

🔑 **ear¹** /ɪə(r)/ *noun* **1** [C] one of the two parts of the body of a person or animal that are used for hearing: *Elephants have large ears.* ○ *He pulled his hat down over his ears.* ○ *Whisper in my ear!* أُذن

2 [sing.] **an ear (for sth)** an ability to recognize or appreciate sounds, especially in music or language: *an ear for music* أُذن موسيقيّة
IDM **play (sth) by ear** to play a piece of music, etc. from memory and without using written notes يعزف قطعة موسيقيّة دون "نوتة"
play it by ear (*informal*) to decide what to do as things happen, instead of planning in advance
يتصرّف وفق ما تقتضيه الظروف
prick up your ears → PRICK²

ear² /ɪə(r)/ *noun* [C] the top part of a plant that produces grain: *an ear of corn* سنبلة

earache /ˈɪəreɪk/ *noun* [U] a pain in your ear: *I've got earache.* ➲ Look at the note at **ache**.
ألم في الأذن

earbud /ˈɪəbʌd/ *noun* [C, usually plural] a very small headphone that is worn inside the ear
سماعات صغيرة للأذنين

eardrum /ˈɪədrʌm/ *noun* [C] a thin piece of skin inside the ear that is tightly stretched and that allows you to hear sound طبلة الأذن

earl /ɜːl/ *noun* [C] a British nobleman of high rank ℹ A woman of the same rank is called a **countess**. "ايرل": نبيل بريطانيّ عالي المركز

🔑 **early** /ˈɜːli/ (**earlier**; **earliest**) *adj, adv* **1** near the beginning of a period of time, a piece of work, a series, etc: *Come in the early afternoon.* ○ *I have to get up early on weekday mornings.* ○ *He died in his early twenties.* ○ *The project is still in its early stages.* ○ *The tunnel should be finished early next year.* مبكّر : باكراً : في أوائل

2 before the usual or expected time: *She arrived five minutes early for her interview.* ○ *Spring is early this year.* مبكّر أو مبكّراً
IDM **at the earliest** not before the date or time mentioned: *I can repair it by Friday at the earliest.* على أقلّ تقدير
the early hours very early in the morning, in the hours after midnight الساعات الأخيرة من الليل
an early/a late night → NIGHT
early on soon after the beginning: *He achieved fame early on in his career.* مبكّراً ، بعد فترة قصيرة

earmark /ˈɪəmɑːk/ *verb* [T] **earmark sb/sth (for sth/sb)** to choose sb or keep sth for a particular job or purpose: *The factory has been earmarked for closure.* يفرد لغرض محدّد

🔑 **earn** /ɜːn/ *verb* [T] **1** to get money by working: *How much does a dentist earn?* ○ *I earn £20 000 a year.* ○ *He earns his living as an artist.* ○ *How much interest will my savings earn* (= produce) *in the bank?* يكسب ، يجني

2 to get sth that you deserve: *The team's victory*

today has earned them a place in the final. ○ *You've earned a holiday.* يستحق ، يستأهل

▸ **earnings** *noun* [plural] the money that a person earns by working: *Average earnings have increased by 5%.* إيراد من العمل

earnest /ˈɜːnɪst/ *adj* serious or determined: *He's such an earnest young man – he never makes a joke.* ○ *They were having a very earnest discussion.* جدّي : عاقد العزم

▸ **earnest** *noun*

IDM **in earnest 1** serious and sincere about what you are going to do: *His mother was worried that he was in earnest about wanting to leave university.* جادّ

2 happening more seriously or with more force than before: *Work began in earnest on the project.* بجدّ

earnestly *adv* in an earnest way بجدّ، جدّياً

earphones /ˈɪəfəʊnz/ *noun* [plural] a piece of equipment that fits over the ears and is used for listening to music, the radio, etc. سمّاعة

earring /ˈɪərɪŋ/ *noun* [C] a piece of jewellery that is worn in or on the lower part of the ear: *Do these earrings clip on or are they for pierced ears?* قرط ، حلَق

earshot /ˈɪəʃɒt/ *noun* [U]

IDM **(be) out of/within earshot** where a person cannot/can hear: *Wait until he's out of earshot before you say anything about him.* خارج مدى السمع ؛ على مسمع من

the earth

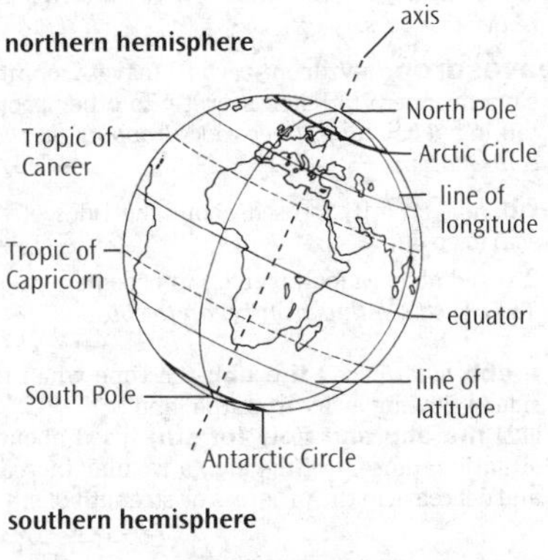

earth¹ /ɜːθ/ *noun* **1** (*also* **the earth**; **the Earth**) [sing.] the world; the planet on which we live: *life on earth* ○ *The earth is protected by the ozone layer.* الكرة الأرضيّة ، العالم

2 [sing.] the surface of the world; land: *The spaceship fell towards earth.* ○ *The earth shook.* الأرض

3 [U] soil (that plants grow in): *The earth is very fertile here.* ➲ Look at the note at **ground**. تربة

IDM **charge, cost, pay, etc. (sb) the earth** (*informal*) to charge, etc. a very large amount of money (يكلّف) مبالغ طائلة

how, why, where, who, etc. on earth/in the world (*informal*) (used for emphasizing sth or expressing surprise): *Where on earth have you been?* بحقّ السماء (أين كنت!)

earth² /ɜːθ/ (*especially US* **ground**) *verb* [T] to make a piece of electrical equipment safer by connecting it to the ground with a wire: *Make sure the plug is earthed.* يؤرّض ، يصل سلكاً بالأرض

▸ **earth** *noun* [C, usually sing.] (*especially Brit*) (*US* **ground**) a wire that makes a piece of electrical equipment safer by connecting it to the ground: *The green and yellow wire is the earth.* موصل أرضي، الأرضي

earthly /ˈɜːθli/ *adj* **1** connected with this world, not heaven: *The monks gave up all their earthly possessions.* دنيوي ، ماديّ

2 (often in questions or negatives) possible: *What earthly use is a gardening book to me? I haven't got a garden!* ممكن

earthquake /ˈɜːθkweɪk/ (*also informal* **quake**) *noun* [C] a sudden violent movement of the earth's surface زلزال

earthworm /ˈɜːθwɜːm/ *noun* [C] a common type of worm that lives in the soil دودة التراب

🔑 **ease¹** /iːz/ *noun* [U] a lack of difficulty: *She answered the questions with ease.* ○ *The ease with which he won the match amazed the spectators.* ➲ Look at **easy**. سهولة ، يُسْر

IDM **(be/feel) at (your) ease** to be/feel comfortable, relaxed, etc: *They were all so kind and friendly that I felt completely at ease.* (يشعر) بالارتياح وعدم الارتباك

🔑 **ease²** /iːz/ *verb* **1** [I,T] to become or make sth less painful or severe: *The pain should ease by this evening.* ○ *What can I take to ease this headache?* ○ *This money will ease their financial problems a little.* ○ *The tension has eased.* يخفّ أو يخفّف (الألم مثلاً)

2 [T] to cause sth to move slowly and gently: *He eased the key into the lock.* يحرّك شيئاً ببطء وعناية بالغة

IDM **ease sb's mind** to make sb feel less worried: *The doctor tried to ease her mind about her son's illness.* يطمئن

PHRV **ease off** to become less severe: *Let's wait until the rain eases off.* يخفّ

ease up to work less hard: *Ease up a bit or you'll make yourself ill!* يخفّف من عمله

easel /ˈiːzl/ *noun* [C] a wooden frame that holds a blackboard or a picture that is being painted حامل السبّورة أو لوحة الرسّام

easily *adv* → EASY¹

🔑 **east** /iːst/ *noun* [sing.] (*abbr* **E**) **1** (*also* **the east**) one of the four main points of the compass; the direction you look towards in order to see the sun rise: *Which way is east?* ○ *a cold wind from the east* ○ *Which county is to the east of Oxfordshire?* شرق ، الشرق

2 the east; **the East** the part of any country, city, etc. that lies further to the east than the other parts: *Norwich is in the East of England.* شرق ، الشرق

s so z zoo ʃ she ʒ vision h how m man n no ŋ sing l leg r red j yes w wet

a b c d e f g h i j k l m n o p q r s t u v w x y z

3 the East the countries of Asia, e.g. China, Japan ➲ Look at **Far East** and **Middle East**. الشرق ، بلاد المشرق

▸ **east** (*also* **East**) *adj* in or towards the east, or from the east: *the East Coast of America* ○ *an east wind* ○ *East London* شرقيّ

east *adv* to or towards the east: *They headed east.* ○ *We live east of the city.* شرقاً ، شرق (المدينة)

easterly /ˈiːstəli/ *adj* **1** to, towards or in the east: *They travelled in an easterly direction.* شرقيّ ، متّجه نحو الشرق

2 (used about winds) coming from the east: *cold easterly winds* (ريح) شرقيّة

eastward /ˈiːstwəd/ *adj* towards the east: *to travel in an eastward direction* متّجه نحو الشرق

eastward (*also* **eastwards**) *adv* towards the east: *The Amazon flows eastwards.* شرقاً ، نحو الشرق

eastbound /ˈiːstbaʊnd/ *adj* travelling or leading towards the east: *The eastbound carriageway of the motorway is blocked.* متّجه أو مؤدٍّ إلى الشرق

Easter /ˈiːstə(r)/ *noun* [U] the Sunday in March or April when Christians celebrate Christ's return to life عيد الفِصح

ˈ**Easter egg** *noun* [C] an egg, usually made of chocolate, that you give as a present at Easter بيضة الفصح (من الشوكولاتة عادة)

🔑 **eastern** (*also* **Eastern**) /ˈiːstən/ *adj* (*abbr* **E**) **1** of, in or from the east of a place: *Eastern Scotland* ○ *the eastern shore of the lake* شرقيّ

2 from or connected with the countries of the East: *Eastern cookery* (= that comes from Asia) شرقيّ أو آسيويّ

eastward *adj, adv* → EAST

🔑 **easy**[1] /ˈiːzi/ *adj* (**easier**; **easiest**) **1** not difficult: *an easy question* ○ *It isn't easy to explain the system.* ○ *The system isn't easy to explain.* سهل ، هيّن

2 without any pain, trouble or worry: *an easy life* ○ *My mind's easier now.* ➲ Look at **ease**. مرتاح ، مطمئن

IDM **free and easy** → FREE[1]

I'm easy (*informal*) I don't mind; whichever you prefer: *'Would you like to go first or second?' 'I'm easy.'* لا فرق عندي ، كما تريد

▸ **easily** *adv* **1** without difficulty: *I can easily ring up and check the time.* بسهولة

2 without doubt: *It's easily his best novel.* دون شكّ

easiness *noun* [U] سهولة ، يُسْر ؛ راحة

easy[2] /ˈiːzi/ *adv* (**easier**; **easiest**)

IDM **easier said than done** more difficult to do than to talk about: *'You should get her to help you.' 'That's easier said than done.'* الكلام أسهل من الفعل

go easy (*informal*) to work less hard: *My doctor advised me to go easy until I'm fully recovered.* يخفّف من عمله

go easy on/with sb/sth (*informal*) **1** to be gentle or less strict with sb: *Go easy on him; he's just a child.* يتساهل مع ، يعامل برفق

2 to avoid using too much of sth: *Go easy with the salt; it's bad for your heart.* يتجنّب الاكثار من ، يخفّف

take it/things easy to relax and not work too hard or worry too much يستريح ، يقلّل من مشاغله

ˌ**easy ˈchair** *noun* [C] a large comfortable chair with arms مقعد منجّد ذو ظهر ومسندَيْن

ˌ**easy-ˈgoing** *adj* (used about a person) calm, relaxed and not easily worried: *Her parents are very easy-going. They let her do what she wants.* هادئ النفس ؛ متساهل

🔑 **eat** /iːt/ *verb* (*pt* **ate** /et; *US* eɪt/; *pp* **eaten** /ˈiːtn/) **1** [I,T] to put food into your mouth, then chew and swallow it: *Have you eaten all the biscuits?* ○ *Eat your dinner up, Joe* (= Finish it all). ○ *She doesn't eat properly. No wonder she's so thin.* يأكل

2 [I] to have a meal: *What time shall we eat?* يتناول الطعام

IDM **have your cake and eat it** → CAKE

PHR V **eat sth away/eat away at sth** to damage or destroy sth gradually: *The sea had eaten away at the cliff.* يحتّ، يأكل

eat out to have a meal in a restaurant: *Would you like to eat out tonight?* يأكل في مطعم

▸ **eater** *noun* [C] a person who eats in a particular way: *My uncle's a big eater* (= he eats a lot). أكِل

eau de cologne /ˌəʊ də kəˈləʊn/ (*also* **cologne**) *noun* [U] a type of perfume that is not very strong عطر خفيف ، كولونيا

eaves /iːvz/ *noun* [plural] the edges of a roof that come out beyond the walls: *There's a bird's nest under the eaves.* افريز ، طنف

eavesdrop /ˈiːvzdrɒp/ *verb* [I] (eavesdro**pp**ing; eavesdro**pp**ed) to listen secretly to other people talking: *They caught her eavesdropping on their conversation.* يسترق السمع

ebb /eb/ *verb* [I] **1** (used about the tides of the sea) to go out ينحسر (الماء)

2 (used about a feeling, etc.) to become weaker: *The crowd's enthusiasm began to ebb.* يتضاءل ، يضعف

▸ **ebb** *noun* [sing.] **the ebb** the time when the tide is flowing away from the land جَزْر

IDM **the ebb and flow (of sth)** (used about a situation, noise, feeling, etc.) a regular increase and decrease in the progress or strength of sth مدّ وجزر ، تقدُّم وتراجع

ebony /ˈebəni/ *noun* [U] a hard black wood خشب الأبنوس

ˈ**e-book** *noun* [C] a book that is displayed on a computer screen or on an electronic device that is held in the hand, instead of being printed on paper كتاب رقمي أو إلكتروني

eccentric /ɪkˈsentrɪk/ *adj* (used about people or their behaviour) strange or unusual: *People said he was mad but I think he was just slightly eccentric.* شاذّ ، غريب الأطوار

▸ **eccentric** *noun* [C] an eccentric person: *She is quite an eccentric.* شخص غريب الأطوار

eccentricity /ˌeksen'trɪsəti/ *noun* [C,U] (*pl.* **eccentricities**) شذوذ ، غرابة الأطوار

ecclesiastical /ɪˌkli:zi'æstɪkl/ *adj* connected with the Christian Church: *ecclesiastical law* كَنَسي

echo /'ekəʊ/ *noun* [C] (*pl.* **echoes**) a sound that is repeated as it is sent back off a surface such as the wall of a cave: *'Is anybody there?' she shouted. '...ere,' came back the echo.* صدى

▸ **echo** *verb* **1** [I] (used about a sound) to be repeated; to come back as an echo: *Their footsteps echoed in the empty church.* يصدي ، يردّد الصدى

2 [T] **echo sth (back)** to repeat or send back a sound: *The tunnel echoed back their calls.* ○ (*figurative*) *The child echoed everything his mother said.* يردّد ، يكرّر

3 [I] **echo (to/with sth)** (used about places) to be full of a particular sound: *The valley echoed with their laughter.* يدوّي بـ ، يملأ أرجاء المكان

eclair /ɪ'kleə(r)/ *noun* [C] a type of long thin cake, usually filled with cream and covered with chocolate فطيرة مليئة بالقشدة

eclipse /ɪ'klɪps/ *noun* [C] **1** an occasion when the moon passes between the earth and the sun or the earth's shadow falls on the moon, cutting off all or some of the light: *a total/partial eclipse of the sun* كسوف ؛ خسوف

2 the loss of a person's importance, success, etc. أفول ، ضياع المجد

▸ **eclipse** *verb* [T] **1** (used about the moon, etc.) to cause an eclipse of the sun, etc. يكسف ؛ يخسف

2 (used about a person) to make another person seem less interesting, important, etc. يبز ، يفوق

eco-friendly /'i:kəʊ frendli/ *adj* not harmful to the environment: *eco-friendly products/fuel* غير ضارّ بالبيئة

ecology /i'kɒlədʒi/ *noun* [U] the relations between living things and their surroundings; the study of this subject علم البيئة

▸ **ecological** /ˌi:kə'lɒdʒɪkl/ *adj*: *an ecological disaster* ○ *The Green Party has tried to make people aware of ecological issues.* بيئي

ecologically /-kli/ *adv* بيئياً ، فيما يتعلّق بالبيئة

ecologist /i'kɒlədʒɪst/ *noun* [C] a expert in ecology عالم البيئة

⚷ **economic** /ˌi:kə'nɒmɪk; ˌekə-/ *adj* **1** (only *before* a noun) connected with the supply of money, trade, industry, etc: *the government's economic policy* ○ *The country faces growing economic problems.* اقتصاديّ

2 producing a profit: *The mine was closed because it was not economic.* ➲ Look at **economical**. It has a different meaning. مربح

▸ **economically** /-kli/ *adv*: *The country was economically very underdeveloped.* اقتصادياً

economical /ˌi:kə'nɒmɪkl; ˌekə-/ *adj* costing less time, money, fuel, etc.; using sth carefully: *an economical car to run* ➲ Look at **economic**. It has a different meaning. مقتصد ، مدبّر ؛ رخيص

▸ **economically** /-kli/ *adv*: *The train service could be run more economically.* بتوفير ، باقتصاد

economics /ˌi:kə'nɒmɪks; ˌekə-/ *noun* [U] the study or principles of the way money, trade and industry are organized: *a degree in economics* ○ *the economics of a company* علم الاقتصاد

economist /ɪ'kɒnəmɪst/ *noun* [C] an expert in economics عالِم اقتصاديّ

economize (*also* **economise**) /ɪ'kɒnəmaɪz/ *verb* [I] **economize (on sth)** to save money, time, resources, etc.; to use less of sth يقتصد ، يوفّر

⚷ **economy** /ɪ'kɒnəmi/ *noun* (*pl.* **economies**) **1** [C] (*also* **the economy**) the operation of a country's money supply, trade and industry: *The economy of the country is based on agriculture.* ○ *There are signs of improvement in the economy.* ○ *the economies of America and Japan* اقتصاد

2 [C,U] careful spending of money, time, resources, etc.; trying to save, not waste sth: *Our department is making economies in the amount of paper it uses.* ○ *For reasons of economy, please turn off all unnecessary lights.* ○ *economy class* (= the cheapest class of air travel) اقتصاد ، توفير

ecstasy /'ekstəsi/ *noun* [C,U] (*pl.* **ecstasies**) a feeling or state of great happiness: *to be in ecstasy* ○ *She went into ecstasies about the ring he had bought her.* نشوة ، شدّة الفرح

▸ **ecstatic** /ɪk'stætɪk/ *adj* extremely happy نشوان ، في غاية الفرح

ecumenical /ˌi:kju:'menɪkl; ˌekju:-/ *adj* connected with the idea of uniting all the different parts of the Christian Church مسكونيّ ، عالمي

eczema /'eksɪmə; *US* ɪg'zi:mə/ *noun* [U] a disease which makes the skin red and itchy اكزيما ، مرض النَملة

ed. (*also* **Ed.**) *abbrev* = EDITED BY; EDITION; EDITOR

eddy /'edi/ *noun* [C] (*pl.* **eddies**) a circular movement of water, wind, dust, etc. دوّامة ، دردور

⚷ **edge**[1] /edʒ/ *noun* [C] **1** the place where sth, especially a surface, ends; the limit: *the edge of a table* ○ *The leaves were brown and curling at the edges.* ○ *I stood at the water's edge.* ○ *to fall off the edge of a cliff* حافّة ، حرف

2 the sharp cutting part of a knife, etc. حدّ

IDM **an/the edge on/over sb/sth** a slight advantage over sb/sth: *She knew she had the edge over the other candidates.* ميزة ، أفضلية

(be) on edge to be nervous, excited or quick to lose your temper: *I'm a bit on edge because I get my exam results today.* ➲ Look at **edgy**. It has a similar meaning. متوتّر الأعصاب ، "منرفز"

edge[2] /edʒ/ *verb* **1** [T] (usually passive) **edge sth (with sth)** to arrange sth along the edge of sth else: *The cloth was edged with lace.* يجعل له حافّة أو حاشية

2 [I,T] **edge (sth/your way) across, along, away, back, etc.** to move slowly and carefully across, etc: *The burglar edged his way along the roof.* ○ *We edged closer to get a better view.* ○ *She*

edged her chair up to the window.
يقترب أو يبتعد تدريجياً : يحرك شيئاً ببطء وعناية

edgeways /ˈedʒweɪz/ (*also* **edgewise** /ˈedʒwaɪz/) *adv*
IDM **get a word in edgeways** → WORD

edgy /ˈedʒi/ *adj* (**edgier**; **edgiest**) (*informal*) nervous, worried or quick to become upset: *You seem very edgy. What's bothering you?*
متوتّر الأعصاب ، مضطرب

edible /ˈedəbl/ *adj* good or safe to eat: *Are these mushrooms edible?* ❶ The opposite is **inedible**.
صالح للأكل

edifice /ˈedɪfɪs/ *noun* [C] (*formal*) a large impressive building بناء ضخم ، صرح

edit /ˈedɪt/ *verb* [T] **1** to prepare a piece of writing to be published, making sure that it is correct, the right length, etc. يحقّق ويعدّ نصّاً للنشر
2 to prepare a film, television or radio programme by arranging filmed or recorded material in a particular order يحرّر أو يعدّ فيلماً
3 to be in charge of a newspaper, magazine, etc. يحرر (جريدة مثلاً)
4 (*computing*) to make changes to text or data on screen ينقّح

⚷**edition** /ɪˈdɪʃn/ *noun* [C] **1** the form in which a book is published: *a paperback/hardback edition* نسخة
2 one of a series of television or radio programmes: *And now for this week's edition of 'Panorama'...* حلقة
3 the number of copies of a book, etc. that are printed at the same time: *the morning edition of a newspaper* طبعة

⚷**editor** /ˈedɪtə(r)/ *noun* [C] **1** a person whose job is to prepare a book, television or radio programme محرّر ؛ منقّح
2 the person who is in charge of a newspaper or part of a newspaper: *the financial editor* ○ *Who is the editor of 'The Times'?* محرّر

editorial /ˌedɪˈtɔːriəl/ *noun* [C] an article in a newspaper, usually written by the editor, giving an opinion on an important subject
المقال الافتتاحي

⚷**educate** /ˈedʒukeɪt/ *verb* [T] to teach or train sb, especially in school: *Young people should be educated to care for their environment.* ○ *All their children were educated at private schools.*
يثقّف ، يعلّم
▸ **educated** *adj* having learnt a lot of things to a high standard: *a highly educated woman*
مثقّف ، متعلّم

⚷**education** /ˌedʒuˈkeɪʃn/ *noun* [C, usually sing., U] the teaching or training of people, especially in schools, etc. to improve their knowledge and develop their skills: *primary, secondary, higher, adult education* ○ *She received an excellent education.* تعليم ، تربية
▸ **educational** /-ʃənl/ *adj* connected with or providing education: *an educational toy, visit, experience, etc.* تعليمي ، تربوي

eel /iːl/ *noun* [C] a long fish that looks like a snake أنقليس ، ثعبان السمك

eerie /ˈɪəri/ *adj* strange and frightening
موحش ، مفزع
▸ **eerily** *adv* بشكل غريب مفزع
eeriness *noun* [U] وحشة ، جو غريب مفزع

⚷**effect** /ɪˈfekt/ *noun* **1** [C,U] **(an) effect (on sb/sth)** a change that is caused by sth; a result: *the effects of acid rain on the lakes and forests* ○ *His words had a strong effect on me.* ○ *Her shouting had little or no effect on him.* ➲ Look at **after-effect** and **side effect**. أثر ، تأثير ، نتيجة
2 [C,U] the impression that a speaker, book, film, etc. gives: *How does the artist create the effect of moonlight?* ○ *He likes to say things just for effect* (= to impress people). وقع ، انطباع
3 effects (*formal*) your personal possessions
أمتعة أو ممتلكات شخصية
IDM **come into effect** (used especially about laws or rules) to begin to be used; to come into operation (قانون) يسري مفعوله
in effect 1 in fact; for all practical purposes: *Though they haven't made an official announcement, she is, in effect, the new director.*
في الواقع ، عملياً
2 (used about a rule, a law, etc.) in operation; in use: *The new rules will be in effect from next season.* ساري المفعول
take effect 1 (used about a drug, etc.) to begin to work; to produce the desired result: *The anaesthetic took effect immediately.*
(دواء) يحدث مفعولاً : يعطي النتيجة المطلوبة
2 (used about a law, etc.) to come into operation: *The ceasefire takes effect from midnight.*
يصبح نافذ المفعول
to this/that effect with this/that meaning: *I told him to leave her alone, or words to that effect.* بهذا المعنى ، بما معناه
▸ **effect** *verb* [T] (*formal*) to cause sth to happen; to have sth as a result: *to effect a change* ➲ Look at **affect**. It has a different meaning.
يُحدث ، يحقّق

⚷**effective** /ɪˈfektɪv/ *adj* **1** producing the result that you want: *Scientists are looking for an effective way to reduce energy consumption.* ○ *a medicine that is effective against the common cold* ❶ The opposite is **ineffective**. مؤثّر ، فعّال
2 making a pleasing impression: *That picture would look more effective on a dark background.* ذو تأثير حسن ، أخّاذ
3 real or actual, although perhaps not official: *The soldiers gained effective control of the town.* فعلي ، حقيقي
▸ **effectively** *adv* **1** in a effective way: *She dealt with the situation effectively.*
بشكل فعّال ، بنجاح
2 in effect; for practical purposes: *It meant that, effectively, they had lost.* في الواقع
effectiveness *noun* [U] فعالية ، نجاح

effeminate /ɪˈfemɪnət/ *adj* (used about a man or his behaviour) like a woman مخنّث

⚷**efficient** /ɪˈfɪʃnt/ *adj* able to work well without

making mistakes or wasting time and energy: *Our secretary is very efficient.* ○ *You must find a more efficient way of organizing your time.* ❶ The opposite is **inefficient**. كفء ، قدير : فعّال
▸ **efficiency** /ɪ'fɪʃnsi/ *noun* [U] فعّالية : كفاءة : قدرة
efficiently *adv* بكفاءة : بِمردود حسن

effluent /'efluənt/ *noun* [U] liquid waste, especially chemicals produced by factories المياه والنفايات القذرة

effort /'efət/ *noun* **1** [U] the use of strength or energy: *They have put a lot of effort into their studies this summer.* ○ *He made no effort to contact his parents.* جهد ، مجهود
2 [C] something that is done with difficulty or the use of energy: *It was a real effort to stay awake in the lecture.* عناء
▸ **effortless** /'efətləs/ *adj* (apparently) needing little or no effort سهل
effortlessly *adv* بسهولة ، دون عناء

EFL /ˌiː ef 'el/ *abbrev* English as a Foreign Language الانكليزية كلغة أجنبية

e.g. /ˌiː 'dʒiː/ *abbrev* for example مثال

egalitarian /iˌgælɪ'teəriən/ *adj* (used about a person, system, society, etc.) following the principle that everyone should have equal rights مؤمن بالمساواة

egg[1] /eg/ *noun* **1** [C] an oval object with a hard shell that contains a young bird, reptile or insect ❶ A female bird **lays** her eggs and then **sits on** them until they **hatch**. بيضة
2 [C,U] an egg from a hen, etc., used as food: *Would you like an egg for breakfast?* ❶ Eggs may be **boiled**, **fried**, **poached** (cooked in water without their shells) or **scrambled**. بيضة
3 [C] the small seed in a female animal that can join with a male seed (a sperm) to make a baby بويضة
IDM **put all your eggs in one basket** to risk everything by depending completely on one thing, plan, etc. يجازف بكل شيء

egg[2] /eg/ *verb*
PHRV **egg sb on (to do sth)** to encourage sb to do sth (bad or dangerous) يحثّ

eggcup /'egkʌp/ *noun* [C] a small cup for holding a boiled egg قدح للبيضة المسلوقة

eggplant /'egplɑːnt; *US* -plænt/ *noun* [C,U] (*especially US*) = AUBERGINE

eggshell /'egʃel/ *noun* [C,U] the hard outside part of an egg قشرة البيضة

ego /'iːgəʊ; *Brit also* 'egəʊ/ *noun* [C] (*pl.* **egos**) the (good) opinion that you have of yourself: *It was a blow to her ego when she lost her job.* الاعتزاز بالنفس : الذات

egocentric /ˌiːgəʊ'sentrɪk; *Brit also* ˌeg-/ *adj* interested only in yourself; selfish مهتمّ بنفسه فقط : أناني

egoism /'iːgəʊɪzəm; *Brit also* 'eg-/ *noun* [U] thinking about yourself too much; selfishness حبّ الذات : أنانية
▸ **egoist** /-ɪst/ *noun* [C] a person who thinks about himself/herself too much; a selfish person المحب لذاته : الأناني
egoistic /-'ɪstɪk/ *adj* مركز على ذاته ، مهتم بنفسه فقط

eh /eɪ/ *interj* (*informal*) **1** (used for asking sb to agree with you): *'Good party, eh?'* "مش كده" ، "موهيك"؟
2 (used for asking sb to repeat sth): *'Did you like the film?' 'Eh?' 'I asked if you liked the film!'* تستعمل لحثّ المستمع على الإجابة

Eid (*also* **Id**) /iːd/ *noun* [C] any of several Muslim festivals, especially the one that celebrates the end of the fast of Ramadan العيد

eiderdown /'aɪdədaʊn/ *noun* [C] a covering for a bed filled with soft feathers (down), usually used on top of blankets ➲ Look at **duvet**. لحاف محشو بالزغب

eight /eɪt/ *number* 8; one more than seven ❶ For examples of how to use numbers in sentences, look at **six**. ثمانية
▸ **eight-** (in compounds) having eight of sth: *an eight-sided coin* ذو ثمانية (أضلاع مثلاً)
eighth /eɪtθ/ *pron, det, adv* 8th; next after seventh ثامن
eighth *noun* [C] the fraction ⅛; one of eight equal parts of sth ➲ Look at the examples at **sixth**. ثُمن

eighteen /ˌeɪ'tiːn/ *number* 18; one more than seventeen ❶ For examples of how to use numbers in sentences, look at **six**. ثمانية عشر
▸ **eighteenth** /ˌeɪ'tiːnθ/ *pron, det, adv* 18th; next after seventeenth ➲ Look at the examples at **sixth**. ثامن عشر

eighty /'eɪti/ *number* 80; one more than seventy-nine ❶ For examples of how to use numbers in sentences, look at **sixty**. ثمانون
▸ **eightieth** /'eɪtiəθ/ *pron, det, adv* 80th, next after seventy- ninth ➲ Look at the examples at **sixth**. الثمانون

either /'aɪðə(r); 'iːðər/ *det, pron* **1** one or the other of two; it does not matter which: *There's cake or ice cream. You can have either.* ○ *You can ask either of us for advice.* ○ *Either of us is willing to help.* أيّ (منهما)
2 both: *It is a pleasant road, with trees on either side.* كِلا
▸ **either** *conj* **either ... or ...** (used when you are giving a choice, usually of two things): *You can have the car in either black or blue.* ○ *Either you leave or I do.* ○ *You can either write or phone.* إمّا هذا أو ذاك
either *adv* **1** (used after two negative statements) also: *I don't like Pat and I don't like Nick much either.* ○ *'I can't remember his name.' 'I can't either.'* ❶ We can also say **neither can I**. ولا..
2 (used for emphasizing a negative statement): *The restaurant is quite good. And it's not expensive either.* كما أنّه ليس

eject /i'dʒekt/ *verb* **1** [T] (often passive) to push or send sb/sth out of a place (usually with force): *The protesters were ejected from the building.* يطرد

2 [I] to make an emergency exit from an aeroplane ينقذف من الطائرة

eke /iːk/ *verb*
IDM **eke out a living** to manage to live with very little money يسدّ رمقه ، يدبّر معيشته
PHRV **eke sth out** to make a small amount of sth last longer يقتصد

elaborate /ɪˈlæbərət/ *adj* very complicated; done or made very carefully: *elaborate plans* معقّد : مفصّل ، متقن
▸ **elaborate** /ɪˈlæbəreɪt/ *verb* [I] **elaborate (on sth)** (*formal*) to give details about sth يفصّل ، يتوسّع

elapse /ɪˈlæps/ *verb* [I] (*formal*) (used about time) to pass يمضي ، ينقضي

elastic /ɪˈlæstɪk/ *noun* [U] material with rubber in it which can stretch مطّاط
▸ **elastic** *adj* **1** (used about material, etc.) able to return to its original size after being stretched مطّاطي : مَرِن

2 (*figurative*) able to be changed; not fixed: *Our rules are quite elastic.* مَرِن

eˌlastic ˈband *noun* [C] = RUBBER BAND

elated /iˈleɪtɪd/ *adj* (*formal*) very happy and excited مبتهج ، جذِل ، نشوان
▸ **elation** /iˈleɪʃn/ *noun* [U] ابتهاج ، جذَل

elbow /ˈelbəʊ/ *noun* [C] **1** the joint where the arm bends in the middle مرفق ، كوع

2 the part of the sleeve of a coat, jacket, etc. that covers the elbow مرفق كُمّ الجاكيت وغيره
▸ **elbow** *verb* [T] to push with the elbows: *She elbowed me out of the way to get to the food first.* يشقّ طريقه بمرفقيه

ˈelbow room *noun* [U] enough space to move freely متّسع كافٍ للحركة

elder /ˈeldə(r)/ *adj* (only *before* a noun) older (of two members of a family): *My elder daughter is at university now but the other one is still at school.* أكبرهما سنّاً
▸ **elder** *noun* **1** [sing.] the older of two people: *Who is the elder of the two?* الأكبر سنّاً

2 **my, etc. elder** [sing.] (*formal*) a person who is older than me, etc: *He is her elder by several years.* الأكبر سنّاً

3 **elders** [plural] older people: *Do children still respect the opinions of their elders?* المسِنّون

elderly /ˈeldəli/ *adj* (used about a person) old
ⓘ This is a polite way of saying 'old'. You can use **the elderly** to refer to old people in general: *The elderly need special care in winter.* كبير السنّ

eldest /ˈeldɪst/ *adj, noun* [C] oldest (of three or more members of a family): *Their eldest child is a boy.* ○ *John's got 4 boys. The eldest has just gone to university.* الأكبر ، البكر

elect /ɪˈlekt/ *verb* [T] **1** **elect sb (to sth)**; **elect sb (as sth)** to choose a Member of Parliament, President, representative, etc. by voting: *He was elected to Parliament in 1970.* ○ *The committee elected her as their representative.* ينتخب

2 **elect to do sth** (*formal*) to decide to do sth يقرّر ، يختار

election /ɪˈlekʃn/ *noun* [C,U] (the time of) choosing a Member of Parliament, President, etc. by voting: *In America, presidential elections are held every four years.* ○ *I will not be standing for election again.* ○ *election results* انتخاب ، الانتخابات

In Britain, **general elections** are held about every five years. Sometimes **by-elections** are held at other times. In each region (**constituency**) voters must choose one from a list of **candidates**.

elector /ɪˈlektə(r)/ *noun* [C] a person who has the right to vote in an election ⓘ **Voter** is a more common word. الناخِب أو المنتخِب
▸ **electoral** /ɪˈlektərəl/ *adj*: *the electoral register/roll* (= the list of electors in an area) انتخابيّ
electorate /ɪˈlektərət/ *noun* [C, with sing. or pl. verb] all the people who can vote in a region, country, etc. الناخبون

electric /ɪˈlektrɪk/ *adj* **1** producing or using electricity: *an electric current* ○ *an electric kettle* كهربائي

2 (*figurative*) very emotional: *The atmosphere in the room was electric.* مكهرَب ، مشحون بالانفعال

electrical /ɪˈlektrɪkl/ *adj* of or about electricity: *an electrical fault* ○ *an electrical appliance* (= a machine that uses electricity) ○ *an electrical engineer* (= a person who produces electrical systems and equipment) كهربائيّ

the eˌlectric ˈchair *noun* [sing.] a chair used for putting criminals to death with a very strong electric current الكرسيّ الكهربائيّ

electrician /ɪˌlekˈtrɪʃn/ *noun* [C] a person whose job is to install and repair electrical systems and equipment عامل كهربائيّ

electricity /ɪˌlekˈtrɪsəti/ *noun* [U] a type of energy that provides heat, light and power to work machines, etc: *Turn that light off. We don't want to waste electricity.* الكهرباء

Electricity is usually **generated** in **power stations**. It may also be produced by **generators** or by **batteries**.

eˌlectric ˈrazor = SHAVER

eˌlectric ˈshock (*also* **shock**) *noun* [C] the effect on the body when an electric current goes through it: *That light switch isn't safe. I got a shock when I touched it.* صدمة كهربائية

electrify /ɪˈlektrɪfaɪ/ *verb* [T] (*pres part* **electrifying**; *3rd pers sing pres* **electrifies**; *pt, pp* **electrified**) **1** to supply sth with electricity: *The railways are being electrified as quickly as possible.* يكهرب ، يشحن بالكهرباء

2 (*figurative*) to make sb excited يثير

electrocute /ɪˈlektrəkjuːt/ *verb* [T] (usually

passive) to kill sb with an electric current that passes through the body: *Don't touch that wire! You'll electrocute yourself.* يصعق أو يقتل بالكهرباء
▸ **electrocution** /ɪˌlektrəˈkjuːʃn/ *noun* [U] الإعدام بالصدمة الكهربائية

electrode /ɪˈlektrəʊd/ *noun* [C] one of two points (terminals) where an electric current enters or leaves a battery, etc. قطب كهربائي

electronic /ɪˌlekˈtrɒnɪk/ *adj* using electronics: *electronic equipment* ○ *Some dictionaries are available in electronic form* (= on a computer disk). إلكتروني
▸ **electronically** /-kli/ *adv* إلكترونياً

ˌelectronic ˈmail = EMAIL

electronics /ɪˌlekˈtrɒnɪks/ *noun* [U] the technology of using silicon chips, etc. to produce computers, radios, etc: *the electronics industry* علم الإلكترونيات

elegant /ˈelɪgənt/ *adj* showing style or good design: *She looked very elegant in her new dress.* ○ *an elegant coat* أنيق
▸ **elegance** /ˈelɪgəns/ *noun* [U] أناقة
elegantly *adv* بأناقة

element /ˈelɪmənt/ *noun* **1** [C] one important part of sth: *Cost is an important element when we're thinking about holidays.* عامل

2 [C, usually sing.] **an element of sth** a small amount of sth: *There was an element of truth in what he said.* شيء من

3 [C] people of a certain type: *The criminal element at football matches causes a lot of trouble.* عنصر

4 [C] one of the basic substances e.g. water, oxygen, gold, etc. عنصر

5 [C] the part of a kettle, an electric heater, etc. that produces heat سلك التسخين (في مدفأة كهربائية مثلاً)

6 the elements [plural] (*formal*) (bad) weather: *exposed to the elements* العوامل الجويّة القاسية

IDM in/out of your element in a situation where you feel comfortable/uncomfortable في (أو خارج) جوّه الملائم

elementary /ˌelɪˈmentri/ *adj* **1** at or in the beginning stages: *an elementary course in English* ○ *a book for elementary students* ابتدائي ، أوّلي

2 basic; not difficult: *elementary physics* أساسيّ ، بسيط

eleˈmentary school *noun* [C] (*US*) a school for children aged six to eleven مدرسة ابتدائية

elephant /ˈelɪfənt/ *noun* [C] a very large grey animal with two long curved teeth (tusks) and a long nose (a trunk) فيل

elevate /ˈelɪveɪt/ *verb* [T] (*formal*) to raise sb/sth to a higher place or position: *an elevated railway* ○ *He was elevated to the Board of Directors.* يرفع ؛ يرقّي
▸ **elevating** *adj* (*formal*) improving the mind; educating: *an elevating book* تثقيفي

elevation /ˌelɪˈveɪʃn/ *noun* **1** [C,U] (*formal*) elevating or being elevated رفع ؛ ترقية

2 [C] the height of a place (above sea level): *The city is at an elevation of 2 000 metres.* ارتفاع

elevator /ˈelɪveɪtə(r)/ *noun* [C] (*US*) = LIFT

eleven /ɪˈlevn/ *number* 11, one more than ten
❶ For examples of how to use numbers in sentences, look at **six**. أحد عشر
▸ **eleventh** /ɪˈlevnθ/ *pron, det, adv* 11th, next after tenth ➲ Look at the examples at **sixth**. الحادي عشر

elf /elf/ *noun* [C] (*pl.* **elves** /elvz/) (in stories) a small creature with pointed ears who has magic powers عفريت صغير

elicit /iˈlɪsɪt/ *verb* [T] **elicit sth (from sb)** (*formal*) to get information, facts, a reaction, etc. from sb يستخلص منه ؛ يحصل على

eligible /ˈelɪdʒəbl/ *adj* **eligible (for sth/to do sth)** having the right qualifications for sth; suitable: *In Britain, you are eligible to vote when you are eighteen.* ○ *an eligible young man* (= a man who might be a suitable husband) مؤهل لِ ؛ صالح

eliminate /ɪˈlɪmɪneɪt/ *verb* [T] **1** to remove sb/sth that is not wanted or needed: *We must try and eliminate the problem.* يزيل ؛ يتخلّص من

2 (often passive) to stop sb going further in a competition, etc: *The school team was eliminated in the first round of the competition.* يُخرِج من مباراة
▸ **elimination** /ɪˌlɪmɪˈneɪʃn/ *noun* [U] قضاء على ، إزالة ؛ إخراج

elite /eɪˈliːt/ *noun* [C, with sing. or pl. verb] a social group that is thought to be the best or most important because of its power, money, intelligence, etc: *the ruling elite* ○ *an intellectual elite* ○ *an elite group* النخبة ، الصفوة
▸ **elitism** /eɪˈliːtɪzəm/ *noun* [U] the belief that elites should be treated in a special way الإيمان بامتياز النخبة
elitist /-tɪst/ *noun* [C], *adj* مفضّل لِ أو مقتصر على الصفوة

elk /elk/ (*pl.* **elk** or **elks**) (*US* **moose**) *noun* [C] a very large deer with large flat horns (antlers) أيّل كبير

elm /elm/ (*also* **ˈelm tree**) *noun* [C] a tall tree with broad leaves شجرة الدردار

elocution /ˌeləˈkjuːʃn/ *noun* [U] the art of speaking clearly (especially in public) فنّ الإلقاء

elongated /ˈiːlɒŋgeɪtɪd; *US* ɪˈlɔːŋ-/ *adj* long and thin طويل ، مطوّل ، ممدود

elope /ɪˈləʊp/ *verb* [I] **elope (with sb)** to run away secretly to get married يفرّ مع حبيب للزواج

eloquent /ˈeləkwənt/ *adj* (*formal*) able to use language and express your opinions well, especially when you speak in public بليغ ، فصيح
▸ **eloquence** /ˈeləkwəns/ *noun* [U] بلاغة ، فصاحة
eloquently *adv* ببلاغة ، بفصاحة

else /els/ *adv* (used after words formed with *any-*, *no-*, *some-* and after question words) **1** in addition: *What else would you like?* ○ *Does anybody* *else* (= any other person) *know about this?* (شيء أو شخص) آخر

2 different: *There's nothing on the television. Let's find something else to do.* ○ *This isn't mine. It must be somebody else's* (= belong to another person). ○ *You'll have to pay. Nobody else* (= no other person) *will.* آخر

3 apart from: *Everybody else* (= everybody apart from me) *is allowed to stay up late.* آخر : الآخرون

IDM or else otherwise; if not: *You'd better go to bed now or else you'll be tired in the morning.* ○ *He's either forgotten or else he's decided not to come.* وإلاّ ؛ وإمّا

elsewhere /ˌelsˈweə(r); *US* -ˈhweər/ *adv* (*formal*) in or to another place: *If she doesn't like it here, she can go elsewhere.* ○ *He's travelled a lot – in Europe and elsewhere.* في أو إلى مكان آخر

ELT /ˌiː el ˈtiː/ *abbrev* English Language Teaching (to non-native speakers) تعليم اللغة الانكليزية

elude /iˈluːd/ *verb* [T] (*formal*) **1** to escape (from sb/sth) (sometimes by using a trick) يتهرّب من ؛ يهرب من

2 to be difficult or impossible to remember: *I remember his face but his name eludes me.* يمتنع على ، يراوغ

elusive /iˈluːsɪv/ *adj* not easy to find, catch or remember (سهل) ممتنع ؛ مراوغ

elves *pl.* of ELF

'em /əm/ *pron* (*informal*) = THEM

emaciated /ɪˈmeɪʃieɪtɪd/ *adj* (used about a person) thin and weak because of illness, lack of food, etc. هزيل

▸ **emaciation** /ɪˌmeɪsiˈeɪʃn/ *noun* [U] هزال

email (*also* **e-mail**) /ˈiːmeɪl/ (*also* **electronic mail**; **mail**) *noun* [U] sending information using a computer التراسل بواسطة الكمبيوتر، بريد الكتروني

▸ **email** *verb* [I, T]: *I'll email the information to you.* يرسل بالبريد الالكتروني

emancipate /ɪˈmænsɪpeɪt/ *verb* [T] to give sb the same legal, social and political rights as other people يحرّر

▸ **emancipation** /ɪˌmænsɪˈpeɪʃn/ *noun* [U] تحرير (المرأة)

embankment /ɪmˈbæŋkmənt/ *noun* [C] a thick wall of earth, stone, etc. that is built to stop a river overflowing or to carry a road or railway جدار أو طريق بمحاذاة نهر

embargo /ɪmˈbɑːɡəʊ/ *noun* [C] (*pl.* **embargoes**) an official order to stop trade with another country: *to impose an oil embargo* ○ *to lift/remove the embargo on the trade in oil* حظر أو حصار اقتصاديّ

embark /ɪmˈbɑːk/ *verb* [I] to get on a ship: *Passengers with cars must embark first.* ❶ The opposite is **disembark**. يصعد إلى سفينة

PHRV embark on sth (*formal*) to start sth (new): *I'm embarking on a completely new career.* يشرع في ؛ يخوض في

▸ **embarkation** /ˌembɑːˈkeɪʃn/ *noun* [C,U] الصعود إلى السفينة

embarrass /ɪmˈbærəs/ *verb* [T] to make sb feel ashamed or uncomfortable: *She was very embarrassed when her child behaved badly in public.* ○ *He felt really embarrassed to be seen in odd socks.* ○ *The Minister's mistake embarrassed the government.* يُحرج ، يُخجل

▸ **embarrassing** *adj* محرج ، مُخجِل

embarrassingly *adv* بصورة محرجة

embarrassment *noun* **1** [U] the feeling you have when you are embarrassed حرج ، إحراج

2 [C] a person or thing that makes you embarrassed مدعاة للإحراج

embassy /ˈembəsi/ *noun* [C] (*pl.* **embassies**) (the official building of) a group of people (diplomats) headed by an ambassador, who are sent to live in a foreign country and represent their government there ➲ Look at **consulate**. سفارة

embed /ɪmˈbed/ *verb* [T] (embe**dd**ing; embe**dd**ed) (usually passive) to fix sth firmly and deeply (in sth else): *The axe was embedded in the piece of wood.* يغرز فيه بإحكام

embezzle /ɪmˈbezl/ *verb* [T] to steal money, etc. that you are responsible for (e.g. in a firm or organization) يختلس

emblem /ˈembləm/ *noun* [C] an object or symbol that represents sth: *The dove is the emblem of peace.* شعار ، رمز

embody /ɪmˈbɒdi/ *verb* [T] (*pres part* **embodying**; *3rd pers sing pres* **embodies**; *pp, pt* **embodied**) (*formal*) **1** to be a very good example of sth: *To me she embodies all the best qualities of a teacher.* يجسِّد ، يمثِّل

2 to include or contain sth: *This latest model embodies many new features.* يحتوي على

embrace /ɪmˈbreɪs/ *verb* **1** [I,T] to take sb into your arms as a sign of love or affection يعانق ، يحتضن

2 [T] (*formal*) to include: *His report embraced all the main points.* يتضمَّن ، يشمل

3 [T] (*formal*) to accept sth eagerly: *She embraced Christianity in her later years.* يعتنق

▸ **embrace** *noun* [C] the act of embracing(1) عناق ، ضمّة إلى الصدر

embroider /ɪmˈbrɔɪdə(r)/ *verb* **1** [I,T] to decorate cloth by sewing with small stitches: *She embroidered flowers on the cushion in gold thread.* يطرِّز

2 [T] to add untrue details to a story, etc. to make it more interesting يبهِّر أو ينمِّق (القصّة)

▸ **embroidery** *noun* [U] decorative sewing with small stitches; something that has been embroidered(1) تطريز

embryo /ˈembriəʊ/ *noun* [C] (*pl.* **embryos** /-əʊz/) an animal or a plant in the early stages of development before birth ➲ Look at **foetus**. جنين

▸ **embryonic** /ˌembriˈɒnɪk/ *adj* جنينيّ ؛ في المرحلة الأولى

emerald /ˈemərəld/ *noun* [C] a bright green precious stone زمرد

▸ **emerald** (*also* ˌ**emerald** ˈ**green**) *adj* bright green زمرّدي

emerge /iˈmɜːdʒ/ *verb* [I] **emerge (from sth)** **1** to appear or come from somewhere (unexpectedly): *A man emerged from the shadows.* ○ (*figurative*) *to emerge strengthened from a difficult experience* يبرز فجأة ، يظهر ؛ يخرج من
2 to become known: *During investigations it emerged that she was lying about her age.* يتّضح ، يتكشّف
▸ **emergence** /-dʒəns/ *noun* [U] ظهور ، انبثاق ، نشوء
emergent /-dʒənt/ *adj* ناشئ، نام

emergency /iˈmɜːdʒənsi/ *noun* [C,U] (*pl.* **emergencies**) a serious event that needs immediate action: *In an emergency phone 999 for help.* ○ *The government has declared a state of emergency.* ○ *an emergency exit* طارئ : حالة طوارئ

eˈmergency room *noun* [C] (*abbr* **ER**) (*US*) = ACCIDENT AND EMERGENCY

emigrate /ˈemɪɡreɪt/ *verb* [I] to leave your own country to go and live in another: *They emigrated to Australia twenty years ago.* يهاجر
▸ **emigrant** /ˈemɪɡrənt/ *noun* [C] a person who has gone to live in another country مهاجر، نازح
emigration /ˌemɪˈɡreɪʃn/ *noun* [C,U] هجرة ، نزوح
➲ Look at **immigrant** and **immigration**.

eminent /ˈemɪnənt/ *adj* (*formal*) (used about a person) famous and important: *an eminent scientist* بارز ، شهير

eminently /ˈemɪnəntli/ *adv* obviously; very: *She is eminently suitable for the job.* بصورة واضحة ، للغاية

emit /iˈmɪt/ *verb* [T] (emi**tt**ing; emi**tt**ed) (*formal*) to send out sth (a smell, a sound, smoke, heat, light, etc.) يصدر ، يطلق
▸ **emission** /iˈmɪʃn/ *noun* [C,U]: *controls on sulphur dioxide emissions from power stations* غاز منطلق ؛ إطلاق

emo /ˈiːməʊ/ *noun* (**pl. emos**) **1** [U] a style of rock music that developed from punk, but has more complicated musical arrangements and deals with more emotional subjects نوع عاطفي من موسيقى الروك
2 [C] a person who likes emo music and often follows emo fashion, wearing tight jeans and having long black hair. Emos are typically supposed to be emotional and sensitive. من هواة موسيقى وأزياء الإيمو

emoticon /ɪˈməʊtɪkɒn/ *noun* [C] (*computing*) a short set of keyboard symbols that represents the expression on sb's face, used in email, etc. to show the feelings of the person sending the message. For example :-) represents a smiling face (when you look at it sideways). رموز (كمبيوتر)

emotion /ɪˈməʊʃn/ *noun* **1** [C] a strong feeling such as love, anger, fear, jealousy, etc. عاطفة
2 [U] strength of feeling: *His voice was filled with emotion.* انفعال
▸ **emotional** /-ʃənl/ *adj* **1** connected with the emotions: *emotional problems* عاطفيّ
2 causing strong feelings: *He gave an emotional speech* مثير للعواطف
3 having strong emotions and showing them openly: *She always gets very emotional when I leave.* ○ *He's a very emotional sort of person.* عاطفيّ ، سريع الانفعال
emotionally /-ʃənəli/ *adv* عاطفياً

emotive /iˈməʊtɪv/ *adj* causing strong emotions: *emotive language* ○ *an emotive issue* انفعاليّ ، مثير للعواطف

empathy /ˈempəθi/ *noun* [U] the ability to imagine how another person is feeling and so understand his/her mood مشاركة وجدانيّة ، تعاطف

emperor /ˈempərə(r)/ (*feminine* **empress**) *noun* [C] the ruler of an empire إمبراطور

emphasis /ˈemfəsɪs/ *noun* [C,U] (*pl.* **emphases** /-siːz/) **1** the force that you give to a word or phrase when you are speaking to show that it is important توكيد
2 emphasis (on sth) (giving) special importance or attention (to sth): *There's a lot of emphasis on science at our school.* ○ *We should really put a greater emphasis on getting our facts right.* (يعطي) أهميّة خاصة

emphasize (*also* **emphasise**) /ˈemfəsaɪz/ *verb* [T] **emphasize (that...)** to put emphasis on sth; stress: *They emphasized that healthy eating is important.* ○ *They emphasized the importance of healthy eating.* يؤكّد ، يشدّد

emphatic /ɪmˈfætɪk/ *adj* having or using emphasis: *an emphatic refusal* مشدّد ، مؤكّد ؛ باتّ
▸ **emphatically** /-kli/ *adv* بلهجة جازمة ؛ مؤكّداً

empire /ˈempaɪə(r)/ *noun* [C] **1** a group of countries that is governed by one country: *the Roman Empire* ➲ Look at **emperor** and **empress**. إمبراطوريّة
2 a group of companies that is controlled by one parent company إمبراطورية (من الشركات)

empirical /ɪmˈpɪrɪkl/ *adj* (*formal*) based on observation and practical experience, not on theory: *empirical evidence* تجريبيّ ، مبنيّ على التجربة

employ /ɪmˈplɔɪ/ *verb* [T] **1 employ sb (in/on sth)**; **employ sb (as sth)** to pay sb to work for you: *He is employed in a chocolate factory.* ○ *She is employed as a lorry driver.* ○ *They employ 600 workers.* ➲ Look at **unemployed**. يوظّف ، يشغّل
2 employ sb/sth (in/on) sth (*formal*) to use: *We must employ all our expertise in solving this problem.* يستخدم
▸ **employee** /ɪmˈplɔɪiː/ *noun* [C] a person who works for sb: *The factory has 500 employees.* موظّف ، مستخدم
employer *noun* [C] a person or company that employs other people: *The car factory is a large employer in this town.* ربّ العمل ؛ موظّف
employment *noun* [U] **1** the state of having a paid job: *She is in/out of employment.* ○ *This bank can give employment to ten extra staff.* ○ *It is difficult to find employment in the north of the country.* ➲ Look at **unemployment** and at the note at **work**[1]. عمل ، شغل ، وظيفة
2 (*formal*) the use of sth: *the employment of force* استخدام

emˈployment agency *noun* [C] a business that helps people to find work وكالة استخدام (لإيجاد وظائف)

empower /ɪmˈpaʊə(r)/ *verb* [T] (usually passive) (*formal*) to give sb power or authority (to do sth) يخوّل ، يمنح سلطة

empress /ˈemprəs/ *noun* [C] **1** a woman who rules an empire إمبراطورة

2 the wife or widow of an emperor إمبراطورة

empty[1] /ˈempti/ *adj* **1** having nothing or nobody inside it: *an empty box* ○ *The bus was half empty.* ○ *That house has been empty for months.* فارغ ، خالٍ

2 without meaning or value: *It was an empty threat* (= it was not meant seriously). ○ *My life feels empty now the children have left home.* فارغ ، لا معنى له

▸ **emptiness** /ˈemptinəs/ *noun* [U] فراغ ، خلاء

empty[2] /ˈempti/ *verb* (*pres part* **emptying**; *3rd pers sing pres* **empties**; *pt, pp* **emptied**) **1** [T] **empty sth (out)** to make sth empty: *'Where can I empty my cup?' 'Oh, empty it into the sink.'* ○ *Empty your pockets out, please.* يفرغ

2 [T] **empty sth (out) (into/onto sth)** to take sth from a container and put it somewhere else: *Empty that milk into the sink. It's gone sour.* ○ *The boy emptied out all his toys onto the floor.* يفرغ في أو على

3 [I] to become empty: *The cinema emptied very quickly once the film was finished.* يفرَغ ، يخلو

ˌempty-ˈhanded *adj* bringing or taking nothing: *She went out to buy a new dress but returned empty-handed.* صفر اليدين

emulate /ˈemjuleɪt/ *verb* [T] (*formal*) to try to do sth as well as, or better than, sb ❶ A less formal word is **copy**. يتشبّه بِ ؛ يضاهي ، يحاكي

enable /ɪˈneɪbl/ *verb* [T] **enable sb/sth to do sth** to make sb/sth able to do sth (by giving him/her/it power, authority, etc.): *The new law has enabled more women to return to work.* يمكّن ؛ يخوّل

enamel /ɪˈnæml/ *noun* [U] **1** a hard, shiny substance used for protecting or decorating metal, etc: *enamel paint* ميناء (لطلي المعادن)

2 the hard white outer covering of a tooth ميناء الأسنان

enc. (*also* **encl.**) *abbrev* = ENCLOSED

enchanted /ɪnˈtʃɑːntɪd; *US* -ˈtʃænt-/ *adj* **1** pleased or delighted: *The audience was enchanted by her singing.* مفتون ؛ مسرور جداً

2 under a magic spell: *an enchanted forest* مسحور

enchanting /ɪnˈtʃɑːntɪŋ; *US* -ˈtʃænt-/ *adj* very nice or pleasant; delightful فاتن ، أخّاذ ، جذّاب

encircle /ɪnˈsɜːkl/ *verb* [T] (*formal*) to make a circle round sth; to surround: *London is encircled by the M25 motorway.* يطوّق ، يحيط بِ

enclose /ɪnˈkləʊz/ *verb* [T] **1 enclose sth (in/with sth)** to surround sth with a wall, fence, etc: *The garden is enclosed by a high hedge.* ○ *He gets very nervous in enclosed spaces.* يسوّر ؛ يحصر

2 to put sth in an envelope, parcel, etc: *Can I enclose a letter with this parcel?* يرفق طيّ رسالة

enclosure /ɪnˈkləʊʒə(r)/ *noun* [C] **1** a piece of land that is enclosed by a wall, fence, etc. فناء مسيّج

2 something that is enclosed in an envelope, parcel, etc. المرفق داخل رسالة

encode /ɪnˈkəʊd/ *verb* [T] to put or write sth in code يرمّز

encore /ˈɒŋkɔː(r)/ *interj* (called out by an audience that wants the performers in a play, concert, etc. to perform sth extra) زِدْنا طرباً! ، أعِد!

▸ **encore** *noun* [C] (a call for) an extra performance at the end of a play, concert, etc. استعادة الأداء (في المسرح)

encounter /ɪnˈkaʊntə(r)/ *verb* [T] **1** (*formal*) to meet sb unexpectedly يصادف ، يلتقي بِ

2 to experience sth (a danger, difficulty, etc.): *I've never encountered any discrimination at work.* ❶ **Meet with** is used as a synonym for encounter in this sense. يواجه

▸ **encounter** *noun* [C] an unexpected (often unpleasant) meeting مجابهة

encourage /ɪnˈkʌrɪdʒ/ *verb* [T] **1 encourage sb/sth (in sth/to do sth)** to give hope, support or confidence to sb: *The teacher encouraged her students to ask questions.* ○ *His friends encouraged him in his attempt to stop smoking.* يشجّع

> The opposite is **discourage**. Note that we say **discourage sb from doing sth**: *The teacher discouraged her students from asking questions.*

2 to make sth happen more easily: *The government wants to encourage new businesses.* يساعد

▸ **encouragement** *noun* [C,U] تشجيع ؛ مساعدة

encouraging *adj* مشجع

encroach /ɪnˈkrəʊtʃ/ *verb* [I] (*formal*) **encroach (on/upon sth)** to take away part of sth or use more of sth than is right: *I do hope that I am not encroaching too much upon your free time.* يتعدّى على ، يتجاوز

encyclopedia (*also* **encyclopaedia**) /ɪnˌsaɪkləˈpiːdiə/ *noun* [C] (*pl.* **encyclopedias**) a book or set of books that gives information about very many subjects, arranged in alphabetical order (i.e. from A to Z) موسوعة

end[1] /end/ *noun* [C] **1** the furthest or last part of sth; the place or time where sth stops: *the end of a road, room, line, piece of string, etc.* ○ *Join the end of the queue.* ○ *My house is at the end of the street.* ○ *The man on the other end of the phone spoke so quietly that I didn't catch his name.* ○ *There are some seats at the far end of the room.* ○ *I'm going on holiday at the end of October.* ○ *He promised to give me an answer by the end of the week.* ○ *She couldn't wait to hear the end of the story.* ➲ Look at the noun **finish**. It is used to mean **end** only in connection with races and competitions. ❶ **End** is sometimes used before another noun: *the end house* ○ *the end seat* نهاية ، آخر

2 a little piece of sth that is left after the rest has been used: *a cigarette end* عُقْب

3 (*formal*) an aim or purpose: *They were prepared to do anything to achieve their ends.* غاية ، هدف

IDM **at an end** (*formal*) finished or used up: *Her career is at an end.* ينتهي

at the end of your tether having no more patience or strength عيل صبره ، طفح الكيل

at a loose end → LOOSE

at your wits' end → WIT

bring sth/come/draw to an end (to cause sth) to finish: *His stay in England was coming to an end and he was thinking about going home again.* ينتهي ؛ ينهي ، يختم

a dead end → DEAD

end to end in a line with the ends touching: *They put the tables end to end.* طرفاً ملاصقاً لطرف ، متلاصقَيْن

get (hold of) the wrong end of the stick → WRONG[1]

in the end at last; finally: *He wanted to get home early but in the end it was midnight before he left.* في النهاية

> The idiom **in the end** refers to time and means 'finally'. **At the end of sth** refers to the last part of a book, film, class, etc., at the point where it is about to finish: *At the end of the meal we had a row about who should pay for it.*

make ends meet to have enough money for your needs: *It's hard for us to make ends meet.* يقتصد حتى لا يتجاوز إمكاناته

a means to an end → MEANS[1]

no end of sth (*informal*) very many or much; a lot of sth: *She has given us no end of trouble.* كثير من ، مقدار لا حدّ له

odds and ends → ODDS

on end (used about time) continuously: *He sits and reads for hours on end.* بلا انقطاع

put an end to sth to stop sth from happening any more يضع حداً لـ

end² /end/ *verb* [I,T] **end (in/with sth)** (to cause sth) to finish: *The road ends here.* ○ *How does this story end?* ○ *The match ended in a draw.* ○ *Most adverbs in English end in -ly.* ○ *I think we'd better end this conversation now.* ينتهي ؛ ينهي

PHRV **end up (as sth)**; **end up (doing sth)** to find yourself in a place/situation that you did not intend or expect: *We got lost and ended up in the centre of town.* ○ *She had always wanted to be a writer but ended up as a teacher.* ○ *There was nothing to eat at home so we ended up going out for fish and chips.* يجد نفسه في ، يؤول مصيره

endanger /ɪn'deɪndʒə(r)/ *verb* [T] to cause danger to sb/sth: *Smoking endangers your health.* يعرِّض للخطر

▸ **endangered** *adj* (used about animals, plants, etc.) in danger of disappearing from the world (becoming extinct): *The panda is an endangered species.* معرَّض للانقراض

endear /ɪn'dɪə(r)/ *verb* [T] **endear sb/yourself to sb** (*formal*) to make sb/yourself liked by sb: *She managed to endear herself to everybody by her kindness.* يحبِّب بـ

▸ **endearing** *adj* محبَّب ، محبِّب

endearingly *adv* بشكل محبَّب ، بصورة تستدرّ العطف

endeavour (*US* **endeavor**) /ɪn'devə(r)/ *verb* [I] (*formal*) **endeavour (to do sth)** to try: *She endeavoured to make the best of a very difficult situation.* يسعى ، يحاول جاهداً

▸ **endeavour** *noun* [C,U] (*formal*) مسعى ، محاولة

endemic /en'demɪk/ *adj* regularly found in a particular country or area, or among a particular group of people: *Malaria is endemic in/to many hot countries.* مستوطِن

ending /'endɪŋ/ *noun* [C] **1** the end (of a story, play, film, etc.): *That film made me cry but I was pleased that it had a happy ending.* نهاية ، خاتمة

2 (*grammar*) the last part of a word, which can change: *When nouns end in -ch or -sh or -x, the plural ending is -es not -s.* نهاية الكلمة

endive /'endaɪv/ *noun* [C,U] (*US*) = CHICORY

endless /'endləs/ *adj* **1** very large in size or amount and seeming to have no end: *The possibilities are endless.* لا حدّ له

2 lasting for a long time and seeming to have no end: *Our plane was delayed for hours and the wait seemed endless.* مستمرّ ، لا نهاية له

▸ **endlessly** *adv* دون توقُّف ؛ دون نهاية

endorse /ɪn'dɔːs/ *verb* [T] **1** to give (official) support or agreement to a plan, statement, decision, etc. يصادق على

2 (*Brit*) to write a note in a driving licence to say that the driver has broken the law يسجِّل عليه مخالفة في شهادة السواقة

▸ **endorsement** *noun* [C,U] تصديق على ؛ مخالفة مرور

'end product *noun* [C] the final product of a manufacturing process or an activity الحصيلة ، المنتوج النهائيّ

endure /ɪn'djʊə(r); *US* -'dʊər/ *verb* (*formal*) **1** [T] to suffer sth painful or uncomfortable: *She endured ten years of loneliness.* ❶ **Endure** is often used in the negative: *My parents can't endure pop music.* In this sense **can't bear** or **can't stand** are less formal. يتحمل ، يعاني

2 [I] to last; continue يدوم ، يستمر

▸ **endurance** /ɪn'djʊərəns; *US* -'dʊə-/ *noun* [U] the ability to endure(1): *You need endurance to play a four-hour match.* جَلَد ، قوة التحمُّل

,end-'user *noun* [C] a person who actually uses a product rather than one who makes or sells it, especially a person who uses a product connected with computers: *Programs are tailored to meet the needs of end-users and their own business environments.* ○ *an end-user application* المستهلك

enemy /'enəmi/ *noun* (*pl.* **enemies**) **1** [C] a person who hates and tries to harm sb/sth: *It's strange that people who used to be friends can become bitter enemies.* ○ *He has made several enemies since his arrival in the school.* ❶ The noun is **enmity**. عدوّ

2 the enemy [with sing. or pl. verb] the army or country that your country is fighting against:

a b c d e f g h i j k l m n o p q r s t u v w x y z

The enemy is/are attacking at daybreak. ○ *enemy forces* العدوّ ، قوات العدوّ

energetic /ˌenəˈdʒetɪk/ *adj* full of or needing energy(1): *Jogging is a very energetic form of exercise.* نشيط ، ذو طاقة حيويّة : متطلِّب طاقة
▸ **energetically** /-kli/ *adv* بهمة ونشاط

energy /ˈenədʒi/ *noun* (*pl.* **energies**) **1** [U] the ability to be very active or do a lot of work without getting tired: *Children are usually full of energy.* ○ *This flu has left me with no energy at all.* طاقة ، قوّة ، نشاط

2 energies [plural] the effort and attention which you give to doing sth: *She devoted all her energies to charity work.* طاقة، طاقات

3 [U] the power that comes from coal, electricity, gas, etc. that is used for driving machines, etc: *nuclear energy* طاقة

enforce /ɪnˈfɔːs/ *verb* [T] **1** to make sure that laws, etc. are obeyed: *How will they enforce the new law?* ينفِّذ القانون

2 to force sth to be done or to happen: *Enforcing discipline by using threats is not often successful.* يفرض (على) ، يطبِّق بالقوة
▸ **enforcement** *noun* [U] تنفيذ (القانون): فرض

engage /ɪnˈgeɪdʒ/ *verb* [T] **1** to occupy sb's thoughts, time, interest, etc: *You need to engage the students' attention right from the start.* يشغل

2 to give work to sb: *They engaged him as a cook.* يشغِّل ، يستخدم

3 to make parts of a machine fit together: *Engage the clutch before selecting a gear.* يُعشِّق (المسنَّنات مثلاً)

PHR V **engage in sth** to take part in sth: *I don't engage in that kind of gossip!* يشترك في ، يشغل وقته

engaged /ɪnˈgeɪdʒd/ *adj* **1 engaged (to sb)** having agreed to get married: *We've just got engaged.* ○ *Susan is engaged to Jim.* مخطوب

2 (*US* **busy**) (used about a telephone) in use: *That line/number is engaged.* ○ *the engaged tone* مشغول

3 (used about a toilet, etc.) in use مشغول

4 engaged (in/on sth) (used about a person) busy doing sth: *They are engaged in talks with the Irish government.* مرتبط، مشغول، منهمك في

engagement /ɪnˈgeɪdʒmənt/ *noun* [C] **1** an agreement to get married; the time when you are engaged: *Their engagement was announced in the paper.* ○ *Their engagement only lasted for six months.* ○ *He broke off their engagement.* خطوبة

2 (*formal*) an arrangement to go somewhere or do sth at a fixed time; an appointment: *a lunch engagement* موعد ، ارتباط

enˈgagement ring *noun* [C] a ring, usually with precious stones in it, that a man gives to a woman on their engagement(1) خاتم الخطوبة

engine /ˈendʒɪn/ *noun* [C] **1** the part of a machine that changes energy (from oil, electricity, etc.) into movement: *This engine runs on diesel.* ○ *a car engine* ○ *a jet engine* ➲ Look at the note at **motor**. محرِّك

2 (*also* **locomotive**) a machine that pulls a railway train قاطرة

engineer¹ /ˌendʒɪˈnɪə(r)/ *noun* [C] **1** a person whose job is to design, build or repair engines, machines, roads, bridges, railways, mines, etc: *a civil, chemical, electrical, mechanical, etc. engineer* مهندس

2 (*US*) a person whose job is to drive a railway engine سائق القطار
▸ **engineering** *noun* [U] (the study of) the work that is done by an engineer: *mechanical engineering* ○ *a degree in engineering* هندسة

engineer² /ˌendʒɪˈnɪə(r)/ *verb* [T] (*formal*) to arrange for sth to happen by careful (secret) planning: *Her promotion was engineered by her father.* يدبِّر أمراً ، يخطِّط ل

English /ˈɪŋglɪʃ/ *noun* **1** [U] the language that is spoken in Britain and the USA and in some other countries: *Do you speak English?* ○ *I've been learning English for 5 years.* ○ *I don't know what 'cadeau' is in English.* اللغة الإنكليزيّة/الإنجليزية

2 the English [with pl. verb] the people of England الإنكليز
▸ **English** *adj* belonging to England, the English people, the English language, etc: *English history* ○ *the English countryside* إنكليزي

> Be careful. The people of Scotland (the Scots) and of Wales (the Welsh) are **British** not English. Look at the note at **United Kingdom**.

ˌEnglish ˈbreakfast *noun* [C] a breakfast that consists of cereals, cooked bacon and eggs, toast and marmalade and tea or coffee, etc. ➲ Look at **continental breakfast**. فطور إنكليزي

Englishman /ˈɪŋglɪʃmən/ *noun* [C] (*pl.* **Englishmen**), **Englishwoman** /ˈɪŋglɪʃwʊmən/ *noun* [C] (*pl.* **Englishwomen**) a person who comes from England or whose parents are English ℹ We normally say: *'I'm English'* not *'I'm an Englishman/-woman.'* رجل إنكليزيّ ؛ امرأة إنكليزية

ˌEnglish ˈmuffin *noun* [C] (*US*) = MUFFIN (1)

engrave /ɪnˈgreɪv/ *verb* [T] **engrave B on A/engrave A with B** to cut patterns or words on metal, stone, etc: *His name is engraved on the cup.* ○ *The cup is engraved with his name.* ينقش ، يحفر على
▸ **engraving** *noun* [C] a picture that is printed from an engraved metal plate صورة مطبوعة عن لوح معدنيّ منقوش

engrossed /ɪnˈgrəʊst/ *adj* **engrossed (in sth)** very interested in sth so that you forget other things: *She was completely engrossed in the play on television.* مستغرق ، منهمك في

enhance /ɪnˈhɑːns; *US* -ˈhæns/ *verb* [T] (*formal*) to improve sth or to make sth look better يزيد من قيمته أو جماله

enigma /ɪˈnɪgmə/ *noun* [C] (*pl.* **enigmas**) a person, thing or situation that is difficult to understand لغز ، شيء غامض

▸ **enigmatic** /ˌenɪɡˈmætɪk/ *adj*
غامض ، محيِّر ، مبهم

⚷ **enjoy** /ɪnˈdʒɔɪ/ *verb* [T] **1 enjoy sth/enjoy doing sth** to get pleasure from: *I really enjoyed that meal – thank you very much.* ○ *Do you enjoy your work?* ○ *He enjoys listening to music while he's driving.* يتمتّع أو يستمتع بِـ

2 enjoy yourself to be happy; to have a good time: *I enjoyed myself at Sue's party last night – did you?* يسرّ ، يقضي وقتاً ممتعاً

▸ **enjoyable** /-əbl/ *adj* giving pleasure: *We spent an enjoyable few days in Scotland.* ممتع ، سارّ

enjoyment *noun* [C,U] pleasure or a thing which gives pleasure: *She gets a lot of enjoyment from travelling.* متعة ، سرور

enlarge /ɪnˈlɑːdʒ/ *verb* [I,T] (to cause sth) to become larger: *I'm going to have this photo enlarged.* يكبر؛ يكبِّر

PHR V **enlarge on sth** to say or write more about sth يتوسع في

▸ **enlargement** *noun* [C,U] making sth larger or sth that has been made larger: *an enlargement of a photo* تكبير ؛ صورة مكبَّرة

enlighten /ɪnˈlaɪtn/ *verb* [T] (*formal*) to give sb more information about sth so that he/she knows the truth يزيده علماً ، ينوِّر

enlist /ɪnˈlɪst/ *verb* **1** [I,T] to join the army, navy or air force; to make sb a member of the army, etc: *They enlisted as soon as war was declared.* ينخرط (في الجيش مثلاً) ، يتجنّد ؛ يجنّد

2 [T] to get help, support, etc: *We need to enlist the support of everybody who works here.* يستعين بِـ ، يطلب العون

enmity /ˈenməti/ *noun* [U] the feeling of hatred towards an enemy عداء ، بغضاء

enormity /ɪˈnɔːməti/ *noun* [sing.] (*formal*) the extent or seriousness of sth; how bad sth is جسامة ، فداحة ، ضخامة

⚷ **enormous** /ɪˈnɔːməs/ *adj* very large or very great: *an enormous building* ○ *enormous pleasure* ○ *There is an enormous amount of work involved in this.* ضخم ، هائل

▸ **enormously** *adv* إلى حدّ كبير ، للغاية

⚷ **enough**[1] /ɪˈnʌf/ *det, pron* **1** as much or as many of sth as necessary: *We've saved enough money to buy a computer.* ○ *Not everybody can have a book – there aren't enough.* ○ *Are there enough chairs?* ○ *If enough of you are interested, we'll arrange a trip to the theatre.* مقدار أو عدد كاف

2 as much or as many as you want: *I've had enough of living in a town* (= I don't want to live in a town any more). ○ *Don't give me any more work. I've got quite enough already.* ما فيه الكفاية

⚷ **enough**[2] /ɪˈnʌf/ *adv* (used *after* verbs, adjectives and adverbs) **1** to the necessary degree; sufficiently: *You don't practise enough.* ○ *He's not old enough to travel alone.* ○ *Does she speak Italian well enough to get the job?* إلى حدّ كافٍ

2 quite, but not very: *She plays well enough, for a beginner.* لا بأس به ، إلى حدّ معقول

IDM **fair enough** → FAIR[2]

funnily, strangely, etc. enough it is funny, etc. that...: *Funnily enough, I thought exactly the same myself.* مما يثير (الضحك أو الدهشة...الخ)

sure enough → SURE

enquire (*also* **inquire**) /ɪnˈkwaɪə(r)/ *verb* (*formal*) [I,T] to ask for information about sth: *We must enquire whether it is possible to get a bus on a Sunday.* ○ *Could you enquire when the trains to Cork leave?* ○ *We need to enquire about hotels in Vienna.* ○ *'Do they take travellers' cheques here?' 'I don't know. I'll enquire.'* يستعلم ، يسأل

PHR V **enquire after sb** to ask about sb's health يستفسر

enquire into sth to study or investigate sth to find out all the facts: *The journalist enquired into the politician's financial affairs.* يستقصي ، يتحرى

▸ **enquirer** (*also* **inquirer**) *noun* [C] a person who enquires المستعلِم ، السائل ، المستقصي

enquiring (*also* **inquiring**) *adj* **1** interested in learning new things: *We should encourage children to have an enquiring mind.* مستطلع ، محبّ للاستطلاع

2 asking for information: *an enquiring look* مستطلِع ، مستفهم

enquiringly (*also* **inquiringly**) *adv* كأنه يسأل سؤالاً : مستفهماً

⚷ **enquiry** (*also* **inquiry**) /ɪnˈkwaɪəri; *US* ˈɪnkwəri/ *noun* (*pl.* **enquiries**) **1** [C] **enquiry (about/concerning sb/sth)** (*formal*) a question that you ask about sth: *I have made some enquiries into English language courses in Oxford.* استفسار ، سؤال

2 [U] the act of asking about sth: *After weeks of enquiry he finally found what he was looking for.* استعلام ، بحث

3 [C] **enquiry (into sth)** an official investigation to find out the cause of sth: *After the accident there were many calls for an enquiry into safety procedures.* تحقيق ، تحرٍّ

enrage /ɪnˈreɪdʒ/ *verb* [T] to make sb very angry يغضب

enrich /ɪnˈrɪtʃ/ *verb* [T] **1** to make sb/sth rich or richer يغْني ، يزيده غنى

2 to improve the quality, flavour, etc. of sth: *These cornflakes are enriched with vitamins/are vitamin-enriched.* يحسّن قيمته (الغذائية مثلاً) ، يغْني

enrol (*US* **enroll**) /ɪnˈrəʊl/ *verb* [I,T] (enrolling; enrolled) **enrol (sb) (in/as sth)** to become or to make sb a member of a club, school, etc: *I've enrolled in my local swimming class.* ○ *They enrolled 100 new students last year.* يتسجّل ؛ يسجّل

▸ **enrolment** (*US* **enrollment**) *noun* [U]: *Enrolment for the course will take place next week.* تسجيل

en route /ˌɒ̃n ˈruːt/ *adv* **en route (from...) (to...); en route (for...)** on the way: *The car broke down when we were en route for Dover.* في الطريق إلى

ensue /ɪnˈsjuː; *US* -ˈsuː/ *verb* [I] (*formal*) to happen after (and often as a result of) sth else ينجم عن ، يتلو

en suite /ɒ̃ swiːt/ *adv, adj* (used about rooms)

a b c d e f g h i j k l m n o p q r s t u v w x y z

forming one unit: *The bedroom has a bathroom en suite.* ○ *an en-suite bathroom* ملحقاً به

ensure (*US* **insure**) /ɪn'ʃʊə(r); -ʃɔ:(r); *US* ɪn-'ʃʊər/ *verb* [T] to make sth certain to happen: *Please ensure that the door is locked before you leave.* يتأكّد ، يتحقّق من

entail /ɪn'teɪl/ *verb* [T] (*formal*) to make sth necessary; to involve: *This is going to entail a lot of hard work.* ○ *The job sounds interesting but I'm not sure what it entails.* يتطلّب ، يستلزم

entangled /ɪn'tæŋgld/ *adj* caught in sth else: *The bird was entangled in the net.* ○ (*figurative*) *I've got myself entangled in some financial problems.* يتشبّك في: يتورّط

enter /'entə(r)/ *verb* **1** [I,T] (*formal*) to come or go into a place: *Don't enter without knocking.* ○ *They all stood up when he entered the room.* ○ (*figurative*) *We have just entered a new phase in international relations.* ❶ Note that **enter** is used without a preposition. **Come into** and **go into** are much more common. ➲ Look at **entrance**, **entrant** and **entry**. يدخل

2 [I,T] **enter (for) sth** to put your name on the list for an exam, race, competition, etc: *I entered that competition in the Sunday paper and I won £20!* يتسجّل ، يدرج أسمه

3 [T] **enter sth (in/into/on/onto sth)** to put names, numbers, details, etc. in a list, book, computer, etc: *Please enter your name in the book.* ○ *I've entered all the data onto the computer.* يسجّل ، يدون

4 [T] to become a member of a school, a college, a profession, an institution, etc: *She entered politics in 1960.* ينخرط في ، يدخل

PHRV **enter into sth 1** to start to think or talk about sth: *I don't want to enter into details now.* يدخل (في التفاصيل) ، يطرق (موضوعاً)

2 to be part of sth: *This is a business matter. Friendship doesn't enter into it.* يدخل ضمن

enter into sth (with sb) to begin sth: *The government has entered into negotiations with the unions.* يبدأ

enterprise /'entəpraɪz/ *noun* **1** [C] something (e.g. a plan or a project) that is new and difficult: *It's a very exciting new enterprise.* مشروع جديد جريء

2 [U] the courage that you need to start such an enterprise: *We need men and women of enterprise and energy.* جرأة ، مبادرة

3 [C,U] a business; the way business is organized: *a new industrial enterprise* ○ *This government supports private enterprise.* مؤسّسة تجاريّة صغيرة : إدارة الأعمال

▸ **enterprising** *adj* having enterprise(2) ❶ The opposite is **unenterprising**. جريء (في المشاريع التجاريّة) : مغامر

entertain /,entə'teɪn/ *verb* **1** [T] to interest and amuse sb: *He entertained us with jokes all evening.* ○ *I find it very hard to keep my class entertained on a Friday afternoon.* يسلّي

2 [I,T] to welcome sb as a guest; to give sb food and drink: *They entertain a lot./They do a lot of entertaining.* يستضيف

▸ **entertainer** *noun* [C] a person who entertains (1) as a job ممثّل هزليّ أو مغنٍ لتسلية الجمهور

entertaining *adj* interesting and amusing مسلٍ ، ممتع

entertainment /,entə'teɪnmənt/ *noun* [C,U] things to do that interest and amuse people: *There isn't much entertainment for young people in this town.* ○ *Entertainments Guide* (= a list in a newspaper of the cinema, theatre, concert, etc. programmes) تسلية ، لهو

enthral (*US* **enthrall**) /ɪn'θrɔ:l/ *verb* [T] (enthralling; enthralled) to hold sb's interest and attention completely: *He was enthralled by her story.* يسحر ، يفتن ، يخلب لبّه

▸ **enthralling** *adj* ساحر ، أخّاذ

enthusiasm /ɪn'θju:ziæzəm; *US* -'θu:-/ *noun* [U] **enthusiasm (for/about sb/sth)** a strong feeling of eagerness or interest: *Jan showed great enthusiasm for the new project.* ○ *There wasn't much enthusiasm when I mentioned the trip to the museum.* حماس

▸ **enthusiast** /ɪn'θju:ziæst; *US* -'θu:-/ a person who is very interested in an activity or subject: *She is a jazz enthusiast.* هاوٍ ، مهتمّ بِ

enthusiastic /ɪn,θju:zi'æstɪk; *US* -θu:-/ *adj* full of enthusiasm متحمّس

enthusiastically /-kli/ *adv* بحماس

entice /ɪn'taɪs/ *verb* [T] to persuade sb to do sth by offering something nice: *Advertisements try to entice people into buying more things than they need.* يغري ، يستهوي

▸ **enticement** *noun* [C,U] شيء مغرٍ ، مغريات : إغراء

enticing *adj* attractive مغرٍ

entire /ɪn'taɪə(r)/ *adj* (only *before* a noun) whole or complete: *Surely she didn't eat the entire cake herself?* ○ *We invited the entire village to the party.* ❶ **Entire** is stronger than **whole**. كامل : كلّ

▸ **entirely** *adv* completely: *I entirely agree with you.* كلّياً

entirety /ɪn'taɪərəti/ *noun* [U]: *We must consider the problem in its entirety* (= as a whole). جملة ، تمام

entitle /ɪn'taɪtl/ *verb* [T] to give sb the right to have or do sth: *I think I'm entitled to a day's holiday – I've worked hard enough.* يخوّل

▸ **entitled** *adj* (used about books, plays, etc.) with the title: *Duncan's first book was entitled 'Aquarium'.* تحت عنوان ، معنْون

entity /'entəti/ *noun* [C] (*pl.* **entities**) something that exists separately from sth else: *The kindergarten and the school are in the same building but they're really separate entities.* كيان ، وحدة مستقلّة

entrance /'entrəns/ *noun* **1** [C] the door, gate or opening where you go into a place: *I'll meet you at the entrance to the theatre.* ❶ **Entry** is used in American English with the same meaning. مدخل

2 [C] **entrance (into/onto sth)** the act of coming or going in: *He made a dramatic entrance*

onto the stage. ⓘ **Entry** can be used with the same meaning. دخول

3 [U] **entrance (to sth)** the right to enter a place: *They were refused entrance to the disco because they were wearing shorts.* ○ *an entrance fee* ⓘ **Entry** is also possible. Look at **admission**, **admittance**. دخول

4 [U] **entrance (into/to sth)** the right to join a club, institution, etc: *You don't need to take an entrance exam to get into university.* ➲ Look at **admission**. قبول ، انتساب

entrant /'entrənt/ *noun* [C] a person who enters a profession, competition, examination, university, etc. مشترك في : متقدِّم إلى : منتسب

entreat /ɪn'triːt/ *verb* [T] (*formal*) to ask sb, with great feeling, to do sth (that may be difficult) يتوسّل ، يترجّى

entrust /ɪn'trʌst/ *verb* [T] **entrust A with B/entrust B to A** (*formal*) to make sb responsible for sth that is given to him/her: *I entrusted Rachel with the arrangements for the party./I entrusted the arrangements for the party to Rachel.* يأتمن على ، يعهد به إلى

entry /'entri/ *noun* (*pl.* **entries**) **1** [C] **entry (into sth)** the act of coming or going in; entering(1): *The thieves forced an entry into the building.* ⓘ **Entrance** is also possible. دخول

2 [U] **entry (to sth)** the right to enter a place: *The immigrants were refused entry at the airport.* ○ *The sign says 'No Entry'.* ○ *an entry visa* ⓘ **Entrance** is also possible. Look at **admission** and **admittance**. دخول

3 [C] (*US*) a door, gate, passage, etc. where you enter a building, etc.; an entrance hall ⓘ **Entrance** is also possible in American English and is the only word used in British English. مدخل

4 [C] **entry (in sth)** one item that is written down in a list, diary, account book, dictionary, etc: *You'll find 'enrolment' at the entry for 'enrol'.* مادّة (مُدْرَجة)

5 [C] **entry (for sth)** a person or thing that is entered for a competition, etc: *There were fifty entries for the Eurovision song contest.* ○ *The winning entry is number 45!* مشترك

envelop /ɪn'veləp/ *verb* [T] (*formal*) to cover or surround sb/sth completely (in sth): *The hills were enveloped in mist.* يغلّف ، يحيط بِ : يغشّي

envelope /'envələʊp; 'ɒn-/ *noun* [C] the paper cover for a letter ظرف أو مظروف

> After writing a letter you **address** the envelope, **seal** it and stick a stamp in the top right-hand corner. Sometimes when you answer an advertisement you are asked to send an **SAE**. This is a 'stamped addressed envelope', addressed to yourself.

enviable /'enviəbl/ *adj* (used about sth that sb else has and that you would like) attractive ⓘ The opposite is **unenviable**. محسود عليه ، مرغوب فيه

envious /'enviəs/ *adj* **envious (of sb/sth)** feeling or showing envy, i.e. wanting sth that sb else has: *She was envious of her sister's success.* حسود

▸ **enviously** *adv* بحسد

environment /ɪn'vaɪrənmənt/ *noun* **1** [C,U] the conditions in which you live, work, etc: *A bad home environment can affect a child's progress at school.* بيئة ، محيط

2 the environment [sing.] the natural world, e.g. land, air, water, etc. in which people, animals and plants live: *We need stronger laws to protect the environment.* البيئة الطبيعيّة

▸ **environmental** /ɪnˌvaɪrən'mentl/ *adj*: *environmental science* بيئي

environmentalist /ɪnˌvaɪrən'mentəlɪst/ *noun* [C] a person who wants to protect the environment المحافظ على البيئة

environmentally /-təli/ *adv*: *These products are environmentally friendly.* بيئياً ، فيما يتعلّق بالبيئة

environs /ɪn'vaɪrənz/ *noun* [plural] (*formal*) the area around a place, especially a town: *Berlin and its environs* ضواحي (المدينة)

envisage /ɪn'vɪzɪdʒ/ *verb* [T] (*formal*) to think of sth as being possible in the future; to imagine: *I don't envisage any problems with this.* يتصوّر، يتخيّل ، يتوقّع

envoy /'envɔɪ/ *noun* [C] a person who is sent by a government with a message to another country مبعوث ، مندوب

envy /'envi/ *noun* [U] **envy (of sb)**; **envy (at/of sth)** the feeling that you have when sb else has sth that you want: *It was difficult for her to hide her envy of her friend's success.* ➲ Look at **enviable** and **envious**. حسد

IDM **the envy of sb** the thing that causes sb to feel envy: *The city's transport system is the envy of many of its European neighbours.* موضع حسد

▸ **envy** *verb* [T] (*pres part* **envying**; *3rd pers sing pres* **envies**; *pt, pp* **envied**) **envy (sb)(sth)** to want sth that sb else has; to feel envy: *I've always envied your good luck.* ○ *I don't envy you that job* (= I'm glad that I don't have it). يحسد

enzyme /'enzaɪm/ *noun* [C] **1** a chemical substance which occurs naturally in living creatures and assists in performing chemical changes, e.g. in processing food in the stomach, without being changed itself أنزيم، خميرة كيميائية

2 a similar substance that is produced artificially, e.g. for use in washing powders: *Washing powders containing enzymes are said to remove stains more efficiently.* أنزيم

epic /'epɪk/ *noun* [C] a long book, poem, film, etc. that describes exciting adventures: *The film 'Glory' is an American Civil War epic.* ملحمة : مؤلّف فنّي بطولي

▸ **epic** *adj* of or like an epic: *an epic struggle* ملحميّ ، بطولي

epidemic /ˌepɪ'demɪk/ *noun* [C] a large number of cases of people or animals suffering from the same disease at the same time: *A flu epidemic broke out in February.* وباء

epilepsy /'epɪlepsi/ *noun* [U] a disease of the

a b c d e f g h i j k l m n o p q r s t u v w x y z

brain that can cause a person to become unconscious (sometimes with violent uncontrolled movements) مرض الصَّرْع

▸ **epileptic** /ˌepɪˈleptɪk/ *adj* connected with or suffering from epilepsy: *an epileptic fit* ○ *She's epileptic.* (نوبة) صرع : مصاب بالصَّرْع

epileptic *noun* [C] a person who suffers from epilepsy المصاب بالصَّرْع

epilogue /ˈepɪlɒɡ/ (*US* **epilog** /-lɔːɡ/) *noun* [C] a short passage that is added at the end of a book, play, etc. and that comments on what has gone before ➲ Look at **prologue.** خاتمة الكتاب أو المسرحيّة

episode /ˈepɪsəʊd/ *noun* [C] **1** one separate event in sb's life, a novel, etc: *That's an episode in my life I'd rather forget.* حادثة ، فصل

2 one part of a TV or radio drama that is broadcast in several parts (a serial): *Don't miss tomorrow's exciting episode.* حلقة

epitaph /ˈepɪtɑːf; *US* -tæf/ *noun* [C] words that are written or said about a dead person, especially words written on a gravestone تأبين مكتوب على القبر

epitome /ɪˈpɪtəmi/ *noun* [sing.] a perfect example of sth عنوان لِ ، مثال ، نموذج

▸ **epitomize** /ɪˈpɪtəmaɪz/ *verb* [T] to be typical of sth يمثّل

epoch /ˈiːpɒk; *US* ˈepək/ *noun* [C] a period of time in history (that is important because of special events, features, etc.) عهد ، عصر

⚷ **equal** /ˈiːkwəl/ *adj* **1** the same in size, amount, value, number, status, etc: *They are equal in weight.* ○ *They are of equal weight.* ○ *Divide it into two equal parts.* ○ *Women are demanding equal pay for equal work.* ○ *We've appointed an Equal Opportunities Officer* (= a person who makes sure that people are treated equally). ⓘ The opposite is **unequal.** متساوٍ ، مساوٍ لِ

2 equal to sth (*formal*) having the strength, ability etc. to do sth: *I'm afraid Bob just isn't equal to the task.* كفء ، قادر

IDM be on equal terms (with sb) to have the same advantages and disadvantages as sb else يكون على قدم المساواة مع

▸ **equal** *noun* [C] a person who has the same ability, rights, etc. as you do: *to treat sb as an equal* ندّ ، مثيل

equal *verb* [T] (equalling; equalled; *US* equaling; equaled) **1** (used about numbers, etc.) to be the same as sth: *44 plus 17 equals 61 is written: 44 + 17 = 61.* يساوي

2 equal sb/sth (in sth) to be as good as sb/sth: *He ran an excellent race, equalling the club record.* ○ *Nowhere quite equals France for food.* يعادل ، يضاهي

equally /ˈiːkwəli/ *adv* **1** to the same degree or extent: *They both worked equally hard.* على حدّ سواء

2 in equal parts: *His money was divided equally between his children.* بالتساوي

3 (used when you are comparing two ideas or commenting on what you have just said) at the same time; but/and also: *I do not think what he did was right. Equally, I can understand why he did it.* في الحين ذاته... ; ولكن

equality /iˈkwɒləti/ *noun* [U] the situation in which everybody has the same rights and advantages; being equal: *equality of opportunity* ⓘ The opposite is **inequality.** المساواة

equalize (*also* **equalise**) /ˈiːkwəlaɪz/ *verb* [I] (*sport*) to reach the same number of points as your opponent: *Wales equalized in the 87th minute to make the score 2 all.* يتعادل مع

equate /iˈkweɪt/ *verb* [T] **equate sth (with sth)** to consider one thing as being the same as sth else: *It is a mistake to equate wealth with happiness.* يساوي بين

equation /ɪˈkweɪʒn/ *noun* [C] (in mathematics) a statement that two quantities are equal: *2x + 5 =11 is an equation.* معادلة

equator (*also* **Equator**) /ɪˈkweɪtə(r)/ *noun* [sing.] the imaginary line around the earth at an equal distance from the North and South Poles: *north/south of the equator* ○ *on the equator* خطّ الاستواء

equestrian /ɪˈkwestriən/ *adj* (*formal*) connected with horse riding: *equestrian events at the Olympic Games* فروسي

equilibrium /ˌiːkwɪˈlɪbriəm; ˌek-/ *noun* [U] **1** a situation in which opposing forces, influences, etc. are balanced and under control: *the need to keep supply and demand in equilibrium.* توازن

2 a state of mind in which feelings and emotions are under control: *He sat down for a while to recover his equilibrium.* هدوء، رباطة جأش

equip /ɪˈkwɪp/ *verb* [T] (equi**pp**ing; equi**pp**ed) **equip sb/sth (with sth) 1** (usually passive) to supply sb/sth with what is needed (for a particular purpose): *We shall equip all schools with new computers in the next year.* ○ *The schools in France are much better equipped than ours.* ○ *The flat has a fully equipped kitchen.* يزوّد ، يجهّز

2 to prepare sb for a particular task: *The course equips students with all the skills necessary to become a chef.* يهيّئ ، يؤهّل

⚷ **equipment** /ɪˈkwɪpmənt/ *noun* [U] the things that are needed for carrying out a particular activity: *office equipment* ○ *sports equipment* ○ *Standard equipment in the car includes power steering and central door locking.* معدّات ، لوازم

> Note that **equipment** is uncountable. We have to say 'a piece of equipment' if we are talking about one item: *a very useful piece of kitchen equipment.*

equity /ˈekwəti/ *noun* **1** [U] the value of the shares issued by a company: *He controls seven per cent of the equity.* قيمة الأسهم

2 equities [plural] ordinary stocks and shares that carry no fixed interest: *invest in equities* ○ *the equities market* سندات أو أسهم عادية

3 [U] the money value of a property after all the

charges on it, e.g. those relating to a mortgage, have been paid قيمة عقار بعد دفع المصاريف المترتبة عليه

equivalent /ɪ'kwɪvələnt/ *adj* **equivalent (to sth)** equal in value, amount, meaning, importance, etc: *The price of British cars is higher than that of equivalent French or German models.* ○ *People in Britain smoked 94 billion cigarettes last year, equivalent to 1680 per person.* مساوٍ ، معادل

▸ **equivalent** *noun* [C] something that is equivalent: *There is no English equivalent to the French 'bon appetit'.* مقابل

ER /ˌiː 'ɑː(r)/ = EMERGENCY ROOM

er /ɜː(r)/ *interj* (used in writing to show that sb cannot decide what to say next): *Well, er, ladies and gentlemen, I, er, I'm very pleased to be here today.* (تشير إلى التردد في الكلام)

era /'ɪərə/ *noun* [C] a period of time in history (that is special for some reason): *We are living in the era of the computer.* عصر ، عهد

eradicate /ɪ'rædɪkeɪt/ *verb* [T] (*formal*) to destroy sth completely يستأصل : يقضي على

▸ **eradication** /ɪˌrædɪ'keɪʃn/ *noun* [U] استئصال ، محو ، قضاء على

erase /ɪ'reɪz; *US* ɪ'reɪs/ *verb* [T] (*formal*) to remove sth (a pencil mark, a recording on tape, etc.): (*figurative*) *He tried to erase the memory of those terrible years from his mind.* ❶ We usually say **rub out** a pencil mark. يمحو

▸ **eraser** /ɪ'reɪzə(r); *US* -sər/ *noun* [C] (*especially US*) = RUBBER (2)

erect[1] /ɪ'rekt/ *adj* **1** standing straight up; upright: *He stood with his head erect.* قائم ، منتصب

2 (used about the penis) stiff and upright because of sexual excitement منتصب

erect[2] /ɪ'rekt/ *verb* [T] (*formal*) to build sth or to put sth in an upright position: *to erect a statue* ○ *Huge TV screens were erected so that everybody could see what was going on.* يقيم ، ينصب : يشيِّد

▸ **erection** /ɪ'rekʃn/ *noun* **1** [U] (*formal*) the act of putting sth in an upright position or of building sth إقامة ، تشييد

2 [C] the hardening of the penis in sexual excitement: *to get/have an erection* انتصاب

ermine /'ɜːmɪn/ *noun* the white winter fur of a stoat, that is sometimes used on the clothes worn by judges, etc: *a gown trimmed with ermine* قاقم، قاقوم

erode /ɪ'rəʊd/ *verb* [T] (usually passive) (used about the sea, the weather, etc.) to destroy sth slowly: *The cliff has been eroded by the sea.* ○ (*figurative*) *Freedom of speech is being eroded.* يحتّ ، يفتّت : يزيل تدريجياً

▸ **erosion** /ɪ'rəʊʒn/ *noun* [U]: *the erosion of the coastline by the sea* حتّ ، تعرية : زوال تدريجي

erotic /ɪ'rɒtɪk/ *adj* causing sexual excitement: *an erotic film, poem, etc.* مثير جنسياً

err /ɜː(r); *US* eər/ *verb* [I] (*formal*) to be or do wrong; to make mistakes: *It is better to err on the side of caution* (= it is better to be too careful rather than not careful enough). يخطئ ؛ يزلّ

errand /'erənd/ *noun* [C] a short journey to take or get sth for sb, e.g. to buy sth from a shop مهمّة صغيرة ، "مشوار" أو "مرسال"

erratic /ɪ'rætɪk/ *adj* (used about a person's behaviour, or about the quality of sth) changing without reason; that you cannot rely on: *Jones is a talented player but he's very erratic* (= sometimes he plays well, sometimes badly). غير منتظم

▸ **erratically** /-kli/ *adv* بصورة غير منتظمة ، بشكل متقلّب

error /'erə(r)/ *noun* **1** [C] a mistake: *The telephone bill was far too high due to a computer error.* ○ *an error of judgement* ○ *to make an error* خطأ ، غلطة

> **Error** is more formal than **mistake**. There are some expressions, e.g. *error of judgement*, *human error* where only **error** can be used.

2 [U] the state of being wrong in behaviour or belief: *The letter was sent to you in error.* ○ *The accident was the result of human error.* خطأ

IDM **trial and error** → TRIAL

erupt /ɪ'rʌpt/ *verb* [I] **1** (used about a volcano) to explode and throw out fire, rock that has melted (lava), etc. يثور أو ينفجر (البركان)

2 (used about violence, anger, etc.) to start suddenly: *The demonstration erupted into violence.* ينقلب فجاة إلى

3 (used about people) to suddenly become very angry: *George erupted when he heard the news.* يثور غضبه

▸ **eruption** /ɪ'rʌpʃn/ *noun* [C,U] ثوران أو انفجار : تفجّر

escalate /'eskəleɪt/ *verb* [I,T] **1** (to cause sth) to become stronger or more serious: *The demonstrations are escalating into violent protest in all the major cities.* ○ *The terrorist attacks escalated tension in the capital.* يتصاعد ، يزداد حدّة : يزيد من

2 (to cause sth) to become greater or higher; to increase: *The cost of housing has escalated in recent years.* يرتفع : يزداد : يرفع

▸ **escalation** /ˌeskə'leɪʃn/ *noun* [C,U] تصاعد : تفاقم : تصعيد

escalator /'eskəleɪtə(r)/ *noun* [C] a moving staircase in a shop, etc. درج أو سلّم متحرّك

escapade /ˌeskə'peɪd/ *noun* [C] an exciting adventure that may be dangerous مغامرة جريئة

escape[1] /ɪ'skeɪp/ *verb* **1** [I] **escape (from sb/sth)** to get away from a place where you do not want to be; to get free: *Two prisoners have escaped.* ○ *A lion escaped from its cage at Bristol Zoo last night.* يهرب ، يفلت من

2 [I] (used about gases or liquids) to find a way out of a container, etc: *There's gas escaping somewhere.* يتسرّب

3 [I,T] to be safe from sth; to avoid sth: *The two men in the other car escaped unhurt in the accident.* ○ *David Smith escaped injury when his*

a b c d e f g h i j k l m n o p q r s t u v w x y z

car skidded off the road. ○ *to escape criticism* ينجو (من) : يتجنّب

4 [T] to be forgotten or not noticed by sb: *His name escapes me.* ○ *to escape sb's notice* (= not be noticed by sb) يغيب عن باله ، يفوته

▸ **escaped** *adj* having escaped from a place: *The escaped prisoners have not been recaptured.* فارّ

escape² /ɪ'skeɪp/ *noun* **1** [C,U] **escape (from sth)** the act of escaping¹ (1,2,3): *There have been twelve escapes from the local prison this year.* ○ *She had a narrow escape when a lorry crashed into her car* (= she was nearly killed or seriously hurt). ○ *Escape from Alcatraz prison was impossible.* فرار ، هروب : نجاة

2 [C] a means of escaping: *a fire escape* مَفَرّ ، مَهْرَب

3 [U, sing.] something that helps you forget your daily life: *For him, listening to music is a means of escape.* ○ *an escape from reality* هروب

escort /'eskɔːt/ *noun* [C] **1** [with sing. or pl. verb] a person or vehicle (or group of people and vehicles) that goes with and protects sb/sth, or that goes with sb/sth as an honour: *a police escort* ❶ Note the phrase **under escort**: *He arrived under military escort.* مرافق ، حَرَس، حراسة

2 (*formal*) a companion for a particular social event مرافق (إلى حفل مثلاً)

▸ **escort** /ɪ'skɔːt/ *verb* [T] **1** to go with sb as an escort: *The President's car was escorted by several police cars.* يرافق ، يحرس

2 to take sb somewhere: *Philip escorted her to the door.* يرافق ، يوصل

Eskimo /'eskɪməʊ/ *noun* [C] (*pl.* **Eskimo** or **Eskimos**) = INUIT

ESL /ˌiː es 'el/ *abbrev* English as a Second Language الانكليزية كلغة ثانية

especial /ɪ'speʃl/ *adj* (only *before* a noun) (*formal*) not usual; special: *This will be of especial interest to you.* خاص ، غير عادي

especially /ɪ'speʃəli/ *adv* **1** (*abbr* **esp.**) to an unusual degree; in particular: *She loves sport, especially tennis.* ○ *The Irish, especially, are proud of their traditions.* ○ *The car is rather small, especially if you have a large family.* ○ *He was very disappointed with his mark in the exam, especially as he had worked so hard for it.* خاصة ، بوجه خاص

2 for a particular purpose: *I made this especially for you.* ❶ **Specially** is also possible with this meaning. It is less formal. خصّيصاً

3 very (much): *It's not an especially difficult exam.* ○ *'Do you like jazz?' 'Not especially.'* كثيراً

espionage /'espiənɑːʒ/ *noun* [U] the system of finding out secret information about another country or organization ➲ Look at **spy**. تجسّس ، جاسوسية

espresso /e'spresəʊ/ *noun* (*pl.* **espressos**) **1** [U] strong black coffee made by forcing steam or boiling water through ground coffee قهوة "اسبرسو"

2 [C] a cup of espresso: *Two espressos, please.* قهوة "اسبرسو"

essay /'eseɪ/ *noun* [C] a short piece of writing on one subject: *to write an essay on tourism* مقال ، موضوع (أدبي)

essence /'esns/ *noun* **1** [sing.] the basic or most important quality of sth: *The essence of the problem is that there is not enough money available.* جوهر ، لبّ

2 [C,U] a substance (usually a liquid) that is taken from a plant or food and that has a strong smell or taste of that plant or food: *vanilla essence* خلاصة ، روح

essential /ɪ'senʃl/ *adj* absolutely necessary; that you must have or do: *Essential medical supplies will be delivered to the area by plane.* ○ *Maths is essential for a career in computers.* ○ *It is essential that all school-leavers should have a qualification.* ○ *It is essential to book in advance if you are travelling by coach.* ○ *Local clubs are an essential part of village life.* ضروري ، أساسيّ

▸ **essential** *noun* [C, usually pl.] something that is necessary or very important: *food, and other essentials such as clothing and heating* مستلزمات

essentially /ɪ'senʃəli/ *adv* basically; really: *The problem is essentially one of money.* جوهرياً : في الحقيقة

establish /ɪ'stæblɪʃ/ *verb* [T] **1** to start sth (especially an organization or institution): *The school was established in 1875.* يؤسّس ، ينشئ

2 to make sth exist: *We must establish good relations with the local newspaper.* يقيم ، يكوّن

3 establish sb/sth (as sth) to place sb/sth in a position permanently: *She has been trying to get established as a novelist for several years.* ○ *The festival has become established as one of the most popular events in the town.* يوطّد قدمه ، يرسّخ

4 to decide sth: *We need to establish our aims before we can go any further.* يقرّ

5 to discover or find proof of sth: *The police are not able to establish where he was at the time of the murder.* يتحقق من : يثْبِت

establishment /ɪ'stæblɪʃmənt/ *noun* **1** [U] the act of starting sth such as an organization or institution: *the establishment of a new government department* تأسيس ، إنشاء

2 [C] a shop or business مؤسّسة

3 the Establishment [sing.] (*Brit*) the people in positions of power in a country, who usually do not support change السلطة الحاكمة

estate /ɪ'steɪt/ *noun* [C] **1** a large area of land in the country that is owned by one person or family: *He owns a large estate in Scotland.* ضيعة ، عزبة ، مِلك

2 (*Brit*) an area of land that has a lot of buildings of the same type on it: *an industrial estate* (= where there are a lot of factories) ○ *a housing estate* وَحْدة (سكنيّة)

3 all the money and property that sb leaves when he/she dies التركات ، مجموع أموال المتوفى

es'tate agent (*US* **Realtor**; **real estate**

agent) *noun* [C] a person who buys and sells houses and land for other people سمسار عقارات ، دلّال

es'tate car (*US* **station wagon**) *noun* [C] a car with a door at the back and a large area for luggage behind the back seat سيّارة "ستيشن"

esteem /ɪ'sti:m/ *noun* [U] (*formal*) great respect; a good opinion of sb احترام ، تبجيل ؛ تقدير

esthetic (*US*) = AESTHETIC

estimate¹ /'estɪmət/ *noun* [C] **1** a guess or judgement about the size, cost, etc. of sth, before you have all the facts and figures: *Can you give me a rough estimate of how many people will be at the meeting?* تخمين ، تقدير

2 a written statement from a builder, etc. giving a price for a particular job مقايسة

estimate² /'estɪmeɪt/ *verb* [T] to calculate the size, cost, etc. of sth approximately, before you have all the facts and figures: *She estimated that the work would take three months.* ○ *The police estimated the crowd at 10 000.* ○ *Work on the new bridge will cost an estimated five million pounds.* يقدّر ، يخمّن

estimation /ˌestɪ'meɪʃn/ *noun* [U] (*formal*) opinion or judgement تقدير ، رأي

estranged /ɪ'streɪndʒd/ *adj* **1** no longer living with your husband/wife: *He's estranged from his wife.* مفترق عن زوجه

2 no longer friendly towards sb who used to be close to you مجافٍ ، متباعد عن

estuary /'estʃuəri; *US* -ʊeri/ *noun* [C] (*pl.* **estuaries**) the wide part (mouth) of a river where it joins the sea مصبّ النهر

etc. *abbrev* et cetera; and so on, and other things of a similar kind: *sandwiches, biscuits, cakes, etc.* إلى آخره، الخ...

eternal /ɪ'tɜ:nl/ *adj* **1** without beginning or end; lasting for ever: *eternal life* (= after death) أبدي ، سرمدي ، خالد

2 happening too often; seeming to last for ever: *I'm tired of these eternal arguments!* دائم ، مستمرّ ، متكرّر

▸ **eternally** /ɪ'tɜ:nəli/ *adv*: *I'll be eternally grateful if you could help me.* إلى الأبد ، دوماً

eternity /ɪ'tɜ:nəti/ *noun* **1** [U] time that has no end; the state or time after death الأبد ، السرمدية ، الأزل

2 an eternity [sing.] (*informal*) a period of time that seems endless: *It seemed like an eternity before the ambulance arrived.* زمن طويل جداً

ethics /'eθɪks/ *noun* **1** [U] the study of what is right and wrong in human behaviour: *Ethics is a branch of philosophy.* علم الأخلاق

2 [plural] beliefs about what is morally right and wrong: *The medical profession has its own code of ethics.* مبادئ أخلاقيّة

▸ **ethical** /'eθɪkl/ *adj* **1** connected with ethics (2): *That is an ethical problem.* أخلاقيّ

2 morally correct: *She had not broken the law but her behaviour had not been ethical.* ❶ The opposite is **unethical**. أخلاقيّ

ethnic /'eθnɪk/ *adj* connected with or typical of a racial group or groups: *ethnic minorities* ○ *ethnic food, music, etc.* إثنيّ ، متعلّق بعرق معيّن

ˌethnic 'cleansing *noun* [U] the policy of forcing people of a certain race or religion to leave an area or country تطهير عرقي

etiquette /'etɪket/ *noun* [U] the rules of polite and correct behaviour آداب السلوك

etymology /ˌetɪ'mɒlədʒi/ *noun* (*pl.* **etymologies**) **1** [U] the study of the origins and history of words and their meanings دراسة أصول الكلمات

2 [C] an explanation of the origin and history of a particular word إيضاح أصل كلمة وتاريخها

EU *abbrev* = EUROPEAN UNION

euphemism /'ju:fəmɪzəm/ *noun* [C,U] (using) a polite word or expression instead of a more direct one when you are talking about sth that is unpleasant or embarrassing: *'Pass away' is a euphemism for 'die'.* تعبير ملطّف ؛ تلطيف تعبير (فظ)

euphoria /ju:'fɔ:riə/ *noun* [U] (*formal*) a strong feeling of happiness نشوة ، ابتهاج شديد

euro /'jʊərəʊ/ *noun* [C] (*pl.* **euros** or **euro**) (*symbol*) a unit of money used in several countries of the European Union يورو

European /ˌjʊərə'pi:ən/ *adj* of or from Europe: *European languages* ○ *the European Championship* أوروبي

▸ **European** *noun* [C] a person from a European country شخص أوروبي

the Euroˌpean 'Union *noun* [sing.] (*abbr* **EU**) an economic and political association of certain European countries الاتحاد الأوربي

euthanasia /ˌju:θə'neɪziə; *US* -'neɪʒə/ *noun* [U] the painless killing of sb who is very old or suffering from a disease that cannot be cured الإماتة الرحيمة

evacuate /ɪ'vækjueɪt/ *verb* [T] to move people from a dangerous place to somewhere safer; to leave a place because it is dangerous: *During the war children were evacuated from London to the country.* ○ *The village had to be evacuated when the river burst its banks.* يُخلي ، يجلو عن

▸ **evacuation** /ɪˌvækju'eɪʃn/ *noun* [C,U] إخلاء ، جلاء عن

evade /ɪ'veɪd/ *verb* [T] **1** to get out of the way of or to escape from sb/sth: *They managed to evade capture and escaped to France.* يتفادى ، يتجنّب ؛ ينجو من

2 to avoid sth: *He was accused of evading income tax.* ○ *I asked her directly, but she evaded the question.* يتهرّب من

❶ The noun is **evasion**.

evaluate /ɪ'væljueɪt/ *verb* [T] (*formal*) to study the facts and then give your opinion about the meaning of sth or about how good sth is: *We evaluated the situation very carefully before we made our decision.* يقيّم ، يقدّر ؛ يثمّن

▸ **evaluation** /ɪˌvælju'eɪʃn/ *noun* [C,U] تقييم ، تقدير

evangelical /ˌiːvæn'dʒelɪkl/ *adj* (of certain Protestant churches) believing that religious ceremony is not as important as faith in Jesus Christ and study of the Bible إنجيلي : متعلّق بالكنيسة البروتستانتية

evaporate /ɪ'væpəreɪt/ *verb* [I] **1** (used about a liquid) to change into steam or a gas and disappear: *The water evaporated in the sunshine.* ➲ Look at **condense**. يتبخّر

2 (used about feelings) to disappear: *All her hopes evaporated when she heard the news.* يزول ، يختفي ، يتبخّر

▸ **evaporation** /ɪˌvæpə'reɪʃn/ *noun* [U] تبخُّر

evasion /ɪ'veɪʒn/ *noun* [C,U] an action, statement, etc. that is used for avoiding sth unpleasant: *He has been sentenced to two years' imprisonment for tax evasion.* ❶ The verb is **evade**. تهرُّب ، تجنُّب : مراوغة

evasive /ɪ'veɪsɪv/ *adj* trying to avoid sth; not direct: *Ann gave an evasive answer.* تهرّبي : مراوغ

eve /iːv/ *noun* [C] the day or evening before a religious festival, important event, etc: *Christmas Eve* عشيّة عيدٍ أو اليوم السابق له

⚷ **even¹** /'iːvn/ *adj* **1** flat, level or smooth: *The game must be played on an even surface.* مستوٍ ، منبسط

2 not changing; regular: *He's very even-tempered – in fact I've never seen him angry.* ثابت : منتظم

3 (used about a competition, etc.) with one side being as good as the other: *The contest was very even until the last few minutes of the game.* متعادل

❶ The opposite for senses **1,2,3** is **uneven**.

4 (used about numbers) that can be divided by two: *4, 6, 8, 10, etc. are even numbers.* ❶ The opposite is **odd**. (عدد) زوجي

IDM be/get even (with sb) to hurt or harm sb who has hurt or harmed you ينتقم أو يثأر من

break even to make neither a loss nor a profit (الشركة) لا تربح ولا تخسر

▸ **evenly** *adv* in an even way: *The match was very evenly balanced.* ○ *Spread the cake mixture evenly in the tin.* على نحو متعادل : بالتساوي ، باستواء

⚷ **even²** /'iːvn/ *adv* **1** (used for emphasizing sth that is surprising): *It isn't very warm here even in summer.* ○ *Even the children helped in the garden.* ○ *He didn't even open the letter* (= so he certainly didn't read it). ○ *I have been so busy that I haven't even had time to read the newspaper.* ○ *I like her very much even though she can be very annoying.* ➲ Look at the note at **although**. حتّى

2 (used when you are comparing things, to make the comparison stronger): *You know even less about it than I do.* ○ *It is even more difficult than I expected.* ○ *We are even busier than yesterday.* حتّى أنه... : بل...

IDM even if (used for saying that what follows 'if' makes no difference): *I wouldn't do it, even if you paid me a thousand pounds.* حتّى لو...

even so (used for introducing a new idea, fact, etc. that is surprising) in spite of that; nevertheless: *There are a lot of spelling mistakes; even so it's quite a good essay.* بالرغم من ذلك

⚷ **evening** /'iːvnɪŋ/ *noun* [C,U] the part of the day between the afternoon and the time that you go to bed: *What are you doing this evening?* ○ *We were out yesterday evening.* ○ *I went to the cinema on Saturday evening.* ○ *Tom usually goes swimming on Wednesday evenings.* ○ *Most people watch television in the evening.* ○ *an evening class* (= a course of lessons for adults that takes place in the evening) مساء

IDM good evening (used when you see sb for the first time in the evening) ❶ Often we just say *Evening*: *'Good evening, Mrs Wilson.' 'Evening, Mr Mills.'* مساء الخير

⚷ **event** /ɪ'vent/ *noun* [C] **1** something that happens, especially sth important or unusual: *an historic event* ○ *The events of the past few days have made things very difficult for the Government.* حدَث ، واقعة

2 one of the races, competitions, etc. in a sports programme: *The next event is the 800 metres.* مسابقة ، مباراة

IDM at all events/in any event whatever happens: *I hope to see you soon, but in any event I'll phone you on Sunday.* على أية حال

in the event of sth (*formal*) if sth happens: *In the event of fire, leave the building as quickly as possible.* في حالة حدوث

▸ **eventful** /-fl/ *adj* full of interesting or important events ❶ The opposite is **uneventful**. مليء بالأحداث ، زاخر

eventual /ɪ'ventʃuəl/ *adj* (only *before* a noun) happening as a result at the end of a period of time or of a process: *It is impossible to say what the eventual cost will be.* نهائيّ : ناجم (عن)

⚷ **eventually** /ɪ'ventʃuəli/ *adv* in the end; at last: *He eventually managed to persuade his parents to let him buy a motor bike.* أخيراً، في النهاية

⚷ **ever** /'evə(r)/ *adv* **1** (used in questions and negative sentences, when you are comparing things, and in sentences with 'if') at any time: *Do you ever wish you were famous?* ○ *Nobody ever comes to see me.* ○ *She hardly ever* (= almost never) *goes out.* ○ *Today is hotter than ever.* ○ *This is the best meal I have ever had.* ○ *If you ever visit England, you must come and stay with us.* في أيّ وقت

2 (used in questions with verbs in the perfect tenses) at any time up to now: *Have you ever been to Spain?* ❶ Notice that when you answer a question like this, you do not use 'ever'. You say, 'Yes, I have' or 'No, I haven't' (or 'No, never'). في عمرك، في وقت من الاوقات

3 (used with a question that begins with 'when', 'where', 'who', 'how', etc., to show that you are surprised or shocked): *How ever did he get back so quickly?* ○ *What ever were you thinking about when you wrote this?* ➲ Look at **whatever**, **whenever**, **however**, etc. (تستعمل تعبيراً عن الاستغراب)

4 ever- (in compounds) always; continuously:

the ever-growing problem of pollution دائماً، بصورة مستمرّة

IDM (as) bad, good, etc. as ever (as) bad, good, etc. as usual or as you expected: *In spite of his problems, Andrew is as cheerful as ever.* كالمعتاد

ever after (used especially at the end of stories) from that moment on for always: *The prince married the princess and they lived happily ever after.* إلى الأبد

ever since (...) all the time from (...) until now: *She has had a car ever since she was at university.* منذ ذلك الحين، منذ

ever so/ever such a (*Brit informal*) very: *He's ever so kind.* ○ *He's ever such a kind man.* جداً

for ever → FOREVER (1)

evergreen /ˈevəgriːn/ *noun* [C], *adj* (a tree, etc.) with green leaves throughout the year ➲ Look at **deciduous.** (نبات) دائم الخضرة

everlasting /ˌevəˈlɑːstɪŋ; *US* -ˈlæst-/ *adj* (*formal*) lasting for ever: *everlasting life* دائم، أبدي

every /ˈevri/ *det* **1** (used with singular nouns) all the people or things in a group of three or more: *She knows every student in the school.* ○ *There are 200 students in the school, and she knows every one of them.* ○ *I've read every book in this house.* ○ *You were out every time I phoned.* كل

2 all that is possible: *You have every chance of success.* ○ *She had every reason to be angry.* كل؛ تامّ

3 (used for saying how often sth happens): *We see each other every day.* ○ *Take the medicine every four hours* (= at 8, 12, 4, etc.). ○ *The milkman comes every other day* (= on Monday, Wednesday, Friday, etc.). ○ *One in every three marriages ends in divorce.* كلّ

everybody /ˈevribɒdi/ (*also* **everyone** /ˈevriwʌn/) *pron* every person; all people: *Is everybody here?* ○ *The police questioned everyone who was at the party.* ○ *I'm sure everybody else* (= all the other people) *will agree with me.* كلّ واحد، الجميع

> **Everyone** is only used about people and is not followed by 'of'. **Every one** means 'each person or thing' and is often followed by 'of': *Every one of his records has been successful.* Look also at the note at **somebody**.

everyday /ˈevrideɪ/ *adj* (only *before* a noun) normal and usual: *The computer is now part of everyday life.* عادي، يومي

everyplace /ˈevripleɪs/ *adv* (*US*) = EVERYWHERE

everything /ˈevriθɪŋ/ *pron* [with sing. verb] **1** each thing; all things: *Sam lost everything in the fire.* ○ *Everything is very expensive in this shop.* ○ *We can leave everything else* (= all the other things) *at my parents' house.* كلّ شيء

2 the most important thing: *Money isn't everything.* أهمّ شيء في الحياة، كلّ شيء

everywhere /ˈevriweə(r)/ (*also* **everyplace**) *adv* in or to every place: *I've looked everywhere, but I still can't find it.* في أو إلى كل مكان

evict /ɪˈvɪkt/ *verb* [T] to force sb (officially) to leave the house or land where he/she is living: *They were evicted for not paying the rent.* يخلي (مستاجراً مثلاً)

▸ **eviction** /ɪˈvɪkʃn/ *noun* [C,U] إخلاء رسمي

evidence /ˈevɪdəns/ *noun* [U] something that gives a reason for believing sth: *There was no evidence of a struggle in the room.* ○ *There was not enough evidence to prove him guilty.* ○ *Her statement to the police was used in evidence against him.* ○ *The witnesses to the accident will be asked to give evidence in court.* ○ *You have absolutely no evidence for what you're saying!* دليل، برهان، بيِّنة

> Note that **evidence** is uncountable. We use **piece** if we are talking about single items that are evidence: *One piece of evidence is not enough to prove somebody guilty.*

IDM (to be) in evidence to be seen; to be noticeable: *When we arrived there was no ambulance in evidence.* يمكن رؤيته، بادٍ للعيان

evident /ˈevɪdənt/ *adj* clear (to the eye or mind); obvious: *It was evident that the damage was very serious.* واضح جليّ؛ ظاهر

▸ **evidently** *adv* **1** it appears that: *Evidently he has decided to leave.* على مايبدو

2 it is obvious that: *She was evidently extremely shocked at the news.* من الواضح أن...؛ بوضوح

evil /ˈiːvl/ *adj* very bad; causing trouble or harm: *Dr Jekyll and the evil Mr Hyde* ○ *In the play Richard is portrayed as an evil king.* شرّير

> Another word for **evil** is **wicked**. These are very strong words. Children are usually described as **naughty** or **mischievous**.

▸ **evil** *noun* [C,U] (*formal*) something that is very bad; wickedness: *The play is about the good and evil in all of us.* ○ *Drugs and alcohol are two of the evils of modern society.* شرّ

IDM the lesser of two evils → LESSER

evoke /ɪˈvəʊk/ *verb* [T] (*formal*) to produce a memory, feeling, etc: *For me, that music always evokes long summer evenings.* ○ *Her article evoked a lot of interest.* يستثير؛ يعيد إلى الذاكرة

evolution /ˌiːvəˈluːʃn; *US* ˌev-/ *noun* [U] **1** the development of living things over many thousands of years from simple early forms: *Darwin's theory of evolution* تطوُّر، نشوء، ارتقاء

2 the process of change and development: *Political evolution is a slow process.* نموّ، تطوّر

evolve /iˈvɒlv/ *verb* **1** [I] (used about living things) to develop from simple early forms يتطوّر، ينشأ، يرتقي

2 [I,T] (*formal*) to develop or to make sth develop: *His style of painting has evolved gradually over the past 20 years.* ○ *The twins have evolved a language of their own.* يتطوّر؛ يبتكر؛ يطوّر

ewe /juː/ *noun* [C] a female sheep ➲ Look at the note at **sheep**. نعجة، شاة

ex- /eks/ *prefix* (in nouns) former: *ex-wife* ○ *ex-president* سابق

a b c d e f g h i j k l m n o p q r s t u v w x y z

exact[1] /ɪɡˈzækt/ *adj* **1** (completely) correct; accurate: *He's in his mid-fifties. Well, 56 to be exact.* ○ *What is the exact time?* ○ *I can't tell you the exact number of people who are coming.* ○ *She's the exact opposite of her sister.* صحيح؛ مضبوط

2 able to work in a way that is completely accurate: *You need to be very exact when you calculate the costs.* دقيق، مضبوط

▸ **exactly** *adv* **1** (used for emphasizing sth) just: *You've arrived at exactly the right moment.* ○ *I found exactly what I wanted.* تماماً، بالضبط

2 (used when you are asking for, or giving, completely correct information): *Where exactly are you going on holiday?* ○ *He took exactly one hour to finish.* بالضبط

3 (used for agreeing with a statement) yes; you are right: *'But I don't think she's old enough to travel on her own.' 'Exactly.'* نعم، هذا صحيح...

IDM **not exactly** (*informal*) **1** not really; not at all: *He's not exactly the most careful driver I know.* في الواقع إنه ليس...

2 (used as an answer to say that sth is almost true): *'So you think I'm wrong?' 'No, not exactly, but ...'* صحيح إلى حدّ ما، "ليس تماماً"

exactness *noun* [U] the quality of being exact دقّة، صِحّة

exact[2] /ɪɡˈzækt/ *verb* [T] (*formal*) to demand and get sth يرغمه على، يأخذ عنوة

▸ **exacting** *adj* needing a lot of care and attention; difficult: *exacting work* متطلّب عناية فائقة؛ صعب

exaggerate /ɪɡˈzædʒəreɪt/ *verb* [I,T] to make sth seem larger, better, worse, etc. than it really is: *Don't exaggerate. I was only two minutes late, not twenty.* ○ *The problems have been greatly exaggerated.* يبالغ، يغالي

▸ **exaggeration** /ɪɡˌzædʒəˈreɪʃn/ *noun* [C,U] making sth seem bigger, etc. than it really is; sth that does this: *It's rather an exaggeration to say that all the students are lazy.* مبالغة، مغالاة

exam /ɪɡˈzæm/ *noun* [C] (*informal*) examination (2): *an English exam* ○ *the exam results* امتحان

examination /ɪɡˌzæmɪˈneɪʃn/ *noun* **1** [C,U] the act of looking at sth carefully: *They made a thorough examination of the car before buying it.* ○ *On close examination, it was found that the passport was false.* ○ *a medical examination* فحص؛ تدقيق

2 (*also informal* **exam**) [C] a written, spoken or practical test of what you know or can do: *I've got an examination in French next week.* ○ *to take/sit an examination* ○ *to pass/fail an examination* ℹ A **test** is less formal and usually shorter than an examination. امتحان

examine /ɪɡˈzæmɪn/ *verb* [T] **1 examine sb/sth (for sth)** to look at sb/sth carefully in order to find out sth: *The detective examined the room for clues.* ○ *I'm going to have my teeth examined next week.* ○ *Please examine your change carefully before you leave the shop.* يفحص؛ يفتّش

2 examine sb (in/on sth) (*formal*) to test what sb knows or can do: *You will be examined on everything that has been studied in the course.* يمتحن، يفحص

▸ **examiner** *noun* [C] a person who tests sb in an examination (2) الممتحِن

example /ɪɡˈzɑːmpl; *US* -ˈzæmpl/ *noun* [C] **1** a thing that shows a general rule about what sth is like: *This dictionary gives many examples of how words are used in sentences.* ○ *I don't quite understand you. Can you give me an example of what you mean?* ○ *This is a typical example of a Victorian house.* مثال

2 a person or thing or a type of behaviour that is good and should be copied: *Joe's bravery should be an example to us all.* مثل، قدوة

IDM **follow sb's example/lead** → FOLLOW

for example (used for giving an illustration of what you are talking about): *In many countries, Italy, for example, family life is much more important than here.* ℹ The short form is **e. g.** مثلاً

set a good, bad, etc. example (to sb) to behave in a way that should/should not be copied: *Parents should always take care when crossing roads in order to set their children a good example.* يكون قدوة (حسنة)

exasperate /ɪɡˈzæspəreɪt/ *verb* [T] to make sb angry; to annoy: *She was exasperated by the lack of progress.* يغضب، يثير السخط؛ يضايق

▸ **exasperating** *adj*: *I spent an exasperating morning trying to arrange our flights.* مثير للغضب؛ مزعج للغاية

exasperation /ɪɡˌzæspəˈreɪʃn/ *noun* [U]: *She finally threw the book across the room in exasperation.* حنق، غضب؛ انزعاج شديد

excavate /ˈekskəveɪt/ *verb* [I,T] **1** to dig a hole in the ground يحفر

2 to uncover objects or buildings from the past by digging in an area of land: *A Roman villa has been excavated in a valley near the village.* يحفر، ينقّب عن الآثار

▸ **excavation** /ˌekskəˈveɪʃn/ *noun* [C,U]: *Excavations on the site have revealed several Roman buildings.* حفريّات؛ تنقيب عن الآثار

exceed /ɪkˈsiːd/ *verb* [T] **1** to be greater than sth: *The price must not exceed £100.* يتجاوز، يزيد عن

2 to go beyond what is allowed or necessary: *He was stopped by the police for exceeding the speed limit.* ➲ Look at **excess** and **excessive**. يتجاوز

▸ **exceedingly** *adv* (*formal*) very: *an exceedingly difficult problem* للغاية، إلى أقصى حدّ

excel /ɪkˈsel/ *verb* [I] (excelling; excelled) (*formal*) **1 excel in/at sth** to be very good at sth يتفوّق، يبرع

2 excel yourself (*Brit*) to do sth even better than you usually do: *Rick's cooking is always good, but this time he really excelled himself.* يتجاوز نفسه أو حدود امكانياته

excellence /ˈeksələns/ *noun* [U] the quality of being very good: *The headteacher said that she wanted the school to be a centre of academic excellence.* تفوّق، امتياز

excellent /'eksələnt/ *adj* very good; of high quality: *He speaks excellent French.* جيّد جداً، ممتاز
▸ **excellently** *adv* بصورةٍ ممتازة، بشكل رائع

except[1] /ɪk'sept/ *prep* **except (for) sb/sth**; **except (that...)** not including sb/sth; apart from the fact that: *The museum is open every day except Mondays.* ○ *Everyone except Tony is going on the trip.* ○ *I can answer all of the questions except for the last one.* ○ *It was a good hotel except that it was rather noisy.* ماعدا، باستثناء

except[2] /ɪk'sept/ *verb* [T] (often passive) **except sb/sth (from sth)** (*formal*) to leave sb/sth out; to not include sb/sth يستثني، يسقط من
▸ **excepting** *prep* not including; except[1] ماعدا، باستثناء

exception /ɪk'sepʃn/ *noun* [C] a person or thing that is not included: *Most of his songs are awful but this one is an exception.* ○ *There's an exception to every rule.* المستثنى من، حالة استثنائيّة، استثناء
IDM **to make an exception (of sb/sth)** to treat sb/sth differently: *We don't usually allow children under 14 but we'll make an exception in your case.* يستثني
with the exception of except for; apart from: *He has won every major tennis championship with the exception of Wimbledon.* ماعدا، باستثناء
without exception in every case; including everybody/everything: *Everybody without exception must take the test.* (الجميع) دون استثناء

exceptional /ɪk'sepʃənl/ *adj* very unusual; unusually good: *You will only be allowed to leave early in exceptional circumstances.* ○ *We have had a really exceptional summer.* استثنائيّ، خارق للعادة، رائع
▸ **exceptionally** /-ʃənəli/ *adv*: *The past year has been exceptionally difficult for us.* بشكل استثنائيّ، بصورة غير معهودة

excerpt /'eksɜːpt/ *noun* [C] a short piece taken from a book, film, piece of music, etc. مقتطف، نُبذة

excess[1] /ɪk'ses/ *noun* [sing.] more of sth than is needed or usual; too much of sth: *An excess of fat in your diet can lead to heart disease.* زيادة، إفراط، فرط
IDM **in excess of** more than: *Her debts are in excess of £1 000.* أكثر من، يزيد عن

excess[2] /'ekses/ *adj* (only *before* a noun) more than is usual or allowed; extra: *There are high charges for excess baggage on planes.* زائد عن المحدّد؛ إضافيّ

excessive /ɪk'sesɪv/ *adj* too much; too great: *I think £200 for a dress is excessive.* مفرط، متجاوز الحدّ
▸ **excessively** *adv*: *I think you are being excessively pessimistic about this.* بإفراط، أكثر من اللازم

exchange[1] /ɪks'tʃeɪndʒ/ *noun* **1** [C,U] giving or receiving sth in return for sth else: *a useful exchange of information* ○ *We can offer free accommodation in exchange for some help in the house.* تبادل، مبادلة، مقايضة
2 [C] an (angry) conversation or argument مُشادّة، جدال
3 [U] the relation in value between kinds of money used in different countries: *What's the exchange rate/rate of exchange for dollars?* صرف أو تحويل العملة
4 [U] money that can be used to pay for goods or services from other countries: *Most of the country's foreign exchange comes from oil.* قطع، عملة أجنبيّة
5 [C] a visit by a group of students or teachers to another country and a return visit by a similar group from that country: *an exchange with a school in France* ○ *an exchange visit* زيارة تبادل (بين طلاب دولتين)
6 = TELEPHONE EXCHANGE ➲ Look at **Stock Exchange**.

exchange[2] /ɪks'tʃeɪndʒ/ *verb* [T] **exchange A for B**; **exchange sth (with sb)** to give or receive sth in return for sth else: *I would like to exchange this skirt for a bigger one.* ○ *Amy and Lisa exchanged addresses with the boys.* ○ *They exchanged glances* (= they looked at each other). يبدّل؛ يبادل؛ يتبادل

excise /'eksaɪz/ *noun* [U] a government tax on certain goods that are produced or sold in a country, e.g. tobacco, alcohol, etc. ➲ Look at **customs**. ضريبة، مكس، رسم

excitable /ɪk'saɪtəbl/ *adj* easily excited سريع الهياج، انفعاليّ

excite /ɪk'saɪt/ *verb* [T] **1** to cause strong feelings (e.g. of happiness or nervousness): *Don't excite the baby too much or we'll never get him off to sleep.* يثير، يهيج؛ ينبّه
2 to cause a reaction in sb: *The programme excited great interest.* يثير

excited /ɪk'saɪtɪd/ *adj* feeling very happy because you are looking forward to sth happening; not calm: *Are you getting excited about your holiday?* ○ *We're all very excited at the thought of moving into our new house.* متحمّس، مبتهج؛ منفعل
▸ **excitedly** *adv* بحماس؛ باهتياج

excitement /ɪk'saɪtmənt/ *noun* **1** [U] the state of being excited; a feeling of pleasure, especially because sth interesting is happening or will happen: *There was great excitement as the winner's name was announced.* ○ *The match was full of excitement until the very last minute.* اهتياج؛ حماس؛ إثارة؛ ابتهاج
2 [C] something that makes you feel excited: *After all the excitements of the last few weeks, it's nice to relax at home for a while.* شيء مثير

exciting /ɪk'saɪtɪŋ/ *adj* causing strong feelings of pleasure and interest: *That's very exciting news.* ○ *Berlin is one of the most exciting cities in Europe.* ❶ The opposite is **unexciting**. مثير، شيّق

exclaim /ɪk'skleɪm/ *verb* [I,T] to say sth suddenly because you are surprised, angry, etc: *'I just don't believe it!' he exclaimed.* يصيح فجأة، يهتف

exclamation /ˌeksklə'meɪʃn/ *noun* [C] a sound or word that expresses sudden pain, anger, surprise, etc: *'Ouch!' is an exclamation.* صيحة أو كلمة تدلّ على الانفعال

a b c d e f g h i j k l m n o p q r s t u v w x y z

ˌ**exclaˈmation mark** (*US* ˌ**exclaˈmation point**) *noun* [C] a mark (!) that is written after an exclamation علامة تعجُّب

exclude /ɪkˈskluːd/ *verb* [T] **1 exclude sb/sth (from sth)** to prevent sb/sth from getting in: *Women are excluded from the temple.* ○ *Try and exclude draughts from the room, and you will save money on your heating bills.* يمنع من الدخول؛ يبعد

2 to decide that sth is not true: *The police had excluded the possibility that the child had run away.* يستبعد

3 to leave out; not include: *The price excludes all extras such as drinks or excursions.* يستثني؛ يسقط

▸ **excluding** *prep* not including: *Lunch costs £10 per person excluding drinks.* باستثناء، دون

exclusion /ɪkˈskluːʒn/ *noun* [U] keeping or leaving sb/sth out منع؛ إبعاد؛ استثناء

exclusive /ɪkˈskluːsɪv/ *adj* **1** (only *before* a noun) for only one person, group, etc.; not to be shared: *This car is for the Director's exclusive use.* ○ *Tonight we are showing an exclusive interview with the new leader of the Labour Party* (= on only one television or radio station). خاص؛ مقصور على (صحيفة واحدة مثلاً)

2 expensive and not welcoming people who are thought to be socially unsuitable: *an exclusive restaurant* ○ *a flat in an exclusive part of the city* مقتصر على النخبة، راقٍ

3 exclusive of sb/sth not including sb/sth; without: *Lunch costs £10 per person exclusive of drinks.* فيما عدا، دونَ

▸ **exclusive** *noun* [C] a newspaper story that is given to and published by only one newspaper مقال يكتب خصّيصاً لجريدة واحدة فقط

exclusively *adv* only; not involving anybody/anything else: *The swimming pool is reserved exclusively for members of the club.* فقط؛ على وجه الحصر

excrement /ˈekskrɪmənt/ *noun* [U] (*formal*) the solid waste matter that is passed from the body through the bowels ➲ Look at **faeces**. غائط؛ براز

excrete /ɪkˈskriːt/ *verb* [T] (*formal*) to pass out waste matter from the body يفرز، يطرح الفضلات

excruciating /ɪkˈskruːʃieɪtɪŋ/ *adj* (used about pain, etc.) very bad (ألم) مبرّح

excursion /ɪkˈskɜːʃn; *US* -ɜːrʒn/ *noun* [C] a short journey or trip (that a group of people make for pleasure): *to go on an excursion* ➲ Look at the note at **travel**. نزهة، رحلة قصيرة

excuse[1] /ɪkˈskjuːs/ *noun* [C] **excuse (for sth/for doing sth)** a reason (that may be true or untrue) that you give in order to explain your behaviour: *There's no excuse for rudeness.* ○ *He always finds a good excuse for not helping with the housework.* ○ *to make an excuse* عذر، حجّة

excuse[2] /ɪkˈskjuːz/ *verb* [T] **1 excuse sb/sth (for sth/for doing sth)** to forgive sb/sth: *Please excuse the interruption but I need to talk to you.* يعذر، يصفح عن

2 to explain sb's bad behaviour and make it seem less bad: *Nothing can excuse such behaviour.* يقدّم عذراً؛ يبرّر

3 excuse sb (from sth) to free sb from a duty, responsibility, etc: *She was excused from PE because of her leg injury.* ○ *She excused herself for arriving late and sat down.* يعفي من

> The expression **excuse me** is used when you interrupt somebody or when you want to start talking to somebody that you don't know: *Excuse me, can you tell me the way to the station?* In US English and sometimes in British English **excuse me** is used when you apologize for something: *Did I tread on your toe? Excuse me.*

▸ **excusable** /ɪkˈskjuːzəbl/ *adj* that can be forgiven ❶ The opposite is **inexcusable**. ممكن أن يغتفر

execute /ˈeksɪkjuːt/ *verb* [T] **1** to kill sb as an official punishment: *He was executed for murder.* يعدم

2 (*formal*) to perform a task, etc. or to carry out a plan ينفّذ

execution /ˌeksɪˈkjuːʃn/ *noun* **1** [C,U] the act of killing sb as an official punishment إعدام

2 [U] (*formal*) carrying out a plan, order, etc. تنفيذ

▸ **executioner** /ˌeksɪˈkjuːʃənə(r)/ *noun* [C] a person whose job is to execute criminals الجلاّد، منفّذ حكم الإعدام

executive /ɪɡˈzekjətɪv/ *adj* **1** (used in connection with people in business, government, etc.) concerned with managing, carrying out decisions, plans, etc: *an executive director of the company* تنفيذيّ

2 (used about goods, buildings, etc.) designed to be used by important business people: *an executive briefcase* مصمّم لكبار رجال الأعمال

▸ **executive** *noun* [C] **1** a person who has an important position in a business: *She's a senior executive in a computer company.* موظّف كبير في شركة، منفّذ

2 the part of an organization which takes important decisions الهيئة الاداريّة

exemplary /ɪɡˈzempləri/ *adj* very good; that can be an example to other people: *exemplary behaviour* ممتاز، نموذجي

exemplify /ɪɡˈzemplɪfaɪ/ *verb* (*pres part* **exemplifying**; *3rd pers sing pres* **exemplifies**; *pt, pp* **exemplified**) [T] to be a typical example of sth يمثّل، يعطي مثلاً عن

exempt /ɪɡˈzempt/ *adj* (not before a noun) **exempt (from sth)** free from having to do sth or pay sth: *Children under 16 are exempt from dental charges.* معفى من

▸ **exempt** *verb* [T] **exempt sb/sth (from sth)** (*formal*) to say officially that sb does not have to do sth or pay sth يعفي من

exemption /ɪɡˈzempʃn/ *noun* [C,U] إعفاء، استثناء

exercise[1] /ˈeksəsaɪz/ *noun* **1** [U] physical or mental activity that keeps you healthy: *The doc-*

tor advised him to take regular exercise. ○ *Swimming is a good form of exercise.* رياضة بدنيّة

2 [C] (often plural) a movement or activity that you do in order to keep healthy or to train sth: *I do keep-fit exercises every morning.* ○ *You need to do some exercises to improve your technique.* تمارين رياضية

3 [C] a piece of work that is intended to help you learn or practise sth: *an exercise on phrasal verbs* تمرين

4 [C] a series of actions that have a particular aim: *The project is an exercise in getting the best results at a low cost.* ممارسة؛ تحقيق ا

5 [U] (*formal*) the use of sth (e.g. a power, right, etc.) ممارسة، استعمال

6 [C] a series of activities by soldiers to practise fighting: *military exercises* تدريبات أو مناورات عسكريّة

⚷**exercise²** /ˈeksəsaɪz/ *verb* **1** [I] to do some form of physical movement in order to stay fit and healthy: *It is important to exercise regularly.* يمارس الرياضة البدنيّة، يتمرّن

2 [T] to make use of sth (e.g. a power, right, etc.): *You should exercise your right to vote.* يمارس، يستخدم

ˈ**exercise book** (*US* **notebook**) a small book for students to write their work in دفتر التمارين

exert /ɪɡˈzɜːt/ *verb* [T] **1** to make use of sth (e.g. influence, strength, etc.): *Parents exert a powerful influence on their children's opinions.* يمارس

2 exert yourself to make an effort: *You won't make any progress if you don't exert yourself a bit more.* يبذل مجهوداً

▸ **exertion** /ɪɡˈzɜːʃn; *US* -ɜːrʒn/ *noun* [C,U] using your body in a way that takes a lot of effort; sth that you do that makes you tired: *I'm tired after the exertions of the past few days.* ○ *At his age physical exertion was dangerous.* إجهاد؛ مجهود

exhale /eksˈheɪl/ *verb* [I, T] (*formal*) to breathe out the air or smoke, etc. in your lungs يزفر، ينفث

exhaust¹ /ɪɡˈzɔːst/ *noun* **1** [C] a pipe (particularly at the back of a car) through which waste gas escapes from an engine or machine (انبوب) العادم

2 [U] the waste gas that escapes from an engine or machine الغاز المنطلق من العادم

exhaust² /ɪɡˈzɔːst/ *verb* [T] **1** to make sb very tired: *The long journey to work every morning exhausted him.* ينهك

2 to use sth up completely; to finish sth: *All the supplies of food have been exhausted.* يستنفد

3 to say everything you can about a subject, etc: *Well, I think we've exhausted that topic.* ينهك الموضوع، لا يترك فيه شيئاً للبحث

▸ **exhausted** *adj* very tired منهَك

exhausting *adj* making sb very tired: *Teaching young children is exhausting work.* منهِك

exhaustion /ɪɡˈzɔːstʃən/ *noun* [U] great tiredness إعياء، إرهاق؛ إنهاك

exhaustive /ɪɡˈzɔːstɪv/ *adj* including everything possible: *This list is certainly not exhaustive.* شامل؛ كامل

exhibit¹ /ɪɡˈzɪbɪt/ *noun* [C] an object that is shown in a museum, etc. شيء معروض

⚷**exhibit²** /ɪɡˈzɪbɪt/ *verb* [T] **1** to show sth to the public: *His paintings have been exhibited in the local art gallery.* يعرض

2 (*formal*) to show sth (e.g. a feeling or quality): *The refugees are exhibiting signs of exhaustion and stress* يبدي

▸ **exhibitor** *noun* [C] a person who shows his/her work to the public العارض

⚷**exhibition** /ˌeksɪˈbɪʃn/ *noun* **1** [C] a collection of objects that are shown to the public: *an exhibition of photographs* ○ *Have you seen the Picasso exhibition?* ○ *the National Exhibition Centre in Birmingham* ❶ Notice the expression **on exhibition**: *Her paintings will be on exhibition in London for the whole of April.* معرض

2 [C] an occasion when a particular skill is shown to the public: *We saw an exhibition of Scottish dancing last night.* عرض

3 [sing.] (*formal*) the act of showing a quality, feeling, etc: *The game was a superb exhibition of football at its best.* إظهار، عرض

exhilarate /ɪɡˈzɪləreɪt/ *verb* [T] (usually passive) to make sb feel very happy, excited, etc: *We felt exhilarated by our walk along the beach.* يُبْهِج؛ يُنْعِش، يشرح الصدر

▸ **exhilarating** *adj* مبهِج، منعِش؛ مثير

exhilaration /ɪɡˌzɪləˈreɪʃn/ *noun* [U] ابتهاج، انتعاش

exile /ˈeksaɪl/ *noun* **1** [U] the state of being forced to live outside your own country (especially for political reasons): *He went into exile after the revolution of 1968.* ○ *They lived in exile in London for many years.* نفي؛ منفى

2 [C] a person who is forced to live outside his/her own country (especially for political reasons): *Trotsky spent his last years as a political exile in Mexico.* ➲ Look at **refugee**. منفيّ

▸ **exile** *verb* [T] (usually passive) to send sb to live in another country (especially for political reasons): *After the revolution the king was exiled.* ينفي، يبعِد عن البلاد

⚷**exist** /ɪɡˈzɪst/ *verb* [I] **1** to be real; to be found in the real world; to live: *Does God exist?* ○ *I don't think that word exists, does it?* ○ *Fish cannot exist out of water.* يكون له وجود، يوجد؛ يعيش

2 exist (on sth) to manage to live: *I don't know how she exists on the wage she earns.* يعيش؛ يبقى حيّاً

▸ **existing** *adj* (only *before* a noun) that is already there or being used; present: *Under the existing law you are not allowed to work in this country.* حاضر، قائم

⚷**existence** /ɪɡˈzɪstəns/ *noun* **1** [U] the state of existing: *This is the oldest human skeleton in existence.* ○ *The country of Yugoslavia came into existence in 1918.* وجود

2 [sing.] a way of living; life: *They lead a*

a b c d e f g h i j k l m n o p q r s t u v w x y z

miserable existence in a tiny flat in London. معيشة، حياة

exit /'eksɪt; 'egzɪt/ *noun* [C] **1** a door or way out of a public building: *an emergency exit* مخرج

2 the act of leaving sth: *When he saw her coming he made a quick exit.* ○ *an exit visa* (= one that allows you to leave a country) خروج

3 a place where traffic can turn off a motorway, roundabout, etc: *At the roundabout take the third exit.* مخرج

▸ **exit** *verb* **1** [I] (*formal*) to go out or away يخرج؛ ينصرف

2 [I, T] (*computing*) to finish using a computer program: *I exited the database and switched off the computer.* يخرج؛ ينهي

exonerate /ɪg'zɒnəreɪt/ *verb* [T] (often passive) (*formal*) to free sb from blame, responsibility etc. يبرِّئ

exorbitant /ɪg'zɔːbɪtənt/ *adj* (*formal*) (used about the cost of sth) much more expensive than it should be باهظ

exotic /ɪg'zɒtɪk/ *adj* unusual or interesting because it comes from a different country or culture: *exotic plants, animals, etc.* غريب، طريف

expand /ɪk'spænd/ *verb* [I,T] to become bigger or to make sth bigger: *Metals expand when they are heated.* ○ *We hope to expand our business this year.* ❶ The opposite is **contract**. يتمدَّد؛ يوسِّع

PHRV **expand on sth** to give more details of a story, plan, point of view, etc. يفصِّل

expanse /ɪk'spæns/ *noun* [C] a large open area (of land, sea, sky, etc.) فسحة واسعة

expansion /ɪk'spænʃn/ *noun* [U] the action of expanding or the state of being expanded: *The rapid expansion of the university has caused a lot of problems.* توسُّع

expansive /ɪk'spænsɪv/ *adj* (*formal*) (used about a person) willing to talk a lot; friendly منفتح، ودود

expatriate /ˌeks'pætriət/ (*also informal* **expat** /ˌeks'pæt/) *noun* [C] a person who lives outside his/her own country مغترِب

expect /ɪk'spekt/ *verb* [T] **1** to think or believe that sb/sth will come or that sth will happen: *She was expecting a letter from the bank this morning but it didn't come.* ○ *I expect that it will rain this afternoon.* ○ *He expected it to be hot in Washington and it was.* ○ *'I'm really disappointed – she forgot my birthday.' 'Well, what did you expect?'* (= it's not surprising) ○ *She's expecting a baby in the spring* (= she's pregnant). ➲ Look at the note at **wait**[1]. يتوقَّع؛ ينتظر

2 expect sth (from sb); expect sb to do sth to hope that you will get sth from sb or that he/she will do what you want: *He expects a high standard of work from everyone.* ○ *Factory workers are often expected to work at nights.* يتوقَّع

3 (not used in the continuous forms) (*Brit*) (used when you think sth is probably true) to suppose: *'Who's eaten all the biscuits?' 'Oh it was Tom, I expect.'* ○ *'Will you be able to help me later on?' 'I expect so.'* يظنّ

▸ **expectancy** /ɪk'spektənsi/ *noun* [U] the state of expecting sth to happen; hope: *a look, feeling, etc. of expectancy* ➲ Look at **life expectancy**. توقُّع، ترقُّب

expectant /ɪk'spektənt/ *adj* expecting sth good; hopeful: *an expectant audience* ○ *expectant faces* ❶ **Expectant** also means 'pregnant' or 'waiting for a baby': *Expectant mothers need a lot of rest.* متوقِّع (خيراً)، متطلِّع؛ (امرأة) حامل

expectantly *adv* بكلِّ تلهُّف

expectation /ˌekspek'teɪʃn/ *noun* (*formal*) **1** [U] the belief that sth will happen: *There's no expectation of the weather getting better for some days yet.* توقُّع

2 [C, usually pl.] hope for the future: *They had great expectations for their daughter, but she didn't really live up to them.* أمل

IDM **against/contrary to (all) expectation(s)** quite different to what was expected: *Contrary to all expectations, Val won first prize.* توقُّع

not come up to (sb's) expectations to be less good than expected: *I'm afraid the hotel did not come up to our expectations.* رجاء، توقُّع

expedient /ɪk'spiːdiənt/ *adj* (*formal*) (used about an action) convenient or helpful for a purpose (but not always good or moral): *Before the election the government thought that it was expedient not to increase taxes.* نفعي

▸ **expediency** /-ənsi/ *noun* [U] نفعيَّة

expedition /ˌekspə'dɪʃn/ *noun* [C] **1** a long journey for a special purpose: *a scientific expedition to Antarctica* رحلة استكشافيَّة

2 a short journey that you make for pleasure: *a shopping expedition* جَوْلة

expel /ɪk'spel/ *verb* [T] (expelling; expelled) **1** to force sb to leave a country, school, club, etc: *The government has expelled all foreign journalists.* ○ *The boy was expelled from school for smoking.* يطرد

2 (*formal*) to send sth out by force: *to expel air from the lungs* ❶ The noun is **expulsion**. ينفث (بقوة)

expend /ɪk'spend/ *verb* [T] (*formal*) to spend or use money, time, care, etc. in doing sth: *I have expended a lot of time and energy on that project.* ينفِق

▸ **expendable** /-əbl/ *adj* (*formal*) not thought of as important or worth saving: *In a war human life is expendable.* يمكن الاستغناء عنه، لاقيمة له

expenditure /ɪk'spendɪtʃə(r)/ *noun* [U, sing.] (*formal*) the act of spending or using money, etc.; the amount of money, etc. which is spent: *Government expenditure on education is very low.* ○ *an expenditure of £2 000* إنفاق؛ نفقات أو مصروف

expense /ɪk'spens/ *noun* **1** [C,U] the cost of sth in time or money: *Running a car is a great expense.* ○ *Expense wasn't important when they were deciding where to go on holiday.* ❶ Note the expressions: **at great expense** (= at a high cost) and **at no expense** (= at no cost). كُلفة

2 expenses [plural] money that is spent for a particular purpose: *You can claim back your travelling expenses.* نفقات

IDM at sb's expense 1 with sb paying; at sb's cost: *My trip is at the company's expense.* نفقة، حساب

2 against sb, so that he/she looks silly: *They were always making jokes at Paul's expense.* (على) حساب؛ ضد

at the expense of sth harming or damaging sth: *He was a successful businessman, but it was at the expense of his family life.* (على) حساب

expensive /ɪk'spensɪv/ *adj* costing a lot of money: *Houses are very expensive in this area.* ○ *It's too expensive.* ❶ The opposite is **inexpensive** or **cheap**. غالٍ

▸ **expensively** *adv* بكلفة غالية

experience /ɪk'spɪəriəns/ *noun* **1** [U] the things that you have done; the knowledge or skill that you get from seeing or doing sth: *We all learn by experience.* ○ *She has five years' teaching experience.* ○ *You need a lot of experience in this job.* ○ *I know from experience what will happen.* خبرة

2 [C] something that has happened to you (often something unusual or exciting): *She wrote a book about her experiences in Africa.* ○ *It's an experience not to be missed.* حادثة هامة، تجربة

▸ **experience** *verb* [T] to have experience of sth; to feel: *It was the first time I'd ever experienced failure.* ○ *to experience pleasure, pain, difficulty, etc.* جرّب؛ يشعر، يعاني

experienced *adj* having the knowledge or skill that is necessary for sth: *He's not a very experienced driver.* ❶ The opposite is **inexperienced**. ذو خبرة

experiment /ɪk'sperɪmənt/ *noun* [C,U] a scientific test or trial that is done in order to prove sth or to get new knowledge: *Researchers often perform experiments on animals.* ○ *It's difficult to do experiments into how people learn languages.* ○ *I'm going to try cycling to work – it's just an experiment.* ○ *We need to prove this theory by experiment.* تجربة

▸ **experiment** *verb* [I] **experiment (on sth) / (with sth)** to do an experiment or to test: *Is it really necessary to experiment on animals?* ○ *We're experimenting with a new timetable this month.* يقوم بتجارب؛ يجرّب

experimental /ɪkˌsperɪ'mentl/ *adj* connected with experiments or new ideas: *We're still at the experimental stage with the new product.* ○ *experimental schools* تجريبي

experimentally /-təli/ *adv* تجريبياً

expert /'ekspɜːt/ *noun* [C] **an expert (at/in/on sth)** a person who has special knowledge or skill: *He's an expert on the history of rock music.* ○ *She's a computer expert.* ○ *Let me try – I'm an expert at parking cars in small spaces.* خبير

▸ **expert** *adj* **expert (at/in/on sth)** with special knowledge or skill: *He's an expert cook.* ○ *I think we should get expert advice on the problem.* اختصاصي

expertly *adv* بشكل محترف، بمهارة

expertise /ˌekspɜː'tiːz/ *noun* [U] special knowledge or skill: *I was amazed at his expertise on the word processor.* خبرة، مهارة

expire /ɪk'spaɪə(r)/ *verb* [I] (used about sth that only lasts for a certain period of time) to come to the end of the time when you can use it: *My passport's expired. I'll have to get it renewed.* ينتهي مفعوله

expiry /ɪk'spaɪəri/ *noun* [U] the end of a period when you can use sth: *The expiry date on this yogurt was 20 November.* انتهاء مدة أو مفعول

explain /ɪk'spleɪn/ *verb* [I,T] **1** to make sth clear or easy to understand: *A dictionary explains the meaning of words.* ○ *She explained how I should fill in the form.* ○ *I don't understand this. Can you explain?* يشرح

2 to give a reason for sth: *'This work isn't very good.' 'I wasn't feeling very well.' 'Oh, that explains it then.'* ○ *That explains why she was looking so miserable.* ○ *The manager explained to the customers why the goods were late.* يفسّر، يعلّل

explanation /ˌeksplə'neɪʃn/ *noun* **1** [U] making sth clear or giving a reason for sth: *That idea needs some explanation.* شرح، ايضاح

2 [C] something that makes a situation clear or understandable: *He could not give a satisfactory explanation for his behaviour.* تعليل، تبرير

explanatory /ɪk'splænətri; *US* -tɔːri/ *adj* giving an explanation: *There are some explanatory notes at the back of the book.* ○ *Those instructions are self-explanatory* (= they don't need explaining). تفسيري، ايضاحي

explicable /ɪk'splɪkəbl; 'ek-/ *adj* (*formal*) (usually used about people's behaviour) that can be explained ❶ The opposite is **inexplicable**. يمكن تفسيره أو تعليله

explicit /ɪk'splɪsɪt/ *adj* **1** clear, not making anything difficult to understand: *I gave you explicit instructions not to touch anything.* ○ *She was quite explicit about her feelings on the subject.* واضح

2 not hiding anything: *Some of the sex scenes in that TV play were very explicit.* صريح

▸ **explicitly** *adv*: *He was explicitly forbidden to stay out later than midnight.* بكلّ وضوح وصراحة

explode /ɪk'spləʊd/ *verb* [I,T] to burst with a loud noise: *The bomb exploded without warning.* ○ *The bomb was taken away and the army exploded it at a safe distance from the houses.* ○ (*figurative*) *My father exploded* (= became very angry) *when I told him how much the car would cost to repair.* ❶ The noun is **explosion**. ينفجر؛ يفجر

exploit¹ /ɪk'splɔɪt/ *verb* [T] **1** to use sth or to treat sb unfairly or selfishly: *This region has been exploited for oil for fifty years.* يستغلّ

2 to develop sth or make the best use of sth: *Solar energy is a source of power that needs to be exploited more fully.* يستثمر، يستخدم

▸ **exploitation** /ˌeksplɔɪ'teɪʃn/ *noun* [U] exploiting or being exploited: *They're only paying £3 an hour? That's exploitation!* استغلال

exploit² /ˈeksplɔɪt/ *noun* [C] a brave or adventurous action عمل بطوليّ، مغامرة

explore /ɪkˈsplɔː(r)/ *verb* [I,T] to travel around a place, etc. in order to learn about it: *They went on an expedition to explore the River Amazon.* ○ *I've never been to Paris before – I'm going out to explore.* ○ (*figurative*) *We need to explore* (= look carefully at) *all the possibilities before we decide.* يستكشف؛ يتحرّى، يتفحّص

▸ **exploration** /ˌekspləˈreɪʃn/ *noun* [C,U] the act of exploring: *space exploration* استكشاف

exploratory /ɪkˈsplɒrətri; *US* -tɔːri/ *adj* done in order to find sth out: *The doctors are doing some exploratory tests to try and find out what's wrong.* استطلاعيّ؛ تمهيدي

explorer *noun* [C] a person who travels round a place in order to find out about it مستكشِف

explosion /ɪkˈspləʊʒn/ *noun* [C] the sudden and violent bursting and loud noise that happen when sth like a bomb explodes: *The explosion may have been caused by a gas leak.* ○ (*figurative*) *the population explosion* (= the sudden increase in the number of people in a country or in the world) انفجار

explosive /ɪkˈspləʊsɪv/ *adj* **1** capable of exploding and therefore dangerous: *Hydrogen is extremely explosive.* متفجّر

2 causing strong feelings or having dangerous effects: *The situation is explosive. We must do all we can to calm people down.* متفجّر، يهدّد بالانفجار

▸ **explosive** *noun* [C] a substance that can explode: *Dynamite and TNT are powerful explosives.* مادّة متفجِّرة

export¹ /ɪkˈspɔːt/ *verb* [I,T] **1** to send goods, etc. to another country, usually for sale: *India exports tea and cotton.* يصدّر

2 (*computing*) to move information from one program to another ينقل مادة من برنامج إلى آخر

▸ **exporter** *noun* [C] a person, firm or country that exports goods: *Which country is the largest exporter of electronic goods?* ❶ The opposites are **import**, **importer**. مصدّر

export² /ˈekspɔːt/ *noun* **1** [U] sending goods to another country for sale: *Most of our goods are produced for export.* ○ *the export trade* تصدير

2 [C, usually pl.] something that is sent to another country for sale: *What are the main exports of Brazil?* ❶ The opposite is **import**. صادرات

expose /ɪkˈspəʊz/ *verb* [T] **1** to make it possible to see sth that is usually hidden: *The rocks are exposed at low tide.* يكشف، يظهِر

2 to put sb/sth or yourself in a situation that could be difficult or dangerous: *Thousands of people were exposed to radiation when the nuclear reactor exploded.* يعرّض

3 to make public the truth about a bad person or situation: *This is an injustice which needs to be exposed.* يكشف، يفضح

4 (in photography) to allow light to reach the film by opening the shutter of the camera يعرّض

5 expose sb to sth to give sb the chance to experience sth: *I like jazz because I was exposed to it as a child.* يتعرّف على؛ يتعرّض

▸ **exposed** *adj* (used about a place) not protected from the wind and bad weather (مكان) مكشوف، معرّض للعوامل الطبيعية

exposure /ɪkˈspəʊʒə(r)/ *noun* **1** [U] being affected or influenced by sth: *Exposure to radiation is almost always harmful.* تعرُّض

2 [U] a harmful condition when a person becomes very cold because he/she has been outside in very bad weather: *The climbers all died of exposure.* التعرّض للعوامل الجويّة القاسية

3 [C,U] the act of making sth public; the thing that is made public: *The minister resigned because of the exposures about his private life.* كَشْف، فضْح: الخفايا المفضوحة

4 [U] attention from newspapers, television, etc.; publicity: *The President's visit has been given a lot of exposure in the media.* دعاية إعلاميّة

5 [C] the amount of film that is exposed(4) when you take one photograph: *How many exposures are there on this film?* (= how many photographs can I take?) صورة

express¹ /ɪkˈspres/ *verb* [T] **1** to show sth such as a feeling or an opinion by words or actions: *I found it very hard to express what I felt about her.* يعبّر

2 express yourself to speak or write: *I don't think she expresses herself very well in that article.* يفصح عن رأيه

express² /ɪkˈspres/ *adj* (only *before* a noun) **1** going or sent quickly: *an express letter* ○ *an express coach* سريع

2 (used about a wish, command, etc.) clearly and openly stated: *It was her express wish that he should have the picture after her death.* صريح، واضح

▸ **express** *adv* by a special service that does sth faster than usual: *We'd better send the parcel express if we want it to get there on time.* (بالبريد) السريع

expressly *adv* **1** clearly; definitely: *I expressly told you not to eat in the classroom.* بشكل واضح

2 for a special purpose; specially: *These scissors are expressly designed for left-handed people.* خصّيصاً

express³ /ɪkˈspres/ (*also* **express train**) *noun* [C] a fast train that does not stop at all stations قطار سريع

expression /ɪkˈspreʃn/ *noun* **1** [C] a number of words that belong together: *You haven't quite got the right expression here.* ○ *a slang expression* ○ *'I'm starving' is an expression meaning 'I'm very hungry'.* عبارة، تعبير

2 [C] the look on a person's face that shows what he/she is thinking or feeling: *He had a puzzled expression on his face.* تعابير الوجه

3 [C,U] putting feelings or thoughts into words or actions; an example of doing this: *Freedom of*

expression (= freedom to say what you think) *is a basic human right.* ○ *These flowers are an expression of our gratitude.* ○ *She read the poem with great expression* (= showing feeling for the meaning of it). الإفصاح عن المشاعر، تعبير

expressive /ɪk'spresɪv/ *adj* showing feelings or thoughts: *That is a very expressive piece of music.* معبِّر
▸ **expressively** *adv* بشكل له معنى

ex'pressway *noun* [C] (*US*) = MOTORWAY

expulsion /ɪk'spʌlʃn/ *noun* [C,U] making sb leave a place or an institution (when he/she does not want to go): *There have been three expulsions from school this year.* ❶ The verb is **expel**. طرْد، إخراج

exquisite /ɪk'skwɪzɪt/ *adj* very beautiful and pleasing: *She has an exquisite face.* ○ *I think that ring is exquisite.* رائع

extend /ɪk'stend/ *verb* **1** [T] to make sth longer or larger (in space or time): *They are planning to extend the motorway as far as Fishguard.* ○ *Could you extend your visit for a few days?* ○ *We're going to extend the sitting room.* يمدّ، يطيل، يوسّع

2 [I] (usually used about space, land, time, etc.) to continue or stretch: *How far does your garden extend?* ○ *This project will extend well into next year.* يمتدّ

3 [T] to stretch out a part of the body: *She extended her hand to her new colleague.* يمُدّ

4 [T] (*formal*) to offer or give sth (such as an invitation or a welcome): *The whole town extended a warm welcome to the president.* يقدّم

extension /ɪk'stenʃn/ *noun* [C] **1** a part which is added to a building: *They've just opened the hospital extension.* بناء ملحق

2 an extra period of time that is given to you by an official: *I've applied for an extension to my work permit.* تمديد

3 (*abbr* **ext.**) a telephone that is connected to a central phone in a house or to a central point (switchboard) in a large office building: *What's your extension number?* ○ *Can I have extension 4342, please?* تليفون فرعي

extensive /ɪk'stensɪv/ *adj* large in area or amount: *The house has extensive grounds.* ○ *Most of the buildings suffered extensive damage.* واسع: واسع النطاق
▸ **extensively** *adv* على نطاق واسع

extent /ɪk'stent/ *noun* [U] the length, area or size of sth: *From the roof we could see the full extent of the park.* ○ *I was amazed at the extent of his knowledge.* ○ *The full extent of the damage is not yet known.* مدى، امتداد

IDM **to a certain/to some extent** (words used to show that sth is only partly true): *I agree with you to a certain extent but there are still a lot of points I disagree with.* حدّ

to what extent how far: *I'm not sure to what extent I believe her.* إلى أيّ حدّ

exterior /ɪk'stɪəriə(r)/ *adj* on the outside: *the exterior walls of a house* ❶ The opposite is **interior**. خارجي
▸ **exterior** *noun* [C] the appearance of sb/sth; the outside of sth: *The exterior of the house is fine but inside it isn't in very good condition.* مظهر خارجي

exterminate /ɪk'stɜːmɪneɪt/ *verb* [T] to kill a large group of people or animals يبيد، يقضي على
▸ **extermination** /ɪkˌstɜːmɪ'neɪʃn/ *noun* [U] إبادة

external /ɪk'stɜːnl/ *adj* **1** connected with the outside of sth: *The cream is for external use only* (= to be used on the skin). خارجي

2 coming from another place: *You will be tested by an external examiner.* ❶ The opposite is **internal**. خارجيّ، (ممتحِن) من جامعة أخرى

extinct /ɪk'stɪŋkt/ *adj* **1** (used about a type of animal, plant, etc.) no longer existing: *Tigers are nearly extinct in the wild.* منقرض، بائد

2 (used about a volcano) no longer active (بركان) خامد
▸ **extinction** /ɪk'stɪŋkʃn/ *noun* [U]: *The panda is in danger of extinction.* انقراض

extinguish /ɪk'stɪŋgwɪʃ/ *verb* [T] (*formal*) to cause sth to stop burning: *The fire was extinguished very quickly.* ○ *The stewardess asked everybody to extinguish their cigarettes.* ❶ A less formal expression is **put out**. يخمِد
▸ **extinguisher** *noun* [C] = FIRE EXTINGUISHER

extort /ɪk'stɔːt/ *verb* [T] **extort sth (from sb)** to get sth by using threats, violence, etc. يبتزّ
▸ **extortion** /ɪk'stɔːʃn/ *noun* [U] ابتزاز

extortionate /ɪk'stɔːʃənət/ *adj* (used about demands, prices, etc.) too great or high: *Three pounds for a cup of coffee? That's extortionate!* ابتزازيّ، (سعر) فاحش

extra /'ekstrə/ *adj, adv* more than is usual: *I'll need some extra money for the holidays.* ○ *The football match went into extra time.* ○ *'What size is this pullover?' 'Extra large.'* ○ *The meal costs £10 and drinks are extra.* ○ *They charge £1 extra if you want to reserve a seat.* ○ *I tried to be extra nice to him yesterday because it was his birthday.* إضافيّ: أكثر من المعتاد
▸ **extra** *noun* [C] **1** something that is or costs extra: *Optional extras such as colour printer, scanner and modem are available on top of the basic package.* علاوة، رسم اضافي

2 a person in a film, etc. who has a small unimportant part, for example in a crowd ممثل يقوم بدور تافه جداً، "كمبارس"

extract /ɪk'strækt/ *verb* [T] to take or get sth out (with force or difficulty): *I think this tooth will have to be extracted.* ○ *I wasn't able to extract an apology from her.* يقتلع، ينتزع؛ يستخرج
▸ **extract** /'ekstrækt/ *noun* [C] a part of a book, piece of music, etc. An extract has often been specially chosen to show sth: *We're reading extracts from modern British novels this term.* مقتطف

extraction /ɪk'strækʃn/ *noun* **1** [U] the act of taking or getting sth out استخراج

2 [C] the removal of a tooth اقتلاع، خلع

3 [U] (*formal*) family origin: *He's an American but he's of Italian extraction.* أصل

extra-curricular /ˌekstrə kəˈrɪkjələ(r)/ *adj* not part of the normal course of studies (curriculum) in a school or college: *The school offers many extra-curricular activities such as sport, music, drama, etc.* (نشاط مدرسيّ) ليس جزءاً من المنهج الدراسيّ المقرّر

extradite /ˈekstrədaɪt/ *verb* [T] to send a person who may be guilty of a crime from the country in which he/she is living to the country which wants to try him/her for the crime: *The suspected terrorists were captured in Spain and extradited to France.* يسلّم مجرماً فاراً إلى دولته

▸ **extradition** /ˌekstrəˈdɪʃn/ *noun* [C,U] تسليم مجرم فارّ إلى دولته

extraordinary /ɪkˈstrɔːdnri; *US* -dəneri/ *adj*

1 very unusual: *She had an extraordinary ability to learn new languages.* خارق

2 very strange (and not what you would expect in a particular situation): *That was extraordinary behaviour for a teacher!* غير مألوف، غريب

▸ **extraordinarily** /ɪkˈstrɔːdnrəli; *US* -dənerəli/ *adv*: *He was an extraordinarily talented musician.* بشكل خارق

extravagant /ɪkˈstrævəgənt/ *adj* **1** spending or costing too much money: *He's terribly extravagant – he never looks at the price of anything.* ○ *an extravagant present* مبذّر؛ مفرط

2 (used about ideas, behaviour, etc.) not controlled, not realistic: *The advertisements made extravagant claims for the new medicine.* مغالٍ، مسرف

▸ **extravagance** /-gəns/ *noun* [C,U] إسراف، تبذير

extravagantly *adv* بإسراف؛ بشكل مبالغ فيه

extreme /ɪkˈstriːm/ *adj* **1** (used about a person and his/her political opinions) not usual or moderate: *She holds extreme views on immigration.* ○ *the extreme left/right* ⓘ This word is used in a disapproving way. متطرّف

2 (only *before* a noun) the greatest or strongest possible: *You must take extreme care when driving at night.* شديد

3 (only *before* a noun) as far away as possible; at the very beginning or at the very end: *Kerry is in the extreme West of Ireland.* اقصى

▸ **extreme** *noun* [C] something that is completely different from or opposite to sth else: *Alex used to be very shy but now she's gone to the opposite extreme.* طرف قصيّ

extremely *adv* very جداً، للغاية

extremity /ɪkˈstreməti/ *noun* [C] (*pl.* **extremities**) the furthest point of sth طرف، نهاية

exˌtreme ˈsport *noun* [C] a very dangerous sport or activity which some people do for fun نوع خطر من الرياضة

extremist /ɪkˈstriːmɪst/ *noun* [C] a person who has extreme (1) political opinions متطرّف

▸ **extremism** *noun* [U] تطرّف

extricate /ˈekstrɪkeɪt/ *verb* [T] to free sb/sth/yourself from a difficult situation or position: *I finally managed to extricate myself from the meeting by saying that I had a train to catch.* يُخلّص (من مأزق)

extrovert /ˈekstrəvɜːt/ *noun* [C] a person who is lively and cheerful and who prefers being with other people to being alone ⓘ The opposite is **introvert**. انبساطيّ، ذو شخصية مفتوحة

exuberant /ɪgˈzjuːbərənt; *US* -ˈzuː-/ *adj* (used about a person and his/her behaviour) full of energy and excitement طافح بالحيويّة

▸ **exuberance** /-rəns/ *noun* [U] حيويّة، بِشر ومَرح

eye¹ /aɪ/ *noun* [C] **1** one of the two organs of the body that we use to see with: *She opened/closed her eyes.* ○ *He is blind in one eye.* ○ *She's got blue eyes.* ○ *an eye operation* عين، مقلة

> If somebody hits you on the eye you might get a **black eye**. When you close both eyes very quickly and open them again you **blink**. To close one eye quickly and open it again is to **wink**.

2 the power of seeing: *He has sharp eyes* (= he can see very well). ○ *She has an eye for detail* (= she notices small details). بصر

3 the part at one end of a needle that the thread passes through ثقب الابرة

IDM **be up to your eyes in sth** (*informal*) to have more of sth than you can easily do or manage: *I can't come out with you tonight – I'm up to my eyes in work.* غارق لأذنيه (في العمل مثلاً)

cast an eye/your eye(s) over sb/sth → CAST²

catch sb's attention/eye → CATCH¹

in the eyes of sb/in sb's eyes in the opinion of sb: *She was still a child in her mother's eyes.* نظر

keep an eye on sb/sth to make sure that sb/sth is safe; to look after sb/sth: *Please could you keep an eye on the house while we are away?* يراقب، يرعى

keep an eye open/out (for sb/sth) to watch or look out for sb/sth: *I've lost my ring – could you keep an eye out for it?* ينظر باحثاً عن شيء

the naked eye → NAKED

see eye to eye with sb to agree with sb; to have the same opinion as sb: *We're good friends but we don't always see eye to eye on political matters.* يوافق في الرأي

set eyes on sb/sth → SET²

turn a blind eye → BLIND¹

with your eyes open knowing what you are doing: *He married her with his eyes open so he can't complain now.* على علم بالعاقبة

eye² /aɪ/ *verb* [T] (*pres part* **eyeing** or **eying**; *pt, pp* **eyed**) to look at sb/sth closely: *She eyed him with suspicion.* يحدّق، يرمق

eyeball /ˈaɪbɔːl/ *noun* [C] the whole of the eye (including the part which is hidden inside the head) العين، مقلة العين

eyebrow /ˈaɪbraʊ/ (*also* **brow**) *noun* [C] the line of hair that is above your eye: *to pluck your eyebrows* حاجب

IDM raise your eyebrows → RAISE[1]

ˈeye-catching *adj* (used about a thing) attracting your attention immediately because it is interesting, bright or pretty ملفت للنظر: أخاذ

eyeglasses /ˈaɪglɑːsɪz; *US* -glæsɪz/ *noun* [plural] (*US*) = GLASSES

eyelash /ˈaɪlæʃ/ (*also* **lash**) *noun* [C] one of the hairs that grow on the edges of your eyelids هدب، رمش

ˈeye level *adj* level with sb's eyes when he/she is standing up: *an eye-level grill* على مستوى البصر

eyelid /ˈaɪlɪd/ (*also* **lid**) *noun* [C] the piece of skin that can move to close your eye جفن
IDM not bat an eyelid → BAT[3]

ˈeye-opener *noun* [C] something that makes you realize the truth about sth: *That television programme about the inner cities was a real eye-opener.* شيء ينبّه إلى حقائق الأمور

eyeshadow /ˈaɪʃædəʊ/ *noun* [U] colour that is put on the skin above the eyes to make them look more attractive ظلّ (لتجميل العيون)

eyesight /ˈaɪsaɪt/ *noun* [U] the ability to see: *good/poor eyesight* بصر

eyesore /ˈaɪsɔː(r)/ *noun* [C] something that is ugly and unpleasant to look at: *All this litter in the streets is a real eyesore.* منظر مؤذ

eyewitness /ˈaɪwɪtnəs/ *noun* [C] = WITNESS (1)

F f

F, f /ef/ *noun* [C] (*pl.* **Fs**; **F's**; **f's**) the sixth letter of the English alphabet: *'Father' begins with (an) 'F'.* الحرف السادس من الابجدية الانكليزية

F *abbrev* = FAHRENHEIT

f (*also* **fem**) *abbrev* = FEMALE; FEMININE

fable /ˈfeɪbl/ *noun* [C] a short story that teaches a lesson (a moral) and that often has animals as speaking characters: *Aesop's fables* أقصوصة ذات مغزى تروى على ألسنة الحيوان

fabric /ˈfæbrɪk/ *noun* **1** [C,U] (a type of) cloth: *cotton fabrics* قماش، نسيج

2 [sing.] the walls, floor, roof, etc. (of a building): *The fabric of the church is in need of repair.* ○ (*figurative*) *The Industrial Revolution changed the fabric* (= the basic structure) *of society.* بنية، بنيان

fabulous /ˈfæbjələs/ *adj* **1** (*informal*) very good; excellent: *It was a fabulous concert.* رائع، ممتاز

2 (used about beauty, wealth, etc.) very great أسطوريّ: هائل

facade /fəˈsɑːd/ *noun* [C] **1** the front wall of a large building that you see from the outside واجهة المبنى

2 something that gives you the wrong impression about a situation: *His good humour was just a facade.* مظهر خارجي

face[1] /feɪs/ *noun* [C] **1** the front part of your head; the expression on it: *Go and wash your face.* ○ *She has a very pretty face.* ○ *He came in with a smile on his face.* ○ *the children's happy faces* وجه

2 the front or one side of sth: *the north face of the mountain* ○ *He put the cards face up/down on the table.* ○ *a clock face* وجه؛ واجهة؛ سطح
IDM face to face (with sb/sth) close to and looking at sb/sth: *She turned the corner and came face to face with the headmaster.* وجهاً لوجه
keep a straight face → STRAIGHT[1]
lose face → LOSE
make/pull faces/a face (at sb/sth) to make an expression that shows that you dislike sb/sth: *When she saw what was for dinner she pulled a face.* تعبير على الوجه ينم عن الاستياء، يكشّر
make/pull faces to make rude expressions with your face: *The children made faces behind the teacher's back.* يسخر منه بحركات على وجهه
save face → SAVE
to sb's face openly and directly: *I wanted to say that I was sorry to her face, not on the phone.* ❶ The opposite is **behind sb's back**. مواجهة، وجهاً لوجه
▸ **faceless** *adj* without individual character: *faceless civil servants* عديم الشخصية

face[2] /feɪs/ *verb* [T] **1** to have or turn the face or front towards sb/sth: *The garden faces south.* ○ *Can you all face the front, please?* ○ *Turn round and face the camera.* يواجه

2 to have to deal with sth unpleasant; to deal with sb in a difficult situation: *They faced a lot of problems when they moved house.* ○ *I can't face another argument.* ○ *He couldn't face going to work yesterday – he felt too ill.* ○ *I didn't know how to face my mother after I'd crashed her car.* يجابه، يواجه

3 to need attention from sb: *Several problems face the government.* ○ *There are several problems facing the government.* يجابه، يواجه

4 (often passive) to force somebody to deal with a situation, etc: *We are faced with a difficult decision.* يتصدّى لـ، يجابه
IDM let's face it (*informal*) we must accept it as true: *Let's face it, your spelling is terrible.* لنعترفْ بالواقع
PHR V face up to sth to accept a difficult or unpleasant situation and do sth about it: *She faced up to the fact that she had no money and went out and got a job.* يجابه
▸ **-faced** (in compounds) with a particular type of face: *red-faced* وجه، محيّا

a b c d e f g h i j k l m n o p q r s t u v w x y z

facecloth /ˈfeɪsklɒθ/ (*also* **flannel**) (*US* **washcloth**) *noun* [C] a small square towel that is used for washing the face, hands, etc. فوطة صغيرة لتنظيف الوجه

facelift /ˈfeɪslɪft/ *noun* [C] a medical operation that makes your face look younger عملية شدّ الوجه

ˈface-saving *adj* done to stop yourself looking silly or losing other people's respect: *In his interview, the captain made face-saving excuses for his team's defeat.* حافظ للكرامة، حافظ لماء الوجه

facet /ˈfæsɪt/ *noun* [C] **1** one part of sth: *There are many facets to this argument* (= points that must be considered). وجه، جانب

2 one side of a precious stone سُطيح أو وُجَيْه في جوهرة

facetious /fəˈsiːʃəs/ *adj* trying to be amusing at an unsuitable time or about an unsuitable subject: *He kept making facetious remarks during the lecture.* سخيف، (تعليق) هزليّ في غير محلّه

▸ **facetiously** *adv* بسخف، مداعباً دعابة سخيفة

ˌface ˈvalue *noun* [C,U] the cost or value that is shown on stamps, coins, etc. قيمة، (طابع مثلاً) من فئة...

IDM **take sb/sth at (its, his, etc.) face value** to accept sb/sth as it, he, etc. appears to be: *Don't take his story at face value. There is something he hasn't told us yet.* (يقبل الشيء) على علاته، كما يبدو في الظاهر

facial /ˈfeɪʃl/ *adj* of or for the face: *a facial expression* وجهي

▸ **facial** *noun* a beauty treatment in which a person's face is cleaned using creams, steam, etc. in order to improve the quality of the skin معالجة تجميليّة للوجه

facile /ˈfæsaɪl; *US* ˈfæsl/ *adj* (used about a remark, argument, etc.) not carefully thought out سطحي

facilitate /fəˈsɪlɪteɪt/ *verb* [T] (*formal*) to make sth possible or easier يسهّل

🔑 **facility** /fəˈsɪləti/ *noun* (*pl.* **facilities**) **1 facilities** [plural] a service, building, piece of equipment, etc. that makes it possible to do sth: *Our town has excellent sports facilities* (e.g. a stadium, swimming pool, etc.). ○ *The room was nice but there were no cooking facilities.* تسهيلات: معدّات: وسائل

2 [C] an extra feature that a machine, etc. may have: *a facility for checking spelling* وسيلة: امكانيّة

facsimile /fækˈsɪməli/ *noun* [C,U] an exact copy of a picture, piece of writing, etc. ➲ Look at **fax**. نسخة طبق الأصل

🔑 **fact** /fækt/ *noun* **1** [C] something that you know has happened or is true: *It is a scientific fact that light travels faster than sound.* ○ *We need to know all the facts before we can decide.* ○ *I know for a fact that Peter wasn't ill yesterday.* ○ *The fact that I am older than you makes no difference at all.* ○ *You must face facts and accept that he has gone.* حقيقة، أمر واقع

2 [U] true things; reality: *The film is based on fact.* ❶ The opposite is **fiction**. حقائق، وقائع

IDM **as a matter of fact** → MATTER[1]

the fact (of the matter) is (that)... the truth is that...: *I would love a car, but the fact is that I just can't afford one.* واقع الأمر

facts and figures (*informal*) detailed information: *Before we make a decision, we need some more facts and figures.* معلومات، تفاصيل

the facts of life the details of sexual behaviour and how babies are born حقائق الحياة: الحقائق المتعلقة بالجنس والحمل وغير ذلك

hard facts → HARD[1]

in (actual) fact 1 (used for emphasizing that sth is true) really; actually: *I thought the lecture would be boring but in actual fact it was rather interesting.* في الحقيقة، في الواقع

2 (used for introducing more detailed information): *It was cold. In fact it was freezing.* على الأصحّ، بالأحرى

faction /ˈfækʃn/ *noun* **1** [C] a small group within a larger one that opposes some of its beliefs or activities: *rival factions within the government.* فئة معارضة

2 [U] films, programmes, plays, books, etc. that combine real events with fiction عمل فنّي يمزج الحقيقة والخيال

🔑 **factor** /ˈfæktə(r)/ *noun* [C] **1** one of the things that influences a decision, situation, etc: *economic factors* ○ *His unhappiness at home was a major factor in his decision to go abroad.* عامل، عنصر

2 (in mathematics) a whole number (except 1) by which a larger number can be divided: *2, 3, 4 and 6 are factors of 12.* قاسم، عامل

🔑 **factory** /ˈfæktri/ (*pl.* **factories**) *noun* [C] a large building or group of buildings where goods are manufactured or put together in large quantities (by machine): *a car factory* ○ *factory workers* معمل، مصنع

factual /ˈfæktʃuəl/ *adj* based on or containing facts: *a factual account of the events* ➲ Look at **fictional**. واقعي، حقيقي

faculty /ˈfæklti/ (*pl.* **faculties**) *noun* [C] **1** one of the natural abilities of a person's body or mind: *the faculty of hearing, sight, etc.* ملكة، مقدرة

2 (*also* **Faculty**) one department in a university, college, etc: *the Faculty of Law* كليّة، قِسم

> **The Faculty** can also mean the teaching staff of a university or college department and is then used with either a singular or a plural verb: *The Faculty has/have been invited to the meeting.*

fad /fæd/ *noun* [C] (*informal*) a fashion, interest, etc. that will probably not last long ميل عابر، "صَرْعة" أو "موضة" لاتدوم

fade /feɪd/ *verb* **1** [I] to become lighter in colour or less strong or fresh: *Jeans fade when you wash them.* ○ *The sun was setting and the light was fading fast.* يبهت، يخفت، يخبو

2 [T] to make sth fade: *Look how the sun has faded these curtains.* يذبل، يبهت (اللون)

3 [I] **fade (away)** to disappear slowly (from

sight, hearing, memory, etc.): *The cheering of the crowd faded away.* ○ *The smile faded from his face.* يتلاشى، يَذبل

faeces (*US* **feces**) /'fiːsiːz/ *noun* [plural] (*formal*) solid waste matter that is passed from the body through the bowels ❶ **Faeces** is used mainly in a medical context. Look at **excrement**. براز، غائط

fag /fæg/ *noun* **1** [C] (*Brit slang*) a cigarette سيجارة

2 [sing.] (*informal*) a piece of work that you do not want to do: *I've got to wash the car. What a fag!* عمل مستثقل

Fahrenheit /'færənhaɪt/ *noun* [U] (*abbr* **F**) the name of a scale which measures temperatures: *Water freezes at 32° Fahrenheit (32°F).* ➲ Look at **Celsius.** فارنهايت

⚷**fail** /feɪl/ *verb* **1** [I,T] to be unsuccessful in sth: *She failed her driving test.* ○ *I feel that I've failed – I'm 29 and I still haven't got a steady job.* ➲ Look at **pass** and **succeed**. يفشل، يخفق

2 [T] (used about an examiner, etc.) to decide that sb is unsuccessful in a test, examination, etc: *The examiners failed half of the candidates.* ❶ The opposite is **pass**. يرسِّب

3 [I] **fail to do sth** to not do sth: *Jimmy failed to arrive on time.* ○ *She never fails to do her homework.* يعجز عن، يقصِّر، يتخلَّف

4 [I,T] to not be enough or not do what people are expecting or wanting: *If the crops fail, people will starve.* ○ *I think the government has failed us.* يَخذُل، يتخلّى عن؛ يفشل

5 [I] (used about health, eyesight, etc.) to become weak: *His health is failing.* يتدهور

6 [I] to stop working: *My brakes failed on the hill but I managed to stop the car.* يتعطّل، ينقطع

▸ **fail** *noun* [C] a failure in an examination ❶ The opposite is a **pass**. رسوب

IDM **without fail** always, even if there are difficulties: *The postman always comes at 8 o'clock without fail.* بكلّ تأكيد؛ دوماً وبدون تقصير

failing¹ /'feɪlɪŋ/ *noun* [C] a weakness or fault: *She's not very patient – that's her only failing.* نقطة ضعف، عَيْب

failing² /'feɪlɪŋ/ *prep* if sth is not possible: *Ask Jackie to go with you, or failing that, try Anne.* في حال عدم حدوث... إن لم...

⚷**failure** /'feɪljə(r)/ *noun* **1** [U] lack of success: *All my efforts ended in failure.* فشل، إخفاق

2 [C] a person or thing that is unsuccessful: *I was a failure as a mother.* ○ *His first attempt at ice skating was a miserable failure.* شخص فاشل؛ خائب

3 [C,U] **failure to do sth** not doing sth that people expect you to do: *I was very disappointed at his failure to come to the meeting.* تخلّف، تقصير

4 [C,U] an example of sth not working or functioning properly: *She died of heart failure.* ○ *There's been a failure in the power supply.* تعطُّل؛ قصور؛ سكتة (قلبيّة)

⚷**faint** /feɪnt/ *adj* **1** (used about things that you can see, hear, feel, etc.) not strong or clear: *a faint light in the distance* ○ *They heard a faint cry, then there was silence.* ○ *There is still a faint hope that they will find more people alive.* خافت، ضعيف

2 (used about people) on the point of losing consciousness; very weak: *I feel faint – I'd better sit down.* واهن؛ على وشك الاغماء

3 (used about actions, etc.) done without much effort: *He made a faint protest.* ضعيف

IDM **not have the faintest/foggiest (idea)** not to know at all: *I haven't the faintest idea where they've gone.* ليست لديه أدنى فكرة...

▸ **faint** *verb* [I] to lose consciousness: *She fainted from shock and loss of blood.* يغمى على

⚷**fair¹** /feə(r)/ *adj* **1** **fair (to/on sb)** treating each person or side equally, according to the law or the rules, etc: *That's not fair – he got the same number of mistakes as I did and he's got a better mark.* ○ *It wasn't fair on her to ask her to stay so late.* ○ *a fair trial* عادل، منصف

2 right, according to what people generally accept as right: *That's a fair price for that house, I think.* ○ *I think it's fair to say that the number of homeless people is increasing.* معقول؛ مشروع

3 quite good, large, etc: *They have a fair chance of success.* ○ *It is a fair-sized house.* لابأس به، معتدل

4 (used about the skin or hair) light in colour: *We think of Germans as having fair hair but a lot of them are dark.* أشقر، أبيض البشرة

5 (used about the weather) good, without rain (طقس) صَحْو

IDM **fair play** equal treatment of both/all sides according to the rules: *The referee is there to ensure fair play during the match.* منصف، مراعٍ للشروط والانظمة

(more than) your fair share of sth (more than) the usual or expected amount of sth: *We've had more than our fair share of trouble this year.* عادل، متوقَّع

▸ **fairness** *noun* [U] the state or quality of being fair عدل، إنصاف

fair² /feə(r)/ *adv* in a fair way: *You must play fair in all team games.* بعدل، بإنصاف

IDM **fair enough** (used for showing that you agree with what sb has suggested): *'I'd rather go on Sunday, if that's all right with you.' 'Fair enough, Sunday is fine.'* موافق، لامانعَ (عندي)

fair³ /feə(r)/ *noun* [C] **1** (*also* **funfair**) a public entertainment which is held outside. At a fair you can ride on machines or try and win prizes at games. Fairs usually travel from town to town. مدينة الملاهي

2 a large exhibition of commercial or industrial goods: *a trade fair* ○ *the Frankfurt book fair* معرض؛ سوق

fairground /'feəgraʊnd/ *noun* [C] a large outdoor area where fairs³ (1) are held أرض يقام عليها معرض أو سوق

ˌfair-'haired *adj* with light-coloured or blond hair أشقر

⚷**fairly** /'feəli/ *adv* **1** in a fair¹ (1) way: *I felt that the*

a b c d e f g h i j k l m n o p q r s t u v w x y z

teacher didn't treat us fairly. ❶ The opposite is **unfairly**. بإنصاف

2 quite, not very: *He is fairly tall.* ○ *We must leave fairly soon.* ➲ Look at the note at **rather**. إلى حدٍّ ما

fairy /ˈfeəri/ *noun* [C] (*pl.* **fairies**) (in stories) a small creature with magical powers جنّية

ˈfairy story *noun* [C] (*pl.* **fairy stories**) (*also* **ˈfairy tale**) a story that is about fairies, magic, etc: *Grimm's fairy tales* قصة عن الجن والسحرة

⚷**faith** /feɪθ/ *noun* **1** [U] **faith (in sb/sth)** strong belief (in sb/sth); trust: *I've got great faith in your ability to do the job* (= I'm sure that you can do it). ○ *I have lost faith in him.* إيمان؛ ثقة

2 [U] strong religious belief: *I've lost my faith.* عقيدة

3 [C] a religion: *the Christian faith* دين

IDM **in good faith** with honest reasons for doing sth: *I bought the car in good faith. I didn't know it was stolen.* بإخلاص؛ بحُسْن نيّة

⚷**faithful** /ˈfeɪθfl/ *adj* **1** not changing; loyal: *Peter has been a faithful friend.* ○ *He was always faithful to his wife* (= he didn't have sexual relations with anyone else). ❶ The opposite is **unfaithful**. مخلص

2 true to the facts; accurate: *a faithful description* أمين؛ مطابق للأصل

▸ **faithfully** /-fəli/ *adv* ❶ **Yours faithfully** is used to end formal letters. المخلص (تستعمل في نهاية الرسائل الرسمية في الانكليزيّة)

faithfulness *noun* [U] إخلاص، وفاء

fake /feɪk/ *noun* [C] **1** a work of art, etc. that seems to be real or genuine but is not: *That's not a real diamond necklace. It's just a fake!* شيء مزيّف؛ زَيف

2 a person who pretends to be sb/sth else in order to deceive people دجّال

▸ **fake** *adj* not real or genuine: *a fake passport* مزيّف

fake *verb* [T] **1** to copy sth in order to deceive people: *He faked his father's signature.* يزيّف

2 to pretend that you are feeling sth that you are not: *I faked surprise when he told me the news.* يلفّق؛ يتظاهر بـ

falafel (*also* **felafel**) /fəˈlæfl/ *noun* [U,C] (*pl.* **falafel** or **falafels**) a Middle Eastern dish consisting of small balls formed from crushed chickpeas, usually eaten with flat bread; one of these balls فلافل

falcon /ˈfɔːlkən; *US* ˈfælkən/ *noun* [C] a small bird of the type that kills and eats other animals (a bird of prey). Falcons can be trained to hunt. باز، صقر

⚷**fall**[1] /fɔːl/ *verb* [I] (*pt* **fell** /fel/; *pp* **fallen** /ˈfɔːlən/) **1** to drop down towards the ground: *He fell off the ladder onto the grass.* ○ *Don't walk along that wall – you might fall.* ○ *Autumn came and the leaves started to fall.* ○ *The rain was falling steadily.* يسقط، يقع

2 fall (down/over) to suddenly stop standing: *She slipped on the ice and fell.* ○ *The little boy fell over and hurt his knee.* يسقط، يهوي

3 (*formal*) to come or happen: *My birthday falls on a Sunday this year.* ○ *In the word 'interesting' the stress falls on the first syllable.* يقع؛ يصادف

4 to hang down: *Her hair fell down over her shoulders.* يتدلّى

5 to become lower or less: *The temperature is falling.* ○ *The price of coffee has fallen again.* ○ *When he heard the bad news, his spirits fell* (= he felt sad). يهبط؛ ينهار

6 to be killed (in battle): *Millions of soldiers fell in the Second World War.* يخرّ (صريعاً)

7 to be defeated: *The Government fell because of the scandal.* يسقط

8 to change into a different state; to become: *He fell asleep on the sofa.* ○ *They fell in love with each other in Spain.* ○ *I must get some new shoes – these ones are falling to pieces.* يصبح؛ يقع (في الحب)

9 to belong to a particular group, type, etc: *Animals fall into two groups, those with backbones and those without.* يقع؛ يصنّف

IDM **fall flat** → FLAT[3]

fall in love → LOVE[1]

fall short (of sth) → SHORT[2]

PHR V **fall apart** to break (into pieces): *My car is falling apart.* يتداعى؛ يصبح خَرِباً أو مهترئاً

fall back on sb/sth to use sb/sth when you are in difficulty: *When the electricity was cut off we fell back on candles.* يلجأ أو يعمد إلى

fall for sb (*informal*) to fall in love with sb يغرم بـ؛ يقع في حبه

fall for sth (*informal*) to be tricked into believing sth that is not true: *He makes excuses and she falls for them every time.* ينخدع

fall out (with sb) to quarrel or fight (with sb) يتخاصم، يتشاجر

fall through to fail or not happen: *Our trip to Japan has fallen through.* يفشل؛ يلغى

⚷**fall**[2] /fɔːl/ *noun* **1** [C] an act of falling (1, 2): *She had a nasty fall from her horse.* كَبْوة، سقطة

2 [C] **a fall (of sth)** the amount of sth that has fallen or the distance that sth has fallen: *We have had a heavy fall of snow.* ○ *a fall of four metres* كمية (المطر) الهاطلة؛ مسافة السقوط

3 [C] a decrease (in value, quantity, etc.): *There has been a sharp fall in the price of oil.* ❶ The opposite is **rise**. انخفاض، هبوط

4 [sing.] **the fall of sth** a (political) defeat: *the fall of the Roman Empire* انهيار، سقوط

5 [C, usually pl.] a waterfall: *Niagara Falls* شلّالات؛ شلّال

fall[3] /fɔːl/ *noun* [C] (*US*) = AUTUMN: *I visited Europe in the fall of 1963.*

fallacy /ˈfæləsi/ *noun* (*pl.* **fallacies**) [C,U] (*formal*) a false or mistaken belief or argument: *It's a fallacy to believe that money brings happiness* (= it's not true). فكرة خاطئة، مغالطة

fallen *pp* of FALL[1]

fallible /ˈfæləbl/ *adj* able or likely to make mistakes: *Even our new computerized system is fall-*

ible. ℹ The opposite is **infallible**.
عرضة للخطأ، غير معصوم

fallout /'fɔːlaʊt/ *noun* [U] radioactive waste matter that is carried in the air after a nuclear explosion الغبار الذري

⚷**false** /fɔːls/ *adj* **1** not true; incorrect: *Bucharest is the capital of Romania – true or false?* ○ *I think the information you have been given is false.* خاطئ؛ كاذب

2 not real; artificial: *false hair, eyelashes, etc.* اصطناعي؛ مستعار

3 based on wrong information or belief: *I got a completely false impression of him from our first meeting.* خاطئ

4 made or done incorrectly in order to deceive people: *This suitcase has a false bottom.* ○ *a false name* مزيف؛ مزوّر

5 not faithful; not loyal: *a false friend* خادع، لايؤتمن

IDM **a false alarm** a warning about a danger that does not happen كاذب

on/under false pretences pretending to be or to have sth in order to deceive people: *She got into the club under false pretences – she isn't a member at all!* كاذب؛ مضلّل

ˌ**false 'teeth** (*also* **dentures**) *noun* [plural] teeth that are made of plastic, etc., worn by a person who has lost his/her natural teeth أسنان اصطناعية

falsify /'fɔːlsɪfaɪ/ *verb* [T] (*pres part* **falsifying**; *3rd pers sing pres* **falsifies**; *pt, pp* **falsified**) (*formal*) to change a document, information, etc. in order to deceive other people يزوّر، يزيّف

falter /'fɔːltə(r)/ *verb* [I] **1** to become weak or move in a weak, unsteady way: *As she began to speak her voice faltered.* ○ *The engine faltered and stopped.* يتعثر؛ يتداعى

2 to lose confidence and hesitate: *Roddick faltered and missed the ball.* يتردد؛ يتلعثم

⚷**fame** /feɪm/ *noun* [U] being known or talked about by many people: *Pop stars achieve fame at a young age.* شهرة، صيت

▸ **famed** *adj* well-known (for sth): *Welsh people are famed for their singing.* ➲ Look at **famous**, which is the more usual word. مشهور

⚷**familiar** /fə'mɪliə(r)/ *adj* **1** (not before a noun) **familiar with sth** having a good knowledge of sth: *People in Europe aren't very familiar with Chinese music.* عليم، ذو إلمام

2 familiar (to sb) well-known (to sb): *Chinese music isn't very familiar to people in Europe.* ○ *It was a relief to see a familiar face in the crowd.* مألوف، معروف

ℹ The opposite for senses **1** and **2** is **unfamiliar**.

3 too friendly and informal: *I was annoyed by the waiter's familiar behaviour.* رافع للكلفة؛ حميم

▸ **familiarity** /fəˌmɪli'ærəti/ *noun* [U] **1** good knowledge of sth: *His familiarity with the area was an advantage.* معرفة (بالشيء)؛ اطّلاع

2 being too friendly and informal رفع الكلفة

familiarize (*also* **familiarise**) /fə'mɪliəraɪz/ *verb* [T] to inform sb/yourself about sth: *I want to familiarize myself with the plans before the meeting.* يتعرّف على معالم شيء؛ يعوّد نفسه على

⚷**family** /'fæməli/ *noun* (*pl.* **families**) **1** [C, with sing. or pl. verb] a group of people who are related to each other عائلة، أسرة

> Sometimes we use 'family' to mean 'parents and their children' (a **nuclear family**), sometimes we use it to include other relatives, e.g. grandparents, aunts, uncles, etc. (an **extended family**). **Family** is used with a singular verb when we are talking about it as a unit: *Almost every family in the village owns a television.* A plural verb is used when we are thinking about the members of a family as individuals: *My family are all very tall.* **Family** can be used before another noun to describe things that are suitable for or that can be used by all the family: *family entertainment* ○ *the family car.*

2 [C,U] children: *Do you have any family?* ○ *We are planning to start a family next year* (= to have our first baby). أولاد؛ أبناء

3 [C] a group of animals, plants, etc. that are related to each other: *Lions belong to the cat family.* فصيلة

IDM **run in the family** to be found very often in a family: *Red hair runs in the family.* وراثي، موروث

'**family name** *noun* [C] the name that is shared by members of a family; surname ➲ Look at the note at **name**[1]. اسم العائلة، كنية، لقب

ˌ**family 'planning** *noun* [U] controlling the number of children in a family by using birth control ➲ Look at **contraception**. تحديد النسل

ˌ**family 'tree** *noun* [C] a diagram that shows the relationships between different members of a family شجرة العائلة

famine /'fæmɪn/ *noun* [C,U] a lack of food in a large area that can cause the death of many people: *There is a severe famine in many parts of Africa.* ○ *The long drought was followed by famine.* مَجاعة

famished /'fæmɪʃt/ *adj* (not before a noun) (*informal*) very hungry: *When's lunch? I'm famished!* "ميّت من الجوع"

⚷**famous** /'feɪməs/ *adj* **famous (for sth)** well-known to many people: *a famous singer* ○ *Glasgow is famous for its museums and art galleries.* ➲ Look at **infamous** and **notorious**, which mean 'famous for being bad'. مشهور

▸ **famously** *adv* (*informal*) very well: *She's getting on famously in the new job.* بشكل ممتاز، بشكل هائل

⚷**fan**[1] /fæn/ *noun* [C] something that is used for making a (cool) wind, e.g. an object made of paper, feathers, etc. in the shape of half a circle or an (electric) machine with large blades that turn around very quickly مروحة

▸ **fan** *verb* [T] (fanning; fanned) **1** to cool sb/sth

a b c d e f g h i j k l m n o p q r s t u v w x y z

by moving the air with a fan or sth like a fan: *She used a newspaper to fan her face.* يهوّي (بالمروحة)

2 to make a fire burn more strongly: *The strong wind really fanned the flames.* يزيد (النار) اشتعالاً

PHRV fan out to spread out: *The police fanned out across the field.* ينتشر

fan² /fæn/ *noun* [C] somebody who admires and is very enthusiastic about a sport, a film star, a singer, etc: *football fans* ○ *He's a Van Morrison fan.* ○ *I'm not a great fan of modern jazz* (= I don't like it very much). معجب؛ نصير

fanatic /fəˈnætɪk/ *noun* [C] a person who is too enthusiastic about sth (especially about religion or politics): *a religious fanatic* ○ *She's a health-food fanatic.* شخص متعصّب

▸ **fanatic** (*also* **fanatical** /-kl/) *adj* feeling very strongly or being too enthusiastic about sth: *He's fanatical about keeping things tidy.* متعصّب

fanatically /-kli/ *adv* بتعصّب؛ بشدّة

fanaticism /-tɪsɪzəm/ *noun* [C,U] تعصّب

ˈfan belt *noun* [C] the belt that drives the fan to cool the engine of a car, etc. حزام مروحة السيارة، سير

fancy¹ /ˈfænsi/ *noun*

IDM take sb's fancy to attract or please sb: *If you see something that takes your fancy I'll buy it for you.* يروق لِ

take a fancy to sb/sth to start liking sb/sth: *I think that Alan's really taken a fancy to you.* يستلطف، يصادف هوى عند

fancy² /ˈfænsi/ *adj* not simple or ordinary: *My father doesn't like fancy food.* ○ *I just want a pair of black shoes – nothing fancy.* غير عادي؛ مُنمّق؛ "مفزلك"

fancy³ /ˈfænsi/ *verb* (*pres part* **fancying**; *3rd pers sing pres* **fancies**; *pt, pp* **fancied**) **1** [T] (*informal*) to like the idea of having or doing sth: *What do you fancy for supper?* ○ *I don't fancy going out in this rain.* يحبّ، يميل إلى

2 [T] (*Brit informal*) to be (sexually) attracted to sb: *Alan keeps looking at you. I think he fancies you.* يشتهي، يجذب جنسياً

3 [I,T] (used for expressing surprise, shock, etc.): *'They're getting married next week.' 'Well, fancy that!'* ○ *Fancy meeting you here!* تصوّر!، تخيل!

4 [T] (*formal*) to think or imagine sth: *He fancied that he heard footsteps behind him.* يتخيّل، يتوهّم

ˌfancy ˈdress *noun* [U] special clothes that you wear to a party at which people dress up to look like a different person (e.g. from history or a story): *We've been invited to a fancy dress party – I'm going as Napoleon.* ○ *It was a Halloween party and everyone went in fancy dress.* تنكري

fanfare /ˈfænfeə(r)/ *noun* [C] a short loud piece of music played on trumpets that is used for introducing sb/sth افتتاح بنفخ الأبواق

fang /fæŋ/ *noun* [C] a long sharp tooth of a dog, poisonous snake, etc. ناب (حيوان أو أفعى)

fantasize (*also* **fantasise**) /ˈfæntəsaɪz/ *verb* [I,T] to imagine sth that you would like to happen: *He liked to fantasize that he had won a gold medal at the Olympics.* يتخيّل: يحلم بِ

fantastic /fænˈtæstɪk/ *adj* **1** (*informal*) very good; excellent: *She's a fantastic swimmer.* ○ *You passed your test. Fantastic!* عظيم؛ هائل، رائع

2 strange and difficult to believe: *a story full of fantastic creatures from other worlds* خيالي؛ عجيب

3 (*informal*) very large or great: *A Rolls Royce costs a fantastic amount of money.* هائل؛ خيالي

▸ **fantastically** /-kli/ *adv* بشكل لا يصدّق؛ بشكل رائع

fantasy /ˈfæntəsi/ *noun* [C,U] (*pl.* **fantasies**) situations that are not true, that you just imagine: *They live in a world of fantasy.* ➲ Look at the note at **imagination**. وهم؛ خيال

FAQ /ˌef eɪ ˈkjuː/ *abbrev* frequently asked questions الأسئلة الشائعة

far¹ /fɑː(r)/ *adj* (**farther** /ˈfɑːðə(r)/ or **further** /ˈfɜːðə(r)/, **farthest** /ˈfɑːðɪst/ or **furthest** /ˈfɜːðɪst/) **1** distant; a long way away: *Let's walk – it's not far.* بعيد

2 (only *before* a noun) more distant (used about one of two ends, sides, etc.): *My friend lives at the far end of the street.* ○ *In the far north, days are short in winter.* أقصى

IDM a far cry from sth/from doing sth an experience that is very different from sth/doing sth مختلف جداً عن

far² /fɑː(r)/ *adv* (**farther** /ˈfɑːðə(r)/ or **further** /ˈfɜːðə(r)/, **farthest** /ˈfɑːðɪst/ or **furthest** /ˈfɜːðɪst/) **1** (at) a distance: *London's not far from here.* ○ *Do you live far from Oxford?* ○ *How far did we walk yesterday?* ○ *Call me if you need me; I won't be far away.* بعيد؛ بعيداً

> **Far** in this sense is usually used in negative sentences and questions. In positive sentences we say **a long way**: *It's a long way from here to the sea.* Some sentences have a negative meaning although they are positive in form. **Far** can be used in them: *Let's get a bus. It's much too far to walk.*

2 a long time: *This story began far back, in 1850.* ○ *We danced far into the night.* زمن بعيد، وقت طويل

3 (before comparative adjectives) very much: *She's far more intelligent than I thought.* ○ *It's far wetter in England than in Italy.* جداً؛ بكثير

IDM as far as to the place mentioned but not further: *We walked as far as the river and then turned back.* حتّى؛ لغاية

as/so far as 1 the same distance as (sb): *I can't swim as far as you.* مسافة، بقدْر

2 to the degree that: *As far as I know, she's not coming, but I may be wrong.* إلى حدّ

as far as I can see (used for introducing your opinion): *As far as I can see, the accident was John's fault, not Ann's.* في حدود علمي

as/so far as sb/sth is concerned on the subject of sb/sth; as sb/sth is affected or influenced by sth: *As far as school work is concerned, he's hopeless.* ○ *As far as I'm concerned* (= in my opinion), *this is the most important point.* فيما يتعلق بِ

by far (used for emphasizing comparative or

superlative words) by a large amount: *Jane is by far the best student in the class.* بمراحل؛ بكثير

far afield far away, especially from where you live or from where you are staying: *We decided to hire a car in order to explore further afield.* بعيداً؛ قصياً

far from doing sth instead of doing sth: *Far from enjoying the film, he fell asleep in the middle.* بدلاً من

far from sth/from doing sth almost the opposite of sth: *He's far from happy* (= he's sad). عكس؛ بالعكس

far from it (*informal*) certainly not; just the opposite: *'Did you enjoy your holiday?' 'No, far from it. It was awful.'* بالعكس تماماً

few and far between → FEW[1]

go far 1 to be enough: *This food won't go very far between three of us* يكفي

2 to be successful in life: *Dan is very talented and should go far.* ينجح في الحياة، له مستقبل باهر

go too far to behave in a way that causes trouble or upsets other people: *He's always been naughty but this time he's gone too far.* يجاوز الحد

so far until now: *So far the weather has been good but it might change.* حتى الآن

faraway /ˈfɑːrəweɪ/ *adj* **1** distant: *He told us stories of faraway countries.* قصيّ، ناءٍ

2 (used about a look in a person's eyes) as if you are thinking of sth else: *She stared out of the window with a faraway look in her eyes.* (نظرة) شاردة

farce /fɑːs/ *noun* [C] **1** a funny play for the theatre full of ridiculous situations مسرحية هزليّة

2 something important or serious that is not organized well or treated with respect: *The trial was a complete farce.* مهزلة

▶ **farcical** /ˈfɑːsɪkl/ *adj* مضحك؛ مهزلي، سخيف

fare[1] /feə(r)/ *noun* [C] the amount of money you pay to travel by bus, train, taxi, etc: *What's the fare to Birmingham?* ○ *Train fares are going up next month.* ❶ Adults pay **full fare**, children pay **half fare**. أجرة السفر

fare[2] /feə(r)/ *noun* [U] food, especially that served at a restaurant, pub or hotel طعام؛ ماكولات

fare[3] /feə(r)/ *verb* [I] (*formal*) to be successful/unsuccessful in a particular situation: *How did you fare in your examination?* (= did you do well or badly?) (تسير الأمور)

the Far 'East China, Japan and other countries in E and SE Asia الشرق الأقصى

farewell /ˌfeəˈwel/ *interj* (*old-fashioned*) goodbye وداعاً، الوداع

▶ **farewell** *noun* [C]: *He said a sad farewell and left.* ○ *a farewell party* وداع

ˌfar-'fetched *adj* not easy to believe: *It's a good book but the story's too far-fetched.* يصعب تصديقه؛ بعيد عن العقل

⚷**farm[1]** /fɑːm/ *noun* [C] an area of land with fields and buildings that is used for growing crops and keeping animals: *In the summer holidays I often work on a farm.* ○ *farm buildings* مزرعة

⚷**farm[2]** /fɑːm/ *verb* [I,T] to use land for growing crops or keeping animals: *He's farming in Scotland.* ○ *She farms 200 acres.* يزرع؛ يَفلَح

▶ **farmer** *noun* [C] a person who owns or manages a farm مزارع

farming *noun* [U] managing a farm or working on it: *Farming is extremely hard work.* زراعة، فلاحة

farmhouse /ˈfɑːmhaʊs/ (*also* **farm**) *noun* [C] the house on a farm where the farmer lives بيت المزارع

farmyard /ˈfɑːmjɑːd/ *noun* [C] an outside area near a farmhouse surrounded by buildings or walls حَوْش أو فناء المزرعة

'far-off *adj* (only *before* a noun) **1** a long distance away: *a far-off land* بعيد، قصيّ

2 a long time ago: *memories of those far-off days* غابر، قديم

ˌfar-'reaching *adj* having, or going to have, a great influence on a lot of other things: *far-reaching changes* عظيم الأثر، بعيد المدى

ˌfar-'sighted *adj* **1** being able to see what will be necessary and making plans for it بعيد النظر

2 (*US*) = LONG-SIGHTED

⚷**farther** /ˈfɑːðə(r)/ *adj, adv* more distant in space or time; a greater distance: *Rome is farther from London than Paris is.* ○ *I can swim farther than you.* ❶ **Farther** is the comparative of **far**. Look at the note at **further**. أبعد؛ مسافة أطول

⚷**farthest** /ˈfɑːðɪst/ (*also* **furthest**) *adj, adv* most distant in space or time; the greatest distance: *the farthest corner of Europe* ○ *Who can swim farthest?* ❶ **Farthest** is the superlative of **far**. الأقصى؛ أطول مسافة

fascinate /ˈfæsɪneɪt/ *verb* [T] to attract or interest sb very much: *He fascinated the children with his magic tricks.* ○ *I was fascinated by that film.* يسحَر، يفتِن

▶ **fascinating** *adj* طريف؛ خلّاب، ساحر

fascination /ˌfæsɪˈneɪʃn/ *noun* [C,U] فتنة؛ سحر؛ افتتان

fascism (*also* **Fascism**) /ˈfæʃɪzəm/ *noun* [U] an extreme right-wing political system: *the rise of fascism in the 1930s* الفاشيّة

▶ **fascist** (*also* **Fascist**) /ˈfæʃɪst/ *noun* [C], *adj* فاشيّ، فاشستي

⚷**fashion** /ˈfæʃn/ *noun* **1** [C,U] the style of dressing or behaving that is the most popular at a particular time: *What is the latest fashion in hairstyles?* ○ *a fashion show, model, etc.* موضة أو مودة؛ زيّ

2 [sing.] the way you do sth: *Watch him. He's been behaving in a very strange fashion.* طريقة، أسلوب

IDM **be in/come into fashion** to be or to become popular as a style: *Jeans are always in fashion.* يكون أو يصير زيّاً دارجاً

be/go out of fashion to be or to become unpopular as a style: *That colour is out of fashion this year.* لم يعد شائعاً، "بطلت موضته"

fashionable /ˈfæʃnəbl/ *adj* following the latest popular style: *a fashionable woman, suit, restaurant, idea, etc.* ❶ The opposite is **unfashionable** or **old-fashioned**.
من الطراز الأحدث، من الموضة الحديثة؛ "على الموضة"
▶ **fashionably** /-əbli/ *adv* آخر موضة، على الموضة

fast¹ /fɑːst; *US* fæst/ *adj* **1** able to move or act at great speed: *a fast car, train, worker, etc.* ➲ Look at the note at **quick**. ❶ There is no noun formed from **fast**. Use **speed**: *The car was travelling very fast./The car was travelling at great speed.* سريع
2 (used about a clock or watch) showing a time that is later than the real time: *I'm early – my watch must be fast.* ○ *The clock is five minutes fast.* ❶ The opposite is **slow**. (ساعة) مقدّمة
▶ **fast** *adv* quickly: *Don't drive so fast.* سريعاً، بسرعة

fast² /fɑːst; *US* fæst/ *adj* **1** (only *after* a noun) firmly fixed: *Peter made the boat fast* (= he tied it to something) *before he got out.* مكين، راسخ
2 (used about colours) not likely to change when washed: *Colour-fast materials can be washed in hot water.* ثابت
▶ **fast** *adv* firmly or deeply: *The children were fast asleep when we got home.* ○ *Our car was stuck fast in the mud.* عميقاً؛ بإحكام

fast³ /fɑːst; *US* fæst/ *verb* [I] to eat no food for a certain time usually for religious reasons: *Muslims fast during Ramadan.* يصوم
▶ **fast** *noun* [C] صَوْم

fasten /ˈfɑːsn; *US* ˈfæsn/ *verb* **1** [T] to fix, join or shut and lock sth firmly: *Please fasten your seat belts.* ○ *Could you fasten this suitcase for me?* يغلق، يوصد
2 [I] to become closed or fixed: *My blouse fastens at the back.* يُقفَل؛ يزرّر
3 [T] **fasten sth (on/to sth)**; **fasten A and B (together)** to attach sth to sth, or two things together: *Fasten this badge on your jacket.* ○ *How can I fasten these pieces of wood together?* يثبّت؛ يلصق
▶ **fastener** /ˈfɑːsnə(r); *US* fæs-/ (*also* **fastening** /ˈfɑːsnɪŋ; *US* ˈfæs-/) *noun* [C] something that fastens things together وسيلة للربط: سحّاب أو سوستة

ˌfast ˈfood *noun* [U] food like hamburgers and chips that can be cooked and eaten quickly in a restaurant or taken away from the restaurant: *a fast-food restaurant* الوجبات السريعة

ˌfast ˈforward *verb* [T] to make a cassette, tape or video go forward quickly without playing it يمرر إلى الأمام

fastidious /fæˈstɪdiəs/ *adj* (used about people) difficult to please, wanting everything to be very clean and tidy نيّق؛ مفرط في التدقيق

fat¹ /fæt/ *adj* (**fatter**; **fattest**) **1** (used about bodies) covered with too much flesh: *You'll get fat if you eat too much.* ❶ The opposite is **thin**. ❶ It is not very polite to describe a person as **fat**. Less direct words are **plump, stout** or **overweight**. سمين
2 (used about a thing) thick or full: *a fat wallet, book, etc.* ثخين؛ ممتلئ

fat² /fæt/ *noun* **1** [U] the greasy substance under the skins of animals and people: *I don't like meat with too much fat on it.* ❶ The adjective is **fatty**. دُهن؛ شَحْم
2 [C,U] the substance we obtain from animals, plants or seeds and use for cooking: *Cook the onions in a little fat.* ○ *Vegetable fats are healthier than animal fats.* دهن؛ دَسَم

fatal /ˈfeɪtl/ *adj* **1** causing or ending in death: *It was a fatal accident – both drivers were killed.* مميت، قاتل
2 causing trouble or a bad result: *She made the fatal mistake of forgetting her passport.* مشؤوم؛ ذو عواقب وخيمة؛ حتمي
▶ **fatally** *adv* بشكل قاتل؛ حتى الموت

fatality /fəˈtæləti/ *noun* [C] (*pl.* **fatalities**) a person's death caused by an accident or in war, etc: *There were no fatalities in the fire.* ضحيّة؛ قتيل

fate /feɪt/ *noun* **1** [U] the power that some people believe controls everything that happens: *It was fate that brought them together again after twenty years.* القضاء والقدَر
2 [C] your future or something that happens to you: *Both men suffered the same fate – they both lost their jobs.* مصير؛ نهاية

fateful /ˈfeɪtfl/ *adj* having an important effect on the future: *a fateful decision* حاسم؛ تترتب عليه نتائج هامة؛ مشؤوم

father /ˈfɑːðə(r)/ *noun* [C] **1** a person's male parent: *John looks exactly like his father.* أب، والد
2 a man who starts something important: *Shakespeare is the father of English drama.* أب؛ مبتدع
3 Father the title of certain priests: *Father O'Reilly* الأب
▶ **fatherhood** /-hʊd/ *noun* [U] the state of being a father: *How are you enjoying fatherhood?* أبوّة
ˈfatherly *adj* like or typical of a father: *Would you like a piece of fatherly advice?* أبويّ

ˌFather ˈChristmas (*also* **Santa Claus**) an old man with a red coat and a long white beard who, children believe, brings presents at Christmas بابا نويل

ˈfather-in-law *noun* [C] (*pl.* **fathers-in-law**) the father of your husband or wife (أبو الزوج أو الزوجة) حمٌ

ˈFather's Day *noun* [C] a day when fathers receive cards and gifts from their children, usually the third Sunday in June يوم الأب

fathom /ˈfæðəm/ *noun* [C] a measure of the depth of water; 6 feet (1.8 metres) قامة، مقياس للعمق يعادل 6 اقدام
▶ **fathom** *verb* [T] (usually in the negative) to understand sth: *I can't fathom what he means.* يسبر؛ يفهم

fatigue /fəˈtiːg/ *noun* [U] **1** great tiredness إعياء

2 weakness in metals caused by a lot of use إجهاد أو كلال

fatten /ˈfætn/ *verb* [T] **fatten sb/sth (up)** to maker sb/sth fatter: *He's fattening the pigs up for market.* يسمِّن

▸ **fattening** *adj* (used about food) that makes people fat: *You shouldn't eat too much chocolate. It's very fattening.* مسمِّن

fatty /ˈfæti/ *adj* (**fattier**; **fattiest**) (used about food) having a lot of fat in or on it دسِم، دهني

faucet /ˈfɔːsɪt/ *noun* [C] (*US*) = TAP[1]

fault /fɔːlt/ *noun* **1** [C] something wrong or not perfect in a person's character or in a thing: *One of my faults is that I'm always late.* ○ *a fault in the electricity supply* ➲ Look at the note at **mistake.** عيب، نقيصة، خلل

2 [U] responsibility for a mistake: *'We're going to be late.' 'Well, it's not my fault – I was ready on time.'* ○ *It will be your own fault if you don't pass your exams.* غلطة؛ ذَنْب

IDM **be at fault** be wrong or responsible for a mistake: *The other driver was at fault – he didn't stop at the traffic lights.* ذَنْب؛ مذْنِب

find fault → FIND[1]

▸ **fault** *verb* [T] to find a fault or mistake in sb/sth: *It was impossible to fault her English.* يعيب، ينتقد

faultless *adj* without any mistakes; perfect: *The pianist gave a faultless performance.* لا عيب فيه، كامل الأوصاف

faulty *adj* (used especially about electricity or machinery) not working properly: *a faulty switch* فيه خَلَل؛ معيب

fauna /ˈfɔːnə/ *noun* [U] all the animals of an area or a period of time: *the flora and fauna of South America* ➲ Look at **flora.** حيوانات حقبة أو منطقة معينة

faux pas /ˌfəʊ ˈpɑː/ *noun* [C] (*pl.* **faux pas** /ˌfəʊ ˈpɑːz/) something you say or do that is embarrassing or offends people زلّة (تحرج اجتماعياً)

favour[1] (*US* **favor**) /ˈfeɪvə(r)/ *noun* **1** [C] something that helps sb: *Would you do me a favour and post this letter for me?* ○ *Could I ask you a favour – could you babysit for us tonight?* معروف، خدمة

2 [U] liking or approval: *In the end the politician won the crowd's favour.* رضاء، استحسان

IDM **be in/out of favour (with sb)** to have/not have a person's approval: *I'm afraid I'm out of favour with my neighbour since our last argument.* مغضوب عليه/(غير) مَرضي عنه

in favour of sb/sth in agreement with: *Are you in favour of private education?* مؤيِّد

in sb's favour to the advantage of sb: *The committee decided in their favour.* لصالحه

favour[2] (*US* **favor**) /ˈfeɪvə(r)/ *verb* [T] **1** to support sb/sth; to prefer: *Which suggestion did they favour?* يؤيِّد؛ يفضّل

2 to treat one person very well and so be unfair to others: *Parents must try not to favour one of their children.* يفضّل؛ يتحيَّز لِ

favourable (*US* **favorable**) /ˈfeɪvərəbl/ *adj* **1** showing liking or approval: *Did you get a favourable report on your work?* ○ *He made a favourable impression on his bank manager.* (تقرير) إيجابي؛ (انطباع) حسن

2 (often used about the weather) suitable or helpful: *Conditions are favourable for skiing today.* مناسب، ملائم

ⓘ The opposite for both senses is **unfavourable.**

▸ **favourably** (*US* **favorably**) /-əbli/ *adv* (أكثر) ملاءمةً؛ إيجابياً؛ بشكل حسن

favourite[1] (*US* **favorite**) /ˈfeɪvərɪt/ *adj* liked more than any other: *What is your favourite colour?* ○ *Who is your favourite singer?* مفضّل

favourite[2] (*US* **favorite**) /ˈfeɪvərɪt/ *noun* [C] **1** a person or thing that you like more than any others: *This restaurant is a great favourite of mine.* ○ *That sweater is my husband's favourite.* (شئ) مفضّل أو محبوب

2 the favourite (especially in horse racing) the horse that is expected to win الحصان المرجّح فوزه

▸ **favouritism** (*US* **favoritism**) /-ɪzəm/ *noun* [U] giving unfair advantages to the people that you like best تحيّز؛ محسوبيّة

fawn[1] /fɔːn/ *noun* [C] a young deer ➲ Look at the note at **deer.** ولد الظبي

fawn[2] /fɔːn/ *adj, noun* [U] (of a) light yellowish-brown colour: *a fawn coat* ○ *Fawn doesn't really suit you.* (لون) طحينيّ، "بيج"

fax /fæks/ *noun* **1** [C,U] a copy of a letter, etc. which you can send by telephone lines using a special machine: *I need an answer today. Send them a fax!* ○ *They contacted us by fax.* فاكس

2 [C] (*also* **ˈfax machine**) the machine that you use for sending faxes: *Have you got a fax?* ○ *What's your fax number?* (جهاز) فاكس

▸ **fax** *verb* [T] **fax sth (to sb)**; **fax sb (sth)** to send sb a fax: *We will fax our order to you tomorrow.* ○ *I've faxed her a copy of the letter.* يرسل بالفاكس

faze /feɪz/ *verb* [T] (*informal*) to make sb anxious or nervous: *He doesn't get fazed by things going wrong.* يقلق، يربك

FBI /ˌef biː ˈaɪ/ *abbrev* (*US*) Federal Bureau of Investigation; the section of the US Justice Department which investigates crimes that are against federal law, such as bank robbery and terrorism مكتب التحقيقات الفدرالي

fear[1] /fɪə(r)/ *noun* [C,U] the feeling that you have when sth dangerous, painful or frightening might happen: *He was shaking with fear after the accident.* ○ *She showed no fear.* ○ *My fears for his safety were unnecessary.* خوف

IDM **no fear** (*informal*) (used when answering a suggestion) certainly not حتماً لا!

▸ **fearful** /-fl/ *adj* **1 fearful (of sth/of doing sth)**; **fearful (that)** anxious or afraid about sth: *You should never be fearful of starting something new.* ➲ Look at **frightened** and the note at **afraid.** These words are much more common. خائف، متخوّف

2 terrible: *the fearful consequences of war* مخيف

fearfully /-fəli/ *adv* بتخوّف، بهلع: جداً
fearfulness *noun* [U] تهيّب، تخوّف
fearless *adj* not afraid; brave جريء، جسور
fearlessly *adv* بجسارة
fearlessness *noun* [U] جراة، جسارة

fear² /fɪə(r)/ *verb* **1** [I,T] to be afraid of sb/sth great or important: *We all fear illness and death.* ○ *We'll get there in time – never fear!* (= don't worry). يخاف، يخشى

2 [T] to feel that something bad might happen: *The government fears that it will lose the next election.* ○ *Thousands of people are feared dead in the earthquake.* ➲ Look at **afraid** and at the note at **frightened**. يخشى: يتوجّس

PHRV **fear for sb/sth** to be worried about sb/sth: *Parents often fear for the safety of their children.* يخاف على

feasible /'fi:zəbl/ *adj* possible to do: *a feasible plan* يمكن تطبيقه: عملي
▸ **feasibility** /ˌfi:zə'bɪləti/ *noun* [U] إمكان تطبيق (مشروع ما)

feast /fi:st/ *noun* [C] a large, special meal (sometimes to celebrate sth) وليمة، مأدبة: عيد
▸ **feast** *verb* [I] يقيم الولائم

feat /fi:t/ *noun* [C] something you do that shows great strength, skill or courage: *The new bridge is a feat of engineering.* مأثرة، عمل بطولي

feather /'feðə(r)/ *noun* [C] one of the light, soft things that grow in a bird's skin and cover its body ريشة

feature /'fi:tʃə(r)/ *noun* [C] **1** an important or noticeable part of sth: *Mountains and lakes are the main features of the landscape of Wales.* ○ *Noise is a feature of city life.* تضريس، مَعْلم (معالم)

2 a part of the face: *Her eyes are her best feature.* قَسَمة (قسمات)

3 a feature (on sth) an important newspaper or magazine article or television programme: *a front-page feature* مقالة صحفية هامة: برنامج تلفزيوني

4 (*also* '**feature film**) a full-length film with a story فيلم رئيسي

▸ **feature** *verb* **1** [T] to include sb/sth as an important part: *The film features many well-known actors.* يبرز

2 [I] **feature in sth** to have a part in sth: *Does marriage feature in your future plans?* يلعب دوراً، يشترك: يَبْرز

featureless *adj* uninteresting; with no features (1) عديم الشخصية: عديم المعالم

February /'februəri; *US* -ueri/ *noun* [C,U] (*abbr* **Feb.**) the second month of the year, coming before March ℹ For examples of the use of the months in sentences, look at **January**. فبراير/شباط

feces (*US*) = FAECES

fed *pt, pp* of FEED¹

federal /'fedərəl/ *adj* **1** organized as a federation: *the Federal Republic of Germany* اتحادي، فيدرالي

2 relating to the central government of a federation: *That is a federal, not a state, law.* اتحادي، فيدرالي

federation /ˌfedə'reɪʃn/ *noun* [C] a political union of states for the control of foreign affairs, defence, etc. by the central (federal) government but with local (state) government for areas such as education اتحاد فيدرالي

fed up /ˌfed 'ʌp/ *adj* (not before a noun) (*informal*) bored or unhappy; tired of sth: *What's the matter? You look really fed up.* ○ *I'm fed up with waiting for the phone to ring.* متضايق: نافد الصبر

fee /fi:/ *noun* [C] **1** (usually plural) the money you pay for professional advice or service from private doctors, lawyers, schools and universities, etc: *We can't afford private school fees.* ➲ Look at the note at **pay¹**. أجر، رسم

2 the cost of an examination, club membership, entrance etc: *How much is the entrance fee?* رسم

feeble /'fi:bl/ *adj* **1** with no energy or power; weak: *a feeble old man* ○ *a feeble cry* ضعيف، واهن، خافت

2 not able to convince sb: *a feeble argument* واهٍ

feed¹ /fi:d/ *verb* (*pt, pp* **fed** /fed/) **1** [T] to give food to a person or an animal: *Don't forget to feed the dog.* ○ *I can't come yet. I haven't fed the baby.* ○ *I've cooked enough to feed us for weeks.* يُطعم

2 [I] (used about animals or babies) to eat: *What do horses feed on in the winter?* يأكل، يتغذى

3 [T] **feed A (with B)**; **feed B into A** to supply sth to sb/sth: *This channel feeds us with news and information 24 hours a day.* ○ *Metal sheets are fed into the machine one at a time.* يُغذّي، يزوّد، يلقم (ماكينة أو آلة)

feed² /fi:d/ *noun* **1** [C] a meal for an animal or a baby: *When's the baby's next feed due?* وجبة، إطعام

2 [U] food for animals عَلَف

feedback /'fi:dbæk/ *noun* [U] information about sth that you have done or made which tells you how good or successful it is: *We need some more feedback from the people who use our textbooks.* صدى العمل

feel¹ /fi:l/ *verb* (*pt, pp* **felt** /felt/) **1** [I] (usually with an adjective) to be in the state that is mentioned: *to feel cold, sick, tired, happy, etc.* ○ *How are you feeling today?* ○ *You'll feel better in the morning.* يَشْعر

2 [I] **feel (to sb) (like sth/sb)** to give an impression of sth: *The hole in my tooth feels much bigger than it is.* ○ *My new coat feels like leather but it's not.* يبدو

3 [T] to learn about sth by touching it with your hands: *Feel this material. Is it silk or cotton?* ○ *I felt her forehead and knew that she had a temperature.* يتحسس باللمس

4 [T] to be aware of sth: *I felt something crawling up my back.* ○ *I could feel myself dropping off to sleep.* يدْرك، يحس

5 [T] to believe or think: *I felt (that) it was a mistake not to ask her advice.* يعتقد

6 [T] to suffer from sth: *Do you feel the cold in winter?* ○ *She felt it badly when her mother died.* يقاسي مِنْ

7 [I] **feel (about) (for sb/sth)** to try to find something with your hands instead of your eyes: *She felt about in the dark for the light switch.* يبحث باللمس، يتلمّس طريقه

8 [I] **feel (to sb) as if/as though** to have or give the impression that: *He felt as if he had been there before.* ○ *My head feels as though it will burst.* ❶ **It** is often used as the subject of **feel** in this sense: *It feels as if it is going to snow soon.* يخال

IDM feel like sth/doing sth to want sth or to want to do sth: *Do you feel like going out?* يَوَدّ

feel² /fiːl/ *noun* [sing.] **1 the feel** the impression something gives you when it is touched; the impression an experience gives you: *You can tell it's wool by the feel.* حِس

2 an act of touching sth in order to learn about it: *Let me have a feel of that material.* جَسّ

feelers /ˈfiːləz/ *noun* [plural] the long thin parts at the front of an insect's head that it uses to feel things with قَرْن اسْتِشْعار

feeling /ˈfiːlɪŋ/ *noun* **1** [C] **a feeling (of sth)** something that you feel in your mind or body: *a feeling of hunger, happiness, fear, success, etc.* إحْساس، شعور

2 feelings [plural] a person's emotions: *I don't want to hurt his feelings* (= make him unhappy). ○ *She's not very good at hiding her feelings.* عواطف

3 [U] the ability to feel in your body: *After the accident he lost all feeling in his legs.* إحْساس

4 [sing.] a belief or idea that you cannot explain exactly: *She had a feeling that something terrible would happen.* ○ *I get the feeling that Ian doesn't like me much.* ○ *I had a nasty feeling that Jan didn't get our message.* إحْساس

5 [U] sympathy or understanding: *She hasn't much feeling for music.* تعاطف

IDM bad/ill feeling unhappy relations between people: *The decision caused a lot of bad feeling at the factory.* نفور، تنافر

have mixed feelings about sb/sth → MIXED

feet *pl.* of FOOT¹

feisty /ˈfaɪsti/ *adj* (**feistier**; **feistiest**) (*informal, approving*) (of people) strong, determined and not afraid of arguing with people شديد الحيوية، قوي الشخصية

felafel = FALAFEL

feline /ˈfiːlaɪn/ *adj* of or like a cat كالقطّة، قِطّي

fell¹ *pt* of FALL¹

fell² /fel/ *noun* [C] an area of mountain country: *the fells of the Lake District* منطقة جبلية

fell³ /fel/ *verb* [T] to cut down a tree يقطع شجرة

fellow¹ /ˈfeləʊ/ *noun* [C] **1** a member of an academic or professional organization, or of certain universities زميل

2 a person who is paid to study a particular thing at a university: *Jill is a research fellow in the biology department.* عضو جمعية أدبية أو علمية

3 (*old-fashioned*) a man: *What's that fellow over there doing?* رَجل

fellow² /ˈfeləʊ/ *adj* (only *before* a noun) another or others like yourself in the same situation: *Her fellow students were all older than her.* زميل، قرين

fellowship /ˈfeləʊʃɪp/ *noun* **1** [U] friendly relations with others زمالة

2 [C] a group or society جماعة

3 [C] the position of a college or university fellow وظيفة جامعية

felt¹ *pt, pp* of FEEL¹

felt² /felt/ *noun* [U] a type of soft cloth made from wool, etc. which has been pressed flat لبّاد

ˌfelt-tip ˈpen (*also* **ˌfelt-ˈtip**, **ˌfelt-tipped ˈpen**) *noun* [C] a type of pen with a tip made of felt قلم لبّاد

female /ˈfiːmeɪl/ *adj* **1** of the sex that can give birth to young: *Please state sex: male or female* (e.g. on a form). أنثى

2 (used about plants and flowers) producing fruit مثْمِرة

▸ **female** *noun* [C] a female animal or plant: *Is your mouse a male or a female?* أنثى حيوان أو نبات

Female and **male** are used only to describe the sex of a creature. To describe the qualities we think of as typical of females and males, we use **feminine** and **masculine**.

feminine /ˈfemənɪn/ *adj* (*abbr* **fem**) **1** of or like a woman: *My daughter always dresses like a boy. She hates looking feminine.* ➲ Look at **masculine** and the note at **female**. عندها أُنوثة: أنثوي

2 (*grammar*) (in English) of the forms of words used to describe females: *'Lioness' is the feminine form of 'lion'.* مؤَنّث

3 (*grammar*) (in certain languages) belonging to a certain grammatical class: *The German word for a flower is feminine.* ➲ Look at **masculine** and **neuter**. مؤَنّث

▸ **femininity** /ˌfeməˈnɪnəti/ *noun* [U] أنوثة، أنثوية

feminism /ˈfemənɪzəm/ *noun* [U] the belief that women should have the same rights and opportunities as men (الحركة) النسوية

▸ **feminist** /ˈfemənɪst/ *noun* [C] a person who believes in and supports the aims of feminism نصير الحركة النسوية

fen /fen/ *noun* [C] an area of low wet land أرض مستنقعية

fence¹ /fens/ *noun* [C] a line of wooden or metal posts joined by wood, wire, metal, etc. to divide land or to keep in animals: *a garden fence* ○ *an electric fence* ○ *a barbed-wire fence* سياج، سور

IDM sit on the fence → SIT

▸ **fence** *verb* [T] to surround land with a fence يسيّج، يسوّر

PHRV **fence sb/sth in** to surround sb/sth with a fence: *They fenced in their garden to make it more private.* يسيّج، يسوّر
fence sth off to separate one area from another with a fence يفصل بسياج، يسيّج، يسوّر

fence² /fens/ *verb* [I] to fight with a long thin sword (a foil) as a sport يبارز

fencing /ˈfensɪŋ/ *noun* [U] the sport of fighting with swords مبارزة

fend /fend/ *verb*
PHRV **fend for yourself** to look after yourself: *It's time Ben left home and learned to fend for himself.* يعيل نفسه
fend sth/sb off to defend yourself from sth/sb: *He fended off the dog with his stick.* ○ *Politicians usually manage to fend off awkward questions.* يحمي نفسه؛ يصدّ

fender /ˈfendə(r)/ *noun* [C] **1** a low metal guard put in front of an open fire to stop coal or wood from falling out حاجز مدفأة
2 (*US*) = WING (4)

fennel /ˈfenl/ *noun* [U] a plant that has a thick round part at the base of the leaves with a strong taste. The base is used as a vegetable and the seeds and leaves are also used in cooking. الشمار

ferment /fəˈment/ *verb* [I,T] to (make sth) change chemically: *The wine is starting to ferment.* يختمر؛ يخمّر
▶ **ferment** /ˈfɜːment/ *noun* [U] a state of excitement and change: *The country is in ferment and nobody's sure what will happen next.* هيجان

fern /fɜːn/ *noun* [C] a green plant with no flowers and a lot of long thin leaves سرخس (نبات)

ferocious /fəˈrəʊʃəs/ *adj* very fierce and violent متوحّش
▶ **ferociously** *adv* بوحشية

ferocity /fəˈrɒsəti/ *noun* [U] violent cruelty وحشيّة

ferret /ˈferɪt/ *noun* [C] a small fierce animal used for hunting rats and rabbits ابن مقرض

ferry /ˈferi/ *noun* [C] (*pl.* **ferries**) a boat that transports people and goods on short journeys: *a car ferry* معدّية (مركب)
▶ **ferry** *verb* [T] (*pres part* **ferrying**; *3rd pers sing pres* **ferries**; *pt, pp* **ferried**) to carry people or goods by boat, plane, car, etc. from one place to another: *Could you ferry us across to the island?* ○ *We have to ferry the children to school every day.* ينقل بمعدّية

fertile /ˈfɜːtaɪl; *US* ˈfɜːrtl/ *adj* **1** (used about land, plants, animals and people) able to produce crops, fruit or young ℹ The opposite is **infertile**. Look at **sterile.** خصب
2 (used about a person's mind) full of ideas: *a fertile imagination* مبدع
▶ **fertility** /fəˈtɪləti/ *noun* [U] the state of being fertile: *Nowadays women can take drugs to increase their fertility* (= their chances of having a child). ℹ The opposite is **infertility**. خصوبة

fertilize (*also* **fertilise**) /ˈfɜːtəlaɪz/ *verb* [T] **1** to put a male seed into an egg, a plant or a female animal so that it starts to develop fruit or young يلقّح
2 to put natural or artificial substances on soil in order to make it more fertile يسمّد
▶ **fertilization** (*also* **fertilisation**) /ˌfɜːtəlaɪˈzeɪʃn; *US* -ləˈz-/ *noun* [U] تلقيح، تسميد
fertilizer (*also* **fertiliser**) *noun* [C,U] a natural or chemical substance that is put on land to make plants grow better سماد

fervent /ˈfɜːvənt/ *adj* showing strong feelings: *She's a fervent believer in women's rights.* متحمّس، جيّاش
▶ **fervently** *adv* بحماس

fervour (*US* **fervor**) /ˈfɜːvə(r)/ *noun* [U] very strong feelings about sth; enthusiasm حماسة، عاطفة جياشة، حمية

fester /ˈfestə(r)/ *verb* [I] **1** (used about a cut or wound) to become infected يتعفّن، يتقيّح
2 (used about an unpleasant situation, feeling or thought) to become more unpleasant or painful ينخر

⚷ **festival** /ˈfestɪvl/ *noun* [C] **1** a day or time when people celebrate sth (especially a religious event): *Christmas is an important Christian festival.* عيد
2 a series of musical or dramatic performances often held regularly in one place: *the Cannes Film Festival* ○ *a jazz festival* مهرجان

festive /ˈfestɪv/ *adj* happy, because people are enjoying themselves: *the festive season* (= Christmas) مرح، بهيج

festivity /feˈstɪvəti/ *noun* (*pl.* **festivities**) **1** [U] being happy and celebrating: *The wedding was followed by three days of festivity.* بهجة
2 festivities [plural] happy events when people celebrate sth: *The festivities went on until dawn.* أعياد، احتفالات

⚷ **fetch** /fetʃ/ *verb* [T] **1** to go for and bring back sb/sth: *Shall I fetch you your coat?/Shall I fetch your coat for you?* ○ *I left my keys on the table; could you fetch them for me?* ○ *It's my turn to fetch the children from school.* يجلب
2 (used about goods) to be sold for the price mentioned: *'How much will your car fetch?' 'It should fetch about £900.'* يباع (بكذا)

fête /feɪt/ *noun* [C] an outdoor event with competitions, entertainment and things to buy, often organized to make money for a particular purpose: *the church fête* مهرجان؛ سوق خيرية

fetus (*US*) = FOETUS

feud /fjuːd/ *noun* [C] a long and serious quarrel between two people or groups عداوة
▶ **feud** *verb* [I] يتعادى

feudal /ˈfjuːdl/ *adj* relating to the system of feudalism إقطاعي

feudalism /ˈfjuːdəlɪzəm/ *noun* [U] the social system which existed in the Middle Ages in Europe, in which people worked and fought for a landowner and received land and protection from him نظام الإقطاع

fever /ˈfiːvə(r)/ *noun* **1** [C,U] a condition of the body when it is too hot because of illness: *A high fever can be dangerous, especially in small children.* ○ *Aspirin can reduce fever.* ❶ When somebody's body is very hot we normally say they **have a temperature**. حُمّى
2 [sing.] (*figurative*) a state of nervous excitement هَيَجان
▶ **feverish** /ˈfiːvərɪʃ/ *adj* **1** showing the signs of a fever محموم
2 showing great excitement مهتاج
feverishly *adv* very quickly and excitedly بهَيَجان

few¹ /fjuː/ *det, adj, pron* (used with a plural noun and a plural verb) not many: *Few people live to be 100.* ○ *There are fewer cars here today than yesterday.* ○ *The few people I have asked thought the same as I do.* ○ *Few of the players played really well.* ○ *Very few of the books were new.* قليل
IDM **few and far between** not happening very often: *Our visits to the theatre are few and far between.* نادر

few² /fjuː/ **a few** *det, pron* (used with a plural noun and a plural verb) a small number of; some: *a few people* ○ *a few letters* ○ *Only a few of the people who applied were suitable.* ○ *She's written lots of books but I've only read a few (of them).* ○ *I knew a few (= some) of the people there.* ➲ Compare with: *I knew few of the people* (= not many). عدد قليل، بعض
IDM **a good few**; **quite a few** quite a lot: *It's been a good few years since I saw him last.* عَديد

ff. *abbrev* (used to indicate that sth starts on a particular page or line and continues for several pages or lines more): *British Politics, p 10ff* حتى الصفحة...

fiancé /fiˈɒnseɪ; *US* ˌfiːɑːnˈseɪ/ *noun* [C] a man to whom a woman is engaged to be married: *This is my fiancé Dave. We got engaged a few weeks ago.* خطيب

fiancée /fiˈɒnseɪ; *US* ˌfiːɑːnˈseɪ/ *noun* [C] a woman to whom a man is engaged to be married: *Can I introduce you to my fiancée?* خطيبة

fiasco /fiˈæskəʊ/ *noun* [C] (*pl.* **fiascos**; *US also* **fiascoes**) an event that does not succeed, often in a way that causes embarrassment: *Our last party was a complete fiasco.* إخفاق تام، فَشَل مخْزٍ

fib /fɪb/ *noun* [C] (*informal*) something you say that is not true; a small lie: *Please don't tell fibs.* كذبة صغيرة
▶ **fib** *verb* [I] (**fibbing**; **fibbed**) to say untrue things, to tell a fib ➲ Look at **lie**. **Fib** is used when the lie does not seem very important. يكذب

fibre (*US* **fiber**) /ˈfaɪbə(r)/ *noun* **1** [C] one of the thin threads which form a natural or artificial substance: *a fibre of cotton* ○ *a muscle fibre* لِيف
2 [C,U] material or a substance made from fibres ❶ **Natural** fibres are, for example, cotton and wool. **Man-made** or **synthetic** fibres are nylon, polyester, etc. مادة ليفيّة
3 [U] the parts of plants (used as food) that your body cannot digest and that are thought to be good for it: *Wholemeal bread is high in fibre.* لِيف (نباتي)، ألياف

fibreglass /ˈfaɪbəɡlɑːs/ (*US* **fiberglass** /ˈfaɪbərɡlæs/) (*also* **glass fibre**) *noun* [U] a material made from plastic and glass fibres, used for making small boats, parts of cars, etc. زجاج ليفي

fickle /ˈfɪkl/ *adj* always changing your mind or your feelings متقلّب

fiction /ˈfɪkʃn/ *noun* [U] stories, novels, etc. which describe events and people that do not really exist: *I don't read much fiction.* قصص، روايات

> Fiction is one type of **literature**. Look at **drama** and **poetry**. The opposite is **non-fiction**. Look at **fact**.

▶ **fictional** /-ʃənl/ *adj* only existing in fiction: *The book gave a fictional account of a doctor's life.* ➲ Look at **factual**. خيالي

fictitious /fɪkˈtɪʃəs/ *adj* invented; not real: *They used fictitious names in the newspaper article.* مُختلَق

fiddle¹ /ˈfɪdl/ *noun* [C] (*informal*) **1** a dishonest action, especially one that is connected with money: *a tax fiddle* احتيال؛ تلاعب (في الحسابات)
2 a violin or an instrument of the violin family كَمان

fiddle² /ˈfɪdl/ *verb* **1** [I] **fiddle (about/around) (with sth)** to play with sth carelessly, nervously or without thinking: *He sat nervously, fiddling with a pencil.* يعْبث
2 [T] (*informal*) to change sth (business accounts, income tax forms, etc.) to gain money: *She fiddled her expenses form.* يغش، يزور
▶ **fiddly** /ˈfɪdli/ *adj* (**fiddlier**; **fiddliest**) (*informal*) difficult to do or manage with your hands (because small or complicated parts are involved) يصعُب عمله أو الإمساك به لدقة أجزائه أو تعقّدها

fidelity /fɪˈdeləti; *US* faɪ-/ *noun* [U] **1** (*formal*) the quality of being faithful ❶ The opposite is **infidelity**. إخلاص
2 (used in connection with texts, translations, reproduction of music, etc.) the quality of being accurate or close to the original ➲ Look at **hi-fi**. أمانة

fidget /ˈfɪdʒɪt/ *verb* [I] **fidget (about) (with sth)** to move about or play with sth in a restless way because you are nervous, bored, etc: *Stop fidget-*

ing! ○ *The children were fidgeting with their books while they waited for the bell to ring.* يتململ

▸ **fidgety** *adj* متململ

field¹ /fi:ld/ *noun* [C] **1** an area of land on a farm, usually surrounded by fences or hedges and used for growing crops or keeping animals in: *a cornfield* ○ *a field of corn* حقل

2 an area of land used for sports, games or some other activity: *a football field* ○ *the playing fields* (= the area of grass in a village or town or belonging to a school where people go to play games, sports, etc.) ○ *an airfield* (= where planes land and take off) ○ *a battlefield* مَلعَب؛ ميدان

3 an area of land where oil, coal or other minerals are found: *a coalfield* ○ *a North Sea oilfield* حقل

4 an area of study or knowledge: *He's an expert in the field of economics.* ○ *That question is outside my field.* مجال؛ ميدان

5 an area affected by or included in sth: *a magnetic field* ○ *It's outside my field of vision* (= I can't see it). حقل

field² /fi:ld/ *verb* **1** [I,T] (to be ready) to catch and throw back the ball (in cricket and baseball) ❶ When one team is **fielding**, the other is **batting**. (في لعبة الكريكيت مثلاً) يتلقف الكرة ثم يعيدها

2 [T] to choose a team for a game of football, cricket, hockey, etc: *New Zealand is fielding an excellent team for the next match.* يشكّل فريق اللاعبين

'field day *noun* [C] a day or time of great excitement: *The newspapers always have a field day when there's a royal wedding.* يوم مشهود

'field event *noun* [C] an athletics event that is not running, e.g. jumping and throwing ➲ Look at **track events**. لعبة من ألعاب الميدان

fieldwork /fi:ldwɜ:k/ *noun* [U] practical research work done outside the classroom, laboratory, etc. عمل ميداني

fiend /fi:nd/ *noun* [C] **1** a devil or a very cruel person شيطان؛ طاغية

2 (*informal*) a person who is unusually fond of or interested in one particular thing: *a health fiend* مَهووس

fiendish /'fi:ndɪʃ/ *adj* **1** very fierce or cruel شيطانيّ؛ وحشيّ

2 clever and complicated: *a fiendish plan* (خطة) جهنمية

▸ **fiendishly** *adv* very, extremely: *fiendishly clever* جداً؛ للغاية

fierce /fɪəs/ *adj* **1** angry and aggressive: *The house was guarded by fierce dogs.* شرس

2 very strong: *fierce competition for jobs* ❶ The noun is **ferocity**. ضارٍ

▸ **fiercely** *adv* بضراوة

fiery /'faɪəri/ *adj* **1** looking like fire ناريّ

2 (used about a person's character or temper) quick to become angry نَزِق

fifteen /ˌfɪf'ti:n/ *number* 15, one more than fourteen ❶ For examples of how to use numbers in sentences, look at **six**. خمسة عَشَر

▸ **fifteenth** /ˌfɪf'ti:nθ/ *pron, det, adv* 15th, next after fourteenth ➲ Look at the examples at **sixth**. الخامس عشر

fifth /fɪfθ/ *pron, det, adv* 5th, next after fourth ➲ Look at **five**. الخامس

▸ **fifth** *noun* [C] the fraction ⅕; one of five equal parts of sth ➲ Look at the examples at **sixth**. خُمس

fifty /'fɪfti/ *number* 50, one more than forty-nine ❶ For examples of how to use numbers in sentences, look at **sixty**. خمسون

▸ **fiftieth** /'fɪftiəθ/ *pron, det, adv* 50th, next after forty-ninth ➲ Look at the examples at **sixth**. الخمسون

ˌfifty-'fifty *adj, adv* (*informal*) equal or equally (between two people, groups, etc.): *You've got a fifty-fifty chance of winning.* ○ *We'll divide the money fifty-fifty.* متساوٍ؛ بالتساوي؛ مناصفةً

fig /fɪg/ *noun* [C] (a type of tree with) a soft sweet fruit full of small seeds that grows in warm countries and is often eaten dried تين، شجرة تين

fig. *abbrev* **1** = FIGURE, ILLUSTRATION: *See diagram at fig 2.*

2 = FIGURATIVE(LY)

fight¹ /faɪt/ *verb* (*pt, pp* **fought** /fɔ:t/) **1** [I,T] **fight (against/with sb/sth) (about/over sth)** to use physical strength, guns, weapons etc. against sb/sth: *Did he fight in the Gulf War?* ○ *What were the boys fighting each other about?* ○ *Have you been fighting with your sister again?* يحارب، يقاتل؛ يتشاجر

2 [I,T] **fight (against sth)** to try very hard to stop or prevent sth: *to fight a fire, a decision, etc.* ○ *to fight against crime, disease, etc.* يكافح، يحارب

3 [I] **fight (for sth/to do sth)** to try very hard to get or keep sth: *to fight for your rights* يناضِل

4 [I] **fight (about/over sth)** to quarrel: *It's not worth fighting about money.* ينازع

PHR V **fight back** to protect yourself by fighting with actions or with words: *If he hits you again, fight back!* يردّ الهجوم؛ يدافع

▸ **fighter** *noun* [C] **1** (*also* **'fighter plane**) a small fast aircraft used for shooting down enemy aircraft طائرة مقاتلة

2 a person who fights in war or in sport (especially a boxer) مقاتل، محارب، ملاكم

fighting *noun* [U] an occasion when people fight: *There has been street fighting in many parts of the city today.* قتال؛ كفاح

fight² /faɪt/ *noun* **1** [C] an act of fighting or a struggle: *Don't get into a fight at school, will you?* ○ *the government's fight against inflation* قتال؛ كفاح

2 [U] the desire to continue trying or struggling: *I've had some bad luck but I've still got plenty of fight in me.* قدرة أو رغبة في القتال

IDM **pick a fight** → PICK¹

figurative /'fɪgərətɪv/ *adj* (used about a word or

an expression) not used with its exact meaning but used for giving an imaginative description or a special effect: *'He exploded at the news' is a figurative use of the verb 'to explode'.* ❶ The opposite is **literal**. مجازي
▸ **figuratively** *adv* مجازاً

figure¹ /ˈfɪɡə(r); *US* ˈfɪɡjər/ *noun* [C] **1** a written sign for a number (0 to 9): *Write the numbers in figures, not words.* ○ *He has a six-figure income/an income in six figures* (= more than £100 000). ○ *Our pay rise is going to be in single figures* (= less than 10 per cent). ○ *double figures* (= more than 10) رقم
2 an amount (in numbers) or a price: *The unemployment figures are lower this month.* ○ *What sort of figure are you thinking of for your house?* ثمن؛ عدد
3 a person (that you cannot see very clearly): *Two figures were coming towards us in the dark.* شخص
4 a person (in a picture or photograph): *There were two figures on the right of the photo that I didn't recognize.* شخص
5 the shape of the human body: *She's got a beautiful slim figure.* ➲ Look at the note at **build**. جسم؛ قوام
6 a well-known or important person: *an important political figure* شخصية
7 a diagram or illustration used in a book to explain sth: *Figure 3 shows the major cities of Italy.* شكل
8 figures arithmetic: *I'm not very good at figures.* حساب
IDM **facts and figures** → FACT
in round figures/numbers → ROUND¹

figure² /ˈfɪɡə(r); *US* ˈfɪɡjər/ *verb* **1** [I] **figure (in sth)** to be included in sth; to be an important part of sth: *Women don't figure much in his novels.* يدخل في نطاق؛ يظهر، يبرز
2 [T] **figure (that)** (*especially US*) to think or guess sth: *I figured he was here because I saw his car outside.* يخمِّن
IDM **it/that figures** (*informal*) that is what I expected يتوقّع
PHRV **figure on sth/on doing sth** (*especially US*) to include sth in your plans: *I figure on arriving in New York on Wednesday.* ينوي
figure sb/sth out to find an answer to sth or to understand sb يفهم

ˌfigure of ˈeight (*US* **figure eight**) *noun* [C] (*pl.* **figures of eight**) something in the shape of an 8 شبيه بالرقم 8

ˌfigure of ˈspeech *noun* [C] (*pl.* **figures of speech**) a word or expression used not with its original meaning but in an imaginative way to make a special effect ➲ Look at **figurative**. استعارة، مجاز

file¹ /faɪl/ *noun* [C] **1** a box or a cover that is used for keeping papers together and in order: *Students are given a file to keep their course notes in.* ملفّ، اضبارة
2 a collection of papers or information kept in a file: *I can't remember what exactly I said in the letter. I'll need to look at the file.* ملف
3 a collection of information or material on one subject that is stored in a computer or on a disk: *to open/close a file* اضبارة
IDM **on file** kept in a file: *We have all the information you need on file.* يدْرَج في ملفّ
the rank and file → RANK
▸ **file** *verb* [T] **file sth (away)** to put in a file: *File these letters under 'Job Applications'.* يصنّف

file² /faɪl/ *noun* [C] a metal tool with a rough surface used for making rough surfaces smooth: *a nail file* مبْرَد
▸ **file** *verb* [I,T] to use a file to cut sth or make sth smooth يبْرُد

file³ /faɪl/ *noun*
IDM **in single file** in a line, one behind the other: *You'll have to go in single file – the path is very narrow.* صفّ
▸ **file** *verb* [I] **file in, out, past, etc.** to walk or march in a line يسير في صف

ˈfile sharing *noun* [U] the practice of sharing computer files with other people over the Internet or another computer network مشاركة الملفات

fill /fɪl/ *verb* **1** [I,T] **fill (sth/sb) (with sth)** to make sth full or to become full: *Can you fill the kettle for me?* ○ *The news filled him with excitement.* ○ *The room filled with smoke within minutes.* يملأ؛ يمتلئ
2 [T] to occupy a position or time: *I'm afraid that teaching post has just been filled* (= somebody has got the job). يَشْغَل
PHRV **fill sth in** (*US also* **fill sth out**) to complete a form, etc. by writing information on it: *Could you fill in the application form, please?* يملأ استمارة
fill (sth) up to become or to make sth completely full: *There weren't many people at first but then the room filled up.* ○ *Fill up the tank, please* (= with petrol). يمتلئ؛ يملأ

fillet (*US* **filet**) /ˈfɪlɪt/ *noun* [C,U] (a piece of) meat or fish with the bones taken out شريحة لحم أو سمك بلا عظم

filling /ˈfɪlɪŋ/ *noun* **1** [C] the material that a dentist uses to fill a hole in a tooth: *a gold filling* مادة حشو الأسنان
2 [C,U] food put inside a sandwich, pie, cake, etc. to make it taste nice طعام في شطيرة
▸ **filling** *adj* (used about food) that makes you feel full يملأ إلى حد التخمة، "شباعي"

ˈfilling station (*US*) = PETROL STATION

film¹ /fɪlm/ *noun* **1** (*US* **movie**) [C] a story, play, etc. shown in moving pictures at the cinema or on television: *There's a good film on at the cinema this week. Do you fancy going?* ○ *the film industry* ○ *the film version of 'Hamlet'* فيلم

Some types of film are **documentary**, **feature**, **horror** films and **westerns**.

2 [C,U] a roll of thin plastic that you use in a camera to take photographs: *a 35-millimetre film*

○ *a black and white film* ○ *a colour film* ○ *Fast film is better in this light.* فيلم تصوير

You **load** a film into a camera and **rewind** it when it is finished. When the film is **developed**, you can have **prints** made from the **negatives**.

3 [usually sing.] a thin layer of a substance or material: *a film of oil* غشاء رقيق؛ غشاوة

film² /fɪlm/ *verb* [I,T] to make a film of an event, story, etc. with a camera: *They're filming in Oxford today.* ○ *A lot of westerns are filmed in Spain.* ○ *The man was filmed stealing from the shop.* يُصوِّر فيلماً سينمائياً

'film star *noun* [C] a person who is a well-known actor or actress in films نجم سينمائي

filter /'fɪltə(r)/ *noun* [C] **1** an apparatus for holding back solid substances from a liquid or gas that passes through it: *a coffee filter* ○ *an oil filter* مرشّح

2 a piece of coloured glass used with a camera to hold back some types of light مرشّح ضوء

▶ **filter** *verb* **1** [T] to pass a liquid through a filter: *Do you filter your water?* يرشّح

2 [I] **filter in, out, through, etc.** to move slowly and/or in small amounts: (*figurative*) *News of her illness filtered through to her friends.* يرشح؛ يتسرّب

filth /fɪlθ/ *noun* [U] **1** disgusting dirt: *The room was covered in filth.* وسَخ

2 extremely rude words, pictures, etc. usually in books, magazines or films بذاءة

▶ **filthy** *adj* (**filthier**; **filthiest**) **1** very dirty: *They got absolutely filthy playing football in the rain.* قذر

2 (used about language, books, films, etc.) extremely rude and unpleasant بذيء؛ فاحش

fin /fɪn/ *noun* [C] a part of a fish, shaped like a thin wing. Fish use fins for swimming. زعْنفة

final /'faɪnl/ *adj* **1** (only *before* a noun) last (in a series): *This will be the final lesson of our course.* ○ *I don't want to miss the final episode of that serial.* أخير

2 not to be changed: *The judge's decision is always final.* نهائي

IDM **the last/final straw** → STRAW

▶ **final** *noun* [C] **1** (*also* **finals**) the last game or match in a series of competitions or sporting events: *I wonder who'll get through to the final at Wimbledon this year?* ○ *The finals of the swimming championship will be held in Cardiff.* ➲ Look at **semi-final**. المباراة النهائية

2 finals the examinations you take in your last year at university: *I'm taking my finals in June.* امتحانات نهائية (قبل التخرّج)

finalist /-nəlɪst/ *noun* [C] a person who is in the final of a competition ➲ Look at **semi-finalist**. مشارك في مباراة نهائية

finalize (*also* **finalise**) *verb* [T] to make firm decisions about plans, dates, etc: *Have you finalized your holiday arrangements yet?* يَحْسِم؛ يقرّر نهائياً

finale /fɪ'nɑːli; *US* -'næli/ *noun* [C] the last part of a piece of music, an opera, show, etc. نهاية عرض فنّي

finally /'faɪnəli/ *adv* **1** (used at the beginning of a sentence when you have a list of things to say, especially in a speech) as a last point: *Finally, I would like to say how much we have all enjoyed this evening.* أخيراً

2 after a long time or delay: *It was getting dark when the plane finally took off.* أخيراً

3 in a definite way so that sth cannot be changed: *We haven't finally decided yet – it depends on the cost.* بشكل نهائي

finance /'faɪnæns; faɪ'næns/ *noun* **1** [U] the money you need to start or support a business, etc: *How will you raise the finance to start your own business?* مال

2 [U] the management of (public) money: *Who is the new Minister of Finance?* ○ *an expert in finance* ماليّة

3 finances [plural] the money a person, company, country, etc. has to spend: *What are our finances like at the moment?* (= how much money have we got?) حالة ماليّة

▶ **finance** *verb* [T] to provide the money to pay for sth: *Your trip will be financed by the company.* يموّل

financial /faɪ'nænʃl; fɪ'nænʃl/ *adj* connected with money: *The business got into financial difficulties.* ○ *New York and Tokyo are important financial centres.* ماليّ

financially *adv* /-ʃəli/ ماليّاً

finch /fɪntʃ/ *noun* [C] a small bird with a strong beak حسّون (طائر)

find¹ /faɪnd/ *verb* [T] (*pt, pp* **found** /faʊnd/) **1** to get back sth that you have lost: *Did you find the pen you lost?* ○ *I can't find my new sweater anywhere.* يجد

2 to discover sth or get sth that you want (after a search): *After six months she finally found a job.* ○ *Did you manage to find a good hotel?* ○ *Scientists haven't yet found a cure for colds.* ○ *They found oil in the North Sea.* ○ *I hope you find an answer to your problem.* يجد

Notice the expressions **find the time, find the money**: *I never seem to find the time to write letters these days.* ○ *We'd like to go on holiday but we can't find the money.*

3 to discover sth by chance: *Tom found a £20 note in the park.* ○ *I've found a piece of glass in this milk.* ○ *We went into the house and found her lying on the floor.* يجد؛ يكتشف

4 to think or to have an opinion about sth (because of your own experience): *I find that book very difficult to understand.* ○ *We didn't find the film at all funny.* ○ *How are you finding life as a student?* ❶ When we are expressing an opinion we say **I think that...** NOT **I find that....** يجد

IDM **find fault (with sb/sth)** to look for things that are wrong with sb/sth and complain about them يتصيد أو يتلمّس الأخطاء؛ يَعيب

find your feet to become confident and independent in a new situation: *Don't worry if the job seems difficult at first – you will soon find your feet.* يقف على قدميه؛ يكتسب مهارة وثقة

find your way (to...) to discover the right route (to a place): *I hope you can find your way home.* يجد طريقه إلى

PHRV **find (sth) out** to get some information by asking or studying: *Have you found out how much the tickets cost?* يستطلع؛ يعرِف؛ يكتشف

find sb out to discover that sb has done sth wrong: *He used a false name for years before they found him out.* يكشّف، يفتضح أمر شخص ما

▶ **finder** *noun* [C] a person that finds sth: *The lucky finder of the buried treasure will win a holiday in Spain.* مُكتشِف

finding *noun* [C] (usually plural) something that is discovered by research or investigation: *the findings of a survey, a report, a committee, etc.* نتائج بحث أو تحقيق

find² /faɪnd/ *noun* [C] a thing or a person that is unusually good or valuable: *That new software is a real find.* لُقْية

fine¹ /faɪn/ *adj* **1** (only *before* a noun) of very good quality, beautiful: *a fine piece of work* ○ *That's the finest painting I've ever seen by that artist.* ممتاز؛ رائع

2 good enough: *'Do you want some more milk in your coffee?' 'No that's fine, thanks.'* ○ *Don't cook anything special – a sandwich will be fine.* ○ *The hotel rooms were fine but the food was awful.* كافٍ، لا بأس به

3 in good health, or happy and comfortable: *'How are you?' 'Fine thanks.'* ○ *'Do you want to change places?' 'No I'm fine here, thanks.'* بصحة جيدة؛ مرتاح

> We do not use meanings **2** and **3** in questions or in the negative form, so you CANNOT say 'Are you fine?' or 'This isn't fine'.

4 (used about weather) bright and sunny; not raining: *Let's hope it stays fine for our barbecue tomorrow.* (طقس) جميل، صحو

5 thin: *That hairstyle's no good for me – my hair's too fine.* ○ *You must use a fine pencil for the diagrams.* ❶ The opposite is **thick**. دقيق: (شَعْر) ناعم

6 made of very small pieces, grains, etc: *Salt is finer than sugar.* ❶ The opposite is **coarse**. دقيق؛ ناعِم

7 difficult to see; very detailed: *The difference in meaning between those two words is very fine.* ○ *I couldn't understand the finer points of his argument.* دقيق جداً (الدرجة الغموض): دقيق التفاصيل

▶ **finely** *adv* **1** into small pieces: *The onions must be finely chopped for this recipe.* (يقطّع) قطعاً صغيرة

2 very delicately: *a finely tuned instrument* (مضبوط) بدِقّة

fine² /faɪn/ *noun* [C] a sum of money that you have to pay for breaking a law or rule: *a parking fine* ○ *You'll get a fine if you park your car there.* ○ *He'll either have to pay a heavy fine or go to prison.* غرامة

▶ **fine** *verb* [T] **fine sb (for sth/for doing sth)** to make sb pay a sum of money because he/she has broken a law or rule: *He was fined £50 for speeding.* يُغرِّم

finger¹ /ˈfɪŋɡə(r)/ *noun* [C] one of the five parts at the end of each hand (or a glove): *little finger, ring finger, middle finger, forefinger (or index finger), thumb* ○ *Children learn to count on their fingers.* إصبع

> Sometimes we think of the thumb as one of the fingers, sometimes we contrast it: *Hold the pen between your finger and thumb.* The 'fingers' on our feet are called **toes**.

IDM **keep your fingers crossed** to hope that sb/sth will be successful or lucky: *I'll keep my fingers crossed for you in your exams.* يتفاءل

➲ Look also at **cross your fingers** at **cross²**.

IDM **snap your fingers** → SNAP¹

finger² /ˈfɪŋɡə(r)/ *verb* [T] to touch or feel sth with your fingers يلمس؛ يتحسّس بالأصابع

fingermark /ˈfɪŋɡəmɑːk/ *noun* [C] a mark on a wall, door, book, etc. made by a dirty finger أثر إصبع

fingernail /ˈfɪŋɡəneɪl/ (*also* **nail**) *noun* [C] the hard parts on the ends of the fingers: *Your fingernails are filthy!* ○ *She always paints her fingernails bright red.* ظُفْر

fingerprint /ˈfɪŋɡəprɪnt/ *noun* [C] the mark made by the skin of a finger, used for identifying people: *The burglar left his fingerprints all over the house.* ○ *The police took the suspect's fingerprints.* بصمة إصبع

fingertip /ˈfɪŋɡətɪp/ *noun* [C] the end of a finger أنمُلة

IDM **have sth at your fingertips** to have sth ready for quick and easy use: *They asked some difficult questions but luckily I had all the facts at my fingertips.* في متناول اليد

finish¹ /ˈfɪnɪʃ/ *verb* **1** [I,T] **finish (sth/doing sth)** to come or bring sth to an end or to reach the end of sth: *What time does the film finish?* ○ *Haven't you finished yet? You've taken ages!* ○ *The Ethiopian runner won the race, and the Kenyans finished second and third.* ○ *Finish your work quickly!* ○ *Have you finished typing that letter?* ينتهي؛ ينهي

2 [T] **finish sth (off/up)** to eat, drink or use the last part of sth: *Finish up your milk, Tom!* ينْهي

3 [T] **finish sth (off)** to complete the last details of sth or make sth perfect: *He's just adding the finishing touches to his painting.* ○ *He stayed up all night to finish off the article he was writing.* يُكمِل

PHRV **finish sb/sth off** (*informal*) to kill sb/sth: *The cat played with the mouse before finishing it off.* ○ (*figurative*) *I was very tired towards the end of the race, and that last hill finished me off.* يقتل

finish with sb/sth 1 to stop needing or using sb/sth: *Don't go away. I haven't finished with you* *yet.* ○ *I'll borrow that book when you've finished with it.* يستغني عن: ينتهي من

2 to end a relationship with sb: *Sally's not going out with David any more – she finished with him last month.* يقاطع، ينهي علاقة

finish² /ˈfɪnɪʃ/ *noun* [C] **1** (used especially about a race) the end: *The last race was a very close finish* (= the runners at the front were close together at the end). ❶ The opposite is **start**. نهاية (سباق)

2 (used especially about wood and furniture) the feel or look that sth has when it has been polished, etc: *This table has a beautiful finish.* صَقْل

finished /ˈfɪnɪʃt/ *adj* **1** (not before a noun) **finished (with sb/sth)** having stopped doing sth, using sth or dealing with sb/sth: *'Are you using the computer?' 'Yes, I won't be finished with it for another hour or so.'* يفرغ من

2 (not before a noun) not able to continue: *The business is finished – there's no more money.* مُنْتَهٍ

3 made; completed: *the finished product, article, etc.* مُكْمَل: في شكله النهائي، مُنْجَز

finite /ˈfaɪnaɪt/ *adj* having a definite limit or a fixed size: *The world's resources are finite.* ❶ The opposite is **infinite**. محدود

fiord = FJORD

fir /fɜː(r)/ (*also* ˈ**fir tree**) *noun* [C] a straight tree that keeps its thin leaves (needles) in winter شجرة التَّنُّوب

ˈ**fir cone** *noun* [C] the fruit of the fir ثمر التنوب

fire¹ /ˈfaɪə(r)/ *noun* **1** [U] hot bright flames produced by sth that is burning: *Many animals are afraid of fire.* نار

2 [C,U] burning that destroys and is out of control: *Firemen struggled for three hours to put out the fire.* ○ *It had been a dry summer so there were many forest fires.* ○ *You need to insure your house against fire.* ○ *The furniture caught fire within seconds* (= started burning). ○ *Did someone set fire to that pile of wood?* ○ *Help! The frying pan's on fire!* حريق

3 [C] burning wood or coal to warm people or cook food: *They lit a fire to keep warm.* ○ *It's cold – don't let the fire go out!* ○ *a camp fire* نار؛ موقد

4 [C] an apparatus for heating a room, etc: *a gas fire* ○ *an electric fire* مدْفأة

5 [U] shooting from guns: *The soldiers were under fire from all sides.* ○ *I could hear gunfire in the distance.* إطلاق نار

IDM **open fire** → OPEN²

fire² /ˈfaɪə(r)/ *verb* **1** [I,T] **fire (sth) (at sb/sth)**; **fire (sth) into sth** to shoot with a gun or shoot bullets, etc. from a gun: *'Fire!' shouted the officer.* ○ *Can you hear the guns firing?* ○ *He fired his gun at the ceiling.* ○ *They fired rubber bullets into the crowd.* يطلق النار

2 [T] (*informal*) to dismiss sb from a job: *He was fired for always being late.* يطرد من عمل

3 [T] **fire sth at sb** to ask questions, or make remarks, quickly and aggressively: *If you stop firing questions at me I might be able to answer!* يمطر وابلاً من الاسئلة، ينهال عليه بـ

4 [T] **fire sb with sth** to produce a strong feeling in sb: *Her speech fired me with determination.* يهيِّج؛ يُلْهِب

▶ **-fired** (in compounds) using the fuel mentioned: *gas-fired central heating* مستخدماً الوقود (المذكور)

ˈ**fire alarm** *noun* [C] a bell or other signal to warn people that there is a fire: *If the fire alarm goes off, leave the building immediately.* انذار حريق

firearm /ˈfaɪərɑːm/ *noun* [C, usually pl.] a gun that you can carry: *Most policemen don't carry firearms.* سلاح ناري

ˈ**fire brigade** (*US* ˈ**fire department**) *noun* [C, with sing. or pl. verb] an organization of people trained to put out (= stop) fires: *Dial 999 to call the fire brigade.* فرقة الإطفاء

ˈ**fire engine** *noun* [C] a special vehicle that carries equipment for fighting large fires عربة الإطفاء

ˈ**fire escape** *noun* [C] a special staircase on the outside of a building that people can escape down if there is a fire سلَّم النجاة من الحريق

ˈ**fire extinguisher** (*also* **extinguisher**) *noun* [C] a metal container with water or chemicals inside that you use for fighting small fires: *Shops and offices have fire extinguishers on every floor.* مطفأة الحريق

firefighter /ˈfaɪəfaɪtə(r)/ *noun* [C] a person whose job is to fight fires إطفائي

firelight /ˈfaɪəlaɪt/ *noun* [U] the light that comes from a fire in a fireplace: *It's quite romantic sitting here in the firelight.* ضوء النار

fireman /ˈfaɪəmən/ *noun* [C] (*pl.* **firemen** /-mən/) a person whose job is to fight fires إطْفائي

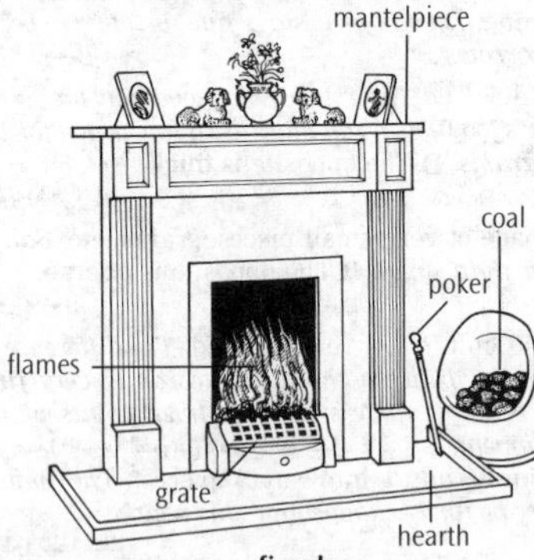

fireplace

fireplace /ˈfaɪəpleɪs/ *noun* [C] the open place in a room (at the bottom of a chimney) where you light a fire موْقِد

fireside /ˈfaɪəsaɪd/ *noun* [C, usually sing.] the part of a room beside the fireplace: *Come and sit by the fireside.* جوار الموقد

ˈfire station *noun* [C] a building where fire engines are kept and firefighters wait to be called
محطة الإطفاء

firewall /ˈfaɪəwɔːl/ *noun* [C] (*computing*) a part of a computer system that is designed to prevent people from getting information without authority but still allows them to receive information that is sent to them
حاجز ناري

firewood /ˈfaɪəwʊd/ *noun* [U] wood used for burning on fires
حَطَب

firework /ˈfaɪəwɜːk/ *noun* [C] a small container with chemicals inside that burns or explodes with coloured lights and bangs, used for entertainment: *Be careful not to burn your fingers when you let off that firework.* ○ *a firework display/party* ℹ **Firework** is often used in the plural: *We went to watch the fireworks in Hyde Park.*
ألعاب ناريّة

ˈfiring squad *noun* [C] a group of soldiers who have been ordered to shoot and kill a prisoner
جنود الإعدام رمياً بالرصاص

firm¹ /fɜːm/ *noun* [C, with sing. or pl. verb] a business company: *Which firm do you work for?* ○ *My firm's moving to Manchester soon.*
شركة

firm² /fɜːm/ *adj* **1** able to stay the same shape when pressed; quite hard: *a firm mattress*
صامد؛ قاسٍ

2 strong or steady or not likely to change: *She kept a firm grip on her mother's hand.* ○ *Have you got a firm date for your holiday yet?* ○ *We've taken a firm decision – we're not going to change it now.* ○ *I've got a firm offer of a job in New York.*
قوي؛ ثابت

3 firm (with sb) insisting that people do what you want: *He's very firm with his children.*
حازم

▶ **firmly** *adv*
بقوة؛ بصلابة؛ باعتقاد راسخ

firmness *noun* [U]
حزم، صمود

first¹ /fɜːst/ *det* coming before all others; that has not happened before: *his first day at school* ○ *their first baby* ○ *the first half of the game* ○ *You've won first prize!* ○ *My first choice is blue, but I'll take green if there's no blue left.* ○ *first impressions* ○ *The first time she went skiing, she broke her leg.* ○ *King Charles I* (= King Charles the First)
أوّل

IDM at first glance/sight when first seen or examined: *At first glance it looked like solid gold.*
للوهلة الأولى

first/last thing → THING

▶ **firstly** *adv* (used to introduce the first point in a list): *They were angry firstly because they had to pay extra, and secondly because no one had told them about it.*
أوّلاً

first² /fɜːst/ *adv* **1** before any others: *Sue arrived first at the party.* ○ *Our team came first in the race* (= we won). ○ *Do you want to go first or second?*
أوّل، قبل الآخرين

2 before doing anything else: *I'll come out later. I've got to finish my homework first.*
قبل أي شيء آخر

3 for the first time: *Where did you first meet your husband?*
لأوّل مرّة

4 at the beginning: *When I first started my job I hated it.*
في البداية

5 (used for introducing the first thing in a list): *There are several people I would like to thank: First, my mother.*
أوّلاً

IDM at first at the beginning: *At first I thought he was joking, but then I realized he was serious.*
في البدء

come first to be more important (to sb) than anything else: *Her family has always come first.*
في المرتبة الأولى

first and foremost more than anything else; most importantly: *He worked in television but he was a stage actor first and foremost.*
أوّلاً وقبل كل شيء

first of all as the first thing (to be done or said): *In a moment I'll introduce our guest speaker, but first of all, let me thank you all for coming.*
قَبْلَ كل شيء

head first → HEAD

first³ /fɜːst/ *noun, pron* **1** [sing.] **the first** the first person or thing, people or things: *Are we the first to arrive?* ○ *You are the first to hear the news.* ○ *They enjoyed the holiday – their first for ten years.*
الأوّل

2 [sing.] an important event that is happening for the first time: *This operation is a first in medical history.*
الأوّل من نوعه

3 [C] **a first (in sth)** (*Brit*) the highest grade of university degree
مرتبة الامتياز (في الجامعة)

ˌfirst ˈaid *noun* [U] medical help that you give to sb who is hurt or ill before the doctor arrives
إسْعاف أوّلي

ˌfirst ˈclass *adj, adv* **1** excellent; of the best quality: *a first-class player* ○ *This book is really first class.*
ممْتاز؛ من الدرجة الأولى

2 giving or using the best and most expensive type of service: *Are the first-class carriages at the front or the back of the train?* ○ *He always travels first class.* ○ *Ten first-class stamps, please.* ○ *If you send the letter first class, it should arrive tomorrow.*
من الدرجة الأولى

ˌfirst ˈcousin = COUSIN

ˌfirst ˈfloor *noun* [C] **1** (*Brit*) the floor of a building above the one on street level (the ground floor): *I live in a flat on the first floor/a first-floor flat.*
طابق أوّل

2 (*US*) the floor of a building on street level
طابق أرضي

ˌfirst ˈgear *noun* [C] the lowest gear on a car, bicycle, etc.
الأوّل (في مغير السرعة في سيارة أو دراجة)

first-hand /ˌfɜːstˈhænd/ *adj, adv* (used about information, experience, a story, etc.) heard, seen or learnt directly, not from other people: *He gave me a first-hand account of the accident* (= he had seen it). ○ *I've experienced the problem first-hand, so I know exactly how you feel.*
مباشَر

ˌfirst ˈminister (*also* **ˌFirst ˈMinister**) *noun* [C] the leader of the ruling political party in some regions or countries, for example in Scotland
الوزير الأوّل

ˈfirst name (*especially US* **given name**) *noun* [C] the name that is given to a child when he/she is born: *'What's Mrs Brown's first name?' 'Alice, I think.'* ○ *Do you know him well enough to call him by his first name?* ➲ Look at the note at **name**[1]. اسم

the ˌfirst ˈperson *noun* [sing.] **1** (*grammar*) the words such as 'I', 'me', 'we', and the verb forms that go with them: *'I am' is the first person singular of the verb 'to be'.* ضمير المتكلم (في القواعد)

2 the style of telling a story as if it happened to you: *The author writes in the first person* (= he writes, 'I...'). (رواية قصة) بضمير المتكلم

ˌfirst-ˈrate *adj* excellent; of the best quality من الطراز الأوّل

fish[1] /fɪʃ/ *noun* (*pl.* **fish** or **fishes**) **1** [C] an animal that lives and breathes in water using its fins and tail for swimming: *How many fish have you caught?* ○ *I went diving on holiday – it was fantastic to see so many different fishes* (= types or species of fish). ❶ The plural form **fish** is more common. **Fishes** is used when we are talking about different types of fish. سمك

2 [U] fish as food: *We're having fresh fish for supper.* لحم السمك

▸ **fishy** *adj* (**fishier**; **fishiest**) **1** of or like a fish, especially in taste or smell: *a fishy smell* سَمَكيّ

2 (*informal*) seeming suspicious or untrue: *The police thought the man's story sounded extremely fishy.* مريب

fish[2] /fɪʃ/ *verb* [I] **1 fish (for sth)** to try to catch fish with rods, nets, etc: *He's fishing for trout.* يصيد سمكاً

> When we are talking about spending time fishing we usually say **go fishing**: *They often go fishing at weekends.*

2 fish for sth to search for sth in water or in a deep or hidden place: *She fished (around) for her keys in the bottom of her bag.* يفتّش عن

PHR V fish for sth to try to get sth you want in an indirect way: *to fish for an invitation* يحتال في الحصول على ما يريد، يتصيّد

fish sth out (of sth) to take or pull sth out (of sth) especially after searching for it: *After the accident they fished the car out of the canal.* ○ *She fished a pair of socks out of the bottom of the cupboard.* يستخرج

ˌfish and ˈchips *noun* [U] fried fish and potato chips often bought already cooked and taken away to eat سمك وبطاطس

> We buy fish and chips at a **fish and chip shop**. The fish is covered with **batter** (a mixture of flour, egg and milk) and **deep-fried**. You find a fish and chip shop in most towns in Britain.

fishcake /ˈfɪʃkeɪk/ *noun* [C] pieces of fish mixed with mashed potato made into a flat round shape, covered with breadcrumbs and fried أقراص مقليّة من لحم السمك

fisherman /ˈfɪʃəmən/ *noun* [C] (*pl.* **fishermen** /ˈfɪʃəmən/) a person who catches fish especially as a job but also as a sport ➲ Look at **angler**. صيّاد سمك

ˌfish ˈfinger (*US* **fish stick**) *noun* [C] a small oblong piece of fish covered in breadcrumbs: *a packet of fish fingers* أصابع من لحم السمك

fishing /ˈfɪʃɪŋ/ *noun* [U] catching fish as a job, sport or hobby: *Fishing is a major industry in Iceland.* ❶ The sport or hobby of fishing is also called **angling**. صيد السمك

ˈfishing rod *noun* [C] a long thin stick with a line and a hook on it for catching fish صنارة صيد السمك

fishmonger /ˈfɪʃmʌŋgə(r)/ *noun* [C] (*Brit*) a person whose job is to sell fish, or a shop that sells fish (= the fishmonger's): *I bought it at the fishmonger's.* بائع سمك

ˌfish ˈstick *noun* [C] (*US*) = FISH FINGER

fist /fɪst/ *noun* [C] a hand with the fingers closed together tightly: *She clenched her fists.* قَبْضة

fit[1] /fɪt/ *adj* (**fitter**; **fittest**) **1 fit for sb/sth**; **fit to do sth** good enough; suitable: *These houses are not fit (for people) to live in.* ○ *Do you think she is fit for the job?* لائق، مناسب

2 fit (for sth/to do sth) in good physical health (especially because of exercise): *He keeps fit by jogging five miles a day.* ○ *I'm afraid you won't be fit enough for work for a long time yet.* ○ *She goes to keep-fit classes.* ❶ The opposite is **unfit**. ذو لياقة بدنية

3 (*Brit informal*) sexually attractive ذو فتنة وإغراء

▸ **fitness** *noun* [U] **1** the condition of being fit (2): *Fitness is important in most sports.* اللياقة البدنيّة

2 fitness for sth/to do sth the quality of being suitable: *The directors were not sure about his fitness for the job.* مناسبة، ملاءمة

fit[2] /fɪt/ *verb* (**fitting**; **fitted**) **1** [I,T] to be the right size or shape for sb/sth: *These jeans don't fit.* ○ *This dress doesn't fit me any more.* ○ *This key doesn't fit the lock.* ○ *My car won't fit into your garage.* يناسب؛ يطابق المقاييس

2 [T] **fit sb/sth in/into/on/onto sth** to find enough space for sb/sth: *Can you fit one more person in the car?* ○ *I can't fit all these books onto the shelf.* يجد مكاناً كافياً

3 [T] to put or fix sth in the right place: *The builders are fitting new windows today.* ○ *I can't fit these pieces of the model together.* يركّب

4 [T] to be or make sb/sth right or suitable: *I don't think Ruth's fitted for such a demanding job.* ○ *That description fits Jim perfectly.* يؤهّل؛ يناسب

PHR V fit sb/sth in; fit sb/sth in/into sth to find time to see sb or to do sth: *The doctor managed to fit me in this morning.* ○ *You're tired because you're trying to fit too much into one day.* يجد الوقت الكافي لشيء ما

fit in (with sb/sth) to be able to live, work, etc. in an easy and natural way (with sb/sth): *The new girl found it difficult to fit in (with the other*

children) at school. ○ *I will happily change my plans to fit in with yours.* ينسجم
▸ **fitted** *adj* made or cut to fit a particular space and fixed there: *fitted cupboards* ○ *a fitted carpet* ○ *a fitted kitchen* (= one with fitted cupboards) مصنوع حسَب المقاس

fit[3] /fɪt/ *noun* [sing.] (usually after an adjective) the way in which sth (e.g. a piece of clothing) fits: *a good, bad, tight, etc. fit* مقاس

fit[4] /fɪt/ *noun* [C] **1** a sudden loss of consciousness with movements that are not controlled and sometimes violent صَرْعَة

2 a sudden (usually short) attack of illness: *a fit of coughing* نوبة مَرَضيّة

3 a sudden period of activity or violent feeling: *a fit of laughter, energy, etc.* ○ *a fit of anger* نوبة: هبّة

fitting[1] /ˈfɪtɪŋ/ *adj* (*formal*) right; suitable مناسِب

fitting[2] /ˈfɪtɪŋ/ *noun* [C, usually pl.] the things that are fixed in a building or on a piece of furniture but that can be changed or moved if necessary ➲ Look at **fixture**. تجهيزات منزلية

⚷ **five** /faɪv/ *number* 5; one more than four ➲ Look at **fifth** (= 5th). ❶ For examples of how to use numbers in sentences, look at **six**. خَمْسة
▸ **five-** (in compounds) having five of the thing mentioned: *a five-day week* ○ *a five-hour flight* ذو خمسة مكوِّنات

fiver /ˈfaɪvə(r)/ *noun* [C] **1** (*Brit informal*) a five pound note; £5: *Can you lend me a fiver?* ورقة ماليّة قيمتها خمسة جنيهات

2 (*US informal*) a five dollar note; $5 ورقة ماليّة قيمتها خمسة دولارات

⚷ **fix**[1] /fɪks/ *verb* [T] **1** to put sth firmly in place so that it will not move: *Can you fix this new handle to the door?* ○ *He fixed the post firmly in the ground.* ○ (*figurative*) *I found it difficult to keep my mind fixed on what they were saying.* يثبِّت

2 fix sth (up) to decide or arrange sth: *We need to fix the price.* ○ *Have you fixed (up) a date for the party?* يحدِّد

3 to repair: *The electrician's coming to fix the cooker.* يصلح

4 (usually passive) (*informal*) to arrange the result of sth in a way that is not honest or fair: *The race was fixed* (= the result was arranged before it happened). يحصل على نتيجة ما بالغش، يزوِّر

5 fix sth (for sb) (*especially US*) to prepare sth (especially food or drink) for sb: *Can I fix you a drink/a drink for you?* يعدّ له (طعاماً أو شراباً)

PHRV fix sb up (with sth) (*informal*) to arrange for sb to have sth: *I can fix you up with a job, a car, a place to stay, etc.* يرتِّب لـ؛ يدبِّر
▸ **fixed** /fɪkst/ *adj* **1** already decided: *a fixed date, rent, price, etc.* محدَّد

2 not changing: *He has such fixed ideas that you can't discuss anything with him.* ○ *She looked at him with a fixed smile.* راسخ؛ لا يتزعزع

IDM (of) no fixed abode/address (with) no permanent place to live: *Smith, of no fixed abode, was found guilty of robbery.* بلا مقرّ دائم

fix[2] /fɪks/ *noun* [C] **1** [usually sing.] (*informal*) a difficult situation: *I was in a real fix – I'd locked the car keys inside the car.* مأزِق

2 (*informal*) an injection of a drug such as heroin زرقة (من مخدِّر)

fixation /fɪkˈseɪʃn/ *noun* [C] a feeling (about sb/sth) that is too strong and not normal هَوَس، تعلّق (مَرَضي)

fixture /ˈfɪkstʃə(r)/ *noun* [C] **1** [usually pl.] a piece of furniture or equipment that is fixed in a house or building and sold with it: *Does the price of the house include fixtures and fittings?* ➲ Look at **fitting**. قطعة أثاث (أو جهاز) ثابتة في بناء

2 a sporting event arranged for a particular day: *a fixture list* ○ *We had to cancel our fixture last week.* موعد محدد لحدَث رياضي

fizz /fɪz/ *verb* [I] to produce many small bubbles and/or make a hissing sound يئزّ، يفور (شراب غازيّ مثلاً)
▸ **fizz** *noun* [U] the bubbles in a liquid and the sound they make: *This lemonade's lost its fizz.* فقاعات الشراب الغازي؛ هسيس، أزيز

fizzy /ˈfɪzi/ *adj* (**fizzier**; **fizziest**) (used about a drink) containing many small bubbles ❶ The opposite is **still**. Look at **sparkling**. (شراب) فوّار

fizzle /ˈfɪzl/ *verb*
PHRV fizzle out to end in a weak or disappointing way: *The game started well but it fizzled out in the second half.* يضمحلّ، يخفق

fjord (*also* **fiord**) /ˈfiːɔːd/ *noun* [C] a long narrow piece of sea between cliffs, especially in Norway فيورد

flabbergasted /ˈflæbəɡɑːstɪd; *US* -ɡæst-/ *adj* (*informal*) extremely surprised مذهول، مشدوه

flabby /ˈflæbi/ *adj* (**flabbier**; **flabbiest**) **1** (used about a person) having too much soft loose flesh مترهِّل

2 (used about muscles, arms, legs, etc.) too soft رَخْو

⚷ **flag**[1] /flæɡ/ *noun* [C] a piece of cloth with a pattern or picture on it, often attached to a pole (flagpole) or rope and used as a symbol of a country, club, etc. or as a signal: *The flag is flying for the Queen's birthday.* ○ *The train will leave when the guard waves his flag.* علَم، راية

⚷ **flag**[2] /flæɡ/ *verb* [I] (fla**gg**ing; fla**gg**ed) to become tired or less strong or active يضعف، يتراخى؛ يفتر

flagrant /ˈfleɪɡrənt/ *adj* (only *before* a noun) easily seen to be bad and shocking صارخ، فاضح

flail /fleɪl/ *verb* [I,T] to wave or swing about without control: *The insect's legs were flailing in the air.* ○ *The drowning child flailed his arms above his head.* يتخبّط، يترنّح؛ يلوّح، يخبط بيديه في الهواء

flair /fleə(r)/ *noun* **1 (a) flair for sth** [sing.] a natural ability to do sth well: *She has a flair for languages* (= she's good at learning them). استعداد فطري، ملكة

2 [U] the quality of being interesting or having style: *That poster is designed with her usual flair.* ذوق فنيّ، مهارة فطريّة

flak /flæk/ *noun* [U] **1** guns shooting at enemy aircraft; fire from those guns: *run into heavy flak* (نيران) المدافع المضادة للطائرات

2 (*informal*) severe criticism: *The plans for the new tax have come in for a lot of flak.* هجوم، انتقاد شديد

flake /fleɪk/ *noun* [C] a small thin piece of sth: *snowflakes* ○ *cornflakes* ○ *soap flakes* نُدفة (ثلج)، رقيقة صغيرة

▶ **flake** *verb* [I] **flake (off)** to come off in flakes: *My skin is very dry – it's beginning to flake (off).* يتقشّر

flamboyant /flæm'bɔɪənt/ *adj* **1** (used about a person) acting in a loud, confident way مُفرِط في ملبسه وفي إظهار الثقة بنفسه

2 very easily noticed: *flamboyant colours* (لون) صارخ

▶ **flamboyance** /-'bɔɪəns/ *noun* [U] إفراط في البَهْرَجة والتنميق

flamboyantly *adv* بأسلوب مبهرَج: بشكل دْرامي

flame /fleɪm/ *noun* [C,U] an area of bright burning gas that comes from sth that is on fire: *The flame of the candle flickered by the open window.* ○ *The house was in flames when the fire engine arrived.* ○ *The piece of paper burst into flame in the fire* (= suddenly began to burn strongly). لَهَب؛ شُعلة

flaming /'fleɪmɪŋ/ *adj* (only *before* a noun) **1** burning brightly: *a flaming torch* ملْتَهِب

2 (used about colours, especially red) very bright: *flaming red hair* ○ *a flaming sunset* زاهٍ، صارخ، فاقع

3 (used about anger, an argument, etc.) violent: *He was in a flaming temper.* محتدم، غاضب، عنيف

4 (*informal*) (used as a mild swear word): *I can't get in – I've lost the flaming key.* الخبيث، الملعون! (تستعمل كشتيمة خفيفة)

flammable /'flæməbl/ *adj* able to burn easily سريع الاشتعال

The opposite is **non-flammable. Inflammable** has the same meaning as flammable and is more common.

flan /flæn/ *noun* [C,U] a round open pie that is filled with cheese, vegetables, fruit, etc. ➲ Look at the note at **pie**. فطيرة مستديرة عليها جبن أو خضار الخ...

flank /flæŋk/ *noun* [C] the side of an animal or of an army ready for battle خاصرة، جنب؛ جناح (الجيش)

▶ **flank** *verb* [T] (usually passive) to be placed at the side or sides of: *The road was flanked by trees.* يحيط من الجانبين

flannel /'flænl/ *noun* **1** [U] a type of soft woollen cloth فانيلا

2 [C] = FACECLOTH

flap¹ /flæp/ *noun* [C] a piece of material that is fixed to sth at one side only, often covering an opening: *a tent flap* ○ *a cat flap* (= in a door for a cat to get through) غطاء سائب (للجيب مثلاً)

IDM **be in/get into a flap** (*informal*) to be in/get into a state of worry or excitement يصاب باضطراب أو قلق

flap² /flæp/ *verb* (fla**pp**ing; fla**pp**ed) **1** [I,T] to move sth up and down or from side to side; to move in this way, especially in the wind: *The sails were flapping in the wind.* ○ *The bird flapped its wings and flew away.* يصفِّق (بجناحيه)، يرفرف

2 [I] (*informal*) to become worried or excited: *You don't need to flap – it's all organized!* يضطرب أو يتشوّش

flare /fleə(r)/ *verb* [I] to burn with a sudden bright flame يتوهّج فجأة

PHR V **flare up 1** (used about a fire) to suddenly burn more fiercely يشتعل، يندلع

2 (used about violence, anger, a person's temper, etc.) to start suddenly or become worse يَحْتَدِم، يستَشيط غضباً

▶ **flare** *noun* **1** [sing.] a sudden bright light or flame شعلة، اندلاع مفاجئ

2 [C] a thing that produces a bright light or flame, used especially as a signal إشارة ضوئية، شُعلة

flared /fleəd/ *adj* (used about trousers and skirts) becoming wider towards the bottom edge متّسع عند الاسفل (سروال مثلاً)

flash¹ /flæʃ/ *noun* **1** [C] a sudden bright light that comes and goes quickly: *a flash of lightning* ومضة، وميض

2 [C] a sudden ability (to guess, understand or imagine sth): *a flash of inspiration* ○ *The idea came to me in a flash.* التماعة (ذكاء)

3 [C,U] a bright light that you use with a camera for taking photographs when the light is not good; the apparatus for producing this light: *My new camera's got a built-in flash.* ○ *The light's not very good. You'll need flash.* "فلاش": ضوء وهّاج ترسله الكاميرا

flash² /flæʃ/ *verb* **1** [I,T] to produce a sudden bright light or to make sth produce it: *The neon sign above the door flashed on and off all night.* ○ *That lorry driver's flashing his lights at us* (= in order to tell us sth). يومض، يرسل ومضات سريعة

2 [I] to move very fast: *I saw something flash past the window.* ○ *Thoughts kept flashing through my mind and I couldn't sleep.* يمرّ كلمْح البَصَر

3 [T] to show sth quickly: *The detective flashed his card and went straight in.* يري شيئاً بسرعة خاطفة

4 [T] to send a particular look towards sb (suddenly, and only for a moment): *He flashed a smile at her and drove away.* يرمي بنظرة

5 [T] to send sth by radio, television, etc: *The news of the disaster was flashed across the world.* يَبْرق، يَبثّ

PHR V **flash back** (used about a person's thoughts) to return suddenly to a time in the past: *Something he said made my mind flash back to my childhood.* يتذكّر الماضي

flashback /'flæʃbæk/ *noun* [C,U] a part of a film, play, etc. that shows sth that happened before the main story رجوع سريع للماضي (في فيلم أو قصة)

'**flash drive** *noun* [C] a small memory device that can be used to store data from a computer and to

move it from one computer to another
"فلاشة"، ذاكرة محمولة

ˈflashlight /ˈflæʃlaɪt/ *noun* [C] (*US*) = TORCH

flashy /ˈflæʃi/ *adj* (**flashier**; **flashiest**) attracting attention by being too bright and smart: *a flashy car* ○ *flashy clothes* صارخ، برّاق

flask /flɑːsk; *US* flæsk/ *noun* [C] **1** a bottle with a narrow neck that is used in a laboratory
قارورة، دورق

2 a small flat bottle used for carrying drink in a pocket زجاجة مشروب كحولي توضع في الجيب

3 = VACUUM FLASK

flat[1] /flæt/ (*especially US* **apartment**) *noun* [C] a set of rooms that is used as a home (usually on one floor in a larger building): *Do you rent your flat or have you bought it?* ○ *That old house has been divided into luxury flats.* شقة

> **Apartment** is much more common in American English. In British English we usually say a **flat**. But we do say apartment when talking about a flat we are renting for a holiday, etc. rather than to live in: *We're renting an apartment in the South of France.* You **rent** a flat from a **landlord/landlady**. The landlord/lady **lets** the flat to you, the **tenant**. The money you have to pay is called **rent**. Your flat may be **furnished** or **unfurnished**. A tall modern building that contains many flats is a **block** of flats. A person who shares the flat with you is your **flatmate**.

flat[2] /flæt/ *adj* (**flatter**; **flattest**) **1** smooth and level, with no parts that are raised above the rest: *The countryside in Essex is quite flat* (= there are not many hills). ○ *I need a flat surface to write this letter on.* ○ *a flat roof* مستوٍ أو مُنبسط

2 not high or deep: *You need flat shoes for walking.* ○ *a flat dish* مسطّح: (حذاء) بدون كعب

3 (used about a tyre) without enough air in it: *This tyre looks flat – has it got a puncture?*
خالٍ من الهواء (إطار سيارة)

4 without much interest or energy: *Things have been a bit flat since Alex left.* فاتر، خامد

5 (used about a drink) not fresh because it has lost its bubbles: *Open a new bottle. That lemonade has gone flat.* مشروب فوّار بَطَل مفعوله

6 (used about a battery) no longer producing electricity; not working: *We couldn't start the car because the battery was completely flat.*
(بطارية) فارغة

7 (*symbol* ♭) (in music) half a tone lower than the stated note: *a symphony in B flat* ➲ Look at **sharp** (9).
منخفض

8 (in music) lower than the correct note: *That last note was flat. Can you sing it again?* ➲ Look at **sharp** (10). نغمة أخفض مما يجب

9 that will not change; firm (used about sth that you say or decide): *He answered our request with a flat 'No!'* (جواب) جازم، قاطع

10 (used about the cost of sth) that is the same for everybody; that is fixed: *We charge a flat fee of £20, however long you stay.* (سعر) ثابت، موحّد

▸ **flatly** *adv* **1** in a way that shows no interest
بفتور

2 in a direct way; absolutely: *He flatly denied the allegations.*
بشكل قاطع

flatten /ˈflætn/ *verb* [I,T] **flatten (sth) (out)** to become flat or to make sth flat: *The countryside flattens out as you get nearer the sea.* ○ *The storms have flattened crops all over the country.*
يتسطّح، يستوي؛ يبسط، يدحو، يفلطح

flat[3] /flæt/ *adv* **1** in a level position: *She lay flat on her back in the sunshine.* ○ *He fell flat on his face in the mud.* مستلقياً، منبطحاً

2 lower than the correct note: *You're singing flat.* ➲ Look at **sharp** (9). (نغمة) أخفض مما يجب

3 (used for emphasizing how quickly sth is done) in exactly the time mentioned and no longer: *She can get up and out of the house in ten minutes flat.* بالضبط، تماماً

IDM **fall flat** (used about a joke, a story, an event, etc.) to fail to produce the effect that you wanted بدون تأثير، بفتور

flat out as fast as possible; without stopping: *He's been working flat out for two weeks and he needs a break.* بهمّة ونشاط، دون توقّف

flat[4] /flæt/ *noun* **1** [C] (*symbol* ♭) (in music) a note which is half a tone lower than the note with the same letter ➲ Look at **sharp**. علامة الخفض (موسيقى)

2 [sing.] **the flat (of sth)** the flat part or side of sth: *the flat of your hand* السطح المنبسط

3 [C] (*especially US*) a tyre on a car, etc. that has no air in it (دولاب) أو إطار فارغ من الهواء

ˌflat-ˈscreen *adj* [only before a noun] a type of television or computer monitor that is very thin when compared with the traditional type: *a flat-sceen television*
شاشة مسطحة

flatter /ˈflætə(r)/ *verb* [T] **1** to praise sb too much because you want to please him/her or because you want to get an advantage for yourself
يطري، يتملّق

2 (usually passive) to give pleasure or honour to sb: *I felt very flattered when they gave me the job.* يرضي غرور شخص بمدحه، يسر

3 flatter yourself (that) to choose to believe sth good about yourself although you may be wrong: *He flatters himself that he speaks fluent French.* يبالغ في تقدير قيمة نفسه

▸ **flattering** *adj* making sb look or sound more attractive or important than he/she really is
يظهر الشخص اكثر جمالاً من حقيقته

flattery *noun* [U] praise that you do not really mean
تملّق

flaunt /flɔːnt/ *verb* [T] to show sth that you are proud of so that other people will admire it
يتباهى بـ، يعرض نفسه متباهياً

flautist /ˈflɔːtɪst/ (*US* **flutist**) *noun* [C] a person who plays the flute
عازف الفلوت

flavour (*US* **flavor**) /ˈfleɪvə(r)/ *noun* [C,U] **1** the taste and smell (of food): *Do you think a little salt would improve the flavour?* ○ *ten different fla-*

vours of yogurt ○ *yogurt in ten different flavours* نكهة

2 the particular quality or character of sth صفة مميزة

▶ **flavour** (*US* **flavor**) *verb* [T] to give flavour to sth: *strawberry-flavoured milkshake* ○ *I flavoured the soup with lemon and parsley.* ينكّه

flavouring (*US* **flavoring**) /ˈfleɪvərɪŋ/ *noun* [C,U] something that you add to food or drink to give it a particular taste مُنكِّه

flaw /flɔː/ *noun* [C] **1** a mark or crack in an object that means that it is not perfect عيب

2 a mistake in sth that makes it not satisfactory: *a flaw in an argument* خطأ، نقص

3 a bad quality in sb's character نقيصة

▶ **flawed** *adj* with a fault or weakness so that it is not perfect معيوب

flawless *adj* perfect لا عيبَ فيه

flax /flæks/ *noun* [U] **1** a small plant with blue flowers, that is grown for its stem and seeds نبات الكتّان

2 the thread that is used for making linen. It comes from the flax plant. خيوط الكتّان

flea /fliː/ *noun* [C] a very small jumping insect without wings that lives on animals, e.g. cats and dogs. Fleas bite people and animals and make them scratch. برغوث

ˈ**flea market** *noun* [C] a market, often in a street, that sells old and used goods سوق لبيع أشياء قديمة أو مستعملة

fleck /flek/ *noun* [C] a tiny mark on sth; a tiny piece of sth نقطة، ذرّة

flee /fliː/ *verb* [I,T] (*pt, pp* **fled** /fled/) to run away or escape from sth: *When the hunter fired his gun the tiger turned and fled.* ○ *The man whom the police want to interview has fled the country.* يفرّ

fleece /fliːs/ *noun* **1** [C] the wool coat of a sheep or goat: *fine thick fleeces* صوف الخراف؛ جزّة

2 [U] a type of fabric that feels like sheep's wool: *a wind-resistant jacket lined with polyester and cotton fleece* قماش يشبه صوف الخروف

3 [C] a type of jacket that is made from this material جاكيت مصنوع من صوف الخروف

fleet /fliːt/ *noun* [C, with sing. or pl. verb] **1** a group of ships or boats that are sailing together أسطول

2 a group of vehicles (especially taxis, buses or aircraft) that are travelling together or owned by one person قافلة (سيارات مثلاً)

⚷ **flesh** /fleʃ/ *noun* [U] **1** the soft part of a human or animal body (between the bones and under the skin) ❶ **Flesh** that we eat is called **meat**. لحم

2 the part of a fruit or vegetable that is soft and can be eaten اللّب (في الثمار)

flew *pt* of FLY[1]

flex[1] /fleks/ (*especially US* **cord**) *noun* [C,U] (a piece of) electric wire inside a plastic tube, used for carrying electricity to electrical equipment ❶ At the end of a flex there is a **plug** which you fit in to a **power point**. سلك كهربائي (معزول)

flex[2] /fleks/ *verb* [T] to bend or move a leg, arm, muscle, etc. in order to exercise it يثني أو يحرّك (الذراعين مثلاً) للتدريب

flexible /ˈfleksəbl/ *adj* **1** able to bend easily without breaking مرن

2 that can change or be changed in order to suit different situations or conditions ❶ The opposite is **inflexible**. مَرِن، قابل للتكيف

▶ **flexibility** /ˌfleksəˈbɪləti/ *noun* [U] مرونة

flick /flɪk/ *verb* **1** [I,T] to move, or to make sth move, with a quick sudden movement: *The frog's tongue flicked out and caught the fly.* ○ *She flicked the switch and the light came on.* يتحرك أو يحرّك بسرعة خاطفة

2 [T] to hit sb/sth lightly and quickly يضرب ضربة خفيفة

PHR V **flick sth away; flick sth off sth** to remove sth with a quick movement of your hand or finger ينقر، ينفض بإصبعه

flick/flip through sth to turn over the pages of a book, magazine, etc. quickly يتصفّح بسرعة

▶ **flick** *noun* [C] a quick sudden movement or light blow نقرة بالإصبع، ضربة خفيفة

flicker /ˈflɪkə(r)/ *verb* [I] **1** (used about a light or a flame) to burn or shine in a weak or unsteady way: *The candle flickered and went out.* (ضوء) يترجرج أو يضطرب

2 to move lightly and quickly up and down or backwards and forwards: *His eyelids flickered for a second and then he lay still.* يرفرف؛ يرف

▶ **flicker** *noun* [C, usually sing.] **1** a flickering movement تذبذب، تردّد

2 a slight feeling of sth: *a flicker of hope* وميض، بصيص؛ شعور خفي

flies /flaɪz/ *noun pl.* of FLY[2]

⚷ **flight**[1] /flaɪt/ *noun* **1** [C] a journey in a plane, etc: *to book a flight* ○ *a direct flight* ○ *a scheduled flight* ○ *a charter flight* ○ *They met on a flight to Australia.* ○ *a manned space flight to Mars* رحلة جوية

2 [C] a plane that takes you on a particular journey: *Flight number 340 from London to New York is boarding now* (= is ready for passengers to get on it). رحلة جوية معيّنة

3 [U] the action of flying: *It's unusual to see swans in flight* (= when they are flying). طيران

4 [C] a number of stairs or steps leading up or down: *a flight of stairs* قِسم متواصل من درجات السلّم

flight[2] /flaɪt/ *noun* [C,U] the act of running away or escaping فرار

IDM **put sb to flight** to make sb run away يهزم، يطرد

ˈ**flight attendant** *noun* [C] a person whose job is to serve and take care of passengers on an aircraft مضيف أو مضيفة طائرة

flimsy /ˈflɪmzi/ *adj* (**flimsier**; **flimsiest**) **1** (used about material) light and thin رقيق

2 (used about an object) not strong; easily broken غير متين

3 weak; not convincing you that it is true: *He gave a flimsy excuse for his absence.* واهٍ

flinch /flɪntʃ/ *verb* [I] **1** to make a slight movement backwards because of sth painful or frightening يجفل

2 flinch from sth/from doing sth to avoid doing sth because it is unpleasant: *She didn't flinch from telling him the whole truth.* يحجم عن

fling[1] /flɪŋ/ *verb* [T] (*pt, pp* **flung** /flʌŋ/) to throw sb/sth suddenly or with great force: *He flung his book on the floor and rushed out.* يطرح، ينبذ

fling[2] /flɪŋ/ *noun* [C] a short period of fun and pleasure علاقة غرامية عابرة؛ فترة متعة قصيرة

flint /flɪnt/ *noun* **1** [U] very hard grey stone that produces small flames (sparks) when you strike it against steel صوّان

2 [C] a small piece of flint or metal that is used to produce sparks (for example in a cigarette lighter) حجر القدّاحة أو الولّاعة

flip /flɪp/ *verb* (flipping; flipped) **1** [I,T] to turn with a quick movement: *She flipped the book open and started to read.* ينقلب أو يقلّب بسرعة

2 [T] to throw sth into the air and make it turn over: *Let's flip a coin to see who starts.* يقذف (قطعة نقود) في الهواء فتتقلّب

3 [I] (*informal*) to become very angry or excited يثور، يجن جنونه

PHR V flick/flip through sth → FLICK

ˈflip-flop *noun* [C] simple open shoe with a thin strap that goes between your big toe and the toe next to it صندل له سير بين الإبهام والأصابع

flippant /ˈflɪpənt/ *adj* not serious or respectful enough about things that are important غير جدّي، أرعن

flipper /ˈflɪpə(r)/ *noun* [C] **1** a flat limb that some sea animals use for swimming زِعنفة

2 a rubber shoe shaped like an animal's flipper that people wear so that they can swim better (especially under water): *a pair of flippers* زعانف مطّاطية تلبس في القدمين

flipping /ˈflɪpɪŋ/ *adj, adv* (*informal*) (used as a mild way of swearing): *When's the flipping bus coming?* الخبيث، ثقيل الدم (شتيمة خفيفة تقال غيظاً)

flirt /flɜːt/ *verb* [I] **1** to behave in a way that suggests you find sb attractive and are trying to attract him/her: *Who was that boy Lucy was flirting with at the party?* يغازل أو يداعب

2 flirt with sth to think about doing sth (but not very seriously) تداعبه فكرة

▸ **flirt** *noun* [C] a person who often flirts لَعوب

flit /flɪt/ *verb* [I] (flitting; flitted) to fly or move quickly from one place to another يطير أو يتنقل بسرعة

float[1] /fləʊt/ *verb* [I] **1** to stay on the surface of a liquid and not sink; to move gently on the surface of a liquid: *Cork floats in water.* ○ *There was something floating near the bank of the river.* يطفو

2 to move slowly through the air: *A leaf floated gently down to the ground.* يسبح في الهواء، يهيم

▸ **floating** *adj* not fixed; not living permanently in one place: *a floating population* (one in which people frequently move from one place to another) ○ *a floating voter* (= a person who does not always vote for the same political party) غير ثابت، متغير

float[2] /fləʊt/ *noun* [C] **1** a light floating object used for helping people learn to swim عوّامة (لمساعدة السباحين)

2 a light floating object used on a fishing line or net عوّامة صنّارة الصيد

3 a lorry or other vehicle that is decorated and used in a procession عربة مفتوحة ومزينة تستعمل في المواكب

flock /flɒk/ *noun* [C] **1** a group of sheep, goats or birds ➲ Look at **herd**. قطيع أو سرب

2 a large number of people: *Flocks of tourists visit London every summer.* جمهور، جموع

▸ **flock** *verb* [I] to gather or go somewhere in large numbers: *People are flocking to the exhibition in large numbers.* يتدفّق؛ يحتشد

flog /flɒg/ *verb* [T] (flogging; flogged) **1** (*Brit informal*) to sell sth يبيع شيئاً للتخلص منه

2 to hit sb hard with a whip or stick as a punishment يجلد

▸ **flogging** *noun* [C,U] hitting sb with a whip or stick as a punishment جَلْد

flood[1] /flʌd/ *verb* [I,T] **1** to fill a place with water; to be filled or overflow with water: *The river burst its banks and flooded the village.* ○ *The river Trent floods almost every year.* يفيض؛ يغمر بالماء

2 (used about a thought, feeling, etc.) to fill sb's mind suddenly: *At the end of the day all his worries came flooding back.* يطغى على (الأفكار)

PHR V flood in to arrive in large numbers: *Entries for the competition have been flooding in.* ينهال على

flood[2] /flʌd/ *noun* [C] **1** (*also* **floods** [plural]) a large amount of water (from a river, the sea, etc.) that covers an area which should be dry: *Many people have been forced to leave their homes because of the floods.* فيضان، طوفان

2 a large number or amount: *She received a flood of letters after the accident.* ○ *The little boy was in floods of tears* (= crying a great deal). سيل، فيض

floodlight /ˈflʌdlaɪt/ *noun* [C] a powerful light that is used for lighting sports grounds, the outside of public buildings, etc. أنوار ساطعة توجّه على المبنى

floodlit /ˈflʌdlɪt/ *adj* lit by floodlights: *a floodlit hockey match* مغمور بالنور

floor[1] /flɔː(r)/ *noun* **1** [C, usually sing.] the flat surface that you walk on indoors: *Don't come in – there's broken glass on the floor!* ○ *There aren't enough chairs so some people will have to sit on the floor.* ○ *to sweep the floor* ○ *a wooden floor* ➲ Look at the note at **ground**. أرض الغرفة

2 [C, usually sing.] the ground or surface at the

bottom of the sea, a forest, etc: *the ocean floor* قاع، قعر

3 [C] a level in a building: *Which floor is the men's department on, please?* طابق، دَوْر

In Britain, the **ground floor** is the floor at street level, and the floor above is the **first floor**. In US English the **first floor** is the floor at street level.

floor² /flɔː(r)/ *verb* [T] to surprise or completely confuse sb with a question or a problem يفحِم، يربك

floorboard /ˈflɔːbɔːd/ *noun* [C] one of the long wooden boards used to make a floor ألواح الأرضية الخشبية

flop /flɒp/ *verb* [I] (flo**pp**ing; flo**pp**ed) **1** to move or fall in a heavy or an awkward way: *I was so tired that all I could do was flop onto the sofa and watch TV.* يرتمي بتثاقل، يتهالك

2 to hang down loosely: *I can't bear my hair flopping in my eyes.* يتهدّل، يتدلّى

3 (used about a book, film, record, etc.) to be unsuccessful with the public يفشل، يخفق

▸ **flop** *noun* [C] something that is not a success; a failure: *Her first novel was very successful but her second was a flop.* محاولة فاشلة

floppy /ˈflɒpi/ *adj* (**floppier**; **floppiest**) soft, loose and hanging downwards; not stiff: *a floppy hat* متدلٍّ، متهدل، مرتخ

ˌfloppy ˈdisk (*also* **floppy**; **diskette**) *noun* [C] a square piece of plastic that can store information for a computer: *Don't forget to back up your files onto a floppy disk.* ➲ Look at **hard disk**. القرص الليّن (في الكمبيوتر)

flora /ˈflɔːrə/ *noun* [plural] all the plants growing in a particular area: *He's studying the flora and fauna* (= the plants and animals) *of South America.* ➲ Look at **fauna**. نباتات منطقة معينة

floral /ˈflɔːrəl/ *adj* decorated with a pattern of flowers, or made with flowers مزهّر، مصنوع من الزهور

florist /ˈflɒrɪst; *US* ˈflɔːr-/ *noun* [C] a person who has a shop that sells flowers ❶ The shop itself is called **the florist's**: *I bought her a bunch of flowers at the florist's.* بائع زهور

flounder¹ /ˈflaʊndə(r)/ *verb* [I] **1** to move with difficulty or to struggle (e.g. when you are trying not to sink in water) يتعثّر، يتخبّط

2 to find it difficult to speak or act in a suitable way (usually in an awkward situation) يتلعثم، يرتبك

flounder² /ˈflaʊndə(r)/ *noun* [C] a small flat sea fish that you can eat سمك بحري مفلطح

flour /ˈflaʊə(r)/ *noun* [U] a fine powder made from wheat or other grain and used for making breads, cakes, biscuits, etc. دقيق، طحين

flourish /ˈflʌrɪʃ/ *verb* **1** [I] to be strong and healthy; to develop in a successful way: *These plants flourish in a sunny position.* ○ *a flourishing new sports centre* يزدهر

2 [T] to wave sth in the air so that people will notice it يلوّح (لجذب الانتباه)

▸ **flourish** *noun* [C, usually sing.] a movement that you make to attract attention حركة مسرحية مصطنعة

flout /flaʊt/ *verb* [T] to refuse to obey or accept sth: *to flout the rules of the organization* ○ *to flout sb's advice* يستهين بـ، يعصي

flow /fləʊ/ *verb* [I] **1** to move in a smooth and continuous way (like water): *This river flows south into the English Channel.* ○ *a fast-flowing stream* ○ *It was three hours before the traffic began to flow normally after the accident.* يسيل أو يجري

2 (used about hair and clothes) to hang down in a loose way: *a long flowing dress.* يتهدّل، يسترسل

▸ **flow** *noun* [sing.] **1** a steady, continuous movement of sth/sb: *Press hard on the wound to stop the flow of blood. There's a steady flow of young people from the country to the towns.* تدفّق

2 a supply of sth: *a flow of information between the school and the parents* جريان؛ إمداد

flower /ˈflaʊə(r)/ *noun* [C] **1** the beautiful coloured part of a plant or tree from which seeds or fruit grow ❶ A flower consists of several **petals**. It grows from a **bud** on the end of a **stem**. زهرة

2 a plant that is grown for its flowers; a flower and its stem: *She grows a lot of flowers but no vegetables.* ○ *a lovely bunch of flowers* نبات مزهر؛ زهرة

We **pick** flowers and **arrange** them in a vase. Flowers that are given or carried on a special occasion are called a **bouquet**.

▸ **flower** *verb* [I] to produce flowers: *This plant flowers in late summer.* يزهر

flowery *adj* **1** covered or decorated with flowers: *a flowery dress, hat, wallpaper, etc.* مزخرف بالأزهار

2 (used about a style of speaking or writing) using long, difficult words (أسلوب) منمّق

ˈflower bed (*also* **bed**) *noun* [C] a piece of ground in a garden or park where flowers are grown مغرس الأزهار، "مَسْكَبَة"، "حوض زهور"

flowerpot /ˈflaʊəpɒt/ *noun* [C] a pot in which a plant can be grown أصيص

flown *pp* of FLY²

fl oz (*pl.* **fl oz**) *abbrev* = FLUID OUNCE(S)

flu /fluː/ (*also formal* **influenza**) *noun* [U] an illness that is like a bad cold but more serious. You usually have a temperature and your arms and legs ache: *The whole family has got flu.* ○ *They're in bed with flu.* انفلونزا، النزلة الوافدة

fluctuate /ˈflʌktʃueɪt/ *verb* [I] **fluctuate (between A and B)** (used about prices and numbers, or people's feelings) to change frequently from one thing to another: *The number of students fluctuates between 100 and 150.* يتقلّب، يتراوح

▸ **fluctuation** /ˌflʌktʃuˈeɪʃn/ *noun* [C,U] تأرجح، تراوح، تقلّب

fluent /ˈfluːənt/ *adj* **1 fluent (in sth)** able to speak or write a language easily and accurately: *After a year in France she was fluent in French.* طلق اللسان

2 (used about speech, reading or writing) expressed in a smooth and accurate way: *He speaks fluent German.* فصيح أو سلس
▸ **fluency** /ˈfluːənsi/ *noun* [U] فصاحة أو طلاقة
fluently *adv* بطلاقة

fluff /flʌf/ *noun* [U] **1** small pieces of waste material (from woollen clothes, etc.) that form into balls and collect under furniture, in the corners of a room, etc. or on people's clothes زَغَب

2 the soft new fur on young animals or birds زَغَب
▸ **fluffy** *adj* (**fluffier**; **fluffiest**) very soft and light like fur: *a fluffy jumper* خفيف أو ناعم؛ منفوش

fluid /ˈfluːɪd/ *noun* [C] a substance that can flow; a liquid: *The doctor told her to drink plenty of fluids.* ○ *body fluids* ○ *cleaning fluids* سائل
▸ **fluid** *adj* **1** able to flow like a liquid سائل أو مائع

2 (used about plans, etc.) able or likely to be changed مَرِن

ˌ**fluid ˈounce** *noun* [C] (*abbr* **fl oz**) a measure of liquid; in Britain, 0.0284 of a litre; in the USA, 0.0295 of a litre. There are 20 fluid ounces in a British pint and 16 fluid ounces in an American pint. وحدة سعة للسوائل

fluke /fluːk/ *noun* [C, usually sing.] (*informal*) something good that happens by accident, not because you have been clever or skilful: *The result was no fluke. The better team won.* مُصادفة، ضربة حظ

flung *pt, pp* of FLING[1]

fluorescent /flɔːˈresnt/ *adj* **1** shining with a particular kind of hard white light: *People often have fluorescent lighting in the kitchen.* (ضوء) نيون أو فلورسنت

2 very bright; seeming to shine: *fluorescent pink socks* متألق أو برّاق

fluoride /ˈflʊəraɪd; *US* ˈflɔːr-/ *noun* [U] a chemical substance that can be added to water or toothpaste to help prevent tooth decay فلوريد

flurry /ˈflʌri/ *noun* [C] (*pl.* **flurries**) **1** a small amount of wind, rain or snow that comes suddenly هطول خفيف مفاجئ (لمطر أو ثلج)

2 a short sudden burst of activity or feelings: *a flurry of excitement* فَوْرة (نشاط) مفاجئة

flush[1] /flʌʃ/ *verb* [I] (used about a person or his/her face) to go red: *Susan flushed and could not hide her embarrassment.* يحمرّ وجهه
▸ **flush** *noun* [C, usually sing.] a rush of blood to the face that makes it look red تورُّد الوجه
flushed *adj* with a hot red face: *You look very flushed. Are you sure you're all right?* متورِّد الوجه

flush[2] /flʌʃ/ *verb* **1** [T] to clean a toilet by pressing or pulling a handle that sends a stream of water into the toilet: *Please remember to flush the toilet.* يشدّ "السيفون" ويشطف المرحاض

2 [I] (used about a toilet) to be cleaned with a stream of water: *The toilet won't flush.* "السيفون" لا يُشَدّ (أي معطّل)

3 [T] **flush sth away, down, etc.** to get rid of sth in a stream of water: *You can't flush tea leaves down the sink – they'll block it.* يشطف بماء متدفق

fluster /ˈflʌstə(r)/ *verb* [T] (usually passive) to make sb feel nervous and confused (because there is too much to do or not enough time): *Don't get flustered – there's plenty of time.* يربك

flute /fluːt/ *noun* [C] a musical instrument like a pipe that you hold sideways and play by blowing over a hole at one side فلوت (آلة موسيقيّة)
▸ **flutist** /ˈfluːtɪst/ *noun* [C] (*US*) = FLAUTIST

flutter /ˈflʌtə(r)/ *verb* **1** [I,T] to move up and down or from side to side quickly and lightly; to make sth move in this way: *The flags were fluttering in the wind.* ○ *The bird fluttered its wings and tried to fly.* يصفِّق بجناحيه، يخفق

2 [I] to move lightly through the air: *The dead leaves fluttered to the ground.* يتراقص، يتمايل

3 [I] when your heart or stomach flutters, you are feeling nervous and excited يرتعد؛ يخفق بشدة
▸ **flutter** *noun* [C, usually sing.] **1** a quick, light movement رعشة، خفقة

2 a state of nervous excitement: *I always get in a flutter before I go on holiday.* اضطراب أو اهتياج

flux /flʌks/ *noun* [U] continuous change; the state of not being settled: *a country in a state of flux* تغيّر مستمر

⚷ **fly[1]** /flaɪ/ *verb* (*pres part* **flying**; *3rd pers sing pres* **flies**; *pt* **flew** /fluː/; *pp* **flown** /fləʊn/) **1** [I] (used about a bird, insect, aircraft, etc.) to move through the air: *This bird has a broken wing and cannot fly.* ○ *I can hear a plane flying overhead.* يطير

2 [I,T] to travel in or to carry sth in an aircraft, etc: *My daughter is flying (out) to Singapore next week.* ○ *Supplies of food were flown (in) to the starving people.* يسافر أو ينقل بالطائرة

3 [I,T] (used about a pilot) to control an aircraft, etc: *You have to have special training to fly a jumbo jet.* يقود طائرة

4 [T] to travel over an area of land or sea by flying: *Concorde could fly the Atlantic in three hours.* يجتاز بالطائرة

5 [I] to move quickly or suddenly: *It's late. I must fly.* ○ *A large stone came flying through the window.* ينطلق بسرعة

6 [I] (used about time) to pass quickly: *The weekend has just flown (by) and now it's Monday again.* يطير، يمضي بسرعة

7 [I,T] to move about in the air; to make sth move about in the air: *The flags are flying.* ○ *Let's go and fly our kite!* ❶ The noun is **flight**. يرفرف؛ يطيِّر
IDM **as the crow flies** → CROW[1]
fly off the handle (*informal*) to become very angry ينفجر غضباً
let fly (at sb/sth) 1 to shout angrily at sb: *My parents really let fly at me when I got home late.* يصرخ غاضباً

2 to attack sb in anger: *She let fly at him with her fists.* ينهال عليه باللكم

fly² /flaɪ/ *noun* [C] (*pl.* **flies**) a small insect with two wings: *There were flies buzzing round the dead cow.* ذبابة

fly³ /flaɪ/ *noun* [C] (*also* **flies** [plural]) a flap of cloth that covers the zip or buttons on the front of a pair of trousers: *Henry, your flies are undone.* فتحة البنطلون الأمامية

flying /ˈflaɪɪŋ/ *adj* able to fly: *flying insects* قادر على الطيران، طائر

IDM **with flying colours** with great success; very well: *Martin passed the exam with flying colours.* ناجح نجاحاً باهراً

get off to a flying start to begin sth well and so get some advantage يبدأ بداية حسنة متفوّقة

▸ **flying** *noun* [U] travelling in a plane, etc: *I don't like flying.* الطيران

ˌflying ˈvisit *noun* [C] a very quick visit: *I can't stop. This is just a flying visit.* زيارة خاطفة

flyover /ˈflaɪəʊvə(r)/ (*US* **overpass**) *noun* [C] a type of bridge that carries a road over another road مَعْبَر فوقي، "كوبري علوي"

FM /ˌef ˈem/ *abbrev* frequency modulation; one of the systems of broadcasting radio signals تضمين التردد (راديو)

foal /fəʊl/ *noun* [C] a young horse ➲ Look at the note at **horse**. مهر، فِلو

foam /fəʊm/ *noun* [U] **1** a mass of small white bubbles that are formed when air and a liquid are mixed together: *white foam on the tops of the waves* رغوة أو زبَد

2 an artificial substance that looks like foam: *shaving foam* مادة مزبدة (صابون الحلاقة مثلاً)

3 (*also* **ˌfoam ˈrubber**) soft rubber or plastic that is used inside seats, cushions, etc. مطّاط اسفنجي

▸ **foam** *verb* [I] to produce foam: *The dog was foaming at the mouth.* يرغي أو يزبد

fob /fɒb/ *verb* (fo**bb**ing; fo**bb**ed)

PHRV **fob sb off (with sth)**; **fob sth off on sb** to try to give sb something that is not suitable or that is not what he/she wants: *Don't try to fob me off with that old car – I want a new one.* ○ *Don't try and fob that old car off on me.* يتخلّص من شخص بالوعود؛ يصرِّف عليه بضاعة رديئة

focal point /ˌfəʊkl ˈpɔɪnt/ *noun* [sing.] the centre of interest or activity مركز الاهتمام، النقطة المركزية

focus /ˈfəʊkəs/ *noun* [C] (*pl.* focuses) **1** the point at which rays of light meet or from which they appear to come بؤرة، محرق

2 [usually sing.] the centre of interest or attention; special attention that is given to sb/sth: *The school used to be the focus of village life.* ○ *Tonight our focus will be on modern jazz.* مركز؛ تركيز

IDM **in focus/out of focus** (used about a photograph or sth in a photograph) clear/not clear: *This photo is so badly out of focus that I can't recognize anyone.* (صورة فوتوغرافية) واضحة/غير واضحة (بسبب حسن أو سوء تركيز العدسة)

▸ **focus** *verb* (focu**ss**ing; focu**ss**ed or focu**s**ing; focu**s**ed) **focus (sth) (on sth) 1** [T] to direct rays of light onto one particular point يركّز أو يجمع في بؤرة

2 [I,T] to be or become able to see clearly; to adjust your eyes so that you can see clearly: *Gradually his eyes focussed.* ○ *She focussed her eyes on the page.* يرى بوضوح، يركّز بصره

3 [I,T] to adjust a camera so that the picture that you are taking will be clear: *I focussed on the person in the middle of the group.* يركّز عدسة الكاميرا

4 [I,T] to give all your attention to sth: *to focus on a problem* ○ *to focus attention on a problem* يركّز اهتمامه على

fodder /ˈfɒdə(r)/ *noun* [U] food that is given to farm animals علَف

foe /fəʊ/ *noun* [C] (*formal*) an enemy عدوّ أو خصم

foetus (*US* **fetus**) /ˈfiːtəs/ *noun* [C] (*pl.* **foetuses**; **fetuses**) a young human or animal that is still developing in its mother's body ❶ An **embryo** is at an earlier stage of development. جنين

fog /fɒg; *US* fɔːg/ *noun* **1** [U] thick cloud that forms close to or just above the land or sea. Fog makes it difficult for us to see: *Patches of dense fog are making driving dangerous.* ○ *The fog had lifted/cleared by midday.* ضباب

> **Fog** is thicker than **mist**. **Haze** is caused by heat. **Smog** is caused by pollution. Look at the note at **weather**.

2 [C] a period of fog: *Thick fogs are common in November.* فترة ضباب

▸ **foggy** *adj* (**foggier**; **foggiest**) used to describe the weather when there is a fog: *a foggy morning* ضبابيّ، مُضبّ

IDM **not have the faintest/foggiest (idea)** → FAINT

foil¹ /fɔɪl/ *noun* [U] metal that has been rolled or beaten into very thin sheets, often used when you are wrapping or cooking food: *tin/aluminium foil* "ورق ألمنيوم"، رقاقة معدنية

foil² /fɔɪl/ *verb* [T] to prevent sb from succeeding or from carrying out his/her plans; to prevent a plan from succeeding: *The prisoners were foiled in their attempt to escape.* يحبِط

foist /fɔɪst/ *verb*

PHRV **foist sth on/upon sb** to force sb to accept sth that he/she does not want يكرِه شخصاً على قبول شيء ما

fold /fəʊld/ *verb* **1** [T] **fold sth (up)** to bend one part of sth over another part in order to make it smaller, tidier, etc: *He folded the letter into three before putting it into the envelope.* ○ *Fold up your clothes neatly, please.* ❶ The opposite is **unfold**. يطوي

2 [I] **fold (up)** to be able to be folded in order to be easier to carry or to store: *This garden table folds up flat.* ○ *a folding bed* ينطوي

3 [I] **fold (up)** (used about a business, a play in the theatre, etc.) to close because it is unsuccessful يتوقّف أو ينتهي (لفشله)

IDM **cross/fold your arms** → ARM[1]

▸ **fold** *noun* [C] **1** the mark or line where sth has been folded ثنية أو طيّة

2 a curved shape that is made by a piece of material, etc. that has been folded: *the folds of a dress* ثنية أو طيّة

folder /ˈfəʊldə(r)/ *noun* [C] **1** a cardboard or plastic cover that is used for holding papers, etc. ملف، محفظة أوراق

2 a collection of information or files on one subject that is stored in a computer or on a disk مجلّد أو إضبارة (في الكمبيوتر)

foliage /ˈfəʊliɪdʒ/ *noun* [U] (*formal*) all the leaves of a tree or plant أوراق النبتة أو الشجرة

folk /fəʊk/ *noun* **1** [plural] (*US* **folks**) (*informal*) people in general: *Some folk are never satisfied.* الناس

2 [plural] a particular type of people: *Old folk often don't like change.* ○ *country folk* زمرة معيّنة من الناس

3 folks [plural] (*informal*) used as a friendly way of addressing more than one person: *What shall we do today, folks?* جماعة، اخوان

4 folks [plural] (*informal*) your parents or close relatives: *How are your folks?* الأهل أو الأقرباء

▸ **folk** *adj* traditional in a community; of a traditional style: *Robin Hood is an English folk hero.* ○ *folk music* ○ *a folk song* شعبي

folklore /ˈfəʊklɔː(r)/ *noun* [U] (the study of) the traditional stories and beliefs of a community الفولكلور أو التقاليد الشعبية

⚷ **follow** /ˈfɒləʊ/ *verb* **1** [I,T] to come, go or happen after sb/sth: *You go first and I'll follow (on) later.* ○ *The dog followed her wherever she went.* ○ *The crash was followed by a scream and then there was silence.* ○ *The news will be followed by a programme on the situation in West Africa.* ○ *We had steak followed by fresh fruit.* يتبَع أو يتلو

2 [T] to go after sb in order to catch him/her: *Go a bit slower! I think the police are following us!* يلحَق أو يقتفي

3 [T] to go along a road, etc; to go in the same direction as sth: *Follow this road for a mile and then turn right at the pub.* ○ *The road follows the river for a few miles.* يسلك؛ يحاذي

4 [T] to accept advice, instructions, an example, etc. and do what you have been told or shown to do: *When lighting fireworks, it is important to follow the instructions carefully.* ○ *She always follows the latest fashions.* يتّبع أو يعمل بِ

5 [I,T] to understand the meaning of sth: *I'm sorry, I don't follow.* ○ *The children couldn't follow the plot of that film.* يتابع، يفهم

6 [T] to watch or listen to sb/sth very carefully: *You'll have to follow what he says very carefully if you want to understand it.* يتابع

7 [T] to take an active interest in sth: *Have you been following the tennis championships?* يتابع

8 [I] **follow (on) (from sth)** to happen as a result of sth; to be the necessary result of sth: *It doesn't follow that old people can't lead active lives.* يصحّ بالضرورة، ينتج منه

9 [T] to happen in the planned or expected way: *The day's events followed the usual pattern.* يسير على ما يرام

IDM **as follows** (used for introducing a list): *The names of the successful candidates are as follows ...* كما يلي:

follow sb's example/lead to do what sb else has done or decided to do يحتذي بِ

follow suit to do the same thing that sb else has just done يحذو حذو

PHR V **follow sth through** to continue doing sth until it is finished يتابع قضية حتى نهايتها

follow sth up 1 to take further action about sth: *You should follow up your letter with a phone call.* يتبع؛ يلاحق

2 to find out more about sth: *We need to follow up the story about the school.* يواصل البحث

▸ **follower** *noun* [C] a person who follows or supports a person, belief, etc. تابع أو مريد

⚷ **following** /ˈfɒləʊɪŋ/ *adj* **1** next (in time): *He was taken ill on Sunday and died the following week.* التالي أو الآتي

2 (in a list) that I will mention now: *Please could you bring the following items to the meeting ...* التالي أو ما يلي

> We can also use **the following** as a noun: *The following are the winners of the competition...*

▸ **following** *noun* [sing.] a group of people who support or admire sth: *Buddhism has quite a large following in Japan.* أتباع أو معجبون

following *prep* after; as a result of: *Following the riots many students have been arrested.* بعدَ أو عقِبَ

ˈ**follow-up** *noun* [C] something that is done to continue sth: *As a follow-up to the television series, the BBC is publishing a book on the subject.* ملحَق

folly /ˈfɒli/ *noun* [C,U] (*pl.* **follies**) (*formal*) a foolish act: *It would be folly to ignore their warnings.* حماقة

fond /fɒnd/ *adj* **1** (not before a noun) **fond of sb/sth**; **fond of doing sth** liking a person or a thing, or liking doing sth: *We're all very fond of Mrs Simpson.* ○ *He's a good cook. I'm especially fond of his chicken casserole.* ○ *I'm not very fond of getting up early.* محبّ لِ، مولع بِ

2 (only *before* a noun) kind and loving: *I have fond memories of both my aunts.* حنون، رقيق

3 (only *before* a noun) wished or hoped for but unlikely to come true: *She had a fond belief that David would come back.* بعيد التحقيق

▸ **fondly** *adv* **1** in a loving way بحنان، بحبّ

2 in a foolish way: *I fondly imagined that you liked me.* بحماقة أو بسذاجة

fondness *noun* [U] a liking for sb/sth ولَع أو شغَف

fondle /ˈfɒndl/ *verb* [T] to touch or stroke sb/sth in a loving way يلمس برقّة، يُداعب

food /fu:d/ *noun* **1** [U] something that people, animals or plants take into their bodies in order to keep them alive and healthy: *There is a shortage of food in some areas.* غذاء، طعام

2 [C,U] a particular type of food that you eat: *baby food* ○ *We eat a lot of health foods.* ○ *food and drink* مأكولات، طعام

ˈ**food mile** *noun* [C] a measurement of the distance food has to be transported from the producer to the consumer and the fuel that this uses: *Cut food miles by buying local produce.* مقياس بيئي (للوقود والمسافة لإيصال الأطعمة إلى المستهلك)

ˈ**food poisoning** *noun* [U] an illness that is caused by eating food that is bad تسمّم من الطعام

ˈ**food processor** *noun* [C] an electric machine that can mix food and also cut or slice food into small pieces آلة كهربائية لتحضير الطعام

foodstuff /ˈfu:dstʌf/ *noun* [C, usually pl.] a substance that is used as food: *There has been a sharp rise in the cost of basic foodstuffs.* مادة غذائية

fool /fu:l/ *noun* [C] a person who is silly or who acts in a silly way: *I felt such a fool when I realized my mistake.* ○ *She was fool enough to believe it when he said that he loved her.* ➲ Look at **April Fool.** أحمق

IDM make a fool of sb/yourself to make sb/yourself look foolish or silly يجعله أضحوكة

▸ **fool** *verb* **1** [T] to trick sb: *Don't be fooled into believing everything that the salesman says.* يخدع

2 [I] to speak without being serious: *You didn't really believe me when I said I was going to America, did you? I was only fooling.* يمزح

PHR V fool about/around to behave in a silly way: *Stop fooling around with that knife or someone will get hurt!* يعبث

foolhardy /ˈfu:lhɑ:di/ *adj* taking unnecessary risks متهوّر أو مخاطر (حماقة)

foolish /ˈfu:lɪʃ/ *adj* **1** silly; not sensible: *I was foolish enough to trust him.* أحمق

2 looking silly or feeling embarrassed: *He felt rather foolish when he couldn't start his motorcycle in front of his friends.* مرتبك؛ سخيف

▸ **foolishly** *adv* بغباء

foolishness *noun* [U] حماقة

foolproof /ˈfu:lpru:f/ *adj* not capable of going wrong or being wrongly used: *Our security system is absolutely foolproof.* (جهاز) غاية في سهولة الاستعمال، مضمون

foot¹ /fʊt/ *noun* [C] (*pl.* **feet** /fi:t/) **1** the lowest part of the leg, below the ankle, on which a person or animal stands: *She rose to her feet* (= she stood up). ○ *What size feet have you got?* ○ *big/small feet* ○ *wide/narrow feet* ○ *She sat by the fire and the dog sat at her feet.* ○ *a foot brake* (= one that is operated by your foot) ❶ When you walk somewhere you go **on foot**. قَدَم

2 the part of a sock, etc. into which you put your foot قدم الجورب

3 (*abbr* **ft**; **ft.**) a measure of length; 30.48 centimetres. There are 12 inches in a foot, and 3 feet in a yard: *'How tall are you?' 'Five foot two (inches).'* ○ *a six-foot high wall* ❶ The plural can be **feet** or **foot**. قدم (مقياس للطول)

4 [sing.] the bottom of sth: *There's a note at the foot of the page.* ○ *sitting at the foot of the stairs* ❶ The opposite is **top**. أسفل أو ذيل؛ سفح (الجبل)

5 [sing.] the end of a bed where the feet go ❶ The opposite is **head**. أسفل أو ذيل (السرير)

IDM find your feet → FIND¹

get/have cold feet → COLD¹

put your foot down (*informal*) to say firmly that sth must (not) happen: *Susan put her foot down and said that the children could only watch an hour of television each evening.* يصرّ

put your foot in it (*informal*) to say or do sth that upsets or embarrasses sb (هفوة) توقع في مأزق

set foot in/on sth → SET²

stand on your own (two) feet to take care of yourself without help; to be independent يعتمد على نفسه

foot² /fʊt/ *verb*

IDM foot the bill (for sth) to pay (for sth) يدفع (الحساب)

footage /ˈfʊtɪdʒ/ *noun* [U] part of a film showing a particular event: *The documentary included footage of the assassination of Kennedy.* مقطع من فيلم

football /ˈfʊtbɔ:l/ *noun* **1** (*also* **soccer**) [U] a game that is played by two teams of eleven players who try to kick a round ball into a goal: *a football pitch* ○ *a football match* (لعبة) كرة القدم

In the US **soccer** is the usual word for this game since Americans use the word **football** to refer to **American Football.**

2 [C] the large round ball that is used in this game كرة القدم

▸ **footballer** *noun* [C] a person who plays football, especially as a professional لاعب كرة القدم

ˈ**football pools** (*also* **the pools**) *noun* [plural] a game in which people bet money on the results of football matches and can win large amounts يانصيب كرة القدم

foothold /ˈfʊthəʊld/ *noun* [C] a place where you can safely put your foot when you are climbing: (*figurative*) *We need to get a foothold in the European market.* موطئ قدم

footing /ˈfʊtɪŋ/ *noun* [sing.] **1** being able to stand firmly on a surface: *He lost his footing on the wet floor and fell.* ○ (*figurative*) *The company is now on a firm footing and should soon show a profit.* رسوخ القدمين؛ أساس وطيد

2 the level or position of sb/sth (in relation to sb/sth else): *to be on an equal footing with sb* مستوى أو مكانة اجتماعية

footnote /ˈfʊtnəʊt/ *noun* [C] an extra piece of information that is added at the bottom of a page in a book تذييل أو حاشية

footpath /ˈfʊtpɑ:θ; *US* -pæθ/ *noun* [C] a path for people to walk on, especially in the country: *a public footpath* ممرّ للمشاة بين الحقول

footprint /ˈfʊtprɪnt/ *noun* [C] a mark that is left by a foot or a shoe أثر قدم

footstep /ˈfʊtstep/ *noun* [C] the sound of sb walking; the mark that a person leaves when walking: *I heard his footsteps in the hall.* خطوة أو وقْع قدم

footwear /ˈfʊtweə(r)/ *noun* [U] boots or shoes أحذية

🔑 **for¹** /fə(r); *strong form* fɔː(r)/ *prep* **1** (showing the person who will receive sth): *Here is a letter for you.* ○ *Save a piece of cake for Mary.* ○ *He made lunch for them.* ○ *She bought some sweets for the children.* لِ، من أجل

2 (showing purpose or use): *What's this gadget for?* ○ *Let's go for a walk.* ○ *Please get me a shampoo for dry hair.* ○ *Shall we have eggs for breakfast?* ○ *What did you do that for?* (= Why did you do that?) من أجل، بغاية

3 (showing where sb/sth is going to): *Is this the train for Glasgow?* ○ *They set off for the shops.* نحو، إلى

4 intended to be used by a particular group or in a particular way: *It's a book for children.* ○ *That chair is for visitors.* ○ *Is the flat for sale?* لِ، من أجل

5 in order to help sb/sth: *What can I do for you?* ○ *You should take some medicine for your cold.* ○ *Doctors are fighting for his life.* ○ *Take care of her for my sake.* لِ، من أجل

6 (showing the price of sth): *I bought this car for £2 000.* ○ *She gave me their old TV for nothing.* بِسعر

7 (showing a reason): *He was sent to prison for robbery.* ○ *I couldn't speak for laughing.* لأنّ...، بسَبَب

8 on the occasion of: *What did they give you for your birthday?* بمناسبة

9 in support of (sb/sth): *Three cheers for the winner!* ○ *Are you for or against shops opening on Sundays?* (مؤيد لـ) ، مع

10 as a representative of (sb/sth): *Who's the MP for Bradford?* ○ *She plays hockey for England.* (ممثل) عن

11 meaning or representing (sb/sth): *What's the 'C' for in 'BBC'?* ○ *What's the Russian for 'window'?* يمثّل، يقابل

12 (after a verb) in order to have or get sth: *She asked me for help.* بِغَرَض الحصول على

13 (after an adjective) when you consider what you could expect: *She's tall for her age.* ○ *It's quite warm for January.* بالنسبة إلى

14 (after a comparative adjective) after sth: *We'll all feel better for a good night's sleep.* بعدَ

15 (used when you give one thing and get sth else back): *I want to exchange this sweater for a larger one.* مقابل، (يبدل) بِـ

16 (showing a length of time): *I'm going away for a few days.* ○ *They have left the town for good* (= they will not return). ○ *He was in prison for 20 years* (= he is not in prison now). ○ *He has been in prison for 20 years* (= he is still in prison). مدّة

> **Since** is used with a point in time for showing when something began: *He has been in prison since 1970.* **Ago** is also used for showing when something began: *He went to prison 20 years ago.*

17 (showing that sth has been arranged to happen at a particular time): *The appointment is for 10.30.* ○ *We've booked our holiday for the second week in July.* في (وقت معين)

18 (showing when sth happens): *I'm warning you for the last time.* ○ *I met him for the second time yesterday.* لِ

19 (showing a distance): *He walked for ten miles.* مسافة

IDM **be (in) for it** (*Brit informal*) to be going to get into trouble or be punished: *If you arrive late again you'll be in for it.* يقع في مشكلة

for all in spite of: *For all his money, he's a very lonely man.* على الرغم من

for ever → FOREVER (1)

for² /fə(r); *strong form* fɔː(r)/ *conj* (*formal*) because: *The children soon lost their way, for they had never been in the forest alone before.* لأن أو بسبب

forbid /fəˈbɪd/ *verb* [T] (*pres part* **forbidding**; *pt* **forbade** /fəˈbæd; *US* fəˈbeɪd/ or **forbad** /fəˈbæd/; *pp* **forbidden** /fəˈbɪdn/) **1 forbid sb to do sth** to order sb not to do sth: *My parents forbade me to see Tim again.* يمنع، يحرِّم

2 to not allow sth: *Smoking is forbidden inside the building.* يمنع

▸ **forbidding** *adj* looking unfriendly or unattractive: *The coast near the village is rather grey and forbidding.* غير جذاب

🔑 **force¹** /fɔːs/ *noun* **1** [U] physical strength or power: *The force of the explosion knocked them to the ground.* ○ *The police used force to break up the demonstration.* قوّة

2 [U] power and influence: *His arguments lost some of their force when they were translated into French.* سلطة أو نفوذ

3 [C] a person or thing that has power or influence: *Britain is no longer a major force in international affairs.* دولة كبرى؛ مركز قوّة

4 [C,U] (*technical*) a power that can cause change or movement: *the force of gravity* قوّة

5 [C, usually sing.] a measure of wind strength: *a force 9 gale* شدّة الريح

6 [C] a group of people who are trained for a particular purpose: *a highly trained workforce* ○ *a UN peace-keeping force* ○ *the police force* قوة منظمة أو هيئة

IDM **bring sth/come into force** to start using a new law, etc.; to start being used: *The government want to bring new anti-pollution legislation into force next year.* تطبيق أو سَريان قانون

in force 1 (used about people) in large numbers: *The police were present in force at the football match.* بأعداد كبيرة

2 (used about a law, rule, etc.) being used: *The*

a b c d e f g h i j k l m n o p q r s t u v w x y z

new laws about rear seat belts in cars are now in force. نافذ المفعول

⚷**force**[2] /fɔːs/ *verb* [T] **1** to make sb do sth that he/she does not want to do: *The bank robber forced the staff and customers to lie on the floor.* ○ *She forced herself to speak to him.* يجبر أو يُرغم

2 to use physical strength to do sth or to move sth: *The window had been forced open.* ○ *We had to force our way through the crowd.* (يفعل شيئا) عَنْوة أو بالقوة

forceful /ˈfɔːsfl/ *adj* strong; powerful: *He has a very forceful personality.* ○ *a forceful speech* قوي الشخصية؛ (خطاب) يؤثِّر في الجمهور

forceps /ˈfɔːseps/ *noun* [plural] a special instrument that looks like a pair of scissors but is not sharp. Forceps are used by doctors for holding things firmly: *a pair of forceps* مِلقط الجرّاح

forcible /ˈfɔːsəbl/ *adj* (only *before* a noun) **1** done using (physical) force: *The police made a forcible entry into the building.* قسري

2 (used about ideas, an argument, etc.) strong; convincing: *a forcible reminder* قوي، مُقنع

▸ **forcibly** /-əbli/ *adv* using force: *The children were forcibly removed from their parents.* قسراً أو عَنوةً

ford /fɔːd/ *noun* [C] a place in a river where the water is shallow and it is easy to walk or drive across مَخاضة (في النهر)

fore /fɔː(r)/ *noun*

IDM **be/come to the fore** to be in or get into an important position so that you are noticed by people في أو إلى المقدّمة

forearm /ˈfɔːrɑːm/ *noun* [C] the lower part of your arm between your elbow and your wrist ساعد

foreboding /fɔːˈbəʊdɪŋ/ *noun* [U, sing.] a strong feeling that danger or trouble is coming نذير بالشرّ، هاجِس

⚷**forecast** /ˈfɔːkɑːst; *US* -kæst/ *verb* [T] (*pt, pp* **forecast** or **forecasted**) to say (with the help of information) what will probably happen in the future: *The Chancellor did not forecast the sudden rise in inflation.* ○ *Rain has been forecast for tomorrow.* يتنبأ أو يتكهّن

▸ **forecast** *noun* [C]: *The weather forecast said it would be fine tomorrow.* تنبؤ؛ نشرة جوية

forecourt /ˈfɔːkɔːt/ *noun* [C] a large open area in front of a building such as a petrol station باحة أمام المبنى

forefinger /ˈfɔːfɪŋɡə(r)/ *noun* [C] the finger next to the thumb ❶ We also say **index finger**. السبّابة

forefront /ˈfɔːfrʌnt/ *noun* [sing.] the leading position; the position at the front: *Our department is right at the forefront of scientific research.* طليعة

forego = FORGO

foregone /ˈfɔːɡɒn; *US* -ˈɡɔːn/ *adj*

IDM **a foregone conclusion** a result that is or was certain to happen مفروغ منه؛ مضمون

foreground /ˈfɔːɡraʊnd/ *noun* [sing.] **the foreground 1** the part of a view, picture, etc. that appears closest to the person looking at it: *Notice the artist's use of colour in the foreground of the picture.* أماميّة (الصورة)

2 a position where you will be noticed most: *He likes to be in the foreground at every meeting.* مقدمة

➲ Look at **background**.

forehand /ˈfɔːhænd/ *noun* [C] a stroke in tennis, etc. that is made with the inside of your hand facing forward ➲ Look at **backhand**. (في التنس) ضربة أمامية

forehead /ˈfɔːhed; *US* ˈfɔːrɪd/ (*also* **brow**) *noun* [C] the flat part of a person's face above the eyes and below the hair جبين

⚷**foreign** /ˈfɒrən; *US* fɔːr-/ *adj* **1** belonging to or connected with a country that is not your own: *a foreign country* ○ *to learn a foreign language* ○ *a foreign coin* أجنبيّ

2 dealing with or involving other countries: *foreign policy* (= government decisions concerning other countries) ○ *the French Foreign Minister* خارجيّ

3 (used about an object or a substance) not belonging where it is: *The X-ray showed up a foreign body* (= object) *in her stomach.* غريب

▸ **foreigner** *noun* [C] a person who belongs to a country that is not your own: *London is full of foreigners in the summer.* أجنبي

the ˌForeign and ˈCommonwealth Office (*abbr* **FCO**) [sing., with sing. or pl. verb] the British government department that deals with relations with other countries. ❶ Many people still refer to this department by its old name, the Foreign Office. وزارة الخارجية والكومنولث

ˌforeign exˈchange *noun* [C,U] the system of buying and selling money from a different country; the place where it is bought and sold: *The pound dropped against the dollar on the foreign exchanges yesterday.* نظام القطع الأجنبي أو إدارته

ˌForeign ˈSecretary *noun* [C] (*pl.* **Foreign Secretaries**) the British government minister who is responsible for dealing with foreign countries ➲ Look at **Home Secretary**. وزير الخارجية

foremost /ˈfɔːməʊst/ *adj* most famous or important; best: *Laurence Olivier was among the foremost actors of the century.* أهمّ؛ في المكان الأوّل

IDM **first and foremost** → FIRST[2]

forename /ˈfɔːneɪm/ *noun* [C] (*formal*) your first name, that is given to you when you are born ➲ Look at the note at **name**[1]. اسم

forensic /fəˈrensɪk; *US* -zɪk/ *adj* connected with the law and finding out about a crime: *The police are carrying out forensic tests to try and find out the cause of death.* ○ *forensic medicine* (طبّ) شرْعي

forerunner /ˈfɔːrʌnə(r)/ *noun* [C] a person or thing that is an early example or a sign of sth that appears or develops later رائد

foresee /fɔːˈsiː/ *verb* [T] (*pt* **foresaw** /fɔːˈsɔː/; *pp*

foreseen /fɔːˈsiːn/) to know or guess that sth is going to happen in the future: *Nobody could have foreseen the result of the election.* ➲ Look at **unforeseen.** يَتنبأ

▸ **foreseeable** /-əbl/ *adj* that can be expected: *These problems were foreseeable.* ○ *The weather won't change in the foreseeable future* (= as far ahead as we can see). مُتوقَّع؛ (في المستقبل) القريب

foresight /ˈfɔːsaɪt/ *noun* [U] the ability to see what will probably happen in the future (and to make wise plans): *My neighbour had the foresight to move house before the new motorway was built.* ➲ Look at **hindsight**. بُعْد نَظر

foreskin /ˈfɔːskɪn/ *noun* [C] the loose piece of skin that covers the end of the penis غُرْلة، قلفة

forest /ˈfɒrɪst; *US* fɔːr-/ *noun* [C,U] a large area of land that is covered with trees: *tropical rain forests* ○ *A large part of Canada is covered in forest.* ○ *a forest fire* ❶ A **forest** is larger than a **wood**. A **jungle** is a forest in a tropical part of the world. غابة

▸ **forestry** *noun* [U] the science of planting and taking care of trees in forests علم الأحراج أو الغابات

forestall /fɔːˈstɔːl/ *verb* [T] to act before sb else in order to prevent him/her from doing sth; to prevent an action from taking place by doing sth that will stop it يحبط باتخاذ اجراءات مسبقة

foretell /fɔːˈtel/ *verb* [T] (*pt, pp* **foretold** /fɔːˈtəʊld/) (*formal*) to say what will happen in the future يَتنبأ

forethought /ˈfɔːθɔːt/ *noun* [U] careful thought about, or preparation for, the future تدبّر؛ نظر في العواقب

foretold *pt, pp* of FORETELL

forever /fərˈevə(r)/ *adv* **1** (*also* **for ever**) for all time; permanently: *I wish the holidays would last forever!* ○ *I realized that our relationship had finished forever.* ○ *My sister always takes forever* (= a very long time) *in the bathroom.* دائماً؛ إلى الأبد

2 (with verbs in the continuous forms) very often: *Our neighbours are forever having noisy parties.* دائماً؛ كثيراً ما

foreword /ˈfɔːwɜːd/ *noun* [C] a piece of writing at the beginning of a book that introduces the book and/or its author مقدّمة (كتاب)

forfeit /ˈfɔːfɪt/ *verb* [T] to lose sth or no longer have sth because you have done sth wrong or because you want to achieve an aim: *Because of his violent behaviour he forfeited the right to visit his children.* يخسر

forgave *pt* of FORGIVE

forge¹ /fɔːdʒ/ *noun* [C] a workshop where metals are heated and shaped, especially one where a blacksmith works making and fitting shoes for horses دكان حدّاد

forge² /fɔːdʒ/ *verb* [T] **1** to make a copy of sth in order to deceive people: *to forge a signature* يُزيِّف

2 to create a relationship with sb/sth: *Our school has forged links with a school in Romania.* يكوِّن (علاقة)

▸ **forgery** /ˈfɔːdʒəri/ *noun* (*pl.* **forgeries**) **1** [U] the crime of copying a document, signature, painting, etc. in order to deceive people تزييف

2 [C] a document, signature, picture, etc. that has been forged: *The painting that had been sold as a Rembrandt was discovered to be a forgery.* مُزيَّف

forge³ /fɔːdʒ/ *verb*

PHR V **forge ahead** to go forward very quickly; to move into the leading position: *It is now time to forge ahead with our plans to open a new shop.* يمضي قدماً؛ يسبق؛ يشق طريقه

forget /fəˈget/ *verb* (*pt* **forgot** /fəˈgɒt/; *pp* **forgotten** /fəˈgɒtn/) **1** [I,T] **forget about sth** to fail to remember sth; to lose the memory of sth: *'Why didn't you come to the party?' 'Oh dear! I completely forgot about it!'* ○ *You never forget how to ride a bicycle.* ○ *I've forgotten what I was going to say.* ○ *I've forgotten the telephone number.* ○ *He forgot that he had invited her to the party.* ○ *I'll never forget meeting my husband for the first time.* ينسى

2 [I,T] to fail to remember to do sth: *Try not to forget about feeding the cat!* ○ *Don't forget to do your homework!* ينسى

3 [T] to fail to bring sth with you: *When my father got to the airport he realized he'd forgotten his passport.* ينسى

> When we are talking about *where* we have forgotten something we have to use the word **leave**. We CANNOT say: *'My father forgot his passport at home'*. We have to say: *'He left his passport at home'*.

4 [T] to stop thinking about sth: *Forget about your work and enjoy yourself!* ○ *'I'm sorry I shouted at you.' 'Forget it.'* (= don't worry about it) يتناسى

5 [T] **forget yourself** to behave without proper control; to behave in a way that is not like the way you usually behave: *When he heard the news he completely forgot himself and kissed everybody in the room!* يذهل؛ ينسى نفسه

▸ **forgetful** /-fl/ *adj* often forgetting things: *My mother's nearly 80 and she's starting to get a bit forgetful.* كثير النسيان

forget-me-not /fəˈget mi nɒt/ *noun* [C,U] a small plant with tiny blue flowers, or a number of these أذن الفأر، لا تنسني

forgive /fəˈgɪv/ *verb* [T] (*pt* **forgave** /fəˈgeɪv/; *pp* **forgiven** /fəˈgɪvn/) **1 forgive sb (sth/for sth/for doing sth)** to stop being angry towards sb or about sth: *I can't forgive his behaviour last night.* ○ *I can't forgive him his behaviour last night.* ○ *I can't forgive him for his behaviour last night.* ○ *I can't forgive him for behaving like that last night.* يعفو، يغفر

2 (used for apologizing politely): *Forgive me for asking, but where did you get that dress?* يَعْذُر

▸ **forgivable** /-əbl/ *adj* that can be forgiven ❶ The opposite is **unforgivable**. مَعْذور؛ مغفور

a b c d e f g h i j k l m n o p q r s t u v w x y z

forgiveness *noun* [U] the act of forgiving عفو؛ غفران

forgiving *adj* ready and willing to forgive غفور

forgo (*also* **forego**) /fɔː'gəʊ/ *verb* [T] (*pt* **forwent** /fɔː'went/; *pp* **forgone** /fɔː'gɒn; *US* -'gɔːn/) to be willing not to have sth nice or sth that you have a right to: *We'll have to forgo a holiday this year if we want to buy a car.* يتنازل عن

forgot *pt* of FORGET

forgotten *pp* of FORGET

fork /fɔːk/ *noun* [C] **1** a small implement with a handle and two or more points (prongs). You use a fork for lifting food to your mouth when eating: *knives, forks and spoons* شوكة

2 a large tool with a handle and three or more points (prongs) that you use for digging the ground شوكة، منكش

3 a place where a road, river, etc. divides into two parts; one of these parts: *After about two miles you'll come to a fork in the road. Take the right fork and keep going for another two miles.* مَفرَق (طرق)

▸ **fork** *verb* [I] **1** (used about a road, river, etc.) to divide into two parts يَتشعَّب

2 to go along the left or right fork of a road: *Fork right up the hill.* ينعطف

PHR V **fork out sth** (*informal*) to pay: *I forked out over £20 for that book.* يدفع

forlorn /fə'lɔːn/ *adj* lonely and unhappy; not cared for بائس

form¹ /fɔːm/ *noun* **1** [C] a particular type of sth or way of doing sth: *Swimming is an excellent form of exercise.* ○ *We never eat meat in any form.* ○ *What form will the meeting take?* (= How will it be organized?) شكل

2 [C,U] the shape of sb/sth: *The articles will be published in book form.* شكل؛ هيئة

3 [C] a piece of paper with questions on it and spaces where you give answers and personal information: *a booking form* ○ *an entry form for a competition* ○ *to fill in an application form* ❶ In American English we fill **out** a form. استمارة

4 [C] a class in a school: *the sixth form* فصل، صف

In Britain, the years at secondary school used to be called **first/second/third, etc. form** but now they are called **Year 7** to **Year 11**. However the last two years of school (for pupils aged between 16 and 18 are still referred to as **the sixth form**.

5 [C] (*grammar*) a way of spelling or changing a word in a sentence: *the irregular forms of the verbs* ○ *The plural form is 'mice'.* صيغة (في قواعد اللغة)

6 [U] the strength or fitness of a sports player, team, etc: *to be in/out of form* ○ *to be on/off form* لياقة (بدنية)

7 [U] the record of how well sb/sth has done sth recently: *On present form the Italian team should win easily.* سِجلّ التفوق

IDM **true to form** → TRUE

form² /fɔːm/ *verb* **1** [T] to make or organize sth: *They formed a group called 'Citizens for Nature'.* ○ *to form a government* ○ *In English we usually form the past tense by adding '-ed'.* يُشكِّل

2 [T] to take the shape of sth: *A sofa bed is a sofa that you can pull out to form a bed.* يكوِّن

3 [I,T] to move into the shape or order mentioned: *The police formed a circle around the house.* يتشكَّل؛ يشكِّل

4 [T] to be the thing mentioned: *Seminars form the main part of the course* (= The main part of the course consists of seminars). يؤلِّف

5 [I,T] to begin to exist or to make sth exist; to begin to have sth: *Buds form on trees in the early spring.* ○ *The rain had formed a huge puddle on the road.* ○ *We formed a very good impression of the school on our first visit.* يتكوَّن؛ يكوِّن

formal /'fɔːml/ *adj* **1** (used about language or behaviour) used when you want to appear serious or official and when you are in a situation in which you do not know the other people very well: *'Yours faithfully' is a formal way of ending a letter.* ○ *She has a very formal manner – she doesn't seem to be able to relax.* ○ *a formal occasion* (= one where you must behave politely and wear the clothes that people think are suitable) رَسْمِي

In this dictionary some words and) phrases are marked *(formal)* or *(informal)*. This will help you to choose the right word for a particular situation. Often there is an informal or neutral word with a similar meaning to a more formal one.

2 public and official: *I shall make a formal complaint to the hospital about the way I was treated.* رسمي

3 (only *before* a noun) obtained in a school or college: *You do not need any formal qualifications for this job but we would like you to have some experience.* مَدرَسي، أكاديمي

▸ **formally** /-li/ *adv* رسمياً

formality /fɔː'mæləti/ *noun* (*pl.* **formalities**) **1** [C] an action that is necessary according to custom or law: *There are certain formalities to attend to before we can give you a visa.* مراسم، اجراء شكلي

If an action is **just a formality**, we mean that people think that it is necessary according to custom or law but that it has no real importance or effect otherwise.

2 [U] careful attention to rules of language and behaviour ترسُّم

format /'fɔːmæt/ *noun* [C] the shape of sth or the way it is arranged or produced: *It's the same book but in a different format.* شكل

▸ **format** *verb* [T] (forma**tt**ing; forma**tt**ed) to arrange sth in a particular format, usually for a computer: *to format a disk* يُشكِّل

formation /fɔː'meɪʃn/ *noun* **1** [U] the making or developing of sth: *the formation of a new government* تشكيل؛ تشكُّل

2 [C,U] an arrangement or pattern (especially of soldiers, aeroplanes, ships, etc.): *A number of planes flew over in formation.* تشكيلة (من جنود أو طائرات ألخ...)

3 [C] a thing that is formed; the particular way in which it is formed: *rock formations* ○ *cloud formations* تكوين؛ تشكيلة

formative /ˈfɔːmətɪv/ *adj* having an important and lasting influence (on sb's character and opinions): *A child's early years are thought to be the most formative ones.* مكوِّن

former¹ /ˈfɔːmə(r)/ *adj* (only *before* a noun) of an earlier time; previous: *Jimmy Carter, the former American President* ○ *Their new neighbour is a former teacher.* ○ *In former times people often had larger families.* سابق

former² /ˈfɔːmə(r)/ *adj, noun* the first (of two people or things just mentioned): *Of the two hospitals in the town – the General and the Royal – the former* (= the General) *has the better reputation.* ❶ The opposite is **the latter**. الأوّل

formerly /ˈfɔːməli/ *adv* in the past; previously: *the country of Myanmar (formerly Burma)* ○ *The hotel was formerly a castle.* ❶ **Used to** is a more common way of expressing the same meaning: *The hotel used to be a castle.* سابقاً

formidable /ˈfɔːmɪdəbl/ *adj* **1** causing you to be rather frightened: *His mother is a rather formidable lady.* هائل

2 difficult to deal with; needing a lot of effort: *Reforming the education system will be a formidable task.* شاقّ

formula /ˈfɔːmjələ/ *noun* [C] (*pl.* **formulas** or **formulae** /-mjəliː/) **1** a group of signs, letters or numbers used in science or mathematics to express a general law or fact: *The formula for carbon monoxide is CO.* ○ *What is the formula for converting miles to kilometres?* صيغة

2 a list of substances used for making sth; the instructions necessary for making sth: *The formula for the new vaccine has not yet been made public.* تركيب

3 a plan of how to get sth or how to do sth: *What is her formula for success?* خُطّة

formulate /ˈfɔːmjuleɪt/ *verb* [T] **1** to prepare and organize a plan or ideas for doing sth: *The Labour Party still has not formulated its policy on Northern Ireland.* يخطّط

2 to express sth (clearly and exactly) يعبر؛ يصيغ

forsake /fəˈseɪk/ *verb* [T] (*pt* **forsook** /fəˈsʊk/; *pp* **forsaken** /fəˈseɪkən/) (*formal*) to leave a person or a place for ever (especially when you should stay) يهجر

fort /fɔːt/ *noun* [C] a strong building that is used for military defence حصن

forth /fɔːθ/ *adv*

IDM **and so forth** and other things like those just mentioned: *The sort of job that you'll be doing is taking messages, making tea and so forth.* وما يشبه ذلك

back and forth → BACK³

forthcoming /ˌfɔːθˈkʌmɪŋ/ *adj* **1** going to happen or appear in the near future: *Look in the local paper for a list of forthcoming events.* آتٍ قريباً

2 (not before a noun) offered or given: *If no money is forthcoming we shall not be able to continue the project.* متوفر، آتٍ قادم

3 (not before a noun) willing to be helpful, give information, etc: *She's never very forthcoming about her future plans.* مستعد للمساعدة أو تقديم المعلومات

forthright /ˈfɔːθraɪt/ *adj* saying clearly and honestly what you think صريح

forthwith /ˌfɔːθˈwɪθ; US -ˈwɪð/ *adv* (*formal*) immediately حالاً

fortieth → FORTY

fortify /ˈfɔːtɪfaɪ/ *verb* [T] (*pres part* **fortifying**; *3rd pers sing pres* **fortifies**; *pt, pp* **fortified**) to make a place stronger and ready for an attack: *to fortify a city* يقوّي

▸ **fortification** /ˌfɔːtɪfɪˈkeɪʃn/ *noun* [C, usually pl.] walls, ditches, etc. that are built to protect a place against attack تحصين

fortnight /ˈfɔːtnaɪt/ *noun* [C, usually sing.] (*Brit*) two weeks: *We're going on holiday for a fortnight.* ○ *a fortnight's holiday* ○ *School finishes in a fortnight/in a fortnight's time* (= two weeks from now). أسبوعان

▸ **fortnightly** *adj, adv* (happening or appearing) once a fortnight: *This magazine is published fortnightly.* كلّ أسبوعين

fortress /ˈfɔːtrəs/ *noun* [C] a castle or other large building that has been made strong so that it is not easy to attack قلعة، حصن

fortunate /ˈfɔːtʃənət/ *adj* lucky: *You were fortunate to have such lovely weather for your holiday.* ○ *It was fortunate that he was at home when you phoned.* ❶ The opposite is **unfortunate**. محظوظ

▸ **fortunately** *adv* by good luck; luckily: *Fortunately the traffic wasn't too bad so I managed to get to the meeting on time.* ○ *Jane arrived late but, fortunately for her, everybody was too busy to notice.* لحسن الحظ

fortune /ˈfɔːtʃuːn/ *noun* **1** [U] the power that affects what happens in a person's life; luck: *Fortune was not on our side that day* (= we were unlucky). قدَر؛ حظ

2 [C, usually pl.] the things (both good and bad) that happen to a person, family, country, etc: *The country's fortunes depend on its industry being successful.* مصائر

3 [C] what is going to happen to a person in the future: *Show me your hand and I'll try to tell your fortune.* مصير؛ بخت

4 [C] a very large amount of money: *I always spend a fortune on presents at Christmas.* ثروة

ˈfortune teller *noun* [C] a person who tells people's fortunes (3) منجّم

forty /ˈfɔːti/ *number* 40, one more than thirty-nine

❶ For examples of how to use numbers in sentences, look at **sixty**. أربعون

▸ **fortieth** /ˈfɔːtiəθ/ *pron, det, adv* 40th, next after thirty-ninth ➲ Look at the examples at **sixth**. الأربعون

forum /ˈfɔːrəm/ *noun* [C] a place or meeting where people can exchange and discuss ideas منتدى عام للمناظرة

⚷ **forward¹** /ˈfɔːwəd/ *adv* **1** (*also* **forwards**) in the direction that is in front of you; towards the front, end or future: *Keep going forward and try not to look back.* ○ *We seem to be going backwards, not forwards.* إلى الأمام، قدماً

2 in the direction of progress; ahead: *The new form of treatment is a big step forward in the fight against AIDS.* نحو الأمام؛ نحو التقدّم

❶ **Forward** is used after many verbs, e.g. **bring, come, look, put**. For the meaning of the expressions look at the verb entries.

IDM **backward(s) and forward(s)** → BACKWARD
put the clock/clocks forward/back → CLOCK¹

⚷ **forward²** /ˈfɔːwəd/ *adj* **1** (only *before* a noun) towards the front or future: *forward planning* (تخطيط) للمستقبل؛ أمامي

2 behaving towards sb in a way that is too confident or too informal: *I hope you don't think I'm being too forward, asking you so many questions.* متجريء

forward³ /ˈfɔːwəd/ *verb* [T] to send a letter, etc. to a new address: *The post office is forwarding all our mail.* يحوّل رسالة (إلى عنوان جديد)

forward⁴ /ˈfɔːwəd/ *noun* [C] an attacking player in a sport such as football لاعب هجوم

ˈ**forwarding address** *noun* [C] a new address to which post should be sent عنوان جديد (يحوّل له البريد)

ˈ**forward-looking** *adj* thinking about or planning for the future; having modern ideas تقدمي، مستقْبلي

forwent *pt of* FORGO

fossil /ˈfɒsl/ *noun* [C] the remains, or a mark, of a prehistoric animal or plant that has been buried in rock for a very long time and that has become hard مستحاثات، أحافير، متحجرات

foster /ˈfɒstə(r); *US* ˈfɔː-/ *verb* [T] **1** to take a child who needs a home into your family and to care for him/her without becoming the legal parents: *to foster a homeless child* يربّي (طفلاً)؛ يتبنّى

The people who do this are **foster parents**. The child is a **foster child**. Look at **adopt**.

2 to help or encourage the development of sth (especially feelings or ideas) يرعى

fought *pt, pp of* FIGHT

foul¹ /faʊl/ *adj* **1** disgusting and dirty (often with a bad smell or taste): *The air in the room was foul and she opened the windows wide.* قذِر، مقرف

2 very bad or unpleasant: *It's been a foul weekend.* ○ *Careful what you say – he's got a foul temper* (= he becomes angry very easily). ○ *What's in this drink? It tastes foul.* كريه؛ شنيع

3 (used about weather) very bad; stormy: *The foul weather prevented our plane from taking off.* (طقس) فظيع؛ عاصف

4 (used about language) very rude; full of swearing بذيء

foul² /faʊl/ *verb* [T] to make sth dirty (with rubbish, waste, etc.): *Dogs must not foul the pavement.* يوسّخ

PHR V **foul sth up** to spoil sth: *The weather really fouled up our holiday.* يفْسِد

foul³ /faʊl/ *noun* [C] (*sport*) an action that is against the rules: *to commit a foul* ○ *He was sent off for a foul on the Juventus goalkeeper.* فاوْل (في الرياضة)

▸ **foul** *verb* [I,T] (*sport*) to be guilty of a foul (against another player): *Owen was fouled inside the area and the referee awarded a penalty.* يرتكب "فاوْل"

ˌ**foul ˈplay** *noun* [U] **1** action that is against the rules of a sport مخالَفة لقوانين اللعب (في الرياضة)

2 violent crime that leads to murder جريمة

found¹ *pt, pp of* FIND

⚷ **found²** /faʊnd/ *verb* [T] **1** to start an organization, institution, etc. especially by providing money: *Oxford has Britain's oldest public museum (founded 1683).* يؤسّس، ينشئ

2 to begin to build a town or establish a country: *Liberia was founded by freed American slaves.* يؤسس

3 (usually passive) to base sth on sth: *Their marriage was founded on mutual respect.* ○ *The book was founded on real life.* يستنِد إلى، يقوم أو يُبنى على

⚷ **foundation** /faʊnˈdeɪʃn/ *noun* **1** [U] the act of founding sth (a building, town, organization, etc.) تأسيس

2 [C] an organization that provides money for a special purpose, e.g. for research or to help people who have a particular problem: *The British Heart Foundation* (= researching the causes of heart disease) مؤسّسة

3 [plural] **foundations** the parts of a building beneath the ground that form its base: *The builders have only just started to lay the foundations of the new school.* أساس، أسُس

4 [C,U] the idea, principle, or fact on which sth is based: *That rumour is completely without foundation* (= it is not true). أساس

founder /ˈfaʊndə(r)/ *noun* [C] a person who founds or establishes sth مؤسّس

ˌ**founder ˈmember** *noun* [C] one of the first members of a club, organization, etc. عضو مؤسّس

foundry /ˈfaʊndri/ *noun* [C] (*pl.* **foundries**) a place where metal or glass is melted and shaped into objects مصهَر، مَسبَك

fountain /ˈfaʊntən; *US* -tn/ *noun* [C] an ornament (in a garden or in a square in a town) that shoots a stream of water into the air. The water that comes out is also called a fountain. نافورة

ˈfountain pen *noun* [C] a type of pen that you fill with ink قلم حبر

four /fɔː(r)/ *number* 4, one more than three ❶ For examples of how to use numbers in sentences, look at **six**. أربعة

IDM on all fours with your hands and knees on the ground; crawling: *The children went through the tunnel on all fours.* زحفاً، على الأربع

▸ **four-** (in compounds) having four of the thing mentioned: *four-legged animals* رباعيّ

fourth /fɔːθ/ *pron, det, adv* 4th, next after third ❶ For ¼ we use the word **quarter**: *a quarter of an hour* (= fifteen minutes). ➲ Look at the examples at **sixth**. رابع

fourthly *adv* (used to introduce the fourth point in a list): *Fourthly (and this point is even more important than the other three), you must speak clearly.* رابعاً

ˌfour-letter ˈword *noun* [C] one of a type of word (often with four letters) that people think is very rude كلمة بذيئة

fourteen /ˌfɔːˈtiːn/ *number* 14, one more than thirteen ❶ For examples of how to use numbers in sentences, look at **six**. أربعة عشر

▸ **fourteenth** /ˌfɔːˈtiːnθ/ *pron, det, adv* 14th, next after thirteenth ➲ Look at the examples at **sixth**. رابع عشر

ˌfour-wheel ˈdrive *adj* having an engine that turns all four wheels ذو دفع رباعي

fowl /faʊl/ *noun* [C] (*pl.* **fowl** or **fowls**) a bird, especially a hen that is kept on a farm طَيْر، دجاجة

fox /fɒks/ *noun* [C] a wild animal with reddish fur that looks like a dog ثعلب

> A fox is often described as **sly** or **cunning**. A female fox is a **vixen**, a young fox is a **cub**.

ˈfox-hunting *noun* [U] a sport in which a fox is hunted by people on horses with dogs (foxhounds) صيد الثعالب

foyer /ˈfɔɪeɪ; *US* ˈfɔɪər/ *noun* [C] an entrance hall in a cinema, theatre, hotel, etc. where people can meet or wait ردْهة

fraction /ˈfrækʃn/ *noun* [C] **1** a small part or amount: *For a fraction of a second I thought the car was going to crash.* جزْء

2 an exact part of a number: *½ and ¼ are fractions.* كَسْر (عَدَد)

▸ **fractionally** /-ʃənəli/ *adv* to a very small degree; slightly: *Alonso was fractionally faster than his nearest rival.* إلى حدٍّ قليل

fracture /ˈfræktʃə(r)/ *noun* [C] a break in sth hard, especially in a bone: *a fracture of the arm* كَسْر (في عظم)

▸ **fracture** *verb* [T] to break sth (especially a bone): *She fell and fractured her ankle.* ○ *a fractured ankle* يكسر

fragile /ˈfrædʒaɪl; *US* -dʒl/ *adj* easily damaged or broken: *This bowl is very fragile. Please handle it carefully.* هَشّ؛ سريع الانكسار

fragment /ˈfrægmənt/ *noun* [C] a small piece (that has broken off sth bigger): *The builders found fragments of Roman pottery on the site.* ○ (*figurative*) *I heard only a fragment of their conversation.* شَظيّة

▸ **fragment** /frægˈment/ *verb* [I,T] (*formal*) to be broken into small pieces; to break sth into small pieces: *The country is becoming increasingly fragmented by civil war.* يتَكسّر؛ يكسّر

fragrance /ˈfreɪgrəns/ *noun* [C,U] a pleasant smell عبير

▸ **fragrant** *adj* having a pleasant smell عطِر

frail /freɪl/ *adj* not strong or healthy: *My aunt is still very frail after her accident.* واهِن

▸ **frailty** /ˈfreɪlti/ *noun* [C,U] (*pl.* **frailties**) moral or physical weakness وَهْن

frame¹ /freɪm/ *noun* [C] **1** a border of wood or metal that goes around the outside of a door, picture, window, etc: *a window frame* إطار

2 [usually pl.] a structure made of plastic or metal that holds the lenses of a pair of glasses إطار

3 the basic structure of a piece of furniture, building, vehicle, etc. onto which other pieces are added: *the frame of a bicycle* هيكل

4 [usually sing.] the shape of a human or animal body: *He has a large frame but he is not fat.* هيكل (جسدي)، بنية

IDM frame of mind a particular state or condition of your feelings; mood: *I'm not in the right frame of mind for a party. I'd prefer to be on my own.* مِزاج

frame² /freɪm/ *verb* [T] **1** to put a border around sth (especially a picture or photograph): *Let's have this photograph framed.* يؤَطِّر، يحيط بإطار

2 (*formal*) to express sth in words, in a particular way: *The question was very carefully framed.* يعبر

3 (usually passive) to give false evidence against sb in order to make him/her seem guilty of a crime: *The man claimed that he had been framed by the police.* يتّهم زوراً

framework /ˈfreɪmwɜːk/ *noun* [C] **1** the basic structure of sth that gives it shape and strength: *A greenhouse is made of glass panels fixed in a metal framework.* هيكل، بنية خارجية

2 a system of rules or ideas which help you decide what to do: *The plan may be changed but it will provide a framework on which we can build.* إطار

franc /fræŋk/ *noun* [C] the unit of money that is used in Switzerland and several other countries, formerly also in France, Belgium and Luxembourg فرنك (نقود)

franchise /ˈfræntʃaɪz/ *noun* **1** [C] official permission to sell a company's goods or services in a particular area: *a franchise for a fast-food restaurant* وكالة شركة

2 [U] (*formal*) the right to vote in elections حق الانتخاب

frank /fræŋk/ *adj* showing your thoughts and feelings openly; saying what you mean; honest: *To be perfectly frank with you, I don't think you'll pass your driving test.* صريح
▸ **frankly** *adv* **1** in a frank manner: *Please tell me frankly what you think about my idea.* بصراحة
2 speaking openly and honestly: *Quite frankly, I'm not surprised at what has happened.* بصدق
frankness *noun* [U]: *She spoke with great frankness about her past life.* صراحة

frankfurter /ˈfræŋkfɜːtə(r)/ (*US* **wiener**) *noun* [C] a type of small smoked sausage سجق ألماني

frantic /ˈfræntɪk/ *adj* **1** in a very emotional state because you are extremely worried or frightened: *frantic with worry* ○ *frantic cries for help* مضطرب
2 very busy or rushed; without organization: *a frantic search for the keys* عَجول
▸ **frantically** /-kli/ *adv*: *They have been working frantically all week trying to get things ready in time.* باستعجال؛ باهتياج

fraternal /frəˈtɜːnl/ *adj* (*formal*) of or like brothers; friendly أخَوي

fraternity /frəˈtɜːnəti/ *noun* (*pl.* **fraternities**) **1** [U] the feeling of friendship between people (like that between brothers) إخاء، أخوّة
2 [C] a group of people who share the same work or interests: *the medical fraternity* إخوان؛ رابطة

fraud /frɔːd/ *noun* **1** [C,U] (an act of) deceiving or tricking sb in order to get money, etc. in a way that is against the law: *The accountant was sent to prison for fraud.* ○ *Millions of pounds are lost every year in credit card frauds.* غش، احتيال
2 [C] a person who deceives or tricks sb by pretending to be sb else غشّاش، محتال
▸ **fraudulent** /ˈfrɔːdjələnt; *US* -dʒʊ-/ *adj* (*formal*) done in order to deceive sb; dishonest: *the fraudulent use of stolen cheques* احتيالي

fraught /frɔːt/ *adj* **1** (not before a noun) filled with sth (unpleasant): *The situation was fraught with danger.* منْذِر
2 (*informal*) (used about people) worried and nervous; (used about a situation) very busy so that people become nervous: *You look fraught – what's the matter?* ○ *Things are usually fraught at work on Monday mornings.* قلق، مضطرب؛ مقلق

fray /freɪ/ *verb* [I,T] (used about cloth, etc.) to become worn so that some threads are loose; to cause cloth to do this: *This shirt is beginning to fray at the cuffs.* ○ *a frayed cuff* ○ (*figurative*) *Nerves began to fray towards the end of the match* (= the players started to get nervous). يَبْلَى؛ يُبلي

freak¹ /friːk/ *noun* [C] **1** a very strange or unusual event: *By some strange freak of nature we had snow in May.* ○ *a freak accident, storm, etc.* أمر عجيب
2 (*informal*) a person who has a very strong interest in sth: *a health freak* هاوٍ ، مهووس بِ
3 a person or animal that is physically abnormal in some way; a person who behaves in a strange way: *The other kids think Ally's a freak because she doesn't watch TV.* شاذّ في مظهره؛ غريب

freak² /friːk/ *verb* [I, T] (*informal*) **freak (sb) out** to react very strongly to sth that makes you feel shocked, frightened, upset, etc. or to make sb react in this way: *She freaked out when she heard the news.* ○ *The film 'Psycho' really freaked me out.* يخض

freckle /ˈfrekl/ *noun* [C, usually pl.] a small brown spot on a person's skin: *A lot of people with red hair have freckles.* نَمَش
▸ **freckled** *adj*: *a freckled face* وجه ذو نَمَش

🔑**free¹** /friː/ *adj* **1** not in prison or in a cage, etc: *After twenty years in prison he was finally set free in 1989.* حُر
2 free (to do sth) not controlled by the government, rules, etc: *There is free movement of people across the border.* ○ *a free press* ○ *You're free this afternoon to do exactly what you want.* حُر
3 free from/of sth not having sth dangerous, unpleasant, etc: *How wonderful to go away for a month, free from all worries and responsibilities.* ○ *free from pain* آمن مِن
4 costing nothing: *Admission to the museum is free/free of charge.* ○ *a free sample* مجّاني
5 not being used: *Do you have a single room free for Saturday night?* شاغِر
6 without appointments; not busy: *I'm afraid Mr Spencer is not free this afternoon.* ○ *I don't get much free time.* غير مشغول، "فاضي"
IDM **free and easy** informal or relaxed: *The atmosphere in our office is very free and easy.* مريح، بدون رسميّات
get, have, etc. a free hand to get, have, etc. permission to make your own decisions about sth مأذون له
of your own free will because you want to, not because sb forces you طَوعاً دون إجبار
▸ **free** *adv* **1** in a free manner: *There is nowhere around here where dogs can run free.* بحرّية
2 without cost or payment: *Children under five usually travel free on trains.* مجّاناً

🔑**free²** /friː/ *verb* [T] **1 free sb/sth (from sth)** to let sb/sth go; to set sb/sth free: *to free a prisoner* ○ *The protesters freed the animals from their cages.* يحرّر
2 free sb/sth of/from sth to take away from sb sth that is unpleasant: *The medicine freed her from pain for a few hours.* يخلّص مِن
3 free sb/sth (from sth) to move sb/sth that is stuck or caught: *The emergency services took three hours to free the man from the wreckage of his car.* ينقذ
4 free sb/sth for sth to make sth available so that it can be used; to put sb in a position in which he/she can do sth: *Cuts in defence spending would free money to spend on education.* يتيح

ˌ**free** ˈ**agent** *noun* [C] a person who can do what

he/she likes because he/she is not responsible to another person حرّ طليق

⚿**freedom** /ˈfriːdəm/ *noun* **1** [U] the state of being free, that is, of not being in prison or under the control of sb else: *The opposition leader was given his freedom after 25 years.* حُرّيّة

2 [C,U] the right to do or say what you want: *You have the freedom to come and go as you please.* ○ *freedom of speech* ○ *the rights and freedoms of the individual* ➲ Look at **liberty**. حرّيّة

3 freedom from sth the state of not having sth unpleasant: *freedom from fear, hunger, pain, etc.* خَلاص، تحرر

ˈ**freedom fighter** *noun* [C] a person who belongs to a group that uses violence to try to remove a government from power مناضل

ˌ**free ˈenterprise** *noun* [U] the operation of trade and business without government control سوق حرّة

freehand /ˈfriːhænd/ *adj, adv* (done) by hand, without the help of an instrument, e.g. a ruler: *a freehand sketch* (بلا آلة) باليَد، يدويّ

ˌ**free ˈkick** *noun* [C] (in football) a kick by a player of one team after a member of the other team has broken a rule ضَرْبة حرّة

freelance /ˈfriːlɑːns; *US* -læns/ (*also* **freelancer**) *noun* [C] a person who works for several different employers and who is paid separately for each piece of work that he/she does عامل مُستَقِل

▸ **freelance** *adj, adv*: *a freelance journalist* ○ *She works freelance.* باستقلال

⚿**freely** /ˈfriːli/ *adv* **1** in a way that is not controlled or limited: *He is the country's first freely elected president for 40 years.* ○ *There are no roadworks on the motorway and traffic is flowing freely.* بحرّيّة

> Note that if you travel **free** it means that you do not have to pay anything. If you can travel **freely** it means that you can go wherever you like.

2 willingly, without hesitating: *I freely admit that I made a mistake.* طَوْعاً

Freemason /ˈfriːmeɪsn/ (*also* **mason**) *noun* [C] a man who belongs to an international secret society whose members help each other and who recognize each other by secret signs ماسوني

Freepost /ˈfriːpəʊst/ *noun* [U] (*Brit*) the system by which the person who sends a letter, etc. does not pay for the cost of postage بريد مجّاني

ˌ**free-ˈrange** *adj* produced by hens that are allowed to move around freely: *free-range eggs* (بيض دجاج) طليق

ˌ**free ˈrunning** *noun* [U] the activity or art of moving through a city by running, jumping and climbing under, around and through things in a way that is as elegant as possible جري في المدن بمصاحبة قفز وتسلق بطريقة رشيقة

freesia /ˈfriːʒə; ˈfriːziə/ *noun* [C] a plant with sweet-smelling yellow, pink or white flowers فريزيا

ˌ**free ˈspeech** *noun* [U] the right to express any opinion in public حرية الكلام

freeway /ˈfriːweɪ/ *noun* [C] (*US*) = MOTORWAY

⚿**freeze** /friːz/ *verb* (*pt* **froze** /frəʊz/; *pp* **frozen** /ˈfrəʊzn/) **1** [I,T] to become hard (and often change into ice) because of extreme cold; to make sth do this: *Water freezes at 0° Celsius.* ○ *Leave the heating on when you're away or the pipes will freeze.* ○ *The ground was frozen solid for most of the winter.* ○ *I've picked ten pounds of raspberries and I'm going to freeze them.* ○ *Raspberries freeze well.* ○ *frozen peas* يَجْمَد؛ يجمّد

2 [I] (used with 'it' to describe extremely cold weather, when water turns into ice): *I think it's going to freeze tonight.* يَجْمَد: تنخفض الحرارة إلى ما دون الصفْر

3 [I,T] (to cause a person) to be very cold or to die from cold: *The two men froze to death on the mountain.* ○ *Turn the heater up a bit – I'm frozen.* يَجْمَد؛ يتجمّد

4 [I] to stop suddenly or become still because you are frightened or shocked: *The terrible scream made her freeze with terror.* يَتَصَلّب، يتسمّر في مكانه

5 [T] to keep wages, prices, fares, etc. at a fixed level for a certain period of time: *Spending on defence has been frozen for one year.* يمنع الازدياد؛ يجمّد

▸ **freeze** *noun* [C] **1** a period of weather when the temperature stays below 0°C (freezing point) فترة برد شديد، فترة جليد

2 the fixing of wages, prices, fares, etc. at a certain level for a certain period of time تجميد (الأسعار مثلاً)

freezing *adj* (*informal*) very cold (not necessarily below 0° Celsius): *Can we turn the central heating on? I'm freezing.* ○ *It's absolutely freezing outside.* (بَرْد) قارس؛ متجمّد

freezer /ˈfriːzə(r)/ (*also* ˌ**deep ˈfreeze**) *noun* [C] a large box or cupboard in which you can store food for a long time at a temperature below 0°C (freezing point) so that it stays frozen ➲ Look at **fridge**. جهاز لتجميد الطعام، "فريزر"

ˈ**freezing point** (*also* **freezing**) *noun* [C,U] the temperature at which water, etc. freezes: *Last night the temperature fell to six degrees below freezing.* درجة حرارة التجمّد

freight /freɪt/ *noun* [U] **1** the method of carrying goods from one place to another: *Your order will be sent by air freight.* شحْن

2 = GOODS (2): *a freight train*

▸ **freighter** *noun* [C] a ship or plane that carries only freight شاحنة (سفينة أو طائرة للشحن فقط)

ˈ**freight car** (*US*) = WAGON

French fry /ˌfrentʃ ˈfraɪ/ *noun* [C] (*pl.* **French fries**) (*especially US*) = CHIP[1] (3)

French window /ˌfrentʃ ˈwɪndəʊ/ (*US* ˌ**French ˈdoor**) *noun* [C] one of a pair of glass

a b c d e f g h i j k l m n o p q r s t u v w x y z

doors that open onto a garden or balcony
باب زجاجيّ يفتح على الحديقة

frenzy /'frenzi/ *noun* [sing., U] a state of great excitement; a period when a person cannot control his/her actions: *The speaker worked the crowd up into a frenzy.* هياج

▸ **frenzied** /'frenzid/ *adj* wild and excited: *a frenzied attack* هائج: مسعور

frequency /'fri:kwənsi/ *noun* (*pl.* **frequencies**)
1 [U] the rate at which sth happens (= the number of times sth happens in a particular period): *Fatal accidents have decreased in frequency in recent years* (= there are fewer of them). تواتر

2 [U] the fact that sth happens often: *The frequency of child deaths from cancer near the nuclear power station is being investigated.* تكرُّر

3 [C,U] the rate at which a sound wave or radio wave vibrates: *high-frequency/low-frequency sounds* ○ *Which frequency does the radio station broadcast on?* ذبذبة

frequent[1] /'fri:kwənt/ *adj* happening often: *There is a frequent bus service from the city centre to the airport.* ❶ The opposite is **infrequent**.
متكرّر، متواتر؛ كثير الحدوث

▸ **frequently** *adv*: *Buses run frequently from the city centre to the airport.* بتواتر؛ كثيراً، تكراراً

frequent[2] /fri'kwent/ *verb* [T] (*formal*) to go to a place often: *He spent most of his evenings in Paris frequenting expensive restaurants.* يتردّد على

fresh /freʃ/ *adj* **1** new or different: *They have decided to make a fresh start in a different town.* ○ *I'm sure he'll have some fresh ideas on the subject.* ○ *I'd like to put on some fresh clothes before we go out.* جديد

2 not old (so there has been no time for any change): *There was fresh blood all over the walls.* ○ *Write a few notes while the lecture is still fresh in your mind.* طازج؛ حديث، قريب العَهْد

3 (used about food, flowers, etc.) made or picked not long ago: *fresh bread* ❶ The opposite for food is **stale**. طازج؛ (زهور) نَضِرة

4 (used about food) not frozen or from a tin: *fresh fruit and vegetables* طازج (غير معلّب)

5 (used about water) not salt; not sea water ❶ A fish that lives in such water is a **freshwater** fish. (ماء) عَذْب

6 (used about the air) clean and cool: *Open the window and let some fresh air in.* (هواء) نقي؛ منعِش

7 (used about the weather) quite cold and windy (طقس) بارد

8 (used about colours, or a person's skin) bright or clear نَضِر، زاهٍ

9 not tired: *I'll think about the problem again in the morning when I'm fresh.* مرْتاح

10 fresh from/out of sth having just finished sth: *Life isn't easy for a young teacher fresh from university.* حديث عهد

IDM **break fresh/new ground** → GROUND[1]

▸ **freshly** *adv* newly; recently: *freshly baked bread* حديثاً

freshness *noun* [U]
نقاء، نظافة؛ جِدّة، حداثة؛ نشاط؛ نضارة

freshen /'freʃn/ *verb* **1** [T] **freshen sth (up)** to make sth cleaner or brighter: *Some new curtains and wallpaper would freshen up this room.*
ينظّف؛ يجدّد، ينْعِش

2 [I] (used about the wind) to become stronger (ريح) تَشتدّ

PHRV **freshen (yourself) up** to wash and make yourself clean and tidy يغسل (وجهه) ويصْلح هِنْدامه

fresher /'freʃə(r)/ *noun* [C] (*Brit informal*) a student who is in his/her first year at university, college, etc. طالب سنة أولى

freshman /'freʃmən/ *noun* [C] (*pl.* **freshmen** /-mən/) (*US*) a student who is in his/her first year at college, high school, university, etc.
طالب سنة أولى

fret /fret/ *verb* [I] (fre**tt**ing; fre**tt**ed) **fret (about/at/over sth)** to be unhappy or worried about sth: *Don't fret. Everything will be all right.* يَقْلَق

friction /'frɪkʃn/ *noun* [U] **1** the rubbing of one surface or thing against another احتكاك

2 disagreement between people or groups: *There is a lot of friction between the older and the younger members of staff.* خلاف

Friday /'fraɪdeɪ/ *noun* [C,U] (*abbr* **Fri.**) the day of the week after Thursday and before Saturday ❶ For examples of the use of the days of the week in sentences, look at **Monday**. (يوم) الجُمُعَة

fridge /frɪdʒ/ (*also formal* **refrigerator**) *noun* [C] a metal container in which food, etc. is kept cold (but not frozen) so that it stays fresh ➲ Look at **freezer**. ثلاّجة، برّاد

friend /frend/ *noun* [C] **1** a person that you know and like (not a member of your family): *Trevor and I are old friends. We were at school together.* ○ *We're only inviting close friends and relatives to the funeral.* ○ *Do you know Helen Wilson? She's my best friend.* ○ *A friend of mine told me about this restaurant.* ○ *One of my friends told me about this restaurant.* ➲ Look at **boyfriend**, **girlfriend** and **penfriend**. صديق

2 a friend of/to sth a helper or supporter of sth: *the Friends of the Churchill Hospital* نصير

IDM **be/make friends (with sb)** to be/become a friend (of sb): *Tony is rather shy and finds it hard to make friends.* يصادق

▸ **friendless** *adj* without friends بلا صديق

friendly /'frendli/ *adj* (**friendlier**; **friendliest**)
1 behaving in a kind and pleasant way; showing kindness and pleasantness: *Everyone here has been very friendly towards us.* ○ *a friendly smile* ○ *a small friendly hotel near the beach* لطيف؛ ودود

2 friendly with sb being the friend of sb: *Nick's become quite friendly with the boy next door.* صديق

▸ **friendliness** *noun* [U] لطف؛ حسْن المعاملة

friendly *noun* [C] a sports match that is not part of a serious competition مباراة وديّة

-friendly (in compounds) supporting or helping

sb/sth: *This software is extremely user-friendly.* معين؛ سَهْل

friendship /ˈfrendʃɪp/ *noun* **1** [U] the state of being friends: *Our relationship is based on friendship, not love.* صداقة

2 [C] a relationship between people who are friends: *The friendships that you make at school often last for life.* صداقة

fright /fraɪt/ *noun* [C,U] a sudden feeling of fear: *That loud bang gave me quite a fright.* ○ *The child cried out in fright.* رعب

frighten /ˈfraɪtn/ *verb* [T] to fill sb with fear: *Sorry, I didn't mean to frighten you.* يُرْعِب

PHR V **frighten sb/sth away/off** to cause a person or animal to go away by frightening him/her/it: *Walk quietly so that you don't frighten the birds away.* يُرْعِب، يهرب، يُجفِل

▶ **frightened** *adj* **1** full of fear or worry: *Frightened children were calling for their mothers.* ○ *He was frightened at the thought of being alone.* ○ *I was frightened that they would think that I was rude.* مَرْعوب، فزع

2 frightened of sb/sth fearing a particular person, thing or situation: *When I was young I was frightened of cats.* ➲ Look at the note at **afraid.** خائف، مذعور

frightening /ˈfraɪtnɪŋ/ *adj* causing fear: *It was a very frightening situation to be in.* ○ *It's frightening how quickly time passes.* ○ *It's frightening that time passes so quickly.* مُرعِب، مخيف

frightful /ˈfraɪtfl/ *adj* (*old-fashioned*) (*especially Brit*) **1** very bad or unpleasant: *The weather this summer has been frightful.* سيء جداً، فظيع

2 (*informal*) (used for emphasizing sth) very bad or great: *We're in a frightful rush.* هائل

▶ **frightfully** /-fəli/ *adv* (*old-fashioned*) very: *I'm frightfully sorry.* جداً

frigid /ˈfrɪdʒɪd/ *adj* (usually used about a woman) disliking sexual activity باردة (جنسياً)

frill /frɪl/ *noun* [C] **1** a special edge for a dress, shirt, etc. which is made by forming many folds in a narrow piece of cloth كَشْكَش، مكَشْكَش

2 [usually pl.] (*figurative*) something that is not necessary but is decorative or pleasant: *We just want a plain simple meal – no frills.* زخرفي: شيء غير أساسي ولكنه مستحَب

▶ **frilly** /ˈfrɪli/ (**frillier**; **frilliest**) *adj* having many frills: *a frilly dress* مكَشْكَش

fringe /frɪndʒ/ *noun* [C] **1** (*US* **bangs** [plural]) the part of your hair that hangs, usually in a straight line, over your forehead: *Your hair looks better with a fringe.* غُرّة

2 a decorative edge on a rug, etc. or on clothes, that is made of loose or hanging threads هُدْب: حاشية تزيينيّة

3 a place, part or position that is a long way from the centre or from what is usual: *the outer fringes of London* ○ *Some people on the fringes of the party are opposed to the policy on Europe.* حاشية: أطراف خارجية

▶ **fringe** *verb*

IDM **be fringed by/with sth** to have sth as a border: *The lake was fringed with pine trees.* يحُدّ بـ

ˈ**fringe benefit** *noun* [C] an extra benefit that is given to an employee in addition to his/her salary: *The fringe benefits of this job include a car and free health insurance.* تعويض (فوق الأجر)

frisk /frɪsk/ *verb* **1** [T] to pass your hands over sb's body in order to search for hidden weapons, drugs, etc. يفتّش (شخصاً)

2 [I] (used about an animal or child) to play and jump about in a lively and happy way يلعب بحبور؛ ينتطّ

▶ **frisky** *adj* (**friskier**; **friskiest**) lively and playful مرح

fritter /ˈfrɪtə(r)/ *verb*

PHR V **fritter sth away (on sth)** to waste time or money on things that are not important يُبدّد

frivolity /frɪˈvɒləti/ *noun* [U] silly behaviour; not acting seriously رعونة؛ عَبَث

frivolous /ˈfrɪvələs/ *adj* not serious; silly: *This is a serious issue. Please don't make frivolous remarks.* أرعن؛ عابث

frizzy /ˈfrɪzi/ *adj* (**frizzier**; **frizziest**) (used about hair) with a lot of very small curls (شعر) أجعد

fro /frəʊ/ *adv*

IDM **to and fro** → TO[3]

frock /frɒk/ *noun* [C] (*old-fashioned*) a dress ثوب، فستان

frog /frɒg; *US* frɔːg/ *noun* [C] a small animal with smooth skin and long legs that are used for jumping. Frogs live in or near water: *the croaking of frogs* ضِفْدع

frogman /frɒgmən; *US* frɔːg-/ *noun* [C] (*pl.* **frogmen** /-mən/) a swimmer who works underwater wearing special rubber clothes and using breathing equipment: *Police frogmen searched the river.* غوّاص

from /frəm; *strong form* frɒm/ *prep* **1** (showing the place where sb/sth starts or started): *Has the bus from London arrived?* ○ *She comes home from work at 7 o'clock.* ○ *Water was dripping from the tap.* ○ *A child fell from the seventh floor of a block of flats.* (مكان البدء) مِنْ

2 (showing the time when sth starts or started): *Peter's on holiday from next Friday.* ○ *The supermarket is open from 8 a.m. till 8 p.m. every day.* ○ *We lived in Wales from 1979 to 1986.* (زمان البدء) مِنْ

3 (showing the person who sent, gave, said, etc. sth): *Have you had a Christmas card from Roy?* ○ *I borrowed this jacket from my sister.* ○ *a phone call from my father* مِن

4 (showing the origin of sb/sth): *'Where do you come from?' 'I'm from Australia.'* ○ *quotations from Shakespeare* ○ *There's a man from the bank to see you.* (مَصْدَر) من

5 (showing the material with which sth is made): *Paper is made from wood.* (مصنوع) مِنْ

6 (showing the distance between two places): *The house is five miles from Oxford.* (يبعد) عن

a b c d e f g h i j k l m n o p q r s t u v w x y z

7 (showing the lower limit in a range of prices, figures, etc.): *Our prices start from £2.50 a bottle.* ○ *Tickets cost from £5 to £15.* (يبدأ) من

8 (showing the state of sb/sth before a change): *The bus fare has gone up from 85p to 95p.* ○ *The article was translated from Russian into English.* ○ *Things have gone from bad to worse.* (يتحوّل: يزداد) مِن

9 (showing that sb/sth is taken away): *Children don't like being separated from their parents for a long period.* ○ *She borrowed the book from the library.* ○ *8 from 12 leaves 4.* (يأخذ) مِن

10 (showing sth that you want to avoid): *There was no shelter from the wind.* ○ *This game will stop you from getting bored.* (يتقي) مِن

11 (showing the reason for sth): *People in the camps are suffering from hunger and cold.* (يقاسي) مِن

12 (showing the difference between two people, places or things): *Can you tell margarine from butter?* ○ *Is Portuguese very different from Spanish?* (يميز) مِن: عن

13 (showing your position or point of view): *There is a wonderful view from the top of the tower.* ○ *From your point of view it would be better to fly to Birmingham rather than to London.* ○ *He always looks at things from his own point of view.* (ينظر) مِن

IDM **from... on** starting at a particular time and continuing for ever: *She never spoke to him again from that day on.* ○ *From now on you must earn your own living.* (نقطة الانطلاق) مِن

🔑**front** /frʌnt/ *noun* **1** [C, usually sing.] the side or surface of sth that is most usually seen or that is most important: *a dress with buttons down the front* ○ *the front of a building* (= the front wall) ○ *a card with flowers on the front* قدّام: الأمام

2 [C, usually sing.] the most forward part of sth or the area that is just outside of or before sb/sth: *Young children should not travel in the front of the car.* ○ *There is a small garden at the front of the house.* قدّام، الجزء الامامي

> **On the front of** means 'on the front surface of sth': *The number is shown on the front of the bus.* **In front of** means 'further forward than another person or thing': *A car has stopped in front of the bus.* **At/In the front of** means 'in the most forward part inside sth': *The driver sits at the front of the bus.* Look at these sentences too: *The teacher usually stands in front of the class.* ○ *The noisy children were asked to sit at the front of the class* (= in the front seats).

3 the front [sing.] the line or area where fighting takes place in a war: *to be sent to the front* جبهة (حرب)

4 [sing.] a way of behaving that hides your true feelings: *His brave words were just a front. He was really feeling very nervous.* ستار

5 [C] (*technical*) (used when talking about the weather) a line or area where warm air and cold air meet: *A cold front is moving in from the north.* جبهة (طقس)

6 [C] a particular area of activity: *Things are difficult on the domestic front at the moment.* مَيدان

IDM **back to front** → BACK[1]

in front ahead of or further forward than sb/sth: *Some of the children ran on in front.* ○ *After three laps the Kenyan runner was in front.* قدّام، في الأمام

in front of 1 in a position further forward than but close to sb/sth: *The bus stops right in front of our house.* ○ *Don't stand in front of the television.* ○ *The book was open in front of her on the desk.* ❶ **In front of** does not mean the same as **opposite**. أمام

2 in the presence of: *I couldn't talk about that in front of my parents.* في حضور

up front (*informal*) as payment before sth is done: *I want half the money up front and half when the job is finished.* دفعة سلفاً

▶ **front** *adj* (only *before* a noun) of or at the front (1,2): *the front door, garden, room, etc.* ○ *front teeth* أماميّ

frontal /ˈfrʌntl/ *adj* (only *before* a noun) from the front: *a frontal attack* أماميّ

frontier /ˈfrʌntɪə(r); *US* frʌnˈtɪər/ *noun* **1** [C] **frontier (between A and B); frontier (with A)** the line where one country joins another; border: *We crossed the frontier between France and Italy.* ○ *France's frontier with Italy* ➲ Look at the note at **border**. حدود

2 the frontiers [plural] the border between what we know and what we do not know: *Scientific research is constantly pushing back the frontiers of our knowledge about the world.* حدود

ˌ**front ˈpage** *noun* [C] the first page of a newspaper, where the most important news is printed الصفحة الأولى

▶ ˈ**front-page** *adj* interesting or important enough to appear on the front page of a newspaper: *front-page news* مستحق للصفحة الأولى (في صحيفة)، هامّ

frost /frɒst; *US* frɔːst/ *noun* **1** [C,U] the weather conditions when the temperature falls below freezing point: *There was a hard frost last night.* ○ *ten degrees of frost* (= minus ten degrees Celsius) صقيع

2 [U] a very thin layer of little pieces of ice that is formed on surfaces when the temperature is below freezing point: *The branches of the trees were white with frost.* صقيع

▶ **frost** *verb* [T] (*especially US*) = ICE[3]

PHRV **frost over/up** to become covered with frost (2): *The window has frosted over/up.* يغطّى بالصقيع

frosted *adj* (used about glass or a window) with a special surface so you cannot see through it (زجاج) مغَبّش

frostbite /ˈfrɒstbaɪt; *US* ˈfrɔːst-/ *noun* [U] injury to the fingers, toes, etc. that is caused by very low temperatures تجمّد الأصابع

frosting /ˈfrɒstɪŋ; *US* ˈfrɔːstɪŋ/ *noun* [U] (*especially US*) = ICING

frosty /ˈfrɒsti; *US* ˈfrɔːsti/ *adj* (**frostier**; **frostiest**) **1** very cold, with frost: *a cold and frosty morning* مكسو بالصقيع: بارد جداً

2 cold and unfriendly: *a frosty welcome* (لقاء) جافّ

froth /frɒθ; *US* frɔːθ/ *noun* [U] a mass of small white bubbles on the top of a liquid, etc. زَبَد، رغوة

▸ **froth** *verb* [I] to have or produce froth: *The mad dog was frothing at the mouth.* يزْبِد، يرغي
frothy *adj* (**frothier**; **frothiest**) مزبِد، ذو رغوة

frown /fraʊn/ *verb* [I] to bring your eyebrows together so that you make lines appear on your forehead. You frown when you are angry or worried: *'You're late', he said, frowning.* يقطّب

PHRV **frown on/upon sth** to think that sth is not good; to disapprove: *Smoking is very much frowned upon these days.* يستَهْجِن

▸ **frown** *noun* [C] an act of frowning: *She read the letter quickly, a worried frown on her face.* تقطيب

froze *pt of* FREEZE

frozen /ˈfrəʊzn/ *pp of* FREEZE: *The pond is frozen. Let's go skating.* ○ *frozen vegetables* ○ *I'm frozen* (= very cold).

fruit /fruːt/ *noun* **1** [C,U] the part of a plant or tree that contains seeds and that is used as food: *Try and eat more fresh fruit and vegetables.* ○ *Marmalade is made with citrus fruit* (= oranges, lemons, grapefruit, etc.). ○ *Is a tomato a fruit or a vegetable?* ○ *fruit juice* فاكهة

> When we say 'a fruit' we mean 'a type of fruit': *Most big supermarkets sell all sorts of tropical fruits.* When we are talking about one individual piece, e.g. a single apple, pear, banana, etc. we must say 'a piece of fruit': *What would you like now? Cheese, or a piece of fruit?* It is more usual to use the uncountable form: *Would you like some fruit?*

2 [C] the part of any plant in which the seed is formed ثمرة

3 the fruits [plural] a good result or a reward for what you have done ثمرات (عمل)

fruitful /ˈfruːtfl/ *adj* producing good results; useful: *fruitful discussions* مثمِر

fruition /fruˈɪʃn/ *noun* [U] the time when a plan, etc. starts to be successful: *After months of hard work, our efforts were coming to fruition.* إثمار

fruitless /ˈfruːtləs/ *adj* producing poor or no results; unsuccessful: *a fruitless search* بلا ثمرة، عقيم

frustrate /frʌˈstreɪt; *US* ˈfrʌstreɪt/ *verb* [T] **1** to cause a person to feel angry or dissatisfied because things are not happening as he/she wants: *It's the lack of money that really frustrates him.* يُثَبِّط

2 (*formal*) to prevent sb from doing sth or sth from happening: *The rescue work has been frustrated by bad weather conditions.* يحْبِط

▸ **frustrated** *adj* angry or dissatisfied, e.g. because you cannot have or do what you want: *In the film she plays a bored, frustrated, middle-aged housewife.* ○ *He felt very frustrated at his lack of progress in learning Chinese.* خائب: محْبَط

frustrating *adj* making you angry or dissatisfied: *I spent a frustrating morning at the Passport Office.* مثبِّط، محبِط

frustration /frʌˈstreɪʃn/ *noun* [C,U] a feeling of anger or dissatisfaction, or sth that causes it: *He felt anger and frustration at not being able to help the starving children.* ○ *Every job has its frustrations.* خيبة: إحباط

fry /fraɪ/ *verb* [I,T] (*pres part* **frying**; *3rd pers sing pres* **fries**; *pt, pp* **fried** /fraɪd/) to be cooked in hot fat or oil; to cook sth in this way: *to fry an egg* ○ *a fried egg* ○ *There was a smell of frying onions in the kitchen.* ينقلي: يَقلي

ˈ**frying pan** (*US* **frypan** /ˈfraɪpæn/) *noun* [C] a flat shallow pan with a long handle that is used for frying food مقْلاة

ft (*also* **ft.**) *abbrev* = FOOT, FEET (3): *a room 10 ft by 6 ft*

fudge[1] /fʌdʒ/ *noun* [U] a soft sweet made from sugar, butter and milk, often with other things added to give flavour: *chocolate/walnut fudge* حلوى تشبه الكراميل

fudge[2] /fʌdʒ/ *verb* [I,T] (*informal*) to say or do sth in a way that is unclear or unsatisfactory, usually because you intend to mislead sb or because you want to avoid making a definite choice: *Politicians are quite adept at fudging (the issue).* يروغ، يتجنب اتخاذ قرار

fuel /ˈfjuːəl/ *noun* **1** [U] material that is burned to produce heat or power: *unleaded fuel* (= petrol without lead in it) ○ *What's the car's fuel consumption?* ○ *Our fuel bills are very high.* وقود

2 [C] a type of fuel: *I think gas is the best fuel for central heating.* وقود

▸ **fuel** *verb* [T] (fuelling; fuelled) ((*US*) fueling; fueled) to provide fuel for sth: (*figurative*) *Her interest in the Spanish language was fuelled by a visit to Spain.* يزوِّد بالوقود: يحثّ: يلهِب حماسه

fugitive /ˈfjuːdʒətɪv/ *noun* [C] a person who is running away or escaping (e.g. from the police) هارب: طريد العدالة
➲ Look at **refugee**.

fulfil (*US* **fulfill**) /fʊlˈfɪl/ *verb* [T] (fulfilling; fulfilled) **1** to perform or carry out a duty, task, etc: *Germany now fulfils a most important role within the European Union.* ينجز: يقوم بـ

2 to make sth that you wish for, or have promised, happen: *He finally fulfilled his childhood dream of becoming a farmer.* ○ *to fulfil an ambition* ○ *The Government has not yet fulfilled its promises on education.* يحقّق

3 to satisfy a need: *The local town can fulfil most of your shopping needs.* يرضي

4 to do or have what is necessary according to a contract, a rule, etc: *The conditions of entry to university in this country are quite difficult to fulfil.* يحقق، يفي

5 fulfil yourself to develop your character and

abilities fully: *She knew that she couldn't fulfil herself without first leaving home.* يُنمّي ذاته؛ يحقق شخصيته

► **fulfilled** *adj* completely satisfied and happy راضٍ

fulfilling *adj* making you feel happy and satisfied: *I found working abroad a very fulfilling experience.* مُرضٍ؛ مسرّ

fulfilment (*US* **fulfillment**) *noun* [U] **1** the act of fulfilling or state of being fulfilled: *Moving into our own home was the fulfilment of a dream.* إرضاء؛ رضى

2 the feeling of satisfaction that you have when you have done sth: *Some women find fulfilment in the home and in bringing up their children.* رضى

full /fʊl/ *adj* **1 full (of sb/sth)** holding or containing as much or as many as possible: *The bin needs emptying. It's full up.* ○ *a full bottle* ○ *I can't get anything else in my suitcase – it's full.* ○ *The bus was full so we had to wait for the next one.* ○ *'Is there any coffee left?' 'Yes, this jar's still half full.'* ○ *(figurative) The children are full of energy.* ○ *(figurative) We need a good night's sleep because we've got a full* (= busy) *day tomorrow.* مليء

2 with a lot of people or things in it: *The room was full of people.* ○ *His work was full of mistakes.* ○ *The streets were full of litter.* مملوء، مكتظّ

3 full (up) having had enough to eat and drink: *No more, thank you. I'm full (up).* شبعان

4 (only *before* a noun) complete; not leaving anything out: *I should like a full report on the accident, please.* ○ *Full details of today's TV programmes are on page 20.* ○ *For the full story, please turn to page 14.* ○ *He took full responsibility for what had happened.* ○ *Please give your full address.* كامل

5 (only *before* a noun) the highest or greatest possible: *She got full marks in her French exam.* ○ *The train was travelling at full speed when it hit the cow on the tracks.* تامّ؛ أقصى (سرعة)

6 full of sb/sth/yourself thinking or talking a lot about a subject or about yourself: *When she got back from holiday she was full of everything they had seen.* ○ *He's very full of himself* (= thinks that he is very important) *since he got that new job.* مهتمّ كليّاً بـ؛ مغترّ بنفسه

7 round in shape: *a full figure* ○ *He's quite full in the face.* (جسم) ممتلئ

8 (used about clothes) made with plenty of material: *a full skirt* فضفاض

IDM **have your hands full** → HAND[1]

in full with nothing missing; completely: *Your money will be refunded in full* (= you will get all your money back). ○ *Please write your name in full.* بالكامل

in full swing at the stage when there is a lot of activity: *When we arrived the party was already in full swing.* في ذروة النشاط

in full view (of sb/sth) in a place where you can easily be seen: *In full view of the guards, he tried to escape over the prison wall.* ○ *in full view of the house* ظاهر، بادٍ للعيان

to the full as much as possible: *to enjoy life to the full* قدر الإمكان

► **full** *adv* directly; straight: *John hit him full in the face.* مباشرة

ˌfull-ˈblown *adj* fully developed: *to have full-blown AIDS* كامل النمو، متطوّر

ˌfull ˈboard *noun* [U] (in a hotel, etc.) with all your meals ➲ Look at **half board** and **bed and breakfast**. (في فندق) إقامة مع كل الوجبات

ˌfull-ˈlength *adj* **1** (used about a picture, mirror, etc.) showing a person from head to foot (صورة) لكامل القامة

2 (used about a dress, skirt, etc.) reaching the ankles: *a full-length ball gown* (ثوب) طويل

3 not shorter than normal: *a full-length film, book, etc.* (كتاب) ذو طول عادي

ˌfull ˈmoon *noun* [sing.] the moon when it appears as a circle ❶ The opposite is a **new moon**. بدْر

ˌfull-ˈscale *adj* **1** (used about a plan, drawing, etc.) of the same size as the original object (مخطّط) بالمقياس الطبيعي

2 using every means that is available: *The police have started a full-scale murder investigation.* شامل

ˌfull ˈstop (*also* **ˌfull ˈpoint**; *especially US* **period**) *noun* [C] a mark (.) that is used when you are writing to show the end of a sentence and in some abbreviations نقطة، علامة وقوف

ˌfull-ˈtime *adj, adv* for a whole of the normal period of work: *He has a full-time job.* ○ *He works full-time.* ○ *We employ 800 full-time and 500 part-time staff.* ➲ Look at **part-time**. (عمل) دوام كامل

fully /ˈfʊli/ *adv* completely; to the highest possible degree: *John's never been fully accepted by the other members of staff.* ○ *I'm fully aware of the problem.* ○ *All our engineers are fully trained.* ○ *a fully automatic camera* كلّياً

ˌfully-ˈfledged *adj* (*US also* **full-fledged**) completely trained or completely developed: *Computer science is now a fully-fledged academic subject.* كامل النضوج

fumble /ˈfʌmbl/ *verb* [I] to use your hands in an awkward way, especially when you are looking for sth: *'It must be here somewhere', she said, fumbling in her pocket for her key.* يتلمّس بتعثّر؛ يتخبّط

fume /fjuːm/ *verb* [I] to feel or show anger: *They were nearly two hours late. By the time they arrived I was absolutely fuming.* يثور

fumes /fjuːmz/ *noun* [plural] smoke or gases that smell unpleasant and that can be harmful if you breathe them in: *Six people died in the fire when they were overcome by smoke and fumes.* دُخان؛ غازات (خانقة)

fun /fʌn/ *noun* [U] pleasure and enjoyment; an activity or a person that gives you pleasure and enjoyment: *There isn't much fun in staying at home on your own.* ○ *Staying at home on your own isn't much fun.* ○ *We had a lot of fun at the party last* *night.* ○ *The party was great fun.* ○ *Have fun!* (= enjoy yourself!) ○ *Sailing can be quite good fun if you don't mind getting wet.* ○ *He was extremely clever but he was also great fun.* بهجة؛ تسلية

Be careful. **Funny** describes something that makes you laugh or that is strange. It is not the same as **fun**: *The party was fun* (= it was enjoyable). ○ *The film was funny* (= it made us laugh).

IDM **(just) for fun/for the fun of it** (just) for amusement or pleasure; not seriously: *I don't need English for my work. I am just learning it for fun.* للتسلية

(just) in fun as a joke: *It was said in fun. They didn't mean to upset you.* للمزاح

make fun of sb/sth to laugh at sb/sth in an unkind way; to make other people do this: *The older children are always making fun of him because of his accent.* يَسْخَر

poke fun at sb/sth → POKE

function /ˈfʌŋkʃn/ *noun* [C] **1** the purpose or special duty of a person or thing: *One function of the school governors is to appoint new teachers.* ○ *The function of the heart is to pump blood through the body.* وظيفة

2 an important social event, ceremony, etc: *The princess attends hundreds of official functions every year.* حفل

▶ **function** *verb* [I] to work; to be in action: *The doctor's new appointments system doesn't seem to be functioning very well.* ○ *Only one engine was still functioning.* يعمل

functional /-ʃənl/ *adj* **1** practical and useful rather than attractive: *cheap functional furniture* عملي

2 working; being used: *The system is now fully functional.* شغّال

ˈ**function key** *noun* [C] a key (3) on a computer which is used to carry out a particular operation (في الكمبيوتر) مفتاح وظيفة

fund /fʌnd/ *noun* **1** [C] a sum of money that is collected for a particular purpose: *They contributed £30 to the disaster relief fund.* صندوق (تمويل)

2 funds [plural] money that is available and can be spent: *The government is making funds available to help pay for the storm damage.* رصيد

▶ **fund** *verb* [T] to provide a project, etc. with money: *The Channel Tunnel was not funded by government money.* يموِّل

fundamental /ˌfʌndəˈmentl/ *adj* important or basic; from which everything else develops: *There will be fundamental changes in the way the school is run.* ○ *There is a fundamental difference between your opinion and mine.* أساسي

▶ **fundamentally** /-təli/ *adv*: *The government's policy has changed fundamentally.* بشكل أساسي

fundamentals *noun* [plural] basic facts or principles أسس

ˈ**fund-raiser** *noun* [C] a person whose job is to find ways of collecting money for a charity or an organization جامع معونات ماليّة

▶ ˈ**fund-raising** *noun* [U]: *fund-raising events* (محاولة) جمع معونات مالية

funeral /ˈfjuːnərəl/ *noun* [C] a ceremony (usually in a church) for burying or burning a dead person: *The funeral will be held next week.* ○ *The mourners at the funeral were all in black.* جنازة

The body of the dead person is carried in a **coffin**, on which there are often **wreaths** of flowers. The coffin is buried in a **grave** or is burned (**cremated**).

ˈ**funeral director** *noun* [C] = UNDERTAKER

funfair /ˈfʌnfeə(r)/ *noun* [C] = FAIR³ (1)

fungus /ˈfʌŋgəs/ *noun* [C,U] (*pl.* **fungi** /-gi; -gaɪ/ or **funguses**) a plant that is not green and that does not have leaves or flowers. One type has a thick stem and a big flat top, another type is like a powder. Fungi grow on other plants, decaying wood or food, etc: *There are many kinds of edible fungi. In Britain we usually only eat the mushroom.* ○ *The roses are covered in fungus.* ➲ Look at **mould** and **toadstool**. فطر

funnel /ˈfʌnl/ *noun* [C] **1** an object that is wide at the top and narrow at the bottom, used for pouring liquid, powder, etc. into a small opening قمع

2 the metal chimney of an engine, a ship, etc. مَدْخنة (سفينة)

funny /ˈfʌni/ *adj* (**funnier**; **funniest**) **1** that makes you smile or laugh: *a funny story* ○ *He's an extremely funny person* (= he can make people laugh). ○ *I didn't think it was very funny when somebody tipped a cup of coffee over me.* مُضحك

2 strange or unusual: *Oh dear, the engine is making a funny noise.* ○ *It's funny how English people never talk on trains.* ○ *What a funny little cottage!* ○ *It's funny that they didn't phone to let us know they couldn't come.* ○ *That's funny – he was here a moment ago and now he's gone.* ○ *Can I sit down for a minute? I feel a bit funny* (= a bit ill). عجيب، غريب

▶ **funnily** /-ɪli/ *adv* **1** (used for expressing surprise at sth strange that has happened): *Funnily enough, my parents weren't at all cross about it.* مِن العجائب، من الغريب

2 in a funny way: *She's breathing very funnily.* بشكل غريب

fur /fɜː(r)/ *noun* **1** [U] the soft thick hair that covers the bodies of some animals فَرْو، فراء

2 [C,U] the skin and hair of an animal that is used for making clothes, etc.; a piece of clothing that is made from this: *These boots are lined with fur.* ○ *a fur coat* ○ *Most of the women were dressed in furs.* فَرْو، فراء

▶ **furry** /ˈfɜːri/ *adj* (**furrier**; **furriest**): *a small furry animal* ذو فَرْو

furious /ˈfjʊəriəs/ *adj* **1 furious (with sb)/(at sth)** very angry: *He was furious with her for losing the keys.* ○ *She was furious at having to catch the train home.* ⓘ The noun is **fury**. هائج، غاضب

2 very strong; violent: *A furious row has broken out over the closing of the school.* عنيف
▸ **furiously** *adv* بعنف؛ باحتداد

furnace /ˈfɜːnɪs/ *noun* [C] a large enclosed fire that is used for heating water, melting metal, burning rubbish, etc. فرن (عالٍ)

furnish /ˈfɜːnɪʃ/ *verb* [T] to put furniture in a room, house, etc: *The room was furnished with antiques.* يؤثّث
▸ **furnished** *adj* having furniture: *She's renting a furnished room in Birmingham.* ❶ The opposite is **unfurnished**. مؤثّث
furnishings *noun* [plural] the furniture, carpets, curtains, etc. in a room, house, etc. أثاث

furniture /ˈfɜːnɪtʃə(r)/ *noun* [U] the movable articles, e.g. tables, chairs, beds, etc. in a room, house or office: *modern/antique/second-hand furniture* أثاث

> Be careful. 'Furniture' is an uncountable noun: *They only got married recently and they haven't got much furniture.* If we are talking about an individual item we must say 'a piece of furniture': *The only nice piece of furniture in the room was an antique desk.*

furrow /ˈfʌrəʊ/ *noun* [C] **1** a line in a field that is made by a plough أخدود
2 a line in a person's face, especially on the forehead تجعيد

furry → FUR

further /ˈfɜːðə(r)/ *adj* **1** more distant or far; farther: *Which is further – Glasgow or Edinburgh?* أبعد
2 more; additional: *Are there any further questions?* ○ *Please let us know if you require any further information.* ○ *I have nothing further to say on the subject.* ○ *The museum is closed until further notice* (= until another announcement is made). إضافي
▸ **further** *adv* **1** at or to a greater distance in time or space; farther: *It's not safe to go any further.* ○ *The hospital is further down the road on the left.* ○ *I can't remember any further back than 1950.* أبعد (في الزمان أو المكان)
2 more; to a greater degree: *Can I have time to consider the matter further?* أكثر

> **Further** and **farther** can both be used when you are talking about distance: *Bristol is further/farther from London than Oxford is.* ○ *I jumped further/farther than you did.* In other senses only **further** can be used: *We need a further week to finish the job.*

IDM **further afield** → FAR AFIELD
further *verb* [T] (*formal*) to help sth to be successful: *to further the cause of peace* يُعين؛ يعزّز

ˌfurther eduˈcation *noun* [U] education for people who have left school (but not at a university) ➲ Look at **higher education**. تعليم إضافي (لمن غادروا المدرسة ولم يدخلوا الجامعة)

furthermore /ˌfɜːðəˈmɔː(r)/ *adv* in addition; also: *We are donating £6 million to the disaster fund. Furthermore, we shall send medical supplies immediately.* فضلاً عن ذلك

furthest /fɜːðɪst/ *adj, adv* = FARTHEST

furtive /ˈfɜːtɪv/ *adj* secret, acting as though you are trying to hide sth because you feel guilty: *a furtive glance at the letter* متستّر؛ مختلس
▸ **furtively** *adv*: *He crept furtively down the stairs and out of the front door.* بتستّر؛ خفيةً

fury /ˈfjʊəri/ *noun* [U] very great anger: *She was speechless with fury.* ❶ The adjective is **furious**. غضب عنيف

fuse[1] /fjuːz/ *noun* [C] **1** a (long) piece of rope, string, etc. that is used for lighting a bomb, etc. فتيل (القنبلة)
2 a device that makes a bomb, etc. explode at a particular time صمام تفجير (زمني)

fuse[2] /fjuːz/ *verb* [I,T] to join together: *Sadness and joy are fused in her poems.* يدمج؛ يندمج

fuse[3] /fjuːz/ *noun* [C] a small piece of wire in an electrical system, machine, etc. that melts and breaks if there is too much power. This stops the flow of electricity and prevents fire or damage: *That plug needs a 15-amp fuse.* ○ *Do you know how to change a fuse?* مصهر (الحماية دارة كهربائية)
▸ **fuse** *verb* [I,T] to stop working because a fuse[3] has melted; to make a piece of electrical equipment do this: *The lights have fused.* ○ *I've fused the lights.* يصهر (مصهر دارة كهربائية)؛ ينصهر

fuselage /ˈfjuːzəlɑːʒ; *US* ˈfjuːsəlɑːʒ/ *noun* [C] the main part of an aeroplane (not the engines, wings or tail) هيكل الطائرة

fusion /ˈfjuːʒn/ *noun* [C,U] the joining together of different things: *the fusion of two political systems* ○ *nuclear fusion* (= a method of releasing nuclear energy) اندماج؛ دمج؛ انصهار

fuss /fʌs/ *noun* **1** [sing., U] unnecessary nervous excitement or activity: *Now get on with your work without making a fuss.* ○ *What's all the fuss about?* اهتياج لاداعي له
2 [sing.] a time when people are angry: *There will be a dreadful fuss if my parents find out that I borrowed the car.* شجار؛ غضب
IDM **make, kick up, etc. a fuss (about/over sth)** to complain strongly يتشكّى
make a fuss of/over sb/sth to pay a lot of attention to sb/sth يدلّل
▸ **fuss** *verb* [I] **1 fuss (about)** to be worried or excited about small things: *Stop fussing. We're not going to be late.* يقلق
2 fuss over sb/sth to pay too much attention to sb/sth: *Stop fussing over all the details.* يفرط في العناية
IDM **not be fussed (about sb/sth)** (*informal*) not to care very much: *'Where do you want to go for lunch?' 'I'm not fussed.'* لا يبالي

fussy /ˈfʌsi/ *adj* (**fussier**; **fussiest**) **1** (used about people) giving too much attention to small details and therefore difficult to please: *He is very fussy about his food* (= there are many things which he does not eat). صعب الإرضاء

2 having too much detail or decoration: *I don't like that pattern. It's too fussy.* مفرط في الزينة أو الزخرفة

futile /'fju:taɪl; *US* -tl/ *adj* (used about an action) having no effect or result; useless: *They made a last futile attempt to make him change his mind.* عبث ؛ بلا جدوى
▶ **futility** /fju:'tɪləti/ *noun* [U]: *the futility of war* عبث

future /'fju:tʃə(r)/ *noun* **1** [sing.] the time that will come after the present: *Who knows what will happen in the future?* ○ *in the near/distant future* (= soon/not soon) ○ *in the immediate future* (= very soon) المستقبل
2 [C] what will happen to sb/sth in the time after the present: *Our children's futures depend on a good education.* ○ *The company's future does not look very hopeful.* ○ *The future of the local school is still undecided.* مستقبل
3 [U] the possibility of being successful: *I could see no future in this country so I left to work abroad.* مستقبل
4 [sing.] (*also* **future tense**) (*grammar*) the tense of a verb that expresses what will happen after the present المستقبل (في علم القواعد)
IDM **in future** from now on: *Please try to be more careful in future.* في المستقبل
▶ **future** *adj* (only *before* a noun) of or happening in the time after the present: *She met her future husband when she was still at school.* ○ *You can keep that book for future reference* (= to look at again later). ○ *What are your future plans?* مقبل؛ مستقبلي

fuzzy /'fʌzi/ *adj* (**fuzzier**; **fuzziest**) not clear: *The photo was rather fuzzy but I could just make out my mother on it.* غير واضح

Gg

G, g /dʒi:/ *noun* [C] (*pl.* **Gs**; **G's**; **g's**) the seventh letter of the English alphabet: *'Girl' begins with (a) 'G'.* الحرف السابع في الابجدية الانكليزية

g *abbrev* = GRAM(S)

gable /'geɪbl/ *noun* [C] the pointed part at the top of an outside wall between two parts of a roof الحائط المثلث للجملون

gad /gæd/ *verb* (**gadding**; **gadded**)
PHRV **gad about/around** (*informal*) to go around from one place to another in order to enjoy yourself يتنزه

gadget /'gædʒɪt/ *noun* [C] (*informal*) a small tool or machine أداة

Gaelic /'geɪlɪk/ *adj, noun* [U] **1** (of) the Celtic language and culture of Ireland لغة ايرلندا وثقافتها
2 /*also* 'gælɪk/ (of) the Celtic language and culture of Scotland لغة اسكوتلندا وثقافتها

gag /gæg/ *noun* [C] **1** a piece of cloth, etc. that is put in or over sb's mouth in order to stop him/her from talking كمامة
2 a joke or funny story نكتة
▶ **gag** *verb* [T] (**gagging**; **gagged**) to put a gag in or over sb's mouth: (*figurative*) *The new laws are an attempt to gag the press.* يكمّم؛ يخرس

gage (*US*) = GAUGE

gaiety /'geɪəti/ *noun* [U] a feeling of happiness and fun حبور

gaily → GAY

gain¹ /geɪn/ *noun* **1** [C,U] an increase in money; (a) profit or advantage: *Shares in the electricity companies have made big gains on the London stock market.* ○ *We didn't make any gain when we sold our house.* ○ *Everything he did was for personal gain.* كسب ، ربح
2 [C] an increase in size, amount or power: *a gain in weight of one kilo* ○ *The Liberal Democrat Party is expected to make gains at the next election.* ازدياد

gain² /geɪn/ *verb* **1** [T] to get or win sth (especially sth that is wanted or needed): *They managed to gain access to secret information.* ○ *He has gained an international reputation as an artist.* ○ *You need to gain more experience before you take your driving test.* يكسب؛ يفوز بِ ؛ ينال
2 [T] to get more of sth: *The train was gaining speed.* ○ *I've gained a lot of weight recently.* يزيد
3 [I] **gain by/from (doing) sth** to get an advantage from sth/from doing sth: *Many people will gain from the changes in the law.* ○ *I've got nothing to gain by staying in this job.* يستفيد
4 [I,T] (used about a clock or watch) to go too fast and show the incorrect time: *My watch gains five minutes a day.* ❶ When a clock gains we say it is **fast**. (ساعة) تقدّم
❶ The opposite for **2**, **3** and **4** is **lose**.
IDM **gain ground** to make progress; to become stronger or more popular: *The Green Party gained ground in the recent elections.* يتقدّم
PHRV **gain in sth** to get more of sth: *He's gained in confidence in the past year.* يزداد
gain on sb/sth to get closer to sb/sth that you are trying to catch يقترب من

gait /geɪt/ *noun* [sing.] the way that sb walks مِشية

gal. *abbrev* = GALLON(S)

gala /'gɑ:lə; *US* 'geɪlə/ *noun* [C] a special social or

a b c d e f g h i j k l m n o p q r s t u v w x y z

sporting occasion: *a gala performance at the National Theatre* ○ *a swimming gala* احتفال ؛ مهرجان

galaxy /ˈɡæləksi/ *noun* [C] (*pl.* **galaxies**) a large group of stars and planets in outer space مجرّة

gale /ɡeɪl/ *noun* [C] a very strong wind: *Several trees blew down in the gale.* ➲ Look at the note at **storm**. ريح عاتية

gallant /ˈɡælənt/ *adj* (*formal*) **1** brave: *a gallant soldier* شجاع ، جسور

2 (used about men) polite to and showing special respect for women لطيف مع النساء

▶ **gallantry** /ˈɡæləntri/ *noun* [U] **1** bravery, especially in a dangerous situation شجاعة ، جسارة

2 polite behaviour towards women (by men) لطف مع النساء

gall bladder /ɡɔːl blædə(r)/ *noun* [C] an organ that is attached to the liver that stores and releases bile. المرارة، الحويصلة الصفراوية

gallery /ˈɡæləri/ *noun* [C] (*pl.* **galleries**) **1** a building or room where works of art are shown to the public: *an art gallery* صالة عرض

2 the highest level of seating in a theatre, etc. شرفة عليا في مسرح

3 a raised area around the sides or at the back of a large hall. People can sit in the gallery and watch what is happening in the hall: *the public gallery* شرفة

⚷ **gallon** /ˈɡælən/ *noun* [C] (*abbr* **gal.**) a measure of liquid; 4.5 litres. There are 8 pints in a gallon. ❶ An American gallon is the same as 3.8 litres. غالون

gallop /ˈɡæləp/ *verb* [I] (used about a horse or a rider) to go at the fastest speed, when the horse's four feet all leave the ground together (الحصان) يعدو

▶ **gallop** *noun* [sing., C] the fastest speed of a horse, etc.; a time when you ride at this speed: [C]: *They went for a gallop over the fields.* عَدْو (الحصان)

gallows /ˈɡæləʊz/ *noun* [C] (*pl.* **gallows**) a wooden framework on which criminals are hanged مشنقة

galore /ɡəˈlɔː(r)/ *adj* (only *after* a noun) in large numbers: *There will be prizes galore at our children's party on Saturday.* بغزارة

⚷ **gamble** /ˈɡæmbl/ *verb* [I,T] to risk money on the result of a card game, horse race, etc. يقامر

PHR V **gamble on sth/on doing sth** to act in the hope that sth will happen although it is possible that it will not: *I wouldn't gamble on the weather staying fine.* يراهن

▶ **gamble** *noun* [C] something you do that is a risk (i.e. you might win sth but you might also lose): *Setting up this business was a bit of a gamble.* مقامرة ؛ مجازفة

IDM **take a gamble (on sth)** to take a chance (on sth or on sth happening) يراهن

gambler /ˈɡæmblə(r)/ *noun* [C] مقامر

gambling /ˈɡæmblɪŋ/ *noun* [U] ميْسِر ، مقامرة

⚷ **game**[1] /ɡeɪm/ *noun* **1** [C] a form of play or sport with rules; a time when you play it: *Let's have a game of chess.* ○ *a game of football, rugby, tennis, etc.* ○ *'Monopoly' is still a very popular game.* ○ *Our next game is against the Oxford Tigers.* ○ *Tonight's game is between Holland and Italy.* ○ *What an exciting game!* ○ *The game ended in a draw.* لعبة

2 [C] a section of a match of tennis, etc: *Roddick won the first game of the second set.* لعبة

3 games [plural] an (international) athletics or sports competition ألعاب ؛ مباريات

4 [C] the set of equipment that you need in order to play a particular (indoor) game: *We usually buy a new board game at Christmas.* أدوات اللعب

5 [C, usually sing.] (*informal*) a way of behaving according to a secret plan: *I wasn't sure what their game was but I didn't trust them.* حيلة

IDM **give the game away** to tell a person sth that you are trying to keep secret: *It was the expression on her face that gave the game away.* يفشي

game[2] /ɡeɪm/ *adj* (used about a person) ready and willing to do sth new, unusual, difficult, etc: *I have never been sailing but I'm game to try.* مستعد ؛ جَريء

game[3] /ɡeɪm/ *noun* [U] wild animals or birds that are hunted for sport or food: *Shooting game is popular in Scotland.* ○ *big game* (= lions, tigers, etc. that are hunted) الطرائد

ˈ**gamekeeper** /ˈɡeɪmkiːpə(r)/ *noun* [C] a person who looks after game[3] on private land حارس الطرائد في أملاك ريفيّة

ˈ**game show** *noun* [C] a television programme in which people play games or answer questions to win prizes برنامج ألعاب ومسابقات

gander /ˈɡændə(r)/ *noun* [C] a male goose ذكر الإوَز

gang /ɡæŋ/ *noun* [C, with sing. or pl. verb] **1** an organized group of criminals: *The police are looking for the gang that committed the robbery.* عصابة

2 a group of young people, especially young men, who sometimes cause trouble: *The phone box was vandalized by a gang of youths.* جماعة شبان عابثين

3 a group of prisoners, building workers, etc. who work together as a team فريق ، جماعة

4 (*informal*) a group of (young) friends: *The whole gang is here tonight.* مجموعة اصحاب ؛ شلّة

▶ **gang** *verb* (*informal*)

PHR V **gang up on sb** to join together with other people in order to act against sb: *She's upset because she says the other kids are ganging up on her.* يتحزّب ضد

gangrene /ˈɡæŋɡriːn/ *noun* [U] the decay of a part of the body because the blood supply to it has been stopped موات (غنغرينا)

gangster /ˈɡæŋstə(r)/ *noun* [C] a member of a gang of criminals رجل عصابات

gangway /ˈɡæŋweɪ/ *noun* [C] **1** a movable

bridge that people use for getting on or off a ship معبَر (جسر بين السفينة والساحل)
2 (*Brit*) a passage that you can walk along between two rows of seats ممر (بين صفّي مقاعد)

gaol, gaoler (*Brit*) = JAIL, JAILER

gap /gæp/ *noun* [C] **a gap (in/between sth)**
1 an empty space in sth or between two things: *The sheep got out through a gap in the fence.* فجْوة
2 an absence of sth; a space where sth should be: *There were several gaps in his story.* ○ *I think our new product should fill a gap in the market.* ○ *Her husband's death left a big gap in her life.* ثغرة
3 a period of time that is not filled or when you are not doing what you normally do: *I returned to teaching after a gap of about five years.* ○ *a gap in the conversation* فترة (انقطاع او صمْت)
4 a difference between people or their ideas: *The gap between the rich and the poor is getting wider.* ○ *the generation gap* (= the difference in opinions between parents and their children) فارق
IDM **bridge a/the gap** → BRIDGE[1]

gape /geɪp/ *verb* [I] **1** to stare at sb/sth with your mouth open يَفْغَر (فمه)
2 to be or become wide open: *There was a gaping hole in the wall after the explosion.* ينفتح

gapper /ˈgæpə(r)/ *noun* [C] a young person who is spending a year working or travelling after leaving school and before going to university طالب يقضي سنة قبل الجامعة في العمل أو السَّفر

ˈ**gap year** *noun* [C] a year that a young person spends working and/or travelling, often between leaving school and starting university: *I'm planning to take a gap year and go backpacking in India.* سنة خارج الدراسة

garage /ˈgærɑːʒ; ˈgærɪdʒ; *US* gəˈrɑːʒ/ *noun* [C]
1 a building where cars, etc. are kept: *The house has a double garage* (= with space for two cars). مرْآب (للسيارة)، كَراج
2 a place where you can have your car serviced or repaired. It may also sell petrol, etc: *a garage mechanic* ➲ Look at **petrol station**. مَشْغَل (للسيارات)، ورشة تصليح

ˌ**garage** ˈ**rock** *noun* [U] a type of rock music played with a lot of energy, often by musicians who are not professionals نوع صاخب من موسيقى الروك للهواة

garbage /ˈgɑːbɪdʒ/ *noun* [U] (*especially US*) = RUBBISH

ˈ**garbage can** *noun* [C] (*US*) = DUSTBIN

garbled /ˈgɑːbld/ *adj* (used about a message, story, etc.) difficult to understand; not clear مشوّش

garden /ˈgɑːdn/ *noun* [C] **1** (*US* **yard**) a piece of land (usually near a house) where flowers and vegetables are grown, usually with a piece of grass (lawn): *Let's have lunch in the garden.* ○ *the back/front garden* ○ *garden flowers* ○ *garden chairs* (= for using in the garden) ➲ Look at the note at **yard**. حديقة

garden equipment

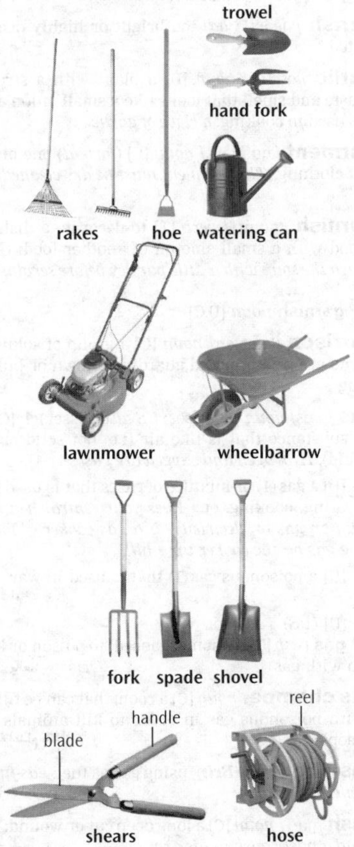

2 gardens [plural] a public park: *the Botanical Gardens* حديقة عامة
▸ **garden** *verb* [I] to work in a garden: *She's been gardening all afternoon.* يعمل في الحديقة
gardener /ˈgɑːdnə(r)/ *noun* [C] a person who works in a garden as a job or for pleasure: *They're keen gardeners.* جَنائني
gardening /ˈgɑːdnɪŋ/ *noun* [U] looking after a garden: *I'm going to do some gardening this afternoon.* ○ *gardening gloves* (= used when you are working in a garden) بستنة

ˈ**garden centre** *noun* [C] a place where plants, seeds, gardening equipment, etc. are sold محل لبيع لوازم البستنة

ˈ**garden party** *noun* [C] (*pl.* **garden parties**) a formal social event that takes place outside (usually in a large garden) on a summer afternoon حفلة في حديقة

a b c d e f g h i j k l m n o p q r s t u v w x y z

gargle /ˈɡɑːɡl/ *verb* [I] to wash your throat with a liquid (which you do not swallow) يتغرغر

garish /ˈɡeərɪʃ/ *adj* too bright or highly decorated (لون) صارخ

garlic /ˈɡɑːlɪk/ *noun* [U] a plant with a strong taste and smell that looks like a small onion and is used in cooking: *a clove of garlic* ثوم

garment /ˈɡɑːmənt/ *noun* [C] (*formal*) one piece of clothing: *This garment must be dry-cleaned.* رداء

garnish /ˈɡɑːnɪʃ/ *verb* [T] to decorate a dish of food with a small amount of another food: *Garnish the soup with a little parsley before serving* يزيّن

▸ **garnish** *noun* [U,C] مزين

garrison /ˈɡærɪsn/ *noun* [C] a group of soldiers who are living in and guarding a town or building حامية

gas /ɡæs/ *noun* (*pl.* gases; *US also* gasses) **1** [C,U] a substance that is like air (i.e. not solid or liquid): *Hydrogen and oxygen are gases.* غاز

2 [U] a gas (1) or mixture of gases that is used for heating, cooking, etc: *Does your central heating run on gas or electricity?* ○ *a gas cooker* ○ *Turn the gas on the cooker up a bit!* غاز

3 [U] a poisonous gas (1) that is used in war غاز سامّ

4 [U] (*US*) = PETROL

▸ **gas** *verb* [T] (gassing; gassed) to poison or kill sb with gas يسمّم بالغاز

ˈ**gas chamber** *noun* [C] a room that can be filled with poisonous gas in order to kill animals or people غرفة إعدام بالغاز

ˌ**gas-ˈfired** *adj* (*Brit*) using gas as fuel: *gas-fired central heating* يعمل بالغاز

gash /ɡæʃ/ *noun* [C] a long deep cut or wound: *He had a nasty gash in his arm.* جرح بليغ

▸ **gash** *verb* [T] to make a long deep cut or wound يجرح جرحاً بليغاً

ˈ**gas mask** *noun* [C] an apparatus that you wear over your face to protect you against poisonous gas قناع الغاز

ˈ**gas meter** *noun* [C] an instrument that measures the amount of gas that you use عدّاد الغاز

gasoline (*also* **gasolene**) /ˈɡæsəliːn/ *noun* [U] (*US*) = PETROL

gasp /ɡɑːsp; *US* ɡæsp/ *verb* **1** [I] to breathe quickly and noisily (e.g. when you have been running fast): *At the end of the race some of the runners were gasping for breath.* يشهق

2 [I] **gasp (at sth)** to breathe in suddenly and noisily because you are surprised or in pain: *She gasped in surprise as she read the letter.* يشهق

3 [T] **gasp sth (out)** to say sth while you are finding it difficult to breathe: *'I can't go on,' he gasped, 'I've got to sit down.'* يتكلم لاهثاً

▸ **gasp** *noun* [C] a quick breath (when you are surprised, in pain, etc.): *Suddenly she gave a gasp of surprise.* شهيق

ˈ**gas station** *noun* [C] (*US*) = PETROL STATION

gastronomic /ˌɡæstrəˈnɒmɪk/ *adj* connected with (good) food متذوق الطعام الفاخر؛ متعلّق بفاخر الطعام

gate /ɡeɪt/ *noun* [C] **1** a movable structure (like a door) that closes an opening in a wall, fence, hedge, etc: *Please keep the garden gate closed.* بوّابة

2 (*also* ˈ**gateway**) an opening in a wall, fence, hedge, etc. that is closed by a gate (1): *Drive through the gates and you'll find the car park on the right.* مدخل ذو بوّابة

3 an entrance or exit at an airport: *Lufthansa Flight 139 to Berlin is now boarding at gate 16.* بوّابة (في مطار)

gateau /ˈɡætəʊ; *US* ɡæˈtəʊ/ *noun* [C] (*pl.* **gateaux** or **gateaus**) a large cake that is usually decorated with cream, fruit, etc. كاتو/جاتو (قطعة حلوى مزينة)

ˈ**gatecrash** /ˈɡeɪtkræʃ/ *verb* [I,T] to go to a private party without being invited يحضر حفلاً بدون دعوة

▸ ˈ**gatecrasher** *noun* [C] طفيلي، ضيف غير مدعو

ˈ**gateway** /ˈɡeɪtweɪ/ *noun* [C] **1** = GATE (2)

2 [sing.] **gateway to sth** the place through which you must pass in order to get to somewhere else: *The port of Dover is England's gateway to Europe.* ○ (*figurative*) *A good education can be the gateway to success.* معبر: ممر

gather /ˈɡæðə(r)/ *verb* **1** [I,T] **gather round (sb/sth)**; **gather sb/sth round (sb/sth)** (used about people) to come together in a group; to make people come together: *A crowd soon gathered at the scene of the accident.* ○ *The children were gathered in a group around the teacher's desk.* يتجمّع: يجمع

2 [T] **gather sth (together/up)** to bring many things together; to collect: *They gathered up all their picnic things and set off home.* ○ *They have gathered together a lot of information on the subject.* ○ *I need some time to gather my thoughts before I can give you an answer.* يجمع

3 [T] to collect plants, fruits, etc. يجمع

4 [T] to understand or find out sth (from sb/sth): *I gather from your letter that you have several years' experience of this kind of work.* ○ *'She's been very ill recently.' 'So I gather.'* يفهم

5 [T] to pull material together into small folds and sew it: *a gathered skirt* يكشكش

6 [I,T] to become greater or to make greater; to increase: *The train is gathering speed.* ○ *In the gathering darkness it was hard to see the ball.* يزداد: يزيد

▸ **gathering** *noun* [C] a time when people come together; a meeting: *a family gathering* اجتماع

gaudy /ˈɡɔːdi/ *adj* (**gaudier**; **gaudiest**) too bright or highly decorated (لون) صارخ: مفرط في البهرجة

gauge (*US also* **gage**) /ɡeɪdʒ/ *noun* [C] **1** an instrument for measuring the amount of sth: *a fuel gauge on a car* (= to show how much petrol is left) معيار، مقياس

2 the distance between the rails on a railway: *a narrow-gauge railway* عرض السكة الحديدية

3 a fact that you can use to judge a situation, sb's feelings, etc. قرينة، دليل

▸ **gauge** *verb* [T] **1** to measure sth يقيس

2 to judge a situation, sb's feelings, etc: *It was difficult to gauge the mood of the audience.* يقدّر

gaunt /gɔːnt/ *adj* (used about a person) very thin because of hunger, illness, etc. هزيل

gauze /gɔːz/ *noun* [U] thin net-like material (often used for covering wounds) شاش

gave *pt* of GIVE

gawp /gɔːp/ *verb* [I] (*informal*) to look or stare (at sb/sth) in a stupid way (with your mouth open) يفغر (فمه)

gay /ɡeɪ/ *adj* **1** sexually attracted to people of the same sex; homosexual ℹ The noun is **gayness**. لوطي

2 (*old-fashioned*) happy and full of fun ℹ The noun is **gaiety**. جَذِل، مَرِح

▸ **gaily** /ˈɡeɪli/ *adv* in a gay (2) manner بجَذَل : بمَرَح

gay *noun* [C] a person, especially a man, who is sexually attracted to people of the same sex; a homosexual اللواط

gaze /ɡeɪz/ *verb* [I] to look steadily for a long time: *She sat at the window gazing silently into space.* يحدّق

▸ **gaze** *noun* [sing.] a long steady look: *She kept her gaze fixed on the man in the front row.* تحديق

GB /ˌdʒiː ˈbiː/ *abbrev* = GREAT BRITAIN

GCSE /ˌdʒiː siː es ˈiː/ *abbrev* (*Brit*) General Certificate of Secondary Education; an examination that schoolchildren in England, Wales and Northern Ireland take when they are about sixteen. They often take GCSEs in five or more subjects. For Scottish examinations, look at SCE. شهادة التعليم الثانوي العام

gear /ɡɪə(r)/ *noun* **1** [C] a set of wheels that fit into another set in order to pass power from one part of a machine to another, e.g. from a car's engine to its wheels: *A car has four (or five) forward gears and a reverse.* مُسنّنات (لنقل الحركة)

2 [U] a particular position of the gears (in a car, etc.) وضع المسننات (في سيارة)

> A car can be **in** or **out of** gear. You use a **low** gear (**first** gear) when you first start moving and then **change** gear as you go faster. For the fastest speeds you use **top** gear.

3 [U] equipment or clothing that you need for a particular activity, etc: *camping gear* معدّات

4 [sing.] (in compounds) an instrument or part of a machine that is used for a particular purpose: *the landing gear of an aeroplane* جهاز او جزء آلة

▸ **gear** *verb*

PHR V **gear sth to/towards sth** (often passive) to make sth suitable for a particular purpose: *There is a special course geared towards the older learner.* مجهز لـ ، مصمَّم لـ

gear up (for sb/sth); gear sb/sth up (for sb/sth) to get ready or to make sb/sth ready: *I was all geared up for the party but it was cancelled at the last minute.* يَستَعِدّ : يعِدّ

gearbox /ˈɡɪəbɒks/ *noun* [C] the metal case that contains the gears (1) of a car, etc. علبة مسنّنات

gearhead /ˈɡɪəhed/ *noun* [C] (*informal*) a person who is very enthusiastic about cars or new technical devices and equipment مولع بالسيّارت أو غيرها من التقنيات

ˈgear lever (*US* **ˈgear shift**) *noun* [C] a stick that is used for changing gear (2) (in a car, etc.) مبدِّل السرعة (في سيارة) : "الفيتيس"

gee /dʒiː/ *interj* (*US*) (used for expressing surprise, pleasure, etc.): *Gee, I'm sorry. I didn't know you'd been ill.* تعبير عن الدهشة أو السرور

geese *pl.* of GOOSE

Geiger counter /ˈɡaɪɡə kaʊntə(r)/ *noun* [C] a device for detecting and measuring radioactive substances عدّاد غايغر

gel /dʒel/ *noun* [C,U] (often in compounds) a thick substance like jelly that is between a liquid and a solid: *hair/shower gel* جل، هلام

gelignite /ˈdʒelɪɡnaɪt/ *noun* [U] a substance that is used for making explosions مادة متفجرة

gem /dʒem/ *noun* [C] **1** a jewel or precious stone جَوْهرة

2 a person or thing that has great value جَوْهرة (إنسان أو شيء)

Gemini /ˈdʒemɪnaɪ/ *noun* [C,U] the third sign of the zodiac, the Twins; a person who was born under this sign برج التوأمين، الجوزاء

Gen. *abbrev* = GENERAL

gender /ˈdʒendə(r)/ *noun* [C,U] **1** (*formal*) the classification of people into two sexes: male and female جنس

2 (*grammar*) (in some languages) the division of nouns, pronouns, etc. into different classes, (e.g. masculine, feminine, neuter); one of these divisions: *There are three genders in German.* ○ *In French the adjective must agree with the noun in number and gender.* المذكر والمؤنث

gene /dʒiːn/ *noun* [C] one of the parts of a cell of a living thing which decide its development. Genes are passed from parents to children. مُوَرِّثة (في علم الوراثة)، جينة حاملة الصفة الوراثية

general[1] /ˈdʒenrəl/ *adj* **1** affecting all or most people, places, things, etc: *Fridges were once a luxury, but now they are in general use.* ○ *That is a matter of general interest.* ○ *The general feeling is that the situation is improving* (= most people think so). ○ *the general public* (= most ordinary people) عامّ

2 (only *before* a noun) not limited to, or describing, one particular part; not detailed: *Your general health is very good.* ○ *The introduction gives you a general idea of what the book is about.*

○ *Let's talk in general terms at first and then get down to details.* عام

3 not limited to one subject or area of study; not specialized: *Children need a good general education.* ○ *The quiz tests your general knowledge.* ○ *a general hospital* عام

4 (often in compounds) with responsibility for the whole of an organization: *The Secretary General of the United Nations* ○ *a general manager* عام

IDM in general in most cases; usually: *In general, standards of hygiene are good.* بشكل عامّ

general[2] /ˈdʒenrəl/ *noun* [C] (*abbr* **Gen.**) an army officer of very high rank: *General Roberts* فريق (ضابط عالٍ في الجيش)

ˌgeneral anaesˈthetic *noun* [C,U] a substance that is given to a patient in hospital before an operation so that he/she becomes unconscious and does not feel any pain ➲ Look at **local anaesthetic**. تخدير عامّ

ˌGeneral Cerˌtificate of ˌSecondary Eduˈcation = GCSE

ˌgeneral eˈlection *noun* [C] an election in which all the voters in a country choose their national parliament انتخابات عامّة

generalize (*also* **generalise**) /ˈdʒenrəlaɪz/ *verb* [I] **1 generalize (about sth) (from sth)** to form an opinion using only a small amount of information: *You can't generalize about English food from only two meals.* يعمّم

2 generalize (about sth) to make a general statement about sth and not look at the details: *You're generalizing, but every case is different.* يعمّم

▸ **generalization** (*also* **generalisation**) /ˌdʒenrəlaɪˈzeɪʃn; *US* -lɪˈz-/ *noun* **1** [U] the act of generalizing تعميم

2 [C] a general statement about sth that does not consider details عمومي

generally /ˈdʒenrəli/ *adv* **1** usually: *She generally cycles to work.* عادة

2 by most people: *He is generally considered to be a good doctor.* لدى أكثر الناس

3 in a general sense, without looking at the details: *Generally speaking, houses in America are bigger than houses in this country.* بشكل عمومي

ˌgeneral pracˈtitioner *noun* [C] = GP

generate /ˈdʒenəreɪt/ *verb* [T] **1** to produce power, heat, electricity, etc. يولّد

2 to cause sth to exist: *I think this new product will generate a lot of income for the company.* يولّد

generation /ˌdʒenəˈreɪʃn/ *noun* **1** [U] the act of generating: *the generation of electricity by water power* توليد

2 [C] a single stage in a family history: *This photograph shows three generations of my family* (= children, parents and grandparents). جيل (في اسرة)

3 [C] all the people in a group or country who were born at about the same time: *My grandmother's generation grew up without electricity or running water.* ○ *future generations* جيل من الناس

Generation is used in the singular with either a singular or plural verb: *The younger generation only seem/seems to be interested in money.*

4 [C] a period of about 25 or 30 years (i.e. the time that a person takes to become an adult): *A generation ago foreign travel was still only possible for a few people.* جيل (زمن)

the geneˈration gap *noun* [sing.] the difference in behaviour, and lack of understanding, between young people and older people فرق بين الأجيال

generator /ˈdʒenəreɪtə(r)/ *noun* [C] a machine that produces electricity مولّد (كهرباء)

generosity /ˌdʒenəˈrɒsəti/ *noun* [U] the quality of being generous كرم

generous /ˈdʒenərəs/ *adj* **1** willing to give more money, help, etc. than is usual or necessary: *It was very generous of your parents to lend us all that money.* كريم

2 larger than usual: *You get very generous portions in that restaurant.* اكبر من المعتاد

▸ **generously** *adv*: *Please give generously.* بسخاء

genetic /dʒəˈnetɪk/ *adj* connected with genes or genetics: *The disease is caused by a genetic defect.* وراثي

▸ **genetically** /-kli/ *adv* بالوراثة

geˌnetically ˈmodified *adj* (*abbr* **GM**) (used about food, plants, etc.) that has been grown from cells whose genes have been changed in an artificial way معدّل جينياً

geˌnetic engiˈneering *noun* [U] changes made by scientists in the genetic structure of plants and animals هندسة وراثية

genetics /dʒəˈnetɪks/ *noun* [U] the scientific study of the way that the development of living things is controlled by features that have been passed on from parents to children ➲ Look at **gene**. علم الوراثة

genial /ˈdʒiːniəl/ *adj* (used about a person) pleasant and friendly دَمِث

genitals /ˈdʒenɪtlz/ *noun* [plural] (*formal*) the external sex organs الاعضاء التناسلية الظاهرة

▸ **genital** /ˈdʒenɪtl/ *adj* تناسلي

genius /ˈdʒiːniəs/ *noun* (*pl.* **geniuses**) **1** [U] very great and unusual ability: *Shakespeare's tragedies show true genius.* عبقرية

2 [C] a person who has very great and unusual ability, especially in a particular subject: *Einstein was a mathematical genius.* عبقري

3 [sing.] **a genius for (doing) sth** great natural ability for (doing) sth: *Our teacher had a genius for explaining difficult things in a simple way.* عبقرية

genocide /ˈdʒenəsaɪd/ *noun* [U] the murder of a nation or race إفناء أمة

genome /ˈdʒiːnəʊm/ *noun* [C] the complete set of genes in a cell or living thing: *the decoding of the human genome* مجين: مجموعة المورثات

genre /ˈʒɒnrə/ *noun* [C] a particular style or type, especially of works of art or literature: *What are the features of the novel as a genre?* نوع ادبي او فنّي

gent /dʒent/ *noun* **1** [C] (*informal*) gentleman رجل مهذّب

2 a/the Gents [sing.] (*Brit informal*) a public toilet for men ➲ Look at the note at **toilet**. مراحيض عامة للرجال

genteel /dʒenˈtiːl/ *adj* paying great (perhaps too much) attention to polite manners مهذّب (أحياناً بإفراط)

▸ **gentility** /dʒenˈtɪləti/ *noun* [U] تهذيب: نُبل

gentle /ˈdʒentl/ *adj* **1** (used about people) kind; calm; touching or treating people or things in a careful way so that they are not hurt: *He was a gentle, patient man who loved playing with his grandchildren.* ○ *'I'll try and be as gentle as I can', said the dentist.* لطيف

2 not rough or violent: *You should be able to take some gentle exercise next week.* ○ *It's just a gentle* (= not steep) *climb to the top of the hill.* خفيف

▸ **gentleness** *noun* [U] لُطف، رقة

gently /ˈdʒentli/ *adv*: *He touched her gently on the shoulder.* ○ *The beach slopes gently down to the sea.* بلُطف: بميل خفيف

gentleman /ˈdʒentlmən/ *noun* [C] (*pl.* **gentlemen** /-mən/) **1** a man who is polite and who behaves well towards other people: *He is a real gentleman.* مهذّب

2 (*formal*) (used when speaking to or about a man or men in a polite way): *Ladies and gentlemen!* (e.g. at the beginning of a speech) ○ *Mrs Flinn, there is a gentleman here to see you.* السيد (كلمة مؤدبة عند الحديث مع رجل او عنه)

3 (*old-fashioned*) a rich man with a high social position: *He likes to think of himself as a country gentleman.* وجيه

ℹ We use **lady** when we are talking about a woman.

genuine /ˈdʒenjuɪn/ *adj* **1** a person or thing that is genuine is exactly what he/she/it seems to be; real: *He thought that he had bought a genuine Rolex watch but it was a cheap fake.* ○ *There are only three genuine Scotsmen in the team.* أصليّ

2 (used about a person or his/her feelings or behaviour) honest; real: *She seems genuine enough but can I trust her?* صادق، حقيقي

▸ **genuinely** *adv*: *I'm genuinely interested in a career in teaching.* بصِدْق

geography /dʒiˈɒɡrəfi/ *noun* [U] **1** the study of the countries of the world, of their natural and physical features and of the cities, industries, etc. that have been made by man جغرافيا

2 the way in which the features of a particular country or place are arranged: *We're studying the geography of Asia.* تضاريس

▸ **geographer** /dʒiˈɒɡrəfə(r)/ *noun* [C] a student of or expert in geography جغرافي

geographic /ˌdʒiːəˈɡræfɪk/ (*also* **geographical** /-ɪkl/) *adj* جغرافي

geographically /-kli/ *adv* جغرافياً

geology /dʒiˈɒlədʒi/ *noun* [U] the study of rocks and soil, and of their development جيولوجيا

▸ **geological** /ˌdʒiːəˈlɒdʒɪkl/ *adj* جيولوجي

geologist /dʒiˈɒlədʒɪst/ *noun* [C] a student of or expert in geology جيولوجي

geometry /dʒiˈɒmətri/ *noun* [U] the study in mathematics of lines, shapes, curves, etc. هندسة

▸ **geometric** /ˌdʒiːəˈmetrɪk/ (*also* **geometrical** /-ɪkl/) *adj* **1** of geometry هندسي

2 consisting of regular shapes and lines: *a geometric design/pattern* منظّم

geometrically /-kli/ *adv* بشكل هندسي

geranium /dʒəˈreɪniəm/ *noun* [C] a garden plant with red, pink or white flowers غرنوقي، إبرة الراعي

geriatrics /ˌdʒeriˈætrɪks/ *noun* [U] the medical treatment of very old people علم المسنّين

▸ **geriatric** *adj*: *a geriatric hospital* خاص بالمسنّين

germ /dʒɜːm/ *noun* **1** [C] a very small living thing that causes disease. Germs can only be seen with a microscope: *This disinfectant kills most germs.* ➲ Look at **bacteria** and **virus**. جرثوم

2 [sing.] **the germ of sth** the beginning of sth that may develop: *the germ of an idea* بذرة

German measles /ˌdʒɜːmən ˈmiːzlz/ (*also* **rubella**) *noun* [U] a mild disease that causes red spots all over the body. It may damage an unborn baby if the mother catches it. الحصبة الألمانية

germinate /ˈdʒɜːmɪneɪt/ *verb* [I,T] (used about a seed of a plant) to start growing; to cause a seed to do this تنبت البذرة: يستنبت

▸ **germination** /ˌdʒɜːmɪˈneɪʃn/ *noun* [U] إنبات

gerund /ˈdʒerənd/ *noun* [C] (*grammar*) a noun, ending in -ing, that has been made from a verb: *In the sentence 'His hobby is collecting stamps', 'collecting' is a gerund.* مصدر مشتق من فعل في الإنكليزية

gesticulate /dʒeˈstɪkjuleɪt/ *verb* [I] to make movements with your hands and arms in order to express sth يلوّح بيديه، يومئ

gesture /ˈdʒestʃə(r)/ *noun* [C] **1** a movement of the hand, head, etc. that expresses sth: *The driver of the car in front made a rude gesture and drove off.* تلويح: إيماءة

2 something that you do that shows other people what you think or feel: *It would be a nice gesture to invite the neighbours in for a meal.* لفتة

▸ **gesture** *verb* [I,T] to point at sth, to make a sign to sb: *She asked them if they were going and gestured towards the door.* يشير

get /ɡet/ *verb* (*pres part* **getting**; *pt* **got** /ɡɒt/; *pp* **got**; *US* **gotten** /ˈɡɒtn/) **1** [T] **have/has got** to have sth: *Have you got a bike?* يملك

2 [I] to become: *It's getting dark.* ○ *She got angry.* يصبح

3 [T] to receive or obtain sth: *I got a letter from my sister.* ○ *What did you get for your birthday?* ○ *He went shopping and got a suit.* ○ *I got a shock when I saw the price.* ○ *She got a job in a travel agency.* ○ *You get a wonderful view from that window.* ○ *I'll do it if I get the time.* يحصل على

4 [T] to fetch or collect sth: *Go and get me a pen, please.* ○ *I'll get the children from school today.* ○ *The police have got* (= caught) *the gang who carried out the robbery.* يجلب

5 [T] to hear or understand sth: *I'm sorry, I didn't get that. Could you repeat it?* يدرك

6 [T] to catch a disease: *She got malaria in Africa.* يصاب (بمرض)

7 [T] to use a form of transport: *I didn't walk – I got the bus.* يركب (في وسيلة نقل)

8 [I] to move somewhere; to reach a place: *We got to Dover at about 10.* ➲ Look at **get in**, **on**, etc. يصل إلى (مكان)

9 [T] to cause sth to be in a particular place: *We couldn't get the piano upstairs.* ينقل إلى

10 [T] to prepare sth; to make sb/sth ready: *He got the breakfast.* يهيئ

11 [I] (used with a past participle) to do sth that you are responsible for: *I'm just getting dressed.* ○ *They've got divorced.* يقوم بـ؛ ينجز

12 [I] to be in a certain situation: *He's got into trouble with the police.* يوجد (في حالة ما)

13 [I] (used in a similar way to the passive) to have sth happen to you: *She got bitten by a dog.* يحصل له

14 [T] to cause sb/sth to do sth or to happen: *I got him to agree to the plan.* ○ *I can't get the television to work.* ○ *She finally got the book finished.* ❶ Note that we also use **get** when we arrange for somebody else to do something: *You must get the car serviced every 10 000 miles* (= at a garage). يتوصل إلى

15 [I] to have the opportunity to do sth: *Did you get to see the Rembrandt exhibition?* يتاح له

IDM **be getting on for ...** to be approaching a certain time or age: *I'm not sure how old he is but he must be getting on for 50.* يقترب من

get somewhere/nowhere (with sb/sth) to make some progress/no progress: *I'm getting nowhere with my research.* يتقدم

❶ For other idioms containing **get**, look at the noun and adjective entries, e.g. for **get rid of** look at **rid**.

PHR V **get about/around** to move or travel to and from many places: *Australia this week, Japan next week – you certainly get around!* يسافر كثيراً

get about/around/round (used about news, a story, etc.) to spread; to become known by many people ينتشر

get sth across (to sb) to succeed in making people understand sth: *The party failed to get its policies across to the voters.* يقنع؛ يفهم

get ahead to progress and be successful in sth, especially a career ينجح، يتقدم

get along → GET ON

get around 1 → GET ABOUT/AROUND

2 → GET ABOUT/AROUND/ROUND

get around sb → GET ROUND/AROUND SB

get around sth → GET ROUND/AROUND STH

get around to sth/doing sth → GET ROUND/AROUND TO STH/DOING STH

get at sb to say unkind or critical things to sb ينتقد

get at sb/sth to succeed in reaching sb/sth: *The pen fell down between my desk and the wall and I couldn't get at it.* يصل الى

get at sth (used only in the continuous tenses) to suggest sth indirectly; to mean sth but not to state it directly: *I'm not quite sure what you're getting at – am I doing something wrong?* يوحي بـ

get away (from...) to succeed in leaving or escaping from sb or a place: *He kept talking to me and I couldn't get away from him.* ○ *The thieves got away in a stolen car.* يفلت من؛ يهرب

get away with sth/with doing sth to do sth bad and not be punished for it: *He lied but he got away with it.* ○ *I don't know how they get away with charging such high prices.* يفلت من العقاب

get back to return to the place where you live or work: *When did you get back from Italy?* يعود

get sth back to be given sth that you had lost or lent: *Can I borrow this book? You'll get it back next week, I promise.* يسترجع

get back to sb to speak to, write to or phone sb later, especially in order to give an answer or deal with sth: *I'll get back to you when I've got some more information.* يستجيب، يردّ على

get back to sth to return to doing sth or talking about sth: *I woke up early and couldn't get back to sleep.* ○ *Let's get back to the point you raised earlier.* يرجع

get behind (with sth) to fail to do or produce sth on time: *We got behind with our rent.* يتأخر

get by (on sth) to manage, often with difficulty, to live, using a certain income: *It's very hard to get by on such a low income.* يدبّر معيشته

get sb down to make sb miserable: *These cold winter days get me down.* يحْزِن

get sth down to make a note of sth; to write sth down: *Did you get the address for the competition down?* يسجِّل

get down to sth/doing sth to start doing or concentrating on sth: *I must get down to answering these letters.* يتفرغ لـ

get in to reach a place: *What time does your train get in?* يَصل

get in; get into sth 1 to climb into a car: *We all got in and Tim drove off.* يدخل

2 to be elected to a political position: *Who do you think will get in at the next election?* يُنتخَب

get sth in to manage to find an opportunity to say or do sth: *He talked all the time and I couldn't get a word in.* يتمكّن من (الكلام)

get into sb (*informal*) (used about a feeling or attitude) to start affecting sb strongly, causing the person to behave in an unusual way: *I wonder what's got into him – he isn't usually unfriendly.* يقْلِق

get into sth to start a particular activity; to become involved in sth: *How did you first get into the music business?* ○ *She has got into the habit of* *turning up late.* ○ *We got into an argument about politics.* يبدأ أو يدخل في

get off (sth) 1 to leave a bus, train, bicycle, etc.; to climb down from a horse ينزل من

2 to leave work with permission at a particular time: *I might be able to get off early today.* يغادر بإذن

get sth off (sth) to remove sth from sth: *My foot was swollen and I couldn't get my shoe off.* ينزع (شيئا من آخر)

get off (with sth) to receive minor or no injuries when serious injury was possible: *She was lucky to get off with only a broken arm in such a bad accident.* يتضرر ضرراً خفيفاً

get (sb) off (with sth) to receive little or no punishment; to help sb to receive little or no punishment: *If you're lucky, you'll get off with a small fine.* ○ *Her lawyer told her that he was confident he would get her off.* ينجو؛ يخلّص

get on 1 to progress or become successful in life, in a career, etc: *After leaving university she was determined to get on.* ينجح

2 to be getting old: *He's getting on – he's over 60, I'm sure.* يشيخ

3 to be getting late: *Time's getting on – we don't want to be late.* يتأخر الوقت

🛈 Senses **2** and **3** are only used in the continuous tenses.

get on/along 1 to make progress: *How are you getting on in your course?* يتقدم

2 to perform in a particular way or to have a good or bad experience in a particular situation: *How did you get on at your interview?* يسلك؛ يصيب نجاحاً أو إخفاقاً

get on/onto sth to climb onto a bus, train, bicycle, horse, etc: *I got on just as the train was about to leave.* ○ *I couldn't get onto the bus because it was full.* يركب

get sth on to put on a piece of clothing: *Get your shoes on, we're going out now.* يلبس

get onto sb (about sth) to speak or write to sb about a particular matter يكلّم أو يكاتب بشأن (كذا)

get on/along with sb; **get on/along (together)** to have a friendly relationship with sb: *Do you get on well with your colleagues?* ○ *We're not close friends but we get on together quite well.* ينسجم مع

get on/along with sth to make progress with sth that you are doing: *How are you getting on with that essay?* يتقدم

get on with sth to continue doing sth, especially after an interruption: *Stop talking and get on with your work!* يواصل

get out (used about a piece of information) to become known, having previously been secret ينفشي (السرّ)

get sth out (of sth) to take sth from its container: *I got my keys out of my bag.* يخرج

get out (of sth) to leave or escape from a place: *My grandmother's very old and she doesn't get out of the house much.* يغادر

get out of sth/doing sth to avoid a duty or doing sth that you have said you will do: *I said I'd go to their party and I can't get out of it now.* يتخلص من

get sth out of sb to obtain sth from sb by force or persuasion: *His parents finally got the truth out of him.* يستخرج

get sth out of sb/sth to gain sth from sb/sth: *I get a lot of pleasure out of music.* يحصل على

get over sth 1 to overcome a problem: *We'll have to get over the problem of finding somewhere to live first.* يتغلب على

2 to recover from sth unpleasant, or from an illness: *He still hasn't got over his wife's death.* ○ *It took her a long time to get over her operation.* ○ *I can't get over how rude he was!* (= I still find it surprising) يشفى من؛ يتقبّل

get sth over with (*informal*) to do and complete sth unpleasant that has to be done: *I'll be glad to get my visit to the dentist's over with.* يتمّ واجباً مقيتاً

get round → GET ABOUT/AROUND/ROUND

get round/around sb (*informal*) to persuade sb to do or agree with sth: *My father says I can't borrow his car but I think I can get round him.* يقنع

get round/around sth to find a way of avoiding or overcoming a problem يتحاشى؛ يجد حلاً

get round/around to sth/doing sth to find the time to do sth, after a delay: *I've been meaning to reply to that letter for ages but I haven't got round to it yet.* يجد الوقت اللازم لـ

get through sth to use or to complete a certain amount or number of sth: *I got through a lot of money at the weekend.* ○ *I got through an enormous amount of work today.* ينفق؛ يكمل

get (sb) through (sth) to be successful in sth (often sth unpleasant); to help sb to be successful: *She got through her final exams easily.* ○ *It was a terrible time financially but I got through it and then things improved.* ○ *Her kindness got me through those awful days.* يجتاز؛ يساعده على اجتياز

get through (to sb) 1 to succeed in making a telephone connection with sb: *I couldn't get through to them because their phone was engaged all day.* ينجح في الاتصال هاتفياً

2 to succeed in making sb understand what you are saying: *They couldn't get through to him that he was completely wrong.* يفهم

get to sb (*informal*) to affect sb in a bad way: *Public criticism is beginning to get to the team manager.* يؤذي

get together (with sb) to meet socially or in order to discuss or do sth: *We should get together one evening.* ○ *Let's get together and talk about it.* يجتمع

get up to rise to a standing position; to stand up: *He got up to let an elderly woman sit down.* يرتقي؛ يقف

get (sb) up to get out of bed or make sb get out of bed: *What time do you have to get up in the morning?* ○ *Could you get me up at 6 tomorrow?* يستيقظ؛ يوقظ

get up to sth 1 to reach a particular point or stage in sth: *We've got up to the last section of our grammar book.* يصل الى مرحلة

2 to do sth, especially sth bad: *I wonder what the children are getting up to?* يَفْعل (شيئاً مؤذياً)

a b c d e f g h i j k l m n o p q r s t u v w x y z

getaway /ˈgetəweɪ/ *noun* [C] an escape (after a crime): *to make a getaway* ○ *a getaway car* هرب

get-together /ˈget təgeðə(r)/ *noun* [C] (*informal*) an informal social meeting or party: *We're having a little get-together on Saturday evening.* اجتماع

ghastly /ˈgɑːstli; *US* ˈgæstli/ *adj* (**ghastlier**; **ghastliest**) **1** causing fear or shock: *a ghastly accident* فظيع
2 (*informal*) very bad, ugly or unpleasant: *a ghastly mistake* ○ *I think these two colours look ghastly together.* شنيع
3 (used about a person) looking pale and ill: *You look ghastly. Do you want to lie down?* شاحب

gherkin /ˈgɜːkɪn/ *noun* [C] a small green cucumber that is preserved in vinegar before being eaten خيار صغير يؤكل مخللاً

ghetto /ˈgetəʊ/ *noun* [C] (*pl.* **ghettoes**) a part of a town where many people of the same race, religion, etc. live, often in poor conditions حي فقير تسكنه أقلية معيّنة

ghost /gəʊst/ (*also* **spectre**; *US* **specter**) *noun* [C] the spirit of a dead person that is seen or heard by sb who is still living: *I don't believe in ghosts.* ○ *The tower is haunted by the ghost of Lady Anne.* ○ *a ghost story* شَبَح
▸ **ghostly** /ˈgəʊstli/ *adj* (**ghostlier**; **ghostliest**) of or like a ghost: *ghostly noises* شبحي

ˈghost town *noun* [C] a town whose inhabitants have all left مدينة مهجورة

ghostwriter /ˈgəʊstraɪtə(r)/ *noun* [C] a person who writes a book, etc. for a famous person (whose name appears as the author) كاتب مستَعار (يُنسَب ما كتبه لسواه)

giant /ˈdʒaɪənt/ *noun* [C] **1** (in children's stories) a person of human shape but enormous size and strength عملاق
2 something that is very large: *the multinational oil giants* (= very large companies) عملاق
▸ **giant** *adj* extremely large; enormous: *a giant new shopping centre* كبير جداً

giddy /ˈgɪdi/ *adj* (**giddier**; **giddiest**) having the feeling that everything is going round and that you are going to fall: *I feel giddy. I must sit down.* دائخ، مصاب بدوار
▸ **giddily** /ˈgɪdɪli/ *adv* دائخاً: مترنحاً
giddiness /ˈgɪdinəs/ *noun* [U] دوار

gift /gɪft/ *noun* [C] **1** something that you give to a person; a present: *wedding gifts* ○ *He made a gift of £500 to charity.* ○ *Their teacher was presented with a gift of flowers and chocolates.* ○ *This week's magazine contains a free gift of some make-up.* ➲ Look at the note at **present**. هدية
2 a gift (for sth/doing sth) natural ability: *She has a gift for saying the right thing at the right time.* موهبة
▸ **gifted** /ˈgɪftɪd/ *adj* having natural ability or great intelligence: *an extremely gifted musician* موهوب

gig /gɪg/ *noun* [C] a performance by pop or jazz musicians حفلة موسيقية

gigabyte /ˈgɪgəbaɪt/ *noun* [C] (*abbr* **Gb**) (*computing*) a unit of computer memory, equal to 2^{30}; (or about a billion bytes) جيغابايت

gigantic /dʒaɪˈgæntɪk/ *adj* extremely large ضخم

giggle /ˈgɪgl/ *verb* [I] to laugh in a silly way because you are amused or nervous يقهقه
▸ **giggle** *noun* [C] a laugh of this kind: *I've got the giggles* (= I can't stop laughing). قهقهة

gilt /gɪlt/ *noun* [U] a thin covering of gold or sth that looks like gold ماء الذهب: شيء مذهّب

gimmick /ˈgɪmɪk/ *noun* [C] something unusual or amusing that is used to attract people's attention (usually so that they buy sth): *They're looking for a new gimmick to advertise the restaurant.* حيلة للفت الأنظار

gin /dʒɪn/ *noun* [C,U] a colourless alcoholic drink that is made from grain and a particular type of berry جِن (مشروب كحولي)

ginger /ˈdʒɪndʒə(r)/ *noun* [U] **1** the hot-tasting root of a plant (used in cooking): *ground ginger* زنجبيل
2 a reddish-orange colour أصهب
▸ **ginger** *adj* **1** flavoured with ginger: *ginger biscuits* مطيَّب بالزنجبيل
2 of a ginger colour: *ginger hair* أصهب

ˌginger ˈale *noun* [U] a non-alcoholic drink that is flavoured with ginger شراب الزنجبيل

gingerbread /ˈdʒɪndʒəbred/ *noun* [U] a sweet cake or biscuit flavoured with ginger كعكة أو بسكوت الزنجبيل

gingerly /ˈdʒɪndʒəli/ *adv* very slowly and carefully so as not to cause harm, make a noise, etc. بحذر

gipsy = GYPSY

giraffe /dʒəˈrɑːf; *US* dʒəˈræf/ *noun* [C] (*pl.* **giraffe** or **giraffes**) an African animal with a very long neck and legs and dark spots on its skin زرافة

girder /ˈgɜːdə(r)/ *noun* [C] a long iron or steel bar that is used in the construction of bridges, large buildings, etc. عارضة معدنية (في البناء)

girl /gɜːl/ *noun* [C] **1** a female child: *the little girl who lives next door* ○ *There are more boys than girls in the class.* بنت
2 a daughter: *They have two boys and a girl.* بنت، ابنة
3 a young woman: *He was eighteen before he became interested in girls.* ○ *The girl at the cash desk was very helpful.* فتاة
4 the girls [plural] female friends of any age: *a night out with the girls* فتيات، صديقات
▸ **girlhood** /ˈgɜːlhʊd/ *noun* [U] the time when sb is a girl سن الصبا أو "البنوتة"
girlish *adj* of or like a girl بنتي، "بناتي"

girlfriend /ˈgɜːlfrend/ *noun* [C] **1** a girl or

woman with whom sb has a romantic and/or sexual relationship حبيبة

2 (*especially US*) a girl or woman's female friend صديقة

ˌGirl ˈGuide (*old-fashioned*) = GUIDE

giro /ˈdʒaɪrəʊ/ *noun* (*pl.* **giros**) (*Brit*) [U] the system for transferring money from one bank, etc. to another الجيرو (نظام نقل المال من بنك لآخر)

gist /dʒɪst/ *noun* **the gist** [sing.] the general meaning of sth rather than all the details: *I know a little Spanish so I was able to get the gist of what he said.* زبدة (الكلام)

give[1] /ɡɪv/ *verb* (*pt* **gave** /ɡeɪv/; *pp* **given** /ˈɡɪvn/)

1 [T] **give sb sth; give sth to sb** to hand sth to sb as a present; to allow sb to have sth as a present: *My parents gave me a watch for my birthday.* ○ *We don't usually give presents to all our nephews and nieces.* ○ *She gave most of her money to cancer research.* يعطي، يهدي

2 [T] **give sb sth; give sth to sb** to hand sth to sb so that he/she can look at it, use it or keep it for a time: *Could you give me that book over there, please?* ○ *I gave my ticket to the lady at the check-in desk.* يعطي، يناول

3 [T] **give sb sth; give sth to sb** to provide sb with sth he/she wants, asks for or pays for: *He was thirsty so I gave him a drink.* ○ *I hope the doctor will give me some new tablets.* ○ *She gives Italian lessons to the people at work.* ○ *He didn't give me the chance to reply.* ○ *Could you give me some help with this essay?* يعطي

4 [T] **give sth to sb/sth** to spend time, etc. on sb/sth: *I can only give you ten minutes.* ○ *We'll have to give some more thought to the matter* (= think about it more). يعطي

5 [T] **give (sb) sth for sth** to pay: *How much would you give me for my old car?* يدفع

6 [T] **give sb sth** to cause sb/sth to have or feel sth: *The news about his father gave him a terrible shock.* ○ *Hard work gives you an appetite.* ○ *That noise is giving me a headache.* ○ *She gave me the impression that she was thinking of leaving her job.* يولِّد، يسبِّب

7 [T] **give sth; give sb sth; give sth to sb/sth** to perform an action: *When the child saw the snow, he gave a shout of delight.* ○ *to give a sigh* ○ *to give a cry of pain* ○ *She gave my hand a squeeze* (= she squeezed it). ○ *They gave us a warm welcome.* ○ *I asked a short question and he gave me a very long answer.* ○ *She gave him a kiss.* يفعل (شيئا)

8 [T] to perform sth in public: *He gave a very interesting lecture on India.* ○ *They're giving* (= having) *a party for their son's eighteenth birthday.* يقدِّم (شيئا أمام الجمهور): يقيم

9 [I] to bend or stretch under pressure: *The branch began to give under his weight.* ينثني: يرتخي: ينهار

IDM **not care/give a damn (about sb/sth)** → DAMN[2]

give or take more or less the number mentioned: *It took us two hours to get here, give or take five minutes.* زائد أو ناقص

give sb to believe/understand (that)... (often passive) to give sb the impression that sth is true: *He gave me to understand that I had got the job.* يوحي

ℹ For other idioms containing **give**, look at the entries for the nouns, adjectives, etc., e.g. **give way** is at **way**.

PHR V **give sb away** (at a wedding in a church) to go with the bride into the church and officially give her to the bridegroom during the marriage ceremony: *Her father gave her away.* يزوِّج، يزف

give sth away to give sth, often sth that you no longer want, to sb without asking for or receiving money in return: *When she got older she gave all her toys away.* ○ *We are giving a shirt away with every suit purchased.* يمنح، يهب

give sth/sb away to show or tell the truth about sth/sb which was secret: *He smiled politely and didn't give away his real feelings.* يفشي

give sb back sth; give sth back (to sb) to return sth to the person from whom you took or borrowed it: *I lent him some books months ago and he still hasn't given them back to me.* يعيد

give sth in to hand sth to the authority collecting it: *I've got to give this essay in to my teacher by Friday.* يسلِّم

give in (to sb/sth) to stop fighting against sb/sth; to accept that you have been defeated يستسلم

give sth off to send sth (e.g. a smell, heat, etc.) out into the air ينشر

give out (used about a machine) to stop working يتعطل

give sth out to hand or pass sth to people: *Could you give out these books to the class, please?* يوزِّع

give up to stop trying to do sth; to accept that you cannot do sth: *They gave up once the other team had scored their third goal.* ○ *Don't give up now, you're improving all the time.* ○ *I give up. What's the answer?* يستسلم

give sb up; give up on sb to stop expecting sb to arrive, succeed, improve or recover: *When he was four hours late, I gave up on him.* ○ *The doctors had given her up when she suddenly started to get better.* يقطع الأمل من

give sth up; give up doing sth to stop doing or having sth that you had done or had regularly before: *I've tried many times to give up smoking.* ○ *Don't give up hope. Things are bound to improve.* يتوقف عن

give yourself/sb up (to sb) to go to the police when they are trying to catch you; to tell the police where sb is: *The suspected murderer gave himself up to the police.* يستسلم (للشرطة)

give sth up (to sb) to give sth to sb who needs or asks for it: *He gave up his seat on the bus to an elderly woman.* يتخلّى عن

give[2] /ɡɪv/ *noun* [U] the quality of being able to bend or stretch a little: *The leather has plenty of give in it.* قابلية الانحناء أو التمدّد قليلاً

IDM **give and take** the willingness, within a relationship, to move towards another person's

a b c d e f g h i j k l m n o p q r s t u v w x y z

point of view because he/she is willing to move towards your point of view: *This dispute can only be settled if there is give and take on both sides.* أخذ وعطاء

given /ˈɡɪvn/ *adj* (only *before* a noun) already stated or fixed: *At a given time they all waved their flags and cheered.* معْطَى

▸ **given** *prep* taking sth into consideration: *Given that you had very little help, I think you did very well.* آخذاً بعين الاعتبار

ˈgiven name *noun* [C] (*especially US*) = FIRST NAME

glacial /ˈɡleɪʃl; ˈɡleɪsiəl/ *adj* **1** caused by ice or a glacier: *a glacial valley* جمودي

2 very cold; like ice: *glacial winds* جليدي

glacier /ˈɡlæsiə(r); *US* ˈɡleɪʃər/ *noun* [C] a mass of ice that moves slowly down a valley نهر جليدي

glad /ɡlæd/ *adj* **1** (not before a noun) **glad (about sth)**; **glad (to do sth/that…)** happy; pleased: *Are you glad about your new job?* ○ *I'm glad to hear he's feeling better.* ○ *I'm glad (that) he's feeling better.* ○ *We'd be glad to see you if you're in the area.* مسرور

> You are usually **glad** or **pleased** about a particular event or situation. **Happy** is used for describing a state, condition of mind, etc. and it *can* be used before the noun it describes: *This kind of music always makes me feel happy.* ○ *She's such a happy child – she's always laughing.*

2 glad (of sth) grateful for sth: *If you are free, I'd be glad of some help.* ممتَن

3 (only *before* a noun) bringing happiness: *I want to be the first to tell her the glad news.* سارّ

▸ **gladden** /ˈɡlædn/ *verb* [T] to make sb glad or happy يسرّ

gladly *adv* (usually used for politely agreeing to a request or accepting an invitation) happily; gratefully: *We will gladly help you if we can.* ○ *She gladly accepted the invitation to stay the night.* بكل سرور

gladness *noun* [U] سرور

glade /ɡleɪd/ *noun* [C] (*formal*) an open space in a forest or wood where there are no trees ℹ **Clearing** is similar in meaning. منطقة بلا اشجار في غابة

gladiator /ˈɡlædieɪtə(r)/ *noun* [C] (in ancient Rome) a man who fought against another man or a wild animal in a public show مصارع (في روما القديمة)

glamour (*US also* **glamor**) /ˈɡlæmə(r)/ *noun* [U] the quality of seeming to be exciting or attractive: *Young people are often attracted by the glamour of city life.* رَوْنَق

▸ **glamorize** (*also* **glamorise**) /ˈɡlæməraɪz/ *verb* [T] to make sth appear more attractive or exciting that it really is: *Television tends to glamorize violence.* يزيِّن

glamorous /ˈɡlæmərəs/ *adj* attractive or full of glamour: *She didn't look very glamorous without her make-up.* ○ *a glamorous job* فاتن

glamorously *adv* بشكل فاتن

glance /ɡlɑːns; *US* ɡlæns/ *verb* [I] to take a quick look: *She glanced round the room to see if they were there.* ○ *He glanced at her and smiled.* ○ *The receptionist glanced down the list of names.* يلمح

PHR V glance off (sth) to hit sth at an angle and move off again in another direction: *The ball glanced off the goalpost and into the net.* يرْتَدّ مائلاً، ينحرف

▸ **glance** *noun* [C] a quick look: *I only had time for a glance at the newspaper.* ○ *They exchanged glances when no one was looking.* ○ *She stole a glance at her watch.* لمحة

IDM at a (single) glance with one look: *I could tell at a glance that something was wrong.* بلمحة واحدة

at first glance/sight → FIRST[1]

gland /ɡlænd/ *noun* [C] a small organ in the body that separates those substances from the blood that will be used by the body or removed from it: *sweat glands* ○ *the poison glands of a snake* ○ *swollen glands* (e.g. in your throat) غدّة

glare /ɡleə(r)/ *noun* **1** [U] strong light that hurts your eyes: *the glare of the sun on snow* ○ *the glare of a car's headlights* ضوء باهر

2 [C] a (long) angry look نظرة غضب، حملقة

▸ **glare** /ɡleə(r)/ *verb* [I] **1** to shine with strong light that hurts your eyes يبهر

2 glare (at sb/sth) to stare at sb angrily: *They stood glaring at each other.* ينظر شزْراً

glaring /ˈɡleərɪŋ/ *adj* **1** (used about a light, etc.) too strong and bright باهر بإفراط

2 angry: *glaring eyes* غاضب

3 great or very noticeable: *a glaring mistake* صارخ

glass /ɡlɑːs; *US* ɡlæs/ *noun* **1** [U] a hard, usually transparent, substance that windows, bottles, etc. are made of: *He cut himself on broken glass.* ○ *a sheet/pane of glass* ○ *In case of emergency, break the glass and press the button.* ○ *a glass jar, dish, etc.* زجاج

2 [C] a drinking container made of glass; the amount of liquid it contains: *a small glass* ○ *Could I have a glass of water, please?* كأس

3 (*also* **glassware** /ˈɡlɑːsweə(r); *US* ˈɡlæs-/) [U] a collection of objects made of glass أشياء زجاجية

▸ **glassful** /-fʊl/ *noun* [C] the amount of liquid that one glass(2) holds ملء كأس

glasses /ˈɡlɑːsɪz; *US* ˈɡlæsɪz/ (*also formal* **spectacles**, *especially Brit informal* **specs**; *US also* **eyeglasses**) *noun* [plural] a pair of lenses in a frame that a person wears in front of his/her eyes (in order to be able to see better): *My sister has to wear glasses.* ○ *I've lost my glasses.* ○ *reading glasses* ○ *dark glasses/sunglasses* ○ *Where's my glasses case?* نظارات

> **Glasses** is more commonly used than **spectacles**. **Specs** is informal. **Glasses** is always plural so we cannot use it with the article *a*. We cannot say: *I need a new glasses.* We can say: *I need a new pair of glasses.*

glass 'fibre = FIBREGLASS

glasshouse /'glɑːshaʊs; *US* 'glæs-/ *noun* [C] a building with glass sides and roof for growing plants ℹ It is also called a **greenhouse**. بيت زجاجي

glassy /glɑːsi; *US* 'glæsi/ *adj* (**glassier**; **glassiest**) **1** looking like glass: *a glassy sea* كالزجاج

2 (used about the eyes) showing no interest or expression: *a glassy stare* (نظرة) فارغة

glaze /gleɪz/ *verb* [T] **1** to fit a sheet of glass into a window, etc. ➲ Look at **double glazing**. يركّب زجاج نافذة

2 glaze sth (with sth) to cover a pot, brick, pie, etc. with a shiny transparent substance (before it is put into an oven): *Glaze the pie with beaten egg.* يطلي بمادة شفّافة لامعة

PHR V glaze over (used about the eyes) to show no interest or expression تشخص عيناه

▸ **glaze** *noun* [C,U] (a substance that gives) a shiny transparent surface on a pot, brick, pie, etc. (مادة تعطي) سطحاً شفّافاً لامعاً

glazed *adj* (used about the eyes, etc.) showing no interest or expression (عينان) شاخصتان

glazier /'gleɪziə(r); *US* -ʒər/ *noun* [C] a person whose job is to fit glass into windows, etc. زجّاج

gleam /gliːm/ *noun* **1** [C, sing.] a soft light (that shines for a short time): *the first gleams of the morning sun* ○ *the gleam of moonlight on the water* وميض

2 [sing.] a brief or sudden show of a quality or emotion: *a gleam of hope, interest, etc.* بارقة (أمل)

▸ **gleam** *verb* [I] **1** to shine softly: *The water of the lake gleamed in the moonlight.* يلمع

2 gleam with sth (used about the face or eyes) to show a particular (happy) emotion: *Their eyes gleamed with enthusiasm.* يلمع

gleaming *adj* shining: *gleaming white teeth* لامع

glee /gliː/ *noun* [U] a feeling of joy or happiness (at sth good that has happened to you or at sth bad that has happened to sb else): *The children laughed with glee at the clown's tricks.* ○ *She couldn't hide her glee when her rival came last in the race.* حبور، غبطة

▸ **gleeful** /-fl/ *adj* مبتهج

gleefully /-fəli/ *adv* بِبهجة

glen /glen/ *noun* [C] a narrow mountain valley (in Scotland or Ireland) وادٍ جبلي ضيق

glib /glɪb/ *adj* **1** (used about a person) speaking quickly and cleverly, in a way that will persuade people but that is not always truthful: *a glib salesman, politician, etc.* حلو اللسان

2 spoken quickly and without hesitation, but not always truthful: *a glib answer, excuse, etc.* (كلام) معسول؛ ارتجالي

ℹ Using the word **glib** shows that you have a low opinion of the person or thing you are describing.

▸ **glibly** *adv* بكلام معسول؛ دون تروٍّ

glibness *noun* [U] كلام معسول؛ عدم تروٍّ

glide /glaɪd/ *verb* [I] **1** to move smoothly without noise or effort: *The dancers glided across the floor.* ○ *The yachts went gliding past.* ينزلق

2 to fly in a glider يطير في طائرة شراعية

▸ **glider** /'glaɪdə(r)/ *noun* [C] a light aircraft without an engine that flies using air currents طائرة شراعية

gliding *noun* [U] the sport of flying in gliders ➲ Look at **hang-gliding**. طيران شراعي

glimmer /'glɪmə(r)/ *verb* [I] to give out a weak unsteady light يَمِض

▸ **glimmer** *noun* [C] **1** a weak unsteady light وميض

2 a weak sign of sth: *a glimmer of hope* بصيص

glimpse /glɪmps/ *noun* [C] **a glimpse (at/of sth)** a quick incomplete view of sb/sth ℹ It is most often used in the phrase **catch a glimpse of**: *I caught a glimpse of myself in the mirror as I walked past.* لمحة

▸ **glimpse** *verb* [T] to get a quick look at sb/sth (often by chance): *I glimpsed Cathy in the crowd, but I don't think she saw me.* يلمح

glint /glɪnt/ *verb* [I] to give out small bright flashes of light: *She thought the diamond was lost until she saw something glinting on the carpet.* ○ *(figurative) His eyes glinted at the thought of all that money.* يتلألأ، يلمع

▸ **glint** *noun* [C]: *the glint of metal in the grass* ○ *(figurative) a glint of anger in his eyes* لَمَعان

glisten /'glɪsn/ *verb* [I] (used about wet surfaces) to shine: *Her eyes glistened with tears.* ○ *Tears glistened in her eyes.* يتألّق، يلمع

glitter /'glɪtə(r)/ *verb* [I] to give out many little flashes of light: *The stars glittered in the frosty sky.* يتلألأ

▸ **glitter** *noun* [U]: *the glitter of jewellery* ○ *(figurative) the glitter of a career in show business* تلألؤ، تألّق

glittering /'glɪtərɪŋ/ *adj* **1** shining brightly with many little flashes of light: *a glittering Christmas tree* متلألئ

2 splendid or successful: *a glittering career, performance, etc.* متألّق

gloat /gləʊt/ *verb* [I] **gloat (about/over sth)** to feel or express pleasure at sth good that has happened to you or at sth bad that has happened to sb else: *Don't gloat – you might be in the same position yourself some time.* يزهو؛ يشْمَت

▸ **gloatingly** *adv* بزهو، بشماتة

⚷**global** /'gləʊbl/ *adj* **1** affecting the whole world: *the global effects of pollution* ○ *global warming* عالمي

2 affecting the whole of a group of facts, possibilities, etc: *We must take a global view of the problem.* شامل

▸ **globally** /-bəli/ *adv* عالمياً

globe /gləʊb/ *noun* **1** [C] a model of the earth, in the shape of a ball, with the continents, etc. shown on it كرة مجسمة (تمثل الأرض)

2 the globe [sing.] the earth: *to travel (all) over the globe* ○ *With the help of television, we can see*

a b c d e f g h i j k l m n o p q r s t u v w x y z

things that are happening on the other side of the globe. الكرة الأرضية

ˌglobe ˈartichoke *noun* [C] = ARTICHOKE

globetrotter /ˈgləʊbtrɒtə(r)/ *noun* [C] (*informal*) a person who travels to many countries جوّاب

globule /ˈglɒbjuːl/ *noun* [C] a small drop or ball of a liquid or melted solid: *There were globules of fat in the soup.* كُرَيَّة

gloom /gluːm/ *noun* [U] **1** a feeling of sadness or hopelessness: *The news brought deep gloom to the village.* غَمّ

2 (near) darkness: *It was hard to see anything in the gloom.* ظُلْمة

▸ **gloomy** /ˈgluːmi/ *adj* (**gloomier**; **gloomiest**) **1** dark (and depressing): *What a gloomy day!* ○ *This dark paint makes the room very gloomy.* مغمّ، كئيب

2 (making sb feel) sad or depressed: *For many young people leaving school, the prospects of finding work are gloomy.* ○ *Don't be so gloomy – cheer up!* قاتم، مكتئب

gloomily /ˈgluːmɪli/ *adv* بغم، بكآبة

gloominess /ˈgluːminəs/ *noun* [U] غمّ، كآبة

glorify /ˈglɔːrɪfaɪ/ *verb* (*pres part* **glorifying**; *3rd pers sing pres* **glorifies**; *pt, pp* **glorified**) [T] **1** (*formal*) to praise sb/sth highly يعظّم

2 to make sb/sth appear better or more important than he/she/it really is: *His biography does not attempt to glorify his early career.* يُفرط في التعظيم

▸ **glorified** /ˈglɔːrɪfaɪd/ *adj* (only *before* a noun) described in a way that makes sb/sth seem better, bigger, more important, etc. than he/she/it really is: *The 'holiday cottage' turned out to be a glorified barn.* معظّم بإفراط، مفخّم

glorious /ˈglɔːriəs/ *adj* **1** having or deserving fame or glory: *a glorious victory* مجيد

2 wonderful or splendid: *What glorious weather!* ○ *a glorious day, view, etc.* بهيّ، رائع

▸ **gloriously** *adv* بصورة رائعة

glory /ˈglɔːri/ *noun* [U] **1** fame or honour that is won by great achievements: *The winning team was welcomed home in a blaze of glory.* مَجْد

2 great beauty: *Autumn is the best time to see the forest in all its glory.* بهاء

▸ **glory** *verb* (*pres part* **glorying**; *3rd pers sing pres* **glories**; *pt, pp* **gloried**)

PHR V **glory in sth** to take (too much) pleasure or pride in sth: *He gloried in his sporting successes.* يزهو

gloss /glɒs/ *noun* [U, sing.] (a substance that gives) brightness or shine on a surface: *the gloss on wood, hair, silk, etc.* ○ *gloss paint* ○ *gloss photographs* ➲ Look at **matt**. لمعان، بريق

▸ **gloss** *verb*

PHR V **gloss over sth** to avoid talking about a problem, mistake, etc. in detail يتغاضى عن التفاصيل

glossy *adj* (**glossier**; **glossiest**) **1** smooth and shiny: *glossy hair* لامع

2 (used about a magazine, etc.) printed on good quality paper and having many colour photographs لامع، صقيل

glossary /ˈglɒsəri/ *noun* [C] (*pl.* **glossaries**) a list of special or unusual words and their meanings (at the end of a book) قائمة مفردات (في آخر الكتاب)

🔑**glove** /glʌv/ *noun* [C] a piece of clothing that covers your hand (and has separate parts for the thumb and each finger): *I need a new pair of gloves for the winter.* ❶ Common types of gloves are **boxing gloves**, **driving gloves**, **rubber gloves**, **leather gloves** and **woollen gloves**. ➲ Look at **mitten**. قفاز

glow /gləʊ/ *verb* [I] **1** to give out light and/or heat without smoke or flames: *A cigarette glowed in the dark.* يتوهج

2 **glow (with sth)** to be warm or red because of excitement, exercise, etc: *to glow with health, enthusiasm, pride, etc.* يتألّق

▸ **glow** *noun* [sing.] **1** a warm light: *the glow of the sky at sunset* وهج

2 a feeling or look of warmth or satisfaction: *a rosy glow on the children's cheeks* تألّق

glowing *adj* giving high praise; favourable: *His teacher wrote a glowing report about his work.* مفعم بالمديح

glowingly *adv* بحماس، باعجاب

glower /ˈglaʊə(r)/ *verb* [I] to look angrily (at sb/sth) ينظر شزراً

glucose /ˈgluːkəʊs/ *noun* [U] a type of sugar that is found in fruit سكّر العنب

🔑**glue** /gluː/ *noun* [U] a thick sticky liquid that is used for joining things together: *You can make glue from flour and water.* ○ *Stick the photo in with glue.* غراء

▸ **glue** *verb* [T] (*pres part* **gluing**) **glue A (to/onto B)**; **glue A and B (together)** to join a thing or things together with glue: *Do you think you can glue the handle back onto the teapot?* يلصق بالغراء

IDM **glued to sth** (*informal*) giving all your attention to sth and unwilling to leave it: *He just sits there every evening glued to the television.* متسمّر، لا يفارق

ˈ**glue-sniffing** *noun* [U] breathing in the chemicals that are given off by glue to get the same effect as that produced by alcohol or drugs استنشاق الغراء (لِلَذّة)

glum /glʌm/ *adj* (**glummer**; **glummest**) (*informal*) sad or disappointed: *What are you looking so glum about?* كئيب، متجهّم

▸ **glumly** *adv* بكآبة

glumness *noun* [U] كآبة

glut /glʌt/ *noun* [C, usually sing.] more of sth than is needed: *The glut of coffee has forced down the price.* فيض

glutton /ˈglʌtn/ *noun* [C] **1** a person who eats too much نهم

2 **a glutton for sth** a person who is willing to have or do more of sth difficult, unpleasant, etc:

She's a glutton for hard work – she never stops. هاوٍ (لشيء صعب أو كريه)

▸ **gluttony** /-təni/ *noun* [U] the habit of eating too much نَهَم

GMO /ˌdʒiː em ˈəʊ/ *noun* [C] **(pl. GMOs)** the abbreviation for genetically modified organism (a plant, etc. that has had its genetic structure changed artificially, so that it will produce more fruit or not be affected by disease) كائن معدّل وراثياً

GMT /ˌdʒiː em ˈtiː/ *abbrev* Greenwich Mean Time; the time system that is used in Britain during the winter and for calculating the time in other parts of the world توقيت غرينتش

gnarled /nɑːld/ *adj* rough and twisted, because of old age or hard work: *The old man had gnarled fingers.* ○ *a gnarled oak tree* كثير العقد

gnash /næʃ/ *verb*

IDM gnash your teeth to feel very angry and upset about sth يَصِرّ (أسنانه): يتميز غيظاً

gnat /næt/ *noun* [C] a small insect like a mosquito, that stings بعوضة

gnaw /nɔː/ *verb* [I,T] **gnaw (at) sth** to bite a bone, etc. many times: *The dog lay on the carpet gnawing its bone.* ○ *(figurative) Fear of the future gnawed away at her all the time.* يقْضم، يقرض

gnome /nəʊm/ *noun* [C] (in children's stories, etc.) a little old man with a beard and a pointed hat who lives under the ground: *a garden gnome* (= a model of a gnome that is used to decorate a garden) قزم خرافي

🔑 **go**[1] /gəʊ/ *verb* [I] (*pres part* **going**; *3rd pers sing pres* **goes**; *pt* **went** /went/; *pp* **gone** /gɒn/; *US* gɔːn/) **1** to move or travel from one place to another: *She always goes home by bus.* ○ *We're going to London tomorrow.* ○ *He went to the cinema yesterday.* ○ *We've still got fifty miles to go.* ○ *How fast does this car go?* يَذْهَب

> **Been** is used as the past participle of **go** when somebody has travelled to a place and has returned. **Gone** means that somebody has travelled to a place but has not yet returned: *I've just been to Berlin. I got back this morning.* ○ *John's gone to Peru. He'll be back in two weeks.*

2 to travel to a place to take part in an activity or do sth: *Are you going to Dave's party?* ○ *Shall we go swimming this afternoon?* ○ *Let's go for a drive.* ○ *My aunt has gone on a cruise.* ○ *They've gone on holiday.* ○ *We went to watch the match.* ○ *I'll go and make the tea.* يَذْهَب

3 to visit or attend a place regularly: *Does Simon go to school yet?* يَذْهَب

4 to leave a place: *I have to go now. It's nearly 4 o'clock.* يغادر، يمضي

5 to lead to or reach a place or time: *Where does this road go to?* ○ *This cut on my hand goes quite deep.* يؤدّي/ يصل إلى

6 to have as its usual place: *Where does this vase go?* يوضع

7 to fit into a space: *My clothes won't all go in one suitcase.* يستوعِب

8 to happen in a particular way; to develop: *How's the new job going?* ○ *My work's going well.* يتقدم، يمشي

9 to work correctly: *This clock doesn't go.* يعمل، يشتغل

10 to become; to reach a particular state: *Her hair is going grey.* ○ *He went blind when he was 20.* ○ *Everybody thought that we had gone mad.* ○ *The baby has gone to sleep.* يصبح

11 to remain in the state mentioned: *Many mistakes go unnoticed.* يظلّ

12 to disappear: *Has your headache gone yet?* يختفي، يزول

13 to become worse or stop working correctly: *The brakes on the car have gone.* يسوء، يتعطّل

14 to look or taste good with sth else: *Does this sweater go with my skirt?* يناسب

15 to have certain words or a certain tune: *How does that song go?* يتألّف من كلمات معيّنة؛ يتنغّم

16 to make a sound: *The bell went early today.* ○ *Cats go 'miaow'.* يصوّت

17 (used about time) to pass: *The last hour went very slowly.* ○ *There's only one minute left to go.* ينقضي

18 (used in the present tense for saying what a person said): *I said, 'How are you, Jim?' and he goes, 'It's none of your business!'* فإذا به يقول

19 (only used in the continuous tenses) to be available: *Are there any jobs going in your department?* متوفّر

20 (used for saying that you do not want sb to do sth bad or stupid): *You can borrow my bike again, but don't go breaking it this time!* ○ *I hope John doesn't go and tell everyone about our plan.* يرباً عن

IDM as people, things, etc. go compared to the average person or thing: *As Chinese restaurants go, it wasn't bad.* بالمقارنة مع

be going to do sth 1 (used for showing what you plan to do in the future): *We're going to sell our car.* ينوي

2 (used for saying that you are sure sth will happen): *It's going to rain soon.* ○ *Oh no! He's going to fall!* سوْف

go all out for sth; **go all out to do sth** to make a great effort to do sth يجهد

have a lot going for you to have many advantages يمتاز

Here goes! (said just before you start to do sth difficult or exciting) هيّا بنا!

to go that is/are left before sth ends: *How long (is there) to go before the end of the lesson?* باقٍ

ℹ For other idioms containing **go**, look at the entries for nouns, adjectives, etc., e.g. **go astray** is at **astray**.

PHRV go about → GO ROUND/AROUND/ABOUT

go about sth to continue to do what you usually do: *We went about our normal routine.* يواصل

go about sth/doing sth to start trying to do sth

a b c d e f g h i j k l m n o p q r s t u v w x y z

difficult: *I wouldn't have any idea how to go about building a house.* يباشر (أمراً صعباً)

go about with sb → GO ROUND/AROUND/ABOUT WITH SB

go against sb to be unfavourable to sb: *The referee's decision went against him.* يعارض؛ يحكم ضدّه

go against sb/sth to do sth that is opposed to sb/sth: *She went against her parents' wishes and married him.* يخالف

go against sth to be opposed or opposite to sth; not to be in agreement with sth: *It goes against my principles to use violence.* يخالف

go ahead to take place after being planned: *Although several members were missing, the meeting went ahead without them.* يحْدث، يقع

go ahead (with sth) to begin to do sth that you have planned يباشر، يبدأ العمل

go along to continue: *The course gets more difficult as you go along.* يتقدم

go along with sb/sth to agree with sb/sth: *I'm happy to go along with whatever you suggest.* يوافق

go around → GO ROUND/AROUND/ABOUT

go around with sb → GO ROUND/AROUND/ABOUT WITH SB

go away 1 to leave the place where you live (e.g. for a holiday) for a period of time of at least one night: *We're going away this weekend and we'll be back on Sunday evening.* يسافر

2 to disappear: *I've tried to remove the stain in the carpet but it won't go away.* يزول

go back (to...) to return (to a place): *It's a wonderful city and I'd like to go back there one day.* يعود

go back (to sth) 1 to return to a previous matter or situation: *Let's go back to the subject we were discussing a few minutes ago.* يرجع

2 to have its origins in a previous period of time: *A lot of the buildings in the village go back to the fifteenth century.* يرجع أصله إلى

go back on sth to break a promise, an agreement, etc: *I promised to help them and I can't go back on it now.* ينكث (بوعْد)

go back to sth/to doing sth to start doing again sth that you had stopped doing: *When the children got a bit older she went back to full-time work.* يباشر من جديد (بعد توقف)

go by 1 (used about time) to pass: *As time went by, her confidence grew.* بمرور الوقت؛ ينقضي، يمضي

2 to pass a place: *She stood at the window watching people go by.* يمرّ

go by sth 1 to obey, follow or be guided by sth: *You can't go by the railway timetables, the trains are very unreliable.* يتّبع: يهتدي، أو يسترشد بِ

2 to form an opinion according to a particular thing: *If experience is anything to go by, they'll be late.* يهتدي بِ

go down 1 (used about a ship, etc.) to sink يغْرَق

2 (used about the sun) to disappear from the sky تغيب الشمس

3 to become lower in price, level, etc.; to fall: *The price of these computers has gone down in the last two years.* ○ *The number of people out of work went down last month.* يهبط، ينخفض

go down (with sb) (used with adverbs, especially 'well' or 'badly' or in questions beginning with 'how') (used about sth that is said, a performance, etc.) to be received by sb: *The film went down well with the critics.* يقدّر؛ يقابل بِ

go down with sth to catch an illness; to become ill with sth: *Ten of our staff have gone down with flu.* يمْرض؛ يصاب بِ

go for sb to attack sb يهاجم

go for sb/sth to be true for a particular person or thing: *We've got financial problems but I suppose the same goes for a great many people.* يصح في

go in (used about the sun) to disappear behind a cloud تحْجب بالسحاب (الشمس)

go in for sth 1 to enter or take part in an examination or competition يشترك (في امتحان أو مسابقة)

2 to start a career in sth: *He has decided to go in for journalism.* يمْتهن

go in for sth/doing sth to do or have sth as a hobby or interest: *He doesn't go in for sport much.* يهتمّ أو يعْنى بِ

go into sth 1 to start working in a certain type of job: *When she left school she went into nursing.* يمْتهن

2 to look at or describe sth in detail: *I haven't got time to go into all the details now.* يدخل في التفاصيل

go off 1 to explode: *A bomb has gone off in the city centre.* ينفجر

2 to make a sudden loud noise: *I woke up when my alarm clock went off.* يقْرع: ينطلق

3 (used about lights, heating, etc.) to stop working: *There was a power cut and all the lights went off.* ينْطفئ

4 (used about food and drink) to become too old to be eaten or drunk; to go bad يفْسد (طعام أو شراب)

5 (used about an event) to take place or happen in a certain way: *I think their wedding went off very well.* يحْدث: يسير

6 to become worse in quality: *I used to like that band but they've gone off recently.* يفقد نكهته أو طعمه

go off sb/sth to stop liking or being interested in sb/sth يعْزف عن

go off with sth to take sth that belongs to sb else: *Who's gone off with my cup?* يأخذ (ما يملكه سواه)

go on 1 (used about lights, heating, etc.) to start working: *I saw the lights go on in the house opposite.* يشتعل

2 (used about time) to pass: *As time went on, she became more and more successful.* ينقضي، يمضي، يمر

3 (used especially in the continuous tenses) to happen or take place: *Can anybody tell me what's going on here?* يحدث، يجري

4 (used about a situation) to continue without changing: *This is a difficult period but it won't go on forever.* يستمر

5 to continue speaking after stopping briefly: *Go on. What happened next?* يواصل كلامه

6 (used as an order for encouraging sb to do sth): *Oh go on, let me borrow your car. I'll bring it back in an hour.* (تقال للإقناع والتشجيع)

go on sth to use sth as information so that you can understand a situation: *There were no witnesses to the crime, so the police had very little to go on.* يسترشد بـ

go on (about sb/sth) to talk about sb/sth for a long time in a boring or annoying way: *She went on and on about the people she works with.* ○ *I know I've made a mistake, there's no need to go on about it.* يطيل في الكلام

go on (at sb) (about sth) to keep complaining about sth: *His parents are always going on at him to dress more smartly.* يشكو باستمرار

go on (with sth) to continue doing sth, perhaps after a pause or break: *She ignored me and went on with her meal.* يتابع

go on doing sth to continue doing sth without stopping or changing: *We don't want to go on living here for the rest of our lives.* يستمرّ

go out 1 to leave the place where you live or work for a short time, returning on the same day: *Let's go out for a meal tonight* (= to a restaurant). ○ *I'm just going out for a walk, I won't be long.* يخرج (من بيته)

2 (used about the tide) to move away from the land: *The sea was a long way away because the tide had gone out.* يبتعد (الجزْر)، ينحسر

3 to stop being fashionable or in use: *That kind of music went out in the seventies.* ○ *Teaching methods like that went out years ago.* يبطل

4 to stop shining or burning: *Suddenly all the lights went out.* ينطفئ

go out with sb; go out (together) to spend time regularly with sb, having a romantic and/or sexual relationship: *He's going out with Jill Brown now.* ○ *They went out together for five years before they got married.* يصاحب، يعاشر

go over sth to look at, think about or discuss sth carefully from beginning to end: *Go over your work before you hand it in.* يمحّص، يراجع بدقة

go round (used especially after 'enough') to be shared among all the people: *In this area, there aren't enough jobs to go round.* يكفي الجميع

go round/around/about 1 (used about a story, a belief, etc.) to pass from person to person: *There's a rumour going round that he's going to resign.* ينتشر

2 (used about an illness) to pass from person to person in a group or area: *There's a virus going round at work.* ينتقل (بالعدوى)

go round (to...) to visit sb's home, usually a short distance away: *I'm going round to Jo's for dinner tonight.* يزور

go round/around/about with sb to spend time and go to places regularly with sb: *Her parents don't like the people she has started going round with.* يصاحب

go through to be completed successfully: *The deal went through as agreed.* ينجز؛ يتم

go through sth 1 to look in or at sth carefully, especially in order to find sth: *I went through all my pockets but I couldn't find my wallet.* يفتش

2 to look at, think about or discuss sth carefully from beginning to end: *Let's go through the arrangements for the trip again.* ○ *We'll start the lesson by going through your homework.* يُدقّق

3 to suffer an unpleasant experience: *I'd hate to go through such a terrible ordeal again.* يقاسي

go through with sth to do sth unpleasant or difficult that you have decided, agreed or threatened to do: *Do you think she'll go through with her threat to leave him?* ينفذ (أمراً صعباً)

go together (used about two or more things) **1** to belong to the same set or group يرافق؛ ينتمي إلى نفس (المجموعة)

2 to look good together يناسب

go towards sth to be used as part of the payment for sth: *The money I was given for my birthday went towards my new bike.* يُنفَق على

go under 1 to sink below the surface of water يغرق

2 (*informal*) (used about a company) to go out of business: *A lot of firms are going under in the recession.* يفْلس

go up 1 to start burning suddenly and strongly: *The car crashed into a wall and went up in flames.* يشْتَعِل

2 to become higher in price, level, amount, etc.; to rise: *Petrol has gone up again.* ○ *The birth rate has gone up by 10%.* يرتفع

go with sth 1 to be included with sth; to happen as a result of sth: *Pressure goes with the job.* يرافق

2 to match or be suitable with sth: *What colour carpet would go with the walls?* يناسب

go without (sth) to manage without having sth: *They went without sleep many nights when the baby was ill.* يبقى دون (نوم مثلاً)

go² /gəʊ/ *noun* (*pl.* **goes** /gəʊz/) **1** [C] a turn to play in a game, etc: *Whose go is it?* ○ *Hurry up – it's your go.* ℹ **Turn** has the same meaning. دوْر (في اللعب)

2 [C] (*informal*) an occasion when you try to do sth: *Andrew passed his driving test first go.* محاولة

3 [U] (*informal*) energy: *He's full of go.* نشاط

IDM **be on the go** (*informal*) to be very active or busy: *I'm exhausted. I've been on the go all day.* دائم الحركة؛ مشغول طول الوقت

to have a go (at sth/doing sth) (*informal*) to try to do sth: *I'm not sure if I can fix it, but I'll have a go.* يحاول

goad /gəʊd/ *verb* [T] **goad sb (into sth/doing sth)** to cause sb to do sth by making him/her angry يحرّض؛ يستفز

'go-ahead *noun* [sing.] permission to do sth: *We've been given the go-ahead for the new building.* إذن، ترخيص

▶ **'go-ahead** *adj* willing to try new ways of doing things مجدِّد؛ فعّال، نشيط

goal /gəʊl/ *noun* [C] **1** (in football, rugby, hockey, etc.) the area between two posts into which the ball must be kicked, hit, etc. for a point to be scored: *Who's in goal for Real Madrid?* مَرْمى

2 a point that is scored when the ball goes into the goal: *Everton won by three goals to two.* ○ *to score a goal* ○ *an own goal* (= when a player kicks, hits, etc. the ball into his/her own goal) هدف

3 your purpose or aim: *I've finally achieved my goal of visiting all the capital cities of Europe.* هدف

▸ **goalless** /ˈɡəʊlləs/ *adj* with no goal scored: *a goalless draw* (مباراة) بلا أهداف

goalkeeper /ˈɡəʊlkiːpə(r)/ (*also informal* **goalie** /ˈɡəʊli/ or **keeper**) *noun* [C] the player who stands in front of the goal(1) and tries to stop the other team from scoring a goal(2): *The goalkeeper made a magnificent save.* حارس المرمى

goalpost /ˈɡəʊlpəʊst/ *noun* [C] one of the two posts that form the sides of a goal. They are joined together by a bar (the crossbar). عمود المرمى

goat

sheep

goat /ɡəʊt/ *noun* [C] a small animal with horns which lives in mountainous areas or is kept on farms for its milk and meat عنزة

gobble /ˈɡɒbl/ *verb* [I,T] (*informal*) **gobble sth (up/down)** to eat quickly and noisily: *He'd gobbled down all his food before I'd started mine.* يلتهم؛ يبتلع

gobbledegook (*also* **gobbledygook**) /ˈɡɒbldiɡuːk/ *noun* [U] (*informal*) official language that is hard to understand لغة (وثائق) رسمية غير مفهومة

ˈ**go-between** *noun* [C] a person who takes messages between two people or groups who do not or cannot meet: *In some countries, marriages are arranged by go-betweens.* وسيط

goblin /ˈɡɒblɪn/ *noun* [C] (in stories) a small ugly creature who plays tricks on people جني قبيح

gobsmacked /ˈɡɒbsmækt/ *adj* (*informal*) so surprised that you are unable to speak معقود اللسان دهشةً

⚷ **god** /ɡɒd/ *noun* **1** (*feminine* **goddess**) [C] a being or force who is worshipped by a group of people and who is believed to have the power to control nature and human affairs: *Mars was the Roman god of war and Venus was the goddess of love.* إله

2 God [sing.] (in Christianity, Islam and Judaism) the creator and ruler of all things: *Do you believe in God?* ○ *Muslims worship God in a mosque.* الله، إله

'God' is used in a number of expressions. (Some people think that it is wrong to use God's name in this way.) **Oh my God!** expresses surprise or shock: *Oh my God! I've won £1000!* We use **thank God** when we are happy and relieved about something: *Thank God you've arrived – I was beginning to think you'd had an accident.* The expression **God forbid!** is used when we say that we don't want something to happen: *'I'm going to invite 50 people to the party'. 'God forbid!'* We use **'for God's sake'** when we are asking somebody to do something and want to sound more urgent or when we are angry with somebody: *For God's sake, shut up!.*

godchild /ˈɡɒdtʃaɪld/ ˈ**god-daughter**, ˈ**god-son** *noun* [C] a person for whom a godparent takes responsibility at a Christian baptism (or christening) فَلْيون، فليونة (ابن أو بنت في العماد عند المسيحيين)

goddess /ˈɡɒdes/ *noun* [C] a female god إلهة

ˈ**godfather** /ˈɡɒdfɑːðə(r)/ ˈ**godmother**, ˈ**godparent** *noun* [C] a person who promises to take responsibility for a child (at his/her baptism or christening) and to make sure that he/she is educated as a Christian عَرّاب، عَرّابة (أب أو أم في العماد عند المسيحيين)

godforsaken /ˈɡɒdfəseɪkən/ *adj* (used about a place) depressing or having nothing of interest كئيب

godsend /ˈɡɒdsend/ *noun* [C] something unexpected that is a great help to you because it comes just when it is needed: *The extra money was a real godsend just before Christmas.* هِبة من السماء

goggle /ˈɡɒɡl/ *verb* [I] to look at sb/sth with wide round eyes (in surprise) يحملق

goggles /ˈɡɒɡlz/ *noun* [plural] special glasses that you wear to protect your eyes from water, wind, dust, etc. ➲ Look at **mask**. نظارات واقية

going[1] /ˈɡəʊɪŋ/ *noun* **1** [sing.] (*formal*) the act of leaving a place; departure: *We were all saddened by his going.* رحيل

2 [U] the rate or speed of travel, progress, etc: *Oxford to London in an hour? That's very good going!* ○ *Three children in four years? That's not bad going!* معدّل (السرعة أو التقدم أو مايشبه ذلك)

3 [U] the condition of a path, the ground, etc: *The mud made the path very hard going.* ○ (*figurative*) *It'll be hard going if we need to finish this by Friday!* ○ (*figurative*) *I'm finding this*

novel very heavy going (= difficult and not very interesting). حالة أرض المسير
IDM get out, go, leave, etc. while the going is good to leave a place or stop doing sth while it is still easy to do so يغادر (مكانا) أو يتوقف (عن عمل شيء) والظروف ملائمة

going² /ˈɡəʊɪŋ/ *adj*
IDM a going concern a successful business (تجارة) ناجحة
the going rate (for sth) the usual cost (of sth): *The going rate for a cleaner is about £6 an hour.* السعر المعتاد

ˌgoings-ˈon *noun* [plural] (*informal*) unusual things that are happening: *The old lady was shocked by the goings-on in the house next door.* أحداث غير مألوفة

go-kart /ˈɡəʊ kɑːt/ (*also* **kart**) *noun* [C] a vehicle like a very small car with no roof or doors, used for racing سيارة سباق بلا سقف أو أبواب

gold /ɡəʊld/ *noun* **1** [U] a precious yellow metal that is used for making coins, jewellery, etc: *Is your bracelet made of gold?* ○ *solid, pure, 22-carat, etc. gold* ○ *What's the price of gold today?* ○ *a gold chain, ring, watch, etc.* ذهب
2 [C] = GOLD MEDAL
IDM (as) good as gold very well-behaved: *The children were as good as gold while you were out.* مهذّب
▸ **gold** *adj* the colour of gold: *The invitation was written in gold letters.* ➲ Look at **golden**. ذهبي

ˈgold dust *noun* [U] gold in the form of powder: (*figurative*) *Good English teachers are like gold dust* (= very hard to find). تِبْر

golden /ˈɡəʊldən/ *adj* made of gold or like gold: *a golden crown* ○ *golden hair* ○ (*figurative*) *a golden* (= excellent) *opportunity* ذهبي

ˌgolden ˈjubilee *noun* [C] a 50th anniversary ➲ Look at **silver jubilee**. يوبيل ذهبي (عيد خمسيني)

ˌgolden ˈwedding *noun* [C] the 50th anniversary of a wedding ➲ Look at **diamond wedding** and **silver wedding**. عيد الزواج الخمسيني

goldfish /ˈɡəʊldfɪʃ/ *noun* [C] (*pl.* **goldfish**) a small orange fish that is kept as a pet in a bowl or pond سمكة ذهبية

ˌgold ˈmedal (*also* **gold**) *noun* [C] the prize for first place in a sports competition: *How many gold medals did we win in the 2004 Olympics?* ➲ Look at **silver medal** and **bronze medal**. ميدالية ذهبية
▸ **ˌgold ˈmedallist** (*US* **gold medalist**) *noun* [C] the winner of a gold medal حائز على ميدالية ذهبية

ˈgold mine *noun* [C] a place where gold is mined منجم ذهب

golf /ɡɒlf/ *noun* [U] a game that is played outdoors on a large area of grass called a golf course and in which you use a stick (a golf club) to hit a small hard ball (a golf ball) into a series of holes (usually 18): *to play a round of golf* ○ *a golf club* (= a club for golfers; the place where they meet and play golf) جولف (لعبة)
▸ **golfer** *noun* [C] a person who plays golf لاعب جولف

golly /ˈɡɒli/ *interj* (*informal*) (used for expressing surprise) عبارة دهشة

gone¹ *pp* of GO

gone² /ɡɒn; *US* ɡɔːn/ *adj* (not before a noun) not present any longer; completely used up: *He stood at the door for a moment, and then he was gone.* ○ *Can I have some more ice cream please or is it all gone?* غير موجود، نافد

> **Gone** meaning 'disappeared' or 'finished' is used with the verb **be**, as in the examples above. When we are thinking about where something has disappeared to, we use *have*: *Nobody knows where John has gone.*

gone³ /ɡɒn/ *prep* later than: *Hurry up! It's gone six already!* (= later than six o'clock) بَعْد

gonna /ˈɡənə/

> **Gonna** is a way of writing 'going to' to show that sb is speaking in an informal way or with a special accent. Do not write 'gonna' yourself (unless you are copying somebody's accent) because it might be marked as a mistake. **Wanna** (= want to) and **gotta** (= got to) are similar.

goo /ɡuː/ *noun* [U] (*informal*) a sticky wet substance مادة رطبة لزجة
▸ **gooey** /ˈɡuːi/ (**gooier**; **gooiest**) *adj* (*informal*) sticky: *gooey cakes* لزج

good¹ /ɡʊd/ *adj* (**better** /ˈbetə(r)/, **best** /best/)
1 of a high quality or standard: *a good book, film, concert, etc.* ○ *The hotel was really good.* ○ *'Why don't you apply for the job?' 'I don't think my English is good enough.'* ○ *The car was in very good condition.* جيد، حَسَن
2 good at sth; good with sb/sth able to do sth or deal with sb/sth well; successful: *Jane's good at chemistry.* ○ *He's very good with children.* ماهر؛ موَفّق
3 pleasant or enjoyable: *It's good to be home again.* ○ *good news, weather, etc.* ○ *Have a good time!* بهيج
4 morally right or well behaved: *She was a very good person – she spent her whole life trying to help other people.* ○ *Were the children good while we were out?* طيِّب
5 good (to sb) kind; helpful: *They were good to me when I was ill.* ○ *It was good of you to come.* لطيف
6 good (for sb/sth) having a positive effect on your health: *Green vegetables are very good for you.* مفيد
7 suitable or favourable: *This beach is very good for surfing.* ○ *I think Paul would be a good person for the job.* ○ *'When shall we meet?' 'Thursday would be a good day for me.'* مناسب
8 (only used before an adjective or noun) great

a b c d e f g h i j k l m n o p q r s t u v w x y z

in number, size, length, etc: *Take a good* (= long and careful) *look at this photograph.* كثير (في العدد أو السعة أو الطول أو ما يشابه ذلك)

9 (only *before* a noun) at least: *We waited for a good ten minutes.* ○ *It's a good three miles to the station.* على الأقل

10 (used when you are pleased about sth): *'Tom's invited us to dinner next week.' 'Oh, good!'* حسَن

IDM **a good/great many** → MANY

as good as almost: *She as good as said I was lying!* ○ *The project is as good as finished.* يكاد؛ تقريباً

in good faith → FAITH

good for you, him, her, etc. (*informal*) (used to show that you are pleased that sb has done sth clever): *Well done! Good for you!* هنيئاً لك أهنئك: مرحى

good gracious, good grief, good heavens, etc. (used for expressing surprise) ➲ Look at the entries for **gracious**, etc. يا للدهشة

good morning/afternoon/evening/night (used for greeting sb) ➲ Look at the entries for **morning**, etc. (صباح أو مساء) الخير

good² /gʊd/ *noun* [U] **1** the quality of being morally right: *the difference between good and evil* ○ *I'm sure there's some good in everybody.* خير

2 something that will help sb/sth; advantage: *She did it for the good of her country.* ○ *I know you don't want to go into hospital, but it's for your own good.* ○ *What's the good of learning French if you have no chance of using it?* خير، فائدة

IDM **be no good (doing sth)** to be of no use or value: *It's no good standing here in the cold. Let's go home.* ○ *This sweater isn't any good. It's too small.* لا فائدة منه؛ لا يصلح

do you good to help or be useful to you: *It'll do you good to meet some new people.* يفيد

for good for ever: *I hope they've gone for good this time!* إلى الأبد

goodbye /ˌgʊdˈbaɪ/ *interj* (said when sb goes or you yourself go): *Goodbye! See you tomorrow!* ○ *We said goodbye to Steven at the airport.* ❶ **Cheerio**, **cheers** and **bye** are other less formal words with the same meaning. ❶ **Goodbye** can also be used as a noun: *We said our goodbyes and left.* وداعاً

Good Friday /ˌgʊd ˈfraɪdeɪ; -di/ *noun* [C] the Friday before Easter when Christians remember the death of Christ الجمعة الحزينة

ˌgood-ˈhumoured (*US* **ˌgood-ˈhumored**) *adj* pleasant and cheerful: *Although there were a lot of complaints, the manager remained polite and good-humoured.* أنيس؛ رائق المزاج

goodies /ˈgʊdiz/ *noun* [plural] (*informal*) **1** good things to eat طيّبات (المآكل)

2 anything that is attractive and that people want to have: *We're giving away lots of free goodies – T-shirts, hats and videos!* ملذات

ˌgood-ˈlooking *adj* (usually used about a person) attractive ➲ Look at the note at **beautiful**. جميل

ˌgood ˈlooks *noun* [plural] an attractive appearance (of a person) جَمال

ˌgood-ˈnatured *adj* friendly or cheerful دَمِث، حسن الطبع

goodness /ˈgʊdnəs/ *noun* [U] **1** the quality of being good طيبَة

2 the quality that helps sb/sth to grow: *Wholemeal bread has more goodness in it than white.* نفع

Goodness is used in a number of expressions. We say **Goodness (me)!** to show that we are surprised. **Thank goodness** expresses happiness and relief: *Thank goodness it's stopped raining!* We say **For goodness' sake** when we are asking somebody to do something and want to sound more urgent or when we are angry with somebody: *For goodness' sake, hurry up!*

goods /gʊdz/ *noun* [plural] **1** things that are for sale: *a wide range of consumer goods* ○ *electrical goods* ○ *stolen goods* بضاعة، سلع

2 (*also* **freight**) things that are carried by train or lorry: *a goods train* ○ *a heavy goods vehicle* (= *HGV*) ❶ **Freight** (not **goods**) is always used in American English. بضاعة؛ شحن

IDM **come up with/deliver the goods** (*informal*) to do what you have promised to do يفي (بوعده)

ˌgood ˈsense *noun* [U] good judgement or intelligence: *He had the good sense to refuse the offer.* حكمة، بصيرة

ˌgood-ˈtempered *adj* not easily made angry حليم

goodwill /ˌgʊdˈwɪl/ *noun* [U] friendly, helpful feelings towards other people: *There is a new atmosphere of goodwill in international politics.* حسن النية

goody /ˈgʊdi/ *noun* [C] (*pl.* **goodies**) (*informal*) a good person in a film, book, etc. ❶ The opposite is **baddy**.

goody-goody /ˈgʊdi gʊdi/ *noun* [C] (*pl.* **goody-goodies**) a person who always behaves well so that other people have a good opinion of him/her ❶ If you call somebody a goody-goody it usually means that you do not like him/her. انسان طيب (بصورة متكلّفة)

gooey → GOO

goof /guːf/ *verb* [I] (*informal*) (*especially US*) to make a silly mistake يخطئ بحماقة

goose /guːs/ *noun* (*pl.* **geese** /giːs/) [C] a large white bird that is like a duck, but bigger. Geese are kept on farms for their meat and eggs. ❶ A male goose is called a **gander** and a young goose is a **gosling**. إوَزّ

gooseberry /ˈgʊzbəri; *US* ˈguːsberi/ *noun* [C] (*pl.* **gooseberries**) a small green fruit that is covered in small hairs and has a sour taste: *a gooseberry bush* عِنَب الثعلب، كِشْمِش شائك

IDM play gooseberry to be present when two lovers want to be alone يلازم عاشقين يرغبان في الانفراد

ˈ**goose pimples** *noun* (*also* ˈ**goose bumps**; **gooseflesh** /ˈɡuːsfleʃ/ [U], *noun* [plural]) small points or lumps which appear on your skin because you are cold or frightened قشعْريرة

gore¹ /ɡɔː(r)/ *noun* [U] the blood that comes from a cut or wound ❶ The adjective is **gory**. دم متجلِّط (على جرح)

gore² /ɡɔː(r)/ *verb* [T] to wound sb with a horn, etc: *She was gored by a bull.* يطعن أو يجرح بالنطح مثلاً

gorge¹ /ɡɔːdʒ/ *noun* [C] a narrow valley with steep sides and a stream or river running through it فجّ (واد عميق ضيق فيه نهر)

gorge² /ɡɔːdʒ/ *verb* [I,T] **gorge (yourself) (on/with sth)** to eat a lot of food يلتهم؛ يملأ بطنه

gorgeous /ˈɡɔːdʒəs/ *adj* (*informal*) very good; wonderful: *What gorgeous weather!* ○ *You look gorgeous in that dress!* رائع

▸ **gorgeously** *adv* بشكل رائع

gorilla /ɡəˈrɪlə/ *noun* [C] a very large black African ape غوريلا

gorse /ɡɔːs/ *noun* [U] a bush with yellow flowers and thin thorny leaves that do not fall off in winter. Gorse often grows on land that is not used or cared for. جولق أوربي

gory /ˈɡɔːri/ *adj* (**gorier**; **goriest**) full of violence and blood: *a gory film* ○ (*figurative*) *He told me all the gory details about the divorce.* دامٍ، مليء بالعنف

gosh /ɡɒʃ/ *interj* (*informal*) (used for expressing surprise, shock, etc.) عبارة دهشة أو صدمة

gosling /ˈɡɒzlɪŋ/ *noun* [C] a young goose وَزّة صغيرة

gospel /ˈɡɒspl/ *noun* **1 Gospel** [sing.] one of the four books in the Bible that describe the life and teachings of Jesus Christ: *St Matthew's/Mark's/Luke's/John's Gospel* إنجيل

2 [U] the truth: *You can't take what he says as gospel.* حقيقة

3 [U] a style of religious music that is especially popular among black American Christians موسيقى دينية يحبها الأمريكان السود

gossip /ˈɡɒsɪp/ *noun* **1** [U] informal talk about other people and their private lives: *Don't believe all the gossip you hear.* ○ *He loves spreading gossip about his neighbours.* نميمة، قيل وقال

2 [C] a conversation (including gossip): *The two neighbours were having a gossip over the fence.* ثرثرة

▸ **gossip** *verb* [I]: *I can't stand here gossiping all day.* يثرثر

ˈ**gossip column** *noun* [C] a part of a newspaper or magazine where you can read about the private lives of famous people صفحة الثرثرة (في جريدة)

got *pt, pp of* GET

Gothic /ˈɡɒθɪk/ *adj* (used about architecture) connected with a style that was common in Europe from the 12th to the 16th centuries. Typical features of Gothic architecture are pointed arches, tall thin pillars, elaborate decoration, etc. قوطي

gotta /ˈɡɒtə/

> **Gotta** is a way of writing 'got to' or 'got a' to show that sb is speaking in an informal way or with a special accent. Do not write 'gotta' yourself (unless you are copying somebody's accent) because it might be marked as a mistake. **Gonna** and **wanna** are similar: *I gotta go* (= I have got to go). ○ *Gotta minute?* (= Have you got a minute?).

gotten (*US*) *pp of* GET

gouge /ɡaʊdʒ/ *verb*

PHR V gouge sth out to take sth out with force (usually with a tool or with your fingers) يقلع

gourmet /ˈɡʊəmeɪ/ *noun* [C] a person who enjoys good food and knows a lot about it: *a gourmet restaurant* ذوّاقة (للطعام)

🔑**govern** /ˈɡʌvn/ *verb* **1** [I,T] to rule or control the public affairs of a country, city, etc: *Britain is governed by the Prime Minister and the Cabinet.* يَحْكُم

2 [T] (often passive) to influence or control sb/sth: *Our decision will be governed by the amount of money we have to spend.* يؤثِّر في

🔑**government** /ˈɡʌvənmənt/ *noun* **1** often **the Government** [C] the group of people who govern a country: *He has resigned from the Government.* ○ *After the Prime Minister's resignation a new government was formed.* ○ *The Government has been overthrown.* ○ *The foreign governments involved are meeting in Geneva.* ○ *government policy, money, ministers, etc.*

> In the singular **government** may be followed by a singular or plural verb. We use a singular verb when we are thinking of the government as one single unit: *The Government welcomes the proposal.* We use a plural verb when we are thinking about all the individual members of the government: *The Government are still discussing the problem.*

❶ Different types of government are: **communist**, **conservative**, **democratic**, **liberal**, **reactionary**, **socialist**, etc. A country or state may also have a **military**, **provisional**, **central** or **federal**, **coalition**, etc. government. Look at **local government** and **opposition**. حكومة

2 [U] the act or method of governing: *Six years of weak government had left the economy in ruins.* حكومة، حكم

IDM in government being the government: *Which party is in government?* حاكم، في الحكم

▸ **governmental** /ˌɡʌvnˈmentl/ *adj*: *a governmental department* ○ *different governmental systems* حكومي

🔑**governor** /ˈɡʌvənə(r)/ *noun* [C] **1** a person who governs a province or state (especially in the USA): *the Governor of New York State* حاكم، محافظ

2 the leader or member of a group of people who govern an organization: *the governor of the Bank of England* ○ *school governors* مدير؛ عضو ادارة

gown /gaʊn/ *noun* [C] **1** a long woman's dress for a special occasion: *a ball gown* ثوب نسائي طويل رسمي

2 a loose piece of clothing that is worn by judges, lawyers, surgeons, etc. جُبّة (القاضي أو المحامي مثلاً)

GP /ˌdʒiː ˈpiː/ *abbrev* general practitioner; a doctor who treats all types of illnesses and works in a practice in a town or village, not in a hospital طبيب عام

grab /græb/ *verb* (gra**bb**ing; gra**bb**ed) **1** [I,T] to take sth suddenly or roughly: *Lily grabbed the toy car from her little brother.* ○ *Don't grab – there's plenty for everybody.* ○ *(figurative) He grabbed the opportunity of a free trip to America.* ○ *(figurative) I grabbed an hour's sleep on the train so I'm not too tired now.* ➲ Look at **snatch**. It is similar in meaning. يَخْطَف، ينتزع

2 [I] **grab at/for sth** to try to get hold of sb/sth: *She grabbed at the branch, missed and fell.* يمسك بِ

▶ **grab** /græb/ *noun* [C]: *She made a grab for the boy but she couldn't stop him falling.* محاولة إمساك

grace /greɪs/ *noun* [U] **1** the ability to move in a smooth and attractive way: *to walk, dance, move, etc. with grace* رشاقة

2 extra time that is allowed for sth: *Payment is due today, but we have been given a week's grace* (= an extra week to pay). مهلة

3 a short prayer of thanks to God before or after a meal: *Father always says grace.* دعاء قبل الطعام

4 His/Her/Your Grace (used when speaking about, or to, a duke, duchess or archbishop) صاحب العطوفة (لقب الدوق والدوقة ورئيس الأساقفة)

IDM **have the grace to do sth** to be polite enough to do sth: *At least she had the grace to apologize for what she did.* يتفضّل (بعمل شيء ما)

with good grace willingly and cheerfully, not showing that you are disappointed: *He accepted the decision with good grace although it wasn't the one that he had been hoping for.* بطيبة خاطر

graceful /ˈgreɪsfl/ *adj* having grace and beauty: *a graceful dancer* ➲ Look at **gracious**. Its meaning is different. رشيق

▶ **gracefully** /-fəli/ *adv*: *She accepted the decision gracefully* (= without showing her disappointment). بطيبة خاطر؛ برشاقة

gracefulness *noun* [U] رشاقة؛ لباقة

graceless /ˈgreɪsləs/ *adj* **1** without grace(1) or beauty عديم الرشاقة

2 rude جلف، وقح

▶ **gracelessly** *adv* دون رشاقة أو لباقة

gracious /ˈgreɪʃəs/ *adj* **1** (used about a person or his/her behaviour) pleasant, kind or polite (to sb of a lower social position): *a gracious smile* عَطوف، مهذّب؛ رقيق

2 (only *before* a noun) (*formal*) (used when speaking about royal people): *by gracious permission of Her Majesty* كريم

3 (only *before* a noun) owned or enjoyed by rich people: *gracious living* مترَف

➲ Look at **graceful**. Its meaning is different.

IDM **good gracious!** (used for expressing surprise: *Good gracious! Is that the time?* عبارة دهشة

▶ **graciously** *adv* بلطف

graciousness *noun* [U] لطف

grade[1] /greɪd/ *noun* [C] **1** the quality or place in a series that sb/sth has: *Which grade of petrol do you need?* ○ *She has passed her violin exams at Grade 6.* ○ *We need to use high-grade materials for this job.* درجة؛ نوع

2 a mark that is given for school work, etc. or in an examination: *He got good/poor grades this term.* ○ *Very few students pass the exam with a grade A.* درجة أو مرتبة

3 (*US*) a class or classes in a school in which all the children are the same age: *My daughter is in the third grade.* صف (في مدرسة)

IDM **make the grade** (*informal*) to reach the expected standard; to succeed يُوفَق، ينجح

grade[2] /greɪd/ *verb* [T] (often passive) to divide things or people into groups, according to their quality or size: *I've graded their work from 1 to 10.* ○ *Students with 90% correct are graded A.* ○ *Eggs are graded by size.* يُصنِّف

ˈ**grade crossing** *noun* [C] (*US*) = LEVEL CROSSING

gradient /ˈgreɪdiənt/ *noun* [C] the steepness of a slope: *The hill has a gradient of 1 in 4* (= 25%). ○ *a steep gradient* تدرُّج (معدَّل الانحدار)

gradual /ˈgrædʒuəl/ *adj* happening slowly or over a long period of time; not sudden: *There has been a gradual increase in the number of people without jobs.* تدريجي

▶ **gradually** /-dʒuəli/ *adv*: *After the storm things gradually got back to normal.* تدريجيًا

graduate[1] /ˈgrædʒuət/ *noun* [C] **1 a graduate (in sth)** a person who holds a (first) degree from a university, etc: *a law graduate/a graduate in law* ○ *a graduate student* (= a student who has already got a first degree and who is studying for a further (postgraduate) degree) ➲ Look at **postgraduate**, **undergraduate** and **bachelor** and the note at **student**. خرّيج (من جامعة)

2 (*US*) a person who has completed a course at a school, college, etc: *a high-school graduate* خريج مدرسة أو كليّة (في أمريكا)

graduate[2] /ˈgrædʒueɪt/ *verb* [I] **1 graduate (in sth) (from sth)** to get a (first) degree from a university, etc. يتخرّج (من جامعة)

2 (*US*) **graduate (in sth) (from sth)** to complete a course at a school, college, etc. يتخرّج (من مدرسة أو كلية)

3 graduate (from sth) to sth to change (from sth) to sth more difficult, important, expensive, etc: *Language learners graduate from using single words to short phrases and sentences.* يرتقي يتدرّج

▸ **graduation** /ˌɡrædʒuˈeɪʃn/ *noun* **1** [U] graduating from a university, etc. تَخرُّج (من جامعة)

2 [sing.] a ceremony in which degree certificates are given to people who have graduated from a university, etc. حفلة تخرُّج

graffiti /ɡrəˈfiːti/ *noun* [U, plural] pictures or writing on a wall, etc. in a public place that are rude, funny or political: *The wall was covered with graffiti.* خَرْبشات جدارية

graft /ɡrɑːft; *US* ɡræft/ *noun* [C] **1** a piece of a living plant that is fixed inside another plant so that it will grow طُعْم (في نبات)

2 a piece of living skin, bone, etc. that is fixed onto a damaged part of a body in a medical operation: *a skin graft* رقعة (في الجراحة)

▸ **graft** *verb* [T] **graft sth onto sth** to fix sth as a graft onto a plant, body, etc. ➲ Look at **transplant**. يطعِّم: يرقِّع

⚷**grain**[1] /ɡreɪn/ *noun* **1** [U] the seeds of wheat, rice, etc. as a product: *The USA is a major producer of grain.* ○ *grain exports* حَبّ (الحنطة أو الرز أو ما يشبه ذلك)

2 [C] a single seed of wheat, rice, etc. حَبّة

3 [C] a very small piece of sth: *a grain of sand, salt, sugar, etc.* ○ (*figurative*) *There isn't a grain of truth in what you say.* حَبّة

grain[2] /ɡreɪn/ *noun* [C] the natural pattern of lines that can be seen or felt in wood, rock, stone, etc: *to cut a piece of wood along/across the grain* تجزّع: اتجاه عروق (الخشب أو الصخر أو الحجر)

IDM **be/go against the grain** to be difficult to do because you do not really think that it is the right thing: *It goes against the grain to say I'm sorry when I'm not sorry at all.* غير طبيعي؛ يتعارض مع رغبة المرء

⚷**gram** (*also* **gramme**) /ɡræm/ *noun* [C] (*abbr* **g**) a measure of weight. There are 1 000 grams in a kilogram. غرام (وزن)

⚷**grammar** /ˈɡræmə(r)/ *noun* **1** [U] the rules of language, e.g. for forming words or joining words together in sentences: *Russian grammar can be difficult for foreign learners.* علم قواعد اللغة

2 [U] the way in which sb uses the rules of language: *You have a good vocabulary, but your grammar needs improvement.* مدى علم شخص بقواعد اللغة

3 [C] a book that describes and explains the rules of grammar: *a French grammar* كتاب قواعد

ˈ**grammar school** *noun* [C] (*Brit*) (especially in the past) a type of secondary school for children from 11 to 18 who are good at academic subjects مدرسة اعدادية في بريطانيا

grammatical /ɡrəˈmætɪkl/ *adj* **1** connected with grammar: *the grammatical rules for forming plurals* متعلّق بقواعد اللغة

2 following the rules of grammar: *The sentence is not grammatical.* ❶ The opposite is **ungrammatical**. نحوي، متفق مع قواعد اللغة

▸ **grammatically** /-kli/ *adv* بشكل متفق مع قواعد اللغة

gramme /ɡræm/ *noun* [C] = GRAM

gramophone /ˈɡræməfəʊn/ *noun* [C] (*Brit old-fashioned*) = RECORD PLAYER: *a gramophone record*

gran /ɡræn/ *noun* [C] (*Brit informal*) = GRANDMOTHER

grand- /ɡrænd/ (used before a noun to show a family relationship) صفة تحدد درجة القرابة

> If you need to distinguish between a grandparent on your mother's and your father's side you can say: *My maternal/paternal grandfather* or *my mother's/father's father.*

⚷**grand**[1] /ɡrænd/ *adj* **1** looking splendid in size or appearance (also used in names): *Our house isn't very grand, but it has a big garden.* ○ *the Grand Canyon* ○ *the Grand Hotel* ❶ The noun is **grandeur**. عظيم

2 seeming to be important or thinking that you are important: *She thinks she's very grand because she drives a Porsche.* عظيم

3 (*informal*) very good or pleasant: *You've done a grand job!* جليل

▸ **grandly** *adv* بعظمة

grandness *noun* [U] عَظمة

grand[2] /ɡrænd/ *noun* [C] (*pl.* **grand**) (*slang*) 1 000 pounds or dollars: *It'll cost you 50 grand!!* ألف (جنيه أو دولار: عبارة عامية)

grandad /ˈɡrændæd/ *noun* [C] (*Brit informal*) = GRANDFATHER

⚷ˈ**grandchild** /ˈɡræntʃaɪld/ ˈ**granddaughter**, ˈ**grandson** *nouns* [C] the daughter or son of your child حفيد أو حفيدة

grandeur /ˈɡrændʒə(r)/ *noun* [U] (*formal*) **1** the quality of being large and impressive: *the grandeur of the Swiss alps* عظمة، أبّهة

2 the feeling of being important شعور بالعظمة

⚷ˈ**grandfather** /ˈɡrænfɑːðə(r)/, ˈ**grandmother** /ˈɡrænmʌðə(r)/, ˈ**grandparent** /ˈɡrænpeərənt/ *nouns* [C] the father or mother of one of your parents جد أو جدة

ˈ**grandfather clock** *noun* [C] a clock that stands on the floor in a tall wooden case ساعة دقاقة في صندوق خشبي كبير

grandiose /ˈɡrændiəʊs/ *adj* bigger or more complicated than necessary: *Their grandiose scheme was completely impractical.* ❶ Using this word about something shows that you do not have a good opinion of it. مُفرط في الكبر أو التعقيد

grandma /ˈɡrænmɑː/ *noun* [C] (*informal*) = GRANDMOTHER

grandpa /ˈɡrænpɑː/ *noun* [C] (*informal*) = GRANDFATHER

ˌ**grand piˈano** *noun* [C] a large flat piano (with horizontal strings) بيانو كبير مسطّح

ˌ**grand ˈslam** *noun* [C] winning all the important

matches or competitions in a particular sport, e. g. rugby or tennis الفوز بالمباريات جميعاً

grandstand /ˈgrændstænd/ *noun* [C] rows of seats (covered by a roof) from which you get a good view of a sports competition, etc. مُدَرَّج رئيسي (في ملعب رياضي)

ˌgrand ˈtotal *noun* [C] the amount that you get when you add several totals together المجموع الكلي

granite /ˈgrænɪt/ *noun* [U] a hard grey rock صَوّان

granny (*also* **grannie**) /ˈgræni/ *noun* [C] (*pl.* **grannies**) (*informal*) = GRANDMOTHER

grant /grɑːnt; *US* grænt/ *verb* [T] **1** (*formal*) to give sb what he/she has asked for: *A visa has been granted to one of our journalists.* ○ *He was granted permission to leave early.* يَمنَح

2 to agree (that sth is true): *I grant you that New York is an interesting place but I still wouldn't want to live there.* يقِر

IDM **take sb/sth for granted** to show too little attention to sb/sth; to not be grateful enough to a person or thing: *In developed countries we take running water for granted.* ○ *She never says thank you – she just takes me for granted.* لا يبالي به

take sth for granted to accept sth as being true: *We can take it for granted that the new students will have at least an elementary knowledge of English.* يصَدّق، يسلّم بأنه صحيح

▸ **grant** *noun* [C] money that is given (by the government, etc.) for a particular purpose: *a student grant* (= to help pay for university education) منحة

granted *adv* (used for saying that sth is true, before you make a comment about it): *'We've never had any problems before.' 'Granted, but this year there are 200 more people coming.'* هذا صحيح ... ولكن

granule /ˈgrænjuːl/ *noun* [C] a small hard piece or grain of sth: *coffee granules* حُبَيبة

grape /greɪp/ *noun* [C] a green or purple berry that grows in bunches on a climbing plant (a vine): *a bunch of grapes*

> Green grapes are usually called 'white' and purple grapes are usually called 'black'. Grapes that have been dried are called **raisins**, **currants** or **sultanas**.

عِنَب

grapefruit /ˈgreɪpfruːt/ *noun* [C] (*pl.* **grapefruit** or **grapefruits**) a large round yellow fruit with a thick skin that is like a big orange but with a sour taste غريبفروت، غريفون، ليمون هندي

the grapevine /ˈgreɪpvaɪn/ *noun* [sing.] the way that news is passed from one person to another: *I heard on/through the grapevine that you are moving.* انتشار الاشاعات

graph /grɑːf; *US* græf/ *noun* [C] a mathematical diagram in which a line or a curve shows the relationship between two quantities, measurements, etc: *a graph showing/to show the number of cars sold each month* ○ *graph paper* مُخَطَّط، رسم بياني

graphs

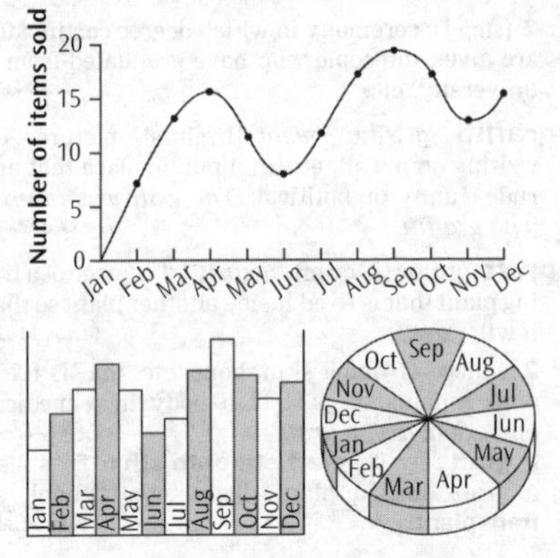

bar chart pie chart

graphic /ˈgræfɪk/ *adj* **1** (only *before* a noun) connected with drawings, letters, diagrams, etc: *graphic design* تخطيطي

2 (used about descriptions) clear and giving a lot of detail: *She described the accident in graphic detail.* واضح ومفصّل، (وصف) حيّ

▸ **graphically** /-kli/ *adv* بشكل واضح ومفصّل

graphics *noun* [plural] the production of drawings, letters, diagrams, etc: *computer graphics* تخطيط

grapple /ˈgræpl/ *verb* [I] **grapple (with sb)** to get hold of sb and struggle or fight with him/her: *She grappled with the thief, but he got away.* ○ (*figurative*) *We have been grappling with this problem all day.* يصارع

grasp /grɑːsp; *US* græsp/ *verb* [T] **1** to take hold of sb/sth suddenly and firmly: *Lisa grasped the child firmly by the hand before crossing the road.* ○ (*figurative*) *to grasp an opportunity* يمْسِك

2 to understand sth: *I don't think you've grasped how serious the situation is.* يدْرِك

PHR V **grasp at sth** to try to seize or grasp sth: *He grasped at the swinging rope, but missed.* يحاول أن يمْسِك

▸ **grasp** *noun* [usually sing.] **1** a firm hold or control over sb/sth: *a strong grasp* مَسْكة، قبضة

2 the ability to get or achieve sth: *Finally their dream was within their grasp.* قيد التحقيق: متناول اليد

3 understanding: *He has a good grasp of English grammar.* فَهم

grasping /ˈgrɑːspɪŋ; *US* ˈgræspɪŋ/ *adj* greedy for money, power, etc. طمّاع

grass /grɑːs; *US* græs/ *noun* **1** [U] the common green plant with thin leaves which covers fields and parts of gardens. Cows, sheep, horses, etc. eat grass: *She lay on the grass and listened to the birds singing.* ○ *Don't walk on the grass.* ○ *I must* *cut the grass at the weekend.* ○ *a blade* (= one leaf) *of grass* ❶ An area of grass in a garden is called a **lawn**. عُشب، حشيش

2 [C] one type of grass: *an arrangement of dried flowers and grasses* عُشب

▸ **grassy** *adj* covered with grass معشب

grasshopper /ˈgrɑːshɒpə(r); *US* ˈgræs-/ *noun* [C] an insect that lives in long grass and that can jump high in the air جرادة

ˌgrass ˈroots *noun* [plural] the ordinary people in an organization and not those who make decisions: *dissatisfaction with party policy at the grass roots* الأعضاء العاديّون؛ القاعدة الشعبية

grate¹ /greɪt/ *noun* [C] the metal frame that holds the wood, coal, etc. in a fireplace; the area surrounding it موقِد

grate² /greɪt/ *verb* **1** [T] to rub food into small pieces using a metal tool (a grater): *Grate the cheese and sprinkle it over the top of the dish.* يبشر

2 [I] to make a sharp unpleasant sound (when two surfaces rub against each other): *The hinges grated as the gate swung back.* يَصِرّ (يولد صوتاً حاداً ومزعجاً)

3 [I] **grate (on sb)** to annoy or irritate: *It's her voice that grates on me.* يضايق

▸ **grater** *noun* [C] a kitchen utensil with a rough surface that is used for grating food مِبشَرة

grateful /ˈgreɪtfl/ *adj* **grateful (to sb) (for sth)**; **grateful (that...)** feeling or showing thanks (to sb): *We are very grateful to you for all the help you have given us.* ○ *He was very grateful that you did as he asked.* ○ *I would be very grateful if you could send me a copy of your brochure.* ❶ The opposite is **ungrateful**. ❶ The noun is **gratitude**. ممتن

▸ **gratefully** /-fəli/ *adv* بامتنان

gratify /ˈgrætɪfaɪ/ *verb* [T] (*pres part* **gratifying**; *3rd pers sing pres* **gratifies**; *pt, pp* **gratified**) (*formal*) (often passive) to give sb pleasure يُرضي، يَسرّ

▸ **gratifying** *adj* مُرضٍ، مسر

grating /ˈgreɪtɪŋ/ *noun* [C] a framework of metal bars that is fixed over a window or over a hole in the road, etc. حاجز مشبَّك

gratitude /ˈgrætɪtjuːd; *US* -tuːd/ *noun* [U] **gratitude (to sb) (for sth)** the feeling of being grateful or thankful: *We should like to express our gratitude to David Stewart for all his help and advice.* ❶ The opposite is **ingratitude**. امتنان

grave¹ /greɪv/ *noun* [C] the place where a dead body is buried: *The coffin was lowered into the grave.* ○ *I put some flowers on the grave.* قبر

grave² /greɪv/ *adj* (*formal*) **1** bad or serious: *These events could have grave consequences for us all.* خطير، سيئ

2 (used about people) sad or serious: *He was looking extremely grave.* جادّ، حزين

❶ The noun is **gravity**. ❶ **Serious** is much more common for both senses.

gravel /ˈgrævl/ *noun* [U] very small stones that are used for making roads, paths, etc. حصى

gravestone /ˈgreɪvstəʊn/ *noun* [C] a stone over a grave that shows the name, etc. of the person who is buried there شاهد (القبر)

graveyard /ˈgreɪvjɑːd/ *noun* [C] an area of land (near a church) where dead people are buried ➲ Look at **cemetery** and **churchyard**. مقبَرة

gravity¹ /ˈgrævəti/ *noun* [U] the natural force that makes things fall to the ground when you drop them: *the force of gravity* الثقالة، الجاذبية الأرضية

gravity² /ˈgrævəti/ *noun* [U] (*formal*) importance or seriousness: *Politicians are only now realizing the gravity of the situation.* ❶ **Seriousness** is more common. ❶ The adjective is **grave**. خطورة، أهمية

gravy /ˈgreɪvi/ *noun* [U] a thin sauce that is made from the juices that come out of meat while it is cooking. Gravy is served with meat, vegetables, etc. ➲ Look at **sauce**. مرق اللحم

gray /greɪ/ *adj, noun* [C,U] (*especially US*) = GREY

graze¹ /greɪz/ *verb* [I] (used about cows, sheep, etc.) to eat grass (that is growing in a field) يرعى

graze² /greɪz/ *verb* [T] **1** to injure your skin because you have scraped it against sth rough: *The child fell and grazed her knee.* يكشط (الجلد)

2 to pass sth and touch it lightly: *The car's tyre grazed the pavement.* يلامس

▸ **graze** *noun* [C] the small wound where the skin has been grazed كشط جلدي

grease /griːs/ *noun* [U] **1** a thick oily substance used, for example, to make engines run smoothly: *engine grease* ○ *grease marks* شحْم؛ مادة دهنية

2 animal fat that has been softened by cooking: *You'll need very hot water to get all the grease off those pans.* دهن

▸ **grease** *verb* [T] to put grease on or in sth: *Grease the tin thoroughly to stop the cake from sticking.* يشحّم؛ يدهن (بالسمن مثلاً)

greasy /ˈgriːsi/ *adj* (**greasier**; **greasiest**) covered with or containing a lot of grease: *greasy fingers* ○ *greasy skin* ○ *greasy food* مدهن

great /greɪt/ *adj* **1** large in amount, degree, size, etc.; a lot of: *We had great difficulty in solving the problem.* ○ *The party was a great success.* ○ *It gives me great pleasure to introduce tonight's guest.* ○ (*formal*) *The town was dominated by the great cathedral.* ➲ Look at the note at **big**. كبير؛ عظيم

2 particularly important; of unusually high quality: *Einstein was perhaps the greatest scientist of the century.* ○ *Alexander the Great* ○ *a great moment in history* عظيم

3 (*informal*) good; wonderful: *We had a great time in Paris.* ○ *It's great to see you again.* ❶ We sometimes use **great** in a sarcastic way, that is, when something is not good at all: *Oh great! I've spilled coffee all over my homework!* رائع

4 (*informal*) (used to emphasize sth) very; very

good: *There was a great big dog in the garden.* ○ *They were great friends.* جداً؛ ممتاز

IDM go to great lengths → LENGTH
a good/great deal → DEAL[1]
a good/great many → MANY

▸ **great** *noun* [C, usually pl.] (*informal*) a person or thing of special ability or importance: *That film is one of the all-time greats.* شخص أو شيئ عظيم

greatly *adv* very much: *She will be greatly missed by friends and family.* كثيراً

greatness *noun* [U] عظمة

great- /greɪt/ (used before a noun to show a family relationship) للدلالة على درجة القرابة

> **Great-** can be added to other words for family members to show another generation: *your great-aunt* (= the aunt of your mother or father) ○ *your great-nephew* (= the son of your nephew or niece) ○ *your great-great-grandfather* (= the grandfather of one of your grandparents).

ˌGreat ˈBritain (*also* **Britain**) (*abbr* **GB**) England, Wales and Scotland ➲ Look at the note at **United Kingdom.** بريطانيا العظمى

ˌgreat-ˈgrandchild, **ˌgreat-ˈgranddaughter**, **ˌgreat-ˈgrandson** *noun* [C] the daughter or son of your grandchild ابن أو ابنة الحفيد أو الحفيدة

ˌgreat-ˈgrandfather, **ˌgreat-ˈgrandmother**, **ˌgreat-ˈgrandparent** *noun* [C] the father or mother of one of your grandparents أب أو أم الجدّ أو الجدّة

greed /griːd/ *noun* [U] **greed (for sth)** a strong desire for more food, money, power, etc. than you really need طمع

▸ **greedy** *adj* (**greedier**; **greediest**) **greedy (for sth)** wanting more food, money, power, etc. than you really need: *Don't be so greedy – you've had three pieces of cake already.* طمّاع، جَشِع

greedily *adv* بطمع؛ بنهم

greediness *noun* [U] طمع

green[1] /griːn/ *adj* **1** of the colour of grass or leaves: *dark/light/pale green* ○ *olive green* ○ *I love the spring when everything's green.* ○ *These bananas aren't ripe yet – they're still green.* أخضر

2 (*informal*) (used about a person) with little experience: *I'm not so green as to believe that!* غِرّ، ساذج

3 pale in the face (because you have had a shock or feel ill): *At the sight of all the blood he turned green and fainted.* شاحب

4 envious (wanting to have what sb else has got): *He was green with envy when he saw his neighbour's new car.* حسود

5 connected with protecting the environment or the natural world: *the Green party* ○ *green products* (= that do not damage the environment) متعلق بحماية الطبيعة

IDM give sb/get the green light (*informal*) to give sb/get permission to do sth يأذن

▸ **greenish** /ˈgriːnɪʃ/ *adj* rather green مخضر

green[2] /griːn/ *noun* **1** [C,U] the colour of grass and leaves: *They were dressed in green.* ○ *The room was decorated in greens and blues.* خَضار، اللون الأخضر

2 greens [plural] green vegetables, e.g. cabbage, that are usually eaten cooked الخُضَر

3 [C] (*Brit*) an area of grass in the centre of a village: *the village green* ساحة معشبة في مركز قرية إنكليزية

4 [C] a flat area of very short grass used in games such as golf: *the green at the 18th hole* مرج أو مَلْعَب معْشب (للعبة الجولف مثلا)

5 Green [C] a member of a green[1](5) political party عضو في حزب يدافع عن البيئة

ˌgreen ˈbelt *noun* [C, U] an area of land around a city where building is not allowed حزام أخضر (منطقة مشجّرة محيطة بمدينة)

ˌgreen ˈcard *noun* [C] a document that allows sb from another country to live and work in the US البطاقة الخضراء

ˌgreen ˈfingers *noun* [plural] (*informal*) the ability to make plants grow well حاذق في الاستنبات: "يده خضراء"

greengage /ˈgriːngeɪdʒ/ *noun* [C] a small yellowish-green plum برقوق أو خَوْخ أخضر

greengrocer /ˈgriːngrəʊsə(r)/ *noun* [C] (*Brit*) a person who sells fruit and vegetables in a small shop (a greengrocer's): *I bought these strawberries at the greengrocer's.* خضري

greenhouse /ˈgriːnhaʊs/ *noun* [C] a building made of glass in which plants are grown بيت زجاجي (للنباتات)

ˈgreenhouse effect *noun* [sing.] the warming of the earth's atmosphere as a result of pollution مفعول البيوت الزجاجية

ˌgreen ˈpepper *noun* [C] → PEPPER (2)

greenwash /ˈgriːnwɒʃ/ *noun* [U] activities by a company or an organization that are intended to make people think that it is concerned about the environment, even if its real business actually harms the environment نشاطات تقوم بها منظمة ما تدّعي كونها صديقة للبيئة

greet /griːt/ *verb* [T] **1** to welcome sb when you meet him/her; to say hello to sb: *He greeted me with a friendly smile.* ○ (*figurative*) *As we entered the house we were greeted by the smell of cooking.* يُحَيّي

2 greet sth with sth (usually passive) to receive sth in a particular way: *The news was greeted with a loud cheer.* يستقبل

▸ **greeting** *noun* [C] **1** the first words you say when you meet sb: *'Hello' and 'Hi' are informal greetings.* تحية

2 [usually pl.] a good wish: *a greetings card* تَمنّيات؛ تحية

gregarious /grɪˈgeəriəs/ *adj* liking to be with other people محبّ للناس، اجتماعيّ

grenade /grəˈneɪd/ *noun* [C] a small bomb that is thrown by hand or fired from a gun: *a hand grenade* قنبلة يدوية

grew *pt of* GROW

grey (*especially US* **gray**) /greɪ/ *adj* **1** of the colour between black and white: *dark/light/pale grey* ○ *He was wearing a grey suit.* ○ *She looked grey with tiredness.* رمادي

2 with grey hair: *He's going grey.* شائب

▸ **grey** (*especially US* **gray**) *noun* [C,U] the colour between black and white الرمادي

greyish (*especially US* **grayish**) *adj* rather grey شبيه بالرمادي

greyhound /ˈgreɪhaʊnd/ *noun* [C] a large thin dog that can run very fast and that is used for racing: *greyhound racing* كلب سَلوقي

grid /grɪd/ *noun* [C] **1** a pattern of lines that cross each other to form squares شبكة

2 a system of squares that are drawn on a map so that the position of any place can be described or found: *a grid reference* خطوط متعامدة على خريطة

3 the system of electricity cables, etc. taking power to all parts of a country: *the National Grid* شبكة كهربائية

gridlock /ˈgrɪdlɒk/ *noun* [U] **1** a situation in which there are so many cars in the streets of a town that the traffic cannot move at all تشابك حركة السير، إستعصاء السير

2 (especially in politics) a situation in which people with different opinions are not able to agree with each other and so no action can be taken معمعة

▸ **gridlocked** *adj* (حركة سير) متشابكة أو متوقفة

grief /griːf/ *noun* [U] **1** great sadness (especially because of the death of sb you love) أسى، لوعة

2 (*informal*) problems and worry هموم

IDM good grief (*informal*) (used for expressing surprise or shock): *Good grief! Whatever happened to you?* يا للدهشة، يا للعجب

grievance /ˈgriːvns/ *noun* [C] **a grievance (against sb)** something that you think is unfair and that you want to complain or protest about: *The workers aired* (= expressed) *their grievances at the meeting.* تَظَلُّم، شكوى

grieve /griːv/ *verb* **1** [I] **grieve (for sb)** to feel great sadness (especially about the death of sb you love): *He is still grieving for his wife.* يَتألّم، يشعر بالفجيعة

2 [T] to cause unhappiness: *It grieves me to have to refuse.* يحْزِن، يؤلم

grill /grɪl/ *noun* [C] **1** a part of a cooker where the food is cooked by heat from above: *Sprinkle with cheese and put under the grill to brown.* مشواة

2 a framework of metal bars that you put food on to cook over a fire or on a barbecue مشواة

▸ **grill** *verb* **1** (*especially US* **broil**) [I,T] to cook under a grill: *grilled steak* ➲ Look at the note at **cook**. يَشْوي

2 [T] (*informal*) to question sb for a long time: *When she got home her parents grilled her about where she had been.* يستجوب طويلاً

grille /grɪl/ *noun* [C] a framework of metal bars that is placed over a window, etc. قضبان حديدية على نافذة

grim /grɪm/ *adj* (**grimmer**; **grimmest**) **1** (used about a person) very serious; not smiling: *The fireman's face was grim when he came out of the burning house.* متجهم

2 (used about a situation, news, etc.) unpleasant or worrying: *We face the grim prospect of even higher inflation.* ○ *The news is grim, I'm afraid.* مزْعِج، مقيت؛ مقلق

3 (used about a place) unpleasant to look at; not attractive: *They lived in a grim block of flats in South London.* بَشِع

4 (*informal*) ill: *I was feeling grim yesterday but I managed to get to work.* مريض

▸ **grimly** *adv* بِتَجهُّم؛ بإصرار

grimace /grɪˈmeɪs; ˈgrɪməs/ *noun* [C] an expression on your face that shows that you are angry or that sth is hurting you: *a grimace of pain* تقطيب، تكشير

▸ **grimace** *verb* [I] to make a grimace: *She grimaced with pain.* يُقطِّب، يكشر

grime /graɪm/ *noun* [U] a thick layer of dirt طبقة من الأوساخ

▸ **grimy** *adj* (**grimier**; **grimiest**) very dirty قذر

grin /grɪn/ *verb* [I] (**grinning**; **grinned**) to smile broadly (so that you show your teeth): *She grinned at me as she came into the room.* يبتسم ابتسامة عريضة

▸ **grin** *noun* [C]: *He came in with a big grin on his face and told us the good news.* ابتسامة عريضة

grind /graɪnd/ *verb* [T] (*pt, pp* **ground** /graʊnd/) **1** to crush sth into very small pieces or into a powder between two hard surfaces: *Wheat is ground into flour.* ○ *ground pepper* يطحن

2 to make sth sharp or smooth by rubbing it on a rough hard surface: *to grind a knife on a stone* يشْحَذ

3 to press sth together or into sth firmly: *Some people grind their teeth while they're asleep.* يحك؛ يَصِرّ (أسنانه مثلاً)

IDM grind to a halt/standstill to stop slowly: (*figurative*) *The talks ground to a halt yesterday.* يتوقف شيئاً فشيئاً

grinder /ˈgraɪndə(r)/ *noun* [C] a machine for grinding: *a coffee grinder* طاحون، مطحنة

grip /grɪp/ *verb* [T] (**gripping**; **gripped**) to take and keep hold of sb/sth firmly: *She gripped my arm in fear.* ○ (*figurative*) *The story really gripped my imagination.* يَقْبِض على

▸ **grip** *noun* **1** [sing.] **a grip (on sb/sth)** a firm hold (on sb/sth): *I relaxed my grip and he ran away.* ○ *You need tyres that give a good grip.* ○ (*figurative*) *The teacher kept a firm grip on the class.* قَبْضَة أو مسكة قوية

2 [C] (*US*) a bag that you use when you are travelling or for sports equipment حقيبة صغيرة

IDM come/get to grips with sth to start dealing with a problem in an effective way: *The government is still trying to get to grips with inflation.* يعالج مشكلة

get/keep/take a grip/hold on yourself (*informal*) to try to behave in a calmer or more sensible way يحتفظ بهدوء أعصابه

a b c d e f g h i j k l m n o p q r s t u v w x y z

gripping *adj* exciting; holding your attention: *a gripping film* خلّاب، مثير

grisly /ˈɡrɪzli/ *adj* (**grislier**; **grisliest**) (used for describing sth that is concerned with death) horrible; terrible: *The detective stared at the grisly remains of the bodies.* ➲ Look at **gruesome**. It is similar in meaning. رهيب، مريع

grit /ɡrɪt/ *noun* [U] **1** small pieces of stone: *I've got some grit/a piece of grit in my shoe.* حصباء، رمل خشن

2 (*informal*) courage; determination جَسارة، جَلَد

▶ **grit** *verb* [T] (gritting; gritted) to cover sth with grit: *The roads are gritted in icy weather.* يغطّي بالرمل الخشن

IDM **grit your teeth** to have courage or determination in a difficult situation: *If things get difficult, you'll have to grit your teeth and keep going.* يجْرُؤ؛ يبدي جلَداً

groan /ɡrəʊn/ *verb* [I] to make a deep sad sound because you are in pain, or to show that you are unhappy or do not approve of sth: *He groaned with pain.* ○ *The children groaned when I told them we were going on a long walk.* ○ *The audience groaned at his terrible jokes.* يئِن

▶ **groan** *noun* [C] the sound that you make when you groan أنين

grocer /ˈɡrəʊsə(r)/ *noun* [C] a person who sells food and other things for the home in a small shop ❶ Note that **the grocer** is the person who runs the shop and **the grocer's** is the shop. ➲ Look at **greengrocer**. سمّان، بقال

⚷ **groceries** /ˈɡrəʊsəriz/ *noun* [plural] food such as flour, sugar, tea, coffee, etc. that is sold by a grocer بضاعة البقّال

groggy /ˈɡrɒɡi/ *adj* (**groggier**; **groggiest**) (*informal*) weak and unable to walk steadily because you feel ill, have not had enough sleep, etc. متوَعك؛ مترنّح

groin /ɡrɔɪn/ *noun* [C] the place where the tops of the legs join the body أُرْبية (ما بين الفخذ والبطن)

groom /ɡruːm/ *noun* [C] **1** a person who looks after horses سائس

2 = BRIDEGROOM

▶ **groom** *verb* [T] **1** to clean or look after an animal by brushing, etc. يتعهد حيواناً بالعناية يفرجن (يعنى بالخيل)

2 (usually passive) to choose and prepare sb for a particular career or job: *He is clearly being groomed for the top job.* يهيّئ (إنسانا لأمر)

groove /ɡruːv/ *noun* [C] a long deep line that is cut in the surface of sth: *the grooves on a record* أخدود

grope /ɡrəʊp/ *verb* [I] **grope (about) (for/after sth)** to search for sth using your hands, as you do in the dark: *He groped for the light switch.* يتحسّس

PHR V **grope (your way) across, along, past, etc. (sth)** to move across, along, past, etc. sth by feeling the way with your hands: *Vic groped his way along the darkened landing and into his bedroom.* يتحسّس طريقه

gross /ɡrəʊs/ *adj* **1** very impolite and unpleasant: *His behaviour was really gross.* فظّ

2 (*formal*) obvious or serious: *There is gross inequality between the rich and the poor.* صارخ؛ واضح

3 total: *gross income* (= before tax, etc. is taken away) ❶ The opposite is **net**. إجْمالي

4 very fat and ugly مفرِط في السمْنة

▶ **grossly** *adv* very: *That is grossly unfair.* جِداً

grotesque /ɡrəʊˈtesk/ *adj* strange or unnatural in a way that is funny or frightening شاذ بشكل مضحك أو مخيف

grotty /ˈɡrɒti/ *adj* (**grottier**; **grottiest**) (*Brit informal*) unpleasant; not nice: *She lives in a grotty flat in London.* بَشِع

⚷ **ground**[1] /ɡraʊnd/ *noun* **1 the ground** [sing.] the solid surface of the earth: *We sat on the ground to eat our picnic.* ○ *He slipped off the ladder and fell to the ground.* ○ *waste ground* (= that is not being used) ○ *ground level* أرض

2 [U] an area or type of soil: *stony ground* تُرْبة، أرض

> The **Earth** is the name of the planet where we live. **Land** is the opposite of sea: *The sailors sighted land./The astronauts returned to Earth.* **Land** is also something that you can buy or sell: *The price of land in Tokyo is extremely high.* When you are outside, the surface under your feet is called **the ground**. When you are inside it is called **the floor**: *Don't sit on the ground. You'll get wet.* ○ *Don't sit on the floor. I'll get another chair.* Plants grow in **earth** or **soil**.

3 [C] a piece of land that is used for a particular purpose: *a sports ground* ○ *a playground* قطعة من الأرض (لغاية ما)

4 grounds [plural] land or gardens surrounding a large building: *the grounds of Buckingham Palace* الحدائق أو الأراضي المحيطة ببناء

5 [U] an area of interest, study, discussion, etc: *The lecture went over the same old ground/ covered a lot of new ground.* موْضوع؛ مادة

6 [C, usually pl.] a reason for sth: *She retired on medical grounds.* ○ *grounds for divorce* أسباب

7 [C, usually sing.] (*US*) = EARTH[2]

IDM **above/below ground** above/below the surface of the earth فوق سطح الأرض أو تحته

break fresh/new ground to make a discovery or introduce a new method or activity: *Scientists are breaking new ground in the field of genetic engineering.* يكتشف؛ يبدِع

gain ground → GAIN[2]

get off the ground (used about a business, scheme, etc.) to make a successful start ينطلق بنجاح

ground[2] /ɡraʊnd/ *verb* [T] **1** to force an aircraft, etc. to stay on the ground: *to be grounded by fog* يمنع (طائرة) من الطيران

2 = EARTH[2]

3 (usually passive) to punish a child by not allowing him/her to go out with friends for a period of time يبقى قابعاً، يحرم من الخروج

▸ **grounding** *noun* [sing.] knowledge of the basic facts or principles of a subject: *This book provides a good grounding in English grammar.* معرفة أسس موضوع

ground³ *pt, pp* of GRIND: *ground rice*

ˌground 'beef *noun* [U] (*US*) = MINCE

ˌground 'floor *noun* [C] the floor of a building that is at ground level: *a ground-floor flat* ➲ Look at the note at **floor**. طابق أرضي

groundless /ˈgraʊndləs/ *adj* without reason: *Our fears were groundless.* بلا سبب، دون مبرر
▸ **groundlessly** *adv* دون مبرر

groundwork /ˈgraʊndwɜːk/ *noun* [U] work that is done in preparation for further work or study عمل تمهيدي

group /gruːp/ *noun* [C] **1** [with sing. or pl. verb] a number of people or things that are together or that are connected: *Our discussion group is/are meeting this week.* ○ *A group of us are planning to meet for lunch.* ○ *Groups of people were standing around in the streets.* ○ *He is in the 40-50 age group.* ○ *Many young people start smoking because of pressure from their peer group* (= people of the same age). ○ *people of many different social groups* ○ *a pressure group* (= a political group that tries to influence the government) ○ *Which blood group* (e.g. A, O, etc.) *do you belong to?* ○ *Divide the class into groups.* ○ *group work* زمرة، مجموعة

2 a number of people who play pop music together: *a pop group* ➲ Look at **band**. فرقة موسيقى حديثة

Group can be used in the singular with either a singular or plural verb. If you are thinking of the members of the group individually, a plural verb is more common.

▸ **group** *verb* [I,T] to form or put into one or more groups: [T]: *Group these words according to their meaning.* يجْمَع، يصنِّف

grouse /graʊs/ *noun* [C] (*pl.* **grouse**) a fat brown bird that lives in hilly areas and that is shot for sport. Grouse can be eaten. طَيْهوج (طائر)

grovel /ˈgrɒvl/ *verb* [I] (grovelling; grovelled; *US* groveling; groveled) to act in a very humble way towards sb who is more important than you or who can give you sth that you want: *to grovel for forgiveness* يَتَذَلَّل
PHR V **grovel about/around** to move around on your hands and knees (usually when you are looking for sth) يَزْحَف

grow /grəʊ/ *verb* (*pt* **grew** /gruː/; *pp* **grown** /grəʊn/) **1** [I] to increase in size or number; to develop into an adult form: *Goodness, haven't you grown!* ○ *a growing child* ○ *You must invest if you want your business to grow.* ○ *The population is growing too fast.* ○ *Plants grow from seeds.* ○ *Kittens soon grow into cats.* يَنْمو

2 [I] (used about plants) to be alive in a particular place: *Palm trees don't normally grow in Britain.* يَنْبُت

3 [T] to cause or allow something to grow: *Mary wants to grow her hair long.* ○ *to grow a beard/ moustache* ○ *My grandfather grows a lot of vegetables in his garden.* يربي، يطلق (شعره)؛ يزرع

4 [I] to become (gradually): *It began to grow dark.* ○ *to grow older, wiser, etc.* ❶ **Get** is also possible and is less formal. يصير (تدريجياً)

PHR V **grow into sth 1** to become (gradually): *She has grown into a very attractive child.* يصير (تدريجياً)

2 to become big enough to fit clothes, etc: *The coat is too big for him, but he will soon grow into it.* يكبر

grow on sb to become more pleasing: *I didn't like it at first, but it's a taste that grows on you.* يصبح مقبولاً أو محبوباً

grow out of sth to become too big or too old for sth: *She's grown out of that dress.* يكبر على (ثيابه مثلاً)

grow up 1 to become mature or adult: *What do you want to be when you grow up?* (= what job do you want to do later?) ○ *Oh, grow up!* (= don't be silly!) يكبر، يصبح راشداً

2 (used about a feeling, etc.) to develop or become strong: *A close friendship has grown up between them.* ينشأ، ينمو؛ يقوى
▸ **growing** *adj* increasing: *a growing problem* متزايد

grown /grəʊn/ *adj* physically adult or mature: *a fully grown elephant* مكتمل النمو، ناضج

growth /grəʊθ/ *noun* **1** [U] growing or development: *A good diet is very important for children's growth.* ○ *a growth industry* (= one that is growing) نموّ

2 [U, sing.] an increase (in sth): *population growth* ○ *There has been a sudden growth in the government's popularity.* ازدياد

3 [C] an abnormal lump that grows in a person's or an animal's body ورم

growl /graʊl/ *verb* [I] (used about dogs and other animals) to make a low noise in the throat to show anger or to give a warning يزمجر، يهرّ
▸ **growl** *noun* [C] زمجرة؛ هرير

ˌgrown-'up *adj* physically or mentally adult or mature: *What do you want to be when you're grown-up?* ○ *She's very grown-up for her age.* ○ *He must be at least 45 – he's got a grown-up daughter.* راشد، ناضج
▸ **'grown-up** *noun* [C] an adult person: *Don't use the cooker unless a grown-up is there to help you.* راشِد، شخص كبير

grub /grʌb/ *noun* **1** [C] the first form that an insect takes (when it has just come out of the egg). Grubs look like short fat worms. يرقة (دودة صغيرة)

2 [U] (*informal*) food طعام

grubby /ˈgrʌbi/ *adj* (**grubbier**; **grubbiest**) (*informal*) dirty قذر

grudge /grʌdʒ/ *verb* [T] **grudge sb sth** to be unwilling to give sth to sb: *I don't grudge him his success – he deserves it.* ➲ Look at **begrudge**. يَضِنّ عليه بـ
▸ **grudge** *noun* [C] **a grudge (against sb)** unfriendly feelings towards sb, because you are

angry about what has happened in the past: *She still bears a grudge against me for what happened in Italy.* حقد
grudging *adj* given or done unwillingly: *grudging thanks* بلا حماسة، مرغم
grudgingly *adv* بلا حماسة، مكرهاً

gruelling (*US* **grueling**) /ˈgruːəlɪŋ/ *adj* difficult and tiring: *a gruelling nine-hour march* منهِك

gruesome /ˈgruːsəm/ *adj* (used about sth concerned with death or injury) very unpleasant or shocking: *A gruesome sight awaited the police when they arrived at the accident.* ➲ Look at **grisly**. It is similar in meaning. فظيع

gruff /grʌf/ *adj* (used about a person or a voice) rough and unfriendly فظّ، خشن
▸ **gruffly** *adv* بفظاظة
gruffness *noun* [U] فظاظة، خشونة

grumble /ˈgrʌmbl/ *verb* [I] to complain or protest in a bad-tempered way; to keep saying that you do not like sth: *The students were always grumbling about the standard of the food.* يتذمّر

People usually **grumble** (or **moan**) when something is not as good as they expect. If they want to take positive action they **complain** to somebody in authority.

▸ **grumble** *noun* [C] a complaint: *I'm tired of listening to your grumbles.* تذمُّر، شكوى

grumpy /ˈgrʌmpi/ *adj* (**grumpier**; **grumpiest**) (*informal*) bad-tempered سيِّئ الطبع: شكّاء، نكد
▸ **grumpily** /-ɪli/ *adv* بتذمر: بنكد
grumpiness *noun* [U] تذمر: نكد

grunt /grʌnt/ *verb* [I,T] to make a noise (a short low sound in the throat) like a pig. People grunt when they do not like sth or are not interested and do not want to talk: *I tried to find out her opinion but she just grunted when I asked her.* ينْخر: يخرج صوتاً من الحنجرة
▸ **grunt** *noun* [C] نخير

Gt (*also* **Gt.**) *abbrev* = GREAT

guarantee /ˌgærənˈtiː/ *noun* [C,U] **1** a written promise by a company that it will repair or replace a product if it goes wrong in a certain period of time: *The watch comes with a year's guarantee.* ○ *It is still under guarantee.* ○ *The guarantee has expired.* ضمان، كفالة
2 a promise that sth will be done or that sth will happen: *The refugees are demanding guarantees about their safety before they return home.* ضَمان
▸ **guarantee** /ˌgærənˈtiː/ *verb* [T] **1** to give a guarantee on a product: *This washing machine is guaranteed for three years.* يضمَن، يكفل
2 to promise that sth will be done or that sth is true: *They have guaranteed delivery within one week.* ○ *The food is guaranteed to be free of additives.* ○ *I can guarantee that you will have a good time.* يَضْمن

guard¹ /gɑːd/ *verb* [T] **1** to keep sb/sth safe from other people; protect: *The building was guarded by men with dogs.* ○ *soldiers guarding the President* يَحْرُس
2 to watch over sb and prevent him/her from escaping: *The prisoner was closely guarded on the way to court.* يَحْرُس
PHR V **guard against sth** to try to prevent sth or stop sth happening: *A good diet helps to guard against disease.* يحمي
▸ **guarded** *adj* (used about an answer, statement, etc.) not saying very much; careful حَذِر
guardedly *adv* بِحَذَر

guard² /gɑːd/ *noun* **1** [C] a person who guards sb/sth: *a border guard* ○ *a security guard* ➲ Look at **warder** and **bodyguard**. حارس
2 [U] the state of being ready to prevent attack or danger: *Soldiers are keeping guard at the gate.* ○ *Who is on guard?* ○ *The prisoner arrived under armed guard.* ○ *a guard dog* حِراسة
3 [sing., with sing. or pl. verb] a group of soldiers, policemen, etc. who guard sb/sth: *the changing of the guard at Buckingham Palace* ○ *a guard of honour* (= for an important person) حَرَس
4 (*US* **conductor**) [C] a person who is in charge of a train حارس القطار
5 [C] (often in compounds) something that covers sth dangerous or protects sth: *a fireguard* ○ *a mudguard* (= over the wheel of a bicycle) غطاء واقٍ
IDM **off/on your guard** unprepared/prepared for an attack, surprise, mistake, etc: *The question caught me off my guard and I didn't know what to say.* محترس: دون احتراس أو على حين غرة

guardian /ˈgɑːdiən/ *noun* [C] **1** a person or institution that guards or protects sth: *The police are the guardians of law and order.* حارس، حامٍ
2 a person who is responsible for a child whose parents are dead وَصيّ

guerrilla (*also* **guerilla**) /gəˈrɪlə/ *noun* [C] a member of a small group of fighters (not an army) who make surprise attacks on the enemy: *guerrilla warfare* جندي في حرب العصابات

guess /ges/ *verb* **1** [I,T] to give an answer or opinion about sth without being sure of all the facts: *Can you guess how much this cost?* ○ *to guess at sb's age* ○ *I'd guess that he's about 45.* يُخمِّن
2 [I,T] to give the correct answer when you are not sure about it; to guess correctly: *He guessed the weight of the cake exactly.* ○ *Did I guess right?* ○ *You'll never guess what Adam just told me!* يَحْزِر
3 [T] (*informal*) (*especially US*) (used when you think that sth is probably true) to suppose: *I guess you're tired after your long journey.* ○ *We ought to leave soon, I guess.* يَظُنّ
4 **guess...!** used to show that you are going to say sth surprising or exciting: *Guess what! He's coming to see us!* ○ *Guess who I've just seen!* يحزر
▸ **guess** *noun* [C] an attempt to give the right answer when you are not sure what it is: *If you don't know the answer, then have a guess!* ○ *My guess is that they've been delayed by the traffic.* ○ *Your guess is as good as mine* (= I don't know). تخمين

IDM at a guess making a guess: *I don't know how far it is, but at a guess I'd say about 50 miles.* تخميناً

guesswork /ˈgeswɜːk/ *noun* [U] an act of guessing: *I arrived at the answer by pure guesswork.* تخمين

guest /gest/ *noun* [C] **1** a person that you invite to your home or to a party, etc: *We are having guests for the weekend.* ○ *wedding guests* ○ *an unexpected guest* ○ *an uninvited guest* ضيف

2 a person that you invite out and pay for at a restaurant, theatre, etc. ضيف، مدعو

3 a person who is staying at a hotel, etc: *This hotel has accommodation for 500 guests.* نزيل فندق

4 a person who is invited to appear on a radio or television show, or to speak at a meeting: *tonight's mystery guest* ○ *a guest speaker* ضيف برنامج (إذاعي)

ˈ**guest house** *noun* [C] a small hotel (sometimes in a private house) فندق صغير

guidance /ˈgaɪdns/ *noun* [U] help or advice: *We need expert guidance on this problem.* إرشاد

guide[1] /gaɪd/ *noun* [C] **1** a person whose job is to show cities, towns, museums, etc. to tourists: *a tour guide* دليل

2 a person who shows the way to others where it is difficult or dangerous: *We found a guide who knew the mountains well.* دليل

3 something that helps you plan what you are going to do: *As a rough guide, add three eggs per pound of flour.* موجِّه؛ مقياس

4 (*also* **guidebook** /ˈgaɪdbʊk/) a book for tourists, etc. that gives information about interesting places, etc. دليل سياحي

5 a book that gives information about a subject: *a guide to English grammar* كتاب دليل

6 Guide (*also old-fashioned* **Girl Guide**; *US* **Girl ˈScout**) a member of an organization for girls that encourages helpfulness and teaches practical skills ➲ Look at **Boy Scout**. فتاة بالكشافة

guide[2] /gaɪd/ *verb* [T] **1** to help a person or a group of people to find the right way or direction to go: *He guided us through the busy streets to our hotel.* ○ *In earlier times sailors were guided by the stars.* يَدُلّ، يرشد؛ يقود

2 to have an influence on sb/sth: *I was guided by your advice.* ➲ Look at the note at **lead**[3](1). يقود؛ يوجه

▸ **guided** *adj* led by a guide: *a guided tour* مستعين بدليل

ˈ**guide dog** *noun* [C] a dog trained to guide a blind person كلب مرشد

guideline /ˈgaɪdlaɪn/ *noun* [C] **1** [usually pl.] advice on what to do about sth (that is given by sb in authority): *The government has issued new guidelines on food safety.* تعليمات

2 something that can be used to help you make a decision or form an opinion: *These figures are a useful guideline when buying a house.* إرشادات توجيهات

guillotine /ˈgɪlətiːn/ *noun* [C] a machine with a heavy sharp blade that is dropped from a great height. The guillotine was used (especially in France) for executing criminals by cutting their heads off. مقصلة

▸ **guillotine** *verb* [T] يُعْدِم بالمقصلة

guilt /gɪlt/ *noun* [U] **1** the feeling that you have when you know that you have done sth wrong: *Now he was dead, she felt terrible guilt at the way she had behaved.* إحساس بالذَّنْب

2 the fact of having broken a law: *His guilt was not proved and so he went free.* ❶ The opposite is **innocence**. ذنب، جرم

3 blame or responsibility for doing sth wrong: *It's difficult to say whether the guilt lies with the parents or the children.* لوم، مسؤولية

▸ **guilty** *adj* (**guiltier**; **guiltiest**) **1 guilty (of sth)** having broken a law; being responsible for doing sth wrong: *She pleaded guilty/not guilty to the crime.* ○ *to be guilty of murder* ❶ The opposite is **innocent**. مذنِب

2 showing or feeling guilt (1): *I feel really guilty about not having written to you for so long.* ○ *a guilty conscience* شاعر بالذنب

guiltily /-ɪli/ *adv* شاعراً بالذنب؛ بصورة مريبة

guinea pig /ˈgɪni pɪg/ *noun* [C] **1** a small furry animal with no tail that is often kept as a pet خنزير هندي

2 a person who is used in an experiment إنسان تجرى عليه تجربة علمية

guitar /gɪˈtɑː(r)/ *noun* [C] a type of musical instrument with strings that you play with the fingers or with a piece of plastic (a plectrum): *an acoustic guitar* (= wooden, with a hollow body) ○ *an electric guitar* (= using electricity, with a solid plastic body) ❶ Note that we say 'play **the** guitar'. قيثارة

▸ **guitarist** /gɪˈtɑːrɪst/ *noun* [C] a person who plays the guitar عازف قيثارة

gulf /gʌlf/ *noun* [C] **1** a part of the sea that is almost surrounded by land: *the Gulf of Mexico* خليج

2 an important or serious difference between people or their opinions: *a wide gulf between people of different generations* فارق؛ هوّة

gull /gʌl/ (*also* **seagull**) *noun* [C] a white or grey seabird with a loud cry نَورس (طائر بحري)

gullible /ˈgʌləbl/ *adj* (used about a person) easily tricked or deceived سهل الانخداع

gulp /gʌlp/ *verb* **1** [T] **gulp sth (down)** to eat or drink sth quickly يَبْلَع بسرعة، يزدرد

2 [I] to make a swallowing movement because you are afraid, surprised, etc. ابتلاع الريق

▸ **gulp** *noun* [C] **1** the act of gulping ازدراد، تجرّع

2 the amount that you can swallow when you gulp: *He took a gulp of coffee and rushed out.* بَلْعة، جرعة

gum¹ /gʌm/ *noun* [C, usually pl.] the hard pink part of the mouth that holds the teeth لثة

gum² /gʌm/ *noun* [U] **1** a substance that you use to stick things together (especially pieces of paper) صَمْغ

2 = CHEWING GUM ➲ Look at **bubblegum**.

▸ **gum** *verb* (gumming; gummed) [T] **gum A to/onto B**; **gum A and B together** to stick sth with gum (1): *The labels were gummed onto the boxes.* يلصق بالصمغ

🔑**gun** /gʌn/ *noun* [C] a weapon that is used for shooting. A gun fires bullets from a metal tube (a barrel): *The robber held a gun to the bank manager's head.* مَدفع، سلاح ناري

> Verbs often used with 'gun' are **load, unload, point, aim, fire**. Different types of gun include a **machine gun, pistol, revolver, rifle, shotgun**.

▸ **gun** *verb* [T] (gunning; gunned)

PHR V **gun sb down** (*informal*) to shoot sb and kill or seriously injure him/her يطلق عليه الرصاص؛ يرديه قتيلاً

gunboat /ˈgʌnbəʊt/ *noun* [C] a small warship that carries heavy guns سفينة حربية صغيرة مزوّدة بمدافع

gunfire /ˈgʌnfaɪə(r)/ *noun* [U] the act of firing a gun or several guns; the sound that it makes: *We were awakened by the sound of gunfire.* نيران المدافع أو الأسلحة النارية

gunge /gʌndʒ/ (*also* **gunk**) /gʌŋk/ *noun* [U] (*informal*) any unpleasant, sticky or dirty substance مادة لزجة مقرفة

gunman /gʌnmən/ *noun* [C] (*pl.* **gunmen** /-mən/) a man who uses a gun to rob or kill people شَقيٌّ مسلّح

gunpoint /ˈgʌnpɔɪnt/ *noun*

IDM **at gunpoint** threatening to shoot: *He held the hostages at gunpoint* (= he said that he would shoot them if they did not obey him). تهديد بإطلاق النار

gunpowder /ˈgʌnpaʊdə(r)/ *noun* [U] an explosive powder that is used in guns and fireworks بارود

gunshot /ˈgʌnʃɒt/ *noun* [C] the firing of a gun or guns or the sound that it makes: *gunshot wounds* طلقة نارية

gurgle /ˈgɜːgl/ *noun* [C] a sound like water draining out of a bath قَرْقَرَة؛ غرغرة

▸ **gurgle** *verb* [I] to make a gurgle or gurgles: *The baby gurgled with pleasure.* يقرقر؛ يغرغر

guru /ˈgʊruː; *US* gəˈruː/ *noun* [C] **1** a spiritual leader or teacher in the Hindu religion مُرْشِد روحيّ عند الهندوس

2 somebody whose opinions you admire and respect, and whose ideas you follow مُرْشِد فكري؛ مثال أعلى

gush /gʌʃ/ *verb* [I] **1 gush (out) (from sth)** (used about a liquid) to flow out suddenly and in great quantities: *Blood gushed from the wound.* يَتدفّق

2 gush over sb/sth to express pleasure or admiration in an exaggerated way يُعبّر عن السرور أو الإعجاب بإفراط

▸ **gush** *noun* [C, usually sing.]: *a sudden gush of water* تدفّق

gushing *adj*: *a gushing stream* ○ *gushing praise* (= given in an exaggerated way) مُتَدَفِّق؛ مفرط

gust /gʌst/ *noun* [C] a sudden rush of wind: *There will be gusts of wind of up to 80 miles per hour.* هبّة ريح فجائية

▸ **gust** *verb* [I] (used about the wind) to blow in gusts تهبّ (الريح) فجأةً

gusto /ˈgʌstəʊ/ *noun*

IDM **with gusto** with great enthusiasm: *We all joined in the singing with gusto.* بحماسة

gut /gʌt/ *noun* **1 guts** [plural] (*informal*) the organs inside your body (especially those in the lower part of the abdomen): *a pain in the guts* أحشاء

2 guts [plural] (*informal*) courage and determination: *It takes guts to admit that you are wrong.* جسارة

3 [C] the tube in the lower part of the body which food passes through ➲ Look at **intestine**, which is a more technical word. يُخْرِج الأحشاء (من حيوان)

▸ **gut** *verb* (gutting; gutted) [T] **1** to remove the guts (1) from an animal, fish, etc. أمعاء

2 to destroy the inside of a building (in a fire): *The warehouse was gutted by fire.* يدمّر داخل المبنى (بالنار مثلاً)

gut *adj* (only *before* a noun) based on emotion or feeling rather than on reason: *a gut feeling/reaction* مستند إلى العاطفة؛ غريزيّ

gutted *adj* (*Brit informal*) extremely sad or disappointed يائس؛ مفجوع

gutter /ˈgʌtə(r)/ *noun* [C] **1** a long metal or plastic pipe that is fixed under the edge of a roof to carry away rainwater مِزْراب، ميزاب؛ مسيل ماء

2 a channel between the road and the pavement that carries away rainwater مَسْرَب على حافّة الطريق؛ بالوعة

🔑**guy** /gaɪ/ *noun* [C] **1** (*informal*) a man or a boy: *He's a nice guy.* ❶ In American English *you guys* is used when speaking to both men and women: *What do you guys want to eat?* رجل أو فتى

2 (*Brit*) a figure of a man, made of straw and dressed in old clothes, that is burned on 5 November in memory of Guy Fawkes ➲ Look at **Bonfire Night**. رجل مصنوع من القش يحرق في الخامس من نوفمبر

guzzle /ˈgʌzl/ *verb* [I,T] (*informal*) to eat or drink greedily يلتهم (طعاما أو شراباً)

gym /dʒɪm/ *noun* (*informal*) **1** (*also formal* **gymnasium**) [C] a large room that contains equipment, e.g. bars, ropes, etc. for doing physical exercises قاعة الألعاب الرياضية (الجمباز)

2 [U] = GYMNASTICS: *gym shoes* ○ *a gym class*

3 a private club where people go to do physical exercise in order to stay or become healthy and fit رياضة بدنية بغرض الرشاقة

gymnasium /dʒɪmˈneɪziəm/ *noun* [C] (*pl.* **gymnasiums** or **gymnasia** /-zɪə/) = GYM (1)

gymnastics /dʒɪmˈnæstɪks/ (*also* **gym**) *noun* [U] physical exercises that are done indoors, often using special equipment such as bars and ropes تمرينات رياضية (جمباز)
▸ **gymnast** /ˈdʒɪmnæst/ *noun* [C] a person who is an expert at gymnastics لاعب جمباز

gynaecology (*US* **gynecology**) /ˌɡaɪnəˈkɒlədʒi/ *noun* [U] the study and treatment of diseases and medical problems that only women have علم الأمراض النسائية
▸ **gynaecologist** (*US* **gynecologist**) *noun* [C] a doctor who has special training in gynaecology طبيب الأمراض النسائية

gypsy (*also* **gipsy**) /ˈdʒɪpsi/ *noun* [C] (*pl.* **gypsies**) (*also* **traveller**) a member of a race of people who spend their lives travelling around from place to place, living in caravans ❶ Many people now find this word offensive. غجري

H h

H, h /eɪtʃ/ *noun* [C] (*pl.* **Hs**; **H's**; **h's**) the eighth letter of the English alphabet: *'Hat' begins with (an) 'H'.* الحرف الثامن من الأبجدية الإنكليزية

ha[1] /hɑː/ *interj* **1** (used for showing that you are surprised or pleased) أوه! (تعبير عن الدهشة أو السرور)
2 (*also* **ha! ha!**) (used in written language to show that sb is laughing) هاها! (تعبير عن الضحك)

ha[2] *abbrev* = HECTARE

⚿ **habit** /ˈhæbɪt/ *noun* **1** [C] something that sb does very often (sometimes almost without thinking about it): *Biting your nails is a horrible habit.* ○ *He's got an annoying habit of coming round just as we're going out.* عادة

> A **habit** is usually something that is done by one person. A **custom** is something that is done by a group, community or nation: *the custom of giving presents at Christmas.*

2 [U] doing sth regularly: *I think I only smoke out of habit now – I don't really enjoy it.* عادة
IDM **be in/get into the habit of doing sth**; **make a habit of sth** to do sth regularly: *I've got into the habit of going for a jog every morning.* ○ *I don't make a habit of listening to gossip.* يتعوّد

habitable /ˈhæbɪtəbl/ *adj* (used about buildings) suitable to be lived in ❶ The opposite is **uninhabitable.** صالح للسكن

habitat /ˈhæbɪtæt/ *noun* [C] the natural home of a plant or an animal موطن : بيئة طبيعيّة

habitation /ˌhæbɪˈteɪʃn/ *noun* [U] (*formal*) living in a place: *These houses are not fit for human habitation.* سُكنى

habitual /həˈbɪtʃuəl/ *adj* **1** doing sth very often: *a habitual liar* معتاد (على)
2 which you always have or do; usual: *He had his habitual cigarette after lunch.* معتاد : معْهود
▸ **habitually** /-tʃuəli/ *adv* عادةً

hack[1] /hæk/ *verb* [I,T] to cut sth using rough strokes with a tool such as a large knife or an axe: *He hacked (away) at the branch of the tree until it fell.* ○ *The explorers hacked their way through the jungle.* يقطع بآلة حادّة (كالفأس مثلاً)

hack[2] /hæk/ *verb* [I,T] **hack (into) (sth)** (*informal*) to use a computer to look at (and change) information that is stored on another computer without permission
يخترق نظام كمبيوتر لسرقة المعلومات، مخترق (كمبيوتر)
▸ **hacker** *noun* [C] (*informal*) a person who uses a computer to look at (and change) information on another computer without permission
من يتسلل ويختلس المعلومات على الكمبيوتر

had[1] *pt, pp* of HAVE[1,2]

had[2] /hæd/ *adj* (*informal*) tricked or deceived: *I've been had. This watch I bought doesn't go.* مخدوع

haemophilia (*US* **hemophilia**) /ˌhiːməˈfɪliə/ *noun* [U] a disease that causes a person to bleed very heavily even from very small injuries because the blood does not thicken (clot) properly. مرض النزيف الدموي ، الناعور
▸ **haemophiliac** (*US* **hemophiliac**) /ˌhiːməˈfɪliæk/ *noun* [C] a person who suffers from haemophilia مصاب بالناعور

haemorrhage (*US* **hemorrhage**) /ˈhemərɪdʒ/ *noun* [C,U] very heavy bleeding نزيف

haemorrhoids (*especially US* **hemorrhoids**) /ˈhemərɔɪdz/ (*also* **piles**) *noun* [plural] painful swellings in the veins near the anus بواسير

haggard /ˈhæɡəd/ *adj* (used about a person) looking tired or worried (وجه) منهَك وشاحب

haggle /ˈhæɡl/ *verb* [I] **haggle (with sb) (over/about sth)** to argue about the price of sth يساوم

hail[1] /heɪl/ *noun* [U] frozen rain that falls in small hard balls (hailstones) ➲ Look at the note at **weather**. برَد
▸ **hail** *verb* [I]: *It is hailing.* يهطل البرَد

hail[2] /heɪl/ *verb* [T] **1** to call or wave to sb/sth: *She raised her umbrella to hail the taxi.* يستوقف (تاكسي مثلا)
2 **hail sb/sth as sth** to say in public that sth is very good: *The book was hailed as a masterpiece.* يحيّي : يمدح

⚿ **hair** /heə(r)/ *noun* **1** [C] one of the long thin things that grow on the skin of people and animals: *There's a hair in my soup.* شَعرة

a b c d e f g h i j k l m n o p q r s t u v w x y z

2 [U] the mass of hairs on a person's head: *He has got short black hair.* شعر

Some special words for the colour of hair are: **auburn**, **blond**, **fair**, **ginger** and **red**. In order to look after or style your hair you may **brush**, **comb**, **wash** (or **shampoo**) it and then **blow-dry** it. You may **part** it (or have **a parting**) in the middle or on one side. When you go to the **hairdresser's** you have your hair **cut**, **blow-dried** or **permed**.

IDM **let your hair down** (*informal*) to relax and enjoy yourself (after being formal): *After the wedding ceremony you can let your hair down at the reception.* يتحرر من الرسميات ، يطلق لنفسه العنان
split hairs → SPLIT
▶ **-haired** (in compounds) having hair of the stated type: *a long-haired rabbit* ذو شعر (طويل)
hairless *adj* without hair بلا شعر
hairy *adj* (**hairier**; **hairiest**) **1** having a lot of hair: *a hairy chest* أشعر ، كثير الشعر
2 (*slang*) dangerous or worrying: *We had a hairy journey down the motorway in freezing fog.* رهيب

hairbrush /ˈheəbrʌʃ/ *noun* [C] a brush that you use on your hair فرشاة شعر

haircut /ˈheəkʌt/ *noun* [C] **1** the cutting of your hair by a hairdresser, etc: *You need to have a haircut.* قصّة شعر ، حلاقة
2 the style in which your hair has been cut: *That haircut really suits you.* قصّة شعر

hairdo /ˈheəduː/ (*informal*) (*pl.* **hairdos**) = HAIRSTYLE

hairdresser /ˈheədresə(r)/ *noun* [C] a person whose job is to cut and style people's hair: *I've made an appointment at the hairdresser's for 10 o'clock.* ❶ A **barber** is a hairdresser who only cuts men's hair. حلاق ، مزيّن

hairdryer (*also* **ˈhairdrier**) /ˈheədraɪə(r)/ *noun* [C] a machine that dries hair by blowing hot air through it آلة تجفيف الشعر

hairpin /ˈheəpɪn/ *noun* [C] a U-shaped pin that is used for holding the hair in place دبّوس شعر

ˌhairpin ˈbend (*US* **ˌhairpin ˈcurve**; **ˌhairpin ˈturn**) *noun* [C] a very sharp bend in a road on a steep hill منعطف حادّ

ˈhair-raising *adj* that makes you very frightened مرعِب ، يقف له شعر الرأس

hairstyle /ˈheəstaɪl/ (*also informal* **hairdo**) *noun* [C] the style in which your hair has been cut or arranged قصّة أو تصفيفة الشعر

haj (*also* **hajj**) /hædʒ/ *noun* [sing.] the pilgrimage to Mecca الحج

halal /ˈhælæl/ *adj* (only *before* a noun) (used about meat) from an animal that has been killed according to Muslim law: *halal meat/food/meals* ○ *a halal butcher (= one who sells halal meat)* حلال

half¹ /hɑːf; *US* hæf/ *noun* [C] (*pl.* **halves** /hɑːvz; *US* hævz/) one of two equal parts of sth: *Two halves make a whole.* ○ *The second half of the book is more exciting.* ○ *No goals were scored in the first half* (= of a match). ❶ The verb is **halve.** نصف
IDM **break, cut, etc. sth in half** to break, etc. sth into two parts ينصّف، يشطر
go half and half with sb; go halves with sb to share the cost of sth with sb يتقاسم مناصفة

half² /hɑːf; *US* hæf/ *det, pron* forming one of two equal parts: *Half of this money is yours.* ○ *He got half his aunt's money when she died.* ○ *half a pint/a half-pint* ○ *half an hour* ○ *Half the people in the office leave at 5.* نصف
IDM **half past...** thirty minutes past an hour on the clock: *half past 6* (= 6.30) (و) نصف

half³ /hɑːf; *US* hæf/ *adv* to the extent of half; not completely: *half full* ○ *The hotel was only half finished.* ○ *I half thought he might come, but he didn't.* ○ *He's half German.* نصف

ˌhalf ˈboard *noun* [U] (in a hotel, etc.) breakfast and an evening meal ➲ Look at **full board** and **bed and breakfast.** (في فندق) مع فطور وعشاء

ˈhalf-brother, **ˈhalf-sister** *noun* [C] a brother or sister with whom you share one parent غير شقيق (أخ أو أخت)

ˌhalf-ˈhearted *adj* without interest or enthusiasm فاتر، غير متحمّس
▶ **ˌhalf-ˈheartedly** *adv* بدون حماس

ˌhalf-ˈprice *adv* at half the usual price بنصف السعر

ˌhalf-ˈterm *noun* [C] a short holiday in the middle of a school term العطلة الانتصافية (في المدرسة)

ˌhalf-ˈtime *noun* [sing.] (in sport) the period of time between the two halves of a match فترة الاستراحة (في المباريات)

ˌhalfˈway *adj, adv* at an equal distance between two places; in the middle of a period of time: *We live halfway between Oxford and Reading.* ○ *They have a break halfway through the morning.* في المنتصف (بين نقطتين)

hall /hɔːl/ *noun* [C] **1** (*also* **hallway**) a room or passage that is just inside the front entrance of a house or public building: *Leave your coat in the hall.* ○ *There is a public telephone in the entrance hall of this building.* ردهة ، بهو
2 a building or large room in which meetings, concerts, dances, etc. can be held: *The end-of-year party will be held in the school hall.* ○ *a concert hall* ➲ Look at **town hall.** قاعة، صالة

hallo = HELLO

ˌhall of ˈresidence *noun* [C] (in colleges, universities, etc.) a building where students live دار الطلبة

Halloween (*also* **Hallowe'en**) /ˌhæləʊˈiːn/ *noun* [sing.] the night before All Saints' Day, 31 October احتفال "هالوين" : الليلة قبل عيد كل القديسين

By tradition Halloween is the time when witches and ghosts are said to appear. Children now dress up as witches, etc. and play tricks on people.

hallucination /həˌluːsɪˈneɪʃn/ *noun* [C,U] seeing sth that is not really there (because you are ill or have taken a drug) هَلْوَسة

hallway /ˈhɔːlweɪ/ *noun* [C,U] → HALL (1)

halo /ˈheɪləʊ/ *noun* [C] (*pl.* **haloes** or **halos**) the circle of light that is drawn around the head of a holy person in a painting هالة

halogen /ˈhælədʒən/ *noun* [C] any of a set of five chemical substances that are not metals and that combine with hydrogen to form strong acid compounds from which simple salts can be made الهالوجين

halt /hɔːlt/ *noun* [sing.] a stop (that does not last very long): *Work came to a halt when the machine broke down.* ○ *to bring sth to a halt* توقّف قصير

IDM **grind to a halt/standstill** → GRIND

▸ **halt** *verb* [I,T] to stop for a short time; to make sth stop يتوقّف أو يوقف لفترة قصيرة

halve /hɑːv; *US* hæv/ *verb* [T] **1** to make sth half as big as it was before: *We aim to halve the number of people on our waiting list in the next six months.* يخفّض إلى النصف

2 to divide sth into two equal parts: *First halve the peach and then remove the stone.* ينصّف ، يشطر

ham /hæm/ *noun* [U] meat from a pig that has been smoked, etc. to keep it fresh جمبون ، لحم فخذ الخنزير

hamburger /ˈhæmbɜːɡə(r)/ *noun* **1** (*also* **burger**) [C] minced meat that has been formed into a flat round shape. Hamburgers are often eaten in a bread roll. همبرغر ، كفتة، أقراص لحمة مفرومة

2 [U] (*US*) = MINCE

hamlet /ˈhæmlət/ *noun* [C] a very small village قرية صغيرة

hammer[1] /ˈhæmə(r)/ *noun* **1** [C] a tool with a heavy metal head that is used for hitting nails, etc. مطرقة

2 the hammer [sing.] a sports event in which a metal ball attached to a wire is thrown رمي المطرقة

hammer[2] /ˈhæmə(r)/ *verb* **1** [I,T] to hit sth with a hammer: *She hammered the nail into the wall.* يطرق ، يضرب بمطرقة

2 [I] to hit sth, making a loud noise: *He hammered on the door until somebody opened it.* يطرق

IDM **hammer sth into sb** to force sb to remember sth by repeating it many times يكرّر الكلام حتى يدخله في ذاكرة شخص

hammer sth out 1 to hammer sth back into the shape that it should be يطرق شيئا إلى شكله الأصلي ، يسوّي بالمطرقة

2 (*figurative*) to succeed in making a plan or agreement after a lot of difficulty: *Eventually a solution was hammered out.* يتوصّل إلى اتفاق

▸ **hammering** /ˈhæmərɪŋ/ *noun* **1** [U] the noise that is made by sb using a hammer or by sb knocking sth many times صوت الطرق

2 [C] (*informal*) a very bad defeat هزيمة نكراء

hammock /ˈhæmək/ *noun* [C] a bed, made of canvas or strong net, which is hung up at both ends. Hammocks are used on board ships or in the garden. أرجوحة من الشبك للنوم

hamper[1] /ˈhæmpə(r)/ *noun* [C] a large basket with a lid that is used for carrying food سَبَت ، سلّة ذات غطاء لنقل الأطعمة

hamper[2] /ˈhæmpə(r)/ *verb* [T] to make sth difficult: *The building work was hampered by bad weather.* يعيق

hamster /ˈhæmstə(r)/ *noun* [C] a small animal that is kept as a pet. Hamsters are like small rats but are fatter and do not have a tail. They store food in the sides of their mouths. مِرْنب: حيوان من فصيلة القوارض

⚷ **hand**[1] /hænd/ *noun* **1** [C] the part of a person's arm below the wrist: *He took the child by the hand.* ○ *She lifted the hot pan out of the oven with her bare hands.* ○ *He held the bird gently in the palm of his hand.* يد

2 a hand [sing.] some help: *I'll give you a hand with the washing-up.* يد المساعدة

3 [C] the pointer on a clock or watch: *the hour/minute/second hand* عقرب (الساعة)

4 [C] a person who works with his/her hands: *farmhands* يد عاملة

5 [C] the set of playing cards that sb has been given in a game of cards مجموعة أوراق اللعب الموزّعة على كل لاعب

IDM **(at) first, second, etc. hand** (used about information that you have received) from sb who was directly/not directly involved: *Did you get this information first hand?* ➲ Look at **second-hand**. (من) مصدر (أولي أو ثانوي أو غير ذلك)

(close/near) at hand (*formal*) near in space or time: *Help is close at hand.* متناول اليد : وشيك

be an old hand (at sth) → OLD

by hand 1 done by a person and not by machine: *I had to do all the sewing by hand.* (مصنوع) باليد

2 not by post: *The letter was delivered by hand.* (يسلّم) باليد

change hands → CHANGE[1]

get, have, etc. a free hand → FREE[1]

get, etc. the upper hand → UPPER

give sb/get a big hand → BIG

hand in hand 1 holding each other's hands يداً بيد

2 (*figurative*) usually happening together; closely connected متلازمان : سوياً

hands off (sb/sth) (*informal*) (used for ordering sb not to touch sth or to leave sth alone) الرجاء عدم اللمس : ارفع يدك عنه

hands up 1 (used in a classroom, etc. for asking people to raise one hand and give an answer): *Hands up, who'd like to go on the trip this afternoon?* (للتلاميذ) ارفعوا أيديكم (قبل الإجابة)

2 (used by a person with a gun to tell other

people to put their hands in the air) ارفع يديك!، سلّم!
have a hand in sth to take part in or share sth: *Even members of staff had a hand in painting and decorating the new office.* يشارك، له يد في
have your hands full to be very busy so that you cannot do anything else مُغرَق بالشغل، مشغول جداً
a helping hand → HELP[1]
hold sb's hand to give help or comfort to sb in a difficult situation يواسي
hold hands (with sb) (used about two people) to hold each other's hands (because you like each other) يمسك يداً بيد
in hand 1 (used about money, etc.) not yet used: *We still have about £50 in hand.* في اليد ، في الجَيْب
2 being dealt with at the moment; under control: *Let's finish the job in hand first before we start something new.* ○ *The situation is in hand.* ➲ Look at **out of hand**. قيد الإعداد ؛ مسيطر عليه
in the hands of sb; in sb's hands in your/sb's possession, control or care: *The document is no longer in my hands.* ○ *The matter is in the hands of a solicitor.* ○ *She is in capable hands.* (الأمر) في يد...
off your hands not your responsibility any more: *Once the children are off our hands we want to go on a world cruise.* خارج نطاق المسؤولية...
on hand available to help or to be used: *There is a teacher on hand to help during your private study periods.* موجود، تحت التصرف
on your hands being your responsibility: *We seem to have a problem on our hands.* (المسؤولية) على عاتق
on the one hand... on the other (hand) (used for showing opposite points of view): *On the one hand, of course, cars are very useful. But on the other, they cause a huge amount of pollution.* من ناحية...ومن ناحية أخرى
out of hand not under control: *Violence at football matches is getting out of hand.* ➲ Look at **in hand**. (يفقد) السيطرة على الموقف
out of your/sb's hands not in your/sb's control: *I can't help you, I'm afraid. The matter is out of my hands.* (ليس الأمر) في يده
shake sb's hand/shake hands (with sb)/ shake sb by the hand → SHAKE[1]
to hand near; within reach: *I'm afraid I haven't got my diary to hand.* في متناول اليد ، قريب
wash your hands of sb/sth → WASH[1]
▶ **-handed** (in compounds) having, using or made for the stated type of hand(s): *heavy-handed* ○ *right-handed* ○ *left-handed scissors* (في التعابير المركبة) ذو يد... ؛ يستعمل باليد (اليسرى)

handful /ˈhændfʊl/ *noun* **1** [C] **a handful (of sth)** as much or as many of sth as you can hold in one hand: *a handful of sand* حفنة
2 [sing.] a small number (of sb/sth): *Only a handful of people came to the meeting.* عدد قليل ؛ حفنة
3 a handful [sing.] (*informal*) a person or an animal that is difficult to control: *The little girl is quite a handful.* صعب المراس

🔑 **hand**[2] /hænd/ *verb* [T] to give or pass sth to sb: *Please hand me the scissors.* ○ *Please hand the scissors to me.* ○ *Could you hand round the biscuits, please?* يناوِل
PHR V **hand sth down (to sb) 1** to pass customs, traditions, etc. from older people to younger ones: *These stories have been handed down from generation to generation.* يورث (من جيل لآخر)
2 to pass clothes, toys, etc. from older children to younger ones in the family يمرِّر (ملابس الطفل الأكبر وغيرها) إلى الطفل الأصغر
hand sth in (to sb) to give sth to sb in authority: *I found a wallet and handed it in to the police.* ○ *She handed in her resignation.* يسلِّم
hand sth on (to sb) to send or give sth to another person: *When you have read the article, please hand it on to another student.* يرسل ؛ يعطي
hand sth out (to sb) to give sth to many people in a group: *Food was handed out to the starving people.* يوزِّع
hand sb over to sb (used at a meeting or on the television, radio, etc.) to let another person speak: *I'm handing you over now to our foreign correspondent.* يعطي الكلام لِ
hand sb/sth over (to sb) to give sb/sth (to sb): *People were tricked into handing over large sums of money.* ○ *The terrorist was handed over to the British police.* يسلِّم

handbag /ˈhændbæg/ (*US* **purse**) *noun* [C] a small bag in which you carry money, keys, etc. حقيبة يد

handbook /ˈhændbʊk/ *noun* [C] a small book that gives useful information and advice about sth دليل ، مرشد ، كتيِّب

handbrake /ˈhændbreɪk/ *noun* [C] a brake in a car, etc. that is operated by hand and that is used when the car is not moving مكبح يدويّ ، فرامل اليد

handcuffs /ˈhændkʌfs/ *noun* [plural] a pair of metal rings that are joined together by a chain and put around the wrists of prisoners قيود ، أصفاد

handicap /ˈhændikæp/ *noun* [C] **1** something that makes doing sth more difficult; a disadvantage: *Not speaking French is going to be a bit of a handicap in my new job.* عائق ، عقبة
2 something physical or mental that means you cannot lead a completely normal life: *The local services for people with a mental handicap have improved greatly.* عائق
3 a disadvantage that is given to a strong competitor in a sports event, etc. so that the other competitors have more chance تنازل اللاعب الأقوى عن بعض النقاط
▶ **handicap** *verb* (handica**pp**ing; handica**pp**ed) [T] (usually passive) to give or be a disadvantage to sb: *They were handicapped by their lack of education.* يعيق
handicapped *adj* (*old-fashioned*) = DISABLED
❶ Many people now find this word offensive. معاق

handicraft /ˈhændikrɑːft; *US* -kræft/ *noun* **1** [C] an activity that needs skill with the hands as well as artistic ability, e.g. sewing حِرفة يدوية

2 handicrafts [plural] the objects that are produced by this activity صناعات يدوية

handkerchief /ˈhæŋkətʃɪf; -tʃiːf/ *noun* (*pl.* **handkerchiefs** or **handkerchieves** /-tʃiːvz/) a square piece of cloth or soft thin paper that you use for blowing your nose ❶ The informal word is **hanky**. ❶ A handkerchief that is made of soft thin paper is also called a **paper handkerchief** or a **tissue**. مِنديل

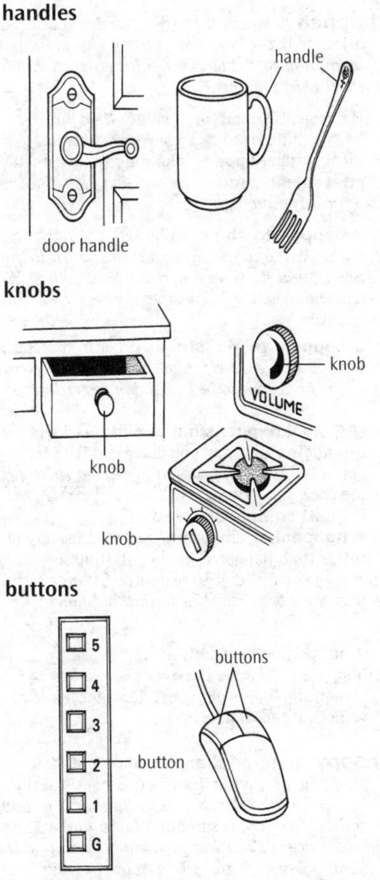

🔑**handle** /ˈhændl/ *noun* [C] a part of sth that is used for holding or opening it: *She turned the handle and opened the door.* ○ *the door handle* ○ *the handle of a frying pan* مقبض ، مَسكة ، يَد

IDM **fly off the handle** → FLY[1]

▶ **handle** *verb* [T] **1** to touch sth with, or hold sth in, your hand(s): *Wash your hands before you handle food.* ○ *Handle with care!* يَلمس ، يمسك

2 to deal with or to control sb/sth: *This port handles 100 million tons of cargo each year.* ○ *I have a problem at work and I don't really know how to handle it.* يتعامل مع ، يتصرّف؛ يعالج

handlebar /ˈhændlbɑː(r)/ *noun* [C, usually pl.] the curved metal bar at the front of a bicycle that you hold when you are riding it مِقوَد الدرّاجة

ˈhand luggage (*especially US* **ˈhand baggage**) *noun* [U] a small bag, etc. that you carry with you onto an aeroplane حقيبة اليد (في السفر بالطائرة)

ˌhandˈmade *adj* made by hand, not by machine (مصنوع) باليد

handout /ˈhændaʊt/ *noun* [C] **1** food, money, etc. given to people who need it badly صدقة

2 a printed sheet or leaflet that is given to a lot of people, to advertise sth or to explain sth in a lesson or lecture أوراق (محاضرة مثلا) توزّع على الطلاب؛ أوراق دعاية

ˌhand-ˈpicked *adj* carefully chosen منتقى باليد ، منتقى بعناية

handrail /ˈhændreɪl/ *noun* [C] a wooden or metal bar that you hold on to when going up or down stairs, or that stops you from falling from high places درابزين للسلّم وغيره

handset /ˈhændset/ *noun* [C] = RECEIVER (1)

ˈhands-free *adj* able to be used without needing to be held in the hand: *hands-free mobile phones* دون المسك باليد

handshake /ˈhændʃeɪk/ *noun* [C] the act of shaking sb's right hand with your own as a greeting مصافحة

handsome /ˈhænsəm/ *adj* **1** (used about a man) good-looking; attractive ➲ Look at the note at **beautiful**. وسيم ؛ جذّاب

2 large or generous: *The company made a handsome profit.* كبير ؛ سخيّ ، (مبلغ) محترم

▶ **handsomely** *adv*: *Her efforts were handsomely rewarded.* بسخاء

ˌhands-ˈon *adj* learnt by you doing sth yourself, not watching sb else do it; practical: *She has hands-on computer experience.* عمليّ: مكتسب بالخبرة اليدوية

handwriting /ˈhændraɪtɪŋ/ *noun* [U] a person's style of writing by hand خط يد

handwritten /ˌhændˈrɪtn/ *adj* written by hand, not typed or printed مكتوب باليد

handy /ˈhændi/ *adj* (**handier**; **handiest**) **1** useful; easy to use: *a handy tip* ○ *a handy gadget* مُفيد ؛ سهل الاستعمال

2 nearby or within easy reach of sth: *Always keep a first-aid kit handy.* ○ *The house is very handy for the shops.* في متناول اليد

IDM **come in handy** to be useful at some time: *Don't throw that box away. It may come in handy.* (سيكون) مفيداً في يوم من الأيام

handyman /ˈhændimæn/ *noun* (*pl.* **handymen** /-men/) a person who is clever at making or mending things رجل ماهر في صنع الأشياء أو في تصليحها

🔑**hang[1]** /hæŋ/ *verb* (*pt, pp* **hung** /hʌŋ/) ❶ The past tense and past participle **hanged** is only used in sense 2.

1 [I,T] to fasten sth or be fastened at the top so that the lower part is free or loose: *Hang your*

coat on the hook. ○ *I hung the washing on the line.* ○ *I left the washing hanging on the line all day.* ○ (*figurative*) *People were hanging out of windows to see the Queen go past.*
يعلّق : ينشر (الغسيل) : يتدلّى

2 [T] to kill sb by putting a rope around their neck and allowing them to drop: *She hanged herself in a fit of depression.* ○ *He was hanged for murder.* يشنق

3 [I] **hang (above/over sb/sth)** to stay in the air (above/over sb/sth): *Smog hung in the air over the city.* ○ (*figurative*) *That essay I've got to write is hanging over me.* يعلق بالهواء ، يخيم (على)

PHR V **hang about/around** (*informal*) to stay in or near a place not doing very much: *I really hate hanging around in airports.*
يبقى في مكان (منتظراً) : يتسكّع

hang on 1 to hold sth tightly: *Keep hanging on. We're very close to you now.* يتشبّث، يتمسّك بِ

2 to wait for a short time: *Hang on a minute. I'm nearly ready.* ○ *The line is engaged. Would you like to hang on or call back later?* ينتظر (قليلا)

hang on to sth 1 to hold sth tightly
يتشبّث، يتمسّك بِ

2 (*informal*) to keep sth: *Let's hang on to the car for another year.* يبقي

hang sth out to put washing, etc. on a clothes line so that it can dry ينشر (الغسيل)

hang up (on sb) (*informal*) to end a telephone conversation by putting down the receiver ➲ Look at the note at **phone**.
يُنهي مخابرة تليفونية بإرجاع السمّاعة

▸ **hanging** *noun* [C,U] death by hanging
الإعدام شنقاً

hang² /hæŋ/ *noun*

IDM **get the hang of sth** (*informal*) to learn how to use or do sth: *It took me a long time to get the hang of my new computer.* يتقن

hangar /ˈhæŋə(r)/ *noun* [C] a big building where aeroplanes are kept حظيرة الطائرات

hanger /ˈhæŋə(r)/ (*also* **ˈcoat hanger**; **ˈclothes hanger**) *noun* [C] a metal, plastic or wooden object with a hook that is used for hanging up clothes in a cupboard علّاقة ملابس

ˌhanger-ˈon *noun* (*pl.* **hangers-on**) a person who tries to be friendly with sb who is rich or important متزلّف

ˈhang-glider *noun* [C] a type of large kite from which a person can hang and fly through the air طائرة شراعية يدوية

▸ **ˈhang-gliding** *noun* [U] the sport of flying using a hang-glider الطيران الشراعي اليدوي

hangman /ˈhæŋmən/ *noun* (*pl.* **hangmen** /-mən/) a person who hangs criminals
جلّاد ، عشْماوي (م)

hangover /ˈhæŋəʊvə(r)/ *noun* [C] a headache and a feeling of sickness that you wake up with if you have drunk too much alcohol the night before خمار السكر

ˈhang-up *noun* [C] (*slang*) something that worries you a lot: *He has a real hang-up about his height.* عقدة

hanker /ˈhæŋkə(r)/ *verb* [I] **hanker after/for sth** to want sth very much (often sth that you cannot easily have) يشتهي : يتوق إلى

hanky (*also* **hankie**) /ˈhæŋki/ *noun* [C] (*pl.* **hankies**) (*informal*) a handkerchief محْرمة ، منديل

haphazard /hæpˈhæzəd/ *adj* without any order or organized plan: *Her system of filing seems to be completely haphazard.* عشوائي ، اعتباطي

▸ **haphazardly** *adv* عشوائياً ، اعتباطياً

happen /ˈhæpən/ *verb* [I] **1** (of an event or situation) to take place: *Can you describe to the police what happened after you left the party?* ○ *How did the accident happen?* يحدث ، يقع

> **Happen** and **occur** are usually used with events that are not planned. **Occur** is more formal than **happen**. **Take place** suggests that an event is planned: *The wedding took place on Saturday June 13th.*

2 **happen to sb/sth** to be what sb/sth experiences: *What do you think has happened to Julie? She should have been here an hour ago.* ○ *What will happen to the business when your father retires?* يحدث، يجري

3 **happen to do sth** to do sth by chance: *I happened to meet him in London yesterday.* ○ *She happened to be in London yesterday, too.*
يُصادف

IDM **as it happens/happened** (used when you are adding to what you have said) by chance; actually: *As it happens, I did remember to bring the book you wanted.* في الواقع ، في الحقيقة

it (just) so happens → so¹

▸ **happening** /ˈhæpənɪŋ/ *noun* [C, usually pl.] a thing that happens; an event (that is usually strange or difficult to explain): *Strange happenings have been reported in that old hotel.*
أحداث غريبة

> A **happening** is usually something that happens by chance. An **event** is usually something that is planned and suggests something special or important.

happy /ˈhæpi/ *adj* (**happier**; **happiest**) **1** feeling, showing or giving pleasure or satisfaction: *a happy childhood* ○ *a happy family* ○ *a happy smile* ○ *The film is sad but it has a happy ending.* ○ *She doesn't feel happy about the salary she's been offered.* ○ *Are you happy in your work?* ○ *I'm not very happy with what you've done.* ○ *Congratulations! I'm very happy for you.* ❶ The opposite is **unhappy**. Look at the note at **glad**.
سعيد : مسرور : سارّ

2 (not before a noun) **happy to do sth** willing; pleased: *I'll be happy to see you any day next week.* مسرور : مستعد

3 **Happy** (used in greetings to wish sb an enjoyable time): *Happy Birthday!* سعيد

4 (only *before* a noun) lucky; fortunate: *He's in the happy position of being able to retire at 50!* ❶ The opposite is **unhappy**. محظوظ

IDM **many happy returns (of the day)** (used

as a greeting to sb on his/her birthday)
عيد ميلاد سعيد

▶ **happily** *adv* **1** in a happy way: *They all lived happily ever after.* ○ *I would happily give up my job if I didn't need the money.* بسعادة : بكل سرور

2 it is lucky that; fortunately: *The police found my handbag and, happily, nothing had been stolen.* لحسن الحظ

happiness *noun* [U]: *Money can't buy happiness.* سعادة

ˌhappy-go-ˈlucky *adj* not worried about life and the future لا يبالي بمشاكل الدنيا ، خلّي البال

harass /ˈhærəs; həˈræs/ *verb* [T] to annoy or put pressure on sb, especially continuously or on many different occasions: *The court ordered him to stop harassing his ex-wife.*
يضايق : يعرّض شخصا للضغط بشكل متكرر

▶ **harassed** *adj* tired and worried because you have too much to do: *Five children came in, followed by a harassed-looking mother.* مرهَق

harassment *noun* [U]: *She accused her boss of sexual harassment.* مضايقة

harbour (*US* **harbor**) /ˈhɑːbə(r)/ *noun* [C] a place on the coast where ships can be tied up (moored) to shelter from the sea: *a busy little fishing harbour* ○ *The weather was too rough for the fishing boats to leave harbour yesterday.* ميناء : مرسى

▶ **harbour** (*US* **harbor**) *verb* [T] **1** to keep sth secret in your mind for a long time: *She began to harbour doubts about the decision.*
يُضمِر، ينطوي على

2 to hide or give shelter to sb/sth bad: *They were accused of harbouring terrorists.* يؤوي (مجرماً)

hard¹ /hɑːd/ *adj* **1** not soft to touch; not easy to break or bend; very firm: *The bed was so hard that I couldn't sleep.* ○ *Diamonds are the hardest known mineral.* قاس : صلْب

2 hard (for sb) (to do sth) difficult to do or understand; not easy: *The first question in the exam was very hard.* ○ *This book is hard to understand./It is a hard book to understand.* ○ *It's hard to know why he made that decision.* ○ *It's hard for young people to find good jobs nowadays.* صعب

3 needing or using a lot of effort: *It's a hard climb to the top of the hill.* ○ *Hard work is said to be good for you.* ○ *We had some long, hard talks before we came to an agreement.* ○ *He's a hard worker.* مجهد ، شاقّ

4 hard (on sb) (used about a person) not feeling or not showing kindness or pity; not gentle: *You have to be hard to succeed in business.* ○ *She used some very hard words to tell him what she thought of him.* ○ *He's much too hard on his children.* قاسٍ

5 (used about conditions) unpleasant or unhappy: *He had a hard time when his parents died.* صعب ، قاسٍ

6 (used about the weather) very cold: *The forecast is for a hard winter.* ❶ The opposite is **mild**. قاسٍ

7 (used about water) containing particular minerals so that soap does not make many bubbles عسير
❶ The opposite is **soft**.

IDM **be hard on sb/sth 1** to hurt sb/sth or to make things difficult: *Managing with very little money can be hard on students.* شاقّ ، مؤذ

2 to be unfair to sb: *It's a bit hard on the people who haven't got a car.* غير منصف

hard facts information that is true, not just people's opinions (حقائق) واقعية

hard luck → LUCK

a hard/rough time → TIME¹

▶ **hardness** *noun* [U] being hard صلابة، صعوبة

hard² /hɑːd/ *adv* **1** with great effort, energy or attention: *He worked hard all his life.* ○ *You'll have to try a bit harder than that.* ○ *She looked hard at the man but she didn't recognize him.*
بجدّ ونشاط : (يحملق) طويلاً

2 with great force; heavily: *It was snowing hard.* ○ *He hit her hard across the face.* بِشدّة

IDM **be hard up** to have very little money: *We're too hard up to afford a holiday this year.*
قليل المال ، فقير

die hard → DIE

hard done by not fairly treated: *He felt very hard done by when he wasn't chosen for the team.* مظلوم : (عومل) بِظلم

hardback /ˈhɑːdbæk/ *noun* [C] a book that has a hard stiff cover ❶ Note the phrase **in hardback**: *I'm afraid this book is only available in hardback.* Look at **paperback**. كتاب ذو غلاف مقوى، مجلد

ˌhard-ˈboiled *adj* (used about an egg) boiled until it is hard inside (بيضة) مسلوقة قاسية

ˌhard ˈcopy *noun* [U,C] information from a computer that has been printed on paper
نسخة مطبوعة

ˈhard core *noun* [sing., with sing. or pl. verb] the members of a group who are the most active
المجموعة المحركة (في منظمة)

ˌhard ˈcurrency *noun* [U] money belonging to a particular country that is easy to exchange
قطع نادر ، عملة صعبة

ˌhard ˈdisk *noun* [C] a piece of hard plastic that is fixed inside a computer and is used for storing data and programs permanently
قرص صلب (في الكمبيوتر)

ˌhard ˈdrug *noun* [C] a drug that is strong and dangerous because people may become dependent on (addicted to) it مخدّر أو مادة تسبب الإدمان

harden /ˈhɑːdn/ *verb* **1** [I,T] to become or to make sth hard or less likely to change: *Allow the icing to harden before decorating the cake.* ○ *The firm has hardened its attitude on this question.*
يتصلّب : يصلّب

2 [T] (usually passive) **harden sb (to sth)** to make sb less sensitive: *a hardened reporter* ○ *a hardened criminal* يقسّي: يمرّس

Harden is only used when hard means 'firm' or 'unkind': *The concrete will harden in 24 hours.* ○ *He hardened himself to the feelings of other people.* **Get harder** is used when hard has

a b c d e f g **h** i j k l m n o p q r s t u v w x y z

another meaning such as 'difficult': *Learning a foreign language gets harder as you get older.*

ˌ**hard-ˈheaded** *adj* not influenced by feelings: *a hard-headed businessman*
لا يتأثر بالعاطفة ، (تاجر) عمليّ

ˌ**hard-ˈhearted** *adj* not being kind to or thinking about other people قاسي القلب

ˌ**hard-ˈhitting** *adj* that talks about or criticizes sb/sth in an honest and very direct way: *a hard-hitting campaign/speech/report* لاذع، موجع

ˌ**hard ˈline** *noun* [sing.] a way of thinking or a plan which will not be changed or influenced by anything: *The government has taken a very hard line on people who drink and drive.*
موقف متزمّت أو متشدد

hardly /ˈhɑːdli/ *adv* **1** only just; almost not; with difficulty: *Speak up – I can hardly hear you.* ○ *She'd hardly gone to sleep than it was time to get up again.* ○ *I can hardly wait for the holidays to begin.* ○ *It hardly matters whether you are there or not.* ○ *Winning this money could hardly have come at a better time.* بالكاد ؛ قلّما ؛ بصعوبة

Note that if 'hardly' is at the beginning of a sentence, the verb follows immediately: *Hardly had she gone to sleep than it was time to get up again.*

2 (used especially before 'any', 'ever', 'anybody', etc.) almost none, never, nobody, etc: *There's hardly any* (= almost no) *coffee left.* ○ *We hardly ever* (= almost never) *go to the theatre nowadays.* ○ *Hardly anybody I knew was at the party.*
بالكاد ؛ تقريباً

3 (used when you are saying that sth is not probable or that it is unreasonable): *He can hardly expect me to do all his washing for him!* ○ *She hasn't written for two years – she's hardly likely to write now* (= it's very improbable that she will write now). من غير المعقول ؛ من غير المحتمل

hardship /ˈhɑːdʃɪp/ *noun* [C,U] difficulty or problems, e.g. because you do not have enough money; the situation in which these difficulties exist: *This new tax is going to cause a lot of hardship.* ○ *Not having a car is going to be a real hardship for us.* مشقّة؛ شدّة، ضيق

ˌ**hard ˈshoulder** *noun* [C] a narrow strip of road at the side of a motorway where cars are allowed to stop in an emergency
كتف الأوتوستراد (للسيارات المتعطلة)

hardware /ˈhɑːdweə(r)/ *noun* [U] **1** tools and equipment that are used in the house and garden: *a hardware shop*
أدوات معدنيّة وخاصة أدوات المنزل والحديقة

2 the machinery of a computer, not the programs written for it ➲ Look at **software**.
اجزاء الكمبيوتر المعدنية

3 heavy machinery or weapons أسلحة ومعدات

ˌ**hard-ˈwearing** *adj* (used about materials, clothes, etc.) strong and able to last for a long time (قماش) متين

ˌ**hard-ˈworking** *adj* working with effort and energy: *a hard-working man*
يعمل بجدّ ونشاط ؛ دؤوب، "شغّيل"

hardy /ˈhɑːdi/ *adj* (**hardier**; **hardiest**) (used about people, animals and plants) able to stand cold weather or difficult conditions
متين ، قوي البنية ، شديد التحمّل

hare /heə(r)/ *noun* [C] an animal like a rabbit but bigger, faster and with longer ears and legs
أرنب بريّ

harem /ˈhɑːriːm; *US* ˈhærəm/ *noun* [C] a number of women living with one man, especially in Muslim societies. The part of the building the women live in is also called a harem. الحريم ؛ جناح الحريم

harissa /ˈærɪsə; *US* həˈriːsə/ *noun* [U] a spicy North African sauce made with peppers and oil هريسة

harm /hɑːm/ *noun* [U] hurt or damage: *Peter ate some of those berries but they didn't do him any harm.* ○ *The tax policy did the Labour party a lot of harm.* ضرر ، أذى

IDM **come to harm** to be hurt or damaged (usually with a negative): *Both the cars were badly damaged but none of the passengers came to any harm.* يُصاب بأذى أو سوء

out of harm's way in a safe place: *Put the medicine out of harm's way where the children can't reach it.* في مكان أمين

there is no harm in doing sth; **it does no harm (for sb) to do sth** there's nothing wrong in doing sth (and something good may result): *I don't think I'll win the competition but there's no harm in trying, is there?* لا (ضرر) من

▸ **harm** *verb* [T] to cause injury or damage; hurt: *Too much sunshine can harm your skin.*
يؤذي ، يضرّ

harmful /ˈhɑːmfl/ *adj* causing harm: *The new drug has no harmful side effects.* مضر ، مؤذٍ

harmless *adj* **1** not able to cause harm; safe: *You needn't be frightened – these insects are completely harmless.* غير مؤذٍ

2 not unpleasant or likely to upset people: *The children can watch that film – it's quite harmless.* غير مسيء ؛ بريء

harmlessly *adv* بدون ضرر ؛ دون تسجيل هدف

harmonica /hɑːˈmɒnɪkə/ *noun* [C] = MOUTH ORGAN

harmonious /hɑːˈməʊniəs/ *adj* **1** without disagreement; peaceful: *Discussions between the two countries have been extremely harmonious.*
منسجم ، متوافق ؛ هادئ

2 (used about musical notes) producing a pleasant sound when played together
متوافق ، متآلف الألحان

▸ **harmoniously** *adv* بانسجام ؛ تدريجياً؛ بشكل جميل

harmonize (*also* **harmonise**) /ˈhɑːmənaɪz/ *verb* [I,T] to fit in well with other things or to make sth fit in: *That new house doesn't really harmonize with the older houses in the street.*
ينسجم ؛ يوفّق

▸ **harmonization** (*also* **harmonisation**)

/ˌhɑːmənaɪˈzeɪʃn; *US* -nɪˈz-/ *noun* [U] توفيق بين ؛ تنسيق

harmony /ˈhɑːməni/ *noun* (*pl.* **harmonies**) **1** [U] a state of agreement (of feelings, interests, opinions, etc.): *There is said to be a lack of harmony within the government.* انسجام ، توافق

2 [C,U] the pleasant combination of different musical notes played or sung together: *They sang in harmony.* ○ *There are some beautiful harmonies in that music.* توافُق (موسيقي) ، تناغم ، هارموني

harness /ˈhɑːnɪs/ *noun* [C] **1** a set of leather straps with which a horse is fastened to a cart, etc. and controlled الأحزمة الجلدية التي تربط الحصان بالعربة

2 a set of straps that fasten sth to a person's body or that stop a small child moving around too much: *a safety harness* أحزمة أمان لتوثيق الطفل مثلاً

▸ **harness** *verb* [T] **1** to put a harness on a horse or to attach a horse to a cart يلجم الحصان ؛ يربط الحصان بالعربة

2 to control sth so that you can use it to produce electricity يخضع ؛ يسخّر لتوليد الكهرباء

harp /hɑːp/ *noun* [C] a large musical instrument which has many strings stretching from the top to the bottom of a frame. You play the harp with your fingers. قيثارة

▸ **harp** *verb*

PHR V **harp on (about) sth** to keep on talking or to talk too much about sth: *He's always harping on about his problems.* يفرط في الكلام: يضرب على وتر واحد

harpist *noun* [C] a person who plays the harp عازف قيثارة

harpoon /hɑːˈpuːn/ *noun* [C] a long thin weapon with a sharp pointed end and a rope attached to it that is thrown or fired when hunting large sea animals حَرْبة لصيد الحيتان وغيرها

harrowing /ˈhærəʊɪŋ/ *adj* making people feel very sad or upset: *The programme showed harrowing scenes of life in the refugee camps.* فظيع ؛ مؤلم، مفجع

harsh /hɑːʃ/ *adj* **1** not thinking of people's feelings; severe or cruel: *a harsh punishment* ○ *The England team came in for some harsh criticism.* ○ *The judge had some harsh words for the journalist's behaviour.* قاسٍ

2 not pleasant to be in: *She grew up in the harsh environment of New York City.* غير محبَّب

3 (used about light or sound or the way sth feels) unpleasantly bright, loud or rough: *a harsh light* شديد ، مزعج؛ مبْهِر

▸ **harshly** *adv* بقسوة ؛ بلا تسامحَ

harshness *noun* قسوة

harvest /ˈhɑːvɪst/ *noun* **1** [C,U] the cutting and picking of crops when they are ripe; the time when this is done: *Farmers always need extra help with the harvest.* ○ *In our country harvest time is usually June.* الحصاد

2 [C] the crops that have been gathered in; the amount or quality of them: *This year's wheat harvest was very poor.* محصول

▸ **harvest** *verb* [I,T] to cut, pick or gather a crop يحصد يجني

➲ Look at **combine harvester**.

has → HAVE[1,2]

has-been /ˈhæz biːn/ *noun* [C] (*informal*) a person or thing that is no longer as famous, successful or important as before (شخص) ولّى عهده

hash /hæʃ/ *noun* [U] a meal of meat cut into small pieces and fried with vegetables وجبة مقليّة من اللحم المفروم والخضار

IDM **make a hash of sth** (*informal*) to do sth badly: *I made a complete hash of the exam.* لخبطة، "تخبيص"

hashish /ˈhæʃiːʃ/ (*also* **hash**) *noun* [U] a drug that is made from a part of the hemp plant and usually smoked or chewed for pleasure حشيش

hasn't *short for* HAS NOT

hassle /ˈhæsl/ *noun* [C,U] (*informal*) **1** a thing or situation that is difficult or that causes problems: *It's going to be a hassle having to change trains with all this luggage.* مشقّة

2 an argument; trouble: *I've decided what to do – please don't give me any hassle about it.* جدال ؛ إزعاج

▸ **hassle** *verb* [T] to bother or annoy sb by telling him/her to do sth: *I wish he'd stop hassling me about decorating the house.* يزعج ، يضايق

haste /heɪst/ *noun* [U] doing things too quickly: *In my haste to get to the airport on time I left my passport at home.* عجَلة

IDM **in haste** quickly; in a hurry: *I am writing in haste to let you know that I will be arriving on Monday.* على عجَل

hasten /ˈheɪsn/ *verb* (*formal*) **1** [T] to make sth happen or be done earlier or more quickly يسرِّع

2 [I] **hasten to do sth** to be quick to do or say sth: *She hastened to apologize.* يسرع

hasty /ˈheɪsti/ *adj* (**hastier**; **hastiest**) **1 hasty (in doing sth/to do sth)** (used about a person) acting or deciding sth too quickly or without enough thought: *Don't be too hasty. This is an important decision.* متسرِّع ؛ متهور

2 said or done too quickly: *He said a hasty 'goodbye' and left.* عجول

▸ **hastily** /-ɪli/ *adv* بسرعة ؛ بلا تحضير

hastiness *noun* [U] عجَلة ، تسرُّع

hat /hæt/ *noun* [C] a covering that you wear on your head, usually when you are outside: *to wear a hat* قبّعة

IDM **old hat** → OLD

hatch[1] /hætʃ/ *noun* [C] **1** an opening in the deck of a ship for loading and unloading cargo باب أرضي (على ظهر السفينة)

2 an opening in a wall between two rooms, especially a kitchen and dining room, which is used for passing food through نافذة صغيرة بين المطبخ وغرفة الطعام

3 the door in a plane or spaceship باب الطائرة

hats

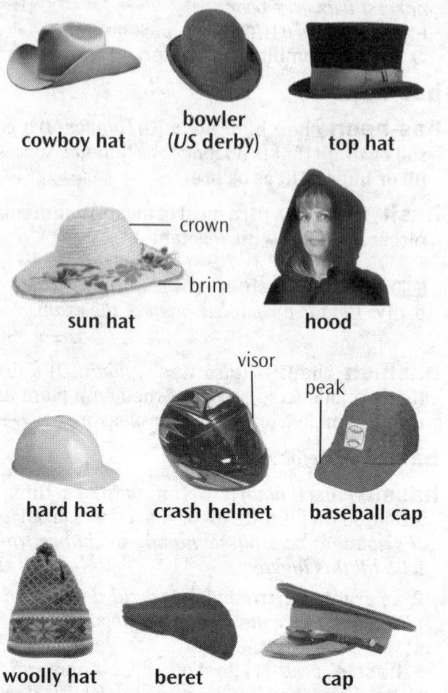

hatch[2] /hætʃ/ *verb* **1** [I] **hatch (out)** (used about a baby bird, insect, fish, etc.) to come out of an egg يخرج من البيضة

2 [T] to make a baby bird, etc. come out of an egg يفقّس

3 [I] (used about an egg) to break open and allow the baby bird, etc. inside to get out يفقس

4 [T] **hatch sth (out)** to think of a plan (usually to do sth bad): *He hatched out a plan to avoid paying any income tax.* يدبّر (مؤامرة) : يحيك (دسيسة)

hatchback /ˈhætʃbæk/ *noun* [C] a car with a large door at the back that opens upwards سيارة ذات باب خلفي يفتح نحو الأعلى

hatchet /ˈhætʃɪt/ *noun* [C] a small axe فأس صغيرة ، بَلْطة

⚷ **hate** /heɪt/ *verb* [T] **1** to have a very strong feeling of dislike (for sb/sth): *She hated her stepmother as soon as she saw her.* ○ *I hate grapefruit.* ○ *I hate to see the countryside spoilt.* ○ *He hates driving at night.* ○ *I hate his/him having to work so hard.* ➲ Look at **detest** and **loathe**. They express an even stronger feeling. يكره، يبغِض

2 (used as a polite way of apologizing for sth you are going to say) to be sorry: *I hate to bother you, but did you pick up my keys by mistake?* يؤسفني أن...

▸ **hate** *noun* **1** [U] a very strong feeling of dislike ℹ Another word for hate is **hatred**. كره ، بُغض

2 [C] a thing that you dislike very much ℹ Often used with **pet** to mean something that you especially dislike: *Plastic flowers are one of my pet hates.* شيء بغيض

hateful /ˈheɪtfl/ *adj* extremely unpleasant; horrible: *It was a hateful thing to say.* كريه ، شنيع

⚷ **hatred** /ˈheɪtrɪd/ *noun* [U] **hatred (for/of sb/sth)** a very strong feeling of dislike ℹ Another word for hatred is **hate**. كُره ، بُغض

ˈ**hat-trick** *noun* [C] (especially in sport) three successes, wins, goals, etc. scored by the same person or team one after the other: *to score a hat-trick* (لاعب واحد يسجّل) ثلاثة أهداف

haughty /ˈhɔːti/ *adj* (**haughtier**; **haughtiest**) proud, and thinking that you are better than other people: *She gave me a haughty look and walked away.* متكبِّر ، متعجرف

▸ **haughtily** /-ɪli/ *adv* بتكبّر ، بتعجرف

haughtiness *noun* [U] تكبر ، تعجرف

haul /hɔːl/ *verb* [T] to pull or drag sth with great effort: *Try to haul yourself up using the rope.* ○ *A lorry hauled the car out of the mud.* يجرّ بعناء ، يسحب بجهد

▸ **haul** *noun* **1** [sing.] the act of hauling جَرّ بعناء

2 [sing.] a distance to be travelled: *It seemed a long haul from the beach back to the hotel.* مسافة

3 [C, usually sing.] an amount gained, especially of fish in a net or stolen goods in a robbery كمية السمك في شبكة الصيد ؛ كمية المسروقات

haulage /ˈhɔːlɪdʒ/ *noun* [U] the transport of goods by road, rail, etc.; the money charged for this نقل البضائع براً: أجرة نقل البضائع براً

haunt /hɔːnt/ *verb* [T] **1** (often passive) (used about a ghost of a dead person) to appear in a place regularly: *The ghost of a woman haunts the castle.* ○ *The house is said to be haunted.* (شبح) يُلازم أو ينتاب مكاناً ما

2 (used about sth unpleasant or sad) to be always in your mind: *His unhappy face has haunted me for years.* يطارد : يراود المخيّلة

▸ **haunt** *noun* [C] a place that a person visits regularly: *This cafe has always been a favourite haunt of mine.* مكان يتردّد المرء عليه ، مثوى

haunting *adj* having a quality that stays in your mind: *a haunting song* لا يفارق الذّهن، ملازم في العقل

⚷ **have**[1] /həv; *strong form* hæv/ *auxiliary verb* (used for forming perfect tenses): *I've seen this film before.* ○ *She's been in England for six months.* ○ *Ian hasn't written to me yet.* ○ *Have you been waiting long?* ○ *They had already told us the news.* (في الإنكليزية) فعل مساعد يستعمل لتشكيل صيغة الماضي

⚷ **have**[2] /hæv/ *verb* (*3rd pers sing pres* **has**; *pt, pp* **had**) **1 have to** (*also* **have got to**) (used for saying that sb must do sth or that sth must happen): *I usually have to work on Saturday mornings.* ○ *Do you have to have a visa to go to America?* ○ *She's got to go to the bank this afternoon.* ○ *Oh good, I haven't got to get up early tomorrow!* ○ *We had to do lots of boring exercises.* ملزَم، يجب عليه

2 (*Brit also* **have got**) to own or possess: *I've*

got a new camera. ○ *They haven't got a car.* ○ *The flat has two bedrooms.* ○ *He's got short dark hair.* ○ *Have you any brothers and sisters?* ○ *We had a lovely house when I was a child.* يملك ؛ عنده

3 (*also* **have got**) to be ill with sth: *She's got a bad cold.* ○ *to have flu, a headache, etc.* ○ *to have Aids, cancer, etc.* يصاب بِ ؛ مصاب بِ

4 (used with many nouns to talk about doing sth): *What time do you have breakfast?* ○ *have a drink, a cigarette, a cup of coffee, a sandwich, etc.* ○ *'Where's Jane?' 'She's having a shower.'* ○ *have an argument, talk, chat, etc.* ○ *We're having a meeting next week.* يتناول ؛ يأخذ ؛ يقوم بِ... الخ

5 (used with many nouns to talk about experiencing sth): *Did you have a nice holiday?* ○ *have fun, a good time, etc.* ○ *have problems, difficulties, etc.* ○ *He's had a terrible shock.* ○ *have an accident, a heart attack, an operation, etc.* (تستعمل مع كثير من الأسماء للتعبير عن حدوث شيء للإنسان)

6 (*also* **have got**) (used with many abstract nouns): *I've got no patience with small children.* ○ *to have the time to do sth* ○ *have power, authority, etc.* له أو عنده (تتبعها أسماء مجرّدة)

7 have sth done to arrange for sth to be done, usually for payment: *I have my hair cut every six weeks.* ○ *You should have your eyes tested.* (تستعمل عندما توكل شخصاً آخر بعمل)

8 have sth done (used when sth unpleasant happens to you): *She had her bag stolen on the underground.* ○ *Charles I had his head cut off.* أصابَ، أناب (تستعمل عند حدوث مكروه)

9 to cause sb/sth to do sth: *The music soon had everyone dancing.* جرّ إلى

IDM have had it (used about things that are completely broken, or dead): *This television has had it. We'll have to buy a new one.* (جهاز) معطّل تماماً

PHR V have (got) sth on 1 to be wearing sth: *She's got a green jumper on.* ○ *What did the man have on?* يرتدي

2 (*informal*) to have an arrangement to do sth: *I've got nothing on on Monday. Are you free then?* ○ *I've got a lot on this week* (= I'm very busy). (عنده مواعيد أو ارتباطات)

haven /ˈheɪvn/ *noun* [C] a place where people or animals can be safe and rest ❶ A **tax haven** is a country where income tax is low. ملجأ ، مَلاذ، مأوى

havoc /ˈhævək/ *noun* [U] a state of confusion or disorder: *The rail strikes created havoc all over the country.* اضطراب ، فوضى

IDM play havoc with sth to damage or upset sth: *The bad weather played havoc with our plans.* يتشوّش ؛ يُخرّب

hawk /hɔːk/ *noun* [C] **1** a type of bird that catches and eats small animals and birds. Hawks have very good eyesight. ❶ Hawks are a type of **bird of prey**. صقر

2 (in politics) a person who supports strong action and the use of force rather than peaceful solutions (في السياسة) صقر ، سياسي غير مسالم

hawthorn /ˈhɔːθɔːn/ *noun* [C, U] a bush or small tree with sharp thorns, white, red or pink flowers and small dark red berries زعرور

hay /heɪ/ *noun* [U] grass that has been cut and dried for use as animal food: *a bale of hay* تبن ؛ قشّ

ˈhay fever *noun* [U] an illness like a bad cold, making a person sneeze a lot ❶ People get hay fever if they are **allergic** to the **pollen** of plants. التحسس الربيعي

haywire /ˈheɪwaɪə(r)/ *adj*

IDM be/go haywire (*informal*) to be or become out of control; to be in a state of disorder يجنّ جنونه ؛ (جهاز) ملخبط تماماً

hazard /ˈhæzəd/ *noun* [C] a danger or risk: *Smoking is a serious health hazard.* مخاطرة ، خطر ؛ مجازفة

▶ **hazard** *verb* [T] to make a guess or to suggest sth that you know may be wrong: *I don't know what he paid for the house but I could hazard a guess.* يخمّن ؛ يقول من باب التخمين

hazardous /ˈhæzədəs/ *adj* dangerous; risky خَطِر

haze /heɪz/ *noun* [C,U] a thin mist caused by heat, dust or smoke ➲ Look at the note at **fog**. غشاوة رقيقة من الغبار أو الدخان

hazel /ˈheɪzl/ *noun* [C] a small tree or bush that produces nuts شجرة البندق

▶ **hazel** *adj* (used especially about eyes) light brown in colour (لون) عسلي

hazelnut /ˈheɪzlnʌt/ *noun* [C] a small nut that you can eat بندقة

hazy /ˈheɪzi/ *adj* (**hazier**; **haziest**) **1** not clear; misty: *The fields were hazy in the early morning sun.* ○ (*figurative*) *I have only a hazy memory of the holiday we spent in France.* مغطى بغشاوة من الضباب ؛ غامض ، غير واضح

2 (used about a person) uncertain, not expressing things clearly: *She's a bit hazy about the details of the trip.* مبهم ؛ متردّد

HDTV /ˌeɪtʃ diː tiː ˈviː/ *noun* [U] the abbreviation for high definition television (technology that produces extremely clear images on a television screen) تلفزيون عالي الجودة

he /hi/ *pron* (the subject of a verb) the male person or animal mentioned earlier: *I spoke to John before he left.* ○ *Look at that little boy – he's going to fall in!* هو

▶ **he** *noun* [sing.] a male animal: *Is your cat a he or a she?* حيوان ذكر

If you want to refer to a person who could be either male or female, there are several ways to do this: **He or she**, **him or her**, and in writing **he/she** or **s/he** can be used: *If you are not sure, ask your doctor. He/she can give you further information.* In informal language you can use **they**, **them** or **their**: *Everybody knows what they want.* ○ *When somebody asks me a question I always try to give them a quick answer.* Or the sentence can be made plural: *A baby cries when s/he is tired* becomes: *Babies cry when they are tired.*

head[1] /hed/ *noun* [C] **1** the part of the body above the neck which has your eyes, nose, mouth and brain in it: *She turned her head to look at him.* ○ *He's in hospital with serious head injuries after the crash.* رأس

In Britain when you **nod** your head it means 'yes' or shows agreement. When you **shake** your head it means 'no' or shows disagreement.

2 a person's mind, brain or mental ability: *Use your head!* (= think!) ○ *A horrible thought entered my head...* ○ *He's got a good head for figures.* رأس ، عقل ، مخ

3 the top, front or most important part or end: *to sit at the head of the table* ○ *Put your name at the head of the paper.* ○ *We were marching right at the head of the procession.* رأس ، أعلى

4 something that is like a head in shape or position: *the head of a hammer* رأس

5 the chief or most important person (in a family, company, country, etc.): *the head of the family* ○ *The Queen is welcoming heads of state from all over the world.* ○ *the head waiter* ○ *I'm afraid I can't answer your question – I'll have to ask head office* (= the most important office) *in London.* رأس ، رئيس

6 = HEADTEACHER: *Who is going to be the new head?*

7 heads the side of a coin with the head of a person on it: *Heads or tails? Heads I go first, tails you do.* (على قطعة نقود) صورة، طرّة

8 a head [sing.] the height or length of one head: *a head taller* ارتفاع بقدر الرأس

9 a head [sing.] (for) one person: *The set menu is £12 a head.* ❶ We also say **per head**. للشخص الواحد

IDM go to sb's head 1 to make sb drunk: *Wine always goes straight to my head.* يدور الخمر برأسه

2 to make sb too proud: *If you keep telling him how clever he is, it will go to his head!* يصاب بالغرور

head first 1 with your head before the rest of your body: *Don't go down the slide head first.* الرأس قبل الرجلين

2 too quickly or suddenly: *Don't rush head first into a decision.* يتسرّع

head over heels 1 turning the body over in a forward direction: *She tripped and fell head over heels.* رأساً على عقب، يتشقلب

2 completely: *Jane's head over heels in love with him.* غارق (في الحب)

hit the nail on the head → HIT[1]

keep your head to stay calm يحافظ على هدوء أعصابه

laugh, scream, etc. your head off to laugh, scream, etc. loudly يغرق في الضحك

lose your head → LOSE

make head or tail of sth to understand sth: *I can't make head or tail of this exercise.* يفهم

off the top of your head → TOP[1]

shake your head → SHAKE[1]

head[2] /hed/ *verb* **1** [T] to be in charge of or to lead sth: *Do you think that he has the experience necessary to head a government?* يرأس ، يترأس

2 [T] to be at the front of a line, top of a list, etc: *to head a procession* ○ *Two names headed the list of possible suspects.* يتقدّم ، يتصدّر : يكون على رأس (القائمة)

3 [T] (often passive) to give a title or some instructions at the top of a piece of writing: *The report was headed 'Private'.* يعَنْوِن

4 [I] to move in the direction mentioned: *The ship headed towards the harbour.* يتوجّه

5 [T] to hit the ball with your head in football: *He headed the ball into the net.* يضرب برأسه

PHR V head for to move towards a place: *It's getting late – I think it's time to head for home.* ○ (*figurative*) *You're heading for trouble if you go on behaving like that.* يتّجه؛ يذهب؛ يقبل على (كارثة)

headache /'hedeɪk/ *noun* [C] **1** a pain in your head: *I've got a splitting* (= very bad) *headache.* ➲ Look at the note at **ache**. صُداع

2 a person or thing that causes worry or difficulty: *Paying the bills is a constant headache.* مصدر متاعب ، وجع رأس

heading /'hedɪŋ/ *noun* [C] the words written as a title at the top of a page or a piece of writing عنوان (في أعلى صفحة)

headland /'hedlənd; -lænd/ *noun* [C] a narrow piece of land that sticks out into the sea رأس

headlight /'hedlaɪt/ (*especially Brit* **'headlamp**) *noun* [C] one of the two large bright lights at the front of a vehicle: *Switch your headlights on – it's getting dark.* مصباح أمامي (في سيّارة)

headline /'hedlaɪn/ *noun* **1** [C] the title of a newspaper article printed in large letters above the story عنوان رئيسي (في صحيفة)

2 the headlines [plural] the main items of news read on television or radio الأخبار الرئيسية

'headlong /'hedlɒŋ/ *adv, adj* **1** with your head before the rest of your body الرأس أولاً ، رأسياً؛ رأسي

2 too quickly; without enough thought: *He rushed headlong into buying the business.* متهور ؛ بتهور

ˌhead 'office *noun* [C,U, with sing. or pl. verb] the main office of a company; the managers who work there: *Their head office is in New York.* ○ *I don't know what head office will think about this proposal.* المكتب الرئيسي

ˌhead of 'state *noun* [C] (*pl.* **heads of state**) the official leader of a country who is sometimes also the leader of the government: *The Queen was joined by the US President and other heads of state from around the world.* رئيس الدولة

ˌhead-'on *adj, adv* with the front of one car, etc. hitting the front of another: *a head-on crash* (اصطدام سيّارتين) وجهاً لوجه

'headphones /'hedfəʊnz/ *noun* [plural] a pair of speakers that fit over each ear and are joined together with a band over the top of your head. Headphones are used for listening to music, radio messages, etc. سمّاعتان على الأذنين

headquarters /ˌhed'kwɔːtəz/ *noun* [plural, with sing. or pl. verb] (*abbr* **HQ**) the central office, etc.

of an organization: *Where is/are the firm's headquarters?* مقر، مركز القيادة

headscarf /ˈhedskɑːf/ *noun* [C] (*pl.* **-scarves**) a square piece of cloth tied around the head by women or girls, usually with a knot under the chin منديل للرأس، "ايشارب"

headset /ˈhedset/ *noun* [C] a piece of equipment that you wear on your head that includes a device for listening (headphones) and/or a device for speaking into (a microphone): *The pilot was talking into his headset.* سماعة وميكرفون

ˌhead ˈstart *noun* [sing.] an advantage that you have from the beginning of a race or competition تسهيل يمنح للمتسابق الأضعف قبل السباق

headstone /ˈhedstəʊn/ *noun* [C] a large stone used to mark the head of a grave, usually with the dead person's name, etc. on it الشاهِد

headstrong /ˈhedstrɒŋ; *US* -strɔːŋ/ *adj* doing what you want, without listening to advice from other people عنيد ، راكب رأسه

headteacher /ˌhedˈtiːtʃə(r)/ (*also* **head**; *US* **principal**) *noun* [C] the teacher in charge of a school; the headmaster or headmistress الناظر، المدرّس الرئيسي

headway /ˈhedweɪ/ *noun*

IDM make headway to go forward or make progress in a difficult situation: *It was impossible for the boat to make any headway against the wind.* تقدُّم

heady /ˈhedi/ *adj* (**headier**,**headiest**) **1** having a quick and exciting effect on the senses: *a heady perfume* ○ *the heady days of her youth* (عطر) نفاذ: مثير

2 (used about alcoholic drinks) likely to make people drunk quickly; potent: *a heady wine* مسكر

3 (used about a person) excited and acting without careful thought: *to be heady with success* مندفع، متهور

heal /hiːl/ *verb* [I,T] **heal (over/up)** to become healthy again; to make sth healthy again: *The cut will heal up in a few days if you keep it clean and dry.* ○ *It takes time to heal a broken leg.* ○ (*figurative*) *Nothing he said could heal the damage done to their relationship.* يلتئم، يشفى : يشفي، يصلح

health /helθ/ *noun* [U] **1** the condition of a person's body or mind: *Fresh fruit and vegetables are good for your health.* ○ *in good/poor health* ○ *Cigarettes carry a government health warning.* ○ *health insurance* صحّة

2 the state of being well and free from illness: *As long as you have your health, nothing else matters.* عافية ، صحّة جيدة

ˈhealth centre *noun* [C] the central surgery and offices for a group of doctors, nurses, etc. who work together ❶ **Health Centres** are not part of hospitals, they are where local doctors and nurses work. مستوصف ، مركز صحّي

ˈhealth food *noun* [C,U] natural food that many people think is especially good for your health because it has been made or grown without adding chemicals مواد الطعام الطبيعية المفيدة للصحة

ˈhealth service *noun* [C] the organization of the medical services of a country ➲ Look at **National Health Service**. دائرة الخدمات الصحّية

ˈhealth spa *noun* [C] a place where people can stay for short periods of time in order to try to improve their health by eating special food, doing physical exercise, etc. منتجع صحي

healthy /ˈhelθi/ *adj* (**healthier**; **healthiest**) **1** not often ill; strong and well: *a healthy child, animal, plant, etc.* موفور الصحّة : قويّ البنية

2 showing good health (of body or mind): *healthy skin and hair* ○ *There was plenty of healthy competition between the brothers.* مُعافى ، سليم : (تنافس) مفيد

3 helping to produce good health: *a healthy climate* صحي

❶ The opposite for all senses is **unhealthy**.

▸ **healthily** *adv* صحياً: بشكل سليم ، بشكل جيد

heap /hiːp/ *noun* [C] **1** a large number or amount of sth which is piled up in an untidy way: *All his clothes are in a heap on the floor!* ○ *a rubbish heap* ➲ Look at the note at **pile**[1]. كومة

2 heaps [plural] (*informal*) a large number or amount; plenty: *There's heaps of time before the train leaves.* ○ *There are heaps of places to go to.* كثير (من) : عدد كبير (من)

IDM heaps better, more, older, etc. (*informal*) much better, etc. بكثير

▸ **heap** *verb* [T] **heap sth (up)** to put things in a pile: *I'm going to heap all the leaves up over there.* ○ *Add six heaped tablespoons of flour* (= in a recipe). يكوّم

hear /hɪə(r)/ *verb* (*pt*, *pp* **heard** /hɜːd/) **1** [I,T] (not used in the continuous forms) to receive sounds with your ears: *Can you speak a little louder – I don't hear very well.* ○ *I'm sorry I'm late – I didn't hear my alarm clock this morning.* يسمع

Compare **hear** and **listen**. To **hear** is to receive a sound by chance or in a passive way with your ears; to **listen** is to make a conscious or active effort to hear something: *I always wake up when I hear the milkman come.* ○ *I love listening to music in the evening.* ○ *Listen! I've got something to tell you.*

2 [T] (not used in the continuous forms) to be told or informed about sth: *I hear that you've been offered a job in Canada.* يسمع : يخبَر

3 [T] (used about a judge, a court, etc.) to listen to the evidence in a trial in order to make a decision about it: *Your case will be heard this afternoon.* يستمع إلى ، ينظر في دعوى قضائية

IDM hear! hear! (used for showing that you agree with what sb has just said, especially in a meeting) عظيم! أحسنت!

won't/wouldn't hear of sth to refuse to allow sth: *I wanted to go to art school but my parents wouldn't hear of it.* يرفض رفضاً قاطعاً

PHR V hear from sb to receive a letter, tele-

phone call, etc. from sb
يتلقى أخباراً (عن طريق رسالة أو غير ذلك)

hear of sb/sth (used especially in questions and negatives) to know or receive information about the existence of a person, place, thing, etc: *Have you heard of the Bermuda Triangle?* يسمع (عن)

🔑 **hearing** /ˈhɪərɪŋ/ *noun* **1** [U] the ability to hear: *Her hearing isn't very good so you need to speak louder.* سمع

2 [U] the distance within which sb can hear: *I'd rather not talk about it within his hearing* (= when he's near enough to hear). (على) مَسْمَع (من)

3 [C] a chance to give your opinion or explain your position: *to get/give sb a fair hearing* فرصة للكلام

4 [C] a trial in a court of law: *Will the press be present at the hearing?* جلسة محاكمة

hearsay /ˈhɪəseɪ/ *noun* [U] things you have heard another person or other people say, which may or may not be true تقوُّلات ؛ سماع عن الآخرين

hearse /hɜːs/ *noun* [C] a large car used for carrying a dead body in a coffin to the funeral سيّارة نقل الموتى

🔑 **heart** /hɑːt/ *noun* **1** [C] the organ inside the chest that sends blood round the body: *When you exercise your heart beats faster.* ○ *heart disease* قلب

2 [C] the centre of a person's feelings: *She has a kind heart* (= she is kind and gentle). ○ *In my heart I knew she was right.* قلب ، سريرة

3 [sing.] the most central part of sth; the middle: *Rare plants can be found in the heart of the forest.* ○ *(figurative) Let's get straight to the heart* (= to the most important part) *of the matter.* قلب ، صَميم

4 [C] a symbol that is shaped like a heart, often red or pink and used to show love: *He sent her a card with a big red heart on it.* قلب (كرمز للحبّ)

5 hearts [plural] the set (suit) of playing cards with red shapes like hearts on them الكبّة أو الكوبة (في ورق اللعب)

6 [C] one of the cards from this suit ورقة كبّة او كوبة

7 [U] complete interest or attention: *He's not working well because his heart isn't in the job.* قلب ، اهتمام، شغف

IDM **after your own heart** (used about people) similar to yourself or of the type you like best (شخص) مطابق لميول المرء

at heart really; in fact: *My father seems strict but he's a very kind man at heart.* في الحقيقة

break sb's heart to make sb very sad يحطم الفؤاد ، يسبِّب حزناً شديداً

by heart by remembering exactly; from memory: *The teacher wanted us to learn the whole poem by heart.* ○ *Learning lists of words off by heart isn't a good way to increase your vocabulary.* عن ظهر قلب

a change of heart → CHANGE²

cross my heart → CROSS²

your heart sinks you suddenly feel disappointed or depressed: *When I saw the queues of people in front of me my heart sank.* يصاب بالكَرْب فجاة

lose heart → LOSE

not have the heart (to do sth) to be unable to do sth unkind: *I didn't have the heart to say no.* لا يطاوعه قلبه

take sth to heart to be greatly affected or upset by sth يتكدّر أو يتأثّر بالأمر تأثراً كبيراً

young at heart → YOUNG

▸ **-hearted** (in compounds) having the type of feelings or character mentioned: *kind-hearted* (في التعابير المركّبة): "طيب القلب" مثلاً

heartless *adj* unkind; cruel: *heartless behaviour* قاسٍ ، لا قلب له

heartlessly *adv* بلا رحمة

heartlessness *noun* [U] قسوة

ˈ**heartache** /ˈhɑːteɪk/ *noun* [C,U] great sorrow or worry; emotional pain أسى ، ألم عميق

ˈ**heart attack** *noun* [C] a sudden serious illness when the heart stops working correctly, sometimes causing death: *She's had a heart attack.* نوبة قلبية

heartbeat /ˈhɑːtbiːt/ *noun* [C] the regular movement of the heart or the sound it makes نبضة ، دقة

heartbreak /ˈhɑːtbreɪk/ *noun* [U] very great unhappiness أسى

▸ ˈ**heartbreaking** *adj* very sad مؤلم ، مفجع

ˈ**heartbroken** (*also* **broken-hearted**) *adj* extremely sad: *Mary was heartbroken at the news of her friend's death.* كسير الفؤاد

hearten /ˈhɑːtn/ *verb* [T] (usually passive) to encourage sb; to make sb feel more cheerful ❶ The opposite is **dishearten.** يشجّع ؛ يبعث على البهجة

heartfelt /ˈhɑːtfelt/ *adj* deeply felt; sincere: *a heartfelt apology* من صميم القلب ؛ مخلص

hearth /hɑːθ/ *noun* [C] the floor of a fireplace or the area in front of it أرضية الموقد أو ما يمتد منها أمامه

heartland /ˈhɑːtlænd/ *noun* [C] the most central or important part of a country, area, etc: *Germany's industrial heartland* قلب ، مركز

ˈ**heart-rending** *adj* causing a strong feeling of pity: *The mother of the missing boy made a heart-rending appeal on television.* مؤثّر ، يقطّع نياط القلب

ˌ**heart-to-ˈheart** *noun* [C] a conversation in which you say openly what you really feel or think: *John's teacher had a heart-to-heart with him and found out what was worrying him.* محادثة صريحة ؛ حديث من القلب إلى القلب

hearty /ˈhɑːti/ *adj* (**heartier**; **heartiest**) **1** showing warm and friendly feelings: *They gave us a hearty welcome when we arrived.* قلبيّ ؛ حارّ ؛ ودي

2 large: *a hearty breakfast* ○ *a hearty appetite* (وجبة) كبيرة

▸ **heartily** /ˈhɑːtɪli/ *adv* **1** in a loud cheerful way: *He joined in heartily with the singing.* بحماس وحبور

2 very much; completely: *I heartily dislike that sort of comment.* كثيراً ؛ كليّاً

heartiness *noun* [U] كمية الوجبة وغناها

🔑 **heat**¹ /hiːt/ *noun* **1** [U] the feeling of sth hot: *Too much heat from the sun is being trapped in the*

Earth's atmosphere. ○ *This fire doesn't give out much heat.* حرارة

2 [sing.] (often with *the*) hot weather: *I like the English climate because I can't stand the heat.* الطقس الحارّ

3 [sing.] a thing that produces heat: *Remove the pan from the heat* (= the cooker). النار (عند الطبخ)، طبّاخ، جهاز طبخ

4 [U] a state or time of anger or excitement: *In the heat of the argument he said a lot of things he didn't mean.* حماة : حدّة

5 [C] one of the first parts of a race or competition. The winners of the heats compete against other winners until the final result is decided: *He won his heat and went through to the final.* سباق تمهيدي

IDM be on heat (used about some female animals) to be ready to mate because it is the right time of the year استحرام ، فترة استعداد أنثى الحيوان للسفاد

heat² /hi:t/ *verb* [I,T] **heat (sth) (up)** to become or to make sth hot or warm: *Wait for the oven to heat up before you put the cake in.* ○ *Old houses are more difficult to heat than modern ones.* ○ *Is it a heated swimming pool?* ○ *The meal is already cooked but it will need heating up.* يسخُن ؛ يُسخِّن ؛ يُدفِئ

▸ **heated** *adj* (used about a person or discussion) angry or excited غاضب، مهتاج : (مناقشة) حامية

heatedly *adv* بحدّة

heater *noun* [C] an apparatus used for heating water or the air in a room, car, etc: *an electric heater* ○ *a water heater* مسخّن (ماء) : مدفأة

heating *noun* [U] a system for heating rooms and buildings: *Our heating goes off at 10 p.m. and comes on again in the morning.* ➲ Look at **central heating**. تدفئة

heath /hi:θ/ *noun* [C] an area of open land that is not used for farming and that is covered with rough plants and grass أرض بور مغطاة بالأعشاب

heathen /ˈhi:ðn/ *noun* [C] (*old-fashioned*) a person who does not belong to one of the major world religions وثني

heather /ˈheðə(r)/ *noun* [U] a small tough plant that grows especially on hills and moors and has small purple, pink or white flowers خَلَنْج

heatwave /ˈhi:tweɪv/ *noun* [C] a period of time when the weather is much hotter than usual موجة حر

heave /hi:v/ *verb* **1** [I,T] to lift or pull sth heavy, using a lot of effort: *Take hold of this rope and heave!* ○ *We heaved the cupboard up the stairs.* يرفع أو يجرّ شيئاً ثقيلاً

2 [T] to throw sth heavy: *He heaved a brick through the window.* يقذف بشيء ثقيل

3 [I] to move up and down or in and out in a heavy but regular way: *His chest was heaving with the effort of carrying the cooker.* (صدره) يعلو ويهبط

4 [I] to experience the tight feeling you get in your stomach when you are just about to vomit: *The sight of all that blood made her stomach heave.* يشعر بالغثيان

IDM heave a sigh to give a big sigh: *He heaved a sigh of relief when he heard the good news.* يتنفس الصعداء، يتنهد تنهداً عميقاً

▸ **heave** *noun* [C,U] a strong pull, push, throw, etc. رَفْعة : جرّة : رَفع : جرّ : قَذْف

heaven /ˈhevn/ *noun* **1** [sing.] the place where it is believed that God and the angels live and good people go when they die: *to go to/be in heaven*

> **Heaven** (often with a capital H) is used in a number of expressions to mean 'God'bid. For the meaning of *for Heaven's sake, Heaven forbid, etc.* look at the entry for **God**. Look also at **hell**.

السّماء

2 the heavens [plural] the sky: *The stars shone brightly in the heavens that night.* السّماء

IDM (good) heavens! (used to express surprise): *Good heavens! I didn't expect to see you!* ياللّه! يا للعجب!

heavenly /ˈhevnli/ *adj* **1** (only *before* a noun) connected with heaven or the sky: *heavenly music* ○ *heavenly bodies* (= the sun, moon, stars, etc.) سماويّ : إلهيّ

2 (*informal*) very pleasant; wonderful رائع : سارّ للغاية

heavy /ˈhevi/ *adj* (**heavier**; **heaviest**) **1** weighing a lot, and difficult to lift or move: *This box is too heavy for me to carry.* ثقيل ، يصعب حمله

2 (used when asking or stating how much sb/sth weighs): *How heavy is your suitcase?* ثقيل

3 larger or stronger than usual: *heavy rain* ○ *heavy traffic* ○ *He felt a heavy blow on the back of his head.* ○ *a heavy smoker* (= a person who smokes a lot) ○ *The sound of his heavy* (= loud and deep) *breathing told her that he was asleep.* (مطر) غزير : (ازدحام) شديد

4 (used about a material or substance) solid or thick: *a heavy soil* ○ *a heavy coat* صلب : سميك، ثقيل

5 (used about food) difficult to digest (= difficult for the body to absorb): *He had a heavy meal and dropped off to sleep in the afternoon.* عَسِر الهضم ، ثقيل

6 full of hard work; (too) busy: *It's been a very heavy day.* ○ *The Queen had a heavy schedule of visits.* (يوم) متعب مليء بالمشاغل

7 serious, difficult or boring: *This book makes very heavy reading.* (كتاب) صعب ، مملّ

8 heavy on sth (*informal*) using a lot of sth: *Don't go so heavy on the garlic.* يفرط في الاستعمال، مسرف في

IDM make heavy weather of sth to make sth seem more difficult than it really is (يزيد من) صعوبة (الشيء)

▸ **heavily** *adv* بغزارة : بشكل ضخم : بصعوبة

heaviness *noun* [U] ثِقَل

ˌheavy ˈindustry *noun* [U] industry that produces materials such as steel or that makes large, heavy objects صناعة ثقيلة

a b c d e f g h i j k l m n o p q r s t u v w x y z

ˌheavy ˈmetal *noun* [U] a style of very loud rock music that is played on electric instruments موسيقى صاخبة تعزف على آلات كهربائية

heavyweight /ˈheviweɪt/ *noun* [C] a boxer weighing over 79.3 kilograms ملاكم من الوزن الثقيل

heck /hek/ *interj, noun* [sing.] (*informal*) (used to express or emphasize annoyance or surprise or to emphasize the amount or size of sth): *Oh heck! I've missed the train!* ○ *How the heck did you know where I was?* ○ *It's a heck of a long way to drive in one day.* (تعبير عن الاستياء أو الاستغراب أو المبالغة)

heckle /ˈhekl/ *verb* [I,T] to interrupt a speaker at a public meeting with difficult questions or rude remarks يقاطع خطيباً بأسئلة وقحة

▸ **heckler** /ˈheklə(r)/ *noun* [C] شخص يقاطع خطيباً بأسئلة وقحة

heckling /ˈheklɪŋ/ *noun* [U] مقاطعة الخطيب بالأسئلة والضوضاء

hectare /ˈhekteə(r)/ *noun* [C] (*abbr* **ha**) a measure of land; 10 000 square metres هكتار

hectic /ˈhektɪk/ *adj* very busy and full of a lot of things that you have to do quickly: *We had a hectic day at the office.* حافل بالمشاغل ، محموم

▸ **hectically** /-kli/ *adv* بشكل جنوني

he'd /hiːd/ *short for* HE HAD; HE WOULD

hedge /hedʒ/ *noun* [C] a row of bushes planted close together at the edge of a garden or field سياج

▸ **hedge** *verb* **1** [T] to put a hedge round a field, garden, etc. يسيّج

2 [I] to avoid giving a direct answer to a question: *Stop hedging and tell us who you're meeting tonight!* يراوغ في الجواب

IDM hedge your bets to protect yourself against losing or making a mistake by supporting more than one person or opinion يراهن على عدة أطراف تفادياً للخسارة

hedgehog /ˈhedʒhɒg; *US* -hɔːg/ *noun* [C] a small brown animal covered with stiff sharp needles (prickles) قنفذ

hedgerow /ˈhedʒrəʊ/ *noun* [C] a row of bushes, etc. forming a hedge especially along a country road or round a field سياج أو صفّ من الشجيرات على طول طريق ريفي

heed /hiːd/ *verb* [T] (*formal*) to pay attention to advice, a warning, etc. يستمع إلى النصيحة

▸ **heed** *noun* (*formal*)

IDM take heed (of sth) to pay careful attention to what sb says: *You should take heed of your doctor's advice.* يصغي : يراعي

🔑**heel** /hiːl/ *noun* [C] **1** the back part of the foot: *These shoes rub against my heels.* كَعْب ، عقِب

2 the part of a sock or stocking that covers your heel كعب

3 the raised part of a shoe under the heel of your foot: *High heels* (= shoes with high heels) *are not practical for long walks.* كعب

4 -heeled having the type of heel mentioned: *high-heeled/low-heeled shoes* ذو كعبٍ عالٍ

IDM head over heels → HEAD[1]

▸ **heel** *verb* [T] to repair the heel of a shoe يصلح أو يجدّد كعب الحذاء

hefty /ˈhefti/ *adj* (**heftier**; **heftiest**) (*informal*) strong, heavy or big: *a hefty young man* ○ *He gave the door a hefty kick and it opened.* ○ *She's earning a hefty salary in London.* ضخم ؛ قويّ ؛ ثقيل

Hegira (*also* **Hejira**, **Hijra**) /ˈhedʒɪrə/ *noun* [sing.] the Muslim era calculated from the date when Muhammad left Mecca for the Medina: *the second century of the Hegira* الهجرة

🔑**height** /haɪt/ *noun* **1** [C,U] the measurement from the bottom to the top of a person or thing: *The nurse is going to check your height and weight.* ○ *She's of medium height.* ○ *We need a fence that's about two metres in height.* ℹ The adjective is **high**. ➲ Look at the note at **tall**. ارتفاع ؛ طول

2 [U] being tall: *He looks older than he is because of his height.* طول القامة

3 [C,U] the distance that sth is above the ground or sea-level: *We are now flying at a height of 6 000 metres.* ℹ A plane **gains** or **loses** height. ارتفاع ، علوّ

4 [C, usually pl.] a high place or area: *I can't go up there. I'm afraid of heights.* مرتفَع

5 [U] the strongest or most important part of sth: *the height of summer* ○ *The tourist season is at its height in July and August.* ذُروة، قمّة

heighten /ˈhaɪtn/ *verb* [I,T] to become or to make sth greater or stronger: *I'm using yellow paint to heighten the sunny effect of the room.* يُقوّي ؛ يزيد من شدته؛ يقوى أو تزيد حدّته

heir /eə(r)/ *noun* [C] the person with the legal right to receive (inherit) money, property or a title when the owner dies: *He's the heir to a large fortune.* ○ *Who is the heir to the throne?* (= Who will become king or queen?) ○ *The queen had no sons so there wasn't an heir.* ℹ A female heir is often called an **heiress** especially when we are talking about somebody who has inherited a very large amount of money. وارث أو وريث

heirloom /ˈeəluːm/ *noun* [C] something valuable that has belonged to the same family for many years قطعة ثمينة تتوارثها العائلة جيلاً بعد جيل

held *pt, pp* of HOLD

helicopter /ˈhelɪkɒptə(r)/ (*also informal* **chopper**) *noun* [C] a small aircraft that can go straight up into the air. Helicopters fly with the help of large spinning blades. هليكوبتر ، طائرة مروحية

he'll /hiːl/ *short for* HE WILL

🔑**hell** /hel/ *noun* **1** [sing.] the place that some religions say bad people will go to when they die: *to go to/be in hell* ➲ Look at **heaven**. جهنّم ، الجحيم

2 [C,U] (*informal*) a situation or place that is very unpleasant, painful or miserable: *He went through hell when his wife left him.* جحيم

3 [U] (*informal*) (used as a swear word to show anger or surprise or to make another expression stronger): *Oh hell, I've forgotten my money!* ○ *Go to hell!* (= go away!) ○ *Who the hell is that at the*

front door?
(تستعمل للتعبير عن الغضب أو الدهشة أو للمبالغة)

IDM a/one hell of a... (*informal*) (used to make an expression stronger or to mean 'very'): *He got into a hell of a fight* (= a terrible fight). ○ *She's a hell of a nice girl.* (تستعمل للمبالغة وأحياناً بمعنى "جداً")

give sb hell (*informal*) to speak to sb very angrily or to treat sb severely
يذيقه الجحيم : (يكلّم شخصاً) بغضب شديد

like hell (*informal*) (used to make an expression stronger): *I'm working like hell* (= very hard) *at the moment.* (تستعمل للمبالغة)

hello (*Brit also* **hallo**, **hullo**) /hə'ləʊ/ *interj* (used for greeting sb, for attracting sb's attention or when you are using the telephone): *Hello, how are you?* ○ *Hello, is anybody there?* ○ *Hello, this is Leeds 4960154.* مرحبا : آلو

Hello is the most common greeting in British English. **Hi** is used in US English. It is also used in British English but is quite informal.

helm /helm/ *noun* [C] the part of a boat or ship that is used to guide it. The helm can be a handle or a wheel. مقبض دفة السفينة

helmet /'helmɪt/ *noun* [C] a type of hard hat that you wear to protect your head: *a crash helmet* ○ *a policeman's helmet* خوذة

help[1] /help/ *verb* **1** [I,T] to do sth for sb in order to be useful or to make a person's work easier: *Can I help?* ○ *Could you help me with the cooking?* ○ *I helped her to organize the party.* ○ *My son's helping in our shop at the moment.* ○ *to help sb off the train, out of a car, across the road, etc.* (= to help sb move in the direction mentioned) يساعد

2 [I,T] to make sth better or easier: *If you apologize to him it might help* (= it might make the situation better). ○ *This medicine should help your headache.* يحسّن الأمر ؛ يخفف

3 [T] **help yourself/sb (to sth)** to take or give sth (especially food and drink): *Help yourself to a drink!* ○ *Shall I help you to the vegetables?* ○ *'Can I borrow your pen?' 'Yes, help yourself.'*
يقدّم أو يتناول (طعاماً أو شراباً)

4 [T] **help yourself to sth** to take sth without asking permission: *Don't just help yourself to my money!* يأخذ دون استئذان

5 [I] (used to get sb's attention when you are in danger or difficulty): *Help! I'm going to fall!*
يطلب النجدة

IDM can/can't/couldn't help sth be able/not be able to stop or avoid doing sth: *It was so funny I couldn't help laughing.* ○ *I just couldn't help myself – I had to laugh.* ○ *He can't help being so small* (= it's not his fault). ○ *The accident couldn't be helped* (= it couldn't be avoided so we must accept that). لا يسعه إلا أن...

a helping hand some help: *My neighbour is always ready to give me a helping hand.*
يساعد ، يمد يد العون

PHRV help (sb) out to help sb in a difficult situation or to give money to help sb: *My parents have promised to help us out with buying the car.* يشارك في حمل العبء ؛ يساعد مالياً

▸ **helper** *noun* [C] a person who helps (especially with work): *The teacher is always looking for extra helpers in the classroom.* مساعد

helping *noun* [C] the amount of food that sb serves: *A large helping of pudding, please!*
حصّة أو "سكبة" من الطعام

help[2] /help/ *noun* **1** [U] the act of helping: *Do you need any help?* ○ *This map isn't much help.* ○ *I'll give you all the help I can.* مساعدة ، عون

2 [sing.] **a help (to sb)** a person or thing that helps: *Your directions were a great help – we found the place easily.* مساعد، معاون

▸ **helpful** /-fl/ *adj* giving help: *helpful advice* ○ *Ask Mr Brown. He's always very helpful.* ❶ The opposite is **unhelpful**. معين ، محبّ للمساعدة : مفيد

helpfully /-fəli/ *adv* للمساعدة : بشكل مفيد

helpfulness *noun* [U] المساعدة : الخدمة

helpless *adj* needing help from other people: *a helpless baby* محتاج للمساعدة : لا حول له ولا قوة

helplessly *adv* بعجز كلّيّ

helplessness *noun* [U] حاجة للمساعدة : عَجْز

helpline /'helplaɪn/ *noun* [C] a telephone service that provides advice and information about particular problems: *to set up/run a helpline*
خط تليفوني لتقديم المساعدة

hem /hem/ *noun* [C] the edge of a piece of cloth (especially on a skirt, dress or trousers) that has been turned under and sewn down
كُفّة (الثوب أو السروال مثلاً)

▸ **hem** *verb* [T] (**hemming**; **hemmed**) to sew a hem on sth يخيط كفّة للثوب

PHRV hem sb in to surround sb and prevent him/her from moving away: *We were hemmed in by the crowd and could not leave.* يحاصر، يطوّق

hemisphere /'hemɪsfɪə(r)/ *noun* [C] **1** the shape of half a ball; half a sphere نصف كرة

2 one half of the earth: *the northern/southern/eastern/western hemisphere* نصف الكرة الأرضية

hemophilia, hemophiliac (*US*) = HAEMOPHILIA, HAEMOPHILIAC

hemorrhage (*US*) = HAEMORRHAGE

hemorrhoids (*especially US*) = HAEMORRHOIDS

hemp /hemp/ *noun* [U] a plant that is used for making rope and rough cloth and for producing the illegal drug cannabis قنب ؛ قنّب هندي

hen /hen/ *noun* [C] **1** a female bird that is often kept on farms for its eggs or its meat: *Our hens haven't laid many eggs this week.* ➲ Look at the note at **chicken**. دجاجة

2 the female of any type of bird: *a hen pheasant* ❶ The male bird is a **cock**. أنثى الطير

hence /hens/ *adv* **1** (*formal*) from here or now: *a week hence* (= in a week's time)
من الآن : من هنا ، من هذا المكان

2 for this reason: *I've got some news to tell you – hence the letter.* لذلك ، لهذا السبب

henceforth /ˌhens'fɔːθ/ (*also* **henceforward** /ˌhens'fɔːwəd/) *adv* (*formal*) from now on; in fu-

a b c d e f g h i j k l m n o p q r s t u v w x y z

ture: *Henceforth all communication should be in writing.* من الآن فصاعداً : فيما بعد

henchman /ˈhentʃmən/ *noun* [C] (*pl.* **henchmen** /-mən/) a person who is employed by a political leader to protect him/her and who may do things that are illegal or violent: *the dictator and his henchmen* أحد أتباع أو حاشية رجل سياسي

henna /ˈhenə/ *noun* [U] a reddish-brown colour (dye) that is obtained from a type of plant. Henna is used to colour and decorate the hair, fingernails, etc. الحناء

henpecked /ˈhenpekt/ *adj* (*informal*) used to describe a husband who always does what his wife tells him to do (زوج) مطيع لأوامر زوجته

hepatitis /ˌhepəˈtaɪtɪs/ *noun* [U] a serious disease of the liver التهاب الكبد

her¹ /hɜː(r)/ *pron* (the object of a verb or preposition) a female person or animal that was mentioned earlier: *He told Sue that he loved her.* ○ *I've got a letter for your mother. Could you give it to her, please?* ○ *That must be her now.* ➲ Look at **she** and the note at **he**. الضمير المتّصل "..ها" في حالة المفعولية

her² /hə(r)/ *det* belonging to a female person or animal that was mentioned earlier: *That's her book. She left it there this morning.* ○ *Fiona has broken her leg.* الضمير المتّصل "..ها" في حالة الملكيّة
▶ **hers** /hɜːz/ *pron* of or belonging to her: *I didn't have a swimsuit but Helen lent me hers.* خاصّتها

herald /ˈherəld/ *noun* [C] a person in former times who gave important messages from a ruler to the people مناد : رسول من الحاكم
▶ **herald** *verb* [T] to be a sign that sb/sth is coming: *The minister's speech heralded a change of policy.* يعلن عن : يبشر بِ
heraldry /ˈherəldri/ *noun* [U] the study of the history of old and important families and their special family symbols (coats of arms) دراسة تاريخ وشعارات النبلاء

herb /hɜːb; *US* ɜːrb/ *noun* [C] a plant whose leaves, seeds, etc. are used in medicine or for giving food more flavour: *Add some herbs, such as rosemary and thyme.* ➲ Look at **spice**. عشبة طبيّة او عطريّة
▶ **herbal** /ˈhɜːbl; *US* ˈɜːrbl/ *adj* made of or using herbs: *herbal tea* ○ *herbal medicine* عشبيّ

herd /hɜːd/ *noun* [C] a large number of animals that live and feed together: *a herd of cattle, deer, elephants, etc.* قطيع
▶ **herd** *verb* [T] to move people or animals forward as if they were in a herd: *The prisoners were herded onto the train.* يسيِّر كالقطيع

here /hɪə(r)/ *adv* **1** (after a verb or a preposition) in, at or to the place where you are or which you are pointing to: *I live here.* ○ *Come (over) here.* ○ *The school is a mile from here.* ○ *Please sign here.* هُنا
2 (used for introducing or drawing attention to sb/sth): *Here is the nine o'clock news.* ○ *Here comes the bus.* ○ *Here we are* (= we've arrived). ○ *'Are the others coming?' 'Yes, here they are now.'*

> Note the word order in the last two examples. We say: *Here are the children* and: *Here they are.* Note also the expression: *Here you are* which is used when we are giving something to somebody: *Here you are – this is that book I was talking about.*

ها (قد وصل) ، ها هو/ها هي....ألخ
3 at this point: *Here the speaker stopped and looked around the room.* عند هذه النقطة
4 (used for emphasizing a noun): *My friend here saw it happen.* ○ *I think you'll find this book here very useful.* (للتأكيد) هنا
IDM **here and there** in various places: *We could see small groups of people here and there along the beach.* هنا وهناك
here goes (*informal*) (used before doing sth exciting, dangerous, etc.): *I've never done a backward dive before, but here goes!* يالله! هيّا بنا!
here's to sb/sth (used for drinking to the health, success, etc. of sb/sth): *Here's to your future happiness!* لنشرب نخب...
neither here nor there not important: *My opinion is neither here nor there. If you like the dress then buy it.* غير مهمّ
▶ **here** *interj* (used for attracting sb's attention, when offering help or when giving sth to sb): *Here! Get down off that wall immediately!* ○ *Here, let me help!* ○ *Here, take this and buy yourself a bar of chocolate.* (نداء للتنبيه) يا.../"وينك"

hereabouts /ˌhɪərəˈbaʊts/ (*US* **hereabout**) *adv* (*formal*) around here بالقرب من هنا

hereafter /ˌhɪərˈɑːftə(r); *US* -ˈæf-/ *adv* (*formal*) (used in legal documents, etc.) from now on; in the future من الآن فصاعداً : في المستقبل

hereditary /həˈredɪtri; *US* -teri/ *adj* passed on from parent to child: *a hereditary disease* ○ *Do you think intelligence is hereditary?* ○ *a hereditary title* (e.g. that of a duke, that is passed from father to son) ➲ Look at **inherit**. وراثيّ ، موروث

heredity /həˈredəti/ *noun* [U] the passing on of physical or mental features from parent to child ➲ Look at **inherit**. وراثة

heresy /ˈherəsi/ *noun* [C,U] (*pl.* **heresies**) a (religious) opinion or belief that is against what is generally accepted to be true in the group you belong to هرطقة ، بدعة : كفر
▶ **heretic** /ˈherətɪk/ *noun* [C] a person who believes a heresy هرطوقيّ ، من أهل البدعة
heretical /həˈretɪkl/ *adj* هرطقي ، منشق عن العقيدة

herewith /ˌhɪəˈwɪð/ *adv* (*formal*) with this letter, etc: *Please fill in the form enclosed herewith.* ضمن هذا ، طيّه

heritage /ˈherɪtɪdʒ/ *noun* [C, usually sing.] the traditions, qualities and cultural achievements of a country that have existed for a long time and that have great importance for the country: *The countryside is part of our national heritage.* ○ *We must preserve our cultural heritage for future generations.* تراث

hermit /ˈhɜːmɪt/ *noun* [C] a person who prefers to live alone, without contact with other people. In former times people became hermits for religious reasons. معتزل للناس ؛ ناسك

hernia /ˈhɜːniə/ (*also* **rupture**) *noun* [C,U] the medical condition when an internal organ (e.g. the bowel) pushes through the wall of muscle which surrounds it فتْق

hero /ˈhɪərəʊ/ *noun* [C] (*pl.* **heroes**) **1** the most important male character in a book, play, film, etc. ➲ Look at **villain**. بطل (فيلم مثلا)

2 a person who has done sth brave or good and who is admired and remembered for it: *sporting heroes* بطل

▸ **heroism** /ˈherəʊɪzəm/ *noun* [U] great courage or bravery بطولة

heroic /həˈrəʊɪk/ *adj* (used about people or their actions) very brave: *a heroic effort* بطولي

▸ **heroically** /-kli/ *adv* كالأبطال ؛ ببطولة

heroin /ˈherəʊɪn/ *noun* [U] a drug (produced from morphine) that is used by doctors to stop pain. Some people take heroin for pleasure and then become addicted to it (= they cannot stop using it) هيروين (عقار مخدِّر)

heroine /ˈherəʊɪn/ *noun* [C] **1** the most important female character in a book, play, film, etc. بطلة (القصة مثلا)

2 a woman who has done sth brave or good and who is admired and remembered for it بطلة

heroism *noun* → HERO

heron /ˈherən/ *noun* [C] a large bird with a long neck and long legs that lives near water مالك الحزين، بَلَشون

herring /ˈherɪŋ/ *noun* [C] (*pl.* **herring** or **herrings**) a small silver fish that swims in large groups (shoals) in the sea and that is used for food ➲ Look at **kipper**. سمك الرنكة

IDM **a red herring** → RED[1]

hers → HER[2]

herself /hɜːˈself/ *pron* **1** (used as the object of a verb or preposition when the female person or animal who does an action is also affected by it): *She hurt herself quite badly when she fell downstairs.* ○ *Val bought herself a pie for lunch.* ○ *Irene looked at herself in the mirror.* نفسها

2 (used for emphasis): *She told me the news herself.* ○ *Has Rosemary done this herself?* (= or did sb else do it for her?) نفسها ، بنفسها

3 in her normal state; healthy: *She's not feeling herself today* (= she's feeling ill). بصحة جيدة

IDM **(all) by herself 1** alone: *She lives by herself.* ➲ Look at the note at **alone**. وحدَها، لوَحدها

2 without help: *I don't think she needs any help – she can change a tyre by herself.* وحدها، لوحدها ، دون مساعدة

(all) to herself without having to share: *Julie has the bedroom to herself now her sister's left home.* لنفسها، دون مشاركة

he's *short for* HE IS, HE HAS

hesitant /ˈhezɪtənt/ *adj* **hesitant to do/about doing sth** slow to speak or act because you are not sure whether you should or not: *I'm very hesitant about criticizing him too much.* ○ *a hesitant manner* متردِّد

▸ **hesitancy** /-ənsi/ *noun* [U] تردُّد

hesitantly *adv* بتردُّد

hesitate /ˈhezɪteɪt/ *verb* [I] **1 hesitate (about/over sth)** to pause before you do sth or before you take a decision, usually because you are uncertain or worried: *He hesitated before going into the room.* ○ *She's still hesitating about whether to accept the job or not.* ○ *Alan replied without hesitating.* يتردّد

2 hesitate (to do sth) to be unwilling to do sth because you are not sure that it is right: *Don't hesitate to phone if you have any problems.* يتردَّد

▸ **hesitation** /ˌhezɪˈteɪʃn/ *noun* [C,U] a time when you wait because you are not sure: *She agreed without a moment's hesitation.* ○ *He continued speaking after a slight hesitation.* تردُّد

heterogeneous /ˌhetərəˈdʒiːniəs/ *adj* (*formal*) made up of different kinds of people or things: *the heterogeneous population of the USA* ❶ The opposite is **homogeneous**. متنافر

heterosexual /ˌhetərəˈsekʃuəl/ *adj* sexually attracted to a person of the other sex (= a man to a woman or a woman to a man) ➲ Look at **bisexual** and **homosexual**. ميّال إلى أفراد الجنس الآخر

▸ **heterosexual** *noun* [C] الميّال إلى أفراد الجنس الآخر

het up /het ˈʌp/ *adj* (not before a noun) **het up (about/over sth)** (*informal*) worried or excited about sth: *What are you getting so het up about?* مهتاج ، منفعل

hew /hjuː/ *verb* [I,T] (*pt* **hewed**; *pp* **hewed** or **hewn** /hjuːn/) (*formal*) to cut sth with an axe, sword, etc: *roughly hewn stone* يقطع بفأس ؛ ينحت ، يحفر

hexagon /ˈheksəgən; *US* -gɒn/ *noun* [C] a shape with six sides شكل سداسيّ، مسدَّس

▸ **hexagonal** /heksˈægənl/ *adj* سداسيّ

hey /heɪ/ *interj* (*informal*) what you shout when you want to attract sb's attention or to show that you are surprised or interested: *Hey, what are you doing here?* ○ *Hey, I like your new bike!* يا هذا!

heyday /ˈheɪdeɪ/ *noun* [sing.] the period when sb/sth was most powerful, successful, rich, etc. أيام العز ، فترة ازدهار ؛ أوْج

HGV /ˌeɪtʃ dʒiː ˈviː/ *abbrev* (*Brit*) heavy goods vehicle, such as a lorry: *He has an HGV licence.* شاحنة نقل ثقيل

hi /haɪ/ *interj* (*informal*) (used as a greeting when you meet sb) hello مرحبا

hibernate /ˈhaɪbəneɪt/ *verb* [I] (used about animals) to spend the winter in a state like deep sleep يسبِت ، ينام الحيوان نومه الشتويّ

▸ **hibernation** /ˌhaɪbəˈneɪʃn/ *noun* [U] إسبات ، نوم شتويّ

hiccup (*also* **hiccough**) /ˈhɪkʌp/ *noun* **1** [C] a sudden, usually repeated, sound that is made in the throat and that you cannot control حازوقة

2 (the) hiccups [plural] a series of hiccups: *Don't eat so fast or you'll get hiccups!* ○ *I had the hiccups.* فواق ، حازوقة

3 [C] a small problem or difficulty: *There's been a slight hiccup in our holiday arrangements but I've got it sorted out now.* مشكلة أو عقبة صغيرة

▸ **hiccup** (*also* **hiccough**) *verb* [I] يصاب بالفواق أو الحازوقة

hide¹ /haɪd/ *verb* (*pt* **hid** /hɪd/; *pp* **hidden** /ˈhɪdn/) **1** [T] to put or keep sb/sth in a place where he/she/it cannot be seen: *Where shall I hide the money?* ○ *You couldn't see Bill in the photo – he was hidden behind John.* ○ *The trees hid the house from view.* يُخبئ ، يخفي

2 [I] to be or get in a place where you cannot be seen or found: *Quick, run and hide!* ○ *The child was hiding under the bed.* ➲ Look also at **hiding²**. يختبئ

3 [T] **hide sth (from sb)** to keep sth secret so that other people do not know about it: *She tried to hide her disappointment from them.* يخفي ، يكتم

hide² /haɪd/ *noun* [C,U] the skin of an animal that will be used for making leather, etc. جلد الحيوان

hide-and-seek /ˌhaɪd n ˈsiːk/ *noun* [U] a children's game in which one person hides and the others try to find him/her لعبة الاستغماية، طمّيمة

hideous /ˈhɪdiəs/ *adj* very ugly or unpleasant: *a hideous sight* ○ *a hideous crime* ○ (*informal*) *That new dress she's got is hideous.* شنيع ، بشع

▸ **hideously** *adv* بشناعة، بشكل قبيح

hideousness *noun* [U] شناعة ، بشاعة

hiding¹ /ˈhaɪdɪŋ/ *noun* [C] (*informal*) a beating that is given as a punishment: *You deserve a good hiding for what you've done.* ضَرْب ، عَلْقة، قتلة

hiding² /ˈhaɪdɪŋ/ *noun* [U]

IDM **be in/go into hiding** to be in or go into a place where you cannot be found: *She escaped from prison and went into hiding.* اختفاء : إختباء

hierarchy /ˈhaɪərɑːki/ *noun* [C] (*pl.* **hierarchies**) a system or organization that has many grades or ranks from the lowest to the highest تراتُب ، تسلسُل هَرَمي

▸ **hierarchical** /ˌhaɪəˈrɑːkɪkl/ *adj* ذو مراتب ، متسلسل هرمياً

hieroglyphics /ˌhaɪərəˈglɪfɪks/ *noun* [plural] the system of writing that was used in ancient Egypt in which a type of picture represents a word or sound الهيروغليفية

hi-fi /ˈhaɪ faɪ/ *noun* (*informal*) electrical equipment for playing recorded music that produces high-quality sound صوت عالي الجودة

▸ **hi-fi** *adj* (only *before* a noun) (في الأجهزة الصوتية) صوت من نوعية ممتازة

higgledy-piggledy /ˌhɪgldi ˈpɪgldi/ *adv, adj* (*informal*) not in any order; mixed up together: *The books were piled up higgledy-piggledy on her desk.* ملخبط ، مشوّش : في هَرَج ومرَج

high¹ /haɪ/ *adj* **1** (used about things) measuring a great amount from the bottom to the top: *high cliffs* ○ *What's the highest mountain in the world?* ○ *high heels* (= on shoes) ○ *The garden wall was so high that we couldn't see over it.* ➲ Look at **height**, **low** and the note at **tall**. عالٍ ، مرتفع

2 having a particular height: *The hedge is one metre high.* ○ *knee-high boots* بالغ ارتفاعه (كذا)

3 at a level which is a long way from the ground, or from sea level: *Keep medicines on a high shelf where children cannot reach them.* ○ *The castle was built on high ground.* عالٍ ، مرتفع

4 above the usual or normal level or amount: *high prices* ○ *at high speed* ○ *a high level of unemployment* ○ *high-quality goods* ○ *He's got a high temperature.* ○ *Oranges are high in vitamin C.* باهظ : رفيع : غنيّ بـ

5 good or favourable: *Her work is of a very high standard.* ○ *He has a high opinion of you.* عالٍ : حسن

6 having an important position or rank: *We shall have to refer the matter to a higher authority.* عالٍ، سامٍ

7 morally good: *high ideals* مُثُل عليا

8 (used about a sound or voice) not deep or low: *She sang the high notes beautifully.* (صوت) حادّ، عالٍ

9 high (on sth) (*informal*) under the influence of drugs, etc. نشوان ، "مكَيِّف"

10 (not before a noun) (used about some kinds of food) beginning to go bad: *That cheese smells a bit high.* (طعام) على وشك الفساد

11 (used about a gear in a car) that allows a faster speed (في السّيارة) نقل مغيِّر السرعة إلى سرعة أعلى

high² /haɪ/ *adv* **1** at or to a high position or level: *The sun was high in the sky.* ○ *I can't jump any higher.* ○ *The plane flew high overhead.* ○ *You should aim high.* عالياً

2 (used about a sound) at a high level: *How high can you sing?* بصوت عالٍ

IDM **high and low** everywhere: *We've searched high and low for the keys.* في كلّ مكان

high³ /haɪ/ *noun* [C] **1** a high level or point: *Profits reached an all-time high last year.* ارتفاع : مستوى عالٍ

2 an area of high atmospheric pressure: *A high over the Atlantic will move towards Britain in the next few days.* منطقة ضغط جويّ عالٍ

3 (*informal*) a feeling of great pleasure or happiness that sb gets from doing sth exciting or being successful: *He was on a high after passing all his exams.* ○ *She talked about the highs and lows of her career.* في غاية السعادة، نشوة

4 (*informal*) a feeling of great pleasure or happiness that may be caused by a drug, etc. نشوة، ثَمَل، حبور (بتاثير الخمر أو المخدّرات)

IDM **on high** (*formal*) (in) a high place, the sky or heaven: *The order came from on high.* (من) فوق ، من سلطة عليا : في السموات

highbrow /ˈhaɪbraʊ/ *adj* interested in or concerned with matters that many people would find too serious to be interesting: *highbrow books* رفيع الثقافة ، فكري

ˈ**high chair** *noun* [C] a special chair with long legs and a little seat and table, for a small child to sit in when eating كرسي إطعام الطفل

ˌ**high-ˈclass** *adj* **1** of especially good quality: *a high-class restaurant* من الدرجة الأولى ، ممتاز

2 (used about a person) having a high (6) position in society ذو منزلة عليا : من طبقة أرستقراطية

ˌ**High ˈCourt** *noun* [C] the most important court of law المحكمة العليا

ˌ**higher eduˈcation** *noun* [U] education at a university or college التعليم العالي

ˌ**high ˈfive** *noun* [C] (*especially US*) an action to celebrate victory or to express happiness in which two people raise one arm each and hit their open hands together ضَرْب الكفّ بكفّ صديق مثلاً ابتهاجاً

ˈ**high jump** *noun* [sing.] the sport in which people try to jump over a bar in order to find out who can jump the highest ➲ Look at **long jump**. القفز العالي

highland /haɪlənd/ *adj* **1** in or connected with mountainous regions: *highland streams* ➲ Look at **lowland**. جبلي ، نجدي

2 the Highlands [plural] the mountainous part of Scotland المناطق الجبلية في اسكتلندا

ˌ**high-ˈlevel** *adj* involving important people: *high-level talks* على مستوى عال

⚷**highlight** /ˈhaɪlaɪt/ *noun* **1** [C] the best or most interesting part of sth: *The highlights of the match will be shown on TV tonight.* أبرز أو أهمّ جزء (في مباراة أو مسرحية)

2 highlights [plural] areas of lighter colour that are put in a person's hair خُصيلات من الشعر تُجعل أفتح لوناً من غيرها

▸ **highlight** *verb* [T] to give special attention to sth: *The report highlighted the need for improved safety at football grounds.* يركّز الأضواء على

highlighter /ˈhaɪlaɪtə(r)/ (*also* ˈ**highlighter pen**) *noun* [C] a special pen used for marking words in a text in a bright colour قلم ملوّن لإبراز الكلمات

⚷**highly** /ˈhaɪli/ *adv* **1** to a high degree; very: *The film was highly amusing.* ○ *The disease is highly contagious.* للغاية ، جداً

2 (very) well or favourably: *I think highly of your work* (= I have a good opinion of it). ○ *a highly paid job* (يقدّر) غاية التقدير : (منصب) ذو راتب عال

ˌ**highly ˈstrung** *adj* (used about a person or animal) very nervous and excitable عصبيّ المزاج ، انفعاليّ

Highness /ˈhaɪnəs/ *noun* [C] a title used when speaking about or to a member of a royal family سمو

ˌ**high-ˈpowered** *adj* **1** (used about things) having great power: *a high-powered engine* ذو طاقة عالية

2 (used about people) important and successful: *high-powered executives* (مدير شركة) ناجح وذو مركز هام

ˌ**high ˈpressure** *noun* [U] the condition of the atmosphere when the pressure of the air is above normal ارتفاع الضغط الجوي

ˈ**high-rise** *adj* (only *before* a noun) (used about a building) very tall and having a lot of floors بناية عالية كثيرة الشقق

ˈ**high school** *noun* [C,U] (*especially US*) a secondary school مدرسة ثانوية

ˈ**high street** *noun* [C] (often used in names) the main street of a town الشارع الرئيسي

ˌ**high-ˈtech** (*also* **hi-tech**) *adj* (*informal*) **1** using a lot of modern equipment, especially computers أحدث تكنولوجيا (خاصة الكمبيوتر)

2 using designs or styles taken from industry, etc; very modern تكنولوجيا حديثة جداً

ˌ**high ˈtide** *noun* [C] the time when the sea comes closest to the shore المدّ (عكس الجَزْر)

⚷**highway** /ˈhaɪweɪ/ *noun* [C] (*especially US*) a main road (between towns) ➲ Look at the note at **road**. طريق رئيسيّ

hijab /hɪˈdʒɑːb/ *noun* [C] a head covering worn in public by some Muslim women حجاب

hijack /ˈhaɪdʒæk/ *verb* [T] to take control of a plane, etc. by force, usually for political reasons: *The plane was hijacked on its flight to Sydney.* يختطف (طائرة مثلا)

▸ **hijacker** *noun* [C] a person who hijacks a plane, etc. مختطف (طائرة)

hijacking *noun* [C,U] an occasion when a plane, etc. is hijacked: *Measures are being taken to prevent hijacking.* اختطاف (طائرة)

hike /haɪk/ *noun* [C] a long walk in the country تجوُل في الريف

▸ **hike** *verb* [I] ❶ **Go hiking** is used when you are talking about spending time hiking: *They went hiking in Wales for their holiday.* يتجوّل في الريف

hiker *noun* [C] متجوّل في المناطق الريفية

hilarious /hɪˈleəriəs/ *adj* very funny مُضحك جداً ، يُميت من الضحك

▸ **hilariously** *adv* (يضحك) بقهقهة مسموعة

hilarity /hɪˈlærəti/ *noun* [U] great amusement or loud laughter جَذَل ، مَرَح صاخب : قهقهة عالية

⚷**hill** /hɪl/ *noun* [C] a high area of land that is not as high (or as rocky) as a mountain: *There was a wonderful view from the top of the hill.* ○ *Tim enjoys walking in the hills.* ○ *I had to push my bike up the hill – it was too steep to ride.* ❶ Note the words **uphill** and **downhill** (*adj, adv*): *an uphill climb* ○ *I like riding downhill on my bike.* تلّ ، هضبة

▸ **hilly** /ˈhɪli/ *adj* (**hillier**; **hilliest**) having many hills: *The country's very hilly around here.* كثير التلال

hillside /ˈhɪlsaɪd/ *noun* [C] the sloping side of a

hill: *a house built on the hillside*
جانب التلّ ، انحدار التلّ

hilltop /ˈhɪltɒp/ *noun* [C] the top of a hill قمة التلّ

hilt /hɪlt/ *noun* [C] the handle of a sword, etc.
مقبض السيف (مثلاً)

IDM **(up) to the hilt** to a high degree or completely: *I'll support you to the hilt.*
حتى النهاية ، كليّة

him /hɪm/ *pron* (the object of a verb or preposition) a male person or animal that was mentioned earlier: *Helen told Ian that she loved him.* ○ *I've got a letter for your father – can you give it to him, please?* ○ (*informal*) *That must be him now.* ➲ Look at the note at **he**.
الضمير المتّصل "..ه" في حالة المفعولية

himself /hɪmˈself/ *pron* **1** (used as the object of a verb or preposition when the male person or animal who does an action is also affected by it): *He cut himself when he was shaving.* ○ *He's bought himself a new sweater.* ○ *John looked at himself in the mirror.*
نفسه

2 (used for emphasis): *He told me the news himself.* ○ *The minister himself came to see the damage.* ○ *Did he write this himself?* (= or did sb else do it for him?) نفسه ، بنفسه

3 in his normal state; healthy: *He's not feeling himself today* (= he's feeling ill). بصحة جيدة

IDM **(all) by himself 1** alone: *He lives by himself.* ➲ Look at the note at **alone**. وحده ، لوحده

2 without help: *He should be able to cook a meal by himself.* وحده، لوحده ، دون مساعدة

(all) to himself without having to share: *Charlie has the bedroom to himself now his brother's left home.* لخاصة نفسه

hind /haɪnd/ *adj* (used about an animal's legs, etc.) at the back ❶ We also say **back legs**. The legs at the front are **front legs** or **forelegs**.
خلفيّ (قائمة حيوان) خلفيّة

hinder /ˈhɪndə(r)/ *verb* [T] to make it more difficult for sb/sth to do sth: *A lot of scientific work is hindered by lack of money.* يعيق ، يعرقل

hindrance /ˈhɪndrəns/ *noun* [C] a person or thing that makes it difficult for you to do sth: *Mark wanted to help me but he was more of a hindrance than a help.* عائق

hindsight /ˈhaɪndsaɪt/ *noun* [U] knowing afterwards why sth bad happened and how you could have stopped it happening: *With hindsight, I wouldn't have lent him the money.* ➲ Look at **foresight**. تفهّم طبيعة الحوادث بعد وقوعها

Hindu /ˌhɪnˈduː; *US* ˈhɪnduː/ *noun* [C] a person whose religion is Hinduism الهندوسي

▶ **Hindu** *adj*: *Hindu beliefs* هندوسي

Hinduism /ˈhɪnduːɪzəm/ *noun* [U] the main religion of India. Hindus believe in many gods and that, after death, people will return to life in a different form. الديانة الهندوسيّة

hinge¹ /hɪndʒ/ *noun* [C] a piece of metal that joins two sides of a box, door, etc. together and allows it to be opened or closed مفصلة (الباب مثلاً)

hinge² /hɪndʒ/ *verb*

PHR V **hinge on sth** to depend on sth: *The future of the project hinges on the meeting today.*
يتوقف على

hint /hɪnt/ *noun* [C] **1** something that you suggest in an indirect way: *She kept looking at her watch as a hint that it was time to go.* تلميح

2 a small amount of sth: *There was a hint of sadness in his voice.* مقدار ضئيل ، أثر : مسحة

3 a piece of advice or information: *The magazine had some helpful hints about how to make your own clothes.* نصيحة ، إرشادات

▶ **hint** *verb* [I,T] to suggest sth in an indirect way: *They only hinted at their great disappointment.* ○ *He hinted that he might be moving to Greece.* يلمح

hip¹ /hɪp/ *noun* [C] the part of the side of your body above your legs and below your waist: *He stood there angrily with his hands on his hips.* ○ *What do you measure round the hips?* ○ *She broke her hip* (= the bone inside her hip) *when she fell.* ورك : مفصل الورك

hip² /hɪp/ *interj*

IDM **hip, hip, hurrah/hurray** (shouted three times when a group wants to show that it is pleased with sb or with sth that has happened): *'Three cheers for David. He's done a great job. Hip, hip...' 'Hurray!'* يعيش...يا!

hippie (*also* **hippy**) /ˈhɪpi/ *noun* [C] (*pl.* **hippies**) a person who rejects the usual values and way of life of western society. Especially in the 1960s, hippies showed that they were different by wearing brightly-coloured clothes, having long hair and taking drugs.
"الهبّي" ، "الوجودي" ، البوهيميّ الرافض لتقاليد المجتمع

hippopotamus /ˌhɪpəˈpɒtəməs/ *noun* [C] (*pl.* **hippopotamuses** /-məsɪz/ or **hippopotami** /-maɪ/) (*also informal* **hippo** /ˈhɪpəʊ/ (*pl.* **hippos**)) a large African river animal with a large head and short legs and thick dark skin
فرس النهر ، سيّد قشطة

hire /ˈhaɪə(r)/ *verb* [T] **1** (*US* **rent**) **hire sth (from sb)** to have the use of sth for a short time by paying for it
يستأجر

> In British English, you **hire** something for a short time: *We hired a car for the day.* ○ *I hired a suit for the wedding* but **rent** something if the period of time is longer: *rent a television, video, etc.* ○ *rent a house, flat, holiday cottage, etc.* In American English **rent** is used in both situations.

2 to give sb a job for a short time: *We'll have to hire somebody to mend the roof.* ❶ In American English **hire** is also used for talking about permanent jobs: *We just hired a new secretary.*
يستخدم ، يكتري : يوظّف

3 (*US* **rent**) **hire sth (out) (to sb)** to allow sb to use sth for a short fixed period in exchange for money: *We hire (out) our vans by the day.* ❶ In British English, **rent** or **let** is used if the period of time is longer: *Mrs Higgs rents out rooms to* *students.* ○ *We let out our house while we were in France for a year.* يؤجّر

▸ **hire** *noun* [U] (the cost of) hiring: *The hire of the hall is £10 an hour.* ○ *Car hire is expensive in this country.* ○ *Bicycles for hire!* ○ *a hire car* استئجار ؛ إيجار

ˌhire ˈpurchase *noun* [U] (*Brit*) (*abbr* **h.p.**; **HP**) a way of buying goods. You do not pay the full price at once but make regular small payments (instalments) until the full amount is paid: *We're buying the video on hire purchase.* شراء بالتقسيط

his /hɪz/ *det* belonging to a male person or animal that was mentioned earlier: *That's his book.* *He left it there this morning.* ○ *Matthew has hurt his shoulder.* الضمير المتّصل "..ه" في حالة الملكيّة

▸ **his** /hɪz/ *pron* of or belonging to him: *This is my book so that one must be his.* ○ *Father has a lot of ties so I borrowed one of his.* ➲ Look at the note at **he**. خاصته

hiss /hɪs/ *verb* **1** [I,T] to make a sound like a very long 's' to show that you are angry or do not like sth: *The goose hissed at me.* ○ *The speech was hissed and booed.*
يهسهس ؛ يفحّ ؛ يهسهس أو يصفّر استنكاراً (للخطيب مثلا)

2 [T] to say sth in an angry hissing voice: *'Stay away from me!' she hissed.* يتكلّم بصوت غاضب أبحّ

▸ **hiss** *noun* [C] هسهسة، فحيح

historian /hɪˈstɔːriən/ *noun* [C] a person who studies history مؤرّخ

historic /hɪˈstɒrɪk; *US* -ˈstɔːr-/ *adj* famous or important in history: *The opening of the Berlin Wall was a historic occasion.* تاريخي، مشهود

historical /hɪˈstɒrɪkl; *US* -ˈstɔːr-/ *adj* **1** connected with history or the study of history: *There is very little historical evidence about the life of Christ.* ○ *This house has great historical interest.* تاريخي

2 that really lived or happened: *Was Robin Hood really a historical figure?* ○ *historical events* حقيقي، تاريخي

▸ **historically** /-kli/ *adv*
من الناحية التاريخية ؛ على مرّ التاريخ

history /ˈhɪstri/ *noun* (*pl.* **histories**) **1** [U] the study of past events and social, political and economic developments: *She has a degree in history.* ○ *History was my favourite subject at school.* ○ *a history teacher* تاريخ

2 [U] events of the past (when you are thinking of them as a whole): *History often repeats itself.* ○ *an important moment in history* ➲ Look at **natural history**. أحداث الماضي، تاريخ

3 [C] a written description of past events: *a new history of Europe* تأريخ

4 [C, usually sing.] the series of events or facts that is connected with a person, place or thing: *There is a history of heart disease in our family.* سلسلة حوادث، تاريخ طويل

> **History** is something true that really happened. A **story** is a description of a series of events that may or may not have happened.

IDM go down in/make history to be or do sth so important that it will be recorded in history: *She made history by becoming the first woman President.* يدخل التاريخ

hit¹ /hɪt/ *verb* [T] (*pres part* **hitting**; *pt, pp* **hit**) **1** to touch sb/sth with a lot of force: *'Don't hit me', she begged.* ○ *The old man was hit by a car while he was crossing the road.* ○ *Someone hit her on the head and stole her handbag.* ○ *to hit a ball with a bat* ○ (*figurative*) *The smell of burning hit her as she entered the room.* ○ (*figurative*) *Things were going really well until we hit this problem.*
يضرب ؛ يصدم ؛ يصيب

> **Strike** is a more formal word than **hit**. **Beat** means to hit many times: *He was badly beaten in the attack.*

2 hit sth (on/against sth) to knock a part of your body, etc. against sth: *Peter hit his head on the low beam.* يرتطم بـ

3 to have a bad effect upon sb/sth: *Inner city areas have been badly hit by unemployment.* ○ *Her father's death has hit her very hard.*
يضرّ بـ، يؤثّر تأثيراً سيّئاً

4 to find or reach sth: *If you follow this road you should hit the motorway in about ten minutes.* ○ *The price of oil hit a new high yesterday.*
يبلغ، يصل

5 [I, T] to suddenly come into sb's mind; to make sb realize or understand sth: *I thought I recognized the man's face and then it hit me – he was my old maths teacher!* خطر لـ

IDM hit it off (with sb) (*informal*) to like sb when you first meet him/her: *When I first met Tony's parents, we didn't really hit it off.*
ينسجم مع شخص

hit the nail on the head to say sth that is exactly right يصيب كبد الحقيقة

PHR V hit back (at sb/sth) to attack (with words) sb who has attacked you: *The Prime Minister hit back at his critics.* يردّ الهجوم (كلامياً)

hit on sth to suddenly find sth by chance: *I finally hit on a solution to the problem.*
يعثر فجأة على

hit out (at sb/sth) to attack sb/sth: *The man hit out at the policeman.* ○ *The newspapers hit out at the company for its poor safety record.* يهاجم

hit² /hɪt/ *noun* [C] **1** the act of hitting sth; a blow: *The ship took a direct hit and sank.* ○ *What a brilliant hit!* (e.g. in a game of cricket or baseball) ➲ Look at **miss**. ضربة موفقة

2 a person or thing that is very popular or successful: *He was quite a hit in America.* ○ *The song was a smash hit.* نجاح باهر

3 a result of a search on a computer, especially on the Internet يتوفق في العثور على

IDM make a hit (with sb) (*informal*) to make a good impression on sb or to cause sb to like you يعطي انطباعاً حسناً، يحرز نجاحاً (معها مثلاً)

ˌhit-and-ˈrun *adj* **1** (used about a car driver) causing an accident and not stopping to see if anybody is hurt
(سائق) فارّ، سائق لا يتوقف بعد التسبّب في حادث

2 (used about a road accident) caused by a hit-and-run driver (حادثة طريق) فرّ مسبّبها

hitch¹ /hɪtʃ/ *verb* **1** [I,T] (*informal*) to get free rides in other people's cars as a way of travelling cheaply: *They hitched a lift in a lorry to London.* يوقف السيّارات المارّة لتأمين سفر مجاني
2 [T] to fasten sth to sth else: *The horses were hitched to the fence.* ○ *to hitch a trailer to the back of a car* يربط ؛ يشدّ إلى

hitch² /hɪtʃ/ *noun* [C] a small problem or difficulty: *The wedding went off without a hitch.* ○ *a technical hitch* مشكلة أو عقبة صغيرة

hitchhike /ˈhɪtʃhaɪk/ *verb* [I] to travel by getting free rides in other people's cars: *He hitchhiked across Europe.* يسافر مجاناً بإيقاف السيّارات المارة
▸ **ˈhitchhiker** *noun* [C] شخص يسافر مجاناً بإيقاف السيّارات المارة

hi-tech /ˌhaɪ ˈtek/ = HIGH-TECH

hitherto /ˌhɪðəˈtuː/ *adv* (*formal*) until now حتى الآن

ˌhit-or-ˈmiss (*also* **ˌhit-and-ˈmiss**) *adj* (*informal*) not well organized; careless: *She works in rather a hit-and-miss way, I'm afraid.* لاعلى التعيين، غير منظّم ؛ غير مكترث

HIV /ˌeɪtʃ aɪ ˈviː/ *abbrev* human immunodeficiency virus; the virus that is believed to cause AIDS فيروس نقص المناعة

hive /haɪv/ *noun* [C] = BEEHIVE

hiya /ˈhaɪjə/ *interj* (*informal*) (used as a greeting when you meet sb) hello مرحبا! أهلاً!

HM (*also* **H.M.**) *abbrev* Her/His Majesty: *HM the Queen* صاحب الجلالة صاحبة الجلالة

hm /hm/ *interj* (used when you are not sure or when you are thinking about sth) "هِمْ": صوت الهمهمة (تعبّر عن التردّد أو التفكّر)

HMS /ˌeɪtʃ em ˈes/ *abbrev* (*Brit*) (for ships in the British Royal Navy) Her/His Majesty's Ship: *HMS Apollo* سفن اسطول صاحبة الجلالة

hoard /hɔːd/ *noun* [C] a store of money, food, etc: *a hoard of treasure* ذخيرة ؛ كنز
▸ **hoard** *verb* [I,T] **hoard (sth) (up)** to collect and store large quantities of sth (often secretly) يدخّر ؛ يكنز

hoarding /ˈhɔːdɪŋ/ (*US* **billboard**) *noun* [C] a large board in the street where advertisements are put لوحة ضخمة في الشارع للإعلان

hoarse /hɔːs/ *adj* **1** (used about a voice) sounding rough and quiet, e.g. because you have a cold: *a hoarse whisper* أجشّ ، مبحوح
2 (used about people) with a hoarse voice: *The spectators shouted themselves hoarse.* مبحوح
▸ **hoarsely** *adv* بصوت أبحّ

hoax /həʊks/ *noun* [C] a trick to make people believe sth that is not true, especially sth unpleasant: *The fire brigade answered the call, but found that it was a hoax.* لعبة صبيانية أو خدعة للإيقاع بشخص

hob /hɒb/ *noun* [C] the flat surface on the top of a cooker that is used for boiling, frying, etc. (في جهاز الطبخ) القسم العلوي المستعمل للطبخ (ليس الفرن)

hobble /ˈhɒbl/ *verb* [I] to walk with difficulty because your feet or legs are hurt: *He hobbled home on his twisted ankle.* يعرج

hobby /ˈhɒbi/ *noun* [C] (*pl.* **hobbies**) something that you do regularly for pleasure in your free time: *The children's hobbies are swimming and stamp collecting.* هواية

hockey /ˈhɒki/ *noun* [U] **1** a game that is played on a field (a pitch) by two teams of eleven players who try to hit a small hard ball into a goal with a curved wooden stick (a hockey stick) ℹ In the US hockey is usually called **field hockey** to distinguish it from **ice hockey**. لعبة الهوكي
2 (*US*) = ICE HOCKEY

hoe /həʊ/ *noun* [C] a garden tool with a long handle that is used for turning the soil and for removing weeds معزق، مِنكاش

hog /hɒg; *US* hɔːg/ *noun* [C] (*US*) a male pig خنزير أهلي
▸ **hog** *verb* [T] (hogging; hogged) (*informal*) to take or keep too much or all of sth in a selfish way: *Don't hog the bathroom when everyone's getting ready to go out!* ○ *The red car was hogging the middle of the road so no one could overtake.* يستأثر بِ

Hogmanay /ˈhɒgməneɪ/ *noun* [C] the Scottish name for New Year's Eve (31 December) and the celebrations that take place then (في اسكتلندا) ليلة رأس السنة

hoist /hɔɪst/ *verb* [T] to raise or lift sth by using ropes, etc: *to hoist a flag, sail, etc.* يرفع بالحبال

hold¹ /həʊld/ *verb* (*pt, pp* **held** /held/) **1** [T] to take sb/sth and keep him/her/it in your hand, etc: *He held a gun in his hand.* ○ *The woman was holding a baby in her arms.* ○ *He manages to write by holding the pen between his teeth.* ○ *Hold my hand. This is a busy road.* يمسك
2 [T] to keep sth in a certain position: *Hold your head up straight.* ○ *Hold the camera still or you'll spoil the picture.* ○ *These two screws hold the shelf in place.* يثبّت؛ يمسك
3 [T] to keep a person in a position or place by force: *The terrorists are holding three men hostage.* ○ *A man is being held at the police station.* يحتجز
4 [I,T] to contain or have space for a particular amount: *The car holds five people.* ○ *How much does this bottle hold?* يتّسع لِ، يستوعب
5 [T] to have sth (usually in an official way): *Does she hold a British passport?* ○ *She holds the world record in the 100 metres.* يحمل ؛ يشغل
6 [T] to have an opinion, etc: *They hold the view that we shouldn't spend any more money.* يرتئي ، يعتقد
7 [I] to remain the same: *I hope this weather holds till the weekend.* ○ *What I said still holds, nothing has changed.* يبقى على حاله ، يدوم
8 [T] to believe that sth is true about a person: *I hold the parents responsible for the child's behaviour.* يعتقد ؛ يعتبر
9 [T] to organize an event: *They're holding a*

party for his fortieth birthday. ○ *The elections will be held in the autumn.* يقيم (حفلة) : يجري

10 [I,T] (when you are telephoning) to wait until the person you are calling is ready: *I'm afraid his phone is engaged. Will you hold the line?* ينتظر (على خطّ التليفون)

11 [T] to have a conversation: *It's impossible to hold a conversation with all this noise.* يتحدّث

IDM **Hold it!** Wait! Don't move! قف! لا تتحرك!

ℹ For other idioms containing **hold**, look at the entries for the nouns, adjectives, etc., e.g. **hold your own** is at **own**.

PHR V **hold sb/sth back 1** to prevent sb/sth from making progress يؤخّر : يعيق

2 to prevent sb/sth from moving forward: *The police tried to hold the crowd back.* يصد ، يرد ، يكبح

hold sth back to not give information: *The police are sure that she is holding something back. She knows much more than she is saying.* يكتم معلومات

hold on 1 to wait: *Hold on. I'll be with you in a minute.* ينتظر

2 to manage in a difficult or dangerous situation: *They managed to hold on until a rescue party arrived.* يصمد

hold on to sb/sth to not let go of sb/sth: *The child held on to his mother. He didn't want her to go.* يتشبّث بِ

hold on to sth to not give or sell sth: *They've offered me a lot of money for this painting, but I'm going to hold on to it.* يحتفظ بِ

hold out to last (in a difficult situation): *How long will our supply of water hold out?* يدوم؛ يصمد، يتحمل

hold sth out to offer sth by moving it towards sb: *He held out a sweet and offered it to the girl.* يقدّم، يعرض على

hold out for sth to continue to ask for sth يصر على مطلوبه ، ينتظر بصبر بغية تحقيق مطلوبه

hold sb/sth up to make sb/sth late: *We were held up by the traffic.* يؤخّر

hold up sth to rob sth, using a gun, etc: *Masked men held up a bank in South London yesterday.* يهدد بالمسدس بغية السرقة ، يسطو مهدداً بسلاح

⚷**hold²** /həʊld/ *noun* **1** [C, sing.] the act or manner of holding sb/sth: *to have a firm hold on the rope* ○ *judo holds* ℹ 'Hold' is often used with the verbs **catch**, **get**, **grab**, **seize**, **take**, etc: *Catch hold of the other side of this sheet and help me to fold it, please.* ○ *I can touch it, but I can't quite get hold of it. It's too far away.* قبضة ، مسكة

2 [sing.] **a hold (on/over sb/sth)** influence or control: *The new government has strengthened its hold on the country.* سيطرة

3 [C] a place where a climber can put his/her hand or foot when climbing ➲ Look at **foothold**. ممسك أو موطئ (عند تسلّق جبل)

IDM **get hold of sb/sth 1** to find sb/sth (that will be useful): *I must try and get hold of a good second-hand bicycle.* يجد ، يقع على

2 to find sb or make contact with sb: *I've been trying to get hold of the complaints department all morning.* يتّصل بِ : يجِد

hold³ /həʊld/ *noun* [C] the part of a ship or plane where goods are carried عنبر (في سفينة) ، مخزن (في طائرة)

holdall /ˈhəʊldɔːl/ (*US* **carry-all**) *noun* [C] a large bag that is used for carrying clothes, etc. when you are travelling حقيبة يد كبيرة لحمل الأمتعة

holder /ˈhəʊldə(r)/ *noun* [C] (often in compounds) **1** a person who has or holds sth: *a ticket holder* ○ *the world record holder in the 100 metres* ○ *holders of British passports* حامل (شهادة مثلا) : حائز على

2 something that contains or holds sth: *a plant-pot holder* وعاء حاوٍ لشيء آخر ، حامل

ˈ**hold-up** *noun* [C] **1** a delay: *What's the hold-up?* تأخير

2 a robbery by people with guns سطو مسلّح

⚷**hole** /həʊl/ *noun* **1** [C] an opening; a hollow or an empty space in sth solid: *The pavement is full of holes.* ○ *There are holes in my socks.* ○ *I've got a hole in my tooth.* ○ (*figurative*) *The repair of the roof has made a big hole in their savings.* حفرة : ثقب : ثغرة

2 [C] the place where an animal lives in the ground or in a tree: *a rabbit hole* جُحْر

3 [sing.] (*informal*) a small dark and unpleasant room, flat, etc: *This place is a hole – you can't live here!* مسكن صغير مظلم ، غرفة مثل "القبر" أو "الجب"

4 [C] (in golf) the hole in the ground that you must hit the ball into. Each section of a golf course is also called a hole: *an eighteen-hole golf course* ○ *Barbara won the seventh hole.* ثقبة (في لعبة الغولف)

⚷**holiday** /ˈhɒlədeɪ/ *noun* **1** [C] a day of rest when people do not go to work, school, etc: *Next Thursday is a holiday in some parts of Germany.* ○ *New Year's Day is a bank/public holiday in Britain.* عطلة

> **Holiday** in this sense is used in both British and American English. A day when you do not go to work is often also called **a day off**: *I'm having two days off next week when we move house.*

2 (*US* **vacation**) [C,U] a period of rest from work or school (often when you go and stay away from home): *We're going to Italy for our summer holidays this year.* ○ *Mr Philips isn't here this week. He's away on holiday.* ○ *I'm going to take a week's holiday in May and spend it at home.* ○ *the school, Christmas, Easter, summer, etc. holidays* إجازة ، عطلة

> In British English **vacation** means the period of time when universities and courts of law are not working: *Maria wants to get a job in the long vacation.* **Leave** is time when you do not go to work for a special reason: *sick leave* ○ *maternity leave* (= when you are having a baby) ○ *unpaid leave.*

ˈ**holiday camp** *noun* [C] (*Brit*) a place that provides accommodation and organized entertainment for people on holiday مكان معدّ للاصطياف : مخيّم سياحي

holidaymaker /ˈhɒlədeɪmeɪkə(r)/ *noun* [C] (*Brit*) a person who is away from home on holiday مصطاف ، سائح

holiness /ˈhəʊlinəs/ *noun* [U] the state of being holy قدسيّة ، قداسة

hollow /ˈhɒləʊ/ *adj* **1** with a hole or empty space inside: *a hollow tree* أجوف

2 (used about a sound) seeming to come from a hollow place: *hollow footsteps in the empty house* (صوت) عميق أو مكتوم

▸ **hollow** *noun* [C] an area that is lower than the surrounding land منخفَض

hollow *verb*

PHR V **hollow sth out** to take the inside part of sth out in order to make sth else: *They hollowed out a tree trunk to make a canoe.* يجوِّف ، يقوِّر

holly /ˈhɒli/ *noun* [U] a plant that has shiny dark-green leaves with prickles and red berries in the winter. It is often used as a Christmas decoration. شجرة الدبق، شرابة الراعي، البهشية

holocaust /ˈhɒləkɔːst/ *noun* [C] a situation where a great many things are destroyed and a great many people die: *a nuclear holocaust* دمار شامل ، مَحْرقة؛ مَجْزرة

hologram /ˈhɒləɡræm/ *noun* [C] an image or picture which appears to stand out from the flat surface it is on when light falls on it هولوغرام: صورة نافرة

holster /ˈhəʊlstə(r)/ *noun* [C] a leather case for a gun that is fixed to a belt or worn under the arm قِراب أو بيت المسدّس

holy /ˈhəʊli/ *adj* (**holier**; **holiest**) **1** connected with God or with religion and therefore very special or sacred: *the Holy Bible* ○ *holy water* ○ *The Koran is the holy book of the Muslims.* مقدّس

2 (used about a person) serving God; pure (رجل) تقيّ مكرس حياته لخدمة الإله

ˌHoly Comˈmunion *noun* [U] = COMMUNION (1)

the ˌHoly ˈGhost (*also* **the ˈHoly ˈSpirit**) *noun* [sing.] Christians believe God consists of three parts: God the Father, God the Son (Jesus Christ) and God the Holy Ghost الروح القدس

home¹ /həʊm/ *noun* **1** [C,U] the place where you live (with your family) or where you feel that you belong: *She left home at the age of 21.* ○ *That old house would make an ideal family home.* ○ *Stephen went abroad and made his home in Canada.* ○ *Now we've got this computer, we'd better find a home for it* (= somewhere to keep it). ➲ Look at the note at **house¹**. بيت ؛ عائلة ؛ مكان إقامة

> Be careful. The preposition *to* is not used before 'home': *It's time to go home.* ○ *She's usually tired when she gets home.* If you want to talk about somebody else's home, you have to say: *at Jane and Andy's* or: *at Jane and Andy's place/house.*

2 [C] a place that provides care for a particular type of person or for animals: *a children's home* (= for children who have no parents to look after them) ○ *an old people's home* ملجأ، مأوى؛ دار

3 [sing.] the place where sth began: *Greece is said to be the home of democracy.* مهْد (الحضارة)

IDM **at home 1** in your house, flat, etc: *Is anybody at home?* ○ *Tomorrow we're staying at home all day.* ❶ In US English **home** is often used without the preposition *at*: *Is anybody home?* في البيت

2 as if you were in your own home; comfortable: *Please make yourself at home.* ○ *They were warm and welcoming and I felt at home straight away.* مرتاح وكأنه في بيته

▸ **homeless** *adj* having no home بلا مأوى ، مشرد

the homeless *noun* [plural] people without a home المشرّدون

homelessness *noun* [U] التشرد

homeward /ˈhəʊmwəd/ *adj* going towards home: *the homeward journey* عائد (إلى البيت أو إلى الوطن)

homewards /-wədz/ *adv* towards home في طريق العودة إلى البيت أو الوطن

home² /həʊm/ *adj* (only *before* a noun) **1** connected with home: *home cooking* ○ *a happy home life* بيتيّ؛ عائلي

2 connected with your own country, not with a foreign country: *The Home Secretary is responsible for home affairs.* ○ *goods for the home market* محليّ ، داخليّ

3 (used in sport) connected with your own sports team or ground: *The home team has a lot of support.* ○ *a home game* ❶ The opposite is **away**. محليّ

home³ /həʊm/ *adv* at, in or to your home or home country: *We must be getting home soon.* ○ *She'll be flying home for Christmas.* في البيت؛ إلى البيت

IDM **bring sth home to sb** to make sb understand sth fully: *Looking at those pictures of hungry children really brought home to me how lucky we are.* يفهم جيداً ، يوضح ؛ يقنع

drive sth home (to sb) → DRIVE¹

homecoming /ˈhəʊmkʌmɪŋ/ *noun* [C,U] the arrival home (especially of sb who has been away for a long time) العودة إلى الوطن

the ˌHome ˈCounties *noun* [plural] the area of Britain around London المقاطعات المحيطة بلندن

ˌhome ecoˈnomics *noun* [U] cooking and other skills needed at home, taught as a subject in school التدبير المنزلي

ˌhome-ˈgrown *adj* (used about fruit and vegetables) grown in your own garden من انتاج حديقة البيت

ˈhomeland /ˈhəʊmlænd/ *noun* [C] the country where you were born or that your parents came from, or to which you feel you belong وَطن

homely /ˈhəʊmli/ *adj* (**homelier**; **homeliest**) **1** (*Brit*) plain and simple but also comfortable or welcoming: *a homely atmosphere* ○ *The farmer's wife was a large homely woman.* (مكان) بسيط لكنه مريح ؛ (جو) عائلي ؛ (امرأة) بسيطة مضيافة

2 (*US*) (used about a person) not very attractive غير جذّاب

ˌ**home-ˈmade** *adj* made at home; not bought in a shop: *home-made cakes* من صنع البيت

the ˈHome Office *noun* [sing.] the department of the British Government that is responsible for affairs inside the country, the police, prisons, etc. The Home Office also decides who can come and live in Britain. وزارة الداخلية البريطانية

homeopathy (*Brit also* **homoeopathy**) /ˌhəʊmiˈɒpəθi/ *noun* [U] the treatment of a disease by giving very small amounts of a drug that would cause the disease if given in large amounts المعالجة المثليّة

▸ **homeopath** (*Brit also* **homoeopath**) /ˈhəʊmiəpæθ/ *noun* [C] a person who treats sick people by using homeopathy معالِج بالطريقة المثليّة
homeopathic (*Brit also* **homoeopathic**) /ˌhəʊmiəˈpæθɪk/ *adj*: *homeopathic medicine* عقار مِثلي

ˈ**home page** *noun* (*computing*) the first of a number of pages of information on the Internet that belongs to a person or an organization. A home page contains connections to other pages of information. صفحة الموقع على الشبكة الدولية

homeroom /ˈhəʊmruːm; -rʊm/ *noun* [C,U] (*US*) a room in a school where students go at the beginning of each school day, so that teachers can check who is in school; the time spent in this room: *Homeroom lasts for ten minutes.* غرفة التفقّد (في مدرسة)

ˌ**Home ˈSecretary** *noun* [C] (*pl.* **Home Secretaries**) the British Government minister who is in charge of the Home Office وزير الداخلية البريطاني

ˈ**homesick** /ˈhəʊmsɪk/ *adj* sad because you are away from home: *She was very homesick for Canada.* مشتاق أو شاعر بالحنين إلى الوطن
▸ ˈ**homesickness** *noun* [U] الحنين إلى الوطن

hometown /ˈhəʊmtaʊn/ *noun* [C] the place where you were born or lived as a child مسقط الرأس

🔑 **homework** /ˈhəʊmwɜːk/ *noun* [U] the work that teachers give to pupils to do away from school: *Have we got any homework?* ○ *We've got a translation to do for homework.* ○ (*figurative*) *The minister had not done his homework and there were several questions that he couldn't answer.* ➲ Look at the note at **housework**. واجب أو فرض مدرسيّ ، وظيفة

homicide /ˈhɒmɪsaɪd/ *noun* [U] the illegal killing of one person by another; murder جريمة قتل
▸ **homicidal** /ˌhɒmɪˈsaɪdl/ *adj* ميّال إلى القتل : قتليّ

homoeopathy = HOMEOPATHY

homogeneous /ˌhɒməˈdʒiːniəs/ *adj* made up of parts that are all of the same type ❶ The opposite is **heterogeneous**. متجانس

homonym /ˈhɒmənɪm/ *noun* [C] a word that is spelt and pronounced like another word but that has a different meaning (كلمات) متطابقة لفظاً مختلفة معنىً

homosexual /ˌhəʊməˈsekʃuəl/ *adj* sexually attracted to people of the same sex لوطي
▸ **homosexual** *noun* [C] a homosexual person اللوطي
homosexuality /ˌhəʊməsekʃuˈæləti/ *noun* [U] الميل للمثل؛ لواطة

Hon (*especially US* **Hon.**) *abbrev* **1** = HONORARY (2) **2** = HONOURABLE (2)

🔑 **honest** /ˈɒnɪst/ *adj* **1** (used about a person) telling the truth; not deceiving people or stealing: *Just be honest – do you like this skirt or not?* ○ *We need somebody who's completely honest for this job.* صادق : أمين

2 showing honest qualities: *an honest face* ○ *I'd like your honest opinion, please.* مخلص ، معبِّر عن الأمانة

❶ The opposite for both senses is **dishonest**.
▸ **honestly** *adv* **1** in an honest way: *He tried to answer the lawyer's questions honestly.* بصدق ، بأمانة

2 (used for emphasizing sth): *I honestly don't know where she has gone.* صدقاً!

3 (used for expressing disapproval): *Honestly! What a mess!* يا إلهي! (تقال تعبيراً عن الاستنكار)

honesty /ˈɒnəsti/ *noun* [U] the quality of being honest ❶ The opposite is **dishonesty**. صدق ، أمانة ، استقامة

honey /ˈhʌni/ *noun* [U] the sweet sticky substance that is made by bees and that people eat: *Would you like honey on your bread?* ❶ **Honey** is also another word for **darling** (used especially in the US). عسل (النحل)

honeycomb /ˈhʌnikəʊm/ *noun* [C,U] the wax structure with many six-sided holes that bees make for keeping their honey and eggs in قرص النحل

honeymoon /ˈhʌnimuːn/ *noun* [C] a holiday that is taken by a man and a woman who have just got married: *We went to Hawaii for our honeymoon.* شهر العسل

honeysuckle /ˈhʌnisʌkl/ *noun* [U] a climbing plant with sweet-smelling yellow or pink flowers صريمة الجدي، سلطان الجبل

honk /hɒŋk/ *verb* [I,T] to sound the horn of a car; to make this sound يزمّر/ يطوّط ببوق السيّارة

honorary /ˈɒnərəri; *US* ˈɒnəreri/ *adj* **1** given as an honour (without the person needing the usual qualifications): *to be awarded an honorary degree* (لقب) فخري

2 often **Honorary** (*abbr* **Hon**) not getting any money for doing a job: *He is the Honorary President.* فخري

🔑 **honour¹** (*US* **honor**) /ˈɒnə(r)/ *noun* **1** [sing.] something that gives pride or pleasure: *It was a great honour to be asked to speak at the conference.* ○ *He did me the honour of mentioning my name in the introduction.* شرف ، فخر

2 [U] the respect from other people that a person, country, etc. gets because of high standards of behaviour and moral character: *a man of*

a b c d e f g h i j k l m n o p q r s t u v w x y z

honour ○ *to fight for the honour of your country* ➲ Look at **dishonour**. احترام : كرامة

3 [C] something that is given to a person officially, to show great respect: *He has been given several honours for his work with handicapped children.* مظهر تكريم ، وسام ، لقب

4 Honours [plural] (*abbr* **Hons**) a type of university degree that is higher than an ordinary degree شهادة جامعية بدرجة شرف

IDM in honour of sb/sth; in sb/sth's honour out of respect for sb/sth: *A party was given in honour of the guests from Bonn.* على شرف

honour² (*US* **honor**) /ˈɒnə(r)/ *verb* [T] **1 honour sb/sth (with sth)** to show great (public) respect for sb/sth or to give sb pride or pleasure: *I am very honoured by the confidence you have shown in me.* يُشرِّف ؛ يُكرِّم

2 to keep a promise to do sth يفي بوعده

honourable (*US* **honorable**) /ˈɒnərəbl/ *adj* **1** acting in a way that makes people respect you; having or showing honour: *The only honourable thing to do was to resign.* ○ *an honourable person* ➲ Look at **dishonourable**. شريف ، جدير بالاحترام

2 the Honourable (*abbr* **Hon**) a title that is given to some high officials, to the children of some noblemen and to Members of Parliament when they are speaking to each other لقب تكريمي يشبه "سيادة" أو "معالي"

▸ **honourably** /-əbli/ *adv* بشرف، بشكل لائق

Hons *abbrev* = HONOURS

hood /hʊd/ *noun* [C] **1** the part of a coat, etc. that you use to cover your head and neck in bad weather قلنسوة المعطف أو البرنس

2 (*especially Brit*) a soft cover for a car, or baby's pram that can be folded down in good weather غطاء أو "كبوت" السيارة أو عربة الطفل

hoody (*also* **hoodie**) /ˈhʊdi/ *noun* [C] (**pl. hoodies**) (*informal*) a jacket or a sweatshirt with a hood رداء ذو قلنسوة

3 (*US*) = BONNET (1)

hoof /huːf/ *noun* [C] (*pl.* **hoofs** or **hooves** /huːvz/) the hard part of the foot of horses and some other animals حافر

hook¹ /hʊk/ *noun* [C] **1** a curved piece of metal, plastic, etc. that is used for catching sth or hanging sth on: *a fish hook* ○ *It fastens with a hook and eye.* ○ *Put your coat on the hook over there.* صِنارة صيد، شص : كُلّاب : كُبْشة

2 (used in boxing) a blow or punch that is given with the elbow bent: *a right hook* (= with the right arm) (في الملاكمة) ضربة خطّاف

IDM off the hook 1 (used about the telephone receiver) not in position, so that telephone calls cannot be received السماعة مرفوعة

2 (*informal*) out of a difficult situation: *My father paid the money I owed and got me off the hook.* (أخرجني من) الورطة

hook² /hʊk/ *verb* **1** [I,T] to fasten sth or to be fastened with a hook or sth like a hook يُثبِّت أو يُثبَّت شيئا بكُلّاب أو ما شابهه

hooks

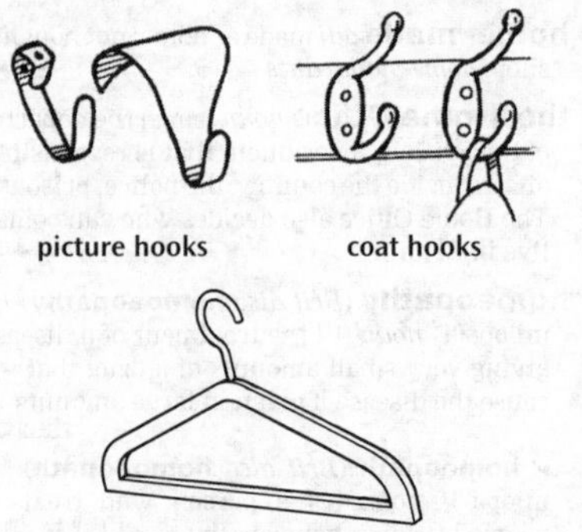

2 [T] to catch hold of sth with a hook or with sth shaped like a hook يلتقط أو يمسك شيئا بكلّاب أو ما شابهه

IDM be/get hooked (on sth) (*informal*) **1** to like (doing) sth very much: *Brian is hooked on computer games.* متعلق بـ، مسحور بـ

2 to be dependent on (addicted to) drugs مدمن على

PHRV hook (sth) up (to sth) to connect sb/sth to a piece of electronic equipment or to a power supply يربط بين عدّة دارات كهربائية

▸ **hooked** *adj* shaped like a hook: *a hooked nose* (أنف) أقنى، معقوف

hooligan /ˈhuːlɪɡən/ *noun* [C] a young person who behaves in a violent and aggressive way in public places: *football hooligans* ➲ Look at **lout** and **yob**. They are similar in meaning. أحد الغوغاء ، شقيّ ، بلطجي، أزعر

▸ **hooliganism** /-ɪzəm/ *noun* [U] غوغائية ، شغب مع عنف

hoop /huːp/ *noun* [C] a large metal or plastic ring طوق كبير من المعدن أو البلاستيك ، طارة

hooray /huˈreɪ/ *interj* = HURRAY

hoot /huːt/ *noun* **1** [C] the sound that is made by an owl, a ship's or car's horn, etc. نعيق البوم : زمّور (سيارة مثلا)

2 [sing.] (*informal*) something that is very funny: *That film is a real hoot!* شيء مضحك جداً

▸ **hoot** *verb* [I,T] to sound the horn of a car or to make a loud noise: *The driver hooted at the dog but it wouldn't move.* ○ *They hooted with laughter at the suggestion.* (سائق) يزمِّر،يطوِّط : يضجّ بالضحك

Hoover™ /ˈhuːvə(r)/ *noun* [C] a vacuum cleaner (used to clean carpets by sucking up the dirt) مكنسة كهربائية ، هوفر

▸ **hoover** *verb* [I,T] to clean a carpet, etc. with a vacuum cleaner: *This carpet needs hoovering.* ○ *We'd better hoover before our visitors arrive.* ينظف/يكنس بمكنسة كهربائية

hooves /huːvz/ *pl.* of HOOF

hop¹ /hɒp/ *verb* [I] (hopping; hopped) **1** (used about a person) to jump on one leg ينطّ على رجل واحدة

2 (used about an animal or bird) to jump with both or all feet together (طائر أو حيوان) يثب، يقفز

3 (*informal*) to go somewhere quickly or for a short time: *Hop upstairs and get my glasses, would you?* يذهب بسرعة ، ينطّ ، "يخطف رِجله"

IDM **hop it!** (*slang*) Go away! إمش! ، إبْعد عني!

PHRV **hop in/into sth; hop out/out of sth** (*informal*) to get in or out of a car, etc. (quickly): *Hop in! I'll give you a lift to town.* يركب أو ينزل بسرعة من سيّارة

hop on/onto sth; hop off sth to get onto/off a bus, etc. (quickly) يصعد أو ينزل بسرعة من أوتوبيس

▸ **hop** *noun* [C] an act of hopping نَطّة ، قفزة

hop² /hɒp/ *noun* **1** [C] a tall climbing plant with flowers جنجل ، حشيشة الدينار

2 **hops** [plural] the flowers of this plant that are used in making beer أزهار الجنجل أو حشيشة الدينار

🔑**hope** /həʊp/ *noun* **1** [C,U] **hope (of/for sth); hope (of doing sth/that...)** the feeling of wanting sth to happen and thinking that it will: *She never gave up hope that a cure for the disease would be found.* ○ *What hope is there for the future?* ○ *There is no hope of finding anybody else alive.* ○ *David has high hopes of becoming an accountant.* أمل

2 [C, usually sing.] a person or thing that gives you hope: *Please can you help me? You're my last hope.* أمل ، رجاء

IDM **in the hope of sth/that...** because you want sth to happen: *I came here in the hope that we could talk privately.* بأمل

▸ **hope** *verb* [I,T] **hope (for sth); hope to do sth; hope (that) sth will happen** to want sth to happen or be true: *I hope that you feel better soon.* ○ *Hoping to hear from you soon* (= at the end of a letter). ○ *'Is it raining?' 'I hope not. I haven't got a coat with me.'* ○ *'Are you coming to London with us?' 'I'm not sure yet but I hope so.'* ○ *We're hoping for snow in January – we're going skiing.* يأمل ، يرجو

hopeful /ˈhəʊpfl/ *adj* **1** thinking that sth that you want to happen will happen: *He's very hopeful about the success of the business.* ○ *The ministers seem hopeful that an agreement will be reached.* آمل ؛ متفائل

2 making you think that sth good will happen: *a hopeful sign* مُشجِّع ، يرجى منه خير

▸ **hopefully** /-fəli/ *adv* **1** in a hopeful way: *She smiled hopefully at me, waiting for my answer.* برجاء ، بتطلّع

2 (*informal*) I/We hope; if everything happens as planned: *Hopefully, we'll be finished by six o'clock.* آملاً أن... ، (إذا سار كل شيء على ما يرام)

hopeless /ˈhəʊpləs/ *adj* **1** giving no hope that sth will be successful or get better: *This is a hopeless situation. There is nothing we can do.* ميؤوس منه

2 **hopeless (at sth)** (*informal*) (used about a person) often doing things wrong; very bad at doing sth: *You're hopeless. You always forget my birthday.* ○ *I'm absolutely hopeless at tennis.* لا أمل في إصلاحه ؛ لا فائدة منه ؛ أخرق

▸ **hopelessly** *adv*: *They were hopelessly lost.* دون أمل (بالنجاة مثلاً)

hopelessness *noun* [U] يأس ، قنوط ؛ انسداد السبل

horde /hɔːd/ *noun* [C] a very large number of people: *There were hordes of people shopping in town on Saturday.* حشد من الناس

horizon /həˈraɪzn/ *noun* [C] the line where the earth and sky appear to meet: *The ship appeared on/disappeared over the horizon.* الأفق

🔑**horizontal** /ˌhɒrɪˈzɒntl; *US* ˌhɔːr-/ *adj* going from side to side, not up and down; flat or level: *The gymnasts were exercising on the horizontal bars.* ➲ Look also at **vertical**. أفقي

▸ **horizontally** /-təli/ *adv* أفقياً

hormone /ˈhɔːməʊn/ *noun* [C] a substance in the body that influences growth and development هرمون

🔑**horn** /hɔːn/ *noun* [C] **1** one of the hard pointed things that cows, goats, etc. have on their heads قرن

2 the thing in a car, etc. that gives a loud warning sound: *Don't sound your horn late at night.* ○ *a foghorn* زمّور أو بوق (السيارة مثلاً)

3 one of the family of brass musical instruments that you play by blowing into them: *a French horn* صور (آلة نفخ موسيقية)، بوق

hornet /ˈhɔːnɪt/ *noun* a large wasp that can give you a painful sting زنبور

IDM **a hornet's nest** angry argument, criticism, etc. involving a lot of people: *His letter to the papers has stirred up/uncovered a real hornet's nest.* عاصفة من السخط والاستياء

horoscope /ˈhɒrəskəʊp; *US* ˈhɔːr-/ *noun* [C] (*also* **stars** [plural]) a statement about what is going to happen to a person in the future, based on the position of the stars and planets when he/she was born: *What does my horoscope for next week say?* ➲ Look at **astrology** and **zodiac**. معرفة البخت من مواقع النجوم والكواكب

horrendous /hɒˈrendəs/ *adj* (*informal*) very bad or unpleasant: *The queues were absolutely horrendous.* فظيع ، مخيف

▸ **horrendously** *adv* للغاية ، بشكل مريع

horrible /ˈhɒrəbl; *US* ˈhɔːr-/ *adj* **1** (*informal*) very bad or unpleasant: *We had a horrible day in London.* ○ *This tastes horrible!* ○ *Don't be so horrible!* ○ *I've got a horrible feeling that I've forgotten something.* شنيع ؛ كريه ؛ مزعج

2 causing fear or shock: *a horrible murder* رهيب ، فظيع

▸ **horribly** /-əbli/ *adv* بشكل مريع ؛ بشكل فظيع

horrid /ˈhɒrɪd; *US* ˈhɔːrɪd/ *adj* (*informal*) very unpleasant or unkind: *We had horrid weather in Italy.* ○ *I'm sorry that I was so horrid last night.* رديء للغاية ، فظيع ؛ مزعج جداً

horrific /həˈrɪfɪk/ *adj* **1** causing fear or shock: *a horrific road accident* رهيب ، مروع

2 (*informal*) very bad or unpleasant: *We had a horrific journey – we were stuck in a traffic jam for two hours.* مزعج للغاية ، (رحلة) ملعونة

a b c d e f g **h** i j k l m n o p q r s t u v w x y z

▸ **horrifically** /-kli/ *adv*: *horrifically expensive* بشكل فاحش ، إلى حدٍّ مخيف

horrify /ˈhɒrɪfaɪ; *US* ˈhɔːr-/ *verb* [T] (*pres part* **horrifying**; *3rd pers sing pres* **horrifies**; *pt, pp* **horrified**) to shock sb greatly: *I was horrified by the conditions they were living in.* يُذهل ، يصدم ؛ يُفزع

▸ **horrifying** *adj* مذهِل ؛ فظيع ، مفْزع

horror /ˈhɒrə(r); *US* ˈhɔːr-/ *noun* **1** [U, sing.] a feeling of great fear or shock: *They watched in horror as the building collapsed.* ○ *She has a horror of rats.* ذهول ، رعب

2 [C] something that makes you feel frightened or shocked: *I'll never forget the horror of what I saw that day.* ○ *the horrors of war* فظاعة ، هَوْل

ˈ**horror film** *noun* [C] a film that entertains people by showing frightening or shocking things فيلم رعْب

hors d'oeuvre /ˌɔː ˈdɜːv/ *noun* [C,U] (*pl.* **hors d'oeuvre** or **hors d'oeuvres** /ˈdɜːv/) small portions of different types of food served as a course at the beginning of a meal مقبِّلات

horse /hɔːs/ *noun* [C] a large animal that is used for riding on or for pulling or carrying heavy loads ⓘ A male horse is a **stallion**, a female horse is a **mare** and a young horse is a **foal**. حصان

IDM **on horseback** sitting on a horse: *Policemen on horseback were controlling the crowds.* ⓘ Police on horseback are also called **mounted police**. راكباً حصاناً

horse chestnut /ˌhɔːs ˈtʃesnʌt/ *noun* [C] **1** a large tree that has leaves divided into seven sections and pink or white flowers (شجرة) قسطل هندي، كستنة بريّة، شاهبلّوط

2 (*also informal* **conker**) the nut from this tree ثمرة القسطلة أو الكستنة البريّة

horsefly /ˈhɔːsflaɪ/ *noun* [C] (*pl.* **-ies**) a large fly that bites horses and cows نعرة: ذبابة الخيل

horseman /ˈhɔːsmən/ *noun* [C] (*pl.* **horsemen** /-mən/) a man who rides a horse (well): *an experienced horseman* فارس ، خيّال

horsepower /ˈhɔːspaʊə(r)/ *noun* [C] (*pl.* **horsepower**) (*abbr* **h.p.; HP**) a measure of the power of an engine, etc: *a ten-horsepower engine* قوة حصان ، حصان بخاري

ˈ**horse racing** (*also* **racing**) *noun* [U] the sport in which a person (jockey) rides a horse in a race to win money ⓘ Horse racing takes place at a **racecourse**. People often **bet** on the results of **horse races**. سباق الخيل

horseradish /ˈhɔːsrædɪʃ/ *noun* [U] a plant with a hot-tasting root which is used for making a cold sauce: *roast beef with horseradish sauce* فجل برّي حار، خردل الألمان

ˈ**horseshoe** /ˈhɔːsʃuː/ (*also* **shoe**) *noun* [C] a U-shaped piece of metal that is fixed to the bottom of a horse's hoof. People believe that horseshoes bring good luck. حدوة ، نعل الحصان

ˈ**horsewoman** /ˈhɔːswʊmən/ *noun* [C] (*pl.* **horsewomen** /-wɪmɪn/) a woman who rides a horse (well): *a good horsewoman* خيّالة ماهرة

horticulture /ˈhɔːtɪkʌltʃə(r)/ *noun* [U] the study of how to grow flowers, fruit and vegetables (علم) البَسْتنة

▸ **horticultural** /ˌhɔːtɪˈkʌltʃərəl/ *adj* بَسْتني ، متعلق بالأزهار والنباتات

hose /həʊz/ (*also* ˈ**hosepipe**) *noun* [C,U] a long rubber or plastic tube that is used for getting water from one place to another, in the garden or when there is a fire خرطوم ماء ، نربيش، بربيش

hospice /ˈhɒspɪs/ *noun* [C] a special hospital where people who are dying are cared for مستشفى خاص يعنى بالمرضى قبيل وفاتهم

hospitable /hɒˈspɪtəbl; ˈhɒspɪtəbl/ *adj* (used about a person) friendly and welcoming to visitors ➲ Look at **inhospitable**. مضياف، كريم

hospital /ˈhɒspɪtl/ *noun* [C] a place where ill or injured people are treated: *He was rushed to hospital in an ambulance.* ○ *to be admitted to/discharged from hospital* مستشفى

> Note the difference between: *My brother works in the local hospital* and: *He's very ill in hospital.* 'In hospital', 'to hospital' are special expressions that are used without 'a' or 'the': *All the people who were hurt in the accident have been taken to hospital.* A person who is being treated in a hospital by **doctors** and **nurses** is a **patient**. If you have an accident you are taken first to the **accident and emergency** department (*US* **emergency room**).

hospitality /ˌhɒspɪˈtæləti/ *noun* [U] looking after guests and being friendly and welcoming towards them: *We're very grateful for your hospitality.* كرم أو حسْن الضيافة

host[1] /həʊst/ *noun* [C] **1** a person who receives and entertains visitors: *He acted as our host and showed us the city.* ○ *It's polite to write a thank-you letter to your host.* ○ *the host country for the next Olympic Games* ➲ Look at **hostess**. المُضيف ، صاحب الدعوة

2 a person who introduces a television or radio show and talks to visiting guests المتحدث مع ضيوف البرنامج (في التلفزيون أو الراديو)

▸ **host** *verb* [T] to act as a host or hostess يستضيف

host[2] /həʊst/ *noun* [C] a large number (of people or things): *I've got a whole host of things I want to discuss with him.* جَمْع ، حشْد : عدد هائل

hostage /ˈhɒstɪdʒ/ *noun* [C] a person who is caught and kept prisoner by a person or group. The hostage may be killed or injured if that person or group does not get what it is asking for: *The hijackers released the women and children but kept the men as hostages.* رهينة

IDM **take/hold sb hostage** to catch/keep sb as a hostage يأخذ رهينة

hostel /ˈhɒstl/ *noun* [C] a place (like a cheap hotel) where people can stay when they are living away from home: *a youth hostel* ○ *a hostel for*

the homeless ○ *a student hostel*
بيت (الشباب) ، دار الطلبة

hostess /ˈhəʊstəs/ *noun* [C] **1** a woman who receives and entertains visitors
المضيفة ، صاحبة الدعوة

2 a woman who introduces a television or radio show and talks to visiting guests
المتحدثة مع ضيوف البرنامج (في التلفزيون أو الراديو)

3 = AIR HOSTESS

hostile /ˈhɒstaɪl; *US* -tl/ *adj* very unfriendly towards sb/sth; not having a good opinion of sb/sth: *a hostile crowd* ○ *They are very hostile to any change.* عدائي ، معاد ، مناوئ

hostility /hɒˈstɪləti/ *noun* **1** [U] being unfriendly towards sb/sth: *She didn't say anything but I could sense her hostility.* عداء ، معاداة

2 [U] thinking that sth is bad: *They didn't try to hide their hostility to the government.*
مناواة ، معارضة : خصومة

3 hostilities [plural] fighting in a war: *Negotiations have led to an end to hostilities.* قتال

hot /hɒt/ *adj* (hotter; hottest) **1** having (quite) a high degree of heat; not cold: *Can I open the window? I'm really hot.* ○ *Be careful. The plates are hot.* ○ *It's hot today, isn't it?* ○ *Do you like this hot weather?* ○ *a hot meal* حارّ : ساخن

You can describe the temperature of sth as **freezing (cold), cold, cool, tepid** (used about water), **warm, hot** or **boiling (hot)**.

2 (used about food) causing a burning feeling in your mouth: *hot curry* حارّ، حرِّيف

3 exciting and popular: *They are one of this year's hot new bands.* يلقى قبولاً حسناً عند العامة

IDM **be hot at/on sth** to know a lot about sth: *Don't ask me. I'm not very hot on British history.* متضلِّع ، خبير

▸ **hot** *verb* (hotting; hotted)

PHR V **hot up** (*Brit informal*) to become more exciting, with more things happening, etc: *The election campaign has really hotted up in the past few days.* يحمى ، يصبح مثيراً

hotly *adv* **1** angrily or with force: *They hotly denied the newspaper reports.* بغضب ؛ بانفعال

2 closely: *The dog ran off, hotly pursued by its owner.* في أعقابه

ˌhot-ˈair balloon *noun* [C] = BALLOON (2)

ˌhot ˈdog *noun* [C] a hot sausage that is eaten in a soft bread roll سندويشة سجق، مقانق

hotel /həʊˈtel/ *noun* [C] a place where you pay to stay (and perhaps have your meals) when you are on holiday or travelling: *We stayed in a really nice hotel in Devon.* ○ *I've booked a double room at the Grand Hotel.* ○ *a two-star hotel* فندق ، اوتيل

You book a **double, single** or **twin-bedded** room at a hotel. When you arrive you **check in** or **register** and when you leave you **check out**. Look at the note at **inn**.

▸ **hotelier** /həʊˈteliə(r); *US* ˌhəʊtelˈjeɪ/ *noun* [C] a person who owns or manages a hotel
صاحب أو مدير فندق

hothouse /ˈhɒthaʊs/ *noun* [C] a heated building, made of glass, where plants are grown ➲ Look at **greenhouse**. بيت زجاجي (لتربية النباتات)

hotline /ˈhɒtlaɪn/ *noun* [C] a special telephone line that people can use to get information or to talk about sth; a direct telephone line between the heads of government in different countries
خطّ تليفوني مباشر

hotly *adv* → HOT

ˌhot-ˈwater bottle *noun* [C] a rubber container that is filled with hot water and put in a bed to warm it كيس ماء ساخن (لتدفئة الفراش مثلاً)

houmous = HUMMUS

hound /haʊnd/ *noun* [C] a type of dog that is used for hunting or racing: *a foxhound* كلب الصَّيد

▸ **hound** *verb* [T] to follow and disturb sb: *The Royal Family are always being hounded by the press.* يتعقّب ويضايق

hour /ˈaʊə(r)/ *noun* **1** [C] a period of 60 minutes: *He worked for three hours after supper.* ○ *The programme lasts about half an hour.* ○ *I've been waiting here for hours.* ○ *I'm going shopping now. I'll be back in about an hour.* ○ *They get paid by the hour.* ○ *How much do you get paid an/per hour?* ○ *a four-hour journey* ساعة (زمنية)

2 the hour [sing.] the time when a new hour starts (= 1 o'clock, 2 o'clock, etc.): *Trains to Reading leave at two minutes past the hour.*
الساعة الكاملة أيّ الواحدة أو الثانية أو الثالثة ألخ....

3 hours [plural] the period of time when sb is working or a shop, etc. is open: *Office hours are usually from 9 a.m. to 5 p.m.* ○ *Visiting hours in the hospital are from 2 to 3 p.m.* ○ *Employees are demanding shorter working hours.*
ساعات العمل ؛ أوقات الزيارة

4 [C] a period of time: *I'm going shopping in my lunch hour.* ○ *The traffic is very bad in the rush hour.* فترة

IDM **at/till all hours** at/till any time: *She stays out till all hours* (= very late). لوقت متأخر جداً

the early hours → EARLY

on the hour at exactly 1, 2, 3, etc. o'clock: *The buses for London leave on the hour.*
في تمام الساعة (كذا) أي دون دقائق تضاف إليها

▸ **hourly** /ˈaʊəli/ *adv* every hour: *Trains run hourly.* كلّ ساعة

hourly *adj* **1** done or happening every hour: *an hourly news bulletin* كلّ ساعة

2 for an hour: *What is your hourly rate of pay?*
(الأجرة) بالساعة

house¹ /haʊs/ *noun* [C] (*pl.* **houses** /ˈhaʊzɪz/) **1** a building that is made for one family to live in: *Is yours a four-bedroomed or a three-bedroomed house?* منزل ، دار ، بيت

Look at **bungalow, cottage** and **flat¹**. Your **home** is the place where you live, even if it is not a house: *Let's go home to my flat.* Your home is also the place where you feel that you belong. A house is just a building: *We've only just moved into our new house and it doesn't feel like home yet.*

> You can **build**, **do up**, **redecorate** or **extend** a house. You may **rent** a house from somebody or **let** it out to somebody else. If you want to **move house** you go to an **estate agent**.

2 [usually sing.] all the people who live in one house: *Don't shout. You'll wake the whole house up.* أهل البيت

3 a building that is used for a particular purpose: *a warehouse* ○ *a public house* مبنى يستخدم لغايات معيّنة

4 a large firm involved in a particular kind of business: *a fashion/publishing house* دار

5 House a group of people who meet to make a country's laws: *the House of Commons* ○ *the Houses of Parliament* ➲ Look at the note at **Parliament**. مجلس

6 [usually sing.] the people at a theatre or cinema, or the area where they sit: *There was a full house for the play this evening.* جمهور المتفرّجين ؛ الصالة

IDM move house → MOVE²

on the house paid for by the pub, restaurant, etc. that you are visiting; free: *Your first drink is on the house.* مجّاناً، على حساب المحل

house² /haʊz/ *verb* [T] **1** to provide sb with a place to live: *The Council must house homeless families.* يسكِن ، يؤوي

2 to contain or keep sth: *Her office is housed in a separate building.* يَحوي ، يَضم

houseboat /ˈhaʊsbəʊt/ *noun* [C] a boat on a river, etc. where sb lives and which usually stays in one place بيت عائم ، مركب يستخدم كبَيْت

housebound /ˈhaʊsbaʊnd/ *adj* unable to leave your house because you are old or ill قعيد البيت

⚷ **household** /ˈhaʊshəʊld/ *noun* [C] all the people who live in one house and the housework, money, organization, etc. that is needed to look after them: *Almost all households have a television.* ○ *household expenses* الأسرة ومستلزماتها

▸ **householder** /-həʊldə(r)/ *noun* [C] a person who rents or owns a house صاحب أو مستأجر بيت

housekeeper /ˈhaʊskiːpə(r)/ *noun* [C] a person who is paid to look after sb else's house and organize the work in it مديرة البيت

housekeeping /ˈhaʊskiːpɪŋ/ *noun* [U] **1** managing and organizing the work in a house إدارة شؤون البيت

2 the money that you need to manage a house ميزانية البيت

the ˌHouse of ˈCommons (*also* **the Commons**) *noun* [with sing. or pl. verb] the group of people (Members of Parliament) who are elected to make new laws in Britain مجلس العموم البريطاني

the ˌHouse of ˈLords (*also* **the Lords**) *noun* [with sing. or pl. verb] the group of people (who are not elected) who meet to discuss the laws that have been suggested by the House of Commons مجلس اللوردات

the ˌHouse of ˌRepreˈsentatives *noun* [sing.] the group of people who are elected to make new laws in the USA ➲ Look at **Congress** and **Senate**. مجلس النوّاب الامريكي

ˈhouse-proud *adj* paying great attention to the care, cleaning, etc. of your house كثير العناية بنظافة البيت وترتيبه

ˌhouse-to-ˈhouse *adj* going to each house: *The police are making house-to-house enquiries.* (زيارة) لكلّ بيت

ˈhouse-warming *noun* [C] a party that you give when you have just moved into a new home حفلة تدشين المسكن الجديد

housewife /ˈhaʊswaɪf/ *noun* [C] (*pl.* **housewives**) a woman who does not have a full-time job outside the home and who spends her time doing housework, cooking, looking after her family, etc. ❶ A man who does this is called a **house husband**. ربّة منزل

housework /ˈhaʊswɜːk/ *noun* [U] the work that is needed to keep a house clean and tidy شُغل البيت ، شؤون المنزل

> Be careful. The word for work that is given to pupils by teachers to be done out of school hours is **homework**.

⚷ **housing** /ˈhaʊzɪŋ/ *noun* [U] houses, flats, etc. for people to live in: *We need more housing that is suitable for elderly people.* ○ *the Council's housing department* مساكن : إسكان

ˈhousing estate *noun* [C] an area where a large number of houses are planned and built at the same time مجموعة كبيرة من البيوت تبنى في وقت واحد

hover /ˈhɒvə(r); *US* ˈhʌvər/ *verb* [I] **1** (used about a bird, etc.) to stay in the air in one place يحوم

2 (used about a person) to wait near sb/sth: *He hovered outside until he could see that she was free.* يحوم ، يتلكّأ

hovercraft /ˈhɒvəkrɑːft; *US* -kræft/ *noun* [C] (*pl.* **hovercraft**) a type of boat that moves over land or water on a cushion of air الحوّامة

⚷ **how** /haʊ/ *adv* **1** (used in questions) in what way: *How do you spell your name?* ○ *Can you show me how to use this machine?* كيف؟

2 (used when you are asking about sb's health): *'How is your mother?' 'She's much better, thank you.'* كيف حال...؟

> You use 'how' only when you are asking about a person's health. When you are asking about a person's character or appearance you say **what ... like**?: *'What is your mother like?' 'Well, she's much taller than me and she's got dark hair.'*

3 (used when you are asking about a thing or a situation): *How was the weather?* ○ *How is your meal?* كيف؟

4 (used in questions before an adjective or adverb when you are asking about the degree, amount, age, etc. of sb/sth): *How old are you?* ○ *How much is that?* ○ *How long did it take to get here?* كَمْ؟، بِكَمْ؟

5 (used for expressing surprise, shock, thanks,

pleasure, etc.): *How sweet of you to remember my birthday.* ○ *How could he have lied to me?* ما (أجمل!) : كيف؟!

IDM **how/what about...?** → ABOUT[2]

how do you do? (*formal*) (used when meeting sb for the first time) تشرّفنا!

Be careful. **How are you?** and **How do you do?** are answered quite differently: *'How do you do?'* is answered with the same words: *'How do you do?'* The answer to: *'How are you?'* depends on how you are feeling: *'I'm fine.'/'Very well.'/'Much better.'* 'How do you do?' is becoming old-fashioned.

▶ **how** *conj* the way in which: *I can't remember how to get there.* كيف

however[1] /haʊ'evə(r)/ *adv* (before an adjective or adverb) to whatever degree: *He won't wear a hat however cold it is.* ○ *You can't catch her however fast you run.* مهما

▶ **however** *conj* in whatever way: *However I sat I couldn't get comfortable.* ○ *You can dress however you like.* كيفما

however *adv* (used in questions for expressing surprise) in what way; how: *However did you manage to find me here?* ○ *However could he afford a car like that?* ❶ When you use only **how** in a question like this there is not so much feeling of surprise. يا للعجب- كيف؟! بأية وسيلة؟

however[2] /haʊ'evə(r)/ *adv* (used for adding a comment on what you have just said) although sth is true: *Sales are poor this month. There may, however, be an increase before Christmas.* لكن ، إلاّ أنّ

howl /haʊl/ *noun* [C] a long loud cry made by a dog or a wolf: (*figurative*) *The Prime Minister's statement met with howls of protest.* نُباح ، عواء ؛ صِياح

▶ **howl** *verb* [I] to make a howl or say sth with a howl: *The wind howled around the house.* يعوي ؛ يصيح : يولول

h.p. (*also* **HP**) /ˌeɪtʃ 'piː/ *abbrev* **1** = HORSEPOWER

2 = HIRE PURCHASE

HQ /ˌeɪtʃ 'kjuː/ *abbrev* = HEADQUARTERS

HR /ˌeɪtʃ 'ɑː(r)/ *abbrev* = HUMAN RESOURCES

hr (*especially US* **hr.**) (*pl.* **hrs** or **hr**) *abbrev* = HOUR

hub /hʌb/ *noun* [C] **1** the round central part of a wheel قَبّ أو سُرّة العجلة

2 the central and most important part of a place or an activity: *the commercial hub of the city* قلب نابض

huddle /'hʌdl/ *verb* [I] **1** to get close to other people because you are cold or frightened: *The campers huddled (together) around the fire.* يتجمع بعضهم إلى بعض ، يتحاضنون

2 huddle (up) to curl your body up and wrap your arms around yourself because you are cold or frightened: *She huddled up in her sleeping bag and tried to get some sleep.* يتكوّر ، يحضن نفسه (من البرد مثلاً)

▶ **huddle** *noun* [C] a small group of people or things that are close together: *They all stood in a huddle, laughing and chatting.* تجمّع صغير (للتحدث سرّياً مثلاً) : كومة، تراكم

huddled *adj*: *We found the children lying huddled together on the ground.* متكوِّر ، متعانق مع ، متجمّع

huff /hʌf/ *noun* [C, usually sing.] a state of bad temper. You go off in a huff when you want to show people how angry you are. ثورة غضب

hug /hʌg/ *verb* [T] (**hugging**; **hugged**) **1** to put your arms around sb to show that you love him/her: *He hugged his mother and sister and got on the train.* يعانق

2 to hold sth close to your body: *She hugged the parcel to her chest as she ran* يحضن

3 (used about a ship, car, etc.) to keep close to sth: *to hug the coast* يلازم ، يسير ملاصقاً ل

▶ **hug** *noun* [C] an act of hugging: *She gave the child a hug and he stopped crying.* معانقة ، حضنة

huge /hjuːdʒ/ *adj* very large: *There is a huge amount of work still to be done.* ○ *a huge building* هائل ، ضخم

▶ **hugely** *adv*: *The play was hugely successful.* بشكل هائل

huh /hʌ/ *interj* (*informal*) (used for expressing anger, surprise, etc. or for asking a question): *They've gone away, huh? They didn't tell me.* أليس كذلك!! (تقال بلهجة الغضب أو الدهشة)

hull /hʌl/ *noun* [C] the body of a ship هيكل السفينة

hullabaloo /ˌhʌləbə'luː/ *noun* [C, usually sing.] a lot of loud noise, e.g. people shouting ضوضاء ، عِياط وزِياط

hullo = HELLO

hum /hʌm/ *verb* (**humming**; **hummed**) **1** [I] to make a continuous low noise like the noise bees make: (*figurative*) *The classroom was humming with activity.* يدنّ كالنحل ؛ يعجّ (بالنشاط)

2 [I,T] to sing with your lips closed: *You can hum the tune if you don't know the words.* يهمهم، يدندن

▶ **hum** *noun* [C, usually sing.] a humming sound: *the hum of distant traffic* دنين ؛ همهمة

human /'hjuːmən/ *adj* connected with people, not with animals or machines; typical of people: *the human body* ○ *The famine caused a terrible loss of human life.* ○ *A human skeleton was found by the building workers.* ○ *The disaster was caused by human error.* ○ *It's only human to be upset in a situation like that.* إنساني ، بَشَريّ

▶ **human** (*also* ˌ**human** '**being**) *noun* [C] a person; a man, woman or child إنسان ، بشر

humanly *adv*: *They did all that was humanly possible to rescue him* (= everything that a human being could possibly do). بشرياً ، ضمن نطاق القدرة البشرية

humane /hjuː'meɪn/ *adj* having or showing kindness or understanding, especially to a person or animal that is suffering: *Zoo animals must be kept in humane conditions.* ❶ The opposite is **inhumane**. إنسانيّ، شَفوق

▶ **humanely** *adv* بشفقة وحنان ، بشكل إنساني

a b c d e f g **h** i j k l m n o p q r s t u v w x y z

humanitarian /hjuːˌmænɪˈteəriən/ *adj* concerned with trying to make people's lives better and reduce suffering محبّ للإنسانيّة : إنساني

humanity /hjuːˈmænəti/ *noun* [U] **1** all the people in the world, thought of as a group; the human race: *crimes against humanity* البشريّة

2 the quality of being kind and understanding: *The prisoners were treated with humanity.* ❶ The opposite is **inhumanity**. إنسانية، رفق

ˌhuman ˈnature *noun* [U] feelings, behaviour, etc. that are common to all people: *It's only human nature to want the best for yourself and your family.* الطبيعة البشريّة

the ˌhuman ˈrace *noun* [sing.] all the people in the world (when you are thinking of them as a group) الجنس البشريّ

ˌhuman reˈsources *noun* [plural] **1** people's skills and abilities, seen as sth a company, an organization, etc. can make use of موارد بشرية

2 (*abbr* **HR**) [with sing. or pl. verb] the department in a company that deals with employing and training people دائرة شؤون الموظفين

ˌhuman ˈrights *noun* [plural] the basic freedoms that all people should have, e.g. the right to say what you think, travel freely, etc. حقوق الإنسان

humble /ˈhʌmbl/ *adj* **1** not thinking that you are better or more important than other people; not proud: *He became very rich and famous but he always remained a very humble man.* ❶ The noun is **humility**. متواضع

2 low in social status; unimportant: *She comes from a humble background.* متواضع : عاديّ

▸ **humble** *verb* [T] to make sb/yourself humble: *a humbling experience* (حادثة) تُبرز نقاط ضعف المرء، تجعله متواضعاً

humbly /ˈhʌmbli/ *adv*: *He apologized very humbly for his behaviour.* بتواضع : بِذِلّة

humid /ˈhjuːmɪd/ *adj* (used about the air or climate) containing a lot of water; damp: *Hong Kong is hot and humid in summer.* رطب

▸ **humidity** /hjuːˈmɪdəti/ *noun* [U] رطوبة

humiliate /hjuːˈmɪlieɪt/ *verb* [T] to make sb feel ashamed: *Did you have to humiliate me in front of all those people?* يهين : يخزي

▸ **humiliating** *adj*: *a humiliating defeat* مهين ، مخزٍ

humiliation /hjuːˌmɪliˈeɪʃn/ *noun* [C,U] خزي : إهانة

humility /hjuːˈmɪləti/ *noun* [U] the quality of being modest or humble, not thinking that you are better than other people تواضع

hummingbird /ˈhʌmɪŋbɜːd/ *noun* [C] a small brightly coloured bird that lives in warm countries and that can stay in one place in the air by beating its wings very fast, making a continuous low sound الطائر الطنان

hummus (*also* **houmous**) /ˈhʊməs; ˈhuːməs/ *noun* [U] a type of food, originally from the Middle East, that is a soft mixture of chickpeas, oil and garlic حِمّص، مسبّحة

⚷ **humorous** /ˈhjuːmərəs/ *adj* amusing or funny: *It's a very humorous book.* ○ *a humorous speaker* مضحك : فكه

▸ **humorously** *adv* بشكل هزليّ : على سبيل الدعابة : بسخرية

⚷ **humour** (*US* **humor**) /ˈhjuːmə(r)/ *noun* [U] **1** the funny or amusing quality or qualities of sb/sth: *It's an awful situation but at least you can see the humour of it.* ○ *It is sometimes hard to understand the humour* (= the jokes) *of another country.* فكاهة ، هزل

2 being able to see when sth is funny and to laugh at things: *Rose has a good sense of humour.* روح الدعابة

▸ **humour** (*US* **humor**) *verb* [T] to keep sb happy by doing what he/she wants: *When she's in a mood like this it's best to humour her.* يداري

-humoured (*US* **-humored**) (in compounds) having or showing a particular mood: *good-humoured* رائق المزاج (مثلاً)

humourless (*US* **humorless**) *adj* not able to see when things are funny جِدّي، تنقصه روح الدعابة

hump /hʌmp/ *noun* [C] a round lump, e.g. on the back of a camel حدبة : سنام

hunch¹ /hʌntʃ/ *noun* [C] (*informal*) a thought or an idea that is based on a feeling rather than on facts or information: *I'm not sure, but I've got a hunch that she's got a new job.* حدس : شعور

hunch² /hʌntʃ/ *verb* [I,T] to bend your back and shoulders forward in a round shape: *They sat there hunched up with the cold.* يحني ظهره وكتفيه

hunchback /ˈhʌntʃbæk/ *noun* [C] a person with a back that has a round lump (hump) on it أحدب

⚷ **hundred** /ˈhʌndrəd/ *number* 100; one more than ninety-nine: *two hundred* ○ *There were a/one hundred people in the room.* ○ *She's a hundred today.* مئة، مائة

> Note that when we are saying a number, e.g. 420, we put 'and' after the word **hundred**: *four hundred and twenty.* The plural **hundreds** is used when we mean 'many' or 'a lot': *The boat cost hundreds of pounds.* ○ *Hundreds of people were left without electricity after the storm.*

▸ **hundredth** /ˈhʌndrədθ/ *pron, det, adv* 100th; next after ninety-ninth (المرّة) المئة

hundredth *noun* [C] the fraction ¹⁄₁₀₀; one of a hundred equal parts of sth جزء من مئة جزء

hundredweight /ˈhʌndrədweɪt/ *noun* [C] (*pl.* **hundredweight**) (*abbr* **cwt.**) a measure of weight; 50.8 kilograms. There are 112 pounds in a hundredweight. ❶ An American hundredweight is 100 pounds (45.4 kilograms). مقياس وزن

hung *pt, pp of* HANG

hunger /ˈhʌŋɡə(r)/ *noun* [U] **1** the wish or need for food: *Hunger is one reason why babies cry.* الجوع

2 a lack of food: *to die of hunger* ➲ Look at **thirst**. جوع : مجاعة

Be careful. You cannot say *I have hunger* in English. You must say: *I am hungry.*

▶ **hunger** *verb (formal)*

PHRV **hunger for/after sb/sth** to have a strong desire for sth يتعطّش إلى ؛ يتوق إلى

ˈ**hunger strike** *noun* [C,U] a time when people (especially prisoners) refuse to eat because they are protesting about sth إضراب عن الطعام

hungry /ˈhʌŋɡri/ *adj* (**hungrier**; **hungriest**) wanting to eat: *I'm hungry. Let's eat soon.* ○ *There were hungry children begging for food in the streets.* ➲ Look at **thirsty**. جائع ، جوعان

IDM **go hungry** to not have any food: *I'd rather go hungry than eat that!* بلا طعام

▶ **hungrily** /ˈhʌŋɡrəli/ *adv* بشراهة

hunk /hʌŋk/ *noun* [C] a large piece of sth: *a hunk of bread* قطعة كبيرة

hunt[1] /hʌnt/ *verb* [I,T] **1** to chase wild animals, etc. in order to catch or kill them either for sport or for food: *Owls hunt at night.* ○ *Are tigers still hunted in India?* ❶ We often use the expression **go hunting** when we are talking about spending time hunting. يصيد ، يتصيّد

2 hunt (for) (sb/sth) to look or search for sb/sth: *I've hunted everywhere for my gloves but I can't find them.* ○ *The police are still hunting the murderer.* يبحث أو يفتّش (عن)

▶ **hunter** *noun* [C] a person or animal that hunts: *(figurative) a bargain hunter* صيّاد

hunting *noun* [U] the chasing and killing of wild animals ➲ Look at **shoot**[1]. الصيد

hunt[2] /hʌnt/ *noun* [C] **1** the act of hunting wild animals, etc: *a fox hunt* صَيْد (الثعالب مثلاً)

2 [usually sing.] the act of searching or looking for sb/sth: *The police have launched a hunt for the missing child.* بحث أو تفتيش (عن)

hurdle /ˈhɜːdl/ *noun* **1** [C] a type of light fence that you jump over in a race حاجز في سباق

2 hurdles [plural] a race over hurdles: *the 200 metres hurdles* سباق الحواجز

3 [C] a problem or difficulty that you must overcome عائق ، عَقَبة

▶ **hurdle** *verb* [I] to jump over a hurdle يقفز فوق حاجز

hurl /hɜːl/ *verb* [T] to throw sth with force يقذف بقوّة

hurray (*also* **hooray**) /həˈreɪ/ (*also* **hurrah** /həˈrɑː/) *interj* (used for expressing great pleasure, approval, etc.): *Hurray! We've won!* ○ *Hip, hip, hurray!* عظيم! يعيش يا!

hurricane /ˈhʌrɪkən; *US* -keɪn/ *noun* [C] a storm with very strong winds ➲ Look at the note at **storm**. زوبعة شديدة

hurry /ˈhʌri/ *noun* [U] a need or wish to do sth quickly: *Take your time. There's no hurry.* ○ *What's the hurry?* استعجال ، عَجَلة

IDM **in a hurry 1** quickly: *She got up late and left in a hurry.* بسرعة ، على عجل

2 wanting to do sth soon: *They are in a hurry to get the job done before the winter.* مستعجِل

in no hurry; **not in any hurry 1** not needing or wishing to do sth quickly: *We weren't in any hurry so we stopped to admire the view.* غير مستعجل

2 (*informal*) unwilling: *I am in no hurry to repeat that experience.* لا أتطلّع إلى ؛ لا أرغب في

▶ **hurry** *verb* (*pres part* **hurrying**; *3rd pers sing pres* **hurries**; *pt, pp* **hurried**) **1** [I] to move or do sth quickly: *Don't hurry. There's plenty of time.* ○ *They hurried back home after school.* ○ *Several people hurried to help.* يسرع

2 [T] to cause sb/sth to do sth or to happen more quickly: *Don't hurry me. I'm going as fast as I can.* ○ *He was hurried into a decision.* يستعجل

PHRV **hurry up** (*informal*) to move or do sth more quickly: *Hurry up or we'll miss the train.* يسرع

hurried *adj* done (too) quickly: *a hurried meal* ❶ The opposite is **unhurried**. سريع ، خاطِف ، على عَجَل

hurriedly *adv* بسرعة ، على عَجَل

hurt /hɜːt/ *verb* (*pt, pp* **hurt**) **1** [T] to cause pain or injury: *Did he hurt himself?* ○ *I fell and hurt my arm.* ○ *(figurative) The new tax will hurt families on low incomes.* يؤذي ؛ يجرح

Compare **hurt**, **injure** and **wound**. A person may be **wounded** by a knife, sword, gun, etc., usually as a result of fighting: *a wounded soldier*. People are usually **injured** in an accident: *Five people were killed in the crash and twelve others were injured*. **Hurt** and **injured** are similar in meaning but **hurt** is more often used when the damage is not very great: *I hurt my leg when I fell off my bike.*

2 [I] to produce a feeling of pain: *My leg hurts.* ○ *It hurts when I lift my leg.* ○ *These shoes hurt; they're too tight.* يؤلم

3 [T] to make sb unhappy; to upset sb: *His unkind remarks hurt her deeply.* يجرح الشعور ؛ يزْعِل

IDM **it won't/wouldn't hurt (sb/sth) (to do sth)** (*informal*) it would be a good thing for sb/sth (to do): *It wouldn't hurt you to leave the car at home and walk.* لا يخسر ، لا يضر

▶ **hurt** *noun* [U] (*formal*) mental pain or suffering معاناة ، عذاب

hurt *adj* **1** injured physically: *No one was seriously hurt in the accident.* يصاب بأذى

2 unhappy because sb has been unkind to you مجروح الشعور، مكسور الخاطر

hurtful /-fl/ *adj* unkind; upsetting: *Don't say such hurtful things to your father!* قاسٍ ؛ مؤلم

hurtle /ˈhɜːtl/ *verb* [I] to move with great speed, perhaps causing danger: *Rocks hurtled down the mountainside.* يندفع بعنف وسرعة

husband /ˈhʌzbənd/ *noun* [C] a man that a woman is married to: *a good husband and father* ○ *Her ex-husband sees the children once a month.* زوج

hush /hʌʃ/ *verb*

PHRV **hush sth up** to stop people knowing about sth; to keep sth secret: *The police managed to hush up the whole affair.* يطمس ؛ يكتم

▶ **hush** *noun* [sing.] silence: *As he rose to speak a hush fell over the audience.* صمت ؛ هدوء تام

ˌ**hush-'hush** *adj* (*informal*) very secret: *Her work is very hush-hush.* سرّي للغاية

husky¹ /'hʌski/ *adj* (**huskier**; **huskiest**) (used about a voice) sounding rough and quiet as if your throat were dry مبحوح ؛ أجشّ

husky² /'hʌski/ *noun* [C] (*pl.* **huskies**) a strong dog with thick fur that is used in teams for pulling heavy loads over snow كلب الاسكيمو

hustle /'hʌsl/ *verb* [T] to push or move sb roughly: *The demonstrators were hustled into police vans.* يدفع (شخصاً) بخشونة ؛ يشقّ طريقه

hut /hʌt/ *noun* [C] a small building with one room, usually made of wood or metal كوخ

hyaena = HYENA

hybrid /'haɪbrɪd/ *noun* [C] an animal or a plant that has parents of two different types: *A mule is a hybrid of a male donkey and a female horse.* ○ *a hybrid flower* هجين، نَغْل

hydrant /'haɪdrənt/ *noun* [C] a pipe in a street from which water can be taken for putting out fires, street-cleaning, etc. مأخذ ماء في شارع (للإطفاء خاصّة)

hydraulic /haɪ'drɔːlɪk/ *adj* worked by water or another liquid moving through pipes, etc: *hydraulic brakes* هيدروليكي: محرك بواسطة الماء

hydroelectric /ˌhaɪdrəʊɪ'lektrɪk/ *adj* **1** using the power of water to produce electricity: *a hydroelectric dam* مائي كهربائي أو هيدروكهربائي

2 (used about electricity) produced by the power of water: *hydroelectric power* (كهرباء) مولّدة بقوة الماء

hydrofoil /'haɪdrəfɔɪl/ *noun* [C] a boat which rises above the surface of the water when it is travelling fast مركب مائي خفيف

hydrogen /'haɪdrədʒən/ *noun* [U] (*symbol* **H**) a light colourless gas. Hydrogen and oxygen form water (H_2O). هيدروجين

hyena (*also* **hyaena**) /haɪ'iːnə/ *noun* [C] a wild animal like a dog that lives in Africa and Asia. Hyenas eat the meat of animals that are already dead and can make a sound like a human laugh. ضبع

hygiene /'haɪdʒiːn/ *noun* [U] (the rules of) keeping yourself and things around you clean, in order to prevent illness: *High standards of hygiene are essential when you are preparing food.* ○ *personal hygiene* النظافة

▶ **hygienic** /haɪ'dʒiːnɪk; *US* ˌhaɪdʒɪ'enɪk; haɪ'dʒenɪk/ *adj* clean, without the germs that cause disease: *hygienic conditions* ❶ The opposite is **unhygienic**. خالٍ من الجراثيم ؛ نظيف

hygienically /-kli/ *adv* بشكل صحي أو سليم

hymn /hɪm/ *noun* [C] a song of praise to God that Christians sing together in church, etc. ترتيلة

hype /haɪp/ *noun* [U] advertisements that tell you how good and important a new product, film, etc. is دعاية، ترويج

▶ **hype** *verb* [T] to exaggerate how good or important sth is: *His much-hyped new movie is released next week.* يبالغ في الدعاية

hypermarket /'haɪpəmɑːkɪt/ *noun* [C] (*Brit*) a very large supermarket that is usually outside a town سوبرماركت ضخم

hyphen /'haɪfn/ *noun* [C] the punctuation mark (-) used for joining two words together (e.g. *left-handed*, *red-hot*) or to show that a word has been divided and continues on the next line الشَرْطة بين جزئي كلمة مركّبة

▶ **hyphenate** /'haɪfəneɪt/ *verb* [T] to write sth with a hyphen: *Do you hyphenate 'girlfriend'?* يضع شَرْطة بين جزئي كلمة مركّبة

hyphenation /ˌhaɪfə'neɪʃn/ *noun* [U] وصل الكلمات المركّبة بشَرْطة

hypnosis /hɪp'nəʊsɪs/ *noun* [U] (the producing of) a state that is like deep sleep where sb's mind and actions can be controlled by another person: *She was questioned under hypnosis.* التنويم المغناطيسي

▶ **hypnotic** /hɪp'nɒtɪk/ *adj*: *The rhythmic dance had a hypnotic effect on the audience.* تنويميّ ؛ منوِّم

hypnotism /'hɪpnətɪzəm/ *noun* [U] using hypnosis التنويم المغناطيسي

hypnotist /'hɪpnətɪst/ *noun* [C] a person who uses hypnosis on other people منوِّم مغناطيسي

hypnotize (*also* **hypnotise**) /'hɪpnətaɪz/ *verb* [T] to use hypnosis on sb ينوّم تنويماً مغناطيسياً

hypochondriac /ˌhaɪpə'kɒndriæk/ *noun* [C] a person who is always worried about his/her health even when there is nothing wrong مريض الوهم ، موَسْوَس على صحته

hypocrisy /hɪ'pɒkrəsi/ *noun* [U] pretending to feel, believe, etc. sth that is different from what you really feel, etc.; saying one thing and doing another نفاق ، رياء

▶ **hypocrite** /'hɪpəkrɪt/ *noun* [C] a person who pretends to have feelings and opinions which he/she does not, in fact, have. Hypocrites say one thing and do another: *What a hypocrite!* المنافق ، المرائي

hypocritical /ˌhɪpə'krɪtɪkl/ *adj* منافِق

hypocritically /-kli/ *adv* بكل نفاق ، رياءً

hypodermic /ˌhaɪpə'dɜːmɪk/ *adj* used for injecting drugs beneath the skin: *a hypodermic needle/syringe* مستعمل للحقن تحت الجِلد

hypothesis /haɪ'pɒθəsɪs/ *noun* [C] (*pl.* **hypotheses** /-siːz/) an idea that is suggested as the possible explanation for sth: *The hypothesis has been put forward that some chemicals used in food can affect children's behaviour.* فرضيّة

▶ **hypothetical** /ˌhaɪpə'θetɪkl/ *adj* based on situations that have not yet happened, not on facts: *That's a hypothetical question because we don't know what the situation will be next year.* افتراضي ، فَرَضي

hypothetically /-kli/ *adv* فَرَضياً ؛ نظرياً

hysteria /hɪ'stɪəriə/ *noun* [U] a state of excitement in which a person or a group of people cannot control their emotions, e.g. cannot stop

laughing, crying, shouting, etc: *mass hysteria*
هستيريا ؛ اهتياج عصبي

▸ **hysterical** /hɪˈsterɪkl/ *adj* **1** caused by or suffering from hysteria: *hysterical laughter* ○ *She was hysterical with grief.*
هستيريّ ؛ مصاب بنوبات عصبية (من الحزن مثلاً)

2 (*informal*) very funny مضحك جداً

hysterically /-kli/ *adv* بهستيريا أو بجنون

hysterics /hɪˈsterɪks/ *noun* [plural] **1** a state of hysteria: *She went into hysterics when they told her the news.* ○ (*informal*) *My father would have hysterics if he knew the truth.* نوبة هستيريا

2 (*informal*) uncontrolled laughter: *The audience was in hysterics.* نوبة ضحك

I i

I, i /aɪ/ *noun* [C] (*pl.* **Is; I's; i's**) the ninth letter of the English alphabet: *'Island' begins with (an) 'I'.*
الحرف التاسع من الأبجدية الإنكليزية

I /aɪ/ *pron* (the subject of a verb) the person who is speaking or writing: *I phoned and said that I was busy.* ○ *I'm not going to fall, am I?* ○ *I'm taller than you, aren't I?* ○ *She and I are planning to go out later.* أنا

ice[1] /aɪs/ *noun* **1** [U] water that has frozen solid: *Do you want ice in your orange juice?* ○ *I slipped on a patch of ice.* ○ *The ice on the lake isn't thick enough for skating.* ○ *The ice quickly melted in the sunshine.* ○ *black ice* (= ice on roads, that cannot be seen easily) جليد ؛ قطع ثلج (في شراب)

2 [C] an ice cream بوظة، جيلاتي، آيس كريم

▸ **iced** /aɪst/ *adj* (used about drinks) very cold مثلّج

icy /ˈaɪsi/ *adj* (**icier**; **iciest**) **1** very cold: *an icy wind* (برد) قارس

2 covered with ice: *icy roads* مغطّى بالجليد

ice[2] /aɪs/ *verb*

PHR V **ice (sth) over/up** to cover or become covered with ice: *The windscreen of the car had iced over in the night.*
يتغطّى أو يغطي بالجليد ؛ يتجمّد أو يجمّد

ice[3] /aɪs/ (*especially US* **frost**) *verb* [T] to cover a cake with icing يغطي الكعكة بمزيج من السكر والبيض ألخ

iceberg /ˈaɪsbɜːɡ/ *noun* [C] a very large block of ice that is floating in the sea: *The ship hit an iceberg and sank.* جبل جليدي (عائم في البحر)

IDM **the tip of the iceberg** → TIP[1]

ˌ**ice-ˈcold** *adj* very cold: *ice-cold drinks* ○ *Your hands are ice-cold.* بارد جداً، "مصقّع"

ˌ**ice ˈcream** *noun* **1** [U] a frozen sweet food that is made from cream (or other types of fat)
بوظة، جيلاتي، آيس كريم

2 [C] a portion of ice cream, usually in paper or a special container (a cone): *Four strawberry ice creams, please.* قطعة آيس كريم

ˈ**ice cube** *noun* [C] a small block of ice that you put in a drink to make it cold
قطعة ثلج (توضع في المشروب)

ˈ**ice hockey** (*US* **hockey**) *noun* [U] a game that is played on ice by two teams who try to hit a small flat rubber object (a puck) into a goal with long wooden sticks لعبة الهوكي على الجليد

ˌ**ice ˈlolly** *noun* [C] (*pl.* **ice lollies**) (*US* **Popsicle**™) a piece of flavoured ice on a stick
عصير فاكهة متجمّد (على عود)، مصّاصة، اسكيمو/ الاسكا

ˈ**ice rink** *noun* [C] = SKATING RINK

ˈ**ice skate** *noun* [C] = SKATE

ˈ**ice-skate** *verb* [I] = SKATE

ˈ**ice skating** *noun* [U] = SKATING (1)

icicle /ˈaɪsɪkl/ *noun* [C] a pointed piece of ice that is formed by water freezing as it falls or runs down from sth دلاة جليدية

icing /ˈaɪsɪŋ/ (*especially US* **frosting**) *noun* [U] a mixture of powdery sugar and egg white or butter, flavouring, etc. that is used for decorating cakes: *chocolate icing*
مزيج من السكّر والبيض وغيره لتغطية المعجنات

icon /ˈaɪkɒn/ *noun* **1** a person or thing that is considered to be a symbol of sth: *Madonna and other pop icons of the 1980s* معبود الجماهير

3 (*also* **ikon**) (computing) a small symbol on a computer screen representing a program, etc. that a user may choose رمز

3 (in the Orthodox Church) a painting, carving, etc., usually on wood, of a holy person أيقونة

ICT /ˌaɪ siː ˈtiː/ *noun* [U] the study of the use of computers, the Internet, video, and other technology as a subject at school (the abbreviation for 'information and communications technology') المعلوماتية والاتصالات

icy *adj* → ICE[1]

I'd /aɪd/ *short for* I HAD, I WOULD

ID /ˌaɪ ˈdiː/ *abbrev* (*informal*) = IDENTIFICATION; IDENTITY

idea /aɪˈdɪə/ *noun* **1** [C] a plan or suggestion: *That's a good idea!* ○ *He's got an idea for a new play.* ○ *I had the bright idea of getting Jane to help me with my homework.* ○ *Has anyone got any ideas of how to tackle this problem?* ○ *It was your idea to invite so many people to the party.*
فكرة ؛ إقتراح

2 [U, sing.] a picture or thought in your mind: *Have you any idea how much this cost?* ○ *You have no idea* (= you can't imagine) *how difficult it was to find a time that suited everybody.* ○ *The programme gave a good idea of what life was like before the war.* فكرة

a b c d e f g h i j k l m n o p q r s t u v w x y z

3 [C] an opinion or belief: *She has her own ideas about how to bring up children.* ○ *Hiding my handbag? If that's your idea of a joke, I don't think it's funny!* رأي

4 the idea [sing.] the aim or purpose of sth: *The idea of the course is to teach the basics of car maintenance.* غاية

IDM **get the idea** to understand: *Right! I think I've got the idea now.* يفهم

get the idea that... to get the feeling or impression that...: *Where did you get the idea that I was paying for this meal?* يظنّ، يخيَّل إليه

have an idea that... to have a feeling or think that...: *I'm not sure but I have an idea that they've gone on holiday.* (لديه) شعور

not have the faintest/foggiest (idea) → FAINT

ideal /aɪˈdiːəl/ *adj* the best possible; perfect: *In an ideal world there would be no poverty.* مثاليّ

▸ **ideal** *noun* [C] **1** an idea or principle that seems perfect to you and that you want to achieve: *She finds it hard to live up to her parents' high ideals.* ○ *socialist ideals* مثل أعلى

2 [usually sing.] a perfect example of a person or thing: *My ideal would be to live in the country and have a flat in London.* حلم ، مبتغى

ideally *adv* **1** perfectly: *They are ideally suited to each other.* تماماً

2 in an ideal situation: *Ideally, no class should be larger than 25.* في عالم مثالي

idealism /aɪˈdiːəlɪzəm/ *noun* [U] the belief that people should have high ideals and live according to them, or that the world can be made perfect: *Young people are usually full of idealism.* ➲ Look at **realism**. المثاليّة ، المذهب المثالي

▸ **idealist** /aɪˈdiːəlɪst/ *noun* [C] a person who has high ideals (but who is sometimes not very practical) المؤمن بالمثاليّة، مثاليّ

idealistic /ˌaɪdiəˈlɪstɪk/ *adj* مثالي، غير عمليّ

idealize (*also* **idealise**) /aɪˈdiːəlaɪz/ *verb* [T] to imagine or show sth as being better than it really is: *Old people often idealize the past.* يضفي عليه صفات مثاليّة ، ينزلها من السماء

identical /aɪˈdentɪkl/ *adj* **1 the identical** the same: *This is the identical room we stayed in last year.* نفسه ، عينه

2 identical (to/with sb/sth) exactly the same as: *I can't see any difference between these two pens – they look identical to me.* مطابق أو مماثل تماماً ؛ متماثلان

▸ **identically** /-kli/ *adv* بشكل متطابق

iˌdentical ˈtwin *noun* [C, usually pl.] one of two children born at the same time from the same mother, and who are of the same sex and look very similar توأمان متطابقان

identify /aɪˈdentɪfaɪ/ *verb* [T] (*pres part* **identifying**; *3rd pers sing pres* **identifies**; *pt, pp* **identified**) **1 identify sb/sth as sb/sth** to recognize or say who or what sb/sth is: *The police need someone to identify the body.* ○ *We must identify the cause of the problem before we look for solutions.* يتعرّف على : يتحقّق من هويّته

2 identify sth with sth to think or say that sth is the same as sth else: *You can't identify nationalism with fascism.* يطابق أو يساوي بين

PHR V **identify with sb** to feel that you understand and share what sb else is feeling: *I found it hard to identify with the woman in the film.* يشارك في الشعور

identify (yourself) with sb/sth to be connected with sb/sth: *She became identified with the new political party.* يصبح اسمه مرتبطاً بـ

▸ **identification** /aɪˌdentɪfɪˈkeɪʃn/ *noun* [U] **1** the act of identifying or being identified: *The identification of the people killed in the explosion was very difficult.* ○ *children's identification with TV heroes* التعرّف على هويّته؛ المشاركة بالشعور والشخصية

2 (*abbr* **ID**) an official paper, etc. that proves who you are: *Do you have any identification?* وثيقة أو بطاقة الهويّة

identity /aɪˈdentəti/ *noun* [C,U] (*pl.* **identities**) (*abbr* **ID**) who or what a person or a thing is: *There are few clues to the identity of the killer.* ○ *The region has its own cultural identity and is demanding more independence.* ○ *The arrest was a case of mistaken identity* (= the wrong person was arrested by the police). ○ *Children of immigrants often suffer from a loss of identity* (= they are not sure which culture they belong to). هويّة ، شخصيّة

iˈdentity card *noun* [C] a card that proves who you are بطاقة الهويّة

ideology /ˌaɪdiˈɒlədʒi/ *noun* [C,U] (*pl.* **ideologies**) a set of ideas which form the basis for a political or economic system: *Marxist ideology* عقيدة ، مذهب

▸ **ideological** /ˌaɪdiəˈlɒdʒɪkl/ *adj* أيديولوجي ، عقائديّ

idiom /ˈɪdiəm/ *noun* [C] a expression with a meaning that you cannot guess from the meanings of the separate words: *The idiom 'bring sth home to sb' means 'make sb understand sth'.* عبارة اصطلاحيّة

▸ **idiomatic** /ˌɪdiəˈmætɪk/ *adj* **1** containing an idiom or idioms: *an idiomatic expression* اصطلاحيّ

2 using language in a way that sounds natural: *He speaks good idiomatic English.* مصطلح عليه ، طبيعي

idiot /ˈɪdiət/ *noun* [C] (*informal*) a stupid or foolish person: *I was an idiot to forget my passport.* أبله ، غبي

▸ **idiotic** /ˌɪdiˈɒtɪk/ *adj* في منتهى الغباء ؛ سخيف

idiotically /-kli/ *adv* بغباء

idle /ˈaɪdl/ *adj* **1** not doing anything; not being used: *She is always busy. She can't bear to be idle.* ○ *The factory stood idle while the machines were being repaired.* عاطل

2 not wanting to work hard; lazy: *He has the ability to succeed but he is just bone* (= very) *idle.* كسول

3 (only *before* a noun) not to be taken seriously because it will not have any result: *an idle promise* فارغ ؛ عقيم

▸ **idleness** *noun* [U] عطالة ؛ كسل

idly /ˈaɪdli/ *adv* عاطلاً ، كسولاً

idol /ˈaɪdl/ *noun* [C] **1** a statue that people worship as a god صنم يعبد : وثَن

2 a person (such as a film star or pop musician) who is admired or loved: *When I was 14, Elvis Presley was my idol.* معبود (الجماهير)

idolize (*also* **idolise**) /ˈaɪdəlaɪz/ *verb* [T] to love or admire sb very much or too much: *He is an only child and his parents idolize him.* يحبّ بإفراط ، يعبد

idyllic /ɪˈdɪlɪk; *US* aɪˈd-/ *adj* very pleasant and peaceful: *We had an idyllic holiday in the West of Ireland.* هادئ وجميل

🔑 **i.e.** /ˌaɪ ˈiː/ *abbrev* that is; in other words: *deciduous trees, i.e. those which lose their leaves in autumn* يعني ذلك، أي

🔑 **if** /ɪf/ *conj* **1** (used in sentences in which one thing happens or is true, depending on whether another thing happens or is true): *If you see him, give him this letter.* ○ *We won't go to the beach if it rains.* ○ *If I had more time, I would learn another language.* ○ *If I had known about the accident, I would have gone to see her in hospital.* ○ *I might see her tomorrow. If not, I'll see her at the weekend.* لو، إنْ، إذا

2 (used after verbs such as 'ask', 'know', 'remember'): *They asked if we would like to go too.* ○ *I can't remember if I posted the letter or not.* ➲ Look at the note at **whether**. إنْ، إذا : فيما إذا

3 (used when you are asking sb to do sth or suggesting sth politely): *If you could just come this way, sir.* ○ *If I might suggest something...* إنْ أمكن...

IDM **as if** → AS

even if → EVEN²

if I were you (used when you are giving sb advice): *If I were you, I'd leave now.* لو كنت مكانك

if only (used for expressing a strong wish): *If only I could drive.* ○ *If only he'd write.* يا ليت

igloo /ˈɪɡluː/ *noun* [C] (*pl.* **igloos**) a small house that is built from blocks of hard snow by people in the Arctic regions بيت من الثلج

ignite /ɪɡˈnaɪt/ *verb* [I,T] (*formal*) to start burning or to make sth start burning: *A spark from the engine ignited the petrol.* يشتعل ، يلتهب : يشعل ، يلهب

▸ **ignition** /ɪɡˈnɪʃn/ *noun* **1** [U] the process of igniting إشعال : اشتعال

2 [C] the electrical system that starts the engine of a car: *to turn the ignition on/off* شرارة الإشعال في السيّارة

ignominious /ˌɪɡnəˈmɪniəs/ *adj* (*formal*) making you feel ashamed: *The team suffered an ignominious defeat.* مشين : مخجِل : شنيع

▸ **ignominiously** *adv* بشكل مخجل

ignorance /ˈɪɡnərəns/ *noun* [U] lack of information or knowledge (about sth): *The workers were in complete ignorance of the management's plans.* ○ *The mistake was due to ignorance.* جهْل

ignorant /ˈɪɡnərənt/ *adj* **1** not knowing about sth: *Many people are ignorant of their rights.* ○ *I'm very ignorant about modern technology, I'm afraid.* جاهل

2 (*informal*) rude or impolite (because you don't know how to behave): *That was a very ignorant remark!* غير لائق ، دالّ على الجهل والسذاجة

🔑 **ignore** /ɪɡˈnɔː(r)/ *verb* [T] to pay no attention to sb/sth: *I said hello to Debby but she totally ignored me* (= acted as though she hadn't seen me). ○ *George ignored his doctor's advice about smoking less.* ❶ Be careful. **Ignore** and **be ignorant** are quite different in meaning. يتجاهل : لا يكترث بِ

ikon = ICON (3)

I'll /aɪl/ *short for* I WILL, I SHALL

🔑 **ill¹** /ɪl/ *adj* **1** (*US* **sick**) (not usually before a noun) not in good health; not well: *I went to bed early because I felt ill but I felt even worse when I woke up.* ○ *I have been ill with flu.* ○ *My mother was taken ill suddenly last week.* ○ *My grandfather is seriously ill in hospital.* ➲ Look at the note at **sick**. مريض

2 (only *before* a noun) bad or harmful: *There should be no ill will* (= bad feelings) *between friends.* ○ *I'm glad to say I suffered no ill effects from all that rich food.* سيّئ : مؤذٍ

ill² /ɪl/ *adv* **1** (often in compounds) badly or wrongly: *You would be ill-advised to drive until you have fully recovered.* خطأً، بصورة سيّئة

2 only with difficulty; not easily: *They could ill afford the extra money for better heating.* بصعوبة

IDM **augur well/ill for sb/sth** → AUGUR

bode well/ill (for sb/sth) → BODE

🔑 **illegal** /ɪˈliːɡl/ *adj* not allowed by the law; not legal: *It is illegal to own a gun without a special licence.* مخالف للقانون ، غير قانوني

▸ **illegally** /-ɡəli/ *adv* بشكل مخالف للقانون

illegible /ɪˈledʒəbl/ *adj* difficult or impossible to read; not legible: *The doctor's handwriting is quite illegible.* (خطّ) تتعذر أو تستحيل قراءته

▸ **illegibly** /-əbli/ *adv* بأسلوب تصعب قراءته

illegitimate /ˌɪləˈdʒɪtəmət/ *adj* **1** (used about a child) born to parents who are not married to each other (ولد) غير شرعي

2 not allowed by law; against the rules غير مشروع : مخالف للقوانين

▸ **illegitimacy** /ˌɪləˈdʒɪtəməsi/ *noun* [U] لا شرعيّة : كون الطفل غير شرعي

ˌill-ˈfated *adj* unlucky سيّئ الحظ ، مشؤوم

illicit /ɪˈlɪsɪt/ *adj* (used about an activity or substance) not allowed by law or by the rules of society: *the illicit trade in ivory* ○ *They were having an illicit affair.* ❶ The usual opposite of illicit is **legal**. غير مشروع : محظور

illiterate /ɪˈlɪtərət/ *adj* **1** not able to read or write; not literate أمّيّ

2 (used about a piece of writing) very badly written عديم الثقافة ، نصف أمّيّ

3 not knowing much about a particular subject: *computer illiterate* ○ *musically illiterate* غير ملمّ بمبادئ علم ما

▸ **illiteracy** /ɪˈlɪtərəsi/ *noun* [U]: *adult illiteracy* الأمّيّة

a b c d e f g h **i** j k l m n o p q r s t u v w x y z

illness /ˈɪlnəs/ *noun* **1** [U] the state of being physically or mentally ill: *In case of illness you can cancel the holiday.* ○ *There is a history of mental illness in the family.* مَرَض

2 [C] a type or period of physical or mental ill health: *Although it is serious, cancer is not always a fatal illness.* ○ *Father is just getting over his illness.* ➲ Look at the note at **disease**. مَرَض

illogical /ɪˈlɒdʒɪkl/ *adj* not sensible or reasonable; not logical: *It seems illogical to me to pay somebody for doing work that you could do yourself.* غير منطقيّ : غير معقول
▸ **illogicality** /ɪˌlɒdʒɪˈkæləti/ *noun* [C,U] (*pl.* **illogicalities**) مخالفة للمنطق
illogically /-kli/ *adv* دون مبرر معقول

ˌill-ˈtreat *verb* [T] to treat sb/sth badly or unkindly: *This cat has been ill-treated.* يسيء المعاملة
▸ **ˌill-ˈtreatment** *noun* [U] سوء المعاملة

illuminate /ɪˈluːmɪneɪt/ *verb* [T] (*formal*) **1** to give light to sth or to decorate sth with lights: *The palace was illuminated by spotlights.* يُنير : يزيّن بالأضواء

2 to explain sth or make sth clear يوضح ، ينوّر
▸ **illuminating** *adj* helping to explain sth or make sth clear: *an illuminating discussion* منير
illumination /ɪˌluːmɪˈneɪʃn/ *noun* **1** [U] the act of illuminating or state of being illuminated إنارة : استنارة

2 illuminations [plural] (*Brit*) bright colourful lights that are used for decorating a street, town, etc. أضواء تزيينيّة ملوّنة

illusion /ɪˈluːʒn/ *noun* **1** [C,U] a false idea, belief or impression: *I have no illusions about the situation – I know it's serious.* فكرة خاطئة ، وَهْم

2 [C] something that your eyes tell you is there or is true but in fact is not: *That line looks longer, but in fact they're the same length. It's an optical illusion.* خِداع بصري
IDM be under an/the illusion (that) to believe wrongly: *I think Peter's under the illusion that he will be the new director.* وَهْم

illustrate /ˈɪləstreɪt/ *verb* [T] **1** to explain or make sth clear by using examples, pictures or diagrams: *These statistics illustrate the point that I was making very well.* يوضح بالأمثلة أو الصور وغيرها

2 to add pictures, diagrams, etc. to a book or magazine: *Most cookery books are illustrated.* يزوّد (كتاباً) بصور أو رسوم
▸ **illustration** /ˌɪləˈstreɪʃn/ *noun* **1** [C] a drawing, diagram or picture in a book or magazine: *colour illustrations* رسم أو صورة في كتاب

2 [U] the activity or art of illustrating تزويد كتاب بالصور : رسم صور إيضاحية

3 [C] an example that makes a point or an idea clear: *Can you give me an illustration of what you mean?* مثال توضيحي

I'm /aɪm/ *short for* I AM

image /ˈɪmɪdʒ/ *noun* [C] **1** a mental picture or idea of sb/sth: *I have an image of my childhood as always sunny and happy.* صورة ذهنية

2 the general impression that a person or organization gives to the public: *Advertising has to create an attractive image for the product it is selling.* انطباع عند الناس

3 a picture or description that appears in a book, film or painting: *horrific images of war* صورة

4 a copy or reflection: *A perfect image of the building was reflected in the lake.* ○ *He's the image of his father* (= he looks exactly like him). صورة ، نسخة عن
▸ **imagery** /ˈɪmɪdʒəri/ *noun* [U] the use of descriptions and comparisons in language in order to have a strong effect on people's imagination and emotions استعارات وتشابيه (في اللغة)

imaginable /ɪˈmædʒɪnəbl/ *adj* (often *after* a noun) that you can think of: *His house was equipped with every luxury imaginable.* يمكن تصوره

imaginary /ɪˈmædʒɪnəri; *US* -əneri/ *adj* existing only in the mind; not real: *Many children have imaginary friends.* وهميّ، خياليّ

imagination /ɪˌmædʒɪˈneɪʃn/ *noun* **1** [C,U] the ability to create mental pictures or new ideas: *He has a lively imagination.* ○ *You need a lot of imagination to see what the building will be like when it's finished.* ○ *She's very clever but she hasn't got much imagination.* خيال : تخيّل

> **Imagination** is a creative quality that a person has. **Fantasy** consists of daydreams about stories and situations that are not related to reality.

2 [C] the part of the mind that uses this ability: *If we really use our imaginations we should find a solution to this problem!* مخيّلة : ملكة الإبداع ، خيال
▸ **imaginative** /ɪˈmædʒɪnətɪv; *US* -əneɪtɪv/ *adj* having or showing imagination: *She's always full of imaginative ideas.* ○ *His writing is highly imaginative.* ❶ The opposite is **unimaginative**. واسع الخيال : مبدع
imaginatively *adv* بِسعة خيال ، بإبداع

imagine /ɪˈmædʒɪn/ *verb* [T] **1** to form a picture or idea of sth in the mind: *Imagine the seaside in summer.* ○ *Imagine that you're lying on a beach.* ○ *It's not easy to imagine your brother as a doctor.* ○ *I can't imagine myself cycling 20 miles a day.* ○ *I can imagine what you felt like.* يتصوّر : يتخيّل

2 to see, hear or think sth that is not true or does not exist: *She's always imagining that she's ill but she's fine really.* يتوهّم

3 to think of sth as probable; to suppose: *I imagine he'll be coming by car.* يظنّ : يفترض

imam (*also* **Imam**) /ɪˈmɑːm/ *noun* [C] (the title of) a religious man who leads the prayers in a mosque إمام

imbalance /ɪmˈbæləns/ *noun* [C] a difference or lack of equality: *an imbalance between our import and export trade* عدم توازن

imbecile /ˈɪmbəsiːl; *US* -sl/ *noun* [C] a stupid person; a fool أبله : غبيّ: أحمق

IMF /ˌaɪ em ˈef/ *abbrev* International Monetary Fund صندوق النقد الدولي

imitate /ˈɪmɪteɪt/ *verb* [T] **1** to copy the behaviour of sb/sth: *Small children learn by imitating their parents.* يقلّد : يحاكي

2 to copy the speech or actions of sb/sth, often in order to be amusing: *She could imitate her mother perfectly.* يقلد

▸ **imitation** /ˌɪmɪˈteɪʃn/ *noun* **1** [C] a copy (of a real thing): *Some artificial flowers are good imitations of real ones.* ○ *This suitcase is made of imitation leather* (= of material that is made to look like leather). ➲ Look at **genuine**. تقليد

2 [C] a copy (of a person's speech or behaviour): *That comedian does very good imitations of politicians.* تقليد

3 [U] the act of copying sth: *Good pronunciation of a language is best learned by imitation.* تقليد

immaculate /ɪˈmækjələt/ *adj* **1** perfectly clean and tidy في غاية النظافة : ناصع

2 without any mistakes; perfect: *an immaculate performance* بلا عيب : كامل الأوصاف

▸ **immaculately** *adv* غاية في حسن الهندام أو النظافة وغير ذلك

immaterial /ˌɪməˈtɪəriəl/ *adj* **immaterial (to sb)** not important: *It's immaterial to me whether we go today or tomorrow.* غير مهم

immature /ˌɪməˈtjʊə(r); *US* -ˈtʊər/ *adj* **1** not fully grown or developed; not mature: *an immature body* غير مكتمل النموّ

2 (used about a person) not behaving as sensibly as you would expect for a person of that age: *Some students are very immature when they go to university.* غير ناضج

ʢ **immediate** /ɪˈmiːdiət/ *adj* **1** happening or done at once or without delay: *I'd like an immediate answer to my proposal.* ○ *The government responded with immediate action.* فوري

2 (only *before* a noun) existing now and needing attention: *Tell me what your immediate needs are.* (حاجة) ماسّة

3 (only *before* a noun) nearest in time, position or relationship: *They won't make any changes in the immediate future.* ○ *You can see the cathedral to your immediate right.* ○ *He has left most of his money to his immediate family* (= parents, children, brothers and sisters). قريب : مباشر

▸ **immediacy** /-əsi/ *noun* [U] the close presence of sth that makes you notice it and become involved in it قرب

immediately *adv* **1** at once; without delay: *Can you come home immediately after work?* ○ *I couldn't immediately see what he meant.* رأساً ، فوراً

2 directly; very closely: *He wasn't immediately involved in the crime.* مباشرة

3 nearest in time or position: *Who's the girl immediately in front of Simon?* ○ *What did you do immediately after the war?* مباشرة

immediately *conj* (*Brit*) as soon as: *I opened the letter immediately I got home.* حال أو فور (وصولي)

immense /ɪˈmens/ *adj* very large or great: *immense difficulties* ○ *She gets immense pleasure from her garden.* هائل : ضخم ، جسيم

▸ **immensely** *adv* extremely; very much: *immensely enjoyable* ○ *'Did you enjoy the party?' 'Yes, immensely.'* للغاية : جداً

immensity /ɪˈmensəti/ *noun* [U] very large size or extent: *the immensity of the universe* جسامة ، ضخامة : لا نهائيّة

immerse /ɪˈmɜːs/ *verb* [T] **1 immerse yourself (in sth)** to involve yourself deeply in sth so that you give it all your attention: *Rachel's usually immersed in a book.* يغرق في (كتاب مثلاً)

2 immerse sth (in sth) to put sth into a liquid so that it is covered يغمر ، يغطّس

immigrant /ˈɪmɪɡrənt/ *noun* [C] a person who has come into a foreign country to live there permanently: *Many immigrants to Britain have come from Asia.* ○ *The government plans to tighten controls to prevent illegal immigrants* (= people coming to live in the country without permission). ○ *London has a high immigrant population.* مهاجر ، مغترب

> Great Britain has many immigrant communities which make it a **multicultural society.** Groups of immigrants or children of immigrants who share a common cultural tradition form an **ethnic minority.**

immigration /ˌɪmɪˈɡreɪʃn/ *noun* [U] **1** entering a country in order to live there permanently: *There are greater controls on immigration than there used to be.* هجرة

2 (*also* **immiˈgration control**) the point at an airport, port, etc. where the passports and documents of people who want to come into a country are checked: *When you leave the plane you have to go through customs and immigration.* قسم الهجرة والجوازات في مطار مثلاً

> There is a verb 'immigrate' but it is very rarely used. We normally use the expression 'be an immigrant' or the verb 'emigrate' which is used in connection with the place that somebody has come from: *'Were you born here in Britain?' 'Yes I was, but my parents emigrated to Britain from Barbados.'* Look at **emigrate**, **emigrant** and **emigration**.

imminent /ˈɪmɪnənt/ *adj* (usually used about sth unpleasant) almost certain to happen very soon: *Heavy rainfall in the south of England means that flooding is imminent.* وشيك ، (كارثة) قريبة الوقوع

▸ **imminently** *adv* وشيكاً ، قريباً جداً

immobile /ɪˈməʊbaɪl; *US* -bl/ *adj* not moving or not able to move: *The hunter stood immobile until the lion had passed.* بلا حراك : عاجز عن الحركة

▸ **immobility** /ˌɪməˈbɪləti/ *noun* [U] the state of being immobile عجز عن الحركة ، جمود

immobilize (*also* **immobilise**) /ɪˈməʊbəlaɪz/ *verb* [T] to prevent sb/sth from moving or working normally: *The railways have been completely immobilized by the strike.* يشلّ عن الحركة

immobilizer (*also* **-iser**) /ɪˈməʊbəlaɪzə(r)/

noun [C] a device in a vehicle that prevents thieves from starting the engine when the vehicle is parked
معطِّل عن الحركة

immoral /ɪ'mɒrəl; *US* ɪ'mɔːrəl/ *adj* wrong or wicked according to the accepted rules of behaviour; not moral: *I think experiments on animals are immoral.* لا أخلاقي؛ منافٍ للآداب العامة
▸ **immorality** /ˌɪmə'ræləti/ *noun* [U]
فساد الأخلاق ، خلاعة
immorally /ɪ'mɒrəli/ *adv* دون إنصاف ودون أخلاق

immortal /ɪ'mɔːtl/ *adj* living or lasting for ever: *Nobody is immortal – we all have to die some time.* ○ (*figurative*) *Shakespeare's immortal plays*
خالد
▸ **immortality** /ˌɪmɔː'tæləti/ *noun* [U] الخلود
immortalize (*also* **immortalise**) /ɪ'mɔːtəlaɪz/ *verb* [T] to give lasting fame to sb/sth (especially in a book, film or painting): *He immortalized their relationship in a poem.* يخلِّد

immune /ɪ'mjuːn/ *adj* **1 immune (to sth)** protected against a certain disease or illness because you have a resistance to it: *You should be immune to measles if you've had it already.* عنده مناعة ، منيع
2 immune (to sth) not affected by sth: *You can say what you like – I'm immune to criticism!*
لا يتأثر بِ، حصين
3 immune (from sth) protected from a danger or punishment: *Young children are immune from prosecution.* عنده حصانة ، حصين
▸ **immunity** /ɪ'mjuːnəti/ *noun* [U] the ability to avoid or be unaffected by disease, criticism, prosecution, etc: *In many countries people have no immunity to diseases like measles.* ○ *Ambassadors to other countries receive diplomatic immunity* (= protection from prosecution, etc.).
مناعة؛ حصانة
immunize (*also* **immunise**) /'ɪmjunaɪz/ *verb* [T] to make sb immune to a disease, usually by giving an injection of a substance (vaccine): *Before visiting certain countries you will need to be immunized against cholera.* ➲ Look at **inoculate** and **vaccinate.** يكسِب مناعة؛ يلقح (ضد مرض)
immunization (*also* **immunisation**) /ˌɪmjunaɪ'zeɪʃn; *US* -nə'z-/ *noun* [C,U]
تلقيح ، تطعيم؛ إكساب مناعة

imp /ɪmp/ *noun* [C] (in stories) a small creature like a little devil عفريت صغير

impact /'ɪmpækt/ *noun* **1** [C, usually sing.] **an impact (on/upon sb/sth)** an effect or impression: *Her speech made a great impact on the audience.* وقع ، تأثير
2 [U] the action or force of one object hitting another: *The impact of the crash threw the passengers out of their seats.* ○ *The bomb exploded on impact* (= when it hit something).
ارتطام؛ قوة الارتطام
▸ **impact** /ɪm'pækt:/ *verb* **1** [I] **impact (on/upon sth)** to have an effect on sth: *Her father's death impacted greatly on her childhood years.*
2 [I,T] **impact (on/upon/with) sth** to hit sth with great force يصدم

impair /ɪm'peə(r)/ *verb* [T] to damage or weaken sth: *Ear infections can result in impaired hearing.* يضرّ بِ؛ يضعِف

impale /ɪm'peɪl/ *verb* [T] **impale sb/sth (on sth)** to stick a sharp pointed object through sb/sth: *The boy fell out of the tree and was impaled on the railings.* "يخوزق" ، يخرق بآلة حادّة

impart /ɪm'pɑːt/ *verb* [T] (*formal*) **1 impart sth (to sb)** to tell: *He rushed home eager to impart the good news.* يخبِر، يطلع على
2 impart sth (to sth) to give a certain quality to sth: *The low lighting imparted a romantic atmosphere to the room.* يضفي

impartial /ɪm'pɑːʃl/ *adj* fair or neutral; not preferring one to another: *The referee must be impartial.* غير متحيز ، حيادي
▸ **impartiality** /ˌɪmˌpɑːʃi'æləti/ *noun* [U]
عدم تحيّز ، حياد
impartially /-ʃəli/ *adv* بدون تحيز؛ بإنصاف

impassable /ɪm'pɑːsəbl; *US* -'pæs-/ *adj* (used about a road, etc.) impossible to travel on because it is blocked: *Flooding and fallen trees have made many roads impassable.* مسدود ، لا يمكن عبوره

impassive /ɪm'pæsɪv/ *adj* (used about a person) showing no emotion or reaction
(شخص) بارد، لا يبدو عليه الانفعال
▸ **impassively** *adv* دون إبداء أية مشاعر، بجمود

impatient /ɪm'peɪʃnt/ *adj* **1 impatient (at sth/with sb)** not able to wait for sb/sth calmly; easily annoyed by sb/sth that seems slow; not patient: *Don't be so impatient – it's your turn next.* ○ *The passengers are getting impatient at the delay.* ○ *It's no good being impatient with small children.* عديم الصبر؛ ضيّق الصدر
2 impatient (to do sth); **impatient (for sth)** (not before a noun) wanting sth to happen soon: *By the time they are sixteen many young people are impatient to leave school.* ○ *At the end of winter we are often impatient for spring to arrive.* متلهِّف أو متحرِّق إلى
▸ **impatience** /ɪm'peɪʃns/ *noun* [U]: *He began to explain for the third time with growing impatience.* نفاد صبر، ضيق؛ تلهُّف
impatiently *adv*
بضيق

impeccable /ɪm'pekəbl/ *adj* perfect; without any mistakes: *impeccable behaviour* ○ *His accent is impeccable.* لا تشوبه شائبة، خالٍ من كل عيب
▸ **impeccably** /-bli/ *adv*
بكل دقّة وإتقان؛ غاية في الأناقة

impede /ɪm'piːd/ *verb* [T] (*formal*) to make it difficult for sb/sth to move or make progress: *The completion of the new motorway has been impeded by bad weather conditions.* يعرقل ، يعيق

impediment /ɪm'pedɪmənt/ *noun* [C] (*formal*)
1 something that makes it difficult for a person or thing to move or progress: *The high rate of tax will be a major impediment to new businesses.*
عائق ، مانع
2 something that makes speaking difficult: *a speech impediment* عيّ أو ثقل لسان

impending /ɪm'pendɪŋ/ *adj* (only *before* a noun) (usually used about sth bad) that will happen soon: *There was a feeling of impending disaster in the air.* (كارثة) وشيكة

impenetrable /ɪmˈpenɪtrəbl/ *adj* **1** impossible to enter or get through: *The jungle was impenetrable.* لا يمكن اختراقه

2 impossible to understand: *an impenetrable mystery* ممتنع ، مغلق

imperative /ɪmˈperətɪv/ *adj* very important or urgent: *It's imperative that you see a doctor immediately.* إلزامي ؛ ضروري ؛ مستعجَل

▸ **imperative** *noun* [C] (*grammar*) the form of the verb that is used for giving orders: *In 'Shut the door!' the verb is in the imperative.* صيغة الأمر (في القواعد)

imperceptible /ˌɪmpəˈseptəbl/ *adj* too small to be seen or noticed; very slight: *The difference between the original painting and the copy was almost imperceptible.* ❶ The verb is **perceive**. لا يُدرك؛ غير ملحوظ : طفيف جداً

▸ **imperceptibly** /-əbli/ *adv*: *Almost imperceptibly winter was turning into spring.* بشكل خفيّ؛ بشكل غير ملحوظ

imperfect /ɪmˈpɜːfɪkt/ *adj* **1** with mistakes or faults; not perfect: *This is a very imperfect system.* معَيب : فيه أخطاء ، غير كامل

2 (only *before* a noun) (*grammar*) used for expressing action in the past that is not completed: *In 'While I was having a bath', the verb is in the imperfect tense.* صيغة الماضي المستمرّ (في قواعد اللغة الإنكليزية)

> We can also use **imperfect** as a noun and say: *The verb is in the imperfect.* It is more usual to call this tense the **past continuous** or **past progressive**.

▸ **imperfectly** *adv* بشكل ناقص ؛ بشكل غير كافٍ

imperial /ɪmˈpɪəriəl/ *adj* **1** connected with an empire or its ruler: *the imperial palace* ○ *imperial power* إمبراطوري

2 belonging to a system of weighing and measuring that was previously used for all goods in the United Kingdom and is still used for some ➲ Look at **metric** and at **inch, foot, yard, ounce, pound, pint** and **gallon**. The entries will tell you what these weights and measures are in metres, kilos and litres. متعلق بالمكاييل البريطانية

imperialism /ɪmˈpɪəriəlɪzəm/ *noun* [U] a political system in which a rich and powerful country controls other countries (colonies) which are not so rich and powerful as itself الاستعمار

▸ **imperialist** /ɪmˈpɪəriəlɪst/ *noun* [C] a person who supports or believes in imperialism استعماري

impersonal /ɪmˈpɜːsənl/ *adj* **1** not showing friendly human feelings; cold in feeling or atmosphere: *A large organization can be very impersonal to work for.* ○ *The hotel room was very impersonal.* (جوّ) غير ودّي : (غرفة) جرداء لا تبعث على الدفء

2 not referring to any particular person: *Can we try to keep the discussion as impersonal as possible, please?* موضوعيّ ، غير شخصيّ

impersonate /ɪmˈpɜːsəneɪt/ *verb* [T] to copy the actions and way of speaking of a person or to pretend to be a different person: *an actress who often impersonates the Queen* ○ *He was arrested for impersonating a policeman.* ينتحل شخصية غيره ؛ يقلّد شخصية شهيرة

▸ **impersonation** /ɪmˌpɜːsəˈneɪʃn/ *noun* [C,U] انتحال شخصية الغير ؛ تقليد الشخصيات الشهيرة

impersonator *noun* [C] ممثّل يتقن تقليد الشخصيات

impertinent /ɪmˈpɜːtɪnənt/ *adj* rude; not showing respect: *I do apologize. It was impertinent of my daughter to speak to you like that.* ❶ The opposite is NOT **pertinent**. It is **polite** or **respectful**. وقح : قليل الأدب

▸ **impertinence** /-əns/ *noun* [U] وقاحة : قلة أدب

impertinently *adv* بوقاحة

imperturbable /ˌɪmpəˈtɜːbəbl/ *adj* (*formal*) not easily worried; calm ❶ The verb is **perturb**. هادئ الأعصاب : لا تهزه الأحداث

impervious /ɪmˈpɜːviəs/ *adj* **1** not allowing water, etc. to pass through (قماش) كتيم، غير منفذ

2 not affected or influenced by sth: *impervious to criticism* صامد (أمام) : لا يتأثر بِ

impetuous /ɪmˈpetʃuəs/ *adj* acting or done quickly and without thinking: *Her impetuous behaviour often got her into trouble.* ❶ A more common word is **impulsive**. متهوِّر ، مندفع : غير متروٍّ

▸ **impetuously** *adv* بتهور، بلا رويّة

impetus /ˈɪmpɪtəs/ *noun* [U, sing.] something that encourages sth else to happen: *I need fresh impetus to start working on this essay again.* دافع ، حافز

impinge /ɪmˈpɪndʒ/ *verb* [I] **impinge on/upon sth** (*formal*) to have an effect on sth; to interfere with sth: *I'm not going to let my job impinge on my home life.* يؤثّر على، يتدخل في

implant /ˈɪmplɑːnt; *US* -plænt/ *noun* [C] something that is put into a part of the body in a medical operation, often in order to make it bigger or a different shape حشوة، زرعة

implausible /ɪmˈplɔːzəbl/ *adj* not easy to believe: *an implausible excuse* غير مقنع : يصعب تصديقه

implement[1] /ˈɪmplɪmənt/ *noun* [C] a tool or instrument (especially for work outdoors): *farm implements* ➲ Look at the note at **tool**. آلة، أداة (زراعية مثلاً)

implement[2] /ˈɪmplɪment/ *verb* [T] to start using a plan, system, etc: *Some teachers are finding it difficult to implement the government's educational reforms.* يطبّق ، يضع موضع التنفيذ

▸ **implementation** /ˌɪmplɪmenˈteɪʃn/ *noun* [U] تنفيذ، تطبيق

implicate /ˈɪmplɪkeɪt/ *verb* [T] **implicate sb (in sth)** (*formal*) to show that sb is involved in sth unpleasant, especially a crime: *A well-known politician was implicated in the scandal.* يتهمه أو يورّطه في جريمة

🔑 **implication** /ˌɪmplɪˈkeɪʃn/ *noun* **1** [C,U] something that is suggested but that is not said openly: *The implication of what she said was that we had*

made a bad mistake. ℹ The verb is **imply**.
مضمون (الكلام)

2 [C] the effect that sth will have on sth else in the future: *The new law will have serious implications for our work.* أثر؛ نتيجة

3 implication (in sth) the fact of being involved, or of involving sb, in sth unpleasant, especially a crime تورّط

implicit /ɪmˈplɪsɪt/ *adj* **1** not expressed directly but understood by the people involved: *We had an implicit agreement that we would support each other.* ➲ Look at **explicit**. ضمنيّ، متعارف عليه ضمناً

2 complete and asking no questions: *I have implicit faith in your ability to do the job.*
مطلق، (إيمان) أعمى

► **implicitly** *adv* completely: *I trust you implicitly.* كلياً؛ مطلقاً

implore /ɪmˈplɔː(r)/ *verb* [T] (*formal*) to ask sb for sth or to do sth. You implore sb when the situation is very serious and you feel desperate: *She implored him not to leave her alone.* ○ *'Don't leave me alone', she implored.* ➲ Look at **beg**. It is similar in meaning. يتوسّل (إلى)، يستعطف

ʞ **imply** /ɪmˈplaɪ/ *verb* [T] (*pres part* **implying**; *3rd pers sing pres* **implies**; *pt, pp* **implied**) to suggest sth in an indirect way or without actually saying it: *He didn't say so – but he implied that I was lying.* ℹ The noun is **implication**. يلمّح؛ يعني ضمناً

impolite /ˌɪmpəˈlaɪt/ *adj* rude; not polite: *I think it was impolite of him to ask you to leave.*
وقح، قليل الأدب

► **impolitely** *adv* بقلّة أدب، بلا تهذيب

ʞ **import**[1] /ɪmˈpɔːt/ *verb* [T] **import sth (from...)**; **import sth (into...)** to buy goods, etc. from a foreign country and bring them into your own country: *This country has to import most of its raw materials.* ○ *imported goods* ○ *Britain imports fruit and vegetables from France, Italy, Spain, etc.* ○ (*figurative*) *We need to import some extra help from somewhere.* ℹ The opposite is **export**.
يستورد

► **importer** *noun* [C]: *Is Britain the world's largest importer of tea?* ℹ The opposite is **exporter**. مستورد

ʞ **import**[2] /ˈɪmpɔːt/ *noun* **1** [C, usually pl.] goods bought from a foreign country for sale or use in your own country: *What are your country's major imports?* ℹ The opposite is **export**.
بضائع مستوردة، واردات

2 [U] (*also* **importation**) the action of importing goods: *The government is introducing new controls on the import of certain goods from abroad.* استيراد

ʞ **important** /ɪmˈpɔːtnt/ *adj* **1** having great value or influence; very necessary: *an important meeting, decision, etc.* ○ *Tomorrow will be the most important day of my life!* ○ *Is money important for happiness?* ○ *It's important not to be late.* ○ *It's important that people should learn at least one foreign language.* ○ *It's important for people to see the results of what they do.* ○ *It was important to me that you were there.* هامّ؛ ضروريّ، لازم

2 (used about a person) having great influence or authority: *He was one of the most important writers of his time.* ○ *I soon got to know who was important in the company and who wasn't.*
مهمّ، ذو شأن، له نفوذ

ℹ The opposite is **unimportant**.

► **importance** /-tns/ *noun* [U] the state of being important; value: *The decision was of great importance to the future of the business.*
أهميّة؛ قيمة

importantly *adv* في نواحٍ هامّة

importation /ˌɪmpɔːˈteɪʃn/ *noun* [U] = IMPORT[2] (2)

ʞ **impose** /ɪmˈpəʊz/ *verb* **1** [T] to make sth be accepted because you are the person with power: *A new tax will be imposed on cigarettes.* ○ *The government should impose restrictions on the use of harmful chemicals.* ○ *Parents should try not to impose their own ideas on their children.* يفرض (على)

2 [I] **impose (on/upon sb/sth)** to ask or expect sb to do sth that may cause extra work or trouble: *I hope I'm not imposing – but could you look after our cats while we're away?* ○ *I hate to impose on you but can you lend me some money?* يثقل على

► **imposition** /ˌɪmpəˈzɪʃn/ *noun* **1** [U] the action of imposing: *the imposition of military rule*
فَرْض

2 [C] an unfair or unpleasant thing that sb has to accept; sth that causes extra work or trouble إثقال (على)

imposing /ɪmˈpəʊzɪŋ/ *adj* making an impression on people because it is big or important: *They lived in a large, imposing house near the park.* رائع

ʞ **impossible** /ɪmˈpɒsəbl/ *adj* **1** not able to be done or to happen; not possible: *It's impossible for me to be there before 12.* ○ *I find it almost impossible to get up in the morning!* ○ *That horse is impossible to control.* ○ *That's impossible!* (= I don't believe it!) مستحيل؛ غير ممكن

2 very difficult to deal with or to make better: *This is an impossible situation!* ○ *He's always been an impossible child.* صعب

► **impossibility** /ɪmˌpɒsəˈbɪləti/ *noun* [C,U] (*pl.* **impossibilities**): *the impossibility of reaching an agreement* ○ *What you are suggesting is a complete impossibility!* استحالة؛ مستحيل

the impossible *noun* [sing.] something that cannot be done: *Don't attempt the impossible!*
المستحيل

impossibly /-əbli/ *adv* extremely: *impossibly complicated* للغاية

impostor /ɪmˈpɒstə(r)/ *noun* [C] a person who pretends to be sb else in order to deceive other people منتحل شخصية كاذبة؛ دعيّ

impotent /ˈɪmpətənt/ *adj* **1** without enough power or influence ℹ The opposite is **powerful**. عاجز عن، لا قوة له، قاصر اليد

2 (used about men) not capable of having sexual intercourse عِنّين، عاجز جنسياً

▸ **impotence** /-əns/ *noun* [U]
عجز جنسيّ ؛ عَجْز، قصور يد

impoverish /ɪm'pɒvərɪʃ/ *verb* [T] (*formal*) to make sb/sth poor or poor in quality ➲ Look at **enrich**.
يفقر؛ يقلّل من شأنه

impracticable /ɪm'præktɪkəbl/ *adj* impossible to use or do in practice: *Your plan is completely impracticable.*
غير قابل للتنفيذ

impractical /ɪm'præktɪkl/ *adj* **1** not sensible or reasonable; not practical: *an impractical suggestion* ○ *It would be impractical to take our bikes on the train.*
غير معقول ؛ غير عمليّ

2 (used about a person) not good at doing ordinary everyday jobs: *He's clever but completely impractical.*
لا يجيد الأشياء العملية

imprecise /ˌɪmprɪ'saɪs/ *adj* not clear or exact; not precise: *imprecise instructions*
غير واضح ؛ غير دقيق

⚷**impress** /ɪm'pres/ *verb* [T] **1 impress sb (with sth)** to make sb feel admiration and respect: *She's always trying to impress people with her new clothes.* ○ *It impressed me that he understood immediately what I meant.*
يترك انطباعاً حسناً

2 (*formal*) **impress sth on/upon sb** to make sth very clear to sb: *I wish you could impress on John that he must pass these exams.*
يوضح لـ ؛ يَطبَع في ذهنه

▸ **impressed** *adj* feeling admiration for sb/sth because you think they are particularly good, interesting, etc.
يعطي انطباعاً حسناً

⚷**impression** /ɪm'preʃn/ *noun* [C] **1** the effect that a person or thing produces on sb else: *She gives the impression of being older than she really is.* ○ *I want to create an impression of light and space in the house.* ○ *Do you think I made a good impression on your parents?*
انطباع

2 an opinion about sb/sth (that is sometimes unclear or wrong): *What's your impression of the new director?* ○ *I'm not sure but I have the impression that Jane's rather unhappy.* ○ *I was under the impression that you were married.*
انطباع أوليّ

3 an amusing imitation of the behaviour or speech of a well-known person: *My brother can do a good impression of the Prime Minister.*
تقليد

4 a mark made by pressing an object hard into a surface
طبعة (أثر يتركه الضغط على سطح ليّن)

impressionable /ɪm'preʃənəbl/ *adj* easy to influence: *Sixteen is a very impressionable age.*
سريع التأثر؛ يَسهل التأثير عليه

⚷**impressive** /ɪm'presɪv/ *adj* causing a feeling of admiration and respect because of importance, size, excellent quality, etc: *an impressive building, speech, etc.* ○ *The way he handled the situation was most impressive.* ❶ The opposite is **unimpressive**.
مثير للإعجاب والاحترام

imprint /'ɪmprɪnt/ *noun* [C] the mark made by pressing an object on a surface: *the imprint of a foot in the sand*
أثر، طبعة (أثر يتركه الضغط على سطح ليّن)

imprison /ɪm'prɪzn/ *verb* [T] (often passive) to put or keep in prison: *He was imprisoned for robbery with violence.*
يسجن

▸ **imprisonment** *noun* [U] the state of being imprisoned: *She was sentenced to five years' imprisonment.* ○ *life imprisonment*
سجن

improbable /ɪm'prɒbəbl/ *adj* not likely to be true or to happen; not probable: *an improbable explanation* ○ *an improbable result* ○ *It is highly improbable that she will arrive tonight.* ➲ Look at **unlikely**.
بعيد الاحتمال أو غير محتمل ؛ يصعب تصديقه

▸ **improbability** /ɪmˌprɒbə'bɪləti/ *noun* [U]
عدم احتمال (حدوث أمر ما) ؛ صعوبة تصديق

improbably /-əbli/ *adv*
بشكل مستبعد ؛ بشكل يصعب تصديقه

impromptu /ɪm'prɒmptjuː; *US* -tuː/ *adj, adv* (done) without being prepared or organized: *an impromptu party*
مرتجَل ؛ ارتجالاً

improper /ɪm'prɒpə(r)/ *adj* **1** rude or not suitable for the situation: *That was a very improper remark!*
غير لائق ؛ في غير محله

2 illegal or not honest: *It seems that she had been involved in improper business deals.*
غير قانوني ؛ غير سليم

3 rude (in a sexual way): *He lost his job for making improper suggestions to several of the women.*
بذيء، غير محتشم

▸ **improperly** *adv*
بشكل غير لائق ؛ على نحو غير قانوني

impropriety /ˌɪmprə'praɪəti/ *noun* [C,U] (*pl.* **improprieties**) (*formal*) the state of being improper; an improper act: *She was unaware of the impropriety of her remark.* ○ *We are certain there were no improprieties in the handling of the deal.*
عدم لياقة ؛ بذاءة ؛ معاملات مشبوهة

⚷**improve** /ɪm'pruːv/ *verb* [I,T] to become or to make sth better: *Your work has greatly improved.* ○ *I hope the weather will improve later on.* ○ *Your vocabulary is excellent but you could improve your pronunciation.*
يتحسّن ؛ يُحَسِّن

PHR V improve on/upon sth to produce sth that is better than sth else: *I think the film improved on the book* (= the film was better than the book). ○ *Nobody will be able to improve on that score* (= nobody will be able to make a higher score).
يدخل تحسيناً على ، ينتج شيئاً أفضل

▸ **improvement** *noun* [C,U] **improvement (on/in sth)** (a) change which makes the quality or condition of sb/sth better: *Housing and public transport are areas which need improvement.*
تحسُّن ؛ تحسين

> We use **improvement in** to talk about something that has got better than it was before: *There's been a considerable improvement in your mother's condition.* **Improvement on** is used when we are comparing two things and one is better than the other: *These marks are an improvement on your previous ones.*

improvise /'ɪmprəvaɪz/ *verb* [I,T] **1** to make, do, or manage sth quickly or without preparation, using what you have: *If you're short of teachers today you'll just have to improvise* (= manage somehow with the people that you've got). يتحايل على مشكلة ، يرتجل

2 to play music, speak or act using your imagination instead of written or remembered material: *It was obvious that the actor had forgotten his lines and was trying to improvise.* ○ *a brilliant improvised speech* يرتجل

▸ **improvisation** /ˌɪmprəvaɪˈzeɪʃn; *US* ɪmˌprɒvəˈzeɪʃn/ *noun* [C,U] the act of improvising ارتجال

impudent /ˈɪmpjədənt/ *adj* (*formal*) very rude; not respectful or polite ❶ A more informal word is **cheeky**. وقح

▸ **impudence** /-əns/ *noun* [U] impudent behaviour or speech وقاحة

impudently *adv* بوقاحة

impulse /ˈɪmpʌls/ *noun* [C] **1** a sudden desire to do sth without thinking about the results: *She felt a terrible impulse to rush out of the house and never come back.* رغبة مفاجئة ، نزوة

2 a single push or signal in a nerve, wire, etc. that causes a reaction: *electrical impulses* نبضة

IDM on (an) impulse without thinking or planning: *Sometimes it's fun to go away on impulse when the weather's nice.* لتوّه، دون سابق تفكير أو تحضير

impulsive /ɪmˈpʌlsɪv/ *adj* likely to act suddenly and without thinking; done without careful thought: *an impulsive character* ○ *an impulsive remark* مندفِع ، متهور: دون تفكير

▸ **impulsively** *adv* بتهور ، دونِ تفكير

impulsiveness *noun* [U] اندفاع ، تهور

impure /ɪmˈpjʊə(r)/ *adj* **1** consisting of more than one substance (and therefore not of good quality); not pure: *impure metals* غير صاف ، مشوب : مغشوش

2 (*old-fashioned*) (used about thoughts and actions connected with sex) not moral; bad غير طاهر ، دَنِس

▸ **impurity** /ɪmˈpjʊərəti/ *noun* (*pl.* **impurities**) **1** [C, usually pl.] a substance that is present in another substance, making it of poor quality: *People are being advised to boil their water because certain impurities have been found in it.* شائبة

2 [U] the state of being impure تلوّث : عدم طهارة : دَنَس

🔑 **in¹** /ɪn/ *adv* ❶ For special uses with many verbs, e.g. **give in**, look at the verb entries.

1 to a position within a particular area: *She opened the door and went in.* ○ *My suitcase is full. I can't get any more in.* ○ *When does the train get in?* (= to the station) إلى داخل أو داخلاً (البيت مثلاً)

2 at home or at work: *She won't be in till late today.* في البيت أو في المكتب

3 (used about the tides of the sea) at the highest point, when the water is closest to the land: *The tide's coming in.* نحو الشاطئ ، (البحر) في حالة مدّ

4 received by sb official: *Entries should be in by 20 March.* (يستلَم من قبل موظف رسمي)

IDM be in for sth to be going to experience sth unpleasant: *He'll be in for a shock when he gets the bill.* (تنتظره أخبار غير سارّة)

be/get in on sth to have a share in sth; to know about sth that is happening: *I'd like to be in on the new project.* (على علم بِ)

have (got) it in for sb (*informal*) to be unpleasant to sb because he/she has done sth to upset you يعامل بجفاء ، يعادي

🔑 **in²** /ɪn/ *prep* ❶ For special uses with many nouns, e.g. **in time**, look at the noun entries.

1 (showing place) within the area of sth; enclosed by sth: *a country in Africa* ○ *a town in France* ○ *an island in the Pacific* ○ *in a box* ○ *I read about it in the newspaper.* ○ *in bed* ○ *She put the keys in her pocket.* ○ *They were working in the garden.* ○ *His wife's in hospital.* في

2 (showing time) during a period of time: *My birthday is in August.* ○ *He was born in 1980.* ○ *You could walk there in about an hour* (= it would take that long to walk there). في

3 (showing time) after a period of time: *I'll be finished in ten minutes.* بعد

4 contained in; forming the whole or part of sth: *There are 366 days in a leap year.* في : ضمن

5 (used for giving the rate of sth): *a new rate of tax of 50p in the pound* ○ *One family in ten owns a dishwasher.* بِ: مِن (ضمن)

6 wearing sth: *They were all dressed in black for the funeral.* ○ *I've never seen you in a suit before.* بِ ، (مرتدياً)

7 (used for saying how things are arranged): *We sat in a circle.* (بشكل)

8 (used for saying how sth is written or expressed): *Please write in pen.* ○ *They were talking in Italian.* بِ

9 (used with feelings): *I watched in horror as the plane crashed to the ground.* بِ

10 (showing the condition or state of sb/sth): *My parents are in poor health.* ○ *This room is in a mess!* ○ *Richard's in love.* في، بِ

11 (showing sb's job or the activity sb is involved in): *He's got a good job in advertising.* ○ *All her family are in politics.* ○ *He's in the army.* في، بِ

in³ /ɪn/ *noun*

IDM the ins and outs (of sth) the details and difficulties (involved in sth): *Will somebody explain the ins and outs of the situation to me?* باطن الأمور وظواهرها، تفاصيل الأمور وخفاياها

in⁴ /ɪn/ *adj* fashionable at the moment: *the in place to go* ○ *Purple is very in this season* آخر صيحة في عالم الموضة

in. (*pl.* **in.** or **ins.**) *abbrev* = INCH: *He is 6 ft 2 in. tall.*

🔑 **inability** /ˌɪnəˈbɪləti/ *noun* [U] **inability (to do sth)** lack of ability, power or skill: *He has a complete inability to listen to other people's opinions.* ❶ The adjective is **unable**. عَجْز ، عدم مقدرة

inaccessible /ˌɪnækˈsesəbl/ *adj* very difficult or impossible to reach or contact: *That beach is inaccessible by car.* ○ (*figurative*) *His books are in-*

accessible to (= cannot be understood by) *the average reader.* صعب المنال : لا يمكن الوصول إليه : يصعب فهمه
▸ **inaccessibility** /ˌɪnækˌsesəˈbɪləti/ *noun* [U] صعوبة الوصول إلى ، مناعة : صعوبة فهم

inaccurate /ɪnˈækjərət/ *adj* not correct; not accurate: *an inaccurate report, description, etc.* خاطئ ، غير صحيح ، مغلوط
▸ **inaccuracy** /ɪnˈækjərəsi/ *noun* (*pl.* **inaccuracies**) **1** [U] being inaccurate: *The inaccuracy of the statistics was immediately obvious.* خطأ
2 [C] an inaccurate statement; a written or spoken mistake: *There are always some inaccuracies in newspaper reports.* عدم صحة : تقرير مغلوط

inaction /ɪnˈækʃn/ *noun* [U] doing nothing; lack of action: *The crisis was blamed on the government's earlier inaction.* قعود عن العمل ، تراخ ، كسل

inactive /ɪnˈæktɪv/ *adj* doing nothing; not active: *The virus remains inactive in the body.* عديم الحركة : غير فعّال؛ ساكن، خامد
▸ **inactivity** /ˌɪnækˈtɪvəti/ *noun* [U] عدم الحركة ، خمول

inadequate /ɪnˈædɪkwət/ *adj* **1** not sufficient; not good enough: *the problem of inadequate housing* غير كاف ، ناقص : غير ملائم
2 (used about a person) not able to deal with a problem or situation, etc.; not confident: *There was so much to learn in the new job that for a while I felt totally inadequate.* غير كفء : قاصر عن حل مشاكله : غير واثق من نفسه
▸ **inadequacy** /ɪnˈædɪkwəsi/ *noun* [C,U] (*pl.* **inadequacies**): *his inadequacy as a parent* ○ *The inadequacies of the health service are often blamed on the government.* عدم كفاية : قصور ، نقص
inadequately /ɪnˈædɪkwətli/ *adv* بشكل ناقص ، بشكل لا يفي بالغرض

inadvertent /ˌɪnədˈvɜːtənt/ *adj* (used about actions) done without thinking, not on purpose; not intentional ساه : غير متعمّد، غير مقصود
▸ **inadvertently** *adv*: *She had inadvertently left the letter where he could find it.* سهواً : عن غير قصد

inadvisable /ˌɪnədˈvaɪzəbl/ *adj* not sensible or wise: *It is inadvisable to go swimming when you have a cold.* غير مستحسن : ليس من الحكمة

inane /ɪˈneɪn/ *adj* without any meaning; silly: *an inane remark* سخيف ، تافه: لا معنى له
▸ **inanely** *adv* بسخف : ببلاهة

inappropriate /ˌɪnəˈprəʊpriət/ *adj* not suitable: *Isn't that dress rather inappropriate for the occasion?* غير لائق ، غير مناسب

inarticulate /ˌɪnɑːˈtɪkjələt/ *adj* **1** (used about a person) not able to express ideas and feelings clearly عاجز عن الإفصاح عن آرائه ومشاعره
2 (used about speech) not clear or well expressed غير واضح
▸ **inarticulately** *adv* بغموض : بشكل غير مفهوم

inasmuch as /ˌɪnəzˈmʌtʃ əz/ *conj* (*formal*) because of the fact that; to the extent that: *We felt sorry for the boys inasmuch as they had not realized that what they were doing was wrong.* نظراً لأنّ: بقدر ما

inattention /ˌɪnəˈtenʃn/ *noun* [U] lack of attention: *a moment of inattention* غفلة ، سهو ، عدم انتباه
▸ **inattentive** /ˌɪnəˈtentɪv/ *adj* not paying attention; not attentive: *One inattentive student can disturb the whole class.* غير منتبه : غافل ، ساه

inaudible /ɪnˈɔːdəbl/ *adj* not loud enough to be heard غير مسموع
▸ **inaudibly** /ɪnˈɔːdəbli/ *adv* (بصوت) غير مسموع

inaugural /ɪˈnɔːgjərəl/ *adj* (only *before* a noun) (used about a speech or meeting that marks the beginning of a new organization, leadership, etc.) first: *the President's inaugural speech* تدشينيّ ، افتتاحي

inaugurate /ɪˈnɔːgjəreɪt/ *verb* [T] **1** to introduce a new official, leader, etc. at a special ceremony: *He will be inaugurated as President next month.* يولّي ، يقلّد مراسم السلطة
2 to start, introduce or open sth new (often at a special ceremony) يدشّن ، يفتتح
▸ **inauguration** /ɪˌnɔːgjəˈreɪʃn/ *noun* [C,U] مراسم تقليد السلطة : افتتاح، تدشين

inbox /ˈɪnbɒks/ *noun* [C] the place on a computer where new email messages are shown: *I have a stack of emails in my inbox.* البريد الوارد (كمبيوتر)

Inc. (*also* **inc**) *abbrev* (*US*) = INCORPORATED

inc. (*also* **incl.**) *abbrev* = INCLUDING; INCLUSIVE

incalculable /ɪnˈkælkjələbl/ *adj* very great; too great to calculate: *an incalculable risk* ○ *incalculable damage* جسيم، بالغ : لا يعدّ ولا يحصى

incapable /ɪnˈkeɪpəbl/ *adj* **1 incapable of sth/doing sth** not able to do sth; not capable of sth/doing sth: *She is incapable of hard work/working hard.* ○ *He's quite incapable of unkindness* (= too nice to be unkind). غير قادر، عاجز (عن)
2 not able to do, manage or organize anything well: *As a doctor, she's totally incapable.* غير كفء

incapacitate /ˌɪnkəˈpæsɪteɪt/ *verb* [T] to make sb unable (to work, live normally, etc.): *They were completely incapacitated by the heat in Spain.* يقعد عن العمل : يشلّ حركته

incarnation /ˌɪnkɑːˈneɪʃn/ *noun* [C] **1** (a person that is) a perfect example of a particular quality مثال ، رمز ، تجسيد
2 a life on earth in a particular form تجسُّد

incendiary /ɪnˈsendiəri; *US* -dieri/ *adj* that causes a fire: *an incendiary bomb* محرق

incense /ˈɪnsens/ *noun* [U] a substance that produces a sweet smell when burnt, used especially in religious ceremonies بَخور

incentive /ɪnˈsentɪv/ *noun* [C,U] **incentive (to do sth)** something that encourages you (to do sth): *The company is offering cash incentives to staff to move to another area.* ○ *There's no incentive for young people to do well at school because there aren't any jobs when they leave.* حافز ، دافع : جائزة تشجيعية

incessant /ɪnˈsesnt/ *adj* never stopping: *incessant rain, noise, etc.* ➲ Look at **continual**. متواصل ، لا ينقطع

a b c d e f g h **i** j k l m n o p q r s t u v w x y z

▸ **incessantly** *adv* بدون انقطاع : باستمرار

incest /ˈɪnsest/ *noun* [U] sexual intercourse between close members of a family, e.g. brother and sister سِفاح القربى ، تعاطي الجنس مع المحارم

▸ **incestuous** /ɪnˈsestjuəs; *US* -tʃuəs/ *adj* **1** involving incest: *an incestuous relationship* (علاقة) جنسية مع المحارم

2 (used about a group of people and their relationships with each other) too close; not open to anyone outside the group: *Life in a small community can be very incestuous.* مغلق ، مفرط في الانعزال عن الآخرين

inch /ɪntʃ/ *noun* [C] (*abbr* **in.**) a measure of length; 2.54 centimetres. There are 12 inches in a foot: *He's 5 foot 10 inches tall.* ○ *Three inches of rain fell last night.* بوصة ، إنش

PHR V **inch forward, past, through, etc.** to move slowly and carefully in the direction mentioned: *He inched forward along the cliff edge.* يحرك أو يتحرك ببطء شديد

incidence /ˈɪnsɪdəns/ *noun* (*formal*) [sing.] the number of times sth (usually sth unpleasant) happens; the rate of sth: *a high incidence of crime, disease, unemployment, etc.* حدوث ، وقوع : معدل أو نسبة الحدوث

incident /ˈɪnsɪdənt/ *noun* [C] (*formal*) **1** an event (especially one that involves violence, danger, something strange, etc.): *There were a number of unpleasant incidents after the football match.* ○ *Various strange incidents had made people suspicious.* ○ *The publishing of the book resulted in a diplomatic incident* (= a dangerous or unpleasant situation between countries). حادث ، حادثة

2 something that happens that is not very important: *There was an amusing incident at work today.* حَدَث ، واقعة بسيطة

incidental /ˌɪnsɪˈdentl/ *adj* happening as part of sth more important; minor: *The incidental expenses of a holiday are often more than expected.* ○ *The book contains various themes that are incidental to the main plot.* عرضيّ ، ثانويّ ؛ طارئ

incidentally /ˌɪnsɪˈdentli/ *adv* (used to introduce extra news, information, etc. that the speaker has just thought of): *Incidentally, that new restaurant you told me about is excellent.* ❶ Another way of saying 'incidentally' is **by the way**. بالمناسبة ، على فكرة

incinerate /ɪnˈsɪnəreɪt/ *verb* [T] (*formal*) to destroy sth completely by burning يُرمِّد ، يحرق حتى يصبح رماداً

▸ **incinerator** /ɪnˈsɪnəreɪtə(r)/ *noun* [C] a container or machine for burning rubbish, etc. محرقة القمامة

incision /ɪnˈsɪʒn/ *noun* [C,U] (*formal*) a cut carefully made into sth (especially into a person's body as part of a medical operation) شَرْط (جراحي) ، حزّ ، شقّ

incite /ɪnˈsaɪt/ *verb* [T] **incite sb (to sth)** to encourage sb to do sth by making him/her very angry or excited: *He was accused of inciting the crowd to violence.* يحرِّض

▸ **incitement** *noun* [C,U]: *He was guilty of incitement to violence.* تحريض

incl. *abbrev* = INCLUDING; INCLUSIVE

inclination /ˌɪnklɪˈneɪʃn/ *noun* [C,U] a feeling that makes sb want to behave in a particular way: *My inclination is to say 'no', but what do you think?* مَيْل : رغبة : نزعة

incline /ɪnˈklaɪn/ *verb* **1** [I,T] to tend to think or behave in a particular way; to make sb do this: *I incline to the view that we should take no action at this stage.* ○ *Lack of money inclines many young people towards crime.* يميل

2 [T] (*formal*) to bend (your head) forward: *They sat round the table, heads inclined, deep in discussion.* يطأطئ (رأسه)

3 [I] **incline towards sth** to lean or slope in the direction of sth: *The land inclines towards the shore.* ينحدر ، يميل نحو

inclined /ɪnˈklaɪnd/ *adj* **1 inclined to do sth** likely to do sth: *She's inclined to change her mind very easily.* عنده استعداد لـ ، ميّال لـ

2 inclined (to do sth) wanting to behave in a particular way: *I know Andrew well so I'm inclined to believe what he says.* ميّال (إلى)

3 inclined to do sth (used to make what is said sound less sure) holding a particular opinion: *I'm inclined to say 'yes', but I'll have to ask James first.* ميّال (إلى) ، في (رأيي)

4 having a natural ability in the subject mentioned: *to be musically inclined* موهوب

include /ɪnˈkluːd/ *verb* [T] **1** to have as one part; to contain (among other things): *The price of the holiday includes the flight, the hotel and taxes.* ○ *The crew included one woman.* ➲ Look at **exclude** and at the note at **contain**. يشمل ، يتضمّن

2 to make sb/sth part (of another group, etc.): *The children immediately included the new girl in their games.* ○ *Everyone was disappointed, myself included.* يضمّ ؛ يضمِّن

▸ **including** /ɪnˈkluːdɪŋ/ *prep* having as a part: *It costs £17.99, including postage and packing.* بما فيه

inclusion /ɪnˈkluːʒn/ *noun* [U]: *The inclusion of all that violence in the film was unnecessary.* إدراج ، تضمين : احتواء

inclusive /ɪnˈkluːsɪv/ *adj* **1 inclusive (of sth)** (used about a price, charge, fee, etc.) including or containing everything; including the thing mentioned: *Is that an inclusive price or are there some extras?* ○ *The rent is inclusive of electricity.* شامل ، متضمن : كلّي

2 (only *after* a noun) including the dates, numbers, etc. mentioned: *You are booked at the hotel from Monday to Friday inclusive* (= including Monday and Friday). ❶ When talking about time **through** is often used in American English instead of **inclusive**: *We'll be away from Friday through Sunday.* متضمّن ، كامل ، (بما فيه التاريخين المذكورين)

incognito /ˌɪnkɒɡˈniːtəʊ; *US* ɪŋˈkɒɡnətəʊ/ *adj, adv* hiding your real name and identity (especially if you are famous and do not want to be recognized): *to travel incognito* متنكّر، متخفٍّ؛ متنكراً؛ بإسم مستعار

incoherent /ˌɪnkəʊˈhɪərənt/ *adj* not clear or easy to understand; not expressing yourself clearly غير مترابط ؛ غير مفهوم

▸ **incoherence** /-əns/ *noun* [U] تفكّك ، عدم تماسك ؛ صعوبة فهم

incoherently *adv* (يتكلم) كلاماً غير مترابط أو غير مفهوم

income /ˈɪnkʌm/ *noun* [C,U] the money you receive regularly as payment for your work or as interest on investments: *It's sometimes difficult for a family to live on one income.* دخْل ، إيراد

> We talk about a **monthly** or an **annual** income. An income may be **high** or **low**. Your **gross** income is the amount you earn before paying tax. Your **net** income is your income after tax. Look at the note at **pay**[1].

ˈincome tax *noun* [U] the tax you pay on the money you earn ضريبة الدخل

incoming /ˈɪnkʌmɪŋ/ *adj* (only *before* a noun) **1** coming in or arriving: *incoming flights, passengers, etc.* ○ *incoming telephone calls* آتٍ ، وارد ، قادم

2 new; recently elected: *the incoming government* جديد ، منتخَب حديثاً

incomparable /ɪnˈkɒmprəbl/ *adj* so good or great that it does not have an equal: *incomparable beauty* ❶ The verb is **compare**. لا يضاهى ، لا نظير له

incompatible /ˌɪnkəmˈpætəbl/ *adj* **incompatible (with sb/sth)** not able to live or work happily with sb; not able to exist in harmony with sb/sth else: *The working hours of the job are incompatible with family life.* غير منسجم مع غيره ، متنافر ، متضارب

▸ **incompatibility** /ˌɪnkəmˌpætəˈbɪləti/ *noun* [C,U] (*pl.* **incompatibilities**) عدم انسجام ، تنافر، تضارب

incompetent /ɪnˈkɒmpɪtənt/ *adj* lacking the necessary skill to do sth well: *He is completely incompetent at his job.* غير كفء ، قليل الخبرة

▸ **incompetence** /-əns/ *noun* [U] عدم كفاءة ، قلة خبرة

incompetently *adv* دون خبرة ، دون الكفاءة المطلوبة

incomplete /ˌɪnkəmˈpliːt/ *adj* having a part or parts missing; not total or complete: *The witness could only give an incomplete account of what had happened.* ○ *His happiness was incomplete without her.* ○ *Unfortunately the jigsaw puzzle was incomplete.* ناقص

▸ **incompletely** *adv* بشكل غير تام ، بشكل ناقص ، جزئياً

incomprehensible /ɪnˌkɒmprɪˈhensəbl/ *adj* impossible to understand: *an incomprehensible explanation* ○ *Her attitude is incomprehensible to the rest of the committee.* يتعذّر فهمه؛ غير مفهوم

inconceivable /ˌɪnkənˈsiːvəbl/ *adj* impossible or very difficult to believe or imagine لا يصدَّق، لا يتصوره العقل

inconclusive /ˌɪnkənˈkluːsɪv/ *adj* not leading to a definite decision or result: *an inconclusive discussion* ○ *inconclusive evidence* (= that doesn't prove anything) (برهان) غير قاطع ؛ غير حاسم

▸ **inconclusively** *adv* دون نتيجة حاسمة ؛ دون التوصّل إلى حل

incongruous /ɪnˈkɒŋgruəs/ *adj* strange; not in harmony; out of place: *He looked very incongruous in his T-shirt and jeans at the ball.* غريب الشكل ؛ غير منسجم ، متنافر

▸ **incongruity** /ˌɪnkɒnˈgruːəti/ *noun* [U] غرابة ؛ عدم انسجام ، تنافر

incongruously *adv* بعدم انسجام ، بشكل لا يتلاءم مع

inconsiderate /ˌɪnkənˈsɪdərət/ *adj* (used about a person) not thinking or caring about the feelings, or needs of other people: *It was inconsiderate of you not to offer her a lift.* ❶ Another word for inconsiderate is **thoughtless**. لا يأبه لمشاعر الآخرين أو مصالحهم ، قليل الإحساس

▸ **inconsiderately** *adv* دون مراعاة مشاعر الآخرين أو مصالحهم

inconsiderateness *noun* [U] عدم مراعاة مشاعر الآخرين أو مصالحهم

inconsistent /ˌɪnkənˈsɪstənt/ *adj* **1** (used about a person) likely to change (in attitude, behaviour, etc.); not reliable: *She's so inconsistent – sometimes her work is good and sometimes it's really awful.* متقلّب ؛ مناقض لنفسه

2 inconsistent (with sth) not in agreement with sth: *These new facts are inconsistent with the earlier information.* متضارب ، متعارض

▸ **inconsistency** /-ənsi/ *noun* [C, U] (*pl.* **inconsistencies**) تضارب ، تناقض ذاتي ، تقلّب

inconsistently *adv* بشكل فيه تضارب أو تناقض

inconspicuous /ˌɪnkənˈspɪkjuəs/ *adj* not easily noticed: *inconspicuous colours such as grey and dark blue* ○ *I tried to make myself as inconspicuous as possible so that no one would ask me a question.* غير ملفت للأنظار ؛ متوارٍ عن العيون

▸ **inconspicuously** *adv* بشكل لا يلفت الأنظار ؛ بعيداً عن العيون

incontinent /ɪnˈkɒntɪnənt/ *adj* unable to control the passing of waste (urine and faeces) from the body مصاب بسلس البول والغائط

▸ **incontinence** /-əns/ *noun* [U] سلس البول والغائط

inconvenience /ˌɪnkənˈviːniəns/ *noun* [C,U] (something that causes) difficulty or discomfort: *We apologize for any inconvenience caused by the delays.* إزعاج ، مضايقة ؛ صعوبة

▸ **inconvenience** *verb* [T] يزعج ، يضايق ؛ يسبّب صعوبات

inconvenient /ˌɪnkənˈviːniənt/ *adj* causing difficulty or discomfort; not convenient: *It's a bit inconvenient at the moment – could you phone again later?* (وقت) غير مناسب ؛ مزعج

▸ **inconveniently** *adv* بشكل غير ملائم ؛ بشكل يسبّب الإزعاج

incorporate /ɪnˈkɔːpəreɪt/ *verb* [T] **incorporate sth (in/into sth)** to make sth part of sth else or to have sth as a part; to include: *I'd like you to incorporate this information into your report.*

a b c d e f g h i j k l m n o p q r s t u v w x y z

○ *The new car incorporates all the most modern safety features.* يضم، يشمل : يدمج

▸ **incorporated** /ɪnˈkɔːpəreɪtɪd/ *adj* (*abbr* **Inc.**; **inc**) (following the name of a company) formed into a business company with legal status (corporation) (شركة) مساهمة

incorrect /ˌɪnkəˈrekt/ *adj* not right or true; not correct: *Incorrect answers should be marked with a cross.* خاطئ، غير صحيح

▸ **incorrectly** *adv* wrongly: *The envelope was incorrectly addressed.* خطأً، بشكل غير صحيح

incorrigible /ɪnˈkɒrɪdʒəbl; *US* -ˈkɔːr-/ *adj* (used about a person or behaviour) very bad; too bad to be corrected or improved: *an incorrigible liar* لا يمكن إصلاحه : راسخ، لا يمكن تغييره

increase[1] /ɪnˈkriːs/ *verb* [I,T] to become or to make sth larger in number or amount: *The number of people working from home will increase steadily during the next decade.* ○ *The rate of inflation has increased by 1% to 7%.* ○ *My employer would like me to increase my hours of work from 25 to 30.* ○ *She increased her speed to overtake the lorry.* ❶ The opposite is **decrease** or **reduce**. يزداد : يزيد

▸ **increasingly** /ɪnˈkriːsɪŋli/ *adv* more and more: *increasingly difficult, important, unhappy, etc.* بازدياد، أكثر فأكثر

increase[2] /ˈɪŋkriːs/ *noun* [C,U] **increase (in sth)** a rise in the number, amount or level of sth: *a steady increase in the number of people taking holidays abroad* ○ *There has been a sharp increase of nearly 50% on last year's figures.* ○ *Doctors expect some further increase in the spread of the disease.* ○ *They are demanding a large wage increase in line with inflation.* ❶ The opposite is **decrease** or **reduction**. ازدياد : زيادة

IDM on the increase becoming larger or more frequent; increasing: *Attacks by dogs on children are on the increase.* في ازدياد

incredible /ɪnˈkredəbl/ *adj* **1** amazing or fantastic; very great: *He earns an incredible salary.* خياليّ، هائل، لا يصدّق

2 impossible or very difficult to believe: *I found his account of the event incredible.* لا يصدّق : يصعب تصديقه

▸ **incredibly** /ɪnˈkredəbli/ *adv* extremely: *We have had some incredibly strong winds recently.* للغاية : بشكل لا يصدّق

incriminate /ɪnˈkrɪmɪneɪt/ *verb* [T] to provide evidence that sb is guilty of a crime: *The police searched the house but found nothing to incriminate the man.* يدين، يتّهم بجريمة

incubate /ˈɪŋkjubeɪt/ *verb* [I,T] **1** (used about eggs) to keep or be kept warm until the young birds come out (hatch) يحضن (البيض)

2 (used about an infectious disease, etc.) to develop: *Some viruses take weeks to incubate.* يحضن (جرثومة) : ينمو

▸ **incubation** /ˌɪŋkjuˈbeɪʃn/ *noun* **1** [U] the process of incubating eggs حضانة

2 [C] (*also* **incuˈbation period**) the period between catching a disease and the time when signs of it (symptoms) appear دور الحضانة

incubator /ˈɪŋkjubeɪtə(r)/ *noun* [C] **1** a heated apparatus used in hospitals for keeping small or weak babies alive حاضنة

2 a similar apparatus for keeping eggs warm until they break open (hatch) حاضنة

incur /ɪnˈkɜː(r)/ *verb* [T] (incurred; incurring) (*formal*) to cause or suffer sth unpleasant as a result of your own actions: *to incur debts/sb's anger, etc.* يجرّ أو يجلب على نفسه

incurable /ɪnˈkjʊərəbl/ *adj* not able to be cured or changed: *an incurable disease* عضال، لا شفاء منه

▸ **incurably** /-əbli/ *adv*: *incurably ill* (مريض) مرضاً عضالاً : بشكل لا شفاء منه

indebted /ɪnˈdetɪd/ *adj* **1 indebted to sb (for sth)** (*formal*) very grateful to sb: *I am deeply indebted to my family and friends for all their help and support.* مَدين لـ (بالشكر)

2 (used about countries, governments, etc.) owing money to other countries or organizations: *a list of the 15 most heavily indebted nations* مديون، مدين

indecent /ɪnˈdiːsnt/ *adj* offending against accepted sexual, moral or social standards of behaviour; not decent غير محتشم : مخلّ بالآداب : بذيء

▸ **indecency** /-nsi/ *noun* [C,U] (*pl.* **indecencies**) قلة احتشام : بذاءة : تحرش جنسيّ

indecently *adv* بشكل غير لائق : دون احتشام

indecision /ˌɪndɪˈsɪʒn/ *noun* [U] being unable to decide: *This indecision about the future is really worrying me.* تردّد

indecisive /ˌɪndɪˈsaɪsɪv/ *adj* (used about a person) not able to make decisions متردّد

▸ **indecisively** *adv* بتردّد

indeed /ɪnˈdiːd/ *adv* **1** (used for agreeing with sth that has just been said or for emphasis) really; certainly: *'Have you had a good holiday?' 'We have indeed.'* نعم، حقاً : بالتأكيد

2 (used for emphasizing a point that has just been made) in fact: *It's important that you come at once. Indeed, it's essential.* في الواقع، وبالأحرى

3 (used for emphasis after 'very' plus an adjective or adverb): *Thank you very much indeed.* ○ *She's very happy indeed.* (تستعمل للتأكيد بمعنى "جداً" أو "للغاية")

4 (used for showing interest, surprise, anger, etc.): *'They were talking about you last night.' 'Were they indeed!'* ○ *'Why did he go without us?' 'Why indeed?'* (تستعمل للتعبير عن الاهتمام أو الدهشة وغير ذلك) ترى لماذا؟ أصحيح هذا؟

indefensible /ˌɪndɪˈfensəbl/ *adj* (used about behaviour, etc.) completely wrong; that cannot be defended or excused شائن : (تصرّف) لا يمكن تبريره

indefinable /ˌɪndɪˈfaɪnəbl/ *adj* difficult or impossible to describe: *There was an indefinable atmosphere of hostility.* غامض : يصعب وصفه

▸ **indefinably** /-əbli/ *adv* بصورة غامضة، دون سبب واضح

indefinite /ɪn'defɪnət/ *adj* not fixed or clear; not definite: *Our plans are still rather indefinite.* غير محدّد ؛ غير واضح ؛ غير نهائي
▸ **indefinitely** *adv* for an indefinite period of time (= you do not know how long it will last): *The meeting was postponed indefinitely.* لأجل غير مسمى

in,definite 'article *noun* [C] (*grammar*) the name used for the words *a* and *an* ➲ Look at **definite article**. (في القواعد) أداة التنكير

indelible /ɪn'deləbl/ *adj* that cannot be removed or washed out: *indelible ink* ○ (*figurative*) *an indelible impression* لا يمحى ، لا يزول
▸ **indelibly** /-əbli/ *adv* بشكل لا يمحى

indent /ɪn'dent/ *verb* [I,T] to start a line of writing further from the left-hand side of the page than the other lines يترك فراغاً في بداية السطر

⚷**independence** /,ɪndɪ'pendəns/ *noun* [U] **independence (from sb/sth)** (used about a person, country, etc.) the state of being free or not controlled by another person, country, etc: *In 1947 India achieved independence from Britain.* ○ *The old lady refused to go into a nursing home because she didn't want to lose her independence.* ○ *financial independence* ❶ On **Independence Day** (4 July) Americans celebrate the day in 1776 when America declared itself independent from Britain. استقلال

⚷**independent** /,ɪndɪ'pendənt/ *adj* **1 independent (of sb/sth)** not dependent on or controlled by another person, country, etc: *Many former colonies are now independent nations.* ○ *to be independent of your parents* ○ *independent schools, television, etc.* (= not dependent on the government for money) مستقل
2 not needing or wanting help: *My son likes travelling on his own – he's very independent for his age.* معتمد على نفسه
3 not influenced by or connected with sb/sth: *Complaints against the police should be investigated by an independent body.* ○ *Two independent opinion polls have obtained similar results.* حياديّ ، لا حزبي
▸ **independently** *adv*: *Scientists working independently of each other have had very similar results in their experiments.* بشكل مستقلٍ (عن بعضهم) ؛ على انفراد

,in-'depth *adj* (usually before noun) very thorough and detailed: *an in-depth discussion/study* ○ *We will be providing in-depth coverage of the election as the results come in.* ○ *Tonight's programme is an in-depth look at the long-term effects of unemployment.* عميق؛ دقيق، مفصّل

indescribable /,ɪndɪ'skraɪbəbl/ *adj* too good or bad to be described: *indescribable poverty, luxury, etc.* يعجز الوصف عنه
▸ **indescribably** /-əbli/ *adv* إلى حدٍّ كبير، إلى حدٍّ لا يوصف

indestructible /,ɪndɪ'strʌktəbl/ *adj* that cannot be easily damaged or destroyed لا يمكن تدميره ، لا يفنى ، صامد أمام الأحداث

⚷**index** /'ɪndeks/ *noun* [C] **1** (*pl.* **indexes**) an alphabetical list of names or subjects at the end of a book فهرس ، مسرد
2 (*pl.* **indexes**) (*also* **'card index**) an alphabetical list of names, books, subjects, etc. written on a series of cards (index cards) بطاقات مفهرسة ، بطاقات مرتّبة أبجدياً
3 (*pl.* **indexes** or **indices**) a way of showing how the price, value, rate, etc. of sth has changed: *the cost-of-living index* مؤشّر
▸ **index** *verb* [T] to make an index or include sth in an index يفهرس ؛ يدرج كلمة في فهرس

'index finger *noun* [C] the finger next to your thumb that is used for pointing ❶ We also say **forefinger**. السبّابة

Indian /'ɪndiən/ *noun* [C], *adj* **1** (a person) from the Republic of India: *Indian food is hot and spicy.* هنديّ
2 = NATIVE AMERICAN: *The Sioux were a famous Indian tribe.* ➲ Look also at **West Indian**.

⚷**indicate** /'ɪndɪkeɪt/ *verb* **1** [T] to show or point to sth: *The receptionist indicated where I should sign.* ○ *The report indicates that children are getting too little exercise.* يدلّ أو يشير إلى
2 [T] to be or give a sign about sth: *If a horse has its ears forward, that indicates that it is happy.* يدلّ على ، ينمّ عن
3 [T] to say sth briefly and in a general way: *The spokesman indicated that an agreement was likely soon.* ينوّه
4 [I,T] to signal that your car, etc. is going to turn: *Why didn't you indicate?* ○ *The lorry indicated left but turned right.* يؤشّر
▸ **indication** /,ɪndɪ'keɪʃn/ *noun* [C,U] something that shows sth; a sign: *There was no indication of a struggle.* ○ *There is every indication that he will make a full recovery.* دليل، علامة، دلالة

indicative /ɪn'dɪkətɪv/ *adj* (*formal*) being or giving a sign of sth: *Is the unusual weather indicative of fundamental climatic changes?* دالّ على

indicator /'ɪndɪkeɪtə(r)/ *noun* [C] **1** something that gives information or shows sth; a sign: *The indicator showed that we had plenty of petrol.* ○ *I've just seen my flight announced on the indicator board.* مؤشّر ؛ لوحة معلومات
2 the flashing light on a car, etc. that shows that it is going to turn right or left المؤشّر الضوئي في سيارة، "غمّازة"

indices *pl.* of INDEX

indictment /ɪn'daɪtmənt/ *noun* [C] **1** a written paper that officially accuses sb of a crime وثيقة الاتّهام
2 (*figurative*) something that shows how bad sth is: *The fact that many children leave school with no qualifications is an indictment of our education system.* إدانة ، دليل على سوء أمر ما

indifference /ɪn'dɪfrəns/ *noun* [U] a lack of interest or feeling (towards sb/sth): *He treated our suggestion with complete indifference.* عدم إكتراث ، لا مبالاة

indifferent /ɪn'dɪfrənt/ *adj* **1 indifferent (to**

a b c d e f g h i j k l m n o p q r s t u v w x y z

sb/sth) not interested in or caring about sb/sth: *How can you remain indifferent when children are suffering?* غير مكترث : عديم الاهتمام

2 of low quality: *The standard of football in the World Cup was rather indifferent.* سيئ نوعاً ما

▸ **indifferently** *adv* بشكل سيئ نوعاً ما

indigenous /ɪnˈdɪdʒənəs/ *adj* (used about people, animals or plants) living or growing in the place where they are from originally
من سكان البلاد الأصليين : بلديّ ، محلي

indigestible /ˌɪndɪˈdʒestəbl/ *adj* (used about food) difficult or impossible to eat and digest
عَسِر الهضم

indigestion /ˌɪndɪˈdʒestʃən/ *noun* [U] pain in the stomach that is caused by difficulty in digesting food: *Onions give me terrible indigestion.*
عسر الهضم

indignant /ɪnˈdɪɡnənt/ *adj* shocked or angry (because sb has said or done sth that you do not like and do not agree with): *They were indignant that they had to pay more for worse services.*
ساخط ، حانق : غاضب

▸ **indignantly** *adv* بحنق : بغضب

indignation /ˌɪndɪɡˈneɪʃn/ *noun* [U] shock and anger: *The growing levels of unemployment have aroused public indignation.* ○ *to express indignation* سخط ، حنق : غضب

⚷ **indirect** /ˌɪndəˈrekt; -daɪˈr-/ *adj* **1** not going in a straight line or using the shortest route; not direct: *We came the indirect route to avoid driving through London.* غير مباشر

2 not directly caused by or connected with sth: *an indirect result* غير مباشر ، عَرَضيّ

3 not mentioning sth openly: *She gave only an indirect answer to my question.* موارب : ملتوٍ

▸ **indirectly** *adv* بشكل غير مباشر

indirectness *noun* [U] مواربة : التواء

ˌ**indirect ˈobject** *noun* [C] (*grammar*) an additional object[1] (4) that is used after some verbs: *In the sentence, 'I wrote him a letter', 'him' is the indirect object.*
(في الإنكليزية) المفعول له أو المفعول غير المباشر

ˌ**indirect ˈspeech** (*also* **reported speech**) *noun* [U] (*grammar*) reporting what sb has said, not using the actual words

> Tim's words were: *'I'll phone again later.'* In indirect speech this becomes: *Tim said that he would phone again later.*

(كلام) منقول عن المتكلّم في صيغة الغائب

indiscreet /ˌɪndɪˈskriːt/ *adj* not careful or polite in what you say or do
غير متحفّظ، غير حكيم فيما يقوله أو يفعله

▸ **indiscreetly** *adv* دون تحفّظ ، دون تبصر

indiscretion /ˌɪndɪˈskreʃn/ *noun* [C,U] behaviour that is indiscreet سلوك طائش : زلة أخلاقيّة

indiscriminate /ˌɪndɪˈskrɪmɪnət/ *adj* not carefully chosen or done with careful thought: *the indiscriminate shooting of civilians*
كيفما اتفق ، جزافيّ : اعتباطيّ

▸ **indiscriminately** *adv*
دون تمييز ، جزافاً ، كيفما اتفق

indispensable /ˌɪndɪˈspensəbl/ *adj* very important, so that it is not possible to be without it; essential or necessary: *A car is indispensable nowadays if you live in the country.*
ضروري جداً ، لا غنى عنه : أساسيّ

indisputable /ˌɪndɪˈspjuːtəbl/ *adj* definitely true; that cannot be proved wrong
(حقيقة) واقعة أو مسلَّم بها: لا جدال فيه

indistinct /ˌɪndɪˈstɪŋkt/ *adj* not clear; not distinct: *indistinct figures, sounds, memories, etc.*
غير واضح ، مشوّش : غامض

▸ **indistinctly** *adv* بشكل غير واضح

indistinguishable /ˌɪndɪˈstɪŋɡwɪʃəbl/ *adj* **indistinguishable (from sth)** appearing to be the same: *From a distance the two colours are indistinguishable.*
لا يمكن التمييز بينهما ؛ (الفرق بينهما) بسيط جداً

⚷ **individual** /ˌɪndɪˈvɪdʒuəl/ *adj* **1** (only *before* a noun) single or particular: *Each individual animal is weighed and measured before being set free.* فردي ، على حدة

2 for or from one person: *an individual portion of butter* (= for one person) ○ *Children need individual attention when they are learning to read.* معدّ لشخص واحد

▸ **individual** *noun* [C] **1** one (single) person: *Are the needs of society more important than the rights of the individual?* فرد

2 (*informal*) a person of the type that is mentioned: *She's an awkward individual.* شخص

individually /-dʒuəli/ *adv* separately; one by one: *The teacher talked to each member of the class individually.* على انفراد ، كلّ على حدة : واحداً واحداً

individuality /ˌɪndɪˌvɪdʒuˈæləti/ *noun* [U] the qualities that make sb/sth different from other people/things: *Young people often try to express their individuality by the way they dress.*
فرديّة ، شخصيّة ، كيان مستقل

indivisible /ˌɪndɪˈvɪzəbl/ *adj* not able to be divided or split into smaller pieces
غير قابل للانقسام ، لا يتجزّأ

indoctrinate /ɪnˈdɒktrɪneɪt/ *verb* [T] to put ideas or beliefs into sb's mind so that they are accepted without criticism: *For 20 years the people have been indoctrinated by the government.* ❶ Using the word **indoctrinate** shows that you disapprove of what is happening.
يلقّن أفكاراً معيّنة ، يرسّخ عقيدة في الأذهان

▸ **indoctrination** /ɪnˌdɒktrɪˈneɪʃn/ *noun* [U]
ترسيخ أفكار معيّنة في الأذهان ، غسل دماغ

⚷ **indoor** /ˈɪndɔː(r)/ *adj* (only *before* a noun) done or used inside a building: *indoor games* ○ *indoor shoes* ○ *an indoor swimming pool* ❶ The opposite is **outdoor**. داخليّ ، (يمارس أو يُستعمل) داخل المبنى

⚷ **indoors** /ˌɪnˈdɔːz/ *adv* in or into a building: *Let's go/stay indoors.* ○ *Oh dear. I've left my sunglasses indoors.* ➲ Look at **outdoors** and **out of doors**. في الداخل ، في البيت : إلى الداخل

induce /ɪnˈdjuːs; *US* -duːs/ *verb* [T] (*formal*) **1** to make or persuade sb to do sth: *Nothing could induce him to change his mind.* يقنع ، يغري ، يستميل

2 to cause or produce sth يسبّب ، يحدث

▶ **inducement** *noun* [C,U] something that is offered to sb to make him/her do sth شيء مغرٍ ؛ دافع، حافز؛ استمالة

indulge /ɪnˈdʌldʒ/ *verb* **1** [T] to allow sb to have or do whatever he/she wants: *You shouldn't indulge that child. It will make him very selfish.* يتساهل مع ، يدلّل

2 [I] **indulge (in sth)**; **indulge yourself (with sth)** to allow yourself to have or do sth for pleasure: *to indulge in self-pity* ○ *I'm going to indulge myself and go shopping for some new clothes.* يطلق العنان لرغباته ، ينغمس في ؛ يتمتّع

▶ **indulgence** /ɪnˈdʌldʒəns/ *noun* **1** [U] the state of having or doing whatever you want: *a life of indulgence* إطلاق العنان للرغبات ، انغماس ؛ تدليل

2 [C] something that you have or do because it gives you pleasure: *A cigar after dinner is my only indulgence.* متعة أو لذة أو تدليل (للنفْس)

indulgent /-ənt/ *adj* allowing sb to have or do whatever he/she wants: *indulgent parents* مفرط في التدليل ، متساهل

indulgently *adv* بتساهل ، بتسامح

⚷ **industrial** /ɪnˈdʌstriəl/ *adj* **1** (only *before* a noun) connected with industry(1): *industrial development* ○ *industrial workers* ○ *coal for industrial purposes* صناعي

2 having a lot of factories, etc: *an industrial region, country, etc.* صناعي

▶ **industrialist** /-ɪst/ *noun* [C] a person who owns or manages a large industrial company صناعي ، من أرباب الصناعة

industrialize (*also* **industrialise**) /-aɪz/ *verb* [T] to develop industries in a country: *Japan was very rapidly industrialized in the late nineteenth century.* ○ *the industrialized nations of the world* يصنّع

industrialization (*also* **industrialisation**) /ɪnˌdʌstriəlaɪˈzeɪʃn; *US* -ləˈz-/ *noun* [U] تصنيع

inˌdustrial ˈaction *noun* [U] the situation when a group of workers go on strike or refuse to work normally, e.g. because they want more money, shorter working hours, etc. إضراب عمّال

industrious /ɪnˈdʌstriəs/ *adj* hard-working مجدّ ، دؤوب

⚷ **industry** /ˈɪndəstri/ *noun* (*pl.* **industries**) **1** [U] the work of making things in factories: *Is British industry being threatened by foreign imports?* ○ *heavy/light industry* الصناعة

2 [C] all the people, buildings, etc. that are involved in producing sth, providing a service, etc: *The new high-tech industries are replacing manufacturing industries in many areas.* ○ *the tourist, catering, entertainment, etc. industry* صناعة (كذا)

inedible /ɪnˈedəbl/ *adj* (*formal*) not suitable to be eaten: *an inedible plant* ○ *The food in the canteen is absolutely inedible.* لا يؤكل

ineffective /ˌɪnɪˈfektɪv/ *adj* not producing the effect or result that you want غير مجدٍ ، عديم التأثير

inefficient /ˌɪnɪˈfɪʃnt/ *adj* not working or producing results in the best way, so that time and money is wasted: *an inefficient way of working* ○ *an inefficient use of space* ○ *Our heating system is very old and extremely inefficient.* ○ *The new manager is very nice but he's very inefficient.* ضعيف المردود ، غير فعّال ؛ غير كفء

▶ **inefficiency** /-nsi/ *noun* [U] عدم كفاءة، عدم فعّالية

inefficiently *adv* بمردود ضعيف ؛ بعدم كفاءة

ineligible /ɪnˈelɪdʒəbl/ *adj* **ineligible (for sth/to do sth)** without the necessary qualifications to do or get sth: *She was ineligible for the job because she wasn't a German citizen.* ○ *ineligible to vote* لا تتوفر فيه الشروط المطلوبة ؛ غير مؤهّل لـ

▶ **ineligibility** /ɪnˌelɪdʒəˈbɪləti/ *noun* [U] عدم توفّر الشروط المطلوبة ؛ عدم أهليّة

inept /ɪˈnept/ *adj* not able to do sth well: *She is totally inept at dealing with people.* أخرق ، غير ماهر

inequality /ˌɪnɪˈkwɒləti/ *noun* [C,U] (*pl.* **inequalities**) (a) difference between groups in society because one has more money, advantages, etc. than the other: *There will be problems as long as inequality between the races exists.* تفاوت ، عدم مساواة

inert /ɪˈnɜːt/ *adj* not able to move or act عاجز عن الحركة ؛ خامل

inertia /ɪˈnɜːʃə/ *noun* [U] **1** a feeling of laziness, when you do not want to do anything كسل ، خمول

2 the physical force that tends to keep things in the position they are in or to keep them moving in the direction they are travelling: (*figurative*) *The inertia of the system makes change very difficult.* العطالة ، القصور الذاتي

inescapable /ˌɪnɪˈskeɪpəbl/ *adj* that cannot be avoided: *an inescapable conclusion* لا مفرّ منه ، محتوم

⚷ **inevitable** /ɪnˈevɪtəbl/ *adj* that cannot be avoided or prevented from happening: *With more cars on the road, traffic jams are inevitable.* ○ *It was inevitable that she would find out the truth one day.* لا بدّ منه ، لا محيد عنه

▶ **inevitability** /ɪnˌevɪtəˈbɪləti/ *noun* [U] حتمية الأمر

the inevitable *noun* [sing.] something that cannot be avoided or stopped from happening ما ليس منه بدّ ، أمر محتوم

inevitably /-əbli/ *adv*: *Building new roads inevitably creates huge problems* (= they cannot be avoided). لا بدّ ، حتماً

inexcusable /ˌɪnɪkˈskjuːzəbl/ *adj* that cannot be allowed or forgiven: *Their behaviour was quite inexcusable.* ○ *inexcusable delays* لا يغتفر ، لا يمكن تبريره

inexhaustible /ˌɪnɪɡˈzɔːstəbl/ *adj* that cannot be finished or used up: *Our energy supplies are not inexhaustible.* لا ينضب ، (مال) لا يفنى

inexpensive /ˌɪnɪkˈspensɪv/ *adj* low in price; not expensive: *an inexpensive camping holiday* رخيص ؛ معتدل السعر

a b c d e f g h i j k l m n o p q r s t u v w x y z

▸ **inexpensively** *adv* دون تكلفة عالية

inexperience /ˌɪnɪkˈspɪəriəns/ *noun* [U] not knowing how to do sth because you have not done it before; lack of experience: *The mistakes were all due to inexperience.* عدم الخبرة : قلّة التجربة

▸ **inexperienced** *adj* not having the knowledge that you get from having done sth before; lacking in experience: *He's too young and inexperienced to be given such responsibility.* عديم الخبرة : قليل التجربة ، غشيم

inexplicable /ˌɪnɪkˈsplɪkəbl/ *adj* that cannot be explained: *Her sudden disappearance is quite inexplicable.* لا يمكن تفسيره

▸ **inexplicably** /ˌɪnɪkˈsplɪkəbli/ *adv* دون سبب : دون مبرر

infallible /ɪnˈfæləbl/ *adj* **1** (used about a person) never making mistakes or being wrong: *Even the most careful typist is not infallible.* معصوم ، لا يخطئ

2 always doing what you want it to do; never failing: *There is no infallible method of birth control.* مضمون ، أكيد المفعول

▸ **infallibility** /ɪnˌfæləˈbɪləti/ *noun* [U] عصمة من الخطأ

infamous /ˈɪnfəməs/ *adj* **infamous (for sth)** famous for being bad: *an infamous dictator* سيّئ السمعة

infancy /ˈɪnfənsi/ *noun* [U] the period when you are a baby or young child: *(figurative) Research in this field is still in its infancy.* طفولة : بداية ، مستهلّ

infant /ˈɪnfənt/ *noun* [C] a baby or very young child: *There is a high rate of infant mortality* (= many children die when they are still babies). ○ *Mrs Davies teaches infants* (= children aged between four and seven). ○ *2 adults, 2 children, 1 infant* (e.g. on an air ticket) ❶ **Baby**, **toddler** or **child** are more common in spoken or informal English. طفل رضيع : طفل صغير

infantile /ˈɪnfəntaɪl/ *adj* of or like a baby or very young child: *infantile* (= very silly) *behaviour* طفليّ ، صبيانيّ ، (تصرف) سخيف لا يليق بالكبار

infantry /ˈɪnfəntri/ *noun* [U, with sing. or pl. verb] soldiers who fight on foot: *The infantry was/were supported by heavy gunfire.* جنود المشاة

ˈinfant school *noun* [C] *(Brit)* a school for children between the ages of four and seven (مدرسة) أطفال

infatuated /ɪnˈfætʃueɪtɪd/ *adj* having a strong but foolish feeling of love for sb/sth that usually does not last long: *The young girl was infatuated with one of her teachers.* مفتون ، مغرم غراماً عابراً

▸ **infatuation** /ɪnˌfætʃuˈeɪʃn/ *noun* [C,U] افتتان ، غرام عابر

🔑 **infect** /ɪnˈfekt/ *verb* [T] (usually passive) to cause sb/sth to have a disease or illness or to become dirty or full of germs: *We must clean the wound before it becomes infected.* ○ *Many thousands of people have been infected with the virus.* ○ *(figurative) Paul's happiness infected the whole family.* يُعدي : يلوّث بالجراثيم

🔑 **infection** /ɪnˈfekʃn/ *noun* **1** [U] making sb ill: *A dirty water supply can be a source of infection.* ○ *There is a danger of infection.* عدوى

2 [C] a disease or illness that is caused by germs: *She is suffering from a chest infection.* ○ *an ear infection* ❶ Infections can be caused by **bacteria** or **viruses**. An informal word for these is **germs**. إصابة ، مرض

🔑 **infectious** /ɪnˈfekʃəs/ *adj* (used about a disease, illness, etc.) that can be easily passed on to another person: *Flu is very infectious.* ○ *(figurative) infectious laughter* ➲ Look at **contagious**. معدٍ ، سريع العدوى

infer /ɪnˈfɜː(r)/ *verb* [T] (inferring; inferred) **infer sth (from sth)** to reach a conclusion from the information you have: *I inferred from our conversation that he was unhappy with his job.* يستنتج

inferior /ɪnˈfɪəriə(r)/ *adj* **inferior (to sb/sth)** low or lower in social position, importance, quality, etc: *I felt very inferior when they started using long words that I didn't understand.* ○ *Cheaper goods are generally of inferior quality.* ❶ The opposite is **superior**. سفليّ ، وضيع ، رديء : من مرتبة أدنى

▸ **inferior** *noun* [C] a person who has a lower social position مرؤوس : شخص أدنى منزلة من غيره

inferiority /ɪnˌfɪəriˈɒrəti; *US* -ˈɔːr-/ *noun* [U] رداءة ، قصور : قلّة

inferiˈority complex *noun* [C] the state of feeling less important, clever, successful, etc. than other people انخفاض المنزلة، (عقدة) نقص

infertile /ɪnˈfɜːtaɪl; *US* -tl/ *adj* **1** (used about land) not able to grow strong healthy plants مجدب ، غير خصيب

2 (used about a person or animal) not able to have a baby or young animal عقيم : (امرأة) عاقر

▸ **infertility** /ˌɪnfɜːˈtɪləti/ *noun* [U]: *treatment for infertility* العقم

infested /ɪnˈfestɪd/ *adj* **infested (with sth)** (used about a building) with large numbers of unpleasant animals or insects in it: *The warehouse was infested with rats.* غاصّ بِ : مبتلى بِ

infiltrate /ˈɪnfɪltreɪt/ *verb* [T] to enter an organization, etc. secretly so that you can find out what it is doing: *The police managed to infiltrate the gang of terrorists.* يتسلّل، يتغلغل، يتسرّب:

▸ **infiltration** /ˌɪnfɪlˈtreɪʃn/ *noun* [C,U] تسرُّب تغلغُل ، تسلُّل

infiltrator /ˈɪnfɪltreɪtə(r)/ *noun* [C] متسلّل

infinite /ˈɪnfɪnət/ *adj* **1** without end or limits: *Supplies of oil are not infinite.* لا نهائي، لا حدّ له: لا ينضب

2 very great: *You need infinite patience for this job.* هائل، قَدْر كبير من

▸ **infinitely** *adv* very much: *Compact discs sound infinitely better than audio cassettes.* إلى حدّ كبير : كثيراً

infinitive /ɪnˈfɪnətɪv/ *noun* [C] *(grammar)* the basic form of a verb ❶ In English the infinitive is sometimes used with and sometimes without *to*: *He can sing.* ○ *He wants to sing.* المصدر (في اللغة الإنكليزية)

infinity /ɪnˈfɪnəti/ *noun* [U] **1** endless space or time اللانهاية

2 (in mathematics) the number that is larger than any other that you can think of اللانهاية، (إلى) ما لانهاية

infirm /ɪnˈfɜːm/ *adj* ill or weak, e.g. because of old age واهن ، ضعيف

▶ **infirmity** /ɪnˈfɜːməti/ *noun* [C,U] (*pl.* **infirmities**) weakness or illness وهن ، ضعف : علّة

infirmary /ɪnˈfɜːməri/ *noun* [C] (*pl.* **infirmaries**) a hospital (used mainly in names): *The Manchester Royal Infirmary* مستشفى ، مشفى

inflamed /ɪnˈfleɪmd/ *adj* (used about a part of the body) red and swollen because of infection or injury (جرح) ملتهب

inflammable /ɪnˈflæməbl/ *adj* that burns easily: *Petrol is highly inflammable.* ➲ Look at **flammable**. It has the same meaning. ❶ The opposite is **non-flammable**. قابل للاشتعال : سريع الالتهاب

inflammation /ˌɪnfləˈmeɪʃn/ *noun* [C,U] redness and swelling in a part of the body, because of infection or injury التهاب

inflate /ɪnˈfleɪt/ *verb* [I,T] (*formal*) to fill sth with air; to become filled with air ❶ The opposite is **deflate**. ينفخ ، يملأ بالهواء : ينتفخ

▶ **inflatable** /-əbl/ *adj* that can or must be filled with air: *an inflatable dinghy/mattress* قابل للنفخ : (قارب) يُنفَخ

inflation /ɪnˈfleɪʃn/ *noun* [U] a general rise in prices: *High wage rises cause inflation.* ○ *the inflation rate/rate of inflation* ○ *Inflation now stands at 3%.* ○ *The government is taking measures to control inflation.* ○ *They've reduced inflation by 2%.* تضخم مالي

inflection (*also* **inflexion**) /ɪnˈflekʃn/ *noun* **1** [U] the act of changing the ending or form of a word to show its grammatical function تصريف (في اللغة)

2 [C] something that is added to a word that changes its grammatical function, e.g. *-ed, -est* أحد أحرف الزيادة التي تغير وظيفة الكلمة

3 [U] the rise and fall of your voice when you are talking ➲ Look at **intonation**. تغيّر طبقة الصوت

inflexible /ɪnˈfleksəbl/ *adj* not able to bend or be bent easily: (*figurative*) *He has a very inflexible attitude to change.* غير مرن ، صلب : عنيد

▶ **inflexibility** /ɪnˌfleksəˈbɪləti/ *noun* [U] عدم مرونة ، جمود : عناد

inflexibly /-əbli/ *adv* بعناد : بعدم مرونة

inflict /ɪnˈflɪkt/ *verb* [T] **inflict sth (on sb)** to force sb to have sth unpleasant or unwanted: *Don't inflict your problems on me – I've got enough of my own.* يفرض على : ينزل (عقوبة) : يبتلي

ˌin-ˈflight *adj* (only *before* a noun) happening or provided during a journey in a plane: *in-flight entertainment* (تسلية) أثناء الرحلة بالطائرة

⚷ **influence** /ˈɪnfluəns/ *noun* **1** [U] **influence (on/over sb/sth)** the power to affect, change or control sb/sth: *I used my influence with the boss to get things changed.* ○ *The fact that he's rich and famous had no influence on our decision.* ○ *Nobody should drive while they are under the influence of alcohol.* نفوذ ، سلطة : تأثير

2 [C] **influence (on sb/sth)** a person or thing that affects or changes sb/sth: *His new friends have been a good influence on him.* تأثير ، أثر

▶ **influence** *verb* [T] to have an effect or influence on sb/sth: *You must decide for yourself. Don't let anyone else influence you.* ○ *Her style of painting has been influenced by Japanese art.* يؤثر على

> **Affect** and **influence** are often very similar in meaning. **Affect** is usually used when the change is physical and **influence** is more often used to describe a change of feeling or attitude: *Some drugs can affect your ability to drive.* ○ *The TV advertisements have influenced my attitude towards road safety.*

influential /ˌɪnfluˈenʃl/ *adj* having power or influence: *an influential politician* ○ *He was influential in getting the hostages set free.* ذو نفوذ : له تأثير

influenza /ˌɪnfluˈenzə/ *noun* [U] (*formal*) = FLU

influx /ˈɪnflʌks/ *noun* [C] a sudden arrival of people or things in large numbers: *the summer influx of visitors from abroad* تدفُّق : سيل (من الزوّار)

⚷ **inform** /ɪnˈfɔːm/ *verb* **1** [T] **inform sb (of/about sth)** to give sb information (about sth): *You should inform the police of the accident.* ○ *Do keep me informed of any changes.* يخبر، يبلّغ، يطلع على

2 [I] **inform on sb** to give information, etc. to the police, etc. about what sb has done wrong: *The wife of the killer informed on her husband.* يبلّغ

▶ **informant** /-ənt/ *noun* [C] a person who gives secret knowledge or information about sb/sth to the police or a newspaper: *The journalist refused to name his informant.* مخبر

informed *adj* having knowledge or information about sth: *Consumers cannot make informed choices unless they are told all the facts.* مطّلع: (اختيار) صحيح يدلّ على معرفة

informer *noun* [C] a person who gives the police, etc. information about what sb has done wrong مخبر، واشٍ

⚷ **informal** /ɪnˈfɔːml/ *adj* relaxed and friendly or suitable for a relaxed occasion; not formal: *I wear a suit to work but more informal clothes at the weekends.* ○ *Don't get dressed up for the party – it'll be very informal.* ○ *The two leaders had informal discussions before the conference began.* غير رسمي

> Some words and expressions in this dictionary are described as *(informal)*. This means that you can use them when you are speaking to friends or people that you know well but that you should not use them in written work, official letters, etc.

▶ **informality** /ˌɪnfɔːˈmæləti/ *noun* [U]: *an atmosphere of informality* عدم الرسميّات ، رفع الكلفة

informally /ɪnˈfɔːməli/ *adv*: *I was told informal-*

ly (= unofficially) *that our plans had been accepted.* بشكل غير رسمي

🔑**information** /ˌɪnfəˈmeɪʃn/ *noun* [U] **information (on/about sb/sth)** knowledge or facts: *For further information please send for our fact sheet.* ○ *Can you give me some information about evening classes in Italian, please?* ○ *The information is fed into the computer and the results are printed out in the form of a graph.*

> The word **information** is uncountable so you CANNOT say: *I need an information.* You can, however, talk about **a bit** or **piece** of information.

معلومات

inforˌmation techˈnology *noun* [U] (*abbr* **IT**) the study or use of computer systems, etc. for collecting, storing and sending out all kinds of information إعلام

informative /ɪnˈfɔːmətɪv/ *adj* giving useful knowledge or information ❶ The opposite is **uninformative**. غني بالمعلومات المفيدة

infrastructure /ˈɪnfrəstrʌktʃə(r)/ *noun* [C,U] the basic structures and systems that are necessary for a country or an organization to function efficiently, e.g. buildings, transport, water and energy resources, and administration أساس، البنية التحتيّة

infrequent /ɪnˈfriːkwənt/ *adj* not happening often: *infrequent visits* قليل الحدوث ، (زيارات) نادرة نوعاً ما

▸ **infrequently** *adv* نادراً ، قليلاً : بشكل غير منتظم

infringe /ɪnˈfrɪndʒ/ *verb* (*formal*) **1** [T] to break a rule, law, agreement, etc. يخرق (القانون) ، يخالف

2 [I] **infringe on/upon sth** to reduce or limit sb's rights, freedom, etc. ينتهك حرمةَ... ، يتعدّى على

▸ **infringement** *noun* [C,U] خرق (القانون) ، مخالفة : تعدٍّ على

infuriate /ɪnˈfjʊərieɪt/ *verb* [T] to make sb very angry يَغيظ ، يجعله يستشيط غضباً

▸ **infuriating** *adj*: *an infuriating habit* مُغيظ : مثير للأعصاب

infuriatingly *adv* بشكل مغيظ : بشكل يثير الأعصاب

ingenious /ɪnˈdʒiːniəs/ *adj* **1** (used about a person) clever at finding answers to problems or at thinking of new things واسع الحيلة ، حاذق

2 (used about a thing or an idea) cleverly made or thought out: *an ingenious plan for making lots of money* بارع

▸ **ingeniously** *adv* ببراعة

ingenuity /ˌɪndʒəˈnjuːəti; *US* -ˈnuː-/ *noun* [U] براعة : دهاء

ingrained /ɪnˈɡreɪnd/ *adj* deeply fixed; difficult to change راسخ ، متأصّل

ingratiate /ɪnˈɡreɪʃieɪt/ *verb* [T] (*formal*) **ingratiate yourself (with sb)** to make yourself liked by doing or saying things that will please people: *He was always trying to ingratiate himself with his teachers.* يحبّب بنفسه؛ يتملّق

▸ **ingratiating** *adj*: *an ingratiating smile* متملّق ، متزلّف : محاول إرضاء الآخرين

ingratiatingly *adv* بتملّق ، بتزلّف : محاولاً إرضاء الآخرين

ingratitude /ɪnˈɡrætɪtjuːd; *US* -tuːd/ *noun* [U] (*formal*) the state of not showing or feeling thanks for sth that has been done for you; a lack of gratitude جحود ، نكران الجميل

🔑**ingredient** /ɪnˈɡriːdiənt/ *noun* [C] one of the items of food you need to make sth to eat: (*figurative*) *The film has all the ingredients of success.* إحدى المواد التي تدخل في إعداد طبخة مثلاً : عنصر مقوّم

inhabit /ɪnˈhæbɪt/ *verb* [T] to live in a place: *Are the Aran Islands still inhabited?* يسكن ، يقطن

▸ **inhabitable** /-əbl/ *adj* that can be lived in: *The house was no longer inhabitable after the fire.* ❶ The opposite is **uninhabitable**. صالح للسكنى

inhabitant /-ənt/ *noun* [C] a person or animal that lives in a place: *How many inhabitants has Paris got?* ○ *The local inhabitants protested at the plans for a new motorway.* ساكن ، قاطن

> When you want to know how many people live in a particular place, you say: *What is the population of...?* not: *How many inhabitants are there in...?*. However, when you answer this question you can say: *The population is 10 000.* or: *It has 10 000 inhabitants.*

inhale /ɪnˈheɪl/ *verb* [I,T] to breathe in: *Be careful not to inhale the fumes from the paint.* يستنشق : يشهق

▸ **inhaler** *noun* [C] a small device containing medicine that you breathe in through your mouth, used by people who have problems with breathing منشقة، جهاز إستنشاق

inherent /ɪnˈhɪərənt; *Brit also* -ˈher-/ *adj* **inherent (in sb/sth)** existing as a natural or permanent feature or quality of sb/sth: *an inherent distrust of foreigners* ○ *the power inherent in the office of President* متأصل؛ ملازم؛ طبيعي، فطري

▸ **inherently** *adv*: *inherently unfair/dishonest* في طبيعته، في حد ذاته

inherit /ɪnˈherɪt/ *verb* [T] **inherit sth (from sb)** **1** to receive property, money, etc. from sb who has died: *I inherited quite a lot of money from my mother. She left me £12 000 when she died.* يرث

2 to receive a quality, disease, etc. from your parents or family: *She has inherited her father's gift for languages.* يرث ، يأخذ عن (أبيه)

▸ **inheritance** /-əns/ *noun* [C,U] the act of inheriting; what you inherit: [U]: *inheritance tax* وراثة : ميراث ، تركة

inhibit /ɪnˈhɪbɪt/ *verb* [T] to prevent sth or make sth happen more slowly: *a drug to inhibit the growth of tumours* يمنع : يثبّط ، يبطئ : يكبت

▸ **inhibited** *adj* not able to express your feelings freely or naturally; not relaxed: *The young man felt shy and inhibited in the roomful of women.* ○ *inhibited about sex* ❶ The opposite is **uninhibited**. مكبوت : مكبوح : خجول

inhibition /ˌɪnhɪˈbɪʃn; ˌɪnɪ-/ *noun* [C,U]: *She has no inhibitions about speaking in front of a large group of people.* مانع ، كابح : خجل

inhospitable /ˌɪnhɒˈspɪtəbl/ *adj* **1** (used about

a person) not friendly or welcoming
غير ودود ، غير مضياف

2 (used about a place) not pleasant to live in: *the inhospitable Arctic regions* (مناخ) قاس

ˌin-ˈhouse *adj* (only *before* a noun) existing or happening within a company or an organization: *an in-house magazine* ○ *in-house language training* داخليّ، داخل (المؤسسة)

inhuman /ɪnˈhjuːmən/ *adj* very cruel, not seeming to be human: *inhuman treatment*
وحشيّ ، غير إنسانيّ

▸ **inhumanity** /ˌɪnhjuːˈmænəti/ *noun* [U] very cruel behaviour: *The twentieth century is full of examples of man's inhumanity to man.*
وحشيّة ، لا إنسانيّة

inhumane /ˌɪnhjuːˈmeɪn/ *adj* very cruel; not caring if people or animals suffer: *the inhumane conditions in which animals are kept on some large farms* وحشي ، قاس ؛ غير رحيم

initial /ɪˈnɪʃl/ *adj* (only *before* a noun) that is at the beginning; first: *My initial reaction was to refuse, but I later changed my mind.* ○ *the initial stages of our survey*
أوّليّ

▸ **initial** *noun* [C, usually pl.] the first letter of a name: *Patricia Anne Morgan's initials are P. A. M.* الحرف الأول من الاسم

initial *verb* [T] (initialling; initialled; *US* initialing; initialed) to mark or sign sth with your initials يوقّع بالأحرف الأولى من اسمه

initially /-ʃəli/ *adv* at the beginning; at first: *I liked the job initially but it soon got quite boring.* في البداية ، في الأول

initiate /ɪˈnɪʃieɪt/ *verb* [T] **1** (*formal*) to start sth: *to initiate a programme of reform*
يضع (برنامجاً)؛ يبدأ ؛ يبتكر

2 initiate sb (into sth) to bring sb into a group by means of a special ceremony or by giving him/her special knowledge: *to initiate somebody into a secret society*
يدخل شخصاً في جمعية سرّية بعد أداء طقوس خاصّة

▸ **initiation** /ɪˌnɪʃiˈeɪʃn/ *noun* [U]
بَدْء ، استهلال ؛ إدخال في جمعية سرّية بطقوس خاصّة

initiative /ɪˈnɪʃətɪv/ *noun* **1** [C] official action that is taken to solve a problem or improve a situation: *a new government initiative to help people start small businesses* قرار حكومي ؛ مبادرة

2 the initiative [sing.] the stronger position because you have done sth first; the advantage: *The enemy forces have lost the initiative.*
مبادهة ، مبادرة

3 [U] the ability to see and do what needs to be done without help from others: *Don't keep asking me how to do it. Use your own initiative.*
روح المبادرة ؛ بصيرة

IDM on your own initiative without being told by sb else what to do بالاعتماد على النفس

take the initiative to be first to do sth: *Let's take the initiative and start organizing things now.* يتّخذ الخطوة الأولى ، مبادأة

inject /ɪnˈdʒekt/ *verb* [T] **1** to put a drug into sb/sth with a needle (syringe): *Something was injected into my arm and I soon fell asleep.* يحقن ، يزرق

2 to add sth: *They injected a lot of money into the business.* يدخل ؛ يضيف

▸ **injection** /ɪnˈdʒekʃn/ *noun* [C,U] **injection (of sth) (into sb/sth)** [C]: *The baby had her first injection yesterday.* ○ *a tetanus injection* [U]: *fuel-injection* حقنة ؛ حقن ؛ إدخال

injunction /ɪnˈdʒʌŋkʃn/ *noun* [C] an official order from a court of law to do/not do sth: *A court injunction prevented the programme from being shown on TV.* إنذار أو أمر قضائي

injure /ˈɪndʒə(r)/ *verb* [T] to harm or hurt a person, animal or part of the body: *David was badly injured in the accident.* ○ *seriously injured* ○ *She fell and injured her back.* ➲ Look at the note at **hurt**. يؤذي ؛ يجرح

▸ **injured** *adj* physically or mentally hurt: *an injured leg* ○ *'Oh, don't be so nasty!' she said in an injured voice.* مجروح ؛ مساء إليه

the injured *noun* [plural] people who have been hurt: *The injured were rushed to hospital.*
المصابون ، الجرحى

injury /ˈɪndʒəri/ *noun* [C,U] (*pl.* **injuries**) harm or hurt done to a person, animal or part of the body: *They escaped from the accident with only minor injuries.* ○ *Injury to the head can be extremely dangerous.* ○ (*figurative*) *injury to your pride, reputation, etc.* جرح ؛ ضرر ، أذى ؛ إصابة

ˈinjury time *noun* [U] (*Brit*) time that is added to the end of a sports match when there has been time lost because of injuries to players
الوقت المستقطَع (في مباراة)

injustice /ɪnˈdʒʌstɪs/ *noun* [C,U] **1** unfairness; a lack of justice: *People are protesting about the injustice of the new tax.* ظلم ، جَوْر

2 an unjust action عمل ظالم ؛ إجحاف

IDM do sb an injustice to judge sb unfairly: *I'm afraid I've done you both an injustice.* عدم إنصاف

ink /ɪŋk/ *noun* [C,U] a coloured liquid that is used for writing, drawing, etc: *Please write in ink, not pencil.*
حِبْر

▸ **inky** /ˈɪŋki/ *adj* made black with ink; very dark: *inky fingers* ملطّخ بالحبر ؛ أسود

inkling /ˈɪŋklɪŋ/ *noun* [sing.] a slight feeling (about sth): *I had an inkling that something was wrong.* شعور خفيف، احساس خفي

inland /ˈɪnlənd/ *adj* in the middle of a country away from the coast or borders: *inland regions, away from the coast* داخليّ ، داخل البلاد

▸ **inland** /ˌɪnˈlænd/ *adv* in or towards the middle of a country: *Goods are carried inland along narrow mountain roads.* إلى داخل البلاد

ˌInland ˈRevenue *noun* [sing.] (*Brit*) the government department that collects taxes
مصلحة ضريبة الدخل

in-laws /ˈɪn lɔːz/ *noun* [plural] (*informal*) your husband's or wife's mother and father or other relations: *My in-laws are coming to lunch on Sunday.* أهل الزوج أو الزوجة

ˌin-line ˈskate *noun* [C] (*also* **Rollerblade**) a type of boot with a line of small wheels attached to the bottom حذاء مدولب (للدحرجة والتزلّج)

▸ ˌ**in-line 'skating** *noun* [U]
التزلّج (بواسطة هذه الأحذية)

inmate /ˈɪnmeɪt/ *noun* [C] one of the people living in an institution such as a prison
نزيل (سجن أو مستشفى الأمراض العقلية)

inn /ɪn/ *noun* [C] (*Brit*) a small hotel or old pub in the country
فندق ريفي صغير؛ حانة ريفيّة

A **hotel** is a place where you can stay, and have your meals if you wish. A **pub** is a place where you go to have a drink. An **inn** is an old pub, usually in the country. Some pubs and inns serve food and some inns have rooms where you can stay.

innate /ɪˈneɪt/ *adj* being a natural quality of sb/sth: *innate ability*
فطري؛ متأصِّل ، من صلب الموضوع

inner /ˈɪnə(r)/ *adj* (only *before* a noun) **1** (of the) inside: *The inner ear is very delicate.* ❶ The opposite is **outer**.
داخليّ

2 (used about a feeling, etc.) that you do not express or show to other people: *Everyone has inner doubts.*
باطني ، في السريرة

▸ **innermost** /-məʊst/ *adj* (only *before* a noun)
1 furthest from the outside
الأعمق

2 (used about a feeling, etc.) most secret or private: *She never told anyone her innermost thoughts.*
من خفايا النفس ، (أفكار) خفيّة

ˌ**inner 'city** *noun* [C] the poor parts of a large city, near the centre, that often have a lot of social problems: *Inner-city schools often have difficulty in attracting good teachers.*
أحياء المدينة الفقيرة

innings /ˈɪnɪŋz/ *noun* [C] (*pl.* **innings**) a period of time in a game of cricket when it is the turn of one player or team to hit the ball (bat)
دور أو جولة في الكريكيت أو البيسبول

innocent /ˈɪnəsnt/ *adj* **1 innocent (of sth)** not having done wrong; not guilty: *An innocent man was arrested by mistake.* ○ *to be innocent of a crime*
بريء

2 not causing harm or intended to upset sb: *He got very aggressive when I asked an innocent question about his past life.*
بريء ، غير مؤذٍ

3 not knowing the bad things in life; believing everything you are told: *Twenty years ago I was still young and innocent.* ○ *She was so innocent as to believe that politicians never lie.*
ساذج ، سليم النيّة

▸ **innocence** /-sns/ *noun* [U]: *The accused man protested his innocence throughout his trial.* ❶ The opposite is **guilt**.
براءة

innocently *adv*
بحسن نيّة؛ بسذاجة ، ببراءة

innocuous /ɪˈnɒkjuəs/ *adj* (*formal*) not causing harm or intended to upset sb: *I made an innocuous remark about teachers and she got really angry.*
عديم الأذى ، لا ضرر منه

▸ **innocuously** *adv*
دون ضرر؛ دون تشويه الموضوع

innovate /ˈɪnəveɪt/ *verb* [I] to introduce sth new; to change
يبتكر ، يبتدع ؛ يجدّد

▸ **innovation** /ˌɪnəˈveɪʃn/ *noun* [C,U] something new that has been introduced: [C]: *technological innovations in industry*
ابتكار ، اختراع

innovative /ˈɪnəvətɪv; ˈɪnəveɪtɪv/ *adj* introducing or using new ideas, ways of doing sth, etc: *There will be a prize for the most innovative design.*
ابداعي، تجديدي

innovator /ˈɪnəveɪtə(r)/ *noun* [C] a person who introduces changes
محدِّد ؛ مبتكر

innumerable /ɪˈnjuːmərəbl; *US* ɪˈnuː-/ *adj* too many to be counted
لا يعدّ ولا يحصى

inoculate /ɪˈnɒkjuleɪt/ *verb* [T] **inoculate sb (with sth) (against sth)** to inject sb with a mild form of a disease. This protects him/her from getting the serious form: *The children have been inoculated against tetanus.* ➲ Look at **immunize** and **vaccinate**.
يلقّح ، يطعّم

▸ **inoculation** /ɪˌnɒkjuˈleɪʃn/ *noun* [C,U]
تلقيح ، تطعيم

inoffensive /ˌɪnəˈfensɪv/ *adj* not upsetting or unpleasant
غير مزعج ؛ غير مؤذٍ ؛ مقبول

inordinate /ɪnˈɔːdɪnət/ *adj* (*formal*) much greater than usual or expected
مفرط ، مجاوز للحدّ ؛

▸ **inordinately** *adv*
إلى حد كبير ؛ بإفراط

inorganic /ˌɪnɔːˈɡænɪk/ *adj* not made of or coming from living things: *Rocks and metals are inorganic substances.*
غير عضوي

input /ˈɪnpʊt/ *noun* [C,U] **input (into/to sth)** what you add to sth to make it better; what you put into sth: *We need some input from teachers into this book.* ○ *The computer breakdown means we have lost the whole day's input.* ➲ Look at **output**.
مساهمة ، مجهود ؛ مدخَلات

▸ **input** *verb* [T] (*pres part* **inputting**; *pt, pp* **input** or **inputted**) to put information into a computer
يدخل (معلومات في الكمبيوتر)

inquest /ˈɪŋkwest/ *noun* [C] an official inquiry to find out about an unexplained death: *to hold an inquest*
تحقيق (لمعرفة سبب الوفاة)

inquire, inquiry = ENQUIRE, ENQUIRY

inquisitive /ɪnˈkwɪzətɪv/ *adj* (*formal*) very interested in finding out about what other people are doing: *Don't be so inquisitive. It's none of your business.*
فضولي

▸ **inquisitively** *adv*
بفضول

inquisitiveness *noun* [U]
فضول

insane /ɪnˈseɪn/ *adj* **1** mad or mentally ill
مجنون

2 very foolish: *You must be insane to leave your job before you've found another one.* ➲ Look at the note at **mad**.
أحمق ، فاقد العقل

▸ **insanely** *adv*: *insanely jealous*
بجنون ، إلى حدّ فظيع

insanity /ɪnˈsænəti/ *noun* [U]
جنون

insanitary /ɪnˈsænətri; *US* -teri/ *adj* (*formal*) likely to cause disease: *The restaurant was closed because of the insanitary conditions of the kitchen.*
غير صحي ؛ غير نظيف

insatiable /ɪnˈseɪʃəbl/ *adj* not able to be satisfied; very great: *an insatiable desire for knowledge* ○ *an insatiable appetite*
لا يشبع ؛ نهِم، جشِع

inscribe /ɪnˈskraɪb/ *verb* [T] (*formal*) **inscribe A (on/in B); inscribe B (with A)** to write or cut (carve) words on sth. You inscribe sth when you want it to be a permanent record: *The book was inscribed with the author's name.* ○ *The names of all the previous champions are inscribed on the cup.* يكتب، يدوِّن : ينقش

▶ **inscription** /ɪnˈskrɪpʃn/ *noun* [C] words that are written or cut on sth: *There was a Latin inscription on the tombstone.* نَقْش ، كتابة

insect /ˈɪnsekt/ *noun* [C] a small animal with six legs and a body which is divided into three parts: *Ants, flies, beetles, butterflies and mosquitoes are all insects.* ○ *an insect bite/sting* ℹ Some other small animals, e.g. spiders, are often also called insects although this is technically incorrect. حشرة

▶ **insecticide** /ɪnˈsektɪsaɪd/ *noun* [C,U] a substance that is used for killing insects ➲ Look at **pesticide**. مبيد الحشرات

insecure /ˌɪnsɪˈkjʊə(r)/ *adj* **1** not supported very well; not safe or secure: *Emily felt very insecure at the top of the ladder.* ○ *The future of the company looks very insecure.* مقلقل ، غير ثابت

2 insecure (about sb/sth) feeling anxious and not sure of yourself; not confident: *Some young people feel lost and insecure when they first leave home.* قلق ، عديم الثقة بالنفس

▶ **insecurely** *adv* بشكل غير ثابت

insecurity /ˌɪnsɪˈkjʊərəti/ *noun* [U]: *Their aggressive behaviour is really a sign of insecurity.* قلَق؛ عدم الثقة بالنفس : تقلقل

insensitive /ɪnˈsensətɪv/ *adj* **1** not knowing or caring how another person feels and whether you have hurt or upset him/her: *Some insensitive reporters tried to interview the families of the accident victims.* عديم الاحساس : غير مراع لشعور الآخرين

2 insensitive (to sth) not able to feel sth: *insensitive to pain, cold, etc.* فاقد الحس ، لا يشعر بِ

▶ **insensitively** *adv* بقلّة احساس : دون اكتراث

insensitivity /ɪnˌsensəˈtɪvəti/ *noun* [U] قلّة إحساس

inseparable /ɪnˈseprəbl/ *adj* not able to be separated from sb/sth: *inseparable friends* ملازِم ، لا ينفصل عن : (صديقان) لا يفترقان

insert /ɪnˈsɜːt/ *verb* [T] (*formal*) to put sth into sth or between two things: *Insert your money and then dial the number.* يدخِل ، يولج : يدرج

▶ **insertion** /ɪnˈsɜːʃn/ *noun* [C,U] إدخال ، ايلاج : إدراج

inshore /ˌɪnˈʃɔː(r)/ *adj, adv* in or towards the part of the sea that is close to the land: *inshore fishermen* ○ *Sharks don't often come inshore.* قرب الساحل ، ساحليّ

inside[1] /ɪnˈsaɪd/ *noun* **1** [C] the inner part or surface of sth: *The insides of the windows need a good clean.* ○ *The door was locked from the inside.* الداخل : السطح الداخلي

2 [sing.] (*also* **insides** /ɪnˈsaɪdz/ [plural]) (*informal*) the stomach: *I've got a pain in my insides.* بطن ، أحشاء

IDM inside out 1 with the inner surface on the outside: *You've got your jumper on inside out.* (يلبس) الداخل إلى الخارج، (يلبسه) بالمقلوب

2 very well, in great detail: *She knows these streets inside out.* (يعرف) تفاصيل الشيء وخفاياه، يعرفه عن ظهر قلب

▶ **inside** *adj* (only *before* a noun) **1** in or on the inner part or surface of sth: *the inside pocket of a jacket* ○ *the inside pages of a newspaper* داخلي

2 (used about information, etc.) told secretly by sb who belongs to a group, organization, etc: *The robbers seemed to have had some inside information about the bank's security system.* (معلومات) من الداخل ، (معلومات) من أهل البيت أنفسهم

insider /ɪnˈsaɪdə(r)/ *noun* [C] a person who is a member of a group or an organization من أهل البيت ، مطّلع (على أسرار شركة مثلاً)

inside[2] /ɪnˈsaɪd/ (*especially US* **inside of**) *prep* **1** in or on the inner part or surface of sb/sth: *Is there anything inside the box?* ○ *It's safer to be inside the house in a thunderstorm.* داخل ، ضمن ، في

2 (*formal*) (used about time) in less than: *Your photos will be ready inside an hour.* في غضون

▶ **inside** *adv* **1** in or to the inner part or surface of sth: *We'd better stay inside until the rain stops.* ○ *It's getting cold. Let's go inside.* ○ *Have a look inside and see what's in it.* في الداخل ؛ إلى الداخل

2 (*slang*) in prison في السجن

ˌinside ˈlane *noun* [C] the part of a wide road or motorway where traffic moves more slowly (في الاوتوستراد) القسم المخصص لحركة المرور الأبطأ

insight /ˈɪnsaɪt/ *noun* [C,U] **insight (into sth)** (an example of) understanding the true nature of sb/sth: *The book gives a good insight into the lives of the poor.* ○ *You need insight into human nature for this job.* بصيرة : معرفة عميقة

insignificant /ˌɪnsɪɡˈnɪfɪkənt/ *adj* of little value or importance: *an insignificant detail* تافه ، لا قيمة له : غير مهم

▶ **insignificance** /-kəns/ *noun* [U] تفاهة ، ضآلة

insignificantly *adv* بتفاهة : (تكلّم كلاماً) لا قيمة له

insincere /ˌɪnsɪnˈsɪə(r)/ *adj* not meaning what you say; not truthful; not sincere: *His apology sounded insincere.* منافق ، مراء : غير مخلص : كاذب

▶ **insincerely** *adv* برياء، كذباً

insincerity /ˌɪnsɪnˈserəti/ *noun* [U] نفاق ، رياء : كذب

insinuate /ɪnˈsɪnjueɪt/ *verb* [T] to suggest sth unpleasant in an indirect way: *She seemed to be insinuating that our work was below standard.* يلمّح ، يدسّ في كلامه

▶ **insinuation** /ɪnˌsɪnjuˈeɪʃn/ *noun* [C,U]: *to make insinuations about sb's honesty* تلميح ، دسّ في الكلام

insipid /ɪnˈsɪpɪd/ *adj* without a strong taste, flavour or colour دون طعم : دون نكهة : باهت : لا روح فيه

insist /ɪnˈsɪst/ *verb* **1** [I,T] **insist (on sth/on doing sth)** to say or demand that you must have or do sth or that sb else must do sth: *He always insists on the best.* ○ *My parents insist that I come home by taxi.* ○ *Dick insisted on coming too.* ○ *'Have another piece of cake.' 'Oh all right, if you insist.'* يصرّ على ، يلحّ

2 [I,T] **insist (on sth)** to say firmly that sth is true (when sb does not believe you): *She insisted*

a b c d e f g h i j k l m n o p q r s t u v w x y z

on her innocence. ○ *James insisted that the accident wasn't his fault.* يصرّ على ؛ يتمسّك برأيه
▸ **insistent** /-ənt/ *adj* saying or demanding that you must have or do sth or that sb else must do sth: *Grandma was most insistent that we should all be there.* ○ *(figurative) We could not ignore the insistent ringing of the telephone.* مصرّ على ، ملحّ
insistence /-əns/ *noun* [U] إصرار ، إلحاح ، تمسّك بالرأي
insistently *adv* بإصرار ؛ بإلحاح ؛ بعناد

insolent /ˈɪnsələnt/ *adj (formal)* rude or impolite: *The school cannot tolerate such insolent behaviour.* وقح
▸ **insolence** /-əns/ *noun* [U] وقاحة
insolently *adv* بوقاحة

insoluble /ɪnˈsɒljəbl/ *adj* **1** impossible to dissolve in a liquid غير قابل للإنحلال
2 not able to be explained or solved: *We faced almost insoluble problems.* (مشكلة) لا حلّ لها

insomnia /ɪnˈsɒmniə/ *noun* [U] inability to sleep أَرَق

inspect /ɪnˈspekt/ *verb* [T] **1 inspect sb/sth (for sth)** to look at sth closely or in great detail: *The detective inspected the room for fingerprints.* يفحص ، يعاين
2 to make an official visit to make sure that rules are being obeyed, work is being done properly, etc: *All food shops should be inspected regularly.* يفتّش
▸ **inspection** /ɪnˈspekʃn/ *noun* [C,U]: *The fire prevention service carries out inspections of all public buildings.* ○ *On inspection, the passport turned out to be false.* فحص ، تمحيص ؛ تفتيش

inspector /ɪnˈspektə(r)/ *noun* [C] **1** an official who inspects(2) sth: *Keep your bus ticket. An inspector may ask to see it.* ○ *a health and safety inspector* مفتّش ؛ مراقب
2 a police officer of middle rank ضابط شرطة

inspiration /ˌɪnspəˈreɪʃn/ *noun* **1** [C,U] **inspiration (to/for sb); inspiration (to do sth)** (a person or thing that causes) a feeling of wanting and being able to do sth good, create a work of art, etc: *The beauty of the mountains was a great source of inspiration to the writer.* ○ *Her example has been an inspiration to many younger women.* مصدر وحي ، مبعث إلهام ؛ وحي، إلهام
2 [C] *(informal)* a (sudden) good idea: *I've had an inspiration – why don't we all go?* فكرة نيّرة (مفاجئة) ؛ وحي

inspire /ɪnˈspaɪə(r)/ *verb* [T] **1** to give sb a feeling of wanting and being able to do sth good, create a work of art, etc: *His novel was inspired by his relationship with his first wife.* يوحي إلى ، يلهم
2 inspire sb (with sth); inspire sth (in sb) to make sb feel, think, etc. sth: *The guide's nervous manner did not inspire much confidence in us.* ○ *to be inspired with enthusiasm* يوحي بِ ، يشعِر بِ ؛ يلهِب
▸ **inspired** *adj* influenced or helped by a particular feeling, thing or person: *The pianist gave an inspired performance.* ○ *a politically inspired killing* ○ *I didn't know the answer. It was just an inspired guess.* ℹ The opposite is **uninspired**. موحى، مستلهم؛ موعز به، ملهَم
inspiring /ɪnˈspaɪərɪŋ/ *adj*: *I'm afraid it was not a very inspiring speech.* ℹ The opposite is **uninspiring**. مبدع ؛ مشجّع

instability /ˌɪnstəˈbɪləti/ *noun* [U] the state of being likely to change: *There are growing signs of political instability.* ℹ The adjective is **unstable**. عدم استقرار

⚷ **install** (*US also* **instal**) /ɪnˈstɔːl/ *verb* [T] **1** to put a piece of equipment, etc. in place so that it is ready to be used: *We are waiting to have our new washing machine installed.* يركّب
2 put sb/sth or yourself in a position or place: *He was installed as President yesterday.* ○ *She installed herself in a deckchair for the afternoon.* ينصّب ؛ يضع ، يجلس
▸ **installation** /ˌɪnstəˈleɪʃn/ *noun* [C,U] تركيب ؛ تنصيب

instalment (*US* **installment**) /ɪnˈstɔːlmənt/ *noun* [C] **1** a single part of a book, television show, etc. that is published or shown regularly over a period of time: *Don't miss next week's exciting instalment.* فصل أو حلقة في مسلسل
2 one of the regular payments that you make for sth. People buy sth in instalments when they do not want to pay the whole amount at once. دفعة ، قسط

⚷ **instance** /ˈɪnstəns/ *noun* [C] an example or case (of sth): *There have been several instances of racial attacks in the area.* ○ *In most instances the drug has no side effects.* حالة
IDM for instance for example: *There are several interesting places to visit around here – Dorchester, for instance.* مثال ؛ مثَلاً

instant¹ /ˈɪnstənt/ *adj* **1** happening suddenly or at once; immediate: *The film was an instant success.* ○ *A new government cannot bring about instant change.* فوري
2 (used about food) able to be prepared quickly and easily, usually by adding hot water: *instant coffee* (طعام) سريع التحضير
▸ **instantly** *adv* at once; immediately: *I asked him a question and he replied instantly.* فوراً ، رأساً

instant² /ˈɪnstənt/ *noun* [usually sing.] **1** a particular point in time: *At that instant I realized I had been tricked.* ○ *Stop doing that this instant!* (= now) لحظة
2 a very short period of time: *Alex thought for an instant and then agreed.* هنيهة

instantaneous /ˌɪnstənˈteɪniəs/ *adj* happening at once or immediately فوري
▸ **instantaneously** *adv* فوراً ، توّاً

⚷ **instead** /ɪnˈsted/ *adv* in the place of sb/sth: *I couldn't go so my husband went instead.* ○ *There's nothing on at the cinema, let's go to the concert instead.* بدلاً من ، عوضاً عن

in'stead of *prep* in the place of: *You should play football instead of just watching it on TV.* ○ *Could I come at 8.00 instead of 7.30?* بدلاً من ، عوضاً عن

instigate /ˈɪnstɪɡeɪt/ *verb* [T] (*formal*) to make sth start to happen يحرّض ، يحثّ
▸ **instigation** /ˌɪnstɪˈɡeɪʃn/ *noun* [U] تحريض ، حثّ

instil (*US* **instill**) /ɪnˈstɪl/ *verb* [T] (instilling; instilled) **instil sth (in/into sb)** to make sb think or feel sth: *Parents should try to instil a sense of responsibility into their children.* يغرس ، يُشرّب ، يلقّن

instinct /ˈɪnstɪŋkt/ *noun* [C,U] the natural force that causes a person or animal to behave in a certain way without thinking or learning about it: *Birds learn to fly by instinct.* ○ *I didn't stop to think. I just acted on instinct.* غريزة ، فطرة ، بديهة
▸ **instinctive** /ɪnˈstɪŋktɪv/ *adj*: *Your instinctive reaction is to run from danger.* غريزي ، فطري ، بديهي
instinctively *adv* بالغريزة ، بالبديهة

institute[1] /ˈɪnstɪtjuːt; *US* -tuːt/ *noun* [C] (a building that contains) an academic society or organization: *the Institute of Science and Technology* معهد

institute[2] /ˈɪnstɪtjuːt; *US* -tuːt/ *verb* [T] (*formal*) to set up or start a system, course of action, etc: *The government has instituted a new scheme for youth training.* ينشئ ، يؤسّس

institution /ˌɪnstɪˈtjuːʃn; *US* -tuːʃn/ *noun* [C]
1 a large organization such as a bank, a university, etc: *the financial institutions in the City of London* مؤسسة ؛ هيئة
2 a building where certain people with special needs live and are looked after: *a mental institution* (= a hospital for the mentally ill) دار (لأغراض معيّنة) ؛ مصحّ (للأمراض العقلية)
3 a social custom or habit that has existed for a long time: *the institution of marriage* عرف ، تقليد
▸ **institutional** /-ʃənl/ *adj* connected with an institution (1,2,3): *The old lady is in need of institutional care.* (عناية) من مؤسّسة مختصة

instruct /ɪnˈstrʌkt/ *verb* [T] **1 instruct sb (in sth)** (*formal*) to teach: *Children must be instructed in road safety before they are allowed to ride a bike on the road.* يعلّم ، يدرّس
2 instruct sb (to do sth) to give an order to sb; to tell sb to do sth: *The soldiers were instructed to shoot above the heads of the crowd.* يعطي تعليمات ؛ يبلغ
▸ **instructor** *noun* [C] a person who teaches (usually not in a school): *a driving instructor* معلّم ، مدرّب

instruction /ɪnˈstrʌkʃn/ *noun* **1** [U] **instruction (in sth)** teaching or being taught: *The staff need instruction in the use of computers.* تعليم ، تدريب
2 [C] an order or direction that tells you what to do or how to do sth: *The guard was under strict instructions not to let anyone in or out.* ○ *The instruction you gave was confusing.* أمر ؛ إرشاد
3 instructions [plural] information on how you should use sth, do sth, etc: *Read the instructions on the back of the packet carefully.* ○ *to follow the instructions* تعليمات ، إرشادات

instructive /ɪnˈstrʌktɪv/ *adj* giving useful information يحوي معلومات مفيدة

instrument /ˈɪnstrəmənt/ *noun* [C] **1** a tool that is used for doing a particular job or task: *surgical instruments* ➲ Look at the note at **tool**. أداة ، آلة ؛ وسيلة
2 something that is used for measuring speed, fuel levels, etc. in a car, plane or ship: *the instrument panel of a plane* عدّاد
3 something that is used for playing music: *'What instrument do you play?' 'The violin.'* آلة موسيقية

Musical instruments may be **stringed** (*violins, guitars, etc.*), **brass** (*horns, trumpets, etc.*) or **woodwind** (*flutes, clarinets, etc.*). **Percussion** instruments include *drums* and *cymbals*.

instrumental /ˌɪnstrəˈmentl/ *adj* **1** (not before a noun) **instrumental in doing sth** helping to make sth happen: *She was instrumental in getting him the job.* له دور فعال
2 for musical instruments without voices: *instrumental music* (لحن) معدّ للآلات الموسيقية (وليس للغناء)

insubordinate /ˌɪnsəˈbɔːdɪnət/ *adj* (*formal*) (used about a person or behaviour) not obedient; not easily controlled عاص ، متمرّد
▸ **insubordination** /ˌɪnsəˌbɔːdɪˈneɪʃn/ *noun* [U] عصيان ، تمرّد

insubstantial /ˌɪnsəbˈstænʃl/ *adj* not large, solid or strong; not substantial: *a hut built of insubstantial materials* ○ *an insubstantial meal* واهٍ ، ضعيف ؛ (وجبة) خفيفة وصغيرة

insufferable /ɪnˈsʌfrəbl/ *adj* (*formal*) (used about a person or behaviour) extremely unpleasant or annoying لا يطاق ، لا يحتمل
▸ **insufferably** /-əbli/ *adv* بشكل لا يحتمل

insufficient /ˌɪnsəˈfɪʃnt/ *adj* **insufficient (for sth/to do sth)** not enough; not sufficient: *The students complained that they were given insufficient time for the test.* غير كافٍ

insular /ˈɪnsjələ(r); *US* -sələr/ *adj* not interested in, or able to accept new people or different ideas منعزل فكرياً ، ضيّق الأفق
▸ **insularity** /ˌɪnsjuˈlærəti; *US* -səˈl-/ *noun* [U] ضيق الأفق ، تعصّب

insulate /ˈɪnsjuleɪt; *US* -səl-/ *verb* [T] to protect or cover sth with a material that prevents electricity, heat or sound from passing through: *You can save a lot of money on heating if your house is well insulated.* يعزل
▸ **insulation** /ˌɪnsjuˈleɪʃn; *US* -səˈl-/ *noun* [U]
1 the material used for insulating sth مادة عازلة
2 the process of insulating or the state of being insulated: *Foam rubber provides good insulation.* عَزْل

insulin /ˈɪnsjəlɪn; *US* -səl-/ *noun* [U] a substance, normally produced by the body itself, which controls the amount of sugar absorbed into the

a b c d e f g h i j k l m n o p q r s t u v w x y z

blood: *a diabetic relying on insulin injections* انسولين

insult /ɪn'sʌlt/ *verb* [T] to speak or act rudely to sb: *I felt very insulted when I didn't even get an answer to my letter.* يهين : يشتم، يسبّ
▶ **insult** /'ɪnsʌlt/ *noun* [C] a rude remark or action: *The drivers were standing in the road yelling insults at each other.* ○ *Some television advertisements are an insult to people's intelligence.* إهانة ، شتيمة
insulting *adj* rude: *A lot of women find his manner quite insulting.* مهين

insuperable /ɪn'su:pərəbl; *Brit also* -'sju:-/ *adj* (*formal*) (used about a problem, etc.) impossible to solve or overcome لا يُذلَّل ، لا يقهر ، (مشكلة) لا حلّ لها

insurance /ɪn'ʃʊərəns; *US* -'ʃɔ:r-/ *noun* **1** [U] **insurance (against sth)** a contract in which, in return for regular payment, a company or the state agrees to pay a sum of money if sth (e.g. illness, death, loss of or damage to property) happens to sb: *Our roof was blown off in the storm but we claimed for it on the insurance.* ○ *Builders should always have insurance against personal injury.* تأمين : ضمان

We **take out** an **insurance policy**. An **insurance premium** is the regular amount you pay to the insurance company. We can take out **life**, **health**, **car**, **travel** and **household insurance**.

2 [U] the business of providing insurance contracts: *He works in insurance.* (شركة) تأمين ، التأمين/الضمان

3 [sing.] **an insurance (against sth)** something you do to protect yourself (against sth unpleasant): *Many people take vitamin pills as an insurance against illness.* وقاية ، احتياط

insure /ɪn'ʃʊə(r); *US* ɪn'ʃʊər/ *verb* [T] **1 insure sb/sth (against sth)** to take out or to provide insurance: *They insured the painting for £10 000 against damage or theft.* ○ *Are you insured against accident and medical expenses on your trip?* يؤمّن

2 (*US*) = ENSURE

insurmountable /,ɪnsə'maʊntəbl/ *adj* (*formal*) (used about a problem, etc.) impossible to solve or overcome لا يُذلّل ، لا يقهر ، (مشكلة) لا حلّ لها

insurrection /,ɪnsə'rekʃn/ *noun* [C,U] (*formal*) violent action against the rulers of a country or the government تمرّد ، عصيان مسلّح

intact /ɪn'tækt/ *adj* (not before a noun) complete; not damaged: *Very few of the buildings remained intact after the earthquake.* سليم ، على حاله الأصلية

intake /'ɪnteɪk/ *noun* [C, usually sing.] **1** (used about food, liquid, air, etc.) the amount that sb/sth takes in or the process of taking it in: *The patient needs to increase his intake of fluid.* كمية الطعام أو الشراب المتناولة

2 the (number of) people who enter an organization or institution during a certain period عدد الملتحقين

intangible /ɪn'tændʒəbl/ *adj* (used about a quality or an idea) difficult to describe, understand or measure; not tangible غير ملموس : يصعب وصفه ، يصعب فهمه

integral /'ɪntɪgrəl/ *adj* essential (in order to make sth complete): *Spending a year in France is an integral part of the university course.* أساسي : متمِّم

integrate /'ɪntɪgreɪt/ *verb* **1** [I,T] **integrate (sb) (into sth/with sth)** to join in and become part of a group or community or to make sb do this: *The government has various schemes to help integrate immigrants into their local communities.* ➲ Look at **segregate**. يَدخل في ، يُشرك : يدمج : يندمج

2 [T] **integrate sth (into sth)**; **integrate A and B/integrate A with B** to join things so that they become one thing or fit together: *The two small schools were integrated to form one larger school.* يدمج
▶ **integration** /,ɪntɪ'greɪʃn/ *noun* [U]: *racial integration* ➲ Look at **segregation**. اندماج عنصري

integrity /ɪn'tegrəti/ *noun* [U] the quality of being honest; firmness of character and moral ideas: *He's a person of great integrity.* استقامة ، نزاهة

intellect /'ɪntəlekt/ *noun* [C,U] the power of the mind to think and to learn العقل ، الفكر ، الذهن

intellectual /,ɪntə'lektʃuəl/ *adj* (only *before* a noun) using or able to use the power of the mind: *The boy's intellectual development was very advanced for his age.* ○ *intellectual people, interests, discussions, etc.* فكري ، ذهني
▶ **intellectual** *noun* [C] a person who is interested in ideas, literature, art, etc: *The cafe was a well-known meeting place for artists and intellectuals.* مفكِّر : مثقَّف
intellectually /,ɪntə'lektʃuəli/ *adv* فكرياً ، نظرياً

intelligence /ɪn'telɪdʒəns/ *noun* [U] **1** the ability to understand, learn and think: *Examinations are not necessarily the best way to measure intelligence.* ○ *a person of normal intelligence* ○ *an intelligence test* ذكاء

2 important information about an enemy country: *to receive intelligence about sb* استخبارات ، تجسّس
▶ **intelligent** /-dʒənt/ *adj* having or showing intelligence; clever: *All their children are very intelligent.* ○ *an intelligent question* ❶ The opposite is **unintelligent**. ذكي : دالّ على الذكاء
intelligently *adv* بشكل يدل على المعرفة أو عمق الفهم؛ بحكمة، بفطنة

intelligible /ɪn'telɪdʒəbl/ *adj* (used especially about speech or writing) possible or easy to understand ❶ The opposite is **unintelligible**. سهل الفهم

intend /ɪn'tend/ *verb* [T] **1** to plan or mean to do sth: *I'm afraid I spent more money than I had intended.* ○ *I intended to telephone but I completely forgot.* ○ *They had intended staying in Wales for two weeks but the weather was so bad that they left* *after one.* ○ *I certainly don't intend to wait here all day!* ❶ The noun is **intention**. ينوي ، يعتزم

2 intend sth for sb/sth; intend sb to do sth to plan, mean or make sth for a particular person or purpose: *You shouldn't have read that letter – it wasn't intended for you.* ○ *This dictionary is intended for intermediate learners of English.* ○ *I didn't intend you to have all the work.* يقصد ، يعني ، يعِدّ لِ

intense /ɪn'tens/ *adj* very great, strong or serious: *intense heat* ○ *intense anger* ○ *an intense* (= very serious) *young man* شديد ، عنيف : جدّي جداً

▸ **intensely** *adv*: *They obviously dislike each other intensely.* بشدّة ، بعنف : إلى حدّ كبير

intensify /ɪn'tensɪfaɪ/ *verb* (*pres part* **intensifying**; *3rd pers sing pres* **intensifies**; *pt, pp* **intensified**) [I,T] to become or to make sth greater or stronger: [T]: *The government has intensified its anti-smoking campaign.* يشدِّد ، يقوِّي : يشتدّ

intensity /-səti/ *noun* [U]: *I wasn't prepared for the intensity of his reaction to the news.* شدّة ، حدّة

intensive /ɪn'tensɪv/ *adj* concentrated on a particular activity or area within a limited amount of time: *an intensive investigation* ○ *The course only lasted a week but it was very intensive.* مركَّز ، مكثَّف

▸ **intensively** *adv* بغزارة : بشدّة

in,tensive 'care *noun* [U] special care for patients who are very seriously ill or injured (or the department that gives this care): *I'm afraid your son's been seriously hurt and he's in intensive care.* عناية مشدّدة

intent /ɪn'tent/ *adj* **1** showing great attention: *He listened to the whole story with an intent expression on his face.* مهتمّ ، مركِّز

2 intent on/upon sth/doing sth determined to do sth or concentrating on sth: *He's always been intent on making a lot of money.* ○ *She was so intent upon her work that she didn't hear me come in.* مصمّم : منكبّ على

▸ **intently** *adv* بِحدّة : باهتمام وتركيز

intention /ɪn'tenʃn/ *noun* [C,U] what sb intends or means to do; a plan or purpose: *It's still not clear what his intentions are when he leaves university.* ○ *Our intention was to leave early in the morning.* ○ *I've got no intention of staying indoors on a nice sunny day like this.* قصْد ، نيّة : هدف

intentional /ɪn'tenʃənl/ *adj* done on purpose, not by chance: *I'm sorry I took your jacket – it wasn't intentional!* ❶ The opposite is **unintentional**. ➲ Look at **deliberate**[1]. It is similar in meaning. متعمَّد ، مقصود

▸ **intentionally** /-ʃənəli/ *adv*: *I can't believe the boys broke the window intentionally.* عَمْداً ، عن قصد

interact /,ɪntər'ækt/ *verb* [I] **1** (used about people) to communicate or mix in a way that has an influence or effect on sb else: *He is studying the way children interact with each other at different ages.* يعامل أو يختلط بالآخرين

2 (of two things) to have an effect on each other يتفاعل

▸ **interaction** /-'ækʃn/ *noun* [C,U] (an example of) co-operation or mixing: *An interaction of two chemicals produced the explosion.* ○ *There is a need for greater interaction among the different departments.* تفاعل : تمازج ، اختلاط

interactive /-'æktɪv/ *adj* **1** that involves people working together and having an influence on each other: *interactive language-learning techniques* تفاعلي

2 (used about computers) involving or allowing direct two-way communication between the computer and the person using it: *interactive computer games* متفاعل : (لعبة) بين الكمبيوتر واللاعب

intercept /,ɪntə'sept/ *verb* [T] to stop or catch sb or sth that is moving from one place to another: *Detectives intercepted him at the airport.* يوقف : يعترض طريقه

▸ **interception** /,ɪntə'sepʃn/ *noun* [C,U] إيقاف : تصدٍ، إنصات خلْسة (لمحادثة لاسلكية)

interchangeable /,ɪntə'tʃeɪndʒəbl/ *adj* able to be used in place of each other without making any difference: *Are these two words interchangeable?* قابل للتبادل مع آخر ، يمكن أن يحلّ محل الآخر

▸ **interchangeably** *adv* مرادفاً لِ : بحيث يمكن استبداله

intercom /'ɪntəkɒm/ *noun* [C] a system of microphones and loudspeakers for communication between people in different parts of a factory, plane, etc: *Please try to contact Mr Pearson on/over the intercom.* شبكة اتصال داخلية ، "انتركوم"

interconnect /,ɪntəkə'nekt/ *verb* [I] to be connected or linked يرتبط

▸ **interconnected** /-tɪd/ *adj* متّصلون مع بعض

intercontinental /,ɪntə,kɒntɪ'nentl/ *adj* between continents: *intercontinental flights* بين القارات : عابر للقارات

intercourse /'ɪntəkɔ:s/ *noun* [U] = SEX (3)

interdependent /,ɪntədɪ'pendənt/ *adj* depending on each other: *Exercise and good health are generally interdependent.* يتوقف كلٌ منهما على الآخر ، معتمدان على بعضهما

▸ **interdependence** /-əns/ *noun* [U] اعتماد كلٍّ على الآخر

interest[1] /'ɪntrəst/ *noun* **1** [U, sing.] **an interest (in sb/sth)** a desire to learn or hear more about sb/sth or to be involved with sb/sth: *She's begun to show a great interest in politics.* ○ *I wish he'd take more interest in his children.* ○ *Don't lose interest now!* اهتمام : رغبة

2 [C] something that you enjoy doing or learning about: *When applying for a job you often have to state your interests and hobbies.* موضوع اهتمام : عمل محبّب

3 [U] the quality that makes sb curious or attracts sb's attention: *I thought this article might be of interest to you.* مثير للاهتمام

4 [C] something that gives a benefit, profit or advantage to sb: *We have your interests at heart.* منفعة ، مصلحة

5 [C] a legal right to share in a business, etc,

a b c d e f g h **i** j k l m n o p q r s t u v w x y z

especially in its profits: *When he retired he sold his interests in the company.* حق أو أسهم في الأرباح

6 [U] **interest (on sth)** the money that you earn from investments or that you pay for borrowing money: *If you invest your capital wisely it will earn a lot of interest.* ○ *We pay 6% interest on our mortgage at the moment.* ○ *The interest rate has never been so high/low.* ○ *Some companies offer interest-free loans.* فائدة : ربح

IDM in sb's interest(s) to sb's advantage: *Using lead-free petrol is in the public interest.* مصلحة

in the interest(s) of sth in order to achieve or protect sth: *In the interest(s) of safety, please fasten your seat belts.* من أجل (مصلحة) ، حفاظاً على...

interest² /ˈɪntrəst/ *verb* [T] **1** to make sb want to learn or hear more about sth or to become involved in sth: *The subject of the talk was one that interests me greatly.* يثير الاهتمام

2 to make sb want to buy, have or do sth: *Can I interest you in our new brochure?* يرغّب

▸ **interested** /-tɪd/ *adj* **1** (not before a noun) **interested (in sth/sb)** wanting to know or hear about sth/sb; or to do or achieve sth: *They weren't interested in my news at all!* ○ *I was interested to hear that you've got a new job. Where is it?* ❶ The opposite is **uninterested**. مهتم

> If you like what you are doing, and want to know or hear more, then you are **interested** in it. The person or thing that makes you feel like this is **interesting**.

2 (only *before* a noun) involved in or affected by (a particular situation, etc.): *I think they should have talked to the interested parties* (= people, groups, etc.) *before they made that decision.* ❶ The opposite is **disinterested**. مشترك ، ذو علاقة ، (الأطراف) المعنيّة

interesting *adj* enjoyable and entertaining to do, think about, talk to, etc.; holding your attention: *an interesting person, book, idea, job, etc.* ○ *It's always interesting to hear about the customs and traditions of other societies.* ❶ The opposite is **uninteresting**. شيّق ، طريف ، ممتع

interestingly *adv* بتشويق : من الطريف أن...

interfere /ˌɪntəˈfɪə(r)/ *verb* [I] **1 interfere (in sth)** to try to take part in sb's affairs, etc. when you and your help are not wanted: *You shouldn't interfere – let your children make their own decisions.* يتداخل ، يتدخّل

2 interfere (with sb/sth) to prevent sth or slow down the progress that sb/sth makes: *Every time the telephone rings it interferes with my work.* يعرقل ، يشوّش

3 interfere (with sth) to touch or alter sth without permission: *Many people feel that scientists shouldn't interfere with nature.* يتدخّل

▸ **interference** /ˌɪntəˈfɪərəns/ *noun* [U] **1 interference (in/with sth)** the act of interfering: *I left home because I couldn't stand my parents' interference in my affairs.* تدخّل

2 noise that prevents the clear reception of radio, television or telephone signals (because of other signals or bad weather) تشويش (إذاعي)

interfering *adj* involving yourself in other people's affairs when you are not wanted متدخّل (في شؤون الآخرين)

interim /ˈɪntərɪm/ *noun*

IDM in the interim in the time between two things happening فاصل زمني ، فترة ، (في) غضون (ذلك)

▸ **interim** *adj* (only *before* a noun) not final or lasting: *an interim arrangement* (= before sth definite can be decided) موقّت

interior /ɪnˈtɪəriə(r)/ *noun* **1** [C, usually sing.] the inner part; inside: *I'd love to see the interior of the castle.* ○ *interior walls* (= ones that are in the inside of a building) ❶ The opposite is **exterior**. داخل المبنى : الداخل

2 the interior [sing.] the part of a country or continent that is not near the coast داخل البلاد

inˌterior deˈsigner *noun* [C] a person whose job is to choose colours, furniture, carpets, etc. to decorate the inside of a house مصمم ديكور

interjection /ˌɪntəˈdʒekʃn/ *noun* [C] **1** (*formal*) something you say that interrupts sb else عبارة تقاطع حديث شخص آخر

2 (*grammar*) a word or phrase that is used as an expression of surprise, pain, pleasure, etc. (e.g. Oh!, Hurray! or Wow!) ➲ Look at **exclamation**. عبارة تدلّ على التعجّب أو الاستحسان أو الألم الخ...

interlude /ˈɪntəluːd/ *noun* [C] a short period of time when an entertainment or activity stops for a break; an interval: *There will now be a 20-minute interlude.* فترة استراحة

intermarry /ˌɪntəˈmæri/ *verb* (*pres part* **intermarrying**; *3rd pers sing pres* **intermarries**; *pt, pp* **intermarried**) [I] (used about people of different races, religions, etc.) to marry each other يتزوج من دين أو عرق آخر

▸ **intermarriage** /ˌɪntəˈmærɪdʒ/ *noun* [U] marriage between people of different races, religions, etc. زواج مختلط

intermediary /ˌɪntəˈmiːdiəri; *US* -dieri/ *noun* [C] (*pl.* **intermediaries**) a person who passes communications between two people or groups, usually in order to help them reach an agreement وسيط

intermediate /ˌɪntəˈmiːdiət/ *adj* **1** coming between two people or things in position, level, etc. في الوسط ، بين الاثنين

2 between two stages (elementary and advanced): *an intermediate student, class, course, book, level, etc.* متوسّط

interminable /ɪnˈtɜːmɪnəbl/ *adj* going on for a very long time or for too long (يبدو وكأنه) لا نهاية له ، طويل وممل

▸ **interminably** /-əbli/ *adv* بشكل لا حدّ له

intermission /ˌɪntəˈmɪʃn/ *noun* [C] (*especially US*) an interval in a film, play, etc. فترة استراحة

intermittent /ˌɪntəˈmɪtənt/ *adj* stopping for a while and then starting again: *There will be intermittent showers.* متقطّع

▸ **intermittently** *adv* بشكل متقطّع

intern¹ /ɪnˈtɜːn/ *verb* [T] (*formal*) to keep sb in

prison for political reasons, especially during a war يعتقل، يحتجز

▶ **internment** *noun* [U] اعتقال

intern² (*also* **interne**) /ˈɪntɜːn/ *noun* [C] (*US*)
1 an advanced student of medicine, whose training is nearly finished and who is working in a hospital to get further practical experience طبيب امتياز (طبيب تحت التدريب)

2 a student or new graduate who is getting practical experience in a job, for example during the summer holiday متدرب

internal /ɪnˈtɜːnl/ *adj* **1** of or on the inside (of a place, person or object): *He was rushed to hospital with internal injuries.* داخلي : باطني

2 (used about political or economic affairs) inside a country; not abroad: *a country's internal affairs* داخلي

3 happening or existing inside a particular organization: *an internal examination* (= one arranged and marked inside a particular school or college) (امتحان مثلاً) تجريه المؤسسة نفسها

ℹ The opposite for all senses is **external**.

▶ **internally** /-nəli/ *adv* on the inside: *This medicine is not to be taken internally* (= not swallowed). داخلياً: عن طريق المعدة

international /ˌɪntəˈnæʃnəl/ *adj* involving two or more countries: *an international agreement, flight, football match, etc.* ○ *international trade, law, etc.* دولي

▶ **international** *noun* [C] a sports match between teams from two different countries or a player in such a match مباراة دولية ، لاعب دولي

internationally /-nəli/ *adv* عالمياً

Internet /ˈɪntənet/ **the Internet** *noun* [sing.] a network that links computers around the whole world ➲ Look also at **ISP**.

انترنت: شبكة الكمبيوتر الدولية

internment *noun* → INTERN¹

interpret /ɪnˈtɜːprɪt/ *verb* **1** [T] **interpret sth (as sth)** to explain or understand the meaning of sth: *I don't know how to interpret his behaviour.* ○ *How would you interpret this part of the poem?* يفسِّر، يؤوِّل

2 [I] to translate what sb is saying into another language: *He'll need somebody to interpret for him.* يترجم (شفوياً)

▶ **interpretation** /ɪnˌtɜːprɪˈteɪʃn/ *noun* [C,U]
1 an explanation or understanding of sth: *He's always putting a wrong interpretation on what I say* (= understanding it wrongly). *What's your interpretation of these statistics?* تفسير، تأويل، فهم

2 the way an actor or musician chooses to perform or understand a character or piece of music: *a modern interpretation of 'Hamlet'* تفهُّم الفنان لدور وأداؤه له

interpreter *noun* [C] a person whose job is to translate what sb is saying immediately into another language: *The president spoke through an interpreter.* ➲ Look at **translator**.

مترجم (شفوياً)

interrelate /ˌɪntərɪˈleɪt/ *verb* [I,T] (usually passive) (*formal*) (used about two or more things) to connect or be connected very closely so that they have an effect on each other

(شيئان) يؤثِّران على بعضهما

▶ **interrelated** *adj* connected with each other مرتبطان ، مترابطان

interrogate /ɪnˈterəgeɪt/ *verb* [T] **interrogate sb (about sth)** to ask sb questions in a thorough and sometimes aggressive way (in order to get information): *The prisoner was interrogated for six hours.* يستجوب ، يحقِّق مع

▶ **interrogation** /ɪnˌterəˈgeɪʃn/ *noun* [C,U] the time when a person is interrogated: *The interrogations took place in a small underground room.* [U]: *The prisoner broke down under interrogation and confessed.* استجواب ، تحقيق

interrogator *noun* [C] a person who interrogates محقِّق ، مستنْطق

interrogative /ˌɪntəˈrɒgətɪv/ *adj* (*grammar*) having the form of a question: *We use 'any' in an interrogative or negative sentence.*

في صيغة الاستفهام ، استفهامي

▶ **interrogative** *noun* [C] (*grammar*) a word used for asking a question: *'Who', 'what' and 'where' are interrogatives.* عبارة استفهام

interrupt /ˌɪntəˈrʌpt/ *verb* **1** [I,T] **interrupt (sb/sth) (with sth)** to make sb stop speaking or doing sth by saying or doing sth yourself: *I'm sorry to interrupt but there's a phone call for you.* ○ *He kept interrupting me with silly questions.*

يُقاطِع

2 [T] to stop sth or make a break in it: *The programme was interrupted by an important news flash.* يقطع ، يوقِف

▶ **interruption** /ˌɪntəˈrʌpʃn/ *noun* **1** [C] something that prevents an activity or situation continuing: *I've had so many interruptions this morning that I've done nothing!* شيء معيق

2 [U] the act of interrupting sb/sth: *She spoke for 20 minutes without interruption.* مقاطعة

intersect /ˌɪntəˈsekt/ *verb* **1** [I,T] (used about roads, lines, etc.) to meet and go across each other يتقاطع مع : يقطع

2 [T] (usually passive) to divide sth by going across it: *The fields were intersected by hedges and streams.* يقسم ، يجزِّئ

▶ **intersection** /ˌɪntəˈsekʃn/ *noun* [C] the place where two or more roads, lines, etc. meet and cross each other: *a dangerous intersection*

نقطة تقاطع: ملتقى طرق

intersperse /ˌɪntəˈspɜːs/ *verb* [T] (usually passive) to put things at various points in sth: *His speech was interspersed with jokes.*

ينثر أو يوزِّع هنا وهناك : (خطاب) تخلَّلته (النكات)

interval /ˈɪntəvl/ *noun* [C] **1** a period of time between two events: *There was a long interval between sending the letter and getting a reply.* ○ *I hope we'll have a few sunny intervals between the showers!* فاصل ، فترة

2 a short break between the parts of a play, film, concert, etc: *There will be two 15-minute intervals when the bar will be open.*

استراحة قصيرة (بين فصول المسرحية مثلاً)

a b c d e f g h i j k l m n o p q r s t u v w x y z

Some words that have a similar meaning to interval are **intermission**, **break**, **recess** and **pause**. In British English we use **interval** for a break in a performance. The US word is **intermission.** A **break** is especially used in connection with periods of work or study e.g. **a lunch/tea break** in an office, factory or school: *The children play outside in the breaks at school.* ○ *You've worked so hard you've earned a break.* In US English a break at school is called **(a) recess.** In British English **recess** is a longer period of time when work or business stops, especially in Parliament or the law courts: *Parliament is in recess.* ○ *the summer recess.* A **pause** is a short temporary stop in action or speech: *After a moment's pause, she answered.*

IDM **at intervals** with time or with spaces between: *I always write home at regular intervals.* ○ *The trees should be planted at two-metre intervals.* من وقت لآخر ؛ فاصل أو مسافة

intervene /ˌɪntəˈviːn/ *verb* [I] **1 intervene (in sth/between A and B)** to act in a way that prevents sth happening or influences the result of sth: *The police had to intervene between the two groups.* ○ *to intervene in a dispute* يتدخّل

2 to say sth that interrupts sb who is speaking: *'Wait a minute,' he intervened.* يقاطع (كلام المتحدِّث)

3 (used about events, etc.) to happen in the meantime or to delay sth: *If no further problems intervene we should be able to finish in time.* يطرأ (خلال ذلك الوقت) ، يعترض

4 (used about time) to come between: *During the months that intervened they wrote to each other nearly every day.* (زمن) يتخلّل

▸ **intervening** *adj* (only *before* a noun) coming or existing between (two events, dates, objects, etc.): *the intervening years* واقع بين (حادثتين أو شيئين)

intervention /ˌɪntəˈvenʃn/ *noun* [C,U] an act of intervening, especially to prevent sth happening: *military intervention in the crisis* تدخّل

⚷ **interview** /ˈɪntəvjuː/ *noun* [C] **1** a meeting at which sb is asked questions to find out if he/she is suitable for a job: *Interviews will be held on June 10th.* ○ *You are invited to attend an interview for the position of assistant sales manager.* مقابلة

2 a meeting at which a journalist asks sb questions in order to find out his/her opinion, etc. (often shown on television or printed in a newspaper): *There was an interview with the Prime Minister on television last night.* ○ *The actress refused to give an interview.* حديث صحفي

▸ **interview** *verb* [T] **1 interview sb (for sth)** to ask sb questions in an interview (to find out if he/she is suitable for a job, etc.): *How many applicants did you interview for the job?* يجري مقابلة

2 interview sb (about sth) (used about a reporter, etc.) to ask sb questions in an interview (to find out his/her opinions, etc.) يجري حديثاً صحفياً

interviewee /ˌɪntəvjuːˈiː/ *noun* [C] a person who is questioned in an interview الشخص المقابَل

interviewer /ˈɪntəvjuːə(r)/ *noun* [C] a person who asks the questions in an interview المقابِل أي من يسأل الأسئلة في المقابلة

intestine /ɪnˈtestɪn/ *noun* [C, usually pl.] the tube in your body that carries food from your stomach الأمعاء

▸ **intestinal** /ɪnˈtestɪnl; ˌɪnteˈstaɪnl/ *adj* معويّ

intimate /ˈɪntɪmət/ *adj* **1** having a very close relationship: *They're intimate friends.* حميم

2 private and personal: *They told each other their most intimate thoughts and secrets.* خاصّ جداً وشخصيّ

3 (used about a place, an atmosphere, etc.) quiet and friendly: *I know an intimate little restaurant we could go to.* (مكان) هادئ يبعث على الراحة والدفء

4 very detailed: *He's lived here all his life and has an intimate knowledge of the area.* (معرفة) عميقة أو دقيقة جداً

▸ **intimacy** /ˈɪntɪməsi/ *noun* [U] the state of being very close: *Their intimacy grew with the years.* ألفة ، صداقة حميمة

intimately *adv* in a close or personal way (يعرفه) معرفة جيدة أو حميمة

intimidate /ɪnˈtɪmɪdeɪt/ *verb* [T] **intimidate sb (into sth/doing sth)** to frighten sb (often in order to make him/her do sth) يُرهب ، يُكرِه شخصاً على عمل ما

▸ **intimidating** *adj* frightening (because of size or difficulty) مرهب

intimidation /ɪnˌtɪmɪˈdeɪʃn/ *noun* [U]: *The rebel troops controlled the area by intimidation.* إرهاب ، تخويف ؛ تهديد

⚷ **into** /ˈɪntə; *before vowels* ˈɪntuː/ *prep* **1** moving to a position inside or in sth: *Come into the house.* ○ *I'm going into town.* إلى، إلى داخل

2 in the direction of sth: *Please speak into the microphone.* باتّجاه، إلى

3 to a point at which you hit sth: *I backed the car into a wall.* (يَصدم) بـ

4 (showing a change): *We're turning the spare room into a study.* ○ *She changed into her jeans.* ○ *The new rules will come into force next year.* (يبدِّل) إلى

5 (used when you are dividing numbers): *4 into 10 won't go.* (في عملية قسمة الأعداد): على (مثلاً عشرة على أربعة)

IDM **be into sth** to be very interested in sth (e.g. as a hobby): *I'm really into canoeing.* مولع بـ، مهتم بـ

intolerable /ɪnˈtɒlərəbl/ *adj* too bad or severe to stand or accept; not tolerable: *The living conditions were intolerable.* ○ *intolerable pain* ℹ The verb is **tolerate**. فظيع ؛ لا يطاق

▸ **intolerably** /-əbli/ *adv* بشكل لا يطاق

intolerant /ɪnˈtɒlərənt/ *adj* **intolerant (of sb/sth)** not able to accept behaviour or opinions that are different from your own; not tolerant قليل التحمّل ؛ غير متسامح

▸ **intolerance** /-əns/ *noun* [U] تعصّب، عدم تسامح

intolerantly *adv* بتعصّب

intonation /ˌɪntəˈneɪʃn/ *noun* [C,U] the rise and

fall of the level of your voice while you are speaking تغيّر طبقة الصوت اثناء الكلام

intoxicated /ɪnˈtɒksɪkeɪtɪd/ *adj* *(formal)*
1 having had too much alcohol to drink; drunk ثَمِل ، سكران ، مخمور
2 very excited: *She was intoxicated by her success.* منتشٍ، ثَمِل
▸ **intoxication** /ɪnˌtɒksɪˈkeɪʃn/ *noun* [U] سُكْر : تأثير الخمر

intranet /ˈɪntrənet/ *noun* [C] a system of computers inside an organization that makes it possible for people who work there to look at the same information and to send information to each other شبكة داخلية

intransitive /ɪnˈtrænsətɪv/ *adj* *(grammar)* (used about a verb) used without an object ❶ Intransitive verbs are marked [I] in this dictionary. (فعل) لازم
▸ **intransitively** *adv* (يستعمل) كفعل لازم

ˈin tray *(US* **ˈin box)** *noun* [C] (in an office) a container on your desk for letters that are waiting to be read or answered (البريد) الوارد

intrepid /ɪnˈtrepɪd/ *adj* *(formal)* (used about people and their actions) brave and without any fear جريء ، جسور

intricate /ˈɪntrɪkət/ *adj* having many small parts put together in a complicated way: *an intricate pattern* ○ *an intricate plot to the story* معقد : عويص
▸ **intricacy** /ˈɪntrɪkəsi/ *noun* **1 intricacies** [plural] the complicated details (of sth): *It's difficult to understand all the intricacies of the situation.* تفاصيل متشابكة
2 [U] the quality of being intricate: *I was impressed by the intricacy of the design.* تعقُّد، تشابك
intricately /-ətli/ *adv* بشكل معقّد؛ بتداخل

intrigue /ɪnˈtriːg/ *verb* [T] to make sb very interested or curious: *The idea intrigues me – tell me more!* يثير الاهتمام ، يثير الفضول
▸ **intrigue** /ˈɪntriːg; ɪnˈtriːg/ *noun* [C,U] the making of a secret plan to do sth bad: [C]: *The book is about political intrigues against the government.* دسيسة ، مكيدة
intriguing *adj* very interesting; fascinating خلّاب، ساحر : مثير للاهتمام

intrinsic /ɪnˈtrɪnsɪk; -zɪk/ *adj* (only *before* a noun) *(formal)* (used about the value or quality of sth) belonging to sth as part of its nature; basic: *The object is of no intrinsic value* (= the material it is made of is not worth anything). جوهريّ ، حقيقيّ : (قيمة الشيء) في حدّ ذاته
▸ **intrinsically** /-kli/ *adv* في حد ذاته ، في جوهره

⚷introduce /ˌɪntrəˈdjuːs; *US* -duːs/ *verb* [T]
1 introduce sb (to sb) to tell two or more people who have not met before what each others' names are so that they can get to know each other: *'Who's that girl over there?' 'Come with me and I'll introduce you to her.'* يقدّم إلى ، يعرِّف على

> In Britain, when we introduce one person to another, there are a number of different ways of doing it, depending on the occasion: *(informal) 'John, meet Mary.'* ○ *(informal) 'Mrs Smith, this is my daughter, Jane.'* ○ *(formal) 'May I introduce you. Dr Waters, this is Mr Jones. Mr Jones, Dr Waters.'* An informal response to an introduction is 'Hello' or 'Nice to meet you.' A formal response is 'How do you do?' The other person also replies: 'How do you do?' When people are introduced they often shake hands.

2 introduce yourself (to sb) to tell sb what your name is so that you can get to know him/her: *He just walked over and introduced himself to me!* يقدّم (نفسه)
3 to tell an audience the name of the person who is going to speak, perform, entertain, etc: *May I introduce my guest on the show tonight...* يقدّم (خطيباً)
4 to announce and give details of a radio or television programme: *The programme was introduced by Charles Gordon.* يقدّم
5 introduce sth (in/into sth) to bring in, use, or take sth to a place for the first time: *The new law was introduced in 2004.* يُدخل أو يستعمل شيئاً للمرة الأولى
6 introduce sb to sth to make sb begin to learn about sth or do sth for the first time: *This pamphlet will introduce you to the basic aims of our society.* يُطلع شخصاً على مبادئ (علم أو غير ذلك) ، يُعرِّف بـ

⚷introduction /ˌɪntrəˈdʌkʃn/ *noun* **1** [U] bringing in or using of sth for the first time: *the introduction of computers into the classroom* إدخال
2 [sing.] **introduction to sth** first experience of sth: *My first job – in a factory – was not a pleasant introduction to work.* مقدّمة
3 [C] the first part of a book or a talk which gives an explanation of the rest of it مقدّمة، تمهيد
4 [C] a book for people who are beginning to study a subject: *'An Introduction to English Grammar'* مدخل
5 [C] the act of telling two or more people each others' names for the first time: *I think I'll get my husband to make the introductions – he's better at remembering names!* ○ *Well, you don't need an introduction to each other, do you?* (= you already know each other) تقديم شخص لآخر

introductory /ˌɪntrəˈdʌktəri/ *adj* happening or said at the beginning in order to give a general idea of what will follow: *an introductory speech, chapter, remark, etc.* تمهيدي

introvert /ˈɪntrəvɜːt/ *noun* [C] a quiet, shy person who is concerned with his/her own thoughts or feelings ❶ The opposite is **extrovert**. انطوائي
▸ **introverted** /ˈɪntrəvɜːtɪd/ *adj* quiet and shy انطوائي

intrude /ɪnˈtruːd/ *verb* [I] **intrude (on/upon sb/sth)** to enter a place or situation without permission or when you are not wanted: *I'm sorry to intrude on your Sunday lunch but...* ○ *You're intruding – this is a private party.* يتطفّل ، يُقحم نفسه
▸ **intruder** *noun* [C] a person who enters a place

a b c d e f g h **i** j k l m n o p q r s t u v w x y z

without permission and often secretly
دخيل ، متطفّل ؛ غريب يخترق حرمة البيت

intrusion /ɪn'truːʒn/ *noun* [C,U] **intrusion (on/upon/into sth)** something that disturbs you or your life when you want to be private
تدخّل ، تطفّل ، اقتحام

▸ **intrusive** /ɪn'truːsɪv/ *adj*
متطفّل ، مقيّد لحريّة أهل البيت

intuition /ˌɪntju'ɪʃn; *US* -tuː-/ *noun* [C,U] the feeling or understanding that makes you believe or know sth without any reason or proof: *She knew, by intuition, about his illness although he never mentioned it.* بديهة ، حَدْس

▸ **intuitive** /ɪn'tjuːɪtɪv; *US* -tuː-/ *adj*
بدهيّ ، حَدْسيّ ، فطريّ

intuitively *adv* بالبديهة ، بالفطرة

Inuit /'ɪnuɪt; -nju-/ *noun* [C] (a member of) the race of people from northern Canada and parts of Alaska and Greenland
أحد سكان المنطقة المتجمدة من امريكا الشمالية وغرينلاند

inundate /'ɪnʌndeɪt/ *verb* [T] (usually passive) **1 inundate sb (with sth)** to give or send sb so many things that he/she can hardly deal with them all: *We were inundated with applications for the job.* يغرق بـ ، يغمر

2 (*formal*) to cover with water; to flood: *After the heavy rains the fields were inundated.*
يغمر ؛ يفيض على ، يجتاح

invade /ɪn'veɪd/ *verb* **1** [I,T] to enter a country with an army in order to attack, conquer it, etc: *They invaded the country with tanks and guns.*
يغزو ، يهجم على

2 [T] (usually passive) to enter in large numbers: *The whole area has been invaded by tourists.* يغزو ؛ يتدفّق على

3 [T] to come in and disturb: *Everywhere you go new motorways invade the countryside.*
يعتدي على ، ينتهك حرمة

▸ **invader** *noun* [C, usually pl.] a person or thing that invades: *They forced back the invaders.* ➲ Look at **invasion**. غازٍ ، معتدٍ

invalid¹ /'ɪnvəlɪd; 'ɪnvəliːd/ *noun* [C] a person who has been very ill for a long time and needs to be looked after by sb else: *He's been an invalid since the accident.* مريض ، عليل ، عاجز

invalid² /ɪn'vælɪd/ *adj* **1** not correct according to reason; not valid: *an invalid argument*
باطل ، غير صحيح

2 not able to be accepted by law; not valid: *I'm afraid your passport is invalid.* لاغٍ ، بطَل مفعوله

invaluable /ɪn'væljuəbl/ *adj* very useful or valuable: *The mobile library is an invaluable service to many people.* ❶ Be careful. Invaluable is not the opposite of valuable. The opposite is **valueless** or **worthless**. لا يقدّر بثمن ، نفيس

invariable /ɪn'veəriəbl/ *adj* not changing
ثابت ، لا يتغيّر

▸ **invariably** /ɪn'veəriəbli/ *adv* almost always: *She invariably arrives late.* بلا استثناء ، تقريباً دائماً

invasion /ɪn'veɪʒn/ *noun* [C,U] a time when the armed forces of one country enter another country in order to attack it: *Germany's invasion of Poland in 1939* ○ (*figurative*) *Such questions are an invasion of privacy.* ❶ The verb is **invade**.
هجوم ، غزو ، اعتداء

🔑 **invent** /ɪn'vent/ *verb* [T] **1** to think of or make sth for the first time: *Laszlo Biro invented the ballpoint pen.* ○ *When was the camera invented?* يخترع ، يبتكر

2 to make up a story, excuse, etc. that is not true: *He had invented the whole story.*
يلفق ، يختلق

▸ **inventive** /ɪn'ventɪv/ *adj* having clever and original ideas ذو فكر مبدع

inventor *noun* [C] a person who invents(1) sth for the first time مخترع

🔑 **invention** /ɪn'venʃn/ *noun* **1** [C] a thing that has been made or designed by sb for the first time: *The microwave oven is a very useful invention.* مخترع

2 [U] the act or process of making or designing sth for the first time: *Books had to be written by hand before the invention of printing.* اختراع

3 [C,U] telling a story or giving an excuse that is not true: *It was obvious that his story about being robbed was (an) invention.* تلفيق

inventory /'ɪnvəntri; *US* -tɔːri/ *noun* [C] (*pl.* **inventories**) a detailed list, e.g. of all the furniture in a house قائمة بالمحتويات ، قائمة الجرد

invert /ɪn'vɜːt/ *verb* [T] (*formal*) to put sth in the opposite order or position to the way it should be or usually is يعكس ، يقلب راساً على عقب

invertebrate /ɪn'vɜːtɪbrət/ *noun* (*biology*) an animal with no backbone حيوان لا فقاري

inˌverted 'commas *noun* [plural] (*Brit*) = QUOTATION MARKS: *to put sth in inverted commas*

🔑 **invest** /ɪn'vest/ *verb* **1** [I,T] to put money in a bank, or use it to buy property or shares in a business, etc. in the hope that you will make a profit: *They invested in the Channel Tunnel project.* ○ *I've invested all my money in the bank.* ○ (*figurative*) *You have to invest a lot of time if you really want to learn a language well.*
يوظّف (مالاً) ، يستثمر ؛ يكرّس (وقتاً)

2 [I] (*informal*) to buy sth (usually sth quite expensive): *Perhaps we should invest in some new garden chairs for the summer.* يشتري ، ينفق مالاً على

▸ **investment** *noun* **1** [U] **investment (in sth)** the act of putting money in a bank, property, business, etc: *The industry needs new capital investment.* ○ *investment in local industry*
توظيف أو استثمار الأموال

2 [C] **investment (in sth)** an amount of money that has been put in a business, etc: *We got a good return on our original investment of £10 000.* ○ *Those shares were a good long-term investment.* المبلغ المستثمر

3 (*informal*) [C] a thing that you have bought: *This coat has been a good investment – I've worn it for three years.* شروة

investor *noun* [C] a person who invests(1) in sth مستثمر

⚷**investigate** /ɪnˈvestɪɡeɪt/ *verb* [I,T] to try to find out all the facts about sth: *A murder was reported and the police were sent to investigate.* ○ *A group of experts are investigating the cause of the crash.* يحقّق في، يتحرّى

▸ **investigation** /ɪnˌvestɪˈɡeɪʃn/ *noun* [C,U] **investigation (into sth)**: *The airlines are going to carry out a thorough investigation into security procedures at airports.* ○ *The matter is still under investigation.* فحص، تحرٍّ؛ تحقيق

investigative /ɪnˈvestɪɡətɪv; *US* -ɡeɪtɪv/ *adj* trying to find out all the facts about sb/sth: *investigative journalism* صحافة استقصائية، صحافة تحقيق

investigator /ɪnˈvestɪɡeɪtə(r)/ *noun* [C] a person who investigates sth محقّق

invigilate /ɪnˈvɪdʒɪleɪt/ *verb* [I,T] (*Brit*) to watch the people taking an examination to make sure that nobody is cheating يراقب في الامتحانات

▸ **invigilator** /ɪnˈvɪdʒɪleɪtə(r)/ *noun* [C] مراقب في الامتحانات

invigorate /ɪnˈvɪɡəreɪt/ *verb* [I,T] to make sb feel fresher, more energetic, etc. ينعش، ينشّط ؛ يقوّي

▸ **invigorating** *adj*: *an invigorating early-morning swim* منعش، منشّط

invincible /ɪnˈvɪnsəbl/ *adj* too strong or powerful to be defeated or beaten لا يقهر، منيع

invisible /ɪnˈvɪzəbl/ *adj* not able to be seen: *bacteria that are invisible to the naked eye* ○ *Frodo put on the magic ring and became invisible.* ○ (*figurative*) *Britain's invisible exports include tourism and insurance.* غير مَرئي، خفي

▸ **invisibility** /ɪnˌvɪzəˈbɪləti/ *noun* [U] خفاء

invisibly *adv* بشكل غير مَرئي

⚷**invite** /ɪnˈvaɪt/ *verb* [T] **invite sb (to/for sth)** to ask sb to come somewhere or to do sth: *We invited all the family to the wedding.* ○ *Shall we invite Louise and Pete for a meal next Saturday?* ○ *Successful candidates will be invited for interview next week.* ○ (*figurative*) *Don't invite thieves by leaving your windows open.* يدعو؛ يشجع، يغري

PHR V **invite sb back 1** to ask sb to return with you to your home: *Shall we invite the others back for coffee after the meeting?* يدعو زملاءه إلى بيته (بعد حضور اجتماع مثلاً)

2 to ask sb to come to your home after you have been a guest at his/her home يردّ الدعوة

invite sb in to ask sb to come into your home يدعو إلى بيته

invite sb over/round (*informal*) to ask sb to come to your home: *I've invited Trevor and his family round for tea on Sunday.* يدعو إلى بيته

ℹ Note that **ask** can be used instead of invite in all senses.

▸ **invitation** /ˌɪnvɪˈteɪʃn/ *noun* **1** [U] inviting or being invited: *Entry is by invitation only.* ○ *a letter of invitation* دعوة

2 [C] **an invitation to sb/sth (to sth/to do sth)** a written or spoken request to go somewhere or do sth: *He has been sent an invitation to the opening ceremony.* ℹ You may **accept** an invitation or **turn it down**. (**Decline** is more formal.) دعوة، بطاقة دعوة

inviting /ɪnˈvaɪtɪŋ/ *adj* attractive and pleasant: *The log fire and smell of cooking were very inviting.* محبّب، سارّ؛ مغرٍ

invoice /ˈɪnvɔɪs/ *noun* [C] an official paper that lists goods or services that you have received and says how much you must pay for them فاتورة (ترسل للمشتري)، قائمة بالحساب

involuntary /ɪnˈvɒləntri; *US* -teri/ *adj* done without wanting or meaning to: *She gave an involuntary gasp of pain as the doctor inserted the needle.* لا إرادي، تلقائي

▸ **involuntarily** /ɪnˈvɒləntrəli; *US* ɪnˌvɒlənˈterəli/ *adv* تلقائياً، عن غير عمد

⚷**involve** /ɪnˈvɒlv/ *verb* [T] **1** to make necessary: *The job involves a lot of travelling.* يقتضي، يتطلّب

2 involve sb/sth in (doing) sth to cause sb/sth to take part in or be concerned with sth: *More than 100 people were involved in the project.* ○ *Please don't involve me in your family arguments.* يشرك، يدخِل في

▸ **involved** *adj* **1** difficult to understand; complicated: *The book has a very involved plot.* معقد؛ صعب الفهم

2 involved (in sth) taking part in sth because you are very interested in it: *I'm very involved in local politics.* منغمس في، شديد الاهتمام

3 involved (with sb) to be emotionally or sexually connected with sb: *She is involved with an older man.* مرتبط بـ، له علاقة مع

involvement *noun* [C,U] ارتباط، علاقة؛ تورُّط

inward /ˈɪnwəd/ *adj* inside your mind, not shown to other people: *my inward feelings* ℹ The opposite is **outward**. مختبئ في السّريرة، باطني

▸ **inward** (*also* **inwards**) *adv* towards the inside or centre: *Stand in a circle facing inwards.* ℹ The opposite is **outward**. نحو الداخل، نحو المركز

inwardly *adv* secretly or privately: *He was inwardly relieved that they could not come.* سرّاً، باطناً

iodine /ˈaɪədiːn; *US* -daɪn/ *noun* [U] a dark-coloured substance that is found in sea water and used in photography and to clean wounds (صبغة) اليود

IOU /ˌaɪ əʊ ˈjuː/ *abbrev* I owe you; a piece of paper that you sign showing that you owe sb some money وثيقة دين موقعة أنا مدان لك

IPA /ˌaɪ piː ˈeɪ/ *abbrev* International Phonetic Alphabet أبجدية علم الصوتيات الدولية

IQ /ˌaɪ ˈkjuː/ *abbrev* intelligence quotient; a measure of a person's intelligence: *to have a high/low IQ* ○ *an IQ of 120* نسبة أو معدل الذكاء

irate /aɪˈreɪt/ *adj* (*formal*) very angry غاضب، حانق

▸ **irately** *adv* بحنق

iris /ˈaɪrɪs/ *noun* [C] **1** the coloured part of the eye القزحية

2 a tall plant with long pointed leaves and large bright yellow or purple flowers نبات السّوسن

Irish /ˈaɪrɪʃ/ *adj* of Ireland, its people, language,

culture, etc: *Irish folk music* ○ *the Irish Republic* ايرلندي

▸ **Irish** *noun* **1 the Irish** [plural] the Irish people الشعب الايرلندي

2 [U] the original language of Ireland: *Few people speak Irish nowadays.* اللغة الايرلندية

Irishman /ˈaɪrɪʃmən/, **Irishwoman** /ˈaɪrɪʃwʊmən/ *noun* [C] (*pl.* **Irishmen** /-mən/, **Irishwomen** /-wɪmɪn/) a man or woman who comes from Ireland رجل أو امرأة من ايرلندا

iron¹ /ˈaɪən; *US* ˈaɪərn/ *noun* [U] (*symbol* **Fe**) a common hard grey metal. Iron is used for making steel and is found in small quantities in food and in blood: *an iron bar* ○ *The roof of the hut was made of corrugated iron.* ○ *a pot made of cast iron* ○ *iron ore* ○ (*figurative*) *The general has an iron* (= very strong) *will.* حديد

iron² /ˈaɪən; *US* ˈaɪərn/ *noun* [C] an electrical instrument with a flat bottom that is heated and used to smooth clothes after you have washed and dried them: *Use a hot iron on cotton and a cool iron on polyester.* ○ *a steam iron* مكواة

▸ **iron** *verb* [I,T] to use an iron to get the creases out of clothes: *Could you iron this dress for me?* ○ *That shirt needs ironing.* ❶ **Do the ironing** is often used instead of iron: *I usually do the ironing on Sunday.* يكوي

ironing *noun* [U] clothes, etc. that need ironing or that have just been ironed: *a large pile of ironing* الملابس المعدة للكي أو التي تمّ كيّها

ironic /aɪˈrɒnɪk/ (*also* **ironical** /aɪˈrɒnɪkl/) *adj* **1** meaning the opposite of what you say: *'Oh, I'm so pleased,' she said in an ironic way.* ➲ Look at **sarcastic**. متهكِّم ، ساخر

2 (used about a situation) strange or amusing because it is unusual or unexpected: *It is ironic that the busiest people are often the most willing to help.* من سخرية القدر

▸ **ironically** /-kli/ *adv* بتهكُّم؛ من سخرية القدر

ˈ**ironing board** *noun* [C] a special table that is used for ironing clothes on منضدة الكي

irony /ˈaɪrəni/ *noun* (*pl.* **ironies**) **1** [U] the way of speaking that shows you are joking or that you mean the opposite of what you say: *'The English are such good cooks,' he said with heavy irony.* تهكُّم، سخرية

2 [C,U] the unusual or unexpected side of a situation, etc. that seems strange or amusing: *The irony was that he was killed in a car accident soon after the end of the war.* سخرية القدَر

irradiate /ɪˈreɪdieɪt/ *verb* [T] to send rays of radioactivity through sth: *Irradiated food lasts longer, but some people think it is not safe.* يعرِّض للإشعاعات

irrational /ɪˈræʃənl/ *adj* not based on reason or clear thought: *an irrational fear of spiders* غير منطقيّ ، مخالف للتفكير السليم

▸ **irrationality** /ɪˌræʃəˈnæləti/ *noun* [U] انعدام المنطق، لاعقلانية

irrationally /ɪˈræʃnəli/ *adv* بشكل خاطئ ، بشكل غير منطقي

irreconcilable /ɪˈrekənsaɪləbl; ɪˌrekənˈsaɪləbl/ *adj* (*formal*) (used about people or their ideas and beliefs) so different that they cannot be made to agree (رأيان مثلاً) متضاربان، لا يمكن التوفيق بينهما

▸ **irreconcilably** /-əbli/ *adv* بحيث لا يمكن التوفيق بينهما

irregular /ɪˈregjələ(r)/ *adj* **1** having parts or sides of different sizes or lengths; not even or regular: *an irregular shape* غير منتظم

2 happening at unequal intervals; not regular: *His visits became more and more irregular.* ○ *an irregular pulse* غير منتظم

3 not allowed according to the rules or social customs: *It is highly irregular for a doctor to give information about patients without their permission.* مخالف للقواعد أو الأصول المرعيّة

4 not following the usual rules of grammar; not regular: *'Caught' is an irregular past tense form.* شاذ ، غير قياسي (في القواعد)

▸ **irregularity** /ɪˌregjəˈlærəti/ *noun* [C,U] (*pl.* **irregularities**) مخالفة ، غشّ ؛ عدم انتظام ؛ تعرج

irregularly *adv* بشكل غير منتظم ؛ على نحو غير قياسي

irrelevant /ɪˈreləvənt/ *adj* not connected with sth or important to it: *That's completely irrelevant to the subject under discussion.* لا علاقة له ، خارج عن الموضوع

▸ **irrelevance** /-əns/ *noun* [U] the state of being irrelevant خروج عن الصدد، عدم علاقة بالموضوع

irrelevancy /-ənsi/ *noun* (*pl.* **irrelevancies**) **1** [U] = IRRELEVANCE

2 [C] something that is irrelevant تعليق (مثلاً) خارج عن الموضوع

irrelevantly *adv* خارجَ الصدد

irreparable /ɪˈrepərəbl/ *adj* not able to be repaired or put right: *Irreparable damage has been done to the forests of Eastern Europe.* لا يمكن إصلاحه : (خسارة) لا تعوّض

▸ **irreparably** *adv* بشكل لا يمكن إصلاحه

irreplaceable /ˌɪrɪˈpleɪsəbl/ *adj* (used about sth very valuable or special) not able to be replaced لا يعوّض، ليس له بديل

irrepressible /ˌɪrɪˈpresəbl/ *adj* not able to be controlled; cheerful: *young people full of irrepressible good humour* زاخر بالحيويّة والنشاط ، لا يُكبح جماحه

▸ **irrepressibly** /-əbli/ *adv* لا إرادياً: بشكل لا يضبَط

irresistible /ˌɪrɪˈzɪstəbl/ *adj* **1** very strong or powerful so that you cannot stop yourself doing or agreeing with sth: *Their arguments were irresistible – I had to agree.* ○ *an irresistible urge to laugh* لا يقاوَم

2 very attractive: *The swimming pool is irresistible on a hot day like this.* ❶ The verb is **resist**. لا يقاوم ، أخّاذ ، جذّاب

▸ **irresistibly** /-əbli/ *adv* بشكل لا يمكن مقاومته : دائما في الذهن

irrespective /ˌɪrɪˈspektɪv/ **irrespective of** *prep* not affected by: *Anybody can take part in the competition, irrespective of age.* بغضّ النظر عن

irresponsible /ˌɪrɪˈspɒnsəbl/ *adj* (used about a person or his/her actions) not thinking about the

effect your actions will have; not responsible: *It is irresponsible to let small children go out alone when it's dark.* مستهتر، لا يفكر في العواقب : غير مسؤول
▸ **irresponsibility** /ˌɪrɪˌspɒnsəˈbɪləti/ *noun* [U] عدم الشعور بالمسؤولية
irresponsibly /-əbli/ *adv* دون التفكير بالعواقب

irreverent /ɪˈrevərənt/ *adj* not feeling or showing respect سفيه ، عديم الاحترام للآخرين
▸ **irreverence** /-əns/ *noun* [U] قلّة احترام، عدم توقير
irreverently *adv* دون احترام ، باستخفاف

irreversible /ˌɪrɪˈvɜːsəbl/ *adj* not able to be stopped or changed: *Once taken, the decision is irreversible.* (حكْم) لا رجوع عنه، لا ينقض

irrigate /ˈɪrɪgeɪt/ *verb* [T] to supply land and crops with water by means of pipes, channels, etc. يروي ، يسقي
▸ **irrigation** /ˌɪrɪˈgeɪʃn/ *noun* [U] ري ، سقاية

irritable /ˈɪrɪtəbl/ *adj* easily made angry سريع الغضب ، سريع الانفعال
▸ **irritability** /ˌɪrɪtəˈbɪləti/ *noun* [U] سرعة الانفعال
irritably /-əbli/ *adv* بضيق ، بانفعال

irritate /ˈɪrɪteɪt/ *verb* [T] **1** to make sb angry; to annoy: *It really irritates me the way he keeps repeating himself.* يغيظ ؛ يزعج
2 to cause a part of the body to be painful or sore: *I don't use soap because it irritates my skin.* يؤلم ، يؤذي ؛ يسبّب حكّة
▸ **irritation** /ˌɪrɪˈteɪʃn/ *noun* [C,U] غيظ ؛ انزعاج ؛ حكّة (جلديّة)

is → BE

ISBN /ˌaɪ es biː ˈen/ *abbrev* International Standard Book Number نظام الترقيم الدولي للكتاب

Islam /ɪzˈlɑːm; *US* ˈɪslɑːm/ *noun* [U] the religion of Muslim people. Islam teaches that there is only one God and that Muhammad is His Prophet. الإسلام ، الدين الإسلامي
▸ **Islamic** /ɪzˈlæmɪk; *US* ɪsˈlɑːmɪk/ *adj*: *Islamic law* إسلامي

island /ˈaɪlənd/ *noun* [C] **1** a piece of land that is surrounded by water: *the tropical islands of the Caribbean* جزيرة
2 = TRAFFIC ISLAND
▸ **islander** *noun* [C] a person who lives on a (small) island: *the Shetland Islanders* ساكن جزيرة (صغيرة)

isle /aɪl/ *noun* [C] an island: *the Isle of Wight* ○ *the British Isles* ❶ **Isle** is most commonly used in names. جزيرة

isn't *short for* IS NOT: *It isn't far now.* ○ *This is enough, isn't it?*

isolate /ˈaɪsəleɪt/ *verb* [T] **isolate sb/sth (from sb/sth)** to put or keep sb/sth apart or separate from other people or things: *Some farms were isolated by the heavy snowfalls.* ○ *We need to isolate all the animals with the disease so that the others don't catch it.* يعزل ، يفرد
▸ **isolated** *adj* **1** not connected with others; separate: *Is this an isolated case or part of a general pattern?* منفصل : منفرد
2 alone or apart from other people or things: *an isolated village deep in the countryside* منعزل
isolation /ˌaɪsəˈleɪʃn/ *noun* [U] being away from other people or things; a feeling of being alone and lonely: *He lived in complete isolation from the outside world.* عزلة ، انعزال
IDM **in isolation (from sb/sth)** alone or separately: *In isolation, each problem does not seem bad, but together they are quite daunting.* انفراد، بمعزل عن

ISP /ˌaɪ es ˈpi/ *abbrev* Internet Service Provider; a company that provides you with an Internet connection and services such as email, etc. موفر خدمات الشبكة الدولية

issue /ˈɪʃuː; ˈɪsjuː/ *noun* **1** [C] a problem or subject for discussion: *I want to raise the issue of overtime pay at the meeting.* ○ *The government cannot avoid the issue of homelessness any longer.* قضيّة ، مسألة : مشكلة
2 [C] one in a series of things that are published or produced: *Do you have last week's issue of this magazine?* ○ *There's usually a special issue of stamps for Christmas.* عدد (من مجلّة) ، إصدار
3 [U] the act of publishing or giving sth to people: *the issue of blankets to the refugees* إصدار ؛ صرْف، توزيع
IDM **make an issue (out) of sth** to give too much importance to a small problem: *OK, we disagree on this but let's not make an issue of it.* يضخّم الأمور ، يعمل من الحبّة قبّة
▸ **issue** *verb* **1** [T] to publish or give out sth for the public to use: *When was the new £5 note issued?* يصدر
2 [T] to give or supply sth to sb: *The new employees were issued with uniforms.* ○ *to issue a visa* يزوّد ، يصْدر
3 [I] (*formal*) to come or go out: *An angry voice issued from the loudspeaker.* ينبثق، يصْدر، ينبعث

IT /ˌaɪ ˈtiː/ *abbrev* = INFORMATION TECHNOLOGY

it[1] /ɪt/ *pron* **1** (used as the subject or object of a verb, or after a preposition) an animal or thing mentioned earlier or that is being talked about now: *Look at that car. It's going much too fast.* ○ *The children went up to the pony and patted it.* ○ *This box is heavy. What's inside it?* ❶ **It** can also refer to a baby whose sex you do not know: *Is it a boy or a girl?* ضمير "هو" أو "هي" أو "ه" أو "ها" لغير العاقل (أو لطفل صغير)
2 (used for identifying a person): *It's your Mum on the phone.* ○ *'Who's that?' 'It's the postman.'* ○ *It's me!* ○ *It's him!* إنه...إنها...الخ
IDM **that's it 1** (used for saying that you have had enough of a situation): *That's it. I'm leaving and I'm not coming back.* خلاص! تحملت الكفاية!
2 that's right: *Just move it a little bit to the right – that's it, you've done it.* "أيوه"! تمام!
▸ **its** /ɪts/ *det* belonging to a thing, animal, etc: *The cat's had its dinner.* ○ *The swimming club held its Annual General Meeting last night.* ضمير الملكية "ه" و"ها" لغير العاقل

it[2] /ɪt/ *pron* **1** (used in the position of the subject or object of a verb when the real subject or object is at the end of the sentence): *It's hard for them to* *talk about their problems.* ○ *It doesn't really matter what time we arrive.* ضمير الغائب المجهول

2 (used in the position of the subject of a verb when you are talking about time, the date, distance, the weather, etc.): *It's nearly half past eight.* ○ *It's Tuesday today.* ○ *It's about 100 kilometres from London.* ○ *It was very cold at the weekend.* ○ *It's raining.*
ضمير يشير إلى الوقت أو التاريخ أو الطقس وغير ذلك

3 (used when you are talking about a situation): *It gets very crowded here in the summer.* ○ *I'll come at 7 o'clock if it's convenient.* ○ *It's a pity they can't come to the party.*
ضمير يُشير إلى وضع ما: (المدينة) مزدحمة: من المؤسف أن...الخ

4 (used for emphasizing a part of a sentence): *It's John who's good at cooking, not me.* ○ *It's your health I'm worried about, not the cost.*
ضمير يستعمل للتأكيد: إنه جون...إنها صحتك...

italics /ɪˈtælɪks/ *noun* [U, plural] the type of writing or printing in which the letters slope forwards: *This sentence and all the example sentences in the dictionary are printed in italics.*
أحرف مطبعية مائلة

▶ **italic** *adj*: *italic handwriting*
كتابة بالأحرف المائلة

itch /ɪtʃ/ *noun* [C] the feeling on your skin that makes you want to rub or scratch it حكّة

▶ **itch** *verb* [I] to have or cause an itch: *My nose is itching.* ○ *The spots itch terribly.* يحكّ

itchy *adj* having or causing an itch
مصاب بالحكّة ؛ يلزمه الحك

itchiness *noun* [U] حكّة

it'd /ˈɪtəd/ *short for* IT HAD, IT WOULD

item /ˈaɪtəm/ *noun* [C] **1** one single thing on a list or in a collection: *Some items arrived too late to be included in the catalogue.* ○ *What is the first item on the agenda?* ○ *an item of clothing*
مادّة ، مفردة ؛ بَنْد

2 a single piece of news: *There was an interesting item about Spain in yesterday's news.* نبأ

▶ **itemize** (*also* **itemise**) /ˈaɪtəmaɪz/ *verb* [T] to make a list of all the items(1) in sth: *an itemized bill*
يفصّل (قائمة الحساب) ، يضع جدولاً مفصّلاً

itinerant /aɪˈtɪnərənt; ɪˈtɪnərənt/ *adj* (only *before* a noun) travelling from place to place: *an itinerant circus family*
متجوّل، متنقّل

itinerary /aɪˈtɪnərəri; *US* -reri/ *noun* [C] (*pl.* **itineraries**) a plan of a journey, route, etc.
بيان بمواعيد وطرق الرحلة

it'll /ˈɪtl/ *short for* IT WILL

it's /ɪts/ *short for* IT IS; IT HAS ❶ Be careful. **It's** is a short way of saying *it is* or *it has*. **Its** means 'belonging to it': *The bird has broken its wing.*

its → IT[1]

itself /ɪtˈself/ *pron* **1** (used as the object of a verb or preposition when the animal or thing that does an action is also affected by it): *The cat was washing itself.* ○ *The company has got itself into financial difficulties.*
في حالة المفعوليّة: نفسه/نفسها (لغير العاقل)

2 (used for emphasis): *The village itself is pretty but the surrounding countryside is rather dull.*
تستعمل للتأكيد: نفسه/نفسها (لغير العاقل)

IDM **(all) by itself 1** without being controlled by a person; automatically: *The central heating comes on by itself before we get up.*
من تلقاء نفسه ، أوتوماتيكيا

2 alone: *The house stood all by itself on the hillside.* ➲ Look at the note at **alone**.
لوحده ، بمفرده

ITV /ˌaɪ tiː ˈviː/ (*Brit*) Independent Television; the group of independent television companies that are paid for by advertising: *watch a film on ITV* ○ *an ITV documentary* شركة التلفزيون المستقلة

I've /aɪv/ *short for* I HAVE

ivory /ˈaɪvəri/ *noun* [U] the hard white substance that an elephant's tusks are made of عاج

ivy /ˈaɪvi/ *noun* [U] a climbing plant that has dark leaves with three or five points نبات اللبلاب

J j

J, j /dʒeɪ/ *noun* [C] (*pl.* **Js**; **J's**; **j's**) the tenth letter of the English alphabet: *'Jam' begins with (a) 'J'.* الحرف العاشر من الأبجدية الإنكليزية

jab /dʒæb/ *verb* [I,T] **1 jab (at sb/sth) (with sth); jab sb/sth (with sth)** to push at sb/sth roughly, usually with sth sharp: *He kept jabbing at his potato with his fork.* ○ *She jabbed me in the ribs with her elbow.* ينخز ؛ ينغز

2 jab sth into sb/sth to push sth roughly into sb/sth: *The robber jabbed a gun into my back and ordered me to move.* يلكز، يكز ؛ يدفع بعنف

▶ **jab** *noun* [C] **1** a sudden rough push with sth sharp نغزة ، وكزة

2 (*informal*) a medical injection: *Have you had your typhoid jab yet?* إبرة(تلقيح) ، حقنة طبية

jack[1] /dʒæk/ *noun* [C] **1** a piece of equipment for lifting a car, etc. off the ground, e.g. so that you can change its wheel مرفاع السيّارة ، عفريتة

2 the card between the ten and the queen in a pack of cards الشاب أو الولد (في ورق اللعب)

jack[2] /dʒæk/ *verb*

PHR V **jack sth in** (*informal*) to stop doing sth: *Jerry got fed up with his job and jacked it in.*
يتوقّف، يترك

jack sth up to lift a car, etc. using a jack
يرفع بمرفاع

jackal /ˈdʒækɔːl/ *noun* [C] a wild animal like a dog that lives in Africa and Asia. Jackals eat the meat of animals that are already dead. ابن آوى

jacket /ˈdʒækɪt/ *noun* [C] **1** a short coat with sleeves: *a tweed sports jacket* ○ *a formal dinner jacket* ➲ Look at **life jacket**. سترة ، جاكيت
2 a cover for a hot-water tank, etc. that stops heat from being lost غلاف سميك عازل ، دثار

jacket poˈtato *noun* [C] (*pl.* **jacket potatoes**) a potato that is cooked in the oven in its skin بطاطا مشويّة بقشرها

jackknife /ˈdʒæknaɪf/ *noun* [C] (*pl.* **jackknives**) a large pocketknife that folds in half when not in use مطواة جيب كبيرة
▸ **jackknife** *verb* [I] (used about a lorry that is in two parts) to bend in the middle in an uncontrolled way (في شاحنة مؤلفة من جزئين) ينطوي أو ينعطف الجزء الخلفي على الأمامي

jackpot /ˈdʒækpɒt/ *noun* [C] the largest prize that you can win in a game أكبر جائزة (في اليانصيب مثلاً)

Jacuzzi™ /dʒəˈkuːzi/ *noun* [C] a special bath with jets of water that make your body feel relaxed جَكوزي

jaded /ˈdʒeɪdɪd/ *adj* tired and overworked مُتْعَب ، مرهق

jagged /ˈdʒæɡɪd/ *adj* rough and uneven with sharp points: *Be careful not to cut yourself – that metal has a jagged edge.* ○ *jagged rocks* مثلّم ، مسنّن الأطراف

jaguar /ˈdʒæɡjuə(r)/ *noun* [C] a large spotted wild cat that comes from Central and South America فهد أمريكي

jail /dʒeɪl/ *noun* [C,U] (a) prison: *She was sent to jail for ten years.* السجن
▸ **jail** *verb* [T] to put sb in prison: *She was jailed for ten years.* يسجن
jailer *noun* [C] a person whose job is to guard prisoners حارس السجن ، سجّان
🛈 In British English **jail** and **jailer** can also be spelt **gaol** and **gaoler**.

jam¹ /dʒæm/ *noun* [U] a sweet substance that you spread on bread, made by boiling fruit and sugar together: *Let's have bread and jam for tea.* ○ *a jar of raspberry jam* ○ *a jam jar* (= a glass container for jam) 🛈 Note that jam made from oranges or lemons is called **marmalade**. مربّى

jam² /dʒæm/ *verb* (jamming; jammed) **1** [T] **jam sb/sth in, under, between, etc. sth** to push or force sb/sth into a place where there is not much room: *There were three of us jammed into a phone box.* ○ *She managed to jam everything into her suitcase.* يحشر أو يكبس (داخل مكان ضيّق)
2 [I,T] **jam (sth) (up)** to fix sth or to be fixed in one position: *Something is jamming up the machine.* ○ *I can't open the door. The lock has jammed.* يسدّ، يوقف؛ يستعصي
3 [T] (usually passive) **jam sth (up)** to fill sth so that it is difficult to move: *All the roads were jammed with cars and people.* يسد ، يحشر
4 [T] to send out signals in order to stop radio programmes, etc. from being received or heard clearly يشوّش البثّ الإذاعي
PHR V **jam sth on** to push on a car's brakes, etc. with force: *I jammed on the brakes as the child ran into the road.* "يفرمل"، يدوس على الفرامل بسرعة هائلة
▸ **jam** *noun* [C] **1** a lot of people or things that are crowded together making it difficult to move: *a traffic jam* توقُّف حركة السير لشدّة الازدحام
2 (*informal*) a difficult situation: *Oh dear. We're in a bit of a jam.* (في) مأزق

Jan. *abbrev* = JANUARY

jangle /ˈdʒæŋɡl/ *verb* [I,T] to make a noise like metal striking against metal; to move sth so that it makes this noise: *The baby smiles if you jangle your keys.* يقرقع ، يخشخش
▸ **jangle** *noun* [U] صلصلة، خشخشة

janitor /ˈdʒænɪtə(r)/ *noun* [C] (*US*) = CARETAKER

January /ˈdʒænjuəri; *US* -jueri/ *noun* [C,U] (*pl.* **Januaries**) (*abbr* **Jan.**) the first month of the year, coming before February: *We're going skiing in January.* ○ *We go skiing every year in January.* ○ *last/next January* ○ *the January before last* ○ *the January after next* ○ *Christine's birthday is (on) January 17* (we say 'January the seventeenth' or 'the seventeenth of January' or, in American English, 'January seventeenth'). ○ *The last two Januaries have been extremely cold.* ○ *January mornings can be very dark.* يناير/كانون الثاني

jar¹ /dʒɑː(r)/ *noun* [C] **1** a container with a lid, usually made of glass and used for keeping food, etc. in: *a jam jar* ○ *a large storage jar for flour* ○ *I can't unscrew the lid of this jar.* مَرْطَبان/بَرْطَمان
2 the food that a jar contains: *a jar of honey* برطمان (عسل)

jar² /dʒɑː(r)/ *verb* (jarring; jarred) **1** [I] **jar (on sb/sth)** to have an unpleasant effect: *The dripping tap jarred on my nerves.* يزْعِج ؛ يوتّر الأعصاب
2 [T] to hurt or damage sth as a result of a sharp knock: *He fell and jarred his back.* يرض ، يضَعْضِع

jargon /ˈdʒɑːɡən/ *noun* [U] special or technical words that are used by a particular group of people and that other people do not understand: *scientific, legal, computer, etc. jargon* مصطلحات مهنة معيّنة

jasmine /ˈdʒæzmɪn/ *noun* [U] a plant with white or yellow sweet-smelling flowers ياسمين

jaundice /ˈdʒɔːndɪs/ *noun* [U] a disease that makes the skin and eyes yellow اليرَقان

javelin /ˈdʒævlɪn/ *noun* [C] a long pointed pole like a spear that is thrown in sports competitions (رمي) الرمح

jaw /dʒɔː/ *noun* **1** [C] either of the bones in your face that contain the teeth: *the lower/upper jaw* فكّ
2 jaws [plural] the mouth (especially of an animal): *The lion was coming towards him with its jaws open.* فم الحيوان ، "أنياب"

a b c d e f g h i j k l m n o p q r s t u v w x y z

jazz /dʒæz/ *noun* [U] a style of popular music with a strong rhythm, originally played by African Americans: *modern/traditional jazz* ○ *a jazz band* موسيقى الجاز
▸ **jazz** *verb*
PHR V **jazz sth up** (*informal*) to make sth brighter, more interesting or lively
ينعش ، يجعله اكثر إشراقاً، يضفي عليه حيويّة

🔑jealous /ˈdʒeləs/ *adj* **1** feeling upset because you think that sb loves another person more than you: *Tim seems to be jealous whenever Sue speaks to another boy!* غيور
2 feeling angry or sad because you want to be like sb else or because you want what sb else has: *He's always been jealous of his older brother.* ○ *I'm very jealous of your new car – how much did it cost?* حسود
▸ **jealously** *adv* بحسَد ؛ بحرص
jealousy /ˈdʒeləsi/ *noun* [C,U] (*pl.* **jealousies**) حسد ؛ غيرة

🔑jeans /dʒiːnz/ *noun* [plural] trousers made of strong, usually blue, cotton cloth (denim): *These jeans are a bit too tight.* ○ *a pair of jeans* بنطلون "جينز"

Jeep™ /dʒiːp/ *noun* [C] a small, strong vehicle suitable for travelling over rough ground سيّارة جيب

jeer /dʒɪə(r)/ *verb* [I,T] **jeer (at sb/sth)** to laugh or shout rudely at sb/sth: *The spectators jeered the losing team.* يضحك أو يصيح مستهزئاً ، يسخر من
▸ **jeer** *noun* [C] an unkind or rude remark or shout ملاحظة ساخرة ؛ صيحة استهزاء

🔑jelly /ˈdʒeli/ *noun* (*pl.* **jellies**) **1** [U, sing.] a transparent soft solid substance that shakes when it is moved: *My legs felt like jelly before the exam* (= not steady because of fear, etc.). هلام
2 (*US* **Jell-O™**) [C,U] a transparent, soft food made with gelatine that shakes when it is moved. Jelly usually has a fruit flavour and is eaten as a pudding. "جيلي"
3 [U] (*especially US*) a type of jam made of fruit juice and sugar نوع من المربّى مصنوع من عصير الفاكهة

jellyfish /ˈdʒelifɪʃ/ *noun* [C] (*pl.* **jellyfish** or **jellyfishes**) a sea animal with a body that looks like colourless jelly. Jellyfish sometimes sting. سمك قنديل البحر أو رئة البحر

jeopardize (*also* **jeopardise**) /ˈdʒepədaɪz/ *verb* [T] to do sth that may damage sth or put it in a dangerous position يعرِّض للخطر

jeopardy /ˈdʒepədi/ *noun*
IDM **in jeopardy** in danger of losing, failing, being injured or damaged, etc.
في خطر (الفشل أو الخسارة وغير ذلك)

jerk /dʒɜːk/ *noun* [C] a sudden pull, push or other movement: *The car started with a jerk and we were off.* رجّة، هزة مفاجئة
▸ **jerk** *verb* **1** [T] to pull sb/sth suddenly and quickly: *She jerked the door open.*
يشدّ بحركة مفاجئة
2 [I] to move with a jerk or a series of jerks: *The lorry jerked from one side to the other over the bumpy road.* يترجرج ؛ يتقدم بطفرات
jerky *adj* متشنِّج ، مرتجّ ، متقطِّع
jerkily /-ɪli/ *adv* بتشنّج ، بشكل مرتجّ ومتقطع

jersey /ˈdʒɜːzi/ *noun* (*pl.* **jerseys**) **1** [C] a piece of clothing made of knitted wool that you wear over a shirt or blouse ➲ Look at **jumper**, **pullover** and **sweater**. These words are more common than **jersey**. Look also at the note at **sweater**.
"كنزة"/"جرزاية"/"جرسي"
2 [U] a soft woollen material used for making clothes قماش الجورسيه الصوفيّ

Jesus /ˈdʒiːzəs/ = CHRIST

jet /dʒet/ *noun* [C] **1** a fast plane with a jet engine طائرة نفّاثة
2 a fast, thin stream of water, gas, etc. coming out of a small hole
فوّارة ماء أو غاز (تنبجس من فتحة ضيقة)

jet-ˈblack *adj* very dark black in colour
أسود فاحِم

ˈjet engine *noun* [C] an engine that makes planes fly by pushing out a stream of hot air and gases at the back محرك نفّاث

ˈjet lag *noun* [U] the tired feeling that people often have after a long journey in a plane to a place where the local time is different
الشعور بالتعب بعد رحلة طويلة لاختلاف التوقيت المحلي
▸ **ˈjet-lagged** *adj* متعب بعد رحلة جويّة

the ˈjet set *noun* [sing.] the group of rich, successful and fashionable people (especially those who travel around the world a lot)
شخصيات المجتمع العصريّ الذين يكثرون من الرحلات عادةً

ˈJet Ski™ *noun* [C] a vehicle with an engine, like a motorcycle, for riding across water التزلج المائي

jetty /ˈdʒeti/ *noun* [C] (*pl.* **jetties**) a stone wall or wooden platform built out into the sea or a river as a landing-place for boats رصيف الميناء

Jew /dʒuː/ *noun* [C] a person whose family was originally from Palestine and whose religion is Judaism; a person who believes in and practises Judaism اليهودي
▸ **Jewish** /ˈdʒuːɪʃ/ *adj*: *He's Jewish.* ○ *a Jewish synagogue* يهودي

jewel /ˈdʒuːəl/ *noun* [C] a valuable stone (e.g. a diamond) or a necklace, ring, etc. with such a stone in it جوهرة ؛ قطعة مجوهرات
▸ **jeweller** (*US* **jeweler**) *noun* [C] a person whose job is to buy, sell, make or repair jewellery and watches: *Take the watch to the jeweller's to see if he can mend it.* صائغ ، جوهري
jewellery (*US* **jewelry**) /ˈdʒuːəlri/ *noun* [U] rings, necklaces, bracelets, etc. that are worn as personal ornaments: *a piece of jewellery* مجوهرات

jig /dʒɪg/ *noun* [C] a lively folk dance رقصة شعبية
▸ **jig** *verb* [I] (jigging; jigged) **jig about/around** to move about in a way that shows that you are excited or impatient يتنطّط

jiggle /ˈdʒɪgl/ *verb* [T] (*informal*) to move sth quickly from side to side يهزهز

jewellery

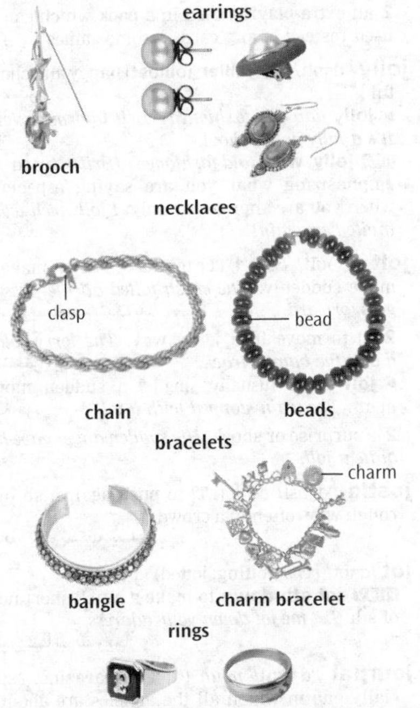

jigsaw /ˈdʒɪɡsɔː/ (*also* **ˈjigsaw puzzle**) *noun* [C] a picture on cardboard or wood that is cut into small pieces. The pieces are then fitted together again as a game. لعبة الصُّور المُقطّعة

jingle /ˈdʒɪŋɡl/ *noun* **1** [sing.] a ringing sound like metal objects gently hitting each other: *the jingle of coins* صلصلة ، خشخشة ؛ جلجلة

2 [C] a short simple tune or song, especially one that is used in an advertisement on television or radio لحن بسيط أو أغنية ترافق الدعايات التجارية، أُرجوزة

▸ **jingle** *verb* **1** [I] to make a gentle ringing sound يجلجل، يرنّ

2 [T] to move sth so that it makes a gentle ringing sound: *He jingled the coins in his pockets.* يُخشخِش بـ ؛ يطنطن

jinx /dʒɪŋks/ *noun* [C, usually sing.] bad luck; a person or thing that is thought to bring bad luck نَحس ؛ جالب للنّحس

▸ **jinx** *verb* [T] (usually passive) (*informal*) to bring bad luck to (sb/sth) ينحس

jitters /ˈdʒɪtəz/ *noun* [plural] (*informal*) extremely nervous or anxious feelings: *Just thinking about the exam gives me the jitters!* ارتعاش عصبي ، نرفزة ، رعب

▸ **jittery** /ˈdʒɪtəri/ *adj* (*informal*) nervous or anxious مرتعش ، مرعوب ، في غاية النرفزة

Jnr *abbrev* (*Brit*) = JUNIOR

⚿**job** /dʒɒb/ *noun* **1** [C] the work that you do regularly to earn money عمَل، شُغْل

We **look for**, **apply for** or **find** a job. A job can be **well paid/highly paid** or **badly paid/low-paid**. A job can be **full-time** or **part-time**, **permanent** or **temporary**. **Job sharing** is becoming popular with people who want to work part-time. Look at the note at **work**[1].

2 [C] a task or a piece of work that may be paid or unpaid: *I always have a lot of jobs to do in the house at weekends.* ○ *The garage has done a good/bad job on our car.* شُغل ؛ مهمّة

3 [C, usually sing.] a function or responsibility: *It's not his job to tell us what we can and can't do.* وظيفة ، مسؤوليّة

IDM **do the job/trick** (*informal*) to get the result that is wanted يفي بالغرض

a good job (*informal*) a good or lucky thing: *It's a good job you reminded me – I had completely forgotten!* لحُسن الحظّ

the job (*informal*) exactly what is needed: *This dress will be just the job for Helen's party.* ملائم جداً

make a bad, good, etc. job of sth to do sth badly, well, etc. يسيء أو يحسن العمل

make the best of a bad job → BEST[3]

out of a job without paid work ℹ A more formal word is **unemployed**. عاطل عن العمل ، بلا عمل

▸ **jobless** *adj* (used about large numbers of people) without paid work عاطل عن العمل

the jobless *noun* [plural] the people who are without work العاطلون عن العمل

joblessness *noun* [U] البطالة

jockey /ˈdʒɒki/ *noun* [C] (*pl.* **jockeys**) a person who rides in horse races, especially as a profession ➲ Look at **disc jockey**. جوكي

jodhpurs /ˈdʒɒdpəz/ *noun* [plural] special trousers that you wear for riding a horse بنطلون خاصّ لركوب الخيل

jog /dʒɒɡ/ *verb* (jogging; jogged) **1** [I] to run slowly, especially as a form of exercise ℹ We often say **go jogging** rather than **jog**: *I go jogging most evenings.* يهرول او يعدو عدواً وئيداً

2 [T] to push or knock sb/sth slightly: *He jogged my arm and I spilled the milk.* يدفع او يصدم برفق

IDM **jog sb's memory** to make sb remember sth: *I've got a photograph that will jog your memory.* ينبّه، ينشط الذاكرة

▸ **jog** *noun* [sing.] **1** a slow run as a form of exercise: *She goes for a jog before breakfast.* هرولة أو عدْو وئيد

2 a slight push or knock دفعة أو صدمة خفيفة

jogger /ˈdʒɒɡə(r)/ *noun* [C] a person who goes jogging for exercise من يهرول أو يعدو بغية الرياضة

⚿**join** /dʒɔɪn/ *verb* **1** [I,T] **join (up) (with sb/sth)** to meet or unite (with sb/sth): *Do the two rivers join (up) at any point?* ○ *Where does this road join the motorway?* ○ *Would you like to join us for a drink?* يلتقي، يتّصل بـ ؛ يجالس (للشراب)

2 [T] to become a member of a club or organization: *James is going to join the army when he leaves school.* ينضمّ إلى ؛ يلتحق بـ

3 [T] to take your place in sth or to take part in

sth: *We'd better go and join the queue if we want to see the film.* ينضمّ إلى ، يقف مع الآخرين

4 [T] **join A onto/to B**; **join A and B (together/up)** to fasten or connect one thing to another: *The Channel Tunnel joins Britain to Europe by rail.* ○ *The two pieces of wood had been carefully joined together.* ○ *We've knocked down the wall and joined the two rooms into one.* يربط أو يصل (بين) شيئين

5 [I,T] **join (with) sb in doing sth/to do sth**; **join together in doing sth/to do sth** to take part with sb (in doing sth for sb else): *I know that everybody here joins me in wishing you the best of luck in your new job.* ○ *The whole school joined together to sing the school song.* يشارك

PHR V **join in (sth/doing sth)** to take part in an activity: *Steve wouldn't join in when everybody else was playing football.* يشترك

join up to become a member of the army, navy or air force يلتحق بـ ، ينخرط

▶ **join** *noun* [C] a place where two things are fixed or joined together وصلة بين شيئين

joiner /ˈdʒɔɪnə(r)/ *noun* [C] a person whose job is to make the wooden parts of a building نجّار (للأبنية)

joint[1] /dʒɔɪnt/ *noun* [C] **1** a part of the body where two bones fit together and are able to bend مفصل

2 the place where two or more things are fastened or connected وصلة

3 a large piece of meat that you cook in the oven: *a joint of lamb* قطعة لحم كبيرة تطبخ في الفرن

joint[2] /dʒɔɪnt/ *adj* (only *before* a noun) shared or owned by two or more people: *Have you and your husband got a joint account?* (= at a bank) ○ *a joint decision* ○ *The joint winners of the competition will each receive £500.* مشترك

▶ **jointly** *adv* معاً ، بالاشتراك مع

joke /dʒəʊk/ *noun* **1** [C] something said or done to make you laugh, especially a funny story: *Have you heard the joke about the three men in a taxi?* ○ *a dirty joke* (= about sex) ○ *I'm sorry, I didn't get that joke. Can you explain it to me?* ℹ A **practical joke** is something you do, not just say. نكتة ؛ دعابة

2 [sing.] a ridiculous person, thing or situation: *The salary he was offered was a joke!* مسخرة

IDM **play a joke/trick on sb** to trick sb in order to amuse yourself or other people "يعمل فيه مقلب"، يعمل عليه حيلة (للمزاح)

see the joke to understand what is funny about a joke or trick يفهم النكتة، يرى الوجه المضحك (من مقلب مثلاً)

take a joke to accept a trick or sth said about you in fun without getting angry يتقبّل المزاح بروح سمحة

▶ **joke** *verb* [I] to say things that are not meant to be serious: *I never joke about religion.* يمزح

IDM **you must be joking** (used to express great surprise) you cannot be serious لا بدّ أنك تمزح! هذا غير معقول

joker /ˈdʒəʊkə(r)/ *noun* [C] **1** a person who likes to make jokes or play tricks المحبّ للمزاح والتنكيت ، "نكتجي"

2 an extra playing card in a pack which can be used instead of any card in some games جوكر

jolly /ˈdʒɒli/ *adj* (**jollier**; **jolliest**) happy and cheerful مرح ، بشوش

▶ **jolly** *adv* (*old-fashioned*) (*Brit informal*) very: *It's a jolly good school.* جداً

IDM **jolly well** (*old-fashioned*) (*Brit*) (used for emphasizing what you are saying especially when you are angry) certainly: *I jolly well won't invite her again!* بكل تأكيد

jolt /dʒəʊlt/ *verb* **1** [T] to shake sth or make it move suddenly: *The crash jolted all the passengers forward.* يخضّ أو يهزّ بعنف؛ يقذف به...

2 [I] to move in a jerky way: *The lorry jolted along the bumpy track.* يتخضخض ، يرتجّ

▶ **jolt** *noun* [usually sing.] **1** a sudden movement: *The train stopped with a jolt.* خضّة ، هزّة

2 a surprise or shock: *His sudden anger gave her quite a jolt.* صدمة

jostle /ˈdʒɒsl/ *verb* [I,T] to push against sb in a rough way (often in a crowd) يتدافع ، يدفع بمنكبيه؛ يصدم

jot /dʒɒt/ *verb* (**jotting**; **jotted**)

PHR V **jot sth down** to make a quick short note of sth: *Let me jot down your address.* يسجّل شيئاً بسرعة وإيجاز

journal /ˈdʒɜːnl/ *noun* [C] **1** a magazine, especially one in which all the articles are about a particular subject: *a medical journal* مجلة دوريّة

2 a written account of what you have done each day: *Have you read his journal of the years he spent in India?* يوميّات

journalism /ˈdʒɜːnəlɪzəm/ *noun* [U] the profession of collecting, writing and publishing news in newspapers and magazines and on television and radio الصحافة

journalist /-nəlɪst/ *noun* [C] a person whose job is to collect, write or publish news, in newspapers and magazines or on television and radio: *a job as a journalist on the local paper* ➲ Look at **reporter**. صحفي

journey /ˈdʒɜːni/ *noun* [C] (*pl.* **journeys**) the act of travelling from one place to another: *Did you have a good journey?* ○ *a two-hour journey* ○ *a twenty-mile journey to work* ○ *We'll have to break the journey* (= stop for a rest).

A journey can include both air and sea travel but to refer specifically to a journey by air we say a **flight** and by sea we say a **voyage** or if it is for pleasure we say a **cruise**.

➲ Look at the note at **travel**. رحلة ، سفرة

jovial /ˈdʒəʊviəl/ *adj* (used about a person) very cheerful and friendly بشوش ، مرح ، ودود

joy /dʒɔɪ/ *noun* **1** [U] a feeling of great happiness: *We'd like to wish you joy and success in your life together.* ○ *to dance, jump, shout, etc. for joy* (= because you feel so happy) فرح ، ابتهاج ، سعادة

Flowers

1

MORE TO EXPLORE

bud
bulb
buttercup
crocus
daisy
dandelion
orchid
petal
seed
stalk
sweet pea
violet

1	**sunflower**	عبّاد الشمس
2	**lily**	نبات الزنبق
3	**water lily**	زنبق الماء
4	**daffodil**	نرجس برّي أو كاذب
5	**snowdrop**	زهرة اللبن الثلجيّة
6	**geranium**	غرنوقي
7	**carnation**	قَرَنْفُل
8	**primrose**	زهرة الربيع
9	**rose**	وردة
10	**poppy**	زهرة الخشخاش
11	**tulip**	خُزامى
12	**pansy**	بنفسج الثالوث

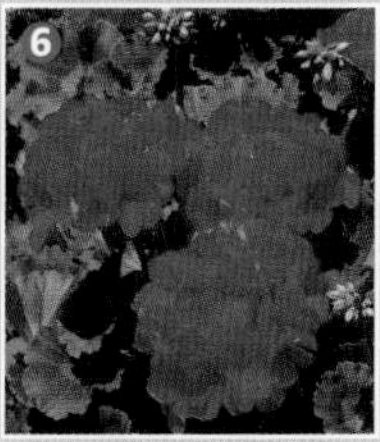

Birds

③

1
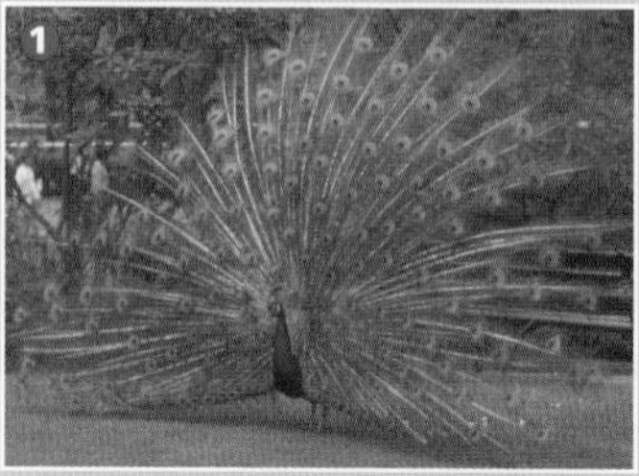

2

④

5

6

7

MORE TO EXPLORE

beak	nest
chick	owl
chicken	penguin
eagle	sparrow
egg	stork
feather	swan
hen	wing

8

9

10

⑪

1 peacock	طاووس
2 turkey	دِيك رومي
3 woodpecker	نقار الخشب
4 pigeon	حمامة
5 budgerigar	طائر صغير من نوع الببغاء
6 hummingbird	الطائر الطنان
7 parrot	ببَغاء
8 goose	إوَز
9 duck	بِطة
10 seagull	نَوْرس
11 kingfisher	صيّاد السمك

Reptiles and fish

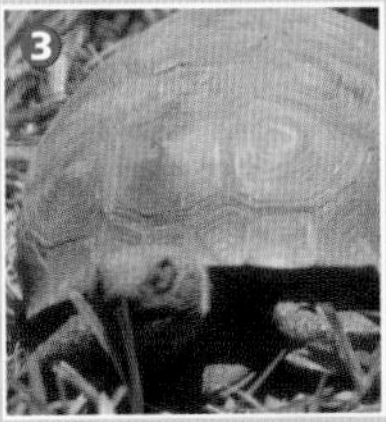

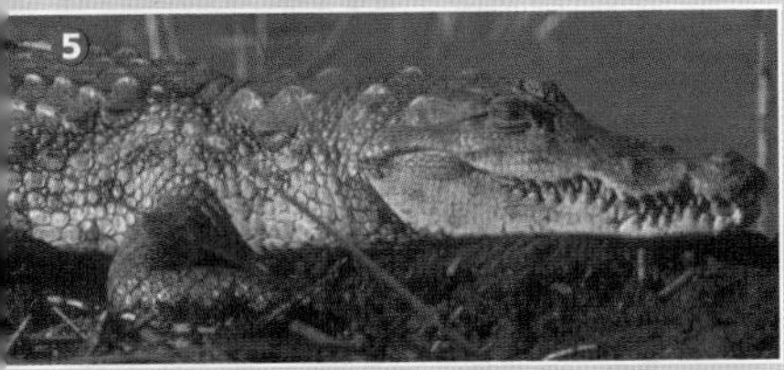

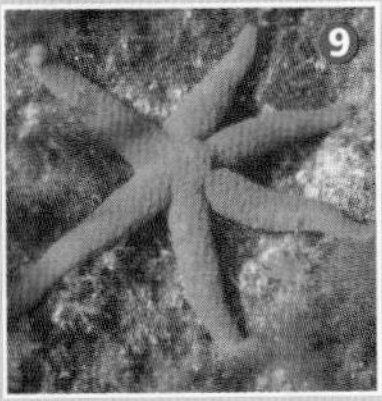

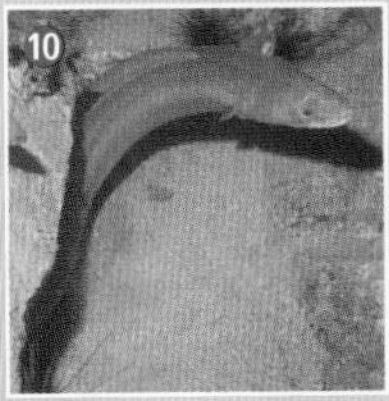

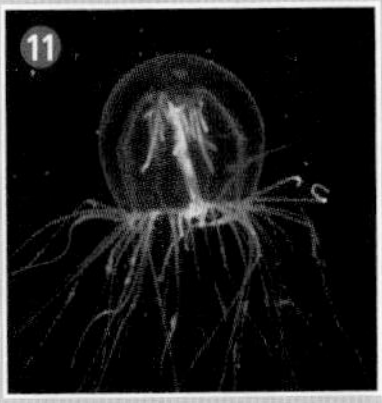

1 **snake** أفعى، حيّة
2 **lizard** سحليّة
3 **tortoise** سُلَحفاة
4 **turtle** سُلَحفاة بحريّة
5 **crocodile** تمساح
6 **salmon** سَلْمون
7 **trout** سمك التروتة
8 **lobster** سرطان البحر
9 **starfish** نجم البحر
10 **eel** ثعبان السمك
11 **jellyfish** سمك قنديل البحر
12 **shark** سمك القِرش

MORE TO EXPLORE

alligator	goldfish	plaice
crab	herring	scale
fin	mussel	shell
freshwater	oyster	shellfish

Animals

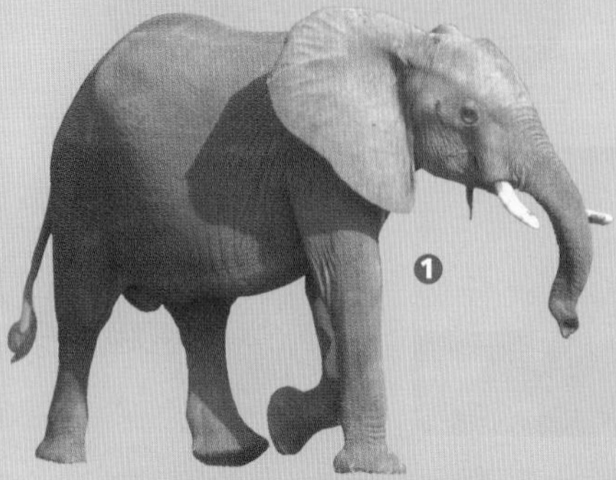

1

❶ **elephant**	فيل
❷ **rhinoceros**	وحيد القرن
❸ **buffalo**	جاموس
❹ **zebra**	حِمار الوحش
❺ **hippopotamus**	فرس النهر
❻ **tiger**	ببْر، نِمر
❼ **giraffe**	زرافة
❽ **leopard**	نِمْر
❾ **lion**	أسد

6

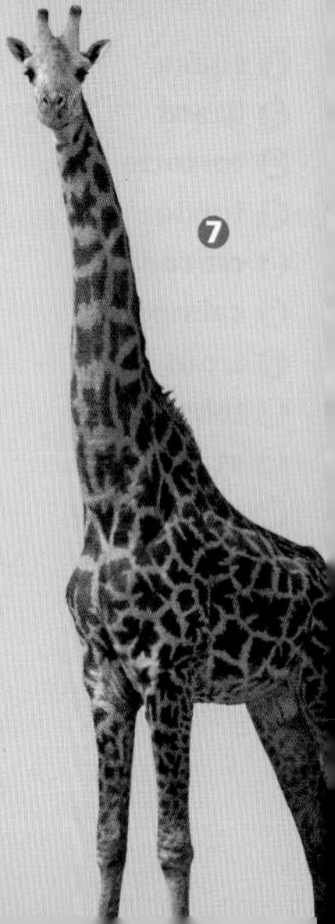

7

MORE TO EXPLORE

endangered
extinct
habitat
hibernate
mammal
pet
prey
species
tame
wild
wildlife
young

1 **seal** حيوان الفُقمة
2 **dolphin** دُلفين
3 **otter** كلب أو ثعلب الماء
4 **polar bear** الدُّب القطبيّ
5 **monkey** قِرد
6 **chimpanzee** الشمبانزي
7 **gorilla** غُوريلا
8 **koala** كُوال (حيوان استراليّ)
9 **bear** دُبّ
10 **wolf** ذِئب
11 **llama** اللامة
12 **deer** أيِّل

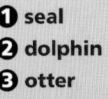

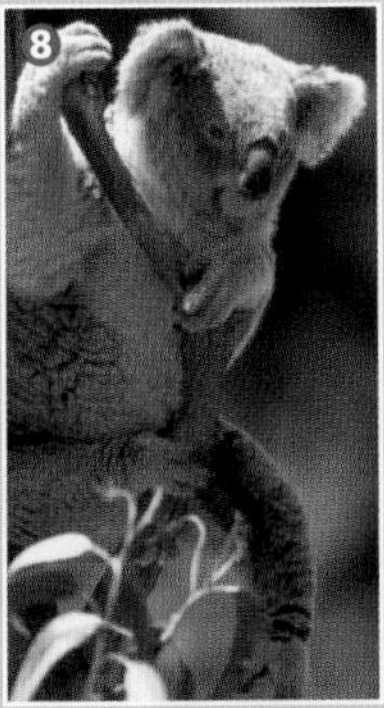

MORE TO EXPLORE

antler	mane
claw	paw
coat	snout
fur	tail
horn	whiskers

Fruit

1

2
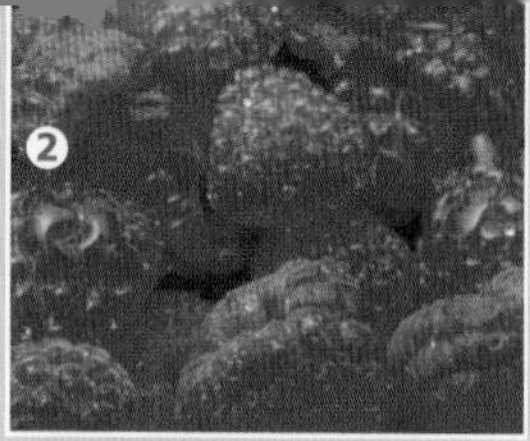

3

4
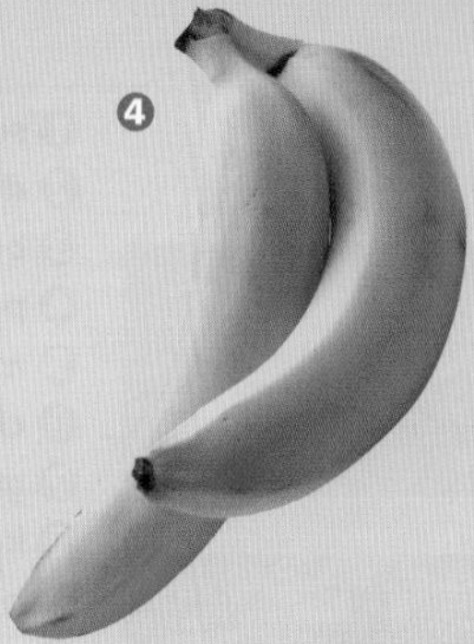

5
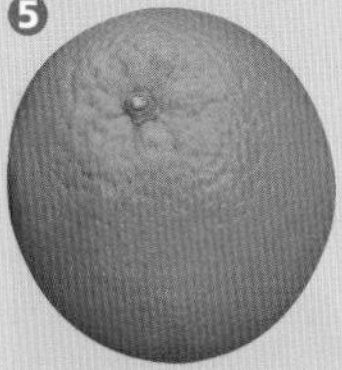

6
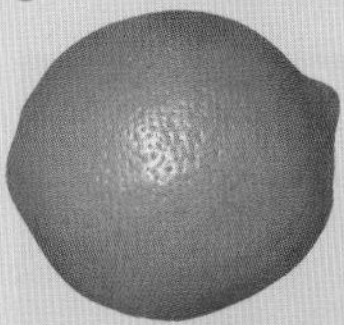

7

8

9
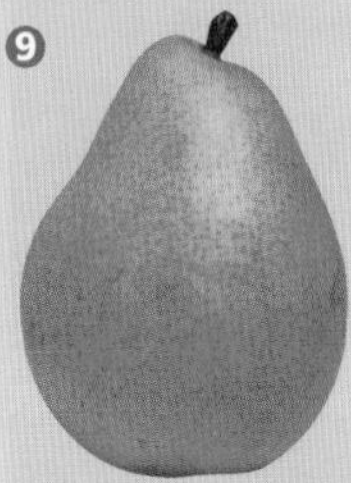

10

11

MORE TO EXPLORE

apricot	pip
blackcurrant	plum
blueberry	redcurrant
core	rind
grapefruit	seed
melon	skin
peach	stalk
peel	stone

12

1 grape	عِنَب
2 raspberry	توت العلّيق
3 lychee	لتشيّة
4 banana	مَوْزة
5 orange	برتقالة
6 lemon	ليمونة، ليمون
7 lime	ليمون مالح
8 strawberry	فراولة، فريز، شليك
9 pear	كمِثرى أو أجاص
10 apple	تفاحة
11 cherry	كَرَز
12 peanut	إحدى حبّات الفستق السودانيّ
13 pineapple	الأناناس

13

Vegetables

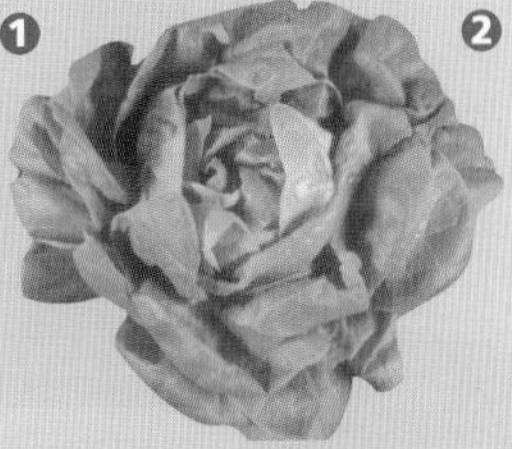

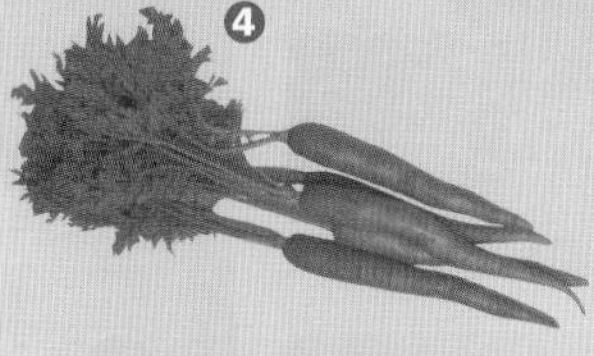

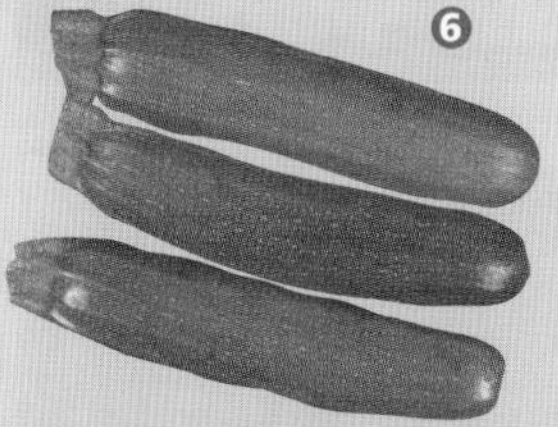
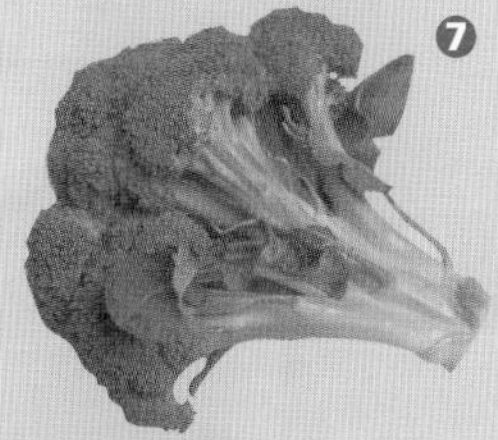

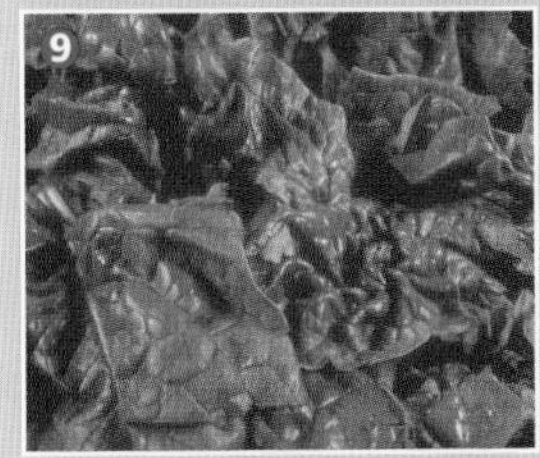
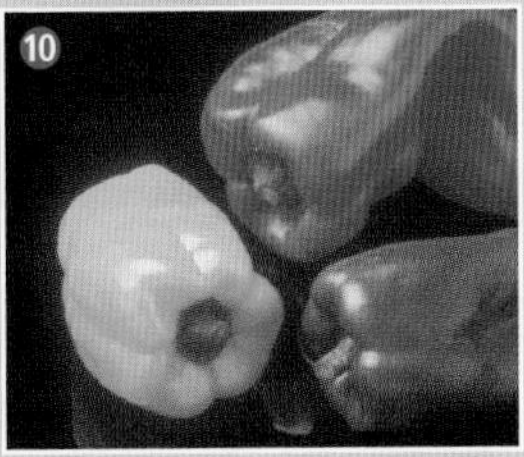
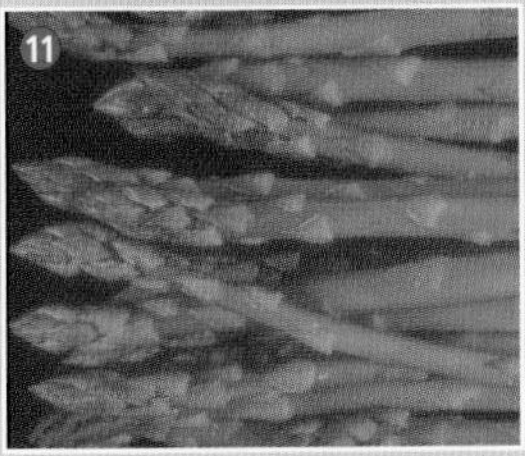
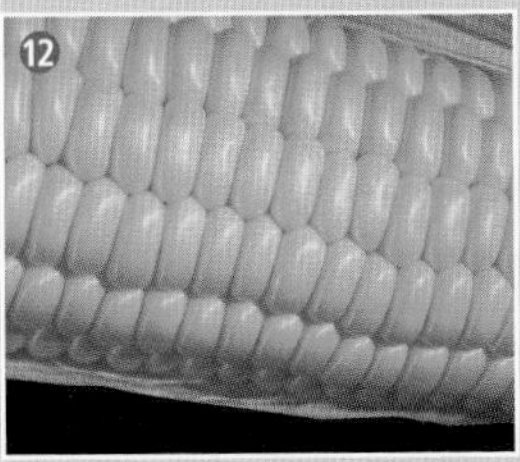

1 **lettuce**	خَسّ
2 **cabbage**	كُرُنْب، مَلْفوف
3 **celery**	الكَرَفْس
4 **carrot**	جَزَر
5 **radish**	فجلة
6 **courgette** (*US* zucchini)	كوسى، قَرْع صيفي
7 **broccoli**	ضرب من القرنبيط
8 **aubergine** (*US* eggplant)	باذِنجان
9 **spinach**	سبانخ
10 **pepper** (*US* bell pepper)	فلفل أو فليفلة (خضراء مثلاً)
11 **asparagus**	(نبات) الهِلْيَون
12 **corn on the cob**	كُوز الذرة

MORE TO EXPLORE

bean	onion
cauliflower	parsley
cucumber	pea
garlic	potato
leek	pumpkin
mushroom	tomato

Homes

1 thatched cottage

بيت سقفه مغطى بالقش أو القصب

2 bungalow

بيت من طابق واحد

3 detached house

بيت غير متصل بجدار غيره

4 semi-detached house

بيت شبه منفصل

5 terraced house

بيت متصِل من كِلا جانبيه

6 farm

مزرعة

7 block of flats

مُجَمّع، بناية كبيرة

MORE TO EXPLORE

back door	front door	patio
balcony	garden	porch
bathroom	hall	roof
bedroom	kitchen	storey
corridor	lounge	upstairs
downstairs	maisonette	yard

Furniture

1
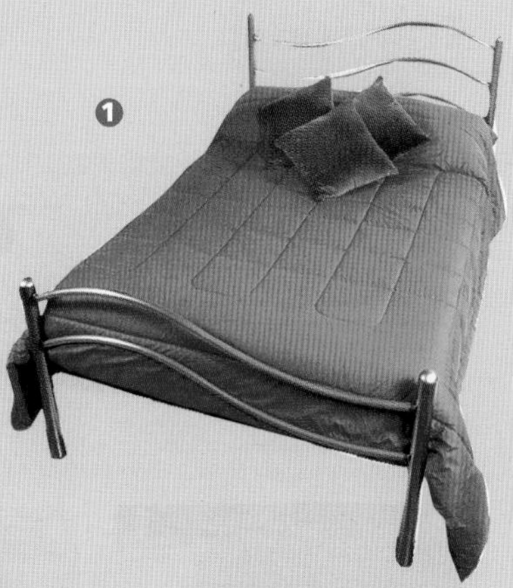

2

4

5

6

7

8

9

10

11

1 bed	سرير
2 sofa	كَنَبة
3 cushion	وسادة
4 armchair	كِرسي مريح ذو مرفقين
5 chair	كرسي
6 stool	كرسي بلا ظهر ولا ذراعين
7 table	طاولة
8 chest of drawers (*US* **bureau**)	خِزانة ذات أدراج
9 coffee table	طاولة القهوة
10 picture frame	إطار
11 rug	سجّادة

MORE TO EXPLORE

bookcase
carpet
cupboard
curtains
desk
mirror
pillow
poster
wardrobe

Transport

1

2

3

4

5

6

7

8

9

10

11

❶ **plane**	طائرة
❷ **helicopter**	هليكوبتر، طائرة مِروَحية
❸ **oil tanker**	ناقلة البترول (وغيره)
❹ **hydrofoil**	مركِب مائي خفيف
❺ **ferry**	مُعدِية (مركب)
❻ **coach**	حافلة
❼ **(double-decker) bus**	باص ذو طابقين
❽ **lorry** (*US* truck)	شاحنة، سيارة شحن
❾ **car**	سيّارة، عربة
❿ **bicycle**	درّاجة
⓫ **train**	قطار

MORE TO EXPLORE

caravan	rail
cyclist	scooter
driver	ship
minibus	subway
moped	taxi
motorcycle	trailer
motorway	underground
people carrier	van

Shops

❶ **grocer's**

بقالة

❷ **baker's**

فُرْن، مَخْبَز

❸ **optician's**

صانع أو بائع الأدوات البصرية

❹ **butcher's**

لحّام، قصّاب، جزّار

❺ **market**

سوق

❻ **flower stall**

كشك لبيع الزهور

❼ **fish and chip shop**

دكان لبيع السمك المقلي والبطاطا

❽ **dry-cleaner's**

محل التنظيف على الناشف

❾ **clothes shop**

دكان لبيع الملابس

❿ **shopping centre** (*US* **shopping mall**)

مركز للتسوُّق

⓫ **garden centre**

محل لبيع لوازم البستنة

MORE TO EXPLORE

bill	chemist's	newsagent
bookshop	counter	receipt
carrier bag	customer	takeaway
change	florist	till
checkout	launderette	trolley

Media

1
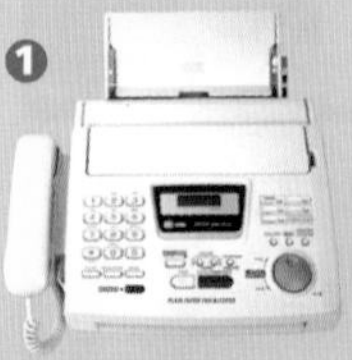

2
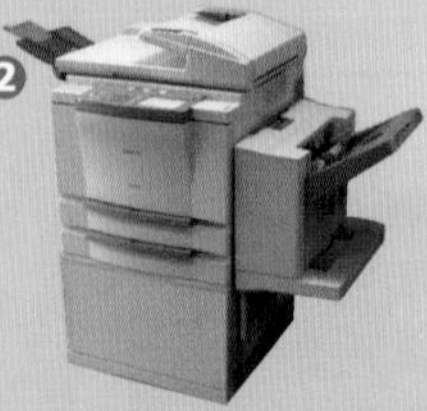

3

4

5
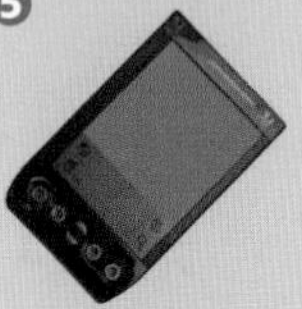

6

7

8

9

10

11

12

13

1 fax machine	(جهاز) فاكس
answering machine	آلة تسجيل الرسائل التليفونيّة
2 photocopier	آلة نسخ
3 laptop	كمبيوتر صغير نقّال
4 scanner	جهاز مسح
5 PDA	كمبيوتر شخصي صغير
6 mobile	تلفون نقال
7 stereo system	جهاز صوتيّ ذو مكبِّرَيْن
8 CD player	جهاز اسطوانة مدمجة
9 headphones	سمّاعتان على الأُذنين
10 personal stereo	استيريو محمول
11 digital camera	آلة تصوير رقمية
12 television	جهاز تلفزيون
13 DVD player	جهاز قرصٍ فيديو رقمي
14 remote control	جهاز التحكم من بُعد

MORE TO EXPLORE

audio	digital	PC
broadband	keypad	radio
cassette	microphone	speaker
computer	pager	WAP

14

Musical instruments

1

2

3

4

1 guitar	قيثارة
2 drums	طبل
3 piano	بيانو، بيان
4 keyboard	الأرغ
5 violin	كَمان
6 viola	كَمان أوسط
7 cello	فيولونسيل: كمنجة كبيرة
8 double bass	أكبر أنواع آلة الكَمان
9 flute	فلوت (آلة موسيقيّة)
10 clarinet	كلارنيت
11 recorder	مزمار خشبيّ يشبه الفلوت
12 saxophone	سكسفون
13 trumpet	بُوق
14 trombone	ترمبون: آلة موسيقية

MORE TO EXPLORE

bassoon	musician
bow	note
brass	oboe
choir	percussion
composer	play
concert	quartet
conductor	score
drum	strings
grand piano	tune
key	woodwind

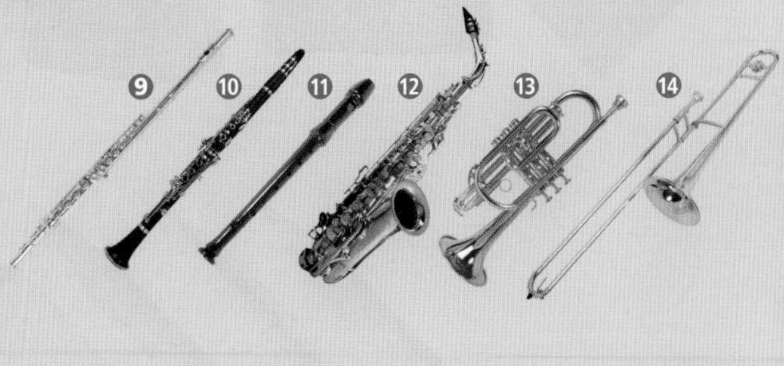

In class

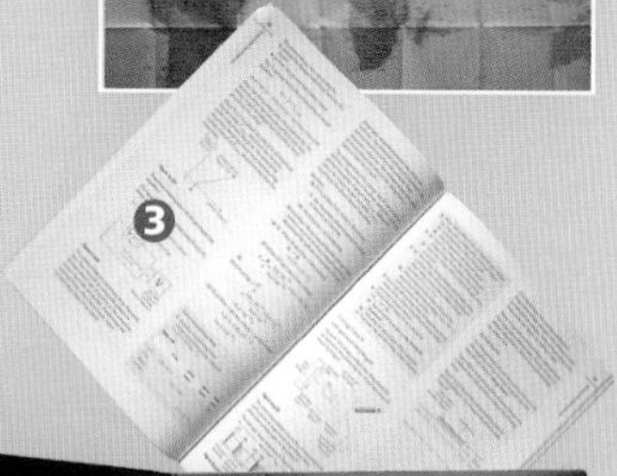

1 **blackboard** (*US* chalkboard) سَبورّة
2 **map** خريطة
3 **textbook** كتاب مدرسيّ
4 **file** ملفّ، اضبارة
5 **exercise book** دفتر التمارين
6 **calculator** آلة حاسبة
7 **pencil case** مَقلَمة
8 **school bag** حقيبة مدرسية
9 **rubber** (*especially US* eraser) ممحاة
10 **pencil sharpener** بَرّاية
11 **pencil** قلم رصاص أو قلم ملوّن
12 **ballpoint (pen)** قلم حبر جاف
13 **felt-tip (pen)** قلم لبّاد
14 **highlighter** قلم ملوّن لإبراز الكلمات
15 **ruler** مسطرة

MORE TO EXPLORE

compasses	set square
dictionary	stapler
noticeboard	timetable
pen	waste-paper basket
register	whiteboard

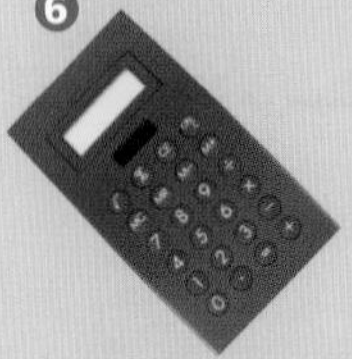

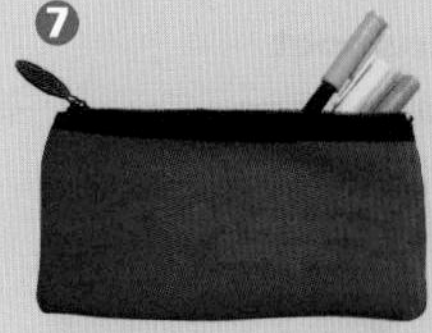

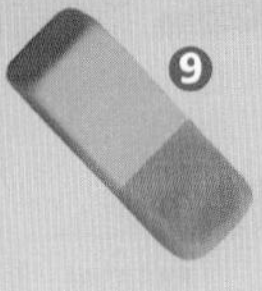

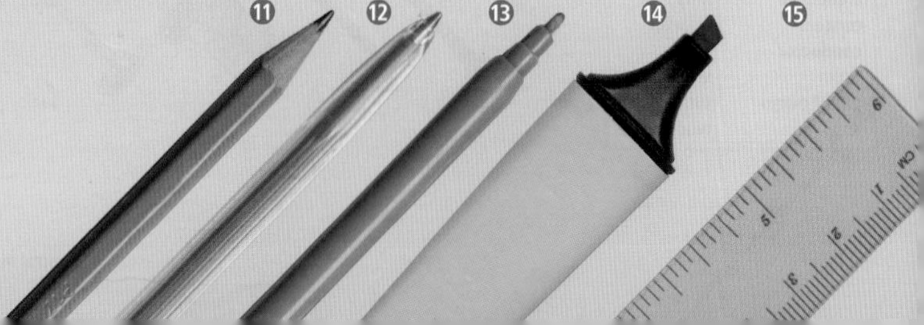

School subjects

❶ **English**	الإنكليزيّة
❷ **biology**	علم الأحياء
❸ **ICT**	المعلوماتية والإتصالات
❹ **art**	الفن؛ أعمال فنيّة
❺ **geography**	الجغرافيا
❻ **music**	الموسيقى
❼ **home economics**	التدبير المنزلي
❽ **maths**	الرياضيّات
❾ **PE**	التربية البدنية

MORE TO EXPLORE

break	physics
chemistry	RE
history	student
homework	teacher
Italian	timetable
lesson	tutor group

Weather and seasons

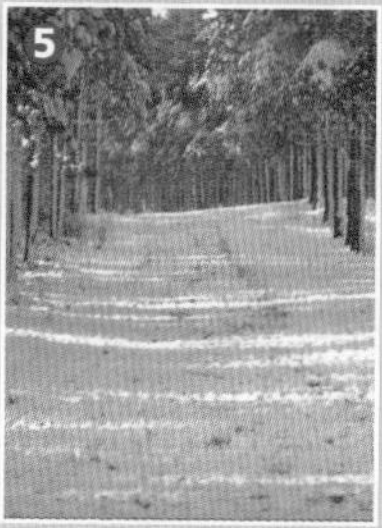

❶ winter	فصل الشِّتاء
❷ spring	فصل الربيع
❸ summer	فصل الصيف
❹ autumn	فصل الخريف
❺ snow	ثلج
❻ sunset	الغروب
❼ clouds	سحاب
❽ rainbow	قوس قزح
❾ lightning	البرق
❿ it's raining	يهطل المطر، تمطر
⓫ it's windy	جو عاصف

MORE TO EXPLORE

boiling	mist
chilly	sleet
fog	storm
freezing	sunny
hail	thunder

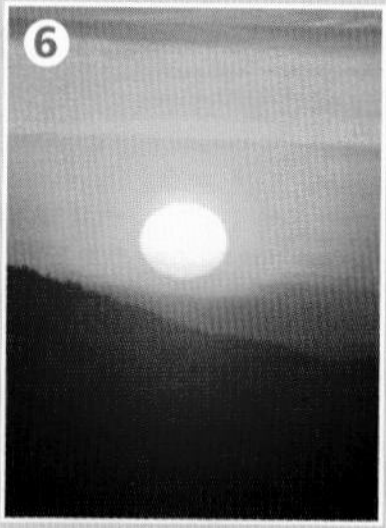

2 [C] a person or thing that gives you great pleasure: *That class is a joy to teach.* مصدر بهجة
▶ **joyful** /-fl/ *adj* very happy: *It was a joyful occasion.* سارّ ، مفرح
joyfully /-fəli/ *adv* بمرح وغبطة
joyfulness *noun* [U] سعادة ، سرور
joyless *adj* unhappy: *a joyless marriage* كئيب ، تعيس

joyride /ˈdʒɔɪraɪd/ *noun* [C] (*informal*) a drive or ride (usually in a stolen car) just for fun and excitement قيادة بتهور لسيّارة غالباً ما تكون مسروقة
▶ **ˈjoyrider** *noun* [C] سائق متهوّر لسيّارة مسروقة
ˈjoyriding *noun* [U] قيادة متهوّرة لسيّارة مسروقة

joystick /ˈdʒɔɪstɪk/ *noun* [C] a handle used for controlling movement on a computer, aircraft, etc. مقبض القيادة في طائرة وما شابهها

JP *abbrev* = JUSTICE OF THE PEACE

Jr. (*Brit also* **Jr**) *abbrev* = JUNIOR

jubilant /ˈdʒuːbɪlənt/ *adj* (*formal*) extremely happy, especially because of a success: *The football fans were jubilant at their team's victory in the cup.* مبتهج (بالنصر)
▶ **jubilation** /ˌdʒuːbɪˈleɪʃn/ *noun* [U] great happiness because of a success ابتهاج (بالنصر)

jubilee /ˈdʒuːbɪliː/ *noun* [C] a day or period when people celebrate because it is a particular number of years after a special event: *It's the company's golden jubilee this year* (= it is fifty years since it was founded). ❶ There is also a **silver** jubilee (25 years) and a **diamond** jubilee (60 years). Look at **anniversary**. اليوبيل (الفضي مثلاً)

Judaism /ˈdʒuːdeɪɪzəm; *US* -diɪzəm/ *noun* [U] the religion of the Jewish people الديانة اليهوديّة

⚷**judge**[1] /dʒʌdʒ/ *noun* [C] **1** a person whose job is to apply the law and decide what punishment should be given to sb found guilty in a court of law: *The judge sentenced the man to three years in prison.* قاضٍ
2 a person who decides who has won a competition: *The judges included several well-known television personalities.* ○ *The judges' decision is final* (= it cannot be changed). محكّم
3 a person who has the ability or knowledge to give an opinion about sth: *You're a good judge of character – what do you think of him?* خبير ، عليم بـ

⚷**judge**[2] /dʒʌdʒ/ *verb* **1** [T] to decide the result or winner (in a competition): *The headmaster will judge the competition.* يقرّر نتيجة مباراة
2 [I,T] to form or give an opinion about sb/sth; to consider: *Judging from what he said, his work is going well.* ○ *Don't judge people by their appearance!* ○ *It's difficult to judge how long the project will take.* ○ *The party was judged a great success by everybody.* يحكم على : يرتئي ، يقدّر : يعتبر
3 [T] to be critical about sb; to decide whether he/she is good or bad: *Don't judge him too harshly – he's had a difficult time.* ينتقد : يحكم على
4 [I,T] to act as a judge, in a court of law: *He said it was the hardest case he had ever had to judge.* يقضي ، يحكم أو يصدر حكماً

⚷**judgement** (*also* **judgment**) /ˈdʒʌdʒmənt/ *noun* **1** [C] an opinion: *What, in your judgement, would be the best course of action?* رأي ، تقدير
2 [C,U] an official decision made by a judge or a court of law: *The man collapsed when the judgment was read out in court.* حكم ، قرار المحكمة
3 [U] the ability to form sensible opinions or to make wise decisions: *He always shows excellent judgement in his choice of staff.* حصافة ، سلامة الرأي ، حسن التقدير

judicial /dʒuˈdɪʃl/ *adj* of a judge, a judgement or a court of law: *a judicial decision* ○ *judicial powers* قضائي

judicious /dʒuˈdɪʃəs/ *adj* (used about a decision or an action) sensible حصيف ، حكيم
▶ **judiciously** *adv* متّسماً بسداد الرأي ، بنضوج ، بفكر ثابت

judo /ˈdʒuːdəʊ/ *noun* [U] a sport from Asia in which two people try to throw each other to the ground. Judo is also a form of self-defence. الجودو

jug /dʒʌg/ (*US* **pitcher**) *noun* [C] a container with a handle used for holding or pouring liquids: *a milk jug* ○ *a jug of water* إبريق

juggle /ˈdʒʌgl/ *verb* [I,T] **1 juggle (with sth)** to keep several objects in the air at the same time by throwing and catching them quickly يشعوذ ، يقذف بكرات في الهواء ويتلقفها بمهارة واحدةً بعد الأخرى
2 juggle (with sth) to keep changing the arrangement of sth in order to get a certain result: *I'll have to juggle my working days round so that I'm free on Mondays.* يلخبط برنامجه ، يعيد تنظيم كل مواعيده وفق المتطلبات الطارئة
▶ **juggler** /ˈdʒʌglə(r)/ *noun* [C] a person who juggles to entertain people مشعوذ

⚷**juice** /dʒuːs/ *noun* [C,U] **1** the liquid that comes from fruit and vegetables: *lemon juice* ○ *I'll have an orange juice, please.* عصير الفاكهة
2 the liquid that comes from a piece of meat when it is cooked المرَق الذي يخرج من اللحم عند طبخه
3 the liquid in the stomach or another part of the body that helps you to digest food عصارة هضميّة

ˈjuice bar *noun* [C] a cafe serving drinks made from freshly squeezed fruit محل عصير فواكه

juicy /ˈdʒuːsi/ *adj* (**juicier**; **juiciest**) **1** containing a lot of juice: *juicy oranges* ريّان ، ماوي
2 (*informal*) used about information) interesting because it is shocking: *Tell me all the juicy details!* (أخبار) ممتعة أو مثيرة لتعلقها بأسرار الناس ، فاضح

jukebox /ˈdʒuːkbɒks/ *noun* [C] a machine in a cafe or bar, that plays music when a coin is put in "الجوكبوكس": جهاز يعزف الموسيقى بوضع قطعة نقد فيه

⚷**July** /dʒuˈlaɪ/ *noun* [C,U] (*pl.* **Julys**) (*abbr* **Jul.**) the seventh month of the year, coming before August ❶ For examples of the use of the months in sentences, look at **January**. يوليو/تمّوز

jumble /ˈdʒʌmbl/ *verb* [T] (usually passive) **jumble sth (up)** to mix things up so that they are untidy or in the wrong place: *I must sort my* *clothes out – they're all jumbled up in the drawer.* ○ (*figurative*) *People from different stages of my life were all jumbled up together in my dream.* يلخبط ، يخلط بدون نظام

▸ **jumble** *noun* **1** [sing.] an untidy group of things; a mess كومة ملخبطة ، خليط من الأشياء

2 [C] (*Brit*) a collection of old things for a jumble sale: *Have you got any jumble you don't want?* أشياء قديمة تباع في سوق خيرية

ˈ**jumble sale** (*US* ˈ**rummage sale**) *noun* [C] a sale of old things that people do not want any more. Clubs, churches, schools and other organizations hold jumble sales to get money: *a jumble sale in the village hall in aid of the school* سوق خيرية لبيع أشياء متبرّع بها

jumbo /ˈdʒʌmbəʊ/ *adj* (*informal*) (only *before* a noun) very large ضخم جداً

▸ **jumbo** *noun* [C] (*pl.* **jumbos**) (*also* ˌ**jumbo** ˈ**jet**) a very large jet aircraft طائرة نفاثة ضخمة

⚷**jump**[1] /dʒʌmp/ *verb* **1** [I] to move quickly off the ground by pushing yourself up with your legs and feet: *to jump into the air, over a stream, off the edge, onto a chair, etc.* ○ *How high can you jump?* ○ *Jump up and down to keep warm.* يقفز

2 [I] to move quickly and suddenly: *The telephone rang and she jumped up to answer it.* ○ *He jumped out of bed when he realized what time it was.* يسرع ، ينطّ

3 [T] to get over sth by jumping: *The dog jumped the fence and ran off down the road.* يتخطّى وثباً ، يثِب فوق (الحاجز)

4 [I] to make a sudden movement because of surprise, fear or excitement: *'Oh, it's only you – you made me jump,' he said.* يفزّ، يجفل

5 [I] **jump (from sth) to sth; jump (by) (sth)** to increase suddenly by a very large amount: *His salary jumped from £15 000 to £25 000 last year.* ○ *Prices jumped (by) 50% in the summer.* يرتفع فجأة ، يقفز

6 [I] **jump from sth to sth** to change suddenly from one subject to another: *The book kept jumping from the present to the past.* ينطّ (من موضوع لآخر)

IDM **climb/jump on the bandwagon** → BANDWAGON

jump the queue to go to the front of a queue of people without waiting for your turn يقف في مقدّمة الطابور مخالفاً دوره

jump to conclusions to decide that sth is true with thinking about it carefully enough يتسرّع في الحكم

PHR V **jump at sth** to accept an opportunity, offer, etc. eagerly: *They asked me if I'd like to go on holiday with them and I jumped at it!* يقبل (عَرْضاً) بحماس ولهفة

⚷**jump**[2] /dʒʌmp/ *noun* [C] **1** an act of jumping: *With a huge jump the horse cleared the hedge.* ➲ Look at **high jump** and **long jump**. قفزة

2 a jump (in sth) a sudden increase in amount, price or value ارتفاع مفاجئ ، قفزة

3 a thing to be jumped over: *The third jump consisted of a five-bar gate.* حاجز

▸ **jumpy** *adj* (*informal*) nervous or anxious: *I always get a bit jumpy if I'm travelling by air.* منرفز ، متوتّر الأعصاب

jumper /ˈdʒʌmpə(r)/ *noun* [C] **1** (*Brit*) a piece of clothing with sleeves, usually made of wool, that you wear on the top part of your body ➲ Look at the note at **sweater**. بلوزة/كنزة من الصوف

2 a person or animal that jumps القافز (في الرياضة) : حيوان نطّاط

junction /ˈdʒʌŋkʃn/ *noun* [C] a place where roads or railway lines meet or join: *Leave the motorway at junction 4 and follow the signs to Bath.* مَفرق ؛ مفترق طرق ؛ ملتقى سكك حديديّة

⚷**June** /dʒuːn/ *noun* [C,U] (*abbr* **Jun.**) the sixth month of the year, coming before July ❶ For examples of the use of the months in sentences, look at **January**. يونيو/حزيران

jungle /ˈdʒʌŋgl/ *noun* [C,U] a thick forest in a hot tropical country: *the jungles of Africa and South America* ➲ Look at the note at **forest**. غابة استوائية

⚷**junior** /ˈdʒuːniə(r)/ *adj* **1 junior (to sb)** having a low or lower position (than sb) in an organization, etc: *a junior officer* ○ *A lieutenant is junior to a captain in the army.* ❶ The opposite is **senior**. ذو مرتبة أدنى

2 Junior (*abbr* **Jnr**; **Jr**; **Jr.**) (used after the name of a son who has the same first name as his father): *Sammy Davies, Junior* الأصغر

3 (*Brit*) of or for children from the ages of about seven to eleven: *She's moving from the infant class to the junior class next term.* خاص بالأحداث: من سن 7 الى 11

▸ **junior** *noun* **1** [C] a person who has a low position in an organization, etc. موظّف صغير

2 [sing.] (with *his, her, your,* etc.) a person who is younger than sb else by the number of years mentioned: *She's two years his junior/his junior by two years.* ➲ Look at **senior**. شخص أصغر منه بِ

3 [C] (*Brit*) a child who goes to junior school: *The juniors are having an outing to a museum today.* تلميذ مدرسة ابتدائية

ˌ**junior** ˈ**high school** *noun* [C,U] (in the US) a school for young people between the ages of 12 and 14 مدرسة متوسطة

ˈ**junior school** *noun* [C] (in Britain) a school for children aged between seven and eleven مدرسة ابتدائية لتلاميذ ما بين 7 و 11

junk /dʒʌŋk/ *noun* [U] (*informal*) things that are old or useless or do not have much value: *There's an awful lot of junk up in the attic – we ought to clear it.* أشياء قديمة تافهة لا فائدة منها ، سَقَط ، كراكيب

ˈ**junk food** *noun* [U] (*informal*) food that is not very good for you but that is ready to eat or easy to prepare: *junk food like crisps and sweets* مأكولات جاهزة تعتبر مضرّة بالصحّة

ˈ**junk mail** *noun* [U] advertising material that is sent to people who have not asked for it دعايات ترسل مجاناً

junta /ˈdʒʌntə; *US* ˈhʊntə/ *noun* [C, with sing. or pl.

verb] a group, especially of military officers, who rule a country by force الفئة العسكرية الحاكمة

Jupiter /ˈdʒuːpɪtə(r)/ *noun* [sing.] the planet that is fifth in order from the sun كوكب المشتري

jurisdiction /ˌdʒʊərɪsˈdɪkʃn/ *noun* [U] legal power or authority; the area in which this power can be used: *That question is outside the jurisdiction of this council.* سلطة قانونيّة ، صلاحيّة ، نطاق السلطة القانونية

juror /ˈdʒʊərə(r)/ *noun* [C] a member of a jury أحد المحلّفين

jury /ˈdʒʊəri/ *noun* [C, with sing. or pl. verb] (*pl.* **juries**) **1** a group of twelve people in a court of law who listen to the facts about a crime and decide whether the accused person is guilty or not guilty: *Do/does the jury have to reach a unanimous decision?* ○ *The jury gave a verdict of not guilty.* هيئة المحلّفين

2 a group of people who decide who is the winner in a competition: *The jury is/are about to announce the winners.* هيئة التحكيم

just[1] /dʒʌst/ *adj* fair and right; reasonable: *I don't think that was a very just decision.* ○ *a just punishment* ❶ The opposite is **unjust**. عادل ؛ مُستحقّ
▸ **justly** *adv* fairly or correctly بعدل ؛ له ما يبرره

⚷**just**[2] /dʒʌst/ *adv* **1** a very short time ago: *She's just been to the shops.* ○ *He'd just returned from France when I saw him.* من برهة ، لتوّه

2 just (about to do sth); just (going to do sth) at this/that moment; now or very soon: *We were just finishing supper when the telephone rang.* ○ *Wait a minute! I'm just coming.* ○ *I was just about to phone my mother when she arrived.* على وشك

3 exactly: *It's just eight o'clock.* ○ *That's just what I meant.* ○ *You're just as clever as he is.* تماماً ، بالضبط

4 at exactly the same time (as); when: *Just as I was beginning to enjoy myself, John said it was time to go.* ○ *Just then the door opened.* في اللحظة ، ما أنْ ، عندما

5 only: *She's just a child.* ○ *It's not just the money, it's the principle of the thing too.* ○ *It was worth it just to see her face as she opened the present.* ○ *Just a minute! I'm nearly ready.* مجرّد ؛ لمجرّد ؛ فقط

6 (often after *only*) almost not; hardly: *I could only just hear what she was saying.* بالكاد ، بشق الأنفس

7 (often with the imperative) (used for getting attention or for emphasis): *Just let me speak for a moment, will you?* ○ *I just don't want to go to the party.* ○ *Just imagine how awful she must feel.* (تستعمل لجذب الانتباه أو للتوكيد)

8 really; absolutely: *The holiday was just wonderful.* حقاً ؛ تماماً

IDM **all/just the same** → SAME[2]

it is just as well (that) it is a good thing: *It's just as well you remembered to bring your umbrella!* ➲ Look also at **(just) as well (to do sth)** at **well**. لحسن الحظ ، أحسنت عملاً أنّك..

just about almost; very nearly: *I've just about finished.* تقريباً ؛ على وشك

just in case in order to be completely prepared or safe: *It might be hot in France – take your shorts just in case.* ربّما يلزم ، استعداداً للطوارئ

just now at this exact moment or during this exact period: *I can't come with you just now – can you wait 20 minutes?* ○ *We haven't got very much money to spend just now.* في هذه اللحظة ؛ في هذه الفترة

just so tidy and correct; exactly as it should be تماماً حسب المطلوب ، بالضبط

⚷**justice** /ˈdʒʌstɪs/ *noun* **1** [U] fair behaviour or treatment: *a struggle for justice* عدل ، إنصاف

2 [U] the law and the way it is used: *a miscarriage of justice* (= a wrong legal decision) العدالة ، القانون

3 [U] the quality of being fair or reasonable: *Everybody realized the justice of what he was saying.* عدالة ؛ صواب

4 [C] (used as a title of a judge): *Mr Justice Smith* سيادة القاضي...، حضرة القاضي فلان

5 [C] (*US*) a judge of a law court قاضٍ

IDM **do yourself justice** to do as well as you should do: *Because of his recent illness he wasn't able to do himself justice in the race.* يستغلّ طاقاته كما يجب ؛ يحقّق الأمل المعقود عليه

do justice to sb/sth; do sb/sth justice to treat sb/sth fairly or to show the real quality of sb/sth: *I don't like him, but to do him justice, he's a very clever man.* ○ *The photograph doesn't do you justice* (= make you look as nice as you are). ينصف ، يقدّره حقّ قدره

ˌJustice of the ˈPeace (*abbr* **JP**) *noun* [C] a person who judges less serious cases in a law court in Britain قاضي صلح

⚷**justify** /ˈdʒʌstɪfaɪ/ *verb* [T] (*pres part* **justifying**; *3rd pers sing pres* **justifies**; *pt, pp* **justified**) to give or be a good reason for sth: *Can you justify your decision?* ○ *Nothing can justify being unkind to children.* يبرّر
▸ **justifiable** /ˈdʒʌstɪfaɪəbl/ *adj* possible to accept because there is a good reason for it: *His action was entirely justifiable.* ❶ The opposite is **unjustifiable**. له ما يبرّره
justifiably /-əbli/ *adv*: *She was justifiably angry and upset.* (غضب) في محلّه
justification /ˌdʒʌstɪfɪˈkeɪʃn/ *noun* [C,U] **justification (for sth/doing sth)** (a) good reason مبرّر ؛ تبرير

jut /dʒʌt/ *verb* (jutting; jutted)
PHR V **jut out** to stand out from sth; to be out of line with the surroundings: *rocks that jut out into the sea* ينتأ ، يبرز

juvenile /ˈdʒuːvənaɪl/ *noun* [C] (*formal*) a child or young person who is not yet adult حَدَث
▸ **juvenile** *adj* **1** (*formal*) of, for or involving young people who are not yet adults: *juvenile crime* متعلق بالأحداث- مثلاً "جرائم الأحداث"

2 childish: *He's twenty but he has a rather juvenile manner.* صبيانيّ

juvenile deˈlinquent *noun* [C] a young person who is guilty of committing a crime جانح حَدَث

a b c d e f g h i j k l m n o p q r s t u v w x y z

juxtapose /ˌdʒʌkstəˈpəʊz/ *verb* [T] (*formal*) to put two people, things, etc. very close together, especially in order to show a contrast: *The artist achieves a special effect by juxtaposing light and dark.* يضع شيئاً بجانب آخر بغية إبراز التضادّ بينهما
▸ **juxtaposition** /ˌdʒʌkstəpəˈzɪʃn/ *noun* [U] تفاوت، تباين : الوجود جنباً إلى جنب : تجاور الأضداد

K k

K, k /keɪ/ *noun* [C] (*pl.* **Ks**; **K's**; **k's**) the eleventh letter of the English alphabet: *'Kate' begins with (a) 'K'.* الحرف الحادي عشر من الأبجدية الإنكليزية

K /keɪ/ *abbrev* (*informal*) = THOUSAND: *She earns 52 K (= £52 000) a year.*

kaffiyeh = KEFFIYEH

kaleidoscope /kəˈlaɪdəskəʊp/ *noun* [C] a toy that consists of a tube containing mirrors and small pieces of coloured glass. When you look into one end of the tube and turn it, you see changing patterns of colours.
المِشكال: منظار النماذج المتغيّرة

kangaroo /ˌkæŋgəˈruː/ *noun* [C] (*pl.* **kangaroos**) an Australian animal that moves by jumping on its strong back legs and that carries its young in a pocket of skin (a pouch) on its stomach حيوان الكنغر

karaoke /ˌkæriˈəʊki/ *noun* [U] a type of entertainment in which a machine plays only the music of popular songs so that people can sing the words themselves
كريوكي (غناء يغنيه الناس وتصدر موسيقاه عن جهاز)

karat (*US*) = CARAT

karate /kəˈrɑːti/ *noun* [U] a style of fighting originally from Japan in which the hands and feet are used as weapons كاراتيه (رياضة يابانيّة)

kart /kɑːt/ *noun* [C] = GO-KART

kayak /ˈkaɪæk/ *noun* [C] a small narrow boat for one person, like a canoe
الكَياك: زورق صغير لشخص واحد
▸ **kayaking** *noun* [U]: *to go kayaking*
ركوب زوارق الكاياك

kebab /kɪˈbæb/ *noun* [C] small pieces of meat, vegetable, etc. that are cooked (and served) on a stick (a skewer) (لحم) كباب

keel /kiːl/ *noun* [C] the wooden or metal bar at the bottom of a boat
رافدة القصّ: عارضة رئيسية في قعر السفينة
▸ **keel** *verb*
PHR V **keel over** to fall over sideways: *Several people keeled over in the heat.*
يتهالك على الأرض ؛ يقع مغشياً عليه

keen /kiːn/ *adj* **1** very interested in sth; wanting to do sth: *They are both keen gardeners.* ○ *I failed the first time but I'm keen to try again.* ○ *She was keen that we should all be there.*
شديد الاهتمام، متحمّس : حريص
2 (used about one of the senses, a feeling, etc.) good or strong: *Foxes have a keen sense of smell.* حادّ، ثاقب
IDM **keen on sb/sth** very interested in or having a strong desire for sb/sth: *He's very keen on jazz.* ○ *Tracey seems very keen on a boy at college.* ○ *I'm not very keen on the idea of going camping.* مولع بـ؛ متلهف
▸ **keenly** *adv* جداً، بشدّة : باهتمام
keenness *noun* [U] حماس ؛ حرص

keep[1] /kiːp/ *verb* (*pt, pp* **kept** /kept/) **1** [I] to continue to be in a particular state or position: *You must keep warm.* ○ *That child can't keep still.* ○ *Remember to keep left when you're driving in Britain.* يبقى
2 [T] to make sb/sth remain in a particular state, place or condition: *Please keep this door closed.* ○ *He kept his hands in his pockets.* ○ *It's hard to keep the children amused when they can't go outside.* ○ *I'm sorry to keep you waiting.* يبقي
3 [T] to continue to have sth, permanently or for a period of time: *You can keep that book – I don't need it any more.* ○ *Can I keep the car until next week?* يحتفظ بـ
4 [T] to have sth in a particular place: *Where do you keep the matches?* يضع، يحتفظ بـ
5 [T] **keep doing sth** to continue doing sth; to do sth again and again: *Keep going until you get to the church and then turn left.* ○ *She keeps asking me silly questions.* يستمرّ، يظلّ
6 [T] to delay sb/sth; to prevent sb from leaving: *Where's the doctor? What's keeping him?*
يؤخّر ؛ يُعيق
7 [T] to support sb financially: *You can't keep a family on the money I earn.* يعيل
8 [T] to own and manage a shop or a restaurant: *Her father keeps a pub in Devon.*
يملك (حانوتا) ويديره
9 [T] to have and look after animals: *They keep ducks on their farm.* يربي
10 [T] to do what you promised or arranged: *Can you keep a promise?* ○ *She didn't keep her appointment at the dentist's.* ○ *to keep a secret* (= not tell it to anyone) يحافظ على، يفي بـ؛ يكتم
11 [T] to write down sth that you want to remember: *Keep a record of how much you spend.* يسجِّل
12 [I] (used about food) to stay fresh: *Drink up all the milk – it won't keep in this weather.*
لا يفسد ؛ يبقى طازجاً
IDM **keep it up** to continue doing sth as well as you are doing it now: *You've made very good progress this year. Keep it up!* يستمرّ في، يحافظ على

ⓘ For other expressions using **keep**, look at the entries for the nouns and adjectives, e.g. **keep count** is at **count**.

PHR V **keep at it/sth** to continue to work on/at sth: *Keep at it – we should be finished soon.* يتابع العمل

keep away from sb/sth to not go near sb/sth: *Keep away from the town centre this weekend.* يتجنّب ؛ يبتعد عن

keep sb/sth back to prevent sb/sth from moving forwards: *The police tried to keep the crowd back.* يمنع من التقدّم ، يصدّ ؛ يكبح

keep sth back (from sb) to refuse to tell sb sth: *I know he's keeping something back; he knows much more than he says.* يخفي معلومات

keep sth down to make sth remain at a low level, to stop sth increasing: *Keep your voice down.* ○ *The government is trying to keep prices down.* يبقي (الأسعار منخفضة) ؛ يمنع الارتفاع

keep sb from sth/from doing sth to prevent sb from doing sth: *His injury kept him from playing in the game yesterday.* يمنع

keep sth from sb to refuse to tell sb sth يكتم عنه معلومات ، يخفي عنه

keep off sth to not approach or go on sth: *Keep off the grass!* يتجنّب ، يبتعد عن

keep sth off (sb/sth) to stop sth touching or going on sb/sth يبعد عن ، يزيح

keep on (doing sth) to continue doing sth; to do sth again and again: *He keeps on interrupting me.* يستمر، يظلّ ؛ يواصل

keep on (at sb) (about sb/sth) to continue talking to sb in an annoying or complaining way: *She kept on at me about my homework until I did it.* يضايق بكثرة الكلام

keep out (of sth) to not enter sth: *The sign said 'Danger – Keep out!'* يبتعد عن ، يتجنّب

keep to sth to not leave sth: *Keep to the path!* ○ *He didn't keep to the subject* (= he started talking about sth else). يلزم

keep sth up 1 to prevent sth from falling down يسند

2 to cause sth to remain at a high level: *We want to keep up standards of education.* يحافظ على المستوى

3 to continue doing sth: *How long can the baby keep up that crying?* يستمر

keep up (with sb) to move at the same speed as sb: *Can't you walk a bit slower? I can't keep up.* يجاري

keep up (with sth) to know about what is happening: *You have to read the latest magazines if you want to keep up.* يتابع الأنباء ، يطّلع على آخر الأحداث

keep² /kiːp/ *noun* [U] food and other things that you need for life: *Gary lives at home and gives his mother £25 a week for his keep.* ○ *to earn your keep* معيشة ، عيش

IDM **for keeps** (*informal*) for always: *Take it. It's yours for keeps.* "على طول" ، إلى الأبد ، بشكل دائم

keeper /ˈkiːpə(r)/ *noun* [C] **1** a person who guards or looks after sth: *a zookeeper* حارس ؛ قيّم

2 (*informal*) = GOALKEEPER

keeping /ˈkiːpɪŋ/ *noun*

IDM **in/out of keeping (with sth) 1** that does/does not look right with sth: *That modern table is out of keeping with the style of the room.* يتمشّى/لا يتمشّى مع ، يلائم/لا يلائم

2 correct or expected according to a rule, belief, etc: *The Council's decision is in keeping with government policy.* تمشياً مع ، يتمشّى مع ؛ يجاري

keffiyeh (*also* **kaffiyeh**) /kəˈfiːjə/ *noun* [C] a square of cloth worn on the head by Arab men and fastened by a band كفيّة

keg /keg/ *noun* [C] a small barrel برميل صغير

kennel /ˈkenl/ *noun* [C] a small house for a dog بيت الكلب

kept *pt, pp* of KEEP¹

kerb (*especially US* **curb**) /kɜːb/ *noun* [C] the line of stones that form the edge of the pavement where it joins the road: *They stood on the kerb waiting to cross the road.* حافّة الرصيف

kernel /ˈkɜːnl/ *noun* [C] **1** the part inside the outer shell of a nut which you can eat or the stone of a fruit لبّ، نواة، عجمة

2 the central or most important part of a subject, problem, etc: *the kernel of her argument* لبّ أو جوهر الموضوع

kerosene (*also* **kerosine**) /ˈkerəsiːn/ *noun* [U] (*US*) = PARAFFIN

ketchup /ˈketʃəp/ *noun* [U] a sauce made from tomatoes that is eaten cold with hot or cold food صلصة مكثفة من الطماطم/البندورة ، "كتش أب"

kettle /ˈketl/ *noun* [C] a container with a lid, handle and spout that is used for boiling water: *Shall I put the kettle on for a cup of tea?* ○ *The kettle's boiling.* غلاّية (لغلي الماء للشاي والقهوة) ، إبريق

🔑**key¹** /kiː/ *noun* [C] **1** a metal object that is used for locking or unlocking a door, etc: *Have you seen my car keys anywhere?* ○ *We need a spare key to the front door.* ○ *a bunch of keys* مفتاح

2 a set of musical notes that is based on one particular note: *The concerto is in the key of A minor.* مفتاح، مقام

3 one of the parts of a piano, computer, etc. that you press with your fingers to make it work أحد مفاتيح أو أصابع البيانو مثلاً

4 a set of answers to exercises or problems: *The key to the crossword will appear in next week's issue.* الحلّ

5 a list of the symbols and signs used in a map or book, showing what they mean مفتاح الرموز

6 [usually sing.] something that helps you achieve or understand sth: *A good education is the key to success.* ○ *This letter holds the key to the mystery.* مفتاح

key² /kiː/ *verb* [T] **key sth (in)** to put information into a computer or give it an instruction by typing on the keyboard: *to key in some data* ○ *First, key in your password.*
يدخل معلومات في الكمبيوتر بالضغط على لوحة المفاتيح

key³ /kiː/ *adj* (only *before* a noun) very important: *Tourism is a key industry in Spain.* رئيسي ؛ هام جداً

keyboard /ˈkiːbɔːd/ *noun* [C] **1** the set of keys¹ (3) on a piano, computer, etc.
لوحة المفاتيح (على الكمبيوتر أو البيانو)

2 [usually pl.] an electrical musical instrument like a small piano الأرغ: آلة موسيقيّة كهربائية تشبه البيانو

keyhole /ˈkiːhəʊl/ *noun* [C] the hole in a lock where you put the key ثقب المفتاح

keypad /ˈkiːpæd/ *noun* [C] a small set of buttons with numbers on used to operate a telephone, television, etc.; the buttons on the right of a computer keyboard لوحة الأرقام

ˈ**key ring** *noun* [C] a ring on which you keep keys حمّالة أو حلقة المفاتيح

kg *abbrev* = KILOGRAM(S)

khaki /ˈkɑːki/ *adj, noun* [U] (of) a dull brownish-yellow colour: *the khaki uniforms of the desert soldiers* اللون الخاكي أو الكاكي

kick¹ /kɪk/ *verb* **1** [T] to hit or move sb/sth with your foot: *She was knocked to the ground and kicked in the stomach.* ○ *He kicked the ball over the top of the net.* يرفس ، يركل

2 [I] to move your foot or feet: *You must kick harder if you want to swim faster.* ○ *The protesters were dragged kicking and screaming into the police vans.*
يدفع بقدمه أو بقدميه ؛ يضرب بقدميه محتجّاً ، يلبط

IDM **make, kick up, etc. a fuss** → FUSS

PHR V **kick off** to start a game of football
يستهلّ مباراة كرة القدم

kick sb out (of sth) (*informal*) to force sb to leave a place: *to be kicked out of university* يطرد

kick² /kɪk/ *noun* [C] **1** an act of kicking: *She gave the door a kick and it closed.* ○ *After one of our players was tripped up, our team got a free kick.*
رفسة ؛ ضربة (قدم)

2 (*informal*) a feeling of great pleasure, excitement, etc: *He gets a real kick out of rock climbing.* ○ *Some young people drive very fast just for kicks.* نشوة ، ابتهاج

ˈ**kick-off** *noun* [C] the start of a game of football: *The kick-off is at 2.30.* موعد ابتداء مباراة كرة القدم

kid¹ /kɪd/ *noun* [C] **1** (*informal*) a child or young person: *How are your kids?* ولد ، طفل

2 kid ˈbrother/ˈsister (*informal*) (*especially US*) younger brother/sister الأخ أو الأخت الأصغر

3 a young goat جَدي

▸ ˈ**kiddy** (*also* **kiddie**) *noun* [C] (*pl.* **kiddies**) (*informal*) a child طفل

kid² /kɪd/ *verb* [I,T] (ki**dd**ing; ki**dd**ed) (*informal*) to trick or deceive sb/yourself; to make a joke about sth: *I didn't mean it. I was only kidding.* ○ *Don't kid yourself Martin, she doesn't really love you.* يمزح ، يمازح ، يضحك على ، يغش

kidnap /ˈkɪdnæp/ *verb* [T] (kidna**pp**ing; kidna**pp**ed; *US* kidna**p**ing; kidna**p**ed) to take sb away by force and demand money for his/her safe return: *The child was kidnapped and £50 000 was demanded for her release.* ➲ Look at **hijack**.
يختطف

▸ **kidnapper** *noun* [C] a person who kidnaps sb مختطِف

kidnapping *noun* [C, U]: *The kidnapping took place just outside his home.* اختطاف

kidney /ˈkɪdni/ *noun* [C] (*pl.* **kidneys**) one of the two parts of the body that separate waste liquid from the blood: *My mother has had a kidney transplant.* كلية، كلوة

kill /kɪl/ *verb* **1** [I,T] to make sb/sth die: *Smoking kills.* ○ *She was killed instantly in the crash.*
يَقتل؛ يَذبح ؛ يقتَل، يموت

> **Murder** means to kill a person on purpose: *This was no accident. The old lady was murdered.* **Assassinate** means to kill for political reasons: *President Kennedy was assassinated.* **Slaughter** and **massacre** mean to kill a large number of people: *Hundreds of people were massacred when the army opened fire on the crowd.* **Slaughter** is also used of killing an animal for food.

2 [T] (*informal*) to cause sb pain; hurt: *My feet are killing me.* يؤلم ألماً شديداً

3 [T] to cause sth to end or fail: *The minister's opposition killed the idea stone dead.* يقضي على

4 [T] (*informal*) **kill yourself/sb** to make yourself/sb laugh a lot: *We were killing ourselves laughing.* يموت ضحكاً

IDM **have an hour, etc. to kill** to have some time when you have nothing to do, usually when you are waiting for sb/sth يقتل (الوقت)

kill time to do sth uninteresting or unimportant to pass the time يقتل أو يمضي الوقت

kill two birds with one stone to do one thing which will achieve two results
يضرب عصفورين بحجر واحد

▸ **kill** *noun* [sing.] **1** the act of killing (an animal): *Lions often make a kill in the evening.*
افتراس

2 an animal or animals that have been killed: *The eagle took the kill back to its young.*
فريسة ، حيوان مصاد ، مجموعة الحيوانات المصادة

killer *noun* [C] a person, animal or thing that kills: *a killer disease* ○ *He's a dangerous killer who may strike again.* قاتِل

killing /ˈkɪlɪŋ/ *noun* [C] an act of killing a person

on purpose; a murder: *There have been a number of brutal killings in the area recently.* جريمة قتل

kilo /'ki:ləʊ/ (*also* **kilogram**; **kilogramme** /'kɪləɡræm/) *noun* [C] (*pl.* **kilos**) (*abbr* **kg**) a measure of weight; 1 000 grams كيلوغرام

kilobyte /'kɪləbaɪt/ *noun* [C] unit for measuring computer memory or information equal to 1 024 bytes كيلوبايت (وحدة قياس ذاكرة الكمبيوتر)

kilometre (*US* **kilometer**) /'kɪləmi:tə(r); kɪ'lɒmɪtə(r)/ *noun* [C] (*abbr* **km**) a measure of length; 1 000 metres كيلومتر

kilt /kɪlt/ *noun* [C] a skirt with many folds (pleats) that is worn by men as part of the national dress of Scotland تنورة يلبسها الرجال في اسكتلندا

kin /kɪn/ *noun* [plural] members of your family; relatives

> Kin is now a formal or old-fashioned word and is rarely used. **Next of kin** however, is still common. It means your closest relative who should be told first if you are injured or killed.

أقرباء ؛ أقرب الأقرباء

kind[1] /kaɪnd/ *noun* [C] a group whose members all have the same qualities: *The concert attracted people of all kinds.* ○ *The concert attracted all kinds of people.* ○ *Many kinds of plant and animal are being lost every year.*

> *Kinds of* may be followed by a singular noun or a plural noun: *There are so many kinds of camera/cameras on the market that it's hard to know which is best.* Sometimes you may hear people say something like: *Those kind/sort of dogs are really dangerous* but this is still thought by many people not to be correct English.

صنف ، نوع

IDM **a kind of** (*informal*) (used for describing sth in a way that is not very clear): *I had a kind of feeling that something would go wrong.* ○ *There's a funny kind of smell in here.* ما يشبه

kind of (*informal*) rather; a little bit: *I'm kind of worried about the interview.* قليلاً ، "شوية"

of a kind 1 very much the same: *The friends were two of a kind – very similar in so many ways.* من نوعيّة واحدة ، من نفس الطّينة

2 of poor quality: *The village has a bus service of a kind – two buses a week!* رديء ، ما يشبه ، ما يمكن تسميته

kind[2] /kaɪnd/ *adj* friendly and thoughtful about what other people want or need: *Would you be kind enough to give Sue a lift to the station?* ○ *It was kind of you to offer, but I don't need any help.* ○ *A present! How kind of you.* ○ *to be kind to children and animals* ❶ The opposite is **unkind**. لطيف

▸ **kindly** *adv* **1** in a kind way: *The nurse smiled kindly.* بلطف ورقّة

2 (used for asking sb to do sth) please: *Would you kindly wait a moment?* ○ *Kindly leave me alone!* رجاءً ، من فضلك

kindness *noun* **1** [U] the quality of being kind: *Be grateful. It was done out of kindness.* رافة ، حسن المعاملة

2 [C] a kind act: *How can I repay your many kindnesses?* فضل ، معروف

ˌ**kind-'hearted** *adj* having a kind nature طيّب القلب ، حنون

kindergarten /'kɪndəɡɑ:tn/ *noun* [C] a school for very young children, aged from about three to five ➲ Look at **nursery school**. روضة أطفال ، مدرسة حضانة

kindly[1] /'kaɪndli/ *adj* (**kindlier**; **kindliest**) kind and friendly: *a kindly face* ○ *kindly advice* عطوف ؛ ودود ، كريم

▸ **kindliness** *noun* [U] عطف ، عناية

kindly[2] → KIND[2]

king /kɪŋ/ *noun* [C] **1** (the title of) a man who rules a country. A king is usually the son or close relative of the previous ruler: *The new king was crowned in Westminster Abbey.* ○ *King Edward VII* ○ (*figurative*) *The lion is the king of the jungle.* ➲ Look at **queen**. ملك

2 one of the four playing cards in a pack with a picture of a king الشايب ، الاختيار (في ورق اللعب)

kingdom /'kɪŋdəm/ *noun* [C] **1** a country that is ruled by a king or queen: *the United Kingdom* مملكة

2 one of the parts of the natural world: *the animal kingdom* مملكة

kingfisher /'kɪŋfɪʃə(r)/ *noun* [C] a bird with a long beak, that catches fish in rivers. The European kingfisher is small and brightly coloured and the American kingfisher is larger and blue-grey in colour. (طائر) صيّاد السمك

'**king-size** (*also* '**king-sized**) *adj* very large: *a king-size bed* (قياس) ملكي ، من حجم كبير

kink /kɪŋk/ *noun* [C] a turn or bend in sth that should be straight: *There's a kink in the hosepipe so the water won't come out.* عقدة ، التواءة، انثناء (في سلك مثلاً)

kiosk /'ki:ɒsk/ *noun* [C] a small hut where newspapers, sweets, cigarettes, etc. are sold كشك (لبيع الصحف وغيرها)

kip /kɪp/ *noun* [sing., U] (*Brit slang*) sleep: *It's time to have a kip.* نوم ، نومة

▸ **kip** *verb* [I] (kip**p**ing; kip**p**ed) (*Brit*) to sleep: *You could kip on the sofa if you like.* ينام

kipper /'kɪpə(r)/ *noun* [C] a type of fish that has been cut open, salted and hung in smoke سمكة رنكة مقدّدة بالتدخين

kiss /kɪs/ *verb* [I,T] to touch sb with your lips as a greeting or to show love or affection: *He kissed her tenderly on the cheek.* ○ *They kissed each other goodbye.* يقبّل

▸ **kiss** *noun* [C] a touch with the lips: *Give Daddy a goodnight kiss.* ○ *a kiss on the lips* قبلة

kit /kɪt/ *noun* **1** [U] the clothes and other things that are needed e.g. by a soldier: *He packed all his kit into a rucksack and set off around Europe.* اللوازم ، العدّة

a b c d e f g h i j k l m n o p q r s t u v w x y z

kitchen utensils

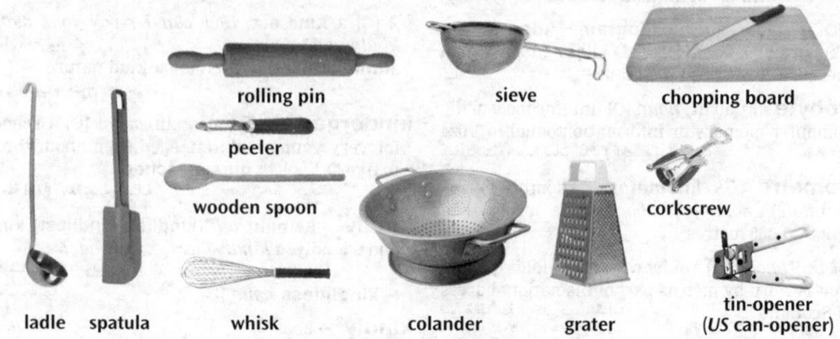

2 [C,U] equipment that you need for a particular sport, activity, situation, etc: *a first-aid kit* ○ *a tool kit* ○ *sports kit* لوازم ، عدّة

3 [C] a set of parts that you buy and put together in order to make sth: *a kit for a model aeroplane*
مجموعة القطع التي يركّب منها نموذج مصغّر (عن طائرة مثلاً)

▸ **kit** *verb* (kitting; kitted)

PHR V **kit sb out/up (with sth)** to give sb all the necessary clothes, equipment, tools, etc. for sth: *Before you go skiing you must get kitted out with all the proper clothing.* يجهز بكل اللوازم

kitchen /ˈkɪtʃɪn/ *noun* [C] a room where food is prepared and cooked: *We usually eat in the kitchen.* ○ *a kitchen cupboard* مطبخ

kite /kaɪt/ *noun* [C] a toy which is a light framework covered with paper or cloth. Kites are flown in the wind on the end of a long piece of string: *Several people were flying kites on the hill.*
طيّارة من ورق

kitesurfing /ˈkaɪtsɜːfɪŋ/ (*also* **kiteboarding**) /ˈkaɪtbɔːdɪŋ/ *noun* [U] the sport of riding on water while standing on a short wide board and being pulled along by wind power, using a large kite ركوب الأمواج بقوة شدّ طيارة ورقية

kitsch /kɪtʃ/ *noun* [U] popular art or design that is lacking in good taste and is too bright or sentimental in style: *kitsch plaster dogs on the mantelpiece* خالٍ من الذوق الفنّي، مبتذل؛ فاقع

kitten /ˈkɪtn/ *noun* [C] a young cat
هريرة ، قطة صغيرة

kitty /ˈkɪti/ *noun* [C] (*pl.* **kitties**) a sum of money that is collected from a group of people and used for a particular purpose: *All the students in the flat put £5 a week into the kitty.*
مبالغ توضع في الحصّالة لتنفق في غايات معيّنة

kiwi /ˈkiːwiː/ *noun* [C] **1** a New Zealand bird with a long beak and short wings that cannot fly
طائر الكيوي

2 (*also* ˈ**kiwi fruit**) a fruit with brown skin that is green inside with black seeds فاكهة الكيوي

km *abbrev* = KILOMETRE(s)

knack /næk/ *noun* [sing.] the ability to do sth (difficult): *Knitting isn't difficult once you've got the knack of it.* مقدرة ؛ مَهارة مكتسَبة

knead /niːd/ *verb* [T] to press and squeeze sth with your hands: *To make bread you mix flour and water into a dough and knead it for ten minutes.* يعجن ، يدلك

knee /niː/ *noun* [C] **1** the place where your leg bends in the middle: *Angie fell and grazed her knee.* ○ *Sue was sitting on her mother's knee.*
ركبة

2 the part of a pair of trousers, etc. that covers the knee: *There's a hole in the knee of those jeans.* ركبة

kneecap /ˈniːkæp/ *noun* [C] the bone that covers the front of the knee الرّضفة ، صابونة الركبة

ˌ**knee-ˈdeep** *adj* deep enough to reach the knees: *The water was knee-deep in places.* واصل إلى الركبة

kneel /niːl/ *verb* [I] (*pt, pp* **knelt** /nelt/ or **kneeled**) **kneel (down)** to go down on one or both knees; to be in this position: *She knelt down to talk to the child.* ○ *to kneel in prayer* يركع ، يجثو

knew *pt* of KNOW

knickers /ˈnɪkəz/ *noun* [plural] (*Brit*) a woman's or girl's underpants ⓘ Note that you talk about *a pair of knickers*: *There's a clean pair of knickers in your drawer.* كَلسون نسائي

knife /naɪf/ *noun* [C] (*pl.* **knives** /naɪvz/) a sharp flat piece of metal (a blade) with a handle. A knife is used for cutting things or as a weapon: *The carving knife is rather blunt.* ○ *Be careful. That bread knife is very sharp.* ○ *Don't use your fingers. Use a knife and fork.* ○ *a pocketknife*
سكّين ، مدية ؛ مطواة

▸ **knife** *verb* [T] to injure sb with a knife: *The young man had been knifed in the chest.*
يطعن بسكّين

knight /naɪt/ *noun* [C] **1** a man who has been given a rank of honour and who can use *Sir* in front of his name رجل منح لقب "سير"

2 a soldier who fought on horseback in the Middle Ages فارس

▸ **knighthood** /-hʊd/ *noun* [C,U] the title or rank of a knight: *He was given a knighthood in last year's Honours List.* لقب أو رتبة "سير"

knit /nɪt/ *verb* [I,T] (kni**tt**ing; kni**tt**ed) to make sth (e.g. an article of clothing) with wool using long needles (2) or a special machine: *Grandma loves knitting.* ○ *I'm knitting a sweater for my nephew.* يحيك، يحبك، يشتغل بالصوف
▶ **-knit** (in compounds) closely joined together: *a closely-knit village community* متماسك
knitting *noun* [U] the act of knitting or sth that is being knitted: *She put down her knitting and yawned.* ○ *I usually do some knitting while I'm watching TV.* حياكة، شغل صوف، تريكو

'knitting needle *noun* [C] = NEEDLE (2)

'knitwear /'nɪtweə(r)/ *noun* [U] articles of clothing that have been knitted: *the knitwear department* تريكو ، ملابس صوفيّة

knob /nɒb/ *noun* [C] **1** a round handle on a door, etc. مِقبض، قبضة
2 a round button on a machine that controls a part of it مفتاح ، زرّ
3 (*Brit*) a (small) round lump: *Grease the pan with a knob of butter.* قطعة صغيرة (من الزبدة مثلاً)

knock¹ /nɒk/ *noun* [C] a sharp blow or the sound it makes: *a nasty knock on the head* ○ *I thought I heard a knock at the door.* ○ (*figurative*) *She has suffered some hard knocks in her life.* ضربة : خبطة ، دقّة

knock² /nɒk/ *verb* **1** [T] to hit sb/sth with a sharp blow: *He knocked the vase onto the floor.* ○ *Be careful not to knock your head when you get up.* ○ *to knock sb unconscious* يضرب : يصدم : يصرع
2 [I] to make a noise by hitting sth: *Someone is knocking at the door.* يطرق ، يدق ، يقرع
3 [T] (*informal*) to say bad or unfavourable things about sb/sth: *That newspaper is always knocking the government.* ينتقد ، يندّد بِ ، يعيب
PHR V **knock about/around** (*informal*) to be in a place: *I'm sure last week's newspaper is knocking around here somewhere.* ○ *I spent a few months knocking around Europe before I went to university.* موجود في مكان ما : يتجوّل
knock sb down to cause sb to fall to the ground/floor: *The old lady was knocked down by a cyclist.* يطرحه أرضاً ، يرمي
knock sth down to destroy a building, etc: *The old houses are to be knocked down to make way for blocks of flats.* يهدم
knock off (sth) (*informal*) to stop doing work, etc: *What time do you knock off?* يفرغ من العمل
knock sth off 1 (*informal*) to reduce a price by a certain amount: *He agreed to knock £10 off the price.* يخفّض السعر
2 (*slang*) to steal sth يسرق ، ينشل
knock sb out 1 to hit sb so that he/she becomes unconscious or cannot get up again for a while: *The punch on the nose knocked him out.* يدوِّخ نتيجة ضربة قويّة : يصرع
2 (used about a drug) to cause sb to sleep ينوّم
knock sb out (of sth) to beat a person or team in a competition so that they do not play any more games in it: *Belgium was knocked out of the European Cup by France.* يهزم خصمه ويخرجه من بقية المباريات
knock sb/sth over to cause sb/sth to fall over: *Be careful not to knock over the drinks.* يوقِع ، يقلب

knocker /'nɒkə(r)/ *noun* [C] a piece of metal on the outside of a door that you knock to attract the attention of the people inside دقاقة أو مقرعة الباب

'knock-on *adj* (*especially Brit*) causing other events to happen one after the other: *An increase in the price of oil has a knock-on effect on other fuels.* متتابع، متواتر

knockout /'nɒkaʊt/ *noun* [C] **1** a blow that causes sb to become unconscious or to be unable to get up again for a while ضربة قاضية
2 a competition in which the winner of each game goes on to the next part but the loser plays no more games مباراة تصفية

knot¹ /nɒt/ *noun* [C] a place where two ends or pieces of rope, string, etc. have been tied together firmly: *to tie/untie a knot* ○ *This knot is very tight – I can't undo it.* عقدة
▶ **knot** *verb* [T] (kno**tt**ing; kno**tt**ed) to tie a knot in sth: *They knotted sheets together and climbed down them.* يربط ، يعقد

knot² /nɒt/ *noun* [C] a measure of the speed of a ship or plane; 1 850 metres per hour عقدة، ميل بحري

know /nəʊ/ *verb* (*pt* **knew** /nju:; *US* nu:/; *pp* **known** /nəʊn/) (not in the continuous tenses) **1** [I,T] to have knowledge or information in your mind: *I don't know much about sport.* ○ *Do you know their telephone number?* ○ *'You've got a flat tyre.' 'I know.'* ○ *Did you know that Jonathan was a keen painter?* ○ *Do you know the whole poem by heart?* ○ *Knowing Katie, she'll be out with her friends.* يعرف ، يعلم
2 [T] to have met or seen sb before: *We've known each other for years.* ❶ Notice the expression **get to know sb**: *Kevin's wife seems very interesting. I'd like to get to know her better.* يعرف ، يتعرّف على
3 [T] to have seen, heard, etc. sth: *I've known him go a whole day without eating.* ○ *It's been known to snow in June.* يعهد ، يعرف ، يصل إلى أسماعه
4 [T] to be familiar with a place: *I don't know this part of London well.* يعرف
5 [T] (often passive) to give sth a particular name; to recognize sb/sth as sth: *Istanbul was previously known as Constantinople.* ○ *She's known as an excellent manager.* ○ *He knows a genuine antique when he sees one.* يعرف بِ : يميّز
6 [T] to speak or understand a language: *I don't know much Spanish.* يعرف
7 [T] to be able to do sth: *Do you know how to use a compass?* ❶ Be careful. You must use **how to**; you CANNOT say: *I know use a compass.* يعرف ، يجيد
8 [T] to have experience of sth: *They have known both wealth and poverty.* ○ *Many people in western countries don't know what it's like to be hungry.* يعرف ، يجرّب، يذوق طعم
IDM **God/goodness/Heaven knows 1** I don't know: *They've ordered a new car but goodness knows how they're going to pay for it.* لا أدري

2 (used for emphasizing sth): *I hope I get an answer soon. Goodness knows, I've waited long enough.* فالله أعلم... فلَقد... في الحقيقة

know better (than that/than to do sth) to have enough sense (not to do sth): *I thought you knew better than to go out in the rain with no coat on.* يعتبر أعقل من أن...

know sb by sight to recognize sb without knowing him/her well يعرفه بالشكل فقط

know sth inside out/like the back of your hand (*informal*) to be very familiar with sth: *I grew up here. I know these woods like the back of my hand.* يعرفه جيداً، يعرفه عن ظهر قلب

know what you are talking about (*informal*) to have knowledge of sth from your own experience يتكلّم عن خبرة

know what's what (*informal*) to have all the important information about sth يعرف كل المعلومات الهامّة عن موضوع ما

let sb know to tell sb; inform sb about sth: *Could you let me know when you've made up your mind?* يعلم، يخبر

you know (used when the speaker is thinking of what to say next): *Well, you know, it's rather difficult to explain.* تعبير يدلّ على التمهّل أو التلكؤ في الكلام

PHRV know of sb/sth to have information about or experience of sb/sth: *Do you know of any pubs around here that serve food?* عنده معلومات أو خبرة في موضوع معين

▸ **know** *noun*

IDM in the know (*informal*) having information that other people do not: *People in the know say that the minister is going to resign.* (مصدر) مطّلع ، مطّلع على معلومات خاصة

'know-all (*especially US* **'know-it-all**) *noun* [C] an annoying person who behaves as if he/she knows everything مدّعي معرفة كل شيء؛ متعالم

'know-how *noun* [U] (*informal*) knowledge of or skill in sth: *We are looking for someone with technical know-how in this field.* مهارة ، خبرة

knowing /ˈnəʊɪŋ/ *adj* showing that you know a lot about sth: *a knowing look* (نظرة) ذات مغزى ، (نظرة) متفهّمة

▸ **knowingly** *adv* **1** on purpose: *I've never knowingly lied to you.* عمداً

2 in a way that shows that you understand: *He smiled knowingly.* بخبث ، بشكل يدلّ على فهم الموقف

⚷**knowledge** /ˈnɒlɪdʒ/ *noun* [U, sing.] information or facts that you have in your mind about sth: *He has extensive knowledge of Ancient Egypt.* ○ *I have a working knowledge of French.* ○ *To my knowledge they are still living there.* ○ *She did it without my knowledge.* معرفة ، علم ، إطّلاع

IDM be common/public knowledge to be known by a lot of people معلومات يعرفها الجميع

▸ **knowledgeable** /-əbl/ *adj* having a lot of knowledge; well-informed: *She's very knowledgeable about history.* واسع الإطّلاع ، خبير

knowledgeably /-əbli/ *adv* عن خبرة ، عن معرفة

knuckle /ˈnʌkl/ *noun* [C] the bones where the fingers join the rest of the hand برجمة ، مفصل بين سُلاميات الأصابع

koala /kəʊˈɑːlə/ (*also* **koˌala ˈbear**) *noun* [C] an Australian animal with thick grey fur that lives in trees and looks like a small bear كُوال (حيوان استرالي)

kohl /kəʊl/ *noun* [U] a black powder that is put around the eyes to make them more attractive. كحل

Koran (*also* **Quran**, **Qur'an**) /kəˈrɑːn; *US* -ˈræn/ *noun* [sing.] **the Koran** the holy book of the Muslims القرآن الكريم

kph /ˌkeɪ piː ˈeɪtʃ/ *abbrev* = KILOMETRES PER HOUR

kW (*also* **kw**) *abbrev* = KILOWATT(s)

L l

L, l /el/ *noun* [C] (*pl.* **Ls**; **L's**; **l's**) the twelfth letter of the English alphabet: *'Lake' begins with (an) 'L'.* الحرف الثاني عشر من الأبجدية الإنكليزية

L /el/ *abbrev* **1** (*Brit*) = LEARNER DRIVER: *L-plates*

2 = LARGE (SIZE)

l *abbrev* **1** = LEFT

2 = LINE

3 = LITRES

Lab *abbrev* = LABOUR PARTY

⚷**label** /ˈleɪbl/ *noun* [C] a piece of paper, etc. on an object which gives information about it: *There is a list of all the ingredients on the label.* ○ (*figurative*) *She hated the label of 'housewife'.* بطاقة أو لصيقة (على زجاجة مثلاً)؛ نعت، لقب

▸ **label** *verb* [T] (labelling; labelled; *US* labeling; labeled) **1** to put a label or labels on sth: *All items of clothing should be clearly labelled with your name.* يضع بطاقات على الحوائج لبيان المحتوى

2 label sb/sth (as) sth to describe sb/sth as sth: *The press had labelled him an extremist.* ينعت ، يلقّب

⚷**laboratory** /ləˈbɒrətri; *US* ˈlæbrətɔːri/ *noun* [C] (*pl.* **laboratories**) (*also informal* **lab**) a room or building that is used for scientific work or for teaching about science: *The blood samples were sent to the laboratory for analysis.* ○ *a physics laboratory* ➲ Look at **language laboratory**. مخبر، مختبر

laborious /ləˈbɔːriəs/ *adj* needing a lot of effort شاقّ ، مُرهِق

▸ **laboriously** *adv* باذلاً جهداً ووقتاً طويلاً

⚷**labour**[1] (*US* **labor**) /ˈleɪbə(r)/ *noun* **1** [U] work, usually of a hard, physical kind: *manual labour* عمل

2 [U] workers, when thought of as a group: *There is a shortage of skilled labour.* ○ *Most of the cotton plantations used slave labour.* ○ *Labour relations* (= between workers and managers) *have improved in recent years.* عمّال ، يد عاملة

3 [C,U] the process of giving birth: *She was in labour for ten hours.* ○ *She had a difficult labour.* مخاض ، ولادة

labour² (*US* **labor**) /ˈleɪbə(r)/ *verb* [I] **1** (*formal*) to work hard: *She laboured on her book for two years.* يكدّ ، يكدح

2 to do sth with difficulty: *The old man laboured up the steep hill.* يبذل جهداً مضنياً ، يرزَح تحت العبء

▶ **laboured** (*US* **labored**) *adj* done slowly or with difficulty: *laboured breathing* مجْهَد ، (تنفس) ثقيل وبصعوبة

labourer (*US* **laborer**) *noun* [C] a person whose job needs hard physical work: *Unskilled labourers are not usually well paid.* ○ *a farm labourer* شغّيل ، فاعل

the ˈLabour Party (*also* **Labour**) *noun* [sing., with sing. or pl. verb] one of the main political parties in Britain. The Labour Party supports the interests of working people: *Labour is/are in government.* ○ *The Labour Party won the election in 1997.* ➲ Look at **Conservative Party** and **Liberal Democrats.** حزب العمّال

ˈlabour-saving *adj* reducing the amount of work needed to do sth: *labour-saving devices* أدوات كهربائية تخفف الجهد المبذول

labrador /ˈlæbrədɔː(r)/ *noun* [C] a type of large yellow or black dog, often used by blind people as a guide لَبرادور: كلب إرشاد المكفوفين

labyrinth /ˈlæbərɪnθ/ *noun* [C] a complicated set of paths and passages, through which it is difficult to find your way: *a labyrinth of corridors* ➲ Look at **maze.** متاهة

lace /leɪs/ *noun* **1** [U] cloth that is made of very fine threads in beautiful patterns: *lace curtains* ○ *a collar made of lace* دانتيل، دنتيلّة

2 [C] a string that is used for tying a shoe, etc: *Do up your laces or you'll trip over them.* شريط أو رباط الحذاء ، قيطان

▶ **lace** *verb* [I,T] **lace (sth) (up)** to fasten sth with a lace(2) يربط بشريط أو قيطان

🔑 lack /læk/ *verb* [T] to have too little or none of sth: *She seems to lack the will to succeed.* يحتاج إلى

IDM be lacking to be needed: *Money is still lacking for the new hospital.* يفتقر إلى ، ينقصه

be lacking in sth not have enough of sth: *He's certainly not lacking in intelligence.* ينقصه

▶ **lack** *noun* [U,sing.] an absence of sth that is needed: *A lack of food forced many people to leave their homes.* فقدان

laconic /ləˈkɒnɪk/ *adj* (*formal*) using few words مقتضَب ، وجيز

▶ **laconically** /-kli/ *adv* باقتضاب وجفاء

lacquer /ˈlækə(r)/ *noun* [U] **1** a type of transparent paint that is put on wood, metal, etc. in order to protect it and make it shiny ورنيش أو طلاء اللّك

2 (*old-fashioned*) a liquid that is put on hair to keep the hairstyle in place سائل يوضع على الشعر لتثبيته

lacy /ˈleɪsi/ *adj* of or like lace مُخرَّم ، مصنوع من أو يشبه الدنتيلّة

lad /læd/ *noun* [C] (*informal*) a boy or young man: *School has changed since I was a lad.* فتى ، غلام

ladder /ˈlædə(r)/ *noun* [C] **1** a piece of equipment that is used for climbing up sth. A ladder consists of two long pieces of metal, wood or rope with steps fixed between them: (*figurative*) *to move up/down the social ladder* سلّم

2 (*US* **run**) a place in a stocking, etc. where it has torn: *Oh no! I've got a ladder in my tights.* تنسيل

laden /ˈleɪdn/ *adj* (not before a noun) having or carrying a lot of sth: *The travellers were laden down with luggage.* ○ (*figurative*) *to be laden with guilt* محمّل ، مثقل بِـ

Ladies /ˈleɪdiz/ *noun* [sing.] (*Brit*) a public toilet for women: *Is there a Ladies near here?* ➲ Look at **Gents** and at the note at **toilet.** تواليت أو دورة مياه للسيدات

ladle /ˈleɪdl/ *noun* [C] a large deep spoon with a long handle, used for serving or transferring liquids: *a soup ladle* مِغرفة

🔑 lady /ˈleɪdi/ *noun* [C] (*pl.* **ladies**) **1** a polite way of saying 'woman': *The old lady next door lives alone.* ○ *a lady doctor* ○ *The lady at reception told me to wait here.* سيّدة

2 a woman who is polite and who behaves well to other people: *A real lady does not scream and shout.* ➲ Look at **gentleman.** سيّدة لبقة محترمة

3 a woman who has a high social position ➲ Look at **lord.** "ليدي"

4 Lady a title that is used before the name of a woman who has a high social position: *Lady Randolph Churchill* ○ *Lady Phillipa Stewart* ➲ Look at **Lord.** الليدي كذا (لقب من ألقاب النبيلات)

IDM ladies and gentlemen (used when you start making a speech to a large group of people) سيّداتي وسادتي

ladybird /ˈleɪdibɜːd/ (*US* **ladybug** /ˈleɪdibʌg/) *noun* [C] a small insect that is red or yellow with black spots حشرة الدعسوقة

ladylike /ˈleɪdilaɪk/ *adj* having or showing suitable behaviour for a lady(2): *That's not a very ladylike way to sit.* محترم ، لائق ، مهذّب

lag /læg/ *verb* [I] (lagging; lagged) **lag (behind) (sb/sth)** to go more slowly than sb/sth: *I'm always lagging behind when we go walking in the mountains.* ○ (*figurative*) *James has been ill and is lagging behind the others at school.* يتخلّف ، يتباطأ ؛ يتوانى

▶ **lag** (*also* **time lag**) *noun* [C] a period of time between two events: *There will be a nine-month lag between the opening of the first part of the*

a b c d e f g h i j k l m n o p q r s t u v w x y z

motorway and its completion. ➲ Look at **jet lag.** فترة بين حدَثين

lager /ˈlɑːɡə(r)/ *noun* [C,U] (a glass or bottle of) a type of light beer نوع من البيرة الخفيفة

lagoon /ləˈɡuːn/ *noun* [C] a salt-water lake بحيرة ماؤها مالح

laid *pt, pp of* LAY[1]

laid-back /ˌleɪd ˈbæk/ *adj* (*informal*) (used about a person) not worried; relaxed: *He's a really laid-back sort of person – he never gets worried about things going wrong.* هادئ الأعصاب ، لا يبالي بمشاكل الحياة

lain *pp of* LIE[2]

lake /leɪk/ *noun* [C] a large area of water that is surrounded by land: *They've gone sailing on the lake.* ○ *Lake Constance* ○ *the Lake District* ❶ A **pond** is smaller than a lake. بحيرة

lamb /læm/ *noun* **1** [C] a young sheep ➲ Look at the note at **sheep.** حَمَل ، خروف صغير

2 [U] the flesh of a lamb when eaten as meat: *lamb chops* ➲ Look at the note at **meat.** لحم الحَمَل (خروف صغير)

lame /leɪm/ *adj* **1** not able to walk properly because of an injury to the leg: *The horse is lame and cannot work.*

> **Lame** is not often used about a person. The verb and noun **limp** are more often used: *He's got a limp.* ○ *You're limping. Have you hurt your leg?*

أعرج

2 (used about an excuse, argument, etc.) not easily believed; weak (عذر) واهٍ

lament /ləˈment/ *verb* [I,T] (*formal*) to feel or express great sadness (about sth) يندب ، يرثي

lamp /læmp/ *noun* [C] a piece of equipment that uses electricity, gas or oil to produce light: *a street lamp* ○ *an oil lamp* ○ *a sunlamp* ○ *a table lamp* مصباح ، سراج ، قنديل

ˈlamp post *noun* [C] a tall pole in a public place with a street lamp on the top عمود الشارع ، عمود كهرباء

lampshade /ˈlæmpʃeɪd/ *noun* [C] a cover for a lamp that makes it look more attractive and makes the light softer غطاء أو شمسيّة المصباح

land[1] /lænd/ *noun* **1** [U] the solid part of the surface of the earth (= not water): *After three months at sea she was glad to reach dry land.* ○ *Penguins can't move very fast on land.* ➲ Look at the note at **ground.** أرض ، برّ ، يابسة

2 [U] a piece of ground: *They have bought a plot of land and plan to build a house on it.* ○ *The moors are public land. You can walk where you like.* قطعة أرض ، أرض

3 [U] ground, soil or earth of a particular kind: *The land is rich and fertile.* ○ *barren land* أرض ، تُربة

4 [C] (*formal*) a country: *She died far from her native land.* ➲ Look at the note at **country.** وطن ، بلاد

land[2] /lænd/ *verb* **1** [I,T] to go onto land or put sth onto land from a ship: *The troops landed on the beaches in Normandy.* ○ *The dockers refused to land the dangerous chemicals.* ينزل أو ينزِل إلى البرّ

2 [I,T] to come down from the air or bring sth down to the ground: *The bird landed on the roof.* ○ *He fell off the ladder and landed on his back.* ○ *The pilot landed the plane safely.* ○ *He is due to land at 3 o'clock.* ➲ Look at **take off.** يحطّ ، يقع (على ظهره مثلاً) : ينْزِل

3 [T] to get sth: *The company has just landed a big contract.* ينجح في الحصول على

PHR V **land up (in...)** (*informal*) to finish in a certain position or situation: *One of the balloons they released landed up in Spain.* ينتهي به الأمر : يحطّ

land sb with sb/sth (*informal*) to give sb a problem or sth difficult to do: *I've been landed with all the organization of the Youth Club disco.* يكلّف بمهمة صعبة ، يحمّل

landfill /ˈlændfɪl/ *noun* **1** [C,U] an area of land where large amounts of waste material are buried أرض طمرت تحتها النفايات

2 [U] waste material that will be buried; the burying of waste material نفايات مطمورة: طمر النفايات

landing /ˈlændɪŋ/ *noun* [C] **1** coming down onto the ground (in a plane): *The plane made an emergency landing in a field.* ○ *a crash landing* ○ *a safe landing* ➲ Look at **take-off.** هبوط الطائرة

2 the area at the top of a staircase or between one staircase and another بسطة السلّم أو الدرَج

ˈlanding page *noun* [C] the part of a website that you reach first when you click on a link on the Internet الصفحة الأولى التي تظهر من الموقع عند النقر على رابط معيّن

ˈlanding stage *noun* [C] a platform for people or things that are going onto or leaving a boat رصيف لنقل الركاب والبضائع من وإلى السفينة

landlady /ˈlændleɪdi/ *noun* [C] (*pl.* **landladies**) **1** a woman who lets a house or room to people for money صاحبة البيت المؤجّر

2 a woman who owns or runs a pub, small hotel, etc. صاحبة حانة أو فندق صغير

landlord /ˈlændlɔːd/ *noun* [C] **1** a person who lets a house or room to people for money صاحب البيت المؤجّر

2 a person who owns or runs a pub, small hotel, etc. صاحب حانة أو فندق صغير

landmark /ˈlændmɑːk/ *noun* [C] **1** an object (often a building) that can be seen easily from a distance: *Big Ben is one of the landmarks on London's skyline.* أحد المعالم البارزة

2 an important stage or change in the development of sth: *The Russian Revolution was a landmark in world history.* طور هام ، نقطة تحوّل

landmine /ˈlændmaɪn/ *noun* [C] a bomb placed on or under the ground, which explodes when vehicles or people move over it لغم أرضي

landscape /ˈlændskeɪp/ *noun* [C] **1** an area of country (when you are thinking about what it looks like): *Heather-covered hills dominate the Scottish landscape.* ○ *an urban landscape* ➲ Look at the note at **scenery**. منظر طبيعي : منظر

2 a picture that shows a view of the countryside صورة تمثل منظراً طبيعياً

landslide /ˈlændslaɪd/ *noun* [C] the sudden fall of earth, rocks, etc. down the side of a mountain: (*figurative*) *a landslide* (= very great) *victory at the election* إنهيال أرضي : (إنتصار) ساحق

lane /leɪn/ *noun* [C] **1** a narrow road in the country: *We found a route through the lanes to avoid the traffic jam on the main road.* طريق ريفيّ ضيّق

2 (often used in names) a narrow street between buildings: *Penny Lane* ممرّ، زقاق

3 a part of a wide road for one line of traffic: *You should look in your mirror and signal before you change lanes.* ○ *a four-lane motorway* ○ *Get into the inside lane. We leave the motorway soon.* أحد أقسام أو مسالك الاوتوستراد

4 a route or path that is regularly used by ships or aeroplanes: *the busy shipping lanes of the English Channel* ممرّ أو طريق (جوي مثلاً)

5 a part of a sports track, swimming pool, etc. for one competitor in a race: *The British athlete is in lane two.* مجرى (في سباق)

language /ˈlæŋgwɪdʒ/ *noun* **1** [U] the system of sounds and writing that human beings use to express their thoughts, ideas and feelings: *written language* ○ *the spoken language* ○ *the language development of young children* لغة

2 [C,U] any system of signs, symbols, movements, etc. that is used to express sth: [C]: *sign language* لغة

3 [C] a form of language that is used by a particular group (usually in one country): *to learn to speak a foreign language* ○ *What is your first language?* ○ *Latin is a dead language.* لغة ، لسان

4 [U] words of a particular type or words that are used by a particular person or group: *bad* (= rude) *language* ○ *legal language* ○ *the language of Shakespeare* لغة : لهجة

ˈ**language laboratory** *noun* [C] (*pl.* **language laboratories**) a room that has special equipment to help you learn a foreign language مختبر لغوي

lanky /ˈlæŋki/ *adj* (used about a person) very tall and thin طويل نحيف

lantern /ˈlæntən/ *noun* [C] a type of light that can be carried. A lantern usually consists of a metal framework with glass sides and a lamp or candle inside. فانوس

lap[1] /læp/ *noun* [C] the flat area that is formed by the upper part of your legs when you are sitting down: *The child sat on his mother's lap and listened to the story.* حجر ، حِضن

lap[2] /læp/ *noun* [C] **1** one journey around a racetrack, etc: *There are three more laps to go in the race.* دورة واحدة حول الملعب (في سباق) ، شوط

2 one part of a long journey مرحلة (في رحلة طويلة)

▸ **lap** *verb* [T] (lapping; lapped) to pass another competitor in a race who is one lap behind you يسبق منافساً في السباق بدورة كاملة

lap[3] /læp/ *verb* (lapping; lapped) **1** [T] **lap sth (up)** (usually used about an animal) to drink sth using the tongue: *The cat lapped up the cream.* يلعَق

2 [I] (used about water) to make gentle sounds as it splashes against sth: *The waves lapped against the side of the boat.* (الموج) يلطم أو يرتطم برفق

PHRV **lap sth up** (*informal*) to listen to or read sth eagerly and accept it as true يتقبل بلهفة ، يتلقّف (المعلومات)

lapel /ləˈpel/ *noun* [C] one of the two parts of the front of a coat or jacket that are folded back قَلْبة ، ثنية قبّة الجاكيت

lapse /læps/ *noun* [C] **1** a short time when you cannot remember sth or you are not thinking about what you are doing: *a lapse of memory* ○ *The crash was the result of a temporary lapse in concentration.* سهوة ، غفلة

2 a piece of bad behaviour that is unlike a person's usual behaviour هفوة ، زلّة

3 a period of time in which you do not do sth, go somewhere, etc: *She returned to work after a lapse of ten years bringing up her family.* ➲ Look at the verb **elapse**. فترة انقطاع

▸ **lapse** *verb* [I] **1** to go into a particular state: *to lapse into silence, a coma, etc.* ينتقل إلى حالة أخرى، يصبح

2 to be lost because it is not used, claimed or paid for: *My membership has lapsed because I forgot to renew it.* يبطل ، ينتهي مفعوله : يسقط حقّه

laptop /ˈlæptɒp/ *noun* [C] a small computer that can work using a battery and that is easily carried كمبيوتر صغير نقّال

larch /lɑːtʃ/ *noun* [C] a tree that has cones and sharp pointed leaves that fall in the winter أرزيّة لاركس

larder /ˈlɑːdə(r)/ *noun* [C] a large cupboard or small room that is used for storing food. خزانة أو غرفة صغيرة لخزن الأطعمة ، بيت المؤونة

large /lɑːdʒ/ *adj* greater in size or amount than is usual: *Have you got this shirt in a large size?* ○ *Large amounts of money are spent on advertising.* ○ *There is a large increase in the numbers of young people going to college.* ➲ Look at the note at **big**. كبير ، ضخم : وافر

IDM **by and large** → BY[1]

▸ **large** *noun*

IDM **at large 1** (used about a criminal, animal, etc.) free: *One of the escaped prisoners is still at large.* طليق ، فار

2 as a whole; in general: *Society at large is becoming more concerned about the environment.* كمجموعة : بصورة عامة

largely *adv* mostly: *His success was largely due to hard work.* إلى حدّ كبير

ˈ**large-scale** *adj* happening over a large area or affecting a lot of people على نطاق واسع

lark /lɑːk/ *noun* [C] a small brown bird that sings beautifully قُبَّرة

laryngitis /ˌlærɪnˈdʒaɪtɪs/ *noun* [U] a mild disease of the throat that makes it difficult to speak التهاب الحنجرة

laser /ˈleɪzə(r)/ *noun* [C] (a piece of equipment that produces) a very strong beam of light. Laser beams are used in weapons and medical operations and can also cut hard substances such as metals. أشعة ليزر

lash[1] /læʃ/ *noun* [C] **1** a blow that is given by a whip: *The prisoner was given twenty lashes.* جَلْدة

2 = EYELASH

lash[2] /læʃ/ *verb* **1** [I,T] to hit (as if) with a whip: *The rain lashed against the windows.* يخبِط ، يصفع

2 [T] to move sth like a whip: *The tiger lashed its tail from side to side.* يهزّ أو يؤرجح غاضباً

3 [T] **lash A to B; lash A and B together** to tie two things together firmly with rope, etc: *The two boats were lashed together.* يوثق، يحكِم الرّبط بحبل

PHR V **lash out (at/against sb/sth)** to suddenly attack sb/sth (with words or by hitting them): *The Prime Minister lashed out at his critics.* ينهال عليه بالضرب أو الشتائم : ينقضّ على...

lash out (on sth) (*informal*) to spend a lot of money on sth: *We've decided to lash out on a foreign holiday next year.* ينفِق بسخاء

lass /læs/ (*also* **lassie** /ˈlæsi/) *noun* [C] (*informal*) a girl or young woman ❶ **Lass** is most commonly used in Scotland and the North of England. صبية، شابّة

lasso /læˈsuː; *US* ˈlæsəʊ/ *noun* [C] (*pl.* **lassos** or **lassoes**) a long rope with a circle (noose) at one end that is used for catching cows and horses وَهَق: حبل في طرفه أنشوطة

▸ **lasso** *verb* [T] يَهِق: يطرح الحبل في عنق الدابّة

last[1] /lɑːst; *US* læst/ *adj* **1** coming at the end; final: *December is the last month of the year.* ○ *Would the last person to leave please turn off the lights?* ○ *Our house is the last one in the row.* ○ *She lived alone for the last years of her life.* أخير : آخر

2 (only *before* a noun) (used about a time, period, event, etc. in the past that is nearest to the present): *I went shopping last Saturday.* ○ *We have been working on the book for the last six months.* ○ *The last time I saw her was in London.*

> **The latest** means 'most recent' or 'new'. **The last** means the one before the present one: *His last novel was a huge success, but the latest one is much less popular.*

الماضي : الأخير ، قبل الأخير : آخر (مرة)

3 (only *before* a noun) only remaining: *This is my last chance to take the exam.* ○ *Who's going to have the last cake?* آخر

4 most unlikely; not suitable: *He's the last person to be trusted with money.* ○ *She's on a diet. Chocolates are the last thing she wants.* غير صالح ، غير مناسب : أقل الأشخاص أو الأشياء صلاحية

IDM **first/last thing** → THING

have, etc. the last word 1 to make the final remark in a discussion or argument (له) الكلمة الأخيرة

2 to make the final decision about sth after a discussion القول الفَصْل

in the last resort; (as) a last resort when everything else has failed; the person or thing that helps when everything else has failed: *In the last resort we can always walk home.* الحل الأخير المتبقّي ، الملاذ الأخير

the last/final straw → STRAW

the last minute/moment the final minute/moment before sth happens: *We arrived at the last minute to catch the train.* ○ *a last-minute change of plan* (في) آخر لحظة

last/next but one, two, etc. one, two, etc. away from the last/next: *I live in the next house but one on the right.* ○ *X is the last letter but two of the alphabet* (= the third letter from the end). الأخير

a week yesterday/last Monday, etc. → WEEK

▸ **lastly** *adv* finally; last of all: *Lastly, I would like to wish you all a Happy New Year.* أخيراً ، في الختام

last[2] /lɑːst; *US* læst/ *adv* **1** at the end; after all the others: *The British athlete came in last.* ○ *Her name is last on the list.* آخراً ، في الذيل ، في المؤخرة

2 on the occasion in the past that is nearest to the present: *When did you last have your eyes checked?* ○ *When I saw her last she seemed very happy.* آخر مرة

IDM **last but not least** (used before the final item in a list) just as important as all the other items: *And last but not least, I'd like to thank you all very much.* أخيراً وليس آخراً

last[3] /lɑːst; *US* læst/ *verb* [I,T] **1** to continue for a period of time: *Do you think this weather will last till the weekend?* ○ *The exam lasts three hours.* يدوم

2 to remain in a good condition: *It's only a cheap radio but it'll probably last a year or so.* يبقى صالحاً ، يخدم

3 (used about the quantity, condition, etc. of sth) to be good enough or sufficient for what sb needs: *The coffee won't last till next week.* ○ *This old coat will have to last another winter. I can't afford a new one.* ○ *I've only got ten pounds to last me till Saturday.* يكفي؛ يتحمّل؛ يخدم

▸ **lasting** *adj* continuing for a long time: *The children's faces left a lasting impression on me.* دائم ، لا يمحى

last[4] /lɑːst; *US* læst/ *noun* [sing.] **1** a person or thing that is last: *Alex was the last to arrive.* آخِر شخص ، آخِر شيء

2 the last (of sb/sth) the only remaining part of sth: *We finished the last of the bread at breakfast so we'd better get some more.* المتبقّي

IDM **at (long) last** in the end; finally: *After months of separation they were together at last.* أخيراً : أخيراً وبعد طول انتظار

'last name *noun* [C] = SURNAME

latch /lætʃ/ *noun* [C] **1** a small metal bar that is used for fastening a door or a gate. You have to lift the latch in order to open the door. مزلاج ، سقّاطة الباب

2 a type of lock for a door that must be opened from the outside with a key قفل الباب الخارجي

IDM on the latch (*Brit*) (used about a door) closed but not locked غير مقفول

▸ **latch** *verb*

PHRV latch on (to sth) (*informal*) to understand: *It took them a while to latch on to what she was talking about.* يفهم ، يدرك

late /leɪt/ *adj, adv* **1** after the usual or expected time: *She was ten minutes late for school.* ○ *The ambulance arrived too late to save him.* ○ *to be late with the rent* ○ *It's never too late to learn.* ○ *to stay up late* ○ *The buses are running late today.* متأخّر

2 near the end of a period of time: *The late nineteenth century was a time of great change.* ○ *in the late morning* ○ *His mother's in her late fifties* (= between 55 and 60). ○ *They are going on holiday in late May.* ○ *We got back home late in the evening.* في أواخر : في وقت متأخّر

3 latest very recent or new: *the latest fashions* ○ *the latest news* ○ *the terrorists' latest attack on the town* ➲ Look at the note at **last**[1]. آخِر

4 (only *before* a noun) no longer alive; dead: *his late wife* الراحل ، المرحوم

IDM at the latest no later than: *I need your report on my desk by Friday at the latest.* على أكثر تقدير ، في أبعد حدّ

an early/a late night → NIGHT

later on at a later time: *Later on you'll probably wish that you'd worked harder at school.* ○ *Bye – I'll see you a bit later on.* بعد فترة من الزمن : فيما بعد

sooner or later → SOON

▸ **latish** /'leɪtɪʃ/ *adj, adv* rather late متأخّر أو متأخّراً بعض الشيء

latecomer /'leɪtkʌmə(r)/ *noun* [C] a person who arrives late من يصل متأخّراً

lately /'leɪtli/ *adv* in the period of time up till now; recently: *What have you been doing lately?* ○ *Hasn't the weather been dreadful lately?* في الآونة الأخيرة ، مؤخّراً

latent /'leɪtnt/ *adj* (usually *before* a noun) existing but not yet active, developed or seen: *latent abilities/talent* كامن

latest /'leɪtɪst/ *noun* [U] (*informal*) the most recent (fashion, news, etc.): *Have you heard the latest?* (= news) ○ *This is the latest in a series of attacks by this terrorist group.* ○ *They have the very latest in new machinery.* أحدث شيء : آخر موضة : آخر الأنباء

latex /'leɪteks/ *noun* [U] **1** a thick white liquid that is produced by some plants and trees, especially rubber trees لبن النبات

2 an artificial substance that is used to make paints, glues and materials لاتكس،مطّاط

lathe /leɪð/ *noun* [C] a machine that shapes pieces of wood, metal, etc. by holding and turning them against a fixed cutting tool مخرطة

lather /'lɑːðə(r); *US* 'læð-/ *noun* [U] white bubbles that you get when you mix soap with water رغوة

Latin /'lætɪn; *US* 'lætn/ *noun* [U] the language that was used in ancient Rome اللغة اللاتينيّة

▸ **Latin** *adj* **1** of or in Latin: *Latin poetry* لاتيني

2 of the countries or people that use languages that developed from Latin, such as French, Italian, Spanish or Portuguese من أصل لاتيني

,Latin A'merican *noun* [C], *adj* (a person who comes) from Latin America (the parts of Central and South America where Spanish or Portuguese is spoken): *Latin American music* (فرد) من أمريكا اللاتينيّة

latitude /'lætɪtjuːd; *US* -tuːd/ *noun* [U] (*abbr* **lat.**) the distance of a place north or south of the equator ℹ Latitude is measured in **degrees**. Look at **longitude**. خطّ العرض الجغرافي

latter /'lætə(r)/ *adj* (*formal*) (only *before* a noun) nearer to the end of a period of time; later: *Interest rates should fall in the latter half of the year.* الأخير : النهائي

▸ **latter** *noun* [sing.], *pron* the second of two people or things that are mentioned: *The options were History and Geography. I chose the latter.* ℹ The first of two people or things that are mentioned is **the former**. الثاني ، الأخير

latterly *adv* (*formal*) lately; recently: *She has taught at the universities of London and Bristol and latterly at Durham.* مؤخّراً : من فترة قصيرة

laugh /lɑːf; *US* læf/ *verb* [I] to make the sounds that show you are happy or amused: *His jokes always make me laugh.* ○ *to laugh out loud* ○ *We laughed till we cried.* يضحك

PHRV laugh at sb/sth 1 to show, by laughing, that you think sb/sth is funny: *The children laughed at the clown.* يضحك من (نكتة مثلاً)

2 to show that you think sb is ridiculous: *Don't laugh at him. He can't help the way he speaks.* يضحك على ، يسخر من

▸ **laugh** *noun* [C] **1** the sound or act of laughing: *Her jokes got a lot of laughs.* ○ *We all had a good laugh at what he'd written.* ضحكة

2 (*informal*) a person or thing that is amusing: *Let's invite Tony. He's a good laugh.* شخص مضحك أو مسلٍ ؛ شيء مسلٍ

IDM for a laugh as a joke: *The boys put a spider in her bed for a laugh.* على سبيل المزاح أو المداعبة

laughable /-əbl/ *adj* (used about sth that is of poor quality) deserving to be laughed at; foolish or ridiculous زري ، مثير للسخرية

laughing /'lɑːfɪŋ; *US* 'læfɪŋ/ *adj* showing amusement or happiness by laughter: *laughing faces* ضاحك ، سعيد

IDM burst out laughing to suddenly start to laugh loudly ينفجر ضاحكاً

'laughing stock *noun* [C] a person or thing that other people laugh at or make fun of (in an unpleasant way) أضحوكة ، هزأة، مَسخرة

a b c d e f g h i j k l m n o p q r s t u v w x y z

laughter /ˈlɑːftə(r); *US* ˈlæf-/ *noun* [U] the sound or act of laughing: *Everyone roared with laughter.* ضحك : قهقهة

launch¹ /lɔːntʃ/ *verb* [T] **1** to send a ship into the water or a rocket, etc. into the sky
ينزل إلى الماء ، يدشّن (سفينة) : يطلق

2 to start sth new or to show sth for the first time: *The enemy launched an attack at midnight.* ○ *to launch a new product onto the market*
يدشّن: يطرح في الأسواق

▸ **launch** *noun* [C, usually sing.] the act of launching a ship, rocket, new product, etc: *The shuttle launch has been delayed by 24 hours.*
تدشين (سفينة) : إطلاق : طَرْح في الأسواق

launch² /lɔːntʃ/ *noun* [C] a large motor boat
زورق ذو محرك ، "لنش"

launderette (*also* **laundrette**) /lɔːnˈdret/ (*US* **laundromat** /ˈlɔːndrəmæt/) *noun* [C] a type of shop where you pay to wash and dry your clothes in washing machines
دكّان مزوّد بالغسالات الكهربائية لاستعمالها مقابل أجر

laundry /ˈlɔːndri/ *noun* (*pl.* **laundries**) **1** [U] clothes, etc. that need washing or that are being washed: *a laundry basket* ⓘ **Do the washing** is more common in spoken British English than 'do the laundry'. الغسيل

2 [C] a business where you send sheets, clothes, etc. to be washed
مصبغة: مكان يختصّ بغسل الملابس وكيّها

laurel /ˈlɒrəl; *US* ˈlɔːr-/ *noun* [C,U] **1** an evergreen bush with dark smooth shiny leaves: *a laurel hedge* الغار

2 laurels [plural] honour and distinction following a great achievement: *She won laurels for her first novel.* مجد، تقدير، شهرة

lava /ˈlɑːvə/ *noun* [U] hot liquid rock that comes out of a volcano حمم بركانية ، لابة

lavatory /ˈlævətri; *US* -tɔːri/ *noun* [C] (*pl.* **lavatories**) **1** a large bowl, joined to a pipe and a drain, used for getting rid of waste that people pass from the body. Another word for 'toilet'.
مرحاض أو تواليت (من البورسلين مثلاً)

2 a room that contains a toilet, washbasin, etc: *Where's the ladies' lavatory, please?* ➲ Look at the note at **toilet**. مرحاض، دورة مياه ، تواليت

lavender /ˈlævəndə(r)/ *noun* [U] a garden plant with purple flowers that smells very pleasant
نبات الخزامى

lavish /ˈlævɪʃ/ *adj* **1** giving or spending generously or in large quantities: *She was always very lavish with her presents.* سخي ، مغدق

2 large in amount or number: *a lavish meal*
غزير ، وافر

▸ **lavish** *verb*

PHR V **lavish sth on sb/sth** to give sth generously or in large quantities to sb: *He lavished expensive gifts on her.* يغدق على

law /lɔː/ *noun* **1** [C] an official rule of a country, etc. that says what a person, company, etc. may or may not do: *Parliament passed a law about wearing seat belts in the back of cars.* قانون

2 the law [U] all the laws in a country, etc: *Stealing is against the law.* ○ *to break the law* ○ *to obey the law* ➲ Look at **legal**. القانون

3 [U] the law(2) as a subject of study or as a profession: *She is studying law.* ○ *My brother works for a law firm in Brighton.* ➲ Look at **legal**. المحاماة ، (كلية) الحقوق

4 [C] (in science) a statement of what always happens in certain circumstances: *the laws of mathematics* ○ *the laws of gravity* قانون

IDM **law and order** a situation in which the law is obeyed: *There has been a breakdown of law and order in this country over the past ten years.* استتباب الأمن ، مراعاة القانون

▸ **lawful** /-fl/ *adj* allowed or recognized by law: *We shall use all lawful means to obtain our demands.* ○ *his lawful wife* ➲ Look at **legal**. ⓘ The opposite is **unlawful**. قانوني ، شرعي

lawless *adj* (used about a person or his/her actions) breaking the law: *a gang of lawless hooligans* متمرّد على السلطة : بِلا قانون ، فوضوي

lawlessness *noun* [U] إخلال بالأمن ، شغب

ˈlaw-abiding *adj* (used about a person) obeying the law: *We are all respectable law-abiding citizens.* مطيع للقانون

lawbreaker /ˈlɔːbreɪkə(r)/ *noun* [C] a person who does not obey the law; a criminal
شخص خارق للقانون ؛ مجرم

ˈlaw court (*also* **court of law**) *noun* [C] a place where a judge or jury decides legal matters (e.g. whether a person is innocent or guilty)

> A **case** is **tried** in a law court. Look at **defence**, **prosecution** and **witness**.

محكمة

lawn /lɔːn/ *noun* [C,U] an area of grass in a garden or park that is regularly cut: *I'm going to mow the lawn this afternoon.* مَرجة : مَخْضَرة

lawnmower /ˈlɔːnməʊə(r)/ *noun* [C] a machine that is used for cutting the grass in a garden
آلة لجزّ الحشيش

ˌlawn ˈtennis *noun* [U] = TENNIS

lawsuit /ˈlɔːsuːt; *Brit also* -sjuːt/ *noun* [C] a legal argument in a court of law that is between two people or groups and not between the police and a criminal دعوى قضائية

lawyer /ˈlɔːjə(r)/ *noun* [C] a person who has studied law and whose job is to give advice on legal matters: *to consult a lawyer* محام

> A **solicitor** is a lawyer who gives legal advice, prepares legal documents, arranges the buying or selling of land, etc. A **barrister** is a lawyer who is qualified to speak for you in a higher court of law. The American term is **attorney**.

lax /læks/ *adj* not having high standards; not strict: *Their security checks are rather lax.*
مُهمِل : غير دقيق ، متهاون

lay¹ /leɪ/ *verb* [T] (*pt, pp* **laid** /leɪd/) **1** to put sb/sth carefully in a particular position or on a surface: *She laid a sheet over the dead body.* ○ *He laid the child gently down on his bed.* ○ *'Don't worry,' she said, laying her hand on my shoulder.* يَضع ، يضجع

2 to put sth in the correct position for a particular purpose: *They're laying new electricity cables in our street.* يمدّ، يَمدّ

3 to prepare sth for use: *The police have laid a trap for him; I think they'll catch him this time.* ○ *Can you lay the table please?* (= put the knives, forks, plates, etc. on it) يَعدّ ، يهيّئ

4 to produce eggs: *Does a snake lay eggs?* يَبيض

5 (used with some nouns to give a similar meaning to a verb): *They laid all the blame on him* (= they blamed him). ○ *to lay emphasis on sth* (= emphasize it) يلقي ؛ يَضع

PHR V **lay sth down** to give sth as a rule: *It's all laid down in the rules of the club.* يسنّ ، يضع ، يرسم

lay off (sb) (*informal*) to stop annoying sb: *Can't you lay off me for a bit?* يَدَعُ شخصاً وشأنه ، يتوقف عن إزعاجه

lay sb off to stop giving work to sb: *They've laid off 500 workers at the car factory.* يسرّح (عاملاً)

lay sth on (*informal*) to provide sth: *They're laying on a trip to London for everybody.* يعدّ ؛ يقدّم

lay sth out 1 to spread out a group of things so that you can see them easily or so that they look nice: *All the food was laid out on a table in the garden.* يمدّ، يبسط ؛ يعرض بشكل جميل

2 to arrange sth in a planned way: *The new shopping centre is very attractively laid out.* يُنظّم

lay² /leɪ/ *adj* (only *before* a noun) **1** a member of a church who is not a priest: *a lay preacher* علمانيّ ، ليس من رجال الكهنوت

2 without special training in or knowledge of a particular subject غير اختصاصيّ

lay³ *pt* of LIE²

layabout /ˈleɪəbaʊt/ *noun* [C] (*Brit informal*) a person who is lazy and does not do much work كسول ، متسكّع ، تَنْبل

lay-by /ˈleɪ baɪ/ (*US* **rest stop**) *noun* [C] (*pl.* **lay-bys**) an area at the side of a road where vehicles can park for a short time out of the way of the traffic موقف استراحة للسّيارات بجانب الطريق

layer /ˈleɪə(r)/ *noun* [C] a thickness or quantity of sth that is on sth else or between other things: *A thin layer of dust covered everything in the room.* ○ *The cake has a layer of jam in the middle.* ○ *It's very cold. You'll need several layers of clothing.* ○ *the top/bottom layer* ○ *the inner/outer layer* طبقة

layman /ˈleɪmən/ *noun* [C] (*pl.* **laymen** /-mən/) (*also* **layperson** /ˈleɪpɜːsn/ (*pl.* **lay people** or **lay persons**)) a person who does not have special training in or knowledge of a particular subject: *a medical reference book for the layman* الرجل العادي (غير المختص)

layout /ˈleɪaʊt/ *noun* [usually sing.] the way in which the parts of sth such as the page of a book, a garden or a building are arranged: *the layout of streets* ○ *the magazine's attractive new page layout* مخطط؛ تصميم؛ ترتيب

laze /leɪz/ *verb* [I] **laze (about/around)** to do very little; to rest or relax: *We just lazed around all afternoon.* يسترخي ، يستريح ؛ لا يقوم بأي عمل

lazy /ˈleɪzi/ *adj* (**lazier**; **laziest**) **1** (used about a person) not wanting to work: *Don't be lazy. Come and give me a hand.* كسول

2 moving slowly or without much energy: *a lazy smile* متراخٍ ، بطيء

3 making you feel that you do not want to do very much: *a lazy summer's afternoon* غير مشجّع على العمل ، يدعو للكسل

▸ **lazily** *adv* متمهلاً ، برِفق ؛ بتكاسل

laziness *noun* [U] كَسَل ، خمول

lb (*US* **lb.**) *abbrev* = POUND(S)¹ (3)

lead¹ /led/ *noun* **1** [U] (*symbol* **Pb**) a soft heavy grey metal. Lead is used in pipes, roofs, etc. معدن الرصاص

2 [C,U] the black substance inside a pencil that makes a mark when you write (قلم) رصاص

lead² /liːd/ *noun* **1** [sing.] a position ahead of other people, organizations, etc: *Britain has taken the lead in developing computer software for that market.* المركز الأول ، (في) الطّليعة

2 the lead [sing.] the first place or position: *The French athlete has gone into the lead.* ○ *Who is in the lead?* المركز الأول

3 [sing.] the distance or amount by which sb/sth is in front of another person or thing: *The company has a lead of several years in the development of the new technology.* مسافة أو مقدار التقدّم على منافس ، تقدّم، سبق

4 [C] the main part or role in a play or show: *Who's playing the lead in the new film?* الدور الرئيسيّ في مسرحية مثلاً

5 [C] a piece of information that may help to give the answer to a problem: *The police are following all possible leads to track down the killer.* معلومات ، دليل أو مفتاح لحلّ لغز

6 [C] a long chain or piece of leather that is attached to the collar around a dog's neck and used for keeping the dog under control: *All dogs must be kept on a lead.* مقود الكلب

7 [C] a piece of wire that is used for carrying electric current سلك أو شريط كهربائي

IDM **follow sb's example/lead** → FOLLOW

lead³ /liːd/ *verb* (*pt, pp* **led** /led/) **1** [T] to go with or in front of a person or animal to show the way or to make them go in the right direction: *The teacher led the children out of the hall and back to the classroom.* ○ *She led the horse into its stable.* ○ *The receptionist led the way to the boardroom.* ○ *to lead sb by the hand* يقود ، يرشد

You usually **guide** a tourist or somebody who needs special help: *to guide visitors around Oxford* ○ *He guided the blind woman to her seat.* If you **direct** somebody, you explain with words how to get somewhere: *Could you direct me to the nearest post office, please?*

2 [T] to influence what sb does or thinks: *He led me to believe he really meant what he said.* يجعل ، يؤثّر على

3 [I] (used about a road or path) to go to a place: *I don't think this path leads anywhere.* يؤدّي أو يفضي إلى

4 [I] **lead to sth** to have sth as a result: *Eating too much sugar can lead to all sorts of health problems.* يؤدّي إلى

5 [T] to have a particular type of life: *They lead a very busy life.* ○ *to lead a life of crime* يعيش حياة...

6 [I,T] **lead (sb/sth) (in sth)** to be the best at sth or to be in first place: *Federer is leading by two sets to love.* ○ *Federer is leading Roddick by two sets to love.* يتقدم على ، يسبق

7 [I,T] to be in control or the leader of sth: *Who is going to lead the discussion?* يقود ، يوجّه

PHR V **lead up to sth** to be an introduction to or cause of sth: *What were the events that led up to the First World War?* يمهّد الطريق ، يؤدّي إلى : يسبّب

leader /ˈliːdə(r)/ *noun* [C] **1** a person who is the head of sth or in charge of sth: *Who is the leader of the Conservative Party?* ○ *a weak/strong leader* ○ *She is a natural leader* (= she knows how to tell other people what to do). زعيم ، قائد ، رئيس

2 the person or team that is best or in first place: *The leader has just finished the third lap.* ○ (*figurative*) *The new brand of shampoo soon became a market leader.* الأوّل (في سباق) : الرائد ، السلعة المفضّلة

▸ **leadership** *noun* **1** [U] the state of being a leader(1): *Who will take over the leadership?* زعامة ، قيادة

2 [U] the qualities that a leader(1) should have صفات القيادة ، حسن القيادة

3 [C, with sing. or pl. verb] a group of leaders(1): *Has/Have the leadership lost touch with ordinary people?* القيادة

leading /ˈliːdɪŋ/ *adj* **1** best or very important: *He's one of the leading experts in this field.* ○ *She played a leading role in getting the business started.* بارز ، هامّ ، رئيسيّ

2 in front or in first place: *Aldridge has been the leading goal scorer this season.* الأوّل ، في المقدّمة

3 that tries to make sb give a particular answer: *The lawyer was warned not to ask the witness leading questions.* (سؤال) ايحائيّ

ˈ**lead story** *noun* [C] (*pl.* **lead stories**) the most important piece of news in a newspaper or news broadcast أهم نبأ (في صحيفة أو في نشرة أخبار)

leaf /liːf/ *noun* [C] (*pl.* **leaves** /liːvz/) one of the thin, flat parts of a plant or tree. Leaves are usually green and grow from a branch but different plants have differently shaped leaves: *autumn leaves* ○ *The leaves rustled in the breeze.* ○ *tea leaves* ورقة : صفحة

▸ **leaf** *verb*

PHR V **leaf through sth** to turn the pages of a book, etc. quickly and without looking at them carefully يتصفّح ، يقلّب صفحات كتاب بعدم اهتمام

leafy *adj* (**leafier**; **leafiest**) **1** having many leaves: *cabbage, spinach, lettuce and other leafy vegetables* كثير الأوراق الخضراء

2 (used about a place) having many trees and plants: *a pleasant leafy suburb* كثير الأشجار

leaflet /ˈliːflət/ *noun* [C] a small printed piece of paper that advertises or gives information about sth. Leaflets are usually given free of charge: *I picked up a leaflet about bus services to Heathrow.* منشور

league /liːɡ/ *noun* [C] **1** a group of sports clubs that compete with each other for a prize: *the football league* ○ *Which team is top of the league at the moment?* ➲ Look at **rugby league**. اتّحاد

2 a group of people, countries, etc. that join together for a particular purpose: *the League of Nations* عصبة

3 (*informal*) a standard of quality or achievement: *He is so much better than the others. They're just not in the same league.* مستوى : كفاءة

IDM **in league (with sb)** having a secret agreement (with sb): *I don't trust them. I'm sure they're in league with each other.* متواطئ مع

leak /liːk/ *noun* [C] **1** a small hole or crack which liquid or gas can get through: *There's a leak in the pipe.* ○ *The roof has sprung a leak.* ثُقب صغير ، خَرق ، فَخت

2 the liquid or gas that gets through such a hole: *I can smell gas. Perhaps there's a leak.* تسرُّب : نَزيز

3 giving away information that should be kept secret تسريب (الأنباء)

▸ **leak** *verb* **1** [I,T] to allow liquid or gas to get through a hole or crack: *The boat was leaking badly.* يتسرّب إليه أو منه

2 [I] (used about liquid or gas) to get through a hole or crack: *Water is leaking in above the window frame.* يتسرّب : (سقف) يدلف

3 [T] **leak sth (to sb)** to give secret information: *The committee's findings were leaked to the press before the report was published.* يسرّب معلومات سرّية

PHR V **leak out** (used about secret information) to become known: *The government did not want the details to leak out.* يتسرّب ، ينكشف

leakage /ˈliːkɪdʒ/ *noun* [C,U] an example of leaking; sth that has been leaked: [C]: *a leakage of dangerous chemicals* تسرُّب : مادة متسرّبة

leaky *adj* having a hole or holes through which liquid or gas can get in or out مثقوب ، سَرِب

lean¹ /liːn/ *adj* **1** (used about a person or animal) thin and in good health نحيف ، ضامر

2 (used about meat) having little or no fat (لحم) قليل الدهن

3 not producing much: *a lean harvest* ضئيل ، شحيح

lean² /liːn/ *verb* (*pt, pp* **leant** /lent/ or **leaned** /liːnd/) **1** [I] to be in a position that is not straight or upright: *He leaned across the table to pick up the phone.* ○ *Don't lean out of the window when the train is moving.* ○ *to lean forwards, backwards, over to one side, etc.* يميل ، ينحني

2 [I] **lean against/on sth** to rest against sth so that it gives support: *She had to stop and lean on the gate.* يتكئ على ، يستند إلى أو على : يعتمد على

3 [T] to put sth against sth: *Please don't lean bicycles against this window.* يسنِد

leap /liːp/ *verb* (*pt, pp* **leapt** /lept/ or **leaped** /liːpt/) [I] **1** to jump high or a long way: *The horse leapt over the wall. ○ The children leapt up and down with excitement.* يقفز ، يَثِب

2 to move quickly: *I leapt upstairs when I heard the scream.* ينط ، يسرِع

PHR V **leap at sth** to accept a chance or offer with enthusiasm: *She leapt at the chance to work in television.* يقبل (عَرْضاً) بتلهف ، يطير من الفرح

▸ **leap** *noun* [C] **1** a big jump: *He took a flying leap at the wall but didn't get over it.* قفزة أو وثبة كبيرة

2 a great change (for the better) or an increase in sth: *The development of penicillin was a great leap forward in the field of medicine.* طفرة : ارتفاع

leapfrog /ˈliːpfrɒg/ *noun* [U] a children's game in which one person bends over and another person jumps over him/her لعبة النَطّة

ˈ**leap year** *noun* [C] one year in every four, in which February has 29 days instead of 28 سنة كبيسة

🔑**learn** /lɜːn/ *verb* (*pt, pp* **learnt** /lɜːnt/ or **learned** /lɜːnd/) **1** [I,T] **learn (sth) (from sb/sth)** to get knowledge, a skill, etc. (from sb/sth): *I'm not very good at driving yet – I'm still learning. ○ Debby is learning to play the piano. ○ to learn a foreign language ○ We're learning how to use the new software. ○ I find it really difficult to learn lists by heart.* يتعلّم

2 [I] **learn (of/about) sth** to get some information about sth; to find out: *I was sorry to learn of your father's death.* يعلَم ، يسمع

3 [T] to understand or realize: *We should have learned by now that we can't rely on her.* يدرك

▸ **learned** /ˈlɜːnɪd/ *adj* **1** (used about a person) having a lot of knowledge from studying: *a learned scholar* علّامة ، واسع الاطّلاع

2 for learned people: *a learned journal* (مجلّة) للمثقفين والمختصّين ، علمي

learner *noun* [C] a person who is learning: *a learner driver ○ books for young learners* الطالب المبتدئ : متعلّم السواقة

learning *noun* [U] knowledge that you get from studying: *men and women of learning* عِلم، معرفة: تعلّم

ˈ**learning difficulties** *noun* [plural] mental problems that people may have from birth, or that may be caused by illness or injury, that affect their ability to learn things عوائق في التعلّم

lease /liːs/ *noun* [C] an official written agreement (a contract) in which land, a building, etc. is let to sb else (a tenant) for a certain period of time in return for rent عقد الايجار

▸ **lease** *verb* [T]: *They lease the land from a local farmer. ○ Part of the building is leased out to tenants.* يؤجِّر

🔑**least**[1] /liːst/ *det, pron* (used as the superlative of *little*) smallest in size, amount, extent, etc: *He's got the least experience of all of us. ○ You've done the most work, and I'm afraid John has done the least.* الأقلّ : الأصغر : الأدنى

🔑**least**[2] /liːst/ *adv* to the smallest extent or degree; less than anybody/anything else: *He's the person who needs help least. ○ I bought the least expensive tickets.* أقلّ من الجميع ، إلى أدنى حدّ : أقلّ (التذاكر) غلاءً

IDM **at least 1** not less than, and probably more: *It'll cost at least £200.* على الأقلّ

2 even if other things are wrong: *It may not be beautiful but at least it's cheap.* على الأقلّ

3 (used for correcting sth that you have just said): *I saw him, at least I think I saw him.* أو بالأحرى ، على الأقلّ

4 (used for saying that sth is the minimum you expect sb to do): *You could at least say you're sorry!* على الأقلّ

last but not least → LAST[2]

least of all especially not: *Nobody should be worried, least of all you.* خاصّة

not in the least not at all: *It doesn't matter in the least.* أبداً ، على الإطلاق

🔑**leather** /ˈleðə(r)/ *noun* [U] the skin of animals which has been specially treated. Leather is used to make shoes, bags, coats, etc: *a leather jacket* جِلد (مدبوغ)

🔑**leave**[1] /liːv/ *verb* (*pt, pp* **left** /left/) **1** [I,T] to go away from sb/sth: *When should we leave for the airport? ○ The train leaves Reading at just after ten. ○ He left his mother in tears. ○ Barry left his wife for another woman.* يغادر : يترك

Notice that if you leave sb/sth it may be permanently or just for a short time: *He leaves home at 8.00 every morning. ○ He left home and went to live in France.* **Depart** is a more formal word and is used about boats, trains, planes, etc: *The 6.15 train for Southampton departs from Platform 3.*

2 [T] to cause or allow sb/sth to stay in a particular place or condition: *Leave the door open, please. ○ Don't leave the iron on when you are not using it. ○ Don't leave your friend outside in the cold. Invite him in.* يترك ، يدع ، يبقي

3 [T] to forget to bring sth with you: *You go on. I've left my keys on the kitchen table. ○ I can't find my glasses. Where could I have left them?* يترك

4 [T] to cause sth to remain as a result: *Don't put that cup on the table. It'll leave a mark.* يترك ، يخلّف

5 [T] not use sth: *Leave some cake for me, please. ○ Is there any bread left?* يبقي على

6 [T] to put sth somewhere: *Val left a message on my answering machine. ○ I left him a note.* يترك

7 [T] to wait until later to do sth: *Let's leave the washing-up till tomorrow.* يترك ، يؤجّل

8 [T] to give sth to sb when you die: *In his will he left everything to his three sons.* يترك ، يوصي بِ

9 [T] to give the care of sb/sth to another person: *I'll leave it to you to organize all the food. ○ He left his assistant in charge when he went away on holiday.* يكلّف ، يعهد إليه بِ

a b c d e f g h i j k **l** m n o p q r s t u v w x y z

IDM **leave sb/sth alone** not touch, bother or speak to sb/sth: *Leave other people's things alone!* ○ *She's very upset. Leave her alone for a few minutes.* يترك ، يدع

leave/let go (of sth) to stop touching or holding sth: *Let go of my arm or I'll scream.* يترك ، يفلت

leave sb in the lurch to leave sb without help in a difficult situation يتخلّى عنه وقت الضيق

leave sth on one side → SIDE¹

PHR V **leave sth behind** to forget to bring sth with you: *I left my gloves behind and now my hands are cold.* ينسى (أن يحضِر) ، يترك

leave sb/sth out (of sth) not include sb/sth: *This doesn't make sense. I think the typist has left out a line.* يغفِل ، يترك (سهواً)

leave² /li:v/ *noun* [U] a period of time when you do not go to work: *Diplomats working abroad usually get a month's home leave each year.* ○ *annual leave* ○ *sick, maternity, etc. leave* ○ *to be on leave* ➲ Look at the note at **holiday**. إجازة

leaves *pl.* of LEAF

lecture /ˈlektʃə(r)/ *noun* [C] **1 a lecture (on/about sth)** a talk or speech to a group of people on a particular subject: *He gave a very interesting lecture on the geology of the Pacific.* ○ *a course of lectures* محاضرة

2 a serious talk to sb that explains what he/she has done wrong or how he/she should behave دَرْس ، محاضرة ، توبيخ

▸ **lecture** *verb* **1** [I] **lecture (on sth)** to give a lecture or lectures (on a particular subject) يحاضِر

2 [T] **lecture sb (about sth)** to talk seriously to sb about what he/she has done wrong or how he/she should behave: *The policeman lectured the boys about the dangers of playing ball games in the road.* يعطي درساً ، يحدِّث جديّاً

lecturer /ˈlektʃərə(r)/ *noun* [C] a person who gives lectures (especially one who teaches at a college or university) محاضِر

led *pt, pp* of LEAD³

ledge /ledʒ/ *noun* [C] a narrow shelf underneath a window, or a narrow piece of rock that sticks out on the side of a cliff or mountain حافّة تحت النافذة : نتوء أو رفّ جبلي

leek /li:k/ *noun* [C] a long thin vegetable that is white at one end with thin green leaves. Leeks taste rather like onions. كُرّاث

left¹ *pt, pp* of LEAVE¹

left² /left/ *adj, adv* on or to the side (of your body) that is towards the west when you face north: *Turn left just past the post office.* ○ *I've hurt my left arm.* ○ *Can you write with your left hand?* يسار ، شمال

▸ **left** *noun* **1** [U] the left side: *In Britain we drive on the left.* ○ *Take the first turning on the left.* الجانب الأيسر ، اليسار

2 the Left [with sing. or pl. verb] political parties or groups that support socialism: *The Left is losing popularity.* (أحزاب) اليسار

ˈleft-hand *adj* (only *before* a noun) of or on the left: *the left-hand side of the road.* ○ *a left-hand drive car* (= where the steering wheel is on the left-hand side) الجانب الأيسر : على الجانب الأيسر

ˌleft-ˈhanded *adj* **1** (used about a person) using the left hand more easily than the right: *Are you left-handed?* أيسر أو أعسر ، عسراوي

2 made for left-handed people to use: *left-handed scissors* صالح ليستعمل باليد اليسرى ، (مِقَص) يسراوي

ˌleft-ˈluggage office (*US* **baggage room**) *noun* [C] the place at a railway station, etc. where you can leave your luggage for a short time مكتب إيداع الامتعة (في محطة مثلاً)

leftovers /ˈleftəʊvəz/ *noun* [plural] food that has not been eaten when a meal has finished ما تبقّى من الطعام

ˌleft ˈwing *noun* [sing., with sing. or pl. verb] the members of a political party, group, etc. that want more social change than the others in their party: *the left wing of the Labour Party* جناح اليسار (في حزب سياسي)

▸ **ˌleft-ˈwing** *adj*: *left-wing extremists* ○ *They're both very left-wing.* يساري

leg /leg/ *noun* [C] **1** the part of the body on which a person or animal stands or walks: *A spider has eight legs.* ○ *long/short legs* ○ *She sat down and crossed her legs.* ○ *Can you balance on one leg?* ○ *See if you can bend your leg at the knee.* ○ (*figurative*) *the leg of a table, chair, etc.* ساق ، رِجْل : قائمة

2 the part of a pair of trousers, shorts, etc. that covers the leg رِجْل

3 one part or section of a journey, competition, etc. شَوط : مرحلة

IDM **pull sb's leg** → PULL¹

stretch your legs → STRETCH¹

legacy /ˈlegəsi/ *noun* [C] (*pl.* **legacies**) money or property that is given to you after sb dies, because he/she wanted you to have it ميراث : تراث

legal /ˈli:gl/ *adj* **1** allowed by law: *It is not legal to own a gun without a licence.* ❶ The opposite is **illegal**. ➲ Look at **lawful** and **legitimate**. قانونيّ ، شرعي

2 (only *before* a noun) using or connected with the law: *legal advice* ○ *to take legal action against sb* ○ *the legal profession* قانونيّ

▸ **legally** /ˈli:gəli/ *adv*: *Schools are legally responsible for the safety of their pupils.* بحكم القانون

legality /li:ˈgæləti/ *noun* [U] the state of being legal: *The legality of the agreement is not certain.* قانونيّة ، شرعيّة

legalize (*also* **legalise**) /ˈli:gəlaɪz/ *verb* [T] to make sth legal يعطي الشيء صفة قانونيّة ، يجيزه شرعاً

legend /ˈledʒənd/ *noun* **1** [C] an old story that may or may not be true: *the legend of Robin Hood* أسطورة

2 [U] such stories when they are grouped together: *According to legend, Robin Hood lived in Sherwood Forest.* الأساطير

3 [C] a famous person or event إنسان أو حَدَث شهير جداً

▶ **legendary** /'ledʒəndri; *US* -deri/ *adj* **1** from a legend or legends: *the legendary heroes of Greek myths* أسطوري

2 very famous: *Michael Jordan, the legendary basketball star* ذائع الصيت

leggings /'legɪŋz/ *noun* [plural] a piece of clothing, usually worn by women, that fits tightly over both legs and reaches from the waist to the ankles بنطلون طويل ملتصق بالجسم تلبسه السيدات عادة : طِماق

legible /'ledʒəbl/ *adj* (used about handwriting or things that are printed) clear enough to be read easily ❶ The opposite is **illegible**. مقروء ، واضح

▶ **legibility** /ˌledʒə'bɪləti/ *noun* [U] وضُوح الخطّ ، سهولة القراءة

legibly /-əbli/ *adv* بِشكل مقروء ، بِخط حسن

legion /'li:dʒən/ *noun* [C] **1** a special military unit, often made up of volunteers serving with the army of another country: *the French Foreign Legion* فرقة عسكرية

2 a large number of people who have something in common: *legions of admirers/photographers* جمع غفير، حشد

legislate /'ledʒɪsleɪt/ *verb* [I] **legislate (for/against sth)** to make a law or laws: *It is very difficult to legislate against racial discrimination.* يُشرِّع ، يسنّ القوانين

▶ **legislation** /ˌledʒɪs'leɪʃn/ *noun* [U] **1** the act of making laws تشريع

2 a group of laws: *The government is introducing new legislation to help small businesses.* مجموعة قوانين

legislative /'ledʒɪslətɪv/ *adj* (*formal*) (only *before* a noun) connected with the act of making laws: *a legislative assembly/body/council* تشريعي

legislature /'ledʒɪsleɪtʃə(r)/ *noun* [C] (*formal*) a group of people who have the power to make and change laws الهيئة التشريعية

legitimate /lɪ'dʒɪtɪmət/ *adj* **1** reasonable or acceptable: *a legitimate excuse/question/concern* معقول ، له ما يبرّره

2 allowed by law: *Could he earn so much from legitimate business activities?* ➲ Look at **lawful** and **legal**. مشروع ، قانوني

3 (*old-fashioned*) having parents who are married to each other ❶ The opposite is **illegitimate**. (طفل) شرعي

▶ **legitimately** *adv* بشكل له ما يبرّره: بشكل معقول

leisure /'leʒə(r); *US* 'li:ʒər/ *noun* [U] the time when you do not have to work; spare time: *Shorter working hours mean that people have more leisure.* ○ *leisure activities* وقت الفراغ

IDM **at your leisure** when you have free time: *Look through the catalogue at your leisure and then order by telephone.* عندما تسمح لك الفرصة ، دون استعجال ، على راحتك

▶ **leisurely** *adj* without hurry: *a leisurely Sunday breakfast* على مَهل ، "على راحتنا"

'leisure centre *noun* [C] (*Brit*) a public building that has sports facilities and other activities for people to do in their free time مركز تشرف عليه البلدية للنشاطات الرياضية وغيرها

⚷ **lemon** /'lemən/ *noun* [C,U] a yellow fruit with sour juice that is used for giving flavour to food and drink: *a slice of lemon* ○ *Add the juice of 2 lemons.* ليمونة : ليمون

lemonade /ˌlemə'neɪd/ *noun* [C,U] **1** (*Brit*) a colourless sweet drink that is fizzy (= has many bubbles in it) ليمونادة غازيّة

2 a drink that is made from fresh lemon juice, sugar and water ليمونادة

'lemon-squeezer *noun* [C] an instrument that is used for pressing the juice out of a lemon عَصّارة ليمون

⚷ **lend** /lend/ *verb* [T] (*pt, pp* **lent** /lent/) **1** to allow sb to use sth for a short time or to give sb money that must be paid back after a certain period of time: *Could you lend me £5 until Friday?* ○ *He lent me his bicycle.* ○ *He lent his bicycle to me.* يُقرِض : يعير

> If a bank, etc. lends you money you must **pay** it **back/repay** it over a fixed period of time with extra payments (called **interest**).

2 lend sth (to sth) (*formal*) to add or give: *to lend advice, support, etc.* ○ *The flowers lent a touch of colour to the room.* يقدِّم : يضفي على

▶ **lender** *noun* [C] a person or organization that lends sth المُقرِض: شخص أو مؤسسة تعطي قروضاً

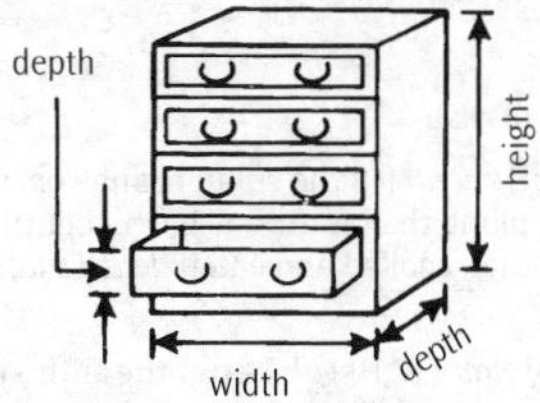

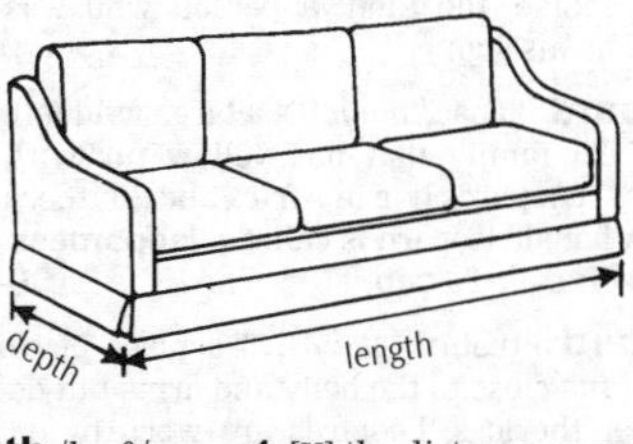

⚷ **length** /leŋθ/ *noun* **1** [U] the distance or amount that sth measures from one end to the other; how long sth is: *to measure the length of a room* ○ *It took an hour to walk the length of Oxford Street.* ○ *The tiny insect is only one millimetre in length.* ○ *the length of a book, letter, etc.* طول

2 [U] the amount of time that sth takes or lasts: *Many people complained about the length of time they had to wait.* طول ، مدّة

3 [C] the length (1) of a swimming pool: *I can swim a length in twenty seconds.* طول

4 [C] a piece of sth (that is long and thin): *a*

length of material, rope, string, etc. قطعة من حبْل أو خيط وما شابه ذلك

IDM **at length** for a long time or in great detail: *We discussed the matter at great length.* مطولاً : بإسهاب

go to great lengths to make more effort than usual in order to achieve sth يبذل قصارى جهده

the length and breadth of sth to or in all parts of sth: *They travelled the length and breadth of India.* (في) طول البلاد وعرضها

▸ **lengthen** *verb* [I,T] to become longer or to make sth longer يَطول ، يمتدّ : يطيل، يمدّد

lengthways (*also* **lengthwise**) *adv* in a direction along the length of sth: *Fold the paper lengthwise.* طولاً، طولياً

lengthy /ˈleŋθi/ *adj* (**lengthier**; **lengthiest**) very long: *lengthy discussions* ○ *Recovery from the illness will be a lengthy process.* طويل الأمد : مطوَل، مسْهَب

lenient /ˈliːniənt/ *adj* (used about a punishment or person who punishes) not strict or severe متساهل ، رحيم

▸ **leniency** /-ənsi/ (*also* **lenience** /-əns/) *noun* [U] تساهل ، تسامح ، رحمة

leniently *adv* بتساهل ، (يعاقب) عقاباً أخف مما يستحق

lens /lenz/ *noun* [C] (*pl.* **lenses**) a piece of glass, etc. that has one or more curved surfaces. Lenses are used in glasses, cameras, telescopes, microscopes, etc.

> Some people wear **contact lenses** to help them see better. You may use a **zoom** or **telephoto lens** on your camera.

عدسة

lent *pt, pp of* LEND

lentil /ˈlentl/ *noun* [C] the small orange or brown seed of a plant that is like a bean. Lentils are dried and then cooked and eaten: *lentil soup* عدسة، عدس

Leo /ˈliːəʊ/ *noun* [C,U] (*pl.* **Leos**) the fifth sign of the zodiac, the Lion; a person who was born under this sign برج الأسد؛ شخص من برج الأسد

leopard /ˈlepəd/ *noun* [C] a large wild animal of the cat family that has yellow fur with dark spots. Leopards live in Africa and Southern Asia. ❶ A female leopard is called a **leopardess** and a baby is called a **cub**. نمْر أو نمرة

leotard /ˈliːətɑːd/ *noun* [C] a piece of clothing that fits close to the body and arms but does not cover the legs. Leotards are worn by dancers, people doing exercises, etc. ثوب يُشبه مايوه سباحة من قطعة واحدة

leper /ˈlepə(r)/ *noun* [C] a person who has leprosy مجذوم

leprosy /ˈleprəsi/ *noun* [U] a serious infectious disease that affects the skin, nerves and flesh. Leprosy can cause fingers and toes to drop off. الجُذام

lesbian /ˈlezbiən/ *noun* [C] a woman who is sexually attracted to other women امرأة سِحاقية أو مُساحِقة

▸ **lesbian** *adj*: *a lesbian relationship* (علاقة) سحاقيّة

lesbianism *noun* [U] سِحاق

less¹ /les/ *det, pron* (used with uncountable nouns) a smaller amount (of): *It took less time than I thought.* ○ *I'm too fat – I must try to eat less.* ○ *It's not far – it'll take less than an hour to get there.* أقلّ: كمية أقلّ: عدد أقلّ

> Many people use **less** with plural nouns: *less cars*, but **fewer** is the form which is still considered to be correct: *fewer cars*.

less² /les/ *adv* to a smaller extent; not so much (as): *He's less intelligent than his brother.* ○ *It rains less in London than in Manchester.* ○ *People work less well when they're tired.* أقلّ

IDM **less and less** becoming smaller and smaller in amount or degree: *I seem to have less and less time for the children.* أقلّ وأقلّ

more or less → MORE²

▸ **less** *prep* taking a certain number or amount away; minus: *You'll earn £10 an hour, less tax.* ناقصاً أو مطروحاً منه

lessen /ˈlesn/ *verb* [I,T] to become less; to make sth less: *Does garlic lessen the risk of heart disease?* يقلّ، يخفّ : يقلّل، يخفّف

lesser /ˈlesə(r)/ *adj, adv* (only *before* a noun) not as great/much as: *He is guilty and so, to a lesser extent, is his wife.* ○ *a lesser-known artist* بدرجة أقلّ

IDM **the lesser of two evils** the better of two bad things أهون الشرّين

lesson /ˈlesn/ *noun* [C] **1** a period of time when you learn or teach sth: *When does the next lesson start?* ○ *How many English lessons do you have a week?* ○ *She gives piano lessons.* ○ *I want to take extra lessons in English conversation.* ○ *a driving lesson* دَرْس؛ حصّة مدرسيّة

2 something that you have learnt or that must be learnt: *I hope we can learn some lessons from this disaster.* درس، عِبرة، موعظة

let¹ /let/ *verb* [T] (*pres part* **letting**; *pt, pp* **let**) **1** to allow or permit sb/sth to do sth; to allow sth to happen: *My parents let me stay out till 11 o'clock.* ○ *How could you let her run away like that?* ○ *He wanted to go on a course but his boss wouldn't let him.* يأذن أو يسمح لِ

> You cannot use **let** in the passive here. You must use **allow** or **permit** and **to**: *They let him take the exam again.* ○ *He was allowed to take the exam again.* Look at the note at **allow**.

2 (used for offering help to sb): *Let me help you carry your bags.* ○ *Let us lend you the money for a new car.* يَدَع

3 (used for making requests or giving instructions): *Don't help him. Let him do it himself.* ○ *If she refuses to come home with us now, let her walk home.* يَدَع، يترك: دَعْه أو دَعها

4 to allow sb/sth to move in a particular direction: *She forgot to let the cat out this morning.* ○ *Open the windows and let some fresh air in.*

○ *They let him out of prison yesterday.* يخرج؛ يُدخِل؛ يطلق سراح...الخ

5 (used for making suggestions about what you and other people can do): *'Let's go to the cinema tonight.' 'Yes, let's.'* ℹ The negative is **let's not** or (in British English only) **don't let's**: *Let's not/Don't let's go to that awful restaurant again.* دعْني أو دعنا...الخ : دعنا لا....

IDM **let alone** and certainly not: *We haven't decided where we're going yet, let alone booked the tickets* ناهيك عن/من؛ وحتماً لم....

let sb/sth go; let go of sb/sth to stop holding sb/sth: *Let me go. You're hurting me!* ○ *I tried to take the book but he wouldn't let go of it.* ○ *Hold the rope and don't let go.* يفلت

let yourself go to allow yourself to behave as you wish; to feel free: *Just relax. Let yourself go!* يأخذ حريته، ينطلق

let yourself/sth go to allow yourself/sth to become untidy, dirty, etc: *She used to be so smart but after her husband died she just let herself go.* يهمل العناية بنفسه

let sb know to give sb a piece of information; to tell sb: *I'll phone you to let you know what time we'll be arriving.* يخبر

let me see; let's see (used when you are thinking or trying to remember sth): *Where did I put the car keys? Let's see. I think I left them by the telephone.* دَعني أفكِّر، "خليني أتذكّر"

let us/let's say for example: *You could work two mornings a week, let's say Tuesday and Friday.* لنَقُل...، لنفرض

PHR V **let sb down** not to do sth that you promised to do for sb; to disappoint sb يخذل

let sb off not to punish sb, or to give sb a lighter punishment than usual: *He expected to go to prison but they let him off with a fine.* يخلي سبيله بحكم خفيف؛ لا يعاقب

let on (about sth) (to sb) to tell sb a secret: *He didn't let on how much he'd paid for the vase.* يطلع ، يفشي

let sth out/down to make clothes larger/longer: *These trousers are too tight. I'll have to let them out.* يوسّع أو يطوّل لباساً

⚷ **let²** /let/ *verb* [T] (*Brit*) to offer a house, flat, etc. for sb to live in, in exchange for rent: *She lets the cottage to holidaymakers in the summer.* ○ *There's a flat to let in our block.* ➲ Look at the note at **hire**. يؤجِّر

lethal /ˈliːθl/ *adj* able to cause death or great damage قاتل، مميت، فتّاك؛ شديد الضرر

▸ **lethally** /ˈliːθəli/ *adv* يسبِّب الموت، (مُشعّ إشعاعاً) فتّاكاً، مسبّباً أضراراً خطيرة

lethargy /ˈleθədʒi/ *noun* [U] the feeling of being very tired and not having any energy خمول ، فتور الهمّة ؛ تبلّد

▸ **lethargic** /ləˈθɑːdʒɪk/ *adj* خمول ، فاتر الهمّة

⚷ **letter** /ˈletə(r)/ *noun* [C] **1** a written or printed sign that represents a sound in a language: *'Z' is the last letter of the English alphabet.* حرف

> Letters may be written or printed as **capitals**, (also **upper case**), or **small** letters (also **lower case**): *Is 'east' written with a capital or a small 'e'?*

letters and cards

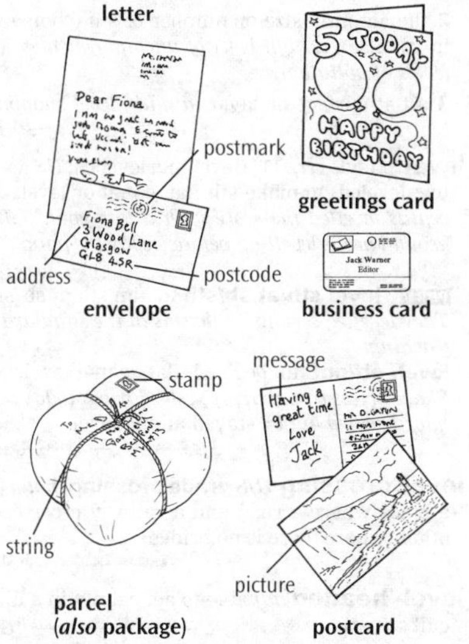

2 a written or printed message. A letter is usually put in an envelope and sent to sb by post: *I have written Denise a letter but I haven't sent it yet.* ○ *Have you had a letter from your son?* ○ *Letters are delivered by the postman.* رسالة ، خطاب/مكتوب

> When you have written a letter you put it in an **envelope**, **address** it, **put/stick** a **stamp** on it and then **post** (*US* **mail**) it. You may **forward** a letter to a person who has moved away.

ˈ**letter box** *noun* [C] **1** a hole in a door or wall through which letters, etc. are delivered صندوق البريد

2 (*US* **mailbox**) a box outside a house or building which letters can be left in when they are delivered صندوق بريد خاص بمبنى

3 = POSTBOX

lettuce /ˈletɪs/ *noun* [C,U] a plant with large green leaves that are eaten raw in salads خَسّ

leukaemia (*US* **leukemia**) /luːˈkiːmiə/ *noun* [U] a serious disease of the blood which often results in death لوكيميا أو سرطان الدم

⚷ **level¹** /ˈlevl/ *adj* **1** with no part higher than any other; flat: *Make sure the shelves are level before you fix them in position.* ○ *Put the tent up on level ground.* ○ *a level teaspoon of sugar* مُسْتوٍ ، على سويّة واحدة ؛ مُنبسِط

2 at the same height, standard or position: *The boy's head was level with his father's shoulder.* ○ *A red car drew level with mine at the traffic lights* (= stopped next to mine). متساوٍ مع؛ موازٍ لـ

⚷ **level²** /ˈlevl/ *noun* [C] **1** the height or position of sth in relation to sth else: *We are at 500 metres above sea level.* ○ *During the flood the water reached knee-level.* ○ *ground level* ○ *She's an* *intermediate-level student.* ○ *top-level discussions* مستوى

2 the amount, size or number of sth (compared to sth else): *a high level of unemployment* ○ *low levels of pollution* نسبة

3 a flat surface or layer: *a multi-level shopping centre* طابق، طبقة

level[3] /ˈlevl/ *verb* [T] (levelling; levelled; *US* leveling; leveled) to make sth flat, equal or level: *Juventus levelled the score with a late goal.* ○ *The ground needs levelling before we lay the patio.* يسوّي، يمهِّد؛ يعادل

PHR V level sth at sb/sth to aim sth at sb/sth: *They levelled serious criticisms at the standard of teaching.* يصوِّب؛ يوجِّه

level off/out to become flat, equal or level: *Share prices rose sharply yesterday but today they have levelled out* (= stayed at one level). يستوي، يتعادل؛ يبقى على مستوى واحد

ˌlevel ˈcrossing (*US* **grade crossing**) *noun* [C] a place where a road and a railway cross each other (where there is no bridge) تقاطع طريق مع سكّة حديديّة

ˌlevel-ˈheaded *adj* able to act calmly in a difficult situation هادئ الأعصاب (وقت المحنة)؛ متّزن

lever /ˈliːvə(r); *US* ˈlevər/ *noun* [C] **1** a bar or tool that is used to lift or open sth when you put pressure or force on one end رافعة، عتلة

2 a handle that you pull or push in order to make a machine, etc. work: *a gear lever* ذراع التشغيل (في آلة)؛ مغيِّر (في سيّارة)

▸ **lever** *verb* [T] to move or lift sth with a lever: *How did ancient man lever those huge lumps of stone into position?* يحرِّك أو يرفع برافعة

leverage /-ərɪdʒ/ *noun* [U] the force or pressure that is put on sth by a lever قوة التحريك أو الرفع (بالرافعة) ، فعالية الرافعة

levy /ˈlevi/ *verb* [T] (*pt, pp* **levied**) **levy sth (on sb)** to officially demand and collect money, etc: *to levy a tax/fine* يفرض أو يجبي (ضريبة)

liability /ˌlaɪəˈbɪləti/ *noun* (*pl.* **liabilities**) **1** [U] **liability (for sth)** the state of being responsible (for sth): *The company cannot accept liability for damage to cars in this car park.* مسؤوليّة

2 [C] (*informal*) a person or thing that can cause a lot of problems, cost a lot of money, etc: *Our car's a real liability – it's always breaking down.* مشكلة كبيرة ، عبء

liable /ˈlaɪəbl/ *adj* (not before a noun) **1 liable to do sth** likely to do sth: *We're all liable to have accidents when we are very tired.* محتمل أن...، قابل لِ، عرضة لِ

2 liable to sth likely to have or suffer from sth: *The area is liable to floods.* معرّض أو عرضة لِ

3 liable (for sth) responsible (in law) (for sth): *Is a wife liable for her husband's debts?* مسؤول قانونياً

liaise /liˈeɪz/ *verb* [I] **liaise (with sb/sth)** (*informal*) to work closely with a person, group, etc. and give him/her/it regular information about what you are doing يكون على صلة دائمة مع

liaison /liˈeɪzn (*US also*) ˈliəzɒn/ *noun* **1** [U] communication between two or more people or groups that work together اتّصال ، ترابط

2 [C] a sexual relationship between two people who are not married to each other علاقة غراميّة

liar /ˈlaɪə(r)/ *noun* [C] a person who tells lies (= who says or writes things that are not true): *She called me a liar.* ➲ Look at the verb and noun **lie**[1]. الكذّاب

Lib Dem *abbrev* = LIBERAL DEMOCRAT

libel /ˈlaɪbl/ *noun* [C,U] something false that is written or printed about sb that would make other people think badly of him/her: *The singer is suing the newspaper for libel.* تشهير ، طعن بِ

▸ **libel** *verb* [T] (libelling; libelled; *US* libeling; libeled) يشهِّر، يطعن بِ

liberal /ˈlɪbərəl/ *adj* **1** willing to accept different opinions or kinds of behaviour; tolerant متحرِّر في تفكيره؛ غير متعصِّب، متسامح

2 generous (used to describe either the person who is giving or the amount that is given): *We were given liberal quantities of food and drink.* سخيّ، وفير

▸ **liberal** *noun* [C] a person who is liberal(1) in his/her way of thinking شخص متحرِّر في تفكيره؛ شخص متسامح

liberalism /-ɪzəm/ *noun* [U] إصلاح تدريجيّ، ليبراليّة؛ تقدّميّة

liberally /-rəli/ *adv* freely or generously بكميات كبيرة؛ بسخاء

the ˌLiberal ˈDemocrats *noun* [plural] a political party in Britain that represents moderate views الحزب الليبراليّ الديمقراطي أو حزب الأحرار

liberate /ˈlɪbəreɪt/ *verb* [T] **liberate sb/sth (from sth)** to set sb/sth free: *France was liberated in 1945.* ○ *to liberate people from poverty* يحرِّر؛ يعتق

▸ **liberated** *adj* not sharing traditional opinions or ways of behaving متحرِّر

liberation /ˌlɪbəˈreɪʃn/ *noun* [U]: *The women's liberation movement wants equal rights for women.* ○ *an army of liberation* تحرير

liberator *noun* [C] a person who liberates محرِّر

liberty /ˈlɪbəti/ *noun* [C,U] (*pl.* **liberties**) the freedom to go where you want, do what you want, etc: *We must defend our civil liberties at all costs.* ○ *loss of liberty* (= being put in prison) حريّة

IDM at liberty (to do sth) free or allowed to do sth: *You are at liberty to leave when you wish.* ○ *I am not at liberty to tell you how I got this information.* حرّ ، له مطلق الحرية أن...: مسموح له

Libra /ˈliːbrə/ *noun* [C,U] the seventh sign of the zodiac, the Scales; a person who was born under this sign برج الميزان؛ شخص من برج الميزان

🔑 **library** /ˈlaɪbrəri; *US* -breri/ *noun* [C] (*pl.* **libraries**) **1** a room or building that contains a collection of books, etc. that can be looked at or borrowed: *My library books are due back tomorrow.* مكتبة (للدراسة)

Most towns and large villages in Britain have a **public library** where you can borrow books and read magazines and newspapers.

2 a private collection of books, etc. مكتبة (عامة مثلاً) ؛ مكتبة خاصّة

▸ **librarian** /laɪˈbreəriən/ *noun* [C] a person who works in or is in charge of a library أمين أو قيّم المكتبة

lice *pl.* of LOUSE

licence (*US* **license**) /ˈlaɪsns/ *noun* **1** [C] an official paper that shows you are allowed to do or have sth: *a driving licence* ○ (*US*) *a driver's license* ○ *A shop needs a licence to sell tobacco.* رخصة

2 [U] (*formal*) freedom to do sth: *The soldiers were given licence to kill if they were attacked.* سماح، ترخيص رسمي

ˈlicence plate (*US* **ˈlicense plate**) *noun* [C] = NUMBER PLATE

license /ˈlaɪsns/ *verb* [T] to give official permission for sth: *Is that gun licensed?* يرخّص بـ، يعطي ترخيصاً رسمياً

lichee = LYCHEE

lick /lɪk/ *verb* [T] to move your tongue across sth: *The child licked the spoon clean.* ○ *I licked the envelope and stuck it down.* يلحس، يلعَق

▸ **lick** *noun* [C]: *Let me have a lick of your ice cream.* لحسة

licorice = LIQUORICE

lid /lɪd/ *noun* [C] **1** the top part of a box, pot, etc. that can be lifted up or taken off ➲ Look at the note at **top**. غطاء (صندوق أو قِدر مثلاً)

2 = EYELID

lie[1] /laɪ/ *verb* [I] (*pres part* **lying**; *pt, pp* **lied**) **lie (to sb) (about sth)** to say or write sth that you know is not true: *He lied about his age in order to join the army.* ○ (*figurative*) *The camera cannot lie.* يكذب

▸ **lie** *noun* [C] a statement that you know is not true: *to tell a lie* ❶ You tell a **white lie** in order not to hurt sb's feelings. Look at **liar** and **fib**. كذبة

ˈlie detector *noun* [C] a piece of equipment that can show if a person is lying or not جهاز لكشف الكذب

lie[2] /laɪ/ *verb* [I] (*pres part* **lying**; *pt* **lay** /leɪ/; *pp* **lain** /leɪn/) **1** to be or put yourself in a flat or horizontal position (so that you are not standing or sitting): *He lay on the sofa and went to sleep.* ○ *to lie on your back/side/front* ○ *The book lay open in front of her.* يستلقي ، يضطجع

Remember that **lie** cannot be used with an object. If you put an object in a flat position you **lay** it down.

2 to be or remain in a certain state or position: *Snow lay thick on the ground.* ○ *The hills lie to the north of the town.* ○ *The factory lay idle during the strike.* ○ *The final decision lies with the managing director.* ○ *They are young and their whole lives lie ahead of them.* يبقى ؛ يقع ؛ يمتد

PHR V **lie about/around** to relax and do nothing: *We just lay around all day on Sunday.* يستريح ، يسترخي أو يتكاسل في بيته

lie back to relax and do nothing while sb else works, etc. يستريح ويترك العمل لغيره

lie down (used about a person) to be or put yourself in a flat or horizontal position so that you can rest: *My head is spinning – I must lie down.* ❶ Note the related expression **have a lie-down**. يستلقي للاستراحة

lie in (*informal*) to stay in bed later than usual ❶ Note the related expression **have a lie-in**. يتأخر في النهوض من الفراش

lieutenant /lefˈtenənt; *US* luːˈt-/ *noun* [C] (*abbr* **Lieut.**; **Lt**) (*US*) (*abbr* **Lt.**) a junior officer in the army or navy ملازم أول

life /laɪf/ *noun* (*pl.* **lives** /laɪvz/) **1** [U] the quality that people, animals or plants have when they are not dead: *Life on earth began in a very simple form.* ○ *Do you believe in life after death?* الحياة

2 [U] living things: *No life was found on the moon.* ○ *There was no sign of life in the deserted house.* ○ *plant life* حياة

3 [C] the existence of an individual person: *He risked his life to save the child.* ○ *Doctors fought all night to save her life.* ○ *Three lives were lost in the fire.* حياة ؛ روح

4 [U] the state of being alive as a human being: *The hostages were rescued without loss of life.* ○ *to bring sb back to life* الروح ، الحياة

5 [C] the period between your birth and death or between your birth and the present: *He worked as a doctor all his life.* ○ *I spent my early life in London.* ○ *to ruin sb's life* حياة

6 [U] the things that you may experience during your life(5): *Life can be hard for a single parent.* ○ *That's life. You can't change it.* ○ *I want to travel and see something of life.* الحياة : تجارب الحياة

7 [U] the period between the present and your death: *She was sent to prison for life.* ○ *life membership of a club* مدى الحياة

8 [C,U] way of living: *They went to America to start a new life.* ○ *They lead a busy life.* ○ *married life* حياة ، معيشة

9 [U] activity; liveliness: *Young children are full of life.* ○ *This town comes to life in the evenings.* حياة ، حيويّة، نشاط

10 [C] the story of sb's life: *He's writing a life of John Lennon.* ترجمة، سيرة حياة

IDM **the facts of life** → FACT

lose your life → LOSE

take your (own) life to kill yourself ينتحر

a walk of life → WALK[2]

a/sb's way of life → WAY[1]

▸ **lifeless** *adj* **1** dead ميّت ، بلا حراك

2 without life(9) or energy عديم الحيويّة ، خامل : مُمل

ˌlife-and-ˈdeath (*also* **ˌlife-or-ˈdeath**) *adj* (only *before* a noun) very serious or dangerous: *a life-and-death struggle* (مسألة) حياة أو موت ، غاية في الأهمية أو الخطورة

lifebelt /ˈlaɪfbelt/ (*also* **lifebuoy** /ˈlaɪfbɔɪ/) *noun* [C] (*Brit*) a ring that is made from light material which will float. A lifebelt is thrown to a person who has fallen into water to stop him/her from sinking. طوق النجاة ، عوامّة

lifeboat /ˈlaɪfbəʊt/ *noun* [C] **1** a small boat that is carried on a large ship and that is used by people to escape from the ship if it is in danger of sinking قارب النجاة

2 a special boat that is used for rescuing people who are in danger at sea زورق الانقاذ

ˈlife cycle *noun* [C] the series of forms or stages of development that a plant, animal, etc. goes through from the beginning of its life to the end الدورة الحياتيّة (لنبات أو حيوان)

ˈlife expectancy *noun* [C,U] (*pl.* **life expectancies**) the number of years that a person is likely to live متوسّط الحياة، متوسط العمر المتوقع

lifeguard /ˈlaɪfgɑːd/ *noun* [C] a person at a beach or swimming pool whose job is to rescue people who are in difficulties in the water المنقِذ (في بركة سباحة مثلاً)

ˈlife jacket *noun* [C] a plastic or rubber sleeveless jacket that can be filled with air. A life jacket is worn by sb to stop him/her from drowning in water. جاكيت أو صِدار النجاة

lifelike /ˈlaɪflaɪk/ *adj* looking like the real person or thing: *The flowers are made of silk but they are very lifelike.* كأنه حقيقي، مطابق للأصل الحيّ ، نابض بالحياة

lifeline /ˈlaɪflaɪn/ *noun* [C] something that is very important for sb and that he/she depends on: *For many old people their telephone is a lifeline.* حبل السلامة

lifelong /ˈlaɪflɒŋ; *US* -lɔːŋ/ *adj* (only *before* a noun) for all of your life: *a lifelong friend* طول العمر ، (دائم) مدى الحياة

ˈlife-size(d) *adj* of the same size as the real person or thing: *a life-sized statue* بالحجم الحقيقي

lifespan /ˈlaɪfspæn/ *noun* [C] the length of time that sb/sth lives, works, lasts, etc. متوسط العمر، عُمْر

ˈlife story *noun* [C] (*pl.* **life stories**) the story of sb's life قصة حياة

lifestyle /ˈlaɪfstaɪl/ *noun* [C] the way that you live: *Getting married often means a sudden change in lifestyle.* أسلوب المعيشة

lifetime /ˈlaɪftaɪm/ *noun* [C] the period of time that sb is alive: *It's a chance of a lifetime. Don't miss it!* عُمر ، حياة

lift /lɪft/ *verb* **1** [T] **lift sb/sth (up)** to move sb/sth to a higher level or position: *He lifted the child up onto his shoulders so that she could see better.* ○ *Lift your arm very gently and see if it hurts.* ○ *It took two men to lift the grand piano.* يرفع

2 [T] to take hold of sb/sth and move him/her/it to a different position: *She lifted the suitcase down from the rack.* ينقل إلى مكان آخر : ينْزل

3 [I] (used about clouds, fog, etc.) to rise up or disappear: *The mist lifted towards the end of the morning.* ينقشع

4 [T] **lift sth (from sb/sth)** (*informal*) to steal or copy sth: *Most of his essay was lifted straight from the textbook.* ➲ Look at **shoplift**. يسرق

5 [T] to end or remove a rule, law, etc: *The ban on public meetings has been lifted.* يرفع (الحظْر) ، يلغي

6 to become or make sb happier: *The news lifted our spirits.* يرفع المعنويات

PHRV **lift off** (used about a rocket) to rise straight up from the ground ينطلق

▶ **lift** *noun* **1** [sing.] lifting or being lifted رفْع ، نقل ، رفْعة

2 [C] (*US* **elevator**) a machine in a large building that is used for carrying people or goods from one floor to another: *It's on the third floor so we'd better take the lift.* مِصعَد كهربائي

3 [C] a free ride in a car, etc: *Can you give me a lift to the station, please?* ○ *I got a lift from a passing car.* توصيلة (بالسيّارة) ، نقلة

4 [sing.] (*informal*) a feeling of happiness or excitement: *Her words of encouragement gave the whole team a lift.* شعور بالابتهاج ، حماس ، رفْع للمعنويّات

IDM **thumb a lift** → THUMB

ˈlift-off *noun* [C] the start of the flight of a rocket: *Only ten seconds to lift-off!* انطلاق (الصاروخ)

ligament /ˈlɪgəmənt/ *noun* [C] a strong band in a person's or animal's body that holds the bones, etc. together رِباط (العضلة بالعظام مثلاً)

light[1] /laɪt/ *noun* **1** [U] the brightness that allows you to see things: *the light of the sun* ○ *The light was too dim for us to read by.* ○ *Strong light is bad for the eyes.* ℹ You may see things by **sunlight**, **moonlight**, **firelight**, **candlelight**, **lamplight**, etc. ضوء ، نور ، ضياء

2 [C] something that produces light, e.g. an electric lamp: *the lights of the city in the distance* ○ *traffic lights* ○ *a neon light* ○ *That car hasn't got its lights on.* ℹ A light may be **on** or **off**. You **put**, **switch** or **turn** a light **on**, **off** or **out**: *Shall I put the light on? It's getting dark in here.* ○ *Please turn the lights out before you leave.* الضوء ، النّور

3 [C] something, e.g. a match, that can be used to light a cigarette, start a fire, etc: *Have you got a light?* وسيلة إشعال: ولاّعة أو كبريت وغير ذلك

IDM **cast light on sth** → CAST[2]

come to light to be found or become known يظهر، يتّضح، يصبح معروفاً

give sb/get the green light → GREEN[1]

in a good, bad, etc. light (used about the way that sth is seen or described by other people) well, badly, etc: *The newspapers often portray his behaviour in a bad light.* بصورة أو مظهر (سيّئ أو حسن)

in the light of because of; considering: *We shall have to change our decision in the light of what you have just said.* على ضوء

set light to sth to cause sth to start burning يُشعل النار

▶ **light** *adj* **1** having a lot of light; not dark: *In summer it's still light at 10 o'clock.* ○ *a light room* مضيء ، منير

2 (used about a colour) pale; not dark: *a light-blue sweater* فاتح اللون

light² /laɪt/ *verb* (*pt, pp* **lit** or **lighted**) **1** [I,T] to begin to burn or to make sth do this: *The gas cooker won't light.* ○ *to light a fire*

> **Lighted** is usually used as an adjective before the noun. **Lit** is used as the past participle of the verb: *Candles were lit in memory of the dead.* ○ *The church was full of lighted candles.*

يَشتعِل؛ يشعل

2 [T] to give light to sth: *The room was lit with one 40-watt bulb.* يضيء ، ينير

PHRV **light up** (used about sb's face, eyes, etc.) to become bright with happiness or excitement يشرق وجهه ، يتهلّل

▶ **lighting** *noun* [U] the quality or type of lights used in a room, building, etc: *Soft lighting helps to make people more relaxed.* ○ *street lighting* الإنارة ، الإضاءة

lights

light³ /laɪt/ *adj* **1** not of great weight; not heavy: *Carry this bag – it's the lightest.* ○ *I've lost weight – I'm five kilos lighter than I used to be.* ○ *light clothes* (= for summer) خفيف

2 not great in amount, degree, etc: *Traffic in London is light on a Sunday.* ○ *a light prison sentence* ○ *a light wind* ○ *a light breakfast* خفيف

3 not using much force; gentle: *a light touch on the shoulder* خفيف، رفيق

4 (used about work, etc.) easy to do: *light exercise* خفيف، سهل

5 not very serious or hard to understand: *light reading* مسلٍ؛ سهل الفهم، خفيف

6 (used about sleep) not deep خفيف

▶ **light** *adv* without much luggage: *to travel light* بأمتعة خفيفة : دون أمتعة

lightly *adv* **1** in a light(3) way: *He touched her lightly on the arm.* برفق

2 only a little; not much: *lightly cooked/spiced/whisked* قليلاً

3 not seriously; without serious thought: *We do not take our customers' complaints lightly.* بدعابة ، بشكل غير جدي

IDM **get off lightly** to avoid serious punishment or trouble: *Some houses were badly damaged in the storms but we got off quite lightly* (= we had very little damage). ينجو من العقاب؛ ينجو من الأذى

lightness *noun* [U] تسلية، دعابة : خفّة

ˈ**light bulb** *noun* [C] = BULB (1)

lighten¹ /ˈlaɪtn/ *verb* [I,T] to become lighter in weight or to make sth lighter: *to lighten a load* يُخفِّف

lighten² /ˈlaɪtn/ *verb* [I,T] to become brighter or to make sth brighter يستبشر ، ينشرح صدره : يفتّح اللون : يضفي جواً من المرح

lighter /ˈlaɪtə(r)/ *noun* [C] = CIGARETTE LIGHTER

ˌ**light-ˈheaded** *adj* feeling dizzy, as if things are going round يشعر بدوار، دائخ

ˌ**light-ˈhearted** *adj* **1** without cares; happy خالي الفؤاد ، خَلي ، سعيد

2 funny; amusing غير جدي

lighthouse /ˈlaɪthaʊs/ *noun* [C] a tall building with a light at the top that guides ships or warns them of dangerous rocks, etc. منارة، فنار

lightning¹ /ˈlaɪtnɪŋ/ *noun* [U] a bright flash of light that appears in the sky during a thunderstorm: *The tree was struck by lightning and burst into flames.* ○ *a flash of lightning* البرق

lightning² /ˈlaɪtnɪŋ/ *adj* (only *before* a noun) very quick or sudden: *a lightning attack* (هجوم) خاطف

lightweight /ˈlaɪtweɪt/ *noun* [C], *adj* **1** (a boxer) weighing between 59 and 61 kilograms من الوزن الخفيف

2 (a person or thing) weighing less than usual: *a lightweight suit for the summer* خفيف الوزن

like¹ /laɪk/ *verb* [T] **1** to find sb/sth pleasant; to be fond of sb/sth: *He's nice. I like him a lot.* ○ *Do you like their new flat?* ○ *I like my coffee with milk.* ○ *I like playing tennis.* ○ *She didn't like it when I shouted at her.* ❶ The opposite is **dislike**. ➲ Look at **likes and dislikes**. يُحبّ؛ يستطيب ، يستحسن

> When **like** means 'have the habit of...' or 'think it's a good thing to...', it is followed by the infinitive: *I like to get up early so that I can go for a run before breakfast.*

2 to want: *Do what you like. I don't care.* يريد ، يرغب، يودّ

> **Would like** is a more polite way to say 'want': *Would you like to come to lunch on Sunday?* ○ *I would like some more cake, please.* ○ *I'd like to speak to the manager.* **Would like** is always followed by the infinitive, never by the *-ing* form.

3 (in negative sentences) to be unwilling to do sth: *I didn't like to disturb you while you were eating.* يحب، يريد

IDM **if you like** (used for agreeing with sb or suggesting sth in a polite way): *'Shall we stop for a rest?' 'Yes, if you like!'* إن شئت!

I like that! (*Brit informal*) (used for saying that

a b c d e f g h i j k **l** m n o p q r s t u v w x y z

sth is not true or not fair): *Well, I like that! She got a present but I didn't.* شيء جميل والله! (تقال تهكماً)
like the look/sound of sb/sth to have a good impression of sb/sth after seeing or hearing about him/her/it يكون انطباعاً حسناً عن، يعجبه
▶ **likeable** (*also* **likable**) /ˈlaɪkəbl/ *adj* (used about a person) easy to like; pleasant لطيف ، أنيس ، محبّب إلى النفس

like² /laɪk/ *prep* **1** similar to sb/sth: *He looks like his father.* ○ *That sounded like thunder.* ○ *Their car is like ours.* ○ *With a coat of paint it will look like new.* ➲ Look at **unlike**. مثل، مشابه لـ

If you want somebody to give a description of something, you ask: **'What's it like?'**: *Tell me about your town. What's it like?*

2 showing what is usual or typical for sb: *It was just like him to be late.* من عادته، (تصرّف) متوقّع منه

Notice the difference in meaning between 'as' and 'like' when used about a person's job, occupation, etc: *Geoff acted as our leader* (= he was our leader). ○ *Geoff acted like our leader* (= but he was, in fact, not our leader).

3 in the same way or manner as sb/sth: *Stop behaving like children.* ○ *That's not right. Do it like this.* مثل
4 for example: *They enjoy most team games, like football and rugby.* مثل، كـَ
IDM like anything (*informal*) very much, fast, hard, etc: *We had to pedal like anything to get up the hill.* كثيراً؛ بشدّة: بسرعة هائلة
▶ **like** *conj* (*informal*) **1** in the same way or manner as: *She can't draw like her sister can.* مثل، مثلما
2 (*informal*) as if: *She acts like she owns the place.* وكأنه
-like (in compounds) in the manner of; similar to: *ladylike* ○ *lifelike* مثل، يشبه، كـَ

like³ /laɪk/ *adj* (*formal*) similar: *We're of like mind* (= we have the same opinion). متشابه ، متماثل

like⁴ /laɪk/ *noun* [sing.] a person or thing that is similar to sb/sth else: *to compare like with like* نظير ، مثيل

likeable *adj* → LIKE¹

likelihood /ˈlaɪklihʊd/ *noun* [U] probability: *There seems very little likelihood of success.* احتمال ، إمكانيّة

likely /ˈlaɪkli/ *adj* (**likelier**; **likeliest**) **1** probable or expected: *Do you think it's likely to rain?* ○ *The boss is not likely to agree.* ○ *It's not likely that the boss will agree.* محتمل ؛ متوقع
2 probably suitable: *a likely candidate for the job* ممكن، ملائم
▶ **likely** *adv*
IDM as likely as not; most/very likely very probably: *They were very late leaving. They will very likely miss the train.* في أغلب الاحتمال
not likely! (*informal*) certainly not حتماً لا! مستحيل!

liken /ˈlaɪkən/ *verb* [T] (*formal*) **liken sth to sth** to compare sth with sth else: *This young artist has been likened to Picasso.* يُشبّه

likeness /ˈlaɪknəs/ *noun* [C,U] (an example of) being alike or similar in appearance: *There is a strong family likeness.* ○ *The portrait is a very good likeness of Grandpa.* تشابه ، شَبَه : صورة زيتية مطابقة للأصل

likes *noun*
IDM likes and dislikes the things that you like or do not like ما يحب الإنسان وما يكره

likewise /ˈlaɪkwaɪz/ *adv* (*formal*) the same: *I intend to send a letter of apology and suggest that you do likewise.* مثل ذلك

liking /ˈlaɪkɪŋ/ *noun*
IDM have a liking for sth to like or be fond of sth: *to have a liking for French cheese* وَلَع ، مَيْل
to your liking (*formal*) the way that you like sth: *I trust that everything is to your liking.* كما يحبّ، حسب ذوقه

lilac /ˈlaɪlək/ *noun* [C,U] a tree or large bush that has large purple or white flowers in spring. The flowers are also called lilac. شجرة الليلاك
▶ **lilac** *adj* of a pale purple colour لون لَيْلَكي

Li-Lo™ /ˈlaɪləʊ/ *noun* [C] (*pl.* **Lilos**) (*Brit*) a plastic or rubber bed that you fill with air when you want to use it. A Li-Lo is used on the beach or for camping. فِراش مطاطي ينفخ عند الحاجة

lily /ˈlɪli/ *noun* [C] (*pl.* **lilies**) a type of plant that grows from a bulb and that has large white or coloured flowers نبات الزنبق

limb /lɪm/ *noun* [C] **1** a leg or an arm of a person طَرَف: ساق أو ذراع
2 one of the main branches of a tree غصن رئيسي

lime¹ /laɪm/ *noun* [U] a white substance that is used for making cement and also for adding to soil to improve its quality كلس ، جير

lime² /laɪm/ (*also* ˈ**lime-tree**) *noun* [C] (*Brit*) a large tree with smooth pale-green leaves and yellow flowers شجرة الزيزفون

lime³ /laɪm/ *noun* **1** [C] a small yellowish-green fruit that tastes like a lemon ليمون مالح
2 [U] (*also* ˌ**lime-ˈgreen**) a yellowish-green colour لون أخضر مائل للصفرة

limelight /ˈlaɪmlaɪt/ *noun*
IDM in the limelight getting a lot of attention from the public: *The pop star was in the limelight wherever he went.* تسلّط عليه الأضواء

limerick /ˈlɪmərɪk/ *noun* [C] a type of humorous poem with five lines. The first two rhyme with the last. شِعر هزلي من خمسة أبيات

limestone /ˈlaɪmstəʊn/ *noun* [U] a type of white rock that is used as a building material and in making cement حجر كلسي، جير

limit¹ /ˈlɪmɪt/ *noun* [C] **1** a point or line that must not be passed: *No lorries are allowed within a three-mile limit of the city centre.* حدّ، تخم
2 the greatest amount of sth that is possible, allowed, etc: *What's the speed limit on this road?*

○ *He was fined for exceeding the speed limit.* ○ *There's a limit to the amount of time I'm prepared to spend on this.* حدّ أقصى

IDM **off limits** (*US*) = OUT OF BOUNDS

within limits as long as it is not too much, great, etc: *I don't mind how much it costs – within limits.* في حدود المعقول

limit² /ˈlɪmɪt/ *verb* [T] **limit sb/sth (to sth)** to keep sb/sth within or below a certain amount, size, degree or area: *In China families are limited to just one child.* ○ *Red squirrels are limited to a few areas in Britain.* يحدِّد، يحصر

▸ **limited** *adj* small in number or amount: *Book early because there are only a limited number of seats available.* محدود

limitation /ˌlɪmɪˈteɪʃn/ *noun* **1** [C,U] controlling sth or making sth smaller; a condition that puts a limit on sth: *There are certain limitations on what we can do.* حدّ، قيْد

2 [plural] **limitations** what you cannot do: *It is important to know your own limitations.* حدود: قصور، موَاطن الضعف

ˌlimited ˈcompany *noun* [C] (*abbr* **Ltd**) a company whose owners need only pay part of the money it owes if it goes bankrupt شركة محدودة

limousine /ˈlɪməziːn; ˌlɪməˈziːn/ (*also informal* **limo** /ˈlɪməʊ/) *noun* [C] a large expensive car that usually has a sheet of glass between the driver and the passengers in the back ليموزين: سيّارة كبيرة فخمة

limp¹ /lɪmp/ *adj* not stiff or strong: *You should put those flowers in water before they go limp.* رَخْو: ذابل، متهلهل

limp² /lɪmp/ *verb* [I] to walk in an uneven way, e.g. because you have hurt your leg or foot: (*figurative*) *After the accident the ship limped back to the harbour.* يعرج، يتمايل: يتقدّم بصعوبة

▸ **limp** *noun* [sing.]: *to walk with a bad limp* عَرَج، تمايل

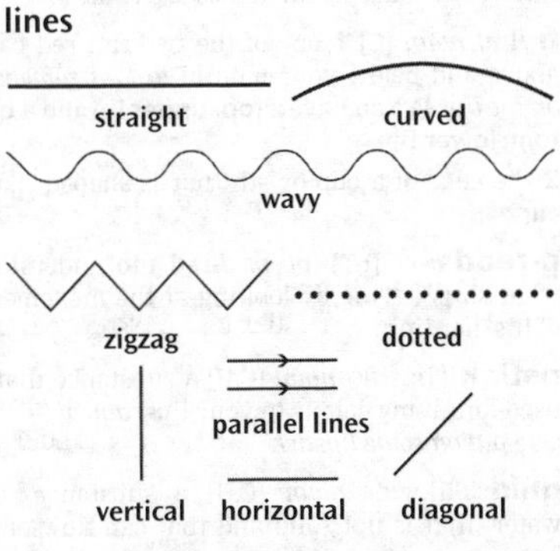

line¹ /laɪn/ *noun* **1** [C] a long thin mark on the surface of sth: *Double yellow lines at the side of the road mean 'no parking'.* ○ *The old lady had lines on her forehead.* ○ *to draw a line* ℹ A line may be **horizontal**, **vertical**, **diagonal**, **parallel** etc, to sth. خطّ، سطر: غَضَن

2 [C] a line on the ground that marks the side or end of a racetrack, sports field, etc: *The ball was definitely over the line.* ○ *the finishing line of a race* حدّ، خطّ

3 [C] a row of people, things, words on a page, etc: *There was a long line of people waiting at the Post Office.* ○ *long lines of houses, all exactly the same* ○ *a five-line poem* ○ *Start each paragraph on a new line.* صفّ: بَيت من الشِّعر؛ سطر

4 (*US*) = QUEUE

5 [C] a piece of rope or string: *Hang out the clothes on the washing line, please.* ○ *a fishing line* مقياس معيّن من حبْل أو خيط

6 [C] a telephone or electricity wire or connection: *I'm sorry – the line is engaged. Can you try again later?* ○ *The strong winds blew down many power lines.* خطّ، سلك

7 [C] a section of railway track: *The accident was caused by a cow on the line.* ○ *a main line* خطّ حديديّ، سكة حديديّة

8 lines [plural] the words that are spoken by an actor in a play, etc: *to learn your lines* كلمات دور الممثّل

9 [sing.] a direction or course of thought or action: *If this policy doesn't work, we'll have to take another line.* ○ *a line of argument* اتّجاه، طريق؛ خطّة

10 [C] a company that provides transport by air, ship, etc: *an airline* شركة خطوط جويّة أو بحرية

11 [sing.] a type of goods in a shop, etc: *a new line in environment-friendly detergents* اتّجاه جديد: مستحضر

12 [C] a route that people move along or send messages, goods, etc. along: *lines of communication* ○ *If you're going there by Underground, check which line you need.* خطّ مواصلات

13 [C] the place where an army is fighting: *a spy working behind enemy lines* جبهة، خطّ العدوّ

IDM **along/on the same, etc. lines** in the way that is mentioned: *We both think along the same lines, so we work well together.* مِنوال، نَحْو، طريقة

draw the line at sth/doing sth → DRAW²

drop sb a line → DROP¹

hold the line to wait on the telephone, e.g. while sb finds the person you want to speak to: *The extension is engaged. Would you like to hold the line or call back later?* ينتظر على خطّ التليفون

in line for sth likely to get sth: *She's next in line for promotion.* دَوْره قادم، الأول على قائمة (الترفيع مثلاً)

in line with sth similar to sth and fitting in with it يتماشى مع، مجارٍ ل

on line connected to a computer system موصول مع شبكة كمبيوتر

stand in line (*US*) to wait in a queue ينتظر في الصف أو الطابور

toe the (party) line → TOE

line² /laɪn/ *verb* [T] **1** (often passive) to mark sth with lines¹ (1): *lined paper* ○ *a face lined with age* يسطِّر: يجعِّد، يغضِّن

2 to make or form a line¹ (3) along sth: *Crowds lined the streets to watch the race.* ○ *a tree-lined avenue* يقف على جانبيّ الطريق، يصطفّ

PHR V **line up (for sth)** (*US*) to form a line or queue (for sth) يقف في صف أو طابور، يصطفّ

line sth up (*informal*) to arrange or organize sth: *What have you got lined up for the weekend?* يرتِّب؛ يعدّ

line³ /laɪn/ *verb* [T] (often passive) to cover the inside surface of sth with a different material: *fur-lined boots* يبطِّن

lineman /ˈlaɪnmən/ *noun* [C] (*pl.* **linemen** /-mən/) (*US*) = LINESMAN

linen /ˈlɪnɪn/ *noun* [U] **1** a type of strong cloth that is made from a natural substance (flax) كتّان

2 sheets, tablecloths, etc. (which often used to be made of linen): *bed linen* بياضات، شراشف وأغطية مائدة

liner¹ /ˈlaɪnə(r)/ *noun* [C] a large ship that carries people, etc. long distances باخرة

liner² /ˈlaɪnə(r)/ *noun* [C] something that is put inside sth else to keep it clean or protect it. A liner is usually thrown away after it has been used: *a dustbin liner* كيس يُبطِّن صفيحة مثلاً يُرمى بعد الاستعمال

linesman /ˈlaɪnzmən/ (*US* **lineman**) (*pl.* **linesmen** /-mən/) *noun* [C] an official person in some games such as football or tennis. The linesman watches to see if a player breaks a rule or if the ball goes over the line¹ (2). المراقب (في لعبة كرة القدم مثلاً)

linger /ˈlɪŋɡə(r)/ *verb* [I] **1** to stay somewhere for a long time يطيل الإقامة ، يمكث طويلاً

2 to take a long time doing sth: *to linger over a meal* يتلكّأ، يتباطأ، يتوانى

lingerie /ˈlænʒəri; *US* ˌlɑːndʒəˈreɪ/ *noun* [U] (used in shops, etc.) women's underclothes ثياب النساء الداخليّة

linguist /ˈlɪŋɡwɪst/ *noun* [C] a person who is good at learning foreign languages; a person who studies or teaches language(s) شخص عنده موهبة لتعلّم اللغات : لغوي: مختص بعلم اللغويات

linguistic /lɪŋˈɡwɪstɪk/ *adj* of language or linguistics لغويّ ؛ متعلق بعلم اللغويات

▶ **linguistics** *noun* [U] the scientific study of language لغويّات ، لسانيّات

lining /ˈlaɪnɪŋ/ *noun* [C,U] material that covers the inside surface of sth: *I've torn the lining of my coat.* بطانة

link /lɪŋk/ *noun* [C] **1** one ring in a chain حلقة

2 a person or thing that connects two other people or things: *There is a strong link between smoking and heart disease.* ○ *Sporting links with South Africa were broken for many years.* ○ *a rail link* صلة، ارتباط؛ صلة الوصل

3 (*computing*) a place in an electronic document that is connected to another electronic document or to another part of the same document: *To visit similar websites to this one, click on the links at the bottom of the page.* حلقات الربط، صلات الوصل

▶ **link** *verb* [T] **link A with B; link A and B (together)** to make or suggest a connection between two or more people or things: *The tunnel links Britain and France.* ○ *The police have evidence that links the priest with a terrorist organization.* ○ *to link arms* يصل، يربط بين؛ يشبك

PHR V **link up (with sb/sth)** to join together (with sb/sth): *All our branches are linked up by computer.* يرتبط بِ، يربط

ˈlink-up *noun* [C] the joining together or connection of two or more things ربْط ، خطّ اتّصال

linoleum /lɪˈnəʊliəm/ (*also informal* **lino** /ˈlaɪnəʊ/) *noun* [U] a type of covering for floors مُشمع الأرضية

lion /ˈlaɪən/ *noun* [C] a large animal of the cat family that lives in Africa and parts of southern Asia. Male lions have a large amount of hair around their head and neck (a mane). ℹ A female lion is called a **lioness** and a young lion is called a **cub**. The noise a lion makes is a **roar**. أسد

lip /lɪp/ *noun* [C] **1** one of the two soft red parts above and below your mouth: *to kiss somebody on the lips* ℹ You have a **top/upper** lip and a **bottom/lower** lip. شفة

2 the edge of a cup or sth that is shaped like a cup حافّة

ˈlip-read *verb* [I,T] (*pt, pp* /-red/) to understand what sb is saying by looking at the movements of his/her lips (الأصمّ مثلاً) يفهم الكلام من حركة الشّفاه

lipstick /ˈlɪpstɪk/ *noun* [C,U] a substance that is used for giving colour to your lips: *a new lipstick* ○ *to put on some lipstick* أحمر الشفاه؛ قلم حمرة

liquid /ˈlɪkwɪd/ *noun* [C,U] a substance, e.g. water, that is not solid and that can flow or be poured سائل ، مائع

▶ **liquid** *adj* in the form of a liquid سائل

liquidate /ˈlɪkwɪdeɪt/ *verb* [T] **1** to close down a business because it has no money left يُصفّي (أعمال شركة)

2 to kill sb يقتل، يقضي على

▸ **liquidation** /ˌlɪkwɪˈdeɪʃn/ *noun* [U]: *to go into liquidation* (= of a business) ○ *the liquidation of political opponents* تصفية (شركة) : القضاء على الخصوم

liquidize (*also* **liquidise**) /ˈlɪkwɪdaɪz/ *verb* [T] to cause sth to become liquid: *He liquidized the vegetables to make soup.* يميّع

▸ **liquidizer** = BLENDER

liquor /ˈlɪkə(r)/ *noun* [U] (*US*) strong alcoholic drinks; spirits مشروبات كحوليّة

liquorice (*also* **licorice**) /ˈlɪkərɪs/ *noun* [U] a black substance, made from a plant, that is used in sweets نبات ومادّة السّوس

lisp /lɪsp/ *noun* [C] an incorrect way of speaking in which 's' sounds like 'th': *He speaks with a slight lisp.* لثغة

▸ **lisp** *verb* [I,T] يلثغ

list /lɪst/ *noun* [C] a series of names, figures, items, etc. that are written or printed one after another: *Can you put butter on your shopping list?* ○ *a checklist of everything that needs to be done* ○ *an alphabetical list* ○ *Your name is third on the waiting list.* قائمة ، جدول

▸ **list** *verb* [T] to make a list of sth; to put or include sth on a list: *to list items in alphabetical order* ○ *Her name is not listed on police files.* يدرج: يضع قائمة بِ

listen /ˈlɪsn/ *verb* [I] **1 listen (to sb/sth)** to pay attention to sb/sth in order to hear him/her/it: *Now please listen carefully to what I have to say.* ○ *to listen to the radio, music, etc.* ➲ Look at the note at **hear**. يصغي ؛ يستمع إلى

2 listen to sb/sth to take notice of or believe what sb says, etc: *I try to give them advice but they never listen to what I tell them.* يصغي (إلى نصيحة)

PHR V **listen (out) for sth** to wait to hear sth: *to listen (out) for a knock on the door* يصيخ السمع

listen in (on/to sth) to listen to sb else's private conversation: *Have you been listening in on my phone calls?* يتنصّت

▸ **listen** *noun* [sing.] (*informal*) the act of listening: *Have a listen and see if you can hear anything.* سَماع، استماع

listener *noun* [C] a person who listens: *He is a good listener* (= he pays attention to you when you are speaking). مستمع؛ شخص حسن الإصغاء

listless /ˈlɪstləs/ *adj* tired and without energy متراخ ، فاتر الهِمّة ، كسول

▸ **listlessly** *adv* بفتور، بملَل

lit *pt, pp* of LIGHT²

liter (*US*) = LITRE

literacy /ˈlɪtərəsi/ *noun* [U] the ability to read and write ➲ Look at **illiteracy**. معرفة القراءة والكتابة

literal /ˈlɪtərəl/ *adj* **1** (used about the meaning of a word or phrase) original or basic: *The adjective 'big-headed' is hardly ever used in its literal sense.* ➲ Look at **figurative** and **metaphorical**. حرفيّ ، (معنى) أصليّ

2 (used about a translation, etc.) translating each word separately without looking at the general meaning (ترجمة) حرفية: كلمة بكلمة

▸ **literally** /ˈlɪtərəli/ *adv* **1** in a literal (2) way: *You can't translate this text literally.* حرفياً ، كلمة بكلمة

2 (*informal*) (used for emphasizing sth): *I literally jumped out of my skin* (= I got a sudden shock). دون أيّ مبالغة ، بالفعل

literary /ˈlɪtərəri; *US* ˈlɪtəreri/ *adj* of or concerned with literature: *literary criticism* ○ *a literary journal* أدبي

literate /ˈlɪtərət/ *adj* able to read and write ℹ The opposite is **illiterate**. ➲ Look at **numerate**. يجيد القراءة والكتابة

literature /ˈlɪtrətʃə(r); *US* -tʃʊər/ *noun* [U] **1** writing that is considered to be a work of art. Literature includes novels, plays and poetry: *French literature* الأدب (شِعر وقصص وغير ذلك)

2 printed material on a particular subject: *Have you got any literature on opening a bank account in Britain?* منشورات ، مطبوعات

litre (*US* **liter**) /ˈliːtə(r)/ *noun* [C] (*abbr* **l**) a measure of liquid: *ten litres of petrol* ○ *a litre bottle* لِتْر

litter /ˈlɪtə(r)/ *noun* **1** [U] pieces of paper, packets, etc. that are left in a public place فضلات ومهملات تترك في الأماكن العامّة

2 [C] all the young animals that are born to one mother at the same time: *a litter of six puppies* بطن

▸ **litter** *verb* [T] to make sth untidy with litter: *The streets were littered with rubbish.* يوسّخ بالمهملات ، يبعثر الأوساخ

ˈ**litter bin** *noun* [C] a container to put litter in صندوق أو سلّة مهملات في مكان عام

ˈ**litter lout** (*US* **litterbug** /ˈlɪtəbʌg/) *noun* [C] a person who drops litter in a public place مَن يرمي المهملات في مكان عام

little¹ /ˈlɪtl/ *adj* **1** not big; small: *There's a little hole in my sock.* ○ *the little hand of the clock* ○ *your little finger/toe*

Little is often used with another adjective: *a little old lady* ○ *a dear little kitten* ○ *What a funny little shop!* Look at the note at **small**.

صغير

2 (used about distance or time) short: *Do you mind waiting a little while?* ○ *It's only a little way.* قصير

3 young: *a little girl/boy* ○ *my little brother* صغير؛ صغير السّن

4 not important: *a little problem* تافه: بسيط

little² /ˈlɪtl/ *det* (with uncountable [U] nouns) not much or not enough: *They have very little money.* ○ *There is little hope that she will recover.* ➲ Look at **less** and **least**. قليل من: ضئيل

▸ **little** *pron* (also as a noun after *the*) a small amount; not enough: *We studied Latin at school but I remember very little.* ○ *The little I know of him has given me a good impression.* قليل، مقدار ضئيل : القليل

little *adv* not much or not enough: *I slept very little last night.* ○ *a little-known author* قليلاً

IDM little by little slowly: *After the accident her strength returned little by little.* بالتدريج ، شيئاً فشيئاً

little³ /ˈlɪtl/ **a little** *det* (with uncountable [U] nouns) a small amount of sth: *I like a little sugar in my tea.* ○ *Could I have a little help, please?* قليل من ، بعض

▶ **a little** *pron* a small amount: *'Is there any butter left?' 'Yes, just a little.'* مقدار قليل

IDM after/for a little after/for a short distance or time: *You must rest for a little.* بعدَ أو لمسافة قصيرة : بعدَ أو لمدة قصيرة

a little *adv* rather: *This skirt is a little too tight.*

ℹ **A little bit** or **a bit** is often used instead of 'a little': *I was feeling a little bit tired so I decided not to go out.* قليلاً ، "شويّة"

live¹ /laɪv/ *adj* **1** having life; not dead: *Have you ever touched a real live snake?* ➲ Look at **alive** and **living**. حيّ ، على قيد الحياة

2 (used about a bomb) that has not yet exploded (قنبلة) معمّرة أي لم تنفجر بعد

3 (used about a wire, etc.) carrying electricity. If you touch sth that is live you will get an electric shock. (سلك) مُكَهْرَب

4 (used about a radio or TV programme) seen or heard as it is happening: *live coverage of the Wimbledon tennis tournament* (بَثّ) حيّ ، (إذاعة) على الهواء مباشرة

5 recorded from a concert, etc., i.e. not made in a studio: *a live recording of Bob Dylan's last concert* (تسجيل) حيّ أي عن حفلة موسيقية

6 (used about an electronic link) functioning correctly, so that it is connected to another document or page on the Internet: *Here are some live links to other aviation-related web pages.* حلقات ربط

▶ **live** *adv* broadcast at the same time as it is happening: *This programme is coming live from Wembley Stadium.* ○ *to go out live on TV* على الهواء ، مباشرةً

live² /lɪv/ *verb* **1** [I] to be or remain alive: *You can't live without water.* ○ *She hasn't got long to live.* ○ *to live to a great age* يحيا ، يعيش

2 [I] to have your home: *Where do you live?* ○ *He still lives with his parents.* يسكن ، يقيم

3 [I,T] to pass or spend your life in a certain way: *to live a quiet life* ○ *They have plenty of money and live well.* يعيش

4 [I] to be able to buy the things that you need: *Many families don't have enough to live.* يقتات ، يعيش

5 [I] to enjoy all the opportunities of life fully: *I want to live a bit before settling down and getting married.* ينعم بالحياة

PHR V live sth down to make people forget sth bad or embarrassing that has happened to you: *They lost 10–nil? They'll never live it down!* ينسي الناس حماقةً ارتكبها في الماضي

live on to continue to live: *After his retirement he lived on for another 25 years.* ○ *(figurative) Mozart is dead but his music lives on.* يبقى حيّاً

live on sth 1 to have sth as your only food: *to live on bread and water* يعيش على

2 to have sth as your income: *I don't know how they live on £8 000 a year!* يعيش

live together to live in the same house, etc. as sb and have a sexual relationship with him/her يساكن ويعاشر معاشرة جنسية

live up to sth to be as good as expected: *Children sometimes find it hard to live up to their parents' expectations.* يحقّق الآمال المعقودة عليه

live with sb = LIVE TOGETHER

live with sth to accept sth unpleasant that you cannot change: *It can be hard to live with the fact that you are getting older.* يتقبّل ، يتعوّد

livelihood /ˈlaɪvlihʊd/ *noun* [C, usually sing.] the way that you earn money: *to lose your livelihood* معيشة ، عَيْش ، قوت

lively /ˈlaɪvli/ *adj* (**livelier**; **liveliest**) full of energy, interest, excitement, etc: *lively children* ○ *There was a lively debate on the route of the new motorway.* ○ *a lively imagination* مليء بالحيويّة : حيّ ؛ (خيال) خصب

liven /ˈlaɪvn/ *verb*

PHR V liven (sb/sth) up to become lively or to make sb/sth lively: *Once the band began to play the party livened up.* ينتعش ، تدبّ فيه الحياة ؛ ينعش

liver /ˈlɪvə(r)/ *noun* **1** [C] the part of your body that cleans your blood الكبد

2 [U] the liver of an animal when it is cooked and eaten as food: *fried liver and onions* كبدة

ˈliver sausage (*US* **liverwurst** /ˈlɪvəwɜːst/) *noun* [U] a type of sausage that contains cooked liver and that is usually eaten cold with bread سجق محشو كبدة مطحونة

lives *pl.* of LIFE

livestock /ˈlaɪvstɒk/ *noun* [U] animals that are kept on a farm, e.g. cows, sheep, etc. المواشي والدواجن

living¹ /ˈlɪvɪŋ/ *adj* **1** alive now: *He has no living relatives.* علي قيد الحياة

2 (used about a language, etc.) still used حيّ

ℹ The opposite for both meanings is **dead**.

living² /ˈlɪvɪŋ/ *noun* **1** [C, usually sing.] a means of earning money to buy the things you need: *What do you do for a living?* معيشة ، كسب المعيشة ، رزق

2 [U] your way or quality of life: *The cost of living has risen in recent years.* ➲ Look at **standard of living.** معيشة

ˈliving room (*especially Brit* **sitting room**) *noun* [C] the room in a house where people sit, relax, watch TV, etc. together غرفة الجلوس

lizard /ˈlɪzəd/ *noun* [C] a small reptile with four legs, rough skin and a long tail. A lizard has a long tongue that it uses for catching insects. عظاية ، سحليّة

llama /ˈlɑːmə/ *noun* [C] a South American animal kept for its soft wool or for carrying loads اللامة

LMS /ˌel em ˈes/ *noun* [C] the abbreviation for learning management system (a software system for managing training and education using the

Internet): *The lecture notes are posted on the college LMS.* نظام إدارة التعلّم الإلكتروني

load¹ /ləʊd/ *noun* [C] **1** something (heavy) that is being or is going to be carried حِمْل ، عبء

2 (often in compounds) the quantity of sth that can be carried: *a lorry load of sand* ○ *bus loads of tourists* حُمُولة

3 loads (of sth) [plural] (*informal*) a lot (of sth): *There are loads of things to do in London in the evenings.* كثير من (الأشياء) ، عدد كبير

IDM **a load of rubbish, garbage, etc.** (*informal*) nonsense كلام فارغ

load² /ləʊd/ *verb* **1** [I,T] to put or have a load or large quantity of sth in or on sb/sth: *Have you finished loading yet?* ○ *Uncle Tim arrived loaded down with presents.* ○ *They loaded the plane with supplies for the refugees.* ○ *Load the washing into the machine and then add the powder.*

يحمّل، يملأ؛ يحمل

2 [I] to receive a load: *The ship is still loading.*

يُحمَّل

3 [T] to put a program or disk into a computer: *First, switch on the machine and load the disk.*

يركّب

4 [T] to put a film in a camera or a bullet in a gun يركّب؛ يحشو

▶ **loaded** *adj* **1** carrying a load محمّل، مثقَل

2 giving an advantage: *The system is loaded in their favour.* راجِح، متحيّز (إلى جانبهم)

3 (*informal*) having a lot of money; rich

ثري، كثير المال

loaf /ləʊf/ *noun* [C] (*pl.* **loaves** /ləʊvz/) bread shaped and baked in one piece: *a loaf of bread* ○ *Two sliced loaves, please.* رغيف من الخبز

loan /ləʊn/ *noun* **1** [C] money, etc. that sb/sth lends you: *to take out a bank loan* ○ *to make a loan to sb* ○ *to pay off a loan* قَرْض ، دَيْن

2 [U] the act of lending sth or state of being lent: *The books are on loan from the library.*

إعارة ، استعارة

▶ **loan** *verb* [T] **loan sth (to sb)** to lend sth: *The painting is loaned from the Louvre for the period of the exhibition.* يُعير

loathe /ləʊð/ *verb* [T] to feel strong hatred or dislike for sb/sth يشمئزّ من : يكره كرهاً شديداً

▶ **loathing** *noun* [U] اشمئزاز ؛ كره

loathsome /-səm/ *adj* (*formal*) causing a strong feeling of dislike يثير الاشمئزاز ؛ كريه

loaves *pl.* of LOAF

lob /lɒb/ *verb* [I,T] (lo**bb**ing; lo**bb**ed) (*sport*) to hit or throw a ball high into the air, so that it lands behind your opponent

يضرب الكرة عالياً في خطّ منحن: يُسقِطها

▶ **lob** *noun* [C] إسقاط الكرة

lobby /ˈlɒbi/ *noun* (*pl.* **lobbies**) **1** [C] the area that is just inside a large building. A lobby often has a reception desk and doors, stairs, lifts, etc. that lead to other parts of the building: *a hotel lobby* بَهو ، ردهة

2 [C, with sing. or pl. verb] a group of people who try to persuade the government, etc. to do or not to do sth: *the anti-abortion lobby*

اللوبي: مجموعة تحاول الضغط على الحكومة

▶ **lobby** *verb* [I,T] (*pres part* **lobbying**; *3rd pers sing pres* **lobbies**; *pt*, *pp* **lobbied**) to try to persuade the government, etc. that sth should or should not be done: *They lobbied the Transport Minister for improved rail services.*

يضغط على

lobe /ləʊb/ *noun* [C] the round soft part at the bottom of your ear شحمة الأذن

lobster /ˈlɒbstə(r)/ *noun* **1** [C] a large shellfish that has eight legs. A lobster is bluish-black but it turns red when it is cooked. سرطان البحر ، كَرْكند

2 [U] a lobster when it is cooked and eaten as food سرطان البحر ، كَرْكند

local /ˈləʊkl/ *adj* of a particular place (near you): *local newspapers* ○ *The local school is the centre of the community.* محلّي

▶ **local** *noun* [C] **1** [usually pl.] a person who lives in a particular place: *One of the locals agreed to be my guide.*

أحد السّكان المحلّيين ، من أهل المنطقة

2 (*Brit informal*) a pub that is near your home where you often go to drink

البار المحليّ الذي اعتاد المرء ارتياده

locally /-kəli/ *adv*: *I do most of my shopping locally.* محلياً ، ضمن حدود هذه المنطقة

ˌlocal anaesˈthetic *noun* [C,U] medicine that is injected into one part of your body so that you do not feel pain there ➲ Look at **general anaesthetic**. تخدير موضعي

ˌlocal auˈthority *noun* [C, with sing. or pl. verb] (*pl.* **local authorities**) the group of people who are responsible for local government in an area السلطة المحليّة

ˈlocal call *noun* [C] a telephone call to sb who is not far away ➲ Look at **long-distance**.

مخابرة محليّة

ˌlocal ˈgovernment *noun* [U] the government of a particular place by a group of people who are elected by the local residents

> The group of elected officials who are in charge of local government is called the **council**. The **local authority** consists of officials who are paid. These officials carry out the decisions that the council has made.

الحكومة المحليّة

localize (*also* **localise**) /ˈləʊkəlaɪz/ *verb* [T] to limit sth to a particular place or area: *localized pain* يحصر ؛ يركّز

locally *adj* → LOCAL

ˈlocal time *noun* [U] the time at a particular place in the world: *We arrive in Singapore at 2 o'clock in the afternoon, local time.* التوقيت المحلي

locate /ləʊˈkeɪt; *US* ˈləʊkeɪt/ *verb* [T] **1** to find the exact position of sb/sth: *The damaged ship has been located and helicopters are arriving to rescue the crew.* يكتشف أو يعيّن مكان شيء مفقود

2 (often passive) to put, build, etc. sth in a particular place: *The railway station is located to the west of the city.* يقع

location /ləʊˈkeɪʃn/ *noun* **1** [C] a place or position: *Several locations have been suggested for the new housing estate.* موقع، مكان

2 [U] finding where sb/sth is: *Police enquiries led to the location of the terrorists' hideout.* إيجاد، عثور على

IDM on location (used about a film, television programme, etc.) made in a suitable place (= not in a studio): *The series was filmed on location in Thailand.* (فيلم صوّر) في مواضع طبيعية

loch /lɒk/ *noun* [C] the Scottish word for a lake: *the Loch Ness monster* بحيرة في اسكتلندا

lock¹ /lɒk/ *noun* [C] **1** something that is used for fastening a door, lid, etc. so that you need a key to open it again: *to turn the key in the lock* ➲ Look at **padlock**. قفل

2 a part of a river or a canal where the level of water changes. Locks have gates at each end and are used to allow boats to move to a higher or lower part of the canal or river. هَويس أو هاويس القناة

lock² /lɒk/ *verb* **1** [I,T] to close or fasten with a lock: *Have you locked the car?* ○ *The door won't lock.* ➲ Look at **unlock**. يقفل؛ ينقفل

2 [T] to put sb/sth inside sth that is locked: *Lock your passport in a safe place.* يُخبّئ في صندوق مقفول

3 [I,T] to fix sth or be fixed in one position: *The wheels locked and the car crashed into the wall.* يستعصي، "يتَدربَس"

PHR V lock sth away to keep sth in a safe or secret place (that is locked) يحفظ شيئاً في مكان أمين مقفل

lock sb in/out to lock a door so that a person cannot get in/out: *All the prisoners are locked in for the night.* ○ *to lock yourself out of your house* يقفل الباب على...

lock (sth) up to lock all the doors, windows, etc. of a building: *Make sure that you lock up before you leave.* يغلق كل النوافذ والأبواب

lock sb up to put sb in prison يسجن، يحبس

locker /ˈlɒkə(r)/ *noun* [C] a small cupboard where personal things can be kept or left. Lockers are found in schools, sports centres, railway stations, etc. خزانة صغيرة خاصّة بالفرد (في مدرسة أو مسبح وغير ذلك)

locket /ˈlɒkɪt/ *noun* [C] a piece of jewellery that is worn around the neck on a chain. A locket is a small case that often contains a photograph. قلادة تحوي صورة أو شيئاً نفيساً

locomotive /ˈləʊkəməʊtɪv/ *noun* [C] = ENGINE (2): *a steam locomotive*

locust /ˈləʊkəst/ *noun* [C] a flying insect from Africa and Asia that moves in very large groups, eating and destroying large quantities of plants جرادة

lodge¹ /lɒdʒ/ *noun* [C] **1** a small house at the gate of a large house بيت الحارس، كوخ البوّاب

2 a house in the country that is used by hunters, sportsmen, etc: *a shooting lodge* بيت ريفيّ يستعمل في موسم الصّيد مثلاً

3 a room at the entrance to a college, block of flats, factory, etc. غرفة البوّاب

lodge² /lɒdʒ/ *verb* **1** [I] (*old-fashioned*) to live at sb's house in return for rent: *He lodged with a family for his first term at university.* يستأجر غرفة عند عائلة

2 [I,T] to become firmly fixed or to make sth do this: *The bullet lodged in her shoulder.* ➲ Look at **dislodge**. يستقرّ؛ يغرز؛ يغيّب (السكّين)

3 [T] (*formal*) **lodge sth (with sb) (against sb/sth)** to make an official statement complaining about sth: *to lodge a complaint* يقدِّم، يودع

▶ **lodger** *noun* [C] a person who pays rent to live in a house as a member of the family مستأجر يقيم مع عائلة

lodging /ˈlɒdʒɪŋ/ *noun* **1** [C,U] a place where you can stay: *The family offered full board and lodging* (= a room and all meals) *in exchange for English lessons.* سكنى، مسكن، إقامة

2 lodgings [plural] a room or rooms in sb's house where you can stay in return for paying rent غرفة مستأجرة في بيت

loft /lɒft; US lɔːft/ *noun* [C] the room or space under the roof of a house or other building: *Our loft has been converted into a bedroom.* ➲ Look at **attic**. غرفة تحت سقف البيت، سقيفة، علّية

log¹ /lɒg; US lɔːg/ *noun* [C] **1** the trunk or large branch of a tree that has been cut or has fallen down جذع شجرة مقطوع، قرمة

2 a small piece of wood for a fire حَطَبة

log² /lɒg; US lɔːg/ (*also* **logbook** /ˈlɒgbʊk; US ˈlɔːg-/) *noun* [C] the official written record of a ship's or an aircraft's journey: *to keep a log* سجل الوقائع (في سفينة أو طائرة)

▶ **log** *verb* [T] (logging; logged) to write sth in the log of a ship or aeroplane يكتب في سجل الوقائع (في سفينة أو طائرة)

PHR V log in/on to start using a computer that is part of a larger system يبدأ العمل على الكمبيوتر

log off/out to finish using a computer that is part of a larger system ينهي العمل على الكمبيوتر

logarithm /ˈlɒgərɪðəm; US ˈlɔːg-/ (*also informal* **log**) *noun* [C] one of a series of numbers arranged in special charts (tables) that allow you to solve mathematical problems by adding or subtracting numbers instead of multiplying or dividing لوغاريتم

loggerheads /ˈlɒgəhedz/ *noun*

IDM at loggerheads (with sb) strongly disagreeing (with sb) على خلاف شديد مع

logic /ˈlɒdʒɪk/ *noun* [U] **1** the science of using reason علم المَنْطق

2 the use of reason: *There is no logic in your argument.* مَنْطق

▶ **logical** /ˈlɒdʒɪkl/ *adj* **1** according to the rules of logic; reasonable: *As I see it, there is only one logical conclusion.* منطقي، معقول

2 able to use logic: *a logical mind* ❶ The opposite is **illogical**. منطقي
logically /-kli/ *adv* منطقياً؛ بشكل معقول

logo /ˈləʊgəʊ/ *noun* [C] a symbol or design that is used as an advertisement by a company or organization. A logo appears on the things the company owns and produces. رمز أو شعار شركة أو مؤسسة

loiter /ˈlɔɪtə(r)/ *verb* [I] to stand somewhere or walk around without any real purpose يتسكّع، يتلكّأ

lollipop /ˈlɒlipɒp/ (*also informal* **lolly** /ˈlɒli/) *noun* [C] a large sweet of boiled sugar on a stick ➲ Look at **ice lolly**. مصّاصة من حلوى السكّر على عود صغير

lone /ləʊn/ *adj* (only *before* a noun) without any other people; alone: *a lone swimmer on the beach* ❶ A parent who looks after his/her child or children alone can be called a **lone parent** or a **single parent**. وحيد ، منفرد
▸ **loner** *noun* [C] (*informal*) a person who likes to be alone محبّ للإنفراد

lonely /ˈləʊnli/ *adj* (**lonelier**; **loneliest**) **1** unhappy because you are not with other people: *to feel sad and lonely* شاعِر بالوحشة ، مستوحش ، وحيد
2 (only *before* a noun) far from other people and places where people live: *a lonely house in the hills* ➲ Look at the note at **alone**. منعزل
▸ **loneliness** *noun* [U] الوحدة ، الانعزال ، الوحشة

lonesome /ˈləʊnsəm/ *adj* (*US*) lonely or making you feel lonely ➲ Look at the note at **alone**. شاعر بالوحشة ؛ موحش، يبعث على الكآبة

long[1] /lɒŋ; *US* lɔːŋ/ *adj* (**longer** /-ŋgə(r)/, **longest** /-ŋgɪst/) measuring a great amount in distance or time: *She has lovely long hair.* ○ *We had to wait a long time.* ○ *a very long journey* ○ *War and Peace is a very long book.* ○ *a long dress* (= down to the floor) ➲ Look at **length**.

Long is also used when you are asking for or giving information about how much something measures in length, distance or time: *How long is the film?* ○ *The insect was only 2 millimetres long.* ○ *a five-mile-long traffic jam*

طويل

IDM **at the longest** not longer than the stated time: *It will take a week at the longest.* على أكثر تقدير
go a long way (used about money, food, etc.) to be used for buying a lot of things, feeding a lot of people, etc: *to make a little money go a long way* (يجعل النقود أو الطعام) يَمدّ أي يكفي لمدة طويلة
in the long run after a long time; in the end: *We ought to buy a new car – it'll be cheaper in the long run.* على المدى البعيد
in the long/short term → TERM

long[2] /lɒŋ; *US* lɔːŋ/ *noun* [U] a long time: *They won't be gone for long.* ○ *It shouldn't take long.* مدة طويلة ، وقت طويل

long[3] /lɒŋ; *US* lɔːŋ/ *adv* **1** for a long time: *She didn't stay long.* ○ *You shouldn't have to wait long.* ○ *I hope we don't have to wait much longer.*

Long and **a long time** are both used as expressions of time. In positive sentences **a long time** is usually used: *They stood there for a long time.* **Long** is only used in positive sentences with another adverb, e.g. 'too', 'enough', 'ago', etc: *We lived here long ago.* ○ *I've put up with this noise long enough. I'm going to make a complaint.* Both **long** and **a long time** can be used in questions: *Were you away long/a long time?* In negative sentences there is sometimes a difference in meaning between **long** and **a long time**: *I haven't been here long* (= I arrived only a short time ago). ○ *I haven't been here for a long time* (= it is a long time since I was last here).

طويلاً ، مدةً طويلة

2 at a time that is distant from a particular point in time: *All that happened long ago.* ○ *We got married long before we moved here.* من زمن بعيد ؛ بزمن طويل
3 for the whole of the time that is mentioned: *The baby cried all night long.* طوالَ (الليل)
IDM **as/so long as** on condition that: *As long as no problems arise we should get the job finished by Friday.* طالما ، شريطة أن
no/not any longer not any more: *They no longer live here.* ○ *They don't live here any longer.* لم يَعدْ (يقطن هنا)

long[4] /lɒŋ; *US* lɔːŋ/ *verb* [I] **long for sth**; **long (for sb) to do sth** to want sth very much: *He longed to hold her in his arms.* يتلهّف إلى ، يتوق
▸ **longing** /ˈlɒŋɪŋ; *US* ˈlɔːŋɪŋ/ *noun* [C,U] a great desire (for sb/sth) شوق ، حنين ، رغبة شديدة
longingly *adv*: *She gazed longingly at the cakes in the shop window.* برغبة شديدة ، بتلهّف

ˌlong-ˈdistance *adj*, *adv* (used about travel or communication) between places that are far from each other: *a long-distance lorry driver* ○ *to phone long-distance* ➲ Look at **local**. لمسافات بعيدة أو طويلة ؛ (مخابرة) خارجيّة

ˌlong-drawn-ˈout *adj* lasting longer than necessary: *long-drawn-out negotiations* مطوّل، يدوم أكثر مما ينبغي

ˈlong-haul *adj* (only *before* a noun) connected with the transport of people or goods over long distances: *a long-haul flight* يقطع مسافات طويلة

longitude /ˈlɒndʒɪtjuːd; *US* -tuːd/ *noun* [U] the distance of a place east or west of a line from the North Pole to the South Pole that passes through Greenwich in England. Longitude is measured in degrees. ➲ Look at **latitude**. خطّ الطول الجغرافي

ˈlong jump *noun* [sing.] the sport in which people try to jump as far as possible ➲ Look at **high jump**. القفز الطويل

ˌlong-ˈlife *adj* lasting for a long time: *a long-life battery* ○ *long-life milk* يدوم مدة طويلة ، طويل الأمد

ˌlong-ˈlived *adj* living or lasting for a long time: *a long-lived dispute* طويل الأمد

ˈlong-range *adj* **1** of or for a long period of time starting from the present: *the long-range weather forecast* بعيد المدى

a b c d e f g h i j k **l** m n o p q r s t u v w x y z

2 that can go or be sent over long distances: *long-range nuclear missiles* بعيد المدى

ˌ**long-ˈsighted** (*US* ˌ**far-ˈsighted**) *adj* able to see things clearly only when they are quite far away ❶ The opposite is **short-sighted** (*US* **near-sighted**). طويل البَصر

ˌ**long-ˈstanding** *adj* that has lasted for a long time: *a long-standing arrangement* طويل العهد ، قديم

ˌ**long-ˈsuffering** *adj* (used about a person) having a lot of troubles that he/she bears without complaining كثير التحمّل لمتاعبه ، صبور على الأذى

ˌ**long-ˈterm** *adj* of or for a long period of time: *long-term planning* طويل الأمد

ˈ**long wave** *noun* [U] (*abbr* **LW**) the system of broadcasting radio using sound waves of 1 000 metres or more ➲ Look at **short wave** and **medium wave**. الموجة الطويلة

ˌ**long-ˈwinded** *adj* (used about sth that is written or spoken) boring because it is too long (خِطاب) مملّ لإفراطه في الطول ، طويل النَّفَس

loo /luː/ *noun* [C] (*Brit informal*) toilet: *I need to go to the loo.* ➲ Look at the note at **toilet**. تواليت ، دورة المياه

⚷ **look**[1] /lʊk/ *verb* **1** [I,T] to turn your eyes in a particular direction (in order to pay attention to sb/sth): *Look carefully at the two pictures and try to spot the differences between them.* ○ *She blushed and looked away.* ○ *to look out of the window* ○ *Look who's come to see us.* ○ *Look where you are going!*

> You can **see** something without paying attention to it: *I saw a girl riding past on a horse.* If you **look** at something you pay attention to it with your eyes: *Look carefully. Can you see anything strange?*

ينظر

2 [I] **look (like sb/sth) (to sb); look (to sb) as if.../as though...** to seem or appear: *You look very smart in that shirt.* ○ *to look tired, ill, sad, well, happy, etc.* ○ *The boy looks like his father.* ○ *The room looks (to me) as if it needs a coat of paint.* ○ *It looks like rain* (= as if it is going to rain). يبدو

3 [I] **look (for sb/sth)** to try to find (sb/sth): *We've been looking for you everywhere. Where have you been?* ○ *'Have you found your watch?' 'No, I'm still looking.'* ○ *to look for work* يبحث أو يفتّش عن

4 [I] to face a particular direction: *Our hotel room looks onto the sea.* يشرف أو يطلّ على

IDM **look good** to seem to be encouraging: *This year's sales figures are looking good.* يُبشِّر بالخير ، يبدو مُشجِّعاً

look here 1 (used for protesting about sth): *Now look here! That's not fair!* اسمع يا هذا! (تقال للاحتجاج)

2 (used for asking sb to pay attention to sth): *Look here everyone. Let's form a committee to decide what to do next.* انتبه أو انتبهوا إليّ

(not) look yourself to (not) look as well or healthy as usual: *What's the matter? You're not looking yourself today.* "مُش على بعضك": يبدو بصحّة جيدة/أو بصحّة منحرفة

PHR V **look after sb/sth/yourself** to be responsible for or take care of sb/sth/yourself: *I want to go back to work if I can find somebody to look after the children.* ○ *The old lady's son looked after all her financial affairs.* يعتني بـ: يتعهّد بِ

look ahead to think about or plan for the future: *Looking ahead a few years, there's going to be a shortage of skilled workers.*

look at sth 1 to examine sth (closely): *My tooth aches. I think a dentist should look at it.* يفحص ، يعاين

2 to think about or study sth: *The government is looking at ways of reducing the number of stray dogs.* يدرس ، يبحث في

3 to read sth: *Could I look at the newspaper when you've finished with it?* يقرأ، يتصفح

4 to consider sth: *Different races and nationalities look at life differently.* ينظر إلى

look back (on sth) to think about sth in your past يعود بأفكاره إلى الماضي

look down on sb/sth (*informal*) to think that you are better than sb/sth: *Don't look down on them just because they haven't been as successful as you.* يستصغِر، يزدري

look forward to sth/doing sth to wait with pleasure for sth to happen (because you expect to enjoy it): *The children are really looking forward to their holiday.* ○ *I'm looking forward to seeing you again.* يتطلّع أو يتشوّق إلى

look into sth to study or investigate sth: *A committee was set up to look into the causes of the accident.* يدرس ، يستقصي

look on to watch sth happening: *All we could do was look on as the house burned.* يتفرّج على ، ينظر إلى (مكتوف الأيدي)

look out to be careful or to pay attention to sth dangerous, etc: *Look out! There's a bike coming.* ينتبه ، يحذَر

look out (for sb/sth) to pay attention in order to see, find or be careful of sb/sth: *Look out for pickpockets!* ينتبه، يحذَر، " خلّي بالك من"...

look round 1 to turn your head in order to see sb/sth يلتفت

2 to look at many things (before buying sth): *She looked round but couldn't find anything she liked.* يتجوّل ويتفحّص أشياء مختلفة قبل الشراء

look round sth to visit a place of interest, etc: *to look round a town/shop/museum* يزور (مكاناً أثرياً) ، يتفرّج على

look through sth to read sth quickly يتصفّح ، يلقي نظرة سريعة على

look to sb for sth; look to sb to do sth to expect sb to do or to provide sth: *He always looked to his father for advice.* ○ *You shouldn't look to the state to support you.* ينتظر من : يلجأ إلى ، يعتمد على

look up 1 to raise your eyes: *She looked up and smiled.* يرفع بصره

2 (*informal*) to improve: *Business is looking up.* يتحسّن ، يزدهر

look sth up to search for information in a book:

to look up a word in a dictionary
يبحث عن معلومات في مرجع

look up to sb to respect or admire sb
يحترم ، يعجب بِ

▸ **look** *interj* (used for asking sb to listen to what you are saying): *Look, William, I know you are busy but could you give me a hand?*
اسمع! (تقال لجذب الانتباه)

-looking (used in compounds to form adjectives) having the stated appearance: *an odd-looking building* ○ *He's very good-looking.*
(غريب) الشكل ؛ (جميل) الطلعة

look² /lʊk/ *noun* **1** [C] the act of looking: *Have a look at this article.* ○ *I knew something was wrong – everybody was giving me funny looks* (= looking at me strangely).
نظرة

2 [C, usually sing.] a search: *I've had a look but I can't find it.*
بحث ، تفتيش

3 [C] the expression or appearance of sb/sth: *He had a worried look on his face.*
تعبير ، سيماء

4 [C] a fashion or style: *The shop has a new look to appeal to younger customers.*
مظهر؛ أسلوب

5 looks [plural] a person's appearance: *He's lucky – he's got good looks and intelligence.*
هيئة ، طلعة ؛ جمال، وَسامة

IDM **by/from the look of sb/sth** judging by the appearance: *It's going to be a fine day by the look of it.*
من المظهر ، كما يبدو

like the look/sound of sb/sth → LIKE¹

'look-in *noun*

IDM **(not) give sb/get/have a look-in** (*informal*) (not) give sb/have a chance to do sth: *The older children spend a lot of time on the computer so the younger ones don't get a look-in.*
يُتيح (أو لا يُتيح) له الفرصة ؛ تسنح (أو لا تسنح) له الفرصة

lookout /'lʊkaʊt/ *noun* [C] a person who watches out for danger
الرقيب، الراصد

IDM **be on the lookout for sb/sth; keep a lookout for sb/sth** = LOOK OUT FOR SB/STH

loom¹ /luːm/ *noun* [C] a machine that is used for making (weaving) cloth by passing pieces of thread across and under other pieces
نَوْل ، منوال

loom² /luːm/ *verb* [I] to appear as a shape that is not clear and in a way that seems frightening: *The mountain loomed (up) in the distance.* ○ (*figurative*) *The threat of war loomed over the country.*
يلوح كشكل مبهم أو مرعب ؛ يُخيِّم على؛ يتراءى

loony /'luːni/ *noun* [C], *adj* (*pl.* **loonies**) (*informal*) (a person who is) crazy or mad
مجنون ، معتوه

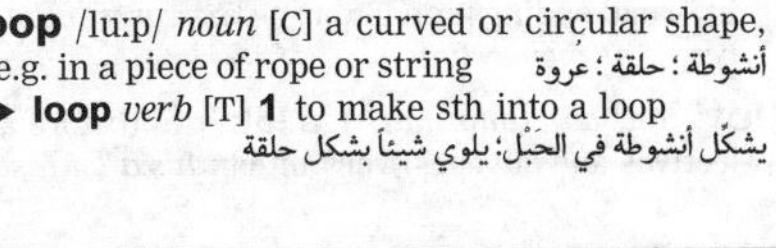

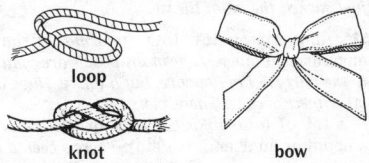

loop /luːp/ *noun* [C] a curved or circular shape, e.g. in a piece of rope or string
أنشوطة ؛ حلقة ؛ عروة

▸ **loop** *verb* [T] **1** to make sth into a loop
يشكّل أنشوطة في الحَبْل؛ يلوي شيئاً بشكل حلقة

2 to fasten or join sth with a loop
يربط شيئاً بأنشوطة ؛ يلُف الخيط حول (إناء مثلاً)

loophole /'luːphəʊl/ *noun* [C] a way of avoiding sth because the words of a rule or law are badly chosen: *a loophole in the tax law*
ثغرة في القانون ، مَهرب

loose /luːs/ *adj* **1** not tied up or shut in sth: *The dog broke loose and ran away.* ○ *She wore her long hair loose.*
طليق ؛ غير مربوط

2 not firmly fixed: *a loose tooth*
مخلخَل ، متقلقِل

3 not contained in sth or joined together: *loose change in your trouser pocket* ○ *some loose sheets of paper*
مفروط ، مبعثر

4 not fitting closely; not tight: *These trousers don't fit. They're much too loose round the waist.*
واسع ، فضفاض

IDM **at a loose end** having nothing to do and feeling bored
شاعر بالوحدة والملل لقلة ما يشغله

▸ **loosely** *adv* in a loose way
بحرّيّة؛ بتصرّف ؛ بشكل سائب

ˌloose-'leaf *adj* (used about a notebook, etc.) with pages that can be removed or added: *a loose-leaf album*
(دفتر) ذو صفحات سائبة أو متحرّكة

loosen /'luːsn/ *verb* [I,T] to become or make sth loose or looser: *to loosen your tie*
يحلّ ، يفكّ

PHRV **loosen (sb/sth) up** to relax or make sb move more easily: *These exercises will help you to loosen up.*
يسترخي ، يرتاح ؛ يليّن

loot /luːt/ *noun* [U] goods that have been stolen
غنيمة ، سَلْب ونَهْب

▸ **loot** *verb* [I,T] to steal things during a war or period of fighting: *Many shops were looted during the riot.*
يسلُب ، ينهب

lop /lɒp/ *verb* [T] (lopping; lopped) to cut branches, etc. off a tree
يقضّب (الشجرة)

PHRV **lop sth off/away** to cut sth off/away
يبتر، يقطع

lopsided /ˌlɒp'saɪdɪd/ *adj* with one side lower or smaller, etc. than the other: *a lopsided smile*
مائل إلى جانب واحد ، (منضدة) غير مستوية

lord /lɔːd/ *noun* **1** [C] a man in a position of authority
صاحب السلطة ، سيِّد، أمير...الخ

2 the Lord [sing.] God; Christ
الله ؛ الرَّب ؛ السيِّد المسيح

3 [C] a nobleman or a man who has been given the title 'Lord': *lords and ladies*
لورد

4 the Lords [with sing. or pl. verb] (*Brit*) (members of) the House of Lords: *The Lords has/have voted against the bill.*
(أعضاء) مجلس اللوردات

5 [C] (*Brit*) used as the title of some high officials or of men who have been made a lord (3): *the Lord Mayor of London* ○ *Lord Derby*
لقب يمنح لبعض كبار الموظفين

6 My Lord (used for addressing a judge, bishop, nobleman, etc.)
لقب يخاطب به القاضي والأسقف وما إليهما

IDM **(Good) Lord** (used for expressing surprise, worry, etc.)
يا إلهي! يا الله!

lordship /'lɔːdʃɪp/ *noun* [C] (used when speaking to or about a judge, bishop, nobleman, etc.): *Their lordships cannot be disturbed.*
سيادة، حضرة؛ عطوفة

the ˌLord's ˈPrayer *noun* [sing.] a very important Christian prayer that was first taught by Christ to his followers (disciples) الصلاة الربّانية

lorry /ˈlɒri; *US* ˈlɔːri/ (*Brit*) *noun* [C] (*pl.* **lorries**) (*especially US* **truck**) a large strong motor vehicle that is used for carrying goods, etc. by road شاحنة ، سيارة شحن

lose /luːz/ *verb* (*pt, pp* **lost** /lɒst; *US* lɔːst/) **1** [T] to be unable to find sth: *I've lost my purse. I can't find it anywhere.* يضيّع، يفقد

2 [T] to no longer have sb/sth: *She lost a leg in the accident.* ○ *He lost his wife last year* (= she died). ○ *to lose your job* يخسر، يفقد

3 [T] to have less of sth: *to lose weight, interest, patience, etc.* ○ *Small shops are losing business to the large supermarkets.* يخسر ، يفقد

4 [I,T] not to win; to be defeated: *The team lost by three goals to two.* ○ *to lose a court case* ○ *Cambridge lost to Oxford in the boat race.* ○ *to lose an argument* يخسر

5 [T] to waste time, a chance, etc: *Hurry up! There's no time to lose.* يضيّع

6 [I,T] to become poorer (as a result of sth): *The company lost on the deal.* يخسر

7 [I,T] (used about a clock, watch, etc.) to go too slowly: *My watch loses two minutes a day.* ⓘ The opposite is **gain**. يقصر، يبطئ

8 [T] (*informal*) to cause sb not to understand sth: *You've totally lost me! Please explain again.* يسيء الشرح فيتعذّر فهمه ، "يضيّع أو يلخبط" مستمعه

IDM **keep/lose your balance** → BALANCE[2]
keep/lose your cool → COOL[1]
keep/lose count → COUNT[2]
keep/lose your temper → TEMPER[1]
keep/lose track of sb/sth → TRACK
lose your bearings → BEARING
lose face to lose the respect of other people يفقد احترامه
lose your head to become confused or very excited يفقد أعصابه ، يرتبك ؛ يهتاج
lose heart to believe that you will be unsuccessful تتثبّط عزيمته، يخشى الإخفاق
lose it to go crazy or suddenly become unable to control your emotions: *I'm afraid I lost it and shouted at Helen.* يفقد أعصابه
lose your life to be killed يقتل ، يموت
lose your place to be unable to find the place in a book, etc. where you stopped reading يضيّع مكانه (مثلاً الصفحة التي كان يقرؤها في الكتاب)
lose sight of sb/sth 1 to no longer be able to see sb/sth يغيب عن النظر
2 to forget sb/sth: *We mustn't lose sight of our original aim.* ينسى : يضيّع
lose your touch to lose a special skill or ability to do sth يفقد لمسته السحرية ، يفقد مهارته في...
lose touch (with sb/sth) to no longer have contact (with sb/sth): *I've lost touch with a lot of my old school friends.* يفقد الصلة (مع صديق قديم مثلاً)
a losing battle a competition, struggle, etc. in which it seems that you will be unsuccessful محاولة يائسة ، معركة فاشلة
win/lose the toss → TOSS

PHRV **lose out (on sth)** (*informal*) to be at a disadvantage: *If a teacher pays too much attention to the bright students, the others lose out.* يخسر ؛ يظلَم

▶ **loser** *noun* [C] a person who is (often) defeated: *He is a bad loser. He always gets cross if I beat him.* الفاشل؛ شخص مخفق

loss /lɒs; *US* lɔːs/ *noun* **1** [U] no longer having sth or not having as much as before; the act of losing sth: *loss of blood, money, etc.* ○ *The loss* (= death) *of his wife was very sad for him.* ○ *The plane crashed with great loss of life.* فقدان ، خسارة

2 [C] a disadvantage: *If she leaves, it will be a big loss to the school.* خسارة

3 [C] the amount of money which is lost by a business: *The firm made a loss of £5 million.* خسارة

IDM **at a loss** not knowing what to do or say مرتبك

lost[1] *pt, pp* of LOSE

lost[2] /lɒst; *US* lɔːst/ *adj* **1** (used about a person or an animal) unable to find the way: *This isn't the right road – we're completely lost!* ○ *Don't get lost!* ضائع ، تائه

2 difficult or impossible to find; missing: *The notice said, 'Lost: a black and white cat in North Street.'* مفقود

3 lost (without) not able to work in an efficient way or to live happily: *I'm lost without my diary!* ○ *He would be lost without his old dog for company.* ضائع ، ملَخبَط ؛ متضايق

4 lost on not noticed or understood: *The humour of the situation was completely lost on Joe and he got quite angry.* ذاهب سدى ؛ غير مفهوم

IDM **get lost** (*slang*) go away: *'Get lost!' she said rudely and walked off.* ابعد عني! ، "روح في داهية!"
a lost cause an ambition or aim that cannot be achieved أمل لا يتحقّق ، قضيّة خاسرة

ˌlost ˈproperty *noun* [U] things that people have lost or left in a public place and that are kept in a special office for the owners to collect (مكتب) المفقودات

lot[1] /lɒt/ *noun* [sing.] ⓘ 'Lot' in this sense is always used in the phrases **the lot**, **all the lot**, **the whole lot**. It can be used with either a singular or plural verb.

1 the whole amount (of sth): *When we opened the bag of potatoes the whole lot was/were bad.* ○ *Just one more suitcase and that's the lot!* الكلّ ، كلّ شيء

2 a whole group (of people): *The manager has just sacked the lot of them!* الجميع

lot[2] /lɒt/ *pron* **a lot**; **lots** (*informal*) a large amount or number: *'How many people are coming to the party?' 'I'm not sure, but a lot!'* ○ *Have another piece of cake. There's lots left.* كثير ؛ عدد كبير

▶ **a lot of** (*also informal* **lots of**) *det* a large amount or number of (sb/sth): *There's been a lot of rain this year.* ○ *Lots of love, Billy.* (= an informal ending for a letter) ○ *There were a lot of people at the meeting.* كثير من ، كمّية كبيرة ؛ عدد كبير

lot[3] /lɒt/ *adv* (*informal*) **1 a lot**; **lots** (before adjectives and adverbs) very much: *It's a lot faster* *now that there's a motorway.* ○ *They see lots more of each other than before.* بكثير ، كثيراً

2 a lot very much or often: *Thanks a lot – that's very kind.* ○ *It generally rains a lot at this time of year.* كثيراً : كثيراً أو غالباً (ما تمطر)

lot⁴ /lɒt/ *noun* **1** [C, with sing. or pl. verb] a group or set (of people or things of the same type): *This lot of clothes needs/need ironing – can you do it?* مجموعة

2 [sing.] the quality or state of a person's life; your fate: *Although things have not been easy for him, he's always been perfectly happy with his lot.* معيشة : حظّ ، نصيب

3 [C] an object or group of objects that are for sale at an auction (= a sale at which the object goes to the person who offers the highest price): *Lot 27: 6 chairs* قطعة أو مجموعة من القطع تُباع في المزاد العلني

4 [C] (*US*) an area of land used for a particular purpose: *a parking lot* (= a car park) قطعة أرض

IDM draw lots → DRAW²

lotion /ˈləʊʃn/ *noun* [C,U] liquid that you use on your hair or skin: *suntan lotion* مستحضر تجميلي أو طبيّ سائل

lottery /ˈlɒtəri/ *noun* [C] (*pl.* **lotteries**) a way of raising money by selling tickets with numbers on them and giving prizes to the people who have bought certain numbers which are chosen by chance يانصيب

loud /laʊd/ *adj* **1** making a lot of noise; not quiet: *He's got such a loud laugh you can hear it next door!* ○ *Can you turn the television down? It's a bit loud.*

> **Loud** is usually used to describe the sound itself or the thing producing the sound: *a loud noise, a loud bang, loud music.* **Noisy** is used to describe a person, animal, place, event, etc. that is very or too loud: *a noisy road, party, etc., noisy neighbours, children, etc.*

(صوت) عال ؛ مدوٍّ ؛ صاخب

2 (used about clothes, colours, behaviour) too bright or noticeable: *Isn't that shirt a bit loud for a formal dinner?* صارخ ؛ صاخب

▶ **loud** *adv* making a lot of noise: *Could you speak a bit louder – the people at the back can't hear.* بصوت عالٍ

IDM ˌout ˈloud so that people can hear it: *Shall I read this bit out loud to you?* بصوت عالٍ (يسمعه الآخرون)

loudly *adv* in a loud way بصوت عالٍ ، بصَخَب

loudness *noun* [U] صخَب ، ضجيج

loudspeaker /ˌlaʊdˈspiːkə(r)/ *noun* [C] **1** an apparatus for making sounds, voices, etc. louder: *The winner of the competition was announced over the loudspeaker.* مكبِّر الصوت

2 (*also* **speaker**) the part of a radio, CD-player, etc. from which the sound comes out مكبِّر الصوت

lounge /laʊndʒ/ *noun* [C] **1** a room in a house or hotel where you can sit comfortably: *Let's go and have coffee in the lounge.* غرفة الجلوس : صالة الجلوس (في فندق)

2 a room at an airport where passengers wait: *the departure lounge* قاعة أو صالة الانتظار

▶ **lounge** *verb* [I] **1** to sit or stand in a lazy way; to relax: *That looks a very comfortable sofa to lounge on.* يقف متراخياً : يسترخي ، يستريح

2 lounge about/around to spend your time in a lazy way, not doing very much: *I wish Ann wouldn't lounge around in her room all day reading magazines.* يتكاسل

louse /laʊs/ *noun* [C] (*pl.* **lice** /laɪs/) a small insect that lives on the bodies of animals and people قملة

lousy /ˈlaʊzi/ *adj* (**lousier**; **lousiest**) (*informal*) very bad: *We had lousy weather on holiday.* ○ *You'll feel lousy tomorrow if you don't get some sleep.* رديء جداً : تعبان، متوعك

lout /laʊt/ *noun* [C] a young man who behaves in a rude, rough or stupid way: *The train was full of louts returning from the football match.* ➲ Look at **hooligan**. It is similar in meaning. جلف ، شقي ، أزعر ، بلطجي

▶ **loutish** *adj* فظّ ، وقح

lovable /ˈlʌvəbl/ *adj* easy to love because attractive and pleasant محبَّب ، قريب إلى القلب

love¹ /lʌv/ *noun* **1** [U] a very strong feeling of affection for sb/sth: *The deep love and understanding between them lasted throughout their lives.* ○ *It was love at first sight.* ○ *I don't think she's marrying him for love!* ○ *Love of one's country is perhaps less important to the young people of today.* ❶ The opposite is **hate** or **hatred**. حُبّ، غرام

2 [U, sing.] a strong feeling of interest in or enjoyment of sth: *a love of adventure* حُبّ ، ولَع

3 [C] a thing in which you are very interested: *His great love was always music.* هَوَس ، شَغَف

4 [C] a person who is loved: *Of course, my love.* ➲ Look at **darling**. حبيب

5 [C] (*Brit informal*) (a friendly way of speaking to sb (often sb you don't know) and used by women, or by men to women or children): *'Hello, love. What can I do for you?'* ❶ Often written **luv**. عزيز ، حبيب

6 [U] (used in tennis) a score of zero: *'15-love', called the umpire.* (في لعبة التنس) عدد النقاط: صفر

7 [U] (*informal*) (a way of ending a letter to a friend or a member of your family): *Lots of love from us all, Denise.* مع خالص حبي ومودتي

IDM be in love (with sb) to have a strong feeling of affection and sexual attraction (for sb): *They're very much in love (with each other).* يعشق ، يهوى

fall in love (with sb) to start to feel a strong affection and attraction for sb: *They fell in love and were married within two months.* يقع في الغرام

give/send sb your love to give/send sb a friendly greeting: *I haven't seen Mary for ages – give her my love, will you?* يسلِّم على ، يحيّي

make love (to sb) to have sex يعاشر معاشرة جنسيّة ، يجامع

love² /lʌv/ *verb* [T] **1** to have a strong feeling of affection for sb/sth: *'Do you love him?' 'Yes, very much.'* ○ *It's wonderful to be loved.* يحب ، يهوى ، يعشق

2 to like very much or to enjoy: *I love the summer!* ○ *My father loves to listen/listening to music.* ○ *'Would you like to come?' 'I'd love to.'* ○ *'What about a drink?' 'I'd love one.'* ○ *We'd love you to come and stay with us.* ○ *The cat loves you stroking her just here.* يحبّ ؛ يودّ

'love affair *noun* [C] a (usually sexual) relationship between two people who love each other but are not married علاقة غرامية

lovely /'lʌvli/ *adj* (**lovelier**; **loveliest**) **1** beautiful or attractive: *a lovely room* ○ *You look lovely with your hair short.* جميل ، جذاب

2 very nice, enjoyable or pleasant: *We had a lovely holiday in Wales.* ○ *It's lovely to see you again.* سار ، ممتع

▸ **loveliness** *noun* [U] جمال ، فتنة

lover /'lʌvə(r)/ *noun* [C] **1** a person who is having a sexual relationship outside marriage. ➲ Look at **mistress**. عشيق ، خليل

2 lovers [plural] (*old-fashioned*) two people who are in love or are having a sexual relationship without being married: *In the evening the park was full of young lovers walking hand in hand.* ○ *It wasn't long before they became lovers.* عاشقان ، عشاق

3 a person who likes or enjoys the thing mentioned: *a music lover* ○ *an animal lover* محبّ لِ ، من عشّاق (الموسيقى)

'love story *noun* [C] (*pl.* **love stories**) a story or novel that is mainly about love قصة غراميّة

loving /'lʌvɪŋ/ *adj* feeling or showing love or care مُحِبّ ، ودود ؛ حنون

▸ **lovingly** *adv* بحب ، بحنان ، برقّة

low¹ /ləʊ/ *adj* **1** not high: *The dog will be able to jump over that fence – it's much too low.* منخفض ، واطئ

2 close to the ground or to the bottom of sth: *Hang that picture a bit higher, it's too low!* منخفض ، واطئ

3 below the usual or normal level or amount: *Temperatures were very low last winter.* ○ *The price of fruit is lower in the summer.* ○ *low wages* منخفض

4 below what is normal in quality, importance or development: *a low standard of living* ○ *low status* منخفض ؛ وضيع ؛ (كائنات عضويّة) دنيا

5 (used about behaviour, etc.) unpleasant; not respectable or honest: *That was a rather low trick to play on you!* منحطّ ، دنيء ، خسيس

6 (used about a sound or voice) deep or soft and quiet: *His voice is already lower than his father's.* منخفض ، خفيض

7 not cheerful or bright: *He's been feeling rather low since his illness.* مكتئب

8 (used about a gear in a car) that allows a slower speed: *You'll need to change into a low gear on this hill.* (في السيّارة) الأول أو الثاني

IDM **high and low** → HIGH²

low² /ləʊ/ *adv* **1** in or to a low position, level, etc.; near the ground or bottom; not high: *He reached down lower and lower – at last he had got it!* ○ *'Whereabouts is the pain? Here?' 'A bit lower down,' she replied.* في وضع منخفض ، إلى مستوى منخفض

2 (in music) with deep notes: *Can you sing a bit lower?* بطبقة صوتية منخفضة

low³ /ləʊ/ *noun* [C] a low point, level, figure, etc: *The pound has fallen to a new low against the dollar.* نقطة منخفضة ، مستوى منخفض

,low-'calorie *adj* (of food and drink) containing very few calories قليل السعرات الحرارية

'low-down *noun* [sing.] (*informal*)

IDM **give sb/get the low-down (on sb/sth)** to tell sb/be told the true facts or secret information (about sb/sth): *Jeremy will give you the low-down on what went on at the meeting.* حقائق ؛ معلومات سريّة

lower¹ /'ləʊə(r)/ *adj* at the bottom of sth; being the bottom part of sth: *She bit her lower lip.* ○ *Write your notes in the lower left-hand corner.* ❶ The opposite is **upper**. أسفل

lower² /'ləʊə(r)/ *verb* [T] **1** to move sb/sth down; *They lowered the boat into the water.* ينزل ؛ يخفض

2 to make sth less in amount or quality: *The virus lowers resistance to other diseases.* يقلّل ؛ يُضعف

❶ The opposite for **1** and **2** is **raise**.

,lower 'case *adj*, *noun* [U] (in) small letters, not capitals: *A lower case R looks like this: r.* ❶ The opposite is **upper case**. (في طباعة اللغات الأوروبية) أحرف صغيرة

,lower 'class *adj* belonging to a low social class ➲ Look at **middle class**, **upper class**, and **working class**. الطبقة الاجتماعية الدنيا

,low-'fat *adj* containing only a very small amount of fat: *low-fat cheese* ○ *a low-fat diet* قليل الدسم

,low-'key *adj* (used about the style of sth) quiet, without a lot of preparation or fuss: *The wedding will be very low-key. We're only inviting ten people.* هادئ وبسيط

lowland /'ləʊlənd/ *noun* [C, usually pl.] a flat area of land usually around sea level: *the lowlands near the coast* ○ *lowland areas* أراضٍ منخفضة

,low-'lying *adj* (used about land) near to sea level; not high واطئ ، منخفض

,low-'paid *adj* not paying or earning much money: *low-paid workers* ذو أجر زهيد ، قليل الدخل

,low-'tech (*also* **,lo-'tech**) *adj* not involving the most modern technology or methods بسيط تكنولوجياً

,low 'tide *noun* [U] the time when the sea is at its lowest level: *At low tide you can walk out to the island.* ❶ The opposite is **high tide**. أدنى مستوى للجَزْر

loyal /'lɔɪəl/ *adj* (used about a person) not changing in your friendship or beliefs; faithful: *a loyal* *friend* ○ *Will you remain loyal to the Conservatives at the next election?* ℹ The opposite is **disloyal**. وفيّ، مخلِص؛ موالٍ

▸ **loyally** /ˈlɔɪəli/ *adv* بولاء

loyalty /ˈlɔɪəlti/ *noun* (*pl.* **loyalties**) **1** [U] the quality of being loyal: *A dog is capable of great loyalty to its master.* وفاء، إخلاص، ولاء

2 [C] a feeling of friendship that makes you faithful towards sth/sb: *I know where my loyalties lie.* ولاء

lozenge /ˈlɒzɪndʒ/ *noun* [C] a sweet that you suck if you have a cough or sore throat أقراص طبيّة تُمصّ كعلاج لالتهاب الحَلْق

L-plate /ˈel pleɪt/ *noun* [C] a sign with a large red letter L (for 'learner') on it, that you fix to a car when you are learning to drive لائحة تحمل الحرف "L" تُثبّت على سيّارة متعلم السواقة

Ltd *abbrev* (*Brit*) = LIMITED COMPANY

lubricant /ˈluːbrɪkənt/ *noun* [C,U] a substance like oil used for making a machine, etc. work smoothly زيت التشحيم؛ مادّة مزْلقة

lubricate /ˈluːbrɪkeɪt/ *verb* [T] to put oil, etc. onto or into sth so that it works smoothly يزيّت (آلة)، يضيف مادّة مزْلقة

▸ **lubrication** /ˌluːbrɪˈkeɪʃn/ *noun* [U] تزييت، تشحيم

lucid /ˈluːsɪd/ *adj* (*formal*) **1** (used about sth that is said or written) clear and easy to understand واضح، سهل الفهم

2 (used about a person's mind) not confused; clear and normal صافي الذهن؛ سليم العقل

▸ **lucidly** *adv* بوضوح

lucidity /luːˈsɪdəti/ *noun* [U] صفاء الذهن، سلامة التفكير

🔑**luck** /lʌk/ *noun* [U] **1** the fact of something happening by chance: *There's no skill in this game – it's all luck.* ○ *to have good, bad, etc. luck* حظّ، مصادفة

2 success or good things that happen by chance: *We'd like to wish you lots of luck in your new career.* ○ *A four-leaved clover is supposed to bring you luck!* حظّ سعيد

IDM **bad luck!; hard luck!** (used to express sympathy): *'Bad luck, darling. You can always try again.'* "معليش" هذا سوء حظّ!

be bad/hard luck (on sb) to be unlucky (for sb): *It was very hard luck on you that he changed his mind at the last minute.* لسوء حظّه...

be in/out of luck to be lucky/unlucky: *I was in luck – the shop had the book I wanted.* محظوظ/غير محظوظ

good luck (to sb) (used to wish that sb is successful): *Good luck! I'm sure you'll get the job.* أتمنى لك التوفيق

worse luck → WORSE

🔑**lucky** /ˈlʌki/ *adj* (**luckier**; **luckiest**) **1** (used about a person) having good luck: *We were very lucky with the weather on holiday* (= it was fine). ○ *I'm very lucky to have such good friends.* محظوظ

2 (used about a situation, event, etc.) having a good result: *It's lucky you reminded me* (= or I would have forgotten). ○ *a lucky escape* من حُسن الحظّ أنّ...؛ ميمون

3 (used about a thing) bringing success or good luck: *a lucky number* ○ *It was not my lucky day* جالب للحظّ

ℹ The opposite for all senses is **unlucky**.

IDM **you'll be lucky** used to tell sb that sth he/she is expecting will probably not happen: *'I was hoping to get a ticket for Saturday.' 'You'll be lucky.'* هذا صعب!

▸ **luckily** /ˈlʌkɪli/ *adv* fortunately: *Luckily, I remembered to bring my umbrella.* لحسن الحظّ

lucrative /ˈluːkrətɪv/ *adj* (*formal*) producing a lot of money مربِح، يدرّ مالاً كثيراً

ludicrous /ˈluːdɪkrəs/ *adj* very silly; ridiculous: *What a ludicrous idea!* سخيف جداً، يدعو إلى السخرية؛ غير معقول

▸ **ludicrously** *adv* بإفراط، بشكل غير معقول

lug /lʌɡ/ *verb* [T] (lugging; lugged) (*informal*) to carry or pull sth with great difficulty يحمل أو يجرّ بعناء

🔑**luggage** /ˈlʌɡɪdʒ/ (*also* **baggage**) *noun* [U] bags, suitcases, etc. used for carrying a person's things on a journey: *'How much luggage are you taking with you?' 'Only one suitcase.'* ○ *We can fit one more piece of luggage in the boot!* ○ *All luggage should be checked in at the airport at least one hour before departure.*

> When flying you will be asked to pay for **excess luggage** if your suitcases weigh more than is allowed. You are only allowed one piece of **hand luggage** that you carry with you on the aeroplane.

حقائب أو أمتعة السفَر

ˈluggage rack *noun* [C] a shelf above the seats in a train or coach for putting your luggage on رفّ الأمتعة (في قطار مثلاً)

lukewarm /ˌluːkˈwɔːm/ *adj* **1** (used about liquids) only slightly warm فاتِر

2 lukewarm (about sb/sth) not showing much interest; not keen: *John's rather lukewarm about going to Iceland for a holiday.* غير متحمس

lull /lʌl/ *verb* [T] **1** to make sb/sth quiet or sleepy: *She sang a song to lull the children to sleep.* يهدّئ، يسكّن؛ يهدْهِد

2 to make sb/sth feel safe, especially by deceiving them: *Our first success lulled us into a false sense of security.* يسكّن قلقه أو يُخدّر أعصابه بوعود زائفة

▸ **lull** *noun* [C, usually sing.] a short period of quiet; a pause in activity: *When she entered the room there was a lull in the conversation.* صمت مفاجئ؛ توقّف مؤقّت

lullaby /ˈlʌləbaɪ/ *noun* [C] (*pl.* **lullabies**) a gentle song that you sing to help a child to go to sleep ترنيمة لتنويم الطفل، "تهليلة"

lumber[1] /ˈlʌmbə(r)/ *noun* [U] (*especially US*) = TIMBER (1)

▸ **lumber** *verb* [T] **lumber sb (with sb/sth)** to give sb a responsibility or job that he/she does

a b c d e f g h i j k l m n o p q r s t u v w x y z

not want: *I've been lumbered with driving the children to school again.* يحمّل، يثقِل على

lumber² /ˈlʌmbə(r)/ *verb* [I] to move in a slow, heavy way: *He heaved himself out of bed and lumbered into the bathroom.* يمشي بتثاقل

luminous /ˈluːmɪnəs/ *adj* shining, especially in the dark: *a luminous watch* برّاق ، متلألئ؛ يضيء في الظلام

lump¹ /lʌmp/ *noun* [C] **1** a piece of sth solid of any size or shape: *a lump of coal* ○ *The sauce was full of lumps.* كتلة صغيرة

2 a hard swelling on or in the body: *You'll have a bit of a lump on your head where you banged it.* تورم ، ورَم

▸ **lump** *verb* [T] **lump sb/sth (together)** to put people or things together; to consider or treat them as being all alike يجمّع، يكوِّم؛ يجمل

lumpy *adj* (**lumpier**; **lumpiest**) full of or covered with lumps (صلصة) مكتّلة/مُخرّزة/مُكلكعة ؛ مغطى بنتوءات صغيرة

lump² /lʌmp/ *verb*

IDM **lump it** (*informal*) to accept sth unpleasant whether you want to or not: *'I don't like this sweater Mum.' 'Well you'll just have to lump it – it's the only one that's clean!'* يقبل شيئاً رغم أنفه

ˌlump ˈsum *noun* [C] an amount of money paid all at once rather than in several smaller amounts: *You'll receive a lump sum when you retire as well as your pension.* مبلغ يدفع دفعة واحدة

lunacy /ˈluːnəsi/ *noun* [U] very foolish behaviour: *It was lunacy to swim so far out to sea.* حماقة ، جنون

lunar /ˈluːnə(r)/ *adj* connected with the moon: *lunar dust* ○ *a lunar spacecraft* قمريّ

lunatic /ˈluːnətɪk/ *noun* [C] **1** (*informal*) a person who behaves in a very foolish way الأحمق؛ شخص طائش

2 (*old-fashioned*) a person who is mad مجنون

▸ **lunatic** *adj* very foolish: *a lunatic idea* ➲ Look at the note at **mad**. أحمق ؛ طائش

ˈlunatic asylum *noun* [C] (*old-fashioned*) a place where mentally ill people were kept in the past مستشفى المجانين

lunch /lʌntʃ/ *noun* [C,U] a meal that you have in the middle of the day: *Hot and cold lunches are served between 12 and 2.* ○ *What would you like for lunch?*

> You might take a **packed lunch** or a **picnic lunch** if you're out for the day. If you're working you might have a **business lunch** (= having a meeting at the same time as eating) or a **working lunch** (= working at the same time as having lunch). For children at school, lunch is usually called **school dinner**. Look at the note at **dinner**.

غداء ، وجبة الغداء

▸ **lunch** *verb* [I] (*formal*) to eat lunch يتغدّى ، يتناول الغداء

luncheon /ˈlʌntʃən/ *noun* **1** [C] a formal meal eaten in the middle of the day: *The opening of the new shopping centre was followed by a luncheon in the town hall.* وجبة غداء رسميّة

2 [U] (*formal*) lunch غداء

ˈlunch hour *noun* [C, usually sing.] the time around the middle of the day when you stop work or school to have lunch: *I went to the shops in my lunch hour.* ساعة الغداء

lunchtime /ˈlʌntʃtaɪm/ *noun* [C,U] the time around the middle of the day when lunch is eaten: *I'll meet you at lunchtime.* فترة الغداء

lung /lʌŋ/ *noun* [C] one of the two parts of the body that are inside your chest and are used for breathing: *lung cancer* رئة

lunge /lʌndʒ/ *noun* [C, usually sing.] a sudden forward movement of the body, especially when trying to attack sb هجمة مفاجئة؛ اندفاع مفاجئ نحو العدوّ

▸ **lunge** *verb* [I]: *He lunged towards me with a knife.* ينقضّ عليه (بسكين مثلاً) ، يندفع نحوه

lurch¹ /lɜːtʃ/ *noun* [sing.]

IDM **leave sb in the lurch** → LEAVE¹

lurch² /lɜːtʃ/ *noun* [C] a sudden movement to one side, especially when out of control: *The ship gave a tremendous lurch as it hit the iceberg.* ميلة مفاجئة ؛ ترنّح ؛ دفعة إلى الجانب

▸ **lurch** *verb* [I] يتمايل ؛ يتخبّط

lure /lʊə(r)/ *noun* [C] the power of attracting sb: *the lure of money, fame, adventure, etc.* سِحْر، إغراء

▸ **lure** *verb* [T] to attract or tempt sb/sth: *Young people are lured to the city by the prospect of a job and money.* يغري

lurid /ˈlʊərɪd/ *adj* **1** shocking, especially because violent or unpleasant: *The newspaper was criticized for its lurid description of the disaster.* فظيع ، مليء بالتفاصيل الرهيبة، مثير

2 having colours that are very or too bright: *a lurid dress in purple and orange* (لون) صارخ ، فاقع

▸ **luridly** *adv* بألوان زاهية

lurk /lɜːk/ *verb* [I] to wait where you cannot be seen, especially when intending to do sth bad: *I thought I saw somebody lurking among the trees.* يكمن ، يتربّص ، يترصّد

luscious /ˈlʌʃəs/ *adj* (used about food) tasting very good لذيذ ، شهيّ

lush /lʌʃ/ *adj* (used about plants) growing very thickly and well (نبات) وافر النموّ ، غزير الإيراق

lust /lʌst/ *noun* **1** [U] strong sexual desire الشهوة الجنسية ، الشَّبَق

2 [C,U] (a) very strong desire to possess or get sth: *a lust for power* رغبة جارفة في الحصول على شيء ، تحرُّق إلى

▸ **lust** *verb* [I] **lust after/for sb/sth** to have a very strong desire for sb/sth: *to lust for power, success, fame, etc.* يشتهي؛ يشبَق ؛ تستولي عليه رغبة جارفة

lustful /-fl/ *adj* full of (sexual) desire: *lustful thoughts* شَبِق؛ شهوانيّ

lustfully /-fəli/ *adv* بشهوانيّة ؛ بشهوة

lute /luːt/ *noun* [C] a musical instrument with strings, played like a guitar. Lutes were used especially in the 14th-17th centuries. العود

luxurious /lʌɡˈʒʊəriəs/ *adj* very comfortable; full of luxury: *a luxurious hotel* مزوّد بأسبابِ الراحة والترف : فخم
▸ **luxuriously** *adv* بترَف ، بتنعم

luxury /ˈlʌkʃəri/ *noun* (*pl.* **luxuries**) **1** [U] great comfort and pleasure, often including the use and enjoyment of expensive and beautiful things: *They are said to be living in Barbados, in the greatest luxury.* ○ *to lead a life of luxury* ○ *a luxury hotel, car, yacht, etc.* رفاهية ، نعيم : فخامة

2 [C] something that is enjoyable and expensive that you do not really need: *A holiday is a luxury we just can't afford this year.* ○ *luxury goods, such as cigars and perfume* ترف ، كماليّات

3 [U, sing.] a pleasure which you do not often have: *It was (an) absolute luxury to do nothing all weekend.* نعيم ، متعة

lychee (*also* **lichee**) /ˌlaɪˈtʃiː; ˈlaɪtʃiː/ *noun* [C] a small Chinese fruit with thick rough reddish skin, white flesh and a large seed inside لتشيَة

lynch /lɪntʃ/ *verb* [T] (used about a crowd of people) to kill sb who is thought to be guilty of a crime, without a legal trial يشنق دون محاكمة

lyric /ˈlɪrɪk/ *adj* (used about poetry) expressing personal feelings (شعر) عاطفيّ
▸ **lyrics** *noun* [plural] the words of a song: *Who wrote the lyrics?* كلمات أغنية

lyrical /ˈlɪrɪkl/ *adj* like a song or a poem, expressing strong personal feelings (شعْر) غنائي ، عاطفي

Mm

M, m /em/ *noun* [C] (*pl.* **Ms**; **M's**; **m's**) the thirteenth letter of the English alphabet: *'Mark' begins with (an) 'M'.* الحرف الثالث عشر من الأبجدية الإنكليزية

M /em/ *abbrev* **1** = MEDIUM (SIZE)

2 (*Brit*) = MOTORWAY

⚷**m** *abbrev* **1** = MALE

2 (*also* **masc**) = MASCULINE

3 = METRE(S): *a 500 m race*

4 = MILLION(S): *population: 10 m*

MA (*US* **M.A.**) /ˌem ˈeɪ/ *abbrev* Master of Arts; a second qualification that you receive when you complete a more advanced course or piece of research in an arts subject at university or college ماجستير الآداب

ma'am /mæm; mɑːm/ *noun* [sing.] (used when speaking to a woman, as a short form for 'madam') ❶ In British English **ma'am** is old-fashioned but it is often used in US English as a polite way of addressing a woman. يا سيدتي ، يا ستّ ، يا هانم

mac (*also* **mack**) /mæk/ (*also old-fashioned* **mackintosh** /ˈmækɪntɒʃ/) *noun* [C] (*especially Brit*) a coat that is made to keep out the rain معطف مطر

macabre /məˈkɑːbrə/ *adj* horrible and frightening because connected with death مرعِب (لأنه متعلّق بالموت)

macaroni /ˌmækəˈrəʊni/ *noun* [U] a type of Italian food made from dried flour and water (pasta) in the shape of hollow tubes معكَرونة/مَكَرونة

⚷**machine** /məˈʃiːn/ *noun* [C] **1** (often in compounds) a piece of equipment with several moving parts, made to perform a particular task: *a washing machine* ○ *Can you operate/work this machine?* ○ *One of the machines has broken down.* ➲ Look at the note at **tool**. آلة

2 a system or organization carefully controlled and organized by a group of people: *It's hard to understand the workings of the party machine* (= a political party). تنظيم : هيئة
▸ **machinery** /məˈʃiːnəri/ *noun* [U] machines in general or the moving parts of a machine: *There's an exhibition of the latest farm machinery.* ○ *the delicate machinery of a watch* الآلات : الأجزاء المتحركة في آلة: آليّة

ma'chine gun *noun* [C] a gun that fires bullets very quickly and continuously رشّاش، مدفع رشّاش

macho /ˈmætʃəʊ/ *adj* (*informal*) (used about a man or his behaviour) very masculine in an aggressive way متباهٍ برجولته ، فحل: (تصرف) رجولي خشن

mackerel /ˈmækrəl/ *noun* (*pl.* **mackerel**) a sea fish that you can eat, that has greenish-blue bands on its body: *smoked mackerel* إسقُمري

mackintosh = MAC

macro /ˈmækrəʊ/ *noun* [C] (*pl.* **macros**) (*computing*) a single instruction that a computer automatically reads as a set of instructions necessary to do a particular task موسِّع (كمبيوتر)

⚷**mad** /mæd/ *adj* (**madder**; **maddest**) **1** with a sick mind; mentally ill: *In the past people who were considered mad were locked up in the most terrible conditions.* معتوه : مريض عقلياً

> It is not usual nowadays to use **mad** or **insane** to describe a person who is not mentally normal. We would use the expression **mentally ill**.

2 very foolish; crazy: *My parents think I'm mad to leave school at 16.* أحمق ، مجنون

3 mad (at/with sb) very angry: *His laziness drives me mad!* ○ *Don't get mad at him. He didn't mean to do it.* غاضب جداً

4 not controlled; wild or very excited: *We're always in a mad rush to get ready in the morning.* ○ *The audience was cheering and clapping like mad* (= very hard). فوضوي : مجنون : هائج : شديد

5 (*informal*) **mad about/on sb/sth** extremely interested in sb/sth: *He's mad on computer games at the moment.* ○ *Steve's mad about Jane* (= he likes her very much). شغوف ، مغرم
▸ **madly** *adv* **1** in a wild or crazy way: *Stop rushing about madly and sit down for a minute!* بجنون ، باهتياج
2 extremely: *They're madly in love.* إلى أقصى حدّ
madness *noun* [U] **1** the state of being mad (1) جنون ، عته
2 foolish behaviour: *It would be madness to take a boat out in such rough weather.* حمق، حماقة

madam /ˈmædəm/ *noun* [sing.] **1** (*formal*) a polite way of speaking to a woman, especially to a customer in a shop: *Can I help you, madam?* ➲ Look at **ma'am** and **sir**. يا سيّدتي ، يا هانم ، يا "مدام"
2 Madam used for beginning a formal letter to a woman when you do not know her name: *Dear Madam, I am writing in reply...* سيّدتي...

mad 'cow disease = BSE

madden /ˈmædn/ *verb* [T] to make sb very angry or annoyed يغيظ ، يجعله يستشيط غضباً
▸ **maddening** /ˈmædnɪŋ/ *adj*: *She has some really maddening habits.* مزعج جداً ، يثير الأعصاب
maddeningly *adv* للغاية : بشكل يثير الأعصاب

made *pt, pp* of MAKE[1]

madman /ˈmædmən/ *noun* [C] (*pl.* **madmen** /-mən/; *feminine* **madwoman** /-wʊmən/; *pl.* **madwomen** /-wɪmɪn/) a person who is mad(1) or who behaves in a foolish way: *Stop behaving like a madman!* ○ *There's a madman trying to overtake a bus on the hill!* مجنون : شخص طائش

🔑 **magazine** /ˌmægəˈziːn; *US* ˈmægəziːn/ *noun* [C] (*also informal* **mag** /mæg/) a type of book with a paper cover which is published every week or month and contains articles, advertisements, photographs and stories by various writers: *a woman's, computer, gardening, etc. magazine* ○ *a magazine article* ○ *How often does this magazine come out?* مجلّة

maggot /ˈmægət/ *noun* [C] an insect that looks like a small worm. Maggots grow from the eggs of flies, which have been laid in meat, cheese, etc. يرقانة قطعاء ، يرقة ، دودة صغيرة

🔑 **magic** /ˈmædʒɪk/ *noun* [U] **1** a secret power that some people believe can make strange or impossible things happen by saying special words or doing special things: *The witch had used her magic to turn the children into frogs.* ➲ Look at **black magic**. السِّحْر
2 the art of performing extraordinary tricks to entertain people سِحْر، شعوذة
3 a special or fascinating quality or sth that has this quality: *I'll never forget the magic of that moment.* ○ *The whole holiday was magic from beginning to end.* سِحْر ، روعة ، فتنة
▸ **magic** *adj* **1** used in or using magic: *a magic spell* سِحريّ
2 wonderful; excellent: *The way she sings is absolutely magic.* رائع ، ساحر ، أخّاذ
magical /-kl/ *adj* **1** that seems to use magic or to produce it: *This is a magical box that makes things disappear.* سِحريّ
2 mysterious and exciting: *Father Christmas has a magical fascination for many children.* سِحريّ ، مثير
magically /-kli/ *adv* بشكل يصعب تفسيره ، بشكل عجيب
magician /məˈdʒɪʃn/ *noun* [C] **1** a person who performs magic tricks to entertain people ➲ Look at **conjurer**. ساحر ، مشعوذ
2 (in stories) a man who has magic power ➲ Look at **wizard**. ساحر

magistrate /ˈmædʒɪstreɪt/ *noun* [C] a judge in the lowest rank of law court that deals especially with less serious crimes حاكم صلح

magnanimous /mægˈnænɪməs/ *adj* generous (especially towards an enemy or a rival that you have beaten) كريم الأخلاق ، شهم ، ذو نخوة

magnet /ˈmægnət/ *noun* [C] a piece of iron that can attract and pick up iron and steel مغناطيس
▸ **magnetic** /mægˈnetɪk/ *adj* **1** having the ability of a magnet to attract iron and steel: *Let's see if this metal is magnetic or not.* مغناطيسي
2 having a quality that strongly attracts people: *a magnetic personality* جذّاب ، يشدّ الانتباه
magnetism /ˈmægnətɪzəm/ *noun* [U] **1** the power of magnets to attract القوة المغناطيسيّة
2 strong personal attraction: *Nobody could resist his magnetism.* جاذبيّة ، سحر الشخصيّة
magnetize (*also* **magnetise**) /ˈmægnətaɪz/ *verb* [T] **1** to make sth become magnetic يُمغْنِط
2 to attract sb strongly يسحر ، يجذب بقوّة

magnificent /mægˈnɪfɪsnt/ *adj* extremely good or beautiful; splendid: *What a magnificent castle!* رائع ؛ فخم ؛ عظيم
▸ **magnificently** *adv* بشكل هائل ؛ بروعة
magnificence /-sns/ *noun* [U] روعة ؛ فخامة ؛ عَظَمة

magnify /ˈmægnɪfaɪ/ *verb* [T] (*pres part* **magnifying**; *3rd pers sing pres* **magnifies**; *pt, pp* **magnified**) **1** to make sth look bigger than it is: *to magnify sth under a microscope* يكبّر؛ يضخّم
2 to make sth seem more important than it really is: *to magnify a problem* يضخّم ، يبالغ في ، يُعظّم
▸ **magnification** /ˌmægnɪfɪˈkeɪʃn/ *noun* [U] تكبير؛ تعظيم

'magnifying glass *noun* [C] a lens that is held in your hand, and used for making things look bigger than they are عدسة مكبّرة

magnitude /ˈmægnɪtjuːd; *US* -tuːd/ *noun* [U] the great size or importance of sth: *the magnitude of the problem* جَسامة ، ضخامة؛ أهمية قصوى

magpie /ˈmægpaɪ/ *noun* [C] a noisy black and white bird that is attracted by, and often takes away, small bright objects عَقْعَق، قُعقُع، كندش

mahogany /məˈhɒgəni/ *noun* [U] hard reddish-brown wood (from a tropical tree) that is used for making expensive furniture خشب الماهوغوني أو الكابلي

maid /meɪd/ *noun* [C] a woman servant in a hotel

or large house: *a chambermaid* ○ *a housemaid* خادمة

maiden /ˈmeɪdn/ *noun* [C] (*old-fashioned*) a girl or unmarried woman فتاة عذراء

ˈ**maiden name** *noun* [C] the surname that a woman had before she got married ➲ Look at the note at **name**[1]. كنية الزوجة قبل الزواج

ˌ**maiden ˈvoyage** *noun* [C] the first journey of a new ship أول رحلة

⚷ **mail** /meɪl/ *noun* [U] **1** the system for collecting and delivering letters and parcels: *to send a parcel by airmail/surface mail* ○ *a mail van* البَريد

2 = POST[3]: *junk mail* (= letters, usually advertising sth, that are sent to people although they have not asked for them) ➲ Look at the note at **post**.

3 = EMAIL

▸ **mail** *verb* [T] (*especially US*) = POST[4]

mailbox /ˈmeɪlbɒks/ *noun* [C] **1** (*US*) = LETTER BOX (2)

2 (*US*) = POSTBOX

3 a computer program that receives and stores email صندوق الرسائل

ˈ**mailing list** *noun* [C] a list of the names and addresses of people to whom advertising material or information is sent قائمة بأسماء وعناوين من تُرسل لهم نشرات

ˈ**mailman** /meɪlmæn/ *noun* [C] (*pl.* **mailmen** /-men/) (*US*) = POSTMAN

ˈ**mail order** *noun* [U] a method of shopping. You choose what you want from a special book (a catalogue) and the goods are then sent to you by post. تسوُّق بواسطة البريد (بعد اختيار الأشياء من كتالوج خاص)

maim /meɪm/ *verb* [T] to hurt sb so badly that part of the body can no longer be used يُعطِّل عُضواً من أعضاء شخص ، "يَعطبه"

⚷ **main**[1] /meɪn/ *adj* (only *before* a noun) most important; chief: *My main reason for wanting to learn English is to get a better job.* ○ *a busy main road* ○ *Do you eat your main meal at midday or in the evening?* ○ *Don't write everything down – just make a note of the main points.* ○ *He doesn't earn very much but he's happy. That's the main thing.* رئيسيّ، الأهمّ

IDM **in the main** (*formal*) generally; mostly: *We found English people very friendly in the main.* على وجه العموم ؛ في الأغلب

▸ **mainly** *adv* mostly: *The students here are mainly from Japan.* في الغالبيّة ؛ في الدرجة الأولى

⚷ **main**[2] /meɪn/ *noun* [C] a large pipe or wire that carries water, gas or electricity to a building or that takes waste water away from it: *The water main has burst.* ❶ Often the form **mains** is used and this can take either a singular or plural verb: *Turn the water off at the mains.* أحد أنابيب توصيل الماء أو الكهرباء أو الغاز للمباني

mainland /ˈmeɪnlænd/ *noun* [sing.] the main part of a country or continent, not including the islands around it: *They took the ferry back from Skye to the mainland.* البرّ الرئيسيّ أو البلاد الرئيسية دون الجزر التابعة لها

ˌ**main ˈline** *noun* [C] the main railway line between two places: *a main-line station* خطّ حديديّ رئيسيّ

mainstay /ˈmeɪnsteɪ/ *noun* [C] (*figurative*) a person or thing that helps sb/sth to work well or to be strong سَنَد، دعامة

mainstream /ˈmeɪnstriːm/ *noun* [sing.] the way that most people think or behave: *The Green Party is not in the mainstream of British politics.* الاتّجاه السائد

⚷ **maintain** /meɪnˈteɪn/ *verb* [T] **1** to continue to have or do sth; to keep sth at the same level or standard: *We need to maintain the quality of our goods but not increase the price.* ○ *to maintain law and order* ○ *to maintain a constant temperature* يُحافظ على

2 to support sb by paying for the things he/she needs: *He has to maintain two children from his previous marriage* يُعيل

3 to keep sth in good condition: *to maintain a road, building, machine, etc.* يَصون ؛ يعتني بِ

4 to say that sth is true: *In the Middle Ages people maintained that the Sun went round the Earth.* يؤكّد ، يزعم

maintenance /ˈmeɪntənəns/ *noun* [U] **1** keeping sth in good condition: *This house needs a lot of maintenance.* ○ *car maintenance* صِيانة

2 money that sb must pay regularly to a former wife, husband or partner especially when they have had children together: *He has to pay maintenance to his ex-wife and children.* نَفقة

maisonette /ˌmeɪzəˈnet/ *noun* [C] a flat on two floors that is part of a larger building شَقّة من طابقين

maize /meɪz/ (*US* **corn**) *noun* [U] a tall plant that produces yellow grains in a large mass (a cob) ➲ Look at **sweet corn**. الذُّرة

majestic /məˈdʒestɪk/ *adj* making a strong impression because it is dignified or beautiful: *a majestic mountain landscape* مَهيب ، رائع ؛ ذو جلال

▸ **majestically** /-kli/ *adv* بِهَيْبة وكبرياء

majesty /ˈmædʒəsti/ *noun* (*pl.* **majesties**) **1** [U] the quality of being grand or dignified like a king or queen: *the splendour and majesty of the palace and its gardens* جَلال ، هَيْبة ؛ روعة

2 Majesty [C] (used when speaking to or about a royal person): *Her Majesty the Queen* جلالة (الملكة)

⚷ **major**[1] /ˈmeɪdʒə(r)/ *adj* (only *before* a noun) great in size, importance, seriousness, etc: *The patient needs major heart surgery.* ○ *a major road* ○ *There haven't been any major problems.* ❶ The opposite is **minor**. هامّ، رئيسي ؛ كبير

▸ **major** *verb*

PHR V **major in sth** (*US*) to study sth as your main subject at college or university يدرس كموضوع رئيسي ، يتخصّص

a b c d e f g h i j k l **m** n o p q r s t u v w x y z

major² /ˈmeɪdʒə(r)/ *noun* [C] an officer of middle rank in the army رائد (رتبة عسكرية)

ˌ**major ˈgeneral** *noun* [C] an officer of high rank in the army لواء (رتبة عسكرية)

majority /məˈdʒɒrəti; *US* -ˈdʒɔːr-/ *noun* (*pl.* **majorities**) **1** [sing.] the largest number or part of sth: *The majority of students in the class come from Japan.* أغلبيّة، أكثريّة : الأغلبية، الأكثرية

Majority is used with either a singular or a plural verb: *The majority is/are in favour of building the new road.* Look at **minority**.

2 [C] **majority (over sb)** the difference in the number of votes in an election for the person/party who came first and the person/party who came second: *He was elected by a majority of almost 5 000 votes.* ❶ If you have an **overall majority** you got more votes than all the other people/parties added together. أغلبيّة

IDM **be in the/a majority** to form the largest number or part of sth: *Women are in the majority in the teaching profession.* أغلبيّة ، أكثريّة

make¹ /meɪk/ *verb* [T] (*pt, pp* **made** /meɪd/) **1** to produce sth or to cause sth to appear: *Can you make me a cup of tea, please?* ○ *They make VW cars in Wolfsburg.* ○ *made in Britain* (= on a label) ○ *What's that shirt made of?* (= what material) ○ *The coffee made a stain on the carpet.* يصنع : يعمل؛ يكوّن

2 (used with nouns) to perform a certain action: *to make a mistake, a noise, a statement, a suggestion, etc.* ○ *to make progress* يعمل ، يقدّم : يتّخذ : يحرز

Often there is a verb with a similar form, e.g. **decide/make a decision**. If you use 'make' + noun, you can use an adjective with it: *He made the right decision.* ○ *They made a generous offer.*

3 to cause a particular action, feeling or situation: *The film made me cry.* ○ *That dress makes you look thin.* ○ *Flying makes him nervous.* ○ *Her remarks made the situation worse.* يجعل

4 to force sb/sth to do sth: *They made him wait at the police station all day.* ❶ In the passive we must use **to**: *He was made to wait at the police station.* يجبر

5 (used with *clear*, *certain* and *sure*): *She made it clear that she didn't agree.* ○ *Make sure you lock the car.* ○ *I made certain I had enough money.* يجعله واضحاً؛ يتأكّد من

6 (used with money, numbers and time): *He makes* (= earns) *£20 000 a year.* ○ *to make a lot of money* ○ *5 and 7 make 12.* ○ *'What do you make the answer?' '28'* ○ *'What's the time?' 'I make it 6.45.'* يكسب؛ يساوي؛ يقدر

7 to have the right qualities to be sth; to make sth perfect: *She'll make a good teacher.* ○ *The beautiful weather really made our holiday.* يكون ؛ يكمّل

8 to give sb a job or elect sb to a position: *She was made Minister of Health.* يعيّن

9 to reach a place; to be able to go somewhere: *We should make Bristol by about 10.* ○ *I'm afraid I can't make the meeting next week.* يَصل إلى ؛ يتمكّن من الحضور

IDM **make do with sth** to use sth that is not good enough because nothing better is available: *If we can't get limes, we'll have to make do with lemons.* يكتفي بـِ ، يستعمل كَبَديل

make it 1 to get to a place (in time); to go to a place you have been invited to: *The train leaves in 5 minutes. We'll never make it!* ○ *I'm afraid I can't make it to your party.* يصل في الوقت المناسب ؛ يحضر

2 to be successful: *She'll never make it as an actress.* ينجح

make the most of sth to get as much pleasure, profit, etc. as possible from sth: *You won't get another chance – make the most of it!* يتمتّع قدر المستطاع ؛ يستغل الفرصة إلى أقصى حدّ

❶ For other expressions with **make**, look at the noun and adjective entries, e.g. for **make love** look at **love**.

PHRV **make for sb/sth** to move towards sb/sth يتّجه أو يندفع نحو

make for sth to help or allow sth to happen: *Arguing all the time doesn't make for a happy marriage.* يساعد؛ يؤدّي إلى

be made for sb/each other to be well suited to sb/each other: *Jim and Alice seem made for each other.* يلائم ملاءمة تامّة ، "خلقا لبعضهما"

make sb/sth into sb/sth to change sb/sth into sb/sth: *She made her spare room into an office.* يحوّل

make sth of sb/sth to understand sb/sth: *I don't know what to make of my boss* (= I can't understand him). يفهم

make off (*informal*) to leave or escape in a hurry ينصرف مسرعاً ؛ يولّي هارباً

make off with sth (*informal*) to steal sth and leave quickly with it: *Someone's made off with my wallet!* يسرق ويولّي هارباً

make sb/sth out 1 to understand sb/sth: *I just can't make him out.* ○ *Can you make this form out?* يفهم

2 to be able to see or hear sb/sth; to manage to read sth: *I could just make out her signature.* يميّز ؛ يقرأ خطاً غير واضح

make sth out to write or complete sth: *She made out a cheque for £100.* يكتب، يحرّر؛ يعدّ (قائمة)

make out that...; make yourself out to be sth to say that sth is true and try to make people believe it: *He made out that he was a millionaire.* ○ *She's not as clever as she makes herself out to be.* يتظاهر

make (yourself/sb) up to put powder, lipstick, etc. on the face يزيّن الوجه ؛ يضع الماكياج

make sth up 1 to form: *the different groups that make up our society* يشكّل

2 to invent sth, often sth that is not true: *to make up an excuse* يخترع ، يلفّق

3 to make a number or an amount complete: *We need one more person to make up our team.* يكمل

make up for sth to do sth that corrects a bad situation: *Her enthusiasm makes up for her lack of experience.* يعوّض

make it up to sb (*informal*) to do sth that shows

that you are sorry for what you have done to sb or that you are grateful for what they have done for you: *I'll make it up to you, I promise.* يقدم هدية مثلاً ليعبر عن أسفه (أو عن شكره)

make (it) up (with sb) to become friends again after a quarrel: *Has she made it up with him yet?* يتصالح مع

make² /meɪk/ *noun* [C] the name of the company that produced sth: *'What make is your television?' 'It's a Sony.'* صُنع شركة كذا ، ماركة

ˈmake-believe *noun* [U] pretending or imagining sth; the things that are imagined: *I don't believe his stories – they're all make-believe.* توهّم ، خيال؛ أشياء خياليّة

makeover /ˈmeɪkəʊvə(r)/ *noun* [C,U] the process of improving the appearance of a person or a place, or of changing the impression that sth gives: *She won a complete makeover in a magazine competition.* تحسين المظهر أو تغييره

maker /ˈmeɪkə(r)/ *noun* [C] a person, company or machine that makes sth: *a film-maker* ○ *If it doesn't work, send it back to the maker.* ○ *an ice-cream maker* الصانع ، المنتج

makeshift /ˈmeɪkʃɪft/ *adj* used for a short time until there is sth better: *The refugees built makeshift shelters out of old cardboard boxes.* موقّت

ˈmake-up *noun* **1** [U] powder, cream, etc. that you put on your face to make yourself more attractive. Actors use make-up to change their appearance when they are acting: *to put on/take off make-up* ○ *She wears a lot of make-up.* ➲ Look at **cosmetics**. The verb is **make (yourself/sb) up**. مستحضرات التجميل ، ماكياج

2 [sing.] a person's character: *He can't help his temper. It's part of his make-up.* شخصيّة ، تكوين

making /ˈmeɪkɪŋ/ *noun* [sing.] the act of doing or producing sth: *breadmaking* ○ *This movie has been three years in the making.* صنع

IDM **be the making of sb** be the reason that sb is successful: *University was the making of Gina.* سبب نجاحه

have the makings of sth to have the necessary qualities for sth: *The book has the makings of a good film.* مقوّمات ، عناصر

maladjusted /ˌmæləˈdʒʌstɪd/ *adj* (used about a person) not able to behave well with other people سيئ التوافق مع المجتمع ، عاجز عن التعامل مع الآخرين

▶ **maladjustment** /ˌmæləˈdʒʌstmənt/ *noun* [U] سوء توافق مع المجتمع ، اضطراب في السلوك الاجتماعي

malaria /məˈleəriə/ *noun* [U] a serious disease that you may get when you have been bitten by a small flying insect (a mosquito) that lives in hot countries الملاريا ، البرداء

male /meɪl/ *adj* belonging to the sex that does not give birth to babies or lay eggs: *A male goat is called a billy.* ➲ Look at the note at **female**. ذَكَر

▶ **male** *noun* [C] a male person or animal الذكر

ˌmale ˈchauvinism *noun* [U] the belief that men are better than women الاعتقاد بتفوّق الرجال

ˌmale ˈchauvinist *noun* [C] المؤمن بتفوّق الرجال

malice /ˈmælɪs/ *noun* [U] a wish to hurt other people حقد ؛ تعمّد الاذى

▶ **malicious** /məˈlɪʃəs/ *adj* حقود؛ سيّئ القصد

maliciously *adv* بنيّة سيئة ؛ بحقد

malignant /məˈlɪɡnənt/ *adj* (used to describe tumours in the body) likely to cause death if not controlled ❶ The opposite is **benign**. (ورم) خبيث

mall /mæl; mɔːl/ *noun* [C] = SHOPPING MALL

mallet /ˈmælɪt/ *noun* [C] a heavy wooden hammer مطرقة خشبيّة

malnutrition /ˌmælnjuːˈtrɪʃn; *US* -nuː-/ *noun* [U] bad health that is the result of not having enough food or enough of the right kind of food سوء التغذية

malt /mɔːlt/ *noun* [U] grain that has been left in water for a long time and then dried. Malt is used for making beer and whisky المَلْت ، المُنْتشة ، شَعير يُنْبَت بالنقع بالماء

maltreat /ˌmælˈtriːt/ *verb* [T] (*formal*) to treat a person or animal cruelly or unkindly يسيء المعاملة

▶ **maltreatment** *noun* [U] سوء المعاملة

malware /ˈmælweə(r)/ *noun* [U] software such as a virus on a computer or computer network that the user does not know about or want برمجيات خبيثة

mammal /ˈmæml/ *noun* [C] an animal of the type that gives birth to live animals and does not lay eggs. Mammals feed their babies on milk from their bodies: *Birds and fish are not mammals but whales and dolphins are.* حيوان من الثدييّات

mammoth /ˈmæməθ/ *adj* very big ضخم ، هائل

man¹ /mæn/ *noun* (*pl.* **men** /men/) **1** [C] an adult male person: *a handsome man in his mid-twenties* ○ *men, women and children* رَجُل

2 [C] a person of either sex, male or female: *All men are equal.* ○ *No man could survive long in such conditions.* شخص ، فَرْد

3 [sing.] the human race; human beings: *Early man lived by hunting and gathering.* ○ *Why is man so destructive?* الإنسان ، الجنس البشري

> Some people do not like the way **man** is used in senses 2 and 3 (or the use of **mankind** to mean 'all men and women') because it seems that women are not included. They prefer to use **humanity**, **the human race**, or **people**.

4 [C] a husband, boyfriend or male lover: *to become man and wife* (= to get married) زوج ؛ حبيب

5 [C, usually pl.] a man of low rank in the army, etc. who takes orders from an officer: *officers and men* جندي ، نفر

6 (*informal*) (used when you are talking to sb): *Hey, man, can you lend me a pound?* يا سيّد ، يا أخي!

IDM **the man in the street** (*Brit*) an ordinary man or woman الرجل العاديّ

the odd man/one out → ODD

▶ **-man** (in compounds) **1** a person who lives in

a particular place: *a Frenchman* ○ *a countryman* (تستعمل كنسبة إلى الأمكنة): فرنسيّ، ريفيّ...

2 a person who has a particular job: *a businessman* ○ *a fireman*
(تستعمل للدلالة على المهنة): رجل أعمال، رجل إطفاء...

man² /mæn/ *verb* [T] (manning; manned) to operate sth or to provide people to operate sth: *to man a boat, gun, telephone, etc.* ○ *When was the first manned space flight?* يشغّل: يزوّد بالرّجال

⚷ **manage** /ˈmænɪdʒ/ *verb* **1** [T] to be in charge or control of sth: *She manages a small advertising business.* يدير

2 [I,T] (often with *can* or *could*) to be able to do sth or to deal with sth: *We are sorry we didn't manage to see you while we were in Scotland.* ○ *I can't manage this suitcase. It's too heavy.* ○ *However did you manage to find us here?* ○ *Paula can't manage next Tuesday* (= she can't come then) *so we'll meet another day.*
يتمكّن؛ يتدبّر؛ يحضر

3 [I] **manage (on sth)**; **manage (without sb/sth)** to have a reasonable way of life: *They live in the country and couldn't manage without a car.* ○ *It's hard for a family to manage on just one income.* يدبر أموره ، يعيش

▶ **manageable** /-əbl/ *adj* not too big or too difficult to control or look after: *a garden of manageable size* (حَجْم) معقول ، في حدود الطاقة

⚷ **management** /ˈmænɪdʒmənt/ *noun* **1** [U] the control or organization of sth: *Good management is the key to success in business.* ○ *management training* الإدارة

2 [C] the people who control a business or company: *The hotel is now under new management.* ❶ In the singular, **management** can be used with a singular or plural verb: *The management is/are considering making some workers redundant.* هيئة الإدارة

⚷ **manager** /ˈmænɪdʒə(r)/ *noun* [C] **1** a man or woman who controls an organization or part of an organization: *Clive's the manager of a shoe shop.* ○ *a bank manager* ○ *a sales manager* ○ *an assistant manager* مدير، رئيس

2 a person who looks after the business affairs of a singer, actor, etc. وكيل أعمال

3 a person who looks after a sports team: *the England team manager* مدير فريق رياضيّ

manageress /ˌmænɪdʒəˈres/ *noun* [C] the woman who is in charge of a shop or restaurant مديرة، رئيسة، صاحبة

managerial /ˌmænəˈdʒɪəriəl/ *adj* connected with the work of a manager: *Do you have any managerial experience?* مديري

ˌ**managing diˈrector** *noun* [C] a person who controls a business or company مدير الشركة

mandarin /ˈmændərɪn/ (*also* ˌ**mandarin ˈorange**) *noun* [C] a type of small orange whose skin comes off easily يوسف أفندي (فاكهة)

mandate /ˈmændeɪt/ *noun* [usually sing.] the power that a group of people has to do sth as a result of winning an election: *The union leaders had a clear mandate from their members to call a strike.* تفويض ، تكليف

mandatory /ˈmændətəri; *US* -ɔːri; (*Brit also*) mænˈdeɪtəri/ *adj* (*formal*) that you must do, have, obey, etc: *The crime carries a mandatory life sentence.* اجباري

mane /meɪn/ *noun* [C] the long hair on the neck of a horse or male lion عرف: شعر الحصان أو الأسد

maneuver (*US*) = MANOEUVRE

mangle /ˈmæŋgl/ *verb* [T] to damage sth greatly so that it is difficult to see what it used to look like: *The motorway was covered with the mangled wreckage of cars and vans.* ❶ **Mangle** is most often used in the passive.
يشوّه الشيء بتمزيقه أو دهسه أو غير ذلك

mango /ˈmæŋgəʊ/ *noun* [C] (*pl.* **mangoes**) a tropical fruit that has a yellowish red skin and is yellow inside فاكهة المنجة أو المنغة

manhole /ˈmænhəʊl/ *noun* [C] a hole in the street with a lid over it through which sb can go to look at the pipes, wires, etc. that are underground فتحة ذات غطاء في الشارع توصل إلى المجاري ونحوها

manhood /ˈmænhʊd/ *noun* [U] the state of being a man rather than a boy: *to reach manhood* الرجولة

mania /ˈmeɪniə/ *noun* **1** [U] a serious mental illness that may cause a person to be very excited or violent جنون يتميّز بالاهتياج والعنف

2 [C] (*informal*) a great enthusiasm for sth: *World Cup mania is sweeping the country.* هَوَس

maniac /ˈmeɪniæk/ *noun* [C] **1** a person who is mad and dangerous: (*figurative*) *to drive like a maniac* مجنون ، معتوه

2 a person who has a great love for sth: *a football maniac* مهووس

manic /ˈmænɪk/ *adj* **1** full of nervous energy or excited activity: *His behaviour became more manic as he began to feel stressed.* ○ *Things are manic* (= very busy) *at work at the moment.*
ممسوس، مهتاج

2 connected with mania(1) مهووس

manicure /ˈmænɪkjʊə(r)/ *noun* [C,U] treatment to make your hands and fingernails look nice تجميل الأظافر ، مانيكور

manifest /ˈmænɪfest/ *verb* [T] (*formal*) **1** to show sth clearly يظهر بوضوح

2 **manifest itself/themselves** to appear: *Mental illness can manifest itself in many forms.* يَظهَر

▶ **manifestation** /ˌmænɪfeˈsteɪʃn/ *noun* [C,U] (*formal*) a sign that sth is happening دليل؛ مظهر؛ إظهار

manifesto /ˌmænɪˈfestəʊ/ *noun* [C] (*pl.* **manifestos**) a written statement by a political party that explains what it hopes to do if it becomes the government in the future بيان سياسيّ

manipulate /məˈnɪpjuleɪt/ *verb* [T] **1** to use or control sth with skill يستعمل شيئاً أو يتحكّم فيه بمهارة

2 to influence sb so that they do or think what you want: *Clever politicians know how to manipulate public opinion*
يتحايل على عقول الآخرين ، يستغل شخصاً بدهاء
▸ **manipulation** /məˌnɪpjuˈleɪʃn/ *noun* [C,U]
تلاعب ؛ استغلال

mankind /mænˈkaɪnd/ *noun* [U] all the people in the world: *A nuclear war would be a threat to all mankind.* ➲ Look at the note at **man**.
الجنس البشريّ

manly /ˈmænli/ *adj* (**manlier**; **manliest**) typical of or suitable for a man: *a deep manly voice*
عنده أو فيه رجولة ؛ رجوليّ
▸ **manliness** *noun* [U] رجولة

ˌ**man-ˈmade** *adj* made by people, not formed in a natural way; artificial: *man-made fabrics such as nylon and polyester* ❶ The opposite is **natural**.
اصطناعي

manner /ˈmænə(r)/ *noun* **1** [sing.] the way that you do sth or that sth happens: *Stop arguing! Let's try to act in a civilized manner.* أسلوب، طريقة

2 [sing.] the way that sb behaves towards other people: *Don't you think that David has got a very arrogant manner?* سلوك ، تصرُّف

3 manners [plural] the way of behaving that is thought to be polite in your society or culture: *In some countries it is bad manners to show the soles of your feet.* ○ *Their children have beautiful table manners.* سلوك، أخلاق، آداب
IDM **all manner of...** every kind of...
مختلف الأصناف ، كلّ أنواع...

mannerism /ˈmænərɪzəm/ *noun* [C] a way of speaking or a movement of part of the body that is typical for a particular person
طريقة كلام أو حركة معيّنة تميِّز الشخص بالذات

manoeuvre (*US* **maneuver**) /məˈnuːvə(r)/ *noun* **1** [C] a movement that needs care or skill: *Parking the car in such a small space would be a tricky manoeuvre.* مناورة

2 [C] something clever that you do in order to win sth, trick sb, etc. خطّة بارعة

3 manoeuvres [plural] a way of training soldiers when large numbers of them practise fighting in battles: *large-scale military manoeuvres* مناورات عسكرية
▸ **manoeuvre** (*US* **maneuver**) *verb* [I,T] to move to a different position using skill: [I]: *The parking space wasn't very big but I managed to manoeuvre into it quite easily.*
يناور ، يستخدم مهاراته للوصول إلى شيء

manor /ˈmænə(r)/ (*also* **manor house**) *noun* [C] a large house in the country that has land around it منزل كبير في الريف تحيط به أراضٍ واسعة

In the Middle Ages the family who lived in the manor house owned all the surrounding land and villages. Look at **feudalism**.

manpower /ˈmænpaʊə(r)/ *noun* [U] the people that you need to do a particular job: *There is a shortage of skilled manpower in the computer industry.* الأيدي العاملة

mansion /ˈmænʃn/ *noun* [C] a very large house بيت كبير فخم

manslaughter /ˈmænslɔːtə(r)/ *noun* [U] the crime of killing sb without intending to do so ➲ Look at **murder**. جريمة قتل غير متعمّد

mantelpiece /ˈmæntlpiːs/ *noun* [C] a shelf that is above a fireplace رفّ فوق الموقد أو المدفأة

manual[1] /ˈmænjuəl/ *adj* using your hands; operated by hand: *Office work can sometimes be more tiring than manual work.* ○ *Does your car have a manual or an automatic gearbox?* ○ *a skilled manual worker*
يدوي
▸ **manually** /-juəli/ *adv* by hand, not automatically (يحرِّك) باليد

manual[2] /ˈmænjuəl/ *noun* [C] a book that explains how to do or operate sth: *a training manual* ○ *Full instructions are given in the owner's manual.* كتيِّب إرشادات ، مرشِد

manufacture /ˌmænjuˈfæktʃə(r)/ *verb* [T] to make sth in large quantities using machines: *a local factory that manufactures high-quality furniture* ○ *manufacturing industries*
ينتج
▸ **manufacture** *noun* [U]: *The manufacture of chemical weapons should be illegal.* إنتاج
manufacturer *noun* [C] a person or company that manufactures sth: *Faulty goods should be returned to the manufacturer.* المنتِج، الشركة المنتجة

manure /məˈnjʊə(r)/ *noun* [U] the waste matter from animals that is put on the ground in order to make plants grow better ➲ Look at **fertilizer**.
زِبْل، سَماد حيوانيّ

manuscript /ˈmænjuskrɪpt/ *noun* [C] **1** a very old book or document that was written by hand مخطوط، مخطوطة

2 a typed or hand-written copy of a book that has not yet been printed مؤلَّف مخطوط لم يطبع بعد

Manx /mæŋks/ *adj* of the Isle of Man, its people or language من سكّان جزيرة مان؛ لغة هذه الجزيرة

many /ˈmeni/ *det, pron* (used with plural nouns or verbs) **1** a large number of people or things: *Many people do not get enough to eat.* ○ *There are too many mistakes in this essay.* ○ *Many of the people at the meeting left early.* ○ *Many of the mistakes were just careless.* عدد كبير

Many in positive sentences sounds quite formal: *Many schools teach computing nowadays.* When speaking or writing informally we usually use **a lot of**: *A lot of schools teach computing nowadays.* In negative sentences and questions, however, **many** can always be used without sounding formal: *I don't know many cheap places to eat.* ○ *Are there many hotels in this town?*

2 (used with 'how' to ask about the number of people or things): *How many children have you got?* ○ *How many mistakes did you make?* ○ *How many came to the meeting?* كم عدد؟

3 many a (used with a singular noun and verb) (*formal*) a large number of: *I've heard him say that many a time.* كثير من ، عدد كبير

IDM **a good/great many** very many عدد كبير جداً

Maori /ˈmaʊri/ *noun* [C] a member of the race of people who were the original inhabitants of New Zealand الماوريّ: أحد سكان نيوزلندا الأصليين
▶ **Maori** *adj* ماوري

map /mæp/ *noun* [C] a drawing or plan of (part of) the surface of the earth that shows countries, rivers, mountains, roads, etc: *a map of the world* ○ *a road map* ○ *a street map of Oxford* ○ *I can't find Cambridge on the map.* ○ *to read a map* ○ *My house is not easy to find so I'll draw you a map.* ❶ A book of maps is called an **atlas**. خريطة، خارطة : مخطّط
▶ **map** *verb* [T] (mapping; mapped) to make a map of a place يرسم أو يضع خريطة

maple /ˈmeɪpl/ *noun* [C] a tree that has leaves with five points and that produces a very sweet liquid: *maple syrup* شجرة القَيْقَب

marathon /ˈmærəθən; US -θɒn/ *noun* [C] a long-distance running race in which people run about 42 kilometres or 26 miles: *Have you ever run a marathon?* ○ *the London Marathon* ○ (*figurative*) *a marathon meeting* (= one that lasts a very long time) سباق الماراثون

marble /ˈmɑːbl/ *noun* **1** [U] a hard attractive stone that is used to make statues and parts of buildings: *a marble statue* ○ *This staircase is made of marble.* الرُّخام ، المرمر
2 [C] a small ball of coloured glass that children play with بِلْية، دَحلة، دعبل
3 marbles [plural] the children's game that you play by rolling marbles along the ground trying to hit other marbles لعبة البلى أو الدحل أو الدعبل

March /mɑːtʃ/ *noun* [C,U] (*abbr* **Mar.**) the third month of the year, coming before April ❶ For examples of the use of the months in sentences, look at **January**. مارس/آذار

march¹ /mɑːtʃ/ *verb* **1** [I] to walk with regular steps (like a soldier): *The President saluted as the troops marched past.* ○ *He marched in and demanded an explanation.* يسير: يخطو كالجنديّ
2 [I] to walk in a large group to protest about sth: *The demonstrators marched through the centre of town.* يسير
3 [T] to cause sb to walk or march somewhere: *The prisoner was marched away.* يأمره بالسَّير

march² /mɑːtʃ/ *noun* [C] **1** an act of marching: *The soldiers were tired after their long march.* سَير (عسكريّ)
2 an organized walk by a large group of people who are protesting about sth: *a peace march* ➲ Look at **demonstration**. مَسيرة ، تظاهرة

mare /meə(r)/ *noun* [C] a female horse or donkey ➲ Look at the note at **horse**. فَرَس، حجر: أنثى الحصان أو الحمار

margarine /ˌmɑːdʒəˈriːn; US ˈmɑːrdʒərɪn/ *noun* [U] a food that looks like butter, made of animal or vegetable fats. Margarine is used for spreading on bread and for cooking. مَرْغَرين/مَرْجَرين

margin /ˈmɑːdʒɪn/ *noun* [C] **1** the empty space at the side of a page in a book, etc: *notes in the margin* ○ *a wide/narrow margin* هامِش
2 the amount of space, time, votes, etc. by which you win sth: *He won the race by a comfortable margin.* فرق ، زيادة
3 an amount of space, time, etc. that is more than you need: *a safety margin* احتياط
4 the amount of profit that a company makes on sth مقدار الربح
▶ **marginal** /-nl/ *adj* small in size or importance: *The differences are marginal.* قليل الأهمية ، صغير
marginally /-nəli/ *adv* a little; slightly: *In most cases costs will increase only marginally.* قليلاً

marijuana (*also* **marihuana**) /ˌmærəˈwɑːnə/ *noun* [U] an illegal drug that is smoked in cigarettes حشيشة الكيف ، قِنّب هندي

marina /məˈriːnə/ *noun* [C] a small harbour for pleasure boats مرفأ صغير لقوارب النزهة

marinade /ˌmærɪˈneɪd/ *noun* [C,U] a mixture of oil, wine, spices, etc. in which fish or meat is left for some time before it is cooked in order to make it more tender or to give it a special taste تتبيلة يترك فيها الطعام مدة

marinate /ˈmærɪneɪt/ (*also* **marinade** /ˈmærɪneɪd/) **marinate sth (in sth)** *verb* to put food in a marinade يتبّل أو ينقع في صلصة خاصة

marine¹ /məˈriːn/ *adj* **1** connected with the sea: *the study of marine life* بحري
2 connected with ships or sailing: *marine insurance* بحري، ملاحي

marine² /məˈriːn/ *noun* [C] a soldier who has been trained to fight on land or at sea من جنود البحريّة

marital /ˈmærɪtl/ *adj* (only *before* a noun) connected with marriage: *marital problems* متعلّق بالزواج ، زوجي

ˌmarital ˈstatus *noun* [U] (*formal*) whether you are married, single, widowed or divorced الوضعيّة العائليّة

maritime /ˈmærɪtaɪm/ *adj* connected with the sea or ships بَحْري : مِلاحيّ

marjoram /ˈmɑːdʒərəm/ *noun* [U] a plant whose sweet-smelling leaves are used in cooking مَرْدَقوش، سَمْسَق، عترة

mark¹ /mɑːk/ *noun* [C] **1** a spot or line that spoils the appearance of sth: *There's a dirty mark on the front of your shirt.* ○ *If you put a hot cup down on the table it will leave a mark.* ➲ Look at **birthmark**. بقعة : أثر
2 something that shows who or what sb/sth is or that gives information about sb/sth: *Crusoe made a mark on a stick for each day that passed.* علامة ، إشارة
3 a written or printed symbol that is a sign of sth: *a question, punctuation, exclamation, etc. mark* علامة ، إشارة
4 a sign of a quality or feeling: *They stood in*

silence for two minutes as a mark of respect. رمز؛ تعبير

5 a number or letter you get for school work that tells you how good your work was: *She got very good marks in the exam.* ○ *The pass mark is 60 out of 100.* ○ *to get full marks* (= everything correct) درجة أو علامة مدرسيّة

6 the level of sth: *The company's sales have now reached the million pound mark.* حدّ

7 a person or an object towards which sth is directed: *The arrow hit/missed its mark.* هدف

IDM **on your marks, get set, go!** (used at the start of a sports race) مكانك -- إستعد -- انطلق!

mark² /mɑːk/ *verb* [T] **1** to put a sign on sth: *We marked the price on all items in the sale.* ○ *The route is marked with yellow arrows.* يُعلِّم على، يضع علامة أو إشارة

2 to spoil the appearance of sth by making a mark on it: *The white walls were dirty and marked.* يخدش، يشوّه

3 to look at school, etc. work that sb has done, show where there are mistakes and give it a number or letter to show how good it is: *Why did you mark that answer wrong?* ○ *He has 100 exam papers to mark before the weekend.* يصحّح (أوراق الامتحان) ، يقدّر الدرجات

4 to show where sth is or where sth happened: *Flowers mark the spot where he died.* يبدي ، يشير إلى

5 to celebrate sth: *The ceremony marked the fiftieth anniversary of the opening of the school.* يحتفل بِ

6 (in sport) to stay close to a player of the opposite team so that he/she cannot play easily يلازم لاعباً خصماً كي يربكه

PHR V **mark sth out** to draw lines to show the position of sth: *Spaces for each car were marked out in the car park.* يرسم ، يخطط، يعلّم

▸ **marked** /mɑːkt/ *adj* clear; noticeable: *There has been a marked increase in vandalism in recent years.* واضح ؛ ملحوظ

marker *noun* [C] something that shows the position of sth: *A marker flag shows where the water is dangerous.* علامة

marking *noun* [C, usually pl.] patterns of colour on an animal or bird التشكيلات الملوّنة على جلد الحيوان أو ريش الطائر

market¹ /ˈmɑːkɪt/ *noun* **1** [C] a place where people go to buy and sell things: *There is a market in the town every Wednesday.* ○ *an open-air/covered market* ○ *Wallingford is an old market town.* ○ *The farmers sell their sheep at the market in Hereford.* ➲ Look at **flea market** and **supermarket.** سوق

2 [U, sing.] the desire to buy a particular thing: *There's no market for very large cars when petrol is so expensive.* طلب

3 [C] a country, area or group of people that may want to buy sth: *The company is hoping to expand into the European Market.* ○ *the home/overseas market* ➲ Look at **black market** and **stock market.** سوق

IDM **on the market** for sale: *This is one of the best automatic cameras on the market.* في السوق

market² /ˈmɑːkɪt/ *verb* [T] to sell sth with the help of advertising يسوّق، يروّج

▸ **marketable** /-əbl/ *adj* able to be sold easily, because people want it رائج، مرغوب

ˌmarket ˈgarden *noun* [C] a farm where vegetables and fruit are grown in large quantities مزرعة خضراوات وفواكه للبيع

marketing /ˈmɑːkɪtɪŋ/ *noun* [U] deciding how sth can be sold most easily, e.g. what price it should be or how it should be advertised: *Effective marketing will lead to increased sales.* ○ *the marketing department* تسويق البضائع

marketplace /ˈmɑːkɪtpleɪs/ (*also* **ˌmarket ˈsquare**) *noun* [C] **1** the place in a town where a market is or used to be held ساحة السوق؛ سوق

2 the activity of competing with other companies to buy and sell goods, services, etc. حركة البيع والشراء

ˌmarket reˈsearch *noun* [U] the study of what people want to buy and why استطلاع عمّا يحبّه المستهلك

marksman /ˈmɑːksmən/ *noun* [C] (*pl.* **marksmen** /-mən/) a person who can shoot very well with a gun الرّامي ، شخص ماهر جداً في الرماية

marmalade /ˈmɑːməleɪd/ *noun* [U] a type of jam that is made from oranges or lemons: *toast and marmalade for breakfast* مَرمَلاد أو مربّى البرتقال ونحوه

maroon /məˈruːn/ *adj* dark brownish-red in colour ➲ Look at **crimson** and **scarlet.** لون أحمر داكن مائل الى البنّيّ

marooned /məˈruːnd/ *adj* in a place that you cannot leave: *The sailors were marooned on a desert island.* متروك أو منقطع في جزيرة نائية

marquee /mɑːˈkiː/ *noun* [C] a very large tent that is used for parties, shows, etc. سرادق ، فسطاط

marriage /ˈmærɪdʒ/ *noun* **1** [C,U] the state of being husband and wife: *They are getting divorced after five years of marriage.* ○ *a happy/an unhappy marriage* ○ *an arranged marriage* (= one where your partner is chosen for you by your parents) ○ *a mixed marriage* (= one between people of different races or religions) زواج

2 [C] a wedding ceremony: *The marriage took place at a registry office in Birmingham.* ❶ The verb is **marry.** ➲ Look at the note at **wedding.** حفلة الزواج ، عقد القِران

married /ˈmærid/ *adj* **1 married (to sb)** having a husband or wife: *a married man/woman/couple* ○ *They've been married for nearly 50 years.* ○ *Shula's married to Mark.* ○ *They're getting married in June.* ❶ The opposite is **unmarried** or **single.** متزوّج

2 (only *before* a noun) of marriage(1): *Married life seems to suit him.* زَوْجيّ

marrow /ˈmærəʊ/ *noun* [C,U] **1** a large vegetable with dark green skin that is white inside الكوسا/الكوسى ؛ كوساية

2 [U] = BONE MARROW

marry /ˈmæri/ *verb* (*pres part* **marrying**; *3rd pers sing pres* **marries**; *pt, pp* **married**) **1** [I,T] to take sb as your husband or wife: *They married when they were very young.* ○ *When did Roger ask you to marry him?* يتزوّج

> **Get married** is more commonly used than **marry**: *When are Sue and Ian getting married?* ○ *They got married in 1982.* ○ *Many people live together without getting married.* ○ *Are you getting married in church or at the registry office?*

2 [T] to join two people together as husband and wife: *We asked the local vicar to marry us.* يزوّج

ℹ The noun is **marriage**.

Mars /mɑːz/ *noun* [sing.] the planet that is fourth in order from the sun and second nearest to the earth ➲ Look at **Martian**. كوكب المرّيخ

marsh /mɑːʃ/ *noun* [C,U] an area of soft wet land مستنقع؛ أرض سبخة

▸ **marshy** *adj* مستنقعي

marshal /ˈmɑːʃl/ *noun* [C] **1** a person who helps to organize or control a large public event: *Marshals are directing traffic in the car park.* موظَّف مسؤول عن تنظيمات الاحتفال

2 (*US*) an officer of high rank in the police or fire department or in a court of law موظف ذو منصب عال في الشرطة أو الإطفاء أو المحكمة

marshmallow /ˌmɑːʃˈmæləʊ; *US* ˈmɑrʃmeləʊ/ *noun* [C,U] a soft pink or white sweet حلوى خاصة طريّة

martial /ˈmɑːʃl/ *adj* (*formal*) connected with war حربي؛ عسكري

ˌmartial ˈarts *noun* [plural] fighting sports such as karate or judo, in which you use your hands and feet as weapons ألعاب الدفاع عن النفس

Martian /ˈmɑːʃn/ *noun* [C] (in stories) a creature that comes from the planet Mars مخلوق قادم من المرّيخ

martyr /ˈmɑːtə(r)/ *noun* [C] **1** a person who is killed because of what he/she believes شهيد

2 a person who does not do or have what he/she wants in order to help other people or to be admired by them: *Don't be such a martyr! You don't have to do all the housework.* من يضحّي برغباته لمصلحة الآخرين ، المؤثِر

▸ **martyrdom** /ˈmɑːtədəm/ *noun* [U] استشهاد : التضحية بالنفس

marvel /ˈmɑːvl/ *noun* [C] a person or thing that is wonderful or that makes you feel surprised: *the marvels of modern technology* ○ *It's a marvel that no one was killed in the accident.* أعجوبة

▸ **marvel** *verb* [I] (marvelling; marvelled; *US* marveling; marveled) (*formal*) to be very surprised at how good, beautiful, etc. sb/sth is: *We marvelled at how much they had been able to do in a short time.* يُدهَش ، يتعجّب

marvellous (*US* **marvelous**) /ˈmɑːvələs/ *adj* very good; wonderful: *Peter was marvellous while I was ill. He took care of everything.* ○ *It's marvellous to have such lovely weather.* رائع؛ بديع

marvellously (*US* **marvelously**) *adv* (رحّبوا بنا ترحيباً) رائعاً؛ بصورة مدهشة

Marxism /ˈmɑːksɪzəm/ *noun* [U] the political and economic thought of Karl Marx, who said that important changes in history were caused by the struggle between social classes ➲ Look at **communism** and **socialism**. الماركسيّة

▸ **Marxist** /ˈmɑːksɪst/ *noun* [C] a person who believes in Marxism الماركسيّ ، من أتباع المذهب الماركسي

Marxist *adj*: *Marxist ideology* ماركسي

marzipan /ˈmɑːzɪpæn; ˌmɑːzɪˈpæn/ *noun* [U] a food that is made of sugar, egg and almonds. Marzipan is used to make sweets or to put on cakes. لَوْزينة، معجونة من اللّوز والسكّر والبيض

mascara /mæˈskɑːrə; *US* -ˈskærə/ *noun* [U] a type of make-up that is used to make your eyelashes look darker and thicker مستحضر لتجميل رموش العين، "مَسْكرة"

mascot /ˈmæskət; -skɒt/ *noun* [C] a person, animal or thing that is thought to bring good luck شخص أو شيء جالب للحظّ

masculine /ˈmæskjəlɪn/ *adj* with the qualities that people think are typical of men ➲ Look at **male** and **manly**, and at **feminine** and the note at **female**. خاصّ بالرجال، مسترجِل؛ مذكّر

> In English grammar **masculine** words refer to male people or animals: *'He' is a masculine pronoun.* In some other languages all nouns are given a gender, either **masculine, feminine** or **neuter**.

▸ **masculinity** /ˌmæskjuˈlɪnəti/ *noun* [U] رجولة ، فحولة

mash /mæʃ/ *verb* [T] to mix or crush sth until it is soft: *mashed potatoes* يهرس

mashup /ˈmæʃʌp/ *noun* [C] a combination of elements from different sources used to create a new song, video, computer file, program, etc. تهجين (التطبيقات الالكترونية)

mask /mɑːsk; *US* mæsk/ *noun* [C] something that you wear that covers your face or part of your face. People wear masks in order to hide or protect their faces or to make themselves look different: *The bank robbers wore stocking masks.* ○ *The doctors and nurses had surgical masks on.* ○ *The children wore animal masks to the party.* ➲ Look at **gas mask** and **goggles**. قناع ، كمامة

▸ **mask** *verb* [T] **1** to cover or hide your face with a mask: *a masked gunman* يغطي وجهه بقناع

2 to hide your feelings: *He masked his anger with a smile.* يخفي مشاعره

masochism /ˈmæsəkɪzəm/ *noun* [U] getting (sexual) pleasure from suffering or pain ➲ Look at **sadism**. الماسوشيّة: التلذّذ عن طريق الشعور بالألم أو العذاب

▸ **masochist** /-kɪst/ *noun* [C] المحِبّ لتعذيب نفسه

masochistic /ˌmæsəˈkɪstɪk/ *adj* تعذيبيّ، مضطهد لنفسه

mason /ˈmeɪsn/ *noun* [C] **1** a person who makes things from stone نحّات أحجار، بنّاء

2 = FREEMASON

▸ **masonry** /ˈmeɪsənri/ *noun* [U] the parts of a building that are made of stone: *The building is old and the masonry is crumbling.* الأجزاء الحجرية في بناء

masquerade /ˌmæskəˈreɪd/ *verb* [I] to pretend to be sb/sth: *Two people, masquerading as doctors, knocked at the door and asked to see the child.* يدّعي ، يتظاهر

Mass (*also* **mass**) /mæs/ *noun* [C,U] the ceremony in some Christian churches when people eat bread and drink wine in order to remember the last meal that Christ had before he died: *to go to Mass* قدّاس

mass /mæs/ *noun* **1** [C] a large amount or number of sth: *The garden was a mass of flowers.* ○ *a dense mass of smoke* ○ *(informal) There were masses of people at the market today.* كميّة كبيرة : حَشْد ، جَمْع غَفير

2 [U] (in physics) the amount of material that sth contains; weight الكتلة

3 the masses [plural] ordinary people when considered as a political group عامّة الشعب، الجماهير

▸ **mass** *adj* (only *before* a noun) involving a large number of people: *a mass murderer* ○ *a mass meeting* جماعي، بالجملة: (اجتماع) شعبيّ حافل

mass *verb* [I,T] to gather together in a mass: *The students massed in the square.* يتجمّع، يحتشّد، يحشد

massacre /ˈmæsəkə(r)/ *noun* [C] the killing of a large number of people or animals مذبحة

▸ **massacre** *verb* [T] ➲ Look at the note at **kill**. يقتل، يذبح

massage /ˈmæsɑːʒ; *US* məˈsɑːʒ/ *noun* [C,U] rubbing or pressing sb's body in order to reduce pain or to help the person move more easily: *to give sb a massage* تدليك ، تمسيد

▸ **massage** *verb* [T] يدلّك ، يمسّد

massive /ˈmæsɪv/ *adj* very big: *a massive increase in prices* هائل، ضخم؛ على نطاق واسع

ˌ**mass ˈmedia** *noun* [plural] the means of communicating with large numbers of people, i.e. newspapers, television and radio وسائل الإعلام

ˌ**mass-proˈduce** *verb* [T] to make large numbers of similar things by machine in a factory ينتج بالجملة

ˌ**mass proˈduction** *noun* [U] إنتاج بالجملة

mast /mɑːst; *US* mæst/ *noun* [C] **1** a tall wooden or metal pole for a flag, ship's sails, etc. صارية/سارية

2 a tall pole that is used for sending out radio or television broadcasts صارية البثّ الإذاعي أو التلفزيونيّ

master¹ /ˈmɑːstə(r); *US* ˈmæs-/ *noun* [C] **1** a man who has people or animals in his control: *The dog ran to his master.* ○ *(figurative) to be master of a difficult situation* ➲ Look at **mistress**. سيّد

2 a person who has great skill at doing sth: *a master builder* حاذق في حرفته ، أُسطى، معلّم

3 (*old-fashioned*) a male teacher (usually in a private school): *the chemistry master* ➲ Look at **mistress** and **headteacher**. أستاذ في مدرسة خاصّة

4 a film or tape from which copies can be made النسخة الأصلية من فيلم وغيره

master² /ˈmɑːstə(r); *US* ˈmæs-/ *verb* [T] **1** to learn how to do sth well: *It takes a long time to master a foreign language.* يتقن ، يجيد

2 to control sth: *to master a situation* يتحكّم في ، يسيطر على

mastermind /ˈmɑːstəmaɪnd; *US* ˈmæs-/ *noun* [C] a very clever person (who planned or organized sth) العقل المدبّر، العقل الموجّه

▸ **mastermind** *verb* [T]: *The police failed to catch the man who masterminded the whole operation.* يخطّط، يدبّر، يدير

masterpiece /ˈmɑːstəpiːs; *US* ˈmæs-/ *noun* [C] a work of art, music, literature, etc. that is of the highest quality: *Tolstoy's masterpiece, War and Peace* تُحفة فنيّة أو أدبية

Master's degree (*also* **Master's**) *noun* [C] a second or higher university degree. You usually get a Master's degree by studying for one or two years after your first degree: *Master of Arts (MA)* ○ *Master of Science (MSc)* ➲ Look at **bachelor**. درجة أو شهادة الماجستير

mastery /ˈmɑːstəri; *US* ˈmæst-/ *noun* [U] **1 mastery (of sth)** great skill at doing sth: *His mastery of the violin was quite exceptional for a child of his age.* إتقان، إجادة

2 mastery (of/over sb/sth) control over sb/sth: *The battle was fought for mastery of the seas.* سيطرة، سيادة

masturbate /ˈmæstəbeɪt/ *verb* [I] to make yourself feel sexually excited by handling and rubbing your sex organs يستمني ، يمارس العادة السريّة

▸ **masturbation** /ˌmæstəˈbeɪʃn/ *noun* [U] الاستمناء ، العادة السّرية

mat¹ /mæt/ *noun* [C] **1** a piece of carpet or other thick material that you put on the floor: *a doormat* ○ *an exercise mat for gymnasts* ○ *a straw mat* ➲ Look at **rug**. سجّادة صغيرة ، بساط

2 a small piece of material that you put under a hot dish, cup, glass, etc: *a table mat* مَفرش صغير يوضع تحت الأطباق وغير ذلك

mat² (*US*) = MATT

match¹ /mætʃ/ *noun* [C] a short piece of wood with a tip that catches fire when it is rubbed against another surface: *to light/strike a match* ○ *a box of matches* عود ثقاب ، عود كبريت

match² /mætʃ/ *noun* **1** [C] an organized game or sports event: *a tennis, football, etc. match* ○ *They beat us last time but we hope to win the return match.* ○ *Game, set and match to Federer!* مباراة

2 [sing.] a person or thing that is as good as or better than sb/sth else: *Carol is no match for her mother when it comes to cooking* (= she doesn't cook as well as her mother). ○ *I think you've met your match in Dave – you won't beat him.* مثيل ، نظير ، ندّ

3 [sing.] **a match (for sb/sth)** something that looks good with sth else, e.g. because it has the same colour or pattern: *Those shoes aren't a very good match with your dress.* ○ (*figurative*) *Bill and Sue are a good match. They should be very happy together.* شيء يتماشى مع ، قرين مناسب

match³ /mætʃ/ *verb* **1** [I,T] to have the same colour or pattern as sth else, or to look nice with sth else: *That blouse doesn't match your skirt.* ○ *We've chosen the curtains but now we need a carpet to match.* يلائم ، ينسجم مع

2 [T] to find sb/sth that is like or suitable for sb/sth else: *The agency tries to match single people with suitable partners.* يوافق بين ، يزاوج

3 [T] to be as good as or better than sb/sth else: *The two teams are very evenly matched.* ○ *Taiwan produces the goods at a price that Europe cannot match.* يعادل ، يكافئ : يضاهي

PHR V **match up** to be the same: *The statements of the two witnesses don't match up.* يطابق ، يماثل

match sth up (with sth) to fit or put sth together (with sth else): *What you have to do is match up each TV personality with his or her pet.* يزاوج ، يطابق بين

match up to sb/sth to be as good as sb/sth: *The film didn't match up to my expectations* (= it wasn't as good as I thought it was going to be). يعادل في الجودة ، يحقّق توقعاته

matchbox /'mætʃbɒks/ *noun* [C] a small box for matches علبة ثقاب أو كبريت

matchstick /'mætʃstɪk/ *noun* [C] the thin wooden part of a match عود (الثقاب)

mate¹ /meɪt/ *noun* [C] **1** (*informal*) a friend or sb you live or work with: *He's an old mate of mine.* ○ *a flatmate* ○ *a classmate* رفيق : زميل

2 (*Brit slang*) (used when speaking to a man): *Hallo mate!* يا سيّد! ، يا أستاذ! ، أخي!

3 one of a male and female pair of animals, birds, etc: *The female sits on the eggs while her mate hunts for food.* أليف ، قرين

4 an officer on a ship ضابط بحريّ (في سفينة تجاريّة)

mate² /meɪt/ *verb* **1** [I] (used about animals and birds) to have sex and produce young: *Pandas rarely mate in zoos.* يتزاوج

2 [T] to bring two animals together so that they can mate يزاوج بين حيوانين

mate³ /meɪt/ *noun* = CHECKMATE

material¹ /mə'tɪəriəl/ *noun* **1** [C,U] a substance that can be used for making or doing sth: *Many African countries export raw materials and import manufactured goods.* ○ *writing materials* (= pens, paper, ink) ○ *This new material is strong but it is also very light.* مادّة

2 [C,U] cloth (for making clothes, etc.): *Is there enough material for a dress?* قماش

3 [U] facts or information that you collect before you write a book, article, etc. معلومات ، موادّ

material² /mə'tɪəriəl/ *adj* **1** connected with real or physical things rather than the spirit or emotions: *We should not value material comforts too highly.* ➲ Look at **spiritual**. ماديّ

2 important: *material evidence* ❶ This word is not common but look at **immaterial**. هامّ ، أساسيّ

materialism /mə'tɪəriəlɪzəm/ *noun* [U] the belief that money and possessions are the most important things in life المذهب الماديّ

▸ **materialist** /mə'tɪəriəlɪst/ *noun* [C] شخص ماديّ ، محبّ للمادّة

materialistic /məˌtɪəriə'lɪstɪk/ *adj* ماديّ

materialize (*also* **materialise**) /mə'tɪəriəlaɪz/ *verb* [I] to become real; to happen: *The pay rise that they had promised never materialized.* يتحقق : يظهر إلى عالم الوجود، يحدث

maternal /mə'tɜːnl/ *adj* **1** of or like a mother: *maternal love* أميّ: متعلق بالأمّ

2 related through your mother's side of the family: *your maternal grandfather* ➲ Look at **paternal**. من ناحية الأم

maternity /mə'tɜːnəti/ *adj* connected with women who are going to have or have just had a baby: *maternity clothes* ○ *the hospital's maternity ward* أمومة

mathematics /ˌmæθə'mætɪks/ *noun* [U] the science or study of numbers, quantities or shapes ❶ The British abbreviation is **maths**, the US is **math**: *Maths is my favourite subject.* الرياضيّات

▸ **mathematical** /ˌmæθə'mætɪkl/ *adj* رياضي

mathematically /-kli/ *adv* من الناحية الحسابية

mathematician /ˌmæθəmə'tɪʃn/ *noun* [C] a person who studies or is an expert in mathematics رياضي ، عالم رياضي

matinee (*also* **matinée**) /'mætɪneɪ; *US* ˌmætn'eɪ/ *noun* [C] an afternoon performance of a play, film, etc. حفلة بعد الظهر ، "ماتينيه"

matrimony /'mætrɪməni; *US* -məʊni/ *noun* [U] (*formal*) the state of being married زواج

▸ **matrimonial** /ˌmætrɪ'məʊniəl/ *adj* زوجي

matron /'meɪtrən/ *noun* [C] **1** a nurse who is in charge of the other nurses in a hospital ❶ **Senior nursing officer** is now more commonly used. رئيسة الممرضات

2 (*old-fashioned*) an older married woman امرأة متزوجة متقدمة في العمر

matt (*US* **mat, matte**) /mæt/ *adj* not shiny: *This paint gives a matt finish.* ➲ Look at **glossy**. غير لامع

matter¹ /'mætə(r)/ *noun* **1** [C] a subject or situation that you must think about and give your attention to: *It's a personal matter and I don't want to discuss it with you.* ○ *They should try to settle matters between themselves before going to court.* ○ *to simplify/complicate matters* قضيّة، مسألة، أمر

2 [U] all physical substances; a substance of a particular kind: *waste matter* ○ *reading matter* مادّة

IDM **as a matter of fact** to tell the truth; in reality: *I like him very much, as a matter of fact.* في الحقيقة

for that matter in addition; as well: *Mick is really fed up with his course. I am too, for that matter.* أيضاً : علاوةً على ذلك

make matters/things worse → WORSE

a matter of sth/doing sth something that needs or requires sth: *Learning a language is largely a matter of practice.* مسألة (تتطلب كذا) ، قضيّة (تدريب)

a matter of course something that you do regularly; the usual practice: *Goods leaving the factory are checked as a matter of course.* روتين عادي ، مسألة طبيعيّة

a matter of life and/or death extremely urgent and important بالغ الأهمية

a matter of opinion a subject on which people do not agree: *'I think the government is doing a good job.' 'That's a matter of opinion.'* مسألة نظر ، مسألة تختلف الآراء فيها

(be) the matter (with sb/sth) to be the reason for unhappiness, pain, problems, etc: *She looks sad. What's the matter with her?* ○ *There seems to be something the matter with the car.* ○ *Eat that food! There's nothing the matter with it.* (شيء يسبّب الحزن أو الانزعاج أو غير ذلك)

no matter who, what, where, etc. whoever, whatever, wherever, etc: *They never listen no matter what you say.* لا يهمّ مَنْ أو ما أو أين...؛ مهما

matter² /ˈmætə(r)/ *verb* [I] to be important: *It doesn't really matter how much it costs.* ○ *Does it matter if we are a little bit late?* ○ *What matters most is giving the children a good start in life.* ○ *Some things matter more than others.* يهمّ ، تكون له أهميّة

> **Matter** is often used in negative sentences, questions and sentences containing *what, who, when, if,* etc. It is not used in the *-ing* forms.

mattress /ˈmætrəs/ *noun* [C] a large soft thing that you lie on to sleep, usually put on a bed: *Don't worry about us – we can sleep on a mattress on the floor.* فَرْشة، حَشيّة

mature¹ /məˈtʃʊə(r); *US* -ˈtʊər/ *adj* **1** fully grown or fully developed: *a mature tree, bird, animal, etc.* ➲ Look at **immature**. تامّ النموّ

2 behaving in a sensible adult way: *Is she mature enough for such responsibility?* ➲ Look at **immature**. ناضج

▸ **maturity** /məˈtʃʊərəti; *US* -ˈtʊə-/ *noun* [U] نضوج : تمام النمو

mature² /məˈtjʊə(r); *US* -ˈtʊər/ *verb* [I] to become mature: *He matured a lot during his two years at college.* ينضج

maul /mɔːl/ *verb* [T] (usually used about a wild animal) to attack and injure sb يهاجم بشراسة ، ينهَش بضراوة

mauve /məʊv/ *adj, noun* [U] reddish purple لون "موف" ، بنفسجي فاتح

maxim /ˈmæksɪm/ *noun* [C] a few words that express a rule for good or sensible behaviour: *Their maxim is: 'If a job's worth doing, it's worth doing well.'* قَوْل ماثور، حِكْمة

maximize (*also* **maximise**) /ˈmæksɪmaɪz/ *verb* [T] **1** to increase sth as much as possible: *to maximize profits* ➲ Look at **minimize**. يزيد إلى الحد الأقصى

2 (*computing*) to increase the size of sth on the computer screen so that it fills the whole screen: *Maximize the window to full screen.* تكبير

maximum /ˈmæksɪməm/ *noun* [sing.] (*abbr* **max**) the greatest amount or level of sth that is possible, allowed, recorded, etc: *The bus can carry a maximum of 40 people.* ○ *£500 is the maximum we can afford.* ○ *to set the dial to maximum* ℹ The opposite is **minimum**. الحدّ الأقصى ، الحدّ الأعلى

▸ **maximum** *adj* (only *before* a noun): *a maximum speed of 120 miles per hour* ○ *a maximum security prison* أقصى ، (سرعة) قصوى

May /meɪ/ *noun* [C,U] the fifth month of the year, coming before June ℹ For examples of the use of the months in sentences, look at **January**. شهر مايو/مايس/أيار

may /meɪ/ *modal verb* (*negative* **may not**) **1** (used for saying that sth is possible): *'Where's Sue?' 'She may be in the garden.'* ○ *You may be right.* ○ *I may be going to China next year.* ○ *They may have forgotten the meeting.* ○ *He may have been driving too fast.* ربّما ، من الممكن

2 (used as a polite way of asking for and giving permission): *May I use your phone?* ○ *You may only borrow books for two weeks.* ممْكن؟؛ يَسْمح لِ

3 (used in the negative as a way of forbidding sb to do sth): *You may not take photographs in the museum.* يمْنع

4 (used for contrasting two facts): *He may be very clever but he can't do anything practical.* قدْ يكون كذا... إلا أنه ، ربّما

5 (*formal*) (used for expressing wishes and hopes): *May God be with you.* (تستعمل للدعاء وللتمني) في رعاية الله!

IDM **may/might as well** → WELL³

maybe /ˈmeɪbi/ *adv* perhaps; possibly: *'Are you going to come?' 'Maybe.'* ○ *There were three, maybe four armed men.* ○ *Maybe I'll accept the invitation and maybe I won't.* ○ *Maybe we ought to try again.* ➲ Look at the note at **perhaps**. ربّما ، من المحتمل

ˈMay Day *noun* [C] 1st May مهرجان الأول من مايو أو الأول من أيار

> **May Day** is traditionally celebrated as a spring festival and in some countries it is also a day for socialist groups to hold meetings and demonstrations.

mayn't /ˈmeɪənt/ *short for* MAY NOT

mayonnaise /ˌmeɪəˈneɪz; *US* ˈmeɪəneɪz/ *noun* [U] a thick yellow sauce made with eggs and oil and often eaten with salad مايونيز

mayor /meə(r); *US* ˈmeɪər/ *noun* [C] a person who is elected to be the leader of the group of people (a council) who manage the affairs of a town or city رئيس البلديّة، المحافظ

▸ **mayoress** /meəˈres; *US* ˈmeɪərəs/ *noun* [C] **1** a mayor who is a woman رئيسة البلديّة

2 the wife of a mayor or a woman who helps the mayor with his official duties زوجة رئيس البلديّة

maze /meɪz/ *noun* [C] a system of paths which is meant to confuse you so that it is difficult to find your way in or out: *We got lost in Hampton Court maze.* ○ (*figurative*) *a maze of winding streets* متاهة

MBA /ˌem biː ˈeɪ/ *abbrev* Master of Business Administration; an advanced university degree in business ماجستير ادارة الأعمال

ˈm-commerce *noun* [U] the business of buying and selling products on the Internet by using mobile phones and other similar technology التجارة الخلوية: البيع والشراء عبر الانترنت باستخدام الهواتف الخلوية

⚷ **me** /mi/ *pron* (used as an object or after the verb *be*) the person who is speaking or writing: *He telephoned me yesterday.* ○ *She wrote to me last week.* ○ *Could you pass me the salt?* ○ *'Somebody's spilt the milk.' 'I'm afraid it was me.'* ○ *'Who's this photograph of?' 'Me.'* ضمير المتكلّم في حالة النصب أو الجرّ

> **It is/was me** is much more common than **it is/was I**, although this can be used in formal speech or writing.

meadow /ˈmedəʊ/ *noun* [C] a field of grass مرج ، أرض معشبة

meagre (*US* **meager**) /ˈmiːɡə(r)/ *adj* too small in amount: *a meagre salary* ○ *The food was good but the portions were meagre.* ضئيل

⚷ **meal** /miːl/ *noun* [C] a certain time when you eat or the food that is eaten at that time: *We're going out for a meal on Friday.* ○ *The pub round the corner serves hot and cold meals.* ○ *Do you have your main meal at lunchtime or in the evening?* ○ *a heavy/light meal* ❶ The main meals of the day are **breakfast**, **lunch** and **dinner**. **Tea** and **supper** are usually smaller meals (but look at the note at **dinner**). A very small meal is called a **snack**. وجبة طعام

mealtime /ˈmiːltaɪm/ *noun* [C] a time at which a meal is usually eaten وقت الطعام

⚷ **mean¹** /miːn/ *verb* [T] (*pt, pp* **meant** /ment/) **1** (not used in the continuous forms) to express, show or have as a meaning: *What does this word mean?* ○ *The bell means that the lesson has ended.* ○ *'What does that symbol mean?' 'Environment-friendly.'* ○ *Does the name 'Charles Bell' mean anything to you?* يعني ، يدلّ على

2 to want or intend to say sth; to refer to sb/sth: *I don't understand what you mean.* ○ *Well, she said 'yes' but I think she really meant 'no'.* ○ *What do you mean by 'a lot of money'?* ○ *I only meant that I couldn't come tomorrow – any other day would be fine.* يقصد

> Note that **mean** cannot be used with the meaning 'to have the opinion that'. We say: *I think that...* or *In my opinion...*: *I think that she'd be silly to buy that car.* **I mean** is often used in conversation when you want to explain something you have just said or to add more information: *What a terrible summer – I mean it's rained almost all the time.* ○ *I think the film will have started – I mean it's past 8 o'clock.* **I mean** is also used to correct something you have just said: *We went there on Tuesday, I mean Thursday.*

3 (not used in the continuous forms) to be important to sb: *This job means a lot to me.* يهمّ

4 (not used in the continuous forms) to make sth likely; to cause: *The shortage of teachers means that classes are larger.* ○ *His new job means him travelling more.* يجعل ، يسبّب

5 (not used in the continuous forms) to be serious or sincere about sth: *He said he loved me but I don't think he meant it!* ○ *I'm never coming back – I mean it!* يعني ؛ يعتزم جدّياً

6 to want or plan to do sth; to intend sth: *I'm sure she didn't mean to upset you.* ○ *She meant the card for both of us.* ○ *I didn't mean you to cook the whole meal!* يعدّ لغرض معين ، يقصد

7 (usually passive) to intend or expect sb/sth to be or do sth: *It was only meant as a joke.* ○ *What's this picture meant to be?* ○ *You're meant to get to work at 9 o'clock.* ○ *That restaurant is meant to be excellent* (= people say that it is). يقصد ؛ يفترض

IDM **mean well** to want to be kind and helpful but usually without success: *My mother means well but I wish she'd stop treating me like a child.* ينوي نوايا حسنة ، يقصد خيراً ، يبغي المساعدة

mean² /miːn/ *adj* **1 mean (with sth)** not willing to give or use sth (especially money); not generous: *It's no good asking him for any money – he's much too mean.* ○ *Don't be mean with the cream.* بخيل ، شحيح

2 mean (to sb) (used about people or their behaviour) unkind: *It was mean of him not to invite you too.* (تصرُّف) غير وديّ ، خسيس

▶ **meanness** *noun* [U] بُخْل ، تقتير

mean³ /miːn/ *adj* (only *before* a noun) average: *What is the mean annual temperature in California?* متوسّط

meander /miˈændə(r)/ *verb* [I] **1** (used about a river, road, etc.) to have a lot of curves and bends يتعرّج ، يتلوّى

2 (used about a person or animal) to walk or travel slowly or without any definite direction يتسكّع ؛ يسير بلا هدف

⚷ **meaning** /ˈmiːnɪŋ/ *noun* **1** [C,U] what sth means or expresses; its sense or intention: *This word has two different meanings in English.* ○ *What do you think is the meaning of the last line of the poem?* معنى ، مدلول

2 [U] purpose or importance: *With his child dead there seemed to be no meaning in life.* هدف ، معنى

▶ **meaningful** /-fl/ *adj* **1** useful, important or interesting: *Most people need a meaningful relationship with another person.* مفيد ، جدّي

2 (used about a look, expression, etc.) trying to express a certain feeling or idea: *They kept giving each other meaningful glances across the table.* ذو مغزى

meaningfully /-fəli/ *adv* بشكل مفيد ؛ جدّياً

meaningless *adj* without meaning, reason or sense: *The figures are meaningless if we have*

nothing to compare them with.
لا معنى له ، لا فائدة منه

🔑**means**[1] /miːnz/ *noun* [C, with sing. or pl. verb] (*pl.* **means**) a method of doing sth: *Have you any means of transport?* (= a car, bicycle, etc.) ○ *Is there any means of contacting your husband?*
وسيلة ، واسطة

IDM **a means to an end** a way of achieving sth where the thing or method you use is not as important as the result مجرّد وسيلة (لتحقيق غاية)

by means of by using: *We got out of the hotel by means of the fire escape.* بواسطة

by no means; not by any means (used for emphasis) not at all: *I'm by no means sure that this is the right thing to do.* أبداً ، على الإطلاق

🔑**means**[2] /miːnz/ *noun* [plural] (*formal*) money or wealth موارد ، دَخْل

meant *pt, pp* of MEAN[1]

meantime /ˈmiːntaɪm/ *noun*

IDM **in the meantime** in the time between two things happening: *The builders haven't finished so in the meantime we're living with my mother.* في هذه الأثناء ، في غضون ذلك

🔑**meanwhile** /ˈmiːnwaɪl; *US* -hwaɪl/ *adv* during the same time or during the time between two things happening: *Peter was at home studying. Tony, meanwhile, was out with his friends.* ○ *The new computer will arrive next week. Meanwhile you'll have to manage without.* في هذه الأثناء

measles /ˈmiːzlz/ *noun* [U] a common infectious disease, especially among children. You have a temperature and your skin is covered in small red spots مرض الحصْبة

> **Measles** looks like a plural noun but it is used with a singular verb: *In many countries measles is a very dangerous disease.*

measly /ˈmiːzli/ *adj* (*informal*) much too small in size, amount or value: *All that work for this measly amount of money!* ضئيل ، تافه

🔑**measure**[1] /ˈmeʒə(r)/ *verb* **1** [I,T] to find the size, weight, etc. of sb/sth often by using an instrument such as a ruler: *to measure the height, width, length, depth, etc. of sth* ○ *Could you measure the table to see if it will fit into our room?* ○ *Height is measured in metres and centimetres.* ○ *Britain now uses the metric system for measuring.* يقيس

2 [I] to be a certain height, width, length, etc: *The room measures five metres across.* ○ *The pool measures 25 metres by 5 metres.*
يبلغ (ارتفاعه، عرضه...الخ)

3 [T] to show or judge the size, amount, etc. of sth: *A speedometer measures speed.* ○ (*figurative*) *How do you measure a person's success?*
يقيس ؛ يُقدِّر

PHR V **measure up (to sth)** to be as good as you need to be or as sb expects you to be: *Did the holiday measure up to your expectations?*
يبلغ المستوى المطلوب ، يعادل ، يتناسب مع

▸ **measurement** *noun* **1** [C] a size, amount, etc. that is found by measuring: *What are the exact measurements of the room?* (= how wide, long, etc. is it?) ○ *What's your waist measurement?* ○ *Let's start by taking your measurements* (= measuring the size of your chest, waist and other parts of the body). مقياس

2 [U] the act of measuring: *I'm not sure how accurate his measurement of the area was.* قياس

🔑**measure**[2] /ˈmeʒə(r)/ *noun* **1** [sing.] (*formal*) a certain amount or quantity; some but not much: *The play achieved a measure of success.*
مقدار ؛ قدْر قليل من ، بعض

2 [sing.] a way of understanding or judging sth: *The school's popularity is a measure of the teachers' success.* معيار

3 [C, usually pl.] an action that is done for a special reason: *The government is taking new measures to reduce inflation.* ○ *As a temporary measure, the road will have to be closed.* ○ *emergency measures* ○ *New safety measures are to be introduced after a child was killed.* إجراء ، تدبير

4 [C] a way of describing the size, amount, etc. of sth: *A metre is a measure of length.* وحدة قياس

🔑**meat** /miːt/ *noun* [U] the flesh of animals or birds that people eat: *She doesn't eat meat – she's a vegetarian.* لحْم

> Some types of meat have different names from the animals they come from. We get **beef** from a cow and **veal** from a calf. **Mutton** comes from a sheep but we get **lamb** from a lamb. For birds and fish there is not a different word. We often call beef, mutton and lamb **red meat**. The meat from birds is called **white meat**. We can **fry**, **grill**, **roast** or **stew** meat. We **carve** a **joint** of meat. Meat can be described as **tough** or **tender**, **lean** or **fatty**. Uncooked meat is **raw**.

meatball /ˈmiːtbɔːl/ *noun* [C] a small ball of minced meat كرة لحم

Mecca /ˈmekə/ *noun* **1** the city in Saudi Arabia where the Prophet Muhammad was born, which is the centre of Islam مكّة المكرّمة

2 [C, usually sing.] **mecca** a place that many people wish to visit because of a particular interest: *Italy is a mecca for art lovers.* قِبلة الأنظار

mechanic /məˈkænɪk/ *noun* [C] a person whose job is to repair and work with machines and tools: *a car mechanic* عامل ميكانيكي

mechanical /məˈkænɪkl/ *adj* **1** connected with, worked by or produced by machines: *a mechanical pump* ○ *mechanical engineering* ○ *a mechanical mind* (= a mind that understands machines) آلي ، ميكانيكي ؛ خبير بالآلات

2 (used about a person's behaviour) done like a machine as if you are not thinking about what you are doing: *He played the piano in a dull and mechanical way.* آليّ ، لا روحَ فيه

▸ **mechanically** /-kli/ *adv* بشكل آلي

mechanics /məˈkænɪks/ *noun* **1 the mechanics** [plural] the way in which sth works or is done: *Don't ask me – I don't understand the mechanics of the legal system.* آليّة ، كيفيّة عمل (جهاز)

a b c d e f g h i j k l **m** n o p q r s t u v w x y z

2 [U] the science of how machines work
علم الميكانيك

mechanism /ˈmekənɪzəm/ *noun* [C] **1** a part of a piece of equipment or a machine that does a certain task: *Our car has an automatic locking mechanism.* جهاز آليّ

2 the way in which sth works or the process by which sth is done: *the mechanism of the heart* ○ *I'm afraid there is no mechanism for dealing with your complaint.*
آليّة ، كيفية عمل (القلب) : طريقة عمل

mechanize (*also* **mechanise**) /ˈmekənaɪz/ *verb* [I,T] to use machines instead of people to do work: *We have mechanized the entire production process.* يدخل استعمال الآلات (بدلاً من الإنسان)

▸ **mechanization** (*also* **mechanisation**) /ˌmekənaɪˈzeɪʃn; *US* -nəˈz-/ *noun* [U]: *Increased mechanization has led to unemployment.*
استخدام الآلات (بدلاً من الإنسان)

Med (*informal*) = MEDITERRANEAN

medal /ˈmedl/ *noun* [C] a flat piece of metal, usually with a design and words on it, which is given to sb for bravery or as a prize in a sporting event: *He was awarded a medal for bravery.* ○ *to win a gold/silver/bronze medal in the Olympics*
وسام ، مدالية

▸ **medallist** (*US* **medalist**) /ˈmedəlɪst/ *noun* [C] a person who has won a medal, especially in sport: *an Olympic gold medallist*
حامل مدالية ، فائز بمدالية

medallion /məˈdæliən/ *noun* [C] a small round piece of metal on a chain which is worn as jewellery around the neck
مداليون ، قطعة مستديرة تلبس في سلسة حول الرقبة

meddle /ˈmedl/ *verb* [I] **meddle (in/with sth)** to take too much interest (in sb's private affairs) or to handle sth that you should not: *She criticized her mother for meddling in her private life.* ○ *Somebody's been meddling with the papers on my desk.* يتدخّل فيما لا يعنيه : يعبث بحوائج غيره

🔑 **media** /ˈmiːdiə/ *noun* [U, with sing. or pl. verb] **the media** television, radio and newspapers used as a means of communication: *The reports in the media have been greatly exaggerated.* وسائل الإعلام

Sometimes **media** is used with a singular verb, although it is a plural noun: *The media always take/takes a great interest in the Royal family.* Look at **mass media** and **the press**.

mediaeval = MEDIEVAL

mediate /ˈmiːdieɪt/ *verb* [I,T] to try to settle a disagreement between two or more people or groups: *As a supervisor she had to mediate between her colleagues and the management.*
يتوسّط (لتسوية خلاف)

▸ **mediation** /ˌmiːdiˈeɪʃn/ *noun* [U]
تسوية الخلاف ، التوسُّط

mediator *noun* [C] وسيط

🔑 **medical** /ˈmedɪkl/ *adj* connected with medicine and the treatment or prevention of illness: *a medical school/student* ○ *Have you had any medical treatment during the last three years?* ○ *Some people take out insurance that pays for private medical care.* ○ *medical research* طبّي

▸ **medical** *noun* [C] an examination of your body by a doctor to check your state of health: *to have a medical* فحص طبّي دقيق

medicated /ˈmedɪkeɪtɪd/ *adj* containing a substance like a medicine: *medicated shampoo*
علاجيّ

medication /ˌmedɪˈkeɪʃn/ *noun* [C,U] medicine that a doctor has given you: *Are you on any medication?* دواء ، عقار طبي

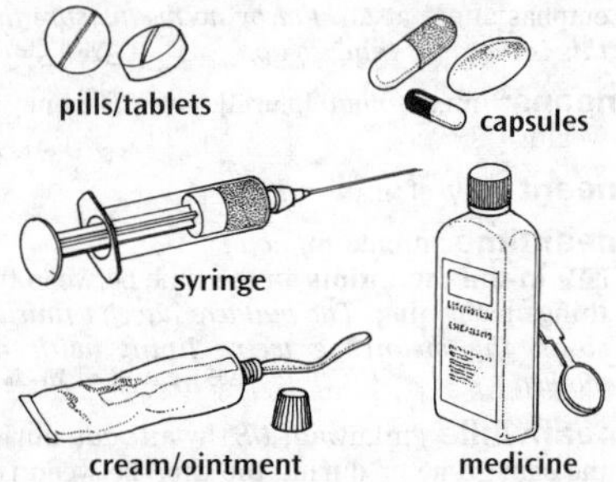

🔑 **medicine** /ˈmedsn; *US* ˈmedɪsn/ *noun* **1** [U] the science of preventing and treating illness: *to study/practise medicine* الطّب

2 [C,U] pills, liquids, etc. that you take in order to treat an illness: *Medicines should be kept out of the reach of children.* ○ *to take medicine* ○ *Did the doctor prescribe any medicine?* ○ *cough medicine* دواء ، علاج

medieval (*also* **mediaeval**) /ˌmediˈiːvl; *US* ˌmiːd-; mɪˈdiːvl/ *adj* of the Middle Ages in European history; i.e. between about 1100 and 1500 AD: *medieval art* متعلّق بالقرون الوسطى

mediocre /ˌmiːdiˈəʊkə(r); ˌmed-/ *adj* of not very high quality: *a mediocre performance*
وَسَط ؛ متوسط الجودة ، بينَ بين

▸ **mediocrity** /ˌmiːdiˈɒkrəti; ˌmed-/ *noun* [U]
كون الشيء متوسط الجودة أو عادياً

meditate /ˈmedɪteɪt/ *verb* **1** [I] to spend time thinking deeply in a special way so that you become calm and peaceful, often as part of religious training يتأمّل

2 [I,T] to think carefully and deeply (about sth): *I've been meditating on what you said last week.* يفكّر ملياً ، يتبصّر

▸ **meditation** /ˌmedɪˈteɪʃn/ *noun* [U] التأمُّل

the Mediterranean /ˌmedɪtəˈreɪniən/ (*also informal* **the Med**) *noun* [sing.] the Mediterranean Sea or the countries around it
البحر الأبيض المتوسّط : بلدان البحر المتوسّط

▸ **Mediterranean** *adj*: *Mediterranean cookery* خاصّ ببلدان البحر المتوسّط

🔑 **medium**[1] /ˈmiːdiəm/ *noun* [C] **1** (*pl.* usually **media**) a means you can use to express or communicate sth: *Many actors feel that the theatre is a more rewarding medium than the cinema.*

➲ Look at **media** and **mass media**.
وسيلة ، واسطة ؛ وسائل الإعلام

2 (*pl.* **mediums**) a person who says that he/she can speak to and take messages from the spirits of dead people وسيط روحي

medium² /ˈmiːdiəm/ *adj* of a size or amount that is neither very large nor very small; average: *She was of medium height and weight.* ○ *Would you like the small, medium or large packet?* ○ *a medium-sized dog* متوسّط

ˈmedium wave *noun* [U] the system of broadcasting radio using sound waves between 100 and 1 000 metres ➲ Look at **long wave** and **short wave**. الموجة المتوسّطة

meek /miːk/ *adj* (used about people) quiet, and doing what other people say without asking questions or arguing: *She seems very meek but she can get very angry.* وديع ؛ مطيع ، خنوع
▸ **meekly** *adv* بخنوع ؛ دون اعتراض
meekness *noun* [U] خنوع ، إطاعة

meet /miːt/ *verb* (*pt*, *pp* **met** /met/) **1** [I,T] to come together by chance or because you have arranged it: *We happened to meet in the middle of Oxford Street!* ○ *Where did you first meet your husband?* ○ *What time shall we meet for lunch?*
يتقابل ، يُصادف ؛ يقابل ، يلتقي بـ

2 [I,T] to be introduced to sb for the first time: *Have you two met before?* يتقابل

3 [T] to go to a place and wait for sb/sth to arrive: *I'll come and meet you at the station.* ○ *A coach will meet your plane and take you to your destination.* يلاقي ، يلقى

4 [I] (used about a group of people) to come together for a special purpose: *Representatives from both countries will meet for talks in London.* ○ *How often does the parish council meet?* يجتمع

5 [T] to be enough for sth; to be able to deal with sth: *The money that I earn is enough to meet our basic needs.* ○ *I'm afraid this piece of work doesn't meet the requirements* (= it's not good enough). ○ *This year is going to be difficult but I'm sure that we can meet the challenge.*
يسدّ الحاجة ، يفي بالغرض؛ يواجه ، يتغلّب على

6 [I,T] to touch, join or make contact with: *The rivers meet in Oxford.* ○ *Can you see where the road meets the motorway on the map?* ○ *His eyes met hers.* يلتقي

IDM **make ends meet** → END¹
there is more to sb/sth than meets the eye sb/sth is more interesting or complex than you might think at first: *Do you think there's more to their relationship than meets the eye?*
ليس الأمر بهذه البساطة ، هناك أشياء أخرى مخفيّة

PHR V **meet up (with sb)** to meet sb, especially after first going in different directions or doing different things: *Let's both do our own shopping and meet up with each other for coffee.*
يقابل أو يلتقي (من جديد) مع

meet with sb (*US*) to meet sb, especially for discussion: *The President met with his advisers early this morning.* يجتمع مع

meet with sth to get a certain answer, reaction or result: *I'm afraid the play did not meet with success.* يقابَل بِـ

meeting /ˈmiːtɪŋ/ *noun* **1** [C] an organized occasion when a number of people come together in order to discuss or decide sth: *The next committee meeting will be held on 19 August.* ○ *We need to have a meeting to discuss these matters.* ○ *I'm afraid Mrs Riley is in a meeting at the moment.* ○ *to attend a meeting* ○ *a public meeting in the town hall* اجتماع

We **call**, **arrange** or **organize** a meeting. We can also **cancel** or **postpone** a meeting.

2 [sing.] the people at a meeting: *The meeting was in favour of the new proposals.* المجتمعون

3 [C] the coming together of two or more people: *Christmas is a time of family meetings and reunions.* ○ *Can you remember your first meeting with your future husband?* التقاء ، اجتماع

mega /ˈmeɡə/ *adj* (*informal*) very large or impressive: *The song was a mega hit last year.* هائل
▸ **mega** *adv*: *They're mega rich.* إلى حدٍ كبير

megabyte /ˈmeɡəbaɪt/ *noun* [C] (*abbr* **MB**) a unit of computer memory, equal to 2^{20} (or about 1 million) bytes: *a 40-megabyte hard disk*
ميغابايت

megaphone /ˈmeɡəfəʊn/ *noun* [C] a piece of equipment that you speak through to make your voice sound louder, especially outside
مُضخّم للصوت على شكل بوق

melancholy /ˈmelənkəli/ *noun* [U] (*formal*) a feeling of sadness which lasts for a long time
المالنخوليا ، الاكتئاب
▸ **melancholy** *adj* مكتئب ، حزين

mellow /ˈmeləʊ/ *adj* **1** (used about colours or sounds) soft, warm and pleasant هادئ ؛ ناعم ، رخيم

2 (used about people) wise, mature or relaxed because of age or experience
ناضج ، عاقل ؛ لطيف المعشر
▸ **mellow** *verb* [I,T]: *The colour of natural stone mellows with age.* ○ *Experience had mellowed her views about many things.* يتعتّق ؛ يلين ، يلطف

melodrama /ˈmelədrɑːmə/ *noun* [C,U] a type of play or novel in which a lot of exciting things happen and in which people's emotions are stronger than in real life
ميلودراما: قصة تبالغ في الأحداث العاطفية المثيرة
▸ **melodramatic** /ˌmelədrəˈmætɪk/ *adj* (used about a person's behaviour) making things seem more exciting and serious than they really are
مفرط في حركاته المسرحية وتهويل الأحداث

melody /ˈmelədi/ *noun* [C] (*pl.* **melodies**) **1** a song or tune: *to play a melody* لَحْن ، أغنية

2 the main tune in a piece of music that is in several parts: *The tenors have the melody here.*
اللحن الرئيسيّ في قطعة موسيقيّة

melon /ˈmelən/ *noun* [C,U] a large round fruit with a thick yellow or green skin and many seeds: *Would you like melon to start, or soup?*
بطّيخ ، جبس ، شمّام

melt /melt/ *verb* **1** [I,T] to change from solid to

a b c d e f g h i j k l **m** n o p q r s t u v w x y z

liquid by means of heat: *When we got up in the morning the snow had melted.* ○ *First melt the butter in a saucepan.* يذوب؛ يُذيب

2 [I] (used about sb's feelings, etc.) to become softer or less strong: *My heart melted when I saw the tiny puppy.* يرقّ ، يلين

PHRV **melt away** to disappear: *The crowd slowly melted away when the speaker had finished.* يختفي ، يتلاشى

melt sth down to heat a metal or glass object until it becomes soft ينصهر ؛ يصهر

ˈmelting pot *noun* [C] a place where large numbers of people from different countries live together: *New York is a melting pot of different nationalities.* البوتقة: ينصهر فيها المهاجرون من جنسيّات مختلفة

member /ˈmembə(r)/ *noun* [C] a person, animal or thing that belongs to a group, club, organization, etc: *All the members of the family were there.* ○ *If you would like to become a member of the club, please let us have your subscription as soon as possible.* ○ *a member of staff* عضو ؛ فرْد

▸ **membership** *noun* **1** [U] the state of being a member of a group, organization, etc: *To apply for membership, please fill in the enclosed form.* ○ *Annual membership costs £200.* عضْوية

2 [C,U] the people who belong to a group, organization, etc: *Membership has fallen in the past year* (= the number of members). ❶ In the singular **membership** can be used with either a singular or a plural verb. عدد الأعضاء

ˌMember of ˈParliament (*also* **Member**) *noun* [C] (*pl.* **Members of Parliament**) (*abbr* **MP**) a person who has been elected to represent people in Parliament عضو البرلمان

membrane /ˈmembreɪn/ *noun* [C] (*formal*) a thin skin which covers or connects parts of a person's or animal's body غِشاء

memento /məˈmentəʊ/ *noun* [C] (*pl.* **mementos** or **mementoes**) something that you keep to remind you of a person, a place or of sth that has happened تذكار

memo /ˈmeməʊ/ *noun* [C] (*pl.* **memos**) (*also formal* **memorandum**) a note sent from one person or office to another within an organization مُذكّرة ، رسالة موجزة بين موظف وآخر في مكتب

memoirs /ˈmemwɑːz/ *noun* [plural] a person's written account of his/her own life and experiences مُذكّرات

memorabilia /ˌmemərəˈbɪliə/ *noun* [U] things that people buy because they are connected with a famous person, event, etc: *Beatles/Titanic/war memorabilia* أشياء تذكارية

memorable /ˈmemərəbl/ *adj* worth remembering or easy to remember because it is special in some way: *The concert was a memorable experience.* لا ينسى ، (يوم) مشهود

▸ **memorably** *adv* بشكل لا ينسى

memorandum /ˌmeməˈrændəm/ *noun* [C] (*pl.* **memoranda** /-də/) (*formal*) = MEMO

memorial /məˈmɔːriəl/ *noun* [C] **memorial (to sb/sth)** something that is built or done to remind people of an event or a person: *a war memorial* (= a statue or cross) ○ *a memorial service* نُصب تذكاري ؛ حفْل تأبيني في كنيسة

memorize (*also* **memorise**) /ˈmeməraɪz/ *verb* [T] to learn sth so that you can remember it exactly: *Actors have to memorize their lines.* يحفظ عن ظهر قلب ، يستظهر

memory /ˈmeməri/ *noun* (*pl.* **memories**) **1** [C] a person's ability to remember things: *a good/bad memory* ○ *A teacher needs to have a good memory for names.* ذاكرة ، تذكُّر

2 [C,U] the part of your mind in which you store things that you remember: *That day remained firmly in my memory for the rest of my life.* ○ *The appointment completely slipped my memory* (= I forgot it). ○ *He played the music from memory* (= without looking at notes or music). الذاكرة

3 [C] something that you remember: *That is one of my happiest memories.* ○ *I have no memories of that time at all.* ○ *childhood memories* ذكرى

4 [C,U] the part of a computer where information is stored: *This computer has a 512MB memory/512MB of memory.* ذاكرة

IDM **in memory of sb/to the memory of sb** in order to remind people of sb who has died: *A service was held in memory of the dead.* تخليداً لذكرى

refresh your/sb's memory → REFRESH

ˈmemory card *noun* [C] an electronic device that can be used to store data, used especially with digital cameras, mobile phones, music players, etc. بطاقة ذاكرة

men *pl.* of MAN

menace /ˈmenəs/ *noun* **1** [C] a danger or threat: *The road is a menace to everyone's safety.* خطَر ، تهديد ؛ شخص مزعج

2 [U] a quality, feeling, etc. that is threatening or frightening: *He spoke with menace in his voice.* تهديد، وَعيد

▸ **menace** *verb* [T] to be likely to hurt sb/sth; to threaten يهدّد ، يتوعّد

menacing *adj* threatening or frightening مُنذِر ، مخيف

mend /mend/ *verb* [T] to put sth that is broken or torn into a good condition again; to repair sth: *Can you mend the hole in this jumper for me?* ○ *This window needs mending – it won't shut properly.* يصلِح ؛ يرمّم ؛ يرفو (الجراب)

▸ **mend** *noun*

IDM **on the mend** (*informal*) to be getting better after an illness or injury; to be recovering: *She's been in bed for a week but she's on the mend now.* يتماثل للشفاء ، صحته آخذة في التحسّن

menial /ˈmiːniəl/ *adj* (used about work) not skilled or important: *a menial job* (عمل) تافه، حقير

meningitis /ˌmenɪnˈdʒaɪtɪs/ *noun* [U] a serious illness which affects the brain and the spine التهاب السحايا

menopause /ˈmenəpɔːz/ *noun* [sing.] **the menopause** the time when a woman stops losing blood once a month (menstruating). This usually happens around the age of 50. سِنّ اليأس

menstruate /ˈmenstrueɪt/ *verb* [I] (*formal*) to lose blood from the uterus about once a month ℹ A less formal way of saying this is **to have periods**. تَحيض ، تطمُث

▸ **menstruation** /ˌmenstruˈeɪʃn/ *noun* [U] the process or time of menstruating الحَيْض ، الطَّمْث ، العادة الشهرية

🔑 **mental** /ˈmentl/ *adj* (only *before* a noun) **1** of or in the mind: *It's fascinating to watch a child's mental development.* ○ *I've got a mental picture of the man but I can't remember his name.* عقلي

2 connected with illness of the mind: *a mental hospital* (مستشفى) الأمراض العقلية

▸ **mentally** /ˈmentəli/ *adv*: *a home for mentally ill people* (المرضى) عقلياً

mentality /menˈtæləti/ *noun* [C] (*pl.* **mentalities**) a type of mind or way of thinking: *I just can't understand his mentality!* ○ *the criminal mentality* عقلية

🔑 **mention** /ˈmenʃn/ *verb* [T] to say or write sth about sb/sth; to talk about sb/sth: *I wouldn't mention her exams to her – she's feeling nervous.* ○ *He mentioned (to me) that he might be late.* ○ *Did she mention what time the film starts?* ○ *Whenever I mention going out together she makes an excuse.* ○ *She mentioned Milton Keynes as a good place for shopping.* يذكر ، يشير إلى

IDM **don't mention it** (used as a polite reply when sb thanks you for sth) I'm pleased to help; not at all: *'Thank you for all your help.' 'Don't mention it.'* "لا داعي للشكر"

not to mention (used for emphasis) and also; as well as: *This is a great habitat for birds, not to mention other wildlife.* إضافةً إلى ، كما أنّه

▸ **mention** *noun* [C,U] a brief remark about sb/sth: *It was odd that there wasn't even a mention of the riots in the newspaper.* ○ *I've heard no mention of a salary rise this year.* ذِكر، إشارة إلى

🔑 **menu** /ˈmenjuː/ *noun* [C] **1** a list of the food that you can choose at a restaurant: *Could we have/see the menu, please?* ○ *I hope there's some soup on the menu.* ○ *The menu here is always excellent* (= there's always a good choice of food). قائمة الطعام

2 a list of choices in a computer program which is shown on the screen (في الكمبيوتر) لائحة

ˈ**menu bar** *noun* [C] a horizontal bar at the top of a computer screen that contains pull-down menus such as 'File',' Edit' and 'Help' شريط القوائم

MEP /ˌem iː ˈpiː/ *abbrev* Member of the European Parliament غضو البرلمان الأوربي

mercenary /ˈmɜːsənəri; *US* -neri/ *adj* interested only in making money: *His motives are entirely mercenary.* مادّي، مالي

▸ **mercenary** *noun* [C] (*pl.* **mercenaries**) a person who fights for any group or country that will pay him/her المرتزق

merchandise /ˈmɜːtʃəndaɪz/ *noun* [U] goods that are for sale بضاعة ، سِلع

merchant /ˈmɜːtʃənt/ *noun* [C] a person whose job is to buy and sell goods, usually of one particular type, in large amounts: *a tea merchant* تاجر

ˌ**merchant ˈnavy** *noun* [C, with sing. or pl. verb] (*pl.* **merchant navies**) all the ships and seamen of a country that are involved in carrying goods for trade السفن التجارية ، الأسطول التجاري

Mercury /ˈmɜːkjəri/ *noun* [sing.] the planet that is nearest to the sun كوكب عطارد

mercury /ˈmɜːkjəri/ *noun* [U] (*symbol* **Hg**) a heavy silver-coloured metal that is usually in liquid form. Mercury is used in thermometers. الزئبق

mercy /ˈmɜːsi/ *noun* [U] kindness or forgiveness (that is shown to sb who has done sth wrong): *The prisoners begged for mercy from the king.* ○ *The rebels were shown no mercy. They were taken out and shot.* رحمة ، رأفة

IDM **at the mercy of sb/sth** having no power against sb/sth strong: *The climbers spent the night on the mountain at the mercy of the wind and rain.* تحت رحمة

▸ **merciful** /-fl/ *adj* feeling or showing mercy: *His death was a merciful release from pain.* رحيم

mercifully /-fəli/ *adv* **1** in a merciful way برحمة وشفقة

2 (*informal*) luckily: *It was bitterly cold but mercifully it was not raining.* لحسن الحظّ

merciless *adj* showing no mercy عديم الرحمة ، قاسي القلب

mercilessly *adv* بعنف ؛ بلا رحمة ولا شفقة

🔑 **mere** /mɪə(r)/ *adj* (only *before* a noun) (used for emphasizing how small or unimportant sth is) nothing more than: *A mere ten per cent of young people in Britain went to university.* مجرّد، ليس إلاّ

IDM **the merest** even a small amount of sth: *The merest smell of the fish market made her feel ill.* حتى أصغر كميّة من...

▸ **merely** *adv* only; just: *I don't want to place an order. I am merely making an enquiry.* فقط ، لا أكثر ولا أقلّ

merge /mɜːdʒ/ *verb* **1** [I] **merge (with/into sth); merge (together)** to become part of sth else: *Three small companies merged into one large one.* ○ *This stream merges with the Thames a few miles downstream.* ○ *Those colours seem to merge into each other.* يندمج ، يتّحد

2 [T] to join things together so that they become one: *We have merged the two classes into one.* يدمج ، يوحّد

▸ **merger** /ˈmɜːdʒə(r)/ *noun* [C,U] the act of joining two or more companies together دمج

meridian /məˈrɪdiən/ *noun* [C] an imaginary line on the surface of the earth from the North Pole to the South Pole that passes through a particular place: *the Greenwich meridian* ➲ Look at **longitude**. خطّ الطول

meringue /məˈræŋ/ *noun* **1** [U] a mixture of sugar and egg whites that is beaten together and

a b c d e f g h i j k l m n o p q r s t u v w x y z

cooked in the oven مزيج من بياض البيض المخفوق مع السكّر يطبخ في الفرن

2 [C] a small cake that is made of meringue كعكة صغيرة من هذا المزيج

merit /ˈmerɪt/ *noun* **1** [U] something that has merit is of high quality: *There is a lot of merit in her ideas.* ○ *a certificate of merit* ○ *a novel of great artistic merit* جدارة ، استحقاق

2 [C, usually pl.] an advantage or a good quality of sb/sth: *What are the merits of this new scheme?* ○ *Each case must be judged separately on its own merits* (= not according to general principles). ميزة ، حسنة

▸ **merit** *verb* [T] (*formal*) to be good enough for sth; to deserve: *This suggestion merits further discussion.* يستحقّ

mermaid /ˈmɜːmeɪd/ *noun* [C] (in stories) a woman who has the tail of a fish instead of legs and who lives in the sea حورية البحر

merry /ˈmeri/ *adj* (**merrier**; **merriest**) **1** happy and cheerful: *merry laughter* ○ *Merry Christmas!* مبتهج ، مَرِح

2 (*informal*) rather drunk "سكران شويّة" ، "مكيّف"

▸ **merrily** /ˈmerəli/ *adv* بمَرَح، بابتهاج

merriment /ˈmerimənt/ *noun* [U] (*formal*) laughter and enjoyment ضحك وسرور ، فَرَح ومَرَح

ˈ**merry-go-round** *noun* [C] = ROUNDABOUT² (2)

mesh /meʃ/ *noun* [C,U] material that is like a net (= made of plastic, wire or rope threads with holes in between): *a fence made of wire mesh* شبكة مصنوعة من البلاستيك أو الأسلاك أو غير ذلك

mesmerize (*also* **mesmerise**) /ˈmezməraɪz/ *verb* [T] to hold sb's attention completely: *The audience seemed to be mesmerized by the speaker's voice.* يسحر ، يسلب لبّه : يمَسْمِر

mess¹ /mes/ *noun* **1** [C, usually sing.] the state of being dirty or untidy: *The kitchen's in a terrible mess!* وسَخ وعدم ترتيب

2 [sing.] a person or thing that is dirty or untidy: *You look a mess! You can't go out like that!* ○ *My hair is a mess.* أشعث ووسِخ ، زريّ الهيئة

3 [sing.] the state of having problems or troubles: *The company is in a financial mess.* ○ *to make a mess of your life* ورطة ، مأزق ، "لخبطة"

▸ **mess** *verb* [T] (*informal*) (*US*) to make sth dirty or untidy: *Don't mess your hands.* يوسِّخ

PHR V **mess about/around 1** to behave in a foolish way يتصرّف تصرفات صبيانية

2 to pass your time in a relaxed way without any real purpose: *We spent Sunday just messing around at home.* يعبث ويضيّع الوقت

mess sb about/around to treat sb in a way that is not fair or reasonable, e.g. by changing your plans without telling him/her: *The builders really messed us around. They never turned up when they promised to.* يعامل شخصاً دون مراعاة لشعوره أو ظروفه : "يلخبط" حياة شخص آخر

mess about/around with sth to touch or use sth in a careless way: *It is dangerous to mess about with fireworks.* يلعب أو يعبث بـ

mess sth up 1 to make sth dirty or untidy يوسّخ : "يلخبط"

2 to do sth badly or spoil sth: *I really messed up the last question in the exam.* يفسد : "يلخبط"

messy *adj* (**messier**; **messiest**) **1** dirty or untidy: *a messy room* وسِخ ، غير مرتّب

2 needing a lot of cleaning up: *Painting the ceiling is a messy job.* موسِخ

3 having or causing problems or trouble: *a messy divorce* محفوف بالمشاكل والمزعجات

mess² /mes/ *noun* [C] the room or building where soldiers eat together: *the officers' mess* غرفة طعام الجنود

message /ˈmesɪdʒ/ *noun* **1** [C] a written or spoken piece of information that is passed from one person to another: *Mr Thomas is not here at the moment. Can I take a message?* ○ *Could you give this message to the headmaster, please?* ○ *to get/receive a message from sb* رسالة مكتوبة أو شفوية

2 [sing.] the main idea of a book, speech, etc: *It was a funny film but it also had a serious message.* مغزى : رسالة ، هدف

IDM **get the message** (*informal*) to understand what sb means even if it is not said directly: *He finally got the message and left Dick and Sarah alone together.* يفهم المقصود : يدرك الموقف

▸ **messaging** *noun* [U]: *a multimedia messaging service* ○ *picture messaging* التراسل

ˈ**message board** *noun* [C] a place on a website where a user can write or read messages: *I posted a question on the message board.* لوحة الاعلانات

messenger /ˈmesɪndʒə(r)/ *noun* [C] a person who carries a message رسول ، ساعٍ

Messiah (*also* **messiah**) /məˈsaɪə/ *noun* [C] a person, e.g. Jesus Christ, who is expected to come and save the world المسيح ، المَهدي الموعود

Messrs /ˈmesəz/ (used as the plural of Mr before a list of men's names and before names of business firms): *Messrs Smith, Brown and Robinson* ○ *Messrs T Brown and Co* السادة

messy → MESS¹

metabolism /məˈtæbəlɪzəm/ *noun* [U,sing.] the chemical processes in plants or animals that change food, minerals, etc. into living matter and produce energy أيْض

metal /ˈmetl/ *noun* [C,U] a type of solid mineral substance, e.g. tin, iron, gold, steel, etc: *Aluminium is a non-magnetic metal.* ○ *to recycle scrap metal* ○ *a metal bar* معدن

▸ **metallic** /məˈtælɪk/ *adj* looking like metal or making a noise like one piece of metal hitting another: *a metallic blue car* ○ *harsh metallic sounds* معدني : شبيه بتألّق المعدن : رنّان

metamorphosis /ˌmetəˈmɔːfəsɪs/ *noun* [C] (*pl.* **metamorphoses** /-əsiːz/) (*formal*) a complete change of form (as part of natural development): *the metamorphosis of a tadpole into a frog* تحوّل

metaphor /ˈmetəfə(r)/ *noun* [C,U] a way of describing sth by comparing it to sth else which has the same qualities (but without using the words 'as' or 'like'). For example, if you say sb is

a 'parrot' you are using a metaphor to express the fact that the person just repeats things without thinking. تعبير مجازيّ ، استعارة ؛ المجاز
▶ **metaphorical** /ˌmetəˈfɒrɪkl; *US* -ˈfɔːr-/ *adj*: *a metaphorical expression* مجازيّ
metaphorically /-kli/ *adv* مجازاً ، على سبيل المَجاز

mete /miːt/ *verb*
PHRV **mete sth out (to sb)** (*formal*) to give a punishment, reward, etc. يأمر بعقاب أو مكافأة ؛ يحدِّد نوع (الجزاء)

meteor /ˈmiːtiə(r)/ *noun* [C] a small piece of rock, etc. in space. When a meteor enters the earth's atmosphere it makes a bright line in the night sky نَيْزَك ، شهاب
▶ **meteoric** /ˌmiːtiˈɒrɪk; *US* -ˈɔːr-/ *adj* very fast or successful: *a meteoric rise to fame* سريع جداً ، (نجاح) خاطف للأبصار

meteorite /ˈmiːtiəraɪt/ *noun* [C] a piece of rock from outer space that hits the earth's surface حجر نيزكيّ، رَجْم

meteorology /ˌmiːtiəˈrɒlədʒi/ *noun* [U] the study of the weather and climate علم الأرصاد الجوّية
▶ **meteorological** /ˌmiːtiərəˈlɒdʒɪkl; *US* ˌmiːtiɔːr-/ *adj*: *the Meteorological Office* متعلق بالأرصاد الجوّية
meteorologist /ˌmiːtiəˈrɒlədʒɪst/ *noun* [C] a person who studies the weather المختصّ بالأرصاد الجوّية

meter¹ /ˈmiːtə(r)/ *noun* [C] a piece of equipment that measures the amount of gas, water, electricity, time, etc. you have used: *The man has come to read the gas meter.* ○ *a parking meter* عدّاد
▶ **meter** *verb* [T] to measure sth with a meter يقيس شيئاً بعدّاد

meter² (*US*) = METRE

method /ˈmeθəd/ *noun* [C] a way of doing sth: *What method of payment do you prefer? Cash, cheque or credit card?* ○ *modern methods of teaching languages* طريقة ، أسلوب
▶ **methodical** /məˈθɒdɪkl/ *adj* having or using a well-organized and careful way of doing sth: *Paul is a very methodical worker.* منظَّم ، منهجيّ
methodically /-kli/ *adv* بطريقة منهجية منظَّمة

Methodist /ˈmeθədɪst/ *noun* [C], *adj* (a member) of a Protestant Church that was started by John Wesley in the 18th century أحد أعضاء الطائفة البروتستانتيّة التي أسسها جون وزلي

meticulous /məˈtɪkjələs/ *adj* giving or showing great attention to detail; very careful شديد التدقيق ؛ كثير الاهتمام بالتفاصيل
▶ **meticulously** *adv* بكل دقّة وعناية

ˈme-time *noun* [U] time when a person who is normally very busy relaxes or does sth they enjoy: *Every working mother needs a little me-time.* وقت (استراحة) لنفسي

metre (*US* **meter**) /ˈmiːtə(r)/ *noun* [C] (*abbr* **m**) a measure of length; 100 centimetres: *A metre is about 39 inches.* ○ *What's the record for the 100 metres?* (=the race) متر

metric /ˈmetrɪk/ *adj* using the system of measurement that is based on metres, grams, litres, etc. (the metric system) ➲ Look at **imperial**. متريّ

metropolis /məˈtrɒpəlɪs/ *noun* [C] a very large city, usually the chief city of a country عاصمة ، حاضرة
▶ **metropolitan** /ˌmetrəˈpɒlɪtən/ *adj* عاصميّ ، منسوب إلى العاصمة

mg *abbrev* = MILLIGRAM(S)

miaow /miˈaʊ/ *noun* [C] one of the sounds that a cat makes مواء الهرّة
▶ **miaow** *verb* [I] to make the sound ➲ Look at **purr**. (الهرّة) تموء

mice *pl.* of MOUSE

mickey /ˈmɪki/ *noun*
IDM **take the mickey (out of sb)** (*informal*) to make sb look silly by laughing at them: *Stop taking the mickey! You can't dance any better yourself.* ➲ Look at **tease**. يسخر من ، يستهزئ بِ

microblogging /ˈmaɪkrəʊblɒɡɪŋ/ *noun* [U] the activity of sending regular short messages, photos or videos over the Internet, either to a selected group of people, or so that they can be viewed by anyone, as a means of keeping people informed about your activities and thoughts التدوين المصغَّر

microchip /ˈmaɪkrəʊtʃɪp/ (*also informal* **chip**) *noun* [C] a very small piece of a special material (silicon) that is used inside a computer, etc. to make it work "ميكروتشيب" ، شطفة ميكرويّة

microcosm /ˈmaɪkrəkɒzəm/ *noun* [C] something that is a small example of sth larger: *Our little village is a microcosm of society as a whole.* عالم مصغَّر

microfinance /ˈmaɪkrəʊfaɪnæns/ *noun* [U] a system of providing services such as lending money and saving for people who are too poor to use banks التمويل الصغرى، التمويل الأصغر

micro-organism /ˌmaɪkrəʊ ˈɔːɡənɪzəm/ *noun* [C] a very small living thing that you can only see with a special piece of equipment (a microscope) حي مجهري

microphone /ˈmaɪkrəfəʊn/ (*also informal* **mike**) *noun* [C] a piece of electrical equipment that is used for making sounds louder or for recording them: *Speak into the microphone so that everyone can hear you.* ميكروفون ، مجهِر الصوت

microprocessor /ˌmaɪkrəʊˈprəʊsesə(r)/ *noun* [C] (*computing*) small unit of a computer that contains all the functions of the central processing unit (= the part of the computer that controls all the other parts of the system) معالج ميكرويّ

microscope /ˈmaɪkrəskəʊp/ *noun* [C] a piece of equipment that makes very small objects look large enough for you to be able to see them: *to examine sth under a microscope* مِجْهَر ، ميكروسكوب
▶ **microscopic** /ˌmaɪkrəˈskɒpɪk/ *adj* too small to be seen without a microscope مِجهَري ، لا يرى إلا بالمِجهَر

microwave /ˈmaɪkrəweɪv/ *noun* [C] **1** a short

a b c d e f g h i j k l m n o p q r s t u v w x y z

electric wave that is used for sending radio messages and for cooking food الموجة الصغرى

2 (*also* ˌ**microwave** ˈ**oven**) a type of oven that cooks or heats food very quickly using microwaves فرن "ميكروويف"

mid /mɪd/ *adj* (only *before* a noun) the middle of: *I'm away from mid June.* ○ *the mid 1950s* منتصف

mid- /mɪd/ (in compounds) in the middle of: *mid-morning coffee* ○ *a mid-air collision* منتصف ، وسط

🔑 **midday** /ˌmɪdˈdeɪ/ *noun* [U] twelve o'clock in the middle of the day; noon: *We just have a light snack at midday.* ➲ Look at **midnight**. الظُّهر ، الساعة الثانية عشرة ظهراً

🔑 **middle** /ˈmɪdl/ *noun* **1 the middle** [sing.] the part, point or position that is at about the same distance from the two ends of sth: *An unbroken white line in the middle of the road means you must not overtake.* ○ *Here's a photo of me with my two brothers. I'm the one in the middle.* منتصف ، وسط

Centre and **middle** are often very similar in meaning but centre is used when you mean the exact middle of something: *How do you find the centre of a circle?* ○ *There was a large table in the middle of the room.* When you are talking about a period of time only **middle** may be used: *The baby woke up in the middle of the night.* ○ *the middle of July*

2 [C] (*informal*) your waist: *I want to lose weight around my middle.* خَصْر

▸ **middle** *adj* (only *before* a noun) in the middle: *I wear my mother's ring on my middle finger.* ○ *There are three houses in a row and ours is the middle one.* أوسط

ˌ**middle** ˈ**age** *noun* [U] the time when you are about 40 to 60 years old: *in late middle age* سنّ الكهولة

ˌ**middle-**ˈ**aged** *adj* of or in middle age: *middle-aged people* كهْل ، في منتصف حياته

the ˌ**Middle** ˈ**Ages** *noun* [plural] the period of European history from about AD1100 to AD1500 العصور الوسطى

ˌ**middle** ˈ**class** *noun* [C] the group of people in society who are between the working class and the upper class. Middle-class people include business people, managers, teachers, doctors, etc: *Most of the people who work here are middle class.* ○ *a comfortable middle-class lifestyle* الطبقة المتوسّطة

the ˌ**Middle** ˈ**East** *noun* [sing.] the group of countries that are situated at the point where Europe, Africa and Asia meet الشّرق الأوسط

middleman /ˈmɪdlmæn/ *noun* [C] (*pl.* **middlemen** /-men/) a person who buys sth from a producer or manufacturer and then sells it to sb else for more money وسيط ، سمسار

ˌ**middle** ˈ**name** *noun* [C] the second of two Christian or given names الاسم الثاني (عند معظم الأوربيّين)

ˈ**middle school** *noun* [C] (*Brit*) a school for children aged between nine and thirteen مدرسة متوسّطة

midfield /ˌmɪdˈfiːld/ *noun* [U,C,sing.] the central part of a sports field; the group of players in this position: *He plays (in) midfield.* ○ *The team's midfield looks strong.* ○ *a midfield player* وسط الملعب أو اللاعبون فيه

midge /mɪdʒ/ *noun* [C] a very small flying insect like a mosquito that can bite people ➲ Look at **gnat**. برْغشة ، ذبابة صغيرة

midget /ˈmɪdʒɪt/ *noun* [C] a very small person قزم

Midlands /ˈmɪdləndz/ *noun* [sing., with sing. or pl. verb] **the Midlands** the central part of England. The Midlands contains the industrial towns of Birmingham, Nottingham, Coventry, etc. المقاطعات الوسطى في إنكلترا

🔑 **midnight** /ˈmɪdnaɪt/ *noun* [U] twelve o'clock at night: *They left the party at midnight.* ○ *The clock struck midnight.* ➲ Look at **midday**. منتصف الليل ، الساعة الثانية عشرة ليلاً

midriff /ˈmɪdrɪf/ *noun* [C] the part of your body between your chest and your waist الجزء الواقع بين الصدر والخصر

midst /mɪdst/ *noun* [U] (after a preposition) the middle part or position: *They realized with a shock that there was an enemy in their midst* (= among them). وسط ، قلب (المنظمة)

midsummer /ˌmɪdˈsʌmə(r)/ *noun* [U] the time around the middle of summer: *a beautiful midsummer/midsummer's evening* منتصف الصيف

midway /ˌmɪdˈweɪ/ *adj, adv* **midway (between sth and sth)** in the middle or halfway (between sth and sth): *Our cottage is midway between Alston and Penrith.* في المنتصف

midweek /ˌmɪdˈwiːk/ *noun* [U] the middle of the week (= Tuesday, Wednesday and Thursday) منتصف الأسبوع

▸ **midweek** *adv*: *If you travel midweek it will be less crowded.* في منتصف الأسبوع

the Midwest /ˌmɪdˈwest/ *noun* [sing.] the northern central part of the USA الجزء الشماليّ المركزيّ في الولايات المتّحدة الامريكيّة

midwife /ˈmɪdwaɪf/ *noun* [C] (*pl.* **midwives** /-waɪvz/) a person who has been trained to help women give birth to babies قابلة ، داية

▸ **midwifery** /ˈmɪdwɪfəri; *US* -waɪf-/ *noun* [U] the work of a midwife القبالة

midwinter /ˌmɪdˈwɪntə(r)/ *noun* [U] the time around the middle of winter منتصف الشتاء

🔑 **might**[1] /maɪt/ *modal verb* (*negative* **might not**; *short form* **mightn't** /ˈmaɪtnt/) **1** (used as the past form of 'may' when you report what sb has said): *He said he might be late* (= his words were, 'I may be late'). صيغة الماضي لفعل may

2 (used for saying that sth is possible): *'Where's William?' 'He might be upstairs.'* ○ *We might be going to Spain on holiday this year.* ○ *She might*

not come if she's very busy. ○ *If I'd have known the film was about Wales, I might have gone to see it* (= but I didn't know, so I didn't go).
ربّما ، من المحتمل

3 (used in formal British English to ask for sth very politely): *I wonder if I might go home half an hour early today?* ○ *Might I say something?*
صيغة مؤدّبة للسؤال: هل من الممكن...

4 (used in formal British English to suggest sth politely): *Might I suggest that we discuss this in private?* ○ *If you need more information, you might try phoning our customer service department.*
صيغة مؤدّبة لتقديم اقتراح: هل من الممكن...

IDM **may/might as well (do sth)** → WELL³

you, etc. might do sth (used when you are angry with sb) you should: *You might tell me if you're going to be late.* ○ *They might at least have phoned if they're not coming.*
كان عليك أن.... كان من اللازم أن..

I might have known (used for saying that you are not surprised that sth has happened): *I might have known he wouldn't help.*
لا أستغرب أن.... كنت أتوقع (ذلك)

might² /maɪt/ *noun* [U] (*formal*) great strength or power: *We pushed with all our might, but the rock did not move.* قوّة ، عظمة ، جبروت

mighty /ˈmaɪti/ *adj* (**mightier**; **mightiest**) very strong or powerful قويّ ، عظيم ، جبّار

▸ **mighty** *adv* (*US informal*) very: *That's mighty kind of you.* جداً ، للغاية

migraine /ˈmiːɡreɪn; *US* ˈmaɪɡreɪn/ *noun* [C,U] a very bad headache that makes you feel sick
الشقيقة ، صداع نصفيّ

migrate /maɪˈɡreɪt; *US* ˈmaɪɡreɪt/ *verb* [I] **1** (used about animals and birds) to travel from one part of the world to another at the same time every year يهاجر

2 to move from one place to go and live and work in another: *Many of the poorer people were forced to migrate to the cities to look for work.*
➲ Look at **emigrate**. يهاجر ، ينزح

▸ **migrant** /ˈmaɪɡrənt/ *noun* [C] a person who goes from place to place in search of work: *migrant workers* نازح لمكان آخر طلباً للعمل

migration /maɪˈɡreɪʃn/ *noun* [C,U]: *the annual migration to the south* هجرة ، نزوح

mike /maɪk/ *noun* [C] (*informal*) = MICROPHONE

milage = MILEAGE

🔑**mild** /maɪld/ *adj* **1** not hard, strong or severe: *a mild soap that is gentle to your skin* ○ *a mild winter* ○ *a mild punishment* لطيف ، معتدل ، خفيف

2 kind and gentle: *He's a very mild man – you never see him get angry.* لطيف ، وديع ، سهل المعشر

3 (used about food) not having a strong taste: *mild cheese* (طعام) غير حارّ ، معتدل التوابل : خفيف المذاق

▸ **mildly** *adv* **1** in a mild way
قليلاً ، إلى حدّ ما ، بشكل خفيف

2 not very; slightly: *I found the talk mildly interesting.* قليلاً ، إلى حدّ ما

mildness *noun* [U] وداعة ، رقّة : هدوء

mildew /ˈmɪldjuː; *US* -duː/ *noun* [U] a tiny white fungus that grows on plants, leather, food, etc. in warm damp conditions: *to spray roses against mildew* فطر العفونة

🔑**mile** /maɪl/ *noun* [C] **1** a measure of length; 1.6 kilometres. There are 1 760 yards in a mile: *The nearest beach is seven miles away.* ○ *It's a seven-mile drive to the sea.* ○ *He ran the mile in less than four minutes.* ○ *My car does 35 miles to the gallon.* ○ *From the top of the hill you can see for miles and miles.* ميل

2 (*also* **miles**) a lot: *to miss a target by a mile* ○ *I'm feeling miles better this morning.*
قدر كبير ؛ مسافة بعيدة

3 miles a long way: *How much further is it? We've walked miles already.* مسافة طويلة

mileage (*also* **milage**) /ˈmaɪlɪdʒ/ *noun* **1** [C,U] the distance that has been travelled (measured in miles): *The car is five years old but it has a low mileage.* المسافة المقطوعة (بالأميال)

2 [U] (*informal*) the amount of use or benefit you get from sth
مقدار الفائدة من شيء ما ؛ مقدار صلاحيته للاستعمال

milestone /ˈmaɪlstəʊn/ *noun* [C] **1** a stone at the side of the road that shows how far it is to the next town
صُوّة ، حجر على حافة الطريق يبيّن المسافة الى مدينة ما

2 a very important event حَدَث هامّ

militant /ˈmɪlɪtənt/ *adj* using or willing to use force or strong pressure to get what you want: *The workers were in a very militant mood.*
قتاليّ ، نضاليّ

▸ **militancy** /-ənsi/ *noun* [U] كفاح ، نضال ؛ عنف

militant *noun* [C] a militant person
مكافح ، مُناضل

🔑**military** /ˈmɪlətri; *US* -teri/ *adj* (only *before* a noun) of or for soldiers, the army, navy, etc: *Do you have military service in your country?* ○ *to take military action* عسكري ، حربي

militia /məˈlɪʃə/ *noun* [C, with sing. or pl. verb] a group of people who are not regular soldiers but who have had military training
"المليشيا" ، المقاومة الشعبيّة

🔑**milk** /mɪlk/ *noun* [U] **1** a white liquid that is produced by women and animals to feed their babies. People drink cows', goats', etc. milk and use it to make butter and cheese: *skimmed, powdered, long-life, low-fat, etc. milk* ○ *Don't use that milk – it's gone sour.* ○ *I don't take milk in my coffee, thank you.* ○ *a bottle of milk* ○ *a milk bottle*
حليب ، لَبَن

2 the juice of some plants or trees that looks like milk: *coconut milk* لَبَن

▸ **milk** *verb* **1** [I,T] to take milk from a cow, goat, etc. يحلب

2 [T] (*figurative*) to get as much money, information, etc. as you can from sb/sth: *The colonists milked the country of its natural resources.*
يستنزف ، يستغلّ إلى أقصى حدّ

ˌ**milk ˈchocolate** *noun* [U] chocolate that is made with milk شوكولا على حليب

milkman /ˈmɪlkmən/ *noun* [C] (*pl.* **milkmen**

/-mən/) a person who delivers milk to people's houses الحلاّب ، بائع الحليب

milkshake /ˈmɪlkʃeɪk/ *noun* [C,U] a drink made of milk, flavouring and sometimes ice cream حليب مخفوق مع بعض الفاكهة أو المنكّهات

milky /ˈmɪlki/ *adj* (**milkier**; **milkiest**) **1** made with milk: *a hot milky drink* معَدّ من الحليب/اللّبن
2 of a pale white colour بِلَوْن الحليب/اللّبن

mill¹ /mɪl/ *noun* [C] **1** a building that contains a large machine that is used for grinding grain into flour: *a windmill* ○ *a water mill* طاحونة
2 a kitchen tool that is used for grinding sth into powder: *a pepper mill* طاحونة ، مطحنة
3 a factory that is used for making certain kinds of material: *a paper mill* ○ *a steel mill* معمل ، مصنع

mill² /mɪl/ *verb* [T] to grind sth in a mill يطحن
PHR V **mill about/around** (*informal*) (used about a large number of people or animals) to move around in one place with no real purpose (حشد من الناس) يحومون أو يدورون هنا وهناك دون هدف معيّن

millennium /mɪˈleniəm/ *noun* [C] (*pl.* **millennia** /-niə-/ or **millenniums**) a period of 1 000 years, especially as calculated before or after the birth of Christ ألف عام، الذكرى الألفية

millet /ˈmɪlɪt/ *noun* [U] grass-like plant whose seeds are used as food for people and birds دخن ، جاوَرس ، ثُمام

milligram (*also* **milligramme**) /ˈmɪligræm/ *noun* [C] (*abbr* **mg**) a measure of weight. There are 1 000 milligrams in a gram. ميليغرام

millilitre (*US* **milliliter**) /ˈmɪliliːtə(r)/ *noun* [C] (*abbr* **ml**) a measure of liquid. There are 1 000 millilitres in a litre. ميليلتر

millimetre (*US* **millimeter**) /ˈmɪlimiːtə(r)/ *noun* [C] (*abbr* **mm**) a measure of length. There are 1 000 millimetres in a metre. ميليمتر

millinery /ˈmɪlɪnəri; *US* -neri/ *noun* [U] making or selling women's hats صناعة أو بيع القبّعات النسائيّة

million /ˈmɪljən/ *number* 1 000 000: *Nearly 60 million people live in Britain.* ○ *Millions are at risk from the disease.* ○ *'How much does it cost?' 'Half a million.'* مليون

Notice that you use million without **s** when you are talking about more than one million: *six million pounds*

▶ **millionth** /ˈmɪljənθ/ *det* 1 000 000th: *the firm's millionth customer* (الزبون) المليون
millionth *noun* [C] one of a million equal parts of sth: *a millionth of a second* جزء من مليون

millionaire /ˌmɪljəˈneə(r)/ *noun* [C] a person who has a million pounds, dollars, etc.; a very rich person مليونير

milometer (*also* **mileometer**) /maɪˈlɒmɪtə(r)/ (*US* **odometer**) *noun* [C] a piece of equipment that measures the distance you have travelled عدّاد المسافة المقطوعة

mime /maɪm/ *noun* [C,U] acting or telling a story without speaking, by using your hands, body and the expressions on your face تمثيل إيمائيّ
▶ **mime** *verb* [I,T] to act or express sth using mime يمثّل تمثيلاً إيمائياً؛ يعبِّر بالإشارات فقط

mimic /ˈmɪmɪk/ *verb* [T] (*pres part* **mimicking**; *pt, pp* **mimicked**) to copy sb's behaviour in an amusing way يُقلّد شخصاً (للتسلية)
▶ **mimic** *noun* [C] a person who can mimic other people شخص يتقن تقليد الآخرين (للتسلية)

min. *abbrev* **1** = MINUTE(S): *fastest time: 6 min.*
2 = MINIMUM: *min. temp 2°*

minaret /ˌmɪnəˈret/ *noun* [C] a tall thin tower, usually forming part of a mosque, from which Muslims are called to prayer مئذنة

mince /mɪns/ *verb* [T] to cut meat into very small pieces using a special machine: *a pound of minced beef* يَفرم (اللحم)
▶ **mince** (*Brit*) (*US* **hamburger**; **ground beef**) *noun* [U] meat that has been cut into very small pieces with a special machine لحم مفروم

mincemeat /ˈmɪnsmiːt/ *noun* [U] a mixture of dried fruit, nuts, sugar, etc. خليط من السكّر والفاكهة المجفّفة المفرومة

ˌmince ˈpie *noun* [C] a small round cake with a mixture of dried fruit, sugar, etc. (mincemeat) inside, traditionally eaten in Britain at Christmas time فطيرة صغيرة محشوة بالفاكهة المجفّفة والسكّر

mind¹ /maɪnd/ *noun* [C,U] the part of your brain that thinks and remembers; your thoughts and intelligence: *He has a brilliant mind.* ○ *Not everybody has the right sort of mind for this work.* عقل ، ذهن
IDM **be out of your mind** (*informal*) to be crazy or mad: *He must be out of his mind to give up a good job like that.* مجنون ، معتوه
bear/keep sb/sth in mind to remember sb/sth: *We'll bear/keep your suggestion in mind for the future.* يتذكّر ، يبقي في ذهنه
change your mind → CHANGE¹
cross your mind → CROSS²
ease sb's mind → EASE²
frame of mind → FRAME¹
have/keep an open mind → OPEN¹
keep your mind on sth to continue to pay attention to sth: *Stop talking and try to keep your mind on your work!* يركز ، ينتبه
make up your mind to decide: *I can't make up my mind which sweater to buy.* يقرر
on your mind worrying you: *Don't bother her with that. She's got enough on her mind already.* مشاكل ، أشياء مقلقة
put/set your/sb's mind at rest to make you/sb stop worrying: *The results of the blood test set his mind at rest.* يطمئِن
slip your mind → SLIP¹
state of mind → STATE¹
take your/sb's mind off sth to help you/sb not to think or worry about sth ينسي ، يسلي

mind² /maɪnd/ *verb* **1** [I,T] (especially in questions, answers, and negative sentences) to feel annoyed, unhappy or uncomfortable: *'Do you* *mind if I smoke?' 'No, not at all.'* ○ *I'm sure Simon won't mind if you don't invite him.* ○ *We've got four children so I hope you won't mind about the mess!* ○ *I don't mind what you do – it's your decision.* ○ *Do you mind having to travel so far to work every day?* ○ *Are you sure your parents won't mind me coming?* ○ *'Would you like tea or coffee?' 'I don't mind.'* (= I'm happy to have either) ○ *I wouldn't mind a holiday in the sun this year!* (= I would like it.) ينزعج : يعترض: يهتمّ

2 [T] (used in a question as a polite way of asking sb to do sth) could you...?: *Would you mind closing the window for me?* ○ *Do you mind driving? I'm feeling rather tired.* هل من الممكن

3 [T] (used as a command) be careful of/about...: *It's a very low doorway so mind your head.* ○ *Mind that step!* ○ *Mind you don't slip on the ice.* احذر!، انتبه إلى

4 [T] to look after or watch sb/sth for a short time: *Could you mind my bag while I go and get us some drinks?* يرعى، ينتبه إلى

IDM **mind you** (used for attracting attention to a point you are making or for giving more information): *Paul seems very tired. Mind you, he has been working very hard recently.* لكن لا تنس...

mind your own business to pay attention to your own affairs, not other people's: *Stop telling me what to do and mind your own business!* لا تتدخل فيما لا يعنيك!

never mind don't worry; it doesn't matter: *'I forgot to post your letter.' 'Never mind, I'll do it later.'* ○ *Never mind about the cost – just enjoy yourself!* "معليش"، لا يهمك!، لا تقلق

PHR V **Mind out** (*informal*) Get out of the way!: *Mind out! There's a bicycle coming.* ابعد عن الطريق!، "حاسب"!، "اوعى"!

▸ **minder** *noun* [C] (especially in compounds) a person whose job is to look after sb/sth: *My son goes to a childminder so that I can work part-time.* راعٍ، مشرف على، حارس

mind-boggling /ˈmaɪnd bɒɡlɪŋ/ *adj* (*informal*) difficult to imagine, understand or believe لا يتصوره العقل

-minded /ˈmaɪndɪd/ *adj* **1** (in compounds) having the type of mind mentioned: *a strong-minded person* ذو عقلٍ...(مستقلّ مثلاً)

2 (in compounds) interested in the thing mentioned: *money-minded* مهتم بـ....(النقود مثلاً)

mindless /ˈmaɪndləs/ *adj* not having or not needing thought or intelligence: *mindless violence* ○ *mindless factory work* أحمق ، لا مبرّر له : (عمل) ميكانيكي لا يتطلّب تفكيراً

⚷ **mine**[1] /maɪn/ *pron* of or belonging to me: *'Whose is this jacket?' 'It's mine.'* ○ *Don't take your car – you can come in mine.* ○ *May I introduce a friend of mine?* (= one of my friends) ➲ Look at **my**. ضمير بمعنى: لي، ملكي، خاصتي

⚷ **mine**[2] /maɪn/ *noun* [C] **1** a hole, or system of holes and passages, that people dig under the ground in order to obtain coal, tin, gold, etc: *a coal mine* منجم

2 a bomb that is hidden under the ground or under water لغم

mine[3] /maɪn/ *verb* **1** [I,T] to dig in the ground for coal, gold, etc.; to get coal, etc. by digging: *Diamonds are mined in South Africa.* ➲ Look at **mining.** يحفر منجماً : يعدّن ، يستخرج المعادن

2 [T] to put hidden mines[2] (2) in an area of land or sea يزرع الألغام

minefield /ˈmaɪnfiːld/ *noun* [C] **1** an area of land or sea where mines[2] (2) have been hidden حقل ألغام

2 a situation that is full of hidden dangers or difficulties وضع متفجر ، وضع محفوف بالمخاطر

miner /ˈmaɪnə(r)/ *noun* [C] a person whose job is to work in a mine to get coal, etc. عامل منجم

⚷ **mineral** /ˈmɪnərəl/ *noun* [C] a natural substance such as coal, salt, oil, etc., especially one that is dug out of the ground for people to use: *a country rich in minerals* معدن

ˈ**mineral water** *noun* [U] water that comes directly from the ground, contains minerals and is thought to be good for your health مياه معدنيّة

mingle /ˈmɪŋɡl/ *verb* [I,T] to mix with another thing or with other people: *The colours slowly mingled together to make a muddy brown.* ○ *His excitement was mingled with fear.* يختلط: يخلط

mini- /ˈmɪni/ (in compounds) very small: *a miniskirt* ○ *minigolf* صغير جداً

miniature /ˈmɪnətʃə(r); *US* ˈmɪnɪətʃʊər/ *noun* [C] a small copy of sth which is much larger صورة مصغّرة جداً

IDM **in miniature** in a very small form في صورة مصغّرة جداً

minibus /ˈmɪnibʌs/ *noun* [C] (*especially Brit*) a small bus, usually for no more than 12 people اوتوبيس أو باص صغير

minimal /ˈmɪnɪməl/ *adj* very small in amount or level: *The project has had minimal support.* ضئيل ، أقلّ ما يمكن

minimize (*also* **minimise**) /ˈmɪnɪmaɪz/ *verb* [T] **1** to make sth as small as possible (in amount or level): *We shall try to minimize the risks to the public.* ❶ The opposite is **maximize**. يقلّل إلى الحدّ الأدنى

2 to make sth small on a computer screen يصغّر

⚷ **minimum** /ˈmɪnɪməm/ *noun* [sing.] the smallest amount or level that is possible or allowed: *I need a minimum of seven hours' sleep.* ○ *The minimum he will accept is £15 000 a year.* ○ *We will try and keep the cost of the tickets to a minimum.* ❶ The opposite is **maximum**. الحدّ الأدنى

▸ **minimum** *adj* (only *before* a noun) the smallest possible or allowed: *What's the minimum age for leaving school in Britain?* ❶ The opposite is **maximum**. أدنى، أقلّ

mining /ˈmaɪnɪŋ/ *noun* [U] (often in compounds) the process or industry of getting coal, metals, salt, etc. out of the ground by digging: *tin mining* ○ *a mining town* صناعة التعدين ، استخراج المعادن

⚷ **minister** /ˈmɪnɪstə(r)/ *noun* [C] **1** (*US* **secre-**

tary) a member of the government, often the head of a government department: *the Minister of Trade and Industry* ➲ Look at **Prime Minister** and **Cabinet Minister**. وزير

2 a priest, especially in a Protestant church ➲ Look at **vicar**. قسيس في الكنيسة البروتستانتية

ministerial /ˌmɪnɪˈstɪəriəl/ *adj* of a government minister or department: *a ministerial decision* وزاري

ministry /ˈmɪnɪstri/ *noun* (*pl.* **ministries**) **1** (*also* **department**) [C] a division of the government responsible for a particular subject: *the Ministry of Defence* ❶ **Department** is the only word used in US English. وزارة

2 the ministry [sing.] the profession of being a priest (in Protestant Churches): *to enter the ministry* (= to become a priest) مهنة القسيس

minivan /ˈmɪnɪvæn/ = PEOPLE CARRIER

mink /mɪŋk/ *noun* [C] a small wild animal whose fur is used for expensive coats: *a mink coat* المنك: حيوان يشبه ابن عرس

minor /ˈmaɪnə(r)/ *adj* **1** not very big, serious or important (when compared with others): *It's only a minor problem. Don't worry.* ○ *She's gone into hospital for a minor operation.* ❶ The opposite is **major**. ضئيل ، صغير ، ثانوي

2 of one of the two types of key¹(2) in which music is usually written: *a symphony in F minor* (في الموسيقى) السلّم الثانوي

▸ **minor** *noun* [C] a person who is not legally an adult ❶ In Britain you are a minor until you are eighteen. القاصِر

minority /maɪˈnɒrəti; *US* -ˈnɔːr-/ *noun* [C] (*pl.* **minorities**) **1** [usually sing., with sing. or pl. verb] the smaller number or part of a group; less than half: *Most women continue to work when they are married. Only a minority stays/stay at home.* ○ *a minority interest* (= of only a small number of people) ❶ The opposite is **majority**. الأقليّة

2 a group of people who are of a different race or religion to most of the people in the community or country where they live: *Schools in Britain need to do more to help children of ethnic minorities.* أقليّة (دينيّة مثلاً)

IDM **be in a/the minority** to be the smaller of two groups: *We take both boys and girls, but girls are in the minority.* ➲ Look at **be in the/a majority**. (من) الأقليّة

mint¹ /mɪnt/ *noun* **1** [U] a small plant (a herb) whose leaves are used for giving a flavour to food, drinks, toothpaste, etc: *lamb with mint sauce* ○ *mint chocolate* النَعنَع أو النعناع

2 [C] a sweet with a strong fresh flavour ❶ Another word is a **peppermint**. "سكر على نعنع"، حلوى منكّهة بالنعناع

▸ **minty** /ˈmɪnti/ *adj* tasting of mint مُنكّه بالنعناع ؛ طعمه نعناع

mint² /mɪnt/ *noun* [sing.] a place where coins and notes are made by the government دار سكّ النقود

▸ **mint** *verb* [T] يسكّ أو يضرب نقوداً

minus /ˈmaɪnəs/ *prep* **1** less; subtract; take away: *Six minus two is four.* ❶ The opposite is **plus**. ناقِص

2 (used about a number) below zero: *The temperature will fall to minus 10.* ناقص ، تحت الصِّفر

3 (*informal*) without: *Are you minus your husband this evening?* بِدون

▸ **minus** *adj* (used with grades given for school work) slightly lower than: *I got A minus (A–) for my essay.* ➲ Look at **plus**. ناقص

minus (*also* **minus sign**) *noun* [C] the sign (-) which is used in mathematics to show that a number is below zero or that you should subtract the second number from the first إشارة السالب في الرياضيّات

minuscule /ˈmɪnəskjuːl/ *adj* very small; tiny صغير أو دقيق جداً

minute¹ /ˈmɪnɪt/ *noun* **1** [C] one of the 60 parts that make up one hour; 60 seconds: *It's five minutes to/past nine.* ○ *He telephoned ten minutes ago.* ○ *Hurry up! The plane leaves in twenty minutes!* ○ *The programme lasts for about fifty minutes.* دقيقة

2 [sing.] a very short time; a moment: *Wait a minute! You've forgotten your notes.* ○ *Have you got a minute to spare? I want to talk to you.* لحظة ، دقيقة

3 the minutes [plural] a written record of what is said and decided at a meeting: *to take the minutes* (= to write them down) وقائع جلسة

IDM **(at) any minute/moment (now)** (*informal*) very soon: *The plane will be landing any minute now.* قريباً جداً ، بعد دقائق

in a minute very soon: *I think it's going to rain in a minute.* قريباً جداً، بعد دقائق

just a minute (*informal*) (used for stopping a person, pausing to think, etc.) to wait for a short time: *Just a minute. Is that your book or mine?* لحظة من فضلك!

the last minute/moment → LAST¹

the minute/moment (that) as soon as: *I'll tell him you rang the minute (that) he gets here.* حالما

up to the minute (*informal*) recent; not old: *For up to the minute information on flight times, phone the following number...* آخر (الأنباء)، أحدث (المعلومات)

minute² /maɪˈnjuːt; *US* -ˈnuːt/ *adj* (**minuter**; **minutest**) **1** very small; tiny: *I couldn't read his writing. It was minute!* صغير أو دقيق جداً

2 very exact or accurate: *She was able to describe the man in minute detail.* دقيق ، بالغ الدقّة

miracle /ˈmɪrəkl/ *noun* [C] a wonderful and extraordinary event that is impossible to explain and that is thought to be caused by God or a god: *Christ performed many miracles, even bringing dead people back to life.* ○ *She's doing her best but nobody can work miracles!* ○ *It will be a miracle if he passes his driving test.* معجزة

▸ **miraculous** /mɪˈrækjələs/ *adj* impossible to explain or understand; extraordinary معجز، خارق للطبيعة

miraculously *adv* بأعجوبة

mirage /ˈmɪrɑːʒ; mɪˈrɑːʒ/ *noun* [C] something

that you think you see in very hot weather but which does not really exist, especially water in a desert سَراب

mirror /ˈmɪrə(r)/ *noun* [C] a piece of special glass that you can look into in order to see yourself or what is behind you: *That dress looks lovely on you. Have a look in the mirror.* ○ *Use your rear mirror before you overtake.* ❶ A mirror **reflects** images. What you see in a mirror is a **reflection.** مرآة
▸ **mirror** *verb* [T] to reflect sth as if in a mirror: *The trees were mirrored in the lake.* يعكس

mirth /mɜːθ/ *noun* [U] (*formal*) amusement or laughter مرح ، فرح، ضحك

misapprehension /ˌmɪsæprɪˈhenʃn/ *noun*
IDM **to be under a/the misapprehension** (*formal*) to have a wrong idea or impression يسيء الفهم

misbehave /ˌmɪsbɪˈheɪv/ *verb* [I] to behave badly يسيء التصرّف ، يسيء السلوك
▸ **misbehaviour** (*US* **misbehavior**) /ˌmɪsbɪˈheɪvjə(r)/ *noun* [U] bad behaviour سوء سلوك

misc. *abbrev* = MISCELLANEOUS

miscalculate /ˌmɪsˈkælkjuleɪt/ *verb* [I,T] to make a mistake in calculating or estimating (a situation or an amount, distance, etc.): *The driver miscalculated the speed at which the other car was travelling.* يخطئ في الحساب ، يخطئ في التقدير
▸ **miscalculation** /ˌmɪskælkjuˈleɪʃn/ *noun* [C,U] سوء حساب ، سوء تقدير

miscarriage /ˈmɪskærɪdʒ/ *noun* [C,U] giving birth to a baby before it is ready to be born, with the result that it cannot live: *She's had several miscarriages.* ➲ Look at **abortion.** إجهاض

miscarry /ˌmɪsˈkæri/ *verb* [I] (*pres part* **miscarrying**; *3rd pers sing pres* **miscarries**; *pt, pp* **miscarried**) **1** to give birth to a baby before it is ready to be born, with the result that it cannot live تجهض
2 (used about a plan, idea, etc.) to fail يخفق ، يفشل

miscellaneous /ˌmɪsəˈleɪniəs/ *adj* of various, different types; mixed: *a box of miscellaneous items for sale* متنوّع ، مختلف

mischief /ˈmɪstʃɪf/ *noun* [U] bad behaviour (usually of children) that is not very serious: *Why are the children so quiet? Are they up to mischief again?* ○ *You can go and see your friends but keep out of mischief this time.* أذى، شرّ

mischievous /ˈmɪstʃɪvəs/ *adj* (usually used about children) fond of having fun in a rather naughty way محبّ للّعب والأذى ، (ولد) شيطان
▸ **mischievously** *adv* بخبث

misconception /ˌmɪskənˈsepʃn/ *noun* [C] a wrong idea or understanding of sth: *It is a popular misconception* (= many people wrongly believe) *that people need meat to be healthy.* فكرة خاطئة ، فهم خاطئ

misconduct /ˌmɪsˈkɒndʌkt/ *noun* [U] (*formal*) bad behaviour, especially by a professional person سوء سلوك

misdemeanour (*US* **misdemeanor**) /ˌmɪsdɪˈmiːnə(r)/ *noun* [C] something slightly bad or wrong that a person does; a minor crime جنحة

miser /ˈmaɪzə(r)/ *noun* [C] a person who loves having a lot of money but hates spending any البخيل

miserable /ˈmɪzrəbl/ *adj* **1** very unhappy; sad: *Oh dear, you look miserable. What's wrong?* ○ *It's a miserable story. Are you sure you want to hear it?* تعيس ، حزين
2 unpleasant (because difficult or uncomfortable): *It's miserable working in such an unfriendly atmosphere.* مزعج
3 too small or of bad quality: *I was offered a miserable salary so I didn't take the job.* ضئيل ، (مبلغ) حقير
▸ **miserably** /-əbli/ *adv* in a miserable way: *I stared miserably out of the window.* ○ *We failed miserably* (= in a disappointing way) *to achieve our aim.* بِشقاء ؛ بشكل مخيب للآمال

misery /ˈmɪzəri/ *noun* [C,U] (*pl.* **miseries**) great unhappiness or lack of comfort; suffering: *There was an expression of pain and misery on his face.* ○ *The period after the war was a time of economic and social misery.* ○ *the miseries of war* تعاسة ، شقاء، معاناة

misfire /ˌmɪsˈfaɪə(r)/ *verb* [I] to fail to have the right result or effect: *The plan misfired.* يُخفق ، يفشل

misfit /ˈmɪsfɪt/ *noun* [C] a person who is or feels different from other people: *He's always lived in a town before so he seems a bit of a misfit in the village.* شخص لا يتكيّف مع مجتمعه

misfortune /ˌmɪsˈfɔːtʃuːn/ *noun* [C,U] (an event, accident, etc. that brings) bad luck or disaster: *Various misfortunes had made her sad and bitter.* ○ *I hope I don't ever have the misfortune to meet him again.* سوء حظ؛ بَليّة؛ نَحْس

misgiving /ˌmɪsˈɡɪvɪŋ/ *noun* [C, U] a feeling of doubt, worry or suspicion: *I had serious misgivings about leaving him on his own in that condition.* شعور بالقلق، ريبة ؛ هاجس

misguided /ˌmɪsˈɡaɪdɪd/ *adj* **1** (used about a person) acting in a way that is not sensible مخطئ؛ مضلّل؛ غير معقول
2 (used about behaviour or opinions) based on wrong ideas or information مُضلّل ؛ مَبنيّ على أفكار خاطئة

mishap /ˈmɪshæp/ *noun* [C,U] an unlucky accident or bad luck that does not have serious results: *to have a slight mishap* حادثة بسيطة ؛ حظّ عاثر

misinform /ˌmɪsɪnˈfɔːm/ *verb* [T] to give sb the wrong information: *It seems that the public have been misinformed about the cause of the disease.* يعطي معلومات خاطئة أو مضلّلة

misinterpret /ˌmɪsɪnˈtɜːprɪt/ *verb* [T] to understand sth wrongly يسيء الفهم
▸ **misinterpretation** /ˌmɪsɪntɜːprɪˈteɪʃn/ *noun*

[C,U] understanding sth in the wrong way: *Parts of the speech were open to misinterpretation* (= easy to misunderstand). سوء الفهم

misjudge /ˌmɪs'dʒʌdʒ/ *verb* [T] to form a wrong opinion of sb/sth or to estimate sth wrongly يخطئ في التقدير ، يخطئ في الحكم على...
▸ **misjudgement** (*also* **misjudgment**) *noun* [C,U] (the forming of) a wrong opinion or idea سوء التقدير؛ حكم خاطئ

mislay /ˌmɪs'leɪ/ *verb* [T] (*pres part* **mislaying**; *3rd pers sing pres* **mislays**; *pt, pp* **mislaid** /-'leɪd/) to lose sth, usually for a short time because you cannot remember where you left it: *I'm afraid I've mislaid my car keys.* يُضيع شيئاً موقتاً، ينسى أين وضع شيئاً ما

mislead /ˌmɪs'li:d/ *verb* [T] (*pt, pp* **misled** /-'led/) to make sb have the wrong idea or opinion: *Don't be misled by his smile – he's not very friendly really.* يضلِّل
▸ **misleading** *adj* giving a wrong idea or impression: *a misleading advertisement* مضلِّل

mismanage /ˌmɪs'mænɪdʒ/ *verb* [T] to manage or organize sth badly or without skill يسيء الإدارة ، يسيء معالجة الأمور
▸ **mismanagement** *noun* [U] سوء إدارة

misplaced /ˌmɪs'pleɪst/ *adj* given to sb/sth that does not deserve to have it: *misplaced loyalty* (مديح) في غير محلّه ، غير مستحَق

misprint /'mɪsprɪnt/ *noun* [C] a mistake in printing خطأ مطبعي

mispronounce /ˌmɪsprə'naʊns/ *verb* [T] to pronounce a word or letter wrongly: *Be careful not to mispronounce 'live' as 'leave'.* يخطئ في اللفظ
▸ **mispronunciation** /ˌmɪsprəˌnʌnsi'eɪʃn/ *noun* [C,U] سوء اللفظ

misread /ˌmɪs'ri:d/ *verb* [T] (*pt, pp* **misread** /-'red/) to read or understand sth wrongly: *He misread my silence as a refusal.* ○ *I misread the bus timetable and missed the last bus home.* يخطئ في القراءة ؛ يخطئ في الفهم

misrepresent /ˌmɪsˌreprɪ'zent/ *verb* [T] (usually passive) to give a wrong description of sb/sth يعطي فكرة خاطئة عن ؛ يشوِّه ، يسيء تمثيل (بلاده)
▸ **misrepresentation** /ˌmɪsˌreprɪzen'teɪʃn/ *noun* [C,U] (a) wrong description: *That's a misrepresentation of what was actually said.* وصف خاطئ ، تحريف

⚷ **Miss** /mɪs/ (used as a title before the name of a girl or unmarried woman): *'Is there a Miss Dean living here?' the postman asked.* ○ *'Dear Miss Harris,' the letter began.* الآنسة

⚷ **miss**[1] /mɪs/ *verb* **1** [T] to not see, hear, understand, etc. sb/sth: *The house is on the corner so you can't miss it.* ○ *There was so much noise that I missed a lot of what the speaker said.* ○ *They completely missed the point of what I was saying.* يفوته (شيء) ، يخطئ
2 [I,T] to not hit, catch, etc. sth: *She tried hard to hit the ball but missed.* ○ *Drive more carefully. You only just missed that car.* يخطئ
3 [T] to feel sad because sb is not with you any more, or because you have not got or cannot do sth that you once had or did: *I'll miss you terribly when you go away.* ○ *I don't miss teaching at all. I prefer my new job.* يشتاق أو يتوق إلى
4 [T] to arrive too late for sth or to fail to be at sth: *Hurry up or you'll miss the bus!* ○ *She'll be very cross if you miss her birthday party.* يفوِّت (الفرصة)، يضيع؛ يقصِّر عن الحضور
5 [T] to notice that you have lost sb/sth: *When did you first miss your handbag?* يفتقد
PHRV **miss sb/sth out** to not include sb/sth: *You've missed out several important points in your report.* يغفل، يحذف
miss out (on sth) to lose a chance to gain sth, enjoy yourself, etc: *You'll miss out on all the fun if you stay at home.* يضيِّع الفرصة ، تفوته (التسلية والمتعة)
▸ **missing** *adj* lost, or not in the right or usual place: *Some of my books are missing – have you seen them?* ○ *The roof has got some tiles missing.* ○ *The little girl has been missing from home for two days.* ○ *a missing person* مفقود ؛ ناقص ؛ غائب

⚷ **miss**[2] /mɪs/ *noun* [C] a failure to hit, catch, etc. sth that you are aiming at: *After several misses he finally managed to hit the target.* رمية خاطئة
IDM **give sth a miss** (*informal*) to decide not to do sth, have sth, go to sth, etc: *I think I'll give the party a miss. I don't feel too well.* يضرب عنه صفحاً ، يقرِّر عدم (الذهاب)
a near miss → NEAR[1]

missile /'mɪsaɪl; *US* 'mɪsl/ *noun* [C] **1** a powerful exploding weapon that can be sent long distances through the air: *nuclear missiles* قذيفة ، صاروخ
2 an object or weapon that is fired from a gun or thrown: *Among the missiles thrown during the riot were broken bottles and stones.* مقذوف ، قذيفة

mission /'mɪʃn/ *noun* [C] **1** an important task or purpose that a person or group of people are sent somewhere to do: *Your mission is to send back information about the enemy's movements.* مهمّة
2 a group of people who are sent abroad to perform a special task: *a British trade mission to China* إرساليّة ، بعثة
3 a special journey made by a space rocket or military aeroplane: *a mission to the moon* رحلة
4 a particular task or duty which you feel that you should do: *Her work with the poor was more than just a job – it was her mission in life.* رسالة ، مهمّة
5 a place where the local people are taught about religion, given medical help, etc. by people who are sent to do this (missionaries). مركز الإرساليّة التبشيريّة

missionary /'mɪʃənri; *US* -neri/ *noun* [C] (*pl.* **missionaries**) a person who is sent abroad to teach about the Christian religion مبشِّر مسيحي

misspell /ˌmɪs'spel/ *verb* [T] (*pt, pp* **misspelled** or **misspelt** /-'spelt/) to spell sth wrongly يخطئ في التهجئة أو الكتابة

misspent /ˌmɪs'spent/ *adj* (of time or money) used in a foolish way; wasted (وقت أو مال) مبدَّد

mist[1] /mɪst/ *noun* **1** [C,U] clouds made of small

drops of water, close to the ground, which make it difficult to see very far; a thin fog: *Early morning mists often mean it will be sunny later on.* ○ *The fields were covered in mist.* ➲ Look at the notes at **fog** and **weather**. ضباب خفيف : غشاوة

2 [U] a very thin layer of tiny drops of water on a window, mirror, etc: *Is the mist on the inside or the outside of the windscreen?* تكاثف بخار الماء

▶ **misty** *adj* (**mistier**; **mistiest**) full of or covered with mist: *a misty day* ➲ Look at **foggy**. مُغطّى بضباب خفيف

mist² /mɪst/ *verb*

PHRV **mist (sth) up** to cover or be covered with mist: *The back window's misted up again. Can you wipe it?* يغطّي بغشاوة ، يغشّي ؛ يتكاثف البخار عليه

🔑 **mistake¹** /mɪˈsteɪk/ *noun* [C,U] something that you think or do that is wrong: *The teacher corrected the mistakes in my essay.* ○ *a spelling mistake* ○ *Waiter! I think you've made a mistake over the bill.* ○ *I think there must be some mistake. My name is Sedgley, not Selley.* ○ *It was a big mistake not to book our flight earlier.* ○ *We made the mistake of asking Paul to look after the house while we were away.* غلطة، خطأ

IDM **by mistake** as a result of a mistake or carelessness: *The terrorists shot the wrong man by mistake.* خطأً، بالغلط، سهواً

> **Error** is more formal than **mistake**: *(formal) Please accept my apologies. I opened your letter in error.* ○ *(informal) I'm sorry. I opened your letter by mistake.* **Fault** indicates who is to blame: *The accident wasn't my fault. The other driver pulled out in front of me.* **Fault** is also used to describe something that is wrong with, or not good about, a person or a thing: *a technical fault* ○ *Laziness is not one of her faults.*

🔑 **mistake²** /mɪˈsteɪk/ *verb* [T] (*pt* **mistook** /mɪˈstʊk/; *pp* **mistaken** /mɪˈsteɪkən/) **1** to be wrong about sth: *to mistake sb's meaning* يخطئ ، يغلط

2 to think (wrongly) that sb/sth is sb/sth else: *I'm sorry. I mistook you for a friend of mine.* يخلط بينه وبين شخص آخر ، يحسبه شخصاً آخر

▶ **mistaken** *adj* wrong; not correct: *I thought the film was a comedy but I must have been mistaken.* ○ *a case of mistaken identity* مُخطئ ، غير صحيح

mistakenly *adv* خطأً

mister /ˈmɪstə(r)/ → MR

mistletoe /ˈmɪsltəʊ/ *noun* [U] a plant with white berries and leaves that are green at all times of the year. Mistletoe grows on trees. الهَدال، الدِبق (نبات طفيلي)

> Mistletoe is used as a decoration inside houses in Britain at Christmas time. There is a tradition of kissing people 'under the mistletoe'.

mistook *pt* of MISTAKE²

mistreat /ˌmɪsˈtriːt/ *verb* [T] to behave badly or cruelly towards a person or animal يسيء المعاملة

▶ **mistreatment** *noun* [U] سوء المعاملة

mistress /ˈmɪstrəs/ *noun* [C] **1** a man's mistress is a woman who is having a (secret) sexual relationship with him ➲ Look at **lover**. عشيقة، خليلة

2 (*old-fashioned*) a female teacher (usually in a private school): *the chemistry mistress* ➲ Look at **master**. مدرِّسة في مدرسة خاصّة

3 a woman who has people or animals in her control ➲ Look at **master**. قيِّمة، مديرة

mistrust /ˌmɪsˈtrʌst/ *verb* [T] to not believe sb/sth; to have no confidence in sb/sth; not to trust: *I always mistrust the information in newspapers.* يَشكّ في؛ لا يصدّق؛ لا يثق في

▶ **mistrust** *noun* [U, sing.] شكّ، عدم ثقة

misty → MIST

misunderstand /ˌmɪsʌndəˈstænd/ *verb* [T] (*pt*, *pp* **misunderstood** /-ˈstʊd/) to understand sb/sth wrongly: *Don't misunderstand me. I'm only trying to do what's best for you.* ○ *I misunderstood the instructions and answered three questions instead of four.* يسيء الفهم

▶ **misunderstanding** *noun* [C,U] not understanding sb/sth properly; an example of this: *There must be some misunderstanding. I ordered spaghetti, not pizza.* ○ *It was all a misunderstanding but we've got it sorted out now.* سوء تفاهم

misuse /ˌmɪsˈjuːz/ *verb* [T] to use sth in the wrong way or for the wrong purpose: *These chemicals can be dangerous if misused.* يسيء الاستعمال؛ يستعمل لأغراض سيئة

▶ **misuse** /ˌmɪsˈjuːs/ *noun* [C,U] using sth in the wrong way or for the wrong purpose: *That project is a misuse of public money.* سوء استعمال؛ استعمال في أغراض سيّئة

mitigate /ˈmɪtɪɡeɪt/ *verb* [T] (*formal*) to make sth less serious, painful, unpleasant, etc. يُخفّف؛ يُسكّن ، يُلطّف

▶ **mitigating** *adj*: *Because of the mitigating circumstances* (= that made the crime seem less bad) *the judge gave her a lighter sentence.* مُخفِّف

mitten /ˈmɪtn/ *noun* [C] a type of glove that has one part for the thumb and another part for the other four fingers: *a pair of mittens* قفّاز بدون أصابع

🔑 **mix¹** /mɪks/ *verb* **1** [T] to put two or more substances together and shake or stir them until they form a new substance: *to mix oil and vinegar together to make a salad dressing* ○ *Mix yellow and blue together to make green.* يمزج ، يخلط

2 [I] to join together to form a separate substance: *Oil and water don't mix.* يمتزج ، يختلط

3 [T] to make sth (by mixing two or more substances together): *to mix cement* يخلط ، يصنع

4 [T] to do or have two or more things at the same time: *to mix business and pleasure* يجمع بين

5 [I] to be with and talk to other people: *He mixes with all types of people at work.* ○ *She is very shy and doesn't mix well.* يخالط، يعاشر

IDM **be/get mixed up in sth** (*informal*) to be/become involved in sth bad or unpleasant يتورّط

PHR V **mix sth up** to put something in the wrong order: *He was so nervous that he dropped his speech and got the pages all mixed up.* يلخبط

mix sb/sth up (with sb/sth) to confuse sb/sth with sb/sth else: *I think you've got us mixed up. I'm Jane and she's Sally.* يخطئ بين شخصين؛ يخلط بين شيئين

mix² /mɪks/ *noun* **1** [C, usually sing.] a group of different types of people or things: *We need a good racial mix in the police force.* مزيج ، مجموعة

2 [C,U] a special powder that contains all the substances needed to make a cake, bread, etc. You add water or another liquid to this powder: *a packet of cake mix* مزيج جاهز (لصنع كاتو مثلاً)

mixed /mɪkst/ *adj* **1** made or consisting of different types of sth: *a mixed salad* ○ *The reaction to our suggestion has been very mixed.* متنوع

2 for both sexes, male and female: *a mixed school* ❶ The opposite is **single-sex**. Look also at **unisex**. مختلط، للجنسين

IDM **have mixed feelings (about sb/sth)** to have some good and some bad feelings about sb/sth; not to be sure about what you think: *I have very mixed feelings about leaving school.* غير متأكد من طبيعة مشاعره؛ عنده مشاعر مختلطة

ˌmixed 'doubles *noun* [U, with sing. or pl. verb] a game of tennis, etc. in which there is a man and a woman on each side (في التنس) زوجي مختلط

ˌmixed 'marriage *noun* [C] a marriage between people of different races or religions زواج مختلط

ˌmixed-'up *adj* (*informal*) confused or unsure about sth/yourself: *He has been very mixed-up since his parents' divorce.* مضطرب، مشوّش

mixer /'mɪksə(r)/ *noun* [C] a machine that is used for mixing sth: *a food mixer* خلّاطة الطعام

mixture /'mɪkstʃə(r)/ *noun* **1** [C,U] something that is made by mixing together two or more substances: *cough mixture* ○ *Put the mixture into a baking tin and cook for half an hour.* مزيج ، خليط

2 [sing.] something that consists of several things that are different from one another: *I stood and stared with a mixture of amazement and horror.* مزيج

'mix-up *noun* [C] (*informal*) a mistake in the planning or organization of sth: *Because of a mix-up at the travel agent's we didn't get our tickets on time.* خطأ، لخبطة

ml *abbrev* (*pl.* **ml** or **mls**) = MILLILITRE(S)

mm *abbrev* = MILLIMETRE(S): *rainfall: 6 mm* ○ *a 35 mm camera*

moan /məʊn/ *noun* [C] a low sound that you make if you are in pain or very sad تأوّه ، أنّة؛ أنين

▸ **moan** *verb* [I] **1** to make the sound of a moan: *to moan with pain* يئن، يتأوّه

2 (*informal*) to keep saying what is wrong about sth; to complain: *The English are always moaning about the weather.* يتشكّى

moat /məʊt/ *noun* [C] a deep ditch that was dug around a castle and filled with water in order to protect the castle خندق مملوء ماءً يحيط بالقلعة

mob /mɒb/ *noun* [C, with sing. or pl. verb] a large crowd of people that may become violent or cause trouble: *The police used tear gas to disperse the angry mob.* جماهير طائشة ، غوغاء

▸ **mob** *verb* [T] (mo**bb**ing; mo**bb**ed) to gather round sb, with a large crowd of people, because you are angry or are very interested in him/her: *The pop star was mobbed as he left the hotel.* يتجمهر حول ، يحدق بِ

mobile /'məʊbaɪl; *US* -bl/ *adj* able to move or be moved easily: *My daughter is much more mobile now she has her own car.* ➲ Look at **immobile**. متنقِّل، متحرِّك، سريع الحركة

▸ **mobility** /məʊ'bɪləti/ *noun* [U] حركة، تحريك

ˌmobile de'vice *noun* [C] any small computing device that will fit into your pocket, such as a PDA or smartphone جهاز نقّال

ˌmobile 'home *noun* [C] a large caravan that sb lives in permanently (not just for holidays) مقطورة كبيرة أو كرافان تستخدم بيتاً

ˌmobile 'phone (*also* **mobile**; **cellphone**; **cellular phone**) *noun* [C] a telephone that you can carry around with you and that works by using radio signals تليفون نقّال، جوّال

mobilize (*also* **mobilise**) /'məʊbəlaɪz/ *verb* **1** [T] to organize sb/sth for a particular purpose: *They mobilized the local residents to oppose the new development.* يجنّد، يعبّئ؛ ينظّم

2 [I,T] to get ready for war يعبّئ

mock¹ /mɒk/ *verb* [I,T] (*formal*) to laugh at sb/sth in an unkind way or to make other people laugh at him/her ❶ **Laugh at** and **make fun of** are less formal and more common. يضحك على ، يسخر من

mock² /mɒk/ *adj* (only *before* a noun) not real or genuine: *We have mock* (= practice) *exams four months before the real ones.* ○ *The houses are built in a mock Georgian style.* غير حقيقي ؛ مقلّد ؛ اصطناعي

'mock-up *noun* [C] a model of sth that shows what the real thing looks like or how it will work نموذج كامل عن الشيء الحقيقي

modal /'məʊdl/ (*also* **modal verb**; **modal auxiliary**) *noun* [C] a verb, e.g. 'might', 'can', 'must' that is used with another verb for expressing possibility, permission, necessity, etc. (في القواعد) فِعل مساعد

mode /məʊd/ *noun* [C] (*formal*) **1** a type of sth or way of doing sth: *a mode of transport* ○ *The mode of life in the village has not changed for 500 years.* طريقة ، أسلوب

2 one of the ways in which a machine can work: *Switch the camera to automatic mode.* وَضْع

model¹ /'mɒdl/ *noun* [C] **1** a copy of sth that is usually smaller than the real thing: *a scale model of the railway station* ○ *a model aeroplane* نموذج مصغّر

2 one of the machines, vehicles, etc. that is made by a particular company: *The latest models are on display at the show.* موديل ، طراز

3 a person or thing that is a good example to

copy: *America's education system has been taken as a model by other countries.* نموذج ، مثال

4 a person who is employed to wear clothes at a fashion show or for magazine photographs: *a male fashion model* عارض أو عارضة أزياء

5 a person who is painted, drawn or photographed by an artist شخص يجلس أمام فنان لرسمه مثلاً

model² /ˈmɒdl/ *verb* (modelling; modelled; *US* modeling; modeled) **1** [T] to try to copy or be like sb/sth: *He modelled himself on his favourite teacher.* ○ *The house is modelled on the Palace of Versailles.* يقلّد، يقتدي بـ؛ يصوغ على غرار

2 [I,T] to wear and show clothes as a model¹ (4): *to model swimsuits* يعرض أو تعرض أزياء

3 [I,T] to make a model¹ (1) of sth يصنع نموذجاً عن شيء

▸ **modelling** (*US* **modeling**) *noun* [U] the work of a fashion model: *a career in modelling* عرض الأزياء

modem /ˈməʊdem/ *noun* [C] a piece of equipment that connects two or more computers together by means of a telephone line so that information can go from one to the other مودِم (كمبيوتر)

moderate¹ /ˈmɒdərət/ *adj* **1** average or not very great in size, amount or degree: *a moderate speed* ○ *We've had a moderate amount of success.* متوسّط

2 (used about a person's political opinions) not very different from those of most other people; not extreme: *to hold moderate views* ➲ Look at **extreme** and **radical**. معتدل ، غير متطرِّف

▸ **moderate** /ˈmɒdərət/ *noun* [C] a person who has moderate political, etc. opinions ➲ Look at **extremist**. شخص ذو آراء معتدلة

moderately *adv* not very; quite: *His career has been moderately successful.* إلى حدٍّ ما

moderate² /ˈmɒdəreɪt/ *verb* [I,T] to become or to make sth less strong or extreme: *The stormy weather has moderated a little.* يعتدل؛ يلطِّف، يهدّئ

moderation /ˌmɒdəˈreɪʃn/ *noun* [U] the quality of being able to control your feelings or actions: *The people reacted violently but their leaders called for moderation.* الاعتدال : ضبط الأعصاب

IDM **in moderation** within limits that are sensible: *Smoking is harmful even in moderation.* باعتدال

🔑 **modern** /ˈmɒdn/ *adj* **1** of the present or recent times: *Pollution is one of the major problems in the modern world.* ○ *Do you prefer modern or classical ballet?* ○ *Radar is very important in modern warfare.* ➲ Look at **ancient** and **traditional**. حديث ، عصري

2 with all the newest methods, equipment, buildings, etc: *It is one of the most modern hospitals in the country.* ➲ Look at **old-fashioned**. حديث ، مزوّد بأحدث الأجهزة

modernize (*also* **modernise**) /ˈmɒdənaɪz/ *verb* [I,T] to become or to make sth suitable for what is needed today: *The railway system is being modernized and high speed trains introduced.* يجدّد، يجعل الشيء ملائماً لمقتضيات العصر الحديث

▸ **modernization** (*also* **modernisation**) /ˌmɒdənaɪˈzeɪʃn; *US* -nɪˈz-/ *noun* [U]: *The house is large but is in need of modernization.* تجديد

ˌmodern ˈlanguage *noun* [C] a language that is spoken now لغة حيّة

modest /ˈmɒdɪst/ *adj* **1** not having or expressing a high opinion of your own qualities or abilities: *She got the best results in the exam but she was too modest to tell anyone.* ➲ Look at **humble** and **proud**. متواضع

2 (used about a woman's clothes) not showing much of the body خجول، محتشم

3 not very large: *They live in a modest little house near the centre of town.* ○ *a modest increase in price* متواضع؛ متوسط

▸ **modestly** *adv* قليلاً؛ بتواضع؛ باحتشام

modesty /ˈmɒdəsti/ *noun* [U] the quality of being modest (1,2) تواضع ، حياء : احتشام

modify /ˈmɒdɪfaɪ/ *verb* [T] (*pres part* **modifying**; *3rd pers sing pres* **modifies**; *pt*, *pp* **modified**) to change sth slightly: *We shall need to modify the existing plan.* يعدِّل، يحوِّر

▸ **modification** /ˌmɒdɪfɪˈkeɪʃn/ *noun* [C,U] a small change: *There have been some small modifications to our original design.* تعديل ، تحوير

module /ˈmɒdjuːl; *US* -dʒuːl/ *noun* [C] a unit that forms part of sth bigger: *The lunar module separated from the spacecraft to land on the moon.* ○ *You must complete three modules* (= courses that you study) *in your first year.* مركبة (قمرية) : وحدة تشكل جزءاً من كلّ

mohair /ˈməʊheə(r)/ *noun* [U] very soft wool that comes from a type of goat صوف الموهير

moist /mɔɪst/ *adj* slightly wet; damp: *Her eyes were moist with tears.* ○ *Keep the soil moist or the plant will die.* ➲ Look at the note at **wet**. رَطْب ، نديّ

▸ **moisten** /ˈmɔɪsn/ *verb* [I,T] to become or to make sth moist يرطب؛ يندّي ، يَبُلّ بعض الشيء

moisture /ˈmɔɪstʃə(r)/ *noun* [U] water in small drops on a surface, in the air, etc. رطوبة ، تكاثف بُخار الماء

molar /ˈməʊlə(r)/ *noun* [C] one of the large teeth at the back of your mouth ضِرس

mold (*US*) = MOULD¹,²

moldy (*US*) = MOULDY

mole¹ /məʊl/ *noun* [C] a small dark spot on a person's skin that never goes away ➲ Look at **freckle**. خال ، شامة

mole² /məʊl/ *noun* [C] **1** a small animal with dark fur that lives underground and is almost blind خُلد ، طوبين

2 (*informal*) a person who works in one organization and gives secret information to another organization or country ➲ Look at **spy**. شخص يتجسس على مؤسّسته

molecule /ˈmɒlɪkjuːl/ *noun* [C] the smallest unit into which a substance can be divided without changing its chemical nature. A molecule consists of one or more atoms. جزيء

molehill /ˈməʊlhɪl/ *noun* [C] a small pile of earth that is made by a mole²(1) while it is digging underground كومة من التراب تتكوّن بعد حفر الخلد جُحْره

molest /məˈlest/ *verb* [T] to seriously annoy sb or to attack sb in a sexual way يُضايق؛ يتحرّش بِ، يتعدّى جنسياً على

molt (*US*) = MOULT

molten /ˈməʊltən/ *adj* (used about metal or rock) made liquid by very great heat: *molten lava* منْصهِر

mom /mɒm/ *noun* [C] (*US informal*) = MUM

moment /ˈməʊmənt/ *noun* **1** [C] a very short period of time: *Would you mind waiting for a moment?* ○ *He hesitated for a few moments and then knocked on the door.* لحظة ، برهة

2 [sing.] a particular point in time: *Just at that moment my mother arrived.* ○ *the moment of birth/death* لحظة

IDM **(at) any minute/moment (now)** → MINUTE¹

at the moment now: *I'm afraid she's busy at the moment. Can I take a message?* في هذه اللحظة ، الآن

for the moment/present for a short time; for now: *I'm not very happy at work but I'll stay there for the moment.* لوقت قصير؛ في الوقت الحاضر

in a moment very soon: *Just wait here. I'll be back in a moment.* بعد قليل

the last minute/moment → LAST¹

the minute/moment (that) → MINUTE¹

momentary /ˈməʊməntri; *US* -teri/ *adj* lasting for a very short time: *a momentary lack of concentration* خاطف ، وجيز جداً

▸ **momentarily** /ˈməʊməntrəli; *US* ˌməʊmənˈterəli/ *adv* for a very short time لبُرهة قصيرة ، لحظةً

momentous /məˈmentəs; məʊˈm-/ *adj* very important: *There have been momentous changes in Eastern Europe in the last few years.* بالغ الأهمية

momentum /məˈmentəm; məʊˈm-/ *noun* [U] strength or speed: *The ball gained momentum as it rolled downhill.* ○ *The environmental movement is gathering momentum.* قوّة، سرعة

momma /ˈmɒmə/ (*also* **mommy** /ˈmɒmi/) *noun* [C] (*US informal*) = MUMMY¹

monarch /ˈmɒnək/ *noun* [C] a king or queen عاهل ، مَلِك او ملكة

▸ **monarchy** /ˈmɒnəki/ *noun* (*pl.* **monarchies**)

1 [sing., U] the system of government or rule by a monarch: [sing.]: *Should Britain abolish the monarchy?* المَلَكيّة، النظام المَلَكي

2 [C] a country that is governed by a monarch ➲ Look at **republic**. دولة مَلَكيّة

monastery /ˈmɒnəstri; *US* -teri/ *noun* [C] (*pl.* **monasteries**) a place where men (monks) live in a religious community ➲ Look at **convent**. دَيْر

Monday /ˈmʌndeɪ/ *noun* [C,U] (*abbr* **Mon.**) the day of the week after Sunday and before Tuesday: *I'm going to see her on Monday.* ○ *I'm going to see her Monday* (in American English and informal British English). ○ *We usually play badminton on Mondays/on a Monday.* ○ *They go to the youth club every Monday.* ○ *'What day is it today?' 'It's Monday.'* ○ *Monday morning/afternoon/evening/night* ○ *last/next Monday* ○ *the Monday before last* ○ *the Monday after next* ○ *a week on Monday/Monday week* (= not next Monday, but the Monday after that) ○ *The museum is open Monday to Friday, 10 till 4.30.* ○ *Did you see that article about Italy in Monday's paper?* يوم الاثنين

monetary /ˈmʌnɪtri; *US* -teri/ *adj* connected with money: *the government's monetary policy* نقدي ، مالي

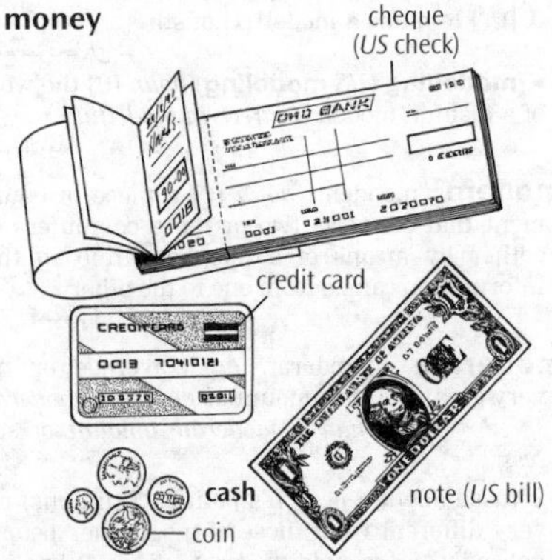

money /ˈmʌni/ *noun* [U] the means of paying for sth or buying sth (= coins or notes): *How much money do you earn a week?* ○ *Young people spend a lot of money on clothes.* ○ *Our holiday cost an awful lot of money.* ○ *Don't change your money at the airport. They charge a lot there.* ○ *If we do the work ourselves we will save a lot of money.* ○ *to borrow/lend money* ○ *My father invested his money in stocks and shares.* ○ *Is this picture worth a lot of money?* ➲ Look also at **pocket money**. نُقود ، فلوس

IDM **get your money's worth** to get full value for the money you have spent: *The meal was expensive but we got our money's worth because there were five courses.* يحصل على قيمة نقوده كاملة ، (السلعة المشتراة) تستحق ثمنها وأكثر

make money to earn money or to make a profit on a business يربح أو يكسب مالاً

ˈmoney box *noun* [C] a box into which you put money that you want to save صندوق لادّخار النقود ، حصّالة

mongrel /ˈmʌŋɡrəl/ *noun* [C] a dog which has parents of different types (breeds) كلب هجين

monitor /ˈmɒnɪtə(r)/ *noun* [C] **1** a machine that shows information or pictures on a screen like a television مرقاب أو شاشة مراقبة

2 a machine that records or checks sth: *A monitor checks the baby's heartbeat.* مرقاب

3 a pupil who has a special job to do in the classroom عريف الصف

▸ **monitor** *verb* [T] **1** to check, record or test sth

regularly for a period of time: *Pollution levels in the lake are being monitored closely.* يرصد ، يراقب

2 to listen to and record foreign radio or television broadcasts يستمع إلى ويسجّل الإذاعات الأجنبية

monk /mʌŋk/ *noun* [C] a man who has decided to leave the ordinary world and live a religious life in a community (monastery) ➲ Look at **nun**. راهب

monkey /ˈmʌŋki/ *noun* [C] (*pl.* **monkeys**) a small, usually brown, animal with a long tail that lives in hot countries and can climb trees ➲ Look at **ape**. **Chimpanzees** and **gorillas** are apes, although people often call them monkeys. قرد، سَعدان

mono /ˈmɒnəʊ/ *adj* (used about recorded music, etc., or a system for playing it) having the sound directed through one channel only ➲ Look at **stereo**. (موسيقى) مسجّلة أو مسموعة على قنال واحد فقط

▸ **mono** *noun* [U]: *The concert was recorded in mono.* تسجيل على قنال واحد أي ليس ستيريو

monolingual /ˌmɒnəˈlɪŋɡwəl/ *adj* using only one language: *This is a monolingual dictionary.* ➲ Look at **bilingual**. (قاموس) ذو لغة واحدة

monologue (*US also* **monolog**) /ˈmɒnəlɒɡ; *US* -lɔːɡ/ *noun* [C] a long speech by one person, e.g. in a play حديث طويل يلقيه ممثّل واحد ، مناجاة النفس

monopolize (*also* **monopolise**) /məˈnɒpəlaɪz/ *verb* [T] to control sth so that other people cannot have or use it: *She completely monopolized the conversation. I couldn't get a word in.* يحتكر

monopoly /məˈnɒpəli/ *noun* [C] (*pl.* **monopolies**) **1** the control of an industry or service by one company: *British Telecom had a monopoly on supplying telephone lines to people's houses.* احتكار

2 a company or organization that controls an industry: *British Rail was a state monopoly.* حصْر ، الحقّ الممنوح لشركة واحدة دون غيرها

monorail /ˈmɒnəʊreɪl/ *noun* [C] a railway in which the train runs on a single track خط حديدي ذو سكّة واحدة

monosyllable /ˈmɒnəsɪləbl/ *noun* [C] a short word, such as 'leg', that has only one syllable كلمة من مقطع واحد فقط

monotonous /məˈnɒtənəs/ *adj* boring and uninteresting because it does not change: *monotonous work* ○ *a monotonous voice* رتيب ، على وتيرة واحدة ، مِملّ

▸ **monotonously** *adv* على وتيرة واحدة : بشكل مملّ

monotony /məˈnɒtəni/ *noun* [U] the state of being boring and uninteresting: *The monotony of the speaker's voice made us all feel sleepy.* رتابة : إملال

monsoon /ˌmɒnˈsuːn/ *noun* [C] the season of heavy rain in Southern Asia, or the wind which brings the rain "المونسون" ، ريح موسمية غزيرة الأمطار

monster /ˈmɒnstə(r)/ *noun* [C] (in stories) a type of animal that is large, ugly and frightening: *Did you see the Loch Ness monster?* ○ *a story of dragons, serpents and other monsters* ○ (*figurative*) *The murderer was described as a dangerous monster.* مخلوق خرافيّ مخيف ؛ وحش

monstrous /ˈmɒnstrəs/ *adj* **1** very bad or unfair: *a monstrous crime* ○ *It's monstrous that she earns less than he does for the same job!* فظيع

2 very large (and often ugly or frightening): *a monstrous block of flats* ○ *a monstrous creature from the sea* ضخم جداً وقبيح

▸ **monstrosity** /mɒnˈstrɒsəti/ *noun* [C] (*pl.* **monstrosities**) something that is ugly (and usually very large): *That new building on the High Street is a monstrosity.* شيء بالغ القبح والضخامة

⚷ **month** /mʌnθ/ *noun* [C] **1** (*also* ˌ**calendar** ˈ**month**) one of the twelve periods of time into which the year is divided, e.g. January: *They are starting work next month.* ○ *We went on holiday last month.* ○ *The rent is £300 a month.* ○ *'When are the exams?' 'Later in the month.'* ○ *at the beginning/end of the month* شهر ، أحد أشهر السنة

2 (*also* ˌ**calendar** ˈ**month**) the period of time from a certain date in one month to the same date in the next, e.g. 13 May to 13 June مدة شهْر

3 a period of about four weeks: *'How long will you be away?' 'For about a month.'* ○ *a three-month course* ○ *The window cleaner will come again in a month/in a month's time.* ○ *I've got a toddler of eighteen months.* شهر

▸ **monthly** *adj, adv* (happening or produced) once a month or every month: *a monthly meeting* ○ *a monthly magazine* ○ *Are you paid weekly or monthly?* شهري

monthly *noun* [C] (*pl.* **monthlies**) a magazine that is published once a month مجلّة شهريّة

monument /ˈmɒnjumənt/ *noun* [C] **1** a building or statue that is built to remind people of a famous person or event نصب تذكاريّ

2 an old building or other place that is of historical importance: *Stonehenge is a famous ancient monument.* أثر، بناء أثري

monumental /ˌmɒnjuˈmentl/ *adj* **1** (used about a building) very large and impressive ضخم

2 very great: *a monumental success* هائل

moo /muː/ *noun* [C] the sound that a cow makes خوار البقر

▸ **moo** *verb* [I] (البقرة) تَخور

⚷ **mood** /muːd/ *noun* **1** [C,U] the way that you feel at a particular time, i.e. if you are happy, sad, etc: *Leave Dad alone for a while. He's in a very bad mood.* ○ *You're in a good mood today!* ○ *a sudden change of mood* ○ *Turn that music down a bit – I'm not in the mood for it.* مزاج، حالة نفسية

2 [C] a time when you are angry or bad-tempered: *Debby's in one of her moods again.* مزاج سيء

3 [sing.] the way that a group of people feel about sth: *The mood of the crowd changed and some stones were thrown.* شعور جماعي

▸ **moody** *adj* (**moodier**; **moodiest**) **1** having moods (1) that change often متقلّب المِزاج

2 bad-tempered or unhappy نكد؛ كئيب

moodily /-ɪli/ *adv* بكآبة؛ بنكد

a b c d e f g h i j k l **m** n o p q r s t u v w x y z

moodiness *noun* [U] تقلُّب المزاج؛ اكتئاب

moon /mu:n/ *noun* **1 the moon** [sing.] the object that shines in the sky at night and that moves round the earth once every 28 days: *The moon's very bright tonight.* ○ *When was the first landing on the moon?* ℹ You may see a **new moon**, a **full moon** or a **crescent moon**. القمر

2 [C] an object like the moon that moves around another planet: *How many moons does Neptune have?* قَمَر، تابع

IDM **once in a blue moon** → ONCE

over the moon (*informal*) very pleased or happy غاية في السرور أو السعادة

moonlight /ˈmu:nlaɪt/ *noun* [U] light that comes from the moon: *The lake looked beautiful in the moonlight.* ضوء القمر

▶ **moonlit** /ˈmu:nlɪt/ *adj* having light from the moon: *a moonlit evening* (ليلة) مقْمِرة

moor[1] /mʊə(r); *Brit also* mɔ:(r)/ (*also* **moorland** /-lənd/) *noun* [C,U] a wild open area of high land that is covered with grass and other low plants أرض براح، أرض مغطاة بالأعشاب والخلنج

moor[2] /mʊə(r); *Brit also* mɔ:(r)/ *verb* [I,T] to fasten a boat to the land or to an object in the water, with a rope or chain يرسي أو يربط القارب بالشاطئ

▶ **mooring** *noun* [C] a place where a boat is moored مرسى

moose /mu:s/ *noun* [C] (*pl.* **moose**) a type of large deer that comes from North America ℹ In northern Europe the same animal is called an **elk**. إلكة ، حيوان من فصيلة الأيليات

mop /mɒp/ *noun* [C] a tool that is used for washing floors. A mop has a long handle and a bunch of thick strings or a sponge at the end. مِمْسَحة بيد طويلة لتنظيف الأرض

▶ **mop** *verb* [T] (mopping; mopped) **1** to clean sth with a mop ينظف الأرض بتلك الممسحة

2 to remove liquid from sth using a dry cloth: *to mop your forehead with a handkerchief* يجفف، يمسح (عرقه) بمنديل

PHRV **mop sth up** to clean unwanted liquid with a mop or dry cloth: *Mop up that tea you've spilt or it'll leave a stain!* ينظف (الشاي المسكوب) بقطعة قماش

mope /məʊp/ *verb* [I] to feel unhappy and not try to do anything to make yourself feel better: *Moping in your room won't make the situation any better.* ينزوي مكتئباً

moped /ˈməʊped/ *noun* [C] a type of small, not very powerful, motorcycle with pedals دراجة بمحرك صغير

moral[1] /ˈmɒrəl; *US* mɔ:rəl/ *adj* **1** concerned with what you believe is the right way to behave: *Some people refuse to eat meat on moral grounds* (= because they believe it to be wrong). ○ *Is the high divorce rate the result of declining moral standards?* ○ *the moral dilemma of whether or not abortion should be allowed* ○ *The state has a moral obligation to house homeless people.* أخلاقي، أدبي

2 having high standards of behaviour: *She has always led a very moral life.* ℹ The opposite is **immoral**. أخلاقي

▶ **morally** /-rəli/ *adv* **1** in a way that is good or right: *to behave morally* بشكل أخلاقي

2 connected with standards of what is right or wrong: *to be morally responsible for sb* (e.g. because it is your duty to look after them) ○ *What he did wasn't illegal but it was morally wrong.* من الناحية الأخلاقيّة

moral[2] /ˈmɒrəl; *US* mɔ:rəl/ *noun* **1** [C] a lesson in the right way to behave that can be learnt from a story or from sth that happens: *The moral of the play is that friendship is more important than money.* عِبرة، موعظة

2 morals [plural] standards or principles of good behaviour مبادئ الأخلاق ، حسْن السلوك

morale /məˈrɑ:l; *US* -ˈræl/ *noun* [U] the way that a group of people feel at a particular time: *The team's morale was high before the match* (= they were confident that they would win). ○ *Low pay in recent years has led to low morale.* الروح المعنوية

morality /məˈræləti/ *noun* [U] whether sth is right or wrong: *There was a lively debate about the morality of abortion.* ℹ The opposite is **immorality**. أخلاقيّة، مراعاة الأخلاق أو مخالفتها

moralize (*also* **moralise**) /ˈmɒrəlaɪz; *US* ˈmɔ:r-/ *verb* [I] **moralize (about/on sth)** to talk or write about what is the right or wrong way to behave يَعِظ، يتحدث عن مبادئ الأخلاق

ˌ**moral supˈport** *noun* [U] help or encouragement that you give to sb (by being with him/her or saying that you agree with him/her): *I went to the dentist's with him just to give him some moral support.* دَعم معنوي

morbid /ˈmɔ:bɪd/ *adj* having or showing great interest in unpleasant things, e.g. disease and death ذو ميل للأشياء الكئيبة مثل الموت والمرض

more[1] /mɔ:(r)/ *det, pron* a larger number of people/things or larger amount of sth; sth in addition to what you already have: *There were more people than I expected.* ○ *I've bought some more plants for the garden.* ○ *We had more time than we thought.* ○ *There's room for three more people.* ○ *I couldn't eat any more.* ○ *Tell me more about your job.* ○ *I've found some more of those magazines you wanted.* عدد أكبر؛ أكثر

IDM **more and more** an increasing amount or number: *There are more and more cars on the road.* أكثر فأكثر ، عدد متزايد من....

more[2] /mɔ:(r)/ *adv* **1** (used to form the comparative of adjectives and adverbs with two or more syllables): *He was more frightened than I was.* ○ *Please write more carefully.* أكثر (خوفاً مثلاً)

2 to a greater extent: *I like him far/much more than his wife.* ○ *This one costs more.* أكثر

IDM **more or less** approximately; almost: *We are more or less the same age.* تقريباً

not any/no more not any longer: *She doesn't live here any more.* لم يعد (يسكن هنا)

what's more (used for adding another fact): *The hotel was awful and what's more it was miles from the beach.* والأسوأ من ذلك ؛ علاوة على ذلك

🔑 **moreover** /mɔːr'əʊvə(r)/ *adv* (*formal*) (used, especially in writing, when you are giving some extra information that supports what you are saying) in addition; also: *This firm did the work very well. Moreover, the cost was not too high.* إضافة إلى ذلك

morgue /mɔːg/ *noun* [C] a building where dead bodies are kept until they are buried or burned ➲ Look at **mortuary**. المشرحة ، مكان تحفظ فيه الجثث

🔑 **morning** /'mɔːnɪŋ/ *noun* [C,U] **1** the early part of the day between the time when the sun rises and midday: *Pat's going to London tomorrow morning.* ○ *Pat stayed with us on Sunday night and went to London the next/the following morning.* ○ *I've been studying hard all morning.* ○ *Dave makes breakfast every morning.* ○ *She only works in the mornings. She's free in the afternoons.* ○ *morning coffee* ○ *the morning paper* صباح ، ضحى

2 the part of the night that is after midnight: *I was woken by a strange noise in the early hours of the morning.* الهزيع الأخير من الليل ، صبح

IDM **good morning** (used when you see sb for the first time in the morning) ❶ Often we just say **Morning**: *'Good morning, Mrs Stevenson.' 'Morning, Mr Johnson.'* صباح الخير!

in the morning 1 during the morning of the next day; tomorrow morning: *I'll try to speak to her about it in the morning.* غداً صباحاً

2 not in the afternoon or evening: *The time of death was about 10.30 in the morning.* قبل الظهر

> When you use the adjectives *early* or *late* before 'morning', 'afternoon' or 'evening' you must use the preposition **in**: *The accident happened in the early morning.* ○ *We arrived in the late afternoon.* With other adjectives, use **on**: *School starts on Monday morning.* ○ *They set out on a cold, windy afternoon.* ○ *The accident happened on the following evening.* No preposition is used before *this, tomorrow, yesterday*: *Let's go swimming this morning.* ○ *I'll phone Liz tomorrow evening.* ○ *We went to the zoo yesterday afternoon.*

moron /'mɔːrɒn/ *noun* [C] (*informal*) a very foolish or stupid person شخص غبيّ جداً ، أبله
▸ **moronic** /mə'rɒnɪk/ *adj* غبيّ جداً ، أبله

morose /mə'rəʊs/ *adj* bad-tempered, and not saying much to other people نكِد، واجم ، مكتئِب

morphine /'mɔːfiːn/ *noun* [U] a drug made from opium that is used for reducing pain (دواء) المورفين

morsel /'mɔːsl/ *noun* [C] a very small piece of food لقمة ؛ كِسرة خبز

mortal /'mɔːtl/ *adj* **1** not living forever: *We are all mortal.* ❶ The opposite is **immortal**. فانٍ ، غير مخلّد

2 (*formal*) that will result in death: *a mortal wound* ➲ Look at **fatal**, which is more common. مميت ، قاتل

3 (*formal*) very great or extreme: *They were in mortal fear of the enemy.* شديد ، هائل

▸ **mortal** *noun* [C] a human being إنسان، بَشَر

mortally /-təli/ *adv* **1** in a way that will result in death: *to be mortally wounded* مؤدياً إلى الموت ، (جُرح) جرحاً مميتاً

2 very; extremely جداً ، للغاية

mortality /mɔː'tæləti/ *noun* [U] **1** the fact that nobody can live forever فناء

2 the number of deaths in a certain period of time or in a certain place: *Infant mortality is high in the region.* عدد الوفيات

mortar¹ /'mɔːtə(r)/ *noun* [U] a mixture of cement, sand and water that you put between bricks when you are building sth مِلاط، مونة

mortar² /'mɔːtə(r)/ *noun* [C] a type of heavy gun مدفع هاون

mortgage /'mɔːgɪdʒ/ *noun* [C] money that you borrow in order to buy a house: *We took out a £40 000 mortgage.* ○ *mortgage repayments* قرض عقاري

> You usually borrow money from a **bank** or a **building society**, who decide what **rate** of **interest** you must pay on the **loan**.

mortician /mɔː'tɪʃn/ *noun* [C] (*US*) = UNDERTAKER

mortuary /'mɔːtʃəri; *US* mɔːtʃʊerɪ/ *noun* [C] (*pl.* **mortuaries**) a place in a hospital, etc. where dead bodies are kept before they are buried or burned ➲ Look at **morgue**. مكان تحفظ فيه الجثث ريثما تدفن

mosaic /məʊ'zeɪɪk/ *noun* [C,U] a picture or pattern that is made by placing together small coloured stones, pieces of glass, etc. فسَيْفساء ، موزاييك

Moslem = MUSLIM

mosque /mɒsk/ *noun* [C] a building where Muslims worship مسجد ، جامع

mosquito /məs'kiːtəʊ; *Brit also* mɒs-/ *noun* [C] (*pl.* **mosquitoes**) a small flying insect found in hot countries. Mosquitoes bite people and animals in order to suck their blood and some types of mosquito spread a very serious disease (malaria). بَعوضة ، ناموسة

moss /mɒs; *US* mɔːs/ *noun* [C,U] a small green plant, with no flowers, that grows in a flat mass in damp places, especially on rocks or trees نبات طُحْلبيّ، طحْلب

🔑 **most¹** /məʊst/ *det, pron* (used as the superlative of *many, much*) **1** greatest in number or amount: *Who picked the most apples?* ○ *The children had the most fun.* ○ *We all worked hard but I did the most.* أكبر عدد ، أكبر مقدار

2 nearly all of a group of people or things: *Most families in this country have a television.* ○ *I like most Italian food.* أغلب ، معظم

> When **most** is followed by a noun which has **the**, **this**, **my**, etc. before it, we must use **most of**: *Most of the people I invited were able to come.* ○ *It rained most of the time we were in Ireland.*

IDM at (the) most not more than a certain number, and probably less: *There were 20 people there, at the most.* على الأكثر

make the most of sth → MAKE[1]

▶ **mostly** *adv* **1** almost all: *The people at work are mostly very nice.* في الغالبية ، على الأغلب

2 usually: *We mostly go shopping in Oxford, not Reading.* عادة ، غالباً

most² /məʊst/ *adv* **1** (used to form the superlative of adjectives and adverbs that have two or more syllables): *It's the most beautiful house I've ever seen.* ○ *I think this machine works the most efficiently.* الأكثر (جمالاً، كفاءة ألخ...)

2 more than anybody/anything else: *What do you miss most when you're abroad?* الأكثر

3 (*formal*) very: *We heard a most interesting talk about Japan.* جداً، للغاية

MOT /ˌem əʊ ˈtiː/ *abbrev* (*Brit*) **1** = MINISTRY OF TRANSPORT

2 (*also* **MOT test**) a test to make sure that vehicles over a certain age are safe to drive: *My car failed its MOT.* شهادة وزارة النقل

motel /məʊˈtel/ *noun* [C] a hotel for people who are travelling by car. In a motel you can usually park your car near your room. نَزْل، فندق على الطريق العام يسهل صفّ السيّارات أمامه

moth /mɒθ; *US* mɔːθ/ *noun* [C] an insect like a butterfly that usually flies at night. Moths do not have such bright colours as butterflies. عُثّة

mothball /ˈmɒθbɔːl; *US* ˈmɔːθ-/ *noun* [C] a small ball made of a chemical substance that protects clothes in cupboards from moths كرة نفتالين، كرة العُثّ

mother /ˈmʌðə(r)/ *noun* [C] the female parent of a person or animal: *an expectant mother* ○ *an unmarried mother* ○ *a foster mother* ○ *Working mothers need good child-care arrangements.* ○ *a mother cow and her calf* ➲ Look at **mum**, **mummy** and **stepmother**. أُم

▶ **mother** *verb* [T] to care for sb as a mother does: *He looked so young and helpless. All the women in the office tried to mother him.* يحنو على (كالأمّ) ، يرعى

motherhood /-hʊd/ *noun* [U] the state of being a mother الأمومة

motherless *adj* having no mother يتيم الأم

motherly *adj* of a mother or like a mother: *She's a motherly sort of person.* أُمومِيّ: حنون ، رؤوم

ˈ**mother country** *noun* [C] (*pl.* **mother countries**) (*formal*) the country where a person was born or grew up مسقط الرأس ، الوطن

ˈ**mother-in-law** *noun* [C] (*pl.* **mothers-in-law**) the mother of your husband or wife حماة

ˈ**Mother's Day** *noun* [C] a day on which mothers traditionally receive cards and gifts from their children, celebrated in Britain on the fourth Sunday in Lent and in the US on the 2nd Sunday in May عيد الأم

ˌ**mother ˈtongue** *noun* [C] the first language that you learned to speak as a child اللغة الأمّ، لغة الطفل الأولى

motif /məʊˈtiːf/ *noun* [C] a picture or pattern on sth: *The blouse has a butterfly motif on each sleeve.* رَسم تزييني

motion /ˈməʊʃn/ *noun* **1** [U] movement or a way of moving: *The swaying motion of the ship made us all feel sick.* ○ *Pull the lever to set the machine in motion.* ➲ Look at **slow motion**. حركة

2 [C] a suggestion that you discuss and vote at a meeting: *The motion was carried/rejected by a majority of eight votes.* اقتراح رسمي

▶ **motion** *verb* [T] to make a movement that tells sb what to do: *The manager motioned me to sit down.* يشير أو يومئ إلى

motionless *adj* not moving بِلا حراك، ساكن

motivate /ˈməʊtɪveɪt/ *verb* [T] **1** to cause sb to act in a particular way: *Her reaction was motivated by fear.* ○ *The attack was politically motivated.* يدفع إلى ، يبعث على

2 to make sb want to do sth (by making it interesting): *Our new teacher certainly knows how to motivate his classes.* يحمّس، يثير اهتمامه

▶ **motivated** *adj*: *highly motivated students* متحمّس، عنده دافع قوي للعمل

motivation /ˌməʊtɪˈveɪʃn/ *noun* [C,U] the need or reason for doing sth; a feeling of interest in doing sth: *I'm suffering from a lack of motivation. My new job is really boring.* باعث نفسيّ ، اهتمام

motive /ˈməʊtɪv/ *noun* [C,U] a reason for doing sth: *Nobody seemed to have a motive for the murder.* باعث ، حافز

motor /ˈməʊtə(r)/ *noun* [C] a machine that changes power into movement: *The washing machine doesn't work. I think something is wrong with the motor.* ○ *to start/turn off a motor* المُحرّك

> **Engine**, not **motor**, is usually used in connection with cars and motorcycles, but sometimes **motor** is also used. Cars are, in fact, sometimes called **motor cars**. **Engines** generally use petrol and **motors** use electricity.

▶ **motor** *adj* (only *before* a noun) connected with vehicles that have an engine or a motor: *a motor boat* ○ *motor racing* ○ *a motor mechanic* ذو محرّك ، (قارب) بخاري : (سباق) سيّارات

motoring /ˈməʊtərɪŋ/ *noun* [U] driving in a car: *to commit a motoring offence* ○ *a motoring holiday* قيادة السيارة ، "سواقة"

motorist /ˈməʊtərɪst/ *noun* [C] a person who drives a car ➲ Look at **pedestrian**. سائق سيّارة

motorized (*also* **motorised**) /ˈməʊtəraɪzd/ *adj* having an engine: *motorized transport* ذو محرك

motorbike /ˈməʊtəbaɪk/ *noun* [C] (*Brit*) = MOTORCYCLE

ˈ**motor boat** *noun* [C] a small fast boat that has an engine قارب بخاريّ ، قارب ذو محرّك

ˈ**motor car** *noun* [C] (*Brit formal*) = CAR (1)

motorcycle /ˈməʊtəsaɪkl/ (*also* **motorbike**) (*Brit informal*) *noun* [C] a large bicycle with an engine درّاجة نارية

▶ ˈ**motorcyclist** /ˈməʊtəsaɪklɪst/ *noun* [C] a person who rides a motorcycle راكب الدرّاجة الناريّة

motorway /ˈməʊtəweɪ/ (*US* **expressway**; **freeway**) *noun* [C] a wide road that is specially built for fast traffic: *to join/leave a motorway* ○ *a motorway service station* "أوتوستراد"، طريق سريع

A motorway has two or three **lanes** on each **carriageway**. On the left of each carriageway there is a **hard shoulder**. Look at the note at **road**.

motto /ˈmɒtəʊ/ *noun* [C] (*pl.* **mottoes**) a short sentence that expresses a rule for a person's or an organization's behaviour: *'Live and let live' that's my motto.* شعار

mould[1] (*US* **mold**) /məʊld/ *noun* **1** [C] a hollow container that you use for making sth into a particular shape. You put a liquid substance into a mould and wait for it to become solid (set) in the shape of the mould. قالب

2 [sing.] a particular type (of person): *She doesn't fit into the usual mould of sales directors.* نموذج : صنف ، نوع معيّن من الناس

▶ **mould** *verb* [T] to make sth into a particular shape or form يصوغ في قالب : يصوغ ، يشكّل

mould[2] (*US* **mold**) /məʊld/ *noun* [U] a soft green substance (a type of fungus) that grows in warm, damp places or on food that has been kept too long عفَن

▶ **mouldy** (*US* **moldy**) *adj*: *The cheese had gone mouldy.* عَفِن

moult (*US* **molt**) /məʊlt/ *verb* [I] (used about an animal or bird) to lose hair or feathers (في الطيور أو الحيوانات) يفقد شعره أو ريشه

mound /maʊnd/ *noun* [C] **1** a large pile of earth; a small hill كومة كبيرة من التراب ، تلّة صغيرة

2 a pile or heap of things: *I've got a mound of papers to work through.* كومة أو كدسة من الأشياء

mount[1] /maʊnt/ *noun* [C] (*abbr* **Mt**) (used in names) a mountain: *Mt Everest* جَبَل (كذا)

mount[2] /maʊnt/ *verb* **1** [T] (*formal*) to go to the top of sth: *to mount the stairs* ○ *He mounted the platform and began to speak.* يصعد

2 [I,T] to get on a horse or bicycle ℹ The opposite is **dismount**. يركب ، يمتطي

3 [I] to increase in level or amount: *The tension mounted as the end of the match approached.* يزداد ، يرتفع ، يشتد

4 [T] to fix sth on or in sth else: *The gas boiler was mounted on the wall.* يركّب، ينصب

5 [T] to organize sth: *to mount an exhibition* ○ *to mount an attack* يقيم: يقوم بِ

PHR V **mount up (to sth)** to increase (often more than you want): *When you're buying food for six people the cost soon mounts up.* يزداد : يتراكم

▶ **mounted** *adj* riding a horse: *mounted police* راكب حصاناً

mounting *adj* increasing: *mounting unemployment* متزايد ، متصاعد

mountain /ˈmaʊntən; *US* -ntn/ *noun* [C] **1** a very high hill: *Which is the highest mountain in the world?* ○ *Have you ever climbed a mountain?* ○ *a steep mountain road* ○ *a range of mountains* جَبَل

2 a large amount of sth: *There is a mountain of unanswered letters on her desk.* جبل ، أكداس هائلة

▶ **mountaineer** /ˌmaʊntəˈnɪə(r)/ *noun* [C] a person who climbs mountains متسلّق الجبال

mountaineering /ˌmaʊntəˈnɪərɪŋ/ *noun* [U] the sport of climbing mountains تسلّق الجبال

mountainous /ˈmaʊntənəs/ *adj* **1** having many mountains: *mountainous countryside* جبلي

2 very large: *The mountainous waves made sailing impossible.* ضخم

ˈ**mountain bike** *noun* [C] a bicycle with a strong frame, wide tyres and many gears, designed for riding on rough ground دراجة جبليّة

ˈ**mountainside** /ˈmaʊntənsaɪd/ *noun* [C] one of the steep sides of a mountain جانب أو منحدر الجبل

mourn /mɔːn/ *verb* [I,T] **mourn (for/over sb/sth)** to feel great sadness, especially because sb has died: *She is still mourning (for) her child.* يتفجّع على: يلبس ملابس الحداد

▶ **mourner** *noun* [C] a person who goes to a funeral as a friend or relative of the person who has died المشترك في جنازة أو ماتم

mournful /-fl/ *adj* sad: *a mournful song* حزين ، نائح ، شجيّ

mournfully /-fəli/ *adv* بِحزن

mourning *noun* [U] a time when people feel or show great sadness because sb has died: *He is in mourning.* الحداد

mouse /maʊs; *US* maʊs/ *noun* [C] (*pl.* **mice** /maɪs/) **1** a small furry animal with a long tail: *The cat has caught a mouse.* ℹ **Mice**, like **rats**, **hamsters**, etc. are members of the **rodent** family. فأر

2 a piece of equipment, attached to a computer, for entering commands without using the keyboard ℹ The mouse controls the **cursor** when you **click** on it. فأر الكمبيوتر

▶ **mouse** *verb*

PHR V ˌ**mouse** ˈ**over sth** (*computing*) to use the mouse to move over sth on a computer screen: *Mouse over the link in the original message.* يشير بالفأرة (في الحاسوب)

ˈ**mouse mat** *noun* [C] a small square of plastic that is the best kind of surface on which to use a computer mouse وسادة الفأر (كمبيوتر)

mousse /muːs/ *noun* [C,U] **1** a type of food that is made by beating together cream and eggs with either sth sweet (e.g. chocolate) or sth savoury (e.g. fish): *a chocolate mousse* ○ *salmon mousse* "موس" : طعام عماده القشدة والبيض المخفوق

2 a substance that is used on hair to give it a particular style or to improve its condition خلطة لتحسين الشعر وتصفيفه

moustache /məˈstɑːʃ/ (*US* **mustache** /ˈmʌstæʃ/) *noun* [C] hair that grows on the top lip, between the mouth and the nose: *Has he got a moustache?* شارِب، شَنَب

mouth[1] /maʊθ/ *noun* [C] (*pl.* **mouths** /maʊðz/)

1 the part of your face that you use for eating and speaking: *Don't speak with your mouth full.* ○ *Open your mouth, please!* ○ *You can close your mouth now.* ○ *Keep your mouth closed when you're eating.* ○ (*figurative*) *They have a low income and five mouths to feed.* فم

2 the place where a river enters the sea مصبّ النهر

▶ **-mouthed** /maʊðd/ (in compounds) **1** having a particular type of mouth: *We stared open-mouthed in surprise.* (في التعابير المركّبة) مثلاً: فاغر الفم

2 having a particular way of speaking: *He's loud-mouthed and ill-mannered.* (للتعبير عن أسلوب الكلام)

mouthful /-fʊl/ *noun* **1** [C] the amount of food or drink that you can put in your mouth at one time لقمة ، ملء الفم من الطعام أو الشراب

2 [sing.] a word or phrase that is long or difficult to say كلمة أو تعبير صعب النطق

mouth² /maʊð/ *verb* [I,T] to move your mouth as if you were speaking but without making any sound يحرك شفتيه دون كلام

'mouth organ (*also* **harmonica**) *noun* [C] a small musical instrument that you play by moving it across your lips while you are blowing هرمونيكا (آلة موسيقيّة)

mouthpiece /'maʊθpi:s/ *noun* [C] **1** the part of a telephone, musical instrument, etc. that you put in or near your mouth الجزء القريب من الفم في سمّاعة التليفون؛ المِبْسَم (في آلة نفخ موسيقيّة)

2 a person, newspaper, etc. that a particular group uses to express its opinions: *Pravda was the mouthpiece of the Soviet government.* الناطق الرسميّ (لحكومة ما)

mouthwash /'maʊθwɒʃ/ *noun* [U] liquid that you use for cleaning your mouth and making it smell nice غسول للفم

'mouth-watering *adj* (used about food) that looks or smells very good شهي ، يسيل له اللعاب

movable /'mu:vəbl/ *adj* that can be moved متحرّك ، متنقّل
➲ Look at **portable**.

move¹ /mu:v/ *noun* [C] **1** a change of place or position: *She sat watching every move I made.* ○ *One false move and I'll shoot!* حركة

2 a change in the place where you live or work: *a move to a bigger house* ○ *I've been in the job for six years and feel it's time for a move.* انتقال إلى مسكن أو عمل آخر

3 action that you take because you want to achieve a particular result: *Moves are being made to secure the release of the hostages.* ○ *Both sides want to negotiate but neither is prepared to make the first move.* ○ *Asking him to help me was a good move.* إجراء ، خطوة

4 a change in the position of a piece in a game like chess دَوْر ، حركة

IDM **be on the move** to be going somewhere: *The car was already on the move.* ○ *The firm is on the move to larger premises.* يتحرك؛ ينتقل إلى مكان آخر

get a move on (*informal*) to hurry: *I'm late. I'll have to get a move on.* يسرع

move² /mu:v/ *verb* **1** [I,T] to change position or to put sth in a different position: *Don't move – there's a bee on your arm.* ○ *Please move your car. It's blocking the drive.* ○ *I thought I heard something moving in the bushes over there.* ○ *They are moving the patient to another hospital.* يتحرك؛ يحرك

2 [I] to go and live in another house, etc: *Our neighbours have sold their house and are moving next week.* ينتقل إلى مسكن جديد

3 [I] to change or make progress: *When the new team of builders arrived things started moving very quickly.* يتقدم، يتحرك

4 [T] to cause sb to have strong feelings (often of sadness): *The reports about the starving children moved many people to tears.* يهزّ المشاعر ، يحزن

5 [I] to take action: *Unless we move quickly lives will be lost.* يتّخذ الخطوات اللازمة ، يقوم بعمل فعّال

6 [I,T] to change the position of a piece in a game like chess يحرك (أحجار الشطرنج)

IDM **get moving** to go, leave or do sth quickly ينصرف؛ يسرع في العمل

get sth moving to cause sth to make progress يسرّع؛ يحرك

move house to move your furniture, etc. to another home ينقل إلى مسكن آخر

PHR V **move across/along/down/over/up** to move further in a particular direction in order to make space for sb/sth else: *The conductor asked the passengers to move down the bus.* يتحرك أو يمشي (إلى الأمام/إلى الخلف أو غيره)

move in to start living in a new house يسكن في منزله الجديد

move off (used about a vehicle) to start a journey; to leave: *Maria waved from the window as the train moved off.* يتحرك، يبدأ رحلته

move out to stop living in a house ينتقل من بيته

▶ **moving** *adj* **1** (only *before* a noun) that moves: *a moving staircase* ○ *It's a computerized machine with few moving parts.* متحرك

2 causing strong feelings: *The film is a moving story about a young boy's fight against cancer.* مثير للمشاعر ، مؤثّر

movement /'mu:vmənt/ *noun* **1** [C,U] an action that involves changing position or place or using the body in some way: *The dancer's movements were smooth and beautifully controlled.* ○ *The man lay still in the long grass, knowing that any movement would be seen by the police.* ○ *the slow movement of the clouds across the sky* حركة

2 [C, usually sing.] **a movement (away from/towards sth)** a general change in the way people think or behave: *There's a slight movement away from the materialism of the 1980s.* اتّجاه، تغيّر في الرأي العام

3 movements [plural] a person's actions or plans during a period of time: *Detectives have been watching the man's movements for several days.* تحركات

4 [C] a group of people who have the same aims or ideas (and who want to persuade other people that they are right): *I support the Animal Rights movement.* حركة

5 [C] one of the main parts of a long piece of music: *a symphony in four movements* حركة

movie /ˈmuːvi/ *noun* (*especially US*) **1** [C] = FILM[1] (1): *Would you like to see a movie?* ○ *a science fiction movie* ○ *a movie director*

2 the movies [plural] = CINEMA: *Let's go to the movies.*

'movie theater *noun* [C] (*especially US*) = CINEMA

mow /məʊ/ *verb* [I,T] (*pt* **mowed**; *pp* **mown** /məʊn/ or **mowed**) to cut grass using a machine or an instrument: *You need to mow the lawn at least once a week.* يجزّ الحشيش (والأعشاب)

▶ **mower** *noun* [C] a machine for cutting grass or crops: *a lawnmower* ○ *an electric mower* آلة جزّ الحشيش (والأعشاب)

MP /ˌem ˈpiː/ *abbrev* (*especially Brit*) = MEMBER OF PARLIAMENT

mpg /ˌem piː ˈdʒiː/ *abbrev* = MILES PER GALLON: *This car does 40 mpg* (= you can drive 40 miles on one gallon of petrol).

mph /ˌem piː ˈeɪtʃ/ *abbrev* = MILES PER HOUR: *a 70 mph speed limit*

Mr /ˈmɪstə(r)/ (used as a title before the name of a man): *Mr (John) Brown* السيّد....

Mrs /ˈmɪsɪz/ (used as a title before the name of a married woman): *Mrs (Jane) Allen* السيّدة.... حرَم...

Ms /məz; mɪz/ (used as a title before the name of a woman, either married or unmarried): *Ms (Emma) Gregg* السيّدة أو الآنسة...

> Some women prefer the title **Ms** to **Mrs** or **Miss**. We can also use it when we do not know whether or not a woman is married.

MSc /ˌem es ˈsiː/ *abbrev* Master of Science; a second qualification that you receive when you complete a more advanced course or piece of research in a science subject at university or college ماجستير في العلوم

Mt *abbrev* = MOUNT: *Mt Everest*

much[1] /mʌtʃ/ *det, pron* (used with uncountable nouns, mainly in negative sentences and questions, or after *as, how, so, too*) a large amount of sth: *I haven't got much money.* ○ *Did you have much difficulty finding the house?* ○ *You've given me too much food.* ○ *How much time have you got?* ○ *I didn't write much.* ○ *Did she say much?* ○ *How much do you want?* ○ *Eat as much as you can.* ○ *'Is there any post?' 'Not much.'* مقدار كبير، كثير

> In statements we usually use **a lot of**, not **much** (which is extremely formal): *I've got a lot of experience.*

IDM not much of a... not very good: *She's not much of a cook.* رديء نوعاً ما: "ليست بطباخة جيّدة"

not up to much → UP

much[2] /mʌtʃ/ *adv* **1** to a great extent or degree: *I don't like her very much.* ○ *We are very much looking forward to meeting you.* ○ *Do you go to the cinema much?* (= very often) ○ *Their house is much nicer than ours.* ○ *You ate much more than me.* كثيراً، بكثير

2 (with past participles used as adjectives) to a great extent or degree: *a much-needed rest* ○ *She was much loved by all her friends.* ➲ Compare: *She was* **very** *popular.* إلى حدّ كبير

IDM much the same very similar: *Polish food is much the same as German.* مثل، مشابه

not much good (at sth) not very good: *I'm not much good at singing.* غير ماهر، لا يجيد

muck[1] /mʌk/ *noun* [U] (*informal*) **1** dirt وسَخ

2 the waste from farm animals, used to make the land more fertile ℹ A more common word is **manure.** سماد حيواني، زبل

muck[2] /mʌk/ *verb*

PHRV muck about/around (*informal*) to behave in a silly way or to waste time: *Stop mucking around and come and help me!* يعبث، يلعب، يضيّع وقته بأعمال صبيانيّة

muck sth up (*informal*) to do sth badly; to spoil sth: *I was so nervous that I completely mucked up my interview.* يلخبط، يفسد

mucus /ˈmjuːkəs/ *noun* [U] (*formal*) a sticky substance that is produced in some parts of the body, especially the nose مخاط

mud /mʌd/ *noun* [U] soft, wet earth: *He came home from the football match covered in mud.* طين، وحل

▶ **muddy** *adj* (**muddier**; **muddiest**) full of or covered in mud: *Take those muddy boots off at the door!* ○ *It's very muddy down by the river.* موحِل

muddle /ˈmʌdl/ *verb* [T] **1 muddle sth (up)** to put things in the wrong place or order or to make them untidy: *Try not to get those papers muddled up – I've got them all in the right order.* "يلَخبِط"، يخلط

2 muddle sb (up) to confuse sb: *Stop muddling me up! I can only answer one question at a time.* يشوّش، يربِك

▶ **muddle** *noun* [C,U] a state of disorder or confusion, in a place or in the mind: *Your room's in a terrible muddle.* ○ *I'm in a complete muddle! Is it Thursday or Friday?* "لخبطة"، فوضى؛ تشويش

muddled *adj* not clear; confused: *He gave me a rather muddled explanation.* مشوّش، "ملَخبَط"

mudguard /ˈmʌdɡɑːd/ *noun* [C] a metal or plastic cover over the wheel of a bicycle, etc. which stops mud and water from splashing up رَفْرَف أو رفراف الدّراجة

muesli /ˈmjuːzli/ *noun* [U] food made of grains, nuts, dried fruit, etc. that you eat with milk for breakfast "ميوزلي": خليط من الحبوب والمكسّرات والفواكه المجففة يؤكل صباحاً

muezzin /muːˈezɪn; mjuː-/ *noun* [C] a man who calls Muslims to prayer, usually from the top of the tower of a mosque مؤذّن

muffin /ˈmʌfɪn/ *noun* [C] (*US* **English muffin**)

1 a type of bread roll often eaten hot with butter كعكة طريّة تشبه القطايف
2 a type of small cake نوع من المعجنات

muffle /ˈmʌfl/ *verb* [T] to make a sound quieter and more difficult to hear: *He put his hand over her mouth to muffle her cries.* يكتم الصوت
▶ **muffled** *adj* (used about sounds) difficult to hear; quiet or not clear: *I could hear muffled voices outside but I couldn't tell what they were saying.* (صوت) مكتوم، غير واضح
muffled up *adj* wrapped up in warm clothes مُلتفّ بملابس مدفئة، متلفّع

muffler (*US*) = SILENCER

mug[1] /mʌg/ *noun* [C] a deep cup with straight sides, used without a saucer; the contents of a mug: *Would you prefer a cup or a mug?* ○ *a mug of coffee* كوز ، فنجان عميق أسطوانيّ الشكل عادة

mug[2] /mʌg/ *verb* [T] (mu**gg**ing; mu**gg**ed) to attack and rob sb in the street يهاجم شخصاً في الشارع لسلب نقوده
▶ **mugger** *noun* [C] a person who attacks sb in this way من يهاجم شخصاً في الشارع بغية سلبه
mugging *noun* [C,U] an occasion when a person is mugged حادث اعتداء على شخص وسلبه، سطو

mug[3] /mʌg/ *noun* [C] (*informal*) a stupid person who is easy to trick or deceive غبي ، ساذج

muggy /ˈmʌgi/ *adj* (used about the weather) too warm and damp (جو) حارّ ورطب ، (جوّ) خانق

mule /mjuːl/ *noun* [C] an animal that has a horse and a donkey as its parents: *to be as stubborn as a mule* ℹ We say that a mule is a **cross** between a horse and a donkey. بَغْل

mull /mʌl/ *verb*
PHR V **mull sth over** to think about sth carefully and for a long time: *Don't ask me for a decision right now. I'll have to mull it over.* يتفكّر في الأمر ، يفكّر مليّاً

mullah /ˈmʌlə; ˈmʊlə/ *noun* [C] a Muslim teacher of religion and holy law ملاّ

multicoloured /ˌmʌltiˈkʌləd/ *adj* consisting of or decorated with many colours, especially bright ones: *a multicoloured dress* متعدد الألوان

multicultural /ˌmʌltiˈkʌltʃərəl/ *adj* for or including people of many different races, languages, religions and customs: *a multicultural society* متعدد الثقافات

multilateral /ˌmʌltiˈlætərəl/ *adj* involving more than two groups of people, countries, etc: *a multilateral agreement* ➲ Look at **unilateral**. متعدّد الجوانب : متعدّد الأطراف

multimedia /ˌmʌltiˈmiːdiə/ *adj* (only *before* a noun) involving several different methods of communication or forms of expression: *a multimedia event, including music, dance, video and a laser show* متعدد الوسائط

multinational /ˌmʌltiˈnæʃnəl/ *adj* involving many countries من دول متعدّدة
▶ **multinational** *noun* [C] a company that has offices or factories in many countries شركة لها فروع في دول عدّة

multiple /ˈmʌltɪpl/ *adj* involving many people or having many parts, types, etc: *a multiple crash on the motorway* ○ *to receive multiple injuries* متعدِّد
▶ **multiple** *noun* [C] a number that contains another number an exact number of times: *12, 18 and 24 are multiples of 6.* (في الرياضيّات) المضاعف

ˌmultiple-ˈchoice *adj* (used about examination questions) showing several different answers from which you have to choose the right one (اختبار) متعدّد الاختيارات

multiple sclerosis /ˌmʌltɪpl skləˈrəʊsɪs/ *noun* [U] (*abbr* **MS**) a serious disease which slowly causes you to lose control of your body and of the ability to move التصلُّب اللُّويحي

multiplex /ˈmʌltɪpleks/ *noun* [C] a large cinema/movie theater with several separate rooms with screens سينما متعددة الصالات

multiplication /ˌmʌltɪplɪˈkeɪʃn/ *noun* [U] the process of multiplying a number: *The children will be tested on addition, subtraction, multiplication and division.* الضرب (في الرياضيّات)

🔑 **multiply** /ˈmʌltɪplaɪ/ *verb* (*pres part* **multiplying**; *3rd pers sing pres* **multiplies**; *pt, pp* **multiplied**) **1** [I,T] **multiply A by B; multiply A and B (together)** to increase a number by the number of times mentioned: *to learn to multiply and divide* ○ *2 multiplied by 4 makes 8* (2 x 4 = 8) ○ *What do you get if you multiply 13 and 11?* ○ *Multiply the two numbers together and you should get the answer.* يضرب (في الرياضيّات)
2 [I,T] to become bigger or greater; to make sth bigger or greater; to increase: *Our profits have multiplied over the last two years.* ○ *Using this method, you can multiply your profit in a very short time.* يزداد ، يتضاعف : يزيد ، يضاعف
3 [I] (used especially about animals) to increase in number by producing large numbers of young يتكاثر

multi-purpose /ˌmʌlti ˈpɜːpəs/ *adj* that can be used for several different purposes: *a multi-purpose tool/machine* متعدد الوظائف أو الاستعمالات

ˌmulti-ˈstorey *noun* [C] a large building with several floors for parking cars in مرآب متعدد الطوابق

multitude /ˈmʌltɪtjuːd; *US* -tuːd/ *noun* [C] (*formal*) a very large number of people or things: *a multitude of difficulties* حشد كبير ، جمع غفير : فَيْض

🔑 **mum** /mʌm/ (*US* **mom** /mɒm/) *noun* [C] (*informal*) mother: *Is that your mum?* ○ *What's for tea, Mum?* ➲ Look at **mummy**. أمّ، ماما

mumble /ˈmʌmbl/ *verb* [I,T] to speak quietly without opening your mouth properly, so that people cannot really hear the words: *I can't hear if you mumble – speak up!* ○ *Last night you kept mumbling something about a car crash in your sleep.* ➲ Look at **mutter**. يغمغم ، يتمتِم

mummy[1] /ˈmʌmi/ *noun* [C] (*pl.* **mummies**) (*US* **mommy**; **momma**) (*informal*) (used by or to children) mother: *Here comes your mummy now.* ماما ، أُمّ

mummy² /ˈmʌmi/ *noun* [C] (*pl.* **mummies**) a dead body of a person or animal which has been preserved by rubbing it with special oils and wrapping it in cloth: *an Egyptian mummy* مومياء

mumps /mʌmps/ *noun* [U] an infectious disease, especially of children. Mumps causes the neck and lower face to swell: *to have/catch (the) mumps* ○ *Mumps usually lasts for about one week.* التهاب الغدّة النكفيّة ، "أبو كعب"

munch /mʌntʃ/ *verb* [I,T] to eat steadily. You usually munch sth hard that makes a noise as you chew it: *He sat there munching an apple and didn't say a word.* يمضغ بصوت مسموع

mundane /mʌnˈdeɪn/ *adj* ordinary; not interesting or exciting: *a mundane life, job, conversation, etc.* عادي ، رتيب

municipal /mjuːˈnɪsɪpl/ *adj* connected with a town or city that has its own local government: *municipal buildings* (= the town hall, public library, etc.) (مجلس) بلدي

munitions /mjuːˈnɪʃnz/ *noun* [plural] military supplies, especially bombs and guns ذخيرة ، أسلحة

mural /ˈmjʊərəl/ *noun* [C] a large picture which is painted on a wall جدارية

murder /ˈmɜːdə(r)/ *noun* **1** [C,U] the crime of killing a person illegally and on purpose: *It is thought that both murders were committed by the same person.* ○ *He was sentenced to life imprisonment for murder.* ○ *the murder victim* ○ *the murder weapon* جريمة قتل ، القتل عمداً

2 [U] (*informal*) a very difficult or unpleasant experience: *It's murder trying to work when it's as hot as this.* "شيء يطلّع الروح" ، شيء فظيع

▸ **murder** *verb* [T] to kill a person illegally and on purpose: *It seems that she was murdered with a knife.* ➲ Look at the note at **kill**. يقتل عمداً

murderer /ˈmɜːdərə(r)/ *noun* [C] a person who has murdered sb قاتل/قاتلة ، مجرم/مجرمة

murderous /ˈmɜːdərəs/ *adj* likely to murder or capable of murder فتّاك ، قاتل ؛ قادر على ارتكاب جريمة قتل

murky /ˈmɜːki/ *adj* (**murkier**; **murkiest**) dark and unpleasant or dirty: *The water in the river looked very murky.* عكِر، داكن؛ قذر

murmur /ˈmɜːmə(r)/ *noun* **1** [C] the sound of words that are spoken quietly: *A murmur of disagreement ran round the room.* غمغمة ، تمتمة ، تذمُّر

2 [sing.] a low, gentle, continuous sound that is often not very clear: *the murmur of the wind in the trees* حفيف ، همهمة ، صوت خافت ناعم

▸ **murmur** *verb* [I,T] to say sth in a low quiet voice: *'I love you,' he murmured.* ○ *Samantha murmured an answer.* يهمس ، يتمتم

muscle /ˈmʌsl/ *noun* [C,U] a piece of flesh inside the body which you can tighten or relax to produce movement: *Don't carry such heavy weights or you'll pull* (= damage) *a muscle.* ○ *Riding a bicycle is good for developing the leg muscles.* ○ *The heart is made of muscle.* عضَلة

muscular /ˈmʌskjələ(r)/ *adj* **1** connected with muscles: *muscular pain* عضَلي

2 having large strong muscles: *a muscular body* مفتول العضلات

museum /mjuˈziəm/ *noun* [C] a building where collections of valuable and interesting objects are kept and shown to the public: *Have you been to the Science Museum in London?* ○ *There's an exhibition of dinosaurs at the Natural History Museum.* متحف

mushroom /ˈmʌʃrʊm; -ruːm/ *noun* [C] a type of plant (a fungus) which grows very quickly, has a flat rounded top on a short stem and can be eaten as a vegetable: *mushrooms with garlic* ○ *mushroom soup* فطر ، عيش الغراب

> A mushroom is a type of **fungus**. Some, but not all, **fungi** can be eaten. **Toadstool** is another name for some types of poisonous fungi.

music /ˈmjuːzɪk/ *noun* [U] **1** an arrangement of sounds in patterns to be sung or played on instruments: *What sort of music do you like?* ○ *classical, folk, pop, rock, etc. music* ○ *Who composed this piece of music?* ○ *That poem has been set to music.* ○ *a music lover* ○ *a music lesson* موسيقى

2 the written signs that represent the sounds of music: *Can you read music?* ○ *I've forgotten my music – can I share yours?* (ورقة) النوتة أو العلامات الموسيقيّة

musical /ˈmjuːzɪkl/ *adj* **1** connected with music: *musical instruments* (= the piano, the violin, the trumpet, etc.) ○ *Would you like our programme of this month's musical events?* موسيقيّ

2 interested in or good at music: *He's very musical.* ○ *a musical child* مغرم بالموسيقى ، ذو موهبة موسيقيّة

3 pleasant to listen to because it is like music: *a musical voice* (صوت) رخيم أو عذب

▸ **musical** *noun* [C] a play or film which has singing and dancing in it مسرحية غنائية ، فيلم غنائيّ

musician /mjuˈzɪʃn/ *noun* [C] **1** a person whose job is to play a musical instrument: *The band consists of ten musicians.* عازف موسيقيّ

2 a person who is good at writing or playing music: *At ten he was already a fine musician.* موسيقار ، ملحّن

Muslim /ˈmʊzlɪm; *US* ˈmʌzləm/ (*also* **Moslem** /ˈmɒzləm/) *noun* [C] a person whose religion is Islam المسلِم

▸ **Muslim** (*also* **Moslem**) *adj*: *Muslim traditions, beliefs, etc.* إسلاميّ

mussel /ˈmʌsl/ *noun* [C] a type of sea animal that lives inside a black shell and can be eaten ميدية ، بلَح البحر

must /məst; *strong form* mʌst/ *modal verb* (*negative* **must not**; *short form* **mustn't** /ˈmʌsnt/) **1** (used for saying that it is necessary that sth happens): *I must remember to go to the bank today.* ○ *Cars must not park in front of the entrance.* ○ *You mustn't take photographs in here. It's forbidden.* ○ *'Must we finish this exercise today?'*

a b c d e f g h i j k l **m** n o p q r s t u v w x y z

'Yes, you must.' ℹ The negative for the last example is *'No, you don't have to'*. يجب، من الضروريّ

2 (used for giving sb advice): *You really must see that film. It's wonderful.* عليك أن... ، أنصحك أن...

3 (used for saying that you are sure that sth is true): *Have something to eat. You must be hungry.* ○ *There's a lot of noise from next door. They must be having a party.* ○ *I can't find my cheque book. I must have left it at home.* ○ *It must have been a great shock when your mother died.* ○ *That car that passed us must have been doing 100 miles an hour.* لا بدّ

▸ **must** *noun* [C] a thing that is absolutely necessary, or that must be seen, done, etc: *This book is a must for all science-fiction fans.* ضرورة حتميّة ، شيء أساسي

mustache (*US*) = MOUSTACHE

mustard /ˈmʌstəd/ *noun* [U] a yellow or brown sauce which is made from the seeds of the mustard plant. The sauce has a very strong taste and is eaten in very small amounts, usually with meat. خَرْدَل

musty /ˈmʌsti/ *adj* (**mustier**; **mustiest**) having an unpleasant stale or damp smell: *The rooms in the old house were dark and musty.* ذو رائحة عَفِنة أو فاسدة

mutant /ˈmjuːtənt/ *noun* [C] a living thing that is different from other living things of the same type because of a change in its basic (genetic) structure مخلوق طافِر

mutate /mjuːˈteɪt/ *verb* **mutate (into sth)** (*technical*) **1** [I, T] to develop or make sth develop a new form or structure, because of a genetic change: *the ability of the virus to mutate into new forms* ○ *mutated genes* يطفر

2 [I] (*formal*) to change into a new form: *Rhythm and blues mutated into rock and roll.* يتحوّل

mutation /mjuːˈteɪʃn/ *noun* [C,U] a change in the basic structure of a living or developing thing; an example of such a change: *Mutations caused by radiation.* طَفرة ، افتجاء : تبدُّل فجائي

muted /ˈmjuːtɪd/ *adj* **1** (used about colours or sounds) not bright or loud; soft (لون) هادئ : (صوت) خافت

2 (used about a feeling or reaction) not strong or not openly expressed: *muted criticism* ○ *a muted response* (انتقاد) غير صريح : مخفّف

mutilate /ˈmjuːtɪleɪt/ *verb* [T] (usually passive) to damage sb's body very badly, often by cutting off parts: *The body was too badly mutilated to be identified.* يمثّل بالجثّة ، يشوّه الجسم ببتر الأطراف وغير ذلك

▸ **mutilation** /ˌmjuːtɪˈleɪʃn/ *noun* [C,U] التمثيل بالجثث

mutiny /ˈmjuːtəni/ *noun* [C,U] (*pl.* **mutinies**) an act that involves a group of people, especially sailors or soldiers, refusing to obey the person who is in command: *There'll be a mutiny if conditions don't improve.* عصيان، تمرد ، فتنة

▸ **mutiny** *verb* [I] (*pres part* **mutinying**; *3rd pers sing pres* **mutinies**; *pt, pp* **mutinied**) **mutiny (against sb/sth)** to refuse to obey your leader or to accept sth يتمرّد أو يثور على

mutter /ˈmʌtə(r)/ *verb* [I,T] to speak in a low, quiet and sometimes rather angry voice that is difficult to hear: *He muttered something about being late for an appointment and left the room.* يغمغم ، يتمتم

mutton /ˈmʌtn/ *noun* [U] the meat from an adult sheep: *a leg/shoulder of mutton* ➲ Look at the note at **meat**. لحم الغنم أو الضأن

mutual /ˈmjuːtʃuəl/ *adj* **1** (used about a feeling or an action) felt or done by both or all the people involved: *We have a mutual agreement* (= we both agree) *to help each other out when necessary.* ○ *I just can't stand her and I'm sure the feeling is mutual* (= she doesn't like me either). متبادل

2 shared by two or more people: *It seems that Jane is a mutual friend of ours.* مشترك

▸ **mutually** /-uəli/ *adv*: *The statements of the two witnesses were mutually exclusive* (= they could not both be true). بشكل متبادل : (الإفادات) الواحدة تُلغي الأخرى

muzzle /ˈmʌzl/ *noun* [C] **1** the nose and mouth of an animal (e.g. a dog or fox) خَطْم

2 a cover made of leather or wire that is put over an animal's nose and mouth so that it cannot bite كمامة

3 the open end of a gun where the bullets come out فوهة البندقيّة

🔑 **my** /maɪ/ *det* **1** of or belonging to me: *This is my husband, Jim.* ○ *It's my turn, not yours!* ○ *My favourite colour is blue.* (ضمير الملكيّة للشخص المتكلّم)

2 (used before a noun or adjective as a way of talking to sb): *My dear Anne, ...* ○ *Goodbye, my darling.* (للمناداة) يا...

3 (used in exclamations): *My goodness! Look at the time.* (تستعمل للتعبير عن التعجب) يا (إلهي!)

🔑 **myself** /maɪˈself/ *pron* **1** (used as the object of a verb or preposition when the person who does an action is also affected by it): *I saw myself in the mirror.* ○ *I felt rather pleased with myself.* نفسي

2 (used for emphasis): *I'll speak to her myself.* ○ *I myself don't agree.* ○ *I'll do it myself* (= if you don't want to do it for me). نفسي ، بنفسي

IDM **(all) by myself 1** alone: *I live by myself.* ➲ Look at the note at **alone**. بمفردي ، لوحدي

2 without help: *I painted the house all by myself.* بمفردي ، دون مساعدة

🔑 **mysterious** /mɪˈstɪəriəs/ *adj* **1** that you do not know about or cannot explain; strange: *Several people reported seeing mysterious lights in the sky.* غريب ، مبهم

2 (used about a person) keeping sth secret or refusing to explain sth: *They're being very mysterious about where they're going this evening.* غامض ، سرّي

▸ **mysteriously** *adv* بشكل خفي : بغموض

🔑 **mystery** /ˈmɪstri/ *noun* (*pl.* **mysteries**) **1** [C] a thing that you cannot understand or explain: *The cause of the accident is a complete mystery.* ○ *Detectives are still trying to solve the mystery of* *his disappearance.* ○ *It's a mystery to me what my daughter sees in her boyfriend.* ○ *It's one of the great mysteries of the natural world.* ○ *a mystery guest, tour, etc.* (= one that you don't know anything about) لغز ، سِرّ

2 [U] the quality of being strange and secret and full of things that are difficult to explain: *novels full of mystery and suspense* ○ *a mystery story* غموض ، خفاء

mystic /ˈmɪstɪk/ *noun* [C] a person who spends his/her life developing the spirit and communicating with God or a god المتصوف؛ شخص روحانيّ

mystical /ˈmɪstɪkl/ (*also* **mystic** /ˈmɪstɪk/) *adj* of the spirit; involving hidden meaning, powers and feelings that are outside our normal everyday experience: *a mystical experience* روحانيّ ؛ صوفيّ ؛ خفيّ وغامض

mysticism /ˈmɪstɪsɪzəm/ *noun* [U] the belief that you can reach complete truth and knowledge of God or gods by prayer, thought and development of the spirit التصوُّف

mystify /ˈmɪstɪfaɪ/ *verb* [T] (*pres part* **mystifying**; *3rd pers sing pres* **mystifies**; *pt, pp* **mystified**) to make sb puzzled or confused: *I was mystified by the strange note. What did it mean?* يحيِّر، يثير الفضول والعَجَب

myth /mɪθ/ *noun* [C] **1** a very old story, especially one about gods and heroes. Myths often explain natural or historical events. أسطورة

2 an idea, belief or story which is untrue or impossible: *The idea that money makes you happy is a complete myth.* خرافة : قصة خياليّة

▸ **mythical** /ˈmɪθɪkl/ *adj* **1** existing only in myths(1): *mythical heroes* أسطوري

2 not real; existing only in the imagination خياليّ ، خرافيّ

mythology /mɪˈθɒlədʒi/ *noun* [U] very old stories and the beliefs contained in them: *Greek and Roman mythology* الأساطير

Nn

N, n /en/ *noun* [C] (*pl.* **Ns; N's** or **n's**) the fourteenth letter of the English alphabet: *'Nicolas' begins with (an) 'N'.* الحرف الرابع عشر من الأبجدية الإنكليزيّة

N (*US also* **No**) *abbrev* = NORTH(ERN)

n. *abbrev* = NOUN

naff /næf/ *adj* (*Brit slang*) lacking taste or style; without any value; not fashionable: *That's a pretty naff idea!* خالٍ من الذوق، تافه؛ موضة قديمة

nag /næg/ *verb* (nagging; nagged) **1** [I,T] **nag (at) sb** to talk to sb continuously in a complaining or critical way: *Stop nagging! I'll do it as soon as I can.* ○ *My parents are always nagging me about working harder.* يطيل في التوبيخ والشكوى ، يُضجر بكثرة النّقْد ، ينقّ

2 [T] to worry or hurt sb continuously: *a nagging doubt in my mind* ○ *a nagging headache* يقلِق أو يؤلم بلا انقطاع

⚿**nail** /neɪl/ *noun* [C] **1** a small thin piece of metal with a point at one end. It is used for holding pieces of wood together, hanging pictures on, etc: *We'll need some small nails, a hammer and some string.* ○ *to hammer in a nail* مسمار

2 the thin hard layer that covers the ends of your fingers and toes: *fingernails* ○ *toenails* ○ *I still bite my nails sometimes when I'm nervous.* ظُفر

IDM **hit the nail on the head** → HIT[1]

▸ **nail** *verb* [T] to fasten sth with a nail or nails: *Do you think we should nail these pieces together or use glue?* يسمِّر ، يثبّت بمسامير

PHRV **nail sb down (to sth)** to make a person say clearly what he/she wants or intends to do: *She says she'll visit us in the summer but I can't nail her down to a definite date.* يجبره على الإفصاح عن نواياه ، يسبر غوره

ˈ**nail brush** *noun* [C] a small brush for cleaning your fingernails فرشاة لتنظيف الأظافر

ˈ**nail file** *noun* [C] a small metal tool with a rough surface that you use for shaping your nails مِبْرَد الأظافر

ˈ**nail scissors** *noun* [plural] small scissors for cutting your nails: *a pair of nail scissors* ○ *Have you got any nail scissors?* مقصّ الأظافر

ˈ**nail varnish** (*Brit*) (*US* ˈ**nail polish**) *noun* [U] a liquid that people paint on their nails to give them colour or to make them shine طلاء الأظافر

naive (*also* **naïve**) /naɪˈiːv/ *adj* without enough experience of the world and too ready to believe what other people say: *I was too naive to really understand what was going on.* ○ *a naive remark* ساذج ، بريء ، بسيط

▸ **naively** (*also* **naïvely**) *adv*: *She naively accepted the first price he offered.* بسذاجة ، دون خِبرة

naivety (*also* **naïvety** /naɪˈiːvəti/) *noun* [U]: *He showed complete naivety in financial matters.* سذاجة ، عدم خبرة

⚿**naked** /ˈneɪkɪd/ *adj* **1** without any clothes on: *He was naked except for a towel.* ➲ Look at **bare** and **nude**. عارٍ ، مجرّد من الثياب

2 (only *before* a noun) not covered (used about sth that is usually covered): *a naked flame* مكشوف

3 (only *before* a noun) openly shown or expressed; easy to see and often shocking: *naked aggression* واضح، صريح ، مكشوف

IDM the naked eye the eye without the help of a microscope or telescope: *Bacteria are too small to be seen with the naked eye.* العين المجرّدة

name¹ /neɪm/ *noun* **1** [C] a word or words by which a person, animal, place or thing is known: *What's your name, please?* ○ *Do you know the name of this flower?* ○ *Has your house got a name or a number?* اسم

Your **first name** (*US* often **given name**) is the name your parents choose for you when you are born. It is very common in Christian countries to call this your **Christian name**. It can also be called your **forename**, although this is more formal and may be found on forms, documents, etc. **Surname** is the word usually used for your **family name** which you are born with. When a woman marries she may change her surname to be the same as her husband's. Her surname before marriage is then called her **maiden name**.

2 [sing.] an opinion that people have of a person or thing; reputation: *That area of London has rather a bad name.* ○ *The company needs to build up a good name for itself.* سمعة ، اسم

3 [C] a famous person: *All the big names in show business were invited to the party.* شخصيّة مشهورة

IDM by name using the name of sb/sth: *It's a big school but the headmaster knows all the children by name.* (يناديه) بالاسم

in the name of sb representing a certain group of people: *Could you write a letter in the name of all the young people in the village?* نيابةً عن ، باسم

in the name of sth because you believe in sth; for the sake of sth: *They acted in the name of democracy.* باسم (الحريّة) ، من أجل

make a name for yourself; make your name to become well known and respected: *It's not easy to make your name as a writer.* يصبح مشهوراً ؛ يربي لنفسه سمعة حسنة

name² /neɪm/ *verb* [T] **1 name sb/sth (after sb)** to give sb/sth a name: *The boy was named James after his grandfather.* ○ *Columbia was named after Christopher Columbus.* ❶ Be careful. When you are talking about being known by a particular name **be called** is used: *The baby is called Dan and his brother is Joe.* يسمّي (وليداً)

2 to say what the name of sb/sth is: *The journalist refused to name the person who had given her the information.* ○ *Can you name all the planets in order?* يسمّي ؛ يصرح باسم

3 to state a date, price, etc: *Have Alex and Julie named a date for their wedding?* يحدّد موعد (زفاف مثلاً)

nameless /ˈneɪmləs/ *adj* **1** without a name or with a name that you do not know or want to say: *the nameless slaves who built the pyramids* دون اسم ؛ مغمور ، نكرة ؛ غير مسمّى

2 not easily described or explained, e.g. because it is so terrible: *the nameless horrors of war* فظيع ، مريع ، يعجز اللسان عن وصفه

namely /ˈneɪmli/ *adv* (used for giving more detail about what you are saying) that is to say: *There is only one person who can overrule the death sentence, namely the President.* (ألا) وهو ، أي ، أعني

namesake /ˈneɪmseɪk/ *noun* [C] a person who has the same name as another سَمِيّ

nanny /ˈnæni/ *noun* [C] (*pl.* **nannies**) (*Brit*) a woman whose job is looking after young children. A nanny usually works at or lives in the child's home. مربيّة أطفال

nap /næp/ *noun* [C] a short sleep that you have during the day قيلولة قصيرة ، إغفاءة

▸ **nap** *verb* [I] (na**pp**ing; na**pp**ed) to have a short sleep يَقيل لمدة قصيرة ، يغفو

nape /neɪp/ *noun* [sing.] the back part of the neck قفا العنق

napkin /ˈnæpkɪn/ *noun* [C] a piece of cloth or paper that you use when you are eating to protect your clothes or for wiping your hands and mouth: *a paper napkin* ➲ Look at **serviette**. فوطة المائدة

nappy /ˈnæpi/ *noun* [C] (*pl.* **nappies**) (*US* **diaper**) a piece of soft thick cloth or paper that a baby or very young child wears around its bottom and between its legs: *Does her nappy need changing?* ○ *disposable nappies* (= that you throw away when they have been used) فوطة أو حفاظ الطفل ، كفولة

narcotic /nɑːˈkɒtɪk/ *noun* [C] a drug that makes you feel sleepy or stops you feeling pain. Some people take narcotics for pleasure and then cannot stop taking them (= they become addicted). مادّة مخدّرة

▸ **narcotic** *adj* مخدِّر

narrate /nəˈreɪt; *US* ˈnæreɪt/ *verb* [T] (*formal*) to tell a story يَرْوِي

▸ **narration** /nəˈreɪʃn/ *noun* [C,U] telling a story; the story that you tell رواية القصص ؛ قصّة

narrative /ˈnærətɪv/ *noun* [C] (*formal*) a story or an account قصة ، سَرْد

narrator *noun* [C] the person who tells a story or explains what is happening in a play, film, etc. الراوي؛ القصّاص

narrow /ˈnærəʊ/ *adj* **1** having only a short distance from side to side: *The bridge is too narrow for two cars to pass.* ❶ The opposite is **wide** or **broad**. ضيّق

2 not large: *a narrow circle of friends* محدود ، صغير

3 by a small amount: *That was a very narrow escape. You were lucky.* ○ *a narrow defeat/victory* بمقدار ضئيل ؛ بمشقّة

▸ **narrow** *verb* [I,T] to become narrow or to make sth narrow: [I]: *The road narrows in 50 metres.* يَضيق ، يصبح ضيّقاً

PHR V narrow sth down to make a list of things smaller: *The police have narrowed down their list of suspects to three.* يقلّل، يضيّق، يختصر

narrowly *adv* only by a small amount: *The driver swerved and narrowly missed hitting the boy.* بقليل ، بقدر ضئيل ، بالكاد

narrowness *noun* [U] ضيق ؛ قصر نظر

ˌnarrow-ˈminded /-ˈmaɪndɪd/ *adj* not willing to

accept new ideas or the opinions of other people if they are not the same as your own متمسك بآرائه ، ضيّق التفكير

nasal /ˈneɪzl/ *adj* connected with the nose أنفيّ

nasty /ˈnɑːsti; *US* ˈnæ-/ *adj* (**nastier**; **nastiest**)
1 ugly or unpleasant: *What's that nasty smell in this cupboard?* ○ *The new furniture looked cheap and nasty.* قبيح : بغيض

2 angry or aggressive: *When she was asked to leave she got really nasty.* ○ *Luke has a really nasty temper.* غاضب ، عدائي ، شرّير

3 unkind: *That was a nasty thing to say to your brother.* قاسٍ ، غير لطيف

4 very bad: *a nasty accident* ○ *a nasty cut on the arm* خطير : بليغ : شديد
▸ **nastily** *adv* بلؤم: بشكل عدائي
nastiness *noun* [U] لؤم ، شرّ: موقف عدائيّ

🔑**nation** /ˈneɪʃn/ *noun* [C] a country or all the people in a country: *The President is going to speak to the nation on television.* ○ *a summit of the leaders of seven nations* دولة: أمّة، شعب

🔑**national** /ˈnæʃnəl/ *adj* concerning all of a nation or country; typical of a particular nation: *Here is today's national and international news.* ○ *a national newspaper* ○ *a young Swede dressed in his national costume* ○ *a national holiday* ➲ Look at **international** and **local**. وطني ، قومي
▸ **national** *noun* [C] (*formal*) a person who comes from a particular country: *There are many British nationals living in Spain.* مواطن
nationally *adv*: *to advertise sth nationally* على نطاق قوميّ ، في كلّ أنحاء الدولة

ˌ**national ˈanthem** *noun* [C] the official song of a country that is played at public events النشيد الوطني

ˌ**National ˈHealth Service** *noun* [sing.] (*abbr* **NHS**) (*Brit*) the system that provides free or cheap medical care for everybody in Britain and that is paid for by taxes: *Can you get glasses on the NHS?* نظام الخدمات الصحيّة المجانية في بريطانيا

ˌ**National Inˈsurance** *noun* [U] (*abbr* **NI**) (*Brit*) the system by which employers and employees pay money to the government so that the government can help people who are ill, unemployed, retired, etc: *National Insurance contributions* تأمين إجباري يدفعه العاملون (في بريطانيا)

nationalism /ˈnæʃnəlɪzəm/ *noun* [U] **1** the strong feeling of love or pride that you feel for your own country. Nationalism often makes people think that their own country is better than others. القومية ، التعصّب القومي

2 the desire of a group of people to form an independent country: *Nationalism is quite strong in Scotland.* الشعور القومي
▸ **nationalist** /ˈnæʃnəlɪst/ *noun* [C] a person who wants a particular group of people to be able to form an independent country: *a Welsh nationalist* القوميّ (أي المنادي بالاستقلال القوميّ) ، الانفصاليّ
nationalistic /ˌnæʃnəˈlɪstɪk/ *adj* having or showing strong feelings of love for or pride in your own country ❶ **Nationalistic** is usually used in a critical way, meaning that a person's feelings of pride are too strong. متطرّف في قوميّته

nationality /ˌnæʃəˈnæləti/ *noun* [C,U] (*pl.* **nationalities**) being a member of a particular nation or country: *Stuart lives in America but he still has British nationality.* ○ *students of many nationalities* ○ *to have dual nationality* (= of two countries) ○ *Am I eligible to take out British nationality?* جنسيّة

nationalize (*also* **nationalise**) /ˈnæʃnəlaɪz/ *verb* [T] to put a company or organization under the control of the state: *The railways were nationalized after the war.* ➲ Look at **privatize**. يؤمّم
▸ **nationalization** (*also* **nationalisation**) /ˌnæʃnəlaɪˈzeɪʃn; *US* -ləˈz-/ *noun* [U] تأميم

ˌ**national ˈpark** *noun* [C] a large area of beautiful land that is protected by the government so that the public can enjoy it حديقة عامّة

ˌ**national ˈservice** *noun* [U] the period of time that a young person must spend in the army, navy, etc. of his/her country: *to do national service* خدمة العَلَم ، خدمة عسكريّة

nationwide /ˌneɪʃnˈwaɪd/ *adj, adv* over the whole of a country: *The police launched a nationwide hunt for the killer.* في كل أنحاء الدولة

native /ˈneɪtɪv/ *noun* [C] **1** a person who was born in a particular place: *She lives in Oxford but she's a native of York.* شخص من مواليد مدينة معينة ، من أبناء (القاهرة)

2 (usually used by white people about non-white people) a person who lives in a particular place: *When European explorers first arrived in South America they were given a warm welcome by the natives.* ❶ Be careful. This sense of **native** is now considered offensive. أحد سكان البلاد الأصليّين

3 an animal or plant that lives or grows naturally in a particular place: *The koala is a native of Australia.* حيوان أو نبات في موطنه الأصليّ
▸ **native** *adj* **1** (only *before* a noun) connected with the place where you were born: *Tadeusz's native land is Poland but he left in 1988.* (وطن) أصليّ

2 (used about an animal or plant) living or growing naturally in a particular place: *There are many grey squirrels in England but they are not a native species.* محلّي ، بلديّ

ˌ**Native Aˈmerican** (*also* **American Indian**) *adj, noun* [C] (of) a member of the race of people who were the original inhabitants of America أحد الهنود الحمر: سكّان أمريكا الأصليّين

ˌ**native ˈspeaker** *noun* [C] a person who learnt a particular language as a very young child: *Are you a native speaker of Dutch?* شخص لغته الأصليّة (كذا)

NATO (*also* **Nato**) /ˈneɪtəʊ/ *abbrev* North Atlantic Treaty Organization; a group of European countries, Canada, the USA and Iceland, who agree to give each other military help if necessary منظمة حلف شمال الأطلسي

natter /ˈnætə(r)/ *verb* [I] (*Brit informal*) to talk a

lot about things that are not very important ➲ Look at **chat**. يثرثر ، "يدردش"
▸ **natter** *noun* [sing.]: *to have a natter* ثرثرة ، "دردشة"

natural /ˈnætʃrəl/ *adj* **1** connected with things that were not made by people: *natural disasters such as earthquakes and floods* ○ *I prefer to see animals in their natural surroundings rather than in zoos.* ○ *Britain's natural resources include coal, oil and gas.* ❶ If somebody dies of **natural causes** they die because they were ill or old, not because they were killed in an accident. طبيعي

2 usual or normal; what you would expect: *It's natural to feel nervous before an interview.* ○ *It's only natural for people to be nervous.* ❶ The opposite is **unnatural**. طبيعي ، من المتوقّع

3 that you had from birth or that was easy for you to learn: *a natural gift for languages* ○ *natural charm* فطري

4 used about parents or their children) related by blood: *She's his stepmother, not his natural mother.* شرعي

ˌnatural ˈhistory *noun* [U] the study of plants and animals التاريخ الطبيعي

naturalist /ˈnætʃrəlɪst/ *noun* [C] a person who studies plants and animals مختصّ في التاريخ الطبيعي

naturalize (*also* **naturalise**) /ˈnætʃrəlaɪz/ *verb* [T] (usually passive) to make sb a citizen of a country where he/she was not born: *Lee was born in Hong Kong but was naturalized after living in Britain for five years.* يجنّس أو يمنح جنسية
▸ **naturalization** (*also* **naturalisation**) /ˌnætʃrəlaɪˈzeɪʃn; *US* -ləˈz-/ *noun* [U] منْح أو اكتساب جنسيّة جديدة

naturally /ˈnætʃrəli/ *adv* **1** in a natural (3) way: *Vera is naturally a very cheerful person.* ○ *Working with computers comes naturally to Nick.* بشكل طبيعيّ ، بطبيعته

2 of course; as you would expect: *The team was naturally upset about its defeat.* من الطبيعيّ ، طبعاً

3 in a way that is normal: *You look very stiff and tense. Try to stand naturally.* ○ *Don't try and impress people. Just act naturally.* بشكل طبيعيّ ، بشكل عاديّ

4 in a way that is not made or done by people: *naturally wavy hair* طبيعيّاً

nature /ˈneɪtʃə(r)/ *noun* **1** [U] all the things in the world that were not made or caused by people: *the forces of nature* (e.g. volcanoes, hurricanes, etc.) ○ *If we destroy too many forests we may upset the balance of nature.* ○ *the wonders of nature* ○ *On holiday we like to get away from civilization and back to nature.* الطبيعة

2 [C,U] the qualities or features of a person or thing: *He's basically honest by nature.* ○ *Our new cat has a very nice nature.* ○ *The nature of my work is secret and I cannot discuss it.* ○ *It's human nature never to be completely satisfied.* ➲ Look also at **second nature**. جوهر الإنسان أو الشيء ، طبيعة : مِزاج

3 [sing.] the type or sort of sth: *I'm not very interested in things of that nature.* طراز : نوع

▸ **-natured** (in compounds) having a particular quality or feature: *good-natured* ذو طبيعة (سمحة) ، ذو خُلق (حسن)

naughty /ˈnɔːti/ *adj* (**naughtier**; **naughtiest**) (used when you are talking to or about a child) not doing what an adult says; badly-behaved; causing trouble: *She's one of the naughtiest children in the class.* ○ *It was very naughty of you not to tell me where you were going.* (ولد) "شقي" أو شيطان، غير مطيع
▸ **naughtily** *adv* بخبث؛ بشكاسة
naughtiness *noun* [U] عدم إطاعة، "شقاوة"

nausea /ˈnɔːziə; *US* ˈnɔːʒə/ *noun* [U] the feeling that you are going to vomit (= bring up food from your stomach): *A wave of nausea came over him at the sight of all the blood.* ➲ Look at **sick** (2). غَثيان
▸ **nauseate** /ˈnɔːzieɪt; *US* ˈnɔːz-/ *verb* [T] to cause sb to feel nausea or strong dislike يسبّب الغثيان ؛ يقزّز النفس
nauseating *adj* يبعث على الاشمئزاز ، مقرِف

nautical /ˈnɔːtɪkl/ *adj* connected with ships, sailors or sailing بحري ، متعلق بالملاحة

naval /ˈneɪvl/ *adj* connected with the navy: *a naval battle* بحري ، متعلّق بالأسطول البَحريّ

navel /ˈneɪvl/ *noun* [C] the small hollow in the middle of your stomach ➲ Look at **umbilical cord**. السرّة

navigable /ˈnævɪgəbl/ *adj* that boats can sail along: *a navigable river* صالح للملاحة

navigate /ˈnævɪgeɪt/ *verb* **1** [I] to use a map, etc. to find out which way a car, ship, plane, etc. should go: *Early explorers used the stars to navigate.* ○ *If you drive, I'll navigate.* يسترشد بالخارطة ليتعرّف طريق رحلته

2 [T] to move or guide a ship, etc. in a particular direction; to find a way through a difficult place: *We managed to navigate the yacht through the rocks.* ○ *Nobody had navigated the Amazon until then.* يقود أو يسيّر سفينة وغيرها (في امكنة صعبة)
▸ **navigation** /ˌnævɪˈgeɪʃn/ *noun* [U] ملاحة
navigator *noun* [C] a person who navigates ملّاح

navy /ˈneɪvi/ *noun* [C] (*pl.* **navies**) **1 the Navy** the organization that controls the warships of a country and the people that work on them: *to join the Navy* البحريّة

> When it is used in the singular **Navy** can take either a singular or a plural verb: *The Navy is/are introducing a new warship this year.* Look at **army**, **air force** and **merchant navy**.

2 a group of warships belonging to a country: *Does Switzerland have a navy?* أسطول بحري

ˌnavy ˈblue (*also* **navy**) *adj*, *noun* [U] dark blue اللون الكحلي، الأزرق الداكن

NB (*also* **N.B.**) /ˌen ˈbiː/ *abbrev* (used before a written note) take special notice of: *NB There is an extra charge for reservations.* ملحوظة هامة، تنبيه

NE *abbrev* = NORTH-EAST

near¹ /nɪə(r)/ *adj* **1** not far in time or distance (from sb/sth): *Let's walk to the library. It's quite near.* ○ *We're hoping to move to Wales in the near future.* ○ *Where's the nearest post office?* ○ *The day of the interview was getting nearer.* قريب

Close and **near** are often the same in meaning but in some phrases only one of them may be used: *a close friend* ○ *the near future* ○ *a close contest.* Look at the note at **next**.

2 closely related to you: *My nearest relative who's still alive is my great-aunt.* قريب، نسيب

IDM a near miss a situation where sth nearly hits you or where sth bad nearly happens: *The bullet flew past his ear. It was a very near miss.* نجاة بأعجوبة

or near(est) offer; **ono** (used when you are selling sth) or an amount that is less than but near the amount that you have asked for: *Motorcycle for sale. £750 ono.* "أو مبلغ قريب من هذا"

near² /nɪə(r)/ *adv, prep* not far in time or distance; close to: *It's a little village near Cardiff.* ○ *I don't want to sit near the window.* ○ *I'd like to live near my parents, if possible.* ○ *Her birthday is very near Christmas.* ○ *I wasn't sitting near enough to see.* ○ *They live quite near.* قربَ، قريباً من، بالقرب

IDM nowhere near far from: *We've sold nowhere near enough tickets to make a profit.* بعيد عن، لا يقارب

near³ /nɪə(r)/ *verb* [I,T] to get closer to sth in time or distance: *The day was nearing when we would have to decide.* ○ *The job is nearing completion.* يقترب

nearby /ˈnɪəbaɪ/ *adj* (only *before* a noun) not far away in distance: *We went out to a nearby restaurant.* قريب، مجاور

Notice that **nearby** is only used before the noun. **Near** cannot be used before a noun in this way: *We went out to a restaurant near our house.* ○ *The restaurant is quite near.*

▸ **nearby** /ˌnɪəˈbaɪ/ *adv* not far away in distance: *A new restaurant has opened nearby.* قريباً من هنا، على مسافة قريبة

nearly /ˈnɪəli/ *adv* almost; not completely or exactly: *It's nearly five years since I've seen him.* ○ *It's nearly time to go.* ○ *Linda was so badly hurt she very nearly died.* ○ *It's not far now. We're nearly there.* ○ *I've nearly finished.* ○ *He earns nearly £20 000 a year.* تقريباً؛ حوالي؛ على وشك

IDM not nearly far from: *It's not nearly as warm as it was yesterday.* لا يقارب، لا يُشابه: بعيد عن

ˌnear-ˈsighted *adj* (*US*) = SHORT-SIGHTED

neat /niːt/ *adj* **1** arranged or done carefully or tidily: *Please keep your room neat and tidy.* ○ *neat rows of figures* مرتَّب، منظَّم

2 (used about a person) liking things to be done or arranged carefully or tidily منظَّم: مهندَم

3 simple but clever: *a neat solution/explanation/idea/trick* مقبول

4 (*US*) good; nice: *That's a really neat car!* جيِّد: جميل

▸ **neatly** *adv* بعناية؛بنظام

neatness *noun* [U] تنظيم: بَراعة

necessarily /ˌnesəˈserəli/ *adv* used to say that sth might be true but is not definitely or always true: *Buying the most expensive CD player doesn't necessarily mean you're getting the best quality.* بالضرورة: في كل الحالات، دائماً

necessary /ˈnesəsəri; *US* -seri/ *adj* needed in order to get sth or to do sth: *A good diet is necessary for a healthy life.* ○ *Don't spend more than £20 unless it's absolutely necessary.* ○ *It's not necessary for you all to come.* ضروريّ، لازم

necessitate /nəˈsesɪteɪt/ *verb* [T] (*formal*) to make sth necessary يستلزم، يستدعي، يستوجب

necessity /nəˈsesəti/ *noun* (*pl.* **necessities**) **1** [U] **necessity (for sth/to do sth)** being necessary; need: *Is there any necessity for change?* ○ *There's no necessity to write every single name down.* ضرورة، لزوم، حاجة

2 [C] something that you must have: *Clean water is an absolute necessity.* ○ *Food, clothing and shelter are all necessities of life.* ضرورة حتميّة، مُستلزم

neck /nek/ *noun* [C] **1** the part of the body that joins your head to your shoulders: *She wrapped a scarf around her neck.* ○ *I've got a stiff neck.* ○ *Giraffes have long necks.* رقبة، عنق

2 the part of a piece of clothing that goes round your neck: *a polo-neck sweater* ○ *a V-neck sweater* قبّة (الثوب)

3 the narrow part of sth that looks like a neck: *the neck of a bottle* عنق (الزجاجة)

IDM be a pain (in the neck) → PAIN

neck and neck (with sb/sth) equal or level: *At the half-way point the two cars were neck and neck.* على سويّة واحدة (في السباق)، متعادلان

up to your neck in sth very deeply involved in sth: *We're up to our necks in work at the moment.* غارق حتى أذنيه (في العمل)

necklace /ˈnekləs/ *noun* [C] a piece of jewellery that you wear around your neck قلادة، طَوْق، عقد

necktie /ˈnektaɪ/ *noun* [C] (*US*) = TIE¹ (1)

nectarine /ˈnektəriːn/ *noun* [C] a type of peach with a smooth skin نوع من الدرّاق (أو الخوخ في مصر)

née /neɪ/ *adj* (used before the surname that a woman had before she got married): *Christine Cowley, née Morgan* ➲ Look at **maiden name**. كُنية سيّدة متزوجة قبل زواجها

need¹ /niːd/ *verb* [T] (not usually used in the continuous forms) **1** to require sth; to think that sth is necessary: *All living things need water.* ○ *I need a new film for my camera.* ○ *Does Bob need any help?* ○ *We've got enough coffee. We don't need any more.* ○ *Can I borrow your dictionary or do you need it?* ○ *She needs three volunteers to bring the food.* ○ *This jumper needs washing/to be washed.* ○ *He needed his eyes tested/testing.* يحتاج إلى، يتطلّب

2 to have to; to be obliged to: *Do we need to buy the tickets in advance?* ○ *I need to ask some*

a b c d e f g h i j k l m **n** o p q r s t u v w x y z

advice. ○ *You didn't need to bring any food but it was very kind of you.* يضطر إلى ، يلزم

Note that the question form of the main verb **need** is **do I need**?, etc. and the past tense is **needed** (question form **did you need**?, etc.; negative **didn't need**).

need² /niːd/ *modal verb* ❶ The present tense is **need** in all persons; the negative is **need not** (**needn't**), and the question form is **need I**?, etc. (not used in the continuous forms; used mainly in questions or negative sentences or with words like *hardly, only, never*) to have to; to be obliged to: *Need we pay the whole amount now?* ○ *You needn't come to the meeting if you're too busy.* ○ *I'll help you any time. You only need ask.* ○ *I hardly need remind you that this is very serious.* (لا) يلزم أو يستدعي ، (هل) يلزم أو يستدعي؟

Need not have or **needn't have** and the past participle means that you did something but it was not necessary: *We needn't have packed our thick clothes. The weather was really warm.* ○ *He needn't have gone to the hospital* (= he went but it wasn't necessary). Compare this with the past tense of the main verb which usually means that the action did not take place: *He didn't need to go to the hospital* (= he didn't go because it wasn't necessary).

need³ /niːd/ *noun* **1** [U, sing.] a situation in which sth is wanted or required: *We are all in need of a rest.* ○ *There is a growing need for low-cost housing in the London area.* ○ *There's no need for you to come if you don't want to.* ○ *Is there any need for all that noise?* ○ *Do phone me if you feel the need to talk to someone.* حاجة ، ضرورة

2 needs [plural] the things that you must have: *He doesn't earn enough to pay for his basic needs.* ○ *Parents must consider their children's emotional as well as their physical needs.* حاجات ، متطلّبات

3 [U] the state of not having enough money: *a campaign to help families in need* فقر ، عوَز

▶ **needless** *adj* that is not necessary: *We had gone through a lot of needless worry. He was safe at home.* ➲ Look at **unnecessary**. لا ضرورة له

needlessly *adv* دون مبرر ، (بقسوة) لا لزوم لها

needle /ˈniːdl/ *noun* [C] **1** a small thin piece of metal with a point at one end and a hole (an eye) at the other that is used for sewing: *to thread a needle with cotton* إبرة الخياطة

2 (*also* **knitting needle**) a long thin piece of metal, plastic or wood with a point at one end that is used for knitting صنّارة الحياكة/التريكو

3 the thin hollow part of a syringe that is used for injecting liquids into your body إبرة جراحيّة

4 something that looks like a needle: *a pine needle* ○ *the needle of a compass* شيء يشبه إبرة الخياطة مثل: إبرة مغناطيسية

➲ Look also at **pins and needles**.

needlework /ˈniːdlwɜːk/ *noun* [U] work that you do by hand using a needle (1). Needlework includes sewing and embroidery. شغل الإبرة، خياطة وتطريز

needy /ˈniːdi/ *adj* (**needier**; **neediest**) not having enough money etc.; poor فقير ، محتاج ، معوِز

negative /ˈnegətɪv/ *adj* **1** (used about a word, phrase or sentence) saying or meaning 'no' or 'not': *a negative sentence* ○ *'Don't you like England?' is a negative question.* ➲ Look at **affirmative**. في صيغة النفي

2 only thinking about the bad qualities of sb/sth: *I'm feeling very negative about my job – in fact I'm thinking about moving.* ❶ The opposite is **positive**. سلبي

3 (used about a medical or scientific test) showing that sth has not happened or has not been found: *The results of the pregnancy test were negative.* ❶ The opposite is **positive**. سلبي

4 (used about a number) less than zero ❶ The opposite is **positive**. سلبي

▶ **negative** *noun* [C] **1** a word, phrase or sentence that says or means 'no' or 'not': *Carol answered in the negative* (= she said no). ○ *'Never', 'neither' and 'nobody' are all negatives.* النفي

2 a piece of film from which we can make a photograph. The light areas of a negative are dark on the final photograph and the dark areas are light: *If you give me the negative, I can have another print made.* الصورة السلبيّة أي الفيلم الفوتوغرافي قبل طبعه

neglect /nɪˈglekt/ *verb* [T] to give too little or no attention or care to sb/sth: *Try hard not to neglect your health even when you are studying for your exams.* يهمل

▶ **neglect** *noun* [U] giving too little care to sb/sth; the state of being neglected: *The house was empty and in a state of total neglect.* إهمال : حالة خراب وقذارة نتيجة الإهمال

neglected *adj* having or showing a lack of care and attention: *Neglected children often get into trouble.* مهمَل ، متروك ، غير معتنى به

negligence /ˈneglɪdʒəns/ *noun* [U] not being careful enough; lack of care: *The accident was a result of negligence.* إهمال، تقصير

negligent /ˈneglɪdʒənt/ *adj* not giving enough care or attention to sth (that you are responsible for) مهمِل، مقصِّر

▶ **negligently** *adv* دونَ عناية كافية : بتراخٍ، بإهمال

negligible /ˈneglɪdʒəbl/ *adj* not important because it is too small تافه ، لا قيمة له ، غير جدير بالذكر

negotiable /nɪˈgəʊʃiəbl/ *adj* that can be decided or changed by discussion: *The price is not negotiable* (= it can't be changed). قابل للمفاوضة أو المساومة ؛ قابل للتعديل

negotiate /nɪˈgəʊʃieɪt/ *verb* **1** [I] to talk to sb in order to decide or agree about sth: *The unions are still negotiating with management about this year's pay claim.* يتفاوض مع

2 [T] **negotiate sth (with sb)** to decide or agree sth by talking about it: *to negotiate an agreement* يفاوض

3 [T] to get over, past or along sth difficult: *The canoeists had to negotiate several rapids on the river.* يتغلب على عقبة بمهارة ، يجتاز مرحلة خطيرة

▶ **negotiator** *noun* [C] a person who negotiates (1, 2) مفاوض

negotiation /nɪˌɡəʊʃiˈeɪʃn/ *noun* [C,U] discussions at which people try to decide or agree sth: *The salary is a matter for negotiation.* ○ *The negotiations were extremely difficult.* ○ *to enter into/break off negotiations* مفاوضة ، مفاوضات

Negro /ˈniːɡrəʊ/ *noun* [C] (*pl.* **Negroes**) a black person ❶ Many people now find this word offensive. زنجي

neigh /neɪ/ *noun* [C] the long high sound that a horse makes صهيل
▶ **neigh** *verb* [I] يصهَل

⚿ **neighbour** (*US* **neighbor**) /ˈneɪbə(r)/ *noun* [C] **1** a person who lives near you: *Don't make too much noise or you'll wake the neighbours.* ○ *our next-door neighbours* جار
2 a person or thing that is near or next to another: *Britain's nearest neighbour is France.* ○ *Try not to look at what your neighbour is writing.* جار ، الشخص أو الشيء المجاور
▶ **neighbourhood** (*US* **neighborhood**) /ˈneɪbəhʊd/ *noun* [C] a particular part of a town and the people who live there: *We've just moved into the neighbourhood and don't know our way around yet.* ○ *a friendly neighbourhood* جيرة، جوار : حَيّ
neighbouring (*US* **neighboring**) /ˈneɪbərɪŋ/ *adj* (only *before* a noun) near or next to: *Farmers from neighbouring villages come into town each week for the market.* مجاور ، قريب
neighbourly (*US* **neighborly**) *adj* friendly and helpful حَسَن الجِوار ، غيور على مصلحة جاره

⚿ **neither** /ˈnaɪðə(r); ˈniːðə(r)/ *det, pron* (used about two people or things) not one and not the other: *Neither team played very well.* ○ *Neither of the teams played very well.* ○ *'Would you like a sandwich? Or a piece of cake?' 'Neither, thank you. I'm not hungry.'* ○ *There were two candidates for the job but neither of them was very good.* لا هذا ولا ذاك ، ولا واحد من....

Notice that **neither** is followed by a singular noun and verb: *Neither day was suitable.* The noun or pronoun that follows **neither of** is in the plural but the verb may be singular or plural: *(formal) Neither of the days is suitable.* ○ *(informal) Neither of the days are suitable.*

▶ **neither** *adv* **1** also not; not either: *I don't eat meat and neither does Tom.* ○ *Stella didn't attend the meeting and neither did Jane.* ○ *'I haven't seen that film.' 'Neither have I.'* وكذلك ، وأيضاً: ولا (أنا)

In this sense **nor** can be used in the same way: *'I haven't seen that film.' 'Nor have I.'* Notice that when you use **not ... either** the order of words is different: *I don't eat meat and Tom doesn't either.* ○ *'I haven't seen that film.' 'I haven't either.'*

2 neither... nor not... and not: *Neither Tom nor I eat meat.* لا (هو) ولا (أنا)

Neither ... nor can be used with a singular or a plural verb: *(formal) Neither Stella nor Jane was at the meeting.* ○ *(informal) Neither Stella nor Jane were at the meeting.*

neon /ˈniːɒn/ *noun* [U] (*symbol* **Ne**) a type of gas that is used for making bright lights and signs: *the neon lights of the city* غاز النيون

⚿ **nephew** /ˈnefjuː/ *noun* [C] the son of your brother or sister, or the son of your husband's or wife's brother or sister ➲ Look at **niece**.
ابن الأخ أو الأخت (أو ابن أخ أو أخت الزوج أو الزوجة)

Neptune /ˈneptjuːn; *US* -tuːn/ *noun* [sing.] the planet that is eighth in order from the sun كوكب نبتون

nerd /nɜːd/ *noun* [C] a person who is not fashionable and has a boring hobby شخص مغرم بهوايات مملّة
▶ **nerdy** *adj* ممل

⚿ **nerve** /nɜːv/ *noun* **1** [C] one of the long thin threads in your body that carry feelings or other messages to and from your brain عَصَب
2 nerves [plural] the ability to stay calm and not get worried: *You need strong nerves for this job.* هدوء أعصاب
3 nerves [plural] the state of being very nervous or worried: *Breathing deeply should help to calm your nerves.* قلق ، توتّر أعصاب
4 [U] the courage that you need to do sth difficult or dangerous: *Racing drivers need a lot of nerve.* ○ *He didn't have the nerve to ask Mandy to go out with him.* ○ *She climbed to the highest diving board but lost her nerve and couldn't jump.* جرأة ، رباطة جأش
5 [U] the rudeness that is needed to do sth: *He had the nerve to ask me to lend him money, and he still owes me £20.* وقاحة ، صفاقة
IDM **get on sb's nerves** (*informal*) to annoy sb or make sb angry: *Turn that music down – it's getting on my nerves.* يثير الأعصاب ، يضايق

ˈ**nerve-racking** *adj* making you very nervous or worried: *Waiting for exam results can be very nerve-racking.* محطِّم للأعصاب ، مثير للقلق

⚿ **nervous** /ˈnɜːvəs/ *adj* **1** connected with the nerves of the body: *a nervous disorder* عصبي
2 worried or afraid: *I'm a bit nervous about travelling on my own.* ○ *I always get nervous just before a match.* ○ *nervous laughter* ○ *She was nervous of giving the wrong answer.* قلق ، خائف ، (ضحكة) عَصبيّة
▶ **nervously** *adv*: *He sat there, biting his fingers nervously.* بعصبيّة
nervousness *noun* [U] عصبيّة : قلق ، خوف

ˌ**nervous** ˈ**breakdown** (*also* **breakdown**) *noun* [C] a time when sb is so depressed that he/she cannot continue living and working normally: *to have a nervous breakdown* انهيار عصبي

ˈ**nervous system** *noun* [C] your brain and all the nerves in your body الجهاز العصبي

⚿ **nest** /nest/ *noun* [C] **1** a round hollow structure that a bird builds to lay its eggs in عُش
2 the home of certain animals or insects: *a wasps' nest* عُش ، مَوكِن

▸ **nest** *verb* [I] to use or build a nest يُعشِّش ، يبني عشّاً

nestle /ˈnesl/ *verb* [I,T] to move yourself or a part of your body into a comfortable position, against a person or sth soft: *The child nestled up against his mother and fell asleep.* ○ *The baby nestled her head on her mother's shoulder.* ○ (*figurative*) *a beautiful village nestling in a river valley* يَستكنّ ؛ يحضن ؛ يؤوي

net¹ /net/ *noun* **1** [U] material that is made of long pieces of string, thread, etc. that are tied together, with spaces between them: *net curtains* (= very thin curtains that are used to stop people from seeing into a room) شبكة

2 [C] a piece of net that is used for a particular purpose: *a tennis net* (= in the centre of the court) ○ *a fishing net* ➲ Look at **safety net**. شبكة لاستعمال خاصّ مثل شبكة التنس أو شبكة الشَّعر

▸ **net** *verb* [T] (netting; netted) to catch sth with a net; to kick a ball into a net يصطاد بشبكة ؛ (في لعبة كرة القدم) يسجِّل هدفاً

net² (*also* **nett**) /net/ *adj* **net (of sth)** from which nothing more needs to be taken away: *What is your net income?* (= after tax, etc. has been paid) ○ *The net weight of the jam is 350g* (= not including the jar). ○ *net profit* ❶ The opposite is **gross**. صافٍ ، (الوزن) الصافي

▸ **net** *verb* [T] (netting; netted) to gain sth as a profit: *The sale of land netted £2 million.* يربح ربحاً صافياً

netball /ˈnetbɔːl/ *noun* [U] a game similar to basketball that is played by two teams of seven players. Each team tries to score goals by throwing a ball through a round net at the top of a pole. Netball is usually played by women. كرة الشبكة

netbook /ˈnetbʊk/ *noun* [C] a small laptop computer, designed especially for using the Internet and email "نت بوك": حاسب صغير محمول لتصفح الانترنت

netting /ˈnetɪŋ/ *noun* [U] material that is made of long pieces of string, thread, wire, etc. that are tied together with spaces between them: *a fence made of wire netting* شبكة

nettle /ˈnetl/ *noun* [C] a wild plant with hairy leaves. Some nettles sting and make your skin red and painful if you touch them: *stinging nettles* نبات القرّاص أو القُرَيص

network /ˈnetwɜːk/ *noun* [C] **1** a complicated system of roads, railway lines, etc: *The underground railway network covers all areas of the capital.* شبكة خطوط ، شبكة مواصلات

2 a group of people or companies, etc. that work together closely: *We have a network of agents who sell our goods all over the country.* شبكة تجاريّة

3 a number of computers that are connected together so that information can be shared شبكة كمبيوترات مرتبطة ببعضها

4 a group of television or radio companies that broadcasts the same programmes in different parts of a country شبكة محطّات إذاعية أو تلفزيونيّة

neurosis /njʊəˈrəʊsɪs; US nʊ-/ *noun* [C] (*pl.* **neuroses** /-ˈəʊsiːz/) a mental illness that causes strong feelings of fear and worry العصاب

neurotic /njʊəˈrɒtɪk; US nʊ-/ *adj* **1** suffering from neurosis مصاب بالعصاب

2 worried about things in a way that is not normal مفرط في القلق

neuter /ˈnjuːtə(r); US ˈnuː-/ *adj* (used about a word) not masculine or feminine according to the rules of grammar (في النحو) ليس بالمذكر ولا بالمؤنث

▸ **neuter** *verb* [T] to remove the sexual parts of an animal ➲ Look at **castrate**. يخصي ، يزيل الأعضاء التناسلية لحيوان

neutral /ˈnjuːtrəl; US ˈnuː-/ *adj* **1** not supporting or belonging to either side in an argument, war, etc: *Switzerland remained neutral during the war.* ○ *The two sides agreed to meet on neutral ground.* محايد، حِيادي

2 having or showing no strong qualities, feelings or colour: *a blouse of a neutral colour that will go with anything* معتدل؛ خفيف؛ قليل أو حياديّ اللون

▸ **neutral** *noun* [U] the position that the gears of a car, etc. are in when no power is sent from the engine to the wheels: *Make sure the car is in neutral before you turn on the engine.* (في السّيارة) حالة انفصال المسنّنات ، الحالة الحياديّة

neutrality /njuːˈtræləti; US nuː-/ *noun* [U] the state of being neutral (1) حياد

neutralize (*also* **neutralise**) *verb* [T] to take away the effect of sth يُبطل مفعول شيء ما

never /ˈnevə(r)/ *adv* **1** at no time; not ever: *I never start work before 9 o'clock.* ○ *I've never been to Portugal.* ○ *After that he never saw his father again.* ○ *We shall never go back to that hotel.* ○ *You should never leave valuables in your car.* ○ *He never ever eats meat.* ○ (*formal*) *Never before has such a high standard been achieved.* أبداً، مطلقاً ، ولا في وقتٍ من الأوقات

2 (used for emphasizing a negative statement): *I never realized she was so unhappy.* ○ *Roy never so much as looked at us* (= he didn't even look at us). أبداً ، قطّ

IDM **never mind** → MIND²

nevertheless /ˌnevəðəˈles/ *adv* in spite of that: *It was a cold, rainy day. Nevertheless, more people came than we had expected.* ○ *She knew that the accident wasn't her fault. She still felt guilty, nevertheless.* بالرغم من ذلك ، مع ذلك

new /njuː; US nuː/ *adj* **1** that has recently been built, made, invented, etc: *There have been record sales of new cars this month.* ○ *Have you seen Tom Cruise's new film?* ○ *a new method of treating mental illness* ○ *Paula came to show us her new baby.* جديد

2 different; other; changed from what was before: *Our new house is much bigger than the old one.* ○ *I've just started reading a new book.* ○ *to make new friends* ○ *The film is about a housewife who dreams of a new life in Greece.* مختلف ، آخر ، جديد

3 new (to sb) that has not been seen, learnt,

etc. before: *This type of machine is new to me.* ○ *to learn a new language* ○ *We've only just arrived here so the area is still new to us.* جديد (بالنسبة لي مثلاً)

4 new (to sth) having just started being or doing sth: *We are new to the area.* ○ *a new parent* ○ *She's new to the job and needs a lot of help.* ○ *a new member of the club* حديث العهد

IDM break fresh/new ground → GROUND[1]

▸ **new-** (in compounds) recently: *a newborn baby* (مولود) جديد

newness *noun* [U] the state of being new جِدّة

ˌNew ˈAge *adj* connected with a way of life that rejects modern Western values and is based on spiritual ideas and beliefs: *a New Age festival* ○ *New Age travellers* (= people in Britain who reject the values of modern society and travel from place to place living in their vehicles) العصر الجديد

newcomer /ˈnjuːkʌmə(r); *US* ˈnuː-/ *noun* [C] a person who has just arrived in a place قادِم جديد

newfangled /ˌnjuːˈfæŋɡld; *US* ˌnuː-/ *adj* new or modern in a way that the speaker dislikes or refuses to accept: *I don't need all these newfangled gadgets in the kitchen.* (جهاز) عصريّ معقد ، (أدوات) "مُفَزْلَكة"

⚷newly /ˈnjuːli/ *adv* (usually before a past participle) recently: *the newly appointed Minister of Health* حديثاً

ˈnewly-wed *noun* [C, usually pl.] a person who has recently got married المتزوج حديثاً

ˌnew ˈmoon *noun* [sing.] the moon when it appears as a thin line ➲ Look at **full moon**. الهلال ، القمر الجديد

⚷news /njuːz; *US* nuːz/ *noun* **1** [U] information about sth that has happened recently: *Have you heard the latest news? Mary and Joe are getting married!* ○ *She writes each Christmas telling us all her news.* ○ *Have you had any news from Malcolm recently?* ○ *That's news to me* (= I didn't know that). ○ *News is coming in of a plane crash in Thailand.* ○ *There will be a further news bulletin at 1 o'clock.* ○ *Our town has been in the news a lot recently* (= a lot has been written in newspapers, etc.). أنباء ، أخبار ؛ نبأ، خبر

> **News** is an uncountable noun. If we are talking about an individual item we must say 'a piece of news': *We had a piece of good news yesterday.*

2 the news [sing.] a regular broadcast of the latest news on the radio and TV: *We always watch the nine o'clock news on television.* ○ *I heard on the news that there's been a plane crash in Thailand.* ○ *the local/national news* نشرة الأنباء أو الأخبار

IDM break the news (to sb) to be the first to tell sb about sth important that has happened يُبلِّغ خبراً جديداً هاماً

newsagent /ˈnjuːzeɪdʒənt; *US* ˌnuːz-/ (*US* **ˈnewsdealer** /ˈnjuːzdiːlə(r); *US* ˌnuːz-/) *noun* [C] a shopkeeper who sells newspapers, magazines, sweets, cigarettes, etc: *I must pop round to the newsagent's* (= the shop) *for my paper.* صاحب محل لبيع الصحف والسجاير وغيرها

newscaster /ˈnjuːzkɑːstə(r); *US* ˌnuːzkæstə(r)/ (*also* **newsreader** /ˈnjuːzriːdə(r); *US* ˌnuːz-/) *noun* [C] a person who reads the news on the radio or on TV مذيع يقرأ الأخبار

newsletter /ˈnjuːzletə(r); *US* ˈnuːz-/ *noun* [C] a printed report about a club or organization that is sent regularly to members and other people who may be interested نشرة دورية

⚷newspaper /ˈnjuːspeɪpə(r); *US* ˈnuːz-/ *noun* **1** (*also* **paper**) [C] large folded pieces of paper printed with news, advertisements and articles on various subjects. Newspapers are printed and sold either daily or weekly: *a daily/weekly/Sunday paper* ○ *a national/local newspaper* ○ *a morning/evening paper* ○ *a newspaper article* ○ *a newspaper headline* صحيفة ، جريدة

2 (*also* **paper**) [C] an organization that produces a newspaper: *Which paper is he from?* مؤسسة صحفيّة

3 [U] the paper on which newspapers are printed: *We wrapped the plates in newspaper so they would not get damaged in the move.* ورق الجرائد

> **Journalists** and **reporters** collect news for newspapers. The **editor** decides what is printed. **Quality** newspapers deal with the news in a serious way. **Tabloids** are popular papers with many more pictures.

ˈnews-stand *noun* [C] (*US*) = BOOKSTALL

ˈnew town *noun* [C] (*Brit*) a town that is planned and built all at one time مدينة بُنيت دفعة واحدة

ˌnew ˈyear *noun* [sing.] the first few days of January: *Happy New Year!* ○ *We will get in touch in the new year.* العام الجديد

ˌNew Year's ˈDay *noun* [U] 1 January رأس السنة ، الأول من يناير/كانون الثاني

ˌNew Year's ˈEve *noun* [U] 31 December ليلة رأس السنة

⚷next[1] /nekst/ *adj* **1** (usually with *the*) coming immediately after sth in order, space or time; closest: *The next bus leaves in twenty minutes.* ○ *She went into hospital on a Sunday and the next day she died.* ○ *Before we all go we'd better set a date for the next meeting.* ○ *the next name on the list* ○ *I must get this finished today because I will be on holiday for the next two weeks.* ○ *How far is it to the next service station?* ○ *Go to the post office and take the next turning on the left.* ○ *I felt dizzy and the next thing I knew I was lying on the ground.* القادم ، التالي، الآتي

> Compare **nearest** and **next**. **The next** means 'the following' in a series of events or places: *When is your next appointment?* ○ *Turn left at the next traffic lights.* (**The**) **nearest** means 'the closest' in time or place: *Where's the nearest supermarket?*

2 (used without *the* before days of the week, months, seasons, years, etc.) the one immediately following the present one: *See you again next*

Monday. ○ Let's go camping next weekend. ○ We are going to Greece next spring. ○ Rachel hopes to get a job abroad next year. (الأسبوع) القادم أو الآتي

IDM last/next but one, two etc. → LAST[1]

▶ **the next** *noun* [sing.] the person or thing that is next (1): *If we miss this train we'll have to wait two hours for the next.* (الشخص أو الشيء) القادم أو التالي

next[2] /nekst/ *adv* after this or that; then: *I wonder what will happen next. ○ I know Joe arrived first, but who came next? ○ It was ten years until I next saw her.* بعد ذلك

ˌnext-ˈbest *adj* not the best, but good enough if you cannot have the best (الاختيار) الثاني بعد الاختيار الأفضل ، (اختيار) لا بأس به

ˌnext ˈdoor *adj, adv* in or into the next house or building: *our next-door neighbours ○ Who lives next door? ○ The school is next door to an old people's home. ○ I'm going next door to borrow some eggs.* في البيت المجاور ، إلى البيت المجاور

ˌnext of ˈkin *noun* [plural, U] your closest living relative or relatives أقرب الأقرباء

> **Next of kin** is used to mean both a single relative and a group of relatives: *My husband is my next of kin. ○ Her next of kin have been informed of her death.*

ˈnext to *prep* **1** at the side of sb/sth; beside: *He sat down next to Pam. ○ There's a public telephone next to the pub.* إلى جانب ، بجانب

2 in a position after sth: *Next to Paris I think my favourite city is Madrid.* بعد

IDM next to nothing almost nothing: *We took £50 but we've got next to nothing left.* لا شيء تقريباً

NHS /ˌen eɪtʃ ˈes/ *abbrev* (*Brit*) *abbrev* = NATIONAL HEALTH SERVICE

nib /nɪb/ *noun* [C] the metal point of a pen where the ink comes out ريشة قلم الحبر

nibble /ˈnɪbl/ *verb* [I,T] to eat sth by taking small bites يقضم قضمات صغيرة ؛ ينقنق

▶ **nibble** *noun* [C]
"لُقم": مأكولات خفيفة مثل المكسّرات والبسكويت..الخ

nice /naɪs/ *adj* **1** pleasant; good: *The weather was quite nice yesterday. ○ Have a nice day! ○ You look very nice today. ○ I'm not eating this – it doesn't taste very nice.* لطيف ؛ سارّ ؛ حسن الهيئة ؛ لذيذ

2 kind; friendly: *What a nice girl! ○ Try and be nice to Julie. She's not feeling very well.*
لطيف ، ودود

IDM nice and ... (*informal*) (used for saying that you like sth): *It's nice and warm by the fire.*
مُحبّب ، سارّ

▶ **nicely** *adv* **1** in a pleasant way: *You can have a biscuit if you ask nicely.* بلطف

2 (*informal*) very well: *This flat will suit us nicely.* كثيراً ، بشكل ملائم جداً

niceness *noun* [U] لُطف ، ظرافة

niche /nɪtʃ; niːʃ/ *noun* [C] **1** a hollow place in a wall, often with a shelf
مشكاة: كَوّة في حائط الغرفة يوضع فيها مصباح أو غير ذلك

2 a job, position, etc. that is suitable for you: *to find your niche in life* العمل الملائم للمرء

nick[1] /nɪk/ *noun* [C] a small cut in sth
حزّ ، ثلم صغير ، خَدْش

IDM in good, bad, etc. nick (*Brit slang*) in a good, bad, etc. state or condition
بحالة حسنة أو سيئة...الخ

in the nick of time only just in time: *The ambulance arrived in the nick of time.*
(وصل) في آخر لحظة قبل فوات الأوان

▶ **nick** *verb* [T] to make a nick or small cut in sb/sth يحز : يجرح جرحاً طفيفاً ، يخدش

nick[2] /nɪk/ *noun* **the nick** [sing.] (*Brit slang*) prison الحبس ، السجن

▶ **nick** *verb* [T] (*Brit informal*) **1 nick sb (for sth)** to arrest sb يلقي القبض على

2 nick sth (from sb/sth) to steal sth يسرق

nickel /ˈnɪkl/ *noun* **1** [U] (*symbol* **Ni**) a hard silver-white metal that is often mixed with other metals معدن النيكل

2 [C] an American or Canadian coin that is worth five cents
قطعة نقود أمريكية أو كندية

nickname /ˈnɪkneɪm/ *noun* [C] an informal name that is used instead of your own name, usually by your family or friends لَقَب : اسم الدلع

nicotine /ˈnɪkətiːn/ *noun* [U] the poisonous chemical substance in tobacco مادّة النيكوتين

niece /niːs/ *noun* [C] the daughter of your brother or sister; the daughter of your husband's or wife's brother or sister ➲ Look at **nephew**.
ابنة الأخ أو الأخت (أو ابنة أخ أو أخت الزوج أو الزوجة)

niggle /ˈnɪgl/ *verb* **1** [I] to pay too much attention to things that are not very important: *It's not worth niggling over a few pence.*
يُفرط في انتقاد التوافه والصغائر

2 [T] to annoy or worry sb: *His untidy habits really niggled her.* يضايق ؛ يقلق

▶ **niggling** /ˈnɪglɪŋ/ *adj* not very serious (but that does not go away): *I've still got niggling doubts about whether we've done the right thing.* (شعور) خفيف يلازم المرء

night /naɪt/ *noun* [C,U] **1** the part of the day when it is dark and when most people sleep: *The nights are short in the summer. ○ a dark night ○ We will be away for a few nights. ○ Did you sleep well last night? ○ a sleepless night ○ The baby cried all night long. ○ It's a long way home. Why don't you stay the night? ○ Owls come out at night.* ليل ؛ ليلة

2 the time between late afternoon and when you go to bed: *Let's go out on Saturday night. ○ He doesn't get home until 8 o'clock at night. ○ I tried to phone Nigel last night but he was out.* مساء

> Note the use of different prepositions with **night**. **At** is most common: *I'm not allowed out after 11 o'clock at night.* **By** is used about something that you usually do in the daytime: *They slept by day and travelled by night.* **In/during** the night is usually used for the night that has just passed: *I woke up twice in the night.* **On** is used when you are talking about one particular night: *On the night of Saturday 30 June.* **Tonight** means the night or evening that will come next: *Where are you staying tonight?*

IDM an early/a late night an evening when you go to bed earlier/later than usual (يأوي إلى فراشه) مبكراً أو متأخراً تلك الليلة

a night out an evening that you spend away from home enjoying yourself سهرة خارج البيت

in the/at dead of night → DEAD

good night (said late in the evening, before you go home or before you go to sleep) تصبح على خير!

▸ **nightly** *adj, adv* (done or happening) every night: *You can see the play nightly, except Sundays, at the Abbey Theatre.* كلّ ليلة

nightclub /ˈnaɪtklʌb/ (*also* **club**) *noun* [C] a place where you can go to eat, drink, dance, etc. until late at night ملهى ليلي

nightdress /ˈnaɪtdres/ (*also informal* **nightie** (*pl.* **nighties**)) *noun* [C] a loose dress that a girl or woman wears in bed ثوب أو قميص النوم

nightingale /ˈnaɪtɪŋgeɪl; *US* -tng-/ *noun* [C] a small brown bird that sings very beautifully العندليب

nightlife /ˈnaɪtlaɪf/ *noun* [U] the entertainment that is available at night in a particular place: *It's a small town with very little nightlife.* الحياة الليليّة، الملاهي الليليّة

nightmare /ˈnaɪtmeə(r)/ *noun* [C] **1** a dream that is frightening: *I had a terrible nightmare last night.* كابوس

2 something that is very unpleasant or frightening: *Travelling in the rush hour can be a real nightmare.* شيء مريع

ˈnight-time *noun* [U] the time when it is dark: *Many women are afraid to go out at night-time.* الليل

nightwatchman /ˈnaɪtwɒtʃmən/ *noun* [C] (*pl.* **nightwatchmen** /-mən/) a person who guards a building at night حارس ليلي

nil /nɪl/ *noun* [U] nothing (used especially about the score in a game): *We won by one goal to nil.* ➲ Look at the note at **zero**. صفْر ، لاشيء

nimble /ˈnɪmbl/ *adj* able to move quickly and lightly: *For a large person she's very nimble on her feet.* خفيف الحركة

▸ **nimbly** /ˈnɪmbli/ *adv* بخفّة ورشاقة

⚿ nine /naɪn/ *number* 9; one more than eight ❶ For examples of how to use numbers in sentences, look at **six**. تسعة

IDM nine to five the hours that you work in most offices: *a nine-to-five job* من التاسعة إلى الخامسة

▸ **ninth** /naɪnθ/ *pron, det, adv* 9th; next after eighth التاسع

ninth *pron, noun* [C] the fraction ⅑; one of nine equal parts of sth تسع ، جزء من تسعة

➲ Look at the examples at **sixth**.

⚿ nineteen /ˌnaɪnˈtiːn/ *number* 19; one more than eighteen ❶ For examples of how to use numbers in sentences, look at **six**. تسعة عشر

▸ **nineteenth** /ˌnaɪnˈtiːnθ/ *pron, det, adv* 19th; next after eighteenth ➲ Look at the examples at **sixth**. التاسع عشر

⚿ ninety /ˈnaɪnti/ *number* 90; one more than 89 ❶ For examples of how to use numbers in sentences, look at **sixty**. تِسعون

▸ **ninetieth** /ˈnaɪntiəθ/ *pron, det, adv* 90th; next after 89th ➲ Look at the examples at **sixth**. التّسعون

nip /nɪp/ *verb* (nipping; nipped) **1** [I,T] to bite or pinch sb/sth lightly: *The dog nipped him on the ankle.* يعضّ عضّاً خفيفاً ; يقرص قرصة خفيفة

2 [I] (*informal*) to move quickly; to hurry: *She nipped round to the shops for some bread and milk.* يذهب مسرعاً (لشراء شيء) ، "يخطف رِجله"

nipple /ˈnɪpl/ *noun* [C] **1** the dark hard part in the centre of a woman's breast from which a baby drinks milk حلمة الثدي

2 the similar part on a man's chest حلمة الثدي(عند الرجل)

nit /nɪt/ *noun* [C] the egg of a small insect that lives in the hair of people or animals صُوابة: بيضة القمل

ˈnit-picking *adj, noun* [U] paying too much attention to small, unimportant details المجادلة في توافه الأمور

nitrogen /ˈnaɪtrədʒən/ *noun* [U] (*symbol* **N**) a gas that has no colour, taste or smell. Nitrogen forms about 80% of the air around the earth. غاز الآزوت أو النتروجين

nitty-gritty /ˌnɪti ˈgrɪti/ *noun* [sing.] **the nitty-gritty** (*informal*) the most important facts, not the small or unimportant details الوقائع الهامّة ، الأشياء الأساسية

No. (*also* **no.**) **1** (*pl.* **Nos; nos**) = NUMBER: *No. 10 Downing Street* ○ *tel no. 51236*

2 (*US*) = NORTH, NORTHERN

⚿ no /nəʊ/ *det* **1** not any; not a: *I have no time to talk now.* ○ *No two days are the same.* ○ *No visitors may enter without a ticket.* ○ *He's no friend of mine.* ○ *There are no jobs for school-leavers in the town.* ○ *No news is good news.* أداة نفي بمعنى: ليس، لا، ما....

2 (used for saying that sth is not allowed): *No smoking.* ○ *No flash photography.* ○ *No parking.* (التدخين) ممنوع

▸ **no** *interj* **1** (used for giving a negative reply or statement): *'Are you ready?' 'No, I'm not.'* ○ *'Would you like something to eat?' 'No, thank you. I'm not hungry.'* ○ *'Can I borrow the car?' 'No, you can't.'* ○ *It's about 70 – no, I'm wrong – 80 kilometres from London.* ○ *No! Don't touch it. It's very hot.* لا ، كلا

> You can also use **no** when you want to agree with a negative statement: *'This programme's not very good.' 'No, you're right. It isn't.'*

2 (used for expressing surprise or shock): *'Mike's had an accident.' 'Oh, no!'* (تقال عند سماع خبر مفجع أو غير متوقّع): لا، مستحيل!

no *adv* not any: *Alice is feeling no better this morning.* ○ *Applications must be returned no later than 31 July.* ليس ؛ لا

nobility /nəʊˈbɪləti/ *noun* **1** [U] the quality of being noble نَبالة ، شهامة

2 the nobility [sing., with sing. or pl. verb] the group of people who belong to the highest social class طبقة النبلاء

noble /ˈnəʊbl/ *adj* **1** honest; brave; that other people should admire: *They made a noble effort in the face of many difficulties.* مخلص ؛ جريء ؛ رائع

2 belonging to the highest social class, with a title: *a noble family* من النبلاء، نبيل

▸ **noble** *noun* [C] (in former times) a person who belonged to the highest social class ➲ Look at **peer**. شخص من النبلاء

nobly /ˈnəʊbli/ *adv*: *He nobly sacrificed his own happiness for that of his family.* بنُبل، بشهامة

⚷ **nobody** /ˈnəʊbədi/ (*also* **no one** /ˈnəʊ wʌn/) *pron* no person; not anybody: *He screamed but nobody came to help him.* ○ *No one else was around.* ○ *There was nobody at home.* لا أحد

None of, not **nobody**, must be used before words like *the, his, her, those*, etc. or before a pronoun: *Nobody remembered my birthday.* ○ *None of my friends remembered my birthday.* ○ *I've asked all my classmates but nobody is free.* ○ *None of them are free.*

▸ **nobody** *noun* [C] (*pl.* **nobodies**) a person who is not very important: *Do you want to be a nobody all your life?* نَكِرة، شخص عديم القيمة

nocturnal /nɒkˈtɜːnl/ *adj* **1** happening in the night: *a nocturnal adventure* ليلي

2 (used about animals and birds) awake and active at night: *Owls are nocturnal birds.* ليلي

nod /nɒd/ *verb* (no**dd**ing; no**dd**ed) [I,T] to move your head down and then up again quickly as a way of saying 'yes' or as a greeting or a sign: *'Would you like to come too?' he asked. She nodded and slowly got up.* ○ *Everybody at the meeting nodded in agreement.* ○ *Nod your head if you understand what I'm saying and shake it if you don't.* ○ *We nodded to each other across the room.* ○ *'Somebody will have to do it,' she said, nodding in my direction.* يومئ برأسه

▸ **nod** *noun* [C]: *Give him a nod to show that you recognize him.* إيماءة بالرأس

ˌ**no-ˈfrills** *adj* including only the basic features, without anything that is unnecessary, especially things added to make sth more attractive or comfortable: *no-frills airlines* دون زخرف، بدون رتوش

ˌ**no-ˈgo area** *noun* [sing.] a place, especially part of a city, where it is very dangerous to go because there is a lot of violence or crime حي اجرام لا يحبّذ دخوله

⚷ **noise** /nɔɪz/ *noun* [C,U] something that you hear; a sound, especially one that is loud, unpleasant or unwanted: *Did you hear a noise downstairs?* ○ *Try not to make a noise if you come home late.* ○ *What an awful noise!* ○ *Why is the engine making so much noise?* ضجيج، ضوضاء

▸ **noiseless** *adj* making no sound هادئ، (جهاز) لا يحدث صوتا

noiselessly *adv* بلا صوت

⚷ **noisy** /ˈnɔɪzi/ *adj* (**noisier**; **noisiest**) making a lot of or too much noise; full of noise: *The clock was so noisy that it kept me awake.* ○ *Are small boys noisier than girls?* ○ *We live on a very noisy road.* ➲ Look at the note at **loud**. مُحدث صوتاً مزعجاً؛ صاخب، كثير الضجيج

▸ **noisily** /-ɪli/ *adv* محدثاً صوتاً مزعجاً؛ بِصَخَب

nomad /ˈnəʊmæd/ *noun* [C] a member of a tribe that travels around to find grass for its animals instead of living in one place أحد أفراد القبائل الرُحل؛ بَدَوِيّ

▸ **nomadic** /nəʊˈmædɪk/ *adj* (قبائل) رُحّل؛ مُحبّ للتنقل والترحال

ˈ**no-man's-land** *noun* [U] land between two armies in a war, between two frontiers, etc. منطقة مجرّدة من السلاح ، المنطقة الحرام

nominal /ˈnɒmɪnl/ *adj* **1** being sth in name only but not in reality: *the nominal leader of the country* (= sb else is really in control) اسمي

2 (used about a price, sum of money, etc.) very small; less than is normal: *Because we were friends he only charged me a nominal fee.* رمزيّ، (سعر) قليل جداً

nominate /ˈnɒmɪneɪt/ *verb* [T] **1 nominate sb/sth (for/as sth)** to suggest that sb/sth should be considered for an official position: *I would like to nominate Don Jones as chairman.* ○ *The novel has been nominated for the Booker prize.* يرشّح

2 nominate sb to/as sth to choose sb for a position: *You may nominate a representative to speak for you.* يعيّن

nomination /ˌnɒmɪˈneɪʃn/ *noun* [C,U] a formal suggestion that sb should be considered for an official position; the appointment of sb to such a position: *The closing date for nominations is September 8th.* ○ *The film has received 10 Oscar nominations.* ○ *His nomination as leader of the party was announced this morning.* ترشيح؛ تعيين

nominee /ˌnɒmɪˈniː/ *noun* [C] a person who is suggested or chosen for a position المرشّح، المعيّن لوظيفة ما

non-aligned /ˌnɒn əˈlaɪnd/ *adj* (used about a country) not supporting any major country or group of countries غير منحاز

nonchalant /ˈnɒnʃələnt/ *adj* not feeling or showing interest or excitement; seeming calm غير مكترث؛ هادئ الأعصاب

▸ **nonchalance** /-ləns/ *noun* [U] عدم اكتراث؛ هدوء الأعصاب

nonchalantly *adv* دون أو بلا مبالاة

non-committal /ˌnɒnkəˈmɪtl/ *adj* not saying or showing exactly what you think, or what you are going to do (جواب) محايد أي غير ملزم

nonconformist /ˌnɒnkənˈfɔːmɪst/ *noun* [C] a person who behaves or thinks differently from most other people in society شخص يختلف في آرائه وسلوكه عن مجتمعه

▸ **nonconformist** *adj* منشَق، مستقل

nondescript /ˈnɒndɪskrɪpt/ *adj* not very interesting; dull عادي، ليس له ما يميزه

⚷ **none** /nʌn/ *pron* not any, not one (of a group of three or more): *'Could you pass me some bread,* *please?' 'I'm afraid there's none left.'* ○ *They gave me a lot of information but none of it was very helpful.* ○ *I've got four brothers but none of them live/lives nearby.* ○ *'Have you brought any books to read?' 'No, none.'* ○ *I went to several shops but none had what I was looking for.* لا أحد؛ لاشيء

When we use **none of** with a plural noun, the verb can be singular, which is formal, or plural, which is informal: *None of the trains is/are going to London.* When we are talking about two people or things we use **neither** not **none**: *Neither of my brothers lives nearby.* Note the difference between **none** and **no**: *I told him that I had no money left.* ○ *When he asked me how much money I had left, I told him that I had none.*

IDM **be none the worse (for sth)** → WORSE

▸ **none** *adv* (with *the* and a comparative adjective) not at all: *We talked for a long time but I'm still none the wiser* (= I don't know any more than before). البتّة، أبداً

nonetheless /ˌnʌnðəˈles/ (*also* ˌ**none the** ˈ**less**) *adv* anyway; in spite of what has just been said: *It won't be easy but they're going to try nonetheless.* ❶ **Nevertheless** has the same meaning. مع ذلك، بالرغم من ذلك؛ على أية حال

non-existent /ˌnɒn ɪɡˈzɪstənt/ *adj* not existing or not available: *In some areas public transport is completely non-existent.* لا وجودَ له

non-fiction /ˌnɒn ˈfɪkʃn/ *noun* [U] writing that is about real people, events and facts مؤلفات عن أشخاص حقيقيين وعن أحداث واقعة

nonplussed /ˌnɒnˈplʌst/ *adj* very surprised or confused مَذهول؛ مضطرب

⚷**nonsense** /ˈnɒnsns; *US* -sens/ *noun* [U] **1** something that sb says or writes that is not true or is just silly: *What you're saying is nonsense.* ○ *Don't talk nonsense!* ○ *It's nonsense to say you aren't good enough to go to university!* ○ *I think that newspaper article is absolute nonsense.* كلام فارغ، هراء

2 foolish or bad behaviour: *The headmaster doesn't allow any nonsense.* شَغَب، تصرّف سيّئ

▸ **nonsensical** /nɒnˈsensɪkl/ *adj* not intelligent or sensible; stupid: *That was a completely nonsensical thing to say.* غير معقول؛ أحمق، غبي

non-smoker /ˌnɒn ˈsməʊkə(r)/ *noun* [C] a person who does not smoke شخص لا يدخن

▸ ˌ**non-**ˈ**smoking** *adj*: *Would you like a seat in the smoking or the non-smoking part of the plane?* (زاوية) لغير المدخّنين

non-starter /ˌnɒn ˈstɑːtə(r)/ *noun* [C] a person, plan or idea that has no chance of success شخص أو مشروع لا أمل في نجاحه؛ فاشل منذ البداية

non-stick /ˌnɒn ˈstɪk/ *adj* (used about a pan, etc.) covered with a substance that prevents food from sticking to it (مقلاة) غير لاصقة

non-stop /ˌnɒn ˈstɒp/ *adj, adv* without a stop or a break: *a non-stop flight to Bombay* ○ *The 9.30 train goes non-stop to Manchester.* ○ *He talked non-stop for two hours about his holiday.* دون توقُّف

non-violence /ˌnɒn ˈvaɪələns/ *noun* [U] the refusal to use force to bring about political or social change سياسة عدم العنف

▸ **non-violent** /-lənt/ *adj* مسالم، غير مؤمن بالعنف

noodle /ˈnuːdl/ *noun* [C, usually pl.] long thin pieces of pasta (= food made of flour, egg and water) that are cooked in boiling water or used in soups رشتة، نوع من المعكرونة الرفيعة

nook /nʊk/ *noun* [C] a small quiet place or corner (in a house, garden, etc.) ركن هادئ منعزل

IDM **every nook and cranny** every part of a place كلّ أرجاء المكان

noon /nuːn/ *noun* [U] 12 o'clock in the middle of the day; midday: *At noon the sun is at its highest point in the sky.* ○ *They arrived around noon and stayed all afternoon.* الظُهر، الساعة الثانية عشرة ظهراً

ˈ**no one** *pron* = NOBODY

noose /nuːs/ *noun* [C] **1** a circle that is tied in the end of a rope and that can be made tighter or looser أنشوطة

2 a circle like this in a rope that is used for hanging a person أنشوطة حبل المشنقة

⚷**nor** /nɔː(r)/ *conj, adv* **1** (used after *neither* or *not*) and not: *I received neither a telephone call nor a letter during the whole six months.* ○ (*formal*) *Not a building nor a tree was left standing.* ولا...، (لا بناء) ولا (شجرة...)

2 (used after a negative statement to add some further information) also not: *The sun hardly shone at all during the first week. Nor during the second, for that matter.* وَ لا...

3 (used before a positive verb to agree with sth negative that has just been said) also not; neither: *'I don't like football.' 'Nor do I.'* ○ *'I couldn't afford to stay there.' 'Nor could I.'* ○ *'We haven't been to America.' 'Nor have we.'* وَ لا (أنا)

norm /nɔːm/ *noun* [C] (often with *the*) a pattern of behaviour that is normal or expected: *Is it the norm in your country for children to leave home before they marry?* القاعدة، السلوك المعتاد، الشيء الطبيعي

⚷**normal** /ˈnɔːml/ *adj* **1** usual, ordinary or what you expect: *I'll pick you up at the normal time.* ○ *If you need to see a doctor outside normal surgery hours, ring the following number.* ○ *I just want to lead a normal life again.* ○ *We're just a normal respectable family.* ○ *It's quite normal to feel angry in a situation like this.* ○ *The amount of traffic was described as normal for a holiday weekend.* ○ *Under normal circumstances the meeting would only have lasted an hour.* معتاد؛ عاديّ؛ متوقّع

2 (used about a person or animal) formed or developed in the usual way: *The child was completely normal at birth.* ➲ Look at **abnormal**. طبيعيّ، سَوِيّ

▸ **normal** *noun* [U] the usual or average state, level, standard, etc: *Your temperature is slightly above normal.* ○ *I hope the situation will soon* *return to normal.* ○ *Things are back to normal at work now.* الحدّ الطبيعي؛ الحالة الطبيعيّة

normality /nɔːˈmæləti/ (*US* **normalcy** /ˈnɔːməlsi/) *noun* [U] the state of being normal الحالة السويّة؛ الوضع الطبيعي

normalize (*also* **normalise**) /ˈnɔːməlaɪz/ *verb* [I,T] (*formal*) to become or make sth normal, good or friendly again يطبّع (العلاقات)

normally /ˈnɔːməli/ *adv* **1** usually: *I normally leave the house at 8 o'clock.* ○ *We don't normally have people round to dinner.* ○ *Normally he gets the bus.* عادةً

2 in a usual or an ordinary way: *The man wasn't behaving normally.* بشكل طبيعي

north /nɔːθ/ *noun* [sing.] (*abbr* **N**; **No.**) **1** (*also* **the north**) one of the four main points of the compass; the direction that is on your left when you face the sunrise: *cold winds from the north* ○ *Which way is north?* الشّمال

2 the north; **the North** the part of any country, city, etc. that lies further towards the north than other parts: *Leeds is in the North of England.* ○ *I live in the north of London.* شمال البلاد

▸ **north** (*also* **North**) *adj* in or towards the north, or from the north: *The new offices will be in North Oxford.* ○ *The north wing of the castle was destroyed in a fire.* ○ *a cold north wind* شماليّ؛ في الشّمال

north *adv* to or towards the north: *We got onto the motorway going north instead of south.* ○ *The house faces north.* ○ *Is Leeds north of Manchester?* شمالاً؛ نحو الشّمال؛ شمال

northerly /ˈnɔːðəli/ *adj* **1** to, towards or in the north: *Keep going in a northerly direction.* شماليّ، متّجه نحو الشّمال

2 (used about a wind) coming from the north (ريح) شماليّة

northward /ˈnɔːθwəd/ *adj* towards the north: *in a northward direction* متّجه نحو الشّمال

northward /ˈnɔːθwəd/ (*also* **northwards**) *adv* towards the north: *Continue northwards out of the city for about five miles.* نحو الشّمال

northbound /ˈnɔːθbaʊnd/ *adj* travelling or leading towards the north: *the northbound carriageway of the motorway* مؤدٍّ إلى الشّمال

ˌnorth-ˈeast *noun* [sing.] (*abbr* **NE**) **1** (*also* **the north-east**) the direction or point of the compass that is between north and east الشّمال الشّرقيّ

2 the north-east; **the North-East** a region that is towards the north-east: *the North-East of France* المنطقة الشّماليّة الشّرقيّة

ˌnorth-ˈeast *adj, adv* in, from or to the north-east of a place or country: *the north-east coast of England* ○ *If you look north-east you can see the sea.* شمال شرقيّ؛ إلى أو من الشّمال الشّرقيّ

▸ **ˌnorth-ˈeasterly** *adj* **1** towards the north-east: *in a north-easterly direction* متّجه نحو الشّمال الشّرقيّ

2 (used about a wind) coming from the north-east (ريح) شماليّة شرقيّة

ˌnorth-ˈeastern *adj* in or from the north-east of a place or country: *north-eastern Africa* شماليّ شرقيّ، من شمال شرقيّ (البلاد)

ˌnorth-ˈeastward (*also* **ˌnorth-ˈeastwards**) *adv* towards the north-east: *Follow the A619 north-eastward.* نحو الشّمال الشّرقيّ

northern (*also* **Northern**) /ˈnɔːðən/ *adj* (*abbr* **N**; **No.**) of, in or from the north of a place: *She has a northern accent.* ○ *in northern Australia* ○ *the northern hemisphere* شماليّ

▸ **northerner** (*also* **Northerner**) /ˈnɔːðənə(r)/ *noun* [C] a person who was born in or who lives in the northern part of a country شخص من شمال البلاد

northernmost /-məʊst/ *adj* furthest north أقصى نقطة في الشّمال

the ˌNorth ˈPole *noun* [sing.] the point on the earth's surface which is furthest north القطب الشّماليّ

ˌnorth-ˈwest *noun* [sing.] (*abbr* **NW**) **1** (*also* **the north-west**) the direction or point of the compass that is between north and west الشّمال الغربيّ

2 the north-west; **the North-West** a region that is towards the north-west: *the North-West of France* المنطقة الشّماليّة الغربيّة

▸ **ˌnorth-ˈwest** *adj, adv* in, from or to the north-west of a place or country: *the north-west coast of Scotland* ○ *If you look north-west you can see the sea.* شمال غربيّ، إلى أو من الشّمال الغربيّ

ˌnorth-ˈwesterly *adj* **1** towards the north-west: *in a north-westerly direction* متّجه نحو الشّمال الغربيّ

2 (used about a wind) coming from the north-west (ريح) شماليّة غربيّة

ˌnorth-ˈwestern *adj* in or from the north-west of a place or country: *north-western Australia* شماليّ غربيّ، من شمال غربيّ (البلاد)

ˌnorth-ˈwestward (*also* **ˌnorth-ˈwestwards**) *adv* towards the north-west: *Follow the A40 north-westward.* نحو الشّمال الغربيّ

nose[1] /nəʊz/ *noun* [C] **1** the part of the face, above the mouth, that is used for breathing and smelling: *a broken nose* ○ *He received a nasty blow on the nose.* ○ *This medicine should stop your nose running.* ○ *Breathe in through your nose and out through your mouth.* ○ *Picking your nose is not a nice habit.* ❶ The adjective is **nasal**. أنف

2 the front part of sth, especially an aeroplane: *The nose of the plane was badly damaged.* مقدّمة، "بوز"

IDM **blow your nose** → BLOW[1]

look down your nose at sb/sth to think that you are better than sb; to think that sth is of poor quality يشمخ بأنفه، يزدري

poke/stick your nose into sth to interfere in sth when you should not: *He's always poking his nose into other people's business!* يتداخل فيما لا يعنيه

turn your nose up at sth to refuse sth because you do not think it is good or do not like it يشمخ بأنفه، يأنف

▸ **-nosed** (in compounds) having a nose of the type mentioned: *red-nosed* ○ *runny-nosed* ذو أنف (أحمر)

nose[2] /nəʊz/ *verb* [I] to go forward slowly and

carefully: *The bus nosed out into the line of traffic.* يتقدّم ببطء شديد وحذر

PHR V nose about/around (*informal*) to look around a private place trying to find sth interesting يشمشم، يتنسّم (الأخبار)

nosebleed /ˈnəʊzbliːd/ *noun* [C] a time when a lot of blood comes from your nose رعاف

nosedive /ˈnəʊzdaɪv/ *verb* [I] to make a fast drop downwards towards the ground: *All of a sudden the plane nosedived.* ينقضّ انقضاضاً عمودياً؛ يهوي رأسياً
▸ **nosedive** *noun* [C] انقضاض عمودي؛ هوِيّ مفاجئ

nostalgia /nɒˈstældʒə/ *noun* [U] a feeling of affection, mixed with sadness, for things that are in the past الحنين إلى الماضي
▸ **nostalgic** /nɒˈstældʒɪk/ *adj* شاعر بالحنين إلى الماضي
nostalgically /-kli/ *adv* بِحَنين

nostril /ˈnɒstrəl/ *noun* [C] one of the two openings at the end of the nose منخَر، أحدى فتحتَيْ الأنف

nosy (*also* **nosey**) /ˈnəʊzi/ *adj* (**nosier**; **nosiest**) too interested in other people's affairs فضوليّ، متطفّل

not /nɒt/ *adv* **1** (used to form the negative with verbs like *be, can, do, have, must, will*, etc. and often shortened to *n't* in speech and informal writing): *It's not/it isn't raining now.* ○ *He's not coming/He isn't coming.* ○ *I'm not coming.* ○ *I cannot/can't see from here.* ○ *You shouldn't have said that.* ○ *He didn't invite me.* ○ *Don't you like spaghetti?* ○ *I hope she will not/won't be late.* ○ *You're German, aren't you?* أداة نفي بمعنى: لا، لم، ليس، لن....
2 (used to give the following word or phrase a negative meaning or to reply in the negative): *He told me not to telephone.* ○ *I remember her but not her sister.* ○ *Not everybody was able to come.* ○ *Not all of the houses are as nice as this one.* ○ *'Whose turn is it to do the shopping?' 'Not mine.'* ○ *'Do you see each other a lot?' 'No, not often.'* ○ *'Are you coming to play tennis?' 'Not now.'* لا، ليس...
3 (used after *be afraid, believe, expect, hope, suppose*, etc., to give a negative reply): *'Do you think they'll get married?' 'I hope not.'* (= I hope that they will not.) ○ *'You can't drive all that way alone.' 'I suppose not.'* ○ *'Did you see her?' 'I'm afraid not.'* لا
4 (used with *or* to give a negative possibility): *Shall we tell her or not?* ○ *I don't know if he's telling the truth or not.* لا
5 (used for saying that sth is not possible or that you do not want to do sth): *'Can I borrow £20?' 'Certainly not!'* ○ *'Are you coming to the theatre with us?' 'I'd rather not, if you don't mind.'* لا
6 (used for showing that you mean the opposite of the word or phrase that follows): *It's not easy* (= it's difficult). ليس، غير(سهل)

IDM not at all 1 (a way of saying 'no' or 'not'): *'Do you mind if I come too?' 'Not at all.'* ○ *The instructions are not at all clear.* لا، غير (واضح)
2 (a way of replying when sb has thanked you): *'Thanks for the present.' 'Not at all, don't mention it.'* لا، أبداً
not only... (but) also (used for emphasizing the fact that there is something more): *They not only have two houses in London, they also have one in France.* ليس...بل

notable /ˈnəʊtəbl/ *adj* deserving to be noticed; interesting or important: *The area is notable for its scenery and wildlife.* هامّ، شهير؛ وجيه؛ جدير بالذكر
▸ **notably** /ˈnəʊtəbli/ *adv* (used for giving an especially important example of what you are talking about): *The house had many drawbacks, most notably its price.* بشكل خاصّ، من أهمّ (هذه العيوب)

notch /nɒtʃ/ *noun* [C] **1** a cut in an edge or surface in the shape of a V قطع صغير على شكل "V"، سِنّ، حَزّ
2 a level on a scale of quality: *This meal is certainly a notch above the last one we had here.* درجة، مستوى
▸ **notch** *verb*

PHR V notch sth up to score or achieve sth: *Lewis notched up his best ever time in the 100 metres.* يحرز نجاحاً؛ يسجّل أهدافاً

note¹ /nəʊt/ *noun* **1** [C] a short letter: *This is just a note to thank you for having us all to stay.* مذكّرة، رسالة قصيرة
2 [C] some words that you write down quickly to help you remember sth: *I'd better make a note of your name and address.* ○ *Keep a note of who has paid and who hasn't.* ○ *The lecturer advised the students to take* (= write down) *notes while he was speaking.* ملاحظة؛ معلومات مسجّلة
3 [C] a short explanation or extra piece of information that is given at the back of a book, etc. or at the bottom or side of a page: *an edition of Shakespeare with student's notes* ○ *See note 5, page 340.* ➲ Look at **footnote**. ملاحظة، تعليق، حاشية
4 [C] (*also* **'banknote**; *US* **bill**) a piece of paper money: *I'd like the money in £10 notes, please.* ورقة نقديّة
5 [C] a single musical sound made by a voice or an instrument: *I can only remember the first few notes of the song.* ○ *high/low notes* نغمة
6 [C] a written sign that represents a musical sound علامة موسيقيّة
7 [sing.] (something that suggests) a certain quality or feeling: *There was a note of embarrassment in her voice.* ○ *The meeting ended on a rather unpleasant note.* شيء من، رنّة؛ روح

IDM compare notes (with sb) → COMPARE

note² /nəʊt/ *verb* [T] **1** to notice or be aware of sth: *He noted a slight change in her attitude towards him.* ○ *Note the fine detail in the painting.* يلاحظ
2 to mention sth: *I'd like to note that the project has so far been extremely successful.* يذكر

PHR V note sth down to write sth down so that you remember it: *The policeman noted down the girl's description of the man.* يكتب، يسجّل
▸ **noted** *adj* **noted (for/as sth)** (*formal*) well known; famous: *The hotel is noted for its food.* مشهور، معروف بـ

a b c d e f g h i j k l m **n** o p q r s t u v w x y z

notebook /ˈnəʊtbʊk/ *noun* [C] **1** (*Brit*) a small book in which you write things that you want to remember مفكّرة، دفتر ملاحظات

2 (*US*) = EXERCISE BOOK

notepad /ˈnəʊtpæd/ *noun* [C] some sheets of paper in a block that are used for writing notes (2) on: *I always keep a notepad by the telephone.* كرّاسة أو كدسة اوراق تستعمل لتدوين الملاحظات

notepaper /ˈnəʊtpeɪpə(r)/ *noun* [U] paper that you write letters on: *a sheet of notepaper* ورق الرسائل

noteworthy /ˈnəʊtwɜːði/ *adj* deserving to be noticed; interesting or important جدير بالذكر، مهمّ؛ طريف

⚷**nothing** /ˈnʌθɪŋ/ *pron* not anything; no thing: *There's nothing in this suitcase.* ○ *Nothing exciting ever happens to me.* ○ *There's nothing to do here.* ○ *There was nothing else to say.* ○ *'What's the matter?' 'Oh, nothing.'* ○ *'Thank you so much for all your help.' 'It was nothing.'* (= nothing of any importance) ➲ Look at the note at **zero**. لا شيء

IDM **be/have nothing to do with sb/sth** to have no connection with sb/sth: *That question has nothing to do with what we're discussing.* ○ *Get out! It's nothing to do with you.* لا علاقة له بِـ؛ ليس من شأنه

come to nothing → COME

for nothing 1 for no good reason or with no good result: *His hard work was all for nothing.* لا داعي له؛ (ذهب) سدًى

2 for no payment; free: *Children under four are allowed in for nothing.* مجّاناً

nothing but only: *He was wearing nothing but a pair of swimming trunks.* مجرّد، فقط

(there's) nothing to it (it's) very easy: *You'll soon learn – there's nothing to it really.* سهل جداً

there is/was nothing for it (but to do sth) there is/was no other action possible: *There was nothing for it but to resign.* ليس هناك خيار آخر

⚷**notice** /ˈnəʊtɪs/ *noun* **1** [C] a written statement giving information or news that is put where everybody can read it: *There's a notice on the board saying that the meeting has been cancelled.* إعلان، إعلام، إشعار

2 [U] a warning that sth is going to happen: *I can't produce a meal at such short notice!* ○ *I wish you had given me more notice that you were going on holiday.* ○ *The swimming pool is closed until further notice* (= until we are told that it will open again). ○ *We've been given a month's notice to leave the flat* (= we have been told we must leave in a month). ○ *My boss has given me a month's notice* (= told me to leave my job in a month). ○ *She handed in her notice last week* (= a letter saying that she is going to leave her job). إشعار، إنذار؛ إنذار بالاستقالة

IDM **come to sb's notice** (*formal*) be seen or heard by sb: *It has come to my notice that you have missed a lot of classes.* يبلغه الخَبَر

take notice (of sth) to act in a way that shows that you know sth is important: *The protests are finally making the government take notice.* يهتمّ

take no notice/not take any notice (of sb/sth) to pay no attention (to sb/sth): *Take no notice of what he said – he was just being silly.* ○ *Some people don't take any notice of speed limits.* لا يهتم، لا يكترث؛ لا يراعي

> If you **don't notice** something, e.g. a speed limit, it means that you don't see it at all. However if you **don't take any notice** of it, it means that you see it but you choose to ignore it.

▸ **notice** *verb* [I,T] to see and be aware of sth: *'What kind of car was the man driving?' 'I'm afraid I didn't notice.'* ○ *Did you notice her eyes? They were the most brilliant blue.* ○ *I noticed (that) he was carrying a black briefcase.* ○ *Did you notice which direction she went in?* ○ *We didn't notice him leave/him leaving.* يلاحظ

noticeable /-əbl/ *adj* easy to see or notice: *The scar from the accident was hardly noticeable.* ○ *a noticeable difference* مرئيّ؛ ملحوظ

noticeably /-əbli/ *adv* بشكل ملحوظ

noticeboard /ˈnəʊtɪsbɔːd/ (*US* ˈ**bulletin board**) *noun* [C] a board on a wall for putting notices (1) on لوحة الاعلانات

notify /ˈnəʊtɪfaɪ/ *verb* [T] (*pres part* **notifying**; *3rd pers sing pres* **notifies**; *pt, pp* **notified**) **notify sb (of sth)** to inform sb (about sth) officially: *The police should be notified of the theft.* ○ *You must notify your landlady that you intend to leave.* يُخبر، يُخطر، يبلّغ

▸ **notification** /ˌnəʊtɪfɪˈkeɪʃn/ *noun* [C,U] إشعار، إخطار، تبليغ

notion /ˈnəʊʃn/ *noun* [C] something that you have in your mind; an idea: *I had a vague notion that I had seen her before.* ○ *You seem to have no notion of how difficult it is going to be.* فكرة

▸ **notional** /ˈnəʊʃənl/ *adj* existing only in the mind; based on a guess not a real figure: *The figures I gave you were only notional.* نظريّ، افتراضيّ؛ وهميّ

notoriety /ˌnəʊtəˈraɪəti/ *noun* [U] the state of being famous for sth bad سوء السمعة، الشهرة بأشياء رديئة

notorious /nəʊˈtɔːriəs/ *adj* **notorious (for/as sth)** well known for sth bad: *a notorious drug dealer* ○ *This road is notorious for the number of accidents on it.* سيّء السمعة، مشهَّر

▸ **notoriously** *adv*: *The British are notoriously bad at learning languages.* (مشهور) بشهرة سيّئة

notwithstanding /ˌnɒtwɪθˈstændɪŋ/ *prep* (*formal*) without being affected by; in spite of: *The plane landed on time, notwithstanding the terrible weather conditions.* على الرغم من

▸ **notwithstanding** *adv* (*formal*) anyway; in spite of this: *He was advised against the deal, but went ahead notwithstanding.* رغماً عن ذلك؛ على أية حال

nought /nɔːt/ *noun* [C] the figure 0: *We say 0.1 'nought point one'.* صِفْر

IDM **noughts and crosses** a game for two players that is played with a pencil and paper.

Each person tries to win by writing three 0s or three Xs in a line. لعبة المربّعات، لعبة الإدريس

noun /naʊn/ *noun* [C] (*grammar*) a word that is the name of a person, place, thing or idea: *'Jane', 'London', 'table' and 'happiness' are all nouns.* ➲ Look at **countable** and **uncountable**. إسم (في القواعد)

nourish /ˈnʌrɪʃ/ *verb* [T] **1** to give a person or animal the right kind of food so that they can grow and be healthy يغذّي

2 (*formal*) to allow a feeling or belief to grow stronger ينمّي

▶ **nourishment** *noun* [U] food that you need to stay healthy تغذية

novel[1] /ˈnɒvl/ *noun* [C] a book that tells a story about people and events that are not real: *the novels of Charles Dickens* ○ *a romantic novel* رواية

▶ **novelist** /ˈnɒvəlɪst/ *noun* [C] a person who writes novels روائي

novel[2] /ˈnɒvl/ *adj* new and different: *That's a novel idea! Let's try it.* مستحدث، مبتكر، جديد

▶ **novelty** /ˈnɒvlti/ *noun* (*pl.* **novelties**) **1** [U] the quality of being new and different: *The novelty of her new job soon wore off.* جِدّة، طرافة

2 [C] something new and unusual: *It was quite a novelty not to have to get up at 7 o'clock.* شيء جديد، شيء غير مألوف

3 [C] a small, cheap object that is sold as a toy or souvenir ألعاب صغيرة أو قطع تذكارية زهيدة الثمن

November /nəʊˈvembə(r)/ *noun* [C,U] (*abbr* **Nov.**) the eleventh month of the year, coming before December ❶ For examples of the use of the months in sentences, look at **January**. شهر نوفمبر/تشرين الثاني

novice /ˈnɒvɪs/ *noun* [C] a person who is new and without experience in a certain job, situation, etc.; a beginner المبتدئ في حرفة أو وظيفة ما

now /naʊ/ *adv* **1** (at) the present time: *We can't go for a walk now – it's pouring with rain.* ○ *Where are you living now?* ○ *It's too late now to do anything about it.* ○ *From now on the nights will be getting longer.* ○ *I've been living with my parents until now.* ○ *Up till now we haven't been able to afford a house of our own.* ○ *He will be on his way home by now.* ○ *You must go to the doctor right now.* الآن، في الوقت الحاضر

2 because of what has happened: *I've lost my pen. Now I'll have to buy a new one.* و لذلك

3 (used to introduce a new subject or to emphasize a request, command, etc., or while pausing to think): *Now this is how it all began.* ○ *Now listen to what he's saying.* ○ *Be quiet, now!* ○ *Now, let me think.* ❶ **Now then** is also used: *Now then, are there any questions?* ○ *Now then, what was I saying?* (تستعمل لذكر موضوع جديد أو للتوكيد)

IDM **(every) now and again/then** occasionally: *We see each other now and then, but not very often.* من حينٍ لآخر

just now → JUST[2]

▶ **now** *conj* **now (that)...** because of the fact that: *Now (that) the children have left home we can move to a smaller house.* بما أنّ...

nowadays /ˈnaʊədeɪz/ *adv* at the present time (when compared with the past): *I don't go to London much nowadays* (= but I did in the past). في هذه الأيّام، في الوقت الحاضر

nowhere /ˈnəʊweə(r)/ *adv* not anywhere; (in or to) no place: *I'm afraid there's nowhere to stay in this village.* ○ *There's nowhere interesting to go round here.* ○ *It's so hot I'm getting nowhere with this work* (= making no progress). ○ *'Don't leave the car there!' 'There's nowhere else to park it.'* لا مكان؛ لا يحرز تقدّماً (في عمله)

IDM **nowhere near** → NEAR[2]

noxious /ˈnɒkʃəs/ *adj* (*formal*) harmful or poisonous: *noxious gases* ضارّ، خبيث؛ سامّ

nozzle /ˈnɒzl/ *noun* [C] a narrow tube that is put on the end of a pipe, etc. to control the liquid or gas coming out فتحة خرطوم الماء مثلاً، "بزبوز"

nr *abbrev* (*Brit*) = NEAR

nuance /ˈnjuːɑːns; *US* ˈnuː-/ *noun* [C] a very small difference in meaning, feeling, sound, etc. فارق بسيط في المعنى، ظل المعنى

nuclear /ˈnjuːkliə(r); *US* ˈnuː/ *adj* **1** connected with the nucleus of an atom: *nuclear physics* نووي

2 connected with the energy that is produced when the nucleus of an atom is split: *nuclear energy* ○ *a nuclear power station* ○ *nuclear weapons* ❶ The opposite is **non-nuclear**. ➲ Look at **atomic**. نووي

ˌnuclear disˈarmament *noun* [U] stopping the use and development of nuclear weapons نزع السلاح النووي

ˌnuclear ˈreactor (*also* **reactor**) *noun* [C] a very large machine that produces nuclear energy مفاعل نووي

nucleus /ˈnjuːkliəs; *US* ˈnuː-/ *noun* [C] (*pl.* **nuclei** /-kliaɪ/) **1** the central part of an atom نواة

2 the central or most important part of sth نواة، مركز، قلب

nude /njuːd; *US* nuːd/ *adj* not wearing any clothes ➲ Look at **bare** and **naked**. عارٍ

▶ **nude** *noun* [C] a picture or photograph of a person who is not wearing clothes صورة عارية

IDM **in the nude** not wearing any clothes عارٍ، مجرّد من ثيابه

nudist /-ɪst/ *noun* [C] a person who likes to be nude, often in groups with other people: *a nudist beach* من أنصار مذهب العري

nudity /ˈnjuːdəti; *US* ˈnuː-/ *noun* [U] the state of being nude عري

nudge /nʌdʒ/ *verb* [T] to touch or push sb/sth with your elbow يكز بمرفقه

▶ **nudge** *noun* [C]: *to give sb a nudge* وكزة بالمرفق

nuisance /ˈnjuːsns; *US* ˈnuː-/ *noun* [C] a person, thing or situation that annoys you or causes you trouble: *My pen's run out. What a nuisance!* ○ *It's*

a b c d e f g h i j k l m n o p q r s t u v w x y z

a nuisance having to queue for everything. إنسان أو شيء مزعج، مضايقة

null /nʌl/ *adj*
IDM null and void (*formal*) not valid in law باطل المفعول

numb /nʌm/ *adj* not able to feel anything; not able to move: *My fingers were numb with cold.* ○ *I'll give you an injection and the tooth will go completely numb.* ○ *He was numb with fear.* فاقد الحس، خَدِر

▸ **numb** *verb* [T] to make sb/sth numb: *The whole family was numbed and shocked by the news.* يفقد الحسّ، يخدّر
numbness *noun* [U]: *The numbness should wear off after a few hours.* فقدان الحسّ، خَدَر

number /ˈnʌmbə(r)/ *noun* **1** [C] a word or symbol that indicates a quantity: *Choose a number between ten and twenty.* ○ *2 is an even number and 3 is an odd number.* ○ *Thirteen is considered to be an unlucky number.* ○ *a three-figure number* (= more than 99 and less than 1 000) ○ *high/low numbers* ○ *cardinal/ordinal numbers* عدد

2 [C] a group of numbers that is used to identify sb/sth: *What is the number of your car?* ○ *a telephone number* رقم

3 [C,U] a quantity or amount: *a large number of visitors* ○ *Pupils in the school have doubled in number in recent years.* ○ *a number of questions* (= several) ○ *We must reduce the number of accidents in the home.* عدد

When **number** has an adjective before it, it is always followed by a plural verb: *A small number of pupils study Latin.*

4 [C] (*abbr* **No.; no.**) (used before a number to show the position of sth in a series): *We live in Croft Road, at number 25.* ○ *room no. 347* ○ *No. 10 (Downing Street) is the official home of the British Prime Minister.* رقم (25 مثلاً)

5 [C] a copy of a magazine, newspaper, etc: *Back numbers of 'New Scientist' are available from the publishers.* عدد (من مجلّة)

6 [C] (*informal*) a song or dance أغنية أو رقصة، "نمرة"

IDM any number of very many: *There are any number of language schools in Oxford.* عدد كبير
in round figures/numbers → ROUND[1]
➲ Look also at **opposite number**.

▸ **number** *verb* **1** [T] to give a number to sth: *It's a country lane and the houses are not numbered.* يرقّم

2 [I] (used for expressing how many people or things there are): *Our forces number 40 000.* يبلغ عدده

ˈnumber plate (*US* **license plate**) *noun* [C] the sign on the front and back of a vehicle that gives its registration number لوحة رقم السيّارة

numeral /ˈnjuːmərəl; *US* ˈnuː-/ *noun* [C] a sign or symbol that represents a quantity: *Roman numerals* رقم، عدد

numerate /ˈnjuːmərət; *US* ˈnuː-/ *adj* having a good basic knowledge of mathematics ➲ Look at **literate**. مُلِمّ بمبادئ الحساب

numerical /njuːˈmerɪkl; *US* nuː-/ *adj* of or shown by numbers: *to put sth in numerical order* عددي

numerous /ˈnjuːmərəs; *US* ˈnuː-/ *adj* (*formal*) very many; existing in large quantities عديد، متعدّد؛ كثير

nun /nʌn/ *noun* [C] a woman who has left the ordinary world and has gone to live in a religious community (convent) ➲ Look at **monk**. راهبة

nurse[1] /nɜːs/ *noun* [C] a person whose job is to look after sick or injured people: *a trained nurse* ○ *a male nurse* ○ *Nurse Mills* ممرّضة، ممرّض

A **community** or **district** nurse visits sick people in their homes to give them the care that they need. A **health visitor** is a nurse who gives help and advice to parents of babies and young children.

nurse[2] /nɜːs/ *verb* **1** [T] to take care of sb who is sick or injured: *She nursed her mother until she died in 1969.* يمرّض، يرعى مريضاً

2 [T] to hold sb/sth in a loving way: *He nursed the child in his arms.* يحتضِن

3 [T] (*formal*) to think a lot about sth: *Dan had long nursed the hope that Paula would marry him.* يشغل تفكيره بـ

4 [I,T] to feed a baby or young animal with milk from the breast; to drink milk from the mother's breast يرضع

▸ **nursing** *noun* [U] the job of being a nurse: *She has decided to go into nursing.* مهنة التمريض

nursery /ˈnɜːsəri/ *noun* [C] (*pl.* **nurseries**) **1** a place where small children and babies are looked after so that their parents can go to work ➲ Look at **crèche**. دار حضانة

2 a place where young plants are grown and sold مشتل، مستَنْبَت

ˈnursery rhyme *noun* [C] a traditional poem or song for children أنشودة أو أغنية أطفال

ˈnursery school *noun* [C] a school for children aged from three to five ➲ Look at **kindergarten**. روضة أطفال

ˈnursing home *noun* [C] a small private hospital, often for old people مستشفى صغير خاص لرعاية المسنّين

nut /nʌt/ *noun* [C] **1** a dry fruit that consists of a hard shell with a seed (kernel) inside. Many types of nut may be eaten: *chopped hazelnuts and almonds* واحدة من المكسّرات مثل الجوز والبندق وغير ذلك

2 a six-sided piece of metal with a round hole in the middle through which you screw a long round piece of metal (bolt). Nuts and bolts are used for fixing things together: *Tighten the nut with a spanner.* عزقة، صمولة

3 (*also* **nutter**) (*slang*) a mad or foolish person شخص أحمق أو مجنون

IDM **do your nut** (*Brit slang*) to be very angry تثور ثائرته، يغضب غضباً شديداً

▸ **nutty** *adj* (**nuttier**; **nuttiest**) **1** containing or tasting of nuts
محتوٍ على مكسّرات؛ ذو طعم شبيه بالجوز أو البندق وغيرها

2 (*informal*) mad or foolish مجنون أو أحمق

nutcrackers /ˈnʌtkrækəz/ *noun* [plural] a tool that you use for breaking open the shell of a nut كسّارة الجوز والبندق وغيرها

nutmeg /ˈnʌtmeg/ *noun* [C,U] a type of spice, used for giving flavour to food جوزة الطِّيب

nutrition /njuˈtrɪʃn; *US* nu:-/ *noun* [U] the food that you eat and the way that it affects your health: *Good nutrition is essential for children's growth.* غذاء، تغذية

▸ **nutritious** /njuˈtrɪʃəs; *US* nu:-/ *adj* (used about a food) very good for you مغذٍّ

nutshell /ˈnʌtʃel/ *noun*

IDM **in a nutshell** using few words: *That, in a nutshell, is the answer to your question.*
بالاختصار، بإيجاز، "في كلمة ونص"

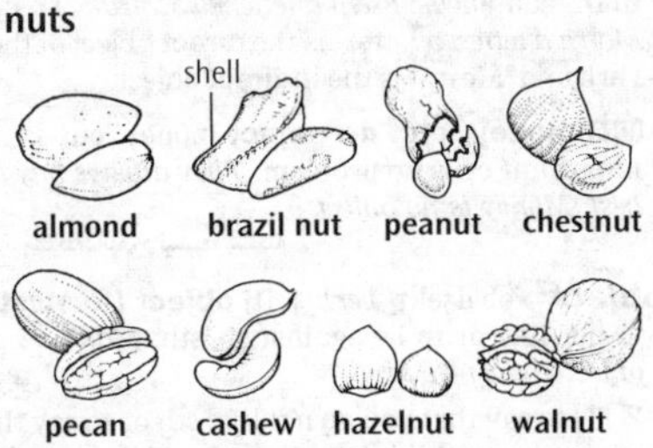

nuzzle /ˈnʌzl/ *verb* [T] to press or rub sb/sth gently with the nose (قط مثلاً) يتمسّح بإنسان بواسطة أنفه

NW *abbrev* = NORTH-WEST

nylon /ˈnaɪlɒn/ *noun* [U] a very strong man-made material that is used for making clothes, rope, brushes, etc: *The blouse is 50% nylon.* نايلون

Oo

O, o /əʊ/ *noun* [C] (*pl.* **Os**; **O's**; **o's**) **1** the fifteenth letter of the English alphabet: *'Orange' begins with (an) 'O'.* الحرف الخامس عشر من الأبجديّة الإنكليزية

2 (used when you are speaking) zero: *My number is five O nine double four* (= 50944). ➲ Look at the note at **zero**. صفْر

O /əʊ/ *interj* (*formal*) = OH

oak /əʊk/ *noun* **1** (*also* ˈ**oak tree**) [C] a type of large tree with hard wood that is common in many northern parts of the world
شجرة البلّوط أو السنديان

2 [U] the wood from the oak tree: *a solid oak table* ❶ The fruit of the oak is an **acorn**.
خشب البلّوط أو السنديان

OAP /ˌəʊ eɪ ˈpi:/ *abbrev* (*Brit*) = OLD-AGE PENSIONER

oar /ɔ:(r)/ *noun* [C] a long pole that is flat at one end and that is used for moving a small boat through water (rowing) ➲ Look at **paddle**.
مجذاف أو مجداف

oasis /əʊˈeɪsɪs/ *noun* [C] (*pl.* **oases** /-si:z/) a place in the desert where there is water and where plants grow واحة

oath /əʊθ/ *noun* [C] **1** a formal promise: *They have to swear an oath of loyalty.* قَسَم، يمين

2 a word or words that are very impolite and that you use when you are really angry ❶ **Swear word** is more common nowadays.
شتيمة، لعنة؛ كلمة بذيئة

IDM **be on/under oath** to have made a formal promise to tell the truth in a court of law
يُقسم قبل الإدلاء بشهادة

oats /əʊts/ *noun* [plural] a type of grain that is used as food for people and animals: *porridge oats* شوفان

obedient /əˈbi:diənt/ *adj* doing what you are told to do: *He was an obedient child and never caused any problems.* ❶ The opposite is **disobedient**. مطيع

▸ **obedience** /-əns/ *noun* [U]: *unquestioning obedience* إطاعة أو طاعة

obediently *adv* مطيعاً، بكل طاعة

obese /əʊˈbi:s/ *adj* (used about people) very fat, in a way that is not healthy بدين، مفرط في السمنة

▸ **obesity** /əʊˈbi:səti/ *noun* [U] سِمنة، بدانة

⚷ **obey** /əˈbeɪ/ *verb* [I,T] to do what you are told to do: *Soldiers are trained to obey orders.* ❶ The opposite is **disobey**. يطيع

obituary /əˈbɪtʃuəri; *US* -tʃueri/ *noun* [C] (*pl.* **obituaries**) an article about a person's life that is printed in a newspaper soon after he/she has died نعي في جريدة يعطي لمحة عن حياة المتوفى

⚷ **object**[1] /ˈɒbdʒɪkt/ *noun* [C] **1** a thing that can be seen and touched: *The shelves were filled with objects of all shapes and sizes.* شيء، جسم ملموس

2 the object of sth a person or thing that causes a feeling, interest, thought, etc.
موضع، مصدر

3 an aim or purpose: *Making money is his sole object in life.* هدف، غاية، غرض

4 (*grammar*) the noun or phrase describing the person or thing that is affected by the action of a verb مفعول به (في النحو)

In the sentences: *I sent a letter to Moira ○ I sent Moira a letter* 'a letter' is the **direct** object of the verb and 'Moira' is the **indirect** object.

IDM money, etc. no object money, etc. is not important or is no problem: *They always buy the best. Money is no object.* عقبة: مشكلة: النقود ليست مشكلة

object² /əbˈdʒekt/ *verb* **1** [I] **object (to sb/sth)** to not like or to be against sb/sth: *Many people object to the new tax.* لا يوافق على

2 [T] to say that you do not like sth or to say that sth is wrong: *'I think that's unfair,' he objected.* يحتجّ أو يعترض على

▸ **objector** *noun* [C] a person who objects to sth المعترض

objection /əbˈdʒekʃn/ *noun* [C,U] a statement or feeling that you do not like or are against sb/sth: *We listed our objections to the proposed new road and sent them to the council.* ○ *My parents have no objection to our marriage.* احتجاج، اعتراض

objectionable /əbˈdʒekʃənəbl/ *adj* very unpleasant مُنفِّر؛ بغيض، كريه

objective¹ /əbˈdʒektɪv/ *adj* not influenced by your own personal feelings (= based only on facts): *Please try and give an objective report of what happened.* ○ *It's hard to be objective about your own strengths and weaknesses.* ❶ The opposite is **subjective**. موضوعيّ، غير متحيّز

▸ **objectively** *adv*: *He is too upset to see things objectively.* بشكل موضوعي

objectivity /ˌɒbdʒekˈtɪvəti/ *noun* [U] موضوعيّة، عدم تحيّز

objective² /əbˈdʒektɪv/ *noun* [C] your aim or purpose: *Our objective is to finish by the end of the year.* ○ *to achieve your objective* هدف، غاية

obligation /ˌɒblɪˈɡeɪʃn/ *noun* **1** [C] something that you must do because it is your duty or because you promised to do it: *We have a moral obligation to help people who are in need.* واجب، التزام

2 [U] having to do sth because it is is your duty: *Unfortunately the shop is under no obligation to give you your money back* (= they do not have to give you your money back). واجب

obligatory /əˈblɪɡətri; *US* -tɔːri/ *adj* (*formal*) that you must do: *It is obligatory to get insurance before you drive a car.* إجباري

oblige /əˈblaɪdʒ/ *verb* **1** [T] (usually passive) to force sb to do sth: *You are not obliged to answer these questions but it would be a great help if you did.* يجبر، يرغِم، يكره

2 [I,T] (*formal*) to do what sb asks; to be helpful: *The service there is excellent. They are always happy to oblige.* يساعد، يآزر؛ يسدي خدمة

▸ **obliged** *adj* (*formal*) grateful: *Thanks for your help. I'm much obliged to you.* ممتنّ، شاكر؛ مَدين لِـ

obliging *adj* friendly and helpful خدوم، محبّ للمساعدة، لطيف

obliterate /əˈblɪtəreɪt/ *verb* [T] (*formal*) to destroy or ruin sth completely يمحو، يزيل من الوجود، يمحق

oblivion /əˈblɪviən/ *noun* [U] **1** the state of having forgotten sth or of not being aware of sth: *I was in a state of complete oblivion.* نسيان، غفلة

2 the state of being forgotten: *His work faded into oblivion after his death.* (طواه) النسيان، أصبح منسياً

oblivious /əˈblɪviəs/ *adj* not noticing or being aware of sth: *The baby slept, oblivious to all that was going on around him.* غافل تماماً عن؛ غير مدرك لِـ

oblong /ˈɒblɒŋ; *US* -lɔːŋ/ *adj, noun* [C] (of) a shape with two long sides and two short sides and four angles of 90° (right angles) ➲ Look at **rectangle**. مستطيل؛ المستطيل

obnoxious /ɒbˈnɒkʃəs/ *adj* very unpleasant كريه، بغيض؛ منفّر

oboe /ˈəʊbəʊ/ *noun* [C] a musical instrument that is made of wood. You play an oboe by blowing through it. أوبو: آلة نفخ موسيقيّة تشبه الناي

obscene /əbˈsiːn/ *adj* (used about words, thoughts, books, pictures, etc.) shocking or disgusting (usually because of the way they talk about or show sex): *an obscene book* ○ (*figurative*) *It's obscene to spend so much on food when millions are starving.* بذيء، فاحش؛ فاضح؛ مقزّز

▸ **obscenity** /əbˈsenəti/ *noun* (*pl.* **obscenities**)
1 [U] the state of being obscene فحش، بذاءة
2 [C] an obscene word or act كلمة بذيئة؛ تصرُّف داعر

obscure /əbˈskjʊə(r)/ *adj* **1** not easy to see or understand: *The reasoning behind his comments was a bit obscure.* غير واضح، غامض، مبهَم

2 not well known: *an obscure Spanish poet* مغمور، غير معروف

▸ **obscure** *verb* [T] to make sth difficult to see or understand: *Our view was obscured by a high fence.* يحجب، يخفي؛ يُبهِم (المعنى)

obscurity /əbˈskjʊərəti/ *noun* [U]: *The artist died penniless and in obscurity.* غموض، عدم وضوح؛ اختفاء من عالم الشُهرة

observance /əbˈzɜːvəns/ *noun* [U] (*formal*) obeying or following a law, custom, ceremony, etc. مراعاة (القانون)

observant /əbˈzɜːvənt/ *adj* good at noticing things: *An observant witness gave the police a description of the men.* ❶ The opposite is **unobservant**. قويّ الملاحظة

observation /ˌɒbzəˈveɪʃn/ *noun* **1** [U] the act of watching sb/sth carefully or the state of being watched carefully: *the observation of animals in their natural surroundings* مراقبة

2 [U] the ability to notice things: *Scientists need good powers of observation.* ملاحظة

3 [C] something that you say or write; a remark: *to make an observation about the weather* ➲ Look at **remark** and **comment**. These words are more common. ملاحظة، تعليق

IDM be under observation to be watched carefully: *The police are keeping the house under observation.* تحت المراقبة

observatory /əbˈzɜːvətri; *US* -tɔːri/ *noun* [C] (*pl.* **observatories**) a building from which scientists can look at the stars, the moon, etc. with telescopes مرصد

observe /əbˈzɜːv/ *verb* [T] **1** to notice sb/sth or watch sb/sth carefully: *A man and a woman were observed leaving by the back door.* ○ *We observed the birds throughout the breeding season.* يشاهد، يلاحظ؛ يراقب

2 (*formal*) to say or remark: *'We're late,' she observed.* يعلّق، يقول، يبدي ملاحظة

3 (*formal*) to obey a law, rule, etc: *to observe the speed limit* يراعي (القانون)

▶ **observer** *noun* [C] **1** a person who watches sb/sth: *Political observers have been predicting trouble for some time.* مراقِب

2 a person who attends a meeting, lesson, etc. to watch and listen but who does not say anything مراقِب (لا يشترك في المناقشات)

obsess /əbˈses/ *verb* [T] (usually passive) to fill sb's mind all the time: *He became obsessed with getting his revenge.* ○ *Alison is obsessed with an older man.* يستحوذ على التفكير، يستولي على كامل العقل

▶ **obsession** /əbˈseʃn/ *noun* **1** [U] the state of being obsessed استحواذ تامّ على التفكير؛ هَوَس

2 [C] a person or thing that obsesses you: *Football is an obsession to some people.* الشُغل الشاغل؛ هَوَس

obsessive /əbˈsesɪv/ *adj* having or showing a way of thinking or behaving that you cannot stop: *He's obsessive about not being late.* ○ *obsessive cleanliness* مفرط في القلق، "مُوَسْوَس": (شعور) متسلّط

obsolete /ˈɒbsəliːt/ *adj* no longer used because it is out of date (تعبير) مهجور؛ باطل الاستعمال؛ من طراز قديم

obstacle /ˈɒbstəkl/ *noun* [C] something that makes it difficult for you to go somewhere or do sth: *Not speaking a foreign language was a major obstacle to her career.* عقبة، عائق

obstetrician /ˌɒbstəˈtrɪʃn/ *noun* [C] a doctor who looks after women who are pregnant طبيب مُولِّد، إخصائي توليد

obstinate /ˈɒbstɪnət/ *adj* not willing to change your mind if you have decided sth: *an obstinate refusal to apologize* ℹ The word **obstinate** is usually used in a critical way. ➲ Look at **stubborn**, which has the same meaning. عنيد

▶ **obstinacy** /ˈɒbstɪnəsi/ *noun* [U] عناد

obstinately *adv* بِعَناد

obstruct /əbˈstrʌkt/ *verb* [T] to stop sb/sth from happening or moving: *Could you move on, please? You're obstructing the traffic if you park there.* يعرقل، يعيق

obstruction /əbˈstrʌkʃn/ *noun* **1** [U] stopping sth from happening or making progress عرقلة، إعاقة

2 [C] a thing that stops sb/sth from moving: *This car is causing an obstruction.* عقبة؛ سَدّ (الطريق)، حائل

obstructive /əbˈstrʌktɪv/ *adj* trying to stop sth from happening معرقِل، معيق، مانع

obtain /əbˈteɪn/ *verb* [T] (*formal*) to get sth: *This book can now be obtained in paperback.* يحصل على؛ ينال

▶ **obtainable** *adj* that can be obtained: *A free leaflet is obtainable from the post office.* ℹ The opposite is **unobtainable**. متوفّر، يمكن الحصول عليه

obvious /ˈɒbviəs/ *adj* easily seen or understood; clear: *It was obvious that he was unwell.* ○ *His disappointment was obvious to everyone.* ○ *an obvious lie* واضح، جليّ

▶ **obviously** *adv* as can easily be seen or understood; clearly: *There has obviously been a mistake.* ○ *Obviously we don't want to spend too much money if we can avoid it.* من الواضح؛ بداهةً

occasion /əˈkeɪʒn/ *noun* **1** [C] a particular time when sth happens: *I have met Bill on two occasions.* مناسبة؛ مرّة

2 [sing.] **occasion (for sth)** the suitable or right time (for sth): *I shall tell her what I think if the occasion arises.* فرصة، مناسبة

> You use **occasion** when you mean the time is right or suitable for something: *I saw them at the funeral, but it was not a suitable occasion for discussing holiday plans.* You use **opportunity** or **chance** when you mean that it is possible to do something: *I was only in Paris for one day and I didn't get the opportunity/chance to visit the Louvre.*

3 [C] a special event, ceremony, etc: *Their wedding was a memorable occasion.* ○ *an official, special, great, etc. occasion* حَدَث هام، احتفال، مناسبة (رسمية)

IDM **on occasion(s)** sometimes أحياناً

occasional /əˈkeɪʒənl/ *adj* done or happening from time to time but not very often: *She rarely goes out – just the occasional visit to her daughter.* حاصل من حينٍ لآخر؛ تصادفي

▶ **occasionally** /-nəli/ *adv*: *We see each other occasionally.* من حينٍ لآخر

occult /ˈɒkʌlt; US əˈkʌlt/ *adj* connected with magic or supernatural powers سِحري، ذو علاقة بالتنجيم وعلوم الغيب؛ سِرّي

▶ **the occult** *noun* [sing.] magic or occult powers, ceremonies, etc. السِّحر والعرافة وما إليهما

occupant /ˈɒkjəpənt/ *noun* [C] (*formal*) a person who lives in or uses a room, house, etc. الساكن أو المقيم (في غرفة مثلاً)

occupation /ˌɒkjuˈpeɪʃn/ *noun* **1** [U] living in a room, house, etc: *The new houses are now ready for occupation.* سكنى، إقامة، شَغْل

2 [C] your job or sth that you do in your free time: *Please state your occupation on the form.* ○ *Fishing is his favourite occupation.* ➲ Look at the note at **work**[1]. مهنة؛ شُغْل؛ هواية

3 [U] the control of a country by the army of another country احتلال

▶ **occupational** /-ʃənl/ *adj* connected with your work: *Accidents are an occupational risk on building sites.* متعلّق بالمهنة، (خطر) ناجم من طبيعة المهنة

occupier /ˈɒkjupaɪə(r)/ *noun* [C] (*formal*) a person who lives in or uses a house, piece of land, etc. الشاغل أو الساكن (في بيت أو غير ذلك)

🔑**occupy** /ˈɒkjupaɪ/ *verb* [T] (*pres part* **occupying**; *3rd pers sing pres* **occupies**; *pt, pp* **occupied**) **1** to live in or use a house, piece of land, etc: *The house next door has not been occupied for some months.* يشغَل، يُقيم في

2 to take control of a building, country, etc. by force: *The rebel forces have occupied the television station.* يحتلّ

3 to fill a space or period of time: *The large table occupied most of the room.* يَشْغَل

4 occupy sb/yourself (in doing sth/with sth) to keep sb/yourself busy: *How does he occupy himself now that he's retired?* يشغَل، يملأ وقت فراغه

▶ **occupied** *adj* **1** being used: *Is this seat occupied?* (مقعد) مشغول، مأخوذ

2 busy: *Looking after the children keeps me fully occupied.* مشغول، منشغل

3 (used about a country or a piece of land) under the control of another country (منطقة) محتلّة

🔑**occur** /əˈkɜː(r)/ *verb* [I] (occurring; occurred) **1** (*formal*) to happen: *The accident occurred late last night.* ➲ Look at the note at **happen**. يحدث، يقع

2 to be or exist: *The virus occurs more frequently in children.* يوجَد

3 occur to sb to come into sb's mind: *It never occurred to John that his wife might be unhappy.* يخطر بالبال

occurrence /əˈkʌrəns/ *noun* [C] something that happens: *Car theft is now a very common occurrence.* حادثة، واقعة

🔑**ocean** /ˈəʊʃn/ *noun* **1** [sing.] the mass of salt water that covers most of the surface of the earth: *the ocean floor* ○ *an ocean-going yacht* محيط

2 [C] **Ocean** one of the five main areas into which the sea is divided: *the Atlantic Ocean* المُحيط (الأطلسيّ مثلاً)

🔑**o'clock** /əˈklɒk/ *adv* (used after the numbers one to twelve for saying what the time is): *Lunch is at twelve o'clock.* الساعة...، في الساعة...

Be careful. **o'clock** can only be used with full hours: *We arranged to meet at 5 o'clock. It's 5.30 already and he's still not here.*

octagon /ˈɒktəgən; *US* -gɒn/ *noun* [C] a shape that has eight straight sides المُثمّن، شكل ذو ثمانية أضلاع

▶ **octagonal** /ɒkˈtægənl/ *adj* مثمّن

octave /ˈɒktɪv/ *noun* [C] the set of eight musical notes that western music is based on (في الموسيقى) الجواب

🔑**October** /ɒkˈtəʊbə(r)/ *noun* [C,U] (*abbr* **Oct.**) the tenth month of the year, coming before November ℹ For examples of the use of the months in sentences, look at **January**. شهر أكتوبر/تشرين الأوّل

octopus /ˈɒktəpəs/ *noun* [C] (*pl.* **octopuses**) a sea animal with a soft body and eight long arms (tentacles) الأخطبوط

🔑**odd** /ɒd/ *adj* **1** strange; unusual: *There's something odd about him.* ○ *It's a bit odd that she didn't phone to say she couldn't come.* غريب، غير عاديّ

2 (used about a number) that cannot be divided by two: *One, three, five and seven are all odd numbers.* ℹ The opposite is **even**. (عدد) مفرد، فرديّ، وَتري

3 being one of a pair, from which the other is missing: *You're wearing odd socks.* مفرَد

4 that remains after other similar things have been used: *He made the bookshelves out of a few odd bits of wood.* متبَقٍّ، زائد

5 (usually used after a number) a little more than: *'How old do you think he is?' 'Well, he must be thirty-odd, I suppose.'* أكثر بقليل، نيِّف (وثلاثون)

6 not regular or fixed: *I do my exercises at odd moments during the day.* غير منتظم، اتّفاقيّ

IDM the odd man/one out one that is different from all the others or that is left behind when all the others are in groups: *Her brothers and sisters were much older than she was. She was always the odd one out.* ○ *'Carrot', 'lettuce', 'tomato' – which is the odd one out?* شخص أو شيء مختلف عن الآخرين؛ شخص أو شيء فائض عن المجموعة

▶ **oddly** *adv* in a strange way: *He's behaving very oddly.* ○ *Oddly enough, the most expensive tickets sold fastest.* بشكل غريب أو شاذّ

oddness *noun* [U] غرابة، شذوذ

oddity /ˈɒdəti/ *noun* (*pl.* **oddities**) **1** [U] the quality of being strange or unusual غرابة، شذوذ

2 [C] a person or thing that is unusual شخص أو شيء غريب

ˌodd ˈjobs *noun* [plural] small jobs of various kinds أعمال صغيرة متنوّعة

oddment /ˈɒdmənt/ *noun* [C, usually pl.] something that remains after the rest has been used فضْلة، بقيّة

odds /ɒdz/ *noun* [plural] the chance or probability that sth will or will not happen: *The odds on him surviving are very slim.* ○ *The odds are against you.* احتمالات، فرَص

IDM against (all) the odds happening although it seemed impossible; in spite of problems or disadvantages: *Graham passed his exam against all the odds.* رغم تضافر كل العوامل ضده: ضد كلّ التوقّعات

odds and ends (*Brit informal*) small things of little value or importance نثريات، خردوات، مجموعة أشياء متنوّعة

odometer /əʊˈdɒmɪtə(r)/ *noun* [C] (*US*) = MILOMETER

odour (*US* **odor**) /ˈəʊdə(r)/ *noun* [C] (*formal*) a smell (often an unpleasant one) رائحة

▶ **odourless** *adj* without a smell عديم الرائحة

🔑**of** /əv; *strong form* ɒv/ *prep* **1** belonging to, relating to, or part of sth: *the roof of the house* ○ *the result of the exam* ○ *the back of the book* ○ *the leader of the party* (أداة إضافة) مثلاً: سقف المنزل

2 relating to a person: *a friend of mine* (= one of my friends) ○ *the poems of Milton* ○ *That was*

nice of her (= she was nice to do that).
(للتعبير عن علاقة شيء بشخص) مثلاً: أشعار ملتون

3 (used for saying what sb/sth is or what a thing contains or consists of): *a woman of intelligence* ○ *the city of Paris* ○ *a glass of milk* ○ *a crowd of people* ○ *It's made of silver.* ○ *a feeling of anger*
ذو؛ من

4 showing sth: *a map of York*
لِ

5 (showing that sb/sth is part of a larger group): *some of the people* ○ *three of the houses*
(جزء من كل): من

6 (with measurements and expressions of time and age): *five miles north of Leeds* ○ *a litre of milk* ○ *the fourth of July* ○ *a girl of 12*
من، (في الثانية عشرة) من (العمر)

7 (with some adjectives): *I'm proud of you.* ○ *She's jealous of her.*
بِ، مِن

8 (with some verbs): *This perfume smells of roses.* ○ *Think of a number.* ○ *It reminds me of you.*
من، بِ

9 (used after a noun which is connected with a verb. The noun after 'of' can be either the subject or the object): *the arrival of the president* (= he arrives) ○ *the murder of the president* (= he is murdered)
(أداة إضافة)

off[1] /ɒf; *US* ɔːf/ *adv, prep* ❶ For special uses with many verbs, e.g. **go off**, look at the verb entries.

1 down or away from a place: *He fell off the ladder.* ○ *We got off the bus.* ○ *I shouted to him but he just walked off.* ○ *I must be off. It's getting late.* ○ *When are you off to Spain?* ○ (*figurative*) *We've got off the subject.*
من؛ عن؛ (ينصرف) إلى؛ بعيداً

2 (used with verbs that mean 'remove'): *She took her coat off.* ○ *He shook the rain off his umbrella.* ○ *Don't leave the top off the toothpaste.*
تستعمل مع أفعال مثل: يخلع، يزيل وما إليهما

3 at a distance from sth: *The Isle of Wight is just off the south coast of England.* ○ *Christmas is still a long way off* (= it is a long time till then).
على مبعدة من، على مسافة (كذا)؛ بعد زمن (طويل)

4 joined to and leading from: *The bathroom is off the main bedroom.*
متصل بِ

5 (used about a machine, a light, etc.) not working or being used: *Please make sure the lights are off.*
(النور أو الجهاز) مطفأ، غير شغّال

6 not present at work, school, etc: *She's off work with a cold.*
منقطع عن (العمل)، غير مداوم

7 when you do not work: *I'm having a day off next week.*
(يوم) إجازة من العمل

8 no longer happening: *The meeting next Monday is off.*
ملغى

9 cheaper; costing a certain amount less: *cars with £400 off* ○ *£400 off the price of a car*
حسْم، تخفيض

10 not eating or using sth: *The baby's off his food.*
كاره أو عائف لِ

IDM **off and on; on and off** sometimes, but not all the time
على نحو متقطّع، من حين لآخر

well/badly off having/not having a lot of money
ميسور، غني؛ معوز، فقير الحال

off[2] /ɒf; *US* ɔːf/ *adj* (not before a noun) **1** no longer fresh (used about food or drink): *The milk's off.*
فاسد

2 (*informal*) unfriendly: *My neighbour was rather off with me today. I wonder if I've upset her.*
فاتر، غير ودود

offal /ˈɒfl; *US* ˈɔːfl/ *noun* [U] the heart, liver, kidneys, etc. of an animal, used as food
فضلات الذبيحة: القلب والكبد والكليتان وغير ذلك

ˈoff chance *noun* [sing.] a slight possibility: *She popped round on the off chance of finding him at home.*
احتمال ضئيل

ˈoff day *noun* [C] (*informal*) a day when things go badly or you do not work well
يوم منحوس؛ يوم لا يسير العمل فيه على ما يرام

ˌoff-ˈduty *adj* not at work: *an off-duty policeman*
خارج أوقات العمل، خارج الدوام

offence (*US* **offense**) /əˈfens/ *noun* **1** [C] **offence (against sth)** (*formal*) a crime; breaking the law: *to commit an offence* ○ *Possessing stolen goods is a criminal offence.* ○ *a minor/serious offence* ○ *She pleaded guilty to five driving offences.*
جرم، مخالفة للقانون

2 [U] **offence (to sb/sth)** annoyance, anger or sadness or sth that causes these feelings: *I didn't mean to cause you any offence.*
إساءة، إهانة؛ إغاظة

IDM **take offence (at sth)** to feel upset or hurt: *Be careful what you say – she takes offence rather easily.*
يستاء، يَغضَب؛ يجرح شعوره

offend /əˈfend/ *verb* **1** [T] (often passive) to hurt sb's feelings; to upset sb: *I hope they won't be offended if I don't come.* ○ *He felt offended that she hadn't written for so long.*
يسيء إلى، يغضِب؛ يجرح شعور...

2 [I] **offend (against sb/sth)** (*formal*) to be wrong or act wrongly according to law, usual behaviour, certain beliefs, etc: *The prisoner had offended* (= committed a crime) *again within days of his release from jail.* ○ *Parts of the book offended against their religious beliefs.*
يرتكب جريمة، يخالف القانون؛ ينتهك حرمة (الدين)

▸ **offender** *noun* [C] **1** (*formal*) a person who commits a crime: *Young offenders should not be sent to adult prisons.* ○ *a first offender*
المرتكب جريمة أو جنحة، المخالف للقانون

2 a person or thing that causes harm or trouble: *When it comes to polluting the North Sea, Britain is the worst offender.*
المسيء

offensive /əˈfensɪv/ *adj* **1** unpleasant; insulting: *an offensive remark* ○ *offensive behaviour* ➲ Look at **inoffensive**.
مسيء، مهين؛ كريه، منفّر

2 (*formal*) used for or connected with attacking: *offensive weapons* ❶ The opposite is **defensive**.
هجومي

▸ **offensive** *noun* [C] an attack
هجوم، اعتداء

IDM **take the offensive** to be the first to attack
يهاجم، يبادئ بالاعتداء

offensively *adv* unpleasantly; rudely: *He was offensively outspoken in his remarks.*
بصورة مسيئة؛ بوقاحة

offer /ˈɒfə(r); *US* ˈɔːf-/ *verb* **1** [T] **offer sth (to sb)** to ask if sb would like sth or to give sb the opportunity to have sth: *He offered his seat on the bus to an old lady.* ○ *I've been offered a job in London.* ○ *She offered me a cigarette.* يقدّم، يَعرض على

2 [I,T] to say or show that you are willing to do sth: *I don't want to do it but I suppose I'll have to offer.* ○ *My brother's offered to help me paint the house.* يبدي استعداده للمساعدة

3 [T] to give or provide sth: *The brochure offers very little information about the surrounding area.* ○ *The job offers plenty of opportunity for travel.* يزوّد بِـ، يعطي

4 [T] to say that you will pay a certain amount: *He offered (me) £2 000 for the car and I accepted.* يعرض سِعراً

▸ **offer** *noun* [C] **1** a statement offering to do sth or give sth to sb: *She accepted my offer of help.* ○ *Thank you for your kind offer.* ❶ We can **make**, **accept**, **refuse** or **withdraw** an offer. عَرْض

2 a low price for sth in a shop, or sth extra that you get when buying sth: *See below for details of our special holiday offer.* تخفيض في الأسعار؛ عروض مغرية

3 an amount of money that you say you will give for sth: *They've made an offer for the house.* ○ *We've turned down* (= refused) *an offer of £90 000.* الثمن المعروض (من قبل الشاري)

IDM on offer 1 for sale or available: *The college has a wide range of courses on offer.* معروض للبيع؛ متوفر

2 for sale at a lower price than usual for a certain time: *This cheese is on offer until next week.* تنزيل في السعر لمدة محدودة

or nearest offer → NEAR[1]

offering /ˈɒfərɪŋ; *US* ˈɔːf-/ *noun* [C] something that is given or produced: *He gave me a box of chocolates as a peace offering.* ○ *The latest offering from the Oxford Youth Theatre is 'Macbeth'.* تقدمة؛ عرض

offhand /ˌɒfˈhænd; *US* ˌɔːf-/ *adj* (used about behaviour) not friendly or polite متعالٍ، غير مؤدّب؛ غير مكترث

▸ **offhand** *adv* without having time to think; immediately: *I can't tell you what it's worth offhand.* رأساً، حالاً؛ ارتجالاً

offhandedly *adv* in an unfriendly way or in a way that shows that you are not interested: *'Oh really?' she said offhandedly, looking at her watch.* دون اهتمام؛ بتعالٍ

⚷ **office** /ˈɒfɪs; *US* ˈɔːf-/ *noun* **1** [C] a room or building where written work is done, especially work connected with a business: *I usually get to the office at about 9 o'clock.* ○ *The firm's head office is in Glasgow.* ○ *office furniture, equipment, etc.* ○ *Please phone again during office hours.* ❶ In America doctors and dentists have **offices**. In Britain they have **surgeries**. مكتب

2 Office [sing.] (often in compounds) a government department, including the people who work there and the work they do: *the Foreign Office* دائرة حكوميّة، مصلحة، وزارة

3 [C] (often in compounds) a room or building that is used for a particular purpose, especially for providing a service: *the tax office* ➲ Look at **booking office**, **box office** and **post office**. مكتب، مصلحة

4 [U] an official position, often as part of a government or other organization: *The chairman holds office for one year.* ○ *The Labour party has been in office since 1997.* منصب؛ حكم

ˈ**office block** *noun* [C] a large building that contains offices, usually belonging to more than one company بناء كله مكاتب

⚷ **officer** /ˈɒfɪsə(r); *US* ˈɔːf-/ *noun* [C] **1** a person who gives the orders to others in the army, navy, etc: *an army, a naval, an air-force officer* ضابط

2 (often in compounds) a person with a position of authority or responsibility in the government or other organization: *a prison officer* موظَّف، موظف رسمي

3 = POLICE OFFICER: *Excuse me, officer, is this the way to Victoria Station?* ➲ Look at the note at **official**.

⚷ **official** /əˈfɪʃl/ *adj* **1** accepted and approved by the government or some other authority: *the official unemployment figures* ○ *The scheme has not yet received official approval.* رسمي، حكومي

2 connected with a position of authority: *official duties* ○ *Her official title is now 'The Princess Royal'.* رسميّ

3 known publicly: *Their engagement is not yet official.* ○ *The official reason for his resignation* (= but perhaps not the real reason) *was that he wanted to spend more time with his family.* علنيّ: (السبب) المعلَن على الناس

❶ The opposite is **unofficial**.

▸ **official** *noun* [C] a person who has a position of authority: *The reception was attended by MPs and high-ranking officials.* ○ *a council official* موظَّف

> An **office worker** is a person who works in an office, at a desk. An **official** is a person who has a position of responsibility in an organization, often the government: *senior government officials*. An **officer** is either a person who gives orders to others in the army, navy, etc. or a policeman or -woman. However, the word is sometimes used like **official**: *She's an executive officer in the Civil Service.*

officialdom /-dəm/ *noun* [U] officials as a group موظَّفو الحكومة، فئة الموظّفين

officially /əˈfɪʃəli/ *adv* **1** as announced publicly but perhaps not strictly true: *Officially we don't accept children under 6, but we'll make an exception in this case.* رسميّاً، علَناً

2 in an official way: *The new school was officially opened last week.* بشكل رسمي

officious /əˈfɪʃəs/ *adj* too ready to tell other people what to do مُقدِّم نصائح وخدمات غير مرغوب فيها، فضوليّ

offing /ˈɒfɪŋ; *US* ˈɔːf-/ *noun*

IDM in the offing likely to appear or happen soon قريب، وشيك، يلوح في الأفق

offline /ˌɒfˈlaɪn/ *adj* not directly controlled by or

connected to a computer or to the Internet غير موصول بكمبيوتر أو بالانترنت

offload /ˌɒfˈləʊd; US ˌɔːf-/ *verb* [T] **offload sb/sth on/onto sb** (*informal*) to give sb/sth that you do not want to sb else يتخلّص من (شيء) بإعطائه للآخرين

ˌ**off-ˈpeak** *adj* available or used at a less popular or busy time: *an off-peak train ticket* صالح للاستعمال خارج أوقات الإقبال الشديد (في السفر مثلاً)

off-putting /ˈɒf pʊtɪŋ; US ˈɔːf-/ *adj* unpleasant or unattractive: *I must say that I find her manner rather off-putting.* غير مستحبّ؛ منفّر

ˈ**off-road** *adj* not on the public road: *an off-road vehicle (= one for driving on rough ground)* خارج الطرق العامة، صالح للطرق الوعرة

offset /ˈɒfset; US ˈɔːf-/ *verb* [T] (**offsetting**; *pt, pp* **offset**) to make the effect of sth less strong or noticeable; to balance: *The disadvantages of the scheme are more than offset by the advantages.* يخفِّف، يلطِّف، يعدل؛ يوازن

offshore /ˌɒfˈʃɔː(r); US ˌɔːf-/ *adj* in the sea not far from the land: *an offshore island* على مقربة من الساحل

offside[1] /ˌɒfˈsaɪd/ *adj, adv* (used about a player in football, etc.) in a position that is not allowed by the rules of the game: *the offside rule* ○ *The Liverpool player seemed to be offside but the goal was allowed.* (في كرة القدم) متسلِّل؛ تسلُّلاً

offside[2] /ˌɒfˈsaɪd; US ˌɔːf-/ *adj* (*Brit*) (used about a car, etc.) on the right side when you are driving: *The front offside tyre is punctured.* (بالنسبة للسائق) جانب السيّارة البعيد عن الرصيف

offspring /ˈɒfsprɪŋ; US ˈɔːf-/ *noun* [C] (*pl.* **offspring**) (*formal*) a child or children; the young of an animal: *Parents can pass many diseases on to their offspring.* نَسل، ذُرّية؛ نَتاج

ˌ**off-ˈwhite** *adj* not pure white أبيض ضارب إلى الصُفرة

⚷ **often** /ˈɒfn; ˈɒftən; US ˈɔːfn/ *adv* **1** many times; frequently: *We often go swimming at the weekend.* ○ *I've often seen him on the train.* ○ *I'm sorry I didn't write very often.* ○ *How often should you go to the dentist?* ○ *Write as often as you can.* كثيراً ما، مراراً

2 in many cases: *Women often go back to work after they have had a baby.* غالباً، في حالات كثيرة

IDM every so often occasionally; from time to time أحياناً؛ بين آنٍ وآخر

more often than not usually: *More often than not the buses are late in the morning.* عادةً؛ في معظم الحالات

ogre /ˈəʊgə(r)/ *noun* [C] **1** (in children's stories) a cruel and frightening giant مارد مرعب شرّير، غول

2 a person who is unpleasant and frightening شخص مرعب منفر

⚷ **oh** (*also formal* **o**) /əʊ/ *interj* **1** (used for introducing a reply or remark, for attracting sb's attention or when pausing to think): *'What time should we leave?' 'Oh, early, I think.'* ○ *'I'm a teacher.' 'Oh? Where?'* ○ *Oh, Simon, take this letter to the post, would you?* ○ *'What time do you think it is?' 'Oh... about 3.30.'* أوه! (تقال قبل البدء في الإجابة أو لجذب الانتباه أو للتفكُّر)

2 (used for expressing surprise, fear, etc.): *'Oh no!' she cried as she began to read the letter.* أوه! (للتعبير عن الدهشة أو الخوف الخ...)

⚷ **oil** /ɔɪl/ *noun* [U] **1** a thick liquid that comes from under the ground and is used as a fuel or to make machines work smoothly: *Britain obtains oil from the North Sea.* ○ *Your bicycle chain needs a little oil.* ○ *Crude oil* (= the raw material) *is transported by tanker to the refinery.* نفط، بترول؛ زيت معدنيّ

2 a thick liquid that comes from animals or plants and is used in cooking: *cooking, vegetable, olive, etc. oil* زيت نباتي أو حيواني

▸ **oil** *verb* [T] to put oil on or into sth, to make it work smoothly يزيّت

oily /ˈɔɪli/ *adj* (**oilier; oiliest**) covered with oil or like oil مغطّى بالزيت؛ زيتيّ، مشابه للزيت

oilfield /ˈɔɪlfiːld/ *noun* [C] an area where oil is found under the ground or the sea حقل نفط أو بترول

ˈ**oil painting** *noun* [C] a painting that has been done using paint made with oil صورة زيتيّة

ˈ**oil slick** (*also* **slick**) *noun* [C] an area of oil that floats on the sea, usually when a ship carrying oil has leaked طبقة من الزيت طافية على البحر، تلوُّث بالزيت

ˈ**oil well** (*also* **well**) *noun* [C] a hole that is made deep in the ground or under the sea in order to obtain oil بئر نفط أو بترول

ointment /ˈɔɪntmənt/ *noun* [C,U] a smooth substance that you put on sore skin or on an injury to help it to heal: *The doctor gave me an ointment to rub in twice a day.* مرهم

⚷ **OK** (*also* **okay**) /ˌəʊˈkeɪ/ *adj, adv* (*informal*) all right; good or well enough: *'Did you have a nice day?' 'Well, it was OK, I suppose.'* ○ *'How's your mother now?' 'OK.'* ○ *If it's okay with you, I'll come at about 7.* حَسَن، لا بأس به، "كُويّس"؛ مناسب

▸ **OK** (*also* **okay**) *interj* yes; all right: *'Would you like to come to the cinema?' 'OK.'* نعم، لا مانع

OK (*also* **okay**) *noun* [sing.] agreement or permission: *My parents have given me the OK to stay out late.* موافقة، سَماح

⚷ **old** /əʊld/ *adj* **1** (used about people, animals, etc.) having lived a long time; not young: *My mother wasn't very old when she died.* ○ *He's only 50 but he looks older.* ○ *to get, grow, become old* متقدّم في السن، عجوز

2 having existed for a long time; not modern: *a beautiful old stone house* ○ *old ideas, traditions, etc.* قديم

3 having been used a lot; not new: *My younger brother gets all my old clothes.* ○ *I'm going to exchange my old car for a new one.* ○ *Oh no, not that old joke again!* مستعمَل؛ قديم

4 (only *before* a noun) former; previous: *I earn more now than I did in my old job.* سابق

5 (used with a period of time or with *how*) of a particular age: *Our car is only a year old.* ○ *My best friend and I have known each other since we*

were five years old. ○ *They have a two-year-old* (= a child who is two years old). ○ *How old are you?* ○ *Are you older or younger than your sister?* ➲ Look at the note at **age**[1]. بالغ من العمر، (كم عمره)

> **Older** and **oldest** are the usual comparative and superlative forms of **old**: *My father's older than my mother.* ○ *That's the oldest story in the world!* **Elder** and **eldest** can be used when comparing the ages of people, especially members of a family. However they cannot be used with *than*. The adjectives are only used *before* the noun.

6 (only *before* a noun) known for a long time (but maybe not old in years): *She's a very old friend of mine. We knew each other at school.* قديم، من زمن طويل

7 (only *before* a noun) (*informal*) (used for expressing friendship and affection): *Good old Tom has solved the problem!* (تُقال تحبُّباً): العزيز...الصديق...

8 (only *before* a noun) (*informal*) (used for emphasizing that sth is not important): *'What time shall I come?' 'Oh, any old time – it doesn't matter.'* في أي (وقت) تشاء

IDM be an old hand (at sth) to be good at sth because you have done it often before مُتمرِّس، "عتيق في الكار"

old hat (*informal*) not new; old-fashioned قديم، متروك، فات زمانه

▸ **the old** *noun* [plural] old people الشُّيوخ، المسنُّون

ˌold ˈage *noun* [U] the part of your life when you are old: *He's enjoying life in his old age.* ➲ Look at **youth**. شيخوخة

ˌold-age ˈpension *noun* [U] money paid by the state to people above a certain age راتب تقاعديّ للمسنّين

▸ **old-age pensioner** (*also* **pensioner**) *noun* [C] (*abbr* **OAP**) a person who gets the old-age pension ❶ Nowadays the expression **senior citizen** is more acceptable. شخص مسنّ يتقاضى راتباً تقاعديّاً، متقاعد

🔑 **ˌold-ˈfashioned** *adj* **1** not modern; not commonly worn, used, etc. now: *a long old-fashioned skirt* (أفكار) بالية؛ (ثوب) من طراز قديم

2 (used about people) believing in old ideas, customs, etc: *My parents are rather old-fashioned about some things.* (شخص) محافظ، لا يجاري العصر الحديث

the ˌOld ˈTestament *noun* [sing.] the first part of the Bible, that tells the history of the Jewish people. العهد القديم

olive /ˈɒlɪv/ *noun* [C] a small green or black fruit with a bitter taste, used for food and oil زيتونة

▸ **olive** (*also* **ˌolive ˈgreen**) *adj* of a colour between yellow and green أخضر مائل إلى الصُّفرة

ˌolive ˈoil *noun* [U] oil obtained from olives and used in cooking or on salads زيت الزيتون

Olympic /əˈlɪmpɪk/ *adj* connected with the Olympic Games: *Who holds the Olympic record for the 1500 metres?* أولمبيّ

the Oˌlympic ˈGames (*also* **the Olympics**) *noun* [plural] the international sports competitions which are organized every four years in a different country: *to win a medal at/in the Olympics* الألعاب الأولمبية

ombudsman /ˈɒmbʊdzmən; -mæn/ *noun* [C] (*pl.* **ombudsmen** /-mən/) a government official who reports on complaints made by ordinary people against public authorities وسيط رسمي بين عامّة الشعب والسلطات المسؤولة

omelette (*also* **omelet**) /ˈɒmlət/ *noun* [C] eggs, mixed and beaten and fried: *A plain omelette and a salad, please.* ○ *a mushroom omelette* بيض مخفوق ومقلي، عجّة بالبيض

omen /ˈəʊmen/ *noun* [C] a sign of sth that will happen in the future: *a good/bad omen* فأل (خير)، نذير (شرّ)

ominous /ˈɒmɪnəs/ *adj* suggesting that sth bad is going to happen: *Those black clouds look ominous.* مُنذِر، مهدِّد بالسّوء

omission /əˈmɪʃn/ *noun* **1** [C] something that has not been included: *There were several omissions on the list of names.* اسم محذوف؛ إغفال، إسقاط

2 [U] the act of not including sb/sth: *The film was criticized for its omission of certain important details.* حذف، إهمال

omit /əˈmɪt/ *verb* [T] (omi**tt**ing; omi**tt**ed) **1** to not include sth: *Several verses of the song can be omitted.* يَحذف، يهمل، يسقط

2 (*formal*) to not do sth: *He omitted to mention the man's name.* يغفل

🔑 **on** /ɒn/ *adv, prep* ❶ For special uses with many verbs and nouns, e.g. **get on, on holiday**, see the verb and noun entries.

1 supported by a surface: *The plates are on the table.* ○ *We sat on the floor.* ○ *Make sure you put the lid on.* على

2 touching or forming part of sth: *There's a mark on your skirt.* ○ *paintings on the wall* ○ *Write it down on a piece of paper.* على

3 in an area of land; near the sea, a river, etc: *on the farm* ○ *We live on a large housing estate.* ○ *a house on the river Thames* في؛ على

4 (showing direction): *on the right/left* على أو إلى (اليمين مثلاً)

5 (used with means of transport): *on the bus, train, plane* ○ *'I got the bus.' 'Where did you get on?'* ○ *We came on foot* (= walking). ○ *on a bicycle* ❶ Note that we say **in** a car. بِ؛ على

6 (with expressions of time): *on August 19th* ○ *on Monday* ○ *on Christmas Day* ○ *What are you doing on your birthday?* في؛ يوم (الإثنين)

7 immediately; soon after: *He telephoned her on his return from New York.* ○ *She began to weep on hearing the news.* فورَ، عندَ

8 (showing that sth continues): *The man shouted at us but we walked on.* ○ *The war went on for five years.* (حَدَث يستمرّ)

9 about sth: *We've got a test on irregular verbs tomorrow.* ○ *a talk on Japan* عن

10 working; being used: *All the lights were on.* ○ *Switch the television on.* (النور) مولع، (الجهاز) شغال

11 happening: *What's on at the cinema?* ○ *We haven't got anything on this weekend.* معروض (في السينما مثلاً): (برنامج) مهيأ أو مرتّب

12 using sth; by means of sth: *I spoke to her on the phone.* ○ *There's a good film on the television tonight.* بـ؛ على

13 wearing sth: *What did she have on?* مرتَدٍ، لابِس

14 having sth with you: *I've got no money on me.* مع

15 using drugs or medicine: *I've been on antibiotics for two weeks.* يتداوى بـ، على

16 receiving a certain amount of money: *I can't support a family on the salary I earn.* على

17 (showing the way sth is spent): *He spends a lot on clothes.* ○ *Don't waste your time on that.* على

18 paid for by sb: *The drinks are on me!* على

IDM **from now/then on** starting from this/that time and continuing: *From then on he never smoked another cigarette.* من الآن فصاعداً؛ منذ ذلك الحين فصاعداً

not on not acceptable: *No, you can't stay out that late. It's just not on.* غير مقبول، غير مسموح به

off and on; on and off → OFF[1]

on and on without stopping: *He just went on and on about his work.* دون توقّف، بلا انقطاع

on at sb talking in a complaining way: *She's always on at me to mend the roof.* يتشكّى، يتذمّر، ينِقّ

once /wʌns/ *adv* **1** one time only; on one occasion: *I've only been to France once.* ○ *once a week, month, year, etc.* ○ *I have the car serviced once every six months.* مرّة واحدة

2 at some time in the past; formerly: *This house was once the village school.* ذات يوم، سابقاً

IDM **all at once** all at the same time or suddenly: *People began talking all at once.* ○ *All at once she got up and left the room.* في نفس الوقت؛ فجأةً

at once 1 immediately; now: *Come here at once!* ○ *I'll telephone at once, before I forget.* حالاً، الآن

2 at the same time: *You can't all go on the slide at once! Take it in turns.* في نفس الوقت

just this once on this occasion only: *'Have a chocolate.' 'Oh, all right. Just this once.'* هذه المرّة فقط

once again/more again, as before: *Spring will soon be here once again.* مرّة أخرى

once and for all now and for the last time: *You've got to make a decision once and for all.* (عليك أن تقرر) الآن ولآخر مرة، بصورة نهائية

once in a blue moon (*informal*) very rarely; almost never: *We live in Glasgow, so I only go to London once in a blue moon.* نادراً جداً

once in a while occasionally but not often من وقت لآخر

once more one more time: *Let's listen to that song once more, shall we?* مرّة أخرى

once upon a time (used at the beginning of a children's story) a long time ago; in the past: *Once upon a time there was a beautiful princess...* في يوم من الأيام، كان يا ما كان

▶ **once** *conj* as soon as; when: *Once you've practised a bit you'll find that it's quite easy.* ○ *Once the meal was finished, the discussions began.* حالما، ما أن؛ عندما

oncoming /ˈɒnkʌmɪŋ/ *adj* (only *before* a noun) coming towards you: *oncoming traffic* (حركة السير) المقبلة نحونا

one[1] /wʌn/ *pron, det, noun* [C] **1** the number 1: *There's only one biscuit left.* ○ *The journey takes one hour.* ○ *If you take one from ten it leaves nine.* ➲ Look at **first**. واحد

2 (used for emphasizing sth) only: *She's the one person I trust.* (الشخص) الوحيد

3 (used when you are talking about a time in the past or future without actually saying which one) a certain: *He came to see me one evening last week.* ○ *We must go and visit them one day.* (في يوم) ما

4 (used with *the other, another* or *other* (s) to make a contrast): *The twins are so alike that it's hard to tell one from the other.* (يصعب تمييز) الواحد (عن الآخر)

5 the same: *We can't all get in the one car.* نفس

6 (*formal*) (used in front of sb's name to show that you do not know the person) a certain: *He worked as an assistant to one Mr Ming.* شخص يعرَف باسم (سميث)

IDM **(all) in one** all together or combined: *It's a bag and a raincoat all in one.* في نفس الوقت

one after another/the other first one, then the next, etc: *One after another the winners went up to get their prizes.* واحداً بعد الآخر

one by one individually or separately: *I'd like to see the three boys one by one.* واحداً فواحداً، كلّ على حدة

one or two a few: *I've borrowed one or two new books from the library.* ○ *Just take one or two – not too many.* بعض، عدد قليل

one[2] /wʌn/ *pron* **1** (used instead of repeating a noun): *I think I'll have an apple. Would you like one?* (تستعمل بدلاً من الاسم): واحد؛ واحدة

2 one of one member (of a certain group): *One of the plates is broken.* ○ *He's staying with one of his friends.* ○ *One of the children is crying.* أحد، واحد من

> **One of** is always followed by a plural noun. The verb is singular because the subject is **one**: *One of our assistants is ill.* ○ *One of the buses was late.*

one[3] /wʌn/ *noun* [C] **1** (used after *this, that, which* or after an adjective which cannot stand alone): *'Which dress do you like?' 'This one.'* ○ *'Can I borrow some books of yours?' 'Yes. Which ones?'* ○ *'This coat's a bit small. You need a bigger one.'* ○ *That idea is a very good one.* (هذا) الواحد؛ (أي) واحدة؛ واحد

2 (used before a group of words that show which person or thing you are talking about): *My house is the one after the post office.* ○ *The girl he's going out with is the one with the red hair.* ○ *If*

you find some questions difficult, leave out the ones you don't understand. الواحد أو الواحدة

3 someone: *She's not one to get upset easily.* شخص، فرد (من نوع معيّن)

one[4] /wʌn/ *pron (formal)* (used for referring to people in general, including the speaker or writer): *One should try not to get annoyed.* ○ *Plenty of exercise makes one fit.* ○ *Fresh fruit is good for one.* ❶ It is very formal to use **one** in this way. In everyday English it is more common to use **you**. المرء، الإنسان

> Note that the possessive form is **one's**: *One must be sure of one's facts before criticizing other people.* **One's** is also the short form of 'one is' or 'one has'.

ˌone ˈanother *pron* each other: *We exchanged news with one another.* ○ *You should listen to one another a bit more.* بعضنا بعضاً، بعضهم بعضاً...الخ

ˌone-ˈoff *noun* [C], *adj* (*informal*) (a thing) that is available or happens only once: *You'll never get a flight at that price again. It was a one-off.* ○ *a one-off opportunity* حادثة أو فرصة وحيدة: فريد من نوعه

oneself /wʌnˈself/ *pron* **1** (used for referring to people in general when *one* is the subject of the sentence): *One can teach oneself to play the piano but it is easier to have lessons.* نفسه

2 (used for emphasizing *one*): *One could easily arrange it all oneself.* بنفسه

IDM **(all) by oneself 1** alone وحدَه، لوحده

2 without help دونَ مساعدة، بنفسه

ˌone-ˈsided *adj* **1** involving one person more than the other: *Her feelings for him seem to be rather one-sided* (= he doesn't feel the same). (حبّ) من جانب واحد فقط

2 unfair; seeing only one side (of an argument, etc.): *I think you're being very one-sided. Think of my point of view.* غير منصف: متحيّز

ˌone-to-ˈone *adj, adv* between only two people: *one-to-one English lessons* (= one teacher to one student) (تدريس) فرديّ

ˌone-ˈway *adv, adj* **1** (used about roads) that you can only drive along in one direction: *a one-way street* (طريق) ذو اتّجاه واحد

2 (used about a ticket) that you can use to travel somewhere but not back again: *I'd like to buy a one-way ticket to the Caribbean!* (تذكرة) ذهاب: ذهاباً

ongoing /ˈɒngəʊɪŋ/ *adj* (only *before* a noun) continuing to exist now: *It's an ongoing problem.* ○ *an ongoing relationship* مستمِر، قائم حتى الآن

onion /ˈʌnjən/ *noun* [C,U] a small white vegetable with many layers and a brown skin. Onions have a strong smell and taste, and are often used in cooking: *a pound of onions* ○ *onion soup* بصَلة: بصَل

online /ˌɒnˈlaɪn/ *adj, adv* controlled by or connected to a computer or to the Internet: *an online ticket booking system* ○ *I'm studying French online.* موصول بكمبيوتر أو بالانترنت

onlooker /ˈɒnlʊkə(r)/ *noun* [C] a person who watches sth happening without taking part in it: *The police were questioning several onlookers about the incident.* من يشاهد حادثاً في الطريق مثلاً، شاهد عيان

only[1] /ˈəʊnli/ *adj* (only *before* a noun) **1** with no others existing or present: *I was the only woman in the bar.* ○ *This is the only dress we have in your size.* وحيد

2 the most suitable or the best: *It's so cold that the only thing to do is to sit by the fire.* أفضل (شيء)

only[2] /ˈəʊnli/ *adv* and no one or nothing else; no more than: *She only likes pop music.* ○ *I've only asked a few friends to the party.* ○ *It was only a little spider.* ○ *It's only one o'clock. There's plenty of time.* فقط: مجرّد

> In written English **only** is usually placed before the word it refers to. In spoken English we can use stress to show which word it refers to and so **only** can have different positions: *I only kissed 'Jane* (= I kissed Jane and no one else). ○ *I only 'kissed Jane* (= I kissed Jane but I didn't do anything else).

IDM **if only** → IF

not only... but also → NOT

only just 1 not long ago: *I've only just started the job.* من فترة قصيرة

2 almost not; hardly: *We only just had enough money to pay for the meal.* بالكاد

only[3] /ˈəʊnli/ *conj* (*informal*) except that; but: *The film was very good, only it was a bit too long.* لكن، إلا أنّ...

ˌonly ˈchild *noun* [C] (*pl.* **only children**) a child who has no brothers or sisters ولد وحيد

onset /ˈɒnset/ *noun* [sing.] the beginning (often of sth unpleasant): *the onset of winter* بدء (شيء غير مستحبّ عادة): هجوم

onslaught /ˈɒnslɔːt/ *noun* [C] **onslaught (on sb/sth)** a fierce attack: *an onslaught on government policy* هجوم عنيف

onto (*also* **on to**) /ˈɒntə; *before vowels* ˈɒntu/ *prep* to a position on sth: *The cat jumped onto the sofa.* ○ *The bottle fell onto the floor.* على

IDM **be onto sb** (*informal*) **1** to have found out about sth illegal that sb is doing: *The police were onto the car thieves.* يكتشف أمره، يفضح أو يكشف (المؤامرة)

2 to talk to sb in order to pass on information or persuade him/her to do sth: *I've been onto the children to tidy their room.* يتكلّم مع، يقنع

be onto sth to have some information, etc. that could lead to an important discovery على وشك اكتشاف شيء هام

onward /ˈɒnwəd/ (*also* **onwards** /ˈɒnwədz/) *adv* **1** and after: *From September onwards it usually begins to get colder.* فصاعداً، وما بعده

2 forward or towards progress: *The road stretched onwards into the distance.* إلى الأمام

ooze /uːz/ *verb* [I,T] to flow slowly out or to allow

sth to flow slowly out: *Blood was oozing from a cut on his head.* ○ *The toast was oozing with butter.* ○ (*figurative*) *She was oozing confidence* (= she was very confident).
ينزّ؛ يسيل؛ ينضَح (بالثقة بالنفس)

op /ɒp/ *noun* [C] (*informal*) = OPERATION (3)

opaque /əʊˈpeɪk/ *adj* **1** that you cannot see through; not transparent: *opaque glass in the door* (زجاج) شافّ أي غير شفاف؛ عاتِم

2 (*formal*) difficult to understand; not clear
عويص؛ مبْهَم

OPEC /ˈəʊpek/ *abbrev* Organization of Petroleum Exporting Countries منظمة الدول المصدرة للنفط

open¹ /ˈəʊpən/ *adj* **1** not closed: *Don't leave the door open.* ○ *an open window* ○ *I can't get this bottle open.* ○ *She stared at me with her eyes wide open.* ○ *The diary was lying open on her desk.* ○ *The curtains were open so that we could see into the room.* مفتوح

2 not keeping feelings and thoughts hidden: *Elena doesn't mind talking about her feelings – she's a very open person.* صريح، غير متحفظ، أمين

3 not hidden or secret: *He looked at him with open dislike.* صريح، واضح

4 with its doors unlocked so that customers can enter: *The bank isn't open till 9.30.* يفتح أبوابه

5 (used about a new building, public area, etc.) ready to be used for the first time: *The new shopping centre will soon be open.* يفتَتح

6 open (to sb/sth) (used about a road, a course of action, etc.) possible to use, do, etc: *After the heavy snow many minor roads were not open to traffic.* سالِك؛ مفتوح

7 (used about clothes) with the buttons not fastened: *His shirt was open at the neck.* مفتوح

8 (only *before* a noun) with few buildings, villages, etc. near (used about an area of land): *open country* (ريف) فسيح، خلاء

9 (only *before* a noun) at a distance from the land (used about an area of sea): *Once we were out in the open sea, the wind got stronger.*
بعيد عن الشاطئ، في عرض البحر

10 (only *before* a noun) not covered: *an open fire* مكشوف

11 open (to sb/sth) that anyone can enter, visit, etc: *The competition is open to everyone.* ○ *The gardens are open to the public in the summer.* مفتوح للجميع

12 not finally decided; still being considered: *Let's leave the details open.*
غير نهائيّ؛ قيدَ البحث؛ معلّق

IDM have/keep an open mind (about/on sth) to be willing to listen to or consider new ideas and suggestions
متقبّل للأفكار الجديدة، منفتح العقل

in the open air outside: *Somehow, food eaten in the open air tastes much better.* في الهواء الطلق

keep an eye open/out (for sb/sth) → EYE¹

open to sth willing to receive sth: *I'm always open to suggestions.* مستعدّ أو متقبّل لـ

with your eyes open → EYE¹

with open arms in a friendly way that shows that you are pleased to see sb or have sth
ترحيب حارّ، (استقبلوه) بالأحضان

▸ **the open** *noun* [sing.] outside or in open country: *After working in an office I like to be out in the open at weekends.* الهواء الطلق؛ الخلاء

IDM bring sth out into the open; come out into the open to make sth known publicly; to be known publicly: *I'm glad our secret has come out into the open at last.* يكشف، يعلن؛ ينكشف، يصبح علنياً

openly *adv* not secretly; honestly: *I think you should discuss your feelings openly with each other.* على المكشوف؛ بصراحة

openness *noun* [U] the quality of being honest and willing to talk: *I was surprised by her openness about her relationship with James.*
صدق؛ صراحة

open² /ˈəʊpən/ *verb* **1** [I,T] to become open or to make sth open: *This window won't open – it's stuck.* ○ *Do you mind if I open this window?* ○ *When I opened my eyes, she was gone.*
ينفتح؛ يفتح

2 [I,T] **open (sth) (out)** to fold out, back, etc: *The book opened at the very page I needed.* ○ *Open your hand – what have you got inside?* ○ *She opened the curtains and looked out.*
ينفتح؛ يفتح

3 [I,T] (used about a shop, office, etc.) to be unlocked so that business, work, etc. can start; to unlock sth: *The shop hasn't opened yet.* ○ *They open the museum an hour later on Sundays.*
ينفتح؛ يفتح

4 [T] to say officially that a new building, etc. is ready for use: *The Mayor will open the college next week.* يفتتح

5 [I,T] to start: *The play opens in London next month.* ○ *The chairman opened the meeting by welcoming everybody.* ○ *I'd like to open a bank account.* يفتتح؛ يستهلّ؛ يفتح

6 [T] to make a road, etc. available for use again: *Snow ploughs have opened many major roads.*
يفتح، يشقّ طريقاً

IDM open fire (at/on sb/sth) to start shooting: *He ordered his men to open fire.* يطلق النار

PHR V open into/onto sth to lead straight to sth: *This door opens onto the garden.*
يؤدّي إلى (الحديقة)، يفتح على (الحديقة)

open out to become wider: *The road opened out and we were able to overtake the tractor.*
يتّسع، يصبح أوسع

open up to talk about what you feel and think
يبوح

open (sth) up 1 to become available or to make sth available: *When I left school, all sorts of opportunities opened up for me.* ○ *Parts of the desert may soon be opened up for farming.*
تنفتح له أبواب الفرص؛ يسمح باستغلاله

2 to open a door: *'Open up,' shouted the police to the man inside.* يفتح الباب

▸ **opener** /ˈəʊpnə(r)/ *noun* [C] (in compounds) a thing that takes the lid, etc. off sth: *a tin-opener* فتّاحة (العلَب)

ˌopen-ˈair *adj* outside; not indoor: *an open-air swimming pool* في الهواء الطلق

ˈopen day *noun* [C] a day when the public can

visit a place that is usually closed to them
يوم تُسمح فيه زيارة العامّة لمكان رسميّ مثلاً

opening /ˈəʊpnɪŋ/ *noun* **1** [sing.] beginning: *The book is famous for its dramatic opening.* افتتاحيّة: مستهَلّ
2 [C] a hole; a way in or out: *We were able to get through an opening in the hedge.* فتحة
3 [C] an opportunity: *There are many new openings for trade with Eastern Europe.* فرصة
4 [C] a job which is available: *We have an opening for a sales manager at the moment.* وظيفة شاغرة
5 [C] a ceremony when a public building, etc. is ready for use: *the opening of the new theatre* حفلة افتتاح
▸ **opening** *adj* (only *before* a noun) first: *the opening chapter of a book* ○ *His opening remarks were rather tactless.* أوّل، افتتاحيّ

ˌ**open-ˈminded** *adj* willing to consider new ideas and opinions
مستعدّ لتقبّل الأفكار الجديدة، مُنفتح العقل

ˌ**open-ˈplan** *adj* (used about a large indoor area) not divided into separate rooms: *an open-plan office* فسيح، غير مقسّم إلى غرف

the ˌ**Open Uniˈversity** *noun* [sing.] (*Brit*) a university whose students study mainly at home. Their work is sent to them by post or email and there are special television and radio programmes for them.
الجامعة المفتوحة أو جامعة الهواء (تُسمع دروسها على الراديو والتلفزيون)

opera /ˈɒprə/ *noun* **1** [C] a play in which the actors (opera singers) sing the words to music: *an opera by Wagner* ○ *a comic opera* أوبرا
2 [U] works of this kind: *Do you like opera?* ○ *grand* (= serious) *opera* ○ *light* (= not serious) *opera* ➲ Look at **soap opera**.
أوبرا (خفيفة أو شعبية وغير ذلك)
▸ **operatic** /ˌɒpəˈrætɪk/ *adj* connected with opera: *operatic music* ذو علاقة بالأوبرا: من نوع الأوبرا

ˈ**opera house** *noun* [C] a theatre where operas are performed دار الأوبرا

operate /ˈɒpəreɪt/ *verb* **1** [I,T] to do business; to manage or direct sth: *The firm operates from its central office in Bristol.* ○ *Many companies operate mail-order services nowadays.* يعمل: يدير، يُشغّل
2 [I] to act or to have an effect: *Several factors were operating to our advantage.* يعمل
3 [I,T] to work, or to make sth work: *I don't understand how this machine operates.* ○ *These switches here operate the central heating.*
يعمل: يشغّل
4 [I] **operate (on sb) (for sth)** to cut open a patient's body in order to deal with a part that is damaged, diseased, etc: *The surgeon is going to operate on her in the morning.* ○ *He was operated on for appendicitis.* يجري عملية جراحيّة

ˈ**operating system** *noun* [C] a computer program that organizes a number of other programs at the same time (في الكمبيوتر) نظام تشغيل

ˈ**operating theatre** (*also* **theatre**) *noun* [C] a room in a hospital where operations (3) are performed غرفة العمليات الجراحيّة

operation /ˌɒpəˈreɪʃn/ *noun* **1** [C] an activity, often highly organized, that involves many people, actions, days, etc: *A rescue operation was mounted to find the missing children.* ○ *military operations* ○ *Building the garden shed was quite a tricky operation.* عمليّة
2 [C] a business company: *a huge international operation* شركة تجاريّة
3 [C] (*also informal* **op**) **operation (on sb) (for sth)**; **operation (to do sth)** cutting open a patient's body in order to deal with a part inside: *The surgeon performed an operation on her for a kidney problem.* ○ *He had an operation to remove some damaged lung tissue.* عمليّة جراحيّة
4 [U] the way in which sth works; working: *The operation of these machines is quite simple.*
كيفية عمل أو سير (الآلة): تشغيل
IDM **be in operation**; **come into operation** to start working or having an effect: *The new tax system will come into operation in the spring.*
يَسري مفعوله، يبدأ تنفيذه

operational /ˌɒpəˈreɪʃənl/ *adj* **1** connected with an operation (1,4) ذو علاقة بسير الآلات والأجهزة
2 ready for use: *The new factory is now fully operational.* جاهز للعمل: (الأسطول) مستعدّ (للهجوم)

operative /ˈɒpərətɪv; *US* -reɪt-/ *adj* (*formal*) working, able to be used; in use: *The new law will be operative from 1 May.* نافذ المفعول: فعّال

operator /ˈɒpəreɪtə(r)/ *noun* [C] **1** a person whose job is to connect telephone calls, for the public or in a particular building: *Dial 100 for the operator.* ○ *a switchboard operator*
عامل أو عاملة مقسَم الهاتف
2 a person whose job is to work a particular machine or piece of equipment: *a computer operator* عامل يُشغّل آلة
3 a person or company that does certain types of business: *a tour operator* صاحب أعمال: شركة

opinion /əˈpɪniən/ *noun* **1** [C] **opinion (of sb/sth)**; **opinion (on/about sth)** what you think about sb/sth: *She asked me for my opinion of her new hairstyle and I told her.* ○ *He has very strong opinions on almost everything.* رأي
2 [U] what people in general think about sth: *Public opinion is in favour of a change in the law.* الرأي العام
IDM **be of the opinion that...** (*formal*) to think or believe that...: *In this case we are of the opinion that you took the right decision.* يَرى: يعتقد
have a good, bad, high, low, etc. opinion of sb/sth to think that sb/sth is good, bad, etc.
يرى: يظنّ: يعتقد
in my, your, etc. opinion I, you, etc. think that...: *In my opinion, you're making a terrible mistake.* في رأيي...
a matter of opinion → MATTER[1]

oˈ**pinion poll** *noun* [C] = POLL[1] (1)

opium /ˈəʊpiəm/ *noun* [U] a drug that is made from the seeds of the poppy flower أفيون

opp. *abbrev* = OPPOSITE

🔑**opponent** /əˈpəʊnənt/ *noun* [C] **1** (in sport or games) a person who plays against sb خَصْم
2 an opponent (of sth) a person who disagrees with sb's actions, plans or beliefs and tries to stop or change them مُعارِض، مناوئ

🔑**opportunity** /ˌɒpəˈtjuːnəti; *US* -ˈtuːn-/ *noun* [C,U] (*pl.* **opportunities**) a chance to do sth that you would like to do; a situation or a time in which it is possible to do sth that you would like to do: *There will be plenty of opportunity for asking questions later.* ○ *I should have gone abroad when I was young – it was a missed opportunity.* ○ *an equal opportunity employer* (= an employer who employs people regardless of sex, colour, etc.) ➲ Look at the note at **occasion**. فرصة؛ مناسبة
IDM take the opportunity to do sth/of doing sth to make use of a chance that you have to do sth: *When we were finally alone, I took the opportunity to ask him a few personal questions.* ينتهز الفرصة

🔑**oppose** /əˈpəʊz/ *verb* [T] to disagree with sb's beliefs, actions or plans and to try to change or stop them: *They opposed the plan to build new houses in the village.* يُعارِض؛ يُقاوِم
▸ **opposed** *adj* **opposed to sth** disagreeing with a plan, action, etc.; believing that sth is morally wrong: *I'm not opposed to the idea but I need more details.* ○ *She has always been opposed to experiments on animals.* مُعارِض
IDM as opposed to (used to emphasize the difference between two things) in contrast with: *Your work will be judged by quality, as opposed to quantity.* بالمقارنة مع، و ليس بِ......

🔑**opposite** /ˈɒpəzɪt/ *adj, adv* **1** in a position directly on the other side of sb/sth; facing: *The two cathedrals are on opposite sides of the river.* ○ *The two families sat at opposite ends of the room to each other.* ○ *You sit there and I'll sit opposite.* ❶ Sometimes **opposite** is used after the noun: *Write your answer in the space opposite.* مُقابِل، مواجِه، متُقابِل
2 as different as possible: *I can't walk with you because I'm going in the opposite direction.* ○ *the opposite sex* (= men for women, women for men) معاكس؛ (الجنس) الآخر
▸ **opposite** *prep* directly on the other side of a space between sth and sth else; facing sb/sth: *I always buy my paper from the shop opposite our flat.* مقابل، مواجه
opposite *noun* [C] the word, thing or person that is as different as possible from sb/sth: *'Hot' is the opposite of 'cold'.* ○ *She's very friendly, whereas her brother is the complete opposite.* عكس، العكس

ˌ**opposite ˈnumber** *noun* [C] a person who does the same job or has the same position in a different company, organization, team, etc: *The Prime Minister met his Italian opposite number.* نظير

🔑**opposition** /ˌɒpəˈzɪʃn/ *noun* [U] **1 opposition (to sb/sth)** the feeling of disagreeing with sth and the action of trying to change it: *Despite strong opposition from local people, the ... was completely rebuilt.* ○ *to express ... ition to sth*
2 the opposition [sing.] the perso... who plays against sb in sport or gar... *manager has told them not to underest... the opposition.* الشخص او الفريق الخصم
3 the Opposition [sing.] the politicians or the political parties that are in Parliament but not in the government: *the leader of the Opposition* ○ *Opposition MPs* المعارضة (في البرلمان)
❶ In numbers **2** and **3**, **opposition** can be used with either a singular or a plural verb.

oppress /əˈpres/ *verb* [T] (usually passive) to rule sb (especially a nation or a part of society) in a way that allows the people no freedom; to control sb in an unjust way, using force يقمع؛ يَضطهِد
▸ **oppressed** *adj* unfairly ruled or treated; not free: *an oppressed minority* مضطهَد
oppression /əˈpreʃn/ *noun* [U] the system or act of oppressing; the state of being oppressed: *a struggle against oppression* سياسة القمع، اضطهاد
oppressive /əˈpresɪv/ *adj* **1** allowing no freedom; controlling by force; unjust: *The military government announced oppressive new laws.* خانق للحرّيات؛ متّسم بالعنف؛ جائر
2 (used especially about heat or the atmosphere) causing you to feel very uncomfortable (حرّ) خانق
oppressor *noun* [C] a person who oppresses حاكم جائر؛ طاغية

opt /ɒpt/ *verb* [T] **opt to do sth** to choose or decide to do sth after thinking about it يختار؛ يقرِّر
PHRV opt for sb/sth to choose sb/sth after you have decided that you do not want the other possibilities يختار، يفضِّل
opt out (of sth) to choose not to take part in sth; to decide to stop being involved in sth: *Schools and hospitals can now opt out of local government control and manage their own finances.* ينسحب من

optical /ˈɒptɪkl/ *adj* connected with the sense of sight: *optical instruments* بَصَري

ˌ**optical ilˈlusion** *noun* [C] something that tricks the eye and makes you believe sth is there or is true when it is not خِداع البَصَر

optician /ɒpˈtɪʃn/ *noun* [C] a person who is qualified to test eyes, sell glasses, etc: *to go to the optician's* (= the shop) أخصائيّ بالنظّارات والأدوات البصرية

optimism /ˈɒptɪmɪzəm/ *noun* [U] the feeling that the future or sth in the future will be good or successful: *There is considerable optimism that the economy will improve.* ❶ The opposite is **pessimism**. تفاؤل
▸ **optimist** /-mɪst/ *noun* [C] a person who is always hopeful that things will be good or successful in the future ❶ The opposite is **pessimist**. المتفائل
optimistic /ˌɒptɪˈmɪstɪk/ *adj* hoping or believing that what happens in the future will be good or successful: *I've applied for the job but I'm not*

very optimistic about my chances of getting it. متفائل، تفاؤلي
ℹ The opposite is **pessimistic**.
optimistically /-kli/ *adv* بتفاؤل

option /ˈɒpʃn/ *noun* **1** [U, sing.] the freedom to choose; choice: *If you're late again, you will give us no option but to dismiss you.* حرية الاختيار، خيار

2 [C] a thing that you choose or can choose; choice: *She looked carefully at all the options before deciding on a career.* خيار؛ إمكانيّة

▸ **optional** /-ʃənl/ *adj* that you can choose or not choose: *an optional subject at school* ○ *an optional extra* (= sth that you can have as an extra thing but must pay for) ℹ The opposite is **compulsory**. اختياري

or /ɔː(r)/ *conj* **1** (used before another possibility or the last of a series of possibilities): *Would you like to sit here or next to the window?* ○ *Are you interested or not?* ○ *For the main course, you can have lamb, beef or fish.* ➲ Look at **either...or**. أو، أم

2 if not; otherwise: *Don't drive so fast or you'll have an accident!* ○ *She must have loved him or she wouldn't have married him.* ℹ **Or else** and **otherwise** can be used with this meaning. وإلاّ

3 (after a negative) and neither; and not: *She hasn't phoned or written to me for weeks.* ○ *I've never been to Italy or Spain.* ➲ Look at **neither... nor**. ولا

4 (used before a word or phrase that explains or comments on what has been said before): *20% of the population, or one in five* ○ *Oxford and Cambridge Universities, or 'Oxbridge' as they are sometimes known* أو، أي

IDM **or else** → ELSE

or so about: *I should think the repairs will cost you £100 or so.* أو نحوَ ذلك

or somebody/something/somewhere (*informal*) (used for showing that you are not sure, cannot remember or do not know which person, thing or place): *She's a computer programmer or something.* ○ *The film was set in Sweden or somewhere.* أو نحوَ ذلك، أو ما يشبه ذلك

> Another phrase that shows that you are not sure is **...or other**: *He muttered something or other about having no time and disappeared.*

oral /ˈɔːrəl/ *adj* **1** spoken, not written: *an oral test* شفهي، شفوي

2 concerning or using the mouth: *oral hygiene* فَمي

▸ **oral** *noun* [C] a spoken examination: *I've got my German oral next week.* امتحان شفهي

orally *adv* **1** using speech, not writing: *Orally her English is good.* من ناحية الكلام والنطق

2 through the mouth and swallowed عن طريق الفمّ

orange /ˈɒrɪndʒ; *US* ˈɔːr-/ *noun* **1** [C] a round fruit with a thick skin, that is divided into sections (segments) inside, and is a colour between red and yellow: *orange juice* برتقالة

2 [U] the colour of this fruit, between red and yellow اللّون البرتقالي

3 [U] a drink made from oranges or with the taste of oranges; a glass of this drink: *freshly squeezed orange* عصير البرتقال

▸ **orange** *adj* having the colour orange: *orange paint* برتقاليّ

ˌorange ˈsquash *noun* [C,U] (*Brit*) a drink made by adding water to an orange-flavoured liquid شراب مُنكّه بالبرتقال

orator /ˈɒrətə(r); *US* ɔːr-/ *noun* [C] (*formal*) a person who is good at making public speeches خطيب مجيد

orbit /ˈɔːbɪt/ *noun* [C,U] the path taken by sth (a planet, a moon, a spacecraft, etc.) going round sth else in space: *to put a satellite into orbit* مدار

▸ **orbit** *verb* [I,T] to move round sth (the moon, the sun, a planet etc.) in orbit يدور (في مداره)؛ يدور حول (الأرض)

orchard /ˈɔːtʃəd/ *noun* [C] a piece of land in which fruit trees are grown: *a cherry orchard* بستان

orchestra /ˈɔːkɪstrə/ *noun* [C] a large group of musicians who play different musical instruments together: *a symphony orchestra* ℹ An orchestra usually plays classical music. Pop music, jazz, etc. are played by a **group** or **band**. أوركسترا، فرقة موسيقيّة

▸ **orchestral** /ɔːˈkestrəl/ *adj* played by or written for an orchestra (موسيقى) تعزفها أوركسترا؛ (لحن) مؤلّف لأوركسترا

orchid /ˈɔːkɪd/ *noun* [C] a plant that has flowers of unusual shapes and bright colours نبات السَّحلب أو الأوركيد

ordeal /ɔːˈdiːl; ˈɔːdiːl/ *noun* [C] a very unpleasant experience: *The woman who was attacked last night is in hospital recovering from her ordeal.* عذاب، محنة، معاناة شديدة

order[1] /ˈɔːdə(r)/ *noun* **1** [C,U] the way in which people or things are arranged in relation to each other: *a list of names in alphabetical order* ○ *a list of dates in chronological order* ترتيب

2 [U] an organized state, when everything is in its right place: *I really must put my notes in order, because I can never find what I'm looking for.* ترتيب، تنظيم

3 [U] the situation in which laws, rules, authority, etc. are obeyed: *Following last week's riots, order has now been restored.* ➲ Look at **disorder**. نظام

4 [C] an instruction or demand that sb must do sth, given by sb who has power over that person: *In the army, you have to obey orders at all times.* أمر

5 [C] a request asking for sth to be made, supplied or delivered: *The company has just received a major export order.* طلب تجاريّ

6 [C] a request for food, drink, etc. in a hotel, restaurant, etc: *Can I take your order now, sir?* طلب

IDM **in order to do sth** with the purpose or intention of doing sth; so that sth can be done: *In order to obtain a passport, you need a birth* *certificate and two photographs.* ○ *We left early in order to avoid the traffic.* كي، حتى

in/into reverse order → REVERSE[1]

in working order (used about machines, etc.) working properly, not broken: *It's an old fridge but it's in perfect working order.* شغّال، في حالة جيّدة

law and order → LAW

out of order 1 (used about a machine, etc.) not working properly or not working at all معطّل، غير شغّال

2 (*informal*) (used about a person's behaviour) unacceptable, because it is rude, etc: *That comment was completely out of order!* منافٍ للذوق، غير لبق، مسيء

order² /ˈɔːdə(r)/ *verb* **1** [T] **order sb (to do sth)** to tell sb to do sth in a strong way which does not permit him/her to refuse, and without saying 'please': *The police ordered the demonstrators to stop.* يأمر

2 [T] to ask for sth to be made, supplied or delivered: *The shop didn't have the book I wanted so I ordered it.* ○ *We've ordered some new chairs for the living room.* يوصي على: يطلب (سلعة)

3 [I,T] to ask for food, drink, etc. in a restaurant, hotel, etc: *Are you ready to order yet, madam?* يطلب (في مطعم مثلاً)

PHRV order sb about/around to keep telling sb what to do and how to do it: *Stop ordering me about! You're not my father.* يتأمّر على، يُعطيه أمراً بعد آخر

ˈ**order form** *noun* [C] a form that is filled in by sb ordering goods استمارة الطَّلب

orderly¹ /ˈɔːdəli/ *adj* **1** well arranged; well organized; tidy: *an orderly office* ○ *an orderly life* منظّم، مرتّب

2 well behaved; peaceful: *The teacher told the pupils to form an orderly queue.* نظاميّ، حَسَن السلوك

orderly² /ˈɔːdəli/ *noun* [C] (*pl.* **orderlies**) a hospital assistant who has not had special training تابع أو عامل في مستشفى

ordinal /ˈɔːdɪnl; *US* -dənl/ (*also* ˌ**ordinal ˈnumber**) *noun* [C] a number that shows the order or position in a series: *'First', 'second', and 'third' are ordinals.* عدد ترتيبي

ordinary /ˈɔːdnri; *US* ˈɔːrdənerɪ/ *adj* normal; not special or unusual or different from others: *It's interesting to see how ordinary people live in other countries.* ○ *They live in an ordinary sort of house.* ℹ The opposite is **extraordinary**. عاديّ

IDM out of the ordinary unusual; different from normal غير عاديّ، غير مألوف؛ فذّ، نادر المثال

▸ **ordinarily** /ˈɔːdnrəli; *US* ˌɔːrdnˈerəlɪ/ *adv* usually; generally: *Ordinarily, I don't work as late as this.* عادةً؛ بشكل عام

ore /ɔː(r)/ *noun* [C,U] rock or earth from which metal can be obtained معدن خام، فِلِزّ

organ¹ /ˈɔːgən/ *noun* [C] a part of the body that has a particular function: *vital organs* (= those such as the heart which help to keep you alive) ○ *sexual organs* عضو

organ² /ˈɔːgən/ *noun* [C] a large musical instrument of the piano family, with pipes through which air is forced. Organs are often found in churches: *a church organ* ○ *organ music* ℹ Note that you play **the** organ: *When did you learn to play the organ?* أرغن

▸ **organist** *noun* [C] a person who plays the organ عازف الأرغن

organic /ɔːˈgænɪk/ *adj* **1** produced by or existing in living things: *You need to add a lot of organic matter to the soil.* ℹ The opposite is **inorganic**. عضويّ

2 (used about food or agricultural methods) produced by or using natural materials, not chemicals: *organic vegetables* ○ *organic farming* (زراعة) عضويّة (أي لا تستعمل المواد الكيماويّة)

organism /ˈɔːgənɪzəm/ *noun* [C] an animal or plant, especially one that is so small that you can only see it with a special instrument (microscope) كائن عضوي

organization (*also* **organisation**) /ˌɔːgənaɪˈzeɪʃn; *US* -nəˈz-/ *noun* **1** [C] an organized group of people who do sth together: *She works for a voluntary organization helping homeless people.* منظّمة

2 [U] the activity of organizing or arranging: *An enormous amount of organization went into the festival.* تنظيم، ترتيب

3 [U] the way in which sth is organized: *The students all complained about the poor organization of their course.* ترتيب المواد في برنامج معيّن

▸ **organizational** (*also* **organisational**) /-ʃənl/ *adj*: *The job requires a high level of organizational ability.* تنظيمي

organize (*also* **organise**) /ˈɔːgənaɪz/ *verb* **1** [T] to plan or arrange an event, an activity, etc: *The school organizes trips to various places of interest.* ينظّم

2 [I,T] to put things into order; to arrange into a system or logical order: *Can you decide what needs doing? I'm hopeless at organizing.* يرتّب؛ ينظّم، ينسّق

▸ **organized** (*also* **organised**) *adj* **1** planned or arranged: *My department is badly organized.* ○ *organized crime* منظّم

2 having a good system; working well: *I wish I was as organized as you are!* منظّم: حَسَن التنسيق

organizer (*also* **organiser**) *noun* [C]: *The organizers of the concert said that it had been a great success.* منظّم

orient¹ /ˈɔːriənt/ *noun* [sing.] **the Orient** (*formal*) the countries of the East or the Far East (China, Japan, etc.) الشّرق، المشرِق

orient² /ˈɔːriənt/ *verb* [T] (*Brit also* **orientate**) **orient yourself** to find out where you are; to become familiar with a place: *When I came out of the station I couldn't orient myself at first.* يحدّد مكان وجوده؛ يتعوّد على المكان

oriental /ˌɔːriˈentl/ *adj* (*old-fashioned*) coming from or belonging to the East or Far East: *oriental languages* ℹ Be careful. When it refers to a person, this word is offensive. It is better to say 'Asian'. شرقي

orientate /ˈɔːriənteɪt/ *verb* [T] = ORIENT[2]

orientated /ˈɔːriənteɪtɪd/ (*also* **oriented** /ˈɔːriəntɪd/) *adj* aimed or directed at a particular type of person or thing: *Our products are male-orientated.* ○ *She's very career-orientated.* موجّه إلى؛ مهتمّ بِ

orienteering /ˌɔːriənˈtɪərɪŋ/ *noun* [U] a sport in which you find your way across country on foot, using a map and compass رياضة استكشاف الطريق سيراً على الأقدام وباستخدام خارطة وبوصلة

🔑 **origin** /ˈɒrɪdʒɪn/ *noun* [C,U] **1** the time when or place where sth first comes into existence; the reason why sth starts: *Could you explain to me the origins of this tradition?* ○ *Many English words are of Latin origin.* أصل؛ مصدر

2 the family, race, class, etc. that a person comes from: *people of African origin* ○ *working-class origins* أصل

🔑 **original** /əˈrɪdʒənl/ *adj* **1** first; earliest (before changes or developments): *The original meaning of this word is different from the meaning it has nowadays.* أصليّ

2 new and interesting; different from others of its type: *There are no original ideas in his work.* جديد، مستحدَث، مبتكَر

3 made or created first, before copies: *'Is that the original painting?' 'No, it's a copy.'* (الصورة) الأصل، أصليّ

▸ **original** *noun* [C] **the original** the first one made or created; not a copy: *Could you make a photocopy and give the original back to me?* الأصل، النموذج الأصليّ

originality /əˌrɪdʒəˈnæləti/ *noun* [U] the quality of being new and interesting أصالة، جدّة، طرافة

originally /-nəli/ *adv* **1** in the beginning; in the first form (before changes or developments): *I'm from London originally, but I left there when I was very young.* أصلاً: في الأصل، في البداية

2 in a way or style that is unlike others: *She has a talent for expressing simple ideas originally.* بأسلوب جديد، بطريقة مبتكَرة

originate /əˈrɪdʒɪneɪt/ *verb* (*formal*) **1** [I] to start or be caused to start: *This game originated in the nineteenth century.* نشأ، بدأ

2 [T] to start or create first: *I wonder who originated the custom of sending birthday cards.* بدأ، ابتدع؛ أوجد

ornament /ˈɔːnəmənt/ *noun* [C] an object that you have because it is attractive, not because it is useful. Ornaments are used to decorate rooms, etc. شيء تزيينيّ، زينة

▸ **ornamental** /ˌɔːnəˈmentl/ *adj* made or put somewhere in order to look attractive, not for any practical use تزيينيّ، زخرفيّ

ornate /ɔːˈneɪt/ *adj* having a lot of decoration: *an ornate building* مزخرف، مبهرَج

ornithology /ˌɔːnɪˈθɒlədʒi/ *noun* [U] the study of birds علم الطّيور

▸ **ornithologist** /ˌɔːnɪˈθɒlədʒɪst/ *noun* [C] a person who studies birds مختصّ بدراسة الطّيور

orphan /ˈɔːfn/ *noun* [C] a child whose parents are dead يتيم

▸ **orphan** *verb* [T] (usually passive) to cause a child to become an orphan: *She was orphaned when she was three and went to live with her grandparents.* ييتّم

orphanage /ˈɔːfənɪdʒ/ *noun* [C] an institution where orphans live and are looked after ميْتَم، دار الأيتام

orthodox /ˈɔːθədɒks/ *adj* **1** generally believed, done or accepted: *orthodox opinions* ○ *orthodox methods* ❶ The opposite is **unorthodox**. تقليديّ، مُتّبع، مجمَع عليه

2 practising the old, traditional beliefs, ceremonies, etc. of certain religions: *an orthodox Jew* ○ *the Greek Orthodox Church* متمسّك بالتقاليد الدينيّة القديمة؛ قويم

ostentatious /ˌɒstenˈteɪʃəs/ *adj* showing wealth, importance, etc. very openly in order to attract attention and impress other people متباهٍ بالثراء والعظَمة، (بيت) مفرط في محاولته لفت الأنظار

▸ **ostentatiously** *adv* بشكلٍ ملفت للأنظار، بإفراط

ostracize (*also* **ostracise**) /ˈɒstrəsaɪz/ *verb* [T] (*formal*) (used about a group of people) to refuse to talk to or be with sb because he/she has done sth that you do not like: *When she left her husband, his family ostracized her.* يقاطِع، ينبذ

ostrich /ˈɒstrɪtʃ/ *noun* [C] a very large African bird with a long neck and long legs, which can run very fast but which cannot fly نَعامة

🔑 **other** /ˈʌðə(r)/ *det, pron* **1** in addition to or different from the one or ones that have already been mentioned or understood: *I hadn't got any other plans that evening so I accepted their invitation.* ○ *How many other students are there in your class?* ○ *If you're busy now, I'll come back some other time.* ○ *I like this jumper but I'm not keen on the colour. Have you got any others?* ○ *Some of my friends went to university, others didn't.* ○ *She doesn't care what other people think.* ❶ **Other** cannot be used after 'an'. Look at **another**. ➲ Look also at **every**. آخر/أخرى

2 (after *the* or a possessive with a singular noun) second of two: *I can only find one sock. Have you seen the other one?* ○ *My glasses broke, but fortunately I had my other pair with me.* الآخر/الأخرى، الثاني/الثانية

3 (after *the* or a possessive with a plural noun) the rest of a group or number of people or things: *Their youngest son still lives with them but their other children have left home.* ○ *I'll have to wear this shirt because all my others are dirty.* الآخر/الأُخرى، الآخرون/الأُخريات

IDM **in other words** saying sth in a different way و بتعبير آخر...

one after another/the other → ONE[1]

the other day, morning, week, etc. recently, not long ago: *An old friend rang me the other day.* مؤخّراً، من مدّة قريبة

other than 1 (usually after a negative) apart from; except (for): *The plane was a bit late but* *other than that the journey was fine.* فيما عدا، باستثناء

2 different(ly) from; not: *I've never seen her other than very smartly dressed.* إلاّ

sb/sth/somewhere or other → OR

otherwise /ˈʌðəwaɪz/ *adv* **1** in all other ways; apart from that: *I'm a bit tired but otherwise I feel fine.* فيما عدا ذلك، من نواحٍ أخرى

2 in a different or another way: *I'm afraid I can't see you next weekend, I'm otherwise engaged* (= I will be busy doing sth else). (مشغول) بشيء آخر، (مرتبط) بموعد آخر

3 of a different type: *I have no opinion, good or otherwise, on this subject.* العكس؛ من أيّ نوع آخر

▸ **otherwise** *conj* (used for stating what would happen if you do not do sth or if sth does not happen) if not: *You have to press the red button, otherwise it won't work.* وإلاّ

otter /ˈɒtə(r)/ *noun* [C] a river animal with brown fur that eats fish قضاعة، كلب أو ثعلب الماء

ouch /aʊtʃ/ *interj* (used when reacting to a sudden feeling of pain): *Ouch! You're hurting me.* آخ! (صرخة ألم)

ought to /ˈɔːt tə; *before vowels and in final position* ˈɔːt tu/ *modal verb* (*negative* **ought not to**; *short form* **oughtn't to** /ˈɔːtnt tə/ before vowels and in final position /ˈɔːtnt tu/) **1** (used for asking for and giving advice about what to do): *What ought I to say to him?* ○ *You ought to read this book. It's really interesting.* ○ *You ought to have come to the meeting. It was very useful.* ينبغي أن، يَحسُن أن

2 (used for telling sb what his/her duty is): *You ought to visit your parents more often.* ○ *She oughtn't to make private phone calls in work time.* ○ *I ought to have helped. I'm sorry.* ○ *He oughtn't to have been driving so fast.* يجب أن، عليك أن

3 (used for saying that you expect sth is true, or that you expect sth to happen/to have happened): *She ought to pass her test.* ○ *They ought to be here by now. They left at six.* ○ *I bought six loaves of bread. That ought to have been enough.* يتوقع؛ كان من المتوقع، كان من اللازم

ounce /aʊns/ *noun* **1** [C] (*abbr* **oz**) a measure of weight; 28.35 grams. There are 16 ounces in a pound: *For this recipe you need four ounces of flour, six ounces of butter...* "أونصة": وحدة وزن إنكليزية

2 [sing.] **an ounce of sth** a very small amount of sth: *He hasn't got an ounce of imagination.* ذرّة، مقدار ضئيل جداً

our /ɑː(r); ˈaʊə(r)/ *det* belonging to or connected with us: *Our house is at the bottom of the road.* ○ *Our teacher is excellent.* ○ *This is our first visit to Britain.* ضمير ملكيّة بمعنى "لنا"

▸ **ours** /ɑːz; ˈaʊəz/ *pron* the one or ones belonging to, connected with or done by us: *Your hi-fi system is exactly the same as ours.* خاصّتنا: "حديقتنا"

ourselves /ɑːˈselvz; aʊəˈselvz/ *pron* **1** (used as the object of a verb or preposition when 'we' do an action and are also affected by it): *We should be angry with ourselves for making such a stupid mistake.* ○ *They asked us to wait so we sat down and made ourselves comfortable.* أنفسنا

2 (used for emphasis): *We haven't got children ourselves, but many of our friends have.* ○ *Do you think we should paint the flat ourselves?* (= or should we ask sb else to do it for us?) أنفسنا، بأنفسنا

IDM **(all) by ourselves 1** without help from anyone else: *We managed to move all our furniture into the new flat by ourselves.* بأنفسنا، دونَ مساعدة

2 not with anyone else; alone: *Now that we're by ourselves, could I ask you a personal question?* لوحدنا
➲ Look at the note at **alone**.

out /aʊt/ *adj, adv* ℹ For special uses with many verbs, e.g. **try sb/sth out**, look at the verb entries.

1 (used for showing movement away from a place): *He opened the box and took a gun out.* ○ *I threw out that old shirt of yours.* ○ *Her ears stick out.* ○ *He opened the window and put his head out.* إلى أو نحو الخارج

2 not at home or in your place of work: *I was out when she called.* ○ *They took me out for a meal when I was in Bristol.* في الخارج، خارجَ البيت أو المكتب؛ إلى (مطعم أو مسرح أو غير ذلك)

3 outside a house, building, etc: *You should be out in the fresh air.* في الهواء الطّلق

4 (used for showing that sth is no longer hidden): *Oh look! The sun's out.* يظهر، يبرز، ينكشف

5 not in fashion: *Short skirts are completely out this season.* بطلت موضته، أصبح طِرازاً قديماً

6 (used about a light or a fire) not on; not burning: *The lights are out. They must be in bed.* (النّور) مطفأ

7 (used when you are calculating sth) making or containing a mistake: *This bill's out by five pounds.* فيه غلَط أو خطأ

8 not possible or acceptable: *I'm afraid Friday is out. I've got a meeting that day.* غير ممكن

9 in a loud voice; clearly: *She cried out in pain.* بصوتٍ عالٍ؛ بوضوح

10 (used about the tide) away from the shore: *Don't swim when the tide is going out.* (البحر) في حالة جَزْر أو انحسار

IDM **be out for sth; be out to do sth** to try hard to get or do sth يعمل جاهداً لـ، يبذل مجهوداً

out-and-out complete: *It was out-and-out war between us.* تامّ، كامل، مطلَق

▸ **out** *verb* [T] to say publicly that sb is homosexual especially when he/she would rather keep it a secret يفضح، يكشف للعيان

outback /ˈaʊtbæk/ *noun* [sing.] the part of a country (especially Australia) which is a long way from where most people live المناطق النائية عن العمران وخاصة في أستراليا

outboard motor /ˌaʊtbɔːd ˈməʊtə(r)/ *noun* [C] an engine that can be attached to a boat محرك يُثبّت في مؤخّرة القارب

ˈout box *noun* [C] the place on a computer where new email messages that you write are stored before you send them البريد الخارج

outbreak /'aʊtbreɪk/ *noun* [C] the sudden beginning or appearance of sth unpleasant (especially disease or violence): *an outbreak of cholera* ○ *outbreaks of fighting* ظهور مفاجئ (لمرض): تفشٍّ، نشوب

outburst /'aʊtbɜːst/ *noun* [C] a sudden expression of a strong feeling, especially anger: *an angry outburst* ثورة (غضب): تفجر، فورة

outcast /'aʊtkɑːst; *US* -kæst/ *noun* [C] a person who is no longer accepted by society or by a group of people: *a social outcast* المنبوذ

outclass /ˌaʊt'klɑːs; *US* -'klæs/ *verb* [T] to be much better than sb/sth, especially in a game or competition يفوق، يمتاز على

outcome /'aʊtkʌm/ *noun* [C, usually sing.] how an event, action or situation ends; the result of sth: *We shall inform you of the outcome of the interview within a week.* نتيجة، حصيلة

outcry /'aʊtkraɪ/ *noun* [C, usually sing.] (*pl.* **outcries**) a strong protest by a large number of people because they disagree with sth: *The public outcry forced the government to change its mind.* احتجاج عنيف

outdated /ˌaʊt'deɪtɪd/ *adj* not useful or common any more; old-fashioned: *A lot of the computer equipment is getting outdated.*
قديم العهد، بَطُل استعماله

outdo /ˌaʊt'duː/ *verb* [T] (*pres part* **outdoing**; *3rd pers sing pres* **outdoes** /-'dʌz/; *pt* **outdid** /-'dɪd/; *pp* **outdone** /-'dʌn/) to do sth better than another person; to be more successful than sb else: *He doesn't want to be outdone by his brother.*
يتفوّق، يمتاز على؛ يفوز على

outdoor /'aʊtdɔː(r)/ *adj* happening, done, or used in the open air (not in a building): *an outdoor job* ○ *outdoor furniture* ❶ The opposite is **indoor**. في الهواء الطلق؛ (مفروشات) للخارج أي للحديقة مثلاً

outdoors /ˌaʊt'dɔːz/ *adv* in the open air; outside a building: *It's a very warm evening so why don't we sit outdoors?* ❶ The opposite is **indoors**.
في الخارج، في الهواء الطلق

outer /'aʊtə(r)/ *adj* **1** on the outside: *the outer layer of skin* خارجيّ

2 far from the inside or the centre: *the outer suburbs of a city* بعيد عن مركز المدينة، خارجيّ

❶ The opposite is **inner**.

outermost /'aʊtəməʊst/ *adj* furthest from the inside or centre; most distant: *the outermost planet in the solar system* ❶ The opposite is **innermost**. أبعد نقطة عن المركز، أبعد

ˌ**outer 'space** *noun* [U] = SPACE (2)

outfit /'aʊtfɪt/ *noun* [C] **1** a set of clothes that are worn together طقم ملابس

2 (*informal*) an organization, a company, etc: *He works for a computer outfit I've never heard of.*
شركة، مؤسّسة

outgoing /'aʊtgəʊɪŋ/ *adj* **1** friendly and interested in other people and new experiences
اجتماعيّ، منطلِق، منفتح

2 leaving a job or a place: *The outgoing headmaster made a short speech.* ○ *Put all the outgoing mail in a pile on that table.* ❶ The opposite is **incoming**.
(الرئيس) المستقيل، (المدير) المغادر؛ (البريد) الصادر

outgoings /'aʊtgəʊɪŋz/ *noun* [plural] the amounts of money that you spend: *Last month my outgoings were greater than my income.*
مصروفات، نفقات

outgrow /ˌaʊt'grəʊ/ *verb* [T] (*pt* **outgrew** /-'gruː/; *pp* **outgrown** /-'grəʊn/) to become too old or too big for sth (especially clothes): *Children outgrow their shoes so quickly.*
يفوق في النموّ: ينمو الطّفل فتصغر ملابسه القديمة؛ يقلع عند كبره عن بعض عادات الصغر

outing /'aʊtɪŋ/ *noun* [C] a short trip for pleasure: *to go on an outing to the zoo* نزهة

outlandish /aʊt'lændɪʃ/ *adj* very strange or unusual: *outlandish clothes* غريب، غير مألوف

outlast /ˌaʊt'lɑːst; *US* -'læst/ *verb* [T] to last or live longer than sb/sth
يصمد أكثر، يدوم أو يعيش أكثر من...

outlaw /'aʊtlɔː/ *noun* [C] (*old-fashioned*) a criminal who is living outside society and trying to avoid being captured: *The film is about a band of outlaws in the Wild West.*
خارج على القانون، طريد العدالة

▶ **outlaw** *verb* [T] to make sth illegal
يحرِّم، يمنع (بحكم القانون)

outlay /'aʊtleɪ/ *noun* [C, usually sing.] money that is spent, especially in order to start a business or a project نفقات البدء بمشروع تجاريّ

outlet /'aʊtlet/ *noun* [C] **1** a hole through which a gas or liquid can escape: (*figurative*) *Gary found an outlet for his energy in playing football.*
مَنْفَذ، مخرج؛ مُتنفَّس

2 a shop, business, etc. that sells goods made by a particular company or of a particular type: *a fast-food outlet* سوق لسلعة تنتجها شركة معيّنة

outline /'aʊtlaɪn/ *noun* [C] **1** a line that shows the shape or outside edge of sb/sth: *She could see the outline of a person through the mist.*
الخطّ الخارجيّ الذي يحدِّد معالم الشّيء

2 the most important facts or ideas about sth: *a brief outline of Indian history*
النقاط الرئيسيّة، مخطَّط، موجز

▶ **outline** *verb* [T] to give the most important facts or ideas about sth يوجِز، يلخِّص

outlive /ˌaʊt'lɪv/ *verb* [T] to live or exist longer than sb/sth: *He outlived his wife by nearly twenty years.* يعمِّر أكثر من، يعيش أو يدوم بعد فناء غيره

outlook /'aʊtlʊk/ *noun* [C] **1** your attitude to or feeling about life: *an optimistic outlook on life.*
نظرة (متفائلة)، موقف

2 outlook (for sth) what will probably happen: *The outlook for the economy is not good.*
المُرتقَب، ما يتوقّع في المستقبل

ˌ**out 'loud** *adv* = ALOUD

outlying /'aʊtlaɪɪŋ/ *adj* (only *before* a noun) far from the centre of a town or city: *The bus service* *to the outlying villages is very poor.* ناءٍ، بعيد عن مركز المدينة، في الضواحي

outmoded /ˌaʊtˈməʊdɪd/ *adj* (only *before* a noun) no longer common or fashionable بطُل استعماله، من طراز قديم

outnumber /ˌaʊtˈnʌmbə(r)/ *verb* [T] (often passive) to be greater in number than sb/sth: *The enemy troops outnumbered us by three to one.* ○ *We were completely outnumbered.* يفوقه عدداً

ˈout of *prep* **1** (used with verbs expressing movement away from the inside of sth): *She took her purse out of her bag.* ○ *to get out of bed* مِن

2 away from, or no longer in, a place or situation: *He's out of the country on business.* ○ *The doctors say she's out of danger.* خارج، زال عنه (الخطر)

3 at a distance from a place: *We live a long way out of London.* على مسافة (بعيدة) خارج

4 (used for saying what you use to make sth): *You could make a table out of this wood.* مِن

5 from among a number: *Nine out of ten people prefer this model.* من

6 (used for saying that you no longer have sth): *We're out of milk.* ○ *I'm out of breath.* ○ *out of work* لم يبقَ (عندنا حليب)؛ يستنفد، يصبح عاطلاً عن العمل

7 (used for saying which feeling causes you to do sth): *I only helped them out of pity.* بدافع

8 from: *I copied the recipe out of a book.* ○ *I prefer to drink tea out of a cup, not a mug.* من؛ بِ

9 (used for saying that sth is not as it should be): *The telephone's out of order.* معطّل

IDM **be/feel out of it** to be/feel lonely and unhappy because you are not included in sth: *I didn't speak the language and I felt rather out of it at the meeting.* يشعر بالعزلة والغربة عن الآخرين، يشعر بأنه دخيل (على الحفلة مثلاً)

out of bounds → BOUNDS

outpatient /ˈaʊtpeɪʃnt/ *noun* [C] a person who goes to see a doctor in hospital but who does not stay there overnight مريض خارجي

output /ˈaʊtpʊt/ *noun* [sing.] **1** the amount that a person or machine produces: *Output has increased in the past year.* نتاج، حصيلة، مردود

2 the information that is given by a computer ➲ Look at **input**. (في الكمبيوتر) مخرجات

outrage /ˈaʊtreɪdʒ/ *noun* **1** [C] something that is very bad or wrong and that causes you to feel great anger: *It's an outrage that such poverty should exist in the 21st century.* إهانة للإنسانيّة، إساءة بالغة

2 [U] great anger: *a feeling of outrage* غضب شديد

▶ **outrage** *verb* [T] (often passive) to make sb feel very angry or upset: *He was outraged at the way he had been treated.* يثور غضبه

outrageous /aʊtˈreɪdʒəs/ *adj* **1** making you very angry: *I refuse to pay such outrageous prices.* (سعر) فاحش، طلب مفرط؛ مثير للغضب

2 very strange or unusual; shocking (زيّ) غريب جداً؛ فاضح

▶ **outrageously** *adv* بصورة فاضحة

outright /ˈaʊtˈraɪt/ *adv* **1** without hiding anything; openly: *She told them outright what she thought about it.* بكل صراحة

2 immediately or completely: *to be killed outright* ○ *They were able to buy the house outright.* فوراً؛ كليّاً؛ (دفع) دفعةً واحدة رأساً

▶ **outright** *adj* (only *before* a noun) complete and clear, without any doubt: *Lester was the outright winner.* تامّ، باتّ، لا شكّ فيه

outset /ˈaʊtset/ *noun*

IDM **at/from the outset (of sth)** at/from the beginning (of sth): *There have been difficulties with this firm right from the outset.* بدء، بداية

outside¹ /ˌaʊtˈsaɪd/ *noun* **1** [C, usually sing.] the outer side or surface of sth: *There is a list of all the ingredients on the outside of the packet.* ○ *to paint the outside of a house* خارج، الجانب أو السطح الخارجيّ

2 [sing.] the area that is near or round a building, etc: *We've only seen the church from the outside.* الخارج، خارج المبنى

IDM **at the outside** at the most: *It will cost £200 at the outside.* على الأكثر، في أقصى حدّ

▶ **outside** /ˈaʊtsaɪd/ *adj* **1** of or on the outer side or surface of sth: *the outside walls of a building* خارجيّ

2 not part of the main building: *Many cottages still have outside toilets.* خارج المبنى، خارجي

3 not connected with or belonging to a particular group or organization: *We can't do all the work by ourselves. We'll need outside help.* (مساعدة) من الغير

4 (used about a chance, possibility, etc.) very small (احتمال) ضئيل

IDM **the outside world** → WORLD

outside² /ˌaʊtˈsaɪd/ (*US also* **outside of**) *prep* **1** in, at or to a place that is not in but close to a building, etc: *Leave your muddy boots outside the door.* خارج

2 not in: *You may do as you wish outside office hours.* ○ *a small village just outside Southampton* خارج (اوقات الدوام)

▶ **outside** *adv* **1** in or to a place that is not in a room: *Please wait outside for a few minutes.* خارج الغرفة

2 in or to a place that is not in a building: *Let's eat outside. The weather's lovely.* ○ *Go outside and see if it's raining.* ➲ Look at **outdoors** and **out of doors** (at the entry for **door**). في الخارج، في الهواء الطَلق؛ إلى الخارج

ˌoutside ˈbroadcast *noun* [C] a television or radio programme that was not made in a studio (برنامج) خارجيّ

ˌoutside ˈlane *noun* [C] the part of a wide road or motorway that is for the fastest cars أسرع قسم من أقسام الطريق السريع أو "الأوتوستراد"

outsider /ˌaʊtˈsaɪdə(r)/ *noun* [C] **1** a person who is not accepted as a member of a particular group دخيل، شخص غريب عن جماعة

2 a person or animal in a race or competition that is not expected to win متسابق لا يتوقّع فوزه

outsize /ˈaʊtsaɪz/ *adj* (often used about clothes) larger than usual (ملابس) أكبر من المقاس العادي

outskirts /ˈaʊtskɜːts/ *noun* [plural] **the outskirts** the parts of a town or city that are furthest from the centre ضواحي المدينة

outspoken /aʊtˈspəʊkən/ *adj* saying exactly what you think or feel: *Linda is very outspoken in her criticism.* صريح، جريء في كلامه
▸ **outspokenness** *noun* [U] صراحة

⚷ **outstanding** /aʊtˈstændɪŋ/ *adj* **1** very good indeed; excellent: *The results in the exams were quite outstanding.* ممتاز؛ رائع؛ بارز
2 not yet paid or done: *Some of the work is still outstanding.* معلّق، غير مبتوت فيه؛ (دَين) لم يسدَّد بعد
▸ **outstandingly** *adv* very well: *Huw played outstandingly.* بشكل رائع

outstretched /ˌaʊtˈstretʃt/ *adj* spread out as far as possible: *outstretched arms* ممدود

ˈ**out tray** (*US* ˈ**out box**) *noun* [C] (in an office) a container on your desk for letters or documents that are waiting to be sent out or passed to sb else البريد الصادر

outward /ˈaʊtwəd/ *adj* (only *before* a noun) **1** (used about a journey) going away from the place that you will return to later ℹ The opposite is **return**. (رحلة) الذهاب
2 of or on the outside: *Her outward good humour hid her inner sadness.* خارجي
▸ **outwardly** *adv* on the outside or surface: *He remained outwardly calm so as not to frighten the children.* ظاهريّاً؛ سطحيّاً
outwards /-wədz/ (*especially US* **outward**) *adv* towards the outside or away from the place where you are: *This door opens outwards.* نحو الخارج

outweigh /ˌaʊtˈweɪ/ *verb* [T] to be more important than sth: *The advantages outweigh the disadvantages.* يفوقه في الأهميّة

outwit /ˌaʊtˈwɪt/ *verb* [T] (outwitting; outwitted) to defeat or get an advantage over sb by being cleverer than him/her يفوقه في الذكاء والحيلة، يتغلّب على خصمه بحسن دهائه

oval /ˈəʊvl/ *adj, noun* [C] shaped like an egg; a shape like that of an egg: *an oval mirror* شكل بيضوي؛ بيضوي

ovary /ˈəʊvəri/ *noun* [C] (*pl.* **ovaries**) one of the two parts of the female body that produce eggs المَبيض (عند الأنثى)

ovation /əʊˈveɪʃn/ *noun* [C] a long period of clapping and applause: *The dancers were given a standing ovation* (= people stood up and clapped). تصفيق حادّ؛ هتاف

⚷ **oven** /ˈʌvn/ *noun* [C] the part of a cooker that has a door. You put things inside an oven to cook them: *Cook in a hot oven for 50 minutes.* ○ *a microwave oven* ℹ You **roast** or **bake** food in an oven. فرن

⚷ **over** /ˈəʊvə(r)/ *adv, prep* ℹ For special uses with many verbs, e.g. **get over sth**, look at the verb entries.
1 directly above sth, but not touching: *There's a painting over the bookcase.* ○ *We jumped when the plane flew over.* فوق؛ فوقَ (الرؤوس)
2 on, and partly or completely covering or touching: *There's a cover over the chair.* ○ *She hung her coat over the back of the chair.* على، فوق
3 down or sideways from an upright position: *He leaned over to speak to the woman next to him.* ○ *I fell over in the street this morning.* (يميل) إلى الجانب؛ (يقع) على الأرض
4 across to the other side of sth: *The dog is jumping over the fence.* ○ *a bridge over the river* من فوق؛ فوق
5 on or to the other side: *She lives over the road.* ○ *Turn the patient over.* في الجانب الآخر؛ إلى الجانب الآخر
6 (used for expressing distance): *He's over in America at the moment.* ○ *Sit down over there.* هناك
7 not used: *There are a lot of cakes left over from the party.* مُتَبَقٍّ
8 above or more than a number, price, etc: *She lived in Athens for over ten years.* ○ *suitable for children aged 10 and over* أكثر من؛ فما فوق
9 (used with *all*) in every part or place: *There was blood all over the place.* ○ *I can't find my glasses. I've looked all over for them.* في كل أنحاء المكان
10 (used for saying that sth is repeated): *You'll have to start all over again* (= from the beginning). ○ *She kept saying the same thing over and over again.* من البداية، من جديد؛ مراراً وتكراراً
11 about; on the subject of: *We quarrelled over money.* على؛ حولَ، فيما يتعلق بِ
12 during: *We met over the Christmas holiday.* خلال، أثناء
▸ **over** *adj* finished: *The exams are all over now.* منتهٍ
over- (used to form verbs, nouns, adjectives and adverbs) too; too much: *They're overexcited.* ○ *I'm overworked.* ○ *He overeats.* مفرط في، زائد عن اللزوم

⚷ **overall**[1] /ˌəʊvərˈɔːl/ *adj* (only *before* a noun) including everything: *The overall cost of the work will be about £200.* كُلي، إجماليّ
▸ **overall** *adv* **1** including everything: *What does the garden measure overall?* كلّياً، بشكل شامل
2 speaking generally about sth: *Overall, I can say that we are pleased with the year's work.* بشكل عامّ

overall[2] /ˈəʊvərɔːl/ *noun* **1** [C] a piece of clothing that is like a coat and that you wear over your clothes to keep them clean when you are working رداء يلبس فوق الملابس العادية لوقايتها من الوسخ
2 overalls (*US* **coveralls**) [plural] a piece of clothing that covers your legs and body (and sometimes your arms) and that you wear over your clothes to keep them clean when you are working رداء من قطعة واحدة يلبسه العمال لوقاية ملابسهم: "عفريتة"، "أوفرول"

overawe /ˌəʊvərˈɔː/ *verb* [T] (usually passive) to cause sb to admire sb/sth and feel a little afraid:

They were rather overawed by the atmosphere in the hall. يرهب

overbalance /ˌəʊvəˈbæləns/ *verb* [I] to fall over or nearly fall over because you cannot stand steadily يفقد توازنه

overboard /ˈəʊvəbɔːd/ *adv* over the side of a boat or ship into the water: *Man overboard!* ○ *She fell overboard and drowned.*
(يسقط) من جانب المركب الى البحر

IDM go overboard (about sb/sth) to be too excited about sb/sth يفرط في؛ يتحمّس حماساً شديداً

overcame *pt* of OVERCOME

overcast /ˌəʊvəˈkɑːst; *US* -ˈkæst/ *adj* (used about the sky) covered with cloud غائم

overcharge /ˌəʊvəˈtʃɑːdʒ/ *verb* [I,T] to ask sb to pay too much money: *The man in the post office overcharged me by 50p.* يتقاضى ثمناً أغلى ممّا ينبغي

overcoat /ˈəʊvəkəʊt/ *noun* [C] a long thick coat that you wear in cold weather معطف، "بالطو"

overcome /ˌəʊvəˈkʌm/ *verb* [T] (*pt* **overcame** /-ˈkeɪm/; *pp* **overcome**) **1** to control or succeed in defeating sb/sth: *She tried hard to overcome her fear of flying.* يتغلّب على، يقهر
2 (usually passive) to cause sb to become weak or ill or to lose control: *He was overcome with emotion and had to leave the room.* ○ *to be overcome by smoke* يغلب، يستولي على؛ يجهد، ينهك

overcrowded /ˌəʊvəˈkraʊdɪd/ *adj* (used about a place) with too many people: *The trains are overcrowded on Friday evenings.* مكتظ، مزدحم

overdo /ˌəʊvəˈduː/ *verb* [T] (*pt* **overdid** /-ˈdɪd/; *pp* **overdone** /-ˈdʌn/) **1** to use or show too much of sth: *He overdid the pepper in the stew.* ○ *You look nice but you overdid the make-up a bit.*
يفرط أو يسرف في
2 to cook sth too long: *The meat was overdone.*
يطبخ الطعام مدةً أطول ممّا ينبغي

IDM overdo it/things to work, etc. too hard; *Exercise is fine but don't overdo it.* يفرط، "يزيدها"!

overdose /ˈəʊvədəʊs/ *noun* [C] an amount of a drug or medicine that is too large and so is not safe: *Hugh killed himself by taking an overdose.*
جرعة دواء أكبر ممّا ينبغي؛ جرعة قاتلة

overdraft /ˈəʊvədrɑːft; *US* -dræft/ *noun* [C] an amount of money that you have spent or want to spend that is greater than the amount you have in your bank account: *We took out an overdraft to pay for the holiday.* ○ *to pay off an overdraft*
مبلغ مسحوب من البنك دون رصيد يغطيه

overdrawn /ˌəʊvəˈdrɔːn/ *adj* having spent more money than you have in your bank account: *Darren is £500 overdrawn.* مَدين للبنك بـ...

overdue /ˌəʊvəˈdjuː; *US* -ˈduː/ *adj* late in arriving, happening, being paid, returned, etc: *Their train is ten minutes overdue.* ○ *Change is long overdue* (= it should have happened before now). متأخّر

overestimate /ˌəʊvərˈestɪmeɪt/ *verb* [T] to think that sb/sth is bigger, better, more expensive, etc. than he/she/it really is: *I overestimated how much we could paint in a day.* ⓘ The opposite is **underestimate**.
يبالغ في تقدير القيمة أو الكمّية أو غير ذلك

overflow /ˌəʊvəˈfləʊ/ *verb* [I,T] to have liquid pouring over the edge; to pour over the edge of sth: *The tap was left on and the bath overflowed.* ○ *After the heavy rains the river overflowed its banks.* يفيض، يطفح

overgrown /ˌəʊvəˈɡrəʊn/ *adj* covered with plants that have not been looked after and that have grown too big: *The garden is neglected and overgrown.* مغطى بالأعشاب والنباتات المهمَلة

overhang /ˌəʊvəˈhæŋ/ *verb* [I,T] (*pt, pp* **overhung**) to stick out from or hang over sth: *I hit my head on an overhanging branch and fell off my bike.* ينتأ، يبرز؛ يتدلّى

overhaul /ˌəʊvəˈhɔːl/ *verb* [T] to look at sth carefully and change or repair it if necessary: *to overhaul an engine*
يفحص (محركاً مثلاً) فحصاً دقيقاً ويصلح ما يلزم
▶ **overhaul** /ˈəʊvəhɔːl/ *noun* [C]: *a complete overhaul of the social security system*
فحص أو دراسة دقيقة شاملة مع إجراء التغييرات اللازمة

overhead /ˈəʊvəhed/ *adj* above your head: *overhead electricity cables* في العالي، فوق الرؤوس
▶ **overhead** /ˌəʊvəˈhed/ *adv*: *A helicopter flew overhead.* في السماء، فوق الرؤوس
overhead /ˈəʊvəhed/ *noun* [U] (*US*) = OVERHEADS

overheads /ˈəʊvəhedz/ *noun* [plural] (*US* **overhead** [U]) money that a company must spend on things like salaries, heat, light, rent, etc.
نفقات عامّة (في شركة)

overhear /ˌəʊvəˈhɪə(r)/ *verb* [T] (*pt, pp* **overheard** /-ˈhɜːd/) to hear what sb is saying when he/she is speaking to sb else and not to you
يسمع (محادثةً) صدفةً

overjoyed /ˌəʊvəˈdʒɔɪd/ *adj* (not before a noun) **overjoyed (at sth/to do sth)** very happy: *We were overjoyed at the news.* مبتهج، يكاد يطير فرحاً

overland /ˈəʊvəlænd/ *adj* not by sea or by air: *an overland journey* بري
▶ **overland** *adv*: *We travelled overland from Paris to China.* برّاً

overlap /ˌəʊvəˈlæp/ *verb* [I,T] (overla**pp**ing; overla**pp**ed) **1** when two things overlap, part of one covers part of the other: *Make sure that the two pieces of material overlap.*
يتراكب، (جزء) يركب على الآخر
2 to be partly the same as sth: *Our jobs overlap to some extent.*
يشتركان في نواحٍ معيّنة؛ متماثل جزئياً مع شيء آخر
▶ **overlap** /ˈəʊvəlæp/ *noun* [C]: *There will be a period of overlap between the new teacher arriving and the old one going.* تراكُب؛ تطابُق؛ تزامُن حدثَيْن

overleaf /ˌəʊvəˈliːf/ *adv* on the other side of the page: *Full details are given overleaf.*
خلفَ هذه الصفحة

overload /ˌəʊvəˈləʊd/ *verb* [T] **1** (often passive) to put too many people or things into or onto sth:

an overloaded vehicle ○ (*figurative*) *to be overloaded with work* يحمّله اكثر من طاقته

2 to put too much electricity through sth: *If you use too many electrical appliances at one time you may overload the system.*
يحمّل الأسلاك الكهربائية اكثر من طاقتها

overlook /ˌəʊvəˈlʊk/ *verb* [T] **1** to have a view over sth: *The sitting room overlooks the river.*
يُشرف أو يطلّ على

2 to fail to see, take notice of or remember sth: *to overlook a spelling mistake* ○ *The local people felt that their opinions had been completely overlooked.* يسهو أو يغفل عن

3 to take no action about sth that sb has done wrong: *I will overlook your behaviour this time but don't let it happen again.*
يتغاضى عن، يغضّ النظر عن

overnight /ˌəʊvəˈnaɪt/ *adj, adv* **1** for or during the night: *an overnight bag* ○ *Why don't you stay overnight?* (حقيبة) تحوي الأشياء الأساسيّة لسفرة قصيرة؛ الليلة

2 (happening) very suddenly: *an overnight success* ○ *She became a star overnight.*
بين ليلةٍ وضحاها، في غمضة عين

overpass /ˈəʊvəpɑːs; *US* -pæs/ *noun* [C] (*US*) = FLYOVER

overpower /ˌəʊvəˈpaʊə(r)/ *verb* [T] to be too strong for sb; to defeat sb because you are stronger than him/her: *The police overpowered the burglars.* ○ *The fireman was overpowered by the heat and smoke.* يتغلّب على، يخضع؛ يسبّب له الإغماء

▸ **overpowering** /ˌəʊvəˈpaʊərɪŋ/ *adj* very strong: *an overpowering smell*
(رائحة) نفّاذة؛ شديد جداً، خانق

overrate /ˌəʊvəˈreɪt/ *verb* [T] (often passive) to have too high an opinion of sb/sth: *I think that the play is greatly overrated.* ❶ The opposite is **underrate**. يبالغ في الإطراء، يبالغ في تقدير قيمة الشيء

override /ˌəʊvəˈraɪd/ *verb* [T] (*pt* **overrode** /-ˈrəʊd/; *pp* **overridden** /-ˈrɪdn/) **1** (used about sb/sth with authority) to pay no attention to a person's decisions or actions: *They overrode my protest and continued with the meeting.*
يتجاهل، لا يحفل بِ؛ يلغي

2 to be more important than sth
يفوق في الأهميّة؛ يطغى على

▸ **overriding** /ˌəʊvəˈraɪdɪŋ/ *adj* (only *before* a noun) more important than anything else
أهمّ من أيّ شيء آخر؛ (طموح) مهيمن أو مسيطر على كلّ الاعتبارات الأخرى

overrule /ˌəʊvəˈruːl/ *verb* [T] (used about sb/sth with authority) to decide that another person's decisions or actions are not valid: *The Home Secretary has the power to overrule the council's decision.* يلغي، يبطل؛ ينقض

overrun /ˌəʊvəˈrʌn/ *verb* (*pt* **overran** /-ˈræn/; *pp* **overrun** /-ˈrʌn/) **1** [T] (often passive) to spread all over an area in great numbers: *The city was overrun by rats.* يجتاح، يكتسح

2 [I,T] to continue later than the expected time: *The meeting overran by 30 minutes.*
يتجاوز الوقت المحدّد، يطول

overseas /ˌəʊvəˈsiːz/ *adj* (only *before* a noun) in, to or from another country (that you have to cross the sea to get to): *There are many overseas students studying in Britain.* أجنبي، من الخارج

▸ **overseas** *adv* in or to another country: *Frank has gone to live overseas.* ○ *People overseas will be able to vote in the election.*
في الخارج، في البلاد الأجنبية؛ ما وراء البحار

oversee /ˌəʊvəˈsiː/ *verb* [T] (*pt* **oversaw** /-ˈsɔː/; *pp* **overseen** /-ˈsiːn/) to watch sth to make sure that it is done properly يراقب، يشرف على

overshadow /ˌəʊvəˈʃædəʊ/ *verb* [T] **1** to cause sth to be less happy: *The celebrations were overshadowed by her illness.* يعكّر، يلقي ظلاً داكناً على

2 to cause sb/sth to seem less important or successful: *Colin always seemed to be overshadowed by his sister.*
(نجاحه) يُقلّل من تفوق (زميله)، يغطّي على، يضعه في المرتبة الثانية

oversight /ˈəʊvəsaɪt/ *noun* [C,U] something that you do not notice or do (that you should have noticed or done): *Through an oversight Len's name did not appear on the list.* سَهْو، خطأ غير مقصود

oversimplify /ˌəʊvəˈsɪmplɪfaɪ/ *verb* [I,T] (*pres part* **oversimplifying**; *3rd pers sing pres* **oversimplifies**; *pt, pp* **oversimplified**) to explain sth in such a simple way that its real meaning is lost يفرط في تبسيط الشّرح حتى أنه يشوّه المعنى

oversleep /ˌəʊvəˈsliːp/ *verb* [I] (*pt, pp* **overslept** /-ˈslept/) to sleep longer than you should have done ينام أكثر مما ينبغي، يتأخر في الاستيقاظ

overtake /ˌəʊvəˈteɪk/ *verb* [I,T] (*pt* **overtook** /-ˈtʊk/; *pp* **overtaken** /-ˈteɪkən/) to go past another person, car, etc. because you are moving faster: *The continuous white line in the middle of the road means you must not overtake.* ○ *I overtook a lorry.* ○ *He overtook me on the bend.* يتجاوز (سيّارة أمامه)

overthrow /ˌəʊvəˈθrəʊ/ *verb* [T] (*pt* **overthrew** /-ˈθruː/; *pp* **overthrown** /-ˈθrəʊn/) to remove a leader or government from power, by using force: *The dictator was overthrown in a military coup.* يطيح بِ، يسقط

▸ **overthrow** /ˈəʊvəθrəʊ/ *noun* [sing.]: *the overthrow of the French monarchy in 1789*
إطاحة، إسقاط

overtime /ˈəʊvətaɪm/ *noun* [U] time that you spend at work after your usual working hours: *Betty did ten hours' overtime last week.* ○ *Do you get paid overtime?* (يعمل) ساعات إضافيّة

▸ **overtime** *adv*: *I have been working overtime for weeks.* زيادةً على ساعات الدوام الرسميّة

overtone /ˈəʊvətəʊn/ *noun* [C, usually pl.] something that is suggested but not expressed openly: *It's a funny play but it has serious overtones.*
معانٍ إضافية دقيقة، معانٍ خفيّة

overture /ˈəʊvətʃʊə(r)/ *noun* **1** [C] a piece of music that is the introduction to an opera, ballet, etc. افتتاحيّة موسيقيّة

2 [C, usually pl.] (*formal*) an act of being friendly towards sb (perhaps because you want sth): *It's time to make some peace overtures to the boss.*
خطوة وديّة؛ تمهيد

overturn /ˌəʊvəˈtɜːn/ *verb* [I,T] to turn over so that the top is at the bottom: *The car overturned but the driver escaped unhurt.* ○ (*figurative*) *to overturn a decision* (= to change it)
ينقلب؛ يقلب؛ يُغيِّر

overweight /ˌəʊvəˈweɪt/ *adj* too heavy or fat: *You're a bit overweight. Perhaps you should go on a diet?* ➲ Look at the note at **fat**[1].
سمين، زائد عن الوزن المرغوب

overwhelm /ˌəʊvəˈwelm/ *verb* [T] (usually passive) **1** to cause sb to feel a very strong emotion: *The new world champion was overwhelmed by all the publicity.* تغمره المشاعر

2 to defeat sb/sth because you have more people يطغى على، يكتسح

▸ **overwhelming** *adj* very great or strong: *Anna had an overwhelming desire to return home.* شديد، عارم، طاغ

overwhelmingly *adv*: *The meeting voted overwhelmingly against the plan.* (بأغلبية) ساحقة

overwork /ˌəʊvəˈwɜːk/ *verb* [I,T] to work too hard or to make sb work too hard: *They are overworked and underpaid.*
يُرهِق نفسه بالعمل؛ يُرهقه بالعمل

▸ **overwork** /ˌəʊvəˈwɜːk/ *noun* [U]
إفراط في العمل؛ إرهاق العمل

⚷**owe** /əʊ/ *verb* [T] **1 owe sth (to sb) (for sth)**; **owe sb for sth** to have to pay money to sb for sth that they have done or given: *We owe the bank £5 000.* ○ *We owe £5 000 to the bank.* ○ *I still owe you for that bread you bought me yesterday.* ○ (*figurative*) *Claudia owes me an explanation.*
مَدين لِ، عليه دَيْن لِ

2 to feel grateful to sb for sth: *I owe you a lot for all you did for me when I was young.*
يدين لِ؛ مُمتنّ لِ

3 owe sth (to sb/sth) to have sth (for the reason given): *She says she owes her success to hard work and determination.* يدين بِ؛ يرجع إلى

owing /ˈəʊɪŋ/ *adj* (not before a noun) not yet paid: *How much is still owing to you?*
(دَيْن) غير مُسَدَّد

▸ **owing to** *prep* because of: *The match was cancelled owing to the bad weather.* بِسبب، نظراً لِ

owl /aʊl/ *noun* [C] a bird that flies at night and that catches and eats small animals. Owls are used as a symbol of wisdom. بومة

⚷**own**[1] /əʊn/ *det, pron* **1** (used to emphasize that sth belongs to a particular person): *I saw him do it with my own eyes.* ○ *Use your own pen. I need mine.* ○ *This is his own house.* ○ *This house is his own.* ○ *Rachel would like her own room* (= she doesn't want to share one). تستعمل للتوكيد: خاصّ بِ

> **Own** cannot be used after *a* or *the*. You CANNOT say: *I would like an own car*. Say: *I would like my own car* or *I would like a car of my own.*

2 (used to show that sth is done or made without help from another person): *The children are old enough to get their own breakfast.* ○ *They grow all their own vegetables.* بنفسه أو بأنفسهم، دون مساعدة

IDM **come into your own** to have your real value recognized: *The mobile phone really comes into its own when you break down on a country road.* تعرف قيمته

get/have your own back (on sb) (*informal*) to hurt or do harm to sb who has hurt or done harm to you ينتقم من، يعامله بالمِثل

hold your own (against sb/sth) to be as strong, good, etc. as sb/sth else
يُجاري في القوة، يصمد

of your, etc. own belonging to you and not to anyone else: *Kate has always wanted a pony of her own.* خاص به، له وحده

(all) on your, etc. own 1 alone: *John lives all on his own.* ➲ Look at the note at **alone**. لوحده

2 without help: *I managed to repair the car all on my own.* دون مساعدة

⚷**own**[2] /əʊn/ *verb* [T] to have sth belonging to you; possess: *We don't own the video. We just rent it.* ○ *Who is this land owned by?* يملك

PHR V **own up (to sth)** (*informal*) to tell sb that you have done sth wrong: *None of the children owned up to breaking the window.* ➲ Look at **confess**. It is more formal. يعترف

⚷**owner** /ˈəʊnə(r)/ *noun* [C] a person who owns sth: *a dog owner* صاحب، مالك

▸ **ownership** *noun* [U] the state of owning sth
ملكيّة

ˌ**own ˈgoal** *noun* [C] **1** a goal that is scored by mistake by a player against his or her own team هدف ذاتي

2 something that you do that achieves the opposite of what you wanted and that brings you a disadvantage يجني على نفسه

ox /ɒks/ *noun* [C] (*pl.* **oxen** /ˈɒksn/) a male cow that has been castrated. Oxen are sometimes used for pulling or carrying heavy loads. ➲ Look at **bull**. ثور مخصيّ

oxygen /ˈɒksɪdʒən/ *noun* [U] (*symbol* **O**) a gas that you cannot see, taste or smell. Plants and animals cannot live and fire cannot burn without oxygen. غاز الأوكسجين

oyster /ˈɔɪstə(r)/ *noun* [C] a shellfish that is eaten as food. Some oysters produce pearls. مَحارة

oz *abbrev* = OUNCE(S)

ozone /ˈəʊzəʊn/ *noun* [U] a form of oxygen
غاز الأوزون

ˌ**ozone-ˈfriendly** *adj* (used about household products, etc.) not containing chemicals that could damage the ozone layer: *Most aerosol sprays are now ozone-friendly.* غير ضارّ بطبقة الأوزون

ˈ**ozone layer** *noun* [sing.] the layer of ozone high above the surface of the earth that helps to protect it from the dangerous rays of the sun: *a hole in the ozone layer* طبقة الأوزون

a b c d e f g h i j k l m n o p q r s t u v w x y z

P p

P, p /piː/ *noun* [C] (*pl.* **Ps**; **P's**; **p's**) the sixteenth letter of the English alphabet: *'Pencil' begins with (a) 'P'.* الحرف السادس عشر من الأبجديّة الإنكليزية

p *abbrev* **1** (*pl.* **pp.**) = PAGE¹: *See p 94* ○ *pp. 63-6*
2 /piː/ (*Brit informal*) = PENNY, PENCE

PA /ˌpiː ˈeɪ/ *abbrev* [C] (*especially Brit*) personal assistant; a person whose job is to type letters, answer the telephone, etc. (a secretary) for just one manager مساعد شخصي

p.a. *abbrev* per annum; in or for a year: *salary £15 000 p.a.* في السنة

pace¹ /peɪs/ *noun* **1** [C] the distance that you move when you take one step: *Take two paces forward and then stop.* خطوة
2 [sing.] the speed at which you do sth or at which sth happens: *Run at a steady pace and you won't get tired so quickly.* ○ *I can't stand the pace of life in London.* سرعة
IDM **keep pace (with sb/sth)** to move or do sth at the same speed as sb/sth else; to change as quickly as sth else is changing: *Wages are not keeping pace with inflation.* يماشي، يساير، يجاري
set the pace to move or do sth at the speed that others must follow
يحدّد سرعة (العمل)، يقود الآخرين (بسرعة معيّنة)

pace² /peɪs/ *verb* [I,T] to walk with slow regular steps: *Fran paced nervously up and down the room, waiting for news.*
يمشي بخطى وئيدة، يذرَع (الغرفة) جيئة وذهاباً

pacemaker /ˈpeɪsmeɪkə(r)/ *noun* [C] **1** a person who sets the pace that others must follow
من يحدّد سرعة الآخرين (في سباق مثلاً)
2 a machine that helps to make a person's heart beat regularly or more strongly منظّم نبضات القلب

pacifier /ˈpæsɪfaɪə(r)/ *noun* [C] (*US*) = DUMMY (2)

pacifism /ˈpæsɪfɪzəm/ *noun* [U] the belief that all wars are wrong and that you should not fight in them مذهب المسالمة، مذهب رفض الحرب
▸ **pacifist** /-ɪst/ *noun* [C] a person who believes in pacifism شخص مسالم، من يرفض الاشتراك بالحروب

pacify /ˈpæsɪfaɪ/ *verb* [T] (*pres part* **pacifying**; *3rd pers sing pres* **pacifies**; *pt, pp* **pacified**) to cause sb who is angry or upset to be calm or quiet يهدّئ، يزيل غضبه، يطيّب خاطره

pack¹ /pæk/ *noun* [C] **1** a number of things that are wrapped or tied together and that you carry on your back or that are carried by an animal: *a packhorse* ➲ Look at **backpack**.
صُرّة، "حملة"، بقجة أمتعة تُحمل على الظهر
2 a packet or group of things that are sold together: *The pack contains a pencil, 10 envelopes and 20 sheets of writing paper.* ○ (*figurative*) *Everything she told me was a pack of lies.*
رزمة، حزمة، مجموعة
3 [with sing. or pl. verb] a group of animals that hunt together: *a pack of wolves* قطيع
4 (*US* **deck**) a complete set of playing cards
ورق اللعب، "كوتشينة"

pack² /pæk/ *verb* **1** [I,T] to put your things into a suitcase, etc. before you go away or go on holiday: *I'll have to pack my suitcase in the morning.* ○ *Have you packed yet?* ○ *Have you packed your toothbrush?*
يحزم الأمتعة، يعدّ حقائبه

Note the expression **do your packing**: *I'll do my packing in the morning.*

2 [I,T] to put things into boxes, in a factory or when you move house يضع في صناديق
ⓘ The opposite for **1** and **2** is **unpack**.
3 [T] (often passive) to fill or crowd: *The train was absolutely packed. We couldn't get a seat.* ○ *an action-packed film* مكتظ، مزدحم، محشوّ
PHR V **pack sth in** (*informal*) to stop doing sth: *I've packed in my job. I'm leaving next month.*
يترك (عمله)، يتوقف أو ينقطع عن
pack sth in; **pack sth in/into sth** to do a lot in a short time: *They packed an awful lot into their three days in Rome.*
يحشو، يملأ، ينجز الكثير في وقت قصير
pack sth out to fill sth with people: *The cinemas are packed out every night.* ملآن، مكتظ، مزدحم
pack up (*informal*) **1** to finish working or doing sth: *There was nothing else to do so we packed up and went home.*
ينهي العمل، يستعدّ للذهاب إلى البيت
2 (used about a machine, engine, etc.) to stop working يتعطّل

package /ˈpækɪdʒ/ *noun* [C] **1** something, or a number of things, wrapped up in paper: *It was a strangely shaped package and no one could guess what was inside.* ➲ Look at the note at **parcel**.
طَرْد، علبة ملفوفة بورق
2 (*US*) = PACKET
3 a number of things that must be bought or accepted together: *a word-processing package* ○ *The strike will go on until the firm offers a better pay and conditions package.*
مجموعة، جملة: صفقة
▸ **package** *verb* [T] to put sth into a packet, box, etc. before it is sold or sent somewhere: *Goods that are attractively packaged sell more quickly.* يضع في علب من الكرتون، يغلّف البضاعة
packaging *noun* [U] all the materials that are used to wrap sth before it is sold or sent somewhere: *Chocolates sometimes have four or five layers of packaging.*
مواد اللّف والحشو (في العلب والصناديق)

ˈ**package holiday** *noun* [C] a holiday that is or-

ganized by a travel agent who arranges your travel and accommodation for you
رحلة سياحيّة تتكفّل بكل شيء

'package store *noun* [C] (*US*) = OFF-LICENCE

,packed 'lunch *noun* [C] sandwiches, etc. that you take with you to work or school
غداء من السندويش ونحوه يؤخذ إلى العمل أو إلى المدرسة

packet /'pækɪt/ (*US* **package**) *noun* [C] a box, bag, etc. in which things are packed to be sold in a shop: *a packet of sweets, cigarettes, biscuits, etc.* ○ *a cigarette packet* ➲ Look at the note at **parcel**.
علبة (سجائر)؛ طرد صغير

packing /'pækɪŋ/ *noun* [U] **1** putting things into a box or suitcase: *I haven't done any packing yet and we're going away this evening.*
وَضْع الأشياء في صناديق؛ إعداد حقائب السّفر

2 soft material that you use when you are packing to stop things from being damaged or broken: *Add £2 to the price for postage and packing.* مواد حشو توضع في الصناديق لصيانة السّلع

'packing case *noun* [C] a wooden box that you put things in before they are transported or stored صندوق خشبي لخزن أو نقل البضائع

pact /pækt/ *noun* [C] a formal agreement between two people, groups or countries
اتّفاق، ميثاق، حلف

pad[1] /pæd/ *noun* [C] **1** a thick piece of soft material, used for cleaning or protecting sth: *Footballers wear shin pads to protect their legs.* ○ *a jacket with shoulder pads* ○ *Press the cotton-wool pad onto the wound to stop the bleeding.*
وسادة رقيقة للوقاية؛ حشوة؛ ضمادة

2 a number of pieces of paper that are fastened together at one end: *a writing pad*
كرّاسة أو رزمة ورق

3 the place from which helicopters and space rockets take off: *a launch pad* منَصّة الإطلاق

4 the soft part on the bottom of the foot of some animals, e.g. dogs, cats, etc. باطن قَدَم (الكلب مثلاً)

pad[2] /pæd/ *verb* [T] (pa**dd**ing; pa**dd**ed) (usually passive) to fill or cover sth with soft material in order to protect it, make it larger or more comfortable, etc: *a padded bra* ○ *Violent prisoners are put in padded cells so they do not hurt themselves.* يحشو؛ يبطّن بمواد طريّة

PHRV **pad sth out** to make a book, speech, etc. longer by adding things that are not necessary
يحشو (خطاباً) ليزيده طولاً، يضيف عبارات لا داعي لها

▶ **padding** *noun* [U] material that you use to pad² sth حشوة؛ بطانة سميكة للوقاية

pad[3] /pæd/ *verb* [I] (pa**dd**ing; pa**dd**ed) **pad about, along, around, etc.** to walk rather quickly and quietly يمشي بخفّة ودون صوت

paddle[1] /'pædl/ *noun* [C] a short pole that is wide at one or both ends and that you use for moving a small boat through water ➲ Look at **oar**.
مجذاف عريض الطرف أو الطرفين

▶ **paddle** *verb* [I,T] to move a small boat through water using a paddle ➲ Look at **row**².
يجذّف قارباً صغيراً

paddle[2] /'pædl/ *verb* [I] to walk with bare feet in shallow water يخوض في الماء حافي القدمين

paddock /'pædək/ *noun* [C] a small field where horses are kept مزرعة صغيرة لترويض الخيول

padlock /'pædlɒk/ *noun* [C] a type of lock that is used for fastening gates, bicycles, etc. قفل

▶ **padlock** *verb* [T] to fasten sth with a padlock يقفل

paediatrician (*US* **pediatrician**) /,piːdiə'trɪʃn/ *noun* [C] a doctor who specializes in looking after sick children طبيب مختص بالأطفال

pagan /'peɪgən/ *adj* having religious beliefs that do not belong to any of the main religions: *Halloween is an ancient pagan festival.* وثَني

page[1] /peɪdʒ/ *noun* [C] (*abbr* **p**) **1** one side of a piece of paper: *The letter was three pages long.* ○ *Start each answer on a new page.* ○ *to turn over the page* ○ *Full flight details are given on page 63.* ○ *the front page of a newspaper.* ○ *the sports page* صفحة

2 one piece of paper in a book, etc: *One page had been torn from her diary.* صفحة

page[2] /peɪdʒ/ *verb* [T] to call sb's name over a loudspeaker in a place where there are a lot of people, so that you can give him/her a message يُنادي شخصاً بواسطة مكبّر الصوت

pageant /'pædʒənt/ *noun* [C] **1** a type of outdoor public entertainment at which there is a procession of people, often dressed up in historical costume مهرجان يمثّل مشاهد تاريخيّة

2 a beauty competition for young women
مسابقة لاختيار ملكة جمال

▶ **pageantry** /'pædʒəntri/ *noun* [U] the feeling and appearance of a grand ceremony when people are dressed in fine colourful clothes: *The pageantry of the Changing of the Guard is very popular with tourists.*
موكب ذو أبّهة بالملابس التقليديّة الزاهية

pager /'peɪdʒə(r)/ *noun* [C] a small machine that you carry, that makes a sound when sb sends you a message جهاز استقبال صغير

paid *pt, pp* of PAY²

,paid-'up *adj* having paid all the money that you owe, e.g. to become a member of sth: *He's a fully paid-up member of Friends of the Earth.*
مُسدّد كلّ ما عليه، مسدّد اشتراكه؛ (عضو) رسميّ (في)

pail /peɪl/ *noun* [C] (*US*) or (*old-fashioned*) a bucket دَلو، سَطْل

pain /peɪn/ *noun* **1** [C,U] the unpleasant feeling that you have when a part of your body has been hurt or when you are ill: *to be in great pain* ○ *I've got a terrible pain in my back.* ○ *to scream with pain* ○ *chest pains* ○ *After I took the tablets, the pain wore off.* ○ *The tablets relieved the pain.* ➲ Look at **ache**. Notice that we usually say: *I've got a headache, etc.* instead of using an expression with 'pain'. ألم، وجع

2 [U] unhappiness that you feel because sth bad has happened or because sb has been unkind: *It*

took me years to get over the pain of my mother's death. ألم، حزن، أسى

IDM be a pain (in the neck) (*informal*) a person, thing or situation that causes you to be angry or annoyed: *Having to clean the ice off the windscreen every morning is a real pain.* شخص مزعج جداً؛ مصدر إزعاج وضيق؛ عناء

▸ **pain** *verb* [T] (*formal*) to cause sb to feel unhappy or upset يؤلم، يحزن؛ يجرح شعوره

pained *adj* showing that you are unhappy or upset: *a pained expression* معبر عن الحزن أو الألم

painful /-fl/ *adj* that causes pain: *A wasp sting can be very painful.* ○ *The break-up of their marriage was very painful for the children.* مؤلم؛ محزن

painfully /-fəli/ *adv*: *Progress is still painfully slow.* للغاية؛ بصورة مزعجة

painless *adj* that does not cause pain: *The animals' death is quick and painless.* غير مؤلم

painlessly *adv* دون ألم

painkiller /ˈpeɪnkɪlə(r)/ *noun* [C] medicine that is used for reducing or removing pain مسكّن للألم

pains /peɪnz/ *noun*

IDM be at (great) pains to do sth to make a special effort to do sth: *He was at pains to hide his true feelings.* يبذل جهداً عظيماً، يحاول جاهداً

take great pains (with/over/to do sth) to take great care with sth or to make a special effort to do sth: *She always takes great pains with her writing.* يعتني عناية كبيرة؛ يبذل مجهوداً كبيراً

▸ **painstaking** /ˈpeɪnzteɪkɪŋ/ *adj* very careful: *The painstaking search of the wreckage gave us clues as to the cause of the crash.* (فحص) دقيق جداً، شديد العناية

painstakingly *adv* بعناية شديدة جداً؛ بصبر ودقّة

🔑 **paint**[1] /peɪnt/ *noun* **1** [U] a liquid that you put onto a surface with a brush in order to give it colour or to protect it: *The door will need two more coats of paint.* ○ *Wet paint!* ○ *spray paint* ○ *The paint was peeling off the walls.* طلاء، دهان

2 [U] coloured liquid that you can use to make a picture: *red paint* ○ *oil paint* طلاء؛ صِباغ، دهان زيتي

3 paints [plural] a collection of tubes, blocks, etc. of paint that an artist uses أصبغة ملوّنة، مجموعة طلاء (زيتي)

🔑 **paint**[2] /peɪnt/ *verb* [I,T] **1** to put paint onto sth: *The bathroom needs painting.* ○ *Wear old clothes when you're painting.* ○ *The walls were painted pink.* يَطلي، يُدهِّن

2 to make a picture of sb/sth using paints: *Vicky paints well.* ○ *to paint a self-portrait* يرسم صورة زيتيّة

paintbox /ˈpeɪntbɒks/ *noun* [C] a box that contains blocks of paint of many colours علبة ألوان

paintbrush /ˈpeɪntbrʌʃ/ *noun* [C] a brush that you use for painting with فرشاة رسم

🔑 **painter** /ˈpeɪntə(r)/ *noun* [C] **1** a person whose job is to paint buildings, walls, etc. دهّان

2 a person who paints pictures ➲ Look at **artist**. رسّام

🔑 **painting** /ˈpeɪntɪŋ/ *noun* **1** [U] the act of painting pictures or buildings طَلي، طِلاء؛ تصوير أو رَسم زيتي

2 [C] a picture that sb has painted: *a famous painting by Van Gogh* ➲ Look at **drawing**. صورة زيتية

paintwork /ˈpeɪntwɜːk/ *noun* [U] a surface that has been painted السطح المدهون

🔑 **pair** /peə(r)/ *noun* **1** [C] two things that are almost the same and that are used together: *a pair of shoes* ○ *a pair of gloves* زوج (من الأحذية)

2 [C] a thing that consists of two parts that are joined together: *a pair of scissors* ○ *a pair of glasses* ○ *two pairs of trousers* شيء مؤلف من قسمين متّصلين مثل المقصّ والبنطلون

3 [C, with sing. or pl. verb] two people or animals that are closely connected with each other: *The pair from Didcot won all their matches easily.* ○ *A pair of blackbirds are nesting in the apple tree.* ➲ Look at **couple**[1]. الزّوجان، الصديقان؛ زوج (من الطيور)

IDM in pairs two at a time: *These earrings are only sold in pairs.* (تُباع) بالزّوج أو زوجاً (أي ليس إفراداً)؛ زوجاً زوجاً

▸ **pair** *verb*

PHR V pair (sb/sth) off (with sb) to form a pair or pairs: *Stop trying to pair me off with your brother – I'm not interested.* يزاوِج، يحاول التقريب بين شخصين

pair up (with sb) to join together with another person or group ينضمّ إلى شخص آخر

pajamas /pəˈdʒæməz/ (*US*) *noun* [plural] = PYJAMAS

pal /pæl/ *noun* [C] (*informal*) a friend رفيق، صديق

🔑 **palace** /ˈpæləs/ *noun* [C] a large house that is or was the home of a king or queen قصر

palate /ˈpælət/ *noun* [C] the top part of the inside of your mouth سقف الفم، سقف الحلق، حنك

🔑 **pale** /peɪl/ *adj* **1** (used about a person or his/her face, etc.) having less colour than usual; rather white: *Are you OK? You look a bit pale.* ℹ The noun is **pallor**. Look at **pallid**. شاحب

2 not bright or strong in colour: *pale yellow* فاتح

palette /ˈpælət/ *noun* [C] a thin board on which an artist mixes colours when painting, with a hole for the thumb to hold it by لوحة مزج الألوان

pall /pɔːl/ *verb* [I] to become uninteresting or annoying يصبح مملاً؛ يصبح مزعجاً

pallid /ˈpælɪd/ *adj* (used about a person or his/her face, etc.) pale or rather white because he/she is ill or frightened شاحب؛ ممتقع الوجه

pallor /ˈpælə(r)/ *noun* [U] the state of being pale or rather white because you are ill or frightened شحوب؛ امتقاع الوجه

palm[1] /pɑːm/ *noun* [C] the flat part of the front of your hand: *Dora held the bird in the palm of her hand.* كفّ، راحة اليد

▸ **palm** *verb*

PHR V palm sb off (with sth) (*informal*) to persuade sb to accept sth that is not true or that is of poor quality: *He tried to palm me off with some story about the train being late.* يخدع، يضحك على

palm sb/sth off (on sb) to get rid of sb/sth that you do not want by giving it to sb else يتخلّص من شخص أو من بضاعة رديئة بالغشّ والاحتيال

palm² /pɑːm/ (*also* **'palm tree**) *noun* [C] a type of tree that grows in hot countries. Palms have no branches and a mass of large leaves at the top: *a date/coconut palm* شجرة نخيل

palmtop /'pɑːmtɒp/ *noun* [C] a computer that is about the same size as your hand كمبيوتر بحجم الكف

paltry /'pɔːltri/ *adj* very small and so not worth very much ضئيل، تافه

pamper /'pæmpə(r)/ *verb* [T] to treat sb very or too kindly يدلّل، يعتني بِ

pamphlet /'pæmflət/ *noun* [C] a thin book with a paper cover that gives you information about sth كُتيّب، كرّاسة

pan /pæn/ *noun* [C] a metal container that is used for cooking: *Cook the spaghetti in a large pan of boiling salted water.* ○ *a frying pan* ○ *All the pots and pans are kept in that cupboard.* طُنجَرة، قدْر، وعاء للطبخ

pancake /'pænkeɪk/ *noun* [C] a type of very thin round cake that is made by frying a mixture of flour, milk and eggs (batter) زلابية، رقائق من العجين المقلي

'Pancake Day (*also* **Shrove Tuesday**) a Tuesday in February when people traditionally eat pancakes. Pancake Day is the day before the period of Lent begins. يوم ثلاثاء يسبق فترة الصّوم عند المسيحيين

panda /'pændə/ *noun* [C] a large black and white animal that looks like a bear and that comes from China. Pandas are very rare nowadays. حيوان الباندا

pandemonium /ˌpændə'məʊniəm/ *noun* [U] a state of great noise and confusion هرج ومرج، صياح وضجيج وفوضى

pander /'pændə(r)/ *verb*

PHR V **pander to sb/sth** to do or say what sb wants even if it is wrong or unpleasant يساير، يحاول إرضاء شخص

p. and p. /ˌpiː ən 'piː/ *abbrev* (*Brit*) postage and packing: *price: £29 incl p. and p.* التغليف وأجور البريد

pane /peɪn/ *noun* [C] a piece of glass in a window, etc: *a pane of glass* ○ *the windowpane* زجاج النافذة؛ لوح زجاجي

panel /'pænl/ *noun* **1** [C, with sing. or pl. verb] a group of people who are chosen to discuss sth, decide sth, answer questions, etc: *All the candidates were interviewed by a panel of four.* ○ *a panel of experts* ○ *a panel game on TV* ○ *What do/does the panel think about the changes in the education system?* هيئة تحكيم؛ لجنة خبراء؛ مجموعة متناقشين

2 [C] a piece of wood, metal or glass that forms part of a door, wall, etc. or that is fixed to it: *They smashed the glass panel in the front door.* لوح خشبي أو معدني أو زجاجي يشكّل جزءاً من باب أو جدار وغير ذلك

3 [C] a surface that contains the equipment for controlling a car, machine, etc: *the instrument panel* لوحة العدّادات (في السّيارة مثلاً)

► **panellist** (*US* **panelist**) /'pænəlɪst/ *noun* [C] a member of a panel (1) عضو تحكيم؛ أحد المشتركين في هيئة مناقشة عامّة

pang /pæŋ/ *noun* [C, usually pl.] a sudden strong feeling (of pain, hunger, guilt, etc.) شعور عنيف مفاجئ بالألم أو الجوع أو الذّنب أو غير ذلك، لذعة، وخز

panic /'pænɪk/ *noun* [C,U] a sudden feeling of fear that makes you do things without thinking carefully about them: *The rumours of war spread panic on the stock market.* ○ *to be in a state of panic* ○ *There was a mad panic when the alarm went off.* هلع مفاجئ يرافقه اضطراب وتصرّفات لا إراديّة

► **panic** *verb* [I] (panicking; panicked) to have a sudden feeling of fear that makes you act without thinking carefully: *Stay calm and don't panic.* يُصاب بهلع مفاجئ، يفزع فجأة ويفقد السيطرة على تصرفاته

panic-stricken /'pænɪk strɪkən/ *adj* very frightened مذعور للغاية، شديد الاضطراب لفزعه

panorama /ˌpænə'rɑːmə; *US* -'ræmə/ *noun* [C] a view over a wide area of land منظر طبيعيّ ممتدّ الأطراف

► **panoramic** /ˌpænə'ræmɪk/ *adj*: *a panoramic view from the top of the hill* (منظر) شامل

pansy /'pænzi/ *noun* [C] (*pl.* **pansies**) a garden plant with a short stem and broad flat flowers of various bright colours بنفسج الثالوث، بانسيه

pant /pænt/ *verb* [I] to take short quick breaths, e.g. after running or because it is very hot يلهث

► **pant** *noun* [C] a short quick breath لهثة؛ لهاث

panther /'pænθə(r)/ *noun* [C] a large wild cat (usually black) النّمِر أو النّمْر

panties /'pæntiz/ *noun* [plural] (*informal*) a small piece of clothing that women and girls wear under their other clothes (from their waists to the top of their legs) ➲ Look at **pants** and **knickers**. سروال نسائيّ داخليّ

pantihose (*also* **pantyhose**) /'pæntihəʊz/ *noun* [plural] (*US*) = TIGHTS

pantomime /'pæntəmaɪm/ *noun* [C] a type of play for children that is usually performed just after Christmas. Pantomimes are based on traditional children's stories. They are funny and have singing and dancing in them. مسرحيّة موسيقيّة للأطفال تمثّل في موسم عيد الميلاد

pantry /'pæntri/ *noun* [C] (*pl.* **pantries**) a small room where food is kept ➲ Look at **larder**. غرفة صغيرة لحفظ المأكولات

pants /pænts/ *noun* [plural] **1** (*Brit*) = UNDERPANTS

2 (*US*) = TROUSERS

paparazzi /ˌpæpə'rætsi/ *noun* [plural] photographers who follow famous people around in order to get pictures of them to sell to a newspaper or magazine مصوّرون صحفيون متطفّلون

papaya /pə'paɪə/ (*also* **pawpaw**) *noun* [C] a

large tropical fruit which is sweet and orange inside and has small black seeds بَبَّايا، ثمر البابايا

🔑**paper** /'peɪpə(r)/ *noun* **1** [U] a material that consists of thin sheets that you use for wrapping things in, writing or drawing on, etc: *a blank piece/sheet of paper* ○ *wallpaper* ○ *Scrap paper can be recycled.* ○ *a brown paper bag* ○ *a paper handkerchief* ❶ Types of paper include **filter**, **tissue**, **toilet** and **writing paper**. ورق

2 [C] = NEWSPAPER: *Where's today's paper?* ○ *a daily paper* ○ *a national/local paper* ❶ You buy a paper at a **paper shop** or **newsagent's**.

3 papers [plural] pieces of paper that have information written on them. Papers are usually important: *If you don't have all your papers with you, you won't be allowed to cross the border.* ○ *The document you want is somewhere in the pile of papers on her desk.* أوراق، وثائق

4 [C] an examination in which you have to write answers to a number of questions: *We have to take three papers in history.* امتحان كتابيّ

5 [C] a piece of writing on a particular subject that is written for or read to specialists مقالة؛ محاضرة، ورقة

IDM on paper 1 in writing: *I've had nothing on paper to say that I've been accepted.* كتابةً، على الورق

2 from what appearances show; in theory: *The scheme sounds fine on paper, but would it work in practice?* نظرياً، ظاهرياً، على الورق

paperback /'peɪpəbæk/ *noun* [C,U] a book that has a paper cover: *The novel is available in paperback.* ○ *a cheap paperback* كتاب غلافه عاديّ أي ورقيّ

'paper boy, **'paper girl** *noun* [C] a boy or girl who delivers newspapers to people's houses غلام أو فتاة يوزعان الصحف على البيوت

'paper clip *noun* [C] a piece of wire or plastic that is used for holding pieces of paper together دبّوس أو شكّالة ورق

paperwork /'peɪpəwɜːk/ *noun* [U] the written work that you do in an office, including writing letters and reports, filling in forms, etc. أعمال كتابيّة

paprika /'pæprɪkə; *US* pə'priːkə/ *noun* [U] a red powder made from a type of sweet pepper and used as a spice فلفل أحمر (غير حار)

par /pɑː(r)/ *noun*

IDM below par (*informal*) not as good or as well as usual تحت المستوى

on a par with sb/sth of an equal level, standard, etc. to sb/sth else على نفس المستوى، نِدّ ل؛ يساوي

parable /'pærəbl/ *noun* [C] a short story (especially in the Bible) that teaches a lesson أقصوصة ذات مغزى اخلاقيّ

parachute /'pærəʃuːt/ *noun* [C] a piece of strong cloth that is folded and fastened with thin ropes to a person's body. A parachute lets the person fall to the ground slowly when they jump from a plane: *a parachute jump* مظلّة، باراشوت

▸ **parachute** *verb* [I] يهبط بالمظلّة

parade /pə'reɪd/ *noun* [C] an occasion when a group of people stand or walk in a procession so that people can look at them: *There used to be a military parade in Red Square on 1 May.* ○ *a fashion parade* عرض؛ استعراضي

paradise /'pærədaɪs/ *noun* **1 Paradise** [sing.] (without *a* or *the*) the place where some people think good people go after they die; heaven الفردوس، الجنّة

2 [C] a perfect place: *This beach is a paradise for windsurfers.* المكان المثاليّ، "جنّة النعيم"

paradox /'pærədɒks/ *noun* [C] **1** a statement that seems to be impossible but that is or may be true: *'A deafening silence' is a paradox.* عبارة متناقضة ظاهرياً

2 a situation that has two or more qualities that you would not expect to find together: *It's a paradox that some countries produce too much food while in other countries people are starving.* تناقض، تنافر

▸ **paradoxical** /ˌpærə'dɒksɪkl/ *adj* متناقض ظاهرياً

paraffin /'pærəfɪn/ (*US* **kerosene**) *noun* [U] a type of oil that is used in heaters, lamps, etc. بارافين، كيروسين، زيت الكاز

paragraph /'pærəgrɑːf; *US* -græf/ *noun* [C] a part of a piece of writing that consists of one or more sentences. A paragraph always starts on a new line. مقطع

🔑**parallel** /'pærəlel/ *adj*, *adv* **1** (used about two lines, etc.) with the same distance between them for all their length: *parallel lines* ○ *The railway runs parallel to the road.* (خطّان) متوازيان؛ موازياً لِ

2 similar: *The two brothers followed parallel careers in different companies.* متماثل، متشابه

▸ **parallel** *noun* **1** [C] (*also* ˌ**parallel 'line**) a line, etc. that is parallel to another الخط الموازي، خط موازٍ لآخر

2 [C,U] a person, thing or situation that is similar to sb/sth else: *Japan's economic success is without parallel in the post-war period.* نظير، مثيل، شبيه

3 [C] an act of comparing sb/sth with sb/sth else: *He drew a parallel between Margaret Thatcher and Winston Churchill.* مقارنة

paralyse (*US* **paralyze**) /'pærəlaɪz/ *verb* [T] **1** to make a person unable to move his/her body or a part of it: *Miriam is paralysed from the waist down.* يشلّ (حركته)

2 to make sb/sth unable to work in a normal way: *The railway system was completely paralysed by the strike.* يشل، يعطّل

paralysis /pə'ræləsɪs/ *noun* [U] **1** the state of being unable to move your body or a part of it شَلَل

2 being unable to work in the normal way: *There has been complete paralysis of the railway system.* شَلَل، توقُّف عن العمل

paramedic /ˌpærə'medɪk/ *noun* [C] a person who has had special training in caring for people who are ill or hurt, but who is not a doctor or nurse موظَّف إسعاف، مساعد

paramilitary /ˌpærəˈmɪlətri; *US* -teri/ *adj* organized in the same way as, but not belonging to, an official army منظَّم على نحو عسكريّ

paramount /ˈpærəmaʊnt/ *adj* (*formal*) most important أساسيّ، رئيسيّ، غاية في الأهميّة

paranoia /ˌpærəˈnɔɪə/ *noun* [U] a type of mental illness in which sb wrongly believes that other people are trying to hurt him/her الشعور بالظلم أو الاضطهاد، جنون الاضطهاد

paranoid /ˈpærənɔɪd/ *adj* wrongly believing that other people are trying to hurt you مصاب بجنون الاضطهاد؛ شديد الارتياب بالآخرين

paraphernalia /ˌpærəfəˈneɪliə/ *noun* [U] a large number of different objects that you need for a particular purpose مجموعة الأدوات والمعدّات اللازمة لغرض معيّن

paraphrase /ˈpærəfreɪz/ *verb* [T] to express sth again using different words so that it is easier to understand يعيد صياغة تعبير (ليَسهل فهمه)
▸ **paraphrase** *noun* [C] صياغة جديدة

parasite /ˈpærəsaɪt/ *noun* [C] a plant or an animal that lives in or on another plant or animal and gets its food from it حيوان أو نبات طفيليّ

paratroops /ˈpærətruːps/ *noun* [plural] soldiers who are trained to drop from an aeroplane by parachute جنود المظلّات، المظليّون

parcel /ˈpɑːsl/ (*US also* **package**) *noun* [C] something that is wrapped in paper and sent by post, or carried: *to wrap/unwrap a parcel* طرد بريديّ؛ علبة ملفوفة، رزمة

A **parcel** (US **package**) is something that is wrapped up and sent by post, etc. A **package** is similar to a parcel but it is usually given by hand. A package may have an unusual shape. A **packet** (US **pack**) is one item or a number of things in a special box, bag, etc. to be sold in a shop. A **pack** is a number of things that are not the same that are sold together: *The pack contains needles, a reel of white cotton and a pair of scissors.* **Packaging** is the material, box, bag, etc. that something is put in before it is sold.

▸ **parcel** *verb* (parcelling; parcelled; *US* parceling; parceled)
PHRV **parcel sth up** to wrap sth up into a parcel يلفّ، يرزم، يهيّئ طرداً بريدياً

parch /pɑːtʃ/ *verb* [T] (usually passive) to make sb/sth very hot, dry or thirsty: *Can I have a drink? I'm parched!* "ميّت من العطش"، ظمآن

pardon¹ /ˈpɑːdn/ *noun* [C,U] an act of forgiving sb. If a prisoner receives a pardon, he/she is released from prison. عفو؛ (أرجو) المعذرة

I beg your pardon is a formal way of saying 'sorry': *Oh, I do beg your pardon. I had no idea this was your seat.* It can also be used when you want to ask somebody to repeat what they have said because you did not understand.

pardon² /ˈpɑːdn/ *verb* [T] **pardon sb (for sth/ for doing sth)** to forgive sb or to say that sb will not be punished يعفو عن، يسامح
▸ **pardon** (*also* ˌ**pardon** ˈ**me**) *interj* (used for asking sb to repeat what he/she has just said because you did not hear or understand it, and also for saying that you are sorry for sth that you have done) آسف، لم أسمع جيداً ما قلت؛ أرجو المعذرة

pardonable /ˈpɑːdnəbl/ *adj* that can be forgiven or excused (ذنب) يمكن الصفح عنه؛ مغفور

parent /ˈpeərənt/ *noun* [C] a mother or father: *Most parents try to bring up their children to be polite.* أحد الوالدَين، الأم أو الأب

A **single parent** is a mother or father who is bringing up their child or children alone, without the other parent. A **foster parent** is a person who looks after a child who is not legally their own.

▸ **parental** /pəˈrentl/ *adj* (only *before* a noun) of a parent or parents: *parental support* أبويّ، نسبة إلى إحد الوالدَين

parenthood /ˈpeərənthʊd/ *noun* [U] the state of being a parent الأبوّة أو الأمومة

paˌrental ˈleave *noun* [U] time when a parent is allowed to be away from work to care for a child إجازة الأم أو الأب من أجل رعاية الطفل

parentheses /pəˈrenθəsiːz/ *noun* [plural] (*especially US*) = BRACKETS (BRACKET 1)

parenthesis /pəˈrenθəsɪs/ *noun*
IDM **in parenthesis** as an extra comment or piece of information كلمة أو جملة معترضة، عبارة بين قوسين

parish /ˈpærɪʃ/ *noun* [C] **1** an area or district which has its own church and priest: *the vicar of a country parish* ○ *the parish church* أبرشيّة، وحدة إدارية لها كنيسة وقسّيس خاص بها
2 a small area which has its own local government مقاطعة صغيرة لها حكومة محليّة
▸ **parishioner** /pəˈrɪʃənə(r)/ *noun* [C] a person who lives in a parish (1), especially one who goes to church there أحد أفراد الأبرشيّة

ˌ**parish** ˈ**council** *noun* [C, with sing. or pl. verb] a division of local government which looks after the interests of a very small area, especially a village ➲ Look at **local government** and **local authority**. مجلس بلدي مسؤول عن قرية وما إليها

park¹ /pɑːk/ *noun* [C] **1** an open area with grass and trees, usually in a town, where anybody can go to walk, play, etc: *a walk in the park* ○ *the park gates* ○ *Hyde Park* حديقة عامّة
2 (*Brit*) the land that surrounds and belongs to a large country house حديقة كبيرة تحيط بقصر ريفيّ
3 (in compounds) a large area of land that is open to the public and is used for special purposes: *a national park* ○ *a theme park* (في التعابير المركّبة): مساحة واسعة من الأرض تستعمل لأغراض معيّنة
4 (*US*) a sports ground or field ملعب رياضيّ

park² /pɑːk/ *verb* [I,T] to stop and leave a car, lorry, etc. somewhere for a time: *You can't park in the centre of town.* ○ *Somebody's parked their car in front of my garage.* يوقِف أو يصفّ السّيارة (في شارع مثلاً)

a b c d e f g h i j k l m n o p q r s t u v w x y z

parka /ˈpɑːkə/ *noun* [C] a warm jacket or coat with a hood سترة أي جاكيت له قلنسوة

parking /ˈpɑːkɪŋ/ *noun* [U] leaving a car, lorry, etc. somewhere for a time; an area where you can do this: *The sign said 'No Parking'.* ○ *There is parking for employees behind the office buildings.* ○ *These parking spaces are reserved for residents.* إيقاف السيّارات؛ موقف للسيّارات

ˈ**parking lot** *noun* [C] (*US*) = CAR PARK

ˈ**parking meter** *noun* [C] a metal post that you put coins into to pay for parking a car in the space beside it عدّاد مثبّت على الرصيف لتسجيل مدة وقوف السيّارة

ˈ**parking ticket** *noun* [C] a piece of paper that orders you to pay money (a fine) for parking your car where it is not allowed تذكرة مُخالَفة (تُعطى لوقوف السّيارة في مكان محظور)

parkour /pɑːˈkʊə(r)/ *noun* [U] the sport of moving through a city by running, jumping and climbing under, around and through things رياضة الجري والقفز والتسلق عبر المدن

parliament /ˈpɑːləmənt/ *noun* **1** [C] the group of people who discuss and make the laws of a country: *The German parliament is called the 'Bundestag'.* ℹ When **parliament** is singular it can be used with either a singular or plural verb. مجلس النوّاب، البرلمان

2 Parliament [sing.] the group of people in the United Kingdom who discuss and make the laws: *the Houses of Parliament* (= the buildings where Parliament meets) ○ *a Member of Parliament (MP)* النوّاب، أعضاء البرلمان

The UK Parliament consists of **The House of Commons** and **The House of Lords**. The House of Commons consists of Members of Parliament, who have been elected to represent areas of the country (called **constituencies**). The House of Lords consists of members of the nobility, bishops and other people who have been appointed, not elected.

▸ **parliamentary** /ˌpɑːləˈmentri/ *adj* (only *before* a noun) connected with parliament: *parliamentary debates* برلماني، نيابي

parody /ˈpærədi/ *noun* [C,U] (*pl.* **parodies**) a piece of writing, speech or music that copies the style of sb/sth in a funny way: *His first novel, 'Snow White', is a parody of a traditional fairy story.* تأليف أدبي أو موسيقي يقلّد آخر بقصد السخرية

▸ **parody** *verb* [T] (*pres part* **parodying**; *3rd pers sing pres* **parodies**; *pt, pp* **parodied**) to make a parody of sb/sth يقلّد قطعة أدبيّة أو موسيقية بقصدَ السخرية

parole /pəˈrəʊl/ *noun* [U] allowing a prisoner to go free before the end of his/her term in prison on condition that he/she continues to behave well: *She's hoping to get parole.* ○ *He's going to be released on parole.* عفو مشروط

parrot /ˈpærət/ *noun* [C] a type of tropical bird with a curved beak and usually with very bright feathers. Parrots that are kept as pets often copy what people say. بَبغاء أو درّة

ˈ**parrot-fashion** *adv* without thinking about or understanding the meaning of sth: *to learn sth parrot-fashion* مثلَ الببغاء، (يكرّر) بلا فَهم

parsley /ˈpɑːsli/ *noun* [U] a plant (herb) with small curly leaves that are used for flavouring or decorating food مقدونس أو بَقدونس

parsnip /ˈpɑːsnɪp/ *noun* [C] a cream-coloured vegetable, shaped like a carrot, that grows under the ground جَزَر أبيض، سيسارون كبير

part[1] /pɑːt/ *noun* **1** [C] (often without *a/an*) **part (of sth)** one of the pieces, areas, periods, divisions, etc. of sth; some, but not all: *Which part of Spain do you come from?* ○ *This part of the church has been rebuilt.* ○ *I enjoyed some parts of the film.* ○ *A large part of my job involves dealing with the public.* ○ *Part of the problem is lack of information.* ○ *a part of the body* ○ *Getting up in the morning is always the hardest part of the day.* جزء، قسم

2 [C] one of the essential pieces that make up a machine: *We always take a box of spare parts for the car with us when we go abroad.* قطعة ميكانيكيّة: قطعة غِيار

3 [C] an amount or quantity (of a liquid or substance): *Use one part of vinegar to three parts of oil.* مقدار

4 [C] a role or character in a play, film, etc: *He played the part of Macbeth.* ○ *a small part in the school play* دَوْر (في مسرحيّة)

5 [C, U] **part (in sth)** a person's share in an activity, event, etc: *Did you have any part in the decision?* نصيب؛ دَوْر؛ مشاركة

IDM **the best/better part of sth** most of sth; more than half of sth, often a period of time: *They've lived here for the best part of forty years.* معظم: معظم الوقت

for the most part usually or mostly: *The countryside is, for the most part, flat and uninteresting.* في أغلب الأحوال

for my, your, etc. part as far as it concerns me, you, etc: *I, for my part, am willing to go.* من ناحيتي،... من ناحيتك...الخ

in part not completely; to some extent: *The accident was, in part at least, the fault of the driver.* جزئيّاً، إلى حدّ ما

on the part of sb/on sb's part made, done or felt by sb: *I'm sorry. It was a mistake on my part.* ○ *There is concern on the part of the teachers that class size will increase.* من طَرَف، من جانب

play a part (in sth) to have a share in sth or to have an effect on sth يلعب دوراً

take part (in sth) to join with other people in an activity: *He was unable to take part in the race because of his recent accident.* ○ *Everybody took part in the discussion.* يشترك، يشارك

▸ **part** *adv* not completely one thing and not completely another: *A mule is part donkey and part horse.* جزئيّاً

partly *adv* to some extent; not completely: *She was only partly responsible for the mistake.* ○ *I love Italy, partly because of the weather, but mostly because of the people.* جزئيّاً، إلى حدّ ما، بعضَ الشيء

part[2] /pɑːt/ *verb* **1** [I,T] **part (from sb); part sb (from sb)** to leave or go away from sb; to separate people or things: *We exchanged telephone numbers when we parted.* ○ *She parted from her husband several years ago.* ○ *He hates being parted from his children for long.* يفترِق عن، يتفرّق؛ يفرِّق

2 [I,T] to divide or separate: *The curtains parted and a face looked out.* يشقّ، يفصل؛ ينفتح

3 [T] to separate the hair on the head with a comb so as to make a clear line: *Don't part your hair in the middle. It looks awful.* ➲ Look at **parting**. يفرق شَعْره

IDM **part company (with sb/sth)** to go different ways or to separate after being together يفترقان، يمضي كلٌ منهما في حال سبيله

PHR V **part with sth** to give or sell sth to sb else: *When we went to live in Italy, we had to part with our horses and dogs.* يتخلّى عن، يمنح شيئاً أو يبيعه

ˌpart exˈchange *noun* [U] a way of buying sth in which you give a used article as part of the payment for a more expensive one مقايضة شيء قديم بشيء جديد مع دفع فرق الثمن

partial /ˈpɑːʃl/ *adj* **1** not complete: *The outing was only a partial success.* جزئي، محدود

2 partial to sb/sth (*old-fashioned*) liking sth very much: *He's very partial to a cigar after dinner.* مولَع أو مغرم بـ

▸ **partiality** /ˌpɑːʃiˈæləti/ *noun* [U] acting unfairly towards one person or side: *The referee was accused of partiality towards the home team.* ℹ The opposite is **impartiality**. ➲ Look at **impartial**. تحيُّز

partially /ˈpɑːʃəli/ *adv* partly; not completely: *The road was partially blocked by a fallen tree.* جزئياً؛ من بعض الوجوه

participate /pɑːˈtɪsɪpeɪt/ *verb* [I] **participate (in sth)** to share or join (in an activity); to take part: *Students are encouraged to participate in sporting activities.* يشترك، يشارك

▸ **participant** /pɑːˈtɪsɪpənt/ *noun* [C] a person who takes part in an activity, etc. المشترك

participation /pɑːˌtɪsɪˈpeɪʃn/ *noun* [U] مشاركة

participle /pɑːˈtɪsɪpl/ *noun* [C] (*grammar*) a word that is formed from a verb and that ends in *-ing* (*present participle*) or *-ed*, *-en*, etc. (*past participle*). Participles are used to form tenses of the verb, or as adjectives: *'Hurrying' and 'hurried' are the present and past participles of 'hurry'.* اسم الفاعل أو اسم المفعول

particle /ˈpɑːtɪkl/ *noun* [C] **1** a very small piece; a bit: *Particles of the substance were examined under a microscope.* جزيئة، ذرّة

2 (*grammar*) a minor word that is not as important as a noun, verb or adjective: *In the phrasal verb 'break down', 'down' is an adverbial particle.* حرف (جرّ مثلاً)، (في القواعد) أداة

⚿ **particular** /pəˈtɪkjələ(r)/ *adj* **1** (only *before* a noun) (used to make it clear that you are talking about one person, thing, time, etc. and not about others): *At that particular time I was working in London. It wasn't until later that I moved to Bristol.* ○ *One particular school, which I won't name, is having a lot of problems.* (في ذلك الوقت) بالذات؛ معيّن

2 (only *before* a noun) special or extra; more than usual: *Are you going to Dublin for any particular reason?* ○ *This article is of particular interest to you.* خاص؛ استثنائي

3 connected with one person or thing and not with others: *Everybody has their own particular problems.* شخصي، خاص

4 (not before a noun) **particular (about/over sth)** difficult to please: *Some people are extremely particular about the coffee they drink.* ➲ Look at **fussy**. صعب الإرضاء، مدقِّق

IDM **in particular 1** especially: *Is there anything in particular you'd like to do this weekend?* خاص؛ بصورة خاصّة

2 (used for giving more detail about sth that you have said): *You must be careful about what you eat. In particular, avoid anything fatty.* و خاصة، ولاسيّما

▸ **particularly** *adv* especially: *I'm particularly interested in European history.* ○ *The meal was excellent, particularly the dessert.* بصورة خاصّة؛ و خاصّة

particulars *noun* [plural] (*formal*) details; facts: *The police took down all the particulars about the missing child.* تفاصيل

parting /ˈpɑːtɪŋ/ *noun* **1** [C,U] saying goodbye to, or being separated from, another person (usually for quite a long time): *the sadness of parting* فِراق؛ وداع

2 [C] the line on your head where you divide your hair and comb it in different directions: *a side parting* فرق الشَّعْر، مَفرق

partition /pɑːˈtɪʃn/ *noun* **1** [C] something that divides a room, etc. into two parts, especially a thin or temporary wall in a house قاطِع، حاجز، جدار داخليّ مؤقّت

2 [U] the division of a country into two or more countries: *the partition of Germany after the war* تقسيم؛ تجزئة

▸ **partition** *verb* [T] يقسّم؛ يجزّئ

⚿ **partner** /ˈpɑːtnə(r)/ *noun* [C] **1** the person that you are married to or have a sexual relationship with شريك الحياة، زوج أو زوجة؛ مُحبّ

2 a person that you are dancing with or playing a game with شريك في الرقص (مراقص) أو في لعبة

3 one of the people who own a business: *a partner in a private medical practice* ○ *business partners* ○ *a junior/senior partner* شريك (في مشروع تجاريّ)

4 a country or organization that has an agreement with another: *Britain's EU partners* دولة أو منظّمة شريكة

▸ **partner** *verb* [T] to be sb's partner in a dance, game, etc. يراقص؛ يكون شريكاً في لعبة ما

partnership /-ʃɪp/ *noun* **1** [U] the state of being a partner or partners, especially in business: *Mary went into partnership with her sister and opened a toy shop in York.* مشاركة، شركة

2 [C] an arrangement or business with two or more partners: *'Does your husband own the firm?' 'Well, it's a partnership.'* ○ *Their partnership has been extremely successful.* مشروع تجاريّ مشاركة،

ˌpart of ˈspeech *noun* [C] (*grammar*) one of the groups that words are divided into, e.g. noun, verb, adjective, etc.
احد اقسام الكلام مثل الأسم والفعل والصّفة وغير ذلك

partridge /ˈpɑːtrɪdʒ/ *noun* [C] (*pl.* **partridges** or **partridge**) a wild bird hunted for food or sport. Partridges have brown feathers, round bodies and short tails. حَجَل، قَبَج

ˌpart-ˈtime *adj, adv* for only a part of the working day or week: *She's got a part-time job.* ○ *I work part-time, about 20 hours a week.* ➲ Look at **full-time.** (دوام) جزئي؛ (يعمل) جزءاً من اليوم أو الأسبوع

party /ˈpɑːti/ *noun* [C] (*pl.* **parties**) **1** a social occasion to which people are invited in order to eat, drink and enjoy themselves: *to have a party* ○ *to go to a party* ○ *a birthday party* ○ *When they moved into the new house they had a house-warming party.* ○ *a garden party* ○ *a farewell party* ○ *a dinner party* حفلة

2 (*also* **Party**) a group of people who have the same political aims and ideas and who are trying to win elections to parliament, etc: *Which party are you going to vote for in the next election?* ○ *a member of the Labour Party* ○ *the Conservative Party conference* ○ *the party leader* ○ *party policy on defence* ○ *a left-wing/right-wing/centre party* ○ *the party in power* (= in government) حزب

> The two main political parties in Great Britain are the **Conservative** (or **Tory**) Party (right-wing) and the **Labour** Party (left-wing). There is also a centre party called the **Liberal Democrats** and some other smaller parties. In the United States the main political parties are the **Republicans** and the **Democrats**.

3 (often in compounds) a group of people who are working, travelling, etc. together: *A search party has set out to try and find the missing child.* ○ *a party of tourists* فريق، فرقة، جماعة

4 (*formal*) a person or group of people forming one side of a legal agreement or argument: *the guilty party* ➲ Look at **third party.**
طَرَف (في نزاع مثلاً)

pass¹ /pɑːs; *US* pæs/ *noun* [C] **1** the act of kicking, hitting or throwing the ball to sb in your own team in various sports تمرير (الكرة)

2 a successful result in an examination: *Grades A, B and C are passes. D and E are fails.*
درجة النجاح في امتحان

3 an official piece of paper that gives you permission to enter or leave a building, travel on a bus or train, etc: *Visitors to the research centre must obtain a pass from the reception desk.* ○ *to show a pass* ○ *a bus pass*
رخصة مرور: رخصة سفر على حافلة أو قطار وغير ذلك

4 a road or way over or through mountains: *The pass was blocked by heavy falls of snow.*
ممر جبلي

pass² /pɑːs; *US* pæs/ *verb* **1** [I,T] to move forward or to the other side of sb/sth; to leave sth behind or on one side as you go past: *The street was crowded and the two buses couldn't pass.* ○ *They passed a police checkpoint.* ○ *Do we pass a postbox on the way to the station?* ○ (*figurative*) *The number of children at the school has passed 500.* يمُرّ، يمرّ بـ: يتجاوز

> The past tense of **pass** is **passed**. It sounds like **past** which is an adjective or a preposition: *The summer months passed slowly.* ○ *The past week was very hot.* ○ *Our house is just past the church.*

2 [I] **pass along, down, etc. (sth)** to go or move in the direction mentioned: *Which towns do we pass through on the way to Bath?* ○ *You pass over a bridge and then the pub is on the right.* يمرّ، يمرّ من

3 [T] **pass sth (to sb)** to pick sth up and give it to sb; to hand sth: *Could you pass (me) the salt, please?* ○ *He passed the bottle to his father.*
يمرر، يناول

4 [T] **pass sth across, around, through, etc. sth** to put or move sth in the direction mentioned: *We'll have to pass the wire through the window.* يدخل؛ يمرِّر شيئاً عبرَ أو حولَ أو غير ذلك

5 [I,T] **pass (sth) (to sb)** to kick, hit or throw the ball to sb on your own team in various sports يرمي أو يمرِّر الكرة إلى لاعب من فريقه

6 [I] (used about time) to go by: *At least a year has passed since I last saw them.* ○ *The time passed very quickly.* يمرّ، يمضي، ينقضي

7 [T] to spend time: *I'll have to think of something to do to pass the time in hospital.*
يُمضي (الوقت)

8 [I,T] to achieve the necessary standard in an examination, test, etc: *Good luck in the exam! I'm sure you'll pass.* ينجح في امتحان

9 [T] to test sb/sth and say that they are good enough: *The examiner passed most of the candidates.* يُنجِّح في امتحان

10 [T] to officially approve a law, proposal, etc: *One of the functions of Parliament is to pass new laws.* يقِرّ (قانوناً)

11 [T] **pass sth (on sb/sth)** to give an opinion, judgement, etc: *The judge passed sentence on the young man* (= said what his punishment would be). يصدِر (حكماً)

12 [I] to be allowed or accepted: *The headmaster won't let that sort of behaviour pass.* ○ *I didn't like what they were saying but I let it pass without comment.* يسمح به، يقبل

IDM **pass the buck (to sb)** to give the responsibility or the blame for sth to sb else
يضع المسؤوليّة أو اللّوم على الآخرين

pass water (*formal*) to urinate يبول

PHR V **pass away** a way of saying 'die': *The old man passed away in his sleep.*
توفّي، انتقل إلى رحمته تعالى

pass by (sb/sth) to go past: *I pass by your house on the way to work.* يمرّ بـ، يمرّ من أمام

pass sth down to give sth (to people who live after you have died): *The family home has been passed down from one generation to the next.*
يتوارث

pass sb/sth off (as sb/sth) to say that a person or a thing is sb/sth that he/she/it is not: *He* *managed to pass the work off as his own.* ينتحل، يدّعي؛ يخدع

pass sth on (to sb) to give sth (to sb else) especially after you have been given it or used it yourself: *Could you pass the message on to Mr Roberts?* يناول، يمرر (رسالة إلى شخص آخر)

pass out to become unconscious; to faint يُغمى عليه

passable /ˈpɑːsəbl; US ˈpæs-/ *adj* **1** good enough but not very good: *My French is not brilliant but it's passable.* لا بأس به، وسَط

2 (not before a noun) (used about roads, rivers, etc.) possible to use or cross; not completely blocked ❶ The opposite is **impassable**. يمكن عبوره، سالك

⚷**passage** /ˈpæsɪdʒ/ *noun* **1** [C] (*also* **ˈpassageway** /ˈpæsɪdʒweɪ/) a long, narrow way through sth, especially one in a building that leads to other rooms; a corridor: *We had to go down a dark passage to reach the bathroom.* ممَر، دهليز

2 [C] a tube in your body which, air, liquid, etc. can pass through: *the nasal passages* قناة

3 [C] a short part of a book, a speech or a piece of music: *The students were given a passage from the novel to study in detail.* مقطع، نص

4 [U] the movement or progress of sb/sth from one place or stage to another: *We watched the ants' slow passage across the road.* عبور، اجتياز

5 [C] a route by sea or a journey by ship: *You are advised to book your passage well in advance.* رحلة بحرية

6 [U] (used about time) the passing: *With the passage of time these rocks will be broken into stones.* مرور (الزمن)

⚷**passenger** /ˈpæsɪndʒə(r)/ *noun* [C] a person who is travelling in a car, bus, train, plane, etc. but who is not driving it or working on it: *Passengers are asked to remain seated until the plane has come to a complete standstill.* ○ *the passenger seat of a car* راكِب، مسافر

passer-by /ˌpɑːsə ˈbaɪ; US ˌpæsər-/ *noun* [C] (*pl.* **passers-by**) a person who is walking past sb/sth (by chance): *None of the passers-by had seen how the accident happened.* أحد المارّة، عابر سبيل

⚷**passing** /ˈpɑːsɪŋ; US ˈpæs-/ *adj* lasting for only a short time; brief: *No, I wasn't serious about going to Italy. It was only a passing thought.* (فكرة) عابرة؛ زائل

▸ **passing** *noun* [U] the process of going by: *the passing of time* مرور (الزمن)

IDM **in passing** done or said quickly, while you are thinking or talking about sth else: *He mentioned the house in passing but he didn't give any details.* بشكلٍ عابر، عَرَضاً، في سياق الكلام

passion /ˈpæʃn/ *noun* **1** [U] very strong sexual love or attraction: *They loved each other but there was no passion in their relationship.* غرام عنيف، حب ملتهب

2 [C,U] (a) very strong feeling, especially of love, hate or anger: *She argued her case with passion.* عاطفة جامحة؛ انفعال قوي

3 [sing.] **a passion for sth** a very strong liking for or interest in sth: *He has a passion for history.* ولَع، شَغَف

passionate /ˈpæʃənət/ *adj* showing or caused by very strong, sometimes sexual feelings: *a passionate believer in democracy* ○ *a passionate speech* ○ *a passionate relationship* ○ *a passionate kiss* شديد الحماس؛ انفعاليّ؛ مشبوب العاطفة، (قبلة) ملتهبة

▸ **passionately** *adv* بعاطفة ملتهِبة؛ بحماسٍ شديد؛ بشدّة

passive /ˈpæsɪv/ *adj* **1** showing no reaction, feeling or interest; not active: *Television encourages people to be passive.* ○ *passive smoking* (= breathing in smoke from other people's cigarettes) سلبيّ؛ هامد، مستكين

2 (used about the form of a verb or a sentence when the subject of the sentence is affected by the action of the verb): *In the sentence 'He was bitten by a dog', the verb is passive.* ❶ You can also say: 'The verb is in the passive'. Look at **active**. مبنيّ للمجهول

▸ **passively** *adv* دون مشاركة فعّالة؛ في صيغة المجهول

⚷**passport** /ˈpɑːspɔːt; US ˈpæs-/ *noun* [C] **1** an official document that identifies you and that you have to show when you enter or leave a country: *Do you have to show your passport at the check-in desk?* جواز سفر

> You **apply for** or **renew** your passport at the **passport office**. This office **issues** new passports.

2 **a passport to sth** a thing that makes it possible to achieve sth: *a passport to success* سبيل؛ وسيلة مضمونة

password /ˈpɑːswɜːd; US ˈpæs-/ *noun* [C] **1** a secret word or phrase that you need to know in order to be allowed into a place كلمة السرّ

2 a secret word that you must type in order to use a computer system: *Please enter your password.* كلمة السر (في الكمبيوتر)

⚷**past**[1] /pɑːst; US pæst/ *adj* **1** already gone; belonging to a time before the present: *in past years, centuries, etc.* ○ *I'd rather forget some of my past mistakes.* ماضي، فائت، سابق

2 (only *before* a noun) just finished; last: *He's had to work very hard during the past year.* ○ *The past few weeks have been very difficult.* فائت، ماضي، أخير

3 (not before a noun) over; finished; no longer existing: *Suddenly his childhood was past and he was a young man.* منقضٍ، منتهٍ، لا وجودَ له

▸ **past** *noun* **1** **the past** [sing.] the time before the present; the things that happened in that time: *The story was set in the distant past.* ○ *We spent the evening talking about the past.* الماضي، الزمن الماضي

2 [C] a person's life before now: *May I ask you a few questions about your past?* ○ *I think his past has been rather unhappy.* ماضي المرء

3 [sing.] (*also* **past tense**) a form of a verb used to describe actions in the past: *The past tense of the verb 'come' is 'came'.* صيغة الماضي

⚷**past**[2] /pɑːst; US pæst/ *prep* **1** (used when telling

the time) after; later than: *It's ten (minutes) past three.* ○ *It's a quarter past seven.*
بعدَ (السابعة) و(الربْع)

2 older than: *She's past 40.* فوقَ، تَجاوز (الأربعين)

3 from one side to the other of sb/sth; further than or on the other side of sb/sth: *He walked straight past me.* ○ *Go past the pub and our house is the second on the right.* ○ *The phone box is just past the village shop.* بعدَ، متجاوزاً

4 beyond the limits or age when you can do sth: *I'm so tired that I'm past caring what we eat.* ○ *She was past the age when she could have children.* متجاوز؛ ما وراء

IDM **not put it past sb (to do sth)** → PUT

past it (*informal*) too old: *I don't think I'll go skiing this year. I'm afraid I'm past it.*
يصبح كبيراً في السن؛ ينقضي زمانه

▸ **past** *adv* by; from one side of sb/sth to another: *The bus went straight past without stopping.* ○ *He waved as he drove past.*
ماراً من أمامنا

pasta /ˈpæstə; *US* ˈpɑːstə/ *noun* [U] a type of food made from a mixture of flour, eggs and water which is cut into various shapes and cooked: *Macaroni is a type of pasta.*
عجينه تصنع منها المعكرونة وما يشبهها

paste¹ /peɪst/ *noun* **1** [C,U] a soft, wet mixture, usually made of a powder and a liquid and sometimes used for sticking things: *wallpaper paste* ○ *Mix the flour and milk into a paste.*
معجون، عجينة؛ معجونة نَشويّة لاصقة، لِزاق

2 [U] (usually in compounds) a soft mixture of food that you can spread onto bread, etc: *fish paste* ○ *chicken paste* طعام وخاصّة لحم مهروس

paste² /peɪst/ *verb* [T] to stick sth to sth else using glue or paste: *He pasted the picture into his book.* يلْصِق، يلزق

pastel /ˈpæstl; *US* pæˈstel/ *adj* (used about colours) pale; not strong (لون) فاتح، خفيف

pasteurized (*also* **pasteurised**) /ˈpɑːstʃəraɪzd; *US* ˈpæs-/ *adj* (used about milk or cream) free from bacteria because it has been heated
(حليب) معقّم، "مُبَستَر"

pastime /ˈpɑːstaɪm; *US* ˈpæs-/ *noun* [C] something that you enjoy doing when you are not working: *What are your favourite pastimes?* ➲ Look at **hobby**. تسلية، هواية لتمضية الوقت

pastoral /ˈpɑːstərəl; *US* ˈpæs-/ *adj* **1** giving advice on personal rather than religious or educational matters: *Each child will have a tutor who is responsible for pastoral care.* (أمور) شخصيّة أو خاصّة

2 connected with the countryside and country life ريفي؛ رَعوي

ˌpast ˈparticiple *noun* [C] the form of a verb that in English ends in -ed, -en, etc. and is used with the verb *have* to form perfect tenses such as *I have eaten* or with the verb *be* to form passive sentences اسم المفعول

ˌpast ˈperfect (*also* **pluperfect**) *noun* [sing.] (*grammar*) the tense of a verb that describes an action that was finished before another event happened: *In the sentence 'After they had finished the meal, they went for a walk', 'had finished' is in the past perfect.* صيغة الماضي التامّ أو الماضي البعيد

pastry /ˈpeɪstri/ *noun* (*pl.* **pastries**) **1** [U] a mixture of flour, fat and water that is used for making pies, etc. and is baked in an oven عجينة الفطائر

2 [C] a small cake made with pastry: *Danish pastries* فطيرة (من المعجّنات)؛ قطعة حلوى من المعجّنات

ˌpast ˈtense *noun* [C] → PAST¹ (3)

pasture /ˈpɑːstʃə(r); *US* ˈpæs-/ *noun* [C,U] a field or land covered with grass, where cattle can feed مرعى، مَرْج

pasty /ˈpæsti/ *noun* [C] (*pl.* **pasties**) a small pie containing meat and/or vegetables: *Cornish pasties* فطيرة صغيرة محشوّة باللحم وغيره

pat¹ /pæt/ *verb* [T] (pa**tt**ing; pa**tt**ed) to hit sb/sth very gently with a flat hand or with sth flat: *'Good dog,' she said, patting him.*
يربت على، يطبطب على

▸ **pat** *noun* [C] a gentle tap with a flat hand or with sth flat: *'Well done,' said the teacher, giving the child a pat on the head.* ربتة، طبطبة خفيفة

IDM **a pat on the back** congratulations for sth good that a person has done تهنئة، ربتة استحسان

pat² /pæt/ *adv* at once; without hesitation: *The answer came back pat.* فوراً، دون تردّد، جاهزاً

▸ **pat** *adj* (only *before* a noun) too quick (used about an answer, comment, etc.)
جاهز، مهيّأ مُسبقاً، على رأس لسانه

patch¹ /pætʃ/ *noun* [C] **1** a piece of material that you use to mend a hole in clothes, etc: *an old pair of jeans with patches on both knees* ○ *to sew a patch on* رقعة

2 a small piece of material that you wear over one eye: *an eye patch* رقعة صغيرة تغطّي العين لوقايتها

3 a patch (of sth) a part of a surface that is different in some way from the area around it: *Drive carefully. There are patches of ice on the roads.* ○ *a damp patch on the ceiling* بقعة، رقعة

4 a small piece of land: *a vegetable patch*
رقعة من الأرض

IDM **a bad patch** a difficult or unhappy period of time فترة عصيبة؛ فترة غير سعيدة

not a patch on sb/sth (*informal*) not nearly as good as sb/sth: *The new singer isn't a patch on the old one.* لا مجال للمقارنة بينهما، أدنى منه بكثير

patch² /pætʃ/ *verb* [T] to put a piece of material over a hole in clothes, etc. or to mend sth by doing this: *to patch a hole in sth* ○ *to patch an old pair of trousers* يرقع

PHR V **patch sth up 1** to mend sth quickly or not very carefully: *The car had been patched up after an accident.* يصلح شيئاً على عجل؛ يصلح كيفما اتّفق

2 to settle a quarrel: *It's time the boys patched up their differences.* يسوّي خلافاً، يتصالح مع

patchwork /ˈpætʃwɜːk/ *noun* **1** [U] a type of sewing in which small pieces of cloth of different colours and patterns are sewn together
رقع من القماش مختلفة الألوان تخاط مع بعضها

2 [sing.] a thing that is made of many different

pieces or parts: *a patchwork of fields*
شيء مؤلف من رقع مختلفة

patchy /'pætʃi/ *adj* (**patchier**; **patchiest**) **1** not all the same or not complete: *His work is patchy* (= some, but not all, of it is good). ○ *I've only got some rather patchy* (= not complete) *information on the subject.*
متفاوت في الجودة؛ (معلومات) متناثرة غير كاملة

2 in small quantities, not everywhere: *patchy fog*
موزّع هنا وهناك، متفرّق

pâté /'pæteɪ; *US* pɑː'teɪ/ *noun* [U] food that is made by mixing up meat, fish or vegetables into a smooth, thick form that you can spread on bread, etc: *liver pâté*
هريسة أو عجين من اللحم أو السمك وغيره، "باتيه"

patent[1] /'peɪtnt; *US* 'pætnt/ *adj* (*formal*) clear; obvious: *a patent lie* واضح، ظاهر، صريح

▸ **patently** *adv* clearly: *She was patently very upset.* ○ *He was patently honest.* بصورة واضحة

patent[2] /'pætnt; 'peɪtnt; *US* 'pætnt/ *noun* [C] an official licence from the government that gives one person or company the right to make or sell a certain product and prevents others from copying it: *a patent on a new invention* براءة اختراع

▸ **patent** *verb* [T] to obtain a patent[2] for sth
يسجّل اختراعاً

patent leather /,peɪtnt 'leðə(r); *US* 'pæt-/ *noun* [U] a type of leather with a hard, shiny surface
جلد لمّاع

paternal /pə'tɜːnl/ *adj* (only *before* a noun) **1** of a father: *the importance of paternal interest and support*
أبوي

2 related through the father's side of the family: *my paternal grandparents* ➲ Look at **maternal**.
قريب من ناحية الأب

paternity /pə'tɜːnəti/ *noun* [U] the state of being a father
أبوّة

path /pɑːθ; *US* pæθ/ *noun* [C] (*pl.* **paths** /pɑːðz; *US* pæðz/) **1** a way across a piece of land that is made by or used by people walking: *The path follows the coastline for several hundred miles.* ○ *the garden path* ○ *Keep to the path or you may get lost.* ○ *Where does this path lead?* ○ (*figurative*) *We're on the path to victory!* ❶ **Pathway** is similar in meaning: *There was a narrow pathway leading down the cliff.* ➲ Look at **footpath**.
طريق، درب، ممرّ، سبيل

2 the line along which sb/sth moves: *the flight path of an aeroplane* ○ *The locusts moved across the country eating everything in their path.*
طريق، ممرّ (جوي)

pathetic /pə'θetɪk/ *adj* **1** causing you to feel pity or sadness: *the pathetic cries of the hungry children* مثير للشفقة، محزن، مؤلم

2 (*informal*) very bad, weak or useless: *What a pathetic performance! The team deserved to lose.* رديء جداً، يرثى له

▸ **pathetically** /-kli/ *adv*
باستعطاف؛ بشكل يرثى له، للغاية

pathological /,pæθə'lɒdʒɪkl/ *adj* **1** connected with pathology مَرَضي

2 (*informal*) caused by feelings that you cannot control; not reasonable: *He's a pathological liar.* ○ *a pathological fear of water*
مرضيّ؛ غير إرادي؛ غير معقول

▸ **pathologically** /-kli/ *adv*
إلى درجة مرضيّة؛ بشكل غير معقول، دون منطق

pathology /pə'θɒlədʒi/ *noun* [U] the scientific study of the diseases of the body علم الأمراض

▸ **pathologist** /pə'θɒlədʒɪst/ *noun* [C] a person who is an expert in pathology, especially one who tries to find out why a person has died
أخصائي في علم الأمراض؛ أخصائيّ في معرفة سبب الوفاة

patience /'peɪʃns/ *noun* [U] **1** **patience (with sb/sth)** the quality of being able to remain calm and not get angry, especially when there is a difficulty or you have to wait a long time: *I'm sorry – I've got no patience with people who don't even try.* ○ *to lose patience with sb* ○ *After three hours of delay our patience was wearing thin.* ❶ The opposite is **impatience**. صبر

2 (*US* **solitaire**) a card game for one player
لعبة ورق (أو كوتشينة) لفرد واحد

patient[1] /'peɪʃnt/ *adj* able to remain calm and not get angry, especially when there is a difficulty or you are waiting for sth: *It's hard to be patient with a screaming child.* ○ *It won't be long now. Just sit there and be patient.* ❶ The opposite is **impatient**. صبور، طويل الأناة

▸ **patiently** *adv*: *to wait patiently* بصبر

patient[2] /'peɪʃnt/ *noun* [C] a person who is receiving medical treatment: *a hospital patient* ○ *a specialist who treats patients with heart problems* ○ *a private patient* (= one who pays for his/her treatment)
مريض

patio /'pætiəʊ/ *noun* [C] (*pl.* **patios** /-əʊz/) an area next to a house where people can sit, eat, etc. outdoors ➲ Look at **veranda** and **terrace**.
باحة صغيرة مرصوفة ملاصقة للبيت

patriot /'pætriət; *US* 'peɪt-/ *noun* [C] a person who loves his/her country
شخص وطنيّ، فرد محبّ لوطنه

▸ **patriotism** /-ɪzəm/ *noun* [U] love of your country الوطنيّة، محبّة الوطن

patriotic /,pætri'ɒtɪk; *US* ,peɪt-/ *adj* having or showing a love for your country
وطنيّ، متحمّس للوطن

▸ **patriotically** /-kli/ *adv* بوطنيّة، بحماس لوطنه

patrol /pə'trəʊl/ *verb* [I,T] (**patrolling**; **patrolled**) to go round a town, building, etc. to make sure that there is no trouble and that nothing is wrong: *Guards patrol the grounds at regular intervals.* يحرس، يتفقّد، يقوم بدوريّة حراسة

▸ **patrol** *noun* [C] **1** the act of patrolling: *The army makes hourly patrols of the area.*
حراسة، خَفَر، عمل الدوريّة

2 a person or group of people that patrols sth: *a police patrol* دوريّة

IDM **on patrol** patrolling sth في دوريّة حراسة

patron /'peɪtrən/ *noun* [C] **1** a person who gives money to artists, musicians, etc. or who supports a good cause: *a patron of the arts* ○ *The princess is* *a patron of the 'Save the Children' fund.* الراعي للفنون والآداب ونحوها

2 a person who goes to a shop, theatre, restaurant, etc: *This car park is for patrons only.* زبون، عميل

patronize (*also* **patronise**) /ˈpætrənaɪz; *US* ˈpeɪt-/ *verb* [T] **1** to treat sb in a friendly way but as if you were better than him/her يُعامل بشيء من الاستعلاء، يتكرّم أو يتعطّف على

2 to go to a shop, theatre, restaurant, etc. (زبون) يعامل أو يتردّد على محلّ تجاريّ مثلاً

▸ **patronizing** (*also* **patronising**) *adj* treating sb in a friendly way but as if you were better than him/her: *I really hate that patronizing smile of hers.* لطيف لكن مع شيء من التعالي، متكرِّم أو متعطِّف

patronizingly (*also* **patronisingly**) *adv* بشيء من التعطف أو التكرّم

ˌ**patron** ˈ**saint** *noun* [C] a saint who is believed to give help and protection to a particular place or to people doing a particular activity: *St David is the patron saint of Wales.* القديس الحامي أو الراعي، الشفيع

patter /ˈpætə(r)/ *noun* [sing.] the sound of many quick light steps or knocks on sth: *the patter of the children's feet on the stairs* وقع أقدام خفيف؛ طرقات خفيفة

▸ **patter** *verb* [I]: *The rain pattered on the windowpane.* يقرع قرعات خفيفة

🔑 **pattern** /ˈpætn/ *noun* [C] **1** an arrangement of lines, shapes, colours, etc. Patterns are often used to decorate clothes, wallpapers, carpets, etc: *china with a flower pattern on it* ○ *a geometrical pattern* أشكال مرسومة، زخرف، رسُوم

2 the way in which sth happens, develops, is arranged, etc: *Her periods of mental illness all followed the same pattern.* ○ *patterns of behaviour* ○ *The second half of the match followed a similar pattern to the first.* طراز، منوال، أسلوب

3 something that helps you to make sth, e.g. a piece of clothing, by showing the shape it should be: *a paper pattern* "بَتْرون": نموذج لتفصيل الملابس مثلاً

▸ **patterned** *adj* having a pattern (1): *patterned curtains* ذو رسوم، ذو زخارف

🔑 **pause** /pɔːz/ *noun* [C] a short stop in sth: *He continued playing for twenty minutes without a pause.* ○ *a pause in the conversation* ➲ Look at the note at **interval**. توقّف قصير

▸ **pause** *verb* [I] **pause (for sth)** to stop for a short time: *to pause for breath* يتوقف برهة؛ يتأنّى

pave /peɪv/ *verb* [T] (often passive) to cover an area of ground with flat stones يرصف، يبلّط

pavement /ˈpeɪvmənt/ *noun* [C] (*US* **sidewalk**) the path at the side of the road that is for people to walk on: *Children should ride on the pavement, not on the road.* رصيف الشارع

pavilion /pəˈvɪliən/ *noun* [C] (*Brit*) a building at a sports ground where players can change their clothes مبنى في ملعب خاصّ بالرياضيين لتبديل ملابسهم

ˈ**paving stone** *noun* [C] a flat piece of stone that is used for covering the ground بلاطة، حجر رصف

paw /pɔː/ *noun* [C] the foot of animals such as dogs, cats, bears, etc. ➲ Look at **hoof**. ❶ Paws have sharp **claws** and soft **pads** underneath. كفّ الحيوان ذي المخالب

▸ **paw** *verb* [I,T] **paw (at) sth** (used about an animal) to touch sb/sth with a paw or foot (كلب مثلاً) يلمس بكفّه

pawn[1] /pɔːn/ *noun* [C] **1** one of the eight pieces in the game of chess that are of least value and importance (في لعبة الشطرنج) بيدق

2 a person who is used or controlled by another person رهينة أو ألعوبة (في يده)

pawn[2] /pɔːn/ *verb* [T] to give sth of value to a pawnbroker in return for money. If you cannot pay back the money after a certain period, the pawnbroker can keep or sell the thing that you gave him/her. يرهن (حلية مثلاً)

pawnbroker /ˈpɔːnbrəʊkə(r)/ *noun* [C] a person who lends money to people when they leave sth of value with him/her سمسار الرهونات، مرتهِن

pawpaw /ˈpɔːpɔː/ (*Brit*) = PAPAYA

🔑 **pay**[1] /peɪ/ *noun* [U] money that you get regularly for work that you have done: *It's a dirty job but the pay is good.* ○ *a pay increase* راتب، أجر

> **Pay** is the general word for money that you get regularly for work that you have done. **Wages** are paid weekly or daily in cash. A **salary** is paid monthly, directly into a bank account. You pay a **fee** for professional services, e.g. to a doctor, lawyer, etc. **Payment** is money that you get for work that you do once or not regularly.

🔑 **pay**[2] /peɪ/ *verb* (*pt, pp* **paid**) **1** [I,T] **pay (sb) (for sth)**; **pay sth (to sb) (for sth)** to give sb money for sth: *She is very well paid.* ○ *Do you want to pay by cheque or by credit card?* ○ *The work's finished but we haven't paid the builders yet.* ○ *to be paid by the hour* ○ *We paid the dealer £3 000 for the car.* يدفع

2 [T] **pay sth (to sb)** to give the money that you owe for sth: *Have you paid the gas bill?* يدفع، يسدّد الحساب

3 [I,T] to make a profit; to be worth doing: *The factory closed down because the owners couldn't make it pay.* ○ *It would pay you to get professional advice before making a decision.* يُفيد، يعود عليه بالنفع؛ يعطي ربحاً

IDM **pay attention (to sb/sth)** to listen carefully to or to take notice of sb/sth يُصغي إلى، يركّز انتباهه على

pay sb a compliment; **pay a compliment to sb** to say that you like sth about sb; to praise sb يلاطف، يجامل؛ يمدح

pay your respects (to sb) (*formal*) to visit sb as a sign of respect يزور شخصاً احتراماً له، يقدّم تحيّاته واحترامه

pay tribute to sb/sth to praise and show your respect for sb/sth يشيد بذكره، يثني على (جهوده)

put paid to sth to destroy or finish sth: *The bad weather put paid to our idea of a picnic.* يدمِّر، يُتلِف، يضع حداً لـ

PHRV **pay sb back sth**; **pay sth back** to give money back to sb that you borrowed from him/

her: *Can you lend me £5? I'll pay you back/I'll pay it back to you on Friday.* يوفي أو يسدّد الدَّين
pay sb back (for sth) to do sth unpleasant to sb who did sth unpleasant to you: *What a mean trick! I'll pay you back one day.* يأخذ بثأره من، يردّ له الصاع صاعين
pay off (*informal*) to be successful: *All their hard work has paid off! The house is finished at last.* يثمر، يعطي نتيجة حسنة؛ يربح
pay sth off to pay all the money that you owe for sth: *to pay off a debt* يسدّد دينَه كاملا
pay up (*informal*) to pay the money that you owe: *If you don't pay up, we'll take you to court.* يسدّد الدَّين

▸ **payable** /ˈpeɪəbl/ *adj* that should or must be paid: *This bill is payable immediately.* ○ *Make the cheque payable to Diane Weller.* واجبٌ دفعه؛ (شيك) مدفوع إلى حساب فلان

payee /ˌpeɪˈiː/ *noun* [C] a person that you must pay money to مستلم المبلغ، الشخص المدفوع له

payment /ˈpeɪmənt/ *noun* **payment (for sth)** **1** [U] paying or being paid: *You get a 5% discount for prompt payment.* ○ *payment of a bill* ○ *I did the work last month but I haven't had any payment yet.* ➲ Look at the note at **pay**[1]. دَفْع؛ دفع الثَّمن؛ أجْر
2 [C] an amount of money that you must pay: *They asked for a payment of £100 as a deposit.* دفعة، مبلغ

PC /ˌpiː ˈsiː/ *abbrev* **1** personal computer اختصار "كمبيوتر شخصي"
2 politically correct: *He offended her with his non-PC language.* (تعبير) مراعٍ للآراء التقدميّة
3 (*pl.* **PCs**) (*Brit*) police constable شُرطي

PDA /ˌpiː diː ˈeɪ/ *noun* [C] a very small computer that is used for storing personal information and creating documents, and that may include other functions such as telephone, fax, connection to the Internet, etc. (abbreviation for 'personal digital assistant') كمبيوتر شخصي صغير

PE /ˌpiː ˈiː/ *abbrev* physical education: *a PE lesson* التربية البدنية

pea /piː/ *noun* [C] a small round green seed that is eaten as a vegetable. A number of peas grow together in a pod. حبّة بازلاء أو بسلّة

peace /piːs/ *noun* [U] **1** the state of not being at war or of not having fighting, disorder, etc: *forty years of peace in Europe* ○ *a peace treaty* ○ *Peace has returned to the streets of Los Angeles.* سلام، سِلْم؛ أمْن؛ هدوء
2 the state of being calm or quiet: *He longed to escape from the city to the peace of the countryside.* ○ *I'm tired – can't you just leave me in peace?* ○ *The noise of lawnmowers disturbed the peace of the afternoon.* هدوء، سكينة

peaceful /ˈpiːsfl/ *adj* **1** not wanting or involving war, fighting or disorder: *a peaceful demonstration* ○ *Nuclear power can be used for peaceful or military purposes.* ○ *a peaceful solution to the conflict* مسالم، سِلْمي
2 calm and quiet: *a peaceful village* هادئ، وادع، مُسْتكِنّ

▸ **peacefully** /-fəli/ *adv* بسلام، دون عنف
peacefulness *noun* [U] هدوء، سكينة

peacetime /ˈpiːstaɪm/ *noun* [U] a period when a country is not at war فترة سِلْم

peach /piːtʃ/ *noun* [C] a soft round fruit with orange-red skin. A peach is soft inside and has a large stone in its centre: *tinned peaches* درّاق (سوريا)، خوخ (مصر)

peacock /ˈpiːkɒk/ *noun* [C] a large bird with beautiful long blue and green tail feathers that it can lift up and spread out like a fan طاووس

peak[1] /piːk/ *noun* [C] **1** the pointed top of a mountain: *snow-covered peaks in the distance* قمة، ذروة
2 the pointed front part of a hat that is above your eyes رفرف القبّعة الأماميّ
3 the highest level, value, rate, etc: *In the early evening demand for electricity is at its peak.* ○ *a man at the peak of his career* ○ *Summer is the peak period for most hotels.* ➲ Look at **off-peak**. أوج، قمّة، ذروة

peak[2] /piːk/ *verb* [I] to reach the highest level, value, rate, etc: *Sales usually peak just before Christmas.* يبلغ الذروة، يصل إلى أعلى نقطة

peal /piːl/ *noun* [C] the loud ringing of a bell or of a set of bells that all have different notes: (*figurative*) *peals of laughter* جلجلة الأجراس

peanut /ˈpiːnʌt/ (*also* **groundnut**) *noun* **1** [C] a nut that grows in a shell under the ground: *roasted and salted peanuts* إحدى حبّات الفستق السوداني
2 peanuts [plural] (*informal*) a very small amount of money مبلغ ضئيل

pear /peə(r)/ *noun* [C] a fruit that has a yellow or green skin and is white inside. Pears are thinner at the top (i.e. where they join onto the tree) than at the bottom. كمّثرى أو أجاص

pearl /pɜːl/ *noun* [C] a small, hard, round, white object that grows inside the shell of an oyster (a type of shellfish). Pearls are used to make jewellery: *a pearl necklace* لؤلؤة

peasant /ˈpeznt/ *noun* [C] (used especially in past times) a person who owns or rents a small piece of land on which he/she grows food and keeps animals in order to feed his/her family ❶ **Peasant** is considered offensive nowadays. فلّاح

peat /piːt/ *noun* [U] a natural substance that is made of decayed plants. Peat is formed underground in cool, wet places. It can be burnt as a fuel or put on the garden to make plants grow better. خُثّ، دندن

pebble /ˈpebl/ *noun* [C] a smooth round stone that is found in or near water حصاة

pecan /ˈpiːkən; prˈkæn; *US* prˈkɑːn/ *noun* [C] a type of nut that we eat باكانية

peck /pek/ *verb* [I,T] **peck (at sth)** (used about a bird) to eat or bite sth with the beak: *The sparrows were pecking around for food.* ○ *Don't touch the bird – it might peck you.* ينقر

a b c d e f g h i j k l m n o p q r s t u v w x y z

▸ **peck** *noun* [C] (*figurative*) *She gave him a quick peck* (= kiss) *on the cheek and then left.* قبلة سريعة

peckish /'pekɪʃ/ *adj* (*informal*) hungry جوعان

peculiar /pɪ'kjuːliə(r)/ *adj* **1** odd or strange: *'Moira left without saying goodbye.' 'How peculiar!'* ○ *There's a very peculiar smell in here.* غريب

2 only belonging to a particular person or found in a particular place: *a fruit peculiar to South East Asia* خاص بِ

▸ **peculiarity** /pɪˌkjuːli'ærəti/ *noun* (*pl.* **peculiarities**) **1** [U] the quality of being strange or odd غرابة

2 [C] something that is strange or odd: *One of his peculiarities is that he never wears socks.* صفة غريبة، صفة غير معتادة

3 [C] sth that only belongs to or is only found in sb/sth صفة مميِّزة لِ، صفة خاصّة بِ

peculiarly *adv* **1** in a peculiar (1) way: *Luke is behaving very peculiarly.* بصورة غريبة

2 especially; very: *The noise of chalk on a blackboard can be peculiarly annoying.* بشكل خاص؛ جداً

3 in a way that is especially typical of sb/sth: *They demonstrated the peculiarly English refusal to take anything seriously.* بشكل مميِّز لِ

pedagogical /ˌpedə'gɒdʒɪkl/ *adj* connected with ways and methods of teaching ذو علاقة بطرق التعليم، تعليمي

pedal /'pedl/ *noun* [C] the part of a bicycle or other machine that you push with your foot in order to make it move or work دوّاسة (الدرّاجة)

▸ **pedal** *verb* [I,T] (pedalling; pedalled; *US* pedaling; pedaled) to push the pedals of a bicycle: *She had to pedal hard to get up the hill.* يحرّك الدوّاسات، يسيِّر الدراجة

pedantic /pɪ'dæntɪk/ *adj* too worried about rules or small details متمسِّك بحرفية القوانين والتفاصيل (دون الروح)؛ متنطِّع

▸ **pedantically** /-kli/ *adv* بتزمُّت، متمسِّكاً بحرفية القانون

pedestal /'pedɪstl/ *noun* [C] the base on which a column, statue, etc. stands قاعدة العمود أو التمثال

pedestrian /pə'destriən/ *noun* [C] a person who is walking in the street (not travelling in a vehicle): *a subway for pedestrians to cross the busy junction* ➲ Look at **motorist**. السائر على قدميه، الماشي

▸ **pedestrian** *adj* **1** of or for pedestrians: *a pedestrian bridge* خاص بالمشاة

2 ordinary; not interesting; dull عاديّ؛ غير شيِّق

peˌdestrian 'crossing (*US* **crosswalk**) *noun* [C] a place for pedestrians to cross the road ➲ Look at **zebra crossing**. طريق أو معبر للمشاة

peˌdestrian 'precinct *noun* [C] a part of a town where there are many shops and where cars are not allowed ساحة تجاريّة لا يسمح فيها بالسيّارات

pedigree /'pedɪgriː/ *noun* [C] **1** the parents, grandparents and other previous family members of an animal. The names of the ancestors are recorded on a document which is also called a 'pedigree'. أصل أو نسب الحيوان

2 a person's background سلالة؛ بيئة الشخص

▸ **pedigree** *adj* of high quality because the parents, grandparents, etc. are all of the same breed and specially chosen أصيل

pee /piː/ *verb* [I] (*informal*) to send out waste water from your body; urinate يبول

▸ **pee** *noun* [sing.] (*informal*) *I'm going to have a pee.* تبويل؛ بَوْل

peek /piːk/ *verb* [I] (*informal*) **peek (at sth)** to look at sth quickly or secretly: *No peeking at the presents before your birthday.* يختلس أو يسترق النظر

▸ **peek** *noun* [sing.]: *I had a quick peek at the answers.* نظرة مختلسة؛ نظرة خاطفة

peel /piːl/ *verb* **1** [T] to take the skin off a fruit or vegetable: *Could you peel the potatoes, please?* يُقشّر

2 [I] to come off in one piece or in small pieces: *Soak the envelope in water and the stamp will peel off easily.* ○ *My nose got sunburnt and now it is peeling* (= the skin is coming off). ○ *The paint is starting to peel off.* ينقشر؛ ينقشر ويتناثر

▸ **peel** *noun* [U] the skin of a fruit or vegetable: *lemon peel* ➲ Look at **rind**. قشرة

peeler /'piːlə(r)/ *noun* [C] (especially in compounds) a device for peeling fruit, vegetables, etc: *a potato peeler* مقشّرة

peep[1] /piːp/ *verb* [I] **1** **peep (at sth)** to look at sth quickly and secretly: *to peep through a keyhole* يختلس النظر (من ثقب المفتاح مثلاً)

2 (used about part of sth) to appear: *The moon is peeping out from behind the clouds.* يلوح، يظهر جزء منه

▸ **peep** *noun* [sing.] a quick or secret look: *Have a peep in the bedroom and see if the baby is asleep.* نظرة سريعة؛ نظرة مختلسة

peep[2] /piːp/ *noun* **1** [sing.] the weak high sound that is made, for example, by a young bird: *There hasn't been a peep out of the children for hours.* زقزقة خافتة، صيء؛ صوت خافت

2 [C] **peep 'peep** the sound that a car's horn makes صوت بوق السيّارة

▸ **peep** *verb* [I] يصيء؛ يصدر صوتاً خافتاً، يزمّر

peer[1] /pɪə(r)/ *noun* [C] **1** a person who is of the same age or rank: *Peer pressure is a great influence on the way people behave.* ندّ

2 (*Brit*) (*feminine* **peeress** /'pɪəres/) a person of noble rank نبيل بريطاني، لورد

▸ **peerage** /'pɪərɪdʒ/ *noun* **1** [with sing. or pl. verb] all the peers (2) in a country مجموعة الأشراف والنبلاء؛ اللوردات

2 [C] the rank of a peer: *a hereditary peerage* رتبة اللورد، رتبة النبيل

peer[2] /pɪə(r)/ *verb* [I] **peer (at sb/sth)** to look closely or carefully at sb/sth, e.g. because you cannot see very well: *I peered outside but it was too dark to see much.* ○ *I had to peer very hard at the handwriting to make out what it said.* يحدّق، ينظر مليّاً

'peer group *noun* [C] a group of people who are of the same age and rank
مجموعة أنداد أي أفراد من نفس العمر والمنزلة

peeved /pi:vd/ *adj* (*informal*) rather angry; annoyed غاضب؛ متضايق، منزعج

peevish /'pi:vɪʃ/ *adj* easily annoyed by things that are not important
ضيق الخلق، سريع الغضب (حتى من التوافه)

▸ **peevishly** *adv* بضيق

peg¹ /peg/ *noun* [C] **1** a piece of wood, metal, etc. on a wall or door that you hang your coat, etc. on: *Your coat is hanging on the peg in the hall.*
مِشجب، علاقة

2 (*also* **tent peg**) a piece of metal that you hammer into the ground to keep one of the ropes of a tent in place وتد معدنيّ لتثبيت الخيمة

3 (*also* **clothes peg**) (*US* **clothespin**) a type of small wooden or plastic object used for fastening clothes to a clothes line مشبك أو شكّالة غسيل

peg² /peg/ *verb* [T] (pegging; pegged) **1** to fix sth with a peg: *He pegged the washing out on the line.* يثبّت بأوتاد؛ يثبّت الغسيل بمشابك

2 to fix or keep sth at a certain level: *Wage increases were pegged at 7%.*
يوقف عند حدّ معيّن، يُثبّت

pelican /'pelɪkən/ *noun* [C] a large water bird that lives in warm countries. A pelican has a large beak that it uses for catching and holding fish. بَجَعة

pellet /'pelɪt/ *noun* [C] a small hard ball that is made from paper, mud, metal, etc: *shotgun pellets* خردقة؛ كُريّة من الورق أو الطين أو المعدن أو غير ذلك

pelt /pelt/ *verb* **1** [T] to attack sb/sth by throwing things: *The speaker was pelted with tomatoes.*
يرجم، يقذفه بِ

2 [I] **pelt (down)** (used about rain) to fall very heavily
يهطل بغزارة

3 [I] to run very fast يعدو، يركض مسرعاً

pelvis /'pelvɪs/ *noun* [C] (*pl.* **pelvises**) the set of wide bones at the bottom of your back, to which your leg bones are joined عظم الحوض، الحوض

▸ **pelvic** /'pelvɪk/ *adj* حوضي

pen¹ /pen/ *noun* [C] an instrument that you use for writing in ink: *a fountain pen* ○ *a ballpoint pen* ○ *a felt-tip pen* قلم حبر وما شابهه

pen² /pen/ *noun* [C] a small piece of ground with a fence around it that is used for keeping animals in
حظيرة، زريبة

penal /'pi:nl/ *adj* (only *before* a noun) connected with punishment by law جزائي، متعلّق بالعقوبات

penalize (*also* **penalise**) /'pi:nəlaɪz/ *verb* [T] **1** to punish sb for breaking a law or rule: *Players must be penalized if they behave badly.* ○ *Motorists who drink and drive should be heavily penalized.* يعاقِب شخصاً لمخالفته القانون

2 to cause sb to suffer a disadvantage: *Children should not be penalized because their parents cannot afford to pay.* يعاقِب، يجعله يقاسي

penalty /'penlti/ *noun* [C] (*pl.* **penalties**) **1** a punishment for breaking a law or rule: *We need stiffer penalties for people who drop litter.* ○ *the death penalty* ○ *No parking. Penalty £25.* عقوبة

2 a disadvantage or sth unpleasant that happens as the result of sth: *I didn't work hard enough and I paid the penalty. I failed all my exams.*
عقوبة، دفْع الثمن، عاقبة وخيمة

3 (in sport) a punishment for one team and an advantage for the other team because a rule has been broken: *The goalkeeper was fouled and the referee awarded a penalty.* ❶ In football, a penalty is a free shot at goal: *If the match ends in a draw, the result will be decided by a penalty shoot-out.*
ضربة جزاء

'penalty area *noun* [C] the marked area in front of the goal in football (في لعبة كرة القدم) منطقة الجزاء

penance /'penəns/ *noun* [C,U] a punishment that you give yourself to show you are sorry for doing sth wrong عقاب للنفس تكفيراً عن ذنب، كفّارة

pence *pl.* of PENNY

pencil /'pensl/ *noun* [C,U] an object that you use for writing or drawing. Pencils are usually made of wood and contain a thin stick of a black or coloured substance: *coloured pencils for children* ○ *Write in pencil, not ink.* قلم رصاص أو قلم ملوّن

▸ **pencil** *verb* [T] (pencilling; pencilled; *US* penciling; penciled) to write or draw with a pencil
يكتب أو يرسم بقلم رصاص أو بقلم ملوّن

'pencil case *noun* [C] a small bag or box that you keep pens, pencils, etc. in مَقلَمة، علبة أقلام

'pencil sharpener *noun* [C] an instrument that you use for making pencils sharp برّاية

pendant /'pendənt/ *noun* [C] an ornament that you wear on a chain around your neck
حِلية تعلّق بسلسلة حول الرقبة

pending /'pendɪŋ/ *adj* (*formal*) waiting to be done or decided: *The judge's decision is still pending.* معلّق، غير مبتوت فيه بعد

▸ **pending** *prep* (*formal*) until: *He took over the leadership pending the elections.* حتّى، إلى حين

pendulum /'pendjələm; *US* -dʒʊləm/ *noun* [C] a string or stick with a heavy weight at the bottom. Some large clocks are worked by a swinging pendulum. نوّاس، بندول

penetrate /'penɪtreɪt/ *verb* [I,T] **1** to make or force a way into or through sth: *The nail hadn't penetrated the skin.* ○ *The car's headlamps could not penetrate the thick fog.* ○ (*figurative*) *We've penetrated the Spanish market.*
يخترق، ينفذ من خلاله

2 to be understood: *I've tried to explain what is going to happen, but I'm not sure if it's penetrated.* يفهم، يدخل في مخّه

▸ **penetrating** *adj* **1** showing the ability to think and understand quickly and well: *a penetrating question* دالّ على الذكاء، ثاقب

2 (used about a voice or sound) loud and carrying for a long way: *a penetrating scream*
(صوت) نافذ، يسمع من بعيد

penetration /ˌpenɪ'treɪʃn/ *noun* [U] the act of penetrating اختراق، نفوذ أو نَفاذ

penfriend /ˈpenfrend/ (*especially US* **pen pal**) *noun* [C] a person that you become friendly with by exchanging letters صديق بالمراسلة

penguin /ˈpeŋɡwɪn/ *noun* [C] a quite large black and white seabird that lives in the Antarctic. Penguins cannot fly. طائر البطريق

penicillin /ˌpenɪˈsɪlɪn/ *noun* [U] a substance that is used as a medicine for preventing and treating diseases caused by bacteria. Penicillin is a type of antibiotic. البنسلين

peninsula /pəˈnɪnsjələ; *US* -nsələ/ *noun* [C] an area of land that is almost surrounded by water: *the Iberian peninsula* (= Spain and Portugal) شبه جزيرة

penis /ˈpiːnɪs/ *noun* [C] the male sex organ that is used for passing waste water and having sex القضيب، العضو المذكّر

penitent /ˈpenɪtənt/ *adj* (*formal*) sorry for having done sth wrong نادم، تائب

penitentiary /ˌpenɪˈtenʃəri/ *noun* [C] (*pl.* **penitentiaries**) (*US*) a prison سجن

penknife /ˈpennaɪf/ *noun* [C] (*pl.* **penknives**) (*also* **pocketknife**) a small knife with one or more blades that fold down into the handle سكين أو مطواة صغيرة للجيب

penniless /ˈpeniləs/ *adj* having no money; poor مفْلِس، لا يملك شروى نقير

penny /ˈpeni/ *noun* [C] (*pl.* **pence** /pens/, **pennies**) **1** (*abbr* **p**) a small brown British coin. There are a hundred pence in a pound: *a fifty-pence piece/coin* بَنْس (بريطاني)

> You use the plural form **pennies** when you are talking about penny coins: *She put five pennies in the slot.* You use **pence** or **p** when you are talking about an amount of money. **P** is more informal than pence.

2 (*US informal*) a cent سِنْت (أمريكيّ)

ˈ**pen pal** *noun* [C] (*especially US*) = PENFRIEND

pension /ˈpenʃn/ *noun* [C] money that is paid regularly to sb who has stopped working (retired) because of old age. Pensions are also paid to people who are widowed or who cannot work because they are ill: *to live on a pension* راتب تقاعديّ

> Almost all men over 65 and women over 60 in Britain receive a pension from the government. This is called a **state pension**. Many people also get a **company pension** from their former employer.

▶ **pensioner** /ˈpenʃənə(r)/ *noun* [C] = OLD-AGE PENSIONER

pentagon /ˈpentəɡən; *US* -ɡɒn/ *noun* [C] a shape that has five straight sides مخمَّس، ذو خمسة أضلاع

pentathlon /penˈtæθlən; -lɒn/ *noun* [C] a sports competition in which each person has to take part in five different events مباراة رياضيّة تتألف من خمسة سباقات مختلفة

penthouse /ˈpenthaʊs/ *noun* [C] an expensive flat at the top of a tall building شقّة فخمة مبنيّة على سطح العمارة

pent up /ˌpent ˈʌp/ *adj* (used about feelings) that you do not express: *pent up anger and frustration* مكبوت، مكظوم

penultimate /penˈʌltɪmət/ *adj* (in a series) the one before the last one: *'Y' is the penultimate letter of the alphabet.* قبلَ الأخير

peony /ˈpiːəni/ *noun* [C] (*pl.* **peonies**) a garden plant with large round pink, red or white flowers فاوانيا، عود الصليب

people /ˈpiːpl/ *noun* **1** [plural] more than one person: *How many people are coming to the party?* ○ *Young people often rebel against their parents.* ○ *What will people say if you go out looking like that?* ○ *He meets a lot of famous people in his job.* أشخاص؛ أناس، ناس

> Be careful. **People** is almost always used instead of the plural form **persons**. **Persons** is very formal and is usually used in legal language, etc: *Persons under the age of sixteen are not permitted to buy cigarettes.* **Folk** is an informal word for people. It is often used when you are talking about older people or people who live in the country: *The old folk have seen many changes in the village over the years.*

2 [C] (*pl.* **peoples**) a nation, race, etc: *The President addressed the American people.* ○ *the French-speaking peoples of the world* شعب

3 [plural] the inhabitants of a particular place: *the people of London* سكّان

4 the people [plural] the ordinary citizens of a country, i.e. not those of high social rank: *a man of the people* عامّة الناس، الشّعب

ˌ**people carrier** (*also* ˌ**people mover**; *US* **minivan**) *noun* [C] a large car, like a van, designed to carry up to eight people سيارة لعائلة كبيرة

pepper /ˈpepə(r)/ *noun* **1** [U] a powder with a hot taste that is used for flavouring food: *salt and pepper* فلفل مسحوق

2 [C] a hollow green, red or yellow vegetable: *stuffed green peppers* فلفل أو فليفلة (خضراء مثلًا)

▶ **pepper** *verb* [T] **1** to put pepper (1) on sth يُبهِّر بالفلفل

2 pepper sb/sth with sth to hit sb/sth many times with sth: *The wall had been peppered with bullets.* يمطره بوابلٍ من...

peppermint /ˈpepəmɪnt/ *noun* **1** [U] a natural substance with a strong flavour that is used in sweets and medicines النعناع أو النعنع البستانيّ

2 [C] (*also* **mint**) a sweet with a peppermint flavour قرص حلوى منكّه بالنعنع

pep talk /ˈpep tɔːk/ *noun* [C] (*informal*) a speech that is given to encourage people or to make them work harder حديث تشجيعيّ، حديث لرفع معنويّات المرء

per /pə(r); *strong form* pɜː(r)/ *prep* for each: *The speed limit is 30 miles per hour.* ○ *To hire a boat costs £5 per hour.* في أو بِ (الساعة)

perceive /pəˈsiːv/ *verb* [T] (*formal*) **1** to notice or realize sth: *Scientists failed to perceive how dangerous the levels of pollutants had become.* يلاحظ؛ يدرك

2 to see or think of sth in a particular way: *I perceived his comments as a criticism.* ❶ The noun is **perception**. يفهم، يرى

per cent (*US* **percent**) /pəˈsent/ *adj, adv* (*symbol* %) in or of each hundred: *There is a ten per cent service charge.* ○ *a two per cent fall in the price of oil* في أو بالمئة

▸ **per cent** (*US* **percent**) *noun* [C, with sing. or pl. verb] (*pl.* **per cent**) (*symbol* %) one part in every hundred: *Nearly ten per cent of all children attend private schools.* ○ *90% of the population owns a television.* ○ *The price of bread has gone up by 50 per cent in two years.* في أو بالمئة

percentage /pəˈsentɪdʒ/ *noun* [C, with sing. or pl. verb] a part of an amount, expressed as a number of hundredths of that amount: *'What percentage of people voted Labour in 1992?' 'About 30 per cent.'* ○ *Please express your answer as a percentage.* نسبة مئويّة

perceptible /pəˈseptəbl/ *adj* (*formal*) that can be seen or felt: *a barely perceptible change in colour* ❶ The opposite is **imperceptible**. ملحوظ، ملموس

▸ **perceptibly** /-əbli/ *adv* بشكل ملحوظ

perception /pəˈsepʃn/ *noun* **1** [U] the ability to notice or understand sth ملاحظة، إدراك، نفاذ البصيرة

2 [C] a particular way of looking at or understanding sth; an opinion: *What is your perception of the situation?* وجهة نظر، فهم

❶ The verb is **perceive**.

perceptive /pəˈseptɪv/ *adj* (*formal*) quick to notice or understand things نافذ البصيرة؛ قويّ الملاحظة؛ مدرك لخفايا الأمور

▸ **perceptively** *adv* بشكل ملحوظ

perch¹ /pɜːtʃ/ *noun* [C] a branch (or a bar in a cage) where a bird sits مَحطّ أو مَجثِم الطائر

▸ **perch** *verb* **1** [I] (used about a bird) to rest from flying on a branch, etc. يحطّ الطائر (على غصن مثلاً)

2 [I,T] to sit, or be put, on the edge of sth: [T]: *The house was perched on the edge of a cliff.* يجثم، يقف على حافة (الجبل)

perch² /pɜːtʃ/ *noun* [C] (*pl.* **perch**) a common fish that you can eat that lives in rivers or lakes فرخ نهري

percussion /pəˈkʌʃn/ *noun* [sing.] **the percussion** [with sing. or pl. verb] the section of an orchestra that consists of the drums and other instruments that you play by hitting them آلات النّقر

perennial /pəˈreniəl/ *adj* that happens often or that lasts for a long time: *the perennial problem of poverty in Britain* متكرّر؛ دائم؛ معمّر

🔑**perfect¹** /ˈpɜːfɪkt/ *adj* **1** as good as can be; without fault: *The car is two years old but it is still in perfect condition.* ○ *Nobody is perfect!* ○ *These shoes are a perfect fit.* ○ *What perfect weather!* ○ *a perfect piece of work* كامل، لا عيبَ فيه

2 perfect (for sb/sth) very suitable or right: *Ken would be perfect for the job.* ○ *Wales is the perfect place for a family holiday.* ○ *the perfect solution to a problem* مثالي؛ الأفضل

3 (used to describe the tense of a verb that is formed with *has/have/had* and the past participle) في صيغة الفعل التامّ

4 (only *before* a noun) complete; total: *What he was saying made perfect sense to me.* ○ *a perfect stranger* تامّ، كلّي، مطلق

▸ **the perfect** *noun* [sing.] the perfect tense: *the present/past perfect* صيغة الفعل التامّ

perfectly *adv* **1** in a perfect way: *He played the piece of music perfectly.* دون عيب؛ بصورة مثاليّة

2 very; completely: *Laura understood perfectly what I meant.* جيّداً؛ تماماً

perfect² /pəˈfekt/ *verb* [T] to make sth perfect: *Hugh is spending a year in France to perfect his French.* يتقن اتقاناً تاماً

perfection /pəˈfekʃn/ *noun* [U] the state of being perfect or without fault: *Perfection is impossible to achieve.* ○ *The steak was cooked to perfection.* الكمال، الحالة المثاليّة

▸ **perfectionist** /-ʃənɪst/ *noun* [C] a person who always does things as well as he/she possibly can and who expects others to do the same شخص يتوخّى الكمال أو غاية الإتقان في عمله

perforate /ˈpɜːfəreɪt/ *verb* [T] to make a hole or holes in sth: *Tear along the perforated line.* يثقب؛ يُثقّب

▸ **perforation** /ˌpɜːfəˈreɪʃn/ *noun* **1** [U] making a hole in sth ثَقب؛ تثقيب

2 [C] a series of small holes in paper, etc. that make it easy for you to tear خطّ مُثقّب (حول الطوابع مثلاً)

🔑**perform** /pəˈfɔːm/ *verb* **1** [T] (*formal*) to do a piece of work or sth that you have been ordered to do: *Doctors performed an emergency operation.* ○ *to perform a task* يقوم بِ، يجري؛ يُنفّذ

2 [I,T] to take part in a play, or to sing, dance, etc. in front of an audience: *She is currently performing at the London Palladium.* ○ *Children performed local dances for the Prince.* ○ *This play has never been performed previously.* يُمثّل؛ يقوم بِ، يؤدّي

3 [I] (used about a machine, etc.) to work: *The car performs badly in cold weather.* يعمل، يشتغل، يسير

▸ **performer** *noun* [C] a person who performs (2) in front of an audience مَن يؤدّي دوراً أمام الجمهور

🔑**performance** /pəˈfɔːməns/ *noun* **1** [sing.] (*formal*) doing sth: *the performance of your duties* تأدية أو أداء، قيام بِ

2 [C] sth that you perform (2) in front of an audience: *The Royal Shakespeare Company is putting on a performance of 'King Lear'.* أداء موسيقيّ أو مسرحي

3 [C] the way in which you do sth, especially how successful you are: *The company's perform-*

a b c d e f g h i j k l m n o p q r s t u v w x y z

ance was disappointing last year. ○ *Germany's fine performance in the World Cup* أداء، مقدار النجاح، فعالية

4 [U] (used about a machine, etc.) the ability to work well: *This car has a high performance engine.* كفاءة؛ قدرة

perfume /ˈpɜːfjuːm; *US also* pərˈfjuːm/ *noun* [C,U] **1** a pleasant smell رائحة زكيّة، عبير

2 a liquid with a sweet smell that you put on your body to make yourself smell nice: *French perfume* عطر؛ طيب

🔑**perhaps** /pəˈhæps; præps/ *adv* (used when you are not sure about sth) maybe; possibly: *Perhaps he isn't coming.* ○ *She was, perhaps, one of the most famous writers of the time.* ○ *'Are you sure that you're doing the right thing?' 'No, perhaps not.'* ○ *If Barnes had played, they might have won. Or perhaps not.* ربما؛ لعلّ؛ هل يمكن

> **Perhaps** and **maybe** are similar in meaning. They are often used to make what you are saying sound more polite: *Perhaps I could borrow your book, if you're not using it?* ○ *Maybe I'd better explain...*

peril /ˈperəl/ *noun* (*formal*) **1** [U] great danger خطر عظيم، تهلكة

2 [C] sth that is very dangerous: *the perils of the sea* خطر، مهلكة

▶ **perilous** /ˈperələs/ *adj* (*formal*) dangerous ❶ **Danger** and **dangerous** are more common. خَطِر، مهلك

perimeter /pəˈrɪmɪtə(r)/ *noun* [C] the outside edge or boundary of an area of land: *the perimeter fence of the army camp* السّور المحيط؛ المحيط

🔑**period** /ˈpɪəriəd/ *noun* [C] **1** a length of time: *The weather tomorrow will be cloudy with sunny periods.* ○ *The scheme will be introduced for a six-month trial period.* ○ *Her son is going through a difficult period at the moment.* ○ *The play is set in the Tudor period in England.* ○ *period costume* (= costume of a particular period) فترة؛ عهد

2 a lesson in school: *We have five periods of English a week.* حصّة مدرسيّة

3 the monthly loss of blood from a woman's body: *period pains* ○ *My period started this morning.* العادة أو الدورة الشهريّة

4 (*especially US*) = FULL STOP

periodic /ˌpɪəriˈɒdɪk/ (*also* **periodical** /-kl/) *adj* happening fairly regularly دَوْريّ، متكرِّر في فترات منتظمة

▶ **periodically** /-kli/ *adv*: *All machines need to be checked periodically.* بشكل دوري، على فترات منتظمة

periodical /ˌpɪəriˈɒdɪkl/ *noun* [C] (*formal*) a magazine that is produced at regular intervals مجلّة دوريّة

perish /ˈperɪʃ/ *verb* [I] (*formal*) to die or be destroyed: *Thousands perished in the war.* يهلك، يموت

▶ **perishable** /-əbl/ *adj* (used about food) that will go bad quickly (طعام) سريع التلف

perjure /ˈpɜːdʒə(r)/ *verb* [T] **perjure yourself** to tell lies in a court of law يُدلي بشهادة كاذبة، يحلف يميناً كاذبة (في المحكمة)

perjury /ˈpɜːdʒəri/ *noun* [U] (*formal*) telling a lie (in a court of law) الإدلاء بشهادة زور (في المحكمة)

perk[1] /pɜːk/ *verb*

PHR V **perk up** to become more cheerful or lively ينتعش، يصبح أكثر بِشْراً، "يفَرْفِش"

perk sb/sth up to make sb/sth more cheerful or lively يُبهِج، ينَشِّط

perk[2] /pɜːk/ *noun* [C] (*informal*) something extra that you get from your employer in addition to your salary: *Travelling abroad is one of the perks of the job.* علاوة أو فائدة إضافية يتمتّع بها الموظّف

perm /pɜːm/ *noun* [C] the treatment of hair with special chemicals in order to make it curly or wavy تجعيد الشّعر بالمواد الكيماويّة، "برمانِنت"

▶ **perm** *verb* [T]: *She has had her hair permed.* يجعِّد الشّعر (عادةً) بمواد كيماويّة

permanence /ˈpɜːmənəns/ *noun* [U] the state of lasting or remaining for a very long time or for ever دوام، بقاء

🔑**permanent** /ˈpɜːmənənt/ *adj* lasting for a long time or for ever; that will not change: *The accident left him with a permanent scar.* ○ *Are you looking for a permanent or a temporary job?* دائم؛ ثابت

▶ **permanently** *adv*: *Has she left permanently?* بشكل دائم

permissible /pəˈmɪsəbl/ *adj* (*formal*) that is allowed (by the rules): *They have been exposed to radiation above the permissible level.* مسموح به؛ مقبول

🔑**permission** /pəˈmɪʃn/ *noun* [U] the act of allowing sb to do sth: *I'm afraid you can't leave without permission.* ○ *Children under 18 need their parents' permission to attend.* ○ *to ask permission for sth* ○ *to give permission for sth* ○ *The refugees have been refused permission to stay in this country.* سماح، إذن، موافقة

> Be careful. **Permission** is uncountable. A piece of paper that says that you are allowed to do something is a **permit**.

permissive /pəˈmɪsɪv/ *adj* having, allowing or showing a lot of freedom, especially in sexual matters: *the permissive society of the 1960s* مُبيح، متساهل وخاصّة في الأمور الجنسيّة

🔑**permit** /pəˈmɪt/ *verb* (*formal*) (permitting; permitted) **1** [T] to allow sth: *Food and drink are not permitted in this building.* ○ *You are not permitted to smoke in the hospital.* ○ *His visa does not permit him to work.* ➲ Look at the note at **allow**. يسمح بِ، يجيز

2 [I,T] to make possible: *Let's have a barbecue at the weekend, weather permitting.* يمكِّن، يتيح الفرصة

▶ **permit** /ˈpɜːmɪt/ *noun* [C] an official paper that says you are allowed to do sth: *a work permit* ترخيص، إذن

perpendicular /ˌpɜːpənˈdɪkjələ(r)/ *adj* **1** at an angle of 90° to sth ➲ Look at **horizontal** and **vertical**. عمودي، رأسي

2 pointing straight up; upright قائم، منتصب

perpetual /pəˈpetʃuəl/ *adj* not stopping or changing: *They lived in perpetual fear of losing their jobs.* ○ *the perpetual roar of traffic* مستمر، دائم

▶ **perpetually** /-tʃuəli/ *adv* always: *People are perpetually complaining about the hospital food.* دائما: باستمرار

perpetuate /pəˈpetʃueɪt/ *verb* [T] (*formal*) to cause sth to continue يديم، يبقي: يخلّد

perplexed /pəˈplekst/ *adj* not understanding sth; confused حائر، مرتبك: مضطرب الذهن

persecute /ˈpɜːsɪkjuːt/ *verb* [T] to cause sb to suffer, especially because of what he/she believes يضطهد

▶ **persecution** /ˌpɜːsɪˈkjuːʃn/ *noun* [C,U]: *the persecution of minorities* اضطهاد

persecutor /ˈpɜːsɪkjuːtə(r)/ *noun* [C] مضطهد

persevere /ˌpɜːsɪˈvɪə(r)/ *verb* [I] **persevere (at/in/with sth)** to continue trying or having sth that is difficult: *The treatment is painful but I'm going to persevere with it.* يواظب، يثابر

▶ **perseverance** /ˌpɜːsɪˈvɪərəns/ *noun* [U]: *It takes a lot of perseverance to become a champion at any sport.* مُثابرة، دأب

persist /pəˈsɪst/ *verb* [I] **1 persist (in sth/in doing sth)** to continue doing sth even though other people say that you are wrong or that you cannot do it: *If you persist in making so much noise, I shall call the police.* ○ *She persists in her belief that he did not kill himself.*
يمعن في، يتمادى: يتشبّث برأيه

2 to continue to exist: *If your symptoms persist you should consult your doctor.* يستمّر

▶ **persistence** /-əns/ *noun* [U] **1** the state of continuing to do sth even though people say that you are wrong or that you cannot do it: *Finally her persistence was rewarded and she got what she wanted.* إصرار، مثابرة: إمعان في

2 the state of continuing to exist: *the persistence of unemployment at high levels* استمرار

persistent /-ənt/ *adj* **1** continuing to do sth even though people say that you are wrong or that you cannot do it: *Some salesmen can be very persistent.* مصِر، لحوح

2 lasting for a long time or happening often: *a persistent cough* ○ *persistent rain*
مستمر، متشبّث: متواصل

persistently *adv* بعناد، باصرار

⚷ **person** /ˈpɜːsn/ *noun* [C] (*pl.* **people** or **persons**)
➲ Look at the note at **people**.

1 a man or woman: *I would like to speak to the person in charge.* شخص، إنسان، مرء

2 one of the three types of pronoun in grammar. *I/we* are the first person, *you* is the second person and *he/she/it/they* are the third person. شخص

IDM in person seeing or speaking to sb face to face, (not speaking on the telephone or writing a letter): *I went to apologize to her in person.*
شخصياً، بنفسه

⚷ **personal** /ˈpɜːsənl/ *adj* **1** (only *before* a noun) of or belonging to a particular person: *Judges should not let their personal feelings influence their decisions.* ○ *The car is for your personal use only.* شخصي، فردي

2 of or concerning your feelings, health, relations with other people, etc: *I should like to speak to you in private. I have something personal to discuss.* ○ *The letter was marked 'personal' so I did not open it.* شخصي، خاص

3 (only *before* a noun) done or made by a particular person: *The Prime Minister made a personal visit to the victims in hospital.*
(اهتمام) شخصي، (زار) بنفسه...

4 speaking about sb's appearance or character in an unpleasant or unfriendly way: *It started as a general discussion but then people started making personal remarks and an argument began.* (نقد) متعلّق بشخصيّة المرء وهيئته وغير ذلك

5 (only *before* a noun) connected with the body: *personal hygiene* جسمي، بَدَني

▶ **personally** /-ənəli/ *adv* **1** in person, not with sb else acting for you: *I should like to deal with this matter personally.* شخصياً، بنفسه

2 (used for expressing your own opinions): *Personally, I think that nurses deserve more money.* في رأيي أنا

3 as a person: *I wasn't talking about you personally – I meant all teachers.* ○ *The ship's captain was held personally responsible for the accident.* بشكل شخصيّ، (لا أنتقدك) أنت بالذات

ˌ**personal comˈputer** = PC (1)

ˈ**personal day** *noun* [C] a day that you take off work for personal reasons, but not because you are ill or on holiday إجازة لأسباب شخصية

⚷ **personality** /ˌpɜːsəˈnæləti/ *noun* (*pl.* **personalities**) **1** [C] the qualities and features of a person: *Joe has a very forceful personality.* الشخصية

2 [C,U] the quality of having a strong, interesting and attractive character; a person who has this quality: *A good entertainer needs a lot of personality.* شخصيّة قويّة: شخصيّة جذّابة

3 [C] a famous person (especially in sport, on television, etc.): *a television personality*
شخصيّة (مهمة)

personalize (*also* **personalise**) /ˈpɜːsənəlaɪz/ *verb* [T] to mark sth with your initials, etc. to show that it belongs to you: *a car with a personalized number plate*
يكتب أو يحفر أسمه على شيء ما للدلالة على ملكيته

ˌ**personal ˈpronoun** *noun* [C] (*grammar*) any of the pronouns *I, me, she, her, he, him, we, us, you, they, them,* etc. أحد الضمائر الشخصيّة

ˌ**personal ˈstereo** *noun* [C] (*pl.* **personal stereos**) a small machine that you carry round with you on which you can listen to CDs, tapes or the radio استيريو محمول

personify /pəˈsɒnɪfaɪ/ *verb* [T] (*pres part* **personifying**; *3rd pers sing pres* **personifies**; *pt, pp* **personified**) **1** to be an example in human form of a particular quality يجسّد، يُمثّل

2 to describe sth as if it were a person, e.g. in a poem يَصِف شيئاً وكأنه إنسان، يضفي صفات إنسانيّة على الجماد

personnel /ˌpɜːsəˈnel/ *noun* **1** [plural] the people who work for a large organization: *The army cannot afford to lose qualified personnel.* هيئة الموظّفين في منظمة كبيرة

2 [U, with sing. or pl. verb] (*also* **personˈnel department**) the department of a large organization that looks after the people who work there دائرة شؤون الموظّفين

perspective /pəˈspektɪv/ *noun* **1** [U] the art of drawing on a flat surface so that some objects appear to be farther away than others: *the laws of perspective* ○ *in/out of perspective* الرّسم المنظوري

2 [C,U] the way that you think about sth; your point of view: *If you go away for a few days you will see everything in a new perspective.* منظور، وجهة نظر

perspire /pəˈspaɪə(r)/ *verb* [I] (*formal*) to lose liquid through your skin ❶ **Sweat** is more informal. يعرَق

▶ **perspiration** /ˌpɜːspəˈreɪʃn/ *noun* [U] **1** the act of perspiring تعرُّق

2 the liquid that you lose through your skin: *a drop of perspiration* عَرَق

🔑 **persuade** /pəˈsweɪd/ *verb* [T] **1 persuade sb (to do sth); persuade sb (into/out of sth)** to cause sb to do sth by giving him/her good reasons: *It was difficult to persuade Louise to change her mind.* ○ *We eventually persuaded Tim into coming with us.* ➲ Look at **dissuade**. يقْنِع

2 persuade sb (of sth) (*formal*) to cause sb to believe sth: *The jury was persuaded of her innocence.* ➲ Look at **convince**. يقْنِع، يستميله إلى رأيه

persuasion /pəˈsweɪʒn/ *noun* **1** [U] persuading or being persuaded: *It took a lot of persuasion to get Alan to agree.* ○ *I suggested going to the beach and the others didn't need much persuasion.* إقناع؛ إقتناع

2 [C] (*formal*) a religious or political belief: *politicians of all persuasions.* معتقَد دينيّ أو سياسيّ

persuasive /pəˈsweɪsɪv/ *adj* able to make sb do or believe sth: *The arguments were very persuasive.* مقْنِع

▶ **persuasively** *adv* بشكل مقْنِع

persuasiveness *noun* [U] القدرة على الإقناع

pertinent /ˈpɜːtɪnənt; *US* -tənənt/ *adj* directly connected with sth: *to ask a pertinent question* وثيق العلاقة بصلب الموضوع

perturb /pəˈtɜːb/ *verb* [T] (often passive) (*formal*) to make sb worried or upset يقلق؛ يشوّش الفكر

pervade /pəˈveɪd/ *verb* [T] to spread to all parts of sth: *The smell from the factory pervaded the whole town.* ينتشر في كلّ مكان، يتفشّى، يعمّ

pervasive /pəˈveɪsɪv/ *adj* that is present in all parts of sth: *a pervasive mood of pessimism* منتشر في كل مكان، عام

perverse /pəˈvɜːs/ *adj* (*formal*) having or showing behaviour that is not reasonable or that upsets other people: *Derek gets perverse pleasure from shocking his parents.* غير معقول؛ معاند، شرّير

▶ **perversely** *adv* بشكل غير طبيعي، بدافع شرّير

perversity *noun* [U] عناد، مشاكسة

perversion /pəˈvɜːʃn; *US* -ʒn/ *noun* [C,U] **1** the changing of sth from right to wrong or good to bad: *That statement is a perversion of the truth.* تشويه (للحقائق)، إفساد

2 sexual behaviour that is unnatural or not acceptable انحراف جنسي

pervert /pəˈvɜːt/ *verb* [T] **1** to change sth so that it becomes bad or is used wrongly: *to pervert scientific knowledge for military purposes* يشوّه، يفْسِد؛ يسيء استعماله

2 to cause sb to think or behave in a way that is not right or natural: *Children should be protected from influences that may pervert them.* يضِلّ، يحرفه عن الطريق السّوي

▶ **pervert** /ˈpɜːvɜːt/ *noun* [C] a person whose sexual behaviour is not natural or normal منحرِف جنسياً

pessimism /ˈpesɪmɪzəm/ *noun* [U] the state of expecting or believing that bad things will happen تشاؤم

▶ **pessimist** /-ɪst/ *noun* [C] a person who always thinks that what is going to happen will be bad متشائم

pessimistic /ˌpesɪˈmɪstɪk/ *adj* متشائم، تشاؤمي

pessimistically /-kli/ *adv* بتشاؤم

➲ Look at **optimism, optimist** and **optimistic**.

pest /pest/ *noun* [C] **1** an insect or animal that destroys plants, food, etc: *pest control* آفة

2 (*informal*) a person or thing that annoys you شخص مزعج جداً

pester /ˈpestə(r)/ *verb* [T] to annoy or bother sb, e.g. by asking him/her sth many times: *to pester sb for money* يضايق بكثرة الحاجه، يضجِر بكثرة أسئلته

pesticide /ˈpestɪsaɪd/ *noun* [C,U] a chemical substance that is used for killing animals or insects that eat food crops ➲ Look at **insecticide**. مبيد الآفات

🔑 **pet** /pet/ *noun* [C] **1** an animal that you keep in your home for company or for pleasure: *a pet lamb* ○ *to keep a pet* حيوان أليف مدلَّل

2 a person who is treated as a favourite: *teacher's pet* الشّخص المفضّل، الحظيّ، المدلّل

▶ **pet** *verb* (petting; petted) **1** [T] to treat an animal with affection, e.g. by stroking it يلاطف، يدلّل، يملّس عليه بحنان

2 [I] (*informal*) (used about two people) to kiss and touch in a sexual way يقبّل، يحتضن (الحبيب)

petal /ˈpetl/ *noun* [C] one of the thin soft coloured parts of a flower تُوَيجيّة

peter /ˈpiːtə(r)/ *verb*

PHRV **peter out** to finish or come to an end gradually: *The flow of water slowed down and finally petered out.* يتلاشى تدريجياً

pet ˈhate *noun* [C] sth that you particularly do not like: *Filling in forms is one of my pet hates.* أبغض الاشياء

petition /pəˈtɪʃn/ *noun* [C] a written document, signed by many people, that asks a government, etc. to do sth: *More than 50 000 people signed the petition protesting about the new road.* عريضة

petrified /ˈpetrɪfaɪd/ *adj* very frightened متسمّر في مكانه ذعراً، خائف جداً

petrol /ˈpetrəl/ (*US* **gas**; **gasoline**) *noun* [U] the liquid that is used as fuel for motor vehicles such as cars and motorbikes: *a petrol pump* ○ *to fill up with petrol* بنزين أو غازولين

petroleum /pəˈtrəʊliəm/ *noun* [U] oil that is found under the surface of the earth and that is used for making petrol and other types of chemical substances نفط أو بترول

ˈ**petrol station** (*also* **filling station**; **service station**; *US* **gas station**) *noun* [C] a place where you can buy petrol and other things for your car محطّة بنزين

petticoat /ˈpetɪkəʊt/ *noun* [C] (*old-fashioned*) a thin piece of women's clothing that is worn under a dress or a skirt تنّورة داخليّة: "شلحة" (سوريا)، "كمبزون"

petty /ˈpeti/ *adj* **1** small or not important: *He didn't want to get involved with the petty details.* ○ *petty crime* تافه، ضئيل، طفيف

2 unkind or unpleasant (for a reason that does not seem very important): *He's tried so hard that it would be petty to criticize him now.* حقير، دنيء؛ قاس

pew /pjuː/ *noun* [C] one of the long seats in a church مقعد خشبي طويل في كنيسة

PGCE *abbrev* (in Britain) Postgraduate Certificate of Education دبلوم تربية

phantom /ˈfæntəm/ *noun* [C] **1** something with the shape of a dead person that seems to appear on earth and behave as if it was alive ❶ **Ghost** is a more common word. شَبَح، طَيْف

2 something that you think exists, but that is not real وَهْم، خيال

pharmaceutical /ˌfɑːməˈsuːtɪkl; *Brit also* -ˈsjuː-/ *adj* connected with the production of medicines منتج للأدوية، صيدلانيّ

pharmacist /ˈfɑːməsɪst/ *noun* [C] = CHEMIST (1)

pharmacy /ˈfɑːməsi/ *noun* (*pl.* **pharmacies**) **1** [U] (the study of) the preparation of medicines الصَّيْدَلة

2 [C] a place where medicines are prepared and given out or sold صيدليّة، "أجزخانة"

> A shop that sells medicine is also called **a chemist's (shop)** in British English or a **drugstore** in American English.

phase /feɪz/ *noun* [C] a period in the development of sth: *the final phase of the hospital building programme* ○ *to enter a new phase* ○ *Julie went through a difficult phase when she started school.* مرحلة، طَور

▶ **phase** *verb*

PHR V **phase sth in** to introduce sth slowly or over a period of time: *The metric system was phased in over several years.* يُطبِّق برنامجاً جديداً بصورة تدريجيّة

phase sth out to take away or remove sth slowly or over a period of time: *The older machines are gradually being phased out and replaced by new ones.* يلغي شيئاً بصورة تدريجيّة

phat /fæt/ *adj* (*US slang*) very good جيد جداً

PhD /ˌpiː eɪtʃ ˈdiː/ *abbrev* Doctor of Philosophy; an advanced university degree that you receive when you complete a piece of research into a special subject: *She has a PhD in History.* ○ *Malcolm Crofts PhD* دكتوراة الفلسفة

pheasant /ˈfeznt/ *noun* [C] (*pl.* **pheasants** or **pheasant**) a type of bird with a long tail. The males have brightly coloured feathers. Pheasants are often shot for sport and are eaten as food. تَدْرُج

phenomenal /fəˈnɒmɪnl/ *adj* unusual because it is so good or so great: *phenomenal success* غير عاديّ، خارق، هائل

▶ **phenomenally** /-nəli/ *adv* بشكل غير عاديّ، بصورة هائلة

phenomenon /fəˈnɒmɪnən; *US* -nɒn/ *noun* [C] (*pl.* **phenomena** /-ɪnə/) something that happens or exists (often sth unusual): *Acid rain is not a natural phenomenon. It is caused by pollution.* ظاهرة؛ واقعة نادرة

phew /fjuː/ (*also* **whew**) *interj* (used to show the sound which expresses tiredness, surprise, relief, shock, etc.): *Phew, it's hot in here!* أف!

philosopher /fəˈlɒsəfə(r)/ *noun* [C] a person who has developed a set of ideas and beliefs about the meaning of life فيلسوف

philosophy /fəˈlɒsəfi/ *noun* (*pl.* **philosophies**) **1** [U] the study of ideas and beliefs about the meaning of life الفلسفة

2 [C] a belief or set of beliefs that tries to explain the meaning of life or give rules about how to behave: *the philosophy of Nietzsche* ○ *Her philosophy is 'If a job's worth doing, it's worth doing well'.* فلسفة، آراء في الحياة

▶ **philosophical** /ˌfɪləˈsɒfɪkl/ (*also* **philosophic**) *adj* **1** of or concerning philosophy: *a philosophical debate* فلسفيّ

2 philosophical (about sth) having or showing a calm, quiet attitude when you are in danger, suffering or disappointed: *He was quite philosophical about failing the exam and says he will try again next year.* رصين: رابط الجأش: مُتقبّل للصعوبات بحكمة

philosophically /-kli/ *adv* برصانة، بهدوء، بتقبّل

phishing /ˈfɪʃɪŋ/ *noun* [U] the activity of tricking people by getting them to give their identity, bank account numbers, etc. over the Internet or by email, and then using these to steal money from them الاصطياد الالكتروني: إحدى تقنيات الاحتيال الالكتروني

phlegm /flem/ *noun* [U] the thick yellow substance that is produced in your nose and your throat when you have a cold بَلْغَم

phlegmatic /fleg'mætɪk/ *adj (formal)* not easily excited or upset; calm
هادئ الأعصاب، بارد الدّم؛ بلغميّ المزاج (عند الأقدمين)

phobia /'fəʊbiə/ *noun* [C] a very strong fear or dislike that you cannot explain خوف مرضي شديد

🔑phone /fəʊn/ *noun (also* **telephone)** **1** [U] an electrical system for talking to sb in another house, town, country, etc. by speaking into a special piece of equipment: *a phone call* ○ *You can book the tickets by phone.* تليفون، هاتف

When you make a phone call you first **pick up the receiver** and **dial** the number. The phone **rings** and the person at the other end **answers** it. If he/she is already using the phone, it is **engaged** (*US* **busy**). When you finish speaking you **put down** the receiver and **ring off**.

2 [C] the piece of equipment that you use when you talk to sb by telephone: *The phone is ringing – could you answer it?* ○ *Could I use your phone?* جهاز التليفون

IDM on the phone/telephone 1 using the telephone: *'Where's Ian?' 'He's on the phone.'*
(يتكلّم) على التليفون

2 having a telephone in your home: *I'll have to write to her because she's not on the phone.*
عنده تليفون

▸ **phone** *(also* **telephone)** *verb* [I,T]: *Did anybody phone while I was out?* ○ *Could you phone the restaurant and book a table?*
يتّصل بالتلفون،يهتف

'phone book *noun* [C] = TELEPHONE DIRECTORY

'phone box *(also* **telephone box)** *noun* [C] a small covered place in a street, etc. that contains a telephone for public use كشك تليفون عمومي

phonecard™ /'fəʊnkɑːd/ *noun* [C] a small plastic card that you can use to pay for calls in a public telephone box بطاقة تليفون

'phone-in *(US* **call-in)** *noun* [C] a radio or television programme during which you can ask a question or give your opinion by telephone
برنامج إذاعيّ أو تلفزيوني يتلقّى مخابرات من المستمعين

'phone number *noun* [C] = TELEPHONE NUMBER

phonetic /fə'netɪk/ *adj* **1** connected with the sounds of human speech متعلّق بأصوات الكلام

2 using a system for writing a language that has a different sign for each sound: *the phonetic alphabet* ممثّل لأصوات اللغة برموز مختلفة

▸ **phonetically** /-kli/ *adv*
(يكتَب) تماماً كما يلفَظ، (يلفَظ) تماماً كما يكتَب

phonetics *noun* [U] the study of the sounds of human speech علم الصوتيّات

phoney *(also* **phony)** /'fəʊni/ *adj* not real; false مزيّف؛ كاذب

▸ **phoney** *(also* **phony)** *noun* [C] *(pl.* **phoneys)** a person who is not what he/she pretends to be دجّال، منتحل شخصية أخرى

phoniness *noun* [U] زيف

🔑photo /'fəʊtəʊ/ *noun* [C] *(pl.* **photos** /-təʊz/) *(informal)* = PHOTOGRAPH

🔑photocopy /'fəʊtəʊkɒpi/ *noun* [C] *(pl.* **photocopies)** a copy of a piece of paper, page in a book, etc. that is made by a special machine (a photocopier) that can photograph sth quickly
نُسخة فوتوغرافيّة

▸ **photocopy** *verb* [I,T] *(pres part* **photocopying**; *3rd pers sing pres* **photocopies**; *pt, pp* **photocopied)** to make a photocopy of sth
يستنسخ، يستخرج نسخة فوتوغرافية

photocopier *noun* [C] a machine that makes photocopies آلة نسخ

🔑photograph /'fəʊtəgrɑːf; *US* -græf/ *(also informal* **photo)** *noun* [C] a picture that is taken with a camera: *to take a photo* ○ *a colour photograph* ○ *She looks younger in real life than she did in the photograph.* ○ *This photo is a bit out of focus.* ○ *to have a photo enlarged* ➲ Look at **negative** and **slide**²(2).
صورة فوتوغرافيّة

▸ **photograph** *verb* [T] to take a photograph of sb/sth
يصوِّر

photographer /fə'tɒgrəfə(r)/ *noun* [C] a person who takes photographs ➲ Look at **cameraman**.
مصوِّر

photographic /ˌfəʊtə'græfɪk/ *adj* connected with photographs or photography: *photographic equipment* فوتوغرافي، متعلّق بالتصوير

photography /fə'tɒgrəfi/ *noun* [U] the skill or process of taking photographs: *wildlife photography* فن التصوير

phrasal verb /ˌfreɪzl 'vɜːb/ *noun* [C] a verb that is combined with an adverb or a preposition to give a new meaning, such as 'look after' or 'put sb off' فعل اصطلاحي: مؤلّف من فعل وحرف جرّ

🔑phrase /freɪz/ *noun* [C] a group of words that are used together. A phrase does not contain a full verb: *'First of all' and 'a bar of chocolate' are phrases.* شبه جملة

▸ **phrase** *verb* [T] to express sth in a particular way: *The statement was phrased so that it would offend no one.* يصوغ فكرة بأسلوب معيّن، يعبّر بشكل ملائم

'phrase book *noun* [C] a book that gives common words and phrases in a foreign language. People use phrase books when they travel abroad to a country whose language they do not know.
قاموس صغير خاص بالمسافرين

🔑physical /'fɪzɪkl/ *adj* **1** of or for your body: *physical exercise* ○ *Parents must consider their children's physical and emotional needs.*
بَدَنيّ، جسديّ أو جسميّ

2 connected with real things that you can touch, or with the laws of nature: *physical geography* ○ *It is a physical impossibility to be in two places at once.* ماديّ، ملموس؛ طبيعيّ

3 connected with physics فيزيائي، طبيعيّ

▸ **physically** /-kli/ *adv*: *to be physically fit* ○ *It will be physically impossible to get to London before ten.* جسديّاً؛ ماديّاً، عمليّاً

physician /fɪ'zɪʃn/ *noun* [C] a doctor, especially one who treats diseases with medicine (= not a surgeon) طبيب

physicist /'fɪzɪsɪst/ *noun* [C] a person who studies physics فيزيائي

🔑physics /'fɪzɪks/ *noun* [U] the scientific study of

natural forces such as light, sound, heat, electricity, pressure, etc. الفيزياء، علم الطبيعة

physiotherapy /ˌfɪziəʊˈθerəpi/ *noun* [U] the treatment of disease or injury by exercise, massage, heat, etc. المعالجة الفيزيائيّة
▸ **physiotherapist** /-pɪst/ *noun* [C] a person who is trained to use physiotherapy معالج فيزيائي

physique /fɪˈziːk/ *noun* [C] the size and shape of a person's body: *a strong muscular physique* بنية أو تكوين الجسم

pianos

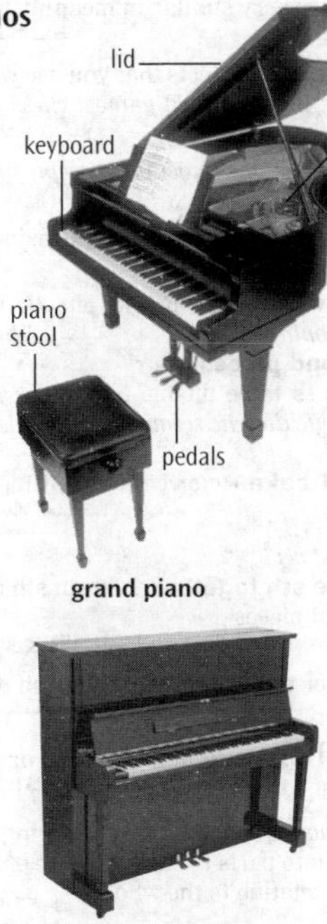

piano /piˈænəʊ/ *noun* [C] (*pl.* **pianos** /-nəʊz/) a large musical instrument that you play by pressing down black and white bars (keys). This causes small hammers to hit strings inside the instrument: *an upright piano* ○ *a grand piano*
ℹ Note that, as with all musical instruments, we play **the** piano. بيانو، بيان
▸ **pianist** /ˈpɪənɪst/ *noun* [C] a person who plays the piano عازف بيانو

pick¹ /pɪk/ *verb* [T] **1** to choose sb/sth from a group of people or things: *She picked her words carefully so as not to upset anybody.* ○ *to be picked to play for the team* ○ *We picked a good day to go to the beach.* ينتقي، يختار

2 to take a flower, fruit or vegetable from the place where it is growing: *I've picked you a bunch of flowers.* ○ *Don't pick wild flowers.* ○ *to go fruit-picking* يقطف

3 to remove a small piece or pieces of sth with your fingers: *Don't pick your nose!* ينتف؛ يخلّل بأصابعه

4 to take sth off sth: *Don't pick all the nuts off the top of the cake.* ○ *She picked a hair off her jacket.* يلتقط

5 to open a lock without a key, e.g. with a piece of wire يفتح قفلاً بطريقة خاصّة بغيةَ السرقة

IDM **have a bone to pick with sb** → BONE

pick a fight (with sb) to start a fight with sb deliberately يتعمّد الشِّجار مع...

pick sb's pocket to steal money, etc. from sb's pocket or bag ينشل (من جيب مثلاً)

PHR V **pick on sb** to behave unfairly or unkindly towards sb يَخص شخصاً بالمضايقة، يعامله معاملة سيّئة

pick sb/sth out to choose or recognize sb/sth from a number of people or things: *I immediately picked Jean out in the photo.* ينتقي من مجموعة، يميّز أو يتعرّف على

pick up to become better; to improve يتحسّن، ينتعِش

pick sb up 1 to collect sb, in a car, etc: *We've ordered a taxi to pick us up at ten.* يأخذ رُكّاباً

2 (*informal*) to start talking to sb you do not know and try to start a sexual relationship with him/her يتودّد إلى أو يحادث شخصاً غريباً بنوايا جنسيّة

3 (used about the police) to stop sb and question them: *The drug dealers were picked up in Dover.* يوقف، يعتقل

pick sb/sth up 1 to take hold of and lift sb/sth: *The phone stopped ringing just as I picked up the receiver.* ○ *Lucy picked up the child and gave him a cuddle.* ○ *Pick those things up off the floor!* يرفع، يلتقط

2 to hear or see sb/sth by means of a radio, television, etc: *In the north of France you can pick up English television programmes.* يلتقط (إذاعة)

pick sth up 1 to learn sth without formal lessons: *Joe picked up a few words of Spanish on holiday.* يتعلّم، "يلقط"

2 to get or find sth: *You can pick up a lot of information about local history by talking to the older residents.* يحصل على

3 to go and get sth; to collect sth: *We must pick up the tickets half an hour before the show begins.* يستلم، يتناول، يأخذ

pick² /pɪk/ *noun* [sing.] **1** the one that you choose; your choice: *You can have whichever cake you like. Take your pick.* الشيء المختار

2 the best of a group: *You can see the pick of the new films at this year's festival.* صفوة، نخبة

pick³ /pɪk/ *noun* [C] (*also* **pickaxe**; *US* **pickax** /ˈpɪkæks/) a tool that consists of a curved iron bar with sharp points at both ends, fixed onto a wooden handle. Picks are used for breaking stones or hard ground. مِعوَل

picket /ˈpɪkɪt/ *noun* [C] a worker or group of workers who stand outside a place of work during a strike and try to persuade other people not to go in عامل أو عمال مضربون يحاولون عدل الآخرين عن الدخول
▸ **picket** *verb* [I,T] يرابط المضربون أمام مكان عملهم

pickle /ˈpɪkl/ *noun* [C,U] food such as fruit and vegetables that is put in vinegar or salt water so

that it can be kept for a long time: *a supper of cold meat and pickles* مخلّل، طرشي
▸ **pickle** *verb* [T]: *pickled onions* يخلّل

pickpocket /ˈpɪkpɒkɪt/ *noun* [C] a person who steals things from other people's pockets or bags in public places نشّال

pickup /ˈpɪkʌp/ *noun* a type of vehicle that has an open part with low sides at the back سيارة "بيك آب"

picky /ˈpɪki/ *adj* (**pickier**; **pickiest**) (*informal*) difficult to please ➲ Look at **fussy**. نيّق، صعب الإرضاء

picnic /ˈpɪknɪk/ *noun* [C] **1** a meal that you eat outdoors (in the country or on a beach, etc.): *a picnic lunch* ○ *We had a picnic on the beach.* وجبة طعام في الهواء الطّلق

2 a trip that you make for pleasure during which you eat a picnic: *It's a lovely day – let's go for a picnic.* نزهة مصحوبة بالطعام: سَيران (سوريا)
▸ **picnic** *verb* [I] (*pres part* **picnicking**; *pt, pp* **picnicked**) يتنزه ويأكل في الهواء الطلق

pictorial /pɪkˈtɔːriəl/ *adj* expressed in pictures مصوّر، تصويريّ

picture /ˈpɪktʃə(r)/ *noun* **1** [C] a painting, drawing or photograph: *Many of Turner's pictures are of the sea.* ○ *to draw/paint a picture* ○ *Look at the picture on page 96 and describe what you see.* ○ *Come and have your picture* (= photograph) *taken.* صورة؛ لوحة، رسم

2 [C] an idea or memory of sth in your mind: *Dickens' novels give a good picture of what life was like in Victorian England.* صورة، فكرة

3 [C] the quality of what you see on a television: *I'm sorry, the television's quite old and the picture isn't very good.* الصورة التلفزيونية

4 [C] (*Brit*) a film (in a cinema) فيلم سينمائيّ

5 the pictures [plural] (*Brit*) the cinema: *We're going to the pictures this evening.* السّينما
▸ **picture** *verb* [T] **1** to imagine sth in your mind: *Kevin used to be so wild. I can't picture him as a father.* يتصور، يتخيّل

2 to make a picture of sb/sth: *The happy couple, pictured above, left for a honeymoon in Bali.* يصور، ينشر صورته

ˈ**picture messaging** *noun* [U] a system of sending images from one mobile phone to another إرسال الصور من هاتف جوال إلى آخر

picturesque /ˌpɪktʃəˈresk/ *adj* (usually used about a place) attractive and interesting: *a picturesque fishing village* جميل كالصّورة، أخّاذ

pie /paɪ/ *noun* [C,U] a type of food. A pastry case is filled with fruit, vegetables or meat and then baked: *apple pie and custard* فطيرة

In Britain a **pie** usually has pastry underneath and on top of the filling. (An American pie may only have pastry underneath). A **tart** or **flan** only has pastry under the filling and is usually sweet. A **quiche** is a type of flan with a savoury filling. Look at **shepherd's pie** and **mince pie**.

piece[1] /piːs/ *noun* [C] **1** an amount or example of sth: *a piece of paper* ○ *a lovely piece of furniture* ○ *Would you like another piece of cake?* ○ *a very good piece of work* ○ *a piece of advice* ○ *a very interesting piece of information* قطعة؛ شيء من، نموذج

2 one of the parts that sth is made of: *She took the model to pieces and started again.* ○ *We need a new three-piece suite* (= a sofa and two chairs). جزء، قطعة

3 one of the parts into which sth breaks: *The plate fell to the floor and smashed to pieces.* ❶ **Bit** and **piece** are very similar in meaning but **bit** is more informal. "حتّة"، "شَقفة"، قطعة

4 one of the small objects that you use when you are playing indoor board games: *chess pieces* إحدى قطع الشطرنج مثلاً

5 a coin: *Does the machine accept fifty-pence pieces?* قطعة نقود

6 an article in a newspaper or magazine مقال أو مقالة

7 a single work of art, music, etc: *He played a piece by Chopin.* قطعة فنيّة: قطعة موسيقيّة

IDM **bits and pieces** → BIT[1]

go to pieces to be unable to control yourself: *When his wife died he seemed to go to pieces.* ينهار، يفقد السيطرة على نفسه

a piece of cake (*informal*) something that is very easy شيء سهل جداً، "لعب عيال"

piece[2] /piːs/ *verb*

PHR V **piece sth together 1** to put sth together from several pieces يلصِق القطع المكسورة مع بعضها، يعيد بناء...

2 to discover the truth about sth from different pieces of information يستنتج من سلسلةٍ من الوقائع

piecemeal /ˈpiːsmiːl/ *adj, adv* done or happening a little at a time تدريجي؛ شيئاً فشيئاً

ˈ**pie chart** *noun* [C] a diagram consisting of a circle divided into parts to show the size of particular parts in relation to the whole رسم بياني دائري

pier /pɪə(r)/ *noun* [C] a large wooden or metal structure that is built out into the sea. Boats can stop at piers so that people can get on or off and goods can be loaded or unloaded. رصيف طويل ممتدّ في البحر

A **pier** in a seaside holiday town is a similar structure which is used as a place of entertainment, with a theatre, amusements, etc.

pierce /pɪəs/ *verb* [T] **1** to make a hole in sth with a sharp point: *She has had her ears pierced.* ○ *The sharp thorns pierced the ball.* يثقب؛ يخترق

2 (used about light or a sound) to be seen or heard suddenly: *A scream pierced the air.* يُرى أو يُسمع فجأة، (صيحة) تخترق أو تشقّ الفضاء
▸ **piercing** *adj* **1** (used about the wind, pain, a loud noise, etc.) strong and unpleasant حادّ، قارس

2 (used about eyes or a look) seeming to know what you are thinking ثاقب، نافذ

piety /ˈpaɪəti/ *noun* [U] strong religious belief ℹ The adjective is **pious**. تقوى، ورَع

pig /pɪɡ/ *noun* [C] **1** a fat animal with short legs and a curly tail خنزير

2 (*informal*) an unpleasant person or one who eats too much شخص كريه أو قذِر، خنزير: شخص نَهِم

▸ **pig** *verb* [T] (pigging; pigged) **pig yourself** to eat or drink too much يأكل بشرَه، يُفرط في الأكل والشُرب

piggyback /ˈpɪɡibæk/ *noun* [C] the way of carrying sb in which he/she rides on your back with his/her arms round your neck and knees round your waist: *to give sb a piggyback* حمْل على الظهر

ˈ**piggy bank** *noun* [C] a small box, often shaped like a pig, that children use for saving money in حصّالة نقود

pigeon /ˈpɪdʒɪn/ *noun* [C] a fat grey bird that often lives in towns حمامة

pigeonhole /ˈpɪdʒɪnhəʊl/ *noun* [C] one of a set of small open boxes that are used for putting papers or letters in أحد أقسام عديدة في خزانة لتصنيف الرسائل والأوراق

ˌ**pig-ˈheaded** *adj* (*informal*) unwilling to change your mind or say that you are wrong ➲ Look at **stubborn** and **obstinate**. They are more formal. عنيد، متشبّث برأيه

piglet /ˈpɪɡlət/ *noun* [C] a young pig خنّوص، خنزير صغير

pigment /ˈpɪɡmənt/ *noun* [C,U] a substance that gives colour to things: *The colour of your skin depends on the amount of pigment in it.* مادّة ملوِّنة، صبغ

pigsty /ˈpɪɡstaɪ/ *noun* [C] (*pl.* **pigsties**) (*also* **sty**; *US* ˈ**pigpen**) a small building where pigs are kept: (*figurative*) *Tidy up your bedroom – it's a pigsty!* زريبة الخنازير: مكان غاية في القذارة

pigtail /ˈpɪɡteɪl/ *noun* [C] a piece of hair that has been divided into three and twisted together (plaited) ضفيرة

pike /paɪk/ *noun* [C] (*pl.* **pike**) a large fish that lives in rivers, lakes, etc. and has very sharp teeth سمك الكراكي

pilchard /ˈpɪltʃəd/ *noun* [C] a small sea fish similar to a herring, that you can eat صابوغة: سمك شبيه بالرنكة

pile[1] /paɪl/ *noun* [C] **1** a number of things lying on top of one another, or an amount of sth that is in a large mass: *He always left his books in a neat pile.* ○ *A large pile of sand blocked the pavement.* ℹ A **pile** may be tidy or untidy. A **heap** is untidy. كومة، كدسة

2 (often plural) (*informal*) a lot of sth: *I've got piles of work to do this evening.* ℹ **Loads of** is also common. اكداس، كثير من...

pile[2] /paɪl/ *verb* [T] **1 pile sth (up)** to put things one on top of the other to form a pile: *Pile them on top of each other.* يكوم، يكدس

2 pile A on(to) B; pile B with A to put a lot of sth on sth: *She piled the papers on the desk.* ○ *The desk was piled with papers.* يكدّس؛ يثقل

PHR V **pile into sth/out of sth** (*informal*) to go in or out of sth in a disorganized way: *All the children tried to pile into the bus at the same time.* يندفعون (إلى السيّارة) دون نظام، يتزاحمون

pile up 1 to increase in quantity: *The problems really piled up while I was away.* يتراكم، يزداد

2 to put sth in a pile: *They piled up the logs at the side of the house.* يكدّس، يكوم

3 (used about several cars, etc.) to crash into each other تتصادم عدّة سيّارات مع بعضها

piles /paɪlz/ *noun* [plural] = HAEMORRHOIDS

ˈ**pile-up** *noun* [C] a crash that involves several cars, etc. حادث تصادم عدّة سيّارات

pilgrim /ˈpɪlɡrɪm/ *noun* [C] a person who travels to a holy place for religious reasons: *Many pilgrims visit Mecca every year.* حاج

▸ **pilgrimage** /-ɪdʒ/ *noun* [C,U] a journey that is made by a pilgrim: *to make a pilgrimage to Lourdes* حِجّة؛ حَج

pill /pɪl/ *noun* **1** [C] a small round piece of medicine that you swallow: *Take one pill, three times a day after meals.* ○ *a sleeping pill* ➲ Look at **tablet**. حبّة دواء

2 the pill (*also* **the Pill**) [sing.] a pill that some women take regularly so that they do not become pregnant: *She is on the pill.* حبّة (أو حبوب) منْع الحمل

pillar /ˈpɪlə(r)/ *noun* [C] **1** a column of stone, wood or metal that is used for supporting part of a building دعامة، عمود

2 an important and active member of sth: *a pillar of the local golf club* رُكن، عماد، عضو هام...

ˈ**pillar box** *noun* [C] (*Brit*) a tall round red box in a public place into which you can post letters, which are then collected by a postman ➲ Look at **postbox**. (في بريطانيا) صندوق البريد

pillion /ˈpɪliən/ *noun* [C] a seat for a passenger behind the driver on a motorcycle المقعد خلف سائق الدرّاجة الناريّة

pillow /ˈpɪləʊ/ *noun* [C] a large cushion that you put under your head when you are in bed ℹ You use a **pillow** in bed. In other places, e.g. on a chair, you use a **cushion**. مِخدّة، وِسادة

pillowcase /ˈpɪləʊkeɪs/ (*also* **pillowslip** /ˈpɪləʊslɪp/) *noun* [C] a cover for a pillow غطاء المِخدّة

pilot /ˈpaɪlət/ *noun* [C] **1** a person who flies an aircraft: *Philip is an airline pilot.* طيّار

2 a person with special knowledge of a difficult area of water, who guides ships through it مُرشد ملاحيّ

▸ **pilot** *adj* (only *before* a noun) done as an experiment or to test sth: *The pilot scheme will run for six months and then we will judge how successful it has been.* تجريبي

pilot *verb* [T] **1** to guide or help sb/sth (through sth) يرشِد، يقود

2 to act as the pilot of a vehicle يقود طائرة؛ يسيِّر سفينة

a b c d e f g h i j k l m n o p q r s t u v w x y z

3 to be the first to test sth that will be used by everyone: *The new exam is being piloted in schools this year.* يجرّب بغرض الاسترشاد

pimp /pɪmp/ *noun* [C] a man who controls prostitutes, finds customers for them and takes part of the money they earn قوّاد

pimple /ˈpɪmpl/ *noun* [C] a small red spot on your skin بَثْرة

PIN /pɪn/ (*also* **ˈPIN number**) *abbrev* Personal Identification Number; a number given to you by your bank so that you can use a plastic card to take out money from a cash machine رقم التعريف الشخصي

pins

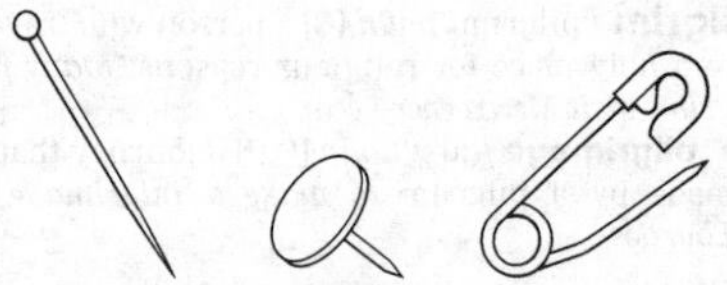

pin — drawing pin (*US* thumbtack) — safety pin

pin¹ /pɪn/ *noun* [C] **1** a short thin piece of metal with a round head at one end and a sharp point at the other. Pins are used for fastening together pieces of cloth, paper, etc. ➲ Look at **drawing pin** and **safety pin**. دبّوس

2 a small piece of wood or metal that is used for a particular purpose: *a hairpin* دبّوس (شَعر مثلاً)، مسمار صغير: خابور

pin² /pɪn/ *verb* [T] (pinning; pinned) **pin sth to/on sth; pin sth together** to fasten sth with a pin or pins: *Could you pin this notice on the board, please?* ○ *The dress is just pinned together. I've not sewn it yet.* ○ (*figurative*) *The policeman held him with his arms pinned to his sides.* ○ (*figurative*) *All our hopes are pinned on him.* يثبّت بمسمار كبس أو بدبّوس، يثبّت؛ يعلّق (آماله) على

PHR V **pin sb/sth against/under sth** to keep sb/sth in one position so that it is impossible to move: *He was pinned under the fallen tree.* ○ *to be pinned against a wall* يسمّر أو يثبّت

pin sb down 1 to cause sb to be unable to move يشلّ حركته

2 to make sb decide sth or say exactly what he/she is going to do: *Can you pin her down and find out what time she will be coming?* يستخلص منه جواباً وافياً

pin sth down to describe or explain exactly what sth is يصف أو يفسّر بدقّة

pinafore /ˈpɪnəfɔː(r)/ *noun* [C] a piece of clothing for the front part of your body that you wear to keep your other clothes clean when you are cooking or doing dirty jobs ➲ Look at **apron**. مريلة أو "مريول" لوقاية الملابس

pincer /ˈpɪnsə(r)/ *noun* **1** [C] one of the two front claws of some shellfish that are used for catching and eating food كلّاب (عند بعض القشريات)

2 pincers [plural] a tool that is used for holding things, pulling nails out of wood, etc. كمّاشة

pinch /pɪntʃ/ *verb* [T] **1** to squeeze a piece of sb's skin tightly between your thumb and first finger: *The lesson was so boring I had to pinch myself to stay awake.* ○ *Paul pinched his brother and made him cry.* يقرص

2 (*informal*) to steal: *Someone's pinched my umbrella.* يسرق

▸ **pinch** *noun* [C] **1** an act of pinching (1): *She gave him a little pinch on the arm.* قرصة

2 the amount of sth that you can pick up with your thumb and first finger: *a pinch of salt* ذرّة او رشّة (ملح)

IDM **at a pinch** if necessary but with some difficulty: *We really need three but we could manage with two at a pinch.* بشيء من الصعوبة

take sth with a pinch of salt to believe that sth is probably not true or completely accurate لا يصدّق تماماً

pinched *adj* (used about sb's face) thin and pale because of illness, cold, etc. (وجه) هزيل شاحب

pine¹ /paɪn/ *noun* **1** [C] (*also* **ˈpine tree**) a tall tree that has thin sharp leaves (needles) and woody fruit (pine cones): *a Swedish pine forest* شجرة الصنوبر

Trees, like the pine, that do not lose their leaves in winter are called **evergreen**.

2 [U] the wood from pine trees (which is often used for making furniture): *a pine table* خشب الصنوبر

pine² /paɪn/ *verb* [I] to be very unhappy because sb has died or gone away or because you cannot have sth that you want: *I hope you haven't been pining for me while I've been away.* يحزن؛ يحنّ إلى؛ يهْزَل

pineapple /ˈpaɪnæpl/ *noun* [C,U] a large juicy fruit that is yellow inside and has a thick brown skin with sharp points. Pineapples grow in hot countries: *pineapple juice* الأناناس

ping /pɪŋ/ *noun* [C] the short high noise that is made by a small bell or by a metal object hitting against sth hard طنّة، رنّة؛ أزيز

▸ **ping** *verb* [I,T]: *The microwave oven will ping when the food is ready.* يطن، يرن؛ يئز

ping-pong /ˈpɪŋpɒŋ/ *noun* [U] (*informal*) = TABLE TENNIS

pink /pɪŋk/ *adj* pale red in colour: *Baby girls are often dressed in pink clothes.* (لون) ورديّ أو زهريّ أو بمبة

▸ **pink** *noun* [U] a pink colour: *The bedroom was decorated in pink.* اللّون الورديّ

pinkish *adj* rather pink مائل إلى الورديّ

pinnacle /ˈpɪnəkl/ *noun* [C] **1** a pointed stone ornament on the top of a church or castle قمة البرج المدبّبة

2 a high rock on a mountain ذُروة الجبل

3 the highest point of sth: *Mary is at the pinnacle of her career.* ذروة، قمّة، أَوْج

pinpoint /ˈpɪnpɔɪnt/ *verb* [T] **1** to find the exact position of sth: *to pinpoint a place on the map* يعيّن الموقع بدقّة بالغة

2 to describe or explain exactly what sth is: *Once the cause of the failure has been pinpointed, we can decide what to do about it.* يحدِّد بدقّة

ˌpins and ˈneedles *noun* [U] (*informal*) the little pains that you get in a part of your body after it has been in one position for too long and when the blood is returning to it: *I've got pins and needles in my hand.* تنميل اليدَين أو القدمَين

pint /paɪnt/ *noun* [C] **1** (*abbr* **pt**) a measure of liquid; 0.57 of a litre. There are 8 pints in a gallon: *a pint of milk* ℹ An American pint is 0.47 of a litre. مكيال للسوائل

2 (*informal*) a pint of beer: *Let's have a pint at the pub.* قدَح من البيرة

ˈpin-up *noun* [C] (*informal*) a picture of an attractive person, in a magazine or pinned on a wall صورة فتاة أو شاب جذّابين تعلَّق على الجدار

pioneer /ˌpaɪəˈnɪə(r)/ *noun* [C] **1** a person who is one of the first to go and live in a particular area: *the pioneers of the American West* أحد المقيمين الأوائل في منطقة ما

2 a person who is one of the first to go somewhere or do sth: *Yuri Gagarin was one of the pioneers of space exploration.* رائد

▶ **pioneer** *verb* [I,T] to be one of the first people or organizations to go somewhere, do sth or develop sth: *The hospital is famous for its pioneering work in heart surgery.* يسبق، يَشقّ طريقاً جديداً

pious /ˈpaɪəs/ *adj* having or showing a deep belief in and love of religion تقيّ، ورِع

▶ **piously** *adv* ℹ The noun is **piety**. بتقى، بورع

pip¹ /pɪp/ *noun* [C] the small seed of an apple, a lemon, an orange, etc. بذرة التفاحة أو الليمونة الخ...

pip² /pɪp/ *verb* (pipping; pipped)

IDM **pip sb at the post** to defeat sb at the last moment or by a small amount يهزم خصمه قُبيل النهاية أو بمقدار قليل

pipe¹ /paɪp/ *noun* [C] **1** a hollow tube that carries gas or liquid: *The burglar climbed up a drainpipe and got in through an open window.* ○ *a gas pipe* ○ *The hot-water pipe has burst.* أنبوب

2 a small tube with a bowl at one end that is used for smoking tobacco: *Does Don smoke a pipe?* غليون

3 a simple musical instrument that consists of a tube with holes. You blow into it to play it. مزمار

4 pipes [plural] = BAGPIPES

pipe² /paɪp/ *verb* **1** [T] to carry liquid or gas in pipes¹(1): *Water is piped to all the houses in the village.* ينقل بالأنابيب؛ يذيع موسيقى عبر أنحاء (المخزن مثلاً)

2 [I,T] to play music on a pipe (3) يزمِّر، يعزف على مزمار

pipeline /ˈpaɪplaɪn/ *noun* [C] a line of pipes¹ (1) that are used for carrying liquid or gas: *The oil pipeline stretches from Iraq to the Turkish coast.* خطّ الأنابيب

IDM **in the pipeline** being planned or prepared في مرحلة الإعداد، "في الطريق"

piper /ˈpaɪpə(r)/ *noun* [C] a person who plays a pipe (3) or the bagpipes الزمّار، العازف على القربة

pirate /ˈpaɪrət/ *noun* [C] **1** a sailor who attacks and robs ships at sea قرصان

2 a person who copies books, videotapes, computer programs, etc. in order to sell them illegally من ينسَخ ويبيع أعمال الآخرين دون ترخيص منهم

▶ **piracy** /ˈpaɪrəsi/ *noun* [U] **1** robbery by pirates القرصنة

2 illegal copying of books, videotapes, etc. نسخ أعمال الآخرين وبيعها دون ترخيص منهم

pirate *verb* [T] to copy a book, video tape, etc. in order to sell it ينسَخ ويبيع أعمال الآخرين دون ترخيص منهم

Pisces /ˈpaɪsiːz/ *noun* [C,U] the twelfth sign of the zodiac, the Fishes; a person who was born under this sign برج الحوت؛ شخص من برج الحوت

pistachio /pɪˈstæʃiəʊ; -ˈstɑːʃiəʊ/ (*also* **pistachio nut**) *noun* [C] (*pl.* **pistachios**) the small green nut of an Asian tree فستق

pistol /ˈpɪstl/ *noun* [C] a small gun that you hold in one hand: *She aimed the pistol and fired.* ○ *a water pistol* ➲ Look at the note at **gun**. مسدَّس

piston /ˈpɪstən/ *noun* [C] a piece of metal in an engine, etc. that fits tightly inside a tube. The piston is moved up and down inside the tube and itself causes other parts of the engine to move. مكبس

pit¹ /pɪt/ *noun* [C] **1** a large hole that is made in the ground: *a gravel pit* حفرة كبيرة في الارض

2 = COAL MINE: *to work down the pit*

3 the pits [plural] the place near a racetrack where cars stop for fuel, new tyres, etc. during a race (في سباق السيّارات) موقف للتزود بالبنزين أو لتبديل العجلة

IDM **be the pits** (*informal*) (*especially US*) to be very bad: *The food in that restaurant is the pits!* أردأ ما يكون!

pit² /pɪt/ *verb* [T] (pitting; pitted) to make shallow holes in the surface of sth: *The front of the building was pitted with bullet marks.* يحفَر، ينقُر، يثقّب

PHRV **pit sb/sth against sb/sth** to test sb/sth against sb/sth else in a fight or competition: *The two strongest teams were pitted against each other in the final.* يختبر قوّته بمباراة خصمه

pita = PITTA

pitch¹ /pɪtʃ/ *verb* **1** [T] to set sth at a particular level: *The talk was pitched at people with far more experience than me.* ○ *a high-pitched voice* يحدِّد مستوى (المحاضرة مثلاً)؛ يعيِّن طبقة الصوت

2 [I,T] (to cause sb/sth) to fall over: *His bike hit a stone and he was pitched forwards over the handlebars.* يقذف بـ، يطرح أرضاً

3 [I] (used about a ship or plane) to move up and down or from side to side تتخبّط (السفينة)، تهتزّ وتتأرجح (الطائرة)

4 [T] to put up a tent or tents: *They pitched camp in the valley.* ينصب (خيمة)

5 [T] to throw sth (often a ball) يرمي، يقذف

PHRV **pitch in** (*informal*) to join in and work

together with other people: *Everybody has to pitch in when we're busy.* يساهم، يشارك

pitch² /pɪtʃ/ *noun* **1** [C] a special area of ground where you play certain sports: *a cricket, football, hockey, etc. pitch* ○ *on/off the pitch* ○ *The fans invaded the pitch when the match ended.* ➲ Look at **court¹**. ملعب رياضي

2 [sing.] the level of sth: *The children's excitement almost reached fever pitch.* درجة، حدّ، مستوى

3 [U] the degree of highness or lowness of a musical note or a voice طبقة الصوت أو النغمة الموسيقية

4 [U] the movement of a ship or an aircraft up or down or from side to side تمايل (السفينة) إلى الأمام وإلى الوراء أو ترنّحها

ˌpitch-ˈblack (*also* **ˌpitch-ˈdark**) *adj* completely dark; with no light at all (ظلام) حالك أو دامس

pitcher /ˈpɪtʃə(r)/ *noun* [C] **1** a large container for holding and pouring liquids ❶ In US English this is the usual word for **jug**. إبريق، كوز

2 (in baseball) the player who throws the ball to a player from the other team, who tries to hit it الرامي (بيسبول)

pitchfork /ˈpɪtʃfɔːk/ *noun* [C] a fork with a long handle and two sharp metal points, that is often used on a farm for lifting and moving cut grass, etc. شوكة القش، مذراة تفريغ

piteous /ˈpɪtiəs/ *adj* (*formal*) that makes you feel pity or sadness مثير للشفقة؛ محزن

▸ **piteously** *adv* بشكل مثير للشفقة

pitfall /ˈpɪtfɔːl/ *noun* [C] an unexpected danger; a mistake that you might easily make خطر غير متوقع، مطبّ؛ زلّة يسهل ارتكابها

pith /pɪθ/ *noun* [U] the white substance inside the skin of an orange, etc. لبّ قشرة البرتقالة (وغيرها) الأبيض

pithy /ˈpɪθi/ *adj* (**pithier**; **pithiest**) expressed in a clear, direct way: *a pithy comment* (تعبير) محكم واضح

pitiful /ˈpɪtɪfl/ *adj* causing you to feel pity or sadness: *the pitiful groans of the wounded soldiers* ➲ Look at **pathetic**. محزن، مثير للشفقة

▸ **pitifully** /-fəli/ *adv*: *The children were pitifully thin.* بشكل مثير للشفقة

pitiless /ˈpɪtiləs/ *adj* having or showing no pity for other people's suffering عديم الرحمة

▸ **pitilessly** *adv* دون رحمة أو شفقة

pitta (*US* **pita**) /ˈpiːtə; *Brit also* ˈpɪtə/ (*also* **ˈpitta bread**; **ˈpita bread**) *noun* [U,C] a type of flat bread in the shape of an oval that can be split open and filled خبز يوناني يشبه خبز بلاد الشام

pity /ˈpɪti/ *noun* **1** [U] a feeling of sadness that you have for sb/sth that is suffering or in trouble: *The dog was in such a terrible state that we took it home with us out of pity.* ○ *The situation is his fault so I don't feel any pity for him.* رحمة أو شفقة

2 [sing.] something that makes you feel a little sad or disappointed: *'You're too late. Emily left five minutes ago.' 'Oh, what a pity!'* ○ *Isn't it a pity that Jane couldn't come after all?* ○ *It would be a pity not to use the car now that we've got it.* ○ *'There's a street map in the car.' 'It's a pity you didn't think of it before.'* شيء مؤسف

IDM **take pity on sb** to help sb who is suffering or in trouble because you feel sorry for him/her يشفق عليه ويساعده

▸ **pity** *verb* [T] (*pres part* **pitying**; *3rd pers sing pres* **pities**; *pt, pp* **pitied**) to feel pity or sadness for sb who is suffering or in trouble: *It is not enough to pity these people; we must try to help them.* ○ *I pity the person who has to clean his room!* يشفق على، يرثي

pitying *adj* showing pity: *a pitying look* مشفق، رؤوف

pivot /ˈpɪvət/ *noun* [C] the central point on which sth balances or turns نقطة الارتكاز

▸ **pivot** *verb* [I] to balance or turn on a central point يتوازن أو يدور حول نقطة الارتكاز

pixie (*also* **pixy**) /ˈpɪksi/ *noun* [C] (*pl.* **pixies**) (in children's stories) a small person (a kind of fairy) who has magic powers جنيّة صغيرة لعوب

pizza /ˈpiːtsə/ *noun* [C,U] a round flat piece of dough (like bread) that is covered with tomatoes, cheese, onions, etc. and cooked in an oven (فطيرة) البيتزا

pl. *abbrev* = PLURAL

placard /ˈplækɑːd/ *noun* [C] a large notice that is fixed onto a wall or carried (in a demonstration, etc.) إعلان كبير في مكان عام؛ يافطة أو لائحة

placate /pləˈkeɪt; *US* ˈpleɪkeɪt/ *verb* [T] to make sb feel less angry يراضي، يهدّئ من غضبه

place¹ /pleɪs/ *noun* [C] **1** a particular position or area: *No one can be in two places at once.* ○ *This is a good place for a picnic.* ○ *The wall was damaged in several places.* ○ *to mark your place in a book* (= where you have read to) ○ *Do you think that lamp is in the right place?* مكان

2 a building, village, town, country, etc: *What is your place of birth?* ○ *Vienna is a very beautiful place.* ○ *a popular meeting place for young people* مكان

3 a seat or position for sb/sth: *They went into the classroom and sat down in their places.* ○ *Go on ahead and save me a place in the queue.* ○ *to lay six places for dinner* متّسع: محل، مكان

> A **place** [C] is a seat or position for sb/sth: *If you arrive first, can you keep a place for me?* A place where you can park your car is also called a **space** [C]. You use **space** [U] and **room** [U] when you are talking about area in general: *This piano takes up a lot of space/room.* ○ *There is enough space/room for three people in the back of the car.*

4 your rank or position in society; your role: *I feel it is not my place to criticize my boss.* منزلة: شأن، مهمّة

5 an opportunity to study at a college, play for a team, etc: *Douglas has got a place to study law at Hull.* ○ *Lucy is now sure of a place in the England team.* قبول في جامعة: انضمام إلى فريق

6 the usual or proper position or occasion for

sth: *The room was tidy. Everything had been put away in its place.* ○ *I saw him at the funeral but it was not the place to discuss business.* المكان المناسب

7 the position of a number after the decimal point: *Your answer should be correct to three decimal places.* مرتبة بعد الفاصلة العشريّة

8 the position that you have at the end of a race, competition, etc: *Clare finished in second place.* ترتيب أو مرتبة

9 (*informal*) the house, etc. where you live: *Why not stay the night at our place?* منزل أو مسكن

IDM **change/swap places (with sb)** to take sb's seat, position, etc. and let him/her have yours: *Let's change places so that you can look out of the window.* يُبدِّل مكانه بمكان غيره

fall, fit, slot, etc. into place (used about sth that is complicated or difficult to understand) to become organized or clear in your mind: *Pete spent two hours working on the timetable before it all fell into place.* يصبح مفهوماً أو واضحاً

in the first, second, etc. place (used when you are explaining or giving reasons for sth) firstly, secondly, etc. أولاً، ثانياً...ألخ

in my, your, etc. place in my, your, etc. situation or position: *If I were in your place I would wait a year before getting married.* (لو كنت) مكانَك...(مثلاً)

in place of sb/sth; in sb/sth's place instead of sb/sth: *The professor was too ill to travel but she sent one of her colleagues in her place.* بَدَلاً من، عوَضاً عن

put yourself in sb else's/sb's place to imagine that you are sb else: *Put yourself in Steve's place and you will realize how worried he must be.* إفرض أنّك فلان، ضع نفسك في مكانه

out of place 1 not in the correct or usual place في غير محلّه

2 not suitable for a particular situation: *I felt very out of place among all those clever people.* ناب، غير لائق

take place to happen: *The ceremony took place in glorious sunshine.* يحدث، يجري

place² /pleɪs/ *verb* [T] **1** to put sth in a particular position or in its usual or proper position: *Dominic placed the cup on the table.* ○ *The chairs had all been placed in neat rows.* ○ *to place an advertisement in a newspaper* ○ (*figurative*) *We placed our trust in you and you failed us.* ○ (*figurative*) *The blame for the disaster was placed firmly on the company.* يَضَع

2 to put sb in a particular position or situation: *His behaviour placed me in a difficult situation.* ○ *to place sb in charge* ○ *Jane was placed third.* يَضَع؛ يعيِّن؛ يرتِّب أو يصنِّف

3 to remember who sb is or where you have seen them before يتذكّر اسم شخص أو أين قابله سابقاً

4 to give an order for sth to a person or company: *We placed an order for 150 T-shirts with a company in York.* يقدّم طلباً لشراء شيء ما

'place name *noun* [C] the name of a city, town, hill, etc. اسم مكان، اسم مدينة أو قرية... الخ

placid /'plæsɪd/ *adj* calm or not easily excited هادئ الطبع، وديع

▸ **placidly** *adv* بهدوء، بِلا اعتراض

plague /pleɪg/ *noun* **1** [C,U] a disease that spreads quickly and kills many people وباء؛ طاعون

2 [C] a large number of unpleasant animals or insects that come into an area at one time: *a plague of ants* أسراب من...

▸ **plague** *verb* [T] to cause sb/sth trouble or discomfort: *The project was plagued by a series of disasters.* يَبتَلي

plaice /pleɪs/ *noun* [C,U] (*pl.* **plaice**) a type of flat sea fish, eaten as food سمك الشبّوط

plain¹ /pleɪn/ *adj* **1** (only *before* a noun) all one colour; without a pattern, etc: *Shall we have a plain or patterned carpet?* سادة أي ذو لون واحد؛ بسيط دون زخرف

2 simple in style: *The rooms are quite plain, but very comfortable.* ○ *My father likes plain English cooking.* ○ *Do you prefer plain* (= dark and strong) *or milk chocolate?* بسيط؛ (شوكولا) سادة دون حليب

3 easy to see, hear or understand; clear: *It was plain that he didn't want to talk about it.* ○ *She made it plain that she didn't want to see me again.* ○ *His instructions were very plain.* واضح، جليّ

4 (used about people, thoughts, actions, etc.) saying what you think; direct and honest: *I'll be plain with you. I don't like the idea.* صريح، صادق

5 (used especially about a woman or girl) not beautiful: *She's a rather plain child.* غير جميلة

▸ **plain** *adv* (*especially US*) completely: *That is plain wrong.* تماماً

plainly *adv* clearly: *Smoke was plainly visible nearly twenty miles away.* ○ *He was plainly very upset.* بوضوح، بشكل جليّ

plain² /pleɪn/ *noun* [C] a large area of flat land with few trees: *the great plains of the American Midwest* سهل

plain³ /pleɪn/ *noun* [C] a simple stitch used in knitting: *knit two plain, one purl* قُطبة عاديّة في حياكة التريكو

ˌplain 'clothes *noun* [plural] (used in connection with the police) ordinary clothes; not uniform: *The detectives were in plain clothes.* ○ *a plain-clothes detective* التحرّي، بوليس بملابس مَدَنيّة

ˌplain 'flour *noun* [U] flour that does not contain a powder, (baking powder) which makes cakes, etc. rise ➲ Look at **self-raising flour**. دقيق أو طحين صرف (أي خال من مسحوق الخميرة)

plaintiff /'pleɪntɪf/ *noun* [C] (*formal*) a person who starts a legal action against sb in a court of law ➲ Look at **defendant**. المدّعي (في القضاء)

plaintive /'pleɪntɪv/ *adj* sounding sad (صوت) شجيّ أو حزين

▸ **plaintively** *adv* بصوت شَجيّ

plait /plæt/ (*US* **braid**) *verb* [T] to twist three or more long thin pieces of hair, rope, etc. over and under each other to make one thick piece يضفر

a b c d e f g h i j k l m n o p q r s t u v w x y z

▶ **plait** *noun* [C] a long piece of hair, rope, etc. that has been plaited: *to wear your hair in a plait/in plaits* ضفيرة

plan /plæn/ *noun* [C] **1** an idea or arrangement for doing or achieving sth in the future: *Have you got any plans for the weekend?* ○ *We usually make our holiday plans in January.* ○ *The firm has no plans to employ more people.* ○ *The best plan is to ask him to meet us on Monday.* خطّة

2 a list, drawing or diagram that shows how sth is to be organized: *Before you start writing an essay, it's a good idea to make a brief plan.* مخطّط

3 a map showing how a particular place is arranged: *a plan of the Safari Park* ○ *a street plan of Berlin* مخطّط، خارطة

4 a drawing that shows a building, part of a building, machine, road, etc. as seen from different positions: *We're getting an architect to draw up some plans for a new kitchen extension.* ○ *You can study the plans for the motorway at the Town Hall.* تصميم

IDM **go according to plan** to happen as planned يسير كلّ شيء على ما يرام

▶ **plan** *verb* (planning; planned) **1** [I,T] to decide, organize or prepare for sth: *to plan for the future* ○ *You need to plan your work more carefully.* يخطّط، يضع خِطّة

2 [I,T] **plan (on sth)** to intend doing sth: *I'm planning on having a holiday in July.* ○ *We're planning to arrive at about 4 o'clock.* ينوي

3 [T] to make a plan of or for sth; to design sth: *You need an expert to help you plan the garden.* ○ *The new shopping centre seems to be very badly planned.* يصمّم

planning *noun* [U] making plans or arrangements: *The project requires careful planning.* ○ *Family planning* (= using contraception) *enables people to control the number of children they have.* تخطيط، تنظيم

plane[1] /pleɪn/ (*also* **aeroplane**; *US* **airplane**) *noun* [C] a vehicle with wings and one or more engines that can fly through the air: *We boarded the plane in Geneva.* ○ *a plane ticket* ○ *Has her plane landed yet?* ○ *a Pan Am plane* ○ *a plane crash* طائرة

plane[2] /pleɪn/ *noun* [C] (*technical*) a flat surface المستوي، سطح مستو

plane[3] /pleɪn/ *noun* [C] a tool used for making the surface of wood smooth by taking very thin pieces off it المسحاج، فارة النجّار

▶ **plane** *verb* [T] يسحج، ينعّم الخشب بالفارة

planet /ˈplænɪt/ *noun* [C] a large body in space (like a star) that moves around the sun or another star: *the natural resources of our planet* (= of the Earth) كوكب

▶ **planetarium** /ˌplænɪˈteəriəm/ *noun* [C] (*pl.* **planetariums**) a building that contains an apparatus for showing the positions and movements of the planets and stars قاعة كبيرة تري مواقع الكواكب والنجوم وحركاتها

plank /plæŋk/ *noun* [C] a long flat piece of wood (that is used for making floors, etc.) لوح خشبيّ طويل

plant

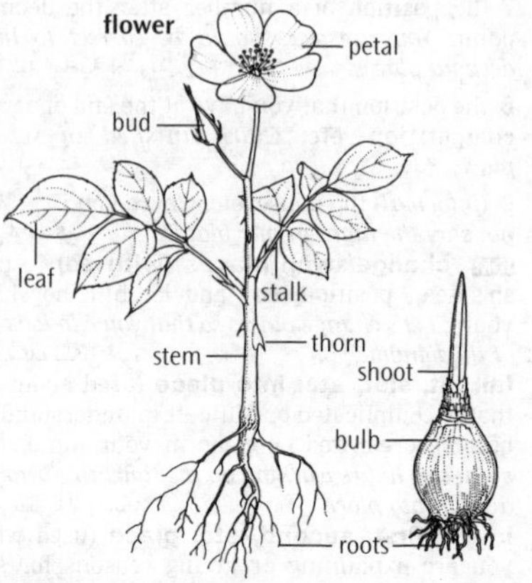

plant[1] /plɑːnt; *US* plænt/ *noun* **1** [C] a living thing that grows in earth and has a stem, leaves and roots: *a tomato plant* ○ *a house plant* (= one that grows in a pot inside a house) ○ *to water the plants* نبات

2 [C] a building where an industrial process takes place; a large factory مصنع أو معمل

plant[2] /plɑːnt; *US* plænt/ *verb* [T] **1** to put plants, seeds, etc. in the ground to grow: *Bulbs should be planted in the autumn.* يزرع، يغرس

2 plant sth (with sth) to cover or supply a garden, area of land, etc. with plants: *It takes a lot of hard work to plan and plant a new garden.* ○ *The field's been planted with wheat this year.* يزود حديقة بالنباتات

3 to put sb/sth firmly in a certain position: *He planted himself in the best seat.* يرسّخ، يثبّت

4 plant sth (on sb) to hide sth somewhere for a secret and usually criminal purpose (sometimes in order to make sb seem guilty of a crime): *The police think that terrorists may have planted the bomb.* ○ *The women claimed that the drugs had been planted on them.* يَدُسّ، يُخفي شيئاً ممنوعاً عند عدوّه ليوقع به

plantation /plɑːnˈteɪʃn/ *noun* [C] **1** a large area of land, especially in a tropical country, where tea, cotton, tobacco, etc. are grown مزرعة كبيرة وخاصّة في بلد استوائيّ

2 an area of land planted with trees: *plantations of fir and pine* مَشْجَرة أو غابة مزروعة

plaque[1] /plæk; plɑːk; *US* plæk/ *noun* [C] a flat piece of stone or metal that is fixed on a wall as a way of remembering a famous person or past event: *a memorial plaque* لوحة على جدار لتخليد ذكرى ما

plaque[2] /plæk; plɑːk; *US* plæk/ *noun* [U] a harmful substance that forms on teeth قُلاح (يتشكّل على الأسنان)

plasma screen /ˌplæzmə ˈskriːn/ *noun* [C] a type of television or computer screen that is larger and thinner than most screens and produces a very clear image شاشة البلازما

plaster /ˈplɑːstə(r); *US* ˈplæs-/ *noun* **1** [U] a soft mixture of sand, water, etc. that becomes hard when it is dry. Plaster is put on walls and ceilings to form a smooth surface.
خليط من الماء والرمل وغيره لتغطية الجدران والسقف

2 (*also* **Band-Aid™**) [C] a small piece of sticky material that is used to cover a cut, etc. on the body: *a waterproof plaster* ℹ Another word for a plaster is a **sticking plaster**.
لصيقة طبيّة لتغطية الجروح

3 [U] a white substance that becomes hard when dry and is used for putting round broken bones, etc. until they mend: *When Alan broke his leg it was in plaster for six weeks.* جص أو جبس
▸ **plaster** *verb* [T] **1** to cover a wall, etc. with plaster (1) يغطّي الحائط مثلاً بطبقة من الأسمنت وغيره
2 to cover sth thickly with sth; to put things onto a surface: *The car was plastered with mud.* ○ *She had plastered her room with posters.* ○ *She had plastered pictures of the singer all over her room.* يطلي بطبقة سميكة، يكسو

plastic /ˈplæstɪk/ *noun* [C,U] a light, artificial material which does not break easily and is used for making many different sorts of objects: *A lot of kitchen utensils are made of plastic.* ○ *Plastics and other synthetic materials are commonly used today.* البلاستيك؛ اللدائن
▸ **plastic** *adj* (used about goods) made of plastic: *plastic cups and spoons* ○ *a plastic bag*
بلاستيكي

ˌplastic ˈsurgery *noun* [U] doing a surgical operation to repair or replace damaged skin or to improve the appearance of a person's face or body: *Several of the fire victims needed plastic surgery.* جراحة تجميليّة

plate /pleɪt/ *noun* **1** [C] a flat, usually round, dish for eating or serving food from: *Put the cake on a plate.* ○ *a plastic plate* ○ *a paper plate*
طبق، صحن

> You eat your main course from a **dinner plate**. You may put bread, etc. on a **side plate**. You usually eat cereal or a pudding from a **bowl**.

2 [C] a thin flat piece of metal or glass
لوح معدنيّ أو زجاجي

3 [C] a flat piece of metal with sth written on it: *I couldn't read the car's number plate.*
لوحة كُتب عليها شيء

4 [U] metal that has a thin covering of gold or silver: *gold plate* مَعدن مموّه بالذهب أو الفضة

5 [C] a picture or photograph in a book that takes up a whole page: *colour plates* لوحة في كتاب

6 [C] a piece of plastic with false teeth fixed to it that fits inside a person's mouth طقم أسنان
▸ **plateful** /-fʊl/ *noun* [C] the amount of food that a plate (1) can hold مِلء طَبَق، طَبَق مليء

plateau /ˈplætəʊ; *US* plæˈtəʊ/ *noun* [C] (*pl.* **plateaus** or **plateaux** /-təʊz/) **1** a large area of high, flat land أرض مرتفعة مستوية السّطح، نَجْد
2 a state where there is little development or change: *House prices seem to have reached a plateau.* مرحلة عدم تغيُّر

platform /ˈplætfɔːm/ *noun* [C] **1** a raised floor in a public place, where people stand to make speeches or to perform منَصّة
2 a flat raised surface, especially the area beside the track at a railway station where passengers get on and off trains: *Which platform does the train to York leave from?* رصيف في محطّة قطار
3 the ideas and aims of a political party, especially as expressed before an election
البرنامج الانتخابي لحزب

platinum /ˈplætɪnəm/ *noun* [U] a valuable grey-ish-white metal that is often used for making jewellery: *a platinum ring* البلاتين

platonic /pləˈtɒnɪk/ *adj* (used about a relationship between two people) not sexual (حبّ) عذري

platoon /pləˈtuːn/ *noun* [C] a small group of soldiers فصيلة عسكريّة

plausible /ˈplɔːzəbl/ *adj* sounding as if it is true; reasonable: *a plausible excuse* ℹ The opposite is **implausible**. مقبول ظاهراً، (يبدو) معقولاً

play¹ /pleɪ/ *verb* **1** [I] to do sth to enjoy yourself; to have fun: *They've been playing on the beach all day.* ○ *He's playing with his new toy.* ○ *Jane's found a new friend to play with.* يلعب، يلهو
2 [I,T] to take part in a sport, game or match: *'What about a game of chess?' 'I'm afraid I don't know how to play.'* ○ *Who's Brazil playing next in the World Cup?* ○ *I play football on Saturdays.*
يلعب (رياضة)
3 [I,T] **play (sth) (with/against sb)**; **play sb (at sth)** to compete against sb in a game or sport: *I usually play against Bob.* ○ *The school plays rugby against other schools nearby.* ○ *She played him at cards and won!* يلاعب؛ يلعب ضد...
4 [T] **play sth (on sb)** to do sth which may surprise or annoy sb for your own amusement: *Schoolchildren often play tricks on their teachers.* يعابث، "يعمل عليه مقلباً"
5 [I,T] to make music with a musical instrument: *My son's learning the piano. He plays very well.* ○ *She played a few notes of the tune on the violin.* ○ *Could you play that piece of music again?* يعزف

> We always use the definite article **the** before the names of musical instruments: *to play the piano* ○ *to learn the trumpet, etc.*

6 [T] to turn on a CD, tape, etc. so that it produces sound: *Shall I play the CD for you again?* يسمع تسجيلاً أو شريطاً
7 [I] (*formal*) to move quickly and lightly: *A smile played on her lips.* يتماوج، يتلألأ؛ (ابتسامة) ترتسم
PHR V **play at sth/being sth** to do sth with little interest or effort: *He's only playing at studying. He'd prefer to get a job now.* ○ *Whatever is that driver playing at?* (= doing)
يعبث، يتسلّى: (ماذا) يعمل!!

play sth back (to sb) to turn on a tape or a film after recording the material on it: *We made a video of the occasion and played it back to all the guests before they left.*
يستمع إلى شريط أو يرى فيلماً بعد تسجيلهما

play sth down to make sth seem less important than it really is: *to play down a crisis*
يقلّل من أهميّة الحادثة

play A off against B to make people compete or argue with each other, especially for your own advantage: *I think she enjoys playing one boyfriend off against the other.* يؤلّب شخصاً على آخر

play on sth to use and take advantage of sb's fears or weaknesses: *This advertising campaign plays on people's fears of illness.* يستغل ضعف

play (sb) up to cause sb trouble or pain: *The car always plays up in wet weather.*
يسبّب المتاعب، يضايق؛ يؤلم

play² /pleɪ/ *noun* [U] **1** activity done for enjoyment only, especially by children: *Young children learn through play.* ○ *Everybody needs a balance of work and play.* اللعب، اللهو

2 the playing of a game or sport; the way it is played: *Bad weather stopped play yesterday.* ○ *rough play* لعب (الرياضة)

We **play** tennis, football, etc. but we CANNOT say **a play** of tennis. We have **a game** of tennis.

IDM fair play → FAIR¹

play³ /pleɪ/ *noun* [C] a story which is written to be performed by actors in the theatre, on television or radio: *Would you like to see/go to a play while you're in London?* ○ *a radio play* ○ *The children always put on a school play at the end of term.* ○ *the opening night of the play* مسرحيّة

Actors **rehearse** a play. A theatre company, drama group, etc. **produces** a play. A play is usually acted on a **stage**.

▶ **play** *verb* [I,T] to act a part in a play: *Simon is going to play Romeo.* يمثّل أو يلعب دوراً

Play a part, role, etc. is often used in a figurative way: *Britain has played an active part in the recent discussions.* ○ *John played a key role in organizing the protest.*

playboy /ˈpleɪbɔɪ/ *noun* [C] a rich man who spends his time enjoying himself and spending money غنيّ منغمس في الملذّات

player /ˈpleɪə(r)/ *noun* [C] **1** a person who plays a game: *a game for four players* ○ *She's an excellent tennis player.* لاعب

2 a person who plays a musical instrument: *a piano player* عازف

3 (*old-fashioned*) an actor ممثّل

playful /ˈpleɪfl/ *adj* **1** done or said in fun; not serious: *a playful remark* مازح، عابث، غير جديّ

2 full of fun; lively: *a playful puppy*
لعوب؛ مليء بالحيويّة

playground /ˈpleɪgraʊnd/ *noun* [C] a public area of land where children can play: *the school playground* ملعب للأطفال

playgroup /ˈpleɪgruːp/ (*also* **playschool**) (*Brit*) *noun* [C] a school for children aged from about two to five حضانة

playing card /ˈpleɪɪŋ kɑːd/ *noun* [C] = CARD (4)

playing field /ˈpleɪɪŋ fiːld/ *noun* [C] a large field used for sports such as cricket and football
ملعب رياضيّ كبير

ˈplay-off *noun* [C] a match between two teams or players who have equal scores, to decide the winner المباراة الفاصلة بين فريقين متعادلين في النقاط

playschool /ˈpleɪskuːl/ *noun* [C] (*Brit*) = PLAYGROUP

plaything /ˈpleɪθɪŋ/ *noun* [C] (*formal*) a toy
العوبة؛ دمية

playtime /ˈpleɪtaɪm/ *noun* [C,U] a period of time when children at school can go outside to play
فترة الاستراحة بين الدروس، فرصة

playwright /ˈpleɪraɪt/ *noun* [C] a person who writes plays مؤلف مسرحيّ

PLC (*also* **plc**) /ˌpiː el ˈsiː/ *abbrev* (*Brit*) = PUBLIC LIMITED COMPANY

plea /pliː/ *noun* [C] **1** a strong request; an appeal: *a last plea for mercy* التماس، رجاء؛ توسّل

2 a statement made by sb in a court of law in which he/she claims to be guilty or not guilty of a certain crime: *a plea of guilty/not guilty*
ردّ المتّهم بالإنكار أو بالإثبات حول جريمة موجّهة إليه

plead /pliːd/ *verb* (*pt, pp* **pleaded**; *US* **pled** /pled/) **1** [I] **plead (with sb) (for sth)** to ask sb for sth in a very strong and serious way: *She pleaded with him not to leave her.* ○ *The hostages' families pleaded for their release.* يتوسّل إلى

2 [T] to give sth as an excuse or explanation for sth: *He pleaded family problems as the reason for his lack of concentration.* يتحجج بـ، يتشفّع بـ

3 [I,T] **plead (for/against sb)** (*formal*) (used especially about a lawyer in a court of law) to support sb's case: *He needs the very best lawyer to plead for him.* يدافع أمام القضاء

4 [T] (*formal*) (used about sb accused of a crime in a court of law) to say that you are guilty or not guilty: *The defendant pleaded not guilty to the charge of theft.* يردّ على تهمة أمام القضاء

pleasant /ˈpleznt/ *adj* nice, enjoyable or friendly: *The weather was very pleasant.* ○ *What a pleasant surprise!* ○ *It must be pleasant to live in such a peaceful place.* ○ *He's a very pleasant young man.* ○ *My father's never very pleasant to my boyfriends.* ❶ The opposite is **unpleasant**.
سارّ، محبّب، لطيف

▶ **pleasantly** *adv* بصورة مريحة أو محبّبة

please /pliːz/ *verb* **1** [I,T] to make sb happy; to satisfy: *The shop assistant was a bit too eager to please.* ○ *I'll put on my best clothes to please my mother.* ○ *That teacher's very difficult to please.*
يرضي، يسرّ

2 [I] (not used as the main verb in a sentence; used after words like *as, what, whatever, anything*, etc.) to want; to choose: *You can't always* *do exactly as you please.* ○ *She has so much money she can buy anything she pleases.* يريد، يشاء

▸ **please** *interj* (used as a polite way of making a request, an inquiry or giving an order): *Come in, please.* ○ *Is this the right road for Brighton, please?* ○ *Please don't spend too much money.* ○ *Sit down, please.* ○ *Two cups of coffee, please.* ℹ We do not use **please** in English when we are giving something to somebody. من فضلك، لطفاً!

IDM **please yourself** to be able to do whatever you want: *Without anyone else to cook for, I can please myself what I eat.* يفعل ما يحلو له

yes, please (used when you are accepting sth politely): *'Sugar?' 'Yes, please.'* نعم، من فضلك!

pleased *adj* (not before a noun) **pleased (with sb/sth); pleased to do sth** happy or satisfied: *John seems very pleased with his new car.* ○ *My parents aren't at all pleased with me at the moment.* ○ *We were very pleased to hear your wonderful news.* ○ *I'm pleased that you've decided to stay another week.* ➲ Look at the note at **glad**. ℹ The opposite is **displeased**. مسرور من؛ راضٍ عن

pleasing *adj* giving pleasure: *The results are very pleasing, I must say.* ℹ The opposite is **displeasing**. سارّ

⚷ **pleasure** /'pleʒə(r)/ *noun* **1** [U] the feeling of being happy or satisfied: *Parents get a lot of pleasure out of watching their children grow up.* ○ *He stood back and looked at his work with obvious pleasure.* ○ *It gives me great pleasure to introduce our next speaker.* سرور، سعادة

2 [U] enjoyment (rather than work): *Are you in Paris on business, or is it for pleasure?* متعة، سرور

3 [C] an event or activity, that you enjoy or that makes you happy: *It's been a pleasure to work with you.* ○ *This car is a pleasure to drive.* ○ *'Thanks for your help.' 'It's a pleasure.'* تجربة سعيدة، فرصة سارّة

IDM **take (no) pleasure in sth/doing sth** to enjoy/not enjoy (doing) sth يتمتّع (أو لا يتمتّع) بِ، يُسَرّ (أو لا يُسَرّ) بِ

with pleasure (used as a polite way of saying that you are happy to accept or agree to sth): *'Could you give me a lift into town?' 'Yes, with pleasure.'* بكلّ سرور

▸ **pleasurable** /'pleʒərəbl/ *adj* (*formal*) enjoyable: *a pleasurable experience* سارّ، ممتِع

pleat /pli:t/ *noun* [C] a fold that is sewn or pressed into a piece of cloth: *a skirt with pleats at the front* ثنية مكويّة (في التنّورة مثلاً)، كَسْرة

pled (*US*) *pt, pp* of PLEAD

pledge /pledʒ/ *noun* [C] a promise or agreement: *The government made a pledge to bring down interest rates.* وعد، عهد

▸ **pledge** *verb* [T] **pledge (sth) (to sb/sth)** to promise to give or do sth: *They pledged their support to us.* ○ *The Government has pledged £250 000 to help the victims of the crash.* ○ *The President pledged to find a peaceful solution.* ○ *The management pledged that an agreement would be reached.* يَعِد، يأخذ على نفسه عهداً

plentiful /'plentɪfl/ *adj* available in large amounts or numbers: *Fruit is plentiful at this time of year.* ➲ Look at **scarce**. وفير، كثير، غزير

⚷ **plenty** /'plenti/ *pron* as much or as many as you need; a lot: *'Shall I get some more coffee?' 'No, we've still got plenty.'* ○ *Make sure you take plenty of warm clothes with you.* ○ *There's still plenty of time to get there.* ○ *Have you brought plenty to drink?* ما فيه الكفاية؛ كثير من...

▸ **plenty** *adv* **1** (before *more*) a lot: *There's plenty more ice cream.* أكثر بكثير

2 (with *big, long, tall*, etc. followed by *enough*): *'This shirt's too small.' 'Well, it looks plenty big enough to me.'* كفاية؛ بما فيه الكفاية

pliable /'plaɪəbl/ *adj* **1** easy to bend or shape: *Plastic is more pliable than wood.* مَرِن أو لَدِن، قابل للثني

2 (used about a person or a person's mind) easy to influence (شخص) سهل الإقناع

pliers /'plaɪəz/ *noun* [plural] a tool that is used for holding things tightly, pulling nails out of wood, cutting wire, etc: *Have you got the/some pliers?* ○ *a pair of pliers* زردية، بِنسة

plight /plaɪt/ *noun* [sing.] (*formal*) a bad or difficult state or situation: *to be in an awful plight* مِحنة؛ ورطة

plimsoll /'plɪmsəl/ *noun* [C] (*Brit*) (*US* **sneaker**) a light shoe made of canvas that is especially used for sports, etc: *a pair of plimsolls* ➲ Look at **trainer**. حذاء قماشي خفيف

plod /plɒd/ *verb* [I] (plo**dd**ing; plo**dd**ed) **plod (along/on) 1** to walk slowly and in a heavy or tired way: *We plodded on through the rain for nearly an hour.* يمشي بجهد وتثاقل، يتخبّط في مشيته

2 to do sth or to work slowly and with difficulty: *I just plod on with the work day after day and never seem to get anywhere.* يعمل بتثاقل وتعب، يجهد ويكدح

plonk[1] /plɒŋk/ *noun* [sing.] (*informal*) a sound of sth dropping heavily: *The tin fell onto the floor with a plonk.* قرقعة، خبطة

▸ **plonk** *adv*: *The lamp fell plonk onto the floor.* بقرقعة شديدة

plonk *verb* [T] **plonk sth (down)** (*informal*) to put sth down or to drop sth heavily: *Just plonk your bag down anywhere.* يُلقي شيئاً ثقيلاً على الأرض، يخبط

plonk[2] /plɒŋk/ *noun* [U] (*informal*) (*Brit*) cheap wine: *Let's open a bottle of plonk!* نبيذ رخيص

plop /plɒp/ *noun* [usually sing.] a sound like that of a smooth object dropping into water: *With a tiny plop the ring disappeared into the water.* صوت شيء يسقط في الماء

▸ **plop** *verb* [I] (plo**pp**ing; plo**pp**ed) to fall with a plop: *The fish plopped back into the water.* يسقط أو يغطس في الماء محدثاً صوتاً

⚷ **plot**[1] /plɒt/ *noun* [C] **1** a secret plan made by several people, to do sth that is wrong: *a plot to kill the president* مؤامرة

2 the events in a story, film, etc. and how they develop: *The play had a very strong plot but the*

a b c d e f g h i j k l m n o **p** q r s t u v w x y z

acting was terrible. ○ *I can't follow the plot of this novel.* حبكة القصّة

▸ **plot** *verb* [I,T] to make a secret plan to do sth: *They were accused of plotting against the government.* ○ *The terrorists had been plotting this campaign for years.* يتآمر على

plot² /plɒt/ *noun* [C] a small piece of land, used for a special purpose: *a vegetable plot* ○ *They're selling two plots of land for development.* قطعة أرض

▸ **plot** *verb* [T] (plo**tt**ing; plo**tt**ed) to mark sth on a map, diagram, graph, etc: *to plot the ship's course on the map* ○ *to plot the figures on a graph* يعيِّن (خطّ الرحلة) على خارطة؛ يرسم خطّاً بيانياً

plough (*US* **plow**) /plaʊ/ *noun* [C] a large tool which is used on a farm and is pulled by a tractor or by an animal. A plough turns the soil over and is used especially before seeds are planted: *a snowplough* (= a tool like a plough that is used for clearing snow from roads) محراث

▸ **plough** (*US* **plow**) *verb* [I,T] to break up and turn over the soil, with a plough: *to plough the fields* ○ (*figurative*) *The book was long and boring but I managed to plough through it* (= read it with difficulty). يحرث، يفلَح؛ يتقدّم بصعوبة

ploy /plɔɪ/ *noun* [C] something that you say or do in order to get what you want or to persuade sb to do sth: *He realized that her kindness had been a ploy to get him to stay.* حيلة

pluck /plʌk/ *verb* **1** [T] to pull sth in order to pick or remove it: *He plucked the letter from my hands.* ○ *to pluck your eyebrows* (= to pull out the hairs you do not want) ينتش: ينتف: يقطف

2 [I,T] **pluck (at sth)** to pull sth, often in order to get attention: *The little girl plucked at her mother's skirt.* يمسك بـ، يجذب (كمّه) ليسترعي انتباهه

3 [T] to pull the feathers out of a chicken, etc. in order to prepare it for cooking ينتف

4 [T] to pull the strings of a musical instrument and let them go again, in order to make music ينقر أوتار آلة موسيقية

IDM **pluck up courage** to try to be brave enough to do sth يستجمع شجاعته

▸ **pluck** *noun* [U] (*informal*) courage شجاعة، جرأة

plucky *adj* (**pluckier**; **pluckiest**) brave شجاع، جسور

plugs

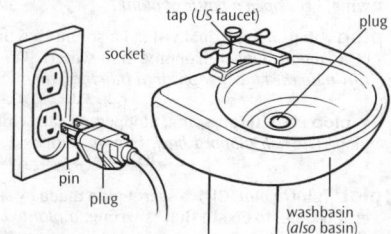

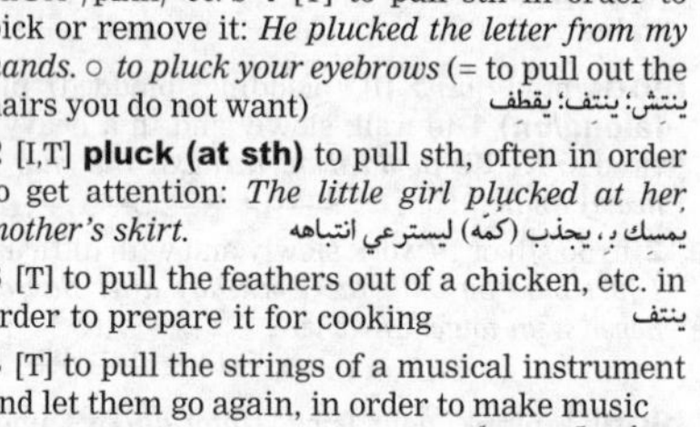

plug /plʌg/ *noun* [C] **1** a plastic or rubber object with two or three metal pins, which connects the wire on a piece of electrical equipment to a point in the wall where there is electricity (a socket) القابِس، "الفيشة أو الفيش"

2 (*informal*) = SOCKET: *I'll get the electrician to fit a plug beside the bed.*

3 a piece of rubber, metal or plastic that fits tightly into a hole (e.g. in a bath, basin, etc.) سدادة (البالوعة مثلاً)، سطام

4 a favourable reference to a book, record, etc. made in public in order to make people buy the thing mentioned دعاية أمام الجمهور لعمل أدبيّ أو فنّي

▸ **plug** *verb* [T] (plu**gg**ing; plu**gg**ed) **1** to fill or block a hole with sth: *He managed to plug the leak in the pipe with a piece of plastic.* يسدّ

2 (*informal*) to praise a book, record, etc. in public in order to make people buy the thing mentioned: *They're really plugging that song on the radio at the moment.* يقوم بدعاية لعمل أدبيّ أو فنّي

PHR V **plug sth in** to connect sth to the electricity supply with a plug (1): *The video isn't plugged in.* ❶ The opposite is **unplug**. يَصل بالكهرباء

plughole /ˈplʌghəʊl/ *noun* [C] (*Brit*) a hole in a bath, sink, etc. into which you put a plug (3) بالوعة المغسلة وغيرها

plum /plʌm/ *noun* [C] a soft, round fruit with red or yellow skin and a stone in the middle خوخ (سوريا)، برقوق (مصر)، عنجاص (عراق)

plumber /ˈplʌmə(r)/ *noun* [C] a person whose job is to put in and repair water pipes, baths, sinks, etc. السبّاك، مصلّح حنفيّات وغيرها

plumbing /ˈplʌmɪŋ/ *noun* [U] **1** all the pipes, water tanks, etc. in a building: *The plumbing in this house is very old and noisy.* مجموعة أنابيب المياه والمجاري في مبنى

2 the work of a person who puts in and repairs the water pipes, tanks, etc. السِّباكة

plume /pluːm/ *noun* [C] **1** a large and often bright feather ريشة كبيرة زاهية اللون

2 something worn in the hair or on a hat, made from feathers or long, thin pieces of material ريش تزيينيّ للشَّعر

3 a quantity of smoke that rises in the air عمود من الدخان

plummet /ˈplʌmɪt/ *verb* [I] (*formal*) to fall suddenly and quickly from a high level or position: *prices plummeted to an all-time low.* ○ *The jet plummeted into a row of houses* ينهار، يهوي

plump¹ /plʌmp/ *adj* (used about a person or an animal) rather fat (but looking nice): *the baby's plump cheeks* ○ *a nice, plump chicken* ممتلئ الجسم (بشكل جذّاب)

plump² /plʌmp/ *verb*

PHR V **plump (oneself/sb/sth) down** to sit down or to put sth down heavily: *She plumped herself down by the fire.* يرتمي بثقل (على المقعد مثلاً): يخبط شيئاً (على الأرض)

plump for sb/sth to choose or decide to have: *I think I'll plump for the roast chicken, after all.* يختار، يقرِّر أن يتناول...

plunder /ˈplʌndə(r)/ *verb* [I,T] to steal things from a place, especially during war or fighting: *They captured the city, killing and plundering as they advanced.* يسلب وينهب (خاصّة أثناء الحرب)
▸ **plunder** *noun* [U] **1** the act of stealing from people or places سلب ونهب
2 the goods that are stolen الغنيمة، الأسلاب

plunge /plʌndʒ/ *verb* **1** [I] **plunge (into sth)** to go, jump, dive, fall, etc. suddenly and with force into sth: *He turned and plunged into the crowd.* ○ *A woman plunged to her death from the cliffs at Beachy Head yesterday.* يندفع فجاة؛ يقتحم؛ يلقي بنفسه في
2 [T] **plunge sth in/into sth** to push sth suddenly and with force into sth: *He plunged the knife into the woman's arm and ran off.* يُغْمِد؛ يقحِم
3 [T] to cause sb/sth to be in the state mentioned: *The country has been plunged into chaos by the first snow of the winter.* يقحِم؛ يغرق
4 [I] **plunge into sth** to suddenly start or become involved in sth: *She was about to plunge into her story when the phone rang.* يدخل في، ينغمس في (العمل)
5 [I] to move suddenly downwards; to decrease: *The horse tripped and plunged to the ground.* ○ *The value of the pound plunged overnight.* يسقط فجاة؛ يتدهور فجاة
▸ **plunge** *noun* [C] a sudden forward or downward movement, a dive, fall or decrease: *a plunge into cold water* ○ *the plunge in house prices* نَطّة أو غطسة في الماء؛ سقوط مفاجئ
IDM **take the plunge** to decide to do sth difficult after thinking about it for quite a long time (وأخيراً قرّر أن) يقوم بهذه المجازفة

pluperfect /ˌpluːˈpɜːfɪkt/ *noun* [sing.] (*grammar*) = PAST PERFECT

plural /ˈplʊərəl/ *noun* [C] (*grammar*) the form of a noun, verb, etc. which refers to more than one person or thing: *The plural of 'man' is 'men'.* ○ *The verb should be in the plural.* صيغة الجمع
▸ **plural** *adj* (*grammar*) referring to more than one person or thing: *A plural noun must be followed by a plural verb.* ➲ Look at **singular**. في صيغة الجمع

plus /plʌs/ *prep* **1** and; added to: *Two plus two is four (2 + 2 = 4).* ➲ Look at **minus**. زائد
2 as well as: *I've got an essay to write this evening plus some reading to do.* إضافة إليه، وأيضاً
▸ **plus** *adj* (only *after* a noun) **1** or more: *He gets a salary of £30 000 plus.* وأكثر
2 (used for marking work done by students) slightly above: *I got a B plus (written 'B+') for my homework.* ➲ Look at **minus**. (عند وضع درجات للطّلاب): "ب+" تعني أعلى قليلاً من "ب"
plus *noun* [C] **1** the sign (+): *He mistook a plus for a minus.* علامة الزائد
2 an advantage: *The job involves a lot of travel, which is a definite plus.* ➲ Look at **minus**. ميزة إضافيّة، حسنة

plush /plʌʃ/ *adj* smart and expensive: *a plush hotel* فَخْم

Pluto /ˈpluːtəʊ/ *noun* [sing.] the planet that is furthest from the sun كوكب بلوتو

plutonium /pluːˈtəʊniəm/ *noun* [U] a radioactive substance used especially as a fuel in nuclear power stations عنصر البلوتونيوم

ply /plaɪ/ *verb* (*pres part* **plying**; *3rd pers sing pres* **plies**; *pt, pp* **plied** /plaɪd/) [I,T] (used about ships, boats, buses, etc.) to travel regularly on a certain route: *ships that ply the Atlantic* (ناقلة) تُسافر على خطّ واحد بانتظام
PHR V **ply sb with sth** to keep giving sb food and drink, or asking sb questions: *He plied her with questions about her work.* يظلّ يقدّم لضيفه طعاماً وشراباً؛ يغرقه بالأسئلة

plywood /ˈplaɪwʊd/ *noun* [U] board made by sticking thin layers of wood on top of each other خشب معاكس أو رقائقيّ، أبلكاش

p.m. /ˌpiː ˈem/ (*US* **P.M.**) *abbrev* after midday: *2 p.m.* (= 2 o'clock in the afternoon) ○ *11.30 p.m.* (= 11.30 in the evening) بعد الظهر

pneumonia /njuːˈməʊniə; *US* nuː-/ *noun* [U] a serious illness of the lungs which makes breathing difficult ذات الرئة

PO /ˌpiː ˈəʊ/ *abbrev* = POST OFFICE

poach[1] /pəʊtʃ/ *verb* [T] **1** to cook an egg without its shell in boiling water: *poached eggs* يسلق بيضة دون قِشرتها
2 to cook food (especially fish) in water or milk that is boiling gently يطبخ (سمكاً مثلاً) في ماء أو حليب يغلي

poach[2] /pəʊtʃ/ *verb* **1** [I,T] to catch or shoot birds, animals or fish on sb else's land without permission يصطاد في أرض غيره دون إذن
2 [T] to take an idea from sb else and use it in an unfair way يسرق أفكار غيره
3 [T] to take members of staff from another company "يسرق" أي يستميل موظفي شركة أخرى للعمل عنده
▸ **poacher** *noun* [C] a person who catches birds, animals or fish on sb else's land without permission مَنْ يصيد في ارض غيره دون اذن

pocket /ˈpɒkɪt/ *noun* [C] **1** a small bag that is sewn inside or on sth you wear and is used for carrying things in: *He always walks with his hands in his trouser pockets.* ○ *a pocket dictionary, calculator, etc.* (= one small enough to fit in your pocket) جَيْب
2 a bag or flap that is fixed to the inside of a car door, suitcase, etc. and used for putting things in: *There are safety instructions in the pocket of the seat in front of you.* جَيْب؛ محفظة
3 a small area or group of sth: *pockets of unemployment* ○ *a pocket of warm air* جَيْب
IDM **pick sb's pocket** → PICK[1]
▸ **pocket** *verb* [T] **1** to put sth in your pocket: *He took the letter and pocketed it quickly.* يضع في جيبه
2 to steal sth or to keep money for yourself يسرق، يضع في جيبه سرقةً

pocketful /-fʊl/ *noun* [C] the amount that a pocket holds مِلء جيب

pocketbook /ˈpɒkɪtbʊk/ *noun* [C] **1** a small book or notebook دفتر جيب

2 (*US*) = WALLET

ˈ**pocket knife** *noun* [C] (*pl.* **pocket knives**) = PENKNIFE

ˈ**pocket money** *noun* [U] an amount of money that parents give a child, usually every week مصروف الجيب للطفل؛ خرجيّة (سوريا)

pod /pɒd/ *noun* [C] the long, green part of some plants, such as peas and beans, that holds the seeds سِنفة، قرن (حبّات الفاصوليا...الخ)

podcast /ˈpɒdkɑːst; *US* ˈpɒdkæst/ *noun* [C] a recording of a radio broadcast or a video that can be taken from the Internet "بودكاست": ملَفّات الوسائط المتعددة

podium /ˈpəʊdiəm/ *noun* [C] a small platform for a speaker, a performer, etc. to stand on مَنصّة، مِنبَر

⚷**poem** /ˈpəʊɪm/ *noun* [C] a piece of writing, often arranged in short lines which rhyme. Poems try to express thoughts and feelings with the help of sound and rhythm: *a Wordsworth poem* ○ *to write a poem* قطعة شِعْر، قصيدة

poet /ˈpəʊɪt/ *noun* [C] a person who writes poems شاعر

poetic /pəʊˈetɪk/ (*also* **poetical** /-kl/) *adj* **1** beautiful and full of imagination شِعْريّ، خياليّ، سحري

2 of or like poets and poetry: *poetic language* (مَيْل) شِعْري

▸ **poetically** /-kli/ *adv* بأسلوب شِعْري

⚷**poetry** /ˈpəʊətri/ *noun* [U] poems, thought of as a group or a form of literature: *Shakespeare's poetry and plays* ○ *poetry and prose* الشِّعْر

poignant /ˈpɔɪnjənt/ *adj* causing sadness or pity: *a poignant memory* مؤثِّر، مؤلم، جارح
▸ **poignancy** /-jənsi/ *noun* [U] (*formal*) the state or quality of being poignant ألم، حدّة؛ شدّة الحزن
poignantly /-jəntli/ *adv* بصورة مؤثِّرة

⚷**point**[1] /pɔɪnt/ *noun* [C, sing.] **1** [C] something that you say as part of a discussion; a particular fact, idea or opinion: *During the meeting she made some interesting points.* ○ *I see your point but I don't agree with you.* نقطة، فكرة، رأي

> We **bring up**, **raise**, **make**, **argue**, **emphasize** and **illustrate** a point.

2 [C] an important idea or thought that needs to be considered: *'Supposing it rains – where shall we have the barbecue?' 'That's a point!'* فكرة تستحقّ الاهتمام

3 the point [sing.] the most important part of what is being said; the main piece of information: *The point is that we can't go on holiday until the car's been repaired.* ○ *She always talks and talks and takes ages to get to the point.* النقطة الهامّة في الموضوع

4 [C] a detail, single item, quality of sb/sth: *What would you say are your strong and your weak points?* (= good and bad qualities) صفة، خاصيّة

5 [sing.] the meaning, reason, purpose, etc. of sth: *What's the point of telephoning her again?* ○ *There's no point in telling my parents all my problems.* غرض، قصد؛ معنى، فائدة

6 [C] (often in compounds) a particular place or position: *We should be reaching the point where the road joins the motorway.* ○ *The library is a good starting point for that sort of information.* ○ *He aimed the gun at a point just above the man's head.* مكان، موضع، نقطة

7 [C] any of the 32 marks on a compass that show direction, especially North, South, East and West إحدى الجهات على البوصلة

8 [C] the thin sharp end of sth: *the point of a pin, needle, pencil, etc.* رأس (الدبّوس مثلاً)

9 points [plural] (*Brit*) a set of rails where a railway line divides into two tracks. Points can be moved to allow a train to use either track. وسيلة تنقل القطار من سكة الى اخرى

10 [C] a small round dot used when writing parts of numbers الفاصلة العشريّة

11 [C] a particular time or moment; a stage of progress, development, etc: *At one point I thought I was going to laugh.* ○ *He has reached the high point of his career.* ○ *the boiling/freezing point of water* وقت، مرحلة؛ درجة (الغليان)

12 [C] a single mark in some games, sports, etc. that you add to others to get the score: *to score a point* ○ *After the first round of the competition Mrs Wilson had scored 32 points.* ○ *Federer has two match points.* (يسجِّل) نقطة

13 [C] a unit of measurement for certain things: *The value of the dollar has fallen by a few points.* نقطة (وحدة قياس)

IDM **beside the point** → BESIDE
have your, etc. points to have some good qualities له بعض الصفات الحسنة، لا باس به
if/when it comes to the point if or when the moment to act or decide comes: *If it comes to the point I will have to tell him what I really think.* (اذا حانَ) او عندما يحين وقت العمل
make a point of doing sth to be especially careful to do sth: *I'll make a point of inviting them to our next party.* يحرص أو يتعمد أن يقوم بعمل ما
on the point of doing sth just going to do sth: *I was on the point of going out when the bell rang.* على وشْك
point of view a way of looking at a situation; an opinion: *You must try to understand other people's points of view.* ○ *From my point of view it would be better to wait a little longer.* وجهة نظر، راي

> Do not confuse **from my point of view** with **in my opinion**. The first means 'from my position in life' i.e. as a woman, child, teacher, etc. The second means 'I think': *From an advertiser's point of view, television is a wonderful medium.* ○ *In my opinion people watch too much television.*

prove your/the case/point → PROVE
a sore point → SORE

stretch a point → STRETCH[1]
sb's strong point → STRONG
take sb's point to understand and accept what sb is saying: *I tried to explain what I meant but I don't think he took my point.* يقتنع؛ يفهم
to the point connected with what is being discussed: *His speech was short and to the point.* في صلب الموضوع
up to a point partly: *I agree with you up to a point.* الى حدّ ما

point[2] /pɔɪnt/ *verb* **1** [I] **point (at/to sb/sth)** to show where sth is or to draw attention to sth using your finger, a stick, etc: *'I'll have that one,' she said, pointing to a big chocolate cake.* يشير إلى، يدلّ على
2 [T] **point sth (at/towards sb/sth)** to aim sth in the direction of sb/sth: *The farmer pointed his gun at the rabbit and fired.* يوجّه، يصوّب
3 [I] to face in a particular direction or to show that sth is in a particular direction: *Go down this road and you'll see the sign pointing towards the motorway.* يتوجّه، يشير إلى
4 [I] **point to sth** to show that sth is likely to exist, happen, be true, etc: *Research points to a connection between smoking and cancer.* يدلّ، يشير
PHRV **point sth out (to sb)** to direct attention to sth; to make clear to sb: *The guide pointed out all the places of interest to us on the way.* ○ *I'd like to point out that we haven't got much time left.* يلفت انتباهه؛ يوضّح
▸ **pointed** *adj* **1** having a point at one end: *a pointed nose* مدبّب، مستدق
2 done or spoken in a way that makes it clear that you are being critical: *She made a pointed comment about people who are always late.* (تعليق) انتقادي
pointedly *adv* متعمّداً، بصورة ذات مغزى

ˌ**point-'blank** *adj, adv* **1** (used about sth that is said) in a way that is very direct and often rather rude; not allowing any discussion: *He told her point-blank to get out of the house.* دونَ لفٍّ ودوران، بصراحة تامّة
2 (used about a shot) from a very close position: *The shot was fired at point-blank range.* (طلقة) من مسافة قريبة جداً

pointer /'pɔɪntə(r)/ *noun* [C] **1** a piece of helpful advice or information: *Could you give me some pointers on how best to tackle the problem?* نصيحة، إرشاد
2 a stick or rod which is used to point to things on a map, etc. المؤشّر
3 a small arrow on a computer screen that you move by moving the mouse السهم

pointless /'pɔɪntləs/ *adj* without any use or purpose: *It's pointless to try and make him agree.* ○ *My whole life seemed pointless after my husband died.* عديم الفائدة؛ بلا هدف
▸ **pointlessly** *adv* دون مبرر، بلا لزوم
pointlessness *noun* [U] بطلان، عدم جدوى

poise /pɔɪz/ *noun* [U] a calm, confident way of behaving رزانة، ثقة بالنّفس
▸ **poised** *adj* **1** not moving but ready to move: *'Shall I call the doctor or not?' he asked, his hand poised above the telephone.* جامد في مكانه لكنه على استعداد للتحرك
2 poised (to do sth) ready to act; about to do sth: *The government is poised to take action if the crisis continues.* على استعداد لـ...؛ على وشك القيام بـ
3 calm and confident متّزن وواثق من نفسه، وَقور

poison /'pɔɪzn/ *noun* [C,U] a substance that kills or harms you if you eat or drink it: *The label on the bottle said, 'Poison. Not to be taken internally.'* ○ *rat poison* ○ *poison gas* سُمّ
▸ **poison** *verb* [T] **1** to give poison to sb/sth; to kill, harm or damage sb/sth with poison: *The police confirmed that the murder victim had been poisoned.* يسمّم، يقتل بالسُّم
2 to put poison in sth: *The cup of coffee had been poisoned.* يدس سمّاً في
3 to spoil or ruin sth: *The quarrel had poisoned their relationship.* يفسد، يسمّم
poisoned *adj* **1** containing poison: *a poisoned drink* مسمّم، مسموم
2 damaged by dangerous substances: *our poisoned water* ملوّث
poisoner /'pɔɪzənə(r)/ *noun* [C] a person who uses poison to murder sb مسمّم، من يقتل بالسمّ
poisoning /'pɔɪzənɪŋ/ *noun* [U] the giving or taking of poison or a dangerous substance: *His death was the result of poisoning.* ○ *food poisoning* (= illness as a result of eating bad food) تسمّم؛ تسميم
poisonous /'pɔɪzənəs/ *adj* **1** causing death or illness if you eat or drink it: *a poisonous plant* سامّ
2 (used about animals, etc.) producing and using poison to attack its enemies: *poisonous snakes, insects, etc.* سامّ
3 very unpleasant: *She wrote him a poisonous letter criticizing his behaviour.* مليء بالحقد والكراهية، يقطر سمّاً

poke /pəʊk/ *verb* [T] **1** to push sb/sth with a finger, stick or other long, thin object: *He poked the insect with his finger to see if it was alive.* ينخَس، يزغَد، ينكش
2 poke sth into, through, out of, down, etc. to push sth quickly into sth or in a certain direction: *'Hello Jane,' she called, poking her head out of the window.* ○ *He poked the stick down the hole to see how deep it was.* يدُسّ، يُدخل؛ يمدّ (رأسه من النافذة)
IDM **poke fun at sb/sth** to make jokes about sb/sth, often in an unkind way يستهزئ أو يسخر من
poke/stick your nose into sth → NOSE[1]
PHRV **poke about/around** (*informal*) to try to find sth by looking behind, under, etc. things: *I noticed that somebody had been poking about in my desk.* يفتّش في كل زاويا وخفايا المكان
poke out of/through sth; poke out/through/up to appear in a certain place in a sudden or surprising way: *A rabbit's head poked up in the middle of the field and then disappeared.* ينطّ فجأة (من داخل الصندوق مثلاً)، يبرز فجأةً
▸ **poke** *noun* [C] a sharp push: *I gave him a poke in the side to wake him up.* نخسة، زغدة

poker /ˈpəʊkə(r)/ *noun* [C] **1** a metal stick for moving the coal or wood in a fire
محراك النّار، بَشكور

2 a type of card game بوكر (لعبة ورق)

poky /ˈpəʊki/ *adj* (**pokier**; **pokiest**) (*informal*) (used about a house, room, etc.) too small: *a poky little office* صغير جداً

polar /ˈpəʊlə(r)/ *adj* (only *before* a noun) of or near the North or South Pole: *the polar regions* قُطبيّ

ˈ**polar bear** *noun* [C] a large white bear that lives in the area near the North Pole الدُّب القطبيّ

pole¹ /pəʊl/ *noun* [C] either of the two points at the exact top and bottom of the earth: *the North/South Pole* القطب (الشماليّ أو الجنوبيّ)

pole² /pəʊl/ *noun* [C] a long, thin piece of wood or metal, used especially to hold sth up: *a flagpole* ○ *a tent pole* عمود؛ سارية

the ˈpole vault *noun* [C] the sport of jumping over a high bar with the help of a long pole القفز بالزانة، القفز العالي

police /pəˈliːs/ *noun* [plural] the official organization whose job is to make sure that people obey the law, and to prevent and solve crime, etc: *Dial 999 if you need to call the police.* ○ *Have the police been informed of the incident?* ○ *a police car* ○ *a police report* ○ *There were over 100 police on duty* (= members of the police). الشّرطة، رجال البوليس

> **Police** is a plural noun, always used with a plural verb. You cannot say 'a police' meaning one man or woman. When we are talking about the organization, we always use **the**: *The police are investigating the murder.*

▸ **police** *verb* [T] to keep control in a place by using the police or a similar official group: *The cost of policing football games is extremely high.* يضبط الأمن (باستخدام البوليس وغيره)

poˌlice ˈconstable (*also* **constable**) *noun* [C] (*abbr* **PC**) a policeman or policewoman of the lowest rank شرطيّ

poˈlice force *noun* [C] (the organization of) all the police officers in a country or area
هيئة أو قُوات البوليس

policeman /pəˈliːsmən/ *noun* [C] (*pl.* **policemen** /-mən/) a man who is a member of the police شرطيّ

poˈlice officer (*also* **officer**) *noun* [C] a policeman or policewoman: *a plain-clothes police officer* (= one who is not wearing uniform) ➲ Look at **detective**. شرطيّ

poˈlice station *noun* [C] an office of a local police force مخفر الشُّرطة، نقطة البوليس

policewoman /pəˈliːswʊmən/ *noun* [C] (*pl.* **-women** /-wɪmɪn/) a woman who is a member of the police شرطيّة

policy¹ /ˈpɒləsi/ *noun* [C,U] (*pl.* **policies**) **policy (on sth)** a plan of action or statement of aims and ideas, especially that of a government, company or other organization: *Labour has a new set of policies on health and education.* ○ *It is company policy not to allow smoking in meetings.* ➲ Look at the note at **politics**. سياسة؛ خُطّة

policy² /ˈpɒləsi/ *noun* [C] (*pl.* **policies**) a document that shows an agreement that you have made with an insurance company: *an insurance policy* عقد أو بوليصة التأمين

polio /ˈpəʊliəʊ/ (*also formal* **poliomyelitis** /ˌpəʊliəʊˌmaɪəˈlaɪtɪs/) *noun* [U] a serious disease which can cause you to lose the power in certain muscles شَلَل الأطفال

polish /ˈpɒlɪʃ/ *verb* [T] to make sth shine by rubbing it and often by putting a special cream or liquid on it: *Don't forget to polish your shoes!* يلمّع، يَصقُل

PHR V **polish sth off** (*informal*) to finish sth quickly: *I'm just going to polish off one or two jobs and then I'll join you.* يُنهي بسرعة؛ يأتي على (الطعام)

▸ **polish** *noun* **1** [U] a cream, liquid, wax, etc. that you put on sth to clean it and make it shine: *a tin of shoe polish* طلاء للتلميع

2 [sing.] an act of polishing: *I'll give the glasses a quick polish before the guests arrive.* تلميع، صقْل

polished *adj* **1** shiny because of polishing: *polished wood floors* مصقول (بالشّمع)، ملمّع

2 (used about a performance, etc.) of a high standard: *The actors gave a polished performance.* (أداء) رائع، من مستوى رفيع

polite /pəˈlaɪt/ *adj* having or showing good manners, e.g. that you are helpful and thoughtful towards other people and do not say or do things that might upset them; not rude: *The assistants in that shop are always very helpful and polite.* ○ *It's polite to say thank you.* ○ *He gave me a polite smile.* ❶ The opposite is **impolite**. مؤدّب، مهذّب

▸ **politely** *adv* بأدب

politeness *noun* [U] أدب، تهذيب

political /pəˈlɪtɪkl/ *adj* **1** connected with politics and government: *The two main political parties are Conservative and Labour.* ○ *She has very strong political opinions.* ○ *a political prisoner* (= one who has been put in prison for criticizing the government) سياسي

2 (used about people) interested or active in politics ذو اهتمام أو نشاط سياسي

▸ **politically** /-kli/ *adv* with regard to politics: *Politically, he's fairly right wing.* سياسيّاً

poˌlitical aˈsylum *noun* [U] protection given by a state to a person who has left his/her own country for political reasons: *to seek political asylum* لجوء سياسي

poˌlitical corˈrectness *noun* [U] the principle of avoiding language and behaviour that may offend particular groups of people
تجنُّب الاساءة للآخرين

poˌlitically corˈrect *adj* (*abbr* **PC**) showing political correctness مراعٍ للآراء التقدميّة، كيِّس

politician /ˌpɒləˈtɪʃn/ *noun* [C] a person whose

job is in politics, especially one who is a member of parliament or of the government: *a Conservative politician* ○ *Politicians of all parties supported the war.* رجل السياسة، سياسي

politics /ˈpɒlətɪks/ *noun* **1** [U, with sing. or pl. verb] the work and ideas that are connected with governing a country, a town, etc: *Are you interested in politics?* ○ *My son wants to go into politics* (= become a politician). ○ *local politics* ○ *Politics has/have never been of great interest to me.* السّياسة

2 [plural] a person's political opinions and beliefs: *His politics are extreme.* الآراء والميول السياسيّة

> A government's **policy** (= plan of action or aim) will depend on its **politics** (= its ideas and beliefs).

3 [U] the scientific study of government: *a degree in politics* العلوم السياسيّة

poll[1] /pəʊl/ *noun* [C] **1** (*also* **opinion poll**) a way of finding out public opinion by asking a number of people their views on sth: *The Conservatives had a five point lead over Labour in the latest poll.* استطلاع الرأي العام، استفتاء

2 (giving votes at) a political election: *The result of the poll is still uncertain.* ○ *The country will go to the polls in June.* تصويت انتخاب؛ اقتراع

poll[2] /pəʊl/ *verb* [T] **1** to ask sb his/her opinion on a subject: *Of those polled, only 20 per cent were in favour of changing the law.* يستطلع (الرأي العام)

2 to receive a certain number of votes in an election: *The Liberal Democrat candidate polled over 3 000 votes.* يحصل على عدد معيّن من الأصوات

▸ **polling** *noun* [U] voting in an election: *Polling takes place today in the Henley by-election.* اقتراع أو انتخاب

ˈ**polling day** *noun* [C] the day when people vote in an election يوم الانتخابات

pollen /ˈpɒlən/ *noun* [U] a fine, usually yellow, powder which is formed in flowers. It makes other flowers of the same type produce seeds when it is carried to them by the wind, insects, etc. غبار الطّلع

pollute /pəˈluːt/ *verb* [T] to make air, rivers, etc. dirty and dangerous: *Almost all of Britain's beaches are polluted.* يلوّث

▸ **pollutant** /-ənt/ *noun* [C] a substance that pollutes air, water, etc. مادّة ملوِّثة

pollution /pəˈluːʃn/ *noun* [U] **1** the act of polluting: *Major steps are being taken to control the pollution of beaches.* تلويث: تلوُّث

2 substances that pollute: *Five years after the disaster the pollution on the coast of Alaska has still not been cleared.* التلوُّث، المواد الملوِّثة

polo /ˈpəʊləʊ/ *noun* [U] a game for two teams of horses and riders. The players try to score goals by hitting a ball with long wooden hammers. لعبة البولو (على الخيل)

ˈ**polo neck** *noun* [C] a high collar (on a sweater, etc.) that is rolled over and that covers most of your neck: *I'd like a jumper with a polo neck.*

ⓘ The sweater itself can also be called a **polo neck**. قبّة عالية تطوى حول العنق؛ بلوزة (صوف) ذات قبّة عالية

polyester /ˌpɒliˈestə(r); *US* ˈpɒliːestər/ *noun* [U] a type of man-made material that is used for making clothes, etc. بوليستر: قماش صناعيّ يشبه النايلون

polystyrene /ˌpɒliˈstaɪriːn/ *noun* [U] a light firm plastic substance that is used for stopping heat from escaping or for packing things so that they do not get broken بوليسترين: مادّة خفيفة عازلة

polythene /ˈpɒlɪθiːn/ *noun* [U] a type of very thin plastic material often used to make bags for food or to keep things dry مادّة تشبه النايلون تصنع منها أكياس حفظ الأطعمة

polyunsaturated /ˌpɒliʌnˈsætʃəreɪtɪd/ *adj* (used about fats and oils) having the type of chemical structure that is thought to be good for your health: *polyunsaturated margarine* حاوٍ بعض المواد الدهنيّة التي يعتقد أنها مفيدة للصحّة

pomp /pɒmp/ *noun* [U] the splendid nature of a public ceremony أُبّهة

pompous /ˈpɒmpəs/ *adj* feeling or showing that you think you are more important than other people, e.g. by using long and important-sounding words ⓘ This word is used in a critical way. مغرور، متَعَجرِف؛ متَشدِّق

pond /pɒnd/ *noun* [C] an area of water that is smaller than a lake بِركة، بحرة

> A **lake** is usually big enough to sail on: *a boating lake.* A **pond** may be big enough for animals to drink from or may be a very small area of water in a garden: *We have a fish pond in our garden.* A **pool** is a much smaller area of water: *When the tide went out, pools of water were left among the rocks.* A **puddle** is a small pool of water made by the rain.

ponder /ˈpɒndə(r)/ *verb* [I,T] **ponder (on/over sth)** to think about sth carefully or for a long time يفكّر مليّاً: يتأمّل

pong /pɒŋ/ *noun* [C] (*Brit informal*) a strong unpleasant smell رائحة كريهة منفِّرة

▸ **pong** (*Brit informal*) *verb* [I] يصدِر رائحة كريهة منفِّرة

pony /ˈpəʊni/ *noun* [C] (*pl.* **ponies**) a type of small horse حصان صغير الجسم، سيسي

ponytail /ˈpəʊniteɪl/ *noun* [C] long hair that is tied at the back of the head and that hangs down like the tail of a horse ذيل الحصان (تسريحة شعر)

ˈ**pony-trekking** *noun* [U] riding horses for pleasure in the country (often for several days, as a holiday) ركوب الخيل في الريف للمتعة

poodle /ˈpuːdl/ *noun* [C] a type of dog with thick curly hair that is often cut into a special pattern نوع من الكلاب يقصّ شعره الأجعد بشكل تزيينيّ

pooh /puː/ *interj* (*informal*) (used when you smell sth unpleasant) أفّ... رائحة كريهة!

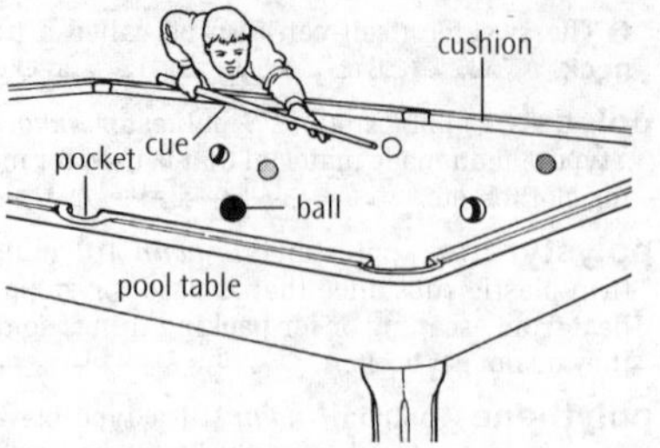

pool

pool¹ /puːl/ *noun* [C] **1** a small shallow area of water: *The heavy rain left pools of water on the pavement.* ○ *rock pools* ➲ Look at **puddle** and at the note at **pond**. بركة

2 a small area of any liquid or of light: *They found her lying in a pool of blood.* ○ *a pool of light* بركة (من الدماء)، بقعة

3 = SWIMMING POOL: *a heated indoor pool* ○ *He swam ten lengths of the pool.*

pool² /puːl/ *noun* **1** [C] a quantity of money, goods, workers, etc. that is shared between a group of people: *There is a pool of cars that anyone in the company can use.*
مجموعة (ممتلكات) يشترك فيها عدد من الناس

2 [U] an indoor game that is played on a table with 16 coloured and numbered balls. Two players try to hit these balls into holes in the table (pockets) with long thin sticks (cues). ➲ Look at **billiards** and **snooker**.
لعبة تشبه البلياردو

3 the pools [plural] = FOOTBALL POOLS

▶ **pool** *verb* [T] to collect money, ideas, etc. from a number of people and share them: *If we pool our ideas we should come up with a good plan.*
يجمّع مالاً أو أفكاراً من عدد من الناس لأغراضهم المشتركة

poor /pʊə(r); *US* pʊər/ *adj* **1** having very little money and a very low standard of living: *The family was too poor to buy proper food.* ○ *We have a duty to help poorer countries.* ❶ The opposite is **rich**. فقير

2 of low quality or in a bad condition: *Paul is in very poor health.* ○ *a poor harvest* ○ *The industry has a poor safety record.* ○ *Attendance at the meeting was poor* (= not as many people came as had been expected). رديء؛ ضعيف

3 (used when you are showing that you feel sorry for sb): *That poor child has lost both her parents.* ○ *Poor Don! He's very upset!*
(الطفل) المسكين!

▶ **the poor** *noun* [plural] people who have little money الفقراء، المساكين

Note that we use **the poor** in the plural. It always means 'poor people' and CANNOT mean 'the poor person'.

poorly¹ /'pʊəli; 'pɔːli/ *adv* not well; badly: *a poorly-paid job* ○ *The science lab is very poorly equipped.* زهيداً؛ بشكل هزيل، بصورة رديئة

poorly² /'pʊəli; 'pɔːli/ *adj* (*informal*) not well; ill: *I'm feeling a bit poorly.* متوعّك الصحة

pop¹ /pɒp/ *noun* **1** [C] a short sharp sound like a small explosion: *There was a loud pop as the cork came out of the bottle.* فرقعة، طقّة

2 [U] (*informal*) a sweet drink with bubbles in it that does not contain alcohol. شراب غازيّ

▶ **pop** *adv*: *The balloon went pop.*
بفرقعة، مُحدثاً صوتاً

pop² /pɒp/ *verb* (popping; popped) [I,T] (to cause sth) to make a short sharp sound like a small explosion: *The balloon popped.* ○ *He popped the balloon.* يفقع أو يطق (البالون)

PHR V **pop across, down, out, etc.** to come or go somewhere quickly or suddenly: *I'm just popping out to the shops.*
يذهب ويرجع بسرعة، "يخطف رجله"

pop sth across, in, into, etc. sth to put or take sth somewhere quickly or suddenly: *He popped his head round the door and said goodbye.* ينبُق أو يبرز فجاة؛ يدخل بسرعة

pop in to make a quick visit: *Why don't you pop in for a cup of tea?* يزور زيارة سريعة

pop out to come out (of sth) suddenly or quickly: (*figurative*) *Her eyes nearly popped out of her head in surprise.*
تجحظ عيناه من الدهشة؛ يقفز من مكانه

pop up (*informal*) to appear or happen when you are not expecting it يحدث أو يظهر دون توقّع

pop³ /pɒp/ *noun* [U] (*informal*) modern music that is most popular among young people: *I like pop and jazz.* ○ *pop music* ○ *a pop group* ➲ Look at **jazz**, **rock³** and **classical**.
موسيقى الشباب والمراهقين الحديثة

pop⁴ /pɒp/ *noun* [C] (*US informal*) father
أب، أبي أو بابا

pop. *abbrev* = POPULATION

popcorn /'pɒpkɔːn/ *noun* [U] a type of corn (maize) that is heated until it bursts and becomes light and fluffy بوشار، فشار

pope /pəʊp/ *noun* [C] the head of the Roman Catholic Church: *Pope Benedict* (قداسة) البابا

poplar /'pɒplə(r)/ *noun* [C] a type of tall straight tree with soft wood شجرة الحور

popper /'pɒpə(r)/ (*also* **press stud**) *noun* [C] (*Brit*) two round pieces of metal or plastic that you press together in order to fasten a piece of clothing كبّاس أو كبسول أو طَبّاق

poppy /'pɒpi/ *noun* [C] (*pl.* **poppies**) a bright red wild flower that has small black seeds: *a roll with poppy seeds on top* زهرة الخشخاش

Popsicle™ /'pɒpsɪkl/ *noun* [C] (*US*) = ICE LOLLY

popular /'pɒpjələ(r)/ *adj* **1** liked by many people or by most people in a group: *Spain is a popular holiday destination.* ○ *He's always been very popular with his pupils.* ❶ The opposite is **unpopular**. محبوب من الناس؛ محبوب من قبل فئة معيّنة

2 for ordinary people (= not for specialists or people with a high level of education): *The*

popular newspapers seem more interested in scandal than news. شعبي

3 (only *before* a noun) of or for a lot of people: *The programme is being repeated by popular demand.* شعبي، (من قِبَل) الجماهير

▸ **popularity** /ˌpɒpjuˈlærəti/ *noun* [U] the quality or state of being liked by many people: *The Green Party has been gaining in popularity recently.* ○ *to lose popularity* شعبيّة

popularize (*also* **popularise**) /ˈpɒpjələraɪz/ *verb* [T] to make sth popular with, or known to, a lot of people: *The film did a lot to popularize her novels.* يعرّف الناس بـ، يروّج

popularly *adv* by many people; generally: *The Conservatives are popularly known as Tories.* عند كثير من الناس؛ بشكل عامّ

populate /ˈpɒpjuleɪt/ *verb* [T] (usually passive) to fill a particular area with people: *Parts of Wales are very thinly populated.* ○ *Britain as a whole is very densely populated.* يؤهل، يعمّره بالسكّان

⚷ **population** /ˌpɒpjuˈleɪʃn/ *noun* **1** [C,U] a number of people who live in a particular place: *What is the population of your country?* ○ *an increase/a fall in population* عدد السكّان

2 [C] all the people who live in a particular area: *The report examines the effects of the changes on the local population.* ○ *The local population is/are very much against the changes.* السكّان، أهالي المنطقة

3 [C] all the people or animals of a particular type that live in an area: *The prison population has greatly increased in recent years.* ○ *the civilian population* (= the people who are not soldiers) ○ *the penguin population of the island* عدد المقيمين في.... فئة، طبقة

> In senses **2** and **3**, **population** is sometimes used in the singular with a plural verb when you are thinking about the individual people who form the population.

porcelain /ˈpɔːsəlɪn/ *noun* [U] a hard white substance that is made by baking clay in an oven. Porcelain is used for making expensive cups, plates, etc. الخزف الصينيّ

porch /pɔːtʃ/ *noun* [C] **1** a covered area at the entrance to a house or church مَدخَل مسقوف

2 (*US*) = VERANDA

pore¹ /pɔː(r)/ *noun* [C] one of the small holes in your skin through which sweat can pass سَمّ (أحد مسامات الجلد)

pore² /pɔː(r)/ *verb*

PHRV **pore over sth** to study or read sth very carefully يمعن التفكير في؛ ينكبّ على (كتابه)

pork /pɔːk/ *noun* [U] meat from a pig لحم خنزير

pornography /pɔːˈnɒɡrəfi/ (*also informal* **porn** /pɔːn/) *noun* [U] books, magazines, films, etc. that describe or show sexual acts in order to cause sexual excitement أفلام ومنشورات جنسيّة، أدب أو فنّ إباحيّ

▸ **pornographic** /ˌpɔːnəˈɡræfɪk/ *adj*: *pornographic films* (أفلام) جنسيّة أو إباحيّة

porous /ˈpɔːrəs/ *adj* allowing liquid or air to pass through slowly: *Sand is a porous material.* نَفوذ، مساميّ

porpoise /ˈpɔːpəs/ *noun* [C] a sea animal that looks like a large fish. It is very similar to a dolphin and also lives in groups. خنزير البحر (من الفصيلة الدلفينيّة)

porridge /ˈpɒrɪdʒ; *US* ˈpɔːr-/ *noun* [U] a food that is made from oats mixed with milk or water and usually eaten for breakfast شوفان يُطبخ مع الحليب أو الماء

⚷ **port¹** /pɔːt/ *noun* **1** [C,U] an area where ships load and unload goods and passengers: *a fishing port* ○ *The fleet spent two days in port.* ○ *The damaged ship reached port safely.* مرفأ أو ميناء

2 [C] a town or city that has a harbour: *Hull is a major port.* مدينة ذات مرفأ، ميناء، ثغر

port² /pɔːt/ *noun* [U] the side of a ship that is on the left when you are facing towards the front of the ship ❶ The opposite is **starboard**. جانب السفينة الأيسر (وانت ناظر إلى مقدّمتها)

portable /ˈpɔːtəbl/ *adj* that can be moved or carried easily: *a portable television set* نقّال، قابل للحمل والنقل

porter /ˈpɔːtə(r)/ *noun* [C] **1** a person whose job is to carry suitcases, etc. at a railway station, airport, etc. حمّال

2 a person whose job is to be in charge of the entrance of a hotel or other large building بوّاب

porthole /ˈpɔːthəʊl/ *noun* [C] a small round window in a ship or an aircraft نافذة السفينة أو الطائرة

portion /ˈpɔːʃn/ *noun* [C] **1** a part or share of sth: *What portion of your salary goes on tax?* ○ *We must both accept a portion of the blame.* جزء، نصيب

2 an amount of food for one person (especially in a restaurant): *Could we have two extra portions of chips, please?* ➲ Look at **helping**. كميّة من الطعام لشخص واحد

portrait /ˈpɔːtreɪt/ *noun* [C] **1** a picture, painting or photograph of a person: *to paint sb's portrait* صورة (زيتيّة مثلاً) تمثّل وجه الشّخص

2 a description of sb/sth in words وَصْف أو صورة عن

portray /pɔːˈtreɪ/ *verb* [T] **1** to make a picture, painting or photograph of sb: *The writer was portrayed sitting at his desk.* يرسم، يصوّر

2 to describe sb/sth in words; to show sb/sth in a particular way: *Dickens portrayed life in 19th century England.* ○ *In many of his novels life is portrayed as being hard and brutal.* يصف، يصوّر

3 to act the part of sb in a play or film: *It's hard for a young actress to portray a very old woman.* يلعب أو يمثّل دوراً

▸ **portrayal** /pɔːˈtreɪəl/ *noun* [C]: *He won an award for his portrayal of King Lear.* تصوير؛ وصف؛ تمثيل دور

⚷ **pose** /pəʊz/ *verb* **1** [I] to sit or stand in a particular position for a painting, photograph, etc: *After* *the wedding we all posed for photographs.* يجلس أو يقف أمام المصوِّر أو الرسّام

2 [I] to behave in a way that makes other people notice you: *They hardly swam at all. They just sat posing at the side of the pool.* يقف أو يجلس بتصنُّع

3 [I] **pose as sb/sth** to pretend to be sb/sth: *The robbers got into the house by posing as telephone engineers.* يتظاهر بأنه...، ينتحل شخصية

4 [T] to set, cause or create sth: *The rise in the cost of living is posing problems for many families.* ○ *to pose a question* يخلق، يسبِّب؛ يطرح (سؤالاً)

▸ **pose** *noun* [C] **1** a position in which you pose, e.g. for a painting or photograph وضع خاصّ (أمام الرسام أو المصوِّر)

2 a way of behaving that is intended to impress people who see you تصنُّع، تظاهر

posh /pɒʃ/ *adj* (*informal*) **1** fashionable and expensive: *We went for a meal in a really posh hotel.* راقٍ وفخم

2 (*Brit*) (used about people) belonging to or typical of a high social class: *He's got a really posh accent.* (لهجة) ارستقراطيّة، من طبقة راقية

⚷**position** /pəˈzɪʃn/ *noun* **1** [C,U] the place where sb/sth is or should be: *The enemy's position was marked on the map.* ○ *That plant's in the wrong position. It doesn't like too much sun.* ○ *All the dancers were in position waiting for the music to begin.* موضع، موقع

2 [C,U] the way in which sb/sth sits, stands or is placed: *I've got a stiff neck. I must have been sitting in an awkward position.* ○ *Turn the switch to the off position.* ○ *He woke in pain every time he changed position.* وَضْع

3 [C] **a position (on sth)** what you think about sth; your opinion: *What is your position on smoking?* موقف؛ رأي

4 [C, usually sing.] a state or situation: *What would you do if you were in my position?* ○ *I'm in a very difficult position.* ○ *I'm sorry, I'm not in a position to help you financially.* وَضْع، حالة

5 [C,U] your place or rank in society, in a group, or in a race or competition: *Max finished the race in second position.* منزلة، مركز؛ ترتيب

6 [C] a job: *There have been over a hundred applications for the position of Sales Manager.* وظيفة

7 [C] the part you play in a team game: *'What position do you play?' 'I'm the goalkeeper.'* مركز

▸ **position** *verb* [T] to put sb/sth in a particular place or position: *Mary positioned herself near the door so she could get out quickly.* يضعه في مكان أو وضع معيَّن

⚷**positive** /ˈpɒzətɪv/ *adj* **1 positive (about sth/ that...)** certain; sure: *Are you positive that this is the woman you saw?* متأكِّد، واثق

2 clear; definite: *There is no positive evidence that he is guilty.* ○ *We must take positive action to stop the situation getting worse.* واضح؛ حاسم

3 helpful or encouraging: *The teacher tried to make positive suggestions.* ○ *Their reaction to my idea was generally positive.* مشجِّع، إيجابي

4 hopeful or confident: *I feel very positive about our team's chances this season.* ○ *Positive thinking will help you to succeed.* متفائل، إيجابيّ؛ واثق

5 (used about a medical or scientific test) showing that sth has happened or is present: *The result of the pregnancy test was positive.* إيجابيّ، إثباتيّ

6 (used about a number) more than zero موجِب

ℹ In senses **3** – **6** the opposite is **negative**.

▸ **positively** *adv* **1** with no doubt, firmly: *I was positively convinced that I was doing the right thing.* حتماً، بكلّ تأكيد؛ بشدّة

2 in a way that shows you are thinking about the good things in a situation, not the bad: *Thinking positively helps many people deal with stress.* بشكل إيجابي

3 (used about a person's way of speaking or acting) in a confident way: *The team played cautiously for the first ten minutes, then continued more positively.* بثقة

4 (*informal*) (used for emphasizing sth) really; extremely: *He wasn't just annoyed – he was positively furious!* حقّاً؛ للغاية

⚷**possess** /pəˈzes/ *verb* [T] **1** (*formal*) to have or own: *They lost everything they possessed in the fire.* ○ *It is illegal to possess a gun without a licence.* يملك

2 to influence sb or to make sb do sth: *Whatever possessed you to say a thing like that!* يسيطر على، يتملّك؛ يعتري

▸ **possessor** *noun* [C] a person who has or owns sth المالك

⚷**possession** /pəˈzeʃn/ *noun* **1** [U] the state of having or owning sth: *He was arrested for possession of an illegal weapon.* ○ *Enemy forces took possession of the hill.* امتلاك، حيازة؛ استيلاء

2 [C, usually pl.] something that you have or own: *Bob packed all his possessions into a suitcase and left without a word.* ○ *to insure your possessions* ممتلكات

IDM **in possession (of sth)** having or owning sth: *Two youths were caught in possession of stolen goods.* في حوزته

possessive /pəˈzesɪv/ *adj* **1** not wanting to share sb/sth: *Dan is so possessive with his toys – he won't let anyone else play with them.* محبّ للتملُّك، مُستأثِر

2 (used in grammar to describe words that show who or what a person or thing belongs to): *'My', 'your', 'his' are possessive adjectives.* ○ *'Mine', 'yours', 'his' are possessive pronouns.* دالّ على الملكيّة

⚷**possibility** /ˌpɒsəˈbɪləti/ *noun* (*pl.* **possibilities**) **1** [U] **possibility (of sth/of doing sth)**; **possibility (that...)** the situation when sth might happen or be true; the state of being possible: *What's the possibility of the weather getting better before the weekend?* ○ *There's not much possibility of the letter reaching you before Saturday.* إمكانيّة، احتمال

2 [C] something that might happen or be true; sth that is possible: *There is a strong possibility*

that the fire was started deliberately. ○ *One possibility would be for you to go by train and for me to come later by car.* أمر ممكن

possible /'pɒsəbl/ *adj* **1** that can happen or be done: *I'll phone you back as soon as possible.* ○ *It is possible to phone directly from your hotel room.* ○ *Could you give me your answer today, if possible?* ○ *The doctors did everything possible to save his life.* ○ *You were warned of all the possible dangers.* ➲ Look at **impossible**. ممكن، مستطاع

2 that may be true or suitable: *There are several possible explanations for her strange behaviour.* ○ *There are four possible candidates for the job.* ➲ Look at **probable**. محتَمل، جائز

▶ **possibly** /-əbli/ *adv* **1** perhaps: *'Will you be free on Sunday?' 'Possibly.'* ○ *Edward phoned to say he would possibly be late home.* ربّما

2 (used for emphasizing sth) according to what is possible: *I will leave as soon as I possibly can.* بقدر الإمكان

post¹ /pəʊst/ *noun* [C] an upright piece of metal or wood that is put in the ground to mark a position or to support sth: *The wooden gate post is rotten.* ○ *a goal post* ○ *Can you see a signpost anywhere?* عمود؛ دعامة

IDM **pip sb at the post** → PIP²

post² /pəʊst/ *noun* [C] **1** a job: *the best candidate for the post* ○ *The post was advertised in the local newspaper.* منصب، وظيفة

2 a place where sb is on duty or is guarding sth: *The soldiers had to remain at their posts all night.* مركز حراسة؛ مقرّ الوظيفة

▶ **post** *verb* [T] **1** to send sb to go and work somewhere: *After two years in London, Rosa was posted to the Tokyo office.* يرسِل موظفاً إلى مقرّ عمل جديد

2 to put sb on guard or on duty in a particular place: *Policemen were posted at the front door of the building.* يَضع حارساً أو جنوداً في موقع ما

posting /-ɪŋ/ *noun* [C] a job in another country that you are sent to do by your employer وظيفة في بلد آخر

post³ /pəʊst/ (*especially US* **mail**) *noun* **1** [U] the system or organization for collecting and delivering letters, parcels, etc: *The document is too valuable to send by post.* ○ *Your cheque is in the post.* البريد؛ النظام البريديّ

2 [sing., U] letters, parcels, etc. that are collected or delivered: *Has the post come yet this morning?* ○ *There wasn't any post for you.* ○ *I'll stop now or I'll miss the post* (= collection). ○ *to open the post* بريد

IDM **by return (of post)** → RETURN²

post⁴ /pəʊst/ (*especially US* **mail**) *verb* [T] to send a letter, parcel, etc. to sb by putting it in a postbox or taking it to a post office: *This letter was posted in Edinburgh yesterday.* يرسِل بالبريد

Post (noun and verb) is more commonly used in British English and **mail** in American English. However, British English uses the noun **mail** quite often. The official name of the Post Office organization is the **Royal Mail**. Note too, the expressions **airmail** and **surface mail**. When we order goods in a letter, we use a **mail-order** service.

postage /'pəʊstɪdʒ/ *noun* [U] the amount that you must pay to send a letter, parcel, etc: *The cost of postage and packing is £2.* أجرة البريد، قيمة الطوابع البريديّة

'postage stamp *noun* [C] = STAMP¹

postal /'pəʊstl/ *adj* connected with the collecting and delivering of letters, parcels, etc: *postal charges* بريدي

'postal code *noun* [C] = POSTCODE

'postal order *noun* [C] a piece of paper that you can buy at a post office that represents a certain amount of money. A postal order is a safe way of sending money by post. حَوالة بريدية

postbox (*Brit*) mailbox (*US*)

postbox /'pəʊstbɒks/ (*also* **letter box**) (*US* **mailbox**) *noun* [C] a box in a public place where you put letters, etc. that you want to send ➲ Look at **pillar box**. صندوق بريد عامّ

postcard /'pəʊstkɑːd/ *noun* [C] a card that you write a message on and send to sb. Postcards often have a picture on one side and are usually sent without an envelope. بطاقة بريديّة

postcode /'pəʊstkəʊd/ (*also* **postal code**) (*US* **zip code**) *noun* [C] a group of letters and/or numbers that you put at the end of an address. The postcode helps the Post Office to sort letters by machine. الرمز البريديّ أو رقم المنطقة

poster /'pəʊstə(r)/ *noun* [C] a large printed picture or a notice in a public place, often used to advertise sth صورة كبيرة أو إعلان في مكان عامّ

posterity /pɒ'sterəti/ *noun* [U] the future and the people who will be alive then: *We should look after our environment for the sake of posterity.* الأجيال القادمة، الخَلَف

postgraduate /ˌpəʊst'grædʒuət/ *noun* [C] a person who is doing further studies at a university after taking his/her first degree ➲ Look at **graduate** and **undergraduate**. طالب دراسات عليا

posthumous /'pɒstjʊməs; *US* 'pɒstʃəməs/ *adj* given or happening after sb has died: *a posthumous medal for bravery* ممنوح بعد وفاته

▸ **posthumously** *adv*: *Her last novel was published posthumously.* بعدَ الوفاة

postman /'pəʊstmən/ *noun* [C] (*pl.* **postmen** /-mən/) (*US* **mailman**) a person whose job is to collect and deliver letters, parcels, etc. ساعي البريد

postmark /'pəʊstmɑːk/ *noun* [C] an official mark over a stamp on a letter, parcel, etc. that says when and where it was posted الختم البريدي

post-mortem /ˌpəʊst 'mɔːtəm/ *noun* [C] a medical examination of a dead body to find out how the person died فحص الجثّة طبياً لتحديد سبب الموت

⚷ **'post office** *noun* [C] **1** a building or part of a shop where you can buy stamps, post parcels, etc. مكتب بريد

2 the Post Office the national organization that is responsible for collecting and delivering letters, parcels, etc. مؤسّسة البريد

'post-office box *noun* [C] (*abbr* **PO box**) a place in a post office where letters, parcels, etc. are kept until they are collected by the person they were sent to صندوق بريد: ص.ب.

postpone /pə'spəʊn/ *verb* [T] to arrange that sth will happen at a later time than the time you had planned; to delay: *The wedding was postponed until August because the bride's mother was ill.* ○ *Because of illness, the concert is postponed until further notice* (= no date for it can be given now). ➲ Look at **cancel**. يؤجّل، يرجئ

▸ **postponement** *noun* [C,U] تأجيل، إرجاء

postscript /'pəʊstskrɪpt/ *noun* [C] (*abbr* **PS**) a short message that you add to the end of a letter after you have signed your name: *PS, I love you.* ملاحظة إضافيّة في أسفل الرسالة

posture /'pɒstʃə(r)/ *noun* **1** [U] the way that a person sits, stands, walks, etc: *Poor posture can lead to backache.* جِلسة، وقفة؛ مشية

2 [C] a position that your body is in: *an upright posture* وضعيّة الجسم

ˌpost-'war *adj* existing or happening in the period after the end of a war: *post-war reconstruction* حاصل في فترة ما بعد الحرب

⚷ **pot**[1] /pɒt/ *noun* [C] **1** a round container that is used for cooking food: *pots and pans* قِدْر

2 a container that you use for a particular purpose: *That plant needs a larger pot.* ○ *a flowerpot* ○ *a teapot* ○ *a pot of paint* إناء لاستعمال معيّن، مثلاً: أصيص، إبريق الخ

3 the amount that a pot contains: *We drank two pots of tea.* (ملء) قدْر؛ (ملء) إبريق

pot[2] /pɒt/ *verb* [T] (po**tt**ing; po**tt**ed) to put a plant into a flowerpot ينقل نبتة إلى أصيص

⚷ **potato** /pə'teɪtəʊ/ *noun* [C,U] (*pl.* **potatoes**) a round vegetable with a brown, yellow or red skin. Potatoes are white or yellow inside. They grow under the ground on the roots of the potato plant: *mashed potato* ○ *potatoes baked in their jackets* ○ *roast potatoes* (= cooked in fat in the oven) ○ *Linda peeled the potatoes for supper.* بطاطس، بطاطا

poˌtato 'crisp (*US* **po'tato chip**) *noun* [C] = CRISP[2]

potent /'pəʊtnt/ *adj* strong or powerful: *a potent drug/drink* قويّ المفعول

▸ **potency** /-nsi/ *noun* [U] تأثير، قوّة

⚷ **potential** /pə'tenʃl/ *adj* (only *before* a noun) that may possibly become sth, happen, be used, etc: *Wind power is a potential source of energy.* ○ *potential customers* ممكن؛ كامن

▸ **potential** *noun* [U] the qualities or abilities that sb/sth has but that may not be fully developed yet: *That boy has great potential as a pianist.* ○ *to realize your full potential* إمكانات، مقدرات كامنة

potentially /-ʃəli/ *adv*: *That machine is in poor condition and is potentially very dangerous.* في الامكان، من المحتمل

pothole /'pɒthəʊl/ *noun* [C] **1** a deep hole in rock that was made by water. Potholes often lead to underground caves. فتحة عميقة في الصخر تؤدّي إلى مغارة تحت الأرض

2 a hole in the surface of a road, etc. حفرة في الطريق

▸ **'potholing** *noun* [U] going down inside potholes and underground caves as a sport هواية النزول إلى مغاور تحت الأرض

'pot plant *noun* [C] a plant that you keep indoors نبات بيتيّ

potter[1] /'pɒtə(r)/ (*US* **putter** /'pʌtər/) *verb* [I] **potter (about/around)** to spend your time doing small jobs in an unhurried way: *Grandpa spends most of the day pottering in the garden.* يقوم بأعمال صغيرة على هينته

potter[2] /'pɒtə(r)/ *noun* [C] a person who makes pots, dishes, etc. (pottery) from baked clay الخزّاف، الفاخوري

▸ **pottery** /'pɒtəri/ *noun* (*pl.* **potteries**) **1** [U] pots, dishes, etc. that are made from baked clay أوانٍ خزفيّة أو فخّارية

2 [U] the activity of making pottery الفاخورة، صنع الأواني الفخّارية

3 [C] a place where pottery is made مصنع الفخّار أو الخزف

potty[1] /'pɒti/ *adj* (**pottier**; **pottiest**) (*Brit informal*) **1** mad or foolish مجنون، أحمق

2 potty about sb/sth liking sb/sth very much مولع أو مغرم بـ

potty[2] /'pɒti/ *noun* [C] (*pl.* **potties**) (*informal*) a pot that children sit on when they are too small to use a toilet قصريّة أو نونيّة للأطفال

pouch /paʊtʃ/ *noun* [C] **1** a small leather bag كيس صغير من الجلد

2 a pocket of skin in which some animals, e.g. kangaroos, carry their babies جيب، جراب

poultry /'pəʊltri/ *noun* **1** [plural] birds, e.g. hens, ducks, geese, turkeys, etc. that are kept for their eggs or their meat: *to keep poultry* الدّواجن

2 [U] the meat from these birds ➲ Look at the note at **meat**. لحم الدّواجن

pounce /paʊns/ *verb* [I] **pounce (on sb/sth)** to

jump or land on sb/sth suddenly in order to attack: *The cat sat motionless, waiting to pounce on the mouse.* ○ *(figurative) He was quick to pounce on any mistakes I made.* ينقضّ على

pound[1] /paʊnd/ *noun* **1** [C] (*also* ˌ**pound ˈsterling**) (*symbol* **£**) the unit of money in Britain; one hundred pence (100p): *Melissa earns £16 000 a year.* ○ *a ten-pound note* ○ *Grandpa sent me a cheque for £25.* ○ *a pound coin* ○ *How many dollars will I get for a pound?* جنيه إسترليني

2 [sing.] **the pound** the value of the British pound on international money markets: *The pound has fallen against the dollar.* ○ *How many pesos are there to the pound?* الجنيه الإسترليني

3 [C] (*abbr* **lb**) a measure of weight; 0.454 of a kilogram. There are 16 ounces in a pound: *The carrots cost 30p a pound.* ○ *The baby weighed six pounds at birth.* ○ *Half a pound of mushrooms, please.* رطل إنكليزي

pound[2] /paʊnd/ *verb* **1** [T] to beat sth with a heavy tool to make it soft or like powder يسحق، يهرس

2 [I] **pound (away) (at/against/on sth)** to hit or beat sth many times: *Great waves pounded against the rocks.* ○ *to pound on a door* ○ *(figurative) My heart was pounding with excitement.* يضرب أو يطرق مرّة بعد مرّة

3 [I] **pound along, down, up, etc.** to move quickly and with heavy steps in a particular direction: *Jason went pounding up the stairs three at a time.* يمشي يخبط الأرض بقدميه

pour /pɔː(r)/ *verb* **1** [I] (used about a liquid) to flow out of or into sth, quickly and steadily, and in large quantities: *Tears were pouring down her cheeks.* ○ *There was blood pouring out of the wound.* ○ *(figurative) People were pouring out of the station.* يسيل، ينهمر، يتدفّق

2 [T] to make sth flow steadily out of or into a container: *I spilled some of the oil when I tried to pour it back into the bottle.* ○ *Pour the sugar into a bowl.* يصبّ، يسكب

3 [T] **pour sth (for sb)** to serve drinks to sb: *Have you poured out the tea?* ○ *Pour me another glass, would you?* يصبّ مشروباً ويقدّمه للضيوف

4 [I] to rain heavily: *The rain poured down all day long.* ○ *I'm not going out. It's pouring.* ينهمل، يهطل مدراراً

PHR V **pour sth out** to speak freely about what you think or feel about sth that has happened to you: *to pour out all your troubles* يبوح بخفايا نفسه

pout /paʊt/ *verb* [I] to push your lips, or your bottom lip, forward to show that you are not pleased about sth يبوّز أو يبرطم

▶ **pout** *noun* [C] برطمة، تبويزة

poverty /ˈpɒvəti/ *noun* [U] the state of having very little money; the state of being poor: *There are millions of people in this country who are living in poverty.* فقر، عَوَز

▶ ˈ**poverty-stricken** *adj* very poor (فقر) مُدقِع، مُعْدِم

powder /ˈpaʊdə(r)/ *noun* **1** [C,U] a dry substance that is in the form of very small particles or grains: *washing powder* ○ *baking powder* مسحوق

2 [U] powder that you use on your skin: *face powder* ○ *talcum powder* مسحوق تجميلي، بودرة

▶ **powder** *verb* [T] to put powder (2) on sb/sth: *to powder a baby after a bath* يرُش بودرة أو ذَرور

powdered *adj* (used about a substance that is usually liquid) dried in the form of a powder: *powdered milk* مجفّف بشكل مسحوق

power /ˈpaʊə(r)/ *noun* **1** [C,U] the ability to do sth: *The minister promised to do everything in her power to make sure the hostages were not harmed.* ○ *He has great powers of observation.* قدرة، طاقة

2 [U] force or strength: *The ship was helpless against the power of the storm.* قوّة، شدّة

3 [U] control or influence over other people: *When did this government come to power?* ○ *the power of the trade unions* ○ *He was greedy for power and money.* ○ *to have sb in your power* سلطة، نفوذ

4 [C] the right or authority to do sth: *Do the police have the power to stop cars without good reason?* سلطة، صلاحيّة

5 [C] a person, organization or country that controls or influences others: *Britain is no longer a world power.* دولة كبرى ذات نفوذ (مثلاً)

6 [U] energy that is used for making machines work, giving light, heat, etc: *nuclear power* ○ *the power supply* ○ *This car has power steering.* طاقة، قوّة محرّكة

▶ **powered** *adj* driven by or having a particular type of energy: *a nuclear-powered submarine* ○ *a high-powered engine* مسيّر بقوة آليّة؛ ذو قدرة (عالية)

ˈ**power cut** *noun* [C] a time when the supply of electricity is cut off انقطاع التيار الكهربائي

powerful /ˈpaʊəfl/ *adj* **1** very strong in a physical way: *That car has a very powerful engine.* ○ *Adrian is a powerful swimmer.* قويّ

2 having a strong effect: *The Prime Minister made a powerful speech.* مقنع، فعّال

3 having a lot of influence over other people: *There was a meeting of some of the most powerful people in the country.* ذو نفوذ

▶ **powerfully** /-fəli/ *adv* (قويّ) جسدياً؛ بقوّة

powerless /ˈpaʊələs/ *adj* **1** without strength or influence لا سلطان له، ضعيف

2 not able to do sth: *I stood and watched him struggle, powerless to help.* عاجز

ˈ**power point** *noun* [C] = SOCKET (1)

ˈ**power station** *noun* [C] a place where electricity is made (generated) محطّة توليد الكهرباء

pp *abbrev* **1** = PAGES

2 /ˌpiː ˈpiː/ (before a signature) on behalf of: *pp J Symonds (signed, for example, by his secretary in his absence)* نيابة عن، عن

PR /ˌpiː ˈɑː(r)/ *abbrev* = PUBLIC RELATIONS

pr *abbrev* = PAIR

practicable /ˈpræktɪkəbl/ *adj* that can be done

successfully: *The scheme is just not practicable. It is too complicated and too expensive.* ❶ The opposite is **impracticable**. ممكن عملياً

practical /ˈpræktɪkl/ *adj* **1** concerned with actually doing sth rather than ideas or theory: *A degree in agriculture is not very useful without practical experience of working on a farm.* ➲ Look at **theoretical**. عمليّ

2 very suitable for a particular purpose; useful: *Plastic tablecloths are practical but they're not very elegant.* صالح لغرض معيّن، مفيد

3 (used about people) making sensible decisions and good at dealing with problems: *We must be practical. It's no good buying a house we cannot afford.* عاقل، واقعي

4 that is likely to succeed: *Your plan just isn't practical.* محتمَل النجاح

❶ The opposite in senses **2**, **3**, **4** is **impractical**.

5 clever at doing things with your hands: *A dentist has to have good practical skills.* ماهر يدوياً

▸ **practical** *noun* [C] (*informal*) a lesson or examination where you do or make sth rather than just writing الدرس أو الامتحان العمليّ

practicality /ˌpræktɪˈkæləti/ *noun* [U] the state of being sensible or possible: *I am not convinced of the practicality of the scheme.* فائدة، إمكانيّة

practically /-kli/ *adv* **1** almost; nearly: *The city centre is practically deserted on Sundays.* ○ *He practically begged me not to go.* تقريباً

2 in a practical way عملياً

ˌpractical ˈjoke *noun* [C] a trick that you play on sb (that involves doing sth that will make him/her look silly) مَقْلب، حيلة بغاية المزاح

practice /ˈpræktɪs/ *noun* **1** [U] the actual doing of sth rather than ideas or theory: *Your suggestion sounds fine in theory, but would it work in practice?* ○ *I can't wait to put what I've learnt into practice.* تطبيق

2 [C,U] (a period of) doing sth many times so that you become good at it: *You need plenty of practice when you're learning to drive.* ○ *His accent should improve with practice.* ○ *The team met for a practice twice a week.* تدريب، تمرين

3 [C,U] (*formal*) the usual way of doing sth; sth that is done regularly: *It is standard practice not to pay bills until the end of the month.* ○ *The practice of banks closing at 3.30 is very annoying.* عادة أو عرف

4 [U] the work of a doctor or lawyer: *Dr Roberts doesn't work in a hospital. He's in general practice* (= he's a family doctor). ممارسة الطّب أو المحاماة

5 [C] the business of a doctor or lawyer: *There are two practices in our local health centre.* عيادة؛ مكتب محاماة

IDM **in/out of practice** having spent/not having spent a lot of time practising sth recently: *I'm not playing very well at the moment. I'm really out of practice.* متدرّب جيّداً؛ ينقصه التدريب

practise (*US* **practice**) /ˈpræktɪs/ *verb* **1** [I,T] to do sth many times so that you become very good at it: *If you want to play a musical instrument well, you must practise every day.* ○ *They practised the dance until it was perfect.* ○ *You need to practise saying 'th' in front of a mirror.* يتمرّن أو يتدرّب

2 [T] to do sth or take part in sth regularly or openly: *For many years people were not allowed to practise their religion.* يمارس

3 [I,T] to work as a doctor or lawyer: *She's practising as a doctor in Leeds.* يزاول مهنة الطب أو المحاماة

▸ **practised** (*US* **practiced**) *adj* very good at sth, because you have had a lot of practice متدرب جيّداً

practitioner /prækˈtɪʃənə(r)/ *noun* [C] (*formal*) a person who works as a doctor or lawyer ➲ Look at **general practitioner**. طبيب أو محام

pragmatic /prægˈmætɪk/ *adj* dealing with problems in a practical way rather than by following theory or principles واقعيّ، عمليّ

prairie /ˈpreəri/ *noun* [C] a very large area of flat land covered in grass with few trees (especially in North America) سَهْب، مرج

praise[1] /preɪz/ *verb* [T] **praise sb/sth (for sth)** to say that sb/sth is good and should be admired: *Her new novel has been highly praised.* ○ *The Prime Minister praised the efforts of the rescue services.* ○ *The fireman was praised for his courage.* يمدح، يثني على

praise[2] /preɪz/ *noun* [U] what you say when you are expressing admiration for sb/sth: *The survivors were full of praise for the paramedics.* ○ *Children respond better to praise than to criticism.* مديح، ثناء

▸ **ˈpraiseworthy** /-wɜːði/ *adj* deserving praise ممدوح، جدير بالثناء

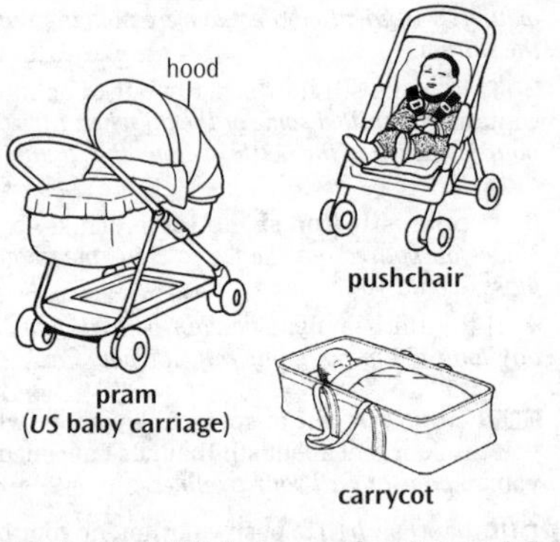

pram /præm/ (*US* **ˈbaby carriage**) *noun* [C] a small carriage for a baby to go out in. A pram has four wheels, a hood and a handle to push it with. عربة الطفل

prance /prɑːns; *US* præns/ *verb* [I] to move about with quick steps, as if you were jumping or dancing, often because you feel proud or pleased with yourself يرقص أو يتنطّط (فَرَحاً)

prat /præt/ *noun* [C] (*slang*) a stupid person: *What a prat!* شخص غبي

prawn /prɔːn/ *noun* [C] a small sea animal with a

shell. Prawns can be eaten as food; they turn pink when you cook them. ➲ Look at **scampi** and **shrimp**. الإربيان أو الجمبري أو القريدس

pray /preɪ/ *verb* [I,T] **pray (to sb) (for sb/sth)** to speak to God or a god in order to give thanks or to ask for sth: *Let us pray.* ○ *They knelt down and prayed for peace.* ○ *They prayed that the war would end soon.* يصلّي؛ يبتهل إلى

prayer /preə(r)/ *noun* **1** [C] the words that you use when you speak to God or a god: *to say your prayers* ○ *The vicar said a prayer for all the people who were ill.* دعاء؛ ابتهال

2 [U] the act of praying: *to kneel in prayer* صلاة

preach /priːtʃ/ *verb* **1** [I,T] to give a talk (a sermon) on a religious subject: *The vicar preached a sermon on the meaning of love.* ○ (*figurative*) *Stop preaching at me! You're no better than I am.* يلقي خطبة دينية، يعظ

2 [T] to say that sth is good and to persuade others to accept it: *I always preach caution in situations like this.* ينصح بـ

▸ **preacher** *noun* [C] a person who gives religious talks (sermons), e.g. in a church الواعظ

precarious /prɪˈkeəriəs/ *adj* not safe or certain; dangerous: *Working on the roof of that building looks very precarious.* مقلْقل؛ خَطِر

▸ **precariously** *adv*: *He balanced the glass precariously on the arm of his chair.* بشكل مقلق

precaution /prɪˈkɔːʃn/ *noun* [C] something that you do in order to avoid danger or problems: *We took the precaution of locking our valuables in the hotel safe.* ○ *precautions against fire* حَيْطة، احتراس

▸ **precautionary** /prɪˈkɔːʃənəri; *US* -neri/ *adj*: *a precautionary measure* وقائيّ أو احتياطيّ

precede /prɪˈsiːd/ *verb* [I,T] (*formal*) to come or go before sb/sth: *The results of the experiment are given in the table on the preceding page.* يتقدّم على، يسبق

precedence /ˈpresɪdəns/ *noun* [U] **precedence (over sb/sth)** the right that sb/sth has to come before sb/sth else because of greater importance: *In business, making a profit seems to take precedence over everything else.* الأولويّة، حقّ الأفضليّة

precedent /ˈpresɪdənt/ *noun* [C,U] something that is considered as an example or rule for what happens later: *We don't want to set a precedent by allowing one person to come in late or they'll all want to do it.* ○ *Such protests are without precedent in recent history.* ➲ Look at **unprecedented**. سابقة

precinct /ˈpriːsɪŋkt/ *noun* **1** [C] (*Brit*) a special area of shops in a town where cars are not allowed: *a shopping precinct* مجمّع تجاري

2 [C] (*US*) a part of a town that has its own police and fire services قسم إداري خاص في مدينة

3 precincts [plural] the area near or around a building, etc: *Security guards patrol the hospital and its precincts.* المنطقة المحيطة ببناء

precious /ˈpreʃəs/ *adj* **1** of great value (usually because it is rare or scarce): *Gold and silver are precious metals.* ○ *In overcrowded Hong Kong, every small piece of land is precious.* ثمين

2 loved very much: *My mother's ring is one of my most precious possessions.* ○ *The painting was very precious to her.* عزيز، غالٍ

precious ˈstone (*also* **stone**) *noun* [C] a stone which is very rare and valuable and often used in jewellery: *diamonds, rubies and other precious stones* حجر ثمين

precipice /ˈpresəpɪs/ *noun* [C] a very steep slope on the side of a mountain: (*figurative*) *The economy is on the edge of a precipice.* جُرْف؛ هاوية

precis /ˈpreɪsiː; *US* preɪˈsiː/ *noun* [C,U] (*pl.* **precis**) a shortened form of a speech or written text that contains only the most important points ➲ Look at **summary**[1]. ملخّص

precise /prɪˈsaɪs/ *adj* **1** clear and accurate: *Try to be precise in your measurements.* ○ *I gave them precise instructions how to get here.* ○ *The answer was 10, or 9.98 to be precise.* ○ *She couldn't be very precise about what her attacker was wearing.* دقيق، مضبوط وواضح

2 (only *before* a noun) exact; particular: *I'm sorry. I can't come just at this precise moment.* (في هذا الوقت) بالذات

3 (used about a person) taking care to get small details right: *He's very precise.* (شخص) دقيق

ℹ In senses **1** and **3** the opposite is **imprecise**.

▸ **precisely** *adv* **1** clearly or exactly: *The time is 10.03 precisely.* ○ *That's precisely what I mean.* ○ *I mean precisely what I say.* تماماً، بالضبط

2 (used before 'because' to emphasize that the reason you are giving is different from the reason that people might expect): *'But he was so friendly.' 'I didn't trust him precisely because he was so friendly.'* خاصّةً (لأنه...)

3 (used for agreeing with a statement) yes, that is right: *'So, if we don't book now, we probably won't get a flight?' 'Precisely.'* بالضبط!، نعم، هذا صحيح

precision /prɪˈsɪʒn/ (*also* **preciseness**) *noun* [U] the quality of being clear or exact: *The plans were drawn with great precision.* إحكام أو ضبط؛ دقّة

precocious /prɪˈkəʊʃəs/ *adj* **1** (used about children) acting in a way that makes them seem older than they really are ℹ This word is often used in a critical way. ناضج قبل الأوان، (طفل) أكبر من عمره

2 developed very early: *a precocious talent for playing the piano* مبكِّر

preconceived /ˌpriːkənˈsiːvd/ *adj* (used about an idea or opinion) formed before you have knowledge or experience: *When I visited Russia last year I soon forgot all my preconceived ideas about the country.* مسبَق، (فكرة) مكونّة سلفاً

preconception /ˌpriːkənˈsepʃn/ *noun* [C] an idea or opinion that you have formed about sb/sth before you have enough knowledge or experience فكرة مسبَقة

a b c d e f g h i j k l m n o **p** q r s t u v w x y z

predator /ˈpredətə(r)/ *noun* [C] an animal that kills and eats other animals حيوان مفترس

predecessor /ˈpriːdɪsesə(r); *US* ˈpredə-/ *noun* [C] **1** the person who was formerly in the job or position that sb else is in now: *The new head teacher is much better than her predecessor.* السَّلَف

2 something that is no longer used and has been replaced by sth else: *Our latest car is more reliable than most of its predecessors.* ➲ Look at **successor**. الشيء السابق

predicament /prɪˈdɪkəmənt/ *noun* [C] a difficult situation محنة، مأزق

predicative /prɪˈdɪkətɪv; *US* ˈpredɪkeɪtɪv/ *adj* (used about an adjective) not used before a noun; coming after a verb such as 'be', 'become', 'get', 'seem', 'look': *You cannot say 'an asleep child' because 'asleep' is a predicative adjective.* صفة تستخدم خبراً (في الإنكليزية)

▸ **predicatively** *adv*: *'Asleep' can only be used predicatively.* كَخَبَر (في النحو)

🔑 **predict** /prɪˈdɪkt/ *verb* [T] to say that sth will happen (often because you have special knowledge): *to predict the results of the election* ○ *Scientists still cannot predict when earthquakes will happen.* ○ *Mrs Jones predicted that all the students would pass the exam, and they did.* يتنبأ

▸ **predictable** /-əbl/ *adj* **1** that was or could be expected متوقَّع، معروف مسبقاً

2 (used about a person) always behaving in the way that is expected: *I knew you were going to say that – you're so predictable.* ❶ The opposite is **unpredictable**. (تصرّف)متوقَّع.

predictably *adv*: *Predictably, all the applause came from the politician's own supporters.* كما هو متوقع

prediction /prɪˈdɪkʃn/ *noun* [C,U] saying what will happen; what sb thinks will happen: *Prediction of the result is extremely difficult.* ○ *The Institute's prediction of economic chaos has been proved correct.* تكهُّن أو تنبُّؤ

predominant /prɪˈdɒmɪnənt/ *adj* most noticeable, powerful or important: *The predominant colour was yellow.* مسيطر، غالب

▸ **predominance** /-əns/ [sing., U] the state of being most important or greatest in number: *There is a predominance of Japanese tourists in Hawaii.* تفوُّق؛ أكثريّة

predominantly *adv* mostly; mainly: *The population of the island is predominantly Spanish.* في الأغلبية، في الدرجة الأولى

predominate /prɪˈdɒmɪneɪt/ *verb* [I] **predominate (over sb/sth)** (*formal*) to be most important or greatest in number: *In the colder regions, pine trees predominate.* يسود، يغلب

preface /ˈprefəs/ *noun* [C] a written introduction to a book that explains what it is about or why it was written مقدّمة، تمهيد

prefect /ˈpriːfekt/ *noun* [C] (*Brit*) an older pupil in a school who has special duties and responsibilities. Prefects often help to make sure that the younger pupils behave properly. عريف (في المدرسة)

🔑 **prefer** /prɪˈfɜː(r)/ *verb* [T] (preferring; preferred) **prefer sth (to sth)** to choose sth rather than sth else; to like sth better: *Would you prefer tea or coffee?* ○ *I prefer skating to skiing.* ○ *You go to the cinema if you want. I'd prefer to stay in tonight.* ○ *Marianne prefers not to walk home on her own at night.* يفضّل

> Notice the different ways that **prefer** can be used: *Helen prefers going by train to flying.* ○ *Helen prefers to go by train rather than to fly.* ○ *My parents would prefer me to study law at university.* ○ *My parents would prefer it if I studied law at university.* ○ *My parents would prefer that I studied law at university.* The last two sentences are more formal.
> Note that **prefer** is generally rather formal. Instead of: *Would you prefer tea or coffee?* we can say: *Would you rather have tea or coffee?* Instead of: *I prefer skating to skiing* we can say: *I like skating better than skiing*.

▸ **preferable** /ˈprefrəbl/ *adj* **preferable (to sth/to doing sth)** better or more suitable: *Going anywhere is preferable to staying at home for the weekend.* ○ *Cold drinks are preferable in hot weather.* أفضل من؛ أنسب

preferably /ˈprefrəbli/ *adv* more suitably; better: *Come round on Sunday morning but preferably not before ten!* من الأفضل، من الأنسب

🔑 **preference** /ˈprefrəns/ *noun* **1** [sing., U] **preference (for sth)** a liking for sth rather than for sth else: *What you wear is entirely a matter of personal preference.* ○ *We have both sparkling and still mineral water. Do you have a preference for one or the other?* تفضيل

2 [U] **preference (to/towards sb)** special treatment that you give to one person or group rather than to others: *When allocating accommodation, we will give preference to families with young children.* ○ *Please list your choices in order of preference* (= put the thing you want most first on the list, and so on). معاملة تفضيليّة؛ الأفضليّة

preferential /ˌprefəˈrenʃl/ *adj* giving or showing preference (2): *I don't see why he should get preferential treatment – I've worked here just as long!* تفضيليّ، (سلوك) متحيّز

prefix /ˈpriːfɪks/ *noun* [C] a word or group of letters that you put at the beginning of a word to change its meaning: *The prefix 'im-' means 'not', e.g. 'impossible'.* ➲ Look at **suffix**. بادئة (في اللغة)

🔑 **pregnant** /ˈpregnənt/ *adj* (used about a woman or female animal) having a baby developing in her body: *Liz is five months pregnant.* ○ *to get pregnant* ❶ It is also possible to say: *Liz is expecting a baby* or: *Liz is going to have a baby.* حبلى، حامل

▸ **pregnancy** /-nənsi/ *noun* (*pl.* **pregnancies**) **1** [U] the state of being pregnant: *You should try to rest during pregnancy.* ○ *a pregnancy test* حَمْل أو حَبَل

2 [C] the period of time when a woman or female animal is pregnant: *to have a difficult pregnancy* فترة الحمل

prehistoric /ˌpriːhɪˈstɒrɪk; *US* -ˈstɔːrɪk/ *adj* of the time before history was written down: *prehistoric cave paintings* حادثٌ ما قبل التاريخ

prejudice /ˈpredʒudɪs/ *noun* [C,U] a strong feeling of like or dislike towards sb/sth that is not based on reason or experience: *racial prejudice* ○ *He has a prejudice against women doctors.* تحيُّز، تحامل

▸ **prejudice** *verb* [T] **1 prejudice sb (against/in favour of sb/sth)** to influence sb; to cause sb to have a prejudice: *The newspaper stories had prejudiced the jury against him.* يجعله يتحيّز ضد أو إلى جانب

2 to hurt or weaken sth: *Your appearance may prejudice your chances of getting the job.* يضرّ بـ

prejudiced *adj* having or showing prejudice: *You can't rely on his opinion – he's prejudiced.* متحيّز

preliminary /prɪˈlɪmɪnəri; *US* -neri/ *adj* coming before sth else that is more important: *After a few preliminary remarks the discussions began.* تمهيديّ

▸ **preliminary** *noun* [C] a thing that you do before sth more important: *Once the preliminaries are over, we can get down to business.* عمل تمهيديّ، مقدمة

prelude /ˈpreljuːd/ *noun* [C] **1** something that comes before sth else or that forms an introduction to sth: *The build-up of troops seemed to be a prelude to war.* تمهيد لـ، مقدّمة

2 a piece of music that forms the first part of a longer piece مقدمة موسيقيّة

premature /ˈpremətʃə(r); *US* ˌpriːməˈtʊər/ *adj* **1** coming or happening before the proper or expected time: *Premature babies* (= babies who are born before the expected time) *need special care.* حادثٌ قبل أوانه: خديج

2 acting or happening too soon: *I think our decision was premature. We should have thought about it for longer.* متسرّع

▸ **prematurely** *adv*: *The shock caused her to go prematurely grey.* قبلَ الأوان

premeditated /ˌpriːˈmedɪteɪtɪd/ *adj* planned in advance: *Was the attack premeditated?* متعمّد، مخطّط له مسبقاً

premier /ˈpremiə(r); *US* ˈpriːmɪər/ *adj* (only *before* a noun) most important; best: *the Premier Division/League* أوّل، أفضل

▸ **premier** *noun* [C] the leader of the government of a country رئيس الوزراء

premiere /ˈpremieə(r); *US* prɪˈmɪər/ *noun* [C] the first performance of a play, film, etc. العرض الأوّل

⚷ **premises** /ˈpremɪsɪz/ *noun* [plural] (*formal*) a building and the land that surrounds it: *Smoking is not allowed on the premises.* المبنى والأرض المحيطة به

premium /ˈpriːmiəm/ *noun* [C] **1** an amount of money that you pay regularly to a company for insurance: *monthly premiums of £25* قسط التأمين

2 an extra payment: *You must pay a premium for express delivery.* دفعة إضافية

premonition /ˌpriːməˈnɪʃn/ *noun* [C] a feeling that sth unpleasant is going to happen هاجِس، واجِس

preoccupation /ˌpriɒkjuˈpeɪʃn/ *noun* **1** [U] **preoccupation (with sth)** the state of thinking or being worried about sth all the time انشغال البال، قلق

2 [C] a thing that you think or worry about all the time: *The family's main preoccupation at that time was finding somewhere to live.* الشُغل الشاغل

preoccupy /priˈɒkjupaɪ/ *verb* [T] (*pres part* **preoccupying**; *3rd pers sing pres* **preoccupies**; *pt, pp* **preoccupied**) to fill sb's mind so that he/she does not think about anything else يشغل الفكر كليّاً

▸ **preoccupied** *adj* not paying attention to sb/sth because you are thinking or worrying about sth else قلق، شارد الذهن

⚷ **preparation** /ˌprepəˈreɪʃn/ *noun* **1** [U] the act of getting sb/sth ready: *Hygiene is essential during the preparation of food.* ○ *exam preparation* تحضير أو تهيء

2 [C, usually pl.] **preparation (for sth/to do sth)** something that you do to get ready for sth: *The wedding preparations are almost complete.* استعدادات

IDM **in preparation (for sth)** in order to get ready for sth: *The team has been training hard in preparation for the big game.* استعداداً لـ

preparatory /prɪˈpærətri; *US* -tɔːri/ *adj* done in order to get ready for sth: *a preparatory course in English for students who wish to study at a British university* تحضيري

pre'paratory school (*also informal* **'prep school**) *noun* [C] **1** (*Brit*) a private school for pupils aged between seven and thirteen. مدرسة ابتدائية

2 (*US*) a private school that prepares students for college or university مدرسة إعدادية

⚷ **prepare** /prɪˈpeə(r)/ *verb* [I,T] **prepare (sb/sth) (for sb/sth)** to get ready or to make sb/sth ready: *Bob helped me prepare for the party.* ○ *I didn't leave myself enough time to prepare for the exam.* ○ *to prepare a meal* ○ *The spokesman read out a prepared statement but refused to answer any questions.* ○ *I'm afraid you're going to have to prepare yourself for a shock.* يستعدّ لـ: يُحضّر

IDM **be prepared for sth** to be ready for sth difficult or unpleasant مستعدّ (للصعوبات)

be prepared to do sth to be willing to do sth: *I am not prepared to stay here and be insulted.* مستعدّ (للقيام بـ)

preposition /ˌprepəˈzɪʃn/ *noun* [C] a word or phrase that is used before a noun or pronoun to show place, time, direction, etc: *'In', 'for', 'to', 'out of', 'on behalf of' are all prepositions.* حرف جرّ

preposterous /prɪˈpɒstərəs/ *adj* silly; ridiculous; not to be taken seriously غير معقول، غاية في السُخف

prerequisite /ˌpriːˈrekwəzɪt/ *noun* [C] **pre-**

a b c d e f g h i j k l m n o p q r s t u v w x y z

requisite (for/of sth) something that is necessary for sth to happen or exist: *Is a good education a prerequisite of success?* متطلَّب أساسيّ

prerogative /prɪˈrɒɡətɪv/ *noun* [C] a special right that sb/sth has: *It is the Prime Minister's prerogative to fix the date of the general election.* حقّ خاص، امتياز

Pres. *abbrev* = PRESIDENT

prescribe /prɪˈskraɪb/ *verb* [T] **1** to say what medicine or treatment you should have; to order medicine on a special form (prescription): *Can you prescribe something for my cough please, doctor?* يَصِف دواءً

2 (*formal*) (used about a person or an organization with authority) to say that sth must be done: *The law prescribes that the document must be signed in the presence of two witnesses.* يقضي بِـ

prescription /prɪˈskrɪpʃn/ *noun* **1** [C,U] a form on which a doctor has written the name of the medicine that you need. You take your prescription to a chemist's and get the medicine there: *a prescription for sleeping pills* ○ *Some medicines are only available on prescription* (= with a prescription from a doctor). وصفة طبيّة، "رشتّة"

2 [U] the act of prescribing sth وصف الأدوية

🔑**presence** /ˈprezns/ *noun* **1** [U] being in a place or with sb: *He apologized to her in the presence of the whole family.* ○ *to request sb's presence at a meeting* ❶ The opposite is **absence**. حضور، وجود

2 [sing.] a number of soldiers or policemen who are in a place for a special reason: *There was a huge police presence at the demonstration.* عدد من البوليس أو الجند

🔑**present¹** /ˈpreznt/ *adj* **1** (not before a noun) being in a particular place: *There were 200 people present at the meeting.* ❶ The opposite is **absent**. حاضر، موجود

2 (only *before* a noun) existing or happening now: *We hope to overcome our present difficulties very soon.* حاليّ

IDM **the present day** modern times: *In some countries traditional methods of farming have survived to the present day.* ○ *present-day attitudes to women* الوقت الحاضر؛ عصريّ

▶ **present** *noun* [sing.] **1 the present** the time now: *We live in the present but we must learn from the past.* الوقت الحاضر

2 the present = PRESENT TENSE

IDM **at present** now: *I'm rather busy at present. Can I call you back later?* الآن

for the moment/present → MOMENT

🔑**present²** /ˈpreznt/ *noun* [C] something that you give to sb or receive from sb; a gift: *The tie was a present from my sister.* ○ *a birthday, wedding, Christmas, etc. present* ○ *I must buy a present for my friend.* ❶ **Gift** is more formal and is often used in shops, catalogues, etc. هديّة

🔑**present³** /prɪˈzent/ *verb* [T] **1 present sb with sth; present sth (to sb)** to give sth to sb, e.g. at a formal ceremony: *All the dancers were presented with flowers.* ○ *Flowers were presented to all the dancers.* ○ *The mayor presented a silver cup to the winner.* يقدّم

2 present sb (to sb) to introduce sb to a person of higher social rank: *to be presented to the Queen* يقدّم إلى

3 to give or show sth: *Good teachers try to present their material in an interesting way.* ○ *to present a report to the board of directors* يقدّم

4 to cause or provide sth: *Learning English presented no problem to him.* ○ *The course aims to present each participant with new challenges.* يسبّب؛ يزوّده بِـ

5 to show a play, etc. to the public: *The Theatre Royal is presenting a new production of 'Ghosts'.* يعرض (مسرحيّة مثلاً)

6 to introduce a television or radio programme or the people who appear on it يقدّم

▶ **presenter** *noun* [C] a person who introduces a television or radio programme مقدّم برنامج إذاعيّ مثلاً

presentable /prɪˈzentəbl/ *adj* quite good, and suitable to be seen in public: *I'm going to wear this dress to the party – it's still quite presentable.* حسن الهيئة؛ مناسب اجتماعيّاً

🔑**presentation** /ˌpreznˈteɪʃn; *US* ˌpriːzen-/ *noun* **1** [U] presenting sth or being presented: *the presentation of new material in a textbook* تقديم، عرض

2 [U] the appearance of sth or the impression that it makes on other people: *Untidy presentation of your work may lose you marks.* مظهر، أسلوب التقديم

3 [C] a formal ceremony at which a prize, etc. is given to sb حفلة تقديم جائزة ونحوها

4 [C] (*formal*) a talk that gives information on a particular subject حديث أو محاضرة

presently /ˈprezntli/ *adv* **1** soon: *I'll be finished presently.* عن قريب

2 after a short time: *Presently I heard the car door shut.* بعد قليل

3 (*especially US*) now: *The management are presently discussing the matter with the unions.* الآن أو حاليّاً

> Notice that when **presently** means 'soon' it usually comes at the end of the sentence and when it means 'after a short time' it usually comes at the beginning of the sentence. When **presently** means 'now' it goes with the verb.

ˌpresent parˈticiple *noun* [C] the form of the verb that ends in *-ing*: *'Going', 'walking' and 'trying' are all present participles.* صيغة اسم الفاعل

ˌpresent ˈperfect *noun* [sing.] the form of a verb that expresses an action done in a time period from the past to the present, formed with the present tense of 'have' and the past participle of the verb المضارع التامّ

ˌpresent ˈtense (*also* **present**) *noun* [C] the tense of the verb that you use when you are talking about what is happening or what exists now صيغة الحاضر

preservation /ˌprezəˈveɪʃn/ *noun* [U] keeping sth in the same or in good condition: *the preservation of law and order* ○ *The society is working for the preservation of wildlife.* حِفظ

preservative /prɪˈzɜːvətɪv/ *noun* [C,U] a substance that is used for keeping food, etc. in good condition مادّة حافظة

preserve /prɪˈzɜːv/ *verb* [T] to keep sth safe or in good condition: *They've managed to preserve most of the wall paintings in the caves.* ○ *You can preserve fruit by making it into jam.* يحفظ

preside /prɪˈzaɪd/ *verb* [I] to be in charge of a discussion, meeting, etc. يترأس أو يرأس

PHR V **preside over sth** to be in control of or responsible for sth: *Our present director has presided over a period of expansion.* يترأس، يكون رئيساً لمدّة ما

presidency /ˈprezɪdənsi/ *noun* (*pl.* **presidencies**) **1 the presidency** [sing.] the position of being president: *to be nominated for the presidency* رئاسة

2 [C] the period of time that sb is president مدّة الرئاسة

president /ˈprezɪdənt/ *noun* [C] **1** (*also* **President**) the leader of the country and head of the government in many countries that do not have a king or queen. A president is usually chosen in an election: *the President of France* ○ *the US president* رئيس الجمهوريّة

2 the person with the highest position in some organizations الرئيس

▸ **presidential** /ˌprezɪˈdenʃl/ *adj* connected with a president متعلّق برئيس الجمهوريّة، رئاسيّ

press¹ /pres/ *noun* **1** [sing.] often **the press** [with sing. or pl. verb] newspapers, and the journalists who work for them. The news departments of television and radio are also part of the press: *The minister refused to speak to the press.* ○ *the local/national press* ○ *a press photographer* ○ *The press support/supports government policy.* الصحافة؛ رجال الصحافة

If a person gets **a good press** it means that he/she is praised by the press. The opposite is **a bad press**.

2 [U] the act of printing books, newspapers, etc: *All details were correct at the time of going to press.* طبْع، نشْر

3 = PRINTING PRESS

4 [C] an act of pushing sth firmly: *With a press of a button you can call up all the information you need.* ○ *This shirt needs a press* (= with an iron). ضغْط؛ كيّ

press² /pres/ *verb* **1** [I,T] to push firmly: *Just press that button and the door will open.* ○ *He pressed the lid firmly shut.* ○ *The child pressed her nose against the window.* يضغط على؛ يكبس

2 [T] to put weight onto sth, e.g. in order to get juice out of it: *to press grapes* ○ *to press wild flowers between the pages of a book* يعصر

3 [T] to make a piece of clothing smooth and smart by using an iron يكوي

4 [T] to hold sb/sth firmly as a sign of love, etc: *She pressed the photo to her chest.* يعانق؛ يضمّ

5 [I,T] **press (sb) (for sth)** to try to get sth or to make sb do sth: *I pressed them to stay for supper.* ○ *to press sb for an answer* ○ *The opposition is pressing for a public inquiry into the accident.* يصرّ أو يلحّ على

6 [T] to try to get sth accepted: *I don't want to press the point, but you do owe me £200.* يلحّ

IDM **be pressed for sth** to not have enough of sth: *I must hurry. I'm really pressed for time.* ينقصه، ليس عنده ما يكفي

PHR V **press across, against, around, etc. (sth)** (used about people) to move in a particular direction by pushing: *The crowd pressed against the wall of policemen.* يدفع بقوة

press ahead/forward/on (with sth) to continue doing sth even though it is difficult or hard work: *They pressed on with the building work in spite of the bad weather.* يواصل العمل بإصرار

▸ **pressing** *adj* that you must do or deal with immediately: *I can't stop now. I have a pressing engagement.* مستعجَل

ˈpress conference *noun* [C] a meeting when a famous or important person answers questions from newspaper and television journalists: *to hold a press conference* مؤتمر صحفيّ

ˈpress stud *noun* [C] = POPPER

ˈpress-up (*US* **ˈpush-up**) *noun* [C] a type of exercise in which you lie on your front on the floor and push your body up with your arms كَبْسة أو ضغطة على الأرض (لتقوية الذراعين)

pressure *noun* **1** [U] the force that is produced when you press on or against sth: *Apply pressure to the cut and it will stop bleeding.* ○ *The pressure of the water caused the dam to crack.* ضغط

2 [C,U] the force that a gas or liquid has when it presses against sth: *high/low blood pressure* ○ *You should check your tyre pressures regularly.* ضغط

3 [C,U] a situation that causes you to be worried or unhappy: *financial pressures* ○ *They moved to the country to escape the pressures of city life.* ضغط، وطأة

IDM **put pressure on sb (to do sth)** to persuade or force sb to do sth: *The press are putting pressure on the minister to resign.* يضغط على، يجبر

under pressure 1 (used about liquid or gas) having great force: *Water is forced out through the hose under pressure.* بقوة عظيمة

2 being forced to do sth: *The workers were under pressure to get the job finished as quickly as possible.* ○ *Anna was under pressure from her parents to leave school and get a job.* يُضيَّق أو يضغط على

▸ **pressure** *verb* [T] = PRESSURIZE

ˈpressure cooker *noun* [C] a large pan with a lid in which you can cook things quickly using steam under high pressure طنجرة البخار، قدر ضغط

ˈpressure group *noun* [C, with sing. or pl. verb] a group of people who are trying to influence what a government or other organization does جماعة تحاول التأثير على الحكومة

pressurize (*also* **pressurise**) /ˈpreʃəraɪz/ (*also* **pressure** /ˈpreʃə(r)/) *verb* [T] **pressurize sb into sth/into doing sth** to use force or influence to make sb do sth: *Some workers were pressurized into taking early retirement.* يكره، يجبر
▸ **pressurized** (*also* **pressurised**) *adj* (used about air in an aircraft, etc.) kept at the pressure at which people can breathe مكيَّف الضغط

prestige /preˈstiːʒ/ *noun* [U] the respect and admiration that people feel for a person because he/she has a high social position or has been very successful: *Nursing isn't a very high-prestige job but it gives you a lot of satisfaction.* مقام، جاه
▸ **prestigious** /preˈstɪdʒəs/ *adj* respected or admired; bringing prestige: *Eton is one of Britain's most prestigious schools.* معتبَر، وجيه

⚷ **presumably** /prɪˈzjuːməbli; *US* -ˈzuː-/ *adv* I imagine; I suppose: *Presumably this rain means the match will be cancelled?* على ما اعتقد

presume /prɪˈzjuːm; *US* -ˈzuːm/ *verb* [T] to think that sth is true even if you do not know for sure; to suppose: *The house looks empty so I presume they are away on holiday.* ○ *The soldiers were missing, presumed dead.* يظن؛ يفترض

presumption /prɪˈzʌmpʃn/ *noun* [C] something that you presume or suppose to be true ظن؛ افتراض

presumptuous /prɪˈzʌmptʃuəs/ *adj* doing sth that you have no right or authority to do: *It was very presumptuous of him to say that I would help without asking me first.* وقح، متجرئ

pretence (*US* **pretense**) /prɪˈtens/ *noun* [U, sing.] an action that makes people believe sth that is not true: *She was unable to keep up the pretence that she loved him.* ○ *to make a pretence of being ill* تظاهر
IDM **on/under false pretences** → FALSE

⚷ **pretend** /prɪˈtend/ *verb* [I,T] to appear to do or be sth, in order to trick or deceive sb: *Frances walked past pretending (that) she hadn't seen me.* ○ *Paul's not really asleep. He's just pretending.* ○ *The children are pretending to be space explorers.* يتظاهر؛ يدّعي

pretentious /prɪˈtenʃəs/ *adj* trying to appear more serious or important than you really are: *a pretentious modern film* ❶ The opposite is **unpretentious**. متظاهر بالأهميّة؛ مدّع

pretext /ˈpriːtekst/ *noun* [C] a reason that you give for doing sth that is not the real reason: *Clive left on the pretext of having an appointment at the dentist's.* ذريعة، حجّة؛ ادّعاء

⚷ **pretty**[1] /ˈprɪti/ *adj* (**prettier**; **prettiest**) pleasant to look at; attractive: *Rachel looks really pretty in that dress.* ○ *What a pretty garden!* مليح، جذّاب، لطيف

> When we are talking about people, we use **pretty** to describe girls and women. To describe men we use **good-looking** or **handsome**. Look at the note at **beautiful**.

▸ **prettily** *adv*: *to smile prettily* بجاذبية، برِقّة
prettiness *noun* [U] جاذبيّة أو مَلاحة

⚷ **pretty**[2] /ˈprɪti/ *adv* (*informal*) quite; rather: *It's pretty cold outside.* ○ *I'm pretty certain that Alex will agree.* ➲ Look at the note at **rather**. إلى حدّ ما، نوعاً ما
IDM **pretty much/nearly/well** almost: *I won't be long. I've pretty well finished.* تقريباً

prevail /prɪˈveɪl/ *verb* [I] **1** to exist or be common: *In some remote areas a lot of superstition still prevails.* يوجد؛ يعم

2 (*formal*) to win or gain control: *In the end justice prevailed and the men were set free.* يسود، يغلب

▸ **prevailing** *adj* (only *before* a noun) **1** most common or general: *the prevailing climate of opinion* شائع، عامّ

2 (used about the wind) most common in a particular area: *The prevailing wind is from the south-west.* سائد

prevalent /ˈprevələnt/ *adj* (*formal*) common in a particular place at a particular time: *The prevalent atmosphere was one of fear.* غالب، سائد

⚷ **prevent** /prɪˈvent/ *verb* [T] **prevent sb/sth (from) (doing sth)** to stop sth happening or to stop sb doing sth: *Everyone hopes the negotiations will prevent a war.* ○ *I don't think that we can prevent them finding out about this.* ○ *Her parents tried to prevent her from going.* ❶ **Prevent** is more formal than **stop**. يمنع
▸ **preventable** /-əbl/ *adj* that can be prevented: *Many accidents are preventable.* يمكن تفاديه

prevention /prɪˈvenʃn/ *noun* [U] the act of preventing sth منع، وقاية

preventive /prɪˈventɪv/ (*also* **preventative** /prɪˈventətɪv/) *adj* intended to stop or prevent sth (especially crime or disease) from happening: *preventive measures to reduce crime* ○ *preventive medicine* وقائيّ، احتياطي

preview /ˈpriːvjuː/ *noun* [C] a chance to see a play, film, etc. before it is shown to the general public عرض خاصّ

⚷ **previous** /ˈpriːviəs/ *adj* coming or happening before or earlier: *Do you have previous experience of this type of work?* ○ *Giles has two children from his previous marriage.* ○ *The previous owners of our house moved to Liverpool.* سابق
▸ **previously** *adv*: *Before I moved to France I had previously worked in Italy and Spain.* سابقاً

prey /preɪ/ *noun* [U] an animal or bird that is killed and eaten by another animal or bird: *Antelope and zebra are prey for lions.* ○ *The eagle is a bird of prey* (= it kills and eats other birds or small animals). فريسة؛ ضحيّة
▸ **prey** *verb*
IDM **prey on sb's mind** to cause sb to worry or think about sth: *The thought that he was responsible for the accident preyed on the train driver's mind.* يعذّب ضميره، يقضّ مضجعه
PHR V **prey on sth** (used about an animal or bird) to kill and eat other animals or birds: *Cats prey on rats and mice.* يفترس

price /praɪs/ *noun* [C] the amount of money that you must pay in order to buy sth: *What's the price of petrol now?* ○ *to charge high/low prices* ○ *We can't afford to buy the car at that price.* ○ *She offered me a fair price for the car.* ○ (*figurative*) *Is pollution the price we have to pay for progress?* سعر؛ ثمن

A **charge** is the amount of money that you must pay for using something: *Is there a charge for parking here?* ○ *admission charges*. You use **cost** when you are talking about paying for services or about prices in general without mentioning an actual sum of money: *The cost of electricity is going up.* ○ *the cost of living*. The **price** of something is the amount of money that you must pay in order to buy it. A shop may **raise/increase**, **reduce/bring down** or **freeze** its prices. The prices **rise/go up** or **fall/go down**.

IDM **at any price** even if the cost is very high or if it will have unpleasant results: *Richard was determined to succeed at any price.* مهما كلفه الأمر

not at any price in no circumstances; never ولا بحال من الأحوال، أبداً

▸ **price** *verb* [T] **1** to fix the price of sth: *The books were priced between £5 and £10.* يحدِّد السعر أو يُسعِّر

2 to mark the price on goods in a shop يضع السعر على السِّلع

priceless *adj* of very great value: *priceless jewels and antiques* ➲ Look at **worthless**, **valuable** and **invaluable**. لا يقدَّر بثمن

pricey /ˈpraɪsi/ *adj* (**pricier**; **priciest**) (*Brit informal*) expensive غالٍ

ˈ**price list** *noun* [C] a list of the prices of the goods that are on sale قائمة الأسعار

prick¹ /prɪk/ *noun* [C] the sharp pain that you feel when sth pricks you: *the sharp prick of a needle* وخزة

prick² /prɪk/ *verb* [T] to make a small hole in sth or to cause sb pain with a sharp point: *You should prick the sausage skins before you cook them.* ○ *Ouch! I pricked myself on that needle.* يثقب؛ يَخِز

IDM **prick up your ears** (used about an animal) to raise the ears in order to listen carefully to sth: (*figurative*) *He pricked up his ears when he heard Mandy's name.* يصغي باهتمام؛ يفتّح آذانه

prickle /ˈprɪkl/ *noun* [C] one of the sharp points on some plants and animals: *Hedgehogs are covered in prickles.* شوكة

▸ **prickle** *verb* [I] to have a feeling of pricking: *His skin prickled with fear.* يتشوَّك؛ يقشعر

prickly /ˈprɪkli/ *adj* (**pricklier**; **prickliest**) **1** covered with prickles: *a prickly bush* شائك

2 (*informal*) (used about a person) easily made angry سريع الغضب

pride /praɪd/ *noun* **1** [U] **pride (in sb/sth)** the feeling of pleasure that you have when you (or people who are close to you) do sth good or own sth good: *Her parents watched with pride as Mary went up to collect her prize.* ○ *to feel pride in your achievement* ℹ The adjective is **proud**. فخر، اعتزاز

2 [sing.] **the pride of sth** a person or thing that is very important or of great value to sb: *The new stadium was the pride of the whole town.* مفخرة

3 [U] the feeling that you are better than other people: *the sin of pride* زهوّ، تكبّر

4 [U] the sense of your own worth or value; self-respect: *You'll hurt his pride if you refuse to accept the present.* كبرياء، عزّة نفس

IDM **take (a) pride in sb/sth** to feel pleased and proud about sth good that sb has done: *The manager took great pride in his team's success.* يفخر أو يعتزّ بِ

take pride in sth/in doing sth to do sth very well or carefully: *I wish you'd take more pride in your work.* يعمل شيئاً بإتقان

▸ **pride** *verb*

PHR V **pride yourself on sth/on doing sth** to feel pleased about sth good or clever that you can do: *Henry prides himself on his ability to cook.* يتفاخر أو يتباهى بِ

priest /priːst/ *noun* [C] **1** a person (usually a man) who performs religious ceremonies in the Christian Church قسِّيس

Priest is a general word and is used in all churches but especially in the Roman Catholic Church. A priest in the Anglican Church is also called a **vicar** or a **clergyman**. A priest in other Protestant churches is also called a **minister**.

2 a person who performs religious ceremonies in some other religions ℹ For sense **2** there is a feminine form **priestess**. كاهن

prim /prɪm/ *adj* (used about a person) always behaving very correctly and easily shocked by anything that is rude متزمِّت اخلاقياً، مفرط في التحشُّم

▸ **primly** *adv* بتكلُّف؛ بدقّة

primary¹ /ˈpraɪməri; *US* -meri/ *adj* most important; main: *Smoking is one of the primary causes of lung cancer.* ○ *A high standard of service should be of primary importance.* رئيسيّ، أساسيّ

▸ **primarily** /ˈpraɪmərəli; *US* praɪˈmerəli/ *adv* more than anything else; mainly: *The course will be aimed primarily at people who have no previous experience.* في الدرجة الأولى

primary² /ˈpraɪməri; *US* -meri/ (*also* **primary eˈlection**) *noun* [C] (*pl.* **primaries**) (*US*) an election in which a political party chooses the person who will be its candidate in a later important election, e.g. for president انتخابات (الرئاسة) الأوليّة

ˌ**primary ˈcolour** *noun* [C] any of the colours red, yellow or blue. You can make any other colour by mixing primary colours in different ways. لون أوليّ

ˌ**primary eduˈcation** *noun* [U] the education of children in their first years at school التعليم الابتدائيّ

ˈ**primary school** *noun* [C] (*Brit*) a school for children aged five to eleven مدرسة ابتدائية

prime¹ /praɪm/ *adj* (only *before* a noun) **1** most important; main: *The prime cause of the com-*

a b c d e f g h i j k l m n o p q r s t u v w x y z

pany's failure was high interest rates. أهمّ أو أوّل، رئيسي

2 of very good quality; best: *prime pieces of beef* ممتاز، أفضل (قطعة)

3 having all the typical qualities: *That's a prime example of what I was talking about.* أفضل (مثال)

prime² /praɪm/ *noun* [sing.] the time when sb is strongest, most beautiful, most successful, etc: *Several of the team are past their prime.* ○ *In his prime, he was a fine actor* ○ *to be in the prime of life* ريْعان، عنفوان

prime³ /praɪm/ *verb* [T] to give sb information in order to prepare him/her for sth: *The politician had been well primed with all the facts before the interview.* يمدّه بالمعلومات الضرورية (قبل المقابلة)

ˌprime ˈminister *noun* [C] the leader of the government in Britain and some other countries رئيس الوزراء

primitive /ˈprɪmətɪv/ *adj* **1** (only *before* a noun) connected with a very early stage of development (particularly of human life): *Primitive man lived in caves and hunted wild animals.* بدائي

2 very simple; not developed: *The washing facilities in the camp were very primitive.* ○ *a primitive shelter made out of bits of wood and cloth* بدائي، بسيط جداً

primrose /ˈprɪmrəʊz/ *noun* [C] a common yellow spring flower زهرة الربيع

prince /prɪns/ *noun* [C] **1** a son or other close male relative of a king or queen أمير

2 the male ruler of a small country حاكم، أمير

princess /prɪnˈses/ *noun* [C] **1** a daughter or other close female relative of a king or queen أميرة

2 the wife of a prince أميرة

principal /ˈprɪnsəpl/ *adj* (only *before* a noun) most important; main: *The principal aim of the talks is to reduce the numbers of weapons.* ○ *the principal characters in a play* أساسي، رئيسي

▸ **principal** *noun* [C] the head of some schools, colleges, etc. رئيس أو مدير كليّة أو مدرسة

principally /-pli/ *adv* mainly; mostly: *Our products are designed principally for the European market.* في الدرجة الأولى

principle /ˈprɪnsəpl/ *noun* **1** [C] a basic general rule or truth about sth: *We believe in the principle of equal opportunity for everyone.* ○ *The course teaches the basic principles of car maintenance.* مبدأ، قاعدة

2 [C,U] a rule for good behaviour, based on what each person believes is right: *She refuses to wear fur. It's a matter of principle with her.* ○ *a person of high moral principles* مبدأ، معتقد

3 [sing.] a law of science: *The system works on the principle that heat rises.* قانون طبيعي، مبدأ علمي

IDM **in principle** in general, but possibly not in detail: *His proposal sounds fine in principle, but there are a few points I'm not happy about.* مبدئياً، بشكل عامّ

on principle because of your moral beliefs or principles (2): *Tessa refuses to eat meat on principle.* طبقاً لمبادئه أو معتقداته

print¹ /prɪnt/ *noun* **1** [U] the letters, words, etc. in a book, newspaper, etc: *The print is too small for me to read without my glasses.* أحرف الطباعة

2 [C] a mark that is made by sth pressing onto sth else: *The police are searching the room for fingerprints.* ○ *footprints in the snow* أثر أو طبعة على شيء

3 [C] a picture that was made by printing صورة مطبوعة

4 [C] a photograph (when it has been printed from a negative): *I ordered an extra set of prints for my friends.* صورة فوتوغرافية

IDM **out of print** (used about a book, etc.) that is not available from the publisher; not being printed any more نفدت طبعته

print² /prɪnt/ *verb* **1** [T] to put words, pictures, etc. onto paper by using a metal or wood surface covered with ink: *How much did it cost to print the posters?* يطبع

2 [I,T] to make a book, newspaper, etc. in this way: *50 000 copies of the textbook were printed.* يطبع

3 [T] to include sth in a book, newspaper, etc: *The newspaper should not have printed the photograph of the crash.* ينشر

4 [I,T] to write with letters that are not joined together: *Children learn to print when they first go to school.* يكتب بأحرف غير متّصلة

5 [T] to put a pattern onto cloth, paper, etc: *printed cotton, wallpaper, etc.* يطبّع قماشاً وغيره

6 [T] to make a photograph from a piece of negative film "يسحب" صورة فوتوغرافية (عن البلّورة)

PHRV **print (sth) out** to print information from a computer onto paper: *I'll just print out this file.* ○ *The computer's printing out the results now.* (الكمبيوتر) يعطي معلومات مطبوعة

▸ **printer** *noun* [C] **1** a person or company that prints books, newspapers, etc. الطابع

2 a machine that prints out information from a computer onto paper: *a laser printer* آلة طابعة

printing *noun* [U]: *the invention of printing by Gutenberg* الطباعة

ˈprinting press (*also* **press**) *noun* [C] a machine that is used for printing books, newspapers, etc. مطبعة

printout /ˈprɪntaʊt/ *noun* [C,U] information from a computer that is printed onto paper نسخة مطبوعة

prior /ˈpraɪə(r)/ *adj* (only *before* a noun) coming before or earlier: *Miss Parker was unable to attend because of a prior engagement.* سابق

▸ **prior to** *prep* (*formal*) before: *Passengers are asked to report to the check-in desk prior to departure.* قبلَ

priority /praɪˈɒrəti; *US* -ˈɔːr-/ *noun* (*pl.* **priorities**) **1** [U] **priority (over sb/sth)** the state of being more important than sb/sth or of coming before sb/sth else: *Families with small children will be given priority.* ○ *Emergency cases take pri-*

ority over other patients in hospital. ○ *On roundabouts in Britain traffic coming from the right has priority.* حقّ الأفضليّة، أولويّة

2 [C] something that is most important or that you must do before anything else: *Our top priority is to get food and water to the refugee camps.* ○ *You must decide what your priorities are.* الشيء الأهمّ، الأمر ذو الأولويّة

prise /praɪz/ (*especially US* **prize**, **pry**) *verb* [T] to use force to open sth, remove a lid, etc: *He prised the door open with an iron bar.* يفتح (الباب مثلا) بِمُخل

⚷ prison /'prɪzn/ (*also* **jail**) *noun* [C,U] a building where criminals are kept as a punishment: *She was sent to a maximum-security prison.* ○ *The terrorists were sent to prison for twenty-five years.* ○ *to escape from prison* ○ *He will be released from prison next month.* ○ *a prison warder* سِجن

> You talk about **prison** (no '**the**') when you are talking about somebody going or being there as a prisoner: *He's in prison.* You talk about **the prison** if you are talking about people going there for a different reason: *The minister visited the prison and said that conditions were poor.* You also use **a** or **the** when more information is given: *a high-security prison.* Look also at **imprison** and **jail**.

⚷ prisoner *noun* [C] a person who is being kept in a prison: *In many prisons, there are three prisoners in a cell.* ○ *a political prisoner* سجين

ˌprisoner of ˈwar *noun* [C] (*pl.* **prisoners of war**) a soldier, etc. who is caught by the enemy during a war and who is kept in a prison until the end of the war أسير حرب

privacy /'prɪvəsi; 'praɪv-/ *noun* [U] the state of being alone or away from other people who may disturb you: *There is not much privacy in large hospital wards.* عزلة، خلوة؛ خصوصيّة

⚷ private /'praɪvət/ *adj* **1** belonging to one particular person or group and not to be used by others: *This is private property. You may not park here.* خاص، خصوصي

2 secret; not to be shared by other people: *a private letter* شخصي، سري

3 with no one else present: *I would like a private interview with the personnel manager.* على انفراد، انفرادي

4 not connected with work or business: *He never discusses his private life with his colleagues at work.* خاص، شخصي

5 owned, done or organized by a person or company, and not by the government: *a private hospital* (= you must pay to go there). ○ *a private school* ○ *a private detective* (= one who is not in the police) ➲ Look at **public**. خاصّ (عكس حكومي)

IDM **in private** with no one else present: *May I speak to you in private?* على انفراد

▸ **private** *noun* [C] a soldier of the lowest rank جندي، نفر

privately *adv* not in public: *She said she agreed but privately she had her doubts.* سِراً، في سِرّه

privatize (*also* **privatise**) /'praɪvətaɪz/ *verb* [T] to change the ownership of an organization from the government to a private company: *The water industry has been privatized.* ❶ The opposite is **nationalize**. يجعل ملكيّته خاصّة، يخصخص

▸ **privatization** (*also* **privatisation**) /ˌpraɪvətaɪ'zeɪʃn; *US* -tə'z-/ *noun* [U] خصخصة

privilege /'prɪvəlɪdʒ/ *noun* **1** [C,U] a special right or advantage that only one person or group has: *Prisoners who behave well enjoy special privileges.* ○ *the wealth and privilege of the upper classes* امتياز، حقّ خاص

2 [C] a special advantage or opportunity that gives you great pleasure: *It was a great privilege to hear her sing in Milan.* فرصة عظيمة

▸ **privileged** *adj* having an advantage or opportunity that most people do not have: *I feel very privileged to be playing for the England team.* محظوظ، ذو امتياز خاص

⚷ prize¹ /praɪz/ *noun* [C] something of value that is given to sb who is successful in a race, competition, game, etc: *She won first prize in the competition.* ○ *He was awarded second prize for his painting.* ○ *a prize-winning novel* جائزة

▸ **prize** *adj* (only *before* a noun) winning, or good enough to win, a prize: *a prize flower display* جدير بجائزة

prize *verb* [T] to consider sth to be very valuable: *This picture is one of my most prized possessions.* يعتزّ بِ

prize² *verb* [T] (*especially US*) = PRISE

pro¹ /prəʊ/ *noun*

IDM **the pros and cons** the reasons for and against doing sth: *We should consider all the pros and cons before reaching a decision.* المحاسن والمساوئ

pro² /prəʊ/ *noun* [C] (*pl.* **pros**) (*informal*) a person who is a professional (2,3): *a golf pro* محترف

probability /ˌprɒbə'bɪləti/ *noun* (*pl.* **probabilities**) **1** [U] the state of being probable or likely: *At that time there seemed little probability of success.* احتمال

2 [C] something that is probable or likely: *Closure of the factory now seems a probability.* أمر محتمل، احتمال

⚷ probable /'prɒbəbl/ *adj* that you expect to happen or to be true; likely: *I suppose it's possible that they might still come but it doesn't seem very probable.* ❶ The opposite is **improbable**. محتمَل

> Notice that **probable** and **likely** mean the same but are used differently: *It's probable that he will be late.* ○ *He is likely to be late.*

▸ **probable** *noun* [C] a person or thing that is likely to be chosen for sth or to win sth: *a probable for the next Olympic team* الشخص المتوقع ترشيحه أو نجاحه

probably /-əbli/ *adv* almost certainly: *I will phone next week, probably on Wednesday.* ○ *'Are you coming to London with us?' 'Probably not.'* على الأغلب؛ على الأرجح

probation /prə'beɪʃn; *US* prəʊ-/ *noun* [U] **1** the

system of keeping an official check on a person who has broken the law instead of sending him/her to prison: *The prisoner was released on probation.* مراقبة سلوك (سجين أُطلق سراحه)

2 a period of time at the start of a new job when you are tested to see if you are really suitable: *a three-month probation period* فترة اختبار أو تجربة

pro'bation officer *noun* [C] a person who keeps an official check on people who are on probation (1) ضابط المراقبة

probe /prəʊb/ *noun* [C] **1** a long thin tool that you use for examining sth that is difficult to reach, especially a part of the body مِسْبَر (طبي)

2 asking questions, collecting facts, etc. in order to find out all the information about sth: *a police probe into illegal financial dealing* تحقيق

▸ **probe** *verb* **1** [T] to examine sth carefully with a probe (1) or sth like it يسبر؛ يجسّ

2 [I,T] **probe (into sth)** to try to find out all the facts about sth يستقصي

probing *adj*: *to ask probing questions* استطلاعيّ، عميق

⚷**problem** /'prɒbləm/ *noun* [C] **1** a difficult situation that you must deal with: *Unemployment causes a lot of social problems.* ○ *I'm facing a lot of problems at work at the moment.* ○ *to have financial problems* ○ *There's a problem with the washing machine. It won't work.* ○ *'Can you fix this for me?' 'No problem.'* ○ *It's a problem finding a good plumber these days.* صعوبة، مشكلة

2 a question that you must solve by thinking about it: *Vicky had ten problems to do for homework.* مسألة

⚷**procedure** /prə'si:dʒə(r)/ *noun* [C,U] the action that you must take in order to do sth in the usual or correct way: *What's the procedure for making a complaint?* إجراء

⚷**proceed** /prə'si:d; prəʊ-/ *verb* [I] **1** to go on to do sth else: *After getting an estimate we can decide whether or not to proceed with the work.* ○ *Once he had calmed down he proceeded to tell us what had happened.* يواصل؛ يستأنف الكلام

2 (*formal*) to continue: *The building work was proceeding according to schedule.* يسير، يمضي

proceedings /prə'si:dɪŋz/ *noun* [plural] **1 proceedings (against sb/for sth)** legal action: *to start divorce proceedings* دعوى قضائية، إجراءات قانونية

2 events that happen, especially at a formal meeting, ceremony, etc: *The proceedings of the council were interrupted by the demonstrators.* أحداث؛ وقائع

proceeds /'prəʊsi:dz/ *noun* [plural] **proceeds (of/from sth)** money that you get when you sell sth, or for sth that you have organized: *The proceeds from the sale will go to charity.* ريْع، عائدات

⚷**process** /'prəʊses; *US* 'prɒses/ *noun* [C] **1** a series of actions that you do for a particular purpose: *the process of producing steel* ○ *We've just begun the complicated process of selling the house.* عمليّة

2 a series of changes that happen naturally: *Trees go though the process of growing and losing leaves every year.* سلسلة من التغيُّرات

IDM **in the process** while you are doing sth else: *We washed the dog yesterday – and we all got very wet in the process.* أثناء هذه العمليّة

in the process of sth/doing sth in the middle of doing sth: *They are in the process of moving house.* منهمك في...

▸ **process** *verb* [T] **1** to change a raw material, e.g. with chemicals, before it is sold or used: *Cheese is processed so that it lasts longer.* ○ *to process a film* (= to develop it so that you can print photographs from it) يعالج (كيميائياً)، يصنّع

2 to deal with information, e.g. on a computer: *When we have collected all the data the computer will process it for us.* ○ *It will take about ten days to process your application.* (في الكمبيوتر) يعالج

processor *noun* [C] a machine that processes food or information: *a food processor* ○ *a word processor* آلة كهربائية لتحضير الأطعمة؛ "كمبيوتر"

procession /prə'seʃn/ *noun* [C,U] a number of people, vehicles, etc. that move slowly in a line, e.g. as part of a ceremony: *to walk in procession* ○ *a funeral procession* موكب

proclaim /prə'kleɪm/ *verb* [T] (*formal*) to make sth known officially or publicly: *The day of the royal wedding was proclaimed a national holiday.* ○ *to proclaim a state of emergency* يعلن؛ ينادي بِ

▸ **proclamation** /ˌprɒklə'meɪʃn/ *noun* [C,U]: *to make a proclamation of war* إعلان؛ بيان أو بلاغ

procure /prə'kjʊə(r)/ *verb* [T] **procure sth (for sb)** (*formal*) to obtain or get sth يستحصِل على

prod /prɒd/ *verb* [I,T] (pro**dd**ing; pro**dd**ed) to push or press sb/sth with your finger or other pointed object: (*figurative*) *Ruth works quite hard but she does need prodding occasionally.* ينخس؛ يحثّ

▸ **prod** *noun* [C]: *He gave the fire a prod with a stick.* نخسة؛ منخَس؛ تذكير

prodding *noun* [U] (*figurative*) *Harold needs a lot of prodding before he will go and see a doctor.* حَثّ

prodigious /prə'dɪdʒəs/ *adj* very great: *He seemed to have a prodigious amount of energy.* هائل، مذهل

prodigy /'prɒdədʒi/ *noun* [C] (*pl.* **prodigies**) a person (especially a child) who is unusually good at sth: *Mozart was a child prodigy.* ➲ Look at **genius**. طفل معجزة (عبقريّ)، أعجوبة

⚷**produce** /prə'dju:s; *US* -'du:s/ *verb* [T] **1** to make or grow sth: *The factory produces 20 000 cars a year.* ○ *East Anglia produced much of the country's wheat.* ○ *The children have produced some beautiful pictures for the exhibition.* ○ *The burning of coal produces carbon dioxide.* ينتج، يصنع

2 to cause sth to happen: *Her remarks produced roars of laughter.* يسبِّب

3 to give birth to a young animal: *Our cat's just produced six kittens!* (أنثى الحيوان) تنتج

4 to show sth so that sb else can look at or examine it: *The inspector got on the bus and*

asked all the passengers to produce their tickets. ○ *to produce evidence in court* يبرز؛ يقدّم

5 to organize a play, film, etc. so that it can be shown to the public: *She is producing 'Romeo and Juliet' at the local theatre.* يخرج

▸ **produce** /ˈprɒdjuːs; *US* -duːs/ *noun* [U] food, etc. that is grown on a farm and sold: *fresh farm produce* ➲ Look at the note at **production**. محصول، منتَجات زراعيّة

producer /prəˈdjuːsə(r); *US* -ˈduː-/ *noun* [C] **1** a person, company or country that makes or grows sth: *Brazil is a major producer of coffee.* منتِج

2 a person who deals with the business side of organizing a play, film, etc. منتج أو مخرج

product /ˈprɒdʌkt/ *noun* [C] **1** something that is made in a factory or that is formed naturally: *Coal was once a major product of South Wales.* ○ *waste products* ○ *We have to find the right product for the market.* ○ *The finished product should look very much like this design.* ➲ Look at the note at **production**. منتَج: منتوج؛ نتيجة

2 product of sth the result of sth: *The industry's problems are the product of government policy.* حصيلة أو نتيجة

3 the amount that you get if you multiply one number by another: *The product of three and five is fifteen.* حاصل الضرب

production /prəˈdʌkʃn/ *noun* **1** [U] the act of making or growing sth: *This farm specializes in the production of organic vegetables.* ○ *mass production* ○ *The price increases were the result of rising production costs.* انتاج

2 [U] the amount of sth that is made or grown: *Saudi Arabia is increasing its production of oil.* منتوج

3 [C] a play, film, etc. مسرحيّة أو فيلم

> Notice that **produce** means food, etc. that comes from a farm and a **product** is something that was made in a factory. A **production** is a play, film, etc: *The label on the bottle says 'Produce of Italy'.* ○ *The company's main products are plastic toys.* ○ *the Bolshoi Ballet's production of Swan Lake*

IDM **in production** being made: *The new car is now in production.* قيد الصنع

on production of sth when you show sth: *You can get a ten per cent discount on production of your membership card.* عند إبراز (البطاقة)

productive /prəˈdʌktɪv/ *adj* **1** that can make or grow sth well or in large quantities: *The company wants to sell off its less productive factories.* ○ *productive land* غزير الانتاج

2 useful (because results come from it): *a productive discussion* ❶ The opposite is **unproductive**. مثمِر، مفيد

productivity /ˌprɒdʌkˈtɪvəti/ *noun* [U] the state of being productive (1) or the amount that sb/sth produces (1): *More efficient methods will lead to greater productivity.* غزارة أو كميّة الانتاج

profess /prəˈfes/ *verb* [T] **1** (*formal*) to say that sth is true (even if it is not): *Marianne professed to know nothing at all about it, but I did not believe her.* يزعم أو يدّعي

2 to say openly that you think or believe sth: *He professed his hatred of war.* يصرّح بـ، يعلِن

profession /prəˈfeʃn/ *noun* [C] **1** a job that requires a lot of training and that is respected by other people: *the medical, legal, teaching, etc. profession* ➲ Look at the note at **work**[1]. مهنة

2 the profession [with sing. or pl. verb] all the people who work in a particular profession: *The legal profession is/are trying to resist the reforms.* أهل مهنة معيّنة

IDM **by profession** as your profession or job: *Graham is an accountant by profession.* مهنته (كذا)

professional /prəˈfeʃənl/ *adj* **1** (only *before* a noun) of or concerning sb who has a profession: *The flat would be ideal for a professional couple.* ○ *Get professional advice from your lawyer before you take any action.* عامل في مهن كالطّب والمحاماة مثلاً

2 doing sth in a way that shows skill, training or care: *The police are trained to deal with every situation in a calm and professional manner.* ○ *Her application was neatly typed and looked very professional.* دالّ عل حسن التدريب والاتقان، حِرَفي

❶ The opposite is **unprofessional**.

3 doing a sport, etc. as a job or for money: *After his success at the Olympic Games he turned professional.* محترِف

4 (used about a sport, etc.) done by people who are paid: *professional football* احترافيّ، محترف

❶ The opposite for **3** and **4** is **amateur**.

▸ **professional** *noun* [C] **1** a person who works in a profession (1) من أصحاب المهن الراقية

2 (*also informal* **pro**) a person who plays or teaches a sport, etc. for money محترِف

3 (*also informal* **pro**) a person who does his/her work with skill and care متقن أو بارع في عمله، "معلّم"

professionalism /-ʃənəlɪzəm/ *noun* [U] the quality of showing great skill or care when you are doing a job: *Although they were students, they performed with great professionalism.* اتقان وبراعة في العمل، حِرَفية

professionally /-ʃənəli/ *adv* **1** in a professional (1,2) way بمهارة وإتقان (كأنه محترف)، بحِرَفية

2 for money, by a professional person: *Rob plays the saxophone professionally.* ○ *to have your photograph taken professionally* كمِهنة؛ من قِبل محترف

professor /prəˈfesə(r)/ *noun* [C] (*abbr* **Prof**) **1** a university teacher of the highest rank: *Professor Brown* ○ *Professor Anthony Clare* ○ *She's professor of English at Bristol University.* استاذ جامعة: بروفيسور

2 (*US*) a teacher at a college or university مدرِّس في كليّة أو جامعة

proficient /prəˈfɪʃnt/ *adj* **proficient (in/at sth/doing sth)** able to do a particular thing well; skilled: *We are looking for someone who is proficient in French.* كفء؛ ماهر أو بارع

▸ **proficiency** /-nsi/ *noun* [U] **proficiency (in sth/doing sth)** the ability to do sth well; skill: *a* *cycling proficiency test* ○ *a certificate of proficiency in English* كفاءة؛ مهارة

profile /ˈprəʊfaɪl/ *noun* [C] **1** a person's face or head seen from the side, not the front المنظر الجانبيّ للوجه

2 a short description of sb/sth that gives useful information: *We're building up a profile of our average customer.* نبذة عن شخص

IDM a high/low profile a way of behaving that does/does not attract other people's attention: *I don't know much about the subject – I'm going to keep a low profile at the meeting tomorrow.* ظهور أو بروز (في المجتمع)؛ توارٍ (عن الانظار)

profit¹ /ˈprɒfɪt/ *noun* [C,U] the money that you make when you sell sth for more than it cost you: *Did you make a profit on your house when you sold it?* ○ *an annual profit of £25 000* ○ *I'm hoping to sell my shares at a profit.* ○ *We won't make much profit in the first year.* ➲ Look at **loss**. ربح

profit² /ˈprɒfɪt/ *verb*

PHRV profit from sth (*formal*) to get some advantage from sth: *Who will profit most from the tax reforms?* يستفيد

profitable /ˈprɒfɪtəbl/ *adj* **1** that makes a profit: *a profitable business* مربح

2 helpful or useful: *We had a very profitable discussion yesterday.* مفيد أو نافع

▸ **profitability** /ˌprɒfɪtəˈbɪləti/ *noun* [U] the state of being profitable (1) فائدة أو نفع؛ كون الشيء مربحاً

profitably /-əbli/ *adv* in a profitable (1,2) way: *to invest money profitably* ○ *to spend your time profitably* بشكل مربح؛ بشكل مفيد

profound /prəˈfaʊnd/ *adj* **1** great; that you feel very strongly: *The experience had a profound influence on her.* عظيم، بالغ الأثر

2 serious; showing knowledge or thought: *She's always making profound statements about the meaning of life.* متعمّق أو عميق؛ جدّي

▸ **profoundly** *adv* very; extremely: *I was profoundly relieved to hear the news.* جداً، للغاية

profuse /prəˈfjuːs/ *adj* (*formal*) produced in great quantity: *profuse apologies* وفير أو غزير

▸ **profusely** *adv*: *She apologized profusely for being late.* ○ *The blood was flowing profusely.* بغزارة؛ بإفراط

program /ˈprəʊɡræm; US -ɡrəm/ *noun* [C] **1** a set of instructions that you give to a computer so that it will carry out a particular task: *to write a program* ○ *to load a program into the computer* برنامج

> When we are talking about computers both the US and the British spelling is **program**. For every other meaning the British spelling is **programme** and the US spelling is **program**.

2 (*US*) = PROGRAMME

▸ **program** *verb* [T] (**programming**; **programmed**; *US also* **programing**; **programed**) to give a set of instructions to a computer يبرْمج

programmer *noun* [C] a person whose job is to write programs for a computer: *a computer programmer* مبرمج

programme (*US* **program**) /ˈprəʊɡræm; US -ɡrəm/ *noun* [C] **1** a show or other item that is broadcast on the radio or television: *a TV/radio programme* ○ *Do you want to watch the programme on Italian cookery at 8 o'clock?* ○ *We've just missed an interesting programme on California.* برنامج إذاعيّ أو تلفزيونيّ

2 a plan of things to do; a scheme: *What's (on) your programme today?* (= what are you going to do today?) ○ *The leaflet outlines the government's programme of educational reforms.* برنامج، منهاج، خطّة

3 a little book or piece of paper which you get at a play, concert, etc. that gives you information about what you are going to see برنامج الحفل

▸ **programme** (*US* **program**) *verb* [T] (**programming**; **programmed**; *US also* **programing**; **programed**) to make sb/sth work or act automatically in a particular way: *The lights are programmed to come on as soon as it gets dark.* يجعله يعمل بشكل آليّ، يبرمج

progress /ˈprəʊɡres; US ˈprɒɡ-/ *noun* [U] **1** movement forwards or towards achieving sth: *The heavy traffic meant that we made very slow progress.* ○ *Anna's making steady progress at school.* ○ *The talks have made very little progress towards solving the problem.* ○ *a progress report* تقدُّم

2 change or improvement in society: *scientific progress* ○ *People who oppose new roads are accused of holding back progress.* تقدّم أو تطوّر

IDM in progress happening: *Silence! Examination in progress.* جارٍ الآن

▸ **progress** /prəˈɡres/ *verb* [I] **1** to become better; to develop (well): *Medical knowledge has progressed rapidly in the last twenty years.* يتقدّم، يتطوّر

2 to move forward; to continue: *I got more and more tired as the evening progressed.* يسير، يتقدم؛ يطول

progression /prəˈɡreʃn/ *noun* [C,U] **progression (from sth) (to sth)** movement forward or a development from one stage to another: *There seems to be no logical progression in your thoughts in this essay.* تتابع، تعاقب

progressive /prəˈɡresɪv/ *adj* **1** using or agreeing with modern methods and ideas: *a progressive school* عصري، تقدمي

2 happening or developing steadily: *a progressive reduction in the number of staff* مطّرد، متوالٍ

▸ **progressively** *adv* steadily; a little at a time: *The situation became progressively worse.* باطّراد؛ تدريجيّاً

proˌgressive ˈtense *noun* [sing.] = CONTINUOUS TENSE

prohibit /prəˈhɪbɪt; US prəʊ-/ *verb* [T] (*formal*) **prohibit sb/sth (from doing sth)** to say that sth is not allowed by law; to forbid: *English law prohibits children under 16 from buying cigar-*

ettes. ○ *That sign means that smoking is prohibited.* يحرِّم؛ يمنع

prohibition /ˌprəʊɪˈbɪʃn; *US* ˌprəʊəˈbɪʃn/ *noun* **1** [C] (*formal*) a law or rule that forbids sth تحريم؛ منع

2 [U] the forbidding of sth: *the prohibition of corporal punishment in schools* تحريم؛ منع

prohibitive /prəˈhɪbətɪv; *US* prəʊ-/ *adj* (used about a price etc.) so high that people cannot afford it: *The price of houses in the centre of town is prohibitive.* (سعر) باهظ أو فاحش

▸ **prohibitively** *adv*: *prohibitively expensive* (باهظ) بحيث لا يمكن شراؤه

project¹ /ˈprɒdʒekt/ *noun* [C] **1** a piece of work, often involving many people, that is planned and organized carefully; a plan for some work: *The new television series was an extremely expensive project.* ○ *a major project to reduce pollution in our rivers* ○ *the Channel Tunnel project* ○ *His latest project is making a pond in the garden.* مشروع

2 a piece of school work in which the student has to collect information about a certain subject and then write about it: *The whole class is doing a project on rainforests.* بحث مدرسي

project² /prəˈdʒekt/ *verb* **1** [T] (usually passive) to plan: *the band's projected world tour* يرسم خطّة

2 [T] (usually passive) to estimate or calculate: *a projected increase of 10%* يقدِّر

3 [T] **project sth (on/onto sth)** to make sth (light, a shadow, a picture from a film, etc.) fall on a surface: *Coloured lights were projected onto the dance floor.* يُسقط

4 [T] to show or represent sb/sth/yourself in a certain way: *The government is trying to project a more caring image.* يعطي صورة معيّنة عن...

5 [I] (*formal*) to stick out: *The balcony projects one metre out from the wall.* ينتأ أو يبرز

projection /prəˈdʒekʃn/ *noun* **1** [C] a guess about a future amount, situation, etc. based on the information you have at present: *sales projections for the next five years* تقدير، تخمين

2 [U] the act of making light, a picture from a film, etc. fall on a surface: *film projection* إسقاط

projector /prəˈdʒektə(r)/ *noun* [C] an apparatus that projects pictures or films onto a screen or wall: *a film projector* ○ *a slide projector* ○ *an overhead projector* جهاز عرض

proliferate /prəˈlɪfəreɪt; *US* prəʊ-/ *verb* [I] (*formal*) to increase quickly in number يتكاثر بسرعة؛ ينتشر

▸ **proliferation** /prəˌlɪfəˈreɪʃn; *US* prəʊ-/ *noun* [U] انتشار؛ تكاثر

prolific /prəˈlɪfɪk/ *adj* (used especially about a writer, artist, etc.) producing a lot: *a prolific writer of short stories* غزير الانتاج

prologue (*US* **prolog**) /ˈprəʊlɒɡ; *US* -lɔːɡ/ *noun* [C] a piece of writing or a speech that introduces the rest of a play, poem, etc. ➲ Look at **epilogue**. خطبة افتتاحية لمسرحيّة؛ تمهيد لقصيدة

prolong /prəˈlɒŋ; *US* -ˈlɔːŋ/ *verb* [T] to make sth last longer: *Careful treatment will prolong the life of the furniture.* يطيل من عمره

▸ **prolonged** *adj* continuing for a long time: *There was a prolonged silence before anybody spoke.* طويل، مديد

prom /prɒm/ *noun* [C] **1** = PROMENADE

2 (*US*) a formal dance that is held by a high school class at the end of a school year حفلة راقصة عند نهاية العام الدراسيّ

promenade /ˌprɒməˈnɑːd; *US* -ˈneɪd/ (*also* **prom**) *noun* [C] a wide path or pavement where people walk beside the sea in a seaside town طريق للتنزّه موازٍ للبحر

prominent /ˈprɒmɪnənt/ *adj* **1** important or famous: *a prominent political figure* ○ *The new party hopes to play a prominent role in political life.* بارز، مشهور

2 noticeable; easy to see: *The church is the most prominent feature of the village.* ملحوظ، بارز

▸ **prominence** /-əns/ *noun* [U] the state of being important or easily noticed: *The newspaper gave the affair great prominence.* أهميّة؛ بروز للعيان

prominently *adv*: *Display your ticket prominently at the front of your car.* بشكل تسهل رؤيته

promiscuous /prəˈmɪskjuəs/ *adj* having sexual relations with many people كثير العلاقات الجنسيّة

▸ **promiscuity** /ˌprɒmɪˈskjuːəti/ *noun* [U] promiscuous behaviour تعدُّد العلاقات الجنسيّة

promise¹ /ˈprɒmɪs/ *noun* **1** [C] a written or spoken statement or agreement that you will or will not do sth: *He made a promise not to tell anyone what he had seen.* ○ *Her parents kept their promise to buy her a pony for her birthday.* ○ *You should never break a promise* (= you should do what you have said you will do). ○ *They both gave me a promise of their complete support.* وعد، عهد

2 [U] signs that you will be able to do sth well or be successful: *He showed great promise as a musician.* بَشائر مستقبل باهر

promise² /ˈprɒmɪs/ *verb* **1** [I,T] to say definitely that you will or will not do sth: *I'll try to be back at 6 o'clock but I can't promise.* ○ *'I'll pay you back tomorrow,' his friend promised.* ○ *She promised that she would write every week.* ○ *She promised not to forget to write.* ○ *Tom promised me that he'd never be late again.* ○ *The finance minister has promised to bring down the rate of inflation by the end of the year.* يَعِد، يقطع على نفسه عهداً

2 [T] **promise sth (to sb)** to say definitely that you will give sth to sb: *My father has promised me a new bicycle.* ○ *Can you promise your support?* يَعِد، يعاهد

3 [T] to show signs of sth, so that you expect it to happen: *It promises to be a lovely day.* يدلّ على، يُبشّر بِ

▸ **promising** *adj* showing signs of being very good or successful: *a promising writer* ذو مستقبل باهر

promote /prəˈməʊt/ *verb* [T] **1** (often passive) to give sb a higher position, more important job, etc: *He's been promoted from assistant manager to manager.* يُرفَع، يرقّي

2 to encourage sth; to help sth to happen or develop: *The meetings of the leaders have helped to promote good relations between the two countries.* ينشّط، يعزّز

3 to advertise sth (in order to increase its sales or popularity): *In order to sell a new product you need to promote it in the right way.* يروج

▸ **promoter** *noun* [C] a person who organizes or provides the money for an event منظِّم أو مموِّل حدث (رياضي مثلاً)

promotion /prəˈməʊʃn/ *noun* **1** [C,U] (the giving or receiving of) a higher position or more important job: *The new job is a promotion for her.* ○ *The job offers a good salary and excellent chances of promotion.* ○ *the team's promotion from Division 2 to Division 1* ترقية، ترفيع

2 [U] making sth successful or popular: *We need to work on the promotion of health, not the treatment of disease.* تشجيع، ترويج

3 [C,U] things that you do in order to advertise a product: *It's all part of a special promotion of the new book.* ○ *Millions of pounds were spent on advertising and promotion.* ترويج

prompt¹ /prɒmpt/ *adj* **1** quick; done without delay: *I received a prompt reply from the solicitor.* ○ *We need a prompt decision on this matter.* فوري، عاجل

2 prompt (in doing sth/to do sth) (used about a person) quick; acting without delay: *We are always prompt in paying our bills.* ○ *She was prompt to point out my mistake.* سريع، غير متوانٍ

▸ **prompt** *adv* exactly: *I'll pick you up at 7 o'clock prompt.* تماماً، بالضبط

promptly *adv* **1** immediately; without delay: *I invited her to dinner and she promptly accepted.* فوراً

2 punctually; at the time that you have arranged: *We arrived promptly at 12 o'clock.* بالضبط

prompt² /prɒmpt/ *verb* **1** [T] to cause sth; to make sb decide to do sth: *Whatever prompted that remark?* ○ *What prompted you to give up your job?* يحثّ أو يدفع إلى، يحدو به إلى

2 [I,T] to help sb to continue speaking or to remind an actor of his/her words: *'And can you tell the court what happened next?' the lawyer prompted.* ○ *The speaker had to be prompted several times.* ○ *We need somebody to prompt at the performance tonight.* يلقّن

▸ **prompting** *noun* [C,U] an act of persuading or reminding sb to do sth: *He apologized without any prompting.* حضّ؛ تذكير

prompt³ /prɒmpt/ *noun* [C] **1** a word or words said to an actor to remind him/her of what to say next: *When she forgot her lines I had to give her a prompt.* تلقين

2 a sign on a computer screen that shows that the computer has finished what it was doing and is ready for more instructions: *Wait for the prompt to come up then type in your password.* اشارة البداية

prone /prəʊn/ *adj* (not before a noun) **prone to sth/to do sth** likely to suffer from sth or to do sth: *Young people are especially prone to this disease.* ○ *This area is very prone to fog in winter.* ○ *to be accident-prone* (= to have a lot of accidents) ○ *He's rather prone to criticize people without thinking first.* عرضة لـ؛ ميّال إلى

prong /prɒŋ/ *noun* **1** each of the two or more long pointed parts of a fork سن، شعبة

2 each of the separate parts of an attack, argument, etc. that sb uses to achieve sth أحد محاور الهجوم

pronoun /ˈprəʊnaʊn/ *noun* [C] (*grammar*) a word that is used in place of a noun or a phrase that contains a noun: *'He', 'it', 'hers', 'me', 'them' are all pronouns.* ضمير (في القواعد)

pronounce /prəˈnaʊns/ *verb* **1** [T] to make the sound of a word or letter: *You don't pronounce the 'b' at the end of 'comb'.* ○ *How do you pronounce your surname?* يلفظ

2 [T] (*formal*) to say in a formal or official way that sb/sth is in a particular state: *The doctors pronounced him fit.* يعلن رسمياً، يعطي حكماً

3 [I,T] **pronounce (on sth)** (*formal*) to give your opinion on sth, especially formally: *I can't pronounce on the quality of the diamond.* ○ *The play was pronounced 'brilliant' by all the critics.* يحكم على، يعطي رأياً

▸ **pronounced** *adj* very noticeable: *His English is excellent although he speaks with a pronounced French accent.* واضح أو ظاهر

pronunciation /prəˌnʌnsiˈeɪʃn/ *noun* **1** [C,U] the way in which a language or a word is pronounced: *The dictionary gives two different pronunciations for this word.* ○ *American pronunciation* التلفُّظ، طريقة اللفظ

2 [U] a person's way of speaking a language: *His grammar is good but his pronunciation is awful!* لفظ أو نطق

proof¹ /pruːf/ *noun* [U] a fact or piece of information which shows that sth is true: *'We need some proof of your identity,' the shop assistant said.* ○ *What proof have we got that what he is saying is true?* ❶ The verb is **prove**. برهان، اثبات

proof² /pruːf/ *adj* (in compounds) able to protect from or to be protected against the thing mentioned: *a soundproof room* ○ *bulletproof glass* مانع أو مضاد أو عازل لـ الخ...

prop¹ *noun* [C] a stick or other object that you use to support sth مسند، دعامة

▸ **prop** *verb* [T] (pro**pp**ing; pro**pp**ed) **1** to support sth or keep sth in position: *I'll use this book to prop the window open* يسند، يثبّت

2 to lean sth against sth else: *He propped his bicycle against the wall.* يسند

PHR V **prop sb/sth up** to put an object under or behind sb/sth in order to give support يدعم، يسند

prop sth up to support sth that would otherwise fail يقوّي أو يسنّد شيئاً متهاوياً

prop² /prɒp/ *noun* [C, usually pl.] a piece of furniture or another object that is used in a play, film, etc. الأثاث والتزيينات المستعملة في إخراج مسرحي

propaganda /ˌprɒpəˈɡændə/ *noun* [U] information and ideas that are made public by a government or large organization, in order to influence people or persuade them about sth: *political propaganda* ○ *anti-German propaganda* دعاية

propel /prəˈpel/ *verb* [T] (propelling; propelled) to move, drive or push sb/sth forward يدفع، يُسَيِّر إلى الأمام

▸ **propeller** *noun* [C] a device with several blades, which turns round very fast in order to make a ship or a plane move مروحة طائرة أو قارب

⚷ **proper** /ˈprɒpə(r)/ *adj* **1** (only *before* a noun) real or genuine: *I've been to stay with my mother but I haven't had a proper holiday this year.* ○ *We haven't got any proper friends around here.* ○ *I didn't see much of the flat yesterday. I'm going to go today and have a proper look.* صحيح، حقيقيّ

2 (only *before* a noun) right, suitable or correct: *That's not the proper way to eat spaghetti!* ○ *If you're going skiing you must have the proper clothes.* ○ *I've got to get these pieces of paper in the proper order.* صحيح؛ مناسب

3 (*formal*) accepted as socially correct: *I think it would be only proper for you to apologize.* ❶ The opposite for **3** is **improper**. لائق

4 (only *after* a noun) real or main: *We travelled through miles of suburbs before we got to the city proper.* حقيقي؛ أصلي

▸ **properly** *adv* **1** correctly; in an acceptable way: *The teacher said I hadn't done my homework properly.* ○ *These shoes don't fit properly.* بشكل صحيح؛ جيّداً

2 in a way that is socially correct; politely ❶ The opposite for **2** is **improperly**. بشكل لائق، بأدب

ˈ**proper name** (*also* ˈ**proper noun**) *noun* [C] (*grammar*) a word which is the name of a particular person or place and begins with a capital letter: *'Mary', 'Rome' and 'the Houses of Parliament' are all proper names.* اسم علَم

⚷ **property** /ˈprɒpəti/ *noun* (*pl.* **properties**) **1** [U] something that belongs to sb; all the things that belong to sb: *'Is this your property?' the policeman asked, pointing to a small brown suitcase.* ○ *The sack contained stolen property.* ○ *private /public property* ○ *When she died she left her entire property to a cousin in America.* ➲ Look at **lost property**. ملك؛ ممتلكات

2 [C] (*formal*) a building and the land around it: *'What sort of property are you hoping to buy?' asked the estate agent.* عقار

3 [U] land and buildings: *to invest your money in property* العقارات

4 [C] a special quality that a substance, etc. has: *Some plants have healing properties.* صفة خاصّة، خاصيّة

prophecy /ˈprɒfəsi/ *noun* [C] (*pl.* **prophecies**) a statement about what is going to happen in the future: *His prophecy that there would be a disaster has come true.* نُبوءة

prophesy /ˈprɒfəsaɪ/ *verb* [T] (*pres part* **prophesying**; *3rd pers sing pres* **prophesies**; *pt, pp* **prophesied**) to say what you think will happen in the future: *to prophesy disaster* ○ *She prophesied that there would be a war.* يتنبأ بِ

prophet /ˈprɒfɪt/ *noun* [C] **1** (*also* **Prophet**) a person who is chosen by God to give his message to people: *the Prophet Muhammad* ○ *the prophets of the Old Testament* نبيّ

2 a person who tells or claims to tell what will happen in the future متنبِّئ

▸ **prophetic** /prəˈfetɪk/ *adj* محقق في المستقبل

⚷ **proportion** /prəˈpɔːʃn/ *noun* **1** [C] a part or share of a whole: *A large proportion of the earth's surface is covered by sea.* جزء أو قسم

2 [C] **proportion (of sth to sth)** the relationship between the size or amount of two things: *I was not impressed by the proportion of teachers to students* (= there were not enough teachers for the number of students). نسبة

3 proportions [plural] the size and shape of sth: *He stood and gazed at the magnificent proportions of the cathedral.* ○ *Political unrest is reaching alarming proportions.* حجم؛ أبعاد

IDM **in proportion** in the correct relation to other things: *to draw sth in proportion* (= so that the parts are balanced as they are in reality) ○ *She's so upset that she can't see the problem in proportion any more* (= it seems more important than it really is). بالمقاييس أو بالنسب الصحيحة

in proportion to sth 1 by the same amount or number as sth else: *Salaries have not risen in proportion to inflation.* بالنسبة إلى

2 compared with: *In proportion to the number of students as a whole, there are very few women.* بالمقارنة مع

out of proportion (to sth) 1 too big, small, etc. in relation to other things غير متناسب مع

2 too great, serious, important, etc. in relation to sth: *His reaction was completely out of proportion to the situation.* ○ *Haven't you got this matter rather out of proportion?* (= you think it's more important than it really is). أكبر أو أهمّ ممّا يجب

proportional /prəˈpɔːʃənl/ *adj* directly linked in size, amount, etc: *The cost will be proportional to the amount used.* متناسب مع

proˌportional ˌrepresenˈtation *noun* [U] a system in which all political parties have a number of representatives in parliament in proportion to the number of votes they receive in an election التمثيل النسبي

⚷ **proposal** /prəˈpəʊzl/ *noun* [C] **1** a plan that is suggested; a scheme: *a new proposal for raising money* ○ *The recent proposal has been rejected.* ○ *May I put forward a proposal that the canteen should serve more salads?* مشروع خطّة، اقتراح

2 an offer of marriage عرض زواج

⚷ **propose** /prəˈpəʊz/ *verb* **1** [T] to suggest sth as a possible plan or action: *I propose a day in the country and lunch at a pub. What do you think?* ○ *Our neighbours proposed that we should go on holiday together.* ○ *John Carter proposed the mo-*

tion (= the idea to be discussed) *at last night's student debate.* يقترح؛ يقدّم مشروعاً

2 [T] to intend; to have as a plan: *What do you propose to do now?* ينوي؛ يخطط

3 [I,T] **propose (to sb)** to ask sb to marry you: *We've been going out for a long time but he still hasn't proposed.* ○ *to propose marriage* يعرض عليها الزواج

4 [T] **propose sb for/as sth** to suggest sb for an official position: *I'd like to propose Denise Roberts for/as Chair.* يرشّح

proposition /ˌprɒpəˈzɪʃn/ *noun* [C] **1** an idea or opinion that sb expresses about sth: *That's a very interesting proposition. But can you prove it?* فكرة، رأي

2 an arrangement or offer, especially in business; a suggestion: *He made me a proposition to buy my share of the company.* ○ *A month's holiday in Spain is an attractive proposition.* عرض؛ اقتراح

3 a problem or task that you must deal with: *Getting the work finished on time is going to be quite a difficult proposition.* مسألة، مهمة

proprietor /prəˈpraɪətə(r)/ (*feminine* **proprietress** /prəˈpraɪətrɪs/) *noun* [C] the owner, especially of a hotel, business, newspaper, etc. صاحب (فندق وغيره)

prose /prəʊz/ *noun* [U] written or spoken language that is not in verse: *to write in prose* ○ *a prose writer* ➲ Look at **poetry**. النثر

prosecute /ˈprɒsɪkjuːt/ *verb* [I,T] **prosecute sb (for sth)** to accuse sb of a crime and to try to prove it in a court of law: *Which of the barristers is prosecuting?* ○ *He was prosecuted for theft.* ➲ Look at **defend**. يقاضي، يقيم دعوى ضده

prosecution /ˌprɒsɪˈkjuːʃn/ *noun* **1** [C,U] (an example of) accusing sb of a crime and trying to prove it in a court of law: *to bring a prosecution against sb for a driving offence* ○ *the Director of Public Prosecutions* ○ *Failure to pay your parking fine will result in prosecution.* مقاضاة، إقامة دعوى ضدّه

2 [sing., with sing. or pl. verb] a person or group of people who try to prove in a court of law that sb is guilty of a crime: *a witness for the prosecution* ○ *The prosecution claim/claims that Lloyd was driving at 100 miles per hour.* ➲ Look at **defence**. جهة الادّعاء

🔑**prospect** /ˈprɒspekt/ *noun* **1** [C,U] **prospect (of sth/of doing sth)** the chance or hope that sth will happen: *There's little prospect of better weather before next week.* ○ *Prospects for peace do not look good.* فرصة: أمل، توقّع

2 [C,U] an idea of what may or will happen: *'We'll have to manage without central heating this winter.' 'What an awful prospect.'* فكرة؛ شيء متوقع

3 prospects [plural] chances of being successful: *The job offers a good salary and excellent prospects.* فرص للنجاح، إمكانيات الترقّي

prospective /prəˈspektɪv/ *adj* likely to be or to happen; possible: *prospective changes in the law* متوقَع، محتمل

prospectus /prəˈspektəs/ *noun* [C] a small book which gives details about a school, college, new business, etc. دليل (جامعة مثلاً)

prosper /ˈprɒspə(r)/ *verb* [I] to be successful, especially financially يزدهر، يغتني

prosperity /prɒˈsperəti/ *noun* [U] the state of being successful, especially financially: *Tourism has brought prosperity to many parts of Spain.* ○ *economic prosperity* ازدهار، غنى

prosperous /ˈprɒspərəs/ *adj* rich and successful: *the prosperous countries of Western Europe* غني، مزدهر

prostitute /ˈprɒstɪtjuːt; *US* -tuːt/ *noun* [C] (*also old-fashioned* **whore**) a person, especially a woman, who earns money by having sex with people مومس

▸ **prostitution** /ˌprɒstɪˈtjuːʃn; *US* -ˈtuːʃn/ *noun* [U] working as a prostitute بغاء

prostrate /prɒˈstreɪt/ *adj* lying flat on the ground, facing downwards منبطح؛ ساجد

protagonist /prəˈtæɡənɪst/ *noun* [C] **1** (*formal*) a major character in a drama: *the leading/chief/main protagonist* بطل المسرحية

2 the main person in a story or a real event بطل القصّة

3 protagonist (of sth) a leader of a movement in a course of action, etc: *a leading protagonist of the conservation movement* زعيم، قائد حركة

🔑**protect** /prəˈtekt/ *verb* [T] **protect sb/sth (against/from sth)** to keep sb/sth safe; to defend sb/sth: *Wear something to protect your head against the sun.* ○ *Parents try to protect their children from danger as far as possible.* ○ *Bats are a protected species* (= they must not be killed). يحمي، يقي

🔑**protection** /prəˈtekʃn/ *noun* [U] **protection (against sth)** (a way of) keeping sb/sth safe so that he/she/it is not harmed or damaged: *the protection of the environment* ○ *Vaccination against measles gives you protection against the disease.* ○ *After the attack he was given police protection.* حماية، وقاية

protective /prəˈtektɪv/ *adj* **1** that prevents sb/sth from being damaged or harmed: *In certain jobs workers need to wear protective clothing.* وقائيّ

2 protective (towards sb) wanting to protect sb and keep him/her safe: *He's been very protective towards his wife since she became ill.* حريص على حماية (أبنائه)

protector /prəˈtektə(r)/ *noun* [C] a person who protects الحامي، المدافع عن

protein /ˈprəʊtiːn/ *noun* [C,U] a substance found in food such as meat, fish and beans. It is important for helping people and animals to grow and be healthy. البروتين

🔑**protest¹** /ˈprəʊtest/ *noun* [C,U] the showing of

disagreement; a statement or action that shows that you do not like or agree with sth: *The union organized a protest against the redundancies.* ○ *The centre has been closed after protests from local residents.* ○ *We've received thousands of letters of protest.* ○ *He resigned in protest against the decision.* ○ *a protest march* احتجاج، شكوى؛ مظاهرة احتجاج

IDM **under protest** not happily or willingly: *Fiona agreed to pay in the end but only under protest.* مع الاحتجاج، دون رضى

🔑**protest²** /prəˈtest/ *verb* **1** [I,T] **protest (about/against/at sth)** to say or show that you do not like or agree with sth: *The prisoner was brought, protesting, into the court room.* ○ *Students have been protesting against the government's decision.* ○ *The children protested loudly at being taken home early.* ○ *Many of the holidaymakers protested about the lack of information at the airport.* ⓘ In American English **protest** is used without a preposition: *They protested the government's handling of the situation.* يحتجّ على؛ يشكو من

2 [T] to say sth firmly: *He protested a total lack of knowledge of the affair.* ○ *He protested that he hadn't been in the country when the robbery took place.* ○ *'That's simply not true,' she protested.* يؤكّد، يصِر على

> **Protest** is stronger and usually used about more serious things than **complain**. You **protest** about something that you feel is not right or fair, you **complain** about the quality of something or about a less serious action: *to protest about the new tax* ○ *to complain about the weather.*

▸ **protester** *noun* [C] a person who protests: *Protesters blocked the road as the minister's car drove up.* متظاهِر

Protestant /ˈprɒtɪstənt/ *noun* [C] a member of the Christian church that separated from the Catholic church in the 16th century: *to be a Protestant* فرد بروتستانتي

▸ **Protestant** *adj*: *The majority of the population is Protestant.* ○ *a Protestant church* ○ *a Protestant area of Belfast* ➲ Look at **Roman Catholic**. بروتستانتي

prototype /ˈprəʊtətaɪp/ *noun* [C] the first model or design of sth from which other forms will be copied or developed النموذج الأصلي

protrude /prəˈtruːd; *US* prəʊ-/ *verb* [I] to stick out from a surface: *protruding teeth* يبرز، ينتأ

🔑**proud** /praʊd/ *adj* **1 proud (of sb/sth); proud (to do sth/that...)** feeling pleased and satisfied about sth that you own or have done, or are connected with: *a proud father of twins* ○ *They are very proud of their new house.* ○ *I feel very proud to be part of such a successful organization.* ○ *You should feel very proud that you have been chosen.* فخور

2 not wanting help from other people: *He was too proud to ask for help.* أبيّ

3 feeling that you are better than other people: *Now she's at university she'll be much too proud to talk to us!* متكبّر

ⓘ The noun is **pride**.

▸ **proudly** *adv*: *'I did all the work myself,' he said proudly.* بفخر، باعتزاز

🔑**prove** /pruːv/ *verb* (*pp* **proved**; *US* **proven**) **1** [T] **prove sth (to sb)** to show that sth is true: *It will be difficult to prove that she was lying.* ○ *to prove sb's innocence to the court* ⓘ The noun is **proof**. يبرهن على، يثبت صحّة شيء

2 [I,T] to be found to be sth: *The job proved more difficult than we'd expected.* ○ *He was proved innocent.* يثبت

3 prove yourself (to sb) to show other people how good you are at doing sth and/or that you are capable of doing sth: *He constantly feels that he has to prove himself to others.* يثبت جدارته

IDM **prove your/the case/point** to show that what you say is true: *No one will believe you unless you have evidence to prove your case.* يثبت صحّة قوله، يؤيِّد بالأدلّة

proven /ˈpruːvn/ *adj* that has been shown to be true: *a proven fact* مبرهَن عليه

proverb /ˈprɒvɜːb/ *noun* [C] a short well-known sentence or phrase that gives advice or a general truth about life: *'A stitch in time saves nine,' is a proverb.* مَثَل سائر

🔑**provide** /prəˈvaɪd/ *verb* [T] **provide sb (with sth); provide sth (for sb)** to give or supply sth to sb: *This book will provide you with all the information you need.* ○ *We are able to provide accommodation for two students.* ○ *The course lasts all day and lunch will be provided.* يزوّد بـ، يقدّم

PHR V **provide for sb** to give sb all that he/she needs to live: *Robin has four children to provide for.* يعيل

provide for sth to make arrangements to deal with sth that might happen in the future: *We did not provide for such a large increase in prices.* يحتاط لـ

🔑**provided** /prəˈvaɪdɪd/ (*also* **provided that**; **providing**; **providing that**) *conj* only if: *She agreed to go and work abroad provided that her family could go with her.* شريطة أن، على شرط

province /ˈprɒvɪns/ *noun* **1** [C] one of the main parts into which some countries are divided for the purposes of government: *Canada has ten provinces.* ➲ Look at **county** and **state¹**. مقاطعة، إقليم

2 the provinces [plural] the part of a country that is not the capital city كلّ المقاطعات عدا العاصمة

provincial /prəˈvɪnʃl/ *adj* **1** (only *before* a noun) of a province or the provinces: *the provincial government* ○ *a provincial town* خاصّ بمقاطعة، إقليمي

2 (used about a person or his/her ideas) typical of the provinces; not modern or fashionable: *provincial attitudes* إقليمي؛ ريفي، من طراز قديم

provision /prəˈvɪʒn/ *noun* **1** [U] the act of giving or supplying sth to sb: *The council is respon-*

a b c d e f g h i j k l m n o **p** q r s t u v w x y z

sible for the provision of education and social services. تقديم؛ إمداد

2 [U] **provision for/against sth** arrangements that you make to deal with sth that might happen in the future: *She made provision for the children in the event of her death.* ترتيبات احتياطيّة

3 provisions [plural] (*formal*) supplies of food and drink مؤونة، مواد غذائيّة

provisional /prəˈvɪʒənl/ *adj* only for the present time, that may be changed: *The provisional date for the next meeting is 18 November.* ○ *a provisional driving licence* (= that you use when you are learning to drive) مؤقّت
▸ **provisionally** /-nəli/ *adv*: *The meeting has been provisionally arranged for 18 November.* مؤقّتاً

provocation /ˌprɒvəˈkeɪʃn/ *noun* **1** [U] the act of trying to make sb angry: *You should never hit children, even under extreme provocation.* استفزاز

2 [C] something that sb does to make you angry: *It was a provocation to call him a liar.* عمل استفزازيّ

provocative /prəˈvɒkətɪv/ *adj* **1** intending to cause anger or argument: *He made a provocative remark about a woman's place being in the home.* استفزازيّ
2 intending to cause sexual excitement مثير جنسياً

provoke /prəˈvəʊk/ *verb* [T] **1 provoke sb (into sth/into doing sth)** to make a person or an animal angry by annoying them: *The cat will scratch if you provoke it.* ○ *The lawyer claimed his client was provoked into acts of violence.* يُغضِب؛ يستفزّ

2 to cause a feeling or reaction: *Edwina's remarks provoked a storm of controversy.* يثير، يُحدث

prow /praʊ/ *noun* [C] the front part of a ship or boat ❶ The back of a ship is the **stern**. مقدمة السفينة

prowess /ˈpraʊɪs/ *noun* [U] (*formal*) skill at doing sth بَراعة

prowl /praʊl/ *verb* [I,T] **prowl (about/around)** (used about an animal that is hunting or a person who is waiting for a chance to steal sth, etc.) to move quietly so that you are not seen or heard: *I could hear someone prowling around outside so I called the police.* ❶ A person or animal that is prowling is **on the prowl**. يتمشى خلسة (طلباً للفريسة)
▸ **prowler** *noun* [C]: *The police arrested a prowler outside the hospital.* متجسّس (ربما بقصد السرقة)، متلصّص

proximity /prɒkˈsɪməti/ *noun* [U] (*formal*) the state of being near to sth: *One advantage is the town's proximity to London.* قُرب

proxy /ˈprɒksi/ *noun* [U] the right that you give to sb to act for you: *to vote by proxy* تفويض، وكالة

prude /pruːd/ *noun* [C] a person who does not like to see or hear anything connected with sex شديد التحشّم، متزمّت
▸ **prudish** /ˈpruːdɪʃ/ *adj* متحشّم

prudent /ˈpruːdnt/ *adj* having or showing careful thought; wise and sensible: *It would be prudent to find out more before you decide.* ❶ The opposite is **imprudent**. عاقل، حكيم؛ متبصّر
▸ **prudence** /-əns/ *noun* [U] حسن التدبير
prudently *adv* بحصافة، بحذَر

prune¹ /pruːn/ *noun* [C] a dried plum خوخة/برقوقة/عنجاصة مجفّفة

prune² /pruːn/ *verb* [T] to cut branches or parts of branches off a tree or bush in order to make it a better shape يقلِّم أو يشذِّب الشّجر

pry /praɪ/ *verb* (*pres part* **prying**; *3rd pers sing pres* **pries**; *pt, pp* **pried**) **1** [I] **pry (into sth)** to try to find out about other people's private affairs: *I don't want to pry – but is everything all right?* يسأل بفضول عن الخصوصيّات
2 [T] (*especially US*) = PRISE

PS /ˌpiː ˈes/ *abbrev* (used for adding sth to the end of a letter) postscript: *Love from Tessa. PS I'll bring the car.* عبارة ملحقة

pseudonym /ˈsjuːdənɪm; *US* ˈsuːdənɪm/ *noun* [C] a name used by an author, etc. that is not his/her real name: *to write under a pseudonym* اسم مستعار

psych /saɪk/ *verb*
PHR V **psych yourself up** (*informal*) to prepare yourself in your mind for sth difficult, e.g. by telling yourself that you will be successful يقوّي نفسه معنوياً لمواجهة صعوبة

psychiatry /saɪˈkaɪətri; *US* sə-/ *noun* [U] the study and treatment of mental illness ➲ Look at **psychology**. الطّب النفسيّ
▸ **psychiatric** /ˌsaɪkiˈætrɪk/ *adj* connected with psychiatry: *a psychiatric hospital* متعلق بالأمراض النفسيّة
psychiatrist /-ɪst/ *noun* [C] a doctor who is trained to treat people with mental illness طبيب نفسيّ أو نفسانيّ

psychic /ˈsaɪkɪk/ *adj* (used about a person or his/her mind) having unusual powers, e.g. knowing what sb else is thinking or being able to see into the future ذو قوى روحانيّة خارقة

psychoanalysis /ˌsaɪkəʊəˈnæləsɪs/ *noun* [U] a way of treating sb with a mental illness by asking about his/her past life and dreams in order to find out what is making him/her ill التحليل النفسيّ
▸ **psychoanalyst** /ˌsaɪkəʊˈænəlɪst/ *noun* [C] a person who uses psychoanalysis to treat people محلّل نفسي
psychoanalyse (*US* **-lyze**) /ˌsaɪkəʊˈænəlaɪz/ *verb* [T] to treat sb with a mental illness using psychoanalysis يعالجه بالتحليل النفسي

psychology /saɪˈkɒlədʒi/ *noun* **1** [U] the study of the mind and the way that people behave: *child psychology* ➲ Look at **psychiatry**. علم النّفس
2 [sing.] the type of mind that a person or group of people has: *If we understood the psychology of*

the killer we would have a better chance of catching him. نفسيّة

▸ **psychological** /ˌsaɪkəˈlɒdʒɪkl/ *adj* **1** connected with the mind or the way that it works: *Has her ordeal caused her long-term psychological damage?* نفسي، عقلي

2 connected with psychology: *psychological tests* نفسي

psychologically /-kli/ *adv*: *Psychologically it was a bad time to be starting a new job.* من الناحية النفسيّة

psychologist /-ɪst/ *noun* [C] a person who is trained in psychology عالم نفس

psychopath /ˈsaɪkəʊpæθ/ *noun* [C] a person who has a serious mental illness and who may hurt or kill other people شخص مضطرب عقلياً يميل إلى العنف أو القتل

psychotherapy /ˌsaɪkəʊˈθerəpi/ *noun* [U] the treatment of people with mental illness by psychological methods rather than with drugs المعالجة النفسيّة

pt *abbrev* (*pl.* **pts**) **1** = PINT: *2 pts milk*

2 = POINT: *The winner scored 10 pts.*

3 = PART

PTO (*also* **pto**) /ˌpiː tiː ˈəʊ/ *abbrev* = PLEASE TURN OVER

⚷ **pub** /pʌb/ (*also formal* **public house**) *noun* [C] (*Brit*) a place where people go to have a drink and meet their friends. Pubs can serve alcoholic drinks and they also often serve food: *He's gone down to the pub.* ○ *We're having a pub lunch.* بار أو حانة

puberty /ˈpjuːbəti/ *noun* [U] the time when a child's body is changing and becoming physically like that of an adult: *to reach puberty* سنّ البلوغ

pubic /ˈpjuːbɪk/ *adj* of the area around the sexual organs: *pubic hair* عانيّ

⚷ **public** /ˈpʌblɪk/ *adj* **1** of or concerning all the people in a country or area: *The rubbish tip is a danger to public health.* ○ *How much public support is there for the government's policy?* ○ *to increase public awareness* ○ *The public announcement urged people to use water carefully.* عامّ؛ من الشّعب أو شعبيّ

2 provided for the use of people in general; not private: *a public library* ○ *a public telephone* ○ *public spending* (= money that the government spends on education, health care, etc.) عامّ

3 known by many people: *We're going to make the news public soon.* ➲ Compare **keep sth secret**. علني، معروف لدى الجميع

IDM be common/public knowledge → KNOWLEDGE

▸ **public** *noun* [sing., with sing. or pl. verb] **1 the public** people in general: *Is Buckingham Palace open to the public?* ○ *The police have asked for help from members of the public.* ○ *The public is/are generally in favour of the new law.* الجمهور، عامّة الناس

2 a group of people who are all interested in sth or who have sth in common: *the travelling public* فئة

IDM in public when other people are present: *This is the first time that Jane has spoken about her experience in public.* علناً، أمام الملأ

publicly /-kli/ *adv*: *The company refused to admit publicly that it had acted wrongly.* علناً

publican /ˈpʌblɪkən/ *noun* [C] a person who owns or manages a pub صاحب بار أو حانة

⚷ **publication** /ˌpʌblɪˈkeɪʃn/ *noun* **1** [U] the act of printing a book, magazine, etc. and making it available to the public: *His latest book has just been accepted for publication.* النشر

2 [C] a book, magazine, etc. that has been published واحد من المطبوعات أو المنشورات

3 [U] the act of making sth known to the public: *the publication of exam results* إعلان، نشر

ˌpublic ˈcompany *noun* [C] (*pl.* **public companies**) (*also* **ˌpublic ˌlimited ˈcompany**) (*abbr* **PLC; plc**) a large company that sells shares (2) in itself to the public شركة مساهمة

ˌpublic conˈvenience *noun* [C] (*Brit*) a toilet in a public place that anyone can use ➲ Look at the note at **toilet**. مرحاض، دورة مياه

ˌpublic ˈhouse *noun* [C] (*formal*) = PUB

⚷ **publicity** /pʌbˈlɪsəti/ *noun* [U] **1** notice or attention from the newspapers, television, etc: *to seek/avoid publicity* شهرة، اهتمام من وسائل الأعلام

2 giving information about sth in order to attract people's attention; advertising: *There has been a lot of publicity for Dustin Hoffman's latest film.* ○ *a publicity campaign* دعاية، إعلان

publicize (*also* **publicise**) /ˈpʌblɪsaɪz/ *verb* [T] to attract people's attention to sth or to give people information about sth: *The event has been well publicized and should attract a lot of people.* يقوم بالدعاية لـ، يروّج

ˌpublic oˈpinion *noun* [U] what people in general think about sth: *Public opinion was in favour of the war.* الرأي العام

ˌpublic reˈlations *noun* (*abbr* **PR**) **1** [plural] the state of the relationship between an organization and the public: *Giving money to local charities is good for public relations.* علاقات عامّة

2 [U] the job of making a company, organization, etc. popular with the public مهمّة العلاقات العامّة

ˌpublic ˈschool *noun* [C] **1** (*Brit*) a private school, especially in England, for children aged between 13 and 18. Parents must pay to send their children to one of these schools. Many of the children at public schools live (board) there during term-time. مدرسة خاصة (في بريطانيا)

2 (in the US, Australia, Scotland and other countries) a local school that any child can go to, that provides free education مدرسة رسميّة (في الولايات المتحدة)

ˌpublic-ˈspirited *adj* willing to help other people and the public in general محبّ لخدمة المجتمع

ˌ**public ˈtransport** *noun* [U] (the system of) buses, trains, etc. that run according to a timetable and that anybody can use: *to travel by public transport* وسائل النقل العامّة

publish /ˈpʌblɪʃ/ *verb* **1** [I,T] to prepare and print a book, magazine, etc. and make it available to the public: *This dictionary was published by Oxford University Press.* ينشر

2 [T] (used about a writer, etc.) to have your work put in a book, magazine, etc: *Dr Fraser has published several articles on the subject.* يؤلّف، ينشر

3 [T] to make sth known to the public: *Large companies must publish their accounts every year.* يعلن

▸ **publisher** *noun* [C] a person or company that publishes books, magazines, etc. النّاشر

publishing *noun* [U] the business of preparing books, magazines, etc. to be printed and sold النّشر

pudding /ˈpʊdɪŋ/ *noun* [C,U] **1** (*Brit*) the sweet part (course) of a meal that is eaten at the end of it: *What's for pudding today?* ℹ **Dessert** is more formal. طبق حلو يؤكل في نهاية الوجبة

2 (*Brit*) sweet food that is made from bread, flour or rice with fat, eggs, milk, etc. and cooked in the oven or over water: *rice pudding* ○ *Christmas pudding* بودنج: حلوى إنكليزية تقليديّة

puddle /ˈpʌdl/ *noun* [C] a small amount of water (especially rain) that has gathered on the ground ➲ Look at **pool**[1]. تجمّع مائي صغير على الأرض، "طابوسة"

puff[1] /pʌf/ *noun* [C] **1** a small amount of air, smoke, wind, etc. that is blown or sent out: *a puff of smoke* نفخة، نفثة؛ هبّة

2 one breath that you take when you are smoking a cigarette or pipe: *to take a puff on a cigarette* سحبة

▸ **puffy** *adj* (used about a part of a person's body) looking soft and swollen: *Your eyes look a bit puffy. Have you been crying?* منتفخ

puff[2] /pʌf/ *verb* **1** [I,T] (to cause air, smoke, wind, etc.) to blow or come out in puffs: *Smoke was puffing out of the chimney.* ○ *Stop puffing smoke in my face.* ينبعث على دفعات؛ ينفث

2 [I,T] to smoke a cigarette, pipe etc: *to puff away at a cigarette* ○ *He sat puffing his pipe.* يدخّن

3 [I] to breathe loudly or quickly, e.g. when you are running: *He was puffing hard as he ran up the hill.* يلهث

PHR V **puff along, in, out, up, etc.** to move in a particular direction with loud breaths or small clouds of smoke: *to puff up the stairs* ○ *The train puffed into the station.*
يلهث بصوت مسموع؛ (القطار) يسير نافثاً دخانه

puff sth out/up to cause sth to become larger by filling it with air ينفخه، يملؤه بالهواء

▸ **puffed** (*also* ˌ**puffed** ˈ**out**) *adj* finding it difficult to breathe, e.g. because you have been running: *She was puffed out after running to catch the bus.* مبهور الأنفاس، منقطع النفس

puffin /ˈpʌfɪn/ *noun* [C] a N Atlantic sea bird with a large brightly-coloured beak طائر البَفِن

puke /pjuːk/ *verb* [I,T] (*informal*) to be sick; to vomit يتقيّأ

▸ **puke** *noun* [U] قيء

pull

push

drag

pull[1] /pʊl/ *verb* **1** [I,T] to use force to move or try to move sb/sth towards yourself: *Ian pulled at the rope to make sure that it was secure.* ○ *to pull sb's hair* ○ *to pull a door open* ○ *You push and I'll pull.* ○ *to pull the trigger of a gun* ○ *I felt someone pull at my sleeve and turned round.* ○ *They managed to pull the child out of the water just in time.* يشدّ، يجرّ، يسحب

2 [T] to move sth in the direction that is described: *She pulled her sweater on/She pulled on her sweater.* ○ *He pulled up his trousers/He pulled his trousers up.* ○ *Pull your chair a bit nearer to the table.* ○ *to pull the curtains* (= across the windows) يرفع؛ يسحب؛ يغلق

3 [T] to move sth behind you in the direction that you are moving: *The train is pulling six coaches.* ○ *That cart is too heavy for one horse to pull.* يجرّ وراءه

4 [T] to damage a muscle, etc. by using too much force يرضّ أو يمزّق عضلة

IDM **make/pull faces/a face** → FACE

pull sb's leg (*informal*) to make fun of sb by trying to make him/her believe sth that is not true يضحك على، يمازح

pull strings to use your influence to gain an advantage يستخدم نفوذه لتحقيق أغراضه

pull your weight to do your fair share of the work يؤدّي نصيبه من العمل

PHR V **pull (sth) away** to move your body or part of it away with force: *She pulled away as he tried to kiss her.* ينفر من، يبتعد عن

pull sth down to destroy a building: *The old cinema has been pulled down.* يهدم

pull in (to sth); **pull into sth 1** (used about a train) to enter a station (القطار) يدخل المحطة

2 (used about a car, etc.) to move to the side of the road in order to stop (السيارة) تتوقف عند جانب الطريق

pull sth off (*informal*) to succeed in sth: *to pull off a business deal* ينجح في (عقد صفقة)

pull out (used about a car, etc.) to move away from the side of the road: *I braked as a car suddenly pulled out in front of me.* (سيارة) تطلع من جانب الطريق إلى وسطه

pull out (of sth) (used about a train) to leave a station (القطار) يغادر المحطة

pull (sb/sth) out (of sth) (to cause sb/sth) to leave sth: *The Americans have pulled their forces out of the island.* ○ *We've pulled out of the deal.* ينسحب أو يسحب

pull sth out to take sth out of a place suddenly or with force: *She walked into the bank and pulled out a gun.* يخرِج فجأة، يشهَر (سكّيناً)

pull yourself together to control your feelings and behave in a calm way: *Pull yourself together and stop crying.* "شدّ حيلك!"، يتمالك نفسه

pull up (to cause a car, etc.) to stop: *to pull up at traffic lights* يتوقّف أو يوقف

pull² /pʊl/ *noun* **1** [C] **a pull (at/on sth)** an act of pulling: *The diver gave a pull on the rope to show she wanted to go back up to the surface.* ○ *He took a long pull on his cigarette.* شَدّ؛ سَحْبة

2 [sing.] a hard climb that takes a lot of effort: *It was a hard pull to the top of the hill.* تسلُّق منهك

'pull date (*US*) = SELL-BY DATE

pulley /'pʊli/ *noun* [C] (*pl.* **pulleys**) a piece of equipment, consisting of a wheel and a rope, that is used for lifting heavy things بَكَرة

pullover /'pʊləʊvə(r)/ *noun* [C] a piece of clothing that is usually made of wool and that covers the top part of your body and your arms. You put on a pullover by pulling it over your head. ➲ Look at the note at **sweater**. بلوفر أو كَنْزة صوفيّة

pulp /pʌlp/ *noun* **1** [U] the soft inner part of some fruits or vegetables لبّ الثمرة

2 [U] a soft substance made from wood that is used for making paper عجينه يصنع منها الورق

3 [sing., U] a soft substance that you make by pressing and mixing sth for a long time: *Crush the strawberries to a pulp.* عجينة، شيء مهروس

pulpit /'pʊlpɪt/ *noun* [C] a raised wooden or stone platform in a church where the priest stands when he/she is speaking to the people there منبر

pulsate /pʌl'seɪt; *US* 'pʌlseɪt/ *verb* [I] to move or shake with strong regular movements: *a pulsating rhythm* ينبض

pulse /pʌls/ *noun* [C, usually sing.] the regular beating in your body as blood is pumped through it by your heart. You can feel your pulse at your wrist, neck, etc: *Your pulse rate increases after exercise.* ○ *to have a strong/weak pulse* ○ *to feel/take sb's pulse* (= to count how many times it beats in one minute) النبض

▸ **pulse** *verb* [I] **pulse (through sth)** to move with strong regular movements ينبض

pulses /'pʌlsɪz/ *noun* [C, plural] the seeds of some plants, e.g. peas, beans, etc. that are cooked and eaten as food: *Some pulses such as lentils and soya beans are very rich in protein.* البقول الحَبيّة، القطاني

pump /pʌmp/ *noun* [C] a machine that is used for forcing a gas or liquid in a particular direction: *Have you got a bicycle pump? My tyre's flat.* ○ *a petrol pump* مضخّة

▸ **pump** *verb* [I,T] to force a gas or liquid to go in a particular direction: *Your heart pumps blood around your body.* يضخ

PHR V **pump sth up** to fill sth with air, e.g. by using a pump: *to pump up a car tyre* ينفخه أو يملؤه بالهواء

pumpkin /'pʌmpkɪn/ *noun* [C,U] a very large round fruit with thick orange-coloured skin that is cooked and eaten like a vegetable: *pumpkin pie* ○ *The children made a lantern out of a pumpkin.* يقطينة

pun /pʌn/ *noun* [C] **pun (on sth)** an amusing use of a word that can have two meanings or of different words that sound the same: *We're banking on them lending us the money – no pun intended!* جناس لفظي، تلاعب لفظيّ طريف

punch¹ /pʌntʃ/ *verb* [T] to hit sb/sth hard with your closed hand (fist): *Annie punched him hard in the stomach and ran away.* يلكم، يضرب

▸ **punch** *noun* [C] a hard blow with your closed hand (fist) لكمة

punch² /pʌntʃ/ *noun* [U] a drink made from wine, fruit juice, sugar, etc. مزيج من النبيذ وعصير الفاكهة وغير ذلك

punch³ /pʌntʃ/ *noun* [C] a machine or tool that you use for making holes in sth: *a ticket punch* ثقّابة، خرّامة

▸ **punch** *verb* [T] to make a hole in sth with a punch: *He punched a hole in the ticket.* ○ *He punched the ticket.* يثقّب، يخرم

punchline /'pʌntʃlaɪn/ *noun* [C] the last and most important words of a joke or story العبارة الهامّة في نهاية نكتة أو قصّة

'punch-up *noun* [C] (*Brit informal*) a fight in which people punch or hit each other تضارُب، تلاكم

punctual /'pʌŋktʃuəl/ *adj* doing sth or happening at the right time; not late: *It is important to be punctual for your classes.* ℹ We often say the train, etc. was **on time** rather than punctual. محافظ على المواعيد؛ حاصلٌ في الوقت المحدّد تماماً

▸ **punctuality** /ˌpʌŋktʃu'æləti/ *noun* [U] دقّة المواعيد

punctually /'pʌŋktʃuəli/ *adv*: *to pay your bills punctually* في مواعيده المحددة

punctuate /'pʌŋktʃueɪt/ *verb* **1** [I,T] to use punctuation marks when you are writing يستخدم علامات الترقيم

2 [T] **punctuate sth (with sth)** to interrupt sth

many times: *Her speech was punctuated with bursts of applause.* يقاطع عدة مرّات

▸ **punctuation** /ˌpʌŋktʃuˈeɪʃn/ *noun* [U] the use of punctuation marks when you are writing الترقيم

ˌpunctuˈation mark *noun* [C] one of the signs that you use when you are writing in order to divide the words into sentences, show that sb is speaking, etc: *Punctuation marks include full stops, commas, question marks and speech marks.* علامة ترقيم

puncture /ˈpʌŋktʃə(r)/ *noun* [C] **1** a bicycle or car tyre that has a hole in it: *Oh, no! My tyre's flat. I must have a puncture.* إطار أو دولاب مثقوب

2 a small hole in a bicycle or car tyre: *If you put the tyre in water you should be able to see where the puncture is.* ثقب

▸ **puncture** *verb* [T] to make a small hole in sth with sth sharp: *That stone must have punctured the tyre.* يثقب

pungent /ˈpʌndʒənt/ *adj* (used about a smell) very strong (رائحة) حادّة أو لاذعة

punish /ˈpʌnɪʃ/ *verb* [T] **punish sb (for sth) (by/with sth)** to cause sb to suffer because he/she has done sth wrong: *They have broken the law and they deserve to be punished.* ○ *The children were severely punished for telling lies.* ○ *Minor offenders should be punished by being made to work for the community.* ○ *Dangerous driving should be punished with imprisonment.* يعاقب

▸ **punishable** /-əbl/ *adj* **punishable (by sth)** (used about a crime, etc.) that you can be punished for doing: *a punishable offence* ○ *In some countries drug smuggling is punishable by death.* مستحقّ العقاب، معاقب

punishing *adj* that makes you very tired or weak: *The Prime Minister had a punishing schedule, visiting five countries in five days.* مُنهِك، شاق

punishment *noun* **1** [U] the act of punishing or the state of being punished: *Do you have capital punishment* (= punishment by death) *in your country?* عقاب، عقوبة

2 [C] a way in which sb is punished: *Ideally, the punishment should fit the crime.* عقوبة

punitive /ˈpjuːnətɪv/ *adj* (*formal*) **1** intended as a punishment: *a punitive expedition against the rebels* تأديبيّ، عقابي

2 very hard or severe: *punitive taxation* شديد، قاس

punk /pʌŋk/ *noun* **1** [U] a type of rock music that was popular in Britain in the late 1970s and early 1980s. Punk music often protests strongly about the way that society is organized. البَنْك: نوع من أنواع موسيقى الشباب

2 [C] a person who likes punk music and often has brightly coloured hair and unusual clothes: *punks wearing torn jeans and safety pins in their ears* واحد من شباب البَنْك بشعره الملوّن وملابسه الغريبة

punt¹ /pʌnt/ *noun* [C] a long shallow boat with a flat bottom and square ends which is moved by pushing the end of a long pole against the bottom of a river قارب طويل يدفع بعصا تمسّ القعر

▸ **punt** *verb* to travel in a punt, especially for pleasure: *They often go punting on the river.* يتنزه في هذا القارب

puny /ˈpjuːni/ *adj* (**punier**; **puniest**) small and weak ضئيل؛ هزيل

pup /pʌp/ *noun* [C] **1** = PUPPY

2 the young of some animals, e.g. seals جَرْو، صغير بعض الحيوانات

pupil¹ /ˈpjuːpl/ *noun* [C] **1** a child in school: *There are 28 pupils in the class.* تلميذ مدرسة

2 a person who is being taught ➲ Look at **student**. تلميذ

pupil² /ˈpjuːpl/ *noun* [C] the round black hole in the middle of the eye بؤبؤ العين

puppet /ˈpʌpɪt/ *noun* [C] **1** a model of a person or animal that you can move by pulling the strings which are attached to it or by putting your hand inside it and moving your fingers دمية تحرّك باليد أو بخيوط، عروسة

2 a person or organization that is controlled by sb else ألعوبة، أداة طيّعة

puppy /ˈpʌpi/ *noun* [C] (*pl.* **puppies**) (*also* **pup**) a young dog جَرْو

purchase¹ /ˈpɜːtʃəs/ *noun* (*formal*) **1** [U] the act of buying sth: *to take out a loan for the purchase of a car* ○ *Please state the date and place of purchase.* شراء

2 [C] something that you buy: *to make a purchase* شَروة

purchase² /ˈpɜːtʃəs/ *verb* [T] (*formal*) to buy sth: *Many employees have the opportunity to purchase shares in the company they work for.* يشتري

▸ **purchaser** *noun* [C] (*formal*) a person who buys sth: *The purchaser of the house agrees to pay a deposit of 10%.* ❶ The opposite is **vendor**. الشاري

purdah /ˈpɜːdə/ *noun* [U] the system in some Muslim and Hindu societies by which women live in a separate part of a house or cover their faces so that men do not see them: *to be in purdah* (وراء) حجاب أو ستار

pure /pjʊə(r)/ *adj* **1** not mixed with anything else: *a pure silk blouse* ○ *She was dressed in pure white.* ○ *Declan is of pure Irish descent.* صاف، خالص؛ قحّ

2 not containing any harmful substances: *the pure mountain air* نقيّ

3 not doing or knowing anything evil or anything that is connected with sex: *a young girl still pure in mind and body* بريء، طاهر

❶ The opposite for **2** and **3** is **impure**.

4 (only *before* a noun) (*informal*) complete: *We met by pure chance.* ○ *a pure waste of time* مَحْض (الصدفة)؛ تامّ

5 (used about a sound) clear صاف

6 (only *before* a noun) (used about an area of learning) concerned only with theory rather than practical uses: *pure mathematics* ❶ The opposite is **applied**. بحْت، تجريدي

▸ **purely** *adv* only or completely: *It's not purely a question of money.* مجرَّد: تماماً

purée /ˈpjʊəreɪ; *US* pjʊəˈreɪ/ *noun* [C,U] a food that you make by cooking a fruit or vegetable and then pressing and mixing it until it is smooth and liquid: *apple purée* طعام مهروس، ربّ (البندورة)

purge /pɜːdʒ/ *verb* [T] to remove people that you do not want from a political party or other organization يطهِّر (الحزب)

▸ **purge** *noun* [C] an action to remove people that you do not want from a political party or other organization: *Stalin's purges* حملة تطهير

purify /ˈpjʊərɪfaɪ/ *verb* [T] (*pres part* **purifying**; *3rd pers sing pres* **purifies**; *pt, pp* **purified**) to remove dirty or harmful substances from sth: *purified water* يصفّي، ينقّي

puritan /ˈpjʊərɪtən/ *noun* [C] a person who thinks that it is wrong to enjoy yourself الداعي إلى نبذ المتعة

▸ **puritan** (*also* **puritanical** /ˌpjʊərɪˈtænɪkl/) *adj*: *a puritan attitude to life* متشدِّد، متقشِّف

purity /ˈpjʊərəti/ *noun* [U] the state of being pure: *to test the purity of the air* ➲ Look at **impurity**. نقاء، صفاء

purl /pɜːl/ *noun* [U] a simple stitch used in knitting: *knit two plain, one purl* قطبة أو غرزة معكوسة

⚷ **purple** /ˈpɜːpl/ *adj* of a reddish-blue colour: *the purple robes of the King* أرجوانيّ

▸ **purple** *noun* [U] a reddish-blue colour اللون الأرجوانيّ

⚷ **purpose** /ˈpɜːpəs/ *noun* **1** [C] the reason for doing or making sth: *The main purpose of this meeting is to decide what we should do about the problem of noise.* ○ *You may only use the telephone for business purposes.* غاية، هدف

2 [U] (*formal*) having an aim or plan and acting according to it: *A good leader inspires people with a sense of purpose.* عزم، هدف في الحياة

IDM **on purpose** not by accident; with a particular intention: *'You've torn a page out of my book!' 'I'm sorry, I didn't do it on purpose.'* ○ *I came a bit early on purpose, to see if I could help you.* عمداً

serve your/the purpose → SERVE

▸ **purposeful** /-fl/ *adj* having a definite aim or plan: *Graham strode off down the street looking purposeful.* قاصد هدفاً معيّناً

purposefully /-fəli/ *adv* حثيثاً: نحو هدف معيّن

purposely *adv* with a particular intention: *I purposely waited till everyone had gone so that I could speak to you in private.* عن عمد، قصداً

purr /pɜː(r)/ *verb* [I] (used about a cat) to make a continuous low sound that shows pleasure (الهرّ) يُخرخر

purse[1] /pɜːs/ *noun* [C] **1** a small bag that you keep money in ➲ Look at **wallet**. كيس نقود، جزدان

2 (*US*) = HANDBAG

purse[2] /pɜːs/ *verb* [T] to press your lips together to show that you do not like sth يزمّ شفتيه

purser /ˈpɜːsə(r)/ *noun* [C] the person on a ship who looks after the accounts and who deals with passengers' problems محاسب السفينة

⚷ **pursue** /pəˈsjuː; *US* -ˈsuː/ *verb* [T] (*formal*) **1** to follow sb/sth in order to catch him/her/it: *The robber ran off pursued by two policemen.* ○ (*figurative*) *The goal that he is pursuing is completely unrealistic.* ❶ **Pursue** is more formal than **chase**. يطارد، يتعقب

2 to continue with sth; to find out more about sth: *to pursue a career in banking* ○ *She didn't seem to want to pursue the discussion so I changed the subject.* يتابع، يواصل؛ يمارس

▸ **pursuer** *noun* [C] a person who pursues(1) sb/sth المطارِد، المتعقِّب

pursuit /pəˈsjuːt; *US* -ˈsuːt/ *noun* **1** [U] the act of pursuing sb/sth: *the pursuit of pleasure* مطاردة، تعقُّب ركض (وراء الملذّات)

2 [C] something that you spend your time doing, either for work or for pleasure: *outdoor pursuits* ○ *leisure pursuits* اهتمام، شغل، حرفة

IDM **in pursuit (of sb/sth)** trying to catch or get sb/sth: *a dog in pursuit of a cat* ○ *He neglected his family in pursuit of his own personal ambitions.* راكض وراءه

pus /pʌs/ *noun* [U] a thick yellowish liquid that may form in a part of your body that has been hurt قيح، صديد

⚷ **push**[1] /pʊʃ/ *verb* **1** [I,T] to use force to move or try to move sb/sth forward or away from you: *You push and I'll pull.* ○ *Christine pushed him into the water.* ○ *to push sb in a wheelchair* ○ *to push a pram* ○ *She pushed the door shut with her foot.* يدفع

2 [I,T] to move forward by pushing sb/sth: *John pushed his way through the crowd.* ○ *to push past sb* يندفع، يشقّ طريقه

3 [I,T] to press or use force, e.g. with your finger, to move sth: *Push the red button if you want the bus to stop.* يضغط على

4 [T] (*informal*) to try to make sb do sth, e.g. by asking or telling him/her many times: *Ella will not work hard unless you push her.* ○ *to push sb for an answer* يحثّ على؛ يلحّ عليه بِ

5 [T] (*informal*) to try to make sth seem attractive, e.g. so that people will buy it: *They are launching a major publicity campaign to push their new product.* يروج

IDM **be pushed for sth** (*informal*) to not have enough of sth: *Hurry up. We're really pushed for time.* ينقصه (المال)، يفتقر إلى، ليس لديه الوقت

PHR V **push ahead (with sth)** to continue with sth يواصل (العمل)، يتقدّم

push for sth to try hard to get sth: *The Opposition are pushing for greater freedom of information.* يسعى للحصول على

push in to join a queue in front of other people who were there before you يأخذ دور غيره في مقدّمة الطابور

▸ **pusher** *noun* [C] a person who sells illegal drugs بائع مخدّرات ممنوعة

⚷ **push**[2] /pʊʃ/ *noun* [C] an act of pushing: *Paul gave the door a push and it opened.* ○ *Can you help me*

a b c d e f g h i j k l m n o p q r s t u v w x y z

give the car a push to get it started? ○ *The car windows opened at the push of a button.* دفعة: ضغطة

IDM **at a push** (*informal*) if it is necessary (but only with difficulty): *We can get ten people round the table at a push.* إذا لزم، عند الاضطرار

give sb the push to end a relationship with sb or to dismiss sb from a job
ينهي علاقته مع: يطرده من العمل

ˈ**push-button** *adj* (only *before* a noun) (used about a machine, etc.) that you work by pushing a button: *a radio with push-button tuning*
يعمل بالضغط على زرّ

pushchair /ˈpʊʃtʃeə(r)/ (*Brit also* **buggy**) *noun* [C] a chair on wheels that you use for pushing a young child in. You can fold up a pushchair when you are not using it. عربة طفل خفيفة وقابلة للطي

pushover /ˈpʊʃəʊvə(r)/ *noun* [C] (*informal*) **1** something that is easy to do or win: *With four of their players injured, the game won't be a pushover for Liverpool.* عمل يسير، نجاح سهل

2 a person who is easy to persuade or convince سهل الإقناع

ˈ**push-up** *noun* [C] (*US*) = PRESS-UP

pushy /ˈpʊʃi/ *adj* (**pushier**; **pushiest**) (*informal*) (used about a person) behaving in a forceful way in order to get an advantage or to make people notice you: *You need to be pushy to be successful in show business.* متجرئ، ناصب نفسه في المقدّمة دائماً

puss /pʊs/ *noun* [C] (used when you are speaking to or calling a cat) بِس بِس! : نداء للقطّة

▶ **pussy** /ˈpʊsi/ *noun* [C] (*pl.* **pussies**) (*informal*) a cat قطّة، هرّة

🔑**put** /pʊt/ *verb* [T] (*pres part* **putting**; *pt, pp* **put**) **1** to move sb/sth so that it is in a particular place or position: *She put the book on the table.* ○ *I put the knife back in the drawer.* ○ *Did you put sugar in my tea?* ○ *When do you put the children to bed?* يضع

2 to fix sth to or in sth else: *Can you put* (= sew) *a button on this shirt?* ○ *We're going to put a new window in this room.* يركّب؛ يخيط

3 to make sb feel or experience sth: *This sort of weather always puts me in a bad mood.* ○ *Your decision puts me in a difficult position.*
يجعل، يضع

4 to say or express sth: *I don't know exactly how to put this, but...*
يعبّر

5 to ask sb a question, make a suggestion, etc: *I'd like to put a question to the minister.* ○ *Can I put a suggestion to you?* يسأل؛ يقدّم اقتراحاً

6 to write sth: *12.30 on Friday? I'll put it in my diary.* ○ *What did you put for question 2?* يكتب

IDM **not put it past sb (to do sth)** (used with *would*) to think sb is capable of doing sth bad: *I wouldn't put it past him to do a thing like that.* لا يستغرب منه هذا التصرّف الرديء

put it to sb that... (*formal*) to suggest to sb that sth is true: *I put it to you that this man is innocent.* يبدي رأيه، يقترح

put together (used after a noun or nouns referring to a group of people or things) combined: *You got more presents than the rest of the family put together.* مجموعة، إذا ضُمّت كلّها إلى بعضها

ℹ For other idioms containing **put**, look at the entries for the nouns, adjectives, etc., e.g. **put an end to sth** is at **end**.

PHR V **put sth across/over** to say sth clearly, so that people can understand it: *He didn't put his ideas across very well at the meeting.*
يعبّر بوضوح

put sth aside to save sth, especially money, to use later يوفّر، يدّخر

put sb away (*informal*) to send sb to prison
يسجن

put sth away to put sth where you usually keep it, e.g. in a cupboard يضع شيئاً في مكانه المعتاد

put sth back 1 to return sth to its place: *to put books back on the shelf* يرجع، يعيد

2 to change the time shown on a clock, etc. to an earlier time: *We have to put the clocks back tonight.* ℹ The opposite is **put sth forward**.
يؤخّر الساعة

3 to change sth to a later time or date; to postpone: *I'll have to put back my dental appointment till next week.* يؤخّر، يؤجّل أو يرجئ

put sth by to save money to use later: *Her grandparents had put some money by for her wedding.* يوفّر، يدّخر

put sb down (*informal*) to say things to make sb seem stupid or foolish: *He's always putting his wife down.* يقلّل من قيمته، يجعله يبدو غبياً

put sth down 1 to place sth, e.g. on the floor, a table, etc: *The policeman persuaded him to put the gun down.* يضع أو يلقي على الأرض

2 (used about a government, an army or the police) to stop sth by force: *to put down a rebellion* يقمع، يخمد

3 to kill an animal because it is old, sick or dangerous: *The dog was put down because it attacked a child.* يقضي على حيوان (لمرضه مثلاً)

put sth down to sth to believe that sth is caused by sth: *The education minister puts the children's reading problems down to bad teaching.* يعزو إلى

put sth forward 1 to change the time shown on a clock, etc. to a later time: *We put the clocks forward in spring.* ℹ The opposite is **put sth back**. يقدّم الساعة

2 to suggest sth: *The minister put forward a plan to help the homeless.* يقدّم اقتراحاً

put yourself/sb forward to suggest that you or a particular person should be considered for a job, etc: *His name was put forward for the position of chairman.* يرشّحه (لوظيفة مثلاً)، يقترح اسمه

put sth in 1 to include a piece of information, etc. in sth that you write: *In your letter, you forgot to put in the time your plane would arrive.*
يذكر أو يضمّن في رسالته

2 to ask for sth in an official manner: *to put in a demand for a wage increase* يقدّم طلباً

put sth in; **put sth into sth/into doing sth** to spend time, etc. on sth: *She puts all her time and energy into her business.* يقضي أو يكرّس وقته

put sb off 1 to make sb dislike a person: *I'm sure he's a very nice person but his accent puts me off.*
ينفّر

2 to say to a person that you can no longer do what you had agreed: *They were coming to stay last weekend but I had to put them off at the last moment.* يرجئ؛ يماطل، يتملّص من

put sb off (sth/doing sth) 1 to cause sb to dislike sth/doing sth: *My first visit to Liverpool put me off the place.* ○ *The accident put me off driving for a long time.* ينفّره من

2 to make sb unable to concentrate: *Don't stare at me – you're putting me off!* يشتّت تفكيره، يربكه

put sth off to turn or switch a light off: *She put off the light and went to sleep.* يطفئ (النور)

put sth off; **put off doing sth** to move sth to a later time; to delay doing sth: *'I've got an appointment.' 'Can't you put it off?.'* ○ *She put off writing her essay until the last minute.* يرجئ أو يؤجّل

put sth on 1 to pretend to be feeling sth; to pretend to have sth: *He's not angry with you really: he's just putting it on.* ○ *She put on a Scottish accent.* يتظاهر بـ، ينتحل؛ يتصنّع

2 to place clothes on your body: *Put on your coat!* ○ *I'll have to put my glasses on.* يرتدي، يلبس

3 to apply sth to your skin, face, etc. يضع

4 to make a piece of electrical equipment, etc. start working, usually by pressing a switch: *It's too early to put the lights on yet.* يشعل (النور)؛ يشغّل (آلة كهربائية)

5 to make sth (e.g. a CD, a tape, etc.) begin to play: *Let's put some music on.* يدير (الراديو مثلاً)

6 to become fatter or heavier (by the amount mentioned): *I put on weight very easily.* ○ *She's put on several pounds since I last saw her.* يسمن، يزداد وزناً

7 to organize or prepare sth for people to see or use: *The school is putting on 'Macbeth'.* ○ *They put on extra trains in the summer.* يعرض ينظّم، يجهز

put sth on sth to add an amount of money, etc. to the cost or value of sth: *The government want to put 50p on the price of a packet of cigarettes.* يزيد في السعر

put sb out 1 to give sb trouble or extra work: *He put his hosts out by arriving very late.* يزعج، يثقل على

2 to make sb upset or angry: *I was quite put out by their selfish behaviour.* يغضب، يكدّر

put sth out 1 to make sth stop burning: *to put out a fire* يخمد (النار)

2 to switch off a light: *They put out the lights and locked the door.* يطفئ (النور)

3 to take sth out of your house and leave it: *to put the rubbish out* يخرج من البيت

4 to give or tell the public sth, often by using the television, radio or newspapers: *The police put out a warning about the escaped prisoner.* يذيع، ينشر في الصحف

put yourself out (*informal*) to do sth for sb, even though it brings you trouble or extra work: *'I'll give you a lift home.' 'I don't want you to put yourself out. I'll take a taxi.'* يتعب أو يزعج نفسه

put sth over → PUT STH ACROSS

put sb through sth to make sb experience sth unpleasant يجعله يعاني، يريه نجوم الظهر

put sb/sth through to make a telephone connection that allows sb to speak to sb: *Could you put me through to flight reservations, please?* يوصله بالشخص المطلوب هاتفياً

put sth to sb to suggest sth to sb; to ask sb sth: *I put the question to her.* يقترح؛ يسأل

put sth together to build or repair sth by joining its parts together: *The furniture comes with instructions on how to put it together.* يركّب، يجمّع

put up sth to offer or give resistance in a fight, etc: *The old lady put up a struggle against her attacker.* يبدي مقاومة

put sb up to give sb food and a place to stay: *She had missed the last train home, so I offered to put her up for the night.* يستضيفه (ليلةً)، ينزله عنده

put sth up 1 to raise or hold sth up: *Put your hand up if you know the answer.* يرفع

2 to build sth: *to put up a fence* يبني، يقيم

3 to fix sth to a wall, etc. so that everyone can see it: *to put up a notice* يعلّق (إعلانا)

4 to increase sth: *Some shops put up their prices just before Christmas.* يرفع، يزيد

put up with sb/sth to suffer sb/sth unpleasant and not complain about it: *I don't know how they put up with this noise.* يتحمّل

putt /pʌt/ *verb* [I,T] (used in golf) to hit the ball gently when it is near the hole يدحرج كرة الغولف برفق لتدخل في الثقب

putter /ˈpʌtə(r)/ *verb* [I] (*US*) = POTTER¹

putty /ˈpʌti/ *noun* [U] a substance that is used for fixing glass into windows. Putty is soft when you use it but it turns hard later. معجونة (لزجاج النوافذ)

puzzle /ˈpʌzl/ *noun* [C] **1** [usually sing.] something that is difficult to understand or explain; a mystery: *The reasons for his action have remained a puzzle to historians.* لغز

2 a game or toy that tests your knowledge, skill, intelligence, etc: *to do a crossword puzzle* ○ *The solution to the puzzle is on page 27.* ○ *a jigsaw puzzle* أحجية، حزّورة

▶ **puzzle** *verb* **1** [T] to cause sb to think hard about sth he/she cannot understand or explain: *The appearance of strange circles in fields of corn has puzzled all the experts.* يحيّر

2 [I] **puzzle over sth** to think hard about sth in order to understand or explain it: *to puzzle over a mathematical problem* يفكر ملياً (لإيجاد حلّ للمسألة مثلاً)

PHR V puzzle sth out to find the answer to sth by thinking hard: *The letter was in Italian and it took us an hour to puzzle out what it said.* يجد الحلّ بعد تفكير عميق

puzzled /ˈpʌzld/ *adj* not able to understand or explain sth: *a puzzled expression* (نظرة) حائرة

pyjamas /pəˈdʒɑːməz/ (*US* **pajamas** /pəˈdʒæməz/) *noun* [plural] loose trousers and a loose jacket or top that you wear in bed ❶ Notice that you use **pyjama** (without an 's') before another noun: *pyjama trousers* بيجاما

pylon /ˈpaɪlən; *US* ˈpaɪlɒn/ *noun* [C] a tall metal

a b c d e f g h i j k l m n o p q r s t u v w x y z

tower that carries heavy electricity wires برج الأسلاك الكهربائية

pyramid /ˈpɪrəmɪd/ *noun* [C] a shape with a flat base and three or four triangular sides هرم

python /ˈpaɪθn; *US* ˈpaɪθɒn/ *noun* [C] a large snake that kills animals by squeezing them very hard أصَلَة: ثعبان كبير

Q q

Q, q /kjuː/ *noun* [C] (*pl.* **Qs**; **Q's**; **q's** /kjuːz/) the seventeenth letter of the English alphabet: *'Queen' begins with (a) 'Q'.* الحرف السابع عشر من الأبجديّة الإنكليزيّة

Q *abbrev* = QUESTION[1] (1): *Qs 1-4 are compulsory.*

qt *abbrev* = QUART(S)

quack /kwæk/ *noun* [C] the sound that a duck makes بطبطة أو "كُواك": صوت البطّة
▶ **quack** *verb* [I] (البطّة) تبطبط أو تصيح

quad bike /ˈkwɒd baɪk/ *noun* [C] a motorcycle with four large wheels, used for riding over rough ground, often for fun دراجة ذات أربع عجلات

quadrangle /ˈkwɒdræŋgl/ (*also informal* **quad**) *noun* [C] a square open area with buildings round it, in a school, college, etc. ساحة مربّعة تحيط بها الأبنية

quadruple /ˈkwɒdrʊpl; *US* kwɒˈdruːpl/ *verb* [I,T] to multiply or be multiplied by four: *Profits have quadrupled in the past ten years.* يضاعِف أو يتضاعف أربع مرّات

quail /kweɪl/ *noun* (*pl.* **quail** or **quails**) [C] a small brown bird whose flesh and eggs are eaten as food السلوى، السُّماني

quaint /kweɪnt/ *adj* attractive or unusual because it seems to belong to the past: *The village has quaint narrow streets leading down to the sea.* جذّاب لقِدَم طرازه وغرابته

quake /kweɪk/ *verb* [I] to shake: *to quake with fear, cold, etc.* يرتجف، يرتعد
▶ **quake** *noun* [C] (*informal*) = EARTHQUAKE

qualification /ˌkwɒlɪfɪˈkeɪʃn/ *noun* **1** [C] an examination that you have passed or a course of study that you have completed: *a teaching qualification* ○ *Please list your qualifications on your CV.* ○ *40 per cent of children left school at 16 with no formal qualifications.* مؤهِّل

2 [C] a skill or quality that you need to do a particular job: *Is there a height qualification for the police force?* مؤهِّل، شرط

3 [C,U] something that limits or weakens the meaning of a general statement: *I can recommend him for the job without qualification.* ○ *She accepted the proposal with only a few qualifications.* قيد، تحفُّظ؛ تعديل

qualify /ˈkwɒlɪfaɪ/ *verb* (*pres part* **qualifying**; *3rd pers sing pres* **qualifies**; *pt, pp* **qualified**) **1** [I] to pass the examination that is necessary to do a particular job; to have the qualities that are necessary for sth: *It takes five years to qualify as a vet.* ○ *A cup of coffee and a sandwich doesn't really qualify as a meal.* يحصل على شهادة مؤهِّلة؛ يوصف بِ

2 [T] to give sb the right to do a particular job: *This exam will qualify me to teach music.* يؤهِّل؛ يخوِّل

3 [I] to be successful in one part of a competition and to go on to the next part: *Our team has qualified for the final.* يترفّع إلى المرحلة الثانية

4 [I,T] to have or give sb the right to have or do sth: *How many years must you work to qualify for a pension?* ○ *Residence in this country does not qualify you to vote.* يستحقّ؛ يخوِّل

5 [T] to limit or weaken the meaning of a general statement: *I must qualify what I said earlier – it wasn't quite true.* يعدِّل، يحدِّد، يخفِّف

▶ **qualified** *adj* **1** having passed an examination or completed a course of study: *Edward is well qualified for this job.* ○ *a fully qualified doctor* مؤهَّل

2 having the skill, knowledge or quality that you need to do sth: *I don't feel qualified to comment – I know nothing about the subject.* كفء، خبير

3 not complete; limited: *My boss gave only qualified approval to the plan.* ℹ The opposite is **unqualified**. محدود؛ مشروط

quality /ˈkwɒləti/ *noun* (*pl.* **qualities**) **1** [U] how good or bad sth is: *This paper isn't very good quality.* ○ *These photos are of poor quality.* ○ *a high-quality magazine* ○ *the quality of life in our cities* نوعيّة

2 [U] a high standard or level: *We aim to provide quality at a reasonable price.* مستوى عالٍ، نوعيّة جيّدة

3 [C] something that is typical of a person or thing: *Vicky has all the qualities of a good manager.* صفة، خاصّة أو خاصيّة

qualm /kwɑːm/ *noun* [C, usually pl.] a feeling of doubt or worry about whether what you are doing is right: *I don't have any qualms about asking them to lend us some money.* شكّ، خشية، تحرّج

quandary /ˈkwɒndəri/ *noun* [C] (*pl.* **quandaries**) a state of not being able to decide what to do; a difficult situation: *to be in a quandary* حيرة؛ مأزق

quantity /ˈkwɒntəti/ *noun* (*pl.* **quantities**) **1** [U] the measurement of sth by stating how much of it there is: *Don't write too much in your essay – quality is more important than quantity.* الكميّة

2 [C,U] a number or an amount: *Add a small quantity of salt.* ○ *It's cheaper to buy goods in quantity* (= in large amounts). ○ *It's cheaper to buy goods in large quantities.* كميّة

IDM an unknown quantity → UNKNOWN

quarantine /ˈkwɒrəntiːn/ *noun* [U] a period of time when a person or animal that has or may have an infectious disease must be kept away from other people or animals: *All dogs brought into the country must be kept in quarantine for six months.* الحجر الصحي

quarrel /ˈkwɒrəl; *US* ˈkwɔːrəl/ *noun* [C] **1** an angry argument or disagreement: *We're always having quarrels about who should do the washing-up.* ➔ Look at **argument** and **fight**. شِجار، خلاف

2 quarrel with sb/sth a reason for complaining about or disagreeing with sb/sth: *I have no quarrel with what has just been said.* اعتراض: سبب للشكوى

▶ **quarrel** *verb* [I] (quarrelling; quarrelled; *US* quarreling; quarreled) **1 quarrel (with sb) (about/over sth)** to have an angry argument or disagreement: *The children are always quarrelling!* ○ *I don't want to quarrel with you about it.* ➔ Look at **argue** and **fight**. يتشاجر مع

2 quarrel with sth to disagree with sth: *I wouldn't quarrel with Moira's description of what happened.* يخالف، يعترض على

quarry[1] /ˈkwɒri; *US* ˈkwɔːri/ *noun* [C] (*pl.* **quarries**) a place where sand, stone, etc. is dug out of the ground ➔ Look at **mine**[2]. مقلع أحجار

▶ **quarry** *verb* [T] (*pres part* **quarrying**; *3rd pers sing pres* **quarries**; *pt, pp* **quarried**) to dig stone, sand, etc. out of the ground: *to quarry for marble* يقتلع الأحجار من مقلع

quarry[2] /ˈkwɒri; *US* ˈkwɔːri/ *noun* [sing.] a person or animal that is being hunted طريد؛ طريدة

quart /kwɔːt/ *noun* [C] (*abbr* **qt**) a measure of liquid; 1.14 litres. There are 2 pints in a quart. ℹ An American quart is 0.94 of a litre. مقياس للسوائل

quarter /ˈkwɔːtə(r)/ *noun* **1** [C] one of four equal parts into which sth is divided: *The programme lasts for three quarters of an hour.* ○ *a mile and a quarter* ○ *to cut an apple into quarters* ربع

2 [sing.] fifteen minutes before or after every hour: *I'll meet you at (a) quarter past six.* ○ *It's (a) quarter to three.* ℹ In American English you say '(a) quarter **after**' and '(a) quarter **of**': *I'll meet you at (a) quarter after six.* ○ *It's a quarter of three.* ربع ساعة

3 [C] a period of three months: *You get a gas bill every quarter.* (فترة) ثلاثة أشهر

4 [C] four ounces of sth; ¼ of a pound: *A quarter of mushrooms, please.* ربع الرطل (أو الباوند) الإنكليزي

5 [C] a part of a town, especially a part where a particular group of people live: *the Chinese quarter of the city* حيّ، حارة

6 [C] a person or group of people who may give help or information or who have certain opinions: *Jim's parents haven't got much money so he can't expect any help from that quarter.* ○ *Racist attitudes still exist in some quarters.* ناحية أو جهة؛ فئة

7 [C] (in America or Canada) a coin that is worth 25 cents (¼ dollar) ربع دولار

8 quarters [plural] a place that is provided for a person (especially a soldier) to live in: *married quarters* (= for soldiers and their families) مسكن (للجنود)

IDM at close quarters → CLOSE[1]

quarter-ˈfinal *noun* [C] one of the four matches between the eight remaining players or teams in a competition. The players that win in the quarter-finals go on to the semi-finals. مباراة ربع نهائية

quarterly /ˈkwɔːtəli/ *adj, adv* (produced or happening) once every three months: *a quarterly magazine* ○ *The committee meets quarterly.* رُبعيّ، مرة كل ثلاثة أشهر

quartet /kwɔːˈtet/ *noun* [C] **1** four people who sing or play music together رباعيّ موسيقي

2 a piece of music for four people to sing or play together رباعيّة: قطعة موسيقية لأربعة عازفين

quartz /kwɔːts/ *noun* [U] a type of hard rock that is used in making very accurate clocks or watches المرو أو الكوارتز

quash /kwɒʃ/ *verb* [T] (*formal*) **1** to declare that an official decision, judgment, etc. is no longer true or legal: *The appeal court quashed the verdict of the lower court.* يلغي، يبطل

2 to stop or defeat sth by force: *to quash a rebellion* يخمد، يقمع

quay /kiː/ *noun* [C] a stone or metal platform in a harbour where boats are loaded and unloaded رصيف الميناء

quayside /ˈkiːsaɪd/ *noun* [sing.] the area of land that is near a quay المنطقة المجاورة لرصيف الميناء

queen /kwiːn/ *noun* [C] **1** (*also* **Queen**) the female ruler of a country: *Queen Victoria reigned for more than fifty years.* ○ *to crown a new queen* ○ *Should the Queen abdicate in favour of her son?* ℹ Queen Elizabeth II is pronounced 'Queen Elizabeth **the Second**'. Look at **king** and **princess**. ملكة

2 (*also* **Queen**) the wife of a king ملكة

3 the largest and most important female in a group of insects: *the queen bee* ملكة

4 one of the four playing cards in a pack with a picture of a queen: *the queen of hearts* البنت (في ورق اللعب)

queen ˈmother *noun* [C] the mother of a king or queen أمّ الملك أو الملكة

quell /kwel/ *verb* [T] to put an end to sth: *to quell a rebellion* ○ *to quell sb's fears* يقمع أو يخمد؛ يهدّئ

quench /kwentʃ/ *verb* [T] to satisfy your feeling of thirst by drinking: *to quench your thirst* يروي (ظمأه)

query /ˈkwɪəri/ *noun* [C] (*pl.* **queries**) a question, especially one asking for information or expressing a doubt about sth: *Does anyone have any queries?* استفسار، استفهام

▸ **query** *verb* [T] (*pres part* **querying**; *3rd pers sing pres* **queries**; *pt, pp* **queried**) to ask a question about sth: *We queried the bill but were told it was correct.* يتشكّك في، يتساءل عن صحّة أمر

quest /kwest/ *noun* [C] (*formal*) a long search for sth that is difficult to find: *the quest for eternal youth* بَحْث، سعي وراء

question¹ /ˈkwestʃən/ *noun* **1** [C] a sentence or phrase that asks for an answer: *Are there any questions on what I've just said?* ○ *Put up your hand if you want to ask a question.* ○ *In the examination, you must answer five questions in one hour.* ○ *What's the answer to Question 5?* سؤال، استفهام

2 [C] a problem or difficulty that needs to be discussed or dealt with: *His resignation raises the question of who will take over from him.* ○ *It's not difficult. It's just a question of finding the time to do it.* ○ *We all agree that more money should be spent on education. The question is where that money is going to come from.* مسألة، قضيّة، مشكلة

3 [U] doubt or uncertainty: *There is no question about Sarah's enthusiasm for the job.* ○ *His honesty is beyond question.* شكّ، ريبة

IDM in question that is being considered or talked about: *The lawyer asked where she was on the night in question.* قيد البحث، المُشار إليه

no question of no possibility of: *I'm afraid there is no question of any new jobs here at present.* لا مجال، لا إمكانيّة

out of the question impossible: *A new car is out of the question. It's just too expensive.* مستحيل

question² /ˈkwestʃən/ *verb* [T] **1** to ask sb a question or questions: *The police questioned him for several hours.* ○ *The interviewers questioned me on my past experience.* يسأل؛ يستجوب

2 to express or feel doubt about sth: *She told me she was from the council so I didn't question her right to be there.* ○ *to question sb's sincerity* يشكّ في

▸ **questionable** /-əbl/ *adj* **1** that is not certain: *It's questionable whether we'll be able to finish in time.* مشكوك فيه، غير مؤكّد

2 that may not be true, suitable or honest: *A lot of money has been spent on very questionable projects.* ○ *questionable motives* مريب

ˈquestion mark *noun* [C] the sign (?) that you use when you write a question علامة استفهام

questionnaire /ˌkwestʃəˈneə(r)/ *noun* [C] a list of questions that are answered by many people. A questionnaire is used to collect information about a particular subject: *to complete/fill in a questionnaire* استبيان

ˈquestion tag (*also* **tag**) *noun* [C] a short phrase at the end of a sentence that changes it into a question: *In the sentence 'It's very expensive, isn't it?', the use of the question tag means that the speaker is asking the listener to agree.* عبارة استفهاميّة في نهاية جملة

queue /kju:/ (*US* **line**) *noun* [C] a line of people, cars, etc. that are waiting for sth or to do sth: *We had to wait in a queue for hours to get tickets.* ○ *to join the end of a queue* طابور أو صفّ

IDM jump the queue → JUMP¹

▸ **queue** *verb* [I] **queue (up) (for sth)** to form a line when you are waiting for sth: *to queue for a bus* ○ *They're queueing up to see the film.* يقف في صفّ أو طابور

quiche /ki:ʃ/ *noun* [C,U] a pie without a top that is filled with a mixture of eggs and milk with cheese, onions, etc. and cooked in the oven. You can eat quiche hot or cold. ➲ Look at the note at **pie**. فطيرة تملأ بمزيج من البيض والحليب والجبن...الخ

quick /kwɪk/ *adj* **1** doing sth at speed or in a short time: *It's quicker to travel by train.* ○ *Neil is a quick worker.* ○ *She was quick to point out all the mistakes I had made.* ○ *Run and get your coat and be quick about it.* سريع

2 done in a short time: *May I make a quick telephone call?* سريع، وجيز

> **Fast** is more often used for describing a person or thing that moves or can move at great speed: *a fast horse, car, runner, etc.* **Quick** is more often used for describing sth that is done in a short time: *a quick decision, breakfast, visit, etc.*

IDM quick/slow on the uptake → UPTAKE

▸ **quick** *adv* (*informal*) quickly: *Come over here quick!* بسرعة، في مدة قصيرة

quickly *adv* at speed or in a short time: *Tom quickly undressed and got into bed.* ○ *The cooker's on fire! Do something quickly!* ○ *I'd like you to get here as quickly as possible.* بسرعة؛ فوراً

quid /kwɪd/ *noun* [C] (*pl.* **quid**) (*Brit informal*) a pound (in money); £1: *It costs a quid.* ○ *The tickets are five quid each.* جنيه إسترليني (عاميّة)

quiet¹ /ˈkwaɪət/ *adj* **1** with very little or no noise: *Be quiet!* ○ *His voice was quiet but firm.* ○ *Please keep the children quiet when I'm on the phone.* ○ *Go into the library if you want to work. It's much quieter in there.* ❶ The opposite is **loud**. ساكن، هادئ

2 without many people or much activity; without anything very exciting happening: *London is very quiet on Sundays.* ○ *'Have you been busy?' 'No, we've had a very quiet day today.'* ○ *a quiet country village* ○ *a quiet life* هادئ، وادع؛ راكد اجتماعياً

3 (used about a person) not saying very much; not attracting other people's attention: *You're very quiet today. Is anything wrong?* صامت، منعزل

IDM keep quiet about sth; keep sth quiet to say nothing about sth: *Would you keep quiet about me leaving until I've told the boss?* يكتم سرّاً، لا يذيع خبراً

▸ **quietly** *adv* in a quiet way: *Try and shut the door quietly!* ○ *'She was my best friend,' Rose said quietly.* ○ *He quietly got up and left the room.* بهدوء، دون أية ضجّة

quietness *noun* [U] هدوء، سكون

quiet² /ˈkwaɪət/ *noun* [U] the state of being quiet: *the peace and quiet of the countryside* هدوء، سكون

IDM **on the quiet** secretly: *She's given up smoking but she still has an occasional cigarette on the quiet.* سراً

quieten /ˈkwaɪətn/ *verb* [T] to make sb/sth quiet يهدّئ؛ يسكت
PHRV **quieten (sb/sth) down** to become quiet or to make sb/sth quiet: *When you've quietened down, I'll tell you what happened.* يهدأ؛ يهدّئ، يسكت

quilt /kwɪlt/ *noun* [C] a cover for a bed that has a thick warm material, e.g. feathers, inside it لحاف ➲ Look at **duvet**.

quintet /kwɪnˈtet/ *noun* [C] **1** a group of five people who sing or play music together الخماسيّ: فرقة من خمسة عازفين
2 a piece of music for five people to sing or play together قطعة موسيقيّة لخمسة عازفين

quirk /kwɜːk/ *noun* [C] **1** a strange habit or type of behaviour عادة غريبة، سلوك شاذّ
2 a strange happening: *By a quirk of fate they met again several years later.* واقعة غريبة، فلتة
▶ **quirky** *adj* (used about a person's behaviour) unusual غريب، شاذّ

quit /kwɪt/ *verb* (*pres part* **quitting**; *pt, pp* **quit**) **1** [I,T] (often used in newspapers, etc.) to leave a job, etc. or to go away from a place: *Tennis star says, 'I felt the time had come to quit.'* ○ *Thousands of people have decided to quit Hong Kong for good.* يكفّ عن عمله؛ يغادر أو ينزح عن
2 [T] (*informal*) to stop doing sth: *to quit smoking* يتوقّف عن، يكفّ
3 [I,T] (*computing*) to close a computer program ينهي أو يغلق

quite /kwaɪt/ *adv* **1** not very; to a certain degree; rather: *The film was quite good.* ○ *Beth plays the piano quite well but she needs more practice.* ○ *My husband quite enjoys cooking.* ○ *They had to wait quite a long time.* ○ *It's quite cold today.* ○ *We still meet up quite often.* ➲ Look at the note at **rather**. نوعاً ما، إلى حدّ ما
2 (used for emphasizing sth) completely; very: *Are you quite sure you don't mind?* ○ *Life in Japan is quite different from here.* ○ *I quite agree – you're quite right.* ○ *To my surprise, the room was quite empty.* تماماً، جداً
3 (used for showing that you agree with or understand sth): *'I feel that we shouldn't spend more than £20.' 'Quite.'* نعم بالضبط، تماماً
IDM **not quite** (used for showing that there is nearly enough of sth, or that it is nearly suitable): *There's not quite enough bread for breakfast.* ○ *These shoes don't quite fit.* ليس تماماً
quite a (used for showing that sth is unusual): *It's quite a climb to the top of the hill.* ○ *That's quite a problem.* إنه حقّاً...، لا يستهان به
quite a few; **quite a lot (of)** not a lot, but a certain amount of sb/sth: *We've received quite a few enquiries.* ○ *They've worked hard but there's still quite a lot left to do.* عدد أو مقدار لا بأس به

quits /kwɪts/ *adj*
IDM **be quits (with sb)** if two people are quits, it means that neither of them owes the other any money: *You give me £2 and then we're quits.* متخالصان، لا دَيْنَ لأحدهما على الآخر

quiver /ˈkwɪvə(r)/ *verb* [I] to tremble or shake: *to quiver with rage, excitement, fear, etc.* يرتجف، يرتعد

quiz /kwɪz/ *noun* [C] (*pl.* **quizzes**) a game or competition in which you must answer questions: *a quiz programme on TV* ○ *a general knowledge quiz* مسابقة، اختبار معلومات

quizzical /ˈkwɪzɪkl/ *adj* (used about a look, smile, etc.) seeming to ask a question (نظرة) متسائلة
▶ **quizzically** /-kli/ *adv* بتساؤل واستغراب

quorum /ˈkwɔːrəm/ *noun* [sing.] the minimum number of people that must be at a meeting before it can make decisions النصاب القانوني

quota /ˈkwəʊtə/ *noun* [C] the number or amount of sth that is allowed or that you must do: *There is a quota on the number of cars that can be imported each year.* ○ *We have a fixed quota of work to get through each day.* عدد أو مقدار محدّد، حصة مخصّصة

quotation /kwəʊˈteɪʃn/ (*also informal* **quote**) *noun* [C] **1** a group of words from a book, speech, play, etc., that you repeat exactly: *That's a quotation from Shakespeare.* عبارة مقتبسة، تضمين
2 the amount that sb thinks a piece of work will probably cost: *You should get a quotation from three different builders.* ➲ Look at **estimate**. تقدير لكلفة العمل؛ تسعير

quoˈtation marks (*also informal* **quotes**; *Brit also* **inverted commas**) *noun* [plural] the signs ('...') or ("...") that you put around a word, a sentence, etc. to show that it is what sb said or wrote, that it is a title or that you are using it in a special way علامتا الاقتباس

quote /kwəʊt/ *verb* **1** [I,T] **quote (sth) (from sb/sth)** to repeat exactly sth that sb else has said or written before: *The interviewer quoted a statement that the minister had made several years earlier.* ○ *to quote from the Bible* ○ *She was quoted as saying that she disagreed with the decision.* ○ *The minister asked the newspaper not to quote him.* يستشهد بِ، يكرّر كلام...
2 [T] to give sth as an example to support what you are saying: *She quoted several reasons why she was unhappy about the decision.* يورد على سبيل المثال، يقدّم (كبرهان)
3 [T] to say what the cost of a piece of work, etc. will probably be: *The catering company quoted us £6.50 a head for a buffet lunch.* يقدّر الكلفة، يسعّر

R r

R, r /ɑː(r)/ *noun* [C] (*pl.* **Rs**; **R's**; **r's**) the eighteenth letter of the English alphabet: *'Rabbit' begins with (an) 'R'.* الحرف الثامن عشر من الأبجديّة الإنكليزيّة

R *abbrev* = RIVER

r *abbrev* = RIGHT

rabbit /ˈræbɪt/ *noun* [C] a small animal with long ears: *a wild rabbit* ○ *a tame rabbit* (= one that you keep as a pet) ○ *a rabbit hutch* (= a cage for rabbits) ℹ The children's word for rabbit is **bunny**. أرنب

rabble /ˈræbl/ *noun* [C] a noisy uncontrolled crowd of people غوغاء، رعاع

rabies /ˈreɪbiːz/ *noun* [U] a serious, usually fatal, disease that can be given to humans by the bite of an animal that has the disease داء أو مرض الكلب

RAC /ˌɑːr eɪ ˈsiː/ *abbrev* (*Brit*) Royal Automobile Club; an organization for motorists. If you are a member of the RAC and your car breaks down, you can phone them and they will send someone to help you. نادي السيارات الملكي

⚷ **race¹** /reɪs/ *noun* **1** [C] **race (against/with sb/sth)** a competition between people, animals, cars, etc. to see which is the fastest: *to run/win/lose a race* ○ *to come first, second, last, etc. in a race* ○ *a five kilometre race* ○ *a horse race* ○ *What a close race!* ○ *Let's have a race to the end of the road.* ○ (*figurative*) *Rescuing victims of the earthquake is now a race against time.* سباق

2 the races [plural] (*Brit*) an occasion when a number of horse races are held in one place: *We're going to the races for the day.* (مشاهدة) سباق الخيل

IDM **rat race** → RAT

⚷ **race²** /reɪs/ *verb* **1** [I,T] **race (against/with sb/sth)** to have a competition with sb/sth to find out who is the fastest: *I'll race you home.* ○ *In the 5 000 metres he'll be racing against some of the finest runners in the country.* يتسابق مع، يسابق

2 [I,T] to go very fast or to move sb/sth very fast: *We raced to catch the bus.* ○ *The child had to be raced to hospital.* يعدو مسرعاً؛ ينقَل بأقصى سرعة

3 [T] to cause an animal or a car, etc. to take part in a race يدخل في سباق

▶ **racing** *noun* [U] **1** = HORSE RACING

2 the sport of taking part in races: *motor racing* ○ *a racing car* ○ *powerboat racing* سباق (السيّارات مثلاً)

⚷ **race³** /reɪs/ *noun* **1** [C,U] one of the groups into which people can be divided according to the colour of their skin, their hair type, the shape of their face, etc: *the different races of South Africa* ○ *a child of mixed race* ○ *People should not be discriminated against on grounds of race, religion or sex.* ➲ Look at **human race**. عنصر، عِرق

2 [C] a group of people who have the same language, customs, history, etc: *the Spanish race* شعب

racecourse /ˈreɪskɔːs/ (*US* **ˈracetrack**) *noun* [C] a place where horse races are held حلبة السباق، مضمار

racehorse /ˈreɪshɔːs/ *noun* [C] a horse that is trained to run in horse races حصان سباق، فرس رهان

ˌrace reˈlations *noun* [plural] the relations between people of different races who live in the same town, area, etc: *Community leaders are working to improve race relations.* العلاقات العنصريّة

racial /ˈreɪʃl/ *adj* connected with people's race; happening between people of different races: *racial tension* ○ *racial discrimination* عنصري، (فروق) عرقيّة

▶ **racially** /-ʃəli/ *adv*: *a racially mixed school* عنصرياً

racism /ˈreɪsɪzəm/ *noun* [U] the belief that some races are better than others and people of other races are not as good as people of your own race; ways of treating people that show this belief: *to take measures to combat racism* العنصريّة؛ التحيُّز العنصري

▶ **racist** /ˈreɪsɪst/ *noun* [C], *adj*: *He's a racist.* ○ *a racist remark* عنصري؛ متحيز عنصرياً

rack¹ /ræk/ *noun* [C] (often in compounds) a sort of shelf, made of bars, that you can put things in or on: *Put your coat in the luggage rack.* ○ *We need a roof rack on the car for all this luggage.* مِنصَب، رفّ؛ حامل ذو فتحات (للصحون مثلاً)

rack² /ræk/ *verb*

IDM **rack your brains** to try hard to think of sth or remember sth: *Steve racked his brains trying to remember where they'd met before.* يرهق مخّه في التفكير

rack³ /ræk/ *noun*

IDM **go to rack and ruin** to be in or get into a bad state because of lack of care متخرّب أو يتخرّب بسبب الإهمال

racket¹ (*also* **racquet**) /ˈrækɪt/ *noun* [C] a piece of sports equipment that you use to hit the ball with in the games of tennis, badminton and squash ℹ Rackets are different from **bats** because they have **strings**. Look also at **club²**(2) and **stick¹**(3). مِضرَب

racket² /ˈrækɪt/ *noun* (*informal*) **1** [sing.] a loud noise: *Stop making that terrible racket!* ضجيج مزعج

2 [C] an illegal way of making money: *a drugs racket* وسيلة غير مشروعة للحصول على المال

radar /ˈreɪdɑː(r)/ *noun* [U] the system for finding out the position of sth that you cannot see, with the help of radio waves الرادار

radiant /ˈreɪdiənt/ *adj* **1** sending out light or heat: *radiant energy* مشعّ للنور أو الحرارة

2 showing great happiness: *a radiant smile* متألّق أو مشرق، يفيض بِشراً وسعادة

radiate /ˈreɪdieɪt/ *verb* **1** [T] to send out heat or light: (*figurative*) *She radiated self-confidence.* يشعّ: يتألّق

2 [I] **radiate from sth** to go out in all directions from a central point: *Narrow streets radiate from the harbour.* ينبعث من المركز في كلّ الاتجاهات، يتشعّع

radiation /ˌreɪdiˈeɪʃn/ *noun* [U] powerful and very dangerous rays that are sent out from certain substances. You cannot see or feel radiation but it can cause serious illness or death: *High levels of radiation have been recorded near the power station.* ○ *to be exposed to radiation* ➲ Look at **radioactive**. إشعاع

radiator /ˈreɪdieɪtə(r)/ *noun* [C] **1** a piece of equipment that is used for heating a room. Radiators are made of metal and filled with hot water. They are usually part of a central heating system: *Turn the radiator down a bit!* المُشِع (الرادياتور)

2 a piece of equipment that is used for keeping an engine cool المبرِّد في السيّارة (الرادياتور)

radical /ˈrædɪkl/ *adj* **1** (used about changes in sth) very great: *The tax system needs radical reform.* ○ *radical change* جذريّ، هائل أو ضخم

2 wanting great social or political change: *The students' demands were too radical to be accepted.* ○ *to hold radical views* ➲ Look at **moderate**[1]. متطرِّف، راديكالي

▸ **radical** *noun* [C] a person who wants great social or political change الراديكاليّ، من يدعو إلى تغيير جذري

radically /-kli/ *adv*: *The First World War radically altered the political map of Europe.* جوهريّاً، جذريّاً

radio /ˈreɪdiəʊ/ *noun* (*pl.* **radios**) **1** [U] the process of sending or receiving messages through the air by electrical signals: *The yachtsman was in contact with the coast by radio.* ○ *a radio signal* لاسلكي، راديو

2 [C] a piece of equipment that is used for receiving and/or sending radio messages or broadcasts (on a ship, plane, etc. or in the house): *a ship's radio* ○ *a portable radio* مذياع، راديو؛ جهاز إرسال واستقبال

> You may **put**, **switch** or **turn** a radio **on** or **off**. You may also **turn** it **up** or **down** to make it louder or quieter.

3 often **the radio** [U, sing.] the broadcasting of programmes for people to listen to on their radios: *I always listen to the radio in the car.* ○ *I heard an interesting report on the radio this morning.* ○ *a radio station, programme, etc.* ○ *national/local radio* الراديو؛ محطة راديو، إذاعة

▸ **radio** *verb* [I,T] (*pt, pp* **radioed**) to send a message by radio: *to radio for help* يرسل إشارة لاسلكيّة

radioactive /ˌreɪdiəʊˈæktɪv/ *adj* sending out powerful and very dangerous rays that are produced when atoms are broken up. These rays cannot be seen or felt but can cause serious illness or death: *the problem of the disposal of radioactive waste from power stations* ➲ Look at **radiation**. مشعّ

▸ **radioactivity** /ˌreɪdiəʊækˈtɪvəti/ *noun* [U] **1** the state of being radioactive إشعاع

2 the energy that is produced by radioactive substances النشاط الإشعاعي

radiographer /ˌreɪdiˈɒɡrəfə(r)/ *noun* [C] a person who is trained to take X-rays for medical purposes مختص في التصوير بالأشعّة

radish /ˈrædɪʃ/ *noun* [C] a small red or white vegetable with a strong taste that you eat raw. A radish is the root of a radish plant. فجلة

radius /ˈreɪdiəs/ *noun* [C] (*pl.* **radii**) /-diaɪ/ **1** the distance from the centre of a circle to the outside edge ➲ Look at **diameter**. نصف قطر الدائرة

2 a circular area that is measured from a point in its centre: *The wreckage of the plane was scattered over a radius of several miles.* مساحة دائريّة (حول كذا)

RAF /ˌɑːr eɪ ˈef/ *abbrev* (*Brit*) Royal Air Force القوات الجوية الملكية

raffle /ˈræfl/ *noun* [C] a way of making money for a good cause by selling tickets with numbers on them. Later some numbers are chosen and the tickets with these numbers on them win prizes. بيع أوراق يانصيب

raft /rɑːft; *US* ræft/ *noun* [C] a type of simple flat boat that you make by tying pieces of wood together طوّافة أو عوّامة، رَمَث

▸ **rafting** the sport or activity of travelling down a river on a raft: *white-water rafting* سفر على رمث

rafter /ˈrɑːftə(r); *US* ˈræf-/ *noun* [C] one of the long pieces of wood that support a roof الرافدة، عارضة تدعم السقف

rag /ræɡ/ *noun* **1** [C,U] a small piece of old cloth that you use for cleaning خِرقة

2 rags [plural] clothes that are very old and torn: *to be dressed in rags* أسمال أو خرق بالية

rage /reɪdʒ/ *noun* [C,U] great anger: *He was trembling with rage.* ○ *to fly into a rage* غضب شديد

▸ **rage** *verb* [I] **1** to show great anger about sth تثور ثائرته، يحتدم غيظاً

2 (used about a battle, disease, storm, etc.) to continue with great force: *The battle raged for several days.* يحتدم؛ يتفشّى؛ يثور

raging *adj* (only *before* a noun) very strong: *a raging headache* شديد، فظيع

ragged /ˈræɡɪd/ *adj* **1** (used about clothes) old and torn (ملابس) رثّة أو ممزّقة

2 not straight; untidy: *a ragged edge* (حافة) مسنّنة أو مثلّمة؛ زري الهيئة

a b c d e f g h i j k l m n o p q r s t u v w x y z

raid /reɪd/ *noun* [C] **raid (on sth) 1** a surprise attack on an enemy: *an air raid* غارة

2 an attack in order to steal sth: *a bank raid* سَطو

3 a surprise visit by the police: *Police found 2 kilos of cocaine during a raid on a London hotel last night.* مداهمة، كبسة

▶ **raid** *verb* [T] to make a raid on a place: *Police raided the club looking for guns.* داهم، أغار على

🔑**rail** /reɪl/ *noun* **1** [C] a bar fixed to a wall, which you can hang things on: *a towel rail* ○ *a curtain rail* قضيب معدنيّ لتعليق الستائر مثلاً

2 [C] a bar, usually of metal or wood, which protects people from falling (on stairs, from a building, etc.): *Hold on to the handrail – these steps are very slippery.* حاجز أو سور، درابزين

3 [C, usually pl.] the tracks that trains run on قضبان أو سكّة حديديّة

4 [U] the railway system; trains as a means of transport: *I much prefer travelling by rail to flying.* ○ *There's going to be a new rail link between Paddington and Liverpool Street stations.* الخطوط الحديدية: القطار

railcard /ˈreɪlkɑːd/ *noun* [C] a special card that allows you to buy train tickets more cheaply if you are an old person, student, etc. بطاقة لشراء تذاكر سفر مخفّضة بالقطار

railing /ˈreɪlɪŋ/ *noun* [C, usually pl.] a fence (around a park, garden, etc.) that is made of metal bars سور من قضبان حديديّة

🔑**railway** /ˈreɪlweɪ/ (*US* **railroad**) *noun* [C] **1** the metal lines on which trains run between one place and another سكّة حديديّة

2 (*also* **railways**) the system that organizes travel by train: *He works on the railways.* ○ *a railway engine* (شركة) الخطوط الحديديّة

ˈ**railway line** *noun* [C] the track for trains to run on; the route by train between two places: *the railway line between London and Bristol* سكّة حديديّة

ˈ**railway station** *noun* [C] = STATION (1)

🔑**rain¹** /reɪn/ *noun* **1** [U] the water that falls from the sky: *The grass is so green in England because we get so much rain.* ○ *Take your umbrella, it looks like rain.* ○ *It's pouring with rain* (= the rain is very heavy). ➲ Look at **shower** (3) and **acid rain** and at the note at **weather**. مطر

2 rains [plural] (in tropical countries) the time of the year when there is a lot of rain: *When the rains come in July, the people move their houses to higher ground.* موسم المطر

IDM (as) right as rain → RIGHT² (6)

🔑**rain²** /reɪn/ *verb* [I] (used with *it*) to fall as rain: *Oh no! It's raining again!* ○ *Is it raining hard?* ○ *We'll go out when it stops raining.* يهطل المطر، تمطر

PHR V rain (sth) off (usually passive) to stop sth happening because it is raining: *I'm sorry but the picnic has been rained off.* يلغي (مباراة مثلاً) بسبب المطر

rainbow /ˈreɪnbəʊ/ *noun* [C] an arch of many colours that sometimes appears in the sky when the sun shines through rain: *all the colours of the rainbow* قوس قزح

ˈ**rain check** *noun* (*US*)

IDM take a rain check on sth (*informal*) to refuse an invitation or offer but say that you might accept it later يطلب تأجيل دعوته إلى موعد آخر

raincoat /ˈreɪnkəʊt/ *noun* [C] a special coat which you wear when it is raining معطف مطر

raindrop /ˈreɪndrɒp/ *noun* [C] a single drop of rain قطرة مطر

rainfall /ˈreɪnfɔːl/ *noun* [U] the total amount of rain that falls in a particular place during a month, year, etc: *The annual rainfall in Cairo is less than 3 cm.* كمية الأمطار

rainforest /ˈreɪnfɒrɪst; *US also* ˈreɪnfɔːrɪst/ *noun* [C] a forest in a tropical part of the world غابة استوائيّة

rainy /ˈreɪni/ (**rainier**; **rainiest**) *adj*: *the rainy season* مَطير أو ممطر

IDM keep/save sth for a rainy day to save money or sth valuable or useful so that you can use it at a later time when you really need to يدّخر لوقت الحاجة

🔑**raise¹** /reɪz/ *verb* [T] **1** to lift sth: *If you want to leave the room raise your hand.* ○ *The captain of the winning team raised the cup in the air.* يرفع

2 to increase sth or to make sth better or stronger: *They've raised their prices a lot since last year.* ○ *The hotel needs to raise its standards.* ○ *There's no need to raise your voice* (= speak angrily). يرفع

3 to get sth; obtain: *We managed to raise nearly £1 000 for the school at the Christmas bazaar.* يجمع

4 to look after a child until he/she is grown up: *You can't raise a family on what I earn.* يربّي، يعيل

5 to make a plant or animal grow so that you can use it: *In New Zealand sheep are raised for meat and wool.* يربّي، يزرع

6 to introduce a subject that needs to be talked about: *I would like to raise the subject of money.* ○ *This raises the question of why nothing was done before.* يطرح (سؤالاً)

7 to cause sth or make sth happen: *The neighbours raised the alarm when they saw smoke coming out of the window.* يطلق (صفّارة الإنذار)، ينبّه أو ينذِر

IDM raise your eyebrows to show that you are surprised or that you do not approve of sth يُظهر الدهشة أو عدم الاستحسان

raise² /reɪz/ *noun* [C] (*US*) = RISE¹ (2)

raisin /ˈreɪzn/ *noun* [C] a dried grape, used in cakes, etc. ➲ Look at **sultana**. زبيب

rake /reɪk/ *noun* [C] a garden tool with a long handle, used for collecting leaves or making the earth smooth مشط البستاني، مدمّة

▸ **rake** *verb* [T] to use a rake on sth: *to rake up the leaves* يسوّي التربة أو يجمّع أوراق الشجر بالمدمّة
PHRV **rake sth up** to start talking about sth that it would be better to forget: *Don't rake up all those old stories again.* ينبش

rally[1] /ˈræli/ *noun* [C] (*pl.* **rallies**) **1** a race for cars or motor bikes سباق سيارات أو درّاجات ناريّة
2 a meeting of people for a political reason: *20 000 people attended the peace rally in Trafalgar Square.* تجمّع
3 the series of strokes in a game of tennis before a point is won (في التنس) سلسلة من الضربات

rally[2] /ˈræli/ *verb* (*pres part* **rallying**; *3rd pers sing pres* **rallies**; *pt, pp* **rallied**) **1** [I] to get stronger: *The pound has rallied against the dollar.* يستردّ قوته، يقوى
2 [I,T] to come together or to bring people together: *The Prime Minister tried to rally the party behind him.* يتجمّع؛ يوحّد، يلمّ شعثهم
PHRV **rally round** to come together to help sb: *When I was in trouble my family rallied round.* يتألّفون حوله لمآزرته

RAM /ræm/ *noun* [U] random access memory; computer memory in which data can be changed or removed and can be looked at in any order: *32 megabytes of RAM* ذاكرة الوصول العشوائية

ram[1] /ræm/ *noun* [C] a male sheep ➲ Look at the note at **sheep**. كبش

ram[2] /ræm/ *verb* [T] (ra**mm**ing; ra**mm**ed) to crash into sth or push sth with great force: *The battleship rammed the submarine.* ينطح، يصدم بقوّة

Ramadan /ˈræmədæn; ˌræməˈdæn/ *noun* [C,U] a period of a month when, for religious reasons, Muslims do not eat anything from sunrise to sunset رمضان

ramble /ˈræmbl/ *verb* [I] **1** to walk in the countryside يتمشّى في الريف
2 ramble (on) (about sth) to talk for a long time in a confused way يتكلّم بشكل غير مترابط
▸ **ramble** *noun* [C] an organized walk in the country, usually for a group of people مشية في الأرياف ضمن مجموعة من الناس
rambling *adj* **1** (used about sth written) not saying things in a clear way; confused مفكّك، مضطرب
2 (used about a building) spreading in many directions مبعثَر الأرجاء، ممتدّ هنا وهناك

ramp /ræmp/ *noun* [C] a sloping path which we can use instead of steps to get from one place to another higher or lower place: *We drove the car up the ramp and onto the ship.* معبر مائل، سطح منحدر

rampage /ræmˈpeɪdʒ/ *verb* [I] to rush from one place to another, breaking things and attacking people: *The football fans rampaged through the town.* يقوم بأعمال العنف والتخريب في الشوارع مثلاً
▸ **rampage** /ˈræmpeɪdʒ/ *noun*
IDM **be/go on the rampage** to rush around breaking things and attacking people يقوم بأعمال العنف والتخريب في الشوارع مثلاً

rampant /ˈræmpənt/ *adj* very common and very difficult to control: *Car theft is rampant in this town.* متفشٍّ؛ تصعب السيطرة عليه

ramshackle /ˈræmʃækl/ *adj* (used about a building or a car, etc.) old and needing repair متضعضع، متداعٍ؛ متخلّع

ran *pt of* RUN[1]

ranch /rɑːntʃ; *US* ræntʃ/ *noun* [C] a large farm, especially in the US or Australia, usually where cows or horses are kept مزرعة كبيرة

rancid /ˈrænsɪd/ *adj* **1** (used about foods containing a lot of fat) tasting or smelling bad because they are old: *rancid oil* زنخ
2 (used about smells or tastes) unpleasant, like old fat: *There was a rancid smell in the kitchen.* زنخ، كريه

random /ˈrændəm/ *adj* chosen by chance: *a random number, selected by a computer* ○ *For the opinion poll they interviewed a random selection of people in the street.* عشوائي
IDM **at random** not in any special order or for any special reason: *He ran through the town shooting people at random.* ○ *The competitors were chosen at random from the audience.* جزافاً، كيفما اتّفق
▸ **randomly** *adv* كيفما اتّفق، دون نظام

randy /ˈrændi/ *adj* (*Brit informal*) sexually excited متهيّج جنسياً، شبق

rang *pt of* RING[2]

range[1] /reɪndʒ/ *noun* **1** [C] different things that belong to the same group: *The course will cover a whole range of topics.* ○ *This shop has a very small range of clothes.* تشكيلة، مجموعة
2 [C] the amount between certain limits: *There's a very wide range of ability in the class.* ○ *That car is outside my price range.* ○ *What's the salary range for this job?* ○ *I don't think this game is suitable for all age ranges.* نطاق، مجال
3 [C] a line of mountains or hills سلسلة جبال
4 [U] the distance that it is possible for sb or sth to travel, see or hear, etc: *Keep out of range of the guns.* ○ *The gunman shot the policeman at close range.* ○ *They can pick up signals at a range of 400 metres.* مدى، مسافة

range[2] /reɪndʒ/ *verb* **1** [I] **range between A and B**; **range from A to B** to stretch from one thing to another, within certain limits: *The ages of the students range from 15 to 50.* يتراوح
2 [T] (usually passive) to arrange things or people in a line يَصُفّ
3 [I] (used about sth that is written or spoken) dealing with a large number of subjects: *The discussion ranged widely but we didn't come to any conclusions.* يتطرّق إلى مواضيع عديدة

rank /ræŋk/ *noun* **1** [C,U] the level of importance that sb has in an organization, particularly the army, or in society: *General is one of the highest ranks in the army.* ○ *She's much higher in rank than I am.* ○ *As a writer, he's absolutely first rank.* رتبة؛ منزلة

2 [C] a group or line of things or people, especially soldiers: *a taxi rank* صفّ (من الجنود)

3 ranks [plural] the ordinary soldiers in the army; the members of any large group: *the ranks of the unemployed* جنود الصف؛ فئة أو صفوف (العاطلين)

IDM the rank and file the ordinary members of an organization الأفراد العاديّون

▶ **rank** *verb* [I,T] to have or to give a place in an order of importance: *She's ranked as one of the world's top players.* ○ *I think Tokyo ranks as one of the world's most expensive cities.* ○ *a high-ranking police officer* يعتبَر؛ يحتلّ مرتبة

ransom /ˈrænsəm/ *noun* [C,U] the money that you must pay to free sb who has been captured by terrorists or criminals: *The kidnappers demanded a ransom of £500 000 for the boy's release.* فدية

IDM hold sb to ransom to capture sb and say that you will not free them until you have received some money ➲ Look at **hostage**. يأخذه رهينة ويطلب الفدية

rap /ræp/ *noun* **1** [C] a knock, on a door or window, etc., which is quick and quite loud طرقة أو قرعة قويّة

2 [C,U] a style or piece of rock music with a strong beat, in which the words of a song are spoken, not sung موسيقى حديثة تتلى فيها الكلمات بوَقْع خاصّ

▶ **rap** *verb* (rapping; rapped) **1** [I,T] to hit sth quickly and lightly, making a noise يطرق أو يقرع بخفّة

2 [T] (*informal*) (used mainly in newspaper headlines) to criticize sb strongly: *Minister raps police over rise in crime.* ينتقد بشدّة

3 [I] to speak the words of a song (a rap) that has music with a very strong beat يتلو كلمات الأغنية بإيقاع خاصّ

rape /reɪp/ *verb* [T] to force a person to have sex يغتصب (جنسيّاً)

▶ **rape** *noun* [C,U] **1** the act of forcing sb to have sex: *to commit rape* اغتصاب

2 destroying sth beautiful: *Industry has been responsible for the rape of the countryside.* إتلاف، تشويه

rapist /ˈreɪpɪst/ *noun* [C] a person who is guilty of rape المغتصِب

rapid /ˈræpɪd/ *adj* happening very quickly or moving with great speed: *She made rapid progress and was soon the best in the class.* ○ *After leaving hospital he made a rapid recovery and was soon back at work.* سريع

▶ **rapidity** /rəˈpɪdəti/ *noun* [U] (*formal*) *The rapidity of change has astonished most people.* سرعة

rapidly *adv* بسرعة

rapids /ˈræpɪdz/ *noun* [plural] the part of a river where the water flows very fast over rocks شلّال

rapture /ˈræptʃə(r)/ *noun* [U] a feeling of great joy or happiness نشوة، طَرَب عظيم

IDM go into raptures (about/over sb/sth) to show that you think that sb/sth is very good: *I didn't like the film much but my boyfriend went into raptures about it.* ينتشي؛ يبالغ في المديح

rare¹ /reə(r)/ *adj* not found or seen very often: *a rare bird, flower, etc.* ○ *It's very rare to have hot weather like this in April.* نادر

▶ **rarely** *adv* not happening often: *People rarely live to be over 100 years old.* قلّما، نادراً

rare² /reə(r)/ *adj* (used about meat) not cooked for very long: *a rare steak* مطبوخ طبخاً خفيفاً

raring /ˈreərɪŋ/ *adj* **raring to do sth** wanting to start doing sth very much: *They were raring to try out the new computer.* ○ *When can we start work on the new project? We're all raring to go* (= very eager to start). متحرّق أو متلهف لبدء العمل

rarity /ˈreərəti/ *noun* (*pl.* **rarities**) **1** [U] being unusual or difficult to find: *The rarity of this stamp increases its value a lot.* ندرة

2 [C] a thing or a person that is not found very often: *Women lorry drivers are still quite a rarity.* شيء نادر

rascal /ˈrɑːskl; *US* ˈræskl/ *noun* [C] a dishonest person or a child who does naughty things ℹ When you call a person a rascal, it usually means that you are not seriously angry with them. شخص وغْد؛ طفل "شيطان"

rash¹ /ræʃ/ *noun* [C, usually sing.] **1** an area of small red spots that appear on your skin when you are ill or have been stung by an insect, plant, etc: *He came out in a rash where the plant had touched him.* طَفح جلديّ

2 a series of unpleasant events of the same kind happening close together: *There has been a rash of attacks on old people this month.* سلسلة أحداث سيّئة

rash² /ræʃ/ *adj* **1** doing things that might be dangerous without thinking about it: *You were very rash to give up your job before you had found another one.* طائش، مستهتر

2 done without much thought: *a rash decision* ○ *a rash promise* (= one which you cannot keep easily) متسرِع

▶ **rashly** *adv* بتسرع، دون تروٍّ

raspberry /ˈrɑːzbəri; *US* ˈræzberɪ/ *noun* [C] (*pl.* **raspberries**) **1** a small, soft, red fruit which grows on bushes: *raspberry jam* توت العلّيق

2 a rude sound that you make with your mouth to show sb that you think they are stupid: *to blow a raspberry at sb* "تضريط" بالفم تعبيراً عن الاستياء

rat /ræt/ *noun* [C] an animal like a large mouse الجرذ

> Rats belong to the family of animals that are called **rodents**. If you call a person a **rat** it means that you have a very low opinion of them.

IDM rat race the way of life in which everyone is rushing to be better or more successful than everyone else تنافس مسعور (للنجاح في الحياة)

rate¹ /reɪt/ *noun* [C] **1** a measurement of one amount or of how fast or how often sth is happening in relation to another amount: *The birth rate* *is falling.* ○ *a rise in the annual rate of inflation from 2 to 3%* ○ *The population increased at the rate of less than 0.5% a year.* ○ *an exchange rate of one pound to two dollars* معدل، نسبة

2 the amount that sth costs or that sb is paid: *The higher rate of income tax is 40%.* ○ *The basic rate of pay is £10 an hour.* ➲ Look at **first-rate** and **second-rate**. قيمة، سعر

IDM at any rate 1 (used when you are giving more exact information about sth): *He said that they would be here by ten. At any rate, I think that's what he said.* على الأصحّ؛ على الأقل

2 whatever else might happen: *Well, that's one good piece of news at any rate.* على أيّة حال

the going rate (for sth) → GOING[2]

rate[2] /reɪt/ *verb* [T] **1** to say how good you think sb/sth is: *She's rated among the best tennis players of all time.* يعتبر، يُعطي مكانة

2 to deserve or to get sth: *The accident wasn't very serious – it didn't rate a mention in the local newspaper.* يستحقّ؛ يحوز على

rather /ˈrɑːðə(r); US ˈræ-/ *adv* quite; to some extent: *It was a rather nice present.* ○ *It was rather a nice present.* ○ *No, I didn't fail the exam, in fact I did rather well.* ○ *I'm afraid I owe her rather a lot of money.* ○ *He spoke rather too quickly for me to understand.* ○ *It's rather a pity that you can't come tomorrow.* ○ *I was rather hoping that you'd be free on Friday.* نوعاً ما، إلى حدّ ما

Fairly, **quite**, **rather** and **pretty** can all mean 'not very', or 'moderately'. **Fairly** is the weakest. **Rather** and **pretty** (informal) are the strongest. **Fairly** is mostly used with words that are positive: *This room was fairly tidy.* **Rather** is used when you are criticizing sth: *This room's rather untidy.* If you use **rather** with a positive word, it sounds as if you are surprised or pleased: *The new teacher is rather nice. I'm surprised – he didn't look very friendly.*

IDM or rather a way of correcting sth you have said, or making it more exact: *She lives in London, or rather she lives in a suburb of London.* وبالأحرى

rather than in the place of; instead of: *I think I'll just have a sandwich rather than a full meal.* بدلاً من

would rather... (than) would prefer to: *'How old are you?' 'I'd rather not say.'* ○ *I would rather go to the cinema than watch television.* يفضّل

rating /ˈreɪtɪŋ/ *noun* [C] **1** a measurement of how popular or how good sth is: *The government's popularity rating has fallen sharply.* تقدير؛ تصنيف

2 usually **the ratings** a measurement of the number of people who have watched a TV programme, etc: *Soap operas are always high in the ratings.* تقدير عدد مشاهدي برنامج تلفزيوني معيّن

ratio /ˈreɪʃiəʊ/ *noun* [C] the relation between two numbers which shows how much bigger one quantity is than another: *The ratio of boys to girls in this class is three to one* (= there are three times as many boys as girls). نسبة

ration /ˈræʃn/ *noun* [C] the amount of food, petrol, etc. that you get when there is not enough for everybody to get as much as they want: *During the war our bread ration was three loaves a week.* الحاجيات المقنّنة، جراية أو حصة محدّدة

▸ **ration** *verb* [T] to give people only a small amount of sth, not as much as they want: *In the desert water is strictly rationed.* يُقنّن، يحدّد كمية (الطعام) المعطاة

rationing *noun* [U]: *In the oil crisis of 1973 the government introduced petrol rationing.* تقنين، تحديد الكميّة المعطاة

rational /ˈræʃnəl/ *adj* **1** (used about a person) able to use thought to make decisions, not just feelings: *We're both rational human beings – let's sit down and talk about the problem.* ❶ The opposite is **irrational**. عاقل

2 based on reason; sensible or logical: *There must be a rational explanation for why he's behaving like this.* معقول، منطقيّ

▸ **rationally** *adv* بشكل معقول أو منطقيّ

rationalize (*also* **rationalise**) /ˈræʃnəlaɪz/ *verb* **1** [I,T] to find reasons that explain why you have done sth (perhaps because you do not like the real reason): *She rationalized her decision to buy the car by saying that it would save money on bus fares.* يبرّر، يسوّغ

2 [T] to make a business, etc. better organized يُحسّن تنظيم (الشركة)، يجعلها أكثر مردوداً

▸ **rationalization** (*also* **rationalisation**) /ˌræʃnəlaɪˈzeɪʃn; US -ləˈz/ *noun* [C,U] تنظيم أفضل، تحسين؛ تبرير

rattle[1] /ˈrætl/ *verb* **1** [I,T] to make a noise like things hitting each other or to shake sth so that it makes this noise: *The windows were rattling all night in the wind.* ○ *He rattled the money in the tin.* يُخشخش؛ يطقطق

2 [T] (*informal*) to make sb unsure and afraid: *The news of his arrival really rattled her.* يُقلِق، يخضّ

PHR V rattle off to say a list of things you have learned very quickly: *She rattled off the names of every player in the team.* يقرأ أو يُسمّع بسرعة كالببغاء

rattle[2] /ˈrætl/ *noun* **1** [C, sing.] a noise made by things hitting each other: *There's a funny rattle coming from the back of the car.* خشخشة؛ قرقعة

2 [C] a toy that a baby can shake to make a noise خشخيشة، شخشيخة

raucous /ˈrɔːkəs/ *adj* (used about people's voices) loud and rough: *raucous laughter* أجشّ، خشن

ravage /ˈrævɪdʒ/ *verb* [T] to damage sth very badly: *The forests were ravaged by the winter storms.* يخرّب، يعيث (فساداً)

rave /reɪv/ *verb* [I] **1 rave (about sb/sth)** (*informal*) to praise sb/sth very much: *Everyone's raving about her latest record!* يفرط في المديح

2 to speak angrily or wildly يتكلّم بغضب؛ يهذي

▸ **raving** *adj* (*informal*) acting in a wild, uncontrolled way: *I think you're all raving mad!* هائج، غاية في الجنون

a b c d e f g h i j k l m n o p q r s t u v w x y z

raven /ˈreɪvn/ *noun* [C] a large black bird, like a crow, that has a harsh voice الغراب

ravenous /ˈrævənəs/ *adj* very hungry جائع جداً، "ميّت من الجوع"
▶ **ravenously** *adv* بِنَهَم؛ في غاية الجوع

ˌrave reˈview *noun* [C] an article in a newspaper, etc. that praises a book, film, record, etc. very much مراجعة شديدة الإطراء (لعمل فنيّ)

ravine /rəˈviːn/ *noun* [C] a narrow deep valley with steep sides شِعْب، وادٍ ضيّق عميق

🔑**raw** /rɔː/ *adj* **1** not cooked: *Raw vegetables are good for your teeth.* نيء، فج
2 in the natural state: *raw sugar* ○ *raw materials* (= that are used to make things with, in factories, etc.) خام
3 used about an injury where the skin has been rubbed away: *There's a nasty raw place on my heel where my shoes have rubbed.* مقشوط الجِلد

ray /reɪ/ *noun* [C] a line of light, heat or energy: *A single ray of light came through a hole in the roof.* ○ *the rays of the sun* ➲ Look at **X-ray**. شعاع
IDM **a ray of hope** a small chance that things will get better بصيص من الأمل

razor /ˈreɪzə(r)/ *noun* [C] a sharp instrument which people use to cut off the hair from their skin (= to shave): *an electric razor* موسى الحلاقة؛ آلة حلاقة (كهربائية)

ˈrazor blade *noun* [C] the thin sharp piece of metal that you put in a razor شفرة

Rd (*especially US* **Rd.**) *abbrev* = ROAD

RE /ɑːr ˈiː/ *noun* [U] the abbreviation for religious education, taught as a subject in schools: *an RE teacher* تربية دينية

🔑**reach** /riːtʃ/ *verb* **1** [T] to arrive at a place or condition: *The letter will reach you on Wednesday.* ○ *We won't reach Dover before 12.* ○ *Tell me when you have reached the end of the book.* ○ *Anyone who has reached the age of 60 knows something about the world.* ○ *Sometimes the temperature reaches 45°C.* ○ *We finally reached an agreement after hours of discussion.* ○ *Have you reached a decision yet?* يصل، يبلغ؛ يتوصّل إلى
2 [I,T] **reach (out) (for sb/sth)** to stretch out your arm to try and touch sth or get sth: *The child reached for her mother.* ○ *The monkey reached out its hand for the banana.* ○ *She reached into her bag for her purse.* يمدّ ذراعه
3 [I,T] to be able to touch sth: *Can you get me that book off the top shelf? I can't reach.* ○ *He couldn't reach the light switch.* ○ *I need a longer ladder. This one won't reach.* يصل إلى، يبلغ
4 [T] to contact sb: *You can reach me at this number.* ○ *She can't be reached until Monday morning.* يتّصل (بشخص)
▶ **reach** *noun* [U] the distance that you can stretch مدى، متناوَل
IDM **beyond/out of (sb's) reach 1** outside the distance that you can stretch your arm: *Keep this medicine out of reach of children.* بعيد المنال، بعيد عن أيدي (الأطفال)
2 not able to be got or done by sb: *A job like that is completely beyond his reach.* بعيد المنال
within (sb's) reach 1 inside the distance that you can stretch your arm: *Always keep a glass of water within reach.* في متناول اليد
2 able to be got or done by sb: *Hewitt led by five games to two – victory was within reach!* في متناول اليد، قابَ قوسين أو أدنى
within (easy) reach of sth not far from sth: *The school is within easy reach of the house.* سهل المنال؛ قريب من

🔑**react** /riˈækt/ *verb* [I] **1 react (to sb/sth)** to do or say sth because of sth that has happened or been said: *The players reacted angrily to the decision.* يردّ، (كيف) يكون ردّ فعله
2 react (against sb/sth) to behave or talk in a way that shows that you do not like the influence of sb/sth (e.g. authority, your family, etc.): *She reacted against the strict way she had been brought up.* يرتدّ أو يثور على

🔑**reaction** /riˈækʃn/ *noun* **1** [C,U] **(a) reaction (to sb/sth)** sth that you do or say because of sth that has happened or been said: *Could we have your reaction to the latest news, Minister?* ○ *a hostile reaction* ○ *I shook him to try and wake him up but there was no reaction.* ردّ فعل؛ تجاوب
2 [C,U] **(a) reaction (against sb/sth)** behaviour that shows that you do not like the influence of sb/sth (e.g. authority, your family, etc.): *Her strange clothes are a reaction against the conservative way she was brought up.* ردّ فعل، معاكسة
3 [C, usually pl.] the physical ability to act quickly when sth happens: *If the other driver's reactions hadn't been so good, there would have been an accident.* ردّ فعل؛ تجاوب
4 a reaction (to sth) a bad effect that your body experiences because of sth that you have eaten, touched or breathed: *She had an allergic reaction to something in the food.* رد فعل
▶ **reactionary** /riˈækʃənri; *US* -əneri/ *adj* trying to prevent (political) progress or change رجعي
reactionary *noun* [C] (*pl.* **reactionaries**) a person who tries to prevent (political) progress or change: *The reactionaries in the party want to bring back hanging.* الفئات الرجعيّة

reactor /riˈæktə(r)/ *noun* [C] = NUCLEAR REACTOR

🔑**read** /riːd/ *verb* (*pt, pp* **read** /red/) **1** [I,T] to look at words and understand them: *In their first years at school, children learn to read and write.* ○ *Don't interrupt me, I'm reading.* ○ *Have you read any good books lately?* ○ *I read an interesting article about Japan recently.* ○ *I read in the paper that they've found a cure for migraine.* يقرأ
2 [I,T] **read (sb) (sth); read sth (to sb)** to say written words to sb: *My father used to read me stories when I was a child.* ○ *Read that sentence to me again, I didn't understand it.* ○ *I hate reading out loud.* يتلو، يقرأ بصوت مسموع
3 [T] to be able to see and understand sth: *I can't read the clock – I haven't got my glasses on.* ○

(*figurative*) *She doesn't know what you're thinking. She can't read your mind.* يرى؛ يفسّر، يقرأ

4 [I] to show sth; to have sth written on it: *The sign read 'Keep Left'.* ○ *What does the thermometer read?* يقول؛ يشير إلى

PHR V **read sth into sth** to think that there is meaning in sth that it may not really have: *Don't read too much into the letter. They're only asking you for an interview, not offering you the job.* يضفي عليه معاني غير مقصودة

read on to continue reading; to read the next part(s) of sth: *If you read on, you'll find that the story gets exciting.* يتابع القراءة

read sth out to read sth to other people يتلو، يسمّع

read sth through to read sth to check details or to look for mistakes: *I read my essay through again before handing it in.* يراجع أو يقرأ بدقّة

▸ **read** /ri:d/ *noun* [sing.] (*informal*) a period or an act of reading: *I had a quick read of the newspaper during breakfast.* ❶ A writer or book that is interesting is **a good read**. قراءة

readable /'ri:dəbl/ *adj* **1** able to be read: *machine-readable data* ➲ Look at **legible**. مقروء

2 easy or pleasant to read سهل القراءة؛ سَلِس

reader /'ri:də(r)/ *noun* [C] **1** a person who reads sth (a particular newspaper, magazine, type of book, etc.) القارئ

2 (with an adjective) a person who reads (in a particular way): *a fast/slow reader* قارئ (بطيء)

3 a book for practising reading كتاب قراءة

▸ **readership** *noun* [sing.] the number of people who regularly read a particular newspaper, magazine, etc. القرّاء

reading /'ri:dɪŋ/ *noun* [U] **1** what you do when you are reading: *I haven't had time to do much reading lately.* ○ *On the form she described her interests as reading and tennis.* ○ *This report makes interesting reading* (= reading it is an interesting thing to do). القراءة

2 the figure or measurement that is shown on an instrument: *a reading of 20°* الرقم الذي يسجّله عدّاد

readjust /ˌri:ə'dʒʌst/ *verb* **1** [I,T] **readjust (to sth)** to get used to being in a situation again that you have been in before: *After her divorce, it took her a long time to readjust to being single again.* يكيّف نفسه من جديد

2 [T] to change the position or organization of sth again in order to make it correct يعدّل، يضبط

▸ **readjustment** *noun* [C,U] the act of readjusting (1,2) تكيُّف أو تكييف؛ تعديل

ˌ**read-only** '**memory** *noun* [U] (*computing*) computer memory that contains instructions or data that cannot be changed or removed ذاكرة معلومات ثابتة

ready /'redi/ *adj* **1** **ready (for sb/sth); ready (to do sth)** prepared and able to be used or to do sth: *Dinner will be ready in ten minutes.* ○ *The car will be ready for you to collect on Friday.* ○ *He isn't ready for his driving test, he hasn't had enough lessons.* ○ *I can't talk now, I'm getting ready to go out.* جاهز؛ مستعدّ

2 **ready to do sth** willing to do sth: *You know me – I'm always ready to help.* مستعدّ، راغب في

3 in a place which makes it possible for you to use or reach it easily and quickly: *Have your money ready before you get on the bus.* جاهز، في متناول اليد

▸ **readily** /-ɪli/ *adv* **1** easily, without difficulty: *Most vegetables are readily available at this time of year.* بسهولة

2 without hesitating: *He readily admitted that he was wrong.* في الحال، دون تردّد

readiness /'redinəs/ *noun* [U] **1** the state of being ready or prepared استعداد، تأهّب

2 willingness: *The bank have indicated their readiness to lend him the money.* رغبة، موافقة

ready *adv* (before a past participle) already; previously: *ready-cooked food* مسبقاً

ˌ**ready-'made** *adj* already prepared and ready for use, not made especially for you: *You can buy ready-made reading glasses now.* ○ (*figurative*) *He always has a ready-made answer to every question.* (ملابس) جاهزة؛ مهيّأ مسبقاً

real /'ri:əl/ *adj* **1** actually existing, not imagined: *The film is based on real life.* ○ *This isn't a real word, I made it up.* واقعي؛ حقيقيّ

2 actually true, not what may appear to be true: *The name he gave to the police wasn't his real name.* ○ *She said she had missed the bus, but that's not the real reason why she was late.* حقيقيّ، صحيح

3 natural, not imitation or artificial: *This shirt is real silk.* طبيعي

4 (used when you are making what you say stronger, usually when you are saying how bad sth is) big; complete: *I made a real effort to be polite.* ○ *Money is a real problem for us at the moment.* كبير، هائل

IDM **the real thing** **1** something genuine, not an imitation: *This painting is just a copy. The real thing is in a gallery.* الأصل الحقيقيّ، النسخة الأصليّة

2 the truest and best example of sth: *She's had boyfriends before but this time she says it's the real thing* (= real love). الشيء الحقيقي أو الصحيح

▸ **real** *adv* (*US informal*) very; really: *It was real kind of you to help me.* جداً، حقّاً

'**real estate** *noun* [U] property that cannot be moved, such as land and buildings أملاك غير منقولة

'**real estate agent** *noun* [C] (*US*) = ESTATE AGENT

realism /'ri:əlɪzəm/ *noun* [U] **1** behaviour that shows that you accept the facts of a situation and are not too influenced by your feelings واقعيّة

2 (in art, literature, etc.) showing things as they really are الواقعيّة (في الأدب والفنّ)

▸ **realist** *noun* [C] a person who accepts the facts of life and situations, and who thinks and behaves according to them: *I'm a realist, I don't expect the impossible.* الواقعي

realistic /ˌri:ə'lɪstɪk/ *adj* **1** accepting the facts of a situation (not believing or making yourself believe that they are different): *Be realistic! You're* *not going to get a job like that without qualifications.* ○ *a realistic price* واقعي، عمليّ

2 showing things as they really are: *a realistic description of the lives of ordinary people in London* حقيقي

3 not real but appearing to be real: *The monsters in the film were very realistic.* مطابق للحقيقة، مقنع

ℹ The opposite for **1**, **2** and **3** is **unrealistic**.

▸ **realistically** /-kli/ *adv*: *Think about your future realistically.* بصورة واقعيّة

reality /ri'æləti/ *noun* (*pl.* **realities**) **1** [U] the way life really is, not the way it may appear to be or what you would like it to be: *It's been a lovely holiday but now it's back to reality.* الحقيقة، واقع الحياة

2 [C] the way sth really is when you experience it: *We had hoped that things would get easy but the reality was very different.* ○ *The realities of living in a foreign country were too much for Susie and she went home.* حقيقة، واقع

3 [C] something that really exists, not sth that is imagined: *Death is a reality that everyone has to face eventually.* حقيقة واقعة

IDM **in reality** in fact, really (not the way sth appears or has been described): *People say this is an exciting city but in reality it's rather boring.* في الحقيقة، في الواقع

re,ality T'V *noun* [U] television shows that are based on real people (not actors) in real situations, presented as entertainment تلفزيون الواقع

realize (*also* **realise**) /'ri:əlaɪz/ *verb* [T] **1** to know and understand that sth is true or that sth has happened: *I'm sorry I mentioned the subject, I didn't realize how much it upset you.* ○ *Do you realize how much work I've done today?* يعلم، يدرك

2 to become aware of sth or that sth has happened, usually some time later: *When I got home, I realized that I had left my keys at the office.* ○ *I'm beginning to realize that this job isn't as easy as I thought it was.* يدرك

3 to make sth (an ambition, hope, etc.) become reality: *She finally realized her ambition to see the Taj Mahal.* يحقّق

▸ **realization** (*also* **realisation**) /,ri:əlaɪ'zeɪʃn; *US* -lə'z-/ *noun* [U] the act of realizing sth: *He was suddenly hit by the realization that he might die.* ○ *Becoming Managing Director was the realization of all her dreams.* إدراك؛ تحقيق

really /'ri:əli/ *adv* **1** actually; in fact; truly: *I couldn't believe it was really happening.* ○ *He said that he was sorry but I don't think he really meant it.* ○ *She wasn't really angry, she was only pretending.* ○ *Is it really true?* في الحقيقة، فعلاً

2 very; very much: *I'm really tired.* ○ *He really enjoys his job.* ○ *Are you really sure?* ○ *I really tried but I couldn't do it.* جداً؛ فعلاً

3 (used as a question for expressing surprise, interest, doubt, etc.): *'She's left her husband.' 'Really? When did that happen?'* ○ *'He's a very happy person.' 'Really? I've never seen him smile.'* صحيح!!

4 (used in questions when you are expecting sb to answer 'No'): *You don't really expect me to believe that, do you?* حقّاً! (تستعمل في الأسئلة التي تتوقع جواباً سلبياً)

realm /relm/ *noun* [C] (*formal*) a country that has a king or queen مملكة

Realtor™ /'ri:əltə(r)/ *noun* [C] (*US*) = ESTATE AGENT

reap /ri:p/ *verb* [T] to cut and collect a crop (corn, wheat, etc.): (*figurative*) *Work hard now and you'll reap the benefits later on.* يحصد، يجني

reappear /,ri:ə'pɪə(r)/ *verb* [I] to appear again or be seen again: *She went upstairs and did not reappear until morning.* يظهر من جديد؛ يعود

▸ **reappearance** /-rəns/ *noun* [C,U] ظهور من جديد

reappraisal /,ri:ə'preɪzl/ *noun* [C,U] the examination of sth (a situation, way of doing sth, etc.) in order to decide whether any changes are necessary إعادة نظر

rear[1] /rɪə(r)/ *noun* [sing.] **1 the rear** the back part: *There are toilets at the front and rear of the plane.* ○ *I only saw him from the rear* (= from behind). الجزء الخلفيّ، الخلف

2 the part of your body that you sit on; bottom العَجز، الدُّبر

IDM **bring up the rear** to be the last one in a race, parade, etc: *At the moment the British runner is bringing up the rear.* في المؤخِّرة

▸ **rear** *adj* (used especially about parts of a car) placed at the back: *the rear window* ○ *rear lights* خلفي

rear[2] /rɪə(r)/ *verb* **1** [T] to care for and educate children: *This generation of children will be reared without fear of war.* يربّي، ينشّئ

2 [T] to look after animals on a farm, etc: *They rear ducks in their garden.* يربّي

3 [I] **rear (up)** (used about horses) to stand on the back legs يشبّ (الحصان)

rearrange /,ri:ə'reɪndʒ/ *verb* [T] **1** to change a plan, appointment, etc. that has been fixed: *The match has been rearranged for next Wednesday.* يغيّر الموعد

2 to change the way that sth is organized or arranged: *We've rearranged the living room to make more space.* يعيد التنظيم، يغيّر الترتيب

reason[1] /'ri:zn/ *noun* **1** [C,U] **reason (for sth/for doing sth)**; **reason (why.../that...)** the cause of sth; sth that explains why sth happens or exists: *What's your reason for being so late?* ○ *Is there any reason why you couldn't tell me this before?* ○ *The reason that I'm phoning you is to ask a favour.* ○ *For some reason or another they can't give us an answer until next week* (= I don't know what the reason is). ○ *She left the job for personal reasons.* سبب

2 [C,U] **reason (for sth) (to do sth)** something that shows that it is right or logical to do sth: *I think we have reason for complaint.* ○ *There is a reason for doing things this way – it's cheaper.* ○ *I chose this colour for a reason* (= the reason was important). ○ *He had no reason to be rude to* *me, I hadn't been rude to him.* ○ *You have every reason* (= you are completely right) *to be angry, considering how badly you've been treated.* ○ *I have reason to believe that you've been lying.* مبرر، موجِب، داعٍ

3 [U] the ability to think and to make sensible decisions: *I tried to persuade him not to drive but he just wouldn't listen to reason.* العقل، سلامة التفكير

IDM (do anything) in/within reason if it is not too extreme or completely unacceptable: *I'll pay anything within reason for a ticket.* في حدود المعقول

make sb see reason to persuade sb not to continue acting in a stupid or extreme way: *They were determined to have a fight and nobody could make them see reason.* يعيده إلى الصواب

reason² /ˈriːzn/ *verb* [T] to form a judgement or opinion, after thinking about sth in a logical way يفكّر، يحكّم العقل

PHRV reason with sb to talk to sb in order to persuade him/her to behave or think in a more reasonable or less extreme way: *The police tried to reason with the gunman but he refused to give them his gun.* يحاول اقناعه

▸ **reasoning** *noun* [U] **reasoning (behind sth)** the process of thinking and making a judgement or decision: *What's the reasoning behind his sudden decision to leave?* التفكير، المنطق

reasonable /ˈriːznəbl/ *adj* **1** (used about people) willing to listen to other people's opinions; not asking too much; fair: *You're not being reasonable – I can't change all my plans for you.* ○ *I tried to be reasonable even though I was very angry.* عاقل؛ منصف

2 (used about actions, decisions, etc.) resulting from good reasons; logical: *That seems a reasonable decision in the circumstances.* معقول، منطقي

3 (used about opinions or about what you expect people to do) not expecting too much; fair: *I think it's reasonable to expect people to keep their promises.* معقول

4 (used about a price) not too high; not higher than it should be: *It was a lovely meal and the bill was very reasonable!* ○ *'How much do you want for the car?' 'About £1 000.' 'Well, that seems a reasonable price.'* معتدل

ℹ The opposite for **1**, **2**, **3** and **4** is **unreasonable.**

5 quite good; not bad: *His work is of a reasonable standard.* لا بأس به، مقبول

6 (used about amounts or numbers) not very large: *They've got a reasonable amount of money but they certainly aren't rich.* لا بأس به، متوسّط

▸ **reasonably** /-əbli/ *adv* **1** fairly or quite (but not very): *The weather was reasonably good but not brilliant.* باعتدال، إلى حدّ معقول

2 in a reasonable way: *If you think about my suggestion reasonably, you'll realize that I'm right.* بصورة معقولة، بشكل منطقي

reassure /ˌriːəˈʃʊə(r); *Brit also* -ˈʃɔː(r)/ *verb* [T] to say or do sth in order to make sb feel less frightened, worried or nervous: *I keep trying to reassure my parents that there are no problems at school, but they just don't believe me.* يطمئن

▸ **reassurance** /-rəns/ *noun* **1** [U] the act of reassuring or being reassured: *I need some reassurance that I'm doing things the right way.* اطمئنان؛ طمأنة

2 [C] something that reassures: *The people in the village are asking for reassurances that the water is fit to drink.* تأكيد، طمأنة

reassuring *adj* causing sb to feel less worried, frightened or nervous مطمئن

reassuringly *adv* بشكل يبعث على الاطمئنان

rebate /ˈriːbeɪt/ *noun* [C] a sum of money that is given back to you (by sb official) because you have paid too much: *a tax rebate* مبلغ تُعيده مؤسسة حكوميّة إلى الدافع

rebel /ˈrebl/ *noun* [C] **1** a person who fights against or refuses to cooperate with authority, society, an order, a law, etc: *At school he had a reputation as a rebel.* ثائر، متمرّد

2 a person who fights against his/her country's government because he/she wants things to change: *During the revolution, the rebels took control of the capital.* ثائر، متمرّد

▸ **rebel** /rɪˈbel/ (rebelling; rebelled) *verb* [I] **rebel (against sb/sth) 1** to fight against authority, society, an order, a law, etc: *She rebelled against her parents by marrying a man she knew they didn't approve of.* يعصي، يتمرّد على

2 to fight against the government in order to bring change يثور على

rebellion /rɪˈbeljən/ *noun* [C,U] fighting against authority or the government: *The rebellion ended in failure when all the leaders were shot.* ○ *Voting against the leader of the party was an act of open rebellion.* عصيان، ثورة

rebellious /rɪˈbeljəs/ *adj* not doing what authority, society, etc. wants you to do: *Why do little children have to turn into rebellious teenagers?* متمرّد، عاصٍ

reboot /ˌriːˈbuːt/ *verb* [I,T] (*computing*) if you reboot a computer or if it reboots, you turn it off and then turn it on again immediately يعيد التشغيل

rebound /rɪˈbaʊnd/ *verb* [I] to hit sth and then go in a different direction: *The ball rebounded off a defender and went into the goal.* ترتدّ (الكرة)

rebuff /rɪˈbʌf/ *noun* [C] an unkind refusal of an offer, etc. صدّ، رَفْض جاف

▸ **rebuff** *verb* [T] يصدّ، يرفض بجفاء

rebuild /ˌriːˈbɪld/ *verb* [T] (*pt, pp* **rebuilt** /ˌriːˈbɪlt/) to build again: *Following the storm, a great many houses will have to be rebuilt.* ○ (*figurative*) *She's trying to rebuild her life now that her husband is dead.* يعيد البناء، يبني من جديد

rebuke /rɪˈbjuːk/ *verb* [T] (*formal*) to speak angrily to sb because he/she has done sth wrong يوبّخ، يؤنّب

▸ **rebuke** *noun* [C] توبيخ، تأنيب

recall /rɪˈkɔːl/ *verb* [T] **1** to remember sth (a fact, event, action, etc.) from the past: *I don't recall* *exactly when I first met her.* ○ *She couldn't recall meeting him before.* يتذكّر

2 to order sb to return; to ask for sth to be returned: *The company has recalled all the fridges that have this fault.* يسترجع

recap /ˌriːˈkæp/ (*informal*) (**recapped**; **recapped**) (*also formal* **recapitulate** /ˌriːkəˈpɪtʃuleɪt/) *verb* [I,T] to repeat or look again at the main points of sth to make sure that they have been understood: *Let's quickly recap what we've done in today's lesson, before we finish.* يُكرّر النقاط الرئيسيّة، يُجمل

recapture /ˌriːˈkæptʃə(r)/ *verb* [I,T] **1** to capture again a person or animal that has escaped يأسره أو يقبض عليه من جديد

2 to create or experience again a feeling or period from the past: *The film brilliantly recaptures the lives of ordinary people in the 1930s.* يستردّ، يستعيد

recede /rɪˈsiːd/ *verb* [I] **1** to move away or seem to move away and begin to disappear: *The coast began to recede into the distance.* ينحسر، يتراجع

If a person's **hairline is receding** or if a person **is receding**, he is losing his hair from the front of the head.

2 (used about a hope, a fear, a chance, etc.) to become smaller or less strong: *The threat of war is receding because negotiations between the two countries have started.* يتضاءل، يضعف

receipt /rɪˈsiːt/ *noun* **1** [C] a piece of paper that is given to show that you have paid for sth: *Keep the receipt in case you want to exchange the pullover.* ○ *Could I have a receipt, please?* إيصال، وصل استلام

2 [U] **receipt (of sth)** (*formal*) the act of receiving: *Payment must be made within seven days of receipt of the goods.* وصول، استلام

receive /rɪˈsiːv/ *verb* [T] **1 receive sth (from sb/sth)** to get or take sth that sb sends or gives to you: *Have you received the parcel I sent you?* ○ *I received a letter from an old friend last week.* يستلم

2 (often passive) to react to sth (news, ideas, work, etc.) in a particular way: *My suggestions at the meeting were received in silence.* يُستَقْبَل

receiver /rɪˈsiːvə(r)/ (*also* **handset**) *noun* [C] **1** the part of a telephone that is used for listening and speaking سمّاعة التليفون

To answer or make a telephone call you **pick up** or **lift** the receiver. To end a telephone call you **put down** or **replace** the receiver or you **hang up**.

2 a piece of TV or radio equipment that changes electronic signals into sounds or pictures: *You need a satellite receiver to get this channel.* مُستَقبِل (راديو او تلفزيون)

recent /ˈriːsnt/ *adj* having happened, been done or produced a short time ago: *In recent years there have been many changes.* ○ *Does this brochure include all the most recent information?* ○ *This is a recent photograph of my daughter.* حديث، قريب العهد

▸ **recently** *adv* **1** a short time ago: *I don't know her very well, I only met her recently.* ○ *She worked here until quite recently.* إلى عهد قريب، حديثاً

2 during a period between not long ago and now: *Have you seen Paul recently?* ○ *She's been feeling ill recently.* مؤخّراً

Recently can refer to both a point in time and a period of time. If it refers to a point in time, use the past simple tense: *He got married recently.* If it refers to a period, use the present perfect or present perfect continuous tense: *I haven't done anything interesting recently.* ○ *She's been working hard recently.* **Lately** can only refer to a period of time. Use only present perfect or present perfect continuous tense: *I've seen a lot of films lately.* ○ *I've been spending too much money lately.*

receptacle /rɪˈseptəkl/ *noun* [C] (*formal*) a container that is used for putting or keeping things in وعاء، إناء

reception /rɪˈsepʃn/ *noun* **1** [U] the place in a hotel or office building where you go to say that you have arrived, to make enquiries, appointments, etc: *Leave your key at reception if you go out, please.* ○ *All visitors must report to reception.* مكتب استقبال أو استعلام

2 [C] a formal party to celebrate sth (especially a wedding) or to welcome an important person: *Their wedding reception was held at a local hotel.* ○ *There will be an official reception at the embassy for the visiting ambassador.* حفلة استقبال

3 [sing.] the way people react to sth: *The play got a mixed reception* (= some people liked it, some people didn't). ○ *The President received a warm reception during his visit to China* (= people showed that they liked him). استقبال

4 [U] the quality of radio or television signals: *TV reception is very poor where we live.* استقبال (إذاعيّ مثلاً)

▸ **receptionist** *noun* [C] a person who works in a hotel, office, etc. answering the phone, dealing with guests, customers, visitors, etc: *a hotel receptionist* موظّف الاستقبال أو الاستعلام

receptive /rɪˈseptɪv/ *adj* **receptive (to sth)** willing to listen to new ideas, suggestions, etc. مُتقبّل (للأفكار الجديدة)

recess /rɪˈses; *US* ˈriːses/ *noun* **1** [C,U] a period when Parliament, etc. is on holiday عطلة (قضائيّة مثلاً)

2 [U] (*US*) a short period of free time between classes at school ➲ Look at the note at **interval**. فترة الاستراحة (بين الحصص المدرسيّة)

recession /rɪˈseʃn/ *noun* [C,U] a period when the business and industry of a country is not successful: *The country is now in recession.* ○ *How long will the recession last?* فترة ركود اقتصاديّ

recharge /ˌriːˈtʃɑːdʒ/ *verb* [I,T] to fill a battery with electrical power; to fill up with electrical power: *He plugged the drill in to recharge it.* ○ *A car battery takes about three hours to recharge.* يعيد شحن البطارية

▸ **rechargeable** /-əbl/ *adj*: *rechargeable batteries* (بطارية) متعددة الشحن

recipe /ˈresəpi/ *noun* [C] **1 a recipe (for sth)** the instructions for cooking or preparing sth to eat. A recipe tells you what to use (the ingredients) and what to do. وصفة أو طريقة تحضير طبق معيّن

2 a recipe for sth the way to get or produce sth: *What's the recipe for a happy marriage?* طريقة، وصفة

recipient /rɪˈsɪpiənt/ *noun* [C] a person who receives sth المستلم

reciprocal /rɪˈsɪprəkl/ *adj* both given and received: *The arrangement is reciprocal. They help us and we help them.* متبادَل

recital /rɪˈsaɪtl/ *noun* [C] a public performance of music or poetry, by one person or a small group: *a piano recital* ➲ Look at **concert**. حفلة موسيقيّة أو شعرية يحييها فرد واحد أو عدة أفراد

recite /rɪˈsaɪt/ *verb* [I,T] to say aloud a piece of writing (especially a poem) or a list from memory: *He can recite the names and dates of all the kings and queens of England.* يتلو، ينشد؛ يسرد

reckless /ˈrekləs/ *adj* not thinking about whether what you are doing is dangerous or might have bad results: *reckless driving* طائش، متهوّر

▸ **recklessly** *adv* بحماقة، دون تفكير بالمخاطر

⚷**reckon** /ˈrekən/ *verb* [T] **1** to believe or consider; to have the opinion: *This is generally reckoned to be the nicest area in the city.* يعتقد، يعتبر

2 (*informal*) to think or suppose: *She's very late now. I reckon she isn't coming.* يظنّ، يحسب

3 to calculate approximately or guess: *I reckon the journey will take about half an hour.* يخمن، يقدر

4 to expect to do sth: *We reckon to sell about twenty of these suits a week.* يتوقع

PHR V **reckon on sth** to expect sth to happen and therefore to base a plan or action on it: *I didn't book in advance because I wasn't reckoning on tickets being so scarce.* يدخل في حسابه

reckon with sb/sth to expect sth; to think about sth as a possible problem: *When they decided to buy a bigger house, they didn't reckon with the enormous cost involved.* يتوقع، يدخل في حسابه

reclaim /rɪˈkleɪm/ *verb* [T] **1 reclaim sth (from sb/sth)** to get back sth that you have lost or put in a place where it is kept for you to collect: *Reclaim your luggage after you have been through passport control.* يسترجع

2 to get back useful materials from waste products: *The aluminium used in cans can be reclaimed and recycled.* يستخلص

3 to make land suitable for use: *The Dutch have reclaimed huge areas of land from the North Sea.* يستصلح

recline /rɪˈklaɪn/ *verb* [I] to lie back or down in order to be more comfortable يستلقي؛ يتكئ

▸ **reclining** *adj* lying back; able to be adjusted so that you can lie back: *The car has reclining seats at the front.* (مقعد) قلّاب أي يميل إلى الوراء للاسترخاء عليه

⚷**recognition** /ˌrekəɡˈnɪʃn/ *noun* [U] the act of recognizing sth or of showing or receiving respect: *He showed no sign of recognition when he passed me in the street.* ○ *She has received public recognition for her services to charity.* تعرُّف على؛ إدراك؛ تقدير (لخدماته)

⚷**recognize** (*also* **recognise**) /ˈrekəɡnaɪz/ *verb* [T] **1 recognize sb/sth (by/from sth)** to know again sb/sth that you have seen or heard before: *I recognized him but I couldn't remember his name.* ○ *This district has changed so much since I was last here that I hardly recognize it now.* يتعرَّف على، يعرف

2 to accept or admit that sth is true: *I recognize that some of my ideas are unrealistic.* يعترف بِ، يقرّ

3 to accept sth officially (usually done by institutions or governments): *My qualifications are not recognized in other countries.* يعترف بِ

4 to show that you think sth that sb has done is good: *The company gave her a special present to recognize her long years of service.* يقدِّر (فضله)

▸ **recognizable** (*also* **recognisable**) /ˈrekəɡnaɪzəbl; ˌrekəɡˈnaɪzəbl/ *adj* able to be recognized مميَّز، يسهل التعرّف عليه

recognizably (*also* **recognisably**) /-əbli/ *adv* بشكل واضح، بصورة مميزة

recoil /rɪˈkɔɪl/ *verb* [I] to react to sb/sth with a feeling of fear, horror, etc: *to recoil from the sight of blood* ينفر؛ يرتدّ خوفاً

recollect /ˌrekəˈlekt/ *verb* [I,T] to remember sth from the past: *I don't recollect exactly when it happened.* يتذكّر

recollection /ˌrekəˈlekʃn/ *noun* **1** [U] **recollection (of sb/sth)** the ability to remember: *I have no recollection of promising to lend you money.* تذكّر

2 [C, usually pl.] something that you remember: *I have only vague recollections of the town where I spent my early years.* ذكرى

⚷**recommend** /ˌrekəˈmend/ *verb* [T] **1** to say that sb/sth is good and that it would be liked or useful: *Which film would you recommend?* ○ *Could you recommend me a good hotel in Paris?* ○ *We hope that you'll recommend this restaurant to all your friends.* ○ *The head of her department recommended her for promotion.* ○ *Doctors don't always recommend drugs as the best treatment for every illness.* يزكّي، يوصي بِ

2 to strongly suggest sth; to tell sb what you strongly believe he/she should do: *My doctor has recommended a long period of rest.* ○ *I recommend that you get some legal advice.* ○ *I wouldn't recommend (your) travelling on your own. It could be dangerous.* ينصح بِ، يقترح

▸ **recommendation** /ˌrekəmenˈdeɪʃn/ *noun* **1**

a b c d e f g h i j k l m n o p q r s t u v w x y z

[C,U] saying that sth is good and will be liked or useful: *I visited Seville on a friend's recommendation and I really enjoyed it.* تزكية

2 [C] a statement about what should be done in a particular situation: *After the train crash, a committee of enquiry made several recommendations on how safety could be improved.* توصية

recompense /'rekəmpens/ *verb* [T] (*formal*) to give money, etc. to sb for special efforts or work or because you are responsible for a loss he/she has suffered: *The airline has agreed to recompense us for the damage to our luggage.* يكافئ؛ يعوِّض على

▸ **recompense** *noun* [sing., U] (*formal*) *I received £900 in recompense for loss of earnings.* تعويض؛ مكافأة

reconcile /'rekənsaɪl/ *verb* [T] **1** (often passive) **reconcile sb (with sb)** to cause people to become friendly with or close to each other again: *After years of not speaking to each other, she and her parents were eventually reconciled.* يصالِح

2 reconcile sth (with sth) to find a way to make two things (ideas, situations, statements, etc.) be possible together, when in fact they seem to oppose each other: *She finds it difficult to reconcile her career ambitions with her responsibilities to her children.* يوفّق بين

3 reconcile yourself to sth to accept an unpleasant situation because there is nothing you can do to change it يرضى بِ، يرضخ لِ

▸ **reconciliation** /ˌrekənˌsɪli'eɪʃn/ *noun* [C,U] becoming friendly or close again (after an argument, etc.): [C]: *to bring about a reconciliation between the two sides* مصالحة، وِفاق

reconnaissance /rɪ'kɒnɪsns/ *noun* [C,U] the study of a place or area for military reasons استطلاع أو استكشاف (لأغراض عسكريّة)

reconsider /ˌriːkən'sɪdə(r)/ *verb* [I,T] to think again about sth (a decision, situation, etc.): *Public protests have forced the government to reconsider their policy.* يعيد النظر في

reconstruct /ˌriːkən'strʌkt/ *verb* [T] **1** to build again sth that has been destroyed or damaged: *The cathedral was reconstructed after the fire.* يعيد بناءَه

2 to get a full description or picture of sth using the facts that are known: *The police are trying to reconstruct the victim's movements on the day of the murder.* يعيد تشكيل (القصّة) أو تمثيل (الحادثة مثلاً)

▸ **reconstruction** /-'strʌkʃn/ *noun* [C,U]: *Reconstruction of the city after the earthquake took years.* ○ *a reconstruction of the crime using actors* إعادة بناء؛ إعادة تمثيل (الجريمة)

ɾ **record**[1] /'rekɔːd; *US* 'rekərd/ *noun* [C] **1 record (of sth)** a written account of what has happened, been done, etc: *The teachers keep records of the children's progress.* ○ *medical records* سِجِل

2 (*also* **disc**) a thin, round piece of plastic which can store music and other sound so that you can play it when you want اسطوانة موسيقيّة

3 the best performance or the highest or lowest level, etc. ever reached in sth, especially in sport: *Who holds the world record for high jump?* ○ *to set a new record* ○ *to break a record* ○ *We've had so little rain this year – I'm sure it must be a record* (= the lowest amount ever). ○ *He did it in record time* (= very fast). ○ *record sales* الرقم القياسي

4 [sing.] the facts, events, etc. that are known (and sometimes written down) about sb/sth: *The police said that the man had a criminal record* (= he had been found guilty of crimes in the past). ○ *This airline has a bad safety record.* سجل (عدليّ)، قيْد

IDM put/set the record straight to correct a misunderstanding by telling sb the true facts يطلعه على الحقائق (لإزالة سوء تفاهم بينهما)

ɾ **record**[2] /rɪ'kɔːd/ *verb* **1** [T] to write sth down, put it into a computer, film it, etc. so that it can be used later and will not be forgotten: *Their childhood is recorded in diaries and photographs of those years.* يسجِّل

2 [I,T] to put music, a film, a programme, etc. onto a cassette or record so that it can be listened to or watched again later: *Quiet, please! We're recording.* ○ *The band has recently recorded a new album.* يسجِّل

'record-breaking *adj* (only *before* a noun) the best, fastest, highest, etc. ever: *We did the journey in record-breaking time.* محطِّم لرقم قياسيّ

recorder /rɪ'kɔːdə(r)/ *noun* [C] **1** a machine for recording sound or pictures or both: *a tape recorder* ○ *a video recorder* آلة تسجيل أو مسجِّلة؛ آلة تسجيل فيديو

2 a type of musical instrument that is often played by children. You play it by blowing through it and covering the holes in it with your fingers. مزمار خشبيّ يشبه الفلوت

ɾ **recording** /rɪ'kɔːdɪŋ/ *noun* **1** [C] sound or pictures that have been put onto a cassette, record or film: *the Berlin Philharmonic's recording of Mahler's Sixth symphony* تسجيل (موسيقيّ مثلاً)

2 [U] the process of making cassettes, records or films: *a recording studio* تسجيل

'record player *noun* [C] a machine that you use for playing records غرامفون، "بيك آب"

recount /rɪ'kaʊnt/ *verb* [T] (*formal*) to tell a story or describe an event: *He recounted the story to us in vivid detail.* يقصّ، يروي، يسرد

recourse /rɪ'kɔːs/ *noun*

IDM have recourse to sb/sth (*formal*) to turn to sb/sth for help يلجأ إلى، يستعين بِ

ɾ **recover** /rɪ'kʌvə(r)/ *verb* **1** [I] **recover (from sth)** to become well again after you have been ill: *It took him two months to recover from the operation.* يتعافى، يستردّ صحّته

2 [I] **recover (from sth)** to get back to normal again after a bad experience, etc: *It took her a long time to recover from her father's death.* يعود إلى حالته السويّة

3 [T] **recover sth (from sb/sth)** to find or get back sth that has been lost or stolen: *Police recovered the stolen goods from a warehouse in South London.* يسترجع، يستردّ

4 [T] to get back a state of health, an ability to do sth, etc: *He needs daily exercise if he's going to recover the use of his legs.* ○ *She recovered consciousness in the ambulance.* يستعيد

recovery /rɪˈkʌvəri/ *noun* **1** [sing., U] **recovery (from sth)** a return to good health after an illness or to a normal state after a difficult period of time: *to make a good, quick, slow, etc. recovery* ○ *Nobody is optimistic about the prospects of economic recovery this year.* شفاء، استرداد الصحة: انتعاش

2 [U] **recovery (of sth/sb)** getting sth/sb back: *He offered a reward for the recovery of the paintings.* استرداد

recreation /ˌrekriˈeɪʃn/ *noun* [C,U] enjoying yourself and relaxing when you are not working; a way of doing this: *What do you do for recreation?* استجمام، تسلية

▸ **recreational vehicle** = CAMPER

recruit /rɪˈkruːt/ *noun* [C] a person who has just joined the army or another organization; a new member مجنّد جديد؛ عضو جديد

▸ **recruit** *verb* [I,T] to get sb to join sth, to work as sth or to help with sth: *to recruit young people to the teaching profession* يجنّد، يشغّل في

recruitment *noun* [U] the process of getting people to join sth or work as sth: *Many companies are having problems with recruitment.* تجنيد؛ إيجاد (موظّفين) جدد

rectangle /ˈrektæŋgl/ *noun* [C] a shape with four straight sides and four angles of 90 degrees (right angles). Two of the sides are usually longer than the other two. المستطيل

▸ **rectangular** /rekˈtæŋgjələ(r)/ *adj* مستطيل

rectify /ˈrektɪfaɪ/ *verb* [T] (*pres part* **rectifying**; *3rd pers sing pres* **rectifies**; *pt, pp* **rectified**) (*formal*) to change sth so that it is right: *All these errors will need to be rectified.* يصحّح، يصلِح ، يقوّم

rector /ˈrektə(r)/ *noun* [C] (in the Church of England) a priest in charge of a certain area (a parish) ➲ Look at **vicar**. قسّيس في الكنيسة الأنكليكانيّة

recuperate /rɪˈkjuːpəreɪt/ *verb* [I] to get well again after an illness or injury يتعافى، يستردّ صحّته

▸ **recuperation** *noun* [U] استجمام، استعادة الصحّة

recur /rɪˈkɜː(r)/ *verb* [I] (recurring; recurred) to happen again or many times: *a recurring problem* ○ *It was a theme that recurred in many of her books.* يتكرّر

▸ **recurrence** /rɪˈkʌrəns/ *noun* [C,U] تكرار، عودة

recurrent /-ənt/ *adj* متكرّر (دوريّاً)

recycle /ˌriːˈsaɪkl/ *verb* [T] **1** to process used objects and materials so that they can be used again: *recycled paper* ○ *Aluminium cans can be recycled.* ○ *We take our empty bottles to the bottle bank for recycling.* يكرّر أو يعالج مادّة لإعادة استخدامها

2 to keep used objects and materials and use them again: *Don't throw away your plastic carrier bags – recycle them!* يستعمل من جديد

▸ **recyclable** /ˌriːˈsaɪkləbl/ *adj* that can be recycled: *Most plastics are recyclable.* قابل للتكرير والاستخدام ثانية

red¹ /red/ *adj* (**redder**; **reddest**) **1** of the colour of blood: *red wine* ○ *The berries on that bush turn bright red in October.* أحمر

We use **crimson**, **maroon** and **scarlet** to describe different shades of red.

2 (used about a person's face) a darker colour than usual because of anger, sadness, shame, etc: *He went bright red when she spoke to him.* ○ *to turn/be/go red in the face* أحمر (الوجه)

3 (used about a person's hair or an animal's fur) of a colour between red, orange and brown: *She's got red hair and freckles.* أحمر

IDM **a red herring** an idea or subject which takes people's attention away from what is really important

قضيّة غير مهمّة تصرف الانتباه عن أخرى خطيرة

red² /red/ *noun* [C,U] the colour of blood: *She was dressed in red* (= in red clothes). اللون الأحمر

IDM **be in the red** (*informal*) to have spent more money than you have in the bank, etc.

مَدين للبنك

red-brick /ˈredbrɪk/ *adj* (*Brit*) (of British universities) started in the late 19th or early 20th century (جامعة بريطانية) حديثة نسبيّاً

ˌred ˈcard *noun* [C] (in football, etc.) a card that is shown to a player who is being sent off the field ➲ Look at **yellow card**.

البطاقة الحمراء (في لعبة كرة القدم)

ˌred ˈcarpet *noun* [sing.] a piece of red carpet that is put out to receive an important visitor; a special welcome for an important visitor

السجادة الحمراء (تمدّ احتفاء بزائر مهمّ)

redcurrant /ˌredˈkʌrənt/ *noun* [C] a small red berry that you can eat: *redcurrant jelly*

كِشْمِش أحمر

redden /ˈredn/ *verb* [I,T] to become red or to make sth red: *She reddened with embarrassment.*

ⓘ **Go red** or **blush** are more common.

يحمرّ؛ يحمّر

reddish /ˈredɪʃ/ *adj* slightly red مائل إلى الحمرة

redeem /rɪˈdiːm/ *verb* [T] **1** to prevent sth from being completely bad: *The redeeming feature of the job is the good salary.* يشفع لـ؛ يقلّل من رداءته

2 redeem yourself to save yourself from blame: *It was all his fault. There's nothing he can say to redeem himself.* يخلّص

3 to get sth back by paying the amount needed يفكّ الرهن

redemption /rɪˈdempʃn/ *noun* [U] (*formal*) being saved or redeemed خلاص؛ فداء، تخليص

IDM **beyond redemption** not able to be saved ميؤوس منه، لا مجال لإصلاحه أو إنقاذه

redevelop /ˌriːdɪˈveləp/ *verb* [T] to build or arrange an area, a town, a building, etc. in a different and more modern way: *They're redeveloping the city centre.* يعيد تنظيم أو بناء منطقة معينة، يجدّدها

▸ **redevelopment** *noun* [U] new building work: *There's a lot of redevelopment going on around us at the moment.* إعادة بناء (منطقة ما)، تنظيم بلديّ جديد

ˌ**red-'handed** /red 'hændɪd/ *adj*
IDM to catch sb red-handed → CATCH[1]

redhead /'redhed/ *noun* [C] a person, especially a woman, who has red hair امرأة حمراء الشَّعر

ˌ**red-'hot** *adj* (used about a metal) so hot that it turns red (حديد) محميّ أو متوهّج بالحرارة

redial /ˌriː'daɪəl/ *verb* [I,T] to call the same number on a telephone that you have just called يعيد تشكيل الرقم التلفوني

redistribute /ˌriːdɪ'strɪbjuːt/ *verb* [T] to share sth among people, groups, etc. in a different way يوزِّع من جديد
▸ **redistribution** /ˌriːdɪstrɪ'bjuːʃn/ *noun* [U] إعادة توزيع

ˌ**red 'pepper** *noun* [C] a red vegetable that is almost empty inside فليفلة حمراء

ˌ**red 'tape** *noun* [U] official rules that seem unnecessary and often cause delay and difficulty in achieving sth الروتين الحكومي

reduce /rɪ'djuːs; *US* -'duːs/ *verb* [T] **1** to make sth less: *The sign said 'Reduce speed now'.* ○ *Doctors have advised us to reduce the amount of fat in our diets.* ❶ The opposite is **increase**. يُخفِّف، يقلِّل

2 reduce sb/sth (from sth) to sth (often passive) to make sb/sth be in the (usually bad) state mentioned: *One of the older boys reduced the little child to tears.* ○ *They were reduced from wealth to poverty almost overnight.* يُحيل إلى، يُنزل؛ يجبر

reduction /rɪ'dʌkʃn/ *noun* **1** [U] making sth less or becoming less; an example of this happening: *a reduction in the numbers of people unemployed* ○ *a reduction in the rate of inflation* تخفيض؛ انخفاض

2 [C] the amount by which sth is made smaller, especially in price: *There were huge price reductions during the sale.* تنزيل

redundant /rɪ'dʌndənt/ *adj* **1** (used about employees) no longer needed for a job and therefore out of work: *When the factory closed 800 people were made redundant.* عاطل (عن العمل)

2 not necessary or wanted فائض عن الحاجة، زائد، لا لزوم له

▸ **redundancy** /-ənsi/ *noun* (*pl.* **redundancies**) **1** [C, usually pl.] a case of having lost your job because there is no work for you: *The firm announced fifty redundancies.* عامل مسرّح من العمل

2 [U] the state of having lost your job because there is no work: *Computers have caused some redundancy but have also created jobs.* ○ *redundancy pay* بطالة أو عطالة

ˌ**red 'wine** *noun* [U] wine that is made from black grapes ➲ Look at **white wine**. نبيذ أحمر

reed /riːd/ *noun* [C,U] a tall plant, like grass, that grows in or near water قَصَبة

reef /riːf/ *noun* [C] a long line of rocks, sand, etc. just below or above the surface of the sea: *a coral reef* حاجز صخري في البحر

reek /riːk/ *noun* [sing.] a strong bad smell رائحة كريهة
▸ **reek** *verb* [I] to smell strongly of sth unpleasant: *His breath reeked of garlic.* تفوح منه رائحة كريهة

reel[1] /riːl/ *noun* [C] a round object that cotton, wire, film for cameras, a fishing line, etc. is wound around: *a cotton reel* بكرة، مِلف، "كَركَر"
▸ **reel** *verb* [T] **reel sth in/out** to wind sth on or off a reel or to pull it towards you using a reel: *to reel out the hosepipe* ○ *to reel in a fish* يلفّ على بكرة، يشدّ (الخيط) من البكرة

PHR V reel sth off to say or repeat sth from memory quickly and without effort: *She reeled off a list of names.* يسرد بسرعة ودون عناء، "يكرّ" الأسماء

reel[2] /riːl/ *verb* [I] **1** to move in an unsteady way: *At the end of the day, they reeled home exhausted.* يترنّح، يكاد يتهاوى

2 (used about the mind) to be unclear or confused: *His mind was reeling at the shock.* يَضطرب، يشْدَه: في دوّامة

ref /ref/ *abbrev* **1** = REFEREE (1)
2 = REFERENCE

refectory /rɪ'fektri/ *noun* [C] (*pl.* **refectories**) a large dining room in a college, school, etc. غرفة الطعام في مدرسة وما شابهها

refer /rɪ'fɜː(r)/ *verb* (refe**rr**ing; refe**rr**ed) **1** [I] **refer to sb/sth** to mention or talk about sb/sth: *When he said 'some students', do you think he was referring to us?* ○ *She always referred to Ben as 'that nice man'.* يشير إلى، يتكلّم عن

2 [I] **refer to sb/sth** to be used to describe sb/sth: *The term 'adolescent' refers to young people between the ages of 12 and 17.* يصف، يشير إلى

3 [I] to be connected with or important for: *The figures in brackets refer to holidays in July.* يتعلّق بِ، يخص

4 [I] **refer to sb/sth** to go to sb/sth or to look at sth for information: *If you don't understand a word you may refer to your dictionaries.* يرجع إلى، يستعين بِ

5 [T] **refer sb/sth to sb/sth** to send or direct sb/sth to sb/sth for help or to be dealt with: *The doctor has referred me to a specialist.* ○ *The dispute was referred to the United Nations.* يحيل إلى

referee /ˌrefə'riː/ *noun* [C] **1** (*also informal* **ref**) the person in football, boxing, etc. who controls the match and prevents the rules from being broken ➲ Look at **umpire**. حَكَم

2 a person who gives information about your character and ability, usually in a letter, for example when you are hoping to be chosen for a job مزكّي، حكم
▸ **referee** *verb* [I,T] to act as a referee: *Who refereed the match?* يحكم في مباراة

reference /'refərəns/ *noun* **1** [C,U] **reference (to sb/sth)** a statement that mentions sb/sth; the act of mentioning sb/sth: *The article made a direct reference to a certain member of the royal* *family.* ○ *Don't make any reference to his behaviour last night.* إشارة إلى، ذِكر

2 [C] a note, especially in a book, etc., that tells you where certain information has been or can be found. هامش؛ مرجع؛ إسناد

3 [C] a statement or letter describing a person's character and ability. When you are applying for a job, you give names as references: *My former employer gave me a good reference.* كتاب تزكية أو توصية (بطالب وظيفة مثلاً)

4 [C] (*abbr* **ref**) (used on business letters, etc.) a special number that identifies a letter, etc: *Please quote our reference when replying.* رقم (كتاب رسمي)

IDM with reference to sb/sth (*formal*) about or concerning sb/sth: *I am writing with reference to your letter of 10 April...* بالإشارة إلى...

'reference book *noun* [C] a book that is used for obtaining information, not for reading right through مرجع

referendum /ˌrefəˈrendəm/ *noun* [C] (*pl.* **referendums** or **referenda** /-də/) an occasion when all the people of a country are able to vote on a particular political question استفتاء عام

refill /ˌriːˈfɪl/ *verb* [T] to fill sth again: *Can I refill your glass?* يملأ ثانية

▸ **refill** /ˈriːfɪl/ *noun* [C] (*informal*) the container which holds the amount that is needed to refill sth: *a refill for a pen* عَبْوة جديدة

refine /rɪˈfaɪn/ *verb* [T] **1** to make a substance pure and free from other substances: *to refine sugar, oil, etc.* يصفّي، يكرِّر

2 to improve sth by changing little details: *to refine a theory* يهذِّب، يصقل

▸ **refined** *adj* **1** that has been improved or made pure: *refined sugar* مكرَّر، مصفَّى

2 (used about a person) having extremely good manners مهذَّب، رقيق الحاشية، ذو ذوق رفيع

ⓘ The opposite for **1** and **2** is **unrefined**.

refinery /-nəri/ *noun* [C] (*pl.* **refineries**) a factory where a certain substance is refined: *an oil refinery* مصفاة، معمل تكرير

refinement /rɪˈfaɪnmənt/ *noun* **1** [C] (often plural) a small change that improves sth: *The new model has electric windows and other refinements.* تحسين (تحسينات)، لمسات جديدة

2 [U] good manners, polite behaviour, etc: *a person of great refinement* تهذيب، رِقّة

⚷ **reflect** /rɪˈflekt/ *verb* **1** [T] to send back light, heat or sound: *The windows reflected the bright morning sunlight.* يعكس

2 [T] **reflect sb/sth (in sth)** (used about a mirror, water, etc.) to send back an image of sb/sth: *She caught sight of herself reflected in the shop window.* يعكس

3 [T] to show or express sth: *The increase in wages will be reflected in prices soon.* يظهر

4 [I,T] **reflect (on/upon sth)** to think, especially deeply: *I really need some time to reflect on what you've said.* يفكِّر مليّاً : يتأمّل

PHRV reflect (well, badly, etc.) on sb/sth to give a particular impression of sb/sth: *It reflects badly on the whole school if some of the pupils misbehave in public.* يعطي صورة (سيئة) عن

reflection (*also* **reflexion**) /rɪˈflekʃn/ *noun* **1** [C] a thing that shows or expresses sth: *His success is a reflection of all the hard work he puts into his job.* دليل على، تعبير عن

2 [sing.] **reflection on/upon sb/sth** a thing that causes a bad impression of sb/sth: *Parents often feel that their children's behaviour is a reflection on themselves.* انعكاس سيِّئ على : خزي

3 [C] an image that you see in a mirror or in water صورة في مرآة

4 [U] (*technical*) the process of sending light, heat or sound back from a surface انعكاس، عكس

5 [C,U] thinking deeply about sth: *A moment's reflection will show you that you are wrong.* تفكير عميق، تأمُّل

IDM on reflection after thinking again: *I think, on reflection, that we were wrong.* بعد إعادة النظر

reflective /rɪˈflektɪv/ *adj* **1** (used about a person, mood, etc.) thoughtful: *a reflective expression* تأمُّلي

2 (used about a surface) reflecting light: *Wear reflective strips when you're cycling at night.* عاكِس

reflector /rɪˈflektə(r)/ *noun* [C] a thing that reflects light, heat or sound العاكس

reflex /ˈriːfleks/ *noun* **1** [C] (*also* **'reflex action**) a sudden movement or action that you make automatically: *'I'm going to tap your knee to test your reflexes,' said the doctor.* فعل انعكاسيّ أو لا إرادي

2 reflexes [plural] the ability to act quickly when necessary: *A good tennis player needs to have excellent reflexes.* ردّ فعل تلقائي

reflexion (*Brit*) = REFLECTION

reflexive /rɪˈfleksɪv/ *adj, noun* [C] (*grammar*) (a word or verb form) showing that the action of a sentence is done to the subject of the sentence: *In the sentence 'He cut himself', 'himself' is a reflexive pronoun.* انعكاسيّ : فِعْل يعود مفعوله على الفاعل

⚷ **reform** /rɪˈfɔːm/ *verb* **1** [T] to change sth in order to make it better: *to reform the examination system* يُصلِح، يعدِّل

2 [I,T] to behave better or fit into society better; to make sb do this: *He's done wrong in the past but he has made serious efforts to reform.* ○ *Our prisons aim to reform criminals, not simply to punish them.* يَنصلِح، يتحسَّن : يصلح

▸ **reform** *noun* [C,U] (a) change in sth in order to make it better: *a major reform to the system* ○ *political reform in Eastern Europe* إصلاح، تحسين

reformer *noun* [C] a person who tries to change society and make it better مصلِح

refrain[1] /rɪˈfreɪn/ *verb* [I] **refrain (from sth)** (*formal*) to stop yourself doing sth; not do sth: *Please refrain from smoking in the hospital.* يمتنع أو يمسك عن، يكفّ عن

refrain[2] /rɪˈfreɪn/ *noun* [C] a part of a song which

a b c d e f g h i j k l m n o p q **r** s t u v w x y z

is repeated, especially at the end of each verse اللازمة (ترديدة موسيقيّة)

refresh /rɪˈfreʃ/ *verb* [T] to make sb/sth feel fresh, strong or full of energy again: *He looked refreshed after a good night's sleep.* ينعش

IDM **refresh your/sb's memory (about sb/sth)** to remind yourself/sb about sb/sth: *Could you refresh my memory about what we said on this point last week?* يذكّر

▸ **refreshing** *adj* **1** interesting, different and enjoyable: *It's refreshing to meet somebody who is so enthusiastic.* ممتع ، سارّ ، مثير

2 making you feel fresh and strong again: *a refreshing swim* منعش ، مجدّد للنشاط

refreshment /rɪˈfreʃmənt/ *noun* **1 refreshments** [plural] light food and drinks that are available at a cinema, theatre or other public event: *Refreshments will be sold during the interval.* مأكولات خفيفة ومرطّبات

2 [U] being refreshed, or the food and drink that makes you feel refreshed: *There will be two stops for refreshment on the coach journey.* ○ *Can I offer you some refreshment?* استراحة ، انتعاش: مرطّبات

refrigerate /rɪˈfrɪdʒəreɪt/ *verb* [T] to put food, etc. in a fridge in order to keep it fresh يضع (الطعام) في ثلاّجة أو برّاد

▸ **refrigerator** /rɪˈfrɪdʒəreɪtə(r)/ *noun* [C] (*formal*) = FRIDGE

refuge /ˈrefjuːdʒ/ *noun* [C,U] **refuge (from sb/sth)** a place that is safe; the protection that this place gives you against sth unpleasant: *a refuge from the heat of the sun* ○ *They took refuge in foreign embassies.* ملجأ، ملاذ

refugee /ˌrefjuˈdʒiː; *US* ˈrefjʊdʒiː/ *noun* [C] a person who has been forced to leave his/her country for political or religious reasons, because there is a war, not enough food, etc: *political refugees* ○ *a refugee camp* لاجئ

refund /rɪˈfʌnd; ˈriːfʌnd/ *verb* [T] to pay back money: *Your travelling expenses will be refunded.* يردّ إليه (ما قد دفعه)

▸ **refund** /ˈriːfʌnd/ *noun* [C] a sum of money that is returned to you, for example if you take goods back to a shop مبلغ مردود (إلى الشاري مثلاً)

refundable /-əbl/ *adj* that will be paid back: *The deposit is not refundable.* (مبلغ) قابل للردّ

refusal /rɪˈfjuːzl/ *noun* **1** [U] not wanting or not being able to do sth or to accept sth: *Refusal to pay the new tax may result in imprisonment.* رفض، امتناع عن

2 [C] a statement or act that shows you will not do or accept sth: *The employers warned that a refusal to return to work would result in people losing their jobs.* ○ *So far we've had ten replies to the invitation: eight acceptances and two refusals.* رفض

refuse[1] /rɪˈfjuːz/ *verb* [I,T] to say or show that you do not want to do, give, accept, etc. sth: *I asked her to come but she refused.* ○ *He refused to listen to what I was saying.* ○ *My application for a grant has been refused.* ○ *We offered her a lift but she refused it.* يرفض

refuse[2] /ˈrefjuːs/ *noun* [U] (*formal*) things that you throw away; rubbish: *household refuse* ○ *the refuse collection* (= when dustbins are emptied) قمامة، فضلات

regain /rɪˈɡeɪn/ *verb* [T] to get sth back that you have lost: *to regain your freedom* ○ *to regain consciousness* يستعيد

regal /ˈriːɡl/ *adj* very splendid; like or suitable for a king or queen ملَكي، فخم

regard[1] /rɪˈɡɑːd/ *verb* [T] **1 regard sb/sth (as sth); regard sb/sth (with sth)** to think of sb/sth (in the way mentioned): *I regard him as my best friend.* ○ *Do you regard this issue as important?* ○ *Her work is highly regarded* (= people have a high opinion of it). ○ *In some villages newcomers are regarded with suspicion.* ينظر إلى، يعتبر

2 (*formal*) to look steadily at sb/sth: *She regarded herself thoughtfully in the mirror.* ينظر بإمعان

IDM **as regards sb/sth** (*formal*) about or concerning sb/sth: *What are your views as regards this proposal?* فيما يتعلّق بـ، حولَ

▸ **regarding** *prep* (*formal*) about or concerning: *Please write if you require further information regarding this matter.* حولَ، بشأن

regard[2] /rɪˈɡɑːd/ *noun* **1** [U] **regard (for sb/sth)** a feeling of admiration for sb/sth: respect: *She obviously has great regard for your ability.* إعجاب؛ احترام؛ تقدير

2 [U] **regard to/for sb/sth** care or consideration for sb/sth: *He shows little regard for other people's feelings.* اعتبار، اكتراث

3 regards [plural] (used especially at the end of a letter) kind thoughts and greetings: *Please give my regards to your parents.* تحيّات

IDM **in/with regard to sb/sth; in this/that/one regard** (*formal*) about sb/sth; concerning this or that: *With regard to the details – these will be finalized later.* ○ *It has been a successful year financially, so in this regard we have been fortunate.* فيما يتعلّق بـ؛ من هذه الناحية

▸ **regardless** *adv* paying no attention to sb/sth: *I suggested she should stop but she carried on regardless.* دون اكتراث

regardless of *prep* paying no attention to sb/sth: *Everybody will receive the same, regardless of how long they've worked here.* بصرف النظر عن

regatta /rɪˈɡætə/ *noun* [C] an event at which there are boat races مهرجان سباق الزوارق

reggae /ˈreɡeɪ/ *noun* [U] a type of West Indian popular music with a strong rhythm "الريجي": موسيقى حديثة ذات ايقاع مميّز

regime /reɪˈʒiːm; ˈreʒiːm/ *noun* [C] a method or system of government: *a military regime* نظام الحكم

regiment /ˈredʒɪmənt/ [C, with sing. or pl. verb] a group of soldiers in the army, under the command of a colonel فوْج (عسكريّ)

▸ **regimental** /ˌredʒɪˈmentl/ *adj* خاصّ بالفوج؛ صارم

regimented /ˈredʒɪmentɪd/ *adj* (*formal*) (too) strictly controlled: *University life is much less* *regimented than life at school.* منضبِط، خاضع لنظام صارم

region /ˈriːdʒən/ *noun* [C] **1** a part of the country or the world; a large area of land: *desert, tropical, polar, etc. regions* ○ *This region of France is very mountainous.* ○ *She is responsible for the organization in the London region.* ➲ Look at the note at **district**. منطقة

2 an area of your body: *He's been having pains in the region of his heart.* ناحية

IDM **in the region of sth** about or approximately: *It must have cost somewhere in the region of £1 000.* ما يقارب، حوالي

▸ **regional** /-nl/ *adj* connected with a particular region: *regional accents* إقليمي؛ محلي

register[1] /ˈredʒɪstə(r)/ *noun* [C] an official list of names, etc. or a book that contains such a list: *The teacher calls the register first thing in the morning.* ○ *the electoral register* (= of people who are able to vote in an election) سِجِلّ، سِجِلّ بالأسماء

register[2] /ˈredʒɪstə(r)/ *verb* **1** [I,T] to put a name on an official list: *I'd like to register for the course in June.* ○ *You should register with a doctor while you're living in England.* ○ *All births, deaths and marriages must be registered.* يتسجّل؛ يسجّل

2 [I,T] to show on a measuring instrument: *The thermometer registered 32°C.* تبلغ (الحرارة)، يشير (الميزان)

3 [T] to show feelings, opinions, etc: *Her face registered intense dislike.* يعبِّر أو ينمّ عن

4 [T] to send a letter or parcel by special (registered) post: *Parcels containing valuable goods should be registered.* يُسجِّل، يرسل بالبريد المسجَّل

ˌregistered ˈpost *noun* [U] a postal service that you pay extra for. If your letter or parcel is lost the post office will make some payment to you. البريد المسجَّل

ˈregister office *noun* [C] = Registry Office

registrar /ˌredʒɪˈstrɑː(r); ˈredʒɪstrɑː(r)/ *noun* [C] **1** a person whose job is to keep official lists, especially of births, marriages and deaths القيِّم على سجلّات الولادة والوفاة والزواج

2 a person who is responsible for admissions, examinations, etc. at a college or university مدير التسجيل (في جامعة مثلاً)

registration /ˌredʒɪˈstreɪʃn/ *noun* [U] the act of putting sth or sb's name on an official list: *Registration for evening classes will take place on 8 September.* تسجيل

regiˈstration number *noun* [C] the numbers and letters on the front and back of a car, etc. that are used to identify it رقم السيّارة

registry /ˈredʒɪstri/ *noun* [C] (*pl.* **registries**) a place where official lists are kept: *the church registry* دائرة أو مكتب السجلّات

ˈregistry office (*also* **register office**) *noun* [C] an office where a marriage can take place and where births, marriages and deaths are officially recorded ➲ Look at the note at **wedding**. مكتب عقد الزواج، مكتب تسجيل الزواج والمواليد والوفيات

regret[1] /rɪˈɡret/ *noun* [C,U] a feeling of sadness about sth that cannot now be changed: *Do you have any regrets that you didn't go to university?* ○ *I accepted his decision to leave with great regret.* ندم، أسف

▸ **regretful** /-fl/ *adj* feeling or expressing sadness نادم، آسف

regretfully /-fəli/ *adv* آسفاً؛ بحزن وأسى

regret[2] /rɪˈɡret/ *verb* [T] (regre**tt**ing; regre**tt**ed) **1** to feel sorry or sad about sth; to wish that you had not done sth: *I hope you won't regret your decision later.* ○ *I soon regretted having been so rude.* ○ *Do you regret what you said to him?* ○ *Everyone regretted his leaving the school.* يندم على، يأسف

2 (*formal*) (used as a way of saying that you are sorry for sth): *I regret to inform you that your application has been unsuccessful.* يأسف

▸ **regrettable** /-əbl/ *adj* that you should feel sorry or sad about مؤسف

regrettably /-əbli/ *adv* **1** in a way that makes you feel sad or sorry ممّا يدعو للأسف أو الحزن

2 it is to be regretted that: *Regrettably, most hotels are not well-equipped for disabled people.* من المؤسف أنّ...، للأسف

regular /ˈreɡjələ(r)/ *adj* **1** having the same amount of space or time between each thing or part: *regular breathing* ○ *Nurses checked her blood pressure at regular intervals.* منتظم

2 happening at the same time each day, week, etc. (as a result of an arrangement or a plan): *We have regular meetings every Thursday.* دوري

3 going somewhere or doing sth often: *a regular customer* ○ *We're regular visitors to Britain.* دائم ، مواظب

4 normal or usual: *Who is your regular dentist?* معتاد

5 evenly shaped: *regular teeth* ○ *a regular geometric pattern* منتظم ؛ منظوم، متّسِق

6 (*grammar*) (used about a noun, verb, etc.) having the usual or expected plural, verb form, etc: *'Walk' is a regular verb.* ➲ Look at **irregular**. (فعل) قياسيّ

▸ **regular** *noun* [C] **1** (*informal*) a person who goes to a particular shop, pub, etc. very often زبون دائم

2 a permanent member of the army, navy, etc. جندي نظامي

regularity /ˌreɡjuˈlærəti/ *noun* [U] the state of being regular انتظام ؛ اطّراد ؛ اتّساق

regularly *adv* **1** at regular times or in a regular way: *to have a car serviced regularly* بشكل منتظم ؛ باطّراد

2 often: *Mr Davis regularly takes part in competitions but this is the first one that he has won.* غالباً ، كثيراً ما

regulate /ˈreɡjuleɪt/ *verb* [T] **1** to control sth by using laws: *a strict law to regulate carbon dioxide emissions from factories* ينظِّم

2 to control a machine, piece of equipment, etc: *Special valves in the radiator allow you to regu-*

a b c d e f g h i j k l m n o p q r s t u v w x y z

late the temperature in each room. يتحكّم في ، يضبط

regulation /ˌreɡjuˈleɪʃn/ *noun* **1** [U] control of sth: *state regulation of agriculture* تنظيم

2 [C, usually pl.] a law or rule that controls how sth is done: *to observe/obey the safety regulations* ○ *It is against the fire regulations to smoke on underground trains.* ○ *The plans must comply with the new EU regulations.* ○ *to enforce a regulation* نظام ، قانون

rehabilitate /ˌriːəˈbɪlɪteɪt/ *verb* [T] to help sb to live a normal life again after an illness, being in prison, etc. يعيد تأهيل فرد

▸ **rehabilitation** /ˌriːəˌbɪlɪˈteɪʃn/ *noun* [U] إعادة تأهيل

rehearse /rɪˈhɜːs/ *verb* [I,T] to practise a play, dance, piece of music, etc. before you perform it to other people يتدرّب على غناء أو أداء مسرحيّ وغير ذلك

▸ **rehearsal** /-sl/ *noun* [C,U] the time when you practise a play, dance, piece of music, etc. before you perform it to other people: *a dress rehearsal* (= when all the actors wear their stage clothes) تجربة مسرحيّة مثلاً، "بروفة"

reign /reɪn/ *noun* [C] the period of time that a king or queen rules a country: *the long reign of Queen Victoria* فترة حكم (الملك)، عهد

▸ **reign** *verb* [I] **1 reign (over sb/sth)** (used about a king or queen) to rule a country: (*figurative*) *the reigning world champion* يحكم ، يتولّى الحكم

2 to be present as the most important feature of a particular situation: *Chaos reigned after the first snow of the winter.* يسود

reimburse /ˌriːɪmˈbɜːs/ *verb* [T] (*formal*) to pay money back to sb: *The company will reimburse you in full for your travelling expenses.* ○ *Your expenses will be reimbursed in full.* يردّ له ما أنفقه

rein /reɪn/ *noun* [C, usually pl.] a long thin piece of leather that you use for controlling a horse. Reins are joined to a bridle which fits over a horses's head. عنان، زمام، رَسَن

reindeer /ˈreɪndɪə(r)/ *noun* [C] (*pl.* **reindeer**) a type of large deer that lives in Arctic regions رنّة ، أيّل يعيش في المناطق القطبيّة

According to tradition, reindeer pull Santa Claus's sledge at Christmas when he brings presents to children.

reinforce /ˌriːɪnˈfɔːs/ *verb* [T] to make sth stronger: *Concrete can be reinforced by putting steel bars inside it.* ○ *evidence to reinforce her argument* يقوّي ، يدعم ، يعزّز

▸ **reinforcement** *noun* **1** [U] the act of supporting or strengthening sth: *The sea wall is weak in places and needs reinforcement.* تقوية ، تدعيم ، تعزيز

2 reinforcements [plural] extra people who are sent to make an army, navy, etc. stronger تعزيزات ، قوات اضافيّة

reinstate /ˌriːɪnˈsteɪt/ *verb* [T] to put sb back into his/her previous job or position يعيد إلى (منصب) سابق

▸ **reinstatement** *noun* [U] إعادة إلى العمل

reject /rɪˈdʒekt/ *verb* [T] to refuse to accept sb/sth: *The plan was rejected as being impractical.* ○ *I've rejected all the candidates for the job except one.* يرفض ؛ ينبذ

▸ **reject** /ˈriːdʒekt/ *noun* [C] a person or thing that is not accepted because he/she/it is not good enough: *Rejects are sold at half price.* شخص مرفوض ؛ سلعة فيها عيب (تباع برخص)

rejection /ˈriːdʒekʃn/ *noun*: *Penny got a rejection from Leeds University.* ○ *There has been total rejection of the new policy.* رَفض

rejoice /rɪˈdʒɔɪs/ *verb* [I] **rejoice (at/over sth)** (*formal*) to feel or show great happiness يبتهج ، يطير فرحاً

▸ **rejoicing** *noun* [U] ابتهاج ، احتفال

rejuvenate /rɪˈdʒuːvəneɪt/ *verb* [T] (often passive) to cause sb/sth to feel or look younger يجدّد ؛ يعيد إليه الشباب

▸ **rejuvenation** /rɪˌdʒuːvəˈneɪʃn/ *noun* [U] تجديد أو تنشيط ، إعادة الشباب إليه

relapse /rɪˈlæps/ *verb* [I] to become worse again after an improvement: *to relapse into bad habits* ينتكس ، يعود إلى حالته السّيئة

▸ **relapse** *noun*: *The patient had a relapse and then died.* نكسة

relate /rɪˈleɪt/ *verb* **1** [T] **relate sth to/with sth** to show a connection between two or more things: *The report relates heart disease to high levels of stress.* يربط (بين)

2 [T] **relate sth (to sb)** (*formal*) to tell a story to sb يروي ، يقصّ

PHR V relate to sb/sth 1 to be concerned with sb/sth; to have sth to do with sb/sth: *That question is very interesting but it doesn't really relate to the subject that we're discussing.* يتعلّق بِ

2 to be able to understand how sb feels: *Some teenagers find it hard to relate to their parents.* يشعر بشعوره ، يفهم حقيقة مشاعره

▸ **related** *adj* **related (to sb/sth) 1** connected with sb/sth: *The rise in the cost of living is directly related to the price of oil.* مرتبط بِ

2 of the same family: *We are related by marriage.* ○ *to be closely/distantly related* قريب أو نسيب

relation /rɪˈleɪʃn/ *noun* **1** [U] **relation (between sth and sth)**; **relation (to sth)** the connection between two or more things: *There seems to be no relation between the cost of the houses and their size.* ○ *The film bore no relation to the book* (= it was very different). علاقة ، صلة

2 [C] a member of your family: *a close/distant relation* ❶ Note the expressions: *'What relation are you to each other?'* and *'Are you any relation to each other?'* قريب أو نسيب

3 relations [plural] the way that people, groups, countries, etc. feel about or behave towards each other: *The police officer stressed that good relations with the community were essential.* ○ *to break off diplomatic relations* علاقات

IDM in/with relation to sb/sth 1 concerning sb/sth: *Many questions were asked, particularly*

in relation to the cost of the new buildings. فيما يتعلق بـ

2 compared with: *Prices are low in relation to those in other parts of Europe.* بالمقارنة مع

ꝉ**relationship** /rɪˈleɪʃnʃɪp/ *noun* [C] **1** the way that people, groups, countries, etc. feel about or behave towards each other: *The police have a poor relationship with the local people.* ○ *The relationship between the parents and the school has improved greatly.* علاقة ، صلة

2 a friendship or love affair: *to have a relationship with sb* ○ *The film describes the relationship between a young man and an older woman.* ○ *a close relationship* علاقة (غراميّة مثلاً)

3 a family connection: *'What is your relationship to Bruce?' 'He is married to my cousin.'* قرابة

4 the connection between two or more things: *Is there a relationship between violence on TV and the increase in crime?* صلة ، ارتباط

ꝉ**relative**[1] /ˈrelətɪv/ *noun* [C] a member of your family: *a close/distant relative* قريب أو نسيب

ꝉ**relative**[2] /ˈrelətɪv/ *adj* **1** when compared to sb/sth else: *They live in relative luxury.* ○ *We're in a period of relative calm after the winds of the past few days.* ○ *It's hard to assess the relative importance of the two jobs.* نسبي

2 (*grammar*) referring to an earlier noun, phrase or sentence: *In the phrase 'the lady who lives next door', 'who' is a relative pronoun.* (في القواعد) اسم موصول

▸ **relatively** *adv* to a certain degree; quite: *Spanish is a relatively easy language.* ○ *It's a small house but the garden is relatively large.* نسبياً ، إلى حد ما

relativity /ˌreləˈtɪvəti/ *noun* [U] **1** (*physics*) Einstein's theory of the universe, which states that all motion is relative and treats time as a fourth dimension related to space نظرية النسبيّة لأينشتاين

2 the state of being relative: *a philosopher who emphasizes the relativity of all perception/progress* النسبيّة

ꝉ**relax** /rɪˈlæks/ *verb* **1** [I,T] to make or become less worried or tense; to spend time not doing very much: *This holiday will give you a chance to relax.* ○ *A hot bath will relax you after a hard day's work.* ○ *They spent the evening relaxing in front of the television.* يسترخي أو يرخي ، يستريح أو يريح

2 [I,T] to make or become less stiff or tight: *You should be able to feel all your muscles relaxing.* يرخي : يسترخي

3 [T] to make rules or laws less strict: *The regulations on importing animals have been relaxed.* يخفّف القيود

▸ **relaxation** /ˌriːlækˈseɪʃn/ *noun* **1** [U] the act of relaxing (1,2,3): *the relaxation of a rule* تخفيف القيود

2 [C,U] sth that you do in order to rest or relax (1): *Everyone needs time for rest and relaxation.* ○ *He paints as a relaxation.* استجمام ، إراحة الأعصاب

relaxed *adj* not worried or tense: *The relaxed atmosphere made everyone feel at ease.* هادئ الأعصاب ، مستريح : (جوّ) غير رسمي

relaxing *adj* pleasant, helping you to rest and become less worried: *a quiet relaxing holiday* مريح للأعصاب ، سارّ لطيف

relay[1] /ˈriːleɪ/ (*also* **ˈrelay race**) *noun* [C] a race in which each member of a team runs, swims, etc. one part of the race: *the 4 x 100m relay* سباق التتابع

IDM **in relays** with one group of people replacing another when the first group has completed a period of work: *The men worked in relays throughout the night to get the building finished.* بالتناوب

relay[2] /ˈriːleɪ; rɪˈleɪ/ *verb* [T] (*pt, pp* **relayed**) **1** to receive and send on a signal or message يرحّل إشارة مستقبَلة

2 (*Brit*) to broadcast a radio or television programme يبثّ برنامجاً بالراديو أو التلفزيون

ꝉ**release** /rɪˈliːs/ *verb* [T] **1** to allow sb/sth to be free: *The hostages will be released before Christmas.* ○ *He's been released from prison.* ○ *The driver of the wrecked car had to be released by firemen.* ○ (*figurative*) *His firm released him for two months so he could take part in the Olympic Games.* يطلق سراحه : يخلّص : يتخلّى عن

2 to stop holding sth: *She released his hand and walked off.* يفلت

3 to move sth from a fixed position: *He released the handbrake and drove off.* يفكّ

4 to allow sth to be known by the public: *The identity of the victim has not been released.* يعلن ، ينشر

5 to make a film, record, etc. available so the public can see or hear it: *Their new single is due to be released next week.* ينزل إلى الأسواق

6 to let substances escape into the air, sea, etc: *The power station releases carbon dioxide into the atmosphere.* يطلق

▸ **release** *noun* **1** [C,U] **release (from sth)** the act of freeing or the state of being freed: *The release of the hostages took place this morning.* ○ *I had a great feeling of release when my exams were finished.* إطلاق سراح ؛ فَرَج

2 [C] a book, film, CD, piece of news, etc. that has been made available to the public: *a press release* ○ *The band played their latest release.* كتاب أو فيلم أو نبأ يصبح متوفراً للجمهور

IDM **on (general) release** being shown or available to the public: *Batman flies into action in a new video out on release this month.* متوفّر في الأسواق ، عرض عامّ لفيلم

relegate /ˈrelɪɡeɪt/ *verb* [T] to put sb/sth into a lower rank or position: *West Ham was relegated to the Second Division* (= in football). يُنزّل إلى مرتبة أدنى

▸ **relegation** /ˌrelɪˈɡeɪʃn/ *noun* [U] تنزيل إلى مرتبة أدنى

relent /rɪˈlent/ *verb* [I] to become less strict or hard, e.g. by allowing sth that you had previously forbidden: *Her parents finally relented and allowed her to go.* يلين ، يرقّ قلبه

▸ **relentless** *adj* not stopping or changing: *a relentless enemy* مستمر؛ عنيد أو مصر
relentlessly *adv*: *The sun beat down relentlessly.* بلا رحمة : بلا هوادة

🔑 **relevant** /ˈreləvənt/ *adj* **relevant (to sb/sth)** **1** connected with what is happening or being talked about: *Please enclose all the relevant documents with your visa application.* ○ *Much of what was said was not directly relevant to my case.* متعلّق بالموضوع
2 important and useful: *Many people feel that poetry is no longer relevant in today's world.* ❶ The opposite is **irrelevant**. مهمّ ، مفيد
▸ **relevance** /-əns/ *noun*: *I honestly can't see the relevance of what he said.* علاقة بالموضوع : صلة ، فائدة

reliable /rɪˈlaɪəbl/ *adj* that you can trust: *Japanese cars are usually very reliable.* ○ *I'm surprised she didn't phone back – she's usually very reliable.* ○ *reliable information* ○ *Is he a reliable witness?* ❶ The opposite is **unreliable**. ➲ Look at the verb **rely**. موثوق ، يمكن الاعتماد عليه
▸ **reliability** /rɪˌlaɪəˈbɪləti/ *noun*: *These cars have a good reputation for reliability.* امكانيّة الاعتماد على
reliably /-əbli/ *adv*: *It has been reliably estimated that £10 million will be needed to complete the project.* بصورة موثوقة

reliance /rɪˈlaɪəns/ *noun* [U] **1 reliance on sb/sth** being able to trust sb/sth: *Don't place too much reliance on her promises.* تصديق ، ثقة
2 not being able to live or work without sb/sth; being dependent on sb/sth: *the country's reliance on imported oil* اتّكال أو اعتماد على
▸ **reliant** /-ənt/ *adj* **reliant on sb/sth** (not before a noun) not being able to live or work without sb/sth: *They are totally reliant on the state for financial support.* ❶ The verb is **rely**. ➲ Look at **self-reliant**. متّكل أو معتمد على

relic /ˈrelɪk/ *noun* [C] something from the past that still exists today أثر (تاريخي)

🔑 **relief** /rɪˈliːf/ *noun* **1** [U, sing.] **relief (from sth)** the feeling that you have when sth unpleasant stops or becomes less strong: *The drugs brought him some relief from the pain.* ○ *What a relief! That awful noise has stopped.* ○ *It was a great relief to know they were safe.* ○ *to breathe a sigh of relief* ○ *To my relief, he didn't argue with my suggestion at all.* شعور بالارتياح ، فَرَج ، راحة
2 [U] money or food that is given to help people who are in trouble: *disaster relief for the flood victims* إعانة أو معونة
3 [U] a reduction in the amount of tax you have to pay حسم في ضريبة الدخل

relieve /rɪˈliːv/ *verb* [T] to make an unpleasant feeling or situation better: *This injection should relieve the pain.* ○ *Four new prisons are being built to relieve overcrowding.* يخفف، يسكّن
PHRV **relieve sb of sth** to take sth away from sb ينشل ، يسرق
▸ **relieved** *adj* pleased because your fear or worry has been taken away: *I was very relieved to hear that you weren't seriously hurt.* شاعر بالارتياح ، مفرّج عنه

🔑 **religion** /rɪˈlɪdʒən/ *noun* **1** [U] the belief in a god or gods who made the world and who can control what happens in it: *I never discuss politics or religion with them.* دين
2 [C] one of the systems of worship that is based on this belief: *the Christian, Muslim, etc. religion* ديانة

🔑 **religious** /rɪˈlɪdʒəs/ *adj* **1** connected with religion: *religious faith* دينيّ
2 having a strong belief in a religion: *a deeply religious person* متديّن
▸ **religiously** *adv* **1** in a religious way دينياً
2 regularly: *She stuck to the diet religiously.* بانتظام ، بحماس مفرط، بلا كَلل ولا مَلل

relinquish /rɪˈlɪŋkwɪʃ/ *verb* [T] (*formal*) to stop having or doing sth ❶ **Give up** is more common. يتنازل أو يتخلى عن

relish /ˈrelɪʃ/ *verb* [T] to enjoy sth or to look forward to sth very much يستمتع بـ ؛ يتلهف إلى

relive /ˌriːˈlɪv/ *verb* [T] to remember sth and imagine that it is happening again يحيا (الحادث) من جديد

reluctant /rɪˈlʌktənt/ *adj* **reluctant (to do sth)** not willing and so rather slow to agree to do sth: *I was rather reluctant to lend him the car because he's such a fast driver.* ممانع ، متردّد
▸ **reluctance** /-əns/ *noun*: *Tony left with obvious reluctance* (= it was clear that he didn't want to go). تردّد ، عدم رغبة
reluctantly *adv* بتردّد ، على مضَض

🔑 **rely** /rɪˈlaɪ/ *verb* [I] (*pres part* **relying**; *3rd pers sing pres* **relies**; *pt, pp* **relied**) **rely on/upon sb/sth (to do sth)** **1** to need sb/sth and not be able to live or work properly without them: *The old lady had to rely on other people to do her shopping for her.* ○ *Many students do not like having to rely on their parents for money.* يعتمد على
2 to trust sb/sth to work or behave well: *You can't rely on the weather in Britain.* ○ *Can I rely on you to keep a secret?* ❶ The noun is **reliance** and the adjective is **reliable**. يثق بـ، يأتمن

🔑 **remain** /rɪˈmeɪn/ *verb* [I] **1** to be left after other people or things have gone: *Today only a few stones remain of the castle.* ○ *to remain behind after class* ○ *They spent the two remaining days of their holidays buying presents to take home.* ○ *Tottenham scored with five minutes of the match remaining.* يبقى
2 to stay or continue in the same place or condition: *They remained silent throughout the trial.* ○ *They're divorced but they remain friends.* ○ *Josef went to live in America but his family remained behind in Europe.* ○ (*figurative*) *Although he seems very pleasant, the fact remains that I don't trust him.* يظلّ ، يبقى

remainder /rɪˈmeɪndə(r)/ *noun* [sing., with sing. or pl. verb] the people, things, etc. that are left after the others have gone away or been dealt with; the rest: *There are seats for twenty people – the remainder must stand.* ○ *They couldn't decide* *what to do for the remainder of the afternoon.* الباقي ، المتبقّي من

remains /rɪˈmeɪnz/ *noun* [plural] **1** what is left behind after other parts have been used or taken away: *The builders found the remains of a Roman mosaic floor.* بقايا

2 (*formal*) a dead body (sometimes one that has been found somewhere a long time after death): *Human remains were discovered in the wood.* بقايا ، رفات

remand /rɪˈmɑːnd; *US* -ˈmænd/ *verb* [T] to order sb to come back to court at a later date: *to remand sb in custody* يعيد المتّهم إلى السجن بانتظار موعد آخر للدعوى

▶ **remand** *noun* [U] the time before a prisoner's trial takes place: *a remand prisoner* الفترة التي تسبق محاكمة سجين

IDM **on remand** (used about a prisoner) waiting for the trial to take place (سجين) بانتظار المحاكمة

remark /rɪˈmɑːk/ *verb* [I,T] **remark (on/upon sb/sth)** to say or write sth; to comment: *'What a strange film,' he remarked.* ○ *Millie remarked that she had found the film very interesting.* ○ *A lot of people have remarked on the similarity between them.* يبدي ملاحظة، يعلّق على

▶ **remark** *noun* [C] something that you say or write; a comment: *a few personal remarks at the end of the letter* ○ *to make a rude remark* ملاحظة ، تعليق

remarkable /-əbl/ *adj* unusual or noticeable: *She certainly is a remarkable woman.* ○ *That is a remarkable achievement for someone so young.* رائع ، جدير بالاعجاب ؛ استثنائي

remarkably /-əbli/ *adv* بشكل يلفت الانتباه

remedy /ˈremədi/ *noun* [C] (*pl.* **remedies**) **remedy (for sth) 1** something that makes you better when you are ill or in pain: *Hot lemon with honey is a good remedy for colds.* دواء ، علاج

2 a way of solving a problem: *There is no easy remedy for unemployment.* معالجة

▶ **remedial** /rɪˈmiːdiəl/ *adj* **1** used to improve sth (e.g. sb's health or a difficult situation) علاجيّ ، إصلاحي

2 helping people who are slow at learning sth: *remedial English classes* ترميمي ، تعويضيّ

remedy *verb* [T] (*pres part* **remedying**; *3rd pers sing pres* **remedies**; *pt, pp* **remedied**) to change or improve sth that is wrong or bad: *to remedy an injustice* يصحّح ؛ يسدّ (النقص) ؛ يداوي

remember /rɪˈmembə(r)/ *verb* **1** [I,T] to have sth in your mind or to bring sth back into your mind: *When did we go to Spain? I just don't remember.* ○ *I'm sorry. I don't remember your name.* ○ *Do you remember the night we first met?* ○ *Remember that we're having visitors tonight.* ○ *I know her face but I can't remember what she's called.* ○ *Can you remember when we bought the stereo?* يتذكّر

If you remember **to do** something, you don't forget to do it: *I remembered to buy the coffee.* ○ *Remember to turn the lights off before you leave.* If you remember **doing** something, you have a picture or memory in your mind of doing it: *Polly remembers seeing her keys on the table yesterday.*

2 [T] to give money, etc. to sb/sth: *to remember sb in your will* يقدّم نقوداً أو ما شابهها إلى ، يكافئ

PHRV **remember sb to sb** to pass greetings from one person to another: *Please remember me to your wife.* ➲ Look at the note at **remind**. يسلّم على ، يقدّم تحياته إلى

remembrance /rɪˈmembrəns/ *noun* [U] (*formal*) the act of remembering and showing respect for sb who is dead: *a service in remembrance of those killed in the war* إحياء ذكرى (الشهداء)

remind /rɪˈmaɪnd/ *verb* [T] **1** to say sth to help sb remember sth: *Can you remind me of your address?* ○ *He reminded the children to wash their hands.* ○ *The doctor reminded me that I should see her again in two months.* يُذكّر ، ينبّه إلى

2 remind sb of sb/sth to cause sb to remember sb/sth: *This song reminds me of Paris.* ○ *You remind me of your father.* يُذكّر

You **remember** something by yourself. If somebody or something **reminds** you of something he/she/it causes you to remember it: *Lucy remembered to say thank you after the party.* ○ *Mother reminded Lucy to say thank you after the party.*

▶ **reminder** *noun* [C] sth that makes you remember sth: *We received a reminder that we hadn't paid the electricity bill.* ○ *Eddie kept the ring as a reminder of happier days.* تذكِرة ؛ رسالة تذكرة

reminisce /ˌremɪˈnɪs/ *verb* [I] **reminisce (about sb/sth)** to talk about (pleasant) things that happened in the past يستعيد ذكريات الماضي

reminiscent /ˌremɪˈnɪsnt/ *adj* (not before a noun) that makes you remember sb/sth; like: *I think that painting is very reminiscent of one by Monet.* مذكّر بِ ، مشابه لِ

remnant /ˈremnənt/ *noun* [C] a piece of sth that remains after the rest has gone الفضلة ، المتبقّي

remorse /rɪˈmɔːs/ *noun* [U] a feeling of sadness because you have done sth wrong: *She was filled with remorse for what she had done.* ➲ Look at **guilt**. تأنيب الضمير ، ندم

▶ **remorseful** /-fl/ *adj* feeling remorse نادم ، معذّب الضمير

remorseless *adj* **1** showing no pity عديم الرحمة

2 not stopping or becoming less strong مصرّ ، عنيد

remorselessly *adv* بلا رحمة ؛ بِلا هوادة

remote /rɪˈməʊt/ *adj* **1** far away from where other people live: *a cottage in a remote area of Scotland* ناءٍ ، بعيد ؛ منعزل

2 far away in time: *the remote past/future* بعيد ، سحيق

3 not very great: *I haven't the remotest idea who could have done such a thing.* ○ *a remote possibility* ضئيل ، طفيف ، (ليست لديه) أدنى فكرة

4 not very friendly: *He seemed rather remote.* جافّ، فاترٍ، غير ودود

▸ **remotely** *adv* (used in negative sentences) to a very small degree; at all: *I'm not remotely interested in your problems.* قليلاً ؛ أبداً ؛ لا من قريب ولا من بعيد

remoteness *noun* [U] بُعد، نأي

re,mote con'trol *noun* [U,C] a system for controlling sth from a distance or a piece of equipment for controlling sth from a distance: *You can change channels on the television by remote control.* ○ *Pass me the remote control – I'll see what's on the other channel.* جهاز التحكّم من بعد

remove /rɪ'mu:v/ *verb* [T] (*formal*) **1 remove sb/sth (from sth)** to take sb/sth off or away: *Please remove your shoes before entering the temple.* ○ *This washing powder will remove most stains.* ○ *to remove doubts, fears, problems, etc.* ○ *I would like you to remove my name from your mailing list.* ❶ **Take off**, **out**, **etc.** is less formal. يزيل ، ينزع

2 remove sb (from sth) to make sb leave his/her job or position: *The person responsible for the error has been removed from his post.* ينحّي ، يعزل

▸ **removal** /-vl/ *noun* **1** [U] taking sb/sth away: *I demanded the removal of my name from the list.* إزالة ، حذف

2 [C,U] an act of moving from one house, etc. to another: *The company has agreed to pay all our removal expenses.* ○ *a removal van* الانتقال إلى مسكن جديد

removed *adj* (not before a noun) far or different from sth: *Hospitals today are far removed from what they were fifty years ago.* مختلف عن

remover *noun* [C,U] a substance that cleans off paint, stains, etc: *a stain remover* مزيل (البقع مثلاً)

renaissance /rɪ'neɪsns; *US* 'renəsɑ:ns/ *noun* **the Renaissance** [sing.] the period in the 14th, 15th and 16th centuries during which there was a renewed interest in art and literature, inspired by a fresh study of ancient Greek art, ideas, etc. عصر النهضة الأوربية

render /'rendə(r)/ *verb* [T] (*formal*) **1** to give help, etc. to sb: *to render sb a service* يقدّم

2 to cause sb/sth to be in a certain condition: *She was rendered speechless by the attack.* يجعل ، يصيّر

rendezvous /'rɒndɪvu:/ *noun* [C] (*pl.* **rendezvous** /-z/) **1 rendezvous (with sb)** a meeting that you have arranged with sb موعد ، لقاء

2 a place where people often meet ملتقى ، مكان اللقاء

renew /rɪ'nju:; *US* -'nu:/ *verb* [T] **1** to give new strength or energy: *After a break he set to work with renewed enthusiasm.* ينعش ، يجدّد الحيويّة

2 to start sth again: *renewed outbreaks of violence* ○ *to renew a friendship* يعاود ، يجدّد

3 to make sth valid for a further period of time: *to renew a contract* يجدّد (العقد مثلاً)

▸ **renewable** /-əbl/ *adj* **1** (used about sources of energy) that will always exist: *renewable resources such as wind and solar power* طاقة متوفّرة

2 that can be continued or renewed for another period of time: *The contract is for two years but it is renewable.* قابل للتجديد

renewal /-'nju:əl; *US* -'nu:əl/ *noun* [C,U] تجديد

renewables /rɪ'nju:əblz/ *noun* [pl.] types of energy that can be replaced naturally such as energy produced from wind or water أنواع الطاقة المتجددة

renounce /rɪ'naʊns/ *verb* [T] (*formal*) to say formally that you no longer have a right to sth or that you no longer want to be connected with sth: *to renounce a claim/title/privilege* ❶ The noun is **renunciation**. يعلن تخلّيه عن ، يتنازل عن ، يتبرّأ من

renovate /'renəveɪt/ *verb* [T] to repair an old building and put it back into good condition يرمّم ، يجدّد مبنى قديماً

▸ **renovation** /,renə'veɪʃn/ *noun*: *The house is in need of complete renovation.* تحسين ، ترميم

rent /rent/ *noun* [C,U] money that you pay regularly for the use of land, a house or a building: *a high/low rent* ○ *How much rent do you pay?* أجرة

▸ **rent** *verb* [T] **1** to pay money for the use of land, a building, a machine, etc: *Do you own or rent your television?* ○ *to rent a holiday cottage* ➲ Look at the note at **hire** (1). يستأجر

2 (*US*) = HIRE (1)

3 rent sth (out) (to sb) to allow sb to use land, a building, a machine, etc. for money: *We could rent out the small bedroom to a student.* ➲ Look at **hire** (3). يؤجّر

4 (*US*) = HIRE (3)

rental /'rentl/ *noun* [C,U] money that you pay when you rent a telephone, television, etc. أجرة جهاز التليفون أو التلفزيون الخ

renunciation /rɪ,nʌnsi'eɪʃn/ *noun* [U] (*formal*) saying that you no longer want sth or believe in sth ❶ The verb is **renounce**. التخلّي أو التنازل عن ؛ الزُّهد في

reorganize (*also* **reorganise**) /ri:'ɔ:gənaɪz/ *verb* [I,T] to organize sth again or in a new way so that it works better يغيّر أو يحسّن التنظيم

▸ **reorganization** (*also* **reorganisation**) /,ri:,ɔ:gənaɪ'zeɪʃn; *US* -nɪ'z-/ *noun* [C,U] إعادة أو تحسين التنظيم

rep /rep/ *abbrev* **1** (*informal*) (*also* **representative**) [C] a person whose job is to travel round a particular area and visit companies, etc., to sell the products of the firm for which he/she works: *a sales rep* ممثّل شركة متجوّل

2 (*US*) **Rep.** = REPRESENTATIVE (IN CONGRESS)

3 (*US*) **Rep.** = REPUBLICAN

repair /rɪ'peə(r)/ *verb* [T] to put sth old or damaged back into good condition: *How much will it cost to repair the car?* ○ (*figurative*) *It's difficult to see how their marriage can be repaired.* ➲ Look at **irreparable**. يصلح ، يرمّم

▸ **repair** *noun* [C,U] something that you do to mend sth that is damaged: *The bridge is under repair.* ○ *The swimming pool is closed for repairs to the roof.* ○ *to be damaged beyond repair* تصليح ، ترميم

IDM in good, bad, etc. repair in a good, bad, etc. condition (البناء) في حالة جيّدة أو سّيئة الخ...

repatriate /ˌriːˈpætrieɪt; *US* -ˈpeɪt-/ *verb* [T] to send sb back to his/her own country يعيد لاجئاً أو متّهماً إلى وطنه

▸ **repatriation** *noun* [C,U] أعادة لاجئ أو متّهم إلى وطنه

repay /rɪˈpeɪ/ *verb* [T] (*pt, pp* **repaid** /rɪˈpeɪd/)
1 repay sth (to sb) to pay back money that you owe to sb: *to repay a debt* يسدّد أو يفي ديْناً

2 repay sb (for sth) to give sth to sb in return for help, kindness, etc: *How can I ever repay you for all you have done for me?* يردّ له المعروف

▸ **repayable** /-əbl/ *adj* that you can or must pay back: *The loan is repayable over three years.* ممكن أو واجب دفعه (خلال مدة كذا)

repayment *noun* **1** [U] paying sth back: *the repayment of a loan* تسديد دَيْن

2 [C] money that you must pay back to sb/sth regularly: *monthly mortgage repayments* تسديد ديْن أو دفعاتٌ بالتقسيط

repeal /rɪˈpiːl/ *verb* [T] (in a parliament) to make a law no longer valid يلغي قانوناً ؛ يبطل

repeat /rɪˈpiːt/ *verb* **1** [I,T] to say, write or do sth more than once: *Don't repeat the same mistake again.* ○ *Could you repeat what you said? I didn't quite catch it.* ○ *'I really don't want to do it,' he repeated.* ○ *The essay is quite good, but you repeat yourself several times* (= you say the same thing more than once). ○ *History often seems to repeat itself.* يكرِّر ؛ يتكرّر

2 [T] to say or write sth that sb else has said or written or that you have learnt: *Repeat each sentence after me.* ○ *Please don't repeat what you've heard here.* ℹ The noun is **repetition**. يعيد ؛ يفشي سرّاً

▸ **repeat** *noun* [C] something that is done, shown, given, etc. again, especially a programme on television إعادة ، برنامج معاد

repeated *adj* (only *before* a noun) done or happening many times: *There have been repeated accidents on this stretch of road.* متكرّر

repeatedly *adv* many times; often تكراراً، مرّة بعد مرّة

repel /rɪˈpel/ *verb* [T] (repelling; repelled) **1** to send or push sb/sth back or away: *The army repelled the enemy attack.* يردّ أو يصدّ

2 to cause sb to feel strong dislike or disgust: *The dirt and smell repelled her.* ℹ The noun is **repulsion**. يُنفّر

▸ **repellent** /-ənt/ *adj* causing a strong feeling of dislike or disgust منفّر

repellent *noun* [C,U] a chemical substance that is used to keep insects, etc. away: *a mosquito repellent* (مستحضر) طارد (للحشرات)

repent /rɪˈpent/ *verb* [I,T] **repent (of sth)** (*formal*) to be very sorry about sth bad that you have done: *to repent of your sins* يتوب ، يندم

▸ **repentance** /-əns/ *noun* [U] توبة ؛ ندم

repentant /-ənt/ *adj* تائب ؛ نادم

repercussion /ˌriːpəˈkʌʃn/ *noun* [C, usually pl.] the unpleasant effect or result of sth you do: *His resignation will have serious repercussions.* عاقبة (وخيمة) ، ردّ فعل أو صدى سيّء

repertoire /ˈrepətwɑː(r)/ *noun* [C] all the plays or music that an actor or a musician knows and can perform مجموعة الألحان أو الأدوار التي يتقنها فنّان

repetition /ˌrepəˈtɪʃn/ *noun* [C,U] doing sth again; sth that you do or that happens again: *We don't want any repetition of what happened on Friday.* ○ *We're trying to avoid a repetition of what happened on Friday.* ℹ The verb is **repeat**. تكرار ، إعادة

▸ **repetitive** /rɪˈpetətɪv/ (*also* **repetitious** /ˌrepɪˈtɪʃəs/) *adj* not interesting because the same thing is repeated many times: *repetitive factory work* متكرّر رتيب ، مملّ لكثرة التكرار فيه

replace /rɪˈpleɪs/ *verb* [T] **1** to take the place of sb/sth: *Teachers will never be replaced by computers in the classroom.* يستبدل ، يحلّ محلّه

2 replace sb/sth (with sb/sth) to exchange sb/sth for sb/sth that is better or newer: *We will replace any goods that are damaged.* يَستبدل

3 to put sth back in the right place: *Please replace the books on the shelves when you have finished with them.* ℹ **Put back** is more common and less formal. يعيد إلى مكانه ، يرجع

▸ **replaceable** /-əbl/ *adj* that can be replaced ℹ The opposite is **irreplaceable**. معوَّض ، يمكن تعويضه أو استبداله

replacement *noun* **1** [U] exchanging sb/sth for sb/sth that is better or newer: *The carpets are in need of replacement.* إبدال بشيء أفضل

2 [C] a person or thing that will take the place of sb/sth: *Mary is leaving next month so we must advertise for a replacement for her.* بديل

replay /ˌriːˈpleɪ/ *verb* [T] **1** to play a sports match, etc. again يلعب مباراة رياضيّة من جديد

2 to play again sth that you have recorded يشاهد أو يستمع إلى ما سجّله سابقاً

▸ **replay** /ˈriːpleɪ/ *noun* [C] **1** a sports match that is played again مباراة معادة

2 something on the television, on a film or a cassette tape that you watch or listen to again: *Now let's see an action replay of that tremendous goal!* استماع أو مشاهدة ثانية لشيء سجّل سابقاً

replica /ˈreplɪkə/ *noun* [C] an exact copy of sth نسخة طبق الأصل

reply /rɪˈplaɪ/ *verb* [I,T] (*pres part* **replying**; *3rd pers sing pres* **replies**; *pt, pp* **replied**) to give an answer: *I wrote to Sue but she hasn't replied.* ○ *'Yes, I will,' she replied.* ○ *I asked Matthew how he had got on at the interview but he replied that it was none of my business.* ○ *to reply to a question* ➲ Look at the note at **answer**. يجيب ، يردّ

▸ **reply** *noun* [C,U] (*pl.* **replies**) (an) answer: *Adrian nodded in reply to my question.* ○ *How many replies did you get to your advertisement?* جواب ، إجابة

report[1] /rɪˈpɔːt/ *verb* **1** [I,T] **report (on sb/sth) (to sb/sth)**; **report sth (to sb)** to say or write what you have seen, heard, done, etc: *All accidents must be reported to the police.* ○ *Several people reported having seen the boy.* ○ *Several* *people reported that they had seen the boy.* يبلِّغ ، يُخبر

2 [I,T] (in a newspaper or on the television or radio) to write or speak about sth that has happened: *Kate reported on the events in China for the BBC.* ○ *The strike was not reported in the newspapers.* ينقل خبراً صحفياً ، يراسل صحيفة

3 [T] **report sb (to sb) (for sth)** to tell a person in authority about sth wrong that sb has done: *She was reported to the head teacher for smoking.* يبلِّغ عن

4 [I] **report (to sb/sth) for sth** to tell sb that you have arrived: *On your arrival, please report to the reception desk.* يعلم بالوصول ؛ يحضر بنفسه

▸ **reporter** *noun* [C] a person who writes about the news in a newspaper or speaks about it on the television or radio ➲ Look at **journalist**. صحفيّ ، مراسل صحفي

report² /rɪˈpɔːt/ *noun* [C] **1** a written or spoken description of what you have seen, heard, done, studied, etc: *a report of a bomb attack in Northern Ireland* ○ *newspaper reports* ○ *an annual report on the company's finances* ○ *a first-hand report* (= from the person who saw what happened) تقرير

2 a written statement about the work of a school pupil: *a school report* تقرير مدرسي

reˌported ˈspeech *noun* [U] = INDIRECT SPEECH

represent /ˌreprɪˈzent/ *verb* [T] **1** to be a picture, sign, example, etc. of sb/sth: *The yellow lines on the map represent minor roads.* ○ *an abstract painting that represents pain* ○ *Each phonetic symbol represents one sound.* ○ *Some people think that having to carry an identity card represents a loss of freedom.* يُمثِّل

2 to describe sb/sth in a particular way: *In the book Susan is represented as a very ordinary person.* يصوِّر ، يمثِّل

3 to be equal to: *A pay rise of 3% represents a drop in income if you take inflation into account.* يساوي ، يعادل

4 to act or speak in the place of sb else; to be the representative of a group or country: *You will need a lawyer to represent you in court.* ○ *The British Ambassador represented the Prime Minister at the funeral.* ينوب عن ، يمثِّل

▸ **representation** /ˌreprɪzenˈteɪʃn/ *noun* **1** [U] representing or being represented: *Minority groups are demanding more representation in Parliament.* ➲ Look at **proportional representation**. تمثيل (برلماني)

2 [C] *(formal)* a picture, sign, etc. of sb/sth صورة (مثلاً) ، رمز ؛ مثال عن

representative /ˌreprɪˈzentətɪv/ *adj* **representative (of sb/sth)** typical of a larger group to which it belongs: *Tonight's audience is not representative of national opinion.* ❶ The opposite is **unrepresentative**. ممثِّل لـ ، نموذجيّ

▸ **representative** *noun* [C] **1** a person who has been chosen to act or speak for sb else or for a group ممثِّل عن ، نائب ، مندوب

2 *(formal)* = REP

repress /rɪˈpres/ *verb* [T] **1** to control an emotion or to try to prevent it from being shown or felt يكبح ، يكبت

2 to prevent an action or a protest يقمع

▸ **repressed** *adj* **1** (used about an emotion) that you do not show (شعور) مكبوت

2 (used about a person) not showing natural, especially sexual, feelings مكبوت جنسياً

repression /rɪˈpreʃn/ *noun*: *Religion is still alive in Eastern Europe after forty years of repression.* قمع ، كبح

repressive /rɪˈpresɪv/ *adj* allowing little freedom: *a repressive government* قمعي ، تعسُّفي

reprieve /rɪˈpriːv/ *verb* [T] to stop or delay the punishment of a prisoner who has been condemned to death يعفو عن محكوم بالإعدام أو يُرجئ تنفيذ الحكم

▸ **reprieve** *noun*: *to grant sb a last-minute reprieve* العفو عن المحكوم؛ إرجاء تنفيذ الإعدام

reprimand /ˈreprɪmɑːnd; *US* -mænd/ *verb* [T] **reprimand sb (for sth)** to tell sb officially that he/she has done sth wrong يوبِّخ (رسميًا)

▸ **reprimand** *noun*: *a severe reprimand* توبيخ شديد اللهجة

reprisal /rɪˈpraɪzl/ *noun* [C,U] punishment, especially by military force, for harm that one group of people does to another: *The army carried out reprisals on the village that had sheltered the rebels.* ○ *Civilian targets were bombed in reprisal.* انتقام ، أخذ بالثأر

reproach /rɪˈprəʊtʃ/ *verb* [T] **reproach sb (for/with sth)** to tell sb that he/she has done sth wrong (or not done sth that he/she ought to have done); to blame: *You've nothing to reproach yourself for. It wasn't your fault.* يلوم ؛ يعاتب ؛ يؤنِّب

▸ **reproach** *noun* [C,U] blame or criticism; a comment, etc. that shows that you do not approve of sth: *His behaviour is beyond reproach* (= cannot be criticized). ○ *Alison felt his reproaches were unjustified.* لوم أو ملامة ؛ عتاب ؛ تأنيب

reproachful /-fl/ *adj*: *a reproachful look* تأنيبيّ ؛ مُعاتِب

reproachfully /-fəli/ *adv* بِلَوم ؛ بعتاب

reproduce /ˌriːprəˈdjuːs/ /-ˈduːs/ *verb* **1** [T] to produce a copy of sth: *It is very hard to reproduce a natural environment in the laboratory.* يستخرج نسخة عن شيء ، يخلق ثانية

2 [I,T] (used about people, animals and plants) to produce young: *Fish reproduce by laying eggs.* يتكاثر ، يتوالد

▸ **reproduction** /ˌriːprəˈdʌkʃn/ *noun* **1** [U] the act or process of reproducing or being reproduced: *Digital recording gives excellent sound reproduction.* ○ *sexual reproduction* تسجيل (صوت مثلاً) ؛ توالد أو تناسل

2 [C] a copy of a painting, etc: *That painting is a reproduction, not an original.* نسخة (وليست الاصل)

reproductive /ˌriːprəˈdʌktɪv/ *adj* connected with the production of young animals, plants, etc: *the male reproductive organs* تناسلي

reproof /rɪˈpruːf/ *noun* [C,U] *(formal)* something that you say to tell sb that you do not approve of what he/she has done تأنيب ؛ عتاب

reptile /ˈreptaɪl; *US* -tl/ *noun* [C] an animal, such as a snake or a crocodile, that has a scaly skin, is cold-blooded and lays eggs حيوان من الزواحف

republic /rɪˈpʌblɪk/ *noun* [C] a country that has an elected government and an elected leader (president): *the Republic of Ireland* جمهوريّة

republican /rɪˈpʌblɪkən/ *adj* connected with or supporting a republic جمهوري

▸ **republican** *noun* [C] **1** a person who supports the system of republican government جمهوريّ ، مؤيّد للنظام الجمهوريّ

2 Republican a member of the Republican Party (one of the two main political parties in the US) ℹ The other main party is the Democratic Party, whose members are called **Democrats.** عضو في الحزب الجمهوريّ (في الولايات المتحدة)

repudiate /rɪˈpjuːdieɪt/ *verb* [T] (*formal*) to say that you will not accept sth يرفض ؛ يتبرأ من

repulsion /rɪˈpʌlʃn/ *noun* [U] a strong feeling of dislike; disgust نفور ، اشمئزاز

repulsive /rɪˈpʌlsɪv/ *adj* that causes a strong feeling of dislike; disgusting منفِّر، كريه : مثير للاشمئزاز

reputable /ˈrepjətəbl/ *adj* that is known to be good: *Make sure that your boiler is fitted by a reputable engineer.* ➲ Look at **disreputable.** حسن السمعة

reputation /ˌrepjuˈteɪʃn/ *noun* [C] **reputation (for sth)** the opinion that people in general have about what sb/sth is like: *to have a good/bad reputation* ○ *The restaurant has a reputation for serving some of the finest food in the country.* ○ *an international reputation* ○ *She began to make her reputation as a novelist in the 1960s.* سمعة ، صيت ، شهرة

reputed /rɪˈpjutɪd/ *adj* generally said to be sth, although it is not certain: *He's reputed to earn more than £100 000 a year.* مزعوم ، مفروض ، معتبر

▸ **reputedly** *adv* على ما يقال

request /rɪˈkwest/ *noun* [C] **request (for sth/that...)** an act of asking for sth: *a request for help* ○ *to make an official request* ○ *to grant/turn down a request* طلب ، التماس

IDM **at sb's request/at the request of sb** because sb asked for it: *Aid was sent to the earthquake victims at the request of the government.* بناءً على طلب...

on request if you ask: *Single rooms are available on request.* عند الطلب

▸ **request** *verb* [T] **request sth (from/of sb)** (*formal*) to ask for sth: *Passengers are requested not to smoke on this bus.* ○ *to request a loan from the bank* ℹ **Request** is more formal than **ask.** يطلب من ؛ يرجو

require /rɪˈkwaɪə(r)/ *verb* [T] **1** to need: *Do you require any assistance?* ○ *a situation that requires tact and diplomacy* ℹ **Require** is more formal than **need.** يحتاج إلى ، يتطلّب

2 (often passive) to demand or order sth: *Passengers are required by law to wear seat belts.* يأمر، يكلّف

▸ **requirement** *noun* [C] something that you need or that is demanded: *They grow enough vegetables for their own requirements.* ○ *university entrance requirements* متطلّب، احتياج

rescue /ˈreskjuː/ *verb* [T] **rescue sb/sth (from sb/sth)** to save sb/sth from a situation that is dangerous or unpleasant: *to rescue sb from drowning* ○ *You rescued me from an embarrassing situation.* ينقذ ، يخلّص

▸ **rescue** *noun* [C,U] an act of rescuing or the state of being rescued: *Ten fishermen were saved in a daring sea rescue off the Welsh coast.* عملية إنقاذ؛ إنقاذ

IDM **come/go to the/sb's rescue** to try to help or rescue sb: *She was attacked in the street and no one came to her rescue.* يهرع للمساعدة ، يحاول إنقاذه

rescuer *noun* [C] a person who rescues sb/sth المنقِذ

research /rɪˈsɜːtʃ; *US* ˈriːsɜːtʃ/ *noun* [U] (*also* **researches** [plural]) **research (into/on sth)** a detailed and careful study of sth to find out more information about it: *Bob is doing research into the practical applications of solar power.* ○ *scientific, medical, historical, etc. research* ○ *Market research has shown that many people now prefer coffee to tea.* بحث (علميّ)

▸ **research** /rɪˈsɜːtʃ/ *verb* [I,T] to study sth carefully and in detail: *Scientists are still researching the possible causes of childhood cancer in the area.* يقوم بأبحاث ، يدرس

researcher *noun* [C] a person who carries out research باحث

resemble /rɪˈzembl/ *verb* [T] to be or look like sb/sth else: *Laura resembles her brother.* يشبِه، يماثل

▸ **resemblance** /rɪˈzembləns/ *noun* [C,U] **resemblance (between A and B)**: *a family resemblance* ○ *The film bore no resemblance to the novel.* شِبه ، تشابه

resent /rɪˈzent/ *verb* [T] to feel angry about sth because you think it is unfair: *Louise bitterly resented being treated differently from the men.* يغتاظ ، يستاء ، يمتعض

▸ **resentful** /-fl/ *adj*: *William felt very resentful at being unfairly criticized.* ممتعض

resentment *noun* [sing.]: *Do you feel any resentment towards her new husband?* امتعاض ، غيظ

reservation /ˌrezəˈveɪʃn/ *noun* **1** [C] a seat, table, room, etc. that you have booked: *I made a reservation for a table for two in the name of Morgan.* حَجز

2 [C,U] a feeling of doubt about sth (such as a plan or an idea): *I would recommend Irene for the job without reservation.* ○ *I don't share your reservations about the flat – I think it's fine.* تحفُّظ

reserve¹ /rɪˈzɜːv/ *verb* [T] **reserve sth (for sb/sth) 1** to keep sth for a special reason or to use at a later time: *The car park is reserved for hotel patrons only.* يخصّص ؛ يحتفظ بشيء لغرض خاص

2 to book a seat, table, room, etc: *to reserve theatre tickets* يحجز

reserve² /rɪˈzɜːv/ *noun* **1** [C, usually pl.] something that you keep for a special reason or to use at a later date: *The US has huge oil reserves.* احتياطيّ (النفط)

2 [C] (in sport) a person who will play in a game if one of the usual members of the team cannot play لاعب احتياطي

3 [C] an area of land where the plants, animals, etc. are protected by law: *a nature reserve* أرض يحمي القانون نباتاتها وحيواناتها

4 [U] the quality of being shy or keeping your feelings hidden: *It took a long time to break down her reserve and get her to relax.* تحفُّظ

IDM **in reserve** that you keep and do not use unless you need to: *Keep some money in reserve for emergencies.* شيء مدّخر ، (مال) احتياطيّ

reserved /rɪˈzɜːvd/ *adj* shy and keeping your feelings hidden: *Fred is very reserved until you get to know him well.* متحفّظ

reservoir /ˈrezəvwɑː(r)/ *noun* [C] a large lake where water to be used in a town or city is stored خزّان ماء

reside /rɪˈzaɪd/ *verb* [I] (*formal*) **reside (in/at...)** to have your home in or at يقيم ، يقطن

residence /ˈrezɪdəns/ *noun* **1** [C] (*formal*) the place where sb (famous or important) lives: *The Prime Minister's official residence is 10 Downing Street.* مقرّ ، مسكن

2 [U] the state of having your home in a particular place: *The family applied to take up permanent residence in the United States.* ○ *a hall of residence for college students* إقامة ؛ سُكنى

⚷ **resident** /ˈrezɪdənt/ *noun* [C] **1** a person who lives in a place: *Local residents have complained of the smell from the factory.* ساكن ، مقيم

2 a person who is staying in a hotel: *The hotel bar is open to non-residents.* نزيل

▸ **resident** *adj* living in a place: *If you are resident abroad, you lose your right to vote.* مقيم

residential /ˌrezɪˈdenʃl/ *adj* **1** (used about a place or an area) that has houses rather than offices, large shops or factories: *residential suburbs* سكنيّ

2 where you live or stay: *This home provides residential care for the elderly.* ○ *a residential course* داخليّ ، سكنيّ

residue /ˈrezɪdjuː; *US* -duː/ *noun* [C, usually sing.] what remains of sth after the main part is taken or used البقيّة ، الفضلة ، المتخلّف

resign /rɪˈzaɪn/ *verb* **1** [I,T] **resign (from sth)** to leave your job or position: *She's threatening to resign if she doesn't get a pay increase.* ○ *He's resigned as chairman of the committee.* ○ *He resigned the chairmanship.* يستقيل

2 [T] **resign yourself to sth/doing sth** to accept sth that is unpleasant but that cannot be changed: *Larry resigned himself to the fact that she was not coming back to him.* يرضخ للأمر الواقع

▸ **resigned** *adj* accepting sth that is unpleasant but that cannot be changed: *a resigned sigh* مستسلم للأمر الواقع

IDM **be, etc. resigned to sth/doing sth** to accept sth that is unpleasant but that cannot be changed: *Ben was resigned to the fact that he would never be a rock star.* متقبّل(للحقيقة)

resignation /ˌrezɪɡˈneɪʃn/ *noun* **1** [C,U] **resignation (from sth)** a letter or statement that says you want to leave your job or position: *to hand in your resignation* ○ *He has threatened resignation many times in the past.* ○ *a letter of resignation* استقالة

2 [U] the state of accepting sth unpleasant that you cannot change استسلام للأمر الواقع

resilient /rɪˈzɪliənt/ *adj* strong enough to recover quickly from damage, illness, a shock, change, etc. مَرِن البنية: سريع في استعادة صحّته أو حيويّته

▸ **resilience** /-əns/ *noun* [U] مرونة

⚷ **resist** /rɪˈzɪst/ *verb* **1** [I,T] to try to stop sth happening or to stop sb from doing sth; to fight against sb/sth: *The trade unions are resisting the introduction of new technology.* ○ *If the enemy attacks, we shall not resist.* ○ *to resist arrest* يقاوم ، يعارض

2 [T] to stop yourself from having or doing sth that you want to have or do: *The cakes looked so delicious that I couldn't resist them.* ○ *I couldn't resist opening my present.* يقاوم

⚷ **resistance** /rɪˈzɪstəns/ *noun* [U] **1 resistance (to sb/sth)** trying to stop sth from happening or to stop sb from doing sth; fighting against sb/sth: *The government troops overcame the resistance of the rebel army.* ○ *There is strong resistance to the plan for a new motorway in the area.* مقاومة ؛ معارضة

2 resistance (to sth) the power in a person's body not to be affected by disease: *People with AIDS have very little resistance to infection.* مقاومة (للمرض)

resistant /rɪˈzɪstənt/ *adj* **resistant (to sth)** **1** not wanting sth and trying to prevent it happening: *resistant to change* مقاوِم ، معارض

2 not harmed by sth: *This watch is water-resistant.* مضادّ لـ ، ضدّ (الماء)

resolute /ˈrezəluːt/ *adj* (used about a person or his/her actions) firm and determined; not willing to change because other people want you to: *a resolute refusal to make any concessions* ❶ **Determined** is more common. حازم ؛ متعنّت

▸ **resolutely** *adv*: *They are resolutely opposed to any change.* بشدّة، بصرامة، بتعنُّت

resolution /ˌrezəˈluːʃn/ *noun* **1** [U] the quality of being firm and determined حزم ، تصميم

2 [C] a firm decision to do or not to do sth: *Rose made a New Year's resolution to give up smoking.* قرار حازم

3 [C] a formal decision that is taken after a vote by a group of people: *The UN resolution condemned the invasion.* قرار

4 solving or settling a problem, dispute, etc. قرار حاسِم

⚷ **resolve** /rɪˈzɒlv/ *verb* (*formal*) **1** [T] to find a solution to a problem: *Most of the difficulties have been resolved.* يحلّ (المشكلة)

2 [I,T] to decide sth and be determined not to change your mind: *Ray resolved never to let the same thing happen again.* يعقد العزم ، يصمّم

resort¹ /rɪˈzɔːt/ *verb* [I] **resort to sth** to do or use sth bad or unpleasant because you feel you have no choice: *People who owe huge amounts of money have had to resort to selling their houses.* يلجأ إلى (السرقة)

resort² /rɪˈzɔːt/ *noun*
IDM in the last resort; (as) a last resort → LAST¹

resort³ /rɪˈzɔːt/ *noun* [C] a place where a lot of people go on holiday: *a seaside resort, such as Blackpool or Brighton* مصيَف ؛ منتجَع

resounding /rɪˈzaʊndɪŋ/ *adj* (only *before* a noun) **1** very loud: *resounding cheers* مدوٍ، مجلجِل
2 (used about a success, etc.) very great: *a resounding victory* باهر ، (نصر) مبين

resource /rɪˈsɔːs; -ˈzɔːs/ /ˈriːsɔːrs/ *noun* [C, usually pl.] something that a person, country, etc. has or can use: *Russia is rich in natural resources such as oil and minerals.* ○ *The video is an excellent resource for teachers.* مورد ، ثروة
▸ **resourceful** /-fl/ *adj* good at finding ways of doing things واسع التدبير ، ذو مواهب عمليّة

respect¹ /rɪˈspekt/ *noun* **1** [U] **respect (for sb/ sth)** the feeling that you have when you admire or have a very high opinion of sb/sth: *They stood in silence for one minute as a mark of respect for the dead.* ○ *to win/lose sb's respect* ➲ Look at **self-respect**. احترام ، تقدير
2 [U] **respect (for sb/sth)** the quality of being polite to sb: *We should all treat older people with more respect.* ❶ The opposite is **disrespect**. احترام ، توقير
3 [U] **respect (for sb/sth)** care for or attention to sb/sth: *The secret police show little respect for human rights.* ○ *Electricity is dangerous and should be treated with respect.* مراعاة ؛ حرص ، حيطة
4 [C] a detail or point: *In what respects do you think things have changed in the last ten years?* ○ *Her performance was brilliant in every respect.* ناحية ، وجه
IDM with respect to sth (*formal*) about or concerning: *I am writing with respect to your recent enquiry.* بشأن ؛ فيما يتعلّق بِـ
pay your respects → PAY²

respect² /rɪˈspekt/ *verb* [T] **1 respect sb/sth (for sth)** to admire or have a high opinion of sb/ sth: *I respect him for his honesty.* يقدّر ، يحترم
2 to show care for or pay attention to sb/sth: *We should respect other people's cultures and values.* ○ *to respect sb's wishes* (= do what they want) يراعي ؛ يحترم

respectable /rɪˈspektəbl/ *adj* **1** considered by society to be good, proper or correct: *a respectable middle-class family* ○ *Wear something respectable to the party!* محترم
2 quite good or large: *a respectable salary* (مبلغ) محترم ؛ (عدد) لا يستهان به

▸ **respectability** /rɪˌspektəˈbɪləti/ *noun* [U] جدارة بالاحترام ، قيمة

respectful /rɪˈspektfl/ *adj* **respectful (to/ towards sb)** showing respect¹ (2) or politeness towards sb/sth: *The crowd listened in respectful silence.* ❶ The opposite is **disrespectful**. خاشع ، وقور ، مؤدّب
▸ **respectfully** /-fəli/ *adv* بتقدير وإعجاب

respective /rɪˈspektɪv/ *adj* (only *before* a noun) belonging separately to each of the people who have been mentioned: *After lunch we all got on with our respective jobs.* خاص بكلّ فرد
▸ **respectively** *adv* in the same order that sb/ sth was mentioned: *German and Italian courses are held in Munich and Rome respectively.* على التوالي ، حسب ترتيب الذِكر

respiration /ˌrespəˈreɪʃn/ *noun* [U] (*formal*) the act of breathing تنفُّس

respite /ˈrespaɪt/ *noun* [sing., U] **respite (from sth)** a short period of rest from sth that is difficult or unpleasant: *There was a brief respite from the fighting.* استراحة قصيرة ، متنفَّس ، مهلة

respond /rɪˈspɒnd/ *verb* [I] **1 respond (to sb/ sth) (with/by sth)** (*formal*) to say or do sth as an answer or reaction to sth: *I wrote to them last week but they haven't responded.* ○ *He responded to my question with a nod.* ○ *The government has responded to criticism by giving an extra £5 million to the National Health Service.* ❶ **Respond** is more formal than **answer** or **reply**. يجيب ، يردّ
2 respond (to sb/sth) to have or show a good or quick reaction to sb/sth: *The patient did not respond well to the new treatment.* يستجيب

response /rɪˈspɒns/ *noun* [C,U] **response (to sb/sth)** an answer or reaction to sb/sth: *I've sent out 20 letters of enquiry but I've had no responses yet.* ○ *The government acted in response to economic pressure.* ○ *He knocked on the door but there was no response.* ○ *Meryl Streep's new film has received a very favourable response.* جواب ؛ ردّ فعل ؛ تجاوب

responsibility /rɪˌspɒnsəˈbɪləti/ *noun* (*pl.* **responsibilities**) **1** [U] **responsibility (for sb/ sth)** the state of being responsible; having to take decisions about sth so that you are blamed if sth goes wrong: *The new job means taking on more responsibility.* ○ *I refuse to take responsibility if anything goes wrong.* ○ *The IRA has admitted responsibility for planting the bomb.* ○ *a minister with special responsibility for women's affairs* مسؤوليّة
2 [U] the quality of being sensible: *I wish that you would show a little more responsibility.* نُضوج ، وعي ، شعور بالمسؤوليّة
3 [C] a job or duty that you must do: *It is John's responsibility to make sure the orders are sent out on time.* ○ *I feel that I have a responsibility to help them – after all, they did help me.* ○ *the responsibilities of parenthood* ○ *The children are my responsibility* (= I am responsible for them). مهمّة ، واجب

responsible /rɪˈspɒnsəbl/ *adj* **1** (not before a

a b c d e f g h i j k l m n o p q r s t u v w x y z

noun) **responsible (for sb/sth)**; **responsible (for doing sth)** having the job or duty of doing or looking after sb/sth (so that you are blamed if sth goes wrong): *The school is responsible for the safety of the children between 9 am and 3 pm.* ○ *The manager is responsible for making sure the shop is run properly.* مسؤول عن

2 (not before a noun) **responsible (for sth)** being the cause of or to blame for sth: *Who was responsible for the accident?* مسؤول ، مؤاخَذ

3 (not before a noun) **responsible (to sb/sth)** having to report to sb/sth with authority or in a higher position about what you have been doing: *Members of Parliament are responsible to the electors.* مسؤول أمام (الناخبين)

4 (used about a person) that you can trust to behave well and sensibly: *All children must be accompanied by a responsible adult.* ❶ The opposite is **irresponsible**. موثوق به ، ناضج ، راشد

5 (used about a job) that is important and that should be done by a person who can be trusted ذو مسؤوليّة

▸ **responsibly** /-əbli/ *adv* in a responsible (4) way: *Please behave responsibly while I am out.* بتعقُّل ، بنضوج ، كشخص مسؤول

responsive /rɪˈspɒnsɪv/ *adj* paying attention to sb/sth and reacting in a suitable or positive way: *By being responsive to changes in the market, the company has had great success.* مستجيب

⚷ **rest¹** /rest/ *verb* **1** [I] to relax, sleep or do nothing after a period of activity or because of illness: *We've been walking for hours. Let's rest here for a while.* ○ *The nurse said we couldn't visit him because he was resting.* يستريح

2 [T] to allow sb/sth to rest (1): *Your knee will get better as you rest it as much as you can.* يريح

3 [I,T] **rest (sth) on/against sth** to place sth in a position where it is supported by sth else; to be in such a position: *She rested her head on his shoulder and went to sleep.* يسند

4 [I] not be talked about any longer: *He didn't want to answer any more questions so I let the subject rest.* يتوقّف : يهدأ ، يرقد

PHRV **rest on sb/sth** to depend or be based on sth: *The whole theory rests on a very simple idea.* يستند إلى ، يعتمد على

⚷ **rest²** /rest/ *noun* [C,U] a period or the action of relaxing, sleeping or doing nothing: *I can't walk any further! I need a rest.* ○ *Try not to worry now. Get some rest and think about it again tomorrow.* ○ *Yes, OK, you're right and I'm wrong. Now give it a rest!* (= Stop talking about it) راحة ، استراحة

IDM **at rest** not moving: *Do not open the door until the vehicle is at rest.* ساكن ، غير متحرّك

come to rest to stop moving: *The car crashed through a wall and came to rest in a field.* يتوقّف عن الحركة

put/set your/sb's mind at rest → MIND¹

▸ **restful** /-fl/ *adj* giving a relaxed, peaceful feeling: *I find this piece of music very restful.* مريح للأعصاب

⚷ **rest³** *noun* **the rest (of sth) 1** [sing.] the part that is left: *We had lunch and spent the rest of the day on the beach.* ○ *If you don't want the rest, I'll eat it.* ○ *She takes no interest in what happens in the rest of the world.* بقيّة ، سائر

2 [plural] the ones that are left; the others: *One of the questions was difficult but the rest were quite easy.* ○ *They were the first people to arrive. The rest came later.* ○ *The rest of our bags are still in the car.* البقيّة ، الآخرون

⚷ **restaurant** /ˈrestrɒnt; *US* -tərɑːnt/ *noun* [C] a place where you can buy and eat a meal: *a Chinese restaurant* ○ *We went out to a restaurant to celebrate my birthday.* ○ *She's taken a job as a waitress in a local restaurant.* ➲ Look at **cafe** and **take-away**. مطعم

restless /ˈrestləs/ *adj* **1** unable to relax or be still because you are bored, nervous or impatient: *The children always get restless on long journeys.* ضَجِر ، متملّمِل : قلق

2 (of a period of time) without sleep or rest: *a restless night* أرق : دون راحة

▸ **restlessly** *adv* باضطراب ، بِقلق شديد

restoration /ˌrestəˈreɪʃn/ *noun* **1** [C,U] the act of returning sth to its original condition: *the restoration of the cathedral* ○ *The house is advertised as 'in need of restoration'.* إصلاح ، ترميم

2 [C,U] the act of bringing sth back into use or existence: *a gradual restoration of democracy to the country* إعادة

3 [U] the act of returning sth to its original owner: *the restoration of territory captured during the war* إعادة

⚷ **restore** /rɪˈstɔː(r)/ *verb* [T] **restore sb/sth (to sb/sth) 1** (*formal*) to give sth that was lost or stolen back to sb يعيد ، يرجع

2 to put sb/sth back into a previous condition or position: *In the recent elections, the former president was restored to power.* يعيد (إلى الحكم)

3 to bring sth back into existence or use: *Following the riots, law and order has been restored.* ○ *Winning their last two games has restored the team's confidence.* يعيد

4 to put sth (a building, a painting, a piece of furniture, etc.) back into a condition that is as close as possible to its original condition: *The castle has been restored and is open to the public.* يصلح ، يرمّم

restrain /rɪˈstreɪn/ *verb* [T] **restrain sb/sth (from sth/from doing sth)** to keep sb or sth under control; to prevent sb or sth from doing sth: *Can't you restrain your dog?* ○ *I had to restrain myself from saying something rude.* يقيّد ، يكبَح ، يضبط

▸ **restrained** *adj* not showing strong feelings; calm متحفّظ؛ ضابط لأعصابه

restraint /rɪˈstreɪnt/ *noun* **1** [U] the quality of behaving in a calm or moderate way: *It took a lot of restraint on my part not to hit him.* ضبط النَّفس ، كبح

2 [C] **restraint (on sb/sth)** a limit or control on sb/sth: *Are there any restraints on what the newspapers are allowed to publish?* ○ *a head*

restraint (= a part of a car seat that stops your head being hurt in an accident)
حدّ ، قيْد : مسند للرأس في السيّارة

restrict /rɪ'strɪkt/ *verb* [T] **1** to limit the number, amount, size, freedom, etc. of sb/sth: *I'm trying to restrict myself to two cups of coffee a day.* ○ *Having small children tends to restrict your freedom.* ○ *There is a plan to restrict the use of cars in the city centre.* يقيّد ، يحصر ، يحدّد

2 to make sb/yourself concentrate on a particular thing or things and not on others: *I suggest that you restrict yourself to dealing with the most urgent matters.* يقصر على

▶ **restricted** *adj* controlled or limited in some way: *Entry to the club is restricted to members only.* ○ *There is only restricted parking available.* مقصور على ؛ محدود

restriction /rɪ'strɪkʃn/ *noun* **restriction (on sth) 1** [U] the act of limiting the freedom of sb/sth: *This ticket permits you to travel anywhere, without restriction.* تقييد ، تحديد

2 [C] something (sometimes a rule or law) that limits the number, amount, size, freedom, etc. of sb/sth: *parking restrictions in the city centre* ○ *The government has imposed restrictions on the number of immigrants permitted to settle in this country.* قيْد

restrictive /rɪ'strɪktɪv/ *adj* limiting; preventing people from doing what they want مقيّد : حَصريّ

'rest room *noun* [C] (*US*) a public toilet in a hotel, shop, restaurant, etc. ➲ Look at the note at **toilet**. دورة مياه

result /rɪ'zʌlt/ *noun* **1** [C,U] **result (of sth)** something that happens because of sth else; the final situation at the end of a series of actions: *The result of our argument was that we never spoke to each other again.* ○ *The traffic was very heavy and as a result I arrived late.* ○ *This wasn't really the result that I was expecting.* نتيجة

2 [C,U] a good effect of an action: *He has tried very hard to find a job, but with no result.* ○ *The treatment is beginning to show results.*
فائدة ، ثمرة

3 [C] the score or final position at the end of a game, competition or election: *Do you know today's football results?* ○ *The results of this week's competition will be published next week.* ○ *The result of the by-election was a win for the Liberal Democrats.* نتيجة

4 [C] the mark or grade given for an examination or test: *exam results* نتيجة

5 [C] something that is discovered by a medical test: *I'm still waiting for the result of my X-ray.*
نتيجة

▶ **result** /rɪ'zʌlt/ *verb* [I] **result (from sth)** to happen or exist because of sth: *Ninety per cent of the deaths resulted from injuries to the head.*
ينتج أو ينجم عن

PHR V **result in sth** to cause sth to happen or exist; to produce as an effect: *There has been an accident on the motorway, resulting in long delays.* يؤدّي إلى ، يسفر عن

resume /rɪ'zuːm/ *verb* [I,T] to begin again or continue after a pause or interruption: *Normal service will resume as soon as possible. We apologize for the delay.* ○ *After the birth of the baby, she resumed her career.* يعاود ، يستأنف

résumé /'rezjumeɪ/ *noun* [C] (*US*) = CURRICULUM VITAE

resumption /rɪ'zʌmpʃn/ *noun* [sing., U] (*formal*) the act of beginning again or continuing after a pause or interruption: *a resumption of diplomatic relations between the two countries*
استئناف ، معاودة

resurrect /ˌrezə'rekt/ *verb* [T] to bring sth that has not been used or has not existed for a long time back into use or existence: *From time to time they resurrect old black and white programmes and show them again on television.*
يحيي ، يبعث من جديد

▶ **resurrection** /ˌrezə'rekʃn/ *noun* **1** [U] the act of resurrecting sth: *There will be no resurrection of previous policies.* إحياء

2 [sing.] (in the Christian and Muslim religions) the return of all dead people to life at the end of the world البعث ، النُّشور

3 the Resurrection [sing.] (in the Christian religion) the return to life of Jesus Christ
قيامة السيد المسيح

resuscitate /rɪ'sʌsɪteɪt/ *verb* [T] to bring sb who has stopped breathing back to life: *Unfortunately, all efforts to resuscitate the patient failed.* ينعِش ، يعيد إلى الحياة (بعد إغماء مثلاً)

▶ **resuscitation** /rɪˌsʌsɪ'teɪʃn/ *noun* [U]
إنعاش ، تنفّس اصطناعيّ

retail /'riːteɪl/ *noun* [U] the selling of goods to the public in shops, etc. (for personal use, not to be sold again): *the recommended retail price* ➲ Look at **wholesale**. البيع بالتجزئة أو المفرّق

▶ **retailer** *noun* [C] a person or company who sells goods in a shop بائع بالتجزئة أو المفرّق

retain /rɪ'teɪn/ *verb* [T] (*formal*) to keep or continue to have; not to lose: *Despite all her problems, she has managed to retain a sense of humour.* ○ *If you wish to leave the stadium and return later, please retain your ticket.* ○ *The village has retained much of its original character.* ○ *These cups retain the heat.* ❶ The noun is **retention**. يحتفظ بـ ، يستبقي

retaliate /rɪ'tælieɪt/ *verb* [I] **retaliate (against sb/sth)** to react to sth unpleasant that sb does to you by doing sth unpleasant in return: *They have announced that they will retaliate against anyone who attacks their country.*
يقابل (الاعتداء) بالمثل ، يثأر من

▶ **retaliation** /rɪˌtæli'eɪʃn/ *noun* [U] **retaliation (against sb/sth)**; **retaliation (for sth)** the act of retaliating: *The terrorist group said that the shooting was in retaliation for recent attacks on nationalists.* الأخذ بالثأر ، انتقام

retention /rɪ'tenʃn/ *noun* [U] the act of keeping sth or of being kept احتفاظ ، استبقاء

rethink /ˌriː'θɪŋk/ *verb* [I,T] (*pt*, *pp* **rethought** /-'θɔːt/) to think about sth again because you probably need to change it: *The government has*

a b c d e f g h i j k l m n o p q r s t u v w x y z

been forced to rethink its economic policy. يعيد النظر في

retina /'retɪnə; *US* 'retənə/ *noun* (*pl.* **retinas** or **retinae** /-ni:/) [usually sing.] the part of the back of the eye that is sensitive to light and sends an image of what is seen to the brain الشبكيّة

retire /rɪ'taɪə(r)/ *verb* [I] **1 retire (from sth)** to leave your job and stop working usually because you have reached a certain age: *She's worried that she won't have enough money to live on when she retires.* ○ *Injury forced him to retire from professional athletics.* يتقاعد ، يعتزل الخدمة

2 (*formal*) to leave and go to a quiet or private place: *We were a bit tired, so we retired to our hotel room after dinner.* يأوي إلى ، ينسحب ، يخلو إلى نفسه

▸ **retired** *adj* having stopped work permanently, usually because of having reached a certain age: *a retired teacher* ○ *He's been very unhappy since he's been retired.* متقاعِد

retirement /rɪ'taɪəmənt/ *noun* **1** [C,U] the act of stopping or being forced to stop working permanently, usually because of reaching a certain age: *What's the age of retirement/retirement age in this country?* ○ *There have been a number of retirements in our department this year.* ○ *She has decided to take early retirement.* ○ *The former world champion has announced his retirement* (= that he is not going to play, etc. again). تقاعد

2 [sing., U] the situation or period after retiring from work: *We all wish you a long and happy retirement.*

> A **pension** is the income received by somebody who has retired. It comes from the State, the employer or both. A **pensioner** or an **old age pensioner** is a person who has retired because of age.

التقاعد

retiring /rɪ'taɪərɪŋ/ *adj* (of a person) shy or quiet منطوٍ على نفسه ، خجول

retort /rɪ'tɔ:t/ *verb* [T] to reply quickly to what sb says, in an angry or amusing way: *'Who asked you for your opinion?' she retorted.* ○ *He retorted that there was no such thing as an honest politician.* يجيب بذكاء وحدّة

▸ **retort** *noun* [C] an angry answer ردّ غاضب؛ ردّ سريع البديهة

retrace /rɪ'treɪs/ *verb* [T] to repeat a past journey, series of events, etc: *I retraced my steps* (= I went back the way I had come) *in an attempt to find my wallet.* يعود بخطواته (أو بذاكرته) إلى الوراء

retract /rɪ'trækt/ *verb* [I,T] (*formal*) to say that sth you have said before is not true or not valid: *When he appeared in court, he retracted the confession he had made to the police.* يسحب (أقواله) ، يتراجع

retreat /rɪ'tri:t/ *verb* [I] **1** (of an army, etc.) to move backwards in order to leave a battle or in order not to become involved in a battle: *The troops were heavily outnumbered and so they were forced to retreat.* ○ *The order was given to retreat.* يتقهقر ، ينسحب
➲ Look at **advance**.

2 to move backwards; to go to a safe or private place: *A neighbour tried to get into the burning house but he was forced to retreat by the intense heat.* ○ (*figurative*) *She seems to retreat into a world of her own sometimes.* يتراجع ؛ يأوي إلى؛ ينزوي

▸ **retreat** *noun* **1** [C,U] the act of retreating: *The invading forces are now in retreat.* ○ *the Minister's retreat from his original opinion* ○ *Psychiatrists say that her behaviour is really a retreat into childhood.* تقهقر : انسحاب ، لجوء

2 [C] a private place where you can go when you want to be quiet or to rest ملاذ ، مكان للخلوة

retribution /ˌretrɪ'bju:ʃn/ *noun* [U] **retribution (for sth)** (*formal*) punishment for a crime: *Public opinion is demanding retribution for the recent acts of terrorism.* عقوبة

retrieve /rɪ'tri:v/ *verb* [T] **1 retrieve sth (from sb/sth)** to get sth back from the place where it was left or lost: *The river police retrieved the body from the canal.* يستردّ ، يسترجع

2 (*computing*) to find information that has been stored: *The computer can retrieve all the data about a particular customer.* يستعيد

3 to make sth (a situation, a mistake, etc.) better; to put sth right: *The team was losing two-nil at half-time but they managed to retrieve the situation in the second half.* يصلح : ينقذ

▸ **retrieval** /-vl/ *noun*: *Retrieval of the bodies from the wreckage of the plane took several hours.* استرداد : استخراج

retrospect /'retrəspekt/ *noun*

IDM **in retrospect** thinking about sth that happened in the past (and often seeing it differently from the way you saw it at the time): *In retrospect, I can see what a stupid mistake it was.* عند إعادة النظر في أحداث الماضي

▸ **retrospective** /ˌretrə'spektɪv/ *adj* **1** looking again at the past: *a retrospective analysis of historical events* عائد إلى الماضي

2 (used about laws, decisions, payments, etc.) applying to the past as well as to the present and future: *Is this new tax law retrospective?* ذو مفعول رجعي

retrospectively *adv* كاستعادةٍ لأحداث الماضي

return[1] /rɪ'tɜ:n/ *verb* **1** [I] **return (to...)**; **return (from...)** to come or go back to a place: *I leave on the 10th and return on the 25th.* ○ *I shall be returning to this country in six months.* ○ *When did you return from Italy?* ○ *He left his home town when he was 18 and never returned.* يرجع ، يعود

2 [I] **return (to sth)** to start doing a previous activity or talking about a previous subject again: *The strike is over and they will be returning to work on Monday.* ○ *We'll return to this subject in next week's lesson.* يعاود

3 [I] **return (to sth/to doing sth)** to come or go back to a previous situation or condition: *It is hoped that train services will return to normal soon.* يعود ، يرجع

4 [I] to come back; to happen again: *If the pain returns, make another appointment to see me.*

○ *I expect that the cold weather will return soon.* يعود ، يرجع

5 [T] **return sth (to sb/sth)** to give, send, put or take sth back: *I've stopped lending him things because he never returns them.* ○ *Application forms must be returned by 14 March.* يعيد ، يرجع

6 [T] to react to sth that somebody does, says or feels by doing, saying, or feeling sth similar: *I've phoned them several times and left messages but they haven't returned any of my calls.* ○ *We'll be happy to return your hospitality if you ever come to our country.* يردّ

7 [T] (in sport) to hit or throw the ball back: *He hit the ball so hard that I couldn't return it.* يردّ

▸ **returnable** /-əbl/ *adj* that can or must be given or taken back: *a non-returnable deposit* ممكن أو واجب إرجاعه

return² /rɪˈtɜːn/ *noun* **1** [sing.] **a return (to/from...)** the act of coming or going back to a place, a previous activity, a previous situation or a previous condition: *I'll contact you on my return* (= when I come back). ○ *Our return flight is at 3 o'clock in the morning.* ○ *He has recently made a return to form* (= started playing well again). عودة ، رجوع

2 [U] the act of giving, sending, putting or taking sth back: *I demand the return of my passport immediately.* إعادة : تسليم

3 [C] (in sport) the act of hitting or throwing the ball back: *She hit a brilliant return.* ردّ

4 [C,U] (*also* **returns** [plural]) the profit from a business or an investment: *They're not expecting any return on their new restaurant for at least a year.* ○ *This account offers high returns on all investments.* ربح ، عائدات

5 [C] (*Brit*) (*also* **return ˈticket**; *US* **round trip**; **round trip ticket**) a ticket to travel to a place and back again: *A day return to Oxford, please.* ○ *I asked for a return but I was given a single by mistake.* تذكرة ذهاب وإياب

IDM **by return (of post)** (*Brit*) immediately; by the next post: *Please enclose a stamped addressed envelope and we will send you a receipt by return.* فوراً ، في أول بريد

in return (for sth) as payment or in exchange (for sth); as a reaction to sth: *Please accept this present in return for all your help.* مقابل، لقاء ، عوضاً عن

many happy returns → HAPPY

reˌturn ˈfare *noun* [C] (*Brit*) the price of a ticket to travel to a place and back again: *Is the return fare cheaper than two singles?* ثمن تذكرة الذهاب والإياب

reunion /ˌriːˈjuːniən/ *noun* **1** [C] a party or occasion when friends or colleagues meet again after they have not seen each other for a long time: *The college holds an annual reunion for former students.* ○ *a family reunion* حفلة لقاء أصدقاء قدامى مثلاً : احتفال باجتماع الشمل

2 [C,U] the act of coming together again after a separation: *The released hostages had an emotional reunion with their families at the airport.* لقاء من جديد ، اجتماع الشمل

reunite /ˌriːjuːˈnaɪt/ *verb* [I,T] **reunite (sb/sth) (with sb/sth)** to come together again; to cause sb/sth to come together again: *The separate regions of the country reunited a few years ago.* ○ *The missing child was found by the police and reunited with his parents.* ○ *The new leader's first task will be to reunite the party.* يتّحد أو يوحّد من جديد

Rev. (*Brit also* **Revd**) *abbrev* = REVEREND

rev /rev/ *noun* [C, usually pl.] (*informal*) REVOLUTION (3): *4 000 revs per minute* دورة المحرّك

▸ **rev** *verb* (revving; revved) **1** [I] **rev (up)** (used about an engine) to turn (quickly); to increase the speed of turning: *I was woken up by the sound of a car revving up outside.* يدور (أو يُدير) محرك السيارة بسرعة كبيرة

2 [T] **rev sth (up)** to increase the speed of an engine (usually before driving the car): *Rev the engine for a while before you drive off.* يزيد سرعة المحرّك

reveal /rɪˈviːl/ *verb* [T] **1 reveal sth (to sb)** to make sth known that was previously secret or unknown: *She revealed that she had serious money problems.* ○ *He refused to reveal any names to the police.* يفْشي ، يبوح بِ

2 to allow sth to be seen that was previously hidden: *The X-ray revealed a tiny fracture in her right hand.* ○ *In a moment, the curtains will open to reveal tonight's star prize.* يكشف ، يظهر

▸ **revealing** *adj* **1** allowing sth (facts previously unknown, secrets, etc.) to be known: *This book provides a revealing insight into the world of politics.* كاشف للأسرار

2 allowing sth to be seen that is usually hidden: *a very revealing swimsuit* كاشف (عن الخفايا)

revel /ˈrevl/ *verb* [I] (revelling; revelled; *US* reveling; reveled)

PHR V **revel in sth/in doing sth** to enjoy sth very much: *He likes being famous and revels in the attention he gets.* يتلذّذ بِ، يجد متعة كبرى في

revelation /ˌrevəˈleɪʃn/ *noun* **1** [C] something that is made known, that was previously secret or unknown (especially sth surprising): *This magazine is full of revelations about the private lives of famous people.* كشْف ، إظهار

2 [sing.] a thing or a person that surprises you and causes you to change your attitude to sb/sth: *It's a horrible house from the outside but the inside is a revelation.* مفاجأة مدهشة ، كشف عن الحقيقة

revenge /rɪˈvendʒ/ *noun* [U] something that you do to punish sb who has hurt you, made you suffer, etc: *He made a fool of me and now I want revenge.* ○ *The attack was an act of revenge.* انتقام ، ثأر

IDM **get/have/take your revenge (on sb) (for sth); take revenge (on sb) (for sth)** to punish sb in return for sth bad that he/she has done to you: *He wants to take revenge on the judge who sent him to prison.* يثأر أو ينتقم من

out of/in revenge (for sth) as a way of punishing sb in return for sth bad he/she has done to you: *The shooting was in revenge for an attack by the nationalists.* انتقاماً من أو لِ

▸ **revenge** *verb* [T] **revenge yourself on sb** to punish sb who has done sth bad to you by doing sth bad in return: *She revenged herself on her enemy.* يثأر أو ينتقم من

revenue /ˈrevənjuː; *US* -ənuː/ *noun* [U, plural] income received by a government, company, etc: *Revenue from income tax rose last year.* ○ *Oil revenues are a vital part of the country's economy.* دَخْل ، رَيْع : عائدات

reverence /ˈrevərəns/ *noun* [U] a feeling of great respect إجلال ، توقير

Reverend /ˈrevərənd/ *adj* **the Reverend** (*abbr* **Rev.**; **Revd**) the title of a Christian priest: *the Reverend Charles Gray* لقب للقسّ: حضرة الأب المبجّل أو الموقّر...

reverent /ˈrevərənt/ *adj* showing respect مهيب ، معبِّر عن التوقير

reversal /rɪˈvɜːsl/ *noun* [C,U] the act of changing sth to the opposite; an occasion when sth changes to the opposite of what is usual or expected: *The government insists that there will be no reversal of policy.* ○ *The decision taken yesterday was a complete reversal of last week's decision.* ○ *a reversal of roles* (= when each person does what the other person was doing) عَكْس : انقلاب أو انعكاس

reverse¹ /rɪˈvɜːs/ *adj* opposite to what is expected or has just been described: *In Germany the reverse situation is true.* عكسيّ ، مضادّ

IDM **in reverse order** starting with the last one and going backwards to the first one: *The results will be announced in reverse order.* بترتيب عكسي

reverse² /rɪˈvɜːs/ *noun* **1** [sing.] the reverse (of sth) the complete opposite of the previous statement or of what is expected: *Of course I don't dislike you – quite the reverse* (= I like you very much). ○ *This should be a relaxing holiday but it's just the reverse.* العكس، النقيض

2 [U] (*also* ˌ**reverse ˈgear**) the control in a car, etc. that allows it to move backwards: *Leave the car in reverse while it's parked on this hill.* ○ *Where's reverse in this car?* المغيِّر إلى الوراء في السيّارة

IDM **in/into reverse** in the opposite order, starting at the end and going backwards to the beginning; in the opposite way to the previous direction بترتيب عكسي ؛ في الاتجاه المعاكس

reverse³ /rɪˈvɜːs/ *verb* **1** [T] to put sth in the opposite position: *Writing is reversed in a mirror.* يعكس ، يقلب

2 [I,T] to go backwards in a car, etc.; to make a car go backwards: *It will probably be easier to reverse into that parking space.* ○ *He reversed his brand new car into a wall.* يتحرّك أو يحرّك السيارة إلى الوراء

3 [T] to change sth to the opposite: *Today's results have reversed the order of the top two teams.* ○ *It's too late to reverse your decision now, you've already signed the contract.* يعكس ، يقلب رأساً على عقب

4 [T] to exchange the positions or functions of two things or people: *My husband and I have reversed roles – he stays at home now and I go to work.* يبادل ؛ يعكس

IDM **reverse (the) charges** to make a telephone call that will be paid for by the person who receives it: *Phone us when you get there, and reverse the charges.* ○ *Could I make a reverse charge call to London, please?* ❶ The US expression is **to call collect**. يحوّل أجرة المخابرة التليفونيّة على المخاطَب

▸ **reversible** /-əbl/ *adj* (used about clothes) that can be worn with either side on the outside: *a reversible coat* (قماش أو معطف) يلبس على الوجهين

revert /rɪˈvɜːt/ *verb* [I] **revert (to sth)** to return to a previous state or to sth that you did previously: *The land will soon revert to jungle if it is not farmed.* ○ *If the experiment is unsuccessful we will revert to the old system.* يعود إلى حالته السابقة، يرتد

review /rɪˈvjuː/ *noun* **1** [C,U] the act of examining or considering sth again in order to decide whether changes are necessary: *There will be a review of your contract after the first six months.* ○ *The system is in need of review.* يراجع ، يعيد النظر في

2 [C] the act of looking back at sth in order to check, remember, or be clear about sth: *a review of the major events of the year* يستعرض

3 [C] a newspaper or magazine article, or an item on television or radio, in which sb gives an opinion on a new book, film, play, etc: *The film got bad reviews.* ○ *a book review* عرض أو نقد (لكتاب مثلاً)

▸ **review** *verb* [T] **1** to examine or consider again in order to decide whether changes are necessary: *Your salary will be reviewed after one year.* يعيد النظر في

2 to look at or think about sth again to make sure that you understand it: *Let's review what we've done in this lesson so far.* يراجع

3 to write an article or to talk on television or radio, giving an opinion on a new book, film, play, etc: *In today's edition our film critic reviews the latest films.* يعرض

reviewer *noun* [C] a person who writes reviews of books, films, etc. ناقد أدبيّ أو فنيّ

revise /rɪˈvaɪz/ *verb* **1** [T] to make changes to sth in order to correct or improve it: *The book has been revised for this new edition.* ○ *I revised my opinion of him when I found out that he had lied.* يُنقّح ، يعدّل

2 [I,T] **revise (for sth)** to read or study again sth that you have learnt, especially when preparing for an exam: *I can't come out tonight. I'm revising for my exam.* ○ *None of the things I had revised came up in the exam.* يراجع (دروسه)

▸ **revision** /rɪˈvɪʒn/ *noun* **1** [C,U] the act of changing sth in order to correct or improve it: *It has been suggested that the whole system is in need of revision.* تنقيح ، تعديل ، إعادة نظر

2 [U] the work of reading or studying again sth you have learnt, especially when preparing for an exam: *I've done a lot of revision for history.* مراجعة

revival /rɪˈvaɪvl/ *noun* **1** [C,U] the act of becoming or making sth strong or popular again: *economic revival* ○ *a revival of interest in traditional farming methods* إنتعاش : إنعاش ، إحياء

2 [C] a new performance of a play that has not been performed for some time: *a revival of the musical 'Kiss me Kate'* إحياء أو إعادة إخراج مسرحية منسيّة

revive /rɪˈvaɪv/ *verb* [I,T] **1** to become or make sb/sth strong or healthy again; to come or to bring sb back to life or consciousness: *Hopes have revived for an early end to the fighting.* ○ *I'm terribly tired but I'm sure a cup of coffee will revive me.* ○ *Attempts were made to revive him but he was already dead.* يفيق أو يفيق ، ينتعش أو ينعِش

2 to become or make sth popular again; to begin to do or use sth again: *Public interest in rugby has revived now that the national team is doing well.* ○ *to revive an old custom* يتجدّد أو يجدّد الاهتمام بِ ، يحيي

revolt /rɪˈvəʊlt/ *verb* **1** [I] **revolt (against sb/sth)** to protest in a group (often violently) against the person or people in power: *A group of generals revolted against the government.* يثور على ، يتمرّد

2 [T] to make sb feel disgusted or ill: *Some of her opinions revolt me.* ○ *The sight and the smell revolted him.* ❶ The noun for this meaning is **revulsion**. يثير الاشمئزاز ، يقزّز النفس

▶ **revolt** *noun* [C,U] the act of revolting (1): *The revolt was quickly put down by the army.* ○ *What started as a small protest has turned into widespread revolt.* ثورة ، تمرُّد

revolting /rɪˈvəʊltɪŋ/ *adj* extremely unpleasant; disgusting: *a revolting smell of fish* ○ *What a revolting colour!* مقرف ، مقزّز للنفس

🔑**revolution** /ˌrevəˈluːʃn/ *noun* **1** [C,U] changing or trying to change the political system by violent action, etc: *the French Revolution of 1789* ○ *a country on the brink of revolution* ثورة : تمرُّد

2 [C] **a revolution (in sth)** a complete change in methods, opinions, etc., often as a result of progress: *a revolution in the treatment of diseases such as cancer* ○ *the Industrial Revolution* ثورة (صناعيّة مثلاً)

3 [C,U] (*also informal* **rev**) a movement around sth; one complete turn around a central point (e.g. in a car engine): *400 revolutions per minute* دورة

▶ **revolutionary** /-ʃənəri; *US* -neri/ *adj* **1** connected with or supporting political revolution: *Revolutionary forces have attacked the president's palace.* ○ *the revolutionary leaders* ثوري

2 producing great changes; very new and different: *a revolutionary new scheme to ban cars from the city centre* (تغيير) جذري : مستحدث

revolutionary *noun* [C] (*pl.* **revolutionaries**) a person who takes part in and supports a revolution ثائر ، شخص ثوري

revolutionize (*also* **revolutionise**) /-ʃənaɪz/ *verb* [T] to change sth completely: *a discovery that could revolutionize the treatment of mental illness* يغيرّ جذرياً ، يحدث ثورة في

revolve /rɪˈvɒlv/ *verb* [I] to move in a circle around a central point; to go round: *The earth revolves around the sun.* ○ *This little wheel should revolve when you switch the engine on.* يدور

PHR V **revolve around sb/sth** to have sb/sth as the most important part: *Her life revolves around the family.* يدور حول ، يتركّز في

▶ **revolving** *adj* designed to work by going round: *revolving doors* دوّار

revolver /rɪˈvɒlvə(r)/ *noun* [C] a type of small gun with a container for bullets that goes round مسدّس

revulsion /rɪˈvʌlʃn/ *noun* [U] a feeling of disgust (because sth is extremely unpleasant) اشمئزاز : نفور

🔑**reward** /rɪˈwɔːd/ *noun* **1** [C,U] something that is given in return for work, effort, etc: *She feels that she has done a lot of work for little or no reward.* ○ *Being a parent is often hard work but it has its rewards.* مكافأة ، أجر ، تعويض

2 [C] an amount of money that is given in exchange for helping the police, returning sth that was lost, etc: *Police are offering a reward for information leading to a conviction.* مكافأة

▶ **reward** *verb* [T] **reward sb (for sth/for doing sth)** to give a reward to sb: *Eventually her efforts were rewarded and she got a job.* ○ *His parents bought him a bicycle to reward him for passing the exams.* يكافئ ، يجزي

rewarding *adj* giving satisfaction: *She finds her work with handicapped children very rewarding.* (عمل) مجزٍ ، مرضٍ للضّمير

rewind /ˌriːˈwaɪnd/ *verb* [T] (*pt, pp* **rewound**) to make a tape go backwards: *Please rewind the tape at the end of the film.* يعيد لفّ الشريط

rewrite /ˌriːˈraɪt/ *verb* [T] (*pt* **rewrote** /-rəʊt/; *pp* **rewritten** /-ˈrɪtn/) to write sth again in a different or better way يعيد كتابة شيء

▶ **rewritable** /-abl/ *adj* able to be used again for different data: *a rewritable CD* يمكن اعادة استخدامه

rhetoric /ˈretərɪk/ *noun* [U] a way of speaking or writing that is intended to impress or influence people بلاغة

▶ **rhetorical** /rɪˈtɒrɪkl; *US* -ˈtɔːr-/ *adj* بلاغيّ

rhetorically /-kli/ *adv* بالكلمات الجوفاء

rheˌtorical ˈquestion *noun* [C] a question that is not really a question because it does not expect an answer سؤال بلاغي أو تقريريّ

rheumatism /ˈruːmətɪzəm/ *noun* [U] an illness that causes pain in muscles and joints الرّثية ، الروماتيزم

rhino /ˈraɪnəʊ/ *noun* [C] (*pl.* **rhinos**) (*informal*) RHINOCEROS

rhinoceros /raɪˈnɒsərəs/ *noun* [C] (*pl.* **rhinoceros** or **rhinoceroses**) a large animal from Africa or Asia, with a thick skin and either one or two horns on its nose الكركدنّ ، وحيد القرن

rhubarb /ˈruːbɑːb/ *noun* [U] a plant with long red stems and very large leaves. The stems can be cooked and eaten as fruit. نبات الراوند ، ريباس

rhyme /raɪm/ *noun* **1** [U] the technique of using

words that have the same sound as each other especially at the ends of lines: *All of his poetry was written in rhyme.* قافية أو سَجْع ، تقفية

2 [C] a word that has the same sound as another: *Can you think of a rhyme for 'peace'?* كلمة من نفس القافية

3 [C] a short piece of writing, or something spoken, in which the words at the end of each line sound the same as the words at the end of previous lines ➲ Look at **nursery rhyme**. شعر ، نظم مقفّى

▸ **rhyme** *verb* **1** [I] to have the same sound as another word; to consist of lines that end with words that sound the same: *'Tough' rhymes with 'stuff'.* ○ *'Book' and 'look' rhyme.* ○ *He thinks that all poetry should rhyme.* يتطابق في القافية ، يتقافى مع

2 [T] to put together words that have the same sound: *You can't rhyme 'face' with 'stays'.* يُقفّي أو يُسجّع

rhythm /ˈrɪðəm/ *noun* [C,U] a regular repeated pattern of sound or movement: *the rhythms of Latin America* ○ *He's a terrible dancer because he has no sense of rhythm.* إيقاع

▸ **rhythmic** /ˈrɪðmɪk/ (*also* **rhythmical** /ˈrɪðmɪkl/) *adj* having rhythm: *the rhythmic qualities of African music* إيقاعي

rhythmically /-kli/ *adv* بحركات إيقاعيّة منتظمة

rib /rɪb/ *noun* [C] one of the curved bones that go round the chest: *He's so thin that you can see his ribs.* ضِلع (في القفص الصدري)

ribbon /ˈrɪbən/ *noun* [C,U] **1** a long, thin piece of cotton, nylon, etc. that is used for tying or decorating sth شريط أو شريطة

2 a long, thin piece of material that contains ink and is used in a typewriter شريط الطباعة (في الآلة الكاتبة)

rice /raɪs/ *noun* [U] the grain from a plant grown in hot, wet countries, that we cook and eat: *Rice or potatoes?* ○ *brown rice* ○ *boiled rice* ○ *rice pudding* (= made by cooking rice in milk and sugar) الأرُزّ

rich /rɪtʃ/ *adj* **1** having a lot of money or property; not poor: *a rich family.* ➲ Look at **wealthy**. غنيّ

2 (not before a noun) **rich in sth** containing a lot of sth: *Oranges are very rich in vitamin C.* غني بِـ

3 able to produce sth in large amounts: *rich soil* غني ، خصب

4 (used about food) containing a lot of fat, oil, sugar, cream, etc: *a rich sauce* ○ *a rich chocolate cake* دَسِم

5 (used about colours, sounds or smells) strong and deep: *a rich purple* زاهٍ ؛ عميق ؛ قوي

▸ **the rich** *noun* [plural] rich people: *The rich are getting richer and the poor are getting poorer.* الأغنياء

richly *adv* **1** extremely well: *She was richly rewarded for her hard work.* جيّداً ؛ بوفرة

2 fully: *His promotion was richly deserved.* كلّياً ، تماماً

richness *noun* [U] دسم ؛ غزارة ؛ زهاء ؛ قوّة

riches /ˈrɪtʃɪz/ *noun* [plural] (*formal*) a lot of money or property; wealth: *Despite all his riches, he was a deeply unhappy man.* مال ، ثروة

rickety /ˈrɪkəti/ *adj* likely to fall or break; not strongly made: *a rickety old fence* متُقلقل ، متخلّع ؛ واهن

ricochet /ˈrɪkəʃeɪ; *US* ˌrɪkəˈʃeɪ/ *verb* [I] (*pt, pp* **ricocheted**; **ricochetted** /-ʃeɪd/) **ricochet (off sth)** (used about a bullet, etc.) to fly away from a surface after hitting it (الرصاصة) ترتدّ أو تنبو

rid /rɪd/ *verb* [T] (*pres part* **ridding**; *pt, pp* **rid**) **rid sb/sth of sb/sth** (*formal*) to make sb/sth free from sb/sth that is unpleasant or unwanted: *They have managed to rid the world of smallpox.* ○ *He was unable to rid himself of his fears and suspicions.* يُخلِّص

IDM **be/get rid of sb/sth** to be/become free of sb/sth or to remove sb/sth: *I didn't enjoy having my family to stay. In fact I was glad to get rid of them.* ○ *I can't get rid of this mark on the carpet.* ○ *Let's get rid of that old chair and buy a new one.* يتخلّص من

riddance /ˈrɪdns/ *noun*

IDM **good riddance (to sb/sth)** (*informal*) (used for expressing pleasure or relief that sb/sth that you do not like has gone) الحمد لله على خلاصنا منه! إلى غير رجعة!

ridden¹ /ˈrɪdn/ *pp of* RIDE²

ridden² /ˈrɪdn/ *adj* (usually in compounds) full of: *She was ridden with guilt.* ○ *She was guilt-ridden.* مثقل بِـ ؛ مفعم بِـ

riddle /ˈrɪdl/ *noun* [C] **1** a type of question that you ask people for fun that has a clever or amusing answer أحجية ، لغز

2 a person, thing or event that you cannot understand شخص غامض

riddled /ˈrɪdəld/ *adj* **riddled with** full of: *The car was riddled with bullet holes.* ○ *This essay is riddled with mistakes.* مثقّب كالمنخل ؛ مليء بِـ

ride¹ /raɪd/ *noun* [C] a journey on a horse or bicycle, or in a car, bus, etc: *They went for a ride in the woods.* ○ *It's only a short bus ride into Oxford.* ○ *Would you like to have a ride in my new car?* ركبة أو ركوب ، رحلة على الحصان أو الدرّاجة أو غير ذلك

IDM **take sb for a ride** (*informal*) to cheat or deceive sb يخدع ، يستغفِل

ride² /raɪd/ *verb* (*pt* **rode** /rəʊd/; *pp* **ridden** /ˈrɪdn/) **1** [I,T] to sit on a horse and be carried along, controlling its movements: *I'm learning to ride at the moment.* ○ *We rode through the woods and over the moor.* ○ *Which horse is Dettori riding in the next race?* ❶ **Go riding** is a common way of talking about riding for pleasure: *She goes riding every weekend.* يركب ، يمتطي

2 [I,T] to sit on a bicycle, etc. and be carried along, controlling its movements: *On Sunday thousands of cyclists rode from London to Oxford to raise money for charity.* ○ *She jumped onto her motor bike and rode off.* ○ *Can John ride a bicycle yet?* يركب

3 [I] to travel as a passenger in a bus, car, etc. يركب

▶ **rider** *noun* [C] a person who rides a horse, bicycle, etc. راكب (الحصان مثلاً)

riding /ˈraɪdɪŋ/ *noun* [U] the sport or hobby of riding a horse: *riding boots* ○ *a riding school* ركوب الخيل

ridge /rɪdʒ/ *noun* [C] **1** a long, narrow piece of high land along the top of hills or mountains: *We walked along the ridge looking down at the view.* سلسلة من أعالي الجبال أو الهضاب ، ظهر (الجبل)

2 a line where two sloping surfaces meet سَنَمة أو حَرْف: مكان التقاء سطحين منحدرين

ridicule /ˈrɪdɪkjuːl/ *noun* [U] unkind laughter or behaviour that is meant to make sb/sth appear silly استهزاء ، سخرية

▶ **ridicule** *verb* [T] to laugh at sb/sth in an unkind way: *The idea was ridiculed by everybody present.* يهزأ بِ ، يسخر من

ridiculous /rɪˈdɪkjələs/ *adj* very silly; foolish: *That's a ridiculous suggestion!* ○ *It's ridiculous to drive so fast along these lanes.* ○ *They're asking a ridiculous* (= very high) *price for that house.* سخيف أو مضحك ، أحمق ؛ (سعر) فاحش

▶ **ridiculously** *adv*: *She's paid a ridiculously low salary for the work she does.* للغاية ، بصورة لا تُصدّق

riding → RIDE

rife /raɪf/ *adj* (not before a noun) (*formal*) (used especially about bad things) very common: *The use of drugs was rife among certain groups of students.* متفشٍ، سائد ، شائع

rifle[1] /ˈraɪfl/ *noun* [C] a long gun that you hold against your shoulder to shoot with ℹ We **load**, **aim** and **fire** a rifle. بندقيّة

rifle[2] /ˈraɪfl/ *verb* [I,T] to search sth usually in order to steal from it: *I caught him rifling through the papers on my desk.* ينقّب أو يُنبِّش (بغية السرقة)

rift /rɪft/ *noun* [C] **1** a serious disagreement between friends, groups, etc: *a growing rift between the brothers* انشقاق

2 a crack or split in sth صَدْع ، شَقّ : انقسام

rig[1] /rɪɡ/ *verb* [T] (rigging; rigged)

PHR V **rig sth up** to make sth quickly, using any materials you can find: *We tried to rig up a shelter, using our rugs and coats.* يصنع شيئاً صنعاً سريعاً مرتجلاً

▶ **rig** *noun* [C] (usually in compounds) a large platform, with special equipment for a certain purpose: *an oil rig* منصّة كبيرة (حول بئر البترول مثلاً)

rigging *noun* [U] the ropes, etc. that support a ship's sails ترتيب الأشرعة والصواري في مركب

rig[2] /rɪɡ/ *verb* (rigging; rigged) to arrange or control an event, etc. in an unfair way, in order to get the result you want: *They claimed that the competition had been rigged.* يغش ، يتلاعب بِ

right[1] /raɪt/ *adj* on or of the side of the body that faces east when a person is facing north; not left: *Do you write with your right hand or your left?* ○ *Your seats are on the right side of the theatre.* يمين

▶ **right** *adv* to the right side; not left: *Turn right at the traffic lights.* يميناً ، على اليمين

right *noun* **1** [U] the right side or direction; not left: *We live in the first house on the right.* ○ *If you look slightly to the right you will see Windsor Castle in the distance.* اليمين

2 the Right [sing., with sing. or pl. verb] the people or political parties who support conservative rather than socialist ideas (أحزاب) اليمين

right[2] /raɪt/ *adj* **1** correct; true: *I'm afraid that's not the right answer.* ○ *Have you got the right time?* ○ *You're quite right – the film does start at 7 o'clock.* ○ *You were right about the weather – it did rain.* صحيح ، صواب

2 best; most suitable: *I don't think this is the right colour for the walls.* ○ *I hope I've made the right decision.* ○ *We wouldn't have missed the boat if we'd left at the right time.* ○ *You have to know the right people if you want to join that golf club.* أفضل ، أنسب : ملائم

3 normal; satisfactory: *Her voice didn't sound quite right on the phone.* عاديّ ، سويّ

4 (used about behaviour, actions, etc.) good; fair or what the law allows: *It's not right to pay people so badly.* ○ *It was right of her to give you the news at once.* ○ *It's never right to steal.* مُصيب ؛ عادِل ؛ شرعيّ

5 (*Brit informal*) (used for emphasizing sth bad) real or complete: *I'll look a right idiot in that hat!* حقيقيّ ، تامّ

IDM **all right** → ALL[2]

get on the right/wrong side of sb → SIDE[1]

on the right/wrong track → TRACK

right (you are)! (*informal*) yes, I will; yes, I agree: *'See you later.' 'Right you are!'* طيّب! نعم! مضبوط!

(as) right as rain healthy or working properly بصحّة جيّدة ؛ بحالة ممتازة

▶ **rightly** *adv* correctly or fairly: *As you rightly said, it's time to decide what we want.* ○ *He's been sacked and quite rightly, I believe.* على صواب ؛ على حقّ ، بعدل

rightness *noun*: *She's always convinced of the rightness of her own opinions.* صحّة ، صواب ؛ شرعيّة ؛ إنصاف

right[3] /raɪt/ *adv* **1** correctly; in a satisfactory way: *Have I spelt your name right?* ○ *Nothing seems to be going right for me at the moment.* بشكل صحيح ؛ بصورة ملائمة ، على ما يرام

2 (used for preparing sb for sth that is about to happen) get ready; listen: *Have you got your seatbelts on? Right, off we go.* طيِّب! إنتبِه أو استعدّ!

3 exactly: *The train was right on time.* تماماً، بالضبط

4 all the way: *Did you watch the film right to the end?* كلّه ، حتى الآخر

5 immediately: *He left right after dinner.* ○ *Wait here a minute – I'll be right back.* فوراً ، حالاً

6 (used in some titles): *the Right Honourable James Smith, Foreign Secretary* ○ *the Right Rev-*

a b c d e f g h i j k l m n o p q r s t u v w x y z

erend Richard Pearson, Bishop of Gloucester (المحترم أو الموقّر) جداً

IDM **right/straight away** → AWAY

right now at this moment; exactly now: *We can't discuss this right now.* في هذه اللحظة ، الآن

serve sb right → SERVE

right⁴ /raɪt/ *noun* **1** [U] what is morally good and fair: *Children learn about right and wrong at a very early age.* ○ *Does right always win in the end?* الخير؛ الحق؛ الصواب

2 [C] a thing that you are allowed to do according to the law: *In Britain everybody has the right to vote at 18.* ○ *Freedom of speech is one of the basic human rights.* ○ *civil rights* (= the rights each person has to political and religious freedom, etc.) حقّ

3 [U] **right to sth/to do sth** a moral authority to do sth: *You have no right to tell me what to do.* سلطة ، حقّ

IDM **be in the right** to be doing what is correct and fair: *You don't need to apologize. You were in the right and he was in the wrong.* يكون على حقّ

by rights according to what is fair or correct: *By rights, half the profit should be mine.* وفقاً للعدل والإنصاف

in your own right because of what you are yourself and not because of other people: *She's a very wealthy lady in her own right* (= not only because she has married somebody who is rich). من الأصل ؛ عن جدارة ؛ بحكم حقوقه الخاصّة

within your rights (to do sth) acting in a reasonable or legal way: *You are quite within your rights to demand to see your lawyer.* من حقّه أنْ...

right⁵ /raɪt/ *verb* [T] **1** to return to a normal position: *The boat tipped over and then righted itself again.* يقوِّم ، يسوّي

2 to correct sth ينصِف ، يصلِح

> This verb is almost always used in this sense with the noun **wrong**: *There are many wrongs that need to be righted.* You do not 'right' a mistake, you **correct** it.

ˈright angle *noun* [C] an angle of 90°: *A square has four right angles.* زاوية قائمة

righteous /ˈraɪtʃəs/ *adj* (*formal*) morally good or fair ➲ Look at **self-righteous**. صالح ، قويم ، بارّ

rightful /ˈraɪtfl/ *adj* (only *before* a noun) (*formal*) fair, proper or legal: *You have a rightful claim to your father's property.* عادل؛ صحيح ؛ شرعي

▸ **rightfully** /-fəli/ *adv* قانوناً أو شرعاً

ˈright-hand *adj* (only *before* a noun) of or on the right of sb/sth: *The postbox is on the right-hand side of the road.* ○ *a sharp right-hand bend* (جانب) أيمن ، واقع على اليمين

ˌright-ˈhanded *adj* using the right hand more than the left for writing, etc. يمينيّ أو أيمن

ˌright-hand ˈman *noun* [C] (*pl.* **right-hand men**) the person you rely on most to help and support you in your work ساعِده الأيمن ، مُساعد لا يستغنى عنه

ˌright of ˈway *noun* (*pl.* **rights of way**) **1** [U] (used in road traffic) the right⁴(2) to continue while other traffic must stop أفضليّة المرور

2 [C] a path across private land that the public may use: *Is there a right of way across this field?* حقّ المرور: ممرّ عام داخل ملك خاص

ˌright ˈwing *noun* [sing.] the people in a political party who support more conservative ideas: *He is on the right wing of the Labour party.* جناح اليمين (في حزب سياسيّ)

ˌright-ˈwing *adj* supporting conservative ideas rather than socialist ones: *a right-wing government* ❶ The opposite is **left-wing**. يمينيّ

rigid /ˈrɪdʒɪd/ *adj* **1** not able or willing to change or be changed; strict: *Some students complained about the rigid rules and regulations at the school.* متزمّت ، متشدّد ، صارم

2 stiff, not easy to bend: *For air travel a rigid suitcase is better than a soft bag.* ○ *She was rigid with fear.* صلب ، قاسٍ ، جامد

▸ **rigidity** /rɪˈdʒɪdəti/ *noun* [U] صلابة ، قساوة

rigidly *adv* stiffly, strictly or without any possibility of change: *You don't have to keep rigidly to what I've written – use your imagination.* بتشدُّد ، بصرامة

rigour (*US*) (*also* **rigor**) /ˈrɪɡə(r)/ *noun* (*formal*)

1 [U] the quality of being strict or severe: *the rigour of the law* صرامة ، تشدُّد

2 [C, usually pl.] severe conditions; difficulties: *the rigours of a hard climate* شدّة البرد ، قسوة ؛ مشاقّ

▸ **rigorous** /ˈrɪɡərəs/ *adj* thorough and careful: *Very rigorous tests have been carried out on the drinking water.* متشدِّد ، بالغ الدقّة

rigorously *adv* بدقّة بالغة ، بشدّة

rigorousness *noun* [U] صعوبة ، شدّة

rim /rɪm/ *noun* [C] an edge at the top or outside of sth that is round: *the rim of a cup* ○ *spectacles with silver rims* حافة مستديرة: حتار أو إطار

rind /raɪnd/ *noun* [C,U] the thick hard skin on the outside of some fruits and some types of cheese قشرة

> **Rind** is hard and is not usually removed with the fingers. We say the **rind** or **peel** of a lemon but only the **peel** of an orange. A fruit with a thinner or softer covering has a **skin**. So bananas, apples, pears, etc. all have **skins**.

ring¹ /rɪŋ/ *noun* [C] **1** a piece of jewellery, a round piece of metal, often of silver or gold, that you wear on your finger: *a wedding ring* ○ *an engagement ring* ○ *a gold, diamond, etc. ring* خاتم

2 (usually in compounds) a round object of any material with a hole in the middle: *a key ring* (= for holding keys) حَلَقة

3 a circle: *Stand in a ring and hold hands.* دائرة ، حَلَقة

4 the space with seats all around it where a performance, match, etc. takes place: *a circus ring* ○ *a boxing ring* حلبة ، حلقة

5 (*US* **burner**) one of the round parts on the top of an electric or gas cooker, on which you can put pans: *an electric cooker with an oven, a grill and four rings* "عين" أو "رأس" لجهاز الطبخ

6 a number of people involved together in sth that is secret or not legal: *a drugs ring* عصابة ، عصبة

▶ **ring** *verb* (*pt, pp* **ringed**) [T] **1** to draw a circle around sth: *Ring the correct answer with your pencil.* يرسم دائرة حول...

2 to surround sb/sth: *The whole area was ringed with police.* يطوّق

ring² /rɪŋ/ *verb* (*pt* **rang** /ræŋ/; *pp* **rung** /rʌŋ/) **1** [I,T] (*especially US* **call**) **ring (sb/sth) (up)** to telephone (sb/sth): *What time will you ring tomorrow?* ○ *I rang up yesterday and booked the hotel.* ○ *Ring the station and ask what time the next train leaves.* يتلفن ، يخابر (بالتليفون)

2 [I,T] to make a sound like a bell or to cause sth to make this sound: *Is that the phone ringing?* ○ *We rang the door bell again and again but nobody answered.* يرن أو يطنّ : يدقّ

3 [I] **ring (for sb/sth)** to ring a bell in order to call sb, ask for sth, etc: *'Did you ring, sir?' asked the flight attendant.* يدقّ الجرس استدعاءً (للخادم مثلاً)

4 [I] to have a certain effect when you hear it: *Her words didn't ring true* (= you felt that you could not believe what she said). يوحي بِ ، يتّسم بِ

5 [I] **ring (with sth)** to be filled with loud sounds: *The music was so loud it made my ears ring.* يطنّ ، يدوي

IDM **ring a bell** to sound familiar or to remind you, not very clearly, of sth: *'Do you know Jane Sykes?' 'Well, her name rings a bell.'* يتذكّر شيئاً بشكل غامض

PHR V **ring (sb) back** to phone sb again: *'I'm afraid Mary isn't in.' 'Oh well, I'll ring back later.'* ○ *I can't talk now – can I ring you back?* يتلْفن مرّة ثانية : يردّ المخابرة

ring in (*Brit*) to telephone a TV or radio show, or the place where you work: *Thousands of people rang in during the programme to pledge money.* ○ *Mandy rang in sick this morning.* يتّصل ببرنامج اذاعي أو تلفزيوني الخ

ring off to end a telephone conversation: *I'd better ring off – supper's ready.* ينهي مخابرة تليفونيّة

ring out to sound loudly and clearly: *A pistol shot rang out.* يدوّي

▶ **ring** *noun* **1** [C] the sound made by a bell: *a ring at the door* دقّة ، طنّة ؛ رنين

2 [sing.] **a ring of sth** a feeling or quality of a particular kind: *What the man said had a ring of truth about it* (= sounded true). طابع ، سمة ، نبرة

IDM **give sb a ring** to telephone sb: *I'll give you a ring in the morning.* يتلْفن ، يخابر

ringleader /ˈrɪŋliːdə(r)/ *noun* [C] a person who leads a group of people who are doing sth wrong or causing trouble: *Who is the ringleader of the group?* رئيس العصابة

ˈring pull *noun* [C] a small piece of metal with a ring attached which is pulled to open cans of food, drink, etc. (حلقة) شدّادة

ˈring road *noun* [C] (*Brit*) a road that is built all around a town so that traffic does not have to go into the town centre (الطريق) المحلّق (حول المدينة)

ringtone /ˈrɪŋtəʊn/ *noun* [C] the sound a telephone makes when sb is calling you. Ringtones are often short tunes, and the word is especially used to refer to the different sounds mobile phones make when they ring. نغم رنين التليفون

rink /rɪŋk/ *noun* [C] = SKATING RINK

rinse /rɪns/ *verb* [T] to wash sth in water in order to remove soap or dirt, etc: *Rinse your hair thoroughly after each shampoo.* ○ *I should rinse the apples before you eat them.* يشطف

▶ **rinse** *noun* **1** [C] an act of rinsing: *Give the bath a good rinse after using it.* شطف

2 [C,U] a liquid used for colouring the hair صباغ (غير دائم) للشّعر

riot /ˈraɪət/ *noun* [C] fighting and noisy violent behaviour by a crowd of people: *Further riots have broken out in Manchester.* ○ *Police have been brought in to deal with the riots.* شغب، اضطرابات

IDM **run riot** to behave in a wild way, without any control: *At the end of the football match, the crowd ran riot.* ○ (*figurative*) *You really let your imagination run riot when you painted that picture.* يهوج ويموج ، ينطلق كالمجنون ؛ يطلق العنان لخياله

▶ **riot** *verb* [I] to take part in a riot: *There is a danger that the prisoners will riot if conditions don't improve.* يثور ، يلجأ إلى الشغب أو إلى العنف

rioter *noun* [C] a person who takes part in a riot أحد الثائرين أو مثيري العنف والشغب

riotous /-əs/ *adj* **1** (*formal*) wild or violent; lacking in control: *The crowd was becoming increasingly riotous.* مائل إلى العنف ، هائج لا يمكن ضبطه

2 wild and full of fun: *a riotous party* معَرْبِد ؛ صاخب ، مليء بالمتعة والتسلية

rip /rɪp/ *verb* (ripping; ripped) **1** [I,T] to tear quickly and sharply: *Oh no! The hem of my dress has ripped!* ○ *He ripped the letter in two and threw it in the bin.* ○ *The blast of the bomb ripped the house apart.* ينشق ؛ يمزّق ، يَشقّ

2 [T] to pull sth quickly and violently: *He ripped the poster from the wall.* ○ *The roof was ripped off in the gale.* ينتش ، يملَخ

3 to move very quickly: *The house was badly damaged when fire ripped through the roof and first floor.* يندفع ، يسرّع

PHR V **rip sb off** (*informal*) to cheat sb by asking too much money for sth يبلص، يطلب سعراً فاحشاً

rip sth up to tear sth into small pieces يمزّق إرباً إرباً

▶ **rip** *noun* [C] a long tear or cut (in material, etc.) شرْط ، شقّ

ripe /raɪp/ *adj* **1** (used about fruit, grain, etc.) ready to be picked and eaten ناضج ، يانع

2 ripe (for sth) ready for sth or in a suitable state for sth: *The conditions were ripe for social change.* يانع ، مستعدّ ؛ (الوقت) ملائم لِ

▶ **ripen** /ˈraɪpən/ *verb* [I,T] to make sth ripe or to become ripe يَنضج أو ينْضِج

ˈrip-off *noun* [C] (*informal*) an act of charging too much money for sth: *Two pounds for a cup of coffee is a rip-off!* بَلص ، سرقة! ، سعر فاحش

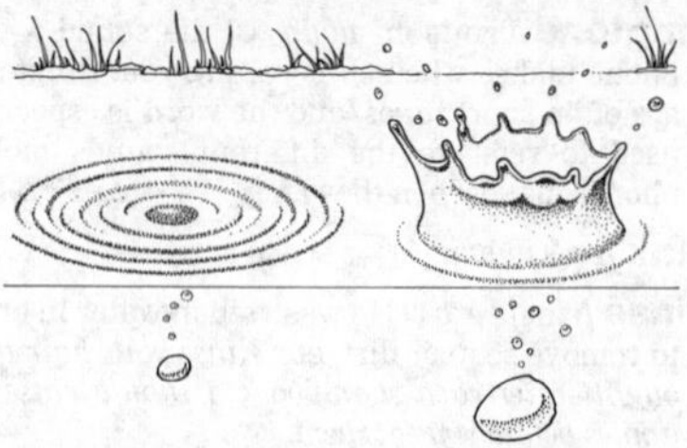

ripple /ˈrɪpl/ *noun* [C] **1** a very small wave or movement on the surface of water: *The breeze sent tiny ripples across the lake.* تمويجة ، تموّج خفيف

2 a sound that gradually becomes louder and then quieter again; a feeling that gradually spreads through a person or a group of people: *A ripple of laughter ran round the room.* هدهدة ، قهقهة ناعمة ، خرير

▸ **ripple** *verb* [I,T] to move gently: *The branches of the trees rippled in the wind.* ○ *The wind rippled the surface of the sea.* يتموّج ؛ يتمايل

rise¹ /raɪz/ *noun* **1** [C] an increase: *There has been a rise in the number of people out of work.* ○ *a sharp price rise* ➲ Look at **drop** and **fall**. ارتفاع ، ازدياد

2 [C] (*US* **raise**) an increase in wages, salary, etc: *I'm hoping to get a rise next April.* ○ *a 10% pay rise* زيادة في الراتب

3 [sing.] the process of becoming more powerful or important: *her meteoric rise to fame/power* ○ *the rise of Fascism in Europe* صعود ، ارتقاء (في عالم الشهرة مثلاً)

IDM **give rise to sth** to cause sth: *The news gave rise to considerable anxiety among many people.* يسبّب ، يؤدّي إلى

rise² /raɪz/ *verb* [I] (*pt* **rose** /rəʊz/; *pp* **risen** /ˈrɪzn/) **1** to move upwards, to become higher or to increase: *Smoke was rising from the chimney.* ○ *Her voice rose in anger* (= became louder). ○ *Do you think inflation will continue to rise?* ○ *The temperature has risen to nearly forty degrees.* ➲ Look at **fall**. يرتفع ، يزداد

2 to stand up: *The audience rose and applauded the singers.* يقف ، ينهض

3 to get out of bed: *They rose at dawn in order to be in London by eight.* ❶ In this sense **get up** is more common. ينهض من فراشه

4 (used about the sun, moon, etc.) to appear above the horizon: *The sun rises in the east and sets in the west.* يشرق ، يبزغ

5 to show (as sth tall above the surroundings): *A range of mountains rose in the distance.* يبرز ، يقف شامخاً

6 to come from: *Shouts of protest rose from the crowd.* يتعالى من ، يصدر عن

7 rise (up) (against sb/sth) to start opposing or fighting people in authority: *The people were afraid to rise up against the dictator.* يتمرّد على ، يقاوم

8 to move to a higher position (in rank, society, career, etc.): *He rose rapidly within the company.* يترفّع ، يترقّى

IDM **rise to the occasion, challenge, task, etc.** to deal with or cope with sth successfully: *Do you think she will rise to the demands of the job?* يثبت أنه كفء ل... ، يعالج الأمور بحنكة

▸ **rising** *noun* [C] fighting by a number of people (against people in authority) ➲ Look also at **uprising**. ثورة ، تمرد

rising *adj* **1** sloping upwards: *The new offices are being built on rising ground outside the town.* (أرض) مرتفعة

2 increasing: *the rising cost of living* متزايد

3 becoming well-known or popular: *a rising young rock star* صاعد

risk /rɪsk/ *noun* **1** [C,U] **risk (of sth/that...)** a possibility (of sth dangerous or unpleasant happening): *You could drive a car without insurance, but it's not worth the risk.* ○ *Scientists say these pesticides pose a risk to wildlife* ○ *Do you think there's any risk of rain?* مجازفة، ضرر أو خطر محتمل

2 [sing.] a dangerous or silly thing to do: *It was an unnecessary risk to overtake that lorry there.* مجازفة ، مخاطرة

3 [sing.] a person or thing that might cause danger: *If he knows your real name he's a security risk.* شخص أو شيء قد يسبّب خطراً

IDM **at your own risk** having the responsibility for whatever may happen: *This building is in a dangerous condition – enter at your own risk.* على مسؤوليّته الخاصّة

at risk in danger: *Small children are most at risk from the disease.* معرّض للخطر

at the risk of (doing sth) with the possibility of (sth unpleasant): *At the risk of interfering, may I offer you some advice?* من المحتمل أن (أتّهم ...)

run the risk (of doing sth) to do sth knowing that the result might be bad or unpleasant; to risk: *If we don't leave early we run the risk of missing the plane.* يعرّض نفسه (للضرر) ؛ يخاطر

take a risk/risks to do sth that you know might fail or be dangerous, etc: *You shouldn't take risks when driving.* ○ *He's very young but I'm prepared to take a risk and give him a job.* يجازف

▸ **risk** *verb* [T] **1** to take the chance of sth unpleasant happening: *If you don't work hard now you risk failing your exams.* يعرّض نفسه لخطر (الرسوب مثلاً)

2 to put sth or yourself in a dangerous position: *The man had risked his life to save the little boy.* يخاطر ، يعرّض للخطر

risky *adj* (**riskier**; **riskiest**) dangerous: *It's risky to drive fast when the roads are icy.* خطِر

rissole /ˈrɪsəʊl/ *noun* [C] a small flat mass of chopped meat and spices that is cooked by frying قرص لحم مقلي

ritual /ˈrɪtʃuəl/ *noun* [C,U] an action, ceremony or process which is usually repeated in the same pattern: *English people often go through the ritual of talking about the weather when they meet.* أحد الطقوس أو الشعائر ؛ عادة متكرّرة

▸ **ritual** *adj* done according to a particular pattern or tradition شعائريّ ، ممثّل لتقليد أو نمط معيّن

ritually /ˈrɪtʃuəli/ *adv* وفق الطقوس والشعائر

rival /ˈraɪvl/ *noun* [C] a person or thing that is competing with another: *They're business rivals.* ○ *It seems that we're rivals for the sales manager's job.* ○ *A rival shop has set up in the same street.* منافس

▸ **rival** *verb* [T] (rivalling; rivalled; *US* rivaling; rivaled) **rival sb/sth (for/in sth)** to be as good as sb/sth: *This novel doesn't rival his earlier writing.* ○ *Nothing rivals skiing for sheer excitement.* ينافس ؛ يباري ، يعادل

rivalry /ˈraɪvlri/ *noun* [C,U] (*pl.* rivalries) competition between people, groups, etc: *There was a lot of rivalry between the sisters.* منافسة

river /ˈrɪvə(r)/ *noun* [C] a large natural stream of water that flows across country: *the River Thames* ○ *a picnic on the bank of the river* نهر

A river **flows** into the sea. Where it joins the sea is the river **mouth**. A boat sails **on** the river. We walk, sail, etc. **up** or **down river**.

riverside /ˈrɪvəsaɪd/ *noun* [sing.] the land beside the banks of a river: *People were strolling along the riverside.* ○ *a riverside hotel* ضفة النهر

rivet[1] /ˈrɪvɪt/ *noun* [C] a metal pin for fastening two pieces of metal together مسمار برشام

rivet[2] /ˈrɪvɪt/ *verb* [T] (usually passive) to interest sb greatly: *I was riveted by her story.* يأسر ، يشدّ الانتباه

▸ **riveting** *adj* extremely interesting: *His speech was absolutely riveting.* ممتع للغاية ، ساحر

roach /rəʊtʃ/ *noun* [C] (*US*) = COCKROACH

road /rəʊd/ *noun* **1** [C] a way between places, with a hard surface which cars, buses, etc. can drive along: *Is this the right road to Beckley?* ○ *Take the London road and turn right at the first roundabout.* ○ *Turn left off the main* (= big, important) *road.* ○ *major/minor roads* ○ *If you get onto the ring road you'll avoid the town centre.* ○ *road signs* ○ *a road junction* طريق ، درب

Roads (*US* **highways**) connect towns and villages: *a road map of England*. A road in a town, city or village that has buildings at the side is often called a **street**. **Street** is not used for roads outside towns: *a street map of London*. However, streets in towns may have the word **Road** as part of their names: *Bayswater Road, London*. **Motorways** (*US* **freeways/expressways**) are roads with two **carriageways**, each with two or three **lanes**, that are built for traffic covering long distances, avoiding towns. **A-roads** are big important roads that link towns. **B-roads** are smaller country roads. **M** on a map stands for **motorway**.

2 Road (*abbr* **Rd**) [sing.] (used in names of roads, especially in towns): *60 Marylebone Road, London* شارع أو جادّة (كذا)

IDM **by road** in a car, bus, etc: *It's going to be a terrible journey by road – let's take the train.* بواسطة السيّارة (و نحوها)

on the road travelling: *We were on the road for 14 hours.* مسافر ، على سفر

roadblock /ˈrəʊdblɒk/ *noun* [C] a barrier put across the road by the police or army to stop traffic متراس ، حاجز يعترض الطريق يقيمه الجيش مثلاً

roadside /ˈrəʊdsaɪd/ *noun* [C, usually sing.] the edge of a road: *We had to stop at the roadside and wait for the engine to cool.* ○ *a roadside café* جانب الطريق

ˈ**road tax** *noun* [C,U] the tax which the owner of a car, etc. must pay to be allowed to drive it on public roads ضريبة يدفعها مالكو السيّارات

roadway /ˈrəʊdweɪ/ *noun* [C] (*formal*) the part of the road used by cars, etc.; not the side of the road قارعة الطريق

roadworks /ˈrəʊdwɜːks/ *noun* [plural] work that involves repairing or building roads: *The sign said 'Slow down. Roadworks ahead.'* (ورشة عمل) إصلاح الطرق

roadworthy /ˈrəʊdwɜːði/ *adj* in good enough condition to be driven on the road صالح للاستخدام على الطرق العامة

roam /rəʊm/ *verb* [I,T] to walk or travel with no particular plan or aim: *Gangs of youths were roaming the streets looking for trouble.* يتجوّل على غير هدى ، يطوف، يسرح

roar /rɔː(r)/ *noun* [C] a loud, deep sound like that made by a lion: *the roar of heavy traffic on the motorway* ○ *roars of laughter* زئير ؛ دوي ، هدير

▸ **roar** *verb* **1** [I] to make a loud, deep sound: *The river roared past, taking trees and rocks with it.* ○ *She roared with laughter at the joke.* يهدر ؛ يقهقه

2 [I] to shout very loudly يصرخ

3 [I] to make the sound that is typical of a lion: *The lion opened its huge mouth and roared.* يزأر ؛ يزمجر

4 [T] **roar sth (out)** to express sth very loudly: *The audience roared its approval.* يصيح

PHR V **roar along, down, past, etc.** to move in the direction mentioned, making a loud, deep sound: *A motorbike roared past us.* ينطلق مزمجراً

roaring /ˈrɔːrɪŋ/ *adj* **1** making a very loud noise: *the roaring waves* هادر ، مدو

2 (used about a fire) burning very well متأجّج

3 very great: *a roaring success* هائل ؛ (تجارة) مزدهرة

roast /rəʊst/ *verb* **1** [I,T] to cook or be cooked in an oven or over a fire: *a smell of roasting meat* ○ *to roast a chicken* ➲ Look at the note at **cook**. يشوي

2 [T] to heat and dry sth: *roasted peanuts* يحمّص

▸ **roast** *adj* (only *before* a noun) cooked by roasting: *roast beef and roast potatoes* مشوي

roast *noun* **1** [C,U] a piece of meat that has been roasted قطعة لحم مشويّة ، شِواء

2 [C] (*especially US*) an outdoor meal at which food is roasted ➲ Look at **barbecue**. وجبة أطعمة مشويّة تعدّ في الهواء الطلق

rob /rɒb/ *verb* [T] (robbing; robbed) **rob sb/sth (of sth) 1** to take sth (money, property, etc.)

from a person or place illegally: *to rob a bank* ○ *Several people on the train were robbed of their money and jewellery.* ➲ Look at the note at **steal**. يسرق ، يسلب

2 to take sth away from sb/sth that they should have: *His illness robbed him of the chance to play for his country.* يحرم من

▸ **robber** *noun* [C] a person who steals from a bank, etc. ➲ Look at the note at **thief**. سارق ، لصّ

robbery /ˈrɒbəri/ *noun* [C,U] (*pl.* robberies) the crime of stealing from a bank, etc: *They were accused of robbery with violence.* ○ *There's been a robbery. They've taken half a million pounds.* سرقة

robe /rəʊb/ *noun* [C] **1** a long, loose piece of clothing رداء ، ثوب

2 (*US*) = DRESSING GOWN

robin /ˈrɒbɪn/ *noun* [C] a small brown bird with a bright red breast أبو الحِنّ أو أبو الحنّاء

robocall /ˈrəʊbəʊkɔːl/ *noun* [C] a phone call from a company that is trying to sell you sth, using an automatic dialling system to call your number and a recorded message اتّصال هاتفي مُسجّل بهدف التسويق

robot /ˈrəʊbɒt/ *noun* [C] a machine that can move and that can be made to do some of the work that a person does. Some robots are made to look like people. الإنسان الميكانيكيّ

robust /rəʊˈbʌst/ *adj* strong and healthy: *a robust child* قويّ البنية

🔑 **rock¹** /rɒk/ *noun* **1** [U] the hard, stony part of the earth: *layers of rock formed over millions of years* صخر

2 [C] a large piece or area of this that sticks out of the sea or the ground: *The ship hit the rocks and started to sink.* صخرة كبيرة : ارض صخريّة

3 [C] a large, separate stone: *The beach was covered with rocks that had broken away from the cliffs.* صخرة

4 [C] (*US*) a small piece of stone that can be picked up: *The boy threw a rock at the dog.* حَجَر ، حصاة

5 [U] (*Brit*) a type of hard sweet made in long, round sticks حلوى صلبة أسطوانية الشكل

IDM **on the rocks 1** (used about drinks) served with ice but no water (مشروب كحوليّ) مع قطع من الثلج

2 (used about a marriage, business, etc.) having problems and likely to fail على وشك الانهيار

▸ **rocky** *adj* (**rockier**; **rockiest**) full of rocks or not level and smooth: *a rocky road* ○ *a rocky coastline* مليء بالصخور، وَعِر

rock² /rɒk/ *verb* **1** [I,T] to move backwards and forwards or from side to side; to make sb/sth do this: *fishing boats rocking gently on the waves* ○ *He rocked the baby in his arms to get her to sleep.* يتهزهز، يتأرجح؛ يهزهز أو يؤرجح؛ يهدهد

2 [T] to shake sth violently: *The city was rocked by a bomb blast.* يرجّ أو يهزّ بعنف

3 [T] to cause shock to sb/sth: *The country was rocked by the news of the riots.* يهزّ ، يصعق (بالخبر)

🔑 **rock³** /rɒk/ (*also* ˈ**rock music**) *noun* [U] a type of pop music with a very strong beat, played on electric guitars, etc: *I prefer jazz to rock.* ○ *a rock singer* ○ *a rock band* موسيقى حديثة قويّة الإيقاع

ˌ**rock and** ˈ**roll** (*also* **rock 'n' roll**) *noun* [U] a type of music with a strong beat that was most popular in the 1950s: *Elvis Presley was the king of rock and roll.* موسيقى "الروك أند رول"

ˌ**rock** ˈ**bottom** *noun* [U] the lowest point: *They say that house prices have reached rock bottom and will soon start to rise again.* ○ *a rock-bottom price* أدنى مستوى، الحضيض

ˈ**rock climbing** *noun* [U] the sport of climbing rocks and mountains with ropes, etc. رياضة تسلّق الجبال والجروف الصخريّة

rocket /ˈrɒkɪt/ *noun* [C] **1** a vehicle shaped like a tube, that is used for travel into space: *a space rocket* ○ *to launch a rocket* صاروخ

2 an object of a similar shape that is used as a weapon and that carries a bomb قنبلة صاروخيّة

3 a firework that shoots high into the air when you light it, and then explodes سهم ناريّ

▸ **rocket** *verb* [I] to increase or rise very quickly يزداد أو يرتفع بسرعة هائلة

rod /rɒd/ *noun* [C] (often in compounds) a thin straight piece of wood or metal: *a fishing rod* عصا ، قضيب ، عود

rode *pt* of RIDE²

rodent /ˈrəʊdnt/ *noun* [C] a type of small animal (such as a rat, a rabbit, a mouse, etc.) which has strong sharp front teeth حيوان قارض

rodeo /ˈrəʊdiəʊ; rəʊˈdeɪəʊ/ *noun* [C] (*pl.* **rodeos**) a contest or performance in which people show their skill in riding wild horses, catching cows, etc. مباراة في ركوب الخيول الجامحة وسَوْق الماشية

roe /rəʊ/ *noun* [U] the eggs or male seed of a fish, which can be eaten as food البَطارخ

rogue /rəʊɡ/ *noun* [C] (*old-fashioned*) a person who is not honest or reliable محتال ، وغد

▸ **rogue** *adj* behaving differently from other similar people or things, often causing damage: *a rogue gene/program* مارِق؛ ضار

🔑 **role** /rəʊl/ *noun* [C] **1** a person's part in a play, film, etc: *She was chosen to play the role of Cleopatra.* ○ *a leading role in the film* دور

2 the position and importance of sb/sth: *During her colleague's illness, she took on the role of supervisor.* ○ *Parents play a vital role in their children's education.* دور ؛ وظيفة

ˈ**role play** *noun* [C,U] an activity, used especially in teaching, in which a person acts a part لعبة تمثيل الأدوار

🔑 **roll¹** /rəʊl/ *noun* [C] **1** something made into the shape of a tube by winding it around itself: *a roll of film* لفّة، "كرّار"

2 a very small loaf of bread for one person: *a roll and butter for breakfast* ○ *a cheese roll* (= a roll filled with cheese) رغيف افرنجي صغير

3 an official list of names: *There are two hun-*

rolls

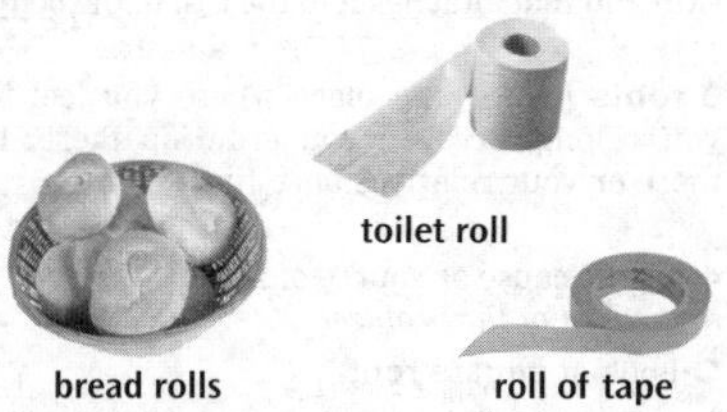

dred children on the school roll. ○ *the electoral roll* (= the list of people who can vote in an election) سجلّ ، قيْد

4 a long, low sound: *a roll of drums* ○ *the roll of thunder* هدير ، دويّ ، قرع

5 a movement from side to side: *the roll of a ship* ترنُّح ، تمايل

roll² /rəʊl/ *verb* **1** [I,T] to move by turning over and over; to make sth move in this way: *The apples fell out of the bag and rolled everywhere.* ○ *We couldn't stop the ball rolling into the river.* ○ *He tried to roll the rock up the hill.* يتدحرج ؛ يُدحرج

2 [I] to move smoothly (on wheels or as if on wheels): *The car began to roll back down the hill.* ○ *Tears were rolling down her cheeks.* ○ *Big black clouds came rolling across the sky.* يدرج ، يسير على دواليب ؛ ينساب

3 [I,T] to turn over or upwards; to make sb/sth do this: *She rolled over and looked up at him.* ○ *We rolled the log over to see what was underneath.* ينقلب؛ يستدير ؛ يقلب ؛ يدير

4 [I,T] **roll (sth) (up)** to make sth into the shape of a ball or tube; to be made into this shape: *He was rolling himself a cigarette.* ○ *The insect rolled up when I touched it.* ❶ The opposite is **unroll**. يلفّ ؛ يلتفّ ؛ يتكوّر

5 [T] to make sth become flat by moving sth heavy over it: *Roll out the pastry* (= using a rolling pin). يملّس ، يمدّ ، يسوّي

6 to rock or swing from side to side: *The ship was beginning to roll in the storm.* ○ *She was rolling about with laughter.* يتمايل ، يترنّح

IDM **be rolling in money/in it** (*slang*) to have a lot of money يمتلك مالاً كثيراً

PHRV **roll in** (*informal*) to arrive in large numbers or quantities: *Offers of help have been rolling in.* يتدفّق

roll up (*informal*) (used about a person or a vehicle) to arrive (often late) يصل (متأخّراً)

roller /ˈrəʊlə(r)/ *noun* [C] **1** a long object in the shape of a tube, which is usually part of a machine or a piece of equipment and can have various uses: *The tins are then crushed between two rollers.* ○ *a roller blind* (= a type of window blind on a roller) اسطوانة ، ملَفّ

2 [usually pl.] small plastic tubes that women wind their hair round to make it curl ملفّات الشَّعر

Rollerblade™ /ˈrəʊləbleɪd/ = IN-LINE SKATE

ˈ**roller coaster** *noun* [C] a type of railway with open carriages, sharp bends and very steep slopes. People go on roller coasters for fun at fairs, etc. (في مدينة الملاهي) قاطرات ترتفع عالياً ثم تهبط بسرعة هائلة

ˈ**roller skate** (*also* **skate**) *noun* [C] a type of shoe with small wheels on the bottom. It allows you to move quickly over a smooth surface: *a pair of roller skates* حذاء ذو دواليب للتزلُّق ، دحروجة
▸ ˈ**roller-skate** *verb* [I] يتزلّق (بحذاء ذي دواليب)
ˈ**roller skating** *noun* [U] رياضة التزلُّق (بأحذية ذات دواليب)

ˈ**rolling pin** *noun* [C] a piece of wood, etc. in the shape of a tube, that you use for making pastry flat and thin before cooking شوبك ، مرقاق العجين

Roman /ˈrəʊmən/ *adj* connected with ancient Rome: *the remains of a Roman villa* ○ *Roman coins* رومانيّ
▸ **Roman** *noun* [C] a citizen of Rome الرومانيّ، شخص من روما

the ˌRoman ˈalphabet *noun* [sing.] the letters A to Z, used especially in West European languages الأبجديّة الرومانيّة أو اللاتينيّة

ˌ**Roman ˈCatholic** (*also* **Catholic**) *noun* [C], *adj* (a member) of the Christian Church which has the Pope as its head: *She's (a) Roman Catholic.* ➲ Look at **Protestant**. أحد أفراد الكنيسة الكاثوليكيّة
▸ ˌ**Roman Caˈtholicism** (*also* **Catholicism**) *noun* [U] the beliefs of the Roman Catholic Church المعتقدات الكاثوليكيّة

romance¹ /rəʊˈmæns/ *noun* **1** [C] a love affair: *The film was about a teenage romance.* قصة غراميّة

2 [U] a feeling or atmosphere of love or of sth new, special and exciting: *The stars were out, the night was warm and romance was in the air.* شعور أو جوّ عاطفي خيالي

3 [C] a novel about a love affair: *She writes historical romances.* رواية غراميّة

ˌ**Roman ˈnumerals** *noun* [plural] the letters used by the ancient Romans as numbers الأرقام الرومانيّة

> Roman numerals, e.g. IV=4 and X=10, are still used sometimes. For example they may be found numbering the pages and chapters of books or on some clocks.

romantic /rəʊˈmæntɪk/ *adj* **1** having or showing ideas about life and love that are emotional rather than real or practical: *He has a romantic idea that he'd like to live on a farm in Scotland.* رومانسي ، خياليّ

2 involving a love affair; describing situations involving love: *Reports of a romantic relationship between the two film stars have been strongly denied.* ○ *a romantic novel* غرامي

3 having a quality that strongly affects your emotions or makes you think about love; showing feelings of love: *a romantic candlelit dinner* ○ *He isn't very romantic – he never says he loves me.* رومانسي، عاطفيّ ، مثير لعاطفة الحبّ
▸ **romantic** *noun* [C] a person who has ideas

a b c d e f g h i j k l m n o p q r s t u v w x y z

that are not based on real life or that are not very practical شخص رومانسي أي يعيش في عالم الخيال
romantically /-kli/ *adv* غرامياً ، عاطفياً
romanticize (*also* **romanticise**) /rəʊ'mæntɪsaɪz/ *verb* [I,T] to make sth seem more interesting, exciting, etc. than it really is يُضفي عليه بريقاً غير حقيقي

romp /rɒmp/ *verb* [I] (used about children and animals) to play in a noisy way with a lot of running, jumping, etc. يقفز ويمرح بصخب
▶ **romp** *noun* [C] لعب ومرح صاخب

roof /ru:f/ *noun* [C] (*pl.* **roofs**) **1** the part of a building, vehicle, etc. which covers the top of it: *the roof of the school* ○ *a flat roof* ○ *The coach had windows in the roof which allowed some air in.* ○ *The library and the sports hall are under one roof* (= in the same building). سقف
2 the highest part of sth: *The roof of the cave had collapsed.* سقف

'**roof rack** *noun* [C] a structure that you fix to the roof of a car and use for carrying luggage or other large objects منصب على ظهر السيّارة

rooftop /'ru:ftɒp/ *noun* [C, usually pl.] the outside of the roofs of buildings: *From the tower we looked down over the rooftops of the city.* سطح المنزل

rook /rʊk/ *noun* [C] a large black bird. Rooks build their nests in groups. زاغ، غراب القيظ، غداف

room /ru:m; rʊm/ *noun* **1** [C] a part of a house or building that is separated from the rest by its own walls, floor and ceiling: *The house has three rooms downstairs and four bedrooms.* ○ *a sitting room* ○ *a dining room* ○ *a spare room* (= for guests) ○ *There is a common room where students can meet and watch television.* ○ *to book a room at a hotel* ○ *a single/double room* غرفة ، حجرة
2 [U] **room (for sb/sth); room (to do sth)** space; enough space: *There isn't room for any more furniture in here.* ○ *The table takes up too much room.* ○ *They're pulling down those old factories to make room for new development.* ○ *There were so many people that there wasn't any room to move.* متّسع ، حيِّز
3 [U] **room (for sth)** the opportunity or need for sth: *There's room for improvement in your work* (= it could be much better). ➲ Look at the note at **place**[1]. مجال ، فرصة ، حاجة
▶ **roomful** /-fʊl/ *noun* [C] the amount or number that a room can contain: *There was a roomful of reporters waiting to interview him.* غرفة مليئة بِ ، مِلء غرفة
roomy *adj* (**roomier**; **roomiest**) having plenty of space: *a roomy house, car, etc.* واسع ، فسيح

'**room-mate** *noun* [C] a person that you share a room with in a flat, etc. ساكن مشارك في حجرة

roost /ru:st/ *noun* [C] a place where birds rest or sleep مجثَم أو مكان مَبيت الطائر

rooster /'ru:stə(r)/ *noun* [C] (*US*) = COCK[1] (1)

root[1] /ru:t/ *noun* **1** [C] the part of a plant that grows under the ground and takes in water and food from the soil جذر
2 [C] the part of a hair or tooth that is under the skin and that attaches it to the rest of the body جذر
3 roots [plural] the place where you feel that you belong, because you grew up there, live there or your relatives once lived there الأصول ، الجذور
4 [C] the cause or source of sth: *Let's try and get to the root of the problem.* مصدر ، أصل
➲ Look at **square root**.

root[2] /ru:t/ *verb*
PHR V **root about/around (for sth)** to search through things, especially in an untidy or careless way: *What are you rooting around in my desk for?* ينبِّش ، يبعثر الأشياء للتفتيش عن شيء
root for sb/sth to give support to sb who is in a competition, etc: *Good luck in the match – we'll all be rooting for you.* يناصر ، يساند
root sb/sth out to find and destroy sth bad completely يجتثّ ، يستأصل

rope

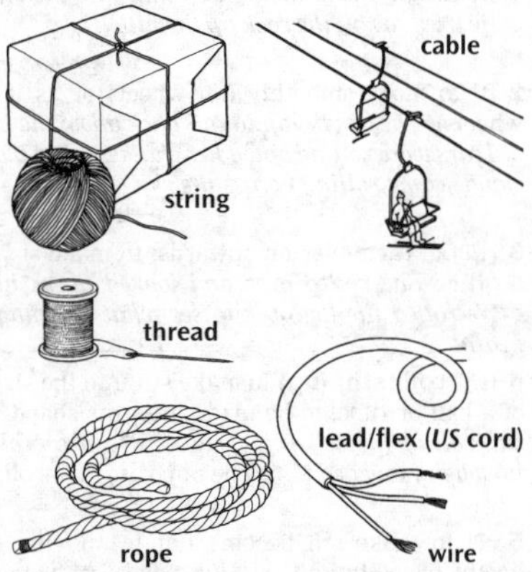

rope /rəʊp/ *noun* [C,U] very thick, strong cord, that is used for tying or lifting heavy things, climbing up, etc: *We need some rope to tie up the boat with.* ○ *a skipping rope* (= one that children use to jump over) حَبْل
▶ **rope** *verb* [T] to tie sb/sth with a rope: *The climbers were roped together when they crossed the glacier.* يربط أو يوثق بالحبال
PHR V **rope sb in (to do sth)** (*informal*) to persuade sb to help in some activity: *I've been roped in to help at the school play.* يُضطَر إلى تقديم المساعدة
rope sth off to put ropes round or across an area in order to keep people out of it يُحيط (مساحة) بالحبال لمنع الدخول اليها

'**rope ladder** *noun* [C] a ladder made of two long ropes and steps of rope, wood or metal سُلَّم من الحبال

rosary /'rəʊzəri/ *noun* [C] (*pl.* **rosaries**) a string of beads used for counting prayers سُبْحة أو مِسبَحة

rose[1] *pt* of RISE[2]

rose² /rəʊz/ *noun* [C] a flower with a sweet smell, that grows on a bush and usually has thorns on its stem وردة

rosemary /ˈrəʊzməri; *US* -meri/ *noun* [U] a bush with narrow sweet-smelling leaves which are used to give flavour to food: *lamb with rosemary and garlic* اكليل الجبل، حصا البان

rosette /rəʊˈzet/ *noun* [C] a large badge made from coloured ribbons. You may get one as a prize in a show or you may wear one to show that you support a sports team, political party, etc. وردية (من الشريط الملوّن)

roster /ˈrɒstə(r)/ *noun* [C] (*especially US*) = ROTA

rostrum /ˈrɒstrəm/ *noun* [C] (*pl.* **rostrums** or **rostra** /ˈrɒstrə/) a platform that sb stands on to make a public speech, etc. منبر الخطابة

rosy /ˈrəʊzi/ *adj* (**rosier**; **rosiest**) **1** deep pink in colour and (used about a person) healthy-looking: *rosy cheeks* وردي ، متورد

2 (used about a situation) full of good possibilities: *The future was looking rosy.* زاهر ، مشرق ، مبشّر بالخير

rot /rɒt/ *verb* (rotting; rotted) **1** [I] to go bad (as part of a natural process); to decay: *Wood will rot in damp conditions.* يتعفّن : يفسد ، ينتخِر

2 [T] to make sth go bad or decay: *Too many sweets will rot your teeth!* يفسّد ، ينخر

▸ **rot** *noun* [U] **1** the condition of being bad or rotten: *The floorboards have got rot in them.* تعفّن : فساد ، تآكل

2 (*old-fashioned, informal*) nonsense: *Don't talk rot!* كلام فارغ!

rota /ˈrəʊtə/ *noun* [C] (*pl.* **rotas**) (*US also* **roster**) a list of people who share a certain job or task and the times that they are each going to do it: *I have a rota with some other mothers for taking the children to school.* قائمة بأسماء المناوبين

rotary /ˈrəʊtəri/ *adj* moving in circles round a central point دوّار ، دَوَراني

rotate /rəʊˈteɪt; *US* ˈrəʊteɪt/ *verb* [I,T] **1** to turn in circles round a central point; to make sth do this: *The earth rotates around the sun.* ○ *You can see the parts that rotate the hands of the clock.* يدور : يدير

2 to happen in turn or in a particular order; to make sth do this: *The position of president is rotated among all the member countries.* يتناوب أو يتعاقب بالدور؛ يجعله متناوباً بالدور

▸ **rotation** /rəʊˈteɪʃn/ *noun* **1** [U] movement in circles: *the earth's rotation* دوران

2 [C] one complete turn around sth: *one rotation every 24 hours* دورة

rotor /ˈrəʊtə(r)/ *noun* [C] a part of a machine that turns round, especially the blades on top of a helicopter جهاز دوّار ، مراوح دوّارة

rotten /ˈrɒtn/ *adj* **1** (used about food and other substances) old and not fresh enough or good enough to use: *rotten vegetables* ○ *Some of the stairs were rotten and not safe.* فاسد ، متعفّن ، نخِر

2 (*informal*) very bad: *We had rotten weather all week.* رديء جداً

3 (*informal*) unfair, unkind or unpleasant: *That was a rotten thing to say to you!* قاسٍ ، مزعج

4 (*informal*) (used for emphasizing that you are angry): *You can keep your rotten job!* (للتعبير عن السخط): (عملك) اللعين!

rottweiler /ˈrɒtwaɪlə(r)/ *noun* [C] a large, often fierce, black and brown dog روتفيلر: كلب كبير يميل إلى الشراسة

rouge /ruːʒ/ *noun* [U] a red powder or cream used for giving more colour to the cheeks أحمر الخدود

rough¹ /rʌf/ *adj* **1** not smooth or level: *It's not easy to walk over such rough ground.* ○ *Her hands were rough with too much work.* وعر ، غير مستوٍ ؛ خشن

2 moving or behaving with too much force and not enough care; not gentle or calm: *There was rather a rough game of football going on.* ○ *The ferry was cancelled because the sea was so rough* (= because of a storm). ○ *I wouldn't walk alone in that part of London at night. It's very rough* (= there is a lot of crime or violence). خشن : هائج : شرس ، خَطِر

3 made or done quickly or without much care; approximately correct: *a rough estimate of what the work would cost* ○ *Can you give me a rough idea of what time you'll be arriving?* تقريبيّ ، غير دقيق

4 (*informal*) rather ill; unwell: *You look a bit rough – are you feeling all right?* منحرف الصحّة ، "تعبان شوية"

IDM **be rough (on sb)** be unpleasant or unlucky (for sb) يصعب عليه ، يقاسي ؛ يصاب بسوء الحظّ

a hard/rough ˈtime → TIME¹

▸ **roughly** *adv* **1** in a violent way; not gently: *He grabbed her roughly by her arm.* بخشونة ، بفظاظة

2 not exactly; approximately: *It took roughly three hours, I suppose.* تقريباً

roughness *noun* [U] the quality or state of being rough: *The roughness of the material irritated my skin.* خشونة ؛ وعورة ؛ شراسة الخ...

rough² /rʌf/ *adv* in a rough way: *One of the boys was told off for playing rough.* بخشونة

IDM **sleep rough** → SLEEP² (3)

rough³ /rʌf/ *noun*

IDM **in rough** in an early form, not finished properly: *Write out your essay in rough first.* في شكله الأولي ، في شكل مسودة

take the rough with the smooth to accept difficult or unpleasant things as well as pleasant things يقبل الحلو والمرّ

rough⁴ /rʌf/ *verb*

IDM **rough it** to live without the usual comforts of life: *You have to rough it a bit when you go camping.* يخشوشِن ، يعيش عيشة بدائيّة

roughage /ˈrʌfɪdʒ/ *noun* [U] the types or parts of food which help you to digest other foods خُشانة: طعام خشن

a b c d e f g h i j k l m n o p q r s t u v w x y z

roughen /ˈrʌfn/ *verb* [T] to make sth rough: *Her skin was roughened by the wind and cold.* يخشّن

round¹ /raʊnd/ *adj* having the shape of a circle or a ball: *a round table* ○ *People used to think the earth was flat, not round.* ○ *He had a fat, round face and fair hair.* مستدير
IDM **in round figures/numbers** given to the nearest 10, 100, 1 000, etc.; not given in exact figures or numbers (عدد) يقرّب إلى العشرة أو أضعافها

round² /raʊnd/ *adv* ❶ For special uses with many verbs, e.g. **come**, **get**, **go**, etc. see the verb entries

1 in a circle or curve to face another way or the opposite way: *She moved her chair round so that she could see out of the window.* ○ *Don't look round but the teacher's just come in.* (يدير) إلى الوراء

2 in a full circle: *The wheels spun round and round but the car wouldn't move.* دورات عديدة

3 measuring or marking a circle or the edge of sth: *You can't get in because there's a fence all round.* حول

4 from one place, person, etc. to another: *Pass the photographs round for everyone to see.* ○ *I've been rushing round all day.* من شخص (أو مكان) لآخر

5 to a particular place, especially where sb lives: *I'll pop round to see you at about 8 o'clock.* إلى بيته

IDM **round about** in the area near a place: *We've been to most of the restaurants round about.* في هذه المنطقة
the other way round in the opposite way or order: *My appointment's at 3 and Leila's is at 3.15 – or was it the other way round?* ❶ **Around** has the same meaning as **round** and is more common in American English. بالعكس

round³ /raʊnd/ *prep* **1** (used about movement) in a circle round a fixed point: *Ellen MacArthur was the youngest person to sail round the world solo.* حول

2 to or on the other side of sth: *There's a postbox just round the corner.* ○ (*figurative*) *It wasn't easy to see a way round the problem* (= a way of solving it). عند الطرف الآخر من...

3 on all sides of sth; surrounding sth: *He had a bandage right round his head.* ○ *We sat round the table, talking late into the night.* حول

4 in the area near a place: *Do you live round here?* قريب من

5 in or to many parts of sth: *Let me show you round the house.* ○ *We drove round France, stopping here and there.* في كل أنحاء

6 round about sth approximately: *We hope to arrive round about 6.* ❶ **Around** has the same meaning as **round** and is more common in American English. حوالى

round⁴ /raʊnd/ *noun* [C] **1** a number or set of events, etc: *a further round of talks with other European countries* سلسلة من...، جولة

2 a regular series of visits, etc., often as part of a job: *The postman's round takes him about three hours.* جولة

3 a number of drinks (one for all the people in a group): *I'll buy the first round.* ○ *It's my round* (=it's my turn to buy the drinks). مشروب يُشرى في بار لكل أفراد "الشلّة"، دَوْر

4 one part of a game or competition: *the third round of the boxing match* ○ *The winners of the first round will go on to the second stage of the competition.* جولة

5 (in golf) one game: *to play a round of golf* شوط أو لعبة في الغولف

6 a bullet or a number of bullets, fired from a gun: *He fired several rounds at us.* طلقة أو طلقات، عيار ناريّ

round⁵ /raʊnd/ *verb* [T] to go round sth: *The police car rounded the corner at high speed.* يدور حول

PHR V **round sth off** to end or complete sth in a satisfactory way: *We rounded off the meal with coffee and chocolates.* يختم، ينهي (نهاية سارّة)
round sb/sth up to gather sb/sth in one place: *The teacher rounded up the children.* يجمّع (في مكان واحد)
round sth up/down to increase/decrease a number, price, etc. to the nearest whole number: *Please round the price up to the nearest penny.* يقرّب الرقم من عدد صحيح

roundabout¹ /ˈraʊndəbaʊt/ *adj* longer than necessary, or usual; not direct: *We got lost and came*

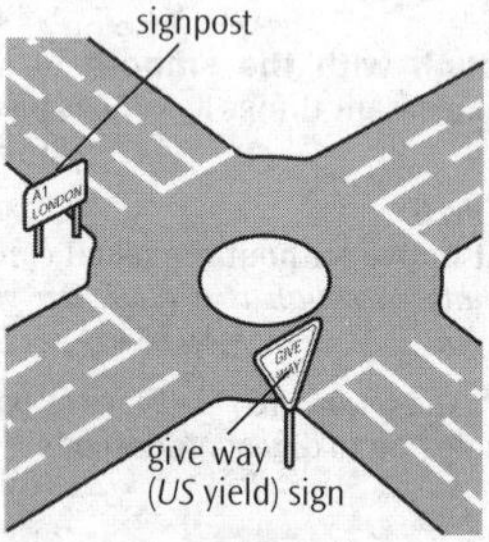

roundabout

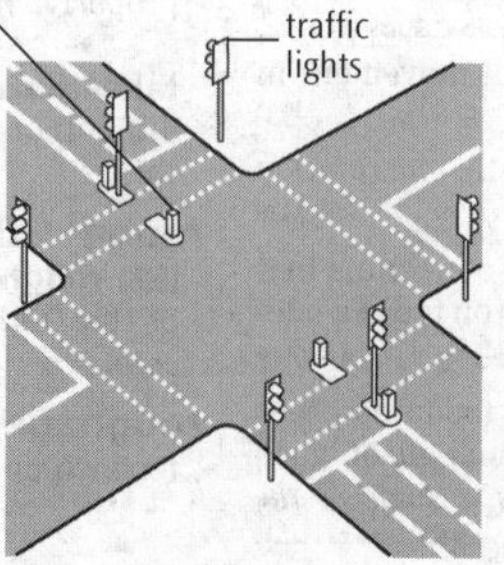

crossroads

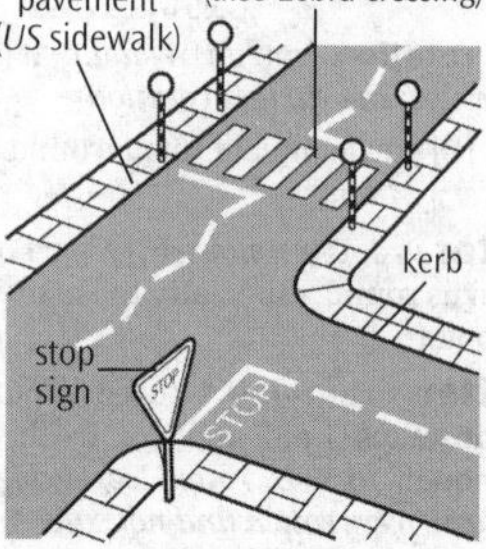

T-junction

by rather a roundabout route. غير مباشر ، (طريق) ملتوٍ

roundabout² /ˈraʊndəbaʊt/ *noun* [C] **1** a circular area where several roads meet. You drive round it until you come to the exit you want: *Give way to traffic that is already on the roundabout.* دوّار

2 (*also* **merry-go-round**; *US* **carousel**) a big round platform at a fair, etc. that turns round and round mechanically. It has model animals, etc. on it for children to ride on: *to have a ride on a roundabout* أرجوحة دوّارة ، "دويخة"

3 a round platform in a playground. Children sit or stand on it and sb pushes it round. منصّة دوّارة يلعب الأطفال عليها

rounders /ˈraʊndəz/ *noun* [U] (*Brit*) a game for two teams played with a bat and ball. Players have to hit the ball and then run round the outside of four posts arranged in a square. لعبة إنكليزية تشبه البيسبول

ˌround ˈtrip *noun* [C] **1** a journey to one or more places and back again, often by a different route رحلة ذهاب وإياب

2 (*US*) = RETURN²(5): *a round-trip ticket*

rouse /raʊz/ *verb* [T] **1** (*formal*) to make sb wake up: *She was sleeping so soundly that I couldn't rouse her.* يوقظ

2 to make sb/sth very angry, excited, interested, etc: *He can get very angry when he's roused.* يهيّج ، يثير ، يحفظ

▸ **rousing** *adj* exciting and powerful: *a rousing speech* مثير

rout /raʊt/ *noun* [C] a complete defeat, ending in disorder اندحار ، هزيمة شنعاء

▸ **rout** *verb* [T] to defeat sb completely يدحر ، يهزمه شرّ هزيمة

⚷ **route** /ruːt; *US* raʊt/ *noun* [C] **1** a way from one place to another: *We took the fastest and most direct route to the coast.* ○ *I got a leaflet about the bus routes from the information office.* ○ *Thousands of people were waiting beside the route that the President's car would take.* طريق ؛ خطّ مواصلات

2 a way of achieving sth: *Hard work is the only route to success.* سبيل ، طريق

⚷ **routine** /ruːˈtiːn/ *noun* **1** [C,U] the fixed and usual way of doing things: *Make exercise part of your daily routine.* ○ *Children like routine. They like to know what to expect.* روتين ، طريقة العمل المعتادة

2 [U] tasks that have to be done again and again and so are boring: *I gave up the job because I couldn't stand the routine.* عمل رتيب مملّ

▸ **routine** *adj* **1** normal and regular; not unusual or special: *The police would like to ask you some routine questions.* معتاد ، اعتيادي ، روتيني

2 boring; not exciting: *It's a very routine job, really.* مملّ ، رتيب

routinely *adv* very often; regularly; as part of a routine: *The machines are routinely checked every two months.* بشكل دوري ، بانتظام

⚷ **row¹** /rəʊ/ *noun* [C] **1** a line of people or things: *a row of books* ○ *The children were all standing in a row at the front of the class.* صفّ

2 a line of seats in a theatre, cinema, etc: *Our seats were in the back row.* ○ *a front-row seat* صفّ

IDM **in a row** one after another; without a break: *It rained solidly for four days in a row.* على التوالي ، دون انقطاع

row² /rəʊ/ *verb* **1** [I,T] to move a boat through the water using oars: *We often go rowing on the lake.* ○ *He rowed the boat slowly down the river.* يجذّف

2 [T] to carry sb/sth in a boat that you row: *Could you row us over to the island?* ينقل في قارب تجذيف

▸ **row** *noun* [sing.] a trip in a boat that you row: *We went for a row on the river.* نزهة في قارب تجذيف

row³ /raʊ/ *noun* **1** [C] a noisy argument between two or more people: *Lucy has had a row with her boyfriend.* مشادّة حادّة ، شجار بصوت عال

2 [C] a public argument especially among politicians: *A row has broken out between the main parties over education.* خلاف ، نزاع

3 [sing.] a loud noise: *What a row! Could you be a bit quieter?* ضجّة ، "دَوْشة"

▸ **row** *verb* [I] to quarrel noisily: *My husband and I are always rowing about money!* يتشاجر (بصوت عال)

rowan /ˈrəʊən; ˈraʊən/ (*also* **ˈrowan tree**) *noun* [C] a type of tree that has red berries in the autumn شجرة السمّن، غبيراء الحابلين

rowdy /ˈraʊdi/ *adj* (**rowdier**; **rowdiest**) noisy and uncontrolled: *rowdy behaviour among a group of football fans* صاخب ، مشاكس ، معربد

▸ **rowdily** *adv* بشجار صاخب

rowdiness *noun* [U] صخب ، مشاكسة ، عربدة

ˈrowing boat (*US* **rowboat** /ˈrəʊbəʊt/) *noun* [C] a small boat that you move through the water using oars قارب تجذيف

⚷ **royal** /ˈrɔɪəl/ *adj* **1** connected with a king, queen or a member of their family: *the royal family* ○ *the royal visit to New Zealand* ملكي

2 (used in the names of organizations) supported by a member of the royal family: *the Royal Society for the Protection of Birds* ملكي

▸ **royal** *noun* [C] (*informal*) a member of the royal family أحد أفراد العائلة المالكة

ˌroyal ˈblue *adj* deep bright blue in colour أزرق غامق

ˌRoyal ˈHighness *noun* [C] (used when you are speaking to or about a member of the royal family): *their Royal Highnesses, the King and Queen of Spain* السموّ الملكي

royalty /ˈrɔɪəlti/ *noun* (*pl.* **royalties**) **1** [U] members of the royal family أفراد العائلة المالكة

2 [C] an amount of money that is paid to the person who wrote a book, piece of music, etc. every time his/her work is sold or performed حصّة يتقاضاها المؤلّف من بيع مؤلّفاته، ريع

rpm /ˌɑː piː ˈem/ *abbrev* = REVOLUTIONS PER MINUTE

RSI /ˌɑːr es ˈaɪ/ *noun* [U] repetitive strain injury;

pain and swelling, especially in the wrists and hands, caused by doing the same movement many times in a job or an activity إجهاد أو ألم العمل المتكرر

RSVP /ˌɑːr es viː ˈpiː/ *abbrev* (used on invitations) please reply الرجاء الردّ

rub /rʌb/ *verb* (ru**bb**ing; ru**bb**ed) **1** [I,T] to move your hand, a cloth, etc. backwards and forwards on the surface of sth while pressing firmly: *Ralph rubbed his hands together to keep them warm.* ○ *Rub hard and the mark should come out.* ○ *The cat rubbed against my leg.* ○ *The cat rubbed its head against my leg.* ○ *He rubbed his face with his hand.* ○ *He rubbed his hand across his face.* ○ *He rubbed the sweat off his face with his hand.* يفرك، يحكّ : يمسح

2 [T] to put a cream, liquid, etc. onto a surface by rubbing (1): *Apply a little of the lotion and rub it into the skin.* يدلّك أو يدعك

3 [I] **rub (on/against sth)** to press on/against sth (often causing pain or damage): *These new shoes are rubbing my heels.* يحتكّ بِ، يضغط على

PHRV **rub off (on/onto sb)** (used about a good quality) to be transferred from one person to another: *Let's hope some of her enthusiasm rubs off onto her brother.* ينتقل إلى، يعدي

rub sth out to remove the marks made by a pencil, chalk, etc. using a rubber, cloth, etc: *That answer is wrong. Rub it out.* يمحو

▶ **rub** *noun* [C] an act of rubbing (1): *Give your shoes a rub before you go out.* مَسْح، صَقْل

rubber /ˈrʌbə(r)/ *noun* **1** [U] a strong substance that is made chemically or from the juice of a tropical tree. Rubber is elastic (= it can stretch and then return to its original shape) and it is also waterproof: *Car tyres are made of rubber.* ○ *foam rubber* ○ *rubber gloves for washing up* المطّاط

2 [C] (*especially US* **eraser**) a small piece of rubber that you use for removing pencil marks from paper ممحاة

3 [C] (*informal*) = CONDOM

▶ **rubbery** /ˈrʌbəri/ *adj* like rubber شبيه بالمطّاط

ˌrubber ˈband (*also* **elastic band**) *noun* [C] a thin circular piece of rubber that is used for holding things together: *Her hair was tied back with a rubber band.* مطّاطة

ˌrubber ˈstamp *noun* [C] a piece of equipment with rubber letters on it that you use for printing a name, date, etc. on a document ختم من المطّاط

▶ **ˌrubber-ˈstamp** *verb* [T] (usually used about sb with authority) to agree to sth without thinking about it carefully يبصم أو يوافق (على شيء) دون اكتراث

rubbish /ˈrʌbɪʃ/ (*US* **garbage**; **trash**) *noun* [U] **1** things that you do not want any more; waste material: *The dustmen collect the rubbish every Monday.* ○ *a rubbish bin* ○ *It's only rubbish – throw it away.* زبالة، قمامة

2 something that you think is bad, silly or wrong: *Don't talk such rubbish.* هراء، كلام فارغ

rubble /ˈrʌbl/ *noun* [U] pieces of broken brick, stone, etc., especially from a damaged building أنقاض

rubella /ruːˈbelə/ *noun* [U] = GERMAN MEASLES

ruby /ˈruːbi/ *noun* [C] (*pl.* **rubies**) a type of precious stone that is red ياقوت

rucksack /ˈrʌksæk/ (*especially US* **backpack**) *noun* [C] a bag that you use for carrying things on your back. You often use a rucksack when you are walking, camping, etc. حقيبة تحمل على الظهر

rudder /ˈrʌdə(r)/ *noun* [C] a piece of wood or metal that is used for controlling the direction of a boat or an aeroplane دَفّة أو سُكّان

rude /ruːd/ *adj* **1** not polite: *It's rude to interrupt when people are speaking.* ○ *He's often rude to his mother.* ○ *I think it was rude of them not to phone and say that they weren't coming.* ➲ Look at **impolite**. عديم الأدب، وقح

2 connected with sex, using the toilet, etc: *a rude joke* ○ *a rude word* بذيء

3 sudden and unpleasant: *If you're expecting any help from him, you're in for a rude shock.* مباغت ومزعج، عنيف

▶ **rudely** *adv* بوقاحة، دون مراعاة للآخرين

rudeness *noun* [U] وقاحة، قلة أدب

rudimentary /ˌruːdɪˈmentri/ *adj* basic or very simple أولي، ابتدائي

ruffle /ˈrʌfl/ *verb* [T] **1** to make sth untidy or no longer smooth: *The bird ruffled up its feathers.* ○ *to ruffle sb's hair* ينفش

2 (often passive) to make sb annoyed or confused يزعج، يربك

rug /rʌg/ *noun* [C] **1** a piece of thick material that covers a small part of a floor ➲ Look at **carpet**. سجّادة، بساط

2 a type of blanket that you put over your legs or around your shoulders بطّانية لتغطية الساقين أو الكتفين

rugby /ˈrʌgbi/ (*also* **ˌrugby ˈfootball**) *noun* [U] a form of football that is played by two teams of 13 or 15 players with an oval ball that can be carried or kicked لعبة الرَّكْبي (أو الرَّجْبي)

> Rugby **League** is a game with 13 players in a team, and Rugby **Union** has 15 players in a team.

rugged /ˈrʌgɪd/ *adj* **1** (used about land) rough and rocky with few plants: *a rugged coastline* وعر

2 (used about a man) looking strong قويّ البنية : صارم خشن

ruin /ˈruːɪn/ *noun* **1** [U] a state of destruction, when sth is completely spoilt: *The city was in a state of ruin.* خراب، دمار

2 [U] the cause or state of having lost all your money, hope of being successful, etc: *Many small companies are facing financial ruin.* انهيار، إفلاس

3 [C] a building, town, etc. that has been badly damaged or destroyed; the parts of a building, town, etc. that are left when it has been almost completely destroyed: *The old house is now a*

ruin. ○ *We went to look at the ruins of the castle.* ○ *the ruins of the ancient city of Pompeii* خراب ؛ آثار ، أطلال

IDM **go to rack and ruin** → RACK[3]

in ruin(s) badly damaged or destroyed: *After the accident her life seemed to be in ruins.* ○ *The city of Berlin was in ruins at the end of the war.* مهدّم ؛ محطّم

▶ **ruin** *verb* [T] **1** to damage sth badly, to destroy: *a ruined building* ○ *The crops were ruined by the late frost.* يتلف ؛ يخرّب

2 to spoil sth so that it is no longer good: *Much of the coast has been ruined by tourism.* ○ *My dress was ruined when I spilled coffee over it.* يتلف ، يخرّب

3 to cause sb to lose all his/her money, hope of being successful, etc: *The cost of the court case nearly ruined them.* يفلس ؛ يحطّم (آماله)

ruinous /ˈruːɪnəs/ *adj* (*formal*) costing much more money than you can afford to spend مجلبة للإفلاس

⚷**rule** /ruːl/ *noun* **1** [C] an official statement that tells you what you can or cannot do, say, etc: *to obey/break a rule* ○ *Do you know the rules of chess?* ○ *It's against the rules to smoke in this area.* ○ *rules and regulations* ❶ A **law** is stronger. You can be officially punished if you break it. نظام ، قاعدة ، قانون

2 [C] (in a language) a description of what is usual or correct: *What is the rule for forming the past tense?* قاعدة

3 [sing.] what is usual: *Large families are the exception rather than the rule nowadays.* الحالة العاديّة ، الأمر الغالب

4 [U] government; control: *Indonesia was formerly under Dutch rule.* ○ *the rule of law* حكم

IDM **as a (general) rule** (*formal*) usually: *Women, as a rule, live longer than men.* عادةً ، كقاعدة عامة

bend the rules → BEND[1]

work to rule a form of industrial protest in which you follow the rules of your employment very closely so that your work takes longer than usual يتقيّد بحرفية الأنظمة كي يبطئ العمل

▶ **rule** *verb* [I,T] **1 rule (over sb/sth)** to have the power over a country, etc: *Britain once ruled over a vast empire.* ○ *The Congress Party ruled India for almost 40 years.* ○ (*figurative*) *His whole life was ruled by his ambition to become Prime Minister.* يحكم ، يسيطر على

2 to make an official decision: *The judge ruled that the police officers had not acted unlawfully.* يقضي ، يحكم

PHR V **rule sb/sth out** to say that sb/sth is not thought to be possible: *The government has ruled out further increases in train fares next year.* يستبعد ، يستثني

⚷**ruler** /ˈruːlə(r)/ *noun* [C] **1** a person who rules a country, etc. حاكم

2 a straight piece of wood, plastic, etc. marked with inches or centimetres, that you use for measuring sth or for drawing straight lines مسطرة

ruling[1] /ˈruːlɪŋ/ *adj* (only *before* a noun) with the most power in an organization, country, etc: *the ruling Nationalist Party in South Africa* مسيطر

ruling[2] /ˈruːlɪŋ/ *noun* [C] an official decision: *a ruling of the European Court of Justice* قرار رسميّ ، حكم

rumble /ˈrʌmbl/ *verb* [I] to make a deep heavy sound: *Thunder was rumbling in the distance.* ○ *I was so hungry that my stomach was rumbling.* يدوّي ؛ يقرقر

▶ **rumble** *noun*: *the distant rumble of thunder* دويّ ؛ قرقرة

rummage /ˈrʌmɪdʒ/ *verb* [I] to move things and make them untidy while you are looking for sth: *Nina rummaged through the drawer looking for the tin-opener.* يبعثر الأشياء مفتّشاً عن شيء

⚷**rumour** (*US* **rumor**) /ˈruːmə(r)/ *noun* [C,U] (a piece of) news or information that many people are talking about but that is possibly not true: *There's a rumour going round that the firm is going to close.* ○ *Rumour has it* (= people are saying) *that Len has resigned.* ○ *to confirm/deny a rumour* (= to say that it is true/not true) إشاعة

▶ **rumoured** (*US* **rumored**) *adj* said in an unofficial way (but perhaps not true): *It is rumoured that they are getting divorced.* ○ *They are rumoured to be getting divorced.* يُقال ، تروج الإشاعة...

rump /rʌmp/ *noun* [C] the back end of an animal: *rump steak* (= meat from the rump) عَجز ، ردف

⚷**run[1]** /rʌn/ *verb* [I,T] (*pres part* **running**; *pt* **ran** /ræn/; *pp* **run**) **1** [I,T] to move using your legs, going faster than when you walk: *I had to run to catch the bus.* ○ *The children came running to meet us.* ○ *She's running in the 100 metres* (= in a race). ○ *I ran nearly ten kilometres this morning.* يركض ، يعدو

2 [I,T] to move, or move sth, quickly in a particular direction: *The car ran downhill and crashed into a wall.* ○ *She ran her finger down the list of passengers.* يسرع ، ينطلق ؛ يزلق بسرعة

3 [I] to go in a particular direction: *The road runs along the side of a lake.* يسير ، يمتدّ

4 [I] (used about water, a liquid, or a river, etc.) to flow: *When it's really cold, my nose runs.* ○ *I can hear a tap running somewhere* (= the water from a tap). يسيل

5 [T] to start water flowing, e.g. in a bath: *She's running the children's bath.* يفتح صنبور الماء مثلاً

6 [I] (used about the colour in material, etc.) to spread (e.g. when the material is washed): *Don't put that red shirt in the washing machine. It might run.* (اللون) ينحلّ أو يفشو

7 [I] (used about buses, trains, etc.) to travel at regular times: *All the trains are running late this morning.* يقوم برحلات منتظمة

8 [I] (used about a machine, an organization, a system, etc.) to work or function: *The engine is running very smoothly now.* يعمل ، يسير

9 [T] to start a machine, etc. and make it work: *Run the engine for a few minutes before you start.*

a b c d e f g h i j k l m n o p q **r** s t u v w x y z

○ *We're running a new computer program today.* يشغّل

10 [T] to organize or be in charge of sth: *They run a restaurant in Bath.* يدير

11 [T] to use and pay for sth: *It costs a lot to run a car.* يمتلك ، يستخدم

12 [I] to be one of the people to be chosen (a candidate) in an election: *He's running for president.* يرشّح

13 [I] to continue for a time: *The play ran for nearly two years in a London theatre.* يدوم ، يستمر

14 [T] to publish sth in a newspaper or magazine: *'The Independent' is running a series of articles on pollution.* ينشر في مجلة أو جريدة

15 run a test/check (on sth) to do a test or check on sth: *They're running checks on the power supply to see what the problem is.* يفحص، يختبر

IDM **be running at** to be at a certain level: *The interest rate is now running at 10%.* يبلغ مستواه

up and running → UP ℹ For other idioms containing **run**, look at the entries for the nouns, adjectives, etc., e.g. **run in the family** is at **family**.

PHR V **run across sb/sth** to meet or find sb/sth by chance يصادف : يعثر على شيء صدفة

run away to escape from somewhere: *He's run away from school.* يهرب

run sb/sth down to criticize sb/sth: *He's always running his children down.* ينتقد

run (sth) down to stop functioning gradually; to make sth do this: *Turn the lights off or you'll run the battery down.* ينهك، يستنفد

run into sb to meet sb by chance يصادف

run into sth to have difficulties or a problem: *If you run into any problems, just let me know.* يواجه (صعوبات وما إليها)

run (sth) into sb/sth to hit sb/sth with a car, etc: *He ran his car into a brick wall.* يرطم ، يصدم

run sth off to copy sth, using a machine يستنسخ (على الناسخة)

run off with sth to take or steal sth: *Who's run off with my pen?* يسرق

run out (of sth) to finish your supply of sth; to come to an end: *We've run out of coffee.* ○ *Time is running out.* يستنفد : ينضب

run sb over to hit sb with a car, etc: *The child was run over as he was crossing the road.* يدهس

run through sth to discuss or read sth quickly: *She ran through the names on the list.* يقرأ أو يناقش شيئاً بسرعة

run² /rʌn/ *noun* **1** [C] an act of running on foot: *Kate goes for a three-mile run every morning.* ○ *a cross-country run* عَدْو ، جري

2 [C] a journey by car, train, etc: *We went for a very pleasant run through the Cotswolds.* رحلة بالسيّارة وغيرها

3 [C] a continuous series of performances of a play, film, etc: *Agatha Christie's 'Mousetrap' has had a run of more than twenty years.* عرض طويل الأمد لمسرحية مثلاً

4 [sing.] a series of similar events or sth that continues for a very long time: *We've had a run of bad luck recently.* سلسلة من (الحوادث)

5 [sing.] **a run on sth** a sudden great demand for sth: *There's always a run on ice cream in the warmer weather.* طلب كبير مفاجئ ، "هجوم"

6 [C] a point in the games of baseball and cricket نقطة في لعبتي البيسبول والكريكيت

7 (*US*) = LADDER (2)

IDM **in the long run** → LONG¹ (2)

on the run hiding or trying to escape from sb/sth: *The escaped prisoner is still on the run.* مختبئ ، فارّ

the ordinary, average, etc. run of sth the ordinary, average, etc. type of sth النوع العادي

runaway /ˈrʌnəweɪ/ *adj* **1** out of control: *a runaway train* فالت ، جامح ؛ شارد

2 happening very easily: *His first novel was a runaway success.* سهل (المنال)

ˌrun-ˈdown *adj* **1** in bad condition: *a run-down block of flats* خَرِب ، غير معتنى به

2 not healthy: *You're looking very run-down.* مُتعَب ، منحرف الصحّة

rung¹ /rʌŋ/ *noun* [C] one of the bars that form the steps of a ladder درجة سُلّم

rung² *pp* of RING²

runner /ˈrʌnə(r)/ *noun* [C] **1** a person or animal that runs, especially in a race: *a long-distance runner* عدّاء

2 a person who takes guns, drugs, etc. illegally from one country to another مهرّب أسلحة أو مخدّرات

ˌrunner-ˈup *noun* [C] (*pl.* **runners-up**) the person or team that finished second in a race or competition الفائز الثاني

running /ˈrʌnɪŋ/ *noun* [U] **1** the act or sport of running: *Ian goes running every morning.* ○ *running shoes* جري ، ركض

2 the management of a business or other organization: *She's not involved in the day-to-day running of the office.* ○ *the running costs of a car* (= petrol, insurance, repairs, etc.) إدارة ، تسيير

IDM **in/out of the running (for sth)** (*informal*) having/not having a good chance of getting or winning sth يحتمل (أو لا يحتمل) فوزه

▶ **running** *adj* **1** (only *before* a noun) not stopping; continuous: *a running battle between two rival gangs* دائم ، مستمرّ

2 (used after a number and a noun) one after another, without a break: *Our school has won the competition for four years running.* متتابع ، على التوالي

3 (only *before* a noun) flowing or available from a tap (used about water): *There is no running water in many villages in India.* (ماء) جارٍ

ˌrunning ˈcommentary *noun* [C] a spoken description of sth while it is happening وصف حيّ للأحداث الجارية

runny /ˈrʌni/ *adj* (**runnier**; **runniest**) (*informal*) **1** containing more liquid than is usual or than you expected: *runny jam* مائع ، غير متجمّد كما يجب

2 (used about your eyes or nose) producing too much liquid: *Their children always seem to have runny noses.* (أنف) كثير السيلان

'run-up *noun* [sing.] the period of time before a certain event: *the run-up to the election* الفترة التي تسبق حدثاً معيناً

runway /'rʌnweɪ/ *noun* [C] a long piece of ground with a hard surface where aircraft take off and land مدرج

rupture /'rʌptʃə(r)/ *noun* [C,U] **1** a sudden breaking or tearing انفجار : تمزق ، فتق

2 = HERNIA

▸ **rupture** *verb* [I,T] to break or tear ينفجر ، يتمزق ؛ ينفتق

rural /'rʊərəl/ *adj* connected with the country, not the town: *a museum of rural life* ○ *They said that the new road would spoil the rural character of the area.* ❶ The opposite is **urban**. ريفي

ruse /ru:z/ *noun* [C] a trick or clever plan خدعة ، تدبيرة

rush[1] /rʌʃ/ *verb* **1** [I] to go or come very quickly: *Don't rush – take your time.* ○ *The children rushed out of school.* ○ *I rushed back home when I got the news.* ○ *Don't rush off – I want to talk to you.* يندفع ، يسرع

2 [I] **rush to do sth** to do sth without delay: *The public rushed to buy shares in the new company.* يسرع

3 [T] to take sb/sth to a place very quickly: *He suffered a heart attack and was rushed to hospital.* ينقل بسرعة

4 [I,T] **rush (sb) (into sth/into doing sth)** to do sth in a hurry or without enough thought; to make sb act in this way: *I'm afraid that we rushed into buying the house – it was a mistake.* ○ *Don't rush your food – there's plenty of time.* ○ *Don't let yourself be rushed into marriage.* يتسرّع ؛ يحثّه على الإسراع

rush[2] /rʌʃ/ *noun* **1** [sing.] a sudden quick movement: *At the end of the match there was a rush for the exits.* اندفاع ، هجوم

2 [sing., U] (a need for) hurry: *I can't stop now. I'm in a terrible rush.* ○ *Don't hurry your meal. There's no rush.* عجلة

3 [sing.] a time when many people try to get sth: *There's been a rush to buy petrol before the price goes up.* تهافت ، هجوم

4 [sing.] a time when there is a lot of activity and people are very busy: *There is always a rush in the shops before Christmas.* حركة ، زحمة

rush[3] /rʌʃ/ *noun* [C] a type of tall grass that grows near water. Rushes can be dried and then used for making chair-seats, baskets, etc. نبات الأسَل أو السَمار

'rush hour *noun* [C] the time each day when the traffic is busy because people are travelling to or from work: *rush-hour traffic* فترة ازدحام الطرق بوسائل المواصلات

rust /rʌst/ *noun* [U] a reddish-brown substance that forms on the surface of iron, etc., caused by the action of air and water صدأ

▸ **rust** *verb* [I,T] to (cause sth to) be attacked by rust: *Some parts of the car had rusted quite badly.* ○ *The sea air had rusted the car quite badly.* يصدأ : يصدئ

rusty *adj* (**rustier**; **rustiest**) **1** covered with rust: *rusty tins* صَدِئ

2 (used about a skill) of poor quality because you have not used it for a long time: *I'm afraid my French is rather rusty.* صدئ أو ضعيف (لقلة الممارسة)

rustic /'rʌstɪk/ *adj* typical of the country (and therefore simple and unspoilt): *The whole area is full of rustic charm.* ○ *The rooms are decorated in a rustic style.* ➲ Look at **rural** and **urban**. ريفيّ : بسيط

rustle /'rʌsl/ *verb* [I,T] to make a sound like dry leaves moving together; to cause sth to make this sound: *There was a rustling noise in the bushes.* ○ *Somebody behind me was rustling his newspaper all through the concert.* يحفّ : يخشخش بـ

PHRV **rustle sb/sth up** (*informal*) to find sb or prepare sth in a short time: *to rustle up a quick snack* يجد (عدداً من الناس) أو يهيئ (وجبة طعام) بسرعة ودون استعداد

▸ **rustle** *noun* [sing.] the sound that dry leaves, etc. make when they move حفيف ، خشخشة

rut /rʌt/ *noun* [C] a deep track that a wheel makes in soft ground أخدود يتركه الدولاب في أرض ليّنة

IDM **be in a rut** to have a boring way of life that is difficult to change يعيش حياة رتيبة مملّة

ruthless /'ru:θləs/ *adj* showing no pity or sympathy towards other people; thinking first about yourself and what you want: *You have to be ruthless to succeed in politics.* عديم الرأفة ، قاسي القلب

▸ **ruthlessly** *adv* بقسوة ، بلا رحمة

ruthlessness *noun* [U] قسوة : بطش

RV /,ɑ: 'vi:/ *noun* [C] recreational vehicle; a large vehicle designed for people to live and sleep in when they are travelling "سيارة الاستجمام"

rye /raɪ/ *noun* [U] a plant that is grown in colder countries for its grain, which is used to make flour نبات الشيلم أو الجاودار

S s

S, s /es/ *noun* [C] (*pl.* **Ss**; **S's**; **s's**) the nineteenth letter of the English alphabet: *'School' begins with (an) 'S'.* الحرف التاسع عشر من الأبجديّة الإنكليزية

S *abbrev* **1** small (size) = SMALL (SIZE)
2 (*US also* **So.**) = SOUTH(ERN)

sabbath /ˈsæbəθ/ *noun* [sing.] (*also* **the Sabbath**) the day of the week for rest and worship in certain religions (Sunday for Christians, Friday for Muslims) يوم الراحة والعبادة

sabotage /ˈsæbətɑːʒ/ *noun* [U] damage that is done on purpose and secretly in order to prevent an enemy or competitor being successful, e.g. by destroying machinery, roads, bridges, etc. or by spoiling plans: *There has been an explosion at the oil refinery, and sabotage is suspected.* تخريب
▸ **sabotage** *verb* [T] to destroy or damage sth by using sabotage: *There are rumours that the plane which crashed has been sabotaged.* يخرّب

saccharin /ˈsækərɪn/ *noun* [U] a very sweet substance that can be used instead of sugar مادّة السكَرين

sachet /ˈsæʃeɪ; *US* sæˈʃeɪ/ *noun* [C] a small (often plastic) packet that contains a small amount of a product: *a sachet of shampoo* ظرف أو كيس صغير

sack[1] /sæk/ *noun* [C] a large bag made from rough heavy material, paper or plastic, used for carrying or storing things (e.g. vegetables, flour, coal, etc.): *sacks of flour* ○ *We threw away several sacks of rubbish when we moved house.* كيس

sack[2] /sæk/ *verb* [T] (*Brit*) to say that sb can no longer work for you (because of bad work, bad behaviour, etc.): *Her boss has threatened to sack her if she's late again.* يعزل من العمل

> We can also say **give sb the sack**. The person **gets** the sack: *Tony's work wasn't good enough and he was given the sack.* ○ *Tony got the sack for poor work.*

sacred /ˈseɪkrɪd/ *adj* **1** connected with God, a god or religion; having a special religious meaning: *sacred music* (= music played in religious services) ○ *The Koran is the sacred book of Muslims.* ديني ؛ مقدس
2 too important and special to be changed or harmed: *a sacred tradition* "مقدّس" لا يجوز مسّه

sacrifice /ˈsækrɪfaɪs/ *noun* **1** [U] the act of offering sth, e.g. an animal that has been killed, to a god تضحية ، تقديم القربان
2 [C] the thing that has been offered in this way: *They killed a lamb as a sacrifice.* ضحيّة ، قربان
3 [C,U] the act of giving up sth that is important or valuable in order to achieve sth; the thing that you give up in this way: *If we're going to have a holiday this year, we'll have to make some sacrifices.* ○ *He was willing to make any sacrifice in order to succeed.* تضحية
▸ **sacrifice** *verb* **1** [I,T] to offer sth to a god, often by killing it يضحّي، يقدّم قرباناً
2 [T] to give up sth important or valuable in order to achieve sth: *to sacrifice your life for your country* ○ *She is not willing to sacrifice her career in order to have children.* يضحّي بـ

sacrilege /ˈsækrəlɪdʒ/ *noun* [U] treating sth that is considered holy or very special without the respect that it deserves تدنيس المقدّسات

sad /sæd/ *adj* (**sadder**; **saddest**) **1** unhappy or causing unhappiness: *I was sad to hear of the death of your father.* ○ *I'm very sad that you don't trust me.* ○ *That's one of the saddest stories I've ever heard!* حزين ؛ محزن
2 bad or unsatisfactory: *It's a sad state of affairs when your best friend doesn't trust you.* رديء ؛ مؤسف
▸ **sadden** /ˈsædn/ *verb* [T] to cause sb to feel sad: *The news of your father's death saddened me greatly.* يحزن
sadly *adv* **1** in a way that shows unhappiness: *He spoke sadly about the death of his father.* بحزن وأسى
2 unfortunately: *I'd love to come to your party but sadly I'm busy that night.* للأسف
3 in a way that is wrong: *If you think that I've forgotten what you did, you're sadly mistaken.* على نحو غير صحيح
sadness *noun* [C,U] the feeling of being sad or a thing that causes unhappiness حزن ، كآبة

saddle /ˈsædl/ *noun* [C] **1** a seat, usually made of leather, that you put on a horse so that you can ride it سرج
2 a seat on a bicycle or motorcycle سرج
▸ **saddle** *verb* [I,T] to put a saddle on a horse, etc. يسرج
PHR V **saddle sb with sth** to give sb a responsibility or task that he/she does not want: *I've been saddled with organizing the office party.* يحمّله مسؤولية لا يرغب فيها

sadism /ˈseɪdɪzəm/ *noun* [U] getting enjoyment or sexual pleasure from being cruel or causing pain الساديّة: التلذّذ بإيلام الآخرين
▸ **sadist** /ˈseɪdɪst/ *noun* [C] a person who gets enjoyment or sexual pleasure from being cruel or causing pain الساديّ: من يتلذّذ بإيلام الآخرين
sadistic /səˈdɪstɪk/ *adj* showing or involving sadism ساديّ
sadistically /-kli/ *adv* بوحشيّة

sae /ˌes eɪ ˈiː/ *abbrev* = STAMPED ADDRESSED ENVELOPE

safari /səˈfɑːri/ *noun* [C,U] a trip, especially in Africa, for hunting or looking at wild animals رحلة للصيد أو لمشاهدة الحيوانات البرّية

safe[1] /seɪf/ *adj* **1 safe (from sb/sth)** free from danger; not able to be hurt: *You shouldn't walk home alone at night. You won't be safe.* ○ *Do you think my car will be safe in this street?* ○ *Keep the papers where they will be safe from fire.* سليم من الأذى ؛ آمِن

2 not causing danger, harm or risk: *Don't sit on that chair, it isn't safe.* ○ *I left my suitcase in a safe place and went for a cup of coffee.* ○ *Is this drug safe for children?* ○ *He hid from the police until it was safe to come out.* ○ *She's a very safe driver.* ○ *I thought it would be a safe investment but I lost everything.* ○ *Is it safe to drink the water here?* ○ *I think it's safe to say that the situation is unlikely to change for some time.* مأمون ، غير مؤذٍ ؛ مضمون

3 not hurt or damaged: *After the accident he checked that all the passengers were safe.* سالم أو سليم

IDM **on the safe side** not taking risks; being very careful: *I think this is enough money to pay for the meal, but I'll take a bit more to be on the safe side.* زيادة في الاطمئنان

safe and sound not hurt or damaged: *The missing child was found safe and sound by the police.* بخير وسلامة

▸ **safely** *adv*: *I rang my parents to tell them I had arrived safely.* (وصل) بالسّلامة

safe[2] /seɪf/ *noun* [C] a strong metal box or cupboard with a special lock that is used for keeping money, jewellery, documents, etc. in صندوق أو خزانة حديديّة

safeguard /'seɪfgɑːd/ *noun* [C] **a safeguard (against sb/sth)** something that protects against possible dangers: *Make a copy of all your computer disks as a safeguard against accidents.* إجراء وقائيّ ، احتياط

▸ **safeguard** *verb* [T] **safeguard sb/sth (against sb/sth)** to keep sth safe; to protect: *When parents get divorced the children's rights must be safeguarded.* يحمي ، يقي

safety /'seɪfti/ *noun* [U] the state of being safe; not being dangerous or in danger: *In the interests of safety, smoking is forbidden.* ○ *road safety* (= the prevention of road accidents) ○ *She has been missing for several days and police now fear for her safety.* ○ *After Chernobyl people questioned the safety of nuclear energy.* ○ *New safety measures have been introduced on trains.* سلامة ؛ أمان

'**safety belt** *noun* [C] = SEAT BELT

'**safety net** *noun* [C] **1** a net that is placed to catch sb who is performing high above the ground if he/she falls شبكة الأمان

2 something that will help you (usually with money) in a difficult situation ذخيرة لوقت الحاجة

'**safety pin** *noun* [C] a metal pin that is used for fastening things together. The pin is bent round and the point goes under a cover so that it cannot be dangerous. دبّوس انكليزي، شكّالة (سوريا)

'**safety valve** *noun* [C] a device in a machine that allows steam, gas, etc. to escape if the pressure becomes too great صمام الأمان

saffron /'sæfrən/ *noun* [U] a bright orange powder that comes from certain crocus flowers, and is used in cooking to give colour and flavour to food زعفران

sag /sæg/ *verb* [I] (sa**gg**ing; sa**gg**ed) to hang loosely or to sink down, especially in the middle: *The skin on your face starts to sag as you get older.* يتهدّل ، يرتخي

saga /'sɑːgə/ *noun* [C] a very long story; a long series of events قصة طويلة جداً: سلسلة طويلة من الأحداث

sage /seɪdʒ/ *noun* [U] a small plant with sweet-smelling greyish-green leaves that are used in cooking: *sage and onion stuffing* ناعمة، مريميّة، قُويسة

Sagittarius /ˌsædʒɪ'teəriəs/ *noun* [C,U] the ninth sign of the zodiac, the Archer; a person who was born under this sign برج الرامي أو القوس

said *pt, pp* of SAY[1]

sail[1] /seɪl/ *noun* **1** [C] a large piece of strong material that is fixed onto a ship or boat. The wind blows against the sail and drives the ship along. شراع

2 [sing.] a trip on water in a ship or boat with a sail: *Would you like to go for a sail in my boat?* رحلة في قارب شراعي

IDM **set sail** → SET[2]

sail[2] /seɪl/ *verb* **1** [I] to travel on water in a ship or boat of any type; to move on water: *On the cruise we sailed all along the coast of Norway.* ○ *I stood at the window and watched the ships sailing by.* يبحر ، يسافر بحراً

2 [I,T] to travel in and control a boat with sails, especially as a sport: *My father is teaching me to sail.* ○ *I've never sailed this kind of yacht before.* يمارس رياضة القوارب الشراعيّة

When you are talking about spending time sailing a boat, the form **go sailing** is very common: *We often go sailing at weekends.*

3 [I] to begin a journey on water: *When does the ship sail?* ○ *We sail for Santander at six o'clock tomorrow morning.* يبحِر، تقلع (السفينة)

4 [I] to move somewhere quickly in a smooth or proud way: *The ball sailed over the fence and into the neighbour's garden.* ○ *Mary sailed into the room and sat down at the head of the table.* ينساب ؛ يسير بكبرياء

IDM **sail through (sth)** to get through a test or exam easily: *He was a clever boy and sailed through all his exams.* يجتاز امتحاناً دون أية صعوبة

sailboard /'seɪlbɔːd/ *noun* [C] = WINDSURFER

sailing /'seɪlɪŋ/ *noun* **1** [U] the sport of being in, and controlling, small boats with sails: *They do a lot of sailing.* رياضة القوارب الشراعيّة

2 [C] a journey made by a ship or boat carrying passengers from one place to another: *Could you tell me the times of sailings to Ostend?* رحلة مائيّة (أو بحريّة)

'sailing boat *noun* [C] a boat that uses a sail or sails قارب أو مركب شراعيّ

sailor /'seɪlə(r)/ *noun* [C] a member of the crew of a ship (usually not an officer): *soldiers, sailors and airmen* بحّار

IDM a good/bad sailor a person who is not often/often sick when travelling on a boat من لا يصاب (أو يصاب) بدوار البحر

saint /seɪnt; snt/ *noun* [C] **1** a very good or holy person who is given special respect after death by the Christian church قدّيس

When it is used as a title **saint** is written with a capital letter: *Saint Patrick*. In the names of places, churches, etc. the short form **St** is usually used: *St Andrew's Church*. Before names **saint** is pronounced /snt/. Look at **patron saint**.

2 a very good, kind person شخص طيّب صالح ؛ وليّ

sake /seɪk/ *noun* [C]

IDM for Christ's, God's, goodness', Heaven's, etc. sake (used as part of a question or order, to make it stronger or to show that you are angry): *Why have you taken so long, for God's sake?* ○ *For Christ's sake, don't be so stupid!* ○ *For goodness' sake, hurry up!* ❶ **For Christ's sake** and **for God's sake** are stronger and may offend some people. (تستعمل للتوكيد أو للتعبير عن الغضب): بحقّ السماء لماذا...

for the sake of sb/sth; for sb's/sth's sake in order to help sb/sth: *Don't go to any trouble for my sake.* ○ *They only stayed together for the sake of their children/for their children's sake.* من أجل ؛ إكراماً لـ

for the sake of sth/of doing sth in order to get or keep sth; for the purpose of sth: *It's not worth complaining for the sake of a few pence.* ○ *You're just arguing for the sake of arguing* (= because you like arguing). من أجل ؛ بغية

salad /'sæləd/ *noun* [C,U] a mixture of vegetables, usually uncooked, that you often eat together with other foods: *All main courses are served with chips or salad.* ○ *I had chicken salad* (= chicken with salad) *for lunch.* ○ *I don't feel like a heavy meal, I think I'll have a salad.* سَلَطة

salary /'sæləri/ *noun* [C,U] (*pl.* **salaries**) the money that a person receives (usually every month) for the work he/she has done: *My salary is paid directly into my bank account.* ○ *a high/low salary* ○ *an increase in salary of £500* ➲ Look at the note at **pay**[1]. راتب أو مرتّب

sale /seɪl/ *noun* **1** [C,U] the act of selling or being sold; the exchange of an item for money; the occasion when sth is sold: *The sale of alcohol to anyone under the age of 18 is forbidden.* ○ *Business is bad. I haven't made a sale all week.* ○ *a sale of used toys* بيع

2 sales [plural] the amount sold: *Sales of personal computers have increased rapidly.* مبيعات

3 sales [U] (*also* **sales department** [C]) the section of a company that is responsible for selling the products قسم المبيعات

4 [C] a time when shops sell things at prices that are lower than usual: *Sale! All this week! Everything at half price.* ○ *I got these trousers cheap in a sale.* ○ *I got several bargains in the sales* (= the period when many shops reduce their prices). الرخصة (السنويّة مثلاً) ، "أوكازيون"

IDM for sale offered for sb to buy: *This painting is not for sale.* معروض للبيع

on sale 1 available for sb to buy, especially in shops: *This week's edition is on sale now at your local newsagents.* متوفّر في الأسواق

2 (*US*) offered at a lower price than usual معروض في الرخصة

'sales clerk (*also* **clerk**) *noun* [C] (*US*) = SHOP ASSISTANT

salesman /seɪlzmən/ (*pl.* **salesmen** /-mən/), **saleswoman** (*pl.* **saleswomen** /-wɪmɪn/), **salesperson** (*pl.* **salespeople** /-pi:pl/) *noun* [C] a person whose job is selling things to people بائع أو بائعة

salient /'seɪliənt/ *adj* (only *before* a noun) most noticeable or important; main: *the salient points of a speech* بارز، مهم؛ رئيسي

saliva /sə'laɪvə/ *noun* [U] the liquid that is produced in the mouth لعاب

salmon /'sæmən/ *noun* [C,U] (*pl.* **salmon**) a large fish with silver skin and pink flesh: *smoked salmon* سمك سليمان ، سَلْمون

salmonella /,sælmə'nelə/ *noun* [U] a type of bacteria that causes food poisoning سَلْمونِلا: بكتريا تسبّب أمراضاً في الإنسان والدواجن

salon /'sælɒn; *US* sə'lɒn/ *noun* [C] a shop where a hairdresser works or where you can have beauty treatment, etc: *a hairdressing salon* ○ *a beauty salon* صالون حلاقة أو تجميل

saloon /sə'lu:n/ *noun* [C] **1** (*US* **sedan**) a car with a fixed roof and a separate area (boot) for luggage سيّارة "صالون"

2 (*US old-fashioned*) a place where you can buy drinks; a bar حانة

salt /sɔ:lt/ *noun* [U] a common white substance that is found in sea water and the earth, that is used especially for flavouring and preserving food: *Season with salt and pepper.* ○ *Pass the salt, please.* ○ *Add a pinch* (= a small amount) *of salt.* ملح

IDM take sth with a pinch of salt → PINCH

▸ **salt** *verb* [T] to put salt on or in sth: *salted peanuts* يملّح

salt *adj* having the taste of or containing salt: *salt water* مالح

salty *adj* (**saltier**; **saltiest**) having the taste of, or containing, salt: *I didn't like the meat, it was too salty.* مالح

saltwater /'sɔ:ltwɔ:tə(r); *Brit also* 'sɒlt-/ *adj* living in the sea: *a saltwater fish* ❶ Fish in rivers are **freshwater** fish. بحريّ ، عائش في المياه المالحة

salute /sə'lu:t/ *noun* [C] **1** a sign that a soldier, etc. makes to show respect, by raising his/her hand to the forehead: *to give a salute* سلام أو تحيّة عسكريّة

2 an action that shows respect for sb: *The next programme is a salute to one of the world's greatest film stars.* تكريم ، تقدير

▶ **salute** *verb* [I,T] to show respect with a salute (1,2): *The soldiers saluted as they marched past the general.* ○ *The soldiers saluted the general.* ○ *This is the day on which we salute those who died in the war.* يحيّي؛ يكرّم

salvage /ˈsælvɪdʒ/ *noun* [U] the act of removing things from a damaged ship, building, etc.; the things that are removed: *a salvage operation* إنقاذ الممتلكات من سفينة غارقة مثلاً : الممتلكات المنقذة

▶ **salvage** *verb* [T] to rescue sth from a damaged building or ship; to rescue sth from a disaster: *They salvaged as much as they could from the house after the fire.* ○ (*figurative*) *The team has only 20 minutes left in which to salvage something from the game.* ينقذ ما تبقى (بعد حريق مثلاً)

salvation /sælˈveɪʃn/ *noun* **1** [U, sing.] a thing or a person that saves sb/sth from danger or a difficult situation إنقاذ، تخليص : منجاة

2 [U] (in the Christian religion) the state of being saved from evil الخلاص

⚷**same**[1] /seɪm/ *adj* **1 the same ... (as sb/sth/that...)** not different, not another or other; exactly the one or ones that you have mentioned before: *My brother and I had the same teacher at school.* ○ *She comes from the same town as me.* ○ *I'm going to wear the same clothes as I wore yesterday.* ○ *Are you the same person that I spoke to on the phone yesterday?* نفسه ، نفس (الأستاذ مثلاً)

2 the same ... (as sb/sth/that...) exactly like the one already mentioned: *I wouldn't buy the same car again* (= the same model of car). ○ *You don't read the same newspaper as me, do you?* ○ *I had the same experience as you some time ago.* ○ *I've had the same experience that you've had.* نفس ، ذات

> We cannot say **a** same ... To express this idea we use **the same sort of**: *I'd like the same sort of job as my father.*

IDM **at the same time 1** together; at one time: *I can't think about more than one thing at the same time.* معاً ، في نفس الوقت

2 on the other hand; however: *It's a very good idea but at the same time it's rather risky.* من ناحية أخرى ؛ إلا أنّه...

on the same wavelength able to understand sb because you have similar ideas and opinions متماثلان في الآراء والمشاعر

▶ **the same** *adv* in the same way; not differently: *We treat all the children in the class the same.* بالتساوي ، بطريقة واحدة

⚷**same**[2] /seɪm/ *pron* **the same (as sb/sth/...)** the same thing, person, situation, etc: *Is there another word that means the same as this?* ○ *Look at what I'm doing and then do the same.* ○ *Things will never be the same again now that my father has died.* نفس (الشيء)

IDM **all/just the same** nevertheless; in spite of this/that; anyway: *I understand what you're saying. All the same, I don't agree with you.* ○ *I don't need to borrow any money but thanks all the same for offering.* مع ذلك ؛ على أية حال

much the same → MUCH[2]

(the) same again (a request to be served or given the same drink as before): *'What would you like to drink?' 'Same again, please.'* نفس المشروب

same here (*informal*) the same thing is also true for me: *'I'm bored.' 'Same here.'* وأنا أيضاً!

(the) same to you (used as an answer when sb wishes you sth or says sth rude to you): *'Have a good weekend.' 'The same to you.'* ○ *'Get lost!' 'Same to you!'* وأنت أيضاً!

⚷**sample** /ˈsɑːmpl; *US* ˈsæmpl/ *noun* [C] **1** a small quantity of sth that is typical of the rest of it: *She sent a sample of her work in an attempt to get a job.* ○ *a blood sample* عيّنة ؛ نموذج

2 a small number of people who are asked questions in order to find out information about a larger group عدد معيّن من الناس

3 a small amount of a product, that is given free to the public in order to show what it is like: *a free sample of a chocolate bar* عيّنة مجّانية ، "مسطرة"

▶ **sample** *verb* [T] to taste or use a small amount of sth (in order to find out what it is like or to decide whether you like it or not): *You are welcome to sample any of our cheeses before making a purchase.* يذوق

sanatorium /ˌsænəˈtɔːriəm/ *noun* [C] (*pl.* **sanatoriums** or **sanatoria**) (*US* **sanitarium** /ˌsænəˈteəriəm/) a type of hospital where patients who need a long period of treatment for an illness can stay مَصَحّ

sanction /ˈsæŋkʃn/ *noun* **1** [U] official permission to do sth ترخيص رسمي

2 [C] a punishment for breaking a rule or law: *Many people feel that the death penalty is the best sanction against murder.* عقاب

3 [C, usually pl.] an action, especially the stopping of trade, that is taken by other countries against a country that has broken an international law: *The sanctions against those countries have now been lifted.* عقوبات اقتصاديّة

▶ **sanction** *verb* [T] to give official permission for sth يجيز ، يسمح رسمياً بِ

sanctuary /ˈsæŋktʃuəri; *US* -ueri/ *noun* (*pl.* **sanctuaries**) **1** [C] a place where birds or animals are protected from hunters and other dangers: *a wildlife sanctuary* حمىً، ملجأ

2 [C,U] a place where sb can be safe from enemies, the police, etc. ملاذ ؛ حرم

⚷**sand** /sænd/ *noun* **1** [U] a powder consisting of very small grains of rock, found in deserts and on beaches: *You need sand to make concrete.* ○ *When we go on holiday all we want is sun, sea and sand.* رمل

2 the sands [plural] a large area of sand مساحة رمليّة واسعة

▶ **sandy** *adj* (**sandier**; **sandiest**) covered with sand or with a lot of sand in it: *miles of sandy beach* ○ *sandy soil* رمليّ

sandal /ˈsændl/ *noun* [C] a type of light, open

shoe with straps that people wear when the weather is warm صندل ، خفّ

sandcastle /ˈsændkɑːsl; *US* -kæsl/ *noun* [C] a pile of sand that looks like a castle, made by children playing on a beach قلعة رمليّة يبنيها الأطفال على الشاطئ

ˈ**sand dune** *noun* [C] = DUNE

sandpaper /ˈsændpeɪpə(r)/ *noun* [U] strong paper with sand on it that is used for rubbing surfaces in order to make them smoother ورق زجاج ، ورق سَنْفَرة

sandwich /ˈsænwɪdʒ; *US* -wɪtʃ/ *noun* [C] two slices of bread with food between them: *a cheese sandwich* ○ *It's going to be a long journey so let's take some sandwiches.* ○ *What's in that sandwich?* شطيرة ، "سندويشة"

▸ **sandwich** *verb* [T] **sandwich sb/sth (between sb/sth)** to place sb/sth in a very narrow space between two other things or people: *I had a most uncomfortable flight, sandwiched between two very large people.* يحشو أو يقحم بين شيئين مثلاً

sane /seɪn/ *adj* **1** (used about a person) mentally normal; not mad: *With a job like mine, it's incredible that I'm still sane!* عاقل ، سليم العقل

2 (used about a person or an idea, a decision, etc.) sensible; showing good judgement: *I had to accept the offer. It was the only sane thing to do.* معقول ؛ حكيم

🛈 The opposite is **insane**. 🛈 The noun is **sanity**.

sang *pt* of SING

sanitarium (*US*) = SANATORIUM

sanitary /ˈsænətri; *US* -teri/ *adj* for or connected with the protection of health, e.g. how human waste is removed: *Sanitary conditions in the refugee camps were terrible.* ➲ Look at **insanitary**. صحّي ، متعلّق بدورات المياه والنظافة

ˈ**sanitary towel** *noun* [C] a thick pad that women use to soak up blood during their period (3) فوطة صحية ، حفاظ

sanitation /ˌsænɪˈteɪʃn/ *noun* [U] a system for protecting public health, especially by removing waste تصريف المجاري والحفاظ على الصحّة العامة

sanity /ˈsænəti/ *noun* [U] **1** the state of being sane (1); the ability to think and behave in a normal way سلامة العقل

2 the quality of being sane (2); sensible or normal thought or behaviour: *I tried to introduce some sanity into the discussion but nobody was willing to listen.* تفكير سليم ، رشد

🛈 The opposite is **insanity**.

sank *pt* of SINK¹

Santa Claus /ˈsæntə klɔːz/ = FATHER CHRISTMAS

sap¹ /sæp/ *noun* [U] the liquid in a plant or tree النسغ

sap² /sæp/ *verb* [T] (sapping; sapped) to make sth weak or to destroy it يوهن ، يستنزف الحيوية ، يقوّض

sapling /ˈsæplɪŋ/ *noun* [C] a young tree غريسة ، فسيلة

sapphire /ˈsæfaɪə(r)/ *noun* [C,U] a bright blue precious stone سفير أو ياقوت أزرق

sarcasm /ˈsɑːkæzəm/ *noun* [U] the use of words or expressions to mean the opposite of what they actually say. People use sarcasm in order to criticize other people or to make them look silly: *'No, you didn't take long to get ready. Only two hours,' she said with heavy sarcasm.* تهكّم ، سخرية

▸ **sarcastic** /sɑːˈkæstɪk/ *adj*: *a sarcastic sense of humour* ○ *a sarcastic comment* ساخر، تهكّمي

sarcastically /-kli/ *adv* بتهكّم أو بسخرية

sardine /ˌsɑːˈdiːn/ *noun* [C] a type of very small fish: *a tin of sardines* سردين

sash /sæʃ/ *noun* [C] a long piece of material that is worn round the waist or over the shoulder, often as part of a uniform, etc. وشاح ، نطاق

SAT™ /ˌes eɪ ˈtiː/ (*US*) Scholastic Aptitude Test, a test taken by high-school students who want to go to a college or university اختبار القابلية للتعلم

Sat. *abbrev* = SATURDAY

sat *pt, pp* of SIT

Satan /ˈseɪtn/ a name for the Devil الشيطان ، إبليس

satchel /ˈsætʃəl/ *noun* [C] a bag, often carried over the shoulder, used by schoolchildren for taking books to and from school حقيبة كتب تحمل عادة على الظهر

satellite /ˈsætəlaɪt/ *noun* [C] **1** a natural object in space that goes round a bigger object, usually a planet تابع

2 a man-made object that has been sent into space and that moves around a planet for a particular purpose: *satellite pictures of today's weather* قمر صناعي

ˈ**satellite dish** (*also* **dish**) *noun* [C] a large, circular piece of equipment that people have on the outside of their houses, that receives signals from a satellite so that they can receive satellite television صحن التقاط

ˈ**satellite television** (*also* ˈ**satellite TV**) *noun* [U] television programmes that are broadcast by means of a satellite 🛈 In order to receive satellite TV you need a satellite **dish**. بثّ تلفزيونيّ بواسطة الأقمار الصناعية

satin /ˈsætɪn; *US* ˈsætn/ *noun* [U] a type of cloth that is smooth and shiny قماش الساتان أو الأطلس

satire /ˈsætaɪə(r)/ *noun* **1** [U] the use of humour to attack a person, an idea or behaviour that you think is bad or foolish الهجاء

2 [C] **satire (on sb/sth)** a piece of writing or a play, film, etc. that uses satire: *a satire on university life* هجاء ، عمل فنيّ هجائيّ

▸ **satirical** /səˈtɪrɪkl/ *adj* using satire: *a satirical magazine* نقديّ أو هجائيّ

satirically /-kli/ *adv* بشكل انتقادي ساخر

🔑 **satisfaction** /ˌsætɪsˈfækʃn/ *noun* **1** [U] the feeling of pleasure that you have when you have done, got or achieved what you wanted: *Emily stood back and looked at her work with a sense of satisfaction.* ○ *We finally made a decision that was* *to everyone's satisfaction* (= that everyone was pleased with). ℹ The opposite is **dissatisfaction**. ارتياح ، رضى

2 [C] something that gives you a feeling of pleasure: *It was a great satisfaction to me to know that I had done the job well.* مبعث سرور

satisfactory /ˌsætɪsˈfæktəri/ *adj* **1** good enough (but not very good): *This piece of work is not satisfactory. Please do it again.* لا بأس به

2 giving satisfaction; suiting a particular purpose: *It will be much more satisfactory if we all travel together.* مُرْضٍ ، مناسب

ℹ The opposite is **unsatisfactory**.

▶ **satisfactorily** /-tərəli/ *adv*: *Work is progressing satisfactorily.* بشكل مرْضٍ

satisfy /ˈsætɪsfaɪ/ *verb* [T] (*pres part* **satisfying**; *3rd pers sing pres* **satisfies**; *pt, pp* **satisfied**) **1** to make sb pleased by doing or giving him/her what he/she wants: *No matter how hard I try, my piano teacher is never satisfied.* ○ *Nothing satisfies him – he's always complaining.* يُرضي ، يسرّ

2 to have or do what is necessary for sth: *She satisfied all the entrance requirements for university.* ○ *I had a quick look inside the parcel just to satisfy my curiosity.*
يفي بشروط معيّنة ؛ يُشبع أو يرضي فضوله

3 satisfy sb (that...) to show or prove to sb that sth is true or has been done: *Once the police were satisfied that they were telling the truth, they were allowed to go.* ○ *She checked the room once again to satisfy herself that everything was ready.* يقنع

▶ **satisfied** *adj* **satisfied (with sb/sth)** pleased because you have had or done what you wanted: *a satisfied smile* ○ *a satisfied customer* ○ *I hope you're satisfied with what you've done!* ℹ The opposite is **dissatisfied**. راضٍ ؛ مقتنع ؛ مكتفٍ

satisfying *adj* pleasing, giving satisfaction: *It was a very satisfying feeling knowing that we'd finished the job on time.* سارّ ؛ باعث على الارتياح

satnav (*also* **sat nav**) /ˈsætnæv/ *noun* [U,C] the abbreviation for satellite navigation (a computer system that uses information obtained from satellites to guide the driver of a vehicle): *The drivers all have satnav in the van.*
(في العربات) جهاز ملاحة يستقبل المعلومات عبر الأقمار الصناعية

satsuma /sætˈsuːmə/ *noun* [C] a type of small orange with a loose skin فاكهة الساتسوما

saturate /ˈsætʃəreɪt/ *verb* [T] **1** to make sth very wet: *Her clothes were completely saturated.* يبلّل ، ينقع ، يشرّب

2 to fill sth completely: *The market is saturated with cheap imports.* يشبع ، يتخم

▶ **saturation** /ˌsætʃəˈreɪʃn/ *noun*: *The market for cars has reached saturation point* (= there can be no more increases in sales). إشباع ؛ نقع ، تشريب

Saturday /ˈsætədeɪ/ *noun* [C,U] (*abbr* **Sat.**) the day of the week after Friday and before Sunday ℹ For examples of the use of the days of the week in sentences, look at **Monday**. يوم السبت

Saturn /ˈsætən/ *noun* [sing.] the planet that is sixth in order from the sun and that has rings around it كوكب زُحَل

sauce /sɔːs/ *noun* [C,U] a thick liquid (that can be hot or cold) that you eat on or with other food: *The chicken was served in a delicious sauce.* ○ *tomato sauce* ○ *In Britain we often eat mint sauce with lamb.* صلصة

> **Gravy** is a type of thin sauce that is made from meat juices and eaten hot with meat.

saucepan /ˈsɔːspən; *US* -pæn/ *noun* [C] a round metal pot that is used for cooking things on top of a stove. A saucepan usually has a lid and one or more handles. قدْر ، طنجرة

saucer /ˈsɔːsə(r)/ *noun* [C] a small round plate that you put under a cup: *a cup and saucer* صحن الفنجان

sauna /ˈsɔːnə/ *noun* [C] **1** a type of bath where you sit in a room that is very hot and full of steam: *to have a sauna* حمّام "سونا"

2 a room or building where there is a sauna: *The apartment block has a swimming pool and sauna.* غرفة حمّام "سونا"

saunter /ˈsɔːntə(r)/ *verb* [I] to walk without hurrying يتهادى ، يمشي الهوينى

sausage /ˈsɒsɪdʒ; *US* ˈsɔːs-/ *noun* [C,U] a mixture of chopped meat, spices, etc. that is made into a long thin shape. Some sausage is eaten cold in slices, other types are cooked and then served whole: *garlic sausage* ○ *liver sausage* ○ *We had sausages and chips for lunch.* سجق ، نقانق

ˌsausage ˈroll *noun* [C] a piece of sausage meat that is covered in pastry
أصابع من العجين محشوة بالنقانق

savage /ˈsævɪdʒ/ *adj* very cruel or fierce: *a savage attack by a big dog* ○ *The book has received some savage criticism.* وحشيّ ؛ ضارٍ ؛ عنيف

▶ **savage** *verb* [T] to attack sb/sth fiercely يهاجم بشراسة

savagely *adv* بشراسة ؛ بوحشيّة

savagery /ˈsævɪdʒri/ *noun*: *The savagery of the punishment disgusted them.* وحشيّة

save /seɪv/ *verb* **1** [T] **save sb/sth (from sth/from doing sth)** to make or keep sb/sth safe from changes, loss, death, etc: *to save sb's life* ○ *to save sb from drowning* ○ *a campaign to save the whale* ○ *We are trying to save the school from closure.* ينقذ ، يحمي

2 [I,T] **save (sth) (up) (for sth)** to keep or not spend money, etc. so that you can use it later: *Carol is saving up for a holiday in Greece.* ○ *We try and save £50 a month.* يدّخر ، يوفّر

3 [T] to keep sth for future use: *I'll be home late so please save me some dinner.* ○ *Save that box. It might come in useful.* ○ *If you get there first, please save me a seat.* يبقي ، يحفظ

4 [T] to store information in a computer by giving it a special instruction: *Don't forget to save the file before you close it.*
(في الكمبيوتر) يدّخر المعلومات

5 [I,T] to prevent the spending or waste of time or money: *You can save on petrol by getting a*

a b c d e f g h i j k l m n o p q r **s** t u v w x y z

smaller car. ○ *This car will save you a lot on petrol.* يوفّر

6 [T] to make sth unnecessary; to make it unnecessary for sb to use sth, spend sth, etc: *You could save yourself a lot of time and effort if you organized your work better.* ○ *Can you lend me your bike? It'll save me having to walk.* يغني عن ، يجنّب

7 [T] to stop a goal being scored in football, etc. يحول دون تسجيل هدف (في مباراة)

IDM keep/save sth for a rainy day → RAINY

save face to prevent yourself losing the respect of other people: *The remarks he made were an attempt to save face in a difficult situation.* يحفظ ماء وجهه ، يحافظ على كرامته

▸ **save** *noun* [C] (in football, etc.) an act of preventing a goal from being scored: *The goal-keeper made a great save.* إنقاذ المرمى (من تسجيل هدف)

saver *noun* [C] a person who saves money for future use: *The rise in interest rates is good news for savers.* مدّخِر

saving /ˈseɪvɪŋ/ *noun* **1** [C] an amount of time, money, etc. that you do not have to use or spend: *The sale price represents a saving of 25%.* توفير

2 savings [plural] money that you have saved for future use: *All our savings are in the bank.* المال المدّخَر

saviour (*US* **savior**) /ˈseɪviə(r)/ *noun* [C] a person who rescues or saves sb/sth from danger, loss, death, etc. ❶ In Christianity Jesus Christ is the **Saviour**. المنقذ ، (في المسيحيّة) المخلّص وهو السيّد المسيح

savoury (*US* **savory**) /ˈseɪvəri/ *adj* (used about food) having a salty or spicy taste; not sweet (طعام) مملّح أو مبهّر

saw[1] *pt of* SEE

saw[2] /sɔː/ *noun* [C] a tool that is used for cutting wood, etc. A saw has a long metal blade with sharp teeth on it: *an electric chainsaw* منشار

▸ **saw** *verb* [I,T] (*pt* **sawed**; *pp* **sawn** /sɔːn/) to cut sth with a saw: *to saw through the trunk of a tree* ○ *Paula sawed the branch off the tree.* ○ *He sawed the log up into small pieces.* ❶ The US past participle is **sawed**. ينشر

sawdust /ˈsɔːdʌst/ *noun* [U] very small pieces of wood that fall like powder when you are sawing نشارة خشب

sax /sæks/ *noun* [C] (*informal*) = SAXOPHONE

saxophone /ˈsæksəfəʊn/ (*also informal* **sax**) *noun* [C] a metal musical instrument that you play by blowing into it. Saxophones are usually used for playing jazz. سكسية أو سكسفون

say[1] /seɪ/ *verb* (*3rd pers sing pres* **says** /sez/; *pt, pp* **said** /sed/) **1** [T] **say sth (to sb)** to speak words: *'Please come back,' she said.* ○ *The teacher said we should hand in our essays on Friday.* ○ *to say goodbye* ○ *to say your prayers* ○ *He said to his mother that he would phone back later.* ○ *They just sat there without saying anything.* ○ *'This isn't going to be easy,' she said to herself* (= she thought). يقول

> **Say** or **tell**? **Say** is often used with the actual words that were spoken or before **that** in indirect speech: *'I'll catch the 9 o'clock train,' he said.* ○ *He said that he would catch the 9 o'clock train.* Notice that you say sth **to** sb: *He said to me that he would catch the 9 o'clock train.* **Tell** is always followed by a noun or pronoun, showing who you were speaking to: *He told me that he would catch the 9 o'clock train.* **Tell**, not **say**, can also be used when you are talking about giving orders or advice: *I told them to hurry up.* ○ *She's always telling me what I ought to do.*

2 [T] (used about a book, notice, etc.) to give information: *What time does it say on that clock?* ○ *The map says the hotel is just past the railway bridge.* يشير إلى : يخبر

3 [I,T] to express a thought, feeling, answer, opinion, etc: *'What time is she coming?' 'I don't know – she didn't say.'* ○ *I should like to say how happy I am to be here today.* ○ *He is said to be very rich* (= people say that he is very rich). ○ *What is the artist trying to say in this painting?* ○ *His angry look said everything about the way he felt.* ○ *Well, what do you say? Do you think it's a good idea?* يعرب عن ، يعبّر عن

4 [T] to suppose sth: *We will need, say, £10 000 for a new car.* ○ *Say you don't get a place at university, what will you do then?* يفرض

IDM go without saying to be clear, so that you do not need to say it: *It goes without saying that the children will be well looked after at all times.* لا داعيَ للقول

that is to say... which means...: *We're leaving on Friday, that's to say in a week's time.* أيْ... ، وهذا معناه

say[2] /seɪ/ *noun* [sing., U] **say (in sth)** the power or right to decide sth: *I'd like to have some say in the arrangements for the party.* رأي ، سلطة

IDM have your say to express your opinion: *Thank you for your comments. Now let somebody else have their say.* يعبّر عن رأيه

saying /ˈseɪɪŋ/ *noun* [C] a well-known phrase that gives advice about sth: *'A stitch in time saves nine' is an old saying.* ➲ Look at **proverb**. مَثَل سائر ، قول مأثور

scab /skæb/ *noun* [C,U] a mass of dried blood that forms over a part of the body where the skin has been cut or broken ➲ Look at **scar**. القِرفة أو قشرة الجرح الجافّة

scaffold /ˈskæfəʊld/ *noun* [C] a platform on which criminals were killed, e.g. by hanging مشنقة

scaffolding /ˈskæfəldɪŋ/ *noun* [U] long metal poles and wooden boards that form a structure which is put next to a building so that builders, painters, etc. can stand and work on it سِقالة

scald /skɔːld/ *verb* [T] to burn sb/sth with very hot liquid يسمط ، يحرق جلده بسائل حار

▸ **scald** *noun* [C] a burn that was caused by very hot liquid سمط ، حرق بسائل حار

scalding *adj*: *scalding hot water* مُحرِق للجلد ، (ماء) حارّ جداً

scales

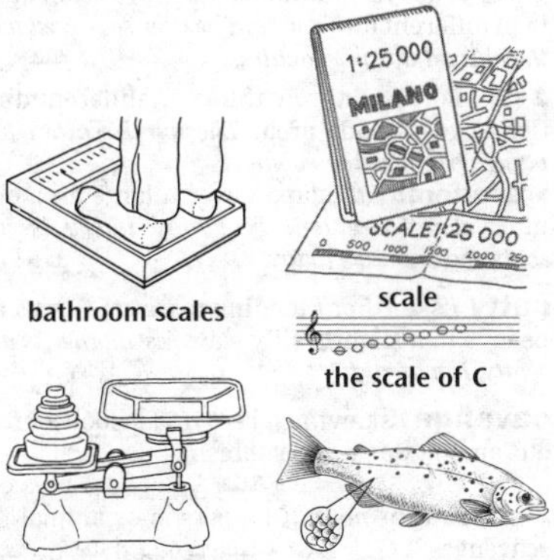

bathroom scales
scale
the scale of C
kitchen scales
fish scales

⚷ **scale**[1] /skeɪl/ *noun* **1** [C] a series of marks on a tool or piece of equipment that you use for measuring sth: *The ruler has one scale in centimetres and one scale in inches.* مقياس مدرّج

2 [C] a series of numbers, amounts, etc. that are used for measuring or fixing the level of sth: *The earthquake measured 6.5 on the Richter scale.* ○ *the new pay scale for nurses* مقياس

3 [C] the relationship between the actual size of sth and its size on a map or plan: *The map has a scale of one centimetre to the kilometre.* ○ *a scale of 1 : 50 000* ○ *We need a map with a larger scale.* ○ *a scale model* ○ *The plan of the building is not drawn to scale* (= the parts of the drawing do not have the same relationship to each other as the parts of the actual building do). مقياس

4 [C,U] the size or extent of sth when compared to other things: *We shall be making the product on a large scale next year.* ○ *I think we have only just realized the scale of the problem* (= how serious it is). نطاق ، مدى

5 [C] a series of musical notes which go up or down in a fixed order. People play or sing scales to practise their musical technique: *the scale of C major* السلّم الموسيقيّ

scale[2] /skeɪl/ *noun* [C] one of the small flat pieces of hard material that cover the body of some fish and animals: *the scales of a snake* حَرْشَفة أو فَلْسة

scale[3] /skeɪl/ *verb* [T] to climb up a high wall, steep cliff, etc. يتسلّق (جداراً عالياً مثلاً)

scales /skeɪlz/ *noun* [plural] a piece of equipment that is used for weighing sb/sth: *I weighed it on the kitchen scales.* ميزان

scalp /skælp/ *noun* [C] the skin on the top of your head that is under your hair جلدة أو فروة الرأس

scalpel /ˈskælpəl/ *noun* [C] a small knife that is used by doctors (surgeons) when they are doing operations مِبضع أو مِشْرَط

scam /skæm/ *noun* [C] (*informal*) a dishonest scheme: *a betting/currency scam* غش، عملية احتيال

scamper /ˈskæmpə(r)/ *verb* [I] (often used about a child or small animal) to run quickly ينطلق راكضاً ؛ يعدو (مذعوراً)

scampi /ˈskæmpi/ *noun* [plural] large prawns that have been fried in a mixture of flour and milk (batter) قريدس كبير مغموس بالدقيق والحليب ومقليّ

scan /skæn/ *verb* [T] (**scanning**; **scanned**) **1** to examine sth carefully because you are looking for sth: *The sailors scanned the horizon for signs of land.* يفحص بدقّة ، يمسح

2 to look at or read sth quickly: *Vic scanned the list until he found his own name.* يتصفّح ، يلقي نظرة عجلى

3 (used about a machine) to examine what is inside a person's body or inside an object such as a suitcase: *Machines scan all the luggage for bombs and guns.* يفحص ، يدقّق في

4 (*computing*) to pass light over a picture or document using a scanner in order to copy it and put it in the memory of a computer: *How do I scan a photo and attach it to an email?* يمسح (تصوير)

▸ **scan** *noun* [C] an act of scanning: *The scan showed the baby was in the normal position.* فحص، مسح طبي، تفرّس

scanner *noun* [C] a machine that scans (3, 4) جهاز مسح؛ مفراس

scandal /ˈskændl/ *noun* **1** [C,U] an action or a situation or behaviour that shocks people; the public feeling that is caused by such behaviour: *The chairman resigned after being involved in a financial scandal.* ○ *There was no suggestion of scandal in his private life.* ○ *The poor state of school buildings is a real scandal.* فضيحة

2 [U] talk about sth bad or wrong that sb has or may have done: *to spread scandal about sb* قيل وقال ، نميمة

▸ **scandalize** (*also* **scandalise**) /ˈskændəlaɪz/ *verb* [T] to cause sb to feel shocked by doing sth that he/she thinks is bad or wrong يروّع بأعماله المُخزية

scandalous /ˈskændələs/ *adj* very shocking or wrong: *It is scandalous that so much money is wasted.* فاضح ، مخزٍ

Scandinavia /ˌskændɪˈneɪviə/ *noun* [U] the group of countries in northern Europe that consists of Denmark, Norway and Sweden. Sometimes Finland and Iceland are also said to be part of Scandinavia. البلدان الاسكندنافية

▸ **Scandinavian** *adj* اسكندنافيّ

scant /skænt/ *adj* (only *before* a noun) not very much; not as much as necessary: *They paid scant attention to my advice.* قليل

scanty /ˈskænti/ *adj* (**scantier**; **scantiest**) too small in size or quality: *We didn't learn much from the scanty information they gave us.* ضئيل ، شحيح : هزيل

▸ **scantily** *adv* بالكاد يغطي الجسم

scapegoat /ˈskeɪpɡəʊt/ *noun* [C] a person who is blamed for sth that sb else has done كبش الفداء

a b c d e f g h i j k l m n o p q r s t u v w x y z

scar /skɑː(r)/ *noun* [C] a mark on the skin that is caused by a cut or wound that has now healed: *The operation didn't leave a very big scar.* ○ (*figurative*) *The city centre still bears the scars of the recent fighting.* ➲ Look at **scab**. أثر الجرح ، ندبة

▸ **scar** *verb* [I,T] (scarring; scarred) to leave a scar on sb/sth: *William's face was scarred for life in the accident.* (جرح) يترك أثراً ، يندب

scarce /skeəs/ *adj* not existing in large quantities; hard to find: *Food for birds and animals is scarce in the winter.* ℹ The opposite is **plentiful**. نادر ، قليل

▸ **scarcity** /ˈskeəsəti/ *noun* [C,U] (*pl.* **scarcities**): *The scarcity of building land has forced the price up.* قلّة ، ندرة

scarcely /ˈskeəsli/ *adv* **1** only just; almost not: *Scarcely had I sat down when the phone rang.* ○ *There was scarcely a car in sight.* ○ *She's not a friend of mine. I scarcely know her.* ➲ Look at **hardly**. بالكاد ؛ يكاد لا...

2 surely not: *You can scarcely expect me to believe that after all you said before.* حتماً لا... ، طبعاً لا...

🔑**scare** /ˈskeə(r)/ *verb* [T] to make a person or an animal frightened: *The sudden noise scared us all.* يُفزع

PHRV **scare sb/sth away/off** to make a person or animal leave or stay away by frightening them: *Don't make any noise or you'll scare the birds away.* يُنفر ، يهرب

▸ **scare** *noun* [C] **1** a feeling of being frightened: *It wasn't a serious heart attack but it gave him a scare.* فزع ، خوف

2 a situation where many people are afraid or worried about sth: *Last night there was a bomb scare in the city centre.* ذعر عام

scared *adj* **scared (of sb/sth)**; **scared (of doing sth/to do sth)** frightened: *Are you scared of the dark?* ○ *She's scared of walking home alone.* ○ *Everyone was too scared to move.* خائف ، فزع

scary /ˈskeəri/ *adj* (**scarier**; **scariest**) (*informal*) rather frightening: *a scary ghost story* ○ *It was a bit scary driving in the mountains at night.* مفزع ، مرعب

scarecrow /ˈskeəkrəʊ/ *noun* [C] a model of a person that is dressed in old clothes and put in a field to frighten away the birds النطّار أو الفزّاعة

scarf /skɑːf/ *noun* [C] (*pl.* **scarfs** /skɑːfs/ or **scarves** /skɑːvz/) **1** a long thin piece of cloth, usually made of wool, that you wear around your neck to keep warm: *He wrapped a scarf around his neck and set off.* "تلفيعة" أو "لفحة"

2 a square piece of cloth that (usually) women wear around their neck or shoulders or over their heads to keep warm or for decoration منديل الرأس ، "ايشارب"

scarlet /ˈskɑːlət/ *adj, noun* [U] (of) a bright red colour ➲ Look at **crimson** and **maroon**. اللون القرمزي

scathing /ˈskeɪðɪŋ/ *adj* expressing a very strong negative opinion about sb/sth; very critical: *a scathing attack on the new leader* ○ *scathing criticism* لاذع ، مقذع

scatter /ˈskætə(r)/ *verb* **1** [I] (used about a group of people or animals) to move away quickly in different directions: *The deer scattered when they heard us approaching.* يتفرّق، يتبعثر

2 [T] to drop or throw things in different directions over a wide area: *The wind scattered the papers all over the room.* يُبعثر

▸ **scattered** *adj* spread over a large area or at intervals: *There will be sunny intervals with scattered showers today.* متفرّق؛ مبعثر

scatty /ˈskæti/ *adj* tending to forget things and behave in a slightly silly way: *My mother is a bit scatty, I'm afraid.* مشتّت الذهن، طائش

scavenge /ˈskævɪndʒ/ *verb* [I,T] to look for food, etc. among waste and rubbish يبحث عن الطعام (وغيره) بين القمامة

▸ **scavenger** *noun* [C] a person or animal that scavenges الباحث عن الطعام (وغيره) بين القمامة، قمّام

scenario /səˈnɑːriəʊ; *US* -ˈnær-/ *noun* [C] (*pl.* **scenarios**) **1** a description of what happens in a play or film النصّ المفصّل لحوادث مسرحيّة أو فيلم

2 one way that things may happen in the future: *The doctor described a scenario in which the disease spread rapidly across the whole country.* سيناريو ، أحد الاحتمالات

🔑**scene** /siːn/ *noun* **1** [C] the place where sth happened: *the scene of a crime, accident, etc.* مسرح أو مكان (الجريمة مثلاً)

2 [C] an occasion when sb expresses great anger or another strong emotion in public: *There was quite a scene when she refused to pay the bill.* ○ *There were emotional scenes at the dockside as the boat pulled away.* شجار أو ثورة غضب في مكان عام

3 [C] one part of a book, play, film, etc. in which the events happen in one place: *The first scene of 'Hamlet' takes place on the castle walls.* مشهد

4 [C,U] what you see around you in a particular place: *Constable painted many scenes of rural life.* ○ *Her new job was no better, but at least it would be a change of scene.* منظر

5 the scene [sing.] the way of life or present situation in a particular area of activity: *The political scene in Eastern Europe is very confused.* ○ *the fashion scene* حياة ، وضع

scenery /ˈsiːnəri/ *noun* [U] **1** the natural features that you see around you in the country: *The scenery is superb in the mountains.* المناظر الطبيعيّة

2 the furniture, painted cloth, boards, etc. that are used on the stage in a theatre: *The scenery is changed during the interval.* المشاهد أو الخلفيّات المستخدمة على المسرح

> We say that an area of the country has beautiful **scenery** when it is attractive to look at. The **landscape** of a particular area is the way the natural features of it are arranged: *Trees and hedges are a typical feature of the British landscape.* You have a **view** of something when you look out of a window or down from a tower:

There was a marvellous view of the sea from our hotel room.

scenic /'si:nɪk/ *adj* having beautiful scenery: *a scenic route through the country lanes* ذو مناظر طبيعيّة جميلة

scent /sent/ *noun* **1** [C,U] a pleasant smell: *This flower has no scent.* عطر ، عبير

2 [U] (*especially Brit*) = PERFUME (2): *a bottle of scent* عطر، طيب

3 [C,U] the smell that an animal leaves behind and that some other animals can follow رائحة ، عبق (رائحة يقتفى أثرها)

▸ **scented** *adj* عطِر أو معطّر

sceptic (*US* **skeptic**) /'skeptɪk/ *noun* [C] a person who doubts that sth is true, right, etc. المتشكّك

▸ **sceptical** (*US* **skeptical**) /-kl/ *adj* **sceptical (of/about sth)** doubting that sth is true, right, etc: *Many doctors are sceptical about the value of alternative medicine.* متشكّك في ، غير متأكّد من

scepticism (*US* **skepticism**) /'skeptɪsɪzəm/ *noun* [U] a general feeling of doubt about sth; a feeling that you are unwilling to believe sth: *They listened with scepticism to the President's promises of reform.* شكّ ، عَجْز عن التصديق

schedule /'ʃedju:l; *US* 'skedʒʊl/ *noun* **1** [C,U] a plan of things that will happen or of work that must be done: *Max has a busy schedule for the next few days.* ○ *to be ahead of/behind schedule* (= to have done more/less than was planned) ○ *to be on schedule* (= to have done the amount that was planned) برنامج ، جدول أعمال

2 (*US*) = TIMETABLE

▸ **schedule** *verb* [T] **schedule sth (for sth)** to arrange for sth to happen or be done at a particular time: *We've scheduled the meeting for Monday morning.* ○ *The train was scheduled to arrive at 10.07.* ○ *Is it a scheduled flight?* (= on the regular timetable) يحدّد موعداً لـ

scheme /ski:m/ *noun* [C] **1** an official plan or system for doing or organizing sth: *a new scheme to provide houses in the area* ○ *Are you paying into a private pension scheme?* مشروع ، خطّة ، برنامج

2 a clever plan to do sth: *He's thought of a new scheme for making money fast.* ➲ Look at **colour scheme**. خطّة

▸ **scheme** *verb* [I,T] to make a secret or dishonest plan يخطّط سرّاً ، يدبّر مكيدة

schizophrenia /ˌskɪtsə'fri:niə/ *noun* [U] a serious mental illness in which a person confuses the real world and the world of the imagination and often behaves in strange and unexpected ways (مرض) انفصام الشخصيّة

▸ **schizophrenic** /ˌskɪtsə'frenɪk/ *adj, noun* [C] (of) a person who is suffering from schizophrenia مصاب بانفصام الشخصيّة

scholar /'skɒlə(r)/ *noun* [C] **1** a person who studies and has a deep knowledge of a particular subject: *a leading Shakespeare scholar* باحث مختصّ بـ ؛ عالم

2 a person who has passed an exam or won a competition and has been given some money (a scholarship) to help pay for his/her studies: *a British Council scholar* ➲ Look at **student**. حائز على منحة دراسيّة

scholarship /'skɒləʃɪp/ *noun* **1** [C] an amount of money that is given to a person who has passed an exam or won a competition, in order to help pay for his/her studies: *to win a scholarship to Yale* منحة دراسيّة

2 [U] serious study; the work of scholars العلم ، الدراسة

school /sku:l/ *noun* **1** [C] the place where children go to be educated: *Paul goes to the local school.* ○ *They're building a new school in our area.* ○ *Do you have to wear school uniform?* ○ *We go on the school bus.* ○ *Every school has several computers.* مدرسة

2 [U] the time you spend at a school; the process of being educated in a school: *Children start school at 5 in Britain and can leave school at 16.* ○ *School starts at 9 o'clock and finishes at about 3.30.* ○ *After school we usually have homework to do.* ○ *Because of the snow there will be no school today.* مدرسة ؛ فترة الدراسة

You talk about **school** (not '**the**') when you are talking about going there for the usual reason (that is, as a pupil or teacher): *Where do your children go to school?* ○ *I enjoyed being at school.* ○ *Do you walk to school?* You talk about **the school** if you are talking about going there for a different reason (for example, as a parent): *I have to go to the school on Thursday to talk to John's teacher.* You must also use **a** or **the** when more information about the school is given: *Pat goes to the local school.* ○ *She teaches at a school in Leeds.*

3 [sing., with sing. or pl. verb] all the pupils and teachers in a school: *The whole school cheered the winner.* كلّ أفراد المدرسة

4 [C] a place where you go to learn a particular subject: *a driving school* ○ *a language school* مدرسة أو معهد

5 [C] (*US*) a college or university كلية أو جامعة

6 [C] a department of a university that teaches a particular subject: *the school of geography at Leeds University* قسم (في جامعة)

7 [C] a group of writers, painters, etc. who have the same ideas or style: *the Flemish school of painting* مدرسة فكريّة أو فنيّة

IDM **a school of thought** the ideas or opinions that one group of people share: *There are various schools of thought on this matter.* مذهب فكري

▸ **schooling** *noun* [U] the time that you spend at school; your education: *Irene's schooling was interrupted because she was ill so often.* فترة التلمذة ؛ دراسة ، تعليم

'school age *noun* [U] the age when a child must go to school, e.g. in Britain, between 5 and 16 سن الدراسة الإجبارية

schoolboy /'sku:lbɔɪ/, **schoolgirl** /'sku:lgɜ:l/ **schoolchild** /'sku:ltʃaɪld/ *noun* [C] a boy/

girl/child who goes to school
ابن أو بنت مدرسة ، تلميذ أو تلميذة مدرسة

schooldays /'sku:ldeɪz/ *noun* [plural] the period of your life when you go to school
أيام التلمذة أو الدراسة

ˌ**school-'leaver** *noun* [C] a person who has just left school من أنهى دراسته المدرسيّة حديثاً

schoolmaster /'sku:lmɑ:stə(r); *US* -mæstər/ (*feminine* **schoolmistress** /'sku:lmɪstrəs/) *noun* [C] (*especially Brit old-fashioned*) a teacher, especially one at a private school
معلّم أو معلّمة (في مدرسة خاصّة)

schoolteacher /'sku:lti:tʃə(r)/ *noun* [C] a person who teaches in a school معلّم

science /'saɪəns/ *noun* **1** [U] the study of and knowledge about the physical world and natural laws: *science and technology* ○ *Modern science has discovered a lot about the origin of life.* ○ *Fewer young people are studying science at university.* ○ *a science teacher* (= one who teaches biology, chemistry or physics) العلم

2 [C,U] one of the subjects into which science can be divided: *Biology, chemistry and physics are all sciences.* ○ *Is mathematics a science?* ❶ The study of people and society is called **social science**. أحد العلوم

▶ **scientist** /'saɪəntɪst/ *noun* [C] a person who studies or teaches science, especially biology, chemistry or physics عالِم

ˌ**science 'fiction** *noun* [U] books, films, etc. about events that take place in the future, especially connected with travel in space
روايات وأفلام الخيال العلمي

scientific /ˌsaɪən'tɪfɪk/ *adj* **1** connected with science: *We need more funding for scientific research.* علمي

2 using the methods that are used in science (1) (= observing facts and testing ideas with experiments): *a scientific study of the way people use language* علميّ ، بطريقة علمية

▶ **scientifically** /-kli/ *adv*: *It will be hard to prove the idea scientifically* (= using the methods of science). بالطرق العلميّة

scissors /'sɪzəz/ *noun* [plural] a tool for cutting things that consists of two flat sharp blades that are joined together مقصّ أو مقراض

Scissors is a plural noun: *These scissors are blunt.* We CANNOT say 'a scissors': we must use the word **pair**: *I need a new pair of scissors.*

scoff /skɒf; *US* skɔ:f/ *verb* [I] **scoff (at sb/sth)** to speak about sb/sth without respect يهزأ من

scold /skəʊld/ *verb* [I,T] (*formal*) **scold sb (for sth/for doing sth)** to speak angrily to sb because he/she has done something bad or wrong: *The teacher scolded her for being late.* ❶ **Tell off** is more common. يوبّخ

scone /skɒn; skəʊn/ *noun* [C] a small plain cake made from fat and flour. You often put butter and jam on scones. كعكة صغيرة تؤكل مع الزبدة والمربّى

scoop /sku:p/ *noun* [C] **1** a tool like a spoon used for picking up ice cream, flour, grain, etc. مغرفة

2 the amount that one scoop contains: *apple pie served with a scoop of ice cream* غَرفة

3 an exciting piece of news that is reported by one newspaper, TV or radio station before it is reported anywhere else سَبْق صحفيّ

▶ **scoop** *verb* [T] **1 scoop sth (out/up)** to make a hole in sth or to take sth out by using a scoop (1) or sth similar: *Scoop out the middle of the pineapple.* يجوّف ، يقوّر

2 scoop sb/sth (up) to move or lift sb/sth using a continuous action: *He scooped up the child and ran.* يغرف؛ ينتشل

3 to win a big or important prize: *The film has scooped all the awards this year.* يحصد، يفوز بِ

4 to get a story before all other newspapers, TV stations, etc. يحقّق سبقاً صحفياً

scooter /'sku:tə(r)/ *noun* [C] **1** a light motorcycle with a small engine درّاجة ناريّة خفيفة

2 a child's toy with two wheels that you stand on and move by pushing one foot against the ground درّاجة يدفعها الطفل برجله

scope /skəʊp/ *noun* **1** [U] **scope (for sth/to do sth)** the chance or opportunity to do sth: *The job offers plenty of scope for creativity.* مجال ، فرصة

2 [sing.] the range of subjects that are being discussed or considered: *The government was unwilling to extend the scope of the inquiry.* ○ *It is not within the scope of this book to discuss these matters in detail.* مدى ، نطاق

scorch /skɔ:tʃ/ *verb* [T] to burn sth slightly so that its colour changes but it is not destroyed: *I scorched my blouse when I was ironing it.* ○ *the scorched landscape of the Arizona desert*
يشيّط ، يسفع ، يحرق حرقاً سطحياً

▶ **scorching** *adj* very hot: *It was absolutely scorching on Tuesday.* حارّ جداً

score[1] /skɔ:(r)/ *noun* **1** [C] the number of points, goals, etc. that sb/sth gets in a game, competition, examination, etc: *What was the final score?* ○ *The score is 3-2 to Liverpool.* ○ *She won the match with a score of 6-4, 6-1.* ○ *The top score in the test was 80%.* نتيجة المباراة ، عدد (الأهداف) المسجّلة

2 scores [plural] very many: *Scores of people have written to offer their support.* أعداد كبيرة

3 [C] the written form of a piece of music
كرّاسة النوتة الموسيقيّة

IDM on that score about that: *Len will be well looked after. Don't worry on that score.*
من هذه الناحية

score[2] /skɔ:(r)/ *verb* [I,T] to get points, goals, etc. in a game, competition, examination, etc: *The team still hadn't scored by half-time.* ○ *Louise scored the highest marks in the exam.* ○ *Alonso scored an easy victory in the new Renault.* ○ *England scored three goals against France.*
يسجّل هدفاً ؛ يحرز (نصراً)

scoreboard /'skɔ:bɔ:d/ *noun* [C] a large board that shows the score during a game, competition, etc. لوحة تظهر النقاط المسجّلة في مباراة

scorn /skɔːn/ *noun* [U] **scorn (for sb/sth)** the strong feeling that you have when you do not respect sb/sth: *She looked at him with scorn and contempt.* ازدراء

▶ **scorn** *verb* [T] **1** to feel or show scorn for sb/sth: *The President scorned his critics.* يزدري

2 to refuse to accept help or advice, especially because you are too proud: *The old lady scorned all offers of help.* يترفع عن ، يأنف من

scornful /-fl/ *adj* feeling or showing scorn: *a scornful look, smile, etc.* مزدرٍ ، محتقِر

scornfully /-fəli/ *adv* بازدراء ، بسخرية

Scorpio /ˈskɔːpiəʊ/ *noun* [C,U] (*pl.* **Scorpios**) the eighth sign of the zodiac, the Scorpion; a person who was born under this sign برج العقرب

scorpion /ˈskɔːpiən/ *noun* [C] a creature which looks like a large insect and lives in warm climates. A scorpion has a long tail with a poisonous sting in it. عقرب

Scot /skɒt/ *noun* [C] a person who comes from Scotland شخص اسكتلندي

Scotch /skɒtʃ/ *noun* **1** [U] a strong alcoholic drink (whisky) that is made in Scotland ويسكي اسكتلندي

2 [C] a glass of Scotch ➲ Look at the note at **Scottish.** كأس من الويسكي

Scots /skɒts/ *adj* of or connected with people from Scotland ➲ Look at the note at **Scottish.** اسكتلندي

Scotsman /ˈskɒtsmən/ (*pl.* **Scotsmen** /-mən/), **Scotswoman** /ˈskɒtswʊmən/ (*pl.* **Scotswomen** /-wɪmɪn/) *noun* [C] a man or woman who comes from Scotland رجل أو امرأة من اسكتلندة

Scottish /ˈskɒtɪʃ/ *adj* of or connected with Scotland, its people, culture, etc. اسكتلندي

> **Scots** is usually only used about the people of Scotland: *a Scots piper.* **Scottish** is used about Scotland and about both people and things that come from Scotland: *Scottish law, dancing, lochs, etc.* ○ *She speaks with a strong Scottish accent.* ○ *the Scottish Highlands.* **Scotch** is used for whisky and some kinds of food. You should not use it for Scottish people.

scoundrel /ˈskaʊndrəl/ *noun* [C] (*old-fashioned*) a man who behaves very badly towards other people, especially by being dishonest وغد ، نصّاب

scour[1] /ˈskaʊə(r)/ *verb* [T] to clean sth by rubbing it hard with sth rough: *to scour dirty pots and pans* يفرك ، يجلو

scour[2] /ˈskaʊə(r)/ *verb* [T] to search a place very carefully because you are looking for sb/sth: *Helen scoured the shops for a suitable dress.* يجوب بحثاً عن ، يفتّش في كل مكان

scourge /skɜːdʒ/ *noun* [C] a person or thing that causes a lot of trouble or suffering: *the scourge of unemployment* بلوى ، عذاب

scout /ˈskaʊt/ *noun* [C] **1** a soldier who is sent on in front of the rest of the group to find out where the enemy is or which is the best route to take الرائد: من يستطلع أمر العدوّ

2 Scout (*also* **Boy Scout**) a member of an organization that teaches boys how to look after themselves and encourages them to help others. Scouts do sport, learn useful skills, go camping, etc. ➲ Look at **Girl Guide.** كشّاف

scowl /skaʊl/ *noun* [C] a look on your face that shows you are angry or in a bad mood ➲ Look at **frown.** عبوسة ، تقطيب

▶ **scowl** *verb* [I] يعبس ، يقطّب

scrabble /ˈskræbl/ *verb* [I] to move your fingers around, trying to find sth or get hold of sth: *She scrabbled about in her purse for some coins.* ينبّش بأصابعه

scramble /ˈskræmbl/ *verb* [I] **1** to climb quickly up or over sth using your hands to help you: *to scramble up a steep hill, over a wall, etc.* يتسلق مسرعاً مستعيناً بيديه ، "يَتَعرْبَش"

2 to move or do something quickly because you are in a hurry: *She scrambled into some clean clothes.* يعجّل في العمل

3 scramble (for sth) to struggle to get sth which a lot of people want: *Everyone was scrambling to get the best bargains.* يتزاحم ، يتدافعون بالمناكب

▶ **scramble** *noun* [sing.] an act of scrambling: *There was a real scramble as everyone rushed for the best seats.* تدافع ، تزاحم شديد

ˌscrambled ˈegg *noun* [U] eggs that are mixed together with milk and then cooked in a pan بيض يخفق مع الحليب ويطبخ

scrap[1] /skræp/ *noun* **1** [C] a small piece or amount of sth: *a scrap of paper* ○ *scraps of food* ○ (*figurative*) *There is not a scrap of truth in what she told me.* قصاصة ، نتفة : فضلات

2 [U] something that you do not want any more but that is made of material that can be used again: *The old car was sold for scrap* (= so the metal could be used again). ○ *scrap paper* سقط المتاع أو خردة تستعمل من جديد

▶ **scrap** *verb* [T] (scra**pp**ing; scra**pp**ed) to get rid of sth that you do not want any more: *the government's decision to scrap nuclear weapons* ○ *I think we should scrap that idea.* يتخلّص من ، يلغي

scrappy *adj* (scrappier; scrappiest) not organized or tidy and so not pleasant to see: *a scrappy letter* مفكّك، مشوّش

scrap[2] /skræp/ *noun* [C] (*informal*) a fight or quarrel which is not very serious صدام ، مهاوشة

scrapbook /ˈskræpbʊk/ *noun* [C] a large book with blank pages that you can stick pictures, newspaper articles, etc. in دفتر تُجمع فيه قصاصات وصور وغير ذلك

scrape[1] /skreɪp/ *verb* **1** [T] **scrape sth (down/out/off)** to make sth clean or smooth by moving a sharp edge across it firmly: *to scrape a pan clean* يجلو ، يفرك

2 [T] to remove sth by moving a sharp edge

across a surface: *Scrape all the mud off your boots before you come in.* يكشط

3 [T] **scrape sth (against/along/on sth)** to damage or hurt sth by rubbing it against sth rough or hard: *Mark fell and scraped his knee.* ○ *Jenny scraped the car against the gatepost.* يجرح ، يكشط ، يخدش

4 [I,T] **scrape (sth) against/along/on sth** rub (sth) against sth and make a sharp unpleasant noise: *The branches scraped against the window.* يحتكّ بِ أو يجرّ محدثاً صوتاً مزعجاً

PHR V **scrape through sth** to succeed with difficulty in doing sth: *to scrape through an exam* (= just manage to pass it) يجتاز امتحاناً بشقّ الأنفس

scrape sth together/up to get or collect sth together with difficulty: *We just managed to scrape enough money together for a week's holiday.* يلملم، يجمّع من هنا وهناك

scrape² /skreɪp/ *noun* [C] **1** an act of scraping or the sound of sth scraping on/against sth: *the scrape of a spoon on a metal pan* كشط : صوت الاحتكاك

2 (*informal*) a difficult situation that was caused by your own foolish behaviour: *The children are always getting into scrapes.* ورطة

ˈscrap heap *noun* [C] a large pile of rubbish كومة نفايات

IDM **on the scrap heap** not wanted any more: *Many of the unemployed feel that they are on the scrap heap.* غير مرغوب فيه ، منبوذ

scrappy → SCRAP¹

scratch¹ /skrætʃ/ *verb* **1** [I,T] to make a mark on a surface or a small wound on a person's skin with sth sharp: *The cat will scratch if you annoy it.* ○ *I've scratched myself quite badly on the rose bush.* ○ *The table was badly scratched.* يخدش

2 [T] to put sth somewhere or to take it away by scratching: *He scratched his name on the top of his desk.* ○ *I tried to scratch the paint off the table.* يحفر (اسمه) على سطح ما : يزيل شيئاً بالخدش

3 [I,T] to rub a part of the body, often to stop it itching: *I put some lotion on his skin to try and stop him scratching.* ○ *Could you scratch my back for me?* ○ *She sat and thought about the problem, scratching her head occasionally.* يحكّ

scratch² /skrætʃ/ *noun* **1** [C] a cut, mark or sound that was made by sb/sth scratching sb/sth else: *There's a scratch on the car door.* ○ *They survived the accident without even a scratch.* خَدْش : حكّ : صوت خربشة

2 [sing.] an act of scratching¹ (3): *The dog had a good scratch.* حكّ

IDM **from scratch** from the very beginning: *I'm learning Spanish from scratch.* من البداية

(be/come) up to scratch (*informal*) to be/become good enough: *Karen's singing isn't really up to scratch.* على المستوى المطلوب ، (ليس) كما يجب

ˈscratch card *noun* [C] a card that you buy that has an area that you scratch off to find out if you have won some money or a prize بطاقة يانصيب تُحكّ

scrawl /skrɔːl/ *verb* [I,T] to write in an untidy and careless way يكتب بعجلة ودون عناية ، يشخبط أو يخربش

▸ **scrawl** *noun*: *Her signature was just a scrawl.* شخبطة أو خربوشة

➲ Look at **scribble**.

scream /skriːm/ *verb* [I,T] **scream (sth) (out) (at sb)** to cry out loudly in a high voice because you are afraid, excited, angry, in pain, etc: *She saw a rat hiding in the corner of the room and screamed.* ○ *'Don't touch that,' he screamed.* ○ *She screamed at the children to stop.* ○ *The horse screamed with pain.* ○ *He clung to the edge of the cliff, screaming for help.* ➲ Look at **shout**. يصرخ ، يصيح

▸ **scream** *noun* **1** [C] a loud cry in a high voice: *a scream of pain* صرخة أو صيحة

2 [sing.] (*informal*) a person or thing that is very funny: *She's a real scream.* شيء أو شخص مضحك جداً

screech /skriːtʃ/ *verb* [I,T] to make an unpleasant loud high sound: *The car's brakes screeched as it came to a halt.* ○ *'Get out of here,' she screeched at him.* ➲ Look at **shriek**. يزعق

▸ **screech** *noun* [sing.] an unpleasant high sound: *the screech of brakes* زعقة أو زعيق

screen /skriːn/ *noun* **1** [C] a flat vertical surface that is used for dividing a room or keeping sb/sth out of sight: *There was only a screen between the two desks.* ○ *The house was hidden by a screen of tall trees.* حاجز ، حائل

2 [C] the blank surface on which films are shown شاشة السينما

3 [C] the glass surface of a television or computer where the picture or information appears شاشة التلفزيون وغيره

4 the screen [sing.] cinema films: *a star of stage and screen* (= a famous actor who appears in both plays and films) أفلام سينمائية

▸ **screen** *verb* [T] **1 screen sb/sth (off) (from sb/sth)** to hide or protect sb/sth from sb/sth: *The bed was screened off while the doctor examined him.* ○ *to screen your eyes from the sun* يستر ، يخفي : يقي

2 screen sb (for sth) to examine or test sb to find out if he/she has a particular disease or if he/she is suitable for a particular job: *All women over 50 should be screened for breast cancer.* ○ *The Ministry of Defence screens all job applicants.* يفحص طبياً : يدقّق في مؤهّلات مرشح ما

3 to show sth on TV or in a cinema: *The programme was too violent to be screened before 9 o'clock.* يعرض على الشاشة

ˈscreen saver *noun* [C] a computer program that replaces what is on the screen with a moving image if the computer is not used for certain amount of time واقي الشاشة

screw /skruː/ *noun* [C] a small piece of metal with a sharp end and a round head used for fixing two things, e.g. pieces of wood, together. A screw is like a nail but you fix it into sth by turning it round with a special tool (a screwdriver). مسمار لولبيّ، برغي ، قلاووظ

▸ **screw** *verb* **1** [T] to fasten sth with a screw or screws: *The bookcase is screwed to the wall.* يثبّت ببراغي أو بمسامير لولبيّة

2 [I,T] to fasten sth, or to be fastened, by turning: *The legs screw into holes in the underside of the seat.* ○ *Make sure that you screw the top of the jar on tightly.* يَثْبت أو يثبّت بالبرم

PHRV **screw sth up 1** to make paper, cloth, etc. into a tight ball: *Joanne screwed up the letter and threw it in the bin.* يكوّر

2 to change the expression on your face by nearly closing your eyes, in pain or because the light is strong يزمّ عينيه أو وجهه

3 (*slang*) to ruin sth or cause sth to fail: *You'd better not screw up this deal.* يفسد ، يخرّب

screwdriver /'skru:draɪvə(r)/ *noun* [C] a tool that you use for turning screws مفكّ (البراغي)

scribble /'skrɪbl/ *verb* [I,T] **1** to write sth quickly and carelessly: *to scribble a note down on a pad* ➲ Look at **scrawl**. يكتب بعجلة ودون عناية

2 to make marks with a pen or pencil that are not letters or pictures: *The children had scribbled all over the walls.* يخربش ، يشخبط

▸ **scribble** *noun* [C,U] something that has been scribbled خربشة أو شخبطة

script /skrɪpt/ *noun* **1** [C] the written form of a play, film, speech, etc. مخطوطة مسرحية أو فيلم وغير ذلك

2 [C,U] a system of writing: *Arabic, Cyrillic, Roman, etc. script* خطّ أو كتابة

scripture /'skrɪptʃə(r)/ *noun* [U] (*also* **the scriptures** [plural]) the holy books of religion, such as the Bible كتاب مقدّس

scroll /skrəʊl/ *noun* [C] a long roll of paper with writing on it درْج ، طومار

▸ **scroll** *verb* [I,T] to move text up or down on a computer screen until you find the part you want يلفّ

'scroll bar /'skrəʊl bɑ:(r)/ *noun* [C] a tool on a computer screen that you use to move the text up and down or left and right عارضة الدرْج (كمبيوتر)

scrounge /'skraʊndʒ/ *verb* [I,T] **scrounge (sth) (from/off sb)** (*informal*) to get sth by asking another person to give it to you instead of making an effort to get it for yourself: *Lucy is always scrounging money off her friends.* يبتزّ أو يستجدي (من أصدقائه مثلا)

scrub¹ /skrʌb/ *noun* [U] small trees and bushes that grow in an area that has poor soil or low rainfall شجيرات في منطقة جافة

scrub² /skrʌb/ *verb* (scru**bb**ing; scru**bb**ed) [I,T] **scrub (sth) (down/out)** to clean sth with soap and water by rubbing it hard, often with a brush: *to scrub down the floor/walls* ينظّف أو يفرك بالماء والصابون

PHRV **scrub sth off** to remove sth by scrubbing: *to scrub the dirt off the walls* يزيل الأوساخ بفرشاة وماء وصابون

▸ **scrub** *noun* [sing.] an act of scrubbing: *This floor needs a good scrub.* فرك ، تنظيف بفرشاة وماء وصابون

scruff /skrʌf/ *noun*

IDM **by the scruff of the/your neck** by the back of the/your neck: *She picked up the puppy by the scruff of the neck.* قفا الرقبة

scruffy /'skrʌfi/ *adj* (**scruffier**; **scruffiest**) dirty and untidy: *He always looks so scruffy.* ○ *scruffy jeans* وسخ زريّ الهيئة

scrum /skrʌm/ *noun* [C] the part of a game of rugby when several players put their heads down in a circle and push against each other in order to try to get the ball (في لعبة الرجبي أو الركبي): تدافع

scruples /'skru:plz/ *noun* [plural] moral beliefs which stop you from doing sth that you think is wrong: *Haven't you any scruples?* ○ *I've got no scruples about asking them for money* (= I don't think it's wrong). تحرّج ، تأنيب الضمير

scrupulous /'skru:pjələs/ *adj* **1** very careful or paying great attention to detail: *a scrupulous investigation into the causes of the disaster* شديد التدقيق

2 careful to do what is right or honest: *Even the most scrupulous businessman might have been tempted.* ❶ The opposite is **unscrupulous**. متورّع ، متمسّك بالأمانة

▸ **scrupulously** *adv*: *scrupulously clean, honest, etc.* إلى أقصى حدّ ، لا تشوبه شائبة

scrutinize (*also* **scrutinise**) /'skru:tənaɪz; *US* -tənaɪz/ *verb* [T] to look at or examine sth carefully يتفحّص ، يمعن النظر في

scrutiny /'skru:təni; *US* skru:tənɪ/ *noun* [U] a careful examination or observation of sb/sth: *The police kept all the suspects under close scrutiny.* تفحّص، تدقيق النظر؛ مراقبة

scuba-diving /'sku:bə daɪvɪŋ/ *noun* [U] swimming underwater using special equipment for breathing الغوص أو السباحة تحت الماء

scuff /skʌf/ *verb* [T] to make a mark on your shoes or with your shoes, e.g. by kicking sth or by dragging your feet along the ground يخدش حذاءه ؛ يترك أثراً بحذائه

scuffle /'skʌfl/ *noun* [C] a fight in which people try to push each other roughly: *There were scuffles between police and demonstrators.* تعارك

sculptor /'skʌlptə(r)/ *noun* [C] a person who makes figures or objects from stone, wood, etc. نحّات

sculpture /'skʌlptʃə(r)/ *noun* **1** [U] the art of making figures or objects from stone, wood, clay, etc. فن النحت

2 [C,U] a work or works of art that were made in this way تمثال ، قطعة منحوتة

scum /skʌm/ *noun* [U] a covering of a dirty or unpleasant substance on the surface of a liquid غُثاء

scurry /'skʌri/ *verb* [I] (*pres part* **scurrying**; *3rd pers sing pres* **scurries**; *pt, pp* **scurried**) to run quickly with short steps; to hurry يفرّ مذعوراً ؛ يتراكض أو يسرع

scuttle /'skʌtl/ *verb* [I] to run quickly with short steps or with the body close to the ground يركض بخطى قصيرة

scythe /saɪð/ *noun* [C] a tool with a long handle and a long curved blade. You use a scythe to cut long grass, corn, etc. محش، محصد

SD card /ˌes ˈdiː kɑːd/ *noun* [C] the abbreviation for secure digital card (= a type of memory card, used with digital cameras, mobile phones, music players, etc.) بطاقة ذاكرة أمينة

SE *abbrev* = SOUTH-EAST

sea /siː/ *noun* [U] **1** often **the sea** the salt water that covers large parts of the surface of the earth: *Do you live by the sea?* ○ *The sea is quite calm/rough today.* ○ *The Thames flows into the sea at Gravesend.* ○ *There were several people swimming in the sea.* ○ *We finally sighted land after we had been at sea for several days.* بحر

2 [C] often **Sea** a particular large area of salt water. A sea may be part of the ocean or may be surrounded by land: *the Mediterranean Sea* ○ *the Black Sea* البحر (الأسود مثلاً)

3 [sing.] (*also* **seas** [plural]) the state or movement of the waves of the sea: *The captain said that we would not sail in heavy seas* (= when the waves are very big). حالة الأمواج أو قوتها

4 [sing.] a large amount of sth: *The square was just a sea of people.* خضمّ ، مقدار هائل

IDM **at sea 1** sailing in a ship: *They spent about three weeks at sea.* في رحلة بحرية

2 not understanding or not knowing what to do: *When I first started this job I was completely at sea.* ضائع ، مذهول ، مرتبك

seabed /ˈsiːbed/ *noun* [C] the floor of the sea قاع البحر

seafood /ˈsiːfuːd/ *noun* [U] fish and shellfish from the sea that can be eaten as food الأسماك والمحارات التي تؤكل

seagull /ˈsiːɡʌl/ *noun* [C] = GULL

seal¹ /siːl/ *noun* [C] a grey animal with short fur that lives in and near the sea and that eats fish. Seals have no legs and swim with the help of short flat limbs (flippers). حيوان الفقمة

seal² /siːl/ *noun* [C] **1** a piece of wax, etc. that you put on an important piece of paper or letter to show that it is genuine and that it has not been opened خَتْم

2 a small piece of paper, metal, plastic, etc. on a packet, bottle, etc. that you must break before you can open it سِدادة ، خَتْم

3 something that stops air or liquid from getting in or out of something: *The seal has worn and oil is escaping.* ○ *the rubber seal in the lid of a jar* مادّة أو أداة مانعة للتسرّب

▶ **seal** *verb* [T] **1 seal sth (up/down)** to close or fasten a parcel, envelope, etc: *The parcel was sealed with tape.* ○ *to seal (down) an envelope* يغلق ، يسدّ

2 seal sth (up) to fill a hole or cover sth so that air or liquid does not get in or out يسدّ ، يمنع التسرُّب

3 to show formally that you have agreed sth: *to seal an agreement*

PHRV **seal sth off** to stop any person or thing from entering or leaving an area or building: *The building was sealed off by the police.* يعزل مكاناً عن الجمهور

ˈ**sea level** *noun* [sing.] the level of the sea when it is halfway between high tide and low tide (used for measuring the height of things on land): *50 metres above/below sea level* مستوى البحر

ˈ**sea lion** *noun* [C] a type of large seal أسد البحر (نوع من الفقمة)

seam /siːm/ *noun* [C] **1** the line where two pieces of cloth are sewn together دَرْز

2 a layer of coal under the ground عِرْق

seaman /ˈsiːmən/ *noun* [C] (*pl.* **seamen** /-mən/) a sailor بحّار

seance /ˈseɪɑ̃s/ *noun* [C] a meeting at which people try to talk to the spirits of dead people جلسة استحضار الأرواح

search /sɜːtʃ/ *verb* [I,T] **search (sb/sth) (for sb/sth)**; **search (through sth)(for sth)** to examine sb/sth carefully because you are looking for something; to look for sth that is missing: *to search sb for drugs* ○ *The police searched the area for clues.* ○ *They are still searching for the missing child.* ○ *She searched through the papers on the desk, looking for the letter.* يفتّش ، يبحث عن

▶ **search** *noun* [C] an act of searching: *the search for the missing boy* تفتيش ، بحث

IDM **in search of sb/sth** looking for sb/sth: *The early explorers went in search of gold.* باحثاً عن

searching *adj* (used about a look, question, etc.) trying to find out the truth: *The customs officers asked a lot of searching questions about our trip.* فاحص ، ثاقب

ˈ**search engine** *noun* [C] (*computing*) a computer program that searches the Internet for information, especially by looking for documents containing a particular word or group of words أداة البحث

searchlight /ˈsɜːtʃlaɪt/ *noun* [C] a powerful lamp whose beam can be turned in any direction, for example to look for enemy aircraft at night نور كشّاف

ˈ**search party** *noun* [C] (*pl.* **search parties**) a group of people who look for sb who is lost or missing: *to send out a search party* جماعة تخرج باحثة عن مفقود

ˈ**search warrant** *noun* [C] an official piece of paper that gives the police the right to search a building, etc. أمر بالتفتيش

seashell /ˈsiːʃel/ *noun* [C] the empty shell of a small animal that lives in the sea صَدَفَة ، قوقع

seashore /ˈsiːʃɔː(r)/ *noun* [U] the part of the land that is next to the sea شاطئ البحر

seasick /ˈsiːsɪk/ *adj* feeling ill because of the movement of a boat or ship: *to feel/get seasick* مصاب بدوار البحر

seaside /ˈsiːsaɪd/ *noun* [sing.] often **the seaside** an area on the coast, especially one where people go on holiday: *It's a lovely day. Let's go to the seaside.* ○ *a seaside hotel* شاطئ البحر

season[1] /ˈsiːzn/ *noun* [C] **1** one of the four periods into which the year is divided (spring, summer, autumn and winter) فصل

2 the period of the year when sth is common or popular or when sth usually happens or is done: *The football season is from August to May.* ○ *the dry/rainy season* ○ *the height of the holiday season* موسم

IDM **in season 1** (used about fresh foods) available in large quantities: *Tomatoes are cheapest when they are in season.* (فاكهة) في موسمها ، متوفر بكميات كبيرة

2 (used about a female animal) ready to mate (أنثى الحيوان) في فترة الاستعداد للجماع

out of season 1 (used about fresh foods) not available in large quantities في غير موسمه ، غير متوفر بكميات كبيرة

2 (of a holiday destination) at the time of year when it is least popular with tourists: *It's much cheaper to go to Spain out of season.* خارج الموسم السياحي

season[2] /ˈsiːzn/ *verb* [T] to add salt, pepper, spices, etc. to food in order to make it taste better يتبّل (الطعام)

seasonal /ˈsiːzənl/ *adj* happening or existing at a particular time of the year: *There are a lot of seasonal jobs in the summer.* موسمي

seasoned /ˈsiːznd/ *adj* having a lot of experience of sth: *a seasoned traveller* محنك، ذو خبرة طويلة

seasoning /ˈsiːzənɪŋ/ *noun* [C,U] salt, pepper, spices, etc. that you add to food to make it taste better تابل (كالملح والفلفل وغيره)

ˈseason ticket *noun* [C] a ticket that allows you to make a particular journey by bus, train, etc. as often as you like for a fixed period of time. تذكرة موسمية

seat[1] /siːt/ *noun* [C] **1** something that you sit on: *Please take a seat* (= please sit down). ○ *the back seat of a car* ○ *The seats for the ballet cost £30 each.* مقعد ، كرسي

2 the part of a chair, etc. that you sit on مقعدة

3 the part of a piece of clothing that covers your bottom مقعدة (البنطلون)

4 a place on a council or in a parliament that you win in an election: *The Conservatives have a majority of 21 seats.* ○ *to win/lose a seat* مقعد

seat[2] /siːt/ *verb* [T] **1** (often passive) (*formal*) to sit down: *Please be seated.* يجلس

2 to have seats or chairs for a particular number of people: *The hall can seat about 500 people.* يتّسع لـ

▸ **seating** *noun* [U] the seats or chairs in a place or the way that they are arranged: *The seating will need to be changed.* ○ *a seating plan* المقاعد أو أماكن الجلوس

ˈseat belt (*also* **ˈsafety belt**) *noun* [C] a belt that you wear in a car or a plane to protect you from injury if there is an accident حزام المقعد ، حزام الأمان

sea urchin /ˈsiː ɜːtʃɪn/ *noun* [C] a small sea creature with a round shell which is covered with spikes قنفذ البحر

seaweed /ˈsiːwiːd/ *noun* [U] a plant that grows in the sea عشب بحري

sec /sek/ *abbrev* = SECOND[3] (2)

sec. /sek/ *noun* [C] (*Brit informal*) = SECOND[3] (1)

secluded /sɪˈkluːdɪd/ *adj* far away from other people, roads, etc.; very quiet: *secluded beaches* ○ *a secluded garden* منعزل ، ناءٍ ؛ هادئ

▸ **seclusion** /sɪˈkluːʒn/ *noun* [U] عزلة ، هدوء

second[1] /ˈsekənd/ *pron, det, adv* 2nd; next after first: *We are going on holiday in the second week in July.* ○ *Birmingham is the second largest city in Britain.* ○ *She poured herself a second cup of tea.* ○ *Our team finished second.* ○ *I came second in the competition.* ثانٍ ، الثاني

▸ **secondly** *adv* (used when you are giving your second reason or opinion) also: *Firstly, I think it's too expensive and secondly, we don't really need it.* ثانياً

second[2] /ˈsekənd/ *noun, pron* **1 the second** [sing.] a person or thing that comes next after the first: *Queen Elizabeth the Second* ○ *the second of January* ○ *January the second* ○ *Terry was the second to arrive.* الثاني

2 [C] **second (in sth)** a second-class university degree: *to get an upper/lower second in physics* المرتبة الثانية

3 [U] the second gear of a car, etc: *Don't try to start the car in second.* (في السيّارة) ناقل الحركة الثاني

4 [C, usually pl.] something that has a small fault and that is sold cheaply: *The clothes are all seconds.* سلعة فيها عيب تباع بسعر أرخص

second[3] /ˈsekənd/ *noun* [C] **1** (*abbr* **sec.**) one of the 60 parts into which a minute is divided ثانية

2 (*also informal* **sec**) a short time: *Wait a second, please.* لحظة

second[4] /ˈsekənd/ *verb* [T] to support sb's proposal or idea at a meeting so that it can then be discussed and voted on يؤيّد اقتراحاً ، يثنّي

second[5] /sɪˈkɒnd/ *verb* [T] **second sb (from sth)(to sth)** to move sb from his/her job for a fixed period of time to do another job: *Our teacher has been seconded to another school for a year.* يعير موظفاً لمدة محدّدة

▸ **secondment** *noun*: *to be on secondment* إعارة (موظف)

secondary /ˈsekəndri; *US* -deri/ *adj* **1** of less importance than sth else: *Other people's opinions are secondary, it's my opinion that counts.* ثانويّ ، غير مهمّ

2 caused by or developing from sth else: *She developed a secondary infection following a bad cold.* ثانوي ، جانبيّ

ˈsecondary school *noun* [C] (*Brit*) a school

for children aged from eleven to eighteen مدرسة ثانوية

ˌ**second 'best** *adj* not quite the best but the next one after the best: *the second-best time in the 100 metres race* الثاني في الأفضلية

▸ ˌ**second-'best** *noun* [U] something that is not as good as the best, or not as good as you would like: *I'm not prepared to accept second-best.* الاختيار الثاني

ˌ**second 'class** *noun* [U] **1** ordinary accommodation in a train, boat, plane, etc: *You can never get a seat in the second class.* سفر في الدرجة الثانية

2 the type of postage that is cheaper but that takes longer than first class طابع بريديّ من المرتبة الثانية

▸ ˌ**second 'class** *adv* using second-class accommodation or postage: *to travel second class* ○ *to send a letter second class* في الدرجة الثانية

ˌ**second-'class** *adj* **1** used about ordinary accommodation in a train, aeroplane, etc: *a second-class ticket* ○ *a second-class compartment* صالح لِ أو موجود في الدرجة الثانية

2 (used about a university degree) of the level that is next after first-class: *a second-class honours degree in geography* من المرتبة الثانية

3 of little importance: *Old people should not be treated as second-class citizens.* قليل الأهميّة

ˌ**second 'cousin** *noun* [C] the child of your mother's or father's cousin أولاد ابن عم (أو خال) الأم أو الأب

ˌ**second 'floor** *noun* [C] the floor in a building that is next above the first floor (= two floors above the ground): *I live on the second floor.* ○ *a second-floor flat* ❶ In American English the second floor is next above the ground. الطابق أو الدور الثاني

'**second hand** *noun* [C] the hand on some clocks and watches that records seconds عقرب الثواني

ˌ**second-'hand** *adj, adv* **1** already used or owned by sb else: *a second-hand car* ○ *I bought this camera second-hand.* مستعمل

2 (used about news or information) that you heard from sb else (= that you did not see or experience yourself) بطريقة غير مباشرة

ˌ**second 'language** *noun* [C] a language that is not your native language but which you learn because it is used, often for official purposes, in your country: *French is the second language of several countries in Africa.* لغة ثانية (بعد اللغة الأم)

'**second name** *noun* [C] **1** a family name or surname اسم العائلة،

2 a second personal name: *His second name is William, after his grandfather.* الاسم الشخصي الثاني

ˌ**second 'nature (to sb)** *noun* [U] something that has become a habit or that you can do easily because you have done it so many times: *With practice, typing becomes second nature.* عادة تمارس بسهولة

ˌ**second-'rate** *adj* of poor quality: *a second-rate poet* من الدرجة الثانية ، رديء

ˌ**second 'thoughts** *noun* [plural] a change of mind or opinion about sth; doubts that you have when you are not sure if you have made the right decision: *On second thoughts, let's go today, not tomorrow.* ○ *I'm having second thoughts about accepting their offer.* إعادة نظر ، تغيير رأي

secrecy /'siːkrəsi/ *noun* [U] the state of being or keeping sth secret: *The negotiations took place in the strictest secrecy.* ○ *I must stress the importance of secrecy in this matter.* سِريّة ، تكتّم

⚷ **secret** /'siːkrət/ *adj* **1 secret (from sb)** that is not or must not be known by other people: *The file was marked 'Top Secret'.* ○ *a secret address* ○ *a secret love affair* سرّي ، مكتوم

2 doing sth that you do not tell anyone else about: *She's got a secret admirer.* خفيّ

▸ **secret** *noun* **1** [C] something that is not or must not be known by other people: *to keep a secret* ○ *to tell sb a secret* ○ *I can't tell you where we're going – it's a secret.* ○ *It's no secret that they don't like each other* (= everybody knows). سِر

2 [sing.] the only way or the best way of doing or achieving sth: *What is the secret of your success* (= how did you become so successful)? سِر، سبب خفي

IDM in secret without other people knowing: *to meet in secret* خفية أو سراً

secretly *adv* without other people knowing: *The government secretly agreed to pay the kidnappers.* ○ *The couple were secretly engaged for years.* سراً

ˌ**secret 'agent** (*also* **agent**) *noun* [C] a person who tries to find out secret information especially about the government of another country ➲ Look at **spy**. جاسوس

⚷ **secretary** /'sekrətri; *US* -rəteri/ *noun* [C] (*pl.* **secretaries**) **1** a person who works in an office. A secretary types letters, answers the telephone, makes appointments, etc: *the director's personal secretary* سكرتير(ة)

2 a person who does similar work for a club or other organization: *The secretary must take the minutes of the meetings.* سكرتير(ة) : أمين السر

3 (*US*) = MINISTER

▸ **secretarial** /ˌsekrə'teəriəl/ *adj* connected with the work that a secretary (1) does: *secretarial skills* سكرتاريّة

ˌ**Secretary of 'State** *noun* [C] **1** (in Britain) the head of one of the main government departments: *the Secretary of State for Defence* وزير

2 (in the US) the head of the government department that deals with foreign affairs وزير الخارجية الأمريكي

secrete /sɪ'kriːt/ *verb* [T] **1** (used about a part of a plant, animal or person) to produce a liquid: *a hormone secreted by the female of the species* يفرز

2 (*formal*) to hide sth in a secret place يخفي ، يخبّئ

▸ **secretion** /sɪ'kriːʃn/ *noun* (*formal*) **1** [C] a liquid that is produced by a plant or an animal إفراز(ات)

2 [U] producing this liquid إفراز

secretive /ˈsiːkrətɪv/ *adj* liking to keep things secret from other people: *Wendy is very secretive about her private life.* متكتّم
▸ **secretively** *adv* بصورة مفرطة في التكتّم
secretiveness *noun* [U] تكتّم

ˌsecret ˈservice *noun* [C] the government department that tries to find out secret information about other countries and governments الاستخبارات، هيئة التجسّس

sect /sekt/ *noun* [C] a group of people who have a particular set of religious or political beliefs. A sect has often broken away from a larger group. طائفة ، فرقة

sectarian /sekˈteəriən/ *adj* connected with one particular sect or the differences between sects: *sectarian violence* طائفي

section /ˈsekʃn/ *noun* [C] **1** one of the parts into which something can be or has been divided: *The final section of the road will be open in June.* ○ *the string section of an orchestra* ○ *the financial section of a newspaper* ○ *The library has an excellent reference section.* قسم ، جزء

2 a view or drawing of sth as if it was cut from the top to the bottom and seen from the side مقطع

sector /ˈsektə(r)/ *noun* [C] **1** a part of the business activity of a country: *The manufacturing sector has declined in recent years.* ○ *the public/private sector* قطاع

2 a part of an area or of a large group of people: *the Christian sector of the city* ○ *All sectors of the community should be consulted before a decision is made.* قطاع

secular /ˈsekjələ(r)/ *adj* not concerned with religion or the church علماني ، دنيوي

secure /sɪˈkjʊə(r)/ *adj* **1** free from worry or doubt, confident: *to feel secure about the future* ○ *Children need to feel secure.* ○ *to be financially secure* ❶ The opposite is **insecure**. مطمئن ، آمن

2 not likely to be lost; safe: *Business is good so his job is secure.* ○ *a secure investment* مضمون ، مأمون

3 not likely to fall or be broken; firmly fixed: *That ladder doesn't look very secure.* راسخ ، ماكن ، ثابت

4 secure (against/from sth) well locked or protected: *Make sure the house is secure before you go to bed.* ○ *a country with secure borders* مغلق بإحكام : محميّ (من الهجوم)

▸ **secure** *verb* [T] **1** to fix or lock sth firmly: *The load was secured with ropes.* ○ *Secure the rope to a tree or a rock.* يوثق ، يثبّت : يغلق بإحكام

2 secure sth (against/from sth) to make sth safe: *The sea wall needs strengthening to secure the town against flooding.* يحمي ، يحصّن

3 to obtain or achieve sth, especially by having to make a big effort: *The company has secured a contract to build ten planes.* يفوز، ينال
securely *adv*: *All doors and windows must be securely fastened.* بإحكام

security /sɪˈkjʊərəti/ *noun* (*pl.* **securities**) **1** [U] the state of feeling safe and being free from worry: *Children need the security of a stable home environment.* ○ *financial security* (= having enough money for your present and future needs) ❶ The opposite is **insecurity**. اطمئنان ، أمان

2 [U] things that you do to protect sb/sth from thieves, attack, war, etc: *Security was tightened at the airport before the president arrived.* ○ *a maximum security prison* (= for dangerous criminals) ○ *the security forces* (= military police, soldiers, etc.) أمن ، إجراءات أمنيّة

3 [C,U] something of value that you use when you borrow money. If you cannot pay the money back then you lose the thing you gave as security: *You may need to use your house as security for the loan.* ضمان ، كفالة

sedan /sɪˈdæn/ *noun* [C] (*US*) = SALOON (1)

sedate¹ /sɪˈdeɪt/ *adj* quiet, calm and well behaved رزين ، هادئ

sedate² /sɪˈdeɪt/ *verb* [T] to give sb a drug or medicine to make him/her calm or sleepy يهدّئ
▸ **sedation** /sɪˈdeɪʃn/ *noun*: *The doctor put her under sedation.* تهدئة ، تنويم
sedative /ˈsedətɪv/ *noun* [C] a drug or medicine that makes you calm or sleepy ➲ Look at **tranquillizer**. مهدّئ

sedentary /ˈsedntri; *US* -teri/ *adj* spending a lot of time sitting down: *a sedentary lifestyle* (عمل) قليل الحركة ، متطلّب جلوساً طويلاً

sediment /ˈsedɪmənt/ *noun* [C,U] a solid substance that forms at the bottom of a liquid راسب

seduce /sɪˈdjuːs; *US* -ˈduːs/ *verb* [T] **1** to persuade sb to do sth they would not usually agree to do: *shops attempting to seduce customers into parting with their money* يغري

2 to persuade sb to have sex with you, especially sb young and without much experience يغوي
▸ **seducer** *noun* [C] a person who seduces (2) sb من يغري أو يغوي
seduction /sɪˈdʌkʃn/ *noun* [C,U] إغراء أو إغواء
seductive /sɪˈdʌktɪv/ *adj* **1** sexually attractive, especially referring to a woman: *a seductive smile* مغرٍ أو مغوٍ

2 very attractive or appealing: *a seductive argument/opinion* (= one which you are tempted to agree with) فتّان ، ساحر : مغرٍ

see /siː/ *verb* (*pt* **saw** /sɔː/; *pp* **seen** /siːn/) **1** [I,T] to become aware of sth, using your eyes: *It was so dark that we couldn't see.* ○ *I can't see the number of that bus without my glasses.* ○ *I've just seen a rat!* ○ *He looked for her but couldn't see her in the crowd.* ➲ Look at the note at **look**¹. يرى ، يبصر

2 [T] to look at or watch a film, play, television programme, etc: *Did you see that programme on Dickens on television last night?* ○ *Have you seen Spielberg's latest film?* يشاهد

3 [T] to get information: *Go and see if the postman has been yet.* ○ *I saw in the paper that they're building a new theatre.* يستخبر : يقرأ ، يعلم

4 [T] to meet or visit sb: *I saw Alan at the*

a b c d e f g h i j k l m n o p q r s t u v w x y z

weekend – we had dinner together. ○ *You should see a doctor about that cough.* ○ *I'm seeing a lot of Paul these days* (= meeting him often).
يزور ، يقابل

5 [T] to go with or accompany sb: *He asked me if he could see me home, but I said no.* يرافق ، يصحب

6 [T] to understand sth; to realize sth: *Do you see what I mean?* ○ *Everybody laughed, but I couldn't see the joke.* ○ *She doesn't see the point in spending so much money on a car.* ○ *I thought he was a gentleman, but now I see I'm wrong.* ○ *'You have to press the return key first.' 'Oh, I see.'*
يفهم ، يدرك

7 [T] to have an opinion about sth: *Lack of money is the problem, as I see it.* ○ *I see things differently now* يرى

8 [T] to imagine: *I can't see her changing her mind now.* يتصوَّر ، يتخيَّل

9 [T] to do what is necessary in a situation; to make sure that sb does sth: *I'll see that he gets the letter.* ○ *Please see that the children clean their teeth.* يقوم بما يلزم ؛ يتأكّد من

10 [T] to be the time when an event happens: *Last year saw huge changes in the education system.* يشهد

IDM **as far as I can see** → FAR[2]

I'll see I'll think about what you have asked me and give you my decision later: *'Can we go swimming today, Dad?' 'I'll see.'* ❶ Also used with **we**: *We'll see.* يفكّر في الأمر

let me see; **let's see** → LET[1]

see if... to try: *I'll see if I can find time to do it.* يحاول

see you around (used for saying goodbye to sb you have made no arrangement to see again) سأراك إن شاء الله!

see you (later) (used for saying goodbye to sb you expect to see soon or later that day) سأراك (اليوم) إذن

you see (used for giving a reason): *She's very unhappy. He was her first real boyfriend, you see.* والسبب أنه...

PHR V **see about sth/doing sth** to deal with sth: *I've got to go to the bank to see about my traveller's cheques.* يعالج أمراً ، يحل قضيّة

see sb off to go with sb to the railway station, the airport, etc. in order to say goodbye to him/her يودّع في المحطّة أو ما إليها

see through sb/sth to be able to see that sb/sth is not what he/she/it appears: *The police immediately saw through his story.* يدرك زيفه

see to sb/sth to do what is necessary in a situation; to deal with sb/sth: *Can you see to the sandwiches for the meeting, please?* يتعهّد بِ

🔑 **seed** /siːd/ *noun* **1** [C,U] the small hard part of a plant from which a new plant of the same kind can grow: *a packet of sunflower seeds* ○ *Grass seed should be sown in the spring.* بذرة أو بزرة

2 [C] a player in a sports competition, especially in tennis, who is expected to finish in a high position at the end of the competition: *Roddick was the top seed.* لاعب متفوّق (وخاصة في التنس)

▶ **seed** *verb* [T] (in a sports competition, especially tennis) to arrange the matches for a good player so that he/she has a better chance of winning; to give a good player a number saying which position you expect him/her to finish in: *Capriati was seeded second at Wimbledon.*
ينظّم المباريات الاوليّة لمصلحة اللاعب المتفوّق ؛ يصنّف لاعباً

seedless *adj* having no seeds: *seedless grapes*
بدون بزر

seedling /ˈsiːdlɪŋ/ *noun* [C] a very young plant that has grown from a seed نبتة ، بادِرة ، شتلة

seedy /ˈsiːdi/ *adj* (**seedier**; **seediest**) looking untidy, dirty, or in bad condition; not respectable: *a seedy nightclub, hotel, etc.*
قذر ، خَرِب ؛ مشبوه أو سيّء السمعة

seeing /ˈsiːɪŋ/ (*also* **seeing that**; **seeing as**) *conj* (*informal*) because: *Seeing as we're going the same way, I'll give you a lift.* بما أنّه... ؛ نظراً ل

🔑 **seek** /siːk/ *verb* [T] (*pt, pp* **sought** /sɔːt/) **1** to try to find or get sth: *Politicians are still seeking a peaceful solution.* يبحث عن ، ينشد

2 seek sth (from sb) to ask sb for sth: *You should seek advice from a solicitor about what to do next.* ○ *to seek help* يطلب ، يلتمس

3 seek (to do sth) to try to do sth: *They are still seeking to find a peaceful solution to the conflict.* يحاول

🔑 **seem** /siːm/ *verb* [I] **seem (to sb) (to be) sth**; **seem like sth** (not used in the continuous tenses) to give the impression of being or doing sth; to appear: *Emma seems like a very nice girl.* ○ *Emma seems to be a very nice girl.* ○ *It seems to me that we have no choice.* ○ *You seem happy today.* ○ *This machine doesn't seem to work.* ○ *It doesn't seem as if/though they will find a solution to the problem.* يبدو ، يظهر

▶ **seeming** *adj* (only *before* a noun) appearing to be sth: *Despite her seeming enthusiasm, Sandra didn't really help much.* ظاهر ، بادٍ ؛ ظاهري

seemingly *adv*: *a seemingly endless list of complaints* ظاهراً ؛ على ما يبدو

seen *pp* of SEE[1]

seep /siːp/ *verb* [I] (used about a liquid) to flow very slowly through sth: *Water started seeping in through small cracks.* ينزّ ، يتسرّب

see-saw /ˈsiːsɔː/ *noun* [C] an outdoor toy for children that consists of a long piece of wood, etc. that is balanced in the middle. One child sits on each end of the see-saw and one goes up while the other is down. لعبة الرجحان

seethe /siːð/ *verb* [I] **1** to be very angry: *I was absolutely seething.* يستشيط غضباً

2 to be very crowded: *The streets were seething with people.* ○ *a seething mass of people* (= a lot of people crowded together) يزخر أو يغصّ بِ

segment /ˈsegmənt/ *noun* [C] **1** a section or part of sth: *a segment of a circle* ○ *a segment of the population* قطعة ، قسم

2 one of the parts into which an orange can be divided فصّ ، "حزّ أو حزّة"

segregate /ˈsegrɪgeɪt/ *verb* [T] **segregate sb/sth (from sb/sth)** to separate one group of people or things from the rest: *The two groups of*

football fans were segregated to avoid trouble. ➲ Look at **integrate**. يفصل ، يعزل
▸ **segregation** /ˌsegrɪˈgeɪʃn/ *noun*: *racial segregation* (= separating people of different races) تفرقة ، فصل

seize /siːz/ *verb* [T] **1** to take hold of sth suddenly and firmly: *The thief seized her handbag and ran off with it.* ○ *to seize sb by the arm* ○ (*figurative*) *I felt myself seized by panic.* يمسك بـ ، يقبض على ، يتملّك

2 to take control or possession of sb/sth: *The police seized 50 kilos of illegal drugs.* ○ *to seize power* ○ *Rebel forces seized the radio station early this morning.* يستولي على ؛ يصادر

PHR V **seize (on/upon) sth** to recognize an opportunity and to use it eagerly: *The Opposition seized upon any opportunity to embarrass the Government.* يغتنم الفرصة

seize up (used about a machine) to stop working because it is too hot, does not have enough oil, etc. يتوقّف عن الحركة ، يستعصي ، "يلصب"

▸ **seizure** /ˈsiːʒə(r)/ *noun* [U] seizing or being seized: *the seizure of 30 kilos of heroin by French police* استيلاء على ؛ مصادرة

seldom /ˈseldəm/ *adv* not often: *There is seldom snow in Athens.* ○ *We very seldom go to the theatre.* نادراً

⚷**select** /sɪˈlekt/ *verb* [T] to choose sb/sth from a number of similar things: *You may select whatever you want from the prizes on display.* ○ *The best candidates will be selected for interview.* ❶ **Select** is more formal than **choose** and suggests that a great deal of care is taken when making the decision. ينتقي ، يختار

▸ **select** *adj* **1** carefully chosen: *a select audience of academics* منتقى، مختار

2 consisting of or available to only a small group of special people: *A university education is no longer the privilege of a select few.* ○ *a select neighbourhood* (= one where the houses are very expensive) مقصور على صفوة الناس : (منطقة) راقية

⚷**selection** /sɪˈlekʃn/ *noun* **1** [U] choosing or being chosen: *All candidates must go through a rigorous selection procedure.* ○ *the selection of the England cricket team* انتقاء ، اختيار

2 [C] a number of people or things that have been chosen: *a selection of hits from the fifties and sixties* مجموعة مختارة

3 [C] a collection of goods in a shop that are for sale: *This shop has a very good selection of toys.* مجموعة من البضائع

selective /sɪˈlektɪv/ *adj* **1** careful when choosing: *She's very selective about who she invites to her parties.* مدقّق في الاختيار

2 of or concerning only some people or things; not general: *selective schools/education* انتقائيّ
▸ **selectively** *adv* بشكل مجزأ ، بصورة انتقائيّة

⚷**self** /self/ (*pl.* **selves** /selvz/) *noun* [C] a person's own nature or qualities: *It's good to see you back to your old self again* (= said to sb who has been ill, sad, worried, etc.). ○ *Her spiteful remark revealed her true self.* نفس ، ذات ، طبيعة

ˌ**self-asˈsured** *adj* = ASSURED
▸ ˌ**self-asˈsurance** *noun* [U] = ASSURANCE (1)

ˌ**self-ˈcatering** *adj* (used about a holiday or accommodation) where meals are not provided for you but you cook them yourself (إقامة) يعِدّ المرء فيها طعامه بنفسه

ˌ**self-ˈcentred** (*US* **self-centered**) *adj* thinking only about yourself and not about other people ➲ Look at **selfish**. أناني

ˌ**self-conˈfessed** *adj* admitting that you are sth or do sth that most people consider to be bad: *a self-confessed drug user* مقر (بذَنْبه)

ˌ**self-ˈconfident** *adj* feeling sure about your own value and abilities واثق بنفسه
▸ ˌ**self-ˈconfidence** *noun*: *Many women lack the self-confidence to apply for senior jobs.* الثقة بالنفس

ˌ**self-ˈconscious** *adj* too worried about what other people think about you: *Men are often very self-conscious about losing their hair.* خجول ، مرتبك ، غير واثق من نفسه
▸ ˌ**self-ˈconsciously** *adv* بعدم ثقة بالنفس ، بارتباك
ˌ**self-ˈconsciousness** *noun* [U] خجل، ارتباك

ˌ**self-conˈtained** *adj* (used about a flat, etc.) having its own private entrance, kitchen, bathroom, etc. مستقلّ ، مكتفٍ ذاتياً

ˌ**self-conˈtrol** *noun* [U] the ability to control your emotions and appear calm even when you are angry, afraid, excited, etc: *to lose/keep your self-control* ضبط النفس ، تمالك الأعصاب

ˌ**self-deˈfence** *noun* [U] the use of force to protect yourself or your property: *Lee is learning karate for self-defence.* ○ *to shoot sb in self-defence* (= because they are about to attack you) الدفاع عن النفس

ˌ**self-deˌtermiˈnation** *noun* [U] **1** the right of a nation, country, etc. to decide what form of government it will have or whether it will be independent of another country or not حق تقرير المصير

2 the right or opportunity of individuals to control their own lives حق الإرادة الشخصية

ˌ**self-emˈployed** *adj* working for yourself and earning money from your own business صاحب مهنة حرّة

ˌ**self-eˈsteem** *noun* [U] a good opinion of your own character and abilities: *a man with high/low self-esteem* ○ *to undermine/raise sb's self-esteem* احترام الذات،الاعتداد بالنفس

ˌ**self-ˈevident** *adj* that does not need proving or explaining; clear بديهي ؛ واضح جلي

ˌ**self-exˈplanatory** *adj* that does not need explaining; clear: *a self-explanatory diagram* ○ *The book's title is self-explanatory.* واضح لا يحتاج إلى تفسير

ˌ**self-inˈdulgent** *adj* allowing yourself to have or do things you enjoy (sometimes when it would be better to control yourself) منقاد لملذّاته ، مُدلّل نفسَه

a b c d e f g h i j k l m n o p q r **s** t u v w x y z

▸ **ˌself-inˈdulgence** *noun* [C,U]
انقياد للأهواء : تدليل النفس

ˌself-ˈinterest *noun* [U] concern for what is best for yourself rather than for other people
مصلحة خاصّة

selfish /ˈselfɪʃ/ *adj* thinking only about your own needs or wishes and not about other people's needs or wishes: *a selfish attitude* ○ *I'm sick of your selfish behaviour!* ❶ The opposite is **unselfish**. أناني
▸ **selfishly** *adv* بأنانيّة
selfishness *noun* [U] أنانيّة

selfless /ˈselfləs/ *adj* (*formal*) thinking about other people's needs or wishes rather than your own: *his years of selfless devotion to his sick wife*
غير أناني ، ايثاري

ˌself-ˈmade *adj* having become rich or successful by your own efforts: *a self-made millionaire*
عصامي

ˌself-ˈpity *noun* [U] the state of thinking too much about your own problems or troubles and feeling how unlucky you are المبالغة في الإشفاق على الذات

ˌself-ˈportrait *noun* [C] a picture that you drew or painted of yourself صورة ذاتيّة ، صورة الفنان بريشته

ˌself-ˈraising flour (*US* **self-rising flour**) *noun* [U] flour that contains a substance that makes it rise up during cooking (used for cakes, etc.) ➲ Look at **plain flour**.
دقيق أضيفت إليه مادّة مخمِّرة

ˌself-reˈliant *adj* not depending on help from sb/sth else معتمد على نفسه

ˌself-reˈspect *noun* [U] the feeling of pride in yourself: *Old people need to keep their dignity and self-respect.* كرامة ، احترام النفس
▸ **ˌself-reˈspecting** *adj* (in negative sentences): *No self-respecting language student* (= nobody who is serious about learning a language) *should be without this book.* معتبَر ، فخور بنفسه

ˌself-ˈrighteous *adj* believing that you are always right and other people are wrong; thinking that you are better than other people
معتقد بصحة آرائه وتفوُّقه
▸ **ˌself-ˈrighteously** *adv* بِتعالٍ
ˌself-ˈrighteousness *noun* [U]
اعتقاد بالتفوّق ، تعالٍ

ˌself-ˈsacrifice *noun* [U] not having or doing what you want, in order to help others
التضحية بالنفس

ˌself-ˈservice *adj* in a self-service shop or restaurant, you serve yourself and then pay at a special desk (cash desk) ذو خدمة ذاتيّة

ˌself-sufˈficient *adj* able to produce or provide everything that you need without help from or having to buy from others مستقلّ أو مكتفٍ ذاتياً

🔑 **sell** /sel/ *verb* (*pt, pp* **sold** /səʊld/) **1** [I,T] **sell (sb) (sth)**; **sell (sth) (to sb)** to give sth to sb who pays for it and is then the owner of it: *We are going to sell our car.* ○ *I sold my guitar for £200.* ○ *Would you sell me your ticket?* ○ *I was too late, the car had already been sold.* ○ *I offered them a lot of money but they wouldn't sell.* ○ *He sold his business at an enormous profit.* يبيع

2 [T] to offer for sale: *Excuse me, do you sell stamps?* يبيع

3 [I] **sell (for/at sth)** to be sold or available for sale at a particular price: *These watches sell at £1 000 each in the shops but you can have this one for £500.* يباع بسعر معيّن

4 [I] to be sold to or bought by many people; to attract buyers: *Her books sell well abroad.*
يباع بكميات كبيرة ، يكثر الإقبال عليه

5 [T] to be sold in a particular quantity: *This newspaper sells over a million copies a day.* يبيع

6 [T] to cause people to want to buy sth; to help sth to attract buyers: *They rely on advertising to sell their products.* يروّج

❶ The noun for **1 – 6** is **sale**.

7 [T] **sell sth to sb** to persuade sb to accept sth; *to sell an idea to sb* يقنع

IDM **be sold on sth** (*informal*) to be very enthusiastic about sth: *She's completely sold on the idea of moving to France* (= she thinks it's a very good idea and wants to do it).
متحمّس لِ ، مقتنع بِ

be sold out (used about tickets for a concert, football game, etc.) to be all sold: *All the tickets were sold out within two hours.* ○ *The concert was sold out weeks ago.* نفدت تذاكر الحفلة

PHR V **sell sth off** to sell sth that is not wanted or is not popular with buyers, often at a low price, in order to get rid of it: *The shops sell their winter clothes off in the spring.* يبيع شيئاً للتخلّص منه

sell out to be sold completely so that no more are available for sale: *By the time I got to the shop, all the newspapers had sold out.*
تنفد البضاعة

sell out (of sth) to sell all of sth so that no more are available to be bought: *I'm afraid we've sold out of the book but we could order a copy for you.* يبيع كلّ ما لديه من سلعة ما

sell up to sell everything you own, especially your house, your business, etc. (in order to start a new life, move to another country, retire, etc.): *When his wife died he sold up and moved to the coast.* يبيع كلّ شيء (ويرحل)

ˈsell-by date (*US* **pull date**) *noun* [C] the date after which an item of food or drink should not be offered for sale مدة انتهاء(بيع طعام أو شراب)

seller /ˈselə(r)/ *noun* [C] **1** (often in compounds) a person or business that sells: *a bookseller*
بائع (كتب مثلاً)

2 something that is sold (especially in the amount described): *This magazine is a big seller in the 25-40 age group.* ➲ Look at **best-seller**.
سلعة (رائجة أو كاسدة)

Sellotape™ /ˈseləteɪp/ *noun* [U] (*Brit*) a type of clear tape that is sold in rolls and used for sticking things شريط من الورق اللاصق الشفّاف
▸ **sellotape** *verb* [T] to put or hold sth together with Sellotape; to attach by using Sellotape
يلصق بهذا الورق

selves *pl.* of SELF

semblance /'sembləns/ *noun* [sing., U] (*formal*) **(a) semblance of sth** the appearance of being sth or of having a certain quality: *After the war, life is now returning to some semblance of normality.* مظهر خارجي : شَبَه ، شكل

semen /'si:men/ *noun* [U] the liquid containing sperm that is produced by the male sex organs المَني أو السائل المنويّ

semester /sɪ'mestə(r)/ *noun* [C] one of the two periods that the school or college year is divided into: *the spring/fall semester* فصل دراسي

semi /'semi/ *noun* [C] (*pl.* **semis** /'semiz/) (*Brit informal*) a semi-detached house بيت متّصل من أحد جوانبه ببيت آخر

semicircle /'semisɜ:kl/ *noun* [C] one half of a circle; something that is arranged in this shape: *I want you all to sit in a semicircle.* نصف دائرة

semicolon /ˌsemi'kəʊlən; *US* 'semik-/ *noun* [C] a mark (;) used in writing or printing for separating parts of a sentence or items in a list فاصلة منقوطة

ˌsemi-de'tached *adj* (used about a house) joined to another house with a shared wall on one side forming a pair of houses (بيت) شبه منفصل

ˌsemi-'final *noun* [C] one of the two matches after which the winners play in the final مباراة نصف نهائيّة

▶ **ˌsemi-'finalist** *noun* [C] a player or team that plays in a semi-final لاعب أو فريق يلعب في مباراة نصف نهائيّة

seminar /'semɪnɑ:(r)/ *noun* [C] **1** a class at a university, college, etc. in which a small group of students discuss or study a subject with a teacher حلقة دراسيّة جامعيّة

2 a short business conference in which working methods, etc. are taught or discussed: *a seminar on becoming self-employed* مؤتمر صغير في إدارة الأعمال

⚷ Senate /'senət/ *noun* [C, with sing. or pl. verb] often **the Senate** one of the two groups of elected politicians who make laws in the government in some countries, e.g. the USA ➲ Look at **Congress** and **House of Representatives**. مجلس الشيوخ ، مجلس الأعيان

▶ **senator** /'senətə(r)/ *noun* [C] often **Senator** (*abbr* **Sen.**) a member of a Senate: *Senator McCarthy* سناتور: عضو في مجلس الشيوخ

⚷ send /send/ *verb* [T] (*pt, pp* **sent** /sent/) **1 send sth/sb (to sb/sth); send (sb) sth** to cause sth/sb to go or be taken somewhere without going there yourself: *to send a letter/parcel* ○ *to send a message to sb* ○ *Don't forget to send me a postcard.* ○ *If you are not satisfied with these goods, send them back within 7 days.* ○ *She sent the children to bed early.* ○ *My company is sending me on a training course next month.* ○ *I asked someone the way to the airport but he sent me in the wrong direction.* ○ *to send sb to prison* ○ *Her parents sent her to a private school when she was 11.* يرسل ، يَبعث

2 to cause sb/sth to move in a particular direction, often quickly or as a reaction that cannot be prevented: *I accidentally pushed the table and sent all the drinks flying.* ○ *This year's poor harvest has sent food prices up.* يقذف ، يدفع

3 cause sb/sth to have a particular feeling or to enter a particular state: *The movement of the train sent me to sleep.* يجعل

IDM give/send sb your love → LOVE[1]

PHRV send for sb/sth to ask for sb to come to you; to ask for sth to be brought or sent to you by telephone, message, letter, etc: *I sent for the manager so that I could make a complaint.* ○ *Quick! Send for a doctor!* يستدعي : يطلب شيئاً (بالتليفون أو برسالة)

send sth in to send sth to a place where it will be officially dealt with: *I sent my application in three weeks ago but I still haven't had a reply.* يقدّم طلباً ، يبعث بأوراق رسميّة

send off (for sth) to write to sb and ask for sth to be sent to you: *Let's send off for some holiday brochures.* يكاتب (شركة مثلاً) طالباً بعض المعلومات...

send sb off (*Brit*) (used about a referee in a sports match) to order a player who has broken a rule to leave the game and not to return: *Two players were sent off for fighting.* يخرج من مباراة

send sth off to post sth: *I'll send the information off today.* يرسِل بالبريد

send sth out 1 to send sth to a lot of different people or places: *We sent out the invitations two months before the wedding.* يرسل للجميع، يوزع

2 to produce sth, for example light, heat, sound, etc: *The sun sends out light and heat.* يرسل للجميع، يوزع ينشر

send sb/sth up (*Brit informal*) to make sb/sth look ridiculous or foolish especially by imitating him/her in a way that is intended to be amusing يقلّد بصورة مضحكة ، يسخر من

sender /'sendə(r)/ *noun* [C] a person who sends sth: *The sender's name appears at the top of the email.* المرسِل

senile /'si:naɪl/ *adj* confused, unable to remember things or to look after yourself properly (because of old age) خَرفان ، هَرِم واهن العقل

▶ **senility** /sə'nɪləti/ *noun* [U] الخَرَف

⚷ senior /'si:niə(r)/ *adj* **senior (to sb) 1** having a high or higher rank in a company, organization, etc: *a senior managerial position* ○ *He's senior to me.* ○ *a meeting of senior government ministers* (منصب) عالٍ : أعلى مرتبة

2 older: *This common room is for the use of senior pupils only.* أقدم : أكبر سناً

3 often **Senior** (*abbr* **Snr; Sr**) (used to show that a person is the parent of sb with the same name): *John Brown Senior* ➲ Look at **junior**. الأكبر ، الأب

▶ **senior** *noun* [C] **1** somebody who is older or of higher rank (than one or more other people): *My oldest sister is ten years my senior.* من هو أكبر سناً أو مقاماً

2 an older pupil at a school طالب في صفّ عالٍ

3 (*US*) a student in the final year of school, college or university طالب في سنة التخرّج

seniority /ˌsi:ni'ɒrəti; *US* -'ɔ:r-/ *noun* [U] the rank or importance that a person has in a company, organization, etc. in relation to others:

The names are listed below in order of seniority. الأولويّة في المركز : الأقدميّة

ˌsenior ˈcitizen *noun* [C] = OLD-AGE PENSIONER

ˌsenior ˈhigh school *noun* [C] (in the US) a school for young people between the ages of 14 and 18 مدرسة ثانوية عليا

sensation /senˈseɪʃn/ *noun* **1** [C] a feeling that is caused by sth affecting the body or part of the body: *a pleasant/unpleasant sensation* ○ *I felt a burning sensation on my skin.* إحساس ، شعور

2 [U] the ability to feel when touching or being touched: *For some time after the accident he had no sensation in his legs.* حسّ أو إحساس

3 [C] a feeling or impression in the mind or body that is not caused by anything definite and may be false: *I had the peculiar sensation that I was floating in the air.* إحساس ، شعور

4 [C] a feeling of great excitement, surprise or interest among a group of people or people in general; something that causes this: *The young American caused a sensation by beating the champion.* ○ *The show got wonderful reviews and was an overnight sensation* (= became famous and popular immediately). ضجّة (بين الناس) ، اهتمام كبير : حدث مثير

▸ **sensational** /-ʃənl/ *adj* **1** causing, or trying to cause, a feeling of great excitement, surprise or interest among people: *sensational events* ○ *the most sensational murder trial this century* ○ *This magazine specializes in sensational stories about the rich and famous.* مثير

2 (*informal*) extremely good; beautiful; very exciting: *You look sensational!* ممتاز ؛ فتّان ؛ مثير للغاية

sensationally /-ʃənəli/ *adv* بصورة مثيرة

sense /sens/ *noun* **1** [C] one of the five natural physical powers that make it possible for a person or animal to get information about the world around: *I've got a cold and I've lost my sense of smell.* حاسّة

2 [U, sing.] the ability to understand or appreciate sth; the ability to recognize what sth is: *She seems to have lost all sense of reality.* ○ *I like him – he's got a great sense of humour.* ○ *I'm always getting lost. I've got absolutely no sense of direction.* إدراك؛ حِسّ لِـ

3 [U, sing.] a natural ability to do or produce sth well: *Good business sense made her a millionaire.* ○ *He's got absolutely no dress sense* (= he dresses very badly). ملكة ، حِسّ

4 [U, sing.] a feeling or consciousness of sth: *I felt a tremendous sense of relief when the exams were finally over.* ○ *She only visits her family out of a sense of duty.* شعور ، إحساس

5 [U] the ability to think or act in a reasonable or sensible way; practical intelligence: *At least he had enough sense to stop when he realized he was making a mistake.* ○ *I think there's a lot of sense in what you're saying.* ➲ Look at **common sense**. سلامة التفكير ، عقل

6 [U] good reason; use or point: *There's no sense in going any further – we're obviously lost.* ○ *What's the sense in making things more difficult for yourself?* فائدة : غاية

7 [C] (used about a word, phrase, etc.) a meaning or possible meaning: *This word has two senses.* ○ *This is an epic film in every sense of the word.* معنى

IDM **in a sense** in one particular way but not in other ways; partly: *In a sense you're right, but there's more to the matter than that.* من ناحية ما : إلى حدّ ما

make sense 1 to be possible to understand; to have a clear meaning: *What does this sentence mean? It doesn't make sense to me.* يفهَم ، يحمل معنى واضحاً

2 (used about an action) to be sensible or logical: *I think it would make sense to wait for a while before making a decision.* يكون معقولاً

make sense of sth to manage to understand sth that is not clear or is difficult to understand: *I can't make sense of these instructions.* يفهم شيئاً عويصاً

talk sense → TALK¹ (6)

▸ **sense** *verb* [T] to realize or become aware of sth; to get the feeling that sth is the case: *I sensed that something was wrong.* يدرك ؛ يحس

senseless /ˈsensləs/ *adj* **1** having no meaning or purpose: *The police described the murder as 'a senseless act of violence'.* لا معنى له

2 unconscious فاقد الوعي

sensibility /ˌsensəˈbɪləti/ *noun* **1** [U,C, usually pl.] the ability to experience feelings deeply and to appreciate beauty, etc: *artistic sensibilities* شعور مرهف

2 sensibilities [plural] the tendency to be easily offended or shocked: *to wound/offend/outrage readers' sensibilities* حساسية، شعور

sensible /ˈsensəbl/ *adj* having or showing the ability to think or act in a reasonable way; having or showing good judgement: *a sensible man* ○ *a sensible decision* ○ *Stop joking and give me a sensible answer.* ○ *I think it would be sensible to leave early, in case there's a lot of traffic.* عاقل ، حكيم ؛ معقول

▸ **sensibly** /-əbli/ *adv*: *Let's sit down and discuss the matter sensibly.* بتعقُّل

Compare **sensible** and **sensitive**. **Sensible** is connected with common sense, reasonable action and good judgement. **Sensitive** is connected with feelings and emotions and with the five senses.

sensitive /ˈsensətɪv/ *adj* **1** easily hurt or damaged; painful, especially if touched: *a new cream for sensitive skin* حسّاس ؛ مرهف الشعور

2 sensitive (about/to sth) easily upset, offended or annoyed, perhaps because of having strong feelings about a particular matter: *Don't be so sensitive! I was only joking.* ○ *She's still a bit sensitive about her divorce.* ○ *He's very sensitive to criticism.* سريع التأثُّر ؛ سريع الاستياء

3 sensitive (to sth) showing that you are aware of and understand people's feelings, problems, etc: *It wasn't exactly sensitive of you to keep*

mentioning the exam. You know she failed it. ○ *to be sensitive to sb's feelings/wishes* مراعٍ لشعور الآخرين

ⓘ The opposite for senses **2** and **3** is **insensitive**.

4 (used about a scientific instrument, a piece of equipment, etc.) able to measure very small changes (مقياس) حسّاس

5 (used about a subject, a situation, etc.) needing to be dealt with carefully because it is likely to cause anger or trouble: *Religion is often a sensitive subject.* ○ *This is a sensitive period in the negotiations between the two countries.* حسّاس

▶ **sensitively** *adv*: *The investigation will need to be handled sensitively.* بعناية ، بمراعاة لظروف معيّنة : برِقّة

sensitivity /ˌsensəˈtɪvəti/ *noun* [U] the quality of being sensitive: *I think your comments showed a complete lack of sensitivity.* حساسية ، مراعاة لشعور الآخرين

sensual /ˈsenʃuəl/ *adj* connected with physical or sexual pleasure: *the sensual rhythms of Latin music* ○ *a life devoted to sensual pleasure and luxury* حسّيّ ، جسديّ ، شهوانيّ

▶ **sensuality** /ˌsenʃuˈæləti/ *noun* [U] الشهوانيّة

sensuous /ˈsenʃuəs/ *adj* giving pleasure to or affecting the mind or body through the senses: *the sensuous feel of pure silk* ممتع للحواس ، حسّيّ

▶ **sensuously** *adv* بصورة ممتعة حسديّاً

sensuousness *noun* [U] اثارة الحواس ، إمتاع الناظر

sent *pt, pp of* SEND

⚷**sentence** /ˈsentəns/ *noun* **1** [C] (*grammar*) a group of words containing a subject and a verb, that expresses a statement, a question, etc. When a sentence is written it begins with a capital letter and ends with a full stop: *a grammatically correct sentence* ○ *You don't need to write a long letter. A couple of sentences will be enough.* جملة

2 [C,U] the punishment given by a judge to sb who has been found guilty of a crime: *20 years in prison was a very harsh sentence.* ○ *He is serving his sentence in a maximum security prison.* ○ *the death sentence* حكْم ، عقوبة

▶ **sentence** *verb* [T] **sentence sb (to sth)** (used about a judge) to tell sb who has been found guilty of a crime what the punishment will be: *The judge sentenced her to three months in prison for shoplifting.* ○ *He was sentenced to life imprisonment for murder.* يحكم على

sentiment /ˈsentɪmənt/ *noun* **1** [C,U] (often plural) an attitude or opinion that is often caused or influenced by emotion: *His comments expressed my sentiments exactly.* ○ *Nationalist sentiment is quite strong throughout the country.* رأي متأثّر بالعاطفة ، موقف ، ميل

2 [U] gentle feelings such as sympathy, love, happy memories, etc. that influence action or behaviour (sometimes in situations where this is not suitable): *There's no room for sentiment in business.* عاطفة

sentimental /ˌsentɪˈmentl/ *adj* **1** caused by or connected with gentle feelings such as sympathy, love, happy memories, etc: *The jewellery had great sentimental value to me.* عاطفيّ ، وجدانيّ

2 having or showing these gentle emotions, sometimes in a silly way: *How can you be sentimental about an old car!* ○ *a sentimental love song* مفرط في العاطفيّة

▶ **sentimentality** /ˌsentɪmenˈtæləti/ *noun* [U] عاطفيّة

sentimentally /-təli/ *adv* بعاطفيّة ، بإحساس عاطفيّ

sentry /ˈsentri/ *noun* [C] (*pl.* **sentries**) a soldier who stands outside a building and guards it حارس ، جندي خفير ، دَيْدَبان

separable /ˈsepərəbl/ *adj* able to be separated قابل للفصل ⓘ The opposite is **inseparable**.

⚷**separate**[1] /ˈseprət/ *adj* **1 separate (from sth/sb)** apart; not joined or together: *You should always keep your cash and credit cards separate.* منفصل

2 different: *A lot of married couples have separate bank accounts.* ○ *We stayed in separate rooms in the same hotel.* منفصل ، مستقل

▶ **separately** *adv* apart; not together; at different times or in different places: *Shall we pay separately or all together?* ○ *Let's deal with each matter separately.* كلّ لوحده ، بشكل منفصل ، على حِدة

⚷**separate**[2] /ˈsepəreɪt/ *verb* **1** [I,T] **separate (sb/sth) (from sb/sth)** to stop being together; to cause people or things to stop being together; to divide people or things: *I think we should separate into two groups.* ○ *The friends separated at the airport.* ○ *I got separated from my friends in the crowd.* ○ *Separate the egg yolk from the white.* ينفصل أو يفترق ؛ يفصل أو يفرّق

2 [T] **separate sb/sth (from sb/sth)** to keep people or things apart, or to be between people or things with the result that they are apart: *I always try to separate business from pleasure.* ○ *When the players started fighting, the referee moved in to separate them.* ○ *The two sides of the city are separated by the river.* ○ *Often the language barrier separates different parts of a community.* يفصل ، يفرّق

3 [I] (used about a married couple, etc.) to stop living together: *His parents separated when he was still a baby.* ينفصل أو يفترق (الزوجان)

▶ **separated** *adj* (used about a married couple) not living together any more but not divorced: *My wife and I are separated.* منفصلان أو مفترقان

⚷**separation** /ˌsepəˈreɪʃn/ *noun* [C,U] **1** the act of separating or being separated; a situation or period of being apart: *Separation from family and friends made me very lonely.* فصل ؛ انفصال ؛ تفرقة ؛ افتراق

2 a legal agreement where a married couple live apart (but do not get a divorce): *a trial separation* انفصال أو تفرقة

⚷**September** /sepˈtembə(r)/ *noun* [C,U] (*abbr* **Sept.**) the ninth month of the year; coming before October ⓘ For examples of the use of the months in sentences, look at **January**. شهر سبتمبر/أيلول

septic /ˈseptɪk/ *adj* infected with poisonous bacteria: *The wound went septic.* متقيّح ، متسمّم ، متعفّن

sequel /ˈsiːkwəl/ *noun* [C] **1** a book, film, etc. that continues the story of the previous one ملحق ، تكملة

2 something that happens after, or is the result of, a previous event نتيجة ، عاقبة

sequence /ˈsiːkwəns/ *noun* **1** [C] a number of things (actions, events, etc.) that happen or come one after another: *the sequence of events leading to war* ○ *Complete the following sequence: 1, 4, 8, 13, …* سلسلة من (الأحداث)

2 [U] the order in which a number of things happen or are arranged: *The photographs are in sequence.* تسلسل ، تتابع أو تعاقب

serene /səˈriːn/ *adj* calm and peaceful: *a serene smile* هادئ ، وادع

▸ **serenely** *adv* بسكينة ، بهدوء بال

serenity /səˈrenəti/ *noun* [U] سكينة : وقار

sergeant /ˈsɑːdʒənt/ *noun* [C] (*abbr* **Sergt**; **Sgt.**; **Sgt**) **1** an officer of low rank in the army or air force رقيب ، عريف

2 an officer in the police with a rank below that of inspector ضابط بوليس ، "شاويش"

serial /ˈsɪəriəl/ *noun* [C] a single story in a magazine or on television or radio that is told in a number of parts over a period of time: *the first part of a six-part drama serial* ➲ Look at the note at **series**. مسلسل : قصّة متسلسلة

▸ **serialize** (*also* **serialise**) /-riəlaɪz/ *verb* [T] to broadcast a story or publish a book in the form of a serial يعرض مسلسلاً : ينشر بشكل متسلسل

ˈ**serial number** *noun* [C] the number marked on sth to identify it and to distinguish it from other things of the same type: *the serial numbers of traveller's cheques* الرقم المتسلسل

⚷**series** /ˈsɪəriːz/ *noun* [C] (*pl.* **series**) **1** a number of things that come one after another and are of the same type or connected: *a series of events* ○ *The orchestra is visiting Britain for a series of concerts next month.* ○ *There has been a series of burglaries in this district recently.* سلسلة

2 a number of programmes on radio or television which have the same main characters and each tell a complete story سلسلة من البرامج (التلفزيونية مثلاً)

> Compare **series** and **serial**. In a **series** each part is a different, complete story involving the same main characters. In a **serial** the same story continues in each part.

⚷**serious** /ˈsɪəriəs/ *adj* **1** (used about problems, situations, etc.) bad; important; causing worry: *a serious accident* ○ *a serious illness* ○ *Pollution is a very serious problem.* ○ *serious crime* خطير : هامّ : مقلِق

2 needing to be treated as important, not just for fun: *Don't laugh, it's a serious matter.* ○ *a serious discussion* هامّ ، جِدّي

3 (used about a person) not joking; thoughtful: *Are you serious about starting your own business* (= are you really going to do it)? ○ *He's terribly serious. I don't think I've ever seen him laugh.* ○ *You're looking very serious. Was it bad news?* جِدّي ، رزين

▸ **seriousness** *noun* [U] the quality of being serious: *It would be unwise to underestimate the seriousness of this situation.* خطورة : جِدّية : أهمّية

⚷**seriously** /ˈsɪəriəsli/ *adv* **1** in a serious way: *Three people were seriously injured in the accident.* ○ *My mother is seriously ill.* ○ *It's time you started to think seriously about the future.* بشكل خطر : بجدّ

2 (used for indicating that you are not joking or that you really mean what you are saying): *Seriously, I do appreciate all your help.* ○ *Seriously, you've got nothing to worry about.* (أكلّمك) جِدّياً

3 (used for expressing surprise at what someone has said and asking whether it is really true): *'I'm 40 today.' 'Seriously? You look a lot younger.'* حقّاً! ، صحيح!

IDM **take sb/sth seriously** to treat sb or sth as important: *He's such a fool that nobody takes him seriously.* ○ *You take everything too seriously! Relax and enjoy yourself.* يعامله بجدّ ، يحمله محمل الجدّ

sermon /ˈsɜːmən/ *noun* [C] a speech on a religious or moral matter that is given as part of a service in church خطبة دينيّة أو موعظة

serrated /səˈreɪtɪd; *US* ˈsereɪtɪd/ *adj* having a row of points in V-shapes along the edge: *a knife with a serrated edge* مسنّن

⚷**servant** /ˈsɜːvənt/ *noun* [C] a person who is paid to work in sb's house, doing work such as cooking, cleaning, etc. ➲ Look at **civil servant**. خادم

⚷**serve** /sɜːv/ *verb* **1** [I,T] to work for a country, a company, an organization, the army, etc; to be useful to sb: *The role of the police is to serve the community.* ○ *She has served on a number of committees.* ○ *During the war, he served in the Army.* ○ *During his long political career he served under three different Prime Ministers.* يخدم ، يعمل

2 [T] to give food or drink to sb during a meal; to take an order and then bring food or drink to sb (in a restaurant, bar, etc.): *Breakfast is served from 7.30 to 9.00 am.* ○ *We waited for half an hour until a waiter finally served us.* يخدم على المائدة ، يقدّم الطعام

3 [I,T] (in a shop) to take a customer's order; to give help, sell goods, etc: *Are you being served?* يخدم الزبائن في متجر : يبيع

4 [T] to provide sb (especially the public) with sth necessary or useful in daily life: *The town is served by three hospitals.* يزوّد (الشعب) بمرافق مفيدة

5 [I,T] **serve (sb) (as sth)** to be good enough for or suitable for a particular purpose; to perform a particular function: *The smallest bedroom serves as my office.* ○ *His pathetic excuses only served to make me even angrier.* يصلح لـ ، يقوم مقام : يعزّز

6 [T] to spend a period of time in prison as punishment: *He is currently serving a ten-year sentence for fraud.* يقضي مدّة في السجن

7 [T] (used about an amount of food) to be enough for a certain number of people: *According to the recipe, this dish serves four.* (وجبة) تكفي (أربعة أشخاص)

8 [I,T] (in tennis and similar sports) to start play by hitting the ball يرسل، يستهلّ اللعب (في التنس مثلاً)

IDM **serve your/the purpose** to have or be what you need: *It's an old car but it will serve our purpose for a few months.* يسدّ الحاجة

serve sb right (used when sth unpleasant happens to sb and you have no sympathy) to be deserved by sb: *'I feel sick.' 'It serves you right for eating so much.'* يستحقّ ، يستاهل

server /'sɜːvə(r)/ *noun* [C] a computer that stores information that a number of computers can share المزوِّد

service /'sɜːvɪs/ *noun* **1** [U] working for a country, a company, an organization, the army, etc: *The minister was thanked for his years of service to the party.* ○ *Military service is no longer compulsory.* ○ *He left the police force after thirty years' service.* خدمة ، عمل

2 [C] a system or organization that provides the public with sth necessary or useful in daily life; the job that an organization does: *the train/bus service* ○ *the postal service* ○ *The airline is starting a new international service.* ○ *We offer a number of financial services.* مصلحة ؛ خدمات

3 [C, usually sing.] one of certain government departments or public institutions: *the National Health Service* ➲ Look at **Civil Service**. هيئة ، مرفق عام ؛ مديريّة

4 the services [plural] the armed forces; the army, navy or air force القوات المسلّحة

5 [U] the work or the quality of work done by sb when serving a customer: *I enjoyed the meal but the service was terrible.* ○ *Is service included in the bill?* ○ *We offer after-sales service on all our photocopiers.* خدمة

6 [C, usually pl.] work done for sb; help given to sb: *He was given an award for his services to the film industry.* خدمات

7 [C,U] the examination (and, if necessary, repair) of a car, machine, etc. to make sure that it is working properly: *We take our car for a service every six months.* فحص (السيّارة) وصيانتها

8 [C] a religious ceremony, usually including prayers, singing, etc: *a funeral service* مراسيم دينيّة (في كنيسة)

9 [C] (in tennis and similar sports) the act of hitting the ball at the start of play; a player's turn to serve: *She's not a bad player but her service is weak.* (في التنس مثلاً): إرسال، "سرفيس" أي استهلال ضرب الكرة

10 services [C] (usually with a plural verb) (*pl.* **services**) a place at the side of a motorway where there is a petrol station, a shop, toilets, a restaurant, etc: *It's five miles to the next services.* خدمات عامّة للمسافرين

▶ **service** *verb* [T] to examine and, if necessary, repair a car, machine, etc: *All cars should be serviced at regular intervals.* يفحص (سيّارة) ويصونها

'service charge *noun* [C] the amount of money that is added to a restaurant bill for the service given by the waiters and waitresses رسم الخدمة

serviceman /'sɜːvɪsmən/ *noun* [C] (*pl.* **-men** /mən/) a man who is a member of the armed forces من أفراد القوات المسلحة

'service station *noun* [C] = PETROL STATION

servicewoman /'sɜːvɪswʊmən/ *noun* [C] (*pl.* **-women** /wɪmɪn/) a woman who is a member of the armed forces من أفراد القوات المسلحة

serviette /ˌsɜːvi'et/ *noun* [C] a square of cloth or paper that you use when you are eating to keep your clothes clean and to wipe your mouth or hands فوطة طعام ، منديل مائدة

session /'seʃn/ *noun* [C] **1** a period of doing a particular activity: *The whole tape was recorded in one session.* ○ *She has a session on a sunbed every week.* جلسة

2 a meeting or series of meetings of an official body (a court, a parliament, etc.) جلسة ، دورة

IDM **in session** (used about an official body) holding a meeting; doing its official work; not on holiday: *Silence! This court is now in session.* منعقد ، مجتمع؛ فترة دوام (في المحاكم مثلاً)

set[1] /set/ *noun* **1** [C] a number of things that belong together: *a set of kitchen knives* ○ *In the first set of questions, you have to fill in the gap.* ○ *a set of instructions* مجموعة ؛ طقم

2 [C] a piece of equipment for receiving television or radio: *a television set* جهاز راديو أو تلفزيون

3 [C] the scenery for a play or film on the stage or in the studio: *a musical with spectacular sets* معدّات المسرح أو الاستوديو

4 [C] (in tennis) a group of games forming part of a match: *game, set and match* (في التنس) مجموعة

set[2] /set/ *verb* (*pres part* **setting**; *pt, pp* **set**) **1** [T] to put sb/sth in a particular position; to place sth somewhere: *He set a large bowl of soup in front of me.* ○ *The hotel is set in beautiful grounds.* يضع ؛ يُقيم

2 [T] (often passive) to place the action of a book, play, film, etc. in a particular time, situation, etc: *The film is set in 16th-century Spain.* تجري حوادثه

3 [T] to cause a particular state or event; to start sth happening: *The new government set the prisoners free.* ○ *The rioters set a number of cars on fire.* ○ *Her comment set him thinking.* يطلق ؛ يجعل

4 [T] to prepare or arrange sth for a particular purpose: *I set my alarm for 6.30.* ○ *to set the table* (= put the plates, knives, forks, etc. on it) ○ *Did you set the video to record that film?* يُعِدّ ، يهيّئ؛ يضبط

5 [T] to fix or establish sth: *Try to set a good example to the younger children.* ○ *Can we set a limit of £100 for the cost of materials?* ○ *They haven't set the date of the next meeting yet.* ○ *He has set a new world record.* يحدّد ؛ يضرب مثلاً ؛ يسجّل

6 [T] to give sb a piece of work: *We've been set a lot of homework this weekend.* يُعطيه أو يفرض عليه عملاً

7 [I] to become firm or hard: *Put the jelly in the fridge for two hours to set.* يتجمّد ، يتصلّب

8 [T] to fix a precious stone, etc. in a piece of jewellery: *The brooch had three diamonds set in gold.* يرصّع بِ

9 [T] to arrange sb's hair while it is wet so that it becomes curly, wavy, etc. يصفّف (الشَعْر)

10 [T] to write music to go with words: *She writes the words of the song and Harry sets them to music.* يلحّن

11 [T] to put a broken bone in a position (and often to fix it in plaster) so that it can heal: *The doctor set her broken leg.* يجبّر

12 [I] (used about the sun, etc.) to go down below the horizon ❶ The opposite is **rise**. تغرب (الشمس)

IDM **put/set your/sb's mind at rest** → MIND[1]

set eyes on sb/sth to see sb/sth: *He loved the house the moment he set eyes on it.* يرى ، يقع نظره على

set foot (in/on sth) to visit, enter or arrive at/ in a place: *No woman has ever set foot in the temple.* يزور ، يطأ المكان

set sail to begin a journey by sea: *Columbus set sail for India.* يبحر ، تقلع (السفينة)

PHR V **set about sth** to start doing sth, especially dealing with a problem or task: *How would you set about tackling this problem?* يَشْرع

set sth aside to keep sth to use later: *I try to set aside part of my wages every week.* يدّخِر

set sb/sth back to delay sb/sth: *The bad weather has set our plans back six weeks.* يؤخّر

set in to arrive and remain for a period of time: *I'm afraid that the bad weather has set in.* يمكث ؛ يدوم

set off to leave on a journey: *We set off at 3 o'clock this morning.* ينطلق ، يبدأ رحلته

set sth off to do sth which starts a reaction: *When this door is opened, it sets off an alarm.* يُطلق

set out to leave on a journey: *They set out at dawn.* ينطلق ، يبدأ رحلته

set out to do sth to decide to achieve sth: *He set out to prove that his theory was right.* يعقد العزم

set (sth) up to start; to establish a business: *The company has set up a new branch in Wales.* ○ *After she qualified as a doctor, she set up in practice in Yorkshire.* يؤسّس ، يقيم

set[3] /set/ *adj* **1** placed in a particular position: *Our house is set back quite a long way from the road.* ○ *deep-set eyes* واقع ، قائم

2 fixed and not changing; firm: *There are no set hours in my job.* ○ *He's getting more and more set in his ways as he gets older* (= with fixed habits and routines which he is unwilling to change). ثابت ؛ متمسّك بِ ؛ متصلّب

3 set (for sth); **set (to do sth)** ready, prepared or likely to do sth: *Okay, I'm all set – let's go!* ○ *I was all set to leave when the phone rang.* ○ *The England team look set for victory.* مستعدّ ؛ متأهّب

IDM **be set against sth/against doing sth** to be opposed to sth: *She's set against moving house.* يعارض

be set on sth/on doing sth to be determined to do sth: *She's set on a career in acting.* ○ *My heart was set on that house* (= I really wanted it). مصمّم على ، (قلبه) معلّق بِ

setback /ˈsetbæk/ *noun* [C] a difficulty or problem that stops you progressing as fast as you would like نكسة

set ˈbook *noun* [C] a book that must be studied in a course for an exam كتاب مقرّر

settee /seˈtiː/ *noun* [C] a long soft seat with a back and arms that more than one person can sit on أريكة، كَنَبَة

setter /ˈsetə(r)/ *noun* [C] a breed of dog with long hair that can be trained to find animals or birds in a hunt: *an Irish/a red setter* نوع من كلاب الصيد

setting /ˈsetɪŋ/ *noun* [C] **1** surroundings; the place where sth happens: *The hotel is in a beautiful setting, close to the sea.* ○ *They decided that the village church would be the perfect setting for their wedding.* موقع ؛ مكان الأحداث

2 one of the positions of the controls of a machine: *Cook it in the oven at a moderate setting.* عيار

settle /ˈsetl/ *verb* **1** [I] to go and live permanently in a new country, an area, a town, etc: *A great many immigrants have settled in this country.* يستقرّ ، يستوطن

2 [T] to reach an agreement about sth; to end an argument; to find a solution to a disagreement: *They settled the dispute without going to court.* يسوّي الخلاف ، يحلّ النزاع

3 [T] to decide or arrange sth finally (e.g. a plan, an action, etc.): *Everything's settled. We leave on the nine o'clock flight on Friday.* مقرّر ، مُنته ، مبتوت فيه

4 [I,T] to get into or put sb into a comfortable position: *I settled in front of the television for the evening.* ○ *She settled herself beside him on the sofa.* يستقرّ في وضع مريح

5 [I,T] to become or to make sb/sth calm or relaxed: *The baby wouldn't settle.* ○ *Have a drink. It might settle your stomach.* يهدأ أو يستريح ؛ يُهدّئ أو يريح

6 [T] to pay sth (a bill, a debt, etc.): *to settle a bill* ○ *The insurance company settled the claim very quickly.* يسدّد حساباً

7 [I] to come to rest after falling on sth; to land: *A flock of birds settled on the roof.* ○ *The snow didn't settle* (= remain on the ground) *for long.* يستقرّ ؛ يحطّ

8 [I] (used about a liquid) to become clear or still يصفو ، يروق ، يترسّب

PHR V **settle down 1** to get into a comfortable position, sitting or lying: *I made a cup of tea and settled down with the newspapers.* يطمئنّ في جلسته

2 to start having a quieter way of life, especially by staying in the same place or getting married, etc: *She had a number of jobs abroad before she eventually settled down.* يستقرّ

3 to become calm and quiet: *Settle down! It's time to start the lesson.* يهدأ، يسكن

settle down to sth to start concentrating on sth: *Before you settle down to your work, could I ask you something?* يبدأ بالتركيز على (عمله)

settle for sth to accept sth that is not as good as you hoped it would be: *You'll have to settle for something cheaper.* يرضى بشيء أدنى من طلبه

settle in/into sth to get used to or start feeling comfortable in a new home, job, etc: *How are the children settling in at their new school?* يتعوّد على ، يستقرّ به الحال

settle on sth to choose sth after considering many different things; to decide on sth يقع اختياره على

settle up (with sb) to pay money that you owe sb يسدّد دَيْناً

settled /'setld/ *adj* **1** not changing or not likely to change: *More settled weather is forecast for the next few days.* ثابت ، غير متقلّب

2 comfortable; feeling that you belong (in a home, a job, a way of life, etc.): *We feel very settled here.* مستقرّ ، مرتاح

settlement /'setlmənt/ *noun* **1** [C,U] (an) agreement, usually official, that ends an argument; the act of reaching this kind of agreement: *The strike lasted for several weeks until a settlement was reached.* تسوية (خلاف)

2 [C] a place that a group of people have built and live in, where few or no people lived before: *a settlement in the jungle* مستوطَنة

settler /'setlə(r)/ *noun* [C] a person who goes to live permanently in a new country, particularly an undeveloped one or one with a small population: *the first settlers in Australia* مستوطِن

'set-up *noun* [usually sing.] **1** a way of organizing sth; a system: *I've only been here a couple of weeks and I don't really know the set-up.* ○ *What's the set-up in your family – who does the cooking?* نظام العمل، ترتيب

2 a situation in which sb tricks you or makes it seem as if you have done sth wrong: *He didn't steal the goods. It was a set-up.* حيلة، فخّ

⚷ **seven** /'sevn/ *number* 7; one more than 6 ❶ For examples of how to use numbers in sentences, look at **six**. سبعة

▸ **seven-** (in compounds) having seven of the thing mentioned: *a seven-sided coin* شيء ذو سبعة (أقسام)

seventh *pron, det, adv* 7th, next after sixth سابع

seventh *noun* [C] the fraction 1/7; one of seven equal parts of sth ➲ Look at the examples at **sixth**. سُبع

⚷ **seventeen** /,sevn'ti:n/ *number* 17; one more than sixteen ❶ For examples of how to use numbers in sentences, look at **six**. سبعة عشر

▸ **seventeenth** /,sevn'ti:nθ/ *pron, det, adv* 17th; next after sixteenth ➲ Look at the examples at **sixth**. سابع عشر

⚷ **seventy** /'sevnti/ *number* 70; one more than sixty-nine ❶ For examples of how to use numbers in sentences, look at **sixty**. سبعون

▸ **seventieth** /'sevntiəθ/ *pron, det, adv* 70th; next after sixty-ninth ➲ Look at the examples at **sixth**. السّبعون

sever /'sevə(r)/ *verb* [T] **1** to break, separate or divide by cutting: *The builders accidentally severed a water pipe.* يكسر ؛ يفصم ، يقطع

2 to end sth (a relationship, etc.): *He has severed all links with his former friends.* يقطع ، يصرم ، ينهي

⚷ **several** /'sevrəl/ *pron, det* more than two but not very many; some: *It took her several days to recover from the shock.* ○ *There were lots of applications for the job – several of them from very well-qualified people.* ○ *I've asked him several times for the money.* عدّة

⚷ **severe** /sɪ'vɪə(r)/ *adj* **1** not kind or gentle: *Such terrible crimes deserve the severest punishment.* ○ *a severe teacher* ○ *a severe expression* ○ *I think your criticism of her work was too severe.* صارم ، قاسٍ

2 very bad; causing unpleasant results or feelings: *The company is in severe financial difficulty.* ○ *a severe cold, headache, illness, pain, etc.* ○ *a severe winter* (= a very cold one) شديد ، فادح : قارس

▸ **severely** *adj*: *The roof was severely damaged in the storm.* ○ *The report severely criticizes the Minister.* بشدّة ؛ بقسوة

severity /sɪ'verəti/ *noun*: *I don't think you realize the severity of the problem.* شدّة ، خطورة ؛ قسوة ، صرامة

⚷ **sew** /səʊ/ *verb* (*pt* **sewed**; *pp* **sewn** /səʊn/ or **sewed**) [I,T] to join pieces of cloth, or to join sth to cloth, using a needle and thread and forming stitches: *I can't sew.* ○ *to sew a new button on a shirt* يَخيط أو يخيِّط

PHR V **sew sth up 1** to join two things by sewing; to repair sth by sewing two things together: *to sew up a hole* ○ *The surgeon sewed up the wound.* يَخيط أو يخيِّط

2 to arrange or organize sth so that it is certain to happen or be successful: *I think we've got the deal sewn up.* يضمن نجاح (الصفقة)

▸ **sewing** *noun* [U] **1** using a needle and thread to make or repair things: *Do you like sewing?* خياطة

2 something that is being sewn: *Have you seen my sewing?* شيء قيد الخياطة

sewage /'su:ɪdʒ; *Brit also* 'sju:-/ *noun* [U] the waste material from people's bodies that is carried away from their homes in water in large underground pipes (sewers) مياه وأوساخ المجاري

sewer /'su:ə(r); *Brit also* 'sju:-/ *noun* [C] an underground pipe that carries waste to a place where it can be treated مجرور (ج مجارير) ، أنبوب الفضلات

'sewing machine *noun* [C] a machine that is used for sewing آلة أو ماكينة خياطة

sewn *pp* of SEW

⚷ **sex** /seks/ *noun* **1** [U] the state of being either male or female: *Applications are welcome from anyone, regardless of sex or race.* ○ *Do you mind what sex your baby is?* جنس

2 [C] one of the two groups consisting of all male

a b c d e f g h i j k l m n o p q r s t u v w x y z

people or all female people: *the male/female sex* ○ *He's always found it difficult to get on with the opposite sex* (= women). جنس

3 (*also formal* **intercourse**; **sexual intercourse**) [U] the physical act in which the sexual organs of two people touch and which can result in a woman having a baby: *to have sex with somebody* ○ *It's against their religion to have sex before marriage.* الجماع، الاتصال الجنسي

4 [U] activities or matters connected with this act: *There's too much sex and violence on TV.* جنس ، علاقات جنسيّة

▶ **sexy** *adj* (**sexier**; **sexiest**) (*informal*) sexually attractive: *a sexy man* ○ *a sexy dress* ➲ Look at **sexual**. جذّاب أو مُثير جنسيّاً

sexism /ˈseksɪzəm/ *noun* [U] treating a person unfairly, or thinking that they are inferior, because of their sex, e.g. thinking that only men can do certain jobs, such as being an engineer التحيّز الجنسي

▶ **sexist** /ˈseksɪst/ *adj* connected with or showing sexism: *a sexist attitude to women* ○ *sexist jokes* متحيّز ضدّ جنس دون الآخر

🔑 **sexual** /ˈsekʃuəl/ *adj* connected with sex: *sexual problems* ○ *the sexual organs* ○ *a campaign for sexual equality* (= a campaign to get fair and equal treatment for both men and women) جنسيّ ؛ تناسليّ

▶ **sexuality** /ˌsekʃuˈæləti/ *noun* [U] the nature of sb's sexual activities or desires: *He found it difficult to come to terms with his sexuality.* طبيعة أو ميول جنسيّة

sexually /-əli/ *adv*: *to be sexually attracted to sb* جنسيّاً

ˌsexual ˈintercourse *noun* [U] (*formal*) = SEX (3)

Sgt. (*Brit also* **Sgt**) *abbrev* = SERGEANT

sh /ʃ/ *interj* be quiet!: *Sh! People are trying to sleep in here.* "هس!"، اسكت!

shabby /ˈʃæbi/ *adj* (**shabbier**; **shabbiest**) **1** in bad condition because of having been used or worn too much: *a shabby suit* رثّ ، بالٍ أو قديم

2 (used about people) dressed in an untidy way; wearing clothes that are in bad condition: *a shabby little man* زريّ الهيئة

3 (used about the way that sb is treated) unfair; not generous مجحف ؛ خسيس

▶ **shabbily** *adv*: *shabbily dressed* ○ *shabbily treated* بإجحاف ؛ بِخسّة

shack /ʃæk/ *noun* [C] a small, roughly built shed or hut كوخ

🔑 **shade** /ʃeɪd/ *noun* **1** [U] an area that is out of direct sunlight and is darker and cooler than areas in the sun: *It was so hot that I had to go and sit in the shade.* ظلّ ، فَيء

> **Shade** [U] is an area or part of a place that is protected from the heat of the sun. **A shadow** [C] is a dark shape made by light shining on a person or object. **Shadow** [U] is an area of darkness in which it is difficult to distinguish things easily.

shadow shade

2 [C] something that keeps out light or makes it less bright: *a lampshade* ظِلّة ، غطاء يقي من النور

3 shades [plural] (*informal*) = SUNGLASSES

4 [C] **a shade (of sth)** a type of a particular colour: *a shade of green* ○ *I'd prefer a darker shade if you have one.* ○ *a pale shade of grey* نوع من أنواع اللّون (الأخضر مثلاً)

5 [C] a small difference or variation in the form or nature of sth: *a word with various shades of meaning* فرق طفيف ؛ ظلّ (المعنى)

6 [sing.] a little bit: *I feel a shade more optimistic now.* قليلاً

▶ **shade** *verb* [T] to protect sth from direct light; to give shade to sth: *The sun was so bright that I had to shade my eyes.* يقي من النّور؛ يظلّل

shading *noun* [U] the use of or the result of using pencil, etc. in part of a picture to create an effect of darkness تظليل

🔑 **shadow** /ˈʃædəʊ/ *noun* **1** [C] a dark shape on a surface that is caused by sth being between light and that surface: *The dog was chasing its own shadow.* ○ *The shadows lengthened as the sun went down.* ○ (*figurative*) *He has always lived in the shadow of his older brother.* ○ (*figurative*) *News of the tragedy cast a shadow over the day.* ظلّ ، خيال

2 [U] an area that is dark because sth prevents direct light from reaching it: *His face was in shadow.* ➲ Look at the note at **shade**. ظلّ ، عتمة

3 [sing.] a very small amount: *There isn't a shadow of doubt that he's lying.* ذرّة

▶ **shadow** *verb* [T] to follow and watch the actions of sb, often secretly: *The police shadowed the suspect for three days.* يتتبّع خلسة ، يلازمه كظلّه متجسّساً

Shadow *adj* (in British politics) belonging to the opposition party, with special responsibility for a particular subject, e.g. education or defence. Shadow ministers would probably become government ministers if their party won the next election: *the Shadow Cabinet* "ظلّيّ" ، (حكومة) الظلّ

shadowy *adj* **1** having many shadows; dark: *a shadowy forest* مظلّل ، معتم

2 difficult to see or identify clearly: *a shadowy figure coming towards me* غامض ، مبهم المعالم

3 mysterious; difficult to know much about: *the shadowy world of the secret police* غامض ، خفيّ

shady /ˈʃeɪdi/ *adj* (**shadier**; **shadiest**) **1** giving shade; giving shelter from the sun: *We ate our picnic in a shady spot.* ظليل

2 (*informal*) not completely honest or legal: *She's made a lot of money from some rather shady deals.* مشبوه

shaft /ʃɑːft; *US* ʃæft/ *noun* [C] **1** a long, narrow hole in which sth can go up and down or enter or leave: *a lift shaft* ○ *a mine shaft* نفق عمودي

2 a bar that connects parts of a machine so that power can pass between them عمود الإدارة (ميكانيك)

shaggy /ˈʃægi/ *adj* (**shaggier**; **shaggiest**) **1** (used about hair, material, etc.) long, thick and untidy أشعث : (فرو) طويل مشعّث

2 covered with long, thick, untidy hair: *a shaggy dog* ذو شعر طويل مشعّث

shake[1] /ʃeɪk/ *verb* (*pt* **shook** /ʃʊk/; *pp* **shaken** /ˈʃeɪkən/) **1** [I,T] to move from side to side or up and down with short, quick movements: *I was so nervous that I was shaking.* ○ *The whole building shakes when big lorries go past.* ○ *(figurative) His voice shook with emotion as he described the tragedy.* ○ *Shake the bottle before taking the medicine.* ○ *She shook him to wake him up.*
يهتزّ ، يرتجف : يهزّ ، يخضّ

2 [T] to disturb or upset sb/sth: *The scandal has shaken the whole country.* يهزّ

3 [T] to cause sth to be less certain; to cause doubt about sth: *Nothing seems to shake her belief that she was right.* يقلقل ، يزعزع (ايمانه)

IDM **shake sb's hand/shake hands (with sb)/shake sb by the hand** to take sb's hand and move it up and down (as a greeting, to show that you have agreed on sth, etc.) يصافح

shake your head to move your head from side to side, as a way of expressing that you mean 'No' يهزّ رأسه بالنفي

PHRV **shake sb/sth off** to escape from sb/sth; to remove by shaking: *I don't seem to be able to shake off this cold.* ○ *Shake the crumbs off the tablecloth.* يتخلّص من : ينفض

shake[2] /ʃeɪk/ *noun* [C] the act of shaking or being shaken physically: *a shake of the head* ○ *You'll have to give the bottle a few shakes.*
هزّة : خضّة

ˈ**shake-up** *noun* [C] a complete change in the structure or organization of sth: *a massive shake-up in the government* تغيير كليّ

shaky /ˈʃeɪki/ *adj* (**shakier**; **shakiest**) **1** shaking or feeling weak because you are frightened or ill مرتعش ، مضطرب : خائر القوى

2 not firm; weak or not very good: *The table's a bit shaky so don't put anything heavy on it.* ○ *They've had a shaky start to the season and have lost most of their games.* مقلقل : ضعيف

▶ **shakily** /-ɪli/ *adv* بارتعاش : خائرَ القوى

shall /ʃəl; *strong form* ʃæl/ *modal verb* (*negative* **shall not**; *short form* **shan't** /ʃɑːnt/) **1** (used with 'I' and 'we' in future tenses, instead of 'will'): *I shall be very happy to see him again.* ○ *We shan't be arriving until ten o'clock.* ○ *At the end of this year, I shall have been working here for five years.* سوف ، سَ...

2 (used for asking for information or advice): *What time shall I come?* ○ *Where shall we go for our holiday?* (تستعمل عند طلب المعلومات أو النصيحة)

3 (used for offering to do sth): *Shall I help you carry that box?* ○ *Shall we drive you home?*
(تستعمل عند عرض المساعدة مثلاً) : هل

4 shall we (used for suggesting that you do sth with the person or people that you are talking to): *Shall we go out for a meal this evening?* هل

5 (*formal*) (used for saying that sth must happen or that sb must/must not do sth): *In the rules it says that a player shall be sent off for using bad language.* ينبغي ، يجب

shallot /ʃəˈlɒt/ *noun* [C] a vegetable like a small onion, with a very strong taste كرّاث أندلسي، قفلوط

shallow /ˈʃæləʊ/ *adj* **1** not deep; with not much distance between top and bottom: *The sea is very shallow here.* ○ *Put in a shallow dish and bake for 20 minutes.* ضحل ، قليل العمق

2 not having or showing serious or deep thought: *a shallow person/book* سطحيّ

▶ **shallowness** *noun* [U] سطحيّة

shame /ʃeɪm/ *noun* **1** [U] the guilty feeling that you have when you think that you have done sth morally wrong, sth that causes other people to have a bad opinion of you, or sth extremely embarrassing: *She was filled with shame at the thought of how she had lied to her mother.* ℹ The adjective that describes this feeling is **ashamed**. خزي

2 [U] the ability to have this feeling: *He doesn't care how he behaves in public. He's got no shame!* خجل ، حياء

3 [U] loss of respect from others; loss of honour: *the shame of defeat* ○ *His actions have brought shame on his whole family.* عار

4 a shame [sing.] a fact or situation that makes you feel disappointed: *It's a shame you can't come. I was looking forward to seeing you.* ○ *'I failed my exam.' 'Oh, what a shame!'* ○ *What a shame you have to leave so soon.* شيء مؤسف

▶ **shame** *verb* [T] to make sb feel ashamed
يخزي ، يخجل : يجلب العار على

shameful /-fl/ *adj* which sb should be ashamed of: *a shameful waste of public money* مخزٍ ، مخجل

shamefully /-fəli/ *adv*: *I think you have behaved shamefully.* بصورة مخزية

shameless *adj* not having or showing the feeling of shame that people would expect you to have in a particular situation: *a shameless display of greed and bad manners*
صفيق الوجه ، قليل الحياء

shamelessly *adv* بكل صفاقة : دون محاولة للتبرير

shampoo /ʃæmˈpuː/ *noun* (*pl.* **shampoos**) **1** [C,U] a liquid that you use for washing your hair: *a shampoo for greasy hair*
شامبو ، مستحضر لغسل الشعر

2 [C] the act of washing sth with shampoo غسل (الشّعر) بالشامبو

▶ **shampoo** *verb* [T] (*pres part* **shampooing**; *3rd pers sing pres* **shampoos**; *pt, pp* **shampooed**) to wash with shampoo يغسل بالشامبو

shamrock /ˈʃæmrɒk/ *noun* [C,U] a plant with three leaves on each stem, which is the national symbol of Ireland نوع من النَفَل يعتبر شعاراً لايرلندا

shan't *short for* SHALL NOT

shanty town /ˈʃænti taʊn/ *noun* [C] a small town or part of a town where poor people live in bad conditions in badly built huts, etc. مدينة الأكواخ الفقيرة ، حيّ الأكواخ و"العشَش"

shapes

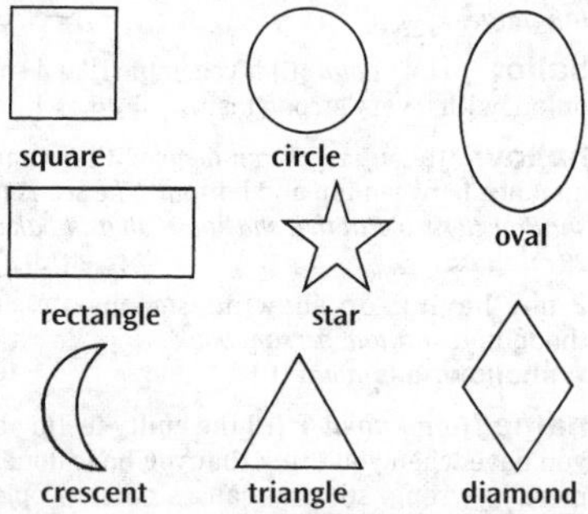

shape¹ /ʃeɪp/ *noun* **1** [C,U] the physical outline or outer form of sth: *a round/square/oblong shape* ○ *an ashtray in the shape of a hand* ○ *clothes to fit women of all shapes and sizes* شكل

2 [C] something that has a particular outline or outer form: *Squares, circles and triangles are all different shapes.* شكل (هندسي)

3 [U] the condition of sb or sth; the good or bad state of sb or sth: *The economy has been in bad shape for some time.* ○ *She was in such bad shape* (= so ill) *that she had to be taken to hospital.* حالة ، وضع

4 [sing.] **the shape (of sth)** the organization, form or structure of sth: *Recent developments have changed the shape of the company.* تنظيم ، بنية

IDM **in shape** healthy and physically fit: *Regular exercise will keep your body in shape.* متمتّع بلياقة بدنيّة

out of shape 1 not in the usual or correct shape: *My sweater's gone out of shape now that I've washed it.* يتغير أو يتشوّه شكله

2 not physically fit: *You're out of shape. You should get more exercise.* غير لائق بدنياً

take shape to start to develop well: *Plans to expand the company are beginning to take shape.* يتبلور ، يتّخذ شكلاً محدّداً

▶ **shapeless** *adj* not having a definite or attractive shape: *a shapeless dress* ليس له شكل محدّد ؛ (ثوب) غير مكسّم

shape² /ʃeɪp/ *verb* [T] **1 shape sth (into sth)** to make sth into a particular form: *Shape the mixture into small balls.* يشكّل

2 to influence the way in which sth develops; to cause sth to have a particular form or nature: *His political ideas were shaped by his upbringing.* يكوّن

▶ **-shaped** (in compounds) having a certain shape; having the shape of the thing mentioned: *an L-shaped room* على شكل (كذا)

share /ʃeə(r)/ *noun* **1** [sing.] **share (of sth)** a part or amount of sth that has been divided between several people: *We each pay a share of the household bills.* ○ *I'm willing to take my share of the blame.* حصّة ، نصيب

2 [C, usually pl.] **shares (in sth)** one of the equal parts into which the ownership of a company is divided. Shares in a company can be bought and sold. سهم

IDM **have, etc. (more than) your fair share of sth** → FAIR¹ (6)

▶ **share** *verb* **1** [T] **share sth (out)** to divide sth and give shares to others: *We shared the pizza between the four of us.* يقتسم

2 [I,T] **share (sth) (with sb)** to have, use, do or pay sth together with another person or other people; to have sth that sb else also has: *I share a flat with four other people.* ○ *There's only one room available so we'll have to share.* ○ *We share the same interests.* يشترك معه (في) ، يشارك

3 [T] **share sth (with sb)** to tell sb about sth; to allow sb to know sth: *Sometimes it helps to share your problems.* يبوح (باحزانه): يشرك معه

shareholder /ˈʃeəhəʊldə(r)/ *noun* [C] an owner of shares in a company مساهِم ، أحد حمَلة الأسهم

sharia (*also* **shariah**) /ʃəˈriːə/ *noun* [U] the system of religious laws that Muslims follow الشريعة الاسلامية

shark /ʃɑːk/ *noun* [C,U] a large, often dangerous, sea fish that has many sharp teeth كلب البحر ، سمك القرش

sharp /ʃɑːp/ *adj* **1** having a fine edge or point; that can cut or make a hole in sth easily: *a sharp knife* ○ *sharp teeth* ❶ The opposite is **blunt**. حادّ

2 (used about a change of direction) very great and sudden: *a sharp rise/fall in inflation* ○ *a sharp bend* (= on a road) حادّ

3 clear; allowing details to be seen clearly: *the sharp outline of the hills* ○ *a sharp contrast between the lives of the rich and the poor* واضح المعالم

4 able to think, act, understand, see or hear quickly: *a sharp mind* ○ *sharp eyesight* حادّ ؛ ثاقب (الذهن) ؛ سريع البديهة

5 (used about actions or movements) quick and sudden: *One short sharp blow was enough to end the fight.* خاطف ؛ قاطع

6 (used about words, remarks, etc.) angry or severe; intended to upset or be critical: *During the debate there was a sharp exchange of views between the two parties.* جارح ، لاذع

7 (used about pain) very strong and sudden: *a*

sharp pain in the chest ⓘ The opposite is **dull**.
حادّ ، مبرِّح

8 (used about sth that affects the senses) not mild or gentle, often causing an unpleasant feeling: *a sharp taste* ○ *a sharp wind*
حرّيف : حامض : لاذع ، قارس

9 (*symbol* ♯) (in music) half a tone higher than the stated note: *in the key of C sharp minor* ➲ Look at **flat**²(7). نصف نغمة أعلى من العلامة الصحيحة

10 (in music) higher than the correct note: *That last note was sharp. Can you sing it again?* ➲ Look at **flat**²(8). (نغمة) أعلى من العلامة الصحيحة
▸ **sharp** *noun* [C] (*symbol* ♯) (in music) a note that is half a tone higher than the note with the same letter ➲ Look at **flat**⁴.
(في الموسيقى) علامة الرفع

sharp *adv* **1** (used about a time) exactly, punctually: *Be here at three o'clock sharp.*
تماماً ، بالضبط

2 in a sharp (2) way: *Go to the traffic lights and turn sharp right.* بحدّة ، (ينعطف) انعطافاً حاداً

3 (in music) slightly higher than the correct note ➲ Look at **flat**³(2). بنغمة أعلى ممّا يجب

sharpen /ˈʃɑːpən/ *verb* [I,T] to become, or to make sth, sharp or sharper: *to sharpen a knife* ○ *The campaign sharpened public awareness of the problem.* يشحذ : يصبح اكثر حدّة

sharpener /ˈʃɑːpnə(r)/ *noun* [C] an object or tool that is used for making sth sharp مِسَنّ : مبراة

sharply *adv* in a sharp way: *The road bends sharply to the left.* ○ *'Mind your own business!' she said sharply.* ○ *Share prices fell sharply this morning.* بحدّة : بشدة

sharpness *noun* [U] حِدّة

shatter /ˈʃætə(r)/ *verb* **1** [I,T] (of glass, etc.) to break into very small pieces: *I dropped the glass and it shattered on the floor.* ○ *The force of the explosion shattered the windows.*
يتحطّم أو يتكسر : يحطِّم أو يكسِّر

2 [T] to destroy completely: *Her hopes were shattered by the news.* يحطِّم ، يقضي على

▸ **shattered** *adj* **1** very upset because of sth shocking that has happened في غاية الكدر والضيق

2 (*informal*) very tired: *I'm absolutely shattered.* منهَك ، مرهق الأعصاب

shave /ʃeɪv/ *verb* [I,T] **shave (sth) (off)** to remove hair from the face or another part of the body with a razor: *I was shaving when the doorbell rang.* ○ *I cut myself shaving this morning.* ○ *When did you shave off your moustache?* يحلق

PHRV **shave sth off (sth)** to cut very thin pieces from a surface (in order to make it smooth or to make it fit sth): *We'll have to shave a bit off the door to make it close properly.* يكشط ، يسحج

▸ **shave** *noun* [C, usually sing.] the act of shaving: *to have a shave* حلاقة

IDM **a close shave/thing** → CLOSE¹

shaven /ˈʃeɪvn/ *adj* having been shaved: *clean-shaven* (= not having a beard or moustache)
حليق ، محلوق

shaver (*also* **electric razor**) *noun* [C] an electric tool that is used for shaving hair
آلة حلاقة كهربائية

shawl /ʃɔːl/ *noun* [C] a large piece of cloth, made of wool, etc. that is worn by a woman round the shoulders or head or that is wrapped round a baby شال

she /ʃi/ *pron* (the subject of a verb) the female person or animal who has already been mentioned: *'What does your sister do?' 'She's a dentist.'* ○ *I asked her a question but she didn't answer.* هي

sheaf /ʃiːf/ *noun* (*pl.* **sheaves** /ʃiːvz/) **1** a number of papers, etc. lying one on top of the other and often tied together: *a sheaf of notes*
ربطة (من الأوراق)

2 a bunch of stalks of corn, wheat, etc. tied together after being cut and left standing up so that they dry حزمة، جرزة، غمرة

shear /ʃɪə(r)/ *verb* [T] (*pt* **sheared**; *pp* **sheared** or **shorn**) to cut the wool off a sheep يجزّ

shears /ʃɪəz/ *noun* [plural] a tool that is like a very large pair of scissors and that is used for cutting things in the garden مِجزّ ، مقص

sheath /ʃiːθ/ *noun* [C] (*pl.* **sheaths** /ʃiːðz/) the cover for a knife or other sharp weapon
غِمْد ، قِراب

she'd /ʃiːd/ *short for* SHE HAD, SHE WOULD

shed¹ /ʃed/ *noun* [C] a small building that is used for keeping things or animals in: *a garden shed* ○ *a bicycle shed* كوخ تخزين : حظيرة

shed² /ʃed/ *verb* [T] (*pres part* **shedding**; *pt, pp* **shed**) **1** to lose sth because it falls off: *This snake sheds its skin every year.* ○ *Autumn is coming and the trees are beginning to shed their leaves.* ○ *A lorry has shed its load.* يطرح ، يسقط

2 to get rid of or remove sth that is not wanted: *She was forced to shed some of her responsibilities through illness.* ○ *Firms in the area have shed thousands of jobs in the past year.* يتخلّص من ، يبطِل

IDM **shed blood** to kill or injure people: *Much blood was shed during the war.* يسفك دما

shed light on sth to make sth clear and easy to understand يلقي ضوءاً على ، يوضِّح

shed tears (*formal*) to cry: *It was a sad occasion and many tears were shed.* يذرف دمعاً

sheep /ʃiːp/ *noun* [C] (*pl.* **sheep**) an animal with a coat of wool that is kept on farms and used for its wool or meat خروف

> A male sheep is a **ram**, a female sheep is a **ewe** and a young sheep is a **lamb**. When sheep make a noise they **bleat**. This is written as **baa**. The meat from sheep is called **mutton**. Look at the note at **meat**.

sheepdog /ˈʃiːpdɒɡ; *US* -dɔːɡ/ *noun* [C] a dog that has been trained to control sheep كلب الراعي

sheepish /ˈʃiːpɪʃ/ *adj* feeling rather ashamed or embarrassed because you have done sth silly: *a sheepish grin* مستحٍ ، خجول : مرتبك
▸ **sheepishly** *adv* مستحياً : بارتباك

sheepskin /ˈʃiːpskɪn/ *noun* [U] the skin of a

a b c d e f g h i j k l m n o p q r **s** t u v w x y z

sheep, including the wool, from which coats, etc. are made جلد الخروف

sheer /ʃɪə(r)/ *adj* **1** (only *before* a noun) complete, absolute; involving nothing else except: *It was sheer luck that I happened to be in the right place at the right time.* ○ *Her success is due to sheer hard work.* مطلق ، تامّ : محض

2 very steep; almost vertical: *Don't walk near the edge. It's a sheer drop to the sea.* شديد الانحدار : شبه عمودي

sheet /ʃiːt/ *noun* [C] **1** a large piece of material used on a bed. Sheets are used in pairs and you sleep between the top and bottom sheet. شَرشَف ، مُلاءة

2 a piece of paper (usually of a particular size) that is used for writing, printing, etc. on: *a sheet of notepaper* ○ *a sheet of A4* ○ *Write each answer on a separate sheet.* ➲ Look at **balance sheet**. طَبَق أو فَرْخ ورق ، ورقة

3 a flat, thin piece of any material, especially glass or metal لوح (زجاج) ، صفيحة (معدن)

sheikh (*also* **sheik**) /ʃeɪk; *US* ʃiːk/ *noun* [C] an Arab ruler شيخ ، حاكم عربي

shelf /ʃelf/ *noun* [C] (*pl.* **shelves** /ʃelvz/) a long flat piece of wood, glass, etc. that is fixed to a wall or in a cupboard, used for standing things on: *I put up a shelf in the kitchen.* ○ *a bookshelf* رفّ

she'll /ʃiːl/ *short for* SHE WILL

shell /ʃel/ *noun* **1** [C,U] a hard covering that protects eggs, nuts and some animals: *a collection of seashells* ○ *an empty shell* ○ *a piece of eggshell* قشرة : صدَفة ، قوقعة

2 [C] the walls of a building that is not finished or that has been seriously damaged by fire, etc. هيكل بناء

3 [C] a metal container filled with explosives that is fired by a large gun قذيفة : خرطوشة ، قنبلة مدفع

▸ **shell** *verb* [T] **1** to take the shell (1) off sth that can be eaten: *to shell peas* يقشّر

2 to fire shells (3) يقذف بالقنابل

shellfish /ˈʃelfɪʃ/ *noun* (*pl.* **shellfish**) **1** [C] a type of animal that lives in water and has a shell المحاريات ، الحيوانات الصدفيّة

2 [U] these animals used as food (أكْل) المحار

shelter /ˈʃeltə(r)/ *noun* **1** [U] **shelter (from sth)** protection from danger or bad weather: *to give somebody food and shelter* ○ *I took shelter under his umbrella.* حماية ، مأوى

2 [C] a small building that gives protection or cover, e.g. from bad weather or attack: *a bus shelter* ○ *an air-raid shelter* ملجأ ، مأوى

▸ **shelter** *verb* **1** [I] **shelter (from sth)** to find protection or shelter: *Let's shelter from the rain under that tree.* ○ *There are 100 refugees sheltering in foreign embassies.* يحتمي

2 [T] **shelter sb/sth (from sb/sth)** to protect sb/sth; to give sb/sth shelter: *The trees shelter the house from the wind.* ○ *The embassy is now sheltering nearly 100 refugees.* يحمي : يؤوي

sheltered *adj* **1** (used about a place) protected from bad weather: *The campers found a sheltered spot for their tent.* محمي من عوامل الطبيعة ، (مكان) لاطٍ

2 protected from unpleasant things in your life: *a sheltered childhood in the country* محميّ ، بعيد عن الفساد

shelve¹ /ʃelv/ *verb* [T] to decide not to continue with a plan, etc: *Plans for a new motorway have been shelved.* يلغي ، يؤجّل (مشروعاً)

shelve² /ʃelv/ *verb* [I] (used about land) to slope in one direction: *The beach shelves down to the sea.* ينحدر (نحو البحر خاصة)

shelves /ʃelvz/ *pl.* of SHELF

shelving /ˈʃelvɪŋ/ *noun* [U] a set of shelves مجموعة من الرفوف

shepherd /ˈʃepəd/ *noun* [C] a person who looks after sheep راعٍ

▸ **shepherd** *verb* [T] to guide and look after people so that they do not get lost: *She shepherded the children onto the train.* يرشد ، يرعى

ˌshepherd's ˈpie *noun* [C] a type of meal made from meat covered with a layer of mashed potato طبق من اللحم والبطاطا المهروسة

sheriff /ˈʃerɪf/ *noun* [C] an officer of the law in an American county ضابط الأمن (في أمريكا)

sherry /ˈʃeri/ *noun* [C,U] (*pl.* **sherries**) a type of strong Spanish wine; a glass of this wine خمر مركّز اسباني الاصل

she's /ʃiːz/ *short for* SHE IS, SHE HAS

Shia (*also* **Shi'a**) /ˈʃɪə/ (*pl.* **Shia** or **Shias**) **1** [U] one of the main branches of Islam الشيعة

2 = SHIITE

shield /ʃiːld/ *noun* [C] **1** a large piece of metal or wood that soldiers used to carry to protect themselves. Now certain policemen carry shields: *riot shields* ترس ، مِجَنّ

2 a person or thing that is used for protection: *The metal door acted as a shield against the explosion.* وقاء ، حاجز واقٍ

3 an object or drawing in the shape of a shield, sometimes used as a school or team badge or as a prize in a sports competition شعار مدرسة أو فريق رياضي

▸ **shield** *verb* [T] **shield sb/sth (against/from sb/sth)** to protect sb/sth from danger or damage: *I shielded my eyes from the bright light with my hand.* يقي ، يحمي ، يستر

shift¹ /ʃɪft/ *verb* **1** [T] to move sb/sth from one position to another: *She shifted the furniture around.* ينقل ، يبدّل

2 [I] to change position or direction: *He shifted uncomfortably in his chair.* ○ (*figurative*) *Public attitudes towards marriage have shifted over the years.* يغير موقعه أو اتجاهه؛ يشهد تحوّلاً

shift² /ʃɪft/ *noun* [C] **1 a shift (in sth)** a change in the position or nature of sth: *There has been a shift in public opinion away from war.* ○ *a shift in policy/a policy shift* تغيُّر في الاتّجاه

2 (in a factory, etc.) a division of the working

day; the group who work this period: *an eight-hour shift* ○ *Firemen do shift work.* ○ *the day/night shift* مناوبة : الفوج المناوب

3 [sing.] one of the keys that you use for writing on a computer, etc., that allows you to write a capital letter: *the shift key* مفتاح الأحرف العالية (في لوحة المفاتيح)

shifty /ˈʃɪfti/ *adj* (**shiftier**; **shiftiest**) (used about a person or his/her appearance) giving the impression that you cannot trust him/her: *shifty eyes* ماكر ، مراوغ

Shiite (*also* **Shi'ite**) /ˈʃiːaɪt/ *noun* [C], *adj* (usually *before* a noun) (a member) of one of the main branches of Islam: *a Shiite Muslim* شيعي

shilling /ˈʃɪlɪŋ/ *noun* [C] a British coin that is no longer in use and that was worth 5p شِلْن

shimmer /ˈʃɪmə(r)/ *verb* [I] to shine with a soft light that seems to be moving: *The tears shimmered in her eyes.* ○ *moonlight shimmering on the sea* يتلألأ، يترقرق

shin /ʃɪn/ *noun* [C] the front part of your leg above your ankle and below your knee قصبة الرِّجل أو الساق : مقدّم الساق

shine /ʃaɪn/ *verb* (*pt, pp* **shone** /ʃɒn; *US* ʃəʊn/)
1 [I] to give out or to reflect light: *moonlight shining on the sea* ○ *The sea shone in the light of the moon.* ○ *(figurative) The child's eyes shone with happiness.* يلمع ، يتألّق

2 [T] to point the light of a torch, etc. at sb/sth: *The policeman shone a torch on the stranger's face.* يسلّط نور المصباح ، يبهر

3 [I] **shine (at/in sth)** to do a school subject, a sport, etc. very well: *She has always shone at languages.* يتفوّق ، يلمع

▸ **shine** *noun* [sing.] **1** brightness, caused by light reflecting, because sth has been polished: *There's a lovely shine on that table.* لَمَعان

2 the act of polishing sth so that it shines: *He gave his shoes a shine.* تلميع ، صقل

shiny *adj* (**shinier**; **shiniest**) bright; reflecting light: *The shampoo leaves your hair soft and shiny.* ○ *a shiny new car* لامع ، برّاق

shingle /ˈʃɪŋgl/ *noun* [U] small pieces of stone lying in a mass on a beach حصى الشاطئ

ˈ**shin pad** *noun* [C] a thick piece of material used to protect the shin when playing football, etc. غطاء واقٍ لقصبة الساق

ship[1] /ʃɪp/ *noun* [C] a large boat used for carrying passengers or cargo by sea: *to travel by ship* ○ *to launch a ship* ○ *The captain went on board ship.* ○ *The ship sails at noon.* ○ *The ship sank.* سفينة

> A **boat** is smaller than a ship. A **liner** is used to carry people for long journeys and a **ferry** is used for short journeys called **crossings**. We use **vessel** in formal English for ship.

ship[2] /ʃɪp/ *verb* [T] (**shipping**; **shipped**) to send or carry sb/sth by ship: *All their furniture was shipped to Australia when they emigrated.* يشحن أو ينقل بحراً

▸ **shipment** *noun* **1** [C] a quantity of goods sent by ship: *a shipment of grain* شحنة

2 [U] the transport of goods by ship: *cargo ready for shipment* الشّحن بحراً

shipping *noun* [U] **1** ships considered as a group or as traffic السفن أو الملاحة (في منطقة ما)

2 the transport of goods by ship الشّحن بحراً

shipbuilding /ˈʃɪpbɪldɪŋ/ *noun* [U] the building of ships بناء السفن

shipwreck /ˈʃɪprek/ *noun* [C,U] an accident at sea in which a ship is destroyed by a storm, rocks, etc. ❶ A person or a ship that has suffered such an accident has been **shipwrecked**. تحطّم أو غرق السفينة

shipyard /ˈʃɪpyɑːd/ *noun* [C] a place where ships are repaired or built حوض (بناء أو إصلاح) السفن

shirk /ʃɜːk/ *verb* [I,T] to avoid doing sth that is difficult or unpleasant: *to shirk your responsibilities* يتهرّب من

shirt /ʃɜːt/ *noun* [C] a piece of clothing made of cotton, etc., worn (especially by men) on the upper part of the body: *He wears a shirt and tie for work.* قميص

> A shirt usually has a **collar** at the neck, long or short **sleeves**, and **buttons** down the front.

shiver /ˈʃɪvə(r)/ *verb* [I] to shake slightly, especially because you are cold or frightened: *shivering with cold/fright* يرتجف ، يرتعد

▸ **shiver** *noun* [C] an act of shivering: *The thought sent a shiver down my spine.* رجفة ، رعشة ، رعدة

shoal /ʃəʊl/ *noun* [C] a large group of fish that feed and swim together سرب أو فوج من السمك

shock[1] /ʃɒk/ *noun* **1** [C,U] the feeling that is caused by sth unpleasant happening suddenly; the situation that causes this feeling: *The sudden noise gave him a shock.* ○ *The bad news came as a shock to her.* ○ *I'm still suffering from shock at the news.* صدمة ، رجّة

2 [C] = ELECTRIC SHOCK: *Don't touch that wire – you'll get a shock.*

3 [C] a violent blow or shaking (from a crash, explosion, etc.): *the shock of the earthquake* صدمة، هزّة عنيفة

4 [U] (in medicine) a condition of extreme weakness caused by damage to the body: *He was in/went into shock after the accident.* صدمة عصبيّة

shock[2] /ʃɒk/ *verb* [T] **1** to cause an unpleasant feeling of surprise in sb: *We were shocked by his death.* ○ *The staff were shocked at the news that the firm was going to close.* يصعق ، يذهل ، يفجع

2 to make sb feel disgust and anger: *The pictures of the starving children shocked the world.* يهزّ ، يغضب

▸ **shocking** *adj* **1** making you feel worried, upset or angry: *a shocking accident* ○ *shocking behaviour* مريع : مفجع : مخجِل

2 (*informal*) (*especially Brit*) very bad: *The weather has been absolutely shocking.* فظيع ، شنيع

shod *pt, pp* of SHOE

shoddy /ˈʃɒdi/ *adj* (**shoddier**; **shoddiest**) made carelessly or with poor quality materials: *shoddy goods* ○ (*figurative*) *He received shoddy treatment* (= he was treated badly). رديء النوع ، غير متقن : (معاملة) سيِّئة

▸ **shoddily** *adv* بشكل غير متقن

shoe /ʃuː/ *noun* [C] **1** a type of covering for the foot, usually made of leather or plastic: *a pair of shoes* ○ *running shoes* ○ *What size are your shoes?* ○ *I tried on a nice pair of shoes but they didn't fit.* ○ *Wait for me – I've just got to do my shoes up.* حذاء

2 = HORSESHOE

▸ **shoe** *verb* [T] (*pt, pp* **shod** /ʃɒd/) to fit a shoe (on a horse) ينعل الحصان

shoelace /ˈʃuːleɪs/ (*especially US* **shoestring**) *noun* [C] a long piece of cord used to fasten a shoe: *to tie/untie a shoelace* شريط الحذاء

shoes

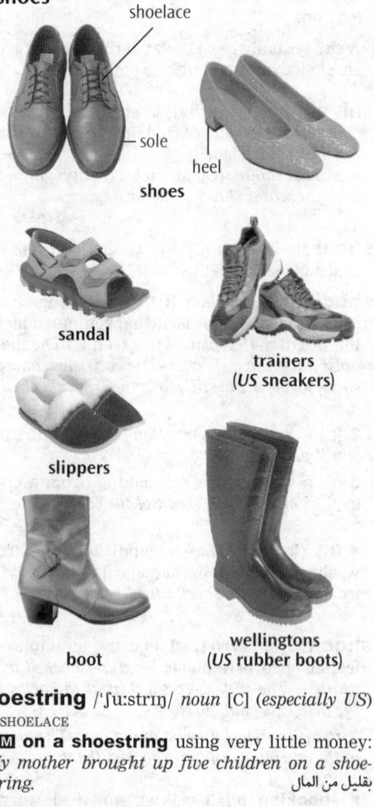

shoestring /ˈʃuːstrɪŋ/ *noun* [C] (*especially US*) = SHOELACE

IDM **on a shoestring** using very little money: *My mother brought up five children on a shoestring.* بقليل من المال

shone *pt, pp* of SHINE

shoo /ʃuː/ *interj* (usually said to animals or small children) Go away! كشْ! هِشْ! إبعد!

▸ **shoo** *verb* (*pt, pp* **shooed**)

PHR V **shoo sb/sth away, off, out, etc.** to make sb/sth go away by saying 'shoo' and waving your hands: *I shooed the birds away from the seeds.* يكشّ أو يهشّ (الطيور مثلاً) ، ينفِّر أو يطرد

shook *pt* of SHAKE¹

shoot¹ /ʃuːt/ *verb* (*pt, pp* **shot** /ʃɒt/) **1** [I,T] **shoot (sth) (at sb/sth)** to fire a gun, etc: *Don't shoot!* ○ *She shot an arrow at the target, but missed it.* يُطلق النار : يرمي بسهم

2 [T] to injure or kill sb/sth with a gun: *The policeman was shot in the arm.* ○ *The soldier was shot dead.* يصيب أو يقتل بالرصاص

3 [I,T] to hunt and kill birds and animals with a gun as a sport: *He goes shooting at the weekends.* يصيد بالبندقيّة

4 [I,T] to move quickly and suddenly in one direction; to make sth move in this way: *The car shot past me at 100 miles per hour.* ○ *She shot him an angry look* (= looked at him very quickly and angrily). ينطلق أو يندفع ، يمرق ؛ يرمي بِ

5 [I] **shoot (down, up, etc. sth)** (of pain) to go very suddenly along part of your body: *The pain shot up my leg.* (ألم) يخز وينتشر فجأة

6 [I] **shoot (at sth)** (in football, etc.) to try to kick or hit the ball into the goal: *He shot at goal but missed.* (في كرة القدم مثلاً) يحاول تسجيل هدف

7 [I,T] to make a film or photograph of sth: *They shot the scene ten times.* يصوّر (مشهداً سينمائياً مثلاً)

PHR V **shoot sb down** to kill sb with a gun يقتل بمسدس أو بندقية

shoot sth down to make an aeroplane, etc. crash to the ground by shooting it: *The helicopter was shot down by a missile.* يسقط (طائرة مثلاً)

shoot up to increase very quickly: *Prices have shot up in the past year.* يرتفع ارتفاعاً سريعاً

shoot² /ʃuːt/ *noun* [C] a new part of a plant or tree فرع جديد للنبتة ، "فرخ" أو "خلف"

shop /ʃɒp/ *noun* [C] **1** (*US* **store**) a building or part of a building where things are bought and sold: *a shoe shop* ○ *a corner shop* (= a local shop, usually at the corner of a street) ○ *When do the shops open?* ○ *a butcher's, baker's, etc. shop* دكّان ، حانوت

We usually say **at the butcher's**, etc. instead of 'at the butcher's shop', etc.

2 = WORKSHOP (1)

IDM **talk shop** → TALK¹

▸ **shop** *verb* [I] (**shopping**; **shopped**) to go to a shop or shops in order to buy things: *I prefer to shop on my own.* ○ *He's shopping for some new clothes.* يتسوّق، يتبضّع

Go shopping is more common than **shop**: *We go shopping every Saturday.* ○ *to go Christmas shopping*

PHR V **shop around (for sth)** to look at the price and quality of an item in different shops before you decide where to buy it: *If you want a bargain you'd better shop around.* يدور على عدة حوانيت قبل الشراء

shopper *noun* [C] a person who is shopping المتسوّق ، الشاري

shopping *noun* [U] **1** the food, clothing, etc. that you have bought in a shop: *Can you help me to put away the shopping?* المشتريات

2 the activity of shopping: *She did the shopping.* ○ *a shopping basket* تسوق ، تبضّع

ˈshop assistant (*US* **sales clerk**; **clerk**) *noun* [C] a person who works in a shop بائع أو بائعة في حانوت

ˌshop ˈfloor *noun* [sing.] (the workers in) an area of a factory where things are made عمّال المصنع : مكان الانتاج في مصنع

shopkeeper /ˈʃɒpkiːpə(r)/ (*US* **storekeeper**) *noun* [C] a person who owns or manages a small shop صاحب الحانوت

shoplift /ˈʃɒplɪft/ *verb* [I,T] to steal sth from a shop while pretending to be a customer (زبون) يسرق بضاعة من حانوت

▸ **shoplifter** *noun* [C]: *Shoplifters will be prosecuted.* ➲ Look at the note at **thief**. من يسرق بضاعة من حانوت

shoplifting *noun* [U]: *He was arrested for shoplifting.* السرقة من الحوانيت

ˈshopping centre *noun* [C] a place where there are many shops, either outside or in a covered building مركز للتسوّق

ˈshopping mall (*also* **mall**) *noun* [C] (*US*) a covered area or building where there are many shops مجمّع مخازن وحوانيت مغطّى

shore /ʃɔː(r)/ *noun* [C,U] the land along the edge of a sea or lake: *The swimmer kept close to the shore.* ○ *The sailors went on shore* (= on land). ❶ **Ashore** is also possible for 'on shore'. شاطئ

shorn *pp* of SHEAR

short¹ /ʃɔːt/ *adj* **1** not measuring much from one end to the other: *a short line* ○ *a short distance* ○ *This essay is rather short.* ○ *short hair* ❶ The opposite is **long**. قصير

2 less than the average height: *a short, fat man* ❶ The opposite is **tall**. قصير القامة

3 not lasting a long time: *a short visit* ○ *She left a short time ago.* ○ *to have a short memory* (= to only remember things that have happened recently) قصير ، قصير الأمد

4 short (of sth) not having enough of what is needed: *Because of illness, the team is two players short.* ○ *Good secretaries are in short supply* (= there are not enough of them). ○ *We're a bit short of money at the moment.* ناقص ، غير كافٍ

5 short for sth used as a shorter way of saying sth: *'Bill' is short for 'William'.* الشكل المختصر لـ

IDM **for short** as a short form: *She's called 'Diana', or 'Di' for short.* اختصاراً

in the long/short term → TERM

in short in a few words; briefly: *Einstein had one of the greatest minds the world has ever known: in short, he was a genius.* بالاختصار

short² /ʃɔːt/ *adv* suddenly: *She stopped short when she saw the accident.* فجأة

IDM **cut sth/sb short** to interrupt: *I tried to explain but he cut me short.* يقاطع

fall short (of sth) not to be enough; not to reach sth: *The pay rise fell short of the workers' demands.* ينقص : يقصّر عن بلوغ الهدف

go short (of sth) to be without enough (of sth): *He made sure his family never went short of food.* ينقصه (شيء)

run short (of sth) to have used up most of sth so there is not much left: *We're running short of coffee.* يستنفد معظم ما عنده

short of sth except for: *He's tried to make money by every means, short of stealing it.* فيما عدا

stop short of sth/doing sth → STOP¹

short³ /ʃɔːt/ *noun* [C] (*informal*) = SHORT CIRCUIT

shortage /ˈʃɔːtɪdʒ/ *noun* [C] a situation where there is not enough of sth: *a food, housing, water, etc. shortage* ○ *a shortage of physics teachers* نقص

shortbread /ˈʃɔːtbred/ *noun* [U] a sweet biscuit made with sugar, flour and butter بسكويت دسم يشبه الغريبة

ˌshort ˈcircuit (*also informal* **short**) *noun* [C] a bad electrical connection that causes a machine to stop working properly دارة قصر ، ماسّ أو تماسّ كهربائيّ

ˌshort-ˈcircuit *verb* [I,T] to have a short circuit or to cause a machine to have one: *The lights short-circuited.* (يَحصَل) أو يحدث تماساً كهربائياً

shortcoming /ˈʃɔːtkʌmɪŋ/ *noun* [C, usually pl.] a fault or weakness: *As a leader, she had many shortcomings.* عيب ، نقص

ˌshort ˈcut *noun* [C] a quicker, easier or more direct way to get somewhere or to do sth: *He took a short cut to school through the park.* طريق مختصر

shorten /ˈʃɔːtn/ *verb* [I,T] to become shorter or to make sth shorter: *I'll have to shorten these trousers – they're much too long.* يَقصُر : يقصّر شيئاً

shortfall /ˈʃɔːtfɔːl/ *noun* [C] **shortfall (in sth)** an amount by which sth is less than what is needed or expected: *a shortfall in the annual budget* ○ *shortfalls in funding* نقص، مقدار النقص

shorthand /ˈʃɔːthænd/ *noun* [U] a method of writing quickly that uses signs or short forms of words: *to write in shorthand* الاختزال

shortlist /ˈʃɔːtlɪst/ *noun* [C] a list of the best people for a job, etc., chosen from a larger number of people القائمة القصيرة (بأسماء المرشّحين لوظيفة)

short-lived /ˌʃɔːt ˈlɪvd; *US* ˈlaɪvd/ *adj* lasting only for a short time قصير الأجل

shortly /ˈʃɔːtli/ *adv* **1** soon; in a short time: *The manager will see you shortly.* بعد قليل : قريباً

2 in an impatient, impolite way: *She spoke rather shortly to the customer.* بجفاء ، بنفاد صبر

shorts /ʃɔːts/ *noun* [plural] **1** a type of short trousers ending above the knee that you wear in hot weather, while playing sports, etc. بنطلون قصير ، "شورت"

a b c d e f g h i j k l m n o p q r **s** t u v w x y z

2 (*US*) men's underpants سروال قصير للرجال

Notice that, because **shorts** is a plural word, we cannot say, for example, 'a new short'. The following are possible: *I need to get some new shorts.* ○ *I need to get a new pair of shorts.*

ˌshort-ˈsighted (*US* **ˌnear-ˈsighted**) *adj* **1** only able to see things clearly when they are close ❶ The opposite is **long-sighted**. قصير البصر

2 not considering what will probably happen in the future: *a short-sighted attitude* قصير النظر ، قليل التبصّر بالعواقب

ˌshort-ˈstaffed *adj* (used of an office, a shop, etc.) not having enough staff بحاجة إلى موظفين اكثر

ˌshort ˈstory *noun* [C] (*pl.* **short stories**) a piece of writing that is shorter than a novel: *a collection of short stories by Thomas Hardy* قصّة قصيرة

ˌshort-ˈterm *adj* lasting for a short period of time from the present: *short-term plans* قصير الأمد

ˈshort wave *noun* [U] (*abbr* **SW**) the system of broadcasting radio using sound waves of less than 100 metres الموجة القصيرة

shot[1] /ʃɒt/ *noun* [C] **1** an act of firing a gun, etc., or the noise that this makes: *to take a shot at the target* ○ *The policeman fired a warning shot into the air.* إطلاق النار : طلقة

2 a shot (at sth/at doing sth) (*informal*) an attempt to do sth: *Let me have a shot at it* (= let me try to do it). محاولة

3 (in sport) an act of kicking or hitting a ball: *to have a shot at goal* ضربة الكرة نحو الهدف

4 a photograph or a picture in a film: *I got some good shots of the runners as they crossed the line.* لقطة سينمائيّة

5 an injection of a drug: *a shot of penicillin* حقنة من مخدّر

6 often **the shot** a heavy metal ball that is thrown as a sport: *to put* (= throw) *the shot* الكلّة ، كرة حديديّة ثقيلة

shot[2] *pt, pp* of SHOOT[1]

shotgun /ˈʃɒtɡʌn/ *noun* [C] a gun used for shooting small animals and birds that fires small metal balls بندقيّة صيد ، بارودة خردق

should /ʃəd; *strong form* ʃʊd/ *modal verb* (*negative* **should not**; *short form* **shouldn't** /ˈʃʊdnt/) **1** (used for saying that it is right for sb to do sth, or for sth to happen): *The police should do something about it.* ○ *Children shouldn't be left on their own.* ينبغي ، يجب

2 (used for giving or asking advice): *You should try that new restaurant.* ○ *He really shouldn't work so hard.* ○ *Should I try again?* عليك بـ ، يجب

3 (used with 'have' to say that sb did the wrong thing): *I'm tired. I shouldn't have gone to bed so late/I should have gone to bed earlier.* كان ينبغي ، كان من اللازم أن...

4 (used for saying that you expect sth is true or will happen): *It's 4.30. They should be in New York by now.* ○ *He should have arrived by now.* لا بدّ أنه (وصل مثلاً)

5 (*formal*) (used with 'I/we' instead of 'would' in 'if' sentences): *I should be most grateful if you could send me...* ساكون...إذا...

6 (used after 'if' and 'in case' when you think that sth is not likely to happen): *If you should decide to accept, please phone us.* ○ *Should you decide to accept...* إنْ ، إذا

7 (used as the past tense of 'shall' when we report what sb says): *He asked me if he should come today* (= Shall I come today?). فيما إذا ، هل

8 (*formal*) (used after 'so that', 'in order that'): *In order that there should be no delay, we took action immediately.* تستعمل بعد "كي" ، "حتى" ، "كي لا"...

9 (used after certain verbs, e.g. when sth is arranged or suggested): *We arranged that they should book the hotel.* ○ *I suggested that he should cancel the meeting.* تستعمل بعد أفعال معيّنة مثل "يقترح" مثلاً

10 (used after certain adjectives): *It's shocking that something like this should happen.* ○ *It's strange that you should mention that...* ○ *Is it important that we should all go?* تستعمل بعد صفات معيّنة

IDM I should... (used when you are giving advice): *I should get to bed early if I were you.* تستعمل عند تقديم نصيحة

I should think my opinion is: *This picture is worth a lot of money, I should think.* اعتقد ، في رأيي

shoulder /ˈʃəʊldə(r)/ *noun* **1** [C] the part of the body between the neck and the top of the arm: *He hurt his shoulder.* ○ *to shrug your shoulders* (= to raise your shoulders, especially as a way of showing that you do not know an answer or that you are not interested) كتف ، عاتق

2 [C] a part of a dress, coat, etc. that covers this part of the body كتف

3 shoulders [plural] the part of your body between your two shoulders: *He carried his little girl on his shoulders.* كتفين ، ظهر

IDM have a chip on your shoulder → CHIP[1]

▸ **shoulder** *verb* [T] **1** to accept the responsibility for sth: *to shoulder the blame/responsibility for sth* يتحمل المسؤولية

2 to push sb/sth with your shoulder: *He shouldered everybody aside and disappeared out of the door.* يدفع بمنكبيه

ˈshoulder bag *noun* [C] a type of bag that you carry over one shoulder with a long strap حقيبة كتف

ˈshoulder blade *noun* [C] either of the two large flat bones on each side of your back, below your shoulders لوح الكتف

shout /ʃaʊt/ *noun* [C] a loud call or cry: *She gave a warning shout.* صيحة

▸ **shout** *verb* **1** [I] **shout (at/to sb); shout (out)** to speak or cry out in a very loud voice: *There's no need to shout – I can hear you.* ○ *The* *teacher shouted angrily at the boys.* ○ *to shout out in pain, excitement, etc.* يصيح ، يصرخ ، يزعق

2 [T] **shout sth (at/to sb); shout sth out** to say sth in a loud voice: *'Look out,' she shouted.* ○ *The captain shouted out instructions to his team.* يصيح ، ينادي بصوت عالٍ

PHR V **shout sb down** to prevent sb from being heard by shouting at them (often in a public meeting): *to shout a speaker down* يكتم صوت الخطيب بصياحات عالية

shove /ʃʌv/ *verb* [I,T] to push with a sudden, rough movement: *They pushed and shoved to the front of the queue.* ○ *The policeman shoved the thief through the door.* ○ (*informal*) *'What should I do with this box?' 'Oh, just shove it over here.'* يدفع بعنف ، "يدفش"

▶ **shove** *noun* [C, usually sing.] a sudden, rough push: *to give sb/sth a shove* دفعة مفاجئة ، "دفشة"

shovel /ˈʃʌvl/ *noun* [C] a tool, like a spade, used for moving earth, snow, sand, etc. مجرفة ، رفش

▶ **shovel** *verb* [I,T] (shovelling; shovelled; *US* shoveling; shoveled) to move sth with a shovel يجرف بالمجرفة

show[1] /ʃəʊ/ *noun* **1** [C] a type of entertainment that has singing, dancing, acting, etc. in the theatre or on television, etc: *a comedy show on TV* ○ *We've booked tickets to see a show in London.* عرض (مسرحيّ مثلاً)

2 [C] a collection of things for people to look at, often in a special large building: *a dog show* ○ *the motor show* (= where new makes of car are displayed) معرض ، عرض

3 [C,U] the outward expression of an emotion that is not what you really feel or that does not have much meaning: *Although she hated him, she put on a show of politeness.* ○ *His bravery is all show* (= he is not as brave as he pretends to be). مظهر ، تظاهر

4 [sing.] a sign of sth: *The parade of weapons was a show of strength by the government.* عرض

IDM **for show** intended to impress people; not to be used: *Those books are only for show – nobody ever reads them.* للمنظر فقط ، للتباهي

on show put in a place where people can see it: *The collection is on show at the British Museum.* معروض للجمهور

show[2] /ʃəʊ/ *verb* (*pt* **showed**; *pp* **shown** /ʃəʊn/ or **showed**) **1** [T] **show sb/sth (to sb)** to make it possible for other people to see sb/sth: *I showed the letter to him.* ○ *I showed him the letter.* ○ *She showed me what she had bought.* ○ *They're showing his latest film at our local cinema.* يري ؛ يعرض

2 [T] to lead or guide sb to a place: *Shall I show you to your room?* ○ *A guide showed us round the museum.* يقود إلى ، يرشد

3 [T] to help sb to do sth by doing it yourself; to explain sth: *Can you show me how to do it?* يري ، يعلّم ، يبيّن

4 [T] to make sth clear; to give information about sth: *Research shows that most people get too little exercise.* ○ *The picture showed the effects of the storm.* يوضح ، يظهِر

5 [I] to be able to be seen; to appear: *Her anger showed in her eyes.* ○ *I've got a hole in my sock but it doesn't show.* يَظهر ، يبدو

6 [T] to allow sth to be seen: *These brown trousers don't show the dirt.* يظهِر

7 [T] to have a particular quality: *She was showing signs of stress.* يبدو عليه

8 [T] to cause people to notice a particular quality: *She was the only one who ever showed him any kindness.* ○ *She didn't want to show what she was really thinking.* يولي ؛ يبدي

PHR V **show (sth) off** (*informal*) to try to impress people by showing them how clever you are or by showing them sth that you are proud of: *John drove his new car very fast in order to show off.* ○ *She wanted to show off her new bike.* يتباهى بِ

show up (*informal*) to arrive, especially when sb is expecting you: *I thought you'd never show up.* يأتي ، يصِل

show (sth) up to allow sth to be seen: *The sunlight shows up those dirty marks on the window.* يظهِر ؛ يبرز

show sb up (*informal*) to make someone feel ashamed or embarrassed by behaving badly: *He showed her up by shouting at the waiter.* يخجل

▶ **showing** *noun* **1** [C] an act of showing a film, etc: *The second showing of the film begins at 8 o'clock.* عرض

2 [sing.] how sb/sth behaves; how successful sb/sth is: *On its present showing, the party should win the election.* سلوك ، مقدار النجاح

ˈ**show business** (*also informal* **showbiz** /ˈʃəʊbɪz/) *noun* [U] the business of entertaining people, in the theatre, in films, on television, etc. عالم الأضواء

showdown /ˈʃəʊdaʊn/ *noun* [C] a final argument at the end of a long disagreement: *The management are preparing for a showdown with the union.* تصفية الحساب بين خصمين ، مجاهرة

shower /ˈʃaʊə(r)/ *noun* [C] **1** a way of washing the body by standing under running water: *He had a shower after the tennis match.* "دوش" أو "دُش"

2 the apparatus used for washing yourself in this way; the small room or part of a bathroom where it is fixed: *The shower doesn't work.* ○ *She's in the shower.* ○ *I'd like a room with a shower, please.* "دوش" أو "دُش" ؛ رشّاش

3 a short period of rain or snow زخّة

4 a lot of very small objects that fall together: *a shower of dust* وابل

▶ **shower** *verb* **1** [T] **shower sb with sth** to cause a great number of very small objects to fall on sb/sth: *to be showered with leaves, dust, water* ○ (*figurative*) *He was showered with praise for his excellent work.* يمطره بِ ، يغدق عليه

2 [I] to have a shower (1) "يأخذ دوش" ، يغتسل تحت "الدش"

showjumping /ˈʃəʊdʒʌmpɪŋ/ *noun* [U] a competition in which people ride horses over a series of fences (jumps) مباراة قفز الخيل فوق الحواجز

shown *pp* of SHOW[2]

ˈ**show-off** *noun* [C] a person who tries to impress others by showing them how clever he/she is: *She's such a show-off.* ℹ This word is used when we are criticizing somebody. شخص متباهٍ بذكائه

showroom /ˈʃəʊruːm; -rʊm/ *noun* [C] a type of shop where goods such as cars and electrical items are displayed صالة العرض

shrank *pt* of SHRINK

shrapnel /ˈʃræpnəl/ *noun* [U] small pieces of metal that are thrown in various directions from an exploding bomb or shell (3) شظيّة

shred /ʃred/ *noun* **1** [C] a small thin piece of material that has been cut or torn off: *He tore the letter to shreds.* قصاصة طويلة رفيعة

2 a shred of sth [sing.] (in negative sentences) a very small amount of sth: *There wasn't a shred of truth in her story.* ذرّة

▸ **shred** *verb* [T] (shre**dd**ing; shre**dd**ed) to tear or cut sth into shreds: *shredded cabbage* يقطّع إلى قطع طويلة رفيعة

shrewd /ʃruːd/ *adj* able to make good decisions because you understand a situation well: *a shrewd thinker* ○ *a shrewd decision* حصيف ، داهية ، ثاقب الرأي

▸ **shrewdly** *adv* بذكاء ، بدهاء

shriek /ʃriːk/ *verb* **1** [I] to give a sudden scream in a high voice: *She shrieked in fright.* ○ *The children were shrieking with laughter.* يزعق ، يصرخ

2 [T] to scream sth in a high voice: *'Stop it!' he shrieked.* يصرخ

▸ **shriek** *noun* [C]: *She gave a loud shriek of pain.* صرخة ، زعقة

shrill /ʃrɪl/ *adj* (used about a sound) high and unpleasant: *a shrill cry* حادّ ، ثاقب للآذان

shrimp /ʃrɪmp/ *noun* [C] a small sea creature with a shell that turns pink when you cook it. Shrimps are smaller than prawns. قريدس ، إربيان

shrine /ʃraɪn/ *noun* [C] a place that is holy for members of a religion, because it is associated with a special person or thing مَزار ، ضريح

shrink /ʃrɪŋk/ *verb* (*pt* **shrank** /ʃræŋk/ or **shrunk** /ʃrʌŋk/; *pp* **shrunk**) [I,T] to become smaller, often after being washed; to make sth smaller: *Oh no! My T-shirt's shrunk!* ○ *I've shrunk my T-shirt. The water must have been too hot.* ○ *Television has shrunk the world.* ○ *The workforce has shrunk to 200.* يتقلّص أو ينكمش ؛ يقلّص أو يصغّر

PHR V **shrink from sth/doing sth** to be unwilling to do sth because you find it unpleasant ينفر من ، يحجم عن

shrivel /ˈʃrɪvl/ *verb* [I,T] (shrive**ll**ing; shrive**ll**ed; *US* shriveling; shriveled) **shrivel (sth) (up)** to dry up and become smaller and wrinkled, usually in hot or dry conditions; to make sth do this يذبل ويتغضّن ، يضمُر ؛ يذبِل ويغضّن

shroud /ʃraʊd/ *noun* [C] a cloth or sheet used to wrap a dead body before it is buried كفن

▸ **shroud** *verb* [T] (usually passive) to cover or

'Oh no! My T-shirt has shrunk!'

'Oh no! My T-shirt has stretched!'

hide sth with sth: *The tops of the mountains were shrouded in mist.* ○ *His past is shrouded in mystery.* يغطّي ، يغشّي ، يكتنف

Shrove Tuesday /ˌʃrəʊv ˈtjuːzdeɪ; *US* ˈtuːz-/ *noun* [C] the day before the beginning of a period called Lent when some Christians do not eat certain foods, etc. ثلاثاء المرافع (تسبق بداية الصوم عند المسيحيّين)

> In some countries the period before Shrove Tuesday is celebrated as **carnival.** In Britain many people eat **pancakes** on this day.

shrub /ʃrʌb/ *noun* [C] a small bush شجيرة ، جَنْبة

▸ **shrubbery** /ˈʃrʌbəri/ *noun* [C] (*pl.* **shrubberies**) an area planted with shrubs جزء من الحديقة مغطّى بالشجيرات

shrug /ʃrʌg/ *verb* [I,T] (shru**gg**ing; shru**gg**ed) to raise your shoulders as a way of showing that you do not know or do not care about sth: *'Who knows?' she said and shrugged.* ○ *'It doesn't matter to me,' he said, shrugging his shoulders.* يهزّ كتفيه (لا مبالاةً مثلاً)

PHR V **shrug sth off** to treat sth as if it is not important to you لا يكترث لـ

▸ **shrug** *noun* [C, usually sing.] a movement of shrugging the shoulders: *He answered his mother with a shrug.* هزّة كتفين

shrunk, shrunken → SHRINK

shudder /ˈʃʌdə(r)/ *verb* [I] to shake with fear, etc: *Just to think about the accident makes me shudder.* ○ *I shudder to think how much this meal is going to cost.* يرتعد ، يرتجف

▶ **shudder** *noun* [C] رعدة ، رجفة

shuffle /ˈʃʌfl/ *verb* **1** [I] to walk by sliding your feet along instead of lifting them from the ground: *The child shuffled past, wearing her mother's shoes.* يجرّ قدميه

2 [I,T] to move your body or feet around because you are uncomfortable or nervous: *The audience were so bored that they began to shuffle in their seats.* يتململ في جلسته

3 [I,T] to mix a pack of playing cards before a game يخلط أوراق اللعب

▶ **shuffle** *noun* [C, usually sing.] **1** a shuffling way of walking جرجرة القدمين

2 an act of shuffling cards خَلْط ورق اللعب

shun /ʃʌn/ *verb* [T] (shu**nn**ing; shu**nn**ed) to avoid sb/sth; to keep away from sb/sth: *The film star shunned publicity.* ○ *The tennis tournament has been shunned by all the world's leading players.* يتجنّب ، يتحاشى ؛ يمتنع عن

shunt /ʃʌnt/ *verb* [T] **1** to move a railway train from one track to another يحوِّل قطاراً من خطّ لآخر

2 to move a person from one place to another: *He was shunted around from one hospital to another.* ينقّل (من مكان لآخر)

⚷**shut** /ʃʌt/ *verb* [I,T] (*pres part* **shutting**; *pt, pp* **shut**) **1** [T] to change the position of sth so that it covers a hole, etc.; to fold sth together; to close: *Could you shut the door, please?* ○ *I can't shut my suitcase.* ○ *Shut your books, please.* ○ *He shut his eyes and tried to go to sleep.* يغلق

2 [I] to move or be moved into a closed position: *This window won't shut properly.* ينغلق

3 [I,T] (used about a shop, restaurant, etc.) to stop being open; to close sth (a shop, restaurant, etc.): *What time do the shops shut on Saturday?* ○ *I shut the shop early and went home.* يغلق

4 [T] to prevent sb/sth from leaving or moving; to trap sth: *She shut herself in her room and refused to come out.* ○ *Tony shut his fingers in the door of the car.* يحبس ؛ يهرس

PHRV **shut sb/sth away** to keep sb/sth in a place where people cannot find or see him/her/it يخبّئ ، يواري عن الأنظار

shut (sth) down (used about a factory, etc.) to be closed for a long time or for ever; to close sth (a factory, etc.) for a long time or for ever: *Financial problems forced the business to shut down.* ○ *They have shut down the factory for reasons of safety.* يغلق

shut sb/sth off (from sth) to keep sb/sth apart from sth: *He shuts himself off from the rest of the world.* يفصل ، يعزل

shut sb/sth out to keep sb/sth out: *He tried to shut out all thoughts of the accident.* يحجب ، يبعد ؛ يوصد الباب في وجهه

shut (sb) up (*informal*) **1** to stop talking; to be quiet: *I wish you'd shut up!* يسكت ، يخرس

2 to make sb stop talking: *Nothing can shut him up once he's started.* يسكّت ، يخرس

shut sb/sth up (in sth) to put sb/sth somewhere and stop them leaving: *He was shut up in prison for nearly ten years.* ➲ Look at the note at **close**. يحبس ، يسجن

▶ **shut** *adj* (not before a noun) **1** in a closed position: *Make sure the door is shut properly before you leave.* مغلق ، موصد

Remember that we can use **closed** before a noun: *a closed door*, but not **shut**.

2 not open to the public: *The restaurant was shut so we went to one round the corner.* مغلَق

shut up! *interj* (*informal*) a way of telling sb (rather rudely) that you want them to be quiet: *Shut up! Can't you see I'm working?* أُسكُت! ؛ إخْرَس!

shutter /ˈʃʌtə(r)/ *noun* [C] **1** a wooden or metal cover that is fixed outside a window and that can be open or shut. A shop's shutter usually slides down from the top of the shop window. دَرفة أو مصراع (خشبيّ) يغطّي النافذة

2 the part at the front of a camera that opens for a very short time to let light in so that a photograph can be taken حجاب ، مصراع ، سديلة

shuttle /ˈʃʌtl/ *noun* [C] a plane, bus or train that travels regularly between two places: *I'm catching the seven o'clock shuttle to Glasgow.* ○ *a shuttle service* وسيلة نقل تسافر بين مدينتين بشكل منتظم

shuttlecock /ˈʃʌtlkɒk/ *noun* [C] the small light object that is hit over a net in the sport of badminton ريشة طائرة: كرة من الفلّين ذات ريش

ˌ**shuttle diˈplomacy** *noun* [U] international talks in which people travel between two or more countries in order to talk to the different governments involved ديبلوماسية المكوك

⚷**shy** /ʃaɪ/ *adj* (**shyer**; **shyest**) nervous and uncomfortable with other people. Shy people do not usually say very much to people they do not know: *She's very shy with strangers.* ○ *a shy smile* خجول

▶ **shy** *verb* (*pres part* **shying**; *3rd pers sing pres* **shies**; *pt, pp* **shied**) [I] (used about a horse) to move back or sideways suddenly in fear يجفل

PHRV **shy away from sth/from doing sth** to avoid doing sth because you are afraid: *He shied away from telling her the truth.* يتجنّب ، يخشى

shyly *adv* in a shy way: *The girl walked shyly into the room.* بحياء ، بخجل

shyness *noun*: *He didn't overcome his shyness till he had left school.* خَجَل ، حياء

sibling /ˈsɪblɪŋ/ *noun* [C] (*formal*) a brother or a sister: *Jealousy between siblings is very common.* ❶ In ordinary language we use **brother(s) and sister(s)**: *Have you got any brothers and sisters?* أخ أو أُخت

⚷**sick** /sɪk/ *adj* **1** not well; ill: *a sick child* ○ *She's been off work sick for the past week.* مريض ، عليل

In British English **to be sick** usually means 'to bring up food from the stomach'. We do not usually say that somebody **is sick**, to mean 'ill'. In American English **be sick** can be used to mean 'be ill': *She's been sick for several weeks now.*

2 feeling ill in your stomach so that any food in it may be thrown up through your mouth: *I feel sick – I think it was that fish I ate.* شاعر بالغثيان

a b c d e f g h i j k l m n o p q r s t u v w x y z

3 sick of sb/sth feeling bored or annoyed because you have had too much of a person or thing: *I'm sick of my job.* ○ *I'm sick of tidying up your mess!* متضايق : متبرم ، سَئِم

4 sick (at/about sth) very annoyed or disgusted by sth: *He felt sick at the sight of so much waste.* متكدِّر : مشمئز النفس

5 (*informal*) cruel or in bad taste: *a sick joke about blind people* لا رحمة فيه : قليل الذوق

IDM be sick to throw up food from the stomach; vomit: *How many times have you been sick?* يتقيأ

make sb sick to make sb very angry: *Oh, stop complaining. You make me sick!* يثير غضبه

sick to death of sb/sth feeling tired of or annoyed by sb/sth: *I'm sick to death of his grumbling.* متضايق أو سئِم للغاية

▶ **sick** *noun* **1** [U] (*informal*) vomit: *There was sick all over the car seat.* قيء

2 the sick [plural] people who are ill المرضى

-sick (in compounds) feeling sick (2) as a result of travelling: *I get carsick on long journeys.* ○ *to be seasick* دوار ، دوخة

sicken /ˈsɪkən/ *verb* [T] to make sb feel disgusted: *Even the smell of the place sickens me.* يقزِّز النفس : يثير الاشمئزاز

▶ **sickening** *adj* disgusting; very unpleasant: *It was a sickening sight.* مقرف ، مقزِّز للنفس

sickle /ˈsɪkl/ *noun* a tool with a curved blade on a short handle, that is used for cutting grass, corn, etc. منجل

ˈsick leave *noun* [U] a period spent away from work, etc. because of illness إجازة مرضيّة

sickly /ˈsɪkli/ *adj* (**sicklier**; **sickliest**) **1** (used about a person) weak, unhealthy and often ill: *a sickly child* واهن ، معلول ، سقيم

2 unpleasant; causing a feeling of sickness (2): *the sickly smell of rotten fruit* كريه : مثير للغثيان

sickness /ˈsɪknəs/ *noun* **1** [U] the state of being ill: *A lot of workers are absent because of sickness.* مرض

2 [U] a feeling in your stomach that may make you throw up food through your mouth: *sickness and diarrhoea* غثيان

3 [C,U] a particular type of illness: *seasickness pills* مرض (كذا)

side[1] /saɪd/ *noun* [C] **1** any of the flat outer surfaces of an object: *A cube has six sides.* ○ *this side up* (= an instruction on a parcel, etc. that tells you which way to store it) ضلع

2 [C] any of the flat outer surfaces of an object except the top or the bottom: *A box has a top, a bottom and four sides.* جانب

3 any of the surfaces of sth except the top, bottom, front or back: *I went round to the side of the building.* ○ *The side of the car was damaged.* جانب

4 the edge or boundary of sth; the area near this: *A triangle has three sides.* ○ *She sat at the side of his bed/at his bedside.* ○ *He waited at the side of the road.* جانب ، طرف

5 either of the two flat surfaces of sth thin: *Write on both sides of the paper.* وجه ، طرف

6 the right or the left part of your body, especially from under your arm to the top of your leg: *She lay on her side.* ○ *The soldier stood with his hands by his sides.* جنب ، خاصرة

7 either of the two parts of a place or object, separated by a real or an imaginary line or boundary: *We drive on the left side of the road in Britain.* ○ *He was sitting at the far side of the room.* ○ *I live on the other side of the city.* ○ *on the other side of the wall* ○ (*figurative*) *She has a generous side to her nature.* جانب: ناحية

8 either of two teams or groups of people who fight or play against each other: *The two sides agreed to stop fighting.* ○ *the winning/losing side* ○ *Whose side are you on?* (= Who do you support?) طرف : فريق

9 the position, opinion or attitude of a person or group of people that is different from that held by another person or group of people: *Do you believe his side of the story?* وجهة نظر ، رؤية

10 your mother's or your father's family: *There is no history of illness on his mother's side.* ناحية ، جانب

IDM get on the right/wrong side of sb to please/annoy sb: *He tried to get on the right side of his new boss.* يرضي : يضايق أو يسيء إلى

on/from all sides; **on/from every side** in/from all directions; generally: *The army was attacked from every side.* ○ *There was agreement on all sides.* من كلّ الجهات أو الأطراف

on the big, small, high, etc. side (*informal*) slightly too big, small, high, etc. كبير/صغير الخ...إلى حدّ ما

on the safe side → SAFE[1] (4)

put sth on/to one side; **leave sth on one side** to leave or keep sth so that you can use it or deal with it later: *You should put some money to one side for the future.* ○ *I'll put this problem on one side until later.* يضعه جانباً: يدّخر

side by side next to each other; close together: *They walked side by side along the road.* جنباً إلى جنب

take sides (with sb) to show that you support one person rather than another: *Parents should never take sides when their children are quarrelling.* يتحيز أو ينحاز

▶ **-sided** (in compounds) having a certain number or type of sides: *a six-sided coin* ذو (ستّة) أضلاع أو جوانب

side[2] /saɪd/ *verb*

PHR V side with sb (against sb) to support sb in an argument: *She always sides with her son against her husband.* يؤيِّد ، يناصر

sideboard /ˈsaɪdbɔːd/ *noun* **1** [C] a type of low cupboard about as high as a table, that is used for storing plates, etc. in a dining room خزانة في غرفة الطعام لحفظ أدوات المائدة -"بوفيه"

2 sideboards (*US* **sideburns** /ˈsaɪdbɜːnz/) [plural] hair that grows down a man's face in front of and below his ears شعر العارضَين، سالف

ˈside effect *noun* [C] the unpleasant effect that sth may have in addition to the effects it is supposed to have: *Unpleasant side effects of the drug may be headaches or sickness.* أثر أو مفعول جانبيّ

sideline /ˈsaɪdlaɪn/ *noun* **1** [C] something that you do in addition to your regular job, usually to earn extra money: *He's an engineer, but he repairs cars as a sideline.* عمل آخر إلى جانب عمل المرء الاساسيّ

2 sidelines [plural] the lines that mark the two long sides of a football pitch or tennis court; the area behind this: *The team's manager was giving orders from the sidelines.* جانبا الملعب

sidelong /ˈsaɪdlɒŋ; *US* -lɔːŋ/ *adj* directed from the side; sideways: *a sidelong glance* جانبيّ : (نظرة) شزراء

ˈ**side order** *noun* [C] a small amount of food ordered in a restaurant to go with the main dish, but served separately طبق جانبيّ

ˈ**side road** *noun* [C] a road which leads from a main road and which is less important or busy طريق أو شارع فرعيّ

ˈ**side street** *noun* [C] a narrow or less important street that usually joins a main street حارة أو طريق فرعيّ

sidetrack /ˈsaɪdtræk/ *verb* [T] to make sb forget what he/she is supposed to be doing or talking about and start doing or talking about sth less important يصرف انتباهه إلى شيء آخر ، يحرفه

⚷ **sideways** /ˈsaɪdweɪz/ *adj, adv* **1** to, towards or from one side: *He jumped sideways to avoid being hit.* ○ *a sideways glance* إلى أو من الجانب ، جانبيّ : شزراً

2 with one of the sides at the top: *We'll have to turn the sofa sideways to get it through the door.* على الجنب ، بالعرض

siding /ˈsaɪdɪŋ/ *noun* [C] a short track at the side of a main railway line تحويلة فرعيّة قصيرة للسكك الحديديّة

sidle /ˈsaɪdl/ *verb* [I] **sidle up/over (to sb/sth)** to move towards sb/sth in a nervous way, as if you do not want anybody to notice you يمشي نحوه مجانبةً وبخجل

siege /siːdʒ/ *noun* [C,U] **1** the situation in which an army surrounds a town in order to capture it. When there is a siege nobody is allowed into or out of the town: *the siege of Troy* حصار

2 a situation in which a building containing a criminal is surrounded by police for a long period of time: *The house was under siege for several hours, until the man released the prisoners.* محاصرة ، محاوطة

siesta /siˈestə/ *noun* [C] a short sleep or rest that people take after lunch, especially in hot countries: *to have/take a siesta* قيلولة

sieve /sɪv/ *noun* [C] a type of kitchen tool that has a metal or plastic net, used for separating solids from liquids or very small pieces of food from large pieces مُنخل ، غربال

▶ **sieve** *verb*: *Sieve the flour before adding it to the mixture.* ينخل ، يغربل

sift /sɪft/ *verb* **1** [T] to pass a fine substance through a sieve: *to sift flour, sugar* ينخل ، يغربل

2 [I,T] **sift (through) sth** (*figurative*) to examine sth very carefully: *It took weeks to sift through all the evidence.* يدقق في ، يمحّص

sigh /saɪ/ *verb* **1** [I] to let out a long, deep breath that shows you are tired, sad, relieved, etc: *She sighed with disappointment at the news.* يتنهد، يتأوّه

2 [I] to make a sound like sighing: *The wind sighed in the trees.* يئنّ ، يهس

3 [T] to say sth with a sigh: *'I'm so tired,' he sighed.* يتأوّه

▶ **sigh** *noun* [C] the act or sound of sighing: *'Well, that's over,' she said, with a sigh of relief.* تنهُّدة؛ تنهُّد : تنفُّس الصعداء

⚷ **sight**[1] /saɪt/ *noun* **1** [U] the ability to see: *He lost his sight in the war* (= he became blind). ○ *My grandmother has very poor sight.* بصر ، نظر

2 [sing.] **sight of sb/sth** the act of seeing sb/sth: *We flew over Paris and had our first sight of the Eiffel Tower.* ○ *Throw that dress out. I can't stand the sight of it any more.* رؤية : منظر

3 [U] a position where sb/sth can be seen: *They waited until the plane was within sight* (= until they could see it) *and then fired.* ○ *She didn't let the child out of her sight.* ○ *'Get out of my sight* (= go away)*!' he shouted, angrily.* مرأى ؛ مدى البصر

4 [C] something that you see: *It was good to be back home, amid all the familiar sights and sounds.* منظر ، مشهد

5 sights [plural] places of interest that are often visited by tourists: *When you come to New York I'll show you the sights.* مشاهد أو معالِم المكان

6 a sight [sing.] (*informal*) a person or thing that looks untidy or that makes you laugh: *Look at that girl with green hair. What a sight!* "أمّا منظر!" ، هيئة زريّة، منظر مثير للسخرية

7 [C, usually pl.] a part of a weapon that you look through in order to aim it: *the sights of a gun* المِهداف أو جهاز التسديد

IDM **at first glance/sight** → FIRST[1]

catch sight/a glimpse of sb/sth → CATCH[1] (9)

in sight likely to happen or come soon: *A peace settlement is in sight.* وشيك

know sb by sight → KNOW (9)

lose sight of sb/sth → LOSE (9)

on sight as soon as sb/sth is seen: *The soldiers were ordered to shoot the enemy on sight.* لدى أو فور رؤيته

▶ **-sighted** (in compounds) having a certain type of eyesight: *I'm short-sighted.* (قصير) البصر أو النظر

sight[2] /saɪt/ *verb* [T] to see sb/sth, especially after looking out for him/her/it: *After many weeks at sea, they sighted land.* ○ *The wanted man has been sighted in Spain.* يرى ، يشاهد ؛ يقع بصره على

▶ **sighting** *noun* [C] an occasion when sb/sth is seen: *the first sighting of a new star* رؤية ، مشاهدة

sightseeing /ˈsaɪtsiːɪŋ/ *noun* [U] visiting the sights of a city, etc. as a tourist: *We did some sightseeing in Rome.* رؤية معالِم المدينة

▶ **sightseer** *noun* [C] a person who does this ➲ Look at **tourist**. متفرج على معالم المدينة، سائح

a b c d e f g h i j k l m n o p q r s t u v w x y z

sign¹ /saɪn/ *noun* [C] **1** a type of shape, mark or symbol that has a particular meaning: *In mathematics, a cross is a plus sign.* علامة ، اشارة

2 a board, notice, etc. that gives you a piece of information, an instruction or a warning: *What does that sign say?* ○ *a road sign* ○ *Follow the signs to Banbury.* إشارة (مرور) ، لافتة

3 a movement that you make with your head, hands or arms that has a particular meaning: *I made a sign for him to follow me.* إشارة ، إيماءة

4 sign (of sth) something that shows that sb/sth is present or exists or may happen: *The patient was showing some signs of improvement.* ○ *There are some signs that things are getting better.* ○ *As we drove into the village there wasn't a sign of life anywhere* (= we couldn't see anyone). علامة ، دليل : آية

5 (*also* **'star sign**; **ˌsign of the 'zodiac**) one of the twelve divisions or symbols of the zodiac أحد بروج الفَلَك

sign² /saɪn/ *verb* [I,T] to write your name on a letter, document, etc. to show that you have written it or that you agree with what it says. When you sign your name you always write it in the same way: *'Could you sign here, please?'* ○ *I forgot to sign the cheque.* ○ *The two presidents signed the treaty.* يوقِّع ، يمضي

PHR V **sign in/out** to write your name to show you have arrived at or left a hotel, club, etc. يسجِّل اسمه عند وصوله أو خروجه

sign sb up to get sb to sign a contract to work for you: *Real Madrid have signed up two new players.* يتعاقد مع

sign up (for sth) to agree formally to do sth: *I've signed up for evening classes.* يتسجَّل في

signal /'sɪɡnəl/ *noun* [C] **1** a sign, action or sound that sends a particular message: *The army waited for the signal to attack.* ○ *The flag went down as a signal for the race to begin.* إشارة

2 a set of lights used to give information to train drivers إشارة (مرور) لسائقي القطارات

3 a series of radio waves, etc. that are sent out or received: *a signal from a satellite* إشارة

▸ **signal** *verb* [I,T] (signalling; signalled; *US* signaling; signaled) to make a signal; to send a particular message using a signal: *She was signalling wildly that something was wrong.* ○ *He signalled his disapproval by leaving the room.* ○ *The policeman signalled to the driver to stop.* يشير ، يومئ، يرسل إشارة : يبدي

signatory /'sɪɡnətri; *US* -tɔːri/ *noun* [C] (*pl.* **signatories**) **signatory (to sth)** (*formal*) any of the people or countries that sign an agreement, etc. الموقِّع على وثيقة وغيرها

signature /'sɪɡnətʃə(r)/ *noun* [C] a person's name, written by himself/herself and always written in the same way: *I couldn't read his signature.* توقيع ، إمضاء

significance /sɪɡ'nɪfɪkəns/ *noun* [U] the importance or meaning of sth: *Few people realized the significance of the discovery.* أهميّة : معنى

significant /sɪɡ'nɪfɪkənt/ *adj* **1** important: *The police said that the time of the murder was extremely significant.* هامّ

2 so large that you notice it: *There has been a significant increase in the number of crimes reported this year.* ملحوظ ، ذو شأن

3 having a particular meaning: *She gave me a significant smile.* ذو مغزى

▸ **significantly** *adv* **1** in a noticeable way: *Attitudes have changed significantly since the 1960s.* بشكل ملحوظ

2 in a way that shows a particular meaning: *He thanked almost everybody but, significantly, he did not mention Terry.* ممّا له دلالته

signify /'sɪɡnɪfaɪ/ *verb* [T] (*pres part* **signifying**; *3rd pers sing pres* **signifies**; *pt, pp* **signified**) (*formal*) **1** to be a sign of sth; to mean: *What do those lights signify?* يدلّ على؛ يعني

2 to express or indicate sth: *He nodded to signify that he agreed.* يعبِّر عن ، يبدي

'sign language *noun* [U] a language used especially by people who cannot hear or speak, using signs instead of spoken words لغة الاشارة

signpost /'saɪnpəʊst/ *noun* [C] a sign at the side of a road that gives information about directions and distances to towns شاخصة، لافتة على جانب طريق المسافرين

Sikh /siːk/ *noun* [C] a member of one of the religions of India (Sikhism) that developed from Hinduism but teaches that there is only one god أحد أفراد طائفة السيخ

▸ **Sikhism** /'siːkɪsm/ *noun* [U] ديانة السيخ

silence /'saɪləns/ *noun* [C,U] **1** [U] complete quietness; no sound: *A loud crash broke the silence.* ○ *There must be silence during examinations.* صمت ، سكون

2 [C] a period when nobody speaks or makes a noise: *There was a silence immediately after the explosion.* ○ *My question was met with an awkward silence.* صمت ، سكوت

3 [U] not making any comments on sth: *I can't understand his silence on the matter.* صمت ، سكوت

IDM **in silence** without talking or making a noise في صمت

▸ **silence** *verb* [T] to make sb/sth be silent or quiet: *He silenced the crowd by raising his hand.* يسكِّت

silencer /'saɪlənsə(r)/ (*US* **muffler**) *noun* [C] **1** the part of a car which reduces the noise made by an exhaust pipe (في السيّارة) خافض أو مخمِدّ الصوت

2 the part of a gun that reduces the noise when it is fired (في المسدّس مثلاً) مخمِّد أو كاتم الصوت

silent /'saɪlənt/ *adj* **1** making no noise; very quiet: *The house was empty and silent.* ساكن، لا صوت فيه

2 not speaking; not using spoken words: *The policeman told her she had the right to remain silent.* ○ *a silent prayer* (= one that is not said out loud) ○ *So far he has remained silent on his future plans.* صامت ، ساكت

3 (of a letter) not pronounced: *The 'b' in 'comb' is silent.* صامت ، غير ملفوظ

▸ **silently** *adv* دونَ صوت ؛ بصمت

silhouette /ˌsɪluˈet/ *noun* [C] the dark outline or black shape of sth seen against a light background شكل ظلّي

▸ **silhouetted** *adj* seen as a silhouette: *the spire of the cathedral, silhouetted against a bright blue sky* ذو شكل ظلّي

silicon /ˈsɪlɪkən/ *noun* [U] (*symbol* **Si**) a substance that exists as a grey solid or as a brown powder and is found in rocks and sand. It is used in making glass. سيليسيوم

ˌ**silicon ˈchip** *noun* [C] a piece of a chemical element (silicon) that is used in computers, etc. رقاقة سيليكون

silicone /ˈsɪlɪkəʊn/ *noun* [U] a chemical containing silicon. There are several different types of silicone, used to make paint, artificial rubber, varnish, etc: *a silicone breast implant* سيليكون

silk /sɪlk/ *noun* [U] the soft smooth cloth that is made from threads produced by an insect (the silkworm): *a silk shirt* حرير

silky /ˈsɪlki/ *adj* (**silkier**; **silkiest**) smooth, soft and shiny; like silk: *silky hair* حريري؛ ناعم كالحرير

sill /sɪl/ *noun* [C] a long thin piece of wood or stone that is at the bottom of a window, either inside or outside: *a window sill* ما يشبه الرَّف عند قاعدة النافذة

silly /ˈsɪli/ *adj* (**sillier**; **silliest**) **1** not showing thought or understanding; foolish: *a silly mistake* ○ *What a silly thing to say!* ○ *Don't be so silly!* سخيف ، أحمق

2 appearing ridiculous, so that people will laugh: *I'm not wearing that hat – I'd look silly in it.* مضحِك

▸ **silliness** *noun* [U] تصرُّفات حمقاء ، سُخْف

silt /sɪlt/ *noun* [U] sand, soil or mud that is carried along by a river and then left somewhere when the river flows more slowly طمي ، غَرين أو غِرْيَن

silver /ˈsɪlvə(r)/ *noun* [U] **1** a valuable grey-white metal that is used for making jewellery, ornaments, coins, etc: *a silver spoon* ○ *That's a nice ring. Is it silver?* فضّة

2 coins made from silver or sth that looks like silver: *Could you change £10 of silver for a £10 note please?* نقود فضيّة

3 objects that are made of silver, e.g. knives, forks, spoons, dishes: *The thieves stole some jewellery and some valuable silver.* فضيّات

▸ **silver** *adj* having the colour of silver: *a silver sports car* فضّي (اللون)

silvery /ˈsɪlvəri/ *adj* having the appearance or colour of silver: *an old lady with silvery hair* ○ *silvery light over the lake* فضّي ؛ شبيه بالفضّة

ˌ**silver ˈjubilee** *noun* [C] the 25th anniversary of an important event اليوبيل الفضّي ، الاحتفال بمرور 25 عاماً على حَدَث معيّن

ˌ**silver ˈmedal** *noun* [C] a small flat round piece of silver that is given to the person or team that comes second in a sports competition: *to win a silver medal at the Olympic Games* ➲ Look at **gold medal** and **bronze medal**. مدالية فضيّة

ˌ**silver ˈmedallist** *noun* [C] a person who wins a silver medal فائز بمدالية فضيّة

ˌ**silver ˈwedding** *noun* [C] the 25th anniversary of a wedding ➲ Look at **golden wedding**. العيد الفضّي للزواج

SIM card /ˈsɪm kɑːd/ *noun* [C] a plastic card inside a mobile phone/cellphone that stores personal information about the person using the phone (SIM is the abbreviation of 'subscriber identification module'.) البطاقة الخاصة (داخل النقّال)

similar /ˈsɪmələ(r)/ *adj* **similar (to sb/sth)** the same in a way or in some ways but not completely the same: *All the books he writes are very similar.* ○ *Your handwriting is very similar to mine.* متشابه ، متماثل ؛ مشابه لـ

▸ **similarly** *adv* also; in a similar way: *The plural of 'shelf' is 'shelves'. Similarly, the plural of 'wolf' is 'wolves'.* كذلك، على نحو مماثل

similarity /ˌsɪməˈlærəti/ *noun* (*pl.* **similarities**) **1** [U] the quality of being similar: *I noticed the similarity in the way the two sisters thought and spoke.* تشابه ، تماثُل

2 [C] a way in which people or things are similar: *Although there are some similarities between the two towns, there are a lot of differences too.* وجه التشابه

simmer /ˈsɪmə(r)/ *verb* [I,T] to cook gently in a liquid that is just below boiling point: *Let the vegetables simmer for a few more minutes.* ○ *Simmer the soup for 30 minutes.* ينطبخ أو يَطبُخ على نار هادئة

simple /ˈsɪmpl/ *adj* **1** easy to understand, do or use; not difficult or complicated: *This dictionary is written in simple English.* ○ *a simple task* ○ *I can't just leave the job. It's not as simple as that.* سهل ؛ بسيط

2 without decoration or unnecessary extra things; plain: *a simple black dress* ○ *The food is simple but perfectly cooked.* بسيط

3 (used about a person or a way of life) natural and uncomplicated: *a simple life in the country* بسيط ، طبيعي

4 unintelligent; slow to understand ساذج ، بطيء الفهم ، بسيط

5 (used for saying that the thing you are talking about is the only thing that is important or true): *I'm not going to buy it for the simple reason that I haven't got enough money.* مجرّد ، محض

▸ **simply** /ˈsɪmpli/ *adv* **1** in a way that makes sth easy to understand: *Could you explain it more simply?* بصورة أسهل ، بشكل أبسط

2 in a plain way; without decoration or unnecessary extra things: *They live simply, with very few luxuries.* ببساطة ؛ دون تنميق

3 (used for emphasis) absolutely; completely: *What a simply marvellous idea!* مطلقاً ، تماماً

4 only; just: *There's no need to get angry. The whole problem is simply a misunderstanding.* مجرّد ، فقط ، ليس إلاّ...

simplicity /sɪmˈplɪsəti/ *noun* [U] **1** the quality of being uncomplicated and easy to understand,

a b c d e f g h i j k l m n o p q r **s** t u v w x y z

do or use: *We all admired the simplicity of the plan.* بساطة ، سهولة

2 the quality of having no decoration or unnecessary extra things; plainness: *I like the simplicity of her paintings.* بساطة ، عدم تنميق

simplify /ˈsɪmplɪfaɪ/ *verb* [T] (*pres part* **simplifying**; *3rd pers sing pres* **simplifies**; *pt, pp* **simplified**) to make sth easier to do or understand; to make sth less complicated: *The process of applying for visas has been simplified.* يبسّط ، يسهّل

▸ **simplification** /ˌsɪmplɪfɪˈkeɪʃn/ *noun* [C,U] تبسيط

simplistic /sɪmˈplɪstɪk/ *adj* making sth that is complicated seem simpler than it really is (تفسير) مفرط في تبسيط الوقائع

simulate /ˈsɪmjuleɪt/ *verb* [T] to create the effect or appearance of sth else: *The astronauts trained in a machine that simulates conditions in space.* يقلّد ، يحاكي ؛ يخلق

▸ **simulation** /ˌsɪmjuˈleɪʃn/ *noun* [C,U] the act of simulating or a simulated form of a real situation, event, etc: *a computer simulation of a nuclear attack* تقليد أو محاكاة : حَدَث مصطنع

simultaneous /ˌsɪmlˈteɪniəs; *US* ˌsaɪm-/ *adj* happening at exactly the same time: *There were simultaneous demonstrations in London, Paris and Rome.* حاصل في نفس الوقت

▸ **simultaneously** *adv* في نفس الوقت ، في آن واحد

sin /sɪn/ *noun* [C,U] an act or way of behaving that breaks a religious law: *He believes it is a sin for two people to live together without being married.* ○ *They confess their sins to the priest every week.* ذنْب ، معصية ، خطيئة ، إثم

▸ **sin** *verb* [I] (sinning; sinned) to do sth that breaks a religious law يذْنب ، يرتكب معصية ، يأثم

sinful /-fl/ *adj* breaking a religious law; immoral أثيم، حرام ؛ فاسق

sinner /ˈsɪnə(r)/ *noun* [C] a person who sins آثم ، خاطئ ، مذنِب

since /sɪns/ *prep* from a particular time in the past until a later time in the past or until now: *It was the first time they'd won since 1974.* ○ *I haven't seen him since last Tuesday.* ○ *Where have you been? I've been waiting for you since 5.30.* ○ *She has had a number of jobs since leaving university.* منذ

> We use both **since** and **for** to talk about how long something has been happening. We use **since** when we are talking about the *beginning* of the period of time, and **for** when we are talking about the *length* of the period of time: *I've known her since 1993.* ○ *I've known her for ten years.*

▸ **since** *conj* **1** from the time when sth happened until a later time in the past or until now: *He hasn't written to us since he arrived in Britain.* ○ *I've been working in a bank ever since I left school.* ○ *It was strange to see my old house again because I hadn't been there since I was a child.* منذ

2 because; as: *Since they've obviously forgotten to phone me, I'll have to phone them.* بما أنّ ، نظراً لـ

since *adv* **1** from a particular time in the past until a later time in the past or until now: *He had come to see us a few weeks earlier but he hadn't been back since.* ○ *We went out for dinner together about six months ago but I haven't seen her since.* ○ *My parents bought this house in 1998 and we've been living here ever since.* منذ ذلك الحين

2 at a time after a particular time in the past: *We were divorced two years ago and she has since married someone else.* ○ *He had left school at the age of 16 and had since got a job in a hotel.* فيما بعد ، بعد ذلك

sincere /sɪnˈsɪə(r)/ *adj* **1** (used about a person) really meaning or believing what you say; honest; not pretending: *Do you think she was being sincere when she said she admired me?* صادق ، مخلص

2 (used about sth that a person says or feels) true; that is really meant: *Please accept our sincere apologies.* ❶ The opposite is **insincere**. خالص

▸ **sincerely** *adv*: *I am sincerely grateful to you for all your help.* ○ *Yours sincerely, ...* (at the end of a formal letter) بصدق ، بإخلاص

sincerity /sɪnˈserəti/ *noun* [U] the quality of being sincere; honesty: *Nobody doubts the sincerity of her political views.* ❶ The opposite is **insincerity**. صدق ، إخلاص

sing /sɪŋ/ *verb* [I,T] (*pt* **sang** /sæŋ/; *pp* **sung** /sʌŋ/) to make musical sounds with the voice: *He always sings when he's in the bath.* ○ *The birds were singing outside my window.* ○ *She sang all her most popular songs at the concert.* يغنّي

▸ **singer** *noun* [C] a person who sings, especially in public مغنٍ

singing *noun* [U] the act of singing: *singing lessons* غناء

singe /sɪndʒ/ *verb* [I,T] (*pres part* **singeing**) to burn or to make sth burn slightly on the edge or tip: *He leaned over the candle and accidentally singed his eyebrows.* يشيّط

single /ˈsɪŋgl/ *adj* **1** (only *before* a noun) only one: *He gave her a single red rose.* ○ *I managed to finish the whole job in a single afternoon.* واحد ، وحيد

2 (only *before* a noun) (used for emphasis when you are thinking about the individual things which together form a group): *You answered every single question correctly. Well done!* تستعمل للتوكيد: (كلّ) واحد (منهم)

3 not married: *Are you married or single?* ○ *a single woman* أعزب أو عزباء

4 (only *before* a noun) for the use of only one person: *I'd like to book a single room, please.* ○ *a single bed* ➲ Look at **double**. لشخص واحد

5 (*also* **one-way**) (only *before* a noun) only to a place, not to a place and back from it (used about a ticket or the cost of a ticket for a journey): *How much is the single fare to Rome, please?* ➲ Look at **return**. (تذكرة) ذهاب فقط

IDM **in single file** → FILE[3]

▸ **single** *noun* **1** [C] a ticket for a journey to a place only, not to a place and back from it: *Two* *singles to Hull, please.* ➲ Look at **return**[2](5). تذكرة ذهاب

2 [C] a bedroom for one person only in a hotel, etc: *The hotel has 25 bedrooms: 10 singles and 15 doubles.* غرفة في فندق لشخص واحد

3 [C] a piece of recorded music, usually popular music, that consists of one song; the tape, CD, etc. that this is recorded onto: *The band releases its new single next week.* ➲ Look at **album**. اسطوانة لأغنية واحدة

4 singles [U, with sing. or pl. verb] a game of tennis, etc. in which one player plays against one other player: *the final of the women's singles.* ➲ Look at **doubles.** مباراة فرديّة (في التنس مثلاً)

single *verb*

PHRV **single sb/sth out (for sth)** to give special attention or treatment to one person or thing from a group: *He singled Sue Taylor out for praise.* يختصّه بِ

singly /ˈsɪŋɡli/ *adv* one by one; individually: *You can buy the tapes either singly or in packs of three.* بالواحد : بشكل افراديّ

ˌsingle-ˈhanded *adj, adv* done by one person, done without help from anybody else: *a single-handed yacht race* فرديّ : دون مساعدة من أحد

ˌsingle-ˈminded *adj* having one clear aim or purpose: *I admired her single-minded determination to win.* عاقد عزمه على هدف معيّن

ˌsingle ˈparent *noun* [C] a parent who looks after his/her child or children alone: *a single-parent family* والد وحيد

singlet /ˈsɪŋɡlət/ *noun* [C] (*Brit*) **1** a piece of clothing for a man, without sleeves, worn under or instead of a shirt قميص تحتاني دون كمّين

2 a similar piece of clothing worn by runners, etc. قميص رياضي دون كمّين

singular /ˈsɪŋɡjələ(r)/ *adj* **1** (*grammar*) in the form that is used for talking about one person or thing only: *'Table' is a singular noun; 'tables' is a plural noun.* مفرد

2 (*formal*) unusual غير عاديّ ، فريد

▸ **singular** *noun* [sing.] (*grammar*) the singular form: *The word 'clothes' has no singular.* ○ *What's the singular of 'people'?* صيغة المفرد

singularly *adv* (*formal*) unusually; particularly: *The government has been singularly unsuccessful in its policy against terrorism.* بصورة غير معتادة : بشكل خاص

sinister /ˈsɪnɪstə(r)/ *adj* making you feel that sth bad will happen; frightening: *a sinister atmosphere* ○ *There's something sinister about him. He frightens me.* مشؤوم ، منذر بشرّ : مرعِب

⚷**sink**[1] /sɪŋk/ *verb* (*pt* **sank** /sæŋk/; *pp* **sunk** /sʌŋk/) **1** [I,T] to go down or make sth go down under the surface or to the bottom of water, etc: *If you throw a stone into water, it sinks.* ○ *The boat sank to the bottom of the sea.* ○ *Three ships were sunk by enemy planes.* ○ *My feet sank into the mud.* يغرَق ، يغوص : يُغرِق

2 [I] to get lower; to fall to a lower position or level: *After a few days the flood water began to sink.* ○ *We watched the sun sink slowly below the horizon.* يهبط ، ينخفض

3 [I] (used about a person) to move or fall to a lower position, usually because you are tired or weak: *I came home very tired and sank into a chair.* يتهالك ، ينهار

4 [I] to decrease in value, number, amount, strength, etc. يهبط ، ينقص ، ينهار

IDM **your heart sinks** → HEART

PHRV **sink in/sink into sth 1** (used about a liquid) to go into sth solid; to be absorbed ينفذ في ؛ يمتص

2 (used about information, an event, an experience, etc.) to be completely understood; to become clear in the mind: *It took a long time for the terrible news to sink in.* يفهم جيّداً ، يتّضح

sink[2] /sɪŋk/ *noun* [C] a basin in a kitchen that is connected to the water supply with pipes and taps and used for washing dishes, vegetables, etc. مغسلة المطبخ

sinus /ˈsaɪnəs/ *noun* [C] (often plural) one of the spaces in the bones of the face that are connected to the nose: *I've got a terrible cold and all my sinuses are blocked.* ○ *a sinus infection* جيب (ج جُيوب)

sip /sɪp/ *verb* [I,T] (sipping; sipped) to drink, taking only a very small amount of liquid into your mouth at a time: *We sat in the sun, sipping lemonade.* يرتشف ، يحتسي

▸ **sip** *noun*: *a sip of water* رشفة

siphon (*also* **syphon**) /ˈsaɪfn/ *verb* [T] **siphon sth into/out of sth; siphon sth off/out** to remove a liquid from a container (or to transfer it from one container to another) through a tube يسحب سائلاً من وعاء بممص أو سيفون

⚷**sir** /sɜː(r)/ *noun* **1** (used as a formal or very polite way of speaking to a man, especially one of higher rank in the armed forces, or a male customer in a restaurant or shop): *You should always address a superior officer as 'sir'.* ○ *I'm afraid we haven't got your size, sir.* ➲ Look at **madam** and **miss.** يا سيّدي

2 Sir, Sirs (used at the beginning of a formal letter to a male person or male people): *Dear Sir...* ○ *Dear Sirs...* ➲ Look at **madam.** تستعمل عند استهلال رسالة رسميّة

3 Sir /sə(r)/ the title that is used in front of the name of a man who has received one of the highest British honours: *Sir Steve Redgrave* "السير" : لقب شرف

siren /ˈsaɪrən/ *noun* [C] a machine that makes a long, loud sound in order to warn people about sth, e.g. on an ambulance, fire engine or police car: *an air-raid siren* صفّارة الإنذار

⚷**sister** /ˈsɪstə(r)/ *noun* [C] **1** a girl or woman who has the same parents as another person: *I've got one brother and two sisters.* ○ *We're sisters.* أخت ، شقيقة

Look at **half-sister** and **stepsister**. In English there is no common word that means 'both brothers and sisters': *Have you got any brothers and sisters?* The word **sibling** is very formal.

2 often **Sister** a senior hospital nurse ممرضة عالية الرتبة

3 Sister a member of certain female religious groups; a nun راهبة

4 a company, organization or ship, etc. that belongs to the same group: *We have a sister company in Japan.* ○ *a sister ship* شقيقة

▸ **sisterly** *adj* of or like a sister: *sisterly love* أُختيّ : كالأخت

'sister-in-law *noun* [C] (*pl.* **sisters-in-law**) **1** the sister of your husband or wife أخت الزوج أو الزوجة

2 the wife of your brother زوجة الأخ

sit /sɪt/ *verb* (*pres part* **sitting**; *pt, pp* **sat** /sæt/) **1** [I] to be in a position on a chair, etc. in which the upper part of your body is upright and your weight is supported at the bottom of your back: *We sat in the garden all afternoon.* ○ *She was sitting on the sofa, talking to her mother.* يجلس ، يقعد

2 [I] **sit (down)** to lower the body into the position of sitting: *Come and sit next to me. I want to talk to you.* يجلس ، يقعد

3 [T] **sit sb (down)** to put sb into a sitting position; make sb sit down: *He picked up his daughter and sat her down on a chair.* ○ *She sat me down and offered me a cup of tea.* يجلس ، يقعد

4 [I] to be in a particular place or position: *The letter sat on the table for several days before anybody opened it.* يبقى ، يقعد

5 [T] (*Brit*) to take an examination: *If I fail, will I be able to sit the exam again?* يقدّم امتحاناً

6 [I] (*formal*) (used about an official group of people) to have a meeting or series of meetings: *Parliament was still sitting at 3 am.* ينعقد

IDM **sit on the fence** to be unwilling to decide between two things يقف محايداً ، يتجنّب الانحياز إلى أحد الطرفين

PHR V **sit about/around** (*informal*) to sit and do nothing active for a period of time: *people sitting around chatting* يجلس لا يعمل شيئاً هامّاً

sit back to relax and not take an active part in what other people are doing: *Sit back and take it easy while I make dinner.* يستريح ، لا يشارك في العمل

sit sth out to stay in a difficult or unpleasant situation until the end, without taking any action يصمد إلى نهاية (جلسة مزعجة)

sit through sth to stay in your seat until sth has finished (especially if it is boring): *I don't think I can sit through another two hours of this film.* يتحمّل ، يبقى إلى نهاية (الحفل)

sit up 1 to move into a sitting position when you have been lying down or leaning back: *Sit up straight or you'll hurt your back!* يجلس (بعد استلقاء) ، يعتدل في جلسته

2 to not go to bed although it is very late: *We sat up all night talking.* يسهر

sitcom /'sɪtkɒm/ (*also formal* **situation comedy**) *noun* [C] (*informal*) situation comedy; a comedy programme on television or radio, based on a number of characters in an amusing situation برنامج هزلي (في التلفزيون مثلاً)

site /saɪt/ *noun* [C] **1** a piece of land that is used or will be used for building on or for another special purpose: *a building site* (= a place where a building is being constructed) ○ *The company is looking for a site for its new offices.* ○ *a caravan site* أرض معدّة للبناء

2 a place where sth happened or existed in the past: *the site of a famous battle between the English and the Scots* مكان ، موقع

▸ **site** *verb* [T] to put or build sth in a particular place: *The new sports centre is to be sited in Church Street.* يقيم ، يبني : يحدّد موقعاً لبناء

sitting /'sɪtɪŋ/ *noun* [C] **1** a period of time during which a meal is served to a number of people, when it is not possible to serve everybody at the same time: *Dinner will be in two sittings.* جلسة

2 a period during which an official group of people meets and does its work جلسة أو اجتماع مجلس

'sitting room *noun* [C] (*especially Brit*) = LIVING ROOM

situated /'sɪtʃueɪtɪd/ *adj* in a particular place or position: *The hotel is conveniently situated close to the beach.* واقع ، قائم

situation /ˌsɪtʃu'eɪʃn/ *noun* [C] **1** the things that are happening in a particular place or at a particular time: *The situation in the north of the country is extremely serious.* ○ *Tim is in a difficult situation at the moment.* ○ *the economic situation* وضع ، حالة

2 the position of a building, town, etc. in relation to the area around it: *The house is in a beautiful situation on the edge of a lake.* موقع

3 (*formal*) a job: *Situations Vacant* (= the part of a newspaper where jobs are advertised) وظيفة ، منصب

ˌsituation 'comedy *noun* [C] (*formal*) = SITCOM

six /sɪks/ *number* 6; one more than five: *The answers are on page six.* ○ *She invited twenty people, but only six came.* ○ *Six (of the pupils) are absent today.* ○ *There are six of us for dinner tonight.* ○ *They have six cats.* ○ *My son is six (years old) next month.* ○ *She lives at 6 Elm Drive.* ○ *a birthday card with a big six on it* ستّة

▸ **six-** (in compounds) having six of the thing mentioned: *a six-day week* ذو ستّة (جوانب مثلاً)

sixth /sɪksθ/ *pron, det, adv* 6th; next after fifth: *I've had five cups of tea already, so this is my sixth.* ○ *This is the sixth time I've tried to phone him.* ○ *Mahler's Sixth Symphony* ○ *George VI* (= George the Sixth) سادس ، السادس

sixth *noun* [C] the fraction ⅙; one of six equal parts of sth سُدْس

sixteen /ˌsɪks'tiːn/ *number* 16; one more than fifteen ❶ For examples of how to use numbers in sentences, look at **six**. ستّة عشر

▸ **sixteenth** /ˌsɪks'tiːnθ/ *pron, det, adv* 16th; next after fifteenth ➲ Look at the examples at **sixth**. سادس عشر ، السادس عشر

ˈsixth form *noun* [C, usually sing., with sing. or pl. verb] (*Brit*) the classes of pupils in the final year(s) of secondary school, usually from the age of 16 to 18 and often studying for A level examinations الفصلان/الصفّان الأخيران في مدرسة ثانويّة

ˈsixth-former *noun* [C] a pupil in the sixth form طالب في السنتين الأخيرتين من الدراسة الثانوية

🔑sixty /ˈsɪksti/ *number* **1** 60; one more than fifty-nine: *Sixty people went to the meeting.* ○ *There are sixty pages in the book.* ○ *He retired at sixty/ when he was sixty.* ستّون

2 the sixties [plural] the numbers, years or temperatures between 60 and 69: *I don't know the exact number of members, but it's in the sixties.* ○ *The most famous pop group of the sixties was The Beatles.* ○ *The temperature tomorrow will be in the high sixties.* الستّينات

IDM in your sixties between the age of 60 and 69: *I'm not sure how old she is but I should think she's in her sixties.* ○ *in your early/mid/late sixties* (في) الستّينات من العمر

▸ **sixtieth** /ˈsɪkstiəθ/ *pron, det, adv* 60th; next after fifty-ninth ➲ Look at the examples at **sixth**. الستّون

🔑size /saɪz/ *noun* **1** [U] the amount by which sth is big or small: *I was surprised at the size of the hotel. It was enormous!* ○ *Their garden is about the same size as ours.* ○ *The planet Uranus is about four times the size of Earth.* حجم : كِبَر

When we ask about the size of something, we usually say, 'How big...?': *How big is your house?* We say, 'What size...?' when we ask about the size of something that is produced in a number of fixed measurements: *What size shoes do you take?*

2 [C] one of a number of fixed measurements in which sth is made: *Have you got this dress in a bigger size?* ○ *What size pizza would you like? Medium or large?* قياس ، مقاس

▸ **size** *verb*

PHRV size sb/sth up to think carefully about sb/sth in order to form an opinion: *She looked at the man in the white suit for a long time, trying to size him up.* يمايزه أو يتفحّصه ليكون رأياً عنه

sizeable (*also* **sizable**) /-əbl/ *adj* quite large: *a sizeable flat* ○ *a sizeable sum of money* كبير ، لا بأس بحجمه

-sized (*also* **-size**) (in compounds) of the size that is mentioned: *a medium-sized flat* ذو حجم (متوسّط)

ˌsize ˈzero *noun* [U,C] (in the US) the smallest size for women's clothes, used to describe women who are extremely thin: *size zero models* ○ *She's a size zero.* (في الولايات المتحدة) المقاس صفر للنساء

sizzle /ˈsɪzl/ *verb* [I] to make the sound of food frying in hot fat: *I could hear the eggs sizzling in the kitchen.* (اللحم المقلي) يئز أو يطش

skate /skeɪt/ *noun* [C] **1** (*also* **ice skate**) a boot with a thick metal blade on the bottom that is used for skating حذاء التزحلق أو التزلّج على الجليد

2 = ROLLER SKATE

ice skates Rollerblades™ roller skates

skateboard

▸ **skate** *verb* [I] **1** (*also* **ice-skate**) to move over ice on skates: *Can you skate?* ○ *They skated across the frozen lake.* ℹ **Go skating** is a common way of talking about skating for pleasure: *We go skating every weekend.* يتزلّج على الجليد

2 = ROLLER-SKATE

skater *noun* [C] a person who skates المتزلّج

skating *noun* **1** (*also* **ice skating**) [U] the activity or sport of moving over ice on skates التزلّج على الجليد

2 = ROLLER SKATING

skateboard /ˈskeɪtbɔːd/ *noun* [C] a narrow board with wheels attached to it that you can stand on and ride دحروجة ، لوح ذو دواليب للتزلّق

▸ **skateboarding** *noun* [U] التزلّق على هذا اللوح

ˈskating rink (*also* **ice rink**; **rink**) *noun* [C] a large area of ice, or a building containing a large area of ice, that is used for skating on حلبة التزلّج

skeleton /ˈskelɪtn/ *noun* [C] the structure formed by all the bones in a human or animal body: *a dinosaur skeleton in the Natural History Museum* ○ *the human skeleton* هيكل عظمي

▸ **skeleton** *adj* (used about an organization, a service, etc.) having the smallest number of people that is necessary for it to operate: *On Sundays, the office is kept open by a skeleton staff.* مقلّص إلى أصغر عدد

skeptic (*US*) = SCEPTIC

sketch /sketʃ/ *noun* [C] **1** a simple, quick drawing without many details: *He drew a rough sketch of the new building on the back of an envelope.* رسم تخطيطيّ ، مخطّط سريع

2 a short description without any details: *a sketch of life in Paris in the 1920s* وصف موجز

3 a short comedy scene, usually part of a television or radio programme فصل أو مشهد كوميديّ قصير

▸ **sketch** *verb* [I,T] to draw a sketch: *I sat on the grass and sketched the castle.* يرسم رسماً تخطيطيّاً سريعاً

sketchy *adj* (**sketchier**; **sketchiest**) not having many or enough details: *He only gave me a sketchy account of the accident.* دون تفاصيل ، إجماليّ أو ناقص

ski /skiː/ *noun* [C] one of a pair of long, flat, narrow pieces of wood, metal or plastic that are fastened to boots and used for moving over snow: *a pair of skis* مزلّج للتزحلق على الثلج

▸ **ski** *verb* [I] (*pres part* **skiing**; *pt, pp* **skied**) to move over snow on skis: *When did you learn to*

a b c d e f g h i j k l m n o p q r s t u v w x y z

ski? ℹ **Go skiing** is a common way of talking about skiing for pleasure: *They go skiing in France every year.* يتزحلق أو يتزلّج على الثلج

ski *adj* connected with skiing: *a ski resort, instructor, etc.* متعلّق بالتزحلق على الثلج

skier /ˈskiːə(r)/ *noun* [C] a person who skis: *a good skier* متزلّج ، متزحلق (على الثلج)

skiing *noun* [U] the activity of moving on skis; the sport of racing on skis رياضة التزلّج على الثلج

skid /skɪd/ *verb* [I] (ski**dd**ing; ski**dd**ed) (used about a vehicle) to be out of control and move or slide sideways on the road: *I skidded on a patch of ice.* يتزحلق ، ينزلق

▸ **skid** *noun*: *The car went into a skid and came off the road.* انزلاق

🔑 **skilful** (*US* **skillful**) /ˈskɪlfl/ *adj* **1** (used about a person) very good at doing sth: *a skilful painter, politician, etc.* ○ *He's very skilful with his hands.* ماهر ، حاذق

2 done very well: *skilful guitar playing* متقَن ، بارع

▸ **skilfully** /-fəli/ *adv*: *The play was skilfully directed by a young student.* ببراعة ؛ بمهارة

🔑 **skill** /skɪl/ *noun* **1** [U] the ability to do sth well, especially because of training, practice, etc: *It takes great skill to make such beautiful jewellery.* ○ *This is an easy game to play. No skill is required.* مهارة ، حذق

2 [C] an ability that is required in order to do a job, an activity, etc. well: *The course will help you to develop your reading and listening skills.* ○ *management skills* ○ *Typing is a skill I have never mastered.* مهارة ، خبرة

▸ **skilled** *adj* **1** (used about a person) having skill; skilful: *a skilled worker* ذو خبرة ، مدرّب ؛ ماهر

2 (used about work, a job etc.) requiring skill or skills; done by people who have been trained: *a highly skilled job* ○ *Skilled work is difficult to find in this area.* متطلّب خبرة ومهارة ؛ ماهر أو ذو خبرة

ℹ The opposite is **unskilled**.

skim /skɪm/ *verb* (ski**mm**ing; ski**mm**ed) **1** [T] to remove sth from the surface of a liquid: *to skim the cream off the milk* يقشد

2 [I,T] to move quickly over a surface, near it but without touching it, or without touching it very often: *The plane flew very low, skimming the tops of the buildings* ○ *I watched a big bird skim across the water.* يمرّ بسرعة قريباً من سطح الشيء، يكاد يلامس

3 [I,T] **skim (through/over) sth** to read sth quickly in order to get the main idea, without paying attention to the details and without reading every word: *I usually just skim through the newspaper in the morning.* يقرأ قراءة سريعة

ˌskimmed ˈmilk *noun* [U] milk from which the cream has been removed حليب (لبن) خالي الدَّسَم

skimp /skɪmp/ *verb* [I,T] **skimp (on sth)** to use or provide less of sth than is necessary يقتصد ، يبخل في ، يقتّر

▸ **skimpy** *adj* (**skimpier**; **skimpiest**) using or having less than is necessary: *a skimpy swimsuit* (= not covering much of the body) شحيح ، غير كاف ، (ثوب) يغطي القليل من الجسم

🔑 **skin** /skɪn/ *noun* [C,U] **1** the natural outer covering of a human or animal body: *to have fair, dark, sensitive, etc. skin* ○ *skin cancer* جلد

2 (often in compounds) the skin of an animal that has been removed from its body and that is often used for making things: *a sheepskin jacket* جلد (الخروف مثلاً)

3 the natural outer covering of some fruits or vegetables; the outer covering of a sausage: *a banana skin* ➲ Look at the note at **rind**. قشرة

4 the thin solid surface that can form on a liquid: *A skin had formed on top of the milk.* قشدة على سطح سائل

IDM **by the skin of your teeth** (*informal*) (used about a successful action) only just; with very little time, space etc. to spare: *I ran into the airport and caught the plane by the skin of my teeth.* بالكاد ، بمعجزة ، في آخر لحظة

have a thick skin → THICK[1]

▸ **skin** *verb* [T] (ski**nn**ing; ski**nn**ed) to remove the skin from sth يسلخ ؛ يقشر

skinny *adj* (skinnier; skinniest) (*informal*) (used about a person) too thin ➲ Look at the note at **thin**. هزيل ، نحيل

skinhead /ˈskɪnhed/ *noun* [C] a young person with shaved or extremely short hair. Skinheads are often associated with violent behaviour. شابّ حليق الرأس

skintight /skɪnˈtaɪt/ *adj* (used about a piece of clothing) fitting very tightly and showing the shape of the body ضيّق جداً

skip[1] /skɪp/ *verb* (ski**pp**ing; ski**pp**ed) **1** [I] to move along quickly and lightly in a way that is similar to dancing, with little jumps and steps, from one foot to the other: *A little girl came skipping along the road.* يقفز بخفّة ، يتنطّط

2 [I] to jump over a rope that you or two other people hold at each end, turning it round and round over the head and under the feet ينطّ فوق الحبل

3 [T] to not go to sth that you should go to; to not have sth that you should have: *I skipped my French class today and went swimming.* ○ *I got up rather late, so I skipped breakfast.* يتغيّب عن ؛ يفوّت

4 [T] (used about part of a book, story, etc.) to miss sth out; to not read or talk about sth and move to the next part: *I think I'll skip the next chapter. It looks really boring.* يتخطّى ، يتجاوز ، يهمل

▸ **skip** *noun* [C] a skipping movement قفزة ، نطّة

skip[2] /skɪp/ *noun* [C] a very large, open metal container for rubbish, often used during building work قادوس معدني كبير لحمل الأنقاض

skipper /ˈskɪpə(r)/ *noun* [C] (*informal*) the captain of a boat or ship, or of a sports team ربّان سفينة ؛ رئيس فريق رياضي

ˈskipping rope *noun* [C] a rope, often with handles at each end, that is used for skipping حَبْل النطّ

skirmish /ˈskɜːmɪʃ/ *noun* [C] a small fight or battle مناوشة

skirt /skɜːt/ *noun* [C] a piece of clothing that is worn by women and girls and that hangs down from the waist: *a short skirt* تنورة ، "جونلة"
▸ **skirt** *verb* [I,T] to go around the edge of sth يحيط بـ ، يسير محاذياً الحافة

PHR V **skirt round sth** to avoid talking about sth directly: *The manager skirted round the subject of our pay increase.* يتجنّب موضوعاً

skittle /ˈskɪtl/ *noun* **1** [C] a wooden object in the shape of a bottle that is used as one of the targets in the game of skittles قنّينة خشبيّة للّعب
2 skittles [U] a game in which players try to knock down as many skittles as possible by throwing or rolling a ball at them لعبة القناني الخشبيّة

skive /skaɪv/ *verb* [I] (*Brit slang*) **skive (off)** to avoid work, especially by staying away from the place of work or leaving it without permission when you should be working: *I don't think he was ill – he was skiving.* يتغيّب عن عمله (مدّعياً المرض مثلاً)

skulk /skʌlk/ *verb* [I] to stay somewhere quietly and secretly, hoping that nobody will notice you, usually because you are planning to do sth bad: *a strange man skulking behind a tree* يتربّص ، يختبئ منتظراً الفرصة

skull /skʌl/ *noun* [C] the bone structure of a human or animal head: *a fractured skull* جمجمة

sky /skaɪ/ *noun* [C,U] (*pl.* **skies**) the space that you can see when you look up from the earth, and where you can see the sun, moon and stars: *a clear blue sky* ○ *I saw a bit of blue sky between the clouds.* السّماء

We usually talk about **the sky**: *I saw a plane high up in the sky.* ○ *The sky's gone very dark. I think it's going to rain.* However, when **sky** follows an adjective, we usually use **a**/**an**: *a cloudless sky* or sometimes the plural form **skies**: *cloudless skies*

skydiving /ˈskaɪdaɪvɪŋ/ *noun* [U] a sport in which you jump from a plane and fall for as long as you safely can before opening your parachute القفز الحّر بالمظلّة

ˌsky-ˈhigh *adj, adv* very high مرتفع جداً ؛ عالياً جداً ، إلى السماء

skyline /ˈskaɪlaɪn/ *noun* [C] the shape that is made by tall buildings, etc. against the sky: *the Manhattan skyline* خطّ الأفق حيث تظهر أمامه أشكال الأبنية وغيرها

skyscraper /ˈskaɪskreɪpə(r)/ *noun* [C] a very tall building ناطحة سحاب

slab /slæb/ *noun* [C] a thick, flat piece of sth: *huge concrete slabs* لوح سميك ، بلاطة

slack /slæk/ *adj* **1** loose; not tightly stretched: *Leave the rope slack.* رخو ، مرتخ
2 (used about a period of business) not busy; not having many customers or much activity: *Trade is very slack here in winter.* راكد ، فاتر
3 not carefully or properly done: *Slack security made terrorist attacks possible.* متراخ ، غير محكم
4 (used about a person) not doing your work carefully or properly: *You've been rather slack about your homework lately.* مهمل

slacken /ˈslækən/ *verb* [I,T] **1** to become or make sth less tight: *The rope slackened and he pulled his hand free.* ○ *After a while she slackened her grip on my arm.* يرتخي ؛ يرخي
2 slacken (sth) (off) to become or make sth slower or less active: *Industrial production has slackened off in recent months.* ○ *His pace slackened towards the end of the race.* يتباطأ، يفتر ؛ يُبطئ أو يضعف

slacks /slæks/ *noun* [plural] (*old-fashioned*) trousers (especially not very formal ones): *a pair of slacks* بنطلون

slag heap /ˈslæg hiːp/ *noun* [C] a hill made of the waste material that remains when metal has been removed from rock كومة خَبَث معدنيّ

slain *pp* of SLAY

slalom /ˈslɑːləm/ *noun* [C] a race (in skiing, canoeing, etc.) along a course on which competitors have to move from side to side between poles سباق متعرّج (في التزلّج مثلاً)

slam /slæm/ *verb* (slam**m**ing; slam**m**ed) **1** [I,T] to shut or make sth shut very loudly and with great force: *I heard the front door slam.* ○ *She slammed her book shut and rushed out of the room.* يغلق بعنف ، يصفق
2 [T] to put sth somewhere very quickly and with great force: *He slammed my letter on the table and stormed out.* ➲ Look at **grand slam**. يرمي بعنف ، "يخبط"

slander /ˈslɑːndə(r); *US* ˈslæn-/ *noun* [C,U] an untrue spoken statement about sb that is intended to damage the good opinion that other people have of him/her; the crime of making this kind of statement: *If you repeat that in public I shall take legal action for slander.* افتراء ، تشويه سمعة ؛ تشهير
▸ **slander** *verb* [T] يفتري (على) ، يشوّه سمعته؛ يشهّر به

slang /slæŋ/ *noun* [U] very informal words and expressions that are more common in spoken language. Slang is sometimes used only by a particular group of people (e.g. schoolchildren, soldiers) and often stays in fashion for a short time. Some slang is not polite: *'Phat' is a slang word for 'good'.* لغة عاميّة ، لغة خاصّة (بالجنود مثلاً)

slant /slɑːnt; *US* slænt/ *verb* **1** [I,T] to lean or make sth lean in a particular direction; to be not straight: *My handwriting slants backwards.* يميل ؛ يميل
2 [T] (usually passive) to describe information, events, etc. in a way that supports a particular group or opinion: *All the political articles in that newspaper are slanted towards the government.* يحرّف ، يميل نحو

▸ **slant** *noun* **1** [sing.] a position that leans in a particular direction ميْل : منحدر

2 [C] a way of thinking about sth, especially one that supports a particular group or opinion: *There is a left-wing slant to all his writing.* ميْل

slanting *adj* leaning in a particular direction; not straight مائل : منحرف

slap /slæp/ *verb* [T] (slap**p**ing; slap**p**ed) **1** to hit sb/sth with the inside of your hand: *She slapped him across the face.* ○ *to slap sb on the back* (= to congratulate him/her) يصفع ، يلطم

2 to put sth onto a surface quickly and carelessly: *to slap some paint onto a wall* يضع بسرعة ودون عناية ، "يلطخ" أو "يلطس"

▸ **slap** *noun*: *I gave him a slap across the face.* صفعة ، لطمة

slap (*also* ˌ**slap-'bang**) *adv* (*informal*) **1** directly and with great force: *I hurried round the corner and walked slap into someone coming the other way.* (يرتطم) مواجهةً وبعنف

2 exactly; right: *The phone rang slap-bang in the middle of my favourite programme.* تماماً ، بالضبط ، "في عزّ"...

slapdash /'slæpdæʃ/ *adj* careless, or done quickly and carelessly: *slapdash building methods* (عمل) سريع غير متقن، "مطصلق"

slapstick /'slæpstɪk/ *noun* [U] a type of comedy that is based on simple jokes, e.g. people falling over or hitting each other مشاهد هزليّة صبيانيّة

'slap-up *adj* (*Brit informal*) (used about a meal) very large and very good (وجبة) كبيرة فاخرة

slash /slæʃ/ *verb* **1** [I,T] **slash (at) sb/sth** to make, or to try to make, a long cut in sth with a violent action: *Several cars have had their tyres slashed in that car park.* يشرط ، يشق

2 [T] to reduce an amount of money, etc. very much: *The price of coffee has been slashed by about 20%.* يخفّض تخفيضاً كبيراً

slat /slæt/ *noun* [C] one of the long narrow pieces of wood, metal or plastic in a cupboard door, venetian blind, etc. صفيحة طويلة ضيقة من الخشب مثلاً

slate /sleɪt/ *noun* **1** [U] a type of dark grey rock that can easily be split into thin flat pieces الأردواز

2 [C] one of the thin flat pieces of slate that are used for covering roofs واحد من ألواح الأردواز التي تغطي السقوف

slaughter /'slɔːtə(r)/ *verb* [T] **1** to kill an animal, usually for food يذبح ، ينحر

2 to kill a large number of people at one time, especially in a cruel way or when they cannot defend themselves: *Men, women and children were slaughtered and whole villages destroyed.* ➲ Look at the note at **kill**. يقتل (بوحشيّة) عدداً من الناس

▸ **slaughter** *noun*: *the slaughter of innocent people during the war* قتْل

slaughterhouse /'slɔːtəhaʊs/ (*also* **abattoir**) *noun* [C] the place where animals are killed for food مسلَخ ، مذبَح

Slav /slɑːv/ *noun* [C] a member of any of the peoples of Central and Eastern Europe who speak Slavic languages السلافي

▸ **Slavic** /'slɑːvɪk/ (*especially Brit* **Slavonic** /slə'vɒnɪk/) *adj* connected with Slavs or their languages, which include Russian, Polish and Czech سلافي

slave /sleɪv/ *noun* [C] (in past times) a person who was owned by another person and had to work for that person عبد ، رقيق

▸ **slave** *verb* [I] **slave (away)** to work very hard يكدح ، يشتغل كالعبد

slavery /'sleɪvəri/ *noun* [U] **1** the system of having slaves: *the abolition of slavery in America* عبوديّة ، امتلاك العبيد

2 the situation of being a slave: *The two boys were captured and sold into slavery.* رقّ ، عبوديّة

slay /sleɪ/ *verb* [T] (*pt* **slew** /sluː/; *pp* **slain** /sleɪn/) to kill violently; to murder: *Many young soldiers were slain in the battle.* ❶ **Slay** is very old-fashioned in British English but is more common in American English. يقتل بوحشيّة : يقتل

sleazy /'sliːzi/ *adj* (**sleazier**; **sleaziest**) (often used about a place) dirty, in poor condition and having an immoral or criminal atmosphere: *a sleazy nightclub* (ناد) قذر رخيص ومشبوه

sledge /sledʒ/ (*US also* **sled** /sled/) *noun* [C] a vehicle without wheels that is used for travelling on snow. You can slide down a hill on a small sledge. Large sledges are often pulled by dogs. ➲ Look at **sleigh** and **toboggan**. زحّافة (على الثلج)

▸ **sledge** *verb* [I] to go down hills on a sledge ينزلق على الثلج راكباً زحّافة

sledgehammer /'sledʒhæmə(r)/ *noun* [C] a large, heavy hammer with a long handle مرزبّة، مطرقة ثقيلة

sleek /sliːk/ *adj* **1** (used about hair or fur) smooth and shiny because it is healthy (شعر) أملس لامع

2 (used about a vehicle) having an elegant, smooth shape: *a sleek new sports car* (سيّارة) أنيقة انسيابيّة الشكل

🔑**sleep**[1] /sliːp/ *noun* **1** [U] the natural condition of rest when your eyes are closed and your mind and body are not active or conscious: *Most people need about eight hours' sleep every night.* ○ *I didn't get much sleep last night.* ○ *Do you ever talk in your sleep?* نوم

2 [sing.] a period of sleep: *You'll feel better after a good night's sleep.* نوم ، نومة

IDM **get to sleep** to succeed in sleeping: *I couldn't get to sleep last night.* ينام ، يغفو

go to sleep 1 to start sleeping; to enter the state of sleep: *He got into bed and soon went to sleep.* ○ *Go to sleep. Everything will seem better in the morning.* ينام ، يغفو

2 (used about an arm, leg, etc.) to lose the sense of feeling in it ينمَل، يخدَر

put (an animal) to sleep to kill an animal that is ill or injured because you want to stop it suffering يميت حيواناً (تخفيفاً عنه مثلاً)

▶ **sleeplessness** *adj* (used about a period, usually the night) without sleep (ليلة) أرقة لا نوم فيها

sleeplessness *noun* [U] ➲ Look at **insomnia.** أرَق ، سهاد

⚷ **sleep²** /sliːp/ *verb* (*pt, pp* **slept** /slept/) **1** [I] to be in a state of sleep for a period of time: *Did you sleep well last night?* ○ *I only slept for a couple of hours last night.* ينام

> We use **to sleep** for talking about sleeping in general, but we use **to be asleep** to talk about being in the state of sleep when something else happens: *I was asleep when the telephone rang.* We use **to go to sleep** to talk about starting to sleep. (NOT: *I slept at ten o'clock last night* but: *I went to sleep at ten o'clock last night.*)

2 [T] (used about a place) to have enough beds for a particular number of people: *an apartment that sleeps four people* يتّسع لـ

IDM **sleep rough** to sleep outside, usually because you have no home ينام في العراء أو أينما كان

PHR V **sleep in** to sleep until later than usual in the morning because you do not have to get up ينام إلى وقت متأخّر

sleep together; **sleep with sb** to have sex with sb (especially sb you are not married to): *Do you think she's slept with him?* يضاجع

sleeper /ˈsliːpə(r)/ *noun* [C] **1** (with an adjective) a person who sleeps in a particular way. If you are a light sleeper you wake up easily: *a light/heavy sleeper* النائم ، شخص ينام نوماً (خفيفاً مثلاً)

2 a bed on a train; a train with beds: *I've booked a sleeper on the night train.* سرير في قطار ؛ عربة نوم في قطار

ˈ**sleeping bag** *noun* [C] a large soft bag that you use for sleeping in when you go camping, etc. كيس النوم ، لحاف على هيئة كيس

ˈ**sleeping pill** *noun* [C] a pill that helps you to sleep حبة منوِّمة

sleepwalk /ˈsliːpwɔːk/ *verb* [I] to walk around while you are asleep يمشي في نومه

sleepy /ˈsliːpi/ *adj* (**sleepier**; **sleepiest**) **1** tired and ready to go to sleep: *These pills might make you feel a bit sleepy.* نعسان

2 (used about a place) very quiet and not having much activity: *a sleepy little village* ناعس ؛ فاتر النشاط

▶ **sleepily** /-ɪli/ *adv* بفتور ونعاس

sleet /sliːt/ *noun* [U] a mixture of rain and snow ➲ Look at the note at **weather**. مزيج من المطر والثلج

⚷ **sleeve** /sliːv/ *noun* [C] one of the two parts of a piece of clothing that cover the arms or part of the arms: *a blouse with long sleeves* كُمّ ، رُدْن

▶ **-sleeved** (in compounds) with sleeves of a particular kind: *a short-sleeved shirt* ذو أكمام (قصيرة مثلاً)

sleeveless *adj* without sleeves دون أكمام

sleigh /sleɪ/ *noun* [C] a vehicle that is used for travelling on snow and that is usually pulled by horses ➲ Look at **sledge**. عربة تجرّها الخيول على الثلج

slender /ˈslendə(r)/ *adj* **1** (used about a person or part of sb's body) thin in an attractive way: *long slender fingers* أهيف ، رشيق ؛ دقيق

2 smaller in amount or size than you would like: *My chances of winning are very slender.* ضئيل ، هزيل

slept *pt, pp of* SLEEP²

slew *pt of* SLAY

⚷ **slice** /slaɪs/ *noun* [C] **1** a flat piece of food that is cut from a larger piece: *a thick/thin slice of bread* شريحة

2 a part of sth: *The directors had taken a large slice of the profits.* حصّة ، قِسم

▶ **slice** *verb* **1** [T] to cut into slices: *Peel and slice the apples.* ○ *thinly sliced bread* يشرِّح ، يقطِّع إلى شرائح

2 [I,T] to cut through or into sth: *He sliced through the rope with a knife.* يحزّ

slick¹ /slɪk/ *adj* **1** done smoothly and well, and seeming to be done without any effort: *The actors gave a slick, highly professional performance.* سَلِس ، مصقول ، بارع

2 clever at persuading people but perhaps not completely honest: *slick advertising* ماهر في الإقناع ، ماكر ، خلّاب

slick² /slɪk/ *noun* [C] = OIL SLICK

⚷ **slide¹** /slaɪd/ *verb* (*pt, pp* **slid** /slɪd/) **1** [I,T] to move or make sth move smoothly along a surface: *She fell over and slid along the ice.* ○ *A large drop of rain slid down the window.* ○ *'Here you are,' he said, sliding the keys across the table.* ○ *a sliding door* (= one that you open by sliding it to one side) ينزلق ؛ يزلق

2 [I,T] to move or make sth move quietly without being noticed: *I slid out of the room when nobody was looking.* ○ *She slid her hand into her pocket and took out a gun.* ينسلّ ؛ يدسّ

3 [I] (used about prices, values, etc.) to go down slowly and continuously: *The pound is sliding against the dollar.* يتدهور تدريجياً

slide² /slaɪd/ *noun* [C] **1** a small piece of photographic film in a plastic or cardboard frame صورة فوتوغرافية شفّافة

> If you shine light through a slide using a **projector** you can make the photograph appear on a **screen**.

2 a small piece of glass that you put sth on when you want to examine it under a microscope الشريحة (الزجاجيّة) المنزلقة

3 a long piece of metal, etc. that children use for sliding down, (e.g. in a playground) زحليقة أو زحلوقة

4 a continuous slow movement down (e.g. of prices, values, levels, etc.): *a slide in the value of the pound* تدهور تدريجيّ ؛ انزلاق

⚷ **slight** /slaɪt/ *adj* **1** very small; not important or serious: *I've got a slight problem, but it's nothing to get worried about.* ○ *a slight change, difference, increase, improvement, etc.* ○ *I haven't the slight-*

est idea (= no idea at all) *what you're talking about.* طفيف ، صغير : تافه

2 (used about a person's body) thin and delicate: *his slight figure* نحيف ، رقيق البنية

IDM not in the slightest not at all: *'Are you angry with me?' 'Not in the slightest.'* لا، أبداً!

▸ **slightly** *adv* a little: *I'm slightly older than her.* قليلاً ، بقليل

slim /slɪm/ *adj* (slimmer; slimmest) **1** thin in an attractive way: *a tall, slim woman* ➲ Look at the note at **thin**. أهيف ، ممشوق ، نحيف

2 not as big as you would like: *Her chances of success are very slim.* ضئيل ، قليل : هزيل

▸ **slim** *verb* [I] (slimming; slimmed) to become or try to become thinner and lighter by eating less food, taking exercise, etc: *'Another piece of cake?' 'No thanks. I'm slimming.'* ➲ Look at **diet**. ينحف : ينحّف نفسه ، يحاول تخفيف وزنه

slime /slaɪm/ *noun* [U] a thick, unpleasant, sticky liquid: *The pond was covered with slime and had a horrible smell.* سائل لزج مقرف

▸ **slimy** /ˈslaɪmi/ *adj* (**slimier**; **slimiest**) **1** covered with slime مغطّى بمادة لزجة زَلِقة

2 (used about a person) very friendly, but in a way that you do not trust or like وَدود بطريقة متزلّفة

sling¹ /slɪŋ/ *noun* [C] a piece of cloth that you put under your arm and tie around your neck to support a broken arm, wrist, etc. حمالة الذراع (المكسورة مثلاً)

sling² /slɪŋ/ *verb* [T] (*pt, pp* **slung**) **1** to put or throw sth somewhere in a rough or careless way: *Don't just sling your clothes on the floor!* يطرح ، يرمي

2 to put sth into a position where it hangs loosely: *She was carrying her bag slung over her shoulder.* يدلّي ، يعلّق

slink /slɪŋk/ *verb* [I] (*pt, pp* **slunk**) to move somewhere slowly and quietly because you do not want anyone to look at you, often when you feel guilty, embarrassed or ashamed ينسلّ ، يملص

slip¹ /slɪp/ *verb* (slipping; slipped) **1** [I] **slip (on sth)** to slide accidentally, lose your balance and fall or nearly fall: *Don't slip on that floor. I've just washed it.* ○ *His foot slipped on the step and he fell down.* يتزحلق ، ينزلق ، يزل

2 [I] to slide accidentally out of the correct position or out of sb's hand: *This hat's too big. It keeps slipping down over my eyes.* ○ *The glass slipped out of my hand and smashed on the floor.* ○ (*figurative*) *I didn't intend to tell them. It just slipped out.* ينزلق : يزِلّ أو يزلق لسانه

3 [I] to move or go somewhere quietly, quickly, and often without being noticed: *While everyone was dancing we slipped away and went home.* ينسلّ ، يملص

4 [T] **slip sth (to sb)**; **slip (sb) sth** to put sth somewhere or give sth quietly and often without being noticed: *She picked up the money and slipped it into her pocket.* يدسّ

5 [I,T] **slip into/out of sth; slip sth on/off** to put on or take off a piece of clothing quickly and easily: *I'm just going to slip into something cooler.* ○ *I slipped off my shoes.* يلبس أو يخلع بخفّة

6 [I] to fall a little (in value, level, etc.): *Sales have been slipping slightly over the last few months.* يهبط قليلاً

IDM let sth slip to tell a secret, some information, etc. without intending to: *He let slip that he had been in prison.* يزلّ لسانه

slip your mind to be forgotten: *I'm sorry, the meeting completely slipped my mind.* يغيب عن ذهنه

PHR V slip up (*informal*) to make a mistake: *I'm afraid somebody must have slipped up. Your name isn't on the list.* يخطئ، يرتكب غلطة

slip² /slɪp/ *noun* [C] **1** an act of slipping (1) زلقة

2 a small mistake: *to make a slip* زلّة ، هفوة

3 a small piece of paper: *I made a note of her name on a slip of paper.* قصاصة ورق

4 a piece of clothing with no sleeves that is worn by a woman under a dress or skirt شلحة (سوريا) ، "كمَبنزون" : تنّورة داخليّة

IDM give sb the slip (*informal*) to escape from sb who is following or chasing you يفلت أو يملص منه

ˌslipped ˈdisc *noun* [C] one of the discs of the spine (in a person's back) that has moved out of its correct position, causing pain انزلاق فقرة

slipper /ˈslɪpə(r)/ *noun* [C] a light, soft shoe that is worn in the house: *a pair of slippers* "شبشب" ، "شحّاطة"، "بابوج"

slippery /ˈslɪpəri/ *adj* (used about a surface or an object) difficult to move over or hold because it is smooth, wet, greasy, etc: *a slippery floor* ○ *The fish was cold and slippery.* زلق

ˈslip road *noun* [C] a road that leads onto or off a motorway طريق جانبي يتّصل بالطريق السريع (الأوتوستراد)

slit /slɪt/ *noun* [C] a long, narrow cut or opening: *We could see into the room through a slit in the curtains.* شق، شرْط

▸ **slit** *verb* [T] (**slitting**; *pt, pp* **slit**) to make a long, narrow cut in sth: *She slit the envelope open with a knife.* ○ *He slit his wrists in a suicide attempt.* يشقّ ، يشرط

slither /ˈslɪðə(r)/ *verb* [I] to slide along in an unsteady or twisting way: *I slithered along the pavement in the snow and ice.* ○ *I saw a snake slithering down a rock.* يتزلّق مترنّحاً : يتلوّى زاحفاً كالحيّة

sliver /ˈslɪvə(r)/ *noun* [C] a small, thin or narrow piece of sth cut or broken off from a larger piece: *slivers of wood* ○ *Please cut me a small sliver of cheese.* شريحة رقيقة: قطعة صغيرة

slob /slɒb/ *noun* [C] (*informal*) (used as an insult) a very lazy or untidy person خمولٌ زريّ الهيئة

slog /slɒg/ *verb* [I] (slogging; slogged) **1 slog (away) at sth** (*informal*) to work hard for a long period at sth difficult or boring: *I've been slogging away at this homework for hours.* يكدّ ويكدح (في عمل مملّ)

2 slog down, up, along, etc. to walk or move

in a certain direction with a lot of effort: *Part of their training involves slogging up and down hills with packs on their backs.* يمشي متحاملاً على نفسه

▶ **slog** *noun* [sing.] a period of long, hard, boring work or a long, tiring journey عمل أو مشي طويل مُضْنٍ

slogan /ˈsləʊɡən/ *noun* [C] a short phrase that is easy to remember and that is used in politics or advertising: *Anti-government slogans had been painted all over the walls.* ○ *'Faster than light' is the advertising slogan for the new car.* شعار ، نداء

slop /slɒp/ *verb* (slo**pp**ing; slo**pp**ed) **1** [I] (used about a liquid) to spill over the edge of its container: *He filled his glass too full and water slopped onto the table.* يندلق ، ينسكب

2 [T] to cause a liquid to do this يدلق ، "يكبكب"

⚿ **slope** /sləʊp/ *noun* **1** [C] a piece of land that goes up or down: *We walked down a slope and came to the river.* ○ *a steep/gentle slope* ○ *ski slopes* منحدر

2 [sing.] the amount that a surface is not level; the fact of not being level: *a slope of 20 degrees* ○ *The slope of the pitch makes it quite difficult to play on.* انحدار

▶ **slope** *verb* [I] to not be level or upright; to have a slope (2): *The road slopes down to the river.* ○ *a sloping roof* ينحدر ، يميل

sloppy /ˈslɒpi/ *adj* (**sloppier**; **sloppiest**) **1** (used about a piece of work, etc.) not done carefully, tidily or thoroughly غير متقَن

2 (used about a person) careless or untidy: *a sloppy worker* عديم العناية بعمله أو بهندامه

3 showing emotions in a silly way; sentimental: *I can't stand sloppy love songs.* مفرط في العاطفيّة

slosh /slɒʃ/ *verb* (*informal*) **1** [I] (used about a liquid) to move around noisily inside a container: *The water sloshed around in the bucket.* يتخضْخَض

2 [T] to put liquid somewhere in a careless and untidy way: *Careful! You're sloshing water all over the floor!* يرشّ أو يرشرش

slot /slɒt/ *noun* [C] **1** a long, straight, narrow opening in a machine, etc: *Put your money into the slot and take the ticket.* فتحة ضيقة (للنقود) في آلة

2 a place in a timetable, system, organization, etc: *Oxford students have been given a new half-hour slot on our local radio station.* حيّز ، حصّة

▶ **slot** *verb* [I,T] (slo**tt**ing; slo**tt**ed) to fit into a particular space: *He slotted a tape into the VCR.* يدخل في حيّز معين

ˈ**slot machine** *noun* [C] a machine that sells drinks, cigarettes, etc. or on which you can play games. You work it by putting money into a slot. آلة تعمل بإسقاط قطعة نقود فيها

slouch /slaʊtʃ/ *verb* [I] to sit, stand or walk in a lazy way, with your head and shoulders hanging down يجلس متراخياً: يقف أو يمشي مطأطئ الرأس

slovenly /ˈslʌvnli/ *adj* lazy, careless and untidy عديم العناية بنفسه وبعمله

⚿ **slow¹** /sləʊ/ *adj* **1** moving, doing sth or happening without much speed; not fast: *The traffic is always very slow in the city centre.* ○ *Haven't you finished your homework yet? You're being very slow!* ○ *a slow improvement in his condition* بطيء

2 slow to do sth; slow (in/about) doing sth not doing sth immediately: *Jane was slow to react to the news.* ○ *They've been rather slow in replying to my letter!* متوانٍ ، متأخّر

3 not busy, lively or exciting: *Business is very slow at the moment.* فاتر ، راكد

4 not quick to learn or understand: *I'm afraid I don't understand what you mean. I must be a bit slow.* ○ *a slow learner* بليد ، بطيء الفهم

5 showing a time that is earlier than the real time: *That clock is five minutes slow* (= it says it is 8.55 when the correct time is 9.00). مؤخّر أو متأخّر

IDM **quick/slow on the uptake** → UPTAKE

▶ **slowly** *adv* at a slow speed; not quickly: *He walked slowly along the street.* ببطء ، على مَهْل

slowness *noun* [U] بطء ؛ تَمهُّل

slow² /sləʊ/ *adv* at a slow speed; slowly ببطء ، على مهل

> It is possible to use **slow** as an adverb, but **slowly** is much more common. However, **slow** is often used in compounds: *slow-moving traffic.* The comparative forms **slower** and **more slowly** are both common: *Could you drive a bit slower/more slowly, please?*

slow³ /sləʊ/ *verb* [I,T] to start to move, do sth or happen at a slower speed; to cause sth to do this: *Jane ran along the path for a few minutes and then slowed to a walk.* يبطئ ، يتمهّل ؛ يُبطِئ

PHR V **slow (sb/sth) down/up** to start to move, do sth or happen at a slower speed; to cause sth to do this: *Can't you slow down a bit? You're driving much too fast.* ○ *These problems have slowed up the whole process.* يبطئ، يتمهّل ؛ يبطِئ ، يؤخِّر

slow ˈmotion *noun* [U] (in a film or on television) a method of making action appear much slower than in real life: *They showed the winning goal again, this time in slow motion.* عرض لقطة سينمائيّة بصورة مبطّأة

sludge /slʌdʒ/ *noun* [U] thick, soft mud وحل ؛ رسابة مياه المجارير

slug /slʌɡ/ *noun* [C] a small animal like a snail without a shell. Slugs have long, slimy bodies, move slowly along the ground and eat plants. بزّاقة

sluggish /ˈslʌɡɪʃ/ *adj* slow-moving; not lively: *This hot weather is making me feel very sluggish.* ○ *sluggish economic growth* قليل الهمّة ، خَمول ؛ بطيء الحركة

slum /slʌm/ *noun* [C] (*also* **the slums** [plural]) an area of a city where living conditions are extremely bad, and where the buildings are dirty and have not been repaired for a long time حيّ فقير قذر مكتظّ بالسكّان

slumber /ˈslʌmbə(r)/ *verb* [I] (*old-fashioned*) to be asleep; to sleep peacefully ينام ؛ يرقد
▶ **slumber** *noun* [C] (*old-fashioned*) sleep: *The princess fell into a deep slumber.* نوم ، سبات

slump /slʌmp/ *verb* [I] **1** to fall or sit down suddenly when your body feels heavy and weak, usually because you are tired or ill: *Her face went very white, and then suddenly she slumped over the table.* يتهاوى ، يتهالك ، يخرّ
2 (used about trade, prices, the value of sth, etc.) to fall suddenly and by a large amount: *The shares slumped 33p to 181p yesterday.* يهبط هبوطاً مفاجئاً
▶ **slump** *noun* [C] **1** a sudden large fall in trade, the value of sth, etc: *a slump in house prices* هبوط كبير مفاجئ
2 a period when a country's economy is doing very badly and there is a lot of unemployment فترة ركود اقتصاديّ

slung *pt, pp* of SLING

slunk *pt, pp* of SLINK

slur /slɜː(r)/ *verb* [T] (slurring; slurred) to speak words in a way that is not clear, often because you are drunk يلفظ بعدم وضوح (لسكْرِه)
▶ **slur** *noun* [C] **a slur (on sb/sth)** a false statement or an insult that could damage sb's reputation: *The suggestion that our teachers are racist is a slur on the good name of the school.* إفتراء ؛ إهانة ، وصمة عار

slurp /slɜːp/ *verb* [I,T] (*informal*) to drink noisily يحتسي بصوت مسموع ، يشفط

slush /slʌʃ/ *noun* [U] snow that has partly melted and that is often watery and dirty ثلج مائع وسخ
▶ **slushy** *adj* (**slushier**; **slushiest**) **1** covered in melting snow: *slushy roads* (رصيف) مغطى بالثلج المائع الوسخ
2 romantic or sentimental in a silly way: *a slushy love song* عاطفي سخيف

slut /slʌt/ *noun* [C] a sexually immoral woman; a very lazy and untidy woman ❶ This word is used as a very strong insult. إمراة فاسقة إو ماجنة ؛ إمراة كسول وَسِخة

sly /slaɪ/ *adj* **1** (used about a person) good at deceiving people or doing things in secret مكّار ؛ دسّاس
2 (used about an action) suggesting that you know sth secret: *a sly smile* ماكر ، خبيث
▶ **slyly** *adv* خلسةً

smack¹ /smæk/ *verb* [T] to hit sb/sth with the inside of your hand: *I never smack my children.* يصفع
▶ **smack** *noun* [C] an act of smacking صفعة

smack² /smæk/ *verb*
PHR V **smack of sth** to make you think that sb/sth has an unpleasant attitude or quality: *Her remarks about your new car smacked of envy.* ينمّ عن ؛ يشتَم منه

🔑 **small** /smɔːl/ *adj* **1** not large in size, number, amount, etc: *a small car, flat, town, etc.* ○ *a small group of people* ○ *a small amount of money* صغير ؛ قليل
2 young: *He has a wife and three small children.* ○ *When I was small we lived in a big old house.* صغير السن
3 not important or serious; slight: *Don't worry. It's only a small problem.* طفيف ، تافه

> **Small** is the most usual opposite of **big** or **large**. **Little** is often used with another adjective to express an emotion, as well as the idea of smallness: *a horrible little man* ○ *a lovely little girl* ○ *a nice little house*. The comparative and superlative forms **smaller** and **smallest** are common, and small is often used with words like 'rather', 'quite' and 'very': *My flat is smaller than yours.* ○ *The village is quite small.* ○ *a very small car*. **Little** is not often used with these words and does not usually have a comparative or superlative form.

▶ **small** *adv* in a small size: *You can fit it all in if you write small.* بحجم صغير

ˈsmall ads *noun* [plural] (*Brit informal*) = CLASSIFIED ADVERTISEMENTS

ˌsmall ˈchange *noun* [U] coins that have a low value قطع نقود قليلة القيمة

ˈsmall hours *noun* [plural] the early morning hours soon after midnight: *We sat up into the small hours discussing the problem.* الهزيع الأخير من الليل

smallpox /ˈsmɔːlpɒks/ *noun* [U] a serious infectious disease that causes a high fever and leaves marks on the skin. In the past many people died from smallpox. الجدري

ˌsmall ˈprint *noun* [U] a part or parts of a legal contract, document, etc. that contain important details that you might not notice: *Make sure you read the small print before you sign anything.* ما يكتب بأحرف صغيرة في وثيقة هامّة

ˌsmall-ˈscale *adj* (used about an organization or activity) not large; limited in what it does: *a small-scale business* صغير ، محدود الإمكانات

ˈsmall talk *noun* [U] polite conversation, e.g. at a party, about unimportant things at social events محادثة للمجاملة

🔑 **smart¹** /smɑːt/ *adj* **1** (used about a person) clean, tidy and well dressed; wearing formal or fairly formal clothes: *You look smart. Are you going somewhere special?* أنيق ، حسن الهندام
2 (used about a piece of clothing, etc.) clean, tidy and new-looking: *a smart suit* أنيق
3 fashionable and usually expensive: *a smart restaurant* راقٍ ، فخم
4 (*especially US*) clever; able to think quickly: *He's not smart enough to be a politician.* ذكيّ ، سريع البديهة
5 (used about a movement or action) quick: *They set off at a smart pace.* سريع ، حثيث
▶ **smarten** /ˈsmɑːtn/ *verb*
PHR V **smarten (yourself/sb/sth) up** to make yourself, sb or sth look smarter يهندِم ؛ يتأنّق

smartly *adv* in a smart way: *She's always smartly dressed.* بأناقة ، بهندام حسن

smart² /smɑːt/ *verb* [I] to feel a stinging pain in your body: *The smoke made her eyes smart.* ○ (*figurative*) *He was still smarting from her insult.* يشعر بألم لاذع : يعاني أو يتألّم

ˈ**smart card** *noun* [C] a plastic card, for example a credit card, on which information can be stored in electronic form "البطاقة الذكية"

smartphone /ˈsmɑːtfəʊn/ *noun* [C] a mobile phone that also has some of the functions of a computer الهاتف الذكي

smash /smæʃ/ *verb* **1** [I,T] **smash sth (up)**; **smash sth open** to break violently into many pieces: *The glass smashed into a thousand pieces.* ○ *The police had to smash the door open.* يتكسّر ، يتحطّم : يكسّر ، يحطّم

2 [T] **smash sth (up)** to crash sth (a car, etc.), usually causing a lot of damage: *I smashed up my father's car.* يحطّم ، يخرّب

3 smash (sth) against, into, through, etc. [I,T] to move with great force in a particular direction: *The car smashed into a tree.* ○ *He smashed his hand through the window.* يندفع ، يصطدم : يضرب بعنف

4 [T] (in tennis) to hit a ball that is high in the air down and over the net, making it travel very fast يكبس: يضرب كرة التنس بشدة وهي في الهواء

▸ **smash** *noun* **1** [sing.] an act or the noise of sth breaking violently: *I heard the smash of breaking glass.* تكسُّر ، تهشّم : صوت التهشّم

2 [C] (*also* ˈ**smash-up**) a car crash حادث اصطدام

3 [C] (in tennis) a way of hitting a ball that is high in the air down and over the net, making it travel very fast كبسة

4 [C] (*also* ˌ**smash** ˈ**hit**) (*informal*) a song, play, film, etc. that is very successful أغنية مثلاً تنجح نجاحاً هائلاً

smashing *adj* (*Brit informal old-fashioned*) extremely good; wonderful: *We had a smashing time at the party.* رائع ، ممتع للغاية

smear /smɪə(r)/ *verb* [T] **smear sth on/over sth/sb**; **smear sth/sb with sth** to spread a sticky substance across sth/sb: *The child had smeared chocolate over his clothes.* ○ *Her face was smeared with grease.* يدهن ، يمسح : يلطّخ

▸ **smear** *noun* [C] **1** a mark made by smearing: *a smear of paint on her dress* لطخة

2 something untrue that is said in a newspaper, etc. about an important person: *He was the victim of a smear campaign.* تشويه سمعة ، افتراء

smell¹ /smel/ *noun* **1** [U] the ability to smell: *Dogs have a very good sense of smell.* حاسّة الشمّ

2 [C] the impression that you get of sth by using your nose; the thing that is smelled: *What's that smell?* ○ *There's a smell of gas.* ○ *a strong smell* رائحة

> **Stink**, **stench**, **odour** and **pong** are all words for unpleasant smells. **Aroma**, **fragrance**, **perfume** and **scent** refer to pleasant smells.

3 [usually sing.] an act of smelling: *Have a smell of this milk; is it all right?* شمّة : شمّ

▸ **smelly** *adj* (**smellier**; **smelliest**) (*informal*) having a bad smell: *smelly feet* ذو رائحة كريهة

smell² /smel/ *verb* (*pt, pp* **smelt** /smelt/ or **smelled**) **1** [T] to notice, identify or examine sb/sth by using your nose: *He could smell something burning.* ○ *Can you smell gas?* يشمّ : يشتمّ

2 [I] to be able to smell: *I can't smell properly because I've got a cold.* يشمّ

3 [I] **smell (of sth)** to have a particular smell: *Dinner smells good!* ○ *This perfume smells of roses.* يفوح منه

4 [I] to have a bad smell: *Your feet smell.* تفوح منه رائحة كريهة

> We do not use **smell** or other verbs of the senses (e.g. **taste**, **see**, **hear**) with the continuous tense. Instead we often use **can**, e.g: *I can smell smoke.*

smile /smaɪl/ *noun* [C] an expression on your face in which the corners of your mouth turn up, showing happiness, pleasure, etc: *to have a smile on your face* ○ *'It's nice to see you,' he said with a smile.* ➲ Look at **beam**, **grin** and **smirk**. ابتسامة

▸ **smile** *verb* **1** [I] **smile (at sb/sth)** to have or give a smile: *She smiled at the camera.* ○ *He was smiling with happiness.* يبتسم

2 [T] to express sth by means of a smile: *I smiled a greeting to them.* يعبّر عن شيء بابتسامة

smiley /ˈsmaɪli:/ *noun* [C] **1** a simple picture of a smiling face that is drawn as a circle with two eyes and a curved mouth رسم لوجه مبتسم

2 a simple picture or series of keyboard symbols :-) that represents a smiling face. The symbols are used, for example, in email or text messages to show that the person sending the message is pleased or joking. رمز يمثل الوجه المبتسم

smirk /smɜːk/ *noun* [C] a silly or unpleasant smile which you have when you are pleased with yourself or think you are very clever ابتسامة غرور

▸ **smirk** *verb* [I] يبتسم بغرور

smock /smɒk/ *noun* [C] a type of long, loose, comfortable shirt ثوب فضفاض

smog /smɒg/ *noun* [U] a mixture of fog and smoke, caused by pollution, that is in the air over some industrial cities ضباب ممزوج بدخان المدن

smoke¹ /sməʊk/ *noun* **1** [U] the gas that you can see in the air when something is burning: *Thick smoke poured from the chimney.* ○ *a room full of cigarette smoke* دخان

2 [C, usually sing.] (*informal*) an act of smoking a cigarette, etc: *He went outside for a quick smoke.* تدخين سيجارة

smoke² /sməʊk/ *verb* **1** [I,T] to breathe in smoke through a cigarette, etc. and let it out again; to have the habit of smoking cigarettes, etc: *Do you mind if I smoke?* ○ *I used to smoke 20 cigarettes a day.* يدخّن

2 [I] to give out smoke: *The factory chimneys were smoking.* ينفث أو يطلق دخاناً

▶ **smoked** *adj* (used of certain types of food) preserved and given a special taste by being hung in smoke: *smoked salmon* مدخَّن

smoker *noun* [C] a person who smokes cigarettes, etc: *She's a chain smoker* (= she finishes one cigarette and then immediately lights another). ❶ The opposite is **non-smoker**. مدخِّن

smoking *noun* [U] the act or habit of smoking cigarettes, etc: *My doctor has advised me to give up smoking.* التدخين

smoky *adj* (**smokier**; **smokiest**) **1** full of smoke; producing a lot of smoke: *a smoky room* ○ *a smoky fire* مليء بالدخان : (مدفأة) مدخِّنة

2 with the smell, taste or appearance of smoke: *This cheese has a smoky flavour.* دخانيّ

smolder (*US*) = SMOULDER

smooth[1] /smuːð/ *adj* **1** having a flat surface with no lumps or holes: *smooth skin* ○ *a smooth piece of wood* أملس ، ناعم

2 (of a liquid mixture) without lumps: *Stir the sauce until it is smooth.* (مزيج) متجانس ناعم

3 (of a journey in a car, etc.) with an even, comfortable movement: *You get a very smooth ride in this car.* مريح ، منساب

4 without difficulties: *The transition from the old method to the new has been very smooth.* سهل ، دون عقبات

5 too pleasant or polite to be trusted ❶ We use this word in a critical way, usually about a man. ملِق ، مفرط في الظرف

IDM **take the rough with the smooth** → ROUGH[3]

▶ **smoothly** *adv* without any difficulty: *My work has been going quite smoothly.* بسهولة ، دون أي صعوبات

smoothness *noun* [U] نعومة ، ملاسة

smooth[2] /smuːð/ *verb* [T] **smooth sth (away, back, down, out, etc.)** to move your hands in the direction mentioned over the surface of sth to make it smooth: *She smoothed her hair away from her face.* ○ *I smoothed the tablecloth out.* يملّس

smoothie /ˈsmuːði/ *noun* **1** [C] a man who dresses well and talks very politely and confidently but who is often not honest or sincere: *I wouldn't trust that smoothie if I were you.* ○ *He's a real smoothie.* رجل معسول اللسان، مصقول

2 a drink made of fruit or fruit juice mixed with milk or ice cream: *a banana smoothie* شراب من الفاكهة والحليب أو ما شابهه

smother /ˈsmʌðə(r)/ *verb* [T] **1** to kill sb by not allowing him/her to breathe: *She was smothered with a pillow.* يكتم أنفاسه ، يخنق

2 to cover sth (with too much of a substance): *He smothered his cake with cream.* يغرقه بِ

3 to stop sth burning by covering it: *to smother the flames with a blanket* يخمد

4 to hide a feeling, etc: *She managed to smother a yawn.* يكتم

smoulder (*US* **smolder**) /ˈsməʊldə(r)/ *verb* [I] to burn slowly without a flame: *a cigarette smouldering in the ashtray.* ○ (*figurative*) *Her eyes were smouldering with rage.* يحترق ببطء دون لهب : يتّقد (من الغضب)

SMS /ˌes em ˈes/ *noun* **1** [U] a system for sending short written messages from one mobile phone to another (the abbreviation for 'short message service') المراسلة التلفونية

2 [C] a message sent by SMS رسالة تلفونية مكتوبة

▶ **SMS** *verb* [T] to send a message to sb by SMS: *He SMSed me every day.* ○ *If you have any comments, just email or SMS.* ○ *She spends her time chatting and SMSing.* يراسل بالتلفون

smudge /smʌdʒ/ *noun* [C] a dirty or untidy mark: *The child's homework was covered in smudges of ink.* لطخة ، لوثة

▶ **smudge** *verb* **1** [T] to make sth dirty or untidy by touching it: *Leave your painting to dry or you'll smudge it.* "يلَغْمِط" ، يلطّخ

2 [I] to become untidy, without a clean line around it: *Her lipstick smudged when she kissed him.* "يتَلغْمَط" ، تزول خطوطه الخارجية

smug /smʌg/ *adj* (**smugger**; **smuggest**) too pleased with yourself: *Don't look so smug.* ❶ We use this word in a critical way. مغتبط أو معتدّ بنفسه

▶ **smugly** *adv* باعتداد ، مسروراً من نفسه

smugness *noun* [U] اعتداد بالنفس

smuggle /ˈsmʌgl/ *verb* [T] to take things into or out of a country in a way which is against the law; to take a person into or out of a place in secret: *The drugs had been smuggled through customs.* ○ *The refugees were smuggled across the border.* يهرِّب

▶ **smuggler** /ˈsmʌglə(r)/ *noun*: *a drug smuggler* مهرِّب

smuggling /ˈsmʌglɪŋ/ *noun* [U] تهريب

snack /snæk/ *noun* [C] a small meal that you eat quickly between main meals: *I had a snack on the train.* وجبة خفيفة

▶ **snack** *verb* [I] (*informal*) to eat a snack instead of a meal or between meals: *I snacked on a chocolate bar instead of having lunch.* يتناول وجبة خفيفة

ˈ**snack bar** *noun* [C] a type of small café where you can buy a snack مقهى تقدِّم وجبات خفيفة

snag[1] /snæg/ *noun* [C] a small difficulty or disadvantage that is often unexpected or hidden: *His offer is very generous – are you sure there isn't a snag?* عقبة غير متوقّعة : مشكلة خفيّة

snag[2] /snæg/ *verb* [T] (snag**g**ing; snag**g**ed) to catch a piece of clothing, etc. on sth sharp and tear it (ثوبه) يعلق بشيء حادّ ويتمزّق

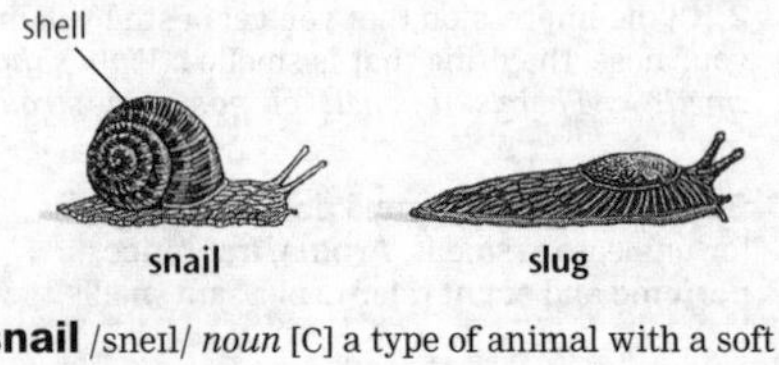

snail /sneɪl/ *noun* [C] a type of animal with a soft

body without legs that is covered by a shell. Snails move very slowly. حلزونة

ˈ**snail mail** *noun* [U] (*informal*) used by people who use email to describe the system of sending letters by ordinary post البريد العادي (عكس الالكتروني)

snake /sneɪk/ *noun* [C] a type of long, thin animal without legs that slides along the ground by moving its body from side to side: *a poisonous snake* ○ *a snakebite* أفعى ، حيّة

▸ **snake** *verb* [I] (*also* **snake its way**) to move like a snake: *The road snakes its way through mountain villages.* يتلوّى

snap¹ /snæp/ *verb* (sna**pp**ing; sna**pp**ed) **1** [I,T] to break suddenly with a sharp noise: *The branch snapped.* ○ *The weight of the snow snapped the branch in two.* ○ (*figurative*) *Suddenly something just snapped and I lost my temper with him.* ينقصف أو ينقصم : يقصف أو يقصم

2 [I,T] to close quickly with a sharp noise: *The lid of the box snapped shut.* ينغلق فجأة محدثاً صوتاً حاداً

3 [I,T] to speak or say sth in a quick angry way: *Why do you always snap at me?* يخاطب بحدة وغضب

4 [I,T] to try to bite sb/sth: *The dog snapped at the child's hand.* ينهش

5 [T] (*informal*) to take a quick photograph of sb/sth يلتقط صورة

IDM **snap your fingers** to make a sharp noise by moving your middle finger quickly against your thumb, especially when you want to attract sb's attention يفرقع بأصابعه

PHR V **snap sth up** to buy or take sth quickly, especially because it is very cheap يتلقّف : تتخاطفه الأيدي

snap² /snæp/ *noun* **1** [C] an act or the sound of snapping: *The piece of wood broke with a snap.* انقصاف أو انقصام : طقّة

2 [C] (*also* **snapshot** /ˈsnæpʃɒt/) a photograph that is taken quickly and informally: *I showed them some holiday snaps.* لقطة أو صورة فوتوغرافية

3 [U] (*Brit*) a type of card game where players call out 'Snap' when two cards that are the same are put down by different players لعبة من ألعاب الورق

▸ **snap** *adj* (*informal*) done quickly and suddenly, often without much careful thought: *a snap decision* خاطف ؛ سريع ودون رويّة

snap *interj* (*Brit*) said when two similar things appear together: *We've got the same skirt on. Snap!* (تقال عند تصادف شيئين متماثلين)

snare /sneə(r)/ *noun* [C] a trap used to catch birds or small animals فخّ ، مصيدة ، شَرَك

▸ **snare** *verb* [T] يوقعه في الفخ أو في الشرَك

snarl /snɑːl/ *verb* [I,T] (used about an animal) to make an angry sound while showing the teeth: *The dog snarled at the stranger.* ○ (*figurative*) *'Get out of here!' he snarled.* يزمجر مكشّراً عن أنيابه

▸ **snarl** *noun* [C, usually sing.] زمجرة

snatch /snætʃ/ *verb* **1** [I,T] to (try to) take or pull sth/sb away quickly: *It's rude to snatch.* ○ *He snatched the gun from her hand.* ○ *My bag was snatched* (= stolen). ○ (*figurative*) *The team snatched a 2-1 victory.* ➲ Look at **grab**. It is similar in meaning. يختطف ، ينتزع

2 [T] to take or get sth quickly when you have just enough time to do so: *I managed to snatch some sleep on the train.* يسترق ، يختلس

PHR V **snatch at sth** to (try to) take hold of sth eagerly: *to snatch at somebody's hand* ○ (*figurative*) *We snatched at every moment we could be together.* يقبض على : ينتهز فرصة

▸ **snatch** *noun* **1** [sing.] an act of snatching (1) at sth: *I made a snatch at the ball.* اختطاف ، انتزاع : خطفة

2 [C, usually pl.] a short part or period of something: *I heard snatches of conversation from the next room.* نُتفة، مقطع قصير

sneak /sniːk/ *verb* **1** [I] **sneak into, out of, past, etc. sth; sneak in, out, away, etc.** to go very quietly in the direction mentioned, so that no one can see or hear you: *Instead of working, he sneaked out to play football.* ○ *The prisoner sneaked past the guards.* ينسلّ ، يتسلّل

2 [T] (*informal*) to take sth secretly or without permission: *She sneaked a chocolate when no one was looking.* يختلس

PHR V **sneak up (on sb/sth)** to approach sb/sth very quietly, especially so that you can surprise him/her/it يقترب منه خلسة

▸ **sneak** *noun* [C] (*informal*) a person who tells an official or a person in authority about the bad things sb has done ℹ This word is used in a critical way. واش ، مخبر "فتّان"

sneaking *adj* (of feelings, etc.) not expressed; secret: *I've a sneaking suspicion that he's lying.* خفي

sneaker /ˈsniːkə(r)/ *noun* [C] (*US*) = TRAINER: *a pair of sneakers*

sneer /snɪə(r)/ *verb* [I] **1** to smile unpleasantly with one side of your mouth raised to show that you dislike sb/sth يبتسم باستخفاف ، يكشّر

2 **sneer (at sb/sth)** to behave or speak as if sth is not good enough for you: *She sneered at his attempts to speak French.* يسخر من

▸ **sneer** *noun* [C] an unpleasant smile or remark ابتسامة أو عبارة استهزاء

sneeze /sniːz/ *noun* [C] a sudden burst of air coming out through your nose and mouth that happens, for example, when you have a cold: *He gave a loud sneeze.* عطسة

▸ **sneeze** *verb* [I] to give a sneeze: *Dust makes me sneeze.* يعطس

snide /snaɪd/ *adj* (of an expression or remark) critical in an unpleasant way (تعليق) لئيم، لاذع

sniff /snɪf/ *verb* **1** [I] to breathe air in through the nose in a way that makes a sound, especially because you have a cold or you are crying: *Stop sniffing and blow your nose.* ينشق

2 [I,T] **sniff (at) sth** to smell sth by sniffing: *'I can smell gas,' he said, sniffing the air.* ○ *The dog sniffed at the bone.* يشمّ ، يتشمّم

▸ **sniff** *noun* [C] an act or the sound of sniffing شمّة : نشقة

sniffle /ˈsnɪfl/ *verb* [I] to sniff continuously, especially because you have a cold or you are crying ينشق باستمرار (بسبب الزكام مثلاً) ، ينخر

snigger /ˈsnɪɡə(r)/ *verb* [I] **snigger (at sb/sth)** to laugh quietly to yourself in an unpleasant way: *They sniggered at his old clothes.* يضحك ضحكة مكتومة ساخرة

▶ **snigger** *noun* [C] ضحكة مكتومة ساخرة

snip[1] /snɪp/ *verb* [I,T] (snipping; snipped) to cut using scissors, with a short quick action يقصّ شيئاً بخفة وسرعة

snip[2] /snɪp/ *noun* [C] **1** a small cut قُصاصة

2 (*Brit informal*) something that is surprisingly cheap: *It's a snip at only £25!* "لقطة"، شروة موفّقة

snippet /ˈsnɪpɪt/ *noun* [C] a small piece of sth, especially information or news نتفة ، نبذة ؛ قُصاصة

snivel /ˈsnɪvl/ *verb* [I] (snivelling; snivelled; *US* sniveling; sniveled) to keep crying in a way that is annoying يبكي وينشق دون توقف

snob /snɒb/ *noun* [C] a person who thinks he/she is better than sb of a lower social class and who admires people who have a high social position متعجرف ، متكبِّر : متشبّه بالأكابر

▶ **snobbery** /ˈsnɒbəri/ *noun* [U] behaviour or attitudes that are typical of a snob تعجرف ، تكبّر؛ تشبّه بالأكابر

snobbish *adj* of or like a snob متعجرف ، شامخ الأنف

snobbishly *adv* بتكبّر مزيّف

snobbishness *noun* [U] تكبّر ، تفاخر بالأصل

snog /snɒɡ/ *verb* (snogging; snogged) [I, T] (*Brit informal*) (used about a couple) to kiss each other for a long period of time قبلة طويلة

snooker /ˈsnuːkə(r)/ *noun* [U] a game in which two players try to hit a number of coloured balls into pockets at the edges of a large table using a long stick (cue): *to play snooker* ➲ Look at **billiards.** لعبة تشبه البلياردو

snoop /snuːp/ *verb* [I] to look around secretly and without permission in order to find out information, etc: *If I catch you snooping around here again, I'll call the police!* يتشمّم حوله ، "يتجسّس"

snooty /ˈsnuːti/ *adj* (**snootier**; **snootiest**) (*informal*) acting in a rude way because you think you are better than other people متعجرف ، شامخ الأنف

snooze /snuːz/ *verb* [I] (*informal*) to have a short sleep, especially during the day يأخذ غفوة أثناء النهار

▶ **snooze** *noun* [C]: *I had a bit of a snooze on the train.* ➲ Look at **nap.** غفوة ، نومة قصيرة

snore /snɔː(r)/ *verb* [I] to breathe noisily through your nose and mouth while you are asleep: *She heard her father snoring in the next room.* يشخر ، يغطّ

▶ **snore** *noun* [C] شخير ، غطيط

snorkel /ˈsnɔːkl/ *noun* [C] a short tube that a swimmer who is just below the surface of the water can use to breathe through ❶ We use **go snorkelling** to talk about swimming like this. انبوب التنفّس (للسبّاح)

snort /snɔːt/ *verb* [I] **1** (used about animals) to make a noise by blowing air through the nose: *The horse snorted in fear.* ينخر ، يزنخر

2 (used about people) to do this as a way of showing that you do not like sth, or that you are impatient ينخر (تعبيراً عن الضجر وغيره)

▶ **snort** *noun* [C] زنخرة ، شخرة

snot /snɒt/ *noun* [U] (*informal*) the liquid produced by the nose مخاط الأنف

snout /snaʊt/ *noun* [C] the long nose of certain animals: *a pig's snout* خطم أو فنطيسة

⚷ **snow**[1] /snəʊ/ *noun* [U] small, soft, white pieces of frozen water that fall from the sky in cold weather: *Three inches of snow fell during the night.* ○ *The snow melted before it could settle* (= stay on the ground). ➲ Look at the note at **weather.** ثلج

⚷ **snow**[2] /snəʊ/ *verb* [I] (used of snow) to fall from the sky: *It snowed all night.* يسقط الثلج ، تثلج

▶ ˌ**snowed ˈin** *adj* not able to leave home or travel because the snow is too deep محصور في بيته (بسبب الثلوج)

ˌ**snowed ˈunder** *adj* with more work, etc. than you can deal with غارق في الأشغال ، مشلول الحركة لكثرة المتطلّبات

snowy *adj* (**snowier**; **snowiest**) with a lot of snow: *snowy weather* ○ *a snowy scene* مكسو بالثلج : كثير الثلج

snowball /ˈsnəʊbɔːl/ *noun* [C] a lump of snow that is pressed into the shape of a ball and used by children for playing كرة ثلج

▶ **snowball** *verb* [I] to quickly grow bigger and bigger or more and more important: *Business has just snowballed so that we can hardly keep up with demand.* يكبر ، يتزايد في الحجم أو القيمة

snowboard /ˈsnəʊbɔːd/ *noun* [C] a type of board that you fasten to both your feet and use for moving down mountains that are covered with snow لوح التزلّج

▶ **snowboarding** *noun* [U]: *Have you ever been snowboarding?* التزلج باستخدام هذا اللوح

snowdrift /ˈsnəʊdrɪft/ *noun* [C] a deep pile of snow that has been made by the wind ركام ثلجيّ كدّسته الرياح

snowdrop /ˈsnəʊdrɒp/ *noun* [C] a type of small white flower that appears at the end of winter زهرة اللبن الثلجيّة

snowfall /ˈsnəʊfɔːl/ *noun* **1** [C] the snow that falls on one occasion: *heavy snowfalls* الثلج الهاطل ، سقوط الثلج

2 [U] the amount of snow that falls in a particular place: *What is the average snowfall in Scotland?* كميّة الثلج

snowflake /ˈsnəʊfleɪk/ *noun* [C] one of the small, soft, white pieces of frozen water that fall together as snow ندفة ثلج

snowman /ˈsnəʊmæn/ *noun* [C] (*pl.* **snowmen**) /-men/ the figure of a person made out of snow, usually by children تمثال من الثلج

snowplough (*US* **snowplow**) /ˈsnəʊplaʊ/ *noun* [C] a type of vehicle that is used to clear snow away from roads or railways جرّافة أو كاسحة ثلج

Snr (*Brit*) *abbrev* = SENIOR

snub /snʌb/ *verb* (snu**bb**ing; snu**bb**ed) [T] to treat sb rudely, e.g. by refusing to look at or speak to him/her: *She snubbed them by not inviting them to the party.* ينتهر ، يصد بجفاء
▶ **snub** *noun*: *When they weren't invited to the party, they felt it was a snub.* صد، استهانة ، خساّة

snuff /snʌf/ *noun* [U] tobacco which people breathe up into the nose in the form of a powder: *to take a pinch of snuff* سعوط ، نشوق ، عاطوس

snuffle /ˈsnʌfl/ *verb* [I] (used of people and animals) to make a noise through your nose: *The dog snuffled around the lamp post.* ينشق بصوت مسموع ، ينخر

snug /snʌɡ/ *adj* (**snugger**; **snuggest**) warm and comfortable: *a snug little room* ○ *The children were snug in bed.* مستكنّ ، دافئ ومريح
▶ **snugly** *adv* **1** warmly and comfortably: *The baby was wrapped snugly in a blanket.* بدفء وراحة ، مستكناً
2 tidily and tightly: *The present fitted snugly into the box.* بكل راحة ؛ بإحكام

snuggle /ˈsnʌɡl/ *verb* [I] **snuggle (up to sb)**; **snuggle (up/down)** to get into a position that makes you feel safe, warm and comfortable, usually next to another person: *She snuggled up to her mother.* ○ *I snuggled down under the blanket to get warm.* يلتصق (بأمّه) التماساً للدفء أو الحماية

so¹ /səʊ/ *adv* **1** (used to emphasize an adjective or adverb, especially when there is a particular result) to the extent (that); to a great degree: *She's so ill (that) she can't get out of bed.* ○ *He was driving so fast that he couldn't stop.* ○ *I haven't enjoyed myself so much for years.* ○ *So many people came to the concert that some couldn't get in.* ➲ Look at the note at **such**. جداً ، إلى حدّ أنّ ...
2 (used in negative sentences for comparing people or things): *She's not so clever as we thought.* بهذا القدر ، إلى هذا الحدّ...
3 very: *You've been so kind. How can I thank you?* جداً
4 (used in place of something that has been said already, to avoid repeating it): *Are you coming by plane? If so,* (= if you are coming by plane) *I can meet you at the airport.* ○ *'I failed, didn't I?' 'I'm afraid so, Susan.'* ذلك ؛ كذلك ، هكذا

> In formal language, you can refer to actions that somebody has mentioned using **do** with **so**: *He asked me to write to him and I did so* (I wrote to him).

5 (not with verbs in the negative) also, too: *He's a teacher and so is his wife.* ○ *'I've been to New York.' 'So have I.'* ○ *I like singing and so does Helen.* ❶ For negative sentences, look at **neither**. أيضاً
6 (used to show that you agree that sth is true, especially when you are surprised): *'It's getting late.' 'So it is. We'd better go.'* حقّاً!! ، يا للغرابة، هذا صحيح!
7 (*formal*) (used when you are showing sb sth) in this way: *Raise your right hand, so.* هكذا
IDM **and so on (and so forth)** (used at the end of a list to show that it continues in the same way): *They sell pens, pencils, paper and so on.* وما إليه ، ونحو ذلك
I told you so (used to tell sb that he/she should have listened to your advice): *'I missed the bus.' 'I told you so. I said you needed to leave earlier.'* لقد قلت لك ذلك!
it (just) so happens (used to introduce a surprising fact) by chance: *It just so happened that we were going the same way, so he gave me a lift.* مصادفةً ، بالصدفة
just so → JUST²
or so (used to show that a number, time, etc. is not exact): *A hundred or so people came to the meeting.* نحو ذلك ، حوالى ذلك
so as to do sth with the intention of doing sth; in order to do sth: *We went early so as to get good seats.* كي ، حتى
so much for (used for expressing that sth is finished or not helpful): *So much for that diet! I didn't lose any weight at all.* لا فائدة منه ، "كلام فاضي"
that is so (*formal*) that is true: *'Mr Jones, you were in Lincoln on May 14. Is that so?' 'That is so.'* هذا صحيح

so² /səʊ/ *conj* **1** with the result that; therefore: *She felt very tired so she went to bed early.* لذلك
2 so (that) with the purpose that; in order that: *She wore dark glasses so that nobody would recognize her.* كي ، لكي ، حتّى
3 (used to show how one part of a story follows another): *So that's how I first met your mother.* وهكذا ، وعلى هذا النحو
IDM **so what?** (*informal*) (showing that you think sth is not important) Why should I care?: *'It's late.' 'So what? We don't have to go to school tomorrow.'* غير مهم! ، "وإيه يعني!"

soak /səʊk/ *verb* **1** [I,T] to become or make sth completely wet: *Leave the dishes to soak for a while.* ○ *I'm going to soak these trousers in hot water to get the stain out.* ينتقع ؛ ينقع
2 [I] **soak into/through sth**; **soak in** (used about a liquid) to pass into or through sth: *Blood had soaked through the bandage.* ينفذ إلى ، يتسرّب، يتفشى
PHRV **soak sth up** to draw sth in (especially a liquid): *I soaked the water up with a cloth.* ○ (*figurative*) *She loves to lie on a beach, soaking up the sunshine.* يمتص ، يتشرّب ؛ يتنعّم بِ
▶ **soaked** /səʊkt/ *adj* (not before a noun) extremely wet: *I got soaked waiting for my bus in the rain.* مبلّل جداً ، مغرق بالماء
soaking /ˈsəʊkɪŋ/ (*also* ˌ**soaking** ˈ**wet**) *adj* extremely wet مبلّل جداً ، يقطر ماءً

ˈ**so-and-so** *noun* [C] (*pl.* **so-and-so's**) (*informal*) **1** a person who is not named: *Imagine a Mrs So-and-so telephones. What would you say?* فلان
2 a person that you do not like: *He's a bad-tempered old so-and-so.* لئيم ، ابن كلب

soap /səʊp/ *noun* [U] a substance that you use for washing and cleaning: *He washed his hands with* *soap.* ○ *a bar of soap* ○ *soap powder* (= for washing clothes) صابون

▸ **soapy** *adj* full of soap: *Wash in plenty of warm soapy water.* كثير الصابون

ˈsoap opera (*also informal* **soap**) *noun* [C] a story about the lives and problems of a group of people which continues every day or several times a week on television or radio مسلسل تلفزيوني أو إذاعي للتسلية

soar /sɔː(r)/ *verb* [I] **1** to fly high in the air: *There were sea birds soaring overhead.* يحلِّق

2 to rise very fast: *The plane soared into the air.* ○ (*figurative*) *Prices are soaring because of inflation.* يحلِّق ، يرتفع : يرتفع ارتفاعاً هائلاً

sob /sɒb/ *verb* [I] (so**bb**ing; so**bb**ed) to cry loudly while taking in sudden, sharp breaths; to speak while you are crying: *The child was sobbing because he'd lost his toy.* ينتحب ، ينشج ، يشهق بالبكاء

▸ **sob** *noun* [C] an act or the sound of sobbing نشجة ، شهقة بكاء : نحيب

sober /ˈsəʊbə(r)/ *adj* **1** (of a person) not affected by alcohol صاحٍ غير ثَمِل

2 (of a person or attitude) serious or thoughtful: *a sober expression* ○ *a sober reminder of just how dangerous drugs can be* جدّي ؛ متزِن

3 (of a colour) not bright or likely to be noticed: *a sober grey suit* (لون) هادئ

▸ **sober** *verb*

PHR V **sober (sb) up** to become, or to make sb, sober (1) يَفيق أو يفيق من سكره ؛ يثوب أو يثيب إلى رشده

sobering *adj* making you feel serious باعث على الجدِّ والرزانة

Soc. *abbrev* = SOCIETY (2)

ˌso-ˈcalled *adj* (used to show that the words you describe sb/sth with are not correct): *Her so-called friends only wanted her money* (= they are not really her friends). المزعوم ، المسمى

soccer /ˈsɒkə(r)/ *noun* [U] = FOOTBALL (1)

sociable /ˈsəʊʃəbl/ *adj* enjoying the company of other people; friendly (شخص) اجتماعيّ ، أنيس ، "معشرانيّ"

social /ˈsəʊʃl/ *adj* **1** concerning the relations between people or groups of people; relating to the organization of society: *The 1980s were a period of social change.* ○ *social problems* اجتماعي

2 concerning the rank of people in society: *We share the same social background.* ○ *social class* اجتماعي

3 to do with meeting people and enjoying yourself: *a social club* ○ *She has a busy social life.* اجتماعيّ

4 (used about animals) living and looking for food together: *Lions are social animals.* اجتماعيّ

▸ **socially** /-ʃəli/ *adv*: *We work together but I don't know him socially.* على المستوى الاجتماعي

ˌsocial ˈbookmarking *noun* [U] a way of bookmarking (= storing and labelling) the addresses of pages on the Internet, using a special service that enables you to make them available to other Internet users خدمة توفر للآخرين مشاركة صفحات الانترنت

socialism /ˈsəʊʃəlɪzəm/ *noun* [U] the political theory and practice that is based on the belief that all people are equal and that wealth should be equally divided الاشتراكيّة

▸ **socialist** /ˈsəʊʃəlɪst/ *noun* [C] a person who believes in socialism; a member of a socialist party الاشتراكيّ

socialist *adj* اشتراكي

ˌsocial ˈnetworking *noun* [U] communication with people who share your interests using a website or other service on the Internet استخدام شبكات التواصل الاجتماعي

ˌsocial ˈscience *noun* [C,U] the study of people in society, including economics, politics and sociology أحد العلوم الاجتماعيّة

ˌsocial seˈcurity (*US* **welfare**) *noun* [U] money paid regularly by the government to people who are poor, old, ill, or who have no job الضمان الجماعيّ أو الاجتماعي

ˌsocial ˈservices *noun* [plural] a group of services organized by local government to help people who have social problems (e.g. with housing, child care, etc.) الخدمات الاجتماعيّة

ˈsocial work *noun* [U] work that involves giving help to people with problems because they are poor, ill, etc. خدمة اجتماعيّة

▸ **ˈsocial worker** *noun* [C] a person whose job is to do social work موظّف في الخدمات الاجتماعية

society /səˈsaɪəti/ *noun* (*pl.* **societies**) **1** [C,U] the people in a country or area, thought of as a group, who have shared customs and laws: *a civilized society* ○ *in Western society* ○ *The aim is to create a classless society in Britain.* ○ *Society's attitude to women has changed considerably this century.* مجتمع

2 [C] (*abbr* **Soc.**) an organization of people who share a particular interest or purpose; a club: *a drama society* ○ *The Royal Society for the Prevention of Cruelty to Animals* جمعيّة

sociology /ˌsəʊsiˈɒlədʒi/ *noun* [U] the study of human societies and social behaviour علم الاجتماع

▸ **sociological** /ˌsəʊsiəˈlɒdʒɪkl/ *adj* متعلّق بعلم الاجتماع ، اجتماعي

sociologist /-dʒɪst/ *noun* [C] a student of or an expert in sociology المتخصص بعلم الاجتماع

sock /sɒk/ *noun* [C] a piece of clothing that you wear on your foot and lower leg, inside your shoe: *a pair of socks* جورب قصير

IDM **pull your socks up** (*Brit informal*) (to try) to work harder, do better, etc. than before يبذل مجهوداً أكبر : "يشدّ حيله"

socket /ˈsɒkɪt/ *noun* [C] **1** (*also* **power point**, *informal* **plug**) a place in a wall where an electrical appliance can be connected to the electricity supply مِقبس أو مأخذ كهربائيّ

2 a hole in a piece of electrical equipment where another piece of equipment can be connected: *an aerial socket on the television* تجويف؛ جبلة أنثية

3 a hollow place where sth fits: *your eye socket* نقرة ، تجويف

soda /'səʊdə/ (*also* **'soda water**) *noun* [C,U] water that has bubbles in it and is used for mixing with other drinks ماء غازيّ

sodium /'səʊdiəm/ *noun* [U] (*symbol* **Na**) a soft silver-white metal that is found naturally only in chemical mixtures (compounds), such as salt الصوديوم

sofa /'səʊfə/ *noun* [C] a comfortable seat with a back and arms. It is long enough for two or more people to sit on: *a sofa bed* (= a sofa that you can pull out to make a bed) كنبة ، أريكة

soft /sɒft; *US* sɔːft/ *adj* **1** not hard or firm: *a soft bed* ○ *The ground is very soft after all that rain.* طري

2 smooth and nice to touch; not rough: *soft skin, hands, etc.* ○ *a soft towel* ناعم

3 (used about sounds, voices, words, etc.) quiet or gentle; not loud or angry: *She spoke in a soft whisper.* رخيم، هادئ

4 (used about light, colours etc.) gentle and pleasant; not bright: *The room was decorated in soft pinks and greens.* هادئ، مريح

5 (used about people and animals) (too) kind and gentle: not hard or strict: *A good manager can't afford to be too soft.* رفيق : متساهل

6 (used about illegal drugs) less dangerous and serious than the type of illegal drugs which can kill people: *soft drugs such as marijuana* (مخدِّر) قليل الخطر

IDM **have a soft spot for sb/sth** (*informal*) to be especially fond of sb/sth: *I've got rather a soft spot for my old teacher.* يحب: له مكانة خاصّة عنده

▶ **softly** *adv* gently or quietly: *'Don't wake the children,' she whispered softly.* برفق : بنعومة : بصوت رخيم

softness *noun* [U] the quality of being soft لين : نعومة : رقّة

ˌsoft 'drink *noun* [C] a cold drink that contains no alcohol مشروب غير كحولي

soften /'sɒfn; *US* 'sɔːfn/ *verb* **1** [I,T] to become softer or gentler; to make sb/sth softer or gentler: *First soften the butter in a bowl.* ○ *The teacher's expression softened as I explained why I was late.* يَلين : يرقّ : يليّن : ينعّم

2 [T] to make sth seem less severe: *to try to soften the effect of bad news* يخفف ، يلطِّف

ˌsoft-'hearted *adj* kind and able to sympathize with other people's feelings ❶ The opposite is **hard-hearted**. رقيق القلب ، عطوف

ˌsoft 'option *noun* [C] the easier thing to do of two or more possibilities, but not always the best one: *The government has taken the soft option of agreeing to their demands.* أسهل مخرج (من مشكلة مثلاً)

ˌsoft-'spoken *adj* having a gentle, quiet voice: *He was a kind, soft-spoken man.* رخيم الصوت

software /'sɒftweə(r)/ *noun* [U] programs that you use to operate a computer: *There's a lot of new educational software available now.* ➲ Look at **hardware**. برامج الكمبيوتر

soggy /'sɒgi/ *adj* (**soggier**; **soggiest**) very wet; having too much liquid in it مثقل بالسائل : مفرط في البلل : (خبز) معجّن

soil /sɔɪl/ *noun* **1** [C,U] the substance that plants, trees, etc. grow in; earth: *poor soil* ➲ Look at the note at **ground**[1]. تربة

2 [U] the land that is part of a country: *to set foot on British soil* (= to arrive in Britain) أرض

▶ **soil** *verb* [T] (*formal*) to make sth dirty يلوِّث ، يوسّخ

solace /'sɒləs/ *noun* [C,U] (*formal*) (something that gives you) comfort or relief when you are sad عزاء ، سلوى

solar /'səʊlə(r)/ *adj* **1** of or relating to the sun: *solar energy* ○ *the solar system* شمسي

2 using the sun's energy: *solar heating* مستخدم الطاقة الشمسيّة

sold *pt, pp* of SELL

solder /'sɒldə(r)/ *verb* [T] to join pieces of metal or wire together using a mixture of metals which is heated and melted يلحم

soldier /'səʊldʒə(r)/ *noun* [C] a member of an army: *The soldiers marched past on their way to battle.* جنديّ

sole[1] /səʊl/ *adj* (only *before* a noun) **1** only; single: *His sole interest is football.* وحيد

2 belonging to one person only; not shared: *Do you have sole responsibility for the accounts?* فرديّ ، مقصور على شخص واحد

▶ **solely** /'səʊlli/ *adv* only: *I agreed to come solely on account of your mother.* فقط ، لمجرّد

sole[2] /səʊl/ *noun* [C] **1** the flat part of your foot that you walk on باطن القدم

2 the part of a shoe or sock that covers the bottom surface of your foot: *These shoes have leather soles and man-made uppers.* نعل الحذاء : أسفل الجورب

sole[3] /səʊl/ *noun* [C,U] (*pl.* **sole**) a small flat sea fish that can be eaten as food سمك موسى

solemn /'sɒləm/ *adj* **1** very serious: *Her solemn face told them that the news was bad.* رصين ، جِدّي ؛ وقور

2 sincere; done or said in a formal way: *to make a solemn promise* ○ *a solemn warning* صادق ؛ رسميّ، جدّي

▶ **solemnity** /sə'lemnəti/ *noun* [U] وقار ، هيبة

solemnly *adv* in a serious or sincere way: *'I have something very important to tell you,' she began solemnly.* بِجدٍ ، برصانة؛ بإخلاص

solicit /sə'lɪsɪt/ *verb* **1** [T] (*formal*) to ask sb for money, help, support, etc: *They tried to solicit support for the proposal.* يلتمس (المعونة مثلاً) : يستعطي

2 [I,T] to approach sb, especially in a public place, and offer sex in return for money (مومس مثلاً) تتصيّد الزبائن

solicitor /sə'lɪsɪtə(r)/ *noun* [C] (*Brit*) a person whose job is to give legal advice, prepare legal documents and speak in the lower courts ➲ Look at the note at **lawyer**. محام

solid /ˈsɒlɪd/ *adj* **1** hard and firm; not in the form of liquid or gas: *It was so cold that the village pond had frozen solid.* ○ *Our central heating runs on solid fuel* (= coal, wood, etc., not gas or electricity). صلب ، جامد

2 having no holes or spaces inside; not hollow: *a solid mass of rock* ○ *The briefcase was packed solid with £50 notes.* أصمّ ، مُصمَت؛ غير أجوف؛ محشوّ للآخر

3 (only *before* a noun) made of the same substance inside and outside: *a solid gold chain* مصنوع من مادّة واحدة : (ذهب) خالص

4 strong, firm and therefore reliable: *a solid little car* متين ؛ وطيد

5 reliable; of sufficient quality and amount: *The police cannot make an arrest without solid evidence.* موثوق به ؛ قويّ

6 (*informal*) without a break or pause: *I was so tired that I slept for twelve solid hours/twelve hours solid.* متواصل

▸ **solid** *noun* [C] **1** a substance or object that is hard; not a liquid or gas: *Liquids become solids when frozen.* مادة صلبة : جسم صلب

2 an object that has length, width and height, not a flat object: *A cube is a solid.* شكل مجسّم

solidity /səˈlɪdəti/ *noun* [U] the quality or state of being solid صلابة : صموت ؛ متانة

solidly *adv* **1** strongly: *a solidly built house* بشكل متين

2 continuously: *It's been raining solidly all day.* بصورة متواصلة

solidarity /ˌsɒlɪˈdærəti/ *noun* [U] the support of one group of people for another, because they agree with their aims: *Many local people expressed solidarity with the strikers.* تضامن ، تآزر

solidify /səˈlɪdɪfaɪ/ *verb* [I] (*pres part* **solidifying**; *3rd pers sing pres* **solidifies**; *pt, pp* **solidified**) to become hard or solid يتجمّد ، يتصلّب

solitary /ˈsɒlətri; *US* -teri/ *adj* **1** living alone, without other people: *She lives a solitary life in a remote part of Scotland.* منفرد ، معتزل

2 done alone: *Writing novels is a solitary occupation.* انفراديّ ، منعزل

3 (only *before* a noun) one on its own with no others around: *a solitary figure walking up the hillside* وحيد

4 (only *before* a noun) only one; single: *I can't think of a solitary example* (= not even one). واحد (فقط) : وحيد

ˌsolitary conˈfinement *noun* [U] a punishment in which a person in prison is kept completely alone الحبس الانفرادي

solitude /ˈsɒlɪtjuːd; *US* -tuːd/ *noun* [U] the state of being alone: *to live in solitude* وَحدة ، عزلة

solo /ˈsəʊləʊ/ *noun* [C] (*pl.* **solos**) a piece of music for only one person to play or sing: *a piano solo* ○ *to sing/play a solo* ➲ Look at **duet**. قطعة موسيقيّة لأداء منفرد

▸ **solo** *adj, adv* (done) alone; by yourself: *a solo flight* ○ *to fly solo* منفرد ؛ منفرداً

soloist *noun* [C] a person who plays or sings a piece of music alone عازف أو مغنٍّ منفرد

soluble /ˈsɒljəbl/ *adj* **1** that will dissolve in liquid: *These tablets are soluble in water.* قابل للانحلال في سائل

2 that has an answer قابل للحلّ

ℹ The opposite is **insoluble**.

solution /səˈluːʃn/ *noun* **1** [C] **a solution (to sth)** a way of solving a problem, dealing with a difficult situation, etc: *a solution to the problem of unemployment* حلّ

2 [C] **solution (to sth)** the answer (to a puzzle, etc.): *The solution to the competition will be published next week.* حلّ

3 [C,U] (a) liquid in which sth solid has been dissolved محلول

solve /sɒlv/ *verb* [T] to find an answer to or a way of dealing with a problem, question, difficulty, etc: *The government is trying to solve the problem of inflation.* ○ *The police have not managed to solve the crime.* ○ *to solve a puzzle, mystery, etc.*

ℹ The noun is **solution**. يحل

solvent /ˈsɒlvənt/ *noun* [C,U] a liquid that can dissolve another substance سائل مُذيب أو حَلول

sombre (*US* **somber**) /ˈsɒmbə(r)/ *adj* **1** dark and dull: *sombre colours* قاتم ، داكن ، عابس

2 sad and serious: *a sombre mood* كئيب ، مغمّ

▸ **sombrely** *adv* بوقار : بشكل يثير الاكتئاب

some /səm; *strong form* sʌm/ *det, pron* **1** a certain amount or number: *We need some butter and some potatoes.* ○ *I don't need any more money – I've still got some.* كميّة أو قليل من

> In negative sentences and in questions we use **any** instead of **some**: *Do we need any butter?* ○ *I need some more money. I haven't got any.* But look at **2** for examples of questions where **some** is used.

2 (used in questions when you expect or want the answer 'yes'): *Would you like some more cake?* ○ *Can I take some of this paper?* شيء من ، بعض

3 (used when you are referring to certain members of a group or certain types of a thing and not all of them): *Some pupils enjoy this kind of work, some don't.* ○ *Some of his books are very exciting.* بعض

4 (*also* **some...or other**) (used for talking about a person or thing whose name you do not know): *There's some woman at the door.* ○ *I read about it in some newspaper or other.* (جريدة) ما

somebody /ˈsʌmbədi/ (*also* **someone** /ˈsʌmwʌn/) *pron* a person (not known or not mentioned by name): *How are you? Somebody said that you'd been ill.* ○ *She's getting married to someone she met at work.* ○ *There's somebody at the door.* ○ *I think you should talk to someone else* (= another person) *about this problem.* شخص أو أحد ما

Somebody, **anybody** and **everybody** are used with a singular verb but are often followed by a plural pronoun (except in formal language): *Somebody is coming.* ○ *Somebody has left their coat behind.* ○ *Has everybody got something to eat?* ○ *I'll see everybody concerned and tell them the news.* The difference between **somebody** and **anybody** is the same as the difference between **some** and **any**. Look at the note at **some**.

'some day *adv* (*also* **someday**) at some time in the future: *I hope you'll come and visit me some-day.* في يوم من الأيام ، يوماً ما

somehow /'sʌmhaʊ/ *adv* **1** in a way that is not known or certain: *The car's broken down but I'll get to work somehow.* ○ *Somehow we had got completely lost.* بطريقة ما

2 for a reason you do not know or understand: *I somehow get the feeling that I've been here before.* لسبب ما

someone /'sʌmwʌn/ *pron* = SOMEBODY

someplace /'sʌmpleɪs/ *adv* (*US*) = SOMEWHERE

somersault /'sʌməsɔːlt/ *noun* [C] a movement in which you roll right over with your feet going over your head: *to do a forward/backward somersault.* شقلبة

something /'sʌmθɪŋ/ *pron* **1** a thing that is not known or not named: *I've got something in my eye.* ○ *Wait a minute – I've forgotten something.* ○ *Would you like something else* (= another thing) *to drink?* شيء ما ، شيء

The difference between **something** and **anything** is the same as the difference between **some** and **any**. Look at the note at **some**.

2 a thing that is helpful, useful or worth considering: *There's something in what your mother says.* شيء مفيد أو مهمّ ؛ شيء من الصحّة

IDM **or something** (*informal*) (used for showing that you are not sure about what you have just said): *'What's his job?' 'I think he's a plumber, or something'.* أو شيء من هذا القبيل

something like similar to: *A loganberry is something like a raspberry.* شبيه بـ

something to do with connected or concerned with: *The programme's something to do with the environment.* يتعلّق بـ ؛ يدور حول

sometime /'sʌmtaɪm/ *adv* (*also* **some time**) at a time that you do not know exactly or have not yet decided: *I'll phone you sometime this evening.* ○ *I must go and see her sometime.* في وقت ما (في المستقبل)

sometimes /'sʌmtaɪmz/ *adv* on some occasions; now and then: *Sometimes I drive to work and sometimes I go by bus.* ○ *I sometimes watch television in the evenings.* أحياناً : من وقت لآخر

somewhat /'sʌmwɒt/ *adv* rather: *We missed the train, which was somewhat unfortunate.* ○ *Somewhat to my surprise, he apologized.* بعض الشيء ، إلى حدٍّ ما

somewhere /'sʌmweə(r)/ (*US also* **someplace**) *adv* **1** at, in, or to a place that you do not know or name exactly: *I've seen your glasses somewhere downstairs.* ○ *'Have they gone to France?' 'No, I think they've gone somewhere else* (= to another place) *this year.'* (في) (إلى) مكان ما

The difference between **somewhere** and **anywhere** is the same as the difference between **some** and **any**. Look at the note at **some**.

2 (used when you do not know the exact time, number, etc.): *Your ideal weight should probably be somewhere around 70 kilos.* تقريباً

son /sʌn/ *noun* [C] a male child ➲ Look at **daughter**. ابن

sonata /sə'nɑːtə/ *noun* [C] a piece of music written for the piano, or another instrument with a piano accompanying it قطعة موسيقيّة تعزف على البيانو أو بمصاحبة آلة أخرى، سوناتا

song /sɒŋ; *US* sɔːŋ/ *noun* **1** [C] a piece of music with words that you sing: *a folk song* أغنية

2 [U] the act of singing: *to burst into song* غناء

3 [C,U] the musical sounds that a bird makes: *birdsong* تغريد

songwriter /'sɒŋraɪtə(r); *US* 'sɔːŋ-/ *noun* [C] a person whose job is to write songs ناظم أغاني

sonic /'sɒnɪk/ *adj* connected with sound-waves صوتي

'son-in-law *noun* [C] (*pl.* **sons-in-law**) your daughter's husband زوج الابنة ، صهر

soon /suːn/ *adv* **1** not long after the present time or the time mentioned: *It will soon be dark.* ○ *He left soon after me.* ○ *We should arrive at your house soon after twelve.* بعد وقت قصير ، بعد قليل

2 early; quickly: *Don't leave so soon. Stay for tea.* ○ *How soon can you get here?* باكراً : مسرعاً

IDM **as soon as** at the moment (that); when: *Phone me as soon as you hear some news.* ○ *I'd like your reply as soon as possible* (= at the earliest possible moment). حالما ، عندما

no sooner ... than immediately when or after: *No sooner had I shut the door than I realized I'd left my keys inside.* ما أن...حتى ، حالما

sooner or later at some time in the future; one day: *I suppose I'll hear from her sooner or later.* عاجلاً أو آجلاً

soot /sʊt/ *noun* [U] black powder that comes from burning things and that collects in chimneys شحّار ، سخام

soothe /suːð/ *verb* [T] **1** to make sb calmer or less upset; to comfort sb: *to soothe a crying child* يهدّئ: يطيّب خاطره

2 to make aches or pains less severe: *The doctor gave me some skin cream to soothe the irritation.* يخفّف ، يسكّن

▸ **soothing** *adj*: *soothing music* ○ *a soothing massage* مهدّئ للأعصاب

soothingly *adv* بتهدئة ، بصورة تبعث على الراحة

sophisticated /sə'fɪstɪkeɪtɪd/ *adj* **1** having or showing a lot of experience of the world and social situations; knowing about things such as fashion, new ideas, etc: *She's a very sophisticated young woman.* ذو خبرة بالحياة ، مصقول ، متحذلق

2 able to understand difficult or complicated things: *Voters are much more sophisticated these days.* محنّك ، ذو خبرة

3 (used about machines, systems, etc.) advanced and complicated: *sophisticated computer equipment* متطوّر ، معقّد

ℹ The opposite is **unsophisticated**.

▸ **sophistication** /səˌfɪstɪˈkeɪʃn/ *noun* [U] تحذلق ؛ دراية بشؤون الحياة

soppy /ˈsɒpi/ *adj* (**soppier**; **soppiest**) (*informal*) full of unnecessary emotion; silly: *a soppy romantic film* مفرط في العاطفيّة ، سخيف

soprano /səˈprɑːnəʊ; *US* -ˈpræn-/ *noun* [C] (*pl.* **sopranos** /-nəʊz/) the highest singing voice; a woman, girl, or boy with this voice أعلى طبقة صوتيّة : مغنّي "السوبرانو"

sorbet /ˈsɔːbeɪ/ *noun* [C,U] a sweet frozen food made from sugar, water and fruit juice, often eaten as a dessert شراب، شربات

sordid /ˈsɔːdɪd/ *adj* **1** unpleasant; not honest or moral: *We discovered the truth about his sordid past.* كريه ؛ دنيء ؛ فاسق

2 dirty and depressing: *a sordid backstreet* قذر ؛ مغم

⚷ **sore** /sɔː(r)/ *adj* aching or painful: *to have a sore throat* ○ *My feet were sore from walking so far.* مؤلم

IDM **a sore point** a subject that is likely to make sb upset or angry when mentioned موضوع اليم

▸ **sore** *noun* [C] a painful place on the body where the skin or flesh is infected قرحة

sorely *adv* (*formal*) very greatly; severely: *You'll be sorely missed when you leave.* بشدّة ؛ بصورة هائلة

soreness *noun* [U]: *You might get some soreness of the skin.* ألم ، حساسية مؤلمة

sorrow /ˈsɒrəʊ/ *noun* (*formal*) **1** [U] great sadness: *I'd like to express my sorrow at the death of your father.* أسى ، حزن

2 [C] an event, etc. that causes great sadness: *His decision to leave home was a great sorrow to his parents.* حادث مؤلم

▸ **sorrowful** /-fl/ *adj* حزين، كئيب؛ محزن

sorrowfully /-fəli/ *adv* بحزن وأسى

⚷ **sorry** /ˈsɒri/ *adj* (**sorrier**; **sorriest**) **1** (not before a noun) **sorry (for/about sth)**; **sorry (to do sth/ that...)** (used for apologizing for sth that you have done): *I'm sorry I've kept you all waiting.* ○ *I'm awfully sorry for spilling that coffee.* ○ *I'm sorry to be so late.* ○ *I'm so sorry that I've disturbed your meal. I'll phone again later.* آسف

2 (not before a noun) **sorry (to do sth/that)**; **sorry (for/about sth)** sad or disappointed: *I was sorry to miss you on Saturday.* ○ *I was sorry not to get the job.* ○ *'Simon's mother died last week.' 'Oh, I am sorry.'* حزين؛ خائب الأمل

3 (used for politely saying 'no' to sth, disagreeing with sth or introducing bad news): *'Would you like to come to supper on Friday?' 'I'm sorry, I'm busy that evening.'* ○ *I'm sorry, I don't agree with you. I think we should accept the offer.* ○ *I'm sorry to tell you that your application has been unsuccessful.* مع الأسف ، يؤسفني أن

4 (only *before* a noun) very bad: *The house was in a sorry state when we first moved in.* رديء جداً، شنيع

IDM **be/feel sorry for sb** to feel sympathy or pity for sb: *I feel very sorry for the families of the victims.* ○ *Stop feeling sorry for yourself!* يشعر بالحزن أو العطف على

▸ **sorry** *interj* **1** (used for apologizing, making excuses, etc.): *Sorry, I didn't see you standing behind me.* ○ *Sorry I'm late – the bus didn't come on time.* المعذرة ، آسف

2 (used for asking sb to repeat sth you have not heard properly): *'My name's Maggie Wiseman' 'Sorry? Maggie who?'* عفواً ، آسف لم أسمع جيّداً

3 (used for correcting yourself when you have said sth wrong): *Take the second turning, sorry, the third turning on the right.* لا...آسف

⚷ **sort¹** /sɔːt/ *noun* **1** [C] a type or kind: *What sort of music do you like?* ○ *That's the sort of car I'd like to have.* ○ *different sorts of people* ○ *She's got all sorts of problems at the moment.* نوع ، صنف

2 [sing.] a type of character; a person: *You can ask him for help – he's a good sort.* شخص ، إنسان

IDM **a sort of sth** (*informal*) a type of sth; sth similar to sth: *Can you hear a sort of ticking noise?* ما يشبه؛ نوع من

sort of (*informal*) rather; in a way: *I feel sort of sick.* ○ *I'd sort of like to go, but I'm not sure.* نوعاً ما ، قليلاً

⚷ **sort²** /sɔːt/ *verb* [T] **1** to put things into different groups or places so that they are properly organized: *I'm just sorting these papers into the correct files.* ○ *The computer will sort the words into alphabetical order.* يصنّف ، يفرز

2 (*informal*) to find an answer to a problem or difficult situation: *I'll have more time when I've got things sorted at home.* يحل مشكلة ؛ يتغلّب على صعوبة

PHR V **sort sth out 1** to tidy or organize sth: *The toy cupboard needs sorting out.* يرتّب ، ينظم

2 to find an answer to a problem: *I haven't found a flat yet but I hope to sort something out soon.* يجد حلا، يتدبّر أمراً

sort through sth to go through a number of things, in order to tidy them or find sth that you are looking for يرتّب ، ينسّق ؛ يفتّش بين حوائجه

so-so /ˌsəʊ ˈsəʊ/ *adj, adv* (*informal*) all right but not particularly good/well: *'How are you?' 'So-so.'* لا بأس ، "نص على نص"

soufflé /ˈsuːfleɪ; *US* suːˈfleɪ/ *noun* [C,U] a type of food made mainly from egg whites, flour and milk, beaten together and baked: *a cheese soufflé* سوفليه: أكلة قوامها بياض البيض المخفوق

sought *pt, pp of* SEEK

ˈ**sought-after** *adj* that people want very much, because it is of high quality or rare مرغوب فيه ، يكثر الإقبال عليه

soul /səʊl/ *noun* **1** [C] the part of a person that is believed to continue to exist after the body is dead: *Christians believe that your soul goes to heaven when you die.* الروح

2 [sing.] the part of a thing or a place that shows its true nature: *You will find the real soul of France in the countryside.* روح

3 [C,U] deep feeling and thought: *The music was performed perfectly but it lacked soul.*
روح ، إحساس ، عمق

4 [C] (used with adjectives expressing affection or pity) person: *She's a kind old soul.*
شخص ، إنسان

5 [sing.] (in negative statements) a person: *There wasn't a soul in sight* (= there was nobody).
شخص ، أحد

6 [U] (*also* **'soul music**) a type of popular Black American music: *a soul singer*
نوع من موسيقى الأمريكيين السود

▶ **soulful** /-fl/ *adj* having or showing deep feeling: *a soulful expression* مفعم بالأحاسيس ، عاطفي
soulless /'səʊlləs/ *adj* without feeling, warmth or interest: *soulless industrial towns*
لا روح فيه ، راكد : كئيب

sound[1] /saʊnd/ *verb* **1** [I] to give a particular impression when heard or heard about; to seem: *That sounds like a child crying.* ○ *She sounded upset and angry on the phone.* ○ *The rain sounds heavy.* ○ *You sound like my mother!* ○ *He sounds a very nice person from his letter.* ○ *Does she sound like the right person for the job?* ○ *It doesn't sound as if he's very reliable.* يبدو من صوته : يبدو أنه

2 [T] to cause sth to make a sound: *to sound the horn of your car* يقرع ، يدق ، يحدث صوتاً

PHRV **sound sb out** to ask sb questions in order to find out what he/she thinks or intends: *Do you mind if I sound you out about these new proposals?* يستطلع رأيه

sound[2] /saʊnd/ *noun* **1** [C] something that you hear or that can be heard: *the sound of voices* ○ *She opened the door without a sound.*
صوت ، ضجة ، حس

2 [U] what you hear; impressions received by hearing: *Light travels faster than sound.* ○ *sound waves* صوت

3 the sound [sing.] the volume on a television, radio, etc: *Can you turn the sound up/down?*
(مفتاح) الصوت

IDM **the sound of sth** the impression that you have of sth when you hear or read about it: *She must be an interesting person, by the sound of it.* انطباع ، هيئة ، مما يبدو

sound[3] /saʊnd/ *adj* **1** healthy and strong; in good condition: *a sound state of health* ○ *The structure of the bridge is basically sound.*
سليم ، في حالة حسنة ، متين

2 sensible; that you can rely on: *sound advice*
معقول ، سديد : موثوق

IDM **safe and sound** → SAFE[1]
▶ **sound** *adv*
IDM **be sound asleep** to be deeply asleep
بعمق ، (ينام) نوماً عميقاً
soundly *adv* thoroughly or deeply: *Our team was soundly beaten this afternoon.* ○ *The children were sleeping soundly.*
كلياً ، تماماً : (نائم) نوماً عميقاً
soundness *noun* [U] سلامة : متانة

'sound effect *noun* [C, usually pl.] sounds other than speech or music that are used in a play, film or computer game to create the required effect
مؤثرات صوتية

soundproof /'saʊndpruːf/ *adj* made so that no sound can get in or out عازل للصوت

soundtrack /'saʊndtræk/ *noun* [C] the recorded sound and music from a film or computer game مدرَج: التسجيل الصوتي لفيلم مثلاً

soup /suːp/ *noun* [U] liquid food made by cooking meat, vegetables, etc. in water: *chicken soup* ○ *a tin of soup* حساء ، شوربة

sour /'saʊə(r)/ *adj* **1** having a sharp taste like that of a lemon: *The apples were very sour.*
حامض ، حاذق

2 (used especially about milk) tasting or smelling unpleasant because it is no longer fresh
محمّض، فاسد

3 having or showing a bad temper; unpleasant: *a sour expression* متجهم ، عابس : نكد

IDM **go/turn sour** to become unpleasant or unsatisfactory: *Their relationship turned sour after a few months.* يتعكّر صفوه ، يفسد

,sour 'grapes pretending to dislike or not to want sth when you secretly want it but cannot have it: *She said she didn't want to come to the party anyway, but I think that was just sour grapes.* حصرم حلب ، قصر ذيل

▶ **sourly** *adv* in a sour (3) way بعبوس ، بنكد ، بحدة
sourness *noun* [U] حموضة

source /sɔːs/ *noun* [C] **1** a place, person or thing where sth comes or starts from or where sth is obtained: *Britain's oil reserves are an important source of income.* ○ *the source of the Nile* (= the place where the river starts) مصدر ، مورد ، منبع

2 a person, book, etc. that supplies information: *Police have refused to reveal the source of their information.* مصدر

south /saʊθ/ *noun* [sing.] (*abbr* **S**; **So.**) **1** (*also* **the south**) one of the four main points of the compass; the direction that is on your right when you face the sunrise: *warm winds from the south* ○ *Which way is south?* جنوب ، الجنوب

2 the south; **the South** the part of any country, city, etc. that lies further towards the south than other parts: *Winchester is in the South of England.* الجنوب ، جنوب البلاد

▶ **south** (*also* **South**) *adj* in or towards the south, or from the south: *the south coast of Cornwall* ○ *The new offices will be in South Oxford.* ○ *a south wind* جنوبي
south *adv* to or towards the south: *If you keep going south, you will soon join the motorway.* ○ *We live just south of Birmingham.* ○ *The house faces south.* جنوب ، جنوباً
southerly /'sʌðəli/ *adj* **1** to, towards or in the south: *Keep going in a southerly direction.*
جنوبي

a b c d e f g h i j k l m n o p q r s t u v w x y z

2 (used about winds) coming from the south: *a southerly wind* (ريح) جنوبيّة

southward /ˈsaʊθwəd/ *adj* towards the south: *in a southward direction* باتّجاه أو نحو الجنوب

southward /ˈsaʊθwəd/ (*also* **southwards**) *adv* towards the south: *We're flying southward at the moment.* جنوباً ، نحو الجنوب

southbound /ˈsaʊθbaʊnd/ *adj* travelling or leading towards the south: *the southbound carriageway of the M1* ذاهب نحو الجنوب

ˌsouth-ˈeast *noun* [sing.] (*abbr* **SE**) **1** (*also* **the south-east**) the direction or point of the compass that is between south and east الجنوب الشرقيّ

2 (*also* **the south-east**; **the South-East**) a region that is towards the south-east: *the South-East of England* جنوب شرقيّ (البلاد)

▶ **ˌsouth-ˈeast** *adj, adv* in, from or to the south-east of a place or country: *the coast of south-east Spain* ○ *Continue south-east for about ten miles.* في جنوب شرقي (البلاد) ؛ من أو نحو الجنوب الشرقيّ

ˌsouth-ˈeasterly *adj* **1** towards the south-east: *in a south-easterly direction* (باتجاه) جنوبيّ شرقيّ

2 (used about a wind) coming from the south-east رياح جنوبيّة شرقيّة

ˌsouth-ˈeastern *adj* in or from the south-east of a place or country: *the south-eastern states of the USA* (الولايات) الجنوبيّة الشرقيّة

ˌsouth-ˈeastward (*also* **ˌsouth-ˈeastwards**) *adv* towards the south-east: *Follow the A423 south-eastward.* باتجاه الجنوب الشرقيّ

🔑 **southern** (*also* **Southern**) /ˈsʌðən/ *adj* (*abbr* **S**; **So.**) of, in or from the south of a place: *Greece is in southern Europe.* ○ *the southern hemisphere* جنوبيّ

▶ **southerner** *noun* [C] a person who was born in or lives in the southern part of a country جنوبيّ، شخص من الجنوب

the ˌSouth ˈPole *noun* [sing.] the point on the surface of the Earth which is furthest south القطب الجنوبيّ

ˌsouth-ˈwest *noun* [sing.] (*abbr* **SW**) **1** (*also* **the south-west**) the direction or point of the compass that is between south and west الجنوب الغربيّ

2 (*also* **the south-west**; **the South-West**) a region that is towards the south-west: *Devon is in the South-West.* الجنوب الغربيّ ، جنوب غربيّ البلاد

▶ **ˌsouth-ˈwest** *adj, adv* in, from or to the south-west of a place or country: *the south-west coast of France* ○ *If you look south-west you can see the sea.* في أو من أو نحو الجنوب الغربيّ

ˌsouth-ˈwesterly *adj* **1** towards the south-west: *in a south-westerly direction* باتجاه جنوبيّ غربيّ

2 (used about a wind) coming from the south-west رياح جنوبيّة غربيّة

ˌsouth-ˈwestern *adj* in or from the south-west of a place or country: *south-western Italy* جنوبيّ غربيّ

ˌsouth-ˈwestward (*also* **ˌsouth-ˈwestwards**) *adv* towards the south-west: *Follow the B409 south-westward.* باتجاه الجنوب الغربيّ

souvenir /ˌsuːvəˈnɪə(r); *US* ˈsuːvənɪər/ *noun* [C] something that you buy and keep to remind you of somewhere you have been on holiday or of a special event تذكار

sovereign /ˈsɒvrɪn/ *noun* [C] a king or queen ملك أو ملكة

▶ **sovereign** *adj* **1** (used about a country) not controlled by any other country; independent (دولة) ذات سيادة، مستقلّ

2 (used about power) without limit; highest (سلطة) مطلقة؛ الأعلى

sovereignty /ˈsɒvrənti/ *noun* [U] the power that a country has to control its own government سيادة، سلطة عليا

sow[1] /saʊ/ *noun* [C] an adult female pig خنزيرة

sow[2] /səʊ/ *verb* [T] (*pt* **sowed**; *pp* **sown** /səʊn/ or **sowed**) **sow A (in B)**; **sow B (with A)** to plant seeds in the ground: *to sow seeds in pots* ○ *to sow a field with wheat* يزرع؛ يبذر

soya bean /ˈsɔɪə biːn/ (*US* **soy bean** /ˈsɔɪ biːn/) *noun* [C] a type of bean that can be cooked and eaten or used to make flour, oil and a sort of milk فول الصويا

ˌsoya ˈsauce (*also* **ˌsoy ˈsauce**) *noun* [U] a dark brown sauce that is made from soya beans and that you add to food to make it taste better صلصة الصويا

spa /spɑː/ *noun* [C] (*pl.* **spas**) **1** a place where mineral water comes out of the ground and where people go to drink this water because it is considered to be healthy ينبوع مياه معدنيّة

2 a place where people can relax and improve their health, with, for example, a swimming pool: *a superb health spa which includes sauna, pool and fitness rooms* منتجع صحّي

🔑 **space** /speɪs/ *noun* **1** [C,U] an area that is empty or not used: *Is there enough space for me to park the car there?* ○ *a parking space* ○ *We're a bit short of space.* ○ *There's a space here for you to write your name.* ○ *wide open spaces* (= empty areas of countryside) ➲ Look at **room** and the note at **place**[1]. فراغ، حيّز، مكان

2 [U] (*also* **ˌouter ˈspace**) the vast area which surrounds the planet Earth and the other planets and stars: *Yuri Gagarin was the first man to go into space.* ○ *space travel* الفضاء الخارجيّ

3 [C, usually sing.] a period of time: *Mandy had been ill three times in the space of four months.* فترة، مدّة

▶ **space** *verb* [T] **space sth (out)** to arrange things so that there are spaces between them يباعد بين، يوزّع على مسافات

spacecraft /ˈspeɪskrɑːft; *US* -kræft/ *noun* [C] (*pl.* **spacecraft**) a vehicle that travels in space مركبة أو سفينة فضائيّة

spaceman /ˈspeɪsmən/ (**-men** /-men/), **spacewoman** /ˈspeɪswʊmən/ (**-women** /-wɪmɪn/) *noun* [C] (**-men**) a person who travels in space رجل الفضاء، رائد/رائدة الفضاء

spaceship /ˈspeɪsʃɪp/ *noun* [C] a vehicle in which people can travel in space مركبة أو سفينة فضائية

spacious /ˈspeɪʃəs/ *adj* having a lot of space or room; large in size واسع، فسيح، كبير
▶ **spaciousness** *noun* [U] اتّساع، وسعة

spade[1] /speɪd/ *noun* [C] a tool that you use for digging. A spade has a long wooden handle and a flat piece of metal (a blade) at one end. ➲ Look at **shovel**. مجراف، رفش، مسحاة، مِر

spade[2] /speɪd/ *noun* **1 spades** [plural] the group (suit) of playing cards with pointed black leaves on them البستوني (في ورق اللعب)

2 [C] one of the cards from this suit ورقة لعب بستوني

spaghetti /spəˈɡeti/ *noun* [U] a type of Italian food (pasta) made from flour and water that looks like long strings: *I'll cook some spaghetti.* سباغيتّي: معكرونة رفيعة

spam /spæm/ *noun* [U] **1** finely chopped cooked meat that has been pressed together in a container, usually sold in cans and served cold in slices نوع من اللحم المعلّب

2 advertising material sent by email to people who have not asked for it بريد متطفّل

span /spæn/ *noun* [C] **1** the length of sth from one end to the other: *the wingspan of a bird* امتداد، طول

2 the length of time that sth lasts or continues: *Young children have a short attention span.* مدّة
▶ **span** *verb* [T] (spanning; spanned) **1** to form a bridge over sth: *The river is spanned by a railway bridge.* يمتدّ كالجسر فوق (طريق مثلاً)

2 to last or continue for a particular period of time: *Her career in politics spanned more than fifty years.* يدوم، يمتد

spaniel /ˈspænjəl/ *noun* [C] a dog with large ears which hang down. There are several breeds of spaniel: *a cocker spaniel* نوع من الكلاب

spank /spæŋk/ *verb* [T] to hit a child on its bottom with an open hand as a punishment يصفع طفلاً على مؤخرته

spanner /ˈspænə(r)/ (*US* **wrench**) *noun* [C] a metal tool with an end shaped so that it can be used for turning nuts مفتاح ربط، مفتاح صواميل

⚷ **spare[1]** /speə(r)/ *adj* **1** not needed now but kept because it may be needed in the future: *The spare tyre is kept in the boot.* ○ *a spare room* احتياطي

2 not used for work: *What do you do in your spare time?* فارغ؛ فائض

3 not being used; free: *Are there any tickets going spare?* خالٍ، شاغر؛ زائد عن الحاجة
▶ **spare** *noun* [C] an extra thing of the same kind that you can use: *The fuse has blown. Where do you keep your spares?* (الشيء) الاحتياطيّ

⚷ **spare[2]** /speə(r)/ *verb* [T] **1** to be able to give sb/sth to sb: *Can you spare any money?* ○ *I am very grateful for you sparing the time to see me.* يستغني عن

2 to not hurt or damage sb/sth: *to spare sb's life* يرحم؛ يستحيي؛ يعفو عن

3 to use as little as possible of sth: *No expense was spared at the wedding.* يقتصد، يوفّر

4 to stop sb from having an unpleasant experience: *I told him what happened but spared him all the details.* يجنّب، يحمي من

IDM **to spare** more than is needed: *There's no time to spare. We must leave straight away.* يدّخر؛ يفيض عن الحاجة
▶ **sparing** /ˈspeərɪŋ/ *adj* (*formal*) using only a little of sth; careful: *Try to be sparing with the salt.* مقلّ، مقتصد
sparingly *adv*: *to use sth sparingly* بتقتير؛ دون إسراف

ˌspare ˈpart *noun* [C] a part for a machine, engine, etc. that you can use to replace an old part which is damaged or broken قطعة غيار، قطعة احتياطيّة

spark /spɑːk/ *noun* [C] **1** a small bright piece of burning material شرارة، ومضة

2 a flash of light that is caused by electricity: (*figurative*) *a spark of anger* شرارة
▶ **spark** *verb*
PHR V **spark sth off** (*informal*) to cause sth: *Eric's comments sparked off a tremendous argument.* يسبّب، يثير

sparkle /ˈspɑːkl/ *verb* [I] to shine with many small points of light: *The river sparkled in the sunlight.* ○ (*figurative*) *Trudy's eyes sparkled with excitement.* يتلألأ
▶ **sparkle** *noun* [C,U] تلألؤ، تألّق
sparkling /ˈspɑːklɪŋ/ *adj* **1** that sparkles: *sparkling blue eyes* متلألئ، برّاق

2 with bubbles in it: *sparkling mineral water* (خمر) فوّار

3 full of life; appearing interesting and intelligent: *a sparkling, witty speech* مفعم بالحيويّة؛ لامع، متوقّد

ˈspark plug (*also* **ˈsparking plug**) *noun* [C] the small piece of equipment that produces sparks in an engine شمعة الإشعال، "بوجية"

sparrow /ˈspærəʊ/ *noun* [C] a small brown bird that is very common عصفور دوري

sparse /spɑːs/ *adj* small in quantity or amount: *a sparse crowd* قليل؛ متناثر؛ غير كثيف
▶ **sparsely** *adv*: *a sparsely populated area* بكثافة قليلة
sparseness *noun* [U] قلّة، تبعثر

spartan /ˈspɑːtn/ *adj* (*formal*) very simple and not comfortable: *spartan living conditions* تقشّفيّ أو متقشّف

spasm /ˈspæzəm/ *noun* [C,U] a sudden tightening of a muscle that you cannot control: *painful muscular spasms in the leg* تشنّج

spat *pt, pp* of SPIT

spate /speɪt/ *noun* [sing.] a sudden large number or amount of sth: *a spate of burglaries in the area* فيض، سيل؛ ازدياد مفاجئ

spatial /ˈspeɪʃl/ *adj* (*formal*) connected with the size or position of sth مكانيّ، حيّزي

spatter /ˈspætə(r)/ *verb* [T] to cover sb/sth with small drops of liquid: *to spatter sb with water* ○ *to spatter water on sb* يرش، يطرطش

spatula /ˈspætʃələ/ *noun* [C] a tool with a wide flat blade used for mixing and spreading things, especially in cooking and painting
ملوَق، سكين بسط المعجون

speak /spiːk/ *verb* (*pt* **spoke** /spəʊk/; *pp* **spoken** /ˈspəʊkən/) **1 speak (to sb) (about sb/sth)** [I] to talk or say things: *I'd like to speak to the manager, please.* ○ *Could you speak more slowly?* ○ *I was so angry I could hardly speak.* يتكلّم

Speak and **talk** have almost the same meaning, although **speak** is slightly more formal. In addition, **talk** is more likely to be used about a conversation, while **speak** is often used when only one person is saying something: *Speaking personally, I'm all in favour of the idea.* ○ *We talked all night.* ○ *I must speak to Ben's parents about his bad behaviour.*

2 [T] to know and be able to use a language: *Does anyone here speak German?* ○ *a French-speaking guide* يتكلّم، يجيد لغة

3 [I] **speak (on/about sth)** to make a speech to a group of people: *Professor Hurst has been invited to speak on American foreign policy.*
يتحدّث، يحاضِر

4 [I] **be speaking (to sb)** (*informal*) (usually in negative sentences) to be friendly with sb: *They had an argument and now they're not speaking to each other.* (لا) يتكلّم مع، (ليس) على ودّ معه

IDM be on speaking terms (with sb) to be friendly with sb (after an argument): *Thankfully they are back on speaking terms again.* يتصالح مع

so to speak (used when you are describing sth in an unusual way or in a way which is not strictly true): *She turned green, so to speak, after watching a television programme about the environment.* إذا صحّ التعبير، مجازاً

speak for itself to be very clear so that no other explanation is needed: *The statistics speak for themselves.* لا حاجة لشرحه، يكون واضحاً جليّاً

speak your mind to say exactly what you think, even though you might offend sb
يفصح عن رأيه بصراحة

PHR V speak for sb to express the thoughts or opinions of sb else: *I cannot speak for my colleagues.* يتكلّم نيابةً عن

speak out (against sth) to say clearly and publicly that you think sth is bad or wrong
يخالفه الرأي علناً، يعترض علناً

speak up to speak louder يرفع صوته

▸ **speaker** *noun* [C] **1** a person who makes a speech to a group of people: *Tonight's speaker is a well-known writer and journalist.*
متحدّث، محاضِر، خطيب

2 (*informal*) = LOUDSPEAKER (2)

3 a person who speaks a particular language: *a Russian speaker* متكلّم، ناطق

spear /spɪə(r)/ *noun* [C] a long pole with a sharp point at one end, used for hunting or fighting
رمح، حربة

spearhead /ˈspɪəhed/ *noun* [C, usually sing.] a person or group that begins or leads an attack, etc. رأس الحربة: من يقود هجوماً وما اليه

▸ **spearhead** *verb* [T] to lead an attack
يقود هجوماً أو حملة

spearmint /ˈspɪəmɪnt/ *noun* [U] a type of leaf with a fresh taste that is used in sweets, etc: *spearmint chewing gum* ➲ Look at **peppermint**. النعنع أو النعناع

special /ˈspeʃl/ *adj* **1** not usual or ordinary; important for some particular reason: *He shouldn't get special treatment just because he is famous.* ○ *a special occasion* ○ *Are you doing anything special tonight?* خاص، غير عاديّ

2 (only *before* a noun) for a particular purpose: *The little boy goes to a special school for the deaf.* ○ *There's a special tool for doing that.* خاص

▸ **special** *noun* [C] something that is not of the usual or ordinary type: *the all-night election special on TV* برنامج استثنائي، شيء أو حدث خاص

specialist /ˈspeʃəlɪst/ *noun* [C] a person with special or deep knowledge of a particular subject: *She's a specialist in diseases of cattle.* ○ *to give specialist advice* أخصّائي أو اختصاصيّ

specially /-ʃəli/ (*also* **especially**) *adv* **1** for a particular purpose or reason: *I made this specially for you.* خصيصاً

2 particularly; very; more than usual: *The hotel was clean but the food was not specially good.* ○ *It's not an especially difficult exam.*
بشكل خاص؛ جداً

speciality /ˌspeʃiˈæləti/ *noun* [C] (*pl.* **specialities**) (*US* **specialty** /ˈspeʃəlti/ (*pl.* **specialties**)) **1** an area of study or a subject that you know a lot about ميدان التخصّص، اختصاص

2 something made by a person, place, business, etc. that is very good and that they are known for: *The cheese is a speciality of the region.*
منتوج مميز، ما يختصّ به (مكان ما مثلاً)

specialize (*also* **specialise**) /ˈspeʃəlaɪz/ *verb* [I] **specialize (in sth)** to give most of your attention to one subject, type of product, etc: *This shop specializes in clothes for taller men.* ○ *a lawyer who specializes in divorce cases* يختص بـ

▸ **specialization** (*also* **specialisation**) /ˌspeʃəlaɪˈzeɪʃn; *US* -ləˈz-/ *noun* [U] تخصّص، اختصاص

specialized (*also* **specialised**) *adj* **1** to be used for a particular purpose: *a specialized system* مخصّص، ذو استعمال معيّن

2 having or needing deep or special knowledge of a particular subject: *We have specialized staff to help you with any problems.* متخصّص

specialty (*US*) = SPECIALITY

species /ˈspiːʃiːz/ *noun* [C] (*pl.* **species**) a group of plants or animals that are very similar to each other and that can breed together: *an endangered species* نوع

specific /spəˈsɪfɪk/ *adj* **1** detailed or exact: *You must give the class specific instructions on what they have to do.* مفصّل، دقيق

2 particular; not general: *Everyone has been given a specific job to do.* معيّن، محدّد

▸ **specifically** /-kli/ *adv*: *a play written specifically for television* ○ *I specifically asked you not to do that.* خصيصاً؛ على وجه التحديد

specification /ˌspesɪfɪˈkeɪʃn/ *noun* [C,U] detailed information about how sth has been or must be built or made: *The kitchen was designed to our own specification.* مواصفات

specify /ˈspesɪfaɪ/ *verb* [T] (*pres part* **specifying**; *3rd pers sing pres* **specifies**; *pt, pp* **specified**) to say or name sth clearly or in detail: *Please specify any dates that you are not available.* ○ *The regulations specify the maximum number of people allowed in.* يعيِّن، يحدِّد

specimen /ˈspesɪmən/ *noun* [C] **1** an example of a particular type of thing, often studied by experts or scientists: *There is a fine specimen of that type of tree in the Botanical Gardens.* نموذج

2 a small amount of sth that is tested for medical or scientific purposes: *Specimens of the patient's blood were tested in the hospital laboratory.* عيِّنة

speck /spek/ *noun* [C] a very small spot or mark: *a speck of dust* ○ *The car was just a tiny speck on the horizon.* نقطة، نمشة، ذرة

speckled /ˈspekld/ *adj* with small marks or spots: *a speckled hen* ○ *speckled eggs* مرقش، منقّط

specs /speks/ *noun* [plural] (*informal*) (*especially Brit*) = GLASSES

spectacle /ˈspektəkl/ *noun* [C] something that is grand, interesting or unusual to look at: *The carnival parade was a magnificent spectacle.* مشهد رائع

spectacles /ˈspektəklz/ *noun* [plural] (*formal*) = GLASSES

spectacular /spekˈtækjələ(r)/ *adj* very grand, interesting or attractive: *The view from the top of the hill is quite spectacular.* ○ *a spectacular display of fireworks* هائل، رائع، أخّاذ
▸ **spectacularly** *adv* بصورة مذهلة، بأبّهة وفخامة

spectator /spekˈteɪtə(r); *US* ˈspekteɪtər/ *noun* [C] a person who watches a show, game, sport, etc. المتفرج، المشاهد

spectre (*US* **specter**) /ˈspektə(r)/ *noun* [C] **1** = GHOST

2 an idea that frightens you because of sth bad that might happen in the future: *the spectre of unemployment* شبح: التخوُّف من

spectrum /ˈspektrəm/ *noun* [C, usually sing.] (*pl.* **spectra** /ˈspektrə/) **1** the set of seven colours into which white light can be separated: *You can see the colours of the spectrum in a rainbow.* الطيف (الضوئيّ)

2 a full or wide range of sth: *speakers representing the whole spectrum of political opinions* مجال: تشكيلة واسعة

speculate /ˈspekjuleɪt/ *verb* **1** [I,T] **speculate (about/on sth)** to think about sth without having all the facts or information: *to speculate about the result of the next election* يخمِّن، يتحزّر

2 [I] to buy and sell with the aim of making money but with the risk of losing it: *to speculate on the stock market* يضارب
▸ **speculator** *noun* [C] مضارب

speculation /ˌspekjuˈleɪʃn/ *noun* [C,U] an act of speculating (1,2): *There was a lot of speculation about the date of the election.* ○ *He bought some shares as a speculation.* تخمين: مضاربة

sped *pt, pp* of SPEED

speech /spiːtʃ/ *noun* **1** [U] the act of speaking or the state of being able to speak: *to lose the power of speech* ○ *freedom of speech* (= to speak your opinions openly) كلام

2 [U] the particular way of speaking of a person or group of people: *She's doing a study of children's speech.* نطق

3 [C] a formal talk that you give to a group of people: *The Chancellor is going to make a speech to city businessmen.* ○ *an after-dinner speech* حديث، خطاب

4 [C] a group of words that one person must say in a play: *the King's speech in Act II* كلام الممثّل في دور ما
▸ **speechless** *adj* not able to speak, e.g. because you are shocked, very angry, etc. معقود اللسان، عاجز عن الكلام

speed /spiːd/ *noun* **1** [U] fast movement: *to gather/pick up speed* ○ *With a final burst of speed, he won the race.* سرعة

2 [C,U] the rate at which sb/sth moves or travels: *The car was travelling at a speed of 40 miles an hour.* ○ *to travel at top speed* سرعة
▸ **speed** *verb* [I] (*pt, pp* **sped** /sped/) **1** to go or move very quickly: *He sped round the corner on his bicycle.* ○ *The holiday seemed to speed by.* يسرع، ينطلق مسرعاً

2 (only used in the continuous tenses) to drive a car, etc. faster than the legal speed limit: *The police said she had been speeding.* يتجاوز السرعة المحدّدة

PHR V **speed (sth) up** (*pt, pp* **speeded**) (to cause sth) to go faster: *Plans to speed up production in the factory.* ○ *The traffic speeded up once it reached the motorway.* يسرِّع: يسرع أو يتسارع

speeding *noun* [U] the act of driving a car, etc. faster than the legal speed limit تجاوز السرعة المحدّدة

speedy *adj* (**speedier**; **speediest**) fast; quick: *a speedy response/reply* سريع، عاجل

speedily *adv* بسرعة، على عجل

speediness *noun* [U] إسراع، عجلة، مبادرة

speedboat /ˈspiːdbəʊt/ *noun* [C] a small fast boat with an engine زورق بخاريّ سريع

ˈspeed hump *noun* [C] a raised area across a road that is put there to make traffic go slower مخفّفات السرعة (في الطريق)

ˈspeed limit *noun* [C, usually sing.] the highest speed that you may drive without breaking the law on a particular piece of road السرعة القصوى

speedometer /spiːˈdɒmɪtə(r)/ *noun* [C] a piece of equipment in a car, etc. that tells you how fast you are travelling عدّاد السرعة

speedway /ˈspiːdweɪ/ *noun* [U] the sport of racing on motor bikes سباق الدرّاجات الناريّة

spell[1] /spel/ *verb* (*pt, pp* **spelt** /spelt/ or **spelled**

/speld/) **1** [I,T] to write or say the letters of a word in the correct order: *I could never spell very well at school.* ○ *How do you spell your surname?* ○ *His name is spelt P-H-I-L-I-P.* يهجّي أو يتهجّى

2 [T] (used about a set of letters) to form a particular word: *A-I-S-L-E spells aisle.* يشكّل لفظة

3 [T] to mean; to have sth as a result: *Another poor harvest would spell disaster for the region.* يعني، يؤدّي إلى

PHR V **spell sth out 1** to write or say the letters of a word or name in the correct order يهجّي أو يتهجّى

2 to explain sth in detail or in a very clear way يشرح بوضوح ودقّة

▶ **spelling** *noun* **1** [C,U] the way that a word is spelt: *'Center' is the American spelling of 'centre'.* تهجئة أو طريقة الكتابة

2 [U] the act of spelling or the state of being able to spell: *Roger is very poor at spelling.* تهجئة، كتابة الكلمات

spell² /spel/ *noun* [C] a short period of time: *a spell of cold weather* فترة قصيرة

spell³ /spel/ *noun* [C] **1** [usually sing.] (in stories, etc.) a state or condition that was caused by magic: *The witch put a spell on the prince.* ○ (*figurative*) *He's completely under her spell.* سِحْر؛ إنسحار

2 a set of words that are believed to have magic power رقية، عبارة سحريّة

spellcheck /ˈspeltʃek/ *verb* [T] to use a computer program to check your writing to see if your spelling is correct يستخدم مدقّق التهجئة

▶ **spellchecker** (*also* **'spell check**) *noun* [C] a computer program that checks your writing to see if your spelling is correct مدقّق التهجئة

spelt *pt, pp* of SPELL¹

spend /spend/ *verb* (*pt, pp* **spent** /spent/) **1** [I,T] **spend (sth) (on sth)** to give or pay money for sth: *How much do you spend on food each week?* ○ *You shouldn't go on spending like that.* ينفِق، يصرف

2 [T] to pass time: *I spent a whole evening writing letters.* ○ *I'm spending the weekend at my parents' house.* ○ *He spent two years in Rome.* يمضي، يقضي

spending /ˈspendɪŋ/ *noun* [U] the giving of large amounts of money by an organization to pay for services such as education: *The government wants to increase spending on health care.* تمويل، إنفاق على

sperm /spɜːm/ *noun* **1** [C] a very small cell that is produced by a male animal and that can join with a female egg to create a new life حُيَيّ مَنَوي، نُطفة

2 [U] the liquid that contains sperms السائل المَنَوي

sphere /sfɪə(r)/ *noun* [C] **1** any round object shaped like a ball كرة

2 an area of interest or activity: *Many countries are having difficulties in the economic sphere.* ميدان، مجال

▶ **spherical** /ˈsferɪkl/ *adj* كرويّ

sphinx /sfɪŋks/ *noun* [C] an ancient Egyptian stone statue of a creature with a human head and the body of a lion lying down أبو الهول

spice /spaɪs/ *noun* **1** [C,U] a substance (especially a powder) that is made from part of a plant and used to give flavour to food: *I use a lot of herbs and spices in my cooking.* ○ *Pepper and paprika are two common spices.* بهار، تابل

2 [U] excitement and interest: *to add spice to a situation* حيويّة؛ طرافة؛ إثارة

▶ **spice** *verb* [T] **spice sth (up) (with sth) 1** to add spice to food يبهّر، يتبّل

2 to add excitement to sth يجعله أكثر حيويّة وإثارة

spicy *adj* (**spicier**; **spiciest**) containing spice: *Indonesian food is rather spicy.* كثير التوابل، مفلفل

spider /ˈspaɪdə(r)/ *noun* [C] a type of small animal (like an insect) with eight legs. Spiders make (spin) special nets (webs) to catch insects for food. عنكبوت

spike /spaɪk/ *noun* [C] a piece of metal, wood, etc. that has a sharp point at one end: *metal railings with spikes on the top* مسمار مدبّب الرأس، شوكة معدنيّة

spill /spɪl/ *verb* [I,T] (*pt, pp* **spilt** /spɪlt/ or **spilled**) (to cause a liquid) to pour out from sth by accident: *I've spilt some coffee on the carpet.* ○ (*figurative*) *There were so many people that the party spilled over into the garden.* يدلق، يكبّ، يريق؛ يفيض

IDM **spill the beans** (*informal*) to tell a person sth when you are supposed to be keeping it secret يفشي سرّاً

spin /spɪn/ *verb* (**spinning**; *pt, pp* **spun** /spʌn/) **1** [I,T] **spin (sth) (round)** (to cause sth) to turn round quickly: *Mary spun round when she heard someone call her name.* ○ *to spin a coin* ○ (*figurative*) *Running up to the top of the tower made my head spin.* يدور بسرعة؛ يفتل؛ يُدير كالدوّامة

2 [I,T] to make thread from a mass of wool, cotton, etc. يغزل

3 [T] to remove water from clothes by spinning(1) them round very fast in a special machine (a spin dryer) يزيل الماء من الغسيل بواسطة آلة سريعة الدوران

PHR V **spin sth out** to make sth last as long as possible: *I managed to spin the discussion out until lunchtime.* يطيل، "يمطمط"

▶ **spin** *noun* [U] an act of spinning(1): *to put some spin on a ball* (= in sports like cricket, tennis, etc.) دوران سريع، فتل

spinach /ˈspɪnɪtʃ; -ɪdʒ/ *noun* [U] a plant with large green leaves that can be cooked and eaten as a vegetable إسفاناخ، سبانخ، رحى

spinal /ˈspaɪnl/ *adj* connected with the bones of the back (the spine) فقري

'spin doctor *noun* [C] (especially in politics) a person who finds ways of talking about difficult situations, mistakes, etc. in a positive way: *The party spin doctors were calling the election defeat a 'great opportunity to rebuild'* مروّج سياسي، مزوّق

ˌspin 'dryer (*also* **ˌspin 'drier**) *noun* [C] a machine that removes water from wet clothes by turning (1) them round and round very fast آلة دوارة (لعصر الماء من الغسيل)

spine /spaɪn/ *noun* [C] **1** the bones of the back of a person or animal; the backbone العمود الفقري
2 one of the sharp points on some plants and animals ➲ Look at **prickle**. شوكة
3 the narrow part of a book that you can see when it is on a shelf عمود أو كعب الكتاب
▶ **spineless** *adj* weak and easily frightened ضعيف الشخصيّة، جبان

ˈspin-off *noun* [C] a useful result that you did not expect فائدة جانبية غير متوقعة

spinster /ˈspɪnstə(r)/ *noun* [C] (*old-fashioned*) a woman who has never been married عانس

Nowadays **single** is the most usual word that is used to describe a man or a woman who is not married.

spiral /ˈspaɪrəl/ *noun* [C] a long curve that moves upwards going round and round a central point حلزون، لولب
▶ **spiral** *adj*: *a spiral staircase* حلزوني، لولبي
spiral *verb* [I] (spiralling; spiralled; *US* spiraling; spiraled) to move upwards or downwards in a spiral, especially very quickly: *Food prices are spiralling up.* يرتفع أو يهبط بشكل حلزوني وبسرعة فائقة

spire /ˈspaɪə(r)/ *noun* [C] a tall pointed tower on the top of a church, etc. برج (كنيسة) ذو قمّة مدبّبة

⚷ **spirit** /ˈspɪrɪt/ *noun* **1** [sing.] the part of a person that is not physical; your thoughts and feelings, not your body: *the power of the human spirit to overcome difficulties* روح
2 [C] the part of a person that many people believe still exists after his/her body is dead: *the spirits of the dead* روح
3 [C] a ghost or being that exists but that does not have a body: *the Holy Spirit* روح؛ طيف
4 [U] energy, strength of mind or liveliness: *The constant setbacks finally broke his spirit.* الروح المعنويّة، الحيويّة
5 [C] the mood or attitude of mind of sb/sth: *the spirit of goodwill at Christmas* ○ *to be in high/low spirits* (= in a happy/sad mood) ○ *Everyone entered into the spirit of the party* (= joined in with enthusiasm). ○ *the 16th-century spirit of exploration* روح، نفسيّة، مزاج
6 [U] the real and intended meaning of a rule, agreement, etc: *Judges should consider the spirit as well as the letter of the law.* الفحوى، المعنى الحقيقيّ المقصود
7 spirits [plural] strong alcoholic drinks, e.g. whisky مشروبات روحيّة، مسكرات قويّة
▶ **spirit** *verb*
PHR V spirit sb/sth away/off to take sb/sth away secretly يختطف خفية
spirited /ˈspɪrɪtɪd/ *adj* lively, energetic or having strength of mind: *The Prime Minister gave a spirited defence of his policies.* ○ *a spirited debate* ذو حيويّة ونشاط؛ حماسي؛ حي
-spirited (in compounds) having a particular mood or attitude of mind: *a group of high-spirited teenagers* ذو روح (عالية مثلاً)

⚷ **spiritual** /ˈspɪrɪtʃuəl/ *adj* **1** concerning your deep thoughts, feelings or emotions: *to fulfil your spiritual needs* ➲ Look at **material**². روحي
2 concerning the Church or religion: *Tibet's exiled spiritual leader, the Dalai Lama* روحي، ديني
▶ **spiritually** /-tʃuəli/ *adv* روحيًا

spiritualism /ˈspɪrɪtʃuəlɪzəm/ *noun* [U] the belief that you can get messages from the spirits (2) of people who are dead الروحانيّة: الاعتقاد بإمكانيّة الاتّصال بالأرواح
▶ **spiritualist** /-ɪst/ *noun* [C] a person who believes in or who is involved with spiritualism روحاني؛ وسيط روحاني

spit /spɪt/ *verb* [I,T] (spitting; *pt, pp* spat /spæt/) **spit (sth) (out)** to send liquid, food, etc. out from your mouth: *No spitting allowed!* ○ *He took one sip of the drink and spat it out.* ❶ In US English the past tense and past participle can also be **spit**. يبصق
▶ **spit** *noun* [U] (*informal*) the liquid in your mouth ➲ Look at **saliva**. لعاب، بصاق

⚷ **spite** /spaɪt/ *noun* [U] the desire to hurt or annoy sb: *He stole her letters out of spite.* ضغينة، نكاية
▶ **in spite of** *prep* used for introducing sth that may be unexpected or surprising: *The match was played in spite of the awful weather.* ○ *In spite of all her hard work, Sue failed her exam.* بالرغم من، رغم
spite *verb* [T] to try to hurt or annoy sb: *I think he only said it to spite me.* يغيظ؛ يؤذي
spiteful /-fl/ *adj* feeling or showing spite (1); unkind: *He's been saying spiteful things about his ex-girlfriend.* مليء بالحقد، مسيء؛ مكايد
spitefully *adv* /-fəli/ بحقد، بكيد، نكاية به

splash /splæʃ/ *verb* [I,T] (to cause a liquid) to fly about in drops and make sb/sth wet: *Rain splashed against the windows.* ○ *The children were splashing each other with water.* ○ *Be careful not to splash paint onto the floor.* يرش؛ يطرطش، يتخبّط في الماء
PHR V splash out (on sth) (*informal*) to spend money on sth that is an expensive luxury or that you do not really need ينفق بسخاء على شيء كمالي
▶ **splash** *noun* [C] **1** an act or sound of splashing: *Paul jumped into the pool with a big splash.* طرطشة، رشاش؛ صوت التخبّط في الماء
2 a mark or spot that was made by sth splashing: *splashes of oil on the cooker* بقعة، لطخة
3 a bright area of colour: *Flowers add a splash of colour to a room.* رقعة زاهية الألوان

splatter /ˈsplætə(r)/ *verb* [I,T] (used about a liquid) to splash and make sb/sth wet or dirty; to make a liquid do this: *The paint was splattered all over the floor.* "يطرطش": يلطّخ

splay /spleɪ/ *verb* [I,T] (to cause sth) to spread out or become wider at one end: *splayed fingers* يمدّ، يبسط؛ ينبسط؛ يتفلطح

splendid /ˈsplendɪd/ *adj* **1** very good; excellent: *What a splendid idea!* ممتاز، رائع
2 of fine or grand appearance: *the splendid royal palace* فخم، بهي

▸ **splendidly** *adv* بشكل رائع

splendour (*US* **splendor**) /ˈsplendə(r)/ *noun* [U] beauty that is grand and that impresses people: *the splendour of the Swiss Alps* بهاء، روعة

splint /splɪnt/ *noun* [C] a piece of wood or metal that is used to keep a broken bone in the right position جبيرة

splinter /ˈsplɪntə(r)/ *noun* [C] a small thin sharp piece of wood, metal or glass that has broken off a larger piece: *I've got a splinter in my finger.* شظيّة؛ كسرة صغيرة

▸ **splinter** *verb* [I,T] to break into small thin sharp pieces يتحطّم (أو يحطّم) إلى قطع صغيرة حادّة

split /splɪt/ *verb* (*pres part* **splitting**; *pt, pp* **split**) **1** [I,T] **split (sth) (up) (into sth)** to break into two or more parts, usually from end to end, making a long line: *My jeans have split.* يفلق أو ينفلق، يشقّ أو ينشقّ

2 [I,T] **split (sb) (up) (into sth)** (to cause people) to divide into different groups: *Let's split into two groups.* ○ *The children have been split into five groups according to their ability.* يقسّم؛ ينقسم

3 [T] to divide or share sth: *We split the cost of the meal between the six of us.* يقسّم

IDM **split the difference** to agree on an amount or figure that is halfway between the two amounts or figures already mentioned يقبل رقماً وسطاً بين عرضين

split hairs to try to find small differences between things that are almost the same ℹ Usually used in a critical way. يماحك في فروقات بسيطة

PHR V **split up (with sb)** to end a marriage or relationship: *He's split up with his girlfriend.* ينفصل عن

▸ **split** *noun* [C] **1** a division in a group: *Disagreement about European policy led to a split within the Conservative party.* انشقاق

2 a long cut or hole in sth شقّ، صدع

ˌsplit ˈsecond *noun* [C] a very short period of time: *It only took me a split second to decide.* برهة وجيزة

splutter /ˈsplʌtə(r)/ *verb* **1** [I,T] to speak with difficulty e.g. because you are very angry or excited: *'How dare you!' she spluttered indignantly.* يجمجم، يتكلّم بصعوبة

2 [I] to make a series of sounds like a person spitting or coughing: *He fell into the pool and came up coughing and spluttering.* يتفّ

▸ **splutter** *noun* [C] جمْجَمة: "تفتفة"

spoil /spɔɪl/ *verb* (*pt*) (*pp* **spoilt** /spɔɪlt/ or **spoiled** /spɔɪld/) **1** [T] to make sth useless or unsuccessful, or not as good as before: *The new office block will spoil the view.* ○ *Our holiday was spoilt by bad weather.* ○ *Eating between meals will spoil your appetite.* يفسد

2 [T] to do too much for sb, especially a child, so that you have a bad effect on his/her character: *a spoilt child* يفرط في التدليل، يفسد

3 [T] to treat sb/yourself very well for a certain period of time in order to make this person/yourself happy: *Why not spoil yourself with one of our new range of beauty products?* (= in an advertisement) يدلّل

▸ **spoils** *noun* [plural] things that have been stolen, or taken in a war or battle غنيمة، سلب

spoilsport /ˈspɔɪlspɔːt/ *noun* [C] a person who tries to stop other people enjoying themselves من يفسد أو يعكّر بهجة الآخرين

spoke¹ /spəʊk/ *noun* [C] one of the thin pieces of metal that connect the centre of a wheel (the hub) to the outside edge (the rim) شعاع الدولاب، بَرْمَق، "سيخ"

spoke² *pt* of SPEAK

spoken *pp* of SPEAK

spokesman /ˈspəʊksmən/ *noun* [C] (*pl.* **spokesmen** /-mən/) a person who is chosen to speak for a group or organization متحدث (رسميّ)، ناطق بلسان

> A woman is called a **spokeswoman**. **Spokesperson** is now often preferred because it can be used for a man or a woman.

sponge /spʌndʒ/ *noun* [C,U] **1** a piece of rubber or plastic (or of a natural substance also called 'sponge'). Sponges have many small holes, soak up water and are used for cleaning things or for washing yourself. اسفنجة

2 [C,U] = SPONGE CAKE

▸ **sponge** *verb* [T] to clean sth with a wet sponge or cloth يمسح أو ينظّف باسفنجة

PHR V **sponge on/off sb** (*informal*) to get money, food, etc. from sb without doing or giving anything in return: *It's about time you stopped sponging off your parents!* يتطفل على، يستدر منه مالاً وغيره

ˈsponge bag *noun* [C] (*Brit*) a bag in which you put soap, toothpaste, etc. when you are travelling حقيبة صغيرة لمستلزمات الحمّام

ˈsponge cake (*also* **sponge**) *noun* [C,U] a light cake made with eggs, flour and sugar, and sometimes fat الكعكة الاسفنجيّة

sponsor /ˈspɒnsə(r)/ *noun* [C] **1** a person or an organization that helps to pay for a special sports event, etc. (usually so that it can advertise its products) راعٍ لبرنامج أو حَدَث رياضي وما إليهما

2 a person who agrees to pay money to a charity if sb else completes a particular activity: *I need sponsors for a bike ride to Brighton in aid of Cancer Research.* متكفّل ماليّاً

▸ **sponsor** *verb* [T] to be a sponsor (1,2) for sb/sth: *A large insurance company is sponsoring the next football tournament.* ○ *a sponsored walk to raise money for children in need* يرعى؛ يتكفّل ماليّاً

> In Britain, it is common to try to raise money for charity by taking part in a **sponsored walk, swim, run**, etc. People ask their friends, family and colleagues to give them a certain amount of money, e.g. 50 pence for each mile that they do and the money is collected afterwards and given to the charity: *Will you sponsor me for a charity swim I'm doing?*

sports equipment

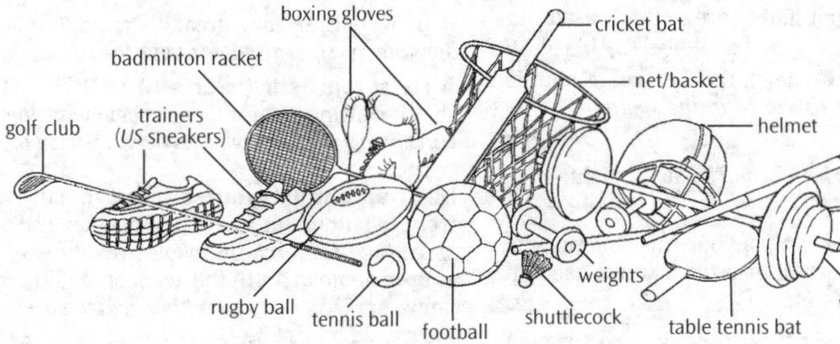

sponsorship *noun* [U]: *Many theatres depend on industry for sponsorship.* رعاية؛ تكفّل مالي

spontaneous /spɒn'teɪniəs/ *adj* done or happening naturally; not planned: *a spontaneous burst of applause* عفوي، تلقائي
▶ **spontaneously** *adv* عفوياً، تلقائياً
spontaneity /ˌspɒntə'neɪəti/ *noun* [U] عفوية

spooky /'spu:ki/ *adj* (**spookier**; **spookiest**) (*informal*) frightening: *It's spooky being in the house alone at night.* مرعب، مُفْزع

spool /spu:l/ *noun* [C] a round object which thread, film, wire, etc. are wound around when you buy them ➲ Look at **reel**[1]. بكرة، ملَفّ، "كرّارية"

⚷ **spoon** /spu:n/ *noun* [C] **1** an object with a round end and a long handle that you use for eating, stirring or serving food: *Give each person a knife, fork and spoon.* ○ *a wooden spoon for cooking* ملعقة
2 (*also* '**spoonful**) the amount that one spoon can hold: *Add two spoonfuls of sugar.* ملء ملعقة
▶ **spoon** *verb* [T] to lift or serve sth with a spoon يغرف أو يسكب بالملعقة

sporadic /spə'rædɪk/ *adj* not done or happening regularly: *There has been sporadic gunfire during the night.* متفرق، متقطّع
▶ **sporadically** /-kli/ *adv* بين آن وآخر

⚷ **sport** /spɔ:t/ *noun* **1** [U] a physical game or activity that you do for exercise or because you enjoy it: *John did a lot of sport when he was at school.* ○ *amateur/professional sport* ○ *And now with the news, sport and weather here's Mark Foster* (= on the radio or on television). رياضة
2 [C] a particular game or type of sport: *Which sports do you like playing?* ○ *the sports page of a newspaper* ○ *winter sports* (= skiing, skating, etc.) لعبة رياضيّة
3 [C] (*informal*) a person who does not get angry or upset if he/she loses a game or if sb plays a joke on him/her ➲ Look at **spoilsport**. من يتقبّل الهزيمة أو الدعابة بروح رياضيّة
▶ **sporting** *adj* connected with sport: *a sporting achievement* رياضي

'**sports car** *noun* [C] a low, fast car often with a roof that you can open سيارة "سباقيّة"

sportsman /'spɔ:tsmən/ *noun* [C] (*pl.* **sportsmen** /-mən/) a man who plays sports: *a keen sportsman* (رجل) رياضي
▶ '**sportsmanlike** *adj* behaving well and fairly when you are playing sport ذو روح رياضيّة متسامحة
'**sportsmanship** *noun* [U] the quality of being sportsmanlike الروح الرياضيّة

sportswoman /'spɔ:tswʊmən/ *noun* [C] (*pl.* **sportswomen** /-wɪmɪn/) a woman who plays sports رياضيّة

⚷ **spot**[1] /spɒt/ *noun* [C] **1** a small round mark of a different colour on sth: *Leopards have dark spots.* ○ *a blue skirt with red spots on it* نقطة، رقطة
2 a small dirty mark on sth: *You've got a spot of gravy on your shirt.* بقعة، لطخة
3 a small red mark on your skin, sometimes caused by a disease: *Many teenagers get spots on their face.* بثرة، حبّة
4 a particular place or area: *a nice spot for a picnic* موضع، بقعة
5 = SPOTLIGHT (1)
6 [usually sing.] **a spot of sth** (*Brit informal*) a small amount of sth: *Can you help me? I'm having a spot of trouble.* قليل من
IDM **have a soft spot for sb/sth** → SOFT
on the spot 1 immediately: *Paul was caught stealing money and was dismissed on the spot.* فوراً
2 at the place where sth happened or where sb/sth is needed: *The fire brigade were on the spot within five minutes.* في مكان الحادث؛ في مكانه
put sb on the spot to make sb answer a difficult question or make a difficult decision without having much time to think يحرجه بسؤال صعب أو قضية يتطلّب تفكيراً طويلاً
▶ **spotted** *adj* marked or covered with spots (1): *a spotted blouse* منقّط؛ مرقّط
spotless *adj* having no spots (2) or marks; very clean: *Her house is always spotless.* نقيّ، ناصع؛ نظيف جداً
spotty *adj* (**spottier**; **spottiest**) having spots (3) on your skin: *a spotty young man* ذو بثور على وجهه

spot[2] /spɒt/ *verb* [T] (**spotting**; **spotted**) to see or notice sb/sth: *I've spotted a couple of spelling mistakes.* يرى، يلاحظ؛ يكتشف

ˌ**spot** '**check** *noun* [C] a test on one of a group of people or things which is not planned or expected اختبار أو تفتيش مفاجئ

spotlight /ˈspɒtlaɪt/ *noun* **1** [C] (*also* **spot**) a lamp that can send a strong beam of light onto a small area. Spotlights are often used in theatres. (في المسرح) نور ساطع مركّز، بقعة ضوء

2 the spotlight [sing.] the centre of public attention or interest: *to be in the spotlight* محطّ الأنظار

ˌspot ˈon *adj* (*Brit informal*) exactly right: *Your estimate was spot on.* مضبوط تماماً

spouse /spaʊs/ *noun* [C] your husband or wife ❶ **Spouse** is a formal or official word, used on forms, documents, etc. زوج أو زوجة

spout /spaʊt/ *noun* [C] a tube or pipe through which liquid comes out: *the spout of a teapot* بزبوز، بلبلة، فوهة؛ ميزاب

▸ **spout** *verb* [I,T] **1** (used about a liquid) to come out from sth with force; to make a liquid do this: *Water spouted out from the broken pipe.* ينبثق، يندفع؛ يضخّ

2 (*informal*) to say sth, using a lot of words, in a way that is not interesting: *She was spouting poetry at me.* يتفوّه بكلام مزعج أو مملّ

sprain /spreɪn/ *verb* [T] to injure part of your body by bending or turning it suddenly: *to sprain your ankle* يلوي (المفصل)، يفكش، يثأ

▸ **sprain** *noun* [C]: *Your wrist isn't broken. It's just a bad sprain.* ليّ، فكش، وثْء

sprang *pt* of SPRING³

sprawl /sprɔːl/ *verb* [I] **1** to sit or lie with your arms and legs spread out in an untidy way: *People lay sprawled out in the sun.* يجلس أو يستلقي باسطاً ذراعيه وساقيه

2 to cover a large area of land (in an unplanned way): *The city sprawls along the coast.* يمتدّ دون نظام

▸ **sprawling** *adj*: *the sprawling city suburbs* منتشر دون نظام

🔑**spray** /spreɪ/ *noun* **1** [U] liquid in very small drops that is blown through the air: *clouds of spray from the waves* رذاذ، رشاش

2 [C,U] liquid in a special container (aerosol) that is forced out under pressure when you push a button: *hairspray* سائل للبخّ

▸ **spray** *verb* [I,T] (used about a liquid) to be sent out in very small drops with great force; to send a liquid out in this way: *The water sprayed out from the hole in the pipe.* ○ *Somebody's sprayed paint on my door!* ○ *Somebody's sprayed my door with paint.* ○ *The crops are regularly sprayed with pesticide.* يترشّش؛ يرشّ، يبخّ

🔑**spread** /spred/ *verb* (*pt, pp* **spread**) **1** [T] **spread sth (out) (on/over sth)** to open sth so that you can see all of it: *Spread out the map on the table so we can all see it!* يبسط، يمدّ

2 [T] **spread A on B; spread B with A** to cover a surface with a soft substance: *to spread jam on bread* ○ *to spread bread with jam* يدهن

3 [I,T] to affect a larger area or a bigger group of people; to make sth do this: *The fire spread rapidly because of the strong wind.* ○ *Rats and flies spread disease.* ينتشر؛ ينشر

4 [I] to continue for a great distance: *The swamp spreads for several miles along the coast.* يمتدّ

5 [T] **spread sth (over sth)** to divide sth so that it continues for a longer period of time: *You can spread your repayments over a period of three years.* يقسّم أو يوزّع

PHR V **spread (sb/yourself) out** to move away from the others in a group of people: *The police spread out to search the whole area.* يتفرّق، يتوزّع

▸ **spread** *noun* **1** [U] the act of spreading sth or being spread: *Dirty drinking water encourages the spread of disease.* انتشار؛ نشر

2 [C,U] soft food that you eat on bread: *Don't eat butter. Use a low-fat spread.* إدام يدهن على الخبز

3 [C] a newspaper or magazine article that covers one or more pages: *a double-page spread* مقالة تملأ صفحة كاملة أو اكثر

spreadsheet /ˈspredʃiːt/ *noun* [C] a computer program for working with rows of numbers, used especially for doing accounts برنامج حسابات (في الكمبيوتر)

spree /spriː/ *noun* [C] (*informal*) a short time that you spend doing sth you enjoy, often doing too much of it: *a shopping/spending spree* وقت للمرح والمتعة، انغماس في المرح والمتعة

sprig /sprɪɡ/ *noun* [C] a small piece of a plant with leaves on it عِرق (زهور)، عسلوج

🔑**spring¹** /sprɪŋ/ *noun* [C] **1** a place where water comes up naturally from under the ground: *a hot spring* نبع أو ينبوع

2 a long piece of thin metal or wire that is bent round and round. After you push or pull a spring it goes back to its original shape and size: *the springs of a bed* نابض، زُنبرك

3 an act of springing³ (1) or jumping up: *With one spring the cat landed on the table.* وثبة، قفزة

▸ **springy** *adj* able to go back to its original shape or size after being pushed, pulled, etc: *soft springy grass* مرن، يعود إلى شكله الأصلي

🔑**spring²** /sprɪŋ/ *noun* [C,U] the season of the year which follows winter and comes before summer. In spring the weather gets warmer and plants begin to grow: *Daffodils bloom in the spring.* ○ *There's a feeling of spring in the air.* الربيع

spring³ /sprɪŋ/ *verb* (*pt* **sprang** /spræŋ/; *pp* **sprung** /sprʌŋ/) [I] **1** to jump or move quickly: *When the alarm went off, Ray sprang out of bed.* ○ *to spring to your feet* ○ (*figurative*) *Everyone sprang to her defence when the boss started criticizing her.* يقفز؛ يهبّ، يسرع إلى

2 to happen suddenly or when not expected: *The door sprang open and Bella walked in.* يحدث فجأة ودون توقّع

3 spring from sth to be the result of sth: *Her behaviour springs from fear.* ينبع من، ينشأ عن

PHR V **spring sth on sb** (*informal*) to tell sb sth that is a surprise or not expected: *I hate to spring this on you, but can you get me those figures by tomorrow?* يفاجئه بـ

spring up to appear or develop quickly or

suddenly: *Children's play areas are springing up everywhere.* يطلع فجأة؛ ينمو بسرعة

springboard /ˈsprɪŋbɔːd/ *noun* [C] a low board that you jump on before diving into water, jumping over sth, etc. It helps you jump higher. خشبة أو منصّة الوثوب

ˌspring-ˈclean *verb* [I, T] to clean a house thoroughly ينظّف البيت تنظيفاً شاملاً

ˌspring ˈonion *noun* [C,U] a type of small onion with a long green central part and leaves بصل أخضر

springtime /ˈsprɪŋtaɪm/ *noun* [U] the period of spring فصل الربيع

sprinkle /ˈsprɪŋkl/ *verb* [T] **sprinkle A (on/onto/over B); sprinkle B (with A)** to throw drops of water or small pieces of sth over a surface: *to sprinkle sugar on a cake* ○ *to sprinkle a cake with sugar* يرش

▸ **sprinkler** /ˈsprɪŋklə(r)/ *noun* [C] a piece of equipment that sends out water in small drops. Sprinklers are used in gardens and for putting out fires in buildings. رشّاشة

sprint /sprɪnt/ *verb* [I,T] to run a short distance as fast as you can يعدو شوطاً قصيراً وبأقصى سرعة

▸ **sprint** *noun* [C] a short run or a short fast race عدو قصير (سريع)

sprout /spraʊt/ *verb* [I,T] (used about a plant) to begin to grow or to produce new leaves: *The seeds are sprouting.* ينمو، ينتش

▸ **sprout** *noun* [C] **1** a new part that has grown on a plant فرخ، شَطْء؛ فسيلة

2 = Brussels sprout

spruce /spruːs/ *verb*

PHR V **spruce (sb/yourself) up** to make sb/yourself clean and tidy يتهندم؛ يهندِم

sprung *pp* of spring³

spud /spʌd/ *noun* [C] (*informal*) a potato بطاطس، بطاطا

spun *pp* of spin

spur /spɜː(r)/ *noun* [C] **1** a sharp piece of metal that a rider wears on the back of his/her boots to help control a horse and to make it go faster مهماز

2 something that encourages you or that makes sth happen more quickly حافز؛ محرِّك

IDM **on the spur of the moment** without planning; suddenly: *I decided to go on the spur of the moment.* على عجل، ارتجالاً، عفوَ الخاطر

▸ **spur** *verb* [T] (spurring; spurred) **1** to make a horse go faster by using spurs يهمز، ينخس (الحصان)

2 spur sb/sth (on/onto sth) to encourage sb or make sb work harder or do sth more quickly: *The general spurred on his men to a fresh attack.* يستحث، يدفع

spurn /spɜːn/ *verb* [T] (*formal*) to refuse sth that sb has offered to you: *to spurn an offer of friendship* يرفض، يأنف من؛ يصدّ

spurt /spɜːt/ *verb* **1** [I,T] (used about a liquid) to come out with great force; to make a liquid do this: *Blood spurted from the wound.* ينبجس، يتفجّر؛ يضخّ

2 [I] to increase your speed or effort يزيد من سرعته؛ يضاعف جهوده

▸ **spurt** *noun* [C] **1** when a liquid comes out in a spurt, it comes out suddenly and with great force دفقة، تفجر، فورة

2 a sudden increase in speed or effort: *She put on a spurt to catch up with the other runners.* إسراع أو جهد مفاجئ

spy /spaɪ/ *noun* [C] (*pl.* **spies**) a person who tries to get secret information about another country, person or organization جاسوس

▸ **spy** *verb* (*pres part* **spying**; *3rd pers sing pres* **spies**; *pt, pp* **spied**) **1** [I] **spy (on sb/sth)** to try to get (secret) information about sb/sth ➲ Look at **espionage**. يتجسّس على

2 [T] (*formal*) to see يرى، يبصِر

Sq. *abbrev* = Square² (2)

sq (*especially US* **sq.**) *abbrev* = square (in measurements)

squabble /ˈskwɒbl/ *verb* [I] to quarrel or argue in a noisy way about sth that is not very important يتنازع (على أمر تافه)

▸ **squabble** *noun* [C] نزاع (على أمر تافه)

squad /skwɒd/ *noun* [C, with sing. or pl. verb] a group of people who work as a team: *the police drugs squad* فرقة، فريق، فصيلة

squadron /ˈskwɒdrən/ *noun* [C, with sing. or pl. verb] a group of soldiers, military ships or aeroplanes, etc. سريّة؛ عمارة؛ سرب

squalid /ˈskwɒlɪd/ *adj* very dirty, untidy and unpleasant: *squalid housing conditions* قذر، بائس، في حال سيّئة

squall /skwɔːl/ *noun* [C] a sudden storm with strong winds عاصفة مفاجئة، عصفة ريح شديدة

squalor /ˈskwɒlə(r)/ *noun* [U] the state of being very dirty, untidy or unpleasant: *to live in squalor* حالة قذارة وبؤس وإهمال

squander /ˈskwɒndə(r)/ *verb* [T] to waste time, money, etc: *Karen squandered her time on TV and computer games.* يبذّر، يبدّد، يبعزق

square¹ /skweə(r)/ *adj* **1** having four straight sides of the same length: *a square tablecloth* مربّع

2 shaped like a square: *a square face* ○ *square shoulders* مربّع

3 not owing any money: *Here is the £10 I owe you. Now we're all square.* غير مدين له، "متخالصان"

4 having equal points (in a game, etc.): *The teams were square at half-time.* متعادل

5 (used for talking about the area of sth): *If a room is 5 metres long and 4 metres wide, its area is 20 square metres.* مربّع

6 (used about sth that is square (1) in shape) having sides of a particular length: *The picture is twenty centimetres square* (= each side is twenty centimetres long). طول ضلع المربّع

IDM **a square meal** a good meal that makes you feel full (وجبة) مشبِعة

▸ **square** (*also* **squarely**) *adv* directly: *to look sb square in the eye* ○ *I think the blame falls squarely on her.* مباشرةً

square² /skweə(r)/ *noun* [C] **1** a shape that has four sides of the same length and four angles of 90 degrees (right angles): *There are 64 squares on a chess board.* المربّع

2 (*also* **Square**) an open space in a town or city that has buildings all around it: *Protesters gathered in the town square.* ○ *the market square* ساحة، ميدان

3 the number that you get when you multiply another number by itself: *Four is the square of two.* ➲ Look at **square root**. مربّع (العدد)

square³ /skweə(r)/ *verb* [I,T] **square (sth) with sth** to agree, or make sth agree, with sth else: *Your conclusion doesn't really square with the facts.* يطابق، يتّفق مع: يجعله متفقاً مع

PHRV **square up (with sb)** to pay sb the money that you owe him/her يسدِّد (دَينَه)

ˌsquare ˈroot *noun* [C] a number that produces another particular number when it is multiplied by itself: *The square root of four is two.* ➲ Look at **square²**(3). الجذر التربيعي

squash¹ /skwɒʃ/ *verb* **1** [T] to damage sth by pressing it hard so that it becomes flat: *My hat got squashed when somebody sat on it.* ○ (*figurative*) *to squash a suggestion* يمعس، يسحق؛ يخمد

2 [I,T] to go into a place, or move sb/sth to a place, where there is not much space: *We all squashed into the back of the car.* ينحشر؛ يحشر

squash² /skwɒʃ/ *noun* **1** [C, usually sing.] a lot of people in a small space: *We can get ten people around the table, but it's a bit of a squash.* زحمة

2 [C,U] (*Brit*) a drink that is made from fruit juice and sugar. You add water to squash before you drink it: *orange squash* شراب (فاكهة)

squash³ /skwɒʃ/ *noun* [U] a game for two people, played in a special room (court). You play squash by hitting a small rubber ball with a racket against any one of the walls of the room: *Let's have a game of squash.* لعبة السكواش

squat¹ /skwɒt/ *verb* [I] (squa**tt**ing; squa**tt**ed) **1** to sit down with your feet on the ground and your legs bent and your bottom just above the ground يقرفص، يجلس القرفصاء

2 to go and live in an empty building without permission from the owner يحتلّ بناء خالياً للسكنى

▸ **squatter** *noun* [C] a person who squats (2) من يحتلّ بناء خالياً للسكنى

squat² /skwɒt/ *adj* short and fat or thick: *a squat and ugly building* قصير وسمين: منخفض وعريض

squawk /skwɔːk/ *verb* [I] (used especially about a bird) to make a loud unpleasant noise ينعق: يطلق صوتاً حادّاً

▸ **squawk** *noun* [C] نعيق: صوت عالٍ حادّ

squeak /skwiːk/ *noun* [C] a short high noise that is not very loud: *the squeak of a mouse* ○ *a little squeak of surprise* صرير؛ صَئي، زقزقة

▸ **squeak** *verb* [I,T] يصرّ؛ يصأى؛ يزقزق أو "يزيّق"

squeaky *adj* (**squeakier**; **squeakiest**): *a squeaky floorboard* ○ *a squeaky voice* ذو صرير؛ ذو صوت حادّ

squeal /skwiːl/ *verb* [I,T] to make a loud high noise that is a sign of pain, fear or enjoyment: *The baby squealed in delight at the new toy.* يزعق أو يصرخ (من الألم أو الفرح أو غيره)

▸ **squeal** *noun* [C]: *The car stopped, with a squeal of tyres.* زعيق؛ صوت رفيع حادّ

A **squeal** is louder and longer than a **squeak** but it is not as loud as a **scream**.

squeamish /ˈskwiːmɪʃ/ *adj* (used about a person) easily upset by sth unpleasant, e.g. the sight of blood شديد الحساسية للأشياء المنفِّرة؛ سريع الغثيان

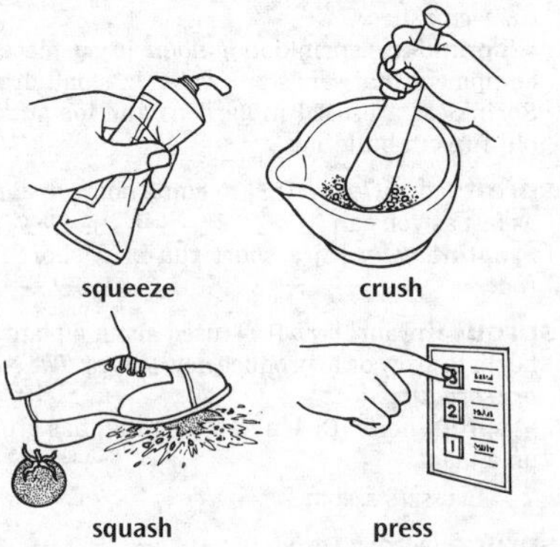

squeeze /skwiːz/ *verb* **1** [T] **squeeze sth (out)**; **squeeze sth (from/out of sth)** to press sth hard for a particular purpose: *She squeezed his hand as a sign of affection.* ○ *to squeeze a tube of toothpaste* ○ *to squeeze an orange/lemon* (= to get the juice) ○ *to squeeze a cloth dry* يعصر؛ يضغط على

2 [I,T] **squeeze (sb/sth) into, through, etc. sth**; **squeeze (sb/sth) through, in, past, etc.** to go or move sth into, through, etc. a place where there is not much space: *Excuse me, please. Can I squeeze past?* ○ *We can squeeze another person into the back of the car.* ○ (*figurative*) *Do you think you can squeeze in another appointment this afternoon?* يخترق الزحام؛ يحشر

▸ **squeeze** *noun* **1** [C] an act of squeezing (1) sb/sth, e.g. as a sign of love or affection: *to give someone a squeeze* ➲ Look at **hug**. حضنة قويّة؛ ضغطة

2 [C] the amount of liquid that you get from squeezing an orange, lemon, etc: *a squeeze of lemon* عصارة ليمونة مثلاً

3 [sing.] a situation where there is not much space: *It was a tight squeeze to get everybody in the car.* زحمة، "حشرة"

4 [C, usually sing.] a difficult situation in which there is not enough money, time, etc: *a government squeeze on spending* تضييق، تحديد

squelch /skweltʃ/ *verb* [I] to make the sound your feet make when you are walking in deep wet mud يحدث صوت التخويض في الوحل

squid /skwɪd/ *noun* [C,U] (*pl.* **squid** or **squids**) a sea animal that we eat with a long soft body and ten long parts (tentacles) حبّار سيبيا

squiggle /ˈskwɪgl/ *noun* [C] (*informal*) a short curly line, e.g. in sb's handwriting خطّ صغير معقوف

squint /ˈskwɪnt/ *verb* [I] **1** to have eyes that do not move together properly and appear to look in different directions at the same time يحول، يكون أحول

2 to look at sth with your eyes almost closed: *to squint in bright sunlight* يضيّق عينيه عند النظر

▶ **squint** *noun* [C] the condition in which your eyes do not move together properly: *to have a squint* حَوَل

squire /ˈskwaɪə(r)/ *noun* [C] (in the past) a man who owned land in a country area ملاّك كبير في الريف

squirm /skwɜːm/ *verb* [I] to move your body in a way which shows you are uncomfortable, ashamed or embarrassed يتلوّى (ألماً أو خجلاً)؛ يتملّص؛ يتململ

squirrel /ˈskwɪrəl; *US* ˈskwɜːrəl/ *noun* [C] a small red or grey animal with a long thick tail that lives in trees and eats nuts سنجاب

squirt /skwɜːt/ *verb* [I,T] (used about a liquid) to be forced out from sth in a thin fast stream; to make a liquid move in this way; to hit sb/sth with a liquid in this way: *I squeezed the bottle and oil squirted out.* ○ *She squirted water at the flames.* ○ *He squirted me with water.* ينبجس من فوهة ضيّقة. "يَنْفُر": يرشّ أو يبخّ

Sr. (*Brit also* **Sr**) *abbrev* = SENIOR

St (*especially US* **St.**) *abbrev* **1** = SAINT

2 = STREET

st. (*Brit also* **st**) *abbrev* = STONE (5)

stab /stæb/ *verb* [T] (sta**bb**ing; sta**bb**ed) to push a knife or other pointed object into sb/sth: *The man had been stabbed in the back.* يطعن

▶ **stab** *noun* [C] **1** an injury that was caused by a knife, etc: *a stab in the back* ○ *a stab wound* طعنة

2 a sudden sharp pain: *a stab of pain* ○ (*figurative*) *a stab of guilt* نخزة ألم مفاجئة؛ وخز

IDM **have a stab at sth/doing sth** (*informal*) to try to do sth: *I'll have a stab at painting your portrait.* محاولة

stabbing *adj* (used about a pain) sudden and strong (ألم) حادّ مفاجئ

stabbing *noun* [C] an occasion when sb stabs sb else: *Following last night's stabbing, police are looking for a tall blond man.* طَعْن بسكّين (مثلاً)

🔑**stable¹** /ˈsteɪbl/ *adj* not likely to move, change or end: *This ladder doesn't seem very stable.* ○ *The patient is in a stable condition.* ○ *a stable relationship* ℹ The opposite is **unstable**. ثابت؛ راسخ؛ مستقرّ

▶ **stability** /stəˈbɪləti/ *noun* [U] the state or quality of being stable: *After so much change we now need a period of stability.* استقرار؛ ثبات؛ توازن

stabilize (*also* **stabilise**) /ˈsteɪbəlaɪz/ *verb* [I,T] to become or to make sth stable ℹ The opposite is **destabilize**. يستقرّ؛ يتوازن؛ يثبّت، يرسّخ؛ يحفظ التوازن

🔑**stable²** /ˈsteɪbl/ *noun* [C] a building where horses are kept اصطبل

stack /stæk/ *noun* [C] **1** a tidy pile of sth: *a stack of plates, books, etc.* كدسة منظّمة، رصيص

2 (often plural) (*informal*) a lot of: *I've still got stacks of work to do.* أكداس من (الشغل)، كثير من

▶ **stack** *verb* [T] **stack sth (up)** to put sth into a pile: *Could you stack those chairs for me?* ينضّد، يكدّس واحداً فوق الآخر

stacked /stækt/ *adj* full of; covered in: *The floor was stacked with books.* مليء بِ، مغطّى بِ

stadium /ˈsteɪdiəm/ *noun* [C] (*pl.* **stadiums** or **stadia** /-diə/) a large sports ground with rows of seats around it: *a football stadium* ○ *the Olympic stadium in Barcelona* ملعب رياضي كبير، "ستاد"

🔑**staff** /stɑːf; *US* stæf/ *noun* [C, usually sing., U] the group of people who work for a particular organization: *The hotel staff were very helpful.* ○ *Two members of staff will accompany the students on the school trip.* ○ *Our London office has a staff of 28.* ○ *All staff must attend the meeting on Friday.* هيئة الموظّفين (في مؤسسة ما)

> We say **a member of staff** (NOT **a staff)** to talk about one person who works for an organization. **Staff** is usually only used in the singular and is usually used with a plural verb: *The staff all speak good English.*

▶ **staff** *verb* [T] (usually passive): *The school is staffed by highly qualified teachers.* يزوّد بموظّفين

staffroom /ˈstɑːfruːm; -rʊm; *US* ˈstæfruːm/ *noun* [C] a room in a school where teachers can go when they are not teaching غرفة المدرسين

stag /stæg/ *noun* [C] an adult male deer أيّل، ذكر الظّبي

🔑**stage¹** /steɪdʒ/ *noun* [C] one part of the progress or development of sth: *The first stage of the course lasts for three weeks.* ○ *I suggest we do the journey in two stages.* ○ *the early stages of the match* ○ *At this stage it's too early to say what will happen.* مرحلة؛ طور

🔑**stage²** /steɪdʒ/ *noun* **1** [C] a raised floor in a theatre or concert hall, etc. on which actors, musicians, etc. perform: *to go on stage* خشبة المسرح

2 the stage [sing.] the world of theatre; the profession of acting: *After starring in several films he has decided to return to the stage.* المسرح، العمل المسرحيّ

▶ **stage** *verb* [T] **1** to organize a performance of a play, concert, etc. for the public يعرض على المسرح، يقدّم للجمهور

2 to organize an event: *They have decided to stage a 24-hour strike.* ينظّم؛ يقوم بِ

ˌ**stage ˈmanager** *noun* [C] the person who is

responsible for the stage and scenery during a theatre performance مدير المسرح

stagger /ˈstægə(r)/ *verb* [I] to walk in an unsteady way, as if you could fall at any moment, e.g. because you are ill or carrying sth heavy يترنّح، يتعثّر وكأنّه على وشك السقوط

▸ **staggered** *adj* **1** very surprised: *I was absolutely staggered when I heard the news.* مصعوق؛ مندهش

2 (used about a set of times, payments, etc.) arranged so that they do not all happen at the same time: *staggered working hours* (= when people start and finish work at different times) متعاقب

staggering *adj* that you find difficult to believe: *a staggering £2 billion profit* مذهل

staggeringly *adv* إلى حدّ كبير؛ بصورة لا تُصدّق

stagnant /ˈstægnənt/ *adj* **1** (used about water) not flowing and therefore dirty and having an unpleasant smell (ماء) راكد، آسِن

2 (used about business, etc.) not active; not developing: *a stagnant economy* راكد

stagnate /stægˈneɪt; *US* ˈstægneɪt/ *verb* [I] to be inactive; not to develop or change: *a stagnating economy* يركد، يجمد

▸ **stagnation** /stægˈneɪʃn/ *noun* [U] ركود، جمود

ˈ**stag night** *noun* [C] (*also* ˈ**stag party** (*pl.* **stag parties**)) a party for men only that is given for a man just before his wedding day حفلة للرجال فقط تُقام قبيل عرس أحدهم

staid /steɪd/ *adj* (used about a person) serious, old-fashioned and rather boring جِدّي ذو عقلية محافظة ومملّ إلى حدّ ما

stain /steɪn/ *verb* [I,T] to leave a coloured mark that is difficult to remove: *Don't spill any of that juice. It'll stain the carpet.* يتلوّث؛ يبقّع، يلوّث، يلطخ

▸ **stain** *noun* [C]: *The blood had left a stain on his shirt.* بقعة، لطخة

ˌ**stained** ˈ**glass** *noun* [U] pieces of coloured glass that are used in church windows, etc: *a stained-glass window* زجاج ملوّن (للنوافذ)

ˌ**stainless** ˈ**steel** *noun* [U] steel that does not stain or rust: *a stainless steel pan* فولاذ لا يصدأ، "ستينلس"

stair /steə(r)/ *noun* **1** **stairs** [plural] a series of steps inside a building that lead from one level to another: *The lift wasn't working so I had to use the stairs.* ○ *at the bottom/top of the stairs* ○ *two flights* (= sets) *of stairs* ○ *I heard somebody coming down the stairs.* ○ *She ran up the stairs.* ➲ Look at **downstairs** and **upstairs**. سلّم، دَرَج

2 [C] one of the steps in this series: *She sat down on the bottom stair to read the letter.* سُلّمة، دَرَجة

staircase /ˈsteəkeɪs/ (*also* **stairway** /ˈsteəweɪ/) *noun* [C] a set of stairs with rails on each side that you can hold on to ➲ Look at **escalator**. سلّم، دَرَج

> Compare **stair** and **step**. **Stairs** or **flights of stairs** are usually inside buildings. **Steps** are usually outside buildings and made of stone or concrete.

stake¹ /steɪk/ *noun* **1** **stakes** [plural] the things that you might win or lose in a game or in a particular situation: *We play cards for money, but never for very high stakes.* رهينة؛ مقدار الرهان

2 [C] a part of a company, etc. that you own, usually because you have invested money in it: *Foreign investors now have a 20% stake in the company.* حصّة في شركة

IDM **at stake** in danger of being lost; at risk: *He thought very carefully about the decision because he knew his future was at stake.* في خطر، عرضة للضياع

▸ **stake** *verb* [T] **stake sth (on sth)** to put your future, etc. in danger by doing sth, because you hope that it will bring you a good result: *He is staking his political reputation on this issue.* يخاطر بـ أو يقامر بـ

IDM **stake a/your claim (to sth)** to say that you have a right to have sth: *Both companies have staked their claim to the same piece of land.* يعلن أو يصرح (عن حقه في)

stake² /steɪk/ *noun* [C] a wooden or metal pole with a point at one end that you push into the ground, e.g. to support a young tree دعامة لنبْتة، رُجْبة، خازوق

stale /steɪl/ *adj* **1** (used about food or air) old and not fresh any more: *The bread had gone stale.* ○ *stale cigarette smoke* غير طازج، بائت

2 not interesting or exciting any more: *She says her marriage has gone stale.* فاتر، قليل الحيويّة والإثارة

stalemate /ˈsteɪlmeɪt/ *noun* [sing., U] a situation in an argument in which neither side can win or make any progress نقطة الجمود (في المفاوضات)

stalk¹ /stɔːk/ *noun* [C] one of the long thin parts of a plant which the flowers, leaves or fruit grow on ساق؛ سويقة؛ عنَيْق

stalk² /stɔːk/ *verb* **1** [T] to follow an animal quietly, closely and secretly in order to catch or kill it: *a lion stalking its prey* يتعقّب خلسة، يترصّد

2 [T] to follow a person over a period of time in a frightening or annoying way: *The actress claimed the man had been stalking her for two years.* يتعقّب خلسة، يترصّد

3 [I] to walk stiffly in an angry or arrogant way: *He got up and stalked angrily out of the room.* يتبختر

stall¹ /stɔːl/ *noun* **1** [C] a small shop with an open front or a table with things for sale in a market, street, etc: *a stall in the market* ○ *a bookstall at the station* كشك، دكّانة صغيرة

2 **stalls** [plural] the level of seats nearest the front in a theatre or cinema المقاعد الأماميّة في مسرح أو سينما

stall² /stɔːl/ *verb* [I,T] **1** (used about a vehicle) to stop suddenly because the engine fails; to make a vehicle do this accidentally: *A bus had stalled in the middle of the road.* ○ *I kept stalling the car.* يتوقّف محرّك السيارة فجأة؛ يوقف المحرّك عن غير قصد

2 to avoid doing sth or to try to stop sth happening until a later time: *I've asked them several times for the money but they keep stalling.* يماطل

stallion /'stæliən/ *noun* [C] an adult male horse, especially one that is kept for breeding ➲ Look at the note at **horse**. فحل الخيل، حصان صالح للتوليد

stalwart /'stɔːlwət/ *adj* loyal and hard-working: *a stalwart member of the Labour Party* شديد الولاء، جادّ في عمله

stamina /'stæmɪnə/ *noun* [U] the ability to do sth that requires a lot of physical or mental effort for a long time: *You need a lot of stamina to run long distances.* جَلَد، قوة الاحتمال

stammer /'stæmə(r)/ *verb* **1** [I] to speak with difficulty and sudden pauses, repeating the same sounds or words again and again, because you have a speech problem or because you are nervous يتلعثم، يتعتع

2 [T] to say sth in this way: *He stammered an apology and left quickly.* يقول شيئاً بلعثمة

▶ **stammer** *noun* [sing.]: *to have a stammer* تعتعة، لعثمة

⚷ **stamp¹** /stæmp/ *noun* [C] **1** (*also* **postage stamp**) a small piece of paper that you stick onto a letter or parcel to show that you have paid for it to be posted: *Three 30p stamps, please.* طابع بريديّ

> In the British postal system, there are two types of stamp for posting letters, etc. to other parts of Britain, **first-class** stamps and **second-class** stamps. Letters with first-class stamps are more expensive and arrive more quickly.

2 a small object that prints some words, a design, the date, etc. when you press it onto a surface: *a date stamp* خَتْم

3 the mark made by a stamp (2): *a stamp in my passport* خَتْم، دمغة

4 the stamp of sth [usually sing.] something that shows a particular quality or that sth was done by a particular person: *Her novels have the stamp of genius.* طابَع خاصّ، سيماء

⚷ **stamp²** /stæmp/ *verb* **1** [I,T] **stamp (on sth)** to put your foot down very heavily on the ground or on sth else: *He stamped on the spider and squashed it.* ○ *It was so cold that I had to stamp my feet to keep warm.* يدوس بقوة على: يضرب الأرض بقدمه

2 [I] to walk with loud heavy steps usually because you are angry: *She stamped around the room, shouting angrily.* يمشي خابطاً الأرض بغضب

3 [T] **stamp A (on B)**; **stamp B (with A)** to print some words, a design, the date, etc. by pressing a small object (a stamp) onto a surface: *to stamp a passport* ○ *The date is stamped on the receipt.* يختم، يمهر، يدمغ

PHR V **stamp sth out** to put an end to sth completely: *The police are trying to stamp out this kind of crime.* يقمع: يمحق

'stamp album *noun* [C] a book in which you put stamps that you have collected ألبوم الطوابع

'stamp collecting *noun* [U] the hobby of collecting stamps هواية جمع الطوابع

,stamped addressed 'envelope *noun* [C] (*abbr* **sae**) an empty envelope with your own name and address and a stamp on it that you send to a company, etc. when you want sth sent back to you ظرف للرد (يعنونه المرسل ويضع عليه طابعاً)

stampede /stæm'piːd/ *verb* [I,T] (used about a group of animals or people) to rush in a particular direction in a wild and uncontrolled way (قطيع أو جمهور) يفرّ بأجمعه فراراً مذعوراً

stance /stæns; stɑːns/ *noun* [C, usually sing.] **1 stance (on sth)** an attitude (especially moral or political) towards sth: *the Prime Minister's stance on foreign affairs* موقف

2 the position in which somebody stands (especially in sport when preparing to hit the ball) وِقفة أو وضعيّة

⚷ **stand¹** /stænd/ *verb* [I,T] (*pt, pp* **stood** /stʊd/) **1** [I] to be on your feet; to be upright: *He was standing near the window.* يقف

2 [I] **stand (up)** to rise to your feet from another position: *He stood up when I entered the room.* يقوم، ينتصب واقفاً

3 [T] to put sb/sth in a particular place or position: *She stood her wet umbrella in the corner of the office.* وقّف

4 [I] to be or to remain in a particular position or situation: *The castle stands on a hill.* ○ *The house has stood empty for ten years.* ○ *He was very critical of the law as it stands* (= as it is now). يقوم؛ يبقى

5 [I] (used about an offer, a decision, etc.) to be or to remain unchanged: *Does your decision still stand?* يظلّ قائماً، يبقى ساري المفعول

6 [I] to be of a particular height, level, amount, etc: *The world record stands at 6.59 metres.* يبلغ

7 [I] to have an opinion or view (about sth): *I don't know where I stand on abortion.* يفكّر، يكوّن رأياً

8 [I] **stand to do sth** to be in a situation where you are likely to do sth: *If he has to sell the company, he stands to lose a lot of money.* يُحتمل أن

9 [I] to be a candidate in an election: *She's standing for the European Parliament.* يترشح

10 [T] (in negative sentences and questions, with *can/could*) to be able to bear sb/sth: *I can't stand that woman – she's so rude.* يتحمّل، يُطيق

11 [T] to buy a meal or drink for sb: *He stood me lunch.* يدفع ثمن وجبة أو مشروب لزميله مثلاً

PHR V **stand around** to stand somewhere not doing anything: *A lot of people were just standing around outside.* يقف متعطلاً

stand aside to move to one side: *People stood aside to let the police pass.* يتنحّى، يقف جانباً

stand back to move back: *The policeman told everybody to stand back.* يرجع إلى الوراء

stand by 1 to be present, but do nothing in a situation: *How can you stand by and let them treat their animals like that?* يقف متفرّجاً لا يساعد

2 to be ready to act: *The police are standing by in case there's trouble.* يقف على أهبة الاستعداد

stand for sth 1 to be a short form of sth: *What does BBC stand for?* يمثّل

2 to support sth (e.g. an idea or opinion): *I hate everything that the party stands for.* يناصر؛ يؤمن بـ

stand in (for sb) to take sb's place for a short time: *Mr Jones is standing in for Miss Evans this week.* يحلّ محلّه موقّتاً

stand out to be easily seen or noticed يبرز، يكون بادياً للعيان

stand up to be or become vertical: *You'll look taller if you stand up straight.* يقف منتصِب القامة

stand sb up (*informal*) to not appear when you have arranged to meet sb, especially a boyfriend or girlfriend: *She never came! I'd been stood up.* يتخلف عن الموعد

stand up for sb/sth to say or do sth which shows that you support sb/sth: *I admire him. He really stands up for his rights.* يدافع عن

stand up to sb/sth to defend yourself against sb/sth that is stronger or more powerful يجابه بجرأة، يدافع عن نفسه

stand[2] /stænd/ *noun* [C] **1** a table or small shop in the street or in a large public building from which you can buy things or get information: *a news-stand ○ a company stand at a trade fair* كشك، منضدة لعرض السلع

2 a piece of furniture that you can put things on or in: *a music stand* حامل؛ مشجب

3 a large building at a sports ground that is open at the front and where people sit or stand in rows to watch the sport قسم المتفرجين في ملعب رياضيّ

IDM **make a stand (against sb/sth)** to defend yourself, your opinion, etc. strongly against sb/sth يدافع بجرأة عن (آرائه)؛ يهاجم

take a stand (on sth) to say publicly what you think and intend to do about sth يتكلّم علناً عن

standard /ˈstændəd/ *noun* [C] **1** a level of quality: *We complained about the low standard of service in the hotel. ○ the high standard of teaching ○ We need to improve educational standards in this country. ○ This work is not up to your usual standard.* مستوى

2 a level of quality that you compare sth else with: *By European standards this is a very expensive city. ○ He is a brilliant player by any standard.* مقياس، معيار

3 [usually pl.] a level of behaviour that is morally acceptable: *Many people are worried about falling standards in modern society.* سلوك، أخلاق

▸ **standard** *adj* **1** of the normal type; without anything special or extra: *This is the standard model of the car. The de luxe version costs more.* عاديّ

2 part of the normal situation; not unusual in any way: *It is standard practice to ask students to fill in this form when they arrive.* متعارف عليه، معتاد

3 (used about language) that people generally accept as normal and correct: *standard English* مصطلح عليه، قياسيّ

4 (used about a book, etc.) that people most often read when they are studying a particular subject: *the standard work on the legal system* أساسيّ؛ نظاميّ

standardize (*also* **standardise**) /ˈstændədaɪz/ *verb* [T] to make things that are different the same: *Safety tests on old cars have been standardized throughout Europe.* يوحّد

▸ **standardization** /stændədaɪˈzeɪʃn/ (*also* **standardisation**) *noun* [U] توحيد

ˌstandard of ˈliving *noun* [C] the level of wealth and comfort that a person, group or country has in everyday life: *There is a higher standard of living in the north than in the south.* ℹ An expression with a similar meaning is **living standards**. This is used in the plural: *Living standards have improved.* مستوى المعيشة

standby /ˈstændbaɪ/ *noun* [C] (*pl.* **standbys**) a person or thing that is ready to be used if necessary: *We always keep candles as a standby in case there is a power cut.* شخص أو شيء احتياطيّ

IDM **on standby** ready; waiting to do sth: *When fighting began, the hospitals were put on standby.* على استعداد

standing /ˈstændɪŋ/ *noun* [U] **1** the opinion that other people (in public life) have of you: *The consequences for Britain's international standing could be extremely serious.* مكانة، منزلة

2 the amount of time during which sth has continued to exist: *a problem of many years' standing* مدّة، فترة

▸ **standing** *adj* continuing to exist; permanent: *I have a standing invitation to go and stay with them whenever I like.* قائم؛ دائم

ˌstanding ˈorder *noun* [C] an instruction to your bank to make a regular payment to sb from your account طلب (أمر) دائم بالدفع

standpoint /ˈstændpɔɪnt/ *noun* [C] a particular way of thinking about sth: *The television programme looked at the problems of education from the standpoint of the teacher.* وجهة نظر

standstill /ˈstændstɪl/ *noun* [sing.] a situation of no movement, progress or activity: *The traffic came to a complete standstill.* توقف تام

IDM **grind to a halt/standstill** → GRIND

stank *pt* of STINK

stanza /ˈstænzə/ *noun* [C] a group of lines that form a unit in some types of poetry; a verse مقطع شِعْري

staple[1] /ˈsteɪpl/ *noun* [C] a small thin piece of bent wire that you push through pieces of paper in order to fasten them together using a special tool (stapler) رَزّة، دبّوس سلكي لضمّ الورق

▸ **staple** *verb* [T]: *Staple the letter to the application form.* يرزّز، يثبّت برَزّة

stapler /ˈsteɪplə(r)/ *noun* [C] رزازة ورق، دبّاسة

staple[2] /ˈsteɪpl/ *adj* (used especially about food) forming the main part of what people eat: *a staple diet of rice and fish* رئيسي

star /stɑː(r)/ *noun* **1** [C] a large ball of burning gas in outer space that you see as a small point of light in the sky at night: *It was a clear night and the stars were shining brightly.* نجم

2 [C] a shape with a number of points sticking out in a regular pattern: *The children decorated the classroom with paper stars.* نجمة

3 [C] a printed shape of this type that is used for indicating a level of quality: *a five-star hotel* نجمة

4 [C] a famous person in acting, music or sport: *a film star* نجم (سينمائي مثلاً)

5 stars [plural] = HOROSCOPE: *Your stars say you're going to be very lucky this month.*

▸ **star** *verb* (starring; starred) **1** [I] **star (in sth)** to be one of the main actors in a play, film, etc: *Gwyneth Paltrow is to star in a new romantic comedy.* يقوم ببطولة فيلم مثلاً

2 [T] to have sb as a star: *The film stars Tom Cruise as a fighter pilot.* يقدّم ممثلاً بدور البطولة

stardom /ˈstɑːdəm/ *noun* [U] the position of being a famous person in acting, music or sport عالم الشهرة والأضواء

starry (starrier; starriest) *adj* full of stars: *a starry night* مليء أو مزادن بالنجوم

starboard /ˈstɑːbəd/ *noun* [U] the side of a ship that is on the right when you are facing towards the front of it ❶ The opposite is **port**. الجانب الأيمن من السفينة

starch /stɑːtʃ/ *noun* [C,U] **1** a white substance with no taste in foods such as potatoes, rice and bread نشاء

2 a substance that is used for making cloth stiff نشاء

▸ **starched** *adj* made stiff with starch: *a starched shirt collar* منشّى

⚷ **stare** /steə(r)/ *verb* [I] **stare (at sb/sth)** to look at sb or sth continuously for a long time because you are interested, surprised, etc: *Everybody stared at his hat.* ○ *He didn't reply, he just stared into the distance.* يحملق، يحدّق

starfish /ˈstɑːfɪʃ/ *noun* a flat sea creature in the shape of a star with five arms نجم البحر

stark /stɑːk/ *adj* **1** very bare and plain and therefore not attractive: *a stark landscape* أجرد، مقفر؛ عارٍ

2 clearly unpleasant: *the stark realities of a life of poverty* قاسٍ، مؤلم

3 very clear: *In stark contrast to the old buildings in the area are five enormous new tower blocks.* واضح، صارخ

▸ **stark** *adv* completely: *stark naked* كلياً

starlight /ˈstɑːlaɪt/ *noun* [U] the light that is given out by stars ضوء النجوم

starling /ˈstɑːlɪŋ/ *noun* [C] a small noisy bird with dark shiny feathers زرزور

starry → STAR

ˈstar sign = SIGN[1] (5)

⚷ **start[1]** /stɑːt/ *verb* **1** [I,T] **start (sth/to do sth/doing sth)** to begin doing sth: *Turn over your exam papers and start now.* ○ *We'll have to start* (= leave) *early if we want to be in Dover by 10.* ○ *Prices start at £5.* ○ *After waiting for an hour, the customers started to complain.* ○ *She started playing the piano when she was six.* ○ *What time do you have to start work in the morning?* يبدأ

2 [I,T] to begin to happen or to make sth begin to happen: *What time does the concert start?* ○ *I'd like to start the meeting now.* ○ *The fight started when the boys were leaving the disco.* ○ *The police think a young woman may have started the fire.* ➲ Look at the note at **begin**. يبدأ؛ يشرع في؛ يسبّب

3 [I,T] **start (sth) (up)** to create a company, an organization, etc.; to be created: *They've decided to start their own business.* ○ *There are a lot of new companies starting up in that area now.* يؤسّس، ينشئ

4 [I,T] **start (sth) (up)** (used about an engine, a car, etc.) to begin to work; to make an engine, a car, etc. begin to work: *The car won't start.* ○ *We heard an engine starting up in the street.* ○ *He got onto his motor bike, started the engine and rode away.* يشتغل؛ يُشغّل

5 [I] to make a sudden, quick movement because you are surprised or afraid: *A loud noise outside made me start.* يجفل

IDM **to start (off) with 1** in the beginning; at first: *To start with everything was fine but then there were problems.* في البداية؛ في الأول

2 (used for giving your first reason for sth): *'Why are you so angry?' 'Well, to start off with you're late, and secondly you've lied to me.'* أولاً

set/start the ball rolling → BALL[1]

PHR V **start off** to begin in a particular way: *I'd like to start off by welcoming you all to Oxford.* يستهلّ (كلامه مثلاً)

start on sth to begin doing sth that needs to be done: *Haven't you started on the washing-up yet?* يشرع في

start out to begin your life, career, etc. in a particular way: *She started out as a teacher in Glasgow.* يبدأ حياته

start over (*US*) to begin again: *I've made a lot of mistakes – I'd better start over.* يبدأ من جديد

⚷ **start[2]** /stɑːt/ *noun* **1** [C, usually sing.] the beginning or first part of sth: *The chairman made a short speech at the start of the meeting.* ○ *I told you it was a bad idea from the start.* بداية، مستهل

2 [C, usually sing.] an act of starting: *We've got a lot of work to do today, so let's make a start.* ○ *a fresh start in life* شروع، بداية

3 the start [sing.] the place where a race starts: *The athletes are now lining up at the start.* مبدأ السباق

4 [C, usually sing.] an advantage that you give to a weaker person at the beginning of a race, game, etc. أفضلية تعطى إلى لاعب أضعف

5 [C, usually sing.] a sudden quick movement that your body makes because you are surprised or afraid جفلة، نفرة

IDM **for a start** (used for giving your first reason for sth): *'Why can't we go on holiday?' 'Well, for a start we can't afford it...'* أولاً

get off to a good, bad, etc. start to start well, badly, etc: *My day got off to a good start – I was told I'd got a pay rise.* يبدأ بداية حسنة (أو سيّئة)

starter /ˈstɑːtə(r)/ *noun* [C] a small amount of food that you eat as the first part of a meal
طبق خفيف يستهلّ الوجبة

ˈ**starting point** *noun* [C] **1** an idea or topic that you use to begin a discussion with نقطة البدء

2 the place where you begin a journey: *This town is a good starting point for a tour of the area.* نقطة الانطلاق

startle /ˈstɑːtl/ *verb* [T] to make sb/sth suddenly surprised or frightened يفزّع؛ يبهت

▸ **startled** *adj*: *He had a startled look on his face.* مبهوت، فزع، مباغت

startling /ˈstɑːtlɪŋ/ *adj* مذهل

starve /stɑːv/ *verb* [I,T] to suffer very badly or die from hunger; to make sb/sth suffer or die in this way: *Millions of people are starving in the poorer countries of the world.* ○ *That winter many animals starved to death.* ○ *You must eat more – you're starving yourself.*
يتضوّر أو يموت جوعاً؛ يُميته جوعاً

IDM **be starved of sth** to suffer because you are not getting enough of sth that you need: *The children had been starved of love for years.*
يعاني من الحرمان

be starving (*informal*) to be extremely hungry: *When will dinner be ready? I'm starving!*
يكاد يموت جوعاً

▸ **starvation** /stɑːˈveɪʃn/ *noun* [U] suffering or death because there is not enough food: *to die of starvation* مجاعة؛ الموت جوعاً

state[1] /steɪt/ *noun* **1** [C] the condition that sb/sth is in at a particular time: *the state of the economy* ○ *a state of shock* ○ *The house is in a terrible state.* حالة، حال

2 [C] (*also* **State**) a country with its own government: *Pakistan has been an independent state since 1947.* ➲ Look at the note at **country**.
دولة

3 [C] (*also* **State**) a part of a country that has its own government: *California is one of the biggest states in the US.* ولاية

4 [U] especially **the State** the government of a country: *the relationship between the Church and the State* ○ *State schools* ○ *heads of State* (= government leaders) الدولة

5 the States [plural] (*informal*) the United States of America: *We lived in the States for about five years.* الولايات المتحدة الأمريكية

6 [U] very formal events and behaviour connected with governments and the leaders of countries: *The Queen is going on a state visit to China.* ○ *The President was driven in state through the streets.* حدث رسميّ؛ أبّهة

IDM **in/into a state** (*informal*) very nervous or upset: *Now don't get into a state! I'm sure everything will be all right.* في حالة اهتياج واضطراب

state of affairs a situation: *This state of affairs must not be allowed to continue.* حالة، وضع

state of mind mental condition: *She's in a very confused state of mind.* حالة نفسيّة، وضع ذهنيّ

state[2] /steɪt/ *verb* [T] to say or write sth, often formally: *Your letter states that you sent the goods on 31 March, but we have never received them.* ○ *As I stated earlier, I do not believe that this information is accurate.* يذكر، يصرّح

▸ **statement** *noun* [C] **1** something that you say or write, often formally: *The Prime Minister will make a statement about the defence cuts today.* ○ *After the accident I had to go to the police station to make a statement.* تصريح، بيان؛ إفادة

2 = BANK STATEMENT

stately /ˈsteɪtli/ *adj* (**statelier**; **stateliest**) formal and dignified: *a stately old building*
فخم، جليل، ذو أبّهة

ˌ**stately ˈhome** *noun* [C] (*Brit*) a large old house that has historical interest and can be visited by the public بيت كبير ذو قيمة تاريخيّة

statesman /ˈsteɪtsmən/ *noun* [C] (*pl.* **statesmen** /-mən/) an important and experienced politician who has earned public respect
سياسيّ محنّك، رجل دولة

static /ˈstætɪk/ *adj* not moving or changing: *House prices are static.* ساكن، ثابت؛ جامد

▸ **static** (*also* ˌ**static elecˈtricity**) *noun* [U] **1** electricity that collects on a surface
الكهرباء الساكنة

2 sudden loud noises on a radio or television, caused by electricity in the atmosphere
تشوُّش (الراديو) بسبب العوامل الجويّة

station /ˈsteɪʃn/ *noun* [C] **1** (*also* **railway station**) a building on a railway line where trains stop so that passengers can get on and off: *I got to the station two minutes before my train left.* ○ *Which station are you getting off at?* محطّة قطار

2 a building from which buses or coaches begin and end journeys: *The coach leaves Victoria Coach Station at 9.30 am.* محطّة انطلاق الباصات

3 a building where a particular service or activity is based: *a fire station* (= where the fire brigade is based) ○ *a petrol station* ○ *a police station* ○ *a power station*
محطّة (بنزين مثلاً)، مركز، نقطة

4 a company that broadcasts programmes on a particular frequency on the radio or on television: *a local radio station* ➲ Look at **channel**.
محطة إذاعة أو تلفزيون

▸ **station** *verb* [T] (often passive) to send soldiers, etc. to a particular place: *During his time in the army, he was stationed in Germany.* ○ *Guards stationed themselves at every entrance to the building.* يرسل (جنديّا) إلى مكان خدمته؛ يرابط

stationary /ˈsteɪʃənri; *US* -neri/ *adj* not moving: *He crashed into the back of a stationary vehicle.* واقف، مستقرّ في محلّه، غير متحرّك

stationery /ˈsteɪʃənri; *US* -neri/ *noun* [U] equipment for writing, e.g. pens, pencils, paper, envelopes أدوات قرطاسيّة

▸ **stationer's** *noun* [C] a shop that sells stationery محل لبيع الأدوات المكتبية، وراّق

ˈ**station wagon** *noun* [C] (*US*) = ESTATE CAR

statistics /stəˈtɪstɪks/ *noun* **1** [plural] numbers that have been collected in order to provide information about sth: *Statistics indicate that 90% of*

stationery

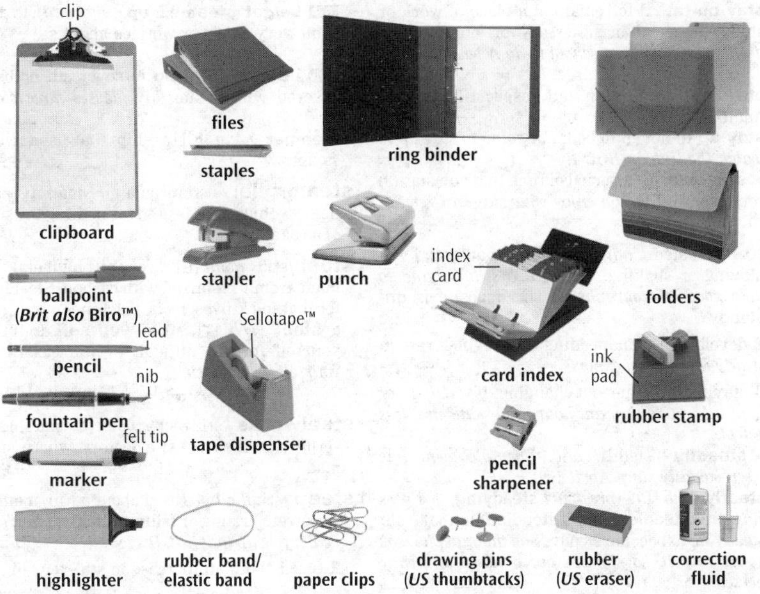

homes in this country have a television. ○ *crime statistics* إحصاءات

2 [U] the science of collecting and analysing these numbers علم الإحصاء

▶ **statistical** /stəˈtɪstɪkl/ *adj*: *statistical information, evidence, etc.* إحصائي

statistically /-kli/ *adv* وفقاً للإحصاءات؛ إحصائياً

⚷ **statue** /ˈstætʃuː/ *noun* [C] the figure of a person or animal, that is made of stone or metal and usually put in a public place: *the Statue of Liberty in New York* تمثال

stature /ˈstætʃə(r)/ *noun* [U] (*formal*) **1** the height of a person: *He's quite small in stature.* قامة

2 the importance that sb has because people have a high opinion of his/her skill or achievement: *Her research has given her considerable stature in the scientific world.* مكانة، قيمة

⚷ **status** /ˈsteɪtəs/ *noun* **1** [sing.] your social or professional position in relation to other people: *Teachers don't have a very high status in this country.* مكانة، مقام

2 [U] a high social position: *The new job gave him much more status.* منزلة رفيعة، جاه

3 [U] your legal position: *Please indicate your name, age and marital status* (= whether you are married or single). الوضع القانوني؛ الحالة العائليّة

status quo /ˌsteɪtəs ˈkwəʊ/ *noun* [sing.] **the status quo** the situation that exists at a particular time الوضع الراهن

ˈ**status symbol** *noun* [C] something that a person owns that shows that he/she has a high position in society رمز للمنزلة الرفيعة

statute /ˈstætʃuːt/ *noun* [C] (*formal*) a rule or law قانون تشريعيّ

▶ **statutory** /ˈstætʃətri; *US* -tɔːri/ *adj* (*formal*) decided by law: *a statutory right* قانونيّ، منصوص عليه قانونياً

staunch /stɔːntʃ/ *adj* believing in sth or supporting sb/sth very strongly; loyal: *a staunch supporter of the Liberal Democrats* شديد الولاء، راسخ العقيدة

stave /steɪv/ *verb*

PHR V **stave sth off** to stop sth unpleasant from happening now, although it may happen at a later time: *to stave off a financial crisis* يدرأ أو يدفع عنه مؤقتاً

⚷ **stay** /steɪ/ *verb* [I] **1** to continue to be somewhere and not go away: *Patrick stayed in bed until 11 o'clock.* ○ *I can't stay long.* ○ *Stay on this road until you get to Wells.* يبقى، يمكث

2 to continue to be in a particular state or situation without change: *I can't stay awake any longer.* ❶ **Remain** and **stay** are similar in meaning but **remain** is more formal. يظلّ، يستمرّ، يبقى

3 to be somewhere as a visitor or guest: *We stayed with friends in France.* ○ *to stay at a hotel* ○ *Can you stay for lunch?* ○ *Why don't you stay the night?* يقيم؛ يمكث

IDM **stay put** (*informal*) to remain in one place: *We like this flat so we'll probably stay put for a few years.* يبقى في مكانه

PHR V **stay behind** to remain in a place after other people have gone لا يغادر مع الآخرين

stay in to remain at home: *I'm going to stay in and watch TV.* يبقى في البيت

stay on (at ...) to remain at a place of work or study longer than necessary or normal: *I've decided to stay on at school to do A levels.* يبقى، يستمر

stay out to remain out, especially late at night يسهر خارج البيت

stay up to not go to bed: *I'm going to stay up to watch the film on BBC 1.* يسهر

▸ **stay** *noun* [C] a period of time that you stay (3) somewhere: *Did you enjoy your stay in Crete?* إقامة

steady /ˈstedi/ *adj* (**steadier**; **steadiest**) **1** not moving or shaking: *You need a steady hand to take good photographs.* ❶ The opposite is **unsteady**. ثابت

2 developing or happening at a regular rate: *a steady increase in exports* مطّرد، منتظم

3 staying the same; not changing: *If you drive at a steady 50 miles an hour, you will use less petrol.* ثابت

▸ **steadily** /ˈstedɪli/ *adv*: *Unemployment has risen steadily since April 1991.* باطّراد

steady *verb* [I,T] (*pres part* **steadying**; *3rd pers sing pres* **steadies**; *pt*, *pp* **steadied**) to make sth steady or to become steady: *She thought she was going to fall, so she put out a hand to steady herself.* يثبّت، يمكّن؛ يثبت؛ يستقرّ

steak /steɪk/ *noun* [C,U] a thick flat piece of meat or fish: *a piece of steak* ○ *a salmon steak* ➲ Look at **chop**[2]. شريحة من اللحم أو السمك

steal /stiːl/ *verb* (*pt* **stole** /stəʊl/; *pp* **stolen** /ˈstəʊlən/) **1** [I,T] **steal (sth) (from sb/sth)** to take sth that belongs to another person secretly and without permission: *The terrorists were driving a stolen car.* يسرق

> You **steal** things, but you **rob** people (of things): *My camera has been stolen!* ○ *I've been robbed!* ○ *They robbed me of all my money!*

➲ Look also at the note at **thief**.

2 [I] **steal away, in, out, etc.** to move somewhere secretly and quietly ينسلّ، ينسحب خلسة

stealth /stelθ/ *noun* [U] (*formal*) behaviour that is secret or quiet: *The terrorists operate by stealth.* تسلّل، خفية

▸ **stealthy** *adj* (**stealthier**; **stealthiest**): *to make a stealthy approach* مسترَق، مختلَس، تسلُّلي

stealthily *adv* خلسةً، تسلّلاً

steam /stiːm/ *noun* [U] **1** the hot gas that water changes into when it boils: *Steam was rising from the coffee.* بخار

2 the power that can be produced from steam: *a steam engine* قوّة بخاريّة محرّكة

IDM **let off steam** (*informal*) to release energy or express strong feeling by behaving in a noisy or uncontrolled way يطلق لنفسه العنان، ينفّس عن مشاعره

run out of steam (*informal*) to have no more energy تنفد طاقته، يتراخى

▸ **steam** *verb* **1** [I] to send out steam: *steaming hot soup* يتصاعد منه البخار

2 [T] to cook sth in steam: *steamed vegetables* يطبخ على البخار

IDM **be/get steamed up** (*informal*) to be/become very angry or worried about sth يغضب؛ يضطرب، ينزعج

PHR V **steam (sth) up** to cover sth or become covered with steam: *My glasses have steamed up.* يغبّش أو يتغبّش بالبخار

steamer *noun* [C] a ship that is driven by steam باخرة، قارب بخاريّ

steamroller /ˈstiːmrəʊlə(r)/ *noun* [C] a big heavy vehicle that is used for making the surface of a road flat محدلة بخاريّة

steel /stiːl/ *noun* [U] a very strong metal that is made from iron mixed with carbon. Steel is used for making knives, tools, machines, etc. فولاذ

▸ **steel** *verb* [T] **steel yourself** to prepare yourself for sth difficult or unpleasant: *Steel yourself for a shock.* يستجمع قواه أو يتأهّب (لسماع أو عمل شيء مزعج)

steelworks /ˈstiːlwɜːks/ *noun* [C, with sing. or pl. verb] (*pl.* **steelworks**) a factory where steel is made مصانع الفولاذ

steep /stiːp/ *adj* **1** (used about a hill, mountain, street, etc.) rising or falling quickly: *I don't think I can cycle up that hill. It's too steep.* شديد الانحدار

2 (used about an increase in sth) very big هائل، كبير جداً

3 (*informal*) too expensive باهظ، غالٍ جداً

▸ **steeply** *adv*: *House prices have risen steeply this year.* بصورة هائلة

steepness *noun* [U] شدة الانحدار؛ غلاء (السعر)

steeped /stiːpt/ *adj* having a lot of; full of: *The city of Oxford is steeped in history.* مفعم بـ؛ منغمس؛ عريق

steeple /ˈstiːpl/ *noun* [C] a church tower that has a pointed top (spire) برج الكنيسة المدبّب

steer /stɪə(r)/ *verb* [I,T] to control the direction that a vehicle is going in, by using a wheel, etc: *Can you push the car while I steer?* ○ *to steer a boat, ship, bicycle, motorbike, etc.* ○ (*figurative*) *She tried to steer the conversation away from the subject of money.* يوجّه؛ يدير الدفّة؛ يقود (سيّارة)

> **Steer** means to control the direction of a vehicle. If you **ride** a bicycle/motorbike or **sail** a boat you steer it and you are also in control of everything else.

▸ **steering** /ˈstɪərɪŋ/ *noun* [U] the mechanical parts that control the direction that a vehicle is going in أجزاء القيادة أو التوجيه في سيّارة

ˈ**steering wheel** (*also* **wheel**) *noun* [C] the wheel in a car, etc. that you use for steering عجلة القيادة

stem[1] /stem/ *noun* [C] **1** one of the long thin parts of a plant which the leaves or flowers grow on ساق النبتة، ساق الزهرة، جذع

2 the main part of a word onto which other parts are added: *'Writ-' is the stem of the words 'write', 'writing', 'written' and 'writer'.* جذر الكلمة

▶ **stem** *verb* (stemming; stemmed)
PHR V **stem from sth** to be caused by sth; to have sth as an origin: *His interest in Egypt stems from the time he spent there when he was a child.* ينشأ عن، ينبع من

stem² /stem/ *verb* [T] (stemming; stemmed) to stop sth that is increasing or spreading يمنع تفشي شيء، يكبح

'stem cell *noun* [C] a basic type of cell which can divide and develop into cells with particular functions. All the different kinds of cells in the human body develop from stem cells خلية جذعيّة

stench /stentʃ/ *noun* [C, usually sing.] a very unpleasant smell رائحة نتن: رائحة خبيثة

step¹ /step/ *verb* [I] (stepping; stepped) to lift one foot and put it down in a different place when you are walking: *Be careful! Don't step in the mud.* ○ *to step forward/back* ○ *Ouch! You stepped on my foot!* يخطو؛ يدوس
PHR V **step down** to give up a position of authority: *Anne is stepping down as chairperson at the end of the year.* يتنازل عن منصبه
step in to become involved in a difficult situation, usually in order to help يتدخّل للمساعدة
step sth up to increase sth: *The Army has decided to step up its security arrangements.* يصعِّد، يزيد، يضاعف

step² /step/ *noun* [C] **1** the act of lifting one foot and putting it down in a different place: *Neil took two steps forwards and then stopped.* ○ *I heard steps outside the window.* خطوة
2 one action in a series of actions that you take in order to achieve sth: *the first step towards peace* خطوة
3 one of the surfaces on which you put your foot when you are going up or down stairs, a ladder, etc: *the top/bottom step* ○ *a flight (= a set) of steps* درجة
➲ Look at the note at **stair**.
IDM **in/out of step (with sb/sth)** moving/not moving your feet at the same time as other people when you are marching, dancing, etc. متوافق (أو غير متوافق) في الخطو مع الآخرين
step by step (used for talking about a series of actions) moving slowly and gradually from one action or stage to the next: *clear step-by-step instructions* خطوة فخطوة، تدريجي
take steps to do sth to take action in order to achieve sth: *to take steps to reduce unemployment* يتّخذ الخطوات اللازمة
watch your step → WATCH²

step- /step-/ (in compounds) related through one parent زوج (الأم) أو زوجة (الأب)

stepbrother /'stepbrʌθə(r)/, **stepsister** /'stepsɪstə(r)/ *noun* [C] the child of your stepmother or stepfather from an earlier marriage أخت أو أخ غير شقيق

stepchild /'steptʃaɪld/ *noun* [C] (*pl.* **stepchildren**) the child of your husband or wife from an earlier marriage ولد الزوج أو الزوجة (من زواج سابق)

stepfather /'stepfɑːðə(r)/ *noun* [C] the man who has married your mother after the death or divorce of your father الرّابّ: زوج الأمّ

stepladder /'steplædə(r)/ *noun* [C] a short ladder with two parts that can stand on its own. You can fold it up when you are not using it. سلّم قصير يطوى

stepmother /'stepmʌðə(r)/ *noun* [C] the woman who has married your father after the death or divorce of your mother الرّابّة: زوجة الأب

'stepping stone *noun* [C] one of a line of flat stones that you can step on in order to cross a river, etc. حجر يداس عليه لعبور الماء

stepson /'stepsʌn/, **stepdaughter** /'stepdɔːtə(r)/ *noun* [C] the child of your husband or wife from an earlier marriage ابن أو بنت الزوج أو الزوجة

stereo /'steriəʊ/ *noun* **1** [U] the system for playing recorded music, speech etc. in which the sound is directed through two channels: *This programme is broadcast in stereo.* نظام صوتيّ ذو قنالَيْن
2 [C] (*also* **'stereo system**) a piece of equipment for playing recorded music, etc. that has two speakers: *a car stereo* ○ *a personal stereo* جهاز صوتيّ ذو مكبّرَيْن
▶ **stereo** *adj*: *a stereo television* ذو قنالَيْن صوتيَّيْن

stereotype /'steriətaɪp/ *noun* [C] a fixed idea about a type of person or thing, which is often not true in reality: *the stereotype of the London businessman as a man with a black hat and umbrella* صورة نمطيّة، فكرة شائعة، صورة ثابتة في الأذهان
▶ **stereotype** *verb* [T] to have or show a fixed idea about a type of person or thing: *In advertisements, women are often stereotyped as housewives.* يقَوْلب: يظهره بنفس الصورة دائماً

sterile /'steraɪl; *US* 'sterəl/ *adj* **1** not able to produce young animals or babies عقيم؛ عاقر
2 completely clean and free from bacteria: *All equipment used during a medical operation must be sterile.* معقّم
3 with no interest or life: *a sterile discussion* لا روح فيه، ممل
▶ **sterility** /stə'rɪləti/ *noun* [U] عقْم

sterilize (*also* **sterilise**) *verb* [T] **1** to make sb/sth completely clean and free from bacteria يُعقِّم
2 (usually passive) to carry out an operation on a person or an animal so that they cannot have babies يعقّم: يجعله عقيماً
sterilization (*also* **sterilisation**) /ˌsterəlaɪ'zeɪʃn; *US* -lə'z-/ *noun* [U] تعقيم

sterling /'stɜːlɪŋ/ *noun* [U] the system of money that is used in Britain: *the pound sterling* الإسترليني، العملة الإنكليزيّة
▶ **sterling** *adj* of very high quality: *sterling work* من النوع الممتاز، رفيع، أصيل

stern¹ /stɜːn/ *adj* very serious and severe; not smiling: *a stern expression* ○ *a stern warning* صارم، متجهّم؛ (تحذير) شديد اللهجة
▶ **sternly** *adv* بشدّة، بصرامة

stern² /stɜːn/ *noun* [C] the back end of a ship or boat ➲ Look at **bow³**. مؤخّرة السفينة أو القارب

steroid /'sterɔɪd; 'stɪərɔɪd/ *noun* [C] a chemical

a b c d e f g h i j k l m n o p q r s t u v w x y z

compound such as a hormone or a vitamin, that is produced naturally in the body. Steroids are also used as drugs. ستيرويد

stethoscope /ˈsteθəskəʊp/ *noun* [C] the piece of equipment that a doctor uses for listening to your breathing and heart سمّاعة الطبيب

stew /stjuː; *US* stuː/ *noun* [C,U] a type of food that you make by cooking meat and/or vegetables in liquid for a long time طعام مطبوخ ببطء في مرق
▸ **stew** *verb* [I,T] to cook sth slowly in liquid: *stewed apple* يطبخ على نار هادئة في المرق

steward /ˈstjuːəd; *US* ˈstuːərd/ *noun* [C] **1** a man who looks after the passengers on an aeroplane, a ship, a train, etc. مضيف
2 a person who helps to organize a large public event, e.g a race مشرف، مدير التنظيم

stewardess /ˌstjʊəˈdes; *US* ˈstuːərdəs/ *noun* [C] **1** (*old-fashioned*) a female flight attendant مضيفة طيران
2 a woman whose job is to take care of the passengers on a ship or train مضيفة

stick¹ /stɪk/ *noun* [C] **1** a small thin piece of wood from a tree عود، قضيب
2 = WALKING STICK
3 (in some sports) a long thin piece of wood that you use for hitting the ball: *a hockey stick* ➲ Look at **bat²**, **club²**(2) and **racket¹**. عصا، مضرب
4 a long thin piece of sth: *a stick of celery* عود؛ إصبع
IDM **get (hold of) the wrong end of the stick** → WRONG¹

stick² /stɪk/ *verb* (*pt, pp* **stuck** /stʌk/) **1** [I,T] **stick (sth) in/into (sth)** to push a pointed object into sth; to be pushed into sth: *Stick a fork into the meat to see if it's ready.* ○ *I can't move. There's a piece of wire sticking in my leg.* يشك، يغرز؛ ينغرز
2 [I,T] to attach sth to sth else or to become attached to sth else by using glue, etc: *to stick a stamp on an envelope* ○ *Jam sticks to your fingers.* يلصق؛ يلتصق
3 [I] **stick (in sth)** (used about sth that can usually be moved) to become fixed in one position so that it cannot be moved: *The car was stuck in the mud.* يعلق
4 [T] (*informal*) to put sth somewhere: *Can you stick these plates on the table?* يضع
5 [T] (*informal*) (often in negative sentences and questions) to stay in a difficult or unpleasant situation: *I can't stick this job much longer.* يواظب؛ يحتمل، يطيق
IDM **poke/stick your nose into sth** → NOSE¹
PHR V **stick around** (*informal*) to stay or wait somewhere يلازم المكان، ينتظر
stick at sth (*informal*) to continue working at sth even when it is difficult يثابر على عمل صعب
stick by sb (*informal*) to continue to give sb help and support even in difficult times يبقى مؤازراً له
stick out (*informal*) to be very noticeable: *The new office block really sticks out from the older buildings around it.* يبرز، يظهر بشكل ملحوظ
stick (sth) out to be further out than sth else or to push sth further out than sth else: *The boy's head was sticking out of the window.* ○ *Don't stick your tongue out.* يبرز، ينتأ؛ يبرز
stick it/sth out (*informal*) to stay in a difficult or unpleasant situation until the end يثابر أو يتحمّل حتى النهاية
stick to sth (*informal*) to continue with sth and not change to anything else: *I'm sticking to orange juice. I prefer it.* يلزم (شيئاً)، يبقى على...
stick together (*informal*) (used about a group of people) to stay friendly and loyal to each other يتّحدون، يتماسكون
stick up to point upwards: *You look funny. Your hair's sticking up!* "يفز"، يقف
stick up for sb/yourself/sth (*informal*) to support or defend sb/yourself/sth: *Don't worry. I'll stick up for you if there's any trouble.* يساند، يدافع عن

sticker /ˈstɪkə(r)/ *noun* [C] a piece of paper with writing or a picture on one side that you can stick onto a car window, book, file, etc. لصيقة عليها كتابة أو صورة

sticky /ˈstɪki/ *adj* (**stickier**; **stickiest**) **1** (used for describing a substance that can stick to sth else, or sth that is covered with this kind of substance): *These sweets are very sticky.* ○ *I've got sticky fingers after eating that ice cream.* ○ *sticky tape* دَبِق
2 (*informal*) (used about a situation) difficult or unpleasant صعب، محرج، شائك

stiff /stɪf/ *adj* **1** (used about material, paper, etc.) quite hard and not easy to bend: *My new shoes feel rather stiff.* صلب، قاسٍ
2 (used about a handle, door, etc.) not easy to turn or move: *This door's very stiff. Can you open it for me?* قاسٍ، متيبس
3 (used about parts of the body) not easy to move: *My arm feels really stiff after playing tennis yesterday.* متيبّس
4 (used about a liquid) very thick; almost solid: *Beat the egg whites until they are stiff.* شبه جامد
5 difficult or strong: *a stiff exam* ○ *stiff opposition to the plan* صعب؛ قوي
6 (used about sb's behaviour) not relaxed or friendly; formal: *She's often a bit stiff with strangers.* جاف، متكلّف؛ رسميّ
7 (used about an alcoholic drink) strong (مشروب كحوليّ) قوي
▸ **stiff** *adv* (*informal*) extremely: *to be bored, frozen, scared, etc. stiff* للغاية، إلى أقصى حدّ
stiffly *adv* in a stiff(6) way: *He smiled stiffly.* بتصنّع؛ بجفاء
stiffness *noun* [U] تصلّب، تيبّس

stiffen /ˈstɪfn/ *verb* **1** [I] (used about a person) to suddenly become very still, usually because you are afraid or angry: *Alison stiffened as she heard a noise outside the door.* يهدأ فجأة، يتسمّر
2 [I,T] to become stiff; to make sth stiff: *a stiffened shirt collar* يتصلّب، يتيبّس؛ يصلّب، ييبّس

stifle /ˈstaɪfl/ *verb* **1** [I,T] to be or to make sb unable to breathe easily: *Richard was almost stifled by the smoke.* يختنق؛ يخنق، يكتم أنفاسه

2 [T] to stop sth from happening, developing or continuing: *Her strict education had stifled her natural creativity.* ○ *to stifle a yawn* يعيق؛ يكبت، يخمِد

▶ **stifling** /ˈstaɪflɪŋ/ *adj*: *The heat was stifling.* خانق

stigma /ˈstɪɡmə/ *noun* [C,U] a bad reputation that sth has because a lot of people have a fixed idea that it is wrong, often unfairly: *There is still a lot of stigma attached to being unemployed.* وصمة عار

still¹ /stɪl/ *adv* **1** (used for talking about sth that started at an earlier time) continuing until now or until the time you are talking about: *Do you still live in London?* ○ *It's still raining.* ○ *In 1984 Rob was still a student.* لا يزال

2 in addition; more: *There are still ten days to go until my holiday.* بعد؛ أكثر

3 (used for making a comparative adjective stronger): *It was very cold yesterday, but today it's colder still.* مع ذلك

4 (used for talking about an action or opinion that you do not expect, because sth else makes it surprising) even so: *He had a bad headache but he still went to the party.* مع ذلك

still² /stɪl/ *adj, adv* **1** without moving: *Stand still! I want to take a photograph!* ثابت، بلا حراك

2 quiet or calm: *The water was perfectly still.* ساكن، هادئ

3 (used about a drink) not containing gas: *still orange* ➲ Look at **fizzy** and **sparkling**. (شراب) غير فوّار

▶ **still** *noun* [C] a single photograph that is taken from a cinema film صورة فوتوغرافية مقتطعة من شريط سينمائي

stillness *noun* [U] the quality of being still: *the stillness of the air on a cold winter's night* سكون، هدوء

stillborn /ˈstɪlbɔːn/ *adj* (used about a baby) dead when it is born مليص: مولود ميتاً

stilt /stɪlt/ *noun* [C] **1** one of two long pieces of wood, with places to rest your feet on, on which you can walk above the ground: *a pair of stilts* إحدى عكّازتين يرتفع عليهما الماشي

2 one of a set of poles that support a building above the ground or water إحدى الركائز التي ترفع البناء فوق الأرض

stilted /ˈstɪltɪd/ *adj* (used about a way of speaking or writing) unnatural and very formal متصنّع، مترسّم

stimulant /ˈstɪmjələnt/ *noun* [C] a drug or medicine that makes you feel more active: *Caffeine is a mild stimulant.* منبّه

stimulate /ˈstɪmjuleɪt/ *verb* [T] **1** to make sth active or more active: *Exercise stimulates the blood circulation.* ○ *The government has decided to cut taxes in order to stimulate the economy.* ينبّه، ينشّط

2 to make sb feel interested and excited about sth: *The teaching he gets doesn't really stimulate him.* يحفز، يذكي حماسه

▶ **stimulating** *adj* interesting and exciting: *a stimulating discussion* شيّق، مثير، منشّط للذهن

stimulation /ˌstɪmjuˈleɪʃn/ *noun* [U] تنشيط، تنبيه، حفز

stimulus /ˈstɪmjələs/ *noun* [C,U] (*pl.* **stimuli** /-laɪ/) something that causes activity, development or interest: *Books provide children with ideas and a stimulus for play.* حافز، دافع

sting¹ /stɪŋ/ *verb* [I,T] (*pt, pp* **stung** /stʌŋ/) **1** (used about an insect, plant, etc.) to make sb/sth feel a sudden pain by pushing sth sharp into their skin and injecting poison into them: *Ow! I've been stung by a bee!* ○ *Be careful. Those plants sting.* يلدغ، يلسع، يقرص

2 to make sb/sth feel a sudden, sharp pain: *Soap stings if it gets in your eyes.* يلسع، يلذع

3 to make sb feel very hurt and upset because of sth you say: *Kate was stung by her father's words.* يجرح أو يؤلم

sting² /stɪŋ/ *noun* [C] **1** the sharp pointed part of some insects and animals that is used for pushing into the skin of a person or another animal and injecting poison إبرة، حمة

2 the pain that you feel when an animal or insect pushes its sting into you: *a wasp sting on the leg* لدغة، لسعة، قرصة

3 a sharp pain that feels like a sting: *the sting of soap in your eyes* لسعة، لذعة

stink /stɪŋk/ *verb* [I] (*pt* **stank** /stæŋk/ or **stunk** /stʌŋk/; *pp* **stunk**) (*informal*) **1** to have a very strong and unpleasant smell: *to stink of fish* تنبعث منه رائحة كريهة

2 to seem to be very bad, unpleasant or dishonest: *The whole business stinks of corruption.* تفوح منه رائحة (الغدر)

▶ **stink** *noun* [C] (*informal*) a very unpleasant smell رائحة كريهة

stint /stɪnt/ *noun* [C] a fixed period of time that you spend doing sth حصّة من العمل، نوبة

stipulate /ˈstɪpjuleɪt/ *verb* [T] (*formal*) to say exactly and officially what must be done: *The law stipulates that all schools must be inspected every three years.* ينصّ (القانون)، يشترط (العقد)

▶ **stipulation** /ˌstɪpjuˈleɪʃn/ *noun* [C,U] (*formal*) *One of the stipulations is that all team members must be British nationals.* شرط؛ اشتراط

stir /stɜː(r)/ *verb* (stirring; stirred) **1** [T] to move a liquid, etc. round and round, using a spoon, etc: *She stirred her coffee with a teaspoon.* يحرّك

2 [I,T] to move or make sb/sth move gently: *The boy stirred in his sleep.* ○ *A sudden wind stirred the leaves.* يتحرّك؛ يحرّك

3 [T] to make sb feel a strong emotion: *The story stirred Carol's imagination.* ○ *a stirring speech* يثير (المشاعر)؛ يهزّ النفوس

PHR V **stir sth up** to cause a strong feeling in other people: *The manager accused him of stirring up trouble.* يهيّج، يثير (الشغب)

▸ **stir** /stɜː(r)/ *noun* **1** [C] the action of stirring: *Give the soup a stir.* تحريكة

2 [sing.] general excitement or shock ضجّة، هزّة في المجتمع

stir-fry /ˈstɜː fraɪ/ *verb* [T] to cook thin strips of vegetables or meat quickly by stirring them in very hot oil: *stir-fried chicken* يقلي بسرعة

▸ **stir-fry** *noun* (*pl.* **-ies**) a hot dish made by stir-frying small pieces of meat, fish and/or vegetables قطع لحم أو خضروات مقلّية بسرعة

stirrup /ˈstɪrəp/ *noun* [C] one of the two metal objects that you put your feet in when you are riding a horse رِكاب

stitch /stɪtʃ/ *noun* [C] **1** one of the small lines of thread that you can see on a piece of material after it has been sewn غرزة، دَرزة، قُطبة

2 one of the small pieces of thread that a doctor uses to sew your skin together if you cut yourself very badly, or after an operation قُطبة، غرزة

3 one of the small circles of wool that you put round a needle when you are knitting قُطبة، غرزة

4 [usually sing.] a sudden pain that you get in the side of your body, e.g. after you have been running نخسة أو وخزة ألم في الخاصرة

IDM **in stitches** (*informal*) laughing so much that you cannot stop (يكاد يموت من الضحك)

▸ **stitch** *verb* [I,T] to sew: *This handle of this bag needs stitching.* يخيط

stoat /stəʊt/ *noun* [C] a small animal with brown fur that turns mainly white in winter. The white fur is called ermine. قاقِم أو قاقوم

stock¹ /stɒk/ *noun* **1** [C,U] the supply of things that a shop, etc. has for sale: *The new shop has a large stock of CDs.* ○ *We'll have to order extra stock if we sell a lot more this week.* المخزون، البضائع الموجودة في محل تجاري

2 [C] a supply or store of sth that is ready to be used: *Food stocks in the village were very low.* ذخيرة، مؤونة

3 [C,U] a share in the capital of a company; money that you lend to a company: *to invest in stocks and shares* سهم تجاري

4 [C,U] a liquid that you use to make soups, sauces, etc. It is made by boiling meat, bones, vegetables, etc. in water. مَرَق لحم أو خضراوات

IDM **in/out of stock** in/not in the supply of things that a shop, etc. has for sale متوفّر (أو غير متوفّر) في المحل التجاري

take stock (of sth) to think about sth very carefully before deciding what to do next: *Let's see how things go for a week or so and then take stock of the situation.* يدرس الموقف

▸ **stock** *adj* (only *before* a noun) (used for describing sth that sb says) used so often that it does not have much meaning: *the usual stock answers* مألوف، "كليشيه"، مبتذل

stock² /stɒk/ *verb* [T] **1** (usually used about a shop) to have a supply of sth: *They stock food from all over the world.* يتاجر بـ، يختزن

2 to provide sth with a supply of sth: *a well stocked bookshop* يجهّز، يموّن

PHR V **stock up (on/with sth)** to collect a large supply of sth for future use: *to stock up with food for the winter* يتموّن، يخزّن

▸ **stockist** *noun* [C] a shop that sells goods made by a particular company وكيل بضاعة معينة

stockbroker /ˈstɒkbrəʊkə(r)/ (*also* **broker**) *noun* [C] a person whose job it is to buy and sell stocks¹ (3) and shares (2) for other people سمسار في البورصة

ˈstock exchange *noun* [C] **1** a place where stocks¹ (3) and shares (2) are bought and sold: *the London Stock Exchange* البورصة: سوق الأوراق الماليّة

2 (*also* **ˈstock market**) the business or activity of buying and selling stocks and shares بورصة: أسعار الأسهم الماليّة

stocking /ˈstɒkɪŋ/ *noun* [C] one of a pair of thin pieces of clothing that fit tightly over a woman's foot and leg: *a pair of stockings* ➲ Look at **tights**. جورب نسائي

stocktaking /ˈstɒkteɪkɪŋ/ *noun* [U] the activity of counting the total supply of things that a shop or business has at a particular time جَرْد المحتويات

stocky /ˈstɒki/ *adj* (used about a person's body) short but strong and heavy قصير ممتلئ الجسم و قويّ

stoic /ˈstəʊɪk/ (*also* **stoical** /-kl/) *adj* (*formal*) suffering pain or difficulty without complaining جَلود على الألم، صبور دون شكوى

▸ **stoically** /-kli/ *adv* بجلَد، دون شكوى

stoicism /ˈstəʊɪsɪzəm/ *noun* [U] تجلُّد، معاناة دون شكوى

stole *pt* of STEAL

stolen *pp* of STEAL

stolid /ˈstɒlɪd/ *adj* (used about a person) showing very little emotion or excitement جامد الإحساس، بطيء التأثُّر

stomach /ˈstʌmək/ (*also informal* **tummy**) *noun* [C] **1** the part of your body where food is digested after you have eaten it معدة

2 the front part of your body below your chest and above your legs: *a fat stomach* ○ *She turned over onto her stomach.* بطن

▸ **stomach** *verb* [T] (*informal*) (usually in negative sentences and questions) to be able to watch, listen to, accept, etc. sth that you think is unpleasant: *I can't stomach too much violence in films.* يتقبّل؛ يتحمّل

ˈstomach ache *noun* [C,U] a pain in your stomach: *I've got terrible stomach-ache.* ➲ Look at the note at **ache**. ألم في المعدة أو في البطن

stomp /stɒmp/ *verb* [I] (*informal*) to walk with heavy steps يمشي بخطى ثقيلة، "يدبّك"

stone /stəʊn/ *noun* **1** [U] a hard solid substance that is found in the ground: *The house was built of grey stone.* ○ *a stone wall* حجر

2 [C] a small piece of rock: *The boy picked up a stone and threw it into the river.* حَجَرة، حصاة

3 [C] = PRECIOUS STONE

4 [C] the hard seed inside some fruits, e.g. peaches, plums, cherries and olives نواة (الثمرة)

5 [C] (*pl.* **stone**) (*abbr* **st.**; **st**) a measure of weight; 6.35 kilograms. There are 14 pounds in a stone. وحدة وزن بريطانيّة

▸ **stone** *verb* [T] to throw stones at sb/sth, e.g. as a punishment: *The two women were stoned to death.* يرجم

stoned *adj* (*slang*) under the influence of drugs "مسطول": "سكران طينة"

stonemason /ˈstəʊnmeɪsn/ *noun* [C] a person who cuts and prepares stone or builds with stone حجّار، بنّاء (بالأحجار)

stonework /ˈstəʊnwɜːk/ *noun* [U] the parts of a building that are made of stone الجزء الحجريّ من مبنى

stony /ˈstəʊni/ *adj* (**stonier**; **stoniest**) **1** (used about the ground) having a lot of stones in it, or covered with stones مليء أو مغطّى بالأحجار

2 not friendly: *There was a stony silence as he walked into the room.* جافّ؛ عدائيّ؛ قاسٍ

stood *pt, pp* of STAND[1]

stool /stuːl/ *noun* [C] a seat that does not have a back or arms: *a piano stool* كرسي بلا ظهر و لا ذراعين

stoop /stuːp/ *verb* [I] to bend your head and shoulders forwards and downwards: *Cathy had to stoop to get through the low doorway.* ينحني

PHRV **stoop to sth/to doing sth** to do sth bad or wrong (that you would normally not do): *I would never stoop to cheating.* يهبط إلى مستوى (كذا)، ينحطّ إلى

▸ **stoop** *noun* [sing.]: *to walk with a stoop* حَنْية الظهر؛ احديداب

stop[1] /stɒp/ *verb* (stop**p**ing; stop**p**ed) **1** [I] to finish moving, happening or operating: *He walked along the road for a bit, and then stopped.* ○ *Does this train stop at Oxford?* ○ *I think the rain has stopped.* ○ *Oh no! My watch has stopped.* يقف، يتوقف

2 [T] to make sb/sth finish moving, happening or operating: *I stopped someone in the street to ask the way to the station.* ○ *Can you stop the car, please?* يوقف

3 [T] to end or finish an activity: *Stop making that terrible noise!* ○ *We stopped work for half an hour to have a cup of coffee.* ○ *It's stopped raining now.* يوقف؛ يقف؛ يكفّ عن

> If you **stop to do** something, you stop in order to do it: *On the way home I stopped to buy a newspaper.* If you **stop doing** something you do not do it any more: *Stop talking and listen to me!*

4 [T] **stop sb/sth (from) doing sth** to make sb/sth end or finish an activity; prevent sb/sth from doing sth: *They built a fence to stop the dog getting out.* ○ *I'm going to go and you can't stop me.* يمنع؛ يوقف

5 [T] to prevent money from being paid: *to stop a cheque* يمنع صرف الشيك

IDM **stop at nothing** to do anything to get what you want, even if it is wrong or dangerous لا يتورّع عن القيام بأيّ شيء

stop short of sth/doing sth to almost do sth, but then decide not to do it at the last minute: *They were very rude but they stopped short of calling her a liar.* يقصر عن

PHRV **stop off (at/in...)** to stop during a journey to do sth: *We stopped off in Paris to see some friends before coming home.* يتوقّف أثناء الرحلة (لغاية ما)

stop[2] /stɒp/ *noun* [C] **1** an act of stopping or state of being stopped: *Our first stop will be in Edinburgh.* ○ *The lift came to a stop on the third floor.* توقف، وقفة

2 the place where a bus, train, etc. stops so that people can get on and off: *a bus stop* موقف

IDM **to put a stop to sth** to prevent sth bad or unpleasant from continuing يضع حداً ل

stopgap /ˈstɒpgæp/ *noun* [C] a person or a thing that does a job for a short time until sb/sth can be found مَنْ أو ما يسدّ الحاجة مؤقتاً

stopover /ˈstɒpəʊvə(r)/ *noun* [C] a short stop in a journey: *a stopover in Singapore on the way to Australia* وقفة قصيرة أثناء رحلة

stoppage /ˈstɒpɪdʒ/ *noun* [C] **1** the act of refusing to work because of a disagreement with your employers; a strike توقُّف عن العمل، إضراب

2 (in sport) an interruption in a game for a particular reason: *The referee added on two minutes' stoppage time at the end of the ninety minutes.* الوقت الضائع

stopper /ˈstɒpə(r)/ *noun* [C] an object that you put into the top of a bottle in order to close it. A stopper can be made of glass, plastic or cork. سدادة

stopwatch /ˈstɒpwɒtʃ/ *noun* [C] a watch which can be started and stopped by pressing a button, so that you can measure exactly how long sth takes ساعة توقيت

storage /ˈstɔːrɪdʒ/ *noun* [U] the keeping of things until they are needed; the place where they are kept: *This room is being used for storage at the moment.* ○ *storage space* ○ *to keep meat in cold storage* خَزْن؛ مكان الخَزْن

store /stɔː(r)/ *noun* **1** [C] a large shop: *She's a sales assistant in a large department store.* ○ *a furniture store* ➲ Look at **chain store**. مخزن كبير، محل تجاري

2 (*US*) = SHOP (1)

3 [C,U] a supply of sth that you keep for future use; the place where it is kept: *a good store of food for the winter* ○ *We'll have to put our furniture into store while we're in Australia.* مونة، ذخيرة؛ مخزن

IDM **in store (for sb/sth)** going to happen in the future: *There's a surprise in store for you when you get home!* في الانتظار

set... store by sth to think that sth has a particular amount of importance or value: *Nigel sets great store by his mother's opinion.* يقدّر؛ يعطيه أهميّة (كبيرة)

▸ **store** *verb* [T] to keep sth or a supply of sth for future use: *to store information on a computer* ○ *The rice is stored in a large building near the village.* يخزن

storekeeper /ˈstɔːkiːpə(r)/ *noun* [C] (*US*) = SHOPKEEPER

storeroom /ˈstɔːruːm; *US* -rʊm/ *noun* [C] a room where things are kept until they are needed مستودع، غرفة تخزين

storey /ˈstɔːri/ (*US* **story**) *noun* [C] (*pl.* **storeys**; *US* **stories**) one floor or level of a building: *The building will be five storeys high.* ○ *a two-storey house* ○ *a multi-storey car park* طابق، دَوْر

stork /stɔːk/ *noun* [C] a large white bird with a long beak, neck and legs. Storks often make their nests on the top of a building. لَقْلَق

storm /stɔːm/ *noun* [C] very bad weather, with heavy rain, strong winds, etc: *Look at those black clouds. I think there's going to be a storm.* ○ *a thunderstorm, snowstorm, etc.* ○ *(figurative) The introduction of the new tax caused a storm of protest.* عاصفة

> **Storm** is the general word for very bad weather. A very strong wind is a **gale**. A storm with very strong winds is a **hurricane**. A storm with a very strong circular wind is called a **cyclone**, **tornado**, **typhoon** or **whirlwind**. A very bad snowstorm is a **blizzard**.

▸ **storm** *verb* **1** [I,T] to enter or leave somewhere in a very angry and noisy way يندفع غاضباً مُزمجراً

2 [T] to attack a building, town, etc. suddenly and violently in order to take control of it: *to storm a castle* يهاجم هجوماً مفاجئاً، ينقضّ على

stormy *adj* (**stormier**; **stormiest**) **1** (used for talking about very bad weather, with strong winds, heavy rain, etc.): *a stormy night* عاصف

2 involving a lot of angry argument and strong feeling: *a stormy debate in Parliament* ○ *a stormy relationship* عنيف، مليء بالنزاع

story¹ /ˈstɔːri/ *noun* [C] (*pl.* **stories**) **1** a description of people and events that are not real: *He always reads the children a bedtime story.* ○ *a detective, fairy, ghost, love, etc. story* ○ *She told us a story about an old woman who lived in a shoe.* قصّة، حكاية

2 an account, especially a spoken one, of sth that has happened: *The police didn't believe his story.* سرد للأحداث

3 a description of true events that happened in the past: *the story of the Russian revolution* ○ *her life story* تاريخ؛ سيرة

4 an article or report in a newspaper or magazine: *The plane crash was the front-page story in most newspapers.* مقالة

story² (*US*) = STOREY

stout /staʊt/ *adj* **1** (used about a person) rather fat بدين، ممتلئ الجسم

2 strong and thick: *stout walking boots* ثخين ومتين

stove /stəʊv/ *noun* [C] **1** the top part of a cooker that is fitted with gas or electric rings: *He put a pan of water to boil on the stove.* جهاز الطبخ

2 a type of heater. A stove is a closed metal box in which you burn wood, coal, etc: *a wood-burning stove* مدفأة

stow /stəʊ/ *verb* [T] **stow sth (away)** to put sth away in a particular place until it is needed يضع أو يخبّئ شيئاً لحين الحاجة

stowaway /ˈstəʊəweɪ/ *noun* [C] a person who hides in a ship or plane so that he/she can travel without paying مسافر بالتهريب

straddle /ˈstrædl/ *verb* [T] **1** (used about a person) to sit or stand with your legs on each side of sth: *to straddle a chair* يجلس أو يقف مفرشخاً (على)

2 (used about a building, bridge, etc.) to be on both sides of sth: *The village straddles the border between the two states.* يقع على طرفَيْ (كذا)

straggle /ˈstrægl/ *verb* [I] **1** to grow or cover sth in an untidy or irregular way: *a straggling moustache* ينمو أو يمتدّ في غير نظام

2 to walk, etc. more slowly than the rest of the group: *The children straggled along behind their parents.* يتلكّأ في السير، يتخلف عن الآخرين

▸ **straggler** /ˈstræglə(r)/ *noun* [C] a person who straggles (2) المتخلّف في سيره عن الآخرين

straggly /ˈstrægli/ *adj* untidy: *long straggly hair* ممتدّ هنا وهناك؛ أشعث

straight¹ /streɪt/ *adj* **1** not bent or curved: *a straight line* ○ *straight hair* (= not curly) ○ *Keep your back straight!* مستقيم

2 (not before a noun) in a level or upright position: *That picture isn't straight.* عموديّ، قائم

3 honest, truthful and direct: *Politicians never give straight answers.* ○ *Are you being straight with me?* صادق، صريح؛ مباشر

4 tidy or organized as it should be مرتّب

5 (*informal*) attracted to people of the opposite sex طبيعي الميول الجنسية

6 (*informal*) used to describe a person who you think is too serious and boring جادّ، صارم

IDM **get sth straight** to make sure that you understand sth completely: *Let's get this straight. You're sure that you've never seen this man before?* يتأكّد من حسن فهمه للموضوع

keep a straight face to stop yourself from smiling or laughing يمنع نفسه من الابتسام أو الضحك

put/set the record straight → RECORD¹

▸ **straighten** /ˈstreɪtn/ *verb* [I,T] **straighten (sth) (up/out)** to become straight or to make sth straight: *The road straightens out at the bottom of the hill.* ○ *to straighten your tie* يستقيم؛ يقوِّم

PHR V **straighten sth out** to remove the confusion or difficulties from a situation يرتّب؛ يمهّد؛ يسوّي

straighten up to stand up straight and tall يقف منتصب القامة

straight² /streɪt/ *adv* **1** in a straight line: *Go straight on for about two miles until you come to some traffic lights.* ○ *He was looking straight ahead.* ○ *to sit up straight* (= with a straight back) على خط مستقيم، "دُغري": منتصباً

2 without stopping; directly: *I took the children straight home after school.* ○ *to walk straight past sb/sth* دون توقّف؛ رأساً

3 in an honest and direct way: *Tell me straight, doctor – is it serious?* من دون مواربة

IDM **go straight** to become honest after being a criminal يتوب، يستقيم

right/straight away → AWAY

straight out in an honest and direct way: *I told Tom straight out that I didn't want to see him any more.* بصدق وصراحة

straightforward /ˌstreɪtˈfɔːwəd/ *adj* **1** easy to do or understand; simple: *straightforward instructions* سهل؛ بسيط

2 honest and open: *a straightforward person* صادق، صريح

strain[1] /streɪn/ *noun* **1** [C,U] the condition of being pulled or stretched too tightly: *The rope finally broke under the strain.* ○ *(figurative) The war has put a great strain on the country's economy.* توتّر؛ جهد؛ عسر ماليّ

2 [C,U] a state of worry and tension: *to be under a lot of strain at work* ○ *Mum's illness has put a strain on the whole family.* إرهاق، توتّر، إجهاد

3 [C] something that makes you feel worried and tense: *I always find exams a terrible strain.* مصدر قلق وتوتّر

4 [C,U] an injury to part of your body that is caused by using it too much: *a back strain* إجهاد

5 one type of animal, plant or disease that is slightly different from the other types فصيلة

strain[2] /streɪn/ *verb* **1** [I,T] to make a great effort to do sth: *Bend down as far as you can without straining.* ○ *I was straining to see what was happening.* يجهد

2 [T] to injure a part of your body by using it too much: *Don't read in the dark. You'll strain your eyes.* ○ *to strain a muscle* يجهد؛ يؤذي

3 [T] to put a lot of pressure on sth: *Money problems have strained their relationship.* يوتّر

4 [T] to separate a solid and a liquid by pouring them into a special container with small holes in it: *This tea hasn't been strained* (= it's full of tea leaves). يصفّي

▸ **strained** *adj* **1** not natural or friendly: *Relations between the two countries are strained.* متوتّر؛ متكلّف

2 worried and tense: *Martin looked tired and strained.* قلق، متوتّر

strait /streɪt/ *noun* [C, usually pl.] **1** a narrow piece of sea that joins two larger seas: *the straits of Gibraltar* مضيق

2 straits [plural] a very difficult situation, especially one caused by having no money: *The factory is in dire straits.* أزمة؛ضائقة مالية

straitjacket /ˈstreɪtdʒækɪt/ *noun* [C] a piece of clothing like a jacket with long arms which is put on people who are considered dangerous to prevent them from behaving violently سترة مقيّدة (لذراعي مريض خطر)

strand /strænd/ *noun* [C] **1** a single piece of cotton, wool, hair, etc. إحدى جدائل الحبل أو الشعر وغيره، "طاق"

2 one part of a story, situation or idea: *At the end of the film all the different strands of the story are brought together.* خيوط (القصّة)

stranded /ˈstrændɪd/ *adj* left in a place that you cannot get away from, e.g. because you have no money or transport "مقطوع" في بلد ما (لأنه فقد نقوده مثلاً)

strange /streɪndʒ/ *adj* **1** unusual or unexpected: *A very strange thing happened to me on the way home.* ○ *a strange noise* ○ *She usually wears jeans. It's really strange to see her in a skirt.* غريب

2 that you have not seen, visited, met, etc. before: *a strange town* ○ *My mother told me not to talk to strange men.* غريب؛ غير مألوف أو معروف

> We do not use **strange** to talk about a person or thing that comes from a different country. Look at **foreign**.

▸ **strangely** *adv*: *The streets were strangely quiet.* ○ *Tim's behaving very strangely at the moment.* بشكل غريب، بغرابة

strangeness *noun* [U] غرابة

stranger /ˈstreɪndʒə(r)/ *noun* [C] **1** a person that you do not know: *I had to ask a complete stranger to help me with my suitcase.* شخص غريب

> We do not use **stranger** to talk about a person who comes from a different country. Look at **foreigner**.

2 a person who is in a place that he/she does not know: *I'm a stranger to this part of the country.* غريب، أجنبيّ

strangle /ˈstræŋgl/ *verb* [T] **1** to kill sb by squeezing his/her neck or throat with your hands, a rope, etc. يخنق

2 to prevent sth from developing يوقف نموّه، يكبت

strap /stræp/ *noun* [C] a long narrow piece of leather, cloth, plastic, etc. that you use for carrying sth or for keeping sth in position: *a watch strap* ○ *a dress with thin shoulder straps* سَيْر؛ شريط؛ حمّالة

▸ **strap** *verb* (stra**pp**ing; stra**pp**ed) [T] to keep sb/sth in position by using a strap or straps: *The racing driver was securely strapped into the car.* يشدّ بحزام، يوثق

strategic /strəˈtiːdʒɪk/ (*also* **strategical**) *adj* **1** helping you to achieve a plan; giving you an advantage استراتيجي

2 connected with a country's plans to achieve success in a war or in its defence system: *strategic planning* استراتيجي

3 (used about bombs and other weapons) intended to hit places of military or economic importance in an enemy country استراتيجي

▸ **strategically** /-kli/ *adv*: *The island is strategically important.* استراتيجياً

strategy /ˈstrætədʒi/ *noun* (*pl.* **strategies**) **1** [C] a plan that you use in order to achieve sth: *a strategy to reduce inflation* خطّة

2 [U] the act of planning how to do or achieve sth: *military strategy* تخطيط، الاستراتيجيّة

straw /strɔː/ *noun* **1** [U] the long stems of plants (e.g. wheat) that are dried and then used for animals to sleep on or for making baskets, mats, etc: *a straw hat* قش

2 [C] one piece of straw قشّة

3 [C] a long plastic or paper tube that you can use for drinking through مصّاصة أو شاروقة، "شلمونة"

IDM the last/final straw an extra problem that is added to a difficult or unpleasant situation, and which makes you think you cannot tolerate the situation any longer ما يطفح الكيل: القشّة الأخيرة

strawberry /ˈstrɔːbəri; *US* -beri/ *noun* [C] (*pl.* **strawberries**) a soft red fruit with small yellow seeds in it: *strawberries and cream* ○ *strawberry jam* فراولة، فريز، شليك

stray /streɪ/ *verb* [I] **1** to go away from the place where you should be for no particular reason: *The sheep had strayed onto the road.* يشرد، يتيه

2 not keeping to the subject you should be thinking about or discussing: *My thoughts strayed for a few moments.* يشرد

▸ **stray** *adj* (only *before* a noun) lost from home: *a stray dog* شارد، ضائع

stray *noun* [C] an animal that is lost from home حيوان شارد

streak /striːk/ *noun* [C] **1 streak (of sth)** a thin line or mark: *The cat had brown fur with streaks of white in it.* خطّ رفيع، "قلم"

2 a part of a person's character that sometimes shows in the way he/she behaves: *a selfish streak* خصلة، مسحة

3 a continuous period of good or bad luck in a game of sport: *a winning/losing streak* سلسلة متواصلة

▸ **streak** *verb* [I] (*informal*) to run fast يعدو مسرعاً

streaked *adj* **streaked (with sth)** having streaks (1) of sth: *black hair streaked with grey* مقلّم، مخطّط

🔑 **stream** /striːm/ *noun* [C] **1** a small river جدول، غدير

2 the constant movement of a liquid or gas: *a stream of blood* سيل: تدفق

3 a constant movement of people or things: *a stream of traffic* سيل، تيّار

4 a large number of things which happen one after another: *a stream of letters, telephone calls, questions, etc.* وابل، سيل

5 a group of schoolchildren who are in the same class because they have similar abilities فئة أو زمرة (تلاميذ)

▸ **stream** *verb* **1** [I] (used about a liquid, gas or light) to flow in large amounts: *Tears were streaming down his face.* ○ *Sunlight was streaming in through the windows.* يسيل، ينحدر

2 [I] (used about people or things) to move somewhere in a continuous flow: *People were streaming out of the station.* يتدفق

3 [T] (usually passive) to put schoolchildren into groups of similar ability يفرز التلاميذ وفقاً لمقدرتهم

streamer *noun* [C] a long piece of coloured paper that you use for decorating a room before a party, etc. شريط ورقي رفيع ملوّن

streamline /ˈstriːmlaɪn/ *verb* [T] **1** to give a vehicle, etc. a long smooth shape so that it will move easily through air or water يعطيه شكلاً انسيابياً

2 to make an organization, process, etc. work better by making it simpler and more efficient: *The company has decided to streamline its production processes.* يبسّط (المنظّمة) ويجعلها اكثر فعالية

🔑 **street** /striːt/ *noun* [C] **1** a road in a town, village or city that has shops, houses, etc. on one or both sides: *to walk along/down the street* ○ *to cross the street* ○ *I met Karen in the street this morning.* ○ *a narrow street* ○ *a street map* ➲ Look at the note at **road**. طريق، شارع

2 Street (*abbr* **St**) [sing.] (used in names of streets): *64 High Street* ○ *to go shopping in Oxford Street* شارع (كذا)

IDM the man in the street → MAN[1]

streets ahead (of sb/sth) (*informal*) much better than sb/sth أفضل منه بكثير

(right) up your street (*informal*) (used about an activity, subject, etc.) exactly right for you because you know a lot about it, like it very much, etc. ملائم له كل الملاءمة

streetcar /ˈstriːtkɑː(r)/ *noun* [C] (*US*) = TRAM

🔑 **strength** /streŋθ/ *noun* **1** [U] the quality of being physically strong; the amount of this quality that you have: *a woman of great physical strength* ○ *He pulled with all his strength but the rock would not move.* قوّة

2 [U] the ability of an object to hold heavy weights or not to break or be damaged easily: *All our suitcases are tested for strength before they leave the factory.* متانة

3 [U] the quality of being powerful: *Germany's economic strength* قوة

4 [U] how strong a feeling or opinion is: *There is great strength of feeling against nuclear weapons in this country.* قوة، شدّة

5 [C,U] the good qualities and abilities of a person or thing: *His greatest strength is his ability to communicate with people.* ○ *the strengths and weaknesses of a plan* نقطة القوة (عنده)

IDM at full strength (used about a group) having the number of people it needs or usually has مكتمل العدد أو النصاب

below strength (used about a group) not having the number of people it needs or usually has أقلّ من العدد المطلوب

on the strength of as a result of information, advice, etc: *She was given the job on the strength of your recommendation.* على أساس، بناءً على

▸ **strengthen** /ˈstreŋθn/ *verb* [I,T] to become stronger or to make sth stronger: *exercises to strengthen your muscles* ○ *Support for the President seems to be strengthening.* يقوى؛ يقوّي

strenuous /ˈstrenjuəs/ *adj* needing or using a lot of effort or energy: *a strenuous effort to improve her English* (جهد) جهيد، عنيف

▸ **strenuously** *adv* بكل طاقته

stress /stres/ *noun* **1** [C,U] a state of worry and tension that is caused by difficulties in your life, having too much work, etc: *He's been under a lot of stress since his wife went into hospital.* ○ *The doctor told her that she was suffering from stress.* ○ *the stresses and strains of life in a big city* إجهاد، إرهاق

2 [U] **stress (on sth)** the special force or emphasis that you give to sth because you think it is important: *There should be more stress on learning foreign languages in schools.* تأكيد، وَضْع أهميّة على

3 [U] the force or emphasis that you put on a word or part of a word when you say it: *In the word 'dictionary' the stress is on the first syllable, 'dic'.* نبرة

4 [C,U] **stress (on sth)** a physical force that may cause sth to bend or break إجهاد، ضغط

▸ **stress** *verb* [T] to give sth special force or emphasis because you think it is important: *The minister stressed the need for a peaceful solution.* ○ *Which syllable is stressed in this word?* يُشدِّد أو يؤكِّد على

stressful /-fl/ *adj* causing stress (1): *a stressful job* مجهِد

stressed /strest/ *adj* **1** too anxious and tired to be able to relax: *He was feeling very stressed and tired* مُجهَد

2 (of a syllable) pronounced with emphasis ❶ The opposite is **unstressed**. (مقطع) منبور

stretch¹ /stretʃ/ *verb* **1** [I,T] to pull sth so that it becomes longer or wider; to become longer or wider in this way: *The artist stretched the canvas tightly over the frame.* ○ *My T-shirt stretched when I washed it.* يمطّ، يشدّ؛ يتمطّط

2 stretch (sth) out [I,T] to push out your arms, legs, etc. as far as possible: *He got out of bed and stretched before going into the bathroom.* ○ *She stretched out on the sofa and fell asleep.* ○ *She stretched out her arm to take the book.* يمدّ، يبسط

3 [I] (used about a piece of land or water, etc.) to cover a large area: *The long white beaches stretch for miles along the coast.* يمتدّ

4 [T] to make use of all the money, ability, time, etc. that sb has available for use: *The test has been designed to really stretch students' knowledge.* يستهلك، يستنفد؛ يمتحن

IDM stretch your legs to go for a walk after sitting down for a long time يتمشّى (بعد جلوس طويل)

stretch a point to agree to sth that you do not normally allow يتساهل؛ يتوسّع في التفسير

stretch² /stretʃ/ *noun* **1** [C] **stretch (of sth)** an area of land or water: *a beautiful stretch of countryside* امتداد؛ مساحة (من الأرض)

2 [C, usually sing.] the act of stretching¹ (2): *Stand up, everybody, and have a good stretch.* تمطُّط؛ تمدُّد

IDM at a stretch without stopping: *six hours at a stretch* دون توقُّف

stretcher /ˈstretʃə(r)/ *noun* [C] a piece of cloth supported by two poles that is used for carrying a person who has been injured in an accident, etc. نقّالة الجرحى، محفّة

strict /strɪkt/ *adj* **1** not allowing people to break rules or behave badly: *Tom's always very strict with his children.* ○ *a strict teacher* ○ *I went to a very strict school.* صارم

2 that must be obeyed completely: *I gave her strict instructions to be home before 9.* مشدّد

3 exactly correct; precise: *a strict interpretation of the law* مضبوط؛ دقيق

▸ **strictly** *adv* in a strict way: *Smoking is strictly forbidden.* بشدّة؛ بصورة صارمة

IDM strictly speaking to be exactly correct or precise: *Strictly speaking, the tomato is not a vegetable. It's a fruit.* على وجه التحديد

stride /straɪd/ *verb* [I] (*pt* **strode** /strəʊd/; *pp* **stridden** /ˈstrɪdn/) to walk with long steps, often because you are feeling very confident or determined: *He strode up to the house and knocked on the door.* يمشي بخطىً واسعة

▸ **stride** *noun* [C] a long step خطوة واسعة

IDM get into your stride to start to do sth confidently and well after an uncertain beginning بدأ يعمل بثقة ومهارة

make great strides to make very quick progress يتقدّم تقدّماً سريعاً

take sth in your stride to deal with a new or difficult situation easily and without worrying يتخطّى صعوبة دون جهد

strident /ˈstraɪdnt/ *adj* (used about a voice or a sound) loud and unpleasant (صوت) عالٍ مزعج

strife /straɪf/ *noun* [U] (*formal*) trouble or fighting between people or groups نزاع، شقاق، صدام

strike¹ /straɪk/ *noun* [C] **1** a period of time when people refuse to go to work, usually because they want more money or better working conditions: *a one-day strike* ○ *to go on strike for better working conditions* ○ *The workers have been on strike for two weeks now.* ○ *to take strike action* إضراب

2 a sudden military attack, especially by aircraft هجوم جوّي مفاجئ، غارة

strike² /straɪk/ *verb* (*pt, pp* **struck** /strʌk/) **1** [T] to hit: *The stone struck me on my face.* ○ *to strike sb with your hand* ○ *The boat struck a rock and began to sink.* ❶ In these three examples it is more common to use the word **hit**: *The stone hit me on my face* but if you are talking about lightning you must use **strike**: *The building had been struck by lightning.* يضرب، يصدم؛ يصيب

2 [I,T] to attack sb/sth suddenly: *The enemy aircraft struck just after 2 am.* ○ *The earthquake struck Kobe in 1995.* يهاجِم فجأة، يضرب

3 [T] **strike sb (as sth)** to give sb a particular impression, often a strong one: *Does anything here strike you as unusual?* يسترعي الانتباه، يترك وقعاً

4 [T] (used about a thought or an idea) to come suddenly into sb's mind: *It suddenly struck me that she would be the ideal person for the job.* يخطر بالبال

5 [T] to produce fire: *to strike a match* يُشعل (عود ثقاب)

6 [I,T] (used about a clock) to ring a bell so that

people know what time it is: *The church clock struck three.* (الساعة) تدقّ

7 [T] to discover gold, oil, etc. يكتشف، يعثر على

8 [I] to go on strike[1] (1): *The workers voted to strike for more money.* يضْرِب

IDM **strike a balance (between A and B)** to find a middle way between two extremes يجد حداً وسطاً بينهما

strike a bargain (with sb) to make an agreement with sb يعقد صفقة أو اتفاقيّة

strike a chord (with sb) to say or do sth that makes other people feel sympathy, excitement, etc. يرضي؛ يصيب وتراً حسّاساً

within striking distance near enough to be reached or attacked easily قريب؛ سهل المنال

PHR V **strike back** to attack sb/sth that has attacked you: *The President threatened to strike back if the army attacked the capital.* يردّ الهجوم

strike up sth (with sb) to start a conversation or friendship with sb يستهلّ (حديثاً مع)؛ يصادق

striker /'straɪkə(r)/ *noun* [C] **1** a person who is on strike[1] (1) مضرب

2 (in football) an attacking player لاعب هجوم، مهاجم

striking /'straɪkɪŋ/ *adj* very noticeable; making a strong impression: *There was a striking similarity between the two men.* لافت للنظر

▸ **strikingly** *adv*: *strikingly attractive* بصورة تسترعي النظر

string[1] /strɪŋ/ *noun* **1** [C,U] the thin cord that you use for tying things, etc; a piece of this: *I need some string to tie round this parcel.* ○ *a ball of string* ○ *a balloon on the end of a string* خيط مصّيص، دوبارة

2 [C] a piece of thin wire, etc. on a musical instrument: *A guitar has six strings.* وتر

3 the strings [plural] the musical instruments in an orchestra, etc. that have strings (2) الآلات الوتريّة في اوركسترا

4 [C] **a string of sth** a line of things that are joined together on the same piece of thread: *a string of beads* حَبْل (لؤلؤ)؛ شيء منظوم في خيط

5 [C] **a string of sth** a series of people, things or events that follow one after another: *a string of visitors* ○ *a string of complaints* سلسلة من

IDM **(with) no strings attached; without strings** with no special conditions: *We will send you a free copy of the magazine, with no strings attached.* دون قيد أو شريط

pull strings → PULL[1]

string[2] /strɪŋ/ *verb* [T] (*pt, pp* **strung** /strʌŋ/) **string sth (up)** to hang up a line of things with a piece of string, etc: *Coloured lights were strung up along the front of the hotel.* يعلّق أو يمدّد (بأسلاك)

PHR V **string sb/sth out** to make people or things form a line with spaces between each person or thing يصفّ (أفراداً) تاركاً مسافات بينهم

string sth together to put words or phrases together to make a sentence, speech, etc. يشكّل جملة

stringent /'strɪndʒənt/ *adj* (used about a law, rule, etc.) very severe and strict صارم، مشدّد

strip /strɪp/ *noun* [C] a long narrow piece of sth: *a strip of paper* ○ *a strip of water* شريط، قطعة طويلة ضيّقة

▸ **strip** *verb* (stripping; stripped) **1** [I,T] **strip (sth) (off)** to take off your clothes; to take off sb else's clothes: *The doctor asked him to strip to the waist.* ○ *I was stripped and searched at the airport by two customs officers.* يتجرّد من ثيابه؛ يجرّده من ثيابه

2 [T] **strip sb/sth (of sth)** to take sth away from sb/sth: *They stripped the house of all its furniture.* ○ *The President has been stripped of most of her power.* يجرِّد

3 [T] **strip sth (off)** to remove sth that is covering a surface: *to strip the paint off a door* يقشط؛ ينزع

stripper *noun* [C] a person whose job is to take off his/her clothes in order to entertain people شخص يتعرّى أمام الجمهور في ملهى

'strip cartoon *noun* [C] (*Brit*) = COMIC STRIP

stripe /straɪp/ *noun* [C] a long narrow band of colour: *Zebras have black and white stripes.* خطّ ملوّن، قلم

▸ **striped** /straɪpt/ *adj* having stripes: *a red-and-white striped dress* مقلّم، ذو خطوط ملوّنة

striptease /'strɪptiːz/ *noun* [C,U] entertainment in which sb takes off his/her clothes, usually to music التعرّي أمام الجمهور في ملهى

strive /straɪv/ *verb* [I] (*pt* **strove** /strəʊv/; *pp* **striven** /'strɪvn/) (*formal*) **strive (for sth)** to try very hard to do or get sth: *The company always strives to satisfy its customers.* يسعى جاهداً

strode *pt* of STRIDE

stroke[1] /strəʊk/ *verb* [T] to move your hand gently over sb/sth: *She stroked his hair affectionately.* ○ *to stroke a dog* يملِّس برفق

stroke[2] /strəʊk/ *noun* **1** [C] one of the movements that you make when you are writing or painting: *a brush stroke* جرّة (قلم)

2 [C] one of the movements that you make when you are swimming, rowing, playing tennis, etc: *a forehand stroke* (= in tennis) ضربة؛ حركة

3 [C,U] one of the styles of swimming: *backstroke* ➲ Look at **crawl**. أحد أنواع السباحة

4 [C] a sudden illness which attacks the brain and can leave a person unable to move part of their body, speak clearly, etc: *to have a stroke* سكتة أو جلطة دماغيّة

5 [sing.] **a stroke of sth** something that happens unexpectedly: *a stroke of luck* شيء غير متوقّع

IDM **at a/one stroke** with a single action: *You can't change people's opinions at a stroke.* بإجراء واحد، بجرّة قلم

not do a stroke (of work) to not do any work at all لا يقوم بأي عمل

stroll /strəʊl/ *noun* [C] a slow walk for pleasure: *to go for a stroll along the beach* تمشٍّ، تنزّه

▸ **stroll** *verb* [I] يتمشّى، يتنزّه

strong /strɒŋ; *US* strɔːŋ/ *adj* **1** (used about a person) physically powerful; able to lift or carry heavy things: *I need someone strong to help me* *move this bookcase.* ○ *to have strong arms, muscles, etc.* قويّ

2 (used about an object) able to hold heavy weights; not easily broken or damaged: *That chair isn't strong enough for you to stand on.* ○ *a pair of strong walking boots* متين

3 intense; felt deeply: *There was strong opposition to the idea.* ○ *strong support for the government's plan* ○ *He has strong views on the subject* (= he will not change them easily). ○ *strong feelings* شديد؛ راسخ

4 powerful and likely to succeed: *She's a strong candidate for the job.* قوي

5 (used about a smell, taste, etc.) powerful and intense: *a strong smell of garlic* ○ *strong tea/ coffee* قويّ؛ مركَّز؛ نفّاذ

6 powerful and moving quickly: *strong winds* شديد؛ عنيف

ℹ In **1 – 6**, the related noun is **strength**.

7 (used after a noun) having a particular number of people: *The army was 50 000 strong.* بالغ عدده

IDM **going strong** (*informal*) continuing, even after a long time: *The company was formed in 1851 and is still going strong.* لا يزال قائماً

sb's strong point something that a person is good at: *Maths is not my strong point.* خير ما يجيده الشخص

▶ **strongly** *adv* very much; to a great degree: *The directors are strongly opposed to the idea.* ○ *to feel very strongly about sth* بشدّة؛ إلى حدّ كبير

strong-'minded *adj* having firm ideas or beliefs مستقل الرأي، راسخ العقيدة

stroppy /'strɒpi/ *adj* (**stroppier**; **stroppiest**) (*Brit slang*) (used about a person) bad-tempered; not helpful شكِس، سيئ الخلق

strove *pt* of STRIVE

struck *pt, pp* of STRIKE²

⚷ **structure** /'strʌktʃə(r)/ *noun* **1** [C,U] the way that the parts of sth are put together or organized: *the structure of the brain* ○ *the political and social structure of a country* تركيب، بنية

2 [C] a building or sth that has been built or made from a number of parts: *The old office had been replaced by a modern glass structure.* بناء، مبنى

▶ **structure** *verb* [T] to arrange sth in an organized way: *a carefully structured English course* ينظِّم، يركِّب وفق نظام معيَّن

structural /'strʌktʃərəl/ *adj*: *Several windows were broken in the explosion but there was no structural damage* (= no damage to the walls, floors, etc.). هيكلي أو بنيوي

⚷ **struggle** /'strʌgl/ *verb* [I] **1** to try very hard to do sth although it is difficult: *We struggled along the road with our heavy suitcases.* ○ *Maria was struggling with her English homework.* يجاهد؛ يكافح

2 to make violent movements when you are trying to escape from sb/sth: *He shouted and struggled but he couldn't get free.* يقاوم، يصارع

PHRV **struggle on** to continue to do sth although it is difficult: *I felt terrible but managed to struggle on to the end of the day.* يصارع؛ يكابر

▶ **struggle** *noun* [C] **1** a fight: *the struggle against terrorism* ○ *He won't give up without a struggle.* نضال، كفاح، صراع

2 [usually sing.] a great effort: *After a long struggle she finally managed to complete the course.* جهاد، جهد كبير

strum /strʌm/ *verb* [I,T] (**strumming**; **strummed**) to play a guitar by moving your hand up and down over the strings يداعب أوتار القيثارة بأنامله

strung *pt, pp* of STRING²

strut /strʌt/ *verb* [I] (**strutting**; **strutted**) to walk in a proud way يتبختر، يختال في مشيته

stub /stʌb/ *noun* [C] a short piece of a cigarette or pencil that remains after the rest of it has been used عُقب (السيجارة مثلاً)

stubble /'stʌbl/ *noun* [U] **1** the short stems that are left in a field after corn, wheat, etc. has been cut جذامة، القشّ المتبقي بعد الحصاد

2 the short hairs that grow on a man's face when he has not shaved for some time شعر الوجه الخشن قبل حلقه

stubborn /'stʌbən/ *adj* not wanting to do what other people want you to do; refusing to change your plans or decisions: *She's too stubborn to apologize.* ○ *a stubborn refusal* عنيد؛ متصلّب في الرأيّ

▶ **stubbornly** *adv* بعناد

stubbornness *noun* [U] عناد؛ مشاكسة

stucco /'stʌkəʊ/ *noun* [U] plaster or cement that is used for covering or decorating walls or ceilings جِصّ؛ زخرفة بالجِص

stuck¹ *pt, pp* of STICK²

stuck² /stʌk/ *adj* **1** not able to move: *This drawer's stuck. I can't open it at all.* مستعصٍ، "عالق"

2 not able to continue with an exercise, etc. because it is too difficult: *If you get stuck, ask your teacher for help.* عاجز عن المتابعة

stud¹ /stʌd/ *noun* [C] **1** a small round earring that you wear through a hole in your ear قُرط يشبه الزرّ الصغير

2 a small round piece of metal on the surface of sth: *a black leather jacket with studs all over it* ○ *the studs on the bottom of football boots* مسمار صغير مفلطح الرأس

▶ **studded** *adj* **studded with sth** covered or decorated with studs or other small objects: *The crown is studded with diamonds.* مزيَّن "بالمسامير": مرصَّع

stud² /stʌd/ *noun* **1** [C,U] a number of horses or other animals that are kept for breeding young animals (of high quality): *to keep a stallion at stud* (= available for breeding) (حصان) أصيل للإنجاب

2 (*also* **'stud farm**) [C] a place where such animals are kept مزرعة خيول الإنجاب

⚷ **student** /'stju:dnt; *US* 'stu:-/ *noun* [C] **1** a person who is studying at a college or university: *Julia is a medical student at Bristol university.* ○ *a full-time/part-time student* ○ *a student teacher* (= a person who is learning to be a teacher) ➲ Look at **graduate** and **undergraduate**. طالب

2 (*especially US*) a person who is studying at school, especially a secondary school: *a 15-year-old high school student* تلميذ مدرسة

studied /ˈstʌdid/ *adj* (*formal*) carefully planned or done, especially when you are trying to give a particular impression مدروس؛ متعمّد

studio /ˈstjuːdiəʊ; *US* ˈstuː-/ *noun* [C] (*pl.* **studios**) **1** a room where an artist or photographer works استوديو؛ مرسم

2 a room or building where radio or television programmes are made استوديو (إذاعي)

3 a room or building where cinema films or records are made: *a recording studio* استوديو (سينمائي)

studious /ˈstjuːdiəs; *US* ˈstuː-/ *adj* (used about a person) spending a lot of time studying مُجِدّ، مجتهد

▸ **studiously** *adv* with great care: *It was a question that I had studiously avoided.* جاهداً؛ بحرص؛ متعمّداً

study¹ /ˈstʌdi/ *noun* (*pl.* **studies**) **1** [U] the act of learning about sth: *One hour every afternoon is left free for quiet study.* دراسة

2 studies [plural] the subjects that you study: *the School of Oriental and African Studies at London University* دراسات

3 [C] scientific research into a particular subject and a book or article that a person writes after studying it: *a scientific study of the causes of heart disease in Britain* دراسة، بحث

4 [C] a room in a house where you go to read, write or study غرفة المكتب (في المنزل)

study² /ˈstʌdi/ *verb* (*pres part* **studying**; *3rd pers sing pres* **studies**; *pt, pp* **studied**) **1** [I,T] to spend time learning about sth: *Leo has been studying hard for his exams.* ○ *to study French at university* يدرس

2 [T] to look at sth very carefully: *to study a map* يدرس، يتفحّص

stuff¹ /stʌf/ *noun* [U] (*informal*) **1** a substance, thing or group of things (used instead of the name of the thing that you are talking about): *What's that green stuff at the bottom of the bottle?* ○ *I bought some computer paper but when I got it home I found it was the wrong stuff.* ○ *The shop was burgled and a lot of stuff was stolen.* مادّة، شيء؛ و أشياء أخرى

2 (used to refer in general to things that people do, say, think. etc.): *I've got lots of stuff to do tomorrow so I'm going to get up early.* ○ *I don't believe all that stuff about him being robbed.* ○ *I like reading and stuff.* اشغال؛ اشياء

stuff² /stʌf/ *verb* **1** [T] **stuff sth (with sth)** to fill sth with sth: *The pillow was stuffed with feathers.* يحشو، يملأ بِ

2 [T] **stuff sth into sth** (*informal*) to put sth into sth quickly or carelessly: *He quickly stuffed a few clothes into a suitcase.* يلقي داخل... يضع دون عناية

3 [I,T] **stuff (yourself) (with sth)** to eat a lot: *The children have been stuffing themselves with sweets and chocolate all afternoon.* يحشو بطنه، يأكل كثيراً

4 [T] **stuff sth (with sth)** to put a mixture of small pieces of food (stuffing) into a chicken, vegetable, etc. before you cook it: *stuffed vine leaves* يحشو

5 [T] to fill the body of a dead bird or animal with special material so that it continues to look as if it is alive يحنّط (طيراً مثلاً)

IDM get stuffed (*slang*) (a rude expression used when you are angry with sb): *He offered to drive me home but I told him to get stuffed.* إذهب إلى الجحيم!

▸ **stuffing** *noun* [U] **1** a mixture of small pieces of food that you put inside a chicken, vegetable, etc. before you cook it حشوة الطعام

2 the material that you put inside cushions, soft toys, etc. حشوة (المخدّة مثلاً)

stuffy /ˈstʌfi/ *adj* (**stuffier**; **stuffiest**) **1** (used of a room, etc.) having air that is not fresh فاسد الهواء

2 (*informal*) (used of a person, of behaviour, etc.) formal and old-fashioned جدّي، مترسّم، من الطراز القديم

stumble /ˈstʌmbl/ *verb* [I] **1** to hit your foot against sth when you are walking or running and almost fall over: *I stumbled as I was getting out of the boat.* يتعثّر

2 to make a mistake when you are speaking, playing music, etc: *The newsreader stumbled over the name of the Russian tennis player.* يتعثّر في كلامه؛ يخطئ (في العزف)

PHR V stumble across/on sb/sth to meet or find sb/sth by chance يعثر عليه صدفة، يقع على

ˈstumbling block *noun* [C] something that causes trouble or a difficulty, so that you cannot get what you want حجر عثرة

stump¹ /stʌmp/ *noun* [C] the part that is left after sth has been cut down, broken off, etc: *a tree stump* أرومة، قرمة؛ عقب

stump² /stʌmp/ *verb* **1** [I] to walk with slow heavy steps يمشي بخطى بطيئة متثاقلة

2 [T] (*informal*) to cause sb to be unable to answer a question or find a solution for a problem: *I was completely stumped by question 14.* يجعله عاجزاً (عن الجواب)

stun /stʌn/ *verb* [T] (**stunning**; **stunned**) **1** to make a person or animal unconscious or confused by hitting him/her/it on the head يدوّخ، يُفقده الوعي

2 to make a person very surprised by giving him/her some unexpected news: *His sudden death stunned his friends and colleagues.* يَصعَق، يُذهِل

▸ **stunned** *adj*: *There was a stunned silence after Margaret announced her resignation.* مصعوق، مذهول

stunning *adj* (*informal*) very attractive or impressive: *a stunning woman* ○ *a stunning view* رائع الجمال، فاتن؛ هائل

stung *pt, pp* of STING[1]

stunk *pp* of STINK

stunt[1] /stʌnt/ *noun* [C] **1** something that you do to get people's attention: *a publicity stunt* شيء مبتكر أو مثير (لجذب الانتباه)

2 a very difficult or dangerous thing that sb does to entertain people or as part of a film: *His latest stunt was walking on a tightrope over Niagara Falls.* ○ *Some actors do their own stunts, others use a stuntman.* حركة بهلوانية بارعة وخطرة

stunt[2] /stʌnt/ *verb* [T] to stop sb/sth growing or developing properly: *A poor diet can stunt a child's growth.* يوقفه عن النموّ

stuntman /ˈstʌntmæn/ (*pl.* **stuntmen** /-men/), **stuntwoman** /ˈstʌntwʊmən/ (*pl.* **stuntwomen** /-wɪmɪn/) *noun* [C] a person who does a stunt[1] (2) in a film in the place of an actor or actress بديل في فيلم يقوم بالأعمال الخطيرة

stupendous /stjuːˈpendəs; *US* stuː-/ *adj* very large, grand or impressive: *a stupendous achievement* هائل، ضخم، مذهل

stupid /ˈstjuːpɪd; *US* ˈstuː-/ *adj* **1** not clever or intelligent; foolish: *Don't be so stupid, of course I'll help you!* ○ *It was stupid of him to trust her.* ○ *He was stupid to trust her.* ○ *a stupid mistake/question/suggestion* غبيّ، أحمق، بليد

2 (only *before* a noun) (*informal*) a word that shows that you do not like sb/sth: *I'm tired of hearing about his stupid car.* (تقال تعبيراً عن السخط): سخيف؛ بغيض

▸ **stupidity** /stjuːˈpɪdəti; *US* stuː-/ *noun* [U] غباء؛ حماقة

stupidly *adv* بغباء، بحماقة

stupor /ˈstjuːpə(r); *US* ˈstuː-/ *noun* [sing., U] the state of being nearly unconscious or being unable to think properly: *a drunken stupor* غيبوبة؛ خَبَل الذهن

sturdy /ˈstɜːdi/ *adj* (**sturdier**; **sturdiest**) strong and healthy; that will not break easily: *a sturdy child* ○ *sturdy shoes* قويّ البنية؛ متين

▸ **sturdily** *adv* بِمتانة

sturdiness *noun* [U] قوة البنية؛ متانة

sturgeon /ˈstɜːdʒən/ *noun* [C] a large fish found in rivers. Sturgeons are eaten as food and also caught for their eggs (called caviar). سمك الحَفْش

stutter /ˈstʌtə(r)/ *verb* [I,T] to have difficulty when you speak, so that you keep repeating the first sound of a word يتعتع، يفأفئ

▸ **stutter** *noun*: *to have a stutter* تعتعة، فأفأة

sty (*also* **stye**) /staɪ/ *noun* [C] (*pl.* **sties** or **styes**) **1** a large and painful spot on the eyelid شحّاذ (العين)، دمّل على الجفن

2 = PIGSTY

style /staɪl/ *noun* **1** [C,U] the way that sth is done, built, etc: *a new style of architecture* ○ *a cathedral in Gothic style* ○ *The Japanese adopted an American-style education system.* طراز، طريقة

2 [C,U] the way that sb usually writes, behaves, etc: *Chekhov's style is very clear and simple.* ○ *I'm afraid going to nightclubs isn't my style.* أسلوب

3 [U] the state of being of very good quality in appearance or behaviour: *a dress with style* ○ *They don't have many parties but when they do, they do it in style.* أناقة؛ فخامة؛ ذوق رفيع

4 [C,U] the fashion, shape or design of sth: *We stock all the latest styles.* ○ *a hairstyle* ○ *Swedish-style pine furniture* طراز، "موضة" أو "مودة"

▸ **stylish** *adj* fashionable and attractive من الطراز الحديث، أنيق

suave /swɑːv/ *adj* (usually used about a man) very polite, charming, and well behaved (sometimes too much so) (رجل) مهذّب رقيق مداهِن أحياناً

subconscious /ˌsʌbˈkɒnʃəs/ (*also* **unconscious**) *noun* [sing.] **the subconscious** the hidden part of your mind that can affect the way that you behave, even though you do not know it exists العقل الباطن، اللاشعور

▸ **subconscious** *adj*: *the subconscious mind* لا شعوري

subconsciously *adv* لا شعورياً

subdivide /ˈsʌbdɪvaɪd/ *verb* [I,T] to divide or be divided into smaller parts يجزّئ، يقسّم

▸ **subdivision** /ˌsʌbdɪˈvɪʒn/ *noun* [C,U] تجزئة، تقسيم

subdue /səbˈdjuː; *US* -ˈduː/ *verb* [T] to defeat or bring sb/sth under control: *to subdue a rebel army* ○ *She tried hard to subdue her emotions.* يُخضِع، يقهر؛ يكبت؛ يخفف

▸ **subdued** /səbˈdjuːd; *US* -ˈduːd/ *adj* **1** not very loud or bright: *subdued lighting* خافت

2 (used about a person) sad or quiet حزين، مستكين

subject[1] /ˈsʌbdʒɪkt; -dʒekt/ *noun* [C] **1** a person or thing that is being considered, shown or talked about: *the subject of an essay* ○ *What are your views on this subject?* ○ *to change the subject* (= start talking about sth else) ○ *I've tried several times to bring up the subject of money.* موضوع

2 an area of knowledge that you study at school, university, etc: *She's studying three subjects at A level: English French and German.* مادّة دراسيّة، موضوع

3 (*grammar*) the person or thing that performs the action described by the verb in a sentence: *In the sentence 'The cat sat on the mat', 'the cat' is the subject.* الفاعل

4 a person from a particular country; a citizen: *a British subject* مواطن، أحد الرعايا

subject[2] /səbˈdʒekt/ *verb*

PHR V **subject sb/sth to sth** to cause sb/sth to experience sth unpleasant يخضِع لِ؛ يعرّض لِ

subject[3] /ˈsʌbdʒekt; -dʒɪkt/ *adj* (not before a noun) **1** controlled by or having to obey sb/sth: *Everyone is subject to the law.* خاضع لِ

2 often experiencing or suffering from sth unpleasant: *The area is subject to regular flooding.* معرّض لِ

3 subject to sth depending on sth as a condi-

a b c d e f g h i j k l m n o p q r s t u v w x y z

tion: *The plan for new housing is still subject to approval by the minister.* متوقّف على

subjective /səb'dʒektɪv/ *adj* influenced by your own feelings and opinions instead of by facts alone: *Try not to be so subjective in your essays.* ❶ The opposite is **objective**.
ذاتيّ، شخصيّ، غير موضوعيّ
▸ **subjectively** *adv* من ناحية شخصيّة، عاطفياً

'subject matter *noun* [U] the idea, problem, etc. that a book, film, play, etc. is about
موضوع (الكتاب أو الفيلم أو غير ذلك)

subjunctive /səb'dʒʌŋktɪv/ *noun* [sing.] the form of a verb that expresses doubt, possibility, a wish, etc. in certain languages
صيغة تعبّر عن الشكّ أو الاحتمال وغير ذلك
▸ **subjunctive** *adj* دالّ على الشكّ أو الاحتمال وغير ذلك

sublime /sə'blaɪm/ *adj* wonderful; having a quality that makes you admire it very much
رائع؛ رفيع، سامٍ
▸ **sublimely** *adv* بصورة لا مثيل لها

submarine /ˌsʌbmə'riːn; *US* 'sʌbməriːn/ *noun* [C] a type of boat that can travel under the water as well as on the surface غوّاصة

submerge /səb'mɜːdʒ/ *verb* [I,T] to go or make sth go under water: *The whale spouted out a jet of water before submerging.* ○ *The fields were submerged by the floods.* يغطس، ينغمر؛ يغطّس، يغمر
▸ **submerged** *adj* under water: *submerged rocks just below the surface* مغمور بالماء

submission /səb'mɪʃn/ *noun* **1** [U] the state of accepting sb else's power or control
خضوع، استسلام، إذعان
2 [C,U] the act of sending a plan or statement to an official organization so that it can be discussed; the plan or statement that you send: *The council requires submission of plans for the new buildings by the end of the year.*
تقديم طلب رسميّ؛ طلب رسمي

submissive /səb'mɪsɪv/ *adj* willing to obey other people خَضوع، طيّع، مذعن

submit /səb'mɪt/ *verb* (submit**t**ing; submit**t**ed) **1** [I] **submit (to sb/sth)** to accept sb/sth's power or control: *After a bitter struggle the rebels were forced to submit.* يخضع، يستسلم
2 [T] **submit sth (to sb/sth)** to give or propose sth to sb/sth so that it can be discussed or considered: *Applications must be submitted by 31 March.* يقدّم (طلباً رسمياً)؛ يحيل إلى

subordinate /sə'bɔːdɪnət; *US* -dənət/ *adj* less important than sth else أقلّ أهميّةً من....
▸ **subordinate** *noun* [C] a person who is of lower rank or position مرؤوس
subordinate /sə'bɔːdɪneɪt; *US* -dəneɪt/ *verb* [T] **subordinate sth (to sth)** to treat sth as less important than sth else يضعه في المرتبة الثانية بعد

suˌbordinate 'clause *noun* [C] (*grammar*) a phrase with a verb that usually begins with a conjunction and that adds information to the main part of the sentence: *In the sentence 'We left early because it was raining', 'because it was raining' is the subordinate clause.*
جملة تابعة (للجملة الرئيسيّة)

subprime /ˌsʌb'praɪm/ *adj* connected with the practice of lending money to people who may not be able to pay the money back, because they have a bad credit rating: *subprime mortgages*
مشكوك فيها، قد لا تستوفى (تقديم قروض)

subscribe /səb'skraɪb/ *verb* [I] **1 subscribe (to sth)** to pay an amount of money regularly in order to receive or use sth: *Which journals does the library subscribe to?* ○ *We subscribe to several sports channels* (= on TV) يشترك في (جريدة مثلاً)
2 subscribe to sth to agree with an idea, belief, etc: *I don't subscribe to the view that all war is wrong.* يؤيّد فكرة، يوافق على
▸ **subscriber** *noun* [C] **1** a person who pays to receive a newspaper or magazine regularly
مشترك
2 a person who uses a particular service: *subscribers to cable television* مشترك
3 a person who has a particular opinion: *I'm not a subscriber to the view that all war is wrong.*
مؤيّد، من أنصار فكرة
subscription /səb'skrɪpʃn/ *noun* [C] an amount of money that you pay to receive a newspaper or magazine regularly or to belong to a particular society or organization قيمة الاشتراك

subsequent /'sʌbsɪkwənt/ *adj* (only *before* a noun) (*formal*) coming after or later: *I thought that was the end of the matter but subsequent events proved me wrong.* تالٍ، لاحق
▸ **subsequently** *adv* afterwards: *The rumours were subsequently found to be untrue.*
وبعد ذلك، لاحقاً

subservient /səb'sɜːviənt/ *adj* **1** (*formal*) too ready to obey other people خانع، متذلّل
2 considered to be less important than sb/sth else ثانويّ في الأهميّة
▸ **subservience** /-əns/ *noun* [U] خضوع، خنوع

subside /səb'saɪd/ *verb* [I] **1** (used about land, a building, etc.) to sink down into the ground
يغور، ينخسف، يهبط
2 to become less strong: *The storm seems to be subsiding.* يهمد، يهدأ
▸ **subsidence** /səb'saɪdns/ *noun* [U] the sinking of land, buildings, etc. انخساف، هبوط

subsidiary /səb'sɪdiəri; *US* -dieri/ *adj* connected to but less important than sth else: *You must study two subsidiary subjects as well as your main subject.* تابع لـ، فرعيّ؛ ثانويّ
▸ **subsidiary** *noun* [C] (*pl.* **subsidiaries**) a business company that belongs to a larger and more important company شركة تابعة

subsidy /'sʌbsədi/ *noun* [C,U] (*pl.* **subsidies**) money that the government, etc. pays to help an organization or to help keep the cost of sth low: *agricultural/state/housing subsidies*
دعم أو إعانة ماليّة (من الحكومة عادة)
▸ **subsidize** (*also* **subsidise**) /'sʌbsɪdaɪz/ *verb* [T] (of a government, etc.) to pay money in order to keep prices or the cost of a service low: *Public*

transport should be subsidized.
"يدعم"، يقدّم معونة ماليّة

subsist /səbˈsɪst/ *verb* [I] *(formal)* to manage to live with very little food or money
يعيش على القليل، يقتات

▶ **subsistence** /-təns/ *noun* [U]: *to live at subsistence level*
عيش، بقاء

substance /ˈsʌbstəns/ *noun* **1** [C] a solid or liquid material: *poisonous substances* ○ *The cloth is coated in a new waterproof substance.*
مادّة

2 [U] the most important points or ideas of sth: *Don't repeat everything. Just tell me the substance of what they said.*
جوهر، زبدة (الكلام)

3 [U] importance, value or truth: *There's little substance to the film but it's very entertaining.*
أهميّة، قيمة

substandard /ˌsʌbˈstændəd/ *adj* of poor quality; not as good as usual or as it should be
دون السويّة المطلوبة

substantial /səbˈstænʃl/ *adj* **1** large in amount: *The storms caused substantial damage.* ○ *a substantial sum of money*
كبير، ضخم

2 large or strong: *The furniture was cheap and not very substantial.*
متين؛ كبير الحجم

▶ **substantially** /-ʃəli/ *adv* **1** by a large amount: *House prices have fallen substantially.*
بمقدار كبير؛ بشكل هائل

2 generally; in most points: *The landscape of Wales has remained substantially the same for centuries.*
بصورة عامّة

substitute /ˈsʌbstɪtjuːt; *US* -tuːt/ *noun* [C] **substitute (for sb/sth)** a person or thing that takes the place of sb/sth else: *One player was injured so the substitute was sent on to play.*
بديل

▶ **substitute** *verb* **1** [T] **substitute sb/sth (for sb/sth)** to put a person or thing in the place of sb/sth else: *You can substitute margarine for butter.*
يستبدِل بـ، يستعيض عن

2 [I] **substitute (for sb/sth)** to be used instead of sb/sth
يحِلّ محلّ

substitution /ˌsʌbstɪˈtjuːʃn; *US* -ˈtuːʃn/ *noun* [C,U]
استبدال، استعاضة

subtitle /ˈsʌbtaɪtl/ *noun* [C, usually pl.] the words at the bottom of the picture on television or at the cinema. The subtitles translate the words of a foreign film or programme or show the words that are spoken, to help deaf people.
الترجمة المطبوعة على الفيلم

subtle /ˈsʌtl/ *adj* **1** not very noticeable; not very strong or bright: *subtle colours* ○ *I noticed a subtle difference in her.*
دقيق، خفيف؛ هادئ

2 very clever and using indirect methods to achieve sth: *Advertisements persuade us to buy things in very subtle ways.*
حاذق، ذو دهاء

▶ **subtlety** /ˈsʌtlti/ *noun* [C,U] *(pl.* **subtleties***)*
رقّة، دقّة؛ حذق

subtly /ˈsʌtli/ *adv*
بشكل خفيف غير ملحوظ

subtract /səbˈtrækt/ *verb* [T] **subtract sth (from sth)** to take one number or quantity away from another: *If you subtract five from nine you get four.*
يطرح

▶ **subtraction** /səbˈtrækʃn/ *noun* [C,U]
عمليّة الطرح؛ طرح

suburb /ˈsʌbɜːb/ *noun* [C] an area where people live that is outside the central part of a town or city: *Most people live in the suburbs and work in the centre of town.* ○ *an industrial suburb*
ضاحية

▶ **suburban** /səˈbɜːbən/ *adj*: *suburban life*
متعلّق بالضواحي؛ مملّ رتيب

> People often think of life in the suburbs as dull, so **suburban** sometime means 'dull and uninteresting'.

suburbia /səˈbɜːbiə/ *noun* [U] the suburbs of towns and cities
الضواحي

subversive /səbˈvɜːsɪv/ *adj* trying to destroy or damage a government, religion or political system by attacking it secretly and in an indirect way
هدّام، تخريبي

▶ **subversive** *noun* [C] a person who is subversive
مخرّب

subvert /səbˈvɜːt/ *verb* [T] to try to destroy or damage a government, religion or political system by attacking it secretly and in an indirect way
يهدم، يخرّب؛ يفسد

▶ **subversion** /səbˈvɜːʃn; *US* -ˈvɜːrʒn/ *noun* [U]
نشاط هدّام؛ تخريب

subway /ˈsʌbweɪ/ *noun* [C] **1** a passage under a busy road or railway that is for people who are walking (pedestrians)
ممرّ تحت الأرض

2 *(US)* = UNDERGROUND

succeed /səkˈsiːd/ *verb* **1** [I] **succeed (in sth/in doing sth)** to manage to achieve what you want; to do well: *Our plan succeeded.* ○ *If you keep on trying you will succeed in the end.* ○ *A good education will help you succeed in life.* ➲ Look at **fail**.
ينجح

2 [I,T] to have a job or important position after sb else: *Tony Blair succeeded John Major as Prime Minister in 1997.*
يخلِف

success /səkˈses/ *noun* **1** [U] achieving what you want; doing well: *Hard work is the key to success.* ○ *Her attempts to get a job for the summer have not met with much success* (= she hasn't managed to do it).
نجاح، توفيق

2 [C] something that achieves what it wants to, or becomes very popular: *You must try to make a success of your marriage.* ○ *The film 'Titanic' was a huge success.* ➲ Look at **failure**.
عمل ناجح

▶ **successful** /-fl/ *adj* having achieved what was wanted; having become popular: *a successful attempt to climb Mount Everest* ○ *a successful actor*
ناجح، موفّق

successfully /-fəli/ *adv*
بنجاح

succession /səkˈseʃn/ *noun* **1** [C] a number of people or things that follow one another: *We've had a succession of hot dry summers.*
سلسلة من؛ تعاقب

2 [U] the right to have an important position after sb else: *Prince William is second in succession to the throne.*
وراثة، خلافة

IDM **in succession** following one after another:

There have been three deaths in the family in quick succession. على التوالي، على التعاقب

successive /sək'sesɪv/ *adj* (only *before* a noun) coming one after the other without a break: *This was their fifth successive win.* متعاقب، متوالٍ

successor /sək'sesə(r)/ *noun* [C] a person who has a job or important position after sb else ➲ Look at **predecessor**. خليفة، خَلَف

succinct /sək'sɪŋkt/ *adj* said clearly, in a few words مختصر مفيد، موجز
▸ **succinctly** *adv* بإيجاز بارع

succulent /'sʌkjələnt/ *adj* (used about food) very good to eat because it is not dry ريّان، كثير العصارة

succumb /sə'kʌm/ *verb* [I] **succumb (to sth)** (*formal*) to stop fighting against sth: *He succumbed to temptation and took another cake.* ○ *to succumb to an illness* (= to die) يرضخ، يخضع؛ يموت

⚷ **such** /sʌtʃ/ *det* **1** (used for referring to sb/sth that you are talking about or that you mentioned earlier) of this or that type: *'Can I speak to Mr Wallis?' 'I'm sorry, there's no such person here.'* ○ *I don't believe in ghosts. There's no such thing.* كهذا: (شخص) بهذا الاسم
2 (used for emphasizing the degree of sth): *It was such a boring film that I fell asleep.* ○ *Let's have lunch in the garden. It's such a lovely day.* ○ *It seems such a long time since we last met.* إلى حدّ كبير؛ إلى هذا الحدّ

> You use **such** before a noun or before a noun that has an adjective in front of it: *Tommy is such a darling!* ○ *Susan is such a good athlete.* You use **so** before an adjective that is used without a noun: *Don't be so silly.* ○ *It was so cold we stayed at home.* Compare: *It was such a cold night that we stayed at home.*

3 (used for talking about the result of sth): *The statement was worded in such a way that it did not upset anyone.* بشكل يؤدّي إلى
▸ **such** *pron* (used for referring to sb/sth that you are talking about or that you mentioned earlier) this or that type of person or thing: *The economic situation is such that we all have less money to spend.* من النوع الذي...
IDM **as such 1** in the exact meaning of the word: *It's not a promotion as such, but it will mean more money.* بالمعنى الحرفيّ للكلمة
2 without anything else; alone: *Poverty as such does not mean unhappiness but it can make life very uncomfortable.* في حدّ ذاته
such as for example: *Fatty foods such as chips are bad for you.* مثل، كـ

⚷ **suck** /sʌk/ *verb* **1** [I,T] to pull a liquid into your mouth, by making your lips into a round shape and pulling your cheeks in: *to suck milk up through a straw* يمص
2 [T] to pull sth in a particular direction, using force: *Vacuum cleaners suck up the dirt.* يشفط، يَشْرق، يمتص
3 [I,T] to have sth in your mouth and keep touching it with your lips and tongue: *All my children sucked their thumbs.* يمصّ

sucker /'sʌkə(r)/ *noun* [C] **1** (*informal*) a person who believes everything that you tell him/her and who is easy to cheat مغفّل، ساذج
2 a part of some plants, animals or insects that is used for helping them stick onto a surface ممص

suction /'sʌkʃn/ *noun* [U] **1** the act of removing air from a space so that another substance is pulled in: *A vacuum cleaner works by suction.* مصّ، امتصاص، شَفْط
2 the act of making two surfaces stick together by removing the air between them: *The hook is attached to the wall by a suction pad.* مص

⚷ **sudden** /'sʌdn/ *adj* done or happening quickly, or when you do not expect it: *a sudden decision* ○ *a sudden loud noise* مفاجئ، مباغت
IDM **all of a sudden** suddenly; unexpectedly: *All of a sudden the lights went out.* فجأة، بغتةً
sudden death a way of deciding who wins a game where the score is equal by playing one more point or game: *a sudden-death play-off* موت مفاجئ: خسارة المباراة
▸ **suddenly** *adv*: *Suddenly, everybody started shouting.* فجأةً
suddenness *noun* [U] فجائيّة، حدوث على حين غرّة

⚷ **sudoku** /ˌsu'dəʊku:; -'dɒk-/ *noun* [C,U] a number puzzle with nine squares, each containing nine smaller squares, in which you have to put the numbers one to nine so that a number appears only once in each of the nine squares and in each row of nine across and down the puzzle سودوكو: لعبة ذكاء شهيرة تعتمد على الأرقام

suds /sʌdz/ *noun* [plural] the bubbles that you get when you mix soap and water رغوة الصابون

sue /su:; *Brit also* sju:/ *verb* [I,T] **sue (sb) (for sth)** to go to a court of law and ask for money from sb because he/she has done sth bad to you, or said sth bad about you يقيم دعوى على، يقاضي

suede /sweɪd/ *noun* [U] a type of soft leather which does not have a smooth surface and feels rather like cloth جلد مخمليّ

suet /'su:ɪt; *Brit also* 'sju:ɪt/ *noun* [U] a type of hard animal fat that is used in cooking شحم يستعمل في الطبخ

⚷ **suffer** /'sʌfə(r)/ *verb* **1** [I,T] to experience sth unpleasant, e.g. pain, sadness, difficulty, etc: *Mary often suffers from severe headaches.* ○ *Our troops suffered heavy losses.* ○ *In a recession it's the poor who suffer most.* يقاسي، يعاني
2 [I] to become worse in quality: *If you have problems at home your work will suffer.* يسوء، يتضرّر
▸ **sufferer** /'sʌfərə(r)/ *noun* [C]: *cancer sufferers* المصاب بـ
suffering /'sʌfərɪŋ/ *noun* [C,U]: *The famine caused great hardship and suffering.* معاناة، ألم

⚷ **sufficient** /sə'fɪʃnt/ *adj* (*formal*) as much as is necessary; enough: *We have sufficient oil reserves*

to last for three months. ℹ The opposite is **insufficient.** كاف
بشكل كافٍ
▸ **sufficiently** *adv*

suffix /ˈsʌfɪks/ *noun* [C] a letter or group of letters that you add at the end of a word, and that change its meaning or the way it is used: *To form the noun from the adjective 'sad', add the suffix 'ness'.* ➲ Look at **prefix**.
لاحقة: مقطع يضاف إلى آخر الكلمة

suffocate /ˈsʌfəkeɪt/ *verb* [I,T] to die because there is no air to breathe; to kill sb in this way يختنق: يخنق
▸ **suffocating** *adj*: *The heat is suffocating.*
خانق
suffocation /ˌsʌfəˈkeɪʃn/ *noun* [U] خنق: اختناق

⚷ **sugar** /ˈʃʊɡə(r)/ *noun* **1** [U] a sweet substance that you get from certain plants: *Do you take sugar in tea?* سكّر
2 [C] one spoonful or lump of sugar (in a cup of tea, coffee, etc.): *Two sugars, please.*
ملعقة أو قطعة سكّر
▸ **sugary** /ˈʃʊɡəri/ *adj* very sweet شديد الحلاوة

⚷ **suggest** /səˈdʒest; *US* səɡˈdʒ-/ *verb* [T] **1 suggest sth (to sb)** to propose a plan or idea for sb to discuss or consider: *Can anybody suggest ways of raising more money?* ○ *Tony suggested going out for a walk.* ○ *Tony suggested that we go out for a walk.* ○ *Tony suggested a walk.* ○ *How do you suggest we get out of this mess?* يقترح
2 to say that a person or thing is suitable, especially a person or thing that you know about from your own experience: *Can you suggest someone for the job?* ○ *Ann suggested Egypt as a good place for a winter holiday.* يقترح، يقدم أسماً
3 to say or show sth in an indirect way: *Are you suggesting the accident was my fault?* ○ *Forecasts suggest that inflation will fall by the end of next year.* يلمّح: يشير إلى
▸ **suggestive** /-ɪv/ *adj* **1** making you think of sth: *music that was suggestive of Asia*
مُذكّر بِ، إيحائيّ أو موحٍ
2 making you think about sex: *a suggestive dance* مثير جنسياً
suggestively *adv* بتلميحات جنسيّة

⚷ **suggestion** /səˈdʒestʃən; *US* səɡˈdʒ-/ *noun* **1** [C] a plan or idea that sb proposes or suggests: *May I make a suggestion?* اقتراح
2 [U] putting an idea into a person's mind; giving advice about what to do: *I came here at my friend's suggestion.* إيعاز: نصيحة
3 [sing.] a small amount or sign of sth: *He spoke with a suggestion of a Scottish accent.*
أثر ضئيل، شيء من

suicide /ˈsuːɪsaɪd; *Brit also* ˈsjuːɪ-/ *noun* **1** [U] the act of killing yourself: *Ben has tried to commit suicide several times.* انتحار
2 [C] an example of this: *There have been nine suicides from this bridge this year.* حادثة انتحار
▸ **suicidal** /ˌsuːɪˈsaɪdl; *Brit also* ˈsjuːɪ-/ *adj* **1** (used about a person) wanting to kill himself/herself: *to feel suicidal* راغب في الانتحار
2 that will probably result in your being killed: *a suicidal risk* انتحاري

⚷ **suit¹** /suːt; *Brit also* sjuːt/ *noun* [C] **1** a formal set of clothes that are made of the same material, consisting of a jacket and either trousers or a skirt بدلة، طقم
2 an article of clothing or set of clothes that you wear for a particular activity: *a tracksuit* ○ *a swimsuit* ○ *a suit of armour* بدلة، طقم، ملابس
3 one of the four sets of thirteen playing cards (= hearts, clubs, diamonds and spades)
أحد النقوش الأربعة في ورق اللعب
IDM **follow suit** → FOLLOW

⚷ **suit²** /suːt; *Brit also* sjuːt/ *verb* **1** [T] to look attractive on sb: *That dress really suits you.*
يلبق بِ، يبدو جميلاً عليه
2 [I,T] to be convenient or suitable for sb/sth: *Would Thursday at 9.30 suit you?* ○ *Living in the country wouldn't suit me at all.* يلائم، يناسب
▸ **suited** *adj* **suited (for/to sb/sth)** suitable or right for sb/sth: *She and her husband are very well suited.* ملائم، مناسب: صالح لِ

⚷ **suitable** /ˈsuːtəbl; *Brit also* ˈsjuːt-/ *adj* **suitable (for sb/sth)** right or convenient for sb/sth: *The film isn't suitable for children.* ○ *I've got nothing suitable to wear for a wedding.* ℹ The opposite is **unsuitable.** ملائم، مناسب
▸ **suitability** /ˌsuːtəˈbɪləti; *Brit also* ˈsjuːt-/ *noun* [U] ملاءمة: صلاحية
suitably /-əbli/ *adv*: *I was suitably dressed for the party.* بشكل مناسب

⚷ **suitcase** /ˈsuːtkeɪs; *Brit also* ˈsjuːt-/ (*also* **case**) *noun* [C] a flat box with a handle that you use for carrying your clothes, etc. in when you are travelling حقيبة سفر

suite /swiːt/ *noun* [C] **1** a set of two or more pieces of furniture of the same style or covered in the same material: *a three-piece suite* (= a sofa and two armchairs) طقم مفروشات
2 a set of rooms in a hotel (= a bedroom, sitting room and bathroom) جناح

suitor /ˈsuːtə(r); *Brit also* ˈsjuː-/ *noun* [C] (*old-fashioned*) a man who wants to marry a particular woman الخاطب، المتقدّم للزواج

sulfur (*US*) = SULPHUR

sulk /sʌlk/ *verb* [I] to be very quiet or bad-tempered because you are angry with sb about sth يحرد، يبوّز
▸ **sulky** *adj* متجهم: مبوز
sulkily /-ɪli/ *adv* بتجهم

sullen /ˈsʌlən/ *adj* looking bad-tempered and not speaking to people: *a sullen face/expression/glare* واجم، مقطّب الجبين
▸ **sullenly** *adv* بعبوس: بوجوم

sulphur (*US* **sulfur**) /ˈsʌlfə(r)/ *noun* [U] (*symbol* S) a yellow substance with a strong unpleasant smell كبريت

sultan (*also* **Sultan**) /ˈsʌltən/ *noun* [C] the ruler in some Muslim countries: *the Sultan of Oman*
سلطان

sultana /sʌl'tɑːnə; *US* -ænə/ *noun* [C] a dried grape with no seeds in it that is used in cooking ➲ Look at **raisin**. زبيب بدون بذر

sultry /'sʌltri/ *adj* (**sultrier**; **sultriest**) **1** (used about the weather) hot and damp حارّ شديد الرطوبة

2 (used about a woman) very sexually attractive مثير جنسياً

🔑**sum** /sʌm/ *noun* [C] **1** a simple problem that involves calculating numbers: *I've got some sums to do for homework.* عملية حسابية

2 an amount of money: *The industry has spent huge sums of money modernizing its equipment.* مبلغ

3 [usually sing.] the amount that you get when you add two or more numbers together: *The sum of two and five is seven.* حاصل الجمع، مجموع

▸ **sum** *verb* (summing; summed)

PHR V **sum (sth) up** to describe in a few words the main ideas of what sb has said or written: *to sum up the main points of an argument* يلخّص، يجْمِل

sum sb/sth up to form an opinion about sb/sth: *He summed the situation up immediately.* يفهم الوضع، يكوّن رأياً

ˌ**summing-'up** *noun* [C] (*pl.* summings-up) a speech in which a judge sums up what has been said in a court of law before a decision (verdict) is reached عرض موجز لوقائع الدعوى

🔑**summary¹** /'sʌməri/ *noun* [C] (*pl.* **summaries**) a short description of the main ideas or events of sth: *A brief summary of the experiment is given at the beginning of the report.* ○ *a news summary* ملخّص، موجز

▸ **summarize** (*also* **summarise**) /'sʌməraɪz/ *verb* [I,T]: *Could you summarize the story so far?* يلخّص

summary² /'sʌməri/ *adj* (*formal*) done quickly and without taking time to think about whether it is the right thing to do: *summary arrests and executions* متسرّع، عاجل، اعتباطيّ

🔑**summer** /'sʌmə(r)/ *noun* [C,U] the second season of the year, after spring and before autumn. Summer is the warmest season of the year: *Are you going away this summer?* ○ *a summer's day* ○ *the summer holidays* فصل الصيف

▸ **summery** /'sʌməri/ *adj*: *summery weather* ○ *a summery dress* صيفي

'**summer house** *noun* [C] a small building in a park or garden where you can sit and relax in good weather بناء صغير في حديقة للجلوس والاستمتاع

summertime /'sʌmətaɪm/ *noun* [U] the season of summer موسم الصيف

summit /'sʌmɪt/ *noun* [C] **1** the top of a mountain قمّة (الجبل)، ذروة

2 an important meeting between the leaders of two or more countries: *the EU summit in Madrid* مؤتمر قمة

summon /'sʌmən/ *verb* [T] **1** (*formal*) to order a person to come to a place: *The boys were summoned to the headmaster's office.* يستدعي

2 summon sth (up) to find strength, courage or some other quality that you need even though it is difficult for you to do so: *She couldn't summon up the courage to leave him.* يستجمع

summons /'sʌmənz/ *noun* [C] (*pl.* **summonses**) an order to go somewhere, especially to a court of law أمر بالحضور (أمام القاضي)

Sun. *abbrev* = SUNDAY

🔑**sun** /sʌn/ *noun* **1 the sun** [sing.] the star that shines in the sky during the day and that gives the earth heat and light: *The sun rises in the east and sets in the west.* ○ *the rays of the sun* الشمس

2 the sun [sing., U] light and heat from the sun: *Don't sit in the sun too long.* ○ *Too much sun can be harmful.* الشمس

IDM **catch the sun** → CATCH¹

▸ **sun** *verb* [T] (sunning; sunned) **sun yourself** sit or lie in the sun (2) in order to enjoy the heat يتشمّس

sunny *adj* (sunnier; sunniest) having a lot of light from the sun: *a sunny garden* ○ *a sunny day* مشمس

sunbathe /'sʌnbeɪð/ *verb* [I] to take off most of your clothes and sit or lie in the sun in order to make your skin go brown يعرّض جسمه للشمس

sunbeam /'sʌnbiːm/ *noun* [C] a line (ray) of sunlight شعاع شمسي

sunburn /'sʌnbɜːn/ *noun* [U] red painful skin which you get after sitting or lying too long in strong sunlight حرق الشمس

▸ '**sunburned** (*also* '**sunburnt**) *adj* suffering from sunburn محروق بالشمس

sundae /'sʌndeɪ; *US* -diː/ *noun* [C] a type of food that consists of ice cream with fruit, nuts, etc. on the top نوع من الجيلاتي/"الآيس كريم"

🔑**Sunday** /'sʌndeɪ/ *noun* [C,U] (*abbr* **Sun.**) the first day of the week, coming before Monday ❶ For examples of the use of the days of the week in sentences, look at **Monday**. يوم الأحد

sundial /'sʌndaɪəl/ *noun* [C] a piece of equipment that uses shadow to show what the time is ساعة شمسيّة، مزولة

sundry /'sʌndri/ *adj* (only *before* a noun) of various kinds: *a shop selling toys, games and sundry gift items* متنوّع، مختلف

IDM **all and sundry** (*informal*) everyone الجميع، كل واحد

sunflower /'sʌnflaʊə(r)/ *noun* [C] a tall plant that has a very large yellow flower with a black centre. The seeds of the plant are used to make cooking oil and margarine. عبّاد الشمس

sung *pp* of SING

sunglasses /'sʌnglɑːsɪz; *US* -glæsiz/ (*also* ˌ**dark 'glasses**) (*also informal* **shades**) *noun* [plural] glasses that have dark glass in them to protect your eyes from bright sunlight نظارة شمسيّة

sunk *pt, pp* of SINK¹

sunken /'sʌŋkən/ *adj* **1** below the water: *a sunken ship* غارق

2 (used about cheeks or eyes) curving inwards and making you look ill غائر

3 at a lower level than the surrounding area: *a luxury bathroom with a sunken bath* غائر في الأرض، مجوّر

sunlight /'sʌnlaɪt/ *noun* [U] the light from the sun نور الشمس
▸ **'sunlit** *adj* having bright light from the sun: *a sunlit terrace* مضيء، منوّر بالشمس

Sunni /'sʊni; 'sʌni/ *noun* (*pl.* **Sunni** or **Sunnis**)
1 [U] one of the main branches of Islam أهل السنّة
2 [C] a member of the Sunni branch of Islam سنّي
▸ **Sunni** *adj* (usually *before* a noun): *a Sunni Muslim* سنّي

sunrise /'sʌnraɪz/ *noun* [C,U] the time when the sun comes up and the day begins: *to get up at sunrise* ➲ Look at **dawn**. الشروق

sunset /'sʌnset/ *noun* [C,U] the time when the sun goes down and night begins: *The park closes at sunset.* ○ *a beautiful sunset* الغروب

sunshine /'sʌnʃaɪn/ *noun* [U] heat and light from the sun: *warm spring sunshine* أشعة الشمس

sunstroke /'sʌnstrəʊk/ *noun* [U] an illness that is caused by spending too much time in strong sunlight ضربة الشمس

suntan /'sʌntæn/ (*also* **tan**) *noun* [C] when you have a suntan, your skin is brown because you have spent time in the sun: *to have a suntan* ○ *suntan oil* اسمرار البشرة من الشمس
▸ **'suntanned** *adj*: *suntanned bodies on the beaches* مسمّر

super /'su:pə(r); *Brit also* 'sju:-/ *adj* (*informal*)
1 very good; wonderful: *We had a super time.* ○ *You've done a super job.* ممتاز، رائع
2 bigger or better than other things which are similar: *a new super computer* الأضخم، الأفضل

superb /su:'pɜ:b; *Brit also* sju:-/ *adj* very good, excellent فائق، ممتاز، رائع
▸ **superbly** *adv* بشكل رائع

supercilious /ˌsu:pə'sɪliəs; *Brit also* ˌsju:-/ *adj* showing that you think that you are better than other people: *a supercilious smile* مترفّع، متكبّر
▸ **superciliously** *adv* بترفّع؛ باستخفاف

superficial /ˌsu:pə'fɪʃl; *Brit also* ˌsju:-/ *adj* **1** (used about people) not caring about serious or important things: *He's a very superficial sort of person.* سطحيّ (في تفكيره)
2 only on the surface, not deep: *Don't worry. It's only a superficial wound.* سطحي
3 not deep, complete or thorough: *a superficial knowledge of the subject* سطحي
▸ **superficiality** /ˌsu:pəˌfɪʃi'æləti; *Brit also* ˌsju:-/ *noun* [U] سطحيّة
superficially /-ʃəli/ *adv* ظاهرياً

superfluous /su:'pɜ:fluəs; *Brit also* sju:-/ *adj* more than is wanted; not needed: *Any further explanation is superfluous.* زائد عن اللزوم

superfood /'su:pəfu:d/ *noun* [C] a type of food that some people think is very good for you and helps to prevent disease غذاء مثالي: أغذية مفيدة جداً و تقي من الأمراض

superhuman /ˌsu:pə'hju:mən; *Brit also* ˌsju:-/ *adj* greater than is usual for human beings: *superhuman strength* يفوق طاقة البشر

superimpose /ˌsu:pərɪm'pəʊz; *Brit also* ˌsju:-/ *verb* [T] **superimpose sth (on sth)** to put sth on top of sth else so that what is underneath can still be seen يركّب أو يضع شيئاً فوق آخر

superintendent /ˌsu:pərɪn'tendənt; *Brit also* ˌsju:-/ *noun* [C] **1** a police officer of high rank: *Detective Superintendent Ron Marsh* ضابط بوليس
2 a person who looks after a large building ناظر، مراقب

superior /su:'pɪəriə(r); *Brit also* sju:-/ *adj* **1** better than usual or than sb/sth else: *He is clearly superior to all the other candidates.* ℹ The opposite is **inferior**. أفضل من، متفوّق على
2 higher in rank: *a superior officer* أعلى مرتبةً
3 thinking that you are better than other people: *There's no need to be so superior.* متعالٍ
▸ **superior** *noun* [C] a person of higher rank or position شخص أعلى مركزاً: رئيس
superiority /su:ˌpɪəri'ɒrəti; *Brit also* sju:-/ *noun* [U]: *the superiority of the new method* تفوّق؛ ترفّع

superlative /su'pɜ:lətɪv; *Brit also* sju-/ *noun* [C] the form of an adjective or adverb that expresses its highest degree: *'Most beautiful', 'best' and 'fastest' are all superlatives.* صيغة منتهى التفضيل

supermarket /'su:pəmɑ:kɪt; *Brit also* 'sju:-/ *noun* [C] a large shop that sells food, drink, things for cleaning your house, etc. You choose what you want from the shelves in a supermarket and pay for everything when you leave. "سوبرماركت"، سوق مركزيّة

supernatural /ˌsu:pə'nætʃrəl; *Brit also* ˌsju:-/ *adj* that cannot be explained by the laws of science: *a creature with supernatural powers* خارق للطبيعة
▸ **the supernatural** *noun* [sing.] things that are supernatural: *I don't believe in the supernatural.* الظواهر الخارقة للطبيعة

supersede /ˌsu:pə'si:d; *Brit also* ˌsju:-/ *verb* [T] to take the place of sb/sth which was present or used before and which has become old-fashioned; *Records were superseded by CDs.* يبطِل، يحلّ محلّ

supersonic /ˌsu:pə'sɒnɪk; *Brit also* ˌsju:-/ *adj* faster than the speed of sound أسرع من الصوت

superstar /'su:pəstɑ:(r); *Brit also* 'sju:-/ *noun* [C] (*informal*) a singer, film star, etc. who is very famous and popular نجم (سينمائيّ) كبير

superstition /ˌsu:pə'stɪʃn; *Brit also* ˌsju:-/ *noun* [C,U] a belief that cannot be explained by reason or science: *According to superstition, it's unlucky to walk under a ladder.* معتقد خرافيّ، خرافة
▸ **superstitious** /-'stɪʃəs/ *adj*: *I never do anything important on Friday the 13th – I'm superstitious.* مؤمن بالخرافات

a b c d e f g h i j k l m n o p q r s t u v w x y z

superstore /'su:pəstɔ:(r); *Brit also* 'sju:-/ *noun* [C] a very large shop that sells food or a wide variety of one type of goods: *a giant superstore on the edge of town* مخزن تجاري ضخم

supervise /'su:pəvaɪz; *Brit also* 'sju:-/ *verb* [I,T] to watch sb/sth to make sure that work, etc. is being done properly and that people are behaving correctly: *Your job is to supervise the building work.* يشرف على، يراقب
▸ **supervision** /ˌsu:pə'vɪʒn; *Brit also* ˌsju:-/ *noun* [U]: *Children should not play here without supervision.* إشراف، مراقبة
supervisor *noun* [C] a person who supervises مشرف، مراقب

supper /'sʌpə(r)/ *noun* [C,U] the last meal of the day, either a cooked meal in the evening or a small meal that you eat quite late, not long before you go to bed ➲ Look at the note at **dinner**. عشاء

supple /'sʌpl/ *adj* that bends or moves easily; not stiff مَرِن، ليِّن
▸ **suppleness** *noun* [U] مرونة

supplement /'sʌplɪmənt/ *noun* [C] **a supplement (to sth)** something that is added to sth else: *There is a £10 supplement for a single room.* مبلغ إضافي؛ ملحق
▸ **supplement** /'sʊplɪment/ *verb* [T] **supplement sth (with sth)** to add sth to sth else: *to supplement your diet with vitamins* يكمِّل، يعزز، يضيف إلى

supplementary /ˌsʌplɪ'mentri; *US* -teri/ *adj* added to sth else; extra: *supplementary exercises at the back of the book* إضافي؛ تكميلي

supply /sə'plaɪ/ *verb* [T] (*pres part* **supplying**; *3rd pers sing pres* **supplies**; *pt, pp* **supplied**) **supply sth (to sb)**; **supply sb (with sth)** to give or provide sth: *The farmer supplies eggs to the surrounding villages.* ○ *He supplies the surrounding villages with eggs.* يزود، يمدّ
▸ **supplier** /sə'plaɪə(r)/ *noun* [C] a person or company that supplies sth المورِّد، المزوِّد
supply *noun* (*pl.* **supplies**) **1** [C] something that is supplied: *The water supply was contaminated.* إمداد
2 [C,U] a store or amount of sth: *Supplies of food were dropped by helicopter.* ○ *In many parts of the country water is in short supply* (= there is not much of it). مؤونة؛ إمداد؛ كمية الشيء

support /sə'pɔ:t/ *verb* [T] **1** to carry the weight of sb/sth: *Large columns support the roof.* يحمل
2 to agree with the aims of sb/sth and to give him/her/it help, money, etc: *I'll support you as much as I can.* ○ *Which political party do you support?* يؤيِّد، يدعم
3 to have a particular sports team as your favourite: *Which football team do you support?* يناصر
4 to show that sth is true or correct: *What evidence do you have to support what you say?* يدعم
5 to give or provide sb with the money he/she needs for food, clothes, etc: *Jim has to support two children from his previous marriage.* يعيل
▸ **support** *noun* **1** [U] **support (for sth)** help that you give to a person or thing (often sth that is encouraging in a difficult situation): *public support for the campaign* ○ *The theatre closed because of lack of support.* ○ *Thank you for your support at this difficult time.* دعم، تأييد
2 [C,U] something that carries the weight of sb/sth: *a roof support* دعامة، عماد
3 [U] money to buy food, clothes, etc: *She has no job, no home and no means of support.* معاش، إعالة
IDM **in support of sb/sth** supporting or agreeing with sb/sth: *Steve spoke in support of the proposal.* مؤيِّداً لـ
supporter *noun* [C] a person who supports a political party, sports team, etc: *football supporters* نصير، مؤيِّد
supportive /sə'pɔ:tɪv/ *adj* giving help or sympathy مساند، مشجِّع، متفهِّم

suppose /sə'pəʊz/ *verb* [T] **1** to think, believe or consider that sth is probable: *I suppose he seems unfriendly because he is shy.* ○ *What do you suppose could have happened?* ○ *I don't suppose that they're coming now.* يظنّ؛ يعتقد
2 to pretend that sth will happen or is true: *Suppose you won a million pounds. What would you do?* يفرض، يفترض
IDM **I suppose 1** (used to show that you are not certain about sth): *I suppose it's all right, but I'm not sure.* ○ *It's about ten years old, I suppose.* أظنّ، على ما أظن
2 (used when you agree with sth, but are not very happy about it): *'Can we give Andy a lift?' 'Yes, I suppose so, if we must.'* طيِّب، لا مانع (تقال بفتور)
be supposed to do sth 1 to be expected to do sth or to have to do sth: *The train was supposed to arrive ten minutes ago.* ○ *This is secret and I'm not supposed to talk about it.* من المفروض أن
2 (*informal*) to be considered or thought to be sth: *I haven't seen it, but it's supposed to be a good play.* ○ *This is supposed to be the oldest pub in London.* يعتبر، يقال إنه
▸ **supposedly** /sə'pəʊzɪdli/ *adv* as people believe or suppose: *Supposedly, this is the place where St George fought the dragon.* على ما يعتقد
supposing *conj* if sth happens or is true: *Supposing the plan goes wrong, what will we do then?* لنفرض

supposition /ˌsʌpə'zɪʃn/ *noun* [C,U] an idea that a person thinks is true but which has not been proved فرضيّة؛ افتراض

suppress /sə'pres/ *verb* [T] **1** to stop sth by using force: *The army suppressed the rebellion.* يقمع، يخمد
2 to stop sth from being seen or known: *to suppress the truth* يخفي، يطمس
3 to stop yourself from expressing your feelings, etc: *to suppress a yawn* ○ *suppressed anger* يكظم، يكبت
▸ **suppression** /sə'preʃn/ *noun* [U] قمع؛ طمس؛ كبت

supreme /suˈpriːm; *Brit also* sjuː-/ *adj* **1** highest in rank or position: *a supreme ruler* الأعلى، الأسمى

2 greatest or most important: *a moment of supreme joy* الأعظم: بالغ الأهميّة

▸ **supremacy** /suˈpreməsi; *Brit also* sjuː-/ *noun* [U] **supremacy (over sb/sth)** the state of being most powerful تفوُّق: سيادة

supremely /suˈpriːmli; *Brit also* sjuː-/ *adv* very: *to be supremely happy* جداً، للغاية

surcharge /ˈsɜːtʃɑːdʒ/ *noun* [C] an extra amount of money that you have to pay for sth: *a surcharge for excess baggage* رسم إضافي

sure /ʃʊə(r); *US* ʃʊər/ *adj* **1** (not before a noun) having no doubt about sth; certain: *You must be sure of your facts before you make an accusation.* ○ *I'm not sure what to do next.* ○ *Craig was sure that he'd made the right decision.* ○ *I think I had my bag when I got off the bus but I'm not sure.* واثق، متأكّد

> **Sure** and **certain** are very similar in meaning. **Sure**, however, cannot be used in the phrase 'It is ... that ...' **Certain** can: *It is certain that there will be an election next year.* With **sure** we must say: *There is sure to be an election next year.*

2 (not before a noun) **sure of sth** certain to get sth: *If you go and see them you can be sure of a warm welcome.* متيقِّن: ضامن

3 **sure to do sth** certain to happen or do sth: *If you work hard you are sure to pass the exam.* متيقِّن، متأكّد

4 that you can trust: *A noise like that is a sure sign of engine trouble.* أكيد

5 (*informal*) (*US* **sure thing**) used to say 'yes' to sb: *'Can I have a look at your newspaper?' 'Sure.'* نعم، بالتأكيد

IDM **Be sure to do sth** Don't forget to do sth: *Be sure to write and tell me what happens.* يتذكّر، لا ينسى

make sure 1 to find out whether sth is in a certain state or has been done: *I must go back and make sure I closed the window.* يتأكّد، يتيقّن

2 to take the action that is necessary to make sth happen: *Make sure you are back home by 11 o'clock.* يتأكّد: يبذل جهده

sure of yourself confident about your opinions, or about what you can do واثق من نفسه

▸ **sure** *adv*

IDM **sure enough** as was expected: *I expected him to be early and sure enough he arrived five minutes before the others.* كما هو متوقّع

surely /ˈʃʊəli; *US* ˈʃʊərli/ *adv* **1** without doubt: *This will surely cause problems.* دون شكّ

2 (used for expressing surprise at sb else's opinions, plans, actions, etc.): *Surely you're not going to walk home in this rain?* ○ *'Tom's looking for another job.' 'Surely not.'* (تعبّر عن الاستغراب)

3 (*US informal*) yes; of course طبعاً، نعم

surf /sɜːf/ *noun* [U] the white part on the top of waves in the sea زبد الأمواج المتخبّطة على الشاطئ

▸ **surf** *verb* **1** [I] to stand or lie on a special board (a surfboard) and ride on a wave towards the shore يمارس رياضة ركوب الأمواج

2 **surf the Net/Internet** to use the Internet يستعمل الشبكة الدولية

surfer *noun* [C] **1** a person who surfs راكب الأمواج

2 (*also* **Net surfer**) a person who spends a lot of time using the Internet مستعمِل الشبكة الدولية

surface /ˈsɜːfɪs/ *noun* **1** [C] the outside part of sth: *the earth's surface* ○ *a new cleaning product for all your kitchen surfaces* سطح

2 [C, usually sing.] the top part of an area of water: *The submarine slowly rose to the surface.* سطح الماء

3 [sing.] the qualities of sb/sth that you see or notice, that are not hidden: *Everybody seems very friendly but there are a lot of tensions beneath the surface.* المظهر الخارجي

▸ **surface** *verb* **1** [T] to cover the surface (1) of sth: *to surface a road with tarmac* يفرش أو يغطّي (بالإسفلت مثلاً)

2 [I] to come to the surface of a liquid: *The submarine surfaced quickly.* يصعد إلى سطح (الماء)

3 [I] (*informal*) to appear again: *All the old arguments surfaced again in the discussion.* يظهر ثانية

ˈ**surface mail** *noun* [U] letters, parcels, etc. that go by road, rail or sea, not by air ➲ Look at **airmail**. البريد العادي (غير الجويّ)

surfeit /ˈsɜːfɪt/ *noun* [sing.] (*formal*) **a surfeit (of sth)** too much of sth كميّة مفرطة: إفراط، تخمة

surfer *noun* → SURF

surge /sɜːdʒ/ *verb* [I] to move forwards with great strength: *The crowd surged forward.* يندفع بقوة هائلة

▸ **surge** *noun* [C, usually sing.] **a surge (of/in sth) 1** a forward movement of a large mass: *a surge forward* ○ (*figurative*) *a surge* (= an increase) *in the demand for electricity* اندفاع الجماهير مثلاً: زيادة مفاجئة

2 a sudden strong feeling: *a surge of pity* موجة، فورة

surgeon /ˈsɜːdʒən/ *noun* [C] a doctor who performs medical operations (surgery): *a brain surgeon* جرّاح

surgery /ˈsɜːdʒəri/ *noun* (*pl.* **surgeries**) **1** [U] medical treatment in which your body is cut open so that part of it can be removed or repaired: *to undergo emergency surgery* ➲ Look at **plastic surgery**. جراحة

2 [C,U] the place or time when a doctor or dentist sees patients: *Her surgery is in Mill Lane.* ○ *Surgery hours are from 9.00 to 11.30 in the morning.* عيادة: مواعيد العيادة

surgical /ˈsɜːdʒɪkl/ *adj* used in surgery (1) or connected with surgery: *surgical instruments* جراحي

▸ **surgically** /-kli/ *adv* جراحياً

surly /ˈsɜːli/ *adj* (**surlier**; **surliest**) unfriendly and rude: *a surly expression* فظّ، سيّئ الخلق، متجهّم

surmount /sə'maʊnt/ *verb* [T] to overcome a problem or difficulty ➲ Look at **insurmountable**. يتغلّب على

surname /'sɜːneɪm/ (*also* **last name**) *noun* [C] the name that you share with other people in your family. Your surname is usually your last name: *'What's your surname?' 'Jones.'* ➲ Look at the note at **name**[1]. كنية أو لقب، اسم العائلة

surpass /sə'pɑːs; *US* -'pæs/ *verb* [T] (*formal*) do sth better than sb/sth else or better than expected يفوق، يبذّ

surplus /'sɜːpləs/ *noun* [C,U] an amount that is extra or more than you need: *the food surplus in Western Europe* الفائض
▶ **surplus** *adj* فائض، زائد عن الحاجة

surprise /sə'praɪz/ *noun* **1** [U] the feeling that you have when sth happens that you do not expect: *They looked up in surprise when she walked in.* ○ *To my surprise the boss agreed.* دهشة

2 [C] something that you did not expect: *What a pleasant surprise to see you again!* ○ *'What's my present?' 'It's a surprise.'* ○ *a surprise visit, attack, etc.* مفاجأة

IDM **take sb by surprise** to happen or do sth when sb is not expecting it: *His remarks took me by surprise.* يفاجئ

▶ **surprise** *verb* [T] **1** to cause sb to feel surprise: *It wouldn't surprise me if you got the job.* يدهِش

2 to attack or find sb suddenly and unexpectedly: *We surprised the burglars just as they were leaving our house.* يباغت

surprised *adj* feeling or showing surprise: *I was very surprised to see Carol there. I thought she was still abroad.* مندهش، مستغرب

surprising *adj* that causes surprise: *It's surprising how many adults can't read or write.* مذهل، مثير للاستغراب

surprisingly *adv* بصورة تثير الدهشة، ممّا يثير الدهشة

surreal /sə'riːəl/ (*also* **surrealistic** /səˌriːə'lɪstɪk/) *adj* very strange, like a dream سريالي، غير واقعي، غريب جداً

surrender /sə'rendə(r)/ *verb* **1** [I,T] **surrender (to sb)** to stop fighting and admit that you have lost يستسلم

2 [T] **surrender sb/sth (to sb)** (*formal*) to give sb/sth to sb else: *The police ordered them to surrender their weapons.* يسلِّم

▶ **surrender** *noun* [C,U] استسلام؛ تسليم

surreptitious /ˌsʌrəp'tɪʃəs/ *adj* done secretly سرّي؛ مختلَس

▶ **surreptitiously** *adv* خلسة، خفية

surrogate /'sʌrəgət/ *noun* [C], *adj* (a person or thing) that takes the place of sb/sth else: *a surrogate mother* (= a woman who has a baby and gives it to another woman who cannot have children) البديل؛ بديل

surround /sə'raʊnd/ *verb* [T] **surround sb/sth (by/with sth)** to be or go all around sb/sth: *The garden is surrounded by a high wall.* ○ *Troops have surrounded the parliament building.* ○ (*figurative*) *He is surrounded by friends.* يحيط ﺑ؛ يطوّق

▶ **surrounding** *adj* (only *before* a noun) that is near or around sth: *Oxford and the surrounding villages* محيط (ﺑ)

surroundings *noun* [plural] everything that is near or around you; the place where you live: *to live in pleasant surroundings* ○ *animals living in their natural surroundings* (= not in zoos) ➲ Look at **environment**. بيئة، محيط، جوار

surveillance /sɜː'veɪləns/ *noun* [U] a careful watch on sb who may have done sth wrong: *The suspect was under police surveillance.* مراقبة، رقابة

survey /sə'veɪ/ *verb* [T] **1** to look at the whole of sth from a distance: *We stood at the top of the hill and surveyed the countryside.* ○ (*figurative*) *Her new book surveys the literature of the twentieth century.* يلقي نظرة فاحصة عن بعد، يستعرض بصورة عامّة

2 to carefully measure and make a map of an area of land يمسح (الأراضي)

3 to examine a building carefully in order to find out if it is in good condition يفحص (البناء)

▶ **survey** /'sɜːveɪ/ *noun* [C] **1** a study of sth: *Surveys have shown that more and more people are getting into debt.* دراسة، استطلاع

2 an act of examining an area of land and making a map of it مَسْح (الأراضي)

3 an act of examining a building in order to find out if it is in good condition فحص (البناء)

survival /sə'vaɪvl/ *noun* **1** [U] the state of continuing to live or exist: *the struggle for survival* بقاء

2 [C] a person or thing that has continued to exist from an earlier time: *The festival is a survival from pre-Christian times.* من بقايا الماضي

survive /sə'vaɪv/ *verb* [I,T] to continue to live or exist, in or after a difficult or dangerous situation: *More than a hundred people were killed in the crash and only five passengers survived.* ○ *to survive a plane crash* ○ *The old man survived all his children* (= lived longer than them). ○ (*figurative*) *She's managed to survive two divorces* (= to deal with them well and to continue with her life). يبقى على قيد الحياة

▶ **survivor** *noun*: [C] *There were five survivors of the crash.* باقٍ على قيد الحياة

susceptible /sə'septəbl/ *adj* (not before a noun) **susceptible to sth** easily influenced, damaged or affected by sb/sth: *People in a new country are highly susceptible to illness.* ○ *The plant is highly susceptible to frost.* سهل التأثر ﺑ؛ حسّاس؛ قابل لِ

suspect /sə'spekt/ *verb* [T] **1** to believe that sth may happen or be true: *The situation is worse than we first suspected.* ○ *Nobody suspected that she was thinking of leaving.* يحسب، يظنّ

2 to have doubts about whether you can trust sb or believe sth: *I rather suspect his motives for offering to help.* يرتاب، يتوجّس

3 **suspect sb (of sth)** to believe that sb is guilty of sth: *I suspect Laura of taking the money.* ○ *She strongly suspected that he was lying.* ➲ Look at **suspicion**. يشتبه أو يشكّ في

▶ **suspect** /ˈsʌspekt/ *noun* [C] a person who is thought to be guilty of a crime المشبوه

suspect /ˈsʌspekt/ *adj* possibly not true or to be trusted: *to have suspect motives* ○ *a suspect parcel* (= one possibly containing a bomb) مريب: مشبوه

suspend /səˈspend/ *verb* [T] **1 suspend sth (from sth)** to hang sth: *to suspend sth from the ceiling* يعلّق: يدلّي
2 to stop or delay sth for a time: *Some rail services were suspended during the strike.* ○ *The young man was given a suspended sentence* (= he will not go to prison unless he commits another crime). يوقف مؤقتاً؛ يرجئ؛ يوقف التنفيذ
3 suspend sb (from sth) to send sb away from his/her school, job, position, etc. for a period of time, usually as a punishment for doing sth bad: *to be suspended from school* ℹ The noun is **suspension**. يفصل مؤقتاً

suspender /səˈspendə(r)/ *noun* **1** [C, usually pl.] (*Brit*) a short piece of elastic that women use to hold up a stocking by its top حمّالة جورب نسائي
2 suspenders [plural] (*US*) = BRACES

suspense /səˈspens/ *noun* [U] the feeling that you have when you are waiting for news or for sth exciting or important to happen: *Don't keep us in suspense. Tell us what happened.* ترقّب قلِق؛ تطلّع متلهّف

suspension /səˈspenʃn/ *noun* [U] **1** delaying sth for a period of time: *the suspension of the train service* إيقاف مؤقّت، إرجاء
2 not being allowed to do your job for a period of time, usually as a punishment: *suspension on full pay* إيقاف أو فصل مؤقّت
3 the parts that are attached to the wheels of a car, etc. that make it more comfortable to ride in مجموعة النوابض الماصّة للصدمات

suspicion /səˈspɪʃn/ *noun* **1** [C,U] a feeling or belief that sth is wrong or that sb has done sth wrong: *He always treats new situations with suspicion.* ○ *She was arrested on suspicion of murder.* ريبة؛ شبهة
2 [C] a feeling that sth may happen or be true: *We have a suspicion that they are not happy together.* شعور، هاجس؛ شكّ
IDM **under suspicion** (used about a person) believed to have done sth wrong مشتبه فيه

suspicious /səˈspɪʃəs/ *adj* **1** that makes you feel or believe that sth is wrong or that sb has done sth wrong: *The old man died in suspicious circumstances.* ○ *It's very suspicious that she was not at home on the evening of the murder.* ○ *a suspicious-looking person* مريب
2 suspicious (of/about sb/sth) not trusting sb/sth: *His strange behaviour made the police suspicious.* مرتاب
▶ **suspiciously** *adv*: *The house was suspiciously quiet* (= as if something was wrong). ○ *to behave suspiciously* بصورة مريبة

sustain /səˈsteɪn/ *verb* [T] **1** to keep sb/sth alive or healthy: *Oxygen sustains life.* ○ *His belief in God sustained him through his long illness.* يمدّ بالحياة، يقوت؛ يقوّي
2 to cause sth to continue for a long period of time: *It's hard to sustain interest for such a long time.* يواصل، يبقي
3 (*formal*) to suffer an injury, etc: *The victim sustained multiple bruises.* يتكبّد، يصاب بـ

SUV /ˌes juː ˈviː/ *noun* [C] a type of large car, often with four-wheel drive and made originally for travelling over rough ground (the abbreviation for 'sport utility vehicle') سيارة كبيرة صالحة للأراضي الوعرة

SW *abbrev* = SOUTH-WEST(ERN)

swagger /ˈswæɡə(r)/ *verb* [I] to walk with a swinging movement that shows that you are too confident or proud of yourself يتبختر، يختال
▶ **swagger** *noun* [sing.] تبختر، اختيال

swallow[1] /ˈswɒləʊ/ *verb* **1** [T] to make food, drink, etc. pass from your mouth down your throat: *It's easier to swallow pills if you take them with water.* ○ (*figurative*) *The rent swallows up most of our monthly income.* يبلع، يبتلع
2 [I] to make a movement in your throat, often because you are afraid or surprised, etc: *She swallowed hard and tried to speak, but nothing came out.* يزدرد ريقه
3 [T] to accept or believe sth, often too easily: *You shouldn't swallow everything they tell you!* يصدّق أو يتقبّل بسهولة
4 [T] to accept an insult, etc. without protest: *I find her criticisms very hard to swallow.* يتقبّل
▶ **swallow** *noun* [C] جرعة، بلعة

swallow[2] /ˈswɒləʊ/ *noun* [C] a small bird that eats insects and has long wings and a forked tail سُنونو

swam *pt* of SWIM

swamp[1] /swɒmp/ *noun* [C,U] (an area of) soft wet land مستنقع، سَبخة

swamp[2] /swɒmp/ *verb* [T] **1** to cover or fill sth with water: *The fishing boat was swamped by enormous waves.* يغمر، يغرّق
2 (usually passive) **swamp sb/sth (with sth)** to give sb so much of sth that they cannot deal with it: *We've been swamped with applications for the job.* يغرقه بسيلٍ من

swan /swɒn/ *noun* [C] a large, usually white, bird with a very long neck that lives on lakes and rivers بَجَعة، وزّة عراقيّة، تَمّ

swap (*also* **swop**) /swɒp/ *verb* [I,T] (swapping; swapped) (*informal*) to give sth for sth else; to exchange: *When we finish these books shall we swap* (= you have my book and I'll have yours)? ○ *Would you swap jobs with me?* ○ *I'd swap my job for hers any day.* يبادل، يقايض؛ يتبادل
IDM **change/swap places (with sb)** → PLACE[1]
▶ **swap** *noun* [C] an act of exchanging: *Let's do a swap.* مبادلة، مقايضة

swarm /swɔːm/ *noun* [C] **1** a large group of insects, especially bees, moving around together سرب: فِرَق النحل

a b c d e f g h i j k l m n o p q r s t u v w x y z

2 a large number of people together
حشد، جمع غفير

▸ **swarm** *verb* [I] to fly or move in large numbers: *When the gates opened the fans swarmed into the stadium.*
يطير (النحل مثلاً) في أسراب؛ يتدفق بأعداد كبيرة

PHR V **swarm with sb/sth** to be too crowded or full: *London is swarming with tourists at the moment.* يعج بـ

swat /swɒt/ *verb* [T] (swa**tt**ing; swa**tt**ed) to hit sth, especially an insect, with sth flat
يضرب أو يخبط (ذبابة مثلاً)

sway /sweɪ/ *verb* **1** [I,T] to move or swing slowly from side to side تمايل، يترنح، يتأرجح

2 [T] to influence sb: *Many people were swayed by his convincing arguments.*
يميل إلى جانبه، يقنع أو يؤثّر في

swear /sweə(r)/ *verb* (*pt* **swore** /swɔː(r)/; *pp* **sworn** /swɔːn/) **1** [I] **swear (at sb/sth)** to use rude or bad language: *He hit his thumb with the hammer and swore loudly.* ○ *There's no point in swearing at the car just because it won't start!* ➲ Look at **curse**. يشتم، يسبّ

2 [I,T] to make a serious promise: *When you give evidence in court you have to swear to tell the truth.* ○ *Will you swear not to tell anyone?* ○ *I could have sworn* (= I'm quite sure) *I heard a knock at the door.* يقسِم، يحلف

PHR V **swear by sb/sth** to believe completely in the value of sth يثق به ثقة عمياء

swear sb in (usually passive) to make sb declare that he/she will accept the responsibility of a new position: *The President will be sworn in next week.* يقسم اليمين قبل تولّيه المنصب

ˈ**swear word** *noun* [C] a word that is considered rude or bad and that may offend people
شتيمة؛ تجديف

sweat /swet/ *noun* [C,U] the liquid that comes out of your skin when you are hot, ill or afraid: *He stopped digging and wiped the sweat from his forehead.* ➲ Look at **perspiration**. عرَق

▸ **sweat** *verb* [I] **1** to produce sweat through your skin يعرق

2 sweat (over sth) to work hard: *I've been sweating over that problem all day.*
يكدّ، يرهق نفسه

sweaty *adj* (**sweatier**; **sweatiest**) **1** wet with sweat: *I was hot and sweaty after the match and needed a shower.* مبلّل بالعرق، عرْقان

2 causing you to sweat: *a hot, sweaty day* معرّق

sweater /ˈswetə(r)/ *noun* [C] a warm piece of clothing with long sleeves, often made of wool, which you put over your head كنزة، "بلوفر"، "جرزاية"

> **Sweater**, **jumper**, **pullover** and **jersey** are all words for the same piece of clothing. They are often made from wool or a similar material. A **sweatshirt** is usually made from cotton and may be worn informally on its own or for sport. A **cardigan** fastens with buttons down the front.

sweatshirt /ˈswet-ʃɜːt/ *noun* [C] a sweater made from thick cotton or a mixture of cotton and another material ➲ Look at the note at **sweater**.
كنزة قطنية سميكة

swede /swiːd/ *noun* [C,U] a large, round, yellow vegetable that grows under the ground
كرَنب لفتيّ، "روتاباج"

sweep[1] /swiːp/ *verb* (*pt, pp* **swept** /swept/) **1** [I,T] to clean by moving dust, dirt, etc. away with a brush: *Could you sweep under the table too?* ○ *Take your shoes off! I've just swept the floor.* ○ *I'm going to sweep the leaves off the path.* ➲ Look at the note at **clean**[2]. يكنس

2 [T] to push, move or remove sb/sth quickly and smoothly: *He swept the money into his pocket and went out.* ○ *The huge waves swept her overboard.* يدفع أو يجرّ بخفة؛ يجرف

3 [I,T] to move quickly and smoothly over the area or in the direction mentioned: *Fire swept through the building.* ○ *The epidemic swept the country within weeks.* يجتاح، يكتسح

4 [I] to move in a proud or impressive way: *Five big black Mercedes swept past us.* ○ *She swept angrily out of the room.* يسير بكبرياء

PHR V **sweep (sth) up** to remove dirt, dust, leaves, etc. using a brush يكنس

sweep[2] /swiːp/ *noun* [C] **1** a long, curving shape or movement: *a bay with a broad sweep of golden sand* امتداد؛ أرجحة

2 [usually sing.] an act of sweeping: *I'd better give the floor a sweep.* كنْس

3 = CHIMNEY SWEEP

IDM **a clean sweep** → CLEAN[1]

sweeper /ˈswiːpə(r)/ *noun* [C] **1** a person or thing that sweeps[1] (1): *road sweepers* ○ *a carpet sweeper* كنّاس؛ مكْنسة

2 (in football) the defending player who plays behind the other defending players and who can come forward to attack اللاعب المكتسِح

sweeping /ˈswiːpɪŋ/ *adj* **1** (used about statements, etc.) too general and perhaps not accurate
تعميمي غير دقيق

2 having a great and important effect: *sweeping reforms* هامّ، ذو اثر بالغ

sweet[1] /swiːt/ *adj* **1** tasting of or like sugar; not sour: *Children usually like sweet things.* ○ *This cake's too sweet.* ➲ Look at **savoury**. حلو المذاق

2 attractive; lovely: *What a sweet little cottage!* ○ *Isn't that little girl sweet?* جذّاب، جميل، حلو

3 (used about a person) kind and thoughtful: *It's very sweet of you to remember my birthday!*
لطيف، ودود

4 (used about a smell or a sound) pleasant: *The garden was full of the sweet smells of summer.* ○ *the sweet sound of children singing*
ذكيّ الرائحة؛ رخيم، عذب

IDM **have a sweet tooth** to like eating sweet things يحبّ المأكولات الحلوة

▸ **sweetly** *adv* in an attractive, kind or pleasant way: *She smiled sweetly.* ○ *sweetly scented flowers* بحلاوة، بلطافة؛ (زهور) عَطِرة

sweetness *noun* [U] حلاوة؛ عذوبة؛ لطف

sweet² /swiːt/ *noun* **1** [C, usually pl.] (*US* **candy**) a small piece of boiled sugar, chocolate, etc., often sold in a packet: *He was sucking a sweet.* ○ *a sweet shop* قطعة حلوى، سكاكر أو مسكّرات

2 [C,U] sweet food often served at the end of a meal: *As a sweet you can have ice cream or chocolate mousse.* ○ *I won't have any sweet, thank you.* ➲ Look at **pudding** and **dessert**. الحلوى (في نهاية الوجبة)

sweetcorn /ˈswiːtkɔːn/ (*US* **corn**) *noun* [U] yellow grains from a tall plant (maize) that taste sweet and are eaten as a vegetable ذرة صفراء سكريّة

sweeten /ˈswiːtn/ *verb* [T] to make sth sweet by adding sugar, honey, etc. يحلّي

▶ **sweetener** /ˈswiːtnə(r)/ *noun* [C,U] a substance used instead of sugar for sweetening food or drink: *artificial sweeteners* مادّة مُحلّية (بدلاً من السكّر)

sweetheart /ˈswiːthɑːt/ *noun* [C] **1** (used when speaking to sb, especially a child, in a very friendly way): *Do you want a drink, sweetheart?* يا حبيبي

2 (*old-fashioned*) a boyfriend or girlfriend: *They were childhood sweethearts.* حبيب، صاحب

swell /swel/ *verb* (*pt* **swelled** /sweld/; *pp* **swollen** /ˈswəʊlən/ or **swelled**) **1** [I,T] **swell (up)** to become or to make sth bigger, fuller or thicker: *After the fall her ankle began to swell up.* ○ *His eyes swelled with tears.* ○ *Heavy rain had swollen the rivers.* ينتفخ، يتورّم؛ ينفخ؛ يرفع المنسوب

2 [I,T] to increase: *The crowd swelled to 600 by the end of the evening.* يزداد

3 [I] (*formal*) (used about feelings or sound) to become stronger or louder suddenly: *Hatred swelled inside him.* يرتفع كموجة عارمة

▶ **swell** *noun* [sing.] the slow movement up and down of the surface of the sea تموّجات البحر

swelling /ˈswelɪŋ/ *noun* **1** [C] a place on the body that is bigger or fatter than usual because of an injury or illness: *a swelling on my knee* ورم

2 [U] the condition of being swollen: *The disease often causes swelling of the ankles and knees.* انتفاخ، تورّم

swelter /ˈsweltə(r)/ *verb* [I] (*informal*) to be much too hot: *It was sweltering in London today.* يشتد الحرّ بشكل لا يطاق؛ يتضايق من الحرّ

swept *pt, pp* of SWEEP¹

swerve /swɜːv/ *verb* [I] to change direction suddenly: *The car swerved to avoid the child.* ينحرف فجأة

▶ **swerve** *noun* [C] انحراف مفاجئ

swift /swɪft/ *adj* quick or fast; happening without delay: *a swift runner* ○ *a swift reaction* سريع؛ عاجل

▶ **swiftly** *adv* بسرعة خاطفة

swig /swɪɡ/ *verb* [I,T] (swi**gg**ing; swi**gg**ed) (*informal*) to take a drink quickly and in large amounts: *He swigged the drink down and poured another glass.* يجرع أو يعبّ (الخمر) بنهم

▶ **swig** *noun* [C] جرعة كبيرة، عبّة (من القارورة)

swill /swɪl/ *verb* [T] **swill sth (out/down)** to wash sth by pouring large amounts of water, etc. into, over or through it يشطف (بالماء)

swim /swɪm/ *verb* (*pres part* **swimming**; *pt* **swam** /swæm/; *pp* **swum** /swʌm/) **1** [I] to move your body through water: *How far can you swim?* ○ *Hundreds of tiny fish swam past.* يسبح

> **Go swimming** is a common way of talking about swimming for pleasure: *We go swimming every Saturday.* ○ *They went swimming before breakfast.* We can also say **go for a swim** when we are talking about one particular occasion: *I went for a swim this morning.*

2 [T] to cover or cross a distance, etc. by swimming: *I swam 25 lengths of the pool.* يسبح، يقطع المسافة سباحةً

3 [I] **be swimming (in/with sth)** to be covered with a lot of liquid: *The salad was swimming in oil.* يسبح في

4 [I] to seem to be moving or turning: *The floor began to swim before my eyes and I fainted.* يميد، يدور

5 [I] (used about your head) to feel unclear or confused: *My head was swimming with so much new information.* يدوخ؛ يرتبك

▶ **swim** *noun*: *Would you like to have a swim?* سباحة، "سبحة"

swimmer *noun* [C]: *a strong swimmer* سبّاح

ˈswimming bath *noun* [C] (*also* **swimming baths** [plural]) a public swimming pool, usually indoors مسبح، حمّام سباحة

ˈswimming costume = SWIMSUIT

ˈswimming pool (*also* **pool**) *noun* [C] a pool that is built especially for people to swim in: *an indoor/outdoor/open-air swimming pool* مسبح

ˈswimming trunks *noun* [plural] a piece of clothing like shorts that a man wears to go swimming: *a pair of swimming trunks* سروال أو "شورت" سباحة للرجال

swimsuit /ˈswmsuːt; *Brit also* -sjuːt/ (*also* **swimming costume**) *noun* [C] a piece of clothing that a woman wears to go swimming ➲ Look at **bikini**. "مايوه" أو لباس سباحة للنساء

swindle /ˈswɪndl/ *verb* [T] **swindle sb/sth (out of sth)** to cheat sb (in order to get money, etc.): *He swindled his sister out of her inheritance.* يحتال عليه، يسلب ماله

▶ **swindle** *noun* [C]: *a tax swindle* احتيال مالي

swindler /ˈswɪndlə(r)/ *noun* [C] a person who swindles محتال، نصّاب

swine /swaɪn/ *noun* **1** [plural] (*old-fashioned*) pigs خنازير

2 [C] (*informal*) a very unpleasant person: *Her husband's an absolute swine.* شخص منحطّ، وغد، جلف

swing¹ /swɪŋ/ *verb* (*pt, pp* **swung** /swʌŋ/) **1** [I,T] to move backwards and forwards or from side to side, while hanging from sth; to make sb/sth move in this way: *The rope was swinging from a*

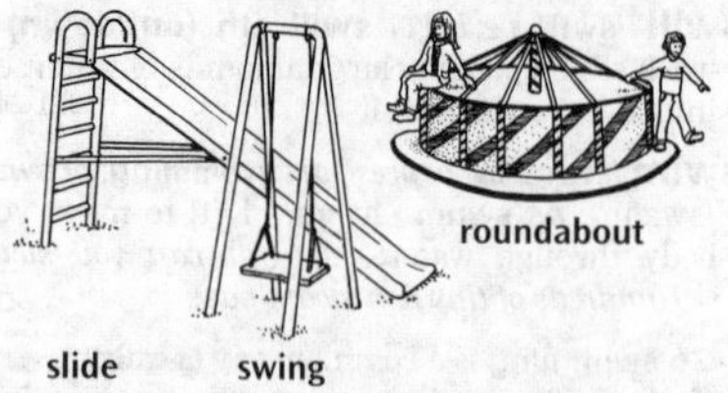

branch. ○ *She sat on the wall, swinging her legs.* يتأرجح؛ يؤرجح

2 [I,T] to move in a curve or to make sb/sth move in this way: *The window swung open and a head peeped out.* ○ *He swung the child up onto his shoulders.* يدور على مفصلة (مثلاً)؛ يرفع بالأرجحة

3 [I] to turn quickly: *She swung round when she heard the door open.* ○ (*figurative*) *His moods swing from one extreme to the other.* يدور على عقبيه، يلتفت بسرعة؛ يتذبذب

4 [I,T] **swing (at sb/sth)** to try to hit sb/sth: *He swung violently at the other man but missed.* يحاول أن يصوِّب ضربةً

🔑**swing²** /swɪŋ/ *noun* **1** [sing.] a swinging movement or action: *He took a swing at the ball.* إهواءة؛ حركة تأرجح

2 [C] a seat that you can swing backwards and forwards on, e.g. in a children's playground أرجوحة

3 [C] a change (in public opinion, etc.): *Opinion polls indicate a significant swing towards the right.* تحوّل؛ ميل

IDM **in full swing** → FULL

swipe /swaɪp/ *verb* **1** [I,T] **swipe (at) sb/sth** (*informal*) to (try to) hit sb/sth in an uncontrolled way: *He swiped at the wasp with a newspaper but missed.* ○ *She swiped the ball into the neighbours' garden.* يضرب أو يخبط كيفما اتفق

2 [T] (*informal*) to steal sth يسرق

3 to pass the part of a plastic card on which information is stored through a special machine for reading it: *The cashier swiped my credit card and handed me the slip to sign.* يسحب، يمرّر (في آلة خاصة)

▸ **swipe** *noun* [C] a careless blow ضربة أو خبطة عشوائيّة

ˈ**swipe card** *noun* [C] a small plastic card on which information is stored which can be read by an electronic machine بطاقة بيانات إلكترونية

swirl /swɜːl/ *verb* [I,T] to move round and round quickly; to make sth do this: *Her long skirt swirled round her legs as she danced.* يدور أو يلتف كالدوامة؛ يدوِّم

▸ **swirl** *noun* [C] دوّامة (من الدخان)

🔑**switch** /swɪtʃ/ *noun* [C] **1** a small button or sth similar that you press up or down in order to turn on electricity: *the light switch* زر أو مفتاح كهربائيّ

2 a sudden change: *a switch in policy* تغيير أو تغيُّر مفاجئ

▸ **switch** *verb* **1** [I,T] **switch (sth) (over) (to sth)** to change or be changed from one thing to another: *We've switched from reading 'The Times' to 'The Independent' now.* ○ *The match has been switched from Saturday to Sunday.* يحوِّل؛ يتحوّل

2 [I,T] **switch (sth) (with sb/sth)**; **switch (sth) (over/round)** to exchange positions, activities, etc: *This week you can have the car and I'll go on the bus, and next week we'll switch over.* ○ *Someone switched the signs round and everyone went the wrong way.* يبدِّل

PHR V **switch (sth) off/on** to press a switch in order to connect/disconnect electric power: *Don't forget to switch off the cooker.* يشعِل أو يطفئ (النور مثلاً)

switchboard /ˈswɪtʃbɔːd/ *noun* [C] the place in a large office, etc. where all the telephone calls are connected مقسم التليفون (في شركة مثلاً)

swivel /ˈswɪvl/ *verb* [I,T] (swivelling; swivelled; *US* swiveling; swiveled) **swivel (sth) (round)** to turn around a central point; to make sth do this: *She swivelled round to face me.* ○ *He swivelled his chair towards the door.* يدور أو يدير (حول محور)

swollen¹ *pp* of SWELL

🔑**swollen²** /ˈswəʊlən/ *adj* thicker or wider than usual: *Her leg was badly swollen after the accident.* منفوخ، متورِّم

swoop /swuːp/ *verb* [I] **1** to fly or move down suddenly: *The bird swooped down on its prey.* ينقضّ على

2 (used especially about the police or the army) to visit or capture sb/sth without warning يداهم

▸ **swoop** *noun* [C] **swoop (on sb/sth)** a swooping movement or a sudden attack: *The troops made a swoop on the capital last night.* انقضاض؛ هجوم مفاجئ، مداهمة

swop = SWAP

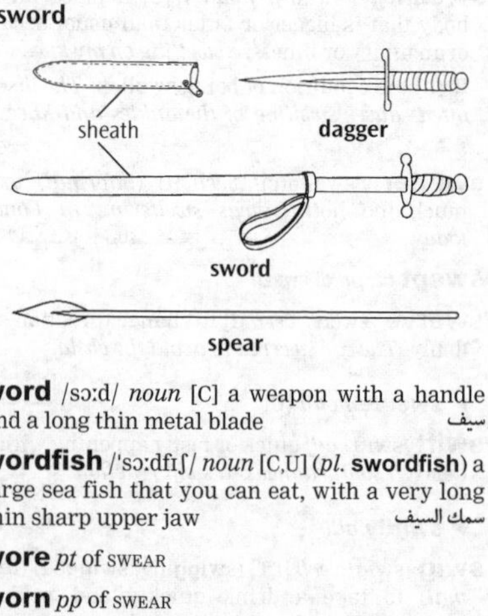

sword /sɔːd/ *noun* [C] a weapon with a handle and a long thin metal blade سيف

swordfish /ˈsɔːdfɪʃ/ *noun* [C,U] (*pl.* **swordfish**) a large sea fish that you can eat, with a very long thin sharp upper jaw سمك السيف

swore *pt* of SWEAR

sworn *pp* of SWEAR

swot /swɒt/ *verb* [I,T] (swotting; swotted) **swot (up) (for/on sth)**; **swot sth up** (*informal*) to study sth very hard, especially to prepare for an

exam: *She's swotting for her A levels.*
يدرس بِجدٍّ شديد (قبل الامتحان)

▸ **swot** *noun* [C] (*informal*) a person who studies too hard
تلميذ يقضي كل وقته في الدراسة

swum *pp* of SWIM

swung *pt, pp* of SWING[1]

sycamore /ˈsɪkəmɔː(r)/ *noun* [C] **1** (*especially Brit*) a large tree of the maple family
شجرة الجميز

2 (*especially US*) a plane tree
الدلب الغربي

syllable /ˈsɪləbl/ *noun* [C] a word or part of a word which contains one vowel sound: *'Mat' has one syllable and 'mattress' has two syllables.*
مقطع (في كلمة)

syllabus /ˈsɪləbəs/ *noun* [C] (*pl.* **syllabuses**) a list of subjects, etc. that are included in a course of study: *Does the syllabus cover modern literature?*
منهج دراسي

⚷ **symbol** /ˈsɪmbl/ *noun* [C] **1 a symbol (of sth)** a sign, object, etc. which represents an idea or an aspect of life: *The cross is the symbol of Christianity.* ○ *Some people think a fast car is a symbol of power and strength.*
رمز، علامة

2 symbol (for sth) a letter, number or sign that has a particular meaning: *O is the symbol for oxygen.*
رمز

▸ **symbolic** /sɪmˈbɒlɪk/ (*also* **symbolical** /-kl/) *adj* used or seen as a symbol: *The violent sea is symbolic of the character's emotions.*
رمزيّ؛ ممثِّل لِ

symbolically /-kli/ *adv*
رمزياً: من ناحيَة المدلول

symbolism /ˈsɪmbəlɪzəm/ *noun* [U] the use of symbols to represent things, especially in art and literature
الرمزيّة (في الفن والأدب)

symbolize (*also* **symbolise**) /ˈsɪmbəlaɪz/ *verb* [T] to be a symbol of sth: *The deepest notes in music often symbolize danger or despair.*
يرمز إلى

symmetry /ˈsɪmətri/ *noun* [U] the state of having two halves that match each other exactly in size, shape, etc.
تناظر، تماثل

▸ **symmetrical** /sɪˈmetrɪkl/**symmetric** *adj* having two halves that are exactly the same in size and shape
متناظر

symmetrically /-kli/ *adv*
بشكل متناظر

⚷ **sympathetic** /ˌsɪmpəˈθetɪk/ *adj* **1** showing that you understand other people's feelings, especially their problems: *When Sandra was ill, everyone was very sympathetic.* ○ *I felt very sympathetic towards him.* ○ *He gave me a sympathetic smile.*
متفهم لمشاعر الآخرين ومشاكلهم، عطوف

> In English, **sympathetic** does not mean 'friendly and pleasant'. If you want to express this meaning, you say a person is **nice**: *I met Alex's sister yesterday. She's very nice.*

2 sympathetic (to sb/sth) being in agreement with or willing to support sb/sth: *I explained our ideas but she wasn't sympathetic to them.*
متعاطف مع، مؤيِّد لِ

ⓘ The opposite is **unsympathetic**.

▸ **sympathetically** /-kli/ *adv*
بعين العطف، بتعاطف

⚷ **sympathy** /ˈsɪmpəθi/ *noun* (*pl.* **sympathies**) **1** [U] **sympathy (for/towards sb)** an understanding of other people's feelings, especially their problems: *Everyone feels great sympathy for the victims of the attack.* ○ *I don't expect any sympathy from you.* ○ *When his wife died he received dozens of letters of sympathy.*
تعاطف، مشاركة في الشعور

2 [plural] feelings of support or agreement: *Some members of the party have nationalist sympathies.*
مشاعر تأييد

IDM in sympathy (with sb/sth) in agreement, showing that you support or approve of sb/sth: *He is not in sympathy with all the ideas of the party.*
موافق، مؤيِّد

▸ **sympathize** (*also* **sympathise**) /ˈsɪmpəθaɪz/ *verb* [I] **sympathize (with sb/sth) 1** to understand and share sb's feelings: *I sympathize with her, but I don't know what I can do to help.*
يشاركه الشعور

2 to be in agreement with sb/sth: *I find it difficult to sympathize with his opinions.*
يشاركه الرأي، يتّفق معه

sympathizer *noun* [C] a person who agrees with and supports an idea or aim: *a Communist sympathizer*
مؤيِّد، مشايع

symphony /ˈsɪmfəni/ *noun* [C] (*pl.* **symphonies**) a long piece of music written for a large orchestra
سمفونية

symptom /ˈsɪmptəm/ *noun* [C] **1** a change in your body that is a sign of illness: *What are the symptoms of flu?*
عَرَض مرضيّ

2 a sign (that sth bad is happening or exists): *The riots are a symptom of a deeper problem.*
دليل منذِر

▸ **symptomatic** /ˌsɪmptəˈmætɪk/ *adj*
دالّ على

synagogue /ˈsɪnəɡɒɡ/ *noun* [C] a building where Jewish people go to pray or to study their religion
كنيس، معبد اليهود

synchronize (*also* **synchronise**) /ˈsɪŋkrənaɪz/ *verb* [T] to make sth happen or work at the same time or speed
يزامن

syndicate /ˈsɪndɪkət/ *noun* [C] a group of people or business companies that join together for a common purpose
نقابة؛ اتحاد (شركات مثلاً)

syndrome /ˈsɪndrəʊm/ *noun* [C] **1** a group of signs or changes in the body that are typical of an illness: *Down's syndrome* ○ *Acquired Immune Deficiency Syndrome (AIDS)*
الأعراض المتلازمة، لَزِمة

2 a group of events, actions attitudes, etc. that are typical of a particular state or condition
أعراض، إمارات

synonym /ˈsɪnənɪm/ *noun* [C] a word or phrase that has the same meaning as another word or phrase in the same language: *'Big' and 'large' are synonyms.*
مرادف، مترادف

▸ **synonymous** /sɪˈnɒnɪməs/ *adj* **synonymous (with sth)** (*figurative*) *Wealth is not always synonymous with happiness.*
مرادف لِ

synopsis /sɪˈnɒpsɪs/ *noun* (*pl.* **synopses** /-siːz/) a summary of a book, play, etc: *The programme gives a brief synopsis of the plot.*
الموجز، الملخّص

a b c d e f g h i j k l m n o p q r s t u v w x y z

syntax /ˈsɪntæks/ *noun* [U] the system of rules for the structure of a sentence
علم النحو، قواعد تركيب الجمَل

synthesis /ˈsɪnθəsɪs/ *noun* (*pl.* **syntheses** /-siːz/) **1** [U] the combining of separate things, especially ideas, to form a complex whole
تركيب؛ تأليف

2 [C] a thing that is produced in this way; a composition: *Her art is a synthesis of modern and traditional techniques.* مركّب؛ مؤلف

synthesizer (*also* **synthesiser**) /ˈsɪnθəsaɪzə(r)/ *noun* [C] an electronic musical instrument that can produce a wide range of different sounds آلة موسيقيّة الكترونية

synthetic /sɪnˈθetɪk/ *adj* made by a chemical process; not natural اصطناعي
▸ **synthetically** /-kli/ *adv* اصطناعياً

syphilis /ˈsɪfɪlɪs/ *noun* [U] a serious disease that passes from one person to another by sexual contact مرض الزهري

syphon = SIPHON

syringe /sɪˈrɪndʒ/ *noun* [C] an instrument that consists of a tube and a needle. It is used for taking a small amount of blood out of the body or for giving injections. محقنة

syrup /ˈsɪrəp/ *noun* [U] **1** thick sweet liquid made by boiling sugar with water or fruit juice: *peaches in syrup* قَطْر، ربّ السكّر

2 thick liquid food made from sugar that you buy in a tin
قَطْر، ربّ السكّر

system /ˈsɪstəm/ *noun* **1** [C] a set of ideas or rules for organizing sth: *We have a new computerized system in the library.* ○ *the metric system* ○ *The government is planning to reform the education system.* نظام

2 [C] a group of things or parts that work together: *a central heating system* جهاز

3 [C] the body of a person or animal; parts of the body that work together: *We must get him to hospital before the poison gets into his system.* ○ *the central nervous system* الجسم؛ جهاز

4 the system [sing.] the traditional methods and rules of a society الجهاز الحكومي أو الاجتماعي

IDM **get sth out of your system** (*informal*) to free yourself of a strong feeling
يتخلّص من شعور معيّن

▸ **systematic** /ˌsɪstəˈmætɪk/ *adj* done using a fixed plan or method: *a systematic search*
نظاميّ، منظَّم، منهجيّ

systematically /-kli/ *adv* بصورة منهجيّة منظَّمة

T t

T, t /tiː/ *noun* [C] (*pl.* **Ts**; **T's**; **t's**) the twentieth letter of the English alphabet: *'Table' begins with (a) 'T'.* الحرف العشرون من الأبجديّة الإنكليزيّة

ta /tɑː/ *interj* (*Brit informal*) thank you شكراً

tab /tæb/ *noun* [C] **1** a small piece of cloth, metal or paper that is fixed to sth to help you open, hold or identify it: *You open the tin by pulling the metal tab.* مِسْكة صغيرة، عروة، لسان

2 (*US*) a bill: *I'll pick up the tab* (= I'll pay the bill). فاتورة الحساب

IDM **keep a tab/tabs on sb/sth** (*informal*) to watch sb/sth carefully; to check sth
يراقب حركاته وسكناته

tabbouleh /təˈbuːleɪ; ˈtæbuːleɪ/ *noun* [U] an Arab dish consisting of crushed wheat with chopped tomatoes, onions and herbs تبّولة

tabby /ˈtæbi/ *noun* [C] (*pl.* **tabbies**) a cat with grey or brown fur and dark stripes
قطّ رماديّ أو بنيّ مع خطوط سوداء

table /ˈteɪbl/ *noun* [C] **1** a piece of furniture with a flat top on one or more legs: *a dining/bedside/kitchen/coffee table* ○ *Could you lay the table for lunch?* (= put the knives, forks, plates, etc. on it) ○ *Don't read the newspaper at the table* (= during the meal). ❶ We put things **on the table** but we sit **at the table** (= around the table). منضدة، طاولة

2 a list of facts or figures, usually arranged in rows down a page: *a table of contents* ○ *Table 3 shows the results.* جدول

tablecloth /ˈteɪblklɒθ; *US* -klɔːθ/ *noun* [C] a piece of cloth that you put over a table, especially when having a meal مفرش أو غطاء المائدة

ˈtable manners *noun* [plural] the way you behave while you are eating آداب المائدة

tablespoon /ˈteɪblspuːn/ *noun* [C] **1** a large spoon used for serving or measuring food
ملعقة كبيرة

2 (*also* **ˈtablespoonful**) (*abbr* **tbsp**; **tbs**) the amount that a tablespoon holds: *Add two tablespoons of sugar.* ملء ملعقة كبيرة

tablet /ˈtæblət/ *noun* [C] a small amount of medicine in solid form, that you swallow: *Take two tablets every four hours.* قرص أو حبّة (دواء)

ˌtablet PˈC™ [C] a small computer that is easy to carry, with a large touch screen and sometimes without a physical keyboard
جهاز لوحي: حاسب محمول ذو شاشة تعمل باللمس

ˈtable tennis (*also informal* **ping-pong**) *noun* [U] a game with rules like tennis in which you hit a light plastic ball across a table with a small round bat كرة الطاولة، "بينغ بونغ"

tabloid /ˈtæblɔɪd/ *noun* [C] a newspaper with small pages, a lot of pictures and short simple articles جريدة صغيرة الحجم مصوّرة

taboo /tə'bu:; *US* tæ'bu:/ *noun* [C] (*pl.* **taboos**) a religious or social custom that forbids certain actions or words شيء محرم، تحريم
▶ **taboo** *adj*: *a taboo subject* محظور، ممنوع

tacit /'tæsɪt/ *adj* (*formal*) understood but not actually said: *They haven't replied. I think that's a tacit admission that they were wrong.* ضمنيّ، مفهوم ضمناً
▶ **tacitly** *adv* ضمناً

tack /tæk/ *noun* **1** [C] a small nail with a broad head مسمار تنجيد، مسمار قباقيبي
2 [U, sing.] a way of achieving sth: *If people won't listen we'll have to try a different tack.* طريقة عمل، سبيل
▶ **tack** *verb* [T] **1** to fasten sth with tacks (1) يثبّت بمسامير تنجيد
2 to sew with loose stitches يسرّج، يخيط بغرزات طويلة
PHRV **tack sth on (to sth)** to put sth extra on the end of sth يلحق بـ، يضيف

tackle /'tækl/ *verb* **1** [T] to deal boldly with sth difficult: *The government must tackle the problem of rising unemployment.* ○ *Firefighters were brought in to tackle the blaze.* يعالج؛ يعارك
2 [I,T] (used in football, etc.) to try to take the ball from sb in the other team يحاول أخذ الكرة
3 [T] (used in rugby, etc.) to stop another player by pulling him down (في الرجبي) يجرّ خصمه إلى الأرض
4 [T] **tackle sb about/over sth** to speak to sb about a difficult subject: *Somebody should tackle Simon about his rudeness.* يحدّثه بصراحة
▶ **tackle** *noun* **1** [C] the act of tackling (2, 3): *a skilful tackle by Walker* محاولة أخذ الكرة
2 [U] the equipment you use in a sport: *fishing tackle* عدّة رياضية، عدّة (الصيد)

tacky /'tæki/ *adj* (**tackier**; **tackiest**) (*informal*)
1 cheap and of poor quality: *tacky souvenirs* رخيص مبتذل
2 (used about paint, glue, etc.) not quite dry; sticky لزج، دبِق

tact /tækt/ *noun* [U] the ability to deal with people without offending or upsetting them: *She handled the situation with tact and diplomacy.* لباقة، كياسة
▶ **tactful** /-fl/ *adj* careful not to say or do things that could offend people: *Talking about his ex-wife like that wasn't very tactful!* لبق
tactfully /-fəli/ *adv* بلباقة، بحسن تصرف
tactless *adj*: *It was rather tactless of you to ask him how old he was.* ○ *a tactless suggestion* غير لبق، قليل الذوق
tactlessly *adv* بعدم لباقة

tactic /'tæktɪk/ *noun* **1** [C, usually pl.] a way of achieving sth: *We must decide what our tactics are going to be at the next meeting.* ○ *I don't think this tactic will work.* طريقة لتحقيق هدف
2 tactics [plural] the skilful arrangement and use of military forces in order to win a battle تخطيط حربي
▶ **tactical** /-kl/ *adj* **1** connected with tactics (2): *a tactical error* تخطيطي
2 designed to bring a future advantage: *a tactical decision* تكتيكيّ، ناظر للمستقبل
tactically /-kli/ *adv* لأسباب تخطيطيّة عسكرية

tadpole /'tædpəʊl/ *noun* [C] a young form of a frog, when it has a large black head and a long tail شرغوف، شرْغ

tag /tæg/ *noun* [C] **1** a small piece of card, material, etc. fastened to sth to give information about it; a label: *a name tag* ○ *How much is this dress? There isn't a price tag on it.* بطاقة بيانية
2 = QUESTION TAG
▶ **tag** *verb* [T] (**tagging**; **tagged**) to fasten a tag to sth: *the electronic tagging of criminals* (attaching a device to sb so that the police know where he/she is) يربط بطاقة بيانية
PHRV **tag along** to follow or go with sb: *The little boy tagged along with the older children when they went to the playground.* يلحق، يرافق

tahini /tɑ:'hi:ni:; tə'h-/ (*also* **tahina** /tɑ:'hi:nə; tə'h-/) *noun* [U] a thick mixture made with crushed sesame seeds, eaten in the Middle East طحينة

tail /teɪl/ *noun* **1** [C] the long thin part at the end of the body of an animal, bird, fish, etc: *The dog barked and wagged its tail.* ذيل، ذنَب
2 [C] a thing like an animal's tail in its shape or position: *the tail of an aeroplane* ذيل مؤخّرة
3 tails [plural] a man's coat, short at the front but with a long, divided piece at the back. It is worn on very formal occasions, such as weddings. سترة رسميّة بذيْل
4 tails [plural] the side of a coin that does not have the head of a person on it: *'We'll toss a coin to decide,' said my father. 'Heads or tails?'* ➲ Look at **heads**. نقش
IDM **make head or tail of sth** → HEAD[1]
▶ **tail** *verb* [T] to follow sb closely, especially to watch where he/she goes, etc. يتعقّبه خفية
PHRV **tail away/off** (*especially Brit*) to become less, smaller, quieter, etc: *His voice tailed off into a whisper.* يتضاءل، يتلاشى

tailor /'teɪlə(r)/ *noun* [C] a person whose job is to make clothes, especially for men خيّاط
▶ **tailor** *verb* [T] (usually passive) **1** to make clothes: *a well-tailored coat* يخيط الملابس
2 to make or design sth for a special purpose: *We specialize in holidays tailored to meet your individual needs.* يكيّف

tailor-'made *adj* very suitable; perfect: *I knew the house was tailor-made for me as soon as I saw it.* وافي الشروط

taint /teɪnt/ *noun* [sing.] (*formal*) a sign of some bad quality or that sth is no longer fresh, pure, etc: *the taint of corruption.* لطخة؛ وصمة
▶ **taint** *verb* [T] (usually passive) to have a bad effect on sth; to spoil sth: *Her reputation was tainted by the scandal.* يفسد؛ يلطّخ، يلوّث

take /teɪk/ *verb* [T] (*pt* **took** /tʊk/; *pp* **taken** /'teɪkən/) **1** to carry sb/sth or to go with sb from one place to another: *Take your coat with you – it's cold.* ○ *Could you take this letter home to your*

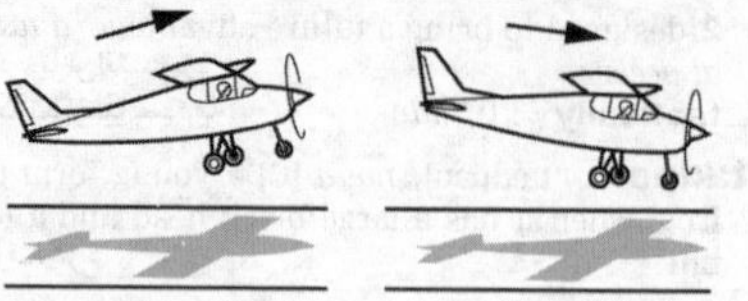

take off   land

parents? ○ *The ambulance took him to hospital.* ○ *I'm taking the children swimming this afternoon.* يأخذ

2 to put your hand round sth and hold it (and move it towards you): *She held out the keys, and I took them.* ○ *He took a sweater out of the drawer.* ○ *She took my hand/me by the hand.* يأخذ، يمسك بـ

3 to remove sth without permission: *Who's taken my pen?* يأخذ

4 to accept or receive sth: *Will you take £2 000 for the car?* ○ *Do you take credit cards?* ○ *I'm not taking the blame for the accident.* ○ *She's not going to take the job.* يقبل

5 to need or require sth: *It takes about an hour to drive to Oxford from here.* ○ *I took three years to learn to drive.* ○ *It took a lot of courage to say that.* يستغرق؛ يحتاج إلى

6 to have enough space for sth: *How many passengers can this bus take?* يستوعب، يتسع لـ

7 to use a form of transport; to go by a particular road: *I always take the train to York.* ○ *Which road do you take to Hove?* يستقلّ، يأخذ

8 to swallow sth: *Take two tablets four times a day.* يتناول، يأخذ

9 to write or record sth: *She took notes during the lecture.* يدوّن

10 to measure sth: *I took his temperature and it was nearly 40.* يقيس

11 (used with nouns to say that sb is performing an action): *Take a look at this article* (= look at it). ○ *We have to take a decision* (= decide). يلقي (نظرة)؛ يتّخذ (قراراً)

12 to photograph sth: *I took some nice photos of the wedding.* يلتقط صورة

13 to have a particular feeling or opinion: *He takes great pleasure in his grandchildren.* ○ *I wish you would take things more seriously.* يشعر؛ يواجه الأمور

14 to understand sth in a particular way: *She took what he said as a compliment.* يفهم، يفسّر، يحمله محملَ...

15 to be able to bear sth: *I find his criticism a bit hard to take.* يتحمّل، يقبل

16 to capture a place by force: *The Allies took the enemy's capital last night.* يستولي على

17 to give lessons to sb: *Who takes you for history?* (= who is your teacher) يعلّم، يدرّس

18 to have a certain size of shoes or clothes: *What size shoes do you take?* يأخذ أو يلبس (مقاساً معيناً)

IDM **I take it (that...)** I suppose: *I take it that you're not coming?* يفترض

take it from me believe me: *Take it from me, she's going to resign.* صدّقني

take a lot out of sb to make sb very tired يرهق، ينهك

take a lot of/some doing to require a lot of work or effort يتطلب مجهوداً كبيراً

ℹ For other idioms containing **take**, look at the entries for the nouns, adjectives, etc., e.g. **take place** is at **place**[1].

PHR V **take after sb** to look or behave like an older member of your family يشبه، يتصرّف (كأبيه مثلاً)

take sth apart to separate sth into the different parts it is made of يفكّك

take sth away 1 to cause a feeling, etc. to disappear: *These aspirins will take the pain away.* يزيل

2 to buy cooked food at a restaurant, etc. and carry it out to eat somewhere else, for example at home يأخذ خارجاً

take sb/sth away (from sb) to remove sb/sth: *She took the scissors away from the child.* يأخذ، يبعد، ينتزع

take sth back 1 to return sth to the place that you got it from يعيد، يرجع

2 to admit that sth you said was wrong يعترف بخطئه، يسحب كلامه

take sth down 1 to remove a structure by separating it into the pieces it is made of: *They took the fence down and put up a wall.* يفكّ؛ يخرب

2 to write down sth that is said يدوّن

take sb in to deceive sb: *I was completely taken in by her story.* يخدع، يغش

take sth in to understand what you see, hear or read: *There was too much in the museum to take in at one go.* يستوعب، يفهم

take off 1 (used about an aeroplane, etc.) to leave the ground and start flying يقلع

2 to become successful or popular يصبح ناجحاً أو مشهوراً

take sb off to copy the way sb speaks or behaves يقلّد

take sth off 1 to remove sth, especially clothes: *Come in and take your coat off.* يخلع، ينزع

2 to have the period of time mentioned as a holiday: *I'm going to take a week off.* يعطّل، يأخذ عطلة

take sb on to start to employ sb: *The firm is taking on new staff.* يشغّل، يوظّف

take sth on to accept or decide to do sth: *He's taken on a lot of extra work.* يأخذ على عاتقه

take sb out to go out with sb (for a social occasion): *I'm taking Sarah out for a meal tonight.* يرافق أو يدعو (فتاة مثلاً) إلى (حفلة)

take sth out to remove a part of the body: *He's having two teeth taken out.* يزيل (جراحياً)، يقتلع

take sth out (of sth) to remove sth: *He took a notebook out of his pocket.* ○ *I need to take some money out of the bank.* يخرج، يسحب

take it out on sb to behave badly towards sb because you are angry or upset about sth, even though it is not this person's fault: *I know you don't feel well but don't take it out on me!* يفشّ خلقه في شخص آخر

take (sth) over to get control of sth or responsibility for sth: *The firm is being taken over by a large company.* ○ *Who's going to take over as assistant when Tim leaves?* يتملك؛ يتولّى عملاً

take to sb/sth to feel a liking for sb/sth: *I took to his parents immediately.* يحب، يميل إلى

take to sth/doing sth to begin doing sth regularly: *We've taken to getting up very late on Sundays.* بدأ يتعوّد (على)

take up sth to use or fill an amount of time or space: *All her time is taken up looking after the new baby.* يشغل، يملأ

take sth up to start doing sth regularly (e.g. as a hobby): *I've taken up yoga recently.* بدأ يمارس (هواية مثلاً)

take sb up on sth 1 to say that you disagree with sth that sb has just said, and ask him/her to explain it: *I must take you up on that last point.* يتحدّى أو يخالف متحدّثاً

2 to accept an offer, etc. that sb has made: *'Come and stay with us any time.' 'We'll take you up on that!'* يقبل (دعوة أو عرضاً)

take sth up with sb to ask or complain about sth: *I'll take the matter up with my MP.* يستوضح؛ يشكو إلى

be taken with sb/sth to find sb/sth attractive or interesting يُفْتَن بِ؛ يجده طريفاً

takeaway /'teɪkəweɪ/ (*US* **takeout** /'teɪkaʊt/) *noun* [C] **1** a restaurant that sells food that you can eat somewhere else: *There's an Indian takeaway in the village.* مطعم يبيع أطعمة للخارج

2 the food that such a restaurant sells: *Let's get a takeaway.* طعام جاهز يشرى من مطعم

'take-off *noun* [C,U] the time when an aeroplane leaves the ground: *The plane is ready for take-off.* إقلاع

takeover /'teɪkəʊvə(r)/ *noun* [C] the act of taking control of sth: *the takeover of a company* ○ *a military takeover* (= in a country) استملاك؛ استيلاء على الحكم

takings /'teɪkɪŋz/ *noun* [plural] the amount of money that a shop, theatre, etc. gets from selling goods, tickets, etc. وارد أو دخل (المتجر مثلاً)

talcum powder /'tælkəm paʊdə(r)/ (*also* **talc** /tælk/) *noun* [U] a soft powder which smells nice. People put it on their skin after a bath. مسحوق التَلْك

tale /teɪl/ *noun* [C] **1** a story about events that are not real: *fairy tales* حكاية، قصّة

2 a report or description of sb/sth that is not necessarily true: *I've heard a lot of tales about the people who live in that house.* إشاعة، قصّة (ملفّقة)

talent /'tælənt/ *noun* [C,U] **talent (for sth)** a natural skill or ability: *She has a talent for painting.* ○ *His work shows great talent.* موهبة

▶ **talented** *adj*: *a talented musician* موهوب

⚷**talk¹** /tɔːk/ *verb* **1** [I] **talk (to/with sb)**; **talk (about/of sb/sth)** to say things; to speak: *I could hear them talking downstairs.* ○ *Can I talk to you for a minute?* ○ *Anne is not an easy person to talk to.* ○ *We need to talk about the plans for the weekend.* ○ *I didn't understand what she was talking about.* ○ *He's been talking of going to Australia for some time now.* ○ *Their little boy is just learning to talk.* ➲ Look at the note at **speak**. يتكلّم، يتحدّث

2 [I] to discuss people's personal affairs: *His strange lifestyle started the local people talking.* ينشر القيل والقال

3 [T] to discuss sth: *Could we talk business after dinner?* يتحدّث عن، يناقش

4 [I] **talk on/about sth** to give a lecture or speech to a group of people about a certain subject: *Mrs Phipps will be talking about Byzantine Art.* يلقي محاضرة أو حديثاً

5 [I] to give information to sb, especially when you do not want to: *'He hasn't talked yet', said the detective, 'but he will.'* يدلي بمعلومات

IDM **know what you are talking about** → KNOW

talk sense to say things that are correct and sensible يتكلّم كلاماً معقولاً

talk shop to talk about work with colleagues outside working hours يتحدّث مع زملائه عن العمل خارج أوقات العمل

PHR V **talk down to sb** to talk to sb as if he/she is less clever, important, etc. than you يكلّمه باستعلاء أو بتنازل

talk sb into/out of doing sth to persuade sb to do/not to do sth: *I didn't really want to go with them, but they talked me into it.* يقنع

▶ **talkative** /'tɔːkətɪv/ *adj* liking or tending to talk a lot ثرثار

⚷**talk²** /tɔːk/ *noun* **1** [C] a conversation or discussion: *Tim and I had a long talk about the problem.* حديث؛ مناقشة

2 talks [plural] formal discussions: *The Foreign Ministers of the two countries will meet for talks next week.* محادثات

3 [U] talking, especially without action, results or the right information: *'Alan says they're going to get married.' 'Don't believe it! It's only talk.'* مجرّد كلام، كلام فارغ

4 [C] a lecture or speech: *He's giving a talk on 'Our changing world'.* محاضرة، حديث

⚷**tall** /tɔːl/ *adj* **1** (used about people or things) of more than average height; not short: *a tall young man* ○ *a tall tree, tower, chimney, etc.* ○ *Nick is taller than his brother.* طويل القامة؛ شاهق أو باسق

2 (used about people) of a particular height: *Claire is five feet tall.* ○ *How tall are you?* ذو طول معيّن

> **Tall** and **high** have similar meanings. We use **tall** to describe the height of people (*He is six foot three inches tall.*), of trees (*A tall oak tree stood in the garden.*) and also sometimes to talk about narrow objects (*the tall skyscrapers of Manhattan*).

tambourine /ˌtæmbə'riːn/ *noun* [C] a small round musical instrument with a skin like a drum and metal discs round the edge. You can hit it or shake it. الدف، الرق

tame /teɪm/ *adj* **1** (used about animals or birds)

not wild or afraid of people: *The birds are so tame they will eat from your hand.* أليف، داجن

2 boring; not interesting or exciting: *After the big city, you must find village life very tame.* مملّ، عديم الحيويّة

▶ **tame** *verb* [T] to bring sth wild under your control يروّض

tamper /ˈtæmpə(r)/ *verb* [I] **tamper with sth** to use, touch, change, etc. sth when you should not: *Don't eat the sweets if the packaging has been tampered with.* يعبث بـ، يتلاعب بـ، يحرّف

tan /tæn/ *noun* **1** [C] = SUNTAN

2 [U] a colour between yellow and brown لونٌ بنّيّ مائل للصفرة

▶ **tan** *adj* of this colour بنّيّ مائل للصفرة

tan *verb* [I,T] (tanning; tanned) to become or to let sth become brown with the effect of sunshine يسمرّ أو يسمّر في الشمس

tanned *adj*: *You're looking very tanned – have you been on holiday?* مسمّر، ملوّح بالشمس

tandem /ˈtændəm/ *noun* [C] a bicycle with seats for two people, one behind the other دراّجة ذات مقعدين واحد خلف الآخر

tang /tæŋ/ *noun* [usually sing.] a sharp taste, flavour or smell: *a sauce with a tang of lemon juice* رائحة أو طعم نفاذ

▶ **tangy** /ˈtæŋi/ *adj*: *a tangy aroma/sauce/flavour* ذو رائحة أو طعم نفاذ

tangent /ˈtændʒənt/ *noun* [C] a straight line that touches a curve but does not cross it مماسّ

IDM **go/fly off at a tangent** to change suddenly from one subject, action, etc. to another يغيرّ اتجاه (الموضوع) فجأة

tangerine /ˌtændʒəˈriːn; *US* ˈtændʒəriːn/ *noun* [C] a fruit like a small sweet orange with a skin that is easy to take off اليوسفيّ، يوسف أفندي

tangible /ˈtændʒəbl/ *adj* clear and definite: *There are tangible benefits in the new system.* ملموس؛ واضح، حقيقيّ

tangle /ˈtæŋgl/ *noun* [C] a confused mass, especially of threads, hair, branches, etc. that cannot easily be separated from each other: *This string's in a tangle.* كتلة متشابكة (من الشّعر مثلاً)

▶ **tangled** *adj*: *The wool was all tangled up.* متشابك، "مشربك"

tank /tæŋk/ *noun* [C] **1** a container for holding liquids or gas: *How many litres does the petrol tank hold?* ○ *a water tank* خزّان، صهريج

2 a large, heavy military vehicle covered with steel and armed with guns, that moves on special wheels دبّابة

▶ **tanker** *noun* [C] **1** a ship for carrying petrol, etc. in large amounts: *an oil tanker* ناقلة البترول (وغيره)

2 (*US* ˈ**tank truck**) a heavy road vehicle with a big round tank for carrying large amounts of oil, milk, etc. سيّارة صهريج

tantalizing (*also* **tantalising**) /ˈtæntəlaɪzɪŋ/ *adj* (used about sth that you cannot have) attractive or tempting: *A tantalizing smell of cooking was coming from the kitchen.* مغرٍ

▶ **tantalizingly** (*also* **tantalisingly**) *adv*: *tantalizingly close* بصورة مغرية

tantamount /ˈtæntəmaʊnt/ *adj* (not before a noun) **tantamount to sth** equal in effect to sth: *Her statement is tantamount to a confession of guilt.* معادل أو مساوٍ لـ

tantrum /ˈtæntrəm/ *noun* [C] a sudden burst of anger, especially in a child نوبة غضب مفاجئة

tap¹ /tæp/ (*US* **faucet**) *noun* [C] a type of handle that you turn to let water, gas, etc. out of a pipe or container: *Turn the hot tap on.* ○ *Don't leave the taps running!* (= turn them off) صنبور، حنفيّة

▶ **tap** *verb* [T] (tapping; tapped) **1** to make use of sth from a supply or reserve: *to tap the skills of young people* يستغلّ؛ يستمد من

2 to fit a piece of equipment to sb's telephone wires so that you can listen to telephone conversations on that line يتجسّس على خطّ تليفوني

tap² /tæp/ *verb* (tapping; tapped) [I,T] **tap (at/on sth); tap sb/sth (on/with sth)** to touch or hit sb/sth quickly and gently: *Their feet were tapping in time to the music.* ○ *They won't hear if you only tap on the door – knock harder!* ○ *She tapped me on the shoulder and said, 'Excuse me, I think you dropped this notebook.'* ينقر؛ يربت

▶ **tap** *noun* [C] a quick gentle blow or the sound it makes: *a tap on the shoulder* نقرة؛ ربتة

ˈ**tap dance** *noun* [C] a dance in which you tap the rhythm with your feet, wearing special shoes رقصُ النقر بالأقدام (كُلاكيه)

tape /teɪp/ *noun* **1** [U] magnetic material used for recording sound, pictures or information: *I've got the whole concert on tape* (= recorded). شريط تسجيل

2 [C] a cassette with magnetic material wound round it, which is used for recording or playing music, videos, etc: *a blank tape* شريط تسجيل؛ شريط فيديو

3 [C,U] a narrow piece of cloth used for tying or labelling things or in sewing, etc: *We have to sew name tapes into school clothes.* شريط قماشيّ

4 [C] a piece of material stretched across a race track to mark where the race finishes الشريط (عند نهاية السباق)

5 [U] sticky paper used for wrapping parcels, covering electric wires, etc: *sticky tape* ○ *insulating tape* شريط (عازل مثلاً)

▶ **tape** *verb* [T] **1** to record sound, music, television programmes, etc. using a cassette: *There's a film on TV tonight that I'd like to tape.* يسجّل

2 **tape sth (up)** to fasten sth with sticky tape يلصق بشريط لاصق

ˈ**tape measure** (*also* **measuring tape**) *noun* [C] a long thin piece of plastic or cloth with centimetres or inches marked on it. It is used for measuring things. شريط القياس

ˈ**tape recorder** *noun* [C] a machine that is used for recording or playing back music or other sounds آلة تسجيل

tapestry /ˈtæpəstri/ *noun* [C,U] (*pl.* **tapestries**) a piece of heavy cloth with pictures or designs sewn on it in coloured thread نسيج سميك مطرّز بالصور

ˈtap water *noun* [U] water that comes out of taps, not water sold in bottles ماء الصنبور

tar /tɑː(r)/ *noun* [U] **1** a thick black sticky liquid that becomes hard when it is cold. It is used for making roads, etc. قطران

2 a similar substance formed by burning tobacco: *low-tar cigarettes* قطران

target /ˈtɑːɡɪt/ *noun* [C] **1** a person or thing that you aim at when shooting or attacking: *Attacks have been launched on military targets such as airfields.* ○ *The bomb missed its target and fell into the sea.* ○ *The politician was a likely target for terrorist attacks.* هدف

2 an object, often a round board with circles on, that you aim at in shooting practice: *I hit the target twice but missed it once.* دريئة، هدف

3 a person or thing that people blame, criticize, laugh at, etc: *The education system has been the target of heavy criticism.* موضع (نقد مثلاً)

4 a result that you are aiming at: *Our target is to raise £10 000 for 'Save the Children'.* ○ *So far we're right on target* (= making the progress we expected). هدف، غاية

▸ **target** *verb* [T] (usually passive) **target sth (at/on sb/sth)** to aim sth: *The product is targeted at teenagers.* يوجه إلى

tariff /ˈtærɪf/ *noun* [C] **1** a tax that has to be paid on goods brought into a country ضريبة جمركيّة

2 a list of prices التعرفة أو قائمة الأسعار

Tarmac™ /ˈtɑːmæk/ *noun* **1** [U] a material used for making the surfaces of roads "تارمك": حصى مقطرن

2 the tarmac [sing.] an area covered with a Tarmac surface: *The plane waited for two hours on the tarmac.* مساحة معبّدة "بالتارمك"

tarnish /ˈtɑːnɪʃ/ *verb* **1** [I,T] (used about a mirror, metal, etc.) to become less bright; to make sth less bright يكمَد: يَفقد أو يفقده بَريقه

2 [T] (used about a reputation) to spoil: *His reputation was tarnished by the scandal.* يلوّث، يشوّه

tarpaulin /tɑːˈpɔːlɪn/ *noun* [C] a large piece of strong, waterproof material that is used for covering things قماش متين مشمّع

tart¹ /tɑːt/ *noun* [C,U] an open pie with a sweet filling such as fruit or jam ➲ Look at the note at **pie**. فطيرة مغطّاة بالفاكهة

tart² /tɑːt/ *noun* [C] (*informal*) a woman or girl who accepts money in return for sex ℹ A more formal word is **prostitute**. مومِس

tartan /ˈtɑːtn/ *noun* [C,U] **1** a traditional Scottish pattern with coloured squares and stripes that cross each other طراز اسكتلندي تقليدي

2 material made from wool with this pattern on it: *a tartan skirt* قماش صوفي من هذا الطراز

task /tɑːsk; *US* tæsk/ *noun* [C] a piece of work that has to be done, especially an unpleasant or difficult one: *Your first task will be to file these letters.* ○ *I found learning Chinese an almost impossible task.* ○ *You have three minutes to complete the three tasks.* ○ *They gave me the task of organizing the school trip.* مهمّة، وظيفة، واجب

taste¹ /teɪst/ *noun* **1** [U] the ability to recognize the flavour of food or drink: *Taste is one of the five senses.* ذوق

2 [C,U] the flavour of food or drink: *I don't like the taste of this coffee.* مذاق، طعم

3 [C, usually sing.] **a taste (of sth)** a small amount of sth to eat or drink: *Have a taste of this cheese to see if you like it.* ○ (*figurative*) *That was my first taste* (= experience) *of success.* مقدار قليل للذَواق؛ تجربة

4 [sing.] **a taste (for sth)** a liking for sth: *She has developed a taste for modern art.* ميل، حبّ

5 [U] the ability to make good choices about whether things are suitable, of good quality, etc: *He has excellent taste in music.* ذوق (فنّي مثلاً)

IDM **(be) in bad taste** (used about sb's behaviour) (to be) unsuitable and unpleasant: *Some of his comments were in very bad taste.* غير لائق، (تصرُّف) قليل الذوق

▸ **tasteful** /-fl/ *adj* attractive and well-chosen: *The furniture was very tasteful.* ذو ذوق سليم

tastefully /-fəli/ *adv* بذوق سليم

tasteless *adj* **1** unattractive; not well-chosen: *She was wearing a lot of rather tasteless jewellery.* تافه، عديم الذوق

2 likely to offend sb: *His joke about the funeral was particularly tasteless.* عديم الذوق، مؤذٍ للشعور

3 having little or no flavour: *We had some tasteless cheese sandwiches for lunch.* عديم الطعم

tasty *adj* (**tastier**; **tastiest**) having a good, strong flavour: *spaghetti with a tasty mushroom sauce* لذيذ، طيّب الطعم

taste² /teɪst/ *verb* **1** [T] to be aware of or recognize the flavour of food or drink: *Can you taste the garlic in this soup?* يستطعم

2 [T] to try a small amount of food and drink; to test: *Can I taste a piece of that cheese to see what it's like?* يذوق مقداراً قليلاً

3 [I] **taste (of sth)** to have a particular flavour: *The pudding tasted of oranges.* ○ *to taste sour, sweet, delicious, etc.* يكون له طعم معيّن

tattered /ˈtætəd/ *adj* old and torn: *a tattered coat* رثّ، ممزّق، مهلهل

tatters /ˈtætəz/ *noun*

IDM **in tatters** badly torn or damaged: *Her dress was in tatters.* ○ (*figurative*) *After the divorce my life seemed to be in tatters.* ممزّق، رثّ: محطّم

tattoo /təˈtuː; *US* tæˈtuː/ *noun* [C] (*pl.* **tattoos**) a picture or pattern on sb's body that is made by pricking his/her skin with a needle and filling the holes with coloured liquid وشْم

▸ **tattoo** *verb* [T] to make a tattoo on sb's body: *She had the word 'love' tattooed on her left hand.* يَشِم

tatty /ˈtæti/ *adj* (**tattier**; **tattiest**) (*informal*) in bad condition: *tatty old clothes* مهلهل، بالٍ

taught *pt, pp* of TEACH

taunt /tɔːnt/ *verb* [T] to try to make sb angry or unhappy by saying unpleasant or cruel things: *They taunted him with the words 'You're scared!'* يعيّر؛ يتهكّم على

▸ **taunt** *noun* [C] تعيير؛ تهكّم

Taurus /ˈtɔːrəs/ *noun* [C,U] the second sign of the zodiac, the Bull; a person who was born under this sign برج الثور؛ شخص من هذا البرج

taut /tɔːt/ *adj* (used about rope, wire, etc.) stretched very tight; not loose مشدود

tavern /ˈtævən/ *noun* [C] (*old-fashioned*) a pub حانة

tax /tæks/ *noun* [C,U] the money that you have to pay to the government so that it can provide public services: *income tax* ○ *You do not have to pay tax on books in this country.* ○ *tax cuts* ضريبة

▸ **tax** *verb* [T] (often passive) **1** to take tax from a sum of money or from the price of goods and services: *Income is taxed at a rate of 25p in the pound.* ○ *Alcohol, cigarettes and petrol are heavily taxed.* يستقطع ضريبة

2 to make a person or an organization pay tax: *Husbands and wives are taxed separately in Britain.* يفرض ضريبة

taxable /-abl/ *adj* on which you have to pay tax: *taxable income* خاضع للضريبة

taxation /tækˈseɪʃn/ *noun* [U] **1** the system by which a government takes money from people so that it can pay for public services: *direct/indirect taxation* فرض الضرائب

2 the amount of money that people have to pay in tax: *to increase/reduce taxation* ○ *high/low taxation* ضريبة

ˌ**tax-ˈfree** *adj* on which you do not have to pay tax معفى من الضريبة

➲ Look at **duty-free**.

taxi[1] /ˈtæksi/ (*also* **cab**; **taxicab** /ˈtæksikæb/) *noun* [C] a car with a driver, whose job is to take you somewhere in exchange for money: *Shall we go by bus or take a taxi?* ○ *I'll phone for a taxi to take us to the airport.* تاكسي، سيارة أجرة

> The amount of money that you have to pay (your **fare**) is shown on a **meter**. People often give the taxi driver a **tip** (= a small extra sum of money that is not included in the fare).

taxi[2] /ˈtæksɪ/ *verb* [I] (used about an aircraft) to move slowly along the ground before or after flying تدرج الطائرة على أرض المطار

taxing /ˈtæksɪŋ/ *adj* difficult; needing a lot of effort: *a taxing problem* شاقّ؛ مرهق

ˈ**taxi rank** (*also* ˈ**taxi stand**; *US* ˈ**cab stand**) *noun* [C] a place where taxis park while they are waiting to be hired موقف سيّارات التاكسي

TB /ˌtiː ˈbiː/ *abbrev* = TUBERCULOSIS

tbsp (*also* **tbs**) (*pl.* **tbsp** or **tbsps**) *abbrev* = TABLESPOONFUL

tea /tiː/ *noun* **1** [U] a hot brown drink that you make by pouring boiling water onto the dried leaves of a bush grown in hot countries such as India and China: *a cup/pot of tea* ○ *I'll make some tea.* ○ *weak/strong tea* شاي

> We usually say '**have** a cup of tea', and *not* '**drink** a cup of tea': *I had three cups of tea this morning.*

2 [U] the dried leaves that are used for making tea: *A packet of Earl Grey tea, please.* شاي

3 [C] a cup of tea: *Two teas and one coffee, please.* فنجان شاي

4 [U] a drink that you make by pouring hot water onto the leaves of other plants: *herb tea* منقوع

5 [C,U] (*especially Brit*) a small afternoon meal of cakes, biscuits etc. and a cup of tea: *The hotel serves afternoon teas.* تناول الشاي مع البسكويت وغيره بعد الظهر

> Some people call their main evening meal **tea**. This is usually eaten at 5 or 6 o'clock. **Supper** and **dinner** are later meals.

IDM **(not) sb's cup of tea** → CUP[1]

ˈ**tea bag** *noun* [C] a small paper bag with tea leaves in it, that you use for making tea كيس شاي

teach /tiːtʃ/ *verb* (*pt, pp* **taught** /tɔːt/) **1** [I,T] to give sb lessons or instructions so that he/she knows how to do sth: *Jeremy is teaching them how to use the computer.* ○ *My mother taught me to play the piano.* ○ *He teaches English to foreign students.* يعلّم، يدرّس

2 [T] to make sb believe sth or behave in a certain way: *The story teaches us that history often repeats itself.* ○ *My parents taught me always to tell the truth.* يعلّم، يلقّن

▸ **teaching** *noun* **1** [U] the work or profession of a teacher: *My son went into teaching and my daughter became a doctor.* ○ *part-time teaching* ○ *teaching methods* تعليم، تدريس

2 [C, usually pl.] ideas and beliefs that are taught by sb/sth: *the teachings of Gandhi* تعاليم

teacher /ˈtiːtʃə(r)/ *noun* [C] a person whose job is to teach, especially in a school or college: *He's a teacher at a primary school.* ○ *a French teacher* مدرّس، معلّم

ˈ**tea cloth** *noun* [C] (*Brit*) = TEA TOWEL

teacup /ˈtiːkʌp/ *noun* [C] a cup that you drink tea from فنجان شاي

ˈ**tea leaf** *noun* [C, usually pl.] one of the small leaves that are left in a cup or pot after you have drunk the tea ورقة شاي

team /tiːm/ *noun* [C] **1** a group of people who play a sport or game together against another group: *a football team* ○ *Are you in the team?* فريق

2 a group of people who work together: *a team of medical workers* فريق، مجموعة

> When **team** is used in the singular, it can be followed by either a singular or a plural verb: *The team play/plays two matches every week.*

PHRV **team up (with sb)** to join sb in order to do sth together ينضمّ إلى

teamwork /ˈtiːmwɜːk/ *noun* [U] the ability of people to work together: *Good teamwork between nurses and doctors is very important.* العمل الجماعي

teapot /ˈtiːpɒt/ *noun* [C] a container that you use for making tea in and for pouring tea into cups. It has a lid, a handle and a small thin tube (a spout) that the tea is poured out of. إبريق الشاي

tear[1] /tɪə(r)/ *noun* [C, usually pl.] a drop of water that comes from your eye when you are crying, etc: *She wiped away his tears.* ○ *I was in tears* (= crying) *at the end of the film.* ○ *The little girl burst into tears* (= suddenly started to cry). دمعة
▸ **tearful** /-fl/ *adj* crying or nearly crying باكٍ؛ على وشك البكاء

tear[2] /teə(r)/ *verb* (*pt* **tore** /tɔː(r)/; *pp* **torn** /tɔːn/)
1 [T] to pull paper, cloth, etc. so that it comes apart, goes into pieces or gets a hole in it: *I tore my shirt on that nail.* ○ *Tear the paper along the dotted line.* ○ *She tore the letter in half.* ○ *I tore a page out of my notebook.* يمزّق، يشق
2 [I] to become torn: *This material doesn't tear easily.* يتمزّق
3 [T] to remove sth by pulling it violently and quickly: *Paul tore the poster down from the wall.* ينتش، ينتزع؛ يهدّ
4 [I] to move very quickly in a particular direction: *An ambulance went tearing past.* يسير بسرعة خاطفة

IDM **wear and tear** → WEAR[2]
PHRV **tear sth apart 1** to pull sth violently into pieces: *The bird was torn apart by the two dogs.* يمزّقه إرْباً
2 to destroy sth completely: *The country has been torn apart by the war.* يدمِّر
tear yourself away (from sb/sth) to make yourself leave sb/sth or stop doing sth: *Tim can't tear himself away from that computer game.* يترك، ينتزع نفسه من
be torn between A and B to find it difficult to choose between two things or people يحتار بين شيئين
tear sth down (used about a building or monument) to bring it to the ground: *They tore down the old houses and built a shopping centre.* يهدم، يهد
tear sth up to pull sth (usually sth made of paper) into pieces: *'I hate this photograph,' she said, tearing it up.* يمزّق إرْباً
▸ **tear** *noun* [C] a hole in paper, cloth, etc. that is caused by tearing شق، مَزْق

ˈ**tear gas** *noun* [U] a type of gas that makes people's eyes fill with tears. It is used by the police, etc. to control large groups of people. غاز مُسيل للدموع

tease /tiːz/ *verb* [I,T] to say unkind or personal things to or about sb because you think it is funny: *Don't pay any attention to those boys. They're only teasing.* ○ *They teased her about being fat.* يضايقه بغية المزاح، يداعب

ˈ**tea shop** (*also* ˈ**tea room**) *noun* [C] a small restaurant which serves tea, coffee, etc., also cakes and light meals مطعم صغير لتناول الشاي والكاتو وغيره

teaspoon /ˈtiːspuːn/ *noun* [C] **1** a small spoon that is used for stirring tea, etc. ملعقة شاي
2 (*also* **teaspoonful** /-fʊl/) (*abbr* **tsp**) the amount that a teaspoon can hold مِلء ملعقة شاي

teatime /ˈtiːtaɪm/ *noun* [C] the time in the afternoon when people usually have tea: *We'll expect to arrive at about teatime.* موعد تناول الشاي بعد الظهر

ˈ**tea towel** (*also* **tea cloth**) *noun* [C] a small towel that is used for drying plates, knives, forks, etc. فوطة لتجفيف الصحون وما إليها

technical /ˈteknɪkl/ *adj* **1** involving detailed knowledge of the machines, materials, systems, etc. that are used in industry or science: *They haven't got the technical knowledge to develop nuclear weapons.* تقْنيّ، تكنيكي
2 (used about sb's practical ability in a particular activity): *The pianist performed with great technical skill but without much feeling.* (مهارة) فنيّة أو تكنيكيّة
3 (only *before* a noun) relating to a particular subject: *the technical terms connected with computers* (مصطلَح) فنّي
▸ **technicality** /ˌteknɪˈkæləti/ *noun* [C] (*pl.* **technicalities**) one of the details of a particular subject or activity نقطة فنيّة (أو تقنيّة)
technically /-kli/ *adv* **1** following a very exact interpretation of facts or laws: *Technically, you should pay by May 1st, but it doesn't matter if it's a few days late.* وفق حَرفية القانون
2 in a way that involves detailed knowledge of the machines, etc. that are used in industry or science: *The country is technically not very advanced.* تقنيّاً
3 (used about sb's practical ability in a particular activity): *technically brilliant* من الناحية الفنيّة (أو التكنيكيّة)

technician /tekˈnɪʃn/ *noun* [C] a person whose work involves practical skills, especially in industry or science: *a laboratory technician* خبير فني

technique /tekˈniːk/ *noun* **1** [C] a particular way of doing sth: *new techniques for teaching languages* أسلوب، طريقة
2 [U] your practical ability in sth مهارة فنيّة

technology /tekˈnɒlədʒi/ *noun* (*pl.* **technologies**) **1** [U] the study and use of science for practical purposes in industry, etc. التكنولوجيا، التقْنيّة
2 [C,U] the scientific knowledge that is needed for a particular industry, etc: *developments in computer technology* تكنولوجيا، معرفة تقْنيّة
▸ **technological** /ˌteknəˈlɒdʒɪkl/ *adj*: *technological developments* فنيّ أو تقني، تكنولوجي
technologist /tekˈnɒlədʒɪst/ *noun* [C] a person who is an expert in technology خبير في التكنولوجيا

teddy /ˈtedi/ (*also* ˈ**teddy bear**) *noun* [C] (*pl.* **teddies**) a toy for children that looks like a bear دمية على هيئة دبّ

a b c d e f g h i j k l m n o p q r s t u v w x y z

tedious /ˈtiːdiəs/ *adj* boring and lasting for a long time: *a tedious train journey* طويل ممل

teem /tiːm/ *verb* [I] **teem with sth** (used about a place) having a lot of people or things moving about in it: *The streets were teeming with people.* يعجّ بـ

teenager /ˈtiːneɪdʒə(r)/ *noun* [C] a person who is between 13 and 19 years old: *Her music is very popular with teenagers.* المراهق

▸ **teenage** /ˈtiːneɪdʒ/ *adj* (only *before* a noun) **1** between 13 and 19 years old: *teenage children* مراهق

2 typical of or suitable for people between 13 and 19 years old: *teenage fashion* خاصّ بالمراهقين

teens /tiːnz/ *noun* [plural] the period of a person's life between the ages of 13 and 19: *to be in your late/early teens* سنّ المراهقة

teeshirt = T-SHIRT

teeth *pl.* of TOOTH

teethe /tiːð/ *verb* [I] (usually used in the continuous forms) (used about a baby) to start growing its first teeth تبزغ أسنانه، يسِنّ أو يسنّن

ˈ**teething troubles** (*also* ˈ**teething problems**) *noun* [plural] the problems that can develop when a person, system, etc. is new "مشاكل التسنين"، الصعوبات الأوليّة

teetotal /ˌtiːˈtəʊtl; *US* ˈtiːtəʊtl/ *adj* (used about a person) never drinking alcohol ممتنع عن المسْكر

▸ **teetotaller** (*US* **teetotaler**) /-tlə(r)/ *noun* [C] a person who never drinks alcohol من لا يتعاطى المسْكِر أبداً

TEFL /ˌtiː iː ef ˈel, ˈtefl/ *abbrev* = TEACHING ENGLISH AS A FOREIGN LANGUAGE

tel. (*also* **Tel.**) *abbrev* = TELEPHONE (NUMBER)

telecommunications /ˌtelikəˌmjuːnɪˈkeɪʃnz/ (*also* **telecoms** /ˈtelikɒmz/) *noun* [plural] the process of communicating over long distances by using electronic equipment, e.g. by radio, television or telephone الاتصالات السلكيّة واللاسلكيّة

telegram /ˈtelɪɡræm/ *noun* [C] (*also old-fashioned* **cable**) a message that you can send very quickly to sb over a long distance. The message is sent for you by a telephone company, etc. and delivered on a printed form برقيّة

telegraph /ˈtelɪɡrɑːf; *US* -ɡræf/ *noun* [U] a system of sending messages by using radio or electrical signals البرق (التلغراف)

ˈ**telegraph pole** *noun* [C] a tall wooden pole that is used for supporting telephone wires عمود البرق أو التلغراف

telemarketing /ˈtelimɑːkɪtɪŋ/ = TELESALES

telepathy /təˈlepəθi/ *noun* [U] the communication of thoughts between people's minds without speaking, etc. تخاطر، تواصل عقليّ

🔑**telephone** /ˈtelɪfəʊn/ = PHONE

▸ **telephonist** /təˈlefənɪst/ *noun* [C] a person whose job is to answer the telephone and make telephone connections in an office or telephone exchange عامل التليفون

ˈ**telephone box** *noun* = PHONE BOX

ˈ**telephone directory** *noun* [C] (*pl.* **telephone directories**) (*also informal* ˈ**phone book**) a book that gives a list of the names, addresses and telephone numbers of the people in a particular area دليل التليفون أو الهاتف

ˈ**telephone exchange** (*also* **exchange**) *noun* [C] a place belonging to a telephone company where telephone lines are connected so that people can speak to each other المقسم العام للتليفون

ˈ**telephone number** (*also informal* ˈ**phone number**) *noun* [C] the number that you dial when you speak to sb on the telephone رقم التليفون

> The number that you dial before the telephone number if you are telephoning a different area or country is called the **code**: *'What's the code for Spain?' '01034.'*

telesales /ˈteliseɪlz/ (*also* **telemarketing**) *noun* [U] a method of selling things by telephone: *He works in telesales.* البيع على التليفون

telescope /ˈtelɪskəʊp/ *noun* [C] an instrument in the shape of a tube with special glass inside it. You look through it to make distant things appear bigger and nearer. ➲ Look at **microscope**. مِقراب، تلسكوب

teletext /ˈtelitekst/ *noun* [U] a service that provides news and other information in written form on television معلومات مكتوبة يقدّمها التليفزيون

🔑**television** /ˈtelɪvɪʒn/ (*also* **TV**; (*Brit informal*) **telly**) *noun* **1** [C] (*also* ˈ**television set**) a piece of electrical equipment in the shape of a box. It has a glass screen which shows programmes with moving pictures and sounds: *to turn the television on/off* جهاز تليفزيون

2 [U] the electrical system and business of sending out programmes so that people can watch them on their television sets: *Television and radio have helped people to learn more about the world they live in.* ○ *cable/satellite television* ○ *She works in television.* تليفزيون

3 [U] the programmes that are shown on a television set: *Paul's watching television.* التليفزيون

IDM on television being shown by television: *What's on television tonight?* (برامج التليفزيون)

▸ **televise** /ˈtelɪvaɪz/ *verb* [T] to show sth on television: *a televised concert* يتلفز: ينقل بالتليفزيون

teleworking /ˈteliwɜːkɪŋ/ *noun* [U] the practice of working from home, communicating with your office, customers and others by telephone, email, etc. مزاولة العمل من المنزل

▸ **teleworker** *noun* [C] a person who works from home, communicating with their office, customers and others by telephone, email, etc. مَن يزاول عمله من المنزل

telex /ˈteleks/ *noun* **1** [U] a system of sending written messages using special machines. The message is typed on a machine in one place, and then sent by telephone to a machine in another place, which immediately prints it out. تِلِكس

2 [C] a machine for sending out such messages; a message that is sent or received by telex ➲ Look at **fax**. جهاز تلِكس

tell /tel/ *verb* (*pt, pp* **told** /təʊld/) **1** [T] **tell sb (sth); tell sth (to sb)** to give information to sb by speaking or writing: *She told me her address but I've forgotten it.* ○ *He wrote to tell me that his mother had died.* ○ *Tell us about your holiday.* ○ *Tell me what you did yesterday.* ○ *to tell the truth/a lie* ○ *to tell a story* ○ *Excuse me, could you tell me where the station is?* ➲ Look at the note at **say**. يخبر، يبلِّغ

2 [T] **tell sb (to do sth)** to order or advise sb to do sth: *The policewoman told us to get out of the car.* ○ *Dad told me not to worry about my exams.* ○ *Please tell me what to do.* ○ *You'll be all right if you do as you're told.* يأمر: ينصح

3 [I,T] to know, see or judge (sth) correctly: *'What do you think Jenny will do next?' 'It's hard to tell.'* ○ *I could tell that he had enjoyed the evening.* ○ *I can't tell which coat is mine. They look exactly the same.* يعرف: يميز

4 [T] (used about a thing) to give information to sb: *This book will tell you all you need to know.* يزوِّد بمعلومات

5 [I] **tell (on sb/sth)** to have a noticeable effect: *Your age is beginning to tell!* تظهر علاماته، يُحدث أثراً ظاهراً

IDM **all told** with everybody or everything counted and included: *The holiday cost over £1 000, all told.* بالتمام والكمال

I told you (so) (*informal*) I warned you that this would happen ألم أقل لك ذلك!

tell A and B apart → APART

tell the time to read the time from a clock or watch يجيد معرفة الساعة؛ يعرف الوقت

PHR V **tell sb off (for sth/for doing sth)** to speak to sb angrily because he/she has done sth wrong يؤنِّب

tell on sb to tell a parent, teacher, etc. about sth bad that sb has done يوشي بـ

▸ **teller** *noun* [C] **1** a person whose job is to receive and pay out money in a bank أمين الصندوق

2 a machine that pays out money automatically: *automatic teller machines* آلة سحب النقود

telling *adj* **1** having a great effect: *a telling argument* قويّ الوقع، شديد الأثر

2 showing your real feelings or thoughts: *a telling remark* فاضح للمشاعر الحقيقيّة

'tell-tale *adj* giving information about sth secret or private: *the tell-tale signs of worry on his face* نامّ عن، كاشف، فاضح

telly /'teli/ *noun* [C,U] (*pl.* **tellies**) (*Brit informal*) = TELEVISION

temp¹ /temp/ *noun* [C] (*informal*) a temporary employee, especially a secretary, who works somewhere for a short period of time when sb else is ill or on holiday سكرتير/ة مؤقّت أو مؤقّتة

temp² (*also* **temp.**) *abbrev* = TEMPERATURE

temper /'tempə(r)/ *noun* **1** [C,U] If you have a temper you are often angry and impatient, and you cannot control your behaviour: *Be careful of Paul. He's got quite a temper!* ○ *You must learn to control your temper.* خُلق، مزاج غاضب

2 [C] the way you are feeling at a particular time: *Leave her alone. She's in a bad temper* (= feeling angry). ○ *I went for a long walk and came back in a better temper.* مزاج

IDM **in a temper** feeling very angry and not controlling your behaviour في حالة غضب شديد

keep/lose your temper to stay calm/to become angry ➲ Look at **bad-tempered**. يتمالك (أو يفقد) أعصابه من الغضب

temperament /'temprəmənt/ *noun* [C,U] a person's character, especially as it affects the way he/she behaves and feels: *to have a calm temperament* مزاج، طبيعة

▸ **temperamental** /ˌtemprə'mentl/ *adj* often and suddenly changing the way you behave متقلِّب الأهواء

temperate /'tempərət/ *adj* (used about a climate) not very hot and not very cold (مناخ) معتدل

temperature /'temprətʃə(r); *US* 'tempərtʃʊər/ *noun* **1** [C,U] how hot or cold sth is: *Heat the oven to a temperature of 200°C.* ○ *Temperatures in some parts of Britain will fall below freezing tomorrow.* ○ *a high/low temperature* درجة الحرارة

2 [C] how hot or cold a person's body is حرارة (الجسم)

IDM **have a temperature** to have a temperature of the body that is higher than normal (when you are ill) (طفل) حرارته مرتفعة

take sb's temperature to measure the temperature of sb's body with a special instrument (thermometer) يقيس حرارة (المريض)

template /'templeɪt/ *noun* [C] a piece of card, metal or thin wood that is made in a particular shape and used as a guide for cutting metal, stone, wood, cloth, etc. قالب أو صفيحة مُعايرة، طبعة

temple¹ /'templ/ *noun* [C] a building where people pray to and worship a god or gods: *a Buddhist temple* معبد، هيكل

temple² /'templ/ *noun* [C] one of the flat parts on each side of your forehead صدغ، فَوْد

tempo /'tempəʊ/ *noun* (*pl.* **tempos** /'tempəʊz/) **1** [sing., U] the speed of an activity or event معدّل السير، سرعة

2 [C,U] (*technical*) the speed of a piece of music سرعة الإيقاع

temporary /'temprəri; *US* -pəreri/ *adj* lasting for a short time; not permanent: *a temporary job* ○ *This arrangement is only temporary.* موقّت

▸ **temporarily** /'temprərəli; *US* ˌtempə'rerəli/ *adv* موقّتاً

tempt /tempt/ *verb* [T] to try to persuade or attract sb to do sth, especially sth that is wrong or silly: *His dream of riches had tempted him into a life of crime.* ○ *She was tempted to stay in bed all*

a b c d e f g h i j k l m n o p q r s t u v w x y z

morning. ○ *I'm very tempted by the idea of working in another country.* يغوي، يغري

▸ **tempting** *adj* attractive: *a tempting offer* ○ *That chocolate cake looks very tempting!* مغرٍ، مستهوٍ

temptation /temp'teɪʃn/ *noun* **1** [U] a feeling that you want to do sth, although you know that it is wrong or silly: *I resisted the temptation to have another cigarette.* إغراء

2 [C] a thing that attracts you to do sth wrong or silly: *All that money is certainly a big temptation.* شيء مغرٍ، غواية

ten /ten/ *number* 10; one more than nine ❶ For examples of how to use numbers in sentences, look at **six**. عَشَرة

▸ **tenth** /tenθ/ *pron, det, adv* 10th; next after ninth عاشِر، العاشِر

tenth *noun* [C] the fraction 1/10; one of ten equal parts ➲ Look at the examples at **sixth**. عُشْر

tenacious /tə'neɪʃəs/ *adj* very determined about sth; not likely to give up or accept defeat: *a tenacious defender of human rights* مُتمسِّك (بحقوقه)، مصرّ؛ عنيد

▸ **tenacity** /tə'næsəti/ *noun* [U] إصرار، عناد

tenant /'tenənt/ *noun* [C] a person who pays money (rent) to the owner of a room, flat, building or piece of land so that he/she can live in it or use it: *The previous tenants of the flat were university students.* ❶ The owner is called a **landlord** or **landlady**. مستأجِر

▸ **tenancy** /-ənsi/ (*pl.* **tenancies**) *noun* [C,U] the use of a room, flat, building or piece of land, for which you pay rent to the owner: *a six-month tenancy* ○ *a tenancy agreement* استئجار

tend¹ /tend/ *verb* [I] **1** to often or normally do or be sth: *Women tend to live longer than men.* ○ *There tends to be a lot of heavy traffic on that road.* ○ *My brother tends to talk a lot when he's nervous.* عادةً، من شأنه أن؛ ينزع إلى

2 (used for giving your opinion in a polite way): *I tend to think that we shouldn't interfere.* (تعبير لبق): من رأيي أن...

▸ **tendency** /'tendənsi/ *noun* [C] (*pl.* **tendencies**) something that a person or thing does; a way of behaving: *He has a tendency to be late for appointments.* ○ *The dog began to show vicious tendencies.* ○ *She seems to have a tendency towards depression.* ○ *There's a growing tendency for people to travel to work by bicycle.* ميل، نزعة

tend² /tend/ *verb* [T] (*formal*) to look after sb/sth: *He tended the child day and night throughout his illness.* يعتني بِ، يرعى

tender¹ /'tendə(r)/ *adj* **1** kind and loving: *She whispered a few tender words in his ear.* رقيق، حنون

2 (used about meat) soft and easy to cut or bite; not tough طريّ، سهل المضغ

3 (used about a part of the body) painful when you touch it مؤلم عند المسّ

4 young and without much experience of life: *She went to live in London at the tender age of 15.* غضّ، ساذج

▸ **tenderly** *adv* برقة، بحنان

tenderness *noun* [U] حنان، رقة؛ حساسية وألم عند المسّ

tender² /'tendə(r)/ *verb* [I,T] (*formal*) to offer or give sth formally: *After the scandal the Foreign Minister was forced to tender her resignation.* ○ *Five different companies tendered for the building contract* (= stated a price for doing the work). يقدِّم رسمياً؛ يقدِّم عطاءً في مناقصة

▸ **tender** (*also* **bid**) *noun* [C] (*technical*) a formal offer to supply goods or do work at a certain price عطاء في مناقصة

tendon /'tendən/ *noun* [C] a strong cord in your body that joins a muscle to a bone وَتَر العضلة

tenement /'tenəmənt/ *noun* [C] a large building that is divided into small flats, especially in a poor area of a city بناء مقسَّم إلى شقق عديدة في حي فقير

tennis /'tenɪs/ (*also* **lawn tennis**) *noun* [U] a game for two or four players who hit a ball to each other over nets with rackets: *Let's play tennis.* ○ *to have a game of tennis* ○ *a tennis match* تنس، كرة المضرب

> In tennis you can play **singles** (a game between two people) or **doubles** (a game between two teams of two people).

tenor /'tenə(r)/ *noun* [C] **1** the highest normal singing voice for a man; a man with this voice: *Pavarotti, the famous Italian tenor* ○ *a lovely tenor voice* أعلى أصوات الرجال في الغناء؛ مغنٍّ بهذا الصوت

2 a musical instrument with the same range as a tenor voice: *a tenor saxophone* آلة موسيقيّة تلائم هذا الصوت

tenpin bowling /ˌtenpɪn 'bəʊlɪŋ/ *noun* [U] a game in which you roll a heavy ball towards ten objects (tenpins) and try to knock them down لعبة الأوتاد العشرة

tense¹ /tens/ *adj* **1** (used about a person) not able to relax because you are worried or nervous: *She looked pale and tense.* متوتِّر الأعصاب، قلِق

2 (used about a person's body) having stiff muscles because you are not relaxed متشنِّج

3 (used about an atmosphere or situation) making people feel worried and not relaxed: *Reporters described the atmosphere in the capital as 'very tense'.* مشحون بالتوتّر

▸ **tense** *verb* [I,T] to become tense or to make your body tense يتوتّر؛ يوتّر

tense² /tens/ *noun* [C,U] (*grammar*) a form of a verb that shows whether sth happens in the past, present or future صيغة الفعل الدالّة على زمن حدوثه

tension /'tenʃn/ *noun* **1** [C,U] the condition of not being able to relax that is caused by worry or nervousness: *I could hear the tension in her voice as she spoke.* توتُّر

2 [C,U] a condition of bad feeling and lack of trust between people, countries, etc: *There are signs of growing tensions between the two countries.* توتُّر

3 [U] (used about a rope, wire, etc.) how tightly it is stretched شدّ، توتُّر

tent /tent/ *noun* [C] a shelter made of nylon or canvas that is held up by poles and ropes. You use a tent to sleep in when you go camping. خيمة

tentacle /'tentəkl/ *noun* [C] a long thin flexible part extending from the body of certain animals, used for feeling or holding things or for moving: *Snails and octopuses have tentacles.* لامسة (ج لوامس)

tentative /'tentətɪv/ *adj* **1** (used about plans, etc.) uncertain; not definite: *I've made a tentative arrangement to meet Paul for lunch next week, but it's not definite yet.* غير مؤكّد، غير نهائي
2 (used about a person or a person's behaviour) not confident about what you are saying or doing: *a tentative smile* متردد، غير واثق من نفسه
▸ **tentatively** *adv* بصورة غير نهائيّة؛ بتردُّد

tenterhooks /'tentəhʊks/ *noun* [plural]
IDM **(be) on tenterhooks** (to be) in a very nervous or excited state because you are waiting to find out what is going to happen على أحرّ من الجَمْر

tenth → TEN

tenuous /'tenjuəs/ *adj* (used about a connection or an idea) very small and weak and possibly not really existing: *My father says we are related to the Churchill family, but actually the link is extremely tenuous.* ضئيل، ضعيف، واهٍ

tenure /'tenjə(r); *US* -jər/ *noun* [U] a legal right to live in a place, hold a job, use land, etc. for a certain time حقّ قانوني لحيازة ملْك أو تولّي وظيفة

tepid /'tepɪd/ *adj* (used about liquids) only slightly warm فاتر

term /tɜːm/ *noun* **1** [C] a word or group of words, especially one that is used in connection with a particular subject: *What exactly do you mean by the term 'racist'?* ○ *a technical term* عبارة، مصطلح
2 terms [plural] **in … terms; in terms of …** (used for indicating which particular way you are thinking about sth or from which point of view): *The flat would be ideal in terms of size, but it is very expensive.* ○ *We must think about this in political terms.* ○ *Let's talk in terms of opening a new office in June* (=let's think about doing this). من ناحية، من حيث؛ حولَ
3 terms [plural] the conditions of an agreement: *Under the terms of the contract you must give a week's notice.* ○ *peace terms* شروط
4 [C,U] a period of time into which a school or university year is divided: *the autumn/spring/summer term* فصل دراسي
5 [C] a period of time for which sth lasts: *The US President is now in his second term of office.* مدة محدّدة، مدّة شَغْل منصب
IDM **be on equal terms (with sb)** → EQUAL
be on good, friendly etc. terms (with sb) to have a friendly relationship with sb يكون على علاقات حسنة مع
come to terms with sth to accept sth unpleasant or difficult يتقبّل أو يتعوّد على وضع سيّئ
in the long/short term over a long/short period of time in the future: *We're aiming at a tax rate of 20% in the long term.* على المدى البعيد (أو القصير)
▸ **term** *verb* [T] to describe sb/sth by using a particular word or expression: *the period of history that is often termed the 'Dark Ages'* يسمّي، يدعو

terminal¹ /'tɜːmɪnl/ *adj* (used about an illness) slowly causing death: *terminal cancer* نهائيّ، مميت
▸ **terminally** /-nəli/ *adv*: *a terminally ill patient* مميتاً، نهائيّاً

terminal² /'tɜːmɪnl/ *noun* **1** [C] a large railway station, bus station or building at an airport where journeys begin and end: *the bus terminal* ○ *British Airways flights depart from Terminal 1.* آخر محطّة
2 a piece of computer equipment (usually a keyboard and screen) that you use for getting information from a central computer or for putting information into it مطراف

terminate /'tɜːmɪneɪt/ *verb* [I,T] (*formal*) to end or to make sth end: *to terminate a contract* يُنْهي؛ ينتهي
▸ **termination** (*formal*) *noun* [U] إنهاء

terminology /ˌtɜːmɪ'nɒlədʒi/ *noun* [C,U] (*pl.* **terminologies**) the special words and expressions that are used in a particular profession, subject or activity: *computer terminology* مصطلحات

terminus /'tɜːmɪnəs/ *noun* [C] (*pl.* **termini** /-naɪ/) the last stop or station at the end of a bus route or railway line آخر محطّة

terrace /'terəs/ *noun* [C] **1** a flat area of stone next to a restaurant or large house where people can have meals, sit in the sun, etc: *lunch on the terrace* ➲ Look at **patio**. شُرفة، سطيحة، مساحة مرصوفة
2 a line of similar houses that are all joined together صفّ من المنازل المتلاصقة
3 [usually pl.] one of a series of steps that are cut into the side of a hill so that crops can be grown there مدرج زراعي
4 [plural] the wide steps that people stand on to watch a football match مدرّجات ملعب كرة القدم

terraced /'terəst/ *adj* **1** (*Brit*) (used about a house) forming part of a line of similar houses that are all joined together متّصل بصفّ من المنازل المتماثلة
2 (used about a hill) having steps cut out of it so that crops can be grown there مدرّج

terracotta /ˌterə'kɒtə/ *noun* [U] **1** clay that has been baked but not glazed, used for making pots, etc: *a terracotta vase* طين نضيج، فخّار
2 the reddish-brown colour of terracotta اللون الآجرّي

terrain /tə'reɪn/ *noun* [U] a type of land: *rough terrain* منطقة، أرض (وعِرة مثلاً)

ter'rain park *noun* [C] an outdoor area with special features designed for winter sports, especially snowboarding (= moving over snow on a

a b c d e f g h i j k l m n o p q r s t u v w x y z

special board)
موقع في الهواء الطلق مخصص للرياضة الشتوية

terrestrial /tə'restriəl/ *adj* **1** (of animals and plants) living on the land or on the ground, rather than in water, in trees or in the air; connected with the planet Earth: *terrestrial life* برّي

2 (of television and broadcasting systems) operating on earth rather than from a satellite
أرضي

terrible /'terəbl/ *adj* **1** very unpleasant or serious: *a terrible accident* ○ *What a terrible thing to do!* فظيع، رهيب

2 ill or very upset: *I feel terrible. I think I'm going to be sick.* ○ *He felt terrible when he realized what he had done.* متوعك؛ منزعج جداً

3 very bad; of poor quality: *The hotel was terrible.* رديء للغاية

4 (only *before* a noun) great: *It was a terrible shame that you couldn't come.* شديد، هائل

▸ **terribly** /-əbli/ *adv* **1** very: *I'm terribly sorry.* جداً، للغاية

2 very badly: *I played terribly.* بصورة رديئة جداً

terrier /'teriə(r)/ *noun* [C] a type of small dog
أحد أنواع الكلاب

terrific /tə'rɪfɪk/ *adj* **1** (*informal*) extremely nice or good; excellent: *You're doing a terrific job!*
ممتاز، رائع

2 (only *before* a noun) very great: *The food was terrific value.* هائل، ضخم

▸ **terrifically** /-kli/ *adv* (*informal*) extremely: *terrifically expensive* للغاية، إلى أقصى حدّ

terrify /'terɪfaɪ/ *verb* [T] (*pres part* **terrifying**; *3rd pers sing pres* **terrifies**; *pt, pp* **terrified**) to frighten sb very much يرعِب، يفزع

▸ **terrified** *adj* **terrified (of sb/sth)** very afraid: *I'm terrified of spiders.* ○ *a terrified face*
فزِع، مرعوب

terrifying /'terɪfaɪɪŋ/ *adj* extremely frightening: *It was a terrifying experience* مفزع، مرعب

territory /'terətri; *US* -tɔːri/ *noun* (*pl.* **territories**) **1** [C,U] an area of land that belongs to one country or ruler: *former French territories in Africa* ○ *to fly over enemy territory*
أرض تابعة لدولة معينة؛ إقليم

2 [C,U] an area that an animal has as its own
إرض يعتبرها الحيوان تابعة له

▸ **territorial** /ˌterə'tɔːriəl/ *adj* (only *before* a noun) connected with the land or area of sea that belongs to a country or ruler: *territorial waters*
إقليمي

terror /'terə(r)/ *noun* **1** [U] very great fear: *He screamed in terror as the rats came towards him.* رعب، ذعر، ارتياع

2 [C] a person or thing that makes you feel afraid: *the terrors of the night* شخص أو شيء مفزع

3 [U] violent action (e.g. bombing, killing) for political purposes: *a terror campaign* إرهاب

▸ **terrorize** (*also* **terrorise**) /'terəraɪz/ *verb* [T] to make sb feel frightened by using or threatening to use violence against him/her
يُرهب، يبثّ الرعب في

terrorism /'terərɪzəm/ *noun* [U] the use of violent action (e.g. bombing, killing) for political purposes: *an act of terrorism* إرهاب

▸ **terrorist** /'terərɪst/ *noun* [C] a person who is involved in terrorism الإرهابيّ

terrorist *adj* إرهابي

terse /tɜːs/ *adj* said in few words and in a not very friendly way: *a terse reply*
مقتضب؛ (جواب) وجيز جافّ

tertiary /'tɜːʃəri; *US* -ʃieri/ *adj* (used about education) after primary and secondary: *a tertiary college* في المرحلة الثالثة

test¹ /test/ *noun* [C] **1** a short examination to measure sb's knowledge or skill in sth: *a spelling test* ❶ When you **take** a test you can either **pass** it (which is good) or **fail** it (which is bad). اختبار

2 a short medical examination of a part of your body: *an eye test* فحص

3 an experiment to find out whether sth works or to find out more information about it: *Tests show that the new drug is safe and effective.* ○ *to carry out/perform/do a test* تجربة

4 a situation or event that shows how good, strong, effective, etc. sb/sth is: *The local elections will be a good test of the government's popularity.* اختبار، مِحك

test² /test/ *verb* [T] **1 test sb/sth (for sth); test sth (on sb/sth)** to try, use or examine sth carefully to find out if it is working properly or what it is like: *These cars have all been tested for safety.* ○ *Do you think drugs should be tested on animals?*
يفحص؛ يختبر، يجرّب

2 to examine a part of the body to find out if it is healthy: *to have your eyes tested* يفحص

3 test sb (on sth) to examine sb's knowledge or skill in sth يختبر

testament /'testəmənt/ *noun* [C, usually sing.] (*formal*) **a testament (to sth)** something that shows that sth else exists or is true: *Puttnam's new film is a testament to his talent and experience.* دليل، برهان

testicle /'testɪkl/ *noun* [C] one of the two male sex organs that produce sperm خُصْيَة

testify /'testɪfaɪ/ *verb* (*pres part* **testifying**; *3rd pers sing pres* **testifies**; *pt, pp* **testified**) [I,T] to make a formal statement that sth is true, especially as a witness in a court of law يدلي بشهادة

testimony /'testɪməni; *US* -məʊni/ *noun* (*pl.* **testimonies**) **1** [C,U] a formal statement that sth is true, especially one that is made in a court of law شهادة

2 [U, sing.] (*formal*) something that shows that sth else exists or is true: *The design was testimony to her architectural skill.* دليل

'test tube *noun* [C] a thin glass tube that is used in chemical experiments أنبوب اختبار

'test-tube baby *noun* [C] (*pl.* **test-tube babies**) a baby that develops from an egg which has been taken out of the mother's body. The egg is fertilized and then put back inside to develop normally. طفل مستولد بالإخصاب في أنبوب

tetanus /ˈtetənəs/ *noun* [U] a serious disease that makes your muscles, especially the muscles of your face, become stiff. It is caused by bacteria entering the body when a cut becomes infected. الكزاز

tether /ˈteðə(r)/ *verb* [T] to tie an animal to sth with a rope, etc. يربط أو يعقل الدابّة
▸ **tether** *noun* [C] حبل طويل تربط به الدابّة لترعى
IDM **at the end of your tether** → END[1]

text /tekst/ *noun* **1** [U] the main written part of a book, newspaper, etc. (not the pictures, notes, index, etc.) متن الكتاب (مثلاً)
2 [C] the written form of a speech, interview, article, etc: *The newspaper printed the complete text of the interview.* نصّ
3 [C] a book or a short piece of writing that people study as part of a literature and language course: *a set text* (= one that has to be studied for an examination) كتاب أو نص مقرّر

textbook /ˈtekstbʊk/ *noun* [C] a book that teaches a particular subject and that is used especially in schools كتاب مدرسي

textile /ˈtekstaɪl/ *noun* [C] (in industry) a material that is made by weaving or knitting: *cotton textiles* نسيج

text message /ˈtekst mesɪdʒ/ *noun* [C] a written message that you send using a mobile phone: *Send a text message to this number to vote.* رسالة تليفون مكتوبة
▸ **text-message** *verb* [T] to send a text message: *I text-messaged him to say we were waiting at the station.* يراسل بالتليفون
text-messaging *noun* [U]: *Too much text-messaging can cause serious injury to the hands.* المراسلة التليفونية

texture /ˈtekstʃə(r)/ *noun* [C,U] the way that sth feels when you touch it: *material with a silky texture* مَلمس: نَسْج

than /ðən; *strong form* ðæn/ *conj, prep* **1** (used when you are comparing two things): *He's taller than me.* ○ *He's taller than I am.* ○ *London is more expensive than Madrid.* ○ *You speak French much better than she does.* مِن
2 (used with 'more' and 'less' before numbers, expressions of time, distance, etc.): *He earns more than £20 000 a year.* مِن
3 (used after 'would rather' to say that you prefer one thing to another): *I'd rather go to France than to Italy.* (يفضّل) على

thank /θæŋk/ *verb* [T] **thank sb (for sth/for doing sth)** to tell sb that you are grateful: *I'm writing to thank you for the present you sent me.* ○ *I'll go and thank him for offering to help.* يشكر

> **Thank you** and **thanks** are both used for telling somebody that you are grateful for something. **Thanks** is more informal: *Thank you very much for your letter.* ○ *'How are you, Rachel?' 'Much better, thanks.'* You can also use **thank you** and **thanks** to accept something that somebody has offered to you: *'Have a piece of cake.' 'Thank you. That would be nice.'* When you want to refuse something you can say **no, thank you** or **no, thanks**: *'Would you like some more tea?' 'No, thanks.'*

IDM **thank God/goodness/heavens** (used for expressing relief): *Thank goodness it's stopped raining.* الحمد لله!
▸ **thankful** /-fl/ *adj* (not before a noun) pleased and grateful: *We were thankful when the winter was over that year.* شاكر، ممتنّ: مسرور
thankfully /-fəli/ *adv* **1** in a pleased or thankful way بامتنان: بارتياح
2 fortunately: *Thankfully, no one was injured.* لحسن الحظ، حمداً لله
thankless *adj* involving hard work that other people do not notice or thank you for: *Being a housewife can sometimes be a thankless task.* بدون مردود، لا يشكر الانسان عليه
thanks *noun* [plural] words which show that you are grateful: *I'd like to express my thanks to all of you for coming here today.* شكْر
IDM **thanks to sb/sth** because of sb/sth: *We're late, thanks to you!* بِسَبَبِه: بفضل...
a vote of thanks → VOTE

Thanksgiving (Day) /ˌθæŋksˈɡɪvɪŋ/ *noun* [U] a public holiday in the USA and in Canada عيد الشُكر

> Thanksgiving Day is on the fourth Tuesday in November in the USA and on the second Monday in October in Canada. It was originally a day when people thanked God for the harvest.

ˈthank you *noun* [C] an expression of thanks: *I'd like to say a big thank you to everybody who worked so hard.* شكر، امتنان

that[1] /ðæt/ *det, pron* (*pl.* **those** /ðəʊz/) **1** (used for describing a person or thing, especially when it is not near the person speaking): *I like that house over there.* ○ *What's that in the road?* ○ *'Could you pass me the book?' 'This one?' 'No, that one over there.'* ذاك، ذلك، تلك
2 (used for talking about a person or thing already known or mentioned): *That was the year we went to Spain wasn't it?* ○ *Can you give me back that money I lent you last week?* ذلك، تلك
IDM **that is (to say)** (used when you are giving more information about sb/sth): *I'm on holiday next week. That's to say, from Tuesday.* وبتعبير أدق
that's that there is nothing more to say or do: *I'm not going and that's that.* و هذا قرار نهائي!، وانتهى الموضوع

that[2] /ðət; *strong form* ðæt/ *pron* (used for introducing a relative clause) the person or thing already mentioned: *I'm reading the book that won the Booker prize.* ○ *The people that live next door are French.* الذي، التي، الذين الخ...

> When **that** is the object of the verb in the relative clause, it is often left out: *I want to see the doctor (that) I saw last week.* ○ *I wore the dress (that) I bought in Paris.*

that[3] /ðət; *strong form* ðæt/ *conj* (used after certain verbs, nouns and adjectives to introduce a new part of the sentence): *She told me that she was leaving.* ○ *I hope that you feel better soon.* ○ *I'm certain that he will come.* ○ *It's funny that you should say that.* إنّ، أنّ

That is often left out in this type of sentence: *I thought (that) you would like it.*

that[4] /ðæt/ *adv* (used with adjectives, adverbs) to that degree or extent: *30 miles? I can't walk that far.* ○ *She can't play the piano that well.* إلى هذا الحدّ، بهذا القدر

thatched /θætʃt/ *adj* (used about a building) having a roof made of straw: *a thatched cottage* (سقف) مصنوع من القشّ

thaw /θɔː/ *verb* [I,T] **thaw (sth) (out)** to become or to make sth become soft or liquid again after freezing: *Is the snow thawing?* ○ *It's starting to thaw* (= the weather is getting warmer). ○ *Always thaw chicken thoroughly before you cook it.* ➲ Look at **melt**. يذوب؛ يذيب
▸ **thaw** *noun* [C, usually sing.] ذوبان

the /ðə; ðɪ; *strong form* ðiː/ *definite article* **1** (used for talking about a person or thing that is already known or that has already been mentioned): *I took the children to the dentist.* ○ *We met the man who bought your house.* ○ *The milk is in the fridge.* الـ... (لام التعريف)

2 (used when there is only one or only one group): *The sun is very strong today.* ○ *Who won the World Cup?* الـ...

3 (used with numbers and dates): *This is the third piece of cake I've had.* ○ *Friday the thirteenth* ○ *I grew up in the sixties.* الـ...

4 (used with adjectives to name a group of people): *the French* ○ *the poor* الـ...

5 (used with a singular noun when you are talking generally about sth): *The dolphin is an intelligent animal.* الـ...

6 (with units of measurement, meaning 'every'): *The car does forty miles to the gallon.* الـ...

7 (with musical instruments): *Do you play the piano?* الـ...

8 most well-known or important: *You don't mean you met the Tom Cruise?* ❶ 'The' is pronounced /ðiː/ in this sense. الـ... (الشهير!)

9 the... the... (used for saying that two things change to the same extent): *The more you eat, the fatter you get.* كلّما

theatre /ˈθɪətə(r)/ (*US* **theater** /ˈθiːətər/) *noun* **1** [C] a building where you go to see plays, musicals, etc: *the Royal Shakespeare Theatre* ○ *I'm going to the theatre this evening* (= to see a play). مسرح

2 [U] plays in general; drama: *He's studying modern Russian theatre.* مؤلفات مسرحيّة

3 [sing., U] the work of acting in or producing plays: *He's worked in the theatre for thirty years.* التمثيل؛ الإخراج المسرحي

4 [C] = OPERATING THEATRE

▸ **theatrical** /θiˈætrɪkl/ *adj* **1** (only *before* a noun) connected with the theatre مسرحي

2 (used about behaviour) unnatural and dramatic because you want people to notice it: *a theatrical gesture* متصنع، تمثيلي

theft /θeft/ *noun* [C,U] the crime of taking sth that belongs to another person secretly and without permission: *There have been a lot of thefts in this area recently.* ○ *The woman was arrested for theft.* ➲ Look at the note at **thief**. سرقة

their /ðeə(r)/ *det* belonging to them: *What colour is their car?* ○ *The children picked up their books and walked to the door.* (دار) هُم...هُنّ
▸ **theirs** /ðeəz/ *pron* of or belonging to them: *Our flat isn't as big as theirs.* خاصّتهم/خاصّتهن

them /ðəm; *strong form* ðem/ *pron* (the object of a verb or preposition) **1** the people, animals or things mentioned earlier: *I'll phone them now.* ○ *'I've got the keys here.' 'Oh good. Give them to me.'* ○ *We have students from several countries but most of them are Italian.* ○ *'Did you post those letters?' 'Oh dear, I forgot about them.'* هم، هنّ، ها

2 (*informal*) him or her: *If anyone phones, tell them I'm busy.* ـه، ها

theme /θiːm/ *noun* [C] **1** a subject of a talk or piece of writing: *The theme of today's discussion will be 'Our changing cities'.* موضوع (الكتاب مثلاً)

2 an idea that is developed or repeated in the work of a writer or artist: *The themes of heaven and hell were very common in paintings of this period.* فكرة متكرّرة في أعمال مؤلّف أو فنّان، "تيما"
▸ **ˈtheme park** *noun* [C] a park with a lot of things to do, see, ride on, etc., which are all based on a single idea حديقة أو مجمّع تسلية

themselves /ðəmˈselvz/ *pron* **1** (used as the object of a verb or preposition when the people or animals who do an action are affected by it): *Helen and Sarah seem to be enjoying themselves.* ○ *People often talk to themselves when they are worried.* أنفسهم، أنفسهن

2 (used for emphasis): *They themselves say that the situation cannot continue.* ○ *Did they paint the house themselves?* (= or did sb else do it for them?) أنفسهم، أنفسهن

IDM (all) by themselves 1 alone: *The boys are too young to go to the shops by themselves.* ➲ Look at the note at **alone**. وحدهم، وحدهن

2 without help: *The children cooked the dinner all by themselves.* بأنفسهم، دون مساعدة

then /ðen/ *adv* **1** (at) that time: *In 1990? I was at university then.* ○ *I'm afraid I'll be on holiday then.* ○ *I haven't seen him since then.* ○ *I'm going tomorrow. Can you wait until then?* (في) ذلك الوقت

2 next; after that: *We're going to France for a week and then down to Spain.* ○ *There was silence for a minute. Then he replied.* بعد ذلك، ثمّ

3 in that case; therefore: *'I don't feel at all well.' 'Then why don't you go to the doctor?'* في هذه الحال، إذنْ

4 (used for emphasis after words like *now*, *OK*, *right*, etc.): *Now then, are we all ready to go?*

○ *Right then, I'll see you tomorrow.* (تستعمل للتأكيد بعد كلمات معيّنة)

IDM **but then (again)**; **then again**; **there again** (used for introducing additional information or information that contrasts with something that has just been said): *The weather forecast says it'll rain but then again it's often wrong.* إلا أنّه

then and there; **there and then** → THERE[1]

thence /ðens/ *adv* (*old-fashioned, formal*) from there من هناك

theology /θiˈɒlədʒi/ *noun* [U] the study of religion علم اللاهوت

▶ **theological** /ˌθiːəˈlɒdʒɪkl/ *adj*: *a theological college* لاهوتي

theoretical /ˌθɪəˈretɪkl/ *adj* **1** based on ideas and principles, not on practical experience: *A lot of university courses are still too theoretical these days.* نظري

2 based on ideas about sth which may not be true in reality: *a theoretical possibility* (= which will probably never happen) افتراضيّ

▶ **theoretically** /-kli/ *adv*: *Theoretically, we could still win, but I don't think we will.* نظريّاً

theory /ˈθɪəri/ *noun* (*pl.* **theories**) **1** [C] an idea or set of ideas that try to explain sth: *the theory about how life on earth began* نظريّة

2 [U] the general ideal or principles of a particular subject: *political theory* مبادئ، أصول

IDM **in theory** as a general idea which may not be true in reality: *Your plan sounds fine in theory, but I don't know if it'll work in practice.* من حيث الفكرة

therapeutic /ˌθerəˈpjuːtɪk/ *adj* **1** helping you to relax and feel better: *I find listening to music very therapeutic.* مريح للأعصاب

2 helping you to recover from an illness: *therapeutic drugs* علاجيّ، استشفائي

therapy /ˈθerəpi/ *noun* [U] treatment to help or cure a mental or physical illness, usually without drugs or operations: *speech therapy* علاج، مداواة

▶ **therapist** /ˈθerəpɪst/ *noun* [C]: *a speech therapist* معالِج، اختصاصيّ بالمعالجة

there[1] /ðeə(r)/ *adv* **1** in, at or to that place: *Could you put the table there, please?* ○ *I like Oxford. My husband and I met there.* ○ *Have you been to Bath? We're going there next week.* ○ *Have you looked under there?* هناك

2 at that point (in a conversation, story, etc.): *Could I interrupt you there for a minute?* هنا، عند هذه النقطة

3 available: *Her parents are always there if she needs help.* موجود، متوفِّر

IDM **be there for sb** to be available to help and support sb when he/she has a problem: *Whenever I'm in trouble, my sister is always there for me.* معين، شخص تجده عند الحاجة

there again → THEN

there and then; **then and there** immediately; at that time and place على الفور؛ توّاً وفي المكان نفسه

there you are 1 (used when you give sth to sb): *There you are. I've bought you a newspaper.* تفضّل، خُذْ!

2 (used when you are explaining sth to sb): *There you are – just press the switch and it starts.* أنظر - الأمر بسيط

3 (used for saying that you are not surprised): *'He's left his wife.' 'There you are, I knew he would.'* ألم أقل لك ذلك!

there[2] /ðə(r); *strong form* ðeə(r)/ *pron* **1** (used as the subject of 'be', 'seem', 'appear', etc. to say that sth exists): *Is there a god?* ○ *There's a man at the door.* ○ *There wasn't much to eat.* ○ *There's somebody singing outside.* ○ *There seems to be a mistake here.* هناك، يوجد

2 (used for calling attention to sth): *Oh look, there's Kate!* ها هو، ها هي

thereabouts /ˌðeərəˈbaʊts/ (*US* **thereabout** /ˈðeərəbaʊt/) *adv* (usually after *or*) somewhere near a number, time or place: *There are 100 students, or thereabouts.* ○ *She lives in Sydney, or thereabouts.* أو ما يقرب من ذلك

thereafter /ðeərˈɑːftə(r); *US* -ˈæf-/ *adv* (*formal*) after that: *You will receive £1 000 in May, and £650 per month thereafter.* بعد ذلك

thereby /ˌðeəˈbaɪ/ *adv* (*formal*) in that way: *We started our journey early, thereby avoiding most of the traffic.* وبذلك، وهكذا

therefore /ˈðeəfɔː(r)/ *adv* for that reason: *The new trains have more powerful engines and are therefore faster.* لذلك، لهذا السبب

therein /ˌðeərˈɪn/ *adv* (*formal*) because of sth that has just been mentioned: *The school is too big. Therein lies the problem.* وفي ذلك، وهنا

thereupon /ˌðeərəˈpɒn/ *adv* (*formal*) immediately after that and often as the result of sth على اثر ذلك

thermal /ˈθɜːml/ *adj* **1** of heat: *thermal energy* حراري

2 (used about clothes) made to keep you warm in cold weather: *thermal underwear* دَفيء، حافظ للدفء

thermometer /θəˈmɒmɪtə(r)/ *noun* [C] an instrument for measuring the temperature of sb's body or of a room (= how hot or cold it is) ميزان أو مقياس الحرارة

Thermos™ /ˈθɜːməs/ *noun* [C] (*pl.* **Thermoses**) (*also* ˈ**Thermos flask**) (*US* ˈ**Thermos bottle**) = VACUUM FLASK

thermostat /ˈθɜːməstæt/ *noun* [C] a device that controls the level of heat in a house or machine by switching it on and off as necessary أداة لتنظيم الحرارة اوتوماتيكياً

thesaurus /θɪˈsɔːrəs/ *noun* [C] (*pl.* **thesauruses**) a book that contains lists of words and phrases with similar meanings قاموس المعاني ومرادفاتها

these → THIS

thesis /ˈθiːsɪs/ *noun* [C] (*pl.* **theses** /ˈθiːsiːz/) **1** a long piece of writing on a particular subject that

you do as part of a university degree
رسالة جامعية؛ أطروحة

2 a statement of an idea or theory نظرية أو فرضيّة

they /ðeɪ/ *pron* (the subject of a verb) **1** the people, animals or things that have been mentioned: *We've got two children. They're both boys.* ○ *'Have you seen my keys?' 'Yes, they're on the table.'*
هما؛ هم؛ هنّ

2 people in general or people whose identity is not known or stated: *They say it's going to be a hard winter.* الناس

3 (used informally instead of *he* or *she*): *Somebody phoned for you but they didn't leave their name.* هو أو هي

they'd /ðeɪd/ *short for* THEY HAD, THEY WOULD

they'll /ðeɪl/ *short for* THEY WILL

they're /ðeə(r)/ *short for* THEY ARE

they've /ðeɪv/ *short for* THEY HAVE

thick[1] /θɪk/ *adj* **1** (used about sth solid) having a large distance between its opposite sides; not thin: *a thick black line* ○ *These walls are very thick.* سميك، ثخين

2 (used for saying what the distance is between the two opposite sides of something): *The ice was six inches thick.* بالغ ثخنه (كذا)

3 having a lot of things close together: *a thick forest* ○ *thick hair* كثيف؛ غزير

4 (used about a liquid) stiff; that doesn't flow easily: *thick cream* ○ *This paint is too thick.*
سميك

🛈 The opposite for **1** to **4** is **thin**.

5 (used about fog, smoke, etc.) difficult to see through كثيف

6 (used about sb's accent) very strong
(لُكْنة) واضحة أو قويّة

7 (*informal*) (used about a person) stupid; not intelligent غبي، بطيء الفهم

IDM have a thick skin to be not easily upset or worried by what people say about you
قليل الإحساس، "مُتَمَسِّح"

▶ **thick** *adv*: *snow lying thick on the ground*
بكثافة

thicken /ˈθɪkən/ *verb* [I,T] to become thicker or to make sth thicker: *Tonight the cloud will thicken and more rain will move in from the south-west.* ○ *Add flour to thicken the sauce.*
يثخُن، يتكاثف؛ يُثخِّن، يكثِّف

thickly *adv*: *Spread the butter thickly.* ○ *a thickly wooded area* بكثافة، بغزارة

thickness *noun* [U] the quality of being thick or how thick sth is: *The children were amazed at the thickness of the castle walls.* ثخن، سماكة؛ كثافة

thick[2] /θɪk/ *noun*

IDM in the thick of sth in the most active or crowded part of sth; very involved in sth: *She always likes to be in the thick of things.*
معمعان، خضَمّ

through thick and thin through difficult times and situations في السرّاء والضرّاء

ˌthick-ˈskinned *adj* not easily worried or upset by what other people say about you: *Politicians have to be thick-skinned.* قليل الإحساس، "متَمَسِّح"

thief /θiːf/ *noun* [C] (*pl.* **thieves** /θiːvz/) a person who steals things from another person
سارق، حرامي

> A **thief** is a general word for a person who steals things, usually secretly and without violence. The name of the crime is **theft**. A **robber** steals from a bank, shop, etc. and often uses violence or threats. A **burglar** steals things by breaking into a house, shop, etc., usually at night, and a **shoplifter** goes into a shop when it is open and takes things without paying. A **mugger** steals from sb in the street and uses violence or threats. Look also at the note at **steal**.

thigh /θaɪ/ *noun* [C] the top part of the leg, above the knee الفخذ

thimble /ˈθɪmbl/ *noun* [C] a small object made of metal or plastic that you wear on the end of your finger to protect it when you are sewing
كُشْتُبان، قمع الخيّاط

thin /θɪn/ *adj* (thinner; thinnest) **1** (used about sth solid) having a small distance between the opposite sides; not thick: *a thin brown book* ○ *a thin cotton shirt* ○ *a thin slice of meat* رقيق، رفيع

2 having very little flesh on the body; not fat: *You need to eat more. You're too thin!* نحيف، نحيل

> **Thin**, **skinny**, **slim** and **underweight** all have a similar meaning. **Thin** is the most general word for describing people who have very little flesh on their bodies. **Slim** is used to describe people who are thin in an attractive way: *You're so slim! How do you do it?* If you say sb is **skinny**, you mean that he/she is too thin and not attractive. **Underweight** is a much more formal word, and is often used for describing people who are too thin in a medical sense: *The doctor says I'm underweight.*

3 (used about a liquid) that flows easily; not stiff or thick: *a thin sauce* غير سميك، (حساء) مائع القوام

4 (used about mist, smoke, etc.) not difficult to see through خفيف

5 having only a few people or things with a lot of space between them: *The population is rather thin in this part of the country.* متناثر، متفرّق

IDM through thick and thin → THICK[2]

vanish, etc. into thin air to disappear completely يختفي كليّاً

wear thin → WEAR[1]

▶ **thin** *adv* thinly: *I don't like bread that's cut too thin.* رقيقاً

thin *verb* [I,T] (thinning; thinned) **thin (sth) (out)** to become thinner or fewer in number; to make sth thinner: *The fog was beginning to thin.* ○ *The trees thin out towards the edge of the forest.* ○ *Thin the sauce by adding milk.*
يخفّ، يرقّ؛ يُرقِّق، يُقلِّل من كثافته

thinly *adv*: *thinly sliced bread* ○ *thinly populated areas* رقيقاً؛ بكثافة قليلة

thing /θɪŋ/ *noun* **1** [C] an object that is not named: *What's that red thing on the table?* ○ *A* *pen is a thing you use for writing with.* ○ *I need to get a few things at the shops.* شيء

2 [C] a quality or state: *There's no such thing as evil* (= it doesn't exist). ○ *The best thing about my job is the way it changes all the time.* شيء، صفة

3 [C] an action, event or statement: *When I get home the first thing I do is have a cup of tea.* ○ *A strange thing happened to me yesterday.* ○ *What a nice thing to say!* عمل؛ حادثة؛ قول

4 [C] a fact, subject, etc: *He told me a few things that I didn't know before.* أمر

5 things [plural] your clothes or personal possessions: *I'll just go and pack my things.* أمتعة خاصة

6 things [plural] the circumstances or conditions of your life: *Things seem to be going very well for him at the moment.* أحوال عامّة، ظروف الحياة

7 [C] (used for expressing your feelings about a person or animal): *Look how thin that cat is! Poor little thing!* مخلوق؛ إنسان

8 the thing [sing.] exactly what is very wanted or needed: *A week in our hotel is just the thing for tired business people.* أفضل شيء، أحسن دواء

IDM **a close shave/thing** → CLOSE[1]

be a good thing (that) be lucky that: *It's a good thing you remembered your umbrella.* لحسن الحظ

do your own thing to do what you want to do, independently of other people يفعل ما يشاء

first/last thing as early/late as possible: *I'll telephone her first thing tomorrow morning.* ○ *I saw him last thing on Friday evening.* في أبكر وقت ممكن؛ آخر شيء مساءً

for one thing (used for introducing a reason for something): *I think we should go by train. For one thing it's cheaper.* أولاً

have a thing about sb/sth (*informal*) to have strong feelings about sb/sth هوس: شعور قويّ (نحو)

make matters/things worse → WORSE

take it/things easy → EASY[2]

think[1] /θɪŋk/ *verb* (*pt, pp* **thought** /θɔːt/) **1** [I] **think (about sth)** to use your mind to consider sth or to form connected ideas: *Think before you speak.* ○ *What are you thinking about?* ○ *He had to think hard* (= a lot) *about the question.* يفكّر

2 [T] to consider or believe; to have as an opinion: *'Do you think it's going to snow?' 'No, I don't think so.'* ○ *'Sue's coming tomorrow, isn't she?' 'Yes, I think so.'* ○ *I think that they've moved to York but I'm not sure.* ○ *What did you think of the film?* ○ *I don't think they are very good musicians.* يظنّ، يَحْسَب

3 [I] **think of/about doing sth** to intend or plan to do sth: *We're thinking of moving house.* ينوي

4 [I] **think about/of sb** to consider the feelings of sb else: *She never thinks about anyone but herself.* يفكّر، يقدّر

5 [T] (used in negative sentences after *can* or *could*) to remember or understand sth: *I couldn't think what he meant.* يذكر، يفهم

6 [T] to expect sth: *The job took longer than we thought.* يتوقّع

IDM **think better of (doing) sth** to decide not to do sth; to change your mind يعدِل عن (رأيه)

think highly, a lot, not much, etc. of sb/sth to have a good, poor, etc. opinion of sb/sth يقدّره (أو لا يقدّره) تقديراً كبيراً

think the world of sb to love and admire sb very much يُعْجَب بشخص إعجاباً شديداً

PHRV **think of sth** to create an idea in your imagination: *Who first thought of the plan?* يفكّر

think sth out to consider carefully all the details of a plan, idea, etc: *a well-thought-out scheme* يتروى، يتبصر

think sth over to consider sth carefully: *I'll think your offer over and let you know tomorrow.* يتروى، يتبصر

think sth up to create sth in your mind; to invent: *to think up a new advertising slogan* يَستحدث، يبتكر

think[2] /θɪŋk/ *noun* [sing.] an act of thinking: *I'm not sure. I'll have to have a think about it.* تفكير

thinker /ˈθɪŋkə(r)/ *noun* [C] a person who thinks about serious and important subjects مفكّر

thinking /ˈθɪŋkɪŋ/ *adj* intelligent and using your mind to think about important subjects: *a newspaper for thinking people* متفكّر، مثقّف

▶ **thinking** *noun* [U] **1** the act of using your mind to think about sth: *clear thinking* تفكير

2 an opinion: *This accident will make them change their thinking on safety matters.* ➲ Look at **wishful thinking**. رأي

third /θɜːd/ *pron, det, adv* 3rd; next after second ➲ Look at the examples at **sixth**. ثالث

▶ **third** *noun* [C] **1** the fraction ⅓; one of three equal parts of sth ثُلث

2 (*Brit*) a grade in final university exams, below first and second class degrees شهادة (جامعية) من الدرجة الثالثة

thirdly *adv* (used to introduce the third point in a list): *We have made savings in three areas: firstly, defence, secondly, education and thirdly, health.* ثالثاً

ˌthird ˈparty *noun* [C] (*pl.* **third parties**) a person who is not one of the two main people or groups involved in sth طرف ثالث

the ˌThird ˈWorld *noun* [sing.] the poorer countries of Asia, Africa and South America ℹ This way of referring to developing countries is sometimes considered offensive. العالم الثالث

thirst /θɜːst/ *noun* **1** [U, sing.] the feeling that you have when you want or need to drink: *Cold tea really quenches your thirst.* ○ *to die of thirst* عَطَش

2 [sing.] **a thirst for sth** a strong desire for sth توق (شديد) لشيء

thirsty /ˈθɜːsti/ *adj* (**thirstier**; **thirstiest**) wanting or needing a drink: *I'm thirsty. Can I have a drink of water, please?* عطشان

▶ **thirstily** /-ɪli/ *adv* بعطش

thirteen /ˌθɜːˈtiːn/ *number* 13; one more than

a b c d e f g h i j k l m n o p q r s t u v w x y z

twelve ℹ For examples of how to use numbers in sentences, look at **six**. ثلاثة عشر، ثلاث عَشْرة

▸ **thirteenth** /ˌθɜːˈtiːnθ/ *pron, det, adv* 13th; next after twelfth ثالث عَشَر، ثالثة عَشْرة

➲ Look at the examples at **sixth**.

thirty /ˈθɜːti/ *number* 30; one more than twenty-nine ℹ For examples of how to use numbers in sentences, look at **sixty**. ثلاثون

▸ **thirtieth** /ˈθɜːtiəθ/ *pron, det, adv* 30th; next after twenty-ninth ➲ Look at the examples at **sixth**. ثلاثون (ترتيباً)

this /ðɪs/ *det, pron* (*pl.* **these** /ðiːz/) **1** (used for talking about sb/sth that is close to you in time or space): *Have a look at this photo.* ○ *These boots are really comfortable. My old ones weren't.* ○ *Is this the book you asked for?* ○ *These are the letters to be filed, not those over there.* هذا، هذه

2 (used for talking about sth that was mentioned or talked about before): *Where did you hear about this?* هذا، هذه؛ ذلك

3 (used for introducing sb or showing sb sth): *Charles, this is my wife, Claudia, and these are our children, David and Vicky.* هذا، هذه

4 (used with days of the week or periods of time) of today or the present week, year, etc: *Are you busy this afternoon?* ○ *this Friday* (= the Friday of this week) هذا، هذه

5 (*informal*) (used when you are telling a story) a certain: *Then this woman said...* (شخص ما)

IDM **this and that**; **this, that and the other** various things: *We chatted about this and that.* هذا وذاك

▸ **this** *adv* (used when you are describing sth) so; as much as this: *The road is not usually this busy.* إلى هذا الحد

thistle /ˈθɪsl/ *noun* [C] a wild plant with purple flowers and sharp points (prickles) on its leaves ℹ The thistle is the national emblem of Scotland. شوك

thorn /θɔːn/ *noun* [C] one of the hard sharp points on the stem of some plants and bushes, e.g. on rose bushes شوكة

▸ **thorny** *adj* **1** having thorns شائك

2 (used about a problem, etc.) difficult عويص

thorough /ˈθʌrə; *US* ˈθʌrəʊ/ *adj* **1** careful and complete: *The police made a thorough search of the house.* شامل

2 doing things in a very careful way, making sure that you look at every detail: *Pam is slow but she is very thorough.* دقيق

▸ **thoroughly** *adv* **1** in a thorough way: *to study a subject thoroughly* بشمول، باتقان

2 completely; very; very much: *We thoroughly enjoyed our holiday.* تماماً

thoroughness *noun* [U] دقّة، شمول

those *pl.* of THAT[1]

though /ðəʊ/ *conj* **1** in spite of the fact that; although: *Though he had very little money, Alex always managed to dress smartly.* ○ *She still loved him even though he had treated her so badly.* رغم، مع أنّ

2 but: *I'll come as soon as I can, though I can't promise to be on time.* غير أنّ

IDM **as if/though** → AS

as though → AS

▸ **though** *adv* (*informal*) however: *I quite like him. I don't like his wife, though.* ➲ Look at the note at **although**. بَيْدَ أنّ

thought[1] *pt, pp* of THINK[1]

thought[2] /θɔːt/ *noun* **1** [U] the act of thinking: *Irene sat, lost in thought, looking at the old photographs.* ○ *I need to give this problem some thought.* تفكير

2 [U] particular ideas or a particular way of thinking: *a change in medical thought on the subject* فِكْر

3 [sing.] an act of being kind or caring about sb/sth: *They sent me flowers. What a kind thought!* اهتمام

4 [C] an idea or opinion: *What are your thoughts on this subject?* ○ *The thought of living alone filled her with fear.* ➲ Look at **second thoughts**. رأي؛ فكرة

IDM **a school of thought** → SCHOOL

▸ **thoughtful** /-fl/ *adj* **1** thinking deeply: *a thoughtful expression* عميق التفكير

2 thinking about what other people want or need: *It was very thoughtful of you to send her some flowers.* حسن الاهتمام

thoughtfully /-fəli/ *adv* بتفكّر، باهتمام

thoughtfulness *noun* [U] تفكّر، اهتمام

thoughtless *adj* not thinking about what other people want or need or what the result of your actions will be طائش، أهوج

thoughtlessly *adv* بطَيْش

thoughtlessness *noun* [U] طَيش

thousand /ˈθaʊznd/ *number* 1 000; one more than nine hundred and ninety-nine ألف

> Notice that you use **thousand** in the singular when you are talking about a number. You use **thousands** when you mean 'a lot': *She earns eighteen thousand pounds a year.* ○ *Thousands of people attended the meeting.*

▸ **thousandth** /ˈθaʊznθ/ *det* 1 000th; next after nine hundred and ninety-ninth الألف (ترتيباً)

thousandth *noun* [C] the fraction 1/1000; one of a thousand equal parts of sth جزء من ألف

thrash /θræʃ/ *verb* **1** [T] to hit sb/sth many times with a stick, whip, etc. يضرب، يجلد

2 [I] **thrash (about/around)** to move your arms, legs, etc. in an uncontrolled way, e.g. because you are in pain يتلوّى (ألماً)

3 [T] to defeat sb easily in a game, competition, etc. يهزم بسهولة

PHR V **thrash sth out** to talk about sth until you reach an agreement يقلّب الأمر (بالمناقشة)؛ يتوصّل إلى نتيجة

▸ **thrashing** *noun* [C] an act of thrashing(1,3) sb/sth ضَرْب، هزيمة

thread /θred/ *noun* **1** [C,U] a long thin piece of cotton, etc. that you use for sewing, etc: *a needle and thread* خيط

2 [C] the connection between ideas, the parts of a story, etc: *I've lost the thread of this argument.* رابطة أو سلسلة الأفكار
▶ **thread** *verb* [T] **1** to put thread through the hole in a needle: *to thread a needle* يُدْخِل الخيط (في ثقب الإبرة)
2 to link things together by putting them onto a string, etc. ينظِم
3 to pass sth narrow through a space and into a particular position: *He threaded the belt through the loops on the trousers.* يدخل
IDM **thread your way through sth** to pass through sth with difficulty, moving around things or people that are in your way يشقّ (طريقه) بصعوبة

threadbare /ˈθredbeə(r)/ *adj* (used about material or clothes) old and very thin رثّ ومهترئ

threat /θret/ *noun* **1** [C,U] a warning that sb may hurt, kill or punish you if you do not do what he/she wants: *Under threat of death he did as they asked.* ○ *to make threats against sb* ○ *to carry out a threat* تهديد
2 [C, usually sing.] a person or thing that may damage sth or hurt sb; something that indicates future danger: *a threat to national security* مهدِّد؛ نذير

threaten /ˈθretn/ *verb* **1** [T] **threaten sb (with sth); threaten (to do sth)** to warn that you may hurt, kill or punish sb if he/she does not do what you want: *to threaten sb with a knife* ○ *She was threatened with dismissal.* ○ *The man threatened to kill her if she didn't tell him where the money was.* يهدِّد
2 [I,T] to seem likely to do sth unpleasant: *The oil slick is threatening the coastline with pollution.* ينذِر
▶ **threatening** *adj* مهدِّد، منذِر بالخطر
threateningly *adv* بتهديد

three /θriː/ *number* 3; one more than two ➲ Look at **third**. ❶ For examples of how to use numbers in sentences, look at **six**. ثلاثة، ثلاث
▶ **three-** (in compounds) having three of the thing mentioned: *a three-bedded room* ذو ثلاثة أو ثلاث

ˌthree-diˈmensional (*also* **3-D**) /ˌθriː ˈdiː/ *adj* having length, width and height: *a three-dimensional model* ذو ثلاثة أبعاد

threshold /ˈθreʃhəʊld/ *noun* [C] **1** the bottom part of a doorway; the entrance to a building: *She stood on the threshold* (= in the entrance). عَتَبة؛ مَدْخَل
2 the time when you are just about to start sth or find sth: *on the threshold of a scientific breakthrough* مستهلّ، على أعتاب
3 the level at which sth starts to happen: *Young children have a very low boredom threshold.* قدرة تحمل

threw *pt* of THROW[1]

thrift /θrɪft/ *noun* [U] the quality of being careful not to spend too much money اقتصاد (في انفاق المال)
▶ **thrifty** *adj* (**thriftier**; **thriftiest**) مقتصد

thrill /θrɪl/ *noun* [C] a sudden strong feeling of pleasure or excitement إثارة
▶ **thrill** *verb* [T] to make sb feel a thrill: *His singing thrilled the audience.* يثير؛ يبهج
thrilled *adj*: *He was absolutely thrilled with my present.* مبتهج للغاية
thriller *noun* [C] a play, film, book, etc. with a very exciting story, often about a crime عمل (فني) مثير ومشوّق
thrilling *adj* very exciting مثير

ˈthrill ride *noun* [C] a ride at an amusement park that makes you feel very excited and frightened at the same time (في مدينة الملاهي) لعبة مثيرة

thrive /θraɪv/ *verb* [I] (*pt* **thrived** or **throve**; *pp* **thrived**) to grow or develop well يزدهر
▶ **thriving** *adj*: *a thriving industry* مزدهر

throat /θrəʊt/ *noun* [C] **1** the front part of your neck: *The attacker grabbed the man by the throat.* حلق
2 the back part of your mouth and the passage down your neck through which air and food pass: *She got a piece of bread stuck in her throat.* ○ *I've got a terrible sore throat.* حنجرة

throb /θrɒb/ *verb* [I] (thro**bb**ing; thro**bb**ed) to make strong regular movements or noises; to beat strongly: *His heart was throbbing.* ○ *Her finger throbbed with pain.* يخفِق، يضرب
▶ **throb** *noun* [sing.]: *the throb of the ship's engines* دَقّة

throne /θrəʊn/ *noun* **1** [C] the special chair where a king or queen sits عرش
2 the throne [sing.] the position of being king or queen: *The Queen came to the throne in 1952.* العرش

throng /θrɒŋ; *US* θrɔːŋ/ *noun* [C] a large crowd of people جمع غفير
▶ **throng** *verb* [I,T] (used about a crowd of people) to move into or fill a particular place: *Crowds thronged to the palace gates.* يتجمّع

throttle /ˈθrɒtl/ *verb* [T] to hold sb tightly by the throat and stop him/her breathing يخنق

through (*US also* **thru**) /θruː/ *prep* **1** from one end or side of sth to the other: *We drove through the centre of London.* ○ *She could see the outline of a tree through the mist.* ○ *to look through a telescope* ○ *James cut through the rope.* ○ *to push through a crowd of people* خلال، عبر
2 from the beginning to the end of sth: *Food supplies will not last through the winter.* ○ *We're halfway through the book.* طِوال، في
3 (*US*) until, and including: *They are staying Monday through Friday.* حتى وبما فيه
4 because of; with the help of: *Errors were made through bad organization.* ○ *David got the job through his uncle.* بسبب؛ بواسطة
▶ **through** (*US also* **thru**) *adv* **1** from one end or side to the other: *The gate was opened and they ran through.* من خلال

On a **through train** you can reach your destination without changing trains. A road with a sign **No through road** is open at only one end.

2 from the beginning to the end of sth: *He read the letter through and handed it back.* من أوله إلى آخره

3 (*Brit*) connected by telephone: *Can you put me through to extension 5678, please?* يصله بـ

PHR V **be through (with sb/sth)** to have finished with sb/sth ينهي (علاقته معها مثلاً)

throughout /θruːˈaʊt/ *adv, prep* **1** in every part: *The house is beautifully decorated throughout.* ○ *The match can be watched live on television throughout the world.* في جميع أنحائه

2 from the beginning to the end of sth: *We didn't enjoy the holiday because it rained throughout.* ○ *Food was scarce throughout the war.* من أوله إلى آخره، في جميع انحائه

throve *pt* of THRIVE

throw[1] /θrəʊ/ *verb* (*pt* **threw** /θruː/; *pp* **thrown** /θrəʊn/) **1** [I,T] to send sth through the air by pushing it out of your hand: *How far can you throw?* ○ *Throw the ball to Wayne.* ○ *Throw Wayne the ball.* ○ *Don't throw stones at people.* يرمي

2 [T] to put sth somewhere quickly or carelessly: *He threw his bag down in a corner.* يلقي

3 [T] to move your body or part of it quickly or suddenly: *Jenny threw herself onto the bed and sobbed.* ○ *Lee threw back his head and roared with laughter.* يطرح، يلقي

4 [T] to cause sb to fall down: *The bus braked and we were thrown to the floor.* يلقي، يرمي

5 [T] (*informal*) to make sb feel upset, confused or surprised: *The question threw me and I didn't know what to reply.* يشوش

6 [T] to put sb in a particular (usually unpleasant) situation: *Many people were thrown out of work in the recession.* يرمي؛ يطرد

7 [T] to send light or shade onto sth: *The house threw a shadow across the lawn.* يلقي

PHR V **throw sth away 1** to get rid of sth that you do not want, e.g. by putting it in a dustbin: *That's rubbish. You can throw it away.* يطرح

2 to waste or not use sth useful: *to throw away a good opportunity* يضيع

throw sth in (*informal*) to include sth else without increasing the price يضيف شيئاً (من غير زيادة في السعر)

throw sb out to force sb to leave يطرد

throw sth out 1 to refuse to accept sb's idea or suggestion ينبذ؛ يرفض

2 = THROW STH AWAY

throw up (*informal*) to send out the food in your stomach through your mouth; to be sick يتقيأ

throw sth up 1 to give up your job, position, studies, etc. يتخلى عن (عمله مثلاً)

2 to produce or show sth: *Our research has thrown up some interesting facts.* يبرز

throw[2] /θrəʊ/ *noun* [C] **1** an act of throwing رَمي، قذف

2 the distance that sb throws sth: *a record throw of 75 metres* رمية

thru (*US*) = THROUGH

thrush /θrʌʃ/ *noun* [C] a bird with a brownish back and brown spots on its breast طائر السمنة

thrust /θrʌst/ *verb* [I,T] (*pt, pp* **thrust**) **1** to push sb/sth/yourself suddenly and with force: *The man thrust her out of the way and ran off.* يدفع

2 to make a sudden forward movement with a knife, etc. يطعَن

PHR V **thrust sb/sth upon sb** to force sb to accept sb/sth يفرض عليه أمراً

▸ **thrust** *noun* **1** [C] a strong push دَفعة

2 [U] the main part or ideas of sth: *The main thrust of our research is to find ways of preventing cancer.* اتجاه

thud /θʌd/ *noun* [C] the low sound that is made when sth heavy falls down صوت ارتطام

▸ **thud** *verb* [I] (thu**dd**ing; thu**dd**ed): *A snowball thudded against the window.* يرتطم محدثاً صوتاً

thug /θʌg/ *noun* [C] a violent person who may harm other people بلطجي، شخص شرير

thumb /θʌm/ *noun* [C] **1** the short thick finger at the side of each hand إبهام (اليد)

2 the part of a glove, etc. that covers your thumb إبهام القفاز

IDM **the thumbs down** a sign or an expression that shows disapproval: *The new proposal was given the thumbs down by the City Council.* تنكيس الابهام اشارة لعدم الموافقة

the thumbs up a sign or an expression that shows approval رفع الابهام موافقةً واستحساناً

▸ **thumb** *verb* [I,T] **thumb (through) sth** to turn the pages of a book, etc. quickly يقلّب (الصفحات بسرعة)

IDM **thumb a lift** to hold out your thumb to cars going past, to ask sb to give you a free ride ➲ Look at **hitchhike**. يشير لسيارة لتوصيله

thumbtack /ˈθʌmtæk/ (*US*) = DRAWING PIN

thump /θʌmp/ *verb* **1** [T] to hit sb/sth with sth heavy, usually your fist يخبط

2 [I] to make a loud sound by hitting or beating heavily: *His heart was thumping with excitement.* يخفق

▸ **thump** *noun* [C] an act or the sound of thumping خبطة، صوت الخبطة

thunder /ˈθʌndə(r)/ *noun* [U] the loud noise that comes after lightning when there is a storm رَعْد

▸ **thunder** *verb* **1** [I] (used with *it*) to make the sound of thunder: *The rain poured down and it started to thunder.* يرعد

2 [I,T] to make a loud noise like thunder: *Traffic thundered across the bridge.* يهدر

thunderstorm /ˈθʌndəstɔːm/ *noun* [C] a storm with thunder and lightning عاصفة رعدية

Thursday /ˈθɜːzdeɪ/ *noun* [C,U] (*abbr* **Thur.**; **Thurs.**) the day of the week after Wednesday and before Friday ℹ For examples of the use of the days of the week, look at **Monday**. يوم الخميس

thus /ðʌs/ *adv* (*formal*) **1** like this; in this way: *Thus began the series of incidents which changed her life.* هكذا: على هذه الصورة
2 because of or as a result of this: *I had been driving very carefully. I was thus very surprised when the police stopped me.* لذلك

thwart /θwɔːt/ *verb* [T] to stop sb doing what he/she planned to do; to prevent sth happening يحول دون، يمنع

thyme /taɪm/ *noun* [U] a plant with sweet-smelling leaves that are used in cooking صعتر أو زعتر

tick¹ /tɪk/ *noun* [C] **1** the regular short sound that a watch or clock makes when it is working تكّة
2 (*informal*) a moment: *Hang on a tick, please.* لحظة
3 (*US* **check**) a mark (✓) that shows sth is correct or has been done: *Put a tick after each correct answer.* علامة

In US English a check mark next to an answer in a piece of writing, etc. shows that sth is **wrong**. In British English it shows that sth is **correct** and a cross (x) is used to indicate a mistake.

▸ **tick** *verb* **1** [I] (used about a clock or watch) to make regular short sounds: *I could hear the clock ticking all night.* يتكْتِك
2 [T] **tick sth (off)** to mark sth with a tick: *Tick off each job on the list when you've finished it.* يضع علامة

PHRV **tick away/by** (used about time) to pass: *The minutes ticked by but there was still no sign of Zoe.* يمر
tick over (*informal*) to continue at a slow rate: *Just keep things ticking over while I'm on holiday.* يعمل على هينته

tick² /tɪk/ *noun* [C] a small insect that sucks blood قرادة

ticket /ˈtɪkɪt/ *noun* [C] **1** a piece of paper or card that shows you have paid for a journey, or to enter a place of entertainment, etc: *a single/return ticket* ○ *two tickets for the concert* ➲ Look at **season ticket**. تذكرة
2 a piece of paper or card that shows the price, size, etc. of sth that is for sale بطاقة
3 an official piece of paper that you get when you have parked in the wrong place, driven too fast, etc. تذكرة مخالفة

tickle /ˈtɪkl/ *verb* **1** [T] to touch sb lightly with your fingers or with sth soft so that he/she laughs: *She tickled the baby's toes.* يدغدغ
2 [I,T] to feel or to cause the sensation of sth touching you lightly: *My nose tickles/is tickling.* ○ *The woollen scarf tickled her neck.* يدغدغ
3 [T] (*informal*) to amuse sb يبهج، يسر
▸ **tickle** *noun* [usually sing.]: *I've got a tickle in my throat.* شعور بحكّة
ticklish /ˈtɪklɪʃ/ *adj* if a person is ticklish, he/she laughs a lot when sb tickles him/her سريع التدغدغ

tidal /ˈtaɪdl/ *adj* connected with the tides in the sea تيّاري، متعلق بالمدّ والجزر

ˌ**tidal wave** *noun* [C] a very large wave in the sea, often caused by earthquakes موجة مديّة

tidbit /ˈtɪdbɪt/ *noun* (*US*) = TITBIT

tide /taɪd/ *noun* [C,U] the regular change in the level of the sea. At high tide the sea is closer to the shore, at low tide it is farther away: *The tide is coming in/going out.* ○ (*figurative*) *The tide* (= of public opinion) *seems to have turned in the government's favour.* مدّ وجَزر
▸ **tide** *verb*
PHRV **tide sb over** to give sb sth to help him/her through a difficult time يعين، يساعد

tidy /ˈtaɪdi/ *adj* (**tidier**; **tidiest**) **1** arranged in good order; neat: *If you keep your room tidy it is easier to find things.* مرتّب
2 (used about a person) liking to keep things neat and in good order: *Mark is a very tidy boy.* منظّم
▸ **tidy** *verb* [I,T] (*pres part* **tidying**; *3rd pers sing pres* **tidies**; *pt, pp* **tidied**) **tidy (sb/sth/yourself) (up)** to make sb/sth/yourself tidy: *We must tidy this room up before the visitors arrive.* يرتّب
PHRV **tidy sth away** to put sth into the drawer, cupboard, etc. where it is kept يحفَظ بنظام
tidily *adv* بترتيب
tidiness *noun* [U] ترتيب، نظام

tie¹ /taɪ/ *noun* [C] **1** (*US* **necktie**) a long thin piece of cloth worn round the neck, especially by men, with a knot at the front. A tie is usually worn with a shirt. ➲ Look at **bow tie**. رباط العنق
2 [usually pl.] something that connects you with a particular group of people: *Our school has ties with another school in America.* ○ *family ties* رابطة، صلة
3 something that limits your freedom: *He never married because he didn't want any ties.* قيد
4 a game or competition in which two or more teams or players get the same score: *There was a tie for first place.* تعادل (في اللعب)

tie² /taɪ/ *verb* (*pres part* **tying**; *3rd pers sing pres* **ties**; *pt, pp* **tied**) **1** [T] to fasten sb/sth or fix sb/sth in position with rope, string, etc: *The prisoner was tied to a chair.* ○ *Kay tied her hair back with a ribbon.* ○ *to tie sth in a knot* ○ *to tie your shoelaces* يربط
2 [I] **tie (with sb) (for sth)** to have the same score as another player or team in a game or competition: *England tied with Italy for third place.* يتعادل
PHRV **tie sb/yourself down** to limit your freedom: *Having young children really ties you down.* يقيّد
tie in (with sth) to agree with other facts or information that you have يتّفق مع، يطابق
tie sb/sth up 1 to fix sb/sth in position with rope, string, etc: *The dog was tied up in the back garden.* يربط
2 (usually passive) to occupy or keep sb busy: *Mr Jones is tied up in a meeting.* مشغول

tier /tɪə(r)/ *noun* [C] one of a number of levels: *a stadium with many tiers of seats* صف، طبقة

tiger /ˈtaɪɡə(r)/ *noun* [C] a large wild cat that has yellow fur with black stripes. Tigers live in Asia. ❶ A female tiger is called a **tigress** and a baby is called a **cub**. نَمِر (شائعاً)، بَبر

⚷**tight** /taɪt/ *adj* **1** firm and difficult to move: *a tight knot* ○ *Keep a tight hold on this rope.* مشدود، وثيق

2 fitting very closely: *These shoes hurt. They're too tight.* ❶ The opposite is **loose**. مشدود، ضيّق

3 (in compounds) not allowing sth to get in or out: *an airtight tin* محكَم الإغلاق (لا يدخله الهواء مثلاً)

4 not having much spare time or space: *My schedule this week is very tight.* مزدحم، مليء

5 stretched or pulled hard: *When you're towing another car, keep the rope between the two cars tight.* مشدود

6 controlled very strictly: *Security is very tight at Heathrow Airport.* محكَم، شديد

▸ **tight** *adv* firmly; closely: *Hold tight please* (= on a bus). بشدّة؛ جيداً

Tightly, not **tight**, is used before a past participle: *The van was packed tight with boxes.* ○ *The van was tightly packed with boxes.*

tighten /ˈtaɪtn/ *verb* [I,T] **tighten (sth) (up)** to become tighter; to make sth tighter: *His grip on her arm tightened.* ○ *He tightened the screws as far as they would go.* يضيق؛ يضيّق، يشدّ

PHRV **tighten up (on sth)** to cause sth to become stricter: *to tighten up the law on the sale of alcohol to children* يشدّد

tightly *adv* firmly; closely: *Screw the lid on tightly.* ○ *She kept her eyes tightly closed.* بإحكام

tightness *noun* [U] شِدّة، إحكام

tightrope /ˈtaɪtrəʊp/ *noun* [C] a rope stretched high above the ground on which people walk, e. g. in a circus حبل البهلوان

tights /taɪts/ (*US* **pantyhose**) *noun* [plural] a piece of thin clothing, usually worn by women, that fits tightly from the waist over the legs and feet: *a pair of tights* ➲ Look at **stocking**. كولان: جوارب نسائيّة متّصلة من الأعلى

tile /taɪl/ *noun* [C] one of the flat, square objects that are arranged in rows to cover roofs, floors, bathroom walls, etc: *The wind had blown several tiles off the roof.* ○ *carpet tiles* قرميدة، بلاطة

▸ **tile** *verb* [T]: *a tiled bathroom* يبلّط

till[1] /tɪl/ *conj, prep* (*informal*) = UNTIL

till[2] /tɪl/ *noun* [C] the machine or drawer where money is kept in a shop, etc. درج (النقود)

tilt /tɪlt/ *verb* [I,T] to have one end or side higher than the other; to put sth in this position: *The front seats of the car tilt forward.* ○ *She tilted her head to one side.* يَميل؛ يميل

▸ **tilt** *noun* [sing.] مَيْل، انحراف

timber /ˈtɪmbə(r)/ *noun* **1** [U] (*especially US* **lumber**) wood that is going to be used for building خشب البناء

2 [C] a large piece of wood: *a ship's timbers* قطعة خشب كبيرة

⚷**time**[1] /taɪm/ *noun* **1** [C] a particular point in the day or night: *What's the time?* ○ *Can your son tell the time yet?* ○ *Can you tell me the times of trains to Bristol, please?* ○ *It's time to go home.* ○ *By the time I get home, Alex will have cooked the dinner.* ساعة، موعد

2 [U] the passing of minutes, hours, days, etc: *As time passed and there was still no news, we got more worried.* زمن، وقت

3 [C,U] an amount of minutes, hours, days, etc: *You're wasting time – get on with your work!* ○ *I'll go by car to save time.* ○ *free time* ○ *We haven't got time to stop now.* ○ *I've been waiting a long time.* وقت

4 [C] a period in the past: *Did you enjoy your time in Spain?* ○ *In Shakespeare's times, few people could read.* فترة؛ عصر

5 [C,U] an occasion when sth happens: *I phoned them three times.* ○ *I'll do it better next time.* ○ *Last time I saw him, he looked ill.* مرّة

6 [C] an event or occasion that you experience in a certain way: *Have a good time tonight!* ○ *We had a terrible time at the hospital.* وقت

7 [sing.] a system for measuring time in a particular part of the world: *Central European Time* ○ *We arrive in Atlanta at eleven, local time.* توقيت

8 [C,U] the number of minutes, etc., taken to complete sth, especially a race: *What was his time in the hundred metres?* الزمن

IDM **all the time** during the time that sb was doing sth or that sth was happening: *I searched everywhere for my keys and they were in the door all the time.* طول الوقت

at a time on each occasion: *The lift can hold six people at a time.* في كلّ مرّة

at one time in the past; previously في الماضي؛ سابقاً

at the same time → SAME[1]

at the time at a particular moment or period in the past: *I agreed at the time but later changed my mind.* حينها

at times sometimes: *At times I wish we'd never had children.* أحياناً

beat time (to sth) → BEAT[1]

before your time before you were born قبل أن تولد

behind the times not modern or fashionable مُتَخلّف، عتيق

for the time being just for the present; not for long في الوقت الحالي

from time to time sometimes; not often من آن لآخر

have a good, great, etc. time to enjoy yourself: *We had a wonderful time at the party.* يبتهج؛ يستمتع بِ

have a hard/rough time to have problems or difficulties يمرّ بظروف عسيرة

have no time for sb/sth to not like sb/sth: *I have no time for people who aren't prepared to work.* لا يحبّ (شخصاً أو شيئاً)

in good time early; at the right time: *We arrived in good time.* مبكراً؛ في الوقت المطلوب
in the nick of time → NICK[1]
in time (for sth/to do sth) not late; at the right time: *Don't worry. We'll get to the station in time for your train.* قبل فوات الأوان؛ في الوقت المطلوب
kill time → KILL
once upon a time → ONCE
on time not late or early في الوقت المحدّد
take your time to do sth without hurrying يتمهّل
tell the time → TELL
time after time; time and (time) again again and again; many times مرّة بعد أخرى؛ مرّات عديدة

time[2] /taɪm/ *verb* [T] **1** to choose or arrange the time that sth happens: *They timed their journey to avoid the rush hour.* يوقّت
2 to measure how long sb/sth takes يقيس (الفترة الزمنية)
▸ **timer** *noun* [C] a person or machine that measures time ضابط الوقت؛ ساعة توقيت
timing *noun* [U] **1** the act of choosing or arranging when sth will happen: *The timing of the meeting is not convenient for many people.* توقيت
2 your skill at choosing or arranging the best time for sth توقيت

'time-consuming *adj* that takes or needs a lot of time مستهلك للوقت

'time lag *noun* [C] = LAG

timeless /'taɪmləs/ *adj* (*formal*) that does not seem to be changed by time خالد، سرمدي

'time limit *noun* [C] a time during which sth must be done أجَل، مدّة معيّنة (للفراغ من عمل)

timely /'taɪmli/ *adj* happening at just the right time: *The accident was a timely reminder of the dangers involved.* يحدث في الوقت المناسب

ˌtime-'poor *adj* having very little or no free time because you work all the time: *products for customers who are time-poor but cash-rich* دائم العمل، ذو وقت ضيق

times /taɪmz/ *prep* (used when you are multiplying one figure by another): *Three times four is twelve.* مضروباً في
▸ **times** *noun* [plural] (used for comparing things): *Tea is three times as/more expensive in Spain than in England* (= if it costs £1 in England it costs £3 in Spain). مرّة

⚷ **timetable** /'taɪmteɪbl/ *noun* [C] (*US* **schedule**) a list that shows the times when sth happens جدول

timid /'tɪmɪd/ *adj* easily frightened; shy هَيوب، خجول
▸ **timidity** /tɪ'mɪdəti/ *noun* [U] تَهيُّب
timidly *adv* بتهيب، بوَجَل

⚷ **tin** /tɪn/ *noun* **1** [U] a soft whitish metal that is often mixed with other metals قصدير
2 (*especially US* **can**) [C] a closed container in which food is stored and sold, made of tin: *a tin of peas* علبة
3 [C] a metal container for food, etc., with a lid: *a biscuit tin* علبة
▸ **tinned** *adj* (used about food) that is in a tin (2) so that you can keep it for a long time: *tinned peaches* معلّب

tinge /tɪndʒ/ *noun* [usually sing.] a small amount of a colour or a feeling: *a tinge of sadness* مَسْحَة
▸ **tinged** *adj*: *Her joy at leaving was tinged with regret.* مشوب بِ

tingle /'tɪŋgl/ *verb* [I] to have a slight stinging or prickling feeling in the skin: *His cheeks tingled as he came in from the cold.* يحسّ بوخز
▸ **tingle** *noun* [C, usually sing.]: *a tingle of excitement* وَخْز

tinker /'tɪŋkə(r)/ *verb* [I] to try to repair or improve sth without having the proper skill or knowledge: *He's been tinkering with the car all afternoon but it still won't start.* يصلِح بغير براعة

tinkle /'tɪŋkl/ *verb* [I] to make a light, ringing sound, like that of a small bell يرن
▸ **tinkle** *noun* [C, usually sing.] رنين

'tin-opener *noun* [C] a tool that you use for opening a tin (2) فتّاحة علَب

tinsel /'tɪnsl/ *noun* [U] strings covered with little pieces of shiny paper, used as a Christmas decoration شرائط لمّاعة للزينة، بهرج

tint /tɪnt/ *noun* [C] a type or shade of a colour: *cream paint with a pinkish tint* لون خفيف
▸ **tint** *verb* [T] to add a little colour to sth: *tinted glass* ○ *She had her hair tinted.* يلوّن بلون خفيف

⚷ **tiny** /'taɪni/ *adj* (**tinier**; **tiniest**) very small: *the baby's tiny fingers* صغير جداً

⚷ **tip**[1] /tɪp/ *noun* [C] the thin or pointed end of sth: *the tips of your toes, fingers, etc.* ○ *the southernmost tip of South America* طرف
IDM **(have sth) on the tip of your tongue** to be about to remember or say sth that you have forgotten for the moment: *Their name is on the tip of my tongue. It'll come back to me in a moment.* على طرف لسانه
the tip of the iceberg a small part of a problem that is much larger الطرف الضئيل الظاهر (من مشكلة كبيرة)

⚷ **tip**[2] /tɪp/ *verb* (**tipping**; **tipped**) **1** [I,T] **tip (sth) (up)** to move so that one side is higher than the other; to make sth move in this way: *When I stood up, the bench tipped up and the person on the other end fell off.* يَميل: يقلِب
2 [I,T] **tip (sth) (over)** to fall or turn over; to make sth turn over: *The tractor turned the corner too fast and the trailer tipped over.* ○ *The baby leaned out of his pushchair and tipped it over.* ينقلب؛ يقلِب
3 [T] to empty or pour sth out of a container: *Tip the dirty water down the drain.* ○ *The child tipped all the toys onto the floor.* يفرِغ، يصب
▸ **tip** *noun* [C] **1** a place where you can take rubbish: *We took the broken furniture to the tip.* مَقْلَب (القمامة)، مزبلة
2 (*informal*) a place that is very dirty or untidy مكان قذر، مكان مهمَل

a b c d e f g h i j k l m n o p q r s t u v w x y z

tip[3] /tɪp/ *verb* (tipping; tipped) to give a small amount of money (in addition to the normal charge) to a waiter, taxi driver, etc. to thank him/her يمنح بقشيشاً
▸ **tip** *noun* [C]: *Service wasn't included so we left a tip for the waitress.* بقشيش

tip[4] /tɪp/ *verb* [T] (tipping; tipped) **tip sb/sth (as sth/to do sth)** to think that sb/sth is likely to do sth: *This horse is tipped to win the race.* ○ *He is widely tipped as the next Prime Minister.* يتوقع
▸ **tip** *noun* [C] a piece of useful advice فكرة مفيدة

tip[5] /tɪp/ *verb* (tipping; tipped)
PHR V **tip sb off** to give sb secret information: *The police had been tipped off and were waiting when the burglars broke in.* يمدّ بمعلومات سرّيّة
▸ **'tip-off** *noun* [C]: *Acting on a tip-off, the police searched the flat for drugs.* معلومات سرّيّة

tiptoe /ˈtɪptəʊ/ *noun*
IDM **on tiptoe** standing or walking on the ends of your toes with your heels off the ground على رؤوس أصابع القدم
▸ **tiptoe** *verb* [I] to walk quietly and carefully on tiptoe يسير بحذر على رؤوس الأصابع

tire[1] /ˈtaɪə(r)/ *verb* **1** [I,T] to feel that you need to rest or sleep; to make sb feel like this: *However hard he works, he never seems to tire.* ○ *The long walk tired us all out.* يتعب؛ يُرهِق
2 [I] **tire of sth/of doing sth** to become bored or not interested in sth/doing sth: *I never tire of this view.* يَمَلّ
tireless *adj* not stopping for rest لا يتعب
▸ **tiresome** /ˈtaɪəsəm/ *adj* (*formal*) that makes you a little angry or bored مُضْجِر، مملّ
tiring /ˈtaɪərɪŋ/ *adj* making you tired: *a long and tiring journey* متعب

tire[2] (*US*) = TYRE

tired /ˈtaɪəd/ *adj* feeling that you need to rest or sleep: *She was tired after a hard day's work.* مُتْعَب، مُرهَق
IDM **be tired of sb/sth/doing sth** to be impatient with or annoyed by sb/sth/doing sth: *I'm tired of this game. Let's play something else.* ○ *I'm tired of listening to the same thing again and again.* يَضْجَر
tired out very tired في غاية التعب
▸ **tiredness** *noun* [U] the state of being tired تَعَب

tissue /ˈtɪʃuː/ *noun* **1** [C,U] the material that the bodies of animals and plants are made of: *brain tissue* ○ *Radiation can destroy the body's tissues.* نسيج
2 [C] a thin piece of soft paper that you use as a handkerchief and throw away after you have used it: *a box of tissues* منديل ورق
3 [U] (*also* **'tissue paper**) thin soft paper that you use for wrapping things that may break ورق لفّ

tit[1] /tɪt/ *noun* [C] a small bird, often with a dark top to the head. There are several types of tit: *a blue tit* طائر القُرقُف أو القُرقُب

tit[2] /tɪt/ *noun*
IDM **tit for tat** something unpleasant that you do to sb because he/she has done sth to you واحدة بواحدة، مثْل بمثْل

tit[3] /tɪt/ *noun* [C] (*slang*) a woman's breast ثدي

titbit /ˈtɪtbɪt/ (*US* **tidbit**) *noun* [C] **1** a small but very nice piece of food قطعة طعام شهي
2 an interesting piece of information معلومة طريفة؛ نبأ مثير

title /ˈtaɪtl/ *noun* [C] **1** the name of a book, play, film, picture, etc. عنوان
2 a word that shows a person's rank or profession: *'Lord', 'Doctor', 'Reverend', 'Mrs' and 'General' are all titles.* لقب
3 the position of champion in a sport: *Sue is playing this match to defend her title* (= to stay champion). لَقَب (البطولة)
▸ **titled** /ˈtaɪtld/ *adj* having a noble rank, e.g. 'Duke' ذو لقب

'title-holder *noun* [C] the champion in a sport: *the current 400-metres title-holder* حامل لَقَب البطولة

'title role *noun* [C] the part in a play or film that is used as the title of it الدور الذي سمّيت به المسرحية أو الفيلم

titter /ˈtɪtə(r)/ *noun* [C] a short silly or nervous laugh كَرْكَرة
▸ **titter** *verb* [I]: *The speaker dropped his notes and the audience tittered.* يكَرْكِر

'T-junction *noun* [C] a place where two roads join to form the shape of a T ملتقى طريقين على شكل T

to[1] /tə; *before vowels* tu; tuː; *strong form* tuː/ *prep* **1** in the direction of; as far as: *She's going to London.* ○ *Turn to the left.* ○ *This road goes to Dover.* ○ *Pisa is to the west of Florence.* ○ *He has gone to school.* إلى؛ نحو
2 (used before the person or thing that receives, sees, etc. sth): *Give that to me.* ○ *You must be kind to animals.* إلى، لِ
3 (nearly) touching sth: *He put his hands to his ears.* ○ *They sat back to back.* (للتعبير عن الملامسة أو شبه الملامسة)
4 (used about time) before: *It's two minutes to three.* إلّا
5 (used before the upper limit of a range): *from Monday to Friday* ○ *from beginning to end* ○ *They sell everything from matches to washing machines.* إلى
6 (used for expressing a reaction to sth): *To my surprise, I saw two strangers coming out of my house.* (للتعبير عن ردّ الفعل)
7 as far as sb is concerned; in sb's opinion: *To me, it was the wrong decision.* (للتعبير عن الرأي)، بالنسبة
8 (used when comparing things): *I prefer Italy to Spain.* (يفضّل) على
9 (used for expressing quantity) for each unit of money, measurement, etc: *How many dollars are there to the euro?* مقابل
10 reaching a particular state: *The meat was*

cooked to perfection. ○ *His speech reduced her to tears* (= made her cry). إلى درجة أو حدّ

to² /tə; *before vowels* tu:; tu:; *strong form* tu:/ (used with verbs to form the infinitive): *I want to go home now.* ○ *Don't forget to write.* ○ *She's learning English in order to get a better job.* ○ *Do you know which button to press?* ○ *I didn't know what to do.* ○ *He asked me to go but I didn't want to.* (مع الأفعال لتكوين المصدر)

to³ /tu:/ *adv* (used about a door) in or into a closed position: *Push the door to.* يغلق الباب
IDM **to and fro** backwards and forwards ذهاباً وإياباً

toad /təʊd/ *noun* [C] a small cold-blooded animal that looks similar to a frog but that is bigger, has a rough skin and lives mainly on land ضفدع الجبل

toadstool /'təʊdstu:l/ *noun* [C] a type of poisonous fungus that looks like a mushroom فطر سامّ

toast¹ /təʊst/ *noun* [U] a thin piece of bread that is heated to make it brown: *toast and marmalade* ○ *fried egg on toast* خبز محمّص
▶ **toast** *verb* [I,T] يحمص
toaster *noun* [C] an electrical machine for making toast محمّصة خبز كهربائية

toast² /təʊst/ *verb* [T] to hold up your glass and wish sb success, happiness, etc. before you drink: *Everyone stood up and toasted the bride and groom.* يشرب نخبه
▶ **toast** *noun* [C]: *a toast to the Queen* نَخْب

tobacco /tə'bækəʊ/ *noun* [U] the substance that people smoke in cigarettes and pipes (the dried leaves of the tobacco plant) تَبْغ
▶ **tobacconist** /tə'bækənɪst/ *noun* [C] a person who sells cigarettes, tobacco, etc. ❶ Note that **the tobacconist** is the person who runs the shop and **the tobacconist's** is the shop. بائع التَّبغ

toboggan /tə'bɒgən/ *noun* [C] a type of flat board, often with metal strips underneath, that people use for travelling downhill on snow for fun ❶ A **toboggan** is a small **sledge**. مِزلَقة

today /tə'deɪ/ *noun* [U], *adv* **1** (on) this day: *Today is Monday.* ○ *What shall we do today?* ○ *School ends a week today* (= on this day next week). ○ *Where is today's paper?* اليوم
2 (in) the present age: *Young people have more freedom today than in the past.* ○ *Today's computers are much smaller than the early models.* (في) الوقت الحاضر، هذه الأيام

toddle /'tɒdl/ *verb* [I] to walk with short unsteady steps, like a young child يَدْرُج
▶ **toddler** /'tɒdlə(r)/ *noun* [C] a child who has only just learnt to walk طفل في بداية مَشيه

toe /təʊ/ *noun* [C] **1** one of the five small parts like fingers at the end of each foot إصبع القدم
2 the part of a sock, shoe, etc. that covers your toes مقدّم الجورب أو الحذاء الخ
▶ **toe** *verb* (*pres part* **toeing**; *pt, pp* **toed**)
IDM **toe the (party) line** to obey the orders of your group, party, etc. يمتثل للأوامر

TOEFL™ /'təʊfl/ *abbrev* (*US*) Test of English as a Foreign Language; the examination for foreign students who want to study at an American university اختبار الانكليزية كلغة أجنبية

toenail /'təʊneɪl/ *noun* [C] one of the hard pieces that cover the end of your toes ظفر إصبع القدم

toffee /'tɒfi; *US* 'tɔ:fi/ *noun* [C,U] a hard sticky sweet that is made by cooking sugar and butter together with milk or water التوفي: حلوى لزجة

together /tə'geðə(r)/ *adv* **1** with each other; in or into the same place as or near to sb/sth else: *Can we have lunch together?* ○ *They walked home together.* ○ *I'll get all my things together tonight because I want to leave early.* ○ *Stand with your feet together.* معاً: جنباً إلى جنب
2 so that two or more things are mixed with, joined to or added to each other: *Mix the butter and sugar together.* ○ *Tie the two ends together.* ○ *Add these numbers together to find the total.* معاً
3 at the same time: *Don't all talk together.* في وقت واحد
IDM **get your act together** → ACT²
together with in addition to; as well as: *I enclose my order together with a cheque for £15.* بالإضافة إلى، علاوةً على
▶ **together** *adj* (*informal*) (used about a person) organized, capable (شخص) منظم؛ كفء
togetherness *noun* [U] a feeling of friendship تآزر

toil /tɔɪl/ *verb* [I] (*formal*) to work very hard or for a long time at sth يكدَح
▶ **toil** *noun* [U] (*formal*) كَدْح

toilet /'tɔɪlət/ *noun* [C] a large bowl with a seat, attached to a drain, that you use when you need to get rid of waste material or water from your body; the room containing this: *I'm going to the toilet.* ○ *Could I use your toilet, please?* ○ *to flush the toilet* مِرْحاض، دورة مياه

> In their houses, British people usually refer to the **toilet** (or, informally, the **loo**). **Lavatory** is a formal and old-fashioned word. In public places the toilets are called the **Ladies** or the **Gents**. You might also see **WC** or **Public Conveniences** on some signs. In US English people talk about the **bathroom** in their houses and the **rest room**, **ladies' room** or **men's room** in public places.

▶ **toiletries** /'tɔɪlətriz/ *noun* [plural] things such as soap, toothpaste, etc. that you use when you are getting washed, doing your hair, etc. أدوات النظافة والزينة

'toilet paper *noun* [U] paper that you use to clean your body after going to the toilet ورق المرحاض

'toilet roll *noun* [C] a long piece of toilet paper rolled round a tube لفة ورق المرحاض

token /'təʊkən/ *noun* [C] **1** something that represents or is a sign of sth else: *Please accept this gift as a token of our gratitude.* علامة، رمز
2 a piece of metal, plastic, etc. that you use for a

particular purpose, often instead of a coin
مسكوكة (معدنية أو بلاستيكية) بديل عن العملة

3 a piece of paper or card that you can use to buy sth of a certain value in a particular shop. Tokens are often given as presents: *a gift token*
➲ Look at **voucher**. قسيمة شراء

▸ **token** *adj* (only *before* a noun) **1** small, but done or given as a sign that sth larger or more serious could follow: *a token payment* رمزي

2 done, chosen, etc. to give the impression that you are interested in sth when you do not intend it sincerely: *There is a token woman on the board.* ○ *The troops put up only token resistance.* صوري

told *pt, pp* of TELL

tolerate /'tɒləreɪt/ *verb* [T] **1** to allow or accept sth that you do not like or agree with: *In a democracy we must tolerate opinions that are different from our own.* يقبل، يسمح بـ

2 to accept or stand sb/sth unpleasant without complaining: *The noise was more than she could tolerate.* يطيق، يحتمل

▸ **tolerable** /'tɒlərəbl/ *adj* of a level that you can tolerate: *Drugs can reduce the pain to a tolerable level.* مُحتَمل

tolerance /'tɒlərəns/ *noun* [U] the ability or willingness to allow or accept sth that is unpleasant or that you do not like or agree with: *religious tolerance* ❶ The opposite is **intolerance**. تسامح

tolerant /-rənt/ *adj* **tolerant (of/towards sb/sth)** having or showing tolerance ❶ The opposite is **intolerant**. متسامح

toleration /ˌtɒlə'reɪʃn/ *noun* [U] = TOLERANCE

toll /təʊl/ *noun* [C] **1** money that you pay to use a road, bridge, etc. رسْم (للمرور في طريق الخ)

2 [usually sing.] the amount of damage done or the number of people who were killed or injured by sth: *The death toll from the earthquake was 35.* خسائر (في الأرواح مثلاً)

IDM take a heavy toll/take its toll (on sth) to cause loss, damage, suffering, etc. يسبّب خسائر فادحة

tom /tɒm/ *noun* [C] = TOMCAT

tomato /tə'mɑːtəʊ; *US* tə'meɪtəʊ/ *noun* [C] (*pl.* **tomatoes**) a soft red fruit that is often eaten raw in salads or cooked as a vegetable: *tomato juice* طماطم، بَندورة

tomb /tuːm/ *noun* [C] a place where a body is buried, often one with a large decorated stone above it قبر، ضريح

tomboy /'tɒmbɔɪ/ *noun* [C] a young girl who likes to play rough games فتاة غلامية (تشبه الصبيان)

tombstone /'tuːmstəʊn/ *noun* [C] a stone over a grave that shows the name of the person who is buried there شاهدة القبر

tomcat /'tɒmkæt/ (*also* **tom**) *noun* [C] a male cat قطّ، هِر

tomorrow /tə'mɒrəʊ/ *noun* [U], *adv* **1** (on) the day after today: *Today is Friday so tomorrow is Saturday.* ○ *The advertisement will appear in tomorrow's papers.* ○ *See you tomorrow.* ○ *I'm going to bed. I've got to get up early tomorrow morning.* ○ *Tomorrow night's concert has been cancelled.* ○ *a week tomorrow* (= a week from tomorrow) غداً

> Notice that we say 'tomorrow morning', 'tomorrow afternoon', etc. not 'tomorrow in the morning', etc.

➲ Look at the note at **morning**.

2 the future: *The schoolchildren of today are tomorrow's workers.* الغد، المستقبل

IDM the day after tomorrow → DAY

ton /tʌn/ *noun* **1** [C] a measure of weight; 2 240 pounds طن

> Do not confuse **ton** and **tonne**. A ton is the same as 1.016 tonnes. An American ton is 2 000 pounds or 0.907 of a tonne.

2 tons [plural] (*informal*) a lot: *tons of homework* أطنان، مقادير كبيرة

tone[1] /təʊn/ *noun* **1** [C,U] the quality of a sound, especially of the human voice: *'Do you know each other?' she asked in a casual tone of voice.* ○ *His tone changed. He was angry now.* نَبْرة

2 [sing.] the general quality or style of sb/sth: *The tone of the meeting was optimistic.* روح

3 [C] one of the shades of a colour: *warm tones of red and orange* درجة شدّة اللون

4 [C] a sound that you hear on the telephone: *the dialling tone* وَنين خطّ التليفون

tone[2] /təʊn/ *verb*

PHRV tone sth down to change sth that you have said, written, etc., to make it seem less strong يُلطف، يُخفّف

ˌtone-'deaf *adj* not able to sing or hear the difference between notes in music ذو اذن موسيقية غير حساسة

tongs /tɒŋz/ *noun* [plural] a tool that looks like a pair of scissors but that you use for holding or picking things up ملْقط

tongue /tʌŋ/ *noun* **1** [C] the soft part inside your mouth that you can move. You use your tongue for speaking, tasting things, etc. لِسان

2 [C,U] the tongue of an animal, e.g. a cow, which can be eaten: *tongue salad* لِسان

3 [C] (*formal*) a language: *your mother tongue* (= the language you learned as a child) لغة

IDM on the tip of your tongue → TIP[1]

put/stick your tongue out to put your tongue outside your mouth, for the doctor to examine or to be rude to sb يُخرج لسانه

(with) tongue in cheek done or said as a joke; not meant seriously على سبيل المزاح

'tongue-tied *adj* not saying anything because you are shy or nervous معقود اللسان (خجلاً أو خوفاً)

'tongue-twister *noun* [C] a phrase or sentence that is difficult to say correctly when you are speaking quickly عاثور لسان: عبارة يصعب نطقها

tonic /'tɒnɪk/ *noun* [C,U] something that makes

you feel stronger, healthier, happier, etc: *A relaxing holiday is a wonderful tonic.* مقوٍّ، منشّط
▸ **'tonic water** (*also* **tonic**) *noun* [U] a type of water with bubbles in it and a rather bitter taste that is often added to alcoholic drinks ماء غازيّ

tonight /tə'naɪt/ *noun* [U], *adv* (on) the evening or night of today: *Tonight is the last night of our holiday.* ○ *tonight's weather forecast* ○ *What's on TV tonight?* ○ *We are staying with friends tonight and travelling home tomorrow.* الليلة، هذه الليلة

tonne /tʌn/ *noun* [C] a measure of weight; 1 000 kilograms ➲ Look at **ton**. طنّ (متري)

tonsil /'tɒnsl/ *noun* [C] one of the two soft lumps in your throat on each side of the back of your tongue لَوْزة الحلق
▸ **tonsillitis** /ˌtɒnsə'laɪtɪs/ *noun* [U] an illness in which the tonsils become very sore التهاب اللوزتين

too /tuː/ *adv* **1** in addition; also: *Red is my favourite colour but I like blue, too.* ○ *Phil thinks you're right and I do too.* أيضاً

> Notice that you say 'There were lions and tigers at the zoo. There were elephants, **too**', but 'There were no zebras and there were no giraffes, **either**.' Look at the note at **also**.

2 (used for expressing surprise or disappointment): *Her purse was stolen. And on her birthday too.* (للتعبير عن الاندهاش أو الشعور بالخيبة)
3 (used before adjectives and adverbs) more than is good, allowed, possible, etc: *These boots are too small.* ○ *It's too cold to go out without a coat.* ○ *It's too long a journey for you to make alone.* ❶ Notice that you cannot say 'It's a too long journey'. (قبل الصفات والظروف للتعبير عن الإفراط)
4 (usually used in negative sentences) very: *The weather is not too bad today.* جداً

took *pt* of TAKE

tools

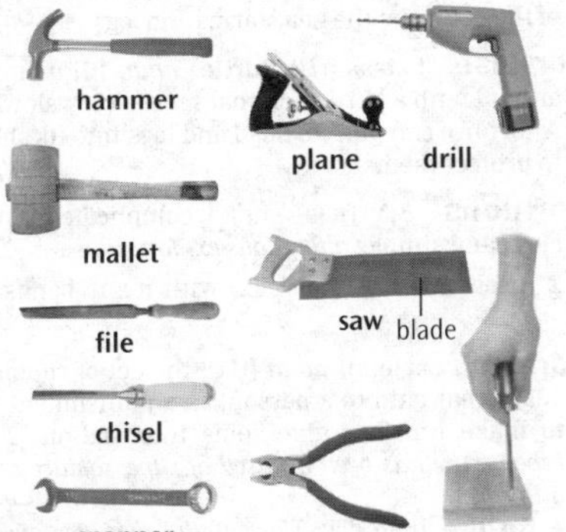

tool /tuːl/ *noun* [C] a piece of equipment that you use to help you do a particular type of job: *Hammers, screwdrivers and saws are all carpenter's tools.* ○ *garden tools* ○ *A laptop is an indispensable tool for a journalist.* أداة

> A **tool** is usually something you can hold in your hand, e.g. a spanner or hammer. An **implement** is often used outside, e.g. for farming or gardening. A **machine** has moving parts and works by electricity, with an engine, etc. An **instrument** is often used for technical or delicate work: *a dentist's instruments* ○ *precision instruments*. A **device** is a more general word for a piece of equipment that you consider to be useful: *The machine has a safety device which switches the power off if there is a fault.*

toolbar /'tuːlbɑː(r)/ *noun* [C] a row of symbols on a computer screen that show the different things that the computer can do لائحة الادوات (كمبيوتر)

toot /tuːt/ *noun* [C] the short sound that a whistle, horn, etc. makes تزميرة
▸ **toot** *verb* [I,T]: *Michael tooted the horn as he drove away.* يزمّر

tooth /tuːθ/ *noun* [C] (*pl.* **teeth** /tiːθ/) **1** one of the hard white parts in your mouth that you use for biting: *to have a tooth out* ○ *The old man took out his false teeth.* ○ *wisdom teeth* سِن

> You **brush/clean** your teeth to remove bits of food. If a tooth is **decayed**, the dentist may **fill** it or **extract** it/ **take** it **out**. If you have had all your teeth out, you can have **false teeth** or **dentures**.

2 one of the long pointed parts of a comb, saw, etc. سِنّ المشط أو المنشار
IDM **by the skin of your teeth** → SKIN
grit your teeth → GRIT
have a sweet tooth → SWEET[1]

toothache /'tuːθeɪk/ *noun* [C,U] a pain in your tooth or teeth ➲ Look at the note at **ache**. وَجَع السِنّ

toothbrush /'tuːθbrʌʃ/ *noun* [C] a small brush with a handle that you use for cleaning your teeth فرشاة الأسنان

toothpaste /'tuːθpeɪst/ *noun* [U] a substance that you put on your toothbrush and use for cleaning your teeth معجون الأسنان

toothpick /'tuːθpɪk/ *noun* [C] a short pointed piece of wood that you use for getting pieces of food out from between your teeth خِلال، عود أسنان

top[1] /tɒp/ *noun* **1** [C] the highest part of sth: *The flat is at the top of the building.* ○ *the top of the stairs* ○ *Start reading at the top of the page.* أعلى
2 [C] the upper surface of sth: *a desk top* سطح
3 [sing.] **the top (of sth)** the highest or most important rank or position: *to be at the top of your profession* قمّة
4 [C] the cover that you put onto sth in order to close it: *Put the tops back on the felt-tip pens or they will dry out.* غطاء

> A **top** or a **cap** is often small and round. You take it off by turning or screwing: *a bottle top* ○ *Unscrew cap to open.* A **lid** may be larger. You can lift it off: *a saucepan lid* ○ *Put the lid back on the box.*

5 [C] a piece of clothing that you wear on the top part of your body: *I need a top to match my new skirt.* "بلوزة" أو قميص وغيرهما
IDM **at the top of your voice** as loudly as possible بأعلى صوتك
get on top of sb (*informal*) to make sb feel sad or depressed: *I've got so much work to do. It's really getting on top of me.* يوقع الكآبة بـ، يوهن العزيمة
off the top of your head (*informal*) without preparing or thinking about sth before you speak عفو الخاطر
on top 1 on or onto the highest point: *There's a pile of books on the desk. Please put this one on top.* فوق (شيء آخر)
2 stronger or better: *Throughout the match Liverpool were on top.* أقوى، أفضل
on top of sb/sth 1 on or onto sb/sth else: *Several demonstrators stood on top of the tank, waving flags and shouting.* فوق، على ظهر
2 in addition to sb/sth else: *On top of all our other problems the car's broken down.* علاوةً على
3 (*informal*) very close to sb/sth: *modern houses built on top of each other* فوق بعضه البعض
over the top (*informal*) (*especially Brit*) stronger or more extreme than necessary "أكثر من اللازم"، مفْرِط
▸ **top** *adj* highest in position, rank or degree: *one of Britain's top businessmen* ○ *at top speed* ○ *the top floor of the building* أعْلى، أقصى

top² /tɒp/ *verb* [T] (**topping**; **topped**) **1** to be or form a top for sth: *cauliflower topped with cheese sauce* يعلو (الشيء)
2 to be higher or greater than sth: *Inflation has topped the 10% mark.* يفوق
PHR V **top (sth) up** to fill sth that is partly empty: *We topped up our glasses.* يملأ، يضيف إلى
▸ **topping** *noun* [C,U] something such as cream or a sauce that is put on the top of food to decorate it or make it taste nicer طبقة علْوية (مثل القشدة أو الصلصة)

top³ /tɒp/ *noun* [C] a child's toy that spins round quickly, balancing on a point خُذْروف: لعبة أطفال

ˌ**top 'hat** *noun* [C] a tall black or grey hat that a man wears on formal occasions قُبّعة رسمية

ˌ**top-'heavy** *adj* heavier at the top than the bottom and likely to fall over (حِمْل) مقلقل لثقل أعلاه

🔑**topic** /'tɒpɪk/ *noun* [C] a subject that you talk, write or learn about موضوع
▸ **topical** /-kl/ *adj* connected with sth that is happening now; that people are interested in now متعلّق بالأمور الراهنة

topmost /'tɒpməʊst/ *adj* (only *before* a noun) highest: *the topmost branches of the tree* الأعلى

topple /'tɒpl/ *verb* **1** [I] **topple (over)** to become unsteady and fall over: *Don't add another book to the pile or it will topple over.* يسقط، يتهاوى
2 [T] to cause a government or leader of a country to lose power: *A coup by the army has toppled the country's president.* يطيح

ˌ**top 'secret** *adj* that must be kept very secret سرّي للغاية

'**top-up** *noun* [C] **1** a payment that you make to increase the amount of money, etc. to the level that is needed: *a phone top-up* (= to buy more time for calls) ○ *Students will have to pay top-up fees* (= fees that are above the basic level). مبلغ اضافي
2 an amount of a drink that you add to a cup or glass in order to fill it again: *Can I give anyone a top-up?* مقدار إضافي

torch /tɔːtʃ/ *noun* [C] **1** (*US* **flashlight**) a small electric light that you carry in your hand. A torch runs on batteries: *Shine the torch under the sofa and see if you can find my ring.* مصباح (جيب) كهربائي
2 a long piece of wood with burning material at the end that you carry to give light شُعْلَة

tore *pt* of TEAR²

torment /'tɔːment/ *noun* [U,C, usually pl.] great pain in your mind or body; sth that causes this pain: *to be in torment* ألم مبرِّح؛ عذاب
▸ **torment** /tɔː'ment/ *verb* [T] to cause sb great pain or unhappiness: *The older boys were always tormenting Richard in the school playground.* ○ *She was tormented by nightmares.* يعَذّب

torn *pp* of TEAR²

tornado /tɔː'neɪdəʊ/ *noun* [C] (*pl.* **tornadoes**) a violent storm with a very strong wind that blows in a circle ➲ Look at the note at **storm**. إعصار

torpedo /tɔː'piːdəʊ/ *noun* [C] (*pl.* **torpedoes**) a bomb, shaped like a tube, that is fired from a ship or submarine and can travel underwater طُرْبيد

torrent /'tɒrənt; *US* 'tɔːr-/ *noun* [C] a strong fast stream of sth, especially water: *When the snow melts, this little river becomes a torrent.* ○ (*figurative*) *She poured out a torrent of abuse at him.* سيل دافق
▸ **torrential** /tə'renʃl/ *adj* (used about rain) very heavy (مطر) منهمر

torso /'tɔːsəʊ/ *noun* [C] (*pl.* **torsos**) the main part of the body, not the head, arms and legs بدَن، جِذْع

tortoise /'tɔːtəs/ (*US* **turtle**) *noun* [C] a small animal with a hard shell that moves very slowly. A tortoise can pull its head and legs into its shell to protect them. سُلَحْفاة

tortuous /'tɔːtʃuəs/ *adj* **1** complicated, not clear and simple: *a tortuous explanation* معقّد
2 (used about a road, etc.) with many bends ملتوٍ

torture /'tɔːtʃə(r)/ *noun* [U,C] the act of causing very great pain to a person, as a punishment or to make him/her give some information: *The rebel army has been accused of rape, torture and murder.* تعذيب
▸ **torture** *verb* [T]: *Most of the prisoners were tortured into making a confession.* ○ (*figurative*) *She was tortured by the thought that the accident was her fault.* يعذّب
torturer /'tɔːtʃərə(r)/ *noun* [C] a person who tortures other people معَذّب

Tory /'tɔːri/ *noun* [C] (*pl.* **Tories**) *adj* a member or supporter of the British Conservative Party; connected with this party: *the Tory Party conference* ➲ Look at the note at **party**. محافظ؛ ذو صلة بحزب المحافظين البريطاني

toss /tɒs; *US* tɔːs/ *verb* **1** [T] to throw sth carelessly, not using all your strength: *Bob opened the letter and tossed the envelope into the paper bin.* يقذف (باهمال)

2 [T] to move your head back quickly: *I asked her to stay but she just tossed her head and walked away.* يحرِّك رأسه للخلف

3 [I,T] to keep moving up and down or from side to side; to make sb/sth do this: *He lay tossing and turning in bed, unable to sleep.* ○ *The rough seas tossed the ship about.* يتحرَّك؛ يقذف، يقلِّب

4 [I,T] **toss (up) (for sth)** to throw a coin into the air in order to decide sth. The person who guesses correctly which side of the coin will face upwards when it lands has the right to choose: *Let's toss to see who does the washing-up.* ○ *to toss a coin* ○ *There's only one cake left. I'll toss you for it.* يقترع (برمي قطعة نقدية)

Look at **heads** and **tails**. These are the names of the two sides of a coin and we say 'heads' or 'tails' when we are guessing which side will face upwards.

▶ **toss** *noun* [C] an act of tossing: *an angry toss of the head* تحريك للخلف

IDM **win/lose the toss** to guess correctly/incorrectly which side of a coin will face upwards when it lands: *Hewitt won the toss and chose to serve first.* يكسب/ يخسر القرعة

tot[1] /tɒt/ *noun* [C] **1** a small child طفل صغير

2 a small glass of a strong alcoholic drink كأس صغير من الكحول

tot[2] /tɒt/ *verb* (totting; totted)

PHRV **tot (sth) up** (*informal*) to add up numbers يجمع (أعداداً)

total /ˈtəʊtl/ *adj* counting everything; complete: *What was the total number of people there?* ○ *a total failure* ○ *They ate in total silence.* كلّي، كامل

▶ **total** *noun* [C] the number that you get when you add two or more numbers or amounts together مجموع

IDM **in total** when you add two or more numbers or amounts together: *The appeal raised £4 million in total.* جملة

total *verb* [T] (totalling; totalled; *US also* totaling; totaled) to add up to a certain amount or number; to make a total of: *His debts totalled more than £10 000.* يبلغ

totally /ˈtəʊtəli/ *adv* completely: *I totally agree with you.* تماماً

totter /ˈtɒtə(r)/ *verb* [I] to stand or move in an unsteady way as if you are going to fall يترنّح

touch[1] /tʌtʃ/ *verb* **1** [I,T] (used about two or more things, surfaces, etc.) to be or go so close together that there is no space between them: *They were sitting so close that their heads touched.* ○ *This bicycle is too big. My feet don't touch the ground.* يلمس

2 [T] to put a part of your body, usually your hand or fingers, onto sb/sth: *Don't touch!* ○ *He touched her gently on the cheek.* ○ *The police asked us not to touch anything.* ○ (*figurative*) *June never touches meat* (= she never eats it). يلمس، يَمَسّ

3 [T] to make sb feel sadness, sympathy, thanks, etc: *a sad story that touched our hearts* ➲ Look at **touched**. يمس، يؤثّر في

4 [T] (in negative sentences) to be as good as sb/sth: *He's a much better player than all the others. No one else can touch him.* يَمَسّ؛ يتوصل له

IDM **touch wood** an expression that people use (often while touching a piece of wood) to prevent bad luck: *I've been driving here for 20 years and I haven't had an accident yet – touch wood!* امسك خشب؛ دُقّ على الخشب

PHRV **touch down** (used about an aircraft) to land يهبط

touch on/upon sth to talk or write about sth for only a short time يتناول باقتضاب

touch[2] /tʌtʃ/ *noun* **1** [C, usually sing.] an act of touching (2) sb/sth: *I felt the touch of her hand on my arm.* لَمْس

2 [U] one of the five senses: the ability to feel: *The sense of touch is very important to blind people.* حاسة اللمس

3 [U] the way sth feels when you touch it: *Marble is cold to the touch.* مَلْمس

4 [C] a small detail: *The flowers on our table were a nice touch.* لَمْسة

5 [sing.] **a touch (of sth)** a small amount of sth: *He's not very ill. It's just a touch of flu.* مس، قليل من

IDM **in/out of touch (with sb)** being/not being in contact with sb by speaking or writing to him/her: *During the year she was abroad, they kept in touch by letter.* على اتصال/على غير اتصال

in/out of touch with sth having/not having recent information about sth: *We're out of touch with what's going on.* على علم/غير علم (بآخر التطورات)

lose touch → LOSE

lose your touch → LOSE

touched /tʌtʃt/ *adj* (not before a noun) made to feel sadness, sympathy, thanks, etc: *We were very touched by your kind offer.* متأثّر

touching /ˈtʌtʃɪŋ/ *adj* that makes you feel sadness, sympathy, thanks, etc: *Romeo and Juliet is a touching story of young love.* مؤثّر

ˈ**touch screen** *noun* [C] (*computing*) a computer screen which shows information when you touch it: *touch-screen technology* شاشة تعمل باللمس

touchy /ˈtʌtʃi/ *adj* **1** easily upset or made angry: *Don't ask about her first marriage. She's very touchy about it.* سريع الاستياء

2 (used about a subject, situation, etc.) that may easily upset people or make them angry مثير للاستياء؛ (موضوع) حسّاس

tough /tʌf/ *adj* **1** not easily broken or cut; very strong: *tough boots* ○ *tough plastic* متين، صُلب

2 not easily weakened by pain or difficulty; very

strong: *You need to be tough to go climbing in winter.* صلب العود، قوي

3 difficult to cut and eat: *This meat is tough.* قاسٍ

4 strict; firm: *The government is introducing tough new laws about drinking and driving.* حازم

5 difficult: *It will be a tough decision to make.* ○ *He's had a very tough time recently.* صعب

6 tough (on sb) (*informal*) unfortunate; bad luck: *That's tough!* ○ *It's tough that she was ill just before she went on holiday.* سوء طالع؛ لسوء حظه

▶ **toughen** /ˈtʌfn/ *verb* [I,T] **toughen (sb/sth) up** to become tough; to make sb/sth tough يقسو؛ يمتّن

toughness *noun* [U] قسوة، متانة

tour /tʊə(r)/ *noun* **1** [C] a journey that you make for pleasure during which you visit many places: *a ten-day coach tour of Scotland* جَوْلة، رحلة

2 [C] a short visit around a city, famous building, etc: *a guided tour round St Paul's Cathedral* ➲ Look at the note at **travel**. طواف، جولة

3 [C,U] a series of visits that you make to play sports matches, give concerts, etc: *The band is currently on tour in America.* جولة

▶ **tour** *verb* [I,T] to go on a journey during which you visit many places: *We spent three weeks touring in southern Spain.* ○ *We toured southern Spain for three weeks.* يتجوّل؛ يقوم برحلة

tourism /ˈtʊərɪzəm/ *noun* [U] the business of providing and arranging holidays and services for people who are visiting a place: *The country's economy relies heavily on tourism.* سياحة

tourist /ˈtʊərɪst/ *noun* [C] a person who visits a place for pleasure: *a foreign tourist* ○ *the Tourist Information Office* سائح

tournament /ˈtʊənəmənt; US ˈtɜːrn-/ *noun* [C] a competition in which many players or teams play games against each other مباراة

tousle /ˈtaʊzl/ *verb* (usually passive) to make sth untidy, especially hair: *a girl with blue eyes and fair tousled hair* يشعّث؛ يلخبط

tow /təʊ/ *verb* [T] to pull a car, etc. along by a rope or chain يجرّ (بحبل مثلاً)، يقطر

▶ **tow** *noun* [sing., U]: *Can you give me a tow?* ○ *a car on tow* سحب، جر

IDM in tow (*informal*) following behind: *He arrived with his wife and five children in tow.* (يجرّ) وراءه

towards /təˈwɔːdz; US tɔːrdz/ (*also* **toward** /təˈwɔːd; US tɔːrd/) *prep* **1** in the direction of sb/sth: *I saw Ken walking towards the station.* ○ *She had her back towards me.* ○ *a first step towards world peace* نحْوَ

2 (used when you are talking about your feelings about sb/sth) in relation to: *Pat felt very protective towards her younger brother.* ○ *What is your attitude towards private education?* تجاه؛ مِنْ

3 as part of the payment for sth: *The money will go towards the cost of a new minibus.* تجاه؛ كجزءٍ من

4 near a time or date: *It gets cool towards evening.* قُبيل

towel /ˈtaʊəl/ *noun* [C] a piece of cloth or paper that you use for drying sb/sth/yourself: *a bath towel* ○ *paper towels* ➲ Look at **sanitary towel** and **tea towel**. فوطة، بشكير

tower /ˈtaʊə(r)/ *noun* [C] a tall narrow building or part of a building such as a church or castle: *the Eiffel Tower* ○ *a church tower* بُرْج

ˈtower block *noun* [C] (*Brit*) a very tall block of flats or offices مجمّع شقق شاهق

town /taʊn/ *noun* **1** [C] a place with many streets and buildings. A town is larger than a village but smaller than a city: *Romsey is a small market town.* بَلَدة، مدينة

2 [sing.] all the people who live in a town: *The whole town was on the streets, waving flags and shouting.* كلّ سكّان المدينة

3 [U] the main part of a town, where the shops, etc. are: *I've got to go into town this afternoon.* (قلب) المدينة

IDM go to town (on sth) (*informal*) to spend a lot of time or money on sth ينفق كثيراً على شيء

ˌtown ˈcouncil *noun* [C] (*Brit*) a group of people who are responsible for the local government of a town مجلس (بلدي)

ˌtown ˈhall *noun* [C] a large building that contains the local government offices and often a large room for public meetings, concerts, etc. دار البلدية

toxic /ˈtɒksɪk/ *adj* poisonous: *Toxic chemicals had leaked into the water.* سامّ

toy¹ /tɔɪ/ *noun* [C] an object for a child to play with: *Here are some toys to keep the children amused.* ○ *toy cars* ○ *a toy soldier* ○ *a toy farm* ○ *a toyshop* لُعْبة

toy² /tɔɪ/ *verb*

PHRV toy with sth 1 to think about doing sth, perhaps not very seriously: *She's toying with the idea of going abroad for a year.* (فكرة) تداعب مخيّلته أو تراوده

2 to move sth about without thinking about what you are doing: *He toyed with his food but hardly ate any of it.* يتشاغل بِ، يعبث

trace¹ /treɪs/ *noun* **1** [C,U] a mark or sign that shows that sb/sth existed or happened: *traces of a bronze age village* ○ *The man disappeared without trace.* أثر

2 [C] a very small amount of sth: *Traces of blood were found under her fingernails.* أثر

trace² /treɪs/ *verb* [T] **1** to find out where sb/sth is by following marks, signs or other information: *The wanted man was traced to an address in Amsterdam.* يقتفي أثر شخص أو شيء

2 to find out or describe the development of sth: *She traced her family tree back to the 16th century.* يتتبّع

3 to make a copy of sth by placing a piece of transparent paper over it and drawing over the lines ينسخ بورقة شفافة

track /træk/ *noun* [C] **1** (usually plural) a line or series of marks that are left behind by a car, a person, an animal, etc: *The hunter followed the tracks of a deer.* ○ *tyre tracks* ➲ Look at **footprint**. أثر، آثار

2 a path or rough road: *The road became just a muddy track.* درب وعر

3 the two metal rails on which a train runs: *The train stopped because there was a tree across the track.* خطّ السكة الحديد

4 a special path, often in a circle, for racing: *a running track* ميدان أو حلْبة

5 one song or piece of music on a cassette, CD or record أغنية، قطعة موسيقية

IDM **keep/lose track of sb/sth** to know/not know what is happening somewhere or to sb/sth: *As a journalist, he has to keep track of events all over the Middle East.* يتابع/ينقطع عن

off the beaten track → BEAT[1]

on the right/wrong track having the right/wrong sort of idea about sth: *That's not the answer but you're on the right track.* في الاتجاه السليم أو الخطأ

▸ **track** *verb* [T] **track sb/sth (to sth)** to follow tracks (1) or signs in order to find sb/sth: *to track enemy planes on a radar screen* يرصد

PHR V **track sb/sth down** to find sb/sth after searching for him/her/it يعثر على

'track events *noun* [plural] athletic events that involve running ➲ Look at **field event**. مباريات الجري

'track record *noun* [C] what a person or an organization has achieved that other people know about منجزات

tracksuit /'træksu:t; *Brit also* -sju:t/ *noun* [C] a suit that consists of loose trousers and a jacket or sweater. You wear a tracksuit for sports practice or when you are relaxing at home. ملابس التمرين الرياضي

tractor /'træktə(r)/ *noun* [C] a large vehicle that is used on farms for pulling heavy pieces of machinery جرّار، تراكتور

trade[1] /treɪd/ *noun* **1** [U] the buying or selling of goods or services: *an international trade agreement* ○ *Trade is not very good* (= not many goods are sold) *at this time of year.* التجارة

2 [C] **trade (in sth)** a particular type of business: *Many seaside resorts depend on the tourist trade.* ○ *We do quite a good trade in second-hand books.* تجارة: "صناعة"

3 [C,U] a job for which you need special skill, especially with your hands: *Jeff is a plumber by trade.* ○ *to learn a trade* ➲ Look at the note at **work**. حِرْفة

trade[2] /treɪd/ *verb* **1** [I] **trade (in sth) (with sb)** to buy or sell goods or services: *The shop was losing money and ceased trading last week.* ○ *More and more countries are trading with China.* ○ *to trade in arms* يتاجر

2 [T] **trade sth for sth** to exchange sth for sth else: *The explorer traded his watch for food.* يبادل، يقايض

PHR V **trade sth in (for sth)** to give sth old in part payment for sth new or newer يبادل (قديماً بجديد كجزء من ثمنه)

▸ **trader** *noun* [C] a person who buys and sells things, especially in a market تاجر

trademark /'treɪdmɑ:k/ *noun* [C] a special mark or name that a company can put on its products and that cannot be used by any other company علامة تجارية

tradesman /treɪdzmən/ *noun* [C] (*pl.* **tradesmen** /-mən/) a person who delivers goods to people's homes or who has a shop بائع يوصل السلع للبيوت، تاجر

,trade 'union (*also* **,trades 'union; union**) *noun* [C] an organization for people who all do the same type of work. Trade unions try to get better pay and working conditions for their members. نقابة

tradition /trə'dɪʃn/ *noun* [C,U] a custom or belief that has continued from the past to the present: *It's a tradition to play tricks on people on 1 April.* ○ *Vienna has a great musical tradition.* ○ *By tradition, the bride's family pays the costs of the wedding.* تقليد، عادة

▸ **traditional** /-ʃənl/ *adj*: *It is traditional to eat turkey at Christmas.* تقليدي

traditionally /-ʃənəli/ *adv* عادةً

traffic /'træfɪk/ *noun* [U] **1** the cars, etc. that are on a road: *heavy/light traffic* ○ *The traffic is at a standstill.* حركة السير أو المرور

2 the movement of ships, aeroplanes, etc: *Cross-channel traffic was affected by a strike at the French ports.* ○ *air traffic controllers* حركة الإبحار أو الطيران

3 traffic (in sth) the illegal buying and selling of sth: *the traffic in arms* تجارة غير مشروعة

▸ **traffic** *verb* [I] (*pres part* **trafficking**; *pt, pp* **trafficked**) **traffic (in sth)** to buy and sell sth illegally: *drug trafficking* يتاجر تجارة غير مشروعة، يهرِّب

'traffic island (*also* **island**) *noun* [C] a raised area in the middle of the road, where you can stand when you are crossing رصيف وسط الشارع

'traffic jam *noun* [C] a long line of cars, etc. that cannot move or that can only move very slowly ازدحام السير

'traffic light *noun* [C, usually pl.] a sign with three coloured lights (red, amber and green) that is used for controlling the traffic at a road junction: *When the traffic lights are red you must stop.* إشارة المرور

'traffic warden *noun* [C] (*Brit*) a person who checks whether cars are parked in the wrong place or for longer than is allowed مراقب السير

tragedy /'trædʒədi/ *noun* (*pl.* **tragedies**) **1** [C,U] an event or a situation that causes great sadness: *A trip to Brighton ended in tragedy for a local couple when they were involved in a car crash on the M23.* ○ *It's a tragedy that so many children leave school without any qualifications.* مأساة

2 [C] a serious play that has a sad ending:

Shakespeare's 'King Lear' is a tragedy. ➲ Look at **comedy**. مسرحية مأساوية، تراجيديا

tragic /ˈtrædʒɪk/ *adj* **1** that causes great sadness: *It's tragic that he died so young.* ○ *a tragic accident* مأساوي، محزن

2 (only *before* a noun) with a sad ending or in the style of tragedy: *a tragic novel* مأساوي، تراجيدي

▸ **tragically** /-kli/ *adv* على نحو مأساوي

trail /treɪl/ *noun* [C] **1** a series of marks in a long line that a person or thing leaves behind: *a trail of muddy footprints* ○ *The storm left behind a trail of destruction.* أثر

2 a path through the country: *a nature trail through the woods* ممر

3 the tracks or smell that you follow when you are hunting sb/sth: *The dogs ran off on the trail of the fox.* ○ (*figurative*) *The burglar got away in a stolen car with the police on his trail.* أثر؛ رائحة

▸ **trail** *verb* **1** [I,T] to be pulled or dragged along behind you; to make sth do this: *Her long hair trailed behind her in the wind.* ○ *Joe sat in the boat trailing a stick in the water.* يتدلّى؛ يُجَرْجِر، يدلي

2 [I] **trail along behind (sb/sth)** to move or walk slowly behind sb/sth else, usually because you are tired يمشي خلفه بتثاقل

3 [I,T] to have a lower score than the other player or team during a game or competition: *At half-time Everton were trailing by two goals to three.* يتخلّف

4 [I] (used about plants) to grow over a surface: *ivy trailing over the wall* ○ (*figurative*) *wires from the stereo trailing across the floor* يمتدّ

trailer /ˈtreɪlə(r)/ *noun* [C] **1** a vehicle with no engine that is pulled by a car, lorry, etc. (عربة) مقطورة

2 (*US*) = CARAVAN (1)

3 a series of short pieces taken from a cinema film and used to advertise it مقتطفات من فيلم للدعاية له

train¹ /treɪn/ *noun* [C] **1** a number of carriages or wagons that are pulled by an engine along a railway line: *a passenger/goods/freight train* ○ *a fast/slow train* ○ *an express/a stopping train* ○ *to catch/get/take a train* ○ *the 12 o'clock train to Bristol* ○ *to get on/off a train* ○ *Hurry up or we'll miss the train.* ○ *You have to change trains at Reading.* ○ *The train pulled into/out of the station.* قطار

> Note that we say **by** train when speaking in general. We say **on the train** when we mean during one particular train journey: *Miranda travels to work by train.* ○ *Yesterday she fell asleep on the train and missed her station.*

2 [usually sing.] a series of thoughts or events that are connected: *A knock at the door interrupted my train of thought.* سلسلة (أفكار أو أحداث)

train² /treɪn/ *verb* **1** [T] **train sb (as sth/to do sth)** to teach a person to do sth which is difficult or which needs practice: *The organization trains guide dogs for the blind.* ○ *There is a shortage of trained teachers.* يدرّب

2 train (as sth) (to do sth) [I] to learn how to do a job: *She's training as an engineer.* ○ *He's training to be a doctor.* يتدرّب

3 [I,T] to prepare for a race or match by exercising; to help a person or an animal to do this: *I'm training for the London Marathon.* ○ *to train racehorses* يتدرّب؛ يدرّب

4 [T] to point a gun, camera, etc. at sb/sth يوجّه

▸ **trainee** /ˌtreɪˈniː/ *noun* [C] a person who is being trained (1): *a trainee manager* تحت التدريب

trainer *noun* [C] **1** a person who teaches people or animals how to do a particular job or skill well, or to do a particular sport: *teacher trainers* ○ *a racehorse trainer* مروِّض، مدرِّب

2 (*US* **sneaker**) [usually pl.] a type of soft shoe that you wear for running حذاء للعدو

training *noun* [U] the preparation for a sport or job: *staff training* ○ *to be in training for the Olympics* تدريب

trait /treɪt/ *noun* [C] a quality; part of sb's character سمة؛ صفة

traitor /ˈtreɪtə(r)/ *noun* [C] a person who is not loyal to his/her country, friends, etc. and harms them ➲ Look at **betray** and at **treason**. خائن

tram /træm/ (*US* **streetcar**) *noun* [C] a type of bus that works by electricity and that runs on special rails in the road ترام، حافلة كهربائية

tramp¹ /træmp/ *noun* [C] a person who has no home or job and who moves from place to place متشرّد

tramp² /træmp/ *verb* [I,T] to walk with slow heavy steps يمشي بتثاقل

▸ **tramp** *noun* [sing.] the sound of people walking with heavy steps وقع الأقدام المتثاقلة

trample /ˈtræmpl/ *verb* [I,T] **trample sb/sth (down)**; **trample on sb/sth** to walk on sb/sth and damage or hurt him/her/it: *The cows trampled the corn.* ○ *The child was trampled to death by the crowd.* ○ *The boys trampled on the flowers.* يدوس

trampoline /ˈtræmpəliːn/ *noun* [C] a piece of equipment for jumping up and down on, made of a piece of strong material fixed to a metal frame by springs ترامبولين: جهاز خاصّ للقفز

trance /trɑːns; *US* træns/ *noun* [C] a condition of the mind in which you do not notice what is going on around you or in which you move and speak as if you were being controlled by another person or force غيبوبة

tranquil /ˈtræŋkwɪl/ *adj* (*formal*) calm and quiet هادئ، ساكن

▸ **tranquillizer** (*also* **tranquilliser**; *US also* **tranquilizer**) *noun* [C] a drug that is used for making people sleepy or calmer مهدّئ، مسكّن

transaction /trænˈzækʃn/ *noun* [C] a piece of business: *financial transactions* صفقة، معاملة تجارية

transatlantic /ˌtrænzətˈlæntɪk/ *adj* to or from

the other side of the Atlantic; across the Atlantic: *a transatlantic flight* عبر (المحيط) الأطلسي

transcend /træn'send/ *verb* [T] (*formal*) to be greater or more important than sb/sth; to go beyond the limits of sth: *Environmental issues transcend national boundaries.* يفوق؛ يتجاوز

transcript /'trænskrɪpt/ *noun* [C] a written copy of what sb said نسخة مكتوبة

transfer[1] /træns'fɜː(r)/ *verb* (transferring; transferred) **1** [I,T] **transfer (sb/sth) (from…) (to…)** to move, or to make sb/sth move, from one place to another: *He has been transferred to our Tokyo branch.* ○ *I want to transfer £1 000 from my deposit to my current account* (= in a bank). ○ *Transfer the data onto a disk.* ينقل، يحوّل

2 [T] to change the ownership of sth from one person to another ينقل (الملكية)

▸ **transferable** /-'fɜːrəbl/ *adj*: *This ticket is not transferable.* قابل لنقل الملكيّة، قابل للتحويل

transfer[2] /'trænsfɜː(r)/ *noun* **1** [C,U] moving or being moved from one place, job or state to another: *Paul is not happy here and has asked for a transfer.* ○ *the transfer of power from a military to a civilian government* نقل، تحويل

2 [U] changing to a different vehicle, route, etc. during a journey تغيير

3 [C] (*US*) a ticket that allows you to travel on two or more buses, etc. during one journey تذكرة تخوّل حاملها التغيير ومواصلة رحلته

4 [C] (*especially Brit*) a piece of paper with a picture or writing on it that you can stick onto another surface by pressing or heating it رسم يمكن طبعه على سطح آخر

transform /træns'fɔːm/ *verb* [T] **transform sb/sth (from sth) (into sth)** to change sb/sth completely: *The arrival of electricity transformed people's lives.* يحوّل (تحويلاً تاماً)

▸ **transformation** /ˌtrænsfə'meɪʃn/ *noun* [C,U] تحوُّل

transfusion /træns'fjuːʒn/ *noun* [C] the act of putting one person's blood into another person's body: *a blood transfusion* نَقْل دم

transistor /træn'zɪstə(r); -'sɪst-/ *noun* [C] **1** a small piece of electrical equipment that is used in radios and televisions ترانزستور

2 (*also* **tranˌsistor 'radio**) a small radio that you can carry easily راديو ترانزستور

transit /'trænzɪt; -sɪt/ *noun* [U] the act of moving or being taken from one place to another: *The goods had been damaged in transit.* نَقْل؛ مرور

transition /træn'zɪʃn/ *noun* [C,U] **transition (from sth) (to sth)** a change from one state or form to another: *the transition from childhood to adolescence* تحوّل، انتقال

▸ **transitional** /-ʃənl/ *adj*: *We're still in a transitional stage.* انتقالي

transitive /'trænsətɪv/ *adj* (*grammar*) (used about a verb) that has a direct object: *In this dictionary transitive verbs are marked* '[T]'. ❶ The opposite is **intransitive**. (فعل) متعدٍّ

translate /træns'leɪt/ *verb* [I,T] **translate (sth) (from sth) (into sth)** to change sth spoken or written from one language to another: *This book has been translated from Czech into English.* ➲ Look at **interpret**. يترجم

▸ **translation** /-'leɪʃn/ *noun* [C,U]: *a word-for-word translation* ○ *an error in translation* ترجمة

translator *noun* [C] a person who translates sth that has been written ➲ Look at **interpreter**. مُترجِم

transmission /træns'mɪʃn/ *noun* **1** [U] sending out or passing on: *the transmission of television pictures by satellite* ○ *the transmission of disease* بَثّ؛ انتشار

2 [C] a TV or radio programme إرسال (تلفزيوني أو إذاعي)

3 [C,U] the set of parts of a car, etc. that take power from the engine to the wheels آلية نقل الحركة

transmit /træns'mɪt/ *verb* [T] (transmitting; transmitted) **1** to send out television or radio programmes, electronic signals, etc: *The match was transmitted live all over the world.* ينقل، يبثّ

2 to send or pass sth from one person or place to another: *a sexually transmitted disease* ينقُل؛ ينتقل

▸ **transmitter** *noun* [C] a piece of equipment that sends out television or radio programmes, electronic signals, etc. جهاز إرسال

transparent /træns'pærənt/ *adj* that you can see through: *Glass is transparent.* ❶ The opposite is **opaque**. شفّاف

▸ **transparency** /-rənsi/ *noun* [C] (*pl.* **transparencies**) a type of photograph that is printed on transparent plastic, or a piece of plastic on which you can write or draw. You look at a transparency by putting it in a special machine (projector) and shining light through it: *a transparency for the overhead projector* ➲ Look at **slide**[2]. صورة شفّافة؛ بلاستيك شفّاف

transplant /træns'plɑːnt; *US* -'plænt/ *verb* [T] **1** to take a plant out of the soil and plant it in another place ينقل نبتة إلى تربة أخرى

2 to take out an organ or other part of sb's body and put it into another person's body يَزْرع عضواً (طب)

▸ **transplant** /'trænsplɑːnt; *US* -plænt/ *noun* [C] an operation in which an organ, etc. is transplanted: *a heart transplant* عملية زرع الأعضاء

transport[1] /træn'spɔːt/ *verb* [T] to move sb/sth from one place to another in a vehicle ينقُل

transport[2] /'trænspɔːt/ (*especially US* **transportation** /ˌtrænspɔː'teɪʃn/) *noun* [U] **1** moving sb/sth from one place to another by vehicle: *road, rail, sea, etc. transport* نَقْل

2 vehicles that you travel in: *Do you have your own transport?* (e.g. a car) ○ *I travel to school by public transport.* وسائل النَّقْل

transvestite /trænz'vestaɪt/ *noun* [C] a person who likes to wear the clothes of sb of the opposite sex من يميل إلى ارتداء ملابس الجنس الآخر

trap /træp/ *noun* [C] **1** a piece of equipment that you use for catching animals: *a mousetrap* ○ *The rabbit's leg was caught in the trap.* ○ *(figurative) He thought of marriage as a trap.* شَرَك، فخّ

2 something that tricks or deceives you: *He fell into the trap of thinking she would always be there.* شَرَك، فخّ

▸ **trap** *verb* [T] (trapping; trapped) **1** to catch an animal, etc. in a trap يوْقع في شرك

2 to keep sb in a place from which he/she cannot move or escape: *The door closed behind them and they were trapped.* ○ *Many people are trapped in low-paid jobs.* يَحْبِس؛ يَنْحَبِس

3 to catch and keep or store sth: *Special glass panels trap heat from the sun.* يَحْبِس

4 trap sb (into sth/into doing sth) to make sb do sth by tricking or deceiving him/her يوْقعه في فخّ أو أُحْبولة

trapdoor /ˈtræpdɔː(r)/ *noun* [C] a door in a floor or ceiling باب في أرض أو سقف الغرفة

trapeze /trəˈpiːz; *US* træ-/ *noun* [C] a bar hanging from two ropes high above the ground, used as a swing by gymnasts and acrobats أرجوحة الألعاب البهلوانيّة

trappings /ˈtræpɪŋz/ *noun* [plural] clothes, possessions, etc. which are signs of a particular rank or position: *a large car, expensive clothes and all the other trappings of success* بهارج (الوظيفة)

trash /træʃ/ *noun* [U] *(US)* = RUBBISH

▸ **trashy** *adj* (**trashier**; **trashiest**) of poor quality: *trashy novels* تافه، سقيم

ˈ**trash can** *noun* [C] *(US)* = DUSTBIN

trauma /ˈtrɔːmə; *US* ˈtraʊmə/ *noun* [C,U] (an event that causes) a state of great unhappiness or shock ➲ Look at **stress**. صدمة نفسيّة

▸ **traumatic** /trɔːˈmætɪk; *US* traʊ-/ *adj*: *Getting divorced can be a traumatic experience.* هائل (الأثر)

travel /ˈtrævl/ *verb* (travelling; travelled; *US* traveling; traveled) **1** [I] to make a journey: *Charles travels a lot on business.* ○ *to travel by sea/air* ○ *They travelled overland from Turkey.* ○ *travelling expenses* ○ *(figurative) News travels fast in the village.* يسافِر

2 [T] to make a journey of a particular distance: *They travelled 60 kilometres to come and see us.* يسافِر، يقْطع مسافة

▸ **travel** *noun* **1** [U] the act of travelling: *Air travel has made the world seem a smaller place.* ○ *a travel book* سفَر، (كتاب) رحلات

2 travels [plural] journeys, especially to places that are far away: *You must have seen lots of interesting places on your travels.* رحلات، أسفار

> **Travel** is an uncountable word and you can only use it to talk about the general activity of moving from place to place: *Foreign travel is very popular these days.* When you talk about going from one particular place to another, you use **journey**. A journey can be long: *the journey across Canada* or short, but repeated: *the journey to work.* A **tour** is a journey or walk during which you visit several places. You may go on a tour round a country, city, place of interest, etc: *a three-week tour around Italy* ○ *a guided tour of the castle.* You often use **trip** when you are thinking about the whole visit (including your stay in a place and the journeys there and back): *They're just back from a trip to Japan. They had a wonderful time.* (but: *'How was your journey?' 'Awful – the plane was delayed!'*) A trip may be short: *a day trip*, or longer: *a trip round the world*, and can be for business or pleasure: *How about a trip to the seaside this weekend?* ○ *He's on a trip to New York to meet a client.* An **excursion** is an organized trip that you go on with a group of people: *The holiday includes a full-day excursion by coach to the Lake District.*

traveller (*US* **traveler**) /ˈtrævələ(r)/ *noun* [C] **1** a person who is travelling or who often travels مسافر؛ رحّالة

2 *(Brit)* a person who travels around the country in a large vehicle and does not have a permanent home anywhere ➲ Look also at **gypsy**. رحّال؛ غجري

ˈ**travel agency** *noun* [C] (*pl.* **travel agencies**) a company that makes travel arrangements for people (booking tickets, making hotel reservations, etc.) وكالة سياحة

ˈ**travel agent** *noun* [C] a person who works in a travel agency وكيل سِياحي

ˈ**traveller's cheque** (*US* ˈ**traveler's check**) *noun* [C] a cheque that you can change into foreign money when you are travelling abroad: *to cash a traveller's cheque* شيك سِياحي

tray /treɪ/ *noun* [C] **1** a flat piece of wood, plastic, metal, etc. with raised edges that you use for carrying food, drink, etc. on: *When she was ill in bed, he took her meals to her on a tray.* صينيّة

2 a shallow container in which you put papers, etc. on a desk طبق

treacherous /ˈtretʃərəs/ *adj* **1** that you cannot trust خائن، غادر

2 full of hidden danger: *The roads are treacherous this morning. There are icy patches.* غير مأمون

▸ **treachery** /ˈtretʃəri/ *noun* [U] the act of causing harm to sb/sth that trusts you خيانة، غَدْر

treacle /ˈtriːkl/ *noun* [U] a thick, dark, sticky liquid that is made from sugar ➲ Look at **syrup**. دِبس السُّكّر

tread /tred/ *verb* (*pt* **trod** /trɒd/; *pp* **trodden** /ˈtrɒdn/) **1** [I] to step or put your foot down: *Don't tread in the puddle!* ○ *He trod on my toe and didn't even say sorry!* ○ *(figurative) We must tread carefully or we'll offend him.* يمشي، يدوس

2 [T] **tread sth (in/down/out)** to press sth with your foot: *The cake crumbs had been trodden into the carpet.* ○ *She planted the seeds and trod the earth down.* يَدْعَس

3 [T] to walk on sth: *He walked down the path he had trodden so many times before.* يسير، يطرق

▸ **tread** *noun* **1** [sing.] the sound you make when you are walking: *the heavy tread of soldiers' boots* وقع (الأقدام)، مشية

2 [C,U] the raised pattern on the outside surface of a tyre مداس الإطار

treason /ˈtriːzn/ *noun* [U] the act of causing harm to your country, e.g. by helping its enemies خيانة

treasure /ˈtreʒə(r)/ *noun* **1** [C,U] a collection of very valuable objects, e.g.things made of gold, silver, etc: *to find buried treasure* كنز

2 [C] something that is very valuable: *the nation's art treasures* كنز

▸ **treasure** *verb* [T] to consider sb/sth to be very special or valuable: *I will treasure those memories forever.* يعز

ˈ**treasure hunt** *noun* [C] a game in which people try to find sth by following special signs (clues) (لعبة) البحث عن الكنز

treasurer /ˈtreʒərə(r)/ *noun* [C] the person who looks after the money that belongs to a club, an organization, etc. أمين الصندوق

treasury /ˈtreʒəri/ *noun* [sing., with sing. or pl. verb] **the Treasury** the government department that controls public money (وزارة) المالية

⚷ **treat** /triːt/ *verb* [T] **1** to act or behave towards sb/sth in a particular way: *Teenagers hate being treated like children.* ○ *You should treat older people with respect.* ○ *to treat sb badly, fairly, etc.* يعامل

2 treat sth as sth to consider sth in a particular way: *The bomb scare was not taken seriously. It was treated as a hoax.* يعتبر

3 to deal with or discuss sth: *This book treats the subject in great detail.* يعالج، يناقش

4 treat sb (for sth) to use medicine or medical care to try to make a sick or injured person well again: *a new drug to treat cancer* ○ *The boy was treated for burns at the hospital.* يعالج، يداوي

5 treat sth (with sth) to put a substance onto sth in order to protect it from damage: *Most vegetables are treated with insecticide.*

6 treat sb/yourself (to sth) to give sb/yourself sth that is very special or enjoyable: *Clare treated the children to an ice cream* (= she paid for them). يستضيف، يدعو إلى (أكلة لذيذة)

▸ **treat** *noun* [C] something that is very special or enjoyable: *I've brought some cream cakes as a treat for tea.* ○ *It's a real treat for me to stay in bed late.* متعة؛ شيء لذيذ

IDM trick or treat → TRICK

⚷ **treatment** /ˈtriːtmənt/ *noun* **1** [U] the way that you behave towards sb or deal with sth: *The treatment of the prisoners of war was very harsh.* معاملة

2 [C,U] the use of medicine or medical care to try to make a sick or injured person well again: *a new treatment for cancer* ○ *In Britain medical treatment is provided free on the NHS.* معالجة

3 [U,C] **treatment (for sth)** a process by which sth is cleaned, protected from damage, etc: *a sewage treatment plant* معاملة، معالجة، تنقية

treaty /ˈtriːti/ *noun* [C] (*pl.* **treaties**) a written agreement between two or more countries: *to sign a peace treaty* معاهدة

treble¹ /ˈtrebl/ *verb* [I,T] to become or to make sth three times bigger: *Prices have trebled in the past ten years.* يصبح أو يجعل ثلاثة أضعاف

▸ **treble** *det*: *This figure is treble the number five years ago.* ثلاثة أضعاف

treble² /ˈtrebl/ *noun* [C] **1** a high singing voice, especially that of a young boy صوت عالي الطبقة

2 a boy who has a high singing voice صبي له هذا الصوت

tree

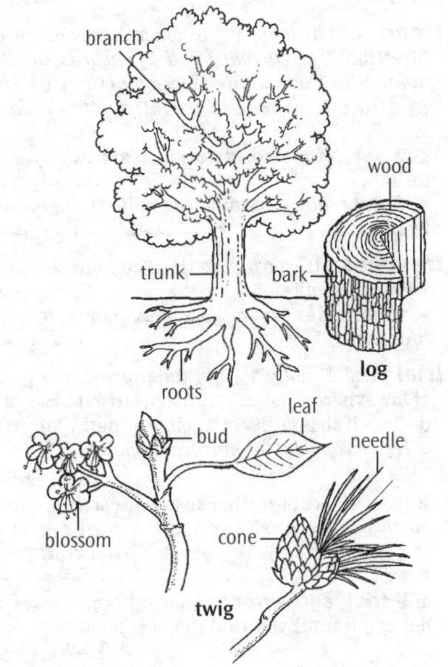

⚷ **tree** /triː/ *noun* [C] a tall plant with a thick wooden stem from which branches grow: *an oak tree* ○ *The house was surrounded by tall trees.* ○ *to climb a tree* ○ *to plant/cut down a tree* شجرة

The stem of a tree is called a **trunk**. The outer surface of this is **bark**. The **branches** grow out from the trunk. A tree may have **leaves** or **needles**. Look at **Christmas tree** and **family tree**.

trek /trek/ *noun* [C] a long hard journey, often on foot رحلة شاقة (على الأقدام)

▸ **trek** *verb* [I] (tre**kk**ing; tre**kk**ed) يقوم برحلة شاقة

tremble /ˈtrembl/ *verb* [I] to shake, e.g. because you are cold, frightened, weak, etc: *She was pale and trembling with shock.* ○ *His hand was trem-*

bling as he picked up his pen to sign. ○ *Sue's voice trembled with excitement.* يرتجف، يرتعش

▸ **tremble** *noun* [C, usually sing.]: *There was a tremble in his voice as he told them the sad news.* رَجْفة، رَعْشة

tremendous /trəˈmendəs/ *adj* **1** very large or great: *a tremendous amount of work* ○ *a tremendous difference* ○ *a tremendous explosion* ضَخْم، هائل

2 (*informal*) very good: *You were tremendous.* رائع

▸ **tremendously** *adv* very; very much: *tremendously exciting* ○ *Prices vary tremendously from one shop to another.* بدرجة هائلة

tremor /ˈtremə(r)/ *noun* [C] a slight shaking or trembling: *a tremor in his voice* ○ *an earth tremor* (= a small earthquake) رَجْفة، رَعْشة؛ هزّة

trench /trentʃ/ *noun* [C] a long narrow hole in the ground for water to flow along or for soldiers to hide in أُخْدود؛ خَنْدق

trend /trend/ *noun* [C] a general movement or direction: *The current trend is towards smaller families.* ○ *There is a trend for people to retire earlier.* ○ *He always followed the latest trends in fashion.* اتجاه، نَزْعة

IDM **set a/the trend** to start a new style or fashion يدخل زيّاً جديداً

▸ **trendy** *adj* (**trendier**; **trendiest**) (*informal*) fashionable حديث، مولع بأحدث الموضات

trespass /ˈtrespəs/ *verb* [I] to go onto sb's land without permission يتعدّى

▸ **trespasser** *noun* [C]: *Trespassers will be prosecuted.* المتَعدي، المتجاوز

trial /ˈtraɪəl/ *noun* **1** [C,U] the process in a court of law where a judge, etc. listens to evidence and decides if sb is guilty of a crime or not: *a fair trial* ○ *He was on trial for murder.* ○ *trial by jury* محاكمة

2 [C,U] an act of testing sb/sth: *New drugs must go through extensive trials.* ○ *a trial period of three months* ○ *We've got the car on trial for a week.* اختبار، تجريب

IDM **trial and error** trying different ways of doing sth until you find the best one (عن طريق) التجربة والخطأ

ˌtrial ˈrun *noun* [C] an occasion when you practise doing sth in order to make sure you can do it correctly later on تجربة، اختبار

triangle /ˈtraɪæŋgl/ *noun* [C] **1** a shape that has three straight sides and three angles: *a right-angled triangle* مثلّث

2 a metal musical instrument in the shape of a triangle that you play by hitting it with a metal stick مثلّث: آلة موسيقية

▸ **triangular** /traɪˈæŋgjələ(r)/ *adj* shaped like a triangle مثلّث الشكل

tribe /traɪb/ *noun* [C] a group of people that have the same language and customs and that are ruled by a chief or chiefs: *the Zulu tribes of South Africa* قبيلة

▸ **tribal** /ˈtraɪbl/ *adj*: *tribal dances* قَبَلي

tribunal /traɪˈbjuːnl/ *noun* [C] a court or group of officials who have the authority to decide who is right in particular types of dispute: *an industrial tribunal* محكمة، هيئة تحكيم

tributary /ˈtrɪbjətri; *US* -teri/ *noun* [C] (*pl.* **tributaries**) a river or stream that flows into a larger river رافد

tribute /ˈtrɪbjuːt/ *noun* **1** [C,U] something that you say or do to show that you respect or admire sb/sth: *A special concert was held as a tribute to the composer on his 80th birthday.* تكريم، تقدير

2 [sing.] **a tribute (to sth)** a sign of how good sb/sth is: *The success of the festival is a tribute to the organizers.* إشادة بكفاءته

IDM **pay tribute to sb/sth** → PAY[2]

trick /trɪk/ *noun* [C] **1** something that you do to deceive sb, in order to make him/her look stupid or to cheat him/her: *The children played a trick on the teacher.* ○ *The thieves got into the house by a trick.* حِيلة

2 a clever or the best way of doing sth: *I can't get the top off this jar. Is there a trick to it?* حيلة، وسيلة

3 an act that uses special skills to make people believe sth which is not true: *The magician performed a trick in which he made a rabbit disappear.* خِدْعة

IDM **do the job/trick** → JOB

trick or treat a tradition in which children dressed as witches, etc. go to people's houses at Halloween. The children may do sth bad to you if you do not give them sweets, money, etc. مناسبة يتنكّر فيها الأطفال ويطلبون الهدايا

▸ **trick** *verb* [T] to deceive sb in order to make him/her do or believe sth: *He tricked me into lending him money.* ○ *Stella was tricked out of her share of the money.* يَخْدَع، يَغُشّ

trickery /-əri/ *noun* [U] the use of a trick (1) in order to deceive sb خِداع، احتيال

trickle /ˈtrɪkl/ *verb* [I] (used about a liquid) to flow in a thin stream: *Tears trickled down his cheek.* ○ (*figurative*) *At first no one came, but then people began to trickle in.* يَقْطُر

▸ **trickle** *noun* [C]: *The stream was only a trickle.* ○ (*figurative*) *The flood of refugees had been reduced to a trickle.* مجرى قليل الماء؛ عدد ضئيل

tricky *adj* (**trickier**; **trickiest**) difficult to do or deal with: *a tricky situation* عويص

tricycle /ˈtraɪsɪkl/ (*also informal* **trike**) *noun* [C] a bicycle that has one wheel at the front and two at the back درّاجة بثلاث عجلات

trifle /ˈtraɪfl/ *noun* **1** [C] something that is of little value or importance تافه، زهيد (القيمة)

2 [C,U] a type of cold dessert made from cake with fruit in jelly covered with custard and cream نوع من الحلواء

IDM **a trifle** (*formal*) rather: *It's a trifle odd that they didn't phone.* بعض الشيء

trigger /ˈtrɪgə(r)/ *noun* [C] the piece of metal that you press to fire a gun: *to pull the trigger* زناد

▸ **trigger** *verb* [T] **trigger sth (off)** to cause sth

to start or happen: *The smoke from her cigarette triggered the fire alarm.* يثير؛ يطلق

trike /traɪk/ *noun* [C] (*informal*) = TRICYCLE

🔑 **trillion** /'trɪljən/ *number* one million million مليون مليون

trilogy /'trɪlədʒi/ *noun* [C] (*pl.* **trilogies**) a group of three books, plays, etc. that form one set ثلاثيّة

trim¹ /trɪm/ *adj* **1** in good order; tidy أنيق، مرتّب

2 not fat: *a trim figure* غير سمين، رشيق

trim² /trɪm/ *verb* [T] (trim**m**ing; trim**m**ed) **1** to cut sth so that it is neat and tidy: *to trim a beard* يشذّب

2 trim sth (off sth/off) to cut sth off because you do not need it: *Trim the fat off the meat.* يزيل

3 trim sth (with sth) to decorate the edge of sth with sth: *a skirt trimmed with lace* يزيّن طرفه

▸ **trim** *noun* [C, usually sing.] an act of cutting sth in order to make it neat and tidy: *My hair needs a trim.* تشذيب

trimming *noun* **1** [C,U] material that you use for decorating the edge of sth زخرفة على الأطراف

2 trimmings [plural] extra things which you add to sth to improve its appearance, taste, etc: *turkey with all the trimmings* ملحقات (للتحسين)

trinity /'trɪnəti/ *noun* [sing.] **the Trinity** (in the Christian religion) the three forms of God: the Father, Jesus the Son and the Holy Spirit الثالوث الأقدس

trio /'triːəʊ/ *noun* (*pl.* **trios**) **1** [C, with sing. or pl. verb] a group of three people who play music or sing together ثلاثي (موسيقي)

2 [C] a piece of music for three people to play or sing قطعة موسيقية (يؤديها ثلاثة موسيقيين)

🔑 **trip** /trɪp/ *verb* (trip**p**ing; trip**p**ed) **1** [I] **trip (over/up)** to knock your foot against sth when you are walking and fall or nearly fall over: *Don't leave your bag on the floor. Someone might trip over it.* ○ *She caught her foot in the root of a tree and tripped up.* يعثر، تزلّ قدمه

2 [T] **trip sb (up)** to cause sb to fall or nearly fall over: *Lee stuck out his foot and tripped John up.* يعثّر، يوقع

PHR V **trip (sb) up** to make a mistake; to make sb say sth that he/she did not want to say: *The journalist asked a difficult question to try to trip the Minister up.* يزلّ؛ يوقعه في الخطأ؛ يزلّ لسانه

▸ **trip** *noun* [C] a journey during which you visit a place and return: *a trip to the mountains* ○ *a business trip to Brussels* ➲ Look at the note at **travel**. رحلة

tripper *noun* [C]: *Brighton was full of day trippers from London.* زائر

triple /'trɪpl/ *adj* **1** made up of three parts: *the triple jump* ثلاثي

2 happening three times or containing three times as much as usual: *a triple world champion* (= one who has won three times) ○ *a triple portion* ثلاث مرّات؛ ثلاثي

▸ **triple** *verb* [I,T] to make sth, or to become, three times greater يضاعف ثلاث مرات

triplet /'trɪplət/ *noun* [C] one of three children or animals that are born to one mother at the same time ➲ Look at **twin**. أحد توائم ثلاثة

tripod /'traɪpɒd/ *noun* [C] a piece of equipment with three legs that you use for putting a camera, etc. on حامل ذو ثلاث قوائم

triumph /'traɪʌmf/ *noun* [C,U] success, especially in a competition or battle; the feeling of joy that you have because of this: *The soldiers returned home in triumph.* ○ *The fans gave a shout of triumph.* ○ *Putting a man on the moon was one of the triumphs of the twentieth century.* نصر؛ فرحة النصر

▸ **triumph** *verb* [I] **triumph (over sb/sth)** to achieve success; to defeat sb/sth: *Hull triumphed over Stoke in the championship.* ○ *Although he was blind, he triumphed over his disability to become an MP.* ينتصر، يهزم

triumphant /traɪ'ʌmfənt/ *adj* feeling or showing great happiness because you have won or succeeded at sth: *a triumphant cheer* مبتهج بالنصر

triumphantly *adv* بمباهاة (المنتصر)

trivial /'trɪviəl/ *adj* of little importance تافه، لا يؤبه له

▸ **triviality** /,trɪvi'æləti/ *noun* [C,U] (*pl.* **trivialities**) تفاهة

trivialize (*also* **trivialise**) /'trɪviəlaɪz/ *verb* [T] to make sth seem unimportant يُتَفِّه (الشيء)، يقلّل من قيمته

trod *pt of* TREAD

trodden *pp of* TREAD

trolleys

shopping trolley   luggage trolley

trolley /'trɒli/ *noun* [C] (*pl.* **trolleys**) a cart on wheels that you use for carrying things: *a supermarket trolley* عربة يد صغيرة لنقل الحاجيات مثلاً

trombone /trɒm'bəʊn/ *noun* [C] a large brass musical instrument that you play by blowing into it and moving a long tube backwards and forwards ترمبون: آلة موسيقية

troop /truːp/ *noun* **1** [C] a large group of people or animals جماعة

2 troops [plural] soldiers جنود

▸ **troop** *verb* [I] to move in a large group: *When the bell rang everyone trooped from one classroom to another.* يحتشد

trophy /'trəʊfi/ *noun* [C] (*pl.* **trophies**) a silver cup, etc. that you get for winning a competition or race جائزة المباراة أو السباق

tropic /ˈtrɒpɪk/ *noun* **1** [C, usually sing.] one of the two lines of latitude that are 23° 27´ north and south of the equator: *the tropic of Cancer* ○ *the tropic of Capricorn* مدار

2 the tropics [plural] the part of the world that is between these two lines, where the climate is hot المنطقة الاستوائية

▸ **tropical** /-kl/ *adj*: *tropical fruit* ○ *tropical rainforest* استوائي

trot /trɒt/ *verb* (trotting; trotted) [I] (used about a horse) to move fairly quickly, lifting the feet quite high off the ground: (*figurative*) *The child trotted along behind his father.* يَخُبّ (في سيره)، يهرول

PHR V **trot sth out** (*informal*) to repeat an old idea rather than thinking of sth new to say: *to trot out the same old story* يكرّر

▸ **trot** *noun* [sing.] the speed that a horse goes when it is trotting; a ride at this speed خَبَب؛ ركوب الحصان خَبَباً

IDM **on the trot** (*informal*) one after another; without a break: *We worked for six hours on the trot.* على التوالي؛ بلا انقطاع

trouble /ˈtrʌbl/ *noun* **1** [C,U] (a situation that causes) problems, difficulty, worry, etc: *If I don't get home by 11 o'clock I'll be in trouble.* ○ *I'm having trouble getting the car started.* ○ *financial troubles* ○ *It's a very good school. The only trouble is it's rather a long way away.* مشكلة، صعوبة

2 [sing., U] extra work or effort: *Let's eat out tonight. It will save you the trouble of cooking.* ○ *Why don't you stay the night with us. It's no trouble.* ○ *I'm sorry to put you to so much trouble.* عناء، تعب

3 [C,U] a situation where people are fighting or arguing with each other: *There's often trouble in town on a Saturday night.* مشاجرة، مشاحنة

4 [U] illness or pain: *I've got back trouble again.* علّة، ألم

IDM **ask for trouble** → ASK

get into trouble to get into a situation which is dangerous or in which you may be punished يتورّط في مشكلة (خطيرة)

go to a lot of trouble (to do sth) to put a lot of work or effort into sth: *They went to a lot of trouble to make us feel welcome.* يبْذُل جهده

take trouble over sth/with sth/to do sth/doing sth to do sth with care يبْذُل عناية (في عمل الشيء)

take the trouble to do sth to do sth even though it means extra work or effort: *He took the trouble to write and thank everyone for his presents.* يتجشّم (عناء)

▸ **trouble** *verb* [T] **1** to cause sb worry, problems, etc. يقْلِق، يزْعِج (بالمشاكل)

2 trouble sb for sth (*formal*) (used when you are politely asking sb for sth or to do sth): *I'm sorry to trouble you, but would you mind answering a few questions?* ○ *Could I trouble you for some change?* يزْعِج

troublesome /-səm/ *adj* that causes trouble (1) مزْعِج

troublemaker /ˈtrʌblmeɪkə(r)/ *noun* [C] a person who often causes trouble (1,3) شخص مثير للمتاعب، مشاغب

trough /trɒf; *US* trɔːf/ *noun* [C] **1** a long narrow container from which farm animals eat or drink مِذْوَد، معلف؛ حوض

2 a low area or point between two higher areas: *a trough of low pressure* مُنْخَفَض

trousers /ˈtraʊzəz/ (*US* **pants**) *noun* [plural] a piece of clothing that covers both legs and reaches from your waist to your ankles بنطلون، سروال

Note that, because **trousers** is a plural word, we cannot say, for example, 'a new trouser'. The following are possible: *I need some new trousers.* ○ *I need a new pair of trousers.* Before another noun the form **trouser** is used: *a trouser leg.*

trout /traʊt/ *noun* [C,U] (*pl.* **trout**) a type of fish that lives in rivers and that is eaten as food سمك التروتة

trowel /ˈtraʊəl/ *noun* [C] **1** a small tool with a flat blade, used for spreading cement, plaster, etc. ملعقة البنّاء، مالَج أو مسْطَرين

2 a small garden tool with a curved blade for lifting plants, digging holes, etc. مقحفة البستاني، مالَج تشتيل

truant /ˈtruːənt/ *noun* [C] a pupil who stays away from school without permission طالب متغيّب

IDM **play truant** to stay away from school without permission يتغيّب (الطالب) بدون إذن

▸ **truancy** /-ənsi/ *noun* [U]: *Truancy is on the increase in some schools.* تغيّب (الطلاب)

truce /truːs/ *noun* [C] an agreement to stop fighting for a period of time ➲ Look at **ceasefire**. هُدْنة

truck /trʌk/ *noun* [C] **1** (*especially US*) = LORRY

2 (*Brit*) an open railway wagon that is used for carrying goods عربة بضاعة في قطار

3 (in compounds) a large heavy vehicle, used for a particular purpose: *a forklift truck* شاحنة

trudge /trʌdʒ/ *verb* [I] to walk with slow, heavy steps, e.g. because you are very tired يمشي بتراخ وإجهاد

true /truː/ *adj* **1** that really happened: *The novel was based on a true story.* حقيقي

2 right or correct; agreeing with fact: *Is it true that Adam is leaving?* ○ *I didn't think the film was at all true to life* (= it didn't show life as it really is). ○ *Read the statements and decide if they are true or false.* صحيح

3 real or genuine: *How do you know when you have found true love?* ○ *the true value of the house* مخْلص؛ حقيقي

4 true (to sth) behaving as expected or as promised: *to be true to your word* (= to do what you promised) صادق، مخْلِص

ℹ The noun is **truth**.

IDM **come true** to happen in the way you hoped

or dreamed: *My dream has come true!* يتحقّق (طبقاً لرغبة الشخص)

true to form typical; as usual: *True to form, Carol started organizing everything straight away.* كما هو متوقّع، كالعادة

truly /ˈtruːli/ *adv* **1** really: *We are truly grateful to you for your help.* ○ *'I'm sorry, truly I am,' he whispered.* حقّاً

2 completely: *With her passport in her hand she at last felt truly American.* تماماً

3 expressing the truth: *I cannot truly say that I was surprised at the news.* حقّاً، صدقاً

Yours truly is often used at the end of a formal letter, especially in American English.

IDM **well and truly** → WELL[1]

trump /trʌmp/ *noun* [C] (in some card games) a card of the suit that has a higher value than the other three suits during a particular game: *Spades are trumps.* ورقة لعب رابحة

ˈ**trump card** *noun* [C] a special advantage that you keep secret until the last moment ورقة رابحة

trumpet /ˈtrʌmpɪt/ *noun* [C] a brass musical instrument that you play by blowing into it. There are three buttons on it which you can press to make different notes. بوق

truncheon /ˈtrʌntʃən/ (*also* **baton**) *noun* [C] (*especially Brit*) a short thick stick that a police officer carries as a weapon هراوة، عصا الشرطيّ

trundle /ˈtrʌndl/ *verb* **1** [I] to move slowly: *A lorry trundled down the hill.* يتحرّك ببطء

2 [T] to push or pull sth along slowly on wheels يدحرج على عجلات

trunk /trʌŋk/ *noun* **1** [C] the thick main stem of a tree جذع، ساق

2 [C] the main part of your body (= not including your head, arms and legs) بدن، جذع

3 [C] a large box, like a large suitcase, that you use for storing or transporting things صندوق

4 [C] an elephant's long nose خُرْطوم (الفيل)

5 trunks [plural] short trousers that men or boys wear when they go swimming سروال سباحة (للرجال)

6 [C] (*US*) = BOOT (2)

trust[1] /trʌst/ *noun* **1** [U] **trust (in sb/sth)** the feeling that you have when you know that you can rely on sb/sth to do what he/she/it is supposed to do: *Our marriage is based on love and trust.* ○ *I put my trust in him, but he failed me.* ثقة

2 [U] responsibility: *As a teacher you are in a position of trust.* ائتمان؛ مسؤوليّة

3 [C,U] an arrangement by which a person or an organization looks after money and property for sb else: *The money was put into a trust for the children.* رعاية، وصاية

IDM **on trust** without having proof; without checking: *I can't prove it. You must take it on trust.* على الثقة، دون تحقيق أو دليل

▶ **trustworthy** *adj* that you can trust جدير بالثقة

trust[2] /trʌst/ *verb* [T] to believe that you can rely on sb/sth to do what he/she/it is supposed to do; to believe that sb/sth will not harm you: *He said the car was safe but I just don't trust him.* ○ *Can I trust you to behave sensibly while I am out?* ○ *You can't trust her with money.* ○ *She is not to be trusted with money.* ○ *I don't trust that dog. It looks dangerous.* يثق بـ، يعتمد على

IDM **Trust sb (to do sth)** It is typical of sb to do sth: *Trust Alice to be late. She's never on time!* تأكّد أنّ، لا شكّ أنه (سيفعل ذلك)

▶ **trusting** *adj* having or showing trust واثق، صدّيق

trustee /trʌˈstiː/ *noun* [C] a person who looks after money or property for sb else وصيّ، قيّم

truth /truːθ/ *noun* (*pl.* **truths** /truːðz/) **1** [U] the state or quality of being true: *There's a lot of truth in what she says.* الصحّة، الحقيقة

2 [sing.] what is true: *Please tell me the truth.* ○ *the whole truth* حقيقة

3 [C] a fact or an idea that is true: *scientific truths* حقيقة

▶ **truthful** /-fl/ *adj* **1** true or correct: *a truthful account* صادق، صحيح

2 (used about a person) who tells the truth; honest صادق، أمين

truthfully /-fəli/ *adv* بصدق

try[1] /traɪ/ *verb* (*pres part* **trying**; *3rd pers sing pres* **tries**; *pt, pp* **tried**) **1** [I] to make an effort to do sth: *I tried to phone you but I couldn't get through.* ○ *She was trying hard not to laugh.* ○ *to try your best/hardest* ○ *I'm sure you can do it if you try.* يحاول

Try and is more informal than **try to**. It cannot be used in the past tense: *I'll try to get there on time.* ○ *(informal) I'll try and get there on time.* ○ *I tried to get there on time, but I was too late.*

2 [T] to do, use or test sth in order to see how good or successful it is: *'I've tried everything but I can't get the baby to sleep.' 'Have you tried taking her out in the pram?'* ○ *Have you ever tried raw fish?* ○ *We tried the door but it was locked.* ○ *He tried several bookshops but none of them stocked the books he wanted.* يجرّب

3 [T] to examine sb in a court of law in order to decide if he/she is guilty of a crime or not: *He was tried for murder.* يحاكِم

PHR V **try sth on** to put on a piece of clothing to see if it fits you properly: *Can I try these jeans on, please?* يقيس أو يجرّب ثوباً

try sb/sth out to test sb/sth by using him/her/it يختبر

▶ **trying** *adj* that makes you tired or angry: *a trying journey* شاق؛ مثير للضيق

try[2] /traɪ/ *noun* [C] (*pl.* **tries**) an occasion when you make an effort to do sth; an attempt: *I don't know if I can move it by myself, but I'll give it a try.* مسعى، محاولة

ˈ**T-shirt** (*also* **tee shirt**) *noun* [C] a shirt with

short sleeves and without buttons or a collar قميص قطني بكُمّين قصيرَين

tsp *abbrev* (*pl.* **tsp** or **tsps**) = TEASPOONFUL(S)

tsunami /tsuːˈnɑːmi/ *noun* [C] an extremely large wave in the sea caused, for example, by an earthquake موجة عاتية

tub /tʌb/ *noun* [C] **1** a large round container with a flat bottom and no lid: *On the terrace there were several tubs with flowers in them.* حوض

2 a small plastic container with a lid that is used for holding food: *a tub of margarine, ice cream, etc.* علبة، وعاء

tuba /ˈtjuːbə; *US* ˈtuː-/ *noun* [C] a large brass musical instrument that makes a low sound التُّوبا: آلة تشبه البوق

tube /tjuːb; *US* tuːb/ *noun* **1** [C] a long hollow pipe made of glass, metal, rubber, etc: *Blood flowed along the tube into the bottle.* ○ *the inner tube of a bicycle tyre* ➲ Look at **test tube**. أنبوب

2 [C] a long thin soft container with a cap at one end made of plastic or metal. Tubes are used for holding soft substances such as toothpaste and you squeeze them to get the substance out. أنبوبة

3 (*Brit informal*) = UNDERGROUND

▸ **tubing** *noun* [U] a long piece of metal, rubber, etc. in the shape of a tube أنبوب معدني أو مطّاطي الخ

tuberculosis /tjuːˌbɜːkjuˈləʊsɪs; *US* tuː-/ *noun* [U] (*abbr* **TB**) a serious disease that especially affects the lungs السُّل، التدرّن الرئوي

TUC /ˌtiː juː ˈsiː/ *abbrev* Trades Union Congress; the association of British trades unions مؤتمر نقابات العمال

tuck /tʌk/ *verb* [T] **1** to put or fold the ends or edges of sth into or round sth else so that it looks tidy: *Tuck your shirt in – it looks untidy like that.* ○ *He tucked the blanket round the old man's knees.* يدْخِل (طرف الثوب مثلاً)، يلفّ

2 to put sth away tidily or in a safe or hidden place: *He tucked his wallet away in his inside pocket.* ○ *The letter was tucked behind a pile of books.* يَدُس

PHRV **tuck sth away** (*informal*) **1** to store sth: *They've got a lot of money tucked away.* يَدّخِر

2 to hide sth: *Their house is tucked away behind the church.* يخْفي؛ يَختَفي

tuck into sth; **tuck in** (*informal*) (*especially Brit*) to eat with pleasure يأكل بشهِيّة

Tuesday /ˈtjuːzdeɪ; *US* ˈtuː-/ *noun* [C,U] (*abbr* **Tue.**; **Tues.**) the day of the week after Monday and before Wednesday ❶ For examples of the use of the days of the week in sentences, look at **Monday**. يوم الثُّلاثاء

tuft /tʌft/ *noun* [C] a small bunch of hair, grass, etc. خُصْلة؛ حزمة

tug /tʌɡ/ *verb* [I,T] (tu**gg**ing; tu**gg**ed) to pull sth hard and quickly يَجْذب بشدة

▸ **tug** *noun* [C] **1** a sudden hard pull: *She gave the rope a tug.* جَذْبة شديدة

2 (*also* **tugboat** /ˈtʌɡbəʊt/) a small strong boat that is used for pulling larger ships into a harbour زورق قَطْر أو سحب

tuition /tjuˈɪʃn; *US* tuː-/ *noun* [U] (*formal*) teaching, especially to a small group of people: *private tuition in Italian* ○ *tuition fees* تدريس، تعليم

tulip /ˈtjuːlɪp; *US* ˈtuː-/ *noun* [C] a brightly-coloured flower, shaped like a small cup, that grows from a bulb in the spring خزامى، توليب

tumble /ˈtʌmbl/ *verb* [I] **1** to fall suddenly in a heavy way, without control: *He tripped and tumbled all the way down the steps.* يهوي، يكبّ (على وجهه)

2 (used about prices, etc.) to become lower: *Hotel prices have tumbled.* يتدهور، ينخفض

3 to move in a particular direction in an untidy way: *I got undressed and tumbled into bed.* ○ *She opened her suitcase and all her things tumbled out of it.* يتعثر، ينْطرح

PHRV **tumble down** to fall down; to collapse: *The walls of the old house were tumbling down.* يتهاوى

▸ **tumble** *noun* [C] a sudden fall سَقْطة

ˌtumble ˈdryer (*also* **ˌtumble-ˈdrier**) *noun* [C] a machine that dries clothes by moving them about in hot air آلة لتجفيف الملابس

tumbler /ˈtʌmblə(r)/ *noun* [C] a drinking glass with straight sides that has no handle or stem كأس

tummy /ˈtʌmi/ *noun* [C] (*pl.* **tummies**) (*informal*) = STOMACH: *I've got (a) tummy ache.*

tumour (*US* **tumor**) /ˈtjuːmə(r); *US* ˈtuː-/ *noun* [C] a mass of diseased cells that are growing abnormally in the body: *a brain tumour* ورم

tumultuous /tjuːˈmʌltʃuəs; *US* tuː-/ *adj* very noisy, because people are excited: *a tumultuous welcome* صاخِب

tuna /ˈtjuːnə; *US* ˈtuːnə/ *noun* (*pl.* **tuna**) **1** [C] a large sea fish سمك التُّونة أو الطون

2 [U] (*also* **ˈtuna fish**) the flesh of this fish, which is often sold in tins التُّونة أو الطون

tune /tjuːn; *US* tuːn/ *noun* [C,U] a series of musical notes that are arranged in a pleasant pattern: *The children played us a tune on their recorders.* ○ *I can't remember the tune of that song.* ○ *a signature tune* (= one that is always played at the beginning of a TV or radio performance) ○ *Some people complain that modern music has no tune to it.* نَغْمة، لحن

IDM **change your tune** → CHANGE[1]

in/out of tune 1 at/not at the correct musical level (pitch): *You're singing out of tune.* بانسجام/من غير انسجام مع الآخرين

2 in/not in agreement with sb/sth: *The President doesn't seem to be in tune with what ordinary people are thinking.* متّفِق/غير متّفق

▸ **tune** *verb* [T] **1** to adjust a musical instrument so that it is at the correct musical level (pitch) يدوزِن (أوتار الآلة)، يناغم

2 to adjust an engine so that it runs well يَضْبِط

IDM **tuned (in) to sth** listening to a particular

radio station: *Stay tuned to this station for the latest news.* يستمع (لإذاعة)

PHRV tune in (to sth) to move the controls of a radio or television so that you can listen to or watch a particular station يَضْبِط (المحرِّك)

tune up to adjust a group of musical instruments so that they play together in tune يؤالف، يناغِم

tuneful /-fl/ *adj* (used about music) pleasant to listen to رخيم، متآلف النغمات

tunic /ˈtjuːnɪk; *US* ˈtuː-/ *noun* [C] **1** the jacket that is part of the uniform of a policeman, soldier, etc. سُترة الشرطي أو الجندي الخ

2 a piece of loose clothing without sleeves that is like a dress ثوب واسع دون كمّين

🔑 **tunnel** /ˈtʌnl/ *noun* [C] a passage under the ground or sea, river, etc: *The train disappeared into a tunnel.* ○ *the Channel Tunnel* نفق

▸ **tunnel** *verb* [I,T] (tunnelling; tunnelled; *US* tunneling; tunneled) to dig a tunnel يحفِر نفقاً

turban /ˈtɜːbən/ *noun* [C] a covering for the head worn by men. A turban is made by wrapping a long piece of cloth around the head. عِمامة

turbine /ˈtɜːbaɪn/ *noun* [C] a machine or an engine that receives its power from a wheel that is turned by the pressure of water, air or gas توربينة

turbulent /ˈtɜːbjələnt/ *adj* **1** in a state of disorder and confusion when things are changing fast هائج، مضطرب

2 (used about water or air) moving in a violent way هائج

turf /tɜːf/ *noun* [U] short thick grass and the layer of soil underneath it خضير: العشب وطبقة التربة تحته

▸ **turf** *verb* [T] to cover ground with turf تغطية الأرض بطبقة عشب

PHRV turf sb out (of sth) (*Brit informal*) to force sb/sth to leave a place يطرد (من مكان)، يزيح

turkey /ˈtɜːki/ *noun* [C,U] (*pl.* **turkeys**) a large bird that is kept on farms. Turkeys are usually eaten at Christmas in Britain and at Thanksgiving in the US. ديك رومي

turmoil /ˈtɜːmɔɪl/ *noun* [C, usually sing., U] a state of great excitement, noise or confusion هيجان

🔑 **turn**[1] /tɜːn/ *verb* **1** [I] to move or go round a fixed point: *The wheels turned faster and faster.* يدور

2 [T] to hold and move sth round a central point; to make sth go round: *She turned the handle on the door.* ○ *Turn the steering wheel to the right.* يُدير

3 [I] to change your position so that you are facing in a different direction: *He turned round when he heard my voice.* يستدير

4 [T] to change the position of sth: *I turned the box upside down.* ○ *He turned the page and started the next chapter.* يقلِب

5 [I,T] to change direction when you are moving: *Go straight on and turn left at the church.* ○ *The car turned the corner.* ○ *He turned the lorry into the yard.* يستدير: يدير

6 [I,T] (to cause sb/sth) to become: *He turned very red when I asked him about the money.* ○ *The fairy waved her wand and the prince turned into a frog.* ○ *She turned him into a frog.* يتحوّل: يحوِّل

ℹ For expressions with **turn**, look at the noun and adjective entries, e.g. for **turn a blind eye**, look at **blind**.

PHRV turn away to stop looking at sb/sth: *She turned away in horror at the sight of the blood.* يشيح بوجهه

turn sb away to refuse to allow a person to go into a place يمنع (من دخول مكان)

turn back to go back in the same direction as you came يعود

turn sb/sth down to refuse an offer, etc. or the person who makes it: *Why did you turn that job down?* ○ *He asked her to marry him, but she turned him down.* يرفض

turn sth down to reduce the sound or heat that sth produces: *Turn the television down!* يخفّض

turn off (sth) to leave one road and go on another: *We turn off the motorway at junction 10.* يفارق

turn sth off to move the switch, etc. on a piece of machinery, etc. to stop it working: *He turned the TV off.* يقفل، يطفئ (النور)

turn sth on to move the switch, etc. on a piece of machinery, etc. to start it working: *Turn the lights on!* يفتح، يشعل (النور)

turn out (for sth) to be present or appear for sth: *Thousands of people turned out to welcome the team home.* يحضر

turn out (to be sth) to be sth in the end: *The weather turned out fine.* ○ *The house that they had promised us turned out to be a tiny flat.* يصبح: يتضح في نهاية الأمر

turn sth out to move the switch, etc. on a light so that it is no longer shining: *Turn the lights out before you go to bed.* يطفئ

turn over 1 to change position so that the other side is facing out or upwards: *He turned over and went back to sleep.* ينقلب

2 (used about an engine) to start or to continue to run يدور، يلف

3 (*Brit*) to change to another programme when you are watching TV يحوِّل

turn sth over 1 to make sth change position so that the other side is facing out or upwards: *You may now turn over your exam papers and begin.* يقلب

2 to keep thinking about sth carefully: *She kept turning over what he'd said in her mind.* يفكر ملياً

turn to sb to go to sb to get help يطلب مساعدته

turn to sth to find a page in a book: *Turn to page 45.* يفتح (صفحة في كتاب)

turn up 1 to arrive: *What time did they finally turn up?* يصل

2 to be found: *I lost my glasses a week ago and they haven't turned up yet.* يعثر عليه

turn sth up to increase the sound or heat that sth produces: *Turn the heating up – it's freezing!* يرفع، يزيد

🔑 **turn**[2] /tɜːn/ *noun* [C] **1** an act of turning sb/sth round: *Give the screw another couple of turns to make sure it is really tight.* دورة

2 a change of direction: *to make a left/right turn* ○ *a U-turn* (= when you turn round and go back in the opposite direction) استدارة

3 a bend or corner in a road, river, etc: *Take the next turn on the left.* منعطف

4 [usually sing.] the time when you must or may do sth: *Please wait in the queue until it is your turn.* دور

5 a change: *The patient's condition has taken a turn for the worse.* تحوّل

IDM do sb a good/bad turn to do sth helpful/unhelpful for sb يساعد/لا يساعد شخصاً

in turn one after the other: *I spoke to each of the children in turn.* على التعاقب

take turns (at sth) to do sth one after the other: *You can't both play on the computer at the same time. You'll have to take turns.* بالتناوب

wait your turn → WAIT[1]

turning /ˈtɜːnɪŋ/ *noun* [C] a place where one road joins or leads off from another: *Take the third turning on the right.* مُنعطَف

▶ **ˈturning point** *noun* [C] a time when an important change happens لحظة حاسمة، نقطة تحوّل

turnip /ˈtɜːnɪp/ *noun* [C,U] a round white vegetable that grows under the ground لِفت

ˈturn-off *noun* [C] the point where a road leads away from a larger or more important one: *This is the turn-off for York.* مُنعرَج، مفرق

turnout /ˈtɜːnaʊt/ *noun* [C, usually sing.] the number of people who go to a meeting, match, etc. الحضور (في اجتماع مثلاً)

turnover /ˈtɜːnəʊvə(r)/ *noun* [sing.] **1** the amount of business that a company does in a particular period of time دورة رأس المال، مقدار المبيعات

2 the rate at which workers leave a company and are replaced by new ones: *a high turnover of staff* معدّل استبدال العمّال

turnstile /ˈtɜːnstaɪl/ *noun* [C] a gate that goes round and that allows one person at a time to enter a place باب دوّار

turpentine /ˈtɜːpəntaɪn/ *noun* [U] a clear liquid with a strong smell that you use for removing paint or for making paint thinner زيت التربنتين

turquoise /ˈtɜːkwɔɪz/ *adj, noun* [U] (of) a greenish-blue colour اللون الفيروزي

turret /ˈtʌrət/ *noun* [C] a small tower on the top of another tower برج صغير

turtle /ˈtɜːtl/ *noun* [C] **1** a reptile with a soft body and a thick shell that lives in the sea سلَحفاة بحريّة

2 (*US*) = TORTOISE

tusk /tʌsk/ *noun* [C] one of the two very long pointed teeth of an elephant, etc. ❶ Elephants' tusks are made of **ivory**. ناب (الفيل مثلاً)

tussle /ˈtʌsl/ *noun* [C] (*informal*) a rough fight, e. g. between two or more people who want to have the same thing صراع، مشادّة

tut /tʌt/ (*also* ˌ**tut-ˈtut**) *interj* the way of writing the sound that people make when they think that sth is bad, foolish, etc. عبارة استهجان

tutor /ˈtjuːtə(r); *US* ˈtuː-/ *noun* [C] **1** a private teacher who teaches one person or a very small group معلّم خصوصي

2 (*Brit*) a teacher who is responsible for a small group of pupils at school, or students at college or university. A tutor advises students on their work or helps them if they have problems in their private life. Sometimes tutors teach small groups. معلّم خصوصي، موجّه

▶ **tutorial** /tjuːˈtɔːriəl; *US* tuː-/ *noun* [C] a lesson given by a tutor (2) to a student or a small group of students درس خصوصي

ˈtutor group *noun* [C] a class in school: *She's in my tutor group at school.* صفّ، فصل

tuxedo /tʌkˈsiːdəʊ/ *noun* [C] (*pl.* **tuxedos** /-dəʊz/) (*also informal* **tux**) (*US*) = DINNER JACKET

TV /ˌtiː ˈviː/ *abbrev* = TELEVISION (SET)

twang /twæŋ/ *noun* [C] the sound that you make when you pull a tight string or wire and then let it go رنّة أو ونّة

▶ **twang** *verb* [I,T] يرن

tweed /twiːd/ *noun* [U] thick woollen cloth with a rough surface التويد: نسيج صوفي خشن

tweet /twiːt/ *noun* [C] **1** the short high sound made by a small bird زقزقة

2 a message sent using the Twitter social networking service رسالة عبر موقع "تويتر" الاجتماعي

tweezers /ˈtwiːzəz/ *noun* [plural] a small tool consisting of two pieces of metal that are joined at one end. You use tweezers for picking up or pulling out very small things: *a pair of tweezers* منتاف، ملقَط

🔑 **twelve** /twelv/ *number* 12; one more than eleven ➲ Look at **dozen**. For examples of how to use numbers in sentences, look at **six**. إثنا عشَر

▶ **twelfth** /twelfθ/ *pron, det, adv* 12th; next after eleventh ➲ Look at the examples at **sixth**. الثاني عشَر؛ جزء من إثني عشَر

🔑 **twenty** /ˈtwenti/ *number* 20; one more than nineteen ❶ For examples of how to use numbers in sentences, look at **sixty**. عشرون

▶ **twentieth** /ˈtwentiəθ/ *pron, det, adv* 20th; next after nineteenth ➲ Look at the examples at **sixth**. العشرون؛ جزء من عشرين

🔑 **twice** /twaɪs/ *adv* two times: *I've been to Egypt twice – once last year and once in 1999.* ○ *The film will be shown twice daily.* ○ *Take the medicine twice a day.* ○ *Prices have risen twice as fast in this country as in Japan.* مرّتان، ضعفان

twiddle /ˈtwɪdl/ *verb* [I,T] to keep turning or moving sth with your fingers يعبث أو يفتل بأصابعه

twig /twɪɡ/ *noun* [C] a small thin branch on a tree or bush غصين

twilight /ˈtwaɪlaɪt/ *noun* [U] the time after the sun has set and before it gets completely dark شفَق، غسَق

🔑 **twin** /twɪn/ *noun* [C] **1** one of two children or animals that are born to the same mother at the same time: *They're very alike. Are they twins?* ○ *a twin brother/sister* ○ *identical twins* توأم

2 one of a pair of things that are the same or very similar: *twin beds* (= two single beds in a room for two people) ○ *a twin-bedded room* صِنْو؛ فردة

▸ **twin** *verb* [T] (twinning; twinned) to join two towns in different countries together in a special relationship: *Oxford is twinned with Bonn.* يُدْخِل (مدينتين) في علاقة توأمة

twinge /twɪndʒ/ *noun* [C] **a twinge (of sth) 1** a sudden thought or feeling: *a twinge of fear* شعور مفاجئ

2 a sudden short pain وَخْزة

twinkle /ˈtwɪŋkl/ *verb* [I] **1** to shine with a light that seems to be moving: *Stars twinkled in the night sky.* يتلألأ، يَبْرق

2 (used about your eyes) to look bright because you are happy تلمع (العينان) فرحاً

▸ **twinkle** *noun* [sing.]: *From the twinkle in her eyes we knew she was joking.* لمعان، بريق

ˌ**twin ˈtown** *noun* [C] one of two towns in different countries that have a special relationship: *Grenoble is Oxford's twin town.* مدينة توأم

twirl /twɜːl/ *verb* **1** [I] to spin or turn around, e.g. when you are dancing يدور

2 [T] to twist or turn sth يدير، يفَتِل

🔑**twist**[1] /twɪst/ *verb* **1** [I,T] to turn yourself or a part of your body: *She twisted round to see where the noise was coming from.* ○ *He kept twisting his head from side to side.* يستدير؛ يدير

2 [I,T] to turn or make sth turn into a shape or position that is not normal: *The metal twisted into strange shapes.* ○ *He twisted his knee while he was playing squash.* يتلوّى؛ يَلْوي

3 [T] to turn sth in a particular direction: *Twist the dial as far as it will go.* ○ *Most containers have twist-off caps.* يَبْرم، يفْتل

4 [I] (used about a road, etc.) to change direction often: *a narrow twisting lane* يتعرّج، يتلوّى

5 [T] to wind sth round and round an object: *I twisted the bandage round her knee.* يلفّ

6 [T] to change the meaning of what sb said: *Journalists often twist your words.* يُشوّه، يُحرِّف

IDM **twist sb's arm** (*informal*) to force or persuade sb to do sth يجبره على فعل شيء

🔑**twist**[2] /twɪst/ *noun* [C] **1** an act of twisting sth: *She killed the chicken with one twist of its neck.* لَيّة

2 a place where sth has become twisted: *Straighten out the wire so that there are no twists in it.* فَتْلة، ثنية

3 a place where a road, river, etc. bends or changes direction: *the twists and turns of the river* التواء، انحناء

4 a change or development (especially one that you do not expect): *an unexpected twist at the end of the book* تطوّر مفاجئ

twit /twɪt/ *noun* [C] (*Brit informal*) a stupid person شخص غبي

twitch /twɪtʃ/ *verb* [I,T] to make a sudden movement; to cause sth to make a sudden movement: *The rabbit twitched and then lay still.* ○ *He twitched his nose.* ينتفض، يرتعش؛ يَنْفض

▸ **twitch** *noun* [C] خلجة، حركة عصبية

twitter /ˈtwɪtə(r)/ *verb* [I] (used about birds) to make a series of short high sounds يغرّد، يشقشق

Twitter™ /ˈtwɪtə(r)/ *noun* [U] a social networking service that allows you to send out short regular messages about what you are doing, that people can access on the Internet or on their mobile/cell phones "تويتر": موقع تفاعل اجتماعي

🔑**two** /tuː/ *number* 2; one more than one ➲ Look at **second**. For examples of how to use numbers in sentences, look at **six**. إثنان

IDM **in two** in or into two pieces: *The plate fell on the floor and broke in two.* إلى قسمين

▸ **two-** (in compounds) having two of the thing mentioned: *a two-week holiday* ثُنائي، يتكوّن من اثنين

tycoon /taɪˈkuːn/ *noun* [C] a person who is very successful in business and who is rich and powerful (شخص) واسع الثراء، من أرباب المال

🔑**type**[1] /taɪp/ *noun* [C] **1 a type (of sth)** a group of people or things that share certain qualities and that are part of a larger group; a kind or sort: *Which type of paint should you use on metal?* ○ *Spaniels are a type of dog.* ○ *There are several different types of apartment to choose from.* ○ *That's just the type of situation that you should avoid.* ○ *You meet all types of people in this job.* ○ *the first building of its type in the world* نوع، صِنْف

2 a person of a particular kind: *He's the careful type.* نوع

> If you say somebody is not **your type** you mean that they are not the sort of person that you would be friendly with. Look at **typical**.

🔑**type**[2] /taɪp/ *verb* [I,T] to write sth using a typewriter, word processor, etc: *Can you type?* ○ *to type a letter* يطبع (على الآلة الكاتبة أو الكمبيوتر)

▸ **type** *noun* [U] the letters that you use when you are typing or printing: *The type is too small to read.* حرف طباعي

typing *noun* [U] **1** the act of typing: *typing skills* طباعة (على الآلة الكاتبة)

2 work that has been or must be typed: *There is still a lot of typing to be done.* نصوص معدّة للطباعة (على الآلة الكاتبة)

typist /ˈtaɪpɪst/ *noun* [C] a person who types, especially as a job طابع (على الآلة الكاتبة)

typewriter /ˈtaɪpraɪtə(r)/ *noun* [C] a machine that you use for writing in print آلة كاتبة

▸ **typewritten** /ˈtaɪprɪtn/ *adj* written using a typewriter or word processor مطبوع على الآلة الكاتبة

typhoid /ˈtaɪfɔɪd/ *noun* [U] a serious disease that can cause death. People get typhoid from bad food or water. حمّى التيفوئيد، الحمّى المعوية

typhoon /taɪˈfuːn/ *noun* [C] a violent tropical storm with very strong winds ➲ Look at the note at **storm**. إعصار استوائي

🔑**typical** /ˈtɪpɪkl/ *adj* **typical (of sb/sth)** having or showing the usual qualities of a particular person, thing or type: *a typical Italian village* ○ *There's no such thing as a typical American* (= they are all different). ○ *It was absolutely typical of him not to reply to my letter.* نموذجي؛ معهود
▸ **typically** /-kli/ *adv* **1** in a typical case: *Typically, it is the girls who offer to help, not the boys.* عادةً، من المعهود
2 in a typical manner: *typically British* على نحو نموذجي

typify /ˈtɪpɪfaɪ/ *verb* [T] (*pres part* **typifying**; *3rd pers sing pres* **typifies**; *pt, pp* **typified**) to be a typical mark or example of sb/sth: *The film typified the Hollywood westerns of that time.* يجسِّد، يمثِّل

typist → TYPE²

tyranny /ˈtɪrəni/ *noun* [U] the cruel and unjust use of power by a person or small group to govern a country or state طغيان، استبداد، ظلم
▸ **tyrannical** /tɪˈrænɪkl/ *adj*: *a tyrannical ruler* متجبِّر، مستبدّ، استبدادي
tyrannize (*also* **tyrannise**) /ˈtɪrənaɪz/ *verb* [I,T] to use power over other people in a cruel and unjust way يستبدّ بـ، يظلم

tyrant /ˈtaɪrənt/ *noun* [C] a cruel ruler who has complete power over the people in his/her country ➲ Look at **dictator**. مستبدّ، طاغية

🔑**tyre** (*US* **tire**) /ˈtaɪə(r)/ *noun* [C] the thick rubber ring that fits around the outside of a wheel: *a flat tyre* ○ *Remember to check your tyre pressure.* عَجَلة: إطار مطاطي

U u

U, u /juː/ *noun* [C] (*pl.* **Us**; **U's**; **u's** /juːz/) the twenty-first letter of the English alphabet: *'Ulcer' begins with (a) 'U'.* الحرف الواحد والعشرون من الأبجدية الإنكليزية

ubiquitous /juːˈbɪkwɪtəs/ *adj* (usually *before* a noun) (*formal*) seeming to be everywhere or in several places at the same time كلّي الوجود: موجود في كل مكان

udder /ˈʌdə(r)/ *noun* [C] the part of a female cow, goat, etc. that hangs like a bag between its legs and produces milk ضَرْع

UEFA /juːˈeɪfə/ *abbrev* Union of European Football Associations: *the UEFA cup* اتحاد روابط كرة القدم الأوروبي

UFO (*also* **ufo**) /ˌjuː ef ˈəʊ; ˈjuːfəʊ/ *abbrev* unidentified flying object, especially a flying saucer صحن طائر

ugh /ɜː/ *interj* (used in writing to express the sound that you make when you think sth is very unpleasant) أُفٍّ (تقال اشمئزازاً)

🔑**ugly** /ˈʌgli/ *adj* (**uglier**; **ugliest**) **1** unpleasant to look at or listen to; unattractive: *an ugly scar on her face* ○ *an ugly modern office block* غير جذّاب؛ بشع، قبيح
2 (used about a situation) dangerous or threatening: *The situation became ugly when people started throwing stones.* ينذر بالشر، خَطِر
▸ **ugliness** *noun* [U] بشاعة، قُبْح

UK (*especially US* **U.K.**) /ˌjuː ˈkeɪ/ *abbrev* = UNITED KINGDOM

ulcer /ˈʌlsə(r)/ *noun* [C] a painful area on your skin or inside your body. Ulcers may produce a poisonous substance and sometimes bleed: *a mouth ulcer* ○ *a stomach ulcer* قَرْحة

ulterior /ʌlˈtɪəriə(r)/ *adj* (*formal*) that you keep hidden or secret: *Why is he suddenly being so nice to me? He must have an ulterior motive.* مُستَتِر، خفيّ

🔑**ultimate** /ˈʌltɪmət/ *adj* (only *before* a noun) **1** being or happening at the end; last or final: *Our ultimate goal is complete independence.* نهائي
2 the greatest, best or worst: *For me the ultimate luxury is to stay in bed till ten o'clock on a Sunday.* أعظم؛ أقصى (الشيء)
▸ **ultimate** *noun* [sing.] **the ultimate (in sth)** (*informal*) the greatest or best: *This new car is the ultimate in comfort.* قمّة، ذروة
ultimately *adv* **1** in the end: *Whatever decision we ultimately take will be in the best interests of the school.* في النهاية
2 at the most basic level: *Ultimately, this discussion is not about quality but about money.* أساساً، جوهرياً

ultimatum /ˌʌltɪˈmeɪtəm/ *noun* [C] (*pl.* **ultimatums**) a warning to a person or country that, if they do not do what you ask, you will use force or take action against them انذار

ultra- /ˈʌltrə/ (in compounds) extremely: *ultra-modern* سابقة معناها جداً أو بإفراط

ultrasound /ˈʌltrəsaʊnd/ *noun* [U] ultrasonic sound: *an ultrasound scan* (صوت) فوق السمعي

ultraviolet /ˌʌltrəˈvaɪələt/ *adj* of a type of light that causes your skin to turn darker and that can be dangerous in large amounts (اشعاع) فوق بنفسجي

umbilical cord /ʌmˌbɪlɪkl ˈkɔːd/ *noun* [C] the tube that connects a baby to its mother before it is born الحبل السُّرّي

🔑**umbrella** /ʌmˈbrelə/ *noun* [C] an object that you carry to keep you dry when it is raining. An umbrella consists of a piece of cloth on a frame and a long handle. You can fold an umbrella up when you are not using it: *to put an umbrella up/down* شمسيّة، مظلّة

umpire /ˈʌmpaɪə(r)/ *noun* [C] a person who watches a game such as tennis or cricket to make sure that the players obey the rules ➲ Look at **referee**. حَكَم
▸ **umpire** *verb* [I,T] يفصل في نزاع، يَحْكم

umpteen /ˌʌmpˈtiːn/ *pron, det* (*informal*) very many; a lot: *I've told you umpteen times to phone me if you're going to be late.* مرّات عديدة جداً، ألف مرّة
▸ **umpteenth** /ˌʌmpˈtiːnθ/ *pron, det*: *For the umpteenth time – phone if you're going to be late!* للمرّة الألف!

UN (*especially US* **U.N.**) /ˌjuː ˈen/ *abbrev* = UNITED NATIONS

⚷ **unable** /ʌnˈeɪbl/ *adj* (not before a noun) **unable to do sth** not having the time, knowledge, skill, etc. to do sth; not able to do sth: *She lay there, unable to move.* ❶ The noun is **inability**. غير قادر، عاجز عن

⚷ **unacceptable** /ˌʌnəkˈseptəbl/ *adj* that you cannot accept or allow غير مقبول، مرفوض
▸ **unacceptably** /-bli/ *adv* بشكل أو لحدٍّ لا يمكن قبوله

unaccompanied /ˌʌnəˈkʌmpənid/ *adj* alone, without sb/sth else going too: *unaccompanied children* غير مصحوب؛ بمفرده

unaffected /ˌʌnəˈfektɪd/ *adj* **1** not changed by sth: *Our department will be unaffected by the decision.* غير متأثّر

2 natural in the way you behave غير متكلّف أو متصنّع، طبيعي

unaided /ʌnˈeɪdɪd/ *adv* without any help بلا مُساعدة، وَحْده

unanimous /juˈnænɪməs/ *adj* **1** (used about a group of people) all agreeing about sth: *The members of the jury were unanimous in their decision.* مجمِع

2 (used about a decision, etc.) agreed by everybody إجماعي
▸ **unanimously** *adv* باتحاد الآراء، بالإجماع

unarmed /ʌnˈɑːmd/ *adj* having no guns, knives, etc.; not armed أعْزَل من السلاح

unashamed /ˌʌnəˈʃeɪmd/ *adj* feeling or showing no guilt غير محرج أو خَجِل
▸ **unashamedly** /ˌʌnəˈʃeɪmɪdli/ *adv*: *The film was unashamedly sentimental.* دون حرَج، بشكل صريح

unassuming /ˌʌnəˈsjuːmɪŋ; *US* ˌʌnəˈsuː-/ *adj* not wishing to be noticed by other people غير مدّعٍ، متواضع

unattached /ˌʌnəˈtætʃt/ *adj* **1** not connected to sb/sth else: *This group is unattached to any political party.* مستقل عن، غير مرتبط

2 not married; without a regular partner غير مرتبط، أعزب

unattended /ˌʌnəˈtendɪd/ *adj* not watched or looked after: *Young children should not be left unattended.* دون مشرف، وحده

unauthorized /ʌnˈɔːθəraɪzd/ *adj* done without permission غير مأذون به، غير مخوّل

unavoidable /ˌʌnəˈvɔɪdəbl/ *adj* that cannot be avoided or prevented حَتْمي، لا مفرّ منه
▸ **unavoidably** /-əbli/ *adv*: *We were unavoidably delayed.* بشكلٍ لا مناص منه

unaware /ˌʌnəˈweə(r)/ *adj* (not before a noun) **unaware (of sb/sth)** not knowing about or not noticing sb/sth: *She seemed unaware of all the trouble she had caused.* غير مُدْرِك لـ، غافل عن
▸ **unawares** /-ˈweəz/ *adv* by surprise; without expecting sth or being prepared for it: *I was taken completely unawares by his suggestion.* على حين غِرّة

unbalanced /ˌʌnˈbælənst/ *adj* **1** (used about a person) rather mad غير متوازن عقلياً، مُختلّ

2 not fair to all ideas or sides of an argument: *an unbalanced newspaper report* غير مُنصف، متحيّز

unbearable /ʌnˈbeərəbl/ *adj* too unpleasant, painful, etc. for you to accept لا يطاق، لا يحتمل
▸ **unbearably** /-əbli/ *adv*: *It was unbearably hot.* لدرجة لا تُطاق

unbeatable /ʌnˈbiːtəbl/ *adj* that cannot be defeated or improved on: *We offer you quality at unbeatable prices.* لا يفوقه أحد أو شيء، لا يقْهر

unbeaten /ʌnˈbiːtn/ *adj* that has not been beaten or improved on: *Her world record remains unbeaten.* غير متفوّق عليه؛ غير مغلوب

unbelievable /ˌʌnbɪˈliːvəbl/ *adj* very surprising; difficult to believe ➲ Look at **incredible**. لا يُصدّق؛ مثير للدهشة
▸ **unbelievably** *adv*: *unbelievably bad* بشكل لا يصدّق

unborn /ˌʌnˈbɔːn/ *adj* not yet born: *Smoking can damage the unborn child.* جنين؛ غير مولود بعد

unbroken /ʌnˈbrəʊkən/ *adj* **1** continuous; not interrupted: *a period of unbroken silence* غير منقطع؛ متواصل

2 that has not been beaten: *His record for the 1500 metres remains unbroken.* غير متفوّق عليه؛ لم يحطّم بعد

uncalled-for /ʌnˈkɔːld fɔː(r)/ *adj* not necessary or right: *That comment was quite uncalled-for.* غير ضروري؛ لا مبرّر له

uncanny /ʌnˈkæni/ *adj* strange and mysterious; that you cannot easily explain غامض؛ غريب

⚷ **uncertain** /ʌnˈsɜːtn/ *adj* **1 uncertain (about/of sth)** not sure; not able to decide: *She was still uncertain of his true feelings for her.* ○ *Chris seemed uncertain about what to do next.* غير متأكد؛ غير واثق

2 not known exactly or not decided: *He's lost his job and his future seems very uncertain.* مُقلقِل، غير مضمون
▸ **uncertainly** *adv*: *Kate stood uncertainly, waiting for someone to speak to her.* في حالة تردّد؛ في حيرة

a b c d e f g h i j k l m n o p q r s t **u** v w x y z

uncertainty /ʌn'sɜːtnti/ *noun* [C,U] (*pl.* **uncertainties**) the state of being uncertain: *Today's decision will put an end to all the uncertainty.* تردّد، شك، حيرة

unchanged /ʌn'tʃeɪndʒd/ *adj* staying the same; not changed: *The town has remained almost unchanged since the eighteenth century.* ثابت على حاله؛ لم يتغيّر

uncharacteristic /ˌʌnˌkærəktə'rɪstɪk/ *adj* not typical or usual غير متوقع؛ غير معهود
▸ **uncharacteristically** /-kli/ *adv* على نحو مخالف للمعهود

uncle /'ʌŋkl/ *noun* [C] **1** the brother of your father or mother: *Uncle Steven* ➲ Look at **aunt**. خال، عمّ

2 the husband of your aunt زوج العمّة أو الخالة

Some children use 'Auntie' or 'Uncle' before the first name of an adult that they know well but who is not related to them.

uncomfortable /ʌn'kʌmftəbl/ *adj* **1** not pleasant to wear, sit in, lie on, etc: *The chairs are hard and very uncomfortable.* غير مريح
2 not able to sit, lie, etc. in a position that is pleasant: *I was very uncomfortable for most of the journey.* غير مرتاح
3 feeling or causing worry or embarrassment: *I felt very uncomfortable when they started arguing in front of me.* محرَج؛ متضايق
▸ **uncomfortably** /-əbli/ *adv* على نحو غير مريح؛ بصورة مزعجة

uncommon /ʌn'kɒmən/ *adj* unusual: *Red squirrels are uncommon in England.* نادر، غير مألوف

uncompromising /ʌn'kɒmprəmaɪzɪŋ/ *adj* not willing to discuss sth or change a decision متصلّب، عنيد

unconcerned /ˌʌnkən'sɜːnd/ *adj* not interested in sth or not worried about it غير قلِق، لا مبالٍ

unconditional /ˌʌnkən'dɪʃənl/ *adj* without limits or conditions: *an unconditional surrender* تامّ، غير مشروط
▸ **unconditionally** /-ʃənəli/ *adv* دونَ قيد أو شرط

unconscious /ʌn'kɒnʃəs/ *adj* **1** in a state that is like sleep. You may be unconscious after an accident if you hit your head: *He was found lying unconscious on the kitchen floor.* فاقد الوعي، مُغمى عليه

2 unconscious of sb/sth not knowing or aware of sb/sth: *He seemed unconscious of everything that was going on around him.* غير مدرك أو واعٍ
3 done, spoken, etc. without you thinking about it or being aware of it: *The article was full of unconscious humour.* غير مقصود
▸ **the unconscious** *noun* [sing.] اللاشعور، العقل الباطن
unconsciously *adv* بشكل غير مقصود؛ بلا وعي
unconsciousness *noun* [U] the state of being unconscious غيبوبة؛ فقدان الوعي

uncontrollable /ˌʌnkən'trəʊləbl/ *adj* that you cannot control: *an uncontrollable urge to giggle* متعذر ضبطه، لا يقاوم
▸ **uncontrollably** *adv* على نحو لا يضبط، خارجَ إرادته

uncool /ˌʌn'kuːl/ *adj* not considered acceptable by fashionable young people: *My kids tell me my hairstyle is really uncool.* طراز قديم، غير رائج

uncountable /ʌn'kaʊntəbl/ *adj* (*grammar*) an uncountable noun cannot be counted and so does not have a plural. In this dictionary uncountable nouns are marked '[U]'. غير معدود، لا يُعدّ

uncover /ʌn'kʌvə(r)/ *verb* [T] **1** to remove the cover from sth يرفع الغطاء
2 to find out or discover sth يكتشف

undecided /ˌʌndɪ'saɪdɪd/ *adj* **1** not having made a decision: *I'm still undecided about whether to take the job or not.* متردّد
2 without any result or decision; not decided: *The future of our jobs is still undecided.* غير مفصول فيه؛ معلّق

undeniable /ˌʌndɪ'naɪəbl/ *adj* clear, true or certain: *The charm of the city is undeniable.* مسلّم به، لا ينكر
▸ **undeniably** /-əbli/ *adv* من غير شك، بكل تأكيد

under /'ʌndə(r)/ *prep* **1** in or to a position that is below or beneath sth: *Put the suitcase under the bed.* ○ *to hide under the table* ○ *The dog crawled under the gate and ran into the road.* تحت

Compare **under**, **below**, **beneath** and **underneath**. You use **under** to say that one thing is directly under another thing. There may be a space between the two things: *The cat is asleep under the table*, or one thing may be touching or covered by the other thing: *I think your letter is under that book.* You can use **below** to say that one thing is in a lower position than another thing when they are both in the same building, on the same hill, on the same part of the body, etc: *They live on the floor below us.* ○ *We could see a few houses below the castle.* ○ *It hurts here – just below the knee.* You use **under** (not **below**) to talk about movement from one side of something to the other side: *We swam under the bridge.* You can use **beneath** to say that one thing is directly under another thing, but **under** is more common. **Beneath** is rather a literary word. You can use **underneath** in place of **under** when you want to emphasize that something is being covered or hidden by another thing: *Have you looked underneath the sofa as well as behind it?*

2 below the surface of sth; covered by sth: *Most of an iceberg is under the water.* ○ *Are you wearing a vest under your shirt?* تحت
3 younger than: *Nobody under eighteen is allowed to buy alcohol.* أصغر من، دونَ
4 less than: *People earning under £10 000 a year will pay no extra tax.* أقلّ من، دون
5 working for or in the control of sb: *This hotel is under new management.* تحت (إشراف)
6 ruled or governed by sb/sth: *The country is*

now under martial law. ○ *Under their new conductor, the orchestra has established an international reputation.* تحت (حكم)، في عهد

7 according to a law, an agreement, a system, etc: *Under English law you are innocent until you are proved guilty.* بموجب، بمقتضى

8 in a particular state or condition: *under the influence of alcohol* ○ *a building under construction* ○ *I was under the impression that Bill was not very happy here.* في طور (التشييد): تحت (تأثير)

9 using a particular name: *to travel under a false name* تحت اسم...

10 found in a particular part of a book, list, etc: *You'll find some information on Budapest under 'Hungary'.* تحت (عنوان معيّن)

▸ **under** *adv* **1** under water: *How long can you stay under for?* تحت سطح الماء

2 less; younger: *The prices quoted are for children aged 12 and under.* أصغر أو أقلّ من؛ دون

under- /ˈʌndə(r)/ (in compounds) **1** lower in rank or position: *the minister's under-secretary* نائب أو وكيل (وزارة مثلاً)

2 not enough: *underdeveloped countries* غير كافٍ؛ غير متطوّر

underclothes /ˈʌndəkləʊðz/ *noun* [plural] = UNDERWEAR

undercover /ˌʌndəˈkʌvə(r)/ *adj* working or happening secretly: *an undercover agent* (= a spy) سرّي

undercut /ˌʌndəˈkʌt/ *verb* [T] (*pres part* **undercutting**; *pt, pp* **undercut**) to sell at a lower price than other shops, etc: *Supermarkets can undercut smaller shops.* يبيع بسعر أرخص

underdog /ˈʌndədɒg; *US* -dɔːg/ *noun* [C] a person who is in a weak position مستضعَف؛ خاسر

underestimate /ˌʌndərˈestɪmeɪt/ *verb* [T] **1** to guess that the amount, etc. of sth will be less than it really is: *We underestimated the amount of food we would need.* يقلّل أو يَبْخس التقدير

2 to think that sb/sth is not as strong, etc. as he/she/it really is: *Don't underestimate your opponent. He's a really good player.* يستهين، لا يقدِّر حقّ قدره

▸ **underestimate** /-mət/ *noun* [C] تقدير أقلّ من الحقيقة

underfoot /ˌʌndəˈfʊt/ *adv* under your feet; where you are walking: *It's very wet underfoot.* على الأرض؛ تحت الأقدام

undergo /ˌʌndəˈgəʊ/ *verb* [T] (*pt* **underwent** /-ˈwent/; *pp* **undergone** /-ˈgɒn; *US* -ˈgɔːn/) to have a difficult or unpleasant experience: *She underwent a five-hour operation at Harefield Hospital.* يمرّ بِ؛ يقاسي؛ يخضع لِ

undergraduate /ˌʌndəˈgrædʒuət/ *noun* [C] a university or college student who has not yet taken his/her first degree ➲ Look at **graduate** and **postgraduate**. طالب جامعي (لم يتخرّج بعد)

⚷**underground** /ˈʌndəgraʊnd/ *adj* **1** under the surface of the ground: *an underground car park* تحت سطح الأرض

2 secret or illegal: *an underground radio station that supports the rebels* سرّي

▸ **underground** /ˌʌndəˈgraʊnd/ *adv* **1** under the surface of the ground: *The cables all run underground.* تحت سطح الأرض

2 into a secret place: *She went underground to escape from the police.* لمكان سرّي، (يختبئ) في مخبأ

underground /ˈʌndəgraʊnd/ (*US* **subway**) *noun* [sing.] an underground railway system: *We travel to work by underground.* ○ *an underground station* ❶ In London the underground railway is called **the underground** or **the tube**. قطار الأنفاق، المترو

undergrowth /ˈʌndəgrəʊθ/ *noun* [U] bushes and plants that grow around and under trees ما ينبت تحت الأشجار أو حولها

underhand /ˌʌndəˈhænd/ *adj* secret or not honest خفيّ؛ غير شريف

underline /ˌʌndəˈlaɪn/ *verb* [T] **1** to draw a line under a word, etc. يضع خطّاً (تحت كلمة)

2 to show sth clearly or to emphasize sth: *This accident underlines the need for greater care.* يؤكّد، يُبْرز

underlying /ˌʌndəˈlaɪɪŋ/ *adj* important but hidden: *the underlying causes of the disaster* أساسي؛ مستَتِر، عميق

undermine /ˌʌndəˈmaɪn/ *verb* [T] to make sth weaker: *The public's confidence in the quality of our drinking water has been undermined.* يضعِف

⚷**underneath** /ˌʌndəˈniːθ/ *prep, adv* under or below: *The coin rolled underneath the chair.* ○ *a flat with a shop underneath* ○ *A blue silk blouse underneath the jacket would look nice.* ○ *This sweater's not very warm but I've got a T-shirt on underneath.* ➲ Look at the note at **under**. أسفل، تحت

▸ **the underneath** *noun* [sing.] the bottom or lowest part of something: *There is a lot of rust on the underneath of the car.* أسفل أو قاع الشيء

underpants /ˈʌndəpænts/ (*Brit also* **pants**) *noun* [plural] a piece of clothing that men or boys wear under their trousers سِروال تحتاني، "كلسون" رجّالي

underpass /ˈʌndəpɑːs; *US* -pæs/ *noun* [C] a road or path that goes under another road, railway, etc. طريق يمرّ تحت طريق آخر

underpay /ˌʌndəˈpeɪ/ *verb* [T] (*pt, pp* **underpaid**) to pay a person too little: *Teachers in this country are underpaid.* يدفع أقلّ مما يجب، يبخس الأجر

underprivileged /ˌʌndəˈprɪvəlɪdʒd/ *adj* having less money, fewer rights, opportunities, etc. than other people in society محدود الامتيازات والفرص؛ فقير

underrate /ˌʌndəˈreɪt/ *verb* [T] to think that sb/sth is less clever, important, good, etc. than he/she/it really is يقلّل من قيمته، لا يقدّره حقّ قدره

undershirt /ˈʌndəʃɜːt/ *noun* [C] (*US*) = VEST

⚷**understand** /ˌʌndəˈstænd/ *verb* (*pt, pp* **understood** /-ˈstʊd/) **1** [I,T] to get the meaning of sb/sth: *I'm not sure that I really understand.*

○ *I didn't understand the instructions.* ○ *Please speak more slowly. I can't understand you.* ○ *He can understand Italian but he can't speak it.* ○ *Can Italians and Spaniards understand each other?* يفهم

2 [T] to know how or why sth happens: *I can't understand why the engine won't start.* يَفْقَه، يدرك السبب

3 [T] to know why sb behaves in a particular way and to feel sympathy: *It's easy to understand why she felt so angry.* ○ *His parents don't understand him.* يشعر بشعوره، يتفهّم

4 [T] (*formal*) to have heard or been told sth: *I understand that you have decided to leave.* يعلم، يبلغ مسامعه

5 [T] to judge a situation, etc: *As far as I understand it, the changes won't affect us.* يقدِّر الموقف

IDM give sb to believe/understand (that) → GIVE[1]

make yourself understood to make your meaning clear: *I can just about make myself understood in Russian.* يعبِّر بوضوح

▸ **understandable** /-əbl/ *adj* that you can understand مفهوم: له ما يبرره؛ ممكن فهمه

understandably /-əbli/ *adv*: *She was understandably angry at the decision.* لا غَرْوَ (أنّ)، لأسباب يمكن فهمها

understanding /ˌʌndəˈstændɪŋ/ *noun* **1** [U] the ability to think or learn about sth: *The book is beyond the understanding of most ten-year-olds.* استيعاب، فهم

2 [U, sing.] knowledge of a subject, how sth works, etc: *A basic understanding of physics is necessary for this course.* إلمام بـ، معرفة

3 [U, sing.] the ability to feel sympathy and trust for sb: *understanding between nations* تفاهم

4 [U] the way in which you think sth is meant: *My understanding of the arrangement is that he will only phone if there is a problem.* (على) حدّ فهمه

5 [C, usually sing.] an informal agreement: *We came to an understanding about the money I owed him.* اتفاق، تفاهم

IDM on the understanding that... only if...; because it was agreed that...: *We let them stay in our house on the understanding that it was only for a short period.* على أساس، على شرط

▸ **understanding** *adj* kind; showing sympathy towards sb متعاطف؛ متفهِّم

understate /ˌʌndəˈsteɪt/ *verb* [T] to say that sth is smaller or less important than it really is يعبِّر عن الشيء بصورة تقلّل من أهميته

▸ **understatement** *noun* [C,U]: *'Is she pleased?' 'That's an understatement. She's delighted.'* تعبير ملطَّف أو مخفَّف

understudy /ˈʌndəstʌdi/ *noun* [C] (*pl.* **understudies**) an actor who learns the role of another actor and replaces him/her if he/she is ill ممثّل بديل

undertake /ˌʌndəˈteɪk/ *verb* [T] (*pt* **undertook** /-ˈtʊk/; *pp* **undertaken** /-ˈteɪkən/) **1** to agree or promise to do sth: *The firm undertook to deliver the machines by Friday.* يلتزم، يتعهد

2 to carry sth out: *The zoo is undertaking a major programme of modernization.* يقوم بِـ

▸ **undertaking** *noun* [C, usually sing.] **1** a piece of work or business: *a risky undertaking* عملية، مشروع

2 undertaking (that.../to do sth) a formal or legal promise (to do sth): (*formal*) *He gave an undertaking that he would not leave the country.* تعهّد، التزام

undertaker /ˈʌndəteɪkə(r)/ (*also* **funeral director**; *US also* **mortician**) *noun* [C] a person whose job is to prepare bodies to be buried and to arrange funerals حانوتي، متعهّد دفن الموتى

undertone /ˈʌndətəʊn/ *noun* [C] **1** a feeling or attitude that is not directly expressed معنى خفيّ، فحوى

2 a low, quiet voice صوت خفيض

undervalue /ˌʌndəˈvælju:/ *verb* [T] to place too low a value on sb/sth يبخس قيمته؛ يستخفّ بأهميته

underwater /ˌʌndəˈwɔ:tə(r)/ *adj, adv* existing, happening or used below the surface of water: *underwater exploration* ○ *an underwater camera* ○ *Can you swim underwater?* تحت الماء

underwear /ˈʌndəweə(r)/ *noun* [U] clothing that is worn next to the skin under other clothes ❶ **Underclothes** has the same meaning and is a plural noun. ملابس داخلية

underweight /ˌʌndəˈweɪt/ *adj* weighing less than is normal or correct ➲ Look at the note at **thin.** أقلّ من الوزن الطبيعي

underworld /ˈʌndəwɜ:ld/ *noun* [sing.] **the underworld** people who are involved in crime عالم الإجرام، العالم السفلي

undesirable /ˌʌndɪˈzaɪərəbl/ *adj* unwanted or unpleasant; likely to cause problems غير مرغوب فيه؛ مضرّ

undid *pt of* UNDO

undignified /ʌnˈdɪgnɪfaɪd/ *adj* clumsy, embarrassing or unsuitable: *Everyone rushed for the food in a most undignified way!* محرج، غير لائق

undivided /ˌʌndɪˈvaɪdɪd/ *adj*

IDM give your undivided attention (to sb/sth) to concentrate fully on sth تعطي شخصاً/شيئاً اهتمامك الكلّي

get/have sb's undivided attention to receive sb's full attention ينال الاهتمام الكلّي من شخص

undo /ʌnˈdu:/ *verb* [T] (*3rd pers sing pres* **undoes**; *pt* **undid**; *pp* **undone**) **1** to open sth that was tied or fastened: *He undid his shoelaces and took off his shoes.* ○ *to undo a knot* يَحلّ، يفكّ

2 to destroy the effect of sth that has already happened: *The damage cannot be undone.* يبطل (المفعول)

▸ **undone** *adj* **1** open; not fastened or tied: *My zip was undone.* محلول، مفكوك

2 not done: *I left the housework undone.* غير مُنْجَز

undoubted /ʌn'daʊtɪd/ *adj* definite; accepted as being true لا جدال في صحّته، مؤكّد
▸ **undoubtedly** *adv* بلا ريب، يقيناً، من غير شك

undress /ʌn'dres/ *verb* **1** [I] to take off your clothes: *I undressed and the doctor examined me.* ⓘ **Get undressed** is more commonly used than **undress**: *He got undressed and had a shower.* يتعرّى، يخلع ملابسه
2 [T] to take off sb's clothes: *She undressed the child and put her into bed.* ينزع أو يخلع (ثياب شخص آخر)
▸ **undressed** *adj* wearing no or few clothes عارٍ؛ شبه عارٍ

undue /ˌʌn'djuː; *US* -'duː/ *adj* more than is necessary or reasonable فوق الحدّ، مفرِط
▸ **unduly** *adv*: *She didn't seem unduly worried by their unexpected arrival.* على نحو مفرط أو غير ملائم

unearth /ʌn'ɜːθ/ *verb* [T] to dig sth up out of the ground; to discover sth that was hidden: *Archaeologists have unearthed a Roman villa.* ○ *(figurative) A journalist unearthed the true facts of the case.* يخرج (شيئاً مدفوناً)؛ يكتشف

unearthly /ʌn'ɜːθli/ *adj* **1** strange or frightening غريب الهيئة؛ مرعب
2 (used about a time) very early or very late: *I can't get up at such an unearthly hour as 5 am!* (وقت) مزعج جداً

uneasy /ʌn'iːzi/ *adj* **1** worried; not feeling relaxed or comfortable قلِق؛ مضطرب
2 not settled; unlikely to last: *an uneasy compromise* غير مستقِرّ؛ متقلقل
▸ **unease** /ʌn'iːz/ (*also* **uneasiness**) *noun* [U] an anxious or uncomfortable feeling تشوّش (البال)، قلق
uneasily /ʌn'iːzɪli/ *adv* باضطراب، بتوجّس

uneconomic /ˌʌnˌiːkə'nɒmɪk; *US* ˌʌnˌek-/ *adj* (used about a company, etc.) not making or likely to make a profit غير مربح

uneconomical /ˌʌnˌiːkə'nɒmɪkl; *US* ˌʌnˌek-/ *adj* wasting money, time, materials, etc. مسرِف
▸ **uneconomically** /-kli/ *adv* بشكل غير مربح

🔑**unemployed** /ˌʌnɪm'plɔɪd/ *adj* not having a job; out of work: *She lost her job six months ago and has been unemployed ever since.* عاطل (عن العمل)؛ بلا عمل
▸ **the unemployed** *noun* [plural] the people who do not have a job: *What does the government do to help the unemployed?* العاطلون عن العمل

🔑**unemployment** /ˌʌnɪm'plɔɪmənt/ *noun* [U] **1** the situation of being unemployed: *If the factory closes, many people face unemployment.* عطالة، بطالة
2 the number of people who are unemployed: *The economy is doing very badly and unemployment is rising.* ○ *unemployment benefit* (= money given by the state) ➲ Look at **dole**. عدد العاطلين عن العمل

unending /ʌn'endɪŋ/ *adj* having or seeming to have no end لا ينتهي، مستديم

unequal /ʌn'iːkwəl/ *adj* **1** different in size, amount, level, etc. متفاوت، غير متساوٍ
2 not fair or balanced: *It was an unequal contest because he's a far better player than me.* غير منصف؛ غير متكافئ
▸ **unequally** /-kwəli/ *adv* على نحو غير متكافئ

uneven /ʌn'iːvn/ *adj* **1** not completely smooth, level or regular: *The sign was painted in rather uneven letters.* غير مستوٍ؛ غير منتظم
2 not always of the same level or quality متفاوت، متباين
▸ **unevenly** *adv*: *The country's wealth is unevenly distributed.* على نحو غير متساوٍ

🔑**unexpected** /ˌʌnɪk'spektɪd/ *adj* not expected and therefore causing surprise: *His death was quite unexpected.* غير متوقع
▸ **unexpectedly** *adv*: *I got there late because I was unexpectedly delayed.* على نحو غير متوقّع

🔑**unfair** /ˌʌn'feə(r)/ *adj* **1 unfair (on/to sb)** not dealing with people as they deserve; not treating each person equally: *It was unfair to blame her for something that was not her fault.* ○ *This law is unfair to women.* مجحف، غير منصف
2 not following the rules and therefore giving an advantage to one person, team, etc: *unfair play* مخادع، فيه غشّ
▸ **unfairly** *adv* على نحو جائر أو ظالم، من دون حقّ
unfairness *noun* [U] تحامل؛ جور، ظلم

unfaithful /ʌn'feɪθfl/ *adj* **unfaithful (to sb/sth)** having a sexual relationship with sb who is not your husband, wife or partner: *She discovered that her husband was being unfaithful to her.* ○ *Have you ever been unfaithful to your husband?* خائن (لعهد الزوجية مثلاً)

unfamiliar /ˌʌnfə'mɪliə(r)/ *adj* **1 unfamiliar (to sb)** not well-known to you: *an unfamiliar part of town* غير مألوف
2 unfamiliar (with sth) not having knowledge or experience of sth ليس له إلمام بـ

unfashionable /ʌn'fæʃnəbl/ *adj* not popular: *unfashionable ideas* ➲ Look at **old-fashioned**. قديم الطراز؛ مهجور

unfit /ʌn'fɪt/ *adj* **1 unfit (for sth/to do sth)** unsuitable or not good enough for sth: *If goods are unfit for use, you should take them back to the shop.* غير صالح (للاستعمال)؛ غير مناسب
2 not in good physical health (especially because you do not get enough exercise): *The doctor said I was overweight and unfit.* عديم اللياقة البدنية

unfold /ʌn'fəʊld/ *verb* [I,T] **1** to open out and become flat; to open out sth that was folded: *The sofa unfolds into a spare bed.* ○ *I unfolded the letter and read it.* ينفتح؛ يفتح
2 to become known, or to allow sth to become known a little at a time: *As the story unfolded, more and more surprising things were revealed.* ينكشف؛ يكشف

unforeseen /ˌʌnfɔː'siːn/ *adj* not expected: *an unforeseen problem* غير متوقّع، طارئ

unforgettable /ˌʌnfəˈgetəbl/ *adj* making such a strong impression that you cannot forget it لا يُنْسى

unfortunate /ʌnˈfɔːtʃənət/ *adj* **1** unlucky: *The unfortunate people who lived near the river lost their homes in the flood.* غير محظوظ، تعيس

2 that you regret: *I would like to apologize for this unfortunate mistake.* مؤسف

▸ **unfortunately** *adv* unluckily; it is a pity that...: *I'd like to help you but unfortunately there's nothing I can do.* لسوء الحظ

unfounded /ʌnˈfaʊndɪd/ *adj* not based on or supported by facts: *He said that the rumour was completely unfounded.* لا أساس له (من الصّحة)

unfriendly /ʌnˈfrendli/ *adj* unpleasant or impolite to sb; not friendly فظ؛ غير وديّ

ungainly /ʌnˈgeɪnli/ *adj* moving in a way that lacks grace غير رشيق

ungrateful /ʌnˈgreɪtfl/ *adj* not feeling or showing thanks (to sb) عاقّ؛ ناكر للجميل، جاحد

▸ **ungratefully** /-fəli/ *adv* بعقوق؛ بجحود

unguarded /ʌnˈgɑːdɪd/ *adj* **1** not protected or guarded غير محروس، سائب

2 careless; saying more than you wanted to: *He admitted the truth in an unguarded moment.* غير حذر، غافل

unhappy /ʌnˈhæpi/ *adj* (**unhappier**; **unhappiest**) **1 unhappy (about sth)** sad or miserable; not happy: *She's terribly unhappy about losing her job.* ○ *a very unhappy childhood* شقيّ؛ غير سعيد

2 unhappy (about/at sth) not satisfied or pleased; worried: *They're unhappy at having to take a pay cut.* قلِق؛ غير راضٍ عن

▸ **unhappily** /-ɪli/ *adv* **1** sadly بشقاء؛ بحزن

2 unfortunately: *Unhappily, we are unable to help.* بكلّ أسف، لسوء الحظ

unhappiness *noun* [U] تعاسة، شقاء

unhealthy /ʌnˈhelθi/ *adj* (**unhealthier**; **unhealthiest**) **1** not having or showing good health: *He looks pale and unhealthy.* معتلّ الصّحة

2 likely to cause illness or poor health: *unhealthy conditions* ضارّ بالصّحة

3 not natural: *an unhealthy interest in torture* غير طبيعي، مَرَضي

unheard /ʌnˈhɜːd/ *adj* not listened to or given attention: *My suggestions went unheard.* غير معتبر، غير مسموع

unheard-of /ʌnˈhɜːd ɒv/ *adj* not known; never having happened before: *Years ago it was unheard-of for women to do jobs like that.* غير مألوف؛ لم يسمع به

unicorn /ˈjuːnɪkɔːn/ *noun* [C] an imaginary animal that looks like a white horse and has one horn growing out of its forehead أحادي القرن: حيوان خرافي

unidentified /ˌʌnaɪˈdentɪfaɪd/ *adj* whose identity is not known: *An unidentified body has been found in the river.* مجهول الهوية

uniform¹ /ˈjuːnɪfɔːm/ *noun* [C,U] the set of clothes worn at work by the members of certain organizations or groups and by some schoolchildren: *Did you have to wear a uniform when you were at school?* ○ *I didn't know he was a policeman because he wasn't in uniform.* لباس رسمي موحّد

▸ **uniformed** *adj*: *uniformed policemen* بزيّ رسمي

uniform² /ˈjuːnɪfɔːm/ *adj* not varying; the same in all cases or at all times متساوٍ؛ على نسق واحد

▸ **uniformity** /ˌjuːnɪˈfɔːməti/ *noun* [U]: *Tests are standardized to ensure uniformity.* تناسق؛ تماثل

unify /ˈjuːnɪfaɪ/ *verb* [T] (*pres part* **unifying**; *3rd pers sing pres* **unifies**; *pt, pp* **unified**) to join or link separate parts together to make one unit, or to make them similar to each other يوحّد

▸ **unification** /ˌjuːnɪfɪˈkeɪʃn/ *noun* [U]: *the unification of Germany* توحيد

unilateral /ˌjuːnɪˈlætrəl/ *adj* done or made by one of the sides involved without the agreement of the other side or sides: *a unilateral declaration of independence* من جانب واحد

▸ **unilaterally** /-rəli/ *adv*: *The decision was taken unilaterally.* من طرف أو جانب واحد

uninhabitable /ˌʌnɪnˈhæbɪtəbl/ *adj* not possible to live in غير صالح للسكنى

uninhibited /ˌʌnɪnˈhɪbɪtɪd/ *adj* behaving in a free and natural way, showing what you feel without worrying what other people think of you منطلق، غير مقيّد بالتقاليد

uninstall /ˌʌnɪnˈstɔːl/ *verb* [T] to remove a program from a computer يزيل (برنامجاً)

unintelligible /ˌʌnɪnˈtelɪdʒəbl/ *adj* impossible to understand مبهم، مستغلق، غير مفهوم

uninterested /ʌnˈɪntrəstɪd/ *adj* **uninterested (in sb/sth)** having or showing no interest in sb/sth: *She seemed uninterested in anything I had to say.* غير مهتمّ

union /ˈjuːniən/ *noun* **1** [U, sing.] the act of joining or the situation of being joined: *the union of the separate groups into one organization* وَحْدة، اتحاد

2 [C] a group of states or countries that have been joined together to form one country or group: *the European Union* اتحاد

3 [C] = TRADE UNION

4 [C] an organization for a particular group of people: *the Athletics Union* رابطة، اتحاد

the ˌUnion ˈJack *noun* [C] the national flag of the United Kingdom, with red and white crosses on a dark blue background علَم المملكة المتحدة

unique /juˈniːk/ *adj* **1** unlike anything else; being the only one of its type: *Shakespeare made a unique contribution to the world of literature.* لا مثيل له، فريد

2 unique to sb/sth connected with only one place, person or thing: *This dance is unique to this region.* خاص بـ

3 (*informal*) very unusual: *There's nothing unique about that sort of crime.* استثنائي، متميز

unisex /'ju:nɪseks/ *adj* designed for and used by both sexes: *unisex fashions* للجنسين، للرجال والنساء

unison /'ju:nɪsn/ *noun*

IDM in unison saying, singing or doing the same thing at the same time as sb else: *'No, thank you,' they said in unison.* ○ *The chorus should be sung in unison.* سوياً: بصوت واحد

unit /'ju:nɪt/ *noun* [C] **1** a single thing which is complete in itself, although it can be part of sth larger: *The book is divided into ten units.* وحْدة

2 a fixed amount or number used as a standard of measurement: *a unit of currency* وحْدة

3 a group of people who perform a certain special function in a larger organization: *the intensive care unit of a hospital* وحْدة، فريق

4 a small machine that performs a particular task or that is part of a larger machine: *The heart of a computer is the central processing unit.* وحْدة، جزء

5 a piece of furniture that fits with other pieces of furniture and has a particular use: *matching kitchen units* وحْدة، قطعة

unite /ju'naɪt/ *verb* **1** [I,T] to join together and act in agreement; to make this happen: *Unless we unite, our enemies will defeat us.* ○ *The leader united the party behind him.* يتّحد؛ يوحّد

2 [I] **unite (in sth/in doing sth)** to join together for a particular purpose: *We should all unite in seeking a solution to this terrible problem.* يتوحد، يتحد

▸ **united** *adj* joined together by a common feeling or aim: *Throughout the crisis, the whole country remained united.* موحّد، متّحد

the U,nited 'Kingdom *noun* (*abbr* **UK**) England, Scotland, Wales and Northern Ireland
ℹ **The UK** includes England, Scotland, Wales and Northern Ireland, but *not* the Republic of Ireland (Eire), which is a separate country. **Great Britain** is England, Scotland and Wales only. **The British Isles** include England, Scotland, Wales, Northern Ireland and the Republic of Ireland. المملكة المتحدة

the U,nited 'Nations *noun* [with sing. or pl. verb] (*abbr* **UN**) the organization formed to encourage peace in the world and to deal with problems between nations الأمم المتحدة

the U,nited 'States (of A'merica) *noun* [with sing. or pl. verb] (*abbr* **US**; **USA**) a large country in North America made up of 50 states and the District of Columbia الولايات المتحدة الأمريكية

unity /'ju:nəti/ *noun* [U] the situation in which people are united or in agreement وحْدة

universal /,ju:nɪ'vɜ:sl/ *adj* connected with, done by or affecting everybody in the world or everybody in a particular group: *The environment is a universal issue.* ○ *There was universal agreement that it was a splendid wedding.* عامّ، عالمي

▸ **universally** /-səli/ *adv* في كلّ مكان، على نحو عام

universe /'ju:nɪvɜ:s/ *noun* [sing.] **the universe** everything that exists, including the planets, stars, space, etc. الكون

university /,ju:nɪ'vɜ:səti/ *noun* [C] (*pl.* **universities**) the highest level of educational institution, in which students study for degrees and in which academic research is done: *Which university did you go to?* ○ *a university lecturer* ○ *He studied at Hull University/the University of Hull.* جامعة

> We use the expressions **at university** and **go to university** without *a* or *the* when we mean that somebody attends the university as a student: *He's hoping to go to university next year*, but not if somebody goes there for any other reason: *I'm going to a conference at the university in July.*

unkind /,ʌn'kaɪnd/ *adj* not friendly or thoughtful; cruel: *That was an unkind thing to say.* قاسٍ، فظّ؛ عديم الرحمة

▸ **unkindly** *adv* بخشونة، بفظاظة

unkindness *noun* [C,U] خشونة، فظاظة، قسوة

unknown /,ʌn'nəʊn/ *adj* **1 unknown (to sb)** not known (by sb): *She left the job for unknown reasons.* ○ *Unknown to the boss, she went home early.* مجهول، غير معلوم

2 not famous or familiar to other people: *an unknown actress* غير معروف، مغمور

IDM an unknown quantity a person or thing that you know very little about شخص أو شيء مجهول الصفات

▸ **unknown** *noun* **1** usually **the unknown** [sing.] a place or thing that you know nothing about: *a fear of the unknown* الغيب، المجهول

2 [C] a person who is not well known: *A complete unknown won the tournament.* شخص مغمور

unleaded /,ʌn'ledɪd/ *adj* not containing lead: *unleaded petrol* لا يحتوي على مادة الرصاص

unless /ən'les/ *conj* if... not; except if: *Unless something unexpected happens, I'll see you next week.* ○ *I was told that unless my work improved, I would lose the job.* ○ *'Would you like a cup of coffee?' 'Not unless you've already made some.'* ○ *Unless anyone has anything else to say, the meeting is closed.* ○ *Don't switch that on unless I'm here.* ○ *That's what I've decided to do – unless there are any objections?* إلاّ إذا، ما لَمْ

unlike /,ʌn'laɪk/ *adj* not like; different from: *She's unlike anyone else I've ever met.* ○ *My new job is completely unlike my previous one.* ○ *The film is not unlike several others I've seen.* مغاير؛ مختلف عن

▸ **unlike** *prep* **1** in contrast to; differing from: *Unlike all the others, I wasn't very keen on the idea.* ○ *He's extremely ambitious, unlike me.* ○ *This is an exciting place to live, unlike my home town.* خلافاً لـ

2 not typical of; unusual for: *It's unlike him to be so rude, he's usually very polite.* على غير (طبيعته، شيمته)

unlikely /ʌn'laɪkli/ *adj* (**unlikelier**; **unlikeliest**)

1 not likely to happen; not expected; not probable: *He is seriously ill and unlikely to recover.* ○ *I suppose she might win but I think it's very unlikely.* ○ *It's unlikely that I'll have any free time next week.* مستبعد الوقوع؛ غير محتمل

2 difficult to believe: *an unlikely excuse* صعب التصديق

unlimited /ʌnˈlɪmɪtɪd/ *adj* without limit; as much or as great as you want مطلق، غير محدود

unload /ˌʌnˈləʊd/ *verb* **1** [I,T] **unload (sth) (from sth)** to take things that have been transported off or out of a vehicle: *to unload goods* ○ *I unloaded the car when I got home from the shops.* يفرّغ (حمولة سيارة مثلاً)

2 [I,T] (used about a vehicle) to have the things removed that have been transported: *Parking here is restricted to vehicles that are loading or unloading.* يقوم بتفريغ الحمولة

3 [T] **unload sb/sth (on/onto sb)** (*informal*) to get rid of sth you do not want or to pass it to sb else يتخلّص من؛ يلقي العبء على عاتق شخص آخر

unlock /ˌʌnˈlɒk/ *verb* [T] to open the lock on sth using a key يفتح (القفل)

unlucky /ʌnˈlʌki/ *adj* (**unluckier**; **unluckiest**) having or causing bad luck; not lucky: *They were unlucky to lose because they played so well.* ○ *Thirteen is often thought to be an unlucky number.* سيئ الحظ، منحوس

▸ **unluckily** *adv* as a result of bad luck; unfortunately: *Unluckily, I arrived just too late to meet them.* لسوء الحظ

unmarried /ˌʌnˈmærid/ *adj* not married; single غير متزوج

unmistakable /ˌʌnmɪˈsteɪkəbl/ *adj* that cannot be mistaken for anything else واضح، لا لَبس فيه

▸ **unmistakably** *adv* بشكل واضح (لا لَبس فيه)

unmoved /ˌʌnˈmuːvd/ *adj* not affected emotionally; feeling no sympathy, pity, sadness etc. غير متأثر، غير منفعل (بالأحداث)

unnatural /ʌnˈnætʃrəl/ *adj* different from what is normal or expected; not natural: *It seemed unnatural for a child to spend so much time alone.* غير معهود؛ غير طبيعي

▸ **unnaturally** /-rəli/ *adv*: *unnaturally quiet* ○ *Not unnaturally, she was delighted by the news.* على نحو غير طبيعي أو مألوف أو متوقّع

unnecessary /ʌnˈnesəsri; *US* -seri/ *adj* not necessary; more than is needed or acceptable: *It was unnecessary to ask because I already knew the answer.* ○ *unnecessary expense* غير ضروري؛ لا موجب له

▸ **unnecessarily** /ˌʌnˈnesəsərəli; *US* ˌʌnˌnesəˈserəli/ *adv*: *unnecessarily rude* بشكل لا موجب له

unnoticed /ˌʌnˈnəʊtɪst/ *adj* not noticed or seen: *All your hard work has not gone unnoticed.* غير ملاحظ؛ غير مقدّر

UNO /ˌjuː en ˈəʊ; ˈjuːnəʊ/ *abbrev* = UNITED NATIONS ORGANIZATION

unobtrusive /ˌʌnəbˈtruːsɪv/ *adj* avoiding being noticed; not attracting attention غير بارز، لا يلفت النظر

unofficial /ˌʌnəˈfɪʃl/ *adj* not accepted or approved by a person or people in authority; not known publicly: *an unofficial strike* ○ *The news of the royal divorce is still unofficial.* غير معلَن، غير رسمي

▸ **unofficially** /-ʃəli/ *adv* على نحو غير رسمي

unorthodox /ʌnˈɔːθədɒks/ *adj* different from what is generally accepted, usual or traditional: *Some of his methods are rather unorthodox.* غير تقليدي

unpack /ˌʌnˈpæk/ *verb* [I,T] to take out the things that were in a bag, suitcase, etc: *When we arrived at the hotel we unpacked and went to the beach.* ○ *to unpack a suitcase* يخرج (الأشياء من الحقيبة الخ)، يفرّغ

unpaid /ˌʌnˈpeɪd/ *adj* **1** not yet paid: *an unpaid bill* غير مسدّد

2 not receiving money for work done: *an unpaid assistant* دون أجر

3 (used about work) done without payment: *unpaid overtime* دون مقابل

unpleasant /ʌnˈpleznt/ *adj* **1** causing you to have a bad feeling; not pleasant: *This news has come as an unpleasant surprise.* كريه؛ مكدّر

2 unfriendly; impolite: *There's no need to get unpleasant, we can discuss this in a friendly way.* قليل الأدب؛ غير ودود

▸ **unpleasantly** *adv* على نحو كريه أو بغيض

unplug /ˌʌnˈplʌg/ *verb* [T] (unplu**gg**ing; unplu**gg**ed) to disconnect a piece of electrical equipment by removing the plug from the socket ❶ The opposite is **plug sth in**. يسحب القابس (الفيش) الكهربائي

unpopular /ʌnˈpɒpjələ(r)/ *adj* **unpopular (with sb)** not popular; not liked by many people غير محبوب؛ غير مقبول لدى الجمهور

▸ **unpopularity** /ˌʌnˌpɒpjəˈlærəti/ *noun* [U]: *What is the reason for her unpopularity?* عدم إقبال (الناس عليه)، عدم شعبيّة

unprecedented /ʌnˈpresɪdentɪd/ *adj* never having happened or existed before غير مسبوق

unprovoked /ˌʌnprəˈvəʊkt/ *adj* not caused by an earlier action: *an unprovoked attack* بدون تحرّش، دون استفزاز

unqualified /ˌʌnˈkwɒlɪfaɪd/ *adj* **1** not having the qualifications or knowledge for sth: *Being unqualified, she found her job opportunities were limited.* ○ *I'm unqualified to offer an opinion on this matter.* غير مؤهّل

2 complete; absolute: *an unqualified success* تامّ، مكتمل؛ مطلق

unquestionable /ʌnˈkwestʃənəbl/ *adj* certain; that cannot be doubted مؤكّد؛ لا يتطرق إليه الشك

▸ **unquestionably** /-əbli/ *adv*: *She is unquestionably the most famous opera singer in the world.* بلا ريب، بلا شك

unravel /ʌnˈrævl/ *verb* (unrave**ll**ing; unrave**ll**ed; *US* unraveling; unraveled) [I,T] **1** (used about threads which are knitted or woven) to come undone: *The knitting I was doing started to unravel.* ينفك، ينحل

2 (used about a complicated story, etc.) to become or to make sth become clear: *Eventually the mystery unravelled and the truth came out.* ينجلي، يتّضح، يحلّ اللغز

unreal /ˌʌnˈrɪəl/ *adj* very strange and seeming to be imagined غير حقيقي، وهمي

unreasonable /ʌnˈriːznəbl/ *adj* **1** not willing to listen to other people; acting without good reasons: *I think she is being totally unreasonable.* عنيد، متصلّب؛ مشتطّ

2 too great, expecting too much: *He makes unreasonable demands on his staff.* مفرط، متجاوز للحد المعقول

▸ **unreasonably** /-əbli/ *adv* على نحو غير معتدل، بشطط

unrelenting /ˌʌnrɪˈlentɪŋ/ *adj* continuously strong, not becoming weaker or stopping: *unrelenting pressure* لا يلين، لا يرحم؛ لا ينقطع

unreserved /ˌʌnrɪˈzɜːvd/ *adj* without limit; complete: *The government's action received the unreserved support of all parties.* غير محدود؛ تام

▸ **unreservedly** /ˌʌnrɪˈzɜːvɪdli/ *adv*: *We apologize unreservedly for our mistake and will refund your money.* مطلقاً، كلياً؛ بدون تحفّظ

unrest /ʌnˈrest/ *noun* [U] a situation in which people are angry or dissatisfied and likely to protest or fight: *social unrest* قلقلة، اضطراب

unrivalled (*US* **unrivaled**) /ʌnˈraɪvld/ *adj* better than any other of the same type; having no rival: *He had an unrivalled knowledge of Greek theology.* لا يضاهى، لا يضارع؛ متفوّق، فذّ

unroll /ʌnˈrəʊl/ *verb* [I,T] to open from a rolled position: *He unrolled the poster and stuck it on the wall.* يبسط، ينشر

unruly /ʌnˈruːli/ *adj* difficult to control; without discipline: *an unruly crowd* منفلت؛ عنيد، عاصٍ

▸ **unruliness** *noun* [U] شغب، انفلات؛ عناد

unsavoury (*US* **unsavory**) /ʌnˈseɪvəri/ *adj* unpleasant; that you do not trust: *a rather unsavoury individual* لا يوثق به؛ بغيض، كريه

unscathed /ʌnˈskeɪðd/ *adj* not hurt, without injury: *He came out of the fight unscathed.* من غير أذى، سالم

unscrew /ˌʌnˈskruː/ *verb* [T] **1** to remove the screws from sth يفك اللولب (البرغي)

2 to open or undo sth by turning it: *Could you unscrew the top of this bottle for me?* يفك، يحلّ

unscrupulous /ʌnˈskruːpjələs/ *adj* willing to be dishonest, cruel or unfair in order to get what you want عديم الضمير، لا يتورع، غير نزيه

unsightly /ʌnˈsaɪtli/ *adj* very unpleasant to look at; ugly: *an unsightly new building* بشع؛ كريه المنظر

unskilled /ˌʌnˈskɪld/ *adj* not having or requiring special skill or training: *an unskilled job* لا يتطلب مهارة أو براعة؛ غير مدرب

unsolicited /ˌʌnsəˈlɪsɪtɪd/ *adj* not asked for: *unsolicited praise* لم يُلتَمس

unsound /ˌʌnˈsaʊnd/ **1** in poor condition; weak: *The building is structurally unsound.* واهن، ضعيف؛ مضرّ؛ لا يوثق به

2 based on wrong ideas and therefore mistaken غير سليم

unstable /ʌnˈsteɪbl/ *adj* **1** likely to fall down or move; not firmly fixed غير مستقرّ؛ متقلقل

2 likely to change or fail: *a period of unstable government* غير مستقرّ

3 (used about a person's moods or behaviour) likely to change suddenly or frequently متقلب (نفسياً)، مختلّ (عاطفياً)

unstuck /ˌʌnˈstʌk/ *adj* no longer stuck together or glued down: *The label on the parcel came unstuck.* مفكّك، غير ملتصق

IDM come unstuck to fail badly; to be unsuccessful يفشل (فشلاً ذريعاً)؛ يخفق

unsure /ˌʌnˈʃʊə(r); *US* -ˈʃʊər/ *adj* **1 unsure of yourself** not feeling confident about yourself: *He's young and still quite unsure of himself.* غير واثق

2 unsure (about/of sth) not certain; having doubts: *I didn't argue because I was unsure of the facts.* مرتاب؛ غير متأكد

unsuspecting /ˌʌnsəˈspektɪŋ/ *adj* not aware of danger: *He came up quietly behind his unsuspecting victim.* غافل

untangle /ˌʌnˈtæŋgl/ *verb* [T] to separate threads which have become tied together in a confused way: *The wires got mixed up and it took me ages to untangle them.* يفكّ التشابك، يحلّ

unthinkable /ʌnˈθɪŋkəbl/ *adj* (used of an event, etc.) impossible to imagine or consider, especially because it is too painful or difficult لا يخطر على البال، لا يتصوّر

unthinking /ʌnˈθɪŋkɪŋ/ *adj* done, said, etc. without thinking carefully بلا رويّة أو تدبّر

▸ **unthinkingly** *adv* من غير تفكير في العواقب، على نحو طائش

untidy /ʌnˈtaɪdi/ *adj* (**untidier**; **untidiest**) **1** not neat or well arranged: *an untidy bedroom* ○ *untidy hair* غير مرتّب

2 (used about a person) not keeping things neat or in good order: *My flatmate is so untidy!* غير مهندم، مهمل، غير منظّم

▸ **untidily** /-ɪli/ *adv* على نحو غير مرتّب، بإهمال

untidiness *noun* [U] قذارة؛ عدم ترتيب، إهمال

untie /ʌnˈtaɪ/ *verb* [T] (*pres part* **untying**; *3rd pers sing pres* **unties**; *pt, pp* **untied**) to undo a knot; to free sb by undoing a rope, etc: *I can't get this knot untied.* يحرّر؛ يَفكّ، يحلّ

until /ənˈtɪl/ (*also* **till** /tɪl/) *conj* up to the time when: *She waited until he had finished.* ○ *Most men work until they're 65.* ○ *We won't leave until the police get here* (= we won't leave before they come). حتّى

▸ **until** (*also* **till**) *prep* up to the time or the event mentioned: *The restaurant is open until mid-*

a b c d e f g h i j k l m n o p q r s t **u** v w x y z

night. ○ *Until that moment she had been happy.* ○ *We can't leave until 10 o'clock* (= we can leave at 10 but not before). إلى (وقت معين)

> We can use **until** in both formal and informal English. **Till** is more common in informal English and is not usually used at the beginning of a sentence. Make sure that you only use **till/until** to talk about a time. We use **as far as** to talk about distance: *I walked as far as the shops.* We use **up to** to talk about a number: *You can take up to 20 kilos of luggage.*

untold /ˌʌnˈtəʊld/ *adj* very great; so big, etc. that you cannot count it: *untold suffering* ○ *untold wealth* لا يمكن تصوّره، لا يعدّ، لا يقدّر

untoward /ˌʌntəˈwɔːd; *US* ʌnˈtɔːrd/ *adj* (*formal*) (used about an event, etc.) unexpected and unpleasant غير متوقّع، غير مستحب

untruth /ˌʌnˈtruːθ/ *noun* [C] (*pl.* **untruths**) /-ˈtruːðz/ (*formal*) something that is not true; a lie: *to tell an untruth* أُكذوبة، كذبة، باطل

▶ **untruthful** /ʌnˈtruːθfl/ *adj*: *I don't like being untruthful.* غير صادق، كاذب

unused[1] /ˌʌnˈjuːzd/ *adj* that has not been used: *an unused stamp* غير مستعمل

unused[2] /ˌʌnˈjuːst/ *adj* (not before a noun) not having any experience of sth; not accustomed to sth: *She was unused to such a lot of attention.* غير متعوّد

⚷ **unusual** /ʌnˈjuːʒuəl/ *adj* **1** not expected or usual: *It's unusual for Joe to be late.* غير مألوف

2 interesting because it is different: *What an unusual hat!* طريف، غريب

▶ **unusually** /-ʒəli/ *adv* **1** more than is common; extremely: *an unusually hot summer* على نحو غير مألوف

2 in a way that is not normal or typical of sb/sth: *Unusually for her, she forgot his birthday.* على غير العادة أو المعهود

unveil /ˌʌnˈveɪl/ *verb* [T] to remove a type of cloth or curtain in order to show a new painting, etc. to the public: *The President unveiled a memorial to those who died in the war.* يميط (الستار)، يكشف

unwanted /ˌʌnˈwɒntɪd/ *adj* not wanted: *an unwanted gift* غير مرغوب فيه

unwarranted /ʌnˈwɒrəntɪd; *US* -ˈwɔːr-/ *adj* that is not deserved or for which there is no good reason لا موجب له، غير مبرّر

unwell /ʌnˈwel/ *adj* (not before a noun) ill; sick: *She's feeling rather unwell.* ➲ Look at the note at **sick**. متوعّك، مريض

unwieldy /ʌnˈwiːldi/ *adj* difficult to move or carry because it is too big, heavy, etc: *an unwieldy parcel* صعب المأخذ (لكبر حجمه أو ثقله الخ)

⚷ **unwilling** /ʌnˈwɪlɪŋ/ *adj* not wanting to do sth but often forced to do it by other people مكره

unwind /ˌʌnˈwaɪnd/ *verb* (*pt, pp* **unwound** /-ˈwaʊnd/) **1** [I,T] (used of sth that is wound round sth else) to become undone or to be pulled out: *The bandage had unwound.* ينْفكّ، يفكّ

2 [I] (*informal*) to relax, especially after working hard: *After a hard day at the office, it takes me a couple of hours to unwind.* يسترخي

unwitting /ʌnˈwɪtɪŋ/ *adj* not realizing sth; not intending to do sth: *an unwitting accomplice to the crime* غير متعمّد

▶ **unwittingly** *adv*: *The bank may have unwittingly broken the law.* دون قصد

unwrap /ʌnˈræp/ *verb* [T] to take off the paper, etc. that covers or protects sth يفتح، يزيل الغلاف

unzip /ˌʌnˈzɪp/ *verb* [T] (*computing*) to return a file to its original size after it has been compressed (= made smaller) يفكّ ضغط (الملف)

⚷ **up** /ʌp/ *prep, adv* ❶ For special uses with many verbs, e.g. **pick sth up**, look at the verb entries.

1 to a high or higher level or position: *The monkey climbed up the tree.* ○ *I carried her suitcase up to the third floor.* ○ *Put your hand up if you know the answer.* ○ *I walked up the hill.* إلى أعلى؛ فوق

2 into an upright position: *Stand up, please.* ○ *Is he up yet?* (= out of bed) ○ *I had to get up early.* منتصباً؛ واقفاً، مستيقظاً

3 (used for showing that an action continues until it is completed): *Eat up, everybody, I want you to finish everything on the table.* (تدلّ على الاستمرار حتى انجاز عمل ما): تماماً، حتى الآخر

4 (used with verbs of closing): *Do up your coat. It's cold.* ○ *She tied the parcel up with string.* (تستعمل مع أفعال تتعلق بالاغلاق)

5 very close to a person or thing: *She ran up to her mother and kissed her.* إلى قرب؛ على مقربة من

6 (used about a period of time) finished: *Stop writing. Your time's up.* انتهى الوقت

7 further along: *I live just up the road.* على بعد معيّن من

8 in a particular direction, usually north: *We're going up to York tomorrow.* نحوَ (الشمال)

9 into pieces: *We chopped the old table up and used it for firewood.* إرْباً إرْباً

10 (used for showing that sth is increasing): *Prices have gone up.* ○ *Turn the volume up.* نحو الأعلى

11 (used about computers) working; in operation: *Are the computers back up yet?* الكمبيوتر شغّال، غير معطّل

IDM **be up for sth 1** to be available to be bought or chosen: *That house is up for sale.* ○ *How many candidates are up for election?* معروض، جاهز لِ؛ متواجد

2 (*informal*) to be enthusiastic about doing sth: *Is anyone up for a swim?* يريد أن يفعل...

be up to sb to be sb's responsibility: *I can't take the decision. It's not up to me.* موكول إليه، يكون مسؤولاً عن

not up to much (*informal*) not very good: *The programme wasn't up to much.* غير جيد

up and down backwards and forwards, or so as to rise and fall: *He was running up and down the road screaming with pain.* جيئة وذهاباً؛ إلى الأعلى وإلى الأسفل

up and running (used about sth new) working

well: *The new system is already up and running.* (الجهاز الجديد) يعمل بصورة حسنة
up to sth 1 as much/many as: *We're expecting up to 100 people at the meeting.* (يصل العدد) إلى
2 as far as now: *Up to now, things have been easy.* حتى
3 capable of sth: *I don't feel up to cooking this evening. I'm too tired.* قادر على
4 doing sth secret and perhaps forbidden: *What are the children up to? Go and see.* يدبّر سرّاً
what's up? (*informal*) what's the matter? ما الأمر، ماذا يحدث؟
▶ **ups** *noun*
IDM **ups and downs** both good and bad luck: *Our marriage is happy but we've had our ups and downs.* تقلّبات الحياة وصروفها

upbringing /ˈʌpbrɪŋɪŋ/ *noun* [sing.] the way a child is treated and taught how to behave by his/her parents: *a religious upbringing* تربية، تنشئة

update /ˌʌpˈdeɪt/ *verb* [T] **1** to make sth more modern يجعل الشيء أكثر حداثة أو عصرية، يحدّث
2 to put the latest information into sth; to give sb the latest information: *Our database of addresses is updated regularly.* ○ *Shall I update you on what happened at the meeting?* يحيط علماً بآخر التطورات
▶ **update** /ˈʌpdeɪt/ *noun* [C]: *an update on a news story* (= the latest information) آخر الأخبار أو التطورات

upgrade /ˌʌpˈɡreɪd/ *verb* [T] to change sth so that it is of a higher standard يرقّي، يرفع، يصعّد
▶ **upgrade** /ˈʌpɡreɪd/ *noun* [C] ترقية، ترفيع

upheaval /ʌpˈhiːvl/ *noun* [C,U] a sudden big change, especially one that causes a lot of trouble تغيّر عنيف؛ اضطراب

uphill /ˌʌpˈhɪl/ *adj, adv* **1** going up a slope, towards the top of a hill: *a long walk uphill* ❶ The opposite is **downhill**. صاعد إلى أعلى الجبل أو الرابية
2 needing a lot of effort: *It was an uphill struggle to find a job.* مجهِد، شاقّ

uphold /ʌpˈhəʊld/ *verb* [T] (*pt, pp* **upheld** /-ˈheld/) to support sth (a decision, etc.) especially when other people are against it: *We must uphold the court's decision.* يتمسك بِ، يساند

upholstered /ˌʌpˈhəʊlstəd/ *adj* (used about a chair, etc.) fitted with a layer of soft material and covered with cloth منجّد

upholstery /-stəri/ *noun* [U] the thick soft materials used to cover chairs, car seats, etc. أقمشة التنجيد

upkeep /ˈʌpkiːp/ *noun* [U] the cost or process of keeping sth in a good condition: *The landlord pays for the upkeep of the building.* كلفة الصيانة، صيانة

upland /ˈʌplənd/ *adj* situated on a hill or mountain: *an upland area* على أرض مرتفعة، نجدي
▶ **upland** *noun* [C, usually pl.] high areas of land أرض مرتفعة، نجد

uplifting /ˌʌpˈlɪftɪŋ/ *adj* producing a feeling of hope and happiness: *an uplifting speech* منعش

upmarket /ˌʌpˈmɑːkɪt/ *adj* (used about products, services, etc.) designed to appeal to or to satisfy people in the higher social classes: *an upmarket restaurant/shop/car* ➲ Look at **downmarket**. راقٍ، رفيع
▶ **upmarket** *adv*: *to go/move upmarket* إلى منزلة أرقى

🔑 **upon** /əˈpɒn/ *prep* (*formal*) = ON

🔑 **upper** /ˈʌpə(r)/ *adj* in a higher position than sth else; situated above sth: *the upper floors of a building* ○ *the upper lip* أعلى؛ علوي
IDM **get, etc. the upper hand** to get into a stronger position than another person; to gain control over sb يهيمن، يتحكّم بِ، يسيطر؛ يسود

ˌupper ˈcase *noun* [U] letters that are written or printed in a large form; capital letters: *'BBC' is written in upper case.* ❶ The opposite is **lower case.** حروف استهلالية

ˌupper ˈclass *adj, noun* [C, with sing. or pl. verb] (of) the social class that is above the middle class; people with a lot of money and land and sometimes special titles الطبقة العليا

uppermost /ˈʌpəməʊst/ *adj* in the highest or most important position: *Concern for her family was uppermost in her mind.* الأسمى، الأعلى

upright /ˈʌpraɪt/ *adj* **1** with a straight back; standing vertically: *Please put the back of your seat in an upright position.* ○ *an upright piano* منتصب، عمودي
2 honest and responsible: *an upright citizen* مستقيم، نزيه
IDM **bolt upright** → BOLT
▶ **upright** *adv* with a straight back; into a vertical position: *to stand upright* منتصباً؛ عمودياً

uprising /ˈʌpraɪzɪŋ/ *noun* [C] a situation in which a group of people start to fight against the people in power in their country: *an armed uprising* تمرّد، ثورة، انتفاضة

uproar /ˈʌprɔː(r)/ *noun* [sing., U] a loud noise of excitement, confusion, anger, etc.; an angry discussion about sth: *The meeting ended in uproar.* ضجيج، صخب
▶ **uproarious** /ʌpˈrɔːriəs/ *adj* very noisy: *uproarious laughter* صاخب

uproot /ˌʌpˈruːt/ *verb* [T] to tear up a plant by the roots: *Strong winds had uprooted the tree.* ○ (*figurative*) *Many people have to uproot themselves when they change jobs* (= leave the place where they have lived for a long time). يستأصل، يجتثّ

upsell /ˈʌpsel/ *verb* [I] to persuade a customer to buy more products or a more expensive product than they originally intended
يرتقي بالمبيعات: يحوّل المستهلك عن طلبه إلى سلعة أثمن أو إلى شراء كميات أكبر

🔑 **upset** /ʌpˈset/ *verb* [T] (*pres part* **upsetting**; *pt, pp* **upset**) **1** to make sb worry or feel unhappy: *The pictures of starving children upset her.*

a b c d e f g h i j k l m n o p q r s t u v w x y z

○ *I was quite upset at losing my purse.* ينزعج: يعكّر (الصفو)، يزعج

2 to make sth go wrong: *to upset someone's plans* يفسد، يربك

3 to knock sth over: *I upset a pot of coffee all over the tablecloth.* يقلب

4 to make sb ill in the stomach: *Rich food usually upsets me.* يوعك المعدة

▸ **upset** /ˈʌpset/ *noun* **1** [C,U] the act of upsetting (1,2) or being upset: *I've had quite a few upsets recently.* مكدر، منغص، شيء مزعج

2 [C] a slight illness in your stomach: *a stomach upset* اضطراب في المعدة

upset /ˌʌpˈset/ *adj* **1** worried and unhappy: *She was looking very upset about something.* قلق، منزعج

2 slightly ill: *I've got an upset stomach.* متوعك

Note that the adjective is pronounced /ˈʌpset/ when it comes before a noun and /ˌʌpˈset/ in other positions in the sentence.

upshot /ˈʌpʃɒt/ *noun* [sing.] **the upshot (of sth)** the final result, especially of a conversation or an event نتيجة (نهائية)، خلاصة

upside down /ˌʌpsaɪd ˈdaʊn/ *adv* **1** with the top part turned to the bottom: *You're holding the picture upside down.* ○ *She was hanging upside down.* على نحو معكوس، بالمقلوب

2 (*informal*) in or into a very untidy state: *He turned the house upside down looking for his keys.* رأسا على عقب

⚷ **upstairs** /ˌʌpˈsteəz/ *adv* to or on the upper floor of a building: *to go upstairs* ○ *She's sleeping upstairs.* إلى أو في دور أعلى (من المبنى)

▸ **upstairs** *adj*: *an upstairs window* في طابق علوي

upstairs *noun* [sing.] (*informal*) **the upstairs** the upper floor of a house: *We're going to paint the upstairs.* الطابق العلوي

upstream /ˌʌpˈstriːm/ *adv* moving against the direction that a river flows: *He found it hard work swimming upstream.* ضد التيار

▸ **upstream** *adj* (not before a noun) situated nearer to the place that a river flows from قرب منبع النهر

upsurge /ˈʌpsɜːdʒ/ *noun* [C, usually sing.] a sudden increase of sth: *an upsurge in violent crime* ارتفاع مفاجئ

uptake /ˈʌpteɪk/ *noun*

IDM **quick/slow on the uptake** quick/slow to understand the meaning of sth: *I gave him a hint but he's slow on the uptake.* سريع/بطئ الفهم أو الاستيعاب

uptight /ˌʌpˈtaɪt/ *adj* (*informal*) **1** nervous: *He gets uptight before an exam.* مرتعب، خائف؛ عصبي

2 angry: *Don't get so uptight – it's only a game.* ساخط، غاضب

ˌup-to-ˈdate *adj* **1** modern: *up-to-date fashions* عصري

2 having the most recent information: *an up-to-date dictionary* حديث

ˌup-to-the-ˈminute *adj* having the most recent information possible: *an up-to-the-minute news report* حاوٍ لأحدث المعلومات

upturn /ˈʌptɜːn/ *noun* [C] an improvement or a gain in sth: *an upturn in support for the government* تحوّل إيجابي، تحسّن

upturned /ˌʌpˈtɜːnd/ *adj* **1** pointing upwards: *an upturned nose* مرفوع إلى أعلى

2 turned upside down: *an upturned boat* مقلوب

⚷ **upward** /ˈʌpwəd/ *adj* moving or directed towards a higher place: *an upward glance* ○ *an upward trend in exports* (= an increase) متّجه نحو الأعلى

▸ **upward** (*also* **upwards** /-wədz/) *adv* moving towards, or in the direction of, a higher place: *I looked upwards.* إلى فوق

upwards of *prep* more than (the number mentioned): *They've invited upwards of a hundred guests.* ما يزيد على

uranium /juˈreɪniəm/ *noun* [U] (*symbol* **U**) a radioactive metal that can be used to produce nuclear energy معْدِن اليورانيوم

Uranus /ˈjʊərənəs; jʊˈreɪnəs/ *noun* [sing.] the planet that is seventh in order from the sun اورانوس: سابع الكواكب السيّارة

⚷ **urban** /ˈɜːbən/ *adj* of a town or city: *urban development* مديني، حضري

⚷ **urge** /ɜːdʒ/ *verb* [T] **1** to try hard to persuade sb to do sth: *I urged him to fight the decision.* يحثّ

2 to advise strongly, especially that sth is necessary: *Drivers are urged to take care on icy roads.* ينصح

3 to force or drive sb/sth in a certain direction: *He urged his horse over the fence.* يدفع (بقوة)

PHR V **urge sb on** to encourage sb: *The captain urged his team on.* يشجّع، يحفز

▸ **urge** *noun* [C] a strong need or desire: *sexual urges* دافع

⚷ **urgent** /ˈɜːdʒənt/ *adj* needing immediate attention: *an urgent message* ○ *It's not urgent; I'll tell you about it later.* مُلحّ، عاجل

▸ **urgency** /-dʒənsi/ *noun* [U]: *a matter of the greatest urgency* أمر مستعجل جدًا

urgently *adv*: *I must see you urgently.* على جناح السرعة، سريعاً

urine /ˈjʊərɪn/ *noun* [U] the yellow liquid that is passed from your body when you go to the toilet بول

▸ **urinate** /ˈjʊərɪneɪt/ *verb* [I] (*formal*) to pass urine from the body يبول

URL /ˌjuː ɑːr ˈel/ *abbrev* uniform/universal resource locator; the address of a World Wide Web page عنوان صفحة انترنت

urn /ɜːn/ *noun* [C] **1** a type of vase, especially one in which the ashes of a dead person are kept جرّة

2 a large metal container used for making a large quantity of tea or coffee and for keeping it hot غلاّية

US /ˌjuː ˈes/ (*also* **USA** /ˌjuː es ˈeɪ/) (*especially US*

U.S., U.S.A.) *abbrev* = UNITED STATES (OF AMERICA)

us /əs; *strong form* ʌs/ *pron* (used as the object of a verb, or after *be*) me and another person or other people; me and you: *Come with us.* ○ *Leave us alone.* ○ *Will you write to us?* ○ *Hello, it's us again!* (ضمير)... نا؛ نحن

usage /ˈjuːsɪdʒ; ˈjuːzɪdʒ/ *noun* **1** [U] the way that sth is used; the amount that sth is used: *With normal usage, the machine should last for years.* استخدام؛ استهلاك

2 [C,U] the way that words are normally used in a language: *a guide to English grammar and usage* استعمال

USB /ˌjuː es ˈbiː/ *abbrev* universal serial bus (the system for connecting other pieces of equipment to a computer): *a USB stick* مسرى تسلسلي عميم

use[1] /juːz/ *verb* [T] (*pres part* **using**; *pt, pp* **used** /juːzd/) **1** when you use sth, you do sth with it for a purpose: *Could I use your phone?* ○ *We used the money to buy a house.* ○ *The building was used as a shelter for homeless people.* ○ *A gun is used for shooting with.* ○ *Use your imagination!* ○ *That's a word I never use.* يستخدم، يستعمل

2 to need or to take sth: *Don't use all the milk.* يستهلك

3 to treat sb/sth in a selfish or unkind way: *He just used me to get what he wanted and then forgot about me.* يستغلّ

PHRV **use sth up** to use sth until no more is left يأتي على الشيء، يستهلك، يستنفد

▸ **usable** /ˈjuːzəbl/ *adj* that can be used قابل للاستعمال، صالح للاستخدام

use[2] /juːs/ *noun* **1** [U] using or being used: *The use of computers is now widespread.* ○ *She kept the money for use in an emergency.* استعمال

2 [C,U] the purpose for which sth is used: *This machine has many uses.* استخدام

3 [U] the ability or permission to use sth: *He lost the use of his hand after the accident.* ○ *She offered them the use of her car.* استخدام أو استفادة من

4 [U] the advantage of sth; how useful sth is: *It's no use studying for an exam at the last minute.* ○ *What's the use of trying?* فائدة؛ جدوى

IDM **come into/go out of use** to start/stop being used يَشيع أو يبطل استعماله

make use of sth/sb to use sth in a way that will give you an advantage يستفيد من، يستغلّ

used[1] /juːzd/ *adj* that has had an owner before: *a garage selling used cars* ❶ Another word with the same meaning is **second-hand**. مستَعْمَل

used[2] /juːst/ *adj* **used to sth/to doing sth** familiar with sth; accustomed to sth: *He's used to the heat.* ○ *I'll never get used to getting up at five.* متعوِّد على

used to /ˈjuːst tə; *before a vowel and in final position* ˈjuːst tuː/ *modal verb* (for talking about sth that happened often or continuously in the past or about a situation which existed in the past): *She used to live with her parents* (= but she doesn't now). ○ *You used to live in Glasgow, didn't you?* ○ *Did you use to smoke?* ○ *I used not to like him.* ○ *He didn't use to speak to me.*
تركيب يدل على الماضي ويقابله بالعربية فعل "كان" مع المضارع

> We usually use **did** to form negatives and questions with **used to**: *I didn't use to like jazz.* ○ *Did she use to be in your class?* The following negative and question forms of **used to** are more formal and not often used: *He used not to drive a car.* ○ *Used they to work here?* Be careful not to confuse **used to** + infinitive, which only refers to the past, with **to be used to (doing) sth**, which can refer to the past, present or future. Compare: *I used to live on my own* (= but now I don't). ○ *I'm used to living on my own* (= I am accustomed to it).

useful /ˈjuːsfl/ *adj* having some practical use; helpful: *a useful tool* ○ *useful advice* نافع، مفيد

IDM **come in useful** to be of practical help, especially in a situation where there is no other help available يساعد على حلّ مشكلة عملية

▸ **usefully** /-fəli/: *Make sure your time is spent usefully.* على نحو نافع أو مفيد

usefulness /-fəlnəs/ *noun* [U] جدوى، استفادة، نَفْع

useless /ˈjuːsləs/ *adj* **1** that does not work well, or is of no use: *This new machine is useless.* ○ *It's useless complaining/to complain; you won't get your money back.* عديم الجدوى، عديم النفع

2 (*informal*) (of a person) weak or not successful at sth: *I'm useless at sport.* فاشل؛ ضعيف

▸ **uselessly** *adv* على نحو عقيم أو غير نافع

uselessness *noun* [U] فشل، عدم الجدوى

user /ˈjuːzə(r)/ *noun* [C] (often in compounds) a person that uses a service, machine, place, etc: *users of public transport* مُستَخدِم

▸ **ˌuser-ˈfriendly** *adj* (used of computers, books, machines, etc.) easy or not too complicated to use سهل الاستخدام

username /ˈjuːzəneɪm/ *noun* [C] (*computing*) the name you use in order to be able to use a computer program or system اسم المستعمِل

usher /ˈʌʃə(r)/ *noun* [C] a person who shows people to their seats in a cinema, church, etc. دليل، مرشد

▸ **usher** *verb* [T] to lead sb carefully in the direction mentioned: *I was ushered to my seat.* يرشد

PHRV **usher sth in** to mark the beginning of sth: *The agreement ushered in a new period of peace for the two countries.* يبشّر بـ

usherette /ˌʌʃəˈret/ *noun* [C] (*especially Brit*) a woman who shows people to their seats in a cinema or theatre دليلة، مرشدة

USP /ˌjuː es ˈpiː/ *abbrev* unique selling proposition/unique selling point; a feature of a product or service that makes it different from all the others that are available and is a reason for people to choose it
المميِّز الذي يجعل سلعة ما فريدة دون بقية السلع

usual /ˈjuːʒuəl/ *adj* happening or used most often: *It's usual for her to work at weekends.* ○ *He* *got home later than usual.* ○ *I sat in my usual seat.* مألوف، معتاد

IDM **as usual** in the way that has often happened before: *Here's Damian, late as usual!* كالعادة، كالعهد (به)

▸ **usually** /'juːʒuəli/ *adv* in the way that is usual; most often: *She's usually home by six.* ○ *Usually, we go out on Saturdays.* من المألوف؛ كثيراً ما، عادة

utensil /juː'tensl/ *noun* [C] a type of tool or object used in the home: *cooking utensils* أداة، وعاء، إناء

uterus /'juːtərəs/ *noun* [C] (*pl.* **uteruses** or, in scientific use, **uteri** /-raɪ/) (*formal*) the part of a woman's body where a baby grows ❶ A less formal word is **womb**. رَحِم

utility /juː'tɪləti/ *noun* (*pl.* **utilities**) **1** [U] (*formal*) the usefulness (of a machine, etc.) فائدة

2 [C] a useful public service, such as the supplying of water or gas مرفق عام

u'tility room *noun* [C] a small room in a house, often next to the kitchen, where people sometimes keep a washing machine, etc. حجرة صغيرة لاستخدامات مختلفة

utilize (*also* **utilise**) /'juːtəlaɪz/ *verb* [T] (*formal*) to make use of sth: *to utilize natural resources* يستغلّ؛ يستعمل

utmost /'ʌtməʊst/ *adj* (only *before* a noun) (*formal*) greatest: *a message of the utmost importance* أقصى

▸ **utmost** *noun* [sing.] the greatest extent, amount, degree, etc. that is possible: *I did my utmost to help.* قصارى (الجهد)

Utopia /juː'təʊpiə/ *noun* [C,U] an imaginary society or place where everything is perfect المجتمع الفاضل، يوطوبيا

▸ **Utopian** /-piən/ *adj* خيالي، مثالي، طوباوي

utter¹ /'ʌtə(r)/ *adj* (only *before* a noun) complete; total: *That's utter nonsense!* ○ *He felt an utter fool.* كامل، مطلق

▸ **utterly** *adv*: *It's utterly impossible.* مطلقاً، على نحو تام

utter² /'ʌtə(r)/ *verb* [T] to speak or make a sound with your mouth: *She left without uttering a word.* يفوه، ينْطِق

▸ **utterance** /'ʌtərəns/ *noun* [C] (*formal*) something that is said لفظة، قول

U-turn /'juː tɜːn/ *noun* [C] **1** a type of movement where a car, etc. turns round so that it goes back in the direction it came دورة إلى الاتجاه المعاكس

2 a sudden change from one plan to a completely different one تحوّل تام ومفاجئ

Vv

V, v /viː/ *noun* [C] (*pl.* **Vs**; **V's**; **v's**) **1** the twenty-second letter of the English alphabet: *'Van' begins with (a) 'V'.* الحرف الثاني والعشرون من الأبجدية الإنكليزية

2 the shape of a V: *The birds were flying in a V.* على شكل هذا الحرف

V *abbrev* = VOLT(s)

v *abbrev* **1** (*pl.* **vv**) = VERSE

2 (*also* **vs**) = VERSUS

3 (*Brit informal*) = VERY: *v good*

vacancy /'veɪkənsi/ *noun* [C] (*pl.* **vacancies**) **1** a room in a hotel, etc. that is not being used: *The sign outside the hotel said 'No Vacancies'.* غرفة شاغرة (في فندق مثلاً)

2 a job that has not been filled: *We have a vacancy for a secretary in our office.* وظيفة شاغرة

vacant /'veɪkənt/ *adj* **1** (of a house, room, seat, etc.) not being used خالٍ

2 (of a job, etc.) not filled: *the 'Situations Vacant' page* (= the page of a newspaper where jobs are advertised) شاغر

3 showing no sign of intelligence or understanding: *a vacant expression* أبله؛ خالٍ من المعنى

▸ **vacantly** *adv*: *She stared vacantly out of the window.* على نحو ساهم، بشرود

🔑 **vacation** /və'keɪʃn; *US* veɪ-/ *noun* **1** [C,U] (*US*) (a) holiday: *The boss is on vacation.* ➲ Look at the note at **holiday**. إجازة

2 [C] any of the holiday periods when a university is closed: *the Easter vacation* عطلة

vaccinate /'væksɪneɪt/ *verb* [T] to give an injection to prevent a person or an animal from getting a disease: *Were you vaccinated against measles as a child?* يطعِّم، يلقّح

▸ **vaccination** /ˌvæksɪ'neɪʃn/ *noun* [C,U] تطعيم، تلقيح

vaccine /'væksiːn; *US* væk'siːn/ *noun* [C] a substance that is given to people in an injection in order to protect them against a disease لِقاح

vacuum /'vækjuəm/ *noun* [C] **1** a space that contains no substance and no air or gas: (*figurative*) *a vacuum in her life* (= a feeling of emptiness) فراغ، خلاء

2 (*informal*) = VACUUM CLEANER

▸ **vacuum** *verb* [I,T] to clean sth using a vacuum cleaner يكنس بالمكنسة الكهربائية

'vacuum cleaner *noun* [C] an electric machine that cleans carpets, etc. by sucking up dirt مكنسة كهربائية

'vacuum flask (*US* **'vacuum bottle**) (*also* **flask**; **Thermos™**) a type of container used for keeping a liquid hot or cold تِرْمس

vagina /və'dʒaɪnə/ *noun* [C] the passage in the

body of a woman or female animal that connects the outer sex organs to the part where a baby grows (the womb) مهْبِل

vague /veɪg/ *adj* **1** not clear or definite: *vague memories of my childhood home* غامض

2 (used about a person) not thinking or understanding clearly: *She looked vague when I tried to explain.* مشوَّش

3 not clearly seen: *a vague shape in the distance* غير واضح، مبهم

▸ **vaguely** *adv* **1** in a way that is not clear; slightly: *Her name is vaguely familiar.* بصورة غامضة؛ بعض الشيء

2 without thinking about what is happening: *He smiled vaguely and walked away.* بشرود

vagueness *noun* [U] إبهام، غموض

vain /veɪn/ *adj* **1** (used about a person) too proud of your appearance, of what you can do, etc. ❶ The noun is **vanity**. مغرور، مزْهو

2 useless; without any hope of success: *a vain attempt* بلا جدوى، عبثاً

IDM in vain without success: *The firemen tried in vain to put out the fire.* بلا طائل

▸ **vainly** *adv* من غير جدوى

vale /veɪl/ *noun* [C] a valley: *the Vale of York* ❶ We use this word in place names and in poetry. وادٍ

valentine /ˈvæləntaɪn/ *noun* [C] **1** (*also* **ˈvalentine card**) a card that you send, usually secretly, to someone you love or like in a romantic way ❶ It is traditional to send these cards on **St Valentine's Day** (14 February). بطاقة غرامية

2 the person you send this card to: *Be my valentine* (= written on a valentine card). حبيبة، حبيب

valiant /ˈvæliənt/ *adj* (*formal*) very brave باسل، شجاع

▸ **valiantly** *adv* ببسالة، بشجاعة

⚿ **valid** /ˈvælɪd/ *adj* **1** that can be used or accepted legally at a certain time: *This passport is valid for one year only.* ساري المفعول، صالح

2 acceptable in a court of law: *a valid contract* شرعي، قانوني

3 (used about a reason, etc.) strong enough to convince sb; acceptable: *I could raise no valid objections to the plan.* مقنع؛ مقبول، سليم

❶ The opposite is **invalid**.

▸ **validity** /vəˈlɪdəti/ *noun* [U]: *the validity of an argument* ○ *the validity of a law* صلاحية، صحّة

⚿ **valley** /ˈvæli/ *noun* [C] the flat land that lies between two lines of mountains or hills and which often has a river flowing through it وادٍ

valour (*US* **valor**) /ˈvælə(r)/ *noun* [U] great bravery, especially in war: *the soldiers' valour in battle* ❶ This word is used in old, formal or poetic writing. إقدام، بسالة، شجاعة

⚿ **valuable** /ˈvæljuəbl/ *adj* **1** worth a lot of money: *Is this ring valuable?* نفيس، قيِّم، ثمين

2 very useful: *a valuable piece of information* نافع، مفيد

❶ The opposite is **valueless** or **worthless**, not **invaluable**.

▸ **valuables** *noun* [plural] the small things that you own that are worth a lot of money, such as jewellery, etc: *Please put your valuables in the hotel safe.* الأشياء النفيسة، نفائس

valuation /ˌvæljuˈeɪʃn/ *noun* [C,U] the act of estimating how much sth is worth تقدير قيمة الشيء، تثمين، تقويم

⚿ **value** /ˈvælju:/ *noun* **1** [U] the usefulness or importance of sth: *the value of education* ○ *of great/little value* أهمية

2 [C,U] the amount of money that sth is worth: *The thieves stole goods with a total value of £10 000.* ○ *The shares have increased in value this month.* ○ *to go up/down in value* ➲ Look at **face value**. قيمة

3 [U] how much sth is worth compared with its price: *The hotel was good value at £40 a night.* قيمة

4 values [plural] a set of beliefs about the way people should behave; moral principles: *the traditional values of Western society* قِيَم

▸ **value** *verb* [T] (*pres part* **valuing**) **1 value sth (at sth)** to decide the amount of money that sth is worth: *The house was valued at £300 000.* يقيِّم، يثمِّن

2 to think sb/sth is very important and worth a lot: *Laura has always valued her independence.* يقدِّر كلَّ التقدير

valueless *adj* without value or use; worthless ➲ Look at **invaluable**. تافه؛ عديم القيمة

ˌvalue ˈadded tax *noun* [U] (*abbr* **VAT**) a tax on the increase in value of sth at each stage of its production ضريبة القيمة المضافة

valve /vælv/ *noun* [C] a mechanical device which controls the flow of air, liquid or gas in a pipe or tube: *a radiator valve* ○ *the valve on a bicycle tyre* صِمام

vampire /ˈvæmpaɪə(r)/ *noun* [C] (in horror stories) a dead person who comes out of his/her grave at night and sucks the blood of living people مصّاص الدماء

⚿ **van** /væn/ *noun* [C] a road vehicle that is used for transporting things ❶ A **van** is smaller than a **lorry** and is always covered. عربة مقفلة لنقل البضائع

vandal /ˈvændl/ *noun* [C] a person who damages property (e.g. cars, shop windows, etc.) intentionally and for no purpose مخرِّب للممتلكات

▸ **vandalism** /-dəlɪzəm/ *noun* [U]: *The police are worried about the recent increase in vandalism.* تخريب ممتلكات الغير

vandalize (*also* **vandalise**) /ˈvændəlaɪz/ *verb* [T] (usually passive) to damage property intentionally and for no purpose يخرِّب ممتلكات الغير

vanilla /vəˈnɪlə/ *noun* [U] a substance from a plant that is used for giving flavour to sweet food: *Strawberry, chocolate or vanilla ice cream?* فانيليا

vanish /ˈvænɪʃ/ *verb* [I] **1** to disappear suddenly and completely: *When he turned round, the two* *men had vanished.* ○ *His fear vanished when he heard his sister's voice outside the door.* يختفي

2 (used about types of things) to disappear little by little over a period of time: *This species of plant is vanishing from the British countryside.* ينقرض؛ يتلاشى

vanity /ˈvænəti/ *noun* [U] the quality of being too proud of your appearance or abilities ℹ The adjective is **vain**. غرور

vapour (*US* **vapor**) /ˈveɪpə(r)/ *noun* [C,U] a substance made of very small drops of liquid which hang together in the air like a cloud or mist: *water vapour* بُخار

variable /ˈveəriəbl/ *adj* not staying the same; changeable متقلّب؛ متغيّر
▸ **variability** /ˌveəriəˈbɪləti/ *noun* [U] تقلّب؛ تغيّر

variant *noun* [C] a different form of sth شكل مختلف؛ نوع من...

🔑 **variation** /ˌveəriˈeɪʃn/ *noun* **1** [C,U] **variation (in sth)** a difference in quality or quantity between a number of things: *There was a lot of variation in the examination results* (= the results were very different from each other). ○ *There may be a slight variation in price from shop to shop.* اختلاف

2 [C] **variation (on/of sth)** something that is almost the same as another thing but has some small differences: *All his films are just variations on a basic theme.* تنويع

🔑 **varied** /ˈveərid/ *adj* having many different kinds of things or activities: *The restaurant has a varied menu of meat, fish and vegetables.* ○ *The work of an English teacher is interesting and varied.* متنوّع

🔑 **variety** /vəˈraɪəti/ *noun* (*pl.* **varieties**) **1** [U] the quality of not being the same: *There's so much variety in my new job. I do something different every day!* تنوّع

2 [C] **a variety (of sth)** a number of different kinds of things: *You can take evening classes in a variety of subjects including photography, Spanish and computing.* نوع، ضَرْب

3 [C] **a variety (of sth)** a type of sth: *a new variety of apple called 'Perfection'* صَنف

🔑 **various** /ˈveəriəs/ *adj* (used for describing things that are different from each other) more than one; several: *Our shop sells hats in various shapes, colours and sizes.* ○ *I decided to leave London for various reasons.* متنوّع، مختلف؛ متعدّد

varnish /ˈvɑːnɪʃ/ *noun* [U] a clear liquid that you paint onto wood or other hard surfaces to protect them and make them shine ➲ Look at **nail varnish**. برنيق، ورنيش
▸ **varnish** *verb* [T] يطّلي بالورنيش

🔑 **vary** /ˈveəri/ *verb* (*pres part* **varying**; *3rd pers sing pres* **varies**; *pt, pp* **varied**) **1** [I] (used about a number of things) to be different from each other: *The hotel bedrooms vary in size from medium to very large.* يتباين

2 [I] to become different; to change: *The price of the holiday varies from £500 to £1 200, depending on the time of year.* يتراوح؛ يختلف

3 [T] to make sth different by changing it often in some way: *I try to vary my work as much as possible so I don't get bored.* ينوّع

vase /vɑːz; *US* veɪs; veɪz/ *noun* [C] a glass or china container used for holding cut flowers مَزْهرِية

vasectomy /vəˈsektəmi/ *noun* [C] (*pl.* **vasectomies**) a small medical operation that prevents a man from having children, by cutting the tube that carries sperm قَطع القناة الدافقة

🔑 **vast** /vɑːst; *US* væst/ *adj* extremely big: *a vast sum of money* ○ *a vast country* واسع، مترامي الأطراف؛ هائل
▸ **vastly** *adv*: *a vastly improved traffic system* للغاية؛ كثيراً

VAT (*also* **Vat**) /ˌviː eɪ ˈtiː; væt/ *abbrev* = VALUE ADDED TAX

vault¹ /vɔːlt/ *noun* [C] **1** a strong underground room in a bank, etc. that is used for keeping money and other valuable things safe قبو، سرداب

2 a room under a church where dead people are buried مدفن (تحت كنيسة)

3 a high roof or ceiling in a church, etc., made from a number of arches joined together at the top عقد؛ سقف مقبّب

vault² /vɔːlt/ *verb* [I,T] **vault (over sth)** to jump over or onto sth in one movement, using your hands or a pole to help you: *The boy vaulted over the wall.* ○ *to pole-vault* يقفز (من فوقه)

VCR /ˌviː siː ˈɑː(r)/ *abbrev* = VIDEO CASSETTE RECORDER

VDU /ˌviː diː ˈjuː/ *abbrev* (*computing*) = VISUAL DISPLAY UNIT

veal /viːl/ *noun* [U] the meat from a young cow (a calf) ➲ Look at the note at **meat**. لحم العجل

veer /vɪə(r)/ *verb* [I] (used about vehicles) to change direction suddenly: *The car veered across the road and hit a tree.* ينحرف

vegan /ˈviːgən/ *noun* [C] a person who does not eat any animal products ➲ Look at **vegetarian**. من لا يأكل أية منتوجات حيوانيّة

🔑 **vegetable** /ˈvedʒtəbl/ *noun* [C] a plant which you eat as food, e.g. potatoes, carrots and onions: *fresh fruit and vegetables* ○ *green vegetables* (= cabbage, lettuce, etc.) ○ *vegetable soup* ○ *a vegetable garden* خُضرة (خضراوات)

vegetarian /ˌvedʒəˈteəriən/ *noun* [C] a person who does not eat meat or fish شخص نباتي

vegetation /ˌvedʒəˈteɪʃn/ *noun* [U] (*formal*) plant life in general; all the plants that are found in a particular place: *tropical vegetation* الحياة النباتية؛ نباتات

vehement /ˈviːəmənt/ *adj* showing strong (often negative) feeling: *a vehement attack on the government* محتدّ، عنيف

🔑 **vehicle** /ˈviːəkl; *US* viːhɪkl/ *noun* [C] (*formal*)

1 something which transports people or things from place to place, especially on land, e.g. cars, bicycles, lorries and buses: *a motor vehicle* عربة، مركبة

2 something which is used for communicating particular ideas or opinions: *This newspaper has become a vehicle for Conservative opinion.* وسيلة (للتعبير عن)

veil /veɪl/ *noun* [C] a piece of thin material for covering the head and face of a woman حجاب، خمار

vein /veɪn/ *noun* **1** [C] one of the tubes which carry blood from all parts of the body to the heart ➲ Look at **artery**. وريد

2 [sing., U] a particular style or quality: *After a humorous beginning, the programme continued in a more serious vein.* نزْعة: أسلوب

Velcro™ /'velkrəʊ/ *noun* [U] a material for fastening parts of clothes together. Velcro is made of nylon and is used in small strips, one rough and one smooth, that stick together. فلكرو: نسيج خاص لتثبيت الملابس

velocity /və'lɒsəti/ *noun* [U] (*technical*) the speed at which sth moves سرعة

velvet /'velvɪt/ *noun* [U] a kind of material made of cotton, silk or nylon with a soft thick surface on one side only مُخْمل، قطيفة

vendetta /ven'detə/ *noun* [C] a serious argument or quarrel which lasts for a long time (especially between an individual and an organization, or between families) عداوة، ثأر

vending machine /'vendɪŋ məʃi:n/ *noun* [C] a machine from which you can buy drinks, cigarettes, etc. by putting coins in it آلة بيع أوتوماتيكية

vendor /'vendə(r)/ *noun* [C] (*formal*) a person who sells sth ➲ Look at **purchaser**. بائع

veneer /və'nɪə(r)/ *noun* [C,U] **1** a thin layer of wood or plastic which you stick onto sth made of cheaper material to give it a better appearance قشرة

2 a veneer (of sth) (*formal*) a part of sb's behaviour or of a situation which hides what it is really like: *a thin veneer of politeness* مظهر خارجيّ خادع

venetian blind /və,ni:ʃn 'blaɪnd/ *noun* [C] a covering for a window that is made of horizontal strips of plastic. You can alter the position of the strips in order to let more or less light into the room. ستار بلاستيكي خاص لتخفيف النور

vengeance /'vendʒəns/ *noun* (*formal*) [U] the act of hurting sb because he/she has hurt you in some way that you think is unjust: *The man wanted vengeance for the death of his wife.* ➲ Look at **revenge**. انتقام، ثأر

IDM with a vengeance with more force and determination than before or than you expected: *After a week of good weather, winter returned with a vengeance today.* بضراوة

venison /'venɪsn/ *noun* [U] the meat from a deer ➲ Look at the note at **meat**. لحم الغزال

venom /'venəm/ *noun* [U] **1** the poisonous fluid that snakes, etc. inject into you when they bite you سمّ (الأفاعي)

2 extreme anger or hatred that you show when you speak ضغينة، سمّ

▸ **venomous** /'venəməs/ *adj* سامّ؛ حقود

vent /vent/ *noun* [C] a hole in the wall of a room or machine which allows air to come in, and smoke, steam or smells to go out: *an air vent* منفذ، مَنْفس

ventilate /'ventɪleɪt; *US* -təleɪt/ *verb* [T] to allow air to move freely in and out of a room or building: *The office is badly ventilated.* يهوّي، يجدد الهواء

▸ **ventilation** /,ventɪ'leɪʃn; *US* -tə'leɪʃn/ *noun* [U]: *There was no ventilation in the room except for one tiny window.* تهوية

venture /'ventʃə(r)/ *noun* [C] a project which is new and often risky, because you cannot be sure that it will succeed: *I wish you luck in your new business venture.* مجازفة

▸ **venture** *verb* [I] to do sth or go somewhere new and risky, when you are not sure what will happen: *The company has decided to venture into computer production as well as design.* ○ *He ventured out into the storm in a thick coat, hat and scarf.* يجازف

venue /'venju:/ *noun* [C] the place where a concert, sports match, conference, etc. happens: *a change of venue* مكان

Venus /'vi:nəs/ *noun* [sing.] the planet that is second in order from the sun and nearest to the earth الزُّهرة

veranda (*also* **verandah**) /və'rændə/ (*US also* **porch**) *noun* [C] a platform attached to the side of a house, with a roof and floor but no outside wall: *to sit on the veranda* ➲ Look at **balcony**, **patio** and **terrace**. فرَندة، شرفة مسقوفة

verb /vɜ:b/ *noun* [C] a word or group of words that is used to indicate an action or a state, e.g. *bring*, *happen* and *be* فعل

verbal /'vɜ:bl/ *adj* (*formal*) **1** spoken, not written: *a verbal warning* شفهي

2 of words, or the use of words: *verbal skill* لفظي، لغوي

▸ **verbally** /'vɜ:bəli/ *adv* لفظياً، شفهياً

verbatim /vɜ:'beɪtɪm/ *adj, adv* exactly as spoken or written; word for word: *a verbatim report* ○ *to report a speech verbatim* حرفيّ: حرفياً، كلمةً كلمة

verdict /'vɜ:dɪkt/ *noun* [C] **1** the decision in a court of law about whether a person is guilty or not guilty, or about the facts of a case[1] (5): *The jury returned a verdict of 'not guilty'.* حكم

2 your opinion or decision about sth, which you tell to other people: *The general verdict was that the restaurant was too expensive.* رأي

verge /vɜ:dʒ/ *noun* [C] the narrow piece of land at the side of a road, that is usually covered in grass: *a grass verge* حافة الطريق العشبية

IDM on the verge of sth/doing sth very near to doing sth, or to sth happening: *on the verge of*

an exciting new discovery ○ on the verge of discovering a cure for AIDS حافّة؛ شفير

▸ **verge** *verb*

PHRV **verge on sth** to be almost the same as sth; to be close to sth: *What they are doing verges on the illegal.* يشرف على، يوشك (أن يكون)

verify /ˈverɪfaɪ/ *verb* [T] (*pres part* **verifying**; *3rd pers sing pres* **verifies**; *pt, pp* **verified**) (*formal*) to check or state that sth is true: *to verify a statement* يثبِت (صحة الشيء)؛ يستوثق من

▸ **verification** /ˌverɪfɪˈkeɪʃn/ *noun* [C,U] اثبات؛ تحقُّق

vermin /ˈvɜːmɪn/ *noun* [plural] small wild animals (e.g. rats) that carry disease and destroy plants and food حيوانات ضارّة

versatile /ˈvɜːsətaɪl; *US* -tl/ *adj* **1** (used about an object) having many different uses: *a versatile tool that drills, cuts or polishes* متعدّد الاستعمالات

2 (used about a person) having many different skills or abilities: *She's so versatile! She can dance, sing, act and play the guitar!* متعدّد القدرات

verse /vɜːs/ *noun* **1** [U] writing arranged in lines which have a definite rhythm and which often rhyme at the end: *He wrote his valentine's message in verse.* شِعْر، نَظْم

2 [C] a group of lines which form one part of a song or poem: *This song has five verses.* بيت (من الشِّعْر)

3 [C] a small part of a chapter of the Koran آية

⚷ **version** /ˈvɜːʃn/ *noun* [C] **1** a thing which is based on sth else but which has some details that are different: *the latest version of the software package ○ the film version of 'Romeo and Juliet'* نُسخة معدّلة

2 a person's description of sth that has happened: *The two drivers gave very different versions of the accident.* رواية، وصف

versus /ˈvɜːsəs/ *prep* **1** (*abbr* **v, vs**) (used in sport for showing that two teams or people are playing against each other): *England versus Argentina* ضِدّ

2 (used for showing that two ideas or things are in opposition to each other, especially when you are trying to choose one of them): *It's a question of quality versus price.* مقابل

⚷ **vertical** /ˈvɜːtɪkl/ *adj* going straight up at an angle of 90° from the ground: *a vertical line ○ The cliff was almost vertical.* رأسي، عمودي

▸ **vertically** /-kli/ *adv* عموديّاً، رأسياً

⚷ **very¹** /ˈveri/ *adv* (used with an adjective or adverb to make it stronger): *very small ○ very slowly ○ very much ○ 'Are you hungry?' 'Not very.'*

> We use **very** with superlative adjectives: *very best, youngest, etc.* but with comparative adjectives we use **much** or **very much**: *much/very much better; much/very much younger*

جدّاً

IDM **very well** (used for showing that you agree to do sth): *Very well, Mrs Dawson, we'll replace your shoes with a new pair.* حسناً

⚷ **very²** /ˈveri/ *adj* (used with a noun for emphasis): *We climbed to the very top of the mountain* (= right to the top). ○ *You're the very person I wanted to talk to* (= exactly the right person). ذات، عين

vessel /ˈvesl/ *noun* [C] **1** (*formal*) a ship or large boat سفينة، مَرْكَب كبير

2 (*old-fashioned*) a container for liquids, e.g. a bottle, cup or bowl إناء، وعاء

vest /vest/ *noun* [C] **1** (*US* **undershirt**) a piece of clothing that you wear under your other clothes, on the top part of your body قميص تحتاني

2 (*US*) = WAISTCOAT

vested interest /ˌvestɪd ˈɪntrəst/ *noun* [C] a strong and often secret reason for doing sth that will bring you an advantage of some kind (e.g. more money or power) مصلحة خاصّة

vestige /ˈvestɪdʒ/ *noun* [C] a small part of sth that remains after the rest of it has gone; a trace: *the last vestige of the old system* أثر

vet¹ /vet/ (*also formal* ˈ**veterinary surgeon**) *noun* [C] a person whose job is to give medical help to sick or injured animals; a doctor for animals: *We took the cat to the vet/to the vet's.* طبيب بيطري

vet² /vet/ *verb* [T] (ve**tt**ing; ve**tt**ed) to examine sb/sth carefully before deciding whether to accept him/her/it or not: *All new employees at the Ministry of Defence are carefully vetted* (= somebody examines the details of their past lives). يفحص، يُدقّق

veteran /ˈvetərən/ *noun* [C] **1** a person who has served in the army, navy or air force, especially during a war محارب قديم

2 a person who has very long experience of a particular job or activity محنّك

ˌ**veteran** ˈ**car** *noun* [C] a car that was made before 1916 ➲ Look at **vintage**. سيارة عريقة: صنعت قبل عام 1916

veterinary /ˈvetrənri; *US* ˈvetərəneri/ *adj* connected with the medical treatment of sick or injured animals: *a veterinary surgeon* ➲ Look at **vet¹**. بيطري

veto /ˈviːtəʊ/ *verb* [T] (*pres part* **vetoing**; *3rd pers sing pres* **vetoes**; *pt, pp* **vetoed**) to refuse to give official permission for an action or a plan, when other people have agreed to it: *The Prime Minister vetoed the proposal to reduce taxation.* ينقض، يرفض

▸ **veto** *noun* (*pl.* **vetoes**) **1** [C,U] the official power to refuse permission for an action or a plan: *Britain used its veto to block the UN resolution. ○ the right of veto* فيتو: حق النقض

2 [C] the act of vetoing on a particular occasion: *the Government's veto of the European Parliament's proposal* فيتو: حق النقض

vexed /vekst/ *adj* causing difficulty, worry, and a lot of discussion: *the vexed question of our growing prison population* مثير للخلاف

⚷ **via** /ˈvaɪə/ *prep* **1** going through a place: *We flew from London to Sydney via Bangkok.* عن طريق

2 by means of; using: *These pictures come to you via our satellite link.* بواسطة

viable /ˈvaɪəbl/ *adj* that will be successful: *I'm afraid your idea is just not commercially viable.* قابل للنجاح

▸ **viability** /ˌvaɪəˈbɪləti/ *noun* [U] القابلية للنجاح أو النمو أو التطبيق

viaduct /ˈvaɪədʌkt/ *noun* [C] a long, high bridge which carries a railway or road across a valley جسر فوق وادٍ (للمواصلات)

vibrant /ˈvaɪbrənt/ *adj* **1** full of life and energy; exciting: *a vibrant city, atmosphere, personality, etc.* مثير، نابض بالحياة

2 (used about colours) bright and strong متألّق

vibrate /vaɪˈbreɪt; *US* ˈvaɪbreɪt/ *verb* [I] to move continuously and very quickly from side to side: *When a guitar string vibrates it makes a sound.* يهتزّ؛ يتذبذب

▸ **vibration** /vaɪˈbreɪʃn/ *noun* [C,U]: *Even at full speed the engine causes very little vibration.* اهتزاز؛ تذبذب

vicar /ˈvɪkə(r)/ *noun* [C] a priest of the Church of England. A vicar looks after a church and the people in the surrounding area (a parish). قسيس الابرشية

▸ **vicarage** /ˈvɪkərɪdʒ/ *noun* [C] the house where a vicar lives مسكن القسيس

vice[1] /vaɪs/ *noun* **1** [U] evil or immoral actions: *The authorities are trying to stamp out vice and corruption.* رذيلة

2 [C] a moral weakness or bad habit: *Greed and envy are terrible vices.* ○ *My only vice is eating too much chocolate.* ➲ Look at **virtue**. نقيصة، نقطة ضعف

vice[2] (*US* **vise**) /vaɪs/ *noun* [C] a tool that you use to hold a piece of wood, metal, etc. firmly while you are working on it مِلزَمة

vice- /vaɪs/ (in compounds) next in importance to the rank mentioned: *Vice-President* ○ *the vice-captain* نائب

vice versa /ˌvaɪs ˈvɜːsə/ *adv* in the opposite way to what has just been said: *We can go on the bus and walk back or vice versa* (= or walk there and come back on the bus). أو العكس، والعكس بالعكس

vicinity /vəˈsɪnəti/ *noun*

IDM in the vicinity (of sth) (*formal*) in the surrounding area: *There's no bank in the immediate vicinity.* قرب، منطقة مجاورة

vicious /ˈvɪʃəs/ *adj* **1** cruel; done in order to hurt sb/sth: *a vicious attack* ضارٍ؛ شرّير

2 (used about an animal) dangerous متوحّش

IDM a vicious circle a situation in which one problem leads to another and the new problem makes the first problem worse حلقة مفرغة، حلقة متفاقمة

▸ **viciously** *adv* بضراوة

⚷ **victim** /ˈvɪktɪm/ *noun* [C] a person or an animal that is injured, killed or hurt by sb/sth: *a murder victim* ○ *The children are often the innocent victims of a divorce.* ضحية

victimize (*also* **victimise**) /ˈvɪktɪmaɪz/ *verb* [T] to punish or make sb suffer unfairly يتجنّى (على)

▸ **victimization** (*also* **victimisation**) /ˌvɪktɪmaɪˈzeɪʃn; *US* -məˈz-/ *noun* [U] تَجَنٍ

victor /ˈvɪktə(r)/ *noun* [C] (*formal*) the person who wins a game, competition, battle, etc. منتصر

Victorian /vɪkˈtɔːriən/ *adj* **1** connected with the time of Queen Victoria (1837-1901): *Victorian houses* متعلّق بعصر الملكة فكتوريا

2 having the qualities of middle-class people during this time (= believing in hard work, religion, strict discipline and moral behaviour) متمسك بالتقاليد "الفكتوريّة"

▸ **Victorian** *noun* [C] a person who lived during this time فكتوري

⚷ **victory** /ˈvɪktəri/ *noun* [C,U] (*pl.* **victories**) success in winning a battle, game, competition, etc: *Hannibal's victory over the Roman army* ○ *The Liberal Democrats won a decisive victory in the by-election.* ○ *He led his team to victory in the 2004 Olympics.* انتصار

▸ **victorious** /vɪkˈtɔːriəs/ *adj*: *the victorious team* (= the one that won) منتصر، ظافر

⚷ **video** /ˈvɪdiəʊ/ *noun* (*pl.* **videos**) **1** [U] the system of recording moving pictures and sound by using a camera, and showing them by using a recorder and a television: *We recorded the wedding on video.* ○ *The film is coming out on video in May.* فيديو

2 [C] a tape or cassette on which you record moving pictures and sound or on which a film or television programme has been recorded: *Would you like to see the video we made on holiday?* ○ *a video rental shop* شريط الفيديو

3 [C] = VIDEO CASSETTE RECORDER

▸ **video** *verb* [T] (*3rd pers sing pres* **videos**; *pres part* **videoing**; *pt, pp* **videoed**) to record moving pictures and sound, or a film or television programme, onto a video (2): *We hired a camera to video the school play.* ○ *I'm going out tonight, so I'll have to video that programme I wanted to watch.* يصوّر أو يسجّل على الفيديو

ˌvideo caˈssette recorder (*also* **ˈvideo recorder**; **video**) (*abbr* **VCR**) a machine that is connected to a television on which you can record or play back moving pictures and sound, or a film or television programme مسجّل الفيديو

videotape /ˈvɪdiəʊteɪp/ *noun* [C,U] tape used for recording moving pictures and sound شريط الفيديو

⚷ **view**[1] /vjuː/ *noun* **1** [U] the ability to be seen from a particular place: *The garden was hidden from view behind a high wall.* ○ *to come into/disappear from view* مرأى

2 [C] what you can see from a particular place. A view usually means sth pleasant to look at, e.g. beautiful natural scenery: *There are breathtaking views from the top of the mountain.* ○ *a room with a sea view* ➲ Look at the note at **scenery**. مشهد، منظر

3 [sing.] the ability to see sth from a particular

place: *A large lorry was blocking her view of the road.* رؤية

4 [C] **a view (about/on sth)** an opinion or idea about sth: *He expressed the view that standards were falling.* ○ *In my view, she has done nothing wrong.* ○ *The poet was jailed for his political views.* ○ *strong views on the subject* وجهة نظر، رأي

IDM have, etc. sth in view (*formal*) to have sth as a plan or idea in your mind ينوي عمل شيء

in full view → FULL

in view of sth because of sth; as a result of sth: *In view of her apology we decided to take no further action.* نظراً لِ

a point of view → POINT[1]

with a view to doing sth (*formal*) with the aim or intention of doing sth بِنيّة أو بقصد عمل شيء

view[2] /vjuː/ *verb* [T] (*formal*) **1 view sth (as sth)** to consider or think about sth: *She viewed holidays as a waste of time.* ○ *He views these changes with suspicion.* يعتبر، يرى

2 to watch or look at sth: *Viewed from this angle, the building looks much taller than it really is.* ينظر

viewer /ˈvjuːə(r)/ *noun* [C] a person who watches television مشاهد

viewpoint /ˈvjuːpɔɪnt/ *noun* [C] = POINT OF VIEW

vigil /ˈvɪdʒɪl/ *noun* [C,U] a period when you stay awake all night for a special purpose: *a candlelit vigil for peace* ○ *All night she kept vigil over the sick child.* سهَر، يقظة

vigilant /ˈvɪdʒɪlənt/ *adj* (*formal*) careful and looking out for danger حَذِر، يقظ

▸ **vigilance** /-əns/ *noun* [U] احتراس، يقظة

vigilante /ˌvɪdʒɪˈlænti/ *noun* [C] a member of an unofficial organization (not the police) that tries to prevent crime in a particular area عضو في منظمة أهليّة لحفظ النظام

vigour (*US* **vigor**) /ˈvɪɡə(r)/ *noun* [U] strength or energy: *After the break we started work again with renewed vigour.* حيوية، نشاط

▸ **vigorous** /ˈvɪɡərəs/ *adj* strong or energetic: *vigorous exercise* نشط، قوي

vigorously *adv*: *Campaigners have protested vigorously about the plans to close the local railway line.* بقوة

vile /vaɪl/ *adj* very bad or unpleasant: *She's in a vile mood.* ○ *a vile smell* كريه

villa /ˈvɪlə/ *noun* [C] a pleasant house with a garden, usually in a warm country. A villa is often used as a holiday house. فيلاّ

village /ˈvɪlɪdʒ/ *noun* **1** [C] a group of houses with other buildings, e.g. a church, shop, school, etc., in a country area. A village is smaller than a town: *a small fishing village* ○ *the village pub* قرية

2 [sing., with sing. or pl. verb] all the people who live in a village: *All the village is/are taking part in the carnival.* أهل القرية

▸ **villager** /ˈvɪlɪdʒə(r)/ *noun* [C] a person who lives in a village قروي

villain /ˈvɪlən/ *noun* [C] **1** an evil person, especially in a book or play: *In the play 'Othello', Iago is the villain.* ➲ Look at **hero**. وغْد

2 (*informal*) a criminal: *The police caught the villains who robbed the bank.* مجرم

vindictive /vɪnˈdɪktɪv/ *adj* being particularly unpleasant to sb; trying to hurt sb more than he/she deserves حقود، انتقامي

vine /vaɪn/ *noun* [C] the climbing plant that grapes grow on كرمة، دالية

vinegar /ˈvɪnɪɡə(r)/ *noun* [U] a liquid with a strong sharp taste that is made from wine, etc. Vinegar is often mixed with oil and put onto salads. خلّ

vineyard /ˈvɪnjəd/ *noun* [C] a piece of land where vines are grown كَرْم

vintage /ˈvɪntɪdʒ/ *noun* [C] the wine that was made in a particular year نبيذ من محصول سنة معينة

▸ **vintage** *adj* **1** (used about wine) that was produced in a particular year and district (نبيذ) مصنوع في سنة ومنطقة معيّنة

2 (used about a car) made between 1917 and 1930 ➲ Look at **veteran car**. سيارة مصنوعة بين 1917 و 1930

3 of very high quality: *a vintage performance by Dustin Hoffman* ممتاز، رائع

vinyl /ˈvaɪnl/ *noun* [C,U] a type of strong plastic that is used for making wall, floor and furniture coverings, book covers, etc. "فينيل": مادة بلاستيكية

viola /viˈəʊlə/ *noun* [C] a musical instrument with strings that looks like a violin but is slightly larger ❶ Note that we play **the** viola. كمان أوسط

violate /ˈvaɪəleɪt/ *verb* [T] **1** to break sth (e.g. a rule or an agreement): *to violate a peace treaty* يخرق

2 to disturb sth, not to respect sth: *to violate sb's privacy, rights, etc.* ينتهك

▸ **violation** /ˌvaɪəˈleɪʃn/ *noun* [C,U]: *violation of human rights* انتهاك

violent /ˈvaɪələnt/ *adj* **1** using physical strength, often in an uncontrolled way, to hurt or kill sb; caused by this behaviour: *a violent man, who abused his children* ○ *The demonstration started peacefully but later turned violent.* ○ *a violent death* عنيف

2 very strong; uncontrolled: *He has a violent temper.* ○ *a violent storm* حادّ، شديد، أهوج

▸ **violence** /-əns/ *noun* [U] **1** violent behaviour: *They threatened to use violence if we didn't give them the money.* ○ *Is there too much violence on TV?* ○ *an act of violence* عُنف

2 great force or energy شدّة

violently *adv* بعُنف

violet /ˈvaɪələt/ *noun* **1** [C] a small plant that grows wild or in gardens and has purple or white flowers and a pleasant smell بَنَفْسجة

2 [U] a bluish purple colour بَنَفْسج

▸ **violet** *adj* بَنَفْسجي

violin /ˌvaɪəˈlɪn/ *noun* [C] a musical instrument

with strings, that you hold under your chin and play with a bow ❶ Note that we play **the** violin. كَمان، كَمَنْجة

VIP /ˌviː aɪ ˈpiː/ *noun* [C] a very important person: *the VIP lounge at the airport* ○ *to give someone the VIP treatment* (= treat sb especially well) شخص مهم جداً

virgin /ˈvɜːdʒɪn/ *noun* [C] a person, especially a girl or woman, who has never had sexual intercourse عذراء، بَتول
▸ **virgin** *adj* that has not yet been used, touched, damaged, etc: *virgin forest* بِكْر
virginity /vəˈdʒɪnəti/ *noun* [U] the state of being a virgin: *to keep/lose your virginity* عذْرة، بتولة

Virgo /ˈvɜːɡəʊ/ *noun* (*pl.* **Virgos**) [C,U] the sixth sign of the zodiac, the Virgin; a person who was born under this sign برج العذراء؛ شخص من هذا البرج

virile /ˈvɪraɪl; *US* ˈvɪrəl/ *adj* (used about a man) strong and having great sexual energy رجولي، فحل
▸ **virility** /vəˈrɪləti/ *noun* [U] the sexual power of men رجولة

virtual /ˈvɜːtʃuəl/ *adj* **1** (only *before* a noun) being almost or nearly sth: *Her disability has made her a virtual prisoner in her own home.* فعلي؛ شبه (سجين)
2 made to appear to exist by computer: *an online 'virtual library'* منقول على الكمبيوتر؛ افتراضي

⚷ **virtually** /ˈvɜːtʃuəli/ *adv*: *The building is virtually finished.* عملياً

ˌ**virtual ˈworld** *noun* [C] images, sounds and text used by a computer to create a world where people can communicate with each other, play games and pretend to live another life عالم افتراضي

virtue /ˈvɜːtʃuː/ *noun* **1** [U] behaviour which shows high moral standards; goodness: *to lead a life of virtue* فضيلة، حسن السيرة
2 [C] a good quality or habit: *Patience is a great virtue.* ➲ Look at **vice**[1]. منقبة، مزيّة
3 [C,U] **the virtue (of sth/of being/doing sth)** an advantage or a useful quality of sth: *This new material has the virtue of being strong as well as very light.* مزيّة
IDM **by virtue of** (*formal*) because of بفضل
▸ **virtuous** /ˈvɜːtʃuəs/ *adj* behaving in a moral or good way فاضل

virtuoso /ˌvɜːtʃuˈəʊzəʊ/ *noun* [C] (*pl.* **virtuosos**) a person who is unusually good at sth (often singing or playing a musical instrument) شخص ماهر؛ موسيقار بارع

virulent /ˈvɪrələnt/ *adj* **1** (used about a poison or a disease) very strong and dangerous: *a particularly virulent form of influenza* خبيث؛ سمّي
2 (*formal*) very strong and full of anger: *a virulent attack on the leader* قاسٍ، لاذع

⚷ **virus** /ˈvaɪrəs/ *noun* [C] (*pl.* **viruses**) **1** a living thing, too small to be seen without a microscope, that causes disease in people, animals and plants: *HIV, the virus that is thought to cause AIDS* ➲ Look at **bacteria** and **germ**. فيروس
2 (*computing*) instructions that are put into a computer program in order to cause errors and destroy information فيروس

visa /ˈviːzə/ *noun* [C] an official mark in your passport that shows you are allowed to enter, leave or travel through a country: *She applied for an extension when her visa expired.* ○ *a tourist visa* تأشيرة

viscount /ˈvaɪkaʊnt/ *noun* [C] a member of the British aristocracy who is higher in rank than a baron but lower than an earl فيكونت

vise (*US*) = VICE[2]

⚷ **visible** /ˈvɪzəbl/ *adj* that can be seen or noticed: *The church tower was visible from the other side of the valley.* ○ *a visible improvement* ❶ The opposite is **invisible**. ظاهر، مرئي
▸ **visibility** /ˌvɪzəˈbɪləti/ *noun* [U] the distance that you can see in particular light or weather conditions: *In the fog, visibility was down to 50 metres.* ○ *poor/good visibility* إمكانية الرؤية
visibly /-əbli/ *adv* noticeably or clearly: *Tom was visibly upset.* على نحو ظاهر، بشكل واضح

⚷ **vision** /ˈvɪʒn/ *noun* **1** [U] the ability to see; sight: *to have good, poor, normal, perfect, etc. vision* نظر، بصر
2 [U] the ability to make great plans for the future: *a statesman of great vision* تصوّر، رؤية
3 [C] a picture in your imagination: *They have a vision of a world without weapons.* ○ *I had visions of being left behind, but in fact the others had waited for me.* حُلم، تخيّل
4 [C] a dreamlike state often connected with a religious experience: *God appeared to Paul in a vision.* رؤيا
5 [U] the picture on a television or cinema screen: *a temporary loss of vision* صورة

⚷ **visit** /ˈvɪzɪt/ *verb* [I,T] to come or go to see a person or place and to spend a short time there: *I don't live here. I'm just visiting.* ○ *We often visit relatives at the weekend.* ○ *She's going to visit her son in hospital.* ○ *When you go to London you must visit the Science Museum.* يزور
▸ **visit** *noun* [C] a short stay with sb or in a particular place: *The Prime Minister is on an official visit to Germany.* ○ *We had a visit from Richard on Sunday.* ○ *They paid us a flying visit* (= a very short one). زيارة

⚷ **visitor** /ˈvɪzɪtə(r)/ *noun* [C] a person who visits sb/sth: *We're not free on Sunday. We're having visitors.* ○ *visitors to London from overseas* زائر

visor /ˈvaɪzə(r)/ *noun* [C] **1** the part of a hard hat (a helmet) that you can pull down to protect your eyes or face واجهة الخوذة
2 a piece of plastic, cloth, etc. on a cap or in a car, which keeps the sun out of your eyes وقاء للعيون من الشمس

visual /ˈvɪʒuəl/ *adj* connected with seeing: *the visual arts* (= painting, sculpture, cinema, etc.) بصري، مرئي

a b c d e f g h i j k l m n o p q r s t u v w x y z

▸ **visualize** (*also* **visualise**) /-aɪz/ *verb* [T] to imagine or have a picture in your mind of sb/sth: *It's hard to visualize what this place looked like before the factory was built.* ○ *I can't visualize Liz as a mother.* يتصور

visually /ˈvɪʒuəli/ *adv*: *to be visually handicapped* (= to be partly or completely blind) بصرياً

ˌvisual ˈaid *noun* [C] a picture, film, map, etc. that helps a pupil to learn sth وسيلة بصرية

ˌvisual disˈplay unit *noun* [C] (*abbr* **VDU**) a screen on which you can see information from a computer شاشة عرض

vital /ˈvaɪtl/ *adj* **1** very important or necessary; essential: *Practice is vital if you want to speak a language well.* ○ *vital information* هام: أساسي

2 full of energy; lively نشيط، مفعم بالحياة

▸ **vitally** /ˈvaɪtəli/ *adv*: *vitally important* على نحو أساسي

vitality /vaɪˈtæləti/ *noun* [U] the state of being lively or full of energy حيوية

vitamin /ˈvɪtəmɪn; *US* ˈvaɪt-/ *noun* [C] one of several substances that are found in certain types of food and that are very important for growth and good health: *Oranges are rich in vitamin C.* ○ *a vitamin deficiency* فيتامين

vivacious /vɪˈveɪʃəs/ *adj* (used about a person, usually a woman) full of energy; lively and cheerful مفعم بالحيوية: مرح

vivid /ˈvɪvɪd/ *adj* **1** (used about light or a colour) strong and bright: *the vivid reds and yellows of the flowers* زاهٍ: قوي

2 having or producing a strong, clear picture in your mind: *a vivid description of his time in the army* ○ *a vivid dream* حي

▸ **vividly** *adv* بوضوح، بصورة حية

vivisection /ˌvɪvɪˈsekʃn/ *noun* [U] doing scientific experiments on live animals تشريح الحيوانات الحية

vixen /ˈvɪksn/ *noun* [C] a female fox ثعلبة: أنثى الثعلب

viz. /vɪz/ *abbrev* (often read out as 'namely') that is to say; in other words ألا وهو، بمعنى

VLE /ˌviː el ˈiː/ *abbrev* virtual learning environment; a software system for teaching and learning using the Internet بيئة التعليم الافتراضي

vocabulary /vəˈkæbjələri; *US* -leri/ *noun* (*pl.* **vocabularies**) **1** [sing.] all the words in a language: *New words are always coming into the vocabulary.* مفردات اللغة

2 [C,U] all the words that sb knows or that are used in a particular book, subject, etc: *He has an amazing vocabulary for a five-year-old.* ○ *There are many ways to increase your English vocabulary.* مفردات (حرفة مثلاً)

vocal /ˈvəʊkl/ *adj* **1** connected with the voice: *vocal music* صوتي

2 expressing your ideas or opinions loudly or freely: *a small but vocal group of protesters* (اعتراض) جهير وصريح

▸ **vocalist** /ˈvəʊkəlɪst/ *noun* [C] a singer, especially in a pop or jazz group مغنٍ

vocation /vəʊˈkeɪʃn/ *noun* [C,U] the feeling that you are especially suited for a particular kind of work, often one which involves helping other people; the ability to do this kind of work: *Peter followed his vocation to become a priest.* ○ *She has no vocation for teaching.* نداء باطني؛ دعوة ربّانية: استعداد طبيعي

▸ **vocational** /-ʃənl/ *adj* connected with the skills or qualifications that you need to do a particular job: *vocational training* مهني

vogue /vəʊg/ *noun* [C, usually sing.] **vogue (for sth)** a current fashion: *a vogue for unusual pets/large families/health foods* ○ *Black is in vogue again.* الموضة الدارجة

voice /vɔɪs/ *noun* **1** [C] the sounds that you make when you speak or sing; the ability to make these sounds: *I heard voices near the house and went out to see who it was.* ○ *She has a beautiful voice* (= she can sing beautifully). ○ *He had a bad cold and lost his voice.* ○ *to speak in a loud, soft, low, hoarse, etc. voice* ○ *Shh! Keep your voice down!* ○ *to raise/lower your voice* ○ *Alan is 13 and his voice is beginning to break* (= to become deep and low like a man's). صوت (الانسان)

2 [U, sing.] **voice (in sth)** (the right to express) your ideas or opinions: *The workers want more voice in the running of the company.* حق التعبير

3 [sing.] (*grammar*) the form of a verb that shows whether a sentence is active or passive: *'Keats wrote this poem' is in the active voice.* ○ *'This poem was written by Keats' is in the passive voice.* صيغة المعلوم أو المجهول (نحو)

IDM **at the top of your voice** → TOP[1]

▸ **voice** *verb* [T] to express your opinions or feelings: *The party voiced its objections to the leader's plans.* يعبّر عن رأي

voicemail /ˈvɔɪsmeɪl/ *noun* [U] an electronic system which can store telephone messages, so that sb can listen to them later مسجّل الرسائل الصوتية

void /vɔɪd/ *noun* [C, usually sing.] (*formal*) an empty space: (*figurative*) *Her death left a void in their lives.* فراغ

▸ **void** *adj* (*formal*) empty; without sth خالٍ: فارغ

IDM **null and void** → NULL

vol. *abbrev* **1** = VOLUME (1): *The Complete Works of Byron, Vol. 2*

2 = VOLUME (2): *vol. 333 ml*

volatile /ˈvɒlətaɪl; *US* -tl/ *adj* **1** (used about a liquid) that can easily change into a gas (سائل) سريع التبخر أو طيّار

2 that can change suddenly: *The situation is still very volatile.* ○ *a volatile personality* متقلّب

volcano /vɒlˈkeɪnəʊ/ *noun* [C] (*pl.* **volcanoes**) a mountain with a hole (a crater) at the top through which steam, hot rocks (lava), fire, etc. sometimes come out: *an active/a dormant/an ex-*

tinct volcano ○ *When did the volcano last erupt?* بُركان

▸ **volcanic** /vɒl'kænɪk/ *adj* بركاني

volley /'vɒli/ *noun* [C] (*pl.* **volleys**) **1** a number of stones, bullets, etc. that are thrown, shot, etc. at the same time: *The soldiers fired a volley over the heads of the crowd.* ○ (*figurative*) *a volley of abuse* وابل (من)

2 (in tennis, etc.) a stroke in which you hit the ball before it touches the ground ضرب الكرة قبل أن تمسّ الأرض

▸ **volley** *verb* [I,T] (in tennis) to hit the ball before it touches the ground يضرب كرة التنس وهي طائرة

volleyball /'vɒlibɔːl/ *noun* [U] a game in which two teams try to hit a ball over a high net with their hands and not let it touch the ground الكرة الطائرة

volt /vəʊlt/ *noun* [C] (*abbr* **V**) a unit for measuring electrical force فولط

▸ **voltage** /'vəʊltɪdʒ/ *noun* [C,U] the electrical force that is measured in volts: *Danger! High voltage.* ○ *The voltage in Europe is 240 volts, but in the United States it is 110 volts.* فولطيّة: جهد كهربائي

volume /'vɒljuːm; *US* -jəm/ *noun* **1** [C] a book, especially one of a set or series: *The library has over 10 000 volumes.* ○ *The dictionary comes in three volumes.* كتاب، مُجلّد

2 [C,U] the amount of space that sth contains or occupies: *What is the volume of this sphere?* ○ *A kilo of feathers is greater in volume than a kilo of gold.* ➲ Look at **area** (2). حجم

3 [U] the quantity or amount of sth: *the volume of traffic on the roads* كميّة، مقدار

4 [U] the strength or degree of sound that sth makes: *to turn the volume on a radio up/down* ارتفاع الصوت

voluntary /'vɒləntri; *US* -teri/ *adj* **1** done or given willingly, not because you have to do it: *Overtime is voluntary where I work and I seldom do any.* ○ *Parents often make voluntary contributions to the school funds.* ℹ Something that you must do is **compulsory**. اختياري، طوعي

2 done or working without payment: *voluntary work at the local hospital* ○ *Voluntary organizations are sending workers to help the refugees.* دون مقابل

▸ **voluntarily** /'vɒləntrəli; *US* ˌvɒlən'terəli/ *adv*: *She left the job voluntarily, she wasn't sacked.* طوعاً

volunteer /ˌvɒlən'tɪə(r)/ *noun* [C] **1** a person who offers or agrees to do sth without being forced or paid to do it متطوّع

2 a person who joins the armed forces without being ordered to متطوّع

▸ **volunteer** *verb* **1** [I,T] **volunteer (sth)**; **volunteer (to do sth)** to offer sth or to do sth which you do not have to do or for which you will not be paid: *They volunteered their services free.* ○ *She frequently volunteers for extra work because she really likes her job.* ○ *One of my friends volunteered to take us all in his car.* يتطوّع لِ، يتبرّع بِ

2 [I] **volunteer (for sth)** to join the armed forces without being ordered to يتطوّع في الجيش

3 [T] to give information, etc. or make a comment or suggestion without being asked to: *I volunteered a few helpful suggestions.* يتبرّع (بتقديم شيء)

vomit /'vɒmɪt/ *verb* [I,T] to bring food, etc. up from the stomach and out of the mouth: *How many times did the patient vomit this morning?* ℹ In everyday British English we say **be sick**: *I ate too much last night and I was sick.* يتقيأ

▸ **vomit** *noun* [U]: *the smell of vomit* قيء، تَقَيّؤ

vote /vəʊt/ *noun* **1** [C] a method of deciding sth by asking people to express their choice and finding out what the majority want: *The democratic way to decide this would be to take a vote.* ○ *Let's have a vote. All those in favour, raise your hands.* تصويت، اقتراع

2 [C] **a vote (for/against sb/sth)** an expression of your choice in an election, etc., which you show by raising your hand or writing on a piece of paper: *The votes are still being counted.* ○ *The Tory candidate got nearly 20 000 votes.* صوت (انتخابي)

3 the vote [sing.] the votes given or received by a certain group in an election: *The Conservatives were elected with 42% of the vote.* الأصوات الانتخابية

4 the vote [sing.] the legal right to vote in political elections: *In some countries, women don't have the vote.* حق التصويت

IDM a vote of thanks a short speech to thank sb, usually a guest at a meeting, dinner, etc: *The club secretary proposed a vote of thanks to the guest speaker.* كلمة شكر

▸ **vote** *verb* **1** [I,T] **vote (for/against sb/sth)**; **vote (on sth)** to show a choice of opinion with a vote: *Who did you vote for in the last general election?* ○ *Very few MPs voted against the new law.* ○ *Now that we've heard everybody's opinion, I think it's time we voted on it.* ○ *They voted to change the rules of the club.* ○ *I voted Liberal Democrat.* يصوّت

2 [T] to choose sb for a particular position or honour: *He was voted best actor.* يختار

3 [T] (*informal*) to decide and state that sth is/was good or bad: *We all voted the trip a success.* يَحْكم، يقْضي

voter *noun* [C] a person who votes or has the right to vote in a political election ناخب

vouch /vaʊtʃ/ *verb* [I] **vouch (for sb/sth)** to state that a person is honest or good or that sth is true or genuine; to guarantee يشهد (بنزاهة شخص مثلاً)؛ يضمن

voucher /'vaʊtʃə(r)/ *noun* [C] (*Brit*) a piece of paper that you can exchange for certain goods or services: *luncheon vouchers* (= ones given by some employers and which can be exchanged at certain restaurants for food) مستند صرف

vow /vaʊ/ *noun* [C] a formal promise (especially

in a religious ceremony): *marriage vows* ○ *a vow of silence* قَسَم، يمين؛ عهد
▸ **vow** *verb* [T] to make a serious promise: *We vowed never to discuss the subject again.* يُقسِم، يحلف، يعاهد

vowel /ˈvaʊəl/ *noun* [C] a sound that you make with your lips and teeth open; the sounds represented in English by the letters 'a', 'e', 'i', 'o' or 'u' ➲ Look at **consonant**. حرف علّة أو حرف لين

voyage /ˈvɔɪɪdʒ/ *noun* [C] a long journey by sea or in space: *Magellan's voyages of discovery* ○ *a spacecraft on a voyage to Jupiter* رِحْلة
▸ **voyager** /ˈvɔɪɪdʒə(r)/ *noun* [C] a person who makes a voyage رحّالة، مسافر

vs *abbrev* = VERSUS

VSO /ˌviː es ˈəʊ/ *abbrev* (*Brit*) Voluntary Service Overseas; a scheme for young people to work in developing countries الخدمة الطوعية خارج بريطانيا

vulgar /ˈvʌlgə(r)/ *adj* **1** not having or showing good taste¹ (5) or good manners; not educated: *a vulgar man/woman* ○ *vulgar furnishings* سوقي، غير مصقول
2 rude or likely to offend people: *a vulgar joke* ○ *a vulgar gesture* بذيء
▸ **vulgarity** /vʌlˈgærəti/ *noun* [C,U] (*pl.* **vulgarities**) فظاظة، سوقيّة

vulnerable /ˈvʌlnərəbl/ *adj* **vulnerable (to sth/sb)** easy to attack, hurt or defeat; open to danger: *Poor organization left the troops vulnerable to enemy attack.* ○ *She felt lonely and vulnerable, living on her own in the big city.* ➲ Look at **invulnerable**. عُرضة للهجوم أو الانهزام؛ عُرْضة للخطر؛ مستضعف
▸ **vulnerability** /ˌvʌlnərəˈbɪləti/ *noun* [U]: *This attack draws attention to the vulnerability of old people living alone.* التعرّض للهجوم أو الخطر

vulture /ˈvʌltʃə(r)/ *noun* [C] a large bird that has no feathers on its head or neck and that eats the flesh of dead animals نَسْر

Ww

W, w /ˈdʌbljuː/ *noun* [C] (*pl.* **Ws**; **W's**; **w's**) the twenty-third letter of the English alphabet: *'Water' begins with (a) 'W'.* الحرف الثالث والعشرون من الأبجدية الإنكليزية

W *abbrev* **1** = WEST(ERN)
2 = WATT(S)

wacky /ˈwæki/ *adj* (**wackier**; **wackiest**) (*informal*) exciting, new and rather crazy: *a wacky comedian* جديد ومثير، (كوميدي) "مجنون"

wad /wɒd/ *noun* [C] **1** a lump or ball of soft material that is used for blocking sth, keeping sth in place, etc: *The nurse used a wad of cotton wool to stop the bleeding.* حَشْوة
2 a large number of papers or banknotes in a pile or rolled together رزمة (من الأوراق المالية)

waddle /ˈwɒdl/ *verb* [I] to walk with short steps, leaning to one side then the other, like a duck: *A small, fat person waddled past.* يتمايل

wade /weɪd/ *verb* [I] to walk with difficulty through fairly deep water, mud, etc: (*figurative*) *She had to wade through three thick books before she could write the essay.* يخوض، يتقدّم بصعوبة

wafer /ˈweɪfə(r)/ *noun* [C] a very thin, crisp biscuit رقاقة

waffle¹ /ˈwɒfl/ *noun* [C] a small, crisp cake, made of flour, eggs and milk, that has a pattern of squares on it and is often eaten warm with a sweet sauce (syrup) وَفْل: نوع من الكعك

waffle² /ˈwɒfl/ *verb* [I] (*Brit informal*) to talk or write for much longer than necessary without saying anything important: *Don't waffle, get to the point.* يلغو، يلقلِق
▸ **waffle** *noun* [U]: *The last two paragraphs of your essay are just waffle.* لغو، لَقْلَقَة

waft /wɒft; *US* wæft/ *verb* [I,T] to move lightly through the air; to make sth move in this way: *The smell of her perfume wafted through the room.* ينبعث؛ يسوق، يحمل

wag /wæg/ *verb* [I,T] (**wagging**; **wagged**) to shake up and down or move from side to side: *The dog wagged its tail.* يَهِزّ

🔑 **wage¹** /weɪdʒ/ *noun* **1** [sing.] the amount of money paid for a week's work: *What's the average wage in this country?* أجر أسبوعي
2 [plural] the pay you receive: *Our wages are paid every Thursday.* أجر

> **Wage** in the singular is mainly used to talk about the amount of money paid, or when the word is combined with another, for example 'wage packet', 'wage rise', etc. **Wages** in the plural means the money itself: *I have to pay the rent out of my wages.* Look at the note at **pay**¹.

wage² /weɪdʒ/ *verb* [T] **wage sth (against/on sb/sth)** to begin and continue sth, especially a war: *to wage war* ○ *The police are waging a campaign against illegal drugs.* يَشُنّ

waggle /ˈwægl/ *verb* [I,T] (*informal*) to move up and down or from side to side with quick, short movements; to make sth move in this way: *Can you waggle your ears?* يهتزّ؛ يهزّ

wagon (*also* **waggon**) /ˈwægən/ *noun* [C] **1** a vehicle with four wheels that is pulled by horses, etc. and used for transporting things عربة نقل
2 (*US* **freight car**) an open railway truck used

for transporting goods: *coal transported in goods wagons* عربة بِضاعة

waif /weɪf/ *noun* [C] a child or an animal who has nowhere to live and is not looked after متشرِّد

wail /weɪl/ *verb* **1** [I,T] to cry or complain in a loud, high voice: *the sound of children wailing* ○ *'Won't somebody help me?' she wailed.* ينتحب؛ يندب

2 [I] to make a sound like this: *sirens wailing in the streets outside* يعْوِل

▸ **wail** *noun* [C] a loud cry of pain or sadness; a sound similar to this: *the wails of a child* ○ *the wail of sirens* نحيب؛ عويل

⚷**waist** /weɪst/ *noun* [C, usually sing.] **1** the part around the middle of the body between the stomach and the hips (and often narrower than them): *What's your waist measurement?* ○ *a 26-inch waist* ○ *She put her arms around his waist.* وَسَط، خَصر

2 the part of a piece of clothing that goes round the waist خَصْر أو كَمَر (التنوّرة مثلاً)

waistcoat /ˈweɪskəʊt; *US* ˈweskət/ (*US* **vest**) *noun* [C] a piece of clothing with buttons down the front and no sleeves that is often worn under a jacket as part of a man's suit صُدْرِيّة

waistline /ˈweɪstlaɪn/ *noun* [C, usually sing.] **1** the measurement or size of the body around the waist: *a slim waistline* قياس الخَصْر

2 the part of a piece of clothing that fits around or close to the waist: *a dress with a high waistline* قصّة الخَصر

⚷**wait¹** /weɪt/ *verb* [I] **1 wait (for sb/sth) (to do sth)** to remain in a particular place, and not do anything until sb/sth arrives or until sth happens: *Wait here. I'll be back in a few minutes.* ○ *Have you been waiting long?* ○ *If I'm a bit late, can you wait for me?* ○ *I wrote to them a few weeks ago and I'm still waiting for a reply.* ○ *I'm waiting to see the doctor.* ○ *He's waiting for them to tell him whether he got the job or not.* ○ *I can't wait* (= I am very keen) *to find out what happens at the end.* ينتظر، يترقّب

> Compare **wait** and **expect**: *I was expecting him to be there at 7.30 but at 8 I was still waiting.* ○ *I'm waiting for the exam results but I'm not expecting to pass.* If you **wait**, you pass the time often doing little else, until sth happens: *I waited outside the theatre until they arrived.* If you **expect** sth, you believe that sth will happen: *I'm expecting a reply from them soon, because it's a month since I wrote.*

2 to be left or delayed until a later time; not to be done or dealt with immediately: *Is this matter urgent or can it wait?* يتأجّل

IDM **keep sb waiting** to make sb wait: *I'm sorry if I've kept you waiting.* يجعله ينتظر

wait and see to wait and find out what will happen (perhaps before deciding to do sth) يتمهّل

wait your turn to wait until the time when you are allowed to do sth ينتظر دوره

PHR V **wait about/around** to stay in a place doing nothing because sb or sth is late يمكث منتظراً

wait behind to stay in a place after others have left it يبقى، يتخلّف

wait in to stay at home because you are expecting sb to come or sth to happen: *I waited in all evening but she didn't phone.* ينتظر في البيت

wait on sb to bring food, drink etc. to sb, usually in a restaurant يَخْدِم

wait up (for sb) to not go to bed because you are waiting for sb to come home: *I won't be back until very late, so don't wait up.* يسهر منتظراً عودة شخص

wait² /weɪt/ *noun* [C, usually sing.] **a wait (for sth/sb)** a period of time when you wait: *a short/long wait* انتظار

⚷**waiter** /ˈweɪtə(r)/ (*feminine* **waitress** /ˈweɪtrəs/) *noun* [C] a person whose job is to take orders from customers and bring food and drink to them in a restaurant, hotel dining room, etc. نادِل، خادم مطعم

ˈ**waiting list** *noun* [C] a list of people who are waiting for sth that will be available in the future: *to put sb's name on the waiting list* قائمة بأسماء المنتظرين دورهم

ˈ**waiting room** *noun* [C] a room at a doctor's surgery, railway station, etc. where people can sit and wait غرفة انتظار

waive /weɪv/ *verb* [T] (*formal*) to state that a rule, etc. need not be obeyed; to give up a right to sth: *The management waived the no-smoking rule in the office for the annual party.* ○ *She signed a contract in which she waived all rights to her husband's money.* يسقِط؛ يتخلّى عن

⚷**wake¹** /weɪk/ *verb* (*pt* **woke** /wəʊk/; *pp* **woken** /ˈwəʊkən/) **1** [I] **wake (up)** to stop being asleep: *I woke early in the morning and got straight out of bed.* ○ *Wake up! It's nearly 8 o'clock!* يستيقظ، يصحو

2 [T] **wake sb (up)** to make sb stop sleeping: *Could you wake me up at 7.30 tomorrow morning, please?* يوقظ

3 [T] **wake sb/sth up** to make sb/sth become more lively or active: *She always has some coffee to wake her up when she gets to work.* يُنعِش، يُنشّط

PHR V **wake up to sth** to become aware of sth: *By the time he had woken up to the danger, it was too late.* ينتبه

▸ **waken** /ˈweɪkən/ *verb* [I,T] (*formal*) to wake up or to make sb/sth wake up: *She wakened from a deep sleep.* ○ *Shh. You'll waken the baby!* يستيقظ؛ يوقظ

wake² /weɪk/ *noun* [C] the track that a moving ship leaves behind on the surface of the water أثر السفينة في الماء

IDM **in the wake of sth** following or happening after sth, often as a result of it: *The floods left a great deal of suffering in their wake.* على أثر، في أعقاب

⚷**walk¹** /wɔːk/ *verb* **1** [I] to move along on foot at a fairly slow speed: *Our little girl is just learning to*

a b c d e f g h i j k l m n o p q r s t u v **w** x y z

walk. ○ *The dog walked in and lay down.* ○ *'How did you get here? By bus?' 'No, I walked.'* ○ *The children ran ahead as we walked to the beach.* ○ *He walked with a limp.* ○ *Are the shops within walking distance?* (= are they close enough to walk to?) يسير، يمشي

2 [I] to move in this way for exercise or pleasure يتمشّى

> **Go walking** is a common way of talking about taking long walks for pleasure: *I often go walking in the Alps in the summer.* Look at the note at **walk**[2].

3 [T] to walk with sb/sth; to guide or help sb to walk: *I'll walk you home if you don't want to go on your own.* ○ *The park was full of people walking their dogs.* يرافق؛ يمشّي

4 [T] to go along or through sth on foot: *He walked the streets all night.* يذرع

PHR V **walk off with sth 1** to win sth easily: *She walked off with all the prizes.* يظفر بـ

2 to steal sth; to take sth that does not belong to you by mistake: *When I got home I realized that I had walked off with her pen.* يسرِق؛ يأخذ (شيئاً) عن طريق الخطأ

walk out (of sth) to leave suddenly and angrily: *She walked out of the meeting in disgust.* يغادر ساخطاً

walk out on sb (*informal*) to leave sb for ever: *He walked out on his wife and children after 15 years of marriage.* يهْجر

walk over sb (*informal*) **1** to defeat sb completely: *He played brilliantly and walked all over his opponent.* يهزم هزيمة ساحقة

2 to deal with sb as if he/she is not important: *I don't know why she lets her husband walk over her like that.* يزدري، يسيء المعاملة

walk up (to sb/sth) to approach (sb/sth): *He walked up to her and asked her if she wanted to dance.* يقترب من

► **walker** *noun* [C] a person who walks: *a fast walker* ○ *This area is very popular with walkers.* ماشٍ

walk[2] /wɔːk/ *noun* **1** [C] a trip on foot for pleasure, exercise, etc: *We went for a walk in the country.* ○ *I'm just going to take the dog for a walk.* نزهة، مَشْية

> We use **go for a walk** when we are talking about a short walk that we take for pleasure. When we mean a long walk, of perhaps a day or more and for which you need special boots, etc., we use **go walking**.

2 [sing.] the time taken to go somewhere on foot; the distance to a place on foot: *The hotel is five minutes' walk from the station.* مسيرة

3 [sing.] a way or style of walking: *He has a funny walk.* مِشْية، طريقة المشي

4 [sing.] the speed of walking: *She slowed to a walk.* سير

5 [C] a route for walking for pleasure: *From here there's a lovely walk through the woods.* ممشى، طريق للنزهة

IDM **a walk of life** a person's position in society: *She has friends from many different walks of life.* مرتبة اجتماعية

walkie-talkie /ˌwɔːki ˈtɔːki/ *noun* [C] (*informal*) a small radio that you can carry with you and use to talk and listen to sb: *The policeman called for help on his walkie-talkie.* جهاز إرسال واستقبال صغير

ˈwalking stick (*also* **stick**) *noun* [C] a stick that you use to lean on if you have difficulty walking عصا المشي، عكّاز

Walkman™ /ˈwɔːkmən/ *noun* [C] (*pl.* **Walkmans**) a small cassette player with earphones that you can carry round with you جهاز "كاسيت" متنقّل

walkover /ˈwɔːkəʊvə(r)/ *noun* [C] an easy win فوز سهل

wall /wɔːl/ *noun* [C] **1** a solid, upright structure made of stone, brick, etc. that is built round an area of land to protect it or to show a boundary: *There is a high wall all around the prison.* حائط، سور

2 one of the sides of a room or building joining the ceiling and the floor: *You could hear the people in the next room talking because the wall was so thin.* ○ *He put the poster up on the wall.* جدار

IDM **up the wall** (*informal*) extremely angry: *She went up the wall when I turned up an hour late.* غاضب للغاية

► **walled** *adj* surrounded by a wall: *an ancient walled city* مسوّر

wallet /ˈwɒlɪt/ (*US* **billfold**; **pocketbook**) *noun* [C] a small, flat, folding case in which you keep banknotes, credit cards, etc. ➲ Look at **purse**[1]. محفظة (نقود)

wallop /ˈwɒləp/ *verb* [T] (*informal*) to hit sb/sth very hard يضرب بشدّة

wallow /ˈwɒləʊ/ *verb* [I] **wallow (in sth) 1** to lie and roll around in water, etc: *I spent an hour wallowing in a hot bath.* يتنعّم بـ؛ يتمرّغ

2 to take great pleasure in sth (a feeling, situation, etc.): *He seems to wallow in self-pity.* يتمتّع، يتلذّذ

wallpaper /ˈwɔːlpeɪpə(r)/ *noun* [U] paper with a pattern on it that you stick to the walls of a room ورق جدران

► **wallpaper** *verb* [I, T]: *We spent the weekend wallpapering the bedroom.* يغطي بورق الجدران

ˌwall-to-ˈwall *adj, adv* (used especially about a carpet) covering the whole floor of a room على كامل الأرضية

wally /ˈwɒli/ *noun* [C] (*pl.* **wallies**) (*Brit informal*) a silly person; a fool سخيف؛ أحمق

walnut /ˈwɔːlnʌt/ *noun* [C] a nut that you can eat, with a hard brown shell that is in two halves جوز

walrus /ˈwɔːlrəs/ *noun* [C] a large animal that lives in the sea in Arctic regions. It is similar to a seal but has two long teeth (tusks) coming out of its face. فرس (أو حصان) البحر

waltz /wɔːls; *US* wɔːlts/ *noun* [C] a dance that you do with a partner, to music which has a rhythm of three beats; the music for this dance: *a Strauss waltz* موسيقى أو رقصة الفالس

▸ **waltz** *verb* [I] **1** to dance a waltz: *They waltzed around the floor.* يرقص الفالس

2 (*informal*) to move easily, carelessly or confidently: *You can't just waltz in and expect your meal to be ready for you.* يسير بخفّة وثقة

wan /wɒn/ *adj* very pale and looking ill or tired شاحب، سقيم

wand /wɒnd/ *noun* [C] a thin stick that magicians, etc. hold when they are doing magic: *I wish I could wave a magic wand and make everything better.* عصا سحرية

🔑**wander** /ˈwɒndə(r)/ *verb* **1** [I,T] to move slowly around a place or to go from place to place with no particular purpose: *We spent a pleasant day wandering around the town.* ○ *He was found in a confused state, wandering the streets.* يتجوّل

2 [I] **wander (away/off)**; **wander (from/off sth)** to leave a place or the path that you were on: *We must stay together while visiting the town, so I don't want anybody to wander off.* ○ (*figurative*) *I seem to have wandered off the subject – what was I talking about?* يتيه

3 [I] (used about sb's mind, thoughts, etc.) to stop concentrating; to be unable to stay on one subject: *The lecture was so boring that my attention began to wander.* ○ *The old man's mind is wandering. He doesn't know where he is any more.* يفقد التركيز؛ يزيغ

wane /weɪn/ *verb* [I] **1** (used about the moon) to appear to become smaller يتناقص، ينمحق

2 to become less powerful, less important, smaller or weaker: *My enthusiasm was waning rapidly.* يضمحلّ يتضاءل

wangle /ˈwæŋgl/ *verb* [T] (*informal*) to get sth by finding a way of persuading or tricking sb: *Somehow he wangled a day off to meet me.* يحتال

wanna /ˈwɒnə/ a way of writing 'want to' or 'want a' to show that sb is speaking in an informal way or with a special accent: *I wanna go home now.* ➲ Look at the note at **gonna**.

🔑**want¹** /wɒnt; *US* wɔːnt/ *verb* [T] **1** to desire; to wish for sth: *He wants a new bike.* ○ *Do you want anything else?* ○ *What do they want for breakfast?* ○ *Is there anything you want to watch on television?* ○ *I don't want to discuss it now.* ○ *I want you to phone me when you get there.* ○ *The boss wants this letter typed.* ○ *I don't want Emma going out on her own at night.* ○ *They want Stevens as captain.* يريد، يرغب في

> **Want** and **would like** are similar in meaning, but 'would like' is more polite: *'I want a drink!' screamed the child.* ○ *'Would you like some more tea, Mrs Jones?'*

2 to need or require sth: *The button on my shirt wants sewing on.* ○ *The house wants a new coat of paint.* يحتاج

3 (*informal*) (used as a warning, as advice, etc.) should or ought to: *He wants to be more careful about what he tells people.* ○ *If you're bored, you want to go out more often.* ينبغي أو يجب أن

4 (usually passive) to need sb to be in a particular place or for a particular reason: *Mrs Lewis, you are wanted on the phone.* ○ *She is wanted by the police* (= the police are looking for her because she is suspected of committing a crime). مطلوب

want² /wɒnt; *US* wɔːnt/ *noun* **1** [C] a desire or need for sth; sth you desire or need: *All our wants were satisfied.* حاجة، رغبة

2 [U, sing.] **want of sth** a lack of sth: *Want of a proper water supply has resulted in disease and death.* ○ *I took the job for want of a better offer.* نَقْص، انعدام

wanton /ˈwɒntən; *US* ˈwɔːn-/ *adj* (used about an action) done in order to hurt sb or damage sth for no good reason تعسفي، (عمل) وحشيّ لا مبرّر له

WAP /wæp/ *abbrev* wireless application protocol; a technology that links devices such as mobile phones to the Internet: *a WAP-enabled phone* وسيلة لوصل (تليفون نقّال مثلاً) مع الانترنت

🔑**war** /wɔː(r)/ *noun* **1** [U] a state of fighting between different countries or groups within countries, using armies and weapons: *war and peace* ○ *The Prime Minister announced that the country was at war.* ○ *to declare war* (= announce that a war has started) ○ *When war broke out, thousands of men volunteered for the army.* ○ *civil war* (= fighting between different groups in one country) حرب

2 [C] a period of military fighting: *the Second World War* ○ *He was killed in the war.* ○ *to fight a war* حرب

3 [C,U] a struggle; very strong competition between groups of people: *a price war among oil companies* صراع؛ منافسة حادّة

4 [sing.] **a war (against sb/sth)** efforts to end sth: *the war against organized crime* حملة

warble /ˈwɔːbl/ *verb* [I] (usually used about a bird) to sing gently, varying the notes up and down يُغرِّد

ward /wɔːd/ *noun* [C] **1** a separate part or room in a hospital, often for a particular group of patients: *the children's ward* جناح، عَنْبَر

2 one of the sections into which a town is divided for elections دائرة انتخابية بلدية

3 a child who is under the protection of a court of law; a child whose parents are dead and who is cared for by another adult (a guardian) قاصر تحت وصاية القضاء؛ يتيم تحت رعاية وصيّ

▸ **ward** *verb*

PHRV **ward sb/sth off** to keep away sb/sth that is dangerous or unpleasant: *They lit a fire to ward off wild animals.* يدفع أو يدرأ (الأذى)

warden /ˈwɔːdn/ *noun* [C] **1** a person whose job is to check that rules are obeyed or to look after the people in a particular place: *a traffic warden* (= a person who checks that cars are not parked in the wrong place) ○ *the warden of a youth hostel* مراقب؛ قيّم

2 (*US*) the governor of a prison آمر أو محافظ السجن

warder /ˈwɔːdə(r)/ *noun* [C] (*Brit*) a prison guard حارس السجن

wardrobe /ˈwɔːdrəʊb/ *noun* [C] **1** a large cupboard in which you can hang your clothes خزانة ثياب

2 a person's collection of clothes: *I need a whole new wardrobe.* مجموعة ملابس

ware /weə(r)/ *noun* **1** [U] (in compounds) made from a particular type of material or suitable for a particular use: *a hardware shop* (= one that sells tools, household equipment, etc.) ○ *an earthenware pot* (مصنوع من مادة معينة)

2 wares [plural] (*old-fashioned*) goods offered for sale سلعة

▶ **warehouse** /ˈweəhaʊs/ *noun* [C] a building where large quantities of goods are stored before being sent to shops مستودع

warfare /ˈwɔːfeə(r)/ *noun* [U] methods of fighting a war; types of war: *guerrilla warfare* ○ *nuclear warfare* حرب

warily *adv* → WARY

warlike /ˈwɔːlaɪk/ *adj* liking to fight or good at fighting: *a warlike nation* حربي، عدواني

warm¹ /wɔːm/ *adj* **1** having a temperature that is fairly high, between cool and hot: *Are you warm enough or would you like me to put the heating on?* ○ *It's quite warm in the sunshine.* ○ *I jumped up and down to keep my feet warm.* ➲ Look at the note at **hot** (1). دافئ

2 (used about clothing) preventing you from getting cold: *Take plenty of warm clothes.* مدفّئ

3 friendly; kind and pleasant; sincere: *I was given a very warm welcome.* وديّ؛ لطيف؛ حارّ

4 creating a pleasant, comfortable feeling: *warm colours* دافئ، مريح

▶ **warmly** *adv*: *warmly dressed* ○ *She thanked him warmly for his help.* على نحو يحفظ الدفء؛ بحرارة

warmth /wɔːmθ/ *noun* [U] **1** a fairly high temperature, or the effect created by this, especially when it is pleasant: *She felt the warmth of the sun on her face.* دِفء، حرارة

2 friendliness or kindness: *I was touched by the warmth of their welcome.* حرارة

warm² /wɔːm/ *verb* [I,T] **warm (sb/sth) (up)** to become or to make sb/sth become warm or warmer: *It was cold earlier but it's beginning to warm up now.* ○ *I sat in front of the fire to warm up.* ○ *There's some meat left over from lunch, so we can warm it up* (= heat it again) *tonight.* يدفأ؛ يُدفّئ؛ يُسخّن

PHR V **warm to/towards sb** to begin to like sb ينشرح صدره (للشخص)

warm to sth to become more interested in sth يتحمّس (للشيء)

warm up to prepare for sth by practising gently: *The team warmed up before the match.* يتهيّأ (للمباراة مثلاً) بالتمرين

warm³ /wɔːm/ *noun* [sing.] **the warm** a warm place or atmosphere: *It's awfully cold out here – I want to go back into the warm.* مكان أو جو دافئ

ˌwarm-ˈhearted *adj* kind and friendly ودود

warming /ˈwɔːmɪŋ/ *noun* [sing.] the process of making sth, or of becoming, warm or warmer: *global warming* ○ *the seasonal warming of the Pacific* تسخين، سخونة

warn /wɔːn/ *verb* [T] **1 warn sb (of sth)**; **warn sb about/against sb/sth**; **warn sb against doing sth** to tell sb to be careful or aware of sth, often unpleasant or dangerous, that exists or might happen: *When I saw the car coming I tried to warn him, but it was too late.* ○ *The government is warning (the public) of possible terrorist attacks.* ○ *The radio warned people about delays on the roads this morning.* ○ *They put up a red flag to warn you against swimming in the sea here.* ○ *She warned me that he was not an easy man to work for.* يحذّر، ينبّه إلى

2 to advise sb (not) to do sth: *I warned you not to trust him.* يحذّر؛ ينصح

▶ **warning** *noun* [C,U] something that tells you to be careful or tells you about sth before it happens: *There was a warning on the gate: 'Beware of the dog'.* ○ *Your employers can't dismiss you without warning.* ○ *He gave me no warning of his arrival.* إنذار، تحذير

warp /wɔːp/ *verb* [I,T] to become bent and out of shape (because of heat or damp); to make sth become like this: (*figurative*) *His view of life had been warped by his unhappy experiences.* يلتوي؛ يلوي

▶ **warped** *adj*: *the killer's warped* (= abnormal) *mind* مشوّه

warpath /ˈwɔːpɑːθ; *US* -pæθ/ *noun*

IDM **(be/go) on the warpath** (*informal*) (to be) very angry and ready to quarrel or fight غاضب ومتحضّر للقتال

warrant /ˈwɒrənt; *US* wɔːr-/ *noun* [C] a written statement that gives sb the authority to do sth: *a search warrant* (= a document that allows the police to search a house) رخصة، إجازة

▶ **warrant** *verb* [T] (*formal*) to make sth seem right or necessary; to deserve sth: *I don't think her behaviour warrants such criticism.* يبرّر؛ يستحق

warranty /ˈwɒrənti; *US* ˈwɔːr-/ *noun* [C,U] (*pl.* **warranties**) a written statement that you get when you buy sth, which promises to repair or replace it if it is broken or does not work ➲ Look at **guarantee**. ضمانة

warrior /ˈwɒriə(r); *US* ˈwɔːr-/ *noun* [C] (*old-fashioned, formal*) a person who fights in battle; a soldier محارب؛ جندي

warship /ˈwɔːʃɪp/ *noun* [C] a ship for use in war سفينة حربية

wart /wɔːt/ *noun* [C] a small hard dry lump that sometimes grows on the face or body ثؤلول

wartime /ˈwɔːtaɪm/ *noun* [U] a period of time

during which there is a war: *wartime Britain* زمن الحرب

wary /ˈweəri/ *adj* (**warier**; **wariest**) **wary (of sb/sth)** careful because you are uncertain or afraid of sth: *He was wary of accepting the suggestion in case it meant more work for him.* حَذِر، محترس
▸ **warily** /-rəli/ *adv* بحَذَر، باحتراس

was → BE

wash[1] /wɒʃ; *US* wɔːʃ/ *verb* **1** [I,T] to clean sb/sth/yourself with water and often soap: *You'll have to wash this jumper by hand.* ○ *Wash and dress quickly or you'll be late!* (= wash yourself). ○ *I'll wash, you dry* (= wash the dishes). ➲ Look at the note at **clean**[2]. يَغسِل
2 [I] (used about water) to flow in the direction mentioned: *I let the waves wash over my feet.* ينساب
3 [T] to carry sth by the movement of water: *The current washed the ball out to sea.* يجرف، يحمل
4 [I] to be able to be washed without being damaged: *Does this material wash well, or does the colour come out?* ينغسل من غير تلف
IDM **wash your hands of sb/sth** to refuse to be responsible for sb/sth any longer يَنْفُض يديه من
PHR V **wash sb/sth away** (used about water) to carry sb/sth away: *The floods had washed away the path.* يَجْرُف؛ يمحو
wash (sth) off to (make sth) disappear from sth by washing: *Go and wash that make-up off!* يُزيل بالغسيل
wash out to be removed from a material by washing: *These grease marks won't wash out.* يزول بالغسيل
wash sth out to wash sth or the inside of sth in order to remove dirt: *I'll just wash out these jeans so that they're ready for tomorrow.* يغسل
wash (sth) up 1 (*Brit*) to wash the plates, knives, forks, etc. after a meal: *Whose turn is it to wash up?* ○ *Don't forget to wash the saucepans up.* يَغسِل (الأواني)
2 (*US*) to wash your face and hands: *Go and wash up quickly and put on some clean clothes.* يَغسِل (الوجه واليدين)
3 (often passive) (used about water) to carry sth to land and leave it there: *Police found the girl's body washed up on the beach.* مَنْجَرِف، ملْقى
▸ **washable** /-əbl/ *adj* that can be washed without being damaged قابل للغسيل

wash[2] /wɒʃ/ *noun* **1** [C, usually sing.] an act of cleaning or being cleaned with water: *I'd better go and have a wash before dinner.* غَسْل، استحمام
2 [sing.] the waves caused by the movement of a ship through water مجرى (السفينة)
IDM **in the wash** being washed: *'Where's my red T-shirt?' 'It's in the wash.'* في الغسيل

washbasin /ˈwɒʃbeɪsn/ (*also* **basin**) *noun* [C] a large bowl for water that has taps and is fixed to a wall, in a bathroom, etc. ➲ Look at **sink**[2]. مغسلة

washcloth /ˈwɒʃklɒθ/ *noun* [C] (*US*) = FACECLOTH

ˌwashed ˈout *adj* tired and pale: *They arrived looking washed out after their long journey.* مُتْعَب وشاحب

washing /ˈwɒʃɪŋ; *US* wɔː-/ *noun* [U] **1** clothes that need to be washed or are being washed: *Could you put the washing in the machine?* ○ *a pile of dirty washing* الغسيل، الملابس الوسخة
2 the act of cleaning clothes, etc. with water: *I usually do the washing on Mondays.* غسيل

ˈwashing machine *noun* [C] an electric machine for washing clothes غسّالة

ˈwashing powder *noun* [U] soap in the form of powder for washing clothes مسحوق غسيل

ˌwashing-ˈup *noun* [U] (*Brit*) the work of washing the plates, knives, forks, etc. after a meal: *I'll do the washing-up.* ○ *washing-up liquid* غسل (الأواني)، "جلّي"

washout /ˈwɒʃaʊt/ *noun* [C] (*informal*) a person or thing that is a complete failure (شخص أو شيء) فاشل

washroom /ˈwɒʃruːm; -rʊm/ *noun* [C] (*US*) a room with a toilet ➲ Look at the note at **toilet**. مِرْحاض

wasn't *short for* WAS NOT

wasp /wɒsp/ *noun* [C] a black and yellow flying insect that can sting زنبور

wastage /ˈweɪstɪdʒ/ *noun* [U] (*formal*) using too much of sth; the amount that is lost تبديد؛ خَسارة

waste[1] /weɪst/ *verb* [T] **1** **waste sth (on sb/sth)** to use or spend sth in a careless way or for sth that is not necessary: *She wastes a lot of money on cigarettes.* ○ *He wasted his time at university because he didn't work hard.* يُبَدِّد، يُهْدِر
2 (usually passive) to be too good, intelligent, etc. for sb/sth: *His humour is wasted on me. I don't understand it.* يذهب هدراً
▸ **wasted** *adj* not necessary or successful: *a wasted journey* مُبَدَّد؛ مُخْفِق

waste[2] /weɪst/ *noun* **1** [sing., U] an action that involves not using sth carefully or using sth in an unnecessary way: *If he gives up acting it will be a waste of great talent.* ○ *The seminar was a waste of time – I'd heard it all before.* تبديد، إضاعة
2 [U] material, food, etc. that is not needed and is therefore thrown away: *nuclear waste* ○ *A lot of household waste can be recycled and reused.* ➲ Look at **rubbish**. نُفاية، فَضْلة
3 wastes [plural] (*formal*) large areas of land that are not lived in and not cultivated: *the wastes of the Sahara desert* قَفْر
IDM **go to waste** to be unused, thrown away and wasted: *I can't bear to see good food going to waste!* يُرْمى كنُفاية، يُهدَر
▸ **wasteful** /-fl/ *adj* using more of sth than necessary; causing waste: *a costly and wasteful advertising campaign* مُسْرِف

waste[3] /weɪst/ *adj* (only *before* a noun) **1** (used about land) not used or not suitable for use; not looked after: *There's an area of waste ground outside the town where people dump their rubbish.* بُور؛ مُهْمَل

2 no longer useful; to be thrown away: *waste material* عديم النفع؛ تالف

ˌ**waste ˈpaper** *noun* [U] paper that is not wanted and is to be thrown away أوراق مهملة

ˌ**waste-ˈpaper basket** (*US* ˈ**wastebasket** /ˈweɪstbɑːskɪt; *US* -bæs-/) *noun* [C] a basket or other container in which you put paper, etc. which is to be thrown away سلّة المهْملات

watch¹ /wɒtʃ/ *noun* [C] a small instrument that shows you what time it is. You wear it on a strap on your wrist: *a gold watch* ○ *a digital watch* ○ *to wind up/set your watch* ○ *My watch is a bit fast/slow* (= shows a time that is later/earlier than the correct time). ساعة يد

watch² /wɒtʃ/ *verb* **1** [I,T] to look carefully at sb/sth: *'Would you like to play too?' 'No thanks. I'll just watch.'* ○ *I watched in horror as the car swerved and crashed.* ○ *I'm watching to see how you do it.* ○ *We watch television most evenings.* ○ *Watch what she does next.* ○ *We went to watch John rowing.* ○ *I watched him open the door and walk away.* ○ *Detectives are watching the suspect day and night.* يشاهد، يراقب

2 [I,T] **watch (for sth)** to pay very careful attention to a situation; to observe: *Doctors are watching for further signs of the disease.* يترقّب؛ يراقب

3 [T] to be careful about sb/sth in order to do the right thing or keep control: *You'd better watch what you say to her. She gets upset very easily.* يحْذَر، يتأنّى

IDM **watch your step 1** to be careful about where you are walking انتبه عند المشي!، "أوعى!"

2 to be careful about how you behave يراعي القواعد و الأصول

PHRV **watch out** to be careful because of possible danger or trouble: *Watch out! There's a car coming.* ○ *If you don't watch out you'll lose your job.* ينتبه

watch out for sb/sth to look carefully and be ready for sb/sth: *Watch out for snakes if you walk through the fields.* يحترس من، ينتبه !

watch over sb/sth to look after or protect sb/sth: *For two weeks she watched over the sick child.* يرْعَى، يسْهر على

watch³ /wɒtʃ/ *noun* [sing.] a person or group of people whose job is to guard and protect a place or a person: *The police put a watch on the suspect's house.* حارس

IDM **keep a close watch on sb/sth** → CLOSE¹

keep watch to guard or to look out for danger يَحرس

▸ **watchful** /-fl/ *adj* careful to notice things متيقّظ

watchdog /ˈwɒtʃdɒg; *US* -dɔːg/ *noun* [C] a person or group whose job is to protect people's rights, especially in relation to large companies: *a consumer watchdog* كلب حراسة؛ حامي حقوق الناس

water¹ /ˈwɔːtə(r)/ *noun* **1** [U] the clear liquid that falls as rain and is in rivers, seas and lakes: *a glass of water* ○ *The bathwater's too hot.* ○ *All the rooms have hot and cold running water.* ○ *The pipe burst and water poured out everywhere.* ○ *drinking water* ○ *tap water* ○ *mineral water* ماء

When water is **heated** to 100° Celsius, it **boils** and becomes **steam**. When steam touches a cold surface, it **condenses** and becomes water again. When water is **cooled** below 0° Celsius, it **freezes** and becomes ice. If the temperature increases, the ice **melts**. When talking about **icy** weather becoming warmer, we say it **thaws**. Frozen food **thaws** or **defrosts** when we take it out of the freezer.

2 [U, plural] a large amount of water, especially the water in a lake, river or sea: *Don't go too near the edge or you'll fall in the water!* ○ *the clear blue waters of the Mediterranean* مياه

3 waters [plural] the sea near a particular country: *The ship was still in British waters.* مياه إقليمية

IDM **pass water** → PASS²

under water 1 in and covered by water: *to swim under water* تحت الماء

2 covered by floods: *After the heavy rain several fields were under water.* يغرقه الفيضان

water² /ˈwɔːtə(r)/ *verb* **1** [T] to give water to plants يسقي

2 [I] (used about the eyes or mouth) to fill with water: *The smoke in the room made my eyes water.* ○ *The food smelled so delicious that it made my mouth water.* تَدمَع (العين)، يتحلّب (الفم)

PHRV **water sth down 1** to add water to a liquid in order to make it weaker يُرَقِّق، يخفّف بالماء

2 to change a statement, report, etc. so that it is weaker يُخَفّف، يلطِّف

watercolour (*US* **watercolor**) /ˈwɔːtəkʌlə(r)/ *noun* **1 watercolours** [plural] paints that are mixed with water, not oil ألوان مائية

2 [C] a picture that has been painted with watercolours لوحة بألوان مائية

watercress /ˈwɔːtəkres/ *noun* [U] a type of plant with bunches of green leaves which have a strong taste and are often eaten in salads قُرّة، جَرْجير

waterfall /ˈwɔːtəfɔːl/ *noun* [C] a stream of water that falls down from a cliff, rock, etc. شلاّل

ˈ**watering can** *noun* [C] a container with a long pipe on one side which is used for watering plants مِرَشّة

ˈ**water lily** *noun* [C] a plant that floats on the surface of water, with large round flat leaves and white, yellow or pink flowers زنبق الماء

waterlogged /ˈwɔːtəlɒgd; *US* -lɔːgd/ *adj* **1** very wet: *Our boots sank into the waterlogged ground.* مشبع بالماء

2 (used about a boat) full of water and likely to sink (قارب) ممتلئ بالماء

watermelon /ˈwɔːtəmelən/ *noun* [C] a large, round fruit with a thick, green skin. It is pink or

red inside with a lot of black seeds.
بطيخ أحمر/ جَبَس/ رقّي

waterproof /ˈwɔːtəpruːf/ *adj* that does not let water go through: *a waterproof anorak*
مانع لنفوذ الماء

watershed /ˈwɔːtəʃed/ *noun* [C] an event or a point which is important because it marks the beginning of sth new (حدث) حاسم أو فاصل

waterski /ˈwɔːtəskiː/ *verb* [I] to move across the surface of water standing on narrow boards (waterskis) and being pulled by a boat
يتزحلق على الماء

watertight /ˈwɔːtətaɪt/ *adj* **1** made so that water cannot get in or out مُحكَم السّد

2 (used about an excuse, an agreement, an argument, etc.) impossible to prove wrong; without any faults: *His alibi for the night of the murder was absolutely watertight.*
لا يمكن دحضه؛ سليم

waterway /ˈwɔːtəweɪ/ *noun* [C] a canal, river, etc. along which boats or ships can travel
طريق مائي

watery /ˈwɔːtəri/ *adj* **1** (used especially about food or drink) containing too much water; thin and weak مذيق، ضعيف

2 weak and pale: *watery sunshine* شاحب

watt /wɒt/ *noun* [C] (*abbr* **W**) a unit of electrical power: *a 60-watt light bulb* الواط: وحدة القوة الكهربائية

wave[1] /weɪv/ *verb* **1** [I,T] **wave (your hand) (at/to sb)** to move your hand from side to side in the air, usually to attract sb's attention or as you meet or leave sb: *She waved to me as the train left the station.* ○ *Who are you waving at?* يلوّح

2 [T] **wave sth (at sb)**; **wave sth (about)** to hold sth in the air and move it from side to side: *The crowd were waving flags as the Queen came out.* ○ *She was talking excitedly and waving her arms about.* يلوّح

3 [T] **wave sth (to sb)** to give a greeting (to sb) by waving your hand: *Wave goodbye to Granny, Tim.* يلوّح

4 [I] to move gently up and down or from side to side: *The branches of the trees waved gently in the breeze.* يهتز

PHR V **wave sth aside** to decide not to pay attention to a comment, etc. because you think it is not important يتجاهل

wave sb/sth away, on, etc. to move your hand in a particular direction to show sb/sth which way to go: *There was a policeman in the middle of the road, waving us on.* يوجّه بالاشارة

wave[2] /weɪv/ *noun* [C] **1** a raised line of water moving on the surface of water, especially the sea: *boats bobbing about on the waves* ○ *A huge wave swept me off my feet.* ○ *We watched the waves roll in and break on the shore.* ○ (*figurative*) *a wave of tourists* موجة

2 a sudden increase or spread of a feeling or type of behaviour: *There has been a wave of sympathy for the refugees.* ○ *A wave of strikes has hit the industry.* ➲ Look at **heatwave**. موجة

3 a form in which some types of energy move, shaped like a wave on the sea: *sound waves* ○ *shock waves from the earthquake* موجة

4 a gentle curve in hair: *Are your waves natural?* ➲ Look at **perm**. تموّج

5 a movement of sth, especially your hand, from side to side in the air: *With a wave of his hand, he said goodbye and left.* تلويح (باليد)

▸ **wavy** *adj* (**wavier**; **waviest**) having curves: *wavy hair* ○ *a wavy line* متموّج

waveband /ˈweɪvbænd/ (*also* **band**) *noun* [C] a set of radio waves of similar length حزمة موجية

wavelength /ˈweɪvleŋθ/ *noun* [C] **1** the distance between two sound waves الطول الموجي

2 the length of wave on which a radio station broadcasts its programmes طول الموجة

IDM **on the same wavelength** → SAME[1]

waver /ˈweɪvə(r)/ *verb* [I] **1** to become weak or uncertain: *He never wavered in his support for her.* يتذبذب؛ يضعف

2 **waver (between sth and sth)** to hesitate, especially when making a decision or choice
يتردّد

3 to move in an unsteady way: *His hand wavered as he reached for the gun.* يضطرب؛ يترنّح

wax /wæks/ *noun* [U] **1** a substance made from fat or oil that melts easily and is used for making candles, polish, etc. شمع

2 a yellow substance like wax that is found in your ears صِملاخ الأذن

waxwork /ˈwækswɜːk/ *noun* [C] **1** a model of sb/sth, especially of a famous person, made of wax تمثال شمعي

2 **waxworks** [with sing. or pl. verb] a place where wax models of famous people are shown to the public متحف الشمع

way[1] /weɪ/ *noun* **1** [C] a path or road along which you can walk or travel: *the way in/out* ➲ Look at **highway**, **motorway** and **railway**. طريق

2 [sing.] the route along which you move or would move if there were space: *There were some cows in the lane, blocking our way.* ○ *Get out of my way!* سبيل، طريق

3 [C, usually sing.] the route you take to reach somewhere: *Can you tell me the way to James Street?* ○ *She lost her way and had to turn back.* ○ *We stopped on the way to Leeds for a meal.* ○ *Can I drive you home? It's on my way.* طريق

4 [sing.] a direction or position: *Look this way!* ○ *That painting is the wrong way up* (= with the wrong edge at the top). ○ *Are you sure these two words are the right way round?* (= in the right order) ○ *Shouldn't you be wearing that hat the other way round?* (= facing in the other direction) ○ *He thought I was older than my sister but in fact it's the other way round* (= the opposite of what he thought). ➲ Look at **back to front**.
ناحية، اتّجاه؛ وضع

5 [sing.] a distance in space or time: *It's a long way from London to Edinburgh.* ○ *The exams are still a long way off.* مسافة؛ مدّة

a b c d e f g h i j k l m n o p q r s t u v w x y z

6 [C] a method, style or manner of doing sth; a habit: *What is the best way to learn a language?* ○ *I've discovered a brilliant way of saving paper!* ○ *There are various ways in which we can help.* ○ *They'll have to find the money one way or another.* ○ *He always does things his way.* ○ *She smiled in a friendly way.* ○ *As you get older, it becomes more difficult to change your ways.* وسيلة؛ طريقة

7 [C] a particular point or part of sth: *In some ways the meeting was very useful.* ○ *In a way, I rather like him.* ○ *Can I help you in any way?* شكل (من الأشكال)، وجه (من الوجوه)

IDM **be set in your ways** to be unable to change your habits, attitudes, etc. ترسّخت فيه عاداته وطبائعه

by the way (used for adding sth to the conversation) on a new subject: *Oh, by the way, I saw Mary in town yesterday.* بالمناسبة

get/have your own way to get or do what you want, although others may want sth else يفعل ما يريد

give way to break or fall down: *The branch of the tree suddenly gave way and came crashing down.* ينكسر، يهوي

give way (to sb/sth) 1 to stop or to allow sb/sth to go first: *Give way to traffic coming from the right.* يفسح

2 to allow sb to have what he/she wants although you did not at first agree with it: *We shall not give way to the terrorists' demands.* يستسلم؛ يذعن

go out of your way (to do sth) to make a special effort to do sth يبْذل خالص جهْده

in a big/small way (used for expressing the size or importance of an activity): *'Have you done any acting before?' 'Yes, but in a very small way.'* (= not very much) على نحو كبير/صغير

in the way 1 blocking the road or path: *I can't get past. There's a big lorry in the way.* يسدّ الطريق

2 not needed or wanted: *I felt rather in the way at my daughter's party.* لا لزوم له

no way (*informal*) definitely not: *'Can I borrow your car?' 'No way!'* حتماً لا!

under way having started and making progress: *Discussions between the two sides are now under way.* ماضٍ قدماً

a/sb's way of life the behaviour and customs that are typical of a person or group of people عادات شخص وتصرفاته

way² /weɪ/ *adv* (*informal*) very far: *I finally found his name way down at the bottom of the list.* أقصى

WC /ˌdʌblju: ˈsi:/ *abbrev* = TOILET

we /wi/ *pron* (the subject of a verb; used for talking about the speaker and one or more other people): *We're going to the theatre.* ○ *We are both very pleased with the house.* ○ *We all left together.* نحْنُ

weak /wi:k/ *adj* **1** (used about the body) having little strength or energy; not strong: *The child was weak with hunger.* ○ *Her legs felt weak.* ○ (*figurative*) *a weak economy* واهن؛ ضعيف

2 likely to break: *That bridge is too weak to take heavy traffic.* ضعيف

3 (used about a person's character) easy to influence; not firm: *He is too weak to be a good leader.* ضعيف الشخصية

4 (used about an argument, excuse, etc.) that does not convince you or seem right; not strong: *She made some weak excuse about washing her hair tonight.* ضعيف؛ واهٍ

5 not easy to see or hear; not definite or strong: *I heard a weak voice whispering for help.* ○ *She gave a weak smile.* واهن؛ باهت

6 (used about liquids) containing a lot of water, not strong in taste: *weak tea* مخفّف، ممدّد

7 weak (at/in/on sth) not able to achieve a high standard in sth: *He's weak at maths.* ○ *His maths is weak.* ضعيف

▸ **weaken** /ˈwi:kən/ *verb* **1** [I,T] to become less strong; to make sb/sth less strong: *The illness had left her weakened.* ○ *The building had been weakened by the earthquake.* يَضْعَف؛ يضْعف

2 [I] to become less certain about sth: *She eventually weakened and allowed them to stay.* يتراخى (في عناده مثلاً)، يتساهل

weakly *adv*: *The little kitten struggled weakly to its feet.* بوَهْن

weakness *noun* **1** [U] the state of being weak: *They were relying on the enemy's weakness in the air.* ضَعْف

2 [C] a fault or lack of strength, especially in a person's character: *It's important to know your own strengths and weaknesses.* ضَعْف

3 [C, usually sing.] **a weakness for sth/sb** a special and often foolish liking for sth/sb: *I have a weakness for chocolate.* موطن ضَعْف

ˈweak form *noun* [C] a way of pronouncing a word when it is not emphasized لفظ كلمة دون نبرة تشديد

wealth /welθ/ *noun* **1** [U] (owning) a lot of money, property, etc: *They were a family of enormous wealth.* ثراء

2 [sing.] **a wealth of sth** a large number or amount of sth: *He has a wealth of experience in this area.* وَفْرة، قَدْر وافر

▸ **wealthy** *adj* (**wealthier**; **wealthiest**) having a lot of money, etc.; rich ثري

wean /wi:n/ *verb* [T] to start feeding a baby or young animal with other food as well as its mother's milk يَفْطِم

weapon /ˈwepən/ *noun* [C] an object which is used for fighting or for killing people, such as a gun, sword, bomb, etc. سلاح

wear¹ /weə(r)/ *verb* (*pt* **wore** /wɔ:(r)/; *pp* **worn** /wɔ:n/) **1** [T] to have clothes, jewellery, etc. on your body: *He was wearing a suit and tie.* ○ *I wear glasses for reading.* ○ *Would you like to wear my necklace?* ○ *to wear your hair short* يَلْبس؛ يَجْعَل (شعره قصيراً مثلاً)

2 [T] to have a certain look on your face: *He was wearing an expression of delight.* يبدو (على الوجه مثلاً)

3 [I] to become thinner or damaged because of being used or rubbed a lot يَبْلَى، يهترئ

4 [T] to make a hole, path, etc. in sth by rubbing, walking, etc: *Put some slippers on or you'll wear a hole in your socks!* يُبْلي

5 [I] to last for a long time without becoming thinner or damaged: *This material wears well.* يَصْمُد

IDM **wear thin** to have less effect because of being used too much: *We've heard that story so often that it's beginning to wear thin.* يَفْقد مفعوله

PHR V **wear (sth) away** to damage sth or to make it disappear over a period of time, by using, touching, etc. it a lot; to disappear or become damaged in this way: *The writing on the floor of the church had worn away over the years.* ○ *The sea had worn the bottom of the cliffs away.* يَبْهت؛ يَحُتّ

wear (sth) down to become or to make sth smaller or shorter يتضاءل؛ يَحُتّ

wear sb/sth down to make sb/sth weaker by attacking, persuading, etc: *They wore him down with constant arguments until he changed his mind.* يُنْهك؛ يضعف

wear off to become less strong or to disappear completely: *The effects of the drug wore off after a few hours.* يزول

wear on (used about time) to pass slowly: *They got to know each other better as the summer wore on.* ينقضي بتثاقل

wear (sth) out to become too thin or damaged to use any more; to cause sth to do this: *Children's shoes wear out very quickly.* ○ *You've worn out two pairs of jeans in the last six months!* يهترئ، يبْلَى؛ يُبْلي

wear sb out to make sb very tired: *She wore herself out walking home with the heavy bags.* يُنْهك ➲ Look at **worn out**.

wear² /weə(r)/ *noun* [U] **1** wearing or being worn; use as clothing: *You'll need jeans and jumpers for everyday wear.* لباس؛ ملابس

2 (usually in compounds) things that you wear; clothes: *menswear* ○ *underwear* ملابس

3 long use which damages the quality or appearance of sth طول الاستعمال

IDM **wear and tear** the damage caused by ordinary use البلى بالاستعمال

the worse for wear → WORSE

weary /ˈwɪəri/ *adj* (**wearier**; **weariest**) tired: *He gave a weary smile.* مُتْعَب

▸ **wearily** /ˈwɪərəli/ *adv* بتعب، بضجر

weariness *noun* [U] تعب، سأم

weasel /ˈwiːzl/ *noun* a small fierce animal with reddish-brown fur, a long thin body and short legs. Weasels kill and eat other small animals. ابن عِرْس

weather¹ /ˈweðə(r)/ *noun* [U] the climate at a certain place and time, how much wind, rain, sunshine, etc. there is and how hot or cold it is: *What was the weather like on holiday?* ○ *We'll go to the seaside if the weather stays fine.* ○ *They say that the weather won't change for the next few days.* طَقْس

> **Rain** is drops of water that fall from the clouds. **Snow** is frozen rain. It is soft and white and often settles on the ground. **Sleet** is rain that is not completely frozen. **Hail** is rain frozen so hard that it feels and sounds like small stones falling. When it is only raining very slightly it is **drizzling**. When it is raining very hard it is **pouring**. **Fog** is like a cloud at ground level. It makes it difficult to see very far ahead. **Mist** is a very thin type of fog. Look also at **storm**.

IDM **make heavy weather of sth** → HEAVY

under the weather (*informal*) not very well متوعِّك

weather² /ˈweðə(r)/ *verb* **1** [T] (used about a ship or a person) to pass safely through a storm or a difficult time يجتاز بسلام، ينجو

2 [I,T] to change in appearance (because of the effect of the sun, air or wind) يلوِّحه الجو، يَبْلَى بتأثير الجو

ˈweather-beaten *adj* made rough and often darker by the sun and wind: *the fishermen's weather-beaten faces* مشْهوب، مسفوع بالشمس والريح

ˈweather forecast *noun* [C] a description of the weather that is expected for the next day or few days نشرة الأحوال الجوية

weave /wiːv/ *verb* [I,T] (*pt* **wove** /wəʊv/ or in sense 2 **weaved**; *pp* **woven** /ˈwəʊvn/ or in sense 2 **weaved**) **1** to make cloth, etc. by passing threads under and over a set of threads that is fixed to a framework (loom): *woven cloth* يَنْسج، يحيك

2 to change direction often when you are moving so that you are not stopped by anything: *He weaved in and out through the traffic.* يشقّ (طريقه) على نحو ملتوٍ

web /web/ *noun* [C] **1** a type of fine net that a spider makes in order to catch small insects: *A spider spins webs.* ➲ Look at **cobweb**. نسيج العنكبوت

2 = THE WORLD WIDE WEB

Web 2.0 /ˌweb tuː pɔɪnt ˈəʊ/ *noun* [U] the developments in the way that people use the Internet that allow users free access and give them more control over the information الجيل الثاني من مواقع الانترنت: يمكِّن المستخدم من الوصول إلى البيانات وتعديلها

webcam /ˈwebkæm/ *noun* [C] (*computing*) a video camera that is connected to a computer so that what it records can be seen on a website as it happens كاميرا موصولة بالكمبيوتر

ˈWeb-enabled *adj* able to be connected to and used with the Internet: *web-enabled phones* قادر على الاتصال بالانترنت

weblog /ˈweblɒɡ/ (*also* **blog**) *noun* [C] (*computing*) a website that belongs to a particular person where they write about things that interest them and list other websites that they think are interesting سجِّل شخصي (انترنت)

ˈweb page *noun* [C] (*computing*) a document that is connected to the World Wide Web and that anyone with an Internet connection can see, usually forming part of a website: *We learned how to create and register a new web page.* صفحة على الانترنت

website /ˈwebsaɪt/ *noun* [C] (*computing*) a place connected to the Internet, where a company, an organization, etc. puts information that can be found on the World Wide Web موقع على الانترنت

we'd /wiːd/ *short for* WE HAD, WE WOULD

wedding /ˈwedɪŋ/ *noun* [C] a marriage ceremony and often the meal or party that follows it (the reception): *I've been invited to his sister's wedding.* ○ *a wedding dress, guest, present, etc.* ○ *a wedding ring* (= one that is placed on the third finger of the left hand during a marriage ceremony and worn to show that a person is married) ○ *a wedding anniversary* عُرْس، زفاف

Look at **golden** and **silver wedding**. **Marriage** is the word for the state of being married to somebody. It can also be used for the ceremony, with the same meaning as **wedding**. The man who is getting married is the **bridegroom**, the woman is the **bride**. Other important people at the ceremony are the **best man** and the **bridesmaids**. A wedding can take place in church (a **church wedding**) or in a **registry office**.

wedge /wedʒ/ *noun* [C] a piece of wood, etc. with one thick and one narrow end that you can push into a space, in order, for example, to keep things apart: *The door was kept open with a wedge.* إسفين

▸ **wedge** *verb* [T] **1** to force sth apart or to prevent sth from moving by using a wedge: *to wedge a door open* يثبّت بإسفين

2 to force sth/sb to fit into a space: *The cupboard was wedged between the table and the door.* يكْبِس (بين شيئين مثلاً)

Wednesday /ˈwenzdeɪ/ *noun* [C,U] (*abbr* **Wed.**) the day of the week after Tuesday and before Thursday ❶ For examples of the use of the days of the week in sentences, look at **Monday**. الأربعاء

wee[1] /wiː/ *adj* little, small: *a wee boy* ○ *I'm a wee bit tired.* ❶ This word is used especially by Scottish people. صغير؛ قليل

wee[2] /wiː/ *noun* [C,U] (*informal*) (used by young children or when you are talking to them) water that you pass from the body; urine: *to need a wee* بول

▸ **wee** *verb* [I] يبول

weed /wiːd/ *noun* **1** [C] a wild plant that is not wanted in a garden because it prevents other plants from growing properly: *Our garden is full of weeds.* عشبة ضارة

2 [U] a mass of tiny green plants that floats on the surface of a pond or river أعشاب مائية طافية

3 [C] (*informal*) a thin, weak person or sb who has a weak character شخص مهزول؛ ضعيف الشخصية

▸ **weed** *verb* [I,T] to remove weeds from a piece of ground, etc. يزيل (العشب الضار)

PHRV **weed sth/sb out** to remove the things or people that you do not think are good enough: *He weeded out all the letters with spelling mistakes in them.* يتخلّص من، يغربل

weedy *adj* (**weedier**; **weediest**) (*informal*) thin and weak in appearance; of weak character: *a small weedy man* مهزول؛ ضعيف الشخصية

week /wiːk/ *noun* [C] **1** a period of seven days (usually beginning on Sunday and ending on Saturday, or beginning on Monday and ending on Sunday): *We arrived last week.* ○ *Can I see you this week? No? How about next week?* ○ *He left two weeks ago.* ○ *I haven't seen her for a week.* ○ *I play tennis twice a week.* ○ *They'll be back in a week/in a week's time.* ○ *I was on holiday the week before last.* ○ *My course ends the week after next.* ❶ A period of two weeks is usually called a **fortnight** in British English. أسبوع

2 the part of the week when people go to work, etc., usually from Monday to Friday: *She works hard during the week so that she can enjoy herself at the weekend.* ○ *I work a 40-hour week.* (أيام) أسبوع العمل

IDM **today, tomorrow, Monday, etc. week** seven days after today, tomorrow, Monday, etc. أسبوع بعد...

week in, week out every week without a rest or change كل أسبوع، باستمرار

a week yesterday, last Monday, etc. seven days before yesterday, Monday, etc: *They got married a week last Saturday.* أسبوع قبل

▸ **weekly** *adj*, *adv* happening or appearing once a week or every week: *We are paid weekly.* ○ *a weekly report* أسبوعي؛ أسبوعياً

weekly *noun* [C] (*pl.* **weeklies**) a newspaper or magazine that is published every week (جريدة أو مجلة) أسبوعية

weekday /ˈwiːkdeɪ/ *noun* [C] any day except Sunday (and usually Saturday): *I only work on weekdays.* يوم من أيام أسبوع العمل

weekend /ˌwiːkˈend; *US* ˈwiːkend/ *noun* [C] Saturday and Sunday: *What are you doing at the weekend?* ❶ In American English we say '**on** the weekend'. نهاية الاسبوع: السبت والأحد

weep /wiːp/ *verb* [I,T] (*pt*, *pp* **wept** /wept/) (*formal*) to let tears fall because of strong emotion; to cry: *She wept at the news of his death.* ○ *to weep for joy* ○ *to weep tears of pity* يبْكي

weigh /weɪ/ *verb* **1** [T] to measure how heavy sth is, especially by using a machine (scales): *I weigh myself every day.* ○ *Can you weigh this parcel for me, please?* يَزِن

2 [T] to have or show a certain weight: *I weigh 56 kilos.* يزن

3 [T] **weigh sth (up)** to consider sth carefully: *You need to weigh up your chances of success.* يفكّر (في الشيء) ملياً

4 [T] **weigh sth (against sb/sth)** to consider whether one thing is better, more important, etc. than another: *We shall weigh the advantages of the plan against the risks.* يوازن

5 [I] **weigh against (sb/sth)** to be considered important when sb/sth is being judged: *She*

didn't get the job because her lack of experience weighed against her. يكون على حساب (الشخص أو الشيء)

PHR V **weigh sb down** to make sb feel worried and sad: *weighed down by cares and responsibilities* يثقل (بالهمّ أو الحزن)

weigh sb/sth down to make it difficult for sb/sth to move (by being heavy): *I was weighed down by heavy shopping.* يثقل؛ ينوء تحت

weigh on sb/sth to make sb worry ⓘ We also say **weigh on sb's mind**: *That problem has been weighing on my mind for a long time.* يقلق

weigh sb up to try and find out what a person is like so that you can form an opinion يتفحّص شخصاً

weight[1] /weɪt/ *noun* **1** [U] the heaviness of sth or the amount that it weighs, especially as measured in kilos, etc: *In two months her weight has increased to 65 kilos.* ○ *I need to lose weight before my holidays* (= become thinner and less heavy). ○ *He's put on weight* (= got fatter). ○ *The weight of the snow broke the branch.* وزن

2 [C] a piece of metal with a certain heaviness that can be used to weigh an amount, especially using scales. Weights are also used by athletes when they are training or in the sport of weightlifting: *a 500-gram weight* ثقل: كرة حديدية؛ سَنْجة

3 [C] a heavy object: *The doctor has told me not to lift heavy weights.* حمل ثقيل

4 [sing.] the worry that is caused by a problem: *Telling her the truth took a weight off his mind.* وطأة

IDM **carry weight** → CARRY
pull your weight → PULL[1]

▸ **weightless** *adj* having no weight, especially when travelling in space عديم الوزن

weightlessness *noun* [U] انعدام الوزن

weighty *adj* (**weightier**; **weightiest**) serious and important: *a weighty question* هامّ، ذو شأن أو وزن

weight[2] /weɪt/ *verb* [T] **1 weight sth (down) (with sth)** to hold sth down with a heavy object or objects: *to weight down a fishing net* يثقّل

2 (usually passive) to organize sth so that a particular person or group has an advantage/a disadvantage: *The system is weighted in favour of people with children.* يجعل شيئاً في أو ضدّ مصلحة فلان

weightlifting /ˈweɪtlɪftɪŋ/ *noun* [U] a sport in which heavy metal objects are lifted رفع الأثقال

weir /wɪə(r)/ *noun* [C] a type of wall that is built across a river to stop or change the direction of the flow of water هدّار: سدّ عبر النهر

weird /wɪəd/ *adj* **1** strange and frightening: *a weird noise* غريب

2 (*informal*) not normal: *weird clothes, ideas, etc.* شاذ، غير مألوف

welcome /ˈwelkəm/ *adj* **1** received with pleasure; giving pleasure: *You're always welcome here.* ○ *welcome news* مرحّب به، سارّ

2 welcome to sth/to do sth allowed to do sth: *You're welcome to use our swimming pool.* مسموح له، مرحّب به

3 we say that sb is welcome to sth if we do not want it ourselves: *Take the car if you want. You're welcome to it. It's always breaking down.* يمنح شيئاً لا يريده صاحبه

IDM **make sb welcome** to receive sb in a friendly way يرحّب بِ

you're welcome you don't need to thank me: *'Thank you for your help.' 'You're welcome.'* لا داعي للشكر

▸ **welcome** *interj* (an expression used for greeting a person who is arriving at a place): *Welcome to London!* ○ *Welcome home!* أهلاً وسهلاً

welcome *noun* [C] a greeting to sb who has arrived: *Let's give a warm welcome to our next guest.* ترحيب

welcome *verb* [T] **1** to greet sb when he/she arrives: *The children rushed to the door to welcome their father.* يرحّب بِ

2 to be pleased about sth and support it: *When I told my parents I wanted to go to university they welcomed the idea.* يرحّب بالفكرة

weld /weld/ *verb* [I,T] to join pieces of metal by heating them and pressing them together يلْحِم

welfare /ˈwelfeə(r)/ *noun* [U] **1** the good health and happiness of a person or group of people: *The doctor is concerned about the child's welfare.* صالح، صحة وسعادة

2 the help and care that is given to people who have problems with health, money, etc: *education and welfare services* رفاه، خدمات اجتماعية

3 (*US*) = SOCIAL SECURITY

ˌwelfare ˈstate *noun* [sing.] (a country which has) a system organized by a government to help people who have no job, who are ill, etc. دولة الرفاه

we'll /wiːl/ *short for* WE SHALL, WE WILL

well[1] /wel/ *adv* (**better** /ˈbetə(r)/, **best** /best/)
1 in a good or satisfactory way: *You speak English very well.* ○ *I hope your work is going well.* ○ *Well done!* (= used when you are praising sth that sb has done) ○ *Did they treat you well?* ○ *The car is running much better since it was serviced.* جيّداً: بصورة حسنة

2 thoroughly, completely or carefully: *Shake the bottle well before opening.* جيّداً: تماماً؛ بعناية

3 (used with *can, could, may* or *ought* to show that sth is probably true): *He might well be right.* على الأرجح

4 (used with *can't* and *couldn't* to show that sth is not sensible or reasonable): *I can't very well refuse to help them after all they've done for me.* بشكل مقبول أو معقول

5 very much: *They arrived home well past midnight.* ○ *This book is well worth reading.* بكثير جداً

IDM **as well (as sb/sth)** in addition (to sb/sth): *Can I come as well?* ○ *He's worked in Japan as well as Italy.* ➲ Look at the note at **also**. أيضاً، فضلاً عن

augur well/ill for sb/sth → AUGUR

be well out of sth to be lucky because you are

not involved in sth: *They're still arguing. I'm glad we're well out of it.* محظوظ لعدم علاقته بشيء ما
bode well/ill (for sb/sth) → BODE
do well 1 to be successful: *Their daughter has done well at university.* يوفَّق، ينجح
2 to be getting better (after an illness): *Mr Brown is doing well after his operation.* يتماثل للشفاء
jolly well → JOLLY
may/might (just) as well (used for saying that sth can or should happen, especially when you have no choice): *I may as well tell you the truth – you'll find out anyway.* يحسن أن
mean well → MEAN[1]
very well → VERY[1]
well and truly completely: *We were well and truly lost.* تماماً
well/badly off → OFF[1]
well off for sth having plenty of sth: *You're well off for space in your office.* عنده ما يكفي (من الشيء)

well[2] /wel/ *adj* (**better** /ˈbetə(r)/, **best** /best/) (not before a noun) **1** (looking or feeling) healthy: *'How are you?' 'I'm very well, thanks.'* ○ *This medicine will make you feel better.* ○ *Get well soon* (= written in a card that you send to somebody who is ill). جيِّد، بصحّة جيِّدة
2 in a satisfactory state: *I hope all is well with you.* حسن، على ما يرام
IDM **all very well (for sb)** (*informal*) (used for showing that you are not happy or do not agree with sth): *It's all very well for her to criticize* (= it's easy for her to criticize) *but it doesn't help the situation.* من السهل أنْ...
(just) as well (to do sth) (used when you are talking about an action that might stop sth bad happening): *It would be just as well to ask his permission.* ➲ Look at **it is just as well (that)** at **just**. تحسباً، من الأفضل

well[3] /wel/ *interj* **1** (used for showing surprise): *Well, look who's here!* عجباً!
2 (used for expressing doubt, hesitation, etc.): *'Do you like it?' 'Well, I'm not really sure.'* ○ *Her new boyfriend seems, well, a little strange.* لا أعرف ما أقول...
3 (used for showing that you are relieved): *Well, thank goodness you've arrived.* الحمد لله!
4 (used when you begin the next part of a story or when you are thinking about what to say next): *Well, the next thing that happened was...* ○ *Well now, let me see...* حسناً، طيِّب!
5 (*also* **oh well**) (used for showing that there is nothing you can do to change a situation): *Oh well, there's nothing we can do about it.* (تعبّر عن الاستسلام للواقع)

well[4] /wel/ *noun* [C] **1** a deep hole in the ground from which water is obtained: *to draw water from a well* بئر
2 = OIL WELL
▶ **well** *verb* [I] **well (out/up)** (used about a liquid) to come to the surface: *Tears welled up in her eyes.* يفيض

ˌwell ˈbalanced *adj* **1** (used about a person) calm and sensible رزين، راجح العقل
2 (used about a meal, etc.) containing enough of the healthy types of food your body needs: *a well-balanced diet* متوازن

ˌwell beˈhaved *adj* behaving in a way that most people think is correct حسَن السلوك

ˈwell-being *noun* [U] a state of being healthy and happy حسْن الحال، سعادة

ˌwell ˈdone *adj* (used about meat, etc.) cooked for a long time مطهو طهياً جيداً

ˌwell ˈdressed *adj* wearing attractive and fashionable clothes أنيق الملبس

ˌwell-ˈearned *adj* that you deserve, especially because you have been working hard مُسْتَحَق

ˌwell ˈfed *adj* having good food regularly جيِّد التغذية

ˌwell inˈformed *adj* knowing a lot about one or several subjects واسع الاطلاع

wellington /ˈwelɪŋtən/ (*also* **ˌwellington ˈboot**, *informal* **welly**) *noun* [C] (*Brit*) one of a pair of long rubber boots that you wear to keep your feet and the lower part of your legs dry: *a pair of wellingtons* حذاء مطاطي عالي الساق، "جزمة"

ˌwell ˈkept *adj* looked after very carefully so that it has a tidy appearance (شيء) معْتنى به

ˌwell ˈknown *adj* known by a lot of people; famous مشهور، معروف

ˌwell ˈmeaning *adj* (used about a person) wanting to be kind or helpful, but often not having this effect حسن النيّة

ˌwell ˈmeant *adj* intended to be kind or helpful but not having this result صادر عن نيّة حسنة

ˌwell-to-ˈdo *adj* wealthy; with a lot of money ثري، ميسور

ˈwell-wisher *noun* [C] somebody who hopes that a person or thing will be successful متمني الخير (لغيره)

welly /ˈweliː/ *noun* [C] (*pl.* **wellies**) (*informal*) = WELLINGTON

Welsh /welʃ/ *adj* of Wales, its people or their language: *the Welsh coast* ○ *He's Welsh. He was born in Cardiff.* ويلزي
▶ **Welsh** *noun* **1** [U] the language of Wales اللغة الويلزية

> Welsh is a Celtic language that English speakers cannot understand unless they have learnt it.

2 the Welsh [plural] the people of Wales الويلزيون، سكان ويلز

went *pt of* GO[1]

wept *pt, pp of* WEEP

we're /wɪə(r)/ *short for* WE ARE

were → BE

west /west/ *noun* [sing.] (*abbr* **W**) **1** (*also* **the west**) one of the four main points of the compass; the direction you look towards in order to see the sun set: *Which way is west?* ○ *Rain is spreading from the west.* ○ *There's a road to the west of here.* الغرب

2 the west; **the West** the part of any country, city, etc. that lies further towards the west than other parts: *I live in the west of Scotland.* ○ *The climate in the West is much wetter than the East.* الجزء الغربي

3 the West the countries of North America and Western Europe الغرب، الدول الغربية

▸ **west** (*also* **West**) *adj* in or towards the west, or from the west: *West London* ○ *the west wind* غربي

west *adv* to or towards the west: *The island is five miles west of here.* ○ *to travel west* غرباً

westerly /'westəli/ *adj* **1** to, towards or in the west: *in a westerly direction* في اتجاه الغرب

2 (used about winds) coming from the west غربي

westward /'westwəd/ *adj* towards the west: *in a westward direction* نحو الغرب، غربي

westward (*also* **westwards**) *adv*: *to fly westwards* غرباً

westbound /'westbaʊnd/ *adj* travelling or leading towards the west: *the westbound carriageway of the motorway* متجه غرباً

the 'West Country *noun* [U] the south-west part of Britain الجزء الجنوبي الغربي من بريطانيا

the ˌWest 'End *noun* [U] (*Brit*) the western part of central London where there are many shops, theatres, cinemas, etc. حي المسارح والسينمات في لندن

⚷ **western** (*also* **Western**) /'westən/ *adj* (*abbr* **W**)
1 in or of the west: *the western United States* في الغرب، غربي

2 from or connected with countries of the West: *the Western way of life* غربي

▸ **western** *noun* [C] a film or book about life in the past in the west of the United States فيلم أو كتاب عن الحياة سابقاً في غرب الولايات المتحدة

westerner *noun* [C] a person who was born or who lives in the West غربي

westernize (*also* **westernise**) /-aɪz/ *verb* [T] to make a country or people more like the West, e.g. in the way people dress and behave: *Young people in our country are becoming westernized through watching American television programmes.* يدخل أساليب الحياة الغربية

the ˌWest 'Indies *noun* [plural, with sing. or pl. verb] a group of islands in the Caribbean Sea that consists of the Bahamas, the Antilles and the Leeward and Windward Islands جزر الهند الغربية

▸ **ˌWest 'Indian** *noun* [C] a person from the West Indies or whose family was originally from the West Indies شخص من جزر الهند الغربية

ˌWest 'Indian *adj*: *the West Indian cricket team* من الهند الغربية

westward *adj, adv* → WEST

⚷ **wet** /wet/ *adj* (**wetter**; **wettest**) **1** covered in a liquid, especially water: *wet clothes* ○ *Don't get your feet wet.* مبتلّ، رطب

> **Moist** means slightly wet. **Damp** is used to describe things that are slightly wet and feel unpleasant because of it: *Don't sit on the grass. It's damp.*

2 (used about the weather, etc.) with a lot of rain: *a wet day* مطير

3 (used about paint, etc.) not yet dry or hard: *The ink is still wet.* نديّ

4 (used about a person) without energy, strength or courage رخْو، خائر

IDM a wet blanket (*informal*) a person who spoils other people's fun, especially because he or she will not join in شخص مفسد للبهجة

wet through extremely wet غارق في البلل

▸ **wet** *noun* [sing.] **the wet** rainy weather: *Come in out of the wet.* بلل، مطر

wet *verb* (*pt, pp* **wet** or **wetted**) [T] **1** to make sth wet يبلّل

2 (used especially of young children) to make yourself or your bed, clothes, etc. wet by urinating: *Joe wet his trousers this morning.* يبول (في فراشه مثلاً)

wetsuit /'wetsuːt; *Brit also* -sjuːt/ *noun* [C] a rubber suit that covers the whole of the body, used by people doing sports in the water or swimming under the water لباس مطاطي ضد الماء

we've /wiːv/ *short for* WE HAVE

whack /wæk/ *verb* [T] (*informal*) to hit sb/sth hard يضرب بشدّة

whale /weɪl/ *noun* [C] a very large animal that lives in the sea and looks like a huge fish (but is, in fact, a mammal) حوت

▸ **whaling** *noun* [U] hunting whales صيد الحيتان

wharf /wɔːf/ *noun* [C] (*pl.* **wharves** /wɔːvz; *US* hwɔːrvz/) a platform made of stone or wood at the side of a river where ships and boats can be tied up رصيف للسفن، رصيف الميناء

⚷ **what** /wɒt/ *det, pron* **1** (used for asking for information about sb/sth): *What time is it?* ○ *What kind of music do you like?* ○ *She asked him what he was doing.* ○ *What's their phone number?* ➲ Look at the note at **which**. ما ، ماذا

2 the things (that); all the...: *What he says is true.* ○ *I believe what he said.* ○ *Is it true what he said?* ○ *I haven't got much, but you can borrow what money I have.* ما

3 (used for showing surprise, pleasure, etc.): *What a beautiful day!* ما (للتعجب)، يا له من!، ماذا!!

> **What** can also be used alone, to express surprise: *'I've just spent a thousand pounds.' 'What!'*

IDM how/what about...? → ABOUT[2]

what for for what purpose; why: *What's this little switch for?* ○ *What did you say that for?* لأي غرض؛ لماذا

what if...? what would happen if...?: *What if the car breaks down?* ماذا يحدث لو

⚷ **whatever** /wɒt'evə(r)/ *adj, pron* **1** any or every; anything or everything: *You can say whatever you like.* ○ *He took whatever help he could get.* أيّ (شيء)؛ كلّ

2 no matter what: *I still love you, whatever you*

may think. ○ *Whatever she says, she doesn't really mean it.* مهما، أيّما

3 (used for expressing surprise or worry) what: *Whatever's the matter?* ○ *Whatever could have happened to them?* ما ، ماذا يا ترى...

IDM or whatever (*informal*) or any other or others of a similar kind: *You don't need to wear anything smart – jeans and a sweater or whatever.* وغير ذلك، وما شابه ذلك

▶ **whatever** (*also* **whatsoever**) *adv* at all: *I've no reason whatever to doubt him.* ○ *'Any questions?' 'None whatsoever.'* مطلقاً، أبداً

wheat /wi:t/ *noun* [U] **1** a type of grain which can be made into flour قمح، حنطة

2 the plant which produces this grain: *a field of wheat* قمح، حنطة

wheel /wi:l/ *noun* **1** [C] a circular object that turns around a rod that is fixed to its centre. Wheels are used to make a car, bicycle, etc. move or to make a machine work عجلة، دولاب

2 [usually sing.] = STEERING WHEEL: *Her husband was at the wheel when the accident happened* (= he was driving).

▶ **wheel** *verb* **1** [T] to push along an object that has wheels; to move sb about in/on a vehicle with wheels: *He wheeled his bicycle up the hill.* ○ *She was wheeled back to her bed on a trolley.* يُدير شيئاً ذا عجلات

2 [I] to fly round in circles: *Birds wheeled above the ship.* يدور

3 [I] to turn round suddenly: *Eleanor wheeled round, with a look of horror on her face.* يستدير

wheelbarrow /'wi:lbærəʊ/ (*also* **barrow**) *noun* [C] a type of small cart with one wheel, two legs and two handles used for carrying small loads, especially in gardens عربة يد بعَجَلة واحدة

wheelchair /'wi:ltʃeə(r)/ *noun* [C] a chair with large wheels that a person who cannot walk can move or be moved about in كرسي المُقْعدين

'wheel clamp *verb* [T] = CLAMP (3)

wheeze /wi:z/ *verb* [I] to breathe noisily with a whistling sound, especially if you have a chest illness يئِزّ (صدر المريض)

when /wen/ *adv* **1** at what time: *When did she arrive?* ○ *I don't know when she arrived.* متى

2 (used for talking about the time at which sth happens or happened): *Sunday is the day when I can relax.* ○ *I last saw her in May, when she was in London.* عندما

▶ **when** *conj* **1** at or during the time that: *He jumped up when the phone rang.* ○ *When we were walking home we saw an accident.* حين، عندما

Notice that we use the present tense after 'when' if we are talking about a future time: *I'll call you when I'm ready.*

2 since; as; considering that: *Why do you want more money when you've got enough already?* بما أنّ؛ في حين

When is used for talking about something that you think will happen, but **if** is used for something you are not sure will happen. Compare: *I'll ask her when she comes* (= you are sure that she will come). ○ *I'll ask her if she comes* (= you are not sure whether she will come or not).

whence /wens/ *adv* (*old-fashioned*) (from) where: *They returned whence they came.* من حيث

whenever /wen'evə(r)/ *conj* at any time; no matter when: *You can borrow my car whenever you want.* ○ *Don't worry. You can give it back the next time you see me, or whenever.* متى ما، كلّما؛ في أي وقت تشاء

▶ **whenever** *adv* (used when you are showing that you are surprised or impatient) when: *Whenever did you find time to do all that cooking?* ○ *Whenever are you going to finish?* متى؟!

where /weə(r)/ *adv, conj* **1** at, in or to what place or position: *Where can I buy a paper?* ○ *I asked him where he lived.* ○ *Where are you going?* أين

2 at, in or to a place or a situation: *the town where you were born* ○ *She ran to where they were standing.* ○ *I know where we can go.* ○ *Where possible, you should travel by bus, not taxi.* حيث

3 at which place: *We came to a village, where we stopped for lunch.* حيث

whereabouts¹ /'weərəbaʊts/ *adv* where; in or near what place: *Whereabouts did you lose your purse?* في أي مكان، أين

whereabouts² /ˌweərə'baʊts/ *noun* [U, with sing. or pl. verb] the place where sb/sth is: *The whereabouts of the stolen painting is/are unknown.* مكان

whereas /weər'æz/ *conj* (used for showing a fact that is different): *He eats meat, whereas she's a vegetarian.* في حين، بينما

whereby /ˌweər'baɪ/ *adv* (*formal*) by which: *These countries have an agreement whereby foreign visitors can have free medical care.* الذي بموجبه أو وفقاً له

whereupon /ˌweərə'pɒn/ *conj* (*formal*) after which: *He fell asleep, whereupon she walked quietly from the room.* عند ذلك، ومن ثمّ

wherever /ˌweər'evə(r)/ *conj* **1** in or to any place: *You can sit wherever you like.* ○ *She comes from Bahia, wherever that is* (= I don't know where it is). أينما: لا أدري أين...

2 everywhere, in all places that: *Wherever I go, he goes.* حيثما

▶ **wherever** *adv* (used for showing surprise): *Wherever did you learn to cook like that?* أين؟!

IDM or wherever or any other place: *The students might be from Sweden, Denmark or wherever.* أو أيّ مكان آخر

whet /wet/ *verb* (whetting; whetted)

IDM whet sb's appetite to make sb want more of sth: *Our short stay in Dublin whetted our appetite to spend more time there.* يثير (الشهية)، يشْحَذ

whether /ˈweðə(r)/ *conj* **1** (used after verbs like 'ask', 'doubt', 'know', etc.) if: *He asked me whether we would be coming to the party.* ما إذا

2 (used for expressing a choice or doubt between two or more possibilities): *I can't make up my mind whether to go or not.* ○ *There was some doubt as to whether she should go.* إن، إذا

> **Whether** and **if** can both be used in sense 1. Only **whether** can be used before 'to' + verb: *Have you decided whether to accept the offer yet?* Only **whether** can be used after a preposition: *the problem of whether to accept the offer.*

IDM **whether or not** (used to say that sth will be true in either of the situations that are mentioned): *We shall play on Saturday whether it rains or not.* ○ *Whether or not it rains, we shall play on Saturday.* سواء

whew = PHEW

whey /weɪ/ *noun* [U] the thin liquid that remains after sour milk has formed curds مصل (اللبن)

which /wɪtʃ/ *det, pron* **1** (used in questions when there are a number of people or things to choose from): *Which cake would you like?* ○ *Which hand do you write with?* ○ *Which is your bag?* ○ *She asked me which colour I preferred.* ○ *I can't remember which of the boys is the older.* أيّ، أيّة

> **Which** or **what**? We use **which** when there is only a limited group to choose from: *Which car is yours? The Ford or the Volvo?* We use **what** when the group is not limited: *What car would you choose, if you could have any one you wanted?*

2 (used for saying what thing or things you are talking about): *We need a car which is reliable.* ○ *Did you see the article which Jenny wrote?* ○ (*formal*) *The situation in which he found himself was very difficult.* الذي، التي

> In less formal English we would write: *The situation which he found himself in was very difficult.* Often the 'which' is left out: *The situation he found himself in...*

3 (used for giving more information about a thing or an animal): *His best film, which won several awards, was about the life of Gandhi.* الذي، التي

> Note that there is a comma before 'which' and at the end of the part of the sentence which it introduces.

4 (used for making a comment on what has just been said): *We had to wait 16 hours for our plane, which was really annoying.* ❶ Note that there is a comma before 'which'. ذلك، وهو (أمر)

whichever /wɪtʃˈevə(r)/ *det, pron* **1** any person or thing: *You can choose whichever book you want.* أيّ، أيّة، ما

2 (used for expressing surprise) which: *Whichever way did you come?* أيّ؟!

whiff /wɪf/ *noun* [sing.] a smell which only lasts for a short time: *He caught a whiff of her perfume.* نَفْحة

while¹ /waɪl/ (*also* **whilst** /waɪlst/) *conj* **1** during the time that; when: *He always phones while we're having lunch.* حينما؛ بينما

2 at the same time as: *He always listens to the radio while he's driving to work.* أثناء

3 (*formal*) (used when you are contrasting two ideas): *Some countries are rich, while others are extremely poor.* بينما

while² /waɪl/ *noun* [sing.] a period of time (usually short): *Let's sit down here for a while.* بُرْهة، مدة قصيرة

IDM **once in a while** → ONCE
worth sb's while → WORTH

▸ **while** *verb*

PHR V **while sth away** to pass time in a lazy or relaxed way: *We whiled away the evening chatting and listening to music.* يمضي الوقت (بتكاسل)

whim /wɪm/ *noun* [C] a sudden idea or desire to do sth (often sth that is not sensible) نَزْوة

whimper /ˈwɪmpə(r)/ *verb* [I] to cry softly, especially with fear or pain يَنْشِج

▸ **whimper** *noun* [C] نشيج

whine /waɪn/ *verb* **1** [I] to make a long high unpleasant sound: *The dog is whining to go out.* يَعْوي

2 [I,T] to complain about sth in an annoying way: *The children were whining all afternoon.* يتذمّر، يتشكّى ويتبكّى

▸ **whine** *noun* [C] عواء؛ تذمّر

whip¹ /wɪp/ *noun* [C] **1** a long thin piece of leather, etc. with a handle, that is used for making animals go faster and for hitting people as a punishment سَوْط

2 an official of a political party who makes sure that all members vote in important debates in Parliament صاحب السوط (في حزب سياسي)

whip² /wɪp/ *verb* (whi**pp**ing; whi**pp**ed) **1** [T] to hit a person or an animal with a whip يضرب بالسوط

2 [T] to mix the white part of an egg, cream, etc. until it is light and stiff: *whipped cream* يَخْفِق

3 [T] (*Brit informal*) to steal sth: *Somebody's whipped my sweater!* يَسْرِق

4 [I,T] (*informal*) to move quickly or suddenly; to make sth move in this way: *He whipped out a pen and made a note of the number.* يُسْرِع؛ يُحرِّك بسرعة؛ يستلّ

PHR V **whip sth up** **1** to cause a strong emotion: *to whip up excitement* يثير

2 (*informal*) to prepare food quickly: *to whip up a quick snack* يعدّ (بسرعة)

whir (*especially US*) = WHIRR

whirl /wɜːl/ *verb* [I,T] to move round very quickly; to make sb/sth move in this way: *The dancers whirled round the room.* ○ *The wind whirled the leaves round and round.* ○ (*figurative*) *I couldn't sleep. My mind was whirling after all the excitement.* ينقل، يدور؛ يُدوِّر

▸ **whirl** *noun* [sing.] **1** the act or sound of whirling: *the whirl of the helicopter's blades* دوران؛ ضجيج

2 a state of confusion: *My head's in a whirl – I'm so excited.* (في حالة) تشوّش

IDM give sth a whirl (*informal*) to try sth يجرّب (الشيء)

whirlpool /ˈwɜːlpuːl/ *noun* [C] a place in a river or the sea where the water moves quickly round and round دوّامة

whirlwind /ˈwɜːlwɪnd/ *noun* [C] a very strong wind that forms a tall column of air moving round and round in a circle as it travels across the land or the sea ➲ Look at the note at **storm**. إعصار، زوبعة

whirr (*especially US* **whir**) /wɜː(r)/ *verb* [I] to make a continuous low sound: *The noise of the fan whirring kept me awake.* يئزّ، يطنّ

▸ **whirr** (*especially US* **whir**) *noun* [C, usually sing.] أزيز، طنين

whisk /wɪsk/ *noun* [C] a tool that you use for beating the white part of an egg, cream, etc. مخفقة

▸ **whisk** *verb* [T] **1** to move sb/sth quickly: *The prince was whisked away in a black limousine.* ينقل أو يأخذ (شيئاً) بخفة ورشاقة

2 to beat eggs, cream, etc. very quickly with a whisk يَخْفِق

whisker /ˈwɪskə(r)/ *noun* **1 whiskers** [plural] the hair that is growing on a man's face لحْية (جانبية)

2 [C] one of the long hairs that grow near the mouth of a mouse, cat, etc. سَبلَة: شارب الفأر أو الهر الخ...

whisky /ˈwɪski/ *noun* (*pl.* **whiskies**) **1** [U] a strong alcoholic drink that is made from grain ويسكي

2 [C] a glass of whisky ❶ In the USA and Ireland the spelling is **whiskey**. كأس من الويسكي

⚷**whisper** /ˈwɪspə(r)/ *verb* [I,T] to speak very quietly to sb, so that other people cannot hear what you are saying يهْمِس

▸ **whisper** *noun* [C]: *to speak in a whisper* هَمْس

⚷**whistle** /ˈwɪsl/ *noun* [C] **1** the long high sound that you make when you force air out between your lips صفير، تَصْفير

2 a simple musical instrument that produces a long high sound: *The referee blew his whistle to stop the game.* صَفّارة

▸ **whistle** *verb* **1** [I,T] to make sounds by forcing air out between your lips or through a whistle: *The girl was whistling as she walked down the street.* ○ *He whistled a tune to himself.* ○ *The referee whistled and the game was over.* يَصْفِر

2 [I] to make a sound like a whistle: *A bullet whistled past his head* (= moved quickly, with the sound of a whistle). يَصفِر، يَئزّ

Whit /wɪt/ *noun* [U] = WHITSUN

⚷**white**[1] /waɪt/ *adj* **1** of the very light colour of snow or milk: *an old lady with white hair* ○ *white coffee* (= with milk) أبيض

2 (used about a person) having pale skin, of European origin أبيض

3 white (with sth) (used about a person) very pale because of illness, fear, etc: *to be white with shock* شاحب

IDM black and white → BLACK[2]

in black and white → BLACK[2]

⚷**white**[2] /waɪt/ *noun* **1** [U] white colour, paint, etc: *She was dressed in white.* بياض؛ اللون الأبيض

2 [C] a person with white skin: *Blacks and Whites in South Africa* الأبيض

3 [C,U] the part of an egg that turns white when it is cooked ❶ The yellow part of an egg is the **yolk**. بياض (أو آح) البيضة

4 [C] the white part of the eye بياض العين

ˌ**white-ˈcollar** *adj* white-collar work is done in an office not a factory, and white-collar workers are people who work in an office (عمل) في مكتب (وليس في مصنع)

ˌ**white ˈelephant** *noun* [sing.] something that you do not need or that is not useful شيء عديم الفائدة

the ˈWhite House *noun* [sing.] **1** the large house in Washington D.C. where the US president lives and works البيت الأبيض

2 used to refer to the US president and the other people in the government who work with him/her البيت الأبيض

ˌ**white ˈlie** *noun* [C] a lie that is not very harmful or serious كذبة بريئة

ˌ**White ˈPaper** *noun* [C] (*Brit*) an official government report on a particular subject that will later be discussed in Parliament بيان أو كتاب أبيض

whitewash /ˈwaɪtwɒʃ/ *noun* [U] a white liquid that you use for painting walls طلاء أبيض (للجدران)، كلْس

▸ **whitewash** *verb* [T] **1** to paint whitewash on a wall يطلي ببياض الكلْس

2 to try to hide sth bad or wrong that you have done يُموّه

ˌ**white-water ˈrafting** *noun* [U] the sport of travelling down a fast rough section of a river, lake, etc. in a rubber boat ركوب الطوافات في مياه عجّاجة

ˌ**white ˈwine** *noun* [U] wine made from green grapes, that is clear or of a very pale yellow colour نبيذ أبيض

Whitsun /ˈwɪtsn/ (*also* **Whit**) *noun* [sing.] the seventh Sunday after Easter and the days close to it أحَد أو عيد العَنْصَرة

whiz (*also* **whizz**) /wɪz/ *verb* [I] (**whizzing**; **whizzed**) (*informal*) to move very quickly, often making a high continuous sound: *The racing cars went whizzing by.* ينطلق بسرعة وهو يئزّ

⚷**who** /huː/ *pron* **1** (used in questions to ask sb's

name, etc.): *Who did this?* ○ *Who did you meet at the party?* ○ *Who did you go with?* مَنْ

2 (used in reported questions and after certain verbs): *She wondered who he was.* ○ *I can't remember who I asked to do this.* مَنْ

3 (used for saying which person or what kind of person you are talking about): *I like people who say what they think.* ○ *That's the man who I met at Ann's party.* ○ *The woman who I work for is very nice.* الذي (وبقية الأسماء الموصولة)

In the last two examples (= when 'who' is the object, or when it is used with a preposition) 'who' can be left out: *That's the man I met at Ann's party.* ○ *The woman I work for is very nice.*

4 used for giving extra information about sb: *My mother, who's over 80, still drives a car.* الذي (وبقية الأسماء الموصولة)

➲ Look at the note at **whom**.

who'd /hu:d/ *short for* WHO HAD, WHO WOULD

whoever /hu:'evə(r)/ *pron* **1** the person who: *Whoever is responsible will have to pay for the damage.* ○ *I want to speak to whoever is in charge.* مَن ، أيّ شخص

2 it does not matter who: *I don't want to see anybody – whoever it is.* أيّ (من)، أيّا كان

3 (used for expressing surprise) who: *Whoever could be phoning so late at night?* مَنْ يا ترى

whole /həʊl/ *adj* **1** complete; full: *We drank a whole bottle of wine.* ○ *a whole month's holiday* كامل

2 not broken or cut: *Snakes swallow their prey whole* (= in one piece). قطعة واحدة

▸ **whole** *noun* [sing.] **1** all that there is of sth: *I spent the whole of the morning cooking.* كُلّ

2 a thing that is complete or full: *Two halves make a whole.* (عدد) صحيح

IDM **as a whole** as one complete thing or unit: *This is true in Britain, but also in Europe as a whole.* جُمْلَة

on the whole generally, but not true in every case: *On the whole I think it's a very good idea.* إجمالاً

wholly /'həʊlli/ *adv* completely; fully: *The government is not wholly to blame for the situation.* كلياً، تماماً

wholefood /'həʊlfu:d/ *noun* [U] food that does not contain artificial substances and chemicals and that is as natural as possible طعام خالٍ من المواد الاصطناعية

wholehearted /ˌhəʊl'hɑ:tɪd/ *adj* complete and without doubt: *to give sb your wholehearted support* كلّي؛ من كل قلبه

▸ **wholeheartedly** *adv*: *We wholeheartedly agree with you.* كلياً: من كل قلبه

wholemeal /'həʊlmi:l/ *adj* (made from flour) that contains all the grain: *wholemeal bread* دقيق كامل: (لم تفصل نخالته)

wholesale /'həʊlseɪl/ *adj*, *adv* **1** connected with buying and selling goods in large quantities: *They get all their building materials wholesale.* بيع بالجملة

2 (usually about sth bad) very great; on a very large scale: *the wholesale destruction of the rainforests* ذريع: على نطاق واسع

wholesome /'həʊlsəm/ *adj* **1** good for your health: *simple wholesome food* صِحّي

2 (used about a person) looking clean and attractive (ذو مظهر) نظيف وجذّاب

3 having a moral effect that is good حكيم؛ سديد

who'll /hu:l/ *short for* WHO WILL

wholly → WHOLE

whom /hu:m/ *pron* (*formal*) **1** (used in questions as the object form of 'who' to ask sb's name, etc.): *Whom did you meet there?* ○ *To whom did you give the money?* مَنْ

2 (used as the object form of 'who' in reported questions and after certain verbs): *He asked me whom I had met.* ○ *I realized to whom I had been speaking.* مَنْ

3 (used for saying which person or what kind of person the object of a verb or preposition is): *A gentleman whom I had never met sat down beside me.* الذي (وبقية الأسماء الموصولة)

4 (used for giving extra information about the object of a verb or preposition): *This is my wife, to whom I owe everything.* الذي (وبقية الأسماء الموصولة)

The use of **whom** instead of **who** as the object pronoun or the pronoun after prepositions is very formal. We usually express a sentence such as: *He asked me with whom I had discussed it.'* as '*He asked me who I had discussed it with.'* (Note the position of the preposition at the end.)

whooping cough /'hu:pɪŋ kɒf/ *noun* [U] a serious disease, especially of children, in which they have a bad cough and make a loud noise when they breathe in after coughing سعال ديكي

whoops /wʊps/ *interj* (*informal*) (used when you have, or nearly have, a small accident): *Whoops! I nearly dropped the cup.* "هوب"!

whoosh /wʊʃ/ *verb* [I] to move very fast, with the sound of air rushing يندفع محدثاً صوتاً

who're /'hu:ə(r)/ *short for* WHO ARE

whore /hɔ:(r)/ *noun* [C] (*old-fashioned*) = PROSTITUTE

who's /hu:z/ *short for* WHO IS, WHO HAS

whose /hu:z/ *det*, *pron* **1** (used in questions when you are asking who sth belongs to) of whom?: *Whose car is that?* ○ *That's a nice coat – I wonder whose it is.* لمن؟

2 of whom; of which: *That's the boy whose mother I met.* ○ *a firm whose most famous product is chocolate* الذي (وبقية الأسماء الموصولة)

who've /hu:v/ *short for* WHO HAVE

why /waɪ/ *adv* for what reason: *Why was she so late?* ○ *I wonder why they went.* ○ *'I'm not staying* *any longer.' 'Why not?'* ○ *Can you tell me the reason why you are so unhappy?* لماذا

IDM **why ever** (used to show that you are surprised or angry): *Why ever didn't you phone?* لم؟

why not (used for making or agreeing to a suggestion): *Why not get fish and chips tonight?* لم لا؟

wick /wɪk/ *noun* [C] the piece of string in the middle of a candle ذبالة، فتيلة

wicked /ˈwɪkɪd/ *adj* **1** morally bad; evil: *The man was described as weak and foolish but not wicked.* ➲ Look at the note at **evil**. خبيث؛ شرّير

2 liking to annoy other people in a way that is not serious: *a wicked sense of humour* لا يخلو من خبث

3 (*slang*) very good ممتع

▶ **wickedly** *adv* بخبث

wickedness *noun* [U] شرّ؛ خبث

⚷**wide** /waɪd/ *adj* **1** measuring a large amount from one side or edge to the other: *The road was not wide enough for two cars to pass.* ○ *a wide river* ❶ The noun is **width**. The opposite is **narrow**. ➲ Look at the note at **broad**. واسع

2 measuring a particular amount from one side or edge to the other: *The box was only 20 centimetres wide.* ○ *How wide is the river?* عريض، واسع

3 covering a large area or range: *You're the nicest person in the whole wide world!* ○ *This shop sells a wide range of goods.* فسيح؛ متنوع

4 fully open: *The children's eyes were wide with excitement.* مفتوح على سعته

5 not near what you wanted to touch or hit: *His first serve was wide* (e.g. in tennis). طائش أو بعيد (عن الهدف)

▶ **wide** *adv* as far or as much as possible; completely: *Open your mouth wide.* ○ *wide awake* ○ *a wide-open door* كاملاً؛ (مفتوح) إلى آخره

widely *adv* **1** to a large degree; a lot: *Their opinions differ widely.* بصورة واسعة؛ كثيراً

2 over a large area or range: *Steve travelled widely in his youth.* على نطاق واسع

widen /ˈwaɪdn/ *verb* [I,T] to become wider; to make sth wider يتّسع؛ يوسّع

ˌ**wide-ˈranging** *adj* covering a large area or many subjects: *a wide-ranging discussion* متنوّع، متعدد (المواضيع)

widespread /ˈwaɪdspred/ *adj* found or happening over a large area; affecting a large number of people: *The storm has caused widespread damage.* شائع، متّسع؛ منتشر

widow /ˈwɪdəʊ/ *noun* [C] a woman whose husband has died and who has not married again أرملة

widowed /ˈwɪdəʊd/ *adj* being a widow or widower: *She's been widowed for ten years now.* يترَمّل

widower /ˈwɪdəʊə(r)/ *noun* [C] a man whose wife has died and who has not married again أرمل

⚷**width** /wɪdθ/ *noun* **1** [C,U] the amount that sth measures from one side or edge to the other: *The room is eight metres in width.* ○ *The carpet is available in two different widths.* عَرْض

2 [C] the distance from one side of a swimming pool to the other عرض المسبح

wield /wiːld/ *verb* [T] to hold and use a weapon: *Some of the men were wielding knives.* يمسك بِ، يستخدم؛ يشهَر

wiener /ˈwiːnə(r)/ *noun* [C] (*US*) = FRANKFURTER

⚷**wife** /waɪf/ *noun* [C] (*pl.* **wives** /waɪvz/) the woman to whom a man is married زوجة، قرينة

wig /wɪg/ *noun* [C] a covering made of real or false hair that you wear on your head, because you are bald or because you want to cover up your own hair شعر مستعار، باروكة

wiggle /ˈwɪgl/ *verb* [I,T] (*informal*) to move from side to side with small quick movements; to make sth do this: *You have to wiggle your hips in time to the music.* يهتز؛ يهز، يأرجح

▶ **wiggle** *noun* [C] (*informal*) *to walk with a wiggle* اهتزاز، أرجحة

wigwam /ˈwɪgwæm; *US* -wɑːm/ *noun* [C] a type of tent that was used by Native Americans in the past خيمة الهنود الحمر

wiki /ˈwɪki/ *noun* [C] a website that allows any user to change or add to the information it contains "ويكي": موقع يسمح للمستخدِم بتعديل أو تغيير محتوياته

⚷**wild** /waɪld/ *adj* **1** living or growing in natural conditions, not looked after by people: *wild animals* بَرّي، وحشي

2 (used about an area of land) not lived on, farmed, etc: *the wild mountain scenery of Wales* قفْر

3 (used about the weather) stormy, with strong winds: *It was a wild night last night.* عاصف

4 (used about a person or his/her behaviour or emotions) not controlled; rather mad: *The crowd went wild with excitement.* ○ *He had a wild look in his eyes.* هائج؛ زائغ

5 wild (about sb/sth) (*informal*) liking sb/sth very much: *I'm not wild about their new house.* متحمس، شديد الاعجاب بِ

6 not carefully done, planned or thought about: *She made rather a wild guess.* طائش، متسرّع

▶ **wild** *noun* **1 the wild** [sing.] natural areas (= not on farms, in zoos, etc.): *the thrill of seeing elephants in the wild* البرّية

2 the wilds [plural] places that are far away from towns: *They live somewhere out in the wilds.* القفار

wildly *adv* in a wild way: *to rush about wildly* باهتياج

wildness *noun* [U] طيش؛ توحش

wilderness /ˈwɪldənəs/ *noun* [C, usually sing.] **1** an area of land with very few signs of human life: *The Antarctic is the last great wilderness.* برّية، قَفْر

2 a place where plants are growing in an uncontrolled way فلاة: أرض مكسوّة بالأعشاب البريّة

wildlife /ˈwaɪldlaɪf/ *noun* [U] wild birds, plants, animals, etc. الحيوانات والنباتات البرّية

wilful (*US also* **willful**) /ˈwɪlfl/ *adj* **1** done on purpose, e.g. to hurt or damage sb/sth: *wilful damage* متعمّد
2 doing exactly what you want, no matter what other people think or say عنيد
▸ **wilfully** /-fəli/ *adv* عمْداً

will[1] /wɪl/ *modal verb* (*short form* **'ll**; *negative* **will not**; *short form* **won't** /wəʊnt/) **1** (used in forming the future tenses): *He will be here soon.* ○ *I'm sure you'll pass your exam.* ○ *I'll be sitting on the beach this time next week.* ○ *Next Sunday, she will have been in England for a year.* سوف
2 (used for showing that sb is willing to do sth, or that sth is able to do sth): *'We need some more milk.' 'OK, I'll get it.'* ○ *Why won't you tell me where you were last night?* ○ *I'll carry your case for you.* ○ *My car won't start.* (للدلالة على الاستعداد أو القدرة)
3 (used for asking sb to do sth): *Will you sit down, please?* هل لك أن...
4 (used for offering sth to sb): *Will you have a cup of tea?* أتريد...
5 (used for talking about sth annoying that sb always or very often does): *He will keep interrupting me when I'm trying to work.* (في التعبير عن أمر مزعج متكرر)

You must put extra stress on 'will' and the short form cannot be used when you want to show that you are annoyed: *He* will *keep interrupting me when I'm trying to work.*

6 (used for saying that you think sth is probably true): *That will be the postman at the door.* (في التعبير عن احتمال صحّة شيء)

will[2] /wɪl/ *verb* [T] to use the power of your mind to do sth or to make sth happen: *He willed himself to carry on to the end of the race.* يحمله على، يجْبِر (نفسه)

will[3] /wɪl/ *noun* **1** [C,U] the power of the mind to choose what actions to take: *Both her children have got very strong wills.* ○ *My father seems to have lost the will to live.* إرادة
2 [sing.] what sb wants or desires: *My mother doesn't want to sell the house and I don't want to go against her will.* رغبة
3 [C] a legal document in which you write down who should have your money and property after your death: *Have you made a will?* ○ *Gran left us some money in her will.* وصيّة
IDM **of your own free will** → FREE[1]
▸ **-willed** (in compounds) having a will (1) of a particular type: *strong-willed* ذو إرادة (قوية مثلاً)

willing /ˈwɪlɪŋ/ *adj* **1** (not before a noun) prepared to do sth; having no objection to doing sth: *Are you willing to help us?* ○ *I'm not willing to take any risks.* مستعدّ؛ راغب
2 ready or eager: *a willing helper* على أُهْبة الاستعداد؛ راغب
▸ **willingly** *adv* طَوعاً، عَنْ رِضا
willingness *noun* [U, sing.] استعداد، قبول

willow /ˈwɪləʊ/ (*also* **'willow tree**) *noun* [C] a tree with thin branches and long thin leaves that grows near water شجرة الصَّفصاف

'will power *noun* [U] strength of mind; the ability to keep trying to succeed, even when sth is difficult: *It takes a lot of will power to give up smoking.* قوة إرادة، عزم

wilt /wɪlt/ *verb* [I] (used about a plant or flower) to bend and start to die, because of heat or lack of water يَذْبُل

wily /ˈwaɪli/ *adj* (**wilier**; **wiliest**) clever at getting what you want داه، ماكر

wimp /wɪmp/ *noun* [C] (*informal*) a weak person شخص ضعيف
▸ **wimpish** *adj* ضعيف، قليل الثقة بالنفس

win /wɪn/ *verb* (*pres part* **winning**; *pt, pp* **won** /wʌn/) **1** [I,T] to be the best, first or strongest in a race, a game, a competition, a battle, an election, etc: *to win a game, match, race, etc.* ○ *Murphy won and Lewis was second.* ○ *I never win at table tennis.* ○ *Which party do you think will win the next election?* يفوز، يَنْتَصِر
2 [T] to get sth as a result of success in a competition, race, etc: *How much did you win?* ○ *Who won the gold medal?* ○ *Labour won the seat from the Conservatives* (= in an election). يربح، ينال

Note that we **earn** (not **win**) money at our job: *I earn £15 000 a year.*

3 [T] to get sth by hard work, great effort, etc: *Her brilliant performance won her a great deal of praise.* ○ *to win support for a plan* يحوز؛ يكسب
IDM **win/lose the toss** → TOSS
you can't win (*informal*) there is no way of being completely successful or of pleasing everybody: *Whatever you do you will upset somebody. You can't win.* لَنْ ترضي الجميع
PHR V **win sb over/round (to sth)** to persuade sb to support or agree with you يستميل
▸ **win** *noun* [C] an act of winning a competition, game, race, etc: *We have had two wins and a draw so far this season.* انتصار، فوز
winner *noun* [C] a person or animal that wins a competition, game, race, etc: *And the winner is...* المنتصر، الفائز
winning *adj*: *The winning ticket is number 65.* فائز

wince /wɪns/ *verb* [I] to make a sudden quick movement (usually twisting the muscles of the face) because of a sharp pain or sth unpleasant يَنْكَمِش وجهه (ألماً)

winch /wɪntʃ/ *noun* [C] a machine that lifts or pulls heavy objects by using a thick chain, etc. that winds round and round a drum وِنْش، رافعة
▸ **winch** *verb* [T] to lift or pull sb/sth using a winch: *The injured climber was winched up into a helicopter.* يرفع برافعة

wind[1] /wɪnd/ *noun* **1** [C,U] (*also* **the wind**) air that is moving across the surface of the earth: *There was a strong wind blowing.* ○ *A gust of* *wind blew his hat off.* ○ *high winds* ○ *a cold north wind* ريح

2 [U] the breath that you need for doing exercise or playing a musical instrument: *She stopped running to get her wind back.* نَفَس

3 [U] air that you swallow when you are eating or drinking; gas that is formed in your stomach غازات أو ريح (المعدة)

IDM get wind of sth to hear about sth that is secret يكتشف، يبلغه (الأمر)، يستشمّ

▸ **windy** *adj* (**windier**; **windiest**) with a lot of wind: *a windy day* عاصف

wind[2] /wɪnd/ *verb* [T] to cause sb to have difficulty in breathing: *The punch in the stomach winded her.* يقطع النَفَس

wind[3] /waɪnd/ *verb* (*pt, pp* **wound** /waʊnd/) **1** [T] to wrap sth long round sth else several times: *Wind the string round your finger or the balloon will fly away.* يلفّ

2 [T] to make sth work or move by turning a key, handle, etc: *He wound the car window down and shouted at the other driver.* ○ *Wind the tape on a bit to the next song.* يدير، يبرم

3 [I] (used about a road, path, etc.) to have a lot of bends or curves in it: *The path winds down the cliff to the sea.* يتعرّج، يتلوّى

PHRV wind down (about a person) to rest and relax after a period of hard work, worry, etc. ➲ Look at **unwind**. يستريح، يسترخي

wind up to be in a place at the end of a journey or in a particular situation after other things have happened: *We wound up in quite a nice hotel near Calais.* ○ *You'll wind up failing your exams if you go on like this.* ينتهي (إلى مكان)، يكون مآله (شيء)

wind sth up to finish, stop or close sth: *The company was losing money and was soon wound up.* يحلّ، ينهي

▸ **winding** *adj* with bends or curves in it: *a winding road through the hills* متعرّج

windfall /ˈwɪndfɔːl/ *noun* [C] an unexpected gift or piece of good luck هِبة أو حظّ غير مرتقب

wind farm /ˈwɪnd fɑːm/ *noun* [C] an area of land on which there are lots of windmills or wind turbines for producing electricity منطقة طواحين هوائية

wind instrument /ˈwɪnd ɪnstrəmənt/ *noun* [C] a musical instrument that you play by blowing through it آلة نفخ

windmill /ˈwɪndmɪl/ *noun* [C] a tall building with long arms (sails) that stick out from it and turn in the wind. Windmills are used for grinding corn, producing electricity, etc. طاحونة هوائية

window /ˈwɪndəʊ/ *noun* [C] **1** the opening in a building, car, etc. that you can see through and that lets light in. A window usually has glass in it: *Open the window. It's hot in here.* ○ *I always keep the downstairs windows closed at night.* ○ *a shop window* ○ *I always try and get a window seat* (= next to a window on a plane). نافذة، شُبّاك

2 the glass in a window: *to break a window* ○ *These windows need cleaning.* زجاج النافذة

3 an area on a computer screen that has a particular type of information in it نافذة (على شاشة الكمبيوتر)

windowpane /ˈwɪndəʊpeɪn/ *noun* [C] one piece of glass in a window لوح زجاج (في نافذة)

ˈ**window-shopping** *noun* [U] looking at things in shop windows without intending to buy anything النظر إلى البضائع المعروضة في الواجهات

windowsill /ˈwɪndəʊsɪl/ (*also* ˈ**window ledge**) *noun* [C] the shelf at the bottom of a window in a building, either inside or outside عتبة النافذة

windpipe /ˈwɪndpaɪp/ *noun* [C] the tube that takes air from the throat to the lungs قصبة هوائية، قصبة الرئة

windscreen /ˈwɪndskriːn/ (*US* ˈ**windshield**) *noun* [C] the window in the front of a car, etc. زجاج أمامي (في السيّارة)

ˈ**windscreen wiper** (*also* **wiper**; *US* ˈ**windshield wiper**) *noun* [C] one of the two moving arms (blades) that remove water, snow, etc. from the windscreen مَسّاحة الزجاج (في السيّارة)

windsurf /ˈwɪndsɜːf/ *verb* [I] to move through water standing on a special board with a sail ℹ We usually say **go windsurfing**: *Have you ever been windsurfing?* يركب الموج (على لوح بِشراع)

▸ ˈ**windsurfer** (*also* **sailboard**) *noun* [C] **1** a board with a sail that you stand on as it moves over the surface of the water, driven by the wind لوح بشِراع

2 a person who rides on a board like this راكب الأمواج

ˈ**windsurfing** *noun* [U] the sport of riding on a windsurfer رياضة ركوب الأمواج

windswept /ˈwɪndswept/ *adj* **1** (used about a place) that often has strong winds: *a windswept coastline* (بقعة) في مهبّ الريح

2 looking untidy because you have been in a strong wind: *windswept hair* متطاير بفعل الريح

wind turbine /ˈwɪnd tɜːbaɪn/ *noun* [C] a type of modern windmill used for producing electricity عَنَفة الرياح، "توربين" الرياح

windy → WIND[1]

wine /waɪn/ *noun* [C,U] an alcoholic drink that is made from grapes (or sometimes other fruit) نبيذ، خمر

ˈ**wine bar** *noun* [C] a place where you can go to drink wine and have sth to eat حانة نبيذ

wing /wɪŋ/ *noun* **1** [C] one of the two parts that a bird, an insect, etc. uses for flying جَناح

2 [C] one of the two long parts that stick out from the side of an aeroplane and support it in the air جَناح (الطائرة)

3 [C] a part of a building that sticks out from the main part or that was added on to the main part: *the maternity wing of the hospital* جَناح (في مستشفى مثلاً)

4 [C] (*US* **fender**) the part of the outside of a car, etc. that covers the top of the wheels رَفرف العجلة

5 [C, usually sing.] a group of people in a political

party that have particular beliefs or opinions: *the right wing of the Conservative Party* ➲ Look at **left wing** and **right wing**. جَناح (في حزب سياسي)

6 [C] (in football, etc.) the part at each side of the area where the game is played: *to play on the wing* جَناح (في ملعب رياضي)

7 [C] (*also* **winger**) (in football, etc.) a person who plays in an attacking position at one of the sides of the field لاعب جناح

8 the wings [plural] (in a theatre) the area at the sides of the stage which cannot be seen by the audience أجْنحة (المسرح)، كواليس

wink /wɪŋk/ *verb* [I] **wink (at sb)** to close and open one eye very quickly, usually as a private signal to sb ➲ Look at **blink**. يَغمِز

▸ **wink** *noun* [C]: *to give sb a wink* ○ *I didn't sleep a wink* (= not at all). غمزة؛ غَمْضَة (عين)

winner, winning → WIN

⚷winter /ˈwɪntə(r)/ *noun* [C,U] the coldest season of the year between autumn and spring: *It snows a lot here in winter.* ○ *a cold winter's day* ○ *We went skiing in France last winter.* ○ *the Winter Olympics* (فصل) الشّتاء

▸ **wintry** /ˈwɪntri/ *adj*: *wintry weather* ○ *a wintry wind* شَتَوي

ˌwinter ˈsports *noun* [plural] sports which take place on snow or ice, e.g. skiing and skating الرياضيات الشتوية

wintertime /ˈwɪntətaɪm/ *noun* [U] the period or season of winter فترة أو فصل الشّتاء

wipe /waɪp/ *verb* [T] **1** to clean or dry sth by rubbing it with a cloth, piece of paper, etc: *Wipe your hands on the towel.* ○ *to wipe your nose on a handkerchief* ○ *Could you wipe the table, please?* ➲ Look at the note at **clean**[2]. يَمْسَح، ينظّف

2 wipe sth from/off sth; wipe sth away/off/up to remove sth by wiping (1): *Wipe the dirt off your shoes.* ○ *He wiped the sweat from his forehead.* ○ *Wipe up the milk you spilled, please.* يَمْسَح، يزيل

PHR V wipe sth out to destroy sth completely: *Whole villages were wiped out in the bombing raids.* يبيد، يمحو

▸ **wipe** *noun* [C] the act of wiping: *He gave the table a quick wipe.* مَسْح، مَسْحَة

wiper *noun* [C] = WINDSCREEN WIPER

⚷wire /ˈwaɪə(r)/ *noun* [C,U] **1** a long thin piece of metal like strong string that is used for fastening things or in fences, cages, etc: *a piece of wire* ○ *barbed wire* ○ *a wire fence* سلك معدني

2 a piece of wire that is used to carry electricity سِلْك كهربائي

▸ **wire** *verb* [T] **1** to fasten or join two things together using wire يَربط بالاسلاك

2 wire sth (up) to connect sth to a supply of electricity by using wires يوصِل بالكهرباء

wiring /ˈwaɪərɪŋ/ *noun* [U] the system of wires that supplies electricity to rooms in a building نظام التوصيل الكهربائي

wireless /ˈwaɪələs/ *noun* [C,U] (*old-fashioned*) communication by radio; a piece of equipment for communicating by radio لاسلكي؛ راديو

▸ **wireless** *adj* not using wires: *wireless communications* دون أسلاك

wiry /ˈwaɪəri/ *adj* (**wirier**; **wiriest**) (used about a person) small and thin but strong نحيف مفتول الجسم

wisdom /ˈwɪzdəm/ *noun* [U] the quality of being wise; the ability to make sensible decisions and judgements because of your knowledge or experience: *a woman of great wisdom* ○ *I doubt the wisdom of taking a decision too early* (= I do not think that it is a good idea). حِكْمة

ˈwisdom tooth *noun* [C] (*pl.* **wisdom teeth**) one of the four teeth at the back of your mouth that appear when you are about 20 years old ضِرْس الحِلْم (العقل)

⚷wise /waɪz/ *adj* having or showing the knowledge or experience to make good or sensible decisions or judgements: *a wise choice* ○ *It would be wiser to wait for a few days.* ○ *a wise old man* صائب، حكيم

▸ **wisely** *adv* بِحكْمة، بتبصر

⚷wish /wɪʃ/ *verb* **1** [T] **wish (that)** (often with a verb in the past tense) to want sth that cannot now happen or that probably will not happen: *I wish (that) I had listened more carefully.* ○ *I wish (that) I knew what was going to happen.* ○ *My father wishes (that) he had gone to university.* ○ *I wish I could help you.* يتمنّى

> Note that in formal English we use **were** instead of **was** with 'I' or 'he/she': *I wish I were rich.* ○ *She wishes she were in a different class.*

2 [I] **wish for sth** to say to yourself that you want sth that can only happen by good luck or magic: *She closed her eyes and wished for her mother to get better.* يتمنّى

3 [T] **wish (to do sth)** (*formal*) to want to do sth: *I wish to make a complaint about one of the doctors.* يَرْغَب، يودّ

4 [T] to say that you hope sb will have sth; to say sth as a greeting: *I rang him up to wish him a happy birthday.* ○ *We wish you all the best for your future career.* يتمنّى؛ يرجو

▸ **wish** *noun* **1** [C] a feeling that you want sth: *a wish for peace* ○ *I have no wish to see her ever again.* ○ *Doctors should respect the patient's wishes.* أُمنية، رَغْبة

2 [C] when you make a wish, you say to yourself secretly that you want to have sth or that you want sth to happen, and you hope that it will: *The prince was granted three wishes by the fairy.* ○ *My wish came true* (= I got what I asked for). أُمْنِية

3 wishes [plural] a hope that sb will be happy or have good luck: *Please give your parents my best wishes.* ○ *Best Wishes* (= at the end of a letter) أُمنيات، تمنيات

ˌwishful ˈthinking *noun* [U] ideas that are based on what you would like, not on facts تفكير ناتج عن الرغبة في حدوث شيء

wisp /wɪsp/ *noun* [C] **1** a small thin bunch of hair, grass, etc. خصلة أو حزمة صغيرة

2 a small amount of smoke خيط رفيع من الدخان

wistful /ˈwɪstfl/ *adj* feeling or showing sadness because you cannot have what you want: *a wistful sigh* كئيب (لعدم نيل ما يريد)

▸ **wistfully** /-fəli/ *adv* بحزن (المتمنّي)، بكآبة (التوّاق لشيء)

wit /wɪt/ *noun* [U] **1** the ability to use words in a clever and amusing way فطنة، سرعة البديهة

2 (*also* **wits** [plural]) cleverness; intelligence: *The game of chess is essentially a battle of wits.* براعة، ذكاء

IDM at your wits' end not knowing what to do or say because you are so worried يحتار في أمره

keep your wits about you to be ready to act in a difficult situation يحسن التصرف في المأزق

▸ **-witted** (in compounds) having a particular type of intelligence: *quick-witted* ذو ذكاء معيّن

witty *adj* (**wittier**; **wittiest**) clever and amusing; using words in a clever way: *a very witty speech* فكِه، ذكيّ الأسلوب

witch /wɪtʃ/ *noun* [C] (in former times and in stories) a woman who is thought to have magic powers that she uses to do bad things. Pictures of witches in stories show them wearing a black cloak and a tall pointed hat. ➲ Look at **wizard**. ساحرة

witchcraft /ˈwɪtʃkrɑːft; *US* -kræft/ *noun* [U] the use of magic powers to do bad things سِحْر

with /wɪð; wɪθ/ *prep* **1** in the company or presence of sb/sth: *I live with my parents.* ○ *Are you coming with us?* ○ *I talked about the problem with my tutor.* ○ *Does this tie go with this shirt?* ○ *Could you put this book with the others?* مع

2 in the care of sb: *We left the keys with the neighbours.* مع

3 having or carrying sth: *a girl with red hair* ○ *a house with a garden* ○ *the man with a suitcase* ذو، له، يحمل

4 using sth: *Cut it with a knife.* ○ *I did it with his help.* بِ

5 (used for expressing what fills, covers, etc. sth): *Fill the bowl with water.* بِ

6 against sb/sth: *He's always arguing with his brother.* ○ *I usually play tennis with my sister.* ضِد

7 agreeing with or supporting sb: *We've got everybody with us on this issue.* مع

8 because of or as a result of sth: *We were shivering with cold.* بسبب

9 (used for expressing how sth happens or is done): *Open this parcel with care.* ○ *to greet sb with a smile* بِ

10 towards, concerning or compared with sb/sth: *Is he angry with us?* ○ *There's a problem with my visa.* ○ *Compared with Canada, England has mild winters.* من، متعلّق بِ، (بالمقارنة) مع

11 including sth: *With wine, the meal cost £25.* مع، بما فيه

12 at the same time as sth: *I can't concentrate with you watching me all the time.* بينما

13 because of sth: *With all the problems we've got, we're not going to finish on time.* بسبب

IDM be with sb to be able to follow what sb is saying: *I'm sorry, I'm not quite with you. Say it again.* يتابع كلامه

withdraw /wɪðˈdrɔː/ *verb* (*pt* **withdrew** /-ˈdruː/; *pp* **withdrawn** /-ˈdrɔːn/) **1** [I,T] **withdraw (sb/sth) (from sth)** (to cause sb/sth) to move back or away: *The troops withdrew from the town.* يَنسَحِب

2 [T] to remove sth or take sth away: *The suspect yogurt has been withdrawn from the shops.* ○ *to withdraw an offer, a statement, etc.* يَسْحَب

3 [T] to take money out of a bank account: *I'd like to withdraw a thousand pounds, please.* ➲ Look at **deposit**. يَسحَب

4 [I] to decide not to take part in sth: *Jackson withdrew from the race at the last minute.* يَنْسَحِب

▸ **withdrawal** /-ˈdrɔːəl/ *noun* **1** [C,U] moving sth back or away: *the withdrawal of troops from the war zone* إنسِحاب

2 [C] the amount of money that you take out of your bank account المبلغ المسحوب

3 [U] the act of stopping doing sth, especially taking a drug: *He was suffering severe withdrawal symptoms.* انقطاع عن مخدّر، وَحْمة إدمان

withdrawn *adj* (used about a person) very quiet and not wanting to talk to other people خجول، منطوٍ على نفسه

wither /ˈwɪðə(r)/ *verb* [I,T] **wither (away) 1** (used about plants) to become dry and die; to make a plant do this: *The plants withered in the hot sun.* يَذْبُل؛ يُذْبِل

2 to become weaker, until it disappears: *This type of industry will wither away in the years to come.* يَضمَحِل

▸ **withering** /ˈwɪðərɪŋ/ *adj* done to make sb feel silly or ashamed: *a withering look* مُخجِل، مُحرِج

withhold /wɪðˈhəʊld/ *verb* [T] (*pt*, *pp* **withheld** /-ˈheld/) (*formal*) **withhold sth (from sb/sth)** to refuse to give sth to sb: *to withhold information from the police* يُمْسِك عنه، يَحْجُب

within /wɪˈðɪn/ *prep* **1** in a period not longer than a particular length of time: *I'll be back within an hour.* خلال

2 within sth (of sth) not further than a particular distance from sth: *The house is within three minutes' walk of the station.* في حدود

3 not outside the limits or range of sb/sth: *Each department must keep within its budget.* ضِمْن

4 (*formal*) inside sb/sth: *The anger was still there deep within him.* (في) داخل

▸ **within** *adv* inside: *Cleaner required. Apply within.* في الداخل

without /wɪˈðaʊt/ *prep* **1** not having, showing or being with sb/sth: *Don't go out without a coat on.* ○ *Pam drinks her coffee without milk.* ○ *After three days without sleep he was exhausted.* ○ *He spoke without much enthusiasm.* ○ *Can you see* *without your glasses?* ○ *Don't leave without me.* مِنْ غير، بلا

2 (used with a verb in the *-ing* form to mean 'not'): *She left without saying goodbye.* دون، مِن غير

withstand /wɪð'stænd/ *verb* [T] (*pt, pp* **withstood** /-'stʊd/) (*formal*) to be strong enough not to break, give up, be damaged, etc: *The troops were too weak to withstand another attack.* يحتمل، يَصْمُد

witness /'wɪtnəs/ *noun* [C] **1** (*also* **eyewitness**) a person who sees sth happen and who can tell other people about it later: *There were two witnesses to the accident.* شاهد عيان

2 a person who appears in a court of law to say what he/she has seen or what he/she knows about sb/sth: *Each witness was cross-examined.* ○ *a witness for the defence/prosecution* شاهد

3 a person who sees sb sign an official document and who then signs it himself/herself شاهد

IDM **bear witness (to sth)** → BEAR[2]

▸ **witness** *verb* [T] **1** to see sth happen and to be able to tell other people about it later: *to witness a murder* يشْهَد، يرى

2 to see sb sign an official document and then sign it yourself: *to witness a will* يشْهَد على

'witness box (*US* **'witness stand**) *noun* [C] the place in a court of law where a witness stands when he/she is giving evidence منصّة الشاهد

witty → WIT

wives *pl.* of WIFE

wizard /'wɪzəd/ *noun* [C] (in stories) a man who is believed to have magic powers ➲ Look at **witch**. ساحِر

wk *abbrev* (*pl.* **wks**) = WEEK

wobble /'wɒbl/ *verb* [I,T] to move from side to side in an unsteady way; to make sb/sth do this: *Put something under the leg of the table. It's wobbling.* ○ *Stop wobbling the desk. I can't write.* يهتزّ؛ يَهزّ

▸ **wobbly** /'wɒbli/ *adj* (*informal*) *a wobbly table* مترَجْرِج، غير مستقرّ

wok /wɒk/ *noun* [C] a large pan that is shaped like a bowl and used for cooking Chinese food مِقلاة صينية كبيرة

woke *pt* of WAKE[1]

woken *pp* of WAKE[1]

wolf /wʊlf/ *noun* [C] (*pl.* **wolves** /wʊlvz/) a wild animal that looks like a dog and that lives and hunts in a group (a pack) ذِئب

woman /'wʊmən/ *noun* [C] (*pl.* **women** /'wɪmɪn/) an adult female person: *men, women and children* ○ *a single/married/divorced woman* ○ *Would you prefer to see a woman doctor?* امرأة

▸ **-woman** (in compounds) a woman who does a particular activity: *a businesswoman* امرأة (تمارس نشاطاً معيناً)

womanhood /-hʊd/ *noun* [U] the state of being a woman أنوثة

womanly *adj* of or like a woman نِسْوي، أنْثوي

womb /wu:m/ *noun* [C] the part of a woman or female animal where a baby grows before it is born الرَحِم

won *pt, pp* of WIN

wonder /'wʌndə(r)/ *verb* **1** [I,T] to want to know sth; to ask yourself questions about sth: *I wonder what the new teacher will be like.* ○ *He hadn't heard from Julia for a week and he began to wonder if she was all right.* ○ *I wonder who that woman over there is.* ○ *It was something that she had been wondering about for a long time.* ○ *Sometimes I wonder how they manage to live on the amount he earns.* يتساءل، يَعْجَب

2 [T] (used when you are asking sb politely to do sth): *I wonder if you could help me.* (ترى) هل يمكنك أن...

3 [I,T] **wonder (at sth)** to feel great surprise or admiration: *We wondered at the speed with which he worked.* ○ *'She was very angry.' 'I don't wonder* (= I'm not surprised). *She had a right to be.'* يَستَغْرِب

▸ **wonder** *noun* **1** [U] a feeling of surprise and admiration: *The children stared in wonder at the acrobats.* استغراب، تعجّب

2 [C] something that causes you to feel surprise or admiration: *the wonders of modern technology* أعجوبة

IDM **it's a wonder (that)...** it's surprising that...: *It's a wonder we managed to get here on time, with all the traffic.* إنه لأمر عجيب أن...

no wonder it is not surprising: *You've been out every evening this week. No wonder you're tired.* لا عجبَ

wonderful /-fl/ *adj* very good; giving great pleasure: *What wonderful weather!* ○ *It's a wonderful opportunity.* ○ *It's wonderful to see you again.* رائع؛ سارّ

wonderfully /-fəli/ *adv* بصورة رائعة

won't *short for* WILL NOT

wood /wʊd/ *noun* **1** [U] the hard material that the trunk and branches of trees are made of: *He chopped some wood for the fire.* ○ *The furniture is made of wood.* الخشب

2 [C] a type of wood: *Pine is a soft wood.* خَشَب

3 [C] (often plural) an area of land that is covered with trees. A wood is smaller than a forest: *a walk in the woods* حَرَجة، غابة

IDM **touch wood** → TOUCH[1]

▸ **wooded** *adj* (used about an area of land) having a lot of trees growing on it: *a heavily wooded valley* مشجَر، محرَج

wooden /'wʊdn/ *adj* made of wood: *wooden toys* خَشَبي

woodland /'wʊdlənd/ *noun* [U] land that has a lot of trees growing on it: *woodland birds* أرض حَرَجية، غابة

woodpecker /'wʊdpekə(r)/ *noun* [C] a bird that climbs trees and taps them rapidly with its beak to find insects نقّار الخشب

woodwind /'wʊdwɪnd/ *noun* [sing., with sing. or

pl. verb] the set of musical instruments that are made of wood and that you play by blowing into them آلات نفخ خشبية

woodwork /ˈwʊdwɜːk/ *noun* [U] **1** the parts of a building that are made of wood (= the doors, stairs, etc.) المنجور

2 the activity or skill of making things out of wood فن المصنوعات الخشبية

woof /wʊf/ *noun* [C] (*informal*) (used for describing the sound (a bark) that a dog makes) نُباح

wool /wʊl/ *noun* [U] **1** the soft thick hair of sheep, goats, etc. صوف، وبَر

2 thick thread or cloth that is made from wool: *The sweater is 50% wool and 50% acrylic.* ○ *knitting wool* ➲ Look at **cotton wool**. صوف

▶ **woollen** (*US* **woolen**) /ˈwʊlən/ *adj* made of wool: *a warm woollen jumper* صوفي

woolly (*US also* **wooly**) /ˈwʊli/ *adj* (**woollier**; **woolliest**) of or like wool: *The dog had a thick woolly coat.* ○ *long woolly socks* صوفي

word /wɜːd/ *noun* **1** [C] a sound or letter or group of sounds or letters that expresses a particular meaning: *What's the Greek word for 'computer'?* ○ *Several words are spelt wrong.* ○ *There are five letters in the word 'apple'.* كلمة

2 [C] a short statement or conversation: *Could I have a word with you in private?* ○ *a few words of thanks* ○ *Don't say a word about this to anyone.* حديث قصير، كلمة

3 [sing.] a promise: *I give you my word that I won't let you down.* وَعْد، عَهْد

IDM **a dirty word** → DIRTY[1]

get a word in edgeways to interrupt when sb else is talking so that you can say sth yourself يقاطع ليقول شيئاً

have, etc. the last word → LAST[1]

in other words → OTHER

put in a (good) word for sb to say sth good about sb to sb else: *If you could put in a good word for me I might stand a better chance of getting the job.* يَمْدَح، يزكّي

take sb's word for it to believe what sb says without any proof يصدّق (ما يقوله شخص آخر) على علاته

word for word 1 repeating sth exactly: *Sharon repeated word for word what he had told her.* (يكرّر) حَرْفيّاً

2 (in a translation) dealing with each word separately, not looking at the general meaning: *a word-for-word translation* حرفي

▶ **word** *verb* [T] (often passive) to choose carefully the words that you use to express sth: *The statement was carefully worded so that nobody would be offended by it.* يصوغ

wording *noun* [sing.] the words that you use to express sth: *The wording of the contract was vague.* صياغة

ˌword-ˈperfect *adj* able to say sth that you have learnt from memory, without making a mistake قادر على الإعادة من الذاكرة دون خطأ

ˈword processing *noun* [U] (*abbr* **WP**) using a word processor معالجة الكلمات

ˈword processor *noun* [C] (*abbr* **WP**) a type of small computer that you can use for writing letters, reports, etc. You can correct or change what you have written before you print it out. معالج الكلمات، كمبيوتر صغير

wore *pt* of WEAR[1]

work[1] /wɜːk/ *noun* **1** [U] something that requires physical or mental effort. You usually do work because you feel you have to, not for pleasure: *Her success is due to sheer hard work.* ○ *Ron never does a stroke of work.* ○ *Much of the heavy work on farms is now done by machines.* ○ *There is still a lot of work to be done.* عَمَل، شُغْل

2 [U] what you do to earn money; the place where you go to earn money: *It is very difficult to find work in this city.* ○ *out of work* (= without a job) ○ *When do you start work?* ○ *I go to work at 8 o'clock.* ○ *The people at work gave me some flowers for my birthday.* عَمَل؛ مكان العمل

> **Work** is an uncountable noun. In some contexts we must use **job**: *I've found work at the hospital.* ○ *I've got a new job at the hospital.*
> **Employment** is the state of having a paid job and is more formal and official than **work** or **job**. It is an uncountable noun: *Many married women are in part-time employment.*
> **Occupation** is the word used on forms to ask what you are or what job you do: *Occupation: student. Occupation: bus driver.* A **profession** is a job that requires special training and higher education: *the medical profession.* A **trade** is a job that you do with your hands and that requires special skill: *He's a carpenter by trade.*

3 [U] something that you are working on or have produced: *a piece of written work* ○ *The teacher marked their work.* ○ *Is this all your own work?* ○ *an exhibition of the work of two young photographers* عَمَل، إنْتاج

4 [C] a book, painting, piece of music, etc: *an early work by Picasso* ○ *the complete works of Shakespeare* عَمَل (فنّي أو أدبي)، مؤلَّف

5 works [plural] the act of building or repairing sth: *Danger! Roadworks ahead.* ورشة شغل، أشغال عامّة

6 works [C, with sing. or pl. verb] a factory: *The steelworks is/are closing down.* مصنع

IDM **get/go/set to work (on sth)** to begin; to make a start (on sth) يَشْرَع؛ يباشِر

work[2] /wɜːk/ *verb* **1** [I,T] to do sth which needs physical or mental effort; to do a job, especially in order to earn money: *My teacher said that I wouldn't pass the exam unless I worked harder.* ○ *I've been working in the garden all day.* ○ *They are working to improve health care in rural areas.* ○ *She's working for a large firm in Glasgow.* ○ *I'd like to work as a newspaper reporter.* ○ *He worked till he was 65, then he retired.* ○ *Doctors often work extremely long hours.* يَعْمَل، يَشْتَغِل

2 [I] (used about a machine, etc.) to do what it is meant to do, correctly; to function: *Our telephone hasn't been working for several days.* ○ *Can you show me how the photocopier works?* يَعْمَل، يَشْتَغِل

3 [I] to have the result or effect that you want; to

be successful: *Your idea sounds good but I don't think it will really work.* يؤدّي (للنتيجة): يتحقّق بنجاح

4 [T] to make yourself/sb/sth work; to use or operate: *He works all his employees very hard.* ○ *Do you know how to work the fax machine?* يدفع للعمل؛ يشغّل

5 [I,T] to produce a particular effect; to help sth to happen: *His reputation as a hard worker had obviously worked in his favour.* يحدِث (أثراً)، يساعد، يفيد

6 [I,T] to move to a new position or state: *Where's the screwdriver? The hinges on the gate have worked loose.* ○ *We worked our way round to the little beach by climbing over the rocks.* ينحَلّ؛ يتحرّك

7 to use materials to make a model, a picture, etc: *He worked the clay into the shape of a horse.* ○ *She usually works in/with oils or acrylics.* يشكّل؛ يعمل بِ

IDM **work to rule** → RULE

PHRV **work out 1** to develop or progress, especially in a good way: *I hope things work out for you.* يسير (سيراً حسناً)

2 to do physical exercises in order to keep your body fit: *We work out to music at my exercise class.* يؤدّي تمرينات (رياضية)

work out (at) to come to a particular result or total after everything has been calculated: *The holiday worked out at around £300 each.* يبلغ

work sb out to understand sb: *I've never been able to work her out.* يفهم

work sth out 1 to find the answer to sth; to solve sth: *I can't work out how to do this.* يجد حلاً؛ يحلّ

2 to calculate sth: *I worked out the total cost.* يحسب

3 to plan sth: *Have you worked out the route through France?* يخطّط

work up to sth to develop or progress to sth: *Start with 15 minutes' exercise and gradually work up to 30.* يزيد، يرفع

work sb/yourself up (into sth) to make sb/yourself become angry, excited, upset, etc: *He had worked himself up into a state of anxiety about his interview.* تساوره (حالة معينة)، يجلب على نفسه

workable /'wɜːkəbl/ *adj* that can be used or that can operate in an efficient way ❶ The opposite is **unworkable.** يمكن تطبيقه، يمكن تشغيله

workaholic /ˌwɜːkə'hɒlɪk/ *noun* [C] a person who loves work and does too much of it مدمن عمل

workbook /'wɜːkbʊk/ (*US* **exercise book**) *noun* [C] a book with questions and exercises in it that you use when you are studying sth كتاب أسئلة وتمارين

🔑**worker** /'wɜːkə(r)/ *noun* [C] **1** (often in compounds) a person who works, especially one who does a particular type of job or belongs to a certain group of people: *factory workers* ○ *an office worker* ○ *immigrant workers* عامل

2 a person who is employed in a business, etc., especially one who does physical work: *manual workers* ○ *Workers' representatives will meet management today to discuss the pay dispute.* عامل، شغّيل

3 a person who works in a particular way: *a slow worker* عامل، شغّيل

workforce /'wɜːkfɔːs/ *noun* [C, with sing. or pl. verb] **1** the total number of people who work in a company, factory, etc. عدد العاملين (في شركة مثلاً)

2 the total number of people in a country who are able to work: *Ten per cent of the workforce is unemployed.* قوة عاملة

🔑**working** /'wɜːkɪŋ/ *adj* (only *before* a noun) **1** employed; having a job: *the problems of child-care for working parents* عامل، موظّف

2 connected with your job: *He stayed with the same company for the whole of his working life.* ○ *The company offers excellent working conditions.* عملي

3 good enough to be used, although it could be improved: *We are looking for someone with a working knowledge of French.* (مستوى معرفة) كاف

IDM **in working order** → ORDER[1]

▸ **workings** *noun* [plural] the way in which a machine, an organization, etc. operates: *It's very difficult to understand the workings of the legal system.* كيفية العمل (أو الأداء)

the ˌworking 'class *noun* [sing.] (*also* **the ˌworking 'classes** [plural]) the group of people in a society who usually do physical work especially in industry, and earn weekly wages: *unemployment among the working class* ○ *a working-class area* ○ *a working-class family* الطبقة العاملة

ˌwork-life 'balance *noun* [sing.] the number of hours per week you spend working, compared with the number of hours you spend with your family, relaxing, etc: *Part-time working is often the best way to improve your work-life balance.* معدّل ساعات العمل إلى ساعات الراحة في أسبوع

workload /'wɜːkləʊd/ *noun* [C] the amount of work that you have to do مقدار العمل

workman /'wɜːkmən/ *noun* [C] (*pl.* **workmen** /-mən/) a man who works with his hands, especially at building or making things عامل يدوي

workmanlike /'wɜːkmənlaɪk/ *adj* of or like a good workman حَسَن الصَّنْعة، متْقَن

workmanship /'wɜːkmənʃɪp/ *noun* [U] the skill that a workman needs or uses to do or make sth well حُسْن الصَّنْعة، بَراعة

ˌwork of 'art *noun* [C] (*pl.* **works of art**) a painting, book, piece of music, etc. of high quality عمل أو أثر فني

workout /'wɜːkaʊt/ *noun* [C] a period of physical exercise, e.g. when you are training for a sport or keeping fit فترة تمرين رياضي

workplace /'wɜːkpleɪs/ *noun* [C] the office, factory, etc. where people work: *the introduction of new technology into the workplace* ○ *These safety standards apply to all workplaces.* مكان العمل

worksheet /'wɜːkʃiːt/ *noun* [C] a piece of paper

with questions or exercises on it that you use when you are studying sth ورقة تمارين

workshop /ˈwɜːkʃɒp/ *noun* [C] **1** (*also* **shop**) a place where things are made or repaired ورْشة، معْمَل

2 a time when a group of people meet and discuss or learn more about a particular subject ورْشة عمل، مُدارسة

workstation /ˈwɜːksteɪʃn/ *noun* [C] (*computing*) the desk and computer that a person works at; one computer that is part of a network مكتب العمل مع كمبيوتر؛ كمبيوتر فرعي

worktop /ˈwɜːktɒp/ (*also* ˈ**work surface**) *noun* [C] a flat surface in a kitchen, etc. that you use for preparing food, etc. on منضدة شغل

world /wɜːld/ *noun* **1** **the world** [sing.] the earth with all its countries and people: *I took a year off work to travel round the world.* ○ *a map of the world* ○ *changes in the world's climate* ○ *the most beautiful place in the world* ○ *English is a world language* (= used all over the world). العالم

2 [sing.] a particular part of the earth: *the western world* ○ *the English-speaking world* ○ *the Arab world* عالَم

3 [sing.] the life and activities of people on earth; their experience: *It is hard to imagine what the world of our grandchildren will be like.* ○ *It's time you learned something about the real world!* ○ *the modern world* عالَم

4 [C] (often in compounds) a particular area of activity or group of people or things: *the world of sport* ○ *the medical world* ○ *the animal world* ○ *the natural world* عالَم، دُنْيا

5 [C] a planet with life on it: *Do you believe there are other worlds out there, like ours?* عالَم

6 [sing.] everybody: *The whole world seemed to know the news before me!* كلّ الناس

IDM **the outside world** people, places, activities, etc. that are beyond the area where you live and your everyday experience العالَم الخارجي

think the world of sb/sth → THINK[1]

a/the world of good (*informal*) a great deal of good; a real benefit: *The holiday has done her the world of good.* فائدة جمّة

▶ **worldly** *adj* **1** connected with ordinary life, not with the spirit: *He left all his worldly possessions to his nephew.* دنيوي

2 having a lot of experience and knowledge of life and people: *a sophisticated and worldly man* ذو خبرة (بالحياة)

ˌ**world-ˈfamous** *adj* known all over the world: *a world-famous writer* مشهور عالميّاً

ˌ**world ˈwar** *noun* [C] a war that involves a lot of important countries: *the Second World War* حرب عالمية

worldwide /ˌwɜːldˈwaɪd/ *adj, adv* (happening) in the whole world: *The situation has caused worldwide concern.* ○ *The product will be marketed worldwide.* عالميّ، على مستوى العالم

the ˌ**World Wide ˈWeb** (*also* **the Web**) *noun* [sing.] a system for finding information on the Internet (في الكمبيوتر) الشبكة العالمية

worm /wɜːm/ *noun* [C] **1** a small animal with a long thin body and no bones or legs: *an earthworm* دودة

2 [plural] a worm that lives inside a person or an animal and may cause disease دودة

▶ **worm** *verb*

PHRV **worm your way/yourself along, through, etc.** to move slowly or with difficulty in the direction mentioned, perhaps by crawling or by moving in between a lot of people or things: *I managed to worm my way through the crowd.* يدِبّ (دبيب الدودة)، ينْسَلّ

worm your way/yourself into sth to win sb's trust, respect or affection, perhaps dishonestly, especially in order to obtain sth you want يتقرّب من شخص بالتزلّف

worn *pp* of WEAR[1]

ˌ**worn ˈout** *adj* **1** too old or damaged to use any more: *a worn-out sweater* بالٍ، مهترئ

2 extremely tired: *I'm worn out. I think I'll go to bed early.* مرْهَق

worry /ˈwʌri/ *verb* (*pres part* **worrying**; *3rd pers sing pres* **worries**; *pt, pp* **worried**) **1** [I] **worry (about sb/sth)** to be anxious (about sb, a problem, an event, etc.): *'Don't worry, Mum,' said Peter, 'I won't be home late.'* ○ *There's nothing to worry about.* ○ *He worries if I don't phone every weekend.* يَقْلق، يَنْزعج

2 [T] **worry sb/yourself (about sb/sth)** to make sb/yourself anxious (about sb/sth): *You look depressed. What's worrying you?* ○ *She worried herself sick when he was away in the army.* يُقْلِق؛ يَقْلق

3 [T] **worry sb (with sth)** to bother or disturb sb: *I'm sorry to worry you with my problems but I really do need some advice.* يضايق، يزْعِج

▶ **worried** *adj* **worried (about sb/sth)**; **worried (that...)** anxious or unhappy: *Don't look so worried. Everything will be all right.* ○ *I'm worried about Jane.* ○ *We were worried stiff* (= extremely worried) *that you might have had an accident.* قلق؛ منْزعج

worry *noun* (*pl.* **worries**) **1** [U] an anxious state or feeling: *His son has caused him a lot of worry recently.* قلَق

2 [C] something that makes you worry; a problem: *financial worries* همّ، مشْكلة

worrying *adj* that makes you worry: *a worrying situation* مقْلق

worse /wɜːs/ *adj* (the comparative of *bad*) **1** not as good as sth else: *The weather in March was worse than in February.* ○ *The food at school seems to be getting worse and worse.* أسوأ

2 (not before a noun) more ill; less well: *The doctors say that he's getting worse.* أسوأ

IDM **be none the worse (for sth)** to be unhurt or undamaged by sth (لم يصَب بأذى)

make matters/things worse to make a situation, problem, etc. even more difficult or dangerous than before (يزيد الأمور سوءاً)

the worse for wear (*informal*) damaged; not in

good condition: *This suitcase looks a bit the worse for wear.* تالف، سيئ الحال

worse luck! (*informal*) unfortunately: *The dentist says I need three fillings, worse luck!* لسوء الحظ

▸ **worse** *adv* (the comparative of *badly*) less well: *She speaks German even worse than I do.* بصورة أسوأ

worse *noun* [U] something that is worse: *The situation was already bad but there was worse to come.* شيء أدهى

worsen /ˈwɜːsn/ *verb* [I,T] to become worse or to make sth worse: *Relations between the two countries have worsened.* يسوء، يتدهور

worship /ˈwɜːʃɪp/ *noun* [U] praying to and showing respect for God or a god: *Different religions have different forms of worship.* ○ *A church is a place of worship.* عبادة

▸ **worship** *verb* (worship**p**ing; worship**p**ed; *US* worshiping; worshiped) **1** [I,T] to pray to and show respect for God or a god: *People travel from all over the world to worship at this shrine.* ○ *In primitive societies people worshipped the sun.* يَعبُد

2 [T] to love or admire sb/sth very much: *She worshipped her husband.* يَعبد، يعجب اعجاباً شديداً

worshipper (*US* **worshiper**) *noun* [C] عابِد

worst /wɜːst/ *adj* (the superlative of *bad*) the least pleasant or suitable: *It's been the worst winter that I can remember.* أسوأ (شيء)

▸ **worst** *adv* (the superlative of *badly*) least well: *A lot of the children behaved badly but my son behaved worst of all!* على أسوأ وجه

worst *noun* [sing.] **the worst** something that is the least satisfactory or desirable: *My parents always expect the worst if I'm late.* أسوأ (شيء)

IDM **at (the) worst** if the worst happens or if you consider sb/sth in the worst way: *The problem doesn't look too serious. At worst we'll have to make a few small changes.* على أسوأ تقدير

if the worst comes to the worst if the worst possible situation develops إذا بلغت الأمور أسوأ حالاتها

worth /wɜːθ/ *adj* **1** having a particular value (in money): *'How much is that house worth?' 'It must be worth at least £300 000.'* قيمة مالية

2 worth doing, etc. (used as a way of recommending or advising): *That museum's really worth visiting if you have time.* ○ *The library closes in five minutes – it's not worth going in now.* ❶ We can say either: *It isn't worth repairing the car* OR: *The car isn't worth repairing.* يستحق

IDM **get your money's worth** → MONEY

worth it enjoyable or useful to do or have, even if it means extra cost, effort, etc: *Don't bother cooking a big meal. It isn't worth it – we're not hungry.* مستحق

worth sb's while helpful, useful or interesting to sb مفيد، ذو قيمة

▸ **worth** *noun* [U] **1** value or usefulness: *She has proved her worth as a member of the team.* قيمة، نَفْع

2 the amount of sth that the money mentioned will buy: *ten pounds' worth of petrol* قيمة (مالية)

3 the amount of sth that will last for the time mentioned: *two days' worth of food* قدر

worthless *adj* **1** having no value or use: *It's worthless – it's only a bit of plastic!* لا قيمة له

2 (used about a person) having bad qualities تافه

worthwhile /ˌwɜːθˈwaɪl/ *adj* enjoyable, useful or satisfying enough to be worth the cost or effort: *Working for so little money just isn't worthwhile.* ○ *Medicine is a very worthwhile career.* مفيد، مستحقّ للجهد المبذول

worthy /ˈwɜːði/ *adj* (**worthier**; **worthiest**)

1 worthy of sth/to do sth good enough for sth, or deserving sth: *The scheme is worthy of our support.* ○ *He felt he was not worthy to accept such responsibility.* مستحقّ، مستأهل

2 deserving respect or consideration: *a worthy leader* ○ *a worthy cause* جدير بالاحترام أو التقدير

would /wəd; *strong form* wʊd/ *modal verb* (*short form* **'d**; *negative* **would not**; *short form* **wouldn't** /ˈwʊdnt/) **1** (used when talking about the result of an event that you imagine): *He would be delighted if you went to see him.* ○ *She'd be stupid not to accept.* ○ *I would have done more if I'd had the time.* (للتعبير عن نتيجة يتصوّرها المتكلم)

2 (used as the past form of 'will' when you report what sb says or thinks): *They said that they would help us.* ○ *She didn't think that he would do a thing like that.* صيغة الماضي لـ will

3 (used for asking sb politely to do sth): *Would you come this way, please?* (للتعبير عن طلب شيء بلطف)

4 (used with 'like' or 'love' as a way of asking or saying what sb wants): *Would you like to come with us?* ○ *I'd love a piece of cake.* يودّ، يحب

5 to be willing to do sth: *She just wouldn't do what I asked her.* (للتعبير عن الاستعداد لفعل شيء)

6 (used after 'wish'): *I wish the sun would come out.* (للتعبير عن التمني مع wish)

7 (used for talking about things that often happened in the past): *When he was young he would often walk in these woods.* (للتعبير عن أشياء غالباً ما حدثت في الماضي)

8 (used for commenting on behaviour that is typical): *You would say that. You always support him.* (للتعليق على تصرف متوقع)

9 (used when you are giving your opinion): *I'd say she's about 40.* (للإعراب عن الرأي)

wound[1] /wuːnd/ *noun* [C] an injury to part of your body, especially a cut, often one received in fighting: *Bathe and bandage the wound.* ○ *a bullet wound* ○ *The wound is healing well.* جرح

▸ **wound** *verb* [T] (usually passive) **1** to injure sb's body with a weapon: *He was wounded in the leg during the war.* ➲ Look at the note at **hurt**. يَجرح

2 (*formal*) to hurt sb's feelings deeply: *I was wounded by his criticism.* يَجرح شعوره

the wounded *noun* [plural] wounded people: *the sick and the wounded* الجَرْحى

wound[2] *pt, pp of* WIND[3]

wove *pt* of WEAVE

woven *pp* of WEAVE

wow /waʊ/ *interj* (*informal*) (used for expressing how much you admire or are pleasantly surprised by sth): *Wow! What a beautiful boat!* (للتعبير عن الاعجاب أو الاندهاش): يا سلام! الله!

WP *abbrev* = WORD PROCESSING; WORD PROCESSOR: *WP skills necessary*

wrangle /ˈræŋgl/ *noun* [C] a noisy or complicated argument جدال

▸ **wrangle** *verb* [I] **wrangle (with sb) (about/over sth)** to argue in a noisy or angry way يجادل

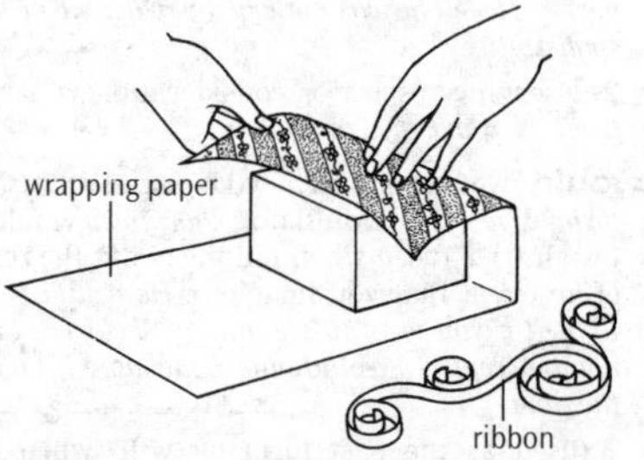

wrap

wrap /ræp/ *verb* [T] (wrapping; wrapped) **1 wrap sth (up) (in sth)** to put paper or cloth around sb/sth as a cover: *to wrap up a present* ○ *The baby was found wrapped in a blanket, on the hospital doorstep.* يلف

2 wrap sth round/around sb/sth to tie sth such as paper or cloth around an object or a part of the body: *The man had a bandage wrapped round his head.* يلف

IDM be wrapped up in sth to be deeply involved and interested in sb/sth: *They were completely wrapped up in each other. They didn't notice I was there.* يستغرق، ينهمك

PHR V wrap (sb/yourself) up to put warm clothes on (sb/yourself) يلف؛ يلتف

▸ **wrapper** *noun* [C] a piece of paper or plastic which covers a sweet, a book, etc. لفافة، غلاف

wrapping *noun* [C,U] paper or cloth that is used for covering or packing sth: *Remove the outer wrapping before heating the pie.* غلاف، غطاء

ˈwrapping paper *noun* [U] paper which is used for wrapping presents: *a sheet of wrapping paper* ورق لف

wrath /rɒθ; *US* ræθ/ *noun* [U] (*old-fashioned, formal*) very great anger غضب شديد

wreak /riːk/ *verb* [T] **wreak sth (on sb/sth)** to carry out or cause sth (a punishment, damage, etc.): *The storm wreaked havoc* (= great damage) *in the forest.* ينزل (عقاباً، اذى الخ)

wreath /riːθ/ *noun* [C] (*pl.* **wreaths** /riːðz/) a circle of flowers and leaves, especially one that you put on sb's grave إكليل

wreck /rek/ *noun* **1** [C] a ship that has sunk or been badly damaged at sea: *Divers searched the wreck.* حطام سفينة

2 [U] the damage or destruction of sth, especially a ship at sea: *the wreck of the Titanic* حطام (سفينة)

3 [C] a car, plane, etc. which has been badly damaged, especially in an accident: *The car was a wreck but the lorry escaped almost without damage.* حطام

4 [C, usually sing.] (*informal*) a person or thing that is in a very bad condition: *a nervous wreck* منهار، كتلة مهشمة

▸ **wreck** *verb* [T] to destroy, damage or spoil sth completely: *Vandals had wrecked the village hall.* ○ *A fishing boat was wrecked in the storms.* ○ *The strike wrecked all our holiday plans.* يتلف، يقوّض

wreckage /ˈrekɪdʒ/ *noun* [U] the broken pieces of sth that has been wrecked حطام

wrench /rentʃ/ *verb* [T] **1 wrench sb/sth (away, off, etc.)** to pull or turn sb/sth strongly and suddenly: *He wrenched the wheel to the left and stopped the car on the grass.* ○ (*figurative*) *The film was so exciting that I could hardly wrench myself away.* ينتزع

2 to injure your ankle, shoulder, etc. by turning it suddenly يلوي، يفكّ، يخلع

▸ **wrench** *noun* **1** [C] a sudden, violent pull or turn: *With a wrench I managed to open the door.* انتزاع، خلعة، شدّة

2 [sing.] an occasion when you feel very sad because you have to leave sb/sth فراق أليم

3 [C] (*US*) = SPANNER

wrestle /ˈresl/ *verb* [I] **1** to fight by trying to get hold of your opponent's body and throw him/her to the ground. People wrestle as a sport. يصارع

2 wrestle with sth to try hard to find an answer to sth; to struggle يغالب؛ يجاهد

▸ **wrestler** /ˈreslə(r)/ *noun* [C] a person who wrestles as a sport مصارع

wrestling /ˈreslɪŋ/ *noun* [U] a sport in which two people fight and try to throw each other to the ground: *a wrestling match* مصارعة

wretch /retʃ/ *noun* [C] (*old-fashioned*) a poor, unhappy person: *The poor wretch was clearly starving.* تعيس

wretched /ˈretʃɪd/ *adj* **1** very unhappy; miserable تعيس؛ شقي

2 (*informal*) (used for expressing anger): *That wretched dog has chewed up my slippers again!* اللعين: في التعبير عن الغضب

wriggle /ˈrɪgl/ *verb* [I,T] **1** to move about, or to move a part of your body, with short, quick movements, especially from side to side: *Sit still and stop wriggling about!* ○ *She wriggled her fingers about in the hot sand.* يحرك أو يتحرك يميناً وشمالاً، يتلوى (كالدودة)

2 to move in the direction mentioned by making quick, turning movements: *The worm wriggled back into the soil.* يتلوّى، يتمعّج

PHR V wriggle out of sth/out of doing sth (*informal*) to avoid sth by making clever excuses: *It's your turn to wash up – you can't wriggle out of it this time!* يتملّص، يتهرّب

wring /rɪŋ/ *verb* [T] (*pt, pp* **wrung** /rʌŋ/) **wring sth (out)** to press and squeeze sth in order to remove water from it يَعْصِر

ˌwringing 'wet *adj* very wet indeed مبتلّ للغاية

wrinkle /ˈrɪŋkl/ *noun* [C] a small line in sth, often one on the skin of your face which you get as you grow older تجعيدة

▸ **wrinkle** *verb* [I,T] to form wrinkles (in sth): *She wrinkled her nose at the smell.* يتجعّد؛ يُقطّب

wrinkled /ˈrɪŋkld/ *adj*: *an old lady with a wrinkled face* متجعّد، متغضّن

wrist /rɪst/ *noun* [C] the part of your body where your arm joins your hand رُسْغ، مِعْصَم

wristwatch /ˈrɪstwɒtʃ/ *noun* [C] a watch on a strap which you wear round your wrist ساعة يد

writ /rɪt/ *noun* [C] a legal order to do or not to do sth, given by a court of law or a person in authority أمر قضائي

write /raɪt/ *verb* (*pt* **wrote** /rəʊt/; *pp* **written** /ˈrɪtn/) **1** [I,T] to make words, letters, etc, especially on paper, using a pen, pencil, etc: *Some children can read and write before going to school.* ○ *I can't write with this pen.* ○ *Write your name and address on the form.* يكتب

2 [T] to create a book, story, song, etc. and write it on paper: *Tolstoy wrote 'War and Peace'.* ○ *He wrote his wife a poem.* ○ *Who wrote the music for that film?* يكتب، يؤلّف

3 [I,T] to write and send a letter, etc. to sb: *Have you written to your mother?* ○ *I'm writing to thank you for the birthday present you sent me.* ○ *She wrote that they were all well and would be home soon.* ○ *They wrote last week, asking us to spend Christmas with them.* ○ *I've written a letter to my son./I've written my son a letter.* ○ *I've written to him.* ❶ In US English we can say: *I've written him.* يكتب إلى، يبعث برسالة

4 [T] **write sth (out) (for sb)** to fill or complete a form, cheque, document, etc. with the necessary information: *I wrote out a cheque for £10.* ○ *The doctor quickly wrote a prescription for me.* يحرّر

PHRV **write back (to sb)** to send a reply to sb يردّ

write sth down to write sth on paper, especially so that you can remember it يسجّل

write in (to sb/sth) (for sth) to write a letter to an organization, etc. to order sth, give an opinion, etc. يطلب خطّياً

write off/away (to sb/sth) (for sth) to write a letter to an organization, etc. to order sth or ask for sth يطلب أو يستفسر خطّياً

write sb/sth off to accept or decide that sb/sth will not be successful or useful: *Don't write him off yet. He could still win.* يَصْرِف النظر عنه (نهائياً)

write sth off to accept that you will not get back an amount of money you have lost or spent: *to write off a debt* يَشْطُب، يسقّط

write sth out to write the whole of sth on paper: *Have you written out the poem in your exercise book?* يكتب (الشيء بكامله)

write sth up to write sth in a complete and final form, often using notes that you have made: *to write up lecture notes* يحرّر (الشيء بشكله النهائي)

➲ Look at **written**.

'write-off *noun* [C] a thing, especially a vehicle, that is so badly damaged that it is not worth repairing (سيارة) حطام؛ خسارة كاملة

writer /ˈraɪtə(r)/ *noun* [C] a person who writes, especially one whose job is to write books, stories, etc. كاتب، مؤلّف

writhe /raɪð/ *verb* [I] to turn and roll your body about: *She lay writhing in pain.* يتلوّى

writing /ˈraɪtɪŋ/ *noun* [U] **1** words that have been written or printed; the way a person writes: *This card's got no writing inside. You can put your own message.* ○ *I can't read your writing, it's too small.* كتابة؛ خطّ

2 the books, etc. that sb has written or the style in which sb writes: *Love is a common theme in his early writing.* ○ *Her writing lacks realism.* كتابات؛ (أُسْلوب) كتابة

3 the activity or job of writing books, etc: *It's difficult to earn much money from writing.* تأليف

IDM **in writing** in written form: *I'll confirm the offer in writing next week.* كتابةً

'writing paper *noun* [U] paper for writing letters on: *writing paper and envelopes* ورق رسائل

written[1] *pp* of WRITE

written[2] *adj* expressed on paper; not just spoken: *a written agreement* ○ *a written test and an oral test* مكتوب؛ تحريري

wrong[1] /rɒŋ; *US* rɔːŋ/ *adj* **1** not true or not correct; not right: *the wrong answer* ○ *What you said was quite wrong.* ○ *You've got the wrong number* (= on the telephone). خطأ؛ غير صحيح

2 not the best; not suitable; not right: *That's the wrong way to hold the bat.* ○ *I think she married the wrong man.* خطأ؛ غير ملائم

3 (not before a noun) **wrong (with sb/sth)** not as it should be; not working properly: *You look upset. Is something wrong?* ○ *What's wrong with the car this time?* ○ *She's got something wrong with her leg.* على غير ما يرام؛ فيه خلل أو علّة

4 **wrong (to do sth)** bad or against the law; not good or right: *The man said that he had done nothing wrong.* ○ *I think it was wrong of us not to invite him.* غير شرعي؛ غير لائق

IDM **get on the right/wrong side of sb** → SIDE

get (hold of) the wrong end of the stick (*informal*) to misunderstand completely what has been said: *You must have got the wrong end of the stick. We're not going there, they are coming here.* يسيء الفهم كلياً

on the right/wrong track → TRACK

▸ **wrong** *verb* [T] (*formal*) to do sth to sb which is bad or unfair: *I wronged her when I said she was lying.* يَظْلِم

wrongful /-fl/ *adj* (*formal*) (only *before* a noun)

not fair, not legal or not moral: *wrongful dismissal (from a job)* تَعسُّفي، غير قانوني

wrongly *adv* in a wrong or mistaken way: *This letter's been wrongly addressed.* ○ *She claimed, quite wrongly, that the handbag was hers.* خطأً، من غير حقّ

The adverb **wrong** is used after a verb or the object of a verb, especially in conversation: *He's spelt my name wrong.* The adverb **wrongly** is especially used before a past participle or a verb: *My name's been wrongly spelt.*

🔑 **wrong**[2] /rɒŋ; *US* rɔːŋ/ *adv* in an incorrect way; not right: *I always pronounce that word wrong.* خطأً، على نحو غير صحيح

IDM **get sb wrong** (*informal*) to misunderstand sb: *Don't get me wrong! I don't dislike him.* يسيء الفهم

go wrong 1 to make a mistake: *I'm afraid we've gone wrong. We should have taken the other road.* يخطئ، يرتكب غلطاً

2 to stop working properly or to stop developing well: *The freezer's gone wrong and all the food has defrosted.* ○ *Everything's gone wrong today.* يتعطّل، يَختلّ

wrong[3] /rɒŋ; *US* rɔːŋ/ *noun* **1** [U] what is bad or against the law: *Children quickly learn the difference between right and wrong.* الخَطأ، الباطل

2 [C] an action or situation which is not fair: *A terrible wrong has been done. Those men should never have gone to prison.* ظُلم

IDM **in the wrong** responsible for sth bad that has happened على خطأ، الحق عليه

wrote *pt* of WRITE

wrung *pt, pp* of WRING

wry /raɪ/ *adj* expressing a mixture of disappointment and amusement: *'Never mind,' she said with a wry grin. 'At least we got one vote.'* ساخر مع إحساس بخيبة أمل

▶ **wryly** *adv* بسخرية وخيبة أمل

wt *abbrev* = WEIGHT: *net wt 454 g*

WWW /ˌdʌbljuː dʌbljuː ˈdʌbljuː/ *abbrev* = WORLD WIDE WEB

X x

X, x /eks/ *noun* [C] (*pl.* **Xs**; **X's**; **x's**) the twenty-fourth letter of the English alphabet: *'Xylophone' begins with (an) 'X'.* الحرف الرابع والعشرون من الأبجدية الإنكليزية

X is used by teachers to show that an answer is wrong. It is also used instead of the name of a person if you do not know or do not want to say the name: *Mr and Mrs X.* At the end of a letter it stands for a kiss: *Lots of love, Mary XX.*

xenophobia *noun* /ˌzenəˈfəʊbiə/ [U] fear or hatred of foreigners الخوف من الاجانب أو كراهيتهم

▶ **xenophobic** *adj* خائف من الاجانب أو كاره لهم

Xerox™ /ˈzɪərɒks/ *noun* [C] **1** a machine that produces photocopies آلة ناسخة (للمستندات مثلاً)

2 a photocopy produced by such a machine: *a Xerox of the letter* نُسخة مصورة

▶ **xerox** *verb* [T] يصوِّر، يستنسخ

XL /ˌeks ˈel/ *abbrev* = EXTRA LARGE (SIZE)

Xmas /ˈkrɪsməs; ˈeksməs/ *noun* [C,U] (*informal*) (used as a short form, especially in writing) Christmas: *a Happy Xmas to all our customers* عيد الميلاد

X-ray /ˈeks reɪ/ *noun* [C] **1** [usually pl.] a kind of radiation that makes it possible to see inside solid objects (e.g. the human body) so that they can be examined and a photograph of them can be made الأشعة السينية

2 a photograph that is made with an X-ray machine: *The X-ray showed that the bone was not broken.* صورة بالأشعة السينية

▶ **X-ray** *verb* [T]: *She had her chest X-rayed.* يصوِّر بالأشعة السينية

xylophone /ˈzaɪləfəʊn/ *noun* [C] a musical instrument that consists of a row of wooden or metal bars of different lengths. You play it by hitting these bars with a small hammer. الخشبية: آلة موسيقية

Y y

Y, y /waɪ/ *noun* [C] (*pl.* **Ys**; **Y's**; **y's**) the twenty-fifth letter of the English alphabet: *'Yawn' begins with (a) 'Y'.* الحرف الخامس والعشرون من الأبجدية الإنكليزية

yacht /jɒt/ *noun* [C] **1** a boat with sails, used for pleasure: *a yacht race* يَخْت (شراعي)
2 a large boat with a motor, used for pleasure: *The harbour was full of millionaires' yachts.* يَخْت (بمحرّك)
▸ **yachting** *noun* [U] the activity or sport of sailing a yacht (رياضة) الإبْحار بِيَخْت

yachtsman /jɒtsmən/ *noun* [C] (*pl.* **-men** /-smən/; *feminine* **yachtswoman** /jɒtswʊmən/) a person who sails a yacht in races or for pleasure: *a round-the-world yachtsman* شخص يُبْحِر أو يتسابق بيخت

yank /jæŋk/ *verb* [I,T] (*informal*) to pull with a sudden quick movement and with great force: *She yanked at the door handle and it came off in her hand.* يَجْذِب بشدّة
▸ **yank** *noun* [C] جذبة عنيفة، انتزاع

yap /jæp/ *verb* [I] (ya**pp**ing; ya**pp**ed) (used about dogs, especially small ones) to bark in an excited way, making short high noises يَنْبَح

⚷**yard** /jɑːd/ *noun* [C] **1** an area, usually of concrete or stone with a wall or fence around it, next to or round a building: *I walked through a yard to get to the back door of the office.* ○ *The children were playing in the school yard.* ○ *a farmyard*
➲ Look at **courtyard** and **churchyard**. فناء، ساحة
2 (*US*) = GARDEN

> In British English the piece of land belonging to a house is a **garden** if it has grass, flowers, etc. and a **yard** if it is made of concrete or stone. In American English this piece of land is a **yard** whether it has grass or not, but if it is large and also has grass it can be called a **garden**.

3 an area, usually without a roof, used for a particular type of work or purpose: *a shipyard* ○ *a builder's yard* فناء، ساحة
4 (*abbr* **yd**) a measure of length; 0.914 of a metre. There are 3 feet (or 36 inches) in a yard: *How do you buy carpet here? By the yard or by the metre?* يارْدة : وحدة قياس

yardstick /ˈjɑːdstɪk/ *noun* [C] a standard by which things can be compared: *Exam results should not be the only yardstick by which pupils are judged.* مقياس

yarn /jɑːn/ *noun* **1** [U] thread (usually of wool or cotton) that is used for knitting, etc. غَزْل (صوفي أو قطني)
2 [C] (*informal*) a story that sb tells, especially one that is exaggerated قصة (تحوي مبالغات)

⚷**yawn** /jɔːn/ *verb* [I] **1** to open your mouth wide and breathe in deeply, especially when you are tired or bored: *'I've only just got up,' she said, yawning.* ○ *I kept yawning all through the lecture.* يتثاءب
2 (used about a hole, etc.) to be wide open: *a yawning hole in the ground where the bomb had exploded* يَنْفَغِر، ينفتح
▸ **yawn** *noun* [C]: *'How much longer will it take?' he said with a yawn.* تثاؤب

yd (*pl.* **yds**) *abbrev* = YARD (4)

⚷**yeah** /jeə/ *interj* (*informal*) yes نعم، ايوه

⚷**year** /jɪə(r); jɜː(r)/ *noun* **1** [C] the time it takes the earth to go once round the sun, about 365 days سَنَة، عام
2 [C] (*also* ˈ**calendar year**) the period from 1 January to 31 December, 365 or 366 days divided into 12 months or 52 weeks: *last year/this year/next year* ○ *The population of the country will be 70 million by the year 2030.* ○ *We go to France at this time every year.* ○ *Interest is paid on this account once a year.* ○ *the year before last/the year after next* ○ *a leap year* (= one that has 366 days) ○ *the New Year* (= the first days of January) سَنَة، عام
3 [C] any period of 12 months, measured from any point: *It's been several years since I last saw him.* ○ *She worked here for twenty years.* ○ *He left school just over a year ago.* ○ *In a year's time, you'll be old enough to vote.* ○ *They've been living in Spain for the last few years.* سَنَة، عام
4 [C] a period of a year in connection with schools, the business world, etc: *The school year runs from September to July.* ○ *the financial year* سَنَة، عام
5 [C] (used in connection with the age of sb/sth) a period of 12 months: *He's ten years old today.* ○ *a six-year-old daughter* ○ *This car is nearly five years old.* ○ *The company is now in its fifth year.* سَنَة، عام

> Note that you say: *He's ten* or: *He's ten years old* but NOT: *He's ten years.* Look at the note at **age**.

6 years [plural] a long time: *It happened years ago.* مدّة طويلة
IDM **all year round** for the whole year: *Most of the hotels are open all year round.* على مدار العام
donkey's years → DONKEY
year after year every year for many years سنة بعد سنة، لسنين عديدة
▸ **yearly** *adj*, *adv* (happening) every year or once a year: *a yearly pay increase* ○ *The conference is held yearly in Sligo.* سنوي؛ سنوياً

yearn /jɜːn/ *verb* [I] **yearn (for sb/sth)**; **yearn (to do sth)** to want sb/sth very much, especially sth that you cannot have يشتاق، يتوق
▸ **yearning** *noun* [C,U] توق، رغْبة (قوية)

a b c d e f g h i j k l m n o p q r s t u v w x y z

yeast /jiːst/ *noun* [U] a substance used for making bread rise and for making beer, wine, etc. خَميرة

yell /jel/ *verb* [I,T] to shout very loudly, often because you are angry, excited or in pain: *There's no need to yell at me, I can hear you perfectly well.* يَصْرُخ، يصيح، يزعق
▸ **yell** *noun* [C] صرخة، زعقة

🔑 **yellow** /ˈjeləʊ/ *adj* having the colour of lemons or butter: *dark/light yellow ○ a bright/pale yellow dress* أصفر
▸ **yellow** *noun* [C,U] the colour yellow; something that has the colour yellow: *a bright shade of yellow ○ the yellows and browns of the autumn leaves* صُفْرة: شيء أصْفَر
yellowish *adj* rather yellow ضارب للصفرة

ˌyellow ˈcard *noun* [C] (used in football) a card that the referee shows to a player as a warning that he/she will be sent off the field if he/she behaves badly again ➲ Look at **red card**. البطاقة الصفراء

ˌyellow ˈline *noun* [C] a yellow line at the side of a road to show that you must not park there خط أصفر (لمنع وقوف السيارات)

ˌYellow ˈPages™ *noun* [plural] a telephone book (on yellow paper) that lists all the business companies, etc. in a certain area, in sections according to the goods or services they provide الصفحات الصفراء: دليل الهاتف التجاري

yelp /jelp/ *noun* [C] a sudden short cry, especially of pain, fear or excitement عواء، نُباح
▸ **yelp** *verb* [I] يعوي، ينبح

🔑 **yes** /jes/ *interj* **1** (used when answering a question to which another possible answer is 'no'): *'Are you having a good time?' 'Yes, thank you' ○ I asked him if he wanted to come and he said yes.* نعم، بَلى

2 (used for saying that a statement is correct or for agreeing with one): *'You spend far too much money.' 'Yes, you're right.'* نعم

3 (used when agreeing to a request): *'May I sit here?' 'Yes, of course.'* نعم، أجل

4 (used when accepting an offer): *'More coffee?' 'Yes, please.'* نعم (من فضلك)

5 (used for showing you have heard sb or will do what they ask): *'Waiter!' 'Yes, madam.'* نعم!

6 (used when saying that a negative statement that sb has made is not true): *'You don't care about anyone but yourself.' 'Yes I do.'* بلى
▸ **yes** *noun* [C] (*pl.* **yeses** /ˈjesɪz/) an answer, statement or vote of 'yes' أصوات الموافقة (في اقتراع)

🔑 **yesterday** /ˈjestədeɪ/ *adv, noun* [C,U] (on) the day before today: *Did you watch the film on TV yesterday? ○ yesterday morning/afternoon/evening ○ I posted the form the day before yesterday* (= if I am speaking on Wednesday, I posted it on Monday). ○ *Did it really happen three weeks ago? It seems like only yesterday. ○ Have you still got yesterday's paper? ○ Yesterday was the best day I've had for ages. ○ I spent the whole of yesterday walking round the shops.* أمس، البارحة

🔑 **yet** /jet/ *adv* **1** (used with negative verbs or in questions for talking about sth that has not happened but that you expect to happen): *We haven't had any serious problems yet. ○ Has it stopped raining yet? ○ There was a pile of work on my desk which I hadn't yet done. ○ I haven't seen that film yet* ❶ In American English: *I didn't see that film yet.* بَعْد، حتى الآن

2 (used with negative verbs) now; as early as this: *You don't have to leave yet – your train isn't for another hour.* الآن؛ في هذا الوقت المبكّر

3 (used especially with *may* or *might*) at some time in the future: *With a bit of luck, they may win yet.* ذات يوم

4 (used after a period of time) longer: *She isn't all that old, she'll live for years yet.* مدة أطول

5 (used with comparatives or 'another' to emphasize the size or amount of sth): *I'm already busy and now I've been given yet more work to do.* رغم ذلك

6 (used with superlatives) until and including now/then; so far: *This is her best film yet.* حتى الآن؛ حتى ذلك الوقت

7 but; in spite of that: *Their plan was simple yet successful.* لكن؛ رغم ذلك

IDM **as yet** until now: *As yet little is known about the disease.* حتى الآن
yet again (used for emphasizing how often sth happens) once more: *I don't want to discuss this yet again!* مرّة أخرى
yet to do, etc. if you have yet to do sth, it means that you have not done it (but may possibly do it in the future): *The final decision has yet to be made.* لا يزال
▸ **yet** *conj* but (when sth is surprising after the first part of the statement): *He seems pleasant, yet there's something about him I don't like.* بَيْدَ أنّ، لكن

yew /juː/ *noun* (*also* **ˈyew tree**) [C] a small tree which has dark green leaves all through the year, and small red berries. Yews are often planted near churches. شجرة الطَّقسوس

YHA /ˌwaɪ eɪtʃ ˈeɪ/ *abbrev* (*Brit*) Youth Hostels Association رابطة بيوت الشباب

yield /jiːld/ *verb* **1** [T] to produce crops, profits or results: *How much wheat does each field yield? ○ Did the experiment yield any new information?* يُنتِج، يُثْمِر

2 [I] **yield (to sb/sth)** (*formal*) to stop resisting sb/sth (so that you do what sb has demanded): *The government refused to yield to the hostage takers' demands.* ❶ **Give in** is less formal. يستسلم، يذعن

3 [T] to allow sb to have control of sth that you were controlling: *The army has yielded power to the rebels.* يسلّم، يتخلى عن

4 [I] **yield to sth** to be replaced by sth, especially sth newer: *Old-fashioned methods have yielded to new technology.* يرضخ؛ ينزاح

5 [I] to bend or break: *The dam finally yielded under the weight of the water.* ينحني؛ ينهار

6 [I] **yield (to sb/sth)** to allow other traffic to go first or to join the road in front of you: *You have to yield to traffic from the left here.* يعطي أفضلية المرور

ℹ In senses **4**, **5** and **6**, **give way** is more common. However, **yield** is the usual American word in sense **6**.

▸ **yield** *noun* [C] the amount that is produced: *Wheat yields were down 5% this year.* ○ *This investment has an annual yield of 12%.* غَلّة: عائد

yo /jəʊ/ *interj* (*especially US slang*) used by some people when they see a friend; hello مرحبا!

yob /jɒb/ *noun* [C] (*also* **yobbo** /ˈjɒbəʊ/ (*pl.* **yobbos**)) (*Brit slang*) a boy or young man who behaves badly in public شاب وقح مشاغب

yoga /ˈjəʊgə/ *noun* [U] a system of exercises for the body, based on Hindu philosophy. Yoga helps you control and relax both your mind and your body. رياضة اليوغا

yogurt (*also* **yoghurt**) /ˈjɒgət; *US* ˈjəʊgərt/ *noun* [C,U] a slightly sour, thick liquid food made from milk with bacteria added to it لبن (زبادي)

yoke /jəʊk/ *noun* [C] a piece of wood fixed across the necks of two animals when they are pulling a cart, etc: (*figurative*) *the yoke of slavery* نِير

yolk /jəʊk/ *noun* [C,U] the yellow part in the middle of an egg: *He ate the yolk and left the white.* المحّ، صفار البيضة

yonks /jɒŋks/ *noun* [U] (*Brit informal*) a very long time: *I haven't been to the theatre for yonks.* مدّة طويلة

🔑**you** /ju/ *pron* **1** (used as the subject or object of a verb, or after a preposition) the person or people being spoken or written to: *You can play the guitar, can't you?* ○ *I've told you about this before.* ○ *Bring your photos with you.* ضمير المُخاطَب

2 (used with a noun, an adjective or a phrase when calling sb sth): *You fool! What do you think you're doing?* (مع اسم أو صفة أو عبارة): أنت يا...

3 a person (not a particular one); people in general: *You don't see many tourists here at this time of year.* ○ *The more you earn, the more tax you pay.* ℹ **One** has the same meaning but is much more formal: *One tries to help as much as one can.* الانسان، المرء

you-all /ˈjuː ɔːl/ *pron* (used in the Southern USA) you ضمير المخاطَب (في جنوب الولايات المتحدة)

you'd /juːd/ *short for* YOU HAD, YOU WOULD

you'll /juːl/ *short for* YOU WILL

🔑**young** /jʌŋ/ *adj* (**younger** /-ŋgə(r)/, **youngest** /-ŋgɪst/) not having lived or existed for very long: *They have two young children.* ○ *The film is about the United States, when it was still a young nation.* ○ *young plants* ○ *I'm a year younger than her.* ○ *My father was the youngest of eight children.* ○ *young fashion* (= for young people) صغير السّن، شابّ

IDM **young at heart** behaving or thinking like a young person, even if you are not young شابّ في تفكيره وتصرفاته

▸ **young** *noun* [plural] **1** young animals: *Swans will attack to protect their young.* صِغار (الحيوان)

2 the young young people when you are thinking about them as a group: *The young of today are the adults of tomorrow.* الشباب

youngish *adj* quite young صغير السّن بعض الشيء

youngster /-stə(r)/ *noun* [C] a young person: *There is very little entertainment for youngsters in this town.* شاب، حَدَث

🔑**your** /jɔː(r); *US* jʊər/ *det* **1** belonging to or connected with the person or people being spoken to: *What's your flat like?* ○ *Thanks for all your help.* ○ *How old are your children now?* ○ *It would be helpful if you could all give me your addresses.* صيغة المِلْكية للمُخاطَب

2 belonging to or connected with people in general: *When your life is as busy as mine, you have little time to relax.* (في التعبير عن تملّك الناس بشكل عام)

3 (used for saying that sth is well known to people in general): *So this is your typical English pub, is it?* (في التعبير عن معرفة شائعة)

4 (*also* **Your**) (used in some titles): *your Majesty* (في بعض صيغ الألقاب)

▸ **yours** /jɔːz; *US* jʊərz/ *pron* **1** belonging to or connected with you: *Is this bag yours or mine?* ○ *I was talking to a friend of yours the other day.* (يملكه المخاطَب): لكَ

2 Yours (used at the end of a letter): *Yours sincerely...* ○ *Yours faithfully...* ○ *Yours truly...* ○ *Yours...* (صيغة في ختام الرسالة)

you're /jʊə(r); jɔː(r)/ *short for* YOU ARE

🔑**yourself** /jɔːˈself; *US* jʊərˈself/ *pron* (*pl.* **yourselves** /-ˈselvz/) **1** (used as the object of a verb or preposition when you are speaking to sb and talking about this person/these people doing an action and also being affected by it): *Be careful or you'll hurt yourself.* ○ *Here's some money. Buy yourselves a present.* ○ *You're always talking about yourself!* نفْسك

2 (used for emphasis): *You yourself told me there was a problem last week.* ○ *Did you repair the car yourselves?* (= or did sb else do it for you?) نفسك أو بنفْسك

3 in your normal state; healthy: *You don't look yourself today.* بصحة جيدة: في حالته المعتادة

IDM **by yourself/yourselves 1** alone: *Do you live by yourself?* بمفردك

2 without help: *You can't cook dinner for ten people by yourself. Let me help you.* لوحدك، دون مساعدة

🔑**youth** /juːθ/ *noun* (*pl.* **youths** /juːðz/) **1** [U] the period of your life when you are young, especially the time between being a child and an adult: *He was quite a good sportsman in his youth.* فترة الشباب

2 [U] the fact or state of being young: *I think that his youth will be a disadvantage in this job.* حداثة السن

3 [C] a young person (usually a young man, and often one that you do not have a good opinion of):

There were gangs of youths standing around on the street corners. حَدَث، فتى

4 the youth [plural, with sing. or pl. verb] young people as a group: *What kind of future does/do the youth of this country have?* الشباب، الشبيبة

▸ **youthful** /-fl/ *adj* **1** having the qualities that are typical of young people: *She was nearly fifty but still full of youthful enthusiasm.* فتيّ، غَضّ، نضير

2 young or relatively young: *a piece of music by the youthful Mozart* شابّ، شاب بعض الشيء

'youth hostel *noun* [C] a type of cheap and simple hotel which people (especially young people) can stay at when they are travelling around on holiday بيت الشباب

you've /juːv/ *short for* YOU HAVE

yo-yo /'jəʊ jəʊ/ *noun* [C] (*pl.* **yo-yos**) a toy which is a round piece of wood or plastic with a string round the middle. You put the string round your finger and can make the yo-yo go up and down it. لعبة اليويو

yr (*especially US* **yr.**) (*pl.* **yrs**) *abbrev* = YEAR

yuck /jʌk/ *interj* (*informal*) (used for saying that you think sth is very unpleasant): *It's filthy! Yuck!* (للتعبير عن الاشمئزاز)

▸ **yucky** *adj* (**yuckier**; **yuckiest**) (*informal*) disgusting; very unpleasant; horrible: *What a yucky colour!* كريه، منَفِّر

yummy /'jʌmi/ *adj* (**yummier**; **yummiest**) (*informal*) tasting very good; delicious لذيذ، شهي

yuppy (*also* **yuppie**) /'jʌpi/ *noun* [C] (*pl.* **yuppies**) a successful young professional person who earns a lot of money and spends it on fashionable things شاب ناجح في عمله مغرم بأحدث الأشياء

Z z

Z, z /zed; *US* ziː/ *noun* [C] (*pl.* **Zs**; **Z's**; **z's**) the twenty-sixth letter of the English alphabet: *'Zero' begins with (a) 'Z'.* ❶ Note the different US pronunciation. الحرف السادس والعشرون من الأبجدية الإنكليزية

zany /'zeɪni/ *adj* funny in an unusual and crazy way: *a zany comedian* مُضحِك بشكل غير مألوف، (تهريج) مجنون

zap /zæp/ *verb* (za**pp**ing; za**pp**ed) (*informal*) **1** [T] to kill sb, usually with a gun or other weapon: *It's a computer game where you have to zap aliens with a laser.* يَقْتُل

2 [I,T] to change television programmes very quickly using a remote control يتنقل عبر البرامج التلفزيونية

zeal /ziːl/ *noun* [U] (*formal*) great energy or enthusiasm: *religious zeal* حَماس

▸ **zealous** /'zeləs/ *adj* using great energy and enthusiasm متحمِّس

zealously *adv* بشدّة، بتفانٍ

zebra /'zebrə; *US* 'ziːbrə/ *noun* [C] (*pl.* **zebra** or **zebras**) an African wild animal that looks like a horse, with black and white stripes all over its body حمار الوحش

,zebra 'crossing *noun* [C] (*Brit*) a place where the road is marked with black and white lines to show that people can cross in safety because cars must stop there to let them over عبور للمشاة

🔑 **zero** /'zɪərəʊ/ *pron* **1** 0; one less than one; nought صِفْر

2 freezing point; 0°C: *The temperature is likely to fall to five below zero (= -5°C).* نقطة التجمّد، الصفر

3 nothing at all; none at all: *My chances of passing the exam are zero.* منعدم؛ لا شيء

> The figure **0** has several different names in British English. **Zero** is most commonly used in scientific or technical contexts. **Nil** is most commonly used in scores in sport (when spoken). **Nought** is used when referring to the figure **0** as part of a number: *a million is one followed by six noughts.* **O** (pronounced 'oh') is most commonly used when speaking numbers such as telephone or bus numbers.

,zero-'carbon *adj* in which the amount of carbon dioxide produced has been reduced to nothing or is balanced by actions that protect the environment: *a zero-carbon house* متوازن في طرح الكربون

zest /zest/ *noun* [U, sing.] **zest (for sth)** a feeling of excitement, pleasure and interest: *She is a very active person, with a great zest for life.* حيوية؛ حماس

zigzag /'zɪgzæg/ *noun* [C] a line with left and right turns, one after the other at sharp angles: *a zigzag path down the cliff* ○ *curtains with a zigzag pattern* خطّ متعرِّج

▸ **zigzag** *verb* [I] (zigza**gg**ing; zigza**gg**ed): *We took a road that zigzagged through the mountains.* يتعرّج

zinc /zɪŋk/ *noun* [U] a silver-grey metal, often put on the surface of iron and steel as protection against water زنك

zip /zɪp/ *noun* [C] (*also* **'zip fastener**; *especially US* **zipper** /'zɪpə(r)/) a device for fastening clothes, bags, etc. which consists of two rows of metal or plastic teeth, one on each side of an opening. You can join these rows together to close the opening: *Your zip's undone!* ○ *Do your zip up.* زمام منْزلق، "سحّاب" أو "سوسته"

▸ **zip** *verb* [T] (zi**pp**ing; zi**pp**ed) **1 zip sth (up)** to fasten sth with a zip: *There was so much in the bag that it was difficult to zip it up.* يغلق بزمام منْزلق

2 (*computing*) to compress a file (= make it smaller) يضغط (الملفات)

'zip code (*also* **'Zip code**) *noun* [C] (*US*) = POSTCODE

zodiac /'zəʊdiæk/ *noun* [sing.] **the zodiac** a diagram of the positions of the planets and stars, which is divided into twelve equal parts (signs) دائرة البروج

> The signs of the zodiac are used in **astrology** and **horoscopes** (often called **The Stars**) in newspapers and magazines. People often refer to the signs and to the influence that they think these have on a person's personality and future: *Which sign of the zodiac are you?* ○ *I'm (a) Leo.*

zone /zəʊn/ *noun* [C] an area that is different from those around it, e.g. because sth special happens there: *the war zone* ○ *We're crossing into a new time zone.* منْطَقَة

zoo /zuː/ *noun* [C] (*pl.* **zoos**) (*also formal* **ˌzoological 'gardens**) a park where many kinds of living (especially wild) animals are kept so that people can look at them: *to go to the zoo* حديقة حيوانات

zoology /zəʊ'ɒlədʒi/ *noun* [U] the scientific study of animals ➲ Look at **botany** and **biology**. علم الحيوان

▸ **zoological** /ˌzəʊə'lɒdʒɪkl/ *adj* متعلّق بعلم الحيوان

zoologist /zəʊ'ɒlədʒɪst/ *noun* [C] a person who studies or is an expert on zoology عالم حيوان

zoom /zuːm/ *verb* [I] to move very quickly and with a loud noise: *A motorcycle zoomed past.* يئزّ؛ يندفع بسرعة

PHR V **zoom in (on sb/sth)** to make an object that you are filming appear bigger by using a special lens: *The camera zoomed in on a face in the crowd.* يركّز العدسة لتكبير الأشياء

'zoom lens *noun* [C] a camera lens that can make an object being photographed appear gradually bigger or smaller so that it seems to be getting closer or further away عدسة "زوم"، عدسة تكبير وتصغير

zucchini /zʊ'kiːni/ *noun* [C] (*pl.* **zucchini**; **zucchinis**) (*especially US*) = COURGETTE

Appendices

Appendix 1
Words that go together

As well as explaining the meaning of a word, ***Oxford Wordpower*** also shows you how to use it correctly in a phrase or sentence.

The example sentences

Do we talk about ***weak*** *cheese* or ***mild*** *cheese*?
Do you ***say*** *a joke* or ***tell*** *a joke*? (It's **mild** and **tell**.)
If you look up a word in the dictionary, the example sentences show you which other words are often used with it:

Write out and **cash** are verbs that are often used with the word **cheque**.

cheque (*US* **check**) /tʃek/ *noun* [C,U] a piece of paper printed by a bank that you can fill in, sign and use to pay for things: *She wrote out a cheque for £20.* ○ *I went to the bank to cash a cheque.* ○ *If there is no money in your account, your cheque will bounce* (= your bank will not pay it). ○ *Can I pay by cheque?* صك أو شيك

Strong, **high**, **cold** and **north** are adjectives that are often used with the word **wind**.

wind¹ /wɪnd/ *noun* **1** [C,U] (*also* **the wind**) air that is moving across the surface of the earth: *There was a strong wind blowing.* ○ *A gust of wind blew his hat off.* ○ *high winds* ○ *a cold north wind* ريح

Practice 1

Match a word in **A** with a word in **B**.
Find the words in **B** in the dictionary and look at the example sentences.

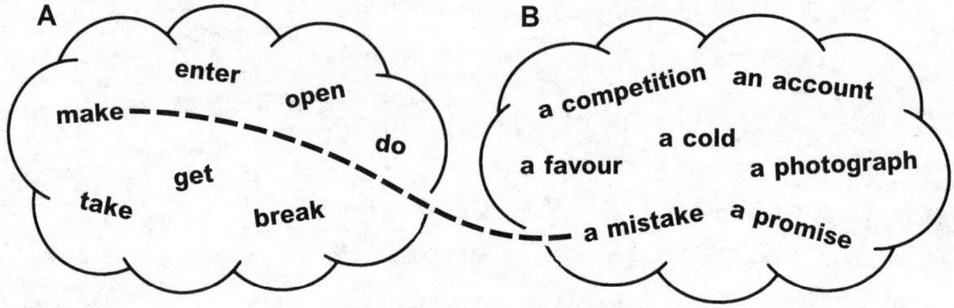

Practice 2

What's the opposite of ...

a weak tea? ....
b curly hair? ....
c dark skin? ....
d calm sea? ....
e a high salary? ....
f heavy traffic? ....
g a mild curry? ....
h an even number? ....

Prepositions and verb patterns

The dictionary also shows you which preposition to use after a noun, verb or adjective, and which construction to use after a verb:

This shows that the preposition that goes with **married** is **to**.

> **married** /ˈmærid/ *adj* **1 married (to sb)** having a husband or wife: *a married man/woman/couple* ○ *They've been married for nearly 50 years.* ○ *Shula's married to Mark.* ○ *They're getting married in June.* ℹ The opposite is **unmarried** or **single**. متزوّج

You can say that you **enjoy something** or that you **enjoy doing something**.

> **enjoy** /ɪnˈdʒɔɪ/ *verb* [T] **1 enjoy sth/enjoy doing sth** to get pleasure from: *I really enjoyed that meal – thank you very much.* ○ *Do you enjoy your work?* ○ *He enjoys listening to music while he's driving.* يتمتّع أو يستمتع بـ

Practice 3

Use the dictionary to complete these sentences with the right preposition.

- **a** Everybody laughed .... the joke.
- **b** We were very pleased .... the hotel.
- **c** She says she's found a solution .... the problem.
- **d** It took her a long time to recover .... the accident.
- **e** Do you believe .... life after death?
- **f** I apologized .... Sam .... breaking the chair.
- **g** She's very proud .... her new motorbike.
- **h** The house is quite close .... the shops.

Practice 4

Complete these sentences with the correct form of the verb in brackets.

- **a** Haven't you **finished** .... (*clean*) your room yet?
- **b** He **keeps** .... (*phone*) me up.
- **c** I've **persuaded** Jan .... (come) to the party.
- **d** Try to **avoid** .... (*make*) mistakes.
- **e** You're not **allowed** .... (*smoke*) in here.
- **f** The bank has **agreed** .... (*lend*) me the money.

Now turn the page upside down and check your answers.

Answers

Practice 1
make a mistake; enter a competition; open an account; do a favour; break a promise; get a cold; take a photograph

Practice 2
a strong tea **e** a low salary
b straight hair **f** light traffic
c fair skin **g** a hot curry
d rough sea **h** an odd number

Practice 3
a at **d** from **g** of
b with **e** in **h** to
c to **f** to, for

Practice 4
a cleaning **d** making
b phoning **e** to smoke
c to come **f** to lend

Appendix 2
Modal verbs

Modal verbs are used with another verb to express possibility, probability, obligation, etc.

The modal verbs **can**, **could**, **may**, **might**, **shall**, **should**, **will**, **would** and **must** are followed by an infinitive without **to**: *I can swim.* These verbs do not change in form (i.e. they have no **-ing**, **-ed** or **-s** forms) and form questions and negatives without **do**:

'Can you hear me?' 'Yes, I can.'

Here are some examples of the use of modal verbs:

Ability

can could be able to

***Can** you ride a bike?*

*He **has been able to** swim for a year.*

*The fire brigade **were able** to rescue the children.*

*The fire brigade **couldn't** rescue the children.*

***I could** run four kilometres without stopping when I was younger.*

*One day people **will be able** to travel to Mars.*

*She **could** have passed the exam if she'd tried harder.*

- Look also at **manage** and **succeed**.

Obligation

must have (got) to

*I **must** go to the bank today.*

*We **have to** give in the essay on Friday.*

*She **had to** wait for him.*

*We **will have to** ring up.*

*He **didn't have to** go to hospital. The test was done at home.*

- Look also at **need** and **suppose**.

Duty

should ought to

*The police **should** do something about it.*

*You **shouldn't** leave children alone.*

*You **ought to** visit your grandparents more often.*

*She **oughtn't to** make private calls in work time.*

*I **shouldn't** have gone to bed so late. I felt very tired the next day.*

*I **ought to** have helped.*

Permission

can could may

***Can** I go now, please?*

*You **can't** go swimming today. I need you to help me at home.*

*Books **may** only be borrowed for two weeks.*

***May** I use your phone?*

***Could** I possibly borrow your car?*

- Look also at **allow** and **let**.

Prohibition

may not must not

You **may not** *take photographs in the museum.*

Cars **must not** *park in front of the entrance.*

- Look also at **allow** and **let**.

Recommendations and advice

must ought to should

You really **must** *see that film. It's wonderful.*

What **ought I to** *say to him?*

You ought to read this book.

You **ought to** *have come with us. It was great!*

He really **shouldn't** *work so hard. He looks exhausted.*

Requests

can could will would

Can *you help me?*

Could *you open the door, please?*

Will *you sit down, please?*

Would *you come this way, please?*

Suggestions and invitations

shall would like

Would *you* **like** *to come with us?*

Shall *I carry that for you?*

Shall *we go out for a meal today?*

- Look also at **let**.

Possibility

can could may might

I **can** *catch a bus from here.*

She **could** *be famous one day.*

Couldn't *you come earlier?*

I **could** *have left my bag in the bank.*

You **may** *be right.*

They **may** *have forgotten the meeting.*

William **might** *be upstairs.*

She **might not** *come if she's very busy.*

If I'd known the film was about Wales, I **might** *have watched it.*

Probability

can't must ought to should will

You **can't** *be hungry – you've just eaten.*

He **couldn't** *have known that.*

Have something to eat. You **must** *be hungry.*

I **must** *have left my book at home.*

It **must** *have been a great shock for you.*

That car **must** *have been doing 100 miles an hour!*

She **ought to** *pass her test. She drives well.*

I bought four bottles. That **ought to** *have been enough.*

He **should** *have arrived by now. I'll ring and check.*

That **will** *be the postman.*

Appendix 3

Phrasal verbs

Phrasal verbs are verbs that consist of two (or three) parts – an ordinary verb and another word (or words) like **in**, **for**, or **off**. They are very common in English. Here are some examples:

lie down **give up** **look for** **get on with**

Some of them are easy to understand (you can guess the meaning of **lie down** if you know the words **lie** and **down**), but many phrasal verbs are more difficult because they have special meanings (you cannot guess that ***give up*** *smoking* means *stop smoking* even if you know the words **give** and **up**).

If you want to find a phrasal verb in the dictionary, look under the first word (to find **give up**, look under **give**). The 'phrasal verbs' section comes after the ordinary meanings of the verb.

Practice 1

Use the dictionary to complete these sentences with the correct word.

a This meat smells horrible. It must have gone ....
(*over, off, past*)

b UK stands .... United Kingdom.
(*out, to, for*)

c I can't work .... how to use this video.
(*up, out, for*)

d Sue came .... the letter while she was tidying her room.
(*to, across, for*)

e I'm sure that story wasn't true. I think Pete made it ....
(*up, for, in*)

f She was offered a job in London, but she decided to turn it ....
(*over, up, down*)

g Oh no, I've run out .... milk. We'll have to buy some more.
(*for, of, with*)

h Can you write .... your address and telephone number, please?
(*down, up, in*)

Now turn the page upside down and check your answers.

Answers

a off **b** for **c** out **d** across **e** up **f** down **g** of **h** down

The four types

There are four main types of phrasal verbs:

1 Phrasal verb *without* an object

The fire **went out**.
My car **broke down** *on the motorway.*

In the dictionary these verbs are written like this:

go out **break down**

2 Phrasal verbs that can be separated by an object

a If the object is a noun, it can either go after both parts of the phrasal verb, or between them:

She **tried on** *the red dress.*
She **tried** *the red dress* **on**.

b If the object is a pronoun, it must go between the two parts of the phrasal verb:

She **tried** *it* **on**.

(NOT ~~She tried on~~ it.)

In the dictionary this verb is written like this: **try sth on**. When you see **sth** or **sb** *between* the two parts of the phrasal verb, you know that they can be separated by an object.

3 Phrasal verbs that cannot be separated by an object

The two parts of the phrasal verb must go together:

John's **looking after** *the children.*

(NOT ~~John's looking the children after.~~)

John's **looking after** *them.*

(NOT ~~John's looking them after.~~)

In the dictionary this verb is written like this: **look after sb**. When you see **sb** or **sth** *after* the two parts of the phrasal verb, you know that they *cannot* be separated by an object.

4 Phrasal verbs with three parts

The three parts of the phrasal verb must go together:

I can't **put up with** *this noise any longer.*

In the dictionary this verb is written like this: **put up with sb/sth**. Again, when you see **sb** or **sth** *after* the three parts of the phrasal verb, you know that they *cannot* be separated by an object.

Practice 2

Complete these sentences by putting the word it in the correct place.
In each sentence you will have to leave one space empty.

a You must be hot with your coat on. Why don't you **take** .... off ....?

b If you don't understand this word, **look** .... up .... in your dictionary.

c He's had a big shock, and it will take him some time to **get** .... over ....

d I was going to do my homework last night, but I'm afraid I didn't **get** round .... to ....

e I thought you'd read the newspaper, so I **threw** .... away ....

f Jill can't come to the meeting tomorrow, so we'll have to **put** .... off .... till next week.

Now turn the page upside down and check your answers.

Answers

a take it off **b** look it up **c** get over it **d** round to it **e** threw it away **f** put it off

Appendix 4
Prefixes and suffixes

Prefixes

a- not: *atypical*
ante- before: *antenatal* (= before birth)
anti- against: *anti-American, antisocial*
auto- self: *autobiography* (= the story of the writer's own life)
bi- two: *bicycle, bilingual* (= using two languages), *bimonthly* (= twice a month or every two months)
cent-, centi- hundred: *centenary* (= the hundredth anniversary), *centimetre* (= one hundredth of a metre)
circum- around: *circumnavigate* (= sail around)
co- with; together: *co-pilot, coexist, cooperation*
con- with; together: *context* (= the words or sentences that come before and after a particular word or sentence)
contra- against; opposite: *contradict* (= say the opposite)
counter- against; opposite: *counterrevolution, counterproductive* (= producing the opposite of the desired effect)
de- taking sth away; the opposite: *defrost* (= removing the layers of ice from a fridge, etc.), *decentralize*
deca- ten: *decathlon* (= a competition involving ten different sports)
deci- one tenth: *decilitre*
dis- reverse or opposite: *displeasure, disembark, discomfort*
e- using electronic communication: *e-commerce*
ex- former: *ex-wife, ex-president*
extra- **1** very; more than usual: *extra-thin, extra-special* **2** outside; beyond: *extraordinary, extraterrestrial* (= coming from somewhere beyond the earth)
fore- **1** before; in advance: *foreword* (= at the beginning of a book) **2** front: *foreground* (= the front part of a picture), forehead
hexa- six: *hexagon* (= a shape with six sides)
in- il-, im-, ir- not: *incorrect, invalid, illegal, illegible, immoral, impatient, impossible, irregular, irrelevant*
inter- between; from one to another: *international, interracial*
kilo- thousand: *kilogram, kilowatt*
maxi- most; very large: *maximum*
mega- million; very large: *megabyte, megabucks* (= a lot of money)
micro- very small: *microchip*
mid- in the middle of: *mid-afternoon, mid-air*
milli- thousandth: *millisecond, millimetre*
mini- small: **miniskirt, mini-series**
mis- bad or wrong; not: **misbehave**, *miscalculate, misunderstand*
mono- one; single: *monolingual* (= using one language), *monorail*
multi- many: *multinational* (= involving many countries)
non- not: *non-alcoholic, nonsense, non-smoker, non-stop*
nona- nine: *nonagon* (= a shape with nine sides)
octa- eight: *octagon* (= a shape with eight sides)
out- more; to a greater degree: *outdo, outrun* (= run faster or better than sb)
over- more than normal; too much: *overeat, oversleep* (= sleep too long)
penta- five: *pentagon* (= a shape with five sides), *pentathlon* (= a competition involving five different sports)
post- after: *post-war*
pre- before: *prepay, preview*
pro- for; in favour of: *pro-democracy, pro-hunting*
quad- four: *quadruple* (= multiply by four), *quadruplet* (= one of four babies born at the same time)
re- again: *rewrite, rebuild*
self- of, to or by yourself: *self-taught*
semi- half: *semicircle, semiconscious*
sept- seven: *septuplet* (one of seven babies born at the same time)
sub- **1** below; less than: *sub-zero* **2** under: *subway, subtitles* (= translations under the pictures of a film)
super- extremely; more than: *superhuman* (= having greater power than humans normally have), *supersonic* (= faster than the speed of sound)
tele- far; over a long distance: *telecommunications, telephoto lens*
trans- across; through: *transatlantic, transcontinental*
tri- three: *triangle, tricycle*
ultra- extremely; beyond a certain limit: *ultramodern*
un- not; opposite; taking sth away: *uncertain, uncomfortable, unsure, undo, undress*
under- not enough: *undercooked*
uni- one; single: *uniform* (= having the same form)
vice- the second most important: *vice-president*

Suffixes

-able, **-ible**,**-ble** (to make adjectives) possible to: *acceptable, noticeable, convertible, divisible* (= possible to divide), *irresistible* (= that you cannot resist)

-age (to make nouns) a process or state: *storage, shortage*

-al (to make adjectives) connected with: *experimental, accidental, environmental*

-ance, **-ence**, **-ancy**, **-ency** (to make nouns) an action, process or state: *appearance, performance, existence, intelligence, pregnancy, efficiency*

-ant,**-ent** (to make nouns) a person who does sth: *assistant, immigrant, student*

-ation (to make nouns) a state or an action: *examination, imagination, organization*

-ble →**able**

-ed (to make adjectives) having a particular state or quality: *bored, patterned*

-ee (to make nouns) a person to whom sth is done: *employee* (= sb who is employed), *trainee* (= sb who is being trained)

-en (to make verbs) to give sth a particular quality; to make sth more ~: *shorten, widen, blacken, sharpen, loosen*, (but note: lengthen)

-ence (**-ency**) →**ance**

-ent →**-ant**

-er (to make nouns) a person who does sth: *rider, painter, banker, driver, teacher*

-ese (to make adjectives) from a place: *Japanese, Chinese, Viennese*

-ess (to make nouns) a woman who does sth as a job: *waitress, actress*

-ful (to make adjectives) having a particular quality: *helpful, useful, beautiful*

-hood (to make nouns) **1** a state, often during a particular period of time: *childhood, motherhood* **2** a group with sth in common: *sisterhood, neighbourhood*

-ian (to make nouns) a person who does sth as a job or hobby: *historian, comedian, politician*

-ible →**-able**

-ical (to make adjectives from nouns ending in -y or -ics) connected with: *economical, mathematical, physical*

-ify (to make verbs) to produce a state or quality: *beautify, simplify, purify*

-ing (to make adjectives) producing a particular state or effect: *interesting*

-ish (to make adjectives) **1** describing nationality or language: *English, Swedish, Polish* **2** like sth: *babyish, foolish* **3** fairly; sort of: *longish, youngish, brownish*

-ist (to make nouns) **1** a person who has studied sth or does sth as a job: *artist, scientist, economist* **2** a person who believes in sth or belongs to a particular group: *capitalist, pacifist, feminist*

-ion (to make nouns) a state or process: *action, connection, exhibition*

-ive (to make adjectives) having a particular quality: *attractive, effective*

-ize, **-ise** (to make verbs) producing a particular state: *magnetize, standardize, modernize, generalize*

-less (to make adjectives) not having sth: *hopeless, friendless*

-like (to make adjectives) similar to: *childlike*

-ly (to make adverbs) in a particular way: *badly, beautifully, completely*

-ment (to make nouns) a state, an action or a quality: *development, arrangement, excitement, achievement*

-ness (to make nouns) a state or quality: *kindness, happiness, weakness*

-ology (to make nouns) the study of a subject: *biology, psychology, zoology*

-or (to make nouns) a person who does sth, often as a job: *actor, conductor, sailor*

-ous (to make adjectives) having a particular quality: *dangerous, religious, ambitious*

-ship (to make nouns) showing status: *friendship, membership, citizenship*

-ward, **-wards** (to make adverbs) in a particular direction: *backward, upwards*

-wise (to make adverbs) in a particular way: *clockwise, edgewise*

-y (to make adjectives) having the quality of the thing mentioned: *cloudy, rainy, fatty, thirsty*

Appendix 5
Word formation

When you find a new word in English, what do you do? Look it up in a **mono**lingual or a **bi**lingual dictionary? Ask a teach**er** or another stud**ent**? Try to **pre**dict the meaning from the rest of the paragraph – the **con**text?

There is another way to try to simpl**ify** difficult words. Often, long words are made from shorter words that you know, combined with a few letters added to the beginning (a **prefix**) or to the end (a **suffix**). Look at the prefixes and suffixes (in dark type) above. They can all be used with many other words, so when you know their meaning, you have the key to a large number of new words.

1 How many sides has an **octagon**?
2 If 1991 was the **bicentenary** of Mozart's death, in which year did he die?
3 Which word is a **monosyllable?**
but **although** **however**
4 Does a **multi-storey car park** have more than one floor?

Numbers Many common words have prefixes that tell us about numbers.

A word that begins with **bi-** shows that there are two of something. A *bicycle* has two wheels (but a *tricycle* has three).

Words for measurements are often made with the prefixes **cent-**, **kilo-**, etc.
100 *centimetres* = 1 metre,
1 *kilogram* = 1000 grams, and so on.

5 If a house was built in the **postwar** period, was it built before or after the war?
6 Would a woman go to **antenatal** classes before or after her baby was born?
7 If your teacher told you to **rewrite** your essay, why would you be angry?

Time A number of prefixes are connected with time, for example **pre-** (before) and **ex-** (former). A *pre-arranged meeting* was arranged beforehand. A divorced man might talk about his *ex-wife*. The *ex-president* is no longer president.

8 Which flies faster than the speed of sound, a **subsonic** plane or a **supersonic** plane?
9 Is a **micro-organism** a very large or very small creature?
10 How do you feel if you have **overeaten** – very full or still hungry?

Size and degree Some common prefixes tell us 'how big' or 'how much'.

A word that begins with **maxi-** is large or the greatest; **mini-** refers to something small (e.g. *mini-skirt*, *minibus*).

Extra- means 'more' – *extra-strong glue* is stronger than usual.

11 Which of the prefixes **un-**, **in-**, **im-**, **il-**, **ir-** would you use to make the opposites of these words?

correct	**certain**	**possible**	**regular**
sure	**legal**	**valid**	**relevant**
patient	**legible**		

Negative Many prefixes change the meaning of a word to its opposite or make it negative. A *non-smoker* does not smoke.The opposite of *happy* is *unhappy*.

Besides **non-** and **un-** we also use **in-** (or before certain letters **im-**, **il-** or **ir-**) in this way. It is important to learn which is the correct prefix to make the opposite of a word.

12 Is an activity that is **extra-curricular** part of the curriculum of a school?
13 Is a flight from London to New York **transatlantic**?

Position These prefixes tell us where something is or happens. For example, **sub-** gives the idea of 'under'. A *subway* goes under the road. We read the *subtitles* under the pictures of a foreign film.

Suffixes

A suffix is added to the end of a word, and it often changes the function of the word. There is one suffix that you probably use very often: **-ly** to make an adjective into an adverb.
He sings beautifully. *The car was badly damaged.*

A suffix can also be added to a noun to make it into an adjective. You can change the noun *Japan* into an adjective describing the nationality of the people who live there by adding **-ese**: *Japan***ese**.

14 Use one of the suffixes **-ation**, **-ment**, **-ness** to make nouns from these verbs and adjectives:

develop	**kind**	**arrange**
imagine	**happy**	**organize**

What happens to the spelling of **happy**?

To make nouns that describe a **state**, an **action** or a **quality** you can add a suffix such as **-ation**, e.g.:
inform + ation → information
examine + ation → examination

There may be small changes in the spelling, e.g. the second 'e' is dropped in examination.

15 Fill the gaps to make words that describe people and their jobs:

- **a** works in a theatre **a_ _ or**
- **b** uses bricks and stone to make houses **b_ _ _ _ er**
- **c** stands in front of the orchestra **c_ _ _ _ _ _ or**
- **d** goes out to discover new countries **e_ _ _ _ _ er**

Other suffixes are used **to make nouns** that describe **people**, for example: **-er**, **-or**, **-ist**, **-ian**, **-ee**, **-ant**, **-ent**. They may be added to a verb to describe the person who does that action, e.g. *rider*, *sailor*, *typist*, or we can add them to nouns to describe someone who works on a particular subject, e.g. *artist*, *historian*.

16 Which verbs can you make from these words using one of the suffixes **-ize**, **-en** and **-ify**? (You may need to change the spelling a little.)

magnet	**beauty**	**sharp**
general	**loose**	**pure**

We can also **make a noun or adjective into a verb** by adding a suffix such as **-ize**, **-en** or **-ify**, e.g.:
modern → modernize
wide → widen
simple → simplify

17 Solve the clues to find these adjectives, which all end in one of the suffixes mentioned:

- **a** practical, that can be used a lot
- **b** having no friends
- **c** easy to see or notice
- **d** needing something to drink

Adjectives can be made with many different suffixes. Some very common ones are:

-able (or sometimes **-ible** or just **-ble**), which often means 'possible to', e.g. *acceptable*, *avoidable*

-y and **-ful**, which often describe qualities, e.g. *cloudy*, *helpful*, *beautiful*

-less, which shows that something is missing, e.g. *hopeless*

Now turn the page upside down and check your answers.

Answers

1 eight **2** 1791 **3** but
4 yes **5** after **6** before
7 because you have to write it again
8 supersonic **9** very small **10** very full
11 incorrect uncertain impossible irregular unsure illegal invalid irrelevant impatient illegible
12 no **13** yes
14 development kindness arrangement imagination happiness organization (the **y** of **happy** becomes an **i**)
15 actor builder conductor explorer
16 magnetize beautify sharpen generalize loosen purify
17 useful friendless noticeable thirsty

Appendix 6
Punctuation

. full stop

A **full stop** (.) (*US* **period**) is used at the end of a sentence, unless the sentence is a question or an exclamation:

We're leaving now.
That's all.
Thank you.

It is also often used after an abbreviation:

Acacia Ave.
a.m.
Walton St.

Note that in email addresses, this is said as **dot**: *www.oup.com = double-u, double-u, double-u, dot o-u-p dot com.*

? question mark

A **question mark** (?) is written at the end of a direct question:

'Who's that man?' Jenny asked.

but not after an indirect question:

Jenny asked who the man was.

! exclamation mark

An **exclamation mark** (!) (*US* **exclamation point**) is used at the end of a sentence which expresses surprise, enthusiasm, shock or horror:

What an amazing story!
How well you look!
Oh no! The cat's been run over!

or after an interjection or a word describing a loud sound:

Bye!
Ow!
Crash!

, comma

A **comma** (,) shows a slight pause in a sentence:

I ran all the way to the station, but I still missed the train.

Although it was cold, the sun was shining.

He did, nevertheless, leave his phone number.

However, we may be wrong.

It is also used before a quotation or direct speech:

Fiona said, 'I'll help you.'

'I'll help you', said Fiona, 'but you'll have to wait till Monday.'

Commas are also used between the items in a list, although they may be omitted before *and*:

It was a cold, rainy day.

This shop sells newspapers, magazines and books.

In relative clauses, commas are used around a phrase which adds some new, but not essential, information. Compare the two sentences:

The boy who had lots of sweets gave some to the boy who had none.

The boy, who had lots of sweets, was already eating.

We cannot understand the first sentence without the information introduced by *who*. However, in the second sentence, the phrase *who had lots of sweets* only adds extra information and is kept separate from the main part of the sentence by commas.

: colon

A **colon** (:) is used to introduce something, such as a long quotation or a list:

There is a choice of main course: roast beef, turkey or omelette.

; semicolon

A **semicolon** (;) is used to separate two contrasting parts of a sentence:

John wanted to go; I did not.

or to separate items in a list where commas have already been used:

The school uniform consists of navy skirt or trousers; grey, white or pale blue shirt; navy jumper or cardigan; grey, blue or white socks.

’ apostrophe

An **apostrophe** (’) shows either that a letter is missing, in short forms such as:

hasn’t, don’t, I’m, he’s

or that a person or thing belongs to somebody:

Peter’s scarf
Jane’s mother
my friend’s car

With some names that end in *s*, another *s* is not always added:

Charles’ book

Notice the position of the apostrophe with singular and plural nouns:

the girl’s keys
(= the keys belonging to the girl)
the girls’ keys
(= the keys belonging to the girls)

“” quotation marks

Quotation marks or **inverted commas** (‘ ’ or “ ”) are used to show the words that somebody said:

‘Come and see,’ said Martin.

‘Oh, no!’ said Martin. ‘Come and see what’s happened.’

Angela shouted, ‘Over here!’

or what somebody thought, when the thoughts are presented like speech:

‘Will they get here on time?’ she wondered.

They are also used around a title, e.g. of a book, play, film, etc:

‘Pinocchio’ was the first film I ever saw.

‘Have you read “Emma”?’ he asked.

- hyphen

A **hyphen** (-) is used to join two words which together form one idea:

a tin-opener
a ten-ton truck

or sometimes to link a prefix to a word:

non-violent
anti-British

and in compound numbers:

thirty-four
seventy-nine

You also write a hyphen at the end of a line if you have to divide a word and write part of it on the next line.

– dash

A **dash** (–) can be used to separate a phrase from the rest of a sentence. It can be used near the end of the sentence before a phrase which sums up the rest of the sentence:

The burglars had taken the furniture, the TV and stereo, the paintings – absolutely everything.

or you can put a dash at the beginning and the end of a phrase which adds extra information:

A few people – not more than ten – had already arrived.

A dash can also show that the speaker has been interrupted in the middle of a sentence:

‘Have you seen –’ ‘Look out!’ she screamed as the ball flew towards them.

( ) brackets

Brackets ( ) (*or especially in US English,* **parentheses**) are also used to keep extra information separate from the rest of the sentence:

Two of the runners (Johns and Smith) finished the race in under an hour.

Numbers or letters used in sentences may also have a bracket after them or brackets around them:

The camera has three main advantages: 1) its compact size 2) its low price and 3) the quality of the photographs.

What would you do if you won a lot of money?
(a) save it
(b) travel round the world
(c) buy a new house
(d) buy presents for your friends

Appendix 7
Computers

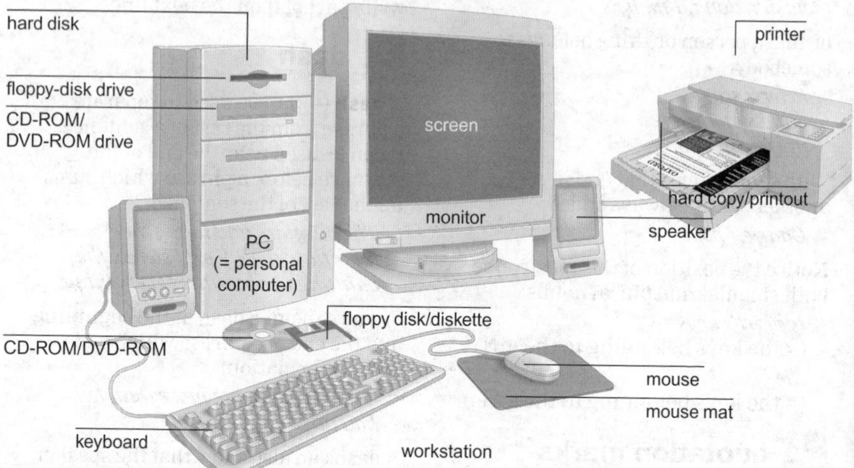

Computers

A computer can **store** and **process** information. This information is called **data** and can be words, numbers or graphics. To process data, the computer uses a **program**, which is a set of instructions stored on the computer's **hard disk**.

To **input data**, you can enter it using the **keyboard**. If you want to store this data, you save it into the computer's memory and you can make a **backup copy** or **print it out** by connecting the computer to a **printer**. Large amounts of information, such as encyclopedias, can be stored on a CD-ROM.

Possible problems:
— the computer won't let you **log in/on**
— you can't **save** your work
— a **bug** in the program
— a **virus** on the network
— the computer **crashes**
— **spam**

On the **screen**, **icons**, which are arranged in a row on a **toolbar**, and **menus** show you what programs and data are stored on the computer and what jobs the computer can do. You use the **mouse** to **click on** an icon and tell the computer what job you want it to do and to move to the part of the screen you want to work on. The **cursor** shows your position on the screen.

Computers can be connected to other computers to form a network. This allows different people to have access to the same information and to communicate with each other using email. To communicate with someone using email, you send your message to their email address.

Can I email you?

Do you have an email address?

My email address is *warnerd@iet.co.uk* (warner d at i-e-t dot co dot U-K) /ˌdɒt ˈkəʊ dɒt juːˈkeɪ/

The **Internet** or the **Net** is an enormous network that covers the world. People who want **to** make information available to the whole world can pay for their own space on the Internet. This is called a **website**. The Web or the

World Wide Web (WWW) is the system which lets you **download information** from the Internet. You can use a **search engine** to **enter** keywords and find all the **websites** that have information about a subject. For example, if you want to write something about the environmental problem of water shortage you can key in the words 'water' and 'shortage' and find websites about the problem. This is called **surfing the Net. Online services** are ones that are available on the Internet.

If you know the **address** of a website you can go directly to it. An example is *http://www.oup.com* (double-u double-u double-u dot o-u-p dot com).

A website can contain many **web pages.** The first page is called the **home page** and it often has a list of answers to **FAQs** (frequently asked questions).

Emails

Informal emails are often short messages between colleagues or friends.

Formal emails can be similar to formal letters without addresses. You do not have to use a particular formula at the end – you can just sign your name. Use the *subject line* to say what your message is about. Use *cc* if you want someone else to read the message.

An email address is written like this: **sam.green@bec.co.uk**

It is said like this:
Sam dot Green at b e c dot co dot u k

Formal email

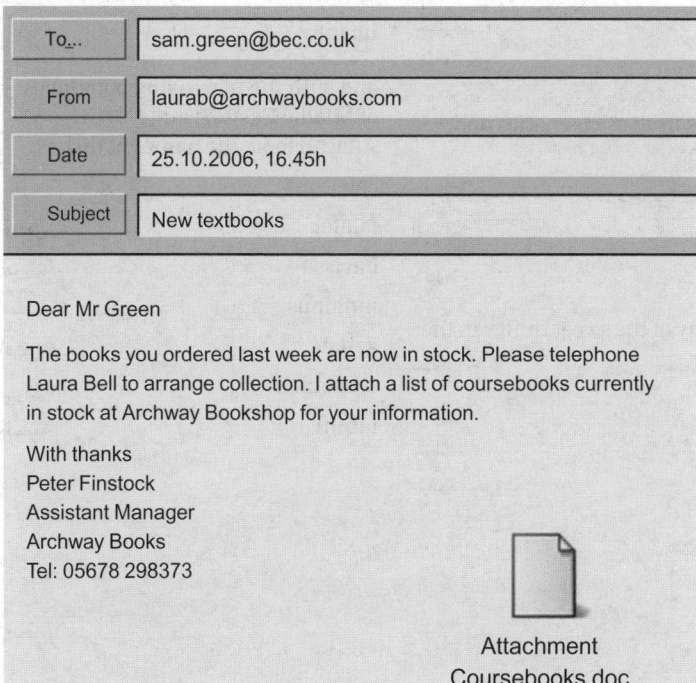

To...	sam.green@bec.co.uk
From	laurab@archwaybooks.com
Date	25.10.2006, 16.45h
Subject	New textbooks

Dear Mr Green

The books you ordered last week are now in stock. Please telephone Laura Bell to arrange collection. I attach a list of coursebooks currently in stock at Archway Bookshop for your information.

With thanks
Peter Finstock
Assistant Manager
Archway Books
Tel: 05678 298373

Attachment
Coursebooks.doc

Appendix 8
Arabic words in English

When people ask in English for 'a coffee with sugar', they probably don't realize that they are using words that have come into English from Arabic. Many very common English words have their origins in Arabic.

Some of them reflect the time when Arab understanding of mathematics was foremost in the world:

algebra (علم) الجبر
zero صِفْر

The names of many items in everyday use come originally from Arabic words:

sofa كَنَبة
mattress حَشيّة، فَرْشة
cotton قطن

—products used as cosmetics and make-up:

mascara "مَسْكَرة"، مستحضر لتجميل رموش العين
henna الحنّاء
kohl كحل

— and many of the sweet things in life:

sugar سكّر
syrup ربّ السكّر، قَطْر
sorbet شراب
carob شجرة الخرّوب

These words became part of English many centuries ago, but Arabic words continue to become used in English. More recently, Arabic words that have become familiar in English include

items of clothing:

burka بُرقع
hijab حجاب
keffiyeh كفيّة

people, especially religious leaders and teachers:

admiral أمير البحر، أميرال
ayatollah آية اللّه
mullah ملاّ
imam إمام

and with the increasing popularity of Middle Eastern and North African food, the names of dishes:

couscous مغربية، كسكس
falafel فلافل
harissa هريسة
hummus مسبّحة، حمّص
kebab (لحم) كباب
tabbouleh تبّولة
tahini طحينة

Appendix 9
Letter writing

When you write a letter you need to think about **layout**, **style** and **content**.

Layout is how your letter looks on the page, where you **put addresses, etc.**

Style is the manner in which you write, i.e. formal or informal.

Content is what you want to say.

Formal letters
A job application letter

Notes	Letter
Your address. Do not put your name here.	34 Cricket Road Exeter EX9 6RT 27 January 2006
All parts of the letter (except for your own address and the date) are lined up on the left hand side of the paper.	Simon Harris Pier Publishing 11 Fish Lane Brighton BR7 9VB
Use the person's title. *Mr*, *Mrs* (married woman), *Miss* (unmarried woman) or *Ms* (any woman, married or single) +	Dear Mr Harris
CV = Curriculum Vitae	I am writing to apply for the post of IT assistant, advertised in the Mail of 13 January. As requested I enclose my CV.
Organize the information in your letter into 3 or 4 paragraphs 1 your reason for writing 2 your skills and experience 3 when you will be available for interview	Before university I worked for a publisher in Exeter for 6 months, where I gained valuable experience. In July I will graduate from York University, where I am studying Business and Spanish. I speak fluent Spanish and good French, and I have excellent computer skills. I would very much like to work for your company and I hope you will consider my application. I am available for interview next week. I look forward to hearing from you.
Use formal words and phrases. Write in full sentences.	
Closing: Use a capital letter. *Yours sincerely* if you know the person's name, *Yours faithfully* if you don't.	Yours sincerely Emma Reyes Emma Reyes

Curriculum Vitae

Curriculum Vitae

Name:	Emma Reyes
Address:	34 Cricket Road Exeter EX9 6RT
Telephone:	0207 544 1002
Date of Birth:	01/07/83
Nationality:	British

Personal Profile

A hard-working and highly motivated person with excellent computer skills as well as experience in business. A good communicator with knowledge of foreign languages. Well organized and able to take responsibility.

Education/Qualifications

2002–2006	University of York, B.A. in Business and Spanish (graduating July 2006)
1994–2001	The Hill School, York 3 A levels: Spanish (A), French (A), Economics (B)

Employment to date

Sept 2001 – Feb 2002
Exoprint Publishing, Exeter. Editorial Assistant (assisted with clerical tasks, data input, etc.)

July – Aug 2003
Vacation work at Seaview Hotel, Dawlish

Sept 2004 – June 2005
Placement at Telegarcia, S.A. Madrid (helped with translation of business letters, dealing with overseas customers, making travel arrangements, etc.)

Skills

- Languages – fluent Spanish, good French
- Computer skills – good knowledge of standard software packages, some experience of programming
- Clean driving licence

Interests

Swimming, travel, photography

References

Available on request

Some useful expressions for formal letters:

—*I am writing to enquire/complain about…*
—*I am writing regarding your advertisement…*
—*I wish to apply for...*
—*I would like to inform you that…*
—*I would be grateful for...*
—*I would be grateful if you could…*
—*Could you send me further details of...?*

Letter of complaint

16 Paddington Lane
Leeds
LS4 7QT
May 16 2006

Seaside Hotel
Harbour Lane
Falmouth
TR12 5LB

Dear Sir or Madam

I am writing to complain about the poor service provided by your hotel, where my friend and I stayed last week.

Explain why you are writing.

First of all, we asked for a room with a view of the sea, but we were given a room at the back of the hotel overlooking the car park. To make matters worse, the bathroom had not been cleaned and when I reported this to your staff they were very slow to take action. Moreover, at breakfast your staff were rude and unhelpful.

Explain what the problem is and describe any action you have already taken.

As a result of all this, we did not enjoy our holiday, and we went home early.

Say what inconvenience it has caused you.

I believe I am entitled to compensation and I expect to receive a refund of at least half our bill. I look forward to hearing from you very soon.

State what you want done about the problem.

Yours faithfully

Elaine Thomas

Elaine Thomas

Informal letters

Your address. Do not put your name here. Date: under your address

Do not write the name or address of the person you are writing to.

27 Wood Avenue,
Oxford,
OX4 7EN

6th July, 2006

Greeting: Dear + first name

Dear Ginny,

How are you? Sorry I haven't been in touch for ages but I've had masses of work! My new job's going really well, though.

Style: Informal. You can use contractions and abbreviations. You don't have to use full sentences.

In fact, I'm writing to ask you a favour. I've been asked to go to a conference in Paris next month and I wondered whether I could stay with you for a couple of nights. It would be great to see you and catch up on all the news!

Hope to hear from you soon.

Closing: Lots of love, Love from, Love (close friends) Best wishes, All the best, Take care (friends/acquaintances)

Love,
Vicky x

PS Put this if you want to add extra information.

PS Love to Alain and the kids!

Appendix 10
The Arab world

Countries

1 Some countries in the Arab world have names in English that come directly from their Arabic names. Their pronunciation in English is, however, often very different from the way they are pronounced in Arabic.

Arabic	English	Pronunciation
البحرين	Bahrain	/bɑːˈreɪn/
العراق	Iraq	/ɪˈrɑːk/
الكويت	Kuwait	/kuˈweɪt/
ليبيا	Libya	/ˈlɪbiə/
عمان	Oman	/əʊˈmɑːn/
قطر	Qatar	/ˈkʌtɑː(r)/
السودان	Sudan	/suˈdɑːn; *US* -ˈdæn/
اليمن	Yemen	/ˈjemən/

2 Other countries have English names that are different from their names in Arabic.

The regions of the world where Arabs live are known as **the Middle East** (e.g. Egypt, Iraq, Jordan) and **North Africa** (e.g. Algeria, Libya, Morocco).

Arabic	English	Pronunciation
الجزائر	Algeria	/ælˈdʒɪəriə/
مصر	Egypt	/ˈiːdʒɪpt/
الأردن	Jordan	/ˈdʒɔːdn/
لبنان	Lebanon	/ˈlebənən; *US* -nɒn/
المغرب	Morocco	/məˈrɒkəʊ/
المملكة العربية السعودية	Saudi Arabia	/ˌsaʊdi əˈreɪbiə/
الصومال	Somalia	/səˈmɑːliə/
سوريا	Syria	/ˈsɪriə/
تونس	Tunisia	/tjuˈnɪziə; *US* tuˈniːʒə/
الإمارات العربية المتحدة	United Arab Emirates	/juˌnaɪtɪd ˌærəb ˈemɪrəts/

Cities

3 Similarly, some cities have the same name in Arabic and English.

Arabic	English	Pronunciation
أبو ظبي	Abu Dhabi	/ˌæbu ˈdɑːbi/
عمان	Amman	/əˈmɑːn/
بغداد	Baghdad	/bægˈdæd/
بيروت	Beirut	/beɪˈruːt/
دبي	Dubai	/d(j)uˈbaɪ/
جدة	Jiddah	/ˈdʒɪdə/
الخرطوم	Khartoum	/kɑːˈtuːm/
مكة	Mecca	/ˈmekə/
مقديشيو	Mogadishu	/ˌmɒgəˈdɪʃu/
مسقط	Muscat	/ˈmʌskæt/
الرباط	Rabat	/rəˈbæt/
الرياض	Riyadh	/riˈjæd; ˈriːɑːd/
تونس	Tunis	/ˈtjuːnɪs/

4 Other cities have a different name in English.

Arabic	English	Pronunciation
الجزائر	Algiers	/ælˈdʒɪəz/
حلب	Aleppo	/æˈlepəʊ/
الاسكندرية	Alexandria	/ˌælɪgˈzɑːndriə/
القاهرة	Cairo	/ˈkaɪərəʊ/
الدار البيضاء	Casablanca	/ˌkæsəˈblæŋkə/
دمشق	Damascus	/dəˈmɑːskəs; -ˈmæskəs/
القدس	Jerusalem	/dʒəˈruːsələm/
الكويت	Kuwait City	/kuˌweɪt ˈsɪti/
طرابلس	Tripoli	/ˈtrɪpəli/

Nationalities

5 The adjectives used to describe nationality in English have a variety of endings, for example:

He is Egyptian. *She is Lebanese.* *They are Iraqi.*

Often the adjective can also be used as a noun to refer to a person from the relevant country:

(adjective) *an Egyptian tradition*
(noun) *She is an Egyptian living in London.*

This is the case with all the nationality words for countries of the Arab world. As a contrast, look at the following cases where different words are needed for the adjective and noun:

He is English. *He is an Englishman.*
She is French. *She is a Frenchwoman.*
the Polish Government *some Poles on holiday*
a Spanish restaurant *a Spaniard from Madrid*

Following is a table of nationality words for some countries of the Arab world:

Country	Nationality (adjective and noun)	Pronunciation
Algeria	Algerian	/æl'dʒɪəriən/
Bahrain	Bahraini	/bɑː'reɪni/
Egypt	Egyptian	/i'dʒɪpʃn/
Iraq	Iraqi	/ɪ'rɑːki/
Jordan	Jordanian	/dʒɔː'deɪniən/
Kuwait	Kuwaiti	/ku'weɪti/
Lebanon	Lebanese [The plural doesn't change.]	/ˌlebə'niːz/
Libya	Libyan	/'lɪbiən/
Morocco	Moroccan	/mə'rɒkən/
Oman	Omani	/əʊ'mɑːni/
Qatar	Qatari	/kʌ'tɑːri/
Saudi Arabia	Saudi (Arabian)	/ˌsaʊdi (ə'reɪbien)/
Somalia	Somali	/sə'mɑːli/
Sudan	Sudanese [The plural doesn't change.]	/ˌsuːdə'niːz/
Syria	Syrian	/'sɪriən/
Tunisia	Tunisian	/tju'nɪziən; *US* tu'niːʒn/
Yemen	Yemeni	/'jeməni/

Geographical features

6 Following are some of the rivers, seas, mountains, etc of the Arab world with their English names:

Arabic	English	Pronunciation
البحر الميت	the Dead Sea	/ðə ˌded 'siː/
البحر الأحمر	the Red Sea	/ðə ˌred 'siː/
البحر الأبيض المتوسط	the Mediterranean Sea	/ðə ˌmedɪtəˌreɪniən 'siː/
الخليج العربي	the Persian Gulf (*also informal* the Gulf)	/ðə ˌpɜːʃn 'gʌlf/
قناة السويس	the Suez Canal	/ðə ˌsuːɪz kə'næl/
نهر النيل	the River Nile	/ðə ˌrɪvə 'naɪəl/
نهر دجلة	the River Tigris	/ðə ˌrɪvə 'taɪgrɪs/
نهر الفرات	the River Euphrates	/ðə ˌrɪvə ju'freɪtiːz/
مضيق جبل طارق	the Strait of Gibraltar	/ðə ˌstreɪt əv dʒɪ'brɔːltə(r)/
شبه الجزيرة العربية	the Arabian Peninsula	/ði əˌreɪbien pə'nɪnsjələ; *US* -sələ/
شبه جزيرة سيناء	Sinai (*also* the Sinai peninsula)	/(ðə) ˌsaɪnaɪ (pə'nɪnsjələ; *US* -sələ)/
الصحراء الكبرى	the Sahara (Desert)	/ðə səˌhɑːrə ('dezət)/
جبل موسى، جبل الطور	Mount Sinai	/ˌmaʊnt 'saɪnaɪ/

Appendix 11

Expressions using numbers

The numbers

1	one	**1st**	first
2	two	**2nd**	second
3	three	**3rd**	third
4	four	**4th**	fourth
5	five	**5th**	fifth
6	six	**6th**	sixth
7	seven	**7th**	seventh
8	eight	**8th**	eighth
9	nine	**9th**	ninth
10	ten	**10th**	tenth
11	eleven	**11th**	eleventh
12	twelve	**12th**	twelfth
13	thirteen	**13th**	thirteenth
14	fourteen	**14th**	fourteenth
15	fifteen	**15th**	fifteenth
16	sixteen	**16th**	sixteenth
17	seventeen	**17th**	seventeenth
18	eighteen	**18th**	eighteenth
19	nineteen	**19th**	nineteenth
20	twenty	**20th**	twentieth
21	twenty-one	**21st**	twenty-first
22	twenty-two	**22nd**	twenty-second
30	thirty	**30th**	thirtieth
40	forty	**40th**	fortieth
50	fifty	**50th**	fiftieth
60	sixty	**60th**	sixtieth
70	seventy	**70th**	seventieth
80	eighty	**80th**	eightieth
90	ninety	**90th**	ninetieth
100	a/one hundred*	**100th**	hundredth
101	a/one hundred and one*	**101st**	hundred and first
200	two hundred	**200th**	two hundredth
1 000	a/one thousand*	**1 000th**	thousandth
10 000	ten thousand	**10 000th**	ten thousandth
100 000	a/one hundred thousand*	**100 000th**	hundred thousandth
1 000 000	a/one million*	**1 000 000th**	millionth

Examples: 697: *six hundred and ninety-seven*
3 402: *three thousand, four hundred and two*
80 534: *eighty thousand, five hundred and thirty-four*

* You use **one hundred, one thousand**, etc., instead of **a hundred, a thousand**, when it is important to stress that you mean one (not two, for example). In numbers over a thousand, you use a comma or a small space: **1,200** or **1 200**

Telephone numbers

In telephone numbers you say each number separately, often with a pause after two or three numbers:
509236 *five o nine – two three six*

You can say *six six* or *double six* for *66*.
02166 *o two one – six six or o two one – double six.*

If you are phoning a number in a different town, you have to use the **area code** before the number:
01865 is the code for Oxford.

If you are phoning somebody in a large firm, you can ask for their extension number. *Extension 4840, please.*

Fractions and decimals

$\frac{1}{2}$	a half	$\frac{1}{3}$	a/one third
$\frac{1}{4}$	a quarter	$\frac{2}{5}$	two fifths
$\frac{1}{8}$	an/one eighth	$\frac{7}{12}$	seven twelfths
$\frac{1}{10}$	a/one tenth	$1\frac{1}{2}$	one and a half
$\frac{1}{16}$	a/one sixteenth	$2\frac{3}{8}$	two and three eighths

0.1 (nought) point one — 1.75 one point seven five
0.25 (nought) point two five — 3.976 three point nine seven six
0.33 (nought) point three three

Percentages and proportions

***90%** of all households have a television.*
***Nine out of ten** households have a television.*
***Nine tenths of** all households have a television.*

Mathematical expressions

+	plus
–	minus
x	times or multiplied by
÷	divided by
=	equals
%	per cent
3^2	three squared
5^3	five cubed
6^{10}	six to the power of ten

Examples:
7 +6 = 13 *seven plus six equals (or is) thirteen*
5 x 8 = 40 *five times eight equals forty*
or *five eights are forty*
or *five multiplied by eight is forty*

Temperature

In Britain, temperatures are now usually given in **degrees Celsius**, (although many people are still more familiar with **Fahrenheit**). In the United States, **Fahrenheit** is used, except in science.

To convert **Fahrenheit** to **Celsius**, subtract 32 from the number, then multiply by 5 and divide by 9:

68°F – 32 = 36 x 5 = 180 ÷ 9 = **20°C**

Examples:
Water freezes at 32°F and boils at 212°F.
The maximum temperature this afternoon will be 15°, and the minimum tonight may reach –5° (minus five).
She had a temperature of 102° last night.

Weight

	Non-metric	Metric
	1 ounce (oz)	= 28.35 grams (g)
16 ounces =	1 pound (lb)	= 0.454 kilogram (kg)
14 pounds =	1 stone (st)	= 6.356 kilograms
8 stone =	1 hundredweight (cwt)	= 50.8 kilograms
20 hundredweight =	1 ton (t)	= 1016.04 kilograms

Examples:
The baby weighed 8 lb 2oz (eight pounds two ounces).
For this recipe you need 750g (seven hundred and fifty grams) of flour.

Length and height

	Non-metric	Metric
	1 inch (in)	= 25.4 millimetres (mm)
12 inches =	1 foot (ft)	= 30.48 centimetres (cm)
3 feet =	1 yard (yd)	= 0.914 metre (m)
1 760 yards =	1 mile	= 1.609 kilometres (km)

Examples:
They were flying at 7 000 feet.
The speed limit is 30 mph (thirty miles per/an hour).
The room is 11'x 9'6" (eleven feet by nine feet six or eleven foot by nine foot six).
She's five feet four (inches).
He's one metre sixty (centimetres).

Area	**Non-metric**	**Metric**
	1 square inch (sq in)	= 6.452 square centimetres (cm^2)
144 square inches =	1 square foot (sq ft)	= 929.03 square centimetres
9 square feet =	1 square yard (sq yd)	= 0.836 square metre (m^2)
4840 square yards =	1 acre	= 0.405 hectare
640 acres =	1 square mile	= 2.59 square kilometres (km^2) or 259 hectares

Examples *an 80-acre country park*
160 000 square miles of the jungle have been destroyed.

Cubic measurements	**Non-metric**	**Metric**
	1 cubic inch (cu in)	= 16 39 cubic centimetres (cc)
1728 cubic inches =	1 cubic foot (cu ft)	= 0.028 cubic metre
27 cubic feet =	1 cubic yard (cu yd)	= 0.765 cubic metre

Example *a car with a 1500 cc engine*

Capacity **GB**	**US**	**Metric**	
20 fluid ounces (fl oz) =	1 pint (pt)	= 1.201 pints	= 0.568 litre (l)
2 pints =	1 quart (qt)	= 1.201 quarts	= 1.136 litres
4 quarts =	1 gallon (gall)	= 1.201 gallons	= 4.546 litres

Examples *I drink a litre of water a day.* *a quart of orange juice*

Dates

8 April 2005 or 8th April 2005 (8/4/05) (Brit)
Her birthday is on the thirteenth of July.
Her birthday is on July the thirteenth.
April 8, 2005 (4/8/05) (US)
Her birthday is July 13th. (US)

Years

1999	*nineteen ninety-nine*	2000	*(the year) two thousand*
1608	*sixteen o eight*	2002	*two thousand and two*
1700	*seventeen hundred*	2015	*twenty fifteen*

Times

There is often more than one way of telling the time:

Half hours

6:30 *six thirty*
half past six
half six (informal)

Other times

5:45	*five forty-five*	*(a) quarter to six*
2:15	*two fifteen*	*(a) quarter past two*
1:10	*one ten*	*ten past one*
3:05	*three o five*	*five past three*
1:55	*one fifty-five*	*five to two*

In American English, *after* is sometimes used instead of *past*, and *of* instead of *to*.

with 5, 10, 20 and 25 the word *minutes* is not necessary, but it is used with other numbers:
10.25 *twenty-five past ten*
10.17 *seventeen minutes past ten*

use o'clock only for whole hours:
It's three o'clock.

Twenty-four hour clock

The twenty-four hour clock is used in official language:
13:52 *thirteen fifty-two (1:52 p.m.)*
22:30 *twenty-two thirty (10.30 p.m.)*

Appendix 12
Irregular verbs

be

present tense	short forms	negative short forms	past tense	present participle
I **am**	I**'m**	**I'm not**	I **was**	**being**
you **are**	you**'re**	you **aren't**	you **were**	
he/she/it **is**	he**'s**/she**'s**/it**'s**	he/she/it **isn't**	he/she/it **was**	*past participle*
we **are**	we**'re**	we **aren't**	we **were**	**been**
you **are**	you**'re**	you **aren't**	you **were**	
they **are**	they**'re**	they **aren't**	they **were**	

do

present tense	negative short forms	past tense
I **do**	I **don't**	**did**
you **do**	you **don't**	*present participle*
he/she/it **does**	he/she/it **doesn't**	**doing**
we **do**	we **don't**	*past participle*
you **do**	you **don't**	**done**
they **do**	they **don't**	

have

present tense	short forms	negative short forms	past tense short forms	past tense
I **have**	I**'ve**	I **haven't**	I**'d**	**had**
you **have**	you**'ve**	you **haven't**	you**'d**	*present participle*
he/she/it **has**	he**'s**/she**'s**/it**'s**	he/she/it **hasn't**	he**'d**/she**'d**/it**'d**	**having**
we **have**	we**'ve**	we **haven't**	we**'d**	*past participle*
you **have**	you**'ve**	you **haven't**	you**'d**	**had**
they **have**	they**'ve**	they **haven't**	they**'d**	

In this list you will find the infinitive form of the verb – the form that appears as a headword in the dictionary – followed by the past tense and the past participle. Where two forms of a past tense or past participle are given, look up the verb in the main part of the dictionary to see whether there is a difference in meaning.

Infinitive	Past tense	Past participle
arise	arose	arisen
awake	awoke	awoken
bear	bore	borne
beat	beat	beaten
become	became	become
begin	began	begun
bend	bent	bent
bet	bet, betted	bet, betted
bid	bid	bidden
bind	bound	bound
bite	bit	bitten
bleed	bled	bled
bless	blessed	blessed
blow	blew	blown
break	broke	broken
breed	bred	bred
bring	brought	brought
broadcast	broadcast	broadcast
build	built	built
burn	burnt, burned	burnt, burned
burst	burst	burst
bust	bust, busted	bust, busted
buy	bought	bought
cast	cast	cast
catch	caught	caught
choose	chose	chosen
cling	clung	clung
come	came	come
cost	cost, costed	cost, costed
creep	crept	crept
cut	cut	cut
deal	dealt	dealt
dig	dug	dug

Infinitive	Past tense	Past participle
dive	dived; (*US*) dove	dived
draw	drew	drawn
dream	dreamt, dreamed	dreamt, dreamed
drink	drank	drunk
drive	drove	driven
eat	ate	eaten
fall	fell	fallen
feed	fed	fed
feel	felt	felt
fight	fought	fought
find	found	found
flee	fled	fled
fling	flung	flung
fly	flew	flown
forbid	forbade	forbidden
forecast	forecast, forecasted	forecast, forecasted
forget	forgot	forgotten
forgive	forgave	forgiven
freeze	froze	frozen
get	got	got; (*US*) gotten
give	gave	given
go	went	gone
grind	ground	ground
grow	grew	grown
hang	hung, hanged	hung, hanged
hear	heard	heard
hide	hid	hidden
hit	hit	hit
hold	held	held
hurt	hurt	hurt
input	input, inputted	input, inputted
keep	kept	kept
kneel	knelt; (*esp US*) kneeled	knelt; (*esp US*) kneeled
know	knew	known
lay	laid	laid
lead	led	led
lean	leant, leaned	leant, leaned
leap	leapt, leaped	leapt, leaped
learn	learnt, learned	learnt, learned
leave	left	left
lend	lent	lent
let	let	let
lie	lay	lain
light	lit, lighted	lit, lighted
lose	lost	lost
make	made	made
mean	meant	meant
meet	met	met
mistake	mistook	mistaken
misunderstand	misunderstood	misunderstood
mow	mowed	mown, mowed
overcome	overcame	overcome
pay	paid	paid
plead	pleaded; (*US*) pled	pleaded; (*US*) pled
prove	proved	proved; (*US*) proven
put	put	put
quit	quit	quit
read	read	read
ride	rode	ridden
ring	rang	rung
rise	rose	risen
run	ran	run
saw	sawed	sawn
say	said	said

Infinitive	Past tense	Past participle
see	saw	seen
seek	sought	sought
sell	sold	sold
send	sent	sent
set	set	set
sew	sewed	sewn, sewed
shake	shook	shaken
shed	shed	shed
shine	shone	shone
shoe	shod	shod
shoot	shot	shot
show	showed	shown, showed
shrink	shrank, shrunk	shrunk
shut	shut	shut
sing	sang	sung
sink	sank	sunk
sit	sat	sat
sleep	slept	slept
slide	slid	slid
sling	slung	slung
slit	slit	slit
smell	smelt, smelled	smelt, smelled
sow	sowed	sown, sowed
speak	spoke	spoken
speed	sped, speeded	sped, speeded
spell	spelt, spelled	spelt, spelled
spend	spent	spent
spill	spilt, spilled	spilt, spilled
spin	spun	spun
spit	spat; (*esp US*) spit	spat; (*esp US*) spit
split	split	split
spoil	spoilt, spoiled	spoilt, spoiled
spread	spread	spread
spring	sprang	sprung
stand	stood	stood
steal	stole	stolen
stick	stuck	stuck
sting	stung	stung
stink	stank, stunk	stunk
stride	strode	stridden
strike	struck	struck
string	strung	strung
strive	strove	striven
swear	swore	sworn
sweep	swept	swept
swell	swelled	swollen, swelled
swim	swam	swum
swing	swung	swung
take	took	taken
teach	taught	taught
tear	tore	torn
tell	told	told
think	thought	thought
throw	threw	thrown
thrust	thrust	thrust
tread	trod	trodden
wake	woke	woken
wear	wore	worn
weave	wove, weaved	woven, weaved
weep	wept	wept
win	won	won
wind[3]	wound	wound
wring	wrung	wrung
write	wrote	written

Appendix 13
Pronunciation

Pronunciation

If two pronunciations for one word are given, both are acceptable. The first form is considered to be more common. A word that is pronounced very differently in American English has the American pronunciation given after a *US* label:

address /əˈdres; *US* ˈædres/

/-/ A hyphen is used in alternative pronunciations when only part of the pronunciation changes. The part that remains the same is replaced by a hyphen:

attitude /ˈætɪtjuːd; *US* -tuːd/

/ˈ/ This mark shows that the syllable after it is said with more force (stress) than the other syllables in the word or group of words. For example, *any* /ˈeni/ has a stress on the first syllable; *depend* /dɪˈpend/ has a stress on the second syllable.

/ˌ/ This mark shows that a syllable is said with more force than other syllables in a word but with a stress that is not as strong as for those syllables marked /ˈ/. So in the word *pronunciation* /prəˌnʌnsiˈeɪʃn/ the main stress is on the syllable /ˈeɪ/ and the secondary stress is on the syllable /ˌnʌn/.

(r) In spoken British English an *r* at the end of a written word (either as the final letter or in an *-re* ending as in *fire*) is not sounded unless another word that begins with a vowel sound follows. For example, the *r* is not heard in *His car was sold*, but it is heard in *His car isn't old*. To show this, words which end in *r* or *re* have (r) at the end of the phonetic spelling in the dictionary:

car /kɑː(r)/

In American English the /r/ is sounded whenever it occurs in the spelling of a word.

Strong and weak forms

Some very common words, e.g. *an, as, that, of* have two or more pronunciations: a *strong* form and one or more *weak* forms. In speech the weak forms are more common. For example, *from* is /frəm/ in *He comes from Spain*. The strong form occurs when the word comes at the end of a sentence or it is given special emphasis. For example, *from* is /frɒm/ in *The ˌpresent's not ˈfrom John, it's ˈfor him.*

Pronunciation in derivatives and compounds

In **compounds** (made up of two or more words) the pronunciation of the individual words is not repeated. The dictionary shows how the compound is stressed by using the marks /ˈ/ and /ˌ/. In ˈ*tin opener* the stress is on the first word. In ˌ*jacket po*ˈ*tato* the secondary stress is on the first syllable of *jacket* and the main stress is on the second syllable of *potato*.

Many **derivatives** are formed by adding a suffix at the end of a word. These are pronounced by simply saying the suffix after the word. For example, *slowly* /ˈsləʊli/ is said by joining the suffix *-ly* /li/ to the word *slow* /sləʊ/.

However, where there is doubt about how a derivative is pronounced, the phonetic spelling is given. The part that remains the same is represented by a hyphen:

mournful /-fl/; mournfully /-fəli/

Other suffixes

-ance, -ence /əns/	-less /ləs /
-er, or /ə(r)/	-ly /li /
-ic /ɪk/	-ment /mənt/
-ics /ɪks/	-ness /nəs/
-ing /ɪŋ/	-ship /ʃɪp/
-ish /ɪʃ/	-tion, sion /ʃən/
-ist /ɪst/	-y /i/